EILIDH ROSS

Æ 46
1610

Willm Shakspere.

THE ILLUSTRATED STRATFORD
STRATFORD
SHAKESPEARE

THE ILLUSTRATED STRATFORD

SHAKESPEARE

CHANCELLOR
PRESS

The Illustrated Stratford Shakespeare first published in Great Britain
in 1992 by Chancellor Press

Reprinted 1983, 1984, 1985, 1986, 1987, 1988, 1989, 1990, 1991,1992

This edition first published in 1993 by Chancellor Press
an imprint of Reed Consumer Books Limited
Michelin House, 81 Fulham Road, London SW3 6RB
and Auckland, Melbourne, Singapore and Toronto

Reprinted 1993

Design and arrangement copyright ©1982 Reed International Books Limited

ISBN 1 85152 381 2

A CIP catalogue record for this book is available at the British Library

Printed in the Slovak Republic
50452/11

CONTENTS

THE PLAYS

THE POEMS

THE SONNETS

THE PLAYS

THE TEMPEST.

DRAMATIS PERSONÆ.

ALONSO, *King of Naples.*
SEBASTIAN, *his Brother.*
PROSPERO, *the right Duke of Milan.*
ANTONIO, *his Brother, the usurping Duke of Milan.*
FERDINAND, *Son to the King of Naples.*
GONZALO, *an honest old Counsellor.*
ADRIAN, } *Lords.*
FRANCISCO, }
CÀLIBAN, *a savage and deformed Slave.*
TRINCULO, *a Jester.*
STEPHANO, *a drunken Butler.*

Master of a Ship, Boatswain, Mariners.
MIRANDA, *Daughter to Prospero.*
ARIEL, *an airy Spirit.*
IRIS, }
CERES, }
JUNO, } *Spirits.*
Nymphs, }
Reapers, }
Other Spirits attending on Prospero.

SCENE—The Sea, with a Ship; afterwards an Island.

ACT I.

SCENE I.—On a Ship at Sea. A tempestuous noise of Thunder and Lightning heard.

Enter a Ship-Master and a Boatswain, severally.

Master.

BOATSWAIN!

Boats. Here, master: what cheer?
Mast. Good, speak to the mariners: fall to 't yarely, or we run ourselves aground: bestir, bestir. [*Exit.*

Enter Mariners.

Boats. Heigh, my hearts! cheerly, cheerly, my hearts! yare, yare. Take in the topsail; tend to the master's whistle.—Blow, till thou burst thy wind, if room enough! 10

Enter ALONSO, SEBASTIAN, ANTONIO, FERDINAND, GONZALO, *and others.*

Alon. Good boatswain, have care. Where's the master? Play the men.
Boats. I pray now, keep below.
Ant. Where is the master, boson?
Boats. Do you not hear him? you mar our labour. Keep your cabins; you do assist the storm.
Gon. Nay, good, be patient.
Boats. When the sea is. Hence! What care these roarers for the name of king? To cabin: silence! trouble us not. 20
Gon. Good, yet remember whom thou hast aboard.
Boats. None that I more love than myself. You are a counsellor: if you can command these elements to silence, and work the peace of the present, we will not hand a rope more; use your authority: if you cannot, give thanks you have lived so long, and make yourself ready in your cabin for the mischance of the hour, if it so hap.—Cheerly, good hearts!—Out of our way, I say. [*Exit.*
Gon. I have great comfort from this fellow: methinks, he hath no drowning mark upon him; his complexion is perfect gallows. Stand fast, good fate, to his hanging! make the rope of his destiny our cable, for our own doth little advantage! If he be not born to be hanged, our case is miserable. [*Exeunt.*

Re-enter Boatswain.

Boats. Down with the topmast: yare; lower, lower. Bring her to try with main-course. [*A cry within.*] A plague upon this howling! they are louder than the weather, or our office.—

Re-enter SEBASTIAN, ANTONIO, *and* GONZALO.

Yet again! what do you here? Shall we give o'er, and drown? Have you a mind to sink? 41
Seb. A pox o' your throat, you bawling, blasphemous, incharitable dog!
Boats. Work you, then.
Ant. Hang, cur, hang! you whoreson, insolent noise-maker, we are less afraid to be drowned than thou art.
Gon. I'll warrant him for drowning, though the ship were no stronger than a nutshell, and as leaky as an unstanched wench. 50
Boats. Lay her a-hold, a-hold! Set her two courses: off to sea again; lay her off.

Enter Mariners, wet.

Mar. All lost! to prayers, to prayers! all lost!
[*Exeunt.*
Boats. What, must our mouths be cold?
Gon. The king and prince at prayers! let's assist them,
For our case is as theirs.
Seb. I am out of patience.
Ant. We are merely cheated of our lives by drunkards.—
This wide-chopp'd rascal,—'would, thou might'st lie drowning,
The washing of ten tides!
Gon. He'll be hang'd yet,
Though every drop of water swear against it, 60
And gape at wid'st to glut him.
[*A confused noise within.*] Mercy on us!—We split, we split!—Farewell, my wife and children!—Farewell, brother!—We split, we split, we split!—
Ant. Let's all sink wi' the king. [*Exit.*
Seb. Let's take leave of him. [*Exit.*

Gon. Now would I give a thousand furlongs of sea for an acre of barren gróund; long heath, brown furze, anything. The wills above be done! but I would fain die a dry death.   70
[*Exit.*

SCENE II.—The Island: before the Cell of PROSPERO.

Enter PROSPERO *and* MIRANDA.

Mira. If by your art, my dearest father, you have

Boats. "What care these roarers for the name of king?"

Put the wild waters in this roar, allay them.
The sky, it seems, would pour down stinking pitch,
But that the sea, mounting to the welkin's cheek,
Dashes the fire out. O! I have suffer'd
With those that I saw suffer: a brave vessel,
Who had no doubt some noble creatures in her,
Dash'd all to pieces. O! the cry did knock
Against my very heart. Poor souls, they perish'd.
Had I been any god of power, I would   10
Have sunk the sea within the earth, or ere
It should the good ship so have swallow'd, and
The fraughting souls within her.
Pro.   Be collected:
No more amazement. Tell your piteous heart,
There's no harm done.
Mira.   O, woe the day!
Pro.   No harm.
I have done nothing but in care of thee,
(Of thee, my dear one! thee, my daughter!) who
Art ignorant of what thou art, nought knowing
Of whence I am; nor that I am more better
Than Prospero, master of a full poor cell,   20
And thy no greater father.
Mira.   More to know
Did never meddle with my thoughts.
Pro.   'T is time
I should inform thee further. Lend thy hand,
And pluck my magic garment from me.—So:
[*Lays down his mantle.*
Lie there, my art.—Wipe thou thine eyes; have comfort.
The direful spectacle of the wrack, which touch'd
The very virtue of compassion in thee,
I have with such provision in mine art
So safely order'd, that there is no soul—
No, not so much perdition as an hair,   30
Betid to any creature in the vessel

Which thou heard'st cry, which thou saw'st sink. Sit down;
For thou must now know further.
Mira.   You have often
Begun to tell me what I am; but stopp'd,
And left me to a bootless inquisition,
Concluding, "Stay, not yet."
Pro.   The hour's now come,
The very minute bids thee ope thine ear;
Obey, and be attentive. Canst thou remember
A time before we came unto this cell?
I do not think thou canst, for then
                        thou wast not   40
Out three years old.
Mira.   Certainly, sir, I can.
Pro. By what? by any other
                        house, or person?
Of anything the image tell me,
                        that
Hath kept with thy remembrance.
Mira.   'T is far off;
And rather like a dream, than an
                        assurance
That my remembrance warrants. Had I not
Four or five women once, that
                        tended me?
Pro. Thou hadst, and more,
        Miranda. But how is it,
That this lives in thy mind?
                What seest thou else
In the dark backward and abysm
                        of time?   50
If thou remember'st aught, ere
                thou cam'st here,
How thou cam'st here, thou
                        may'st.
Mira.   But that I do not.
Pro. Twelve year since, Mi-
        randa, twelve year since,
Thy father was the Duke of Milan, and
A prince of power.
Mira.   Sir, are not
                you my father?
Pro. Thy mother was a piece of virtue, and
She said—thou wast my daughter; and thy father
Was Duke of Milan, and his only heir
A princess;—no worse issued.
Mira.   O, the heavens!
What foul play had we, that we came from thence? 60
Or blessed was't, we did?
Pro.   Both, both, my girl:
By foul play, as thou say'st, were we heav'd thence;
But blessedly holp hither.
Mira.   O! my heart bleeds
To think o' the teen that I have turn'd you to,
Which is from my remembrance. Please you, further.
Pro. My brother, and thy uncle, call'd Antonio,—
I pray thee, mark me,—that a brother should
Be so perfidious!—he whom, next thyself,
Of all the world I lov'd, and to him put
The manage of my state; as, at that time,   70
Through all the signiories it was the first,
And Prospero the prime duke; being so reputed
In dignity and, for the liberal arts,
Without a parallel: those being all my study,
The government I cast upon my brother,
And to my state grew stranger, being transported,
And rapt in secret studies. Thy false uncle—
Dost thou attend me?
Mira.   Sir, most heedfully.
Pro. Being once perfected how to grant suits,
How to deny them, who to advance, and who 80
To trash for over-topping, new created
The creatures that were mine, I say, or chang'd them,
Or else new form'd them: having both the key
Of officer and office, set all hearts i' the state
To what tune pleas'd his ear; that now he was
The ivy, which had hid my princely trunk,
And suck'd my verdure out on't.—Thou attend'st not.
Mira. O good sir! I do.

Pro.   I pray thee, mark me.
I thus neglecting worldly ends, all dedicated
To closeness, and the bettering of my mind   90
With that, which, but by being so retir'd,
O'er-priz'd all popular rate, in my false brother
Awak'd an evil nature: and my trust,
Like a good parent, did beget of him
A falsehood, in its contrary as great
As my trust was; which had, indeed, no limit,
A confidence sans bound. He being thus lorded,
Not only with what my revenue yielded,
But what my power might else exact,—like one,
Who having, unto truth, by telling of it,   100
Made such a sinner of his memory,
To credit his own lie,—he did believe
He was indeed the duke; out o' the substitution,
And executing the outward face of royalty,
With all prerogative: hence his ambition growing,—
Dost thou hear?
    Mira.   Your tale, sir, would cure deafness.
    Pro. To have no screen between this part he play'd,
And him he play'd it for, he needs will be
Absolute Milan. Me, poor man, my library
Was dukedom large enough: of temporal royalties 110
He thinks me now incapable; confederates
(So dry he was for sway) wi' the King of Naples,
To give him annual tribute, do him homage,
Subject his coronet to his crown, and bend
The dukedom, yet unbow'd, (alas, poor Milan!)
To most ignoble stooping.
    Mira.   O the heavens!
    Pro. Mark his condition, and the event; then tell me
If this might be a brother.
    Mira.   I should sin
To think but nobly of my grandmother:
Good wombs have borne bad sons.
    Pro.   Now the condition.   121
This King of Naples, being an enemy
To me inveterate, hearkens my brother's suit;
Which was, that he in lieu o' the premises,
Of homage, and I know not how much tribute,
Should presently extirpate me and mine
Out of the dukedom, and confer fair Milan,
With all the honours, on my brother: whereon,
A treacherous army levied, one midnight
Fated to the purpose, did Antonio open
The gates of Milan; and, i' the dead of darkness,   130
The ministers for the purpose hurried thence
Me, and thy crying self.
    Mira.   Alack, for pity!
I, not rememb'ring how I cried out then,
Will cry it o'er again: it is a hint,
That wrings mine eyes to 't.
    Pro.   Hear a little further,
And then I 'll bring thee to the present business
Which now 's upon us; without the which this story
Were most impertinent.
    Mira.   Wherefore did they not
That hour destroy us?
    Pro.   Well demanded, wench:
My tale provokes that question. Dear, they durst not,
So dear the love my people bore me, nor set   141
A mark so bloody on the business; but
With colours fairer painted their foul ends.
In few, they hurried us aboard a bark,
Bore us some leagues to sea; where they prepar'd
A rotten carcass of a boat, not rigg'd,
Nor tackle, sail, nor mast; the very rats
Instinctively have quit it, there they hoist us,
To cry to the sea that roar'd to us: to sigh
To the winds, whose pity, sighing back again,   150
Did us but loving wrong.
    Mira.   Alack! what trouble
Was I then to you!
    Pro.   O, a cherubin
Thou wast, that did preserve me. Thou didst smile,
Infused with a fortitude from heaven,
When I have deck'd the sea with drops full salt,
Under my burden groan'd; which rais'd in me
An undergoing stomach, to bear up
Against what should ensue.
    Mira.   How came we ashore?

Pro. By Providence divine.
Some food we had, and some fresh water, that   160
A noble Neapolitan, Gonzalo,
Out of his charity, (who being then appointed
Master of this design) did give us; with

Ari. "All hail, great master; great sir, hail!"

Rich garments, linens, stuffs, and necessaries,
Which since have steaded much: so, of his gentleness,
Knowing I lov'd my books, he furnish'd me,
From my own library, with volumes that
I prize above my dukedom.
    Mira.   'Would I might
But ever see that man!
    Pro.   Now I arise.—
Sit still, and hear the last of our sea-sorrow.   170
Here in this island we arriv'd; and here
Have I, thy schoolmaster, made thee more profit
Than other princess' can, that have more time
For vainer hours, and tutors not so careful.
    Mira. Heavens thank you for 't! And now, I pray
                    you, sir,
For still 't is beating in my mind, your reason
For raising this sea-storm?
    Pro.   Know thus far forth.—
By accident most strange, bountiful Fortune,
Now my dear lady, hath mine enemies
Brought to this shore; and by my prescience   180
I find my zenith doth depend upon
A most auspicious star, whose influence
If now I court not, but omit, my fortunes
Will ever after droop. Here cease more questions.
Thou art inclin'd to sleep; 't is a good dulness,
And give it way:—I know thou canst not choose.—
                    [Miranda *sleeps.*
Come away, servant, come! I am ready now.
Approach, my Ariel: come!

Enter Ariel.

    Ari. All hail, great master; grave sir, hail! I come
To answer thy best pleasure; be 't to fly,   190
To swim, to dive into the fire, to ride
On the curl'd clouds: to thy strong bidding task
Ariel, and all his quality.

Pro.   Hast thou, spirit,
Perform'd to point the tempest that I bade thee?
Ari. To every article.
I boarded the king's ship; now on the beak,
Now in the waist, the deck, in every cabin,
I flam'd amazement: sometimes, I'd divide,
And burn in many places; on the topmast,   200
The yards and bowsprit, would I flame distinctly,
Then meet, and join. Jove's lightnings, the pre-
   cursors
O' the dreadful thunder-claps, more momentary
And sight-outrunning were not: the fire, and cracks
Of sulphurous roaring the most mighty Neptune
Seem to besiege, and make his bold waves tremble,
Yes, his dread trident shake.
Pro.   My brave spirit!
Who was so firm, so constant, that this coil
Would not infect his reason?
Ari.   Not a soul
But felt a fever of the mad, and play'd
Some tricks of desperation. All, but mariners,   210
Plung'd in the foaming brine, and quit the vessel,
Then all a-fire with me: the king's son, Ferdinand,
With hair up-staring (then like reeds, not hair),
Was the first man that leap'd; cried, "Hell is empty,
And all the devils are here."
Pro.   Why, that's my spirit!
But was not this nigh shore?
Ari.   Close by, my master.
Pro. But are they, Ariel, safe?
Ari.   Not a hair perish'd;
On their sustaining garments not a blemish,
But fresher than before; and, as thou bad'st me,
In troops I have dispers'd them 'bout the isle.   220
The king's son have I landed by himself,
Whom I left cooling of the air with sighs,
In an odd angle of the isle, and sitting,
His arms in this sad knot.
Pro.   Of the king's ship
The mariners, say, how thou hast dispos'd,
And all the rest o' the fleet?
Ari.   Safely in harbour
Is the king's ship; in the deep nook, where once
Thou call'dst me up at midnight to fetch dew
From the still-vex'd Bermoothes; there she's hid:
The mariners all under hatches stow'd;   230
Whom, with a charm join'd to their suffer'd labour,
I have left asleep: and for the rest o' the fleet
Which I dispers'd, they all have met again,
And are upon the Mediterranean flote,
Bound sadly home for Naples,
Supposing that they saw the king's ship wrack'd,
And his great person perish.
Pro.   Ariel, thy charge
Exactly is perform'd; but there's more work.
What is the time o' the day?
Ari.   Past the mid season.
Pro. At least two glasses. The time 'twixt six and
   now   240
Must by us both be spent most preciously.
Ari. Is there more toil? Since thou dost give me
   pains,
Let me remember thee what thou hast promis'd,
Which is not yet perform'd me.
Pro.   How now? moody?
What is 't thou canst demand?
Ari.   My liberty.
Pro. Before the time be out? no more!
Ari.   I pr'ythee,
Remember, I have done thee worthy service;
Told thee no lies, made thee no mistakings, serv'd
Without or grudge, or grumblings. Thou didst promise
To bate me a full year.
Pro.   Dost thou forget   250
From what a torment I did free thee?
Ari.   No.
Pro. Thou dost; and think'st it much, to tread
   the ooze
Of the salt deep,
To run upon the sharp wind of the north,
To do me business in the veins o' th' earth,
When it is bak'd with frost.

Ari.   I do not, sir.
Pro. Thou liest, malignant thing! Hast thou forgot
The foul witch Sycorax, who, with age and envy,
Was grown into a hoop? hast thou forgot her?
Ari. No, sir.
Pro.   Thou hast. Where was she born? speak;
   tell me.   260
Ari. Sir, in Argier.
Pro.   O! was she so? I must,
Once in a month, recount what thou hast been,
Which thou forgett'st. This damn'd witch, Sycorax,
For mischiefs manifold, and sorceries terrible
To enter human hearing, from Argier,
Thou know'st, was banish'd: for one thing she did,
They would not take her life. Is not this true?
Ari. Ay, sir.
Pro. This blue-ey'd hag was hither brought with
   child,
And here was left by the sailors: thou, my slave   270
As thou report'st thyself, wast then her servant:
And, for thou wast a spirit too delicate
To act her earthy and abhorr'd commands,
Refusing her grand hests, she did confine thee,
By help of her more potent ministers,
And in her most unmitigable rage,
Into a cloven pine; within which rift
Imprison'd, thou didst painfully remain
A dozen years; within which space she died,
And left thee there, where thou didst vent thy groans
As fast as mill-wheels strike. Then was this island
(Save for the son which she did litter here,   282
A freckled whelp, hag-born) not honour'd with
A human shape.
Ari.   Yes; Caliban, her son.
Pro. Dull thing, I say so; he, that Caliban,
Whom now I keep in service. Thou best know'st
What torment I did find thee in: thy groans
Did make wolves howl, and penetrate the breasts
Of ever-angry bears. It was a torment
To lay upon the damn'd, which Sycorax   290
Could not again undo: it was mine art,
When I arriv'd and heard thee, that made gape
The pine, and let thee out.
Ari.   I thank thee, master.
Pro. If thou more murmur'st, I will rend an oak,
And peg thee in his knotty entrails, till
Thou hast howl'd away twelve winters.
Ari.   Pardon, master:
I will be correspondent to command,
And do my spriting gently.
Pro.   Do so, and after two days
I will discharge thee.
Ari.   That's my noble master!
What shall I do? say what? what shall I do?   300
Pro. Go, make thyself like a nymph o' the sea: be
   subject
To no sight but thine and mine; invisible
To every eye-ball else. Go, take this shape,
And hither come in 't: go, hence, with diligence.
                           [*Exit* ARIEL.
Awake, dear heart, awake! thou hast slept well;
Awake!
Mira. The strangeness of your story put
Heaviness in me.
Pro.   Shake it off. Come on:
We'll visit Caliban, my slave, who never
Yields us kind answer.
Mira.   'T is a villain, sir,   310
I do not love to look on.
Pro.   But, as 't is,
We cannot miss him: he does make our fire,
Fetch in our wood, and serves in offices
That profit us.—What ho! slave! Caliban!
Thou earth, thou! speak.
Cal. [*Within.*]   There's wood enough within.
Pro. Come forth, I say, there's other business for
   thee:
Come, thou tortoise! when!

       Re-enter ARIEL, *like a water-nymph.*
Fine apparition! My quaint Ariel,
Hark in thine ear.

Ari.   My lord, it shall be done.   [*Exit.*
Pro. Thou poisonous slave, got by the devil himself
Upon thy wicked dam, come forth !   321

Enter CALIBAN.

Cal. As wicked dew as e'er my mother brush'd
With raven's feather from unwholesome fen,
Drop on you both ! a south-west blow on ye,
And blister you all o'er !
Pro. For this, be sure, to-night thou shalt have
cramps,
Side-stitches that shall pen thy breath up ; urchins
Shall forth, at vast of night, that they may work
All exercise on thee : thou shalt be pinch'd
As thick as honey-comb, each pinch more stinging 330
Than bees that made them.
Cal.   I must eat my dinner.
This island 's mine, by Sycorax my mother,
Which thou tak'st from me. When thou camest first,
Thou strok'dst me, and mad'st much of me ; wouldst
give me
Water with berries in 't ; and teach me how
To name the bigger light, and how the less,
That burn by day and night : and then I lov'd thee,
And show'd thee all the qualities o' th' isle,
The fresh springs, brine-pits, barren place, and fertile.
Cursed be I that did so !—All the charms   340
Of Sycorax, toads, beetles, bats, light on you !
For I am all the subjects that you have,
Which first was mine own king ; and here you sty me,
In this hard rock, whiles you do keep from me
The rest o' the island.
Pro.   Thou most lying slave,
Whom stripes may move, not kindness ! I have us'd
thee
Filth as thou art, with human care ; and lodg'd thee
In mine own cell, till thou didst seek to violate
The honour of my child.
Cal. O ho ! O ho !—'would it had been done !   350
Thou didst prevent me ; I had peopled else
This isle with Calibans.
Pro.   Abhorred slave,
Which any print of goodness wilt not take,
Being capable of all ill ! I pitied thee,
Took pains to make thee speak, taught thee each hour
One thing or other : when thou didst not, savage,
Know thine own meaning, but wouldst gabble like
A thing most brutish, I endow'd thy purposes
With words that made them known ; but thy vile
race,
Though thou didst learn, had that in 't which good
natures   360
Could not abide to be with : therefore wast thou
Deservedly confin'd into this rock,
Who hadst deserv'd more than a prison.
Cal. You taught me language : and my profit on 't
Is, I know how to curse. The red plague rid you
For learning me your language !
Pro.   Hag-seed, hence !
Fetch us in fuel ; and be quick, thou 'rt best,
To answer other business. Shrugg'st thou, malice ?
If thou neglect'st, or dost unwillingly
What I command, I 'll rack thee with old cramps ; 370
Fill all thy bones with aches ; make thee roar,
That beasts shall tremble at thy din.
Cal.   No, 'pray thee !—
[*Aside.*] I must obey : his art is of such power,
It would control my dam's god, Setebos,
And make a vassal of him.
Pro.   So, slave ; hence ! [*Exit* CALIBAN.

Re-enter ARIEL, *invisible, playing and singing ;*
FERDINAND *following him.*

ARIEL'S SONG.

Come unto these yellow sands,
    And then take hands :
Court'sied when you have, and kiss'd,—
    The wild waves whist,—
Foot it featly here and there ;   380
And, sweet sprites, the burden bear.
    Hark ! hark !

Burden. Bowgh, wowgh.
    The watch-dogs bark :
Burden. Bowgh, wowgh.
    Hark, hark ! I hear
The strain of strutting chanticleer
Cry, Cock-a-diddle-dow.

Fer. Where should this music be ? i' the air, or the
earth ?—
It sounds no more ;—and sure, it waits upon   390
Some god o' the island. Sitting on a bank,
Weeping again the king my father's wreck,
This music crept by me upon the waters,
Allaying both their fury, and my passion,
With its sweet air : thence I have follow'd it,
Or it hath drawn me rather : but 't is gone.—
No, it begins again.

ARIEL *sings.*

Full fathom five thy father lies ;
    Of his bones are coral made ;
Those are pearls that were his eyes :   400
    Nothing of him that doth fade,
But doth suffer a sea-change
    Into something rich and strange.
Sea-nymphs hourly ring his knell :
                    [*Burden.* Ding-dong.
Hark ! now I hear them,—ding-dong, bell.

Fer. The ditty does remember my drown'd father.—
This is no mortal business, nor no sound
That the earth owes.—I hear it now above me.
Pro. The fringed curtains of thine eye advance, 410
And say, what thou seest yond.
Mira.   What is 't ? a spirit ?
Lord, how it looks about ! Believe me, sir,
It carries a brave form :—but 't is a spirit.
Pro. No, wench : it eats and sleeps, and hath such
senses
As we have, such. This gallant, which thou seest,
Was in the wrack ; and but he 's something stain'd
With grief, that 's beauty's canker, thou might'st call
him
A goodly person. He hath lost his fellows,
And strays about to find them.
Mira.   I might call him
A thing divine, for nothing natural   420
I ever saw so noble.
Pro. [*Aside.*]   It goes on, I see,
As my soul prompts it.—Spirit, fine spirit ! I 'll free
thee
Within two days for this.
Fer.   Most sure, the goddess
On whom these airs attend !—Vouchsafe, my prayer
May know if you remain upon this island,
And that you will some good instructions give,
How I may bear me here ; my prime request,
Which I do last pronounce, is, O you wonder !
If you be maid, or no ?
Mira.   No wonder, sir ;
But certainly a maid.
Fer.   My language ! heavens !— 430
I am the best of them that speak this speech,
Were I but where 't is spoken.
Pro.   How ! the best ?
What wert thou, if the King of Naples heard thee ?
Fer. A single thing, as I am now, that wonders
To hear thee speak of Naples. He does hear me,
And that he does I weep : myself am Naples ;
Who with mine eyes, ne'er since at ebb, beheld
The king, my father, wrack'd.
Mira.   Alack, for mercy !
Fer. Yes, faith, and all his lords ; the Duke of
Milan,
And his brave son, being twain.
Pro.   The Duke of Milan,
And his more braver daughter could control thee, 441
If now 't were fit to do 't.—[*Aside.*] At the first sight
They have chang'd eyes :—delicate Ariel,
I 'll set thee free for this !—[*To him.*] A word, good
sir ;
I fear, you have done yourself some wrong : a word.
Mira. Why speaks my father so ungently ? This

Is the third man that e'er I saw; the first
That e'er I sigh'd for. Pity move my father
To be inclin'd my way!
    Fer.   O! if a virgin,

The name thou ow'st not; and hast put thyself
Upon this island as a spy, to win it
From me, the lord on 't.
    Fer.   No, as I am a man.

Fer.   "Most sure, the goddess
On whom these airs attend!"

And your affection not gone forth, I 'll make you   450
    The Queen of Naples.
    Pro.   Soft, sir: one word more.—
[*Aside.*] They are both in either's powers: but this
    swift business
I must uneasy make, lest too light winning
Make the prize light. [*To him.*] One word more:
    I charge thee,
That thou attend me. Thou dost here usurp

    Mira. There's nothing ill can dwell in such a temple:
If the ill spirit have so fair a house,   460
Good things will strive to dwell with 't.
    Pro. [*To* FERD.] Follow me.—
Speak not you for him; he 's a traitor.—Come.
I 'll manacle thy neck and feet together;
Sea-water shalt thou drink, thy food shall be
The fresh-brook muscles, wither'd roots, and husks
Wherein the acorn cradled. Follow.

Fer.   No;
I will resist such entertainment, till
Mine enemy has more power.
        [He draws, and is charmed from moving.
Mira.   O, dear father!
Make not too rash a trial of him, for   470
He 's gentle, and not fearful.
Pro.   What! I say:
My foot my tutor?—Put thy sword up, traitor;
Who mak'st a show, but dar'st not strike, thy
        conscience
Is so possess'd with guilt: come from thy ward,
For I can here disarm thee with this stick,
And make thy weapon drop.
   Mira.   'Beseech you, father!
Pro. Hence! hang not on my garments.
   Mira.   Sir, have pity.
I 'll be his surety.
   Pro.   Silence! one word more
Shall make me chide thee, if not hate thee. What!
An advocate for an impostor? hush!   480
Thou think'st there is no more such shapes as
      he,
Having seen but him and Caliban: foolish wench!
To the most of men this is a Caliban,
And they to him are angels.
   Mira.   My affections

Are then most humble: I have no ambition
To see a goodlier man.
   Pro. [*To* Ferd.]   Come on; obey:
Thy nerves are in their infancy again,
And have no vigour in them.
   Fer.   So they are:
My spirits, as in a dream, are all bound up.
My father's loss, the weakness which I feel,   490
The wrack of all my friends, nor this man's threats,
To whom I am subdued, are but light to me,
Might I but through my prison once a day
Behold this maid: all corners else o' the earth
Let liberty make use of; space enough
Have I in such a prison.
   Pro.   It works.—Come on.—
Thou hast done well, fine Ariel!—[*To* Ferd.] Follow
      me.—
[*To* Ariel.] Hark, what thou else shalt do me.
   Mira.   Be of comfort.
My father 's of a better nature, sir,
Than he appears by speech: this is unwonted,   500
Which now came from him.
   Pro.   Thou shalt be as free
As mountain winds; but then exactly do
All points of my command.
   Ari.   To the syllable.
   Pro. Come, follow.—Speak not for him. [*Exeunt.*

ACT II.

Scene I.—Another Part of the Island.

Enter Alonso, Sebastian, Antonio, Gonzalo, Adrian, Francisco, *and others.*

   Gonzalo.
BESEECH you, sir, be merry: you have
      cause
(So have we all) of joy, for our escape
Is much beyond our loss. Our hint of woe
Is common: every day, some sailor's wife,
The master of some merchant, and the merchant,
Have just our theme of woe; but for the miracle,
I mean our preservation, few in millions
Can speak like us: then wisely, good sir, weigh
Our sorrow with our comfort.
   Alon.   Pr'ythee, peace.
   Seb. He receives comfort like cold porridge. 10
   Ant. The visitor will not give him o'er so.
   Seb. Look; he 's winding up the watch of his wit:
by-and-by it will strike.
   Gon. Sir,—
   Seb. One:—tell.
   Gon. When every grief is entertain'd, that 's offer'd,
Comes to the entertainer—
   Seb. A dollar.
   Gon. Dolour comes to him, indeed: you have spoken
truer than you purposed.   20
   Seb. You have taken it wiselier than I meant you
should.
   Gon. Therefore, my lord,—
   Ant. Fie, what a spendthrift is he of his tongue!
   Alon. I pry'thee, spare.
   Gon. Well, I have done. But yet—
   Seb. He will be talking.

   Ant. Which, of he or Adrian, for a good wager,
first begins to crow?
   Seb. The old cock.   30
   Ant. The cockrel.
   Seb. Done. The wager?
   Ant. A laughter.
   Seb. A match!
   Adr. Though this island seem to be desert,—
   Seb. Ha, ha, ha! So, you 're paid.
   Adr. Uninhabitable, and almost inaccessible,—
   Seb. Yet—
   Adr. Yet—
   Ant. He could not miss it.   40
   Adr. It must needs be of subtle, tender, and delicate
temperance.
   Ant. Temperance was a delicate wench.
   Adr. The air breathes upon us here most sweetly.
   Seb. As if it had lungs, and rotten ones.
   Ant. Or as 't were perfumed by a fen.
   Gon. Here is everything advantageous to life.
   Ant. True; save means to live.
   Seb. Of that there 's none, or little.   50
   Gon. How lush and lusty the grass looks! how
green!
   Ant. The ground, indeed, is tawny.
   Seb. With an eye of green in 't.
   Ant. He misses not much.
   Seb. No; he doth but mistake the truth totally.
   Gon. But the rarity of it is, which is indeed almost
beyond credit—
   Seb. As many vouch'd rarities are.   59
   Gon. That our garments, being, as they were,
drenched in the sea, hold, notwithstanding, their
freshness, and glosses; being rather new-dyed, than
stain'd with salt water.

Ant. If but one of his pockets could speak ; would it not say, he lies?

Seb. Ay, or very falsely pocket up his report.

Gon. Methinks, our garments are now as fresh as when we put them on first in Afric, at the marriage of the king's fair daughter Claribel to the King of Tunis.   70

Seb. 'T was a sweet marriage, and we prosper well in our return.

Adr. Tunis was never graced before with such a paragon to their queen.

Gon. Not since Widow Dido's time.

Ant. Widow? a pox o' that! How came that widow in? Widow Dido!

Seb. What if he had said, Widower Æneas too? Good Lord, how you take it!

Adr. Widow Dido, said you? you make me study of that : she was of Carthage; not of Tunis.   81

Gon. This Tunis, sir, was Carthage.

Adr. Carthage?

Gon. I assure you, Carthage.

Ant. His word is more than the miraculous harp.

Seb. He hath rais'd the wall, and houses too.

Ant. What impossible matter will he make easy next?

Seb. I think he will carry this island home in his pocket, and give it his son for an apple.   90

Ant. And sowing the kernels of it in the sea, bring forth more islands.

Gon. Ay?

Ant. Why, in good time.

Gon. Sir, we were talking, that our garments seem now as fresh, as when we were at Tunis at the marriage of your daughter, who is now queen.

Ant. And the rarest that e'er came there.

Seb. Bate, I beseech you, Widow Dido.

Ant. O! Widow Dido ; ay, Widow Dido.   100

Gon. Is not, sir, my doublet as fresh as the first day I wore it? I mean, in a sort.

Ant. That sort was well fish'd for.

Gon. When I wore it at your daughter's marriage?

Alon. You cram these words into mine ears, against The stomach of my sense. 'Would I had never Married my daughter there! for, coming thence, My son is lost ; and, in my rate, she too, Who is so far from Italy remov'd, I ne'er again shall see her. O thou, mine heir   110 Of Naples and of Milan! what strange fish Hath made his meal on thee?

Fran.   Sir, he may live. I saw him beat the surges under him, And ride upon their backs : he trod the water, Whose enmity he flung aside, and breasted The surge most swoln that met him : his bold head 'Bove the contentious waves he kept, and oar'd Himself with his good arms in lusty stroke To the shore, that o'er his wave-worn basis bow'd, As stooping to relieve him. I not doubt,   120 He came alive to land.

Alon.   No, no ; he 's gone.

Seb. Sir, you may thank yourself for this great loss That would not bless our Europe with your daughter, But rather lose her to an African ; Where she, at least, is banish'd from your eye, Who hath cause to wet the grief on 't.

Alon.   Pr'ythee, peace.

Seb. You were kneel'd to, and importun'd otherwise By all of us ; and the fair soul herself Weigh'd, between lothness and obedience, at Which end o' the beam she 'd bow. We have lost your son,   130 I fear, for ever : Milan and Naples have More widows in them, of this business' making, Than we bring men to comfort them : The fault 's your own.

Alon. So is the dearest of the loss.

Gon.   My Lord Sebastian, The truth you speak doth lack some gentleness, And time to speak it in ; you rub the sore, When you should bring the plaster.

Seb.   Very well.

Ant. And most chirurgeonly.

Gon. It is foul weather in us all, good sir,   140 When you are cloudy.

Seb.   Foul weather?

Ant.   Very foul.

Gon. Had I plantation of this isle, my lord,—

Ant. He 'd sow 't with nettle-seed.

Seb.   Or docks, or mallows.

Gon. And were the king on 't, what would I do?

Seb. Scape being drunk, for want of wine.

Gon. I' the commonwealth I would by contraries Execute all things, for no kind of traffic Would I admit ; no name of magistrate ; Letters should not be known ; riches, poverty, And use of service, none ; contract, succession,   150 Bourn, bound of land, tilth, vineyard, none ; No use of metal, corn, or wine, or oil : No occupation, all men idle, all ; And women too, but innocent and pure ; No sovereignty :—

Seb. Yet he would be king on 't.

Ant. The latter end of his commonwealth forgets the beginning.

Gon. All things in common nature should produce, Without sweat or endeavour : treason, felony,   160 Sword, pike, knife, gun, or need of any engine, Would I not have ; but nature should bring forth, Of its own kind, all foison, all abundance, To feed my innocent people.

Seb. No marrying 'mong his subjects?

Ant. None, man ; all idle ; whores, and knaves.

Gon. I would with such perfection govern, sir, To excel the golden age.

Seb.   'Save his majesty!

Ant. Long live Gonzalo!

Gon.   And, do you mark me, sir?—

Alon. Pr'ythee ; no more : thou dost talk nothing to me.   171

Gon. I do well believe your highness ; and did it to minister occasion to these gentlemen, who are of such sensible and nimble lungs, that they always use to laugh at nothing.

Ant. 'T was you we laugh'd at.

Gon. Who, in this kind of merry fooling, am nothing to you : so you may continue, and laugh at nothing still.

Ant. What a blow was there given!   180

Seb. An it had not fallen flat-long.

Gon. You are gentlemen of brave mettle : you would lift the moon out of her sphere, if she would continue in it five weeks without changing.

Enter ARIEL, *invisible; solemn music playing.*

Seb. We would so, and then go a bat-fowling.

Ant. Nay, good my lord, be not angry.

Gon. No, I warrant you ; I will not adventure my discretion so weakly. Will you laugh me asleep, for I am very heavy?

Ant. Go sleep, and hear us.   190

          [*All sleep but* ALON., SEB., *and* ANT.

Alon. What! all so soon asleep? I wish mine eyes Would, with themselves, shut up my thoughts : I find, They are inclin'd to do so.

Seb.   Please you, sir, Do not omit the heavy offer of it : It seldom visits sorrow ; when it doth, It is a comforter.

Ant.   We two, my lord, Will guard your person while you take your rest, And watch your safety.

Alon.   Thank you. Wondrous heavy.—   [ALONSO *sleeps.* Exit ARIEL.

Seb. What a strange drowsiness possesses them!

Ant. It is the quality o' the climate.

Seb.   Why   200 Doth it not then our eyelids sink? I find not Myself dispos'd to sleep.

Ant.   Nor I : my spirits are nimble. They fell together all, as by consent ; They dropp'd, as by a thunder-stroke. What might, Worthy Sebastian—O! what might—no more :— And yet, methinks, I see it in thy face, What thou shouldst be. The occasion speaks thee, and

My strong imagination sees a crown
Dropping upon thy head.
  Seb.   What! art thou waking?
  Ant. Do you not hear me speak?
  Seb.   I do; and, surely,
It is a sleepy language, and thou speak'st   211
Out of thy sleep. What is it thou didst say?
This is a strange repose, to be asleep
With eyes wide open; standing, speaking, moving,
And yet so fast asleep.
  Ant.   Noble Sebastian,
Thou let'st thy fortune sleep, die rather; wink'st
Whiles thou art waking.
  Seb.   Thou dost snore distinctly:
There 's meaning in thy snores.
  Ant. I am more serious than my custom: you
Must be so too, if heed me; which to do,   220
Trebles thee o'er.
  Seb.   Well: I am standing water.
  Ant. I 'll teach you how to flow.
  Seb.   Do so: to ebb
Hereditary sloth instructs me.
  Ant.   O!
If you but knew, how you the purpose cherish,
Whiles thus you mock it! how, in stripping it,
You more invest it! Ebbing men, indeed,
Most often do so near the bottom run
By their own fear, or sloth.
  Seb.   Pr'ythee, say on.
The setting of thine eye, and cheek, proclaim
A matter from thee, and a birth, indeed,   230
Which throes thee much to yield.
  Ant.   Thus, sir.
Although this lord of weak remembrance, this,
(Who shall be of as little memory,
When he is earth'd) hath here almost persuaded
(For he 's a spirit of persuasion, only
Professes to persuade) the king, his son 's alive,
'T is as impossible that he 's undrown'd,
As he that sleeps here, swims.
  Seb.   I have no hope
That he 's undrown'd.
  Ant.   O! out of that no hope,
What great hope have you! no hope, that way, is 240
Another way so high a hope, that even
Ambition cannot pierce a wink beyond,
But doubts discovery there. Will you grant with me,
That Ferdinand is drown'd?
  Seb.   He 's gone.
  Ant.   Then, tell me,
Who 's the next heir of Naples?
  Seb.   Claribel.
  Ant. She that is Queen of Tunis; she that dwells
Ten leagues beyond man's life; she that from Naples
Can have no note, unless the sun were post,
(The man i' the moon 's too slow) till new-born chins
Be rough and razorable; she, from whom   250
We all were sea-swallow'd, though some cast again;
And by that destiny to perform an act,
Whereof what 's past is prologue, what to come,
In yours and my discharge.
  Seb.   What stuff is this!—How say you?
'T is true, my brother's daughter 's Queen of Tunis;
So is she heir of Naples; 'twixt which regions
There is some space.
  Ant.   A space whose every cubit
Seems to cry out, "How shall that Claribel
Measure us back to Naples? Keep in Tunis,
And let Sebastian wake!"—Say, this were death 260
That now hath seiz'd them; why, they were no worse
Than now they are. There be that can rule Naples
As well as he that sleeps; lords that can prate
As amply and unnecessarily,
As this Gonzalo; I myself could make
A chough of as deep chat. O, that you bore
The mind that I do! what a sleep were this
For your advancement! Do you understand me?
  Seb. Methinks, I do.
  Ant.   And how does your content
Tender your own good fortune?
  Seb.   I remember, 270
You did supplant your brother Prospero.

  Ant.   True:
And look how well my garments sit upon me;
Much feater than before. My brother's servants
Were then my fellows, now they are my men.
  Seb. But, for your conscience—
  Ant. Ay, sir; where lies that? if it were a kibe,
'T would put me to my slipper; but I feel not
This deity in my bosom: twenty consciences,
That stand 'twixt me and Milan, candied be they,
And melt, ere they molest! Here lies your brother,—

  Ant.   "Draw together;
And when I rear my hand, do you the like,
To fall it on Gonzalo."

No better than the earth he lies upon,   281
If he were that which now he 's like, that 's dead,—
Whom I, with this obedient steel, three inches of it,
Can lay to bed for ever; whiles you, doing thus,
To the perpetual wink for aye might put
This ancient morsel, this Sir Prudence, who
Should not upbraid our course: for all the rest,
They 'll take suggestion as a cat laps milk;
They 'll tell the clock to any business that
We say befits the hour.
  Seb.   Thy case, dear friend, 290
Shall be my precedent: as thou got'st Milan,
I 'll come by Naples. Draw thy sword: one stroke
Shall free thee from the tribute which thou pay'st,
And I the king shall love thee.
  Ant.   Draw together;
And when I rear my hand, do you the like,
To fall it on Gonzalo.
  Seb.   O! but one word.
                   [They converse apart.

    Music. Re-enter ARIEL, *invisible.*

  Ari. My master through his art foresees the danger
That you, his friend, are in; and sends me forth
(For else his project dies) to keep them living.
                  [Sings in GONZALO'S *ear.*
    While you here do snoring lie,   300
    Open-ey'd Conspiracy
      His time doth take.
    If of life you keep a care,
    Shake off slumber, and beware:
      Awake! Awake!

Ant. Then let us both be sudden.
Gon.   Now, good angels,
Preserve the king.   [*They wake.*
Alon. Why, how now, ho! awake! Why are you
     drawn?
Wherefore this ghastly looking?
Gon.   What's the matter?
Seb. Whiles we stood here securing your repose, 310
Even now, we heard a hollow burst of bellowing
Like bulls, or rather lions : did it not wake you?
It struck mine ear most terribly.
Alon.   I heard nothing.
Ant. O! 't was a din to fright a monster's ear,
To make an earthquake : sure, it was the roar
Of a whole herd of lions.
Alon.   Heard you this, Gonzalo?
Gon. Upon mine honour, sir, I heard a humming,
And that a strange one too, which did awake me.
I shak'd you, sir, and cry'd ; as mine eyes open'd,
I saw their weapons drawn.—There was a noise, 320
That's verity : 't is best we stand upon our guard,
Or that we quit this place. Let's draw our weapons.
Alon. Lead off this ground, and let's make further
     search
For my poor son.
Gon.   Heavens keep him from these beasts,
For he is, sure, i' the island.
Alon.   Lead away.   [*Exeunt.*
Ari. Prospero, my lord, shall know what I have
     done :
So, king, go safely on to seek thy son.   [*Exit.*

SCENE II.—Another Part of the Island.

Enter CALIBAN, *with a burden of wood.*
A noise of Thunder heard.

Cal. All the infections that the sun sucks up
From bogs, fens, flats, on Prosper fall, and make
     him
By inch-meal a disease! His spirits hear me,
And yet I needs must curse ; but they 'll nor pinch,
Fright me with urchin-shows, pitch me i' the mire,
Nor lead me, like a firebrand, in the dark
Out of my way, unless he bid 'em ; but
For every trifle are they set upon me :
Sometime like apes, that moe and chatter at me,
And after, bite me ; then like hedge-hogs, which   10
Lie tumbling in my bare-foot way, and mount
Their pricks at my foot-fall : sometime am I
All wound with adders, who with cloven tongues
Do hiss me into madness.—Lo, now! lo!
Here comes a spirit of his, and to torment me,
For bringing wood in slowly : I 'll fall flat :
Perchance, he will not mind me.   17

Enter TRINCULO.

Trin. Here's neither bush nor shrub to bear off any
weather at all, and another storm brewing ; I hear it
sing i' the wind : yond same black cloud, yond huge
one, looks like a foul bombard that would shed his
liquor. If it should thunder, as it did before, I know
not where to hide my head : yond same cloud cannot
choose but fall by pailfuls.—What have we here? a
man or a fish? Dead or alive? A fish : he smells like
a fish ; a very ancient and fish-like smell ; a kind of,
not of the newest, Poor-John. A strange fish! Were
I in England now (as once I was), and had but this
fish painted, not a holiday fool there but would give a
piece of silver : there would this monster make a man :
any strange beast there makes a man. When they
will not give a doit to relieve a lame beggar, they
will lay out ten to see a dead Indian. Legg'd like a
man! and his fins like arms! Warm ; o' my troth!
I do now let loose my opinion, hold it no longer ; this
is no fish, but an islander, that hath lately suffered by
a thunder-bolt. [*Thunder.*] Alas! the storm is come
again : my best way is to creep under his gaberdine ;
there is no other shelter hereabout : misery acquaints
a man with strange bedfellows. I will here shroud,
till the dregs of the storm be past.   41

Enter STEPHANO, *singing ; a bottle in his hand.*

Ste.   *I shall no more to sea, to sea,
          Here shall I die a-shore.—*

This is a very scurvy tune to sing at a man's funeral.
Well, here's my comfort.   [*Drinks.*

*The master, the swabber, the boatswain, and I,
   The gunner, and his mate,
Lov'd Mall, Meg, and Marian, and Margery,
   But none of us car'd for Kate ;
For she had a tongue with a tang,   50
   Would cry to a sailor, Go hang :
She lov'd not the savour of tar, nor of pitch,
Yet a tailor might scratch her where-e'er she did itch ;
   Then to sea, boys, and let her go hang.*

This is a scurvy tune too ; but here's my comfort.
                              [*Drinks.*

Cal. Do not torment me : O!
Ste. What's the matter? Have we devils here? Do
you put tricks upon us with savages, and men of Inde?
Ha! I have not scap'd drowning, to be afeard now of
your four legs ; for it hath been said, As proper a man
as ever went on four legs cannot make him give
ground : and it shall be said so again, while Stephano
breathes at nostrils.   63
Cal. The spirit torments me : O!
Ste. This is some monster of the isle, with four legs,
who hath got, as I take it, an ague. Where the devil
should he learn our language? I will give him some
relief, if it be but for that : if I can recover him, and
keep him tame, and get to Naples with him, he 's a
present for any emperor that ever trod on neat's-
leather.   71
Cal. Do not torment me, pr'ythee : I 'll bring my
wood home faster.
Ste. He 's in his fit now, and does not talk after the
wisest. He shall taste of my bottle : if he have never
drunk wine afore, it will go near to remove his fit.
If I can recover him, and keep him tame, I will not
take too much for him : he shall pay for him that hath
him, and that soundly.   79
Cal. Thou dost me yet but little hurt ; thou wilt
anon, I know it by thy trembling : now Prosper works
upon thee.
Ste. Come on your ways : open your mouth ; here is
that which will give language to you, cat. Open your
mouth : this will shake your shaking, I can tell you,
and that soundly : you cannot tell who 's your friend ;
open your chaps again.   87
Trin. I should know that voice. It should be—but
he is drowned, and these are devils. O! defend me!—
Ste. Four legs, and two voices! a most delicate
monster. His forward voice, now, is to speak well
of his friend ; his backward voice is to utter foul
speeches, and to detract. If all the wine in my bottle
will recover him, I will help his ague. Come,—Amen!
I will pour some in thy other mouth.
Trin. Stephano!
Ste. Doth thy other mouth call me? Mercy! mercy!
This is a devil, and no monster : I will leave him ; I
have no long spoon.   99
Trin. Stephano!—if thou beest Stephano, touch me,
and speak to me, for I am Trinculo :—be not afeard,—
thy good friend Trinculo.
Ste. If thou beest Trinculo, come forth. I 'll pull
thee by the lesser legs : if any be Trinculo's legs, these
are they. Thou art very Trinculo indeed! How
cam'st thou to be the siege of this moon-calf? Can he
vent Trinculos?   107
Trin. I took him to be killed with a thunder-stroke.
—But art thou not drowned, Stephano? I hope now,
thou art not drowned. Is the storm overblown? I
hid me under the dead moon-calf's gaberdine for
fear of the storm. And art thou living, Stephano?
O Stephano! two Neapolitans scap'd.
Ste. Pr'ythee, do not turn me about : my stomach is
not constant.
Cal. These be fine things, an if they be not sprites.
That 's a brave god, and bears celestial liquor :
I will kneel to him.   118
Ste. How didst thou scape? How cam'st thou hither?

swear by this bottle, how thou cam'st hither. I escaped upon a butt of sack, which the sailors heaved overboard, by this bottle! which I made of the bark of a tree, with mine own hands, since I was cast a-shore.

Cal. I'll swear, upon that bottle, to be thy true subject, for the liquor is not earthly.

Ste. Here: swear then how thou escap'dst.

Trin. Swam a-shore, man, like a duck. I can swim like a duck, I'll be sworn.

Ste. Here, kiss the book. Though thou canst swim like a duck, thou art made like a goose.   130

Trin. O Stephano! hast any more of this?

Ste. The whole butt, man: my cellar is in a rock by the sea-side, where my wine is hid. How now, mooncalf? how does thine ague?

Cal. Hast thou not dropped from heaven?

Ste. Out o' the moon, I do assure thee: I was the man in the moon, when time was.

Cal. I have seen thee in her, and I do adore thee: My mistress show'd me thee, and thy dog, and thy bush.

Ste. Come, swear to that; kiss the book: I will furnish it anon with new contents: swear.   141

Trin. By this good light, this is a very shallow monster:—I afeard of him!—a very weak monster.—The man i' the moon!—a most poor credulous monster. —Well drawn, monster, in good sooth.

Cal. I'll show thee every fertile inch o' the island, And I will kiss thy foot. I pr'ythee, be my god.

Trin. By this light, a most perfidious and drunken monster; when his god's asleep, he'll rob his bottle.

Cal. I'll kiss thy foot: I'll swear myself thy subject.

Ste. Come on, then; down, and swear.   151

Trin. I shall laugh myself to death at this puppy-headed monster. A most scurvy monster: I could find in my heart to beat him,—

Ste. Come, kiss.

Trin. —but that the poor monster's in drink. An abominable monster!

Cal. I'll show thee the best springs; I'll pluck thee berries; I'll fish for thee, and get thee wood enough. A plague upon the tyrant that I serve!   160 I'll bear him no more sticks, but follow thee, Thou wondrous man.

Trin. A most ridiculous monster, to make a wonder of a poor drunkard!

Cal. I pr'ythee, let me bring thee where crabs grow; And I with my long nails will dig thee pig-nuts; Show thee a jay's nest, and instruct thee how To snare the nimble marmoset: I'll bring thee To clustering filberts, and sometimes I'll get thee   169 Young scamels from the rock. Wilt thou go with me?

Ste. I pr'ythee now, lead the way, without any more talking.—Trinculo, the king and all our company else being drowned, we will inherit here.—Here; bear my bottle.—Fellow Trinculo, we'll fill him by-and-by again.

Cal. [*Sings drunkenly.*]
        Farewell, master; farewell, farewell.

Ste. "Come, swear to that; kiss the book: I will furnish it anon with new contents: swear."

Trin. A howling monster, a drunken monster.

Cal.   No more dams I'll make for fish;
                Nor fetch in firing
                    At requiring,   180
            Nor scrape trencher, nor wash dish;
            'Ban, 'Ban, Ca—Caliban
            Has a new master—get a new man.

Freedom, hey-day! hey-day, freedom! freedom! hey day, freedom!

Ste. O brave monster! lead the way.   [*Exeunt.*

ACT III.

Scene I.—Before Prospero's Cell.

Enter Ferdinand, *bearing a log.*

Ferdinand.

HERE be some sports are painful, and their labour Delight in them sets off: some kinds of baseness Are nobly undergone; and most poor matters Point to rich ends. This my mean task Would be as heavy to me, as odious; but The mistress which I serve quickens what's dead, And makes my labours pleasures; O, she is

Ten times more gentle than her father's crabbed; And he's compos'd of harshness. I must remove Some thousands of these logs, and pile them up,   10 Upon a sore injunction: my sweet mistress Weeps when she sees me work; and says, such baseness Had never like executor. I forget: But these sweet thoughts do even refresh my labours; Most busiest when I do it.

Enter Miranda; *and* Prospero *at a distance.*

Mira.   Alas, now, pray you,

Work not so hard: I would, the lightning had
Burnt up those logs that you are enjoin'd to pile.
Pray, set it down, and rest you: when this burns,
'T will weep for having wearied you.   My father
Is hard at study; pray now, rest yourself: 20
He's safe for these three hours.
    Fer.   O most dear mistress!
The sun will set, before I shall discharge
What I must strive to do.
    Mira.   If you 'll sit down,
I 'll bear your logs the while.   Pray, give me that:
I 'll carry it to the pile.

    Mira.   "If you 'll sit down,
I 'll bear your logs the while.   Pray, give me that:
I 'll carry it to the pile."

    Fer.   No, precious creature:
I had rather crack my sinews, break my back,
Than you should such dishonour undergo,
While I sit lazy by.
    Mira.   It would become me
As well as it does you; and I should do it
With much more ease, for my good will is to it,   30
And yours it is against.
    Pro.   Poor worm! thou art infected:
This visitation shows it.
    Mira.   You look wearily.
    Fer. No, noble mistress; 'tis fresh morning with
me,
When you are by at night.   I do beseech you,
Chiefly that I might set it in my prayers,
What is your name?
    Mira.   Miranda—O my father!
I have broke your hest to say so.
    Fer.   Admir'd Miranda!
Indeed the top of admiration; worth
What's dearest to the world!   Full many a lady
I have eye'd with best regard; and many a time   40
The harmony of their tongues hath into bondage
Brought my too diligent ear: for several virtues
Have I lik'd several women; never any
With so full soul, but some defect in her
Did quarrel with the noblest grace she ow'd,
And put it to the foil: but you, O you!
So perfect, and so peerless, are created
Of every creature's best.
    Mira.   I do not know
One of my sex; no woman's face remember,
Save, from my glass, mine own; nor have I seen   50
More that I may call men, than thou, good friend,

And my dear father: how features are abroad,
I am skill-less of; but, by my modesty
(The jewel in my dower), I would not wish
Any companion in the world but you;
Nor can imagination form a shape,
Besides yourself, to like of.   But I prattle
Something too wildly, and my father's precepts
I therein do forget.
    Fer.   I am, in my condition,
A prince, Miranda; I do think, a king;   60
(I would, not so!) and would no more endure
This wooden slavery, than to suffer
The flesh-fly blow my mouth.—Hear my soul speak
The very instant that I saw you, did
My heart fly to your service; there resides,
To make me slave to it: and for your sake,
Am I this patient log-man.
    Mira.   Do you love me?
    Fer. O heaven! O earth! bear witness to this sound,
And crown what I profess with kind event,
If I speak true; if hollowly, invert   70
What best is boded me, to mischief! I,
Beyond all limit of what else i' the world,
Do love, prize, honour you.
    Mira.   I am a fool,
To weep at what I am glad of.
    Pro.   Fair encounter
Of two most rare affections!   Heavens rain grace
On that which breeds between them!
    Fer.   Wherefore weep you?
    Mira. At mine unworthiness, that dare not offer
What I desire to give; and much less take,
What I shall die to want.   But this is trifling;
And all the more it seeks to hide itself,   80
The bigger bulk it shows.   Hence, bashful cunning!
And prompt me, plain and holy innocence!
I am your wife, if you will marry me;
If not, I 'll die your maid: to be your fellow
You may deny me; but I 'll be your servant,
Whether you will or no.
    Fer.   My mistress, dearest,
And I thus humble ever.
    Mira.   My husband then?
    Fer. Ay, with a heart as willing
As bondage e'er of freedom: here 's my hand.
    Mira. And mine, with my heart in 't: and now fare-
well,   90
Till half an hour hence.
    Fer.   A thousand thousand!
               [*Exeunt* FERD. *and* MIRA.
    Pro. So glad of this as they I cannot be,
Who are surpris'd withal; but my rejoicing
At nothing can be more.   I 'll to my book;
For yet, ere supper-time, must I perform
Much business appertaining.   [*Exit.*

SCENE II.—Another Part of the Island.

Enter CALIBAN *with a bottle;* STEPHANO *and*
TRINCULO *following.*

    Ste. Tell me not:—when the butt is out, we will
drink water; not a drop before: therefore bear up,
and board 'em.—Servant-monster, drink to me.
    Trin. Servant-monster? the folly of this island!
They say, there 's but five upon this isle: we are three
of them; if the other two be brained like us, the state
totters.
    Ste. Drink, servant-monster, when I bid thee: thy
eyes are almost set in thy head.   9
    Trin. Where should they be set else? he were a
brave monster indeed, if they were set in his tail.
    Ste. My man-monster hath drowned his tongue in
sack: for my part, the sea cannot drown me: I swam,
ere I could recover the shore, five-and-thirty leagues,
off and on, by this light.—Thou shalt be my lieutenant,
monster, or my standard.
    Trin. Your lieutenant, if you list; he 's no standard.
    Ste. We 'll not run, monsieur monster.
    Trin. Nor go neither; but you 'll lie, like dogs, and
yet say nothing neither.   20

Ste. Moon-calf, speak once in thy life, if thou beest a good moon-calf.

Cal. How does thy honour? Let me lick thy shoe. I'll not serve him, he is not valiant.

Trin. Thou liest, most ignorant monster: I am in case to justle a constable. Why, thou deboshed fish thou, was there ever man a coward, that hath drunk so much sack as I to-day? Wilt thou tell a monstrous lie, being but half a fish, and half a monster?

Cal. Lo, how he mocks me! wilt thou let him, my lord?   31

Trin. Lord, quoth he!—that a monster should be such a natural!

Cal. Lo, lo, again! bite him to death, I pr'ythee.

Ste. Trinculo, keep a good tongue in your head: if you prove a mutineer, the next tree!—The poor monster's my subject, and he shall not suffer indignity.

Cal. I thank my noble lord. Wilt thou be pleas'd to hearken once again to the suit I made to thee?   40

Ste. Marry will I; kneel and repeat it, I will stand, and so shall Trinculo.

Enter ARIEL, *invisible.*

Cal. As I told thee before, I am subject to a tyrant; a sorcerer, that by his cunning hath cheated me of the island.

Ari. Thou liest.

Cal.   Thou liest, thou jesting monkey, thou; I would, my valiant master would destroy thee: I do not lie.

Ste. Trinculo, if you trouble him any more in his tale, by this hand, I will supplant some of your teeth.

Trin. Why, I said nothing.   51

Ste. Mum then, and no more.—[*To* CAL.] Proceed.

Cal. I say, by sorcery he got this isle; From me he got it: if thy greatness will, Revenge it on him—for, I know, thou dar'st; But this thing dare not.

Ste. That's most certain.

Cal. Thou shalt be lord of it, and I'll serve thee.

Ste. How now shall this be compassed? Canst thou bring me to the party?   60

Cal. Yea, yea, my lord: I'll yield him thee asleep, Where thou may'st knock a nail into his head.

Ari. Thou liest; thou canst not.

Cal. What a pied ninny's this! Thou scurvy patch! I do beseech thy greatness, give him blows, And take his bottle from him: when that's gone, He shall drink nought but brine; for I'll not show him Where the quick freshes are.

Ste. Trinculo, run into no further danger: interrupt the monster one word further, and, by this hand, I'll turn my mercy out of doors, and make a stock-fish of thee.   72

Trin. Why, what did I? I did nothing. I'll go further off.

Ste. Didst thou not say, he lied?

Ari. Thou liest.

Ste. Do I so? take thou that. [*Strikes him.*] As you like this, give me the lie another time.

Trin. I did not give the lie.—Out o' your wits, and hearing too?—A pox o' your bottle! this can sack and drinking do.—A murrain on your monster, and the devil take your fingers!   82

Cal. Ha, ha, ha!

Ste. Now, forward with your tale. Pr'ythee, stand further off.

Cal. Beat him enough: after a little time, I'll beat him too.

Ste.   Stand further.—Come, proceed.

Cal. Why, as I told thee, 't is a custom with him I' the afternoon to sleep: there thou may'st brain him, Having first seiz'd his books; or with a log   90 Batter his skull, or paunch him with a stake, Or cut his wezand with thy knife. Remember, First to possess his books; for without them He's but a sot, as I am, nor hath not One spirit to command: they all do hate him As rootedly as I. Burn but his books;

He has brave utensils (for so he calls them), Which, when he has a house, he'll deck withal: And that most deeply to consider is The beauty of his daughter; he himself   100 Calls her a nonpareil: I never saw a woman, But only Sycorax my dam, and she; But she as far surpasseth Sycorax, As great'st does least.

Ste.   Is it so brave a lass?

Cal. Ay, lord; she will become thy bed, I warrant, And bring thee forth brave brood.

Ste. Monster, I will kill this man: his daughter and I will be king and queen; (save our graces!) and Trinculo and thyself shall be viceroys.—Dost thou like the plot, Trinculo?   110

Trin. Excellent.

Ste. Give me thy hand: I am sorry I beat thee; but, while thou livest, keep a good tongue in thy head.

Cal. Within this half hour will he be asleep; Wilt thou destroy him then?

Ste.   Ay, on mine honour.

Ari. This will I tell my master.

Cal. Thou mak'st me merry: I am full of pleasure. Let us be jocund: will you troll the catch You taught me but while-ere?   120

Ste. At thy request, monster, I will do reason, any reason. Come on, Trinculo, let us sing.   [*Sings.*

Flout 'em, and scout 'em; and scout 'em, and flout 'em; Thought is free.

Cal. That's not the tune.

[ARIEL *plays the tune on a tabor and pipe.*

Ste. What is this same?

Trin. This is the tune of our catch, played by the picture of Nobody.

Ste. If thou beest a man, show thyself in thy likeness: if thou beest a devil, take 't as thou list.   130

Trin. O, forgive me my sins!

Ste. He that dies, pays all debts: I defy thee.— Mercy upon us.

Cal. Art thou afeard?

Ste. No, monster, not I.

Cal. Be not afeard; the isle is full of noises, Sounds, and sweet airs, that give delight, and hurt not. Sometimes a thousand twangling instruments Will hum about mine ears; and sometime voices, That, if I then had wak'd after long sleep,   140 Will make me sleep again: and then, in dreaming, The clouds, methought, would open, and show riches Ready to drop upon me, that when I wak'd I cry'd to dream again.

Ste. This will prove a brave kingdom to me, where I shall have my music for nothing.

Cal. When Prospero is destroyed.

Ste. That shall be by-and-by: I remember the story.

Trin. The sound is going away: let's follow it, and after do our work.   151

Ste. Lead, monster; we'll follow.—I would, I could see this taborer: he lays it on.

Trin. Wilt come? I'll follow, Stephano. [*Exeunt.*

SCENE III.—*Another Part of the Island.*

Enter ALONSO, SEBASTIAN, ANTONIO, GONZALO, ADRIAN, FRANCISCO, *and others.*

Gon. By 'r lakin, I can go no further, sir; My old bones ache: here's a maze trod, indeed, Through forth-rights and meanders! By your patience, I needs must rest me.

Alon.   Old lord, I cannot blame thee, Who am myself attach'd with weariness, To the dulling of my spirits: sit down, and rest. Even here I will put off my hope, and keep it No longer for my flatterer: he is drown'd,

Whom thus we stray to find, and the sea mocks
Our frustrate search on land. Well, let him go.   10
   Ant. [*Aside to* SEB.] I am right glad that he's so
       out of hope.
Do not, for one repulse, forego the purpose

Solemn and strange music; and PROSPERO *above,
invisible. Enter several strange shapes bringing
in a banquet: they dance about it with gentle
actions of salutation; and, inviting the* KING,
&c., to eat, they depart.

ARIEL APPEARING AS A HARPY.

That you resolv'd to effect.
   Seb. [*Aside to* ANT.]   The next advantage
Will we take throughly.
   Ant. [*Aside to* SEB.]   Let it be to-night;
For, now they are oppress'd with travel, they
Will not, nor cannot, use such vigilance,
As when they are fresh.
   Seb. [*Aside to* ANT.]   I say, to-night: no more.

   Alon. What harmony is this? my good friends, hark!
   Gon. Marvellous sweet music!
   Alon. Give us kind keepers, heavens! What were
       these?   20
   Seb. A living drollery. Now I will believe
That there are unicorns; that in Arabia
There is one tree, the phœnix' throne; one phœnix
At this hour reigning there.

Ant. I 'll believe both ;
And what does else want credit, come to me,
And I 'll be sworn 't is true : travellers ne'er did lie,
Though fools at home condemn them.
  Gon. If in Naples
I should report this now, would they believe me?
If I should say, I saw such islanders
(For, certes, these are people of the island), 30
Who, though they are of monstrous shape, yet, note,
Their manners are more gentle-kind, than of
Our human generation you shall find
Many, nay, almost any.
  Pro. [*Aside.*] Honest lord,
Thou hast said well ; for some of you there present
Are worse than devils.
  Alon. I cannot too much muse,
Such shapes, such gesture, and such sound, expressing
(Although they want the use of tongue) a kind
Of excellent dumb discourse.
  Pro. [*Aside.*] Praise in departing.
  Fran. They vanish'd strangely.
  Seb. No matter, since
They have left their viands behind, for we have
    stomachs.— 41
Will 't please you taste of what is here?
  Alon. Not I.
  Gon. Faith, sir, you need not fear. When we were
    boys,
Who would believe that there were mountaineers
Dew-lapp'd like bulls, whose throats had hanging at
    them
Wallets of flesh ? or that there were such men,
Whose heads stood in their breasts ? which now we
    find,
Each putter-out of five for one will bring us
Good warrant of.
  Alon. I will stand to, and feed,
Although my last : no matter, since I feel 50
The best is past.—Brother, my lord the duke,
Stand to, and do as we.

Thunder and lightning. Enter ARIEL *like a harpy,
claps his wings upon the table, and, with a quaint
device, the banquet vanishes.*

  Ari. You are three men of sin, whom Destiny
(That hath to instrument this lower world,
And what is in 't) the never-surfeited sea
Hath caus'd to belch up you, and, on this island
Where man doth not inhabit ; you 'mongst men
Being most unfit to live. I have made you mad;
And even with such like valour men hang and drown
Their proper selves.
  [*Seeing* ALON., SEB., *&c., draw their swords.*
    You fools ! I and my fellows 60
Are ministers of fate : the elements,
Of whom your swords are temper'd, may as well
Wound the loud winds, or with bemock'd-at stabs
Kill the still-closing waters, as diminish

One dowle that 's in my plume : my fellow-ministers
Are like invulnerable. If you could hurt,
Your swords are now too massy for your strengths,
And will not be uplifted. But, remember,
(For that 's my business to you) that you three
From Milan did supplant good Prospero; 70
Him, and his innocent child : for which foul deed
The powers, delaying, not forgetting, have
Incens'd the seas and shores, yea, all the creatures,
Against your peace. Thee of thy son, Alonso,
They have bereft ; and do pronounce by me :
Lingering perdition (worse than any death
Can be at once) shall step by step attend
You, and your ways ; whose wraths to guard you from
(Which here, in this most desolate isle, else falls 80
Upon your heads), is nothing, but heart's sorrow,
And a clear life ensuing.

*He vanishes in thunder : then, to soft music, enter the
Shapes again, and dance with mocks and mows,
and carry out the table.*

  Pro. [*Aside.*] Bravely the figure of this harpy hast
    thou
Perform'd, my Ariel ; a grace it had, devouring.
Of my instruction hast thou nothing bated,
In what thou hadst to say : so, with good life
And observation strange, my meaner ministers
Their several kinds have done. My high charms
    work,
And these, mine enemies, are all knit up
In their distractions : they now are in my power ; 90
And in these fits I leave them, while I visit
Young Ferdinand (whom they suppose is drown'd),
And his and my lov'd darling. [*Exit* PROSPERO.
  Gon. I' the name of something holy, sir, why stand
    you
In this strange stare?
  Alon. O, it is monstrous ! monstrous !
Methought, the billows spoke, and told me of it ;
The winds did sing it to me ; and the thunder,
That deep and dreadful organ-pipe, pronounc'd
The name of Prosper : it did bass my trespass.
Therefore my son i' thee ooze is bedded ; and 100
I 'll seek him deeper than e'er plummet sounded,
And with him there lie mudded. [*Exit.*
  Seb. But one fiend at a time,
I 'll fight their legions o'er.
  Ant. I 'll be thy second.
    [*Exeunt* SEB. *and* ANT.
  Gon. All three of them are desperate : their great
    guilt,
Like poison given to work a great time after,
Now gins to bite the spirits.—I do beseech you,
That are of suppler joints, follow them swiftly,
And hinder them from what this ecstasy
May now provoke them to.
  Adr. Follow, I pray you. [*Exeunt.*

ACT IV.

SCENE I.—Before PROSPERO's Cell.

Enter PROSPERO, FERDINAND, *and* MIRANDA.

Prospero.
F I have too austerely punish'd you,
Your compensation makes amends; for I
Have given you here a thread of mine own
    life,
Or that for which I live; whom once again
I tender to thy hand. All thy vexations
Were but my trials of thy love, and thou
Hast strangely stood the test: here, afore
    Heaven,
I ratify this my rich gift. O Ferdinand!
Do not smile at me that I boast her off,
For thou shalt find she will outstrip all
    praise   10
And make it halt behind her.
    Fer.   I do believe it,
Against an oracle.
    Pro. Then, as my gift, and thine own acquisition
Worthily purchas'd, take my daughter: but
If thou dost break her virgin-knot before
All sanctimonious ceremonies may,
With full and holy rite, be minister'd,
No sweet aspersion shall the heavens let fall
To make this contract grow, but barren hate,
Sour-ey'd disdain, and discord, shall bestrew   20
The union of your bed with weeds so loathly,
That you shall hate it both: therefore, take heed,
As Hymen's lamps shall light you.
    Fer.   As I hope
For quiet days, fair issue, and long life,
With such love as 't is now,—the murkiest den,
The most opportune place, the strong'st suggestion
Our worser Genius can, shall never melt
Mine honour into lust, to take away
The edge of that day's celebration,
When I shall think, or Phœbus' steeds are founder'd,
Or night kept chain'd below.
    Pro.   Fairly spoke.   31
Sit then, and talk with her; she is thine own.—
What, Ariel, my industrious servant Ariel!

Enter ARIEL.

Ari. What would my potent master? here I am.
Pro. Thou and thy meaner fellows your last service
Did worthily perform, and I must use you
In such another trick. Go, bring the rabble,
O'er whom I give thee power, here, to this place:
Incite them to quick motion; for I must
Bestow upon the eyes of this young couple   40
Some vanity of mine art: it is my promise,
And they expect it from me.
    Ari.   Presently?
Pro. Ay, with a twink.
Ari. Before you can say, "come," and "go,"
And breathe twice, and cry, "so so·"
Each one, tripping on his toe,
Will be here with mop and mow.
Do you love me, master? no?
Pro. Dearly, my delicate Ariel. Do not approach,
Till thou dost hear me call.
Ari.   Well, I conceive. [*Exit.*
Pro. Look, thou be true. Do not give dalliance   51
Too much the rein: the strongest oaths are straw
To the fire i' the blood. Be more abstemious,
Or else good night your vow.
    Fer.   I warrant you, sir;
The white-cold virgin snow upon my heart
Abates the ardour of my liver.
    Pro.   Well.—
Now come, my Ariel! bring a corollary,
Rather than want a spirit: appear, and pertly.—
No tongue, all eyes; be silent.   [*Soft music.*

Enter IRIS.

Iris. Ceres, most bounteous lady, thy rich leas   60
Of wheat, rye, barley, vetches, oats, and pease;
Thy turfy mountains, where live nibbling sheep,
And flat meads thatch'd with stover, them to keep;
Thy banks with pioned and twilled brims,
Which spongy April at thy hest betrims,
To make cold nymphs chaste crowns; and thy broom-
    groves,
Whose shadow the dismissed bachelor loves,
Being lass-lorn; thy pole-clipt vineyard;
And thy sea-marge, steril, and rocky-hard,
Where thou thyself dost air; the queen o' the sky, 70
Whose watery arch and messenger am I,
Bids thee leave these, and with her sovereign grace,
Here on this grass-plot, in this very place,
To come and sport: her peacocks fly amain:
Approach, rich Ceres, her to entertain.

Enter CERES.

Cer. Hail, many-colour'd messenger, that ne'er
Dost disobey the wife of Jupiter;
Who with thy saffron wings upon my flowers
Diffusest honey-drops, refreshing showers;
And with each end of thy blue bow dost crown   80
My bosky acres, and my unshrubb'd down,
Rich scarf to my proud earth; why hath thy queen
Summon'd me hither, to this short-grass'd green?
Iris. A contract of true love to celebrate,
And some donation freely to estate
On the bless'd lovers.
Cer.   Tell me, heavenly bow,
If Venus, or her son, as thou dost know,
Do now attend the queen? Since they did plot
The means that dusky Dis my daughter got,
Her and her blind boy's scandal'd company
I have forsworn.
Iris.   Of her society
Be not afraid: I met her deity
Cutting the clouds towards Paphos, and her son
Dove-drawn with her. Here thought they to have
    done
Some wanton charm upon this man and maid,
Whose vows are, that no bed-rite shall be paid
Till Hymen's torch be lighted; but in vain:
Mars's hot minion is return'd again;
Her waspish-headed son has broke his arrows,
Swears he will shoot no more, but play with sparrows,
And be a boy right out.
Cer.   Highest queen of state,   101
Great Juno comes: I know her by her gait.

Enter JUNO.

Jun. How does my bounteous sister? Go with me,
To bless this twain, that they may prosperous be,
And honour'd in their issue.

Song.

Jun. Honour, riches, marriage-blessing,
Long continuance, and increasing,
Hourly joys be still upon you!
Juno sings her blessings on you.

Cer. Earth's increase, foison plenty,   110
Barns and garners never empty;
Vines with clust'ring bunches growing;
Plants with goodly burden bowing;
Spring come to you, at the farthest,
In the very end of harvest!
Scarcity and want shall shun you;
Ceres' blessing so is on you.

Fer. This is a most majestic vision, and
Harmonious charmingly. May I be bold
To think these spirits?
Pro.   Spirits, which by mine art
I have from their confines call'd, to enact   121
My present fancies.
Fer.   Let me live here ever:
So rare a wonder'd father, and a wife,
Makes this place Paradise.
[Juno and Ceres whisper, and send
Iris on employment.
Pro.   Sweet, now, silence!
Juno and Ceres whisper seriously;
There's something else to do. Hush, and be
mute,
Or else our spell is marr'd.
Iris. You nymphs, call'd Naiads, of the wan-
dering brooks,
With your sedg'd crowns, and ever-harmless
looks,
Leave your crisp channels, and on this green
land   130
Answer your summons: Juno does command.
Come, temperate nymphs, and help to celebrate
A contract of true love: be not too late.

Enter certain Nymphs.

You sun-burnt sicklemen, of August weary,
Come hither from the furrow, and be merry.
Make holiday: your rye-straw hats put on,
And these fresh nymphs encounter every one
In country footing.

*Enter certain Reapers, properly habited: they join
with the Nymphs in a graceful dance; towards
the end whereof Prospero starts suddenly, and
speaks; after which, to a strange, hollow, and confused noise, they heavily vanish.*

Pro. [Aside.] I had forgot that foul conspiracy
Of the beast Caliban, and his confederates,   140
Against my life; the minute of their plot
Is almost come.—[To the Spirits.] Well done.—Avoid;
—no more.
Fer. This is strange: your father's in some passion
That works him strongly.
Mira.   Never till this day,
Saw I him touch'd with anger so distemper'd.
Pro. You do look, my son, in a mov'd sort,
As if you were dismay'd: be cheerful, sir.
Our revels now are ended. These our actors,
As I foretold you, were all spirits, and
Are melted into air, into thin air: 150
And, like the baseless fabric of this vision,
The cloud-capp'd towers, the gorgeous palaces,
The solemn temples, the great globe itself,
Yea, all which it inherit, shall dissolve,
And, like this insubstantial pageant faded,
Leave not a rack behind. We are such stuff
As dreams are made on, and our little life
Is rounded with a sleep.—Sir, I am vex'd:
Bear with my weakness; my old brain is troubled:
Be not disturb'd with my infirmity.   160
If you be pleas'd, retire into my cell,
And there repose: a turn or two I'll walk,
To still my beating mind.
Fer., Mira.   We wish your peace. [Exeunt.
Pro. Come with a thought!—I thank thee.—Ariel,
come!

Enter Ariel.

Ari. Thy thoughts I cleave to. What's thy plea-
sure?
Pro.   Spirit,
We must prepare to meet with Caliban.
Ari. Ay, my commander: when I presented Ceres,
I thought to have told thee of it; but I fear'd,
Lest I might anger thee.
Pro. Say again, where didst thou leave these
varlets?   170
Ari. I told you, sir, they were red-hot with
drinking:
So full of valour, that they smote the air
For breathing in their faces; beat the ground

THE DANCE OF THE REAPERS.

For kissing of their feet, yet always bending
Towards their project. Then I beat my tabor,
At which, like unback'd colts, they prick'd their ears,
Advanc'd their eyelids, lifted up their noses,
As they smelt music: so I charm'd their ears,
That, calf-like, they my lowing follow'd, through
Tooth'd briers, sharp furzes, pricking goss, and
thorns,   180
Which enter'd their frail shins: at last I left them
I' the filthy-mantled pool beyond your cell,
There dancing up to the chins, that the foul lake
O'erstunk their feet.
Pro.   This was well done, my bird.
Thy shape invisible retain thou still:
The trumpery in my house, go, bring it hither,
For stale to catch these thieves.
Ari.   I go, I go.   [Exit.
Pro. A devil, a born devil, on whose nature
Nurture can never stick; on whom my pains,
Humanely taken, all, all lost, quite lost;   190
And as with age his body uglier grows,
So his mind cankers. I will plague them all,
Even to roaring.

Re-enter Ariel, loaden with glistering apparel, &c.

Come, hang them on this line.

Prospero and Ariel remain invisible. Enter
Caliban, Stephano, and Trinculo, all wet.

Cal. Pray you, tread softly, that the blind mole
may not
Hear a foot fall; we now are near his cell.
Ste. Monster, your fairy, which, you say, is a harmless fairy, has done little better than played the Jack
with us.
Trin. Monster, I do smell all horse-piss, at which my
nose is in great indignation.   200
Ste. So is mine. Do you hear, monster? If I should
take a displeasure against you, look you,—

Trin. Thou wert but a lost monster.
Cal. Good my lord, give me thy favour still.
Be patient, for the prize I 'll bring thee to
Shall hoodwink this mischance : therefore, speak
    softly ;
All 's hush'd as midnight yet.
    Trin. Ay, but to lose our bottles in the pool,—

Trin. Do, do : we steal by line and level, an 't like
your grace.   240
Ste. I thank thee for that jest ; here 's a garment
for 't : wit shall not go unrewarded, while I am
king of this country. " Steal by line and level," is
an excellent pass of pate ; there 's another garment
for 't.

CALIBAN, STEPHANO, AND TRINCULO HUNTED BY HOUNDS.

Ste. There is not only disgrace and dishonour in
that, monster, but an infinite loss.   210
    Trin. That 's more to me than my wetting : yet this
is your harmless fairy, monster.
    Ste. I will fetch off my bottle, though I be o'er ears
for my labour.
    Cal. Pr'ythee, my king, be quiet. Seest thou here,
This is the mouth o' the cell : no noise, and enter :
Do that good mischief, which may make this island
Thine own for ever, and I, thy Caliban,
For aye thy foot-licker.
    Ste. Give my thy hand. I do begin to have bloody
thoughts.   221
    Trin. O King Stephano ! O peer ! O worthy
Stephano ! look, what a wardrobe here is for thee !
    Cal. Let it alone, thou fool : it is but trash.
    Trin. O, ho, monster ! we know what belongs to a
frippery :—O King Stephano !
    Ste. Put off that gown, Trinculo : by this hand, I 'll
have that gown.
    Trin. Thy grace shall have it.
    Cal. The dropsy drown this fool ! what do you mean,
To dote thus on such luggage ? Let 's alone,   231
And do the murder first : if he awake,
From toe to crown he 'll fill our skins with pinches ;
Make us strange stuff.
    Ste. Be you quiet, monster.—Mistress line, is not
this my jerkin ? Now is the jerkin under the line :
now, jerkin, you are like to lose your hair, and prove
a bald jerkin.

Trin. Monster, come, put some lime upon your
fingers, and away with the rest.
    Cal. I will have none on 't : we shall lose our
    time,
And all be turn'd to barnacles, or to apes
With foreheads villainous low.   250
    Ste. Monster, lay-to your fingers : help to bear this
away, where my hogshead of wine is, or I 'll turn you
out of my kingdom. Go to ; carry this.
    Trin. And this.
    Ste. Ay, and this.

*A noise of hunters heard. Enter divers Spirits, in
    shape of hounds, and hunt them about :* PROSPERO
    and ARIEL *setting them on.*

Pro. Hey, Mountain, hey !
    Ari. Silver, there it goes, Silver !
    Pro. Fury, Fury ! there, Tyrant, there ! hark, hark !
    [CAL., STE., *and* TRIN. *are driven out.*
Go, charge my goblins that they grind their joints
With dry convulsions ; shorten up their sinews   260
With aged cramps, and more pinch-spotted make
    them,
Than pard or cat o' mountain.
    Ari.   Hark ! they roar.
    Pro. Let them be hunted soundly. At this hour
Lie at my mercy all mine enemies :
Shortly shall all my labours end, and thou
Shalt have the air at freedom : for a little
Follow, and do me service.   [*Exeunt.*

ACT V.

Scene I.—Before the Cell of Prospero.

Enter Prospero in his magic robes; and Ariel.

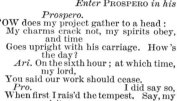

Prospero.
NOW does my project gather to a head :
My charms crack not, my spirits obey,
    and time
Goes upright with his carriage. How 's
    the day?
    Ari. On the sixth hour ; at which time,
    my lord,
You said our work should cease.
    Pro.   I did say so,
When first I rais'd the tempest. Say, my
    spirit,
How fares the king and 's followers?
    Ari.   Confin'd together
In the same fashion as you gave in
    charge ;
Just as you left them : all prisoners, sir,
In the line-grove which weather-fends
    your cell ;   10
They cannot budge till your release. The
    king,
His brother, and yours, abide all three distracted,
And the remainder mourning over them,
Brimful of sorrow and dismay ; but chiefly
Him that you term'd, sir, the good old lord, Gonzalo :
His tears run down his beard, like winter's drops
From eaves of reeds. Your charm so strongly works
    them,
That if you now beheld them, your affections
Would become tender.
    Pro.   Dost thou think so, spirit?
    Ari. Mine would, sir, were I human.
    Pro.   And mine shall.
Hast thou, which art but air, a touch, a feeling   21
Of their afflictions, and shall not myself,
One of their kind, that relish all as sharply
Passion as they, be kindlier mov'd than thou art?
Though with their high wrongs I am struck to the
    quick,
Yet, with my nobler reason, 'gainst my fury
Do I take part. The rarer action is
In virtue than in vengeance : they being penitent,
The sole drift of my purpose doth extend
Not a frown further. Go, release them, Ariel.   30
My charms I 'll break, their senses I 'll restore,
And they shall be themselves.
    Ari.   I 'll fetch them, sir. [*Exit.*
    Pro. Ye elves of hills, brooks, standing lakes, and
    groves ;
And ye, that on the sands with printless foot
Do chase the ebbing Neptune, and do fly him,
When he comes back ; you demi-puppets, that
By moonshine do the green-sour ringlets make,
Whereof the ewe not bites ; and you, whose pastime
Is to make midnight mushrooms ; that rejoice
To hear the solemn curfew ; by whose aid   40
(Weak masters though ye be) I have bedimm'd
The noontide sun, call'd forth the mutinous winds,
And 'twixt the green sea and the azur'd vault
Set roaring war : to the dread rattling thunder
Have I given fire, and rifted Jove's stout oak
With his own bolt : the strong-bas'd promontory
Have I made shake ; and by the spurs pluck'd up
The pine and cedar : graves, at my command,
Have waked their sleepers, op'd, and let them forth
By my so potent art. But this rough magic   50

I here abjure ; and, when I have requir'd
Some heavenly music (which even now I do),
To work mine end upon their senses, that
This airy charm is for, I 'll break my staff,
Bury it certain fathoms in the earth,
And, deeper than did ever plummet sound,
I 'll drown my book.   [*Solemn music.*

*Re-enter Ariel : after him, Alonso, with a frantic
gesture, attended by Gonzalo ; Sebastian and
Antonio in like manner, attended by Adrian
and Francisco : they all enter the circle which
Prospero had made, and there stand charmed ;
which Prospero observing, speaks.*

A solemn air, and the best comforter
To an unsettled fancy, cure thy brains,
Now useless, boil'd within thy skull ! There stand,   60
For you are spell-stopp'd.—
Holy Gonzalo, honourable man,
Mine eyes, even sociable to the show of thine,
Fall fellowly drops.—The charm dissolves apace ;
And as the morning steals upon the night,
Melting the darkness, so their rising senses
Begin to chase the ignorant fumes that mantle
Their clearer reason.—O good Gonzalo !
My true preserver, and a loyal sir
To him thou follow'st, I will pay thy graces   70
Home, both in word and deed.—Most cruelly
Didst thou, Alonso, use me and my daughter :
Thy brother was a furtherer in the act ;—
Thou 'rt pinch'd for 't now, Sebastian.—Flesh and
    blood,
You brother mine, that entertain'd ambition,
Expell'd remorse and nature ; who, with Sebastian
(Whose inward pinches therefore are most strong),
Would here have kill'd your king ; I do forgive thee,
Unnatural though thou art.—Their understanding
Begins to swell, and the approaching tide   80
Will shortly fill the reasonable shores,
That now lie foul and muddy. Not one of them,
That yet looks on me, or would know me.—Ariel,
Fetch me the hat and rapier in my cell ; [*Exit Ariel.*
I will disease me, and myself present,
As I was sometime Milan.—Quickly, spirit ;
Thou shalt ere long be free.

*Ariel re-enters, singing, and helps to attire
Prospero.*

    *Ari. Where the bee sucks, there suck I :
        In a cowslip's bell I lie ;
        There I couch when owls do cry.   90
        On the bat's back I do fly
        After summer merrily.
        Merrily, merrily, shall I live now,
        Under the blossom that hangs on the bough.*

    Pro. Why, that 's my dainty Ariel ! I shall miss
    thee ;
But yet thou shalt have freedom :—so, so, so.—
To the king's ship, invisible as thou art :
There shalt thou find the mariners asleep
Under the hatches ; the master, and the boatswain,
Being awake, enforce them to this place,   100
And presently, I pr'ythee.
    Ari. I drink the air before me, and return
Or e'er your pulse twice beat.   [*Exit Ariel.*

Gon. All torment, trouble, wonder, and amazement
Inhabits here : some heavenly power guide us
Out of this fearful country !
   Pro.   Behold, sir king,
The wronged Duke of Milan, Prospero.
For more assurance that a living prince
Does now speak to thee, I embrace thy body ;
And to thee, and thy company, I bid   110
A hearty welcome.

Pro. "For more assurance that a living prince
Does now speak to thee, I embrace thy body."

   Alon.   Whe'r thou beest he, or no,
Or some enchanted trifle to abuse me,
As late I have been, I not know : thy pulse
Beats as of flesh and blood ; and, since I saw thee,
The affliction of my mind amends, with which,
I fear, a madness held me. This must crave
(An if this be at all) a most strange story.
Thy dukedom I resign ; and do entreat
Thou pardon me my wrongs. — But how should Prospero
Be living, and be here ?
   Pro.   First, noble friend,   120
Let me embrace thine age, whose honour cannot
Be measur'd, or confin'd.
   Gon.   Whether this be,
Or be not, I 'll not swear.
   Pro.   You do yet taste
Some subtleties o' the isle, that will not let you
Believe things certain.—Welcome, my friends all.—
[*Aside to* SEB. *and* ANT.] But you, my brace of lords,
were I so minded,
I here could pluck his highness' frown upon you,
And justify you traitors : at this time
I will tell no tales.
   Seb. [*Aside.*]   The devil speaks in him.
   Pro.   No.—
For you, most wicked sir, whom to call brother   130
Would even infect my mouth, I do forgive
Thy rankest fault ; all of them ; and require
My dukedom of thee, which perforce, I know,
Thou must restore.
   Alon.   If thou beest Prospero,
Give us particulars of thy preservation :
How thou hast met us here, who three hours since
Were wrack'd upon this shore ; where I have lost
(How sharp the point of this remembrance is !)
My dear son Ferdinand.
   Pro.   I am woe for 't, sir.
   Alon. Irreparable is the loss, and patience   140
Says it is past her cure.
   Pro.   I rather think,
You have not sought her help ; of whose soft grace,
For the like loss I have her sovereign aid,
And rest myself content.
   Alon.   You the like loss ?
   Pro. As great to me, as late ; and, supportable

To make the dear loss, have I means much weaker
Than you may call to comfort you, for I
Have lost my daughter.
   Alon.   A daughter ?
O heavens ! that they were living both in Naples,
The king and queen there ! that they were, I wish 150
Myself were mudded in that oozy bed
Where my son lies. When did you lose your daughter ?
   Pro. In this last tempest. I perceive, these lords
At this encounter do so much admire,
That they devour their reason, and scarce think
Their eyes do offices of truth, their words
Are natural breath : but, howsoe'er you have
Been justled from your senses, know for certain,
That I am Prospero, and that very duke
Which was thrust forth of Milan ; who most strangely
Upon this shore, where you were wrack'd, was landed,   161
To be the lord on 't. No more yet of this ;
For 't is a chronicle of day by day,
Not a relation for a breakfast, nor
Befitting this first meeting. Welcome, sir ;
This cell 's my court : here have I few attendants,
And subjects none abroad : pray you, look in.
My dukedom since you have given me again,
I will requite you with as good a thing ;
At least, bring forth a wonder, to content ye   170
As much as me my dukedom.

The entrance of the cell opens, and discovers FER-
DINAND *and* MIRANDA *playing at chess.*

   Mira. Sweet lord, you play me false.
   Fer.   No, my dearest love,
I would not for the world.
   Mira. Yes, for a score of kingdoms you should wrangle,
And I would call it fair play.
   Alon.   If this prove
A vision of the island, one dear son
Shall I twice lose.
   Seb.   A most high miracle !
   Fer. Though the seas threaten, they are merciful :
I have curs'd them without cause.
                 [FERD. *kneels to* ALON.
   Alon.   Now, all the blessings 180
Of a glad father compass thee about !
Arise, and say how thou cam'st here.
   Mira.   O wonder !
How many goodly creatures are there here !
How beauteous mankind is ! O brave new world,
That has such people in 't !
   Pro.   'T is new to thee.
   Alon. What is this maid, with whom thou wast at play ?
Your eld'st acquaintance cannot be three hours :
Is she the goddess that hath sever'd us,
And brought us thus together ?
   Fer.   Sir, she is mortal ;
But, by immortal Providence, she 's mine :
I chose her, when I could not ask my father 190
For his advice, nor thought I had one. She
Is daughter to this famous Duke of Milan,
Of whom so often I have heard renown,
But never saw before ; of whom I have
Receiv'd a second life ; and second father
This lady makes him to me.
   Alon.   I am hers.
But O ! how oddly will it sound, that I
Must ask my child forgiveness.
   Pro.   There, sir, stop :
Let us not burden our remembrances with
A heaviness that 's gone.
   Gon.   I have inly wept, 200
Or should have spoke ere this. Look down, you gods,
And on this couple drop a blessed crown,
For it is you that have chalk'd forth the way,
Which brought us hither !
   Alon.   I say, Amen, Gonzalo.
   Gon. Was Milan thrust from Milan, that his issue
Should become kings of Naples ? O ! rejoice
Beyond a common joy, and set it down
With gold on lasting pillars. In one voyage

Did Claribel her husband find at Tunis ;
And Ferdinand, her brother, found a wife,   210
Where he himself was lost ; Prospero his dukedom,
In a poor isle ; and all of us, ourselves,
When no man was his own.
  Alon. [*To* FERD. *and* MIR.] Give me your hands :
Let grief and sorrow still embrace his heart
That doth not wish you joy !
  Gon.   Be it so : Amen.

Re-enter ARIEL, *with the Master and Boatswain
amazedly following.*

O look, sir ! look, sir ! here is more of us.
I prophesied, if a gallows were on land,
This fellow could not drown.—Now, blasphemy,
That swear'st grace o'erboard, not an oath on shore ?
Hast thou no mouth by land ? What is the news ? 220
  Boats. The best news is, that we have safely found
Our king, and company : the next, our ship,
Which but three glasses since we gave out split,
Is tight, and yare, and bravely rigg'd, as when
We first put out to sea.
  Ari. [*Aside to* PRO.] Sir, all this service
Have I done since I went.
  Pro. [*Aside to* ARI.]   My tricksy spirit !
  Alon. These are not natural events ; they strengthen
From strange to stranger.—Say, how came you hither ?
  Boats. If I did think, sir, I were well awake,
I'd strive to tell you. We were dead of sleep,   230
And (how, we know not) all clapp'd under hatches,
Where, but even now, with strange and several noises
Of roaring, shrieking, howling, jingling chains,
And more diversity of sounds, all horrible,
We were awak'd ; straightway, at liberty :
Where we, in all her trim, freshly beheld
Our royal, good, and gallant ship ; our master
Capering to eye her : on a trice, so please you,
Even in a dream, were we divided from them,
And were brought moping hither.
  Ari. [*Aside to* PRO.]   Was't well done ?
  Pro. [*Aside to* ARI.] Bravely, my diligence ! Thou
    shalt be free.   241
  Alon. This is as strange a maze as e'er men trod ;
And there is in this business more than nature
Was ever conduct of : some oracle
Must rectify our knowledge.
  Pro.   Sir, my liege,
Do not infest your mind with beating on
The strangeness of this business : at pick'd leisure,
Which shall be shortly, single I'll resolve you
(Which to you shall seem probable) of every
These happen'd accidents ; till when, be cheerful, 250
And think of each thing well.—[*Aside to* ARI.] Come
    hither, spirit :
Set Caliban and his companions free ;
Untie the spell. [*Exit* ARIEL.] How fares my
    gracious sir ?
There are yet missing of your company
Some few odd lads, that you remember not.

Re-enter ARIEL, *driving in* CALIBAN, STEPHANO, *and*
TRINCULO, *in their stolen apparel.*

  Ste. Every man shift for all the rest, and let no man
take care for himself, for all is but fortune.—Coragio !
bully-monster, coragio !
  Trin. If these be true spies which I wear in my
head, here's a goodly sight.   260

  Cal. O Setebos ! these be brave spirits, indeed.
How fine my master is ! I am afraid
He will chastise me.
  Seb.   Ha, ha !
What things are these, my Lord Antonio ?
Will money buy them ?
  Ant.   Very like : one of them
Is a plain fish, and, no doubt, marketable.
  Pro. Mark but the badges of these men, my lords,
Then say, if they be true.—This misshapen knave,
His mother was a witch ; and one so strong
That could control the moon, make flows and ebbs, 270
And deal in her command, without her power.
These three have robb'd me ; and this demi-devil
(For he's a bastard one) had plotted with them
To take my life : two of these fellows you
Must know, and own ; this thing of darkness I
Acknowledge mine.
  Cal.   I shall be pinch'd to death.
  Alon. Is not this Stephano, my drunken butler ?
  Seb. He is drunk now : where had he wine ?
  Alon. And Trinculo is reeling ripe : where should they
Find this grand liquor that hath gilded 'em ? 280
How cam'st thou in this pickle ?
  Trin. I have been in such a pickle, since I saw you
last, that, I fear me, will never out of my bones : I
shall not fear fly-blowing.
  Seb. Why, how now, Stephano ?
  Ste. O ! touch me not : I am not Stephano, but a
cramp.
  Pro. You'd be king of the isle, sirrah ?
  Ste. I should have been a sore one then.
  Alon. [*Pointing to* CAL.] This is a strange thing as
e'er I look'd on.   290
  Pro. He is as disproportion'd in his manners
As in his shape.—Go, sirrah, to my cell ;
Take with you your companions : as you look
To have my pardon, trim it handsomely.
  Cal. Ay, that I will ; and I'll be wise hereafter,
And seek for grace. What a thrice-double ass
Was I, to take this drunkard for a god,
And worship this dull fool !
  Pro.   Go to ; away !
  Alon. Hence, and bestow your luggage where you
    found it.
  Seb. Or stole it, rather. [*Exeunt* CAL., STE., *and* TRIN.
  Pro. Sir, I invite your highness, and your train, 301
To my poor cell, where you shall take your rest
For this one night ; which, part of it, I'll waste
With such discourse, as, I not doubt, shall make it
Go quick away ; the story of my life,
And the particular accidents gone by,
Since I came to this isle : and in the morn,
I'll bring you to your ship, and so to Naples,
Where I have hope to see the nuptial
Of these our dear-belov'd solemnised :—   310
And thence retire me to my Milan, where
Every third thought shall be my grave.
  Alon.   I long
To hear the story of your life, which must
Take the ear strangely.
  Pro.   I'll deliver all ;
And promise you calm seas, auspicious gales,
And sail so expeditious, that shall catch
Your royal fleet far off.—My Ariel,—chick,—
That is thy charge ; then to the elements !
Be free, and fare thou well !—Please you, draw near.
                                 [*Exeunt.*

EPILOGUE.

Spoken by PROSPERO.

Now my charms are all o'erthrown,
And what strength I have's mine own ;
Which is most faint : now, 'tis true,
I must be here confin'd by you,
Or sent to Naples. Let me not,
Since I have my dukedom got,
And pardon'd the deceiver, dwell
In this bare island, by your spell ;
But release me from my bands,
With the help of your good hands.   10

Gentle breath of yours my sails
Must fill, or else my project fails,
Which was to please. Now I want
Spirits to enforce, art to enchant ;
And my ending is despair,
Unless I be reliev'd by prayer,
Which pierces so, that it assaults
Mercy itself, and frees all faults.
As you from crimes would pardon'd be,
Let your indulgence set me free.   20

THE TWO GENTLEMEN OF VERONA.

DRAMATIS PERSONÆ.

DUKE OF MILAN, *Father to Silvia.*
VALENTINE, } *the Two Gentlemen.*
PROTEUS, }
ANTONIO, *Father to Proteus.*
THURIO, *a foolish Rival to Valentine.*
EGLAMOUR, *Agent for Silvia in her escape.*
SPEED, *a clownish Servant to Valentine.*
LAUNCE, *the like to Proteus.*
PANTHINO, *Servant to Antonio.*

Host, *where Julia lodges.*
Outlaws *with Valentine.*

JULIA, *beloved of Proteus.*
SILVIA, *beloved of Valentine.*
LUCETTA, *Waiting-woman to Julia.*

Servants, Musicians.

SCENE—Sometimes in VERONA, sometimes in MILAN, and on the frontiers of MANTUA.

ACT I.

SCENE I.—An open Place in Verona.

Enter VALENTINE *and* PROTEUS.

Valentine.

CEASE to persuade, my loving Proteus :
Home-keeping youth have ever homely wits.
Were't not affection chains thy tender days
To the sweet glances of thy honour'd love,
I rather would entreat thy company,
To see the wonders of the world abroad,
Than, living dully sluggardis'd at home,
Wear out thy youth with shapeless idleness.
But since thou lov'st, love still, and thrive therein,
Even as I would, when I to love begin.   10
Pro. Wilt thou be gone? Sweet Valentine, adieu.
Think on thy Proteus, when thou haply seest
Some rare note-worthy object in thy travel :
Wish me partaker in thy happiness,
When thou dost meet good hap ; and in thy danger,
If ever danger do environ thee,
Commend thy grievance to my holy prayers,
For I will be thy beadsman, Valentine.
Val. And on a love-book pray for my success.
Pro. Upon some book I love, I'll pray for thee.   20
Val. That's on some shallow story of deep love,
How young Leander cross'd the Hellespont.
Pro. That's a deep story of a deeper love,
For he was more than over shoes in love.
Val. 'T is true ; for you are over boots in love,
And yet you never swum the Hellespont.
Pro. Over the boots? nay, give me not the boots.
Val. No, I will not, for it boots thee not.
Pro.   What?
Val. To be in love, where scorn is bought with groans ;
Coy looks, with heart-sore sighs ; one fading moment's mirth,   30
With twenty watchful, weary, tedious nights :
If haply won, perhaps, a hapless gain ;
If lost, why then a grievous labour won :
However, but a folly bought with wit,
Or else a wit by folly vanquished.
Pro. So, by your circumstance you call me fool.
Val. So, by your circumstance, I fear, you'll prove.

Pro. 'T is love you cavil at : I am not Love.
Val. Love is your master, for he masters you ;
And he that is so yoked by a fool,   40
Methinks, should not be chronicled for wise.
Pro. Yet writers say, as in the sweetest bud
The eating canker dwells, so eating love
Inhabits in the finest wits of all.
Val. And writers say, as the most forward bud
Is eaten by the canker ere it blow,
Even so by love the young and tender wit
Is turn'd to folly ; blasting in the bud,
Losing his verdure even in the prime,
And all the fair effects of future hopes.   50
But wherefore waste I time to counsel thee,
That art a votary to fond desire?
Once more adieu. My father at the road
Expects my coming, there to see me shipp'd.
Pro. And thither will I bring thee, Valentine.
Val. Sweet Proteus, no ; now let us take our leave.
To Milan let me hear from thee by letters,
Of thy success in love, and what news else
Betideth here in absence of thy friend ;
And I likewise will visit thee with mine.   60
Pro. All happiness bechance to thee in Milan !
Val. As much to you at home ! and so, farewell.
                                          [*Exit.*

Pro. He after honour hunts, I after love :
He leaves his friends to dignify them more ;
I leave myself, my friends, and all, for love.
Thou, Julia, thou hast metamorphos'd me ;
Made me neglect my studies, lose my time,
War with good counsel, set the world at nought,
Made wit with musing weak, heart sick with thought.

Enter SPEED.

Speed. Sir Proteus, save you. Saw you my master?
Pro. But now he parted hence to embark for Milan.
Speed. Twenty to one then, he is shipp'd already,
And I have play'd the sheep in losing him.   73
Pro. Indeed, a sheep doth very often stray,
An if the shepherd be awhile away.
Speed. You conclude, that my master is a shepherd then, and I a sheep?
Pro. I do.
Speed. Why, then my horns are his horns, whether I wake or sleep.   80

Pro. A silly answer, and fitting well a sheep.
Speed. This proves me still a sheep.
Pro. True, and thy master a shepherd.
Speed. Nay, that I can deny by a circumstance.
Pro. It shall go hard, but I 'll prove it by another.
Speed. The shepherd seeks the sheep, and not the sheep the shepherd; but I seek my master, and my master seeks not me: therefore, I am no sheep.
Pro. The sheep for fodder follow the shepherd, the shepherd for food follows not the sheep; thou for wages followest thy master, thy master for wages follows not thee: therefore, thou art a sheep.   92
Speed. Such another proof will make me cry "baa."
Pro. But dost thou hear? gav'st thou my letter to Julia?
Speed. Ay, sir: I, a lost mutton, gave your letter to her, a laced mutton; and she, a laced mutton, gave me, a lost mutton, nothing for my labour.
Pro. Here 's too small a pasture for such store of muttons.   100
Speed. If the ground be overcharg'd, you were best stick her.
Pro. Nay, in that you are astray: 't were best pound you.
Speed. Nay, sir, less than a pound shall serve me for carrying your letter.
Pro. You mistake: I mean the pound,—a pinfold.
Speed. From a pound to a pin? fold it over and over,
'T is threefold too little for carrying a letter to your lover.
Pro. But what said she? [SPEED *nods.*] Did she nod?   110
Speed. I.
Pro. Nod, I? why, that 's noddy.
Speed. You mistook, sir: I say she did nod; and you ask me, if she did nod; and I say, I.
Pro. And that set together, is noddy.
Speed. Now you have taken the pains to set it together, take it for your pains.
Pro. No, no; you shall have it for bearing the letter.
Speed. Well, I perceive I must be fain to bear with you.   120
Pro. Why, sir, how do you bear with me?
Speed. Marry, sir, the letter very orderly; having nothing but the word noddy for my pains.
Pro. Beshrew me, but you have a quick wit.
Speed. And yet it cannot overtake your slow purse.
Pro. Come, come; open the matter in brief: what said she?
Speed. Open your purse, that the money, and the matter, may be both at once deliver'd.
Pro. Well, sir, here is for your pains. What said she?   131
Speed. Truly, sir, I think you 'll hardly win her.
Pro. Why? Couldst thou perceive so much from her?
Speed. Sir, I could perceive nothing at all from her; no, not so much as a ducat for delivering your letter. And being so hard to me that brought your mind, I fear she 'll prove as hard to you in telling your mind. Give her no token but stones, for she 's as hard as steel.
Pro. What! said she nothing?   140
Speed. No, not so much as—"Take this for thy pains." To testify your bounty, I thank you, you have testern'd me; in requital whereof, henceforth carry your letters yourself. And so, sir, I 'll commend you to my master.
Pro. Go, go, be gone, to save your ship from wrack, Which cannot perish, having thee aboard, Being destin'd to a drier death on shore.—
I must go send some better messenger:
I fear my Julia would not deign my lines,   150
Receiving them from such a worthless post. [*Exeunt.*

SCENE II.—The Same. JULIA's Garden.

Enter JULIA *and* LUCETTA.

Jul. But say, Lucetta, now we are alone, Wouldst thou then counsel me to fall in love?

Luc. Ay, madam; so you stumble not unheedfully.
Jul. Of all the fair resort of gentlemen, That every day with parle encounter me, In thy opinion, which is worthiest love?
Luc. Please you, repeat their names, I 'll show my mind
According to my shallow simple skill.
Jul. What think'st thou of the fair Sir Eglamour?
Luc. As of a knight well-spoken, neat and fine;   10
But, were I you, he never should be mine.
Jul. What think'st thou of the rich Mercatio?
Luc. Well of his wealth; but of himself, so, so.
Jul. What think'st thou of the gentle Proteus?
Luc. Lord, Lord! to see what folly reigns in us!
Jul. How now! what means this passion at his name?
Luc. Pardon, dear madam: 't is a passing shame, That I, unworthy body as I am, Should censure thus on lovely gentlemen.
Jul. Why not on Proteus, as of all the rest?   20
Luc. Then thus,—of many good I think him best.
Jul. Your reason?
Luc. I have no other but a woman's reason:
I think him so, because I think him so.
Jul. And would'st thou have me cast my love on him?
Luc. Ay, if you thought your love not cast away.
Jul. Why, he of all the rest hath never mov'd me.
Luc. Yet he of all the rest, I think, best loves ye.
Jul. His little speaking shows his love but small.
Luc. Fire that 's closest kept burns most of all.   30
Jul. They do not love that do not show their love.
Luc. O! they love least, that let men know their love.
Jul. I would I knew his mind.
Luc.   Peruse this paper, madam.
Jul. "To Julia." Say, from whom?
Luc.   That the contents will show.
Jul. Say, say, who gave it thee?
Luc. Sir Valentine's page; and sent, I think, from Proteus.
He would have given it you, but I, being in the way, Did in your name receive it: pardon the fault, I pray.
Jul. Now, by my modesty, a goodly broker! Dare you presume to harbour wanton lines?   40
To whisper and conspire against my youth? Now, trust me, 't is an office of great worth, And you an officer fit for the place.
There, take the paper: see it be return'd; Or else return no more into my sight.
Luc. To plead for love deserves more fee than hate.
Jul. Will ye be gone?
Luc.   That you may ruminate.   [*Exit.*
Jul. And yet, I would I had o'erlook'd the letter.
It were a shame to call her back again, And pray her to a fault for which I chid her.   50
What fool is she, that knows I am a maid, And would not force the letter to my view! Since maids, in modesty, say "No" to that Which they would have the proffer'd construe, "Ay."
Fie, fie! how wayward is this foolish love, That, like a testy babe, will scratch the nurse, And presently, all humbled, kiss the rod.
How churlishly I chid Lucetta hence, When willingly I would have had her here: How angrily I taught my brow to frown,   60
When inward joy enforc'd my heart to smile. My penance is, to call Lucetta back, And ask remission for my folly past.—
What ho! Lucetta!

Re-enter LUCETTA.

Luc.   What would your ladyship?
Jul. Is it near dinner-time?
Luc.   I would it were;
That you might kill your stomach on your meat, And not upon your maid.
Jul. What is 't that you took up so gingerly?
Luc. Nothing.

Jul. Why didst thou stoop then?
Luc.   To take a paper up
That I let fall.
Jul.   And is that paper nothing?   71
Luc. Nothing concerning me.
Jul. Then let it lie for those that it concerns.
Luc. Madam, it will not lie where it concerns,
Unless it have a false interpreter.
Jul. Some love of yours hath writ to you in rhyme.
Luc. That I might sing it, madam, to a tune:
Give me a note: your ladyship can set.
Jul. As little by such toys as may be possible:
Best sing it to the tune of "Light o' love."   80
Luc. It is too heavy for so light a tune.
Jul. Heavy? belike, it hath some burden then.
Luc. Ay; and melodious were it, would you sing
        it.
Jul. And why not you?
Luc.   I cannot reach so high.
Jul. Let's see your song.—How now, minion!
Luc. Keep tune there still, so you will sing it out:
And yet, methinks, I do not like this tune.
Jul. You do not?
Luc.   No, madam; it is too sharp.
Jul. You, minion, are too saucy.
Luc.   Nay, now you are too flat,
And mar the concord with too harsh a descant: 90
There wanteth but a mean to fill your song.
Jul. The mean is drown'd with your unruly base.
Luc. Indeed, I bid the base for Proteus.
Jul. This babble shall not henceforth trouble me.
Here is a coil with protestation!—   [*Tears the letter.*
Go, get you gone, and let the papers lie:
You would be fingering them to anger me.
Luc. She makes it strange, but she would be best
        pleas'd
To be so anger'd with another letter.   [*Exit.*
Jul. Nay, would I were so anger'd with the same!
O hateful hands! to tear such loving words: 101
Injurious wasps, to feed on such sweet honey,
And kill the bees that yield it with your stings!
I'll kiss each several paper for amends.
Look, here is writ—"kind Julia."—Unkind Julia!
As in revenge of thy ingratitude,
I throw thy name against the bruising stones,
Trampling contemptuously on thy disdain.
And here is writ—"love-wounded Proteus."—
Poor wounded name! my bosom, as a bed,   110
Shall lodge thee, till thy wound be throughly heal'd;

Jul. "Be calm, good wind, blow not a word away."

And thus I search it with a sovereign kiss.
But twice, or thrice, was Proteus written down:
Be calm, good wind, blow not a word away,
Till I have found each letter in the letter.

Except mine own name; that some whirlwind bear
Unto a ragged, fearful-hanging rock,
And throw it thence into the raging sea!
Lo! here in one line is his name twice writ,—
"Poor forlorn Proteus; passionate Proteus   120
To the sweet Julia:"—that I'll tear away;
And yet I will not, sith so prettily
He couples it to his complaining names.
Thus will I fold them one upon another:
Now kiss, embrace, contend, do what you will.

Re-enter LUCETTA.

Luc. Madam,
Dinner is ready, and your father stays.
Jul. Well, let us go.
Luc. What! shall these papers lie like tell-tales
        here?
Jul. If you respect them, best to take them up.   130
Luc. Nay, I was taken up for laying them down;
Yet here they shall not lie, for catching cold.
Jul. I see, you have a month's mind to them.
Luc. Ay, madam, you may say what sights you
        see;
I see things too, although you judge I wink.
Jul. Come, come; will't please you go?   [*Exeunt.*

———

SCENE III.—The Same. A Room in ANTONIO'S House.

Enter ANTONIO *and* PANTHINO.

Ant. Tell me, Panthino, what sad talk was that,
Wherewith my brother held you in the cloister?
Pant. 'T was of his nephew Proteus, your son.
Ant. Why, what of him?
Pant.   He wonder'd, that your lordship
Would suffer him to spend his youth at home,
While other men, of slender reputation,
Put forth their sons to seek preferment out:
Some, to the wars, to try their fortune there;
Some, to discover islands far away;
Some, to the studious universities.   10
For any, or for all these exercises,
He said that Proteus, your son, was meet,
And did request me to importune you
To let him spend his time no more at home,
Which would be great impeachment to his age,
In having known no travel in his youth.
Ant. Nor need'st thou much importune me to that
Whereon this month I have been hammering.
I have consider'd well his loss of time,
And how he cannot be a perfect man,   20
Not being tried and tutor'd in the world:
Experience is by industry achiev'd,
And perfected by the swift course of time.
Then, tell me, whither were I best to send him?
Pant. I think, your lordship is not ignorant,
How his companion, youthful Valentine,
Attends the emperor in his royal court.
Ant. I know it well.
Pant. 'T were good, I think, your lordship sent him
        thither.
There shall he practise tilts and tournaments,   30
Hear sweet discourse, converse with noblemen,
And be in eye of every exercise,
Worthy his youth, and nobleness of birth.
Ant. I like thy counsel: well hast thou advis'd;
And, that thou may'st perceive how well I like it,
The execution of it shall make known.
Even with the speediest expedition
I will dispatch him to the emperor's court.
Pant. To-morrow, may it please you, Don Alphonso,
With other gentlemen of good esteem,   40
Are journeying to salute the emperor,
And to commend their service to his will.
Ant. Good company; with them shall Proteus
        go:
And, in good time.—Now will we break with him.

Enter PROTEUS.

Pro. Sweet love! sweet lines! sweet life!
Here is her hand, the agent of her heart;

Here is her oath for love, her honour's pawn.
O ! that our fathers would applaud our loves,
To seal our happiness with their consents !
O heavenly Julia !   50
   Ant. How now ! what letter are you reading there ?
   Pro. May 't please your lordship, 't is a word or two
Of commendations sent from Valentine,
Deliver'd by a friend that came from him.
   Ant. Lend me the letter : let me see what news.
   Pro. There is no news, my lord, but that he writes
How happily he lives, how well belov'd,
And daily graced by the emperor :
Wishing me with him, partner of his fortune.
   Ant. And how stand you affected to his wish ?   60
   Pro. As one relying on your lordship's will,
And not depending on his friendly wi-h.
   Ant. My will is something sorted with his wish.
Muse not that I thus suddenly proceed,
For what I will, I will, and there an end.
I am resolv'd, that thou shalt spend some time
With Valentinus in the emperor's court :
What maintenance he from his friends receives,
Like exhibition thou shalt have from me.
To-morrow be in readiness to go :   70
Excuse it not ; for I am peremptory.

   Pro. My lord, I cannot be so soon provided :
Please you, deliberate a day or two.
   Ant. Look, what thou want'st shall be sent after
    thee :
No more of stay ; to-morrow thou must go.—
Come on, Panthino : you shall be employ'd
To hasten on his expedition.
          [*Exeunt* ANTONIO *and* PANTHINO.
   Pro. Thus have I shunn'd the fire for fear of burn-
    ing,
And drench'd me in the sea, where I am drown'd.
I fear'd to show my father Julia's letter,   80
Lest he should take exceptions to my love ;
And, with the vantage of mine own excuse,
Hath he excepted most against my love.
O ! how this spring of love resembleth
The uncertain glory of an April day,
Which now shows all the beauty of the sun,
And by-and-by a cloud takes all away.

Re-enter PANTHINO.

   Pant. Sir Proteus, your father calls for you :
He is in haste ; therefore, I pray you, go.
   Pro. Why, this it is : my heart accords thereto,   90
And yet a thousand times it answers, No.   [*Exeunt.*

ACT II.

SCENE I.—Milan. A Room in the DUKE'S Palace.

Enter VALENTINE *and* SPEED.

   Speed. SIR, your glove.
   Val. Not mine ; my gloves are on.
   Speed. Why, then this may be yours, for this is but one.
   Val. Ha ! let me see : ay, give it me, it 's mine.—
Sweet ornament, that decks a thing divine !
Ah Silvia ! Silvia !
   Speed. Madam Silvia ! Madam Silvia !
   Val. How now, sirrah ?
   Speed. She is not within hearing, sir.
   Val. Why, sir, who bade you call her ?
   Speed. Your worship, sir ; or else I mistook.   10
   Val. Well, you 'll still be too forward.
   Speed. And yet I was last chidden for being too slow.
   Val. Go to, sir. Tell me, do you know Madam Silvia ?
   Speed. She that your worship loves ?
   Val. Why, how know you that I am in love ?
   Speed. Marry, by these special marks. First, you have learn'd, like Sir Proteus, to wreath your arms, like a malcontent ; to relish a love-song, like a robin-redbreast ; to walk alone, like one that had the pestilence ; to sigh, like a school-boy that had lost his A B C ; to weep, like a young wench that had buried her grandam ; to fast, like one that takes diet ; to watch, like one that fears robbing ; to speak puling, like a beggar at Hallowmas. You were wont, when

you laugh'd, to crow like a cock ; when you walk'd, to walk like one of the lions ; when you fasted, it was presently after dinner ; when you look'd sadly, it was for want of money ; and now you are metamorphosed with a mistress, that, when I look on you, I can hardly think you my master.   30
   Val. Are all these things perceived in me ?
   Speed. They are all perceived without ye.
   Val. Without me ? they cannot.
   Speed. Without you ? nay, that 's certain ; for, without you were so simple, none else would : but you are so without these follies, that these follies are within you, and shine through you like the water in an urinal, that not an eye that sees you, but is a physician to comment on your malady.
   Val. But, tell me, dost thou know my lady Silvia ? 40
   Speed. She, that you gaze on so, as she sits at supper ?
   Val. Hast thou observed that ? even she I mean.
   Speed. Why, sir, I know her not.
   Val. Dost thou know her by my gazing on her, and yet know'st her not ?
   Speed. Is she not hard-favour'd, sir ?
   Val. Not so fair, boy, as well-favour'd.
   Speed. Sir, I know that well enough.
   Val. What dost thou know ?   50
   Speed. That she is not so fair, as (of you) well-favour'd.
   Val. I mean, that her beauty is exquisite, but her favour infinite.
   Speed. That 's because the one is painted, and the other out of all count.
   Val. How painted ? and how out of count ?
   Speed. Marry, sir, so painted to make her fair, that no man counts of her beauty.
   Val. How esteem'st thou me ? I account of her beauty.   61

Speed. You never saw her since she was deform'd.
Val. How long hath she been deform'd?
Speed. Ever since you loved her.
Val. I have loved her ever since I saw her, and still I see her beautiful.
Speed. If you love her, you cannot see her.
Val. Why?
Speed. Because Love is blind. O! that you had mine eyes; or your own eyes had the lights they were wont to have, when you chid at Sir Proteus for going ungartered!   72
Val. What should I see then?
Speed. Your own present folly, and her passing deformity; for he, being in love, could not see to garter his hose; and you, being in love, cannot see to put on your hose.
Val. Belike, boy, then you are in love; for last morning you could not see to wipe my shoes.
Speed. True, sir; I was in love with my bed. I thank you, you swinged me for my love, which makes me the bolder to chide you for yours.   82
Val. In conclusion, I stand affected to her.
Speed. I would you were set, so your affection would cease.
Val. Last night she enjoined me to write some lines to one she loves.
Speed. And have you?
Val. I have.
Speed. Are they not lamely writ?   90
Val. No, boy, but as well as I can do them.—Peace! here she comes.
Speed. O excellent motion! O exceeding puppet! Now will he interpret to her.

Enter SILVIA.

Val. Madam and mistress, a thousand good-morrows.
Speed. O! 'give ye good even: here's a million of manners.
Sil. Sir Valentine and servant, to you two thousand.   100
Speed. He should give her interest, and she gives it him.
Val. As you enjoin'd me, I have writ your letter
Unto the secret nameless friend of yours;
Which I was much unwilling to proceed in,
But for my duty to your ladyship.
Sil. I thank you, gentle servant. 'T is very clerkly done.
Val. Now trust me, madam, it came hardly off;
For, being ignorant to whom it goes,   110
I writ at random, very doubtfully.
Sil. Perchance you think too much of so much pains?
Val. No, madam: so it stead you, I will write, Please you command, a thousand times as much. And yet,—
Sil. A pretty period. Well, I guess the sequel; And yet I will not name it;—and yet I care not;— And yet take this again;—and yet I thank you, Meaning henceforth to trouble you no more.   120
Speed. And yet you will; and yet another yet.
Val. What means your ladyship? do you not like it?
Sil. Yes, yes: the lines are very quaintly writ, But since unwillingly, take them again.
Nay, take them.
Val. Madam, they are for you.
Sil. Ay, ay; you writ them, sir, at my request, But I will none of them; they are for you.
I would have had them writ more movingly.   130
Val. Please you, I 'll write your ladyship another.
Sil. And when it 's writ, for my sake read it over: And, if it please you, so; if not, why, so.
Val. If it please me, madam; what then?
Sil. Why, if it please you, take it for your labour: And so good morrow, servant.   [*Exit.*
Speed. O jest unseen, inscrutable, invisible,
As a nose on a man's face, or a weathercock on a steeple!
My master sues to her, and she hath taught her suitor,

He being her pupil, to become her tutor.   140
O excellent device! was there ever heard a better, That my master, being scribe, to himself should write the letter?
Val. How now, sir! what, are you reasoning with yourself?
Speed. Nay, I was rhyming: 't is you that have the reason.
Val. To do what?
Speed. To be a spokesman from Madam Silvia.
Val. To whom?
Speed. To yourself. Why, she wooes you by a figure.   151
Val. What figure?
Speed. By a letter, I should say.
Val. Why, she hath not writ to me?
Speed. What need she, when she hath made you write to yourself? Why, do you not perceive the jest?
Val. No, believe me.
Speed. No believing you, indeed, sir: but did you perceive her earnest?   160
Val. She gave me none, except an angry word.
Speed. Why, she hath given you a letter.
Val. That 's the letter I writ to her friend.
Speed. And that letter hath she deliver'd, and there an end.
Val. I would it were no worse!
Speed. I 'll warrant you, 't is as well:
For often have you writ to her, and she, in modesty, Or else for want of idle time, could not again reply; Or fearing else some messenger, that might her mind discover,   170
Herself hath taught her love himself to write unto her lover.
All this I speak in print, for in print I found it.—Why muse you, sir? 't is dinner-time.
Val. I have dined.
Speed. Ay, but hearken, sir: though the chameleon Love can feed on the air, I am one that am nourish'd by my victuals, and would fain have meat. O! be not like your mistress: be moved, be moved.   [*Exeunt.*

SCENE II.—Verona. A Room in JULIA'S House.

Enter PROTEUS *and* JULIA.

Pro. Have patience, gentle Julia.
Jul. I must, where is no remedy.
Pro. When possibly I can, I will return.
Jul. If you turn not, you will return the sooner. Keep this remembrance for thy Julia's sake.
                          [*Giving a ring.*
Pro. Why, then we 'll make exchange: here, take you this.
Jul. And seal the bargain with a holy kiss.
Pro. Here is my hand for my true constancy; And when that hour o'erslips me in the day, Wherein I sigh not, Julia, for thy sake,   10
The next ensuing hour some foul mischance Torment me for my love's forgetfulness.
My father stays my coming; answer not.
The tide is now: nay, not thy tide of tears; That tide will stay me longer than I should.
                          [*Exit* JULIA.
Julia, farewell.—What! gone without a word? Ay, so true love should do: it cannot speak; For truth hath better deeds than words to grace it.

Enter PANTHINO.

Pant. Sir Proteus, you are stay'd for.
Pro.   Go; I come, I come.— Alas! this parting strikes poor lovers dumb.   20
                          [*Exeunt.*

SCENE III.—The Same. A Street.

Enter LAUNCE, *leading a dog.*

Launce. Nay, 't will be this hour ere I have done weeping: all the kind of the Launces have this very fault. I have received my proportion, like the prodigious son, and am going with Sir Proteus to the imperial's court. I think Crab, my dog, be the sourest-natured dog that lives: my mother weeping, my father wailing, my sister crying, our maid howling, that cannot be so, neither:—yes, it is so, it is so; it hath the worser sole. This shoe, with the hole in it, is my mother, and this my father. A vengeance on 't! there 't is : now, sir, this staff is my sister ; for, look you, she is as white as a lily, and as small as a wand :

Sil. " Why, if it please you, take it for your labour."

our cat wringing her hands, and all our house in a great perplexity, yet did not this cruel-hearted cur shed one tear. He is a stone, a very pebble-stone, and has no more pity in him than a dog; a Jew would have wept to have seen our parting : why, my grandam, having no eyes, look you, wept herself blind at my parting. Nay, I 'll show you the manner of it. This shoe is my father:—no, this left shoe is my father ;—no, no, this left shoe is my mother ;—nay, this hat is Nan, our maid : I am the dog ;—no, the dog is himself, and I am the dog,—O ! the dog is me, and I am myself : ay, so, so. Now come I to my father ; " Father, your blessing :" now should not the shoe speak a word for weeping : now should I kiss my father ; well, he weeps on. Now come I to my mother ; —O, that she could speak now, like a wood woman !— well, I kiss her ; why, there 't is, here 's my mother's breath up and down. Now come I to my sister ; mark the moan she makes: now, the dog all this while sheds not a tear, nor speaks a word; but see how I lay the dust with my tears.   33

Enter PANTHINO.

Pant. Launce, away, away, aboard: thy master is shipped, and thou art to post after with oars. What's the matter? why weep'st thou, man? Away, ass; you'll lose the tide, if you tarry any longer.

Launce. "But see how I lay the dust with my tears."

Launce. It is no matter if the tied were lost; for it is the unkindest tied that ever any man tied.
Pant. What's the unkindest tide?   40
Launce. Why, he that's tied here, Crab, my dog.
Pant. Tut, man, I mean thou 'lt lose the flood; and, in losing the flood, lose thy voyage; and, in losing thy voyage, lose thy master; and, in losing thy master, lose thy service; and, in losing thy service.—Why dost thou stop my mouth?
Launce. For fear thou shouldst lose thy tongue.
Pant. Where should I lose my tongue?
Launce. In thy tale.
Pant. In thy tail?   50
Launce. Lose the tide, and the voyage, and the master, and the service, and the tied. Why, man, if the river were dry, I am able to fill it with my tears; if the wind were down, I could drive the boat with my sighs.
Pant. Come, come, away, man: I was sent to call thee.
Launce. Sir, call me what thou dar'st.
Pant. Wilt thou go?
Launce. Well, I will go.   60
[*Exeunt.*

SCENE IV.—Milan. A Room in the DUKE's Palace.

Enter VALENTINE, SILVIA, THURIO, *and* SPEED.

Sil. Servant!
Val. Mistress?
Speed. Master, Sir Thurio frowns on you.
Val. Ay, boy, it's for love.
Speed. Not of you.
Val. Of my mistress then.
Speed. 'T were good you knock'd him.
Sil. Servant, you are sad.
Val. Indeed, madam, I seem so.
Thu. Seem you that you are not?   10

Val. Haply, I do.
Thu. So do counterfeits.
Val. So do you.
Thu. What seem I that I am not?
Val. Wise.
Thu. What instance of the contrary?
Val. Your folly.
Thu. And how quote you my folly?
Val. I quote it in your jerkin.
Thu. My jerkin is a doublet.   20
Val. Well, then, I 'll double your folly.
Thu. How?
Sil. What, angry, Sir Thurio! do you change colour?
Val. Give him leave, madam: he is a kind of chameleon.
Thu. That hath more mind to feed on your blood, than live in your air.
Val. You have said, sir.
Thu. Ay, sir, and done too, for this time.
Val. I know it well, sir: you always end ere you begin.   31
Sil. A fine volley of words, gentlemen, and quickly shot off.
Val. 'T is indeed, madam, we thank the giver.
Sil. Who is that, servant?
Val. Yourself, sweet lady; for you gave the fire. Sir Thurio borrows his wit from your ladyship's looks, and spends what he borrows kindly in your company.
Thu. Sir, if you spend word for word with me, I shall make your wit bankrupt.   40
Val. I know it well, sir: you have an exchequer of words, and, I think, no other treasure to give your followers; for it appears by their bare liveries, that they live by your bare words.
Sil. No more, gentlemen, no more. Here comes my father.

Enter the DUKE.

Duke. Now, daughter Silvia, you are hard beset. Sir Valentine, your father's in good health:
What say you to a letter from your friends
Of much good news?
Val.   My lord, I will be thankful   50
To any happy messenger from thence.
Duke. Know you Don Antonio, your countryman?
Val. Ay, my good lord; I know the gentleman
To be of worth, and worthy estimation,
And not without desert so well reputed.
Duke. Hath he not a son?
Val. Ay, my good lord; a son, that well deserves
The honour and regard of such a father.
Duke. You know him well?
Val. I know him as myself; for from our infancy   60
We have convers'd, and spent our hours together:
And though myself have been an idle truant,
Omitting the sweet benefit of time
To clothe mine age with angel-like perfection,
Yet hath Sir Proteus, for that 's his name,
Made use and fair advantage of his days:
His years but young, but his experience old;
His head unmellow'd, but his judgment ripe;
And, in a word (for far behind his worth
Come all the praises that I now bestow),   70
He is complete in feature, and in mind,
With all good grace to grace a gentleman.
Duke. Beshrew me, sir, but, if he make this good,
He is as worthy for an empress' love,
As meet to be an emperor's counsellor.
Well, sir, this gentleman is come to me
With commendation from great potentates;
And here he means to spend his time awhile.
I think, 't is no unwelcome news to you.
Val. Should I have wish'd a thing, it had been he.
Duke. Welcome him then according to his worth.
Silvia, I speak to you; and you, Sir Thurio:—   82
For Valentine, I need not cite him to it.
I 'll send him hither to you presently.   [*Exit.*
Val. This is the gentleman, I told your ladyship,
Had come along with me, but that his mistress
Did hold his eyes lock'd in her crystal looks.
Sil. Belike, that now she hath enfranchis'd them,
Upon some other pawn for fealty.

Val. Nay, sure, I think, she holds them prisoners
     still.   90
Sil. Nay, then he should be blind ; and, being blind,
How could he see his way to seek out you ?
Val. Why, lady, Love hath twenty pair of eyes.
Thu. They say, that Love hath not an eye at all.
Val. To see such lovers, Thurio, as yourself :
Upon a homely object Love can wink.

       Enter PROTEUS.

Sil. Have done, have done. Here comes the gen-
     tleman.
Val. Welcome, dear Proteus !—Mistress, I beseech
     you,
Confirm his welcome with some special favour.
Sil. His worth is warrant for his welcome hither,
If this be he you oft have wish'd to hear from.   101

Val. And how do yours?
Pro.   I left them all in health.
Val. How does your lady, and how thrives your
     love ?
  Pro. My tales of love were wont to weary you :
I know, you joy not in a love-discourse.
  Val. Ay, Proteus, but that life is alter'd now :
I have done penance for contemning Love ;
Whose high imperious thoughts have punish'd me
With bitter fasts, with penitential groans,
With nightly tears, and daily heart-sore sighs ;   230
For, in revenge of my contempt of Love,
Love hath chas'd sleep from my enthralled eyes,
And made them watchers of mine own heart's sorrow.
O gentle Proteus ! Love 's a mighty lord,
And hath so humbled me, as, I confess,
There is no woe to his correction,

Sil. " His worth is warrant for his welcome hither."

Val. Mistress, it is. Sweet lady, entertain him
To be my fellow-servant to your ladyship.
  Sil. Too low a mistress for so high a servant.
  Pro. Not so, sweet lady ; but too mean a servant
To have a look of such a worthy mistress.
  Val. Leave off discourse of disability.--
Sweet lady, entertain him for your servant.
  Pro. My duty will I boast of, nothing else.
  Sil. And duty never yet did want his meed.   110
Servant, you are welcome to a worthless mistress.
  Pro. I 'll die on him that says so, but yourself.
  Sil. That you are welcome.
  Pro.   That you are worthless.

       Enter a Servant.

  Serv. Madam, my lord, your father, would speak
     with you.
  Sil. I wait upon his pleasure. [*Exit Servant.*]
Come, Sir Thurio,
Go with me.—Once more, new servant, welcome :
I 'll leave you to confer of home-affairs ;
When you have done, we look to hear from you.
  Pro. We 'll both attend upon your ladyship.
      [*Exeunt* SILVIA, THURIO, *and* SPEED.
  Val. Now, tell me, how do all from whence you
     came ?   120
  Pro. Your friends are well, and have them much
     commended.

Nor to his service no such joy on earth !
Now, no discourse, except it be of love ;
Now can I break my fast, dine, sup, and sleep,
Upon the very naked name of love.   140
  Pro. Enough ; I read your fortune in your eye.
Was this the idol that you worship so ?
  Val. Even she ? and is she not a heavenly saint ?
  Pro. No, but she is an earthly paragon.
  Val. Call her divine.
  Pro.   I will not flatter her.
  Val. O ! flatter me, for love delights in praises.
  Pro. When I was sick you gave me bitter pills,
And I must minister the like to you.
  Val. Then speak the truth by her: if not divine,   150
Yet let her be a principality,
Sovereign to all the creatures on the earth.
  Pro. Except my mistress.
  Val.   Sweet, except not any,
Except thou wilt except against my love.
  Pro. Have I not reason to prefer mine own ?
  Val. And I will help thee to prefer her too :
She shall be dignified with this high honour,—
To bear my lady's train, lest the base earth
Should from her vesture chance to steal a kiss,
And, of so great a favour growing proud,
Disdain to root the summer-swelling flower,   160
And make rough winter everlastingly.
  Pro. Why, Valentine, what braggardism is this ?

Val. Pardon me, Proteus : all I can, is nothing
To her, whose worth makes other worthies nothing.
She is alone.
   Pro.   Then let her alone.
   Val. Not for the world. Why, man, she is mine
      own,
And I as rich in having such a jewel
As twenty seas, if all their sand were pearl,
The water nectar, and the rocks pure gold.
Forgive me, that I do not dream on thee,   170
Because thou seest me dote upon my love.
My foolish rival, that her father likes,
Only for his possessions are so huge,
Is gone with her along, and I must after,
For love, thou know'st, is full of jealousy.
   Pro. But she loves you ?
   Val. Ay, and we are betroth'd ; nay, more, our
      marriage-hour.
With all the cunning manner of our flight,
Determin'd of : how I must climb her window,
The ladder made of cords, and all the means   180
Plotted, and 'greed on, for my happiness.
Good Proteus, go with me to my chamber,
In these affairs to aid me with thy counsel.
   Pro. Go on before ; I shall enquire you forth.
I must unto the road, to disembark
Some necessaries, that I needs must use,
And then I 'll presently attend you.
   Val. Will you make haste ?
   Pro. I will.   [*Exit* VALENTINE.
Even as one heat another heat expels,   190
Or as one nail by strength drives out another,
So the remembrance of my former love
Is by a newer object quite forgotten.
Is it mine eye, or Valentinus' praise,
Her true perfection, or my false transgression,
That makes me, reasonless, to reason thus ?
She 's fair, and so is Julia that I love,—
That I did love, for now my love is thaw'd,
Which, like a waxen image 'gainst a fire,
Bears no impression of the thing it was.   200
Methinks, my zeal to Valentine is cold,
And that I love him not, as I was wont :
O ! but I love his lady too too much :
And that 's the reason I love him so little.
How shall I dote on her with more advice,
That thus without advice begin to love her ?
'T is but her picture I have yet beheld,
And that hath dazzled my reason's light ;
But when I look on her perfections,
There is no reason but I shall be blind.   210
If I can check my erring love, I will ;
If not, to compass her I 'll use my skill.   [*Exit.*

SCENE V.—The Same. A Street.

Enter SPEED *and* LAUNCE.

Speed. Launce ! by mine honesty, welcome to
Padua !
   Launce. Forswear not thyself, sweet youth, for I
am not welcome. I reckon this always, that a man
is never undone, till he be hang'd ; nor never welcome
to a place, till some certain shot be paid, and the
hostess say, " Welcome !"
   Speed. Come on, you madcap, I 'll to the ale-house
with you presently ; where for one shot of five pence
thou shalt have five thousand welcomes. But, sirrah,
how did thy master part with Madam Julia ?   11
   Launce. Marry, after they closed in earnest, they
parted very fairly in jest.
   Speed. But shall she marry him ?
   Launce. No.
   Speed. How then ? Shall he marry her ?
   Launce. No, neither.
   Speed. What, are they broken ?
   Launce. No, they are both as whole as a fish.
   Speed. Why then, how stands the matter with
them ?   21
   Launce. Marry, thus: when it stands well with
him, it stands well with her.

   Speed. What an ass art thou ! I und⁀rstand thee not.
   Launce. What a block art thou, that thou canst not.
My staff understands me.
   Speed. What thou say'st ?
   Launce. Ay, and what I do too : look thee, I 'll but
lean, and my staff understands me.
   Speed. It stands under thee, indeed.   30
   Launce. Why, stand-under and under-stand is all
one.
   Speed. But tell me true, will 't be a match ?
   Launce. Ask my dog : if he say, ay, it will ; if he
say, no, it will ; if he shake his tail, and say nothing,
it will.
   Speed. The conclusion is then, that it will.
   Launce. Thou shalt never get such a secret from
me, but by a parable.
   Speed. 'T is well that I get it so. But, Launce, how
say'st thou, that my master is become a notable lover ?
   Launce. I never knew him otherwise.   42
   Speed. Than how ?
   Launce. A notable lubber, as thou reportest him
to be.
   Speed. Why, thou whoreson ass, thou mistak'st me.
   Launce. Why, fool, I meant not thee ; I meant thy
master.
   Speed. I tell thee, my master is become a hot lover.
   Launce. Why, I tell thee, I care not though he burn
himself in love. If thou wilt go with me to the ale-
house, so ; if not, thou art an Hebrew, a Jew, and
not worth the name of a Christian.   53
   Speed. Why ?
   Launce. Because thou hast not so much charity
in thee, as to go to the ale with a Christian. Wilt
thou go ?
   Speed. At thy service.   [*Exeunt.*

SCENE VI.—The Same. An Apartment in the Palace.

Enter PROTEUS.

   Pro. To leave my Julia, shall I be forsworn ;
To love fair Silvia, shall I be forsworn ;
To wrong my friend, I shall be much forsworn ;
And even that power which gave me first my oath,
Provokes me to this threefold perjury :
Love bade me swear, and Love bids me forswear.
O sweet-suggesting Love ! if thou hast sinn'd,
Teach me, thy tempted subject, to excuse it.
At first I did adore a twinkling star,
But now I worship a celestial sun.   10
Unheedful vows may heedfully be broken ;
And he wants wit that wants resolved will
To learn his wit to exchange the bad for better.—
Fie, fie, unreverend tongue ! to call her bad,
Whose sovereignty so oft thou hast preferr'd
With twenty thousand soul-confirming oaths.
I cannot leave to love, and yet I do ;
But there I leave to love, where I should love.
Julia I lose, and Valentine I lose :
If I keep them, I needs must lose myself ,   20
If I lose them, thus find I, by their loss,
For Valentine, myself ; for Julia, Silvia.
I to myself am dearer than a friend,
For love is still most precious in itself ;
And Silvia (witness Heaven that made her fair !)
Shows Julia but a swarthy Ethiop.
I will forget that Julia is alive,
Remembering that my love to her is dead ;
And Valentine I 'll hold an enemy,
Aiming at Silvia, as a sweeter friend.   30
I cannot now prove constant to myself
Without some treachery used to Valentine :—
This night, he meaneth with a corded ladder
To climb celestial Silvia's chamber-window ;
Myself in counsel, his competitor.
Now, presently I 'll give her father notice
Of their disguising and pretended flight ;
Who, all enrag'd, will banish Valentine,
For Thurio, he intends, shall wed his daughter ;
But, Valentine being gone, I 'll quickly cross   40
By some sly trick blunt Thurio's dull proceeding.

Love, lend me wings to make my purpose swift,
As thou hast lent me wit to plot this drift !   [*Exit.*

Scene VII.—Verona. A Room in Julia's House.

Enter Julia *and* Lucetta.

Jul. Counsel, Lucetta ; gentle girl, assist me ;
And, e'en in kind love, I do conjure thee,
Who art the table wherein all my thoughts
Are visibly character'd and engrav'd,
To lesson me ; and tell me some good mean,
How, with my honour, I may undertake
A journey to my loving Proteus.
Luc. Alas ! the way is wearisome and long.
Jul. A true-devoted pilgrim is not weary   10
To measure kingdoms with his feeble steps ;
Much less shall she, that hath Love's wings to fly,
And when the flight is made to one so dear,
Of such divine perfection, as Sir Proteus.
Luc. Better forbear, till Proteus make return.
Jul. O ! know'st thou not, his looks are my soul's
     food ?
Pity the dearth that I have pined in,
By longing for that food so long a time.
Didst thou but know the inly touch of love,
Thou wouldst as soon go kindle fire with snow,
As seek to quench the fire of love with words.   20
Luc. I do not seek to quench your love's hot fire,
But qualify the fire's extreme rage,
Lest it should burn above the bounds of reason.
Jul. The more thou damm'st it up, the more it
     burns.
The current, that with gentle murmur glides,
Thou know'st, being stopp'd, impatiently doth rage ;
But, when his fair course is not hindered,
He makes sweet music with the enamell'd stones,
Giving a gentle kiss to every sedge
He overtaketh in his pilgrimage ;   30
And so by many winding nooks he strays
With willing sport to the wild ocean.
Then, let me go, and hinder not my course.
I 'll be as patient as a gentle stream,
And make a pastime of each weary step,
Till the last step have brought me to my love ;
And there I 'll rest, as, after much turmoil,
A blessed soul doth in Elysium.
Luc. But in what habit will you go along ?
Jul. Not like a woman ; for I would prevent   40
The loose encounters of lascivious men.

Gentle Lucetta, fit me with such weeds
As may beseem some well-reputed page.
Luc. Why, then your ladyship must cut your hair
Jul. No, girl ; I 'll knit it up in silken strings
With twenty odd-conceited true-love knots :
To be fantastic, may become a youth
Of greater time than I shall show to be.
Luc. What fashion, madam, shall I make your
     breeches ?
Jul. That fits as well as—" Tell me, good my lord,   50
What compass will you wear your farthingale ? "
Why, even what fashion thou best lik'st, Lucetta.
Luc. You must needs have them with a codpiec
     madam.
Jul. Out, out, Lucetta ! that will be ill-favour'd.
Luc. A round hose, madam, now 's not worth a pin,
Unless you have a codpiece to stick pins on.
Jul. Lucetta, as thou lov'st me, let me have
What thou think'st meet, and is most mannerly.
But tell me, wench, how will the world repute me
For undertaking so unstaid a journey ?   60
I fear me, it will make me scandalis'd.
Luc. If you think so, then stay at home, and go not.
Jul. Nay, that I will not.
Luc. Then never dream on infamy, but go.
If Proteus like your journey, when you come,
No matter who 's displeas'd, when you are gone.
I fear me, he will scarce be pleas'd withal.
Jul. That is the least, Lucetta, of my fear.
A thousand oaths, an ocean of his tears,
And instances of infinite of love,   70
Warrant me welcome to my Proteus.
Luc. All these are servants to deceitful men.
Jul. Base men, that use them to so base effect ;
But truer stars did govern Proteus' birth :
His words are bonds, his oaths are oracles ;
His love sincere, his thoughts immaculate ;
His tears pure messengers sent from his heart ;
His heart as far from fraud, as heaven from earth.
Luc. Pray Heaven, he prove so, when you come to
     him !
Jul. Now, as thou lov'st me, do him not that wrong
To bear a hard opinion of his truth :   81
Only deserve my love by loving him,
And presently go with me to my chamber,
To take a note of what I stand in need of,
To furnish me upon my longing journey.
All that is mine I leave at thy dispose,
My goods, my lands, my reputation ;
Only, in lieu thereof, dispatch me hence.
Come, answer not, but to it presently :
I am impatient of my tarriance.   90
     [*Exeunt.*

ACT III.

Scene I.—Milan. An Antechamber in the Duke's Palace.

Enter Duke, Thurio, *and* Proteus.

Duke.
SIR Thurio, give us leave, I pray, awhile :
     We have some secrets to confer about.—
          [*Exit* Thurio.
Now, tell me, Proteus, what 's your will
     with me ?
Pro. My gracious lord, that which I
     would discover,
     The law of friendship bids me to conceal ;
But, when I call to mind your gracious favours
Done to me, undeserving as I am,

My duty pricks me on to utter that
Which else no worldly good should draw from me.
Know, worthy prince, Sir Valentine, my friend,   10
This night intends to steal away your daughter
Myself am one made privy to the plot.
I know you have determin'd to bestow her
On Thurio, whom your gentle daughter hates ;
And should she thus be stol'n away from you,
It would be much vexation to your age.
Thus, for my duty's sake, I rather chose
To cross my friend in his intended drift

Than, by concealing it, heap on your head
A pack of sorrows, which would press you down,   20
Being unprevented, to your timeless grave.
   Duke. Proteus, I thank thee for thine honest care,
Which to requite, command me while I live.
This love of theirs myself have often seen,
Haply, when they have judg'd me fast asleep;
And oftentimes have purpos'd to forbid
Sir Valentine her company, and my court;
But, fearing lest my jealous aim might err,
And so unworthily disgrace the man
(A rashness that I ever yet have shunn'd),   30
I gave him gentle looks; thereby to find
That which thyself hast now disclos'd to me.
And, that thou may'st perceive my fear of this,
Knowing that tender youth is soon suggested,
I nightly lodge her in an upper tower,
The key whereof myself have ever kept;
And thence she cannot be convey'd away.
   Pro. Know, noble lord, they have devis'd a mean
How he her chamber-window will ascend,
And with a corded ladder fetch her down;   40
For which the youthful lover now is gone,
And this way comes he with it presently,
Where, if it please you, you may intercept him.
But, good my lord, do it so cunningly,
That my discovery be not aimed at;
For love of you, not hate unto my friend,
Hath made me publisher of this pretence.
   Duke. Upon mine honour, he shall never know
That I had any light from thee of this.
   Pro. Adieu, my lord: Sir Valentine is coming.   50
                                   [*Exit.*

        Enter VALENTINE.

   Duke. Sir Valentine, whither away so fast?
   Val. Please it your grace, there is a messenger
That stays to bear my letters to my friends,
And I am going to deliver them.
   Duke. Be they of much import?
   Val. The tenor of them doth but signify
My health, and happy being at your court.
   Duke. Nay, then no matter: stay with me awhile.
I am to break with thee of some affairs,
That touch me near, wherein thou must be secret.   60
'T is not unknown to thee, that I have sought
To match my friend, Sir Thurio, to my daughter.
   Val. I know it well, my lord; and, sure, the match
Were rich and honourable; besides, the gentleman
Is full of virtue, bounty, worth, and qualities
Beseeming such a wife as your fair daughter.
Cannot your grace win her to fancy him?
   Duke. No, trust me: she is peevish, sullen, froward,
Proud, disobedient, stubborn, lacking duty;
Neither regarding that she is my child,   70
Nor fearing me as if I were her father:
And, may I say to thee, this pride of hers,
Upon advice, hath drawn my love from her;
And, where I thought the remnant of mine age
Should have been cherish'd by her child-like duty,
I now am full resolv'd to take a wife,
And turn her out to who will take her in:
Then, let her beauty be her wedding-dower;
For me and my possessions she esteems not.
   Val. What would your grace have me to do in this?
   Duke. There is a lady in Verona here,   81
Whom I affect; but she is nice, and coy,
And nought esteems my aged eloquence:
Now, therefore, would I have thee to my tutor
(For long agone I have forgot to court;
Besides, the fashion of the time is chang'd),
How, and which way, I may bestow myself,
To be regarded in her sun-bright eye.
   Val. Win her with gifts, if she respect not words.
Dumb jewels often, in their silent kind,   90
More than quick words do move a woman's mind.
   Duke. But she did scorn a present that I sent her.
   Val. A woman sometimes scorns what best con-
        tents her.
Send her another; never give her o'er,
For scorn at first makes after-love the more.
If she do frown, 't is not in hate of you,

But rather to beget more love in you;
If she do chide, 't is not to have you gone,
For why the fools are mad, if left alone.
Take no repulse, whatever she doth say;   100
For, "get you gone" she doth not mean, "away."
Flatter, and praise, commend, extol their graces;
Though ne'er so black, say they have angels' faces.
That man that hath a tongue, I say, is no man,
If with his tongue he cannot win a woman.
   Duke. But she I mean is promis'd by her friends
Unto a youthful gentleman of worth,
And kept severely from resort of men,
That no man hath access by day to her.
   Val. Why, then, I would resort to her by night.   110
   Duke. Ay, but the doors be lock'd, and keys kept
        safe,
That no man hath recourse to her by night.
   Val. What lets but one may enter at her window?
   Duke. Her chamber is aloft, far from the ground,
And built so shelving, that one cannot climb it
Without apparent hazard of his life.
   Val. Why then, a ladder quaintly made of cords,
To cast up, with a pair of anchoring hooks,
Would serve to scale another Hero's tower,
So bold Leander would adventure it.   120
   Duke. Now, as thou art a gentleman of blood,
Advise me where I may have such a ladder.
   Val. When would you use it? pray, sir, tell me that.
   Duke. This very night; for Love is like a child,
That longs for everything that he can come by.
   Val. By seven o'clock I'll get you such a ladder.
   Duke. But hark thee; I will go to her alone.
How shall I best convey the ladder thither?
   Val. It will be light, my lord, that you may bear it
Under a cloak that is of any length.   130
   Duke. A cloak as long as thine will serve the turn?
   Val. Ay, my good lord.
   Duke.   Then, let me see thy cloak:
I'll get me one of such another length.
   Val. Why, any cloak will serve the turn, my lord.
   Duke. How shall I fashion me to wear a cloak?—
I pray thee, let me feel thy cloak upon me.—

     Duke. "And here an engine fit for my proceeding!"

What letter is this same? What's here?—"To Silvia?"
And here an engine fit for my proceeding!
I'll be so bold to break the seal for once.   [*Reads.*
" *My thoughts do harbour with my Silvia nightly;*   140
  And slaves they are to me, that send them flying:
O! could their master come and go as lightly,
  Himself would lodge, where senseless they are lying.
My herald thoughts in thy pure bosom rest them;
  While I, their king, that thither them importune,
Do curse the grace that with such grace hath bless'd
    them,
  Because myself do want my servants' fortune:

I curse myself, for they are sent by me,
That they should harbour where their lord should be."
What 's here ?   150
" Silvia, this night I will enfranchise thee."
'T is so ; and here 's the ladder for the purpose.
Why, Phaethon (for thou art Merops' son),
Wilt thou aspire to guide the heavenly car,
And with thy daring folly burn the world ?
Wilt thou reach stars, because they shine on thee ?
Go, base intruder ! overweening slave !
Bestow thy fawning smiles on equal mates,
And think my patience, more than thy desert,
Is privilege for thy departure hence.   160
Thank me for this, more than for all the favours,
Which, all too much, I have bestow'd on thee :
But if thou linger in my territories
Longer than swiftest expedition
Will give thee time to leave our royal court,
By Heaven, my wrath shall far exceed the love
I ever bore my daughter, or thyself.
Be gone : I will not hear thy vain excuse :
But, as thou lov'st thy life, make speed from hence.
                                          [*Exit* DUKE.
Val. And why not death, rather than living tor-
     ment ?   170
To die is to be banish'd from myself ;
And Silvia is myself : banish'd from her,
Is self from self ; a deadly banishment.
What light is light, if Silvia be not seen ?
What joy is joy, if Silvia be not by ?
Unless it be, to think that she is by,
And feed upon the shadow of perfection.
Except I be by Silvia in the night,
There is no music in the nightingale ;
Unless I look on Silvia in the day,   180
There is no day for me to look upon.
She is my essence ; and I leave to be,
If I be not by her fair influence
Foster'd, illumin'd, cherish'd, kept alive.
I fly not death, to fly his deadly doom :
Tarry I here, I but attend on death ;
But, fly I hence, I fly away from life.

            Enter PROTEUS *and* LAUNCE.

Pro. Run, boy ; run, run, and seek him out.
Launce. So-ho ! so-ho !
Pro. What seest thou ?   190
Launce. Him we go to find : there 's not a hair on 's
head, but 'tis a Valentine.
Pro. Valentine ?
Val. No.
Pro. Who then ? his spirit ?
Val. Neither.
Pro. What then ?
Val. Nothing.
Launce. Can nothing speak ? master, shall I strike ?
Pro. Who wouldst thou strike ?   200
Launce. Nothing.
Pro. Villain, forbear.
Launce. Why, sir, I 'll strike nothing : I pray you,—
Pro. Sirrah, I say, forbear.—Friend Valentine, a
word.
Val. My ears are stopp'd, and cannot hear good
     news,
So much of bad already hath possess'd them.
Pro. Then in dumb silence will I bury mine
For they are harsh, untuneable, and bad.
Val. Is Silvia dead ?
Pro. No, Valentine.   210
Val. No Valentine, indeed, for sacred Silvia !—
Hath she forsworn me ?
Pro. No, Valentine.
Val. No Valentine, if Silvia, hath forsworn me !—
What is your news ?
Launce. Sir, there is a proclamation that you are
vanish'd.
Pro. That thou art banish'd : O ! that is the news,
From hence, from Silvia, and from me, thy friend.
Val. O ! I have fed upon this woe already,   220
And now excess of it will make me surfeit.
Doth Silvia know that I am banished ?

Pro. Ay, ay ; and she hath offer'd to the doom
(Which, unrevers'd, stands in effectual force)
A sea of melting pearl, which some call tears :
Those at her father's churlish feet she tender'd,
With them, upon her knees, her humble self,
Wringing her hands, whose whiteness so became
     them,
As if but now they waxed pale for woe :
But neither bended knees, pure hands held up,   230
Sad sighs, deep groans, nor silver-shedding tears,
Could penetrate her uncompassionate sire ;
But Valentine, if he be ta'en, must die.
Besides, her intercession chaf'd him so,
When she for thy repeal was suppliant,
That to close prison he commanded her,
With many bitter threats of biding there.
Val. No more ; unless the next word that thou
     speak'st
Have some malignant power upon my life
If so, I pray thee, breathe it in mine ear,   240
As ending anthem of my endless dolour.
Pro. Cease to lament for that thou canst not help,
And study help for that which thou lament'st.
Time is the nurse and breeder of all good.
Here if thou stay, thou canst not see thy love ;
Besides, thy staying will abridge thy life.
Hope is a lover's staff ; walk hence with that,
And manage it against despairing thoughts.
Thy letters may be here, though thou art hence ;
Which, being writ to me, shall be deliver'd   250
Even in the milk-white bosom of thy love.
The time now serves not to expostulate :
Come, I 'll convey thee through the city-gate,
And, ere I part with thee, confer at large
Of all that may concern thy love-affairs.
As thou lov'st Silvia, though not for thyself,
Regard thy danger, and along with me !
Val. I pray thee, Launce, an if thou seest my boy,
Bid him make haste, and meet me at the north gate.
Pro. Go, sirrah, find him out. Come, Valentine. 260
Val. O my dear Silvia ! hapless Valentine !
                    [*Exeunt* VALENTINE *and* PROTEUS.
Launce. I am but a fool, look you, and yet I have
the wit to think that my master is a kind of a knave ; but
that 's all one, if he be but one knave. He lives not
now, that knows me to be in love : yet I am in love ;
but a team of horse shall not pluck that from me, nor
who 'tis I love ; and yet 'tis a woman : but what
woman, I will not tell myself ; and yet 'tis a milkmaid ; yet 'tis not a maid, for she hath had gossips ;
yet 'tis a maid, for she is her master's maid, and
serves for wages. She hath more qualities than a
water-spaniel, which is much in a bare Christian.
Here is the cate-log [*pulling out a paper*] of her
conditions. *Imprimis,* "She can fetch and carry."
Why, a horse can do no more : nay, a horse cannot
fetch, but only carry ; therefore is she better than a
jade. *Item,* "She can milk," look you ; a sweet virtue
in a maid with clean hands.

                    Enter SPEED.

Speed. How now, Signior Launce ? what news with
your mastership ?   280
Launce. With my master's ship ? why, it is at sea.
Speed. Well, your old vice still ; mistake the word.
What news, then, in your paper ?
Launce. The blackest news that ever thou heard'st.
Speed. Why, man, how black ?
Launce. Why, as black as ink.
Speed. Let me read them.
Launce. Fie on thee, jolthead ! thou canst not
read.
Speed. Thou liest, I can.   290
Launce. I will try thee. Tell me this : who begot
thee ?
Speed. Marry, the son of my grandfather.
Launce. O illiterate loiterer ! it was the son of thy
grandmother. This proves, that thou canst not read.
Speed. Come, fool, come : try me in thy paper.
Launce. There, and Saint Nicholas be thy speed !
Speed. Imprimis, "She can milk."
Launce. Ay, that she can.

Speed. Item, "She brews good ale."   300
Launce. And thereof comes the proverb,—Blessing
of your heart, you brew good ale.
Speed. Item, "She can sew."
Launce. That's as much as to say, Can she so ?
Speed. Item, "She can knit."
Launce. What need a man care for a stock with a
wench, when she can knit him a stock ?
Speed. Item, "She can wash and scour."
Launce. A special virtue ; for then she need not be
wash'd and scour'd.   310
Speed. Item, "She can spin."
Launce. Then may I set the world on wheels, when
she can spin for her living.
Speed. Item, "She hath many nameless virtues."
Launce. That's as much as to say, bastard virtues ;
that, indeed, know not their fathers, and therefore
have no names.
Speed. Here follow her vices.
Launce. Close at the heels of her virtues.
Speed. Item, "She is not to be kissed fasting, in
respect of her breath."   321
Launce. Well, that fault may be mended with a
breakfast. Read on.
Speed. Item, "She hath a sweet mouth."
Launce. That makes amends for her sour breath.
Speed. Item, "She doth talk in her sleep."
Launce. It's no matter for that, so she sleep not in
her talk.
Speed. Item, "She is slow in words."
Launce. O villain, that set this down among her
vices ! To be slow in words is a woman's only virtue.
I pray thee, out with 't, and place it for her chief
virtue.
Speed. Item. "She is proud."
Launce. Out with that too : it was Eve's legacy, and
cannot be ta'en from her.
Speed. Item, "She hath no teeth."
Launce. I care not for that neither, because I love
crusts.
Speed. Item, "She is curst."   340
Launce. Well ; the best is, she hath no teeth to bite.
Speed. Item, "She will often praise her liquor."
Launce. If her liquor be good, she shall : if she will
not, I will ; for good things should be praised.
Speed. Item, "She is too liberal."
Launce. Of her tongue she cannot, for that's writ
down she is slow of ; of her purse she shall not, for
that I'll keep shut ; now, of another thing she may,
and that cannot I help. Well, proceed.
Speed. Item, "She hath more hair than wit, and
more faults than hairs, and more wealth than faults."
Launce. Stop there ; I'll have her : she was mine,
and not mine, twice or thrice in that last article. Re-
hearse that once more.
Speed. Item, "She hath more hair than wit,"—
Launce. More hair than wit,—it may be : I'll prove
it : the cover of the salt hides the salt, and therefore
it is more than the salt : the hair, that covers the wit,
is more than the wit, for the greater hides the less.
What's next ?   360
Speed. —"And more faults than hairs,"—
Launce. That's monstrous : O, that that were out !
Speed. —"And more wealth than faults."
Launce. Why, that word makes the faults gracious.
Well, I'll have her ; and if it be a match, as nothing is
impossible,—
Speed. What then ?
Launce. Why, then will I tell thee,—that thy master
stays for thee at the north gate.
Speed. For me ?   370
Launce. For thee ! ay ; who art thou ? he hath stay'd
for a better man than thee.
Speed. And must I go to him ?
Launce. Thou must run to him, for thou hast stay'd
so long, that going will scarce serve the turn.
Speed. Why didst not tell me sooner ? pox of your
love-letters !   [*Exit.*
Launce. Now will he be swing'd for reading my
letter. An unmannerly slave, that will thrust himself into secrets.—I'll after, to rejoice in the boy's
correction.   [*Exit.*

SCENE II.—The Same.   An Apartment in the DUKE'S
Palace.

Enter DUKE *and* THURIO ; PROTEUS *behind.*

Duke. Sir Thurio, fear not but that she will love
        you,
Now Valentine is banish'd from her sight.
Thu. Since his exile she hath despis'd me most ;
Forsworn my company, and rail'd at me,
That I am desperate of obtaining her.
Duke. This weak impress of love is as a figure
Trenched in ice, which with an hour's heat
Dissolves to water, and doth lose his form.
A little time will melt her frozen thoughts,
And worthless Valentine shall be forgot.—   10
How now, Sir Proteus ? Is your countryman,
According to our proclamation, gone ?
Pro. Gone, my good lord.
Duke. My daughter takes his going grievously.
Pro. A little time, my lord, will kill that grief.
Duke. So I believe ; but Thurio thinks not so.
Proteus, the good conceit I hold of thee
(For thou hast shown some sign of good desert),
Makes me the better to confer with thee.
Pro. Longer than I prove loyal to your grace,   20
Let me not live to look upon your grace.
Duke. Thou know'st how willingly I would effect
The match between Sir Thurio and my daughter.
Pro. I do, my lord.
Duke. And also, I think, thou art not ignorant
How she opposes her against my will.
Pro. She did, my lord, when Valentine was here.
Duke. Ay, and perversely she perseers so.
What might we do to make the girl forget
The love of Valentine, and love Sir Thurio ?   30
Pro. The best way is, to slander Valentine
With falsehood, cowardice, and poor descent ;
Three things that women highly hold in hate.
Duke. Ay, but she 'll think that it is spoke in hate.
Pro. Ay, if his enemy deliver it :
Therefore, it must, with circumstance, be spoken
By one whom she esteemeth as his friend.
Duke. Then you must undertake to slander him.
Pro. And that, my lord, I shall be loth to do :
'T is an ill office for a gentleman,   40
Especially, against his very friend.
Duke. Where your good word cannot advantage him,
Your slander never can endamage him :
Therefore, the office is indifferent,
Being entreated to it by your friend.
Pro. You have prevail'd, my lord. If I can do it
By aught that I can speak in his dispraise,
She shall not long continue love to him.
But say, this weed her love from Valentine,
It follows not that she will love Sir Thurio.   50
Thu. Therefore, as you unwind her love from him,
Lest it should ravel and be good to none,
You must provide to bottom it on me ;
Which must be done, by praising me as much
As you in worth dispraise Sir Valentine.
Duke. And, Proteus, we dare trust you in this
        kind,
Because we know, on Valentine's report,
You are already Love's firm votary,
And cannot soon revolt, and change your mind.
Upon this warrant shall you have access   60
Where you with Silvia may confer at large ;
For she is lumpish, heavy, melancholy,
And for your friend's sake, will be glad of you,
Where you may temper her by your persuasion,
To hate young Valentine, and love my friend.
Pro. As much as I can do I will effect.
But you, Sir Thurio, are not sharp enough ;
You must lay lime to tangle her desires
By wailful sonnets, whose composed rhymes
Should be full fraught with serviceable vows.   70
Duke. Ay,
Much is the force of heaven-bred poesy.
Pro. Say, that upon the altar of her beauty
You sacrifice your tears, your sighs, your heart.
Write, till your ink be dry, and with your tears
Moist it again ; and frame some feeling line,

That may discover such integrity :
For Orpheus' lute was strung with poets' sinews,
Whose golden touch could soften steel and stones,
Make tigers tame, and huge leviathans   80
Forsake unsounded deeps to dance on sands.
After your dire-lamenting elegies,
Visit by night your lady's chamber-window
With some sweet concert : to their instruments
Tune a deploring dump ; the night's dead silence
Will well become such sweet-complaining grievance.
This, or else nothing, will inherit her.

Duke. This discipline shows thou hast been in love.
Thu. And thy advice this night I 'll put in practice.
Therefore, sweet Proteus, my direction-giver,   90
Let us into the city presently,
To sort some gentlemen well skill'd in music.
I have a sonnet that will serve the turn
To give the onset to thy good advice.
Duke. About it, gentlemen !
Pro. We 'll wait upon your grace till after supper,
And afterward determine our proceedings.
Duke. Even now about it ! I will pardon you.
                     [*Exeunt.*

ACT IV.

Scene I.--A Forest, between Milan and Verona.

Enter certain Outlaws.

1 Outlaw.
FELLOWS, stand fast : I see a
   passenger.
2 Out. If there be ten, shrink
   not, but down with 'em.

Enter Valentine *and* Speed.

3 Out. Stand, sir, and throw us
   that you have about you;
If not, we 'll make you sit, and
   rifle you.
Speed. Sir, we are undone. These are the villains
That all the travellers do fear so much.
Val. My friends,—
1 Out. That 's not so, sir : we are your enemies.
2 Out. Peace ! we 'll hear him.
3 Out. Ay, by my beard, will we ; for he is a proper
   man.   10
Val. Then know, that I have little wealth to lose.
A man I am cross'd with adversity ;
My riches are these poor habiliments,
Of which if you should here disfurnish me,
You take the sum and substance that I have.
2 Out. Whither travel you ?
Val. To Verona.
1 Out. Whence came you ?
Val. From Milan.
3 Out. Have you long sojourn'd there ?   20
Val. Some sixteen months ; and longer might have
   stay'd,
If crooked fortune had not thwarted me.
1 Out. What ! were you banish'd thence ?
Val. I was.
2 Out. For what offence ?
Val. For that which now torments me to rehearse.
I kill'd a man, whose death I much repent ;
But yet I slew him manfully in fight,
Without false vantage, or base treachery.
1 Out. Why, ne'er repent it, if it were done so.   30
But were you banish'd for so small a fault ?
Val. I was, and held me glad of such a doom.
2 Out. Have you the tongues ?
Val. My youthful travel therein made me happy,
Or else I often had been miserable.
3 Out. By the bare scalp of Robin Hood's fat friar,
This fellow were a king for our wild faction.
1 Out. We 'll have him. Sirs, a word.
Speed. Master, be one of them :
It is an honourable kind of thievery.   40
Val. Peace, villain !
2 Out. Tell us this : have you anything to take to ?

Val. Nothing, but my fortune.
3 Out. Know then, that some of us are gentlemen,
Such as the fury of ungovern'd youth
Thrust from the company of awful men :
Myself was from Verona banished
For practising to steal away a lady,
An heir, and near allied unto the duke.
2 Out. And I from Mantua, for a gentleman,   50
Who, in my mood, I stabb'd unto the heart.

3 Out. "Say, ay, and be the captain of us all."

1 Out. And I for such-like petty crimes as these.
But to the purpose ; for we cite our faults,
That they may hold excus'd our lawless lives ;
And, partly, seeing you are beautified
With goodly shape, and by your own report
A linguist, and a man of such perfection,
As we do in our quality much want—
2 Out. Indeed, because you are a banish'd man,
Therefore, above the rest, we parley to you.   60
Are you content to be our general ?
To make a virtue of necessity,
And live, as we do, in this wilderness ?
3 Out. What say'st thou ? wilt thou be of our consort ?
Say, ay, and be the captain of us all.

We 'll do thee homage, and be rul'd by thee,
Love thee as our commander, and our king.

1 Out. But if thou scorn our courtesy, thou diest.

2 Out. Thou shalt not live to brag what we have
offer'd.

Val. I take your offer, and will live with you ; 70
Provided that you do no outrages
On silly women, or poor passengers.

3 Out. No ; we detest such vile, base practices.
Come, go with us : we 'll bring thee to our crews,
And show thee all the treasure we have got,
Which, with ourselves, all rest at thy dispose.
                                    [*Exeunt.*

SCENE II.—Milan. The Court of the Palace.

Enter PROTEUS.

Pro. Already have I been false to Valentine,
And now I must be as unjust to Thurio.
Under the colour of commending him,
I have access my own love to prefer :
But Silvia is too fair, too true, too holy,
To be corrupted with my worthless gifts.
When I protest true loyalty to her,
She twits me with my falsehood to my friend ;
When to her beauty I commend my vows,
She bids me think how I have been forsworn, 10
In breaking faith with Julia whom I lov'd :
And, notwithstanding all her sudden quips,
The least whereof would quell a lover's hope,
Yet, spaniel-like, the more she spurns my love,
The more it grows, and fawneth on her still.
But here comes Thurio. Now must we to her window,
And give some evening music to her ear.

Enter THURIO, *and Musicians.*

Thu. How now, Sir Proteus? are you crept before
us ?

Pro. Ay, gentle Thurio ; for you know that love
Will creep in service where it cannot go. 20

Thu. Ay ; but I hope, sir, that you love not here.

Pro. Sir, but I do ; or else I would be hence.

Thu. Who ? Silvia ?

Pro.   Ay, Silvia,—for your sake.

Thu. I thank you for your own. Now, gentlemen,
Let 's tune, and to it lustily awhile.

Enter Host and JULIA, *behind ;* JULIA *in boy's
clothes.*

Host. Now, my young guest ; methinks you 're allicholly : I pray you, why is it ?

Jul. Marry, mine host, because I cannot be merry.

Host. Come, we 'll have you merry. I 'll bring you
where you shall hear music, and see the gentleman
that you ask'd for. 31

Jul. But shall I hear him speak ?

Host. Ay, that you shall.

Jul. That will be music.   [*Music plays.*

Host. Hark ! hark !

Jul. Is he among these ?

Host. Ay ; but peace ! let 's hear 'em.

SONG.

Who is Silvia ? what is she,
    That all our swains commend her ?
Holy, fair, and wise is she ; 40
    The heaven such grace did lend her
    That she might admired be.

Is she kind, as she is fair ?
    For beauty lives with kindness :
Love doth to her eyes repair,
    To help him of his blindness ;
And, being help'd, inhabits there.

Then to Silvia let us sing,
    That Silvia is excelling ;
She excels each mortal thing 50
    Upon the dull earth dwelling ;
To her let us garlands bring.

Host. How now ! are you sadder than you were
before ? How do you, man ? the music likes you not.

Jul. You mistake : the musician likes me not.

Host. Why, my pretty youth ?

Jul. He plays false, false.

Host. How ? out of tune on the strings ?

Jul. Not so ; but yet so false, that he grieves my
very heartstrings. 60

Host. You have a quick ear.

Jul. Ay ; I would I were deaf ! it makes me have a
slow heart.

Host. I perceive, you delight not in music.

Jul. Not a whit, when it jars so.

Host. Hark ! what fine change is in the music.

Jul. Ay, that change is the spite.

Host. You would have them always play but one
thing ?

Jul. I would always have one play but one thing. 70
But, host, doth this Sir Proteus, that we talk on,
Often resort unto this gentlewoman ?

Host. I tell you what Launce, his man, told me,—
he lov'd her out of all nick.

Jul. Where is Launce ?

Host. Gone to seek his dog ; which, to-morrow, by
his master's command, he must carry for a present to
his lady.

Jul. Peace ! stand aside : the company parts.

Pro. Sir Thurio, fear not you : I will so plead 80
That you shall say my cunning drift excels.

Thu. Where meet we ?

Pro.   At Saint Gregory's well.

Thu.   Farewell.
                [*Exeunt* THURIO *and Musicians.*

Enter SILVIA *above, at her window.*

Pro. Madam, good even to your ladyship.

Sil. I thank you for your music, gentlemen.
Who is that that spake ?

Pro. One, lady, if you knew his pure heart's truth,
You would quickly learn to know him by his voice.

Sil. Sir Proteus, as I take it.

Pro. Sir Proteus, gentle lady, and your servant.

Sil. What is your will ?

Pro.   That I may compass yours.

Sil. You have your wish : my will is even this, 91
That presently you hie you home to bed.
Thou subtle, perjur'd, false, disloyal man !
Think'st thou, I am so shallow, so conceitless,
To be seduced by thy flattery,
That hast deceiv'd so many with thy vows ?
Return, return, and make thy love amends.
For me, by this pale queen of night I swear,
I am so far from granting thy request,
That I despise thee for thy wrongful suit, 100
And by-and-by intend to chide myself,
Even for this time I spend in talking to thee.

Pro. I grant, sweet love, that I did love a lady ;
But she is dead.

Jul. [*Aside.*] 'T were false, if I should speak it ;
For, I am sure, she is not buried.

Sil. Say, that she be ; yet Valentine, thy friend,
Survives, to whom, thyself art witness,
I am betroth'd ; and art thou not asham'd
To wrong him with thy importunacy ? 110

Pro. I likewise hear, that Valentine is dead.

Sil. And so, suppose, am I ; for in his grave,
Assure thyself, my love is buried.

Pro. Sweet lady, let me rake it from the earth.

Sil. Go to thy lady's grave, and call hers thence ;
Or, at the least, in hers sepulchre thine.

Jul. [*Aside.*] He heard not that.

Pro. Madam, if your heart be so obdurate,
Vouchsafe me yet your picture for my love,
The picture that is hanging in your chamber : 120
To that I 'll speak, to that I 'll sigh and weep ;
For, since the substance of your perfect self
Is else devoted, I am but a shadow,
And to your shadow will I make true love.

Jul. [*Aside.*] If 't were a substance, you would, sure,
    deceive it,
And make it but a shadow, as I am.

Sil. I am very loth to be your idol, sir ;
But, since your falsehood shall become you well
To worship shadows, and adore false shapes,
Send to me in the morning, and I'll send it.   130
And so, good rest.

SCENE III.—The Same.

Enter EGLAMOUR.

Egl. This is the hour that Madam Silvia
Entreated me to call, and know her mind.

Sil. " I am very loth to be your idol, sir."

Pro.   As wretches have o'ernight,
That wait for execution in the morn.
           [*Exeunt* PROTEUS, *and* SILVIA.
   Jul. Host, will you go ?
   Host. By my halidom, I was fast asleep.
   Jul. Pray you, where lies Sir Proteus ?
   Host. Marry, at my house. Trust me, I think, 't is
almost day.
   Jul. Not so ; but it hath been the longest night
That e'er I watch'd, and the most heaviest. [*Exeunt.*

There 's some great matter she 'd employ me in.—
Madam, madam !

Enter SILVIA *above, at her window.*

   Sil. Who calls ?
   Egl.   Your servant, and your friend ;
One that attends your ladyship's command.
   Sil. Sir Eglamour, a thousand times good morrow.
   Egl. As many, worthy lady, to yourself.
According to your ladyship's impose,

I am thus early come, to know what service   10
It is your pleasure to command me in.
  Sil. O Eglamour, thou art a gentleman
(Think not I flatter, for I swear I do not),
Valiant, wise, remorseful, well accomplish'd.
That art not ignorant what dear good will
I bear unto the banish'd Valentine,
Nor how my father would enforce me marry
Vain Thurio, whom my very soul abhors.
Thyself hast lov'd ; and I have heard thee say,
No grief did ever come so near thy heart,   20
As when thy lady and thy true love died,
Upon whose grave thou vow'dst pure chastity.
Sir Eglamour, I would to Valentine,
To Mantua, where, I hear, he makes abode ;
And, for the ways are dangerous to pass,
I do desire thy worthy company,
Upon whose faith and honour I repose.
Urge not my father's anger, Eglamour,
But think upon my grief, a lady's grief,
And on the justice of my flying hence,   30
To keep me from a most unholy match,
Which heaven and fortune still rewards with plagues.
I do desire thee, even from a heart
As full of sorrows as the sea of sands,
To bear me company, and go with me :
If not, to hide what I have said to thee,
That I may venture to depart alone.
  Egl. Madam, I pity much your grievances ;
Which since I know they virtuously are plac'd,
I give consent to go along with you ;   40
Recking as little what betideth me,
As much I wish all good befortune you.
When will you go?
  Sil.   This evening coming.
  Egl. Where shall I meet you?
  Sil.   At Friar Patrick's cell,
Where I intend holy confession.
  Egl. I will not fail your ladyship.
Good morrow, gentle lady.
  Sil. Good morrow, kind Sir Eglamour.   [*Exeunt.*

SCENE IV.—The Same.

Enter LAUNCE *with his dog.*

  Launce. When a man's servant shall play the cur
with him, look you, it goes hard : one that I brought
up of a puppy ; one that I saved from drowning,
when three or four of his blind brothers and sisters
went to it. I have taught him, even as one would
say precisely, "Thus I would teach a dog." I was
sent to deliver him as a present to Mistress Silvia
from my master, and I came no sooner into the
dining-chamber, but he steps me to her trencher, and
steals her capon's leg. O! 'tis a foul thing, when a
cur cannot keep himself in all companies. I would
have, as one should say, one that takes upon him
to be a dog indeed, to be, as it were, a dog at all
things. If I had not had more wit than he, to take
a fault upon me that he did, I think verily, he had
been hang'd for 't: sure as I live, he had suffer'd for 't:
you shall judge. He thrusts me himself into the
company of three or four gentleman-like dogs under
the duke's table : he had not been there (bless the
mark) a pissing while, but all the chamber smelt
him. "Out with the dog!" says one ; "What cur
is that ?" says another ; "Whip him out," says the
third ; "Hang him up," says the duke. I, having
been acquainted with the smell before, knew it was
Crab, and goes me to the fellow that whips the dogs :
"Friend," quoth I, "you mean to whip the dog ?"
"Ay, marry, do I," quoth he. "You do him the more
wrong," quoth I ; "'t was I did the thing you wot of."
He makes me no more ado, but whips me out of the
chamber. How many masters would do this for his
servant? Nay, I'll be sworn, I have sat in the stocks
for puddings he hath stolen, otherwise he had been
executed ; I have stood on the pillory for geese he
hath kill'd, otherwise he had suffer'd for 't : thou
think'st not of this now.—Nay, I remember the trick

you served me, when I took my leave of Madam
Silvia. Did not I bid thee still mark me, and do as I
do ? When didst thou see me heave up my leg, and
make water against a gentlewoman's farthingale ?
Didst thou ever see me do such a trick ?   40

Enter PROTEUS *and* JULIA.

  Pro. Sebastian is thy name ? I like thee well,
And will employ thee in some service presently.
  Jul. In what you please : I will do what I can.
  Pro. I hope thou wilt.—How now, you whoreson
peasant !
Where have you been these two days loitering ?
  Launce. Marry, sir, I carried Mistress Silvia the
dog you bade me.
  Pro: And what says she to my little jewel ?
  Launce. Marry, she says, your dog was a cur ; and
tells you, currish thanks is good enough for such a
present.   51
  Pro. But she receiv'd my dog ?
  Launce. No, indeed, did she not. Here have I
brought him back again.
  Pro. What ! didst thou offer her this from me ?
  Launce. Ay, sir : the other squirrel was stolen from
me by the hangman's boys in the market-place ; and
then I offer'd her mine own, who is a dog as big as ten
of yours, and therefore the gift the greater.
  Pro. Go get thee hence, and find my dog again,   60
Or ne'er return again into my sight.
Away, I say ! Stay'st thou to vex me here ?
A slave that still an end turns me to shame.   [*Exit* LAUNCE.
Sebastian, I have entertained thee,
Partly, that I have need of such a youth,
That can with some discretion do my business,
For 't is no trusting to yond foolish lout ;
But, chiefly, for thy face, and thy behaviour,
Which (if my augury deceive me not)
Witness good bringing up, fortune, and truth :   70

Pro. "Go presently, and take this ring with thee."

Therefore know thee, for this I entertain thee.
Go presently, and take this ring with thee :
Deliver it to Madam Silvia.
She lov'd me well, deliver'd it to me.
  Jul. It seems, you lov'd not her, to leave her token.
She 's dead, belike ?
  Pro.   Not so : I think, she lives.
  Jul. Alas !
  Pro. Why dost thou cry, Alas ?
  Jul. I cannot choose but pity her.
  Pro. Wherefore shouldst thou pity her ?   80
  Jul. Because, methinks, that she lov'd you as well
As you do love your lady Silvia.
She dreams on him, that has forgot her love ;
You dote on her, that cares not for your love.

'T is pity, love should be so contrary;
And thinking on it makes me cry, Alas!
  Pro. Well, give her that ring, and therewithal
This letter:—that 's her chamber.—Tell my lady,
I claim the promise for her heavenly picture.
Your message done, hie home unto my chamber, 90
Where thou shalt find me sad and solitary.   [*Exit.*
  Jul. How many women would do such a message?
Alas, poor Proteus! thou hast entertain'd
A fox to be the shepherd of thy lambs.
Alas, poor fool! why do I pity him,
That with his very heart despiseth me?
Because he loves her, he despiseth me;
Because I love him, I must pity him.
This ring I gave him when he parted from me,
To bind him to remember my good will;   100
And now am I (unhappy messenger!)
To plead for that which I would not obtain;
To carry that which I would have refus'd,
To praise his faith which I would have disprais'd.
I am my master's true-confirmed love,
But cannot be true servant to my master,
Unless I prove false traitor to myself.
Yet will I woo for him; but yet so coldly,
As, heaven it knows, I would not have him speed.

    Enter SILVIA, *attended.*

Gentlewoman, good day. I pray you, be my mean 110
To bring me where to speak with Madam Silvia.
  Sil. What would you with her, if that I be she?
  Jul. If you be she, I do entreat your patience
To hear me speak the message I am sent on.
  Sil. From whom?
  Jul. From my master, Sir Proteus, madam.
  Sil. O! he sends you for a picture?
  Jul. Ay, madam.
  Sil. Ursula, bring my picture there.
          [*A picture brought.*
Go, give your master this: tell him from me,   120
One Julia, that his changing thoughts forget,
Would better fit his chamber, than this shadow.
  Jul. Madam, please you peruse this letter. –
Pardon me, madam, I have unadvis'd
Deliver'd you a paper that I should not:
This is the letter to your ladyship.
  Sil. I pray thee, let me look on that again.
  Jul. It may not be: good madam, pardon me.
  Sil. There, hold.
I will not look upon your master's lines: 130
I know, they are stuff'd with protestations,
And full of new-found oaths, which he will break
As easily as I do tear his paper.
  Jul. Madam, he sends your ladyship this ring.
  Sil. The more shame for him that he sends it me;
For I have heard him say a thousand times,
His Julia gave it him at his departure.
Though his false finger have profan'd the ring,
Mine shall not do his Julia so much wrong.
  Jul. She thanks you.   140
  Sil. What say'st thou?
  Jul. I thank you, madam, that you tender her.
Poor gentlewoman! my master wrongs her much.
  Sil. Dost thou know her?
  Jul. Almost as well as I do know myself:
To think upon her woes, I do protest,
That I have wept a hundred several times.
  Sil. Belike, she thinks, that Proteus hath forsook
    her.
  Jul. I think she doth, and that 's her cause of sorrow.
  Sil. Is she not passing fair?   150
  Jul. She hath been fairer, madam, than she is.
When she did think my master lov'd her well,
She, in my judgment, was as fair as you;
But since she did neglect her looking-glass,
And threw her sun-expelling mask away,
The air hath starv'd the roses in her cheeks,
And pinch'd the lily-tincture of her face,
That now she is become as black as I.

  Sil. How tall was she?
  Jul. About my stature; for, at Pentecost,   160
When all our pageants of delight were play'd,
Our youth got me to play the woman's part,
And I was trimm'd in Madam Julia's gown,
Which served me as fit, by all men's judgments,
As if the garment had been made for me:
Therefore, I know she is about my height.
And at that time I made her weep agood,
For I did play a lamentable part.
Madam, 't was Ariadne, passioning
For Theseus' perjury and unjust flight;   170
Which I so lively acted with my tears,
That my poor mistress, moved therewithal,
Wept bitterly, and 'would I might be dead,
If I in thought felt not her very sorrow.
  Sil. She is beholding to thee, gentle youth.
Alas, poor lady! desolate and left!—
I weep myself, to think upon thy words.
Here, youth; there is my purse: I give thee this
For thy sweet mistress' sake, because thou lov'st her.
Farewell.   180
          [*Exit* SILVIA, *attended.*

Jul. "Here is her picture."

  Jul. And she shall thank you for 't, if e'er you know
    her.—
A virtuous gentlewoman, mild, and beautiful!
I hope my master's suit will be but cold,
Since she respects my mistress' love so much.
Alas, how love can trifle with itself!
Here is her picture. Let me see: I think,
If I had such a tire, this face of mine
Were full as lovely as is this of hers;
And yet the painter flatter'd her a little,
Unless I flatter with myself too much.   190
Her hair is auburn, mine is perfect yellow:
If that be all the difference in his love,
I 'll get me such a colour'd periwig.
Her eyes are grey as glass, and so are mine:
Ay, but her forehead 's low, and mine 's as high.
What should it be, that he respects in her,
But I can make respective in myself,
If this fond Love were not a blinded god?
Come, shadow, come, and take this shadow up,
For 't is thy rival. O thou senseless form!   200
Thou shalt be worship'd, kiss'd, lov'd, and ador'd,
And, were there sense in this idolatry,
My substance should be statue in thy stead.
I 'll use thee kindly for thy mistress' sake,
That us'd me so, or else, by Jove I vow,
I should have scratch'd out your unseeing eyes,
To make my master out of love with thee.   [*Exit.*

ACT V.

SCENE I.—The Same. An Abbey.

Enter EGLAMOUR.

Eglamour.
THE sun begins to gild the western sky,
And now it is about the very hour,
That Silvia at Friar Patrick's cell should
        meet me.
She will not fail; for lovers break not
        hours,
Unless it be to come before their time
So much they spur their expedition.

Enter SILVIA.

See, where she comes.—Lady, a happy
        evening!
Sil. Amen, amen! go on, good Eglamour,
Out at the postern by the abbey-wall.
I fear, I am attended by some spies.   10
Egl. Fear not : the forest is not three leagues off ;
If we recover that, we are sure enough.   [*Exeunt.*

SCENE II.—The Same.—A Room in the DUKE'S Palace.

Enter THURIO, PROTEUS, *and* JULIA.

Thu. Sir Proteus, what says Silvia to my suit ?
Pro. O, sir ! I find her milder than she was ;
And yet she takes exceptions at your person.
Thu. What ! that my leg is too long ?
Pro. No, that it is too little.
Thu. I'll wear a boot to make it somewhat rounder.
Jul. [*Aside.*] But love will not be spurr'd to what it
        loathes.
Thu. What says she to my face ?
Pro. She says it is a fair one.
Thu. Nay, then the wanton lies : my face is black. 10
Pro. But pearls are fair, and the old saying is,
Black men are pearls in beauteous ladies' eyes.
Jul. [*Aside.*] 'T is true, such pearls as put out ladies'
        eyes :
For I had rather wink than look on them.
Thu. How likes she my discourse ?
Pro. Ill, when you talk of war.
Thu. But well, when I discourse of love and peace ?
Jul. [*Aside.*] But better, indeed, when you hold
        your peace.
Thu. What says she to my valour ?
Pro. O, sir ! she makes no doubt of that.   20
Jul. [*Aside.*] She needs not, when she knows it
        cowardice.
Thu. What says she to my birth ?
Pro. That you are well deriv'd.
Jul. [*Aside.*] True ; from a gentleman to a fool.
Thu. Considers she my possessions ?
Pro. O! ay ; and pities them.
Thu. Wherefore ?
Jul. [*Aside.*] That such an ass should owe them.
Pro. That they are out by lease.
Jul. Here comes the duke.   30

Enter DUKE.

Duke. How now, Sir Proteus ? how now, Thurio ?
Which of you saw Sir Eglamour of late ?

Thu. Not I.
Pro.   Nor I.
Duke.   Saw you my daughter ?
Pro.   Neither.
Duke. Why, then
She's fled unto that peasant Valentine,
And Eglamour is in her company.
'T is true ; for Friar Laurence met them both,
As he in penance wander'd through the forest ;
Him he knew well, and guess'd that it was she,
But, being mask'd, he was not sure of it ;   40
Besides, she did intend confession
At Patrick's cell this even, and there she was not.
These likelihoods confirm her flight from hence.
Therefore, I pray you, stand not to discourse,
But mount you presently ; and meet with me
Upon the rising of the mountain-foot,
That leads towards Mantua, whither they are fled.
Dispatch, sweet gentlemen, and follow me.   [*Exit.*
Thu. Why, this it is to be a peevish girl,
That flies her fortune when it follows her.   50
I'll after, more to be reveng'd on Eglamour,
Than for the love of reckless Silvia.   [*Exit.*
Pro. And I will follow, more for Silvia's love,
Than hate of Eglamour, that goes with her.   [*Exit.*
Jul. And I will follow, more to cross that love,
Than hate for Silvia, that is gone for love.   [*Exit.*

SCENE III.—The Forest.

Enter SILVIA, *and Outlaws.*

1 Out. Come, come ;
Be patient, we must bring you to our captain.
Sil. A thousand more mischances than this one
Have learn'd me how to brook this patiently.
2 Out. Come, bring her away.
1 Out. Where is the gentleman that was with her ?
3 Out. Being nimble-footed, he hath outrun us ;
But Moyses and Valerius follow him.
Go thou with her to the west end of the wood ;
There is our captain. We 'll follow him that 's fled : 10
The thicket is beset ; he cannot scape.
1 Out. Come, I must bring you to our captain's cave.
Fear not ; he bears an honourable mind,
And will not use a woman lawlessly.
Sil. O Valentine ! this I endure for thee.   [*Exeunt.*

SCENE IV.—Another Part of the Forest.

Enter VALENTINE.

Val. How use doth breed a habit in a man !
This shadowy desert, unfrequented woods,
I better brook than flourishing peopled towns.
Here can I sit alone, unseen of any,
And to the nightingale's complaining notes
Tune my distresses, and record my woes.
O! thou that dost inhabit in my breast,
Leave not the mansion so long tenantless,
Lest, growing ruinous, the building fall,

And leave no memory of what it was!   10
Repair me with thy presence, Silvia!
Thou gentle nymph, cherish thy forlorn swain!—
What halloing, and what stir, is this to-day?
These are my mates, that make their wills their law,
Have some unhappy passenger in chase.
They love me well; yet I have much to do,
To keep them from uncivil outrages.
Withdraw thee, Valentine: who's this comes here?
                                        [*Steps aside.*

Enter PROTEUS, SILVIA, *and* JULIA.

Pro. Madam, this service I have done for you
(Though you respect not aught your servant doth), 20
To hazard life, and rescue you from him
That would have forc'd your honour and your love.
Vouchsafe me, for my meed, but one fair look;
A smaller boon than this I cannot beg,
And less than this, I am sure, you cannot give.
Val. How like a dream is this I see and hear!
Love, lend me patience to forbear awhile.
Sil. O miserable, unhappy that I am!
Pro. Unhappy were you, madam, ere I came;
But by my coming I have made you happy.   30
Sil. By thy approach thou mak'st me most unhappy.
Jul. [*Aside.*] And me, when he approacheth to
your presence.
Sil. Had I been seized by a hungry lion,
I would have been a breakfast to the beast,
Rather than have false Proteus rescue me.
O Heaven! be judge, how I love Valentine,
Whose life's as tender to me as my soul;
And full as much (for more there cannot be)
I do detest false perjur'd Proteus.
Therefore be gone: solicit me no more.   40
Pro. What dangerous action, stood it next to death,
Would I not undergo for one calm look!
O! 'tis the curse in love, and still approv'd,
When women cannot love, where they're belov'd.
Sil. When Proteus cannot love, where he's belov'd.
Read over Julia's heart, thy first best love,
For whose dear sake thou didst then rend thy fait'
Into a thousand oaths; and all those oaths
Descended into perjury to love me.
Thou hast no faith left now, unless thou'dst two, 50
And that's far worse than none: better have none
Than plural faith, which is too much by one.
Thou counterfeit to thy true friend!
Pro.   In love,
Who respects friend?
Sil.   All men but Proteus.
Pro. Nay, if the gentle spirit of moving words
Can no way change you to a milder form,
I'll woo you like a soldier, at arms' end,
And love you 'gainst the nature of love: force you.
Sil. O Heaven!
Pro.   I'll force thee yield to my desire.
Val. Ruffian, let go that rude uncivil touch;   60
Thou friend of an ill fashion!
Pro.   Valentine!
Val. Thou common friend, that's without faith or
love
(For such is a friend now); treacherous man!
Thou hast beguil'd my hopes: nought but mine eye
Could have persuaded me. Now I dare not say,
I have one friend alive: thou wouldst disprove me.
Who should be trusted now, when one's right hand
Is perjur'd to the bosom? Proteus,
I am sorry I must never trust thee more,
But count the world a stranger for thy sake.   70
The private wound is deepest. O time most accurst!
'Mongst all foes, that a friend should be the worst!
Pro. My shame and guilt confounds me.—
Forgive me, Valentine. If hearty sorrow
Be a sufficient ransom for offence,
I tender 't here: I do as truly suffer
As e'er I did commit.
Val.   Then I am paid;
And once again I do receive thee honest.
Who by repentance is not satisfied,
Is nor of heaven, nor earth; for these are pleas'd. 80
By penitence the Eternal's wrath's appeas'd:

And, that my love may appear plain and free,
All that was mine in Silvia I give thee.
Jul. O me unhappy!   [*Faints.*
Pro. Look to the boy.
Val. Why, boy! why, wag! how now? what is the
matter?
Look up; speak.
Jul.   O good sir! my master charg'd me
To deliver a ring to Madam Silvia,
Which, out of my neglect, was never done.
Pro. Where is that ring, boy?
Jul.   Here 't is: this is it. [*Gives a ring.*
Pro. How! let me see.   91
Why, this is the ring I gave to Julia.
Jul. O! cry you mercy, sir; I have mistook:
This is the ring you sent to Silvia.
                            [*Shows another ring.*
Pro. But, how cam'st thou by this ring?
At my depart I gave this unto Julia.

Pro. "But, how cam'st thou by this ring?"

Jul. And Julia herself did give it me;
And Julia herself hath brought it hither.
Pro. How? Julia!
Jul. Behold her that gave aim to all thy oaths, 100
And entertain'd them deeply in her heart:
How oft hast thou with perjury cleft the root!
O Proteus! let this habit make thee blush:
Be thou asham'd, that I have took upon me
Such an immodest raiment; if shame live
In a disguise of love.
It is the lesser blot, modesty finds,
Women to change their shapes, than men their minds.
Pro. Than men their minds! 'tis true. O Heaven!
were man   110
But constant, he were perfect: that one error
Fills him with faults; makes him run through all the
sins:
Inconstancy falls off, ere it begins.
What is in Silvia's face, but I may spy
More fresh in Julia's, with a constant eye?
Val. Come, come, a hand from either.
Let me be blest to make this happy close:
'T were pity two such friends should be long foes.
Pro. Bear witness, Heaven, I have my wish for ever.
Jul. And I mine.

Enter Outlaws, with DUKE *and* THURIO.

Outlaws. A prize! a prize! a prize!   120
Val. Forbear: forbear, I say; it is my lord the
duke.—
Your grace is welcome to a man disgrac'd,
Banished Valentine.
Duke.   Sir Valentine!
Thu. Yonder is Silvia; and Silvia's mine.
Val. Thurio, give back, or else embrace thy death.

Come not within the measure of my wrath :
Do not name Silvia thine ; if once again,
Verona shall not hold thee.　Here she stands :
Take but possession of her with a touch ;
I dare thee but to breathe upon my love.　　130
　Thu. Sir Valentine, I care not for her, I.
I hold him but a fool that will endanger
His body for a girl that loves him not :
I claim her not, and therefore she is thine.
　Duke. The more degenerate and base art thou,
To make such means for her as thou hast done,
And leave her on such slight conditions.
Now, by the honour of my ancestry,
I do applaud thy spirit, Valentine,
And think thee worthy of an empress' love.　　140
Know then, I here forget all former griefs,
Cancel all grudge, repeal thee home again.—
Plead a new state in thy unrivall'd merit,
To which I thus subscribe : Sir Valentine,
Thou art a gentleman, and well deriv'd ;
Take thou thy Silvia, for thou hast deserv'd her.
　Val. I thank your grace ; the gift hath made me
　　　happy.
I now beseech you, for your daughter's sake
To grant one boon that I shall ask of you.

　Duke. I grant it for thine own, whate'er it be.　150
　Val. These banish'd men, that I have kept withal,
Are men endued with worthy qualities :
Forgive them what they have committed here,
And let them be recall'd from their exile.
They are reformed, civil, full of good,
And fit for great employment, worthy lord.
　Duke. Thou hast prevail'd ; I pardon them, and
　　　thee :
Dispose of them, as thou know'st their deserts.
Come, let us go : we will include all jars
With triumphs, mirth, and rare solemnity.　　160
　Val. And as we walk along, I dare be bold
With our discourse to make your grace to smile.
What think you of this page, my lord ?
　Duke. I think the boy hath grace in him : he blushes.
　Val. I warrant you, my lord, more grace than
　　　boy.
　Duke. What mean you by that saying ?
　Val. Please you, I 'll tell you as we pass along,
That you will wonder what hath fortuned.—
Come, Proteus ; 't is your penance but to hear
The story of your loves discovered :　　170
That done, our day of marriage shall be yours ;
One feast, one house, one mutual happiness. [*Exeunt.*

THE MERRY WIVES OF WINDSOR.

DRAMATIS PERSONÆ.

SIR JOHN FALSTAFF.
FENTON.
SHALLOW, *a Country Justice.*
SLENDER, *Cousin to Shallow.*
FORD, } *Two Gentlemen dwelling at Windsor.*
PAGE, }
WILLIAM PAGE, *a Boy, Son to Mr. Page.*
SIR HUGH EVANS, *a Welsh Parson.*
DOCTOR CAIUS, *a French Physician.*
Host of the Garter Inn.

BARDOLPH, PISTOL, NYM, *Followers of Falstaff.*
ROBIN, *Page to Falstaff.*
SIMPLE, *Servant to Slender.*
RUGBY, *Servant to Doctor Caius.*
MISTRESS FORD.
MISTRESS PAGE.
ANNE PAGE, *her Daughter, in love with Fenton.*
MISTRESS QUICKLY, *Servant to Doctor Caius.*

Servants to Page, Ford, &c.

SCENE—WINDSOR, and the Parts adjacent.

ACT I.

SCENE I.—Windsor. Before PAGE'S House.

Enter Justice SHALLOW, SLENDER, *and Sir* HUGH EVANS.

Shallow.
Sir Hugh, persuade me not; I will make a Star-chamber matter of it: if he were twenty Sir John Falstaffs, he shall not abuse Robert Shallow, esquire.

Slen. In the county of Gloster, justice of peace, and *coram.*

Shal. Ay, cousin Slender, and *cust-alorum.* 9

Slen. Ay, and *ratolorum* too; and a gentleman born, master parson; who writes himself *armigero;* in any bill, warrant, quittance, or obligation, *armigero.*

Shal. Ay, that I do; and have done any time these three hundred years.

Slen. All his successors, gone before him, hath done 't; and all his ancestors, that come after him, may: they may give the dozen white luces in their coat. 21

Shal. It is an old coat.

Eva. The dozen white louses do become an old coat well; it agrees well, passant; it is a familiar beast to man, and signifies love.

Shal. The luce is the fresh fish; the salt fish is an old coat.

Slen. I may quarter, coz?

Shal. You may, by marrying.

Eva. It is marring, indeed, if he quarter it. 30

Shal. Not a whit.

Eva. Yes, per-lady: if he has a quarter of your coat, there is but three skirts for yourself, in my simple conjectures. But that is all one: if Sir John Falstaff have committed disparagements unto you, I am of the church, and will be glad to do my benevolence, to make atonements and compromises between you.

Shal. The Council shall hear it: it is a riot.

Eva. It is not meet the Council hear a riot; there is no fear of Got in a riot. The Council, look you, shall desire to hear the fear of Got, and not to hear a riot: take your vizaments in that. 42

Shal. Ha! o' my life, if I were young again, the sword should end it.

Eva. It is petter that friends is the sword, and end it: and there is also another device in my prain, which,

Shal. Ha! o' my life, if I were young again, the sword should end it."

peradventure, prings goot discretions with it. There is Anne Page, which is daughter to Master George Page, which is pretty virginity.

Slen. Mistress Anne Page? She has brown hair, and speaks small, like a woman. 51

Eva. It is that fery person for all the 'orld: as just as you will desire, and seven hundred pounds of monies, and gold, and silver, is her grandsire, upon his death's-bed (Got deliver to a joyful resurrections!) give, when she is able to overtake seventeen years old. It were a goot motion, if we leave our pribbles and prabbles, and desire a marriage between Master Abraham and Mistress Anne Page.

Shal. Did her grandsire leave her seven hundred pound? 61

Eva. Ay, and her father is make her a petter penny.

Shal. I know the young gentlewoman; she has good gifts.

Eva. Seven hundred pounds, and possibilities, is good gifts.

Shal. Well, let us see honest Master Page. Is Falstaff there? 68

Eva. Shall I tell you a lie? I do despise a liar as I do despise one that is false; or, as I despise one that is not true. The knight, Sir John, is there; and, I beseech you, be ruled by your well-willers. I will peat the door for Master Page. [*Knocks.*] What, hoa! Got pless your house here!

Page. [*Within.*] Who's there?

Eva. Here is Got's plessing, and your friend, and Justice Shallow; and here young Master Slender, that, peradventures, shall tell you another tale, if matters grow to your likings.

Enter PAGE.

Page. I am glad to see your worships well. I thank you for my venison, Master Shallow. 81

Shal. Master Page, I am glad to see you: much good do it your good heart. I wished your venison better; it was ill kill'd.—How doth good Mistress Page?—and I thank you always with my heart, la; with my heart.

Page. Sir, I thank you.

Sial. Sir, I thank you; by yea and no, I do.

Page. I am glad to see you, good Master Slender.

Slen. How does your fallow greyhound, sir? I heard say, he was outrun on Cotsall. 91

Page. It could not be judged, sir.

Slen. You'll not confess, you'll not confess.

Shal. That he will not.—'T is your fault, 't is your fault.—'T is a good dog.

Page. A cur, sir.

Shal. Sir, he's a good dog, and a fair dog; can there be more said? he is good, and fair. Is Sir John Falstaff here?

Page. Sir, he is within; and I would I could do a good office between you. 101

Eva. It is spoke as a Christians ought to speak.

Shal. He hath wrong'd me, Master Page.

Page. Sir, he doth in some sort confess it.

Shal. If it be confess'd, it is not redress'd: is not that so, Master Page? He hath wrong'd me; indeed, he hath;—at a word, he hath;—believe me:—Robert Shallow, esquire, saith, he is wrong'd.

Page. Here comes Sir John.

Enter Sir JOHN FALSTAFF, BARDOLPH, NYM, *and* PISTOL.

Fal. Now, Master Shallow, you'll complain of me to the king? 111

Shal. Knight, you have beaten my men, killed my deer, and broke open my lodge.

Fal. But not kiss'd your keeper's daughter?

Shal. Tut, a pin! this shall be answered.

Fal. I will answer it straight:—I have done all this.—That is now answer'd.

Shal. The Council shall know this.

Fal. 'T were better for you, if it were known in counsel: you'll be laughed at. 120

Eva. Pauca verba, Sir John; good worts.

Fal. Good worts? good cabbage.—Slender, I broke your head: what matter have you against me?

Slen. Marry, sir, I have matter in my head against you; and against your cony-catching rascals, Bardolph, Nym, and Pistol. They carried me to the tavern, and made me drunk, and afterwards picked my pocket.

Bard. You Banbury cheese!

Slen. Ay, it is no matter. 130

Pist. How now, Mephostophilus?

Slen. Ay, it is no matter.

Nym. Slice, I say! pauca, pauca; slice! that's my humour.

Slen. Where's Simple, my man?—can you tell, cousin?

Eva. Peace! I pray you. Now let us understand: there is three umpires in this matter, as I understand; that is—Master Page, fidelicet, Master Page; and

there is myself, fidelicet, myself; and the three party is, lastly and finally, mine host of the Garter. 141

Page. We three, to hear it, and end it between them.

Eva. Fery goot: I will make a prief of it in my note-book; and we will afterwards 'ork upon the cause, with as great discreetly as we can.

Fal. Pistol!

Pist. He hears with ears.

Eva. The tevil and his tam! what phrase is this, "He hears with ear?" Why, it is affectations. 150

Fal. Pistol, did you pick Master Slender's purse?

Slen. Ay, by these gloves, did he (or I would I might never come in mine own great chamber again else), of seven groats in mill-sixpences, and two Edward shovel-boards, that cost me two shilling and two pence a-piece of Yed Miller, by these gloves.

Fal. Is this true, Pistol?

Eva. No; it is false, if it is a pick-purse.

Pist. Ha, thou mountain-foreigner!—Sir John and master mine,

I combat challenge of this latten bilbo: 160
Word of denial in thy labras here;
Word of denial: froth and scum, thou liest.

Slen. By these gloves, then 't was he.

Nym. Be avised, sir, and pass good humours. I will say, "marry trap," with you, if you run the nuthook's humour on me; that is the very note of it.

Slen. By this hat, then he in the red face had it; for though I cannot remember what I did when you made me drunk, yet I am not altogether an ass.

Fal. What say you, Scarlet and John? 170

Bard. Why, sir, for my part, I say, the gentleman had drunk himself out of his five sentences.

Eva. It is his five senses: fie, what the ignorance is!

Bard. And being fap, sir, was, as they say, cashier'd; and so conclusions pass'd the careires.

Slen. Ay, you spake in Latin then too; but 't is no matter. I'll ne'er be drunk whilst I live again, but in honest, civil, godly company, for this trick: if I be drunk, I'll be drunk with those that have the fear of God, and not with drunken knaves. 180

Eva. So Got 'udge me, that is a virtuous mind.

Fal. You hear all these matters denied, gentlemen; you hear it.

Enter ANNE PAGE, *with wine; Mistress* FORD *and Mistress* PAGE *following.*

Page. Nay, daughter, carry the wine in; we'll drink within. [*Exit* ANNE PAGE.

Slen. O Heaven! this is Mistress Anne Page.

Page. How now, Mistress Ford?

Fal. Mistress Ford, by my troth, you are very well met: by your leave, good mistress. [*Kissing her.*

Page. Wife, bid these gentlemen welcome.—Come, we have a hot venison pasty to dinner: come, gentlemen, I hope we shall drink down all unkindness. 192

[*Exeunt all but* SHALLOW, SLENDER, *and* EVANS.

Slen. I had rather than forty shillings, I had my Book of Songs and Sonnets here.

Enter SIMPLE.

How now, Simple! Where have you been? I must wait on myself, must I? You have not the Book of Riddles about you, have you?

Sim. Book of Riddles! why, did you not lend it to Alice Shortcake upon All-hallowmas last, a fortnight afore Michaelmas? 200

Shal. Come, coz; come, coz; we stay for you. A word with you, coz; marry, this, coz: there is, as 't were, a tender, a kind of tender, made afar off by Sir Hugh here: do you understand me?

Slen. Ay, sir, you shall find me reasonable: if it be so, I shall do that that is reason.

Shal. Nay, but understand me.

Slen. So I do, sir.

Eva. Give ear to his motions, Master Slender. I will description the matter to you, if you be capacity of it. 211

Slen. Nay, I will do as my cousin Shallow says. I pray you pardon me; he's a justice of peace in his country, simple though I stand here.

Eva. But that is not the question; the question is concerning your marriage.

Shal. Ay, there's the point, sir.

Eva. Marry, is it, the very point of it; to Mistress Anne Page.

Eva. Nay, Got's lords and his ladies, you must speak possitable, if you can carry her your desires towards her.   232

Shal. That you must. Will you, upon good dowry, marry her?

Anne. "The dinner is on the table; my father desires your worships' company."

Slen. Why, if it be so, I will marry her upon any reasonable demands.   221

Eva. But can you affection the 'oman? Let us command to know that of your mouth, or of your lips; for divers philosophers hold, that the lips is parcel of the mouth: therefore, precisely, can you carry your good will to the maid?

Shal. Cousin Abraham Slender, can you love her?

Slen. I hope, sir, I will do as it shall become one that would do reason.

Slen. I will do a greater thing than that, upon your request, cousin, in any reason.

Shal. Nay, conceive me, conceive me, sweet coz: what I do, is to pleasure you, coz. Can you love the maid?   239

Slen. I will marry her, sir, at your request: but if there be no great love in the beginning, yet Heaven may decrease it upon better acquaintance, when we are married, and have more occasion to know one another: I hope, upon familiarity will grow more contempt: but if you say, "marry her," I will marry her; that I am freely dissolved, and dissolutely.

Eva. It is a fery discretion answer; save, the faul is in the 'ort dissolutely: the 'ort is, according to our meaning, resolutely.—His meaning is good.

Shal. Ay, I think my cousin meant well.　　250

Slen. Ay, or else I would I might be hanged, la!

Re-enter ANNE PAGE.

Shal. Here comes fair Mistress Anne.—'Would I were young, for your sake, Mistress Anne!

Anne. The dinner is on the table; my father desires your worships' company.

Shal. I will wait on him, fair Mistress Anne.

Eva. Od's plessed will! I will not be absence at the grace.　　　　　[*Exeunt* SHALLOW *and* EVANS.

Anne. Will 't please your worship to come in, sir?

Slen. No, I thank you, forsooth, heartily; I am very well.　　　　261

Anne. The dinner attends you, sir.

Slen. I am not a-hungry, I thank you, forsooth.—Go, sirrah, for all you are my man, go, wait upon my cousin Shallow. [*Exit* SIMPLE.] A justice of peace sometime may be beholding to his friend for a man. —I keep but three men and a boy yet, till my mother be dead; but what though? yet I live like a poor gentleman born.

Anne. I may not go in without your worship: they will not sit, till you come.　　　　271

Slen. I' faith, I 'll eat nothing; I thank you as much as though I did.

Anne. I pray you, sir, walk in.

Slen. I had rather walk here, I thank you. I bruised my shin th' other day with playing at sword and dagger with a master of fence (three veneys for a dish of stewed prunes); and, by my troth, I cannot abide the smell of hot meat since.—Why do your dogs bark so? be there bears i' the town?　　　　280

Anne. I think, there are, sir; I heard them talked of.

Slen. I love the sport well; but I shall as soon quarrel at it as any man in England. You are afraid, if you see the bear loose, are you not?

Anne. Ay, indeed, sir.

Slen. That 's meat and drink to me, now: I have seen Sackerson loose twenty times, and have taken him by the chain; but, I warrant you, the women have so cried and shriek'd at it, that it pass'd: but women, indeed, cannot abide 'em; they are very ill-favoured rough things.　　　　291

Re-enter PAGE.

Page. Come, gentle Master Slender, come; we stay for you.

Slen. I 'll eat nothing, I thank you, sir.

Page. By cock and pie, you shall not choose, sir. Come, come.

Slen. Nay, pray you, lead the way.

Page. Come on, sir.

Slen. Mistress Anne, yourself shall go first.

Anne. Not I, sir; pray you, keep on.　　　300

Slen. Truly, I will not go first: truly, la! I will not do you that wrong.

Anne. I pray you, sir.

Slen. I 'll rather be unmannerly, than troublesome. You do yourself wrong, indeed, la!　　[*Exeunt.*

SCENE II.—The Same.

Enter Sir HUGH EVANS *and* SIMPLE.

Eva. Go your ways, and ask of Doctor Caius' house, which is the way; and there dwells one Mistress Quickly, which is in the manner of his nurse, or his dry nurse, or his cook, or his laundry, his washer, and his wringer.

Sim. Well, sir.

Eva. Nay, it is petter yet.—Give her this letter; for it is a 'oman that altogether 's acquaintance with Mistress Anne Page: and the letter is, to desire and require her to solicit your master's desires to Mistress

Anne Page: I pray you, be gone. I will make an end of my dinner: there 's pippins and cheese to come.

　　　　　　　　[*Exeunt.*

SCENE III.—A Room in the Garter Inn.

Enter FALSTAFF, *Host,* BARDOLPH, NYM, PISTOL,
and ROBIN.

Fal. Mine host of the Garter!

Host. What says my bully-rook? Speak scholarly, and wisely.

Fal. Truly, mine host, I must turn away some of my followers.

Host. Discard, bully Hercules; cashier: let them wag; trot, trot.

Fal. I sit at ten pounds a week.

Host. Thou 'rt an emperor, Cæsar, Keisar, and Pheezar. I will entertain Bardolph; he shall draw, he shall tap: said I well, bully Hector?　　　11

Fal. Do so, good mine host.

Host. I have spoke; let him follow.—Let me see thee froth, and lime: I am at a word; follow.

　　　　　　　　[*Exit Host.*

Fal. Bardolph, follow him. A tapster is a good trade: an old cloak makes a new jerkin; a withered serving-man, a fresh tapster. Go; adieu.

Bard. It is a life that I have desired. I will thrive.

　　　　　　　　[*Exit.*

Pist. O base Gongarian wight! wilt thou the spigot wield?　　　20

Nym. He was gotten in drink; is not the humour conceited? His mind is not heroic, and there 's the humour of it.

Fal. I am glad I am so acquit of this tinder-box: his thefts were too open; his filching was like an unskilful singer, he kept not time.

Nym. The good humour is to steal at a minim's rest.

Pist. Convey, the wise it call. Steal! foh! a fico for the phrase!

Fal. Well, sirs, I am almost out at heels.　　　30

Pist. Why, then let kibes ensue.

Fal. There is no remedy; I must cony-catch, I must shift.

Pist. Young ravens must have food.

Fal. Which of you know Ford of this town?

Pist. I ken the wight: he is of substance good.

Fal. My honest lads, I will tell you what I am about.

Pist. Two yards, and more.　　　38

Fal. No quips now, Pistol! Indeed, I am in the waist two yards about; but I am now about no waste; I am about thrift. Briefly, I do mean to make love to Ford's wife: I spy entertainment in her; she discourses, she carves, she gives the leer of invitation: I can construe the action of her familiar style; and the hardest voice of her behaviour, to be Englished rightly, is, "I am Sir John Falstaff's."

Pist. He hath studied her well, and translated her well, out of honesty into English.

Nym. The anchor is deep: will that humour pass?

Fal. Now, the report goes, she has all the rule of her husband's purse; she hath a legion of angels.　　51

Pist. As many devils entertain; and "To her, boy," say I.

Nym. The humour rises; it is good: humour me the angels.

Fal. I have writ me here a letter to her; and here another to Page's wife, who even now gave me good eyes too, examin'd my parts with most judicious œiliads: sometimes the beam of her view gilded my foot, sometimes my portly belly.　　　60

Pist. Then did the sun on dunghill shine.

Nym. I thank thee for that humour.

Fal. O! she did so course o'er my exteriors with such a greedy intention, that the appetite of her eye did seem to scorch me up like a burning-glass. Here 's another letter to her: she bears the purse too; she is a region in Guiana, all gold and bounty. I will be cheaters to them both, and they shall be exchequers to me: they shall be my East and West Indies, and I will trade to them both. Go, bear thou this letter to

Mistress Page; and thou this to Mistress Ford. We
will thrive, lads, we will thrive.   72
  Pist. Shall I Sir Pandarus of Troy become,
And by my side wear steel? then, Lucifer take all!
  Nym. I will run no base humour: here, take the
humour-letter. I will keep the haviour of reputation.
  Fal. [*To* ROBIN.] Hold, sirrah, bear you these letters
tightly:
Sail like my pinnace to these golden shores.—

Pist. "Shall I Sir Pandarus of Troy become, and by my side wear steel?"

Rogues, hence! avaunt! vanish like hailstones, go;
Trudge, plod away o' the hoof; seek shelter, pack! 80
Falstaff will learn the humour of the age,
French thrift, you rogues: myself, and skirted page.
                    [*Exeunt* FALSTAFF *and* ROBIN.
  Pist. Let vultures gripe thy guts! for gourd and
fullam holds,
And high and low beguile the rich and poor.
Tester I'll have in pouch, when thou shalt lack,
Base Phrygian Turk.
  Nym. I have operations, which be humours of
revenge.
  Pist. Wilt thou revenge?
  Nym. By welkin, and her star.   90
  Pist. With wit, or steel?
  Nym. With both the humours, I:
I will discuss the humour of this love to Page.
  Pist. And I to Ford shall eke unfold,
    How Falstaff, varlet vile,
    His dove will prove, his gold will hold,
    And his soft couch defile.
  Nym. My humour shall not cool: I will incense
Page to deal with poison; I will possess him with
yellowness, for the revolt of mien is dangerous: that
is my true humour.   101
  Pist. Thou art the Mars of malcontents: I second
thee; troop on.   [*Exeunt.*

SCENE IV.—A Room in Doctor CAIUS's House.

Enter Mistress QUICKLY, SIMPLE, *and* RUGBY.

  Quick. What, John Rugby!—I pray thee, go to the
casement, and see if you can see my master, Master
Doctor Caius, coming: if he do, i' faith, and find

anybody in the house, here will be an old abusing of
God's patience, and the king's English.
  Rug. I'll go watch.
  Quick. Go; and we'll have a posset for't soon at
night, in faith, at the latter end of a sea-coal fire.
[*Exit* RUGBY.] An honest, willing, kind fellow, as
ever servant shall come in house withal; and, I
warrant you, no tell-tale, nor no breed-bate: his worst
fault is, that he is given to prayer; he is something
peevish that way, but nobody but has his
fault; but let that pass. Peter Simple you
say your name is?
  Sim. Ay, for fault of a better.
  Quick. And Master Slender's your master?
  Sim. Ay, forsooth.
  Quick. Does he not wear a great round
beard, like a glover's paring-knife?   20
  Sim. No, forsooth: he hath but a little wee
face, with a little yellow beard, a Cain-
coloured beard.
  Quick. A softly-sprighted man, is he not?
  Sim. Ay, forsooth; but he is as tall a man
of his hands, as any is between this and his
head: he hath fought with a warrener.
  Quick. How say you?—O! I should re-
member him: does he not hold up his head,
as it were? and strut in his gait?   30
  Sim. Yes, indeed, does he.
  Quick. Well, Heaven send Anne Page no
worse fortune! Tell Master Parson Evans,
I will do what I can for your master: Anne
is a good girl, and I wish—

            Re-enter RUGBY.

  Rug. Out, alas! here comes my master.
  Quick. We shall all be shent. Run in here,
good young man; go into this closet. [*Shuts*
SIMPLE *in the closet.*] He will not stay long.
—What, John Rugby! John, what, John, I
say!—Go, John, go inquire for my master; I
doubt, he be not well, that he comes not home.
[*Sings.*] *And down, down, adown-a, &c.*

            Enter Doctor CAIUS.

  Caius. Vat is you sing? I do not like dese
toys. Pray you, go and vetch me in my
closet *un boitier vert;* a box, a green-a box: do intend
vat I speak? a green-a box.
  Quick. Ay, forsooth; I'll fetch it you. [*Aside.*] I
am glad he went not in himself: if he had found the
young man, he would have been horn-mad.   50
  Caius. Fe, fe, fe, fe! ma foi, il fait fort chaud. Je
m'en vais à la cour,—la grande affaire.
  Quick. Is it this, sir?
  Caius. Ouy; mettez le au mon pocket; dépêchez,
quickly.—Vere is dat knave Rugby?
  Quick. What, John Rugby! John!
  Rug. Here, sir.
  Caius. You are John Rugby, and you are Jack
Rugby: come, take-a your rapier, and come after my
heel to de court.   60
  Rug. 'Tis ready, sir, here in the porch.
  Caius. By my trot, I tarry too long.—Od's me!
Qu'ay j'oublié? dere is some simples in my closet, dat
I will not for the varld I shall leave behind.
  Quick. [*Aside.*] Ah me! he'll find the young man
there, and be mad.
  Caius. O diable! diable! vat is in my closet?—
Villainy! larron! [*Pulling* SIMPLE *out.*] Rugby; my
rapier!
  Quick. Good master, be content.   70
  Caius. Verefore shall I be content-a?
  Quick. The young man is an honest man.
  Caius. Vat shall de honest man do in my closet?
dere is no honest man dat shall come in my closet.
  Quick. I beseech you, be not so phlegmatic; hear
the truth of it: he came of an errand to me from
Parson Hugh.
  Caius. Vell.
  Sim. Ay, forsooth, to desire her to—
  Quick. Peace, I pray you.   80
  Caius. Peace-a your tongue!— Speak-a your tale.

Sim. To desire this honest gentlewoman, your maid, to speak a good word to Mistress Anne Page for my master, in the way of marriage.

Quick. This is all, indeed, la; but I 'll ne'er put my finger in the fire, and need not.

Caius. Sir Hugh send-a you?—Rugby, *baillez* me some paper: tarry you a little-a while.   [*Writes.*

Quick. I am glad he is so quiet: if he had been thoroughly moved, you should have heard him so loud, and so melancholy.—But notwithstanding, man,

Caius. "You jack'nape, give-a dis letter to Sir Hugh."

I 'll do you your master what good I can: and the very yea and the no is, the French doctor, my master, —I may call him my master, look you, for I keep his house; and I wash, wring, brew, bake, scour, dress meat and drink, make the beds, and do all myself;—

Sim. 'T is a great charge, to come under one body's hand.   98

Quick. Are you avis'd o' that? you shall find it a great charge: and to be up early and down late;—but notwithstanding, to tell you in your ear (I would have no words of it), my master himself is in love with Mistress Anne Page: but notwithstanding that, I know Anne's mind; that 's neither here nor there.

Caius. You jack'nape, give-a dis letter to Sir Hugh; by gar, it is a shallenge: I will cut his troat in de park; and I vill teach a scurvy jack-a-nape priest to meddle or make.—You may be gone; it is not good you tarry here:—by gar, I vill cut all his two stones; by gar, he shall not have a stone to trow at his dog. 110   [*Exit* SIMPLE.

Quick. Alas! he speaks but for his friend.

Caius. It is no matter-a for dat:—do not you tell-a me, dat I shall have Anne Page for myself?—By gar, I vill kill de Jack priest; and I have appointed mine host of de *Jartiere* to measure our weapon.—By gar, I will myself have Anne Page.

Quick. Sir, the maid loves you, and all shall be well. We must give folks leave to prate: what, the good-jer!

Caius. Rugby, come to the court vit me.—By gar, if I have not Anne Page, I shall turn your head out of my door.—Follow my heels, Rugby.   122
    [*Exeunt* CAIUS *and* RUGBY.

Quick. You shall have An fool's-head of your own. No, I know Anne's mind for that: never a woman in Windsor knows more of Anne's mind than I do, nor can do more than I do with her, I thank Heaven.

Fent. [*Within.*] Who 's within there? ho!

Quick. Who 's there, I trow? Come near the house, I pray you.   150

Enter FENTON.

Fent. How now, good woman? how dost thou?

Quick. The better, that it pleases your good worship to ask.

Fent. What news? how does pretty Mistress Anne?

Quick. In truth, sir, and she is pretty, and honest, and gentle; and one that is your friend, I can tell you that by the way; I praise Heaven for it.

Fent. Shall I do any good, think'st thou? Shall I not lose my suit?   140

Quick. Troth, sir, all is in his hands above; but notwithstanding, Master Fenton, I 'll be sworn on a book, she loves you.—Have not your worship a wart above your eye?

Fent. Yes, marry, have I; what of that?

Quick. Well, thereby hangs a tale.—Good faith, it is such another Nan;—but, I detest, an honest maid as ever broke bread:—we had an hour's talk of that wart.—I shall never laugh but in that maid's company;—but, indeed, she is given too much to allicholly and musing. But for you—well, go to.   151

Fent. Well, I shall see her to-day. Hold, there 's money for thee; let me have thy voice in my behalf: if thou seest her before me, commend me.

Quick. Will I? i' faith, that we will; and I will tell your worship more of the wart, the next time we have confidence, and of other wooers.

Fent. Well, farewell; I am in great haste now.
    [*Exit.*

Quick. Farewell to your worship.—Truly, an honest gentleman: but Anne loves him not; for I know Anne's mind as well as another does.—Out upon 't! what have I forgot?   [*Exit.*

ACT II.

SCENE I.—Before Page's House.

Enter Mistress Page, with a letter.

Mrs. Page.

HAT! have I scaped love-letters in the
holiday-time of my beauty, and am I
now a subject for them? Let me see.
　　　　　　　　　　　　　　　[*Reads.*

"Ask me no reason why I love you;
for though Love use Reason for his
physician, he admits him not for his
counsellor. You are not young, no more
am I: go to then, there's sympathy;
you are merry, so am I: ha! ha! then,
there's more sympathy; you love sack,
and so do I: would you desire better
sympathy? Let it suffice thee, Mistress Page, (at the
least, if the love of a soldier can suffice) that I love
thee. I will not say, pity me, 'tis not a soldier-like
phrase; but I say, love me. By me,
　　　　　Thine own true knight,
　　　　　By day or night,
　　　　　Or any kind of light,
　　　　　With all his might
　　　For thee to fight, JOHN FALSTAFF." 20
What a Herod of Jewry is this!—O wicked, wicked
world!—one that is well nigh worn to pieces with age,

Mrs. Page. "I was then frugal of my mirth."

to show himself a young gallant! What an unweighed
behaviour hath this Flemish drunkard picked (with
the devil's name!) out of my conversation, that he
dares in this manner assay me? Why, he hath not
been thrice in my company.—What should I say to
him?—I was then frugal of my mirth:—Heaven forgive me!—Why, I'll exhibit a bill in the parliament
for the putting down of men. How shall I be revenged
on him? for revenged I will be, as sure as his guts are
made of puddings. 32

Enter Mistress FORD.

Mrs. Ford. Mistress Page! trust me, I was going to
your house.

Mrs. Page. And, trust me, I was coming to you.
You look very ill.

Mrs. Ford. Nay, I'll ne'er believe that: I have to
show to the contrary.

Mrs. Page. Faith, but you do, in my mind.

Mrs. Ford. Well, I do then; yet, I say, I could show
you to the contrary. O Mistress Page! give me some
counsel. 42

Mrs. Page. What's the matter, woman?

Mrs. Ford. O woman! if it were not for one trifling
respect, I could come to such honour.

Mrs. Page. Hang the trifle, woman; take the
honour. What is it?—dispense with trifles;—what is
it?

Mrs. Ford. If I would but go to hell for an eternal
moment or so, I could be knighted. 50

Mrs. Page. What?—thou liest.—Sir Alice Ford!—
These knights will hack; and so, thou shouldst not
alter the article of thy gentry.

Mrs. Ford. We burn daylight:—here, read, read;
—perceive how I might be knighted.—I shall think
the worse of fat men, as long as I have an eye to make
difference of men's liking: and yet he would not
swear; praised women's modesty, and gave such
orderly and well-behaved reproof to all uncomeli-
ness, that I would have sworn his disposition would
have gone to the truth of his words; but they do
no more adhere and keep place together, than the
Hundredth Psalm to the tune of "Green Sleeves."
What tempest, I trow, threw this whale, with so
many tuns of oil in his belly, ashore at Windsor? How
shall I be revenged on him? I think, the best way
were to entertain him with hope, till the wicked fire
of lust have melted him in his own grease.—Did you
ever hear the like? 69

Mrs. Page. Letter for letter, but that the name of
Page and Ford differs!—To thy great comfort in this
mystery of ill opinions, here's the twin-brother of thy
letter: but let thine inherit first; for, I protest, mine
never shall. I warrant, he hath a thousand of these
letters, writ with blank space for different names,
(sure more) and these are of the second edition. He
will print them, out of doubt; for he cares not what
he puts into the press, when he would put us two: I
had rather be a giantess, and lie under Mount Pelion.
Well, I will find you twenty lascivious turtles, ere one
chaste man. 81

Mrs. Ford. Why, this is the very same; the very
hand, the very words. What doth he think of us?

Mrs. Page. Nay, I know not: it makes me almost
ready to wrangle with mine own honesty. I'll entertain myself like one that I am not acquainted withal;
for, sure, unless he know some strain in me, that I
know not myself, he would never have boarded me in
this fury.

Mrs. Ford. Boarding call you it? I'll be sure to
keep him above deck. 91

Mrs. Page. So will I: if he come under my hatches,
I'll never to sea again. Let's be revenged on him:
let's appoint him a meeting; give him a show of comfort in his suit; and lead him on with a fine-baited
delay, till he hath pawned his horses to mine host of
the Garter.

Mrs. Ford. Nay, I will consent to act any villainy
against him, that may not sully the chariness of our

honesty. O, that my husband saw this letter! it would give eternal food to his jealousy.   101

Mrs. Page. Why, look, where he comes; and my good man too: he's as far from jealousy, as I am from giving him cause; and that, I hope, is an unmeasurable distance.

Mrs. Ford. You are the happier woman.

Mrs. Page. Let's consult together against this greasy knight. Come hither.   [*They retire.*

Enter FORD, PISTOL, PAGE, *and* NYM.

Ford. Well, I hope, it be not so.

Pist. Hope is a curtail dog in some affairs: 110 Sir John affects thy wife.

Ford. Why, sir, my wife is not young.

Pist. "Sir John affects thy wife."

Pist. He woos both high and low, both rich and poor,
Both young and old, one with another, Ford.
He loves the gally-mawfry: Ford, perpend.

Ford. Love my wife?

Pist. With liver burning hot: prevent, or go thou,
Like Sir Actæon he, with Ringwood at thy heels.
O! odious is the name.

Ford. What name, sir?   120

Pist. The horn, I say. Farewell:
Take heed; have open eye, for thieves do foot by night:
Take heed, ere summer comes, or cuckoo-birds do sing.—
Away, Sir Corporal Nym.—
Believe it, Page; he speaks sense.   [*Exit.*

Ford. I will be patient: I will find out this.

Nym. [*To* PAGE.] And this is true; I like not the humour of lying. He hath wronged me in some humours: I should have borne the humoured letter to her; but I have a sword, and it shall bite upon my necessity. He loves your wife; there's the short and the long. My name is Corporal Nym: I speak, and I avouch 't is true:—my name is Nym, and Falstaff loves your wife.—Adieu. I love not the humour of bread and cheese; and there's the humour of it. Adieu.   [*Exit.*

Page. The humour of it, quoth 'a! here's a fellow frights humour out of his wits.

Ford. I will seek out Falstaff.

Page. I never heard such a drawling, affecting rogue.   140

Ford. If I do find it:—well.

Page. I will not believe such a Cataian, though the priest o' the town commended him for a true man.

Ford. 'T was a good sensible fellow: well.

Page. How now, Meg?

Mrs. Page. Whither go you, George?—Hark you.

Mrs. Ford. How now, sweet Frank? why art thou melancholy?

Ford. I melancholy! I am not melancholy.—Get you home, go.   150

Mrs. Ford. 'Faith, thou hast some crotchets in thy head now.—Will you go, Mistress Page?

Mrs. Page. Have with you.—You 'll come to dinner, George?—[*Aside to Mrs.* FORD.] Look, who comes yonder: she shall be our messenger to this paltry knight.

Mrs. Ford. Trust me, I thought on her: she 'll fit it.

Enter Mistress QUICKLY.

Mrs. Page. You are come to see my daughter Anne?

Quick. Ay, forsooth; and, I pray, how does good Mistress Anne?   160

Mrs. Page. Go in with us, and see; we have an hour's talk with you.
          [*Exeunt Mrs.* PAGE, *Mrs.* FORD, *and Mrs.* QUICKLY.

Page. How now, Master Ford?

Ford. You heard what this knave told me, did you not?

Page. Yes; and you heard what the other told me.

Ford. Do you think there is truth in them?

Page. Hang 'em, slaves; I do not think the knight would offer it: but these that accuse him, in his intent towards our wives, are a yoke of his discarded men; very rogues, now they be out of service.   171

Ford. Were they his men?

Page. Marry, were they.

Ford. I like it never the better for that.—Does he lie at the Garter?

Page. Ay, marry, does he. If he should intend this voyage towards my wife, I would turn her loose to him; and what he gets more of her than sharp words, let it lie on my head.   179

Ford. I do not misdoubt my wife, but I would be loath to turn them together. A man may be too confident: I would have nothing lie on my head: I cannot be thus satisfied.

Page. Look, where my ranting host of the Garter comes. There is either liquor in his pate, or money in his purse, when he looks so merrily.—How now, mine host?

Enter Host *and* SHALLOW.

Host. How now, bully-rook! thou 'rt a gentleman.—Cavalero-justice, I say.

Shal. I follow, mine host, I follow.—Good even, and twenty, good Master Page. Master Page, will you go with us? we have sport in hand.   192

Host. Tell him, cavalero-justice; tell him, bully-rook.

Shal. Sir, there is a fray to be fought between Sir Hugh, the Welch priest, and Caius, the French doctor.

Ford. Good mine host o' the Garter, a word with you.

Host. What say'st thou, my bully-rook?   199
          [*They go aside.*

Shal. [*To* PAGE.] Will you go with us to behold it? My merry host hath had the measuring of their weapons, and, I think, hath appointed them contrary places; for, believe me, I hear, the parson is no jester. Hark, I will tell you what our sport shall be.

Host. Hast thou no suit against my knight, my guest-cavalier?

Ford. None, I protest: but I 'll give you a pottle of burnt sack to give me recourse to him, and tell him, my name is Brook, only for a jest.

Host. My hand, bully: thou shalt have egress and regress; said I well? and thy name shall be Brook. It is a merry knight. Will you go, mynheers?   212

Shal. Have with you, mine host.

Page. I have heard, the Frenchman hath good skill in his rapier.

Shal. Tut, sir! I could have told you more: in these times you stand on distance, your passes, stoccadoes, and I know not what: 't is the heart, Master Page; 't is here, 't is here. I have seen the time, with my long sword, I would have made you four tall fellows skip like rats.   221

Host. Here, boys, here, here! shall we wag?

Page. Have with you.—I had rather hear them scold than fight. [*Exeunt Host,* SHALLOW, *and* PAGE.

Ford. Though Page be a secure fool, and stands so firmly on his wife's frailty, yet I cannot put off my opinion so easily. She was in his company at Page's house, and what they made there, I know not. Well, I will look further into 't; and I have a disguise to sound Falstaff. If I find her honest, I lose not my labour; if she be otherwise, 't is labour well bestowed. [*Exit.*

SCENE II.—A Room in the Garter Inn.

Enter FALSTAFF *and* PISTOL.

Fal. I will not lend thee a penny.

Pist. Why, then the world 's mine oyster,
Which I with sword will open.

Fal. Not a penny. I have been content, sir, you should lay my countenance to pawn: I have grated upon my good friends for three reprieves for you and your coach-fellow Nym; or else you had looked through the grate, like a geminy of baboons. I am damned in hell for swearing to gentlemen, my friends, you were good soldiers, and tall fellows; and when Mistress Bridget lost the handle of her fan, I took 't upon mine honour thou hadst it not. 12

Pist. Didst thou not share? hadst thou not fifteen pence?

Fal. Reason, you rogue, reason: think'st thou, I 'll endanger my soul gratis? At a word, hang no more about me, I am no gibbet for you:—go:—a short knife and a throng:—to your manor of Pickt-hatch, go.—You 'll not bear a letter for me, you rogue!—you stand upon your honour!—Why, thou unconfinable baseness, it is as much as I can do, to keep the terms of my honour precise. I, I, I myself sometimes, leaving the fear of Heaven on the left hand, and hiding mine honour in my necessity, am fain to shuffle, to hedge, and to lurch; and yet you, rogue, will ensconce your rags, your cat-a-mountain looks, your red-lattice phrases, and your bold-beating oaths, under the shelter of your honour! You will not do it, you?

Pist. I do relent: what would thou more of man?

Enter ROBIN.

Rob. Sir, here 's a woman would speak with you.

Fal. Let her approach. 30

Enter Mistress QUICKLY.

Quick. Give your worship good morrow.

Fal. Good morrow, good wife.

Quick. Not so, an 't please your worship.

Fal. Good maid, then.

Quick. I 'll be sworn; as my mother was, the first hour I was born.

Fal. I do believe the swearer. What with me?

Quick. Shall I vouchsafe your worship a word or two?

Fal. Two thousand, fair woman; and I 'll vouchsafe thee the hearing.

Quick. There is one Mistress Ford, sir:—I pray, come a little nearer this ways.—I myself dwell with Master Doctor Caius.

Fal. Well, on: Mistress Ford, you say,—

Quick. Your worship says very true:—I pray your worship, come a little nearer this ways.

Fal. I warrant thee, nobody hears: mine own people, mine own people.

Quick. Are they so? Heaven bless them, and make them his servants! 51

Fal. Well: Mistress Ford;—what of her?

Quick. Why, sir, she 's a good creature. Lord, Lord! your worship 's a wanton: well, Heaven forgive you, and all of us, I pray!

Fal. Mistress Ford;—come, Mistress Ford,—

Quick. Marry, this is the short and the long of it. You have brought her into such a canaries, as 't is wonderful: the best courtier of them all, when the court lay at Windsor, could never have brought her to such a canary; yet there has been knights, and lords, and gentlemen, with their coaches; I warrant you, coach after coach, letter after letter, gift after gift; smelling so sweetly, all musk, and so rushling, I warrant you, in silk and gold; and in such alligant terms; and in such wine and sugar of the best, and the fairest, that would have won any woman's heart, and, I warrant you, they could never get an eye-wink of her.—I had myself twenty angels given me this morning; but I defy all angels, (in any such sort, as they say) but in the way of honesty:—and, I warrant you, they could never get her so much as sip on a cup with the proudest of them all; and yet there has been

Fal. " But what says she to me? be brief, my good she-Mercury."

earls, nay, which is more, pensioners; but, I warrant you, all is one with her.

Fal. But what says she to me? be brief, my good she-Mercury.

Quick. Marry, she hath received your letter, for the which she thanks you a thousand times; and she gives you to notify, that her husband will be absence from his house between ten and eleven. 81

Fal. Ten and eleven.

Quick. Ay, forsooth; and then you may come and see the picture, she says, that you wot of: Master Ford, her husband, will be from home. Alas! the sweet woman leads an ill life with him; he 's a very jealousy man; she leads a very frampold life with him, good heart.

Fal. Ten and eleven.—Woman, commend me to her; I will not fail her. 90

Quick. Why, you say well. But I have another messenger to your worship: Mistress Page hath her hearty commendations to you too;—and let me tell you in your ear, she 's as fartuous a civil modest wife, and one (I tell you) that will not miss you morning nor evening prayer, as any is in Windsor, whoe'er be the other: and she bade me tell your worship, that her husband is seldom from home, but she hopes there will come a time. I never knew a woman so dote upon a man: surely, I think you have charms, la; yes, in truth. 101

Fal. Not I, I assure thee; setting the attraction of my good parts aside, I have no other charms.

Quick. Blessing on your heart for 't!

Fal. But, I pray thee, tell me this: has Ford's wife, and Page's wife, acquainted each other how they love me?

Quick. That were a jest, indeed!—they have not so little grace, I hope:—that were a trick, indeed! But Mistress Page would desire you to send her your little page, of all loves: her husband has a marvellous infection to the little page; and, truly, Master Page is an honest man. Never a wife in Windsor leads a better life than she does: do what she will, say what she will, take all, pay all, go to bed when she list, rise when she list, all is as she will; and, truly, she deserves it, for if there be a kind woman in Windsor, she is one. You must send her your page; no remedy.

Fal. Why, I will.   120

Quick. Nay, but do so, then: and, look you, he may come and go between you both; and, in any case, have a nayword, that you may know one another's mind, and the boy never need to understand anything: for 't is not good that children should know any wickedness; old folks, you know, have discretion, as they say, and know the world.

Fal. Fare thee well: commend me to them both. There's my purse; I am yet thy debtor.—Boy, go along with this woman. [*Exeunt* QUICKLY *and* ROBIN.] This news distracts me.   131

Pist. This punk is one of Cupid's carriers.— Clap on more sails; pursue, up with your fights: Give fire! She is my prize, or ocean whelm them all! [*Exit.*

Fal. Say'st thou so, old Jack? go thy ways; I'll make more of thy old body than I have done. Will they yet look after thee? Wilt thou, after the expense of so much money, be now a gainer? Good body, I thank thee: let them say, 't is grossly done; so it be fairly done, no matter.   140

Enter BARDOLPH.

Bard. Sir John, there's one Master Brook below would fain speak with you, and be acquainted with you; and hath sent your worship a morning's draught of sack.

Fal. Brook is his name?

Bard. Ay, sir.

Fal. Call him in. [*Exit* BARDOLPH.] Such Brooks are welcome to me, that o'erflow such liquor. Ah! ha! Mistress Ford and Mistress Page, have I encompassed you? go to; *via!*   150

Re-enter BARDOLPH, *with* FORD *disguised.*

Ford. Bless you, sir.

Fal. And you, sir: would you speak with me?

Ford. I make bold to press with so little preparation upon you.

Fal. You're welcome. What's your will?—Give us leave, drawer.   [*Exit* BARDOLPH.

Ford. Sir, I am a gentleman that have spent much: my name is Brook.

Fal. Good Master Brook, I desire more acquaintance of you.   160

Ford. Good Sir John, I sue for yours; not to charge you; for I must let you understand, I think myself in better plight for a lender than you are; the which hath something embolden'd me to this unseasoned intrusion, for, they say, if money go before, all ways do lie open.

Fal. Money is a good soldier, sir, and will on.

Ford. Troth, and I have a bag of money here troubles me: if you will help to bear it, Sir John, take all, or half, for easing me of the carriage.   170

Fal. Sir, I know not how I may deserve to be your porter.

Ford. I will tell you, sir, if you will give me the hearing.

Fal. Speak, good Master Brook; I shall be glad to be your servant.

Ford. Sir, I hear you are a scholar,—I will be brief with you,—and you have been a man long known to me, though I had never so good means, as desire, to make myself acquainted with you. I shall discover a thing to you, wherein I must very much lay open mine own imperfection; but, good Sir John, as you have one eye upon my follies, as you hear them unfolded, turn another into the register of your own, that I may pass with a reproof the easier, sith you yourself know, how easy it is to be such an offender.

Fal. Very well, sir; proceed.

Ford. There is a gentlewoman in this town, her husband's name is Ford.

Fal. Well, sir.   190

Ford. I have long loved her, and, I protest to you, bestowed much on her; followed her with a doting observance; engrossed opportunities to meet her; fee'd every slight occasion, that could but niggardly give me sight of her; not only bought many presents to give her, but have given largely to many, to know what she would have given. Briefly, I have pursued her, as love hath pursued me, which hath been, on the wing of all occasions: but whatsoever I have merited, either in my mind, or in my means, meed, I am sure, I have received none, unless experience be a jewel; that I have purchased at an infinite rate, and that hath taught me to say this:

Love like a shadow flies, when substance love pursues;
Pursuing that that flies, and flying what pursues.

Fal. Have you received no promise of satisfaction at her hands?

Ford. Never.

Fal. Have you importuned her to such a purpose?

Ford. Never.   210

Fal. Of what quality was your love then?

Ford. Like a fair house, built upon another man's ground; so that I have lost my edifice, by mistaking the place where I erected it.

Fal. To what purpose have you unfolded this to me?

Ford. When I have told you that, I have told you all. Some say, that though she appear honest to me, yet in other places she enlargeth her mirth so far, that there is shrewd construction made of her. Now, Sir John, here is the heart of my purpose: you are a gentleman of excellent breeding, admirable discourse, of great admittance, authentic in your place and person, generally allowed for your many war-like, court-like, and learned preparations.

Fal. O, sir!

Ford. Believe it, for you know it.—There is money; spend it, spend it; spend more; spend all I have, only give me so much of your time in exchange of it, as to lay an amiable siege to the honesty of this Ford's wife: use your art of wooing, win her to consent to you; if any man may, you may as soon as any.   233

Fal. Would it apply well to the vehemency of your affection, that I should win what you would enjoy? Methinks, you prescribe to yourself very preposterously.

Ford. O! understand my drift. She dwells so securely on the excellency of her honour, that the folly of my soul dares not present itself: she is too bright to be looked against. Now, could I come to her with any detection in my hand, my desires had instance and argument to commend themselves; I could drive her then from the ward of her purity, her reputation, her marriage-vow, and a thousand other her defences, which now are too too strongly embattled against me. What say you to't, Sir John?

Fal. Master Brook, I will first make bold with your money; next, give me your hand; and last, as I am a gentleman, you shall, if you will, enjoy Ford's wife.

Ford. O good sir!   252

Fal. I say you shall.

Ford. Want no money, Sir John; you shall want none.

Fal. Want no Mistress Ford, Master Brook; you shall want none. I shall be with her (I may tell you) by her own appointment; even as you came in to me, her assistant, or go-between, parted from me: I say, I shall be with her between ten and eleven; for at that time the jealous rascally knave, her husband, will be forth. Come you to me at night; you shall know how I speed.   263

Ford. I am blest in your acquaintance. Do you know Ford, sir?

Fal. Hang him, poor cuckoldly knave! I know him not.—Yet I wrong him, to call him poor: they say, the jealous wittolly knave hath masses of money, for the which his wife seems to me well-favoured. I will use her as the key of the cuckoldly rogue's coffer, and there's my harvest-home.   271

Ford. I would you knew Ford, sir, that you might avoid him, if you saw him.

Fal. Hang him, mechanical salt-butter rogue! I will stare him out of his wits; I will awe him with my cudgel: it shall hang like a meteor o'er the cuckold's horns. Master Brook, thou shalt know I will predominate over the peasant, and thou shalt lie with his wife.—Come to me soon at night.—Ford's a knave, and I will aggravate his style; thou, Master Brook, shalt know him for a knave and cuckold.— Come to me soon at night.   [*Exit.*

Ford. What a damned Epicurean rascal is this!— My heart is ready to crack with impatience.—Who says, this is improvident jealousy? my wife hath sent to him, the hour is fixed, the match is made. Would any man have thought this?—See the hell of having a false woman! my bed shall be abused, my coffers ransacked, my reputation gnawn at; and I shall not only receive this villainous wrong, but stand under the adoption of abominable terms, and by him that does me this wrong. Terms! names!—Amaimon sounds well; Lucifer, well; Barbason, well: yet they are devils' additions, the names of fiends: but cuckold! wittol-cuckold! the devil himself hath not such a name. Page is an ass, a secure ass; he will trust his wife, he will not be jealous: I will rather trust a Fleming with my butter, Parson Hugh the Welchman with my cheese, an Irishman with my aqua-vitæ bottle, or a thief to walk my ambling gelding, than my wife with herself: then she plots, then she ruminates, then she devises: and what they think in their hearts they may effect, they will break their hearts but they will effect. Heaven be praised for my jealousy!—Eleven o'clock the hour: I will prevent this, detect my wife, be revenged on Falstaff, and laugh at Page. I will about it; better three hours too soon, than a minute too late. Fie, fie, fie! cuckold! cuckold! cuckold!   [*Exit.*

SCENE III.—Windsor Park.

Enter CAIUS *and* RUGBY.

Caius. Jack Rugby!

Rug. Sir.

Caius. Vat is de clock, Jack?

Rug. 'T is past the hour, sir, that Sir Hugh promised to meet.

Caius. By gar, he has save his soul, dat he is no come: he has pray his Pible vell, dat he is no come. By gar, Jack Rugby, he is dead already, if he be come.

Rug. He is wise, sir; he knew your worship would kill him, if he came.   11

Caius. By gar, de herring is no dead, so as I vill kill him. Take your rapier, Jack; I vill tell you how I vill kill him.

Rug. Alas, sir! I cannot fence.

Caius. Villainy, take your rapier.

Rug. Forbear; here's company.

Enter HOST, SHALLOW, SLENDER, *and* PAGE.

Host. 'Bless thee, bully doctor.

Shal. 'Save you, Master Doctor Caius.

Page. Now, good master doctor!

Slen. Give you good morrow, sir.   20

Caius. Vat be all you, one, two, tree, four, come for?

Host. To see thee fight, to see thee foin, to see thee

traverse, to see thee here, to see thee pass thy punto, thy stock, thy reverse, thy distance, thy montant. Is he dead, my Ethiopian? is he dead, my Francisco? ha, bully! What says my Æsculapius? my Galen? my heart of elder? ha! is he dead, bully-stale? is he dead?   30

Caius. By gar, he is de coward Jack priest of the vorld; he is not show his face.

Host. Thou art a Castilian, King Urinal: Hector of Greece, my boy.

Caius. I pray you, bear vitness that me have stay six or seven, two, tree hours for him, and he is no come.

Shal. He is the wiser man, master doctor: he is a curer of souls, and you a curer of bodies; if you should fight, you go against the hair of your professions. Is it not true, Master Page?   41

Page. Master Shallow, you have yourself been a great fighter, though now a man of peace.

Shal. Bodykins, Master Page, though I now be old, and of the peace, if I see a sword out, my finger itches to make one. Though we are justices, and doctors, and churchmen, Master Page, we have some salt of our youth in us; we are the sons of women, Master Page.

Page. 'T is true, Master Shallow.   59

Shal. It will be found so, Master Page. Master Doctor Caius, I am come to fetch you home. I am sworn of the peace: you have showed yourself a wise physician, and Sir Hugh hath showen himself a wise and patient churchman. You must go with me, master doctor.

Host. Pardon, guest-justice:—a word, Monsieur Mock-water.

Caius. Mock-vater! vat is dat?

Host. Mock-water in our English tongue is valour, bully.   61

Caius. By gar, then I have as much mock-vater as de Englishman.—Scurvy jack-dog priest! by gar, me vill cut his ears.

Host. He will clapper-claw thee tightly, bully.

Caius. Clapper-de-claw! vat is dat?

Host. That is, he will make thee amends.

Caius. By gar, me do look, he shall clapper-de-claw me; for, by gar, me vill have it.

Host. And I will provoke him to 't, or let him wag.

Caius. Me tank you for dat.   71

Host. And moreover, bully,—but first, master guest, and Master Page, and eke Cavalero Slender, go you through the town to Frogmore.   [*Aside to them.*

Page. Sir Hugh is there, is he?

Host. He is there: see what humour he is in, and I will bring the doctor about by the fields. Will it do well?

Shal. We will do so.

Page, Shal., and Slen. Adieu, good master doctor.   [*Exeunt* PAGE, SHALLOW, *and* SLENDER.

Caius. By gar, me vill kill de priest; for he speak for a jack-an-ape to Anne Page.   82

Host. Let him die. Sheathe thy impatience: throw cold water on thy choler. Go about the fields with me through Frogmore; I will bring thee where Mistress Anne Page is, at a farmhouse a-feasting, and thou shalt woo her. Cried I aim? said I well?

Caius. By gar, me tank you vor dat: by gar, I love you; and I shall procure-a you de good guest, de earl, de knight, de lords, de gentlemen, my patients.   90

Host. For the which I will be thy adversary toward Anne Page: said I well?

Caius. By gar, 't is good; vell said.

Host. Let us wag then.

Caius. Come at my heels, Jack Rugby   [*Exeunt.*

ACT III.

Scene I.—A Field near Frogmore.

Enter Sir Hugh Evans and Simple.

Evans.

PRAY you now, good Master Slender's serving-man, and friend Simple by your name, which way have you looked for Master Caius, that calls himself doctor of physic?

Sim. Marry, sir; the Pitty-ward, the park-ward, every way; old Windsor way, and every way but the town way.

Eva. I most fehemently desire you, you will also look that way. 10

Sim. I will, sir.   [*Retiring.*

Eva. Pless my soul! how full of cholers I am, and trempling of mind!—I shall be glad, if he have deceived me.—How melancholies I am!—I will knog his urinals about his knave's costard, when I have good opportunities for the 'ork:—pless my soul!   [*Sings.*

To shallow rivers, to whose falls
Melodious birds sing madrigals; 20
There will we make our peds of roses,
And a thousand fragrant posies.
To shallow—

Mercy on me! I have a great dispositions to cry.

Melodious birds sing madrigals;—
When as I sat in Pabylon,—
And a thousand vagram posies.
To shallow—

Sim. [*Coming forward.*] Yonder he is coming, this way, Sir Hugh. 30

Eva. He 's welcome.—

To shallow rivers, to whose falls—

Heaven prosper the right!—What weapons is he?

Sim. No weapons, sir. There comes my master, Master Shallow, and another gentleman, from Frogmore, over the stile, this way.

Eva. Pray you, give me my gown; or else keep it in your arms.

Enter Page, Shallow, and Slender.

Shal. How now, master parson? Good morrow, good Sir Hugh. Keep a gamester from the dice, and a good student from his book, and it is wonderful. 41

Slen. Ah, sweet Anne Page!

Page. 'Save you, good Sir Hugh.

Eva. 'Pless you from his mercy sake, all of you!

Shal. What! the sword and the word? do you study them both, master parson?

Page. And youthful still, in your doublet and hose, this raw rheumatic day!

Eva. There is reasons and causes for it.

Page. We are come to you to do a good office, master parson. 51

Eva. Fery well: what is it?

Page. Yonder is a most reverend gentleman, who, belike having received wrong by some person, is at most odds with his own gravity and patience that ever you saw.

Shal. I have lived fourscore years, and upward; I never heard a man of his place, gravity, and learning, so wide of his own respect.

Eva. What is he? 60

Page. I think you know him; Master Doctor Caius, the renowned French physician.

Eva. Got's will, and his passion of my heart! I had as lief you would tell me of a mess of porridge.

Page. Why?

Eva. He has no more knowledge in Hibbocrates and Galen,—and he is a knave besides; a cowardly knave, as you would desires to be acquainted withal.

Page. I warrant you, he 's the man should fight with him. 70

Slen. O, sweet Anne Page!

Host. "Peace, I say! hear mine host of the Garter."

Shal. It appears so, by his weapons.—Keep them asunder:—here comes Doctor Caius.

Enter Host, Caius, and Rugby.

Page. Nay, good master parson, keep in your weapon.

Shal. So do you, good master doctor.

Host. Disarm them, and let them question: let them keep their limbs whole, and hack our English.

Caius. I pray you, let-a me speak a word vit your ear: verefore vill you not meet-a me? 80

Eva. Pray you, use your patience : in good time.

Caius. By gar, you are de coward, de Jack dog, John ape.

Eva. Pray you, let us not be laughing-stogs to other men's humours; I desire you in friendship, and I will one way or other make you amends.—I will knog your urinals about your knave's cogscomb for missing your meetings and appointments.

Caius. Diable!—Jack Rugby,—mine host de *Jartiere*, have I not stay for him to kill him? have I not, at de place I did appoint? 91

Eva. As I am a Christians soul, now, look you, this is the place appointed. I'll be judgment by mine host of the Garter.

Host. Peace, I say! Gallia and Guallia, French and Welch, soul-curer and body-curer.

Caius. Ay, dat is very good: excellent.

Host. Peace, I say! hear mine host of the Garter.

Am I politic? am I subtle? am I a Machiavel? Shall I lose my doctor? no; he gives me the potions and the motions. Shall I lose my parson? my priest? my Sir Hugh? no; he gives me the proverbs and the no-verbs.—Give me thy hand, terrestrial; so.—Give me thy hand, celestial; so.—Boys of art, I have deceived you both; I have directed you to wrong places: your hearts are mighty, your skins are whole, and let burnt sack be the issue.—Come, lay their swords to pawn.—Follow me, lad of peace; follow, follow, follow.

Shal. Trust me, a mad host.—Follow, gentlemen, follow.   110

Slen. O, sweet Anne Page!

[*Exeunt* SHALLOW, SLENDER, PAGE, *and Host.*

Caius. Ha! do I perceive dat? have you make-a de *sot* of us? ha, ha!

Eva. This is well; he has made us his vlouting-stog. —I desire you, that we may be friends, and let us knog our prains together to be revenge on this same scall, scurvy, cogging companion, the host of the Garter.   118

Caius. By gar, vit all my heart. He promise to bring me vere is Anne Page: by gar, he deceive me too.

Eva. Well, I will smite his noddles.—Pray you, follow.   [*Exeunt.*

SCENE II.—A Street in Windsor.

Enter Mistress PAGE *and* ROBIN.

Mrs. Page. Nay, keep your way, little gallant: you were wont to be a follower, but now you are a leader. Whether had you rather lead mine eyes, or eye your master's heels?

Rob. I had rather, forsooth, go before you like a man, than follow him like a dwarf.

Mrs. Page. O! you are a flattering boy: now, I see, you 'll be a courtier.

Enter FORD.

Ford. Well met, Mistress Page. Whither go you?

Mrs. Page. Truly, sir, to see your wife: is she at home?   11

Ford. Ay; and as idle as she may hang together, for want of company. I think, if your husbands were dead, you two would marry.

Mrs. Page. Be sure of that,—two other husbands.

Ford. Where had you this pretty weathercock?

Mrs. Page. I cannot tell what the dickens his name is my husband had him of.—What do you call your knight's name, sirrah?

Rob. Sir John Falstaff.   20

Ford. Sir John Falstaff!

Mrs. Page. He, he; I can never hit on 's name.— There is such a league between my good man and he! Is your wife at home, indeed?

Ford. Indeed, she is.

Mrs. Page. By your leave, sir: I am sick, till I see her.   [*Exeunt Mrs.* PAGE *and* ROBIN.

Ford. Has Page any brains? hath he any eyes? hath he any thinking? Sure, they sleep; he hath no use of them. Why, this boy will carry a letter twenty miles, as easy as a cannon will shoot point-blank twelve score. He pieces out his wife's inclination; he gives her folly motion and advantage: and now she 's going to my wife, and Falstaff's boy with her. A man may hear this shower sing in the wind:—and Falstaff's boy with her!—Good plots!—they are laid; and our revolted wives share damnation together. Well; I will take him, then torture my wife, pluck the borrowed veil of modesty from the so seeming Mistress Page, divulge Page himself for a secure and wilful Actæon; and to these violent proceedings all my neighbours shall cry aim. [*Clock strikes.*] The clock gives me my cue, and my assurance bids me search; there I shall find Falstaff. I shall be rather praised for this than mocked; for it is as positive as the earth is firm, that Falstaff is there: I will go.

Enter PAGE, SHALLOW, SLENDER, *Host, Sir* HUGH EVANS, CAIUS, *and* RUGBY.

Page, Shal., &c. Well met, Master Ford.

Ford. Trust me, a good knot. I have good cheer at home, and I pray you all go with me.

Shal. I must excuse myself, Master Ford.   50

Slen. And so must I, sir: we have appointed to dine with Mistress Anne, and I would not break with her for more money than I 'll speak of.

Shal. We have lingered about a match between Anne Page and my cousin Slender, and this day we shall have our answer.

Slen. I hope, I have your good will, father Page.

Page. You have, Master Slender; I stand wholly for you:—but my wife, master doctor, is for you alto-gether.   60

Caius. Ay, by gar; and de maid is love-a me: my nursh-a Quickly tell me so mush.

Host. What say you to young Master Fenton? he capers, he dances, he has eyes of youth, he writes verses, he speaks holiday, he smells April and May: he will carry 't, he will carry 't; 't is in his buttons; he will carry 't.

Page. Not by my consent, I promise you. The gentleman is of no having: he kept company with the wild prince and Poins; he is of too high a region; he knows too much. No, he shall not knit a knot in his fortunes with the finger of my substance: if he take her, let him take her simply; the wealth I have waits on my consent, and my consent goes not that way.

Ford. I beseech you, heartily, some of you go home with me to dinner: besides your cheer, you shall have sport; I will show you a monster.—Master doctor, you shall go:—so shall you, Master Page,—and you, Sir Hugh.   80

Shal. Well, fare you well.—We shall have the freer wooing at Master Page's.

[*Exeunt* SHALLOW *and* SLENDER.

Caius. Go home, John Rugby; I come anon.

[*Exit* RUGBY.

Host. Farewell, my hearts. I will to my honest knight Falstaff, and drink canary with him. [*Exit.*

Ford. [*Aside.*] I think, I shall drink in pipe-wine first with him; I 'll make him dance. Will you go, gentles?

All. Have with you, to see this monster. [*Exeunt.*

SCENE III.—A Room in FORD'S House.

Enter Mistress FORD *and Mistress* PAGE.

Mrs. Ford. What, John! what, Robert!

Mrs. Page. Quickly, quickly. Is the buck-basket—

Mrs. Ford. I warrant.—What, Robin, I say!

Enter Servants with a basket.

Mrs. Page. Come, come, come.

Mrs. Ford. Here, set it down.

Mrs. Page. Give your men the charge: we must be brief.

Mrs. Ford. Marry, as I told you before, John, and Robert, be ready here hard by in the brew-house; and when I suddenly call you, come forth, and (without any pause, or staggering) take this basket on your shoulders: that done, trudge with it in all haste, and carry it among the whitsters in Datchet-mead, and there empty it in the muddy ditch, close by the Thames side.

Mrs. Page. You will do it?

Mrs. Ford. I have told them over and over; they lack no direction. Be gone, and come when you are called.   [*Exeunt Servants.*

Mrs. Page. Here comes little Robin.   20

Enter ROBIN.

Mrs. Ford. How now, my eyas-musket? what news with you?

Rob. My master, Sir John, is come in at your back-door, Mistress Ford, and requests your company.

Mrs. Page. You little Jack-a-Lent, have you been true to us?

Rob. Ay, I 'll be sworn. My master knows not of your being here; and hath threatened to put me into

everlasting liberty, if I tell you of it, for he swears
he 'll turn me away.   30
Mrs. Page. Thou 'rt a good boy; this secrecy of
thine shall be a tailor to thee, and shall make thee
a new doublet and hose.—I 'll go hide me.
Mrs. Ford. Do so.—Go tell thy master, I am alone.
[*Exit* ROBIN.]—Mistress Page, remember you your cue.
Mrs. Page. I warrant thee : if I do not act it, hiss
me.   [*Exit.*
Mrs. Ford. Go to then : we 'll use this unwholesome
humidity, this gross watery pumpion ;—we 'll teach
him to know turtles from jays.   40

Enter FALSTAFF.

Fal. Have I caught my heavenly jewel? Why, now
let me die, for I have lived long enough : this is the
period of my ambition. O this blessed hour !
Mrs. Ford. O sweet Sir John !
Fal. Mistress Ford, I cannot cog, I cannot prate,
Mistress Ford. Now shall I sin in my wish : I would
thy husband were dead. I 'll speak it before the best
lord, I would make thee my lady.
Mrs. Ford. I your lady, Sir John ! alas, I should be
a pitiful lady.   50
Fal. Let the court of France show me such another.
I see how thine eye would emulate the diamond : thou
hast the right arched beauty of the brow, that becomes the ship-tire, the tire-valiant, or any tire of
Venetian admittance.
Mrs. Ford. A plain kerchief, Sir John : my brows
become nothing else ; nor that well neither.
Fal. By the Lord, thou art a tyrant to say so : thou
wouldst make an absolute courtier ; and the firm
fixture of thy foot would give an excellent motion to
thy gait, in a semi-circled farthingale. I see what
thou wert, if Fortune thy foe were not, Nature thy
friend : come, thou canst not hide it.
Mrs. Ford. Believe me, there 's no such thing in
me.
Fal. What made me love thee? let that persuade
thee, there 's something extraordinary in thee. Come;
I cannot cog, and say thou art this and that, like a
many of these lisping hawthorn-buds, that come like
women in men's apparel, and smell like Bucklersbury
in simple-time : I cannot ; but I love thee, none but
thee, and thou deservest it.   72
Mrs. Ford. Do not betray me, sir. I fear, you love
Mistress Page.
Fal. Thou mightst as well say, I love to walk by the
Counter-gate, which is as hateful to me as the reek of
a lime-kiln.
Mrs. Ford. Well, Heaven knows, how I love you ;
and you shall one day find it.
Fal. Keep in that mind ; I 'll deserve it.   80
Mrs. Ford. Nay, I must tell you, so you do, or else
I could not be in that mind.
Rob. [*Within.*] Mistress Ford ! Mistress Ford !
here's Mistress Page at the door, sweating, and blow-
ing, and looking wildly, and would needs speak with
you presently.
Fal. She shall not see me. I will ensconce me
behind the arras.
Mrs. Ford. Pray you, do so : she 's a very tattling
woman.—   [FALSTAFF *hides himself.*

Re-enter Mistress PAGE *and* ROBIN.

What 's the matter? how now !   91
Mrs. Page. O Mistress Ford ! what have you done?
You 're shamed, you are overthrown, you 're undone
for ever.
Mrs. Ford. What 's the matter, good Mistress
Page?
Mrs. Page. O well-a-day, Mistress Ford ! having an
honest man to your husband, to give him such cause
of suspicion !
Mrs. Ford. What cause of suspicion?   100
Mrs. Page. What cause of suspicion?—Out upon
you ! how am I mistook in you !
Mrs. Ford. Why, alas ! what 's the matter?
Mrs. Page. Your husband's coming hither, woman,
with all the officers in Windsor, to search for a gentle-
man, that, he says, is here now in the house, by your

consent, to take an ill advantage of his absence. You
are undone.
Mrs. Ford. 'T is not so, I hope.   109
Mrs. Page. Pray Heaven it be not so, that you have
such a man here ; but 't is most certain your husband 's
coming, with half Windsor at his heels, to search for
such a one : I come before to tell you. If you know
yourself clear, why, I am glad of it : but if you have a
friend here, convey him out. Be not amazed ; call all
your senses to you : defend your reputation, or bid
farewell to your good life for ever.
Mrs. Ford. What shall I do?—There is a gentleman,
my dear friend ; and I fear not mine own shame so
much as his peril : I had rather than a thousand
pound he were out of the house.   121
Mrs. Page. For shame ! never stand "you had
rather," and "you had rather :" your husband 's here
at hand ; bethink you of some conveyance : in the house
you cannot hide him.—O, how have you deceived me !
—Look, here is a basket : if he be of any reasonable
stature, he may creep in here ; and throw foul linen
upon him, as if it were going to bucking : or, it is
whiting-time, send him by your two men to Datchet-
mead.   130
Mrs. Ford. He 's too big to go in there. What shall
I do?

Re-enter FALSTAFF.

Fal. Let me see 't, let me see 't ! O, let me see 't ! I 'll
in, I 'll in.—Follow your friend's counsel.—I 'll in.
Mrs. Page. What ! Sir John Falstaff? Are these
your letters, knight?
Fal. I love thee: help me away ; let me creep in
here ; I 'll never—
  [*He gets into the basket ; they cover him*
    with foul linen.
Mrs. Page. Help to cover your master, boy. Call
your men, Mistress Ford.—You dissembling knight !
Mrs. Ford. What, John ! Robert ! John !   141
                    [*Exit* ROBIN.

Re-enter Servants.

Go take up these clothes here, quickly ; where 's the
cowl-staff? look, how you drumble : carry them to the
laundress in Datchet-mead ; quickly, come.

Enter FORD, PAGE, CAIUS, *and* Sir HUGH EVANS.

Ford. Pray you, come near : if I suspect without
cause, why, then make sport at me, then let me be
your jest ; I deserve it.—How now ? whither bear you
this?
Serv. To the laundress, forsooth.   149
Mrs. Ford. Why, what have you to do whither they
bear it? You were best meddle with buck-washing.
Ford. Buck? I would I could wash myself of the
buck ! Buck, buck, buck? Ay, buck ; I warrant you,
buck, and of the season too, it shall appear. [*Exeunt
Servants with the basket.*] Gentlemen, I have dreamed
to-night : I 'll tell you my dream. Here, here, here be
my keys : ascend my chambers, search, seek, find out :
I 'll warrant, we 'll unkennel the fox.—Let me stop
this way first :—so, now uncape.
Page. Good Master Ford, be contented : you wrong
yourself too much.   161
Ford. True, Master Page.—Up, gentlemen ; you
shall see sport anon : follow me, gentlemen.   [*Exit.*
Eva. This is fery fantastical humours, and jealousies.
Caius. By gar, 't is no de fashion of France : it is
not jealous in France.
Page. Nay, follow him, gentlemen : see the issue of
his search.   [*Exeunt* PAGE, CAIUS, *and* EVANS.
Mrs. Page. Is there not a double excellency in this?
Mrs. Ford. I know not which pleases me better,
that my husband is deceived, or Sir John.   171
Mrs. Page. What a taking was he in, when your
husband asked who was in the basket!
Mrs. Ford. I am half afraid he will have need of
washing ; so, throwing him into the water will do him
a benefit.
Mrs. Page. Hang him, dishonest rascal ! I would
all of the same strain were in the same distress.
Mrs. Ford. I think, my husband hath some special

suspicion of Falstaff's being here; for I never saw
him so gross in his jealousy till now.   181
  Mrs. Page. I will lay a plot to try that; and we will
yet have more tricks with Falstaff: his dissolute
disease will scarce obey this medicine.
  Mrs. Ford. Shall we send that foolish carrion, Mistress Quickly, to him, and excuse his throwing into
the water; and give him another hope, to betray him
to another punishment?
  Mrs. Page. We'll do it: let him be sent for to-
morrow eight o'clock, to have amends.   190

Re-enter FORD, PAGE, CAIUS, *and Sir* HUGH EVANS.

  Ford. I cannot find him: may be, the knave bragged
of that he could not compass.
  Mrs. Page. Heard you that?
  Mrs. Ford. You use me well, Master Ford, do you?
  Ford. Ay, I do so.
  Mrs. Ford. Heaven make you better than your
thoughts!
  Ford. Amen.
  Mrs. Page. You do yourself mighty wrong, Master
Ford.   200
  Ford. Ay, ay; I must bear it.
  Eva. If there be anypody in the house, and in the
chambers, and in the coffers, and in the presses,
Heaven forgive my sins at the day of judgment!
  Caius. By gar, nor I too, dere is no bodies.
  Page. Fie, fie, Master Ford! are you not ashamed?
What spirit, what devil suggests this imagination? I
would not have your distemper in this kind for the
wealth of Windsor Castle.
  Ford. 'T is my fault, Master Page: I suffer for it. 210
  Eva. You suffer for a pad conscience: your wife
is as honest a' omans as I will desires among five
thousand, and five hundred too.
  Caius. By gar, I see 't is an honest woman.
  Ford. Well; I promised you a dinner.—Come,
come, walk in the park: I pray you, pardon me; I
will hereafter make known to you, why I have done
this.—Come, wife:—come, Master Page: I pray you
pardon me; pray heartily, pardon me.   219
  Page. Let 's go in, gentlemen; but, trust me, we 'll
mock him. I do invite you to-morrow morning to
my house to breakfast; after, we 'll a-birding together:
I have a fine hawk for the bush. Shall it be so?
  Ford. Anything.
  Eva. If there is one, I shall make two in the company.
  Caius. If there be one or two, I shall make a deturd.
  Ford. Pray you, go, Master Page.
  Eva. I pray you now, remembrance to-morrow on
the lousy knave, mine host.   230
  Caius. Dat is good; by gar, vit all my heart.
  Eva. A lousy knave! to have his gibes, and his
mockeries!   [*Exeunt.*

SCENE IV.—*A Room in* PAGE'S *House.*

Enter FENTON *and* ANNE PAGE.

  Fent. I see, I cannot get thy father's love;
Therefore, no more turn me to him, sweet Nan.
  Anne. Alas! how then?
  Fent.   Why, thou must be thyself.
He doth object, I am too great of birth,
And that my state being gall'd with my expense,
I seek to heal it only by his wealth.
Besides these, other bars he lays before me,—
My riots past, my wild societies;
And tells me, 't is a thing impossible
I should love thee, but as a property.   10
  Anne. May be, he tells you true.
  Fent. No, Heaven so speed me in my time to come!
Albeit, I will confess, thy father's wealth
Was the first motive that I woo'd thee, Anne:
Yet, wooing thee, I found thee of more value
Than stamps in gold, or sums in sealed bags;
And 't is the very riches of thyself
That now I aim at.
  Anne.   Gentle Master Fenton,
Yet seek my father's love; still seek it, sir:

If opportunity and humblest suit   20
Cannot attain it, why, then,—hark you hither.
                              [*They converse apart.*

Anne. "This is my father's choice."

Enter SHALLOW, SLENDER, *and Mistress* QUICKLY.

  Shal. Break their talk, Mistress Quickly: my kins-
man shall speak for himself.
  Slen. I 'll make a shaft or a bolt on 't. 'Slid, 't is but
venturing.
  Shal. Be not dismay'd.
  Slen. No, she shall not dismay me: I care not for
that,—but that I am afeard.
  Quick. Hark ye; Master Slender would speak a
word with you.   30
  Anne. I come to him.—This is my father's choice.
O! what a world of vile ill-favour'd faults
Looks handsome in three hundred pounds a year!
  Quick. And how does good Master Fenton? Pray
you, a word with you.
  Shal. She 's coming; to her, coz. O boy! thou hadst
a father!
  Slen. I had a father, Mistress Anne: my uncle can
tell you good jests of him.—Pray you, uncle, tell
Mistress Anne the jest, how my father stole two
geese out of a pen, good uncle.   41
  Shal. Mistress Anne, my cousin loves you.
  Slen. Ay, that I do; as well as I love any woman in
Glostershire.
  Shal. He will maintain you like a gentlewoman.
  Slen. Ay, that I will, come cut and long-tail, under
the degree of a squire.
  Shal. He will make you a hundred and fifty pounds
jointure.   49
  Anne. Good Master Shallow, let him woo for himself.
  Shal. Marry, I thank you for it; I thank you for
that good comfort. She calls you, coz: I 'll leave you.
  Anne. Now, Master Slender.
  Slen. Now, good Mistress Anne.
  Anne. What is your will?
  Slen. My will? od's heartlings! that 's a pretty jest,
indeed. I ne'er made my will yet, I thank Heaven; I
am not such a sickly creature, I give Heaven praise.
  Anne. I mean, Master Slender, what would you
with me?   60
  Slen. Truly, for mine own part, I would little or
nothing with you. Your father, and my uncle, have

made motions: if it be my luck, so; if not, happy man be his dole! They can tell you how things go better than I can: you may ask your father; here he comes.

Enter PAGE *and Mistress* PAGE.

Page. Now, Master Slender!—Love him, daughter Anne.—
Why, how now? what does Master Fenton here?
You wrong me, sir, thus still to haunt my house:
I told you, sir, my daughter is dispos'd of.
Fent. Nay, Master Page, be not impatient.   70
Mrs. Page. Good Master Fenton, come not to my child.
Page. She is no match for you.
Fent. Sir, will you hear me?
Page.   No, good Master Fenton.—
Come, Master Shallow; come, son Slender, in.—
Knowing my mind, you wrong me, Master Fenton.
          [*Exeunt* PAGE, SHALLOW, *and* SLENDER.
Quick. Speak to Mistress Page.
Fent. Good Mistress Page, for that I love your daughter
In such a righteous fashion as I do,
Perforce, against all checks, rebukes, and manners,
I must advance the colours of my love,   81
And not retire: let me have your good will.
Anne. Good mother, do not marry me to yond fool.
Mrs. Page. I mean it not; I seek you a better husband.
Quick. That's my master, master doctor.
Anne. Alas! I had rather be set quick i' the earth,
And bowl'd to death with turnips.
Mrs. Page. Come, trouble not yourself.—Good Master Fenton,
I will not be your friend, nor enemy: 90
My daughter will I question how she loves you,
And as I find her, so am I affected.
Till then, farewell, sir: she must needs go in;
Her father will be angry.
          [*Exeunt Mrs.* PAGE *and* ANNE.
Fent. Farewell, gentle mistress.—Farewell, Nan.
Quick. This is my doing, now.—Nay, said I, will you cast away your child on a fool, and a physician? look on Master Fenton.—This is my doing.
Fent. I thank thee; and I pray thee, once to-night
Give my sweet Nan this ring. There's for thy pains.
          [*Exit.*
Quick. Now, Heaven send thee good fortune! A kind heart he hath: a woman would run through fire and water for such a kind heart. But yet I would my master had Mistress Anne; or I would Master Slender had her; or, in sooth, I would Master Fenton had her. I will do what I can for them all three, for so I have promised, and I'll be as good as my word; but speciously for Master Fenton. Well, I must of another errand to Sir John Falstaff from my two mistresses: what a beast am I to slack it!   110
          [*Exit.*

SCENE V.—A Room in the Garter Inn.

Enter FALSTAFF *and* BARDOLPH.

Fal. Bardolph, I say,—
Bard. Here, sir.
Fal. Go fetch me a quart of sack; put a toast in 't.
[*Exit* BARDOLPH.] Have I lived to be carried in a basket, like a barrow of butcher's offal, and to be thrown in the Thames? Well, if I be served such another trick, I'll have my brains ta'en out, and buttered, and give them to a dog for a new year's gift. The rogues slighted me into the river with as little remorse as they would have drowned a blind bitch's puppies, fifteen i' the litter; and you may know by my size, that I have a kind of alacrity in sinking: if the bottom were as deep as hell, I should down. I had been drowned, but that the shore was shelvy and shallow; a death that I abhor, for the water swells a man, and what a thing should I have been, when I had been swelled! I should have been a mountain of mummy.

Re-enter BARDOLPH *with the wine.*

Bard. Here's Mistress Quickly, sir, to speak with you.   20
Fal. Come, let me pour in some sack to the Thames water, for my belly's as cold, as if I had swallowed snowballs for pills to cool the reins. Call her in.
Bard. Come in, woman.

Enter Mistress QUICKLY.

Quick. By your leave.—I cry you mercy: give your worship good morrow.
Fal. Take away these chalices. Go, brew me a pottle of sack finely.
Bard. With eggs, sir?
Fal. Simple of itself; I'll no pullet-sperm in my brewage. [*Exit* BARDOLPH.]—How now?   31
Quick. Marry, sir, I come to your worship from Mistress Ford.
Fal. Mistress Ford! I have had ford enough: I was thrown into the ford; I have my belly full of ford.
Quick. Alas the day! good heart, that was not her fault: she does so take on with her men; they mistook their erection.
Fal. So did I mine, to build upon a foolish woman's promise.   40
Quick. Well, she laments, sir, for it, that it would yearn your heart to see it. Her husband goes this morning a-birding: she desires you once more to come to her between eight and nine. I must carry her word quickly: she'll make you amends, I warrant you.
Fal. Well, I will visit her: tell her so; and bid her think, what a man is: let her consider his frailty, and then judge of my merit.
Quick. I will tell her.
Fal. Do so. Between nine and ten, say'st thou?   50
Quick. Eight and nine, sir.
Fal. Well, be gone: I will not miss her.
Quick. Peace be with you, sir.   [*Exit.*
Fal. I marvel, I hear not of Master Brook: he sent me word to stay within. I like his money well. O! here he comes.

Enter FORD.

Ford. Bless you, sir.
Fal. Now, Master Brook; you come to know what hath passed between me and Ford's wife?
Ford. That, indeed, Sir John, is my business.   60
Fal. Master Brook, I will not lie to you. I was at her house the hour she appointed me.
Ford. And sped you, sir?
Fal. Very ill-favouredly, Master Brook.
Ford. How so, sir? Did she change her determination?
Fal. No, Master Brook; but the peaking Cornuto her husband, Master Brook, dwelling in a continual 'larum of jealousy, comes me in the instant of our encounter, after we had embraced, kissed, protested, and, as it were, spoke the prologue of our comedy; and at his heels a rabble of his companions, thither provoked and instigated by his distemper, and, forsooth, to search his house for his wife's love.
Ford. What, while you were there?
Fal. While I was there.
Ford. And did he search for you, and could not find you?   78
Fal. You shall hear. As good luck would have it, comes in one Mistress Page; gives intelligence of Ford's approach; and in her invention and Ford's wife's distraction, they conveyed me into a buck-basket.
Ford. A buck-basket!
Fal. By the Lord, a buck-basket: rammed me in with foul shirts and smocks, socks, foul stockings, and greasy napkins; that, Master Brook, there was the rankest compound of villainous smell, that ever offended nostril.
Ford. And how long lay you there?   90
Fal. Nay, you shall hear, Master Brook, what I have suffered, to bring this woman to evil for your good. Being thus crammed in the basket, a couple of Ford's knaves, his hinds, were called forth by their mistress, to carry me in the name of foul clothes to

Datchet Lane : they took me on their shoulders; met the jealous knave their master in the door, who asked them once or twice what they had in their basket. I quaked for fear, lest the lunatic knave would have searched it; but fate, ordaining he should be a cuckold, held his hand. Well; on went he for a search, and away went I for foul clothes. But mark the sequel, Master Brook : I suffered the pangs of three several deaths : first, an intolerable fright, to be detected with a jealous rotten bell-wether; next, to be compassed, like a good bilbo, in the circumference of a peck, hilt to point, heel to head ; and then, to be stopped in, like a strong distillation, with stinking clothes that fretted in their own grease : think of that,—a man of my kidney,—think of that ; that am as subject to heat as butter ; a man of continual dissolution and thaw : it was a miracle, to scape suffocation. And in the height of this bath, when I was more than half stewed in grease, like a Dutch dish, to be thrown into the Thames, and cooled, glowing hot, in that surge, like a horse-shoe; think of that,—hissing hot,—think of that, Master Brook.

Ford. In good sadness, sir, I am sorry that for my sake you have suffered all this. My suit then is desperate ; you 'll undertake her no more ?   120

Fal. Master Brook, I will be thrown into Ætna, as I have been into Thames, ere I will leave her thus. Her husband is this morning gone a-birding : I have received from her another embassy of meeting ; 'twixt eight and nine is the hour, Master Brook.

Ford. 'T is past eight already, sir.

Fal. Is it ? I will then address me to my appointment. Come to me at your convenient leisure, and you shall know how I speed, and the conclusion shall be crowned with your enjoying her : adieu. You shall have her, Master Brook ; Master Brook, you shall cuckold Ford.   [*Exit.*

Ford. Hum : ha ! is this a vision ? is this a dream ? do I sleep ? Master Ford, awake ! awake, Master Ford ! there 's a hole made in your best coat, Master Ford. This 't is to be married : this 't is to have linen, and buck-baskets.—Well, I will proclaim myself what I am : I will now take the lecher; he is at my house : he cannot scape me ; 't is impossible he should : he cannot creep into a halfpenny purse, nor into a pepper-box ; but, lest the devil that guides him should aid him, I will search impossible places. Though what I am I cannot avoid, yet to be what I would not, shall not make me tame : if I have horns to make one mad, let the proverb go with me,—I 'll be horn-mad.

[*Exit.*

ACT IV.

SCENE I.—The Street.

Enter Mistress PAGE, Mistress QUICKLY, and WILLIAM.

Mrs. Page. IS he at Master Ford's already, think'st thou ?

Quick. Sure, he is by this, or will be presently ; but truly, he is very courageous mad about his throwing into the water. Mistress Ford desires you to come suddenly.

Mrs. Page. I 'll be with her by-and-by : I 'll but bring my young man here to school. Look, where his master comes ; 't is a playing-day, I see.   11

Enter Sir HUGH EVANS.

How now, Sir Hugh ? no school to-day ?

Eva. No ; Master Slender is let the boys leave to play.

Quick. Blessing of his heart !

Mrs. Page. Sir Hugh, my husband says, my son profits nothing in the world at his book : I pray you, ask him some questions in his accidence.

Eva. Come hither, William ; hold up your head ; come.   20

Mrs. Page. Come on, sirrah ; hold up your head ; answer your master, be not afraid.

Eva. William, how many numbers is in nouns ?

Will. Two.

Quick. Truly, I thought there had been one number more, because they say, Od's nouns.

Eva. Peace your tattlings !—What is *fair*, William ?

Will. *Pulcher.*

Quick. Polecats ! there are fairer things than polecats, sure.   30

Eva. You are a very simplicity 'oman : I pray you, peace.—What is *lapis*, William ?

Will. A stone.

Eva. And what is a stone, William ?

Will. A pebble.

Eva. No, it is *lapis :* I pray you remember in your prain.

Will. *Lapis.*

Eva. That is good, William. What is he, William, that does lend articles ?   40

Will. Articles are borrowed of the pronoun ; and be thus declined, *Singulariter, nominativo, hic, haec, hoc.*

Eva. *Nominativo, hig, hag, hog ;*—pray you, mark : *genitivo, hujus.* Well, what is your accusative case ?

Will. *Accusativo, hinc.*

Eva. I pray you, have your remembrance, child : *accusativo, hung, hang, hog.*

Quick. Hang-hog is Latin for bacon, I warrant you.

Eva. Leave your prabbles, 'oman.—What is the focative case, William ?

Will. O—*vocativo, O.*

Eva. Remember, William ; focative is, *caret.*

Quick. And that 's a good root.

Eva. 'Oman, forbear.

Mrs. Page. Peace !

Eva. What is your genitive case plural, William ?

Will. Genitive case ?

Eva. Ay.

Will. Genitive,—*horum, harum, horum.*   60

Quick. Vengeance of Jenny's case ! fie on her !—Never name her, child, if she be a whore.

Eva. For shame, 'oman !

Quick. You do ill to teach the child such words.—He teaches him to hick and to hack, which they 'll do fast enough of themselves ; and to call whorum,—fie upon you !

Eva. 'Oman, art thou lunatics ? hast thou no understandings for thy cases, and the numbers of the genders ? Thou art as foolish Christian creatures as I would desires.   71

Mrs. Page. Pr'ythee, hold thy peace.

Eva. Show me now, William, some declensions of your pronouns.

Will. Forsooth, I have forgot.

Eva. It is *qui, quæ, quod ;* if you forget your *quies,* your *quæs,* and your *quods,* you must be preeches. Go your ways, and play ; go.

Eva. "Remember, William ; focative is, *caret.*"

Mrs. Page. He is a better scholar than I thought he was.   80

Eva. He is a good sprag memory. Farewell, Mistress Page.

Mrs. Page. Adieu, good Sir Hugh. [*Exit Sir* HUGH.] Get you home, boy.—Come, we stay too long.
                             [*Exeunt.*

SCENE II.—A Room in FORD's House.

Enter FALSTAFF *and Mistress* FORD.

Fal. Mistress Ford, your sorrow hath eaten up my sufferance. I see, you are obsequious in your love, and I profess requital to a hair's breadth ; not only, Mistress Ford, in the simple office of love, but in all the accoutrement, complement, and ceremony of it. But are you sure of your husband now ?

Mrs. Ford. He 's a-birding, sweet Sir John.

Mrs. Page. [*Within.*] What ho ! gossip Ford ! what ho !

Mrs. Ford. Step into the chamber, Sir John.   10
                          [*Exit* FALSTAFF.

Enter Mistress PAGE.

Mrs. Page. How now, sweetheart ? who 's at home besides yourself ?

Mrs. Ford. Why, none but mine own people.

Mrs. Page. Indeed ?

Mrs. Ford. No, certainly.—[*Aside.*] Speak louder.

Mrs. Page. Truly, I am so glad you have nobody here.

Mrs. Ford. Why ?   18

Mrs. Page. Why, woman, your husband is in his old lunes again : he so takes on yonder with my husband ; so rails against all married mankind ; so curses all Eve's daughters, of what complexion soever ; and so buffets himself on the forehead, crying, "Peer out, peer out !" that any madness I ever yet beheld seemed but tameness, civility, and patience, to this his distemper he is in now. I am glad the fat knight is not here.

Mrs. Ford. Why, does he talk of him ?   28

Mrs. Page. Of none but him ; and swears, he was carried out, the last time he searched for him, in a basket : protests to my husband he is now here, and hath drawn him and the rest of their company from their sport, to make another experiment of his

suspicion. But I am glad the knight is not here ; now he shall see his own foolery.

Mrs. Ford. How near is he, Mistress Page ?

Mrs. Page. Hard by ; at street end : he will be here anon.

Mrs. Ford. I am undone ! the knight is here.   39

Mrs. Page. Why, then you are utterly shamed, and he 's but a dead man. What a woman are you !—Away with him, away with him : better shame than murder.

Mrs. Ford. Which way should he go ? how should I bestow him ? Shall I put him into the basket again ?

Re-enter FALSTAFF.

Fal. No, I 'll come no more i' the basket. May I not go out, ere he come ?

Mrs. Page. Alas, three of Master Ford's brothers watch the door with pistols, that none shall issue out ; otherwise you might slip away ere he came. But what make you here ?   51

Fal. What shall I do ?—I 'll creep up into the chimney.

Mrs. Ford. There they always use to discharge their birding-pieces.

Mrs. Page. Creep into the kiln-hole.

Fal. Where is it ?

Mrs. Ford. He will seek there, on my word. Neither press, coffer, chest, trunk, well, vault, but he hath an abstract for the remembrance of such places ; and goes to them by his note : there is no hiding you in the house.   62

Fal. I 'll go out then.

Mrs. Page. If you go out in your own semblance, you die, Sir John. Unless you go out disguised,—

Mrs. Ford. How might we disguise him ?

Mrs. Page. Alas the day ! I know not. There is no woman's gown big enough for him ; otherwise he might put on a hat, a muffler, and a kerchief, and so escape.   70

Fal. Good hearts, devise something : any extremity, rather than a mischief.

Mrs. Ford. My maid's aunt, the fat woman of Brentford, has a gown above.

Mrs. Page. On my word, it will serve him ; she 's as big as he is, and there 's her thrummed hat, and her muffler too.—Run up, Sir John.

Mrs. Ford. Go, go, sweet Sir John : Mistress Page and I will look some linen for your head.   79

Mrs. Page. Quick, quick : we 'll come dress you straight ; put on the gown the while. [*Exit* FALSTAFF.

Mrs. Ford. I would, my husband would meet him in this shape : he cannot abide the old woman of Brentford ; he swears, she 's a witch ; forbade her my house, and hath threatened to beat her.

Mrs. Page. Heaven guide him to thy husband's cudgel, and the devil guide his cudgel afterwards !

Mrs. Ford. But is my husband coming ?

Mrs. Page. Ay, in good sadness, is he ; and talks of the basket too, howsoever he hath had intelligence. 90

Mrs. Ford. We 'll try that ; for I 'll appoint my men to carry the basket again, to meet him at the door with it, as they did last time.

Mrs. Page. Nay, but he 'll be here presently : let 's go dress him like the witch of Brentford.

Mrs. Ford. I 'll first direct my men, what they shall do with the basket. Go up, I 'll bring linen for him straight.   [*Exit.*

Mrs. Page. Hang him, dishonest varlet ! we cannot misuse him enough.   100

We 'll leave a proof, by that which we will do,
W;ves may be merry, and yet honest too :
We do not act, that often jest and laugh ;
'T is old but true, "Still swine eat all the draff."
                               [*Exit.*

Re-enter Mistress FORD *with two Servants.*

Mrs. Ford. Go, sirs, take the basket again on your shoulders : your master is hard at door ; if he bid you set it down, obey him. Quickly ; despatch.   [*Exit.*

1 Serv. Come, come, take it up.

2 Serv. Pray Heaven, it be not full of knight again.

1 Serv. I hope not ; I had as lief bear so much lead. 110

Enter FORD, PAGE, SHALLOW, CAIUS, *and Sir*
HUGH EVANS.

Ford. Ay, but if it prove true, Master Page, have
you any way then to unfold me again?—Set down the

Shal. Indeed, Master Ford, this is not well; indeed.
Ford. So say I too, sir.

Re-enter Mistress FORD.

Come hither, Mistress Ford; Mistress Ford, the honest

Ford. "Out of my door, you witch, you nag, you baggage, you polecat, you ronyon: out! out!"

basket, villains.—Somebody call my wife.—Youth in
a basket!· O you panderly rascals! there's a knot, a
ging, a pack, a conspiracy against me: now shall the
devil be shamed.—What, wife, I say!—Come, come
forth.—Behold what honest clothes you send forth to
bleaching.

Page. Why, this passes! Master Ford, you are not
to go loose any longer; you must be pinioned.   120

Eva. Why, this is lunatics; this is mad as a mad
dog.

woman, the modest wife, the virtuous creature, that
hath the jealous fool to her husband!—I suspect without cause, mistress, do I?

Mrs. Ford. Heaven be my witness, you do, if you
suspect me in any dishonesty.   130

Ford. Well said, brazen-face; hold it out.—Come
forth, sirrah.   [*Pulls the clothes out of the basket.*

Page. This passes!

Mrs. Ford. Are you not ashamed? let the clothes
alone.

Ford. I shall find you anon.

Eva. 'T is unreasonable. Will you take up your wife's clothes? Come away.

Ford. Empty the basket, I say.

Mrs. Ford. Why, man, why,— 110

Ford. Master Page, as I am a man, there was one conveyed out of my house yesterday in this basket: why may not he be there again? In my house I am sure he is: my intelligence is true; my jealousy is reasonable.—Pluck me out all the linen.

Mrs. Ford. If you find a man there, he shall die a flea's death.

Page. Here 's no man.

Shal. By my fidelity, this is not well, Master Ford; this wrongs you. 150

Eva. Master Ford, you must pray, and not follow the imaginations of your own heart: this is jealousies.

Ford. Well, he 's not here I seek for.

Page. No, nor nowhere else, but in your brain.

Ford. Help to search my house this one time: if I find not what I seek, show no colour for my extremity; let me for ever be your table-sport; let them say of me, "As jealous as Ford, that searched a hollow walnut for his wife's leman." Satisfy me once more; once more search with me. 160

Mrs. Ford. What ho! Mistress Page! come you and the old woman down; my husband will come into the chamber.

Ford. Old woman! What old woman 's that?

Mrs. Ford. Why, it is my maid's aunt of Brentford.

Ford. A witch, a quean, an old cozening quean! Have I not forbid her my house? She comes of errands, does she? We are simple men; we do not know what 's brought to pass under the profession of fortune-telling. She works by charms, by spells, by the figure, and such daubery as this is, beyond our element: we know nothing.—Come down, you witch, you hag you; come down, I say. 173

Mrs. Ford. Nay, good, sweet husband.—Good gentlemen, let him not strike the old woman.

Re-enter FALSTAFF *in woman's clothes, led by Mistress* PAGE.

Mrs. Page. Come, Mother Prat; come, give me your hand.

Ford. I'll prat her.—Out of my door, you witch, [*beats him*] you hag, you baggage, you polecat, you ronyon: out! out! I'll conjure you, I'll fortune-tell you. [*Exit* FALSTAFF.

Mrs. Page. Are you not ashamed? I think, you have killed the poor woman. 183

Mrs. Ford. Nay, he will do it.—'T is a goodly credit for you.

Ford. Hang her, witch!

Eva. By yea and no, I think, the 'oman is a witch indeed: I like not when a 'oman has a great peard; I spy a great peard under her muffler. 189

Ford. Will you follow, gentlemen? I beseech you, follow: see but the issue of my jealousy. If I cry out thus upon no trail, never trust me when I open again.

Page. Let 's obey his humour a little further. Come, gentlemen.

[*Exeunt* FORD, PAGE, SHALLOW, *and* EVANS.

Mrs. Page. Trust me, he beat him most pitifully.

Mrs. Ford. Nay, by the mass, that he did not; he beat him most unpitifully, methought.

Mrs. Page. I'll have the cudgel hallowed, and hung o'er the altar: it hath done meritorious service.

Mrs. Ford. What think you? May we, with the warrant of womanhood, and the witness of a good conscience, pursue him with any further revenge? 202

Mrs. Page. The spirit of wantonness is, sure, scared out of him: if the devil have him not in fee-simple, with fine and recovery, he will never, I think, in the way of waste, attempt us again.

Mrs. Ford. Shall we tell our husbands how we have served him? 208

Mrs. Page. Yes, by all means; if it be but to scrape the figures out of your husband's brains. If they can find in their hearts the poor unvirtuous fat knight shall be any further afflicted we two will still be the ministers.

Mrs. Ford. I'll warrant, they'll have him publicly shamed, and, methinks, there would be no period to the jest, should he not be publicly shamed.

Mrs. Page. Come, to the forge with it then; shape it: I would not have things cool. [*Exeunt.*

SCENE III.—A Room in the Garter Inn.

Enter Host and BARDOLPH.

Bard. Sir, the Germans desire to have three of your horses: the duke himself will be to-morrow at court, and they are going to meet him.

Host. What duke should that be, comes so secretly? I hear not of him in the court. Let me speak with the gentlemen; they speak English?

Bard. Ay, sir; I'll call them to you.

Host. They shall have my horses, but I'll make them pay; I'll sauce them: they have had my house a week at command; I have turned away my other guests: they must come off; I'll sauce them. Come. [*Exeunt.*

SCENE IV.—A Room in FORD'S House.

Enter PAGE, FORD, *Mistress* PAGE, *Mistress* FORD, *and Sir* HUGH EVANS.

Eva. 'T is one of the pest discretions of a 'oman as ever I did look upon.

Page. And did he send you both these letters at an instant?

Mrs. Page. Within a quarter of an hour.

Ford. Pardon me, wife. Henceforth do what thou wilt;
I rather will suspect the sun with cold
Than thee with wantonness: now doth thy honour stand,
In him that was of late an heretic,
As firm as faith.

Page.   'T is well, 't is well; no more. 10
Be not as extreme in submission
As in offence;
But let our plot go forward: let our wives
Yet once again, to make us public sport,
Appoint a meeting with this old fat fellow;
Where we may take him, and disgrace him for it.

Ford. There is no better way than that they spoke of.

Page. How? to send him word they'll meet him in the park at midnight? Fie, fie! he'll never come. 19

Eva. You say, he has been thrown in the rivers, and has been grievously peaten, as an old 'oman: methinks, there should be terrors in him, that he should not come; methinks, his flesh is punished, he shall have no desires.

Page. So think I too.

Mrs. Ford. Devise but how you'll use him when he comes,
And let us two devise to bring him thither.

Mrs. Page. There is an old tale goes, that Herne the hunter,
Sometime a keeper here in Windsor Forest,
Doth all the winter-time, at still midnight, 30
Walk round about an oak, with great ragg'd horns;
And there he blasts the tree, and takes the cattle;
And makes milch-kine yield blood, and shakes a chain
In a most hideous and dreadful manner:
You have heard of such a spirit; and well you know,
The superstitious idle-headed eld
Received, and did deliver to our age,
This tale of Herne the hunter for a truth.

Page. Why, yet there want not many, that do fear
In deep of night to walk by this Herne's oak. 40
But what of this?

Mrs. Ford.   Marry, this is our device;
That Falstaff at that oak shall meet with us,
Disguis'd like Herne, with huge horns on his head.

Page. Well, let it not be doubted but he'll come:
And in this shape when you have brought him thither,
What shall be done with him? what is your plot?

Mrs. Page. That likewise have we thought upon,
          and thus:
Nan Page my daughter, and my little son,
And three or four more of their growth, we 'll dress
Like urchins, ouphes, and fairies, green and white, 50
With rounds of waxen tapers on their heads,
And rattles in their hands. Upon a sudden,
As Falstaff, she, and I, are newly met,
Let them from forth a sawpit rush at once
With some diffused song : upon their sight,
We two in great amazedness will fly :
Then let them all encircle him about,
And, fairy-like, to-pinch the unclean knight ;
And ask him, why, that hour of fairy revel,
In their so sacred paths he dares to tread,   60
In shape profane.
Mrs. Ford.   And till he tell the truth,
Let the supposed fairies pinch him sound,
And burn him with their tapers.
Mrs. Page.   The truth being known,
We 'll all present ourselves, dis-horn the spirit,
And mock him home to Windsor.
Ford.   The children must
Be practised well to this, or they 'll ne'er do 't.
Eva. I will teach the children their behaviours ; I
will be like a jack-an-apes also, to burn the knight
with my taber.
Ford. That will be excellent. I 'll go buy them
          vizards.   70
Mrs. Page. My Nan shall be the queen of all the
          fairies,
Finely attired in a robe of white.
Page. That silk will I go buy ;—[*aside*] and in that
          tire
Shall Master Slender steal my Nan away,
And marry her at Eton.—Go send to Falstaff straight.
Ford. Nay, I 'll to him again in name of Brook ;
He 'll tell me all his purpose. Sure, he 'll come.
Mrs. Page. Fear not you that. Go, get us pro-
          perties,
And tricking for our fairies.
Eva. Let us about it : it is admirable pleasures, and
fery honest knaveries.   81
          [*Exeunt* PAGE, FORD, *and* EVANS.
Mrs. Page. Go, Mistress Ford,
Send Quickly to Sir John, to know his mind.
          [*Exit Mrs.* FORD.
I 'll to the doctor : he hath my good will,
And none but he, to marry with Nan Page.
That Slender, though well landed, is an idiot;
And he my husband best of all affects :
The doctor is well money'd, and his friends
Potent at court : he, none but he, shall have her,
Though twenty thousand worthier come to crave her.
          [*Exit.*

SCENE V.—A Room in the Garter Inn.

Enter Host and SIMPLE.

Host. What wouldst thou have, boor? what, thick-
skin? speak, breathe, discuss; brief, short, quick,
snap.
Sim. Marry, sir, I come to speak with Sir John
Falstaff from Master Slender.
Host. There 's his chamber, his house, his castle, his
standing-bed, and truckle-bed : 't is painted about with
the story of the Prodigal, fresh and new. Go, knock
and call : he 'll speak like an Anthropophaginian unto
thee : knock, I say.   10
Sim. There 's an old woman, a fat woman, gone up
into his chamber : I 'll be so bold as stay, sir, till she
come down ; I come to speak with her, indeed.
Host. Ha! a fat woman? the knight may be robbed?
I 'll call.—Bully knight ! Bully Sir John ! speak from
thy lungs military : art thou there? it is thine host,
thine Ephesian, calls.
Fal. [*Above.*] How now, mine host!
Host. Here 's a Bohemian-Tartar tarries the coming
down of thy fat woman. Let her descend, bully, let
her descend ; my chambers are honourable : fie !
privacy ? fie !   22

Enter FALSTAFF.

Fal. There was, mine host, an old fat woman even
now with me, but she 's gone.
Sim. Pray you, sir, was 't not the wise woman of
Brentford ?
Fal. Ay, marry, was it, muscle-shell : what would
you with her ?
Sim. My master, sir, Master Slender, sent to her,
seeing her go through the streets, to know, sir,
whether one Nym, sir, that beguiled him of a chain,
had the chain, or no.   32
Fal. I spake with the old woman about it.
Sim. And what says she, I pray, sir?
Fal. Marry, she says, that the very same man, that
beguiled Master Slender of his chain, cozened him of
it.
Sim. I would, I could have spoken with the woman

Host. " Where be my horses? speak well of them, varletto."

herself : I had other things to have spoken with her
too, from him.   40
Fal. What are they ? let us know.
Host. Ay, come ; quick.
Sim. I may not conceal them, sir.
Host. Conceal them, or thou diest.
Sim. Why, sir, they were nothing but about Mistress
Anne Page ; to know, if it were my master's fortune
to have her, or no.
Fal. 'T is, 't is his fortune.
Sim. What, sir ?
Fal. To have her,—or no. Go ; say, the woman told
me so.   51
Sim. May I be bold to say so, sir ?
Fal. Ay, sir : like who more bold.
Sim. I thank your worship. I shall make my
master glad with these tidings.   [*Exit.*
Host. Thou art clerkly, thou art clerkly, Sir John.
Was there a wise woman with thee ?
Fal. Ay, that there was, mine host ; one, that hath
taught me more wit than ever I learned before in my
life : and I paid nothing for it neither, but was paid
for my learning.   61

Enter BARDOLPH.

Bard. Out, alas, sir ! cozenage ; mere cozenage !
Host. Where be my horses? speak well of them,
varletto.
Bard. Run away with the cozeners ; for so soon as
I came beyond Eton, they threw me off from behind
one of them in a slough of mire ; and set spurs,
and away, like three German devils, three Doctor
Faustuses.
Host. They are gone but to meet the duke, villain.
Do not say, they be fled : Germans are honest men. 71

Enter Sir HUGH EVANS.

Eva. Where is mine host?

Host. What is the matter, sir?

Eva. Have a care of your entertainments : there is a friend of mine come to town, tells me, there is three cousin-germans, that has cozened all the hosts of Readings, of Maidenhead, of Colebrook, of horses and money. I tell you for good will, look you : you are wise, and full of gibes and vlouting-stogs, and 't is not convenient you snould be cozened. Fare you well. 80
        [*Exit.*

Enter Doctor CAIUS.

Caius. Vere is mine host *de Jartiere?*

Host. Here, master doctor, in perplexity, and doubtful dilemma.

Caius. I cannot tell vat is dat ; but it is tell-a me, dat you make grand preparation for a duke *de Jarmany :* by my trot, dere is no duke, dat de court is know to come. I tell you for good vill : adieu. [*Exit.*

Host. Hue and cry, villain! go.—Assist me, knight; I am undone.—Fly, run, hue and cry, villain! I am undone!   [*Exeunt Host and* BARDOLPH.

Fal. I would all the world might be cozened, for I have been cozened, and beaten too. If it should come to the ear of the court how I have been transformed, and how my transformation hath been washed and cudgelled, they would melt me out of my fat, drop by drop, and liquor fishermen's boots with me : I warrant, they would whip me with their fine wits, till I were as crest-fallen as a dried pear. I never prospered since I forswore myself at primero. Well, if my wind were but long enough to say my prayers, I would repent.   101

Enter Mistress QUICKLY.

Now, whence come you?

Quick. From the two parties, forsooth.

Fal. The devil take one party, and his dam the other, and so they shall be both bestowed. I have suffered more for their sakes, more than the villainous inconstancy of man's disposition is able to bear.

Quick. And have not they suffered? Yes, I warrant; speciously one of them : Mistress Ford, good heart, is beaten black and blue, that you cannot see a white spot about her.   111

Fal. What tell'st thou me of black and blue? I was beaten myself into all the colours of the rainbow ; and I was like to be apprehended for the witch of Brentford : but that my admirable dexterity of wit, my counterfeiting the action of an old woman, deliver'd me, the knave constable had set me i' the stocks, i' the common stocks, for a witch.   118

Quick. Sir, let me speak with you in your chamber ; you shall hear how things go, and, I warrant, to your content. Here is a letter will say somewhat. Good hearts! what ado here is to bring you together! Sure, one of you does not serve Heaven well, that you are so crossed.

Fal. Come up into my chamber [*Exeunt.*

SCENE VI.—Another Room in the Garter Inn.

Enter FENTON *and Host.*

Host. Master Fenton, talk not to me : my mind is heavy ; I will give over all.

Fent. Yet hear me speak. Assist me in my purpose, And, as I am a gentleman, I 'll give thee A hundred pound in gold more than your loss.

Host. I will hear you, Master Fenton ; and I will, at the least, keep your counsel.

Fent. From time to time I have acquainted you With the dear love I bear to fair Anne Page ;
Who, mutually, hath answer'd my affection, 10
So far forth as herself might be her chooser,
Even to my wish. I have a letter from her
Of such contents as you will wonder at ;
The mirth whereof so larded with my matter,
That neither singly can be manifested,
Without the show of both ;—wherein fat Falstaff
Hath a great scene : the image of the jest
I 'll show you here at large. Hark, good mine host :
To-night at Herne's oak, just 'twixt twelve and one,
Must my sweet Nan present the fairy queen ; 20
The purpose why, is here ; in which disguise,
While other jests are something rank on foot,
Her father hath commanded her to slip
Away with Slender, and with him at Eton
Immediately to marry : she hath consented.
Now, sir,
Her mother, even strong against that match,
And firm for Doctor Caius, hath appointed
That he shall likewise shuffle her away,
While other sports are tasking of their minds, 30
And at the deanery, where a priest attends,
Straight marry her : to this her mother's plot
She, seemingly obedient, likewise hath
Made promise to the doctor.—Now, thus it rests :
Her father means she shall be all in white ;
And in that habit, when Slender sees his time
To take her by the hand, and bid her go,
She shall go with him :—her mother hath intended,
The better to denote her to the doctor,
(For they must all be mask'd and vizarded) 40
That quaint in green she shall be loose enrob'd,
With ribands pendent, flaring 'bout her head ;
And when the doctor spies his vantage ripe,
To pinch her by the hand ; and on that token
The maid hath given consent to go with him.

Host. Which means she to deceive? father or mother?

Fent. Both, my good host, to go along with me :
And here it rests,—that you 'll procure the vicar
To stay for me at church 'twixt twelve and one, 50
And, in the lawful name of marrying,
To give our hearts united ceremony.

Host. Well, husband your device : I 'll to the vicar.
Bring you the maid, you shall not lack a priest.

Fent. So shall I evermore be bound to thee ;
Besides, I 'll make a present recompense. [*Exeunt.*

ACT V.

SCENE I.—A Room in the Garter Inn.

Enter FALSTAFF and Mistress QUICKLY.

Falstaff.

P'RYTHEE, no more prattling :—go :—
I 'll hold. This is the third time ;
I hope, good luck lies in odd numbers. Away, go. They say, there is
divinity in odd numbers, either in
nativity, chance, or death.—Away.

Quick. I 'll provide you a chain,
and I 'll do what I can to get you a
pair of horns.

Fal. Away, I say ; time wears :
hold up your head, and mince. 11
[*Exit Mrs.* QUICKLY.

Enter FORD.

How now, Master Brook ? Master
Brook, the matter will be known to-night, or never.
Be you in the park about midnight, at Herne's oak,
and you shall see wonders.

Ford. Went you not to her yesterday, sir, as you
told me you had appointed ?

Fal. I went to her, Master Brook, as you see, like
a poor old man ; but I came from her, Master Brook,
like a poor old woman. That same knave Ford, her
husband, hath the finest mad devil of jealousy in him,
Master Brook, that ever governed frenzy. I will tell
you :—he beat me grievously, in the shape of a woman ;
for in the shape of man, Master Brook, I fear not
Goliah with a weaver's beam, because I know also,
life is a shuttle. I am in haste : go along with me ;
I 'll tell you all, Master Brook. Since I plucked geese,
played truant, and whipped top, I knew not what it
was to be beaten, till lately. Follow me : I 'll tell you
strange things of this knave Ford, on whom to-night
I will be revenged, and I will deliver his wife into
your hand.—Follow. Strange things in hand, Master
Brook : follow. [*Exeunt.*

SCENE II.—Windsor Park.

Enter PAGE, SHALLOW, and SLENDER.

Page. Come, come : we 'll couch i' the castle-ditch,
till we see the light of our fairies.—Remember, son
Slender, my daughter.

Slen. Ay, forsooth ; I have spoke with her, and we
have a nay-word, how to know one another. I come
to her in white, and cry, "mum ;" she cries, "budget ;"
and by that we know one another.

Shal. That 's good too : but what needs either your
"mum," or her "budget ?" the white will decipher
her well enough.—It hath struck ten o'clock. 10

Page. The night is dark ; light and spirits will become it well. Heaven prosper our sport ! No man
means evil but the devil, and we shall know him by
his horns. Let 's away ; follow me. [*Exeunt.*

SCENE III.—The Street in Windsor.

Enter Mistress PAGE, Mistress FORD, and Doctor CAIUS.

Mrs. Page. Master doctor, my daughter is in green :
when you see your time, take her by the hand, away

with her to the deanery, and dispatch it quickly. Go
before into the park : we two must go together.

Caius. I know vat I have to do. Adieu.

Mrs. Page. Fare you well, sir. [*Exit* CAIUS.] My
husband will not rejoice so much at the abuse of Falstaff, as he will chafe at the doctor's marrying my
daughter : but 't is no matter ; better a little chiding,
than a great deal of heart-break. 10

Mrs. Ford. Where is Nan now, and her troop of
fairies ? and the Welch devil, Hugh ?

Mrs. Page. They are all couched in a pit hard by
Herne's oak, with obscured lights ; which, at the very
instant of Falstaff's and our meeting, they will at
once display to the night.

Mrs. Ford. That cannot choose but amaze him.

Mrs. Page. If he be not amazed, he will be mocked ;
if he be amazed, he will every way be mocked.

Mrs. Ford. We 'll betray him finely. 20

Mrs. Page. Against such lewdsters, and their
lechery,
Those that betray them do no treachery.

Mrs. Ford. The hour draws on : to the oak, to the
oak ! [*Exeunt.*

SCENE IV.—Windsor Park.

Enter Sir HUGH EVANS, and Fairies.

Eva. Trib, trib, fairies : come : and remember your
parts. Be pold, I pray you ; follow me into the pit,
and when I give the watch-ords, do as I pid you.
Come, come · trib, trib. [*Exeunt.*

SCENE V.—Another Part of the Park.

Enter FALSTAFF disguised, with a buck's head on.

Fal. The Windsor bell hath struck twelve ; the
minute draws on. Now, the hot-blooded gods assist
me !—Remember, Jove, thou wast a bull for thy
Europa ; love set on thy horns.—O powerful love !
that, in some respects, makes a beast a man ; in some
other, a man a beast.—You were also, Jupiter, a swan,
for the love of Leda :—O, omnipotent love ! how near
the god drew to the complexion of a goose !—A fault
done first in the form of a beast ;—O Jove, a beastly
fault ! and then another fault in the semblance of a
fowl : think on 't, Jove ; a foul fault.—When gods have
hot backs, what shall poor men do ? For me, I am
here a Windsor stag ; and the fattest, I think, i' the
forest : send me a cool rut-time, Jove, or who can
blame me to piss my tallow ? Who comes here ? my
doe ?

Enter Mistress FORD and Mistress PAGE.

Mrs. Ford. Sir John ? art thou there, my deer ? my
male deer ? 18

Fal. My doe with the black scut ?—Let the sky rain
potatoes ; let it thunder to the tune of "Green Sleeves ;"
hail kissing-comfits, and snow eringoes ; let there
come a tempest of provocation, I will shelter me here.
[*Embracing her.*

Mrs. Ford. Mistress Page is come with me, sweet-
heart.

Fal. Divide me like a bribed buck, each a haunch :
I will keep my sides to myself, my shoulders for the

fellow of this walk, and my horns I bequeath your
husbands. Am I a woodman? ha! Speak I like
Herne the hunter?—Why, now is Cupid a child of
conscience; he makes restitution. As I am a true
spirit, welcome.　　　　　　　　　[*Noise within.*

Mrs. Page. Alas! what noise?　　　　　　32
Mrs. Ford. Heaven forgive our sins!
Fal. What should this be?
Mrs. Ford. ⎱ Away, away!　　　[*They run off.*
Mrs. Page. ⎰
Fal. I think, the devil will not have me damned,
lest the oil that is in me should set hell on fire; he
would never else cross me thus.

Enter Sir HUGH EVANS, *like a Satyr;* ANNE PAGE,
*as the Fairy Queen, attended by her Brother and
others, dressed like Fairies, with waxen tapers on
their heads.*

Anne. Fairies, black, grey, green, and white,
You moonshine revellers, and shades of night,　40
You orphan heirs of fixed destiny,
Attend your office, and your quality.—
Crier Hobgoblin, make the fairy oyes.

Hobgoblin. Elves, list your names: silence, you
　　airy toys!
Cricket, to Windsor chimneys shalt thou leap:
Where fires thou find'st unrak'd, and hearths unswept,
There pinch the maids as blue as bilberry:
Our radiant queen hates sluts, and sluttery.

Fal. They are fairies; he that speaks to them shall die:
I'll wink and couch. No man their works must eye.
　　　　　　　　[*Lies down upon his face.*

Eva. Where's Bead?—Go you, and where you find
　　a maid,　　　　　　　　　　　51
That, ere she sleep, has thrice her prayers said,
Raise up the organs of her fantasy,
Sleep she as sound as careless infancy;
But those as sleep and think not on their sins,
Pinch them, arms, legs, backs, shoulders, sides, and
　　shins.

Anne. About, about!
Search Windsor Castle, elves, within and out:
Strew good luck, ouphes, on every sacred room,
That it may stand till the perpetual doom,　　60
In state as wholesome, as in state 't is fit,
Worthy the owner, and the owner it.
The several chairs of order look you scour
With juice of balm, and every precious flower:
Each fair instalment, coat, and several crest,
With loyal blazon, ever more be blest!
And nightly, meadow-fairies, look, you sing,
Like to the Garter's compass, in a ring:
The expressure that it bears, green let it be,
More fertile-fresh than all the field to see;　　70
And *Honi soit qui mal y pense,* write
In emerald tufts, flowers purple, blue, and white;
Like sapphire, pearl, and rich embroidery,
Buckled below fair knighthood's bending knee:
Fairies use flowers for their charactery.
Away! disperse! But, till 't is one o'clock,
Our dance of custom, round about the oak
Of Herne the hunter, let us not forget.

Eva. Pray you, lock hand in hand: yourselves in
　　order set;
And twenty glow-worms shall our lanterns be　80
To guide our measure round about the tree.
But, stay! I smell a man of middle-earth.

Fal. Heavens defend me from that Welch
lest he transform me to a piece of cheese!

Hobgoblin. Vile worm, thou wast o'erlook'd even
　　in thy birth.

Anne. With trial-fire touch me his finger-end:
If he be chaste, the flame will back descend,
And turn him to no pain; but if he start,
It is the flesh of a corrupted heart.

Hobgoblin. A trial! come.

Eva. 　　　　　　Come, will this wood take fire?
　　　　　　[*They burn him with their tapers.*

Fal. Oh, oh, oh!　　　　　　　　91

Anne. Corrupt, corrupt, and tainted in desire!
About him, fairies, sing a scornful rhyme;
And, as you trip, still pinch him to your time.

SONG.

Fie on sinful fantasy!
Fie on lust and luxury!
Lust is but a bloody fire,
Kindled with unchaste desire,
Fed in heart; whose flames aspire,
As thoughts do blow them higher and higher.　100
Pinch him, fairies, mutually;
Pinch him for his villainy;
Pinch him, and burn him, and turn him about,
Till candles, and star-light, and moonshine be out.

During this song, the Fairies pinch FALSTAFF.
Doctor CAIUS *comes one way, and steals away a
Fairy in green;* SLENDER *another way, and takes
off a Fairy in white; and* FENTON *comes, and
steals away* ANNE PAGE. *A noise of hunting is
made within. All the Fairies run away.* FALSTAFF
pulls off his buck's head, and rises.

Enter PAGE, FORD, *Mistress* PAGE, *and Mistress*
FORD. *They lay hold on him.*

Page. Nay, do not fly: I think, we have watch'd
　　you now.
Will none but Herne the hunter serve your turn?

Mrs. Page. I pray you, come; hold up the jest no
　　higher.—
Now, good Sir John, how like you Windsor wives?
See you these, husband? do not these fair yokes
Become the forest better than the town?　　110

Ford. Now, sir, who's a cuckold now?—Master
Brook, Falstaff's a knave, a cuckoldly knave; here
are his horns, Master Brook: and, Master Brook, he
hath enjoyed nothing of Ford's but his buck-basket,
his cudgel, and twenty pounds of money, which must
be paid to Master Brook: his horses are arrested for
it, Master Brook.

Mrs. Ford. Sir John, we have had ill luck; we
could never meet. I will never take you for my love
again, but I will always count you my deer.　120

Fal. I do begin to perceive, that I am made an ass.

Ford. Ay, and an ox too; both the proofs are extant.

Fal. And these are not fairies? I was three or four
times in the thought, they were not fairies; and yet
the guiltiness of my mind, the sudden surprise of my
powers, drove the grossness of the foppery into a
received belief, in despite of the teeth of all rhyme
and reason, that they were fairies. See now, how
wit may be made a Jack-a-Lent, when 't is upon ill
employment!　　　　　　　　　　130

Eva. Sir John Falstaff, serve Got, and leave your
desires, and fairies will not pinse you.

Ford. Well said, fairy Hugh.

Eva. And leave you your jealousies too, I pray you.

Ford. I will never mistrust my wife again, till thou
art able to woo her in good English.

Fal. Have I laid my brain in the sun, and dried it,
that it wants matter to prevent so gross o'er-reaching
as this? Am I ridden with a Welch goat too? shall I
have a coxcomb of frize? 'T is time I were choked
with a piece of toasted cheese.　　　　　144

Eva. Seese is not good to give putter: your pelly is
all putter.

Fal. Seese and putter! have I lived to stand at the
taunt of one that makes fritters of English? This
is enough to be the decay of lust, and late-walking
through the realm.

Mrs. Page. Why, Sir John, do you think, though
we would have thrust virtue out of our hearts by the
head and shoulders, and have given ourselves without
scruple to hell, that ever the devil could have made
you our delight?　　　　　　　　　152

Ford. What, a hodge-pudding? a bag of flax?

Mrs. Page. A puffed man?

Page. Old, cold, withered, and of intolerable entrails?

Ford. And one that is as slanderous as Satan?

Page. And as poor as Job?

Ford. And as wicked as his wife?

Eva. And given to fornications, and to taverns, and
sack, and wine, and metheglins, and to drinkings, and
swearings, and starings, pribbles and prabbles?　162

Fal. Well, I am your theme: you have the start of me; I am dejected; I am not able to answer the Welch flannel. Ignorance itself is a plummet o'er me: use me as you will.

Ford. Marry, sir, we'll bring you to Windsor, to one Master Brook, that you have cozened of money, to whom you should have been a pander: over and above that you have suffered, I think, to repay that money will be a biting affliction. 171

Page. Yet be cheerful, knight: thou shalt eat a posset to-night at my house; where I will desire thee to laugh at my wife, that now laughs at thee. Tell her, Master Slender hath married her daughter.

Mrs. Page. [Aside.] Doctors doubt that: if Anne Page be my daughter, she is, by this, Doctor Caius' wife.

Enter SLENDER.

Slen. Whoo, ho! ho! father Page! 180

Page. Son, how now? how now, son? have you despatched?

Slen. Despatched!—I'll make the best in Glostershire know on 't; would I were hanged, la, else.

Page. Of what, son?

Slen. I came yonder at Eton to marry Mistress Anne Page, and she's a great lubberly boy: if it had not been i' the church, I would have swinged him, or he should have swinged me. If I did not think it had been Anne Page, would I might never stir, and 't is a postmaster's boy. 193

Page. Upon my life, then, you took the wrong.

Slen. What need you tell me that? I think so, when I took a boy for a girl: if I had been married to him, for all he was in woman's apparel, I would not have had him.

Page. Why, this is your own folly. Did not I tell you, how you should know my daughter by her garments? 202

Slen. I went to her in white, and cried, "mum," and she cried, "budget," as Anne and I had appointed; and yet it was not Anne, but a postmaster's boy.

Mrs. Page. Good George, be not angry: I knew of your purpose; turned my daughter into green; and indeed, she is now with the doctor at the deanery, and there married. 209

Enter Doctor CAIUS.

Caius. Vere is Mistress Page? By gar, I am cozened; I ha' married *un garçon*, a boy; *un paysan*, by gar, a boy: it is not Anne Page; by gar, I am cozened.

Mrs. Page. Why, did you take her in green?

Caius. Ay, bv gar, and 't is a boy: by gar, I'll raise all Windsor. [*Exit.*

Ford. This is strange. Who hath got the right Anne?

Page. My heart misgives me. Here comes Master Fenton. 220

Enter FENTON *and* ANNE PAGE.

How now, Master Fenton?

Anne. Pardon, good father! good my mother, pardon!

Page. Now, mistress; how chance you went not with Master Slender?

Mrs. Page. Why went you not with master doctor, maid?

Fent. You do amaze her: hear the truth of it.
You would have married her most shamefully,
Where there was no proportion held in love.

Anne. "Pardon, good father! good my mother, pardon!"

The truth is, she and I, long since contracted, 230
Are now so sure, that nothing can dissolve us.
The offence is holy that she hath committed,
And this deceit loses the name of craft,
Of disobedience, or unduteous title,
Since therein she doth evitate and shun
A thousand irreligious cursed hours,
Which forced marriage would have brought upon her.

Ford. Stand not amaz'd: here is no remedy.—
In love, the heavens themselves do guide the state:
Money buys lands, and wives are sold by fate. 240

Fal. I am glad, though you have ta'en a special stand to strike at me, that your arrow hath glanced.

Page. Well, what remedy? Fenton, Heaven give thee joy.
What cannot be eschew'd, must be embrac'd.

Fal. When night-dogs run, all sorts of deer are chas'd.

Mrs. Page. Well, I will muse no further. Master Fenton,
Heaven give you many, many merry days.—
Good husband, let us every one go home,
And laugh this sport o'er by a country fire;
Sir John and all.

Ford.   Let it be so.—Sir John, 250
To Master Brook you yet shall hold your word;
For he, to-night, shall lie with Mistress Ford.

[*Exeunt.*

MEASURE FOR MEASURE.

DRAMATIS PERSONÆ.

VINCENTIO, *the Duke.*
ANGELO, *the Deputy.*
ESCALUS, *an ancient Lord.*
CLAUDIO, *a young Gentleman.*
LUCIO, *a Fantastic.*
Two other like Gentlemen.
Provost.
THOMAS, } *Two Friars.*
PETER, }
A Justice.
VARRIUS.
ELBOW, *a simple Constable.*

FROTH, *a foolish Gentleman.*
Clown.
ABHORSON, *an Executioner.*
BARNARDINE, *a dissolute Prisoner.*

ISABELLA, *Sister to Claudio.*
MARIANA, *betrothed to Angelo.*
JULIET, *beloved of Claudio.*
FRANCISCA, *a Nun.*
MISTRESS OVERDONE, *a Bawd.*

Lords, Officers, Citizens, Boy, and Attendants.

SCENE—VIENNA.

ACT I.

SCENE I.—An Apartment in the DUKE'S Palace.

Enter DUKE, ESCALUS, *Lords, and Attendants.*

Duke.

ESCALUS!

Escal. My lord.

Duke. Of government the properties to
    unfold,
Would seem in me to affect speech and
    discourse;
Since I am put to know, that your own
    science
Exceeds, in that, the lists of all advice
My strength can give you: then no more
    remains,
But that, to your sufficiency, as your worth is able,
And let them work. The nature of our people,
Our city's institutions, and the terms   10
For common justice, you 're as pregnant in,
As art and practice hath enriched any
That we remember. There is our commission,
From which we would not have you warp.—Call
    hither,
I say, bid come before us Angelo.—[*Exit an Attendant.*
What figure of us think you he will bear?
For, you must know, we have with special soul
Elected him our absence to supply,
Lent him our terror, dress'd him with our love,
And given his deputation all the organs   20
Of our own power. What think you of it?
Escal. If any in Vienna be of worth
To undergo such ample grace and honour,
It is Lord Angelo.
Duke.   Look, where he comes.

Enter ANGELO.

Ang. Always obedient to your grace's will,
I come to know your pleasure.
Duke.   Angelo,
There is a kind of character in thy life,
That, to the observer, doth thy history
Fully unfold. Thyself and thy belongings
Are not thine own so proper, as to waste   30
Thyself upon thy virtues, they on thee.

Heaven doth with us, as we with torches do,
Not light them for themselves; for if our virtues
Did not go forth of us, 't were all alike
As if we had them not. Spirits are not finely touch'd,
But to fine issues; nor Nature never lends

Duke. "In our remove, be thou at full ourself."

The smallest scruple of her excellence,
But, like a thrifty goddess, she determines
Herself the glory of a creditor,
Both thanks and use. But I do bend my speech   40
To one that can my part in him advertise;
Hold, therefore, Angelo:—
In our remove, be thou at full ourself;
Mortality and mercy in Vienna
Live in thy tongue and heart. Old Escalus,
Though first in question, is thy secondary.
Take thy commission.

Ang.   Now, good my lord,
Let there be some more test made of my metal,
Before so noble and so great a figure
Be stamp'd upon it.
Duke.   No more evasion :   50
We have with a leaven'd and prepared choice
Proceeded to you ; therefore take your honours.
Our haste from hence is of so quick condition,
That it prefers itself, and leaves unquestion'd
Matters of needful value. We shall write to you,
As time and our concernings shall importune,
How it goes with us ; and do look to know
What doth befall you here. So, fare you well :
To the hopeful execution do I leave you
Of your commissions.
Ang.   Yet, give leave, my lord,   60
That we may bring you something on the way.
Duke. My haste may not admit it ;
Nor need you, on mine honour, have to do
With any scruple : your scope is as mine own,
So to enforce, or qualify the laws
As to your soul seems good. Give me your hand ;
I 'll privily away : I love the people,
But do not like to stage me to their eyes.
Though it do well, I do not relish well
Their loud applause, and Aves vehement,   70
Nor do I think the man of safe discretion,
That does affect it. Once more, fare you well.
Ang. The heavens give safety to your purposes !
Escal. Lead forth, and bring you back in happi-
ness !
Duke. I thank you. Fare you well.   [*Exit.*
Escal. I shall desire you, sir, to give me leave
To have free speech with you ; and it concerns me
To look into the bottom of my place :
A power I have, but of what strength and nature
I am not yet instructed.   80
Ang. 'T is so with me. Let us withdraw together,
And we may soon our satisfaction have
Touching that point.
Escal.   I 'll wait upon your honour. [*Exeunt.*

Scene II.—A Street.

Enter Lucio *and two Gentlemen.*

Lucio. If the duke, with the other dukes, come not
to composition with the King of Hungary, why then,
all the dukes fall upon the king.
1 Gent. Heaven grant us its peace, but not the King
of Hungary's !
2 Gent. Amen.
Lucio. Thou concludest like the sanctimonious
pirate, that went to sea with the Ten Commandments, but scraped one out of the table.
2 Gent. " Thou shalt not steal ? "   10
Lucio. Ay, that he razed.
1 Gent. Why, 't was a commandment to command
the captain and all the rest from their functions :
they put forth to steal. There 's not a soldier of us all,
that, in the thanksgiving before meat, doth relish the
petition well that prays for peace.
2 Gent. I never heard any soldier dislike it.
Lucio. I believe thee ; for, I think, thou never wast
where grace was said.
2 Gent. No ? a dozen times at least.   20
1 Gent. What, in metre ?
Lucio. In any proportion, or in any language.
1 Gent. I think, or in any religion.
Lucio. Ay ; why not ? Grace is grace, despite of all
controversy : as for example, thou thyself art a wicked
villain, despite of all grace.
1 Gent. Well, there went but a pair of shears
between us.
Lucio. I grant ; as there may between the lists and
the velvet : thou art the list.   30
1 Gent. And thou the velvet : thou art good velvet :
thou art a three-pil'd piece, I warrant thee. I had as
lief be a list of an English kersey, as be pil'd, as thou
art pil'd, for a French velvet. Do I speak feelingly
now ?

Lucio. I think thou dost ; and, indeed, with most
painful feeling of thy speech : I will, out of thine own
confession, learn to begin thy health ; but, whilst I
live, forget to drink after thee.
1 Gent. I think, I have done myself wrong, have I not ?
2 Gent. Yes, that thou hast, whether thou art
tainted, or free.   42
Lucio. Behold, behold, where Madam Mitigation
comes !
1 Gent. I have purchased as many diseases under
her roof, as come to—
2 Gent. To what, I pray ?
Lucio. Judge.
2 Gent. To three thousand dollars a year.
1 Gent. Ay, and more.   50
Lucio. A French crown more.
1 Gent. Thou art full of error : I am sound.
Lucio. Nay, not as one would say, healthy ; but
so sound as things that are hollow : thy bones are
hollow ; impiety has made a feast of thee.

Enter Bawd.

1 Gent. How now ? Which of your hips has the
most profound sciatica ?
Bawd. Well, well ; there 's one yonder arrested,
and carried to prison, was worth five thousand of
you all.   61
2 Gent. Who 's that, I pray thee ?
Bawd. Marry, sir, that 's Claudio ; Signior Claudio.
1 Gent. Claudio to prison ! 't is not so.
Bawd. Nay, but I know, 't is so : I saw him arrested ;
saw him carried away ; and, which is more, within
these three days his head is to be chopped off.
Lucio. But, after all this fooling, I would not have
it so. Art thou sure of this ?
Bawd. I am too sure of it ; and it is for getting
Madam Julietta with child.   71
Lucio. Believe me, this may be : he promised to
meet me two hours since, and he was ever precise in
promise-keeping.
2 Gent. Besides, you know, it draws something near
to the speech we had to such a purpose.
1 Gent. But most of all, agreeing with the proclamation.
Lucio. Away : let 's go learn the truth of it.
          [*Exeunt* Lucio *and Gentlemen.*
Bawd. Thus : what with the war, what with the
sweat, what with the gallows, and what with poverty,
I am custom-shrunk.   82

Enter Clown.

How now ? what 's the news with you ?
Clo. Yonder man is carried to prison.
Bawd. Well : what has he done ?
Clo. A woman.
Bawd. But what 's his offence ?
Clo. Groping for trouts in a peculiar river.
Bawd. What, is there a maid with child by him ?
Clo. No ; but there 's a woman with maid by him.
You have not heard of the proclamation, have you ?
Bawd. What proclamation, man ?   92
Clo. All houses in the suburbs of Vienna must be
pluck'd down.
Bawd. And what shall become of those in the city ?
Clo. They shall stand for seed : they had gone down
too, but that a wise burgher put in for them.
Bawd. But shall all our houses of resort in the
suburbs be pull'd down ?
Clo. To the ground, mistress.   100
Bawd. Why, here 's a change, indeed, in the commonwealth ! what shall become of me ?
Clo. Come ; fear not you : good counsellors lack no
clients : though you change your place, you need not
change your trade ; I 'll be your tapster still. Courage !
there will, be pity taken on you ; you that have worn
your eyes almost out in the service, you will be considered.
Bawd. What 's to do here, Thomas Tapster ? Let 's
withdraw.   110
Clo. Here comes Signior Claudio, led by the provost
to prison : and there 's Madam Juliet.   [*Exeunt.*

SCENE III.—The Same.

Enter Provost, CLAUDIO, JULIET, *and Officers.*

Claud. Fellow, why dost thou show me thus to the world?
Bear me to prison, where I am committed.
  Prov. I do it not in evil disposition,
But from Lord Angelo by special charge.
  Claud. Thus can the demi-god Authority
Make us pay down for our offence by weight.—
The words of Heaven;—on whom it will, it will;
On whom it will not, so: yet still 't is just.

Enter LUCIO *and two Gentlemen.*

  Lucio. Why, how now, Claudio? whence comes this restraint?
  Claud. From too much liberty, my Lucio, liberty: 10
As surfeit is the father of much fast,
So every scope by the immoderate use
Turns to restraint. Our natures do pursue,
Like rats that ravin down their proper bane,
A thirsty evil, and when we drink, we die.
  Lucio. If I could speak so wisely under an arrest, I would send for certain of my creditors. And yet, to say the truth, I had as lief have the foppery of freedom, as the morality of imprisonment.—What 's thy offence, Claudio?
  Claud. What but to speak of would offend again.   22
  Lucio. What, is it murder?
  Claud. No.
  Lucio. Lechery?
  Claud. Call it so.
  Prov. Away, sir; you must go.
  Claud. One word, good friend.—Lucio, a word with you.
                              [*Takes him aside.*
  Lucio. A hundred, if they 'll do you any good.
Is lechery so look'd after?   30
  Claud. Thus stands it with me: upon a true contract,
I got possession of Julietta's bed:
You know the lady; she is fast my wife,
Save that we do the denunciation lack
Of outward order: this we came not to,
Only for propagation of a dower
Remaining in the coffer of her friends,
From whom we thought it meet to hide our love,
Till time had made them for us. But it chances,
The stealth of our most mutual entertainment   40
With character too gross is writ on Juliet.
  Lucio. With child, perhaps?
  Claud.   Unhappily, even so.
And the new deputy now for the duke,—
Whether it be the fault and glimpse of newness,
Or whether that the body public be
A horse whereon the governor doth ride,
Who, newly in the seat, that it may know
He can command, lets it straight feel the spur;
Whether the tyranny be in his place,
Or in his eminence that fills it up,   50
I stagger in,—but this new governor
Awakes me all the enrolled penalties,
Which have, like unscour'd armour, hung by the wall
So long, that nineteen zodiacs have gone round,
And none of them been worn; and, for a name,
Now puts the drowsy and neglected act
Freshly on me: 't is surely for a name.
  Lucio. I warrant. it is: and thy head stands so tickle
on thy shoulders, that a milkmaid, if she be in love,
may sigh it off. Send after the duke, and appeal to him.
  Claud. I have done so, but he 's not to be found. 61
I pr'ythee, Lucio, do me this kind service.
This day my sister should the cloister enter,
And there receive her approbation:

Acquaint her with the danger of my state;
Implore her, in my voice, that she make friends
To the strict deputy; bid herself assay him:
I have great hope in that; for in her youth
There is a prone and speechless dialect,
Such as moves men; beside, she hath prosperous art,
When she will play with reason and discourse,   71
And well she can persuade.
  Lucio. I pray, she may: as well for the encouragement of the like, which else would stand under

Claud. "I pr'ythee, Lucio, do me this kind service."

grievous imposition, as for the enjoying of thy life, who I would be sorry should be thus foolishly lost at a game of tick-tack. I 'll to her.
  Claud. I thank you, good friend Lucio.
  Lucio. Within two hours,—
  Claud.   Come, officer; away! [*Exeunt.*

SCENE IV.—A Monastery.

Enter DUKE *and Friar* THOMAS.

  Duke. No, holy father; throw away that thought:
Believe not that the dribbling dart of love
Can pierce a complete bosom. Why I desire thee
To give me secret harbour, hath a purpose
More grave and wrinkled, than the aims and ends
Of burning youth.
  Fri.   May your grace speak of it?
  Duke. My holy sir, none better knows than you
How I have ever lov'd the life remov'd,
And held in idle price to haunt assemblies,
Where youth, and cost, and witless bravery keeps. 10
I have deliver'd to Lord Angelo
(A man of stricture and firm abstinence)
My absolute power and place here in Vienna,
And he supposes me travell'd to Poland;
For so I have strew'd it in the common ear,
And so it is receiv'd. Now, pious sir,
You will demand of me, why I do this?
  Fri. Gladly, my lord.
  Duke. We have strict statutes, and most biting laws,
(The needful bits and curbs to headstrong steeds)   20
Which for this fourteen years we have let sleep;
Even like an o'ergrown lion in a cave,
That goes not out to prey. Now, as fond fathers,
Having bound up the threat'ning twigs of birch,
Only to stick it in their children's sight

For terror, not to use, in time the rod
Becomes more mock'd than fear'd ; so our decrees,
Dead to infliction, to themselves are dead,
And liberty plucks justice by the nose ;
The baby beats the nurse, and quite athwart   30
Goes all decorum.
 Fri.   It rested in your grace
To unloose this tied-up justice, when you pleas'd ;
And it in you more dreadful would have seem'd,
Than in Lord Angelo.

Duke.   "And to behold his sway,
I will, as 't were a brother of your order,
Visit both prince and people."

 Duke.   I do fear, too dreadful :
Sith 't was my fault to give the people scope,
'T would be my tyranny to strike and gall them
For what I bid them do : for we bid this be done,
When evil deeds have their permissive pass,
And not the punishment. Therefore, indeed, my
  father,
I have on Angelo impos'd the office,   40
Who may, in the ambush of my name, strike home,
And yet my nature never in the fight,
To do it slander. And to behold his sway,
I will, as 't were a brother of your order,
Visit both prince and people : therefore, I pr'ythee,
Supply me with the habit, and instruct me
How I may formally in person bear me
Like a true friar. More reasons for this action,
At our more leisure shall I render you ;
Only, this one :—Lord Angelo is precise ;   50
Stands at a guard with envy ; scarce confesses
That his blood flows, or that his appetite
Is more to bread than stone : hence shall we see,
If power change purpose, what our seemers be.
             [*Exeunt.*

    Scene V.—A Nunnery.

   Enter Isabella *and* Francisca.
 Isab. And have you nuns no further privileges ?
 Fran. Are not these large enough ?
 Isab. Yes, truly : I speak not as desiring more,
But rather wishing a more strict restraint
Upon the sisterhood, the votarists of Saint Clare.
 Lucio. [*Within.*] Ho ! Peace be in this place !
 Isab.   Who 's that which calls ?
 Fran. It is a man's voice. Gentle Isabella,
Turn you the key, and know his business of him :
You may, I may not ; you are yet unsworn.
When you have vow'd, you must not speak with men,
But in the presence of the prioress :   11
Then, if you speak, you must not show your face,
Or, if you show your face, you must not speak.
He calls again : I pray you, answer him. [*Exit.*

 Isab. Peace and prosperity ! Who is 't that calls ?

     Enter Lucio.
 Lucio. Hail, virgin, if you be, as those cheek-roses
Proclaim you are no less ! Can you so stead me,
As bring me to the sight of Isabella,
A novice of this place, and the fair sister
To her unhappy brother Claudio ?   20
 Isab. Why her unhappy brother ? let me ask,
The rather, for I now must make you know
I am that Isabella, and his sister.
 Lucio. Gentle and fair, your brother kindly
  greets you.
Not to be weary with you, he 's in prison.
 Isab. Woe me ! for what ?
 Lucio. For that, which, if myself might be his
  judge,
He should receive his punishment in thanks :
He hath got his friend with child.
 Isab. Sir, make me not your story.
 Lucio.   It is true.   30
I would not, though 't is my familiar sin
With maids to seem the lapwing, and to jest,
Tongue far from heart, play with all virgins so :
I hold you as a thing ensky'd, and sainted
By your renouncement, an immortal spirit,
And to be talk'd with in sincerity,
As with a saint.
 Isab. You do blaspheme the good in mocking
  me.
 Lucio. Do not believe it. Fewness and truth, 't is
  thus :
Your brother and his lover have embrac'd :   40
As those that feed grow full ; as blossoming time,
That from the seedness the bare fallow brings
To teeming foison, even so her plenteous womb
Expresseth his full tilth and husbandry.
 Isab. Some one with child by him ?—My cousin
  Juliet ?
 Lucio. Is she your cousin ?
 Isab. Adoptedly ; as school-maids change their names
By vain, though apt, affection.
 Lucio.   She it is.
 Isab. O ! let him marry her.
 Lucio.   This is the point.
The duke is very strangely gone from hence,   50
Bore many gentlemen, myself being one,
In hand, and hope of action ; but we do learn,
By those that know the very nerves of state,
His givings-out were of an infinite distance
From his true-meant design. Upon his place,
And with full line of his authority,
Governs Lord Angelo ; a man whose blood
Is very snow-broth ; one who never feels
The wanton stings and motions of the sense,
But doth rebate and blunt his natural edge   60
With profits of the mind, study and fast.
He (to give fear to use and liberty,
Which have, for long, run by the hideous law,
As mice by lions) hath pick'd out an act,
Under whose heavy sense your brother's life
Falls into forfeit : he arrests him on it,
And follows close the rigour of the statute,
To make him an example. All hope is gone,
Unless you have the grace by your fair prayer
To soften Angelo ; and that 's my pith of business   70
'Twixt you and your poor brother.
 Isab. Doth he so seek his life ?
 Lucio.   Has censur'd him
Already ; and, as I hear, the provost hath
A warrant for his execution.
 Isab. Alas ! what poor ability 's in me
To do him good ?
 Lucio.   Assay the power you have.
 Isab. My power, alas ! I doubt,—
 Lucio.   Our doubts are traitors,
And make us lose the good we oft might win,
By fearing to attempt. Go to Lord Angelo,
And let him learn to know, when maidens sue,   80
Men give like gods ; but when they weep and kneel,
All their petitions are as freely theirs
As they themselves would owe them.

Isab. I'll see what I can do.
Lucio.   But speedily.
Isab. I will about it straight,
No longer staying but to give the mother
Notice of my affair.   I humbly thank you:

Commend me to my brother; soon at night
I'll send him certain word of my success.
Lucio. I take my leave of you.
Isab.   Good sir, adieu.   90
                                          [*Exeunt.*

ACT II.

SCENE I.—A Hall in Angelo's House.

Enter ANGELO, ESCALUS, *a Justice, Provost, Officers, and other Attendants.*

       Angelo.
WE must not make a scarecrow of the law,
Setting it up to fear the birds of prey,
And let it keep one shape, till custom
    make it
Their perch, and not their terror.
  Escal.   Ay, but yet
Let us be keen, and rather cut a little,
Than fall, and bruise to death.   Alas! this gentleman,
Whom I would save, had a most noble father.
Let but your honour know
(Whom I believe to be most strait in virtue),
That, in the working of your own affections,   10
Had time coher'd with place, or place with wishing,
Or that the resolute acting of your blood
Could have attain'd the effect of your own purpose,
Whether you had not, sometime in your life,
Err'd in this point, which now you censure him,
And pull'd the law upon you.
  Ang.   'T is one thing to be tempted, Escalus,
Another thing to fall.   I not deny,
The jury, passing on the prisoner's life,
May in the sworn twelve have a thief or two   20
Guiltier than him they try; what's open made to
    justice,
That justice seizes: what know the laws,
That thieves do pass on thieves?   'T is very pregnant,
The jewel that we find, we stoop and take it,
Because we see it; but what we do not see,
We tread upon, and never think of it.
You may not so extenuate his offence
For I have had such faults; but rather tell me,
When I, that censure him, do so offend,
Let mine own judgment pattern out my death,   30
And nothing come in partial.   Sir, he must die.
  Escal. Be it as your wisdom will.
  Ang.   Where is the provost?
  Prov. Here, if it like your honour.
  Ang.   See that Claudio
Be executed by nine to-morrow morning.
Bring him his confessor, let him be prepar'd;
For that's the utmost of his pilgrimage.
                                   [*Exit Provost.*
  Escal. Well, Heaven forgive him, and forgive us all!
Some rise by sin, and some by virtue fall:
Some run from brakes of vice, and answer none,
And some condemned for a fault alone.   40

Enter ELBOW *and Officers, with* FROTH *and Clown.*

  Elb. Come, bring them away.   If these be good
people in a commonweal, that do nothing but use their
abuses in common houses, I know no law: bring them
away.
  Ang. How now, sir!   What's your name, and what's
the matter?
  Elb. If it please your honour, I am the poor duke's
constable, and my name is Elbow: I do lean upon

justice, sir; and do bring in here before your good
honour two notorious benefactors.   50
  Ang. Benefactors!   Well; what benefactors are
they? are they not malefactors?
  Elb. If it please your honour, I know not well what
they are; but precise villains they are, that I am sure
of, and void of all profanation in the world, that good
Christians ought to have.
  Escal. This comes off well: here's a wise officer.
  Ang. Go to: what quality are they of?   Elbow is
your name? why dost thou not speak, Elbow?
  Clo. He cannot, sir: he's out at elbow.   60
  Ang. What are you, sir?
  Elb. He, sir? a tapster, sir; parcel-bawd; one that
serves a bad woman, whose house, sir, was, as they say,
pluck'd down in the suburbs; and now she professes
a hot-house, which, I think, is a very ill house too.
  Escal. How know you that?
  Elb. My wife, sir, whom I detest before Heaven and
your honour,—
  Escal. How! thy wife?
  Elb. Ay, sir; whom, I thank Heaven, is an honest
woman,—   71
  Escal. Dost thou detest her therefore?
  Elb. I say, sir, I will detest myself also, as well as
she, that this house, if it be not a bawd's house, it is
pity of her life, for it is a naughty house.
  Escal. How dost thou know that, constable?
  Elb. Marry, sir, by my wife; who, if she had been a
woman cardinally given, might have been accused in
fornication, adultery, and all uncleanliness there.
  Escal. By the woman's means?   80
  Elb. Ay, sir, by Mistress Overdone's means; but as
she spit in his face, so she defied him.
  Clo. Sir, if it please your honour, this is not so.
  Elb. Prove it before these varlets here, thou honour-
able man, prove it.
  Escal. [*To* ANGELO.] Do you hear how he misplaces?
  Clo. Sir, she came in great with child, and longing
(saving your honour's reverence) for stew'd prunes.
Sir, we had but two in the house, which at that very
distant time stood, as it were, in a fruit-dish, a dish
of some three-pence: your honours have seen such
dishes; they are not China dishes, but very good
dishes.   93
  Escal. Go to, go to: no matter for the dish, sir.
  Clo. No, indeed, sir, not of a pin; you are therein in
the right; but to the point.   As I say, this Mistress
Elbow, being, as I say, with child, and being great-
bellied, and longing, as I said, for prunes, and having
but two in the dish, as I said, Master Froth here, this
very man, having eaten the rest, as I said, and, as
I say, paying for them very honestly;—for, as you
know, Master Froth, I could not give you three-pence
again.   103
  Froth. No, indeed.
  Clo. Very well: you being then, if you be remember'd, cracking the stones of the foresaid prunes,—

Froth. Ay, so I did, indeed.

Clo. Why, very well: I telling you then, if you be remember'd, that such a one, and such a one, were past cure of the thing you wot of, unless they kept very good diet, as I told you,— 111

Froth. All this is true.

Clo. Why, very well then,—

Escal. Come ; you are a tedious fool : to the purpose. —What was done to Elbow's wife, that he hath cause to complain of ? Come me to what was done to her.

Clo. Sir, your honour cannot come to that yet.

Escal. No, sir, nor I mean it not. 119

Clo. Sir, but you shall come to it, by your honour's leave. And, I beseech you, look into Master Froth here, sir ; a man of fourscore pound a year, whose father died at Hallowmas.—Was 't not at Hallowmas, Master Froth?

Froth. All-Hallownd eve.

Clo. Why, very well : I hope here be truths. He, sir, sitting, as I say, in a lower chair, sir ;—'t was in the Bunch of Grapes, where, indeed, you have a delight to sit ; have you not?

Froth. I have so, because it is an open room, and good for winter. 131

Clo. Why, very well then : I hope here be truths.

Ang. This will last out a night in Russia, When nights are longest there. I 'll take my leave, And leave you to the hearing of the cause, Hoping you 'll find good cause to whip them all.

Escal. I think no less. Good morrow to your lordship. [*Exit* ANGELO.] Now, sir, come on : what was done to Elbow's wife, once more?

Clo. Once, sir ? there was nothing done to her once.

Elb. I beseech you, sir, ask him what this man did to my wife. 142

Clo. I beseech your honour, ask me.

Escal. Well, sir, what did this gentleman to her?

Clo. I beseech you, sir, look in this gentleman's face. —Good Master Froth, look upon his honour ; 't is for a good purpose. Doth your honour mark his face?

Escal. Ay, sir, very well.

Clo. Nay, I beseech you, mark it well.

Escal. Well, I do so. 150

Clo. Doth your honour see any harm in his face?

Escal. Why, no.

Clo. I 'll be supposed upon a book, his face is the worst thing about him. Good then ; if his face be the worst thing about him, how could Master Froth do the constable's wife any harm? I would know that of your honour.

Escal. He's in the right. Constable, what say you to it ?

Elb. First, an it like you, the house is a respected house ; next, this is a respected fellow, and his mistress is a respected woman. 162

Clo. By this hand, sir, his wife is a more respected person than any of us all.

Elb. Varlet, thou liest : thou liest, wicked varlet. The time is yet to come that she was ever respected with man, woman, or child.

Clo. Sir, she was respected with him, before he married with her.

Escal. Which is the wiser here? Justice, or Iniquity?—Is this true? 171

Elb. O thou caitiff! O thou varlet! O thou wicked Hannibal! I respected with her, before I was married to her ?—If ever I was respected with her, or she with me, let not your worship think me the poor duke's officer. Prove this, thou wicked Hannibal, or I 'll have mine action of battery on thee.

Escal. If he took you a box o' th' ear, you might have your action of slander too.

Elb. Marry, I thank your good worship for it. What is 't your worship's pleasure I shall do with this wicked caitiff? 182

Escal. Truly, officer, because he hath some offences in him, that thou wouldst discover if thou couldst, let him continue in his courses, till thou know'st what they are.

Elb. Marry, I thank your worship for it.—Thou seest, thou wicked varlet, now, what's come upon thee : thou art to continue ; now, thou varlet, thou art to continue. 190

Escal. Where were you born, friend ?

Froth. Here in Vienna, sir.

Escal. Are you of fourscore pounds a year ?

Froth. Yes, an 't please you, sir.

Escal. So.—What trade are you of, sir ?

Clo. A tapster ; a poor widow's tapster.

Escal. Your mistress' name ?

Clo. Mistress Overdone.

Escal. Hath she had any more than one husband?

Clo. Nine, sir ; Overdone by the last. 200

Escal. Nine!—Come hither to me, Master Froth. Master Froth, I would not have you acquainted with tapsters ; they will draw you, Master Froth, and you will hang them. Get you gone, and let me hear no more of you.

Froth. I thank your worship. For mine own part, I never come into any room in a taphouse, but I am drawn in.

Escal. Well : no more of it, Master Froth : farewell. [*Exit* FROTH.]—Come you hither to me, master tapster. What 's your name, master tapster? 211

Clo. Pompey.

Escal. What else ?

Clo. Bum, sir.

Escal. 'Troth, and your bum is the greatest thing about you, so that, in the beastliest sense, you are Pompey the Great. Pompey, you are partly a bawd, Pompey, howsoever you colour it in being a tapster. Are you not ? come, tell me true : it shall be the better for you. 220

Clo. Truly, sir, I am a poor fellow that would live.

Escal. How would you live, Pompey? by being a bawd ? What do you think of the trade, Pompey ? is it a lawful trade ?

Clo. If the law would allow it, sir.

Escal. But the law will not allow it, Pompey ; nor it shall not be allowed in Vienna.

Clo. Does your worship mean to geld and splay all the youth of the city.

Escal. No, Pompey. 230

Clo. Truly, sir, in my poor opinion, they will to 't then. If your worship will take order for the drabs and the knaves, you need not to fear the bawds.

Escal. There are pretty orders beginning, I can tell you : it is but heading and hanging.

Clo. If you head and hang all that offend that way but for ten year together, you 'll be glad to give out a commission for more heads. If this law hold in Vienna ten year, I 'll rent the fairest house in it after three-pence a bay. If you live to see this come to pass, say, Pompey told you so. 241

Escal. Thank you, good Pompey ; and, in requital of your prophecy, hark you :—I advise you, let me not find you before me again upon any complaint whatsoever ; no, not for dwelling where you do : if I do, Pompey, I shall beat you to your tent, and prove a shrewd Cæsar to you. In plain dealing, Pompey, I shall have you whipt. So, for this time, Pompey, fare you well.

Clo. I thank your worship for your good counsel : [*aside*] but I shall follow it, as the flesh and fortune shall better determine. 252

Whip me ? No, no ; let carman whip his jade ; The valiant heart 's not whipt out of his trade.

[*Exit.*

Escal. Come hither to mé, Master Elbow ; come hither, master constable. How long have you been in this place of constable?

Elb. Seven year and a half, sir.

Escal. I thought, by the readiness in the office, you had continued in it some time. You say, seven years together ? 261

Elb. And a half, sir.

Escal. Alas ! it hath been great pains to you. They do you wrong to put you so oft upon 't. Are there not men in your ward sufficient to serve it ?

Elb. Faith, sir, few of any wit in such matters. As they are chosen, they are glad to choose me for them : I do it for some piece of money, and go through with all.

Escal. Look you bring me in the names of some six
or seven, the most sufficient of your parish.   271
Elb. To your worship's house, sir?
Escal. To my house.   Fare you well. [*Exit* ELBOW.
What's o'clock, think you?
Just. Eleven, sir.
Escal. I pray you home to dinner with me.
Just. I humbly thank you.
Escal. It grieves me for the death of Claudio;
But there's no remedy.
Just. Lord Angelo is severe.
Escal.   It is but needful: 280
Mercy is not itself, that oft looks so;
Pardon is still the nurse of second woe.
But yet, poor Claudio!—There is no remedy.
Come, sir.   [*Exeunt.*

SCENE II.—Another Room in the Same.

Enter Provost, and a Servant.

Serv. He's hearing of a cause: he will come straight.
I'll tell him of you.
Prov.   Pray you, do. [*Exit Servant.*] I'll know
His pleasure; may be, he will relent.   Alas!
He hath but as offended in a dream!
All sects, all ages smack of this vice, and he
To die for it!—

Enter ANGELO.

Ang.   Now, what's the matter, provost?
Prov. Is it your will Claudio shall die to-morrow?
Ang. Did I not tell thee, yea? hadst thou not order?
Why dost thou ask again?
Prov.   Lest I might be too rash.
Under your good correction, I have seen,   10
When, after execution, judgment hath
Repented o'er his doom.
Ang.   Go to; let that be mine:
Do you your office, or give up your place,
And you shall well be spar'd.
Prov.   I crave your honour's pardon.
What shall be done, sir, with the groaning Juliet?
She's very near her hour.
Ang.   Dispose of her
To some more fitter place, and that with speed.

Re-enter Servant.

Serv. Here is the sister of the man condemn'd,
Desires access to you.
Ang.   Hath he a sister?
Prov. Ay, my good lord; a very virtuous maid,   20
And to be shortly of a sisterhood,
If not already.
Ang.   Well, let her be admitted. [*Exit Servant.*
See you the fornicatress be remov'd:
Let her have needful, but not lavish, means;
There shall be order for't.

Enter LUCIO *and* ISABELLA.

Prov.   God save your honour!
Ang. Stay a little while.—[*To* ISAB.] You're wel-
come: what's your will?
Isab. I am a woful suitor to your honour,
Please but your honour hear me.
Ang.   Well; what's your suit?
Isab. There is a vice, that most I do abhor,   30
And most desire should meet the blow of justice,
For which I would not plead, but that I must;
For which I must not plead, but that I am
At war 'twixt will and will not.
Ang.   Well; the matter?
Isab. I have a brother is condemn'd to die:
I do beseech you, let it be his fault,
And not my brother.
Prov. [*Aside.*] Heaven give thee moving graces!
Ang. Condemn the fault, and not the actor of it?
Why, every fault's condemn'd ere it be done.
Mine were the very cipher of a function,
To fine the faults, whose fine stands in record,   40
And let go by the actor.
Isab.   O just, but severe law!
I had a brother then.—Heaven keep your honour!

Lucio. [*To* ISAB.] Give't not o'er so: to him again,
entreat him;
Kneel down before him, hang upon his gown;
You are too cold: if you should need a pin,
You could not with more tame a tongue desire it.
To him, I say!
Isab. Must he needs die?
Ang.   Maiden, no remedy.
Isab. Yes; I do think that you might pardon him,
And neither Heaven, nor man, grieve at the mercy. 50
Ang. I will not do't.
Isab.   But can you, if you would?
Ang. Look; what I will not, that I cannot do.
Isab. But might you do't, and do the world no
wrong,
If so your heart were touch'd with that remorse
As mine is to him?
Ang.   He's sentenc'd: 't is too late.
Lucio. [*To* ISAB.] You are too cold.
Isab. Too late? why, no; I, that do speak a word,
May call it back again.   Well, believe this,
No ceremony that to great ones 'longs,
Not the king's crown, nor the deputed sword,   60
The marshal's truncheon, nor the judge's robe,
Become them with one half so good a grace
As mercy does.
If he had been as you, and you as he,
You would have slipp'd like him; but he, like you,
Would not have been so stern.
Ang.   Pray you, be gone.
Isab. I would to Heaven I had your potency,
And you were Isabel! should it then be thus?
No; I would tell what 't were to be a judge,
And what a prisoner.
Lucio. [*To* ISAB.] Ay, touch him; there's the vein. 70
Ang. Your brother is a forfeit of the law,
And you but waste your words.
Isab.   Alas! alas!
Why, all the souls that were were forfeit once;
And He that might the vantage best have took,
Found out the remedy.   How would you be,
If He, which is the top of judgment, should
But judge you as you are?   O, think on that,
And mercy then will breathe within your lips
Like man new-made!
Ang.   Be you content, fair maid,
It is the law, not I, condemns your brother: 80
Were he my kinsman, brother, or my son,
It should be thus with him: he must die to-morrow.
Isab. To-morrow? O, that's sudden! Spare him,
spare him!
He's not prepar'd for death.   Even for our kitchens
We kill the fowl of season: shall we serve Heaven
With less respect than we do minister
To our gross selves?   Good, good my lord, bethink
you:
Who is it that hath died for this offence?
There's many have committed it.
Lucio. [*To* ISAB.]   Ay, well said.
Ang. The law hath not been dead, though it hath
slept: 90
Those many had not dar'd to do that evil,
If the first, that did the edict infringe,
Had answer'd for his deed: now, 't is awake,
Takes note of what is done, and, like a prophet,
Looks in a glass, that shows what future evils,
Either new, or by remissness new-conceiv'd,
And so in progress to be hatch'd and born,
Are now to have no successive degrees,
But, ere they live, to end.
Isab.   Yet show some pity.
Ang. I show it most of all, when I show justice; 100
For then I pity those I do not know,
Which a dismiss'd offence would after gall,
And do him right, that, answering one foul wrong,
Lives not to act another.   Be satisfied:
Your brother dies to-morrow: be content.
Isab. So you must be the first that gives this sen-
tence,
And he that suffers.   O! it is excellent
To have a giant's strength, but it is tyrannous
To use it like a giant.

Lucio. [*To* Isab.] That's well said.
Isab. Could great men thunder 110
As Jove himself does, Jove would ne'er be quiet,
For every pelting, petty officer

His glassy essence,—like an angry ape, 120
Plays such fantastic tricks before high heaven,
As make the angels weep; who, with our spleens,
Would all themselves laugh mortal.

Isab. " To-morrow ? O, that 's sudden ! Spare him, spare him ! "

Would use his heaven for thunder; nothing but thun-
    der.—
Merciful Heaven!
Thou rather with thy sharp and sulphurous bolt
Splitt'st the unwedgeable and gnarled oak,
Than the soft myrtle; but man, proud man!
Drest in a little brief authority,
Most ignorant of what he's most assur'd,

Lucio. [*To* Isab.] O, to him, to him, wench! He
    will relent:
He 's coming; I perceive 't.
    Prov. [*Aside.*]   Pray Heaven, she win him!
    Isab. We cannot weigh our brother with our-
    self:
Great men may jest with saints: 't is wit in them,
But in the less foul profanation.

Lucio. [*To* ISAB.] Thou 'rt in the right, girl: more
　　　o' that.
Isab. That in the captain's but a choleric word, 130
Which in the soldier is flat blasphemy.
Lucio. [*To* ISAB.] Art avis'd o' that? more on 't.
Ang. Why do you put these sayings upon me?
Isab. Because authority, though it err like others,
Hath yet a kind of medicine in itself,
That skins the vice o' the top. Go to your bosom;
Knock there, and ask your heart, what it doth know
That 's like my brother's fault: if it confess
A natural guiltiness, such as is his,
Let it not sound a thought upon your tongue 140
Against my brother's life.
Ang. [*Aside.*]　　　　　　She speaks, and 't is
Such sense, that my sense breeds with it. Fare you
　　　well.
Isab. Gentle my lord, turn back.
Ang. I will bethink me.—Come again to-morrow.
Isab. Hark, how I 'll bribe you. Good my lord, turn
　　　back.
Ang. How, bribe me?
Isab. Ay, with such gifts, that Heaven shall share
　　　with you.
Lucio. [*To* ISAB.] You had marr'd all else.
Isab. Not with fond shekels of the tested gold,
Or stones, whose rates are either rich or poor 150
As fancy values them; but with true prayers,
That shall be up at heaven, and enter there
Ere sunrise: prayers from preserved souls,
From fasting maids, whose minds are dedicate
To nothing temporal.
Ang.　　　　　　Well; come to me to-morrow.
Lucio. [*To* ISAB.] Go to; 't is well: away!
Isab. Heaven keep your honour safe!
Ang. [*Aside.*]　　　　　　Amen:
For I am that way going to temptation,
Where prayers cross.
Isab.　　　　　　At what hour to-morrow
Shall I attend your lordship?
Ang.　　　　　　At any time 'fore noon. 160
Isab. 'Save your honour!
　　　　　[*Exeunt* LUCIO, ISABELLA, *and Provost.*
Ang. From thee; even from thy virtue!—
What 's this? what 's this? Is this her fault, or mine?
The tempter, or the tempted, who sins most?
Ha!
Not she, nor doth she tempt; but it is I,
That, lying by the violet in the sun,
Do, as the carrion does, not as the flower,
Corrupt with virtuous season. Can it be,
That modesty may more betray our sense 170
Than woman's lightness? Having waste ground
　　　enough,
Shall we desire to raze the sanctuary,
And pitch our evils there? O, fie, fie, fie!
What dost thou, or what art thou, Angelo?
Dost thou desire her foully for those things
That make her good? O, let her brother live!
Thieves for their robbery have authority,
When judges steal themselves. What! do I love her,
That I desire to hear her speak again,
And feast upon her eyes? What is 't I dream on? 180
O cunning enemy, that, to catch a saint,
With saints dost bait thy hook! Most dangerous
Is that temptation, that doth goad us on
To sin in loving virtue. Never could the strumpet,
With all her double vigour, art and nature,
Once stir my temper; but this virtuous maid
Subdues me quite.—Ever, till now,
When men were fond, I smil'd, and wonder'd how.
　　　　　[*Exit.*

- - -

SCENE III.—A Room in a Prison.

Enter DUKE, *disguised as a Friar, and Provost.*

Duke. Hail to you, provost; so I think you are.
Prov. I am the provost. What 's your will, good
　　　friar?
Duke. Bound by my charity, and my bless'd order,
I come to visit the afflicted spirits

Here in the prison: do me the common right
To let me see them, and to make me know
The nature of their crimes, that I may minister
To them accordingly.
Prov. I would do more than that, if more were
　　　needful.　　　　　　　　　　　　　　　　　10
Look, here comes one: a gentlewoman of mine,
Who, falling in the flames of her own youth,
Hath blister'd her report. She is with child,
And he that got it, sentenc'd—a young man
More fit to do another such offence,
Than die for this.

Enter JULIET.

Duke. When must he die?
Prov.　　　　　　As I do think, to-morrow.—
[*To* JULIET.] I have provided for you: stay awhile,
And you shall be conducted.
Duke. Repent you, fair one, of the sin you carry?
Juliet. I do, and bear the shame most patiently. 20
Duke. I 'll teach you how you shall arraign your
　　　conscience,
And try your penitence, if it be sound,
Or hollowly put on.
Juliet.　　　　　　I 'll gladly learn.
Duke. Love you the man that wrong'd you?
Juliet. Yes, as I love the woman that wrong'd him.
Duke. So then, it seems, your most offenceful act
Was mutually committed?
Juliet.　　　　　　Mutually.
Duke. Then was your sin of heavier kind than his.
Juliet. I do confess it, and repent it, father.
Duke. 'T is meet so, daughter: but lest you do repent,
As that the sin hath brought you to this shame; 31
Which sorrow is always toward ourselves, not Heaven,
Showing, we would not spare Heaven as we love it,
But as we stand in fear.
Juliet. I do repent me, as it is an evil,
And take the shame with joy.
Duke.　　　　　　There rest.
Your partner, as I hear, must die to-morrow,
And I am going with instruction to him.
Grace go with you! *Benedicite!*　　　[*Exit.*
Juliet. Must die to-morrow! O, injurious love, 40
That respites me a life, whose very comfort
Is still a dying horror!
Prov.　　　　　　'T is pity of him. [*Exeunt.*

- - -

SCENE IV.—A Room in ANGELO'S House.

Enter ANGELO.

Ang. When I would pray and think, I think and pray
To several subjects: Heaven hath my empty words,
Whilst my invention, hearing not my tongue,
Anchors on Isabel: Heaven in my mouth
As if I did but only chew his name,
And in my heart the strong and swelling evil
Of my conception. The state, whereon I studied,
Is like a good thing, being often read,
Grown sear'd and tedious; yea, my gravity,
Wherein (let no man hear me) I take pride, 10
Could I, with boot, change for an idle plume,
Which the air beats for vain. O place! O form!
How often dost thou with thy case, thy habit,
Wrench awe from fools, and tie the wiser souls
To thy false seeming!—Blood, thou art blood:
Let 's write good angel on the devil's horn,
'T is not the devil's crest.

Enter a Servant.

How now! who 's there?
Serv.　　　　　　One Isabel, a sister,
Desires access to you.
Ang.　　　　　　Teach her the way. [*Exit Servant.*
O heavens!　　　　　　　　　　　　　　　　　20
Why does my blood thus muster to my heart,
Making both it unable for itself,
And dispossessing all my other parts
Of necessary fitness?
So play the foolish throngs with one that swoons;

Come all to help him, and so stop the air
By which he should revive: and even so
The general, subject to a well-wish'd king,
Quit their own part, and in obsequious fondness
Crowd to his presence, where their untaught love   30
Must needs appear offence.

Enter ISABELLA.

How now, fair maid?
    Isab.   I am come to know your pleasure.
    Ang. That you might know it, would much better
        please me,
Than to demand what 't is.   Your brother cannot
        live.
    Isab. Even so.—Heaven keep your honour!
                          [*Retiring.*
    Ang. Yet may he live awhile; and, it may be,
As long as you, or I: yet he must die.
    Isab. Under your sentence?
    Ang. Yea.
    Isab. When, I beseech you? that in his reprieve,   40
Longer or shorter, he may be so fitted,
That his soul sicken not.
    Ang. Ha! fie, these filthy vices! It were as good
To pardon him, that hath from nature stolen
A man already made, as to remit
Their saucy sweetness, that do coin Heaven's image
In stamps that are forbid: 't is all as easy
Falsely to take away a life true made,
As to put metal in restrained means,
To make a false one.   50
    Isab. 'T is set down so in heaven, but not in earth.
    Ang. Say you so? then, I shall pose you quickly.
Which had you rather, that the most just law
Now took your brother's life, or, to redeem him,
Give up your body to such sweet uncleanness
As she that he hath stain'd?
    Isab.   Sir, believe this,
I had rather give my body than my soul.
    Ang. I talk not of your soul. Our compell'd sins
Stand more for number than for accompt.
    Isab.   How say you?
    Ang. Nay, I'll not warrant that; for I can speak   60
Against the thing I say.   Answer to this:—
I, now the voice of the recorded law,
Pronounce a sentence on your brother's life:
Might there not be a charity in sin,
To save this brother's life?
    Isab.   Please you to do 't,
I'll take it as a peril to my soul:
It is no sin at all, but charity.
    Ang. Pleas'd you to do 't, at peril of your soul,
Were equal poise of sin and charity.
    Isab. That I do beg his life, if it be sin,   70
Heaven let me bear it! you granting of my suit,
If that be sin, I'll make it my morn-prayer
To have it added to the faults of mine,
And nothing of your answer.
    Ang.   Nay, but hear me.
Your sense pursues not mine: either you are ignorant,
Or seem so, craftily; and that's not good.
    Isab. Let me be ignorant, and in nothing good,
But graciously to know I am no better.
    Ang. Thus wisdom wishes to appear most bright,
When it doth tax itself: as these black masks   80
Proclaim an enshield beauty ten times louder
Than beauty could, display'd.—But mark me;
To be received plain, I'll speak more gross:
Your brother is to die.
    Isab. So.
    Ang. And his offence is so, as it appears
Accountant to the law upon that pain.
    Isab. True.
    Ang. Admit no other way to save his life,
(As I subscribe not that, nor any other,
But in the loss of question) that you, his sister,   90
Finding yourself desir'd of such a person,
Whose credit with the judge, or own great place,
Could fetch your brother from the manacles
Of the all-building law, and that there were
No earthly mean to save him, but that either
You must lay down the treasures of your body

To this suppos'd, or else to let him suffer,
What would you do?
    Isab. As much for my poor brother, as myself: 100
That is, were I under the terms of death,
The impression of keen whips I'd wear as rubies,
And strip myself to death, as to a bed
That longing have been sick for, ere I'd yield
My body up to shame.

Ang. "He shall not, Isabel, if you give me love."

    Ang.   Then must your brother die.
    Isab. And 't were the cheaper way.
Better it were, a brother died at once,
Than that a sister, by redeeming him,
Should die for ever.
    Ang. Were not you then as cruel as the sentence
That you have slander'd so?   111
    Isab. Ignomy in ransom, and free pardon,
Are of two houses: lawful mercy
Is nothing kin to foul redemption.
    Ang. You seem'd of late to make the law a tyrant;
And rather prov'd the sliding of your brother
A merriment, than a vice.
    Isab. O, pardon me, my lord! it oft falls out,
To have what we would have, we speak not what we
        mean.
I something do excuse the thing I hate,   120
For his advantage that I dearly love.
    Ang. We are all frail.
    Isab.   Else let my brother die,
If not a fedary, but only he,
Owe and succeed thy weakness.
    Ang. Nay, women are frail too.
    Isab. Ay, as the glasses where they view them-
        selves,
Which are as easy broke as they make forms.
Women!—Help Heaven! men their creation mar
In profiting by them. Nay, call us ten times frail,
For we are soft as our complexions are,   130
And credulous to false prints.
    Ang.   I think it well;
And from this testimony of your own sex,
(Since, I suppose, we are made to be no stronger,
Than faults may shake our frames) let me be bold:
I do arrest your words. Be that you are,

That is, a woman ; if you be more, you 're none ;
If you be one (as you are well express'd
By all external warrants), show it now,
By putting on the destin'd livery.
   Isab. I have no tongue but one : gentle my lord, 140
Let me entreat you speak the former language.
   Ang. Plainly conceive, I love you.
   Isab. My brother did love Juliet ; and you tell me,
That he shall die for 't.
   Ang. He shall not, Isabel, if you give me love.
   Isab. I know, your virtue hath a license in 't,
Which seems a little fouler than it is,
To pluck on others.
   Ang.   Believe me, on mine honour,
My words express my purpose.
   Isab. Ha ! little honour to be much believ'd, 150
And most pernicious purpose !—Seeming, seeming !—
I will proclaim thee, Angelo ; look for 't :
Sign me a present pardon for my brother,
Or with an outstretch'd throat I 'll tell the world
Aloud what man thou art.
   Ang.   Who will believe thee, Isabel?
My unsoil'd name, the austereness of my life,
My vouch against you, and my place i' the state,
Will so your accusation overweigh,
That you shall stifle in your own report,
And smell of calumny. I have begun, 160
And now I give my sensual race the rein :

Fit thy consent to my sharp appetite ;
Lay by all nicety, and prolixious blushes,
That banish what they sue for ; redeem thy **brother**
By yielding up thy body to my will,
Or else he must not only die the death,
But thy unkindness shall his death draw out
To lingering sufferance. Answer me to-morrow,
Or, by the affection that now guides me most,
I 'll prove a tyrant to him. As for you, 170
Say what you can, my false o'erweighs your true.
                             [*Exit.*
   Isab. To whom should I complain? Did I tell this,
Who would believe me ? O perilous mouths !
That bear in them one and the selfsame tongue,
Either of condemnation or approof,
Bidding the law make court'sy to their will,
Hooking both right and wrong to the appetite,
To follow as it draws. I 'll to my brother :
Though he hath fallen by prompture of the blood,
Yet hath he in him such a mind of honour, 180
That, had he twenty heads to tender down
On twenty bloody blocks, he 'd yield them up,
Before his sister should her body stoop
To such abhorr'd pollution.
Then, Isabel, live chaste, and, brother, die :
More than our brother is our chastity.
I 'll tell him yet of Angelo's request,
And fit his mind to death, for his soul's rest.   [*Exit.*

ACT III.

SCENE I.—A Room in the Prison.

Enter DUKE, *as a Friar,* CLAUDIO, *and Provost.*

   Duke.
O, then you hope of pardon from Lord
      Angelo?
   Claud. The miserable have no other
      medicine,
But only hope.
I have hope to live, and am prepar'd to
      die.
   Duke. Be absolute for death ; either
      death, or life,
Shall thereby be the sweeter. Reason
      thus with life :—
If I do lose thee, I do lose a thing
That none but fools would keep ; a
      breath thou art,
Servile to all the skyey influences,
That do this habitation, where thou
      keep'st, 10
Hourly afflict. Merely, thou art death's fool ;
For him thou labour'st by thy flight to shun,
And yet runn'st toward him still. Thou art not
    noble ;
For all the accommodations that thou bear'st
Are nurs'd by baseness. Thou art by no means
    valiant ;
For thou dost fear the soft and tender fork
Of a poor worm. Thy best of rest is sleep,
And that thou oft provok'st ; yet grossly fear'st
Thy death, which is no more. Thou art not thyself ;
For thou exist'st on many a thousand grains 20
That issue out of dust. Happy thou art not ;
For what thou hast not, still thou striv'st to get,
And what thou hast, forgett'st. Thou art not certain ;
For thy complexion shifts to strange effects,

After the moon. If thou art rich, thou 'rt poor ;
For, like an ass, whose back with ingots bows,
Thou bear'st thy heavy riches but a journey,
And death unloads thee. Friend hast thou none ;
For thine own bowels, which do call thee sire,
The mere effusion of thy proper loins, 30
Do curse the gout, serpigo, and the rheum,
For ending thee no sooner. Thou hast nor youth, nor
    age,
But, as it were, an after-dinner's sleep,
Dreaming on both ; for all thy blessed youth
Becomes as aged, and doth beg the alms
Of palsied eld : and when thou art old and rich,
Thou hast neither heat, affection, limb, nor beauty,
To make thy riches pleasant. What 's yet in this,
That bears the name of life ? Yet in this life
Lie hid more thousand deaths, yet death we fear, 40
That makes these odds all even.
   Claud.   I humbly thank you.
To sue to live, I find I seek to die,
And, seeking death, find life : let it come on.
   Isab. [*Without.*] What, ho ! Peace here ; grace and
    good company !
   Prov. Who 's there? come in : the wish deserves a
    welcome.
   Duke. Dear sir, ere long I 'll visit you again.
   Claud. Most holy sir, I thank you.

Enter ISABELLA.

   Isab. My business is a word or two with Claudio.
   Prov. And very welcome. Look, signior ; here 's
    your sister.
   Duke. Provost, a word with you.
   Prov.   As many as you please. 50

Duke. Bring me to hear them speak, where I may
  be conceal'd.   [*Exeunt* Duke *and Provost.*
Claud. Now, sister, what 's the comfort?
Isab. Why, as all comforts are; most good, most
  good, indeed.
Lord Angelo, having affairs to heaven,
Intends you for his swift ambassador,
Where you shall be an everlasting leiger:
Therefore, your best appointment make with speed;
To-morrow you set on.
Claud.   Is there no remedy?
Isab. None, but such remedy, as to save a head
To cleave a heart in twain.
Claud.   But is there any?   60
Isab. Yes, brother, you may live:
There is a devilish mercy in the judge,
If you 'll implore it, that will free your life,
But fetter you till death.
Claud.   Perpetual durance?
Isab. Ay, just; perpetual durance: a restraint,
Though all the world's vastidity you had,
To a determin'd scope.
Claud.   But in what nature?
Isab. In such a one as, you consenting to 't,
Would bark your honour from that trunk you bear,
And leave you naked.
Claud.   Let me know the point.   70
Isab. O, I do fear thee, Claudio; and I quake,
Lest thou a feverous life shouldst entertain,
And six or seven winters more respect
Than a perpetual honour. Dar'st thou die?
The sense of death is most in apprehension,
And the poor beetle, that we tread upon,
In corporal sufferance finds a pang as great
As when a giant dies.
Claud.   Why give you me this shame?
Think you I can a resolution fetch
From flowery tenderness? If I must die,   80
I will encounter darkness as a bride,
And hug it in mine arms.
Isab. There spake my brother: there my father's
    grave
Did utter forth a voice. Yes, thou must die:
Thou art too noble to conserve a life
In base appliances. This outward-sainted deputy,
Whose settled visage and deliberate word
Nips youth i' the head, and follies doth emmew,
As falcon doth the fowl, is yet a devil;
His filth within being cast, he would appear   90
A pond as deep as hell.
Claud.   The princely Angelo?
Isab. O, 't is the cunning livery of hell,
The damned'st body to invest and cover
In princely guards! Dost thou think, Claudio?—
If I would yield him my virginity,
Thou mightst be freed.
Claud.   O heavens! it cannot be.
Isab. Yes, he would give it thee, from this rank
    offence,
So to offend him still. This night 's the time
That I should do what I abhor to name,
Or else thou diest to-morrow.
Claud.   Thou shalt not do 't.   100
Isab. O! were it but my life,
I'd throw it down for your deliverance
As frankly as a pin.
Claud.   Thanks, dear Isabel.
Isab. Be ready, Claudio, for your death to-morrow.
Claud. Yes. Has he affections in him,
That thus can make him bite the law by the nose,
When he would force it? Sure, it is no sin;
Or of the deadly seven it is the least.
Isab. Which is the least?
Claud. If it were damnable, he, being so wise,   110
Why would he for the momentary trick
Be perdurably fin'd?—O Isabel!
Isab. What says my brother?
Claud.   Death is a fearful thing.
Isab. And shamed life a hateful.
Claud. Ay, but to die, and go we know not where;
To lie in cold obstruction, and to rot;
This sensible warm motion to become

A kneaded clod; and the delighted spirit
To bathe in fiery floods, or to reside
In thrilling regions of thick-ribbed ice;   120
To be imprison'd in the viewless winds,
And blown with restless violence round about
The pendant world; or to be worse than worst
Of those that lawless and incertain thoughts
Imagine howling!—'t is too horrible.
The weariest and most loathed worldly life,

Isab. "I 'll pray a thousand prayers for thy death,
No word to save thee."

That age, ache, penury, and imprisonment
Can lay on nature, is a paradise
To what we fear of death.
Isab. Alas! alas!
Claud.   Sweet sister, let me live.   130
What sin you do to save a brother's life,
Nature dispenses with the deed so far,
That it becomes a virtue.
Isab.   O you beast!
O faithless coward! O dishonest wretch!
Wilt thou be made a man out of my vice?
Is 't not a kind of incest, to take life
From thine own sister's shame? What should I
    think?
Heaven shield, my mother play'd my father fair;
For such a warped slip of wilderness
Ne'er issu'd from his blood. Take my defiance: 140
Die; perish! Might but my bending down
Reprieve thee from thy fate, it should proceed.
I 'll pray a thousand prayers for thy death,
No word to save thee.
Claud. Nay, hear me, Isabel.
Isab.   O, fie, fie, fie!
Thy sin 's not accidental, but a trade.
Mercy to thee would prove itself a bawd:
'T is best that thou diest quickly.   [*Going.*
Claud.   O hear me, Isabella!

Re-enter Duke.

Duke. Vouchsafe a word, young sister; but one
  word.   150
Isab. What is your will?
Duke. Might you dispense with your leisure, I
  would by-and-by have some speech with you: the

satisfaction I would require, is likewise your own benefit.

Isab. I have no superfluous leisure : my stay must be stolen out of other affairs ; but I will attend you awhile.   158

Duke. [*Aside to* CLAUDIO.] Son, I have overheard what hath passed between you and your sister. Angelo has never the purpose to corrupt her ; only he hath made an assay of her virtue, to practise his judgment with the disposition of natures. He, having the truth of honour in her, hath made him that gracious denial which he is most glad to receive : I am confessor to Angelo, and I know this to be true ; therefore prepare yourself to death. Do not satisfy your resolution with hopes that are fallible : to-morrow you must die. Go ; to your knees, and make ready.   170

Claud. Let me ask my sister pardon. I am so out of love with life, that I will sue to be rid of it.

Duke. Hold you there : farewell.   [*Exit* CLAUDIO.

Re-enter Provost.

Provost, a word with you.

Prov. What 's your will, father ?

Duke. That now you are come, you will be gone. Leave me awhile with the maid : my mind promises with my habit, no loss shall touch her by my company.

Prov. In good time.   [*Exit.*

Duke. The hand that hath made you fair hath made you good : the goodness that is cheap in beauty makes beauty brief in goodness ; but grace, being the soul of your complexion, shall keep the body of it ever fair. The assault, that Angelo hath made to you, fortune hath convey'd to my understanding ; and, but that frailty hath examples for his falling, I should wonder at Angelo. How will you do to content this substitute, and to save your brother ?   188

Isab. I am now going to resolve him. I had rather my brother die by the law, than my son should be unlawfully born. But O, how much is the good duke deceived in Angelo ! If ever he return, and I can speak to him, I will open my lips in vain, or discover his government.

Duke. That shall not be much amiss ; yet, as the matter now stands, he will avoid your accusation : he made trial of you only.—Therefore, fasten your ear on my advisings : to the love I have in doing good a remedy presents itself. I do make myself believe, that you may most uprighteously do a poor wronged lady a merited benefit, redeem your brother from the angry law, do no stain to your own gracious person, and much please the absent duke, if, peradventure, he shall ever return to have hearing of this business.

Isab. Let me hear you speak further. I have spirit to do anything that appears not foul in the truth of my spirit.

Duke. Virtue is bold, and goodness never fearful. Have you not heard speak of Mariana, the sister of Frederick, the great soldier who miscarried at sea ?   211

Isab. I have heard of the lady, and good words went with her name.

Duke. She should this Angelo have married ; was affianced to her by oath, and the nuptial appointed : between which time of the contract, and limit of the solemnity, her brother Frederick was wrecked at sea, having in that perish'd vessel the dowry of his sister. But mark how heavily this befell to the poor gentlewoman : there she lost a noble and renowned brother, in his love toward her ever most kind and natural ; with him the portion and sinew of her fortune, her marriage-dowry ; with both, her combinate husband, this well-seeming Angelo.

Isab. Can this be so ? Did Angelo so leave her ?

Duke. Left her in her tears, and dried not one of them with his comfort ; swallowed his vows whole, pretending in her discoveries of dishonour : in few, bestowed her on her own lamentation, which she yet wears for his sake, and he, a marble to her tears, is washed with them, but relents not.   231

Isab. What a merit were it in death to take this poor maid from the world ! What corruption in this life, that it will let this man live !—But how out of this can she avail ?

Duke. It is a rupture that you may easily heal ; and the cure of it not only saves your brother, but keeps you from dishonour in doing it.

Isab. Show me how, good father.   239

Duke. This fore-named maid hath yet in her the continuance of her first affection : his unjust unkindness, that in all reason should have quenched her love, hath, like an impediment in the current, made it more violent and unruly. Go you to Angelo : answer his requiring with a plausible obedience : agree with his demands to the point ; only refer yourself to this advantage,—first, that your stay with him may not be long, that the time may have all shadow and silence in it, and the place answer to convenience. This being granted in course,—and now follows all,— we shall advise this wronged maid to stead up your appointment, go in your place ; if the encounter acknowledge itself hereafter, it may compel him to her recompense ; and here by this is your brother saved, your honour untainted, the poor Mariana advantaged, and the corrupt deputy scaled. The maid will I frame, and make fit for his attempt. If you think well to carry this, as you may, the doubleness of the benefit defends the deceit from reproof. What think you of it ?   260

Isab. The image of it gives me content already, and, I trust, it will grow to a most prosperous perfection.

Duke. It lies much in your holding up. Haste you speedily to Angelo : if for this night he entreat you to his bed, give him promise of satisfaction. I will presently to Saint Luke's ; there, at the moated grange, resides this dejected Mariana : at that place call upon me, and despatch with Angelo, that it may be quickly.   270

Isab. I thank you for this comfort. Fare you well, good father.   [*Exeunt.*

SCENE II.—The Street before the Prison.

Enter DUKE, *as a Friar ; to him* ELBOW, *Clown, and Officers.*

Elb. Nay, if there be no remedy for it, but that you will needs buy and sell men and women like beasts, we shall have all the world drink brown and white bastard.

Duke. O heavens ! what stuff is here ?

Clo. 'T was never merry world, since, of two usuries, the merriest was put down, and the worser allow'd by order of law a furr'd gown to keep him warm ; and furr'd with fox and lamb-skins too, to signify that craft, being richer than innocency, stands for the facing.   11

Elb. Come your way, sir.—'Bless you, good father friar.

Duke. And you, good brother father. What offence hath this man made you, sir ?

Elb. Marry, sir, he hath offended the law : and, sir, we take him to be a thief too, sir ; for we have found upon him, sir, a strange picklock, which we have sent to the deputy.

Duke. Fie, sirrah : a bawd, a wicked bawd !   20
The evil that thou causest to be done,
That is thy means to live. Do thou but think
What 't is to cram a maw, or clothe a back,
From such a filthy vice : say to thyself,
From their abominable and beastly touches
I drink, I eat, array myself, and live.
Canst thou believe thy living is a life,
So stinkingly depending ? Go mend, go mend.

Clo. Indeed, it does stink in some sort, sir ; but yet, sir, I would prove—   30

Duke. Nay, if the devil have given thee proofs for sin,
Thou wilt prove his. Take him to prison, officer ;
Correction and instruction must both work,
Ere this rude beast will profit.

Elb. He must before the deputy, sir ; he has given him warning. The deputy cannot abide a whoremaster: if he be a whoremonger, and comes before him, he were as good go a mile on his errand.

Duke. That we were all, as some would seem to be, From our faults, as faults from seeming, free!　40

Elb. His neck will come to your waist,—a cord, sir.

Clo. I spy comfort: I cry, bail. Here's a gentle-man, and a friend of mine.

Enter LUCIO.

Lucio. How now, noble Pompey? What, at the wheels of Cæsar? Art thou led in triumph? What, is there none of Pygmalion's images, newly made woman, to be had now, for putting the hand in the pocket and extracting it clutch'd? What reply? Ha? What say'st thou to this tune, matter, and method? Is 't not drown'd i' the last rain? Ha? What say'st thou, trot? Is the world as it was, man? Which is the way? Is it sad, and few words, or how? The trick of it?　53

Duke. Still thus, and thus: still worse!

Lucio. How doth my dear morsel, thy mistress? Procures she still? Ha?

Clo. Troth, sir, she hath eaten up all her beef, and she is herself in the tub.

Lucio. Why, 'tis good; it is the right of it; it must be so: ever your fresh whore, and your powder'd bawd: an unshunn'd consequence; it must be so. Art going to prison, Pompey?　62

Clo. Yes, faith, sir.

Lucio. Why, 'tis not amiss, Pompey. Farewell. Go; say, I sent thee thither. For debt, Pompey, or how?

Elb. For being a bawd, for being a bawd.

Lucio. Well, then imprison him. If imprisonment be the due of a bawd, why, 't is his right: bawd is he, doubtless, and of antiquity too; bawd-born. Farewell, good Pompey. Commend me to the prison, Pompey. You will turn good husband now, Pompey; you will keep the house.　73

Clo. I hope, sir, your good worship will be my bail.

Lucio. No, indeed, will I not, Pompey; it is not the wear. I will pray, Pompey, to increase your bondage: if you take it not patiently, why, your mettle is the more. Adieu, trusty Pompey.—'Bless you, friar.

Duke. And you.

Lucio. Does Bridget paint still, Pompey? Ha?　80

Elb. Come your ways, sir; come.

Clo. You will not bail me then, sir?

Lucio. Then, Pompey, nor now. — What news abroad, friar? What news?

Elb. Come your ways, sir; come.

Lucio. Go to kennel, Pompey; go. [*Exeunt* ELBOW, *Clown, and Officers.*] What news, friar, of the duke?

Duke. I know none. Can you tell me of any?

Lucio. Some say, he is with the emperor of Russia; other some, he is in Rome: but where is he, think you?　91

Duke. I know not where; but wheresoever, I wish him well.

Lucio. It was a mad fantastical trick of him, to steal from the state, and usurp the beggary he was never born to: he puts transgression to 't.

Duke. He does well in 't.

Lucio. A little more lenity to lechery would do no harm in him: something too crabbed that way, friar.

Duke. It is too general a vice, and severity must cure it.　102

Lucio. Yes, in good sooth, the vice is of a great kindred: it is well allied; but it is impossible to extirp it quite, friar, till eating and drinking be put down. They say, this Angelo was not made by man and woman, after this downright way of creation: is it true, think you?

Duke. How should he be made, then?　109

Lucio. Some report, a sea-maid spawn'd him; some, that he was begot between two stock-fishes. But it is certain, that when he makes water, his urine is congeal'd ice: that I know to be true; and he is a motion generative, that 's infallible.

Duke. You are pleasant, sir, and speak apace.

Lucio. Why, what a ruthless thing is this in him, for the rebellion of a codpiece to take away the life of a man? Would the duke, that is absent, have done this? Ere he would have hang'd a man for the getting a hundred bastards, he would have paid for the nursing a thousand. He had some feeling of the sport: he knew the service, and that instructed him to mercy.　123

Lucio. "A very superficial, ignorant, unweighing fellow."

Duke. I never heard the absent duke much detected for women: he was not inclined that way.

Lucio. O, sir, you are deceived.

Duke. 'T is not possible.

Lucio. Who? not the duke? yes, your beggar of fifty, and his use was to put a ducat in her clack-dish. The duke had crotchets in him: he would be drunk too; that let me inform you.　131

Duke. You do him wrong, surely.

Lucio. Sir, I was an inward of his. A shy fellow was the duke; and, I believe, I know the cause of his withdrawing.

Duke. What, I pr'ythee, might be the cause?

Lucio. No,—pardon:—'t is a secret must be lock'd within the teeth and the lips; but this I can let you understand,—the greater file of the subject held the duke to be wise.　140

Duke. Wise? why, no question but he was.

Lucio. A very superficial, ignorant, unweighing fellow.

Duke. Either this is envy in you, folly, or mistaking: the very stream of his life, and the business he hath helmed, must, upon a warranted need, give him a better proclamation. Let him be but testimonied in his own bringings-forth, and he shall appear to the envious a scholar, a statesman, and a soldier. There-fore, you speak unskilfully; or, if your knowledge be more, it is much darken'd in your malice.　151

Lucio. Sir, I know him, and I love him.

Duke. Love talks with better knowledge, and know-ledge with dearer love.

Lucio. Come, sir, I know what I know.

Duke. I can hardly believe that, since you know not what you speak. But, if ever the duke return (as our prayers are he may), let me desire you to make your answer before him: if it be honest you have spoke, you have courage to maintain it. I am bound to call upon you; and, I pray you, your name?　161

Lucio. Sir, my name is Lucio, well known to the duke.

Duke. He shall know you better, sir, if I may live to report you.

Lucio. I fear you not.

Duke. O! you hope the duke will return no more, or you imagine me too unhurtful an opposite. But, indeed, I can do you little harm: you'll forswear this again.

Lucio. I'll be hang'd first: thou art deceived in me, friar. But no more of this. Canst thou tell, if Claudio die to-morrow, or no?   172

Duke. Why should he die, sir?

Lucio. Why? for filling a bottle with a tun-dish. I would, the duke we talk of were return'd again: this ungenitur'd agent will unpeople the province with continency; sparrows must not build in his house-eaves, because they are lecherous. The duke yet would have dark deeds darkly answer'd; he would never bring them to light: 'would he were return'd! Marry, this Claudio is condemn'd for untrussing. Farewell, good friar: I pr'ythee, pray for me. The duke, I say to thee again, would eat mutton on Fridays. He's now past it; yet, and I say to thee, he would mouth with a beggar, though she smelt brown bread and garlic: say, that I said so. Farewell.   [*Exit.*

Duke. No might nor greatness in mortality
Can censure scape: back-wounding calumny
The whitest virtue strikes. What king so strong.
Can tie the gall up in the slanderous tongue?   190
But who comes here?

Enter ESCALUS, *Provost, Bawd, and Officers.*

Escal. Go: away with her to prison!

Bawd. Good my lord, be good to me: your honour is accounted a merciful man; good my lord.

Escal. Double and treble admonition, and still forfeit in the same kind? This would make mercy swear, and play the tyrant.

Prov. A bawd of eleven years' continuance, may it please your honour.   199

Bawd. My lord, this is one Lucio's information against me. Mistress Kate Keepdown was with child by him in the duke's time: he promised her marriage; his child is a year and a quarter old, come Philip and Jacob; I have kept it myself, and see how he goes about to abuse me!

Escal. That fellow is a fellow of much license:—let him be called before us.—Away with her to prison! Go to; no more words.   [*Exeunt Bawd and Officers.*] Provost, my brother Angelo will not be alter'd; Claudio must die to-morrow. Let him be furnished with divines, and have all charitable preparation: if my brother wrought by my pity, it should not be so with him.   213

Prov. So please you, this friar hath been with him, and advised him for the entertainment of death.

Escal. Good even, good father.

Duke. Bliss and goodness on you.

Escal. Of whence are you?

Duke. Not of this country, though my chance is now To use it for my time: I am a brother   220
Of gracious order, late come from the See,
In special business from his holiness.

Escal. What news abroad i' the world?

Duke. None, but that there is so great a fever on goodness, that the dissolution of it must cure it: novelty is only in request; and it is as dangerous to be aged in any kind of course, as it is virtuous to be constant in any undertaking. There is scarce truth enough alive to make societies secure, but security enough to make fellowships accurs'd. Much upon this riddle runs the wisdom of the world. This news is old enough, yet it is every day's news. I pray you, sir, of what disposition was the duke?   233

Escal. One that, above all other strifes, contended especially to know himself.

Duke. What pleasure was he given to?

Escal. Rather rejoicing to see another merry, than merry at anything which profess'd to make him rejoice: a gentleman of all temperance. But leave we him to his events, with a prayer they may prove prosperous, and let me desire to know how you find Claudio prepared. I am made to understand, that you have lent him visitation.   243

Duke. He professes to have received no sinister measure from his judge, but most willingly humbles himself to the determination of justice; yet had he framed to himself, by the instruction of his frailty, many deceiving promises of life, which I, by my good leisure, have discredited to him, and now is he resolved to die.   250

Escal. You have paid the heavens your function, and the prisoner the very debt of your calling. I have labour'd for the poor gentleman to the extremest shore of my modesty; but my brother justice have I found so severe, that he hath forced me to tell him, he is indeed—Justice.

Duke. If his own life answer the straitness of his proceeding, it shall become him well; wherein if he chance to fail, he hath sentenced himself.

Escal. I am going to visit the prisoner. Fare you well.   261

Duke. Peace be with you!
              [*Exeunt* ESCALUS *and Provost.*
He who the sword of heaven will bear
Should be as holy as severe;
Pattern in himself to know,
Grace to stand, and virtue go;
More nor less to others paying,
Than by self-offences weighing.
Shame to him, whose cruel striking
Kills for faults of his own liking!   270
Twice treble shame on Angelo,
To weed my vice, and let his grow!
O, what may man within him hide,
Though angel on the outward side!
How may likeness made in crimes,
Making practice on the times,
To draw with idle spiders' strings
Most pond'rous and substantial things!
Craft against vice I must apply.   280
With Angelo to-night shall lie
His old betrothed, but despised:
So disguise shall, by the disguised,
Pay with falsehood false exacting,
And perform an old contracting.   [*Exit.*

ACT IV.

Scene I.—A Room in Mariana's House.

Mariana discovered sitting; a Boy singing.

Song.

TAKE, O! take those lips away,
That so sweetly were forsworn;
And those eyes, the break of day,
Lights that do mislead the morn:
But my kisses bring again,
     bring again,
Seals of love, but seal'd in vain,
     seal'd in vain.

Mari. Break off thy song, and haste thee
   quick away:
Here comes a man of comfort, whose
   advice   10
Hath often still'd my brawling discontent.—[*Exit Boy.*

Enter Duke, *disguised as before.*

I cry you mercy, sir; and well could wish
You had not found me here so musical:
Let me excuse me, and believe me so,
My mirth it much displeas'd, but pleas'd my woe.
Duke. 'T is good: though music oft hath such a
   charm,
To make bad good, and good provoke to harm.
I pray you, tell me, hath anybody inquired for me
here to-day? much upon this time have I promis'd
here to meet.   20
Mari. You have not been inquired after: I have sat
here all day.
Duke. I do constantly believe you.—The time is come,
even now. I shall crave your forbearance a little:
may be, I will call upon you anon, for some advantage
to yourself.
Mari. I am always bound to you.   [*Exit.*

Enter Isabella.

Duke. Very well met, and welcome.
What is the news from this good deputy?
Isab. He hath a garden circummur'd with brick, 30
Whose western side is with a vineyard back'd;
And to that vineyard is a planched gate,
That makes his opening with this bigger key;
This other doth command a little door,
Which from the vineyard to the garden leads;
there have I made my promise upon the heavy middle
of the night to call upon him.
Duke. But shall you on your knowledge find this
   way?
Isab. I have ta'en a due and wary note upon 't:
With whispering and most guilty diligence,   40
In action all of precept, he did show me
The way twice o'er.
Duke.   Are there no other tokens
Between you 'greed, concerning her observance?
Isab. No, none, but only a repair i' the dark;
And that I have possess'd him my most stay
Can be but brief: for I have made him know,
I have a servant comes with me along,
That stays upon me; whose persuasion is,
I come about my brother.
Duke.   'T is well borne up.
I have not yet made known to Mariana
A word of this.—What, ho! within! come forth.   50

Re-enter Mariana.

I pray you, be acquainted with this maid:
She comes to do you good.

Isab.   I do desire the like.
Duke. Do you persuade yourself that I respect you?
Mari. Good friar, I know you do, and have found it.
Duke. Take then this your companion by the hand,
Who hath a story ready for your ear.
I shall attend your leisure: but make haste;
The vaporous night approaches.
Mari.   Will 't please you walk aside?
   [*Exeunt* Mariana *and* Isabella.
Duke. O place and greatness! millions of false eyes 60
Are stuck upon thee. Volumes of report
Run with these false and most contrarious quests
Upon thy doings: thousand escapes of wit
Make thee the father of their idle dream,
And rack thee in their fancies!

Re-enter Mariana *and* Isabella.

   Welcome! How agreed?
Isab. She 'll take the enterprise upon her, father,
If you advise it.
Duke.   It is not my consent,
But my entreaty too.
Isab.   Little have you to say,
When you depart from him, but, soft and low,
"Remember now my brother."
Mari.   Fear me not.   70
Duke. Nor, gentle daughter, fear you not at all.
He is your husband on a pre-contract:
To bring you thus together, 't is no sin,
Sith that the justice of your title to him
Doth flourish the deceit. Come, let us go:
Our corn 's to reap, for yet our tithe 's to sow.
   [*Exeunt.*

Scene II.—A Room in the Prison.

Enter Provost and Clown.

Prov. Come hither, sirrah. Can you cut off a man's
head?
Clo. If the man be a bachelor, sir, I can; but if he
be a married man, he is his wife's head, and I can
never cut off a woman's head.
Prov. Come, sir: leave your snatches, and yield
me a direct answer. To-morrow morning are to die
Claudio and Barnardine. Here is in our prison a
common executioner, who in his office lacks a helper:
if you will take it on you to assist him, it shall redeem
you from your gyves; if not, you shall have your full
time of imprisonment, and your deliverance with an
unpitied whipping, for you have been a notorious
bawd.
Clo. Sir, I have been an unlawful bawd, time out of
mind; but yet I will be content to be a lawful hangman. I would be glad to receive some instruction
from my fellow partner.
Prov. What ho, Abhorson! Where's Abhorson,
there?   20

Enter Abhorson.

Abhor. Do you call, sir?
Prov. Sirrah, here's a fellow will help you to-
morrow in your execution. If you think it meet,
compound with him by the year, and let him abide
here with you; if not, use him for the present, and
dismiss him. He cannot plead his estimation with
you: he hath been a bawd.

Abhor. A bawd, sir? Fie upon him! he will discredit our mystery.   29
Prov. Go to, sir; you weigh equally: a feather will
turn the scale.   [*Exit.*
Clo. Pray, sir, by your good favour (for, surely, sir,
a good favour you have, but that you have a hanging
look), do you call, sir, your occupation a mystery?
Abhor. Ay, sir; a mystery.
Clo. Painting, sir, I have heard say, is a mystery;
and your whores, sir, being members of my occupation, using painting, do prove my occupation a
mystery; but what mystery there should be in
hanging, if I should be hang'd, I cannot imagine.   40
Abhor. Sir, it is a mystery.
Clo. Proof?
Abhor. Every true man's apparel fits your thief.
Clo. If it be too little for your thief, your true man
thinks it big enough; if it be too big for your thief,
your thief thinks it little enough: so, every true man's
apparel fits your thief.

Re-enter Provost.

Prov. Are you agreed?
Clo. Sir, I will serve him; for I do find, your hangman is a more penitent trade than your bawd: he doth
oftener ask forgiveness.   51
Prov. You, sirrah, provide your block and your axe
to-morrow, four o'clock.
Abhor. Come on, bawd; I will instruct thee in my
trade: follow.
Clo. I do desire to learn, sir; and, I hope, if you
have occasion to use me for your own turn, you shall
find me yare; for, truly, sir, for your kindness I owe
you a good turn.
Prov. Call hither Barnardine and Claudio: 60
                [*Exeunt Clown and* ABHORSON.
The one has my pity; not a jot the other,
Being a murderer, though he were my brother.

Enter CLAUDIO.

Look, here's the warrant, Claudio, for thy death:
'T is now dead midnight, and by eight to-morrow
Thou must be made immortal. Where's Barnardine?
Claud. As fast lock'd up in sleep, as guiltless labour,
When it lies starkly in the traveller's bones:
He will not wake.
Prov.   Who can do good on him?
Well, go; prepare yourself. But hark, what noise?
                         [*Knocking within.*
Heaven give your spirits comfort! [*Exit* CLAUDIO.]
By-and-by.—   70
I hope it is some pardon, or reprieve,
For the most gentle Claudio.—

Enter DUKE, disguised as before.

                            Welcome, father.
Duke. The best and wholesom'st spirits of the night
Envelop you, good provost! Who call'd here of late?
Prov. None, since the curfew rung.
Duke. Not Isabel?
Prov.   No.
Duke.   They will, then, ere 't be long.
Prov. What comfort is for Claudio?
Duke. There's some in hope.
Prov.   It is a bitter deputy.
Duke. Not so, not so: his life is parallel'd
Even with the stroke and line of his great justice. 80
He doth with holy abstinence subdue
That in himself, which he spurs on his power
To qualify in others: were he meal'd with that
Which he corrects, then were he tyrannous;
But this being so, he's just.—[*Knocking within.*] Now
            are they come.—   [*Exit Provost.*
This is a gentle provost: seldom, when
The steeled gaoler is the friend of men.   [*Knocking.*
How now? What noise? That spirit's possessed
            with haste,
That wounds the unsisting postern with these strokes.

Re-enter Provost.

Prov. There he must stay, until the officer   90
Arise to let him in; he is call'd up.

Duke. Have you no countermand for Claudio yet,
But he must die to-morrow?
Prov.   None, sir, none.
Duke. As near the dawning, provost, as it is,
You shall hear more ere morning.
Prov.   Happily
You something know; yet, I believe, there comes
No countermand: no such example have we.
Besides, upon the very siege of justice,
Lord Angelo hath to the public ear
Profess'd the contrary.

Enter a Messenger.

                 This is his lordship's man.   100
Duke. And here comes Claudio's pardon.
Mess. My lord hath sent you this note; and by me
this further charge, that you swerve not from the
smallest article of it, neither in time, matter, or other
circumstance. Good morrow; for, as I take it, it is
almost day.
Prov. I shall obey him.   [*Exit Messenger.*
Duke. [*Aside.*] This is his pardon, purchas'd by such
            sin,
For which the pardoner himself is in;
Hence hath offence his quick celerity,   110
When it is borne in high authority.
When vice makes mercy, mercy's so extended,
That for the fault's love is the offender friended.—
Now, sir, what news?
Prov. I told you: Lord Angelo, belike thinking me
remiss in mine office, awakens me with this unwonted
putting-on; methinks strangely, for he hath not used
it before.
Duke. Pray you, let's hear.   119
Prov. [*Reads.*] "Whatsoever you may hear to the
contrary, let Claudio be executed by four of the clock;
and, in the afternoon, Barnardine. For my better
satisfaction, let me have Claudio's head sent me by
five. Let this be duly performed; with a thought,
that more depends on it than we must yet deliver.
Thus fail not to do your office, as you will answer it
at your peril."—What say you to this, sir?
Duke. What is that Barnardine, who is to be
executed in the afternoon?
Prov. A Bohemian born, but here nursed up and
bred; one that is a prisoner nine years old.   131
Duke. How came it, that the absent duke had not
either deliver'd him to his liberty, or executed him? I
have heard, it was ever his manner to do so.
Prov. His friends still wrought reprieves for him:
and, indeed, his fact, till now in the government of
Lord Angelo, came not to an undoubtful proof.
Duke. It is now apparent?
Prov. Most manifest, and not denied by himself.
Duke. Hath he borne himself penitently in prison?
How seems he to be touch'd?   141
Prov. A man that apprehends death no more dreadfully, but as a drunken sleep; careless, reckless, and
fearless of what's past, present, or to come: insensible
of mortality, and desperately mortal.
Duke. He wants advice.
Prov. He will hear none. He hath evermore had
the liberty of the prison: give him leave to escape
hence, he would not: drunk many times a day, if not
many days entirely drunk. We have very oft awaked
him, as if to carry him to execution, and show'd him
a seeming warrant for it: it hath not moved him
at all.   153
Duke. More of him anon. There is written in your
brow, provost, honesty and constancy: if I read it
not truly, my ancient skill beguiles me; but in the
boldness of my cunning I will lay myself in hazard.
Claudio, whom here you have warrant to execute, is
no greater forfeit to the law, than Angelo who hath
sentenced him. To make you understand this in a
manifested effect, I crave but four days' respite, for
the which you are to do me both a present and a
dangerous courtesy.   163
Prov. Pray, sir, in what?
Duke. In the delaying death.
Prov. Alack! how may I do it, having the hour
limited, and an express command, under penalty, to

deliver his head in the view of Angelo? I may make my case as Claudio's, to cross this in the smallest. 169

Duke. By the vow of mine order, I warrant you: if my instructions may be your guide, let this Barnardine be this morning executed, and his head borne to Angelo.

Prov. Angelo hath seen them both, and will discover the favour.

Duke. O! death's a great disguiser, and you may add to it. Shave the head, and tie the beard; and

Duke. "This is a thing that Angelo knows not, for he this very day receives letters of strange tenor."

say, it was the desire of the penitent to be so bared before his death: you know, the course is common. If anything fall to you upon this, more than thanks and good fortune, by the saint whom I profess, I will plead against it with my life. 182

Prov. Pardon me, good father: it is against my oath.

Duke. Were you sworn to the duke, or to the deputy?

Prov. To him, and to his substitutes.

Duke. You will think you have made no offence, if the duke avouch the justice of your dealing.

Prov. But what likelihood is in that? 190

Duke. Not a resemblance, but a certainty. Yet since I see you fearful, that neither my coat, integrity, nor my persuasion, can with ease attempt you, I will go further than I meant, to pluck all fears out of you. Look you, sir; here is the hand and seal of the duke: you know the character, I doubt not, and the signet is not strange to you.

Prov. I know them both. 198

Duke. The contents of this is the return of the duke: you shall anon over-read it at your pleasure, where you shall find, within these two days he will be here. This is a thing that Angelo knows not; for he this very day receives letters of strange tenor; perchance, of the duke's death; perchance, entering into some monastery; but, by chance, nothing of what is writ. Look, the unfolding star calls up the shepherd. Put not yourself into amazement how these things should be: all difficulties are but easy when they are known. Call your executioner, and off with Barnardine's head: I will give him a present shrift, and advise him for a better place. Yet you are amazed, but this

shall absolutely resolve you. Come away; it is almost clear dawn.   *[Exeunt.*

SCENE III.—Another Room in the Same.

Enter Clown.

Clo. I am as well acquainted here, as I was in our house of profession: one would think, it were Mistress Overdone's own house, for here be many of her old customers. First, here's young Master Rash; he's in for a commodity of brown paper and old ginger, ninescore and seventeen pounds, of which he made five marks, ready money: marry, then, ginger was not much in request, for the old women were all dead. Then is there here one Master Caper, at the suit of Master Three-pile the mercer, for some four suits of peach-colour'd satin, which now peaches him a beggar. Then have we here young Dizzy, and young Master Deep-vow, and Master Copper-spur, and Master Starve-lackey the rapier-and-dagger-man, and young Drop-heir that kill'd lusty Pudding, and Master Forthright the tilter, and brave Master Shoetie the great traveller, and wild Half-can that stabb'd Pots, and, I think, forty more; all great doers in our trade, and are now for the Lord's sake.

Enter ABHORSON.

Abhor. Sirrah, bring Barnardine hither. 20

Clo. Master Barnardine! you must rise and be hang'd, Master Barnardine.

Abhor. What, ho, Barnardine!

Bar. [Within.] A pox o' your throats! Who makes that noise there? What are you?

Clo. Your friends, sir; the hangman. You must be so good, sir, to rise and be put to death.

Bar. [Within.] Away, you rogue, away! I am sleepy.

Abhor. Tell him, he must awake, and that quickly too. 31

Clo. Pray, Master Barnardine, awake till you are executed, and sleep afterwards.

Abhor. Go in to him, and fetch him out.

Clo. He is coming, sir, he is coming: I hear his straw rustle.

Abhor. Is the axe upon the block, sirrah?

Clo. Very ready, sir.

Enter BARNARDINE.

Bar. How now, Abhorson? what's the news with you? 40

Abhor. Truly, sir, I would desire you to clap into your prayers; for, look you, the warrant's come.

Bar. You rogue, I have been drinking all night: I am not fitted for 't.

Clo. O, the better, sir; for he that drinks all night, and is hang'd betimes in the morning, may sleep the sounder all the next day.

Abhor. Look you, sir; here comes your ghostly father. Do we jest now, think you? 49

Enter DUKE, disguised as before.

Duke. Sir, induced by my charity, and hearing how hastily you are to depart, I am come to advise you, comfort you, and pray with you.

Bar. Friar, not I: I have been drinking hard all night, and I will have more time to prepare me, or they shall beat out my brains with billets. I will not consent to die this day, that's certain.

Duke. O, sir, you must; and, therefore, I beseech you,
Look forward on the journey you shall go.

Bar. I swear, I will not die to-day for any man's persuasion. 60

Duke. But hear you,—

Bar. Not a word: if you have anything to say to me, come to my ward; for thence will not I to-day.   *[Exit.*

Enter Provost.

Duke. Unfit to live, or die. O gravel heart!—
After him, fellows: bring him to the block.
      [Exeunt ABHORSON and Clown.

Prov. Now, sir, how do you find the prisoner?
Duke. A creature unprepar'd, unmeet for death;
And, to transport him in the mind he is,
Were damnable.
Prov.   Here in the prison, father,
There died this morning of a cruel fever   70
One Ragozine, a most notorious pirate,
A man of Claudio's years; his beard and head
Just of his colour. What if we do omit
This reprobate, till he were well inclin'd,
And satisfy the deputy with the visage
Of Ragozine, more like to Claudio?
Duke. O, 'tis an accident that Heaven provides!
Despatch it presently: the hour draws on
Prefix'd by Angelo. See this be done,
And sent according to command, whiles I   80
Persuade this rude wretch willingly to die.
Prov. This shall be done, good father, presently.
But Barnardine must die this afternoon;
And how shall we continue Claudio,
To save me from the danger that might come,
If he were known alive?
Duke.   Let this be done,—
Put them in secret holds, both Barnardine and
     Claudio;
Ere twice the sun hath made his journal greeting
To yonder generation, you shall find
Your safety manifested.   90
Prov. I am your free dependant.
Duke.   Quick, despatch.
And send the head to Angelo.   [*Exit Provost.*
Now will I write letters to Angelo,
(The provost, he shall bear them) whose contents
Shall witness to him, I am near at home,
And that, by great injunctions, I am bound
To enter publicly: him I'll desire
To meet me at the consecrated fount,
A league below the city; and from thence,
By cold gradation and well-balanc'd form,   100
We shall proceed with Angelo.

Re-enter Provost.

Prov. Here is the head; I'll carry it myself.
Duke. Convenient is it. Make a swift return,
For I would commune with you of such things
That want no ear but yours.
Prov.   I'll make all speed. [*Exit.*
Isab. [*Within.*] Peace, ho, be here!
Duke. The tongue of Isabel.—She's come to know,
If yet her brother's pardon be come hither;
But I will keep her ignorant of her good,
To make her heavenly comforts of despair,   110
When it is least expected.

Enter ISABELLA.

Isab.   Ho! by your leave.
Duke. Good morning to you, fair and gracious
     daughter.
Isab. The better, given me by so holy a man.
Hath yet the deputy sent my brother's pardon?
Duke. He hath releas'd him, Isabel, from the world.
His head is off, and sent to Angelo.
Isab. Nay, but it is not so.
Duke. It is no other: show your wisdom, daughter,
In your close patience.
Isab. O, I will to him, and pluck out his eyes!   120
Duke. You shall not be admitted to his sight.
Isab. Unhappy Claudio! Wretched Isabel!
Injurious world! Most damned Angelo!
Duke. This nor hurts him, nor profits you a jot:
Forbear it therefore; give your cause to Heaven.
Mark what I say, which you shall find
By every syllable a faithful verity.
The duke comes home to-morrow;—nay, dry your
     eyes;
One of our covent, and his confessor,
Gives me this instance: already he hath carried   130
Notice to Escalus and Angelo,
Who do prepare to meet him at the gates,
There to give up their power. If you can, pace your
     wisdom
In that good path that I would wish it go;

And you shall have your bosom on this wretch,
Grace of the duke, revenges to your heart,
And general honour.
Isab.   I am directed by you.
Duke. This letter then to Friar Peter give;
'T is that he sent me of the duke's return:
Say, by this token, I desire his company   140
At Mariana's house to-night. Her cause, and yours,
I'll perfect him withal, and he shall bring you
Before the duke; and to the head of Angelo
Accuse him home, and home. For my poor self,
I am combined by a sacred vow,
And shall be absent. Wend you with this letter.
Command these fretting waters from your eyes
With a light heart: trust not my holy order,
If I pervert your course.—Who's here?

Enter LUCIO.

Lucio. Good even. Friar, where is the provost? 150
Duke. Not within, sir.
Lucio. O pretty Isabella, I am pale at mine heart, to
see thine eyes so red: thou must be patient. I am
fain to dine and sup with water and bran; I dare not
for my head fill my belly: one fruitful meal would
set me to't. But, they say, the duke will be here to-
morrow. By my troth, Isabel, I loved thy brother:
if the old fantastical duke of dark corners had been at
home, he had lived.   [*Exit* ISABELLA.
Duke. Sir, the duke is marvellous little beholding
to your reports; but the best is, he lives not in them.
Lucio. Friar, thou knowest not the duke so well as
I do: he's a better woodman than thou takest him
for.
Duke. Well, you'll answer this one day. Fare ye
well.
Lucio. Nay, tarry; I'll go along with thee. I can
tell thee pretty tales of the duke.
Duke. You have told me too many of him already,
sir, if they be true; if not true, none were enough. 170
Lucio. I was once before him for getting a wench
with child.
Duke. Did you such a thing?
Lucio. Yes, marry, did I; but I was fain to forswear
it: they would else have married me to the rotten
medlar.
Duke. Sir, your company is fairer than honest.
Rest you well.   178
Lucio. By my troth, I'll go with thee to the lane's
end. If bawdy talk offend you, we'll have very little
of it. Nay, friar, I am a kind of burr; I shall stick.
         [*Exeunt.*

SCENE IV.—A Room in ANGELO'S House.

Enter ANGELO *and* ESCALUS.

Escal. Every letter he hath writ hath disvouch'd
other.
Ang. In most uneven and distracted manner. His
actions show much like to madness: pray Heaven, his
wisdom be not tainted! and why meet him at the
gates, and re-deliver our authorities there?
Escal. I guess not.
Ang. And why should we proclaim it in an hour
before his entering, that if any crave redress of
injustice, they should exhibit their petitions in the
street?   11
Escal. He shows his reason for that: to have a
despatch of complaints and to deliver us from devices
hereafter, which shall then have no power to stand
against us.
Ang. Well, I beseech you, let it be proclaim'd:
Betimes i' the morn, I'll call you at your house.
Give notice to such men of sort and suit,
As are to meet him.
Escal.   I shall, sir: fare you well. [*Exit.*
Ang. Good night.—   20
This deed unshapes me quite, makes me unpregnant,
And dull to all proceedings. A deflower'd maid,
And by an eminent body, that enforc'd
The law against it!—But that her tender shame
Will not proclaim against her maiden loss,

How might she tongue me! Yet reason dares her no:
For my authority bears a credent bulk,
That no particular scandal once can touch,
But it confounds the breather. He should have liv'd, 30
Save that his riotous youth, with dangerous sense,
Might in the times to come have ta'en revenge,
By so receiving a dishonour'd life
With ransom of such shame. 'Would yet he had
    liv'd!
Alack! when once our grace we have forgot,
Nothing goes right: we would, and we would not.
                                                    [*Exit.*

SCENE V.—Fields without the Town.

Enter DUKE, *in his own habit, and Friar* PETER.
Duke. These letters at fit time deliver me.
                                        [*Giving letters.*
The provost knows our purpose, and our plot.
The matter being afoot, keep your instruction,
And hold you ever to your special drift,
Though sometimes you do blench from this to that,
As cause doth minister. Go, call at Flavius' house,
And tell him where I stay: give the like notice
To Valentius, Rowland, and to Crassus,
And bid them bring the trumpets to the gate;
But send me Flavius first.
Fri. Pet.   It shall be speeded well. 10
    Enter VARRIUS.   [*Exit.*
Duke. I thank thee, Varrius; thou hast made good
    haste.
Come, we will walk: there's other of our friends
Will greet us here anon, my gentle Varrius. [*Exeunt.*

SCENE VI.—Street near the City Gate.

Enter ISABELLA *and* MARIANA.

Isab. To speak so indirectly I am loath:
I would say the truth; but to accuse him so,
That is your part: yet I'm advis'd to do it,
He says, to 'vailful purpose.

Mari.   Be rul'd by him.
Isab. Besides, he tells me, that, if peradventure
He speak against me on the adverse side,
I should not think it strange; for 'tis a physic,
That's bitter to sweet end.

Fri. Pet. "Come, I have found you out a stand most fit."

Mari. I would, Friar Peter—
Isab.   O, peace! the friar is come.

    Enter Friar PETER.

Fri. Pet. Come, I have found you out a stand most
    fit,   10
Where you may have such vantage on the duke,
He shall not pass you. Twice have the trumpets
    sounded:
The generous and gravest citizens
Have hent the gates, and very near upon
The duke is ent'ring: therefore hence, away. [*Exeunt.*

ACT V.

SCENE I.—A Public Place near the City Gate.

MARIANA (*veiled*), ISABELLA, *and* PETER, *at a distance. Enter* DUKE, VARRIUS, *Lords;*
ANGELO, ESCALUS, LUCIO, *Provost, Officers and Citizens, at several doors.*

Duke.
    Y very worthy cousin, fairly met:—
        Our old and faithful friend, we are glad to
            see you.
    Ang. and Escal. Happy return be to
        your royal grace!
    Duke. Many and hearty thankings to
        you both.
    We have made inquiry of you; and we
        hear
    Such goodness of your justice, that our
        soul
    Cannot but yield you forth to public
        thanks,
Forerunning more requital.
Ang.   You make my bonds still greater.

Duke. O! your desert speaks loud; and I should
    wrong it,
To lock it in the wards of covert bosom,   10
When it deserves with characters of brass
A forted residence 'gainst the tooth of time
And razure of oblivion. Give me your hand,
And let the subject see, to make them know
That outward courtesies would fain proclaim
Favours that keep within.—Come, Escalus;
You must walk by us on our other hand,
And good supporters are you.

    Friar PETER *and* ISABELLA *come forward.*
Fri Pet. Now is your time. Speak loud, and kneel
    before him.
Isab. Justice, O royal duke! Vail your regard 20

Upon a wrong'd, I would fain have said, a maid!
O worthy prince! dishonour not your eye
By throwing it on any other object,
Till you have heard me in my true complaint,
And given me justice, justice, justice, justice!

Duke. Relate your wrongs: in what? by whom?
Be brief.
Here is Lord Angelo shall give you justice:
Reveal yourself to him.

Isab. 　　　　　　　O worthy duke!
You bid me seek redemption of the devil.
Hear me yourself; for that which I must speak 30
Must either punish me, not being believ'd,
Or wring redress from you. Hear me, O, hear me, here!

Ang. My lord! her wits, I fear me, are not firm:
She hath been a suitor to me for her brother,
Cut off by course of justice,—

Isab. 　　　　　　　By course of justice!
Ang. And she will speak most bitterly and strange.
Isab. Most strange, but yet most truly, will I speak.
That Angelo 's forsworn, is it not strange?
That Angelo 's a murderer, is 't not strange? 40
That Angelo is an adulterous thief,
An hypocrite, a virgin-violator,
Is it not strange, and strange?

Duke. 　　　　Nay, it is ten times strange.
Isab. It is not truer he is Angelo,
Than this is all as true as it is strange;
Nay, it is ten times true; for truth is truth
To the end of reckoning.

Duke. 　　　　Away with her.—Poor soul!
She speaks this in the infirmity of sense.

Isab. O prince, I conjure thee, as thou believ'st
There is another comfort than this world,
That thou neglect me not, with that opinion 50
That I am touch'd with madness. Make not impossible
That which but seems unlike. 'T is not impossible,
But one, the wicked'st caitiff on the ground,
May seem as shy, as grave, as just, as absolute,
As Angelo; even so may Angelo,
In all his dressings, characts, titles, forms,
Be an arch-villain. Believe it, royal prince:
If he be less, he 's nothing; but he 's more,
Had I more name for badness.

Duke. 　　　　　By mine honesty,
If she be mad, as I believe no other, 60
Her madness hath the oddest frame of sense,
Such a dependency of thing on thing,
As e'er I heard in madness.

Isab. 　　　　　　O gracious duke!
Harp not on that; nor do not banish reason
For inequality; but let your reason serve
To make the truth appear, where it seems hid,
And hide the false, seems true.

Duke. 　　　　Many that are not mad,
Have, sure, more lack of reason.—What would you
say?

Isab. I am the sister of one Claudio,
Condemn'd upon the act of fornication 70
To lose his head; condemn'd by Angelo.
I, in probation of a sisterhood,
Was sent to by my brother; one Lucio
As then the messenger—

Lucio. 　　　That 's I, an 't like your grace.
I came to her from Claudio, and desir'd her
To try her gracious fortune with Lord Angelo,
For her poor brother's pardon.

Isab. 　　　　　　That 's he, indeed.
Duke. You were not bid to speak.

Lucio. 　　　　　　No, my good lord;
Nor wish'd to hold my peace.

Duke. 　　　　　I wish you now then:
Pray you, take note of it; and when you have 80
A business for yourself, pray Heaven, you then
Be perfect.

Lucio. I warrant your honour.
Duke. The warrant 's for yourself: take heed to it.
Isab. This gentleman told somewhat of my tale,—
Lucio. Right.
Duke. It may be right; but you are in the wrong
To speak before your time.—Proceed.

Isab. 　　　　　　　　　I went
To this pernicious caitiff deputy.

Duke. That 's somewhat madly spoken.
Isab. 　　　　　　　　Pardon it: 91
The phrase is to the matter.

Duke. Mended again: the matter;—proceed.
Isab. In brief,—to set the needless process by,
How I persuaded, how I pray'd, and kneel'd,
How he refell'd me, and how I replied,
(For this was of much length) the vile conclusion
I now begin with grief and shame to utter.
He would not, but by gift of my chaste body
To his concupiscible intemperate lust,
Release my brother; and, after much debatement, 100
My sisterly remorse confutes mine honour,
And I did yield to him. But the next morn betimes,
His purpose surfeiting, he sends a warrant
For my poor brother's head.

Duke. 　　　　　This is most likely!
Isab. O, that it were as like as it is true!
Duke. By Heaven, fond wretch! thou know'st not
what thou speak'st,
Or else thou art suborn'd against his honour,
In hateful practice. First, his integrity
Stands without blemish; next, it imports no reason, 110
That with such vehemency he should pursue
Faults proper to himself: if he had so offended,
He would have weigh'd thy brother by himself,
And not have cut him off. Some one hath set you on:
Confess the truth, and say by whose advice
Thou cam'st here to complain.

Isab. 　　　　　　And is this all?
Then, O! you blessed ministers above,
Keep me in patience; and, with ripen'd time,
Unfold the evil which is here wrapt up
In countenance!—Heaven shield your grace from
woe,
As I, thus wrong'd, hence unbelieved go! 120

Duke. I know, you 'd fain be gone.—An officer!
To prison with her.—Shall we thus permit
A blasting and a scandalous breath to fall
On him so near us? This needs must be a practice.
Who knew of your intent, and coming hither?

Isab. One that I would were here, Friar Lodowick.
Duke. A ghostly father, belike.—Who knows that
Lodowick?

Lucio. My lord, I know him: 't is a meddling friar;
I do not like the man: had he been lay, my lord,
For certain words he spake against your grace 130
In your retirement, I had swing'd him soundly.

Duke. Words against me? This' a good friar,
belike!
And to set on this wretched woman here
Against our substitute!—Let this friar be found.

Lucio. But yesternight, my lord, she and that friar,
I saw them at the prison. A saucy friar,
A very scurvy fellow.

Fri. Pet. 　　　　Blessed be your royal grace!
I have stood by, my lord, and I have heard
Your royal ear abus'd. First, hath this woman
Most wrongfully accus'd your substitute, 140
Who is as free from touch or soil with her,
As she from one ungot.

Duke. 　　　　We did believe no less.
Know you that Friar Lodowick, that she speaks of?

Fri. Pet. I know him for a man divine and holy;
Not scurvy, nor a temporary meddler,
As he 's reported by this gentleman;
And, on my trust, a man that never yet
Did, as he vouches, misreport your grace.

Lucio. My lord, most villainously: believe it.
Fri. Pet. Well; he in time may come to clear himself, 150
But at this instant he is sick, my lord,
Of a strange fever. Upon his mere request,
Being come to knowledge that there was complaint
Intended 'gainst Lord Angelo, came I hither,
To speak, as from his mouth, what he doth know
Is true, and false; and what he with his oath,
And all probation, will make up full clear,
Whensoever he 's convented. First, for this woman,
To justify this worthy nobleman,

So vulgarly and personally accus'd,   160
Her shall you hear disproved to her eyes,
Till she herself confess it.
  Duke. Good friar, let's hear it.
    [ISABELLA *is carried off guarded; and*
       MARIANA *comes forward.*
Do you not smile at this, Lord Angelo?—
O heaven, the vanity of wretched fools!—
Give us some seats.—Come, cousin Angelo;
In this I'll be impartial: be
      you judge
Of your own cause.—Is this the
      witness, friar?
First, let her show her face, and
      after speak.
  Mari. Pardon, my lord, I will
      not show my face,
Until my husband bid me.
  Duke. What, are you
      married?   170
  Mari. No, my lord.
  Duke. Are you a maid?
  Mari. No, my lord.
  Duke. A widow then?
  Mari. Neither, my lord.
  Duke. Why, you
Are nothing then: neither
    maid, widow, nor
    wife.
  Lucio. My lord, she may be
a punk; for many of them are
neither maid, widow, nor wife?
  Duke. Silence that fellow: I
    would, he had some
    cause
To prattle for himself.
  Lucio. Well, my lord.
  Mari. My lord, I do confess
    I ne'er was married;
And, I confess, besides, I am
    no maid: 181
I have known my husband, yet
    my husband knows
    not
That ever he knew me.
  Lucio. He was drunk then,
my lord: it can be no better.
  Duke. For the benefit of silence, 'would thou wert
so too!
  Lucio. Well, my lord.
  Duke. This is no witness for Lord Angelo.
  Mari. Now I come to 't, my lord.   190
She that accuses him of fornication,
In selfsame manner doth accuse my husband;
And charges him, my lord, with such a time,
When, I'll depose, I had him in mine arms,
With all the effect of love.
  Ang. Charges she more than me?
  Mari. Not that I know.
  Duke. No? you say, your husband.
  Mari. Why, just, my lord, and that is Angelo,
Who thinks, he knows, that he ne'er knew my body,
But knows, he thinks, that he knows Isabel's.   200
  Ang. This is a strange abuse.—Let's see thy face.
  Mari. My husband bids me; now I will unmask.
                    [*Unveiling.*
This is that face, thou cruel Angelo,
Which once, thou swor'st, was worth the looking on:
This is the hand, which, with a vow'd contract,
Was fast belock'd in thine: this is the body
That took away the match from Isabel,
And did supply thee at thy garden-house
In her imagin'd person.
  Duke. Know you this woman?
  Lucio. Carnally, she says.
  Duke. Sirrah, no more.   210
  Lucio. Enough, my lord.
  Ang. My lord, I must confess, I know this woman;
And five years since there was some speech of marriage
Betwixt myself and her, which was broke off,
Partly, for that her promised proportions
Came short of composition; but, in chief,

Mari.   "As this is true,
Let me in safety raise me from my knees,
Or else for ever be confixed here,
A marble monument."

For that her reputation was disvalued
In levity: since which time of five years
I never spake with her, saw her, nor heard from her,
Upon my faith and honour.
  Mari. Noble prince,   220
As there comes light from heaven, and words from
    breath,
As there is sense in truth, and truth in virtue,
I am affianc'd this man's wife, as strongly
As words could make up vows: and, my good lord,
But Tuesday night last gone, in his garden-house,
He knew me as a wife. As this is true,
Let me in safety raise me from my knees,
Or else for ever be confixed here,
A marble monument.
  Ang. I did but smile till now:
Now, good my lord, give me the scope of justice; 230
My patience here is touch'd. I do perceive,
These poor informal women are no more
But instruments of some more mightier member,
That sets them on. Let me have way, my lord,
To find this practice out.
  Duke. Ay, with my heart;
And punish them to your height of pleasure.—
Thou foolish friar, and thou pernicious woman,
Compact with her that's gone, think'st thou, **thy
    oaths,**
Though they would swear down each particular saint,
Were testimonies against his worth and credit,   240
That's seal'd in approbation?—You, Lord Escalus,
Sit with my cousin: lend him your kind pains
To find out this abuse, whence 't is deriv'd.—
There is another friar that set them on;
Let him be sent for.
  Fri. Pet. 'Would he were here, my lord; for he,
    indeed,
Hath set the women on to this complaint.
Your provost knows the place where he abides,
And he may fetch him.
  Duke. Go, do it instantly.— [*Exit Provost.*
And you, my noble and well-warranted cousin,   251
Whom it concerns to hear this matter forth,
Do with your injuries as seems you best,
In any chastisement: I for a while will leave **you;**

But stir not you, till you have well determin'd
Upon these slanderers.

Escal. My lord, we 'll do it thoroughly. [*Exit*
DUKE.]--Signior Lucio, did not you say, you knew
that Friar Lodowick to be a dishonest person?

Lucio. Cucullus non facit monachum: honest in
nothing, but in his clothes; and one that hath spoke
most villainous speeches of the duke.   262

Escal. We shall entreat you to abide here till he
come, and enforce them against him. We shall find
this friar a notable fellow.

Lucio. As any in Vienna, on my word.

Escal. Call that same Isabel here once again: I
would speak with her. [*Exit an Attendant.*] Pray
you, my lord, give me leave to question; you shall see
how I 'll handle her.   270

Lucio. Not better than he, by her own report.

Escal. Say you?

Lucio. Marry, sir, I think, if you handled her
privately, she would sooner confess: perchance,
publicly she 'll be ashamed.

Escal. I will go darkly to work with her.

Lucio. That's the way; for women are light at
midnight.

Re-enter Officers, with ISABELLA.

Escal. [*To* ISAB.] Come on, mistress. Here's a
gentlewoman denies all that you have said.   280

Lucio. My lord, here comes the rascal I spoke of;
here, with the provost.

Escal. In very good time:--speak not you to him,
till we call upon you.

Lucio. Mum.

Enter DUKE, disguised as a Friar, and Provost.

Escal. Come, sir. Did you set these women on to
slander Lord Angelo? they have confess'd you did.

Duke. 'T is false.

Escal. How! know you where you are?

Duke. Respect to your great place! and let the devil
Be sometime honour'd for his burning throne.-- 291
Where is the duke? 't is he should hear me speak.

Escal. The duke's in us, and we will hear you
speak:
Look you speak justly.

Duke.   Boldly, at least.--But, O, poor souls!
Come you to seek the lamb here of the fox?
Good night to your redress. Is the duke gone?
Then is your cause gone too. The duke's unjust,
Thus to retort your manifest appeal,
And put your trial in the villain's mouth,
Which here you come to accuse.   300

Lucio. This is the rascal: this is he I spoke of.

Escal. Why, thou unreverend and unhallow'd friar!
Is 't not enough, thou hast suborn'd these women
To accuse this worthy man, but, in foul mouth,
And in the witness of his proper ear,
To call him villain?
And then to glance from him to the duke himself,
To tax him with injustice?--Take him hence;
To the rack with him--we 'll touse you joint by joint,
But we will know his purpose.--What! unjust?   310

Duke. Be not so hot; the duke
Dare no more stretch this finger of mine, than he
Dare rack his own: his subject am I not,
Nor here provincial. My business in this state
Made me a looker-on here in Vienna,
Where I have seen corruption boil and bubble,
Till it o'er-run the stew: laws for all faults,
But faults so countenanc'd, that the strong statutes
Stand like the forfeits in a barber's shop,
As much in mock as mark.   320

Escal. Slander to the state! Away with him to
prison.

Ang. What can you vouch against him, Signior
Lucio?
Is this the man that you did tell us of?

Lucio. 'T is he, my lord.--Come hither, goodman
baldpate: do you know me?

Duke. I remember you, sir, by the sound of your
voice: I met you at the prison, in the absence of the
duke.

Lucio. O! did you so? And do you remember what
you said of the duke?   330

Duke. Most notedly, sir.

Lucio. Do you so, sir? And was the duke a flesh-
monger, a fool, and a coward, as you then reported
him to be?

Duke. You must, sir, change persons with me, ere
you make that report: you, indeed, spoke so of
him; and much more, much worse.

Lucio. O thou damnable fellow! Did not I pluck
thee by the nose, for thy speeches?

Duke. I protest, I love the duke as I love myself. 340

Ang. Hark, how the villain would close now, after
his treasonable abuses.

Escal. Such a fellow is not to be talk'd withal:--
away with him to prison.--Where is the provost?--
Away with him to prison. Lay bolts enough upon
him, let him speak no more.--Away with those giglots
too, and with the other confederate companion.
[*The Provost lays hand on the* DUKE.

Duke. Stay, sir; stay awhile.

Ang. What! resists he? Help him, Lucio.   349

Lucio. Come, sir; come, sir; come, sir; foh! sir.
Why, you bald-pated, lying rascal! you must be
hooded, must you? show your knave's visage, with
a pox to you! show your sheep-biting face, and be
hang'd an hour. Will't not off?
[*Pulls off the Friar's hood, and discovers
the* DUKE.

Duke. Thou art the first knave that e'er made a
duke.--
First, provost, let me bail these gentle three.--
[*To* LUCIO.] Sneak not away, sir; for the friar and
you
Must have a word anon.--Lay hold on him.

Lucio. This may prove worse than hanging.

Duke. [*To* ESCAL.] What you have spoke, I pardon;
sit you down.   360
We 'll borrow place of him.--[*To* ANG.] Sir, by your
leave.
Hast thou or word, or wit, or impudence,
That yet can do the office? If thou hast,
Rely upon it till my tale be heard,
And hold no longer out.

Ang.   O my dread lord!
I should be guiltier than my guiltiness,
To think I can be undiscernible,
When I perceive your grace, like power divine,
Hath look'd upon my passes. Then, good prince,
No longer session hold upon my shame,   370
But let my trial be mine own confession:
Immediate sentence then, and sequent death,
Is all the grace I beg.

Duke.   Come hither, Mariana.--
Say, wast thou e'er contracted to this woman?

Ang. I was, my lord.

Duke. Go take her hence, and marry her instantly.--
Do you the office, friar; which consummate,
Return him here again.--Go with him, provost.
[*Exeunt* ANGELO, MARIANA, *Friar* PETER,
and Provost.

Escal. My lord, I am more amaz'd at his dishonour,
Than at the strangeness of it.

Duke.   Come hither, Isabel. 380
Your friar is now your prince: as I was then
Advertising and holy to your business,
Not changing heart with habit, I am still
Attorney'd at your service.

Isab.   O, give me pardon,
That I, your vassal, have employ'd and pain'd
Your unknown sovereignty!

Duke.   You are pardon'd, Isabel:
And now, dear maid, be you as free to us.
Your brother's death, I know, sits at your heart;
And you may marvel, why I obscur'd myself,
Labouring to save his life, and would not rather 390
Make rash remonstrance of my hidden power,
Than let him so be lost. O most kind maid!
It was the swift celerity of his death,
Which I did think with slower foot came on,
That brain'd my purpose: but, peace be with him!
That life is better life, past fearing death,

Than that which lives to fear. Make it your comfort,
So happy is your brother.
    Isab.   I do, my lord.

  Re-enter ANGELO, MARIANA, *Friar* PETER, *and*
                Provost.

  Duke. For this new-married man, approaching here,

"An Angelo for Claudio, death for death!"
Haste still pays haste, and leisure answers leisure,
Like doth quit like, and Measure still for Measure. 410
Then, Angelo, thy fault thus manifested,—
Which, though thou wouldst deny, denies thee van-
      tage,—
We do condemn thee to the very block,

Duke. "Thou art the first knave that e'er made a duke."

Whose salt imagination yet hath wrong'd   400
Your well-defended honour, you must pardon
For Mariana's sake. But, as he adjudg'd your brother,
(Being criminal, in double violation
Of sacred chastity, and of promise-breach,
Thereon dependent, for your brother's life)
The very mercy of the law cries out
Most audible, even from his proper tongue,

Where Claudio stoop'd to death, and with like haste.—
Away with him.
    Mari.   O my most gracious lord!
I hope you will not mock me with a husband.
    Duke. It is your husband mock'd you with a husband.
Consenting to the safeguard of your honour,
I thought your marriage fit; else imputation,
For that he knew you, might reproach your life, 420

And choke your good to come. For his possessions,
Although by confiscation they are ours,
We do instate and widow you withal,
To buy you a better husband.
   Mari.   O my dear lord!
I crave no other, nor no better man.
   Duke. Never crave him: we are definitive.
   Mari. Gentle my liege,—   [*Kneeling.*
   Duke.   You do but lose your labour.
Away with him to death.—[*To* LUCIO.]
            Now, sir, to you.
   Mari. O my good lord!—Sweet
         Isabel, take my part:
Lend me your knees, and all my life
         to come   430
I'll lend you, all my life to do you
         service.
   Duke. Against all sense you do im-
         portune her:
Should she kneel down in mercy of
         this fact,
Her brother's ghost his paved bed
         would break,
And take her hence in horror.
   Mari.   Isabel,
Sweet Isabel, do yet but kneel by
         me:
Hold up your hands, say nothing, I'll
         speak all.
They say, best men are moulded out
         of faults,
And, for the most, become much
         more the better
For being a little bad: so may my
         husband.   440
O Isabel! will you not lend a knee?
   Duke. He dies for Claudio's death.
   Isab.   Most bounteous sir,
           [*Kneeling.*
Look, if it please you, on this man condemn'd,
As if my brother liv'd. I partly think,
A due sincerity govern'd his deeds,
Till he did look on me: since it is so,
Let him not die. My brother had but justice,
In that he did the thing for which he died:
For Angelo,
His act did not o'ertake his bad intent;   450
And must be buried but as an intent
That perish'd by the way. Thoughts are no sub-
      jects,
Intents but merely thoughts.
   Mari.   Merely, my lord.
   Duke. Your suit's unprofitable: stand up, I say.—
I have bethought me of another fault.—
Provost, how came it Claudio was beheaded
At an unusual hour?
   Prov.   It was commanded so.
   Duke. Had you a special warrant for the deed?
   Prov. No, my good lord: it was by private
      message.
   Duke. For which I do discharge you of your
      office: 460
Give up your keys.
   Prov.   Pardon me, noble lord:
I thought it was a fault, but knew it not,
Yet did repent me, after more advice;
For testimony whereof, one in the prison,
That should by private order else have died,
I have reserv'd alive.
   Duke.   What's he?
   Prov.   His name is Barnardine.
   Duke. I would thou hadst done so by Claudio.—
Go fetch him hither: let me look upon him.
           [*Exit Provost.*
   Escal. I am sorry, one so learned and so wise
As you, Lord Angelo, have still appear'd,   470
Should slip so grossly, both in the heat of blood,
And lack of temper'd judgment afterward.
   Ang. I am sorry that such sorrow I procure;
And so deep sticks it in my penitent heart,
That I crave death more willingly than mercy:
'T is my deserving, and I do entreat it.

Re-enter Provost, BARNARDINE, CLAUDIO, *muffled,
and* JULIET.

   Duke. Which is that Barnardine?
   Prov.   This, my lord.
   Duke. There was a friar told me of this man.—
Sirrah, thou art said to have a stubborn soul,
That apprehends no further than this world,   480
And squar'st thy life according. Thou 'rt condemned;

Duke.   "Dear Isabel,
I have a motion much imports your good."

But, for those earthly faults, I quit them all,
And pray thee, take this mercy to provide
For better times to come.—Friar, advise him:
I leave him to your hand.—What muffled fellow's
      that?
   Prov. This is another prisoner that I sav'd,
That should have died when Claudio lost his head,
As like almost to Claudio as himself.
           [*Unmuffles* CLAUDIO.
   Duke. [*To* ISAB.] If he be like your brother, for his
      sake
Is he pardon'd; and for your lovely sake   490
Give me your hand, and say you will be mine,
He is my brother too. But fitter time for that.
By this Lord Angelo perceives he 's safe:
Methinks, I see a quick'ning in his eye.—
Well, Angelo, your evil quits you well:
Look that you love your wife; her worth, worth
      yours.—
I find an apt remission in myself,
And yet here 's one in place I cannot pardon.—
[*To* LUCIO.] You, sirrah, that knew me for a fool, a
      coward,
One all of luxury, an ass, a madman: 500
Wherein have I so deserv'd of you,
That you extol me thus?
   Lucio. 'Faith, my lord, I spoke it but according
to the trick. If you will hang me for it, you may;
but I had rather it would please you, I might be
whipp'd.
   Duke. Whipp'd first, sir, and hang'd after.—
Proclaim it, provost, round about the city,
If any woman 's wrong'd by this lewd fellow
(As I have heard him swear himself there 's one   510
Whom he begot with child), let her appear,
And he shall marry her: the nuptial finish'd,
Let him be whipp'd and hang'd.
   Lucio. I beseech your highness, do not marry me to
a whore! Your highness said even now, I made you
a duke: good my lord, do not recompense me in
making me a cuckold.
   Duke. Upon mine honour, thou shalt marry her.
Thy slanders I forgive; and therewithal

Remit thy other forfeits.—Take him to prison, 520
And see our pleasure herein executed.
   Lucio. Marrying a punk, my lord, is pressing to
death, whipping, and hanging.
   Duke. Slandering a prince deserves it.—
She, Claudio, that you wrong'd, look you restore.
Joy to you, Mariana!—love her, Angelo:
I have confess'd her, and I know her virtue.—
Thanks, good friend Escalus, for thy much goodness:
There's more behind that is more gratulate.

Thanks, provost, for thy care, and secrecy; 530
We shall employ thee in a worthier place.—
Forgive him, Angelo, that brought you home
The head of Ragozine for Claudio's:
The offence pardons itself.—Dear Isabel,
I have a motion much imports your good;
Whereto if you'll a willing ear incline,
What's mine is yours, and what is yours is mine.—
So, bring us to our palace; where we'll show
What's yet behind, that's meet you all should know.
                                          [*Exeunt.*

THE COMEDY OF ERRORS.

DRAMATIS PERSONÆ.

SOLINUS, *Duke of Ephesus.*
ÆGEON, *a Merchant of Syracuse.*
ANTIPHOLUS of *Ephesus,* ⎰ *Twin Brothers, Sons to*
ANTIPHOLUS of *Syracuse,* ⎱ *Ægeon and Æmilia.*
DROMIO of *Ephesus,* ⎰ *Twin Brothers, Attendants*
DROMIO of *Syracuse,* ⎱ *on the two Antipholuses.*
BALTHAZAR, *a Merchant.*
ANGELO, *a Goldsmith.*
A Merchant, *Friend to Antipholus of Syracuse.*

A Merchant *trading with Angelo.*
PINCH, *a Schoolmaster.*

ÆMILIA, *Wife to Ægeon.*
ADRIANA, *Wife to Antipholus of Ephesus.*
LUCIANA, *her Sister.*
LUCE, *Servant to Adriana.*
A Courtesan.

Gaoler, Officers, *and other Attendants.*

SCENE--EPHESUS.

ACT I.

SCENE I.—A Hall in the DUKE's Palace.

Enter DUKE, ÆGEON, *Gaoler, Officers, and other Attendants.*

Ægeon.

PROCEED, Solinus, to procure my fall,
  And by the doom of death end woes and
    all.
  Duke. Merchant of Syracusa, plead no
    more.
I am not partial, to infringe our laws:
The enmity and discord, which of late
Sprung from the rancorous outrage of
    your duke
  To merchants, our well-dealing country-
    men,—
  Who, wanting gilders to redeem their
    lives,
Have seal'd his rigorous statutes with their bloods,—
Excludes all pity from our threat'ning looks. 10
For, since the mortal and intestine jars
'Twixt thy seditious countrymen and us,
It hath in solemn synods been decreed,
Both by the Syracusians and ourselves,
To admit no traffic to our adverse towns:
Nay, more, if any, born at Ephesus,
Be seen at Syracusian marts and fairs;
Again, if any Syracusian born
Come to the bay of Ephesus, he dies,
His goods confiscate to the duke's dispose; 20
Unless a thousand marks be levied,
To quit the penalty, and to ransom him.
Thy substance, valued at the highest rate,
Cannot amount unto a hundred marks;
Therefore, by law thou art condemn'd to die.
  Æge. Yet this my comfort: when your words are
    done,
My woes end likewise with the evening sun.
  Duke. Well, Syracusian; say, in brief, the cause
Why thou departedst from thy native home,
And for what cause thou cam'st to Ephesus. 30
  Æge. A heavier task could not have been impos'd
Than I to speak my griefs unspeakable;
Yet, that the world may witness, that my end
Was wrought by nature, not by vile offence,
I'll utter what my sorrow gives me leave.
In Syracusa was I born, and wed
Unto a woman, happy but for me,
And by me too, had not our hap been bad.
With her I liv'd in joy: our wealth increas'd

By prosperous voyages I often made   40
To Epidamnum; till my factor's death,
And the great care of goods at random left,
Drew me from kind embracements of my spouse:
From whom my absence was not six months old,
Before herself (almost at fainting under
The pleasing punishment that women bear)
Had made provision for her following me,
And soon, and safe, arrived where I was.
There had she not been long, but she became
A joyful mother of two goodly sons;   50
And, which was strange, the one so like the other,
As could not be distinguish'd but by names.
That very hour, and in the self-same inn,
A meaner woman was delivered
Of such a burden, male twins, both alike.
Those, for their parents were exceeding poor,
I bought, and brought up to attend my sons.
My wife, not meanly proud of two such boys,
Made daily motions for our home return:
Unwilling I agreed; alas! too soon   60
We came aboard.
A league from Epidamnum had we sail'd,
Before the always-wind-obeying deep
Gave any tragic instance of our harm:
But longer did we not retain much hope:
For what obscured light the heavens did grant
Did but convey unto our fearful minds
A doubtful warrant of immediate death;
Which, though myself would gladly have embrac'd,
Yet the incessant weepings of my wife,   70
Weeping before for what she saw must come,
And piteous plainings of the pretty babes,
That mourn'd for fashion, ignorant what to fear,
Forc'd me to seek delays for them and me.
And this it was,—for other means was none.
The sailors sought for safety by our boat,
And left the ship, then sinking-ripe, to us.
My wife, more careful for the latter-born,
Had fasten'd him unto a small spare mast,
Such as seafaring men provide for storms: 80
To him one of the other twins was bound,
Whilst I had been like heedful of the other.
The children thus dispos'd, my wife and I,
Fixing our eyes on whom our care was fix'd,
Fasten'd ourselves at either end the mast;.

And floating straight, obedient to the stream,
Were carried towards Corinth, as we thought.
At length the sun, gazing upon the earth,
Dispers'd those vapours that offended us,
And by the benefit of his wished light   90
The seas wax'd calm, and we discovered
Two ships from far making amain to us;
Of Corinth that, of Epidaurus this:
But ere they came,—O, let me say no more!
Gather the sequel by that went before.
  Duke. Nay, forward, old man; do not break off so;
For we may pity, though not pardon thee.
  Æge. O, had the gods done so, I had not now
Worthily term'd them merciless to us!
For, ere the ships could meet by twice five leagues,
We were encounter'd by a mighty rock;   101
Which being violently borne upon,
Our helpful ship was splitted in the midst;
So that in this unjust divorce of us
Fortune had left to both of us alike
What to delight in, what to sorrow for.
Her part, poor soul! seeming as burdened
With lesser weight, but not with lesser woe,
Was carried with more speed before the wind,
And in our sight they three were taken up   110
By fishermen of Corinth, as we thought.
At length another ship had seized on us;
And, knowing whom it was their hap to save,
Gave healthful welcome to their shipwrack'd guests;
And would have reft the fishers of their prey,
Had not their bark been very slow of sail;
And therefore homeward did they bend their course.—
Thus have you heard me sever'd from my bliss,
That by misfortunes was my life prolong'd,
To tell sad stories of my own mishaps.   120
  Duke. And, for the sake of them thou sorrowest for,
Do me the favour to dilate at full
What hath befall'n of them, and thee, till now.
  Æge. My youngest boy, and yet my eldest care,
At eighteen years became inquisitive
After his brother; and importun'd me,
That his attendant (so his case was like,
Reft of his brother, but retain'd his name)
Might bear him company in the quest of him;
Whom whilst I labour'd of a love to see,   130
I hazarded the loss of whom I lov'd.
Five summers have I spent in farthest Greece,
Roaming clean through the bounds of Asia,
And, coasting homeward, came to Ephesus;
Hopeless to find, yet loath to leave unsought
Or that, or any place that harbours men.
But there must end the story of my life;
And happy were I in my timely death,
Could all my travels warrant me they live.
  Duke. Hapless Ægeon, whom the fates have mark'd   141
To bear the extremity of dire mishap!
Now, trust me, were it not against our laws,
Against my crown, my oath, my dignity,
Which princes, would they, may not disannul,
My soul should sue as advocate for thee.
But though thou art adjudged to the death,
And passed sentence may not be recall'd
But to our honour's great disparagement,
Yet will I favour thee in what I can:
Therefore, merchant, I'll limit thee this day,   150
To seek thy help by beneficial help:
Try all the friends thou hast in Ephesus;
Beg thou, or borrow, to make up the sum,
And live; if no, then thou art doom'd to die.—
Gaoler, take him to thy custody.
  Gaol. I will, my lord.
  Æge. Hopeless, and helpless, doth Ægeon wend,
But to procrastinate his lifeless end.   [*Exeunt.*

SCENE II.—A Public Place.

Enter ANTIPHOLUS *of Syracuse,* DROMIO *of Syracuse,*
and a Merchant.

  Mer. Therefore, give out you are of Epidamnum,
Lest that your goods too soon be confiscate.

This very day, a Syracusian merchant
Is apprehended for arrival here;
And, not being able to buy out his life
According to the statute of the town,
Dies ere the weary sun set in the west.
There is your money that I had to keep.
  Ant. S. Go bear it to the Centaur, where we host,
And stay there, Dromio, till I come to thee.   10
Within this hour it will be dinner-time:
Till that, I'll view the manners of the town,
Peruse the traders, gaze upon the buildings,
And then return and sleep within mine inn;
For with long travel I am stiff and weary.
Get thee away.
  Dro. S. Many a man would take you at your word,
And go indeed, having so good a mean.   [*Exit.*
  Ant. S. A trusty villain, sir, that very oft,
When I am dull with care and melancholy,   20
Lightens my humour with his merry jests.
What, will you walk with me about the town,
And then go to my inn, and dine with me?
  Mer. I am invited, sir, to certain merchants,
Of whom I hope to make much benefit;
I crave your pardon. Soon at five o'clock,
Please you, I'll meet with you upon the mart,
And afterwards consort you till bed-time:
My present business calls me from you now.
  Ant. S. Farewell till then. I will go lose myself, 30
And wander up and down to view the city.
  Mer. Sir, I commend you to your own content.
                                        [*Exit.*
  Ant. S. He that commends me to mine own content,
Commends me to the thing I cannot get.
I to the world am like a drop of water,
That in the ocean seeks another drop;
Who, falling there to find his fellow forth,
Unseen, inquisitive, confounds himself:
So I, to find a mother, and a brother,
In quest of them, unhappy, lose myself.   40

Enter DROMIO *of Ephesus.*

Here comes the almanac of my true date.
What now? How chance thou art return'd so soon?
  Dro. E. Return'd so soon! rather approach'd too
late.
The capon burns, the pig falls from the spit,
The clock hath strucken twelve upon the bell;
My mistress made it one upon my cheek:
She is so hot, because the meat is cold;
The meat is cold, because you come not home;
You come not home, because you have no stomach;
You have no stomach, having broke your fast;   50
But we, that know what 'tis to fast and pray,
Are penitent for your default to-day.
  Ant. S. Stop in your wind, sir. Tell me this, I
pray:
Where have you left the money that I gave you?
  Dro. E. O! sixpence, that I had o' Wednesday
last,
To pay the saddler for my mistress' crupper;
The saddler had it, sir; I kept it not.
  Ant. S. I am not in a sportive humour now.
Tell me, and dally not, where is the money?
We being strangers here, how dar'st thou trust   60
So great a charge from thine own custody?
  Dro. E. I pray you, jest, sir, as you sit at dinner.
I from my mistress come to you in post;
If I return, I shall be post indeed,
For she will score your fault upon my pate.
Methinks, your maw, like mine, should be your
clock,
And strike you home without a messenger.
  Ant. S. Come, Dromio, come; these jests are out of
season:
Reserve them till a merrier hour than this.
Where is the gold I gave in charge to thee?   70
  Dro. E. To me, sir? why, you gave no gold to me.
  Ant. S. Come on, sir knave; have done your foolish-
ness,
And tell me how thou hast dispos'd thy charge.
  Dro. E. My charge was but to fetch you from the
mart

Home to your house, the Phœnix, sir, to dinner.
My mistress, and her sister, stay for you.
   Ant. S. Now, as I am a Christian, answer me,
In what safe place you have bestow'd my money;
Or I shall break that merry sconce of yours,
That stands on tricks when I am undispos'd.   80
Where is the thousand marks thou hadst of me?
   Dro. E. I have some marks of yours upon my pate;
Some of my mistress' marks upon my shoulders,
But not a thousand marks between you both.
If I should pay your worship those again,
Perchance, you will not bear them patiently.
   Ant. S. Thy mistress' marks! what mistress, slave,
     hast thou?
   Dro. E. Your worship's wife, my mistress at the
     Phœnix;
She that doth fast till you come home to dinner,
And prays that you will hie you home to dinner.   90
   Ant. S. What, wilt thou flout me thus unto my
     face,
Being forbid? There, take you that, sir knave.
                           [*Strikes him.*
   Dro. E. What mean you, sir? for God's sake, hold
     your hands.
Nay, an you will not, sir, I 'll take my heels.   [*Exit.*
   Ant. S. Upon my life, by some device or other
The villain is o'er-raught of all my money.
They say, this town is full of cozenage;
As, nimble jugglers that deceive the eye,
Dark-working sorcerers that change the mind,

Soul-killing witches that deform the body,   100
Disguised cheaters, prating mountebanks,

Ant. S. "There, take you that, sir knave."

And many such-like liberties of sin:
If it prove so, I will be gone the sooner.
I 'll to the Centaur, to go seek this slave:
I greatly fear, my money is not safe.   [*Exit.*

ACT II.

SCENE I.—House of ANTIPHOLUS of Ephesus.

Enter ADRIANA *and* LUCIANA.

Adriana.

NEITHER my husband, nor the slave re-
   turn'd,
   That in such haste I sent to seek his
     master!
Sure, Luciana, it is two o'clock.
   Luc. Perhaps, some merchant hath in-
     vited him,
And from the mart he 's somewhere gone
     to dinner.
Good sister, let us dine, and never fret:
   A man is master of his liberty:
Time is their master; and, when they see time,
They 'll go, or come: if so, be patient, sister.
   Adr. Why should their liberty than ours be more?   10
   Luc. Because their business still lies out o' door.   11
   Adr. Look, when I serve him so, he takes it ill.
   Luc. O! know he is the bridle of your will.
   Adr. There 's none but asses will be bridled so.
   Luc. Why, headstrong liberty is lash'd with woe.
There 's nothing situate under heaven's eye
But hath his bound, in earth, in sea, in sky:
The beasts, the fishes, and the winged fowls,
Are their males' subjects, and at their controls.
Men, more divine, the masters of all these,   20
Lords of the wide world, and wild wat'ry seas,
Indued with intellectual sense and souls,
Of more pre-eminence than fish and fowls,
Are masters to their females, and their lords:
Then, let your will attend on their accords.
   Adr. This servitude makes you to keep unwed.
   Luc. Not this, but troubles of the marriage-bed.

   Adr. But, were you wedded, you would bear some
     sway.
   Luc. Ere I learn love, I 'll practise to obey.
   Adr. How if your husband start some other where?
   Luc. Till he come home again, I would forbear.   31
   Adr. Patience unmov'd, no marvel though she
     pause;
They can be meek that have no other cause.
A wretched soul, bruis'd with adversity,
We bid be quiet, when we hear it cry;
But were we burden'd with like weight of pain,
As much, or more, we should ourselves complain;
So thou, that hast no unkind mate to grieve thee,
With urging helpless patience wouldst relieve me:
But if thou live to see like right bereft,   40
This fool-begg'd patience in thee will be left.
   Luc. Well, I will marry one day, but to try.—
Here comes your man: now is your husband nigh.

Enter DROMIO *of Ephesus.*

   Adr. Say, is your tardy master now at hand?
   Dro. E. Nay, he is at two hands with me, and that
my two ears can witness.
   Adr. Say, didst thou speak with him? Know'st thou
     his mind?
   Dro. E. Ay, ay; he told his mind upon mine ear.
Beshrew his hand, I scarce could understand it.
   Luc. Spake he so doubtfully, thou couldst not feel
his meaning?   51
   Dro. E. Nay, he struck so plainly, I could too well
feel his blows; and withal so doubtfully, that I could
scarce understand them.

Adr. But say, I pr'ythee, is he coming home?
It seems, he hath great care to please his wife.
 Dro. E. Why, mistress, sure my master is horn-
  mad.
 Adr. Horn-mad, thou villain!
 Dro. E. I mean not cuckold-mad; but, sure, he is
  stark mad.
When I desir'd him to come home to dinner, 60
He ask'd me for a thousand marks in gold:
"'Tis dinner-time," quoth I; "My gold!" quoth he:
"Your meat doth burn," quoth I; "My gold!" quoth
  he:
"Will you come home?" quoth I; "my gold!" quoth
  he:
"Where is the thousand marks I gave thee, villain?"

Luc. "Ere I learn love, I'll practise to obey."

"The pig," quoth I, "is burn'd;" "My gold!" quoth
  he:
"My mistress, sir," quoth I; "Hang up thy mis-
  tress!
I know not thy mistress: out on thy mistress!"
 Luc. Quoth who?
 Dro. E. Quoth my master: 70
"I know," quoth he, "no house, no wife, no mis-
  tress."
So that my errand, due unto my tongue,
I thank him, I bear home upon my shoulders;
For, in conclusion, he did beat me there.
 Adr. Go back again, thou slave, and fetch him
  home.
 Dro. E. Go back again, and be new beaten home?
For God's sake, send some other messenger.
 Adr. Back, slave, or I will break thy pate across.
 Dro. E. And he will bless that cross with other
  beating.
Between you I shall have a holy head. 80
 Adr. Hence, prating peasant! fetch thy master
  home.
 Dro. E. Am I so round with you, as you with me,
That like a football you do spurn me thus?
You spurn me hence, and he will spurn me hither:
If I last in this service, you must case me in leather.
              [Exit.
 Luc. Fie, how impatience lowereth in your face!
 Adr. His company must do his minions grace,
Whilst I at home starve for a merry look.
Hath homely age the alluring beauty took
From my poor cheek? then he hath wasted it: 90
Are my discourses dull? barren my wit?
If voluble and sharp discourse be marr'd,
Unkindness blunts it, more than marble hard.
Do their gay vestments his affections bait?
That's not my fault; he's master of my state.
What ruins are in me, that can be found
By him not ruin'd? then is he the ground
Of my defeatures. My decayed fair

A sunny look of his would soon repair;
But, too unruly deer, he breaks the pale, 100
And feeds from home: poor I am but his stale.
 Luc. Self-harming jealousy!—fie! beat it hence.
 Adr. Unfeeling fools can with such wrongs dis-
  pense.
I know his eye doth homage otherwhere,
Or else, what lets it but he would be here?
Sister, you know, he promis'd me a chain:
'Would that alone alone he would detain,
So he would keep fair quarter with his bed!
I see, the jewel best enamelled
Will lose his beauty: and though gold 'bides still, 110
That others touch, yet often touching will
Wear gold; and no man, that hath a name,
But falsehood and corruption doth it shame.
Since that my beauty cannot please his eye,
I'll weep what's left away, and weeping die.
 Luc. How many fond fools serve mad jealousy!
              [Exeunt.

Scene II.—A Public Place.

Enter Antipholus *of Syracuse.*

 Ant. S. The gold I gave to Dromio is laid up
Safe at the Centaur; and the heedful slave
Is wander'd forth, in care to seek me out.
By computation, and mine host's report,
I could not speak with Dromio, since at first
I sent him from the mart. See, here he comes.

Enter Dromio *of Syracuse.*

How now, sir? is your merry humour alter'd?
As you love strokes, so jest with me again.
You know no Centaur? You receiv'd no gold?
Your mistress sent to have me home to dinner? 10
My house was at the Phœnix? Wast thou mad,
That thus so madly thou didst answer me?
 Dro. S. What answer, sir? when spake I such a
  word?
 Ant. S. Even now, even here, not half an hour
  since.
 Dro. S. I did not see you since you sent me hence,
Home to the Centaur, with the gold you gave me.
 Ant. S. Villain, thou didst deny the gold's receipt,
And toldst me of a mistress, and a dinner;
For which, I hope, thou feltst I was displeas'd.
 Dro. S. I am glad to see you in this merry vein. 20
What means this jest? I pray you, master, tell me.
 Ant. S. Yea, dost thou jeer, and flout me in the
  teeth?
Think'st thou, I jest? Hold, take thou that, and that.
            [Beating him.
 Dro. S. Hold, sir, for God's sake! now your jest is
  earnest:
Upon what bargain do you give it me?
 Ant. S. Because that I familiarly sometimes
Do use you for my fool, and chat with you,
Your sauciness will jet upon my love,
And make a common of my serious hours.
When the sun shines, let foolish gnats make sport, 30
But creep in crannies, when he hides his beams.
If you will jest with me, know my aspect,
And fashion your demeanour to my looks,
Or I will beat this method in your sconce.
 Dro. S. Sconce, call you it? so you would leave bat-
tering, I had rather have it a head: an you use these
blows long, I must get a sconce for my head, and
ensconce it too; or else I shall seek my wit in my
shoulders. But, I pray, sir, why am I beaten?
 Ant. S. Dost thou not know? 40
 Dro. S. Nothing, sir, but that I am beaten.
 Ant. S. Shall I tell you why?
 Dro. S. Ay, sir, and wherefore; for, they say, every
why hath a wherefore.
 Ant. S. Why, first,—for flouting me, and then,
  wherefore,—
For urging it the second time to me.
 Dro. S. Was there ever any man thus beaten out of
  season,

When, in the why, and the wherefore, is neither
    rhyme nor reason?—
Well, sir, I thank you.
    Ant. S. Thank me, sir? for what?   50
    Dro. S. Marry, sir, for this something, that you gave
me for nothing.
    Ant. S. I'll make you amends next, to give you
nothing for something. But say, sir, is it dinner-
time?
    Dro. S. No, sir: I think, the meat wants that I
have.
    Ant. S. In good time, sir; what's that?
    Dro. S. Basting.
    Ant. S. Well, sir, then 't will be dry.   60
    Dro. S. If it be, sir, I pray you eat none of it.
    Ant. S. Your reason?
    Dro. S. Lest it make you choleric, and purchase me
another dry basting.
    Ant. S. Well, sir, learn to jest in good time : there's
a time for all things.
    Dro. S. I durst have denied that, before you were so
choleric.
    Ant. S. By what rule, sir?
    Dro. S. Marry, sir, by a rule as plain as the plain
bald pate of father Time himself.   71
    Ant. S. Let 's hear it.
    Dro. S. There 's no time for a man to recover his
hair that grows bald by nature.
    Ant. S. May he not do it by fine and recovery?
    Dro. S. Yes, to pay a fine for a periwig, and recover
the lost hair of another man.
    Ant. S. Why is Time such a niggard of hair, being,
as it is, so plentiful an excrement?
    Dro. S. Because it is a blessing that he bestows on
beasts : and what he hath scanted men in hair, he
hath given them in wit.   82
    Ant. S. Why, but there 's many a man hath more
hair than wit.
    Dro. S. Not a man of those, but he hath the wit to
lose his hair.
    Ant. S. Why, thou didst conclude hairy men plain
dealers without wit.
    Dro. S. The plainer dealer, the sooner lost : yet he
loseth it in a kind of jollity.   90
    Ant. S. For what reason?
    Dro. S. For two ; and sound ones too.
    Ant. S. Nay, not sound, I pray you.
    Dro. S. Sure ones then.
    Ant. S. Nay, not sure, in a thing falsing.
    Dro. S. Certain ones then.
    Ant. S. Name them.
    Dro. S. The one, to save the money that he spends
in tiring ; the other, that at dinner they should not
drop in his porridge.   100
    Ant. S. You would all this time have proved, there
is no time for all things.
    Dro. S. Marry, and did, sir ; namely, no time to
recover hair lost by nature.
    Ant. S. But your reason was not substantial, why
there is no time to recover.
    Dro. S. Thus I mend it : Time himself is bald, and
therefore, to the world's end, will have bald followers.
    Ant. S. I knew, 'twould be a bald conclusion. But
soft ! who wafts us yonder?   111

    Enter ADRIANA *and* LUCIANA.

    Adr. Ay, ay, Antipholus, look strange, and frown :
Some other mistress hath thy sweet aspects,
I am not Adriana, nor thy wife.
The time was once, when thou unurg'd wouldst
    vow
That never words were music to thine ear,
That never object pleasing in thine eye,
That never touch well-welcome to thy hand,
That never meat sweet-savour'd in thy taste,
Unless I spake, or look'd, or touch'd, or carv'd to
    thee.   120
How comes it now, my husband, O ! how comes it,
That thou art then estranged from thyself?
Thyself I call it, being strange to me,
That, undividable, incorporate,

Am better than thy dear self's better part.
Ah, do not tear away thyself from me ;
For know, my love, as easy may'st thou fall
A drop of water in the breaking gulf,
And take unmingled thence that drop again,
Without addition or diminishing,   130
As take from me thyself, and not me too.
How dearly would it touch thee to the quick,
Shouldst thou but hear I were licentious,
And that this body, consecrate to thee,
By ruffian lust should be contaminate!
Wouldst thou not spit at me, and spurn at me,
And hurl the name of husband in my face,
And tear the stain'd skin off my harlot-brow,
And from my false hand cut the wedding-ring,
And break it with a deep-divorcing vow?   140
I know thou canst ; and therefore, see thou do it.
I am possess'd with an adulterate blot ;
My blood is mingled with the crime of lust
For, if we two be one, and thou play false,
I do digest the poison of thy flesh,
Being strumpeted by thy contagion.
Keep then fair league and truce with thy true bed ;
I live distain'd, thou undishonoured.
    Ant. S. Plead you to me, fair dame? I know you
    not.
In Ephesus I am but two hours old,   150
As strange unto your town, as to your talk ;
Who, every word by all my wit being scann'd,
Want wit in all one word to understand.
    Luc. Fie, brother : how the world is chang'd with
    you !
When were you wont to use my sister thus?
She sent for you by Dromio home to dinner.
    Ant. S. By Dromio?
    Dro. S. By me?
    Adr. By thee ; and this thou didst return from
    him,—
That he did buffet thee, and, in his blows,   160
Denied my house for his, me for his wife.
    Ant. S. Did you converse, sir, with this gentle-
    woman?
What is the course and drift of your compact?
    Dro. S. I, sir? I never saw her till this time.
    Ant. S. Villain, thou liest; for even her very
    words
Didst thou deliver to me on the mart.
    Dro. S. I never spake with her in all my life.
    Ant. S. How can she thus then call us by our
    names,
Unless it be by inspiration?
    Adr. How ill agrees it with your gravity,   170
To counterfeit thus grossly with your slave,
Abetting him to thwart me in my mood !
Be it my wrong, you are from me exempt,
But wrong not that wrong with a more contempt.
Come, I will fasten on this sleeve of thine ;
Thou art an elm, my husband, I a vine,
Whose weakness, married to thy stronger state,
Makes me with thy strength to communicate :
If aught possess thee from me, it is dross,
Usurping ivy, brier, or idle moss ;   180
Who, all for want of pruning, with intrusion
Infect thy sap, and live on thy confusion.
    Ant. S. To me she speaks; she moves me for her
    theme !
What, was I married to her in my dream,
Or sleep I now, and think I hear all this?
What error drives our eyes and ears amiss?
Until I know this sure uncertainty,
I 'll entertain the offer'd fallacy.
    Luc. Dromio, go bid the servants spread for dinner.
    Dro. S. O, for my beads ! I cross me for a sinner.
This is the fairy land : O, spite of spites !   191
We talk with goblins, owls, and elvish sprites.
If we obey them not, this will ensue,
They 'll suck our breath, or pinch us black and blue.
    Luc. Why prat'st thou to thyself, and answer'st
    not?
Dromio, thou drone, thou snail, thou slug, thou sot !
    Dro. S. I am transformed, master, am I not?
    Ant. S. I think thou art, in mind, and so am I.

Dro. S. Nay, master, both in mind and in my
  shape.
Ant. S. Thou hast thine own form.
Dro. S.   No, I am an ape.
Luc. If thou art chang'd to aught, 't is to an ass. 201

And shrive you of a thousand idle pranks.— 210
Sirrah, if any ask you for your master,
Say, he dines forth, and let no creature enter.—
Come, sister.—Dromio, play the porter well.
 Ant. S. Am I in earth, in heaven, or in hell?

Ant. S. "Plead you to me, fair dame? I know you not."

Dro. S. 'T is true; she rides me. and I long for
  grass.
'T is so, I am an ass; else it could never be,
But I should know her, as well as she knows me.
 Adr. Come, come; no longer will I be a fool,
To put the finger in the eye and weep,
Whilst man and master laugh my woes to scorn.
Come, sir, to dinner.—Dromio, keep the gate.—
Husband. I'll dine above with you to-day,

Sleeping or waking? mad, or well advis'd?
Known unto these, and to myself disguis'd?
I'll say as they say, and persever so,
And in this mist at all adventures go.
 Dro. S. Master, shall I be porter at the gate?
 Adr. Ay; and let none enter. lest I break your
  pate.   220
 Luc. Come, come, Antipholus; we dine too late.
             [*Exeunt.*

ACT III.

SCENE I.—The Same.

Enter ANTIPHOLUS *of Ephesus*, DROMIO *of Ephesus*, ANGELO, *and* BALTHAZAR.

Antipholus of Ephesus.

GOOD Signior Angelo, you must excuse us all ;
 My wife is shrewish, when I keep not hours.
Say, that I linger'd with you at your shop
To see the making of her carcanet,
And that to-morrow you will bring it home.
But here's a villain, that would face me down
He met me on the mart, and that I beat him,
 And charg'd him with a thousand marks in gold :
And that I did deny my wife and house.—
Thou drunkard, thou, what didst thou mean by this ?
Dro. E. Say what you will, sir, but I know what I know.   11
That you beat me at the mart, I have your hand to show :
If the skin were parchment, and the blows you gave were ink,
Your own handwriting would tell you what I think.
Ant. E. I think, thou art an ass.
Dro. E.   Marry, so it doth appear,
By the wrongs I suffer, and the blows I bear.
I should kick, being kick'd, and being at that pass,
You would keep from my heels, and beware of an ass.
Ant. E. You are sad, Signior Balthazar : 'pray God, our cheer
May answer my good will, and your good welcome here.   20
Bal. I hold your dainties cheap, sir, and your welcome dear.
Ant. E. O Signior Balthazar, either at flesh or fish,
A table-full of welcome makes scarce one dainty dish.
Bal. Good meat, sir, is common ; that every churl affords.
Ant. E. And welcome more common, for that's nothing but words.
Bal. Small cheer and great welcome makes a merry feast.
Ant. E. Ay, to a niggardly host, and more sparing guest :
But though my cates be mean, take them in good part ;
Better cheer may you have, but not with better heart.
But soft ! my door is lock'd. Go bid them let us in.   30
Dro. E. Maud, Bridget, Marian, Cicely, Gillian, Jin !
Dro. S. [*Within.*] Mome, malt-horse, capon, coxcomb, idiot, patch !
Either get thee from the door, or sit down at the hatch.
Dost thou conjure for wenches, that thou call'st for such store,
When one is one too many ? Go get thee from the door.
Dro. E. What patch is made our porter ?—My master stays in the street.
Dro. S. [*Within.*] Let him walk from whence he came, lest he catch cold on's feet.
Ant. E. Who talks within there ? ho ! open the door.
Dro. S. [*Within.*] Right, sir : I'll tell you when, an you'll tell me wherefore.

Ant. E. Wherefore ? for my dinner : I have not din'd to-day.   40
Dro. S. [*Within.*] Nor to-day here you must not ; come again when you may.
Ant. E. What art thou that keep'st me out from the house I owe ?
Dro. S. [*Within.*] The porter for this time, sir, and my name is Dromio.
Dro. E. O villain ! thou hast stolen both mine office and my name :
The one ne'er got me credit, the other mickle blame.
If thou hadst been Dromio to-day in my place,
Thou wouldst have chang'd thy face for a name, or thy name for an ass.
Luce. [*Within.*] What a coil is there ! Dromio, who are those at the gate ?
Dro. E. Let my master in, Luce.
Luce. [*Within.*]   Faith no ; he comes too late ;
And so tell your master.
Dro. E.   O Lord ! I must laugh.—   50
Have at you with a proverb :—Shall I set in my staff ?
Luce. [*Within.*] Have at you with another : that's, —When ? can you tell ?
Dro. S. [*Within.*] If thy name be called Luce, Luce, thou hast answer'd him well.
Ant. E. Do you hear, you minion ? you'll let us in, I hope ?
Luce. [*Within.*] I thought to have ask'd you.
Dro. S. [*Within.*]   And you said, no.
Dro. E. So ; come, help : well struck ! there was blow for blow.
Ant. E. Thou baggage, let me in.
Luce. [*Within.*]   Can you tell for whose sake ?
Dro. E. Master, knock the door hard.
Luce. [*Within.*]   Let him knock till it ache.
Ant. E. You'll cry for this, minion, if I beat the door down.
Luce. [*Within.*] What needs all that, and a pair of stocks in the town ?   60
Adr. [*Within.*] Who is that at the door, that keeps all this noise ?
Dro. S. [*Within.*] By my troth, your town is troubled with unruly boys.
Ant. E. Are you there, wife ? you might have come before.
Adr. [*Within.*] Your wife, sir knave ? go get you from the door.
Dro. E. If you went in pain, master, this knave would go sore.
Ang. Here is neither cheer, sir, nor welcome : we would fain have either.
Bal. In debating which was best, we shall part with neither.
Dro. E. They stand at the door, master : bid them welcome hither.
Ant. E. There is something in the wind, that we cannot get in.
Dro. E. You would say so, master, if your garments were thin.   70
Your cake there is warm within ; you stand here in the cold :
It would make a man mad as a buck to be so bought and sold.
Ant. E. Go fetch me something : I'll break ope the gate.

Dro. S. [*Within.*] Break any breaking here, and
  I 'll break your knave's pate.
Dro. E. A man may break a word with you, sir, and
  words are but wind ;
Ay, and break it in your face, so he break it not be-
  hind.
Dro. S. [*Within.*] It seems, thou wantest breaking.
  Out upon thee, hind !
Dro. E. Here 's too much out upon thee ! I pray
  thee, let me in.
Dro. S. [*Within.*] Ay, when fowls have no feathers,
  and fish have no fin.
Ant. E. Well, I 'll break in. Go borrow me a crow.

Dro. E. "Master, knock the door hard."

Dro. E. A crow without feather? master, mean you
  so ?   81
For a fish without a fin, there 's a fowl without a
  feather.
If a crow help us in, sirrah, we 'll pluck a crow to-
  gether.
Ant. E. Go get thee gone : fetch me an iron crow.
Bal. Have patience, sir ; O ! let it not be so :
Herein you war against your reputation,
And draw within the compass of suspect
The unviolated honour of your wife.
Once this,—your long experience of her wisdom,
Her sober virtue, years, and modesty,   90
Plead on her part some cause to you unknown ;
And doubt not, sir, but she will well excuse
Why at this time the doors are made against you.
Be rul'd by me : depart in patience,
And let us to the Tiger all to dinner ;
And about evening come yourself alone,
To know the reason of this strange restraint.
If by strong hand you offer to break in,
Now in the stirring passage of the day,
A vulgar comment will be made of it ;   100
And that supposed by the common rout
Against your yet ungalled estimation,
That may with foul intrusion enter in,

And dwell upon your grave when you are dead :
For slander lives upon succession ;
For ever housed, where it gets possession.
Ant. E. You have prevail'd. I will depart in quiet,
And, in despite of mirth, mean to be merry.
I know a wench of excellent discourse, —
Pretty and witty, wild and yet, too, gentle,— 110
There will we dine : this woman that I mean,
My wife (but, I protest, without desert)
Hath oftentimes upbraided me withal :
To her will we to dinner.—Get you home,
And fetch the chain ; by this, I know, 't is made ;
Bring it, I pray you, to the Porpentine ;
For there 's the house : that chain will I bestow
(Be it for nothing but to spite my wife)
Upon mine hostess there. Good sir, make haste.
Since mine own doors refuse to entertain me, 120
I 'll knock elsewhere, to see if they 'll disdain me.
Ang. I 'll meet you at that place, some hour hence.
Ant. E. Do so. This jest shall cost me some expense.
                            [*Exeunt.*

Scene II.—The Same.

Enter Luciana *and* Antipholus *of Syracuse.*

Luc. And may it be that you have quite forgot
A husband's office ? Shall, Antipholus,
Even in the spring of love, thy love-springs rot ?
Shall love, in building, grow so ruinous ?
If you did wed my sister for her wealth,
Then for her wealth's sake use her with more kind-
        ness :
Or, if you like elsewhere, do it by stealth ;
Muffle your false love with some show of blindness ;
Let not my sister read it in your eye ;
Be not thy tongue thy own shame's orator ; 10
Look sweet, speak fair, become disloyalty ;
Apparel vice like virtue's harbinger ;
Bear a fair presence, though your heart be tainted ;
Teach sin the carriage of a holy saint ;
Be secret-false : what need she be acquainted ?
What simple thief brags of his own attaint ?
'T is double wrong, to truant with your bed,
And let her read it in thy looks at board :
Shame hath a bastard fame, well managed ;
Ill deeds are doubled with an evil word. 20
Alas, poor women ! make us but believe,
Being compact of credit, that you love us ;
Though others have the arm, show us the sleeve ;
We in your motion turn, and you may move us.
Then, gentle brother, get you in again :
Comfort my sister, cheer her, call her wife.
'T is holy sport to be a little vain,
When the sweet breath of flattery conquers strife.
Ant. S. Sweet mistress (what your name is else, I
    know not,
Nor by what wonder you do hit of mine), 30
Less in your knowledge, and your grace, you show not,
Than our earth's wonder ; more than earth divine.
Teach me, dear creature, how to think and speak :
Lay open to my earthy-gross conceit,
Smother'd in errors, feeble, shallow, weak,
The folded meaning of your words' deceit.
Against my soul's pure truth, why labour you
To make it wander in an unknown field ?
Are you a god ? would you create me new ?
Transform me then, and to your power I 'll yield. 40
But if that I am I, then well I know,
Your weeping sister is no wife of mine,
Nor to her bed no homage do I owe :
Far more, far more, to you do I decline.
O, train me not, sweet mermaid, with thy note,
To drown me in thy sister's flood of tears.
Sing, siren, for thyself, and I will dote :
Spread o'er the silver waves thy golden hairs,
And as a bed I 'll take thee, and there lie ;
And, in that glorious supposition, think, 50
He gains by death, that hath such means to die :
Let Love, being light, be drowned if she sink !
Luc. What ! are you mad, that you do reason so ?
Ant. S. Not mad, but mated ; how, I do not know.

Luc. It is a fault that springeth from your eye.
Ant. S. For gazing on your beams, fair sun, being by.
Luc. Gaze where you should, and that will clear your sight.
Ant. S. As good to wink, sweet love, as look on night.
Luc. Why call you me love? call my sister so.
Ant. S. Thy sister's sister.
Luc. That's my sister.
Ant. S. No; 60
It is thyself, mine own self's better part;
Mine eye's clear eye, my dear heart's dearer heart;
My food, my fortune, and my sweet hope's aim,
My sole earth's heaven, and my heaven's claim.
Luc. All this my sister is, or else should be.

Luc. "O, soft, sir! hold you still."

Ant. S. Call thyself sister, sweet, for I aim thee.
Thee will I love, and with thee lead my life:
Thou hast no husband yet, nor I no wife.
Give me thy hand.
Luc. O, soft, sir! hold you still:
I'll fetch my sister, to get her good will. 70
[*Exit.*

Enter DROMIO *of Syracuse, hastily.*

Ant. S. Why, how now, Dromio? where runn'st thou so fast?
Dro. S. Do you know me, sir? am I Dromio? am I your man, am I myself?
Ant. S. Thou art Dromio, thou art my man, thou art thyself.
Dro. S. I am an ass, I am a woman's man, and besides myself.
Ant. S. What woman's man? and how besides thyself? 80
Dro. S. Marry, sir, besides myself, I am due to a woman; one that claims me, one that haunts me, one that will have me.
Ant. S. What claim lays she to thee?
Dro. S. Marry, sir, such claim as you would lay to your horse; and she would have me as a beast: not that, I being a beast, she would have me; but that she, being a very beastly creature, lays claim to me.
Ant. S. What is she? 89
Dro. S. A very reverend body; ay, such a one as a man may not speak of, without he say, sir-reverence. I have but lean luck in the match, and yet she is a wondrous fat marriage.
Ant. S. How dost thou mean a fat marriage?
Dro. S. Marry, sir, she's the kitchen-wench, and all grease; and I know not what use to put her to, but to make a lamp of her, and run from her by her own light. I warrant, her rags, and the tallow in them, will burn a Poland winter: if she lives till dooms-day, she'll burn a week longer than the whole world.
Ant. S. What complexion is she of? 101

Dro. S. Swart, like my shoe, but her face nothing like so clean kept: for why she sweats; a man may go over shoes in the grime of it.
Ant. S. That's a fault that water will mend.
Dro. S. No, sir; 'tis in grain: Noah's flood could not do it.
Ant. S. What's her name?
Dro. S. Nell, sir; but her name and three quarters, that is, an ell and three quarters, will not measure her from hip to hip. 111
Ant. S. Then she bears some breadth?
Dro. S. No longer from head to foot, than from hip to hip: she is spherical, like a globe; I could find out countries in her.
Ant. S. In what part of her body stands Ireland?
Dro. S. Marry, sir, in her buttocks: I found it out by the bogs.
Ant. S. Where Scotland?
Dro. S. I found it by the barrenness, hard in the palm of the hand. 121
Ant. S. Where France?
Dro. S. In her forehead; armed and reverted, making war against her hair.
Ant. S. Where England?
Dro. S. I look'd for the chalky cliffs, but I could find no whiteness in them: but I guess, it stood in her chin, by the salt rheum that ran between France and it.
Ant. S. Where Spain? 130
Dro. S. Faith, I saw it not; but I felt it hot in her breath.
Ant. S. Where America, the Indies?
Dro. S. O! sir, upon her nose, all o'er embellished with rubies, carbuncles, sapphires, declining their rich aspect to the hot breath of Spain, who sent whole armadoes of caracks to be ballast at her nose.
Ant. S. Where stood Belgia, the Netherlands?
Dro. S. O! sir, I did not look so low. To conclude, this drudge, or diviner, laid claim to me; call'd me Dromio; swore, I was assured to her; told me what privy marks I had about me, as the mark of my shoulder, the mole in my neck, the great wart on my left arm, that I, amazed, ran from her as a witch.
And, I think, if my breast had not been made of faith, and my heart of steel,
She had transform'd me to a curtail-dog, and made me turn i' the wheel.
Ant. S. Go hie thee presently post to the road:—
An if the wind blow any way from shore,
I will not harbour in this town to-night:—
If any bark put forth, come to the mart, 150
Where I will walk till thou return to me.
If every one knows us, and we know none,
'T is time, I think, to trudge, pack, and be gone.
Dro. S. As from a bear a man would run for life,
So fly I from her that would be my wife. [*Exit.*
Ant. S. There's none but witches do inhabit here,
And therefore 't is high time that I were hence.
She that doth call me husband, even my soul
Doth for a wife abhor; but her fair sister,
Possess'd with such a gentle sovereign grace, 160
Of such enchanting presence and discourse,
Hath almost made me traitor to myself:
But, lest myself be guilty to self-wrong,
I'll stop mine ears against the mermaid's song.

Enter ANGELO.

Ang. Master Antipholus?
Ant. S. Ay, that's my name.
Ang. I know it well, sir. Lo, here is the chain.
I thought to have ta'en you at the Porpentine;
The chain unfinish'd made me stay thus long.
Ant. S. What is your will that I shall do with this?
Ang. What please yourself, sir: I have made it for you. 171
Ant. S. Made it for me, sir? I bespoke it not.
Ang. Not once, nor twice, but twenty times you have.
Go home with it, and please your wife withal;
And soon at supper-time I'll visit you,
And then receive my money for the chain.

Ant. S. I pray you, sir, receive the money now,
For fear you ne'er see chain, nor money, more.
Ang. You are a merry man, sir. Fare you well.
                                   [Exit.
Ant. S. What I should think of this, I cannot
    tell;   180

But this I think, there's no man is so vain,
That would refuse so fair an offer'd chain.
I see, a man here needs not live by shifts,
When in the streets he meets such golden gifts.
I'll to the mart, and there for Dromio stay:
If any ship put out, then straight away.   *[Exit.*

ACT IV.

SCENE I.—The Same.

Enter a Merchant, ANGELO, *and an Officer.*

Merchant.

YOU know, since Pentecost the sum is due,
And since I have not much importun'd
    you;
Nor now I had not, but that I am bound
To Persia, and want gilders for my
    voyage:
Therefore make present satisfaction,
Or I'll attach you by this officer.
    Ang. Even just the sum, that I do
        owe to you,
Is growing to me by Antipholus;
And, in the instant that I met with you,
He had of me a chain: at five o'clock   10
I shall receive the money for the same.
Pleaseth you walk with me down to his house,
I will discharge my bond, and thank you too.

Enter ANTIPHOLUS *of Ephesus and* DROMIO *of
Ephesus.*

Off. That labour may you save: see where he
    comes.
Ant. E. While I go to the goldsmith's house, go
    thou
And buy a rope's end, that will I bestow
Among my wife and her confederates,
For locking me out of my doors by day.—
But soft, I see the goldsmith.—Get thee gone;
Buy thou a rope, and bring it home to me.   20
Dro. E. I buy a thousand pound a year: I buy a
    rope!   *[Exit.*
Ant. E. A man is well holp up that trusts to you:
I promised your presence, and the chain;
But neither chain, nor goldsmith, came to me.
Belike, you thought our love would last too long,
If it were chain'd together, and therefore came not.
Ang. Saving your merry humour, here's the note
How much your chain weighs to the utmost caract,
The fineness of the gold, and chargeful fashion,
Which doth amount to three odd ducats more   30
Than I stand debted to this gentleman:
I pray you, see him presently discharg'd,
For he is bound to sea, and stays but for it.
Ant. E. I am not furnish'd with the present money;
Besides, I have some business in the town.
Good signior, take the stranger to my house,
And with you take the chain, and bid my wife
Disburse the sum on the receipt thereof:
Perchance, I will be there as soon as you.
Ang. Then you will bring the chain to her your-
    self?   40
Ant. E. No; bear it with you, lest I come not time
    enough.
Ang. Well, sir, I will. Have you the chain about
    you?

Ant. E. An if I have not, sir, I hope you have,
Or else you may return without your money.
Ang. Nay, come, I pray you, sir, give me the chain:
Both wind and tide stay for this gentleman,
And I, to blame, have held him here too long.
Ant. E. Good Lord! you use this dalliance, to
    excuse
Your breach of promise to the Porpentine.
I should have chid you for not bringing it,   50
But, like a shrew, you first begin to brawl.
Mer. The hour steals on: I pray you, sir, despatch.
Ang. You hear, how he importunes me: the
    chain—
Ant. E. Why, give it to my wife, and fetch your
    money.
Ang. Come, come; you know, I gave it you even
    now.
Either send the chain, or send me by some token.
Ant. E. Fie! now you run this humour out of
    breath.
Come, where's the chain? I pray you, let me see it.
Mer. My business cannot brook this dalliance.
Good sir, say, whe'r you'll answer me, or no: 60
If not, I'll leave him to the officer.
Ant. E. I answer you! what should I answer you?
Ang. The money that you owe me for the chain.
Ant. E. I owe you none, till I receive the chain.
Ang. You know, I gave it you half an hour since.
Ant. E. You gave me none: you wrong me much to
    say so.
Ang. You wrong me more, sir, in denying it:
Consider how it stands upon my credit.
Mer. Well, officer, arrest him at my suit.
Off. I do,   70
And charge you in the duke's name to obey me.
Ang. This touches me in reputation.—
Either consent to pay this sum for me,
Or I attach you by this officer.
Ant. E. Consent to pay thee that I never had?
Arrest me, foolish fellow, if thou dar'st.
Ang. Here is thy fee: arrest him, officer.—
I would not spare my brother in this case,
If he should scorn me so apparently.
Off. I do arrest you, sir. You hear the suit.   80
Ant. E. I do obey thee, till I give thee bail.—
But, sirrah, you shall buy this sport as dear
As all the metal in your shop will answer.
Ang. Sir, sir, I shall have law in Ephesus,
To your notorious shame, I doubt it not.

Enter DROMIO *of Syracuse.*

Dro. S. Master, there is a bark of Epidamnum,
That stays but till her owner comes aboard,
And then, sir, she bears away. Our fraughtage, sir,
I have convey'd aboard, and I have bought

The oil, the balsamum, and aqua-vitæ.   90
The ship is in her trim : the merry wind
Blows fair from land ; they stay for nought at all,
But for their owner, master, and yourself.
   Ant. E. How now? a madman! Why, thou peevish
      sheep,
What ship of Epidamnum stays for me?
   Dro. S. A ship you sent me to, to hire waftage.
   Ant. E. Thou drunken slave, I sent thee for a rope;
And told thee to what purpose, and what end.
   Dro. S. You sent me for a rope's end as soon.
You sent me to the bay, sir, for a bark.   100
   Ant. E. I will debate this matter at more leisure,
And teach your ears to list me with more heed.
To Adriana, villain, hie thee straight;

Ang. "Here is thy fee: arrest him, officer."

Give her this key, and tell her, in the desk
That 's cover'd o'er with Turkish tapestry,
There is a purse of ducats : let her send it.
Tell her, I am arrested in the street,
And that shall bail me. Hie thee, slave, be gone.
On, officer, to prison till it come.
   [*Exeunt Merchant,* ANGELO, *Officer, and* ANT. E.
   Dro. S. To Adriana! that is where we din'd,   110
Where Dowsabel did claim me for her husband :
She is too big, I hope, for me to compass.
Thither I must, although against my will,
For servants must their masters' minds fulfil.   [*Exit.*

SCENE II.—The Same.

Enter ADRIANA *and* LUCIANA.

   Adr. Ah! Luciana, did he tempt thee so?
Mightst thou perceive austerely in his eye
That he did plead in earnest? yea or no?
Look'd he or red or pale? or sad or merrily?
What observation mad'st thou, in this case,
Of his heart's meteors tilting in his face?
   Luc. First he denied you had in him no right.
   Adr. He meant, he did me none: the more my
      spite.
   Luc. Then swore he, that he was a stranger here.
   Adr. And true he swore, though yet forsworn he
      were.   10
   Luc. Then pleaded I for you.
   Adr.   And what said he?
   Luc. That love I begg'd for you, he begg'd of me.
   Adr. With what persuasion did he tempt thy love?
   Luc. With words that in an honest suit might
      move.
First, he did praise my beauty; then, my speech.
   Adr. Didst speak him fair?
   Luc.   Have patience, I beseech.
   Adr. I cannot, nor I will not hold me still:

My tongue, though not my heart, shall have his will.
He is deformed, crooked, old, and sere,
Ill-fac'd, worse bodied, shapeless everywhere;   20
Vicious, ungentle, foolish, blunt, unkind,
Stigmatical in making, worse in mind.
   Luc. Who would be jealous then of such a one?
No evil lost is wail'd when it is gone.
   Adr. Ah! but I think him better than I say
And yet would herein others' eyes were worse.
Far from her nest the lapwing cries away :
My heart prays for him, though my tongue do curse.

Enter DROMIO *of Syracuse.*

   Dro. S. Here, go : the desk! the purse! sweet now,
      make haste.
   Luc. How hast thou lost thy breath?
   Dro. S.   By running fast.
   Adr. Where is thy master, Dromio? is he well?   31
   Dro. S. No, he 's in Tartar limbo, worse than hell :
A devil in an everlasting garment hath him,
One whose hard heart is button'd up with steel;
A fiend, a fairy, pitiless and rough;
A wolf, nay, worse, a fellow all in buff;
A back-friend, a shoulder-clapper, one that counter-
      mands
The passages of alleys, creeks, and narrow lands :
A hound that runs counter, and yet draws dry-foot
      well;
One that, before the judgment, carries poor souls to
      hell.   40
   Adr. Why, man, what is the matter?
   Dro. S. I do not know the matter : he is 'rested on
      the case.
   Adr. What, is he arrested? tell me at whose suit.
   Dro. S. I know not at whose suit he is arrested
      well :
But is in a suit of buff which 'rested him, that can I
      tell.
Will you send him, mistress, redemption, the money
      in his desk?
   Adr. Go fetch it, sister. [*Exit* LUCIANA.]—This I
      wonder at,
That he, unknown to me, should be in debt :—
Tell me, was he arrested on a band?
   Dro. S. Not on a band, but on a stronger thing;   50
A chain, a chain. Do you not hear it ring?
   Adr. What, the chain?
   Dro. S. No, no, the bell. 'Tis time that I were
      gone :
It was two ere I left him, and now the clock strikes
      one.
   Adr. The hours come back! that did I never hear.
   Dro. S. O yes; if any hour meet a sergeant, a' turns
      back for very fear.
   Adr. As if Time were in debt! how fondly dost thou
      reason!
   Dro. S. Time is a very bankrout, and owes more
      than he 's worth, to season.
Nay, he 's a thief too : have you not heard men say,
That Time comes stealing on by night and day?   60
If Time be in debt and theft, and a sergeant in the
      way,
Hath he not reason to turn back an hour in a day?

Re-enter LUCIANA.

   Adr. Go, Dromio: there 's the money, bear it
      straight,
And bring thy master home immediately.—
Come, sister; I am press'd down with conceit;
Conceit, my comfort, and my injury.   [*Exeunt.*

SCENE III.—The Same.

Enter ANTIPHOLUS *of Syracuse.*

   Ant. S. There 's not a man I meet but doth salute
      me,
As if I were their well-acquainted friend;
And every one doth call me by my name.
Some tender money to me, some invite me;
Some other give me thanks for kindnesses;

Some offer me commodities to buy :
Even now a tailor call'd me in his shop,
And show'd me silks that he had bought for me,
And, therewithal, took measure of my body.
Sure, these are but imaginary wiles,   10
And Lapland sorcerers inhabit here.

Enter DROMIO *of Syracuse.*

Dro. S. Master, here's the gold you sent me for.—
What have you got the picture of old Adam new-
apparell'd ?
Ant. S. What gold is this ? What Adam dost thou
mean ?
Dro. S. Not that Adam that kept the Paradise, but
that Adam that keeps the prison : he that goes in the
calf's skin that was kill'd for the Prodigal : he that
came behind you, sir, like an evil angel, and bid you
forsake your liberty.   20
Ant. S. I understand thee not.
Dro. S. No ? why, 'tis a plain case : he that went,
like a bass-viol, in a case of leather ; the man, sir, that,
when gentlemen are tired, gives them a fob, and 'rests
them ; he, sir, that takes pity on decayed men, and
gives them suits of durance ; he that sets up his rest to
do more exploits with his mace, than a morris-pike.
Ant. S. What, thou mean'st an officer ?
Dro. S. Ay, sir, the sergeant of the band ; he that
brings any man to answer it, that breaks his band ;
one that thinks a man always going to bed, and says,
"God give you good rest ! "   32
Ant. S. Well, sir, there rest in your foolery. Is
there any ship puts forth to-night ? may we be gone ?
Dro. S. Why, sir, I brought you word an hour since,
that the bark Expedition put forth to-night ; and then
were you hindered by the sergeant to tarry for the
hoy Delay. Here are the angels that you sent for to
deliver you.
Ant. S. The fellow is distract, and so am I,   40
And here we wander in illusions.
Some blessed power deliver us from hence !

Enter a Courtesan.

Cour. Well met, well met, Master Antipholus.
I see, sir, you have found the goldsmith now :
Is that the chain you promis'd me to-day ?
Ant. S. Satan, avoid ! I charge thee, tempt me not !
Dro. S. Master, is this Mistress Satan ?
Ant. S. It is the devil.
Dro. S. Nay, she is worse, she is the devil's dam,
and here she comes in the habit of a light wench : and
thereof comes that the wenches say, "God damn
me," that's as much as to say, "God make me a light
wench." It is written, they appear to men like angels
of light : light is an effect of fire, and fire will burn ;
ergo, light wenches will burn. Come not near her.
Cour. Your man and you are marvellous merry,
sir. Will you go with me ? we'll mend our dinner
here.
Dro. S. Master, if you do, expect spoon-meat, or
bespeak a long spoon.   60
Ant. S. Why, Dromio ?
Dro. S. Marry, he must have a long spoon that
must eat with the devil.
Ant. S. Avoid, thou fiend ! what tell'st thou me of
supping ?
Thou art, as you are all, a sorceress :
I conjure thee to leave me, and be gone.
Cour. Give me the ring of mine you had at dinner,
Or for my diamond the chain you promis'd,
And I'll be gone, sir, and not trouble you.
Dro. S. Some devils ask but the parings of one's
nail,   70
A rush, a hair, a drop of blood, a pin,
A nut, a cherry-stone ;
But she, more covetous, would have a chain.
Master, be wise : an if you give it her,
The devil will shake her chain, and fright us with it.
Cour. I pray you, sir, my ring, or else the chain.
I hope you do not mean to cheat me so.
Ant. S. Avaunt, thou witch ! Come, Dromio, let us
go.

Dro. S. "Fly pride," says the peacock : mistress,
that you know. [*Exeunt* ANT. S. *and* DRO. S.
Cour. Now, out of doubt, Antipholus is mad,   80
Else would he never so demean himself.
A ring he hath of mine worth forty ducats,
And for the same he promis'd me a chain :
Both one and other he denies me now.
The reason that I gather he is mad,
Besides this present instance of his rage,
Is a mad tale he told to-day at dinner,
Of his own doors being shut against his entrance.
Belike, his wife, acquainted with his fits,
On purpose shut the doors against his way.   90
My way is now, to hie home to his house,
And tell his wife, that, being lunatic,
He rush'd into my house, and took perforce
My ring away. This course I fittest choose,
For forty ducats is too much to lose.
                                                   [*Exit.*

SCENE IV.—The Same.

Enter ANTIPHOLUS *of Ephesus and the Officer.*

Ant. E. Fear me not, man ; I will not break away :
I'll give thee, ere I leave thee, so much money,
To warrant thee, as I am 'rested for.
My wife is in a wayward mood to-day,
And will not lightly trust the messenger.
That I should be attach'd in Ephesus,
I tell you, 'twill sound harshly in her ears.

Enter DROMIO *of Ephesus with a rope's end.*

Here comes my man : I think he brings the money.—
How now, sir ? have you that I sent you for ?
Dro. E. Here's that, I warrant you, will pay them
all.   10
Ant. E. But where's the money ?
Dro. E. Why, sir, I gave the money for the rope.
Ant. E. Five hundred ducats, villain, for a rope ?
Dro. E. I'll serve you, sir, five hundred at the rate.
Ant. E. To what end did I bid thee hie thee home ?
Dro. E. To a rope's end, sir ; and to that end am I
return'd.
Ant. E. And to that end, sir, I will welcome you.
                                               [*Beating him.*
Off. Good sir, be patient.
Dro. E. Nay, 'tis for me to be patient ; I am in
adversity.   21
Off. Good now, hold thy tongue.
Dro. E. Nay, rather persuade him to hold his hands.
Ant. E. Thou whoreson, senseless villain !
Dro. E. I would I were senseless, sir, that I might
not feel your blows.
Ant. E. Thou art sensible in nothing but blows, and
so is an ass.
Dro. E. I am an ass, indeed ; you may prove it by
my long ears. I have serv'd him from the hour of my
nativity to this instant, and have nothing at his hands
for my service but blows. When I am cold, he heats
me with beating ; when I am warm, he cools me with
beating : I am wak'd with it, when I sleep ; rais'd
with it, when I sit ; driven out of doors with it, when
I go from home ; welcomed home with it, when I
return : nay, I bear it on my shoulders, as a beggar
wont her brat, and, I think, when he hath lamed me,
I shall beg with it from door to door.   39
Ant. E. Come, go along : my wife is coming yonder.

Enter ADRIANA, LUCIANA, *the Courtesan, and*
PINCH.

Dro. E. Mistress, *respice finem,* respect your end ;
or rather the prophecy, like the parrot, "Beware the
rope's end."
Ant. E. Wilt thou still talk ?   [*Beats him.*
Cour. How say you now ? is not your husband
mad ?
Adr. His incivility confirms no less.—
Good Doctor Pinch, you are a conjurer ;
Establish him in his true sense again,
And I will please you what you will demand.

Luc. Alas, how fiery and how sharp he looks!   50
Cour. Mark, how he trembles in his ecstasy!
Pinch. Give me your hand, and let me feel your
        pulse.
Ant. E. There is my hand, and let it feel your ear.

Whilst upon me the guilty doors were shut,
And I denied to enter in my house?
  Adr. O husband, God doth know, you din'd at home;
Where 'would you had remain'd until this time,
Free from these slanders, and this open shame!

Pinch.   "I conjure thee by all the saints in heaven."

Pinch. I charge thee, Satan, hous'd within this man,
To yield possession to my holy prayers,
And to thy state of darkness hie thee straight:
I conjure thee by all the saints in heaven.
  Ant. E. Peace, doting wizard, peace! I am not mad.
  Adr. O, that thou wert not, poor distressed soul!
  Ant. E. You minion, you, are these your customers?
Did this companion with the saffron face   61
Revel and feast it at my house to-day,

  Ant. E. Dined at home! Thou, villain, what say'st
        thou?
  Dro. E. Sir, sooth to say you did not dine at home.
  Ant. E. Were not my doors lock'd up, and I shut
        out?   70
  Dro. E. Perdy, your doors were lock'd, and you shut
        out.
  Ant. E. And did not she herself revile me there?
  Dro. E. Sans fable, she herself revil'd you there.

Ant. E. Did not her kitchen-maid rail, taunt, and
scorn me?
Dro. E. Certes, she did; the kitchen-vestal scorn'd
you.
Ant. E. And did not I in rage depart from thence?
Dro. E. In verity, you did:—my bones bear witness,
That since have felt the vigour of his rage.
Adr. Is't good to soothe him in these contraries?
Pinch. It is no shame: the fellow finds his vein,   80
And, yielding to him, humours well his frenzy.
Ant. E. Thou hast suborn'd the goldsmith to arrest
me.
Adr. Alas, I sent you money to redeem you,
By Dromio here, who came in haste for it.
Dro. E. Money by me? heart and good will you
might,
But, surely, master, not a rag of money.
Ant. E. Went'st not thou to her for a purse of
ducats?
Adr. He came to me, and I deliver'd it.
Luc. And I am witness with her that she did.
Dro. E. God and the rope-maker bear me witness,
That I was sent for nothing but a rope!   91
Pinch. Mistress, both man and master is possess'd:
I know it by their pale and deadly looks.
They must be bound, and laid in some dark room.
Ant. E. Say, wherefore didst thou lock me forth
to-day?
And why dost thou deny the bag of gold?
Adr. I did not, gentle husband, lock thee forth.
Dro. E. And, gentle master, I receiv'd no gold;
But I confess, sir, that we were lock'd out.
Adr. Dissembling villain! thou speak'st false in
both.   100
Ant. E. Dissembling harlot! thou art false in all,
And art confederate with a damned pack,
To make a loathsome abject scorn of me;
But with these nails I'll pluck out these false eyes,
That would behold in me this shameful sport.
Adr. O, bind him, bind him! let him not come
near me.
Pinch. More company!—the fiend is strong within
him.
Luc. Ah me! poor man, how pale and wan he
looks!

Enter three or four, and bind ANTIPHOLUS *of
Ephesus and* DROMIO *of Ephesus.*

Ant. E. What, will you murder me? Thou gaoler,
thou,
I am thy prisoner: wilt thou suffer them   110
To make a rescue?
Off.   Masters, let him go:
He is my prisoner, and you shall not have him.
Pinch. Go bind this man, for he is frantic too.
Adr. What wilt thou do, thou peevish officer?
Hast thou delight to see a wretched man
Do outrage and displeasure to himself?
Off. He is my prisoner: if I let him go,
The debt he owes will be requir'd of me.
Adr. I will discharge thee, ere I go from thee.
Bear me forthwith unto his creditor,   120
And, knowing how the debt grows, I will pay it.
Good master doctor, see him safe convey'd
Home to my house.—O most unhappy day!
Ant. E. O most unhappy strumpet!
Dro. E. Master, I am here enter'd in bond for you.
Ant. E. Out on thee, villain! wherefore dost thou
mad me?
Dro. E. Will you be bound for nothing? be mad,
good master;
Cry, the devil!
Luc. God help, poor souls! how idly do they talk!
Adr. Go bear him hence.—Sister, go you with me.—
[*Exeunt* PINCH *and Assistants with* ANT. E.
and DRO. E.
Say now, whose suit is he arrested at?   131
Off. One Angelo, a goldsmith; do you know him?

Adr. I know the man. What is the sum he owes?
Off. Two hundred ducats.
Adr.   Say, how grows it due?
Off. Due for a chain your husband had of him.
Adr. He did bespeak a chain for me, but had it
not.
Cour. Whenas your husband, all in rage, to-day
Came to my house, and took away my ring
(The ring I saw upon his finger now),
Straight after did I meet him with a chain.   110

Off. "Away! they'll kill us."

Adr. It may be so, but I did never see it.—
Come, gaoler, bring me where the goldsmith is:
I long to know the truth hereof at large.

Enter ANTIPHOLUS *of Syracuse, with his rapier
drawn, and* DROMIO *of Syracuse.*

Luc. God, for thy mercy! they are loose again.
Adr. And come with naked swords. Let's call
more help,
To have them bound again.
Off.   Away! they'll kill us.
[*Exeunt* ADRIANA, LUCIANA, *Courtesan,
and Officer.*
Ant. S. I see, these witches are afraid of swords.
Dro. S. She that would be your wife now ran from
you.
Ant. S. Come to the Centaur; fetch our stuff from
thence:
I long, that we were safe and sound aboard.   150
Dro. S. Faith, stay here this night, they will surely
do us no harm; you saw they speak us fair, give us
gold. Methinks they are such a gentle nation, that
but for the mountain of mad flesh that claims marriage of me, I could find in my heart to stay here still,
and turn witch.
Ant. S. I will not stay to-night for all the town;
Therefore away, to get our stuff aboard.   [*Exeunt.*

ACT V.

SCENE I.—The Same. Before an Abbey.

Enter Merchant and ANGELO.

Angelo. AM sorry, sir, that I have hinder'd you ;
But, I protest, he had the chain of me,
Though most dishonestly he doth deny it.
Mer. How is the man esteem'd here in
    the city ?
Ang. Of very reverend reputation, sir,
Of credit infinite, highly belov'd,
Second to none that lives here in the city :
His word might bear my wealth at any
    time.
Mer. Speak softly : yonder, as I think,
    he walks.

*Enter ANTIPHOLUS of Syracuse and
DROMIO of Syracuse.*

Ang. 'T is so ; and that self chain about his neck, 10
Which he forswore most monstrously to have.
Good sir, draw near to me, I 'll speak to him.—
Signior Antipholus, I wonder much
That you would put me to this shame and trouble ;
And not without some scandal to yourself,
With circumstance and oaths, so to deny
This chain, which now you wear so openly :
Beside the charge, the shame, imprisonment,
You have done wrong to this my honest friend ;
Who, but for staying on our controversy, 20
Had hoisted sail, and put to sea to-day.
This chain you had of me : can you deny it ?
Ant. S. I think, I had ; I never did deny it.
Mer. Yes, that you did, sir, and forswore it too.
Ant. S. Who heard me to deny it, or forswear it ?
Mer. These ears of mine, thou know'st, did hear
    thee.
Fie on thee, wretch ! 't is pity that thou liv'st
To walk where any honest men resort.
Ant. S. Thou art a villain to impeach me thus.
I 'll prove mine honour and mine honesty 30
Against thee presently, if thou dar'st stand.
Mer. I dare, and do defy thee for a villain.
    [*They draw.*

Enter ADRIANA, LUCIANA, Courtesan, and others.

Adr. Hold ! hurt him not, for God's sake ! he is
    mad.—
Some get within him, take his sword away.
Bind Dromio too, and bear them to my house.
Dro. S. Run, master, run ; for God's sake take a
    house !
This is some priory ;—in, or we are spoil'd.
    [*Exeunt ANT. S. and DRO. S. to the Abbey.*

Enter the Abbess.

Abb. Be quiet, people. Wherefore throng you
    hither ?
Adr. To fetch my poor distracted husband hence.
Let us come in, that we may bind him fast, 40
And bear him home for his recovery.
Ang. I knew, he was not in his perfect wits.
Mer. I am sorry now, that I did draw on him.
Abb. How long hath this possession held the man ?
Adr. This week he hath been heavy, sour, sad,
And much different from the man he was ;
But, till this afternoon, his passion
Ne'er brake into extremity of rage.
Abb. Hath he not lost much wealth by wrack of
    sea ?
Buried some dear friend ? Hath not else his eye 50
Stray'd his affection in unlawful love ?
A sin prevailing much in youthful men,
Who give their eyes the liberty of gazing.
Which of these sorrows is he subject to ?
Adr. To none of these, except it be the last ;
Namely, some love, that drew him oft from home.
Abb. You should for that have reprehended him.
Adr. Why, so I did.
Abb.   Ay, but not rough enough.
Adr. As roughly as my modesty would let me.
Abb. Haply, in private.
Adr.   And in assemblies too. 60
Abb. Ay, but not enough.
Adr. It was the copy of our conference.
In bed, he slept not for my urging it :
At board, he fed not for my urging it :
Alone, it was the subject of my theme ;
In company, I often glanced it :
Still did I tell him it was vile and bad.

Abb. "And therefore came it that the man was mad.'

Abb. And therefore came it that the man was mad :
The venom clamours of a jealous woman
Poison more deadly than a mad dog's tooth. 70
It seems, his sleeps were hinder'd by thy railing,
And thereof comes it that his head is light.
Thou say'st, his meat was sauc'd with thy upbraid-
    ings :
Unquiet meals make ill digestions ;
Thereof the raging fire of fever bred :
And what 's a fever but a fit of madness ?
Thou say'st, his sports were hinder'd by thy brawls :
Sweet recreation barr'd, what doth ensue
But moody and dull melancholy,
Kinsman to grim and comfortless despair, 80
And at their heels a huge infectious troop

Of pale distemperatures, and foes to life ?
In food, in sport, and life-preserving rest
To be disturb'd, would mad or man or beast.
The consequence is then, thy jealous fits
Have scar'd thy husband from the use of wits.
  Luc. She never reprehended him but mildly,
When he demean'd himself rough, rude, and wildly.—
Why bear you these rebukes, and answer not ?
  Adr. She did betray me to my own reproof.—   90
Good people, enter, and lay hold on him.
  Abb. No ; not a creature enters in my house.
  Adr. Then, let your servants bring my husband
     forth.
  Abb. Neither : he took this place for sanctuary,
And it shall privilege him from your hands,
Till I have brought him to his wits again,
Or lose my labour in assaying it.
  Adr. I will attend my husband, be his nurse,
Diet his sickness, for it is my office,
And will have no attorney but myself,   100
And therefore let me have him home with me.
  Abb. Be patient ; for I will not let him stir,
Till I have us'd the approved means I have,
With wholesome syrups, drugs, and holy prayers,
To make of him a formal man again.
It is a branch and parcel of mine oath,
A charitable duty of my order ;
Therefore depart, and leave him here with me.
  Adr. I will not hence, and leave my husband here ;
And ill it doth beseem your holiness   110
To separate the husband and the wife.
  Abb. Be quiet, and depart : thou shalt not have
     him.   [*Exit.*
  Luc. Complain unto the duke of this indignity.
  Adr. Come, go : I will fall prostrate at his feet,
And never rise, until my tears and prayers
Have won his grace to come in person hither,
And take perforce my husband from the abbess.
  Mer. By this, I think, the dial points at five :
Anon, I 'm sure, the duke himself in person
Comes this way to the melancholy vale,   120
The place of death and sorry execution,
Behind the ditches of the abbey here.
  Ang. Upon what cause ?
  Mer. To see a reverend Syracusian merchant,
Who put unluckily into this bay
Against the laws and statutes of this town,
Beheaded publicly for his offence.
  Ang. See, where they come : we will behold his
     death.
  Luc. Kneel to the duke before he pass the abbey.

Enter Duke, *attended ;* Ægeon *bareheaded ; with
    the Headsman and other Officers.*

  Duke. Yet once again proclaim it publicly,   130
If any friend will pay the sum for him,
He shall not die, so much we tender him.
  Adr. Justice, most sacred duke, against the abbess !
  Duke. She is a virtuous and a reverend lady :
It cannot be that she hath done thee wrong.
  Adr. May it please your grace, Antipholus, my
     husband,—
Whom I made lord of me, and all I had,
At your important letters,—this ill day
A most outrageous fit of madness took him,
That desperately he hurried through the street,   140
(With him his bondman, all as mad as he)
Doing displeasure to the citizens
By rushing in their houses, bearing thence
Rings, jewels, anything his rage did like.
Once did I get him bound, and sent him home,
Whilst to take order for the wrongs I went,
That here and there his fury had committed.
Anon, I wot not by what strong escape,
He broke from those that had the guard of him,
And with his mad attendant and himself,   150
Each one with ireful passion, with drawn swords,
Met us again, and, madly bent on us,
Chas'd us away ; till, raising of more aid,
We came again to bind them. Then they fled
Into this abbey, whither we pursued them ;
And here the abbess shuts the gates on us,

And will not suffer us to fetch him out,
Nor send him forth, that we may bear him hence.
Therefore, most gracious duke, with thy command,
Let him be brought forth, and borne hence for help.
  Duke. Long since thy husband serv'd me in my
     wars,   161
And I to thee engag'd a prince's word,
When thou didst make him master of thy bed,
To do him all the grace and good I could.—
Go, some of you, knock at the abbey-gate,
And bid the lady abbess come to me.
I will determine this, before I stir.

Enter a Servant.

  Serv. O mistress, mistress ! shift and save yourself.
My master and his man are both broke loose,
Beaten the maids a-row, and bound the doctor,   170
Whose beard they have sing'd off with brands of fire ;
And ever as it blazed they threw on him
Great pails of puddled mire to quench the hair.
My master preaches patience to him, and the while
His man with scissors nicks him like a fool ;
And, sure, unless you send some present help,
Between them they will kill the conjurer.
  Adr. Peace, fool ! thy master and his man are here,
And that is false thou dost report to us.
  Serv. Mistress, upon my life, I tell you true ;   180
I have not breath'd almost, since I did see it.
He cries for you, and vows, if he can take you,
To scorch your face, and to disfigure you.
                     [*Cry within.*
Hark, hark, I hear him, mistress : fly, be gone.
  Duke. Come, stand by me ; fear nothing. Guard
     with halberds !
  Adr. Ah me, it is my husband ! Witness you,
That he is borne about invisible :
Even now we hous'd him in the abbey here,
And now he 's there, past thought of human reason.

Enter Antipholus *of* Ephesus *and* Dromio *of
    Ephesus.

  Ant. E. Justice, most gracious duke ! O ! grant me
     justice,   190
Even for the service that long since I did thee,
When I bestrid thee in the wars, and took
Deep scars to save thy life ; even for the blood
That then I lost for thee, now grant me justice.
  Æge. Unless the fear of death doth make me dote,
I see my son Antipholus, and Dromio !
  Ant. E. Justice, sweet prince, against that woman
     there !
She whom thou gav'st to me to be my wife,
That hath abused and dishonour'd me,
Even in the strength and height of injury.   200
Beyond imagination is the wrong
That she this day hath shameless thrown on me.
  Duke. Discover how, and thou shalt find me just.
  Ant. E. This day, great duke, she shut the doors
     upon me,
While she with harlots feasted in my house.
  Duke. A grievous fault. Say, woman, didst thou
     so ?
  Adr. No, my good lord : myself, he, and my sister,
To-day did dine together. So befall my soul,
As this is false he burdens me withal.
  Luc. Ne'er may I look on day, nor sleep on night,
But she tells to your highness simple truth.   211
  Ang. O perjur'd woman ! They are both forsworn :
In this the madman justly chargeth them.
  Ant. E. My liege, I am advised what I say :
Neither disturbed with the effect of wine,
Nor heady-rash provok'd with raging ire,
Albeit my wrongs might make one wiser mad.
This woman lock'd me out this day from dinner :
That goldsmith there, were he not pack'd with her,
Could witness it, for he was with me then ;   220
Who parted with me to go fetch a chain,
Promising to bring it to the Porpentine,
Where Balthazar and I did dine together.
Our dinner done, and he not coming thither,
I went to seek him : in the street I met him,
And in his company that gentleman.

There did this perjur'd goldsmith swear me down,
That I this day of him receiv'd the chain,
Which, God he knows, I saw not ; for the which
He did arrest me with an officer.   230
I did obey, and sent my peasant home
For certain ducats : he with none return'd.
Then fairly I bespoke the officer,
To go in person with me to my house.
By the way we met
My wife, her sister, and a rabble more
Of vile confederates : along with them
They brought one Pinch, a hungry lean-fac'd villain,
A mere anatomy, a mountebank,
A threadbare juggler, and a fortune-teller,   240
A needy, hollow-ey'd, sharp-looking wretch,
A living dead man.   This pernicious slave,
Forsooth, took on him as a conjurer,
And gazing in mine eyes, feeling my pulse,
And with no face, as 't were, outfacing me,
Cries out, I was possess'd.   Then, altogether
They fell upon me, bound me, bore me thence,
And in a dark and dankish vault at home
There left me and my man, both bound together ;
Till, gnawing with my teeth my bonds in sunder,   250
I gain'd my freedom, and immediately
Ran hither to your grace, whom I beseech
To give me ample satisfaction
For these deep shames, and great indignities.
Ang. My lord, in truth, thus far I witness with him,
That he din'd not at home, but was lock'd out.
Duke. But had he such a chain of thee, or no?
Ang. He had, my lord ; and when he ran in here,
These people saw the chain about his neck.
Mer. Besides, I will be sworn, these ears of mine   261
Heard you confess you had the chain of him,
After you first forswore it on the mart,
And, thereupon, I drew my sword on you ;
And then you fled into this abbey here,
From whence, I think, you are come by miracle.
Ant. E. I never came within these abbey-walls,
Nor ever didst thou draw thy sword on me.
I never saw the chain.   So help me Heaven,
As this is false you burden me withal.
Duke. Why, what an intricate impeach is this !   270
I think, you all have drunk of Circe's cup.
If here you hous'd him, here he would have been ;
If he were mad, he would not plead so coldly ; —
You say, he din'd at home ; the goldsmith here
Denies that saying.—Sirrah, what say you?
Dro. E. Sir, he din'd with her there, at the Por-
                                                      pentine.
Cour. He did, and from my finger snatch'd that
                                                      ring.
Ant. E. 'T is true, my liege ; this ring I had of her.
Duke. Saw'st thou him enter at the abbey here ?
Cour. As sure, my liege, as I do see your grace.   280
Duke. Why, this is strange. — Go call the abbess
                                                      hither. —
I think you are all mated, or stark mad.
                              [*Exit an Attendant.*
Æge. Most mighty duke, vouchsafe me speak a
                                                      word.
Haply, I see a friend will save my life,
And pay the sum that may deliver me.
Duke. Speak freely, Syracusian, what thou wilt.
Æge. Is not your name, sir, call'd Antipholus,
And is not that your bondman Dromio?
Dro. E. Within this hour I was his bondman, sir :
But he, I think, gnaw'd in two my cords :   290
Now am I Dromio, and his man unbound.
Æge. I am sure you both of you remember me.
Dro. E. Ourselves we do remember, sir, by you ;
For lately we were bound, as you are now.
You are not Pinch's patient, are you, sir?
Æge. Why look you strange on me? you know me
                                                      well.
Ant. E. I never saw you in my life, till now.
Æge. O! grief hath chang'd me, since you saw me
                                                      last ;
And careful hours, with Time's deformed hand,
Have written strange defeatures in my face :   300
But tell me yet, dost thou not know my voice?

Ant. E. Neither.
Æge. Dromio, nor thou?
Dro. E.   No, trust me, sir, nor I.
Æge. I am sure thou dost.
Dro. E. Ay, sir, but I am sure I do not ; and what-
soever a man denies, you are now bound to believe
him.
Æge. Not know my voice !   O, time's extremity,
Hast thou so crack'd and splitted my poor tongue
In seven short years, that here my only son   310
Knows not my feeble key of untun'd cares?
Though now this grained face of mine be hid
In sap-consuming winter's drizzled snow,
And all the conduits of my blood froze up,
Yet hath my night of life some memory,
My wasting lamps some fading glimmer left,
My dull deaf ears a little use to hear :
All these old witnesses (I cannot err)
Tell me thou art my son Antipholus.
Ant. E. I never saw my father in my life.   320
Æge. But seven years since, in Syracusa, boy,
Thou know'st we parted.   But, perhaps, my son,
Thou sham'st to acknowledge me in misery.
Ant. E. The duke, and all that know me in the
                                                      city,
Can witness with me that it is not so.
I ne'er saw Syracusa in my life.
Duke. I tell thee, Syracusian, twenty years
Have I been patron to Antipholus,
During which time he ne'er saw Syracusa.
I see, thy age and dangers make thee dote.   330

Enter ABBESS, *with* ANTIPHOLUS *of Syracuse and*
                DROMIO *of Syracuse.*

Abb. Most mighty duke, behold a man much
                  wrong'd.   [*All gather to see them.*
Adr. I see two husbands, or mine eyes deceive me.
Duke. One of these men is Genius to the other ;
And so of these : which is the natural man,
And which the spirit? who deciphers them?
Dro. S. I, sir, am Dromio : command him away.
Dro. E. I, sir, am Dromio : pray, let me stay.
Ant. S. Ægeon art thou not? or else his ghost?
Dro. S. O, my old master! who hath bound him
                                                      here?
Abb. Whoever bound him. I will loose his bonds,
And gain a husband by his liberty.—   341
Speak, old Ægeon, if thou be'st the man
That hadst a wife once called Æmilia,
That bore thee at a burden two fair sons.
O ! if thou be'st the same Ægeon, speak,
And speak unto the same Æmilia !
Æge. If I dream not, thou art Æmilia.
If thou art she, tell me, where is that son
That floated with thee on the fatal raft?
Abb. By men of Epidamnum, he, and I,   350
And the twin Dromio, all were taken up :
But, by-and-by, rude fishermen of Corinth
By force took Dromio and my son from them,
And me they left with those of Epidamnum.
What then became of them, I cannot tell ;
I to this fortune that you see me in.
Duke. Why, here begins his morning story right.
These two Antipholuses, these two so like,
And these two Dromios, one in semblance,--
Besides her urging of her wrack at sea :—   360
These are the parents to these children,
Which accidentally are met together.
Antipholus, thou cam'st from Corinth first ?
Ant. S. No, sir, not I : I came from Syracuse.
Duke. Stay, stand apart : I know not which is
                                                      which.
Ant. E. I came from Corinth, my most gracious
                                                      lord.
Dro. E. And I with him.
Ant. E. Brought to this town by that most famous
                                                      warrior,
Duke Menaphon, your most renowned uncle.   369
Adr. Which of you two did dine with me to-day?
Ant. S. I, gentle mistress.
Adr.   And are not you my husband?
Ant. E. No ; I say nay to that.

Ant. S. And so do I ; yet did she call me so ;
And this fair gentlewoman, her sister here,
Did call me brother.—What I told you then,
I hope, I shall have leisure to make good,
If this be not a dream I see and hear.
    Ang. That is the chain, sir, which you had of me.
    Ant. S. I think it be, sir : I deny it not.
    Ant. E. And you, sir, for this chain arrested me.
    Ang. I think I did, sir : I deny it not.   381
    Adr. I sent you money, sir, to be your bail,
By Dromio ; but I think, he brought it not.
    Dro. E. No, none by me.

And you the calendars of their nativity,
Go to a gossips' feast, and joy with me :
After so long grief such festivity !
    Duke. With all my heart : I 'll gossip at this feast.
        [*Exeunt* Duke, Abbess, Ægeon, Courtesan,
                Merchant, Angelo, *and Attendants.*
    Dro. S. Master, shall I fetch your stuff from ship-
        board?
    Ant. E. Dromio, what stuff of mine hast thou em-
        bark'd ?   410
    Dro. S. Your goods, that lay at host, sir, in the
        Centaur.

Abb. " Most mighty duke, behold a man much wrong'd. '

Ant. S. This purse of ducats I receiv'd from you,
And Dromio, my man, did bring them me.
I see, we still did meet each other's man,
And I was ta'en for him and he for me,
And thereupon these errors are arose.
    Ant. E. These ducats pawn I for my father here.
    Duke. It shall not need : thy father hath his life.
    Cour. Sir, I must have that diamond from you.   392
    Ant. E. There, take it ; and much thanks for my
        good cheer.
    Abb. Renowned duke, vouchsafe to take the pains
To go with us into the abbey here,
And hear at large discoursed all our fortunes
And all that are assembled in this place.
That by this sympathised one day's error
Have suffer'd wrong, go keep us company,
And we shall make full satisfaction.   400
Thirty-three years have I but gone in travail
Of you, my sons ; and till this present hour
My heavy burden ne'er deliver'd.—
The duke, my husband, and my children both,

    Ant. S. He speaks to me. — I am your master,
        Dromio,
Come, go with us ; we 'll look to that anon.
Embrace thy brother there ; rejoice with him.
        [*Exeunt* Ant. S., Ant. E., Adr., *and* Luc.
    Dro. S. There is a fat friend at your master's
        house,
That kitchen'd me for you to-day at dinner :
She now shall be my sister, not my wife.
    Dro. E. Methinks, you are my glass, and not my
        brother :
I see by you I am a sweet-faced youth.
Will you walk in to see their gossiping?   420
    Dro. S. Not I, sir ; you are my elder.
    Dro. E. That 's a question : how shall we try it ?
    Dro. S. We 'll draw cuts for the senior : till then,
        lead thou first.
    Dro. E. Nay, then thus :
We came into the world like brother and brother ;
And now let 's go hand in hand, not one before
        another.   [*Exeunt.*

MUCH ADO ABOUT NOTHING.

DRAMATIS PERSONÆ.

DON PEDRO, *Prince of Arragon.*
JOHN, *his bastard Brother.*
CLAUDIO, *a young Lord of Florence.*
BENEDICK, *a young Lord of Padua.*
LEONATO, *Governor of Messina.*
ANTONIO, *his Brother.*
BALTHAZAR, *Servant to Don Pedro.*
BORACHIO, CONRADE, } *Followers of John.*
DOGBERRY, VERGES, } *Two Officers.*

FRIAR FRANCIS.
A Sexton.
A Boy.

HERO, *Daughter to Leonato.*
BEATRICE, *Niece to Leonato.*
MARGARET, URSULA, } *Gentlewomen attending on Hero.*

Messengers, Watchmen, and Attendants.

SCENE—MESSINA.

ACT I.

SCENE I.—Before LEONATO'S House.

Enter LEONATO, HERO, BEATRICE, *and others, with a Messenger.*

Leonato.

LEARN in this letter, that Don Pedro of Arragon comes this night to Messina.

Mess. He is very near by this: he was not three leagues off when I left him.

Leon. How many gentlemen have you lost in this action?

Mess. But few of any sort, and none of name.

Leon. A victory is twice itself, when the achiever brings home full numbers. I find here, that Don Pedro hath bestowed much honour on a young Florentine, called Claudio.

Mess. Much deserved on his part, and equally remembered by Don Pedro. He hath borne himself beyond the promise of his age, doing in the figure of a lamb the feats of a lion: he hath, indeed, better bettered expectation than you must expect of me to tell you how.   20

Leon. He hath an uncle here in Messina will be very much glad of it.

Mess. I have already delivered him letters, and there appears much joy in him; even so much, that joy could not show itself modest enough without a badge of bitterness.

Leon. Did he break out into tears?

Mess. In great measure.

Leon. A kind overflow of kindness. There are no faces truer than those that are so washed: how much better is it to weep at joy, than to joy at weeping!   31

Beat. I pray you, is Signior Montanto returned from the wars, or no?

Mess. I know none of that name, lady: there was none such in the army of any sort.

Leon. What is he that you ask for, niece?

Hero. My cousin means Signior Benedick of Padua.

Mess. O, he is returned, and as pleasant as ever he was.   39

Beat. He set up his bills here in Messina, and challenged Cupid at the flight; and my uncle's fool, reading the challenge, subscribed for Cupid, and challenged him at the bird-bolt.—I pray you, how

Beat. "But how many hath he killed?"

many hath he killed and eaten in these wars? But how many hath he killed? for, indeed, I promised to eat all of his killing.

Leon. Faith, niece, you tax Signior Benedick too much; but he'll be meet with you, I doubt it not.

Mess. He hath done good service, lady, in these
wars.   50
  Beat. You had musty victual, and he hath holp to
eat it: he is a very valiant trencher-man; he hath an
excellent stomach.
  Mess. And a good soldier too, lady.
  Beat. And a good soldier to a lady; but what is he
to a lord?
  Mess. A lord to a lord, a man to a man; stuffed
with all honourable virtues.
  Beat. It is so, indeed: he is no less than a stuffed
man; but for the stuffing,—well, we are all mortal. 60
  Leon. You must not, sir, mistake my niece. There
is a kind of merry war betwixt Signior Benedick and
her: they never meet, but there's a skirmish of wit
between them.
  Beat. Alas! he gets nothing by that. In our last
conflict four of his five wits went halting off, and now
is the whole man governed with one; so that if he
have wit enough to keep himself warm, let him bear
it for a difference between himself and his horse; for
it is all the wealth that he hath left to be known a
reasonable creature.—Who is his companion now?
He hath every month a new sworn brother.   72
  Mess. Is 't possible?
  Beat. Very easily possible: he wears his faith but
as the fashion of his hat; it ever changes with the
next block.
  Mess. I see, lady, the gentleman is not in your
books.
  Beat. No; an he were, I would burn my study.
But, I pray you, who is his companion? Is there no
young squarer now, that will make a voyage with
him to the devil?   82
  Mess. He is most in the company of the right noble
Claudio.
  Beat. O Lord! he will hang upon him like a disease:
he is sooner caught than the pestilence, and the taker
runs presently mad. God help the noble Claudio!
if he have caught the Benedick, it will cost him a
thousand pound ere he be cured.
  Mess. I will hold friends with you, lady.   90
  Beat. Do, good friend.
  Leon. You will never run mad, niece.
  Beat. No, not till a hot January.
  Mess. Don Pedro is approached.

Enter Don PEDRO, JOHN, CLAUDIO, BENEDICK,
      BALTHAZAR, *and others.*

  D. Pedro. Good Signior Leonato, you are come to
meet your trouble: the fashion of the world is to
avoid cost, and you encounter it.
  Leon. Never came trouble to my house in the likeness of your grace: for trouble being gone, comfort
should remain, but when you depart from me, sorrow
abides, and happiness takes his leave.   101
  D. Pedro. You embrace your charge too willingly.
I think, this is your daughter.
  Leon. Her mother hath many times told me so.
  Bene. Were you in doubt, sir, that you asked her?
  Leon. Signior Benedick, no; for then were you a
child.
  D. Pedro. You have it full, Benedick: we may
guess by this what you are, being a man.—Truly, the
lady fathers herself.—Be happy, lady, for you are like
an honourable father.   111
  Bene. If Signior Leonato be her father, she would
not have his head on her shoulders for all Messina, as
like him as she is.
  Beat. I wonder that you will still be talking, Signior
Benedick: nobody marks you.
  Bene. What, my dear Lady Disdain! are you yet
living?
  Beat. Is it possible disdain should die, while she
hath such meet food to feed it, as Signior Benedick?
Courtesy itself must convert to disdain, if you come
in her presence.   122
  Bene. Then is courtesy a turncoat. But it is cer-
tain, I am loved of all ladies, you only excepted; and
I would I could find in my heart that I had not a hard
heart; for, truly, I love none.
  Beat. A dear happiness to women: they would else

have been troubled with a pernicious suitor. I thank
God, and my cold blood, I am of your humour for
that: I had rather hear my dog bark at a crow, than
a man swear he loves me.   131
  Bene. God keep your ladyship still in that mind: so
some gentleman or other shall scape a predestinate
scratched face.
  Beat. Scratching could not make it worse, an 't were
such a face as yours were.
  Bene. Well, you are a rare parrot-teacher.
  Beat. A bird of my tongue is better than a beast of
yours.
  Bene. I would, my horse had the speed of your
tongue, and so good a continuer. But keep your way
o' God's name, I have done.   142
  Beat. You always end with a jade's trick: I know
you of old.
  D. Pedro. This is the sum of all: Leonato,—Signior
Claudio, and Signior Benedick,—my dear friend
Leonato hath invited you all. I tell him we shall
stay here at the least a month, and he heartily prays
some occasion may detain us longer: I dare swear he
is no hypocrite, but prays from his heart.   150
  Leon. If you swear, my lord, you shall not be for-
sworn.—Let me bid you welcome, my lord: being re-
conciled to the prince your brother, I owe you all duty.
  John. I thank you: I am not of many words, but I
thank you.
  Leon. Please it your grace lead on?
  D. Pedro. Your hand, Leonato: we will go together.
                    [*Exeunt all but* BENEDICK *and* CLAUDIO.
  Claud. Benedick, didst thou note the daughter of
Signior Leonato?
  Bene. I noted her not; but I looked on her.   160
  Claud. Is she not a modest young lady?
  Bene. Do you question me, as an honest man should
do, for my simple true judgment; or would you have
me speak after my custom, as being a professed tyrant
to their sex?
  Claud. No; I pray thee, speak in sober judgment.
  Bene. Why, i' faith, methinks she's too low for a
high praise, too brown for a fair praise, and too little
for a great praise: only this commendation I can
afford her, that were she other than she is, she were
unhandsome, and being no other but as she is, I do
not like her.   172
  Claud. Thou thinkest, I am in sport: I pray thee,
tell me truly how thou lik'st her.
  Bene. Would you buy her, that you inquire after
her?
  Claud. Can the world buy such a jewel?
  Bene. Yea, and a case to put it into. But speak you
this with a sad brow, or do you play the flouting Jack,
to tell us Cupid is a good hare-finder, and Vulcan a
rare carpenter? Come, in what key shall a man take
you, to go in the song?   182
  Claud. In mine eye she is the sweetest lady that
ever I looked on.
  Bene. I can see yet without spectacles, and I see
no such matter: there's her cousin, an she were not
possessed with a fury, exceeds her as much in beauty,
as the first of May doth the last of December. But I
hope, you have no intent to turn husband, have you?
  Claud. I would scarce trust myself, though I had
sworn the contrary, if Hero would be my wife.   191
  Bene. Is 't come to this, i' faith? Hath not the world
one man, but he will wear his cap with suspicion?
Shall I never see a bachelor of threescore again? Go
to, i' faith; an thou wilt needs thrust thy neck into a
yoke, wear the print of it, and sigh away Sundays.
Look, Don Pedro is returned to seek you.

Re-enter Don PEDRO.

  D. Pedro. What secret hath held you here, that you
followed not to Leonato's?
  Bene. I would your grace would constrain me to
tell.   201
  D. Pedro. I charge thee on thy allegiance.
  Bene. You hear, Count Claudio: I can be secret as
a dumb man, I would have you think so; but on my
allegiance,—mark you this, on my allegiance:—he is
in love. With who?—now that is your grace's part.—

Mark, how short his answer is :—with Hero, Leonato's short daughter.

Claud. If this were so, so were it uttered.

Bene. Like the old tale, my lord ; it is not so, nor 't was not so ; but, indeed, God forbid it should be so. 212

Claud. If my passion change not shortly, God forbid it should be otherwise.

D. Pedro. Amen, if you love her ; for the lady is very well worthy.

Claud. You speak this to fetch me in, my lord.

D. Pedro. By my troth, I speak my thought.

Claud. And in faith, my lord, I spoke mine.

Bene. And by my two faiths and troths, my lord, I spoke mine. 221

Claud. That I love her, I feel.

D. Pedro. That she is worthy, I know.

Bene. That I neither feel how she should be loved, nor know how she should be worthy, is the opinion that fire cannot melt out of me : I will die in it at the stake.

D. Pedro. Thou wast ever an obstinate heretic in the despite of beauty.

Claud. And never could maintain his part, but in the force of his will. 231

Bene. That a woman conceived me, I thank her ; that she brought me up, I likewise give her most humble thanks : but that I will have a recheat winded in my forehead, or hang my bugle in an invisible baldrick, all women shall pardon me. Because I will not do them the wrong to mistrust any, I will do myself the right to trust none ; and the fine is (for the which I may go the finer), I will live a bachelor.

D. Pedro. I shall see thee, ere I die, look pale with love. 241

Bene. With anger, with sickness, or with hunger my lord ; not with love : prove, that ever I lose more blood with love, than I will get again with drinking, pick out mine eyes with a ballad-maker's pen, and hang me up at the door of a brothel-house for the sign of blind Cupid.

D. Pedro. Well, if ever thou dost fall from this faith, thou wilt prove a notable argument.

Bene. If I do, hang me in a bottle like a cat, and shoot at me ; and he that hits me, let him be clapped on the shoulder, and called Adam. 252

D. Pedro. Well, as time shall try :
" In time the savage bull doth bear the yoke."

Bene. The savage bull may ; but if ever the sensible Benedick bear it, pluck off the bull's horns, and set them in my forehead ; and let me be vilely painted, and in such great letters as they write, " Here is good horse to hire," let them signify under my sign,—
" Here you may see Benedick the married man." 260

Claud. If this should ever happen, thou wouldst be horn-mad.

D. Pedro. Nay, if Cupid have not spent all his quiver in Venice, thou wilt quake for this shortly.

Bene. I look for an earthquake too then.

D. Pedro. Well, you will temporise with the hours. In the meantime, good Signior Benedick, repair to Leonato's : commend me to him, and tell him, I will not fail him at supper ; for, indeed, he hath made great preparation. 270

Bene. I have almost matter enough in me for such an embassage ; and so I commit you—

Claud. To the tuition of God : from my house, if I had it,—

D. Pedro. The sixth of July : your loving friend, Benedick.

Bene. Nay, mock not, mock not. The body of your discourse is sometime guarded with fragments, and the guards are but slightly basted on neither : ere you flout old ends any further, examine your conscience, and so I leave you. [*Exit.*

Claud. My liege, your highness now may do me good. 283

D. Pedro. My love is thine to teach : teach it but how,
And thou shalt see how apt it is to learn
Any hard lesson that may do thee good.

Claud. Hath Leonato any son, my lord ?

D. Pedro. No child but Hero, she 's his only heir. Dost thou affect her, Claudio ?

Claud. O ! my lord,
When you went onward on this ended action, 290
I look'd upon her with a soldier's eye,
That lik'd, but had a rougher task in hand,
Than to drive liking to the name of love ;
But now I am return'd, and that war-thoughts
Have left their places vacant, in their rooms
Come thronging soft and delicate desires,
All prompting me how fair young Hero is,
Saying, I lik'd her ere I went to wars.

D. Pedro. Thou wilt be like a lover presently,
And tire the hearer with a book of words. 300
If thou dost love fair Hero, cherish it,
And I will break with her, and with her father,
And thou shalt have her. Was 't not to this end,
That thou begann'st to twist so fine a story ?

Claud. How sweetly do you minister to love,
That know love's grief by his complexion !
But lest my liking might too sudden seem,
I would have salv'd it with a longer treatise.

D. Pedro. What need the bridge much broader than the flood ?
The fairest grant is the necessity. 310
Look, what will serve is fit : 't is once, thou lovest,
And I will fit thee with the remedy.
I know we shall have revelling to-night :
I will assume thy part in some disguise,
And tell fair Hero I am Claudio ;
And in her bosom I 'll unclasp my heart,
And take her hearing prisoner with the force
And strong encounter of my amorous tale :
Then, after, to her father will I break ;
And, the conclusion is, she shall be thine. 320
In practice let us put it presently. [*Exeunt.*

SCENE II.—A Room in LEONATO'S House.

Enter LEONATO *and* ANTONIO.

Leon. How now, brother ? Where is my cousin, your son ? Hath he provided this music ?

Ant. He is very busy about it. But, brother, I can tell you strange news that you yet dreamt not of.

Leon. Are they good ?

Ant. As the event stamps them ; but they have a good cover ; they show well outward. The prince and Count Claudio, walking in a thick-pleached alley in my orchard, were thus much overheard by a man of mine : the prince discovered to Claudio that he loved my niece your daughter, and meant to acknowledge it this night in a dance ; and, if he found her accordant, he meant to take the present time by the top, and instantly break with you of it.

Leon. Hath the fellow any wit, that told you this ?

Ant. A good sharp fellow : I will send for him, and question him yourself. 17

Leon. No, no : we will hold it as a dream, till it appear itself ; but I will acquaint my daughter withal, that she may be the better prepared for an answer, if peradventure this be true. Go you, and tell her of it. [*Several persons cross the stage.*] Cousins, you know what you have to do.—O, I cry you mercy, friend ; go you with me, and I will use your skill.—Good cousin, have a care this busy time. [*Exeunt.*

SCENE III.—Another Room in LEONATO'S House.

Enter JOHN *and* CONRADE.

Con. What the good-year, my lord ! why are you thus out of measure sad ?

John. There is no measure in the occasion that breeds ; therefore the sadness is without limit.

Con. You should hear reason.

John. And when I have heard it, what blessing brings it ?

Con. If not a present remedy, yet a patient sufferance.

John. I wonder, that thou, being (as thou say'st thou art) born under Saturn, goest about to apply a moral medicine to a mortifying mischief. I cannot hide what I am: I must be sad when I have cause, and smile at no man's jests; eat when I have stomach, and wait for no man's leisure; sleep when I am drowsy, and tend on no man's business: laugh when I am merry, and claw no man in his humour.

Con. Yea; but you must not make the full show of this, till you may do it without control-ment. You have of late stood out against your brother, and he hath ta'en you newly into his grace; where it is impossible you should take true root, but by the fair weather that you make yourself: it is needful that you frame the season for your own harvest.

John. I had rather be a canker in a hedge, than a rose in his grace; and it better fits my blood to be disdained of all, than to fashion a carriage to rob love from any: in this, though I cannot be said to be a flattering honest man, it must not be denied but I am a plain-dealing villain. I am trusted with a muzzle, and enfranchised with a clog; therefore I have decreed not to sing in my cage. If I had my mouth, I would bite; if I had my liberty, I would do my liking: in the meantime, let me be that I am, and seek not to alter me.   40

Con. Can you make no use of your discontent?

John. I make all use of it, for I use it only. Who comes here? What news, Borachio?

Enter BORACHIO.

Bora. I came yonder from a great supper: the prince, your brother, is royally entertained by Leonato, and I can give you intelligence of an intended marriage.

John. Will it serve for any model to build mischief on? What is he for a fool that betroths himself to unquietness?   52

Bora. Marry, it is your brother's right hand.

John. Who? the most exquisite Claudio?

Bora. Even he.

John. A proper squire! And who, and who? which way looks he?

Bora. Marry, on Hero, the daughter and heir of Leonato.

John. A very forward March-chick! How came you to this?   61

Bora. Being entertained for a perfumer, as I was smoking a musty room, comes me the prince and Claudio, hand in hand, in sad conference: I whipt me behind the arras, and there heard it agreed upon, that the prince should woo Hero for

Bora. "I whipt me behind the arras."

himself, and having obtained her, give her to Count Claudio.

John. Come, come; let us thither: this may prove food to my displeasure. That young start-up hath all the glory of my overthrow: if I can cross him any way, I bless myself every way. You are both sure, and will assist me?   73

Con. To the death, my lord.

John. Let us to the great supper: their cheer is the greater, that I am subdued. 'Would the cook were of my mind!—Shall we go prove what's to be done?

Bora. We'll wait upon your lordship.   [*Exeunt.*

ACT II.

SCENE I.—A Hall in LEONATO's House.

Enter LEONATO, ANTONIO, HERO, BEATRICE, *and others.*

Leonato.
WAS not Count John here at supper?

Ant. I saw him not.

Beat. How tartly that gentleman looks! I never can see him, but I am heart-burned an hour after.

Hero. He is of a very melancholy dis-position.

Beat. He were an excellent man that were made just in the midway between him and Benedick: the one is too like an image, and says nothing; and the other too like my lady's eldest son, evermore tattling.   12

Leon. Then, half Signior Benedick's tongue in Count John's mouth, and half Count John's melancholy in Signior Benedick's face,—

Beat. With a good leg, and a good foot, uncle, and money enough in his purse, such a man would win any woman in the world,—if he could get her good will.

Leon. By my troth, niece, thou wilt never get thee a husband, if thou be so shrewd of thy tongue.   26

Ant. In faith: she's too curst.

Beat. Too curst is more than curst: I shall lessen God's sending that way, for it is said, "God sends a curst cow short horns;" but to a cow too curst he sends none.

Leon. So, by being too curst, God will send you no horns?

Beat. Just, if he send me no husband; for the which blessing, I am at him upon my knees every morning and evening. Lord! I could not endure a husband with a beard on his face: I had rather lie in the woollen. 32

Leon. You may light on a husband that hath no beard.

Beat. What should I do with him? dress him in my apparel, and make him my waiting-gentlewoman? He that hath a beard is more than a youth, and he that hath no beard is less than a man; and he that is more than a youth is not for me; and he that is less than a man, I am not for him: therefore I will even take sixpence in earnest of the bear-ward, and lead his apes into hell. 42

Leon. Well then, go you into hell?

Beat. No; but to the gate; and there will the devil meet me, like an old cuckold, with horns on his head, and say, "Get you to heaven, Beatrice, get you to heaven; here's no place for you maids:" so deliver I up my apes, and away to Saint Peter: for the heavens, he shows me where the bachelors sit, and there live we as merry as the day is long. 50

Ant. [*To* HERO.] Well, niece, I trust, you will be ruled by your father.

Beat. Yes, faith; it is my cousin's duty to make courtesy, and say, "Father, as it please you:" but yet for all that, cousin, let him be a handsome fellow, or else make another courtesy, and say, "Father, as it please me."

Leon. Well, niece, I hope to see you one day fitted with a husband. 59

Beat. Not till God make men of some other metal than earth. Would it not grieve a woman to be over-mastered with a piece of valiant dust? to make an account of her life to a clod of wayward marl? No, uncle, I'll none: Adam's sons are my brethren; and, truly, I hold it a sin to match in my kindred.

Leon. Daughter, remember what I told you: if the prince do solicit you in that kind, you know your answer.

Beat. The fault will be in the music, cousin, if you be not woo'd in good time: if the prince be too important, tell him, there is measure in everything, and so dance out the answer. For hear me, Hero: wooing, wedding, and repenting, is as a Scotch jig, a measure, and a cinque-pace: the first suit is hot and hasty, like a Scotch jig, and full as fantastical; the wedding, mannerly modest, as a measure, full of state and ancientry; and then comes repentance, and with his bad legs falls into the cinque-pace faster and faster, till he sink into his grave.

Leon. Cousin, you apprehend passing shrewdly. 80

Beat. I have a good eye, uncle: I can see a church by daylight.

Leon. The revellers are entering, brother. Make good room!

Enter Don PEDRO, CLAUDIO, BENEDICK, BALTHAZAR, JOHN, BORACHIO, MARGARET, URSULA, *and others, masked.*

D. Pedro. Lady, will you walk about with your friend?

Hero. So you walk softly, and look sweetly, and say nothing, I am yours for the walk; and especially, when I walk away.

D. Pedro. With me in your company? 90

Hero. I may say so, when I please.

D. Pedro. And when please you to say so?

Hero. When I like your favour; for God defend, the lute should be like the case!

D. Pedro. My visor is Philemon's roof; within the house is Jove.

Hero. Why, then your visor should be thatch'd.

D. Pedro.   Speak low, if you speak love.

[*Takes her aside.*

Balth. Well, I would you did like me.

Marg. So would not I, for your own sake; for I have many ill qualities.

Balth. Which is one? 100

Marg. I say my prayers aloud.

Balth. I love you the better: the hearers may cry Amen.

Marg. God match me with a good dancer!

Balth. Amen.

Marg. And God keep him out of my sight, when the dance is done!—Answer, clerk.

Balth. No more words: the clerk is answered.

Urs. I know you well enough: you are Signior Antonio. 110

Ant. At a word, I am not.

Urs. I know you by the waggling of your head.

Ant. To tell you true, I counterfeit him.

Urs. You could never do him so ill-well, unless you were the very man. Here's his dry hand up and down: you are he, you are he.

Ant. At a word, I am not.

Urs. Come, come: do you think I do not know you by your excellent wit? Can virtue hide itself? Go to, mum, you are he: graces will appear, and there's an end. 121

Beat. Will you not tell me who told you so?

Bene. No, you shall pardon me.

Beat. Nor will you not tell me who you are?

Bene. Not now.

Beat. That I was disdainful, and that I had my good wit out of the "Hundred Merry Tales."—Well, this was Signior Benedick that said so.

Bene. What's he?

Beat. I am sure, you know him well enough. 130

Bene. Not I, believe me.

Beat. Did he never make you laugh?

Bene. I pray you, what is he?

Beat. Why, he is the prince's jester: a very dull fool, only his gift is in devising impossible slanders: none but libertines delight in him; and the commendation is not in his wit, but in his villainy, for he both pleases men, and angers them, and then they laugh at him and beat him. I am sure, he is in the fleet: I would he had boarded me! 140

Bene. When I know the gentleman, I'll tell him what you say.

Beat. Do, do: he'll but break a comparison or two on me; which, peradventure, not marked, or not laughed at, strikes him into melancholy; and then there's a partridge wing saved, for the fool will eat no supper that night. [*Music within.*] We must follow the leaders.

Bene. In every good thing.

Beat. Nay, if they lead to any ill, I will leave them at the next turning. 151

[*Dance. Then exeunt all but* JOHN, BORACHIO, *and* CLAUDIO.

John. Sure, my brother is amorous on Hero, and hath withdrawn her father to break with him about it. The ladies follow her, and but one visor remains.

Bora. And that is Claudio: I know him by his bearing.

John. Are not you Signior Benedick?

Claud. You know me well: I am he.

John. Signior, you are very near my brother in his love: he is enamoured on Hero. I pray you, dissuade him from her; she is no equal for his birth: you may do the part of an honest man in it.

Claud. How know you he loves her?

John. I heard him swear his affection.

Bora. So did I too; and he swore he would marry her to-night.

John. Come, let us to the banquet.

[*Exeunt* JOHN *and* BORACHIO.

Claud. Thus answer I in name of Benedick,
But hear these ill news with the ears of Claudio. 170
'Tis certain so:—the prince woos for himself.
Friendship is constant in all other things,
Save in the office and affairs of love:
Therefore, all hearts in love use their own tongues;
Let every eye negotiate for itself,
And trust no agent; for beauty is a witch,
Against whose charms faith melteth into blood.
This is an accident of hourly proof,
Which I mistrusted not. Farewell, therefore, Hero!

Re-enter Benedick.

Bene. Count Claudio?
Claud. Yea, the same.   180
Bene. Come, will you go with me?

Bene. Why, that's spoken like an honest drover:
so they sell bullocks. But did you think, the prince
would have served you thus?
Claud. I pray you, leave me.
Bene. Ho! now you strike like the blind man:

D. Pedro. "Lady, will you walk about with your friend?"

Claud. Whither?
Bene. Even to the next willow, about your own
business, count. What fashion will you wear the
garland of? About your neck, like an usurer's chain,
or under your arm, like a lieutenant's scarf? You
must wear it one way, for the prince hath got your
Hero.
Claud. I wish him joy of her.   190

't was the boy that stole your meat, and you'll beat
the post.
Claud. If it will not be, I'll leave you.   [*Exit.*
Bene. Alas, poor hurt fowl! Now will he creep into
sedges.—But, that my Lady Beatrice should know me,
and not know me! The prince's fool!—Ha! it may be,
I go under that title, because I am merry.—Yea; but
so I am apt to do myself wrong: I am not so reputed:

it is the base, though bitter disposition of Beatrice, that puts the world into her person, and so gives me out. Well, I 'll be revenged as I may.

Re-enter Don PEDRO.

D. Pedro. Now, signior, where 's the count? Did you see him?

Bene. Troth, my lord, I have played the part of Lady Fame. I found him here as melancholy as a lodge in a warren. I told him, and, I think, I told him true, that your grace had got the good will of this young lady; and I offered him my company to a willow-tree, either to make him a garland, as being forsaken, or to bind him up a rod, as being worthy to be whipped.

D. Pedro. To be whipped! What 's his fault?

Bene. The flat transgression of a school-boy; who, being overjoy'd with finding a birds' nest, shows it his companion, and he steals it.   220

D. Pedro. Wilt thou make a trust a transgression? The transgression is in the stealer.

Bene. Yet it had not been amiss, the rod had been made, and the garland too; for the garland he might have worn himself, and the rod he might have bestow'd on you, who, as I take it, have stolen his birds' nest.

D. Pedro. I will but teach them to sing, and restore them to the owner.

Bene. If their singing answer your saying, by my faith, you say honestly.   231

D. Pedro. The Lady Beatrice hath a quarrel to you: the gentleman, that danced with her, told her she is much wronged by you.

Bene. O! she misused me past the endurance of a block: an oak, but with one green leaf on it, would have answered her: my very visor began to assume life, and scold with her. She told me, not thinking I had been myself, that I was the prince's jester; that I was duller than a great thaw; huddling jest upon jest, with such impossible conveyance, upon me, that I stood like a man at a mark, with a whole army shooting at me. She speaks poniards, and every word stabs: if her breath were as terrible as her terminations, there were no living near her; she would infect to the north star. I would not marry her, though she were endowed with all that Adam had left him before he transgressed: she would have made Hercules have turned spit, yea, and have cleft his club to make the fire too. Come, talk not of her; you shall find her the infernal Até in good apparel. I would to God, some scholar would conjure her, for, certainly, while she is here, a man may live as quiet in hell, as in a sanctuary; and people sin upon purpose, because they would go thither; so, indeed, all disquiet, horror, and perturbation follow her.

Enter CLAUDIO, BEATRICE, HERO, and LEONATO.

D. Pedro. Look, here she comes.

Bene. Will your grace command me any service to the world's end? I will go on the slightest errand now to the Antipodes, that you can devise to send me on: I will fetch you a toothpicker now from the farthest inch of Asia; bring you the length of Prester John's foot; fetch you a hair of the Great Cham's beard; do you any embassage to the Pigmies, rather than hold three words' conference with this harpy. You have no employment for me?

D. Pedro. None, but to desire your good company.

Bene. O God, sir, here 's a dish I love not: I cannot endure my Lady Tongue.   [*Exit.*

D. Pedro. Come, lady, come; you have lost the heart of Signior Benedick.   271

Beat. Indeed, my lord, he lent it me awhile; and I gave him use for it, a double heart for his single one: marry, once before he won it of me with false dice, therefore your grace may well say I have lost it.

D. Pedro. You have put him down, lady; you have put him down.

Beat. So I would not he should do me, my lord, lest I should prove the mother of fools. I have brought Count Claudio, whom you sent me to seek.   280

D. Pedro. Why, how now, count? wherefore are you sad?

Claud. Not sad, my lord.

D. Pedro. How then? sick?

Claud. Neither, my lord.

Beat. The count is neither sad, nor sick, nor merry, nor well; but civil, count, civil as an orange, and something of that jealous complexion.

D. Pedro. I' faith, lady, I think your blazon to be true; though, I 'll be sworn, if he be so, his conceit is false. Here, Claudio, I have wooed in thy name, and fair Hero is won; I have broke with her father, and his good will obtained; name the day of marriage, and God give thee joy!

Leon. Count, take of me my daughter, and with her my fortunes: his grace hath made the match, and all grace say Amen to it!

Beat. Speak, count, 't is your cue.

Claud. Silence is the perfectest herald of joy: I were but little happy, if I could say how much.–Lady, as you are mine, I am yours: I give away myself for you, and dote upon the exchange.   302

Beat. Speak, cousin: or, if you cannot, stop his mouth with a kiss, and let him not speak neither.

D. Pedro. In faith, lady, you have a merry heart.

Beat. Yea, my lord; I thank it, poor fool, it keeps on the windy side of care.–My cousin tells him in his ear, that he is in her heart.

Claud. And so she doth, cousin.

Beat. Good Lord, for alliance!–Thus goes every one to the world but I, and I am sun-burnt. I may sit in a corner, and cry heigh-ho for a husband!   312

D. Pedro. Lady Beatrice, I will get you one.

Beat. I would rather have one of your father's getting. Hath your grace ne'er a brother like you? Your father got excellent husbands, if a maid could come by them.

D. Pedro. Will you have me, lady?

Beat. No, my lord, unless I might have another for working-days: your grace is too costly to wear every day.–But, I beseech your grace, pardon me; I was born to speak all mirth, and no matter.   322

D. Pedro. Your silence most offends me, and to be merry best becomes you; for, out of question, you were born in a merry hour.

Beat. No, sure, my lord, my mother cried; but then there was a star danced, and under that was I born. –Cousins, God give you joy!

Leon. Niece, will you look to those things I told you of?   330

Beat. I cry you mercy, uncle.–By your grace's pardon.   [*Exit.*

D. Pedro. By my troth, a pleasant-spirited lady.

Leon. There 's little of the melancholy element in her, my lord: she is never sad, but when she sleeps; and not ever sad then, for I have heard my daughter say, she hath often dreamed of unhappiness, and waked herself with laughing.

D. Pedro. She cannot endure to hear tell of a husband.

Leon. O! by no means, she mocks all her wooers out of suit.   341

D. Pedro. She were an excellent wife for Benedick.

Leon. O Lord! my lord, if they were but a week married, they would talk themselves mad.

D. Pedro. Count Claudio, when mean you to go to church?

Claud. To-morrow, my lord. Time goes on crutches, till love have all his rites.

Leon. Not till Monday, my dear son, which is hence a just seven-night; and a time too brief too, to have all things answer my mind.   351

D. Pedro. Come, you shake the head at so long a breathing; but, I warrant thee, Claudio, the time shall not go dully by us. I will, in the interim, undertake one of Hercules' labours, which is, to bring Signior Benedick and the Lady Beatrice into a mountain of affection, the one with the other. I would fain have it a match; and I doubt not but to fashion it, if you three will but minister such assistance as I shall give you direction.   360

Leon. My lord, I am for you, though it cost me ten nights' watchings.

Claud. And I, my lord.

D. Pedro. And you too, gentle Hero?

Hero. I will do any modest office, my lord, to help my cousin to a good husband.

D. Pedro. And Benedick is not the unhopefullest husband that I know. Thus far can I praise him : he is of a noble strain, of approved valour, and confirmed honesty. I will teach you how to humour your cousin, that she shall fall in love with Benedick ;—and I, with your two helps, will so practise on Benedick, that, in despite of his quick wit and his queasy stomach, he shall fall in love with Beatrice. If we can do this, Cupid is no longer an archer : his glory shall be ours, for we are the only love-gods. Go in with me, and I will tell you my drift.   [*Exeunt.*

SCENE II.—Another Room in LEONATO'S House.

Enter JOHN *and* BORACHIO.

John. It is so : the Count Claudio shall marry the daughter of Leonato.

Bora. Yea, my lord ; but I can cross it.

John. Any bar, any cross, any impediment will be medicinable to me : I am sick in displeasure to him, and whatsoever comes athwart his affection ranges evenly with mine. How canst thou cross this marriage?

Bora. Not honestly, my lord ; but so covertly that no dishonesty shall appear in me.

John. Show me briefly how.   10

Bora. I think, I told your lordship, a year since, how much I am in the favour of Margaret, the waiting-gentlewoman to Hero.

John. I remember.

Bora. I can, at any unseasonable instant of the night, appoint her to look out at her lady's chamber-window.

John. What life is in that, to be the death of this marriage?   19

Bora. The poison of that lies in you to temper. Go you to the prince your brother : spare not to tell him, that he hath wronged his honour in marrying the renowned Claudio (whose estimation do you mightily hold up) to a contaminated stale, such a one as Hero.

John. What proof shall I make of that?

Bora. Proof enough to misuse the prince, to vex Claudio, to undo Hero, and kill Leonato. Look you for any other issue?

John. Only to despite them, I will endeavour anything.   30

Bora. Go then ; find me a meet hour to draw Don Pedro and the Count Claudio alone : tell them, that you know that Hero loves me ; intend a kind of zeal both to the prince and Claudio (as in love of your brother's honour, who hath made this match, and his friend's reputation, who is thus like to be cozened with the semblance of a maid), that you have discovered thus. They will scarcely believe this without trial : offer them instances, which shall bear no less likelihood than to see me at her chamber-window, hear me call Margaret Hero ; hear Margaret term me Claudio ; and bring them to see this the very night before the intended wedding : for in the meantime I will so fashion the matter, that Hero shall be absent, and there shall appear such seeming truth of Hero's disloyalty, that jealousy shall be call'd assurance, and all the preparation overthrown.

John. Grow this to what adverse issue it can, I will put it in practice. Be cunning in the working this, and thy fee is a thousand ducats.   50

Bora. Be you constant in the accusation, and my cunning shall not shame me.

John. I will presently go learn their day of marriage.   [*Exeunt.*

SCENE III.—LEONATO'S Garden.

Enter BENEDICK.

Bene. Boy !

Enter a Boy.

Boy. Signior.

Bene. In my chamber-window lies a book ; bring it hither to me in the orchard.

Boy. I am here already, sir.

Bene. I know that ; but I would have thee hence, and here again. [*Exit Boy.*] I do much wonder, that one man, seeing how much another man is a fool when he dedicates his behaviours to love, will, after he hath laughed at such shallow follies in others, become the argument of his own scorn by falling in love : and such a man is Claudio. I have known, when there was no music with him but the drum and the fife ; and now had he rather hear the tabor and the pipe : I have known, when he would have walked ten mile afoot to see a good armour ; and now will he lie ten nights awake, carving the fashion of a new doublet. He was wont to speak plain, and to the purpose, like an honest man, and a soldier ; and now is he turn'd orthographer : his words are a very fantastical banquet, just so many strange dishes. May I be so converted, and see with these eyes? I cannot tell ; I think not : I will not be sworn, but love may transform me to an oyster ; but I 'll take my oath on it, till he have made an oyster of me, he shall never make me such a fool. One woman is fair, yet I am well ; another is wise, yet I am well ; another virtuous, yet I am well ; but till all graces be in one woman, one woman shall not come in my grace. Rich she shall be, that 's certain ; wise, or I 'll none ; virtuous, or I 'll never cheapen her ; fair, or I 'll never look on her ; mild, or come not near me ; noble, or not I for an angel ; of good discourse, an excellent musician, and her hair shall be of what colour it please God. Ha ! the prince and Monsieur Love ! I will hide me in the arbour.   [*Withdraws.*

Enter Don PEDRO, LEONATO, *and* CLAUDIO, *followed by* BALTHAZAR *and Musicians.*

D. Pedro. Come, shall we hear this music?

Claud. Yea, my good lord. How still the evening is, As hush'd on purpose to grace harmony !

D. Pedro. See you where Benedick hath hid himself?

Claud. O, very well, my lord : the music ended,   41 We 'll fit the kid-fox with a pennyworth.

D. Pedro. Come, Balthazar, we 'll hear that song again.

Balth. O ! good my lord, tax not so bad a voice To slander music any more than once.

D. Pedro. It is the witness still of excellency, To put a strange face on his own perfection.— I pray thee, sing, and let me woo no more.

Balth. Because you talk of wooing, I will sing ; Since many a wooer doth commence his suit   50 To her he thinks not worthy ; yet he wooes, Yet will he swear he loves.

D. Pedro.   Nay, pray thee, come : Or, if thou wilt hold longer argument, Do it in notes.

Balth.   Note this before my notes ; There 's not a note of mine that 's worth the noting.

D. Pedro. Why, these are very crotchets that he speaks ; Note, notes, forsooth, and noting !   [*Music.*

Bene. [*Aside.*] Now, divine air ! now is his soul ravish'd !—Is it not strange, that sheeps' guts should hale souls out of men's bodies?—Well, a horn for my money, when all 's done.   61

Balth. [*Sings.*]

Sigh no more, ladies, sigh no more,
     Men were deceivers ever ;
One foot in sea, and one on shore ;
     To one thing constant never :
          Then sigh not so,
          But let them go,
And be you blithe and bonny,
Converting all your sounds of woe
     Into, Hey nonny, nonny.   70

Sing no more ditties, sing no mo
     Of dumps so dull and heavy ;
The fraud of men was ever so,
     Since summer first was leavy.
          Then sigh not so, &c.

D. Pedro. By my troth, a good song.

Balth. And an ill singer, my lord.

D. Pedro. Ha? no, no; faith, thou singest well
enough for a shift.　　　　79

Bene. [*Aside.*] An he had been a dog that should
have howled thus, they would have hang'd him; and
I pray God, his bad voice bode no mischief! I had as

Balth. "'Sigh no more, ladies, sigh no more.'"

lief have heard the night-raven, come what plague
could have come after it.

D. Pedro. Yea, marry; dost thou hear, Balthazar?
I pray thee, get us some excellent music, for to-morrow
night we would have it at the Lady Hero's chamber-
window.

Balth. The best I can, my lord.　　　　89

D. Pedro. Do so: farewell. [*Exeunt* BALTHAZAR
and Musicians.] Come hither, Leonato: what was it
you told me of to-day? that your niece Beatrice was in
love with Signior Benedick?

Claud. O, ay.—[*Aside to* PEDRO.] Stalk on, stalk on;
the fowl sits.—I did never think that lady would have
loved any man.

Leon. No, nor I neither; but most wonderful, that
she should so dote on Signior Benedick, whom she
hath in all outward behaviours seemed ever to abhor.

Bene. [*Aside.*] Is't possible? Sits the wind in that
corner?　　　　101

Leon. By my troth, my lord, I cannot tell what to
think of it, but that she loves him with an enraged
affection: it is past the infinite of thought.

D. Pedro. May be, she doth but counterfeit.

Claud. 'Faith, like enough.

Leon. O God! counterfeit! There was never counterfeit of passion came so near the life of passion, as
she discovers it.　　　　109

D. Pedro. Why, what effects of passion shows she?

Claud. [*Aside.*] Bait the hook well: this fish will bite.

Leon. What effects, my lord? She will sit you,—you
heard my daughter tell you how.

Claud. She did, indeed.

D. Pedro. How, how, I pray you? You amaze me:
I would have thought her spirit had been invincible
against all assaults of affection.

Leon. I would have sworn it had, my lord; especially
against Benedick.

Bene. [*Aside.*] I should think this a gull, but that

the white-bearded fellow speaks it: knavery cannot,
sure, hide himself in such reverence.　　　　122

Claud. [*Aside.*] He hath ta'en the infection: hold it up.

D. Pedro. Hath she made her affection known to
Benedick?

Leon. No, and swears she never will: that's her
torment.

Claud. 'Tis true, indeed; so your daughter
says: "Shall I," says she, "that have so oft encountered him with scorn, write to him that I love
him?"　　　　131

Leon. This says she, now, when she is beginning
to write to him; for she'll be up twenty times a
night, and there will she sit in her smock, till she
have writ a sheet of paper.—My daughter tells us
all.

Claud. Now you talk of a sheet of paper, I remember a pretty jest your daughter told us of.

Leon. O!—when she had writ it, and was reading
it over, she found Benedick and Beatrice between
the sheet?—　　　　141

Claud. That.

Leon. O! she tore the letter into a thousand half-
pence; railed at herself, that she should be so immodest to write to one that she knew would flout
her:—"I measure him," says she, "by my own
spirit; for I should flout him, if he writ to me: yea,
though I love him, I should."

Claud. Then down upon her knees she falls,
weeps, sobs, beats her heart, tears her hair, prays,
curses:—"O sweet Benedick! God give me patience!"　　　　152

Leon. She doth indeed: my daughter says so; and
the ecstacy hath so much overborne her, that my
daughter is sometimes afeard she will do a desperate
outrage to herself. It is very true.

D. Pedro. It were good, that Benedick knew of
it by some other, if she will not discover it.

Claud. To what end? He would but make a sport
of it, and torment the poor lady worse.　　　　160

D. Pedro. An he should, it were an alms to hang
him. She's an excellent sweet lady, and, out of all
suspicion, she is virtuous.

Claud. And she is exceeding wise.

D. Pedro. In everything, but in loving Benedick.

Leon. O! my lord, wisdom and blood combating in
so tender a body, we have ten proofs to one, that blood
hath the victory. I am sorry for her, as I have just
cause, being her uncle and her guardian.　　　　169

D. Pedro. I would, she had bestowed this dotage on
me; I would have daff'd all other respects, and made
her half myself. I pray you, tell Benedick of it, and
hear what a' will say.

Leon. Were it good, think you?

Claud. Hero thinks surely, she will die; for she
says, she will die if he love her not, and she will die
ere she make her love known, and she will die if he
woo her, rather than she will bate one breath of her
accustomed crossness.　　　　179

D. Pedro. She doth well: if she should make
tender of her love, 'tis very possible he'll scorn it;
for the man, as you know all, hath a contemptible
spirit.

Claud. He is a very proper man.

D. Pedro. He hath, indeed, a good outward happiness.

Claud. Before God, and in my mind, very wise.

D. Pedro. He doth, indeed, show some sparks that
are like wit.

Leon. And I take him to be valiant.　　　　190

D. Pedro. As Hector, I assure you: and in the
managing of quarrels you may say he is wise; for
either he avoids them with great discretion, or undertakes them with a most Christian-like fear.

Leon. If he do fear God, he must necessarily keep
peace: if he break the peace, he ought to enter into a
quarrel with fear and trembling.

D. Pedro. And so will he do; for the man doth
fear God, howsoever it seems not in him by some
large jests he will make. Well, I am sorry for your
niece. Shall we go seek Benedick, and tell him of
her love?　　　　202

Claud. Never tell him, my lord : let her wear it out with good counsel.

Leon. Nay, that's impossible : she may wear her heart out first.

D. Pedro. Well, we will hear further of it by your daughter : let it cool the while. I love Benedick well, and I could wish he would modestly examine himself, to see how much he is unworthy to have so good a lady. 211

Leon. My lord, will you walk? dinner is ready.

Claud. [*Aside.*] If he do not dote on her upon this, I will never trust my expectation.

D. Pedro. [*Aside.*] Let there be the same net spread for her ; and that must your daughter and her gentlewoman carry. The sport will be, when they hold one an opinion of another's dotage, and no such matter : that's the scene that I would see, which will be merely a dumb-show. Let us send her to call him in to dinner. 221

[*Exeunt Don* PEDRO, CLAUDIO, *and* LEONATO.

Bene. [*Advancing from the arbour.*] This can be no trick : the conference was sadly borne.—They have the truth of this from Hero. They seem to pity the lady : it seems, her affections have their full bent. Love me! why, it must be requited. I hear how I am censured : they say, I will bear myself proudly, if I perceive the love come from her ; they say, too, that she will rather die than give any sign of affection.— I did never think to marry.—I must not seem proud.— Happy are they that hear their detractions, and can put them to mending. They say, the lady is fair : 'tis a truth, I can bear them witness ; and virtuous : 'tis so, I cannot reprove it ; and wise, but for loving me. By my troth, it is no addition to her wit, nor no great argument of her folly, for I will be horribly in love with her. I may chance have some odd quirks and remnants of wit broken on me, because I have railed so long against marriage ; but doth not the appetite alter? A man loves the meat in his youth, that he cannot endure in his age. Shall quips, and sentences, and these paper bullets of the brain, awe a man from the career of his humour? No ; the world must be peopled. When I said I would die a bachelor, I did not think I should live till I were married.—Here comes Beatrice. By this day, she's a fair lady : I do spy some marks of love in her.

Enter BEATRICE.

Beat. Against my will I am sent to bid you come in to dinner.

Bene. Fair Beatrice, I thank you for your pains. 250

Beat. I took no more pains for those thanks, than

Bene. "This can be no trick."

you take pains to thank me : if it had been painful, I would not have come.

Bene. You take pleasure then in the message?

Beat. Yea, just so much as you may take upon a knife's point, and choke a daw withal.—You have no stomach, signior : fare you well. [*Exit.*

Bene. Ha! "Against my will I am sent to bid you come in to dinner;"—there's a double meaning in that. "I took no more pains for those thanks, than you took pains to thank me,"—that's as much as to say, any pains that I take for you is as easy as thanks.—If I do not take pity of her, I am a villain ; if I do not love her, I am a Jew. I will go get her picture. [*Exit.*

ACT III.

SCENE I.—LEONATO'S Garden.

Enter HERO, MARGARET, *and* URSULA.

Hero.

GOOD Margaret, run thee to the parlour ;
There shalt thou find my cousin Beatrice
Proposing with the prince and Claudio :
Whisper her ear, and tell her, I and
    Ursula
Walk in the orchard, and our whole dis-
    course
Is all of her ; say, that thou overheardst
    us,
And bid her steal into the pleached
    bower,
Where honeysuckles, ripen'd by the
    sun,
Forbid the sun to enter ; like favourites,
Made proud by princes, that advance their pride 10
Against that power that bred it.—There will she hide
    her,

To listen our propose. This is thy office ;
Bear thee well in it, and leave us alone.

Marg. I'll make her come, I warrant you, presently.
[*Exit.*

Hero. Now, Ursula, when Beatrice doth come,
As we do trace this alley up and down,
Our talk must only be of Benedick :
When I do name him, let it be thy part
To praise him more than ever man did merit.
My talk to thee must be, how Benedick 20
Is sick in love with Beatrice : of this matter
Is little Cupid's crafty arrow made,
That only wounds by hearsay.

Enter BEATRICE, *behind.*
                           Now begin ;
For look where Beatrice, like a lapwing, runs
Close by the ground, to hear our conference.

Urs. The pleasant'st angling is to see the fish
Cut with her golden oars the silver stream,
And greedily devour the treacherous bait:
So angle we for Beatrice; who even now
Is couched in the woodbine coverture.   30
Fear you not my part of the dialogue.
    Hero. Then go we near her, that her ear lose
        nothing
Of the false sweet bait that we lay for it.—
No, truly, Ursula, she is too disdainful;
I know, her spirits are as coy and wild
As haggards of the rock.
    Urs.   But are you sure
That Benedick loves Beatrice so entirely?
    Hero. So says the prince, and my new-trothed lord.
    Urs. And did they bid you tell her of it, madam?
    Hero. They did entreat me to acquaint her of it; 40
But I persuaded them, if they lov'd Benedick,
To wish him wrestle with affection,
And never to let Beatrice know of it.
    Urs. Why did you so? Doth not the gentleman
Deserve as full as fortunate a bed,
As ever Beatrice shall couch upon?
    Hero. O god of love! I know, he doth deserve
As much as may be yielded to a man;
But Nature never fram'd a woman's heart
Of prouder stuff than that of Beatrice: 50
Disdain and scorn ride sparkling in her eyes,
Misprising what they look on; and her wit
Values itself so highly, that to her
All matter else seems weak. She cannot love,
Nor take no shape nor project of affection,
She is so self-endeared.
    Urs.   Sure, I think so;
And therefore, certainly, it were not good
She knew his love, lest she make sport at it.
    Hero. Why, you speak truth. I never yet saw man,
How wise, how noble, young, how rarely featur'd, 60
But she would spell him backward: if fair-fac'd,
She would swear the gentleman should be her sister;
If black, why, Nature, drawing of an antick,
Made a foul blot; if tall, a lance ill-headed;
If low, an agate very vilely cut;
If speaking, why, a vane blown with all winds;
If silent, why, a block moved with none.
So turns she every man the wrong side out,

BEATRICE IN THE BOWER.

And never gives to truth and virtue that
Which simpleness and merit purchaseth.   70
    Urs. Sure, sure, such carping is not commendable.
    Hero. No; not to be so odd, and from all fashions,

As Beatrice is, cannot be commendable.
But who dare tell her so? If I should speak,
She would mock me into air: O! she would laugh me
Out of myself, press me to death with wit.

Urs. "O! do not do your cousin such a wrong."

Therefore let Benedick, like cover'd fire,
Consume away in sighs, waste inwardly:
It were a better death than die with mocks,
Which is as bad as die with tickling.   80
    Urs. Yet tell her of it: hear what she will say.
    Hero. No; rather I will go to Benedick,
And counsel him to fight against his passion.
And, truly, I'll devise some honest slanders
To stain my cousin with. One doth not know,
How much an ill word may empoison liking.
    Urs. O! do not do your cousin such a wrong.
She cannot be so much without true judgment
(Having so swift and excellent a wit,
As she is priz'd to have), as to refuse   90
So rare a gentleman as Signior Benedick.
    Hero. He is the only man of Italy,
Always excepted my dear Claudio.
    Urs. I pray you, be not angry with me, madam,
Speaking my fancy: Signior Benedick,
For shape, for bearing, argument, and valour,
Goes foremost in report through Italy.
    Hero. Indeed, he hath an excellent good name.
    Urs. His excellence did earn it, ere he had it.—
When are you married, madam?   100
    Hero. Why, every day;—to-morrow. Come, go in:
I'll show thee some attires, and have thy counsel,
Which is the best to furnish me to-morrow.
    Urs. [*Aside.*] She's lim'd, I warrant you: we have
            caught her, madam.
    Hero. [*Aside.*] If it prove so, then loving goes by
            haps:
Some Cupid kills with arrows, some with traps.
                    [*Exeunt* HERO *and* URSULA.
    Beat. [*Advancing.*] What fire is in mine ears? Can
        this be true?

Stand I condemn'd for pride and scorn so much?
Contempt, farewell! and maiden pride, adieu!
No glory lives behind the back of such.   110
And, Benedick, love on: I will requite thee,
Taming my wild heart to thy loving hand.
If thou dost love, my kindness shall incite thee
To bind our loves up in a holy band;
For others say thou dost deserve, and I
Believe it better than reportingly.   [*Exit.*

SCENE II.—A Room in LEONATO's House.

Enter Don PEDRO, CLAUDIO, BENEDICK, *and*
LEONATO.

D. Pedro. I do but stay till your marriage be consummate, and then go I toward Arragon.

Claud. I'll bring you thither, my lord, if you'll vouchsafe me.

D. Pedro. Nay; that would be as great a soil in the new gloss of your marriage, as to show a child his new coat, and forbid him to wear it. I will only be bold with Benedick for his company; for, from the crown of his head to the soul of his foot, he is all mirth: he hath twice or thrice cut Cupid's bowstring, and the little hangman dare not shoot at him. He hath a heart as sound as a bell, and his tongue is the clapper; for what his heart thinks, his tongue speaks.

Bene. Gallants, I am not as I have been.

Leon. So say I: methinks, you are sadder.

Claud. I hope he be in love.

D. Pedro. Hang him, truant! there's no true drop of blood in him, to be truly touch'd with love. If he be sad, he wants money.

Bene. I have the toothache.   20

D. Pedro. Draw it.

Bene. Hang it!

Claud. You must hang it first, and draw it afterwards.

D. Pedro. What! sigh for the toothache?

Leon. Where is but a humour, or a worm?

Bene. Well, every one can master a grief, but he that has it.

Claud. Yet say I, he is in love.   29

D. Pedro. There is no appearance of fancy in him, unless it be a fancy that he hath to strange disguises; as, to be a Dutchman to-day, a Frenchman to-morrow, or in the shape of two countries at once, as a German from the waist downwards, all slops, and a Spaniard from the hip upward, no doublet. Unless he have a fancy to this foolery, as it appears he hath, he is no fool for fancy, as you would have it appear he is.

Claud. If he be not in love with some woman, there is no believing old signs. He brushes his hat o' mornings; what should that bode?   40

D. Pedro. Hath any man seen him at the barber's?

Claud. No, but the barber's man hath been seen with him, and the old ornament of his cheek hath already stuffed tennis-balls.

Leon. Indeed, he looks younger than he did, by the loss of a beard.

D. Pedro. Nay, he rubs himself with civet: can you smell him out by that?

Claud. That's as much as to say, the sweet youth's in love.   50

D. Pedro. The greatest note of it is his melancholy.

Claud. And when was he wont to wash his face?

D. Pedro. Yea, or to paint himself? for the which, I hear what they say of him.

Claud. Nay, but his jesting spirit, which is now crept into a lute-string, and now governed by stops.

D. Pedro. Indeed, that tells a heavy tale for him. Conclude, conclude, he is in love.

Claud. Nay, but I know who loves him.

D. Pedro. That would I know too: I warrant, one that knows him not.   61

Claud. Yes, and his ill conditions; and, in despite of all, dies for him.

D. Pedro. She shall be buried with her face upwards.

Bene. Yet is this no charm for the toothache.—Old

signior, walk aside with me: I have studied eight or nine wise words to speak to you, which these hobby-horses must not hear.

[*Exeunt* BENEDICK *and* LEONATO.

D. Pedro. For my life, to break with him about Beatrice.   71

Claud. 'T is even so. Hero and Margaret have by this played their parts with Beatrice, and then the two bears will not bite one another when they meet.

Enter JOHN.

John. My lord and brother, God save you.

D. Pedro. Good den, brother.

John. If your leisure served, I would speak with you.

D. Pedro. In private?

John. If it please you; yet Count Claudio may hear, for what I would speak of concerns him.   80

D. Pedro. What's the matter?

John. [*To* CLAUD.] Means your lordship to be married to-morrow?

D. Pedro. You know, he does.

John. I know not that, when he knows what I know.

Claud. If there be any impediment, I pray you, discover it.

John. You may think, I love you not: let that appear hereafter, and aim better at me by that I now will manifest. For my brother, I think, he holds you well, and in dearness of heart hath holp to effect your ensuing marriage; surely, suit ill spent, and labour ill bestowed!

D. Pedro. Why, what's the matter?

John. I came hither to tell you; and circumstances shortened (for she has been too long a talking of), the lady is disloyal.

Claud. Who? Hero?

John. Even she: Leonato's Hero, your Hero, every man's Hero.   100

Claud. Disloyal?

John. The word is too good to paint out her wickedness; I could say, she were worse: think you of a worse title, and I will fit her to it. Wonder not till further warrant: go but with me to-night, you shall see her chamber-window entered, even the night before her wedding-day: if you love her then, to-morrow wed her; but it would better fit your honour to change your mind.

Claud. May this be so?   110

D. Pedro. I will not think it.

John. If you dare not trust that you see, confess not that you know. If you will follow me, I will show you enough; and when you have seen more, and heard more, proceed accordingly.

Claud. If I see anything to-night why I should not marry her to-morrow: in the congregation, where I should wed, there will I shame her.

D. Pedro. And, as I wooed for thee to obtain her, I will join with thee to disgrace her.   120

John. I will disparage her no further, till you are my witnesses: bear it coldly but till midnight, and let the issue show itself.

D. Pedro. O day untowardly turned!

Claud. O mischief strangely thwarting!

John. O plague right well prevented! So will you say, when you have seen the sequel.   [*Exeunt.*

SCENE III.—A Street.

Enter DOGBERRY *and* VERGES, *with the Watch.*

Dogb. Are you good men and true?

Verg. Yea, or else it were pity but they should suffer salvation, body and soul.

Dogb. Nay, that were a punishment too good for them, if they should have any allegiance in them, being chosen for the prince's watch.

Verg. Well, give them their charge, neighbour Dogberry.

Dogb. First, who think you the most desartless man to be constable?   10

1 Watch. Hugh Oatcake, sir, or George Seacoal, for they can write and read.

Dogb. Come hither, neighbour Seacoal. God hath blessed you with a good name: to be a well-favoured man is the gift of fortune, but to write and read comes by nature.

2 Watch. Both which, master constable,—

Dogb. You have: I knew it would be your answer. Well, for your favour, sir, why, give God thanks, and make no boast of it; and for your writing and reading, let that appear when there is no need of such vanity. You are thought here to be the most senseless and fit man for the constable of the watch; therefore bear you the lantern. This is your charge. You shall comprehend all vagrom men: you are to bid any man stand, in the prince's name.

2 Watch. How, if a' will not stand?

Dogb. Why, then take no note of him, but let him go; and presently call the rest of the watch together, and thank God you are rid of a knave.　　　　30

Verg. If he will not stand when he is bidden, he is none of the prince's subjects.

Dogb. True, and they are to meddle with none but the prince's subjects.—You shall also make no noise in the streets; for, for the watch to babble and talk is most tolerable, and not to be endured.

2 Watch. We will rather sleep than talk: we know what belongs to a watch.

Dogb. Why, you speak like an ancient and most quiet watchman, for I cannot see how sleeping should offend; only, have a care that your bills be not stolen. Well, you are to call at all the ale-houses, and bid those that are drunk get them to bed.

2 Watch. How, if they will not?

Dogb. Why, then let them alone till they are sober: if they make you not then the better answer, you may say, they are not the men you took them for.

2 Watch. Well, sir.

Dogb. If you meet a thief, you may suspect him, by virtue of your office, to be no true man; and, for such kind of men, the less you meddle or make with them, why, the more is for your honesty.　　　　52

2 Watch. If we know him to be a thief, shall we not lay hands on him?

Dogb. Truly, by your office you may; but, I think, they that touch pitch will be defiled. The most peaceable way for you, if you do take a thief, is, to let him show himself what he is, and steal out of your company.

Verg. You have been always called a merciful man, partner.　　　　61

Dogb. Truly, I would not hang a dog by my will; much more a man who hath any honesty in him.

Verg. If you hear a child cry in the night, you must call to the nurse, and bid her still it.

2 Watch. How, if the nurse be asleep and wi'l not hear us?

Dogb. Why, then depart in peace, and let the child wake her with crying; for the ewe that will not hear her lamb when it baes, will never answer a calf when he bleats.　　　　71

Verg. 'T is very true.

Dogb. This is the end of the charge. You, constable, are to present the prince's own person: if you meet the prince in the night, you may stay him.

Verg. Nay, by 'r lady, that, I think, a' cannot.

Dogb. Five shillings to one on 't, with any man that knows the statues, he may stay him: marry, not without the prince be willing; for, indeed, the watch ought to offend no man, and it is an offence to stay a man against his will.　　　　81

Verg. By 'r lady, I think, it be so.

Dogb. Ha, ha, ha! Well, masters, good night: an there be any matter of weight chances, call up me. Keep your fellows' counsels and your own, and good night. Come, neighbour.

2 Watch. Well, masters, we hear our charge: let us go sit here upon the church-bench till two, and then all to bed.

Dogb. One word more, honest neighbours. I pray you, watch about Signior Leonato's door; for the wedding being there to-morrow, there is a great coil to-night. Adieu, be vigitant, I beseech you.

[*Exeunt* DOGBERRY *and* VERGES.

Enter BORACHIO *and* CONRADE.

Bora. What! Conrade!

Watch. [*Aside.*] Peace! stir not.

Bora. Conrade, I say!

Con. Here, man, I am at thy elbow.

Bora. Mass, and my elbow itched; I thought, there would a scab follow.

Con. I will owe thee an answer for that; and now forward with thy tale.　　　　101

Bora. Stand thee close then under this penthouse, for it drizzles rain, and I will, like a true drunkard, utter all to thee.

Watch. [*Aside.*] Some treason, masters; yet stand close.

Bora. Therefore know, I have earned of Don John a thousand ducats.

Con. Is it possible that any villainy should be so dear?

Bora. Thou shouldst rather ask, if it were possible any villainy should be so rich; for when rich villains have need of poor ones, poor ones may make what price they will.　　　　113

Con. I wonder at it.

Bora. That shows thou art unconfirmed. Thou knowest, that the fashion of a doublet, or a hat, or a cloak, is nothing to a man.

Con. Yes, it is apparel.

Bora. I mean, the fashion.

Con. Yes, the fashion is the fashion.　　　　120

Bora. Tush! I may as well say, the fool's the fool. But seest thou not what a deformed thief this fashion is?

Watch. [*Aside.*] I know that Deformed; a' has been a vile thief this seven year; a' goes up and down like a gentleman. I remember his name.

Bora. Didst thou not hear somebody?

Con. No: 't was the vane on the house.　　　　128

Bora. Seest thou not, I say, what a deformed thief this fashion is? how giddily a' turns about all the hot bloods between fourteen and five-and-thirty? sometime, fashioning them like Pharaoh's soldiers in the reechy painting; sometime, like god Bel's priests in the old church-window; sometime, like the shaven Hercules in the smirched worm-eaten tapestry, where his codpiece seems as massy as his club?

Con. All this I see, and I see that the fashion wears out more apparel than the man. But art not thou thyself giddy with the fashion too, that thou hast shifted out of thy tale into telling me of the fashion?

Bora. Not so neither; but know, that I have to-night wooed Margaret, the Lady Hero's gentlewoman, by the name of Hero: she leans me out at her mistress' chamber-window, bids me a thousand times good night,—I tell this tale vilely:—I should first tell thee, how the prince, Claudio, and my master, planted, and placed, and possessed by my master Don John, saw afar off in the orchard this amiable encounter.

Con. And thought they Margaret was Hero?　　　　149

Bora. Two of them did, the prince and Claudio; but the devil, my master, knew she was Margaret; and partly by his oaths, which first possessed them, partly by the dark night, which did deceive them, but chiefly by my villainy, which did confirm any slander that Don John had made, away went Claudio enraged; swore he would meet her, as he was appointed, next morning at the temple, and there, before the whole congregation, shame her with what he saw over-night, and send her home again without a husband.　　　　160

1 Watch. We charge you in the prince's name, stand.

2 Watch. Call up the right master constable. We have here recovered the most dangerous piece of lechery, that ever was known in the commonwealth.

1 Watch. And one Deformed is one of them: I know him, a' wears a lock.

Con. Masters, masters!

2 Watch. You 'll be made bring Deformed forth, I warrant you.　　　　170

Con. Masters,—

1 Watch. Never speak: we charge you, let us obey you to go with us.

Bora. We are like to prove a goodly commodity, being taken up of these men's bills.

Con. A commodity in question, I warrant you. Come, we 'll obey you.   [*Exeunt.*

1 *Watch.* " We charge you in the prince's name, stand."

SCENE IV.—A Room in LEONATO'S House.

Enter HERO, MARGARET, *and* URSULA.

Hero. Good Ursula, wake my cousin Beatrice, and desire her to rise.

Urs. I will, lady.

Hero. And bid her come hither.

Urs. Well.   [*Exit.*

Marg. Troth, I think, your other rebato were better.

Hero. No, pray thee, good Meg, I 'll wear this.

Marg. By my troth 's not so good; and I warrant, your cousin will say so.

Hero. My cousin 's a fool, and thou art another. I 'll wear none but this.   11

Marg. I like the new tire within excellently, if the hair were a thought browner; and your gown 's a most rare fashion, i' faith. I saw the Duchess of Milan's gown, that they praise so.

Hero. O, that exceeds, they say.

Marg. By my troth 's but a night-gown in respect of yours: cloth o' gold, and cuts, and laced with silver, set with pearls down sleeves, side sleeves, and skirts round, underborne with a bluish tinsel; but for a fine, quaint, graceful, and excellent fashion, yours is worth ten on 't.   22

Hero. God give me joy to wear it, for my heart is exceeding heavy!

Marg. 'T will be heavier soon by the weight of a man.

Hero. Fie upon thee! art not ashamed?

Marg. Of what, lady? of speaking honourably? Is not marriage honourable in a beggar? Is not your lord honourable without marriage? I think, you would have me say, saving your reverence,—a husband: an bad thinking do not wrest true speaking, I 'll offend nobody. Is there any harm in—the heavier for a husband? None, I think, an it be the right husband, and the right wife; otherwise 't is light, and not heavy: ask my Lady Beatrice else; here she comes.

Enter BEATRICE.

Hero. Good morrow, coz.

Beat. Good morrow, sweet Hero.

Hero. Why, how now? do you speak in the sick tune?

Beat. I am out of all other tune, methinks.   40

Marg. Clap us into "Light o' love;" that goes without a burden: do you sing it, and I 'll dance it.

Beat. Yea, "Light o' love," with your heels! —then, if your husband have stables enough, you 'll see he shall lack no barns.

Marg. O illegitimate construction! I scorn that with my heels.

Beat. 'T is almost five o'clock, cousin: 't is time you were ready. By my troth, I am exceeding ill.—Heigh-ho!   51

Marg. For a hawk, a horse, or a husband?

Beat. For the letter that begins them all, H.

Marg. Well, an you be not turned Turk, there 's no more sailing by the star.

Beat. What means the fool, trow?

Marg. Nothing I; but God send every one their heart's desire!

Hero. These gloves the count sent me, they are an excellent perfume.   60

Beat. I am stuffed, cousin, I cannot smell.

Marg. A maid, and stuffed! there 's goodly catching of cold.

Beat. O, God help me! God help me! how long have you profess'd apprehension?

Marg. Ever since you left it. Doth not my wit become me rarely?

Beat. It is not seen enough, you should wear it in your cap.—By my troth, I am sick.

Marg. Get you some of this distilled Carduus Benedictus, and lay it to your heart: it is the only thing for a qualm.   72

Hero. There thou prick'st her with a thistle.

Beat. Benedictus! why Benedictus? you have some moral in this Benedictus.

Marg. Moral? no, by my troth, I have no moral meaning; I meant, plain holy-thistle. You may think, perchance, that I think you are in love: nay, by 'r lady, I am not such a fool to think what I list; nor I list not to think what I can; nor indeed, I cannot think, if I would think my heart out of thinking, that you are in love, or that you will be in love, or that you can be in love. Yet Benedick was such another, and now is he become a man: he swore he would never marry; and yet now, in despite of his heart, he eats his meat without grudging: and how you may be converted, I know not, but, methinks, you look with your eyes as other women do.

Beat. What pace is this that thy tongue keeps?

Marg. Not a false gallop.   90

Re-enter URSULA.

Urs. Madam, withdraw: the prince, the count, Signior Benedick, Don John, and all the gallants of the town, are come to fetch you to church.

Hero. Help to dress me, good coz, good Meg, good Ursula.   [*Exeunt.*

SCENE V.—Another Room in LEONATO'S House.

Enter LEONATO, *with* DOGBERRY *and* VERGES.

Leon. What would you with me, honest neighbour?

Dogb. Marry, sir, I would have some confidence with you, that decerns you nearly.

Leon. Brief, I pray you; for, you see, it is a busy time with me.

Dogb. Marry, this it is, sir.

Verg. Yes, in truth it is, sir.

Leon. What is it, my good friends?

Dogb. Goodman Verges, sir, speaks a little off the matter: an old man, sir, and his wits are not so blunt, as, God help, I would desire they were; but, in faith, honest as the skin between his brows.   12

Verg. Yes, I thank God, I am as honest as any man living, that is an old man, and no honester than I.

Dogb. Comparisons are odorous: palabras, neighbour Verges.

Leon. Neighbours, you are tedious.

Dogb. It pleases your worship to say so, but we are the poor duke's officers; but, truly, for mine own part, if I were as tedious as a king, I could find in my heart to bestow it all of your worship.　　　　21

Leon. All thy tediousness on me? ha!

Dogb. Yea, an 't were a thousand pound more than 'tis; for I hear as good exclamation on your worship, as of any man in the city, and though I be but a poor man, I am glad to hear it.

Verg. And so am I.

Leon. I would fain know what you have to say.

Verg. Marry, sir, our watch to-night, excepting your worship's presence, have ta'en a couple of as arrant knaves as any in Messina.　　　　31

Dogb. A good old man, sir; he will be talking: as they say, when the age is in, the wit is out. God help us! it is a world to see!—Well said, i' faith, neighbour Verges:—well, God's a good man: an two men ride of a horse, one must ride behind.—An honest soul, i' faith, sir: by my troth he is, as ever broke bread; but, God is to be worshipped: all men are not alike; alas, good neighbour!

Leon. Indeed, neighbour, he comes too short of you.

Dogb. Gifts that God gives.　　　　41

Leon. I must leave you.

Dogb. One word, sir. Our watch, sir, have, indeed, comprehended two aspicious persons, and we would have them this morning examined before your worship.

Leon. Take their examination yourself, and bring it me: I am now in great haste, as may appear unto you.

Dogb. It shall be suffigance.

Leon. Drink some wine ere you go. Fare you well.

Enter a Messenger.

Mess. My lord, they stay for you to give your daughter to her husband.　　　　52

Leon. I'll wait upon them: I am ready.

　　　　[*Exeunt* LEONATO *and Messenger.*

Dogb. Go, good partner, go; get you to Francis Seacoal; bid him bring his pen and inkhorn to the gaol: we are now to examination these men.

Verg. And we must do it wisely.

Dogb. We will spare for no wit, I warrant you; here's that shall drive some of them to a *non-com:* only get the learned writer to set down our excommunication, and meet me at the gaol.　　[*Exeunt.*

ACT IV.

Scene I.—The Inside of a Church.

Enter Don Pedro, John, Leonato, *Friar* Francis, Claudio, Benedick, Hero, Beatrice, *&c.*

　　　　Leonato.
OME, Friar Francis, be brief: only to the plain form of marriage, and you shall recount their particular duties afterwards.

Fri. You come hither, my lord, to marry this lady?

Claud. No.

Leon. To be married to her; friar, you come to marry her.

Fri. Lady, you come hither to be married to this count?　　　　11

Hero. I do.

Fri. If either of you know any inward impediment, why you should not be conjoined, I charge you on your souls to utter it.

Claud. Know you any, Hero?

Hero. None, my lord.

Fri. Know you any, count?

Leon. I dare make his answer; none.

Claud. O, what men dare do! what men may do! what men daily do, not knowing what they do!　　21

Bene. How now! Interjections? Why then, some be of laughing, as, ah! ha! he!

Claud. Stand thee by, friar.—Father, by your leave: Will you with free and unconstrained soul Give me this maid, your daughter?

Leon. As freely, son, as God did give her me.

Claud. And what have I to give you back, whose worth May counterpoise this rich and precious gift?

D. Pedro. Nothing, unless you render her again.　30

Claud. Sweet prince, you learn me noble thankfulness.—
There, Leonato, take her back again:
Give not this rotten orange to your friend;
She's but the sign and semblance of her honour.—

Behold, how like a maid she blushes here:
O, what authority and show of truth
Can cunning sin cover itself withal!
Comes not that blood, as modest evidence,
To witness simple virtue? Would you not swear,
All you that see her, that she were a maid,　　40
By these exterior shows? But she is none:
She knows the heat of a luxurious bed;
Her blush is guiltiness, not modesty.

Leon. What do you mean, my lord?

Claud.　　　　　　　　Not to be married,
Not to knit my soul to an approved wanton.

Leon. Dear my lord, if you, in your own proof,
Have vanquish'd the resistance of her youth,
And made defeat of her virginity,—

Claud. I know what you would say: if I have known her,
You'll say, she did embrace me as a husband,　50
And so extenuate the 'forehand sin:
No, Leonato,
I never tempted her with word too large;
But, as a brother to his sister, showed
Bashful sincerity, and comely love.

Hero. And seem'd I ever otherwise to you?

Claud. Out on thee, seeming! I will write against it:
You seem to me as Dian in her orb,
As chaste as is the bud ere it be blown;
But you are more intemperate in your blood　60
Than Venus, or those pamper'd animals
That rage in savage sensuality.

Hero. Is my lord well, that he doth speak so wide?

Claud. Sweet prince, why speak not you?

D. Pedro.　　　　　　　What should I speak?
I stand dishonour'd, that have gone about
To link my dear friend to a common stale.

Leon. Are these things spoken, or do I but dream?

John. Sir, they are spoken, and these things are true.

Bene. This looks not like a nuptial.
Hero.   True! O God!
Claud. Leonato, stand I here?   70
Is this the prince? Is this the prince's brother?
Is this face Hero's? Are our eyes our own?

Claud. To make you answer truly to your name. 80
    Hero. Is it not Hero? Who can blot that name
With any just reproach?
    Claud.   Marry, that can Hero:
Hero itself can blot out Hero's virtue.

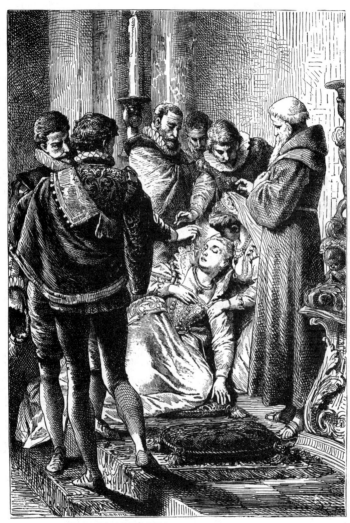

Beat. "Why, how now, cousin! wherefore sink you down?"

Leon. All this is so; but what of this, my lord?
Claud. Let me but move one question to your
            daughter,
And, by that fatherly and kindly power
That you have in her, bid her answer truly.
    Leon. I charge thee do so, as thou art my child.
    Hero. O God, defend me! how am I beset!—
What kind of catechising call you this?

What man was he talk'd with you yesternight
Out at your window, betwixt twelve and one?
Now, if you are a maid, answer to this.
    Hero. I talk'd with no man at that hour, my lord.
    D. Pedro. Why, then are you no maiden.—Leonato,
I am sorry you must hear: upon mine honour,
Myself, my brother, and this grieved count,   90
Did see her, hear her, at that hour last night,

Talk with a ruffian at her chamber-window ;
Who hath, indeed, most like a liberal villain,
Confess'd the vile encounters they have had
A thousand times in secret.
 John. Fie, fie : they are not to be nam'd, my lord,
Not to be spoke of ;
There is not chastity enough in language,
Without offence to utter them. Thus, pretty lady,
I am sorry for thy much misgovernment. 100
 Claud. O Hero ! what a Hero hadst thou been,
If half thy outward graces had been placed
About thy thoughts, and counsels of thy heart !
But, fare thee well, most foul, most fair ! farewell,
Thou pure impiety, and impious purity !
For thee I'll lock up all the gates of love,
And on my eyelids shall conjecture hang,
To turn all beauty into thoughts of harm,
And never shall it more be gracious.
 Leon. Hath no man's dagger here a point for me ?
       [HERO *swoons.*
 Beat. Why, how now, cousin ! wherefore sink you
   down ?   111
 John. Come, let us go. These things, come thus to
   light,
Smother her spirits up.
   [*Exeunt Don* PEDRO, JOHN, *and* CLAUDIO.
 Bene. How doth the lady ?
 Beat.   Dead, I think :—help, uncle !—
Hero ! why, Hero ! — Uncle ! — Signior Benedick ! —
  Friar !
 Leon. O fate ! take not away thy heavy hand :
Death is the fairest cover for her shame,
That may be wish'd for.
 Beat.   How now, cousin Hero ?
 Fri. Have comfort, lady.
 Leon. Dost thou look up ?
 Fri.   Yea ; wherefore should she not ?
 Leon. Wherefore ? Why, doth not every earthly
   thing   121
Cry shame upon her ? Could she here deny
The story that is printed in her blood ?—
Do not live, Hero ; do not ope thine eyes ;
For did I think thou wouldst not quickly die,
Thought I thy spirits were stronger than thy shames,
Myself would, on the rearward of reproaches,
Strike at thy life. Griev'd I, I had but one ?
Chid I for that at frugal Nature's frame ?
O, one too much by thee ! Why had I one ? 130
Why ever wast thou lovely in my eyes ?
Why had I not with charitable hand
Took up a beggar's issue at my gates ;
Who smirched thus, and mir'd with infamy,
I might have said, " No part of it is mine,
This shame derives itself from unknown loins ?"
But mine, and mine I lov'd, and mine I prais'd,
And mine that I was proud on ; mine so much,
That I myself was to myself not mine,
Valuing of her ; why, she—O ! she is fallen 140
Into a pit of ink, that the wide sea
Hath drops too few to wash her clean again,
And salt too little, which may season give
To her foul-tainted flesh !
 Bene.   Sir, sir, be patient.
For my part, I am so attir'd in wonder,
I know not what to say.
 Beat. O, on my soul, my cousin is belied !
 Bene. Lady, were you her bedfellow last night ?
 Beat. No, truly, not ; although, until last night,
I have this twelvemonth been her bedfellow. 150
 Leon. Confirm'd, confirm'd ! O, that is stronger
   made,
Which was before barr'd up with ribs of iron !
Would the two princes lie ? and Claudio lie,
Who lov'd her so, that, speaking of her foulness,
Wash'd it with tears ? Hence from her, let her die.
 Fri. Hear me a little ;
For I have only been silent so long,
And given way unto this course of fortune,
By noting of the lady : I have mark'd
A thousand blushing apparitions   160
To start into her face ; a thousand innocent shames
In angel whiteness beat away those blushes ;

And in her eye there hath appear'd a fire,
To burn the errors that these princes hold
Against her maiden truth.—Call me a fool ;
Trust not my reading, nor my observation,
Which with experimental seal doth warrant
The tenor of my book ; trust not my age,
My reverence, calling, nor divinity,
If this sweet lady lie not guiltless here 170
Under some biting error.
 Leon.   Friar, it cannot be.
Thou seest, that all the grace that she hath left,
Is, that she will not add to her damnation
A sin of perjury : she not denies it.
Why seek'st thou then to cover with excuse
That which appears in proper nakedness ?
 Fri. Lady, what man is he you are accus'd of ?
 Hero. They know that do accuse me, I know none.
If I know more of any man alive,
Than that which maiden modesty doth warrant, 180
Let all my sins lack mercy !—O my father !
Prove you that any man with me convers'd
At hours unmeet, or that I yesternight
Maintain'd the change of words with any creature,
Refuse me, hate me, torture me to death.
 Fri. There is some strange misprision in the princes.
 Bene. Two of them have the very bent of honour ;
And if their wisdoms be misled in this,
The practice of it lives in John the bastard,
Whose spirits toil in frame of villainies. 190
 Leon. I know not. If they speak but truth of her,
These hands shall tear her ; if they wrong her honour,
The proudest of them shall well hear of it.
Time hath not yet so dried this blood of mine,
Nor age so eat up my invention,
Nor fortune made such havoc of my means,
Nor my bad life reft me so much of friends,
But they shall find, awak'd in such a kind,
Both strength of limb, and policy of mind,
Ability in means, and choice of friends, 200
To quit me of them thoroughly.
 Fri.   Pause awhile,
And let my counsel sway you in this case.
Your daughter here the princes left for dead ;
Let her awhile be secretly kept in,
And publish it, that she is dead indeed :
Maintain a mourning ostentation ;
And on your family's old monument
Hang mournful epitaphs, and do all rites
That appertain unto a burial.
 Leon. What shall become of this ? what will this do ?
 Fri. Marry, this, well carried, shall on her behalf
Change slander to remorse ; that is some good : 212
But not for that dream I on this strange course,
But on this travail look for greater birth.
She dying, as it must be so maintain'd,
Upon the instant that she was accus'd,
Shall be lamented, pitied and excus'd
Of every hearer ; for it so falls out,
That what we have we prize not to the worth,
Whiles we enjoy it, but being lack'd and lost, 220
Why, then we rack the value ; then we find
The virtue, that possession would not show us,
Whiles it was ours.—So will it fare with Claudio :
When he shall hear she died upon his words,
The idea of her life shall sweetly creep
Into his study of imagination,
And every lovely organ of her life
Shall come apparell'd in more precious habit,
More moving, delicate, and full of life,
Into the eye and prospect of his soul, 230
Than when she liv'd indeed :—then shall he mourn,
(If ever love had interest in his liver)
And wish he had not so accused her ;
No, though he thought his accusation true.
Let this be so, and doubt not but success
Will fashion the event in better shape
Than I can lay it down in likelihood.
But if all aim but this be levell'd false,
The supposition of the lady's death
Will quench the wonder of her infamy : 240
And, if it sort not well, you may conceal her,
As best befits her wounded reputation.

In some reclusive and religious life,
Out of all eyes, tongues, minds, and injuries.
Bene. Signior Leonato, let the friar advise you:
And though, you know, my inwardness and love
Is very much unto the prince and Claudio,
Yet, by mine honour, I will deal in this
As secretly and justly, as your soul
Should with your body.
Leon.   Being that I flow in grief, 250
The smallest twine may lead me.
Fri. 'T is well consented: presently away,
For to strange sores strangely they strain the cure.—
Come, lady, die to live: this wedding-day,
Perhaps, is but prolong'd: have patience, and endure.
        [*Exeunt Friar,* Hero, *and* Leonato.
Bene. Lady Beatrice, have you wept all this while?
Beat. Yea, and I will weep a while longer.
Bene. I will not desire that.
Beat. You have no reason; I do it freely.
Bene. Surely, I do believe your fair cousin is
wronged.   261
Beat. Ah, how much might the man deserve of me
that would right her!
Bene. Is there any way to show such friendship?
Beat. A very even way, but no such friend.
Bene. May a man do it?
Beat. It is a man's office, but not yours.
Bene. I do love nothing in the world so well as you.
Is not that strange?   269
Beat. As strange as the thing I know not. It were
as possible for me to say, I loved nothing so well as
you; but believe me not, and yet I lie not: I confess
nothing, nor I deny nothing.—I am sorry for my
cousin.
Bene. By my sword, Beatrice, thou lovest me.
Beat. Do not swear by it, and eat it.
Bene. I will swear by it, that you love me; and I
will make him eat it, that says I love not you.
Beat. Will you not eat your word?
Bene. With no sauce that can be devised to it. I
protest, I love thee.   281
Beat. Why then, God forgive me!
Bene. What offence, sweet Beatrice?
Beat. You have stayed me in a happy hour: I was
about to protest, I loved you.
Bene. And do it with all thy heart.
Beat. I love you with so much of my heart, that
none is left to protest.
Bene. Come, bid me do anything for thee.
Beat. Kill Claudio.   290
Bene. Ha! not for the wide world.
Beat. You kill me to deny it. Farewell.
Bene. Tarry, sweet Beatrice.
Beat. I am gone, though I am here.—There is no
love in you.—Nay, I pray you, let me go.
Bene. Beatrice,—
Beat. In faith, I will go.
Bene. We 'll be friends first.
Beat. You dare easier be friends with me, than fight
with mine enemy.   300
Bene. Is Claudio thine enemy?
Beat. Is he not approved in the height a villain,
that hath slandered, scorned, dishonoured my kins-
woman?—O, that I were a man!—What! bear her in
hand until they come to take hands, and then with
public accusation, uncovered slander, unmitigated
rancour,—O God, that I were a man! I would eat his
heart in the market-place.
Bene. Hear me, Beatrice,—
Beat. Talk with a man out at a window!—a proper
saying.   311
Bene. Nay, but, Beatrice,—
Beat. Sweet Hero!—she is wronged, she is slandered,
she is undone.
Bene. Beat—
Beat. Princes, and counties! Surely, a princely
testimony, a goodly count, count-confect; a sweet
gallant, surely! O, that I were a man for his sake!
or that I had any friend would be a man for my sake!
But manhood is melted into courtesies, valour into
compliment, and men are only turned into tongue, and
trim ones too: he is now as valiant as Hercules, that

only tells a lie, and swears it.—I cannot be a man with
wishing, therefore I will die a woman with grieving.
Bene. Tarry, good Beatrice. By this hand, I love
thee.
Beat. Use it for my love some other way than
swearing by it.
Bene. Think you in your soul the Count Claudio
hath wronged Hero?   330
Beat. Yea, as sure as I have a thought, or a soul.
Bene. Enough! I am engaged, I will challenge him.

Beat. "Nay, I pray you, let me go.'

I will kiss your hand, and so I leave you. By this
hand, Claudio shall render me a dear account. As you
hear of me, so think of me. Go, comfort your cousin:
I must say she is dead; and so, farewell.   [*Exeunt.*

Scene II.—A Prison.

Enter Dogberry, Verges, *and Sexton, in gowns;
and the Watch, with* Conrade *and* Borachio.

Dogb. Is our whole dissembly appeared?
Verg. O! a stool and a cushion for the sexton.
Sexton. Which be the malefactors?
Dogb. Marry, that am I and my partner.
Verg. Nay, that 's certain: we have the exhibition
to examine.
Sexton. But which are the offenders that are to be
examined? let them come before master constable.
Dogb. Yea, marry, let them come before me.—What
is your name, friend?   10
Bora. Borachio.
Dogb. Pray, write down Borachio.—Yours, sirrah?
Con. I am a gentleman, sir, and my name is Conrade.
Dogb. Write down master gentleman Conrade.—
Masters, do you serve God?
Con., Bora. Yea, sir, we hope.
Dogb. Write down, that they hope they serve God:
—and write God first; for God defend but God should
go before such villains!—Masters, it is proved already
that you are little better than false knaves, and it will
go near to be thought so shortly. How answer you for
yourselves?   22
Con. Marry, sir, we say we are none.
Dogb. A marvellous witty fellow, I assure you; but
I will go about with him.—Come you hither, sirrah; a
word in your ear, sir: I say to you, it is thought you
are false knaves.
Bora. Sir, I say to you, we are none.
Dogb. Well, stand aside.—'Fore God, they are both
in a tale. Have you writ down, that they are none? 30
Sexton. Master constable, you go not the way to
examine: you must call forth the watch that are their
accusers.
Dogb. Yea, marry, that 's the eftest way.—Let the

watch come forth.—Masters, I charge you, in the prince's name, accuse these men.

1 Watch. This man said, sir, that Don John, the prince's brother, was a villain.

Dogb. Write down—Prince John a villain.—Why, this is flat perjury, to call a prince's brother villain. 40

Bora. Master constable,—

Dogb. Pray thee, fellow, peace: I do not like thy look, I promise thee.

Sexton. What heard you him say else?

2 Watch. Marry, that he had received a thousand ducats of Don John, for accusing the Lady Hero wrongfully.

Dogb. Flat burglary as ever was committed.

Verg. Yea, by the mass, that it is.

Sexton. What else, fellow?   50

1 Watch. And that Count Claudio did mean, upon his words, to disgrace Hero before the whole assembly, and not marry her.

Dogb. O villain! thou wilt be condemned into everlasting redemption for this.

Sexton. What else?

2 Watch. This is all.

Sexton. And this is more, masters, than you can deny. Prince John is this morning secretly stolen away: Hero was in this manner accused, in this very manner refused, and, upon the grief of this, suddenly died. Master constable, let these men be bound, and brought to Leonato's: I will go before, and show him their examination.   [*Exit.*

Dogb. Come, let them be opinioned.

Verg. Let them be in the hands—

Con. Off, coxcomb!

Dogb. God's my life! where's the sexton? let him write down the prince's officer, coxcomb.—Come, bind them.—Thou naughty varlet!   ;0

Con. Away! you are an ass; you are an ass.

Dogb. Dost thou not suspect my place? Dost thou not suspect my years?—O, that he were here to write me down an ass!—but, masters, remember, that I am an ass; though it be not written down, yet forget not

Dogb. "Dost thou not suspect my place? Dost thou not suspect my years?"

that I am an ass.—No, thou villain, thou art full of piety, as shall be proved upon thee by good witness. I am a wise fellow; and, which is more, an officer; and, which is more, a householder; and, which is more, as pretty a piece of flesh as any in Messina; and one that knows the law, go to; and a rich fellow enough, go to; and a fellow that hath had losses; and one that hath two gowns, and everything handsome about him. Bring him away. O, that I had been writ down an ass!   [*Exeunt.*

ACT V.

SCENE I.—Before LEONATO'S House.

Enter LEONATO and ANTONIO.

Antonio.
IF you go on thus, you will kill yourself;
And 't is not wisdom thus to second grief
Against yourself.

Leon.   I pray thee, cease thy counsel,
Which falls into mine ears as profitless
As water in a sieve. Give not me counsel;
Nor let no comforter delight mine ear,
But such a one whose wrongs do suit with mine:
Bring me a father that so lov'd his child,
Whose joy of her is overwhelm'd like mine,
And bid him speak of patience: 10
Measure his woe the length and breadth of mine,
And let it answer every strain for strain;
As thus for thus, and such a grief for such,
In every lineament, branch, shape, and form:
If such a one will smile, and stroke his beard,
And—sorrow, wag!—cry hem, when he should groan;
Patch grief with proverbs; make misfortune drunk
With candle-wasters: bring him yet to me,
And I of him will gather patience.
But there is no such man; for, brother, men   20
Can counsel, and speak comfort to that grief
Which they themselves not feel; but, tasting it,

Their counsel turns to passion, which before
Would give preceptial medicine to rage,
Fetter strong madness in a silken thread,
Charm ache with air, and agony with words.
No, no; 't is all men's office to speak patience
To those that wring under the load of sorrow,
But no man's virtue, nor sufficiency,
To be so moral, when he shall endure   30
The like himself. Therefore give me no counsel:
My griefs cry louder than advertisement.

Ant. Therein do men from children nothing differ.

Leon. I pray thee, peace! I will be flesh and blood;
For there was never yet philosopher,
That could endure the toothache patiently,
However they have writ the style of gods,
And made a push at chance and sufferance.

Ant. Yet bend not all the harm upon yourself;
Make those that do offend you suffer too.   40

Leon. There thou speak'st reason: nay, I will do so.
My soul doth tell me Hero is belied;
And that shall Claudio know; so shall the prince,
And all of them, that thus dishonour her.

Enter Don PEDRO and CLAUDIO.

Ant. Here comes the prince and Claudio hastily.

D. Pedro. Good den, good den.

Claud.   Good day to both of you.
Leon. Hear you, my lords,—
D. Pedro.   We have some haste, Leonato.
Leon. Some haste, my lord!—well, fare you well,
   my lord :—
Are you so hasty now?—well, all is one.
D. Pedro. Nay, do not quarrel with us, good old man.
Ant. If he could right himself with quarrelling,   51
Some of us would lie low.
Claud.   Who wrongs him?
Leon. Marry, thou dost wrong me; thou, dissembler
   thou.—
Nay, never lay thy hand upon thy sword;
I fear thee not.
Claud.   Marry, beshrew my hand,
If it should give your age such cause of fear.
In faith, my hand meant nothing to my sword.

Claud. " In faith, my hand meant nothing to my sword."

Leon. Tush, tush, man! never fleer and jest at
   me :
I speak not like a dotard, nor a fool,
As, under privilege of age, to brag   60
What I have done being young, or what would do,
Were I not old. Know, Claudio, to thy head,
Thou hast so wrong'd mine innocent child and me,
That I am forc'd to lay my reverence by,
And with grey hairs, and bruise of many days,
Do challenge thee to trial of a man.
I say, thou hast belied mine innocent child :
Thy slander hath gone through and through her heart,
And she lies buried with her ancestors,
O! in a tomb where never scandal slept,   70
Save this of hers, fram'd by thy villainy.
Claud. My villainy?
Leon.   Thine, Claudio; thine, I say.
D. Pedro. You say not right, old man.
Leon.   My lord, my lord,
I 'll prove it on his body, if he dare,
Despite his nice fence, and his active practice,
His May of youth, and bloom of lustihood.
Claud. Away! I will not have to do with you.
Leon. Canst thou so daff me? Thou hast kill'd my
   child :
If thou kill'st me, boy, thou shalt kill a man.
Ant. He shall kill two of us, and men indeed: 80
But that 's no matter; let him kill one first ;—
Win me and wear me ;—let him answer me.—
Come, follow me, boy! come, sir boy, come, follow me.
Sir boy, I 'll whip you from your foining fence ;
Nay, as I am a gentleman, I will.
Leon. Brother,—
Ant. Content yourself. God knows, I lov'd my
   niece ;

And she is dead ; slander'd to death by villains,
That dare as well answer a man, indeed,
As I dare take a serpent by the tongue.   90
Boys, apes, braggarts, Jacks, milksops !--
Leon.   Brother Antony,—
Ant. Hold you content. What, man! I know them,
   yea,
And what they weigh, even to the utmost scruple :
Scambling, outfacing, fashion-mong'ring boys,
That lie, and cog, and flout, deprave and slander,
Go antickly, and show outward hideousness,
And speak off half a dozen dangerous words,
How they might hurt their enemies, if they durst ;
And this is all !
Leon. But, brother Antony,—
Ant.   Come, 't is no matter :
Do not you meddle, let me deal in this.   101
D. Pedro. Gentlemen both, we
   will not wake your pa-
   tience.
My heart is sorry for your daugh-
   ter's death ;
But, on my honour, she was
   charg'd with nothing
But what was true, and very full
   of proof.
Leon. My lord, my lord !—
D. Pedro. I will not hear you.
Leon.   No?
Come, brother, away.—I will be
   heard.—
Ant. And shall, or some of us
   will smart for it.
         [*Exeunt* Leonato *and*
                  Antonio.

Enter Benedick.

D. Pedro. See, see : here comes
   the man we went to seek.
Claud. Now, signior, what news?
Bene. Good day, my lord.   111
D. Pedro. Welcome, signior :
you are almost come to part
almost a fray.
Claud. We had like to have
had our two noses snapped off
with two old men without teeth.
D. Pedro. Leonato and his brother. What think'st
thou? Had we fought, I doubt we should have been
too young for them.   120
Bene. In a false quarrel there is no true valour. I
came to seek you both.
Claud. We have been up and down to seek thee ;
for we are high-proof melancholy, and would fain
have it beaten away. Wilt thou use thy wit?
Bene. It is in my scabbard ; shall I draw it?
D. Pedro. Dost thou wear thy wit by thy side ?
Claud. Never any did so, though very many have
been beside their wit.—I will bid thee draw, as we do
the minstrels ; draw to pleasure us.   130
D. Pedro. As I am an honest man, he looks pale.—
Art thou sick, or angry ?
Claud. What! courage, man! What though care
killed a cat, thou hast mettle enough in thee to kill
care.
Bene. Sir, I shall meet your wit in the career, an
you charge it against me.—I pray you, choose another
subject.
Claud. Nay, then give him another staff : this last
was broke cross.   140
D. Pedro. By this light, he changes more and more.
I think he be angry indeed.
Claud. If he be, he knows how to turn his girdle.
Bene. Shall I speak a word in your ear ?
Claud. God bless me from a challenge !
Bene. You are a villain.—I jest not. I will make it
good how you dare, with what you dare, and when
you dare.—Do me right, or I will protest your
cowardice. You have killed a sweet lady, and her
death shall fall heavy on you. Let me hear from you.
Claud. Well, I will meet you, so I may have good
cheer.   152

D. Pedro. What, a feast? a feast?

Claud. I' faith, I thank him; he hath bid me to a calf's-head and a capon, the which if I do not carve most curiously, say my knife's naught.—Shall I not find a woodcock too?

Bene. Sir, your wit ambles well: it goes easily.

D. Pedro. I'll tell thee how Beatrice praised thy wit the other day. I said, thou hadst a fine wit. "True," said she, "a fine little one." "No," said I, "a great wit." "Right," says she, "a great gross one." "Nay," said I, "a good wit." "Just," said she, "it hurts nobody." "Nay," said I, "the gentleman is wise." "Certain," said she, "a wise gentleman." "Nay," said I, "he hath the tongues." "That I believe," said she, "for he swore a thing to me on Monday night, which he forswore on Tuesday morning: there's a double tongue; there's two tongues." Thus did she, an hour together, trans-shape thy particular virtues; yet at last she concluded with a sigh, thou wast the properest man in Italy.

Claud. For the which she wept heartily, and said she cared not.

D. Pedro. Yea, that she did; but yet, for all that, an if she did not hate him deadly, she would love him dearly. The old man's daughter told us all. 180

Claud. All, all; and moreover, God saw him when he was hid in the garden.

D. Pedro. But when shall we set the savage bull's horns on the sensible Benedick's head?

Claud. Yea, and text underneath, "Here dwells Benedick the married man!" 189

Bene. Fare you well, boy: you know my mind. I will leave you now to your gossip-like humour: you break jests as braggarts do their blades, which, God be thanked, hurt not.— My lord, for your many courtesies I thank you: I must discontinue your company. Your brother, the bastard, is fled from Messina: you have, among you, killed a sweet and innocent lady. For my Lord Lackbeard there, he and I shall meet; and till then, peace be with him. [*Exit.*

D. Pedro. He is in earnest. 202

Claud. In most profound earnest; and, I'll warrant you, for the love of Beatrice.

D. Pedro. And hath challenged thee?

Claud. Most sincerely.

D. Pedro. What a pretty thing man is, when he goes in his doublet and hose, and leaves off his wit!

Claud. He is then a giant to an ape; but then is an ape a doctor to such a man. 210

D. Pedro. But, soft you; let me be: pluck up, my heart, and be sad! Did he not say, my brother was fled?

Enter DOGBERRY, VERGES, *and the Watch, with* CONRADE *and* BORACHIO.

Dogb. Come you, sir: if justice cannot tame you, she shall ne'er weigh more reasons in her balance. Nay, an you be a cursing hypocrite once, you must be looked to.

D. Pedro. How now! two of my brother's men bound? Borachio one?

Claud. Hearken after their offence, my lord! 220

D. Pedro. Officers, what offence have these men done?

Dogb. Marry, sir, they have committed false report; moreover, they have spoken untruths; secondarily, they are slanders; sixth and lastly, they have belied a lady; thirdly, they have verified unjust things; and, to conclude, they are lying knaves.

D. Pedro. First, I ask thee what they have done; thirdly, I ask thee what's their offence; sixth and lastly, why they are committed; and, to conclude, what you lay to their charge. 231

Claud. Rightly reasoned, and in his own division; and, by my troth, there's one meaning well suited.

D. Pedro. Who have you offended, masters, that you are thus bound to your answer? this learned constable is too cunning to be understood. What's your offence?

Bora. Sweet prince, let me go no further to mine answer: do you hear me, and let this count kill me. I have deceived even your very eyes: what your wisdoms could not discover, these shallow fools have brought to light; who, in the night, overheard me confessing to this man, how Don John your brother incensed me to slander the Lady Hero; how you were brought into the orchard, and saw me court Margaret in Hero's garments; how you disgraced her, when you should marry her. My villainy they have upon record, which I had rather seal with my death, than

Dogb. "Marry, sir, they have committed false report."

repeat over to my shame. The lady is dead upon mine and my master's false accusation; and, briefly, I desire nothing but the reward of a villain. 250

D. Pedro. Runs not this speech like iron through your blood?

Claud. I have drunk poison whiles he utter'd it.

D. Pedro. But did my brother set thee on to this?

Bora. Yea; and paid me richly for the practice of it.

D. Pedro. He is compos'd and fram'd of treachery.— And fled he is upon this villainy.

Claud. Sweet Hero! now thy image doth appear In the rare semblance that I loved it first.

Dogb. Come, bring away the plaintiffs: by this time our sexton hath reformed Signior Leonato of the matter. And, masters, do not forget to specify, when time and place shall serve, that I am an ass. 262

Verg. Here, here comes master Signior Leonato, and the sexton too.

Re-enter LEONATO, ANTONIO, *and the Sexton.*

Leon. Which is the villain? Let me see his eyes, That when I note another man like him, I may avoid him. Which of these is he?

Bora. If you would know your wronger, look on me.

Leon. Art thou the slave, that with thy breath hast kill'd Mine innocent child?

Bora. Yea, even I alone. 270

Leon. No, not so, villain; thou beliest thyself: Here stand a pair of honourable men, A third is fled, that had a hand in it.— I thank you, princes, for my daughter's death: Record it with your high and worthy deeds. 'T was bravely done, if you bethink you of it.

Claud. I know not how to pray your patience,
Yet I must speak. Choose your revenge yourself;
Impose me to what penance your invention
Can lay upon my sin : yet sinn'd I not,   280
But in mistaking.
      D. Pedro.   By my soul, nor I ;
And yet, to satisfy this good old man,
I would bend under any heavy weight
That he 'll enjoin me to.
      Leon. I cannot bid my daughter live
That were impossible : but, I pray you both,
Possess the people in Messina here,
How innocent she died ; and, if your love
Can labour aught in sad invention,
Hang her an epitaph upon her tomb,   290
And sing it to her bones : sing it to-night.—
To-morrow morning come you to my house,
And since you could not be my son-in-law,
Be yet my nephew. My brother hath a daughter,
Almost the copy of my child that 's dead,
And she alone is heir to both of us :
Give her the right you should have given her cousin,
And so dies my revenge.
      Claud.   O noble sir,
Your over-kindness doth wring tears from me.
I do embrace your offer ; and dispose   300
From henceforth of poor Claudio.
      Leon. To-morrow then I will expect your coming ;
To-night I take my leave.—This naughty man
Shall face to face be brought to Margaret,
Who, I believe, was pack'd in all this wrong,
Hir'd to it by your brother.
      Bora.   No, by my soul, she was not ;
Nor knew not what she did, when she spoke to me ;
But always hath been just and virtuous,
In anything that I do know by her.   309
      Dogb. Moreover, sir, which, indeed, is not under
white and black, this plaintiff here, the offender, did
call me ass : I beseech you, let it be remembered in his
punishment. And also, the watch heard them talk of
one Deformed : they say, he wears a key in his ear,
and a lock hanging by it, and borrows money in God's
name ; the which he hath used so long, and never
paid, that now men grow hard-hearted, and will lend
nothing for God's sake. Pray you, examine him upon
that point.   320
      Leon. I thank thee for thy care and honest pains.
      Dogb. Your worship speaks like a most thankful
and reverend youth, and I praise God for you.
      Leon. There 's for thy pains.
      Dogb. God save the foundation !
      Leon. Go, I discharge thee of thy prisoner, and I
thank thee.
      Dogb. I leave an arrant knave with your worship ;
which I beseech your worship to correct yourself for
the example of others. God keep your worship ; I
wish your worship well : God restore you to health.
I humbly give you leave to depart, and if a merry
meeting may be wished, God prohibit it !—Come,
neighbour. [*Exeunt* DOGBERRY, VERGES, *and Watch.*
      Leon. Until to-morrow morning, lords, farewell.
      Ant. Farewell, my lords : we look for you to-morrow.
      D. Pedro. We will not fail.
      Claud.   To-night I 'll mourn with Hero.
            [*Exeunt Don* PEDRO *and* CLAUDIO.
      Leon. Bring you these fellows on. We 'll talk with
            Margaret,
How her acquaintance grew with this lewd fellow.
                              [*Exeunt.*

SCENE II.—LEONATO'S Garden.

Enter BENEDICK *and* MARGARET, *meeting.*

      Bene. Pray thee, sweet Mistress Margaret, deserve
well at my hands by helping me to the speech of
Beatrice.
      Marg. Will you then write me a sonnet in praise of
my beauty ?
      Bene. In so high a style, Margaret, that no man
living shall come over it ; for, in most comely truth,
thou deservest it.

      Marg. To have no man come over me ? why, shall
I always keep below stairs ?   10
      Bene. Thy wit is as quick as the greyhound's mouth ;
it catches.
      Marg. And yours as blunt as the fencer's foils,
which hit, but hurt not.
      Bene. A most manly wit. Margaret ; it will not hurt
a woman : and so, I pray thee, call Beatrice. I give
thee the bucklers.
      Marg. Give us the swords, we have bucklers of our
own.
      Bene. If you use them, Margaret, you must put in
the pikes with a vice ; and they are dangerous
weapons for maids.   22
      Marg. Well, I will call Beatrice to you, who, I
think, hath legs.
      Bene. And therefore will come.   [*Exit* MARG.
      [*Singing.*]   *The god of love,*
                              That sits above,
            And knows me, and knows me,
                  How pitiful I deserve,—

I mean, in singing ; but in loving, Leander the good
swimmer, Troilus the first employer of panders, and a
whole book full of these quondam carpet-mongers,
whose names yet run smoothly in the even road of a
blank verse, why, they were never so truly turned
over and over as my poor self in love. Marry, I
cannot show it in rhyme ; I have tried : I can find out
no rhyme to "lady" but "baby," an innocent rhyme ;
for "scorn," "horn," a hard rhyme ; for "school,"
"fool," a babbling rhyme,—very ominous endings.
No, I was not born under a rhyming planet, nor I
cannot woo in festival terms.   41

Enter BEATRICE.

Sweet Beatrice, wouldst thou come when I called
thee ?
      Beat. Yea, signior ; and depart when you bid me.
      Bene. O, stay but till then !
      Beat. "Then" is spoken ; fare you well now :—and
yet, ere I go, let me go with that I came ; which is,
with knowing what hath passed between you and
Claudio.
      Bene. Only foul words ; and thereupon I will kiss
thee.   51
      Beat. Foul words is but foul wind, and foul wind is
but foul breath, and foul breath is noisome ; therefore
I will depart unkissed.
      Bene. Thou hast frighted the word out of his right
sense, so forcible is thy wit. But, I must tell thee
plainly, Claudio undergoes my challenge, and either I
must shortly hear from him, or I will subscribe him a
coward. And, I pray thee now, tell me, for which of
my bad parts didst thou first fall in love with me ? 60
      Beat. For them all together ; which maintained so
politic a state of evil, that they will not admit any
good part to intermingle with them. But for which
of my good parts did you first suffer love for me ?
      Bene. Suffer love ! a good epithet. I do suffer love,
indeed, for I love thee against my will.
      Beat. In spite of your heart, I think. Alas, poor
heart ! If you spite it for my sake, I will spite it for
yours ; for I will never love that which my friend
hates.   70
      Bene. Thou and I are too wise to woo peaceably.
      Beat. It appears not in this confession : there 's not
one wise man among twenty that will praise himself.
      Bene. An old, an old instance, Beatrice, that lived
in the time of good neighbours. If a man do not
erect in this age, his own tomb ere he dies, he shall
live no longer in monument, than the bell rings, and
the widow weeps.
      Beat. And how long is that, think you ?   79
      Bene. Question :—why, an hour in clamour, and a
quarter in rheum : therefore is it most expedient for
the wise (if Don Worm, his conscience, find no
impediment to the contrary), to be the trumpet of
his own virtues, as I am to myself. So much for
praising myself, who, I myself will bear witness, is
praiseworthy And now tell me, how doth your
cousin ?

Beat. Very ill.

Bene. And how do you?

Beat. Very ill too.　　90

Bene. Serve God, love me, and mend. There will I leave you too, for here comes one in haste.

Enter URSULA.

Urs. Madam, you must come to your uncle. Yonder's old coil at home: it is proved, my Lady Hero hath been falsely accused, the prince and Claudio mightily abused; and Don John is the author of all, who is fled and gone. Will you come presently?

Beat. Will you go hear this news, signior?

Beat. "Will you go hear this news, signior?"

Bene. I will live in thy heart, die in thy lap, and be buried in thy eyes; and, moreover, I will go with thee to thy uncle's.　　[*Exeunt.*

SCENE III.—The Inside of a Church.

Enter Don PEDRO, CLAUDIO, *and Attendants, with music and tapers.*

Claud. Is this the monument of Leonato?

Atten. It is, my lord.

Claud. [*Reads from a scroll.*]

　"*Done to death by slanderous tongues*
　　Was the Hero that here lies:
　Death, in guerdon of her wrongs,
　　Gives her fame which never dies.
　So the life, that died with shame,
　　Lives in death with glorious fame."

Hang thou there upon the tomb,
Praising her when I am dumb.—　　10
Now, music, sound, and sing your solemn hymn.

SONG.

　Pardon, goddess of the night,
　Those that slew thy virgin knight;
　For the which, with songs of woe,
　Round about her tomb they go.
　Midnight, assist our moan;
　Help us to sigh and groan,
　　Heavily, heavily:
　Graves, yawn, and yield your dead,
　Till death be uttered,　　20
　　Heavily, heavily.

Claud. Now, unto thy bones good night!
Yearly will I do this rite.

D. Pedro. Good morrow, masters: put your torches out.
The wolves have prey'd; and look, the gentle day,
Before the wheels of Phœbus, round about
Dapples the drowsy east with spots of grey.
Thanks to you all, and leave us: fare you well.

Claud. Good morrow, masters: each his several way.

D. Pedro. Come, let us hence, and put on other weeds;　　30
And then to Leonato's we will go.

Claud. And Hymen now with luckier issue speed's,
Than this, for whom we render'd up this woe!

　　　　　　　　　　[*Exeunt.*

SCENE IV.—A Room in LEONATO'S House.

Enter LEONATO, ANTONIO, BENEDICK, MARGARET, BEATRICE, URSULA, *Friar* FRANCIS, *and* HERO.

Fri. Did I not tell you she was innocent?

Leon. So are the prince and Claudio, who accus'd her
Upon the error that you heard debated:
But Margaret was in some fault for this,
Although against her will, as it appears
In the true course of all the question.

Ant. Well, I am glad that all things sort so well.

Bene. And so am I, being else by faith enforc'd
To call young Claudio to a reckoning for it.

Leon. Well, daughter, and you gentlewomen all,　　10
Withdraw into a chamber by yourselves,
And, when I send for you, come hither mask'd:
The prince and Claudio promis'd by this hour
To visit me. [*Exeunt Ladies.*]—You know your office, brother:
You must be father to your brother's daughter,
And give her to young Claudio.

Ant. Which I will do with confirm'd countenance.

Bene. Friar, I must entreat your pains, I think.

Fri. To do what, signior?

Bene. To bind me, or undo me; one of them.—　　20
Signior Leonato, truth it is, good signior,
Your niece regards me with an eye of favour.

Leon. That eye my daughter lent her: 'tis most true.

Bene. And I do with an eye of love requite her.

Leon. The sight whereof, I think, you had from me,
From Claudio, and the prince. But what's your will?

Bene. Your answer, sir, is enigmatical:
But, for my will, my will is, your good will
May stand with ours, this day to be conjoin'd
In the state of honourable marriage:—　　30
In which, good friar, I shall desire your help.

Leon. My heart is with your liking.

Fri.　　　　　　　　And my help.
Here come the prince and Claudio.

Enter Don PEDRO *and* CLAUDIO, *with Attendants.*

D. Pedro. Good morrow to this fair assembly.

Leon. Good morrow, prince; good morrow, Claudio:
We here attend you. Are you yet determin'd
To-day to marry with my brother's daughter?

Claud. I'll hold my mind, were she an Ethiop.

Leon. Call her forth, brother: here's the friar ready.

　　　　　　　　　　[*Exit* ANTONIO.

D. Pedro. Good morrow, Benedick. Why, what's the matter,　　40
That you have such a February face,
So full of frost, of storm, and cloudiness?

Claud. I think, he thinks upon the savage bull.—
Tush! fear not, man, we'll tip thy horns with gold,
And all Europa shall rejoice at thee,
As once Europa did at lusty Jove,
When he would play the noble beast in love.

Bene. Bull Jove, sir, had an amiable low:
And some such strange bull leap'd your father's cow,
And got a calf in that same noble feat,　　50
Much like to you, for you have just his bleat.

Re-enter ANTONIO, *with the Ladies masked.*

Claud. For this I owe you, here come other reckonings.
Which is the lady I must seize upon?

Ant. This same is she, and I do give you her.
Claud. Why, then she 's mine.—Sweet, let me see
   your face.
Leon. No, that you shall not, till you take her hand
Before this friar, and swear to marry her.

One Hero died defil'd ; but I do live,
And, surely as I live, I am a maid.
   D. Pedro. The former Hero ! Hero that is dead !
Leon. She died, my lord, but whiles her slander liv'd.
Fri. All this amazement can I qualify :

Claud. "Give me your hand before this holy friar :
I am your husband, if you like of me."

Claud. Give me your hand before this holy friar :
I am your husband, if you like of me.
   Hero. And when I liv'd, I was your other wife : 60
                                              [*Unmasking.*
And when you lov'd, you were my other husband.
   Claud. Another Hero ?
   Hero.   Nothing certainer.

When after that the holy rites are ended,
I 'll tell you largely of fair Hero's death :
Meantime, let wonder seem familiar,
And to the chapel let us presently.
   Bene. Soft and fair, friar.—Which is Beatrice ?
   Beat. I answer to that name. [*Unmasking.*] What
      is your will ?

70

Bene. Do not you love me?

Beat. Why, no; no more than reason.

Bene. Why, then, your uncle, and the prince, and Claudio, have been deceived: they swore you did.

Beat. Do not you love me?

Bene. Troth, no; no more than reason.

Beat. Why, then my cousin, Margaret, and Ursula, Are much deceiv'd; for they did swear you did.   81

Bene. They swore that you were almost sick for me.

Beat. They swore that you were well-nigh dead for me.

Bene. 'T is no such matter.—Then, you do not love me?

Beat. No, truly, but in friendly recompense.

Leon. Come, cousin, I am sure you love the gentleman.

Claud. And I 'll be sworn upon 't, that he loves her; For here 's a paper, written in his hand, A halting sonnet of his own pure brain, Fashion'd to Beatrice.

Hero.   And here 's another,   90 Writ in my cousin's hand, stol'n from her pocket, Containing her affection unto Benedick.

Bene. A miracle! here 's our own hands against our hearts.—Come, I will have thee; but, by this light, I take thee for pity.

Beat. I would not deny you;—but, by this good day, I yield upon great persuasion, and, partly, to save your life, for I was told you were in a consumption.

Bene. Peace! I will stop your mouth.

D. Pedro. How dost thou, Benedick, the married man?   101

Bene. I 'll tell thee what, prince; a college of wit-crackers cannot flout me out of my humour. Dost thou think, I care for a satire, or an epigram? No: if a man will be beaten with brains, a' shall wear nothing handsome about him. In brief, since I do purpose to marry, I will think nothing to any purpose that the world can say against it; and therefore never flout at me for what I have said against it, for man is a giddy thing, and this is my conclusion.—For thy part, Claudio, I did think to have beaten thee; but, in that thou art like to be my kinsman, live unbruised, and love my cousin.

Claud. I had well hoped, thou wouldst have denied Beatrice, that I might have cudgelled thee out of thy single life, to make thee a double-dealer; which, out of question, thou wilt be if my cousin do not look exceeding narrowly to thee.

Bene. Come, come, we are friends.—Let 's have a dance ere we are married, that we may lighten our own hearts, and our wives' heels.   121

Leon. We 'll have dancing afterward.

Bene. First, of my word; therefore play, music!-Prince, thou art sad; get thee a wife, get thee a wife: there is no staff more reverend than one tipped with horn.

Enter a Messenger.

Mess. My lord, your brother John is ta'en in flight, And brought with armed men back to Messina.

Bene. Think not on him till to-morrow: I 'll devise thee brave punishments for him.—Strike up, pipers.

[*Dance. Exeunt.*

LOVE'S LABOUR'S LOST.

DRAMATIS PERSONÆ.

FERDINAND, *King of Navarre.*
BIRON, ⎫
LONGAVILLE, ⎬ *Lords attending on the King.*
DUMAINE, ⎭
BOYET, ⎫ *Lords attending on the Princess of*
MERCADE, ⎬   *France.*
DON ADRIANO DE ARMADO, *a fantastical Spaniard.*
SIR NATHANIEL, *a Curate.*
HOLOFERNES, *a Schoolmaster.*
DULL, *a Constable.*
COSTARD, *a Clown.*

MOTH, *Page to Armado.*
A *Forester.*

PRINCESS OF FRANCE.
ROSALINE, ⎫
MARIA, ⎬ *Ladies attending on the Princess.*
KATHARINE, ⎭
JAQUENETTA, *a Country Wench.*

*Officers and Others, Attendants on the King and
    Princess.*

SCENE—NAVARRE.

ACT I.

SCENE I.—Navarre. A Park, with a Palace in it.

Enter the KING, BIRON, LONGAVILLE, *and* DUMAINE.

King.
LET fame, that all hunt after in their
    lives,
Live register'd upon our brazen tombs,
And then grace us in the disgrace of
    death,
When, spite of cormorant devouring
    time,
The endeavour of this present breath
    may buy
That honour, which shall bate his scythe's
    keen edge,
And make us heirs of all eternity.
Therefore, brave conquerors!—for so you are,
That war against your own affections,
And the huge army of the world's desires,— 10
Our late edict shall strongly stand in force :
Navarre shall be the wonder of the world ;
Our court shall be a little academe,
Still and contemplative in living art.
You three, Biron, Dumaine, and Longaville,
Have sworn for three years' term to live with me,
My fellow-scholars, and to keep those statutes
That are recorded in this schedule here :
Your oaths are pass'd, and now subscribe your names,
That his own hand may strike his honour down, 20
That violates the smallest branch herein.
If you are arm'd to do, as sworn to do,
Subscribe to your deep oaths, and keep it too.

Long. I am resolv'd : 't is but a three years' fast.
The mind shall banquet, though the body pine :
Fat paunches have lean pates ; and dainty bits
Make rich the ribs, but bankerout the wits.

Dum. My loving lord, Dumaine is mortified.
The grosser manner of these world's delights
He throws upon the gross world's baser slaves : 30
To love, to wealth, to pomp, I pine and die,
With all these living in philosophy.

Biron. I can but say their protestation over,
So much, dear liege, I have already sworn,
That is, to live and study here three years.
But there are other strict observances,
As, not to see a woman in that term,—

Which, I hope well, is not enrolled there :
And, one day in a week to touch no food,
And but one meal on every day beside ; 40
The which, I hope, is not enrolled there :
And then, to sleep but three hours in the night,
And not be seen to wink of all the day,
(When I was wont to think no harm all night,
And make a dark night too of half the day)—
Which, I hope well, is not enrolled there.
O ! these are barren tasks, too hard to keep,
Not to see ladies, study, fast, not sleep.

King. Your oath is pass'd to pass away from these.

Biron. Let me say no, my liege, an if you please. 50
I only swore to study with your grace,
And stay here in your court for three years' space.

Long. You swore to that, Biron, and to the rest.

Biron. By yea and nay, sir, then I swore in jest.—
What is the end of study ? let me know.

King. Why, that to know which else we should
    not know.

Biron. Things hid and barr'd, you mean, from com-
    mon sense ?

King. Ay, that is study's god-like recompense.

Biron. Come on then, I will swear to study so,
To know the thing I am forbid to know ; 60
As thus,—to study where I well may dine,
When I to feast expressly am forbid ;
Or study where to meet some mistress fine,
When mistresses from common sense are hid ;
Or, having sworn too hard-a-keeping oath,
Study to break it, and not break my troth.
If study's gain be thus, and this be so,
Study knows that which yet it doth not know.
Swear me to this, and I will ne'er say no.

King. These be the stops that hinder study quite, 70
And train our intellects to vain delight.

Biron. Why, all delights are vain ; but that most
    vain,
Which, with pain purchas'd, doth inherit pain :
As, painfully to pore upon a book,
To seek the light of truth ; while truth the while
Doth falsely blind the eyesight of his look.
Light, seeking light, doth light of light beguile :

So, ere you find where light in darkness lies,
Your light grows dark by losing of your eyes.
Study me how to please the eye indeed,   80
By fixing it upon a fairer eye;
Who dazzling so, that eye shall be his heed,
And give him light that it was blinded by.
Study is like the heaven's glorious sun,
That will not be deep-search'd with saucy looks:
Small have continual plodders ever won,
Save base authority from others' books.
These earthly godfathers of heaven's lights,
That give a name to every fixed star,
Have no more profit of their shining nights,   90
Than those that walk, and wot not what they are.
Too much to know is to know nought but fame;
And every godfather can give a name.
    King. How well he 's read, to reason against reading!
    Dum. Proceeded well, to stop all good proceeding!
    Long. He weeds the corn, and still lets grow the
            weeding.
    Biron. The spring is near, when green geese are
            a-breeding.
    Dum. How follows that?
    Biron.   Fit in his place and time.
    Dum. In reason nothing.
    Biron.   Something then in rhyme.
    King. Biron is like an envious sneaping frost,   100
That bites the first-born infants of the spring.
    Biron. Well, say I am: why should proud summer
            boast,
Before the birds have any cause to sing?
Why should I joy in an abortive birth?
At Christmas I no more desire a rose,
Than wish a snow in May's new-fangled shows;
But like of each thing that in season grows.
So you, to study now it is too late,
Climb o'er the house to unlock the little gate.
    King. Well, sit you out: go home, Biron: adieu! 110
    Biron. No, my good lord; I have sworn to stay with
            you:
And, though I have for barbarism spoke more,
Than for that angel knowledge you can say,
Yet confident I 'll keep what I have swore,
And bide the penance of each three years' day.
Give me the paper: let me read the same;
And to the strict'st decrees I 'll write my name.
    King. How well this yielding rescues thee from
            shame!
    Biron. [*Reads.*] "Item, That no woman shall come
within a mile of my court."—Hath this been proclaim'd?
    Long. Four days ago.   121
    Biron. [*Reads.*] "On pain
of losing her tongue."—Who devis'd this penalty?
    Long. Marry, that did I.
    Biron. Sweet lord, and why?
    Long. To fright them hence with that dread penalty.
    Biron. A dangerous law against gentility!
    [*Reads.*] "Item, If any man be seen to talk with
a woman within the term of three years, he shall
endure such public shame as the rest of the court
can possibly devise."—   131
This article, my liege, yourself must break;
For, well you know, here comes in embassy
The French king's daughter with yourself to speak,—
A maid of grace, and complete majesty,—
About surrender-up of Aquitain
To her decrepit, sick, and bed-rid father:
Therefore, this article is made in vain,
Or vainly comes the admired princess hither.
    King. What say you, lords? why, this was quite
            forgot.   140
    Biron. So study evermore is overshot:
While it doth study to have what it would,
It doth forget to do the thing it should;
And when it hath the thing it hunteth most,
'T is won, as towns with fire; so won, so lost.
    King. We must of force dispense with this decree:
She must lie here on mere necessity.
    Biron. Necessity will make us all forsworn
Three thousand times within this three years' space;
For every man with his affects is born,   150
Not by might master'd, but by special grace.

If I break faith, this word shall speak for me,
I am forsworn on mere necessity.—
So to the laws at large I write my name; [*Subscribes.*
And he that breaks them in the least degree,
Stands in attainder of eternal shame.
Suggestions are to others as to me;
But, I believe, although I seem so loath,
I am the last that will last keep his oath.
But is there no quick recreation granted?   160
    King. Ay, that there is.   Our court, you know, is
            haunted
With a refined traveller of Spain;
A man in all the world's new fashion planted,
That hath a mint of phrases in his brain;
One, whom the music of his own vain tongue
Doth ravish like enchanting harmony;
A man of complements, whom right and wrong
Have chose as umpire of their mutiny:
This child of fancy, that Armado hight,

Biron. "This article, my liege, yourself must break."

For interim to our studies, shall relate   170
In high-born words the worth of many a knight
From tawny Spain, lost in the world's debate.
How you delight, my lords, I know not, I;
But, I protest, I love to hear him lie,
And I will use him for my minstrelsy.
    Biron. Armado is a most illustrious wight,
A man of fire-new words, fashion's own knight.
    Long. Costard, the swain, and he shall be our
            sport;
And so to study, three years is but short.

            Enter DULL, *with a letter, and* COSTARD.

    Dull. Which is the duke's own person?   180
    Biron. This, fellow.   What wouldst?
    Dull. I myself reprehend his own person, for I am
his grace's tharborough: but I would see his own
person in flesh and blood.
    Biron. This is he.
    Dull. Signior Arm—Arm—commends you. There 's
villainy abroad: this letter will tell you more.
    Cost. Sir, the contempts thereof are as touching me.
    King. A letter from the magnificent Armado.
    Biron. How low soever the matter, I hope in God
for high words.   191
    Long. A high hope for a low heaven: God grant us
patience!
    Biron. To hear, or forbear laughing?
    Long. To hear meekly, sir, and to laugh moderately;
or to forbear both.
    Biron. Well, sir, be it as the style shall give us
cause to climb in the merriness.
    Cost. The matter is to me, sir, as concerning

Jaquenetta. The manner of it is, I was taken with the manner. 201
Biron. In what manner?
Cost. In manner and form following, sir; all those three: I was seen with her in the manor-house, sitting with her upon the form, and taken following her into the park; which, put together, is in manner and form following. Now, sir, for the manner,—it is the manner of a man to speak to a woman; for the form,—in some form.
Biron. For the following, sir? 210
Cost. As it shall follow in my correction; and God defend the right!
King. Will you hear this letter with attention?
Biron. As we would hear an oracle.
Cost. Such is the simplicity of man to hearken after the flesh.
King. [*Reads.*] "Great deputy, the welkin's vicegerent, and sole dominator of Navarre, my soul's earth's God, and body's fostering patron,"—
Cost. Not a word of Costard yet. 220
King. "So it is,"—
Cost. It may be so; but if he say it is so, he is, in telling true, but so,—
King. Peace!
Cost. —be to me, and every man that dares not fight.
King. No words!
Cost. —of other men's secrets, I beseech you.
King. "So it is, besieged with sable-coloured melancholy, I did commend the black-oppressing humour to the most wholesome physic of thy health-giving air; and, as I am a gentleman, betook myself to walk. The time when? About the sixth hour; when beasts most graze, birds best peck, and men sit down to that nourishment which is called supper. So much for the time when. Now for the ground which; which, I mean, I walked upon: it is ycleped thy park. Then for the place where; where, I mean, I did encounter that obscene and most preposterous event, that draweth from my snow-white pen the ebon-coloured ink, which here thou viewest, beholdest, surveyest, or seest. But to the place where;—it standeth north-north-east and by east from the west corner of thy curious-knotted garden: there did I see that low-spirited swain, that base minnow of thy mirth,"— 245
Cost. Me.
King. —"that unletter'd small-knowing soul,"—
Cost. Me.
King. —"that shallow vassal,"—
Cost. Still me. 250
King. —"which, as I remember, hight Costard,"—
Cost. O! me.
King. —"sorted and consorted, contrary to thy established proclaimed edict and continent canon, with—with—O! with—but with this I passion to say wherewith,"—
Cost. With a wench.
King. —"with a child of our grandmother Eve, a female; or, for thy more sweet understanding, a woman. Him I (as my ever-esteemed duty pricks me on) have sent to thee, to receive the meed of punishment, by thy sweet grace's officer, Antony Dull, a man of good repute, carriage, bearing, and estimation." 264
Dull. Me, an't shall please you: I am Antony Dull.
King. —"For Jaquenetta (so is the weaker vessel called), which I apprehended with the aforesaid swain, I keep her as a vessel of thy law's fury; and shall, at the least of thy sweet notice, bring her to trial. Thine, in all complements of devoted and heart-burning heat of duty,   DON ADRIANO DE ARMADO." 271
Biron. This is not so well as I looked for, but the best that ever I heard.
King. Ay, the best for the worst.—But, sirrah, what say you to this?
Cost. Sir, I confess the wench.
King. Did you hear the proclamation?
Cost. I do confess much of the hearing it, but little of the marking of it.
King. It was proclaimed a year's imprisonment, to be taken with a wench. 281

Cost. I was taken with none, sir: I was taken with a damosel.
King. Well, it was proclaimed damosel.
Cost. This was no damosel neither, sir: she was a virgin.
King. It is so varied too, for it was proclaimed virgin.
Cost. If it were, I deny her virginity: I was taken with a maid. 290
King. This maid will not serve your turn, sir.
Cost. This maid will serve my turn, sir.
King. Sir, I will pronounce your sentence: you shall fast a week with bran and water.
Cost. I had rather pray a month with mutton and porridge.
King. And Don Armado shall be your keeper.—
My Lord Biron, see him deliver'd o'er:
And go we, lords, to put in practice that
Which each to other hath so strongly sworn. 300
    [*Exeunt* KING, LONGAVILLE, *and* DUMAINE.
Biron. I'll lay my head to any good man's hat,
These oaths and laws will prove an idle scorn.—
Sirrah, come on.
Cost. I suffer for the truth, sir: for true it is, I was taken with Jaquenetta, and Jaquenetta is a true girl; and therefore, welcome the sour cup of prosperity! Affliction may one day smile again, and till then, sit thee down, sorrow!   [*Exeunt.*

SCENE II.—ARMADO'S *House in the Park.*

Enter ARMADO *and* MOTH.

Arm. Boy, what sign is it, when a man of great spirit grows melancholy?
Moth. A great sign, sir, that he will look sad.
Arm. Why, sadness is one and the self-same thing, dear imp.
Moth. No, no; O Lord! sir, no.
Arm. How canst thou part sadness and melancholy, my tender juvenal?
Moth. By a familiar demonstration of the working, my tough senior. 10
Arm. Why tough senior? why tough senior?
Moth. Why tender juvenal? why tender juvenal?
Arm. I spoke it, tender juvenal, as a congruent epitheton appertaining to thy young days, which we may nominate tender.
Moth. And I, tough senior, as an appertinent title to your old time, which we may name tough.
Arm. Pretty, and apt.
Moth. How mean you, sir? I pretty, and my saying apt? or I apt, and my saying pretty? 20
Arm. Thou pretty, because little.
Moth. Little pretty, because little. Wherefore apt?
Arm. And therefore apt, because quick.
Moth. Speak you this in my praise, master?
Arm. In thy condign praise.
Moth. I will praise an eel with the same praise.
Arm. What, that an eel is ingenious?
Moth. That an eel is quick.
Arm. I do say, thou art quick in answers. Thou heatest my blood. 30
Moth. I am answered, sir.
Arm. I love not to be crossed.
Moth. [*Aside.*] He speaks the mere contrary: crosses love not him.
Arm. I have promised to study three years with the duke.
Moth. You may do it in an hour, sir.
Arm. Impossible.
Moth. How many is one thrice told?
Arm. I am ill at reckoning: it fitteth the spirit of a tapster. 41
Moth. You are a gentleman, and a gamester, sir.
Arm. I confess both: they are both the varnish of a complete man.
Moth. Then, I am sure, you know how much the gross sum of deuce-ace amounts to.
Arm. It doth amount to one more than two.
Moth. Which the base vulgar do call three.
Arm. True.

Moth. Why, sir, is this such a piece of study? Now, here is three studied, ere you 'll thrice wink; and how easy it is to put years to the word three, and study three years in two words, the dancing horse will tell you.   54

Arm. A most fine figure!

Moth. [*Aside.*] To prove you a cypher.

Arm. I will hereupon confess I am in love; and, as it is base for a soldier to love, so am I in love with a base wench. If drawing my sword against the humour of affection would deliver me from the reprobate thought of it, I would take desire prisoner, and ransom him to any French courtier for a new-devised courtesy. I think scorn to sigh: methinks, I should outswear Cupid. Comfort me, boy. What great men have been in love?   65

Moth. Hercules, master.

Arm. Most sweet Hercules!—More authority, dear boy, name more; and, sweet my child, let them be men of good repute and carriage.

Moth. Samson, master: he was a man of good carriage, great carriage, for he carried the town-gates on his back, like a porter, and he was in love. 72

Arm. O well-knit Samson! strong-jointed Samson! I do excel thee in my rapier, as much as thou didst me in carrying gates. I am in love too. Who was Samson's love, my dear Moth?

Moth. A woman, master.

Arm. Of what complexion?

Moth. Of all the four, or the three, or the two, or one of the four.   80

Arm. Tell me precisely of what complexion.

Moth. Of the sea-water green, sir.

Arm. Is that one of the four complexions?

Moth. As I have read, sir; and the best of them too.

Arm. Green, indeed, is the colour of lovers; but to have a love of that colour, methinks, Samson had small reason for it. He, surely, affected her for her wit.

Moth. It was so, sir, for she had a green wit.

Arm. My love is most immaculate white and red.

Moth. Most maculate thoughts, master, are masked under such colours.   91

Arm. Define, define, well-educated infant.

Moth. My father's wit, and my mother's tongue, assist me!

Arm. Sweet invocation of a child; most pretty, and pathetical!

Moth. If she be made of white and red,
　　　Her faults will ne'er be known;
　　For blushing cheeks by faults are bred,
　　　And fears by pale-white shown: 100
　　Then, if she fear, or be to blame,
　　　By this you shall not know;
　　For still her cheeks possess the same,
　　　Which native she doth owe.

A dangerous rhyme, master; against the reason of white and red.

Arm. Is there not a ballad, boy, of the King and the Beggar?

Moth. The world was very guilty of such a ballad some three ages since; but I think, now 't is not to be found; or, if it were, it would neither serve for the writing, nor the tune.   112

Arm. I will have that subject newly writ o'er, that I may example my digression by some mighty precedent. Boy, I do love that country girl, that I took in the park with the rational hind Costard: she deserves well.

Moth. [*Aside.*] To be whipped; and yet a better love than my master.

Arm. Sing, boy: my spirit grows heavy in love. 120

Moth. And that's great marvel, loving a light wench.

Arm. I say, sing.

Moth. Forbear till this company be past.

Enter DULL, COSTARD, *and* JAQUENETTA.

Dull. Sir, the duke's pleasure is, that you keep Costard safe: and you must let him take no delight, nor no penance, but a' must fast three days a week. For this damsel, I must keep her at the park; she is allowed for the day-woman. Fare you well.

Arm. I do betray myself with blushing.—Maid. 130

Jaq. Man.

Arm. I will visit thee at the lodge.

Jaq. That's hereby.

Arm. I know where it is situate.

Jaq. Lord, how wise you are!

Arm. I will tell thee wonders.

Jaq. With that face?

Arm. I love thee.

Jaq. So I heard you say.

Arm. And so farewell.   140

Jaq. Fair weather after you!

Dull. Come, Jaquenetta, away.

　　　　　　　　[*Exeunt* DULL *and* JAQUENETTA.

Arm. Villain, thou shalt fast for thy offences, ere thou be pardoned.

Jaq. "Lord, how wise you are!"

Cost. Well, sir, I hope, when I do it, I shall do it on a full stomach.

Arm. Thou shalt be heavily punished.

Cost. I am more bound to you than your fellows, for they are but lightly rewarded.

Arm. Take away this villain: shut him up.   150

Moth. Come, you transgressing slave: away!

Cost. Let me not be pent up, sir: I will fast, being loose.

Moth. No, sir; that were fast and loose: thou shalt to prison.

Cost. Well, if ever I do see the merry days of desolation that I have seen, some shall see—

Moth. What shall some see?

Cost. Nay, nothing, Master Moth, but what they look upon. It is not for prisoners to be too silent in their words; and therefore I will say nothing: I thank God I have as little patience as another man, and therefore I can be quiet.   163

　　　　　　　　[*Exeunt* MOTH *and* COSTARD.

Arm. I do affect the very ground, which is base, where her shoe, which is baser, guided by her foot, which is basest, doth tread. And how can that be true love, which is falsely attempted? Love is a familiar; Love is a devil: there is no evil angel but Love. Yet was Samson so tempted, and he had an excellent strength: yet was Solomon so seduced, and he had a very good wit. Cupid's butt-shaft is too hard for Hercules' club, and therefore too much odds for a Spaniard's rapier. The first and second cause will not serve my turn; the passado he respects not, the duello he regards not: his disgrace is to be called boy, but his glory is to subdue men. Adieu, valour! rust, rapier! be still, drum! for your manager is in love; yea, he loveth. Assist me some extemporal god of rhyme, for, I am sure, I shall turn sonneter. Devise, wit; write, pen; for I am for whole volumes in folio.   [*Exit.*

ACT II.

Scene I.—Another Part of the Park.　A Pavilion and Tents at a distance.

Enter the Princess of France, Rosaline, Maria, Katharine, Boyet, *Lords, and other Attendants.*

Boyet.
NOW, madam, summon up your dearest spirits :
Consider whom the king your father sends,
To whom he sends, and what's his embassy :
Yourself, held precious in the world's esteem,
To parley with the sole inheritor
Of all perfections that a man may owe,
Matchless Navarre ; the plea of no less weight
Than Aquitain, a dowry for a queen.
Be now as prodigal of all dear grace,
As Nature was in making graces dear, 10
When she did starve the general world beside,
And prodigally gave them all to you.
　Prin. Good Lord Boyet, my beauty, though but mean,
Needs not the painted flourish of your praise :
Beauty is bought by judgment of the eye,
Not utter'd by base sale of chapmen's tongues.
I am less proud to hear you tell my worth,
Than you much willing to be counted wise
In spending your wit in the praise of mine.
But now to task the tasker.—Good Boyet, 20
You are not ignorant, all-telling fame
Doth noise abroad, Navarre hath made a vow,
Till painful study shall outwear three years,
No woman may approach his silent court :
Therefore to us seemeth it a needful course,
Before we enter his forbidden gates,
To know his pleasure ; and in that behalf,
Bold of your worthiness, we single you
As our best-moving fair solicitor.
Tell him, the daughter of the King of France, 30
On serious business, craving quick despatch,
Importunes personal conference with his grace.
Haste, signify so much ; while we attend,
Like humble-visag'd suitors, his high will.
　Boyet. Proud of employment, willingly I go.
　Prin. All pride is willing pride, and yours is so.—
　　　　　　　　　　　　　　[Exit Boyet.
Who are the votaries, my loving lords,
That are vow-fellows with this virtuous duke ?
　1 Lord. Longaville is one.
　Prin.　　　　Know you the man ?
　Mar. I know him, madam : at a marriage-feast, 40
Between Lord Perigort and the beauteous heir
Of Jaques Falconbridge solemnised
In Normandy, saw I this Longaville.
A man of sovereign parts he is esteem'd ;
Well fitted in the arts, glorious in arms :
Nothing becomes him ill, that he would well.
The only soil of his fair virtue's gloss,
If virtue's gloss will stain with any soil,
Is a sharp wit match'd with too blunt a will ;
Whose edge hath power to cut, whose will still wills
It should none spare that come within his power. 51
　Prin. Some merry mocking lord, belike : is 't so ?
　Mar. They say so most that most his humours know.

　Prin. Such short-liv'd wits do wither as they grow.
Who are the rest ?
　Kath. The young Dumaine, a well-accomplish'd youth,
Of all that virtue love for virtue lov'd :
Most power to do most harm, least knowing ill,
For he hath wit to make an ill shape good,
And shape to win grace though he had no wit. 65
I saw him at the Duke Alençon's once ;
And much too little of that good I saw
Is my report to his great worthiness.
　Ros. Another of these students at that time
Was there with him : if I have heard a truth,
Biron they call him ; but a merrier man,
Within the limit of becoming mirth,
I never spent an hour's talk withal.
His eye begets occasion for his wit ;
For every object that the one doth catch, 70
The other turns to a mirth-moving jest,
Which his fair tongue (conceit's expositor)
Delivers in such apt and gracious words,
That aged ears play truant at his tales,
And younger hearings are quite ravished ;
So sweet and voluble is his discourse.
　Prin. God bless my ladies ! are they all in love,
That every one her own hath garnished
With such bedecking ornaments of praise ?
　Lord. Here comes Boyet.

Re-enter Boyet.

　Prin.　　　　Now, what admittance, lord ? 80
　Boyet. Navarre had notice of your fair approach ;
And he and his competitors in oath
Were all address'd to meet you, gentle lady,
Before I came.　Marry, thus much I have learnt,
He rather means to lodge you in the field,
Like one that comes here to besiege his court,
Than seek a dispensation for his oath,
To let you enter his unpeopled house.
Here comes Navarre.　　　　*[The Ladies mask.*

Enter King, Longaville, Dumaine, Biron, *and Attendants.*

　King. Fair princess, welcome to the court of Navarre. 90
　Prin. Fair, I give you back again ; and welcome I have not yet : the roof of this court is too high to be yours, and welcome to the wide fields too base to be mine.
　King. You shall be welcome, madam, to my court.
　Prin. I will be welcome then.　Conduct me thither.
　King. Hear me, dear lady ; I have sworn an oath.
　Prin. Our Lady help my lord ! he 'll be forsworn.
　King. Not for the world, fair madam, by my will.
　Prin. Why, will shall break it ; will, and nothing else. 100
　King. Your ladyship is ignorant what it is.
　Prin. Were my lord so, his ignorance were wise,
Where now his knowledge must prove ignorance.
I hear, your grace hath sworn out house-keeping :
'T is deadly sin to keep that oath, my lord,
And sin to break it.

But pardon me, I am too sudden-bold :
To teach a teacher ill beseemeth me.
Vouchsafe to read the purpose of my coming,
And suddenly resolve me in my suit. [*Gives a paper.*
King. Madam, I will, if suddenly I may.   111
Prin. You will the sooner that I were away,
For you'll prove perjur'd, if you make me stay.
Biron. Did not I dance with you in Brabant once ?
Ros. Did not I dance with you in Brabant once ?
Biron. I know you did.
Ros.   How needless was it then
To ask the question !
Biron.   You must not be so quick.
Ros. 'T is 'long of you, that spur me with such
    questions.
Biron. Your wit's too hot, it speeds too fast, 't will
    tire.
Ros. Not till it leave the rider in the mire.   120
Biron. What time o' day ?
Ros. The hour that fools should ask.
Biron. Now fair befall your mask !
Ros. Fair fall the face it covers !
Biron. And send you many lovers !
Ros. Amen, so you be none.
Biron. Nay, then will I be gone.
King. Madam, your father here doth intimate
The payment of a hundred thousand crowns ;
Being but the one-half of an entire sum,   130
Disbursed by my father in his wars.
But say, that he, or we, (as neither have)
Receiv'd that sum, yet there remains unpaid
A hundred thousand more ; in surety of the which,
One part of Aquitain is bound to us,
Although not valued to the money's worth.
If then the king your father will restore
But that one-half which is unsatisfied,
We will give up our right in Aquitain,
And hold fair friendship with his majesty.   140
But that, it seems, he little purposeth,
For here he doth demand to have repaid
A hundred thousand crowns ; and not demands,
On payment of a hundred thousand crowns,
To have his title live in Aquitain ;
Which we much rather had depart withal,
And have the money by our father lent,
Than Aquitain, so gelded as it is.
Dear princess, were not his requests so far
From reason's yielding, your fair self should make 150
A yielding, 'gainst some reason, in my breast,
And go well satisfied to France again.
Prin. You do the king my father too much wrong,
And wrong the reputation of your name,
In so unseeming to confess receipt
Of that which hath so faithfully been paid.
King. I do protest, I never heard of it ;
And if you prove it, I'll repay it back,
Or yield up Aquitain.
Prin.   We arrest your word.
Boyet, you can produce acquittances   160
For such a sum, from special officers
Of Charles his father.
King.   Satisfy me so.
Boyet. So please your grace, the packet is not come,
Where that and other specialities are bound :
To-morrow you shall have a sight of them.
King. It shall suffice me : at which interview,
All liberal reason I will yield unto.
Meantime, receive such welcome at my hand,
As honour, without breach of honour, may
Make tender of to thy true worthiness.   170
You may not come, fair princess, in my gates ;
But here without you shall be so receiv'd,
As you shall deem yourself lodg'd in my heart,
Though so denied fair harbour in my house.
Your own good thoughts excuse me, and farewell :
To-morrow shall we visit you again.
Prin. Sweet health and fair desires consort your
    grace !
King. Thy own wish wish I thee in every place !
                [*Exeunt* KING *and his Train.*
Biron. Lady, I will commend you to mine own
    heart.

Ros. 'Pray you, do my commendations ; I would be
glad to see it.   181
Biron. I would you heard it groan.
Ros. Is the fool sick ?
Biron. Sick at the heart.
Ros. Alack ! let it blood.
Biron. Would that do it good ?
Ros. My physic says, ay.
Biron. Will you prick 't with your eye ?
Ros. No *point*, with my knife.
Biron. Now, God save thy life !   190
Ros. And yours from long living !
Biron. I cannot stay thanksgiving.   [*Retiring.*
Dum. Sir, I pray you, a word. What lady is that
    same ?
Boyet. The heir of Alençon, Rosaline her name.
Dum. A gallant lady. Monsieur, fare you well.
                                    [*Exit.*
Long. I beseech you a word. What is she in the
    white ?
Boyet. A woman sometimes, an you saw her in the
    light.
Long. Perchance, light in the light. I desire her
    name.
Boyet. She hath but one for herself ; to desire that,
    were a shame.
Long. Pray you, sir, whose daughter ?   200
Boyet. Her mother's, I have heard.
Long. God's blessing on your beard !
Boyet. Good sir, be not offended.
She is an heir of Falconbridge.
Long. Nay, my choler is ended.
She is a most sweet lady.
Boyet. Not unlike, sir ; that may be.   [*Exit* LONG.
Biron. What's her name in the cap ?
Boyet. Katharine, by good hap.
Biron. Is she wedded, or no ?   210
Boyet. To her will, sir, or so.
Biron. O ! you are welcome, sir. Adieu.
Boyet. Farewell to me, sir, and welcome to you.
                [*Exit* BIRON.—*Ladies unmask.*
Mar. That last is Biron, the merry mad-cap lord :
Not a word with him but a jest.
Boyet.   And every jest but a word.
Prin. It was well done of you to take him at his
    word.
Boyet. I was as willing to grapple, as he was to board.
Mar. Two hot sheeps, marry !
Boyet.   And wherefore not ships ?
No sheep, sweet lamb, unless we feed on your lips.
Mar. You sheep, and I pasture : shall that finish
    the jest ?   220
Boyet. So you grant pasture for me.
                        [*Offering to kiss her.*
Mar.   Not so, gentle beast.
My lips are no common, though several they be.
Boyet. Belonging to whom ?
Mar.   To my fortunes and me.
Prin. Good wits will be jangling ; but, gentles, agree.
The civil war of wits were much better used
On Navarre and his book-men, for here 't is abused.
Boyet. If my observation (which very seldom lies),
By the heart's still rhetoric, disclosed with eyes,
Deceive me not now, Navarre is infected.
Prin. With what ?   230
Boyet. With that which we lovers entitle, affected.
Prin. Your reason ?
Boyet. Why, all his behaviours did make their retire
To the court of his eye, peeping thorough desire :
His heart, like an agate, with your print impressed
Proud with his form, in his eye pride expressed :
His tongue, all impatient to speak and not see,
Did stumble with haste in his eyesight to be ;
All senses to that sense did make their repair,
To feel only looking on fairest of fair.   240
Methought, all his senses were lock'd in his eye,
As jewels in crystal for some prince to buy ;
Who, tend'ring their own worth, from where they
    were glass'd,
Did point you to buy them, along as you pass'd.
His face's own margent did cote such amazes,
That all eyes saw his eyes enchanted with gazes.

I'll give you Aquitain, and all that is his,
An you give him for my sake but one loving kiss.
  Prin. Come to our pavilion : Boyet is dispos'd.
  Boyet. But to speak that in words, which his eye
    hath disclos'd.   250
I only have made a mouth of his eye,
By adding a tongue, which I know will not lie.
  Ros. Thou art an old love-monger, and speak'st
    skilfully.

  Mar. He is Cupid's grandfather, and learns news
    of him.
  Ros. Then was Venus like her mother, for her
    father is but grim.
  Boyet. Do you hear, my mad wenches?
  Mar.   No.
  Boyet.   What then, do you see?
  Ros. Ay, our way to be gone.
  Boyet.   You are too hard for me.
                                        [*Exeunt.*

ACT III.

SCENE I.—Another Part of the Same.

Enter ARMADO *and* MOTH.

  Armado.
WARBLE, child : make passionate
    my sense of hearing.
  Moth. [*Singing.*] Concolinel —
  Arm. Sweet air ! — Go, tenderness of years : take this key, give
enlargement to the swain, bring
him festinately hither ; I must
employ him in a letter to my
love.
  Moth. Master, will you win
your love with a French brawl?
  Arm. How meanest thou? brawling in French?
  Moth. No, my complete master ; but to jig off a
tune at the tongue's end, canary to it with your feet,
humour it with turning up your eyelids, sigh a note,
and sing a note ; sometime through the throat, as if you
swallowed love with singing love ; sometime through
the nose, as if you snuffed up love by smelling love ;
with your hat, penthouse-like, o'er the shop of your
eyes ; with your arms crossed on your thin belly-doublet, like a rabbit on a spit ; or your hands in your
pocket, like a man after the old painting ; and keep
not too long in one tune, but a snip and away. These
are complements, these are humours, these betray
nice wenches, that would be betrayed without these,
and make them men of note, (do you note me?) that
most are affected to these.
  Arm. How hast thou purchased this experience?
  Moth. By my penny of observation.
  Arm. But O,—but O,—   30
  Moth. —the hobby-horse is forgot.
  Arm. Callest thou my love hobby-horse?
  Moth. No, master ; the hobby-horse is but a colt,
and your love, perhaps, a hackney. But have you
forgot your love?
  Arm. Almost I had.
  Moth. Negligent student ! learn her by heart.
  Arm. By heart, and in heart, boy.
  Moth. And out of heart, master : all those three I
will prove.   40
  Arm. What wilt thou prove?
  Moth. A man, if I live ; and this, by, in, and with-
out, upon the instant : by heart you love her, because
your heart cannot come by her ; in heart you love her,
because your heart is in love with her ; and out of
heart you love her, being out of heart that you cannot
enjoy her.
  Arm. I am all these three.
  Moth. And three times as much more, and yet
nothing at all.   50
  Arm. Fetch hither the swain : he must carry me a
letter.

  Moth. A message well sympathised : a horse to be
ambassador for an ass.
  Arm. Ha, ha ! what sayest thou?
  Moth. Marry, sir, you must send the ass upon the
horse, for he is very slow-gaited. But I go.

Arm. "What wilt thou prove?"

  Arm. The way is but short. Away !
  Moth. As swift as lead, sir.
  Arm. Thy meaning, pretty ingenious?   60
Is not lead a metal heavy, dull, and slow?
  Moth. Minime, honest master ; or rather, master,
    no.
  Arm. I say, lead is slow.
  Moth.   You are too swift, sir, to say so :
Is that lead slow which is fir'd from a gun?
  Arm. Sweet smoke of rhetoric !
He reputes me a cannon ; and the bullet, that's he :—
I shoot thee at the swain.
  Moth.   Thump then, and I flee. [*Exit.*
  Arm. A most acute juvenal ; voluble and free of
    grace !

By thy favour, sweet welkin; I must sigh in thy
    face:
Most rude melancholy, valour gives thee place.   70
My herald is return'd.

     Re-enter MOTH *with* COSTARD.

  Moth. A wonder, master! here's a Costard broken
    in a shin.
  Arm. Some enigma, some riddle : come,—thy *l'en-*
    voy;—begin.
  Cost. No egma, no riddle, no *l'envoy!* no salve in
the mail, sir. O, sir, plantain, a plain plantain! no
l'envoy, no *l'envoy :* no salve, sir, but a plantain.
  Arm. By virtue, thou enforcest laughter; thy silly
thought, my spleen; the heaving of my lungs pro-
vokes me to ridiculous smiling: O, pardon me, my
stars! Doth the inconsiderate take salve for *l'envoy,*
and the word *l'envoy* for a salve?   81
  Moth. Do the wise think them other? is not *l'envoy*
a salve?
  Arm. No, page: it is an epilogue or discourse, to
    make plain
Some obscure precedence that hath tofore been sain.
I will example it:
    The fox, the ape, and the humble-bee,
    Were still at odds, being but three.
There's the moral. Now the *l'envoy.*
  Moth. I will add the *l'envoy.* Say the moral again.
  Arm. The fox, the ape, and the humble-bee,   91
    Were still at odds, being but three.
  Moth. Until the goose came out of door,
    And stay'd the odds by adding four.
Now will I begin your moral, and do you follow with
my *l'envoy.*
    The fox, the ape, and the humble-bee,
    Were still at odds, being but three.
  Arm. Until the goose came out of door,
    Staying the odds by adding four.   100
  Moth. A good *l'envoy,* ending in the goose. Would
you desire more?
  Cost. The boy hath sold him a bargain, a goose,
    that's flat.—
Sir, your pennyworth is good, an your goose be fat.—
To sell a bargain well, is as cunning as fast and loose:
Let me see, a fat *l'envoy;* ay, that's a fat goose.
  Arm. Come hither, come hither. How did this
    argument begin?
  Moth. By saying that a Costard was broken in a
    shin.
Then call'd you for the *l'envoy.*
  Cost. True, and I for a plantain: thus came your
    argument in;   110
Then the boy's fat *l'envoy,* the goose that you bought,
And he ended the market.
  Arm. But tell me; how was there a Costard broken
in a shin?
  Moth. I will tell you sensibly.
  Cost. Thou hast no feeling of it, Moth: I will speak
that *l'envoy.*
  I, Costard, running out, that was safely within,
    Fell over the threshold, and broke my shin.
  Arm. We will talk no more of this matter.   120
  Cost. Till there be more matter in the shin.
  Arm. Sirrah Costard, I will enfranchise thee.
  Cost. O! marry me to one Frances?—I smell some
l'envoy, some goose in this.
  Arm. By my sweet soul, I mean, setting thee at
liberty, enfreedoming thy person: thou wert immured,
restrained, captivated, bound.
  Cost. True, true, and now you will be my purgation,
and let me loose.   129
  Arm. I give thee thy liberty, set thee from durance;
and, in lieu thereof, impose one nothing but this:
bear this significant to the country maid Jaquenetta.
There is remuneration; for the best ward of mine
honour is rewarding my dependents. Moth, follow.
                                [*Exit.*
  Moth. Like the sequel, I.—Signior Costard, adieu.
  Cost. My sweet ounce of man's flesh! my incony
Jew!—   [*Exit* MOTH.
Now will I look to his remuneration. Remuneration!
O! that's the Latin word for three farthings: three

farthings, remuneration.—"What's the price of this
inkle? a penny :—No, I'll give you a remuneration :"
why, it carries it.—Remuneration!—why, it is a fairer
name than French crown. I will never buy and sell
out of this word.   143

     Enter BIRON.

  Biron. O, my good knave Costard! exceedingly well
met.
  Cost. Pray you, sir, how much carnation ribbon
may a man buy for a remuneration?
  Biron. What is a remuneration?
  Cost. Marry, sir, halfpenny farthing.
  Biron. O! why then, three-farthing-worth of silk.
  Cost. I thank your worship. God be wi' you.   151
  Biron. O, stay, slave! I must employ thee :
As thou wilt win my favour, good my knave,
Do one thing for me that I shall entreat.
  Cost. When would you have it done, sir?
  Biron. O! this afternoon.

        Biron. "There's thy guerdon: go."

  Cost. Well, I will do it, sir. Fare you well.
  Biron. O! thou knowest not what it is.
  Cost. I shall know, sir, when I have done it.
  Biron. Why, villain, thou must know first.   160
  Cost. I will come to your worship to-morrow
morning.
  Biron. It must be done this afternoon. Hark, slave,
it is but this :—
The princess comes to hunt here in the park,
And in her train there is a gentle lady;
When tongues speak sweetly, then they name her
    name,
And Rosaline they call her : ask for her,
And to her white hand see thou do commend
This seal'd-up counsel. There's thy guerdon: go. 170
                       [*Gives him money.*
  Cost. Gardon.—O! sweet gardon! better than re-
muneration; eleven-pence farthing better. Most
sweet gardon!—I will do it, sir, in print.—Gardon—
remuneration!   [*Exit.*
  Biron. O!—And I, forsooth, in love! I, that have
been love's whip;
A very beadle to a humorous sigh;
A critic, nay, a night-watch constable;
A domineering pedant o'er the boy,
Than whom no mortal so magnificent!   180
This wimpled, whining, purblind, wayward boy;
This senior-junior, giant-dwarf, Dan Cupid,
Regent of love-rhymes, lord of folded arms,
The anointed sovereign of sighs and groans,
Liege of all loiterers and malcontents,
Dread prince of plackets, king of codpieces,
Sole imperator, and great general
Of trotting paritors : (O my little heart!)
And I to be a corporal of his field,

And wear his colours like a tumbler's hoop! 190
What! I love! I sue! I seek a wife!
A woman, that is like a German clock,
Still a repairing, ever out of frame,
And never going aright, being a watch,
But being watch'd that it may still go right!
Nay, to be perjur'd, which is worst of all;
And, among three, to love the worst of all;
A whitely wanton with a velvet brow,
With two pitch-balls stuck in her face for eyes;
Ay, and, by heaven, one that will do the deed, 200
Though Argus were her eunuch and her guard;
And I to sigh for her! to watch for her!
To pray for her! Go to; it is a plague
That Cupid will impose for my neglect
Of his almighty dreadful little might.
Well, I will love, write, sigh, pray, sue, and groan:
Some men must love my lady, and some Joan. [*Exit.*

ACT IV.

SCENE I.—Another Part of the Same.

Enter the PRINCESS, ROSALINE, MARIA, KATHARINE, BOYET, *Lords, Attendants, and a Forester.*

Princess.

WAS that the king, that spurr'd his horse so hard
Against the steep uprising of the hill?
Boyet. I know not; but I think, it was not he.
Prin. Whoe'er he was, he show'd a mounting mind.
Well, lords, to-day we shall have our despatch;
On Saturday we will return to France.—
Then, forester, my friend, where is the bush,
That we must stand and play the murderer in?
For. Hereby, upon the edge of yonder coppice;
A stand where you may make the fairest shoot. 10
Prin. I thank my beauty, I am fair that shoot,
And thereupon thou speak'st the fairest shoot.
For. Pardon me, madam, for I meant not so.
Prin. What, what? first praise me, and again say,
    no?
O short-liv'd pride! Not fair? alack for woe!
For. Yes, madam, fair.
Prin.   Nay, never paint me now:
Where fair is not, praise cannot mend the brow.
Here, good my glass, take this for telling true.
    [*Giving him money.*
Fair payment for foul words is more than due.
For. Nothing but fair is that which you inherit. 20
Prin. See, see! my beauty will be sav'd by merit.
O heresy in fair, fit for these days!
A giving hand, though foul, shall have fair praise.—
But come, the bow:—now mercy goes to kill,
And shooting well is then accounted ill.
Thus will I save my credit in the shoot:
Not wounding, pity would not let me do 't;
If wounding, then it was to show my skill,
That more for praise than purpose meant to kill.
And, out of question, so it is sometimes: 30
Glory grows guilty of detested crimes,
When, for fame's sake, for praise, an outward part,
We bend to that the working of the heart;
As I for praise alone now seek to spill
The poor deer's blood, that my heart means no ill.
Boyet. Do not curst wives hold that self-sovereignty
Only for praise' sake, when they strive to be
Lords o'er their lords?
Prin. Only for praise; and praise we may afford
To any lady that subdues a lord. 40

Enter COSTARD.

Prin. Here comes a member of the commonwealth.
Cost. God dig-you-den all. Pray you, which is the head lady?
Prin. Thou shalt know her, fellow, by the rest that have no heads.
Cost. Which is the greatest lady, the highest?
Prin. The thickest, and the tallest.
Cost. The thickest, and the tallest? it is so; truth is truth.
An your waist, mistress, were as slender as my wit,
One o' these maids' girdles for your waist should be fit.
Are not you the chief woman? you are the thickest here. 51
Prin. What's your will, sir? what's your will?
Cost. I have a letter from Monsieur Biron to one
    Lady Rosaline.
Prin. O, thy letter, thy letter! he's a good friend of mine.
Stand aside, good bearer.—Boyet, you can carve;
Break up this capon.
Boyet.   I am bound to serve.—
This letter is mistook; it importeth none here:
It is writ to Jaquenetta.
Prin.   We will read it, I swear.
Break the neck of the wax, and every one give ear. 59
Boyet. [*Reads.*] "By heaven, that thou art fair, is most infallible; true, that thou art beauteous; truth itself, that thou art lovely. More fairer than fair, beautiful than beauteous, truer than truth itself, have commiseration on thy heroical vassal! The magnanimous and most illustrate King Cophetua set eye upon the pernicious and indubitate beggar Zenelophon, and he it was that might rightly say, *Veni, vidi, vici;* which to anatomise in the vulgar (O base and obscure vulgar!), *videlicet,* he came, saw, and overcame: he came, one; saw, two; overcame, three. Who came? the king; why did he come? to see; why did he see? to overcome. To whom came he? to the beggar; what saw he? the beggar; who overcame he? the beggar. The conclusion is victory: on whose side? the king's. The captive is enriched: on whose side? the beggar's. The catastrophe is a nuptial: on whose side? the king's?—no, on both in one, or one in both. I am the king, for so stands the comparison; thou the beggar, for so witnesseth thy lowliness. Shall I command thy love? I may. Shall I enforce thy love? I could. Shall I entreat thy love? I will. What shalt thou exchange for rags? robes; for tittles? titles; for thyself? me. Thus, expecting thy reply, I profane my lips on thy foot, my eyes on thy picture, and my heart on thy every part.
    Thine, in the dearest design of industry,
        DON ADRIANO DE ARMADO."
Thus dost thou hear the Nemean lion roar
'Gainst thee, thou lamb, that standest as his prey;
Submissive fall his princely feet before. 90

And he from forage will incline to play.
But if thou strive, poor soul, what art thou then
Food for his rage, repasture for his den.
    Prin. What plume of feathers is he that indited
        this letter?
What vane? what weathercock? did you ever hear
    better?

    Prin. To whom shouldst thou give it?
    Cost.   From my lord to my lady.
    Prin. From which lord to which lady?
    Cost. From my Lord Biron, a good master of mine,
To a lady of France, that he call'd Rosaline.
    Prin.   Thou hast mistaken his letter.—Come, lords,
    away. –

Prin. "What plume of feathers is he that indited this letter?"

    Boyet. I am much deceiv'd, but I remember the
        style.
    Prin. Else your memory is bad, going o'er it ere-
        while.
    Boyet. This Armado is a Spaniard, that keeps here
        in court;
A phantasm, a Monarcho, and one that makes sport
To the prince, and his book-mates.
    Prin.   Thou, fellow, a word.
Who gave thee this letter?
    Cost.   I told you; my lord. 101

Here, sweet, put up this: 't will be thine another day.
                 [*Exeunt* PRINCESS *and Train.*
    Boyet. Who is the suitor? who is the suitor?
    Ros.   Shall I teach you to know?
    Boyet. Ay, my continent of beauty.
    Ros.   Why, she that bears the bow.
Finely put off!   110
    Boyet. My lady goes to kill horns; but if thou
        marry,
Hang me by the neck, if horns that year miscarry.
Finely put on!

Ros. Well then, I am the shooter.
Boyet.   And who is your deer?
Ros. If we choose by the horns, yourself : come not
     near.
Finely put on, indeed !—
Mar. You still wrangle with her, Boyet, and she
     strikes at the brow.
Boyet. But she herself is hit lower. Have I hit her
     now ?
Ros. Shall I come upon thee with an old saying,
that was a man when King Pepin of France was a
little boy, as touching the hit it ?   121
Boyet. So I may answer thee with one as old, that
was a woman when Queen Guinever of Britain was a
little wench, as touching the hit it.

Ros.   Thou canst not hit it, hit it, hit it,
           Thou canst not hit it, my good man.
Boyet.   An I cannot, cannot, cannot,
           An I cannot, another can.

                         [*Exeunt* Ros. *and* KATH.
Cost. By my troth, most pleasant : how both did fit it !
Mar. A mark marvellous well shot, for they both
     did hit it.   130
Boyet. A mark ! O ! mark but that mark : a mark,
     says my lady.
Let the mark have a prick in 't to mete at, if it may be.
Mar. Wide o' the bow-hand : i' faith, your hand is
     out.
Cost. Indeed, a' must shoot nearer, or he 'll ne'er hit
     the clout.
Boyet. An if my hand be out, then belike your hand
     is in.
Cost. Then will she get the upshot by cleaving the
     pin.
Mar. Come, come, you talk greasily ; your lips grow
     foul.
Cost. She 's too hard for you at pricks, sir : chal-
     lenge her to bowl.
Boyet. I fear too much rubbing. Good night, my
     good owl.   [*Exeunt* BOYET *and* MARIA.
Cost. By my soul, a swain ! a most simple clown !
Lord, Lord ! how the ladies and I have put him down !
O' my truth, most sweet jests ! most incony vulgar wit !
When it comes so smoothly off, so obscenely, as it
     were, so fit.   143
Armado o' the one side,—O, a most dainty man !
To see him walk before a lady, and to bear her fan !
To see him kiss his hand ! and how most sweetly a'
     will swear !—
And his page o' t' other side, that handful of wit !
Ah, heavens, it is a most pathetical nit !
Sola, sola !   [*Shouting within.*
                                     [*Exit* COSTARD.
 ——

SCENE II.—The Same.

Enter HOLOFERNES, *Sir* NATHANIEL, *and* DULL.

Nath. Very reverend sport, truly : and done in the
testimony of a good conscience.
Hol. The deer was, as you know, *sanguis,*—in
blood ; ripe as the pomewater, who now hangeth like
a jewel in the ear of *coelo,*—the sky, the welkin, the
heaven ; and anon falleth like a crab, on the face of
terra,—the soil, the land, the earth.
Nath. Truly, Master Holofernes, the epithets are
sweetly varied, like a scholar at the least : but, sir,
I assure ye, it was a buck of the first head.   10
Hol. Sir Nathaniel, *haud credo.*
Dull. 'T was not a *haud credo,* 't was a pricket.
Hol. Most barbarous intimation ! yet a kind of insinuation, as it were, *in via,* in way of explication ;
facere, as it were, replication, or, rather, *ostentare,* to
show, as it were, his inclination,—after his undressed,
unpolished, uneducated, unpruned, untrained, or
rather unlettered, or, ratherest, unconfirmed fashion,
—to insert again my *haud credo* for a deer.
Dull. I said, the deer was not a *haud credo :* 't was
a pricket.   21
Hol. Twice-sod simplicity, *bis coctus !*—
O, thou monster Ignorance, how deformed dost thou
     look !

Nath. Sir, he hath never fed of the dainties that
     are bred in a book ;
He hath not eat paper, as it were ; he hath not drunk
ink : his intellect is not replenished ; he is only an
animal, only sensible in the duller parts ;
And such barren plants are set before us, that we
     thankful should be
(Which we of taste and feeling are) for those parts that
     do fructify in us more than he ;
For as it would ill become me to be vain, indiscreet,
     or a fool,   30
So, were there a patch set on learning, to see him in
     a school :
But, *omne bene,* say I ; being of an old father's mind,
Many can brook the weather, that love not the wind.
Dull. You two are book-men : can you tell by your
     wit,
What was a month old at Cain's birth, that 's not five
     weeks old as yet ?
Hol. Dictynna, goodman Dull ; Dictynna, goodman
     Dull.
Dull. What is Dictynna ?
Nath. A title to Phœbe, to Luna, to the moon.
Hol. The moon was a month old when Adam was
     no more ;
And raught not to five weeks, when he came to five-
     score.   40
The allusion holds in the exchange.
Dull. 'T is true indeed : the collusion holds in the
exchange.
Hol. God comfort thy capacity ! I say, the allusion
holds in the exchange.
Dull. And I say, the pollusion holds in the exchange,
for the moon is never but a month old ; and I say
beside, that 't was a pricket that the princess kill'd.
Hol. Sir Nathaniel, will you hear an extemporal
epitaph on the death of the deer ? and, to humour
the ignorant, I have call'd the deer the princess
kill'd, a pricket.   52
Nath. Perge, good Master Holofernes, *perge ;* so it
     shall please you to abrogate scurrility.
Hol. I will something affect the letter ; for it argues
     facility.

The preyful princess pierc'd and prick'd a pretty
     pleasing pricket ;
Some say, a sore ; but not a sore, till now made
     sore with shooting.
The dogs did yell ; put l to sore, then sorel jumps
     from thicket ;
Or pricket sore, or else sorel ; the people fall a-
     hooting.
If sore be sore, then l to sore makes fifty sores ; O
     sore l !
Of one sore I an hundred make, by adding but one
     more l.   60

Nath. A rare talent !
Dull. If a talent be a claw, look how he claws him
with a talent.
Hol. This is a gift that I have, simple, simple ; a
foolish extravagant spirit, full of forms, figures,
shapes, objects, ideas, apprehensions, motions, re-
volutions : these are begot in the ventricle of memory,
nourished in the womb of *pia mater,* and delivered
upon the mellowing of occasion. But the gift is good
in those in whom it is acute, and I am thankful for it.
Nath. Sir, I praise the Lord for you, and so may
my parishioners ; for their sons are well tutored by
you, and their daughters profit very greatly under
you : you are a good member of the commonwealth.
Hol. Mehercle ! if their sons be ingenious, they shall
want no instruction ; if their daughters be capable,
I will put it to them. But, *vir sapit qui pauca*
loquitur. A soul feminine saluteth us.

Enter JAQUENETTA *and* COSTARD.

Jaq. God give you good morrow, master person.
Hol. Master person,—*quasi* pers-on. An if one
should be pierced, which is the one ?   81
Cost. Marry, master schoolmaster, he that is likest
to a hogshead.
Hol. Of piercing a hogshead ! a good lustre of

conceit in a turf of earth; fire enough for a flint, pearl enough for a swine: 'tis pretty; it is well.

Jaq. Good master person, be so good as read me this letter. It was given me by Costard, and sent me from Don Armado: I beseech you, read it.

Hol. Fauste, precor gelidâ quando pecus omne sub umbrâ Ruminat, and so forth. Ah, good old Mantuan! I may speak of thee as the traveller doth of Venice: 93

> *Venetia, Venetia,*
> *Chi non ti vede, non ti pretia.*

Old Mantuan! old Mantuan! who understandeth thee not, loves thee not.—*Ut, re, sol, la, mi, fa.*—Under pardon, sir, what are the contents? or, rather, as Horace says in his—What, my soul, verses?   100

Nath. Ay, sir, and very learned.

Hol. Let me hear a staff, a stanza, a verse: *lege, domine.*

> *Nath. If love make me forsworn, how shall I swear*
>   *to love?*
> *Ah, never faith could hold, if not to beauty vowed!*
> *Though to myself forsworn, to thee I'll faithful prove;*
> *Those thoughts to me were oaks, to thee like osiers*
>   *bowed.*
> *Study his bias leaves, and makes his book thine eyes,*
>   *Where all those pleasures live, that art would com-*
>   *prehend:*
> *If knowledge be the mark, to know thee shall suffice.*
>   *Well learned is that tongue, that well can thee*
>   *commend;*   110
> *All ignorant that soul, that sees thee without wonder;*
>   *Which is to me some praise, that I thy parts*
>   *admire.*
> *Thy eye Jove's lightning bears, thy voice his dreadful*
>   *thunder,*
>   *Which, not to anger bent, is music, and sweet fire.*
> *Celestial as thou art, O! pardon love this wrong,*
> *That sings heaven's praise with such an earthly*
>   *tongue!*

Hol. You find not the apostrophes, and so miss the accent: let me supervise the canzonet. Here are only numbers ratified; but, for the elegancy, facility, and golden cadence of poesy, *caret.* Ovidius Naso was the man: and why, indeed, Naso, but for smelling out the odoriferous flowers of fancy, the jerks of invention? *Imitari* is nothing, so doth the hound his master, the ape his keeper, the tired horse his rider. But, damosella, virgin, was this directed to you?   125

Jaq. Ay, sir, from one Monsieur Biron, one of the strange queen's lords.

Hol. I will overglance the superscript. "To the snow-white hand of the most beauteous Lady Rosaline." I will look again on the intellect of the letter, for the nomination of the party writing to the person written unto: "Your ladyship's in all desired employment, BIRON." Sir Nathaniel, this Biron is one of the votaries with the king; and here he hath framed a letter to a sequent of the stranger queen's, which, accidentally, or by the way of progression, hath miscarried.—Trip and go, my sweet; deliver this paper into the royal hand of the king: it may concern much. Stay not thy compliment, I forgive thy duty; adieu.   140

Jaq. Good Costard, go with me.—Sir, God save your life!

Cost. Have with thee, my girl.

                         [*Exeunt* COST. and JAQ.

Nath. Sir, you have done this in the fear of God, very religiously; and, as a certain father saith,—

Hol. Sir, tell not me of the father; I do fear colourable colours. But, to return to the verses: did they please you, Sir Nathaniel?   149

Nath. Marvellous well for the pen.

Hol. I do dine to-day at the father's of a certain pupil of mine; where if before repast it shall please you to gratify the table with a grace, I will, on my privilege I have with the parents of the foresaid child or pupil, undertake your *ben venuto;* where I will prove those verses to be very unlearned, neither

savouring of poetry, wit, nor invention. I beseech your society.

Nath. And thank you too; for society (saith the text) is the happiness of life.   159

Hol. And, certes, the text most infallibly concludes it.—[*To* DULL.] Sir, I do invite you too: you shall not say me nay: *pauca verba.* Away! the gentles are at their game, and we will to our recreation.   [*Exeunt.*

Hol. "Was this directed to you?"

SCENE III.—Another Part of the Same.

Enter BIRON, *with a paper.*

Biron. The king he is hunting the deer; I am coursing myself: they have pitch'd a toil; I am toiling in a pitch,—pitch that defiles. Defile! a foul word. Well, sit thee down, sorrow! for so, they say, the fool said, and so say I, and I the fool. Well proved, wit! By the Lord, this love is as mad as Ajax: it kills sheep; it kills me, I a sheep. Well proved again o' my side! I will not love; if I do, hang me: i' faith, I will not. O! but her eye,—by this light, but for her eye, I would not love her! yes, for her two eyes. Well, I do nothing in the world but lie, and lie in my throat. By heaven, I do love, and it hath taught me to rhyme, and to be melancholy; and here is part of my rhyme, and here my melancholy. Well, she hath one o' my sonnets already: the clown bore it, the fool sent it, and the lady hath it: sweet clown, sweeter fool, sweetest lady! By the world, I would not care a pin if the other three were in. Here comes one with a paper: God give him grace to groan!

                         [*Gets up into a tree.*

Enter the KING, *with a paper.*

King. Ay me!   20

Biron. [*Aside.*] Shot, by heaven!—Proceed, sweet Cupid: thou hast thump'd him with thy bird-bolt under the left pap.—In faith, secrets!—

> *King.* [*Reads.*] *So sweet a kiss the golden sun gives*
>   *not*
> *To those fresh morning drops upon the rose,*
> *As thy eyebeams, when their fresh rays have smote*
> *The night of dew that on my checks down flows:*
> *Nor shines the silver moon one half so bright*
> *Through the transparent bosom of the deep,*
> *As doth thy face through tears of mine give light;*   30
> *Thou shin'st in every tear that I do weep:*
> *No drop but as a coach doth carry thee,*
> *So ridest thou triumphing in my woe.*
> *Do but behold the tears that swell in me,*
>   *And they thy glory through my grief will show:*
> *But do not love thyself; then thou wilt keep*
> *My tears for glasses, and still make me weep.*
> *O queen of queens, how far dost thou excel,*
> *No thought can think, nor tongue of mortal tell.*

How shall she know my griefs? I'll drop the paper.
Sweet leaves, shade folly. Who is he comes here? 41
                                    [*Steps aside.*

Enter LONGAVILLE, *with a paper.*

[*Aside.*] What, Longaville! and reading! listen, ear.
  Biron. [*Aside.*] Now, in thy likeness, one more fool
    appear!
  Long. Ay me! I am forsworn.
  Biron. [*Aside.*] Why, he comes in like a perjure,
    wearing papers.
  King. [*Aside.*] In love, I hope : sweet fellowship
    in shame !
  Biron. [*Aside.*] One drunkard loves another of the
    name.
  Long. Am I the first that have been perjur'd so?
  Biron. [*Aside.*] I could put thee in comfort : not by
    two that I know.
Thou mak'st the triumviry, the corner-cap of society,
The shape of Love's Tyburn, that hangs up sim-
    plicity.   51
  Long. I fear these stubborn lines lack power to move.
O sweet Maria, empress of my love !
These numbers will I tear, and write in prose.
  Biron. [*Aside.*] O ! rhymes are guards on wanton
    Cupid's hose :
Disfigure not his slop.
  Long.   This same shall go.
                              [*He reads the sonnet.*

Did not the heavenly rhetoric of thine eye,
  'Gainst whom the world cannot hold argument,
Persuade my heart to this false perjury ?
Vows for thee broke deserve not punishment.   60
A woman I forswore ; but I will prove,
  Thou being a goddess, I forswore not thee :
My vow was earthly, thou a heavenly love ;
Thy grace, being gain'd, cures all disgrace in me.
Vows are but breath, and breath a vapour is :
  Then thou, fair sun, which on my earth dost shine,
Exhal'st this vapour-vow ; in thee it is :
  If broken, then it is no fault of mine,
If by me broke. What fool is not so wise,
To lose an oath, to win a paradise ?   70

  Biron. [*Aside.*] This is the liver-vein, which makes
flesh a deity ;
A green goose, a goddess : pure, pure idolatry.
God amend us, God amend ! we are much out o' the
    way.

Enter DUMAINE, *with a paper.*

  Long. By whom shall I send this?—Company! stay.
                                    [*Steps aside.*
  Biron. [*Aside.*] All hid, all hid ; an old infant play.
Like a demi-god here sit I in the sky,
And wretched fools' secrets heedfully o'er-eye.
More sacks to the mill ! O heavens ! I have my wish :
Dumaine transform'd : four woodcocks in a dish !
  Dum. O most divine Kate !   80
  Biron. [*Aside.*] O most profane coxcomb !
  Dum. By heaven, the wonder of a mortal eye !
  Biron. [*Aside.*] By earth, she is but corporal ; there
    you lie.
  Dum. Her amber hairs for foul have amber coted.
  Biron. [*Aside.*] An amber-colour'd raven was well
    noted.
  Dum. As upright as the cedar.
  Biron. [*Aside.*]   Stoop, I say :
Her shoulder is with child.
  Dum.   As fair as day.
  Biron. [*Aside.*] Ay, as some days ; but then no sun
    must shine.
  Dum. O, that I had my wish !
  Long. [*Aside.*]   And I had mine !
  King. [*Aside.*] And I mine too, good Lord !   90
  Biron. [*Aside.*] Amen, so I had mine. Is not that
    a good word ?
  Dum. I would forget her ; but a fever she
Reigns in my blood, and will remember'd be.
  Biron. [*Aside.*] A fever in your blood ? why, then
    incision
Would let her out in saucers : sweet misprision !

  Dum. Once more I'll read the ode that I have writ.
  Biron. [*Aside.*] Once more I'll mark how love can
    vary wit.

  Dum. *On a day, alack the day !*
    Love, whose month is ever May,
    Spied a blossom, passing fair,   100
    Playing in the wanton air :
    Through the velvet leaves the wind,
    All unseen, 'gan passage find ;
    That the lover, sick to death,
    Wish'd himself the heaven's breath.
    Air, quoth he, thy cheeks may blow ;
    Air, would I might triumph so !
    But alack ! my hand is sworn,
    Ne'er to pluck thee from thy thorn :
    Vow, alack ! for youth unmeet,   110
    Youth so apt to pluck a sweet.
    Do not call it sin in me,
    That I am forsworn for thee ;
    Thou for whom Jove would swear
    Juno but an Ethiop were ;
    And deny himself for Jove,
    Turning mortal for thy love.

This will I send, and something else more plain,
That shall express my true love's fasting pain.
O, 'would the king, Biron, and Longaville,   120
Were lovers too! Ill, to example ill,
Would from my forehead wipe a perjur'd note ;
For none offend, where all alike do dote.
  Long. [*Advancing.*] Dumaine, thy love is far from
    charity,
That in love's grief desir'st society :
You may look pale, but I should blush, I know,
To be o'erheard, and taken napping so.
  King. [*Advancing.*] Come, sir, you blush ; as his
    your case is such ;
You chide at him, offending twice as much :
You do not love Maria ; Longaville   130
Did never sonnet for her sake compile,
Nor never lay his wreathed arms athwart
His loving bosom, to keep down his heart.
I have been closely shrouded in this bush,
And mark'd you both, and for you both did blush.
I heard your guilty rhymes, observ'd your fashion,
Saw sighs reek from you, noted well your passion :
Ay me ! says one ; O Jove ! the other cries ;
One, her hairs were gold, crystal the other's eyes :
[*To* LONG.] You would for paradise break faith and
    troth ;   140
[*To* DUMAINE.] And Jove for your love would in-
    fringe an oath.
What will Biron say, when that he shall hear
Faith infringed, which such zeal did swear?
How will he scorn ! how will he spend his wit !
How will he triumph, leap, and laugh at it !
For all the wealth that ever I did see,
I would not have him know so much by me.
  Biron. Now step I forth to whip hypocrisy.—
                              [*Descends from the tree.*
Ah, good my liege, I pray thee, pardon me :
Good heart ! what grace hast thou, thus to reprove
These worms for loving, that art most in love ?   151
Your eyes do make no coaches ; in your tears
There is no certain princess that appears :
You'll not be perjur'd, 'tis a hateful thing :
Tush ! none but minstrels like of sonneting.
But are you not asham'd ? nay, are you not,
All three of you, to be thus much o'ershot ?
You found his moth ; the king your moth did see ;
But I a beam do find in each of three.
O ! what a scene of foolery have I seen,   160
Of sighs, of groans, of sorrow, and of teen !
O me ! with what strict patience have I sat,
To see a king transformed to a gnat !
To see great Hercules whipping a gig,
And profound Solomon tuning a jig,
And Nestor play at push-pin with the boys,
And critic Timon laugh at idle toys !
Where lies thy grief? O ! tell me, good Dumaine :
And, gentle Longaville, where lies thy pain ?

And where my liege's? all about the breast ;–   170
A caudle, ho!
King.   Too bitter is thy jest.
Are we betray'd thus to thy over-view?
Biron. Not you to me, but I betray'd by you :
I, that am honest ; I, that hold it sin
To break the vow I am engaged in ;
I am betray'd, by keeping company
With men like you, men of inconstancy.
When shall you see me write a thing in rhyme ?

Biron. " But are you not asham'd ? "

Or groan for Joan? or spend a minute's time
In pruning me? When shall you hear that I   180
Will praise a hand, a foot, a face, an eye,
A gait, a state, a brow, a breast, a waist,
A leg, a limb?—
King.   Soft ! Whither away so fast ?
A true man, or a thief, that gallops so ?
Biron. I post from love ; good lover, let me go.

Enter JAQUENETTA *and* COSTARD.

Jaq. God bless the king !
King.   What present hast thou there ?
Cost. Some certain treason.
King.   What makes treason here ?
Cost. Nay, it makes nothing, sir.
King.   If it mar nothing neither,
The treason and you go in peace away together.
Jaq. I beseech your grace, let this letter be read :
Our person misdoubts it ; it was treason, he said.   191
King. Biron, read it over.   [BIRON *reads the letter.*
Where hadst thou it ?
Jaq. Of Costard.
King. Where hadst thou it ?
Cost. Of Dun Adramadio, Dun Adramadio.
King. How now ! what is in you ? why dost thou
tear it ?
Biron. A toy, my liege, a toy : your grace needs not
fear it.
Long. It did move him to passion, and therefore
let 's hear it.
Dum. [*Picking up the pieces.*] It is Biron's writing,
and here is his name.   200
Biron. [*To* COSTARD.] Ah, you whoreson logger-
head ! you were born to do me shame.—
Guilty, my lord, guilty ! I confess, I confess.
King. What ?
Biron. That you three fools lack'd me, fool, to make
up the mess ;
He, he, and you, and you, my liege, and I,
Are pick-purses in love, and we deserve to die.
O ! dismiss this audience, and I shall tell you more.
Dum. Now the number is even.
Biron.   True, true ; we are four.—
Will these turtles be gone ?
King.   Hence, sirs ; away !
Cost. Walk aside the true folk, and let the traitors
stay.   [*Exeunt* COSTARD *and* JAQUENETTA.

Biron. Sweet lords, sweet lovers, O ! let us embrace.
As true we are, as flesh and blood can be :   212
The sea will ebb and flow, heaven show his face ;
Young blood doth not obey an old decree :
We cannot cross the cause why we are born ;
Therefore, of all hands must we be forsworn.
King. What, did these rent lines show some love of
thine ?
Biron. Did they ? quoth you. Who sees the heavenly
Rosaline,
That, like a rude and savage man of Inde,
At the first opening of the gorgeous east,   220
Bows not his vassal head, and, stricken blind,
Kisses the base ground with obedient breast ?
What peremptory, eagle-sighted eye
Dares look upon the heaven of her brow,
That is not blinded by her majesty ?
King. What zeal, what fury hath inspir'd thee now ?
My love, her mistress, is a gracious moon,
She an attending star, scarce seen a light.
Biron. My eyes are then no eyes, nor I Biron.
O ! but for my love, day would turn to night.   230
Of all complexions the cull'd sovereignty
Do meet, as at a fair, in her fair cheek ;
Where several worthies make one dignity,
Where nothing wants that want itself doth seek.
Lend me the flourish of all gentle tongues,—
Fie, painted rhetoric ! O ! she needs it not :
To things of sale a seller's praise belongs ;
She passes praise ; then praise too short doth blot.
A wither'd hermit, five-score winters worn,
Might shake off fifty, looking in her eye :   240
Beauty doth varnish age, as if new-born,
And gives the crutch the cradle's infancy.
O ! 't is the sun, that maketh all things shine !
King. By heaven, thy love is black as ebony.
Biron. Is ebony like her ? O wood divine !
A wife of such wood were felicity.
O ! who can give an oath ? where is a book ?
That I may swear beauty doth beauty lack,
If that she learn not of her eye to look :
No face is fair, that is not full so black.   250
King. O paradox ! Black is the badge of hell,
The hue of dungeons, and the scowl of night ;
And beauty's crest becomes the heavens well.
Biron. Devils soonest tempt, resembling spirits of
light.
O ! if in black my lady's brows be deck'd,
It mourns, that painting, and usurping hair,
Should ravish doters with a false aspect ;
And therefore is she born to make black fair.
Her favour turns the fashion of the days ;
For native blood is counted painting now,   260
And therefore red, that would avoid dispraise,
Paints itself black, to imitate her brow.
Dum. To look like her are chimney-sweepers black.
Long. And since her time are colliers counted
bright.
King. And Ethiops of their sweet complexion
crack.
Dum. Dark needs no candles now, for dark is
light.
Biron. Your mistresses dare never come in rain,
For fear their colours should be wash'd away.
King. 'T were good, yours did ; for, sir, to tell you
plain,
I 'll find a fairer face not wash'd to-day.   270
Biron. I 'll prove her fair, or talk till doomsday here.
King. No devil will fright thee then so much as she.
Dum. I never knew man hold vile stuff so dear.
Long. [*Showing his shoe.*] Look, here 's thy love :
my foot and her face see.
Biron. O ! if the streets were paved with thine eyes,
Her feet were much too dainty for such tread.
Dum. O vile ! then, as she goes, what upward lies
The street should see, as she walk'd overhead.
King. But what of this ? Are we not all in love ?
Biron. O ! nothing so sure ; and thereby all for-
sworn.   280
King. Then leave this chat : and, good Biron, now
prove
Our loving lawful, and our faith not torn.

Dum. Ay, marry, there; some flattery for this evil.
Long. O! some authority how to proceed;
Some tricks, some quillets, how to cheat the devil.
Dum. Some salve for perjury.
Biron. O! 't is more than need.—
Have at you then, affection's men-at-arms:
Consider, what you first did swear unto,—
To fast,—to study,—and to see no woman:
Flat treason 'gainst the kingly state of youth. 290
Say, can you fast? your stomachs are too young,
And abstinence engenders maladies.
And where that you have vow'd to study, lords,
In that each of you have forsworn his book,
Can you still dream, and pore, and thereon look?
For when would you, my lord, or you, or you,
Have found the ground of study's excellence,
Without the beauty of a woman's face?
From women's eyes this doctrine I derive:
They are the ground, the books, the academes, 300
From whence doth spring the true Promethean fire.
Why, universal plodding prisons up
The nimble spirits in the arteries,
As motion, and long-during action, tires
The sinewy vigour of the traveller.
Now, for not looking on a woman's face,
You have in that forsworn the use of eyes,
And study too, the causer of your vow;
For where is any author in the world,
Teaches such beauty as a woman's eye? 310
Learning is but an adjunct to ourself,
And where we are, our learning likewise is:
Then, when ourselves we see in ladies' eyes,
Do we not likewise see our learning there?
O! we have made a vow to study, lords,
And in that vow we have forsworn our books:
For when would you, my liege, or you, or you,
In leaden contemplation have found out
Such fiery numbers, as the prompting eyes
Of beauty's tutors have enrich'd you with? 320
Other slow arts entirely keep the brain,
And therefore, finding barren practisers,
Scarce show a harvest of their heavy toil:
But love, first learned in a lady's eyes,
Lives not alone immured in the brain,
But, with the motion of all elements,
Courses as swift as thought in every power,
And gives to every power a double power,
Above their functions and their offices.
It adds a precious seeing to the eye; 330
A lover's eyes will gaze an eagle blind:
A lover's ear will hear the lowest sound,
When the suspicious head of theft is stopp'd:
Love's feeling is more soft, and sensible,

Than are the tender horns of cockled snails:
Love's tongue proves dainty Bacchus gross in taste.
For valour, is not Love a Hercules,
Still climbing trees in the Hesperides?
Subtle as Sphinx; as sweet, and musical,
As bright Apollo's lute, strung with his hair; 340
And, when Love speaks, the voice of all the gods
Make heaven drowsy with the harmony.
Never durst poet touch a pen to write,
Until his ink were temper'd with Love's sighs;
O! then his lines would ravish savage ears,
And plant in tyrants mild humility.
From women's eyes this doctrine I derive:
They sparkle still the right Promethean fire;
They are the books, the arts, the academes,
That show, contain, and nourish all the world; 350
Else none at all in aught proves excellent.
Then, fools you were these women to forswear,
Or, keeping what is sworn, you will prove fools.
For wisdom's sake, a word that all men love,
Or for love's sake, a word that loves all men,
Or for men's sake, the authors of these women,
Or women's sake, by whom we men are men,
Let us once lose our oaths, to find ourselves,
Or else we lose ourselves, to keep our oaths.
It is religion to be thus forsworn; 360
For charity itself fulfils the law;
And who can sever love from charity?
King. Saint Cupid, then! and, soldiers, to the
field!
Biron. Advance your standards, and upon them,
lords!
Pell-mell, down with them! but be first advis'd,
In conflict that you get the sun of them.
Long. Now to plain-dealing: lay these glozes by.
Shall we resolve to woo these girls of France?
King. And win them too: therefore, let us devise
Some entertainment for them in their tents. 370
Biron. First, from the park let us conduct them
thither;
Then, homeward, every man attach the hand
Of his fair mistress. In the afternoon
We will with some strange pastime solace them,
Such as the shortness of the time can shape;
For revels, dances, masks, and merry hours,
Forerun fair Love, strewing her way with flowers.
King. Away, away! no time shall be omitted,
That will be time, and may by us be fitted.
Biron. Allons! Allons!—Sow'd cockle reap'd no
corn; 380
And justice always whirls in equal measure:
Light wenches may prove plagues to men forsworn;
If so, our copper buys no better treasure. [*Exeunt.*

ACT V.

Scene I.—Another Part of the Same.

Enter Holofernes, *Sir* Nathaniel, *and* Dull.

Holofernes.
*A*TIS *quod sufficit.*
  Nath. I praise God for you, sir: your
reasons at dinner have been sharp and
sententious; pleasant without scurrility,
witty without affection, audacious without impudency, learned without opinion,
and strange without heresy. I did converse this *quondam* day with a companion of the king's, who is intituled,
nominated, or called, Don Adriano de Armado. 10

Hol. Novi hominem tanquam te: his humour is
lofty, his discourse peremptory, his tongue filed, his
eye ambitious, his gait majestical, and his general
behaviour vain, ridiculous, and thrasonical. He is
too picked, too spruce, too affected, too odd, as it
were, too peregrinate, as I may call it.
  Nath. A most singular and choice epithet.
  [*Draws out his table-book.*
  Hol. He draweth out the thread of his verbosity
finer than the staple of his argument. I abhor such
fanatical phantasms, such insociable and point-device

companions; such rackers of orthography, as to speak
dout, fine, when he should say doubt; det, when he
should pronounce debt,—d, e, b, t, not d, e, t; he
clepeth a calf, caulf; half, haulf; neighbour *vocatur*
nebour; neigh abbreviated ne. This is abhominable
(which he would call abominable), it insinuateth me
of insanie: *ne intelligis, domine?* to make frantic,
lunatic.

Nath. Laus Deo, bone intelligo.

Hol. Bone?—*bone* for *bene: Priscian* a little
scratch'd; 't will serve.   31

Enter ARMADO, MOTH, *and* COSTARD.

Nath. Videsne quis venit?
Hol. Video, et gaudeo.
Arm. [*To* MOTH.] Chirrah!
Hol. Quare chirrah, not sirrah?
Arm. Men of peace, well encounter'd.
Hol. Most military sir, salutation.
Moth. They have been at a great feast of languages,
and stolen the scraps.   39
Cost. O! they have lived long on the alms-basket of
words. I marvel thy master hath not eaten thee for
a word; for thou art not so long by the head as *hono-
rificabilitudinitatibus:* thou art easier swallowed
than a flap-dragon.
Moth. Peace! the peal begins.
Arm. [*To* HOL.] Monsieur, are you not letter'd?
Moth. Yes, yes, he teaches boys the horn-book.—
What is a, b, spelt backward with the horn on his
head?
Hol. Ba, *pueritia,* with a horn added.   50
Moth. Ba! most silly sheep, with a horn.—You hear
his learning.
Hol. Quis, quis, thou consonant?
Moth. The third of the five vowels, if you repeat
them; or the fifth, if I.
Hol. I will repeat them;—a, e, i.
Moth. The sheep: the other two concludes it;—o, u.
Arm. Now, by the salt wave of the Mediterranean,
a sweet touch, a quick venew of wit! snip, snap, quick
and home: it rejoiceth my intellect; true wit!   60
Moth. Offer'd by a child to an old man; which is
wit-old.
Hol. What is the figure? what is the figure?
Moth. Horns.
Hol. Thou disputest like an infant: go, whip thy gig.
Moth. Lend me your horn to make one, and I will
whip about your infamy *circum circa.* A gig of a
cuckold's horn!   68
Cost. An I had but one penny in the world, thou
shouldst have it to buy gingerbread. Hold, there is
the very remuneration I had of thy master, thou halfpenny purse of wit, thou pigeon-egg of discretion.
O! an the heavens were so pleased, that thou wert but
my bastard, what a joyful father wouldst thou make
me! Go to; thou hast it *ad dunghill,* at the fingers'
ends, as they say.
Hol. O! I smell false Latin; dunghill for *unguem.*
Arm. Arts-man, *præambula:* we will be singled
from the barbarous. Do you not educate youth at the
charge-house on the top of the mountain?   80
Hol. Or *mons,* the hill.
Arm. At your sweet pleasure, for the mountain.
Hol. I do, sans question.
Arm. Sir, it is the king's most sweet pleasure and
affection, to congratulate the princess at her pavilion
in the posteriors of this day, which the rude multitude call the afternoon.
Hol. The posterior of the day, most generous sir, is
liable, congruent, and measurable for the afternoon:
the word is well cull'd, chose; sweet and apt, I do assure you, sir; I do assure.   91
Arm. Sir, the king is a noble gentleman, and my
familiar, I do assure ye, very good friend.—For
what is inward between us, let it pass;—I do beseech
thee, remember thy courtesy,—I beseech thee, apparel thy head;—and among other importunate and
most serious designs,—and of great import indeed,
too,—but let that pass;—for I must tell thee, it will
please his grace (by the world) sometime to lean upon

my poor shoulder, and with his royal finger, thus,
dally with my excrement, with my mustachio: but,
sweet heart, let that pass. By the world, I recount no
fable: some certain special honours it pleaseth his
greatness to impart to Armado, a soldier, a man of
travel, that hath seen the world: but let that pass.—
The very all of all is,—but, sweet heart, I do implore
secrecy,—that the king would have me present the
princess, sweet chuck, with some delightful ostentation, or show, or pageant, or antick, or fire-work.
Now, understanding that the curate and your sweet
self are good at such eruptions, and sudden breaking out of mirth, as it were, I have acquainted you
withal, to the end to crave your assistance.

Arm. "But, sweet heart, I do implore secrecy."

Hol. Sir, you shall present before her the Nine
Worthies.—Sir Nathaniel, as concerning some entertainment of time, some show in the posterior of this
day, to be rendered by our assistance,—at the king's
command, and this most gallant, illustrate, and
learned gentleman,—before the princess, I say, none
so fit as to present the Nine Worthies.   120
Nath. Where will you find men worthy enough to
present them?
Hol. Joshua, yourself; myself, or this gallant gentleman, Judas Maccabæus; this swain (because of his
great limb or joint) shall pass Pompey the Great; the
page, Hercules.
Arm. Pardon, sir; error: he is not quantity enough
for that Worthy's thumb: he is not so big as the end
of his club.
Hol. Shall I have audience? he shall present Hercules in minority: his *enter* and *exit* shall be strangling a snake; and I will have an apology for that
purpose.
Moth. An excellent device! so, if any of the audience
hiss, you may cry, "Well done, Hercules! now thou
crushest the snake!" that is the way to make an
offence gracious, though few have the grace to do it.
Arm. For the rest of the Worthies?—
Hol. I will play three myself.
Moth. Thrice-worthy gentleman!   140
Arm. Shall I tell you a thing?
Hol. We attend.
Arm. We will have, if this fadge not, an antick.
I beseech you, follow.
Hol. Via!—Goodman Dull, thou hast spoken no
word all this while.
Dull. Nor understood none neither, sir.
Hol. Allons! we will employ thee.
Dull. I'll make one in a dance, or so; or I will play
On the tabor to the Worthies, and let them dance the
hay.   150
Hol. Most dull, honest Dull. To our sport, away!
       [*Exeunt.*

Scene II.—Another Part of the Same. Before the
PRINCESS'S Pavilion.

Enter the PRINCESS, KATHARINE, ROSALINE, *and*
MARIA.

Prin. Sweet hearts, we shall be rich ere we depart,
If fairings come thus plentifully in:
A lady wall'd about with diamonds!—
Look you, what I have from the loving king.
Ros. Madam, came nothing else along with that?
Prin. Nothing but this? yes; as much love in rhyme,
As would be cramm'd up in a sheet of paper,
Writ on both sides the leaf, margin and all,
That he was fain to seal on Cupid's name.
Ros. That was the way to make his godhead wax;
For he hath been five thousand years a boy. 11
Kath. Ay, and a shrewd unhappy gallows too.
Ros. You'll ne'er be friends with him: he kill'd
your sister.
Kath. He made her melancholy, sad, and heavy;
And so she died: had she been light, like you,
Of such a merry, nimble, stirring spirit,
She might have been a grandam ere she died;
And so may you, for a light heart lives long.
Ros. What's your dark meaning, mouse, of this
light word? 20
Kath. A light condition in a beauty dark.
Ros. We need more light to find your meaning out.
Kath. You'll mar the light by taking it in snuff;
Therefore, I'll darkly end the argument.
Ros. Look, what you do, you do it still i' the dark.
Kath. So do not you, for you are a light wench.
Ros. Indeed, I weigh not you, and therefore light.
Kath. You weigh me not?—O! that's you care not
for me.
Ros. Great reason; for, past cure is still past care.
Prin. Well bandied both; a set of wit well play'd.
But, Rosaline, you have a favour too: 30
Who sent it? and what is it?
Ros.   I would you knew:
An if my face were but as fair as yours,
My favour were as great: be witness this.
Nay, I have verses too, I thank Biron.
The numbers true; and, were the numbering too,
I were the fairest goddess on the ground:
I am compar'd to twenty thousand fairs.
O! he hath drawn my picture in his letter.
Prin. Anything like?
Ros. Much in the letters, nothing in the praise. 40
Prin. Beauteous as ink: a good conclusion.
Kath. Fair as a text B in a copy-book.
Ros. 'Ware pencils! ho! let me not die your debtor,
My red dominical, my golden letter:
O, that your face were not so full of O's!
Prin. A pox of that jest! and I beshrew all shrows!
But, Katharine, what was sent to you from fair
Dumaine?
Kath. Madam, this glove.
Prin.   Did he not send you twain?
Kath. Yes, madam; and, moreover,
Some thousand verses of a faithful lover: 50
A huge translation of hypocrisy,
Vilely compil'd, profound simplicity.
Mar. This, and these pearls to me sent Longaville:
The letter is too long by half a mile.
Prin. I think no less. Dost thou not wish in heart,
The chain were longer, and the letter short?
Mar. Ay, or I would these hands might never part.
Prin. We are wise girls to mock our lovers so.
Ros. They are worse fools to purchase mocking so.
That same Biron I'll torture ere I go. 60
O! that I knew he were but in by the week!
How I would make him fawn, and beg, and seek,
And wait the season, and observe the times,
And spend his prodigal wits in bootless rhymes,
And shape his service wholly to my hests,
And make him proud to make me proud that jests!
So portent-like would I o'ersway his state,
That he should be my fool, and I his fate.
Prin. None are so surely caught, when they are
catch'd,

As wit turn'd fool: folly, in wisdom hatch'd, 70
Hath wisdom's warrant, and the help of school,
And wit's own grace to grace a learned fool.
Ros. The blood of youth burns not with such excess,
As gravity's revolt to wantonness.
Mar. Folly in fools bears not so strong a note,
As foolery in the wise, when wit doth dote;
Since all the power thereof it doth apply,
To prove, by wit, worth in simplicity.

Enter BOYET.

Prin. Here comes Boyet, and mirth is in his face.
Boyet. O! I am stabb'd with laughter. Where's
her grace? 80
Prin. Thy news, Boyet?
Boyet.   Prepare, madam, prepare!
Arm, wenches, arm! encounters mounted are
Against your peace. Love doth approach disguis'd,
Armed in arguments: you'll be surpris'd.
Muster your wits; stand in your own defence;
Or hide your heads like cowards, and fly hence.

Boyet. "Arm, wenches, arm!"

Prin. Saint Denis to Saint Cupid! What are they,
That charge their breath against us? say, scout, say.
Boyet. Under the cool shade of a sycamore,
I thought to close mine eyes some half an hour, 90
When, lo! to interrupt my purpos'd rest,
Toward that shade I might behold addrest
The king and his companions: warily
I stole into a neighbour thicket by,
And overheard what you shall overhear;
That by-and-by disguis'd they will be here.
Their herald is a pretty knavish page,
That well by heart hath conn'd his embassage:
Action, and accent, did they teach him there;
"Thus must thou speak, and thus thy body bear:"100
And ever and anon they made a doubt,
Presence majestical would put him out;
"For," quoth the king, "an angel shalt thou see;
Yet fear not thou, but speak audaciously."
The boy replied, "An angel is not evil;
I should have fear'd her, had she been a devil."
With that all laugh'd, and clapp'd him on the
shoulder,
Making the bold wag by their praises bolder.
One rubb'd his elbow, thus, and fleer'd, and swore,
A better speech was never spoke before; 110
Another, with his finger and his thumb,
Cry'd "*Via!* we will do't, come what will come;"
The third he caper'd, and cried, "All goes well;"
The fourth turn'd on the toe, and down he fell.
With that, they all did tumble on the ground,
With such a zealous laughter, so profound,
That in this spleen ridiculous appears,
To check their folly, passion's solemn tears.

Prin. But what, but what, come they to visit us?
Boyet. They do, they do ; and are apparell'd thus,—
Like Muscovites, or Russians : as I guess, 121
Their purpose is, to parle, to court, and dance ;
And every one his love-feat will advance
Unto his several mistress ; which they 'll know
By favours several which they did bestow.
Prin. And will they so? the gallants shall be
　　task'd,
For, ladies, we will every one be mask'd,
And not a man of them shall have the grace,
Despite of suit, to see a lady's face.—
Hold, Rosaline, this favour thou shalt wear, 130
And then the king will court thee for his dear :
Hold, take thou this, my sweet, and give me thine,
So shall Biron take me for Rosaline.—
And change you favours, too ; so shall your loves
Woo contrary, deceiv'd by these removes.
Ros. Come on then : wear the favours most in sight.
Kath. But in this changing what is your intent?
Prin. The effect of my intent is, to cross theirs :
They do it but in mocking merriment ;
And mock for mock is only my intent. 140
Their several counsels they unbosom shall
To loves mistook ; and so be mock'd withal,
Upon the next occasion that we meet,
With visages display'd, to talk and greet.
Ros. But shall we dance, if they desire us to 't ?
Prin. No ; to the death, we will not move a foot ;
Nor to their penn'd speech render we no grace ;
But, while 't is spoke, each turn away her face.
Boyet. Why, that contempt will kill the speaker's
　　heart.
And quite divorce his memory from his part. 150
Prin. Therefore I do it ; and, I make no doubt,
The rest will ne'er come in, if he be out.
There 's no such sport, as sport by sport o'erthrown ;
To make theirs ours, and ours none but our own :
So shall we stay, mocking intended game,
And they, well mock'd, depart away with shame.
　　　　　　　　　　[*Trumpets sound within.*
Boyet. The trumpet sounds : be mask'd, the maskers
　　come.　　　　　　　　　[*The Ladies mask.*

Enter the KING, BIRON, LONGAVILLE, *and* DUMAINE,
in Russian habits, and masked ; MOTH, *Musicians,
and Attendants.*

Moth. " All hail, the richest beauties on the earth !"
Boyet. Beauties no richer than rich taffata.
Moth. " A holy parcel of the fairest dames, 160
　　　　　　　　[*The Ladies turn their backs to him.*
That ever turn'd their—backs—to mortal views !"
Biron. " Their eyes," villain, " their eyes."
Moth. " That ever turn'd their eyes to mortal
　　views !"
Out"—
Boyet. True ; " out," indeed.
Moth. " Out of your favours, heavenly spirits,
　　vouchsafe
Not to behold "—　　　　　　　　[*The Ladies mask.*
Biron. " Once to behold," rogue.
Moth. " Once to behold with your sun-beamed eyes,
　　with your sun-beamed eyes "— 170
Boyet. They will not answer to that epithet ;
You were best call it daughter-beamed eyes.
Moth. They do not mark me, and that brings me
　　out.
Biron. Is this your perfectness? be gone, you rogue.
Ros. What would these strangers? know their
　　minds, Boyet.
If they do speak our language, 't is our will
That some plain man recount their purposes.
Know what they would.
Boyet. 　　　　What would you with the princess?
Biron. Nothing but peace, and gentle visitation.
Ros. What would they, say they? 180
Boyet. Nothing but peace, and gentle visitation.
Ros. Why, that they have ; and bid them so be
　　gone.
Boyet. She says, you have it, and you may be gone.
King. Say to her, we have measur'd many miles..
To tread a measure with her on this grass.

Boyet. They say, that they have measur'd many a
　　mile,
To tread a measure with you on this grass.
Ros. It is not so. Ask them how many inches
Is in one mile : if they have measur'd many,
The measure then of one is easily told. 190
Boyet. If, to come hither, you have measur'd miles,
And many, miles, the princess bids you tell,
How many inches do fill up one mile.
Biron. Tell her, we measure them by weary steps.
Boyet. She hears herself.
Ros. 　　　　　　　How many weary steps,
Of many weary miles you have o'ergone,
Are number'd in the travel of one mile?
Biron. We number nothing that we spend for you :
Our duty is so rich, so infinite,
That we may do it still without accompt. 200
Vouchsafe to show the sunshine of your face,
That we, like savages, may worship it.
Ros. My face is but a moon, and clouded too.
King. Blessed are clouds, to do as such clouds do !
Vouchsafe, bright moon, and these thy stars, to
　　shine
(Those clouds removed) upon our watery eyne.
Ros. O vain petitioner ! beg a greater matter ;
Thou now request'st but moonshine in the water.
King. Then, in our measure vouchsafe but one
　　change.
Thou bidd'st me beg ; this begging is not strange. 210
Ros. Play, music, then ! nay, you must do it soon.
　　　　　　　　　　　　　[*Music plays.*
Not yet ;—no dance :—thus change I like the moon.
King. Will you not dance? How come you thus
　　estrang'd ?
Ros. You took the moon at full, but now she 's
　　changed.
King. Yet still she is the moon, and I the man.
Yet music plays : vouchsafe some motion to it.
Ros. Our ears vouchsafe it.
King. 　　　　　　　But your legs should do it.
Ros. Since you are strangers, and come here by
　　chance,
We 'll not be nice : take hands :—we will not dance.
King. Why take we hands then?
Ros. 　　　　　　　　Only to part friends.—
Court'sy, sweet hearts ; and so the measure ends. 221
King. More measure of this measure : be not nice.
Ros. We can afford no more at such a price.
King. Prize you yourselves? What buys your
　　company ?
Ros. Your absence only.
King. 　　　　　　　That can never be.
Ros. Then cannot we be bought ; and so adieu.
Twice to your visor, and half once to you !
King. If you deny to dance, let 's hold more chat.
Ros. In private then.
King. 　　　　　　I am best pleas'd with that.
　　　　　　　　　　　[*They converse apart.*
Biron. White-handed mistress, one sweet word
　　with thee. 230
Prin. Honey, and milk, and sugar : there are three.
Biron. Nay then, two treys, (an if you grow so
　　nice)
Metheglin, wort, and malmsey.—Well run, dice !
There 's half a dozen sweets.
Prin. 　　　　　　　Seventh sweet, adieu.
Since you can cog, I 'll play no more with you.
Biron. One word in secret.
Prin. 　　　　　　　Let it not be sweet.
Biron. Thou griev'st my gall.
Prin. 　　　　　　　Gall? bitter.
Biron. 　　　　　　　　　Therefore meet.
　　　　　　　　　　　[*They converse apart.*
Dum. Will you vouchsafe with me to change a
　　word ?
Mar. Name it.
Dum. 　　　Fair lady,—
Mar. 　　　　　Say you so? Fair lord,—
Take that for your fair lady.
Dum. 　　　　　Please it you, 240
As much in private, and I 'll bid adieu.
　　　　　　　　　　　[*They converse apart.*

Kath. What, was your visor made without a
  tongue?
Long. I know the reason, lady, why you ask.
Kath. O, for your reason! quickly, sir ; I long.
Long. You have a double tongue within your
  mask,
And would afford my speechless visor half.
Kath. Veal, quoth the Dutchman.—Is not veal a
  calf?
Long. A calf, fair lady?
Kath.   No, a fair lord calf.
Long. Let 's part the word.
Kath.   No, I 'll not be your half :
Take all, and wean it : it may prove an ox.   250
Long. Look, how you butt yourself in these sharp
  mocks.
Will you give horns, chaste lady? do not so.
Kath. Then die a calf, before your horns do grow.
Long. One word in private with you, ere I die.
Kath. Bleat softly then : the butcher hears you cry.
                  [*They converse apart.*
Boyet. The tongues of mocking wenches are as
  keen
As is the razor's edge invisible,
Cutting a smaller hair than may be seen ;
Above the sense of sense, so sensible
Seemeth their conference : their conceits have wings
Fleeter than arrows, bullets, wind, thought, swifter
  things.   261
Ros. Not one word more, my maids : break off,
  break off.
Biron. By heaven, all dry-beaten with pure scoff!
King. Farewell, mad wenches : you have simple
  wits.
   [*Exeunt* KING, *Lords,* MOTH, *Music, and
      Attendants.*
Prin. Twenty adieus, my frozen Muscovites.—
Are these the breed of wits so wonder'd at ?
Boyet. Tapers they are, with your sweet breaths
  puff'd out.
Ros. Well-liking wits they have ; gross, gross ; fat,
  fat.
Prin. O poverty in wit, kingly-poor flout!
Will they not, think you, hang themselves to-night,
Or ever, but in visors, show their faces ?   271
This pert Biron was out of countenance quite.
Ros. O ! they were all in lamentable cases !
The king was weeping-ripe for a good word.
Prin. Biron did swear himself out of all suit.
Mar. Dumaine was at my service, and his sword :
No point, quoth I : my servant straight was mute.
Kath. Lord Longaville said, I came o'er his heart ;
And trow you, what he call'd me ?
Prin.   Qualm, perhaps.
Kath. Yes, in good faith.
Prin.   Go, sickness as thou art!
Ros. Well, better wits have worn plain statute-caps.
But will you hear? the king is my love sworn.   282
Prin. And quick Biron hath plighted faith to me.
Kath. And Longaville was for my service born.
Mar. Dumaine is mine, as sure as bark on tree.
Boyet. Madam, and pretty mistresses, give ear.
Immediately they will again be here
In their own shapes ; for it can never be,
They will digest this harsh indignity.
Prin. Will they return ?
Boyet.   They will, they will, God knows ;
And leap for joy, though they are lame with blows :
Therefore, change favours ; and, when they repair,
Blow like sweet roses in this summer air.   293
Prin. How blow? how blow? speak to be under-
  stood.
Boyet. Fair ladies, mask'd, are roses in their bud :
Dismask'd, their damask sweet commixture shown,
Are angels vailing clouds, or roses blown.
Prin. Avaunt, perplexity ! What shall we do,
If they return in their own shapes to woo ?
Ros. Good madam, if by me you 'll be advis'd,   300
Let 's mock them still, as well known, as disguis'd.
Let us complain to them what fools were here,
Disguis'd like Muscovites, in shapeless gear ;
And wonder, what they were, and to what end

Their shallow shows, and prologue vilely penn'd,
And their rough carriage so ridiculous,
Should be presented at our tent to us.
Boyet. Ladies, withdraw ; the gallants are at hand.
Prin. Whip to our tents, as roes run over land.
  [*Exeunt* PRIN., ROS., KATH., *and* MAR.

Enter the KING, BIRON, LONGAVILLE, *and* DUMAINE,
    in their proper habits.

King. Fair sir, God save you ! Where is the prin-
  cess ?   310
Boyet. Gone to her tent. Please it your majesty,
Command me any service to her thither ?
King. That she vouchsafe me audience for one
  word.
Boyet. I will ; and so will she, I know, my lord.
                         [*Exit.*
Biron. This fellow pecks up wit, as pigeons peas,
And utters it again when God doth please.
He is wit's pedlar, and retails his wares
At wakes, and wassails, meetings, markets, fairs ;
And we that sell by gross, the Lord doth know,
Have not the grace to grace it with such show.   320
This gallant pins the wenches on his sleeve :
Had he been Adam, he had tempted Eve.
He can carve too, and lisp : why, this is he,
That kiss'd away his hand in courtesy ;
This is the ape of form, monsieur the nice,
That, when he plays at tables, chides the dice
In honourable terms : nay, he can sing
A mean most meanly, and in ushering,
Mend him who can : the ladies call him, sweet ;
The stairs, as he treads on them, kiss his feet.   330
This is the flower that smiles on every one,
To show his teeth as white as whales-bone ;
And consciences, that will not die in debt,
Pay him the due of honey-tongued Boyet.
King. A blister on his sweet tongue, with my heart,
That put Armado's page out of his part !

Enter the PRINCESS, *ushered by* BOYET ; ROSALINE,
  MARIA, KATHARINE, *and Attendants.*

Biron. See where it comes !—Behaviour, what wert
  thou,
Till this man show'd thee? and what art thou now?
King. All hail, sweet madam, and fair time of day!
Prin. Fair, in all hail, is foul, as I conceive.   340
King. Construe my speeches better, if you may.
Prin. Then wish me better : I will give you leave.
King. We came to visit you, and purpose now
To lead you to our court : vouchsafe it then.
Prin. This field shall hold me, and so hold your
  vow :
Nor God, nor I, delights in perjur'd men.
King. Rebuke me not for that which you provóke ;
The virtue of your eye must break my oath.
Prin. You nickname virtue ; vice you should have
  spoke ;
For virtue's office never breaks men's troth.   350
Now, by my maiden honour, yet as pure
As the unsullied lily, I protest,
A world of torments though I should endure,
I would not yield to be your house's guest ;
So much I hate a breaking cause to be
Of heavenly oaths, vow'd with integrity.
King. O ! you have liv'd in desolation here,
Unseen, unvisited, much to our shame.
Prin. Not so, my lord ; it is not so, I swear :
We have had pastimes here, and pleasant game.   360
A mess of Russians left us but of late.
King. How, madam ? Russians ?
Prin.   Ay, in truth, my lord ;
Trim gallants, full of courtship, and of state.
Ros. Madam, speak true.—It is not so, my lord :
My lady (to the manner of the days)
In courtesy gives undeserving praise.
We four, indeed, confronted were with four
In Russian habit : here they stay'd an hour,
And talk'd apace ; and in that hour, my lord,
They did not bless us with one happy word.   370
I dare not call them fools ; but this I think,
When they are thirsty, fools would fain have drink.

Biron. This jest is dry to me.—Fair, gentle sweet,
Your wit makes wise things foolish : when we greet,
With eyes best seeing, heaven's fiery eye,
By light we lose light : your capacity
Is of that nature, that to your huge store
Wise things seem foolish, and rich things but poor.
Ros. This proves you wise and rich, for in my eye,—
Biron. I am a fool, and full of poverty.　380
Ros. But that you take what doth to you belong,
It were a fault to snatch words from my tongue.
Biron. O! I am yours, and all that I possess.
Ros. All the fool mine?
Biron.　　　　　　　I cannot give you less.
Ros. Which of the visors was it that you wore?
Biron. Where? when? what visor? why demand
　　you this?
Ros. There, then, that visor; that superfluous case,
That hid the worse, and show'd the better face.
King. We are descried : they 'll mock us now down-
　　right.
Dum. Let us confess, and turn it to a jest.　390
Prin. Amaz'd, my lord? Why looks your highness
　　sad?
Ros. Help! hold his brows! he 'll swoond. Why
　　look you pale?—
Sea-sick, I think, coming from Muscovy.
Biron. Thus pour the stars down plagues for per-
　　jury.
Can any face of brass hold longer out?—
Here stand I, lady; dart thy skill at me;
Bruise me with scorn, confound me with a flout;
Thrust thy sharp wit quite through my ignorance;
Cut me to pieces with thy keen conceit;
And I will wish thee never more to dance,　400
Nor never more in Russian habit wait.
O! never will I trust to speeches penn'd,
Nor to the motion of a school-boy's tongue;
Nor never come in visor to my friend;
Nor woo in rhyme, like a blind harper's song;
Taffata phrases, silken terms precise,
Three-pil'd hyperboles, spruce affectation,
Figures pedantical : these summer-flies
Have blown me full of maggot ostentation.
I do forswear them; and I here protest,　410
By this white glove, (how white the hand, God knows)
Henceforth my wooing mind shall be express'd
In russet yeas, and honest kersey noes :
And, to begin,—wench, so God help me, la!
My love to thee is sound, sans crack or flaw.
Ros. Sans SANS, I pray you.
Biron.　　　　　　　Yet I have a trick
Of the old rage :—bear with me, I am sick;
I'll leave it by degrees. Soft! let us see :—
Write "Lord have mercy on us" on those three;
They are infected, in their hearts it lies;　420
They have the plague, and caught it of your eyes :
These lords are visited; you are not free,
For the Lord's tokens on you do I see.
Prin. No, they are free that gave these tokens to us.
Biron. Our states are forfeit : seek not to undo us.
Ros. It is not so. For how can this be true,
That you stand forfeit, being those that sue?
Biron. Peace! for I will not have to do with you.
Ros. Nor shall not, if I do as I intend.
Biron. Speak for yourselves : my wit is at an end.
King. Teach us, sweet madam, for our rude trans-
　　gression　431
Some fair excuse.
Prin.　　　　　The fairest is confession.
Were you not here, but even now, disguis'd?
King. Madam, I was.
Prin.　　　　　And were you well advis'd?
King. I was, fair madam.
Prin.　　　　　When you then were here,
What did you whisper in your lady's ear?
King. That more than all the world I did respect her.
Prin. When she shall challenge this, you will re-
　　ject her.
King. Upon mine honour, no.
Prin.　　　　　Peace! peace! forbear!
Your oath once broke, you force not to forswear.　440
King. Despise me, when I break this oath of mine.

Prin. I will; and therefore keep it.—Rosaline,
What did the Russian whisper in your ear?
Ros. Madam, he swore, that he did hold me dear
As precious eyesight, and did value me
Above this world; adding thereto, moreover,
That he would wed me, or else die my lover.
Prin. God give thee joy of him! the noble lord
Most honourably doth uphold his word.
King. What mean you, madam? by my life, my
　　troth,　450
I never swore this lady such an oath.
Ros. By heaven, you did; and to confirm it plain,
You gave me this : but take it, sir, again.
King. My faith, and this, the princess I did give :
I knew her by this jewel on her sleeve.
Prin. Pardon me, sir, this jewel did she wear;
And Lord Biron, I thank him, is my dear.—
What! will you have me, or your pearl again?
Biron. Neither of either; I remit both twain.—
I see the trick on 't :—here was a consent,　460
Knowing aforehand of our merriment,
To dash it like a Christmas comedy.
Some carry-tale, some please-man, some slight zany,
Some mumble-news, some trencher-knight, some
　　Dick,
That smiles his cheek in years, and knows the trick
To make my lady laugh when she's dispos'd,
Told our intents before; which once disclos'd,
The ladies did change favours, and then we,
Following the signs, woo'd but the sign of she.
Now, to our perjury to add more terror,　470
We are again forsworn,—in will, and error.
Much upon this it is;—[*to* BOYET] and might not you
Forestall our sport, to make us thus untrue?
Do not you know my lady's foot by the squire,
And laugh upon the apple of her eye?
And stand between her back, sir, and the fire,
Holding a trencher, jesting merrily?
You put our page out : go, you are allow'd;
Die when you will, a smock shall be your shroud.
You leer upon me, do you? there 's an eye,　480
Wounds like a leaden sword.
Boyet.　　　　　Full merrily
Hath this brave manage, this career, been run.
Biron. Lo, he is tilting straight! Peace! I have
　　done.

Enter COSTARD.

Welcome, pure wit! thou partest a fair fray.
Cost. O Lord, sir, they would know,
Whether the three Worthies shall come in, or no.
Biron. What, are there but three?
Cost.　　　　　No, sir; but it is vara fine,
For every one pursents three.
Biron.　　　　　And three times thrice is nine.
Cost. Not so, sir; under correction, sir, I hope, it is
　　not so.
You cannot beg us, sir, I can assure you, sir; we know
　　what we know :　490
I hope, sir, three times thrice, sir,—
Biron.　　　　　Is not nine.
Cost. Under correction, sir, we know whereuntil it
doth amount.
Biron. By Jove, I always took three threes for nine.
Cost. O Lord! sir, it were pity you should get your
living by reckoning, sir.
Biron. How much is it?
Cost. O Lord! sir, the parties themselves, the actors,
sir, will show whereuntil it doth amount : for mine
own part, I am, as they say, but to perfect one man
in one poor man,—Pompion the Great, sir.　501
Biron. Art thou one of the Worthies?
Cost. It pleased them to think me worthy of Pompion
the Great : for mine own part, I know not the degree
of the Worthy, but I am to stand for him.
Biron. Go, bid them prepare.
Cost. We will turn it finely off, sir : we will take
　　some care.　[*Exit.*
King. Biron, they will shame us; let them not
　　approach.
Biron. We are shame-proof, my lord; and 't is some
policy

To have one show worse than the king's and his
    company.   510
King. I say, they shall not come.
Prin. Nay, my good lord, let me o'errule you now.
That sport best pleases, that doth least know how :
Where zeal strives to content, and the contents
Die in the zeal of them which it presents,
Their form confounded makes most form in mirth ;
When great things labouring perish in their birth.
  Biron. A right description of our sport, my lord.

    Enter ARMADO.

  Arm. Anointed, I implore so much expense of thy
royal sweet breath, as will utter a brace of words. 520
  [ARMADO *converses with the* KING, *and delivers*
    a paper to him.
  Prin. Doth this man serve God ?
  Biron. Why ask you ?
  Prin. He speaks not like a man of God's making.
  Arm. That's all one, my fair, sweet, honey monarch ;
for, I protest, the schoolmaster is exceeding fantastical ; too, too vain ; too, too vain : but we will put
it, as they say, to *fortuna della guerra.* I wish you
the peace of mind, most royal couplement ! [*Exit.*
  King. Here is like to be a good presence of Wor-
thies. He presents Hector of Troy ; the swain, Pom-
pey the Great ; the parish curate, Alexander ; Armado's
page, Hercules ; the pedant, Judas Maccabæus. 532
And if these four Worthies in their first show thrive,
These four will change habits, and present the other
five.
  Biron. There is five in the first show.
  King. You are deceived, 'tis not so.
  Biron. The pedant, the braggart, the hedge-priest,
the fool, and the boy :—
Abate throw at novum, and the whole world again
Cannot pick out five such, take each one in his vein.
  King. The ship is under sail, and here she comes
amain. 541

    Enter COSTARD *armed, for Pompey.*

  Cost. "I Pompey am,"—
  Boyet.   You lie, you are not he.
  Cost. "I Pompey am,"—
  Boyet.   With libbard's head on knee.
  Biron. Well said, old mocker : I must needs be
friends with thee.
  Cost. "I Pompey am, Pompey surnam'd the Big,"—
  Dum. The Great.
  Cost. It is "Great," sir ;—"Pompey surnam'd the
Great ;"
That oft in field, with targe and shield, did make my
  foe to sweat :
And travelling along this coast, I here am come by
  chance,
And lay my arms before the legs of this sweet lass of
  France." 550
If your ladyship would say, "Thanks, Pompey," I
  had done.
  Prin. Great thanks, great Pompey.
  Cost. 'Tis not so much worth ; but I hope, I was
perfect. I made a little fault in "Great."
  Biron. My hat to a halfpenny, Pompey proves the
best Worthy.

    Enter Sir NATHANIEL *armed, for Alexander.*

  Nath. "When in the world I liv'd, I was the world's
    commander ;
By east, west, north, and south, I spread my con-
  quering might :
My 'scutcheon plain declares, that I am Alisander."
  Boyet. Your nose says, no, you are not ; for it
stands too right.
  Biron. Your nose smells, no, in this, most tender-
smelling knight. 560
  Prin. The conqueror is dismay'd. Proceed, good
Alexander.
  Nath. "When in the world I liv'd, I was the world's
  commander ;"—
  Boyet. Most true ; 'tis right : you were so, Alisander.
  Biron. Pompey the Great,—
  Cost. Your servant, and Costard.

  Biron. Take away the conquerer, take away Alisander.
  Cost. [*To* NATH.] O! sir, you have overthrown
Alisander the conqueror. You will be scraped out of
the painted cloth for this : your lion, that holds his
poll-axe sitting on a close-stool, will be given to Ajax :
he will be the ninth Worthy. A conqueror, and
afeard to speak ? run away for shame, Alisander.
[NATH. *retires.*] There, an't shall please you : a
foolish mild man ; an honest man, look you, and soon
dash'd ! He is a marvellous neighbour, faith, and
a very good bowler ; but, for Alisander, alas ! you
see, how 'tis ; — a little o'erparted.—But there are
Worthies a-coming will speak their mind in some
other sort.
  Prin. Stand aside, good Pompey. 580

    Enter HOLOFERNES *armed, for Judas, and* MOTH
      armed, for Hercules.

  Hol. "Great Hercules is presented by this imp,
Whose club kill'd Cerberus, that three-headed *canus ;*
And, when he was a babe, a child, a shrimp,
Thus did he strangle serpents in his *manus.*
Quoniam he seemeth in minority,
Ergo I come with this apology.—
Keep some state in thy *exit,* and vanish.—
" Judas I am,"—
  Dum. A Judas !
  Hol. Not Iscariot, sir.— 590
" Judas I am, ycleped Maccabæus."
  Dum. Judas Maccabæus clipt, is plain Judas.
  Biron. A kissing traitor.—How art thou prov'd
    Judas ?
  Hol. "Judas I am,"—
  Dum. The more shame for you, Judas.
  Hol. What mean you, sir ?
  Boyet. To make Judas hang himself.
  Hol. Begin, sir : you are my elder.
  Biron. Well follow'd : Judas was hang'd on an elder. 600
  Hol. I will not be put out of countenance.
  Biron. Because thou hast no face.
  Hol. What is this ?
  Boyet. A cittern-head.
  Dum. The head of a bodkin.
  Biron. A death's face in a ring.
  Long. The face of an old Roman coin, scarce seen.
  Boyet. The pummel of Cæsar's falchion.
  Dum. The carv'd-bone face on a flask.
  Biron. St. George's half-cheek in a brooch.
  Dum. Ay, and in a brooch of lead. 610
  Biron. Ay, and worn in the cap of a tooth-drawer.
And now, forward ; for we have put thee in coun-
  tenance.
  Hol. You have put me out of countenance.
  Biron. False : we have given thee faces.
  Hol. But you have outfac'd them all.
  Biron. An thou wert a lion, we would do so.
  Boyet. Therefore, as he is an ass, let him go.
And so adieu, sweet Jude ! nay, why dost thou stay ?
  Dum. For the latter end of his name.
  Biron. For the ass to the Jude ? give it him :—Jud-as,
  away. 620
  Hol. This is not generous, not gentle, not humble.
  Boyet. A light for Monsieur Judas ! it grows dark,
he may stumble.
  Prin. Alas, poor Maccabæus, how hath he been
baited !

    Enter ARMADO *armed, for Hector.*

  Biron. Hide thy head, Achilles : here comes Hector
in arms.
  Dum. Though my mocks come home by me, I will
now be merry.
  King. Hector was but a Trojan in respect of this.
  Boyet. But is this Hector ?
  King. I think Hector was not so clean-timber'd. 630
  Long. His leg is too big for Hector's.
  Dum. More calf, certain.
  Boyet. No ; he is best indued in the small.
  Biron. This cannot be Hector.
  Dum. He's a god or a painter ; for he makes faces.

Arm. "The armipotent Mars, of lances the almighty,
Gave Hector a gift,"—
Dum. A gilt nutmeg.
Biron. A lemon.
Long. Stuck with cloves.   640
Dum. No, cloven.
Arm. Peace!
"The armipotent Mars, of lances the almighty,
Gave Hector a gift, the heir of Ilion;
A man so breath'd, that certain he would fight ye,
From morn till night, out of his pavilion.
I am that flower,"—
Dum.   That mint.
Long.   That columbine.
Arm. Sweet Lord Longaville, rein thy tongue.
Long. I must rather give it the rein, for it runs
against Hector.   650
Dum. Ay, and Hector's a greyhound.
Arm. The sweet war-man is dead and rotten: sweet
chucks, beat not the bones of the buried: when he
breathed, he was a man.—But I will forward with my
device. Sweet royalty, bestow on me the sense of
hearing.   [BIRON *whispers* COSTARD.
Prin. Speak, brave Hector: we are much delighted.
Arm. I do adore thy sweet grace's slipper.
Boyet. Loves her by the foot.
Dum. He may not by the yard.   660
Arm. "This Hector far surmounted Hannibal,"—
Cost. The party is gone: fellow Hector, she is gone;
she is two months on her way.
Arm. What meanest thou?
Cost. Faith, unless you play the honest Trojan, the
poor wench is cast away: she's quick; the child brags
in her belly already: 'tis yours.
Arm. Dost thou infamonise me among potentates?
Thou shalt die.
Cost. Then shall Hector be whipp'd for Jaquenetta
that is quick by him, and hang'd for Pompey that is
dead by him.   672
Dum. Most rare Pompey!
Boyet. Renowned Pompey!
Biron. Greater than great, great, great, great Pompey! Pompey the Huge!
Dum. Hector trembles.
Biron. Pompey is moved.—More Atés, more Atés!
stir them on! stir them on!
Dum. Hector will challenge him.   680
Biron. Ay, if he have no more man's blood in's belly
than will sup a flea.
Arm. By the north pole, I do challenge thee.
Cost. I will not fight with a pole, like a northern
man: I'll slash; I'll do it by the sword.—I pray you,
let me borrow my arms again.
Dum. Room for the incensed Worthies!
Cost. I'll do it in my shirt.
Dum. Most resolute Pompey!
Moth. Master, let me take you a button-hole lower.
Do you not see, Pompey is uncasing for the combat?
What mean you? you will lose your reputation.   692
Arm. Gentlemen, and soldiers, pardon me; I will
not combat in my shirt.
Dum. You may not deny it: Pompey hath made the
challenge.
Arm. Sweet bloods, I both may and will.
Biron. What reason have you for't?
Arm. The naked truth of it is, I have no shirt. I go
woolward for penance.   700
Boyet. True, and it was enjoin'd him in Rome for
want of linen; since when, I'll be sworn, he wore
none but a dishclout of Jaquenetta's, and that he
wears next his heart for a favour.

Enter Monsieur MERCADE, a Messenger.

Mer. God save you, madam.
Prin. Welcome, Mercade,
But that thou interrupt'st our merriment.
Mer. I am sorry, madam; for the news I bring
Is heavy in my tongue.—The king your father—
Prin. Dead, for my life!   710
Mer. Even so: my tale is told.

Biron. Worthies, away! The scene begins to cloud.
Arm. For mine own part, I breathe free breath. I
have seen the day of wrong through the little hole of
discretion, and I will right myself like a soldier.
     [*Exeunt Worthies.*
King. How fares your majesty?
Prin. Boyet, prepare: I will away to-night.
King. Madam, not so; I do beseech you, stay.
Prin. Prepare, I say.—I thank you, gracious lords,
For all your fair endeavours; and entreat,   720
Out of a new-sad soul, that you vouchsafe
In your rich wisdom to excuse, or hide,
The liberal opposition of our spirits:
If over-boldly we have borne ourselves
In the converse of breath, your gentleness
Was guilty of it. Farewell, worthy lord!
A heavy heart bears not a humble tongue.
Excuse me so, coming so short of thanks
For my great suit so easily obtain'd.
King. The extreme part of time extremely forms
All causes to the purpose of his speed;   731
And often, at his very loose, decides
That which long process could not arbitrate:
And though the mourning brow of progeny
Forbid the smiling courtesy of love
The holy suit which fain it would convince;
Yet, since love's argument was first on foot,
Let not the cloud of sorrow justle it
From what it purpos'd; since, to wail friends lost,
Is not by much so wholesome, profitable,   740
As to rejoice at friends but newly found.
Prin. I understand you not: my griefs are dull.
Biron. Honest plain words best pierce the ear of
     grief;
And by these badges understand the king.
For your fair sakes have we neglected time,
Play'd foul play with our oaths. Your beauty, ladies,
Hath much deform'd us, fashioning our humours
Even to the opposed end of our intents;
And what in us hath seem'd ridiculous,—
As love is full of unbefitting strains;   750
All wanton as a child, skipping, and vain;
Form'd by the eye, and, therefore, like the eye,
Full of strange shapes, of habits, and of forms,
Varying in subjects, as the eye doth roll
To every varied object in his glance:
Which party-coated presence of loose love
Put on by us, if, in your heavenly eyes,
Have misbecom'd our oaths and gravities,
Those heavenly eyes, that look into these faults,
Suggested us to make. Therefore, ladies,   760
Our love being yours, the error that love makes
Is likewise yours: we to ourselves prove false,
By being once false, for ever to be true
To those that make us both,—fair ladies, you:
And even that falsehood, in itself a sin,
Thus purifies itself, and turns to grace.
Prin. We have receiv'd your letters full of love;
Your favours, the ambassadors of love;
And, in our maiden council, rated them
At courtship, pleasant jest, and courtesy,   770
As bombast, and as lining to the time.
But more devout than this, in our respects,
Have we not been; and therefore met your loves
In their own fashion, like a merriment.
Dum. Our letters, madam, show'd much more than
     jest.
Long. So did our looks.
Ros.   We did not cote them so.
King. Now, at the latest minute of the hour,
Grant us your loves.
Prin.   A time, methinks, too short
To make a world-without-end bargain in.
No, no, my lord, your grace is perjur'd much,   780
Full of dear guiltiness; and therefore this.—
If for my love (as there is no such cause)
You will do aught, this shall you do for me:
Your oath I will not trust; but go with speed
To some forlorn and naked hermitage,
Remote from all the pleasures of the world;
There stay, until the twelve celestial signs
Have brought about their annual reckoning.

If this austere insociable life
Change not your offer made in heat of blood ; 790
If frosts, and fasts, hard lodging, and thin weeds,
Nip not the gaudy blossoms of your love,
But that it bear this trial, and last love ;
Then, at the expiration of the year,
Come challenge me, challenge me by these deserts,
And by this virgin palm, now kissing thine,

You are attaint with faults and perjury ;
Therefore, if you my favour mean to get, 810
A twelvemonth shall you spend, and never rest,
But seek the weary beds of people sick.]
 Dum. But what to me, my love ? but what to me ?
 Kath. A wife !—A beard, fair health, and honesty ;
With three-fold love I wish you all these three.
 Dum. O! shall I say, I thank you, gentle wife ?

Prin. " Was not that Hector ? "

I will be thine ; and, till that instant, shut
My woful self up in a mourning house,
Raining the tears of lamentation
For the remembrance of my father's death. 800
If this thou do deny, let our hands part :
Neither intitled in the other's heart.
 King. If this, or more than this, I would deny,
To flatter up these powers of mine with rest
The sudden hand of death close up mine eye.
Hence ever then my heart is in thy breast.
 Biron. And what to me, my love ? and what to
  me ?
 Ros. You must be purged too, your sins are rank :

 Kath. Not so, my lord. A twelvemonth and a day
I 'll mark no words that smooth-fac'd wooers say :
Come when the king doth to my lady come ;
Then, if I have much love, I 'll give you some. 820
 Dum. I'll serve thee true and faithfully till then.
 Kath. Yet swear not, lest you be forsworn again.
 Long. What says Maria ?
 Mar.   At the twelvemonth's end,
I'll change my black gown for a faithful friend.
 Long. I'll stay with patience ; but the time is long.
 Mar. The liker you ; few taller are so young.
 Biron. Studies my lady ? mistress, look on me.
Behold the window of my heart, mine eye.

What humble suit attends thy answer there;
Impose some service on me for thy love.   830
Ros. Oft have I heard of you, my Lord Biron,
Before I saw you, and the world's large tongue
Proclaims you for a man replete with mocks;
Full of comparisons and wounding flouts,
Which you on all estates will execute,
That lie within the mercy of your wit:
To weed this wormwood from your fruitful brain.
And, therewithal, to win me, if you please,
Without the which I am not to be won,
You shall this twelvemonth term, from day to day, 840
Visit the speechless sick, and still converse
With groaning wretches; and your task shall be,
With all the fierce endeavour of your wit,
To enforce the pained impotent to smile.
Biron. To move wild laughter in the throat of death?
It cannot be; it is impossible:
Mirth cannot move a soul in agony.
Ros. Why, that's the way to choke a gibing spirit,
Whose influence is begot of that loose grace
Which shallow laughing hearers give to fools.   850
A jest's prosperity lies in the ear
Of him that hears it, never in the tongue
Of him that makes it: then, if sickly ears,
Deaf'd with the clamours of their own dear groans,
Will hear your idle scorns, continue then,
And I will have you, and that fault withal;
But, if they will not, throw away that spirit,
And I shall find you empty of that fault,
Right joyful of your reformation.
Biron. A twelvemonth? well, befall what will befall,
I'll jest a twelvemonth in an hospital.   861
Prin. [*To the* KING.] Ay, sweet my lord: and so I
          take my leave.
King. No, madam; we will bring you on your way.
Biron. Our wooing doth not end like an old play;
Jack hath not Jill: these ladies' courtesy
Might well have made our sport a comedy.
King. Come, sir, it wants a twelvemonth and a day,
And then 't will end.
Biron.   That's too long for a play.

Enter ARMADO.

Arm. Sweet majesty, vouchsafe me,—
Prin. Was not that Hector?   870
Dum. The worthy knight of Troy.
Arm. I will kiss thy royal finger, and take leave.
I am a votary: I have vowed to Jaquenetta to hold
the plough for her sweet love three years. But, most
esteemed greatness, will you hear the dialogue that
the two learned men have compiled in praise of the
owl and the cuckoo? it should have followed in the
end of our show.
King. Call them forth quickly; we will do so.
Arm. Holla! approach.   880

Enter HOLOFERNES, NATHANIEL, MOTH, COSTARD, *and others.*

This side is Hiems, Winter, this Ver, the Spring; the
one maintaind by the owl, the other by the cuckoo.
Ver, begin.

SONG.

SPRING.

I.

When daisies pied, and violets blue,
  And lady-smocks all silver-white,
And cuckoo-buds of yellow hue,
  Do paint the meadows with delight,
The cuckoo then, on every tree,
Mocks married men, for thus sings he,
          Cuckoo;   890
Cuckoo, cuckoo,—O word of fear
Unpleasing to a married ear!

II.

When shepherds pipe on oaten straws,
  And merry larks are ploughmen's clocks,
When turtles tread, and rooks, and daws,
  And maidens bleach their summer smocks,
The cuckoo then, on every tree,
Mocks married men, for thus sings he,
          Cuckoo;
Cuckoo, cuckoo,—O word of fear,   900
Unpleasing to a married ear!

WINTER.

III.

When icicles hang by the wall,
  And Dick the shepherd blows his nail,
And Tom bears logs into the hall,
  And milk comes frozen home in pail,
When blood is nipp'd, and ways be foul
Then nightly sings the staring owl,
          To-who;
Tu-whit, to-who, a merry note,
While greasy Joan doth keel the pot.   910

IV.

When all aloud the wind doth blow,
  And coughing drowns the parson's saw,
And birds sit brooding in the snow,
  And Marian's nose looks red and raw,
When roasted crabs hiss in the bowl,
Then nightly sings the staring owl,
          To-who;
Tu-whit, to-who, a merry note,
While greasy Joan doth keel the pot.

Arm. The words of Mercury are harsh after the
songs of Apollo. You, that way: we, this way.   921
          [*Exeunt.*

A MIDSUMMER-NIGHT'S DREAM.

DRAMATIS PERSONÆ.

THESEUS, *Duke of Athens.*
EGEUS, *Father to Hermia.*
LYSANDER, } *In love with Hermia.*
DEMETRIUS, }
PHILOSTRATE, *Master of the Revels to Theseus.*
QUINCE, *a Carpenter.*
SNUG, *a Joiner.*
BOTTOM, *a Weaver.*
FLUTE, *a Bellows-mender.*
SNOUT, *a Tinker.*
STARVELING, *a Tailor.*

HIPPOLYTA, *Queen of the Amazons.*

HERMIA, *in love with Lysander.*
HELENA, *in love with Demetrius.*

OBERON, *King of the Fairies.*
TITANIA, *Queen of the Fairies.*
PUCK, *or Robin Good-fellow.*
PEASE-BLOSSOM, }
COBWEB, }
MOTH, } *Fairies.*
MUSTARD-SEED. }

Other Fairies attending their King and Queen.
Attendants on Theseus and Hippolyta.

SCENE—ATHENS, *and a Wood not far from it.*

ACT I.

SCENE I.—Athens. A Room in the Palace of THESEUS.

Enter THESEUS, HIPPOLYTA, PHILOSTRATE, *and Attendants.*

Theseus.
NOW, fair Hippolyta, our nuptial hour
  Draws on apace: four happy days bring in
Another moon; but, O, methinks, how slow
This old moon wanes! she lingers my desires,
Like to a step-dame, or a dowager,
Long withering out a young man's revenue.
  Hip. Four days will quickly steep themselves in nights;
Four nights will quickly dream away the time;
And then the moon, like to a silver bow
New-bent in heaven, shall behold the night   11
Of our solemnities.
  The.   Go, Philostrate,
Stir up the Athenian youth to merriments;
Awake the pert and nimble spirit of mirth:
Turn melancholy forth to funerals;
The pale companion is not for our pomp.—
                [*Exit* PHILOSTRATE.
Hippolyta, I woo'd thee with my sword,
And won thy love doing thee injuries;
But I will wed thee in another key,
With pomp, with triumph, and with revelling.   20

Enter EGEUS, HERMIA, LYSANDER, *and* DEMETRIUS.

  Ege. Happy be Theseus, our renowned duke!
  The. Thanks, good Egeus: what's the news with thee?
  Ege. Full of vexation come I, with complaint
Against my child, my daughter Hermia.—
Stand forth, Demetrius.--My noble lord,
This man hath my consent to marry her.—
Stand forth, Lysander;—and, my gracious duke,

This man hath bewitch'd the bosom of my child:
Thou, thou, Lysander, thou hast given her rhymes,
And interchang'd love-tokens with my child: 30
Thou hast by moonlight at her window sung,
With feigning voice, verses of feigning love;
And stol'n the impression of her fantasy
With bracelets of thy hair, rings, gawds, conceits,
Knacks, trifles, nosegays, sweetmeats (messengers
Of strong prevailment in unharden'd youth):
With cunning hast thou filch'd my daughter's heart,
Turn'd her obedience, which is due to me,
To stubborn harshness.—And, my gracious duke,
Be it so she will not here before your grace   40
Consent to marry with Demetrius,
I beg the ancient privilege of Athens,
As she is mine, I may dispose of her;
Which shall be either to this gentleman,
Or to her death, according to our law
Immediately provided in that case.
  The. What say you, Hermia? be advis'd, fair maid.
To you your father should be as a god;
One that compos'd your beauties; yea, and one
To whom you are but as a form in wax,   50
By him imprinted, and within his power
To leave the figure, or disfigure it.
Demetrius is a worthy gentleman.
  Her. So is Lysander.
  The.   In himself he is:
But, in this kind, wanting your father's voice,
The other must be held the worthier.
  Her. I would, my father look'd but with my eyes!
  The. Rather your eyes must with his judgment look.
  Her. I do entreat your grace to pardon me.
I know not by what power I am made bold,   60
Nor how it may concern my modesty,
In such a presence here, to plead my thoughts:
But I beseech your grace, that I may know
The worst that may befall me in this case,
If I refuse to wed Demetrius.

The. Either to die the death, or to abjure
For ever the society of men.
Therefore, fair Hermia, question your desires;
Know of your youth, examine well your blood,
Whether, if you yield not to your father's choice,   70
You can endure the livery of a nun,
For aye to be in shady cloister mew'd,
To live a barren sister all your life,
Chanting faint hymns to the cold fruitless moon.

The. "Hippolyta, I woo'd thee with my sword."

Thrice blessed they, that master so their blood,
To undergo such maiden pilgrimage:
But earthlier happy is the rose distill'd,
Than that which, withering on the virgin thorn,
Grows, lives, and dies, in single blessedness.
Her. So will I grow, so live, so die, my lord,   80
Ere I will yield my virgin patent up
Unto his lordship, whose unwished yoke
My soul consents not to give sovereignty.
The. Take time to pause: and by the next new
          moon,
The sealing-day betwixt my love and me
For everlasting bond of fellowship,
Upon that day either prepare to die,
For disobedience to your father's will,
Or else to wed Demetrius, as he would;
Or on Diana's altar to protest,   90
For aye, austerity and single life.
Dem. Relent, sweet Hermia;—and, Lysander, yield
Thy crazed title to my certain right.
Lys. You have her father's love, Demetrius;
Let me have Hermia's: do you marry him.
Ege. Scornful Lysander! true, he hath my love,
And what is mine my love shall render him;
And she is mine, and all my right of her
I do estate unto Demetrius.
Lys. I am, my lord, as well deriv'd as he,   100
As well possess'd; my love is more than his;
My fortunes every way as fairly rank'd

(If not with vantage), as Demetrius';
And, which is more than all these boasts can be,
I am belov'd of beauteous Hermia.
Why should not I then prosecute my right?
Demetrius, I'll avouch it to his head,
Made love to Nedar's daughter, Helena,
And won her soul; and she, sweet lady, dotes,
Devoutly dotes, dotes in idolatry,   110
Upon this spotted and inconstant man.
The. I must confess, that I have heard so much,
And with Demetrius thought to have spoke thereof;
But, being over-full of self-affairs,
My mind did lose it.—But, Demetrius, come;
And come, Egeus: you shall go with me,
I have some private schooling for you both.—
For you, fair Hermia, look you arm yourself
To fit your fancies to your father's will,
Or else the law of Athens yields you up   120
(Which by no means we may extenuate)
To death, or to a vow of single life.—
Come, my Hippolyta: what cheer, my love?—
Demetrius, and Egeus, go along:
I must employ you in some business
Against our nuptial, and confer with you
Of something nearly that concerns yourselves.
Ege. With duty and desire we follow you.
          [*Exeunt* THES., HIP., EGE., DEM., *and Train.*
Lys. How now, my love? Why is your check so
          pale?
How chance the roses there do fade so fast?   130
Her. Belike, for want of rain, which I could well
Beteem them from the tempest of mine eyes.
Lys. Ah me! for aught that ever I could read,
Could ever hear by tale or history,
The course of true love never did run smooth;
But, either it was different in blood,—
Her. O cross! too high to be enthrall'd to low!
Lys. Or else misgraffed, in respect of years,—
Her. O spite! too old to be engag'd to young!
Lys. Or else it stood upon the choice of friends,—
Her. O hell! to choose love by another's eyes!   141
Lys. Or, if there were a sympathy in choice,
War, death, or sickness did lay siege to it,
Making it momentany as a sound,
Swift as a shadow, short as any dream,
Brief as the lightning in the collied night,
That, in a spleen, unfolds both heaven and earth,
And ere a man hath power to say,—behold!
The jaws of darkness do devour it up:
So quick bright things come to confusion.   150
Her. If then true lovers have been ever cross'd,
It stands as an edict in destiny:
Then let us teach our trial patience,
Because it is a customary cross,
As due to love as thoughts, and dreams, and
          sighs,
Wishes, and tears, poor fancy's followers.
Lys. A good persuasion: therefore, hear me,
          Hermia.
I have a widow aunt, a dowager
Of great revenue, and she hath no child:
From Athens her house remote seven leagues;   160
And she respects me as her only son.
There, gentle Hermia, may I marry thee,
And to that place the sharp Athenian law
Cannot pursue us. If thou lov'st me then,
Steal forth thy father's house to-morrow night,
And in the wood, a league without the town
(Where I did meet thee once with Helena,
To do observance to a morn of May),
There will I stay for thee.
Her.   My good Lysander!
I swear to thee by Cupid's strongest bow,   170
By his best arrow with the golden head,
By the simplicity of Venus' doves,
By that which knitteth souls, and prospers loves,
And by that fire which burn'd the Carthage queen,
When the false Trojan under sail was seen,
By all the vows that ever men have broke,
In number more than ever women spoke:
In that same place thou hast appointed me,
To-morrow truly will I meet with thee.

Lys. Keep promise, love. Look, here comes
Helena.   18)

Enter HELENA.

Her. God speed fair Helena! Whither away?
Hel. Call you me fair? that fair again unsay.
Demetrius loves your fair: O happy fair!
Your eyes are lode-stars, and your tongue's sweet
air
More tuneable than lark to shepherd's ear,
When wheat is green, when hawthorn buds appear.
Sickness is catching: O, were favour so,
Yours would I catch, fair Hermia! ere I go;
My ear should catch your voice, my eye your eye,
My tongue should catch your tongue's sweet melody.
Were the world mine, Demetrius being bated,   191
The rest I 'll give to be to you translated.
O ! teach me how you look, and with what art
You sway the motion of Demetrius' heart.
Her. I frown upon him, yet he loves me still.
Hel. O, that your frowns would teach my smiles
such skill!
Her. I give him curses, yet he gives me love.
Hel. O, that my prayers could such affection
move !
Her. The more I hate, the more he follows me.
Hel. The more I love, the more he hateth me.   200
Her. His folly, Helena, is no fault of mine.
Hel. None, but your beauty : 'would that fault were
mine !
Her. Take comfort: he no more shall see my
face ;
Lysander and myself will fly this place.—
Before the time I did Lysander see,
Seem'd Athens as a paradise to me :
O then, what graces in my love do dwell,
That he hath turn'd a heaven unto a hell !
Lys. Helen, to you our minds we will unfold.
To-morrow night, when Phœbe doth behold   210
Her silver visage in the wat'ry glass,
Decking with liquid pearl the bladed grass,
(A time that lovers' flights doth still conceal)
Through Athens' gates have we devis'd to steal.
Her. And in the wood, where often you and I
Upon faint primrose-beds were wont to lie,
Emptying our bosoms of their counsel sweet,
There my Lysander and myself shall meet ;
And thence, from Athens, turn away our eyes,
To seek new friends and stranger companies.   220
Farewell, sweet playfellow : pray thou for us,
And good luck grant thee thy Demetrius !—
Keep word, Lysander : we must starve our sight
From lovers' food, till morrow deep midnight.
Lys. I will, my Hermia. [*Exit* HERM.]—Helena,
adieu :
As you on him, Demetrius dote on you !   [*Exit.*
Hel. How happy some o'er other some can be !
Through Athens I am thought as fair as she ;
But what of that? Demetrius thinks not so ;
He will not know what all he do know ;   230
And as he errs, doting on Hermia's eyes,
So I, admiring of his qualities.
Things base and vile, holding no quantity,
Love can transpose to form and dignity.
Love looks not with the eyes, but with the mind,
And therefore is wing'd Cupid painted blind.
Nor hath Love's mind of any judgment taste ;
Wings, and no eyes, figure unheedy haste :
And therefore is Love said to be a child,
Because in choice he is so oft beguil'd.   240
As waggish boys in game themselves forswear,
So the boy Love is perjur'd every where ;
For ere Demetrius look'd on Hermia's eyne,
He hail'd down oaths that he was only mine ;
And when this hail some heat from Hermia felt,
So he dissolv'd, and showers of oaths did melt.
I will go tell him of fair Hermia's flight :
Then to the wood will he, to-morrow night,
Pursue her ; and for this intelligence
If I have thanks, it is a dear expence :   250
But herein mean I to enrich my pain,
To have his sight thither, and back again.   [*Exit.*

SCENE II.—The Same. A Room in QUINCE'S House.

Enter QUINCE, SNUG, BOTTOM, FLUTE, SNOUT, *and*
STARVELING.

Quin. Is all our company here?
Bot. You were best to call them generally, man by
man, according to the scrip.
Quin. Here is the scroll of every man's name, which
is thought fit, through all Athens, to play in our interlude before the duke and duchess on his wedding-day
at night.
Bot. First, good Peter Quince, say what the play
treats on ; then read the names of the actors, and so
grow to a point.   10
Quin. Marry, our play is—The most lamentable
comedy, and most cruel death of Pyramus and Thisby.
Bot. A very good piece of work, I assure you, and

Bot. "This is Ercles' vein, a tyrant's vein."

a merry.—Now, good Peter Quince, call forth your
actors by the scroll. Masters, spread yourselves.
Quin. Answer, as I call you.—Nick Bottom, the
weaver.
Bot. Ready. Name what part I am for, and proceed.
Quin. You, Nick Bottom, are set down for Pyramus.
Bot. What is Pyramus? a lover, or a tyrant?   20
Quin. A lover, that kills himself most gallantly for
love.
Bot. That will ask some tears in the true performing
of it : if I do it, let the audience look to their eyes ; I
will move storms, I will condole in some measure.
To the rest :—yet my chief humour is for a tyrant : I
could play Ercles rarely, or a part to tear a cat in, to
make all split.

"The raging rocks,
And shivering shocks,   30
Shall break the locks
Of prison gates :
And Phibbus' car
Shall shine from far,
And make and mar
The foolish Fates."

This was lofty!—Now name the rest of the players.—
This is Ercles' vein, a tyrant's vein ; a lover is more
condoling.
Quin. Francis Flute, the bellows-mender.   40
Flu. Here, Peter Quince.
Quin. You must take Thisby on you.
Flu. What is Thisby? a wandering knight?
Quin. It is the lady that Pyramus must love.
Flu. Nay, faith, let me not play a woman : I have
a beard coming.

Quin. That's all one. You shall play it in a mask, and you may speak as small as you will.

Bot. An I may hide my face, let me play Thisby too. I'll speak in a monstrous little voice:—"Thisne, Thisne,"—"Ah, Pyramus, my lover dear! thy Thisby dear, and lady dear!"   52

Quin. No, no; you must play Pyramus, and, Flute, you Thisby.

Bot. Well, proceed.

Quin. Robin Starveling, the tailor.

Star. Here, Peter Quince.

Quin. Robin Starveling, you must play Thisby's mother.—Tom Snout, the tinker.

Snout. Here, Peter Quince.   60

Quin. You, Pyramus's father; myself, Thisby's father.—Snug, the joiner, you, the lion's part;—and, I hope, here is a play fitted.

Snug. Have you the lion's part written? pray you, if it be, give it me, for I am slow of study.

Quin. You may do it extempore, for it is nothing but roaring.

Bot. Let me play the lion too. I will roar, that I will do any man's heart good to hear me: I will roar, that I will make the duke say, "Let him roar again, let him roar again."   71

Quin. An you should do it too terribly, you would fright the duchess and the ladies, that they would shriek; and that were enough to hang us all.

All. That would hang us, every mother's son.

Bot. I grant you, friends, if that you should fright the ladies out of their wits, they would have no more discretion but to hang us; but I will aggravate my voice so, that I will roar you as gently as any sucking dove: I will roar you an't were any nightingale.   80

Quin. You can play no part but Pyramus; for Pyramus is a sweet-faced man; a proper man, as one shall see in a summer's day; a most lovely, gentleman-like man; therefore, you must needs play Pyramus.

Bot. Well, I will undertake it. What beard were I best to play it in?

Quin. Why, what you will.

Bot. I will discharge it in either your straw-colour beard, your orange-tawny beard, your purple-in-grain beard, or your French-crown-colour beard, your perfect yellow.   91

Quin. Some of your French crowns have no hair at all, and then you will play bare-faced.— But, masters, here are your parts; and I am to entreat you, request you, and desire you, to con them by to-morrow night, and meet me in the palace wood, a mile without the town, by moonlight: there will we rehearse; for if we meet in the city, we shall be dogged with company, and our devices known. In the meantime I will draw a bill of properties, such as our play wants. I pray you, fail me not.   101

Bot. We will meet; and there we may rehearse more obscenely, and courageously. Take pains; be perfect; adieu.

Quin. At the duke's oak we meet.

Bot. Enough; hold, or cut bowstrings.   [*Exeunt.*

ACT II.

SCENE I.—A Wood near Athens.

Enter a Fairy and PUCK *from opposite sides.*

    Puck.
HOW now, spirit! whither wander you?
Fai. Over hill, over dale,
    Thorough bush, thorough brier,
    Over park, over pale,
    Thorough flood, thorough fire,
    I do wander every where,
    Swifter than the moon's sphere;
    And I serve the fairy queen,
    To dew her orbs upon the green:
    The cowslips tall her pensioners be;
    In their gold coats spots you see;   11
    Those be rubies, fairy favours,
    In those freckles live their savours:
I must go seek some dew-drops here,
And hang a pearl in every cowslip's ear.
Farewell, thou lob of spirits: I'll be gone;
Our queen and all her elves come here anon.

Puck. The king doth keep his revels here to-night.
Take heed, the queen come not within his sight;
For Oberon is passing fell and wrath,   20
Because that she as her attendant hath
A lovely boy, stol'n from an Indian king:
She never had so sweet a changeling;
And jealous Oberon would have the child
Knight of his train, to trace the forests wild;
But she, perforce, withholds the loved boy,
Crowns him with flowers, and makes him all her joy.
And now they never meet in grove, or green,
By fountain clear, or spangled starlight sheen,
But they do square; that all their elves, for fear,   30
Creep into acorn cups, and hide them there.

Fai. Either I mistake your shape and making quite,

Puck. "I am that merry wanderer of the night."

Or else you are that shrewd and knavish sprite,
Call'd Robin Good-fellow. Are you not he,
That frights the maidens of the villagery;
Skim milk, and sometimes labour in the quern,
And bootless make the breathless housewife churn;

And sometime make the drink to bear no barm ;
Mislead night-wanderers, laughing at their harm ?
Those that Hobgoblin call you, and sweet Puck,   40
You do their work, and they shall have good luck.
Are not you he ?
   Puck.   Thou speak'st aright ;
I am that merry wanderer of the night.
I jest to Oberon, and make him smile,
When I a fat and bean-fed horse beguile,
Neighing in likeness of a filly foal :
And sometime lurk I in a gossip's bowl,
In very likeness of a roasted crab ;
And, when she drinks, against her lips I bob,
And on her wither'd dewlap pour the ale.   50
The wisest aunt, telling the saddest tale,
Sometime for three-foot stool mistaketh me ;
Then slip I from her bum, down topples she,
And " tailor " cries, and falls into a cough ;
And then the whole quire hold their hips, and laugh,
And waxen in their mirth, and neeze, and swear
A merrier hour was never wasted there.—
But room, fairy : here comes Oberon.
   Fai. And here my mistress.—'Would that he were
       gone !

SCENE II.

Enter OBERON *from one side, with his Train, and*
   TITANIA *from the other, with hers.*
   Obe. Ill met by moonlight, proud Titania.
   Tita. What, jealous Oberon ! Fairies, skip hence :
I have forsworn his bed and company.
   Obe. Tarry, rash wanton. Am not I thy lord ?
   Tita. Then I must be thy lady ; but I know
When thou hast stol'n away from fairy land,
And in the shape of Corin sat all day,
Playing on pipes of corn, and versing love
To amorous Phillida. Why art thou here,
Come from the farthest steep of India,   10
But that, forsooth, the bouncing Amazon,
Your buskin'd mistress and your warrior love,
To Theseus must be wedded ? and you come
To give their bed joy and prosperity.
   Obe. How canst thou thus, for shame, Titania,
Glance at my credit with Hippolyta,
Knowing I know thy love to Theseus ?
Didst thou not lead him through the glimmering night
From Perigenia, whom he ravished ?
And make him with fair Ægle break his faith,   20
With Ariadne, and Antiopa ?
   Tita. These are the forgeries of jealousy :
And never, since the middle summer's spring,
Met we on hill, in dale, forest, or mead,
By paved fountain, or by rushy brook,
Or in the beached margin of the sea,
To dance our ringlets to the whistling wind,
But with thy brawls thou hast disturb'd our sport.
Therefore the winds, piping to us in vain,
As in revenge, have suck'd up from the sea   30
Contagious fogs ; which, falling in the land,
Have every pelting river made so proud,
That they have overborne their continents :
The ox hath therefore stretch'd his yoke in vain,
The ploughman lost his sweat, and the green corn
Hath rotted, ere his youth attain'd a beard :
The fold stands empty in the drowned field,
And crows are fatted with the murrain flock :
The nine men's morris is fill'd up with mud ;
And the quaint mazes in the wanton green   40
For lack of tread are undistinguishable :
The human mortals want their winter here :
No night is now with hymn or carol blest ;—
Therefore the moon, the governess of floods,
Pale in her anger, washes all the air,
That rheumatic diseases do abound :
And thorough this distemperature we see
The seasons alter : hoary-headed frosts
Fall in the fresh lap of the crimson rose ;
And on old Hiems' thin and icy crown,   50
An odorous chaplet of sweet summer buds
Is, as in mockery, set. The spring, the summer,

The childing autumn, angry winter, change
Their wonted liveries ; and the mazed world,
By their increase, now knows not which is which.
And this same progeny of evils comes
From our debate, from our dissension :
We are their parents and original.
   Obe. Do you amend it then ; it lies in you.
Why should Titania cross her Oberon ?   60
I do but beg a little changeling boy,
To be my henchman.
   Tita.   Set your heart at rest,
The fairy land buys not the child of me.
His mother was a votaress of my order :
And, in the spiced Indian air, by night,
Full often hath she gossip'd by my side,
And sat with me on Neptune's yellow sands,
Marking the embarked traders on the flood ;
When we have laugh'd to see the sails conceive,
And grow big-bellied, with the wanton wind ;   70
Which she, with pretty and with swimming gait
Following, (her womb then rich with my young
       squire)
Would imitate, and sail upon the land,
To fetch me trifles, and return again,
As from a voyage, rich with merchandise.
But she, being mortal, of that boy did die ;
And for her sake I do rear up her boy,
And for her sake I will not part with him.
   Obe. How long within this wood intend you stay ?
   Tita. Perchance, till after Theseus' wedding-day.
If you will patiently dance in our round,   81
And see our moonlight revels, go with us ;
If not, shun me, and I will spare your haunts.
   Obe. Give me that boy, and I will go with thee.
   Tita. Not for thy fairy kingdom.—Fairies, away !
We shall chide downright, if I longer stay.
              [*Exit* TITANIA, *with her Train.*
   Obe. Well, go thy way : thou shalt not from this
       grove,
Till I torment thee for this injury.—
My gentle Puck, come hither : thou remember'st
Since once I sat upon a promontory,   90
And heard a mermaid on a dolphin's back
Uttering such dulcet and harmonious breath,
That the rude sea grew civil at her song,
And certain stars shot madly from their spheres,
To hear the sea-maid's music.
   Puck.   I remember.
   Obe. That very time I saw (but thou couldst not),
Flying between the cold moon and the earth,
Cupid all arm'd : a certain aim he took
At a fair vestal throned by the west,
And loos'd his love-shaft smartly from his bow,   100
As it should pierce a hundred thousand hearts.
But I might see young Cupid's fiery shaft
Quench'd in the chaste beams of the wat'ry moon,
And the imperial votaress passed on,
In maiden meditation, fancy-free.
Yet mark'd I where the bolt of Cupid fell :
It fell upon a little western flower,
Before milk-white, now purple with love's wound,
And maidens call it Love-in-idleness.
Fetch me that flower ; the herb I show'd thee once :   111
The juice of it, on sleeping eyelids laid,
Will make or man or woman madly dote
Upon the next live creature that it sees.
Fetch me this herb ; and be thou here again,
Ere the leviathan can swim a league.
   Puck. I 'll put a girdle round about the earth
In forty minutes.   [*Exit.*
   Obe.   Having once this juice,
I 'll watch Titania when she is asleep,
And drop the liquor of it in her eyes :
The next thing then she waking looks upon   120
(Be it on lion, bear, or wolf, or bull,
On meddling monkey, or on busy ape),
She shall pursue it with the soul of love.
And ere I take this charm off from her sight
(As I can take it with another herb),
I 'll make her render up her page to me.—
But who comes here ? I am invisible,
And I will overhear their conference.

Enter DEMETRIUS, HELENA *following him.*

Dem. I love thee not, therefore pursue me not.
Where is Lysander, and fair Hermia?
The one I 'll slay, the other slayeth me.
Thou toldst me, they were stol'n into this wood;
And here am I, and wood within this wood,
Because I cannot meet my Hermia.
Hence! get thee gone, and follow me no more.
Hel. You draw me, you hard-hearted adamant:
But yet you draw not iron, for my heart
Is true as steel: leave you your power to draw,
And I shall have no power to follow you.
Dem. Do I entice you? do I speak you fair?   110
Or, rather, do I not in plainest truth
Tell you I do not, nor I cannot love you?
Hel. And even for that do I love you the more.
I am your spaniel; and, Demetrius,
The more you beat me, I will fawn on you:
Use me but as your spaniel, spurn me, strike me,
Neglect me, lose me; only give me leave,
Unworthy as I am, to follow you.
What worser place can I beg in your love
(And yet a place of high respect with me),   150
Than to be used as you use your dog?
Dem. Tempt not too much the hatred of my spirit,
For I am sick when I do look on thee.
Hel. And I am sick when I look not on you.
Dem. You do impeach your modesty too much,
To leave the city, and commit yourself
Into the hands of one that loves you not;
To trust the opportunity of night,
And the ill counsel of a desert place,
With the rich worth of your virginity.   160
Hel. Your virtue is my privilege for that.
It is not night, when I do see your face,
Therefore I think I am not in the night;
Nor doth this wood lack worlds of company,
For you, in my respect, are all the world:
Then how can it be said I am alone,
When all the world is here to look on me?
Dem. I 'll run from thee, and hide me in the brakes,
And leave thee to the mercy of wild beasts.
Hel. The wildest hath not such a heart as you.   170
Run when you will, the story shall be chang'd;
Apollo flies, and Daphne holds the chase:
The dove pursues the griffin; the mild hind
Makes speed to catch the tiger. Bootless speed,
When cowardice pursues, and valour flies!
Dem. I will not stay thy questions: let me go;
Or, if thou follow me, do not believe
But I shall do thee mischief in the wood.
Hel. Ay, in the temple, in the town, the field,
You do me mischief. Fie, Demetrius!   180
Your wrongs do set a scandal on my sex.
We cannot fight for love, as men may do;
We should be woo'd, and were not made to woo.
I 'll follow thee, and make a heaven of hell,
To die upon the hand I love so well.
                              [*Exeunt* DEMETRIUS *and* HELENA.
Obe. Fare thee well, nymph: ere he do leave this
                                             grove,
Thou shalt fly him, and he shall seek thy love.—

Re-enter PUCK.

Hast thou the flower there? Welcome, wanderer.
Puck. Ay, there it is.
Obe.   I pray thee, give it me.
I know a bank where the wild thyme blows,   190
Where oxlips, and the nodding violet grows;
Quite over-canopied with luscious woodbine,
With sweet musk-roses, and with eglantine:
There sleeps Titania, some time of the night,
Lull'd in these flowers with dances and delight;
And there the snake throws her enamell'd skin,
Weed wide enough to wrap a fairy in:
And with the juice of this I 'll streak her eyes,
And make her full of hateful fantasies.
Take thou some of it, and seek through this grove. 200
A sweet Athenian lady is in love
With a disdainful youth: anoint his eyes;
But do it, when the next thing he espies

May be the lady. Thou shalt know the man
By the Athenian garments he hath on.
Effect it with some care, that he may prove
More fond on her, than she upon her love.
And look thou meet me ere the first cock crow.
Puck. Fear not, my lord, your servant shall do so.
                                             [*Exeunt.*

SCENE III.—Another Part of the Wood.

Enter TITANIA, *with her Train.*

Tita. Come, now a roundel, and a fairy song;
Then, for the third part of a minute, hence:
Some, to kill cankers in the musk-rose buds;
Some, war with rear-mice for their leathern wings,
To make my small elves coats; and some, keep back
The clamorous owl, that nightly hoots, and wonders
At our quaint spirits. Sing me now asleep;
Then to your offices, and let me rest.

FAIRIES' SONG.

I.

1 Fai. *You spotted snakes, with double tongue,*
  Thorny hedge-hogs, be not seen;   10
Newts, and blind-worms, do no wrong;
  Come not near our fairy queen.

Chorus.

Philomel, with melody
Sing in our sweet lullaby;
Lulla, lulla, lullaby; lulla, lulla, lullaby:
    Never harm,
    Nor spell nor charm,
Come our lovely lady nigh;
So, good night, with lullaby.

II.

2 Fai. *Weaving spiders, come not here;*
  Hence, you long-legg'd spinners, hence;   20
Beetles black, approach not near;
  Worm, nor snail, do no offence.

Chorus.

Philomel, with melody, &c.

1 Fai. Hence, away! now all is well.
  One, aloof, stand sentinel.
              [*Exeunt Fairies.* TITANIA *sleeps.*

Enter OBERON, *and squeezes the flower on* TITANIA'S
                                             eyelids.

Obe. What thou seest, when thou dost wake,
  Do it for thy true-love take;
  Love, and languish for his sake:
  Be it ounce, or cat, or bear,
  Pard, or boar with bristled hair,   30
  In thy eye that shall appear
  When thou wak'st, it is thy dear.
  Wake when some vile thing is near.   [*Exit.*

Enter LYSANDER *and* HERMIA.

Lys. Fair love, you faint with wandering in the
                                             wood;
And, to speak troth, I have forgot our way:
We 'll rest us, Hermia, if you think it good,
And tarry for the comfort of the day.
Her. Be it so, Lysander: find you out a bed,
For I upon this bank will rest my head.
Lys. One turf shall serve as pillow for us both: 40
One heart, one bed, two bosoms, and one troth.
Her. Nay, good Lysander; for my sake, my dear,
Lie further off yet: do not lie so near.
Lys. O, take the sense, sweet, of my innocence!
Love takes the meaning in love's conference.
I mean, that my heart unto yours is knit,
So that but one heart we can make of it:
Two bosoms interchained with an oath;
So then, two bosoms, and a single troth.
Then, by your side no bed-room me deny,   50
For, lying so, Hermia, I do not lie.
Her. Lysander riddles very prettily.

Now much beshrew my manners and my pride,
If Hermia meant to say Lysander lied.
But, gentle friend, for love and courtesy
Lie further off; in human modesty

Enter PUCK.

Puck. Through the forest have I gone,
But Athenian found I none,

Obe. "What thou seest, when thou dost wake,
Do it for thy true-love take."

Such separation as may well be said
Becomes a virtuous bachelor and a maid,
So far be distant; and good night, sweet friend.
Thy love ne'er alter till thy sweet life end!   60
  Lys. Amen, amen, to that fair prayer say I;
And then end life, when I end loyalty!
Here is my bed: sleep give thee all his rest!
  Her. With half that wish the wisher's eyes be
      press'd!   [*They sleep.*

On whose eyes I might approve
This flower's force in stirring love.
Night and silence?—Who is here?
Weeds of Athens he doth wear: 70
This is he, my master said,
Despised the Athenian maid;
And here the maiden, sleeping sound
On the dank and dirty ground.
Pretty soul! she durst not lie

Near this lack-love, this kill-courtesy.
Churl, upon thy eyes I throw
All the power this charm doth owe.
When thou wak'st, let love forbid
Sleep his seat on thy eyelid.   80
So awake when I am gone;
For I must now to Oberon.   [*Exit.*

Puck. "Through the forest have I gone."

Enter DEMETRIUS *and* HELENA, *running.*

Hel. Stay, though thou kill me, sweet Demetrius.
Dem. I charge thee, hence, and do not haunt me
    thus.
Hel. O! wilt thou darkling leave me? do not so.
Dem. Stay, on thy peril: I alone will go.   [*Exit.*
Hel. O! I am out of breath in this fond chase.
The more my prayer, the lesser is my grace.
Happy is Hermia, wheresoe'er she lies;
For she hath blessed and attractive eyes.   90
How came her eyes so bright? Not with salt tears:
If so, my eyes are oftener wash'd than hers.
No, no, I am as ugly as a bear;
For beasts, that meet me, run away for fear;
Therefore, no marvel, though Demetrius
Do, as a monster, fly my presence thus.
What wicked and dissembling glass of mine
Made me compare with Hermia's sphery eyne?—
But who is here?—Lysander! on the ground?
Dead, or asleep?—I see no blood, no wound.— 100
Lysander, if you live, good sir, awake.

Lys. [*Awaking.*] And run through fire I will, for
    thy sweet sake.
Transparent Helena! Nature here shows art,
That through thy bosom makes me see thy heart.
Where is Demetrius? O, how fit a word
Is that vile name to perish on my sword!
Hel. Do not say so, Lysander; say not so.
What though he love your Hermia? Lord! what
    though?
Yet Hermia still loves you: then be content.
Lys. Content with Hermia! No: I do repent 110
The tedious minutes I with her have spent.
Not Hermia, but Helena I love.
Who will not change a raven for a dove?
The will of man is by his reason sway'd;
And reason says you are the worthier maid.
Things growing are not ripe until their season:
So I, being young, till now ripe not to reason;
And touching now the point of human skill,
Reason becomes the marshal to my will,
And leads me to your eyes; where I o'erlook 120
Love's stories, written in love's richest book.
Hel. Wherefore was I to this keen mockery
    born?
When, at your hands, did I deserve this scorn?
Is 't not enough, is 't not enough, young man,
That I did never, no, nor never can,
Deserve a sweet look from Demetrius' eye,
But you must flout my insufficiency?
Good troth, you do me wrong, good sooth, you do,
In such disdainful manner me to woo.
But fare you well: perforce I must confess, 130
I thought you lord of more true gentleness.
O, that a lady of one man refus'd
Should of another therefore be abus'd!   [*Exit.*
Lys. She sees not Hermia.—Hermia, sleep thou
    there;
And never may'st thou come Lysander near.
For, as a surfeit of the sweetest things
The deepest loathing to the stomach brings;
Or, as the heresies, that men do leave,
Are hated most of those they did deceive:
So thou, my surfeit, and my heresy, 140
Of all be hated, but the most of me.
And, all my powers, address your love and might
To honour Helen, and to be her knight.   [*Exit.*
Her. [*Awaking.*] Help me, Lysander, help me! do
    thy best,
To pluck this crawling serpent from my breast.
Ah me, for pity!—what a dream was here!
Lysander, look, how I do quake with fear.
Methought a serpent eat my heart away,
And you sat smiling at his cruel prey.—
Lysander! what, remov'd? Lysander! lord! 150
What, out of hearing? gone? no sound, no word?
Alack! where are you? speak, an if you hear;
Speak, of all loves! I swoon almost with fear.
No?—then I well perceive you are not nigh:
Either death, or you, I'll find immediately. [*Exit.*

ACT III.

SCENE I.—The Same.   TITANIA lying asleep.

Enter QUINCE, SNUG, BOTTOM, FLUTE, SNOUT, *and* STARVELING.

Bottom.

ARE we all met?

Quin. Pat, pat; and here's a marvellous convenient place for our rehearsal. This green plot shall be our stage, this hawthorn-brake our tiring-house; and we will do it in action, as we will do it before the duke.

Bot. Peter Quince,—

Quin. What say'st thou, bully Bottom?   11

Bot. There are things in this comedy of "Pyramus and Thisby," that will never please. First, Pyramus must draw a sword to kill himself, which the ladies cannot abide. How answer you that?

Snout. By 'r lakin, a parlous fear.

Star. I believe, we must leave the killing out, when all is done.

Bot. Not a whit: I have a device to make all well. Write me a prologue; and let the prologue seem to say, we will do no harm with our swords, and that Pyramus is not killed indeed: and, for the more better assurance, tell them, that I, Pyramus, am not Pyramus, but Bottom the weaver. This will put them out of fear.

Quin. Well, we will have such a prologue, and it shall be written in eight and six.

Bot. No, make it two more: let it be written in eight and eight.   30

Snout. Will not the ladies be afeard of the lion?

Star. I fear it, I promise you.

Bot. Masters, you ought to consider with yourselves: to bring in, God shield us! a lion among ladies, is a most dreadful thing; for there is not a more fearful wild-fowl than your lion living, and we ought to look to it.

Snout. Therefore, another prologue must tell he is not a lion.

Bot. Nay, you must name his name, and half his face must be seen through the lion's neck; and he himself must speak through, saying thus, or to the same defect:—"Ladies," or, "Fair ladies, I would wish you," or, "I would request you," or, "I would entreat you, not to fear, not to tremble: my life for yours. If you think I come hither as a lion, it were pity of my life: no, I am no such thing: I am a man as other men are;" and there, indeed, let him name his name, and tell them plainly he is Snug, the joiner.

Quin. Well, it shall be so. But there is two hard things: that is, to bring the moonlight into a chamber; for you know, Pyramus and Thisby meet by moonlight.   52

Snug. Doth the moon shine that night we play our play?

Bot. A calendar, a calendar! look in the almanac; find out moonshine, find out moonshine.

Quin. Yes, it doth shine that night.

Bot. Why, then you may leave a casement of the great chamber-window, where we play, open; and the moon may shine in at the casement.   60

Quin. Ay; or else one must come in with a bush of thorns and a lanthorn, and say, he comes to disfigure, or to present, the person of Moonshine. Then, there is another thing: we must have a wall in the great chamber; for Pyramus and Thisby, says the story, did talk through the chink of a wall.

Snug. You can never bring in a wall.—What say you, Bottom?

Bot. Some man or other must present Wall; and let him have some plaster, or some loam, or some rough-cast about him, to signify wall; and let him hold his fingers thus, and through that cranny shall Pyramus and Thisby whisper.

Quin. If that may be, then all is well. Come, sit down, every mother's son, and rehearse your parts. Pyramus, you begin. When you have spoken your speech, enter into that brake; and so every one according to his cue.

Enter PUCK *behind.*

Puck. What hempen home-spuns have we swaggering here,
So near the cradle of the fairy queen?   80
What, a play toward? I 'll be an auditor;
An actor too, perhaps, if I see cause.

Quin. Speak, Pyramus.—Thisby, stand forth.

Pyr. "Thisby, the flowers of odious savours sweet,"—

Quin. Odours, odours.

Pyr. —"odours savours sweet:
So hath thy breath, my dearest Thisby, dear.
But, hark, a voice! stay thou but here awhile,
And by and by I will to thee appear."   [*Exit.*

Puck. A stranger Pyramus than e'er play'd here!   90   [*Exit.*

This. Must I speak now?

Quin. Ay, marry, must you; for you must understand, he goes but to see a noise that he heard, and is to come again.

This. "Most radiant Pyramus, most lily-white of hue,
Of colour like the red rose on triumphant brier,
Most brisky juvenal, and eke most lovely Jew,
As true as truest horse, that yet would never tire,
I 'll meet thee, Pyramus, at Ninny's tomb."

Quin. Ninus' tomb, man. Why, you must not speak that yet; that you answer to Pyramus. You speak all your part at once, cues and all.—Pyramus, enter: your cue is past; it is, "never tire."

Re-enter PUCK, *and* BOTTOM *with an ass's head.*

This. O!—"As true as truest horse, that yet would never tire."—

Pyr. "If I were fair, Thisby, I were only thine."—

Quin. O monstrous! O strange! we are haunted. Pray, masters! fly, masters! help!   [*Exeunt Clowns.*

Puck. I 'll follow you, I'll lead you about a round,
Through bog, through bush, through brake, through brier:
Sometime a horse I 'll be, sometime a hound,   110
A hog, a headless bear, sometime a fire;
And neigh, and bark, and grunt, and roar, and burn,
Like horse, hound, hog, bear, fire, at every turn.   [*Exit.*

Bot. Why do they run away? this is a knavery of them, to make me afeard.

Re-enter SNOUT.

Snout. O Bottom! thou art changed: what do I see on thee?   [*Exit.*

Bot. What do you see? you see an ass-head of your own, do you?   119

Re-enter QUINCE.

Quin. Bless thee, Bottom! bless thee! thou art translated.   [*Exit.*
Bot. I see their knavery. This is to make an ass of me, to fright me, if they could. But I will not stir from this place, do what they can. I will walk up and down here, and I will sing, that they shall hear I am not afraid.   [*Sings.*

> The ousel-cock, so black of hue,
>   With orange-tawny bill,
> The throstle with his note so true,
>   The wren with little quill.   130

Tita. [*Awaking.*] What angel wakes me from my flowery bed?
Bot. The finch, the sparrow, and the lark,
>   The plain-song cuckoo gray,
> Whose note full many a man doth mark,
>   And dares not answer, nay;

for, indeed, who would set his wit to so foolish a bird? who would give a bird the lie, though he cry "cuckoo" never so?
Tita. I pray thee, gentle mortal, sing again:
Mine ear is much enamour'd of thy note;   140
So is mine eye enthralled to thy shape;
And thy fair virtue's force, perforce, doth move me,
On the first view, to say, to swear, I love thee.
Bot. Methinks, mistress, you should have little reason for that: and yet, to say the truth, reason and love keep little company together now-a-days. The more the pity, that some honest neighbours will not make them friends. Nay, I can gleek upon occasion.
Tita. Thou art as wise as thou art beautiful.   150
Bot. Not so, neither; but if I had wit enough to get out of this wood, I have enough to serve mine own turn.
Tita. Out of this wood do not desire to go:
Thou shalt remain here, whether thou wilt or no.
I am a spirit of no common rate;
The summer still doth tend upon my state;
And I do love thee: therefore, go with me;
I'll give thee fairies to attend on thee,
And they shall fetch thee jewels from the deep,   160
And sing while thou on pressed flowers dost sleep:
And I will purge thy mortal grossness so,
That thou shalt like an airy spirit go.—
Pease-blossom! Cobweb! Moth! and Mustard-seed!

Enter Four Fairies.

1. *Fai.* Ready.
2. *Fai.*   And I.
3. *Fai.*   And I.
4. *Fai.*   Where shall we go?
Tita. Be kind and courteous to this gentleman:
Hop in his walks, and gambol in his eyes;
Feed him with apricocks, and dewberries,
With purple grapes, green figs, and mulberries.
The honey-bags steal from the humble-bees,   170
And for night-tapers crop their waxen thighs,
And light them at the fiery glow-worm's eyes,
To have my love to bed, and to arise;
And pluck the wings from painted butterflies,
To fan the moonbeams from his sleeping eyes.
Nod to him, elves, and do him courtesies.
1. *Fai.* Hail, mortal!
2. *Fai.* Hail!
3. *Fai.* Hail!
4. *Fai.* Hail!   180
Bot. I cry your worships mercy, heartily.—I beseech your worship's name.
Cob. Cobweb.
Bot. I shall desire you of more acquaintance, good Master Cobweb. If I cut my finger, I shall make bold with you.—Your name, honest gentleman?
Peas. Pease-blossom.
Bot. I pray you, commend me to Mistress Squash, your mother, and to Master Peascod, your father. Good Master Pease-blossom, I shall desire you of more acquaintance too.—Your name, I beseech you, sir?

Mus. Mustard-seed.
Bot. Good Master Mustard-seed, I know your patience well: that same cowardly, giant-like oxbeef hath devoured many a gentleman of your house. I promise you, your kindred hath made my eyes water ere now. I desire you more acquaintance, good Master Mustard-seed.
Tita. Come, wait upon him: lead him to my bower.
The moon, methinks, looks with a watery eye;   200
And when she weeps, weeps every little flower,
Lamenting some enforced chastity.
Tie up my love's tongue, bring him silently. [*Exeunt.*

SCENE II.—Another Part of the Wood.

Enter OBERON.

Obe. I wonder, if Titania be awak'd;

Obe. "I wonder, if Titania be awak'd."

Then, what it was that next came in her eye,
Which she must dote on in extremity.

Enter PUCK.

Here comes my messenger.—How now, mad spirit?
What night-rule now about this haunted grove?
Puck. My mistress with a monster is in love.
Near to her close and consecrated bower,
While she was in her dull and sleeping hour,
A crew of patches, rude mechanicals,   10
That work for bread upon Athenian stalls,
Were met together to rehearse a play,
Intended for great Theseus' nuptial day.
The shallowest thick-skin of that barren sort,
Who Pyramus presented in their sport,
Forsook his scene, and enter'd in a brake,
When I did him at this advantage take;
An ass's nowl I fixed on his head:
Anon, his Thisbe must be answered,
And forth my mimic comes. When they him spy,   20
As wild geese that the creeping fowler eye,
Or russet-pated choughs, many in sort,
Rising and cawing at the gun's report,

Sever themselves, and madly sweep the sky;
So, at his sight, away his fellows fly,
And, at our stamp, here o'er and o'er one falls:
He murder cries, and help from Athens calls.
Their sense thus weak, lost with their fears thus
   strong,
Made senseless things begin to do them wrong;
For briers and thorns at their apparel snatch;
Some, sleeves, some, hats, from yielders all things
   catch.   30
I led them on in this distracted fear,
And left sweet Pyramus translated there;
When in that moment (so it came to pass)
Titania wak'd, and straightway lov'd an ass.
  Obe. This falls out better than I could devise.
But hast thou yet latch'd the Athenian's eyes
With the love-juice, as I did bid thee do?
  Puck. I took him sleeping, (that is finish'd too)
And the Athenian woman by his side,
That, when he wak'd, of force she must be ey'd. 40

       Enter DEMETRIUS *and* HERMIA.

  Obe. Stand close: this is the same Athenian.
  Puck. This is the woman; but not this the man.
  Dem. O! why rebuke you him that loves you so?
Lay breath so bitter on your bitter foe.
  Her. Now I but chide; but I should use thee worse,
For thou, I fear, hast given me cause to curse.
If thou hast slain Lysander in his sleep,
Being o'er shoes in blood, plunge in the deep,
And kill me too.
The sun was not so true unto the day,   50
As he to me. Would he have stol'n away
From sleeping Hermia? I'll believe as soon,
This whole earth may be bor'd, and that the moon
May through the centre creep, and so displease
Her brother's noontide with the Antipodes.
It cannot be but thou hast murder'd him;
So should a murderer look, so dead, so grim.
  Dem. So should the murder'd look, and so should I,
Pierc'd through the heart with your stern cruelty;
Yet you, the murderer, look as bright, as clear, 60
As yonder Venus in her glimmering sphere.
  Her. What's this to my Lysander? where is he?
Ah, good Demetrius, wilt thou give him me?
  Dem. I had rather give his carcass to my hounds.
  Her. Out, dog! out, cur! thou driv'st me past the
   bounds
Of maiden's patience. Hast thou slain him then?
Henceforth be never numbered among men!
O! once tell true, tell true, e'en for my sake;
Durst thou have look'd upon him, being awake,
And hast thou kill'd him sleeping? O brave touch! 70
Could not a worm, an adder, do so much?
An adder did it; for with doubler tongue
Than thine, thou serpent, never adder stung.
  Dem. You spend your passion on a mispris'd mood:
I am not guilty of Lysander's blood,
Nor is he dead, for ought that I can tell.
  Her. I pray thee, tell me then, that he is well.
  Dem. An if I could, what should I get therefore?
  Her. A privilege, never to see me more.—
And from thy hated presence part I so;   80
See me no more, whether he be dead or no. *[Exit.*
  Dem. There is no following her in this fierce vein:
Here, therefore, for a while I will remain.
So sorrow's heaviness doth heavier grow
For debt that bankrupt sleep doth sorrow owe;
Which now in some slight measure it will pay,
If for his tender here I make some stay. [*Lies down.*
  Obe. What hast thou done? thou hast mistaken
   quite,
And laid the love-juice on some true-love's sight:
Of thy misprision must perforce ensue   90
Some true-love turn'd, and not a false turn'd true.
  Puck. Then fate o'er-rules, that, one man holding
   troth,
A million fail, confounding oath on oath.
  Obe. About the wood go swifter than the wind,
And Helena of Athens look thou find:
All fancy-sick she is, and pale of cheer
With sighs of love, that cost the fresh blood dear.

By some illusion see thou bring her here:
I'll charm his eyes against she do appear.
  Puck. I go, I go; look how I go;   100
Swifter than arrow from the Tartar's bow. [*Exit.*
  Obe.   Flower of this purple die,
    Hit with Cupid's archery,
    Sink in apple of his eye.
    When his love he doth espy,
    Let her shine as gloriously
    As the Venus of the sky.—
    When thou wak'st, if she be by,
    Beg of her for remedy.

       Re-enter PUCK.

  Puck. Captain of our fairy band,   110
    Helena is here at hand,

Her. "And from thy hated presence part I so."

    And the youth, mistook by me,
    Pleading for a lover's fee.
    Shall we their fond pageant see?
    Lord, what fools these mortals be!
  Obe.   Stand aside: the noise they make
    Will cause Demetrius to awake.
  Puck.   Then will two at once woo one;
    That must needs be sport alone;
    And those things do best please me, 120
    That befall preposterously.

    Enter LYSANDER *and* HELENA.

  Lys. Why should you think that I should woo in
   scorn?
Scorn and derision never come in tears:
Look, when I vow, I weep; and vows so born,
In their nativity all truth appears.
How can these things in me seem scorn to you,
Bearing the badge of faith to prove them true?
  Hel. You do advance your cunning more and more.
When truth kills truth, O devilish-holy fray!
These vows are Hermia's: will you give her o'er?
Weigh oath with oath, and you will nothing weigh:
Your vows, to her and me, put in two scales,
Will even weigh, and both as light as tales.
  Lys. I had no judgment, when to her I swore.
  Hel. Nor none, in my mind, now you give her o'er. 130
  Lys. Demetrius loves her, and he loves not you.

Dem. [*Awaking.*] O Helen, goddess, nymph, perfect,
   divine!
To what, my love, shall I compare thine eyne?
Crystal is muddy. O! how ripe in show
Thy lips, those kissing cherries, tempting grow! 140
That pure congealed white, high Taurus' snow,
Fann'd with the eastern wind, turns to a crow,
When thou hold'st up thy hand. O, let me kiss
This princess of pure white, this seal of bliss!
  Hel. O spite! O hell! I see, you all are bent
To set against me, for your merriment:
If you were civil and knew courtesy,
You would not do me thus much injury.
Can you not hate me, as I know you do,
But you must join in souls to mock me too? 150
If you were men, as men you are in show,
You would not use a gentle lady so;
To vow, and swear, and superpraise my parts,
When, I am sure, you hate me with your hearts.
You both are rivals, and love Hermia,
And now both rivals, to mock Helena.
A trim exploit, a manly enterprise,
To conjure tears up in a poor maid's eyes
With your derision! none of noble sort
Would so offend a virgin, and extort 160
A poor soul's patience, all to make you sport.
  Lys. You are unkind, Demetrius; be not so;
For you love Hermia; this, you know, I know:
And here, with all good will, with all my heart,
In Hermia's love I yield you up my part;
And yours of Helena to me bequeath,
Whom I do love, and will do till my death.
  Hel. Never did mockers waste more idle breath.
  Dem. Lysander, keep thy Hermia; I will none:
If e'er I lov'd her, all that love is gone. 170
My heart to her but as guest-wise sojourn'd,
And now to Helen is it home return'd,
There to remain.
  Lys.   Helen, it is not so.
  Dem. Disparage not the faith thou dost not know,
Lest to thy peril thou aby it dear.—
Look, where thy love comes: yonder is thy dear.

Enter HERMIA.

  Her. Dark night, that from the eye his function
   takes,
The ear more quick of apprehension makes;
Wherein it doth impair the seeing sense,
It pays the hearing double recompense.— 180
Thou art not by mine eye, Lysander, found;
Mine ear, I thank it, brought me to thy sound.
But why unkindly didst thou leave me so?
  Lys. Why should he stay, whom love doth press to
   go?
  Her. What love could press Lysander from my
   side?
  Lys. Lysander's love, that would not let him bide,
Fair Helena, who more engilds the night
Than all yon fiery O's and eyes of light.
Why seek'st thou me? could not this make thee
   know,
The hate I bear thee made me leave thee so? 190
  Her. You speak not as you think: it cannot be.
  Hel. Lo! she is one of this confederacy.
Now I perceive they have conjoin'd all three,
To fashion this false sport in spite of me.
Injurious Hermia! most ungrateful maid!
Have you conspir'd, have you with these contriv'd
To bait me with this foul derision?
Is all the counsel that we two have shar'd,
The sisters' vows, the hours that we have spent,
When we have chid the hasty-footed time 200
For parting us,—O! is all forgot?
All school-days' friendship, childhood innocence?
We, Hermia, like two artificial gods,
Have with our needles created both one flower,
Both on one sampler, sitting on one cushion,
Both warbling of one song, both in one key,
As if our hands, our sides, voices, and minds,
Had been incorporate. So we grew together,
Like to a double cherry, seeming parted,
But yet an union in partition; 210

Two lovely berries moulded on one stem;
So, with two seeming bodies, but one heart;
Two of the first, like coats in heraldry,
Due but to one, and crowned with one crest.
And will you rend our ancient love asunder,
To join with men in scorning your poor friend?
It is not friendly, 't is not maidenly:
Our sex, as well as I, may chide you for it,
Though I alone do feel the injury.
  Her. I am amazed at your passionate words. 220
I scorn you not: it seems that you scorn me.
  Hel. Have you not set Lysander, as in scorn,
To follow me, and praise my eyes and face,
And made your other love, Demetrius,
(Who even but now did spurn me with his foot)
To call me goddess, nymph, divine, and rare,
Precious, celestial? Wherefore speaks he this
To her he hates? and wherefore doth Lysander
Deny your love, so rich within his soul,
And tender me, forsooth, affection, 230
But by your setting on, by your consent?
What though I be not so in grace as you,
So hung upon with love, so fortunate,
But miserable most to love unlov'd,
This you should pity rather than despise.
  Her. I understand not what you mean by this.
  Hel. Ay, do, persever, counterfeit sad looks,
Make mouths upon me when I turn my back;
Wink at each other; hold the sweet jest up:
This sport, well carried, shall be chronicled. 240
If you have any pity, grace, or manners,
You would not make me such an argument,
But, fare ye well: 't is partly mine own fault,
Which death, or absence, soon shall remedy.
  Lys. Stay, gentle Helena! hear my excuse:
My love, my life, my soul, fair Helena!
  Hel. O excellent!
  Her.   Sweet, do not scorn her so.
  Dem. If she cannot entreat, I can compel.
  Lys. Thou canst compel no more than she entreat:
Thy threats have no more strength than her weak
   prayers.— 250
Helen, I love thee; by my life, I do:
I swear by that which I will lose for thee,
To prove him false, that says I love thee not.
  Dem. I say, I love thee more than he can do.
  Lys. If thou say so, withdraw, and prove it too.
  Dem. Quick, come,—
  Her.   Lysander, whereto tends all this?
  Lys. Away, you Ethiop!
  Dem.   No, no, sir:—
Seem to break loose; take on, as you would follow;
But yet come not. You are a tame man, go!
  Lys. Hang off, thou cat, thou burr! vile thing, let
   loose, 260
Or I will shake thee from me like a serpent.
  Her. Why are you grown so rude? what change is
   this,
Sweet love?
  Lys.   Thy love? out, tawny Tartar, out!
Out, loathed medicine! O hated potion, hence!
  Her. Do you not jest?
  Hel.   Yes, sooth; and so do you.
  Lys. Demetrius, I will keep my word with thee.
  Dem. I would, I had your bond; for, I perceive,
A weak bond holds you: I 'll not trust your word.
  Lys. What! should I hurt her, strike her, kill her
   dead?
Although I hate her, I 'll not harm her so. 270
  Her. What! can you do me greater harm than
   hate?
Hate me! wherefore? O me! what news, my love?
Am not I Hermia? Are not you Lysander?
I am as fair now, as I was erewhile.
Since night you lov'd me; yet, since night you left me.
Why, then you left me (O, the gods forbid!)
In earnest, shall I say?
  Lys.   Ay, by my life;
And never did desire to see thee more.
Therefore, be out of hope, of question, of doubt;
Be certain, nothing truer: 't is no jest, 280
That I do hate thee, and love Helena.

Her. O me !—you juggler ! you canker-blossom !
You thief of love ! what, have you come by night,
And stol'n my love's heart from him ?
Hel.   Fine, i' faith !
Have you no modesty, no maiden shame,
No touch of bashfulness ? What, will you tear
Impatient answers from my gentle tongue ?
Fie, fie ! you counterfeit, you puppet you !
Her. Puppet ! why so ? Ay, that way goes the
    game.
Now I perceive that she hath made compare   290
Between our statures : she hath urg'd her height,
And with her personage, her tall personage,
Her height, forsooth, she hath prevail'd with him.—
And are you grown so high in his esteem,
Because I am so dwarfish, and so low ?
How low am I, thou painted maypole ? speak ;
How low am I ? I am not yet so low,
But that my nails can reach unto thine eyes.
Hel. I pray you, though you mock me, gentlemen,
Let her not hurt me : I was never curst ;   300
I have no gift at all in shrewishness ;
I am a right maid for my cowardice :
Let her not strike me. You, perhaps, may think,
Because she is something lower than myself,
That I can match her.
Her.   Lower ! hark, again.
Hel. Good Hermia, do not be so bitter with me.
I evermore did love you, Hermia,
Did ever keep your counsels, never wrong'd you ;
Save that, in love unto Demetrius,
I told him of your stealth unto this wood.   310
He follow'd you ; for love, I follow'd him ;
But he hath chid me hence, and threaten'd me
To strike me, spurn me, nay, to kill me too :
And now, so you will let me quiet go,
To Athens will I bear my folly back,
And follow you no further. Let me go :
You see how simple and how fond I am.
Her. Why, get you gone. Who is 't that hinders
    you ?
Hel. A foolish heart, that I leave here behind.
Her. What, with Lysander ?
Hel.   With Demetrius.   320
Lys. Be not afraid : she shall not harm thee, Helena.
Dem. No, sir ; she shall not, though you take her
    part.
Hel. O ! when she is angry, she is keen and shrewd.
She was a vixen, when she went to school ;
And, though she be but little, she is fierce.
Her. Little again ? nothing but low and little ?—
Why will you suffer her to flout me thus ?
Let me come to her.
Lys.   Get you gone, you dwarf ;
You minimus, of hindering knot-grass made ;
You bead, you acorn.
Dem.   You are too officious   330
In her behalf that scorns your services.
Let her alone ; speak not of Helena ;
Take not her part, for if thou dost intend
Never so little show of love to her,
Thou shalt aby it.
Lys.   Now she holds me not ;
Now follow, if thou dar'st, to try whose right,
Of thine or mine, is most in Helena.
Dem. Follow ? nay, I 'll go with thee, cheek by jole.
    [*Exeunt* LYSANDER *and* DEMETRIUS.
Her. You, mistress, all this coil is 'long of you.
Nay, go not back.
Hel.   I will not trust you, I,   340
Nor longer stay in your curst company.
Your hands than mine are quicker for a fray ;
My legs are longer though, to run away.   [*Exit.*
Her. I am amaz'd, and know not what to say.
                                            [*Exit.*
Obe. This is thy negligence : still thou mistak'st,
Or else committ'st thy knaveries wilfully.
Puck. Believe me, king of shadows, I mistook.
Did not you tell me, I should know the man
By the Athenian garments he had on ?
And so far blameless proves my enterprise,   350
That I have 'nointed an Athenian's eyes ;

And so far am I glad it so did sort,
As this their jangling I esteem a sport.
Obe. Thou seest, these lovers seek a place to fight :·
Hie therefore, Robin, overcast the night ;
The starry welkin cover thou anon
With drooping fog, as black as Acheron ;
And lead these testy rivals so astray,
As one come not within another's way.
Like to Lysander sometime frame thy tongue,   360
Then stir Demetrius up with bitter wrong ;
And sometime rail thou like Demetrius ;
And from each other look thou lead them thus,
Till o'er their brows death-counterfeiting sleep
With leaden legs and batty wings doth creep :
Then crush this herb into Lysander's eye ;
Whose liquor hath this virtuous property,
To take from thence all error with his might,
And make his eyeballs roll with wonted sight.
When they next wake, all this derision   370
Shall seem a dream, and fruitless vision ;
And back to Athens shall the lovers wend,
With league whose date till death shall never end.
Whiles I in this affair do thee employ,
I 'll to my queen, and beg her Indian boy ;
And then I will her charmed eye release
From monster's view,·and all things shall be peace.
Puck. My fairy lord, this must be done with haste,
For night's swift dragons cut the clouds full fast,
And yonder shines Aurora's harbinger ;   380
At whose approach, ghosts, wandering here and
    there,
Troop home to churchyards : damned spirits all,
That in crossways and floods have burial,
Already to their wormy beds are gone ;
For fear lest day should look their shames upon,
They wilfully themselves exile from light,
And must for aye consort with black-brow'd night.
Obe. But we are spirits of another sort.
I with the morning's love have oft made sport ;
And, like a forester, the groves may tread,   390
Even till the eastern gate, all fiery-red,
Opening on Neptune with fair blessed beams,
Turns into yellow gold his salt green streams.
But, notwithstanding, haste ; make no delay :
We may effect this business yet ere day.   [*Exit.*
Puck.   Up and down, up and down ;
    I will lead them up and down :
    I am fear'd in field and town ;
    Goblin, lead them up and down.
Here comes one.   400

Re-enter LYSANDER.

Lys. Where art thou, proud Demetrius ? speak thou
    now.
Puck. Here, villain ! drawn and ready. Where art
    thou ?
Lys. I will be with thee straight.
Puck.   Follow me then
To plainer ground. [*Exit* LYS. *as following the voice.*

Re-enter DEMETRIUS.

Dem.   Lysander, speak again.
Thou runaway, thou coward, art thou fled ?
Speak ! In some bush ? Where dost thou hide thy
    head ?
Puck. Thou coward ! art thou bragging to the stars,
Telling the bushes that thou look'st for wars,
And wilt not come ? Come, recreant ; come, thou
    child ;
I 'll whip thee with a rod : he is defil'd,   410
That draws a sword on thee.
Dem.   Yea ; art thou there ?
Puck. Follow my voice : we 'll try no manhood here.
                                            [*Exeunt.*

Re-enter LYSANDER.

Lys. He goes before me, and still dares me on ;
When I come where he calls, then he is gone.
The villain is much lighter-heel'd than I ·
I follow'd fast, but faster he did fly ;
That fallen am I in dark uneven way,
And here will rest me. [*Lies down.*] Come, thou gentle
    day !

For if but once thou show me thy grey light,
I'll find Demetrius, and revenge this spite.   420
                                              [*Sleeps.*

Re-enter PUCK and DEMETRIUS.

Puck. Ho! ho! ho! Coward, why com'st thou
    not?
Dem. Abide me, if thou dar'st; for well I wot,
Thou runn'st before me, shifting every place,
And dar'st not stand, nor look me in the face.
Where art thou now?
  Puck.   Come hither: I am here.
Dem. Nay, then thou mock'st me. Thou shalt buy
    this dear,
If ever I thy face by day-light see:
Now, go thy way. Faintness constraineth me
To measure out my length on this cold bed:
By day's approach look to be visited.   430
                              [*Lies down and sleeps.*

Re-enter HELENA.

Hel. O weary night, O long and tedious night,
Abate thy hours: shine, comforts, from the east,
That I may back to Athens, by day-light,
From these that my poor company detest.
And sleep, that sometimes shuts up sorrow's eye,
Steal me awhile from mine own company. [*Sleeps.*
Puck. Yet but three? Come one more;
Two of both kinds make up four.
Here she comes, curst and sad.

Cupid is a knavish lad,   440
Thus to make poor females mad.

Re-enter HERMIA.

Her. Never so weary, never so in woe,
Bedabbled with the dew, and torn with briers:
I can no further crawl, no further go;
My legs can keep no pace with my desires.
Here will I rest me till the break of day.
Heavens shield Lysander, if they mean a fray!
                                          [*Lies down.*
Puck.   On the ground
        Sleep sound:
        I'll apply   450
        To your eye,
  Gentle lover, remedy.
        [*Squeezing the juice on* LYS.'s *eye.*
        When thou wak'st,
        Thou tak'st
        True delight
        In the sight
  Of thy former lady's eye:
  And the country proverb known,
  That every man should take his own,
  In your waking shall be shown: 460
        Jack shall have Jill;
        Nought shall go ill;
  The man shall have his mare again,
        And all shall be well.
[*Exit* PUCK.—DEMETRIUS, HELENA, *&c. sleep.*

ACT IV.

SCENE I.—The Same.

Enter TITANIA *and* BOTTOM, *Fairies attending;* OBERON *behind unseen.*

Titania.
COME, sit thee down upon this flowery
        bed,
While I thy amiable cheeks do coy,
And stick musk-roses in thy sleek
        smooth head,
And kiss thy fair large ears, my gentle
        joy.
Bot. Where's Pease-blossom?
Peas. Ready.
Bot. Scratch my head, Pease-blossom.—Where's
Monsieur Cobweb?
Cob. Ready.   9
Bot. Monsieur Cobweb; good monsieur, get your
weapons in your hand, and kill me a red-hipped
humble-bee on the top of a thistle; and, good
monsieur, bring me the honey-bag. Do not fret
yourself too much in the action, monsieur; and,
good monsieur, have a care the honey-bag break
not: I would be loath to have you over-flown with
a honey-bag, signior.—Where's Monsieur Mustard-
seed?
Must. Ready.
Bot. Give me your neif, Monsieur Mustard-seed.
Pray you, leave your courtesy, good monsieur.   20
Must. What's your will?
Bot. Nothing, good monsieur, but to help Cavalery
Cobweb to scratch. I must to the barber's, monsieur;
for, methinks, I am marvellous hairy about the face;
and I am such a tender ass, if my hair do but tickle
me, I must scratch.

Tita. What, wilt thou hear some music, my sweet
love?
Bot. I have a reasonable good ear in music: let's
have the tongs and the bones.   30
Tita. Or, say, sweet love, what thou desir'st to eat.
Bot. Truly, a peck of provender: I could munch
your good dry oats. Methinks, I have a great desire
to a bottle of hay: good hay, sweet hay, hath no fellow.
Tita. I have a venturous fairy that shall seek
The squirrel's hoard, and fetch thee new nuts.
Bot. I had rather have a handful or two of dried
peas. But, I pray you, let none of your people stir
me: I have an exposition of sleep come upon me.
Tita. Sleep thou, and I will wind thee in my arms.
Fairies, be gone, and be all ways away.   41
                                      [*Exeunt Fairies.*
So doth the woodbine the sweet honey-suckle
Gently entwist; the female ivy so
Enrings the barky fingers of the elm.
O, how I love thee! how I dote on thee! [*They sleep.*

Enter PUCK.

Obe. [*Advancing.*] Welcome, good Robin. Seest
        thou this sweet sight?
Her dotage now I do begin to pity;
For, meeting her of late behind the wood,
Seeking sweet savours for this hateful fool,
I did upbraid her, and fall out with her;   50
For she his hairy temples then had rounded
With coronet of fresh and fragrant flowers;
And that same dew, which sometime on the buds

Was wont to swell like round and orient pearls,
Stood now within the pretty flowerets' eyes,
Like tears that did their own disgrace bewail.
When I had at my pleasure taunted her,
And she in mild terms begg'd my patience,

And think no more of this night's accidents,
But as the fierce vexation of a dream.
But first I will release the fairy queen.   70
     Be, as thou wast wont to be;
     See, as thou wast wont to see:

Tita. " O, how I love thee! how I dote on thee!"

I then did ask of her her changeling child:
Which straight she gave me, and her fairy sent   60
To bear him to my bower in fairy land.
And now I have the boy, I will undo
This hateful imperfection of her eyes:
And, gentle Puck, take this transformed scalp
From off the head of this Athenian swain,
That, he awaking when the other do,
May all to Athens back again repair,

    Dian's bud o'er Cupid's flower
    Hath such force and blessed power.
Now, my Titania! wake you, my sweet queen.
  Tita. My Oberon! what visions have I seen!
Methought, I was enamour'd of an ass.
  Obe. There lies your love.
  Tita.   How came these things to pass?
O, how mine eyes do loathe his visage now!
  Obe. Silence awhile.—Robin, take off this head.—

Titania, music call; and strike more dead   80
Than common sleep of all these five the sense.
  Tita. Music, ho! music! such as charmeth sleep.
  Puck. Now, when thou wak'st, with thine own
           fool's eyes peep.
  Obe. Sound, music! Come, my queen, take hands
           with me,
And rock the ground whereon these sleepers be.
Now thou and I are new in amity,
And will to-morrow midnight solemnly
Dance in Duke Theseus' house triumphantly,
And bless it to all fair prosperity.   90
There shall the pairs of faithful lovers be
Wedded, with Theseus, all in jollity.
  Puck.   Fairy king, attend, and mark,
      I do hear the morning lark.
  Obe.   Then, my queen, in silence sad,
      Trip we after the night's shade;
      We the globe can compass soon,
      Swifter than the wandering moon.
  Tita. Come, my lord; and in our flight
      Tell me how it came this night,   100
      That I sleeping here was found
      With these mortals on the ground. [*Exeunt.*
                  [*Horns sound within.*

Enter THESEUS, HIPPOLYTA, EGEUS, *and Train.*

  The. Go, one of you, find out the forester;
For now our observation is perform'd:
And since we have the vaward of the day,
My love shall hear the music of my hounds.—
Uncouple in the western valley: let them go!—
Despatch, I say, and find the forester.—
We will, fair queen, up to the mountain's top,
And mark the musical confusion   110
Of hounds and echo in conjunction.
  Hip. I was with Hercules and Cadmus once,
When in a wood of Crete they bay'd the bear
With hounds of Sparta: never did I hear
Such gallant chiding; for, besides the groves,
The skies, the fountains, every region near
Seem'd all one mutual cry. I never heard
So musical a discord, such sweet thunder.
  The. My hounds are bred out of the Spartan kind,
So flew'd, so sanded; and their heads are hung   120
With ears that sweep away the morning dew;
Crook-knee'd, and dew-lapp'd like Thessalian bulls;
Slow in pursuit, but match'd in mouth like bells,
Each under each. A cry more tuneable
Was never halloo'd to, nor cheer'd with horn,
In Crete, in Sparta, nor in Thessaly:
Judge, when you hear.—But, soft! what nymphs are
      these?
  Ege. My lord, this is my daughter here asleep;
And this, Lysander; this Demetrius is;
This Helena, old Nedar's Helena: 130
I wonder of their being here together.
  The. No doubt, they rose up early, to observe
The rite of May, and, hearing our intent,
Came here in grace of our solemnity.—
But speak, Egeus, is not this the day
That Hermia should give answer of her choice?
  Ege. It is, my lord.
  The. Go, bid the huntsmen wake them with their
      horns.
     [*Horns, and shout within.* DEMETRIUS, LYSAN-
      DER, HERMIA, *and* HELENA, *wake and start up.*
  The. Good morrow, friends. Saint Valentine is
      past;
Begin these wood-birds but to couple now?
  Lys. Pardon, my lord.   110
         [*He and the rest kneel to* THESEUS.
  The.   I pray you all, stand up.
I know, you two are rival enemies:
How comes this gentle concord in the world,
That hatred is so far from jealousy,
To sleep by hate, and fear no enmity?
  Lys. My lord, I shall reply amazedly,
Half 'sleep, half waking: but as yet, I swear,
I cannot truly say how I came here;
But, as I think, (for truly would I speak,—
And now I do bethink me, so it is)   150

I came with Hermia hither:'our intent
Was to be gone from Athens, where we might
Without the peril of the Athenian law—
  Ege. Enough, enough! my lord, you have enough.
I beg the law, the law, upon his head.
They would have stol'n away; they would, Demetrius,
Thereby to have defeated you and me;
You, of your wife, and me, of my consent,
Of my consent that she should be your wife.
  Dem. My lord, fair Helen told me of their stealth,
Of this their purpose hither, to this wood;   161
And I in fury hither follow'd them,
Fair Helena in fancy following me.
But, my good lord, I wot not by what power
(But by some power it is) my love to Hermia,
Melted as doth the snow, seems to me now
As the remembrance of an idle gawd,
Which in my childhood I did dote upon;
And all the faith, the virtue of my heart,

Bot. "I have had a most rare vision."

The object and the pleasure of mine eye,   170
Is only Helena. To her, my lord,
Was I betroth'd ere I saw Hermia:
But, like in sickness, did I loathe this food;
But, as in health, come to my natural taste,
Now do I wish it, love it, long for it,
And will for evermore be true to it.
  The. Fair lovers, you are fortunately met.
Of this discourse we more will hear anon.—
Egeus, I will overbear your will,
For in the temple, by and by with us,   180
These couples shall eternally be knit.
And, for the morning now is something worn,
Our purpos'd hunting shall be set aside.
Away, with us, to Athens: three and three,
We 'll hold a feast in great solemnity.—
Come, Hippolyta.
     [*Exeunt* THESEUS, HIPPOLYTA, EGEUS, *and Train.*
  Dem. These things seem small and undistinguish-
      able,
Like far-off mountains turned into clouds.
  Her. Methinks, I see these things with parted eye,
When every thing seems double.
  Hel.   So methinks: 190
And I have found Demetrius, like a jewel,
Mine own, and not mine own.
  Dem.   Are you sure
That we are awake? It seems to me
That yet we sleep, we dream.—Do not you think

The duke was here, and bid us follow him?
Her. Yea, and my father.
Hel.   And Hippolyta.
Lys. And he did bid us follow to the temple.
Dem. Why then, we are awake. Let 's follow him;
And by the way let us recount our dreams. [*Exeunt.*
Bot. [*Waking.*] When my cue comes, call me, and
I will answer:—my next is, "Most fair Pyramus."—
Hey, ho!—Peter Quince! Flute, the bellows-mender!
Snout, the tinker! Starveling! God 's my life! stolen
hence, and left me asleep. I have had a most rare
vision. I have had a dream,—past the wit of man
to say what dream it was: man is but an ass, if he go
about to expound this dream. Methought I was—
there is no man can tell what. Methought I was,
and methought I had,—but man is but a patched fool,
if he will offer to say what methought I had. The
eye of man hath not heard, the ear of man hath not
seen, man's hand is not able to taste, his tongue to
conceive, nor his heart to report, what my dream was.
I will get Peter Quince to write a ballad of this dream:
it shall be called Bottom's Dream, because it hath no
bottom; and I will sing it in the latter end of a play,
before the duke: peradventure, to make it the more
gracious, I shall sing it at her death.   [*Exit.*

SCENE II.—Athens. A Room in QUINCE'S House.

Enter QUINCE, FLUTE, SNOUT, *and* STARVELING.

Quin. Have you sent to Bottom's house? is he come
home yet?
Star. He cannot be heard of. Out of doubt, he is
transported.
Flu. If he come not, then the play is marred. It
goes not forward, doth it?
Quin. It is not possible: you have not a man in all
Athens able to discharge Pyramus, but he.

Flu. No; he hath simply the best wit of any handi-
craft man in Athens.   10
Quin. Yea, and the best person too; and he is a very
paramour for a sweet voice.
Flu. You must say, paragon: a paramour is, God
bless us! a thing of naught.

Enter SNUG.

Snug. Masters, the duke is coming from the temple,
and there is two or three lords and ladies more married.
If our sport had gone forward, we had all been made
men.
Flu. O sweet bully Bottom! Thus hath he lost sixpence a day during his life; he could not have 'scaped
sixpence a day: an the duke had not given him sixpence a day for playing Pyramus, I 'll be hanged;
he would have deserved it: sixpence a day in Pyramus, or nothing.

Enter BOTTOM.

Bot. Where are these lads? where are these hearts?
Quin. Bottom!—O most courageous day! O most
happy hour!
Bot. Masters, I am to discourse wonders; but ask
me not what, for, if I tell you, I am no true Athenian:
I will tell you every thing, right as it fell out.   30
Quin. Let us hear, sweet Bottom.
Bot. Not a word of me. All that I will tell you is,
that the duke hath dined. Get your apparel together,
good strings to your beards, new ribbons to your
pumps: meet presently at the palace; every man look
o'er his part; for, the short and the long is, our play
is preferred. In any case, let Thisby have clean linen,
and let not him that plays the lion pare his nails,
for they shall hang out for the lion's claws. And,
most dear actors, eat no onions, nor garlic, for we are
to utter sweet breath, and I do not doubt, but to hear
them say, it is a sweet comedy. No more words:
away! go; away!   [*Exeunt.*

ACT V.

SCENE I.—The Same. An Apartment in the Palace of THESEUS.

Enter THESEUS, HIPPOLYTA, PHILOSTRATE, *Lords, and Attendants.*

Hippolyta.
'IS strange, my Theseus, that these lovers
            speak of.
The. More strange than true: I never
            may believe
These antick fables, nor these fairy toys.
Lovers and madmen have such seething
            brains,
Such shaping fantasies, that apprehend
More than cool reason ever comprehends.
The lunatic, the lover, and the poet,
Are of imagination all compact:
One sees more devils than vast hell can
            hold;
That is the madman: the lover, all as frantic,   10
Sees Helen's beauty in a brow of Egypt:
The poet's eye, in a fine frenzy rolling,
Doth glance from heaven to earth, from earth to
            heaven;
And, as imagination bodies forth
The forms of things unknown, the poet's pen
Turns them to shapes, and gives to airy nothing

A local habitation, and a name.
Such tricks hath strong imagination,
That, if it would but apprehend some joy,
It comprehends some bringer of that joy: 20
Or in the night, imagining some fear,
How easy is a bush suppos'd a bear?
Hip. But all the story of the night told over,
And all their minds transfigur'd so together,
More witnesseth than fancy's images,
And grows to something of great constancy,
But, howsoever, strange, and admirable.
The. Here come the lovers, full of joy and mirth.

Enter LYSANDER, DEMETRIUS, HERMIA, *and*
HELENA.

Joy, gentle friends! joy, and fresh days of love,
Accompany your hearts!
Lys.   More than to us   30
Wait in your royal walks, your board, your bed!
The. Come now; what masques, what dances shall
            we have,
To wear away this long age of three hours,

Between our after-supper, and bed-time?
Where is our usual manager of mirth?
What revels are in hand? Is there no play,
To ease the anguish of a torturing hour?
Call Philostrate.
  Phil.   Here, mighty Theseus.
  The. Say, what abridgment have you for this
      evening?
What masque, what music? How shall we beguile 40
The lazy time, if not with some delight?
  Phil. There is a brief how many sports are ripe;
Make choice of which your highness will see first.
                          [*Giving a paper.*

Phil. "There is a brief how many sports are ripe."

  The. [*Reads.*] " The battle with the Centaurs, to be
      sung
By an Athenian eunuch to the harp."
We'll none of that: that have I told my love,
In glory of my kinsman Hercules.
" The riot of the tipsy Bacchanals,
Tearing the Thracian singer in their rage."
That is an old device; and it was play'd   50
When I from Thebes came last a conqueror.
" The thrice three Muses mourning for the death
Of Learning, late deceas'd in beggary."
That is some satire keen, and critical,
Not sorting with a nuptial ceremony.
" A tedious brief scene of young Pyramus,
And his love Thisbe; very tragical mirth."
Merry and tragical! Tedious and brief!
That is, hot ice, and wonderous strange snow.
How shall we find the concord of this discord? 60
  Phil. A play there is, my lord, some ten words long,
Which is as brief as I have known a play;
But by ten words, my lord, it is too long,
Which makes it tedious; for in all the play
There is not one word apt, one player fitted.
And tragical, my noble lord, it is,
For Pyramus therein doth kill himself.
Which when I saw rehears'd, I must confess,
Made mine eyes water; but more merry tears
The passion of loud laughter never shed. 70
  The. What are they that do play it?
  Phil. Hard-handed men, that work in Athens here,
Which never labour'd in their minds till now,
And now have toil'd their unbreath'd memories
With this same play, against your nuptial.

  The. And we will hear it.
  Phil.   No, my noble lord;
It is not for you: I have heard it over,
And it is nothing, nothing in the world,
Unless you can find sport in their intents,
Extremely stretch'd and conn'd with cruel pain, 80
To do you service.
  The.   I will hear that play:
For never anything can be amiss,
When simpleness and duty tender it.
Go, bring them in;—and take your places, ladies.
                       [*Exit* PHILOSTRATE.
  Hip. I love not to see wretchedness o'ercharg'd,
And duty in his service perishing.
  The. Why, gentle sweet, you shall see no such
      thing.
  Hip. He says, they can do nothing in this kind.
  The. The kinder we, to give them thanks for no-
      thing.
Our sport shall be to take what they mistake: 90
And what poor duty cannot do,
Noble respect takes it in might, not merit.
Where I have come, great clerks have purposed
To greet me with premeditated welcomes;
Where I have seen them shiver and look pale,
Make periods in the midst of sentences,
Throttle their practis'd accent in their fears,
And, in conclusion, dumbly have broke off,
Not paying me a welcome. Trust me, sweet,
Out of this silence, yet, I pick'd a welcome; 100
And in the modesty of fearful duty
I read as much, as from the rattling tongue
Of saucy and audacious eloquence.
Love, therefore, and tongue-tied simplicity,
In least speak most, to my capacity.

          Re-enter PHILOSTRATE.
  Phil. So please your grace, the Prologue is addrest.
  The. Let him approach.   [*Flourish of trumpets.*

          Enter the Prologue.
  Prol. "If we offend, it is with our good will.
That you should think, we come not to offend,
But with good will. To show our simple skill, 110
That is the true beginning of our end.
Consider then, we come but in despite.
We do not come as minding to content you,
Our true intent is. All for your delight,
We are not here. That you should here repent you,
The actors are at hand; and, by their show,
You shall know all, that you are like to know."
  The. This fellow doth not stand upon points.
  Lys. He hath rid his prologue like a rough colt; he
knows not the stop. A good moral, my lord: it is not
enough to speak, but to speak true. 121
  Hip. Indeed, he hath played on this prologue like a
child on a recorder, a sound, but not in government.
  The. His speech was like a tangled chain,
Nothing impair'd, but all disordered.
Who is next?

Enter PYRAMUS *and* THISBE, *Wall, Moonshine, and*
       Lion, as in dumb-show.

  Prol. "Gentles, perchance, you wonder at this
      show;
But wonder on, till truth make all things plain.
This man is Pyramus, if you would know;
This beauteous lady Thisby is, certain. 130
This man, with lime and rough-cast, doth present
Wall, that vile Wall, which did these lovers sunder:
And through Wall's chink, poor souls, they are content
To whisper, at the which let no man wonder.
This man, with lantern, dog, and bush of thorn,
Presenteth Moonshine; for, if you will know,
By moonshine did these lovers think no scorn
To meet at Ninus' tomb, there, there to woo.
This grisly beast, which Lion hight by name,
The trusty Thisby, coming first by night, 140
Did scare away, or rather did affright;
And, as she fled, her mantle she did fall,
Which Lion vile with bloody mouth did stain.
Anon comes Pyramus, sweet youth and tall,

And finds his trusty Thisby's mantle slain :
Whereat with blade, with bloody blameful blade,
He bravely broach d his boiling bloody breast ;
And Thisby, tarrying in mulberry shade,

And this the cranny is, right and sinister,
Through which the fearful lovers are to whisper."
  The. Would you desire lime and hair to speak
better ?

Pyr. " I see a voice : now will I to the chink."

His dagger drew, and died. For all the rest,
Let Lion, Moonshine, Wall, and lovers twain,   150
At large discourse, while here they do remain."
  [*Exeunt Prol.,* THISBE, *Lion, and Moonshine.*
  The. I wonder, if the lion be to speak.
  Dem. No wonder, my lord : one lion may when
many asses do.
  Wall. " In this same interlude it doth befall,
That I, one Snout by name, present a wall ;
And such a wall, as I would have you think,
That had in it a cranny'd hole, or chink,
Through which the lovers, Pyramus and Thisby,
Did whisper often very secretly.   160
This lime, this rough-cast, and this stone, doth show
That I am that same wall : the truth is so ;

  Dem. It is the wittiest partition that ever I heard
discourse, my lord.
  The. Pyramus draws near the wall : silence !

Enter PYRAMUS.

  Pyr. " O grim-look'd night ! O night with hue so
    black !   170
O night, which ever art, when day is not !
O night ! O night ! alack, alack, alack !
I fear my Thisby's promise is forgot.—
And thou, O wall ! O sweet, O lovely wall !
That stand'st between her father's ground and mine ;
Thou wall, O wall ! O sweet and lovely wall !
Show me thy chink to blink through with mine eyne.
    [*Wall holds up his fingers.*

Thanks, courteous wall: Jove shield thee well for this!
But what see I? No Thisby do I see.
O wicked wall! through whom I see no bliss; 180
Curs'd be thy stones for thus deceiving me!"
The. The wall, methinks, being sensible, should curse again.
Pyr. No, in truth, sir, he should not.—"Deceiving me," is Thisby's cue: she is to enter now, and I am to spy her through the wall. You shall see, it will fall pat as I told you.—Yonder she comes.

Enter THISBE.

This. "O wall, full often hast thou heard my moans,
For parting my fair Pyramus and me:
My cherry lips have often kiss'd thy stones, 190
Thy stones with lime and hair knit up in thee."
Pyr. "I see a voice: now will I to the chink,
To spy an I can hear my Thisby's face.
Thisby!"
This. "My love! thou art my love, I think."
Pyr. "Think what thou wilt, I am thy lover's grace;
And like Limander am I trusty still."
This. "And I like Helen, till the Fates me kill."
Pyr. "Not Shafalus to Procrus was so true."
This. "As Shafalus to Procrus, I to you." 200
Pyr. "O! kiss me through the hole of this vile wall."
This. "I kiss the wall's hole, not your lips at all."
Pyr. "Wilt thou at Ninny's tomb meet me straightway?"
This. "'Tide life, 'tide death, I come without delay."
Wall. "Thus have I, Wall, my part discharged so;
And, being done, thus Wall away doth go."
[*Exeunt Wall,* PYRAMUS *and* THISBE.
The. Now is the mural down between the two neighbours.
Dem. No remedy, my lord, when walls are so wilful to hear without warning. 210
Hip. This is the silliest stuff that e'er I heard.
The. The best in this kind are but shadows, and the worst are no worse, if imagination amend them.
Hip. It must be your imagination then, and not theirs.
The. If we imagine no worse of them than they of themselves, they may pass for excellent men. Here come two noble beasts in, a moon and a lion.

Enter Lion and Moonshine.

Lion. "You, ladies, you, whose gentle hearts do fear
The smallest monstrous mouse that creeps on floor, 220
May now, perchance, both quake and tremble here,
When lion rough in wildest rage doth roar.
Then know, that I, one Snug the joiner, am
A lion fell, nor else no lion's dam:
For, if I should as lion come in strife
Into this place, 't were pity on my life."
The. A very gentle beast, and of a good conscience.
Dem. The very best at a beast, my lord, that e'er I saw.
Lys. This lion is a very fox for his valour. 230
The. True; and a goose for his discretion.
Dem. Not so, my lord; for his valour cannot carry his discretion, and the fox carries the goose.
The. His discretion, I am sure, cannot carry his valour, for the goose carries not the fox.' It is well: leave it to his discretion, and let us listen to the moon.
Moon. "This lantern doth the horned moon present."
Dem. He should have worn the horns on his head.
The. He is no crescent, and his horns are invisible within the circumference. 240
Moon. "This lantern doth the horned moon present;
Myself the man i' the moon do seem to be."
The. This is the greatest error of all the rest. The man should be put into the lantern: how is it else the man i' the moon?
Dem. He dares not come there for the candle; for, you see, it is already in snuff.
Hip. I am aweary of this moon: 'would, he would change!
The. It appears by his small light of discretion, that

he is in the wane; but yet, in courtesy, in all reason, we must stay the time. 252
Lys. Proceed, Moon.
Moon. All that I have to say, is, to tell you, that the lantern is the moon; I, the man in the moon; this thorn-bush, my thorn-bush; and this dog, my dog.
Dem. Why, all these should be in the lantern; for all these are in the moon. But, silence! here comes Thisbe.

Enter THISBE.

This. "This is old Ninny's tomb. Where is my love?" 261
Lion. "Oh"—
[*The Lion roars.*—THISBE *runs off.*
Dem. Well roared, Lion.
The. Well run, Thisbe.
Hip. Well shone, Moon.—Truly, the moon shines with a good grace.
[*The Lion tears* THISBE'S *mantle, and exit.*
The. Well moused, Lion.
Dem. And then came Pyramus.
Lys. And so the lion vanished.

Enter PYRAMUS.

Pyr. "Sweet moon, I thank thee for thy sunny beams: 270
I thank thee, moon, for shining now so bright,
For, by thy gracious, golden, glittering streams,
I trust to taste of truest Thisby's sight.
      But stay;—O spite!
      But mark, poor knight,
   What dreadful dole is here?
      Eyes, do you see?
      How can it be?
   O dainty duck! O dear!
      Thy mantle good, 280
      What! stain'd with blood?
   Approach, ye Furies fell!
      O Fates! come, come;
      Cut thread and thrum;
   Quail, crush, conclude, and quell!"
The. This passion, and the death of a dear friend, would go near to make a man look sad.
Hip. Beshrew my heart, but I pity the man.
Pyr. "O, wherefore, Nature, didst thou lions frame,
Since lion vile hath here deflour'd my dear? 290
Which is—no, no—which was the fairest dame,
That liv'd, that lov'd, that lik'd, that look'd with cheer.
      Come, tears, confound;
      Out, sword, and wound
   The pap of Pyramus:
      Ay, that left pap,
      Where heart doth hop:—
   Thus die I, thus, thus, thus!
      Now am I dead,
      Now am I fled; 300
   My soul is in the sky:
      Tongue, lose thy light!
      Moon, take thy flight!
   Now die, die, die, die, die."
[*Dies.—Exit Moonshine.*
Dem. No die, but an ace, for him; for he is but one.
Lys. Less than an ace, man, for he is dead; he is nothing.
The. With the help of a surgeon, he might yet recover, and yet prove an ass.
Hip. How chance Moonshine is gone, before Thisbe comes back and finds her lover? 311
The. She will find him by starlight.—Here she comes, and her passion ends the play.

Enter THISBE.

Hip. Methinks, she should not use a long one for such a Pyramus: I hope she will be brief.
Dem. A moth will turn the balance, which Pyramus, which Thisbe, is the better; he for a man, God warrant us; she for a woman, God bless us.
Lys. She hath spied him already with those sweet eyes. 320
Dem. And thus she moans, *videlicet:—*
This. "Asleep, my love?
      What, dead, my dove?

O Pyramus, arise!
   Speak, speak! Quite dumb?
   Dead, dead? A tomb
Must cover thy sweet eyes.
   These lily lips,
   This cherry nose,
These yellow cowslip cheeks,   330
   Are gone, are gone,
   Lovers, make moan!
His eyes were green as leeks.
   O Sisters Three,
   Come, come to me,
With hands as pale as milk;
   Lay them in gore,
   Since you have shore
With shears his thread of silk.
   Tongue, not a word.—   340
   Come, trusty sword;

THE BERGOMASK.

Come, blade, my breast imbrue:
   And farewell, friends.—
   Thus Thisby ends:
   Adieu, adieu, adieu."   [*Dies.*
The. Moonshine and Lion are left to bury the dead.
Dem. Ay, and Wall too.
Bot. No, I assure you; the wall is down, that
parted their fathers. Will it please you to see the
epilogue, or to hear a Bergomask dance between two
of our company?   351
The. No epilogue, I pray you; for your play needs
no excuse. Never excuse, for when the players are
all dead, there need none to be blamed. Marry, if he
that writ it had play'd Pyramus, and hanged himself in
Thisbe's garter, it would have been a fine tragedy; and
so it is, truly, and very notably discharged. But come,
your Bergomask: let your epilogue alone. [*A dance.*
The iron tongue of midnight hath told twelve.—
Lovers, to bed: 't is almost fairy time.   360
I fear we shall outsleep the coming morn,
As much as we this night have overwatch'd.
This palpable-gross play hath well beguil'd
The heavy gait of night.—Sweet friends, to bed.—
A fortnight hold we this solemnity,
In nightly revels, and new jollity.   [*Exeunt.*

SCENE II.
Enter PUCK.

Puck. Now the hungry lion roars,

And the wolf behowls the moon;
Whilst the heavy ploughman snores,
   All with weary task fordone.
Now the wasted brands do glow,
   Whilst the screech-owl, screeching loud,
Puts the wretch, that lies in woe,
   In remembrance of a shroud.
Now it is the time of night,
   That the graves, all gaping wide,   10
Every one lets forth his sprite,
   In the church-way paths to glide:
And we fairies, that do run
   By the triple Hecate's team,
From the presence of the sun,
   Following darkness like a dream,
Now are frolic; not a mouse
Shall disturb this hallow'd house:
I am sent with broom before,
   To sweep the dust behind the door.   20

Enter OBERON *and* TITANIA, *with
their Train.*

Obe. Through the house give glim-
     mering light,
   By the dead and drowsy fire;
   Every elf, and fairy sprite,
   Hop as light as bird from
     brier;
And this ditty after me
Sing, and dance it trippingly.
Tita. First, rehearse your song by
     rote,
   To each word a warbling note:
   Hand in hand, with fairy grace,
   Will we sing, and bless this
     place.   30
     [*Song and dance.*
Obe. Now, until the break of day,
Through this house each fairy
     stray.
To the best bride-bed will we,
   Which by us shall blessed be;
And the issue there create
   Ever shall be fortunate.
So shall all the couples three
   Ever true in loving be
And the blots of Nature's hand
   Shall not in their issue stand: 40
Never mole, hare-lip, nor scar,
Nor mark prodigious, such as are
Despised in nativity,
Shall upon their children be.
With this field-dew consecrate,
Every fairy take his gait,
And each several chamber bless,
Through this palace with sweet peace,
Ever shall in safety rest,
And the owner of it blest.   50
   Trip away!
   Make no stay;
Meet me all by break of day.
     [*Exeunt* OBERON, TITANIA, *and Train.*
Puck. If we shadows have offended,
Think but this, and all is mended,
That you have but slumber'd here,
While these visions did appear.
And this weak and idle theme,
No more yielding but a dream,
Gentles, do not reprehend: 60
If you pardon, we will mend.
And, as I 'm an honest Puck,
If we have unearned luck
Now to 'scape the serpent's tongue,
We will make amends ere long:
Else the Puck a liar call.
So, good night unto you all.
Give me your hands, if we be friends,
And Robin shall restore amends.   [*Exit.*

THE MERCHANT OF VENICE.

DRAMATIS PERSONÆ.

DUKE OF VENICE.
PRINCE OF MOROCCO, } *Suitors to Portia.*
PRINCE OF ARRAGON, }
ANTONIO, *the Merchant of Venice.*
BASSANIO, *his Friend.*
GRATIANO, }
SOLANIO, } *Friends to Antonio and Bassanio.*
SALARINO, }
LORENZO, *in love with Jessica.*
SHYLOCK, *a Jew.*
TUBAL, *a Jew, his Friend.*

LAUNCELOT GOBBO, *a Clown.*
OLD GOBBO, *Father to Launcelot.*
LEONARDO, *Servant to Bassanio.*
BALTHAZAR, } *Servants to Portia.*
STEPHANO, }

PORTIA, *a rich Heiress.*
NERISSA, *her Waiting-maid.*
JESSICA, *Daughter to Shylock.*

*Magnificoes of Venice, Officers of the Court of Justice,
Gaoler, Servants, and other Attendants.*

SCENE—Partly at VENICE, and partly at BELMONT.

ACT I.

SCENE I.—Venice. A Street.

Enter ANTONIO, SALARINO, and SOLANIO.

Antonio.

IN sooth, I know not why I am so sad.
It wearies me : you say, it wearies you ;
But how I caught it, found it, or came by it,
What stuff 't is made of, whereof it is born,
I am to learn ;
And such a want-wit sadness makes of me,
That I have much ado to know myself.
  Salar. Your mind is tossing on the ocean,
There, where your argosies with portly sail,
Like signiors and rich burghers on the flood,
Or, as it were, the pageants of the sea,   11
Do overpeer the petty traffickers,
That curt'sy to them, do them reverence,
As they fly by them with their woven wings.
  Solan. Believe me, sir, had I such venture forth,
The better part of my affections would
Be with my hopes abroad. I should be still
Plucking the grass to know where sits the wind,
Peering in maps for ports, and piers, and roads ;
And every object that might make me fear   20
Misfortune to my ventures, out of doubt,
Would make me sad.
  Salar.   My wind, cooling my broth,
Would blow me to an ague, when I thought
What harm a wind too great might do at sea.
I should not see the sandy hour-glass run,
But I should think of shallows and of flats,
And see my wealthy Andrew, decks in sand,
Vailing her high-top lower than her ribs,
To kiss her burial. Should I go to church,   30
And see the holy edifice of stone,
And not bethink me straight of dangerous rocks,
Which touching but my gentle vessel's side,
Would scatter all her spices on the stream,
Enrobe the roaring waters with my silks,
And, in a word, but even now worth this,
And now worth nothing? Shall I have the thought
To think on this, and shall I lack the thought,
That such a thing bechanc'd would make me sad?
But tell not me : I know, Antonio   40
Is sad to think upon his merchandise.

  Ant. Believe me, no. I thank my fortune for it,
My ventures are not in one bottom trusted,
Nor to one place ; nor is my whole estate

Salar. "Why, then you are in love."

Upon the fortune of this present year :
Therefore, my merchandise makes me not sad.
  Salar. Why, then you are in love.
  Ant.   Fie, fie !

Salar. Not in love neither? Then let's say you are
    sad,
Because you are not merry; and 't were as easy
For you to laugh, and leap, and say you are merry,
Because you are not sad. Now, by two-headed Janus,
Nature hath fram'd strange fellows in her time: 51
Some that will evermore peep through their eyes,
And laugh, like parrots, at a bag-piper;
And other of such vinegar aspect,
That they 'll not show their teeth in way of smile,
Though Nestor swear the jest be laughable.

    Enter BASSANIO, LORENZO, *and* GRATIANO.

    Solan. Here comes Bassanio, your most noble kins-
    man,
Gratiano, and Lorenzo. Fare you well:
We leave you now with better company.
    Salar. I would have stay'd till I had made you
    merry, 60
If worthier friends had not prevented me.
    Ant. Your worth is very dear in my regard.
I take it, your own business calls on you,
And you embrace the occasion to depart.
    Salar. Good morrow, my good lords.
    Bass. Good signiors both, when shall we laugh?
    say, when?
You grow exceeding strange: must it be so?
    Salar. We 'll make our leisures to attend on yours.
                [*Exeunt* SALARINO *and* SOLANIO.
    Lor. My lord Bassanio, since you have found
    Antonio,
We two will leave you; but at dinner-time, 70
I pray you, have in mind where we must meet.
    Bass. I will not fail you.
    Gra. You look not well, signior Antonio;
You have too much respect upon the world:
They lose it that do buy it with much care.
Believe me, you are marvellously chang'd.
    Ant. I hold the world but as the world, Gratiano;
A stage, where every man must play a part,
And mine a sad one.
    Gra.   Let me play the fool:
With mirth and laughter let old wrinkles come, 80
And let my liver rather heat with wine,
Than my heart cool with mortifying groans.
Why should a man, whose blood is warm within,
Sit like his grandsire cut in alabaster?
Sleep when he wakes, and creep into the jaundice
By being peevish? I tell thee what, Antonio,—
I love thee, and it is my love that speaks,—
There are a sort of men, whose visages
Do cream and mantle, like a standing pond,
And do a wilful stillness entertain, 90
With purpose to be dress'd in an opinion
Of wisdom, gravity, profound conceit;
As who should say, "I am Sir Oracle,
And, when I ope my lips, let no dog bark!"
O! my Antonio, I do know of these,
That therefore only are reputed wise,
For saying nothing; when, I am very sure,
If they should speak, would almost damn those ears,
Which, hearing them, would call their brothers fools.
I 'll tell thee more of this another time: 100
But fish not, with this melancholy bait,
For this fool-gudgeon, this opinion.—
Come, good Lorenzo.—Fare ye well awhile:
I 'll end my exhortation after dinner.
    Lor. Well, we will leave you then till dinner-time.
I must be one of these same dumb wise men,
For Gratiano never lets me speak.
    Gra. Well, keep me company but two years moe,
Thou shalt not know the sound of thine own tongue.
    Ant. Farewell: I 'll grow a talker for this gear. 110
    Gra. Thanks, i' faith; for silence is only commendable
In a neat's tongue dried, and a maid not vendible.
             [*Exeunt* GRATIANO *and* LORENZO.
    Ant. Is that anything now?
    Bass. Gratiano speaks an infinite deal of nothing,
more than any man in all Venice. His reasons are as
two grains of wheat hid in two bushels of chaff: you
shall seek all day ere you find them; and when you
have them, they are not worth the search.

    Ant. Well; tell me now, what lady is the same
To whom you swore a secret pilgrimage, 120
That you to-day promis'd to tell me of?
    Bass. 'Tis not unknown to you, Antonio,
How much I have disabled mine estate,
By something showing a more swelling port
Than my faint means would grant continuance:
Nor do I now make moan to be abridg'd
From such a noble rate; but my chief care
Is to come fairly off from the great debts,
Wherein my time, something too prodigal,
Hath left me gaged. To you, Antonio, 130
I owe the most, in money and in love;
And from your love I have a warranty
To unburthen all my plots and purposes,
How to get clear of all the debts I owe.
    Ant. I pray you, good Bassanio, let me know it;
And if it stand, as you yourself still do,
Within the eye of honour, be assur'd,
My purse, my person, my extremest means,
Lie all unlock'd to your occasions.
    Bass. In my school-days, when I had lost one shaft,
I shot his fellow of the self-same flight 141
The self-same way with more advised watch,
To find the other forth; and by adventuring both,
I oft found both. I urge this childhood proof,
Because what follows is pure innocence.
I owe you much, and, like a wilful youth,
That which I owe is lost; but if you please
To shoot another arrow that self way
Which you did shoot the first, I do not doubt,
As I will watch the aim, or to find both, 150
Or bring your latter hazard back again,
And thankfully rest debtor for the first.
    Ant. You know me well, and herein spend but
    time,
To wind about my love with circumstance;
And, out of doubt, you do me now more wrong,
In making question of my uttermost,
Than if you had made waste of all I have:
Then, do but say to me what I should do,
That in your knowledge may by me be done,
And I am prest unto it: therefore, speak. 160
    Bass. In Belmont is a lady richly left,
And she is fair, and, fairer than that word,
Of wondrous virtues. Sometimes from her eyes
I did receive fair speechless messages.
Her name is Portia; nothing undervalued
To Cato's daughter, Brutus' Portia;
Nor is the wide world ignorant of her worth,
For the four winds blow in from every coast
Renowned suitors; and her sunny locks
Hang on her temples like a golden fleece; 170
Which makes her seat of Belmont Colchos' strand;
And many Jasons come in quest of her.
O my Antonio! had I but the means
To hold a rival place with one of them,
I have a mind presages me such thrift,
That I should questionless be fortunate.
    Ant. Thou know'st, that all my fortunes are at sea;
Neither have I money, nor commodity
To raise a present sum: therefore, go forth;
Try what my credit can in Venice do: 180
That shall be rack'd, even to the uttermost,
To furnish thee to Belmont, to fair Portia.
Go, presently inquire, and so will I,
Where money is, and I no question make,
To have it of my trust, or for my sake. [*Exeunt.*

    SCENE II.—Belmont. An Apartment in PORTIA'S
             House.

    Enter PORTIA *and* NERISSA.

    Por. By my troth, Nerissa, my little body is aweary
of this great world.
    Ner. You would be, sweet madam, if your miseries
were in the same abundance as your good fortunes
are. And yet, for aught I see, they are as sick that
surfeit with too much, as they that starve with
nothing. It is no mean happiness, therefore, to be

seated in the mean: superfluity comes sooner by
white hairs, but competency lives longer.

Por. Good sentences, and well pronounced.   10

Ner. They would be better, if well followed.

Por. If to do were as easy as to know what were
good to do, chapels had been churches, and poor men's
cottages princes' palaces. It is a good divine that
follows his own instructions: I can easier teach
twenty what were good to be done, than be one of the
twenty to follow mine own teaching. The brain may
devise laws for the blood; but a hot temper leaps o'er
a cold decree: such a hare is madness, the youth, to
skip o'er the meshes of good counsel, the cripple. But
this reasoning is not in the fashion to choose me a
husband.—O me! the word choose! I may neither
choose whom I would, nor refuse whom I dislike; so
is the will of a living daughter curbed by the will of a
dead father.—Is it not hard, Nerissa, that I cannot
choose one, nor refuse none?   26

Por. "God made him, and therefore let him pass for a man."

Ner. Your father was ever virtuous, and holy men
at their death have good inspirations; therefore, the
lottery, that he hath devised in these three chests, of
gold, silver, and lead, (whereof who chooses his meaning, chooses you) will, no doubt, never be chosen by
any rightly, but one who you shall rightly love. But
what warmth is there in your affection towards any
of these princely suitors that are already come?

Por. I pray thee, over-name them, and as thou
namest them, I will describe them; and, according to
my description, level at my affection.

Ner. First, there is the Neapolitan prince.   38

Por. Ay, that's a colt, indeed, for he doth nothing
but talk of his horse; and he makes it a great appro-
priation to his own good parts, that he can shoe him
himself. I am much afraid, my lady his mother
played false with a smith.

Ner. Then is there the county Palatine.

Por. He doth nothing but frown, as who should
say, "An you will not have me, choose." He hears
merry tales, and smiles not: I fear he will prove the
weeping philosopher when he grows old, being so full
of unmannerly sadness in his youth. I had rather be
married to a death's-head with a bone in his mouth,
than to either of these. God defend me from these
two!   52

Ner. How say you by the French lord, Monsieur Le
Bon?

Por. God made him, and therefore let him pass for
a man. In truth, I know it is a sin to be a mocker;
but, he! why, he hath a horse better than the Neapolitan's, a better bad habit of frowning than the count
Palatine: he is every man in no man; if a throstle
sing, he falls straight a capering: he will fence with
his own shadow. If I should marry him, I should
marry twenty husbands. If he would despise me, I
would forgive him; for if he love me to madness, I
shall never requite him.   64

Ner. What say you then to Faulconbridge, the
young baron of England?

Por. You know, I say nothing to him, for he understands not me, nor I him: he hath neither Latin,
French, nor Italian; and you will come into the court
and swear, that I have a poor penny-worth in the
English. He is a proper man's picture; but, alas!
who can converse with a dumb-show? How oddly he
is suited! I think, he bought his doublet in Italy, his
round hose in France, his bonnet in Germany, and
his behaviour every where.

Ner. What think you of the Scottish lord, his neighbour?

Por. That he hath a neighbourly charity in him;
for he borrowed a box of the ear of the Englishman,
and swore he would pay him again, when he was
able: I think, the Frenchman became his surety, and
sealed under for another.   82

Ner. How like you the young German, the duke of
Saxony's nephew?

Por. Very vilely in the morning, when he is sober,
and most vilely in the afternoon, when he is drunk:
when he is best, he is a little worse than a man; and
when he is worst, he is little better than a beast. An
the worst fall that ever fell, I hope I shall make shift
to go without him.   90

Ner. If he should offer to choose, and choose the
right casket, you should refuse to perform your
father's will, if you should refuse to accept him.

Por. Therefore, for fear of the worst, I pray thee,
set a deep glass of Rhenish wine on the contrary
casket, for, if the devil be within, and that temptation
without, I know he will choose it. I will do anything,
Nerissa, ere I will be married to a sponge.

Ner. You need not fear, lady, the having any of
these lords: they have acquainted me with their
determinations; which is, indeed, to return to their
home, and to trouble you with no more suit, unless
you may be won by some other sort than your father's
imposition, depending on the caskets.

Por. If I live to be as old as Sibylla, I will die as
chaste as Diana, unless I be obtained by the manner
of my father's will. I am glad this parcel of wooers
are so reasonable; for there is not one among them
but I dote on his very absence, and I pray God grant
them a fair departure.   110

Ner. Do you not remember, lady, in your father's
time, a Venetian, a scholar, and a soldier, that came
hither in company of the marquess of Montferrat?

Por. Yes, yes; it was Bassanio: as I think, so was
he called.

Ner. True, madam: he, of all the men that ever my
foolish eyes looked upon, was the best deserving a fair
lady.

Por. I remember him well, and I remember him
worthy of thy praise.   120

Enter a Servant.

How now? what news?

Serv. The four strangers seek for you, madam, to
take their leave; and there is a forerunner come from
a fifth, the prince of Morocco, who brings word, the
prince, his master, will be here to-night.

Por. If I could bid the fifth welcome with so good
heart, as I can bid the other four farewell, I should be
glad of his approach: if he have the condition of a
saint, and the complexion of a devil, I had rather he
should shrive me than wive me.   130

Come, Nerissa.—Sirrah, go before.—
Whiles we shut the gate upon one wooer, another
      knocks at the door.   [*Exeunt.*

SCENE III.—Venice. A public Place.

Enter BASSANIO *and* SHYLOCK.

Shy. Three thousand ducats,—well.

Bass. Ay, sir, for three months.

Shy. For three months,—well.

Bass. For the which, as I told you, Antonio shall be
bound.

Shy. Antonio shall become bound,--well.
Bass. May you stead me ? Will you pleasure me ?
Shall I know your answer ?
Shy. Three thousand ducats for three months, and
Antonio bound.   10
Bass. Your answer to that.
Shy. Antonio is a good man.
Bass. Have you heard any imputation to the contrary ?
Shy. Ho ! no, no, no, no :--my meaning, in saying
he is a good man, is to have you understand me, that
he is sufficient ; yet his means are in supposition. He
hath an argosy bound to Tripolis, another to the
Indies ; I understand moreover upon the Rialto, he
hath a third at Mexico, a fourth for England, and
other ventures he hath squandered abroad. But ships
are but boards, sailors but men : there be land-rats,
and water-rats, water-thieves, and land-thieves, I
mean, pirates : and then, there is the peril of waters,
winds, and rocks. The man is, notwithstanding,
sufficient. Three thousand ducats :--I think, I may
take his bond.
Bass. Be assured you may.
Shy. I will be assured I may ; and, that I may be
assured, I will bethink me. May I speak with
Antonio ?   31
Bass. If it please you to dine with us.
Shy. Yes, to smell pork ; to eat of the habitation
which your prophet, the Nazarite, conjured the devil
into. I will buy with you, sell with you, talk with
you, walk with you, and so following ; but I will not
eat with you, drink with you, nor pray with you.
What news on the Rialto ?--Who is he comes here ?

Enter ANTONIO.

Bass. This is Signior Antonio.
Shy. [*Aside.*] How like a fawning publican he
looks !   40
I hate him for he is a Christian :
But more, for that, in low simplicity,
He lends out money gratis, and brings down
The rate of usance here with us in Venice.
If I can catch him once upon the hip,
I will feed fat the ancient grudge I bear him.
He hates our sacred nation ; and he rails,
Even there where merchants most do congregate,
On me, my bargains, and my well-won thrift,
Which he calls interest. Cursed be my tribe,   50
If I forgive him !
Bass.   Shylock, do you hear ?
Shy. I am debating of my present store,
And, by the near guess of my memory,
I cannot instantly raise up the gross
Of full three thousand ducats. What of that ?
Tubal, a wealthy Hebrew of my tribe,
Will furnish me. But soft ! how many months
Do you desire ?--[*To* ANTONIO.] Rest you fair, good
signior ;
Your worship was the last man in our mouths.
Ant. Shylock, albeit I neither lend nor borrow,   60
By taking, nor by giving of excess,
Yet, to supply the ripe wants of my friend,
I 'll break a custom.--Is he yet possess'd,
How much ye would ?
Shy.   Ay, ay, three thousand ducats.
Ant. And for three months.
Shy. I had forgot :--three months ; you told me so.
Well then, your bond ; and let me see. But hear you :
Methought, you said, you neither lend nor borrow
Upon advantage.
Ant.   I do never use it.
Shy. When Jacob graz'd his uncle Laban's sheep,--
This Jacob from our holy Abram was   71
(As his wise mother wrought in his behalf)
The third possessor ; ay, he was the third,--
Ant. And what of him ? did he take interest ?
Shy. No ; not take interest ; not, as you would say,
Directly interest : mark what Jacob did.
When Laban and himself were compromis'd,
That all the eanlings which were streak'd and pied,
Should fall as Jacob's hire, the ewes, being rank,
In end of autumn turned to the rams ;   80

And when the work of generation was
Between these woolly breeders in the act,
The skilful shepherd peel'd me certain wands,
And, in the doing of the deed of kind,
He stuck them up before the fulsome ewes,
Who, then conceiving, did in eaning time
Fall party-colour'd lambs, and those were Jacob's.
This was a way to thrive, and he was blest :
And thrift is blessing, if men steal it not.
Ant. This was a venture, sir, that Jacob serv'd for ;
A thing not in his power to bring to pass,   91
But sway'd and fashion'd by the hand of Heaven.
Was this inserted to make interest good ?
Or is your gold and silver ewes and rams ?
Shy. I cannot tell : I make it breed as fast.--
But note me, signior.
Ant.   Mark you this, Bassanio,
The devil can cite Scripture for his purpose.
An evil soul, producing holy witness,
Is like a villain with a smiling cheek,
A goodly apple rotten at the heart.   100
O, what a goodly outside falsehood hath !
Shy. Three thousand ducats ;--'tis a good round
sum.
Three months from twelve, then let me see the rate.
Ant. Well, Shylock, shall we be beholding to you ?
Shy. Signior Antonio, many a time and oft,
In the Rialto, you have rated me
About my moneys, and my usances :
Still have I borne it with a patient shrug ;
For sufferance is the badge of all our tribe.
You call me misbeliever, cut-throat dog,   110
And spit upon my Jewish gaberdine,
And all for use of that which is mine own.
Well then, it now appears, you need my help :
Go to then ; you come to me, and you say,
" Shylock, we would have moneys : " you say so ;
You, that did void your rheum upon my beard,
And foot me as you spurn a stranger cur
Over your threshold : moneys is your suit.
What should I say to you ? Should I not say,
" Hath a dog money ? Is it possible,   120
A cur can lend three thousand ducats ? " or
Shall I bend low, and in a bondman's key,
With bated breath, and whispering humbleness,
Say this :--
" Fair sir, you spit on me on Wednesday last ;
You spurn'd me such a day ; another time
You call'd me dog ; and for these courtesies
I 'll lend you thus much moneys ? "
Ant. I am as like to call thee so again,
To spit on thee again, to spurn thee too.   130
If thou wilt lend this money, lend it not
As to thy friends ; for when did friendship take
A breed of barren metal of his friend ?
But lend it rather to thine enemy :
Who, if he break, thou may'st with better face
Exact the penalty.
Shy.   Why, look you, how you storm !
I would be friends with you, and have your love,
Forget the shames that you have stain'd me with,
Supply your present wants, and take no doit
Of usance for my moneys, and you 'll not hear me. 140
This is kind I offer.
Ant. This were kindness.
Shy.   This kindness will I show.
Go with me to a notary, seal me there
Your single bond ; and, in a merry sport,
If you repay me not on such a day,
In such a place, such sum or sums as are
Express'd in the condition, let the forfeit
Be nominated for an equal pound
Of your fair flesh, to be cut off and taken
In what part of your body pleaseth me.   150
Ant. Content, in faith : I 'll seal to such a bond
And say there is much kindness in the Jew.
Bass. You shall not seal to such a bond for me :
I 'll rather dwell in my necessity.'
Ant. Why, fear not, man ; I will not forfeit it :
Within these two months, that 's a month before
This bond expires, I do expect return
Of thrice three times the value of this bond.

Shy. O father Abram ! what these Christians are,
Whose own hard dealings teaches them suspect   160
The thoughts of others !—Pray you, tell me this :
If he should break his day, what should I gain
By the exaction of the forfeiture ?
A pound of man's flesh, taken from a man,
Is not so estimable, profitable neither,
As flesh of muttons, beefs, or goats. I say,
To buy his favour, I extend this friendship :
If he will take it, so ; if not, adieu ;
And, for my love, I pray you, wrong me not.
    Ant. Yes, Shylock, I will seal unto this bond.   170

Shy. Then meet me forthwith at the notary's.
Give him direction for this merry bond,
And I will go and purse the ducats straight,
See to my house, left in the fearful guard
Of an unthrifty knave, and presently
I will be with you.
    Ant.   Hie thee, gentle Jew. [*Exit* SHYLOCK.
This Hebrew will turn Christian : he grows kind.
    Bass. I like not fair terms, and a villain's mind.
    Ant. Come on : in this there can be no dismay ;
My ships come home a month before the day.   180
                                          [*Exeunt.*

ACT II.

SCENE I.—Belmont. An Apartment in PORTIA'S House.

Enter the Prince of MOROCCO, *and his Followers ;* PORTIA, NERISSA, *and others of her Train.*
Flourish cornets.

Morocco.
DISLIKE me not for my complexion,
The shadow'd livery of the burnish'd sun,
To whom I am a neighbour, and near bred.
Bring me the fairest creature northward
                                       born,
Where Phœbus' fire scarce thaws the icicles,
And let us make incision for your love,
To prove whose blood is reddest, his or mine.
I tell thee, lady, this aspect of mine
Hath fear'd the valiant : by my love, I swear,
The best-regarded virgins of our clime   10
Have lov'd it too. I would not change this
                                       hue,
Except to steal your thoughts, my gentle queen.
    Por. In terms of choice I am not solely led
By nice direction of a maiden's eyes :
Besides, the lottery of my destiny
Bars me the right of voluntary choosing ;
But, if my father had not scanted me,
And hedg'd me by his wit, to yield myself
His wife who wins me by that means I told you,
Yourself, renowned prince, then stood as fair,   20
As any comer I have look'd on yet,
For my affection.
    Mor.   Even for that I thank you :
Therefore, I pray you, lead me to the caskets,
To try my fortune. By this scimitar,—
That slew the Sophy, and a Persian prince
That won three fields of Sultan Solyman,—
I would outstare the sternest eyes that look,
Outbrave the heart most daring on the earth,
Pluck the young suckling cubs from the she-bear,
Yea, mock the lion when he roars for prey,   30
To win thee, lady. But, alas the while !
If Hercules and Lichas play at dice,
Which is the better man, the greater throw
May turn by fortune from the weaker hand :
So is Alcides beaten by his page ;
And so may I, blind fortune leading me,
Miss that which one unworthier may attain,
And die with grieving.
    Por.   You must take your chance ;
And either not attempt to choose at all,
Or swear before you choose,—if you choose wrong,   40
Never to speak to lady afterward
In way of marriage : therefore be advis'd.
    Mor. Nor will not : come, bring me unto my chance.

Por. First, forward to the temple : after dinner
Your hazard shall be made.
    Mor.   Good fortune then,
To make me blest, or cursed'st among men !
                          [*Cornets, and exeunt.*

Mor. "Even for that I thank you."

SCENE II.—Venice. A Street.

Enter LAUNCELOT GOBBO.

Laun. Certainly, my conscience will serve me to
run from this Jew my master. The fiend is at mine
elbow, and tempts me, saying to me,—"Gobbo,
Launcelot Gobbo, good Launcelot," or "good Gobbo,"
or "good Launcelot Gobbo, use your legs, take the
start, run away." My conscience says,—"No ; take

heed, honest Launcelot; take heed, honest Gobbo;"
or, as aforesaid, "honest Launcelot Gobbo; do not
run; scorn running with thy heels." Well, the most
courageous fiend bids me pack: "Via!" says the
fiend; "away!" says the fiend; "for the heavens,
rouse up a brave mind," says the fiend, "and run."
Well, my conscience, hanging about the neck of my
heart, says very wisely to me,—"My honest friend
Launcelot, being an honest man's son,"—or rather an
honest woman's son;—for, indeed, my father did
something smack,—something grow to,—he had a
kind of taste:—well, my conscience says, "Launcelot,
budge not." "Budge," says the fiend: "budge not,"
says my conscience. "Conscience," say I, "you
counsel well;" "fiend," say I, "you counsel well:"
to be ruled by my conscience, I should stay with the
Jew my master, who (God bless the mark!) is a kind
of devil; and, to run away from the Jew, I should be

Gob. "Master, young gentleman, I pray you, which is the way
to Master Jew's?"

ruled by the fiend, who, saving your reverence, is the
devil himself. Certainly, the Jew is the very devil
incarnation, and, in my conscience, my conscience is
but a kind of hard conscience to offer to counsel me
to stay with the Jew. The fiend gives the more
friendly counsel: I will run, fiend; my heels are at
your commandment; I will run.   31

Enter Old GOBBO, *with a basket.*

Gob. Master, young man, you; I pray you, which is
the way to Master Jew's?

Laun. [*Aside.*] O heavens! this is my true-begotten
father, who, being more than sand-blind, high gravel-
blind, knows me not:—I will try confusions with him.

Gob. Master, young gentleman, I pray you, which
is the way to Master Jew's?

Laun. Turn up on your right hand at the next
turning, but at the next turning of all, on your left;
marry, at the very next turning, turn of no hand, but
turn down directly to the Jew's house.   42

Gob. By God's sonties, 't will be a hard way to hit.
Can you tell me, whether one Launcelot, that dwells
with him, dwell with him, or no?

Laun. Talk you of young Master Launcelot?—
[*Aside.*] Mark me now; now will I raise the waters.—
[*To him.*] Talk you of young Master Launcelot?

Gob. No master, sir, but a poor man's son: his
father, though I say it, is an honest exceeding poor
man; and, God be thanked, well to live.   51

Laun. Well, let his father be what 'a will, we talk
of young Master Launcelot.

Gob. Your worship's friend, and Launcelot, sir.

Laun. But I pray you, *ergo,* old man, *ergo,* I beseech you, talk you of young Master Launcelot?

Gob. Of Launcelot, an 't please your mastership.

Laun. Ergo, Master Launcelot. Talk not of Master
Launcelot, father; for the young gentleman (according to Fates and Destinies, and such odd sayings,
the Sisters Three, and such branches of learning) is,
indeed, deceased; or, as you would say, in plain terms,
gone to heaven.   63

Gob. Marry, God forbid! the boy was the very staff
of my age, my very prop.

Laun. Do I look like a cudgel, or a hovel-post, a
staff, or a prop?—Do you know me, father?

Gob. Alack the day! I know you not, young gentleman; but, I pray you, tell me, is my boy (God rest his
soul!) alive, or dead?   70

Laun. Do you not know me, father?

Gob. Alack, sir, I am sand-blind; I know you not.

Laun. Nay, indeed, if you had your eyes, you might
fail of the knowing me: it is a wise father that knows
his own child. Well, old man, I will tell you news of
your son. [*Kneels.*] Give me your blessing: truth will
come to light; murder cannot be hid long, a man's
son may, but in the end truth will out.

Gob. Pray you, sir, stand up. I am sure you are
not Launcelot, my boy.   80

Laun. Pray you, let 's have no more fooling about
it, but give me your blessing: I am Launcelot, your
boy that was, your son that is, your child that shall be.

Gob. I cannot think you are my son.

Laun. I know not what I shall think of that; but I
am Launcelot, the Jew's man, and, I am sure, Margery,
your wife, is my mother.

Gob. Her name is Margery, indeed: I 'll be sworn,
if thou be Launcelot, thou art mine own flesh and
blood. Lord worshipp'd might he be! what a beard
hast thou got! thou hast got more hair on thy chin,
than Dobbin my phill-horse has on his tail.   92

Laun. It should seem then that Dobbin's tail grows
backward: I am sure he had more hair of his tail,
than I have of my face, when I last saw him.

Gob. Lord! how art thou changed! How dost thou
and thy master agree? I have brought him a present.
How 'gree you now?

Laun. Well, well; but, for mine own part, as I have
set up my rest to run away, so I will not rest till I
have run some ground. My master 's a very Jew:
give him a present! give him a halter: I am famish'd
in his service; you may tell every finger I have with
my ribs. Father, I am glad you are come: give me
your present to one Master Bassanio, who, indeed,
gives rare new liveries. If I serve not him, I will run
as far as God has any ground.—O rare fortune! here
comes the man:—to him, father; for I am a Jew, if I
serve the Jew any longer.   109

Enter BASSANIO, *with* LEONARDO, *and other
Followers.*

Bass. You may do so;—but let it be so hasted, that
supper be ready at the farthest by five of the clock.
See these letters delivered: put the liveries to making,
and desire Gratiano to come anon to my lodging.
    [*Exit a Servant.*

Laun. To him, father.

Gob. God bless your worship!

Bass. Gramercy. Wouldst thou aught with me?

Gob. Here 's my son, sir, a poor boy,—

Laun. Not a poor boy, sir, but the rich Jew's man,
that would, sir,—as my father shall specify,—

Gob. He hath a great infection, sir, as one would
say, to serve—   121

Laun. Indeed, the short and the long is, I serve the
Jew, and have a desire,—as my father shall specify,—

Gob. His master and he (saving your worship's
reverence) are scarce cater-cousins,—

Laun. To be brief, the very truth is, that the Jew,
having done me wrong, doth cause me,—as my father,
being, I hope, an old man, shall frutify unto you,—

Gob. I have here a dish of doves, that I would
bestow upon your worship; and my suit is,—   130

Laun. In very brief, the suit is impertinent to
myself, as your worship shall know by this honest
old man; and, though I say it, though old man, yet
poor man, my father.

Bass. One speak for both.—What would you?
Laun. Serve you, sir.
Gob. That is the very defect of the matter, sir.
Bass. I know thee well: thou hast obtain'd thy suit.
Shylock, thy master, spoke with me this day,
And hath preferr'd thee; if it be preferment, 140
To leave a rich Jew's service, to become
The follower of so poor a gentleman.
Laun. The old proverb is very well parted between
my master Shylock and you, sir: you have the grace
of God, sir, and he hath enough.
Bass. Thou speak'st it well.—Go, father, with thy
son.—
Take leave of thy old master, and inquire
My lodging out.—[*To his Followers.*] Give him a livery
More guarded than his fellows': see it done. 149
Laun. Father, in.—I cannot get a service,—no; I
have ne'er a tongue in my head.—Well; [*looking on
his palm*] if any man in Italy have a fairer table,
which doth offer to swear upon a book,—I shall have
good fortune.—Go to; here's a simple line of life!
here's a small trifle of wives: alas! fifteen wives is
nothing: eleven widows, and nine maids, is a simple
coming-in for one man; and then, to 'scape drowning
thrice, and to be in peril of my life with the edge of a
feather-bed:—here are simple 'scapes! Well, if Fortune be a woman, she's a good wench for this gear.—
Father, come; I'll take my leave of the Jew in the
twinkling of an eye. 162
      [*Exeunt* LAUNCELOT *and Old* GOBBO.
Bass. I pray thee, good Leonardo, think on this.
These things being bought, and orderly bestow'd,
Return in haste, for I do feast to-night
My best-esteem'd acquaintance: hie thee; go.
Leon. My best endeavours shall be done herein.

Enter GRATIANO.

Gra. Where is your master?
Leon.   Yonder, sir, he walks. [*Exit.*
Gra. Signior Bassanio!
Bass. Gratiano! 170
Gra. I have a suit to you.
Bass.   You have obtain'd it.
Gra. You must not deny me. I must go with you
to Belmont.
Bass. Why, then you must; but hear thee, Gratiano.
Thou art too wild, too rude, and bold of voice;—
Parts, that become thee happily enough,
And in such eyes as ours appear not faults;
But where thou art not known, why, there they show
Something too liberal. Pray thee, take pain
To allay with some cold drops of modesty 180
Thy skipping spirit, lest, through thy wild behaviour,
I be misconstrued in the place I go to,
And lose my hopes.
Gra.   Signior Bassanio, hear me:
If I do not put on a sober habit,
Talk with respect, and swear but now and then,
Wear prayer-books in my pocket, look demurely,
Nay more, while grace is saying, hood mine eyes
Thus with my hat, and sigh, and say amen,
Use all the observance of civility,
Like one well studied in a sad ostent 190
To please his grandam, never trust me more.
Bass. Well, we shall see your bearing.
Gra. Nay, but I bar to-night; you shall not gage me
By what we do to-night.
Bass.   No, that were pity.
I would entreat you rather to put on
Your boldest suit of mirth, for we have friends
That purpose merriment. But fare you well:
I have some business.
Gra. And I must to Lorenzo, and the rest;
But we will visit you at supper-time. 200
      [*Exeunt.*

SCENE III.—The Same. A Room in SHYLOCK'S
House.

Enter JESSICA *and* LAUNCELOT.
Jes. I am sorry, thou wilt leave my father so

Our house is hell, and thou, a merry devil,
Didst rob it of some taste of tediousness.
But fare thee well; there is a ducat for thee:
And, Launcelot, soon at supper shalt thou see
Lorenzo, who is thy new master's guest;
Give him this letter; do it secretly;
And so farewell: I would not have my father
See me in talk with thee. 9
Laun. Adieu!—tears exhibit my tongue.—Most
beautiful pagan,—most sweet Jew! If a Christian did
not play the knave, and get thee, I am much deceived.
But, adieu! these foolish drops do somewhat drown
my manly spirit: adieu!
Jes. Farewell, good Launcelot.— [*Exit* LAUNCELOT.
Alack, what heinous sin is it in me,
To be asham'd to be my father's child!
But though I am a daughter to his blood,
I am not to his manners. O Lorenzo!
If thou keep promise, I shall end this strife, 20
Become a Christian, and thy loving wife. [*Exit.*

SCENE IV.—The Same. A Street.

Enter GRATIANO, LORENZO, SALARINO, *and* SOLANIO.

Lor. Nay, we will slink away in supper-time,
Disguise us at my lodging, and return
All in an hour.
Gra. We have not made good preparation.
Salar. We have not spoke us yet of torch-bearers.
Solan. 'Tis vile, unless it may be quaintly order'd,
And better, in my mind, not undertook.
Lor. 'Tis now but four o'clock: we have two hours
To furnish us.—

Enter LAUNCELOT, *with a letter.*

      Friend Launcelot, what's the news?
Laun. An it shall please you to break up this, it
shall seem to signify. [*Giving a letter.*
Lor. I know the hand: in faith, 'tis a fair hand; 12
And whiter than the paper it writ on,
Is the fair hand that writ.
Gra.   Love-news, in faith.
Laun. By your leave, sir.
Lor. Whither goest thou?
Laun. Marry, sir, to bid my old master, the Jew, to
sup to-night with my new master, the Christian.
Lor. Hold here, take this.—Tell gentle Jessica,
I will not fail her:—speak it privately; go.— 20
      [*Exit* LAUNCELOT.
Gentlemen,
Will you prepare you for this masque to-night?
I am provided of a torch-bearer.
Salar. Ay, marry, I'll be gone about it straight.
Solan. And so will I.
Lor.   Meet me, and Gratiano,
At Gratiano's lodging some hour hence.
Salar. 'Tis good we do so.
      [*Exeunt* SALARINO *and* SOLANIO.
Gra. Was not that letter from fair Jessica?
Lor. I must needs tell thee all. She hath directed,
How I shall take her from her father's house; 30
What gold and jewels she is furnish'd with;
What page's suit she hath in readiness.
If e'er the Jew her father come to Heaven,
It will be for his gentle daughter's sake;
And never dare misfortune cross her foot,
Unless she do it under this excuse,
That she is issue to a faithless Jew.—
Come, go with me: peruse this, as thou goest.
Fair Jessica shall be my torch-bearer. [*Exeunt.*

SCENE V.—The Same. Before SHYLOCK'S House.

Enter SHYLOCK *and* LAUNCELOT.
Shy. Well, thou shalt see, thy eyes shall be thy
judge,
The difference of old Shylock and Bassanio:—
What, Jessica!—thou shalt not gormandize,

As thou hast done with me ;—what, Jessica !—
And sleep and snore, and rend apparel out.—
Why, Jessica, I say !
    Laun.   Why, Jessica !
    Shy. Who bids thee call ? I do not bid thee call.

Look to my house.—I am right loath to go :
There is some ill a brewing towards my rest,
For I did dream of money-bags to-night.
    Laun. I beseech you, sir, go : my young master doth
expect your reproach.   20

Shy. "Jessica, my girl, look to my house."

    Laun. Your worship was wont to tell me, I could
do nothing without bidding.

Enter JESSICA.

    Jes. Call you ? What is your will ?   10
    Shy. I am bid forth to supper, Jessica :
There are my keys.—But wherefore should I go ?
I am not bid for love ; they flatter me :
But yet I 'll go in hate, to feed upon
The prodigal Christian.—Jessica, my girl,

    Shy. So do I his.
    Laun. And they have conspired together :—I will
not say, you shall see a masque ; but if you do, then it
was not for nothing that my nose fell a bleeding on
Black-Monday last, at six o'clock i' the morning, falling out that year on Ash-Wednesday was four year
in the afternoon.
    Shy. What ! are there masques ?—Hear you me,
        Jessica :
Lock up my doors ; and when you hear the drum,

And the vile squeaking of the wry-neck'd fife,   30
Clamber not you up to the casements then,
Nor thrust your head into the public street
To gaze on Christian fools with varnish'd faces,
But stop my house's ears, I mean my casements:
Let not the sound of shallow foppery enter
My sober house.—By Jacob's staff, I swear,
I have no mind of feasting forth to-night;
But I will go.—Go you before me, sirrah:
Say, I will come.
   Laun. I will go before, sir.—Mistress, look out at
window, for all this;   41
         There will come a Christian by,
         Will be worth a Jewess' eye.   [*Exit.*
   Shy. What says that fool of Hagar's offspring? ha!
   Jes. His words were "Farewell, mistress;" nothing
      else.
   Shy. The patch is kind enough, but a huge feeder,
Snail-slow in profit, and he sleeps by day
More than the wild-cat: drones hive not with me;
Therefore I part with him, and part with him
To one that I would have him help to waste   50
His borrow'd purse.—Well, Jessica, go in:
Perhaps I will return immediately.
Do, as I bid you: shut doors after you:
Fast bind, fast find;
A proverb never stale in thrifty mind.   [*Exit.*
   Jes. Farewell; and if my fortune be not crost,
I have a father, you a daughter, lost.   [*Exit.*

SCENE VI.—The Same.

Enter GRATIANO *and* SALARINO, *masqued.*

   Gra. This is the penthouse, under which Lorenzo
Desir'd us to make stand.
   Salar.   His hour is almost past.
   Gra. And it is marvel he outdwells his hour,
For lovers ever run before the clock.
   Salar. O! ten times faster Venus' pigeons fly
To seal love's bonds new-made, than they are wont
To keep obliged faith unforfeited!
   Gra. That ever holds: who riseth from a feast
With that keen appetite that he sits down?
Where is the horse that doth untread again   10
His tedious measure with the unbated fire
That he did pace them first? All things that are,
Are with more spirit chased than enjoy'd.
How like a younker, or a prodigal,
The scarfed bark puts from her native bay,
Hugg'd and embraced by the strumpet wind!
How like the prodigal doth she return,
With over-weather'd ribs, and ragged sails,
Lean, rent, and beggar'd by the strumpet wind!

Enter LORENZO.

   Salar. Here comes Lorenzo:—more of this here-
after.   20
   Lor. Sweet friends, your patience for my long
abode;
Not I, but my affairs have made you wait:
When you shall please to play the thieves for wives,
I'll watch as long for you then.—Approach;
Here dwells my father Jew.—Ho! who's within!

Enter JESSICA *above, in boy's clothes.*

   Jes. Who are you? Tell me for more certainty,
Albeit I'll swear that I do know your tongue.
   Lor. Lorenzo, and thy love.
   Jes. Lorenzo, certain; and my love, indeed,
For who love I so much? And now who knows,   30
But you, Lorenzo, whether I am yours?
   Lor. Heaven, and thy thoughts are witness that
      thou art.
   Jes. Here, catch this casket: it is worth the pains.
I am glad 't is night, you do not look on me,
For I am much asham'd of my exchange;
But love is blind, and lovers cannot see
The pretty follies that themselves commit;
For if they could, Cupid himself would blush
To see me thus transformed to a boy.

   Lor. Descend, for you must be my torch-bearer.   40
   Jes. What! must I hold a candle to my shames?
They in themselves, good sooth, are too too light.
Why, 't is an office of discovery, love,
And I should be obscur'd.
   Lor.   So are you, sweet,
Even in the lovely garnish of a boy.
But come at once;
For the close night doth play the runaway,
And we are stay'd for at Bassanio's feast.
   Jes. I will make fast the doors, and gild myself
With some more ducats, and be with you straight.   50
                   [*Exit from above.*
   Gra. Now, by my hood, a Gentile, and no Jew.
   Lor. Beshrew me, but I love her heartily;
For she is wise, if I can judge of her,
And fair she is, if that mine eyes be true,
And true she is, as she hath prov'd herself;
And therefore, like herself, wise, fair, and true,
Shall she be placed in my constant soul.

Enter JESSICA.

What, art thou come?—On, gentlemen; away!
Our masquing mates by this time for us stay.
        [*Exit with* JESSICA *and* SALARINO.

Enter ANTONIO.

   Ant. Who's there?   60
   Gra. Signior Antonio?
   Ant. Fie, fie, Gratiano! where are all the rest?
'T is nine o'clock; our friends all stay for you.
No masque to-night: the wind is come about;
Bassanio presently will go aboard:
I have sent twenty out to seek for you.
   Gra. I am glad on 't: I desire no more delight,
Than to be under sail and gone to-night.   [*Exeunt.*

SCENE VII.—Belmont.   An Apartment in PORTIA'S House.

Enter PORTIA, *with the Prince of* MOROCCO, *and both their Trains.*

   Por. Go, draw aside the curtains, and discover
The several caskets to this noble prince.—
Now make your choice.
   Mor. The first, of gold, who this inscription bears:
"Who chooseth me, shall gain what many men
     desire."
The second, silver, which this promise carries:
"Who chooseth me, shall get as much as he deserves."
This third, dull lead, with warning all as blunt:
"Who chooseth me, must give and hazard all he
     hath."
How shall I know if I do choose the right?   10
   Por. The one of them contains my picture, prince:
If you choose that, then I am yours withal.
   Mor. Some god direct my judgment? Let me see.
I will survey the inscriptions back again:
What says this leaden casket?
"Who chooseth me, must give and hazard all he
     hath."
Must give—for what? for lead? hazard for lead?
This casket threatens. Men that hazard all,
Do it in hope of fair advantages:
A golden mind stoops not to shows of dross;   20
I'll then nor give, nor hazard, aught for lead.
What says the silver, with her virgin hue?
"Who chooseth me, shall get as much as he deserves."
As much as he deserves?—Pause there, Morocco,
And weigh thy value with an even hand.
If thou be'st rated by thy estimation,
Thou dost deserve enough; and yet enough
May not extend so far as to the lady;
And yet to be afeard of my deserving,
Were but a weak disabling of myself.   30
As much as I deserve!—Why, that 's the lady:
I do in birth deserve her, and in fortunes,
In graces, and in qualities of breeding;
But more than these in love I do deserve.
What if I stray'd no further, but chose here?—

Let's see once more this saying grav'd in gold :
"Who chooseth me, shall gain what many men
   desire."
Why, that's the lady : all the world desires her ;
From the four corners of the earth they come,
To kiss this shrine, this mortal-breathing saint.   40
The Hyrcanian deserts, and the vasty wilds
Of wild Arabia, are as throughfares now,
For princes to come view fair Portia :
The watery kingdom, whose ambitious head
Spits in the face of heaven, is no bar
To stop the foreign spirits, but they come,
As o'er a brook, to see fair Portia.
One of these three contains her heavenly picture.
Is 't like, that lead contains her? 'T were damnation,
To think so base a thought : it were too gross   50
To rib her cerecloth in the obscure grave.
Or shall I think in silver she's immur'd,
Being ten times undervalued to tried gold?
O sinful thought ! Never so rich a gem
Was set in worse than gold. They have in England
A coin, that bears the figure of an angel
Stamped in gold, but that's insculp'd upon ;
But here an angel in a golden bed
Lies all within.—Deliver me the key :
Here do I choose, and thrive I as I may !   60
  Por. There, take it, prince ; and if my form lie
   there,
Then I am yours.   [*He unlocks the golden casket.*
  Mor.   O hell ! what have we here ?
A carrion death, within whose empty eye
There is a written scroll. I 'll read the writing.
[*Reads.*] "All that glisters is not gold :
    Often have you heard that told :
    Many a man his life hath sold,
    But my outside to behold :
    Gilded tombs do worms infold.
    Had you been as wise as bold,   70
    Young in limbs, in judgment old,
    Your answer had not been inscroll'd :
    Fare you well ; your suit is cold."
  Cold, indeed, and labour lost :
    Then, farewell, heat ; and, welcome, frost.—
Portia, adieu. I have too griev'd a heart,
To take a tedious leave : thus losers part.   [*Exit.*
  Por. A gentle riddance.—Draw the curtains : go.
Let all of his complexion choose me so.   [*Exeunt.*

SCENE VIII.—Venice. A Street.

Enter Salarino *and* Solanio.

  Salar. Why, man, I saw Bassanio under sail :
With him is Gratiano gone along ;
And in their ship, I 'm sure, Lorenzo is not.
  Solan. The villain Jew with outcries rais'd the
   duke,
Who went with him to search Bassanio's ship.
  Salar. He came too late, the ship was under sail :
But there the duke was given to understand,
That in a gondola were seen together
Lorenzo and his amorous Jessica.
Besides, Antonio certified the duke,   10
They were not with Bassanio in his ship.
  Solan. I never heard a passion so confus'd,
So strange, outrageous, and so variable,
As the dog Jew did utter in the streets :
"My daughter !—O my ducats !—O my daughter !
Fled with a Christian !—O my christian ducats !
Justice ! the law ! my ducats, and my daughter !
A sealed bag, two sealed bags of ducats,
Of double ducats, stol'n from me by my daughter !
And jewels ! two stones, two rich and precious stones,
Stol'n by my daughter !—Justice ! find the girl !   21
She hath the stones upon her, and the ducats !"
  Salar. Why, all the boys in Venice follow him,
Crying, his stones, his daughter, and his ducats.
  Solan. Let good Antonio look he keep his day,
Or he shall pay for this.
  Salar.   Marry, well remember'd.
I reason'd with a Frenchman yesterday,

Who told me, in the narrow seas that part
The French and English, there miscarried
A vessel of our country, richly fraught.   20
I thought upon Antonio when he told me,
And wish'd in silence that it were not his.

Solan. "'My daughter !—O my ducats !—O my daughter !'"

  Solan. You were best to tell Antonio what you
   hear ;
Yet do not suddenly, for it may grieve him.
  Salar. A kinder gentleman treads not the earth.
I saw Bassanio and Antonio part.
Bassanio told him, he would make some speed
Of his return : he answer'd—"Do not so ;
Slubber not business for my sake, Bassanio,
But stay the very riping of the time ;   40
And for the Jew's bond, which he hath of me,
Let it not enter in your mind of love.
Be merry, and employ your chiefest thoughts
To courtship, and such fair ostents of love
As shall conveniently become you there."
And even there, his eye being big with tears,
Turning his face, he put his hand behind him,
And with affection wondrous sensible
He wrung Bassanio's hand ; and so they parted.
  Solan. I think, he only loves the world for him. 50
I pray thee, let us go, and find him out,
And quicken his embraced heaviness
With some delight or other.
  Salar.   Do we so.   [*Exeunt.*

SCENE IX.—Belmont. An Apartment in Portia's
House.

Enter Nerissa, *with a Servitor.*

  Ner. Quick, quick, I pray thee, draw the curtain
   straight.
The prince of Arragon hath ta'en his oath,
And comes to his election presently.

Enter the Prince of Arragon, Portia, *and their
Trains. Flourish cornets.*

  Por. Behold, there stand the caskets, noble prince.
If you choose that wherein I am contain'd,
Straight shall our nuptial rites be solemniz'd ;
But if you fail, without more speech, my lord,
You must be gone from hence immediately.
  Ar. I am enjoin'd by oath to observe three things : 10
First, never to unfold to anyone
Which casket 't was I chose : next, if I fail
Of the right casket, never in my life

To woo a maid in way of marriage:
Lastly,
If I do fail in fortune of my choice,
Immediately to leave you and be gone.
   Por. To these injunctions every one doth swear,
That comes to hazard for my worthless self.
   Ar. And so have I address'd me. Fortune now
To my heart's hope!—Gold, silver, and base lead.
"Who chooseth me, must give and hazard all he
      hath :"
You shall look fairer, ere I give, or hazard.   20
What says the golden chest? ha! let me see :—
"Who chooseth me, shall gain what many men
    desire."
What many men desire :—that many may be meant
By the fool multitude, that choose by show,
Not learning more than the fond eye doth teach,
Which pries not to the interior, but, like the martlet,
Builds in the weather on the outward wall,
Even in the force and road of casualty.
I will not choose what many men desire,
Because I will not jump with common spirits,   30
And rank me with the barbarous multitudes.
Why, then, to thee, thou silver treasure-house ;
Tell me once more what title thou dost bear :
"Who chooseth me, shall get as much as he deserves."
And well said too ; for who shall go about
To cozen fortune, and be honourable,
Without the stamp of merit ? Let none presume
To wear an undeserved dignity.
O! that estates, degrees, and offices,
Were not deriv'd corruptly! and that clear honour 40
Were purchas'd by the merit of the wearer !
How many then should cover, that stand bare ;
How many be commanded, that command ;
How much low peasantry would then be glean'd
From the true seed of honour ; and how much
    honour
Pick'd from the chaff and ruin of the times,
To be new-varnish'd! Well, but to my choice :
"Who chooseth me, shall get as much as he deserves."
I will assume desert.—Give me a key for this,
And instantly unlock my fortunes here.   50
             [*He opens the silver casket.*
   Por. Too long a pause for that which you find
    there.
   Ar. What 's here? the portrait of a blinking idiot,
Presenting me a schedule ! I will read it.
How much unlike art thou to Portia !
How much unlike my hopes, and my deservings !

"Who chooseth me, shall have as much as he
    deserves."
Did I deserve no more than a fool's head ?
Is that my prize ? are my deserts no better ?
   Por. To offend, and judge, are distinct offices,
And of opposed natures.
   Ar.   What is here ?   60
[*Reads.*] " The fire seven times tried this :
    Seven times tried that judgment is
    That did never choose amiss.
    Some there be that shadows kiss ;
    Such have but a shadow's bliss.
    There be fools alive, I wis,
    Silver'd o'er ; and so was this.
    Take what wife you will to bed,
    I will ever be your head ;
    So be gone : you are sped."   70
Still more fool I shall appear
By the time I linger here :
With one fool's head I came to woo,
But I go away with two.—
Sweet, adieu. I 'll keep my oath,
Patiently to bear my wroth.
            [*Exeunt* ARRAGON *and Train.*
   Por. Thus hath the candle sing'd the moth.
O, these deliberate fools ! when they do choose,
They have the wisdom by their wit to lose.
   Ner. The ancient saying is no heresy :—   80
Hanging and wiving goes by destiny.
   Por. Come, draw the curtain, Nerissa.

        Enter a Messenger.

   Mess. Where is my lady ?
   Por.   Here ; what would my lord ?
   Mess. Madam, there is alighted at your gate
A young Venetian, one that comes before
To signify the approaching of his lord,
From whom he bringeth sensible regreets ;
To wit, (besides commends, and courteous breath)
Gifts of rich value ; yet I have not seen
So likely an ambassador of love.   90
A day in April never came so sweet,
To show how costly summer was at hand,
As this fore-spurrer comes before his lord.
   Por. No more, I pray thee : I am half afeard
Thou wilt say anon he is some kin to thee.
Thou spend'st such high-day wit in praising him.—
Come, come, Nerissa ; for I long to see
Quick Cupid's post, that comes so mannerly.
   Ner. Bassanio, Lord love, if thy will it be! [*Exeunt.*

ACT III.

SCENE I.—Venice. A Street.

Enter SOLANIO *and* SALARINO.

         Solano.
NOW, what news on the Rialto ?
   Salar. Why, yet it lives there uncheck'd, that Antonio hath a ship of rich
lading wrack'd on the narrow seas ; the
Goodwins, I think they call the place : a
very dangerous flat, and fatal, where the
carcasses of many a tall ship lie buried,
as they say, if my gossip Report be an honest woman
of her word.   9
   Solan. I would she were as lying a gossip in that,
as ever knapped ginger, or made her neighbours
believe she wept for the death of a third husband.
But it is true, without any slips of prolixity, or crossing the plain highway of talk, that the good Antonio,
the honest Antonio,—O, that I had a title good enough
to keep his name company !—
   Salar. Come, the full stop.
   Solan. Ha !—what say'st thou ?—Why, the end is,
he hath lost a ship.   19
   Salar. I would it might prove the end of his losses.
   Solan. Let me say amen betimes, lest the devil

cross my prayer ; for here he comes in the likeness
of a Jew.

Enter SHYLOCK.

How now, Shylock ? what news among the merchants ?
Shy. You knew, none so well, none so well as you,
of my daughter's flight.
Salar. That 's certain : I, for my part, knew the
tailor that made the wings she flew withal.
Salan. And Shylock, for his own part, knew the
bird was fledg'd ; and then it is the complexion of
them all to leave the dam.   31
Shy. She is damned for it.
Salar. That 's certain, if the devil may be her judge.
Shy. My own flesh and blood to rebel !
Solan. Out upon it, old carrion ! rebels it at these
years ?
Shy. I say, my daughter is my flesh and blood.
Salar. There is more difference between thy flesh
and hers, than between jet and ivory ; more between
your bloods, than there is between red wine and
rhenish. But tell us, do you hear whether Antonio
have had any loss at sea or no ?   42
Shy. There I have another bad match : a bankrupt,
a prodigal, who dare scarce show his head on the
Rialto ;—a beggar, that used to come so smug upon
the mart.—Let him look to his bond : he was wont to
call me usurer ;—let him look to his bond : he was wont
to lend money for a Christian courtesy ;—let him look
to his bond.
Salar. Why, I am sure, if he forfeit, thou wilt not
take his flesh : what 's that good for ?   51
Shy. To bait fish withal : if it will feed nothing else,
it will feed my revenge. He hath disgraced me, and
hindered me half a million, laughed at my losses,
mocked at my gains, scorned my nation, thwarted my
bargains, cooled my friends, heated mine enemies ;
and what 's his reason ? I am a Jew. Hath not a Jew
eyes ? hath not a Jew hands, organs, dimensions,
senses, affections, passions ? fed with the same food,
hurt with the same weapons, subject to the same
diseases, healed by the same means, warmed and
cooled by the same winter and summer, as a Christian
is ? If you prick us, do we not bleed ? if you tickle us,
do we not laugh ? if you poison us, do we not die ?
and if you wrong us, shall we not revenge ? If we are
like you in the rest, we will resemble you in that. If a
Jew wrong a Christian, what is his humility ? revenge.
If a Christian wrong a Jew, what should his sufferance be by Christian example ? why, revenge. The
villany you teach me, I will execute ; and it shall go
hard but I will better the instruction.   71

Enter a Servant.

Serv. Gentlemen, my master Antonio is at his house,
and desires to speak with you both.
Salar. We have been up and down to seek him.
Solan. Here comes another of the tribe : a third
cannot be matched, unless the devil himself turn Jew.
[*Exeunt* SOLANIO, SALARINO, *and Servant.*

Enter TUBAL.

Shy. How now, Tubal ? what news from Genoa ?
hast thou found my daughter ?
Tub. I often came where I did hear of her, but cannot find her.   80
Shy. Why, there, there, there, there ! a diamond
gone, cost me two thousand ducats in Frankfort.
The curse never fell upon our nation till now ; I never
felt it till now :—two thousand ducats in that, and
other precious, precious jewels.—I would, my daughter
were dead at my foot, and the jewels in her ear !
'would she were hearsed at my foot, and the ducats in
her coffin ! No news of them ?—Why, so ;—and I know
not what 's spent in the search : why, thou—loss upon
loss ! the thief gone with so much, and so much to find
the thief, and no satisfaction, no revenge ; nor no ill
luck stirring, but what lights o' my shoulders ; no sighs,
but o' my breathing ; no tears, but o' my shedding. 93
Tub. Yes, other men have ill luck too. Antonio, as I
heard in Genoa,—
Shy. What, what, what ? ill luck, ill luck ?

Tub. —hath an argosy cast away, coming from Tripolis.
Shy. I thank God ! I thank God ! Is it true ? is it true ?
Tub. I spoke with some of the sailors that escaped
the wrack.   101
Shy. I thank thee, good Tubal.—Good news, good
news ! ha ! ha !—Where ? in Genoa ?
Tub. Your daughter spent in Genoa, as I heard, one
night, fourscore ducats.
Shy. Thou stick'st a dagger in me. I shall never see
my gold again. Fourscore ducats at a sitting ! fourscore ducats !
Tub. There came divers of Antonio's creditors in
my company to Venice, that swear he cannot choose
but break.
Shy. I am very glad of it : I 'll plague him ; I 'll torture him ; I am glad of it.
Tub. One of them showed me a ring, that he had of
your daughter for a monkey.
Shy. Out upon her ! Thou torturest me, Tubal : it
was my turquoise ; I had it of Leah, when I was a
bachelor : I would not have given it for a wilderness
of monkeys.   120
Tub. But Antonio is certainly undone.
Shy. Nay, that 's true, that 's very true. Go, Tubal,
fee me an officer, bespeak him a fortnight before. I
will have the heart of him, if he forfeit ; for were he
out of Venice, I can make what merchandise I will.
Go, Tubal, and meet me at our synagogue : go, good
Tubal ; at our synagogue, Tubal.   [*Exeunt.*

SCENE II.—Belmont.   An Apartment in PORTIA'S
                        House.

Enter BASSANIO, PORTIA, GRATIANO, NERISSA, *and
                        Attendants.*

Por. I pray you, tarry : pause a day or two,
Before you hazard ; for, in choosing wrong,
I lose your company : therefore, forbear awhile.
There 's something tells me (but it is not love),
I would not lose you ; and you know yourself,
Hate counsels not in such a quality.
But lest you should not understand me well,
(And yet a maiden hath no tongue but thought)
I would detain you here some month or two,
Before you venture for me. I could teach you   10
How to choose right, but then I am forsworn ;
So will I never be : so may you miss me ;
But if you do, you 'll make me wish a sin,
That I had been forsworn. Beshrew your eyes,
They have o'erlook'd me, and divided me :
One half of me is yours, the other half yours,—
Mine own, I would say ; but if mine, then yours,
And so all yours ! O ! these naughty times
Put bars between the owners and their rights ;
And so, though yours, not yours.—Prove it so,   20
Let fortune go to hell for it,—not I.—
I speak too long ; but 't is to peise the time,
To eke it, and to draw it out in length,
To stay you from election.
Bass.   Let me choose ;
For, as I am, I live upon the rack.
Por. Upon the rack, Bassanio ? then confess
What treason there is mingled with your love.
Bass. None, but that ugly treason of mistrust,
Which makes me fear the enjoying of my love.
There may as well be amity and life   30
'Tween snow and fire, as treason and my love.
Por. Ay, but, I fear, you speak upon the rack,
Where men enforced do speak anything.
Bass. Promise me life, and I 'll confess the truth.
Por. Well then, confess, and live.
Bass.   Confess, and love,
Had been the very sum of my confession.
O happy torment, when my torturer
Doth teach me answers for deliverance !
But let me to my fortune and the caskets.
              [*Curtain drawn from before the caskets.*
Por. Away then.   I am lock'd in one of them :   40
If you do love me, you will find me out.—

Nerissa, and the rest, stand all aloof.—
Let music sound, while he doth make his choice;
Then, if he lose, he makes a swan-like end,
Fading in music: that the comparison
May stand more proper, my eye shall be the stream,
And watery death-bed for him. He may win;
And what is music then? then music is
Even as the flourish when true subjects bow
To a new-crowned monarch: such it is,   50
As are those dulcet sounds in break of day,
That creep into the dreaming bridegroom's ear,
And summon him to marriage. Now he goes,
With no less presence, but with much more lov
Than young Alcides, when he did redeem
The virgin tribute paid by howling Troy
To the sea-monster: I stand for sacrifice;
The rest aloof are the Dardanian wives,
With bleared visages, come forth to view
The issue of the exploit. Go, Hercules!   60
Live thou, I live:—with much, much more dismay
I view the fight, than thou that mak'st the fray.

A Song, whilst BASSANIO *comments on the caskets
to himself.*

   Tell me, where is fancy bred,
   Or in the heart, or in the head?
   How begot, how nourished?
     Reply, reply.
   It is engender'd in the eyes,
   With gazing fed; and fancy dies
   In the cradle where it lies.
   Let us all ring fancy's knell: 70
   I'll begin it.—Ding, dong, bell.
All.   *Ding, dong, bell.*

Bass. So may the outward shows be least them-
   selves:
The world is still deceiv'd with ornament.
In law, what plea so tainted and corrupt,
But, being season'd with a gracious voice,
Obscures the show of evil? In religion,
What damned error, but some sober brow
Will bless it, and approve it with a text,
Hiding the grossness with fair ornament?   80
There is no vice so simple, but assumes
Some mark of virtue on his outward parts.
How many cowards, whose hearts are all as false
As stairs of sand, wear yet upon their chins
The beards of Hercules and frowning Mars,
Who, inward search'd, have livers white as milk;
And these assume but valour's excrement,
To render them redoubted. Look on beauty,
And you shall see 't is purchas'd by the weight;
Which therein works a miracle in nature,   90
Making them lightest that wear most of it:
So are those crisped snaky golden locks,
Which make such wanton gambols with the wind,
Upon supposed fairness, often known
To be the dowry of a second head,
The scull that bred them, in the sepulchre.
Thus ornament is but the guiled shore
To a most dangerous sea; the beauteous scarf
Veiling an Indian beauty; in a word,
The seeming truth which cunning times put on   100
To entrap the wisest. Therefore, thou gaudy gold,
Hard food for Midas, I will none of thee;
Nor none of thee, thou pale and common drudge
'Tween man and man: but thou, thou meagre lead,
Which rather threat'nest than dost promise aught,
Thy plainness moves me more than eloquence,
And here choose I. Joy be the consequence!
Por. How all the other passions fleet to air,
As doubtful thoughts, and rash-embrac'd despair,
And shuddering fear, and green-ey'd jealousy!   110
O love! be moderate; allay thy ecstacy;
In measure rain thy joy; scant this excess:
I feel too much thy blessing; make it less,
For fear I surfeit!
Bass.   What find I here?
            [*Opening the leaden casket.*
Fair Portia's counterfeit! What demi-god
Hath come so near creation? Move these eyes?
Or whether, riding on the balls of mine,

Seem they in motion? Here are sever'd lips,
Parted with sugar breath; so sweet a bar
Should sunder such sweet friends. Here, in her hairs,
The painter plays the spider, and hath woven   121
A golden mesh to entrap the hearts of men
Faster than gnats in cobwebs; but her eyes!—
How could he see to do them? having made one,
Methinks, it should have power to steal both his,
And leave itself unfurnish'd: yet look, how far
The substance of my praise doth wrong this shadow
In underprizing it, so far this shadow
Doth limp behind the substance.—Here's the scroll,
The continent and summary of my fortune.   130
[*Reads.*] " You that choose not by the view,
    Chance as fair, and choose as true!
    Since this fortune falls to you,
    Be content, and seek no new.
    If you be well pleas'd with this,
    And hold your fortune for your bliss,
    Turn you where your lady is,
    And claim her with a loving kiss."
A gentle scroll.—Fair lady, by your leave;
              [*Kissing her.*
I come by note, to give and to receive.   140
Like one of two contending in a prize,
That thinks he hath done well in people's eyes,
Hearing applause, and universal shout,
Giddy in spirit, still gazing, in a doubt
Whether those peals of praise be his or no;
So, thrice fair lady, stand I, even so,
As doubtful whether what I see be true,
Until confirm'd, sign'd, ratified by you.
Por. You see me, Lord Bassanio, where I stand,
Such as I am: though for myself alone   150
I would not be ambitious in my wish,
To wish myself much better; yet for you
I would be trebled twenty times myself;
A thousand times more fair, ten thousand times more
   rich;
That only to stand high in your account,
I might in virtues, beauties, livings, friends,
Exceed account: but the full sum of me
Is sum of nothing; which, to term in gross,
Is an unlesson'd girl, unschool'd, unpractis'd:
Happy in this, she is not yet so old   160
But she may learn; happier than this,
She is not bred so dull but she can learn;
Happiest of all is, that her gentle spirit
Commits itself to yours to be directed,
As from her lord, her governor, her king.
Myself, and what is mine, to you, and yours,
Is now converted: but now I was the lord
Of this fair mansion, master of my servants,
Queen o'er myself; and even now, but now,
This house, these servants, and this same myself, 170
Are yours, my lord. I give them with this ring,
Which when you part from, lose, or give away,
Let it presage the ruin of your love,
And be my vantage to exclaim on you.
Bass. Madam, you have bereft me of all words:
Only my blood speaks to you in my veins;
And there is such confusion in my powers
As after some oration, fairly spoke
By a beloved prince, there doth appear
Among the buzzing pleased multitude;   180
Where every something, being blent together,
Turns to a wild of nothing, save of joy,
Express'd, and not express'd. But when this ring
Parts from this finger, then parts life from hence:
O! then be bold to say, Bassanio's dead.
Ner. My lord and lady, it is now our time,
That have stood by and seen our wishes prosper,
To cry, good joy. Good joy, my lord and lady!
Gra. My lord Bassanio, and my gentle lady,
I wish you all the joy that you can wish;   190
For, I am sure, you can wish none from me;
And, when your honours mean to solemnize
The bargain of your faith, I do beseech you,
Even at that time I may be married too.
Bass. With all my heart, so thou canst get a wife.
Gra. I thank your lordship, you have got me one.
My eyes, my lord, can look as swift as yours,—

You saw the mistress, I beheld the maid;
You lov'd, I lov'd; for intermission
No more pertains to me, my lord, than you.   200
Your fortune stood upon the caskets there,
And so did mine too, as the matter falls;

Gra. We'll play with them the first boy for a
thousand ducats.
Ner. What! and stake down?
Gra. No; we shall ne'er win at that sport, and
stake down.—

Bass. "Thy plainness moves me more than eloquence."

For wooing here, until I sweat again,
And swearing, till my very roof was dry
With oaths of love, at last, if promise last,
I got a promise of this fair one here,
To have her love, provided that your fortune
Achiev'd her mistress.
Por.   Is this true, Nerissa?
Ner. Madam, it is, so you stand pleas'd withal.
Bass. And do you, Gratiano, mean good faith?   210
Gra. Yes, 'faith, my lord.
Bass. Our feast shall be much honour'd in your
marriage.

But who comes here? Lorenzo, and his infidel?
What! and my old Venetian friend Solanio?
        Enter LORENZO, JESSICA, *and* SOLANIO.
Bass. Lorenzo, and Solanio, welcome hither,
If that the youth of my new interest here   220
Have power to bid you welcome.—By your leave,
I bid my very friends and countrymen,
Sweet Portia, welcome.
Por.   So do I, my lord:
They are entirely welcome.
Lor. I thank your honour.—For my part, my lord,
My purpose was not to have seen you here;

But meeting with Solanio by the way,
He did entreat me, past all saying nay,
To come with him along.   I did, my lord,
  Solan.
And I have reason for it.—Signior Antonio   230
Commends him to you.   [*Gives* BASSANIO *a letter.*
  Bass.   Ere I ope his letter,
I pray you, tell me how my good friend doth.
  Solan. Not sick, my lord, unless it be in mind ;
Nor well, unless in mind : his letter there
Will show you his estate. [BASSANIO *reads the letter.*
  Gra. Nerissa, cheer yon stranger ; bid her welcome.
Your hand, Solanio. What's the news from Venice ?
How doth that royal merchant, good Antonio ?
I know, he will be glad of our success ;
We are the Jasons, we have won the fleece.   240
  Solan. I would you had won the fleece that he hath
     lost !
  Por. There are some shrewd contents in yon same
     paper,
That steal the colour from Bassanio's cheek :
Some dear friend dead, else nothing in the world
Could turn so much the constitution
Of any constant man. What, worse and worse ?—
With leave, Bassanio ; I am half yourself,
And I must freely have the half of anything
That this same paper brings you.
  Bass.   O sweet Portia !   250
Here are a few of the unpleasant'st words
That ever blotted paper. Gentle lady,
When I did first impart my love to you,
I freely told you, all the wealth I had
Ran in my veins,—I was a gentleman :
And then I told you true, and yet, dear lady,
Rating myself at nothing, you shall see
How much I was a braggart. When I told you,
My state was nothing, I should then have told you,
That I was worse than nothing ; for, indeed,
I have engag'd myself to a dear friend,   260
Engag'd my friend to his mere enemy,
To feed my means. Here is a letter, lady ;
The paper as the body of my friend,
And every word in it a gaping wound,
Issuing life-blood.—But is it true, Solanio ?
Have all his ventures fail'd ? What, not one hit ?
From Tripolis, from Mexico, and England,
From Lisbon, Barbary, and India ?
And not one vessel 'scape the dreadful touch
Of merchant-marring rocks ?
  Solan.   Not one, my lord.   270
Besides, it should appear, that if he had
The present money to discharge the Jew,
He would not take it. Never did I know
A creature, that did bear the shape of man,
So keen and greedy to confound a man.
He plies the duke at morning, and at night,
And doth impeach the freedom of the state,
If they deny him justice : twenty merchants,
The duke himself, and the magnificoes
Of greatest port, have all persuaded with him ;   280
But none can drive him from the envious plea
Of forfeiture, of justice, and his bond.
  Jes. When I was with him, I have heard him swear
To Tubal, and to Chus, his countrymen,
That he would rather have Antonio's flesh,
Than twenty times the value of the sum
That he did owe him ; and I know, my lord,
If law, authority, and power deny not,
It will go hard with poor Antonio.
  Por. Is it your dear friend that is thus in trouble ?
  Bass. The dearest friend to me, the kindest man,
The best-condition'd and unwearied spirit   292
In doing courtesies ; and one in whom
The ancient Roman honour more appears,
Than any that draws breath in Italy.
  Por. What sum owes he the Jew ?
  Bass. For me, three thousand ducats.
  Por.   What, no more ?
Pay him six thousand, and deface the bond :
Double six thousand, and then treble that,
Before a friend of this description   300
Shall lose a hair through Bassanio's fault.

First, go with me to church, and call me wife,
And then away to Venice to your friend ;
For never shall you lie by Portia's side
With an unquiet soul. You shall have gold
To pay the petty debt twenty times over :
When it is paid, bring your true friend along.
My maid Nerissa and myself, meantime,
Will live as maids and widows. Come, away !
For you shall hence upon your wedding-day.   310
Bid your friends welcome, show a merry cheer ;
Since you are dear bought, I will love you dear.—
But let me hear the letter of your friend.
  Bass. [*Reads.*] "Sweet Bassanio, my ships have all
miscarried, my creditors grow cruel, my estate is
very low, my bond to the Jew is forfeit ; and since, in
paying it, it is impossible I should live, all debts are
cleared between you and I, if I might but see you at
my death. Notwithstanding, use your pleasure : if
your love do not persuade you to come, let not my
letter."   321
  Por. O love, despatch all business, and be gone.
  Bass. Since I have your good leave to go away,
I will make haste ; but till I come again,
No bed shall e'er be guilty of my stay,
Nor rest be interposer 'twixt us twain.   [*Exeunt.*

SCENE III.—Venice. A Street.

Enter SHYLOCK, SALARINO, ANTONIO, *and Gaoler.*

  Shy. Gaoler, look to him : tell not me of mercy.
This is the fool that lent out money gratis.—
Gaoler, look to him.
  Ant.   Hear me yet, good Shylock.
  Shy. I'll have my bond ; speak not against my
     bond.
I have sworn an oath that I will have my bond.
Thou call'dst me dog before thou hadst a cause,
But, since I am a dog, beware my fangs.
The duke shall grant me justice.—I do wonder,
Thou naughty gaoler, that thou art so fond
To come abroad with him at his request.   10
  Ant. I pray thee, hear me speak.
  Shy. I'll have my bond ; I will not hear thee speak :
I'll have my bond, and therefore speak no more.
I'll not be made a soft and dull-ey'd fool,
To shake the head, relent, and sigh, and yield
To Christian intercessors. Follow not ;
I'll have no speaking ; I will have my bond.   [*Exit,*
  Salar. It is the most impenetrable cur,
That ever kept with men.
  Ant.   Let him alone :
I'll follow him no more with bootless prayers.   20
He seeks my life ; his reason well I know.
I oft deliver'd from his forfeitures
Many that have at times made moan to me ;
Therefore he hates me.
  Salar.   I am sure, the duke
Will never grant this forfeiture to hold.
  Ant. The duke cannot deny the course of law ;
For the commodity that strangers have
With us in Venice, if it be denied,
Will much impeach the justice of the state ;
Since that the trade and profit of the city   30
Consisteth of all nations. Therefore, go :
These griefs and losses have so bated me,
That I shall hardly spare a pound of flesh
To-morrow to my bloody creditor.—
Well, gaoler, on.—Pray God, Bassanio come
To see me pay his debt, and then I care not ! [*Exeunt.*

SCENE IV.—Belmont. A Room in PORTIA'S House.

Enter PORTIA, NERISSA, LORENZO, JESSICA, *and*
     BALTHAZAR.

  Lor. Madam, although I speak it in your presence,
You have a noble and a true conceit
Of god-like amity ; which appears most strongly
In bearing thus the absence of your lord.

But, if you knew to whom you show this honour,
How true a gentleman you send relief,
How dear a lover of my lord, your husband,
I know, you would be prouder of the work,
Than customary bounty can enforce you.
  Por. I never did repent for doing good,   10
Nor shall not now : for in companions
That do converse and waste the time together,
Whose souls do bear an equal yoke of love,
There must be needs a like proportion
Of lineaments, of manners, and of spirit ;
Which makes me think, that this Antonio,
Being the bosom lover of my lord,
Must needs be like my lord. If it be so,
How little is the cost I have bestow'd,
In purchasing the semblance of my soul   20
From out the state of hellish cruelty !
This comes too near the praising of myself ;
Therefore, no more of it : hear other things.—
Lorenzo, I commit into your hands
The husbandry and manage of my house,
Until my lord's return : for mine own part,
I have toward heaven breath'd a secret vow
To live in prayer and contemplation,
Only attended by Nerissa here,
Until her husband and my lord's return.   30
There is a monastery two miles off,
And there we will abide. I do desire you
Not to deny this imposition,
The which my love, and some necessity,
Now lays upon you.
  Lor.   Madam, with all my heart :
I shall obey you in all fair commands.
  Por. My people do already know my mind,
And will acknowledge you and Jessica
In place of Lord Bassanio and myself.
So fare you well, till we shall meet again.   40
  Lor. Fair thoughts, and happy hours, attend on
       you !
  Jes. I wish your ladyship all heart's content.
  Por. I thank you for your wish, and am well pleas'd
To wish it back on you : fare you well, Jessica.—
               [*Exeunt* JESSICA *and* LORENZO.
Now, Balthazar,
As I have ever found thee honest-true,
So let me find thee still. Take this same letter,
And use thou all the endeavour of a man
In speed to Padua : see thou render this
Into my cousin's hand, doctor Bellario ;   50
And, look, what notes and garments he doth give thee,
Bring them, I pray thee, with imagin'd speed
Unto the traject, to the common ferry
Which trades to Venice. Waste no time in words,
But get thee gone : I shall be there before thee.
  Bal. Madam, I go with all convenient speed. [*Exit.*
  Por. Come on, Nerissa : I have work in hand,
That you yet know not of. We'll see our husbands,
Before they think of us.
  Ner.   Shall they see us ?
  Por. They shall, Nerissa ; but in such a habit,   60
That they shall think we are accomplished
With that we lack. I'll hold thee any wager,
When we are both accoutred like young men,
I'll prove the prettier fellow of the two ;
And wear my dagger with the braver grace ;
And speak between the change of man and boy,
With a reed voice ; and turn two mincing steps
Into a manly stride ; and speak of frays,
Like a fine bragging youth ; and tell quaint lies,
How honourable ladies sought my love,   70
Which I denying, they fell sick and died ;
I could not do withal ;—then I'll repent,
And wish, for all that, that I had not kill'd them.
And twenty of these puny lies I'll tell,
That men shall swear, I have discontinued school
Above a twelvemonth. I have within my mind
A thousand raw tricks of these bragging Jacks,
Which I will practise.
  Ner.   Why, shall we turn to men ?
  Por. Fie, what a question's that,
If thou wert near a lewd interpreter !   80
But come : I'll tell thee all my whole device

When I am in my coach, which stays for us
At the park gate ; and therefore haste away,
For we must measure twenty miles to-day. [*Exeunt.*

SCENE V.—The Same. A Garden.

Enter LAUNCELOT *and* JESSICA.

  Laun. Yes, truly ; for, look you, the sins of the
father are to be laid upon the children ; therefore, I
promise you, I fear you. I was always plain with
you, and so now I speak my agitation of the matter :
therefore, be of good cheer ; for, truly, I think, you
are damned. There is but one hope in it that can do
you any good, and that is but a kind of bastard hope
neither.
  Jes. And what hope is that, I pray thee ?
  Laun. Marry, you may partly hope that your father
got you not, that you are not the Jew's daughter.   11
  Jes. That were a kind of bastard hope, indeed : so
the sins of my mother should be visited upon me.
  Laun. Truly then I fear you are damned both by
father and mother : thus when I shun Scylla, your
father, I fall into Charybdis, your mother. Well, you
are gone both ways.
  Jes. I shall be saved by my husband ; he hath made
me a Christian.   19
  Laun. Truly, the more to blame he : we were
Christians enow before ; e'en as many as could well
live one by another. This making of Christians will
raise the price of hogs : if we grow all to be pork-
eaters, we shall not shortly have a rasher on the coals
for money.
  Jes. I'll tell my husband, Launcelot, what you say :
here he comes.

Enter LORENZO.

  Lor. I shall grow jealous of you shortly, Launcelot,
if you thus get my wife into corners.   29
  Jes. Nay, you need not fear us, Lorenzo : Launcelot
and I are out. He tells me flatly, there is no mercy
for me in heaven, because I am a Jew's daughter :
and he says, you are no good member of the commonwealth, for, in converting Jews to Christians, you
raise the price of pork.
  Lor. I shall answer that better to the commonwealth,
than you can the getting up of the negro's belly : the
Moor is with child by you, Launcelot.
  Laun. It is much, that the Moor should be more
than reason ; but if she be less than an honest woman,
she is, indeed, more than I took her for.   41
  Lor. How every fool can play upon the word ! I
think, the best grace of wit will shortly turn into
silence, and discourse grow commendable in none
only but parrots.—Go in, sirrah : bid them prepare for
dinner.
  Laun. That is done, sir ; they have all stomachs.
  Lor. Goodly Lord, what a wit-snapper are you !
then bid them prepare dinner.
  Laun. That is done too, sir ; only, cover is the word.
  Lor. Will you cover then, sir ?   51
  Laun. Not so, sir, neither ; I know my duty.
  Lor. Yet more quarrelling with occasion ? Wilt
thou show the whole wealth of thy wit in an instant ?
I pray thee, understand a plain man in his plain
meaning : go to thy fellows, bid them cover the table,
serve in the meat, and we will come in to dinner.
  Laun. For the table, sir, it shall be served in ; for
the meat, sir, it shall be covered ; for your coming in
to dinner, sir, why, let it be as humours and conceits
shall govern.   [*Exit.*
  Lor. O dear discretion, how his words are suited !
The fool hath planted in his memory   63
An army of good words ; and I do know
A many fools, that stand in better place,
Garnish'd like him, that for a tricksy word
Defy the matter. How cheer'st thou, Jessica ?
And now, good sweet, say thy opinion :
How dost thou like the Lord Bassanio's wife ?
  Jes. Past all expressing. It is very meet,   70
The Lord Bassanio live an upright life,

For, having such a blessing in his lady,
He finds the joys of heaven here on earth ;
And, if on earth he do not mean it, then
In reason he should never come to heaven.
Why, if two gods should play some heavenly match,
And on the wager lay two earthly women,
And Portia one, there must be something else
Pawn'd with the other, for the poor rude world
Hath not her fellow.

Lor.   Even such a husband   80
Hast thou of me, as she is for a wife.
  Jes. Nay, but ask my opinion too of that.
  Lor. I will anon ; first, let us go to dinner.
  Jes. Nay, let me praise you, while I have a stomach.
  Lor. No, pray thee, let it serve for table-talk ;
Then howsoe'er thou speak'st, 'mong other things
I shall digest it.
  Jes.   Well, I 'll set you forth.   [*Exeunt.*

ACT IV.

Scene I.—Venice. A Court of Justice.

Enter the Duke ; *the Magnificoes ;* Antonio, Bassanio, Gratiano, Salarino, Solanio, *and others.*

Duke.
WHAT, is Antonio here?
  Ant. Ready, so please your grace.
  Duke. I am sorry for thee : thou art
    come to answer
A stony adversary, an inhuman wretch
Uncapable of pity, void and empty
From any dram of mercy.
  Ant.   I have heard,
Your grace hath ta'en great pains to qualify
His rigorous course ; but since he stands obdurate,
And that no lawful means can carry me
Out of his envy's reach, I do oppose   10
My patience to his fury, and am arm'd
To suffer with a quietness of spirit,
The very tyranny and rage of his.
  Duke. Go one, and call the Jew into the court.
  Salar. He's ready at the door. He comes, my lord.

Enter Shylock.

  Duke. Make room, and let him stand before our
    face.—
Shylock, the world thinks, and I think so too,
That thou but lead'st this fashion of thy malice
To the last hour of act ; and then, 't is thought,
Thou 'lt show thy mercy and remorse more strange,
Than is thy strange apparent cruelty ;   21
And where thou now exact'st the penalty,
Which is a pound of this poor merchant's flesh,
Thou wilt not only loose the forfeiture,
But touch'd with human gentleness and love,
Forgive a moiety of the principal ;
Glancing an eye of pity on his losses,
That have of late so huddled on his back,
Enow to press a royal merchant down,
And pluck commiseration of his state   30
From brassy bosoms, and rough hearts of flint,
From stubborn Turks and Tartars, never train'd
To offices of tender courtesy.
We all expect a gentle answer, Jew.
  Shy. I have possess'd your grace of what I purpose ;
And by our holy Sabbath have I sworn,
To have the due and forfeit of my bond :
If you deny it, let the danger light
Upon your charter, and your city's freedom.
You 'll ask me, why I rather choose to have   40
A weight of carrion flesh, than to receive
Three thousand ducats? I 'll not answer that :
But, say, it is my humour : is it answer'd?
What if my house be troubled with a rat,
And I be pleas'd to give ten thousand ducats
To have it baned? What, are you answer'd yet?
Some men there are love not a gaping pig ;

Some, that are mad if they behold a cat ;
And others, when the bagpipe sings i' the nose,
Cannot contain their urine : for affection,
Master of passion, sways it to the mood   50
Of what it likes, or loathes. Now, for your answer.
As there is no firm reason to be render'd,
Why he cannot abide a gaping pig ;
Why he, a harmless necessary cat ;
Why he, a woollen bagpipe ; but of force
Must yield to such inevitable shame,
As to offend himself, being offended ;
So can I give no reason, nor I will not,
More than a lodg'd hate, and a certain loathing,   60
I bear Antonio, that I follow thus
A losing suit against him. Are you answer'd?
  Bass. This is no answer, thou unfeeling man,
To excuse the current of thy cruelty.
  Shy. I am not bound to please thee with my answer.
  Bass. Do all men kill the things they do not love?
  Shy. Hates any man the thing he would not kill?
  Bass. Every offence is not a hate at first.
  Shy. What! wouldst thou have a serpent sting thee
    twice?
  Ant. I pray you, think you question with the Jew.
You may as well go stand upon the beach,   71
And bid the main flood bate his usual height ;
You may as well use question with the wolf,
Why he hath made the ewe bleat for the lamb ;
You may as well forbid the mountain pines
To wag their high tops, and to make no noise,
When they are fretted with the gusts of heaven ;
You may as well do any thing most hard,
As seek to soften that (than which what's harder?)
His Jewish heart.—Therefore, I do beseech you,   80
Make no more offers, use no further means ;
But with all brief and plain conveniency,
Let me have judgment, and the Jew his will.
  Bass. For thy three thousand ducats here is six.
  Shy. If every ducat in six thousand ducats
Were in six parts, and every part a ducat,
I would not draw them,—I would have my bond.
  Duke. How shalt thou hope for mercy, rendering
    none?
  Shy. What judgment shall I dread, doing no wrong?
You have among you many a purchas'd slave,   90
Which, like your asses, and your dogs, and mules,
You use in abject and in slavish parts,
Because you bought them : —shall I say to you,
Let them be free ; marry them to your heirs?
Why sweat they under burdens? let their beds
Be made as soft as yours, and let their palates
Be season'd with such viands? You will answer :
The slaves are ours.—So do I answer you :

The pound of flesh, which I demand of him,
Is dearly bought, 't is mine, and I will have it.   100
If you deny me, fie upon your law!
There is no force in the decrees of Venice.
I stand for judgment: answer; shall I have it?
Duke. Upon my power I may dismiss this court,
Unless Bellario, a learned doctor,
Whom I have sent for to determine this,
Come here to-day.
Salar. My lord, here stays without
A messenger with letters from the doctor,
New come from Padua.
Duke. Bring us the letters: call the messenger.   110
Bass. Good cheer, Antonio! What, man, courage
yet!
The Jew shall have my flesh, blood, bones, and all,
Ere thou shalt lose for me one drop of blood.
Ant. I am a tainted wether of the flock,
Meetest for death: the weakest kind of fruit

Shy. " To cut the forfeiture from that bankrupt there."

Drops earliest to the ground, and so let me.
You cannot better be employ'd, Bassanio,
Than to live still, and write mine epitaph.

Enter NERISSA, *dressed like a lawyer's clerk.*
Duke. Came you from Padua, from Bellario?   119
Ner. From both, my lord. Bellario greets your
grace. [*Presents a letter.*
Bass. Why dost thou whet thy knife so earnestly?
Shy. To cut the forfeiture from that bankrupt there.
Gra. Not on thy sole, but on thy soul, harsh Jew,
Thou mak'st thy knife keen; but no metal can,
No, not the hangman's axe, bear half the keenness
Of thy sharp envy. Can no prayers pierce thee?
Shy. No, none that thou hast wit enough to make.
Gra. O, be thou damn'd, inexorable dog,
And for thy life let justice be accus'd!
Thou almost mak'st me waver in my faith,   130
To hold opinion with Pythagoras,
That souls of animals infuse themselves
Into the trunks of men: thy currish spirit
Govern'd a wolf, who, hang'd for human slaughter,
Even from the gallows did his fell soul fleet,
And whilst thou lay'st in thy unhallow'd dam,
Infus'd itself in thee; for thy desires
Are wolfish, bloody, starv'd, and ravenous.
Shy. Till thou canst rail the seal from off my bond,
Thou but offend'st thy lungs to speak so loud.   140

Repair thy wit, good youth, or it will fall
To cureless ruin.—I stand here for law.
Duke. This letter from Bellario doth commend
A young and learned doctor to our court.—
Where is he?
Ner. He attendeth here hard by,
To know your answer, whether you 'll admit him.
Duke. With all my heart:—some three or four of
you,
Go give him courteous conduct to this place.
Meantime, the court shall hear Bellario's letter.   119
Clerk. [*Reads.*] " Your grace shall understand, that,
at the receipt of your letter, I am very sick; but in the
instant that your messenger came, in loving visitation
was with me a young doctor of Rome; his name is
Balthazar. I acquainted him with the cause in controversy between the Jew and Antonio, the merchant:
we turned o'er many books together: he is furnish'd
with my opinion; which, better'd with his own
learning, the greatness whereof I cannot enough commend, comes with him, at my importunity, to fill up
your grace's request in my stead. I beseech you, let
his lack of years be no impediment to let him lack a
reverend estimation, for I never knew so young a
body with so old a head. I leave him to your gracious
acceptance, whose trial shall better publish his commendation."
Duke. You hear the learn'd Bellario, what he writes:
And here, I take it, is the doctor come.—

Enter PORTIA, *dressed like a doctor of laws.*
Give me your hand. Came you from old Bellario?
Por. I did, my lord.
Duke. You are welcome: take your place.
Are you acquainted with the difference   170
That holds this present question in the court?
Por. I am informed throughly of the cause.—
Which is the merchant here, and which the Jew?
Duke. Antonio and old Shylock, both stand forth.
Por. Is your name Shylock?
Shy. Shylock is my name.
Por. Of a strange nature is the suit you follow;
Yet in such rule, that the Venetian law
Cannot impugn you, as you do proceed.—
[*To* ANTONIO.] You stand within his danger, do you
not?
Ant. Ay, so he says.
Por. Do you confess the bond?   180
Ant. I do.
Por. Then must the Jew be merciful.
Shy. On what compulsion must I? tell me that.
Por. The quality of mercy is not strain'd,
It droppeth as the gentle rain from heaven
Upon the place beneath: it is twice bless'd;
It blesseth him that gives, and him that takes.
'T is mightiest in the mightiest, it becomes
The throned monarch better than his crown:
His sceptre shows the force of temporal power,
The attribute to awe and majesty,   190
Wherein doth sit the dread and fear of kings;
But mercy is above this sceptred sway,
It is enthroned in the hearts of kings,
It is an attribute to God himself,
And earthly power doth then show likest God's,
When mercy seasons justice. Therefore, Jew,
Though justice be thy plea, consider this,—
That in the course of justice none of us
Should see salvation: we do pray for mercy,
And that same prayer doth teach us all to render   200
The deeds of mercy. I have spoke thus much,
To mitigate the justice of thy plea,
Which if thou follow, this strict court of Venice
Must needs give sentence 'gainst the merchant there.
Shy. My deeds upon my head! I crave the law,
The penalty and forfeit of my bond.
Por. Is he not able to discharge the money?
Bass. Yes, here I tender it for him in the court;
Yea, twice the sum: if that will not suffice,
I will be bound to pay it ten times o'er,   210
On forfeit of my hands, my head, my heart.
If this will not suffice, it must appear
That malice bears down truth. And I beseech you,

Wrest once the law to your authority :
To do a great right, do a little wrong,
And curb this cruel devil of his will.
    Por. It must not be. There is no power in Venice
Can alter a decree established :
'T will be recorded for a precedent,
And many an error, by the same example,   220
Will rush into the state. It cannot be.
    Shy. A Daniel come to judgment ! yea, a Daniel !—
O wise young judge, how I do honour thee !
    Por. I pray you, let me look upon the bond.
    Shy. Here 't is, most reverend doctor ; here it is.
    Por. Shylock, there 's thrice thy money offer'd thee.
    Shy. An oath, an oath, I have an oath in heaven.
Shall I lay perjury upon my soul ?
No, not for Venice.
    Por.   Why, this bond is forfeit,
And lawfully by this the Jew may claim   230
A pound of flesh, to be by him cut off
Nearest the merchant's heart.—Be merciful ;
Take thrice thy money : bid me tear the bond.
    Shy. When it is paid according to the tenour. —
It doth appear you are a worthy judge ;
You know the law, your exposition
Hath been most sound : I charge you by the law,
Whereof you are a well-deserving pillar,
Proceed to judgment. By my soul I swear,   240
There is no power in the tongue of man
To alter me. I stay here on my bond.
    Ant. Most heartily I do beseech the court
To give the judgment.
    Por.   Why then, thus it is :—
You must prepare your bosom for his knife.
    Shy. O noble judge ! O excellent young man !
    Por. For the intent and purpose of the law
Hath full relation to the penalty,
Which here appeareth due upon the bond.
    Shy. 'T is very true. O wise and upright judge !
How much more elder art thou than thy looks !   250
    Por. Therefore, lay bare your bosom.
    Shy.   Ay, his breast ;
So says the bond :—doth it not, noble judge ?—
Nearest his heart : those are the very words.
    Por. It is so. Are there balance here to weigh
The flesh ?
    Shy. I have them ready.
    Por. Have by some surgeon, Shylock, on your
        charge,
To stop his wounds, lest he do bleed to death.
    Shy. Is it so nominated in the bond ?
    Por. It is not so express'd ; but what of that ?   260
'T were good you do so much for charity.
    Shy. I cannot find it : 't is not in the bond.
    Por. You, merchant, have you anything to say ?
    Ant. But little : I am arm'd, and well prepar'd.—
Give me your hand, Bassanio : fare you well.
Grieve not that I am fallen to this for you ;
For herein Fortune shows herself more kind
Than is her custom : it is still her use.
To let the wretched man outlive his wealth,
To view with hollow eye, and wrinkled brow,   270
An age of poverty ; from which lingering penance
Of such misery doth she cut me off.
Commend me to your honourable wife ;
Tell her the process of Antonio's end ;
Say how I lov'd you, speak me fair in death ;
And, when the tale is told, bid her be judge,
Whether Bassanio had not once a love.
Repent not you that you shall lose your friend,
And he repents not that he pays your debt ;
For, if the Jew do cut but deep enough,   280
I 'll pay it instantly with all my heart.
    Bass. Antonio, I am married to a wife,
Which is as dear to me as life itself ;
But life itself, my wife, and all the world,
Are not with me esteem'd above thy life :
I would lose all, ay, sacrifice them all,
Here to this devil, to deliver you.
    Por. Your wife would give you little thanks for
        that,
If she were by to hear you make the offer.
    Gra. I have a wife, whom, I protest, I love :   290

I would she were in heaven, so she could
Entreat some power to change this currish Jew.
    Ner. 'T is well you offer it behind her back ;
The wish would make else an unquiet house.
    Shy. These be the Christian husbands ! I have a
        daughter ;
'Would any of the stock of Barrabas
Had been her husband, rather than a Christian !
We trifle time ; I pray thee, pursue sentence.
    Por. A pound of that same merchant's flesh is thine:
The court awards it, and the law doth give it.   300
    Shy. Most rightful judge !
    Por. And you must cut this flesh from off his breast :
The law allows it, and the court awards it.
    Shy. Most learned judge !—A sentence ! Come,
        prepare !
    Por. Tarry a little : there is something else.—
This bond doth give thee here no jot of blood ;
The words expressly are, a pound of flesh :
Take then thy bond, take thou thy pound of flesh ;
But, in the cutting it, if thou dost shed
One drop of Christian blood, thy lands and goods   310
Are, by the laws of Venice, confiscate
Unto the state of Venice.
    Gra. O upright judge !—Mark, Jew :—O learned
        judge !
    Shy. Is that the law ?
    Por.   Thyself shalt see the act ;
For, as thou urgest justice, be assur'd,
Thou shalt have justice, more than thou desirest.
    Gra. O learned judge !—Mark, Jew :—a learned
        judge !
    Shy. I take this offer then : pay the bond thrice,
And let the Christian go.
    Bass.   Here is the money.
    Por. Soft !   320
The Jew shall have all justice ;—soft !—no haste :—
He shall have nothing but the penalty.
    Gra. O Jew ! an upright judge, a learned judge !
    Por. Therefore, prepare thee to cut off the flesh.
Shed thou no blood ; nor cut thou less, nor more,
But just a pound of flesh : if thou tak'st more,
Or less, than a just pound,—be it but so much
As makes it light, or heavy, in the substance,
Or the division of the twentieth part
Of one poor scruple, nay, if the scale do turn   330
But in the estimation of a hair,
Thou diest, and all thy goods are confiscate.
    Gra. A second Daniel, a Daniel, Jew !
Now, infidel, I have thee on the hip.
    Por. Why doth the Jew pause ? take thy forfeiture.
    Shy. Give me my principal, and let me go.
    Bass. I have it ready for thee : here it is.
    Por. He hath refus'd it in the open court :
He shall have merely justice, and his bond.
    Gra. A Daniel, still say I ; a second Daniel !—   340
I thank thee, Jew, for teaching me that word.
    Shy. Shall I not have barely my principal ?
    Por. Thou shalt have nothing but the forfeiture,
To be so taken at thy peril, Jew.
    Shy. Why, then the devil give him good of it !
I 'll stay no longer question.
    Por.   Tarry, Jew :
The law hath yet another hold on you.
It is enacted in the laws of Venice,
If it be prov'd against an alien,
That, by direct or indirect attempts,   350
He seek the life of any citizen,
The party, 'gainst the which he doth contrive,
Shall seize one half his goods : the other half
Comes to the privy coffer of the state ;
And the offender's life lies in the mercy
Of the duke only, 'gainst all other voice.
In which predicament, I say, thou stand'st ;
For it appears by manifest proceeding,
That, indirectly and directly too,
Thou hast contriv'd against the very life   360
Of the defendant, and thou hast incurr'd
The danger formerly by me rehears'd.
Down, therefore, and beg mercy of the duke.
    Gra. Beg, that thou may'st have leave to hang
        thyself ;

And yet, thy wealth being forfeit to the state,
Thou hast not left the value of a cord;
Therefore, thou must be hang'd at the state's charge.
  Duke. That thou shalt see the difference of our
     spirit,

  Ant. So please my lord the duke, and all the court,
To quit the fine for one half of his goods;   381
I am content, so he will let me have
The other half in use, to render it,
Upon his death, unto the gentleman

Por. "Thou diest, and all thy goods are confiscate."

I pardon thee thy life before thou ask it.
For half thy wealth, it is Antonio's: 370
The other half comes to the general state,
Which humbleness may drive unto a fine.
  Por. Ay, for the state; not for Antonio.
  Shy. Nay, take my life and all; pardon not that:
You take my house, when you do take the prop
That doth sustain my house; you take my life,
When you do take the means whereby I live.
  Por. What mercy can you render him, Antonio?
  Gra. A halter gratis; nothing else, for God's sake!

That lately stole his daughter:
Two things provided more,—that, for this favour,
He presently become a Christian;
The other, that he do record a gift,
Here in the court, of all he dies possess'd,
Unto his son Lorenzo, and his daughter.   390
  Duke. He shall do this, or else I do recant
The pardon, that I late pronounced here.
  Por. Art thou contented, Jew? what dost thou say?
  Shy. I am content.
  Por.   Clerk, draw a deed of gift.

Shy. I pray you, give me leave to go from hence.
I am not well. Send the deed after me,
And I will sign it.
 Duke.   Get thee gone, but do it.
Gra. In christening thou shalt have two godfathers;
Had I been judge, thou shouldst have had ten more,
To bring thee to the gallows, not the font.   400
       [*Exit* SHYLOCK.
Duke. Sir, I entreat you home with me to dinner.
Por. I humbly do desire your grace of pardon:
I must away this night toward Padua,
And it is meet I presently set forth.
 Duke. I am sorry, that your leisure serves you not.
Antonio, gratify this gentleman,
For, in my mind, you are much bound to him.
  [*Exeunt* DUKE, *Magnificoes, and Train.*
 Bass. Most worthy gentleman, I and my friend
Have by your wisdom been this day acquitted
Of grievous penalties; in lieu whereof,   410
Three thousand ducats, due unto the Jew,
We freely cope your courteous pains withal.
 Ant. And stand indebted, over and above,
In love and service to you evermore.
 Por. He is well paid, that is well satisfied;
And I, delivering you, am satisfied,
And therein do account myself well paid.:
My mind was never yet more mercenary.
I pray you, know me, when we meet again:
I wish you well, and so I take my leave.   420
 Bass. Dear sir, of force I must attempt you further:
Take some remembrance of us, as a tribute,
Not as a fee. Grant me two things, I pray you;
Not to deny me, and to pardon me.
 Por. You press me far, and therefore I will yield.
Give me your gloves, I 'll wear them for your sake;
And, for your love, I 'll take this ring from you.—
Do not draw back your hand; I 'll take no more;
And you in love shall not deny me this.
 Bass. This ring, good sir?—alas, it is a trifle;   430
I will not shame myself to give you this.
 Por. I will have nothing else but only this;
And now, methinks, I have a mind to it.
 Bass. There 's more depends on this than on the
  value.
The dearest ring in Venice will I give you,
And find it out by proclamation:
Only for this, I pray you, pardon me.
 Por. I see, sir, you are liberal in offers.
You taught me first to beg, and now, methinks,
You teach me how a beggar should be answer'd.   440
 Bass. Good sir, this ring was given me by my wife;
And, when she put it on, she made me vow,
That I should neither sell, nor give, nor lose it.
 Por. That 'scuse serves many men to save their
  gifts.
An if your wife be not a mad-woman,
And know how well I have deserv'd this ring,
She would not hold out enemy for ever,
For giving it to me. Well, peace be with you.
    [*Exeunt* PORTIA *and* NERISSA.
 Ant. My lord Bassanio, let him have the ring:
Let his deservings, and my love withal,   450
Be valued 'gainst your wife's commandment.
 Bass. Go, Gratiano; run and overtake him;
Give him the ring, and bring him, if thou canst,
Unto Antonio's house.—Away! make haste.
       [*Exit* GRATIANO.

Come, you and I will thither presently,
And in the morning early will we both
Fly toward Belmont. Come, Antonio.   [*Exeunt.*

Por. "Away! make haste: thou know'st where I will tarry."

SCENE II.—The Same. A Street.

Enter PORTIA *and* NERISSA.

 Por. Inquire the Jew's house out, give him this
  deed,
And let him sign it. We 'll away to-night,
And be a day before our husbands home.
This deed will be well welcome to Lorenzo.

Enter GRATIANO.

 Gra. Fair sir, you are well o'erta'en.
My lord Bassanio, upon more advice,
Hath sent you here this ring, and doth entreat
Your company at dinner.
 Por.   That cannot be.
His ring I do accept most thankfully,
And so, I pray you, tell him: furthermore,   10
I pray you, show my youth old Shylock's house.
 Gra. That will I do.
 Ner.   Sir, I would speak with you.—
[*To* PORTIA.] I 'll see if I can get my husband's ring,
Which I did make him swear to keep for ever.
 Por. Thou may'st, I warrant. We shall have old
  swearing,
That they did give the rings away to men;
But we 'll outface them, and outswear them too.
Away! make haste: thou know'st where I will tarry.
 Ner. Come, good sir; will you show me to this
  house?   [*Exeunt.*

ACT V.

Scene I.—Belmont. The Avenue to Portia's House.

Enter Lorenzo *and* Jessica.

Lorenzo.
THE moon shines bright.—In such a night
  as this,
When the sweet wind did gently kiss the
  trees,
And they did make no noise, in such a
  night,
Troilus, methinks, mounted the Trojan
  walls,
And sigh'd his soul toward the Grecian
  tents,
Where Cressid lay that night.
Jes.   In such a night
Did Thisbe fearfully o'ertrip the dew ;
And saw the lion's shadow ere himself,
And ran dismay'd away.
Lor.   In such a night
Stood Dido with a willow in her hand   10
Upon the wild sea-banks, and wav'd her love
To come again to Carthage.
Jes.   In such a night
Medea gather'd the enchanted herbs
That did renew old Æson.
Lor.   In such a night
Did Jessica steal from the wealthy Jew,
And with an unthrift love did run from Venice,
As far as Belmont.
Jes.   In such a night
Did young Lorenzo swear he lov'd her well,
Stealing her soul with many vows of faith,
And ne'er a true one.
Lor.   In such a night   20
Did pretty Jessica, like a little shrew,
Slander her love, and he forgave it her.
Jes. I would out-night you, did no body come ;
But, hark, I hear the footing of a man.

Enter Stephano.

Lor. Who comes so fast in silence of the night ?
Steph. A friend.
Lor. A friend ? what friend ? your name, I pray you,
  friend ?
Steph. Stephano is my name ; and I bring word,
My mistress will before the break of day
Be here at Belmont : she doth stray about   30
By holy crosses, where she kneels and prays
For happy wedlock hours.
Lor.   Who comes with her ?
Steph. None, but a holy hermit, and her maid.
I pray you, is my master yet return'd ?
Lor. He is not, nor we have not heard from
  him.—
But go we in, I pray thee, Jessica,
And ceremoniously let us prepare
Some welcome for the mistress of the house.

Enter Launcelot.

Laun. Sola, sola ! wo ha, ho ! sola, sola !
Lor. Who calls ?   40
Laun. Sola ! did you see Master Lorenzo, and
Mistress Lorenzo ? sola, sola !
Lor. Leave halloing, man ; here.
Laun. Sola ! where ? where ?
Lor. Here.
Laun. Tell him, there 's a post come from my master,

with his horn full of good news : my master will be
here ere morning.   [*Exit.*
Lor. Sweet soul, let 's in, and there expect their
  coming.
And yet no matter ;—why should we go in ?   50
My friend Stephano, signify, I pray you,
Within the house, your mistress is at hand ;
And bring your music forth into the air.—
                     [*Exit* Stephano.
How sweet the moonlight sleeps upon this bank !
Here we will sit, and let the sounds of music
Creep in our ears : soft stillness, and the night,
Become the touches of sweet harmony.
Sit, Jessica : look, how the floor of heaven
Is thick inlaid with patines of bright gold.
There 's not the smallest orb, which thou behold'st,   60
But in his motion like an angel sings,
Still quiring to the young-ey'd cherubins ;
Such harmony is in immortal souls ;
But, whilst this muddy vesture of decay
Doth grossly close it in, we cannot hear it.

Enter Musicians.

Come, ho ! and wake Diana with a hymn :
With sweetest touches pierce your mistress' ear,
And draw her home with music.   [*Music.*
Jes. I am never merry when I hear sweet music.
Lor. The reason is, your spirits are attentive :   70
For do but note a wild and wanton herd,
Or race of youthful and unhandled colts,
Fetching mad bounds, bellowing and neighing loud,
Which is the hot condition of their blood ;
If they but hear perchance a trumpet sound,
Or any air of music touch their ears,
You shall perceive them make a mutual stand,
Their savage eyes turn'd to a modest gaze,
By the sweet power of music : therefore, the poet
Did feign that Orpheus drew trees, stones, and floods ;
Since nought so stockish, hard, and full of rage,   81
But music for the time doth change his nature.
The man that hath no music in himself,
Nor is not mov'd with concord of sweet sounds,
Is fit for treasons, stratagems, and spoils ;
The motions of his spirit are dull as night,
And his affections dark as Erebus.
Let no such man be trusted.—Mark the music.

Enter Portia *and* Nerissa, *at a distance.*

Por. That light we 'see is burning in my hall.
How far that little candle throws his beams !   90
So shines a good deed in a naughty world.
Ner. When the moon shone, we did not see the
  candle.
Por. So doth the greater glory dim the less :
A substitute shines brightly as a king,
Until a king be by ; and then his state
Empties itself, as doth an inland brook
Into the main of waters. Music ! hark !
Ner. It is your music, madam, of the house.
Por. Nothing is good, I see, without respect.
Methinks, it sounds much sweeter than by day.   100
Ner. Silence bestows that virtue on it, madam.
Por. The crow doth sing as sweetly as the lark,
When neither is attended ; and, I think,
The nightingale, if she should sing by day,

When every goose is cackling, would be thought
No better a musician than the wren.
How many things by season season'd are
To their right praise, and true perfection !—
Peace, ho ! the moon sleeps with Endymion,
And would not be awak'd !
  Lor.   That is the voice,   110
Or I am much deceiv'd, of Portia.
  Por. He knows me, as the blind man knows the
        cuckoo,
By the bad voice.
  Lor.   Dear lady, welcome home.
  Por. We have been praying for our husbands'
        welfare,
Which speed, we hope, the better for our words.
Are they return'd ?
  Lor.   Madam, they are not yet ;
But there is come a messenger before,
To signify their coming.
  Por.   Go in, Nerissa :
Give order to my servants, that they take
No note at all of our being absent hence ;—   120
Nor you, Lorenzo ;—Jessica, nor you.
                       [*A tucket sounded.*
  Lor. Your husband is at hand : I hear his trumpet.
We are no tell-tales, madam ; fear you not.
  Por. This night, methinks, is but the day-light sick ;
It looks a little paler : 'tis a day,
Such as the day is when the sun is hid.

   Enter BASSANIO, ANTONIO, GRATIANO, *and their*
               Followers.

  Bass. We should hold day with the Antipodes,
If you would walk in absence of the sun.
  Por. Let me give light, but let me not be light ;
For a light wife doth make a heavy husband,   130
And never be Bassanio so for me :
But God sort all !—You are welcome home, my lord.
  Bass. I thank you, madam. Give welcome to my
        friend :
This is the man, this is Antonio,
To whom I am so infinitely bound.
  Por. You should in all sense be much bound to him,
For, as I hear, he was much bound for you.
  Ant. No more than I am well acquitted of.
  Por. Sir, you are very welcome to our house :
It must appear in other ways than words,   140
Therefore, I scant this breathing courtesy.
  Gra. [*To* NERISSA.] By yonder moon, I swear, you
        do me wrong ;
In faith, I gave it to the judge's clerk :
'Would he were gelt that had it, for my part,
Since you do take it, love, so much at heart.
  Por. A quarrel, ho, already ! what's the matter ?
  Gra. About a hoop of gold, a paltry ring
That she did give me ; whose posy was
For all the world like cutlers' poetry
Upon a knife, " Love me, and leave me not."   150
  Ner. What talk you of the posy, or the value ?
You swore to me, when I did give it you,
That you would wear it till your hour of death,
And that it should lie with you in your grave :
Though not for me, yet for your vehement oaths,
You should have been respective, and have kept it.
Gave it a judge's clerk ! no, God's my judge,
The clerk will ne'er wear hair on his face, that had it.
  Gra. He will, an if he live to be a man.
  Ner. Ay, if a woman live to be a man.   160
  Gra. Now, by this hand, I gave it to a youth,
A kind of boy, a little scrubbed boy,
No higher than thyself, the judge's clerk ;
A prating boy, that begg'd it as a fee :
I could not for my heart deny it him.
  Por. You were to blame, I must be plain with you,
To part so slightly with your wife's first gift ;
A thing stuck on with oaths upon your finger,
And so riveted with faith unto your flesh.
I gave my love a ring, and made him swear   170
Never to part with it ; and here he stands :
I dare be sworn for him, he would not leave it,
Nor pluck it from his finger for the wealth
That the world masters. Now, in faith, Gratiano,

You give your wife too unkind a cause of grief :
An't were to me, I should be mad at it.
  Bass. [*Aside.*] Why, I were best to cut my left hand
        off,
And swear I lost the ring defending it.
  Gra. My lord Bassanio gave his ring away
Unto the judge that begg'd it, and, indeed,   180
Deserv'd it too ; and then the boy, his clerk,
That took some pains in writing, he begg'd mine ;
And neither man, nor master, would take aught
But the two rings.
  Por.   What ring gave you, my lord ?
Not that, I hope, which you receiv'd of me.
  Bass. If I could add a lie unto a fault,
I would deny it ; but you see, my finger
Hath not the ring upon it : it is gone.
  Por. Even so void is your false heart of truth.
By heaven, I will ne'er come in your bed   190
Until I see the ring.
  Ner.   Nor I in yours,
Till I again see mine.
  Bass.   Sweet Portia,
If you did know to whom I gave the ring,
If you did know for whom I gave the ring,
And would conceive for what I gave the ring,
And how unwillingly I left the ring,
When nought would be accepted but the ring,
You would abate the strength of your displeasure.
  Por. If you had known the virtue of the ring,   200
Or half her worthiness that gave the ring,
Or your own honour to contain the ring,
You would not then have parted with the ring.
What man is there so much unreasonable,
If you had pleas'd to have defended it
With any terms of zeal, wanted the modesty
To urge the thing held as a ceremony ?
Nerissa teaches me what to believe :
I'll die for't, but some woman had the ring.
  Bass. No, by mine honour, madam, by my soul,   210
No woman had it ; but a civil doctor,
Which did refuse three thousand ducats of me,
And begg'd the ring, the which I did deny him,
And suffer'd him to go displeas'd away,
Even he that had held up the very life
Of my dear friend. What should I say, sweet lady ?
I was enforc'd to send it after him :
I was beset with shame and courtesy ;
My honour would not let ingratitude
So much besmear it. Pardon me, good lady,   220
For, by these blessed candles of the night,
Had you been there, I think, you would have begg'd
The ring of me to give the worthy doctor.
  Por. Let not that doctor e'er come near my house.
Since he hath got the jewel that I lov'd,
And that which you did swear to keep for me,
I will become as liberal as you :
I'll not deny him any thing I have ;
No, not my body, nor my husband's bed.
Know him I shall, I am well sure of it :
Lie not a night from home ; watch me like Argus ;
If you do not, if I be left alone,   231
Now, by mine honour, which is yet mine own,
I'll have that doctor for my bedfellow.
  Ner. And I his clerk ; therefore, be well advis'd,
How you do leave me to mine own protection.
  Gra. Well, do you so : let not me take him then ;
For, if I do, I'll mar the young clerk's pen.
  Ant. I am the unhappy subject of these quarrels.
  Por. Sir, grieve not you ; you are welcome notwith-
        standing.
  Bass. Portia, forgive me this enforced wrong ;   240
And in the hearing of these many friends
I swear to thee, even by thine own fair eyes,
Wherein I see myself,—
  Por.   Mark you but that !
In both my eyes he doubly sees himself ;
In each eye, one :—swear by your double self,
And there's an oath of credit.
  Bass.   Nay, but hear me.
Pardon this fault, and by my soul I swear,
I never more will break an oath with thee.
  Ant. I once did lend my body for his wealth,

Which, but for him that had your husband's ring, 250
Had quite miscarried : I dare be bound again,
My soul upon the forfeit, that your lord
Will never more break faith advisedly.
  Por. Then you shall be his surety.   Give him this,
And bid him keep it better than the other.
  Ant. Here, Lord Bassanio ; swear to keep this ring.
  Bass. By heaven ! it is the same I gave the doctor.
  Por. I had it of him : pardon me, Bassanio,
For, by this ring, the doctor lay with me.
  Ner. And pardon me, my gentle Gratiano,   260
For that same scrubbed boy, the doctor's clerk,
In lieu of this last night did lie with me.
  Gra. Why, this is like the mending of highways
In summer, where the ways are fair enough.
What ! are we cuckolds, ere we have deserv'd it ?
  Por. Speak not so grossly.—You are all amaz'd :
Here is a letter, read it at your leisure ;
It comes from Padua, from Bellario :
There you shall find. that Portia was the doctor ;
Nerissa there, her clerk.   Lorenzo here   270
Shall witness, I set forth as soon as you,
And even but now return'd : I have not yet
Enter'd my house.—Antonio, you are welcome ;
And I have better news in store for you,
Than you expect : unseal this letter soon ;
There you shall find, three of your argosies
Are richly come to harbour suddenly.
You shall not know by what strange accident
I chanced on this letter.
  Ant.   I am dumb.

  Bass. Were you the doctor, and I knew you not ?
  Gra. Were you the clerk that is to make me
    cuckold ?   281
  Ner. Ay ; but the clerk that never means to do it,
Unless he live until he be a man.
  Bass. Sweet doctor, you shall be my bedfellow :
When I am absent, then lie with my wife.
  Ant. Sweet lady, you have given me life and living,
For here I read for certain that my ships
Are safely come to road.
  Por.   How now, Lorenzo ?
My clerk hath some good comforts too for you.
  Ner. Ay, and I 'll give them him without a fee.—
There do I give to you and Jessica,   291
From the rich Jew, a special deed of gift,
After his death, of all he dies possess'd of.
  Lor. Fair ladies, you drop manna in the way
Of starved people.
  Por.   It is almost morning,
And yet, I am sure, you are not satisfied
Of these events at full.   Let us go in ;
And charge us there upon inter'gatories,
And we will answer all things faithfully.
  Gra. Let it be so : the first inter'gatory,   300
That my Nerissa shall be sworn on, is,
Whether till the next night she had rather stay,
Or go to bed now, being two hours to day :
But were the day come, I should wish it dark,
Till I were couching with the doctor's clerk.
Well, while I live, I 'll fear no other thing
So sore, as keeping safe Nerissa's ring.   [*Exeunt.*

AS YOU LIKE IT.

DRAMATIS PERSONÆ.

DUKE, *living in exile.*
FREDERICK, *his Brother, Usurper of his dominions.*
AMIENS, }
JAQUES, } *Lords attending upon the exiled Duke.*
LE BEAU, *a Courtier.*
CHARLES, *a Wrestler.*
OLIVER, }
JAQUES, } *Sons of Sir Rowland de Bois.*
ORLANDO, }
ADAM, }
DENNIS, } *Servants to Oliver.*
TOUCHSTONE, *a Clown.*

SIR OLIVER MAR-TEXT, *a Vicar.*
CORIN, }
SILVIUS, } *Shepherds.*
WILLIAM, *a Country Fellow, in love with Audrey.*
HYMEN.

ROSALIND, *Daughter to the exiled Duke.*
CELIA, *Daughter to Frederick.*
PHEBE, *a Shepherdess.*
AUDREY, *a Country Wench.*

Lords, Pages, Foresters, and Attendants.

The *SCENE* lies, first, near OLIVER'S House ; afterwards, in the Usurper's Court, and in the Forest of ARDEN.

ACT I.

SCENE I.—An Orchard, near OLIVER'S House.

Enter ORLANDO *and* ADAM.

Orlando.

AS I remember, Adam, it was upon this fashion bequeathed me by will but poor a thousand crowns ; and, as thou say'st, charged my brother on his blessing to breed me well : and there begins my sadness. My brother Jaques he keeps at school, and report speaks goldenly of his profit : for my part, he keeps me rustically at home, or, to speak more properly, stays me here at home unkept ; for call you that keeping for a gentleman of my birth, that differs not from the stalling of an ox ? His horses are bred better ; for, besides that they are fair with their feeding, they are taught their manage, and to that end riders dearly hired : but I, his brother, gain nothing under him but growth, for the which his animals on his dunghills are as much bound to him as I. Besides this nothing that he so plentifully gives me, the something that Nature gave me, his countenance seems to take from me : he lets me feed with his hinds, bars me the place of a brother, and, as much as in him lies, mines my gentility with my education. This is it, Adam, that grieves me ; and the spirit of my father, which I think is within me, begins to mutiny against this servitude. I will no longer endure it, though yet I know no wise remedy how to avoid it.

Adam. Yonder comes my master, your brother.

Orl. Go apart, Adam, and thou shalt hear how he will shake me up. 30

Enter OLIVER.

Oli. Now, sir ! what make you here ?

Orl. Nothing : I am not taught to make anything.

Oli. What mar you then, sir ?

Orl. Marry, sir, I am helping you to mar that which God made, a poor unworthy brother of yours, with idleness.

Oli. Marry, sir, be better employed, and be naught awhile.

Orl. Shall I keep your hogs, and eat husks with them ? What prodigal portion have I spent, that I should come to such penury ? 41

Oli. Know you where you are, sir ?

Orl. O ! sir, very well : here, in your orchard.

Oli. Know you before whom, sir ?

Orl. Ay, better than him I am before knows me. I know, you are my eldest brother ; and, in the gentle condition of blood, you should so know me. The courtesy of nations allows you my better, in that you are the first-born ; but the same tradition takes not away my blood, were there twenty brothers betwixt us. I have as much of my father in me, as you ; albeit, I confess, your coming before me is nearer to his reverence. 53

Oli. What, boy !

Orl. Come, come, elder brother, you are too young in this.

Oli. Wilt thou lay hands on me, villain ?

Orl. I am no villain : I am the youngest son of Sir Rowland de Bois ; he was my father, and he is thrice a villain, that says, such a father begot villains. Wert thou not my brother, I would not take this hand from thy throat, till this other had pulled out thy tongue for saying so : thou hast railed on thyself. 63

Adam. [*Coming forward.*] Sweet masters, be patient : for your father's remembrance, be at accord.

Oli. Let me go, I say.

Orl. I will not, till I please : you shall hear me. My father charged you in his will to give me good education : you have trained me like a peasant, obscuring and hiding from me all gentleman-like qualities : the spirit of my father grows strong in me, and I will no longer endure it ; therefore, allow me such exercises as may become a gentleman, or give me the poor allottery my father left me by testament : with that I will go buy my fortunes.

Oli. And what wilt thou do ? beg, when that is spent ? Well, sir, get you in : I will not long be troubled with you ; you shall have some part of your will. I pray you, leave me.

Orl. I will no further offend you, than becomes me for my good.   81
Oli. Get you with him, you old dog.
Adam. Is old dog my reward? Most true, I have lost my teeth in your service.—God be with my old master! he would not have spoke such a word.
                              [*Exeunt* ORLANDO *and* ADAM.
Oli. Is it even so? begin you to grow upon me? I will physic your rankness, and yet give no thousand crowns neither. Holla, Dennis!

            Enter DENNIS.

Den. Calls your worship?
Oli. Was not Charles, the duke's wrestler, here to speak with me?   91
Den. So please you, he is here at the door, and importunes access to you.
Oli. Call him in. [*Exit* DENNIS.]—'T will be a good way; and to-morrow the wrestling is.

            Enter CHARLES.

Cha. Good-morrow to your worship.
Oli. Good Monsieur Charles, what's the new news at the new court?   98
Cha. There's no news at the court, sir, but the old news: that is, the old duke is banished by his younger brother the new duke, and three or four loving lords have put themselves into voluntary exile with him, whose lands and revenues enrich the new duke; therefore, he gives them good leave to wander.
Oli. Can you tell, if Rosalind, the duke's daughter, be banished with her father?
Cha. O! no; for the duke's daughter, her cousin, so loves her,—being ever from their cradles bred together,—that she would have followed her exile, or have died to stay behind her. She is at the court, and no less beloved of her uncle than his own daughter; and never two ladies loved as they do.   112
Oli. Where will the old duke live?
Cha. They say, he is already in the forest of Arden, and a many merry men with him; and there they live like the old Robin Hood of England. They say, many young gentlemen flock to him every day, and fleet the time carelessly, as they did in the golden world.
Oli. What,—you wrestle to-morrow before the new duke?   120
Cha. Marry, do I, sir; and I came to acquaint you with a matter. I am given, sir, secretly to understand, that your younger brother, Orlando, hath a disposition to come in disguised against me to try a fall. To-morrow, sir, I wrestle for my credit, and he that escapes me without some broken limb shall acquit him well. Your brother is but young, and tender; and, for your love, I would be loath to foil him, as I must for my own honour if he come in: therefore, out of my love to you, I came hither to acquaint you withal, that either you might stay him from his intendment, or brook such disgrace well as he shall run into, in that it is a thing of his own search, and altogether against my will.   131
Oli. Charles, I thank thee for thy love to me, which, thou shalt find, I will most kindly requite. I had myself notice of my brother's purpose herein, and have by underhand means laboured to dissuade him from it; but he is resolute. I'll tell thee, Charles, it is the stubbornest young fellow of France, full of ambition, an envious emulator of every man's good parts, a secret and villainous contriver against me his natural brother: therefore, use thy discretion. I had as lief thou didst break his neck as his finger; and thou wert best look to 't; for if thou dost him any slight disgrace, or if he do not mightily grace himself on thee, he will practise against thee by poison, entrap thee by some treacherous device, and never leave thee till he hath ta'en thy life by some indirect means or other; for, I assure thee (and almost with tears I speak it), there is not one so young and so villainous this day living. I speak but brotherly of him; but should I anatomise him to thee as he is, I must blush and weep, and thou must look pale and wonder.   154
Cha. I am heartily glad I came hither to you. If he come to-morrow, I'll give him his payment: if ever

he go alone again, I'll never wrestle for prize more; and so, God keep your worship!   [*Exit.*
Oli. Farewell, good Charles.—Now will I stir this gamester. I hope, I shall see an end of him; for my soul, yet I know not why, hates nothing more than he: yet he's gentle; never schooled, and yet learned; full of noble device; of all sorts enchantingly beloved, and, indeed, so much in the heart of the world, and especially of my own people, who best know him, that I am altogether misprised. But it shall not be so long; this wrestler shall clear all: nothing remains, but that I kindle the boy thither, which now I'll go about.
                                                    [*Exit.*

SCENE II.—A Lawn before the DUKE'S Palace.

            Enter ROSALIND *and* CELIA.

Cel. I pray thee, Rosalind, sweet my coz, be merry.
Ros. Dear Celia, I show more mirth than I am mistress of, and would you yet I were merrier? Unless you could teach me to forget a banished father, you must not learn me how to remember any extraordinary pleasure.
Cel. Herein I see, thou lovest me not with the full weight that I love thee. If my uncle, thy banished father, had banished thy uncle, the duke, my father, so thou hadst been still with me, I could have taught my love to take thy father for mine: so wouldst thou, if the truth of thy love to me were so righteously tempered, as mine is to thee.   13
Ros. Well, I will forget the condition of my estate, to rejoice in yours.
Cel. You know, my father hath no child but I, nor none is like to have; and, truly, when he dies, thou shalt be his heir: for what he hath taken away from thy father perforce, I will render thee again in affection: by mine honour, I will; and when I break that oath, let me turn monster. Therefore, my sweet Rose, be merry.   22
Ros. From henceforth I will, coz, and devise sports. Let me see; what think you of falling in love?
Cel. Marry, I pr'ythee, do, to make sport withal: but love no man in good earnest; nor no further in sport neither, than with safety of a pure blush thou may'st in honour come off again.
Ros. What shall be our sport then?
Cel. Let us sit, and mock the good housewife, Fortune, from her wheel, that her gifts may henceforth be bestowed equally.   32
Ros. I would, we could do so; for her benefits are mightily misplaced, and the bountiful blind woman doth most mistake in her gifts to women.
Cel. 'T is true, for those that she makes fair, she scarce makes honest; and those that she makes honest, she makes very ill-favouredly.
Ros. Nay, now thou goest from Fortune's office to Nature's: Fortune reigns in gifts of the world, not in the lineaments of Nature.   41
Cel. No: when Nature hath made a fair creature, may she not by Fortune fall into the fire?—Though Nature hath given us wit to flout at Fortune, hath not Fortune sent in this fool to cut off the argument?

            Enter TOUCHSTONE.

Ros. Indeed, there is Fortune too hard for Nature, when Fortune makes Nature's natural the cutter-off of Nature's wit.   48
Cel. Peradventure, this is not Fortune's work neither, but Nature's; who, perceiving our natural wits too dull to reason of such goddesses, hath sent this natural for our whetstone: for always the dulness of the fool is the whetstone of the wits.—How now, wit? whither wander you?
Touch. Mistress, you must come away to your father.
Cel. Were you made the messenger?
Touch. No, by mine honour; but I was bid to come for you.
Ros. Where learned you that oath, fool?   60
Touch. Of a certain knight, that swore by his honour they were good pancakes, and swore by his honour

the mustard was naught: now, I 'll stand to it, the pancakes were naught, and the mustard was good, and yet was not the knight forsworn.

Cel. How prove you that, in the great heap of your knowledge?

Ros. Ay, marry: now unmuzzle your wisdom.

Touch. Stand you both forth now: stroke your chins, and swear by your beards that I am a knave. 70

Touch. "No, by mine honour; but I was bid to come for you.

Cel. By our beards, if we had them, thou art.

Touch. By my knavery, if I had it, then I were; but if you swear by that that is not, you are not forsworn: no more was this knight, swearing by his honour, for he never had any; or, if he had, he had sworn it away before ever he saw those pancakes, or that mustard.

Cel. Pr'ythee, who is 't that thou mean'st?

Touch. One that old Frederick, your father, loves.

Cel. My father's love is enough to honour him enough. Speak no more of him: you 'll be whipped for taxation, one of these days. 81

Touch. The more pity, that fools may not speak wisely, what wise men do foolishly.

Cel. By my troth, thou say'st true; for since the little wit that fools have was silenced, the little foolery that wise men have makes a great show. Here comes Monsieur Le Beau.

Enter LE BEAU.

Ros. With his mouth full of news.

Cel. Which he will put on us, as pigeons feed their young. 90

Ros. Then shall we be news-cramm'd.

Cel. All the better: we shall be the more marketable. *Bon jour, Monsieur Le Beau:* what 's the news?

Le Beau. Fair princess, you have lost much good sport.

Cel. Sport? Of what colour?

Le Beau. What colour, madam? How shall I answer you?

Ros. As wit and fortune will. 100

Touch. Or as the Destinies decree.

Cel. Well said: that was laid on with a trowel.

Touch. Nay, if I keep not my rank,—

Ros. Thou losest thy old smell.

Le Beau. You amaze me, ladies: I would have told you of good wrestling, which you have lost the sight of.

Ros. Yet tell us the manner of the wrestling.

Le Beau. I will tell you the beginning; and, if it please your ladyships, you may see the end, for the best is yet to do: and here, where you are, they are coming to perform it. 112

Cel. Well, the beginning, that is dead and buried.

Le Beau. There comes an old man, and his three sons,—

Cel. I could match this beginning with an old tale.

Le Beau. Three proper young men, of excellent growth and presence;—

Ros. With bills on their necks,—"Be it known unto all men by these presents,"— 120

Le Beau. The eldest of the three wrestled with Charles, the duke's wrestler; which Charles in a moment threw him, and broke three of his ribs, that there is little hope of life in him: so he served the second, and so the third. Yonder they lie, the poor old man, their father, making such pitiful dole over them, that all the beholders take his part with weeping.

Ros. Alas!

Touch. But what is the sport, monsieur, that the ladies have lost? 131

Le Beau. Why, this that I speak of.

Touch. Thus men may grow wiser every day! it is the first time that ever I heard breaking of ribs was sport for ladies.

Cel. Or I, I promise thee.

Ros. But is there any else longs to see this broken music in his sides? is there yet another dotes upon rib-breaking?—Shall we see this wrestling, cousin?

Le Beau. You must, if you stay here; for here is the place appointed for the wrestling, and they are ready to perform it. 142

Cel. Yonder, sure, they are coming: let us now stay and see it.

Flourish. Enter Duke FREDERICK, *Lords,* ORLANDO, CHARLES, *and Attendants.*

Duke F. Come on: since the youth will not be entreated, his own peril on his forwardness.

Ros. Is yonder the man?

Le Beau. Even he, madam.

Cel. Alas! he is too young: yet he looks successfully.

Duke F. How now, daughter, and cousin! are you crept hither to see the wrestling? 151

Ros. Ay, my liege, so please you give us leave.

Duke F. You will take little delight in it, I can tell you, there is such odds in the men. In pity of the challenger's youth I would fain dissuade him, but he will not be entreated. Speak to him, ladies; see if you can move him.

Cel. Call him hither, good Monsieur Le Beau.

Duke F. Do so: I 'll not be by. [DUKE *goes apart.*

Le Beau. Monsieur the challenger, the princess' call for you. 161

Orl. I attend them, with all respect and duty.

Ros. Young man, have you challenged Charles the wrestler?

Orl. No, fair princess; he is the general challenger: I come but in, as others do, to try with him the strength of my youth.

Cel. Young gentleman, your spirits are too bold for your years. You have seen cruel proof of this man's strength: if you saw yourself with your eyes, or knew yourself with your judgment, the fear of your adventure would counsel you to a more equal enterprise. We pray you, for your own sake, to embrace your own safety, and give over this attempt.

Ros. Do, young sir: your reputation shall not therefore be misprised. We will make it our suit to the duke, that the wrestling might not go forward. 177

Orl. I beseech you, punish me not with your hard thoughts, wherein I confess me much guilty, to deny so fair and excellent ladies anything. But let your fair eyes and gentle wishes go with me to my trial: wherein if I be foiled, there is but one shamed that was never gracious; if killed, but one dead that is willing to be so. I shall do my friends no wrong, for

I have none to lament me; the world no injury, for in it I have nothing; only in the world I fill up a place, which may be better supplied when I have made it empty.

Orl. Ready, sir; but his will hath in it a more modest working.

Duke F. You shall try but one fall.

Cha. No, I warrant your grace, you shall not entreat

Ros.   "Gentleman,
Wear this for me, one out of suits with fortune,
That could give more, but that her hand lacks means."

Ros. The little strength that I have, I would it were with you.   190
Cel. And mine, to eke out hers.
Ros. Fare you well. Pray Heaven, I be deceived in you!
Cel. Your heart's desires be with you.
Cha. Come, where is this young gallant, that is so desirous to lie with his mother earth?

him to a second, that have so mightily persuaded him from a first.   202
Orl. You mean to mock me after: you should not have mocked me before; but come your ways.
Ros. Now, Hercules be thy speed, young man!
Cel. I would I were invisible, to catch the strong fellow by the leg. [CHARLES *and* ORLANDO *wrestle.*
Ros. O excellent young man!

Cel. If I had a thunderbolt in mine eye, I can tell
who should down.   [CHARLES *is thrown. Shout.*
Duke F. No more, no more.   211
Orl. Yes, I beseech your grace: I am not yet well
breathed.
Duke F. How dost thou, Charles?
Le Beau. He cannot speak, my lord.
Duke F. Bear him away.   [CHARLES *is borne out.*]
- What is thy name, young man?
Orl. Orlando, my liege; the youngest son of Sir
Rowland de Bois.
Duke F. I would thou hadst been son to some man
else.
The world esteem'd thy father honourable,   220
But I did find him still mine enemy:
Thou shouldst have better pleas'd me with this deed,
Hadst thou descended from another house.
But fare thee well; thou art a gallant youth.
I would thou hadst told me of another father.
          [*Exeunt Duke* FREDERICK, *Train, and* LE BEAU.
Cel. Were I my father, coz, would I do this?
Orl. I am more proud to be Sir Rowland's son,
His youngest son;—and would not change that calling,
To be adopted heir to Frederick.
Ros. My father lov'd Sir Rowland as his soul,   230
And all the world was of my father's mind.
Had I before known this young man his son,
I should have given him tears unto entreaties,
Ere he should thus have ventur'd.
Cel.   Gentle cousin,
Let us go thank him, and encourage him:
My father's rough and envious disposition
Sticks me at heart.—Sir, you have well deserv'd:
If you do keep your promises in love
But justly, as you have exceeded all promise,
Your mistress shall be happy.
Ros.   Gentleman,   240
          [*Giving him a chain from her neck.*
Wear this for me, one out of suits with fortune,
That could give more, but that her hand lacks
          means.—
Shall we go, coz?
Cel.   Ay.—Fare you well, fair gentleman.
Orl. Can I not say, I thank you? My better parts
Are all thrown down, and that which here stands up
Is but a quintain, a mere lifeless block.
Ros. He calls us back. My pride fell with my
          fortunes:
I'll ask him what he would.—Did you call, sir?—
Sir, you have wrestled well, and overthrown
More than your enemies.
Cel.   Will you go, coz?   250
Ros. Have with you.—Fare you well.
          [*Exeunt* ROSALIND *and* CELIA.
Orl. What passion hangs these weights upon my
          tongue?
I cannot speak to her, yet she urg'd conference.
O poor Orlando! thou art overthrown.
Or Charles, or something weaker, masters thee.

Re-enter LE BEAU.

Le Beau. Good sir, I do in friendship counsel you
To leave this place. Albeit you have deserv'd
High commendation, true applause, and love,
Yet such is now the duke's condition,
That he misconstrues all that you have done.   260
The duke is humorous: what he is, indeed,
More suits you to conceive, than I to speak of.
Orl. I thank you, sir; and, pray you, tell me this:
Which of the two was daughter of the duke,
That here was at the wrestling?
Le Beau. Neither his daughter, if we judge by
          manners:
But yet, indeed, the smaller is his daughter:
The other is daughter to the banish'd duke,
And here detain'd by her usurping uncle,
To keep his daughter company; whose loves   270
Are dearer than the natural bond of sisters.
But I can tell you, that of late this duke
Hath ta'en displeasure 'gainst his gentle niece,
Grounded upon no other argument,
But that the people praise her for her virtues,

And pity her for her good father's sake;
And, on my life, his malice 'gainst the lady
Will suddenly break forth.—Sir, fare you well:
Hereafter, in a better world than this,
I shall desire more love and knowledge of you.   280
Orl. I rest much bounden to you: fare you well.
          [*Exit* LE BEAU.
Thus must I from the smoke into the smother;
From tyrant duke unto a tyrant brother.—
But heavenly Rosalind!   [*Exit.*

SCENE III.—A Room in the Palace.

Enter CELIA *and* ROSALIND.

Cel. Why, cousin, why, Rosalind!—Cupid have
mercy!—Not a word?

Cel. "Why, cousin, why, Rosalind!—Cupid have mercy!—Not
a word?"

Ros. Not one to throw at a dog.
Cel. No, thy words are too precious to be cast away
upon curs, throw some of them at me: come, lame me
with reasons.
Ros. Then there were two cousins laid up, when the
one should be lamed with reasons, and the other mad
without any.
Cel. But is all this for your father?   10
Ros. No, some of it is for my child's father: O, how
full of briars is this working-day world!
Cel. They are but burs, cousin, thrown upon thee in
holiday foolery: if we walk not in the trodden paths,
our very petticoats will catch them.
Ros. I could shake them off my coat: these burs are
in my heart.
Cel. Hem them away.
Ros. I would try, if I could cry hem, and have him.
Cel. Come, come; wrestle with thy affections.   20
Ros. O! they take the part of a better wrestler than
myself.
Cel. O, a good wish upon you! you will try in time,
in despite of a fall.—But, turning these jests out of
service, let us talk in good earnest. Is it possible, on
such a sudden, you should fall into so strong a liking
with old Sir Rowland's youngest son?
Ros. The duke my father lov'd his father dearly.

Cel. Doth it therefore ensue, that you should love
his son dearly? By this kind of chase, I should hate
him, for my father hated his father dearly; yet I hate
not Orlando.   32
Ros. No, 'faith, hate him not, for my sake.
Cel. Why should I not? doth he not deserve well?
Ros. Let me love him for that; and do you love
him, because I do.—Look, here comes the duke.
Cel. With his eyes full of anger.

Enter Duke FREDERICK, *with Lords.*

Duke F. Mistress, despatch you with your safest
    haste,
And get you from our court.
Ros.   Me, uncle?
Duke F.   You, cousin:
Within these ten days if that thou be'st found   40
So near our public court as twenty miles,
Thou diest for it.
Ros.   I do beseech your grace,
Let me the knowledge of my fault bear with me.
If with myself I hold intelligence,
Or have acquaintance with mine own desires,
If that I do not dream, or be not frantic
(As I do trust I am not), then, dear uncle,
Never so much as in a thought unborn
Did I offend your highness.
Duke F.   Thus do all traitors:
If their purgation did consist in words,   50
They are as innocent as grace itself.
Let it suffice thee, that I trust thee not.
Ros. Yet your mistrust cannot make me a traitor.
Tell me, whereon the likelihood depends.
Duke F. Thou art thy father's daughter; there's
    enough.
Ros. So was I when your highness took his duke-
    dom;
So was I when your highness banish'd him.
Treason is not inherited, my lord;
Or, if we did derive it from our friends,
What's that to me? my father was no traitor.   60
Then, good my liege, mistake me not so much,
To think my poverty is treacherous.
Cel. Dear sovereign, hear me speak.
Duke F. Ay, Celia: we stay'd her for your sake;
Else had she with her father rang'd along.
Cel. I did not then entreat to have her stay:
It was your pleasure, and your own remorse.
I was too young that time to value her;
But now I know her: if she be a traitor,
Why, so am I; we still have slept together,
Rose at an instant, learn'd, play'd, eat together; 70
And wheresoe'er we went, like Juno's swans,
Still we went coupled, and inseparable.
Duke F. She is too subtle for thee; and her smooth-
    ness,
Her very silence, and her patience,
Speak to the people, and they pity her.
Thou art a fool: she robs thee of thy name;
And thou wilt show more bright, and seem more
    virtuous,
When she is gone. Then, open not thy lips:

Firm and irrevocable is my doom   80
Which I have pass'd upon her. She is banish'd.
Cel. Pronounce that sentence then on me, my liege:
I cannot live out of her company.
Duke F. You are a fool.—You, niece, provide your-
    self:
If you outstay the time, upon mine honour,
And in the greatness of my word, you die.
            [*Exeunt Duke* FREDERICK *and Lords.*
Cel. O my poor Rosalind! whither wilt thou go?
Wilt thou change fathers? I will give thee mine.
I charge thee, be not thou more griev'd than I am.
Ros. I have more cause.
Cel.   Thou hast not, cousin. 90
Pr'ythee, be cheerful: know'st thou not, the duke
Hath banish'd me, his daughter?
Ros.   That he hath not.
Cel. No? hath not? Rosalind lacks then the love
Which teacheth thee that thou and I am one.
Shall we be sunder'd? shall we part, sweet girl?
No: let my father seek another heir.
Therefore, devise with me how we may fly,
Whither to go, and what to bear with us:
And do not seek to take your change upon you,
To bear your griefs yourself, and leave me out;   100
For, by this heaven, now at our sorrows pale,
Say what thou canst, I'll go along with thee.
Ros. Why, whither shall we go?
Cel. To seek my uncle in the forest of Arden.
Ros. Alas, what danger will it be to us,
Maids as we are, to travel forth so far!
Beauty provoketh thieves sooner than gold.
Cel. I'll put myself in poor and mean attire,
And with a kind of umber smirch my face.
The like do you: so shall we pass along,   110
And never stir assailants.
Ros.   Were it not better,
Because that I am more than common tall,
That I did suit me all points like a man?
A gallant curtle-axe upon my thigh,
A boar-spear in my hand; and, in my heart
Lie there what hidden woman's fear there will,
We'll have a swashing and a martial outside;
As many other mannish cowards have,
That do outface it with their semblances.
Cel. What shall I call thee, when thou art a man? 120
Ros. I'll have no worse a name than Jove's own
    page,
And therefore look you call me Ganymede.
But what will you be call'd?
Cel. Something that hath a reference to my state:
No longer Celia, but Aliena.
Ros. But, cousin, what if we essay'd to steal
The clownish fool out of your father's court?
Would he not be a comfort to our travel?
Cel. He'll go along o'er the wide world with me;
Leave me alone to woo him. Let's away,   130
And get our jewels and our wealth together,
Devise the fittest time, and safest way
To hide us from pursuit that will be made
After my flight. Now go we in content
To liberty, and not to banishment.   [*Exeunt.*

ACT II.

SCENE I.—The Forest of Arden.

Enter DUKE *Senior,* AMIENS, *and other Lords, like foresters.*

Duke Senior.
NOW, my co-mates, and brothers in exile,
Hath not old custom made this life
        more sweet
Than that of painted pomp? Are not
        these woods
More free from peril than the en-
        vious court?
Here feel we but the penalty of Adam,
The seasons' difference; as the icy
        fang,
And churlish chiding of the winter's
        wind,
Which when it bites, and blows upon
        my body,
Even till I shrink with cold, I smile,
        and say,
This is no flattery: these are coun-
        sellors   10
That feelingly persuade me what I am.
Sweet are the uses of adversity,
Which, like the toad, ugly and venomous,
Wears yet a precious jewel in his head;
And this our life, exempt from public haunt,
Finds tongues in trees, books in the running brooks,
Sermons in stones, and good in everything.
Ami. I would not change it. Happy is your grace,
That can translate the stubbornness of fortune
Into so quiet and so sweet a style.   20
Duke S. Come, shall we go and kill us venison?
And yet it irks me, the poor dappled fools,
Being native burghers of this desert city,
Should, in their own confines, with forked heads,
Have their round haunches gor'd.
1 Lord.   Indeed, my lord,
The melancholy Jaques grieves at that;
And, in that kind, swears you do more usurp,
Than doth your brother that hath banish'd you.
To-day my Lord of Amiens and myself
Did steal behind him, as he lay along   30
Under an oak, whose antique root peeps out
Upon the brook that brawls along this wood;
To the which place a poor sequester'd stag,
That from the hunter's aim had ta'en a hurt,
Did come to languish: and, indeed, my lord,
The wretched animal heav'd forth such groans,
That their discharge did stretch his leathern coat
Almost to bursting; and the big round tears
Cours'd one another down his innocent nose
In piteous chase: and thus the hairy fool,   40
Much marked of the melancholy Jaques,
Stood on the extremest verge of the swift brook,
Augmenting it with tears.
Duke S.   But what said Jaques?
Did he not moralise this spectacle?
1 Lord. O! yes, into a thousand similes.
First, for his weeping into the needless stream;
"Poor deer," quoth he, "thou mak'st a testament
As worldlings do, giving thy sum of more
To that which had too much." Then, being there
        alone,
Left and abandon'd of his velvet friends;   50
"'T is right," quoth he; "thus misery doth part
The flux of company." Anon, a careless herd,
Full of the pasture, jumps along by him,

And never stays to greet him: "Ay," quoth Jaques,
"Sweep on, you fat and greasy citizens;
'T is just the fashion: wherefore do you look
Upon that poor and broken bankrupt there?"
Thus most invectively he pierceth through
The body of the country, city, court,
Yea, and of this our life; swearing, that we   60
Are mere usurpers, tyrants, and what's worse,
To fright the animals, and to kill them up
In their assign'd and native dwelling-place.
Duke S. And did you leave him in this contempla-
        tion?
2 Lord. We did, my lord, weeping and commenting
Upon the sobbing deer.
Duke S.   Show me the place.
I love to cope him in these sullen fits,
For then he's full of matter.
2 Lord. I'll bring you to him straight. [*Exeunt.*

SCENE II.—A Room in the Palace.

Enter Duke FREDERICK, *Lords, and Attendants.*

Duke F. Can it be possible that no man saw them?
It cannot be: some villains of my court
Are of consent and sufferance in this.
1 Lord. I cannot hear of any that did see her.
The ladies, her attendants of her chamber,
Saw her a-bed; and, in the morning early,
They found the bed untreasur'd of their mistress.
2 Lord. My lord, the roynish clown, at whom so oft
Your grace was wont to laugh, is also missing.
Hesperia, the princess' gentlewoman,   10
Confesses, that she secretly o'erhead
Your daughter and her cousin much commend
The parts and graces of the wrestler,
That did but lately foil the sinewy Charles;
And she believes, wherever they are gone,
That youth is surely in their company.
Duke F. Send to his brother: fetch that gallant
        hither;
If he be absent, bring his brother to me,
I'll make him find him. Do this suddenly,
And let not search and inquisition quail   20
To bring again these foolish runaways. [*Exeunt.*

SCENE III.—Before OLIVER'S House.

Enter ORLANDO *and* ADAM, *meeting.*

Orl. Who's there?
Adam. What! my young master?—O my gentle
        master!
O my sweet master! O you memory
Of old Sir Rowland! why, what make you here?
Why are you virtuous? why do people love you?
And wherefore are you gentle, strong, and valiant?
Why would you be so fond to overcome
The bony priser of the humorous duke?
Your praise is come too swiftly home before you.
Know you not, master, to some kind of men   10
Their graces serve them but as enemies?
No more do yours: your virtues, gentle master,

Are sanctified and holy traitors to you.
O, what a world is this, when what is comely
Envenoms him that bears it !
  Orl. Why, what's the matter?
  Adam.   O unhappy youth !
Come not within these doors : within this roof
The enemy of all your graces lives.
Your brother—(no, no brother : yet the son—
Yet not the son—I will not call him son   20
Of him I was about to call his father)—
Hath heard your praises, and this night he means
To burn the lodging where you use to lie,
And you within it : if he fail of that,
He will have other means to cut you off.
I overheard him, and his practices.
This is no place ; this house is but a butchery :
Abhor it, fear it, do not enter it.
  Orl. Why, whither, Adam, wouldst thou have me go?
  Adam. No matter whither, so you come not here. 30

Orl. "Why, whither, Adam, wouldst thou have me go?"

  Orl. What ! wouldst thou have me go and beg my food,
Or with a base and boisterous sword enforce
A thievish living on the common road?
This I must do, or know not what to do ;
Yet this I will not do, do how I can.
I rather will subject me to the malice
Of a diverted blood, and bloody brother.
  Adam. But do not so. I have five hundred crowns,
The thrifty hire I sav'd under your father,
Which I did store, to be my foster-nurse,   40
When service should in my old limbs lie lame,
And unregarded age in corners thrown.
Take that ; and He that doth the ravens feed,
Yea, providently caters for the sparrow,
Be comfort to my age ! Here is the gold :
All this I give you. Let me be your servant :
Though I look old, yet I am strong and lusty ;
For in my youth I never did apply
Hot and rebellious liquors in my blood ;   50
Nor did not with unbashful forehead woo
The means of weakness and debility ;
Therefore my age is as a lusty winter,
Frosty, but kindly. Let me go with you :
I'll do the service of a younger man
In all your business and necessities.

  Orl. O good old man ! how well in thee appears
The constant service of the antique world,
When service sweat for duty, not for meed !
Thou art not for the fashion of these times,
Where none will sweat but for promotion,   60
And having that, do choke their service up
Even with the having : it is not so with thee.
But, poor old man, thou prun'st a rotten tree,
That cannot so much as a blossom yield,
In lieu of all thy pains and husbandry.
But come thy ways, we'll go along together,
And ere we have thy youthful wages spent,
We'll light upon some settled low content.
  Adam. Master, go on, and I will follow thee
To the last gasp with truth and loyalty.   70
From seventeen years, till now almost fourscore,
Here lived I, but now live here no more.
At seventeen years many their fortunes seek ;
But at fourscore it is too late a week :
Yet fortune cannot recompense me better,
Than to die well, and not my master's debtor. [*Exeunt.*

SCENE IV.—The Forest of Arden.

Enter ROSALIND *in boy's clothes,* CELIA *dressed like a shepherdess, and* TOUCHSTONE.

  Ros. O Jupiter ! how weary are my spirits !
  Touch. I care not for my spirits, if my legs were not weary.
  Ros. I could find in my heart to disgrace my man's apparel, and to cry like a woman ; but I must comfort the weaker vessel, as doublet and hose ought to show itself courageous to petticoat : therefore, courage, good Aliena !   8
  Cel. I pray you, bear with me : I can go no further.
  Touch. For my part, I had rather bear with you than bear you : yet I should bear no cross, if I did bear you ; for I think you have no money in your purse.
  Ros. Well, this is the forest of Arden.
  Touch. Ay, now am I in Arden ; the more fool I : when I was at home, I was in a better place ; but travellers must be content.
  Ros. Ay, be so, good Touchstone.—Look you ; who comes here ? a young man, and an old, in solemn talk.

Enter CORIN and SILVIUS.

  Cor. That is the way to make her scorn you still.
  Sil. O Corin, that thou knew'st how I do love her ! 20
  Cor. I partly guess, for I have lov'd ere now.
  Sil. No, Corin ; being old, thou canst not guess,
Though in thy youth thou wast as true a lover
As ever sigh'd upon a midnight pillow :
But if thy love were ever like to mine,
As sure I think did never man love so,
How many actions most ridiculous
Hast thou been drawn to by thy fantasy?
  Cor. Into a thousand that I have forgotten.
  Sil. O ! thou didst then ne'er love so heartily.
If thou remember'st not the slightest folly
That ever love did make thee run into,
Thou hast not lov'd :
Or if thou hast not sat, as I do now,
Wearing thy hearer in thy mistress' praise,
Thou hast not lov'd :
Or if thou hast not broke from company,
Abruptly, as my passion now makes me,
Thou hast not lov'd.—O Phebe, Phebe, Phebe ! [*Exit.*
  Ros. Alas, poor shepherd ! searching of thy wound,
I have by hard adventure found mine own.   41
  Touch. And I mine. I remember, when I was in love I broke my sword upon a stone, and bid him take that for coming a-night to Jane Smile ; and I remember the kissing of her batlet, and the cow's dugs that her pretty chopped hands had milked ; and I remember the wooing of a peascod instead of her, from whom I took two cods, and, giving her them again, said with weeping tears, "Wear these for my sake." We, that are true lovers, run into strange capers ; but as all is

mortal in nature, so is all nature in love mortal in
folly.   52
  Ros. Thou speakest wiser than thou art 'ware of.
  Touch. Nay, I shall ne'er be 'ware of mine own wit,
till I break my shins against it.
  Ros. Jove, Jove! this shepherd's passion
    Is much upon my fashion.
  Touch. And mine; but it grows something stale
with me.
  Cel. I pray you, one of you question yond man,   60
If he for gold will give us any food:
I faint almost to death.
  Touch. Holla, you clown!

Sil. "O Corin, that thou knew'st how I do love her!"

  Ros.   Peace, fool: he's not thy kinsman.
  Cor. Who calls?
  Touch. Your betters, sir.
  Cor. Else are they very wretched.
  Ros.   Peace, I say.—
Good even to you, friend.
  Cor. And to you, gentle sir; and to you all.
  Ros. I pr'ythee, shepherd, if that love, or gold,
Can in this desert place buy entertainment,   70
Bring us where we may rest ourselves, and feed.
Here's a young maid with travel much oppress'd,
And faints for succour.
  Cor.   Fair sir, I pity her,
And wish, for her sake more than for mine own,
My fortunes were more able to relieve her;
But I am shepherd to another man,
And do not shear the fleeces that I graze;
My master is of churlish disposition,
And little recks to find the way to heaven
By doing deeds of hospitality.   80
Besides, his cote, his flocks, and bounds of feed,
Are now on sale: and at our sheepcote now,
By reason of his absence, there is nothing
That you will feed on; but what is, come see,
And in my voice most welcome shall you be.
  Ros. What is he that shall buy his flock and pasture?
  Cor. That young swain that you saw here but ere-
while,
That little cares for buying anything.
  Ros. I pray thee, if it stand with honesty,
Buy thou the cottage, pasture, and the flock,   90
And thou shalt have to pay for it of us.
  Cel. And we will mend thy wages. I like this place,
And willingly could waste my time in it.
  Cor. Assuredly, the thing is to be sold.

Go with me: if you like, upon report,
The soil, the profit, and this kind of life,
I will your very faithful feeder be,
And buy it with your gold right suddenly.   [*Exeunt.*

SCENE V.—*Another Part of the Forest.*

Enter AMIENS, JAQUES, *and others.*

SONG.

  Ami.   *Under the greenwood tree,*
     Who loves to lie with me,
     And turn his merry note
     Unto the sweet bird's throat,
 Come hither, come hither, come hither:
    Here shall he see
    No enemy,
  But winter and rough weather.

  Jaq. More, more! I pr'ythee, more.   9
  Ami. It will make you melancholy, Monsieur Jaques.
  Jaq. I thank it. More! I pr'ythee more. I can
suck melancholy out of a song, as a weasel sucks
eggs. More! I pr'ythee, more.
  Ami. My voice is ragged; I know I cannot please
you.
  Jaq. I do not desire you to please me; I do desire
you to sing. Come, more; another stanza. Call you
'em stanzas?
  Ami. What you will, Monsieur Jaques.
  Jaq. Nay, I care not for their names; they owe me
nothing. Will you sing?   21
  Ami. More at your request than to please myself.
  Jaq. Well then, if ever I thank any man, I'll thank
you: but that they call compliment is like the encounter of two dog-apes; and when a man thanks me
heartily, methinks I have given him a penny, and he
renders me the beggarly thanks. Come, sing; and
you that will not, hold your tongues.
  Ami. Well, I'll end the song.—Sirs, cover the while:
the duke will drink under this tree.—He hath been all
this day to look you.   31
  Jaq. And I have been all this day to avoid him. He
is too disputable for my company: I think of as many
matters as he, but I give Heaven thanks, and make
no boast of them. Come, warble; come.

SONG.

  Who doth ambition shun, [*All together here.*
  And loves to live i' the sun,
  Seeking the food he eats,
  And pleas'd with what he gets,
 Come hither, come hither, come hither: 40
    Here shall he see
    No enemy,
  But winter and rough weather.

  Jaq. I'll give you a verse to this note, that I made
yesterday in despite of my invention.
  Ami. And I'll sing it.
  Jaq. Thus it goes—

    If it do come to pass,
    That any man turn ass,
    Leaving his wealth and ease,   50
    A stubborn will to please,
 Ducdame, ducdame, ducdame:
    Here shall he see
    Gross fools as he,
  An if he will come to me.

  Ami. What's that *ducdame?*
  Jaq. 'Tis a Greek invocation to call fools into a circle.
I'll go sleep if I can; if I cannot, I'll rail against all
the first-born of Egypt.   59
  Ami. And I'll go seek the duke: his banquet is
prepared.   [*Exeunt severally.*

SCENE VI.—*Another Part of the Forest.*

Enter ORLANDO *and* ADAM.

  Adam. Dear master, I can go no further: O! I die

for food. Here lie I down, and measure out my grave.
Farewell, kind master.
   Orl. Why, how now, Adam! no greater heart in
thee? Live a little; comfort a little; cheer thyself a
little. If this uncouth forest yield anything savage,
I will either be food for it, or bring it for food to thee.
Thy conceit is nearer death than thy powers. For my
sake be comfortable, hold death awhile at the arm's
end, I will here be with thee presently, and if I bring
thee not something to eat, I will give thee leave to die;
but if thou diest before I come, thou art a mocker of
my labour. Well said! thou look'st cheerily; and I'll
be with thee quickly.—Yet thou liest in the bleak air:
come, I will bear thee to some shelter, and thou shalt
not die for lack of a dinner, if there live anything in
this desert. Cheerly, good Adam.   [*Exeunt.*

SCENE VII.—Another Part of the Forest.

A table set out. Enter DUKE Senior, AMIENS, *Lords,
and others.*

   Duke S. I think he be transform'd into a beast,
For I can nowhere find him like a man.
   1 *Lord.* My lord, he is but even now gone hence:
Here was he merry, hearing of a song.
   Duke S. If he, compact of jars, grow musical,
We shall have shortly discord in the spheres.—
Go, seek him: tell him, I would speak with him.
   1 *Lord.* He saves my labour by his own approach.

Enter JAQUES.

   Duke S. Why, how now, monsieur! what a life
     is this,
That your poor friends must woo your company?   10
What, you look merrily.
   Jaq. A fool, a fool!—I met a fool i' the forest,
A motley fool—a miserable world!—
As I do live by food, I met a fool,
Who laid him down and bask'd him in the sun,
And rail'd on Lady Fortune in good terms,
In good set terms, and yet a motley fool.
"Good morrow, fool," quoth I:—"No, sir," quoth he,
"Call me not fool, till Heaven hath sent me fortune."
And then he drew a dial from his poke,   20
And looking on it with lack-lustre eye,
Says very wisely, "It is ten o'clock:
Thus may we see," quoth he, "how the world wags:
'T is but an hour ago since it was nine,
And after one hour more 't will be eleven;
And so from hour to hour we ripe and ripe,
And then from hour to hour we rot and rot,
And thereby hangs a tale." When I did hear
The motley fool thus moral on the time,
My lungs began to crow like chanticleer,   30
That fools should be so deep-contemplative;
And I did laugh, sans intermission,
An hour by his dial.—O noble fool!
A worthy fool! Motley 's the only wear.
   Duke S. What fool is this?
   Jaq. O worthy fool!—One that hath been a courtier,
And says, if ladies be but young and fair,
They have the gift to know it; and in his brain,
Which is as dry as the remainder biscuit
After a voyage, he hath strange places cramm'd   40
With observation, the which he vents
In mangled forms.—O, that I were a fool!
I am ambitious for a motley coat.
   Duke S. Thou shalt have one.
   Jaq.   It is my only suit;
Provided that you weed your better judgments
Of all opinion that grows rank in them,
That I am wise. I must have liberty
Withal, as large a charter as the wind,
To blow on whom I please; for so fools have:
And they that are most galled with my folly,   50
They most must laugh. And why, sir, must they so?
The way is plain as way to parish church:
He, that a fool doth very wisely hit,
Doth very foolishly, although he smart,
Not to seem senseless of the bob; if not,

The wise man's folly is anatomis'd
Even by the squandering glances of the fool.
Invest me in my motley: give me leave
To speak my mind, and I will through and through
Cleanse the foul body of the infected world,   60
If they will patiently receive my medicine.
   Duke S. Fie on thee! I can tell what thou wouldst
     do.
   Jaq. What, for a counter, would I do but good?
   Duke S. Most mischievous foul sin, in chiding sin:
For thou thyself hast been a libertine,
As sensual as the brutish sting itself;
And all the embossed sores, and headed evils,
That thou with license of free foot hast caught,
Wouldst thou disgorge into the general world.
   Jaq. Why, who cries out on pride,   70
That can therein tax any private party?
Doth it not flow as hugely as the sea,
Till that the weary very means do ebb?
What woman in the city do I name,
When that I say, the city-woman bears
The cost of princes on unworthy shoulders?
Who can come in, and say that I mean her,
When such a one as she, such is her neighbour?
Or what is he of basest function,
That says, his bravery is not on my cost,   80
Thinking that I mean him, but therein suits
His folly to the mettle of my speech?
There then; how then? what then? Let me see
     wherein
My tongue hath wrong'd him: if it do him right,
Then he hath wrong'd himself; if he be free,
Why, then my taxing like a wild-goose flies,
Unclaim'd of any man.—But who comes here?

Enter ORLANDO, *with his sword drawn.*

   Orl. Forbear, and eat no more.
   Jaq.   Why, I have eat none yet.
   Orl. Nor shalt not, till necessity be serv'd.
   Jaq. Of what kind should this cock come of?   90
   Duke S. Art thou thus bolden'd, man, by thy dis-
     tress,
Or else a rude despiser of good manners,
That in civility thou seem'st so empty?
   Orl. You touch'd my vein at first: the thorny point
Of bare distress hath ta'en from me the show
Of smooth civility; yet am I inland bred,
And know some nurture. But forbear, I say:
He dies that touches any of this fruit,
Till I and my affairs are answered.
   Jaq. An you will not be answered with reason, 100
I must die.
   Duke S. What would you have? Your gentleness
     shall force,
More than your force move us to gentleness.
   Orl. I almost die for food, and let me have it.
   Duke S. Sit down and feed, and welcome to our
     table.
   Orl. Speak you so gently? Pardon me, I pray you:
I thought, that all things had been savage here,
And therefore put I on the countenance
Of stern commandment. But whate'er you are,
That in this desert inaccessible,   110
Under the shade of melancholy boughs,
Lose and neglect the creeping hours of time,
If ever you have look'd on better days,
If ever been where bells have knoll'd to church,
If ever sat at any good man's feast,
If ever from your eyelids wip'd a tear,
And know what 't is to pity, and be pitied,
Let gentleness my strong enforcement be:
In the which hope, I blush, and hide my sword.
   Duke S. True is it that we have seen better days, 120
And have with holy bell been knoll'd to church,
And sat at good men's feasts, and wip'd our eyes
Of drops that sacred pity hath engender'd;
And therefore sit you down in gentleness,
And take upon command what help we have,
That to your wanting may be minister'd.
   Orl. Then, but forbear your food a little while
Whiles, like a doe, I go to find my fawn,
And give it food. There is an old poor man,

Who after me hath many a weary step   130
Limp'd in pure love : till he be first suffic'd,—
Oppress'd with two weak evils, age and hunger,—
I will not touch a bit.
  Duke S.   Go find him out,
And we will nothing waste till you return.

They have their exits and their entrances :
And one man in his time plays many parts,
His acts being seven ages. At first, the infant,
Muling and puking in the nurse's arms.
Then, the whining school-boy, with his satchel,
And shining morning face, creeping like snail

Orl. " Forbear, and eat no more."

  Orl. I thank ye, and be bless'd for your good com-
        fort !   [*Exit.*
  Duke S. Thou seest, we are not all alone unhappy :
This wide and universal theatre
Presents more woful pageants than the scene
Wherein we play in.
  Jaq.   All the world 's a stage,
And all the men and women merely players :   140

Unwillingly to school. And then, the lover,
Sighing like furnace, with a woful ballad
Made to his mistress' eyebrow. Then, a soldier,   150
Full of strange oaths, and bearded like the pard,
Jealous in honour, sudden and quick in quarrel,
Seeking the bubble reputation
Even in the cannon's mouth. And then, the justice,
In fair round belly, with good capon lin'd,

With eyes severe, and beard of formal cut,
Full of wise saws and modern instances ;
And so he plays his part.   The sixth age shifts
Into the lean and slipper'd pantaloon,
With spectacles on nose, and pouch on side ;
His youthful hose well sav'd, a world too wide   160
For his shrunk shank ; and his big manly voice,
Turning again toward childish treble, pipes
And whistles in his sound.   Last scene of all,
That ends this strange eventful history,
Is second childishness, and mere oblivion ;
Sans teeth, sans eyes, sans taste, sans everything.

Re-enter ORLANDO, *with* ADAM.

Duke S. Welcome. Set down your venerable burden,
And let him feed.
Orl.   I thank you most for him.
Adam. So had you need :
I scarce can speak to thank you for myself.   170
Duke S. Welcome ; fall to : I will not trouble you
As yet to question you about your fortunes.
Give us some music ; and, good cousin, sing.

                    SONG.

Ami.   *Blow, blow, thou winter wind,*
           Thou art not so unkind
               As man's ingratitude ;

           Thy tooth is not so keen,
           Because thou art not seen,
               Although thy breath be rude.
Heigh, ho ! sing, heigh, ho ! unto the green holly :
Most friendship is feigning, most loving mere folly.
           Then, heigh, ho ! the holly !   182
           This life is most jolly.

           Freeze, freeze, thou bitter sky,
           That dost not bite so nigh
               As benefits forgot :
           Though thou the waters warp,
           Thy sting is not so sharp
               As friend remember'd not.
Heigh, ho ! sing, &c.   190

Duke S. If that you were the good Sir Rowland's
               son,
As you have whisper'd faithfully, you were,
And as mine eye doth his effigies witness
Most truly limn'd, and living in your face,
Be truly welcome hither.   I am the duke,
That lov'd your father.   The residue of your fortune,
Go to my cave and tell me.—Good old man,
Thou art right welcome as thy master is.
Support him by the arm.—Give me your hand,
And let me all your fortunes understand.   200
                                              [*Exeunt.*

ACT III.

SCENE I.—A Room in the Palace.

Enter Duke FREDERICK, OLIVER, *and Attendants.*

Duke Frederick.
NOT see him since? Sir, sir, that
          cannot be:
But were I not the better part
          made mercy,
I should not seek an absent argu-
          ment
Of my revenge, thou present. But
          look to it :
Find out thy brother, wheresoe'er
          he is ;
Seek him with candle ; bring him,
          dead or living,
Within this twelvemonth, or turn thou no more
To seek a living in our territory.
Thy lands,·and all things that thou dost call thine,
Worth seizure, do we seize into our hands,   10
Till thou canst quit thee by thy brother's mouth,
Of what we think against thee.
Oli. O, that your highness knew my heart in this !
I never lov'd my brother in my life.
Duke F. More villain thou.—Well, push him out of
          doors ;
And let my officers of such a nature
Make an extent upon his house and lands.
Do this expediently, and turn him going.   [*Exeunt.*

———

SCENE II.—The Forest of Arden.

Enter ORLANDO, *with a paper.*

Orl. Hang there, my verse, in witness of my love :
And thou, thrice-crowned queen of night, survey
With thy chaste eye, from thy pale sphere above,
Thy huntress' name, that my full life doth sway.
O Rosalind ! these trees shall be my books,
And in their barks my thoughts I 'll character,
That every eye, which in this forest looks,
Shall see thy virtue witness'd everywhere.
Run, run, Orlando : carve on every tree
The fair, the chaste, and unexpressive she.   10
                                                [*Exit.*

Enter CORIN *and* TOUCHSTONE.

Cor. And how like you this shepherd's life, Master
Touchstone ?
Touch. Truly, shepherd, in respect of itself, it is a
good life, but in respect that it is a shepherd's life, it
is naught.   In respect that it is solitary, I like it very
well ; but in respect that it is private, it is a very vile
life.   Now, in respect it is in the fields, it pleaseth
me well ; but in respect that it is not in the court, it is
tedious.   As it is a spare life, look you, it fits my
humour well ; but as there is no more plenty in it, it
goes much against my stomach.   Hast any philosophy
in thee, shepherd ?   22
Cor. No more, but that I know, the more one
sickens, the worse at ease he is ; and that he that
wants money, means, and content, is without three
good friends ; that the property of rain is to wet, and
fire to burn ; that good pasture makes fat sheep, and
that a great cause of the night is lack of the sun ; that
he that hath learned no wit by nature nor art may
complain of good breeding, or comes of a very dull
kindred.   31
Touch. Such a one is a natural philosopher. Wast
ever in court, shepherd ?
Cor. No, truly.
Touch. Then thou art damned.
Cor. Nay, I hope,—

Touch. Truly, thou art damned, like an ill-roasted egg, all on one side.

Cor. For not being at court? Your reason.   39

Touch. Why, if thou never wast at court, thou never saw'st good manners; if thou never saw'st good manners, then thy manners must be wicked; and wickedness is sin, and sin is damnation. Thou art in a parlous state, shepherd.

Cor. Not a whit, Touchstone: those that are good manners at the court are as ridiculous in the country, as the behaviour of the country is most mockable at the court. You told me, you salute not at the court, but you kiss your hands: that courtesy would be uncleanly, if courtiers were shepherds.   50

Touch. Instance, briefly; come, instance.

Cor. Why, we are still handling our ewes, and their fells, you know, are greasy.

Touch. Why, do not your courtier's hands sweat? and is not the grease of a mutton as wholesome as the sweat of a man? Shallow, shallow. A better instance, I say; come.

Cor. Besides, our hands are hard.

Touch. Your lips will feel them the sooner: shallow again. A more sounder instance; come.   60

Cor. And they are often tarred over with the surgery of our sheep; and would you have us kiss tar? The courtier's hands are perfumed with civet.

Touch. Most shallow man! Thou worms-meat, in respect of a good piece of flesh, indeed!—Learn of the wise, and perpend: civet is of a baser birth than tar; the very uncleanly flux of a cat. Mend the instance, shepherd.

Cor. You have too courtly a wit for me: I'll rest.

Touch. Wilt thou rest damned? God help thee, shallow man! God make incision in thee! thou art raw.   72

Cor. Sir, I am a true labourer: I earn that I eat, get that I wear; owe no man hate, envy no man's happiness; glad of other men's good, content with my harm; and the greatest of my pride is, to see my ewes graze and my lambs suck.

Touch. That is another simple sin in you, to bring the ewes and the rams together, and to offer to get your living by the copulation of cattle; to be bawd to a bell-wether, and to betray a she-lamb of a twelvemonth, to a crooked-pated, old, cuckoldly ram, out of all reasonable match. If thou be'st not damned for this, the devil himself will have no shepherds: I cannot see else how thou shouldst scape.

Cor. Here comes young Master Ganymede, my new mistress's brother.

Enter ROSALIND, *reading a paper.*

Ros.   From the east to western Ind,
        No jewel is like Rosalind.
        Her worth, being mounted on the wind,   90
        Through all the world bears Rosalind.
        All the pictures, fairest lin'd,
        Are but black to Rosalind.
        Let no face be kept in mind,
        But the fair of Rosalind.

Touch. I'll rhyme you so eight years together, dinners, and suppers, and sleeping hours excepted: it is the right butter-women's rank to market.

Ros. Out, fool!

Touch. For a taste:—   100

        "If a hart do lack a hind,
        Let him seek out Rosalind.
        If the cat will after kind,
        So, be sure, will Rosalind.
        Winter garments must be lin'd,
        So must slender Rosalind.
        They that reap must sheaf and bind,
        Then to cart with Rosalind.
        Sweetest nut hath sourest rind,
        Such a nut is Rosalind.   110
        He that sweetest rose will find,
        Must find love's prick, and Rosalind."

This is the very false gallop of verses: why do you infect yourself with them?

Ros. Peace! you dull fool: I found them on a tree.

Touch. Truly, the tree yields bad fruit.

Ros. I'll graff it with you, and then I shall graff it with a medlar: then it will be the earliest fruit i' the country; for you'll be rotten ere you be half ripe, and that's the right virtue of the medlar.   120

Touch. You have said; but whether wisely or no, let the forest judge.

Ros. Peace!
Here comes my sister, reading: stand aside.

Touch. "This is the very false gallop of verses."

Enter CELIA, *reading a paper.*

Cel. Why should this a desert be?
        For it is unpeopled? No;
        Tongues I'll hang on every tree,
        That shall civil sayings show.
        Some, how brief the life of man
        Runs his erring pilgrimage,   130
        That the stretching of a span
        Buckles in his sum of age.
        Some, of violated vows
        'Twixt the souls of friend and friend:
        But upon the fairest boughs,
        Or at every sentence' end,
        Will I Rosalinda write;
        Teaching all that read, to know
        The quintessence of every sprite
        Heaven would in little show.   140
        Therefore Heaven Nature charg'd
        That one body should be fill'd
        With all graces wide enlarg'd:
        Nature presently distill'd
        Helen's cheek, but not her heart,
        Cleopatra's majesty,
        Atalanta's better part,
        Sad Lucretia's modesty.
        Thus Rosalind of many parts
        By heavenly synod was devis'd,   150
        Of many faces, eyes, and hearts,
        To have the touches dearest priz'd.
        Heaven would that she these gifts should have,
        And I to live and die her slave.

Ros. O most gentle Jupiter!—what tedious homily of love have you wearied your parishioners withal, and never cried, "Have patience, good people!"

Cel. How now? back-friends.—Shepherd, go off a little:—go with him, sirrah.   159

Touch. Come, shepherd, let us make an honourable retreat; though not with bag and baggage, yet with scrip and scrippage.

              [*Exeunt* CORIN *and* TOUCHSTONE.

Cel. Didst thou hear these verses?

Ros. O! yes, I heard them all, and more too; for some of them had in them more feet than the verses would bear.

Cel. That's no matter: the feet might bear the verses.

Ros. Ay, but the feet were lame, and could not bear themselves without the verse, and therefore stood lamely in the verse. 171

Cel. But didst thou hear without wondering, how thy name should be hanged and carved upon these trees?

Ros. I was seven of the nine days out of the wonder, before you came; for look here what I found on a palm-tree: I was never so be-rhymed since Pythagoras' time, that I was an Irish rat, which I can hardly remember.

Cel. Trow you, who hath done this? 180

Ros. Is it a man?

Cel. And a chain, that you once wore, about his neck. Change you colour?

Ros. I pr'ythee, who?

Cel. O Lord, Lord! it is a hard matter for friends to meet; but mountains may be removed with earth-quakes, and so encounter.

Ros. Nay, but who is it?

Cel. Is it possible?

Ros. Nay, I pr'ythee, now, with most petitionary vehemence, tell me who it is. 191

Cel. O, wonderful, wonderful, and most wonderful wonderful! and yet again wonderful! and after that, out of all whooping!

Ros. Good my complexion! dost thou think, though I am caparison'd like a man, I have a doublet and hose in my disposition? One inch of delay more is a South Sea of discovery; I pr'ythee, tell me, who is it, quickly, and speak apace. I would thou couldst stammer, that thou mightst pour this concealed man out of thy mouth, as wine comes out of a narrow-mouth'd bottle; either too much at once, or none at all. I pr'ythee, take the cork out of thy mouth, that I may drink thy tidings.

Cel. So you may put a man in your belly.

Ros. Is he of God's making? What manner of man? Is his head worth a hat, or his chin worth a beard?

Cel. Nay, he hath but a little beard.

Ros. Why, God will send more, if the man will be thankful. Let me stay the growth of his beard, if thou delay me not the knowledge of his chin. 211

Cel. It is young Orlando, that tripp'd up the wrestler's heels and your heart, both in an instant.

Ros. Nay, but the devil take mocking: speak sad brow, and true maid.

Cel. I' faith, coz, 't is he.

Ros. Orlando?

Cel. Orlando. 218

Ros. Alas the day! what shall I do with my doublet and hose?—What did he, when thou saw'st him? What said he? How look'd he? Wherein went he? What makes he here? Did he ask for me? Where remains he? How parted he with thee, and when shalt thou see him again? Answer me in one word.

Cel. You must borrow me Gargantua's mouth first: 't is a word too great for any mouth of this age's size. To say, ay, and no, to these particulars is more than to answer in a catechism.

Ros. But doth he know that I am in this forest, and in man's apparel? Looks he as freshly as he did the day he wrestled? 231

Cel. It is as easy to count atomies, as to resolve the propositions of a lover: but take a taste of my finding him, and relish it with good observance. I found him under a tree, like a dropped acorn.

Ros. It may well be call'd Jove's tree, when it drops forth such fruit.

Cel. Give me audience, good madam.

Ros. Proceed.

Cel. There lay he, stretch'd along like a wounded knight. 241

Ros. Though it be pity to see such a sight, it well becomes the ground.

Cel. Cry, holla! to thy tongue, I pr'ythee; it curvets unseasonably. He was furnish'd like a hunter.

Ros. O ominous! he comes to kill my heart.

Cel. I would sing my song without a burden: thou bring'st me out of tune.

Ros. Do you not know I am a woman? when I think, I must speak. Sweet, say on. 250

Cel. You bring me out.—Soft! comes he not here?

Ros. 'T is he: slink by, and note him.

[ROSALIND *and* CELIA *retire.*

Enter ORLANDO *and* JAQUES.

Jaq. I thank you for your company; but, good faith, I had as lief have been myself alone.

Orl. And so had I; but yet, for fashion sake, I thank you too for your society.

Jaq. Good bye, you: let's meet as little as we can.

Orl. I do desire we may be better strangers.

Jaq. I pray you, mar no more trees with writing love-songs in their barks. 261

Orl. I pray you, mar no more of my verses with reading them ill-favouredly.

Jaq. Rosalind is your love's name?

Orl. Yes, just.

Jaq. I do not like her name.

Orl. There was no thought of pleasing you, when she was christened.

Jaq. What stature is she of?

Orl. Just as high as my heart. 270

Jaq. You are full of pretty answers. Have you not been acquainted with goldsmiths' wives, and conn'd them out of rings?

Orl. Not so; but I answer you right painted cloth, from whence you have studied your questions.

Jaq. You have a nimble wit: I think 't was made of Atalanta's heels. Will you sit down with me? and we two will rail against our mistress the world, and all our misery.

Orl. I will chide no breather in the world, but my-self, against whom I know most faults. 281

Jaq. The worst fault you have, is to be in love.

Orl. 'T is a fault I will not change for your best virtue. I am weary of you.

Jaq. By my troth, I was seeking for a fool when I found you.

Orl. He is drown'd in the brook: look but in, and you shall see him.

Jaq. There I shall see mine own figure.

Orl. Which I take to be either a fool, or a cypher. 290

Jaq. I'll tarry no longer with you. Farewell, good Signior Love.

Orl. I am glad of your departure. Adieu, good Monsieur Melancholy.

[*Exit* JAQUES.—ROSALIND *and* CELIA *come forward.*

Ros. [*Aside to* CELIA.] I will speak to him like a saucy lackey, and under that habit play the knave with him.—Do you hear, forester?

Orl. Very well: what would you?

Ros. I pray you, what is 't o'clock?

Orl. You should ask me, what time o' day: there's no clock in the forest. 301

Ros. Then, there is no true lover in the forest; else sighing every minute, and groaning every hour, would detect the lazy foot of Time as well as a clock.

Orl. And why not the swift foot of Time? had not that been as proper?

Ros. By no means, sir. Time travels in divers paces with divers persons. I'll tell you, who Time ambles withal, who Time trots withal, who Time gallops withal, and who he stands still withal. 310

Orl. I pr'ythee, who doth he trot withal?

Ros. Marry, he trots hard with a young maid, be-tween the contract of her marriage, and the day it is solemnised: if the interim be but a se'nnight, Time's pace is so hard that it seems the length of seven years.

Orl. Who ambles Time withal?

Ros. With a priest that lacks Latin, and a rich man that hath not the gout; for the one sleeps easily, because he cannot study; and the other lives merrily, because he feels no pain: the one lacking the burden of lean and wasteful learning; the other knowing no burden of heavy tedious penury. These Time ambles withal. 323

Orl. Who doth he gallop withal?

Ros. With a thief to the gallows; for though he go

as softly as foot can fall, he thinks himself too soon there.

Orl. Who stays it still withal?

Ros. With lawyers in the vacation; for they sleep between term and term, and then they perceive not how Time moves. 331

Orl. Where dwell you, pretty youth?

Ros. With this shepherdess, my sister; here in the skirts of the forest, like fringe upon a petticoat.

Orl. Are you native of this place?

Ros. As the cony, that you see dwell where she is kindled.

Orl. Your accent is something finer than you could purchase in so removed a dwelling. 339

Ros. I have been told so of many: but, indeed, an old religious uncle of mine taught me to speak, who was in his youth an inland man; one that knew courtship too well, for there he fell in love. I have heard him read many lectures against it; and I thank God, I am not a woman, to be touched with so many giddy offences, as he hath generally taxed their whole sex withal.

Orl. Can you remember any of the principal evils that he laid to the charge of women? 349

Ros. There were none principal: they were all like one another, as half-pence are; every one fault seeming monstrous, till its fellow fault came to match it.

Orl. I pr'ythee, recount some of them.

Ros. No; I will not cast away my physic but on those that are sick. There is a man haunts the forest, that abuses our young plants with carving Rosalind on their barks; hangs odes upon hawthorns, and elegies on brambles; all, forsooth, deifying the name of Rosalind: if I could meet that fancy-monger, I would give him some good counsel, for he seems to have the quotidian of love upon him. 361

Orl. I am he that is so love-shaked. I pray you, tell me your remedy.

Ros. There is none of my uncle's marks upon you: he taught me how to know a man in love; in which cage of rushes, I am sure, you are not prisoner.

Orl. What were his marks?

Ros. A lean cheek, which you have not; a blue eye, and sunken, which you have not; an unquestionable spirit, which you have not; a beard neglected, which you have not:—but I pardon you for that, for simply, your having in beard is a younger brother's revenue.— Then, your hose should be ungartered, your bonnet unbanded, your sleeve unbuttoned, your shoe untied, and everything about you demonstrating a careless desolation. But you are no such man: you are rather point-device in your accoutrements; as loving yourself, than seeming the lover of any other.

Orl. Fair youth, I would I could make thee believe I love. 380

Ros. Me believe it? you may as soon make her that you love believe it; which, I warrant, she is apter to do, than to confess she does; that is one of the points in the which women still give the lie 'to their consciences. But, in good sooth, are you he that hangs the verses on the trees, wherein Rosalind is so admired?

Orl. I swear to thee, youth, by the white hand of Rosalind, I am that he, that unfortunate he.

Ros. But are you so much in love as your rhymes speak? 391

Orl. Neither rhyme nor reason can express how much.

Ros. Love is merely a madness; and, I tell you, deserves as well a dark house and a whip as madmen do; and the reason why they are not so punished and cured, is, that the lunacy is so ordinary, that the whippers are in love too. Yet I profess curing it by counsel.

Orl. Did you ever cure any so? 400

Ros. Yes, one; and in this manner. He was to imagine me his love, his mistress; and I set him every day to woo me: at which time would I, being but a moonish youth, grieve, be effeminate, changeable, longing, and liking; proud, fantastical, apish, shallow, inconstant, full of tears, full of smiles; for every passion something, and for no passion truly anything,

as boys and women are, for the most part, cattle of this colour; would now like him, now loathe him; then entertain him, then forswear him; now weep for him, then spit at him; that I drave my suitor from his mad humour of love, to a living humour of madness, which was, to forswear the full stream of the world, and to live in a nook merely monastic. And thus I cured him; and this way will I take upon me to wash your liver as clean as a sound sheep's heart, that there shall not be one spot of love in 't.

Ros. "There is none of my uncle's marks upon you.'

Orl. I would not be cured, youth.

Ros. I would cure you, if you would but call me Rosalind, and come every day to my cote, and woo me.

Orl. Now, by the faith of my love, I will. Tell me where it is. 422

Ros. Go with me to it, and I 'll show it you; and, by the way, you shall tell me where in the forest you live. Will you go?

Orl. With all my heart, good youth.

Ros. Nay, you must call me Rosalind.—Come, sister, will you go? [*Exeunt.*

SCENE III.—Another Part of the Forest.

Enter TOUCHSTONE *and* AUDREY; JAQUES *behind, observing them.*

Touch. Come apace, good Audrey: I will fetch up your goats, Audrey. And how, Audrey? am I the man yet? doth my simple feature content you?

Aud. Your features? Lord warrant us! what features?

Touch. I am here with thee and thy goats, as the most capricious poet, honest Ovid, was among the Goths.

Jaq. [*Aside.*] O knowledge ill-inhabited, worse than Jove in a thatched house! 10

Touch. When a man's verses cannot be understood, nor a man's good wit seconded with the forward child Understanding, it strikes a man more dead than a great reckoning in a little room.—Truly, I would the gods had made thee poetical.

Aud. I do not know what poetical is. Is it honest in deed and word? Is it a true thing?

Touch. No, truly, for the truest poetry is the most feigning; and lovers are given to poetry, and what they swear in poetry, may be said, as lovers they do feign.   21·
Aud. Do you wish then, that the gods had made me poetical?
Touch. I do, truly; for thou swear'st to me, thou art honest: now, if thou wert a poet, I might have some hope thou didst feign.
Aud. Would you not have me honest?
Touch. No, truly, unless thou wert hard-favour'd, for honesty coupled to beauty, is to have honey a sauce to sugar.   30
Jaq. [*Aside.*] A material fool.
Aud. Well, I am not fair, and therefore I pray the gods make me honest.
Touch. Truly, and to cast away honesty upon a foul slut were to put good meat into an unclean dish.
Aud. I am not a slut, though I thank the gods I am foul.
Touch. Well, praised be the gods for thy foulness: sluttishness may come hereafter. But be it as it may be, I will marry thee; and to that end, I have been with Sir Oliver Mar-text, the vicar of the next village, who hath promised to meet me in this place of the forest, and to couple us.   43
Jaq. [*Aside.*] I would fain see this meeting.
Aud. Well, the gods give us joy!
Touch. Amen. A man may, if he were of a fearful heart, stagger in this attempt; for here we have no temple but the wood, no assembly but horn-beasts. But what though? Courage! As horns are odious, they are necessary. It is said,—many a man knows no end of his goods: right; many a man has good horns, and knows no end of them. Well, that is the dowry of his wife: 't is none of his own getting. Horns? Even so.—Poor men alone?—No, no; the noblest deer hath them as huge as the rascal. Is the single man therefore blessed? No: as a walled town is more worthier than a village, so is the forehead of a married man more honourable than the bare brow of a bachelor; and by how much defence is better than no skill, by so much is a horn more precious than to want. Here comes Sir Oliver.   61

Enter Sir OLIVER MAR-TEXT.

Sir Oliver Mar-text, you are well met: will you despatch us here under this tree, or shall we go with you to your chapel?
Sir Oli. Is there none here to give the woman?
Touch. I will not take her on gift of any man.
Sir Oli. Truly, she must be given, or the marriage is not lawful.
Jaq. [*Coming forward.*] Proceed, proceed: I'll give her.   70
Touch. Good even, good Master What-ye-call 't: how do you, sir? You are very well met: God 'ild you for your last company. I am very glad to see you.—Even a toy in hand here, sir.—Nay; pray, be cover'd.
Jaq. Will you be married, motley?
Touch. As the ox hath his bow, sir, the horse his curb, and the falcon her bells, so man hath his desires; and as pigeons bill, so wedlock would be nibbling.   79
Jaq. And will you, being a man of your breeding, be married under a bush, like a beggar? Get you to church, and have a good priest that can tell you what marriage is: this fellow will but join you together as they join wainscot; then one of you will prove a shrunk panel, and, like green timber, warp, warp.
Touch. [*Aside.*] I am not in the mind but I were better to be married of him than of another; for he is not like to marry me well, and not being well married, it will be a good excuse for me hereafter to leave my wife.   90
Jaq. Go thou with me, and let me counsel thee.
Touch. Come, sweet Audrey:
We must be married, or we must live in bawdry.
Farewell, good Master Oliver! Not,—
                O sweet Oliver!
                O brave Oliver!
        Leave me not behind thee:

but,—
                Wind away,
                Begone, I say,   100
        I will not to wedding with thee.
[*Exeunt* JAQUES, TOUCHSTONE, *and* AUDREY.
Sir Oli. 'T is no matter: ne'er a fantastical knave of them all shall flout me out of my calling.   [*Exit.*

SCENE IV.—Another Part of the Forest. Before a Cottage.

Enter ROSALIND *and* CELIA.

Ros. Never talk to me: I will weep.
Cel. Do, I pr'ythee; but yet have the grace to consider, that tears do not become a man.
Ros. But have I not cause to weep?
Cel. As good cause as one would desire: therefore weep.
Ros. His very hair is of the dissembling colour.
Cel. Something browner than Judas's. Marry, his kisses are Judas's own children.
Ros. I' faith, his hair is of a good colour.   10
Cel. An excellent colour: your chestnut was ever the only colour.
Ros. And his kissing is as full of sanctity as the touch of holy bread.
Cel. He hath bought a pair of cast lips of Diana: a nun of winter's sisterhood kisses not more religiously; the very ice of chastity is in them.
Ros. But why did he swear he would come this morning, and comes not?
Cel. Nay, certainly, there is no truth in him.   20
Ros. Do you think so?
Cel. Yes: I think he is not a pick-purse, nor a horse-stealer; but for his verity in love, I do think him as concave as a covered goblet, or a worm-eaten nut.
Ros. Not true in love?
Cel. Yes, when he is in; but I think he is not in.
Ros. You have heard him swear downright, he was.
Cel. *Was* is not *is :* besides, the oath of a lover is no stronger than the word of a tapster; they are both the confirmers of false reckonings. He attends here in the forest on the duke your father.   31
Ros. I met the duke yesterday, and had much question with him. He asked me, of what parentage I was: I told him, of as good as he; so he laughed, and let me go. But what talk we of fathers, when there is such a man as Orlando?
Cel. O, that's a brave man! he writes brave verses, speaks brave words, swears brave oaths, and breaks them bravely, quite traverse, athwart the heart of his lover; as a puny tilter, that spurs his horse but on one side, breaks his staff like a noble goose. But all's brave, that youth mounts, and folly guides.—Who comes here?   43

Enter CORIN.

Cor. Mistress, and master, you have oft inquir'd
After the shepherd that complain'd of love,
Who you saw sitting by me on the turf,
Praising the proud disdainful shepherdess
That was his mistress.
Cel.   Well, and what of him?
Cor. If you will see a pageant truly play'd,
Between the pale complexion of true love,   50
And the red glow of scorn and proud disdain,
Go hence a little, and I shall conduct you,
If you will mark it.
Ros.   O! come, let us remove:
The sight of lovers feedeth those in love.—
Bring us to this sight, and you shall say
I'll prove a busy actor in their play.   [*Exeunt.*

SCENE V.—Another Part of the Forest.

Enter SILVIUS *and* PHEBE.

Sil. Sweet Phebe, do not scorn me; do not, Phebe;
Say that you love me not; but say not so
In bitterness. The common executioner.

Whose heart the accustom'd sight of death makes
   hard,
Falls not the axe upon the humbled neck,
But first begs pardon : will you sterner be
Than he that dies and lives by bloody drops ?

    Enter ROSALIND, CELIA, *and* CORIN, *behind.*

  Phe. I would not be thy executioner :
I fly thee, for I would not injure thee.
Thou tell'st me, there is murder in my mine eye :   10
'T is pretty, sure, and very probable,
That eyes—that are the frail'st and softest things,
Who shut their coward gates on atomies,—
Should be call'd tyrants, butchers, murderers !
Now I do frown on thee with all my heart ;
And if mine eyes can wound, now let them kill thee ;
Now counterfeit to swoon, why, now fall down ;
Or, if thou canst not, O, for shame, for shame !
Lie not, to say mine eyes are murderers.
Now show the wound mine eye hath made in thee : 20
Scratch thee but with a pin, and there remains
Some scar of it ; lean upon a rush,
The cicatrice and capable impressure
Thy palm some moment keeps, but now mine eyes,
Which I have darted at thee, hurt thee not,
Nor, I am sure, there is no force in eyes
That can do hurt.
  Sil.   O dear Phebe,
If ever (as that ever may be near)
You meet in some fresh cheek the power of fancy,
Then shall you know the wounds invisible   30
That love's keen arrows make.
  Phe.   But till that time
Come not thou near me ; and when that time comes,
Afflict me with thy mocks, pity me not,
As till that time I shall not pity thee.
  Ros. [*Advancing.*] And why, I pray you ? Who
       might be your mother,
That you insult, exult, and all at once,
Over the wretched ? What though you have no
      beauty
(As, by my faith, I see no more in you
Than without candle may go dark to bed),
Must you be therefore proud and pitiless ?   40
Why, what means this ? Why do you look on me ?
I see no more in you, than in the ordinary
Of nature's sale-work.—Od 's my little life !
I think she means to tangle my eyes too.
No, 'faith, proud mistress, hope not after it :
'T is not your inky brows, your black silk hair,
Your bugle eye-balls, nor your cheek of cream,
That can entame my spirits to your worship.—
You foolish shepherd, wherefore do you follow her,
Like foggy south, puffing with wind and rain ?   50
You are a thousand times a properer man,
Than she a woman : 't is such fools as you,
That make the world full of ill-favour'd children.
'T is not her glass, but you, that flatters her ;
And out of you she sees herself more proper,
Than any of her lineaments can show her.—
But, mistress, know yourself : down on your knees,
And thank Heaven, fasting, for a good man's love ;
For I must tell you friendly in your ear,
Sell when you can : you are not for all markets.   60
Cry the man mercy ; love him ; take his offer :
Foul is most foul, being foul to be a scoffer.
So, take her to thee, shepherd.—Fare you well.
  Phe. Sweet youth, I pray you, chide a year together.
I had rather hear you chide, than this man woo.
  Ros. He 's fallen in love with your foulness, and
she 'll fall in love with my anger. If it be so, as fast
as she answers thee with frowning looks, I 'll sauce
her with bitter words.—Why look you so upon me ?
  Phe. For no ill will I bear you.   70

  Ros. I pray you, do not fall in love with me,
For I am falser than vows made in wine :
Besides, I like you not.—If you will know my house,
'T is at the tuft of olives, here hard by.—
Will you go, sister ?—Shepherd, ply her hard.--
Come, sister.—Shepherdess, look on him better,
And be not proud : though all the world could see,
None could be so abus'd in sight as he.
Come, to our flock.
          [*Exeunt* ROSALIND, CELIA, *and* CORIN.
  Phe. Dead shepherd ! now I f'nd thy saw of might :
" Who ever lov'd, that lov'd not at first sight ?"   81
  Sil. Sweet Phebe,—
  Phe.   Ha ! what say'st thou, Silvius ?
  Sil. Sweet Phebe, pity me.
  Phe. Why, I am sorry for thee, gentle Silvius.
  Sil. Wherever sorrow is, relief would be :
If you do sorrow at my grief in love,
By giving love your sorrow and my grief
Were both extermin'd.
  Phe. Thou hast my love : is not that neighbourly ?
  Sil. I would have you.
  Phe.   Why, that were covetousness.   90
Silvius, the time was that I hated thee,
And yet it is not that I bear thee love ;
But since that thou canst talk of love so well,
Thy company, which erst was irksome to me,
I will endure, and I 'll employ thee too ;
But do not look for further recompense,
Than thine own gladness that thou art employ'd.
  Sil. So holy, and so perfect is my love,
And I in such a poverty of grace,
That I shall think it a most plenteous crop   100
To glean the broken ears after the man
That the main harvest reaps : loose now and then
A scatter'd smile, and that I 'll live upon.
  Phe. Know'st thou the youth that spoke to me ere-
      while ?
  Sil. Not very well ; but I have met him oft ;
And he hath bought the cottage, and the bounds,
That the old carlot once was master of.
  Phe. Think not I love him, though I ask for him.
'T is but a peevish boy :—yet he talks well :—
But what care I for words ? yet words do well,   110
When he that speaks them pleases those that hear.
It is a pretty youth :—not very pretty :—
But, sure, he 's proud ; and yet his pride becomes him.
He 'll make a proper man : the best thing in him
Is his complexion ; and faster than his tongue
Did make offence, his eye did heal it up.
He is not very tall ; yet for his years he 's tall.
His leg is but so so ; and yet 't is well.
There was a pretty redness in his lip ;
A little riper, and more lusty red   120
Than that mix'd in his cheek : 't was just the dif-
      ference
Betwixt the constant red, and mingled damask.
There be some women, Silvius, had they mark'd him
In parcels, as I did, would have gone near
To fall in love with him ; but, for my part,
I love him not, nor hate him not ; and yet
Have more cause to hate him than to love him :
For what had he to do to chide at me?
He said, mine eyes were black, and my hair black ;
And, now I am remember'd, scorn'd at me.   130
I marvel, why I answer'd not again :
But that 's all one ; omittance is no quittance.
I 'll write to him a very taunting letter.
And thou shalt bear it ; wilt thou, Silvius ?
  Sil. Phebe, with all my heart.
  Phe.   I 'll write it straight ;
The matter 's in my head, and in my heart :
I will be bitter with him, and passing short.
Go with me, Silvius.   [*Exeunt.*

ACT IV.

SCENE I.—The Forest of Arden.

Enter ROSALIND, CELIA, and JAQUES.

Jaques.
PR'YTHEE, pretty youth, let me be better acquainted with thee.

Ros. They say, you are a melancholy fellow.

Jaq. I am so: I do love it better than laughing.

Ros. Those that are in extremity of either are abominable fellows, and betray themselves to every modern censure worse than drunkards. 10

Jaq. Why, 't is good to be sad and say nothing.

Ros. Why then, 't is good to be a post.

Jaq. I have neither the scholar's melancholy, which is emulation; nor the musician's, which is fantastical; nor the courtier's, which is proud; nor the soldier's, which is ambitious; nor the lawyer's, which is politic; nor the lady's, which is nice; nor the lover's, which is all these; but it is a melancholy of mine own, compounded of many simples, extracted from many objects, and, indeed, the sundry contemplation of my travels; which, by often rumination, wraps me in a most humorous sadness. 23

Ros. A traveller! By my faith, you have great reason to be sad. I fear, you have sold your own lands, to see other men's; then, to have seen much, and to have nothing, is to have rich eyes and poor hands.

Jaq. Yes, I have gained my experience.

Ros. And your experience makes you sad. I had rather have a fool to make me merry, than experience to make me sad; and to travel for it too! 32

Enter ORLANDO.

Orl. Good day, and happiness, dear Rosalind.

Jaq. Nay, then, God be wi' you, an you talk in blank verse. [*Exit.*

Ros. Farewell, Monsieur Traveller. Look you lisp, and wear strange suits; disable all the benefits of your own country; be out of love with your nativity; and almost chide God for making you that countenance you are: or I will scarce think you have swam in a gondola.—Why, how now, Orlando! where have you been all this while? You a lover?—An you serve me such another trick, never come in my sight more.

Orl. My fair Rosalind, I come within an hour of my promise.

Ros. Break an hour's promise in love! He that will divide a minute into a thousand parts, and break but a part of the thousandth part of a minute in the affairs of love, it may be said of him, that Cupid hath clapped him o' the shoulder, but I 'll warrant him heart-whole. 52

Orl. Pardon me, dear Rosalind.

Ros. Nay, an you be so tardy, come no more in my sight: I had as lief be woo'd of a snail.

Orl. Of a snail?

Ros. Ay, of a snail; for though he comes slowly, he carries his house on his head, a better jointure, I think, than you make a woman. Besides, he brings his destiny with him. 60

Orl. What 's that?

Ros. Why, horns; which such as you are fain to be beholding to your wives for: but he comes armed in his fortune, and prevents the slander of his wife.

Orl. Virtue is no horn-maker, and my Rosalind is virtuous.

Ros. And I am your Rosalind.

Cel. It pleases him to call you so; but he hath a Rosalind of a better leer than you.

Ros. Come, woo me, woo me; for now I am in a holiday humour, and like enough to consent.—What would you say to me now, an I were your very very Rosalind?

Orl. I would kiss before I spoke.

Ros. Nay, you were better speak first; and when you were gravelled for lack of matter, you might take occasion to kiss. Very good orators, when they are out, they will spit; and for lovers, lacking (God warn us!) matter, the cleanliest shift is to kiss.

Orl. How if the kiss be denied? 80

Ros. Then she puts you to entreaty, and there begins new matter.

Orl. Who could be out, being before his beloved mistress?

Ros. Marry, that should you, if I were your mistress, or I should think my honesty ranker than my wit.

Orl. What, of my suit?

Ros. Not out of your apparel, and yet out of your suit. Am not I your Rosalind? 90

Orl. I take some joy to say you are, because I would be talking of her.

Ros. Well, in her person, I say—I will not have you.

Orl. Then, in mine own person, I die.

Ros. No, 'faith, die by attorney. The poor world is almost six thousand years old, and in all this time there was not any man died in his own person, *videlicet,* in a love-cause. Troilus had his brains dashed out with a Grecian club; yet he did what he could to die before, and he is one of the patterns of love. Leander, he would have lived many a fair year, though Hero had turned nun, if it had not been for a hot midsummer-night; for, good youth, he went but forth to wash him in the Hellespont, and, being taken with the cramp, was drowned, and the foolish chroniclers of that age found it was—Hero of Sestos. But these are all lies: men have died from time to time, and worms have eaten them, but not for love.

Orl. I would not have my right Rosalind of this mind, for, I protest, her frown might kill me. 110

Ros. By this hand, it will not kill a fly. But come, now I will be your Rosalind in a more coming-on disposition; and ask me what you will, I will grant it.

Orl. Then love me, Rosalind.

Ros. Yes, 'faith will I; Fridays, and Saturdays, and all.

Orl. And wilt thou have me?

Ros. Ay, and twenty such.

Orl. What say'st thou?

Ros. Are you not good? 120

Orl. I hope so.

Ros. Why then, can one desire too much of a good thing?—Come, sister, you shall be the priest, and marry us.—Give me your hand, Orlando.—What do you say, sister?

Orl. Pray thee, marry us.
Cel. I cannot say the words.
Ros. You must begin,—" Will you, Orlando,"—
Cel. Go to.—Will you, Orlando, have to wife this
Rosalind?   130
Orl. I will.
Ros. Ay, but when?
Orl. Why, now, as fast as she can marry us.
Ros. Then you must say,—" I take thee, Rosalind,
for wife."
Orl. I take thee, Rosalind, for wife.

Cel. " Will you, Orlando, have to wife this Rosalind?"

Ros. I might ask you for your commission; but,—I
do take thee, Orlando, for my husband:—there's a
girl goes before the priest; and certainly, a woman's
thought runs before her actions.   140
Orl. So do all thoughts: they are winged.
Ros. Now tell me how long you would have her,
after you have possessed her.
Orl. For ever, and a day.
Ros. Say a day, without the ever. No, no, Orlando:
men are April when they woo, December when they
wed; maids are May when they are maids, but the
sky changes when they are wives. I will be more
jealous of thee than a Barbary cock-pigeon over his
hen; more clamorous than a parrot against rain;
more new-fangled than an ape; more giddy in my
desires than a monkey: I will weep for nothing, like
Diana in the fountain, and I will do that when you
are disposed to be merry; I will laugh like a hyen,
and that when thou art inclined to sleep.
Orl. But will my Rosalind do so?
Ros. By my life, she will do as I do.
Orl. O! but she is wise.   158
Ros. Or else she could not have the wit to do this:
the wiser, the waywarder. Make the doors upon a
woman's wit, and it will out at the casement; shut
that, and 't will out at the key-hole; stop that, 't will
fly with the smoke out at the chimney.
Orl. A man that had a wife with such a wit, he
might say,—" Wit, whither wilt?"
Ros. Nay, you might keep that check for it, till you
met your wife's wit going to your neighbour's bed.
Orl. And what wit could wit have to excuse that?
Ros. Marry, to say,—she came to seek you there.

You shall never take her without her answer, unless
you take her without her tongue: O! that woman
that cannot make her fault her husband's occasion,
let her never nurse her child herself, for she will breed
it like a fool.
Orl. For these two hours, Rosalind, I will leave
thee.
Ros. Alas, dear love! I cannot lack thee two hours.
Orl. I must attend the duke at dinner: by two
o'clock I will be with thee again.   179
Ros. Ay, go your ways, go your ways.—I knew
what you would prove; my friends told me as much,
and I thought no less:—that flattering tongue of
yours won me:—'t is but one cast away, and so,—
come, death!—Two o'clock is your hour?
Orl. Ay, sweet Rosalind.
Ros. By my troth, and in good earnest, and so God
mend me, and by all pretty oaths that are not dangerous, if you break one jot of your promise, or come
one minute behind your hour, I will think you the
most pathetical break-promise, and the most hollow
lover, and the most unworthy of her you call Rosalind,
that may be chosen out of the gross band of the un-
faithful. Therefore, beware my censure, and keep
your promise.
Orl. With no less religion, than if thou wert indeed
my Rosalind: so, adieu.
Ros. Well, Time is the old justice that examines all
such offenders, and let Time try. Adieu.   198
                                        [*Exit* ORLANDO.
Cel. You have simply misused our sex in your love-
prate. We must have your doublet and hose plucked
over your head, and show the world what the bird
hath done to her own nest.
Ros. O! coz, coz, coz, my pretty little coz, that thou
didst know how many fathom deep I am in love!
But I cannot be sounded: my affection hath an unknown bottom, like the bay of Portugal.
Cel. Or, rather, bottomless; that as fast as you
pour affection in, it runs out.   208
Ros. No; that same wicked bastard of Venus, that
was begot of thought, conceived of spleen, and born
of madness, that blind rascally boy, that abuses every
one's eyes, because his own are out, let him be judge
how deep I am in love.—I'll tell thee, Aliena, I cannot
be out of the sight of Orlando. I'll go find a shadow,
and sigh till he come.
Cel. And I'll sleep.   [*Exeunt.*

SCENE II.—Another Part of the Forest.

Enter JAQUES *and Lords, like foresters.*

Jaq. Which is he that killed the deer?
1 Lord. Sir, it was I.
Jaq. Let's present him to the duke, like a Roman
conqueror; and it would do well to set the deer's
horns upon his head for a branch of victory.—Have
you no song, forester, for this purpose?
2 Lord. Yes, sir.
Jaq. Sing it: 't is no matter how it be in tune, so it
make noise enough.

SONG.

What shall he have, that kill'd the deer?   10
His leather skin, and horns to wear.
   Then sing him home.
Take thou no scorn, to wear the horn;
It was a crest ere thou wast born.
   Thy father's father wore it,
   And thy father bore it:
The horn, the horn, the lusty horn,
Is not a thing to laugh to scorn.   [*Exeunt.*

SCENE III.—Another Part of the Forest.

Enter ROSALIND *and* CELIA.

Ros. How say you now? Is it not past two o'clock?
and here much Orlando!
Cel. I warrant you, with pure love, and troubled

brain, he hath ta'en his bow and arrows, and is gone
forth—to sleep. Look, who comes here.

Enter SILVIUS.

Sil. My errand is to you, fair youth.—
My gentle Phebe did bid me give you this:
       [Giving a letter.
I know not the contents; but, as I guess
By the stern brow, and waspish action,
Which she did use as she was writing of it, 10
It bears an angry tenor. Pardon me,
I am but as a guiltless messenger.
 Ros. Patience herself would startle at this letter,
And play the swaggerer: bear this, bear all.
She says, I am not fair; that I lack manners;
She calls me proud, and that she could not love me,
Were man as rare as phœnix. Od's my will!
Her love is not the hare that I do hunt:
Why writes she so to me?—Well, shepherd, well;
This is a letter of your own device. 20
 Sil. No, I protest; I know not the contents:
Phebe did write it.
 Ros.   Come, come, you are a fool,
And turn'd into the extremity of love.
I saw her hand: she has a leathern hand,
A freestone-colour'd hand: I verily did think
That her old gloves were on, but 't was her hands:
She has a housewife's hand; but that's no matter.
I say, she never did invent this letter;
This is a man's invention, and his hand.
 Sil. Sure, it is hers. 30
 Ros. Why, 't is a boisterous and a cruel style,
A style for challengers: why, she defies me,
Like Turk to Christian. Woman's gentle brain
Could not drop forth such giant-rude invention,
Such Ethiop words, blacker in their effect
Than in their countenance.—Will you hear the letter?
 Sil. So please you; for I never heard it yet,
Yet heard too much of Phebe's cruelty.
 Ros. She Phebes me. Mark how the tyrant writes.
 " Art thou god to shepherd turn'd, 40
  That a maiden's heart hath burn'd?"—
Can a woman rail thus?
 Sil. Call you this railing?
 Ros. " Why, thy godhead laid apart,
  Warr'st thou with a woman's heart?"
Did you ever hear such railing?—
 " Whiles the eye of man did woo me,
  That could do no vengeance to me."—
Meaning me a beast.—
 " If the scorn of your bright eyne 50
Have power to raise such love in mine,
Alack! in me what strange effect
Would they work in mild aspect?
Whiles you chid me, I did love;
How then might your prayers move?
He that brings this love to thee,
Little knows this love in me:
And by him seal up thy mind;
Whether that thy youth and kind
Will the faithful offer take 60
Of me, and all that I can make;
Or else by him my love deny,
And then I'll study how to die."
 Sil. Call you this chiding?
 Cel. Alas, poor shepherd!
 Ros. Do you pity him? no; he deserves no pity.—
Wilt thou love such a woman?—What, to make thee
an instrument, and play false strains upon thee? not
to be endured!—Well, go your way to her, (for I see,
love hath made a tame snake,) and say this to
her:—that if she love me, I charge her to love thee;
if she will not, I will never have her, unless thou
entreat for her.—If you be a true lover, hence, and
not a word, for here comes more company.
       [Exit SILVIUS.

Enter OLIVER.

 Oli. Good morrow, fair ones. Pray you, if you
  know,
Where in the purlieus of this forest stands
A sheepcote, fenc'd about with olive-trees?
 Cel. West of this place, down in the neighbour
  bottom:
The rank of osiers, by the murmuring stream,
Left on your right hand, brings you to the place. 80
But at this hour the house doth keep itself;
There's none within.
 Oli. If that an eye may profit by a tongue,
Then should I know you by description;
Such garments, and such years:—" The boy is fair,
Of female favour, and bestows himself
Like a ripe sister: the woman low,
And browner than her brother." Are not you
The owner of the house I did inquire for?
 Cel. It is no boast, being ask'd, to say, we are. 90
 Oli. Orlando doth commend him to you both;
And to that youth, he calls his Rosalind,
He sends this bloody napkin. Are you he?
 Ros. I am. What must we understand by this?
 Oli. Some of my shame; if you will know of me,
What man I am, and how, and why, and where
This handkercher was stain'd.
 Cel.   I pray you, tell it.
 Oli. When last the young Orlando parted from
  you,
He left a promise to return again
Within an hour; and, pacing through the forest, 100
Chewing the food of sweet and bitter fancy,
Lo, what befell! he threw his eye aside,
And, mark, what object did present itself!
Under an old oak, whose boughs were moss'd with
  age,
And high top bald with dry antiquity,
A wretched ragged man, o'ergrown with hair,
Lay sleeping on his back: about his neck
A green and gilded snake had wreath'd itself,
Who with her head, nimble in threats, approach'd
The opening of his mouth: but suddenly, 110
Seeing Orlando, it unlink'd itself,
And with indented glides did slip away
Into a bush; under which bush's shade
A lioness, with udders all drawn dry,
Lay couching, head on ground, with catlike watch,
When that the sleeping man should stir; for 't is
The royal disposition of that beast,
To prey on nothing that doth seem as dead.
This seen, Orlando did approach the man,
And found it was his brother, his elder brother. 120
 Cel. O! I have heard him speak of that same
  brother;
And he did render him the most unnatural
That liv'd 'mongst men.
 Oli.   And well he might so do,
For well I know he was unnatural.
 Ros. But, to Orlando.—Did he leave him there,
Food to the suck'd and hungry lioness?
 Oli. Twice did he turn his back, and purpos'd so;
But kindness, nobler ever than revenge,
And nature, stronger than his just occasion,
Made him give battle to the lioness, 130
Who quickly fell before him: in which hurtling
From miserable slumber I awak'd.
 Cel. Are you his brother?
 Ros.   Was it you he rescu'd?
 Cel. Was 't you that did so oft contrive to kill
  him?
 Oli. 'T was I; but 't is not I. I do not shame
To tell you what I was, since my conversion
So sweetly tastes, being the thing I am.
 Ros. But, for the bloody napkin?
 Oli.   By-and-by.
When from the first to last, betwixt us two,
Tears our recountments had most kindly bath'd, 140
As, how I came into that desert place:—
In brief, he led me to the gentle duke,
Who gave him fresh array, and entertainment,
Committing me unto my brother's love:
Who led me instantly unto his cave,
There stripp'd himself; and here, upon his arm,
The lioness had torn some flesh away,
Which all this while had bled; and now he fainted,
And cried, in fainting, upon Rosalind.
Brief, I recover'd him, bound up his wound; 150

And, after some small space, being strong at heart,
He sent me hither, stranger as I am,

Oli. "He sent me hither, stranger as I am,
To tell this story, that you might excuse
His broken promise."

To tell this story, that you might excuse
His broken promise; and to give this napkin,

Dy'd in his blood, unto the shepherd youth
That he in sport doth call his Rosalind.

[ROSALIND *swoons.*

Cel. Why, how now, Ganymede? sweet Ganymede!

Oli. Many will swoon when they do look on
blood.

Cel. There is more in it.—Cousin!—Ganymede!

Oli. Look, he recovers. 160

Ros. I would I were at home.

Cel. We 'll lead you thither.—
I pray you, will you take him by the arm?

Oli. Be of good cheer, youth.—You a man? You
lack a man's heart.

Ros. I do so, I confess it. Ah, sirrah! a body
would think this was well counterfeited. I pray
you, tell your brother hôw well I counterfeited.
Heigh-ho!—

Oli. This was not counterfeit: there is too great
testimony in your complexion, that it was a passion of
earnest. 171

Ros. Counterfeit, I assure you.

Oli. Well then, take a good heart, and counterfeit
to be a man.

Ros. So I do; but, i' faith, I should have been a
woman by right.

Cel. Come; you look paler and paler: pray you,
draw homewards.—Good sir, go with us.

Oli. That will I, for I must bear answer back,
How you excuse my brother, Rosalind. 180

Ros. I shall devise something. But, I pray you,
commend my counterfeiting to him.—Will you go?

[*Exeunt.*

ACT V.

SCENE I.—The Forest of Arden.

Enter TOUCHSTONE *and* AUDREY.

Touchstone.

WE shall find a time, Audrey: patience,
gentle Audrey.

Aud. 'Faith, the priest was good
enough, for all the old gentleman's
saying.

Touch. A most wicked Sir Oliver,
Audrey; a most vile Mar-text. But,
Audrey, there is a youth here in the
forest lays claim to you.

Aud. Ay, I know who 't is: he hath no interest in
me in the world. Here comes the man you mean. 11

Enter WILLIAM.

Touch. It is meat and drink to me to see a clown.
By my troth, we that have good wits have much to
answer for: we shall be flouting; we cannot hold.

Will. Good even, Audrey.

Aud. God ye good even, William.

Will. And good even to you, sir.

Touch. Good even, gentle friend. Cover thy head,
cover thy head, nay, pr'ythee, be covered. How old
are you, friend? 20

Will. Five-and-twenty, sir.

Touch. A ripe age. Is thy name William?

Will. William, sir.

Touch. A fair name. Wast born i' the forest here?

Will. Ay, sir, I thank God.

Touch. Thank God;—a good answer. Art rich?

Will. 'Faith, sir, so, so.

Touch. So, so, is good, very good, very excellent
good: and yet it is not; it is but so, so. Art thou
wise? 30

Will. Ay, sir, I have a pretty wit.

Touch. Why, thou say'st well. I do now remember
a saying, "The fool doth think he is wise, but the
wise man knows himself to be a fool." The heathen
philosopher, when he had a desire to eat a grape,
would open his lips when he put it into his mouth,
meaning thereby, that grapes were made to eat, and
lips to open. You do love this maid?

Will. I do, sir.

Touch. Give me your hand. Art thou learned? 40

Will. No, sir.

Touch. Then learn this of me. To have, is to have;
for it is 'a figure in rhetoric, that drink, being poured
out of a cup into a glass, by filling the one doth empty
the other; for all your writers do consent, that *ipse* is
he: now, you are not *ipse*, for I am he.

Will. Which he, sir? 47

Touch. He, sir, that must marry this woman.
Therefore, you clown, abandon,—which is in the
vulgar, leave,—the society,—which in the boorish is,
company,—of this female,—which in the common is,
woman; which together is, abandon the society of this
female, or, clown, thou perishest; or, to thy better
understanding, diest; or, to wit, I kill thee, make thee
away, translate thy life into death, thy liberty into
bondage. I will deal in poison with thee, or in bastinado, or in steel: I will bandy with thee in faction; I

will o'errun thee with policy; I will kill thee a
hundred and fifty ways: therefore tremble, and
depart.   60
Aud. Do, good William.
Will. God rest you merry, sir.   [*Exit.*

Enter CORIN.

Cor. Our master and mistress seek you: come,
away, away!
Touch. Trip, Audrey, trip, Audrey.—I attend, I
attend.   [*Exeunt.*

SCENE II.—Another Part of the Forest.

Enter ORLANDO and OLIVER.

Orl. Is 't possible, that on so little acquaintance you
should like her? that, but seeing, you should love her?
and, loving, woo? and, wooing, she should grant?
and will you persever to enjoy her?
Oli. Neither call the giddiness of it in question, the
poverty of her, the small acquaintance, my sudden
wooing, nor her sudden consenting; but say with me,
I love Aliena; say with her, that she loves me; consent with both, that we may enjoy each other: it shall
be to your good; for my father's house, and all the
revenue that was old Sir Rowland's, will I estate upon
you, and here live and die a shepherd.   12
Orl. You have my consent. Let your wedding be
to-morrow: thither will I invite the duke, and all his
contented followers. Go you, and prepare Aliena;
for, look you, here comes my Rosalind.

Enter ROSALIND.

Ros. God save you, brother.
Oli. And you, fair sister.   [*Exit.*
Ros. O! my dear Orlando, how it grieves me to see
thee wear thy heart in a scarf.   20
Orl. It is my arm.
Ros. I thought thy heart had been wounded with
the claws of a lion.
Orl. Wounded it is, but with the eyes of a lady.
Ros. Did your brother tell you how I counterfeited
to swoon, when he showed me your handkercher?
Orl. Ay, and greater wonders than that.   27
Ros. O! I know where you are.—Nay, 'tis true:
there was never anything so sudden, but the fight of
two rams, and Cæsar's thrasonical brag of—"I came,
saw, and overcame:" for your brother and my sister
no sooner met, but they looked; no sooner looked,
but they loved; no sooner loved, but they sighed; no
sooner sighed, but they asked one another the reason;
no sooner knew the reason, but they sought the
remedy: and in these degrees have they made a pair
of stairs to marriage, which they will climb incontinent, or else be incontinent before marriage. They
are in the very wrath of love, and they will together:
clubs cannot part them.   40
Orl. They shall be married to-morrow, and I will
bid the duke to the nuptial. But, O! how bitter a
thing it is to look into happiness through another
man's eyes! By so much the more shall I to-morrow
be at the height of heart-heaviness, by how much I
shall think my brother happy in having what he
wishes for.
Ros. Why then, to-morrow I cannot serve your turn
for Rosalind?
Orl. I can live no longer by thinking.   50
Ros. I will weary you then no longer with idle
talking. Know of me then (for now I speak to some
purpose), that I know you are a gentleman of good
conceit. I speak not this, that you should bear a
good opinion of my knowledge, insomuch I say, I
know you are; neither do I labour for a greater
esteem than may in some little measure draw a belief
from you, to do yourself good, and not to grace me.
Believe then, if you please, that I can do strange
things. I have, since I was three years old, conversed with a magician, most profound in his art,
and yet not damnable. If you do love Rosalind so
near the heart as your gesture cries it out, when your
brother marries Aliena, shall you marry her. I know

into what straits of fortune she is driven; and it is
not impossible to me, if it appear not inconvenient to
you, to set her before your eyes to-morrow, human as
she is, and without any danger.
Orl. Speak'st thou in sober meaning?   69
Ros. By my life, I do; which I tender dearly,
though I say I am a magician. Therefore, put you in
your best array, bid your friends, for if you will be
married to-morrow, you shall, and to Rosalind, if you
will. Look, here comes a lover of mine, and a lover
of hers.

Enter SILVIUS and PHEBE.

Phe. Youth, you have done me much ungentleness,
To show the letter that I writ to you.
Ros. I care not, if I have: it is my study
To seem despiteful and ungentle to you.
You are there follow'd by a faithful shepherd: 80
Look upon him, love him; he worships you.
Phe. Good shepherd, tell this youth what 'tis to
                          love.
Sil. It is to be all made of sighs and tears;
And so am I for Phebe.
Phe. And I for Ganymede.
Orl. And I for Rosalind.
Ros. And I for no woman.
Sil. It is to be all made of faith and service;
And so am I for Phebe.
Phe. And I for Ganymede.   90
Orl. And I for Rosalind.
Ros. And I for no woman.
Sil. It is to be all made of fantasy,
All made of passion, and all made of wishes;
All adoration, duty, and observance;
All humbleness, all patience, and impatience;
All purity, all trial, all observance;
And so am I for Phebe.
Phe. And so am I for Ganymede.
Orl. And so am I for Rosalind.   100
Ros. And so am I for no woman.
Phe. [*To* ROSALIND.] If this be so, why blame you
                          me to love you?
Sil. [*To* PHEBE.] If this be so, why blame you me
                          to love you?
Orl. If this be so, why blame you me to love you?
Ros. Who do you speak to, "Why blame you me to
                          love you?"
Orl. To her, that is not here, nor doth not hear.
Ros. Pray you, no more of this: 'tis like the howling
of Irish wolves against the moon.—[*To* SILVIUS.] I will
help you, if I can:—[*To* PHEBE.] I would love you, if I
could.—To-morrow meet me all together.—[*To* PHEBE.]
I will marry you, if ever I marry woman, and I 'll be
married to-morrow:—[*To* ORLANDO.] I will satisfy you,
if ever I satisfied man, and you shall be married to-
morrow:—[*To* SILVIUS.] I will content you, if what
pleases you contents you, and you shall be married
to-morrow.—[*To* ORLANDO.] As you love Rosalind,
meet:—[*To* SILVIUS.] As you love Phebe, meet: and
as I love no woman, I 'll meet.—So, fare you well: I
have left you commands.
Sil. I 'll not fail, if I live.   120
Phe. Nor I.
Orl. Nor I.   [*Exeunt.*

SCENE III.—Another Part of the Forest.

Enter TOUCHSTONE and AUDREY.

Touch. To-morrow is the joyful day, Audrey: to-
morrow will we be married.
Aud. I do desire it with all my heart, and I hope it
is no dishonest desire, to desire to be a woman of the
world. Here come two of the banished duke's pages.

Enter two Pages.

1 Page. Well met, honest gentleman.
Touch. By my troth, well met. Come, sit, sit, and
a song.
2 Page. We are for you: sit i' the middle.
1 Page. Shall we clap into 't roundly, without

hawking, or spitting, or saying we are hoarse, which
are the only prologues to a bad voice?   12
   2 Page. I' faith, i' faith; and both in a tune, like two
gipsies on a horse.

Between the acres of the rye,
   With a hey, and a ho, and a hey nonino,
These pretty country folks would lie,
   In spring time, &c.

Ros. "You are there follow'd by a faithful shepherd:
Look upon him, love him; he worships you."

SONG.

It was a lover, and his lass,
   With a hey, and a ho, and a hey nonino,
That o'er the green corn-field did pass,
   In the spring time, the only pretty ring time,
When birds do sing, hey ding a ding, ding;
   Sweet lovers love the spring.   20

This carol they began that hour,
   With a hey, and a ho, and a hey nonino,
How that a life was but a flower
   In spring time, &c.

And therefore take the present time,
   With a hey, and a ho, and a hey nonino,   30
For love is crowned with the prime
   In spring time, &c.

Touch. Truly, young gentlemen, though there was no great matter in the ditty, yet the note was very untuneable.

1 Page. You are deceived, sir: we kept time; we lost not our time.

Touch. By my troth, yes; I count it but time lost to hear such a foolish song. God be wi' you; and God mend your voices. Come, Audrey.   40
                                                   [*Exeunt.*

SCENE IV.—Another Part of the Forest.

Enter DUKE *Senior,* AMIENS, JAQUES, ORLANDO, OLIVER, *and* CELIA.

Duke S. Dost thou believe, Orlando, that the boy Can do all this that he hath promised?

Orl. I sometimes do believe, and sometimes do not, As those that fear; they hope, and know they fear.

Enter ROSALIND, SILVIUS, *and* PHEBE.

Ros. Patience once more, whiles our compact is urg'd.—

[*To the* DUKE.] You say, if I bring in your Rosalind, You will bestow her on Orlando here?

Duke S. That would I, had I kingdoms to give with her.

Ros. [*To* ORLANDO.] And you say, you will have her, when I bring her?

Orl. That would I, were I of all kingdoms king.   10

Ros. [*To* PHEBE.] You say, you 'll marry me, if I be willing?

Phe. That will I, should I die the hour after.

Ros. But if you do refuse to marry me, You 'll give yourself to this most faithful shepherd?

Phe. So is the bargain.

Ros. [*To* SILVIUS.] You say, that you 'll have Phebe, if she will?

Sil. Though to have her and death were both one thing.

Ros. I have promis'd to make all this matter even. Keep you your word, O duke! to give your daughter;— You yours, Orlando, to receive his daughter;—   20 Keep you your word, Phebe, that you 'll marry me, Or else, refusing me, to wed this shepherd;— Keep your word, Silvius, that you 'll marry her, If she refuse me:—and from hence I go, To make these doubts all even.
                      [*Exeunt* ROSALIND *and* CELIA.

Duke S. I do remember in this shepherd-boy Some lively touches of my daughter's favour.

Orl. My lord, the first time that I ever saw him, Methought he was a brother to your daughter; But, my good lord, this boy is forest-born,   30 And hath been tutor'd in the rudiments Of many desperate studies by his uncle, Whom he reports to be a great magician, Obscured in the circle of this forest.

Jaq. There is, sure, another flood toward, and these couples are coming to the ark. Here comes a pair of very strange beasts, which in all tongues are called fools.

Enter TOUCHSTONE *and* AUDREY.

Touch. Salutation and greeting to you all.

Jaq. Good my lord, bid him welcome. This is the motley-minded gentleman, that I have so often met in the forest: he hath been a courtier, he swears.   42

Touch. If any man doubt that, let him put me to my purgation. I have trod a measure; I have flattered a lady; I have been politic with my friend, smooth with mine enemy; I have undone three tailors; I have had four quarrels. and like to have fought one.

Jaq. And how was that ta'en up?

Touch. 'Faith, we met, and found the quarrel was upon the seventh cause.   50

Jaq. How seventh cause?—Good my lord, like this fellow.

Duke S. I like him very well.

Touch. God 'ild you, sir; I desire you of the like. I press in here, sir, amongst the rest of the country copulatives, to swear, and to forswear, according as marriage binds, and blood breaks.—A poor virgin,

sir, an ill-favoured thing, sir, but mine own: a poor humour of mine, sir, to take that no man else will. Rich honesty dwells like a miser, sir, in a poor house, as your pearl in your foul oyster.   61

Duke S. By my faith, he is very swift and sententious.

Touch. According to the fool's bolt, sir, and such dulcet diseases.

Jaq. But, for the seventh cause, how did you find the quarrel on the seventh cause?

Touch. Upon a lie seven times removed.—Bear your body more seeming, Audrey.—As thus, sir. I did dislike the cut of a certain courtier's beard: he sent me word, if I said his beard was not cut well, he was in the mind it was: this is called the "retort courteous." If I sent him word again it was not well cut, he would send me word he cut it to please himself: this is called the "quip modest." If again, it was not well cut, he disabled my judgment: this is called the "reply churlish." If again, it was not well cut, he would answer, I spake not true: this is called the "reproof valiant." If again, it was not well cut, he would say, I lie: this is called the "countercheck quarrelsome:" and so to the "lie circumstantial," and the "lie direct."   82

Jaq. And how oft did you say, his beard was not well cut?

Touch. I durst go no further than the "lie circumstantial," nor he durst not give me the "lie direct;" and so we measured swords, and parted.

Jaq. Can you nominate in order now the degrees of the lie?   89

Touch. O sir, we quarrel in print; by the book, as you have books for good manners: I will name you the degrees. The first, the retort courteous; the second, the quip modest; the third, the reply churlish; the fourth, the reproof valiant; the fifth, the countercheck quarrelsome; the sixth, the lie with circumstance; the seventh, the lie direct. All these you may avoid, but the lie direct; and you may avoid that too, with an *if*. I knew when seven justices could not take up a quarrel; but when the parties were met themselves, one of them thought but of an *if*, as *if you said so, then I said so;* and they shook hands and swore brothers. Your *if* is the only peace-maker; much virtue in *if*.   103

Jaq. Is not this a rare fellow, my lord? he 's as good at anything, and yet a fool.

Duke S. He uses his folly like a stalking-horse, and under the presentation of that, he shoots his wit.

Enter HYMEN, *leading* ROSALIND *in woman's clothes, and* CELIA.

Still Music.

Hym.   Then is there mirth in heaven,
        When earthly things made even
            Atone together.   110
        Good duke, receive thy daughter,
        Hymen from heaven brought her;
            Yea, brought her hither,
        That thou mightst join her hand with his,
        Whose heart within her bosom is.

Ros. [*To* DUKE S.] To you I give myself, for I am yours.

[*To* ORLANDO.] To you I give myself, for I am yours.

Duke S. If there be truth in sight, you are my daughter.

Orl. If there be truth in sight, you are my Rosalind.

Phe. If sight and shape be true,   120 Why then, my love adieu!

Ros. [*To* DUKE S.] I 'll have no father, if you be not he:—

[*To* ORLANDO.] I 'll have no husband, if you be not he:—

[*To* PHEBE.] Nor ne'er wed woman, if you be not she.

Hym. Peace, ho! I bar confusion.
        'T is I must make conclusion
            Of these most strange events:
        Here 's eight that must take hands,
        To join in Hymen's bands,
            If truth holds true contents.   130

[*To* ORLANDO *and* ROSALIND.] You and you
    no cross shall part:
[*To* OLIVER *and* CELIA.] You and you are
    heart in heart:
[*To* PHEBE.] You to his love must accord,
    Or have a woman to your lord:
[*To* TOUCHSTONE *and* AUDREY.] You and
    you are sure together,
As the winter to foul weather.
Whiles a wedlock-hymn we sing,
Feed yourselves with questioning,
That reason wonder may diminish,
How thus we met, and these things finish.

        SONG.

Wedding is great Juno's crown: 141
  O blessed bond of board and bed!
'T is Hymen peoples every town;
  High wedlock then be honoured.
Honour, high honour, and renown,
  To Hymen, god of every town!

Duke S. O my dear niece! welcome thou art to me:
Even daughter, welcome in no less degree.
  Phe. [*To* SILVIUS.] I will not eat my word, now
    thou art mine;
Thy faith my fancy to thee doth combine.   150

     Enter JAQUES DE BOIS.

  Jaq. de B. Let me have audience for a word or two.
I am the second son of old Sir Rowland,
That bring these tidings to this fair assembly.—
Duke Frederick, hearing how that every day
Men of great worth resorted to this forest,
Address'd a mighty power, which were on foot
In his own conduct, purposely to take
His brother here, and put him to the sword.
And to the skirts of this wild wood he came,
Where, meeting with an old religious man,   160
After some question with him, was converted
Both from his enterprise, and from the world;

His crown bequeathing to his banish'd brother,
And all their lands restor'd to them again,
That were with him exil'd. This to be true,
I do engage my life.
  Duke S.   Welcome, young man;
Thou offer'st fairly to thy brothers' wedding:
To one, his lands withheld; and to the other,
A land itself at large, a potent dukedom.
First, in this forest, let us do those ends   170
That here were well begun, and well begot;
And after, every of this happy number,
That have endur'd shrewd days and nights with us,
Shall share the good of our returned fortune,
According to the measure of their states.
Meantime, forget this new-fall'n dignity,
And fall into our rustic revelry.—
Play, music! and you brides and bridegrooms all,
With measure heap'd in joy, to the measures fall.
  Jaq. Sir, by your patience.—If I heard you rightly,
The duke hath put on a religious life,   181
And thrown into neglect the pompous court?
  Jaq. de B. He hath.
  Jaq. To him will I: out of these convertites
There is much matter to be heard and learn'd.—
[*To* DUKE S.] You to your former honour I bequeath;
Your patience, and your virtue, well deserve it:—
[*To* ORLANDO.] You to a love, that your true faith doth
    merit:—
[*To* OLIVER.] You to your land, and love, and great
    allies:
[*To* SILVIUS.] You to a long and well-deserved bed:—
[*To* TOUCHSTONE.] And you to wrangling; for thy
    loving voyage   191
Is but for two months victuall'd.—So, to your pleasures:
I am for other than for dancing measures.
  Duke S. Stay, Jaques, stay.
  Jaq. To see no pastime, I:—what you would have,
I 'll stay to know at your abandon'd cave.   [*Exit.*
  Duke S. Proceed, proceed: we will begin these rites,
As we do trust they 'll end in true delights. [*A dance.*

EPILOGUE.

Ros. It is not the fashion to see the lady the epilogue;
but it is no more unhandsome, than to see the lord the
prologue. If it be true that good wine needs no bush,
'tis true that a good play needs no epilogue; yet to good
wine they do use good bushes, and good plays prove
the better by the help of good epilogues. What a case
am I in then, that am neither a good epilogue, nor
cannot insinuate with you in the behalf of a good
play? I am not furnished like a beggar, therefore to
beg will not become me: my way is, to conjure you;
and I 'll begin with the women. I charge you, O
women! for the love you bear to men, to like as much
of this play as please you: and I charge you, O men!
for the love you bear to women (as I perceive by your
simpering, none of you hates them), that between you
and the women, the play may please. If I were a
woman, I would kiss as many of you as had beards
that pleased me, complexions that liked me, and
breaths that I defied not; and, I am sure, as many as
have good beards, or good faces, or sweet breaths,
will, for my kind offer, when I make curtsy, bid me
farewell.   [*Exeunt.*

THE TAMING OF THE SHREW.

DRAMATIS PERSONÆ.

A Lord.
CHRISTOPHER SLY, *a Tinker.* ⎱ *Persons in the*
Hostess, Page, Players, Hunts- ⎰ *Induction.*
men, and Servants.

BAPTISTA, *a rich Gentleman of Padua.*
VINCENTIO, *an old Gentleman of Pisa.*
LUCENTIO, *Son to Vincentio.*
PETRUCHIO, *a Gentleman of Verona.*
GREMIO, ⎱ *Suitors to Bianca.*
HORTENSIO, ⎰

TRANIO, ⎱ *Servants to Lucentio.*
BIONDELLO, ⎰
GRUMIO, ⎱ *Servants to Petruchio.*
CURTIS, ⎰
A Pedant.

KATHARINA, ⎱ *Daughters to Baptista.*
BIANCA, ⎰
Widow.

Tailor, Haberdasher, and Servants attending on
Baptista and Petruchio.

SCENE—Sometimes in PADUA, and sometimes in PETRUCHIO'S House in the Country.

INDUCTION.

SCENE I.—Before an Ale-house on a Heath.

Enter Hostess and SLY.

Sly. I 'LL pheese you, in faith.
Host. A pair of stocks, you rogue!
Sly. Y' are a baggage: the Slys are no
rogues; look in the chronicles, we came
in with Richard Conqueror. Therefore,
paucas pallabris; let the world slide.
Sessa!
Host. You will not pay for the glasses
you have burst?
Sly. No, not a denier. Go by, Saint
Jeronimy: go to thy cold bed, and warm
thee. 12
Host. I know my remedy: I must go
fetch the thirdborough. [*Exit.*
Sly. Third, or fourth, or fifth borough,
I'll answer him by law. I ll not budge
an inch, boy: let him come, and kindly.
[*Lies down on the ground, and falls asleep.*

Wind Horns. Enter a Lord from hunting, with
Huntsmen and Servants.

Lord. Huntsman, I charge thee, tender well my
hounds:
Brach Merriman, the poor cur is emboss'd,
And couple Clowder with the deep-mouth'd brach. 20
Saw'st thou not, boy, how Silver made it good
At the hedge-corner, in the coldest fault?
I would not lose the dog for twenty pound.
1 Hun. Why, Belman is as good as he, my lord;
He cried upon it at the merest loss,
And twice to-day pick'd out the dullest scent:
Trust me, I take him for the better dog.
Lord. Thou art a fool: if Echo were as fleet,
I would esteem him worth a dozen such.
But sup them well, and look unto them all: 30
To-morrow I intend to hunt again.
1 Hun. I will, my lord.
Lord. What's here? one dead, or drunk? See, doth
he breathe?
2 Hun. He breathes, my lord. Were he not
warm'd with ale,
This were a bed but cold to sleep so soundly.
Lord. O monstrous beast! how like a swine he
lies!
Grim death, how foul and loathsome is thine image!
Sirs, I will practise on this drunken man.
What think you, if he were convey'd to bed,
Wrapp'd in sweet clothes, rings put upon his fingers,
A most delicious banquet by his bed, 41
And brave attendants near him when he wakes,
Would not the beggar then forget himself?
1 Hun. Believe me, lord, I think he cannot choose.
2 Hun. It would seem strange unto him when he
wak'd.
Lord. Even as a flattering dream, or worthless
fancy.
Then take him up, and manage well the jest.
Carry him gently to my fairest chamber,
And hang it round with all my wanton pictures;
Balm his foul head with warm distilled waters, 50
And burn sweet wood to make the lodging sweet.
Procure me music ready when he wakes,
To make a dulcet and a heavenly sound;
And if he chance to speak, be ready straight,
And, with a low submissive reverence,
Say, "What is it your honour will command?"
Let one attend him with a silver basin,
Full of rose-water, and bestrew'd with flowers;
Another bear the ewer, the third a diaper,
And say, "Will 't please your lordship cool your
hands?" 60
Some one be ready with a costly suit,
And ask him what apparel he will wear;
Another tell him of his hounds and horse,
And that his lady mourns at his disease.
Persuade him, that he hath been lunatic;
And, when he says he is —, say, that he dreams,
For he is nothing but a mighty lord.
This do, and do it kindly, gentle sirs:
It will be pastime passing excellent,
If it be husbanded with modesty. 70
1 Hun. My lord, I warrant you, we will play our
part,
As he shall think, by our true diligence,
He is no less than what we say he is.

Lord. Take him up gently, and to bed with him,
And each one to his office when he wakes.—
        [SLY *is borne out. A trumpet sounds.*
Sirrah, go see what trumpet 't is that sounds :—
                        [*Exit Servant.*
Belike, some noble gentleman, that means,
Travelling some journey, to repose him here.—

           Re-enter Servant.

How now ? who is it ?
  Serv.   An it please your honour,
Players that offer service to your lordship.   80
Lord. Bid them come near.

           Enter Players.

         Now, fellows, you are welcome.
Players. We thank your honour.
Lord. Do you intend to stay with me to-night ?
A Play. So please your lordship to accept our
     duty.
Lord. With all my heart.—This fellow I remember,
Since once he play'd a farmer's eldest son :—
'T was where you woo'd the gentlewoman so well.
I have forgot your name ; but, sure, that part
Was aptly fitted, and naturally perform'd.
A Play. I think, 't was Soto that your honour
     means.   90
Lord. 'T is very true : thou didst it excellent.
Well, you are come to me in happy time,
The rather for I have some sport in hand,
Wherein your cunning can assist me much.
There is a lord will hear you play to-night ;
But I am doubtful of your modesties,
Lest over-eying of his odd behaviour,
(For yet his honour never heard a play,)
You break into some merry passion,
And so offend him ; for I tell you, sirs,   100
If you should smile he grows impatient.
A Play. Fear not, my lord : we can contain our-
     selves,
Were he the veriest antick in the world.
Lord. Go, sirrah, take them to the buttery,
And give them friendly welcome every one :
Let them want nothing that my house affords.—
         [*Exeunt Servant and Players.*
[*To a Servant.*] Sirrah, go you to Barthol'mew my
     page,
And see him dress'd in all suits like a lady :
That done, conduct him to the drunkard's chamber ;
And call him madam, do him obeisance.   110
Tell him from me, as he will win my love,
He bear himself with honourable action,
Such as he hath observ'd in noble ladies
Unto their lords by them accomplished :
Such duty to the drunkard let him do,
With soft low tongue, and lowly courtesy ;
And say, " What is 't your honour will command,
Wherein your lady, and your humble wife,
May show her duty, and make known her love ?"
And then, with kind embracements, tempting kisses,
And with declining head into his bosom,   121
Bid him shed tears, as being overjoy'd
To see her noble lord restor'd to health,
Who, for this seven years, hath esteemed him
No better than a poor and loathsome beggar.
And if the boy have not a woman's gift,
To rain a shower of commanded tears,
An onion will do well for such a shift,
Which, in a napkin being close convey'd,
Shall in despite enforce a watery eye.   130
See this despatch'd with all the haste thou canst :
Anon I 'll give thee more instructions. [*Exit Servant.*
I know, the boy will well usurp the grace,
Voice, gait, and action of a gentlewoman :
I long to hear him call the drunkard husband,
And how my men will stay themselves from laughter,
When they do homage to this simple peasant.
I 'll in to counsel them : haply, my presence
May well abate the over-merry spleen,
Which otherwise would grow into extremes.   140
                              [*Exeunt.*

SCENE II.—A Bed-chamber in the Lord's House.

SLY *is discovered in a rich night-gown, with Attendants ; some with apparel, others with basin, ewer,
and other appurtenances. Enter Lord, dressed
like a servant.*

Sly. For God's sake, a pot of small ale !
1 Serv. Will 't please your lordship drink a cup of
     sack ?
2 Serv. Will 't please your honour taste of these
     conserves ?
3 Serv. What raiment will your honour wear to-day ?
Sly. I am Christophero Sly ; call not me honour,
nor lordship : I ne'er drank sack in my life ; and if
you give me any conserves, give me conserves of beef.
Ne'er ask me what raiment I 'll wear, for I have no
more doublets than backs, no more stockings than
legs, nor no more shoes than feet ; nay, sometime,
more feet than shoes, or such shoes as my toes look
through the overleather.   12
Lord. Heaven cease this idle humour in your
     honour !
O, that a mighty man, of such descent,
Of such possessions, and so high esteem,
Should be infused with so foul a spirit !
Sly. What ! would you make me mad ? Am not I
Christopher Sly, old Sly's son, of Burton Heath, by
birth a pedlar, by education a card-maker, by trans-
mutation a bear-herd, and now by present profession
a tinker ? Ask Marian Hacket, the fat ale-wife of
Wincot, if she know me not : if she say I am not
fourteen pence on the score for sheer ale, score me
up for the lyingest knave in Christendom. What ! I
am not bestraught. Here's—
1 Serv. O ! this it is that makes your lady mourn.
2 Serv. O ! this it is that makes your servants droop.
Lord. Hence comes it that your kindred shuns your
     house,
As beaten hence by your strange lunacy.
O noble lord, bethink thee of thy birth ;   30
Call home thy ancient thoughts from banishment,
And banish hence these abject lowly dreams.
Look how thy servants do attend on thee,
Each in his office ready at thy beck :
Wilt thou have music ? hark ! Apollo plays,   [*Music.*
And twenty caged nightingales do sing :
Or wilt thou sleep ? we 'll have thee to a couch
Softer and sweeter than the lustful bed
On purpose trimm'd up for Semiramis.
Say thou wilt walk, we will bestrew the ground :   40
Or wilt thou ride, thy horses shall be trapp'd,
Their harness studded all with gold and pearl.
Dost thou love hawking ? thou hast hawks will soar
Above the morning lark : or wilt thou hunt ?
Thy hounds shall make the welkin answer them,
And fetch shrill echoes from the hollow earth.
1 Serv. Say thou wilt course, thy greyhounds are as
     swift
As breathed stags, ay, fleeter than the roe.
2 Serv. Dost thou love pictures ? we will fetch thee
     straight
Adonis painted by a running brook,   50
And Cytherea all in sedges hid,
Which seem to move and wanton with her breath,
Even as the waving sedges play with wind.
Lord. We 'll show thee Io as she was a maid,
And how she was beguiled and surpris'd,
As lively painted as the deed was done.
3 Serv. Or Daphne roaming through a thorny wood,
Scratching her legs, that one shall swear she bleeds ;
And at that sight shall sad Apollo weep,
So workmanly the blood and tears are drawn.   60
Lord. Thou art a lord, and nothing but a lord :
Thou hast a lady, far more beautiful
Than any woman in this waning age.
1 Serv. And, till the tears that she hath shed for
     thee,
Like envious floods, o'erran her lovely face,
She was the fairest creature in the world ;
And yet she is inferior to none.
Sly. Am I a lord ? and have I such a lady ?
Or do I dream ? or have I dream'd till now ?

I do not sleep; I see, I hear, I speak; 70
I smell sweet savours, and I feel soft things.-
Upon my life, I am a lord indeed,
And not a tinker, nor Christopher Sly.—
Well, bring our lady hither to our sight;
And once again, a pot o' the smallest ale.
  2 *Serv.* Will 't please your mightiness to wash your
    hands?
  [*Servants present a ewer, basin, and napkin.*
O, how we joy to see your wit restor'd!
O, that once more you knew but what you are!
These fifteen years you have been in a dream,
Or, when you wak'd, so wak'd as if you slept. 80
  Sly. These fifteen years! by my fay, a goodly nap.
But did I never speak of all that time?
  1 *Serv.* O! yes, my lord, but very idle words;—
For though you lay here in this goodly chamber,
Yet would you say, ye were beaten out of door,
And rail upon the hostess of the house,
And say you would present her at the leet,
Because she brought stone jugs and no seal'd quarts.
Sometimes you would call out for Cicely Hacket.
  Sly. Ay, the woman's maid of the house. 90
  3 *Serv.* Why, sir, you know no house, nor no such
    maid,
Nor no such men, as you have reckon'd up,—
As Stephen Sly, and old John Naps of Greece,
And Peter Turf, and Henry Pimpernell,
And twenty more such names and men as these,
Which never were, nor no man ever saw.
  Sly. Now, Lord be thanked for my good amends!
  All. Amen.
  Sly. I thank thee; thou shalt not lose by it.

Enter the Page, as a lady, with Attendants.

  Page. How fares my noble lord? 100
  Sly. Marry, I fare well, for here is cheer enough.
Where is my wife?
  Page. Here, noble lord: what is thy will with
    her?
  Sly. Are you my wife, and will not call me husband?
My men should call me lord: I am your goodman.

  Page. My husband and my lord, my lord and
    husband;
I am your wife in all obedience.
  Sly. I know it well.—What must I call her?
  Lord. Madam.
  Sly. Al'ce madam, or Joan madam? 110
  Lord. Madam, and nothing else: so lords call ladies.
  Sly. Madam wife, they say that I have dream'd
And slept above some fifteen year or more.
  Page. Ay, and the time seems thirty unto me,
Being all this time abandon'd from your bed.
  Sly. 'T is much.—Servants, leave me and her alone.—
Madam, undress you, and come now to bed.
  Page. Thrice noble lord, let me entreat of you
To pardon me yet for a night or two;
Or if not so, until the sun be set: 120
For your physicians have expressly charg'd,
In peril to incur your former malady,
That I should yet absent me from your bed.
I hope this reason stands for my excuse.
  Sly. Ay, it stands so, that I may hardly tarry so
long; but I would be loath to fall into my dreams again:
I will therefore tarry, in despite of the flesh and the
blood.

Enter a Servant.

  Serv. Your honour's players, hearing your amend-
    ment,
Are come to play a pleasant comedy; 130
For so your doctors hold it very meet,
Seeing too much sadness hath congeal'd your blood,
And melancholy is the nurse of frenzy:
Therefore, they thought it good you hear a play,
And frame your mind to mirth and merriment,
Which bars a thousand harms, and lengthens life.
  Sly. Marry, I will; let them play it. Is not a com-
monty a Christmas gambol, or a tumbling-trick?
  Page. No, my good lord: it is more pleasing stuff.
  Sly. What, household stuff? 140
  Page. It is a kind of history.
  Sly. Well, we 'll see 't. Come, madam wife, sit by
    my side,
And let the world slip: we shall ne'er be younger.
  [*They sit down.*

ACT I.

SCENE I.—Padua. A Public Place.

Enter LUCENTIO *and* TRANIO.

  Lucentio.
RANIO, since for the great desire I had
  To see fair Padua, nursery of arts,
  I am arriv'd for fruitful Lombardy,
  The pleasant garden of great Italy;
  And, by my father's love and leave, am
    arm'd
  With his good will, and thy good company,
  My trusty servant, well approv'd in all;
  Here let us breathe, and haply institute
  A course of learning, and ingenious
    studies.
  Pisa, renowned for grave citizens, 10
  Gave me my being, and my father first,
A merchant of great traffic through the world,
Vincentio, come of the Bentivolii.
Vincentio's son, brought up in Florence,
It shall become, to serve all hopes conceiv'd,
To deck his fortune with his virtuous deeds:
And therefore, Tranio, for the time I study,
Virtue, and that part of philosophy
Will I apply, that treats of happiness 20
By virtue specially to be achiev'd.
Tell me thy mind; for I have Pisa left,
And am to Padua come, as he that leaves
A shallow plash, to plunge him in the deep,
And with satiety seeks to quench his thirst.
  Tra. Mi perdonate, gentle master mine,
I am in all affected as yourself,
Glad that you thus continue your resolve,
To suck the sweets of sweet philosophy.
Only, good master, while we do admire 30
This virtue, and this moral discipline,
Let 's be no stoics, nor no stocks, I pray;

Or so devote to Aristotle's checks,
As Ovid be an outcast quite abjur'd.
Balk logic with acquaintance that you have.
And practise rhetoric in your common talk :
Music and poesy use to quicken you.
The mathematics, and the metaphysics,
Fall to them, as you find your stomach serves you.
No profit grows, where is no pleasure ta'en.—
In brief, sir, study what you most affect.   40
 Luc. Gramercies, Tranio, well dost thou advise.
If, Biondello, thou wert come ashore,
We could at once put us in readiness,
And take a lodging fit to entertain
Such friends as time in Padua shall beget.
But stay awhile : what company is this?
 Tra. Master, some show, to welcome us to town.

Enter BAPTISTA, KATHARINA, BIANCA, GREMIO, *and*
 HORTENSIO. LUCENTIO *and* TRANIO *stand aside.*

 Bap. Gentlemen, importune me no further,
For how I firmly am resolv'd you know ;
That is, not to bestow my youngest daughter,   50
Before I have a husband for the elder.
If either of you both love Katharina,
Because I know you well, and love you well,
Leave shall you have to court her at your pleasure.
 Gre. [*Aside.*] To cart her rather : she's too rough
   for me.—
There, there, Hortensio, will you any wife?
 Kath. [*To* BAP.] I pray you, sir, is it your will
To make a stale of me amongst these mates?
 Hor. Mates, maid! how mean you that? no mates
   for you,
Unless you were of gentler, milder mould.   60
 Kath. I' faith, sir, you shall never need to fear :
I wis, it is not half way to her heart;
But, if it were, doubt not her care should be
To comb your noddle with a three-legg'd stool,
And paint your face, and use you like a fool.
 Hor. From all such devils, good Lord, deliver us!
 Gre. And me too, good Lord!
 Tra. Hush, master! here is some good pastime to-
   ward :
That wench is stark mad, or wonderful froward.
 Luc. But in the other's silence do I see   70
Maid's mild behaviour and sobriety.
Peace, Tranio!
 Tra. Well said, master : mum! and gaze your fill.
 Bap. Gentlemen, that I may soon make good
What I have said,—Bianca, get you in :
And let it not displease thee, good Bianca,
For I will love thee ne'er the less, my girl.
 Kath. A pretty peat! it is best
Put finger in the eye,—an she knew why.
 Bian. Sister, content you in my discontent.—   80
Sir, to your pleasure humbly I subscribe :
My books, and instruments, shall be my company,
On them to look, and practise by myself.
 Luc. Hark, Tranio! thou may'st hear Minerva
   speak.
 Hor. Signior Baptista, will you be so strange?
Sorry am I, that our good will effects
Bianca's grief.
 Gre.   Why, will you mew her up,
Signior Baptista, for this fiend of hell,
And make her bear the penance of her tongue?
 Bap. Gentlemen, content ye ; I am resolv'd.—   90
Go in, Bianca.   [*Exit* BIANCA.
And for I know, she taketh most delight
In music, instruments, and poetry,
Schoolmasters will I keep within my house,
Fit to instruct her youth.—If you, Hortensio,
Or Signior Gremio, you, know any such,
Prefer them hither ; for to cunning men
I will be very kind, and liberal
To mine own children in good bringing-up ;
And so farewell. Katharina, you may stay,   99
For I have more to commune with Bianca. [*Exit.*
 Kath. Why, and I trust, I may go too ; may I not?
What! shall I be appointed hours, as though, belike,
I knew not what to take, and what to leave? Ha!
          [*Exit.*

 Gre. You may go to the devil's dam : your gifts are
so good, here's none will hold you.—Their love is not
so great, Hortensio, but we may blow our nails together, and fast it fairly out : our cake's dough on both
sides. Farewell :—yet, for the love I bear my sweet
Bianca, if I can by any means light on a fit man to
teach her that wherein she delights, I will wish him
to her father.   112
 Hor. So will I, Signior Gremio : but a word, I pray.
Though the nature of our quarrel yet never brook'd
parle, know now, upon advice, it toucheth us both,—
that we may yet again have access to our fair mistress, and be happy rivals in Bianca's love,—to labour
and effect one thing specially.
 Gre. What's that, I pray?
 Hor. Marry, sir, to get a husband for her sister.   120
 Gre. A husband! a devil.
 Hor. I say, a husband.
 Gre. I say, a devil. Think'st thou, Hortensio,
though her father be very rich, any man is so very a
fool to be married to hell?
 Hor. Tush, Gremio! though it pass your patience
and mine, to endure her loud alarums, why, man,
there be good fellows in the world, an a man could
light on them, would take her with all faults, and
money enough.   130
 Gre. I cannot tell ; but I had as lief take her dowry
with this condition,—to be whipped at the high-cross
every morning.
 Hor. 'Faith, as you say, there's small choice in
rotten apples. But, come; since this bar in law makes
us friends, it shall be so far forth friendly maintained,
till by helping Baptista's eldest daughter to a husband,
we set his youngest free for a husband, and then have
to't afresh.—Sweet Bianca!—Happy man be his dole!
He that runs fastest gets the ring. How say you,
Signior Gremio?   141
 Gre. I am agreed : and 'would I had given him the
best horse in Padua to begin his wooing, that would
thoroughly woo her, wed her, and bed her, and rid
the house of her. Come on.
      [*Exeunt* GREMIO *and* HORTENSIO.
 Tra. [*Advancing.*] I pray, sir, tell me, is it possible,
That love should of a sudden take such hold?
 Luc. O Tranio! till I found it to be true,
I never thought it possible, or likely ;
But see! while idly I stood looking on,   150
I found the effect of love in idleness :
And now in plainness do confess to thee,—
That art to me as secret, and as dear,
As Anna to the Queen of Carthage was,—
Tranio, I burn, I pine ; I perish, Tranio,
If I achieve not this young modest girl.
Counsel me, Tranio, for I know thou canst :
Assist me, Tranio, for I know thou wilt.
 Tra. Master, it is no time to chide you now ;
Affection is not rated from the heart :   160
If love have touch'd you, nought remains but so,—
Redime te captum, quam queas minimo.
 Luc. Gramercies, lad ; go forward ; this contents;
The rest will comfort, for thy counsel's sound.
 Tra. Master, you look'd so longly on the maid,
Perhaps you mark'd not what's the pith of all.
 Luc. O! yes, I saw sweet beauty in her face,
Such as the daughter of Agenor had,
That made great Jove to humble him to her hand,
When with his knees he kiss'd the Cretan strand.   170
 Tra. Saw you no more! mark'd you not, how her
   sister
Began to scold, and raise up such a storm,
That mortal ears might hardly endure the din?
 Luc. Tranio, I saw her coral lips to move,
And with her breath she did perfume the air :
Sacred, and sweet, was all I saw in her.
 Tra. Nay, then, 'tis time to stir him from his
   trance.—
I pray, awake, sir : if you love the maid,
Bend thoughts and wits to achieve her. Thus it
   stands :
Her elder sister is so curst and shrewd,   180
That, till the father rid his hands of her,
Master, your love must live a maid at home ;

And therefore has he closely mew'd her up,
Because she will not be annoy'd with suitors.
Luc. Ah, Tranio, what a cruel father's he!
But art thou not advis'd, he took some care
To get her cunning schoolmasters to instruct her?
Tra. Ay, marry, am I, sir; and now 't is plotted.
Luc. I have it, Tranio.
Tra.   Master, for my hand,
Both our inventions meet and jump in one.   190
Luc. Tell me thine first.
Tra.   You will be schoolmaster,
And undertake the teaching of the maid:
That's your device.
Luc.   It is: may it be done?
Tra. Not possible; for who shall bear your part,
And be in Padua, here, Vincentio's son;
Keep house, and ply his book, welcome his friends,
Visit his countrymen, and banquet them?
Luc. Basta, content thee; for I have it full.
We have not yet been seen in any house,
Nor can we be distinguished by our faces,   200
For man or master: then, it follows thus:—
Thou shalt be master, Tranio, in my stead,
Keep house, and port, and servants, as I should.
I will some other be; some Florentine,
Some Neapolitan, or meaner man of Pisa.
'T is hatch'd, and shall be so:—Tranio, at once
Uncase thee, take my colour'd hat and cloak:
When Biondello comes, he waits on thee;
But I will charm him first to keep his tongue.
Tra. So had you need.   [*They exchange habits.*
In brief, sir, sith it your pleasure is,   211
And I am tied to be obedient
(For so your father charg'd me at our parting;
"Be serviceable to my son," quoth he,
Although, I think, 't was in another sense),
I am content to be Lucentio,
Because so well I love Lucentio.
Luc. Tranio, be so, because Lucentio loves,
And let me be a slave, to achieve that maid
Whose sudden sight hath thrall'd my wounded eye.

Enter BIONDELLO.

Here comes the rogue.—Sirrah, where have you
been?   221
Bion. Where have I been? Nay, how now? where
are you?
Master, has my fellow Tranio stol'n your clothes,
Or you stol'n his, or both? pray, what 's the news?
Luc. Sirrah, come hither: 't is no time to jest,
And therefore frame your manners to the time.
Your fellow Tranio here, to save my life,
Puts my apparel and my countenance on,
And I for my escape have put on his;
For in a quarrel, since I came ashore,   230
I kill'd a man, and fear I was descried.
Wait you on him, I charge you, as becomes,
While I make way from hence to save my life.
You understand me?
Bion.   I, sir? ne'er a whit.
Luc. And not a jot of Tranio in your mouth:
Tranio is chang'd into Lucentio.
Bion. The better for him; 'would I were so too!
Tra. So could I, 'faith, boy, to have the next wish
after,
That Lucentio indeed had Baptista's youngest
daughter.
But, sirrah, not for my sake, but your master's, I
advise   240
You use your manners discreetly in all kind of
companies:
When I am alone, why, then I am Tranio;
But in all places else, your master, Lucentio.
Luc. Tranio, let 's go.—
One thing more rests, that thyself execute:—
To make one among these wooers: if thou ask me why,
Sufficeth, my reasons are both good and weighty.
[*Exeunt.*
1 Serv. My lord, you nod; you do not mind the
play.
Sly. Yes, by Saint Anne, do I. A good matter,
surely: comes there any more of it?   250

Page. My lord, 't is but begun.
Sly. 'T is a very excellent piece of work, madam
lady: 'would 't were done!

SCENE II.—*The Same. Before* HORTENSIO'S *House.*

Enter PETRUCHIO *and* GRUMIO.

Pet. Verona, for a while I take my leave,
To see my friends in Padua; but, of all,

Pet. "'Faith, sirrah, an you 'll not knock, I 'll wring it."

My best beloved and approved friend,
Hortensio; and, I trow, this is his house.—
Here, sirrah Grumio! knock, I say.
Gru. Knock, sir! whom should I knock? is there
any man has rebused your worship?
Pet. Villain, I say, knock me here soundly.
Gru. Knock you here, sir? why, sir, what am I,
sir, that I should knock you here, sir?   10
Pet. Villain, I say, knock me at this gate;
And rap me well, or I 'll knock your knave's pate.
Gru. My master is grown quarrelsome.—I should
knock you first,
And then I know after who comes by the worst.
Pet. Will it not be?
'Faith, sirrah, an you 'll not knock, I 'll wring it:
I 'll try how you can *sol, fa,* and sing it.
[*He wrings* GRUMIO *by the ears.*
Gru. Help, masters, help! my master is mad.
Pet. Now, knock when I bid you: sirrah! villain!

Enter HORTENSIO.

Hor. How now? what 's the matter?—My old
friend Grumio, and my good friend Petruchio!—How
do you all at Verona?   22
Pet. Signior Hortensio, come you to part the fray?
Con tutto il core ben trovato, may I say.

Hor. Alla nostra casa ben venuto; molto honorato
signior mio Petruchio.
Gru. Rise, Grumio, rise : we will compound this quarrel.
Gru. Nay, 'tis no matter, sir, what he 'leges in
Latin.—If this be not a lawful cause for me to leave
his service,—look you, sir,—he bid me knock him, and
rap him soundly, sir: well, was it fit for a servant to
use his master so; being, perhaps, (for aught I see)
two-and-thirty,—a pip out?   33
Whom, 'would to God, I had well knock'd at first,
Then had not Grumio come by the worst.
Pet. A senseless villain!—Good Hortensio,
I bade the rascal knock upon your gate,
And could not get him for my heart to do it.
Gru. Knock at the gate?—O heavens!
Spake you not these words plain,—"Sirrah, knock
me here,   40
Rap me here, knock me well, and knock me soundly?"
And come you now with knocking at the gate?
Pet. Sirrah, be gone, or talk not, I advise you.
Hor. Petruchio, patience: I am Grumio's pledge.
Why, this' a heavy chance 'twixt him and you,
Your ancient, trusty, pleasant servant Grumio.
And tell me now, sweet friend, what happy gale
Blows you to Padua, here, from old Verona?
Pet. Such wind as scatters young men through the
world,   50
To seek their fortunes further than at home,
Where small experience grows. But, in a few,
Signior Hortensio, thus it stands with me:
Antonio, my father, is deceas'd,
And I have thrust myself into this maze,
Haply to wive, and thrive, as best I may.
Crowns in my purse I have, and goods at home,
And so am come abroad to see the world.
Hor. Petruchio, shall I then come roundly to thee,
And wish thee to a shrewd ill-favour'd wife?
Thou'dst thank me but a little for my counsel;   60
And yet I 'll promise thee she shall be rich,
And very rich:—but thou 'rt too much my friend,
And I 'll not wish thee to her.
Pet. Signior Hortensio, 'twixt such friends as we
Few words suffice; and therefore, if thou know
One rich enough to be Petruchio's wife
(As wealth is burthen of my wooing dance),
Be she as foul as was Florentius' love,
As old as Sibyl, and as curst and shrewd
As Socrates' Xanthippe, or a worse: 70
She moves me not, or not removes, at least,
Affection's edge in me,—were she as rough
As are the swelling Adriatic seas:
I come to wive it wealthily in Padua;
If wealthily, then happily in Padua.
Gru. Nay, look you, sir, he tells you flatly what his
mind is: why, give him gold enough and marry him
to a puppet, or an aglet-baby; or an old trot with ne'er
a tooth in her head, though she have as many diseases
as two-and-fifty horses: why, nothing comes amiss,
so money comes withal.   81
Hor. Petruchio, since we are stepp'd thus far in,
I will continue that I broach'd in jest.
I can, Petruchio, help thee to a wife
With wealth enough, and young, and beauteous,
Brought up as best becomes a gentlewoman:
Her only fault, and that is faults enough,
Is, that she is intolerable curst,
And shrewd, and froward; so beyond all measure,
That, were my state far worser than it is,   90
I would not wed her for a mine of gold.
Pet. Hortensio, peace! thou know'st not gold's
effect.—
Tell me her father's name, and 't is enough:
For I will board her, though she chide as loud
As thunder, when the clouds in autumn crack.
Hor. Her father is Baptista Minola,
An affable and courteous gentleman;
Her name is Katharina Minola,
Renown'd in Padua for her scolding tongue.
Pet. I know her father, though I know not her,   100
And he knew my deceased father well.
I will not sleep, Hortensio, till I see her;
And therefore let me be thus bold with you,

To give you over at this first encounter,
Unless you will accompany me thither.
Gru. I pray you, sir, let him go while the humour
lasts. O' my word, an she knew him as well as I do,
she would think scolding would do little good upon
him. She may, perhaps, call him half a score knaves,
or so; why, that 's nothing: an he begin once, he 'll
rail in his rope-tricks. I 'll tell you what, sir,—an she
stand him but a little, he will throw a figure in her
face, and so disfigure her with it, that she shall have
no more eyes to see withal than a cat. You know him
not, sir.
Hor. Tarry, Petruchio, I must go with thee,
For in Baptista's keep my treasure is:
He hath the jewel of my life in hold,
His youngest daughter, beautiful Bianca,
And her withholds from me, and other more   120
Suitors to her, and rivals in my love;
Supposing it a thing impossible,

Gre. "And see you read no other lectures to her."

For those defects I have before rehears'd,
That ever Katharina will be woo'd:
Therefore this order hath Baptista ta'en,
That none shall have access unto Bianca,
Till Katharine the curst have got a husband.
Gru. Katharine the curst!
A title for a maid of all titles the worst.
Hor. Now shall my friend Petruchio do me grace,
And offer me, disguis'd in sober robes,   131
To old Baptista as a schoolmaster
Well seen in music, to instruct Bianca;
That so I may, by this device, at least
Have leave and leisure to make love to her,
And unsuspected court her by herself.

Enter GREMIO, *and* LUCENTIO *disguised, with books
under his arm.*

Gru. Here 's no knavery! See, to beguile the old
folks, how the young folks lay their heads together!
Master, master, look about you: who goes there? ha!
Hor. Peace, Grumio: 't is the rival of my love. 140
Petruchio, stand by awhile.
Gru. A proper stripling, and an amorous!
                                            [*They retire.*
Gre. O! very well; I have perus'd the note.
Hark you, sir; I 'll have them very fairly bound:

All books of love, see that at any hand,
And see you read no other lectures to her.
You understand me.—Over and beside
Signior Baptista's liberality,
I'll mend it with a largess.—Take your papers, too,
And let me have them very well perfum'd,   150
For she is sweeter than perfume itself,
To whom they go to. What will you read to her?
    Luc. Whate'er I read to her, I'll plead for you,
As for my patron, stand you so assur'd,
As firmly as yourself were still in place;
Yea, and perhaps with more successful words
Than you, unless you were a scholar, sir.
    Gre. O, this learning! what a thing it is!
    Gru. O, this woodcock! what an ass it is!
    Pet. Peace, sirrah!   160
    Hor. Grumio, mum!—[*Coming forward.*] God save
            you, Signior Gremio!
    Gre. And you're well met, Signior Hortensio. Trow
            you,
Whither I am going?—To Baptista Minola.
I promis'd to inquire carefully
About a schoolmaster for the fair Bianca;
And, by good fortune, I have lighted well
On this young man; for learning, and behaviour,
Fit for her turn; well read in poetry,
And other books,—good ones, I warrant ye.
    Hor. 'T is well: and I have met a gentleman,   170
Hath promis'd me to help me to another,
A fine musician to instruct our mistress:
So shall I no whit be behind in duty
To fair Bianca, so belov'd of me.
    Gre. Belov'd of me, and that my deeds shall prove.
    Gru. And that his bags shall prove.
    Hor. Gremio, 't is now no time to vent our love.
Listen to me, and if you speak me fair,
I'll tell you news indifferent good for either.
Here is a gentleman, whom by chance I met,   180
Upon agreement from us to his liking,
Will undertake to woo curst Katharine;
Yea, and to marry her, if her dowry please.
    Gre. So said, so done, is well.—
Hortensio, have you told him all her faults?
    Pet. I know, she is an irksome, brawling scold:
If that be all, masters, I hear no harm.
    Gre. No, say'st me so, friend? What countryman?
    Pet. Born in Verona, old Antonio's son:
My father dead, my fortune lives for me;   190
And I do hope good days and long to see.
    Gre. O! sir, such a life, with such a wife, were
            strange!
But if you have a stomach, to 't o' God's name:
You shall have me assisting you in all.
But will you woo this wild-cat?
    Pet.   Will I live?
    Gru. Will he woo her? ay, or I'll hang her.
    Pet. Why came I hither, but to that intent?
Think you, a little din can daunt mine ears?
Have I not in my time heard lions roar?
Have I not heard the sea, puff'd up with winds,   200
Rage like an angry boar, chafed with sweat?
Have I not heard great ordnance in the field,
And heaven's artillery thunder in the skies?
Have I not in a pitched battle heard
Loud 'larums, neighing steeds, and trumpets' clang?
And do you tell me of a woman's tongue,
That gives not half so great a blow to hear
As will a chestnut in a farmer's fire?
Tush! tush! fear boys with bugs.
    Gru.   For he fears none.
    Gre. Hortensio, hark.   210
This gentleman is happily arriv'd,
My mind presumes, for his own good, and ours.
    Hor. I promis'd we would be contributors,
And bear his charge of wooing, whatsoe'er.

    Gre. And so we will, provided that he win her.
    Gru. I would, I were as sure oi a good dinner.

Enter TRANIO, *bravely apparelled; and* BIONDELLO.

    Tra. Gentlemen, God save you! If I may be bold,
Tell me, I beseech you, which is the readiest way
To the house of Signior Baptista Minola?
    Gre. He that has the two fair daughters:—is 't he
            you mean?   220
    Tra. Even he.—Biondello!
    Gre. Hark you, sir: you mean not her too?
    Tra. Perhaps, him and her, sir: what have you to do?
    Pet. Not her that chides, sir, at any hand, I pray.
    Tra. I love no chiders, sir.—Biondello, let's away.
    Luc. [*Aside.*] Well begun, Tranio.
    Hor.   Sir, a word ere you go.
Are you a suitor to the maid you talk of, yea, or no?
    Tra. An if I be, sir, is it any offence?
    Gre. No; if without more words you will get you
            hence.
    Tra. Why, sir, I pray, are not the streets as free   230
For me, as for you?
    Gre.   But so is not she.
    Tra. For what reason, I beseech you?
    Gre. For this reason, if you'll know,
That she's the choice love of Signior Gremio.
    Hor. That she's the cho-en of Signior Hortensio.
    Tra. Softly, my masters! if you be gentlemen,
Do me this right; hear me with patience.
Baptista is a noble gentleman,
To whom my father is not all unknown;
And were his daughter fairer than she is,   240
She may more suitors have, and me for one.
Fair Leda's daughter had a thousand wooers;
Then, well one more may fair Bianca have,
And so she shall. Lucentio shall make one,
Though Paris came in hope to speed alone.
    Gre. What! this gentleman will out-talk us all.
    Luc. Sir, give him head: I know, he'll prove a
            jade.
    Pet. Hortensio, to what end are all these words?
    Hor. Sir, let me be so bold as ask you,
Did you yet ever see Baptista's daughter?   250
    Tra. No, sir; but hear I do, that he hath two,
The one as famous for a scolding tongue,
As is the other for beauteous modesty.
    Pet. Sir, sir, the first's for me; let her go by.
    Gre. Yea, leave that labour to great Hercules,
And let it be more than Alcides' twelve.
    Pet. Understand you this of me: in sooth,
The youngest daughter, whom you hearken for,
Her father keeps from all access of suitors,
And will not promise her to any man,   260
Until the elder sister first be wed;
The younger then is free, and not before.
    Tra. If it be so, sir, that you are the man
Must stead us all, and me among the rest;
And if you break the ice, and do this feat,
Achieve the elder, set the younger free
For our access,—whose hap shall be to have her
Will not so graceless be, to be ingrate.
    Hor. Sir, you say well, and well you do conceive;
And since you do profess to be a suitor,   270
You must, as we do, gratify this gentleman,
To whom we all rest generally beholding.
    Tra. Sir, I shall not be slack: in sign whereof,
Please ye we may contrive this afternoon,
And quaff carouses to our mistress' health;
And do as adversaries do in law,
Strive mightily, but eat and drink as friends.
    Gru., Bion. O excellent motion! Fellows, let's be
            gone.
    Hor. The motion's good indeed, and be it so.—
Petruchio, I shall be your *ben venuto.*   280
                                            [*Exeunt.*

ACT II.

SCENE I.—The Same. A Room in BAPTISTA's House.

Enter KATHARINA and BIANCA.

Bianca.
GOOD sister, wrong me not, nor wrong
  yourself,
To make a bondmaid and a slave of me :
That I disdain ; but for these other gawds,
Unbind my hands, I'll pull them off
  myself,
Yea, all my raiment, to my petticoat ;
Or what you will command me, will I do,
So well I know my duty to my elders.
  Kath. Of all thy suitors, here I charge
  thee, tell
Whom thou lov'st best : see thou dis-
  semble not.
  Bian. Believe me, sister, of all the men alive,   10
I never yet beheld that special face
Which I could fancy more than any other.
  Kath. Minion, thou liest. Is 't not Hortensio ?
  Bian. If you affect him, sister, here I swear,
I 'll plead for you myself, but you shall have him.

  Kath. O ! then, belike, you fancy riches more
You will have Gremio to keep you fair.
  Bian. Is it for him you do envy me so ?
Nay, then you jest ; and now I well perceive,
You have but jested with me all this while.   20
I pr'ythee, sister Kate, untie my hands.
  Kath. If that be jest, then all the rest was so.
                            [Strikes her.

Enter BAPTISTA.

  Bap. Why, how now, dame ! whence grows this
  insolence ?—
Bianca, stand aside :—poor girl ! she weeps.—
Go ply thy needle ; meddle not with her.—
For shame, thou hilding of a devilish spirit,
Why dost thou wrong her that did ne'er wrong thee ?
When did she cross thee with a bitter word ?

  Kath. Her silence flouts me, and I 'll be reveng'd.
                       [Flies after BIANCA.
  Bap. What ! in my sight ?—Bianca, get thee in.   30
                           [Exit BIANCA.
  Kath. What ! will you not suffer me ? Nay, now I see,
She is your treasure, she must have a husband ;
I must dance bare-foot on her wedding-day,
And, for your love to her, lead apes in hell.
Talk not to me : I will go sit and weep,
Till I can find occasion of revenge.   *[Exit.*
  Bap. Was ever gentleman thus griev'd as I ?—
But who comes here ?

Enter GREMIO, with LUCENTIO in the habit of a mean man ; PETRUCHIO, with HORTENSIO as a musician ; and TRANIO, with BIONDELLO bearing a lute and books.

  Gre. Good morrow, neighbour Baptista.
  Bap. Good morrow, neighbour Gremio. God save
you, gentlemen !   41
  Pet. And you, good sir. Pray,
      have you not a daughter,
Call'd Katharina, fair, and virtuous ?
  Bap. I have a daughter, sir, call'd
    Katharina.
  Gre. You are too blunt : go to it
    orderly.
  Pet. You wrong me, Signior
    Gremio : give me leave. —
I am a gentleman of Verona, sir,
That, hearing of her beauty, and her
    wit,
Her affability, and bashful modesty,
Her wondrous qualities, and mild
    behaviour,   50
Am bold to show myself a forward
    guest
Within your house, to make mine
    eye the witness
Of that report which I so oft have
    heard.
And, for an entrance to my enter-
    tainment,
I do present you with a man of mine,
        [Presenting HORTENSIO.
Cunning in music and the mathe-
    matics,
To instruct her fully in those sciences,
Whereof, I know, she is not ignorant.
Accept of him, or else you do me wrong :
His name is Licio, born in Mantua.   60
  Bap. You 're welcome, sir ; and he, for your good
sake.
But for my daughter Katharine, this I know,
She is not for your turn, the more my grief.
  Pet. I see, you do not mean to part with her,
Or else you like not of my company.
  Bap. Mistake me not ; I speak but as I find.
Whence are you, sir ? what may I call your name ?
  Pet. Petruchio is my name, Antonio's son ;
A man well known throughout all Italy.
  Bap. I know him well : you are welcome for his sake.
  Gre. Saving your tale, Petruchio, I pray,   71
Let us, that are poor petitioners, speak too.
Backare ! you are marvellous forward.

'Bap. "Why, how now, dame ! whence grows this insolence ?"

Pet. O! pardon me, Signior Gremio; I would fain
be doing.
Gre. I doubt it not, sir; but you will curse your
wooing.—
Neighbour, this is a gift very grateful, I am sure of it.
To express the like kindness, myself that have been
more kindly beholding to you than any, freely give
unto you this young scholar [*presenting* LUCENTIO],
that hath been long studying at Rheims; as cunning
in Greek, Latin, and other languages, as the other in
music and mathematics. His name is Cambio: pray
accept his service.   83
Bap. A thousand thanks, Signior Gremio; welcome,
good Cambio.—[*To* TRANIO.] But, gentle sir, methinks,
you walk like a stranger: may I be so bold to know
the cause of your coming?
Tra. Pardon me, sir, the boldness is mine own,
That, being a stranger in this city here,
Do make myself a suitor to your daughter,   90
Unto Bianca, fair, and virtuous.
Nor is your firm resolve unknown to me,
In the preferment of the eldest sister.
This liberty is all that I request,—
That, upon knowledge of my parentage,
I may have welcome 'mongst the rest that woo,
And free access and favour as the rest.
And, toward the education of your daughters,
I here bestow a simple instrument,
And this small packet of Greek and Latin books: 100
If you accept them, then their worth is great.
Bap. Lucentio is your name? of whence, I pray?
Tra. Of Pisa, sir; son to Vincentio.
Bap. A mighty man of Pisa; by report
I know him well: you are very welcome, sir.—
[*To* HOR.] Take you the lute, [*to* LUC.] and you the
set of books;
You shall go see your pupils presently.
Holla, within!

Enter a Servant.

Sirrah, lead these gentlemen
To my daughters; and tell them both,
These are their tutors: bid them use them well.   110
[*Exit Servant, with* HORTENSIO, LUCENTIO,
and BIONDELLO.
We will go walk a little in the orchard,
And then to dinner.   You are passing welcome,
And so I pray you all to think yourselves.
Pet. Signior Baptista, my business asketh haste,
And every day I cannot come to woo.
You knew my father well, and in him, me,
Left solely heir to all his lands and goods,
Which I have better'd rather than decreas'd:
Then tell me,—if I get your daughter's love,
What dowry shall I have with her to wife?   120
Bap. After my death, the one half of my lands;
And in possession twenty thousand crowns.
Pet. And, for that dowry, I'll assure her of
Her widowhood, be it that she survive me,
In all my lands and leases whatsoever.
Let specialties be therefore drawn between us,
That covenants may be kept on either hand.
Bap. Ay, when the special thing is well obtain'd,
That is, her love; for that is all in all.
Pet. Why, that is nothing; for I tell you, father, 130
I am as peremptory as she proud-minded;
And where two raging fires meet together,
They do consume the thing that feeds their fury:
Though little fire grows great with little wind,
Yet extreme gusts will blow out fire and all;
So I to her, and so she yields to me,
For I am rough, and woo not like a babe.
Bap. Well may'st thou woo, and happy be thy
speed!
But be thou arm'd for some unhappy words.
Pet. Ay, to the proof, as mountains are for winds,
That shake not, though they blow perpetually.   141

Re-enter HORTENSIO, *with his head broken.*

Bap. How now, my friend? why dost thou look so
pale?
Hor. For fear, I promise you, if I look pale.

Bap. What, will my daughter prove a good
musician?
Hor. I think, she'll sooner prove a soldier:
Iron may hold her, but never lutes.
Bap. Why, then thou canst not break her to the
lute?
Hor. Why, no, for she hath broke the lute to me.
I did but tell her she mistook her frets,
And bow'd her hand to teach her fingering,   150
When, with a most impatient, devilish spirit,
"Frets call you these?" quoth she; "I'll fume with
them:"
And with that word she struck me on the head,
And through the instrument my pate made way;
And there I stood amazed for a while,
As on a pillory, looking through the lute,
While she did call me rascal fiddler,
And twangling Jack, with twenty such vile terms,
As had she studied to misuse me so.
Pet. Now, by the world, it is a lusty wench!   160
I love her ten times more than e'er I did:
O, how I long to have some chat with her!
Bap. Well, go with me, and be not so discomfited:
Proceed in practice with my younger daughter;
She's apt to learn, and thankful for good turns.—
Signior Petruchio, will you go with us,
Or shall I send my daughter Kate to you?
Pet. I pray you do; I will attend her here,
[*Exeunt* BAPTISTA, GREMIO, TRANIO, *and*
HORTENSIO.
And woo her with some spirit when she comes.
Say, that she rail; why, then I'll tell her plain, 170
She sings as sweetly as a nightingale:
Say, that she frown; I'll say, she looks as clear
As morning roses newly wash'd with dew:
Say, she be mute, and will not speak a word;
Then I'll commend her volubility,
And say, she uttereth piercing eloquence:
If she do bid me pack, I'll give her thanks,
As though she bid me stay by her a week:
If she deny to wed, I'll crave the day
When I shall ask the banns, and when be married.—
But here she comes; and now, Petruchio, speak.   181

Enter KATHARINA.

Good morrow, Kate, for that's your name, I hear.
Kath. Well have you heard, but something hard of
hearing:
They call me Katharine, that do talk of me.
Pet. You lie, in faith; for you are call'd plain Kate,
And bonny Kate, and sometimes Kate the curst;
But Kate, the prettiest Kate in Christendom;
Kate of Kate Hall, my super-dainty Kate,
For dainties are all cates: and therefore, Kate,
Take this of me, Kate of my consolation:—   190
Hearing thy mildness prais'd in every town,
Thy virtues spoke of, and thy beauty sounded,
Yet not so deeply as to thee belongs,
Myself am mov'd to woo thee for my wife.
Kath. Mov'd! in good time: let him that mov'd
you hither,
Remove you hence. I knew you at the first,
You were a movable.
Pet.   Why, what's a movable?
Kath. A joint-stool.
Pet.   Thou hast hit it: come, sit on me.
Kath. Asses are made to bear, and so are you.
Pet. Women are made to bear, and so are you.   200
Kath. No such jade as bear you, if me you mean.
Pet. Alas, good Kate! I will not burden thee;
For, knowing thee to be but young and light,—
Kath. Too light for such a swain as you to catch,
And yet as heavy as my weight should be.
Pet. Should be? should buz.
Kath.   Well ta'en, and like a buzzard.
Pet. O slow-wing'd turtle! shall a buzzard take thee?
Kath. Ay, for a turtle, as he takes a buzzard.
Pet. Come, come, you wasp; i'faith, you are too
angry.
Kath. If I be waspish, best beware my sting.   210
Pet. My remedy is then, to pluck it out.
Kath. Ay, if the fool could find it where it lies.

Pet. Who knows not where a wasp does wear his
    sting?
In his tail.
    Kath.   In his tongue.
    Pet.   Whose tongue?
    Kath. Yours, if you talk of tails; and so farewell.
    Pet. What! with my tongue in your tail? nay, come
    again:
Good Kate, I am a gentleman.
    Kath.   That I 'll try. [*Striking him.*
    Pet. I swear I 'll cuff you, if you strike
    again.
    Kath. So may you lose your arms:
If you strike me, you are no gentleman,
And if no gentleman, why, then no
    arms.   221
    Pet. A herald, Kate? O! put me in
    thy books.
    Kath. What is your crest? a coxcomb?
    Pet. A combless cock, so Kate will be
    my hen.
    Kath. No cock of mine; you crow too
    like a craven.
    Pet. Nay, come, Kate, come; you must
    not look so sour.
    Kath. It is my fashion when I see a
    crab.
    Pet. Why, here 's no crab, and there-
    fore look not sour.
    Kath. There is, there is.
    Pet. Then show it me.
    Kath.   Had I a glass, I would.
    Pet. What, you mean my face?
    Kath.   Well aim'd
    of such a young one.   231
    Pet. Now, by Saint George, I am too
    young for you.
    Kath. Yet you are wither'd.
    Pet.   'T is with cares.
    Kath.   I care not.
    Pet. Nay, hear you, Kate: in sooth, you 'scape not so.
    Kath. I chafe you, if I tarry: let me go.
    Pet. No, not a whit: I find you passing gentle.
'T was told me, you were rough, and coy, and sullen,
And now I find report a very liar;
For thou art pleasant, gamesome, passing courteous,
But slow in speech, yet sweet as spring-time flowers,
Thou canst not frown, thou canst not look askance,
Nor bite the lip, as angry wenches will;   242
Nor hast thou pleasure to be cross in talk;
But thou with mildness entertain'st thy wooers,
With gentle conference, soft and affable.
Why does the world report that Kate doth limp?
O slanderous world! Kate, like the hazel-twig,
Is straight, and slender; and as brown in hue
As hazel-nuts, and sweeter than the kernels.
O! let me see thee walk: thou dost not halt.   250
    Kath. Go, fool, and whom thou keep'st command.
    Pet. Did ever Dian so become a grove,
As Kate this chamber with her princely gait?
O! be thou Dian, and let her be Kate,
And then let Kate be chaste, and Dian sportful.
    Kath. Where did you study all this goodly speech?
    Pet. It is extempore, from my mother-wit.
    Kath. A witty mother! witless else her son.
    Pet. Am I not wise?
    Kath.   Yes; keep you warm.
    Pet. Marry, so I mean, sweet Katharine, in thy
    bed.   260
And therefore, setting all this chat aside,
Thus in plain terms:—your father hath consented
That you shall be my wife; your dowry 'greed on;
And, will you, nill you, I will marry you.
Now, Kate, I am a husband for your turn;
For, by this light, whereby I see thy beauty,
Thy beauty that doth make me like thee well,
Thou must be married to no man but me:
For I am he am born to tame you, Kate,
And bring you from a wild Kate to a Kate   270
Conformable, as other household Kates.
Here comes your father: never make denial;
I must and will have Katharine to my wife.

Re-enter BAPTISTA, GREMIO, *and* TRANIO.

    Bap. Now, Signior Petruchio, how speed you with
    my daughter?
    Pet. How but well, sir? how but well?
It were impossible I should speed amiss.
    Bap. Why, how now, daughter Katharine? in your
    dumps?
    Kath. Call you me daughter? now, I promise you,
You have show'd a tender fatherly regard,

Bap. "God send you joy, Petruchio! 't is a match."

To wish me wed to one half lunatic;   280
A mad-cap ruffian, and a swearing Jack,
That thinks with oaths to face the matter out.
    Pet. Father, 't is thus:—yourself and all the world,
That talk'd of her, have talk'd amiss of her.
If she be curst, it is for policy,
For she 's not froward, but modest as the dove;
She is not hot, but temperate as the morn;
For patience she will prove a second Grissel,
And Roman Lucrece for her chastity;
And to conclude,—we have 'greed so well together,
That upon Sunday is the wedding-day.   291
    Kath. I 'll see thee hang'd on Sunday first.
    Gre. Hark, Petruchio: she says, she 'll see thee
    hang'd first.
    Tra. Is this your speeding? nay then, good night
    our part.
    Pet. Be patient, gentlemen, I choose her for myself:
If she and I be pleas'd, what 's that to you?
'T is bargain'd 'twixt us twain, being alone,
That she shall still be curst in company.
I tell you, 't is incredible to believe
How much she loves me. O, the kindest Kate!   300
She hung about my neck, and kiss on kiss
She vied so fast, protesting oath on oath,
That in a twink she won me to her love.
O! you are novices: 't is a world to see,
How tame, when men and women are alone,
A meacock wretch can make the curstest shrew.—
Give me thy hand, Kate: I will unto Venice,
To buy apparel 'gainst the wedding-day.—
Provide the feast, father, and bid the guests;
I will be sure, my Katharine shall be fine.   310
    Bap. I know not what to say; but give me your
    hands:
God send you joy, Petruchio! 't is a match.
    Gre., Tra. Amen, say we: we will be witnesses.
    Pet. Father, and wife, and gentlemen, adieu.
I will to Venice; Sunday comes apace.
We will have rings, and things, and fine array;
And kiss me, Kate, we will be married o' Sunday.
    [*Exeunt* PETRUCHIO *and* KATHARINA, *severally.*

Gre. Was ever match clapp'd up so suddenly?
Bap. 'Faith, gentlemen, now I play a merchant's part,
And venture madly on a desperate mart. 320
  Tra. 'T was a commodity lay fretting by you :
'T will bring you gain, or perish on the seas.
  Bap. The gain I seek is—quiet in the match.
  Gre. No doubt but he hath got a quiet catch.—
But now, Baptista, to your younger daughter.
Now is the day we long have look'd for :
I am your neighbour, and was suitor first.
  Tra. And I am one, that love Bianca more
Than words can witness, or your thoughts can guess.
  Gre. Youngling, thou canst not love so dear as I. 330
  Tra. Grey-beard, thy love doth freeze.
  Gre.   But thine doth fry.
Skipper, stand back : 't is age, that nourisheth.
  Tra. But youth, in ladies' eyes that flourisheth.
  Bap. Content you, gentlemen ; I 'll compound this strife :
'T is deeds must win the prize ; and he, of both,
That can assure my daughter greatest dower,
Shall have Bianca's love.—
Say, Signior Gremio, what can you assure her?
  Gre. First, as you know, my house within the city
Is richly furnished with plate and gold : 340
Basins, and ewers, to lave her dainty hands;
My hangings all of Tyrian tapestry ;
In ivory coffers I have stuff'd my crowns ;
In cypress chests my arras, counterpoints,
Costly apparel, tents, and canopies,
Fine linen, Turkey cushions boss'd with pearl,
Valance of Venice gold in needlework,
Pewter and brass, and all things that belong
To house, or housekeeping : then, at my farm,
I have a hundred milch-kine to the pail, 350
Sixscore fat oxen standing in my stalls,
And all things answerable to this portion.
Myself am struck in years, I must confess ;
And if I die to-morrow, this is hers,
If whilst I live she will be only mine.
  Tra. That " only " came well in.—Sir, list to me :
I am my father's heir and only son :
If I may have your daughter to my wife,
I 'll leave her houses three or four as good,
Within rich Pisa walls, as any one 360
Old Signior Gremio has in Padua ;
Besides two thousand ducats by the year
Of fruitful land, all which shall be her jointure.—
What, have I pinch'd you, Signior Gremio?
  Gre. Two thousand ducats by the year of land !
My land amounts not to so much in all :
That she shall have ; besides an argosy,
That now is lying in Marseilles' road.—
What, have I chok'd you with an argosy?
  Tra. Gremio, 't is known, my father hath no less 370
Than three great argosies, besides two galliasses,
And twelve tight galleys : these I will assure her,
And twice as much, whate'er thou offer'st next.
  Gre. Nay, I have offer'd all, I have no more ;
And she can have no more than all I have :—
If you like me, she shall have me and mine.
  Tra. Why, then the maid is mine from all the world,
By your firm promise. Gremio is out-vied.
  Bap. I must confess, your offer is the best ;
And, let your father make her the assurance, 380
She is your own ; else, you must pardon me :
If you should die before him, where 's her dower?
  Tra. That 's but a cavil : he is old, I young.
  Gre. And may not young men die, as well as old?
  Bap. Well, gentlemen,
I am thus resolv'd.—On Sunday next, you know,
My daughter Katharine is to be married :
Now, on the Sunday following shall Bianca
Be bride to you, if you make this assurance ;
If not, to Signior Gremio : 390
And so I take my leave, and thank you both. [*Exit.*
  Gre. Adieu, good neighbour.—Now I fear thee not :
Sirrah, young gamester, your father were a fool
To give thee all, and, in his waning age,
Set foot under thy table. Tut ! a toy !
An old Italian fox is not so kind, my boy. [*Exit.*
  Tra. A vengeance on your crafty wither'd hide !
Yet I have faced it with a card of ten.
'T is in my head to do my master good :—
I see no reason, but suppos'd Lucentio 400
Must get a father, call'd—suppos'd Vincentio ;
And that 's a wonder : fathers, commonly,
Do get their children ; but in this case of wooing,
A child shall get a sire, if I fail not of my cunning.
                                [*Exit.*

ACT III.

Scene I.—A Room in Baptista's House.

Enter Lucentio, Hortensio, *and* Bianca.

  Lucentio.
FIDDLER, forbear : you grow too forward, sir.
Have you so soon forgot the entertainment
Her sister Katherine welcom'd you withal?
  Hor. But, wrangling pedant, this is
The patroness of heavenly harmony :
Then give me leave to have prerogative ;
And when in music we have spent an hour,
Your lecture shall have leisure for as much.
  Luc. Preposterous ass, that never read so far
To know the cause why music was ordain'd !
Was it not to refresh the mind of man, 11
After his studies, or his usual pain ?
Then give me leave to read philosophy,
And while I pause serve in your harmony.
  Hor. Sirrah, I will not bear these braves of thine.
  Bian. Why, gentlemen, you do me double wrong,
To strive for that which resteth in my choice.
I am no breeching scholar in the schools ;
I 'll not be tied to hours, nor 'pointed times,
But learn my lessons as I please myself. 20
And, to cut off all strife, here sit we down :—
Take you your instrument, play you the whiles ;
His lecture will be done, ere you have tun'd.
  Hor. You 'll leave his lecture, when I am in tune?
                            [*Retires.*
  Luc. That will be never :—tune your instrument.
  Bian. Where left we last ?
  Luc. Here, madam :—
      Hic ibat Simois ; hic est Sigeia tellus ;
      Hic steterat Priami regia celsa senis.
  Bian. Construe them. 30

Luc. Hic ibat, as I told you before,—Simois, I am
Lucentio,—hic est, son unto Vincentio of Pisa,—
Sigeia tellus, disguised thus to get your love;—Hic
steterat, and that Lucentio that comes a-wooing,—
Priami, is my man Tranio,—regia, bearing my port,
—celsa senis, that we might beguile the old pantaloon.
  Hor. [Returning.] Madam, my instrument's in tune.

Bian. "O fie! the treble jars."

Bian. Let's hear. [HOR. plays.] O fie! the treble
      jars.
  Luc. Spit in the hole, man, and tune again.
  Bian. Now let me see if I can construe it :   40
Hic ibat Simois, I know you not;—hic est Sigeia
tellus, I trust you not;—Hic steterat Priami, take
heed he hear us not;—regia, presume not;—celsa
senis, despair not.
  Hor. Madam, 'tis now in tune.
  Luc.   All but the base.
  Hor. The base is right; 'tis the base knave that
      jars.
How fiery and forward our pedant is!
Now, for my life, the knave doth court my love :
Pedascule, I'll watch you better yet.
  Bian. In time I may believe, yet I mistrust.   50
  Luc. Mistrust it not; for, sure, Æacides
Was Ajax, call'd so from his grandfather.
  Bian. I must believe my master; else, I promise
      you,
I should be arguing still upon that doubt :
But let it rest.—Now, Licio, to you.
Good masters, take it not unkindly, pray,
That I have been thus pleasant with you both.
  Hor. [To LUCENTIO.] You may go walk, and give
      me leave awhile :
My lessons make no music in three parts.
  Luc. Are you so formal, sir? [Aside.] Well, I must
      wait,   60
And watch withal; for, but I be deceiv'd,
Our fine musician groweth amorous.
  Hor. Madam, before you touch the instrument,
To learn the order of my fingering,
I must begin with rudiments of art;
To teach you gamut in a briefer sort,
More pleasant, pithy, and effectual,
Than hath been taught by any of my trade :
And there it is in writing, fairly drawn.
  Bian. Why, I am past my gamut long ago.   70
  Hor. Yet read the gamut of Hortensio.
  Bian. [Reads.]
      "Gamut I am, the ground of all accord,
        A re, to plead Hortensio's passion ;
      B mi, Bianca, take him for thy lord,
        C fa ut, that loves with all affection:
      D sol re, one cliff, two notes have I:
        E la mi, show pity, or I die."
Call you this gamut? tut! I like it not :
Old fashions please me best; I am not so nice,
To change true rules for odd inventions.   80

Enter a Servant.

  Serv. Mistress, your father prays you leave your
      books,
And help to dress your sister's chamber up :
You know, to-morrow is the wedding-day.
  Bian. Farewell, sweet masters both : I must be
      gone.   [Exeunt BIANCA and Servant.
  Luc. 'Faith, mistress, then I have no
          cause to stay.   [Exit.
  Hor. But I have cause to pry into
      this pedant :
Methinks, he looks as though he were
      in love.
Yet if thy thoughts, Bianca, be so
      humble,
To cast thy wandering eyes on every
      stale,
Seize thee that list : if once I find thee
      ranging,   90
Hortensio will be quit with thee by
      changing.   [Exit.

SCENE II.—The Same. Before
          BAPTISTA'S House.

Enter BAPTISTA, GREMIO, TRANIO,
    KATHARINA, BIANCA, LUCENTIO,
    and Attendants.

  Bap. Signior Lucentio, this is the
      'pointed day,
That Katharine and Petruchio should be married,
And yet we hear not of our son-in-law.
What will be said? what mockery will it be,
To want the bridegroom, when the priest attends
To speak the ceremonial rites of marriage !
What says Lucentio to this shame of ours?
  Kath. No shame but mine : I must, forsooth, be
      forc'd
To give my hand, oppos'd against my heart,
Unto a mad-brain rudesby, full of spleen ;   10
Who woo'd in haste, and means to wed at leisure.
I told you, I, he was a frantic fool,
Hiding his bitter jests in blunt behaviour ;
And to be noted for a merry man,
He'll woo a thousand, 'point the day of marriage,
Make friends, invite 'them, and proclaim the banns ;
Yet never means to wed where he hath woo'd.
Now must the world point at poor Katharine,
And say,—" Lo, there is mad Petruchio's wife,
If it would please him come and marry her."   20
  Tra. Patience, good Katharine, and Baptista too.
Upon my life, Petruchio means but well,
Whatever fortune stays him from his word :
Though he be blunt, I know him passing wise ;
Though he be merry, yet withal he's honest.
  Kath. 'Would Katharine had never seen him
      though !
      [Exit, weeping, followed by BIANCA and others.
  Bap. Go, girl; I cannot blame thee now to weep,
For such an injury would vex a very saint,
Much more a shrew of thy impatient humour.

Enter BIONDELLO.

  Bion. Master, master! old news, and such news as
you never heard of !   31
  Bap. Is it new and old too? how may that be?
  Bion. Why, is it not news to hear of Petruchio's
coming?
  Bap. Is he come?
  Bion. Why, no, sir.
  Bap. What then?
  Bion. He is coming.
  Bap. When will he be here?
  Bion. When he stands where I am, and sees you
there.   41
  Tra. But, say, what to thine old news?
  Bion. Why, Petruchio is coming, in a new hat, and
an old jerkin : a pair of old breeches, thrice turned ; a
pair of boots that have been candle-cases, one buckled,
another laced ; an old rusty sword ta'en out of the

town-armoury, with a broken hilt, and chapeless;
with two broken points: his horse hipped, with an old
mothy saddle, and stirrups of no kindred; besides,
possessed with the glanders, and like to mose in the
chine; troubled with the lampass, infected with the
fashions, full of windgalls, sped with spavins, rayed
with the yellows, past cure of the fives, stark spoiled
with the staggers, begnawn with the bots, swayed in
the back, and shoulder-shotten; ne'er-legged before,
and with a half-checked bit, and a head-stall of sheep's
leather; which, being restrained to keep him from
stumbling, hath been often burst, and now repaired
with knots; one girth six times pieced, and a woman's
crupper of velure, which hath two letters for her name
fairly set down in studs, and here and there pieced
with packthread.   62
Bap. Who comes with him?
Bion. O, sir! his lackey, for all the world capari-
soned like the horse; with a linen stock on one leg,
and a kersey boot-hose on the other, gartered with a
red and blue list; an old hat, and "the humour of
forty fancies" pricked in 't for a feather: a monster,
a very monster in apparel, and not like a Christian
footboy, or a gentleman's lackey.   70
Tra. 'T is some odd humour pricks him to this
                fashion;
Yet oftentimes he goes but mean-apparell'd.
Bap. I am glad he is come, howsoe'er he comes.
Bion. Why, sir, he comes not.
Bap. Didst thou not say, he comes?
Bion. Who? that Petruchio came?
Bap. Ay, that Petruchio came.
Bion. No, sir; I say, his horse comes, with him on
his back.
Bap. Why, that 's all one.   80
Bion.   Nay, by Saint Jamy,
       I hold you a penny,
       A horse and a man
       Is more than one,
       And yet not many.

        Enter PETRUCHIO *and* GRUMIO.

Pet. Come, where be these gallants? who 's at
home?
Bap. You are welcome, sir.
Pet.   And yet I come not well.
Bap. And yet you halt not.
Tra.   Not so well apparell'd,
As I wish you were.
Pet. Were it better, I should rush in thus.   90
But where is Kate? where is my lovely bride?—
How does my father?—Gentles, methinks you frown:
And wherefore gaze this goodly company,
As if they saw some wondrous monument,
Some comet, or unusual prodigy?
Bap. Why, sir, you know, this is your wedding-day.
First were we sad, fearing you would not come;
Now sadder, that you come so unprovided.
Fie! doff this habit, shame to your estate,
An eyesore to our solemn festival.   100
Tra. And tell us what occasion of import
Hath all so long detain'd you from your wife,
And sent you hither so unlike yourself?
Pet. Tedious it were to tell, and harsh to hear:
Sufficeth, I am come to keep my word,
Though in some part enforced to digress;
Which, at more leisure, I will so excuse
As you shall well be satisfied withal.
But, where is Kate? I stay too long from her:
The morning wears, 't is time we were at church.   110
Tra. See not your bride in these unreverent
                robes.
Go to my chamber: put on clothes of mine.
Pet. Not I, believe me: thus I 'll visit her.
Bap. But thus, I trust, you will not marry her.
Pet. Good sooth, even thus; therefore ha' done
       with words:
To me she 's married, not unto my clothes.
Could I repair what she will wear in me,
As I can change these poor accoutrements,
'T were well for Kate, and better for myself.
But what a fool am I to chat with you,   120

When I should bid good-morrow to my bride,
And seal the title with a lovely kiss!
        [*Exeunt* PETRUCHIO, GRUMIO, *and* BIONDELLO
Tra. He hath some meaning in his mad attire.
We will persuade him, be it possible,
To put on better ere he go to church.
Bap. I 'll after him, and see the event of this. [*Exit.*
Tra. But to her love concerneth us to add
Her father's liking: which to bring to pass,
As I before imparted to your worship,
I am to get a man,—whate'er he be,   130
It skills not much, we 'll fit him to our turn,—
And he shall be Vincentio of Pisa,
And make assurance, here in Padua,
Of greater sums than I have promised.
So shall you quietly enjoy your hope,
And marry sweet Bianca with consent.
Luc. Were it not that my fellow-schoolmaster
Doth watch Bianca's steps so narrowly,
'T were good, methinks, to steal our marriage;
Which once perform'd, let all the world say no,   140
I 'll keep mine own, despite of all the world.
Tra. That by degrees we mean to look into,
And watch our vantage in this business.
We 'll over-reach the grey-beard, Gremio,
The narrow-prying father, Minola,
The quaint musician, amorous Licio;
All for my master's sake, Lucentio.

                Re-enter GREMIO.

Signior Gremio, came you from the church?
Gre. As willingly as e'er I came from school.
Tra. And is the bride, and bridegroom, coming
                home?   150
Gre. A bridegroom say you? 't is a groom indeed,
A grumbling groom, and that the girl shall find.
Tra. Curster than she? why, 't is impossible.
Gre. Why, he 's a devil, a devil, a very fiend.
Tra. Why, she 's a devil, a devil, the devil's dam.
Gre. Tut! she 's a lamb, a dove, a fool to him.
I 'll tell you, Sir Lucentio: when the priest
Should ask, if Katharine should be his wife,
"Ay, by gogs-wouns," quoth he; and swore so loud,
That, all amaz'd, the priest let fall the book;   160
And, as he stoop'd again to take it up,
This mad-brain'd bridegroom took him such a cuff,
That down fell priest and book, and book and priest:
"Now take them up," quoth he, "if any list."
Tra. What said the wench, when he arose again?
Gre. Trembled and shook; for why, he stamp'd, and
                swore,
As if the vicar meant to cozen him.
But after many ceremonies done,
He calls for wine:—"A health!" quoth he; as if
He had been aboard, carousing to his mates   170
After a storm:—quaff'd off the muscadel,
And threw the sops all in the sexton's face;
Having no other reason,
But that his beard grew thin and hungerly,
And seem'd to ask him sops as he was drinking.
This done, he took the bride about the neck,
And kiss'd her lips with such a clamorous smack,
That, at the parting, all the church did echo.
And I, seeing this, came thence for very shame;
And after me, I know, the rout is coming: 180
Such a mad marriage never was before.
Hark, hark! I hear the minstrels play.   [*Music.*

Enter PETRUCHIO, KATHARINA, BIANCA, BAPTISTA,
        HORTENSIO, GRUMIO, *and Train.*

Pet. Gentlemen and friends, I thank you for your
        pains.
I know, you think to dine with me to-day,
And have prepar'd great store of wedding cheer;
But, so it is, my haste doth call me hence,
And therefore here I mean to take my leave.
Bap. Is 't possible you will away to-night?
Pet. I must away to-day, before night come.
Make it no wonder: if you knew my business,   190
You would entreat me rather go than stay.—
And, honest company, I thank you all,
That have beheld me give away myself

To this most patient, sweet, and virtuous wife.
Dine with my father, drink a health to me,
For I must hence : and farewell to you all.
   Tra. Let us entreat you stay till after dinner.

   Pet.   Grumio, my horse!
   Gru. Ay, sir, they be ready : the oats have eaten
the horses.
   Kath. Nay, then,

Pet. "Come, where be these gallants? who's at home?"

   Pet. It may not be.
   Gre.   Let me entreat you.
   Pet. It cannot be.
   Kath.   Let me entreat you.
   Pet. I am content.
   Kath.   Are you content to stay?   200
   Pet. I am content you shall entreat me stay,
But yet not stay, entreat me how you can.
   Kath. Now, if you love me, stay.

Do what thou canst, I will not go to-day ;
No, nor to-morrow, nor till I please myself.
The door is open, sir, there lies your way,
You may be jogging whiles your boots are green ;   210
For me, I 'll not be gone, till I please myself.—
'T is like you 'll prove a jolly surly groom,
That take it on you at the first so roundly.
   Pet. O, Kate ! content thee : pr'ythee, be not
      angry.

Kath. I will be angry. What hast thou to do?—
Father, be quiet; he shall stay my leisure.
  Gre. Ay, marry, sir, now it begins to work.
  Kath. Gentlemen, forward to the bridal dinner.
I see, a woman may be made a fool,
If she had not a spirit to resist.   220
  Pet. They shall go forward, Kate, at thy command.—
Obey the bride, you that attend on her:
Go to the feast, revel and domineer,
Carouse full measure to her maidenhead,
Be mad and merry, or go hang yourselves.
But for my bonny Kate, she must with me.
Nay, look not big, nor stamp, nor stare, nor fret;
I will be master of what is mine own.
She is my goods, my chattels; she is my house,
My household stuff, my field, my barn,   230
My horse, my ox, my ass, my anything;
And here she stands; touch her whoever dare,
I'll bring mine action on the proudest he
That stops my way in Padua.—Grumio,
Draw forth thy weapon; we're beset with thieves:

Rescue thy mistress, if thou be a man.—
Fear not, sweet wench; they shall not touch thee,
         Kate:
I'll buckler thee against a million.
           [*Exeunt* PETRUCHIO, KATHARINA, *and*
                      GRUMIO.
  Bap. Nay, let them go, a couple of quiet ones.
  Gre. Went they not quickly, I should die with
     laughing.   240
  Tra. Of all mad matches never was the like!
  Luc. Mistress, what's your opinion of your sister?
  Bian. That, being mad herself, she's madly mated.
  Gre. I warrant him, Petruchio is Kated.
  Bap. Neighbours and friends, though bride and
     bridegroom wants
For to supply the places at the table,
You know, there wants no junkets at the feast.—
Lucentio, you shall supply the bridegroom's place,
And let Bianca take her sister's room.   249
  Tra. Shall sweet Bianca practise how to bride it?
  Bap. She shall, Lucentio.—Come, gentlemen, let's
     go.   [*Exeunt.*

ACT IV.

SCENE I.—A Hall in PETRUCHIO'S Country House.

Enter GRUMIO.

  Grumio.

FIE, fie, on all tired jades, on all mad masters, and all foul ways! Was ever man so beaten? was ever man so rayed? was ever man so weary? I am sent before to make a fire, and they are coming after to warm them. Now, were not I a little pot, and soon hot, my very lips might freeze to my teeth, my tongue to the roof of my mouth, my heart in my belly, ere I should come by a fire to thaw me; but, I, with blowing the fire, shall warm myself, for, considering the weather, a taller man than I will take cold. Holla, ho! Curtis!   14

  Enter CURTIS.

  Curt. Who is that calls so coldly?
  Gru. A piece of ice: if thou doubt it, thou may'st slide from my shoulder to my heel, with no greater a run but my head and my neck. A fire, good Curtis.   20
  Curt. Is my master and his wife coming, Grumio?
  Gru. O! ay, Curtis, ay; and therefore fire, fire; cast on no water.
  Curt. Is she so hot a shrew as she's reported?
  Gru. She was, good Curtis, before this frost; but, thou know'st, winter tames man, woman, and beast, for it hath tamed my old master, and my new mistress, and myself, fellow Curtis.
  Curt. Away, you three-inch fool! I am no beast.   29
  Gru. Am I but three inches? why, thy horn is a foot; and so long am I at the least. But wilt thou make a fire, or shall I complain on thee to our mistress, whose hand (she being now at hand) thou shalt soon feel, to thy cold comfort, for being slow in thy hot office?

  Curt. I pr'ythee, good Grumio, tell me, how goes the world?
  Gru. A cold world, Curtis, in every office but thine; and, therefore, fire. Do thy duty, and have thy duty, for my master and mistress are almost frozen to death.
  Curt. There's fire ready; and therefore, good Grumio, the news.   42
  Gru. Why, "Jack, boy! ho, boy!" and as much news as thou wilt.
  Curt. Come, you are so full of cony-catching.
  Gru. Why, therefore, fire: for I have caught extreme cold. Where's the cook? is supper ready, the house trimmed, rushes strewed, cobwebs swept; the serving-men in their new fustian, their white stockings, and every officer his wedding-garment on? Be the Jacks fair within, the Jills fair without, the carpets laid, and everything in order?   52
  Curt. All ready; and therefore, I pray thee, news.
  Gru. First, know, my horse is tired; my master and mistress fallen out.
  Curt. How?
  Gru. Out of their saddles into the dirt; and thereby hangs a tale.
  Curt. Let's ha't, good Grumio.
  Gru. Lend thine ear.   60
  Curt. Here.
  Gru. There.   [*Striking him.*
  Curt. This is to feel a tale, not to hear a tale.
  Gru. And therefore 't is called a sensible tale; and this cuff was but to knock at your ear, and beseech listening. Now I begin:— *Imprimis*, we came down a foul hill, my master riding behind my mistress,—
  Curt. Both of one horse?
  Gru. What's that to thee?
  Curt. Why, a horse.   70
  Gru. Tell thou the tale:—but hadst thou not crossed me, thou shouldst have heard how her horse fell, and she under her horse; thou shouldst have heard, in

how miry a place; how she was bemoiled; how he left
her with the horse upon her; how he beat me because
her horse stumbled; how she waded through the dirt
to pluck him off me; how he swore; how she prayed,
that never prayed before; how I cried; how the
horses ran away; how her bridle was burst; how I
lost my crupper;—with many things of worthy
memory, which now shall die in oblivion, and thou
return unexperienced to thy grave.   82

Gru. "And thereby hangs a tale."

Curt. By this reckoning he is more shrew than she.
Gru. Ay; and that thou and the proudest of you all
shall find, when he comes home. But what talk I of
this?—Call forth Nathaniel, Joseph, Nicholas, Philip,
Walter, Sugarsop, and the rest: let their heads be
sleekly combed, their blue coats brushed, and their
garters of an indifferent knit: let them curtsy with
their left legs, and not presume to touch a hair of my
master's horsetail, till they kiss their hands. Are they
all ready?   92
Curt. They are.
Gru. Call them forth.
Curt. Do you hear? ho! you must meet my master,
to countenance my mistress.
Gru. Why, she hath a face of her own.
Curt. Who knows not that?
Gru. Thou, it seems, that callest for company to
countenance her.   100
Curt. I call them forth to credit her.
Gru. Why, she comes to borrow nothing of them.

Enter several Servants.

Nath. Welcome home, Grumio.
Phil. How now, Grumio?
Jos. What, Grumio!
Nich. Fellow Grumio!
Nath. How now, old lad?
Gru. Welcome, you;—how now, you;—what, you;
—fellow, you;—and thus much for greeting. Now,
my spruce companions, is all ready, and all things
neat?   111
Nath. All things is ready. How near is our master?
Gru. E'en at hand, alighted by this; and therefore
be not—Cock's passion, silence!—I hear my master.

Enter PETRUCHIO *and* KATHARINA.

Pet. Where be these knaves? What! no man at
          door,
To hold my stirrup, nor to take my horse?
Where is Nathaniel, Gregory, Philip?—

All Serv. Here, here, sir; here, sir.
Pet. Here, sir! here, sir! here, sir! here, sir!
You logger-headed and unpolish'd grooms!   126
What, no attendance? no regard? no duty?—
Where is the foolish knave I sent before?
Gru. Here, sir; as foolish as I was before.
Pet. You peasant swain! you whoreson malt-horse
          drudge!
Did I not bid thee meet me in the park,
And bring along these rascal knaves with thee?
Gru. Nathaniel's coat, sir, was not fully made,
And Gabriel's pumps were all unpink'd i' the heel;
There was no link to colour Peter's hat,
And Walter's dagger was not come from sheathing:
There were none fine, but Adam, Ralph, and Gregory;
The rest were ragged, old, and beggarly;   132
Yet, as they are, here are they come to meet you.
Pet. Go, rascals, go, and fetch my supper in.—
          [*Exeunt Servants.*
[*Sings.*] *Where is the life that late I led—*
Where are those--? Sit down, Kate, and welcome.
Soud, soud, soud, soud!

Re-enter Servants, with supper.

Why, when, I say?—Nay, good sweet Kate, be merry.
Off with my boots, you rogues, you villains! When?
[*Sings.*] *It was the friar of orders grey,*   140
     As he forth walked on his way:—
Out, you rogue! you pluck my foot awry:
Take that, and mend the plucking of the other.—
          [*Strikes him.*
Be merry, Kate.—Some water, here; what, ho!—
Where's my spaniel Troilus?—Sirrah, get you hence,
And bid my cousin Ferdinand come hither:—
          [*Exit Servant.*
One, Kate, that you must kiss, and be acquainted
          with.—
Where are my slippers?—Shall I have some water?

Enter a Servant with a basin and ewer.

Come, Kate, and wash, and welcome heartily.—
You whoreson villain! will you let it fall?   150
          [*Strikes him.*
Kath. Patience, I pray you; 't was a fault unwilling.
Pet. A whoreson, beetle-headed, flap-ear'd knave!
Come, Kate, sit down; I know you have a stomach.
Will you give thanks, sweet Kate, or else shall I?
What's this? mutton?
1 Serv.   Ay.
Pet.   Who brought it?
1 Serv.   I.
Pet. 'T is burnt; and so is all the meat.
What dogs are these!—Where is the rascal cook?
How durst you, villains, bring it from the dresser,
And serve it thus to me that love it not?
There, take it to you, trenchers, cups, and all.   160
          [*Throws the meat, &c., at them.*
You heedless joltheads, and unmanner'd slaves!
What! do you grumble? I'll be with you straight.
Kath. I pray you, husband, be not so disquiet:
The meat was well, if you were so contented.
Pet. I tell thee, Kate, 't was burnt and dried away,
And I expressly am forbid to touch it,
For it engenders choler, planteth anger;
And better 't were, that both of us did fast,
Since, of ourselves, ourselves are choleric,
Than feed with such over-roasted flesh.   170
Be patient, to-morrow 't shall be mended,
And for this night we'll fast for company.
Come, I will bring thee to thy bridal chamber.
          [*Exeunt* PETRUCHIO, KATHARINA, *and* CURTIS.
Nath. Peter, didst ever see the like?
Peter. He kills her in her own humour.

Re-enter CURTIS.

Gru. Where is he?
Curt. In her chamber,
Making a sermon of continency to her:
And rails, and swears, and rates, that she, poor soul,
Knows not which way to stand, to look, to speak,   180
And sits as one new-risen from a dream.
Away, away! for he is coming hither.   [*Exeunt.*

Re-enter PETRUCHIO.

Pet. Thus have I politicly begun my reign,
And 't is my hope to end successfully.
My falcon now is sharp, and passing empty,
And, till she stoop, she must not be full-gorg'd,
For then she never looks upon her lure.
Another way I have to man my haggard,
To make her come, and know her keeper's call;

Scene II.—Padua. Before BAPTISTA'S House.

Enter TRANIO *and* HORTENSIO.

Tra. Is 't possible, friend Licio, that Mistress Bianca
Doth fancy any other but Lucentio?
I tell you, sir, she bears me fair in hand.
Hor. Sir, to satisfy you in what I have said,
Stand by, and mark the manner of his teaching.
           [*They stand aside.*

Pet. " There, take it to you, trenchers, cups, and all."

That is, to watch her, as we watch these kites, 190
That bate, and beat, and will not be obedient.
She eat no meat to-day, nor none shall eat;
Last night she slept not, nor to-night she shall not:
As with the meat, some undeserved fault
I 'll find about the making of the bed;
And here I 'll fling the pillow, there the bolster,
This way the coverlet, another way the sheets:—
Ay, and amid this hurly, I intend,
That all is done in reverent care of her;
And, in conclusion, she shall watch all night: 200
And, if she chance to nod, I 'll rail and brawl,
And with the clamour keep her still awake.
This is a way to kill a wife with kindness;
And thus I 'll curb her mad and headstrong humour.
He that knows better how to tame a shrew,
Now let him speak : 't is charity to show. [*Exit.*

Enter BIANCA *and* LUCENTIO.

Luc. Now, mistress, profit you in what you read?
Bian. What, master, read you? first resolve me
  that.
Luc. I read that I profess, the Art to Love.
Bian. And may you prove, sir, master of your art!
Luc. While you, sweet dear, prove mistress of my
  heart.   [*They retire.*
Hor. [*Coming forward.*] Quick proceeders, marry!
  Now tell me, I pray, 11
You that durst swear that your Mistress Bianca
Lov'd none in the world so well as Lucentio.
Tra. O despiteful love! unconstant womankind!—
I tell thee, Licio, this is wonderful.
Hor. Mistake no more : I am not Licio,
Nor a musician, as I seem to be,

But one that scorns to live in this disguise,
For such a one, as leaves a gentleman,
And makes a god of such a cullion. 20
Know, sir, that I am call'd Hortensio.
  Tra. Signior Hortensio, I have often heard
Of your entire affection to Bianca ;
And since mine eyes are witness of her lightness,
I will with you, if you be so contented,
Forswear Bianca and her love for ever.
  Hor. See, how they kiss and court!—Signior Lu-
    centio,
Here is my hand, and here I firmly vow
Never to woo her more ; but do forswear her,
As one unworthy all the former favours 30
That I have fondly flatter'd her withal.
  Tra. And here I take the like unfeigned oath,
Never to marry with her, though she would entreat.
Fie on her ! see, how beastly she doth court him.
  Hor. 'Would all the world, but he, had quite for-
    sworn !
For me, that I may surely keep mine oath,
I will be married to a wealthy widow,
Ere three days pass, which hath as long lov'd me,
As I have lov'd this proud disdainful haggard.
And so farewell, Signior Lucentio.— 40
Kindness in women, not their beauteous looks,
Shall win my love :—and so I take my leave,
In resolution as I swore before.
  [*Exit* HORTENSIO.—LUCENTIO *and* BIANCA *advance.*
  Tra. Mistress Bianca, bless you with such grace,
As 'longeth to a lover's blessed case !
Nay, I have ta'en you napping, gentle love,
And have forsworn you, with Hortensio.
  Bian. Tranio, you jest. But have you both for-
    sworn me ?
  Tra. Mistress, we have.
  Luc.   Then we are rid of Licio.
  Tra. I' faith, he 'll have a lusty widow now, 50
That shall be woo'd and wedded in a day.
  Bian. God give him joy !
  Tra. Ay, and he 'll tame her.
  Bian.   He says so, Tranio.
  Tra. 'Faith, he is gone unto the taming-school.
  Bian. The taming-school ! what, is there such a
    place ?
  Tra. Ay, mistress, and Petruchio is the master ;
That teacheth tricks eleven and twenty long,
To tame a shrew, and charm her chattering tongue.

    Enter BIONDELLO, *running.*

  Bion. O master, master ! I have watch'd so long
That I 'm dog-weary ; but at last I spied 60
An ancient angel coming down the hill,
Will serve the turn.
  Tra.   What is he, Biondello?
  Bion. Master, a mercatant, or a pedant,
I know not what ; but formal in apparel,
In gait and countenance surely like a father.
  Luc. And what of him, Tranio?
  Tra. If he be credulous, and trust my tale,
I 'll make him glad to seem Vincentio,
And give assurance to Baptista Minola,
As if he were the right Vincentio. 70
Take in your love, and then let me alone.
  [*Exeunt* LUCENTIO *and* BIANCA.

    Enter a Pedant.

  Ped. God save you, sir !
  Tra.   And you, sir ! you are welcome.
Travel you far on, or are you at the furthest ?
  Ped. Sir, at the furthest for a week or two ;
But then up further, and as far as Rome,
And so to Tripoli, if God lend me life.
  Tra. What countryman, I pray ?
  Ped.   Of Mantua.
  Tra. Of Mantua, sir ?—marry, God forbid !
And come to Padua, careless of your life ?
  Ped. My life, sir ! how, I pray ? for that goes hard.
  Tra. 'T is death for any one in Mantua 81
To come to Padua. Know you not the cause ?
Your ships are stay'd at Venice ; and the duke,
For private quarrel 'twixt your duke and him,

Hath publish'd and proclaim'd it openly.
'T is marvel ; but that you are but newly come,
You might have heard it else proclaim'd about.
  Ped. Alas, sir ! it is worse for me than so ;
For I have bills for money by exchange
From Florence, and must here deliver them. 90
  Tra. Well, sir, to do you courtesy,
This will I do, and this I will advise you.—
First, tell me, have you ever been at Pisa ?
  Ped. Ay, sir, in Pisa have I often been ;
Pisa, renowned for grave citizens.
  Tra. Among them, know you one Vincentio ?
  Ped. I know him not, but I have heard of him :
A merchant of incomparable wealth.
  Tra. He is my father, sir ; and, sooth to say,
In countenance somewhat doth resemble you. 100
  Bion. [*Aside.*] As much as an apple doth an oyster,
    and all one.
  Tra. To save your life in this extremity,
This favour will I do you for his sake ;
And think it not the worst of all your fortunes,
That you are like to Sir Vincentio.
His name and credit shall you undertake,
And in my house you shall be friendly lodg'd.
Look, that you take upon you as you should !
You understand me, sir ;—so shall you stay
Till you have done your business in the city. 110
If this be courtesy, sir, accept of it.
  Ped. O ! sir, I do ; and will repute you ever
The patron of my life and liberty.
  Tra. Then go with me, to make the matter good.
This, by the way, I let you understand :
My father is here look'd for every day,
To pass assurance of a dower in marriage
'Twixt me and one Baptista's daughter here :
In all these circumstances I 'll instruct you.
Go with me, to clothe you as becomes you. 120
                          [*Exeunt.*

    SCENE III.—A Room in PETRUCHIO'S House.

    Enter KATHARINA *and* GRUMIO.

  Gru. No, no, forsooth ; I dare not, for my life.
  Kath. The more my wrong, the more his spite
    appears.
What, did he marry me to famish me ?
Beggars, that come unto my father's door,
Upon entreaty, have a present alms ;
If not, elsewhere they meet with charity :
But I, who never knew how to entreat,
Nor never needed that I should entreat,
Am starv'd for meat, giddy for lack of sleep ;
With oaths kept waking, and with brawling fed. 10
And that which spites me more than all these wants,
He does it under name of perfect love ;
As who should say, if I should sleep, or eat,
'T were deadly sickness, or else present death.
I pr'ythee go, and get me some repast ;
I care not what, so it be wholesome food.
  Gru. What say you to a neat's foot ?
  Kath. 'T is passing good : I pr'ythee let me have it.
  Gru. I fear, it is too choleric a meat.
How say you to a fat tripe, finely broil'd ? 20
  Kath. I like it well : good Grumio, fetch it me.
  Gru. I cannot tell ; I fear, 't is choleric.
What say you to a piece of beef, and mustard ?
  Kath. A dish that I do love to feed upon.
  Gru. Ay, but the mustard is too hot a little.
  Kath. Why, then the beef, and let the mustard
    rest.
  Gru. Nay, then I will not : you shall have the
    mustard,
Or else you get no beef of Grumio.
  Kath. Then both, or one, or anything thou wilt.
  Gru. Why, then the mustard without the beef. 30
  Kath. Go, get thee gone, thou false deluding slave,
                      [*Beats him.*
That feed'st me with the very name of meat.
Sorrow on thee, and all the pack of you,
That triumph thus upon my misery !
Go, get thee gone, I say.

Enter Petruchio, *with a dish of meat, and*
Hortensio.

Pet. How fares my Kate? What, sweeting, all
     amort?
Hor. Mistress, what cheer?
Kath.   'Faith, as cold as can be.
Pet. Pluck up thy spirits; look cheerfully upon me.
Here, love; thou seest how diligent I am,
To dress thy meat myself, and bring it thee :   40
               [*Sets the dish on a table.*
I am sure, sweet Kate, this kindness merits thanks.
What! not a word? Nay then, thou lov'st it not,
And all my pains is sorted to no proof.—
Here, take away this dish.
Kath.   I pray you, let it stand.
Pet. The poorest service is repaid
     with thanks,
And so shall mine, before you touch
     the meat.
Kath. I thank you, sir.
Hor. Signior Petruchio, fie! you are
     to blame.
Come, Mistress Kate, I'll bear you
     company.
Pet. [*Aside.*] Eat it up all, Hortensio,
     if thou lov'st me.—   50
Much good do it unto thy gentle heart!
Kate, eat apace.—And now, my honey
     love,
Will we return unto thy father's house,
And revel it as bravely as the best,
With silken coats, and caps, and golden
     rings,
With ruffs, and cuffs, and farthingales,
     and things ;
With scarfs, and fans, and double
     change of bravery,
With amber bracelets, beads, and all
     this knavery.
What, hast thou din'd? The tailor stays thy leisure,
To deck thy body with his ruffling treasure.   60

Enter Tailor.

Come, tailor, let us see these ornaments;
Lay forth the gown.—

Enter Haberdasher.

                 What news with you, sir?
Hab. Here is the cap your worship did bespeak.
Pet. Why, this was moulded on a porringer;
A velvet dish :—fie, fie! 'tis lewd and filthy.
Why, 'tis a cockle or a walnut-shell,
A knack, a toy, a trick, a baby's cap:
Away with it! come, let me have a bigger.
Kath. I'll have no bigger: this doth fit the time,
And gentlewomen wear such caps as these.   70
Pet. When you are gentle, you shall have one too;
And not till then.
Hor. [*Aside.*]   That will not be in haste.
Kath. Why, sir, I trust, I may have leave to speak,
And speak I will; I am no child, no babe:
Your betters have endur'd me say my mind,
And, if you cannot, best you stop your ears.
My tongue will tell the anger of my heart
Or else my heart, concealing it, will break :
And, rather than it shall, I will be free
Even to the uttermost, as I please, in words.   80
Pet. Why, thou say'st true: it is a paltry cap,
A custard-coffin, a bauble, a silken pie.
I love thee well, in that thou lik'st it not.
Kath. Love me, or love me not, I like the cap,
And it I will have, or I will have none.
               [*Exit Haberdasher.*
Pet. Thy gown? why, ay:—come, tailor, let us
     see't.
O, mercy, God! what masking stuff is here?
What's this? a sleeve? 'tis like a demi-cannon :
What! up and down, carv'd like an apple-tart?
Here's snip, and nip, and cut, and slish, and slash,   90
Like to a censer in a barber's shop.—
Why, what, o' devil's name, tailor, call'st thou this?

Hor. [*Aside.*] I see, she's like to have neither cap
     nor gown.
Tai. You bid me make it orderly and well,
According to the fashion and the time.
Pet. Marry, and did: but if you be remember'd,
I did not bid you mar it to the time.
Go, hop me over every kennel home,
For you shall hop without my custom, sir.
I'll none of it: hence! make your best of it.   100
Kath. I never saw a better-fashion'd gown,
More quaint, more pleasing, nor more commendable.
Belike, you mean to make a puppet of me.
Pet. Why, true; he means to make a puppet of
     thee.

Pet. " Why, what, o' devil's name, tailor, call'st thou this?"

Tai. She says, your worship means to make a
     puppet of her.
Pet. O monstrous arrogance! Thou liest, thou
     thread,
Thou thimble,
Thou yard, three-quarters, half-yard, quarter, nail!
Thou flea, thou nit, thou winter-cricket thou!—
Brav'd in mine own house with a skein of thread?   110
Away! thou rag, thou quantity, thou remnant,
Or I shall so be-mete thee with thy yard,
As thou shalt think on prating whilst thou liv'st!
I tell thee, I, that thou hast marr'd her gown.
Tai. Your worship is deceiv'd: the gown is made
Just as my master had direction.
Grumio gave order how it should be done.
Gru. I gave him no order; I gave him the stuff.
Tai. But how did you desire it should be made?
Gru. Marry, sir, with needle and thread.   120
Tai. But did you not request to have it cut?
Gru. Thou hast faced many things.
Tai. I have.
Gru. Face not me: thou hast braved many men;
brave not me: I will neither be faced nor braved. I
say unto thee,—I bid thy master cut out the gown;
but I did not bid him cut it to pieces: *ergo*, thou liest.
Tai. Why, here is the note of the fashion to
testify.
Pet. Read it.   130
Gru. The note lies in's throat, if he say I said so.
Tai. "*Imprimis*, a loose-bodied gown."
Gru. Master, if ever I said loose-bodied gown, sew
me in the skirts of it, and beat me to death with a
bottom of brown thread. I said, a gown.
Pet. Proceed.
Tai. "With a small compassed cape."
Gru. I confess the cape.
Tai. "With a trunk sleeve."
Gru. I confess two sleeves.   140
Tai. "The sleeves curiously cut."
Pet. Ay, there's the villainy.
Gru. Error i' the bill, sir; error i' the bill. I com-
manded the sleeves should be cut out, and sewed up

again; and that I'll prove upon thee, though thy little finger be armed in a thimble.

Tai. This is true, that I say: an I had thee in place where, thou shouldst know it.

Gru. I am for thee straight: take thou the bill, give me thy mete-yard, and spare not me. 150

Hor. God-a-mercy, Grumio, then he shall have no odds.

Pet. Well, sir, in brief, the gown is not for me.

Gru. You are i' the right, sir: 't is for my mistress.

Pet. Go, take it up unto thy master's use.

Gru. Villain, not for thy life! Take up my mistress' gown for thy master's use!

Pet. Why, sir, what's your conceit in that?

Gru. O, sir, the conceit is deeper than you think for. Take up my mistress' gown to his master's use! 160 O, fie, fie, fie!

Pet. [*Aside.*] Hortensio, say thou wilt see the tailor paid.—
Go take it hence; be gone, and say no more.

Hor. Tailor, I'll pay thee for thy gown to-morrow: Take no unkindness of his hasty words. Away, I say; commend me to thy master.
[*Exit Tailor.*

Pet. Well, come, my Kate; we will unto your father's, Even in these honest mean habiliments. Our purses shall be proud, our garments poor: For 't is the mind that makes the body rich; 170 And as the sun breaks through the darkest clouds, So honour peereth in the meanest habit. What, is the jay more precious than the lark, Because his feathers are more beautiful? Or is the adder better than the eel, Because his painted skin contents the eye? O! no, good Kate; neither art thou the worse For this poor furniture, and mean array. If thou account'st it shame, lay it on me; And therefore frolic: we will hence forthwith, 180 To feast and sport us at thy father's house.—
Go, call my men, and let us straight to him; And bring our horses unto Long Lane end; There will we mount, and thither walk on foot.—
Let's see; I think, 't is now some seven o'clock, And well we may come there by dinner-time.

Kath. I dare assure you, sir, 't is almost two, And 't will be supper-time, ere you come there.

Pet. It shall be seven, ere I go to horse. Look, what I speak, or do, or think to do, 190 You are still crossing it.—Sirs, let 't alone: I will not go to-day; and ere I do, It shall be what o'clock I say it is.

Hor. Why, so this gallant will command the sun.
[*Exeunt.*

SCENE IV.—Padua. Before BAPTISTA'S House.

Enter TRANIO, *and the Pedant dressed like* VINCENTIO.

Tra. Sir, this is the house: please it you, that I call?

Ped. Ay, what else? and, but I be deceived, Signior Baptista may remember me, Near twenty years ago, in Genoa, Where we were lodgers at the Pegasus.

Tra. 'T is well; and hold your own, in any case, With such austerity as 'longeth to a father.

Enter BIONDELLO.

Ped. I warrant you. But, sir, here comes your boy; 'T were good he were school'd.

Tra. Fear you not him. Sirrah Biondello, 10 Now do your duty throughly, I advise you: Imagine 't were the right Vincentio.

Bion. Tut! fear not me.

Tra. But hast thou done thy errand to Baptista?

Bion. I told him, that your father was at Venice, And that you look'd for him this day in Padua.

Tra. Thou 'rt a tall fellow: hold thee that to drink. Here comes Baptista.—Set your countenance, sir.—

Enter BAPTISTA *and* LUCENTIO.

Signior Baptista, you are happily met.—

Sir, this is the gentleman I told you of. 20 I pray you, stand good father to me now, Give me Bianca for my patrimony.

Ped. Soft, son!—
Sir, by your leave: having come to Padua To gather in some debts, my son Lucentio Made me acquainted with a weighty cause Of love between your daughter and himself: And, for the good report I hear of you, And for the love he beareth to your daughter, And she to him,—to stay him not too long, 30 I am content, in a good father's care, To have him match'd; and, if you please to like No worse than I, upon some agreement, Me shall you find ready and willing With one consent to have her so bestow'd; For curious I cannot be with you, Signior Baptista, of whom I hear so well.

Bap. Sir, pardon me in what I have to say: Your plainness, and your shortness please me well. Right true is it, your son Lucentio here 40 Doth love my daughter, and she loveth him, Or both dissemble deeply their affections; And, therefore, if you say no more than this, That like a father you will deal with him, And pass my daughter a sufficient dower, The match is made, and all is done: Your son shall have my daughter with consent.

Tra. I thank you, sir. Where then do you know best, We be affied, and such assurance ta'en, As shall with either part's agreement stand? 50

Bap. Not in my house, Lucentio; for, you know, Pitchers have ears, and I have many servants. Besides, old Gremio is hearkening still, And, happily, we might be interrupted.

Tra. Then at my lodging, an it like you: There doth my father lie, and there this night We'll pass the business privately and well. Send for your daughter by your servant here; My boy shall fetch the scrivener presently. The worst is this,—that, at so slender warning, 60 You're like to have a thin and slender pittance.

Bap. It likes me well:—Cambio, hie you home, And bid Bianca make her ready straight; And, if you will, tell what hath happened: Lucentio's father is arriv'd in Padua, And how she's like to be Lucentio's wife.

Luc. I pray the gods she may, with all my heart!

Tra. Dally not with the gods, but get thee gone.—
Signior Baptista, shall I lead the way? Welcome: one mess is like to be your cheer. 70 Come, sir; we will better it in Pisa.

Bap. I follow you.
[*Exeunt* TRANIO, *Pedant, and* BAPTISTA.

Bion. Cambio!—

Luc. What say'st thou, Biondello?

Bion. You saw my master wink and laugh upon you?

Luc. Biondello, what of that?

Bion. 'Faith, nothing; but he has left me here behind, to expound the meaning or moral of his signs and tokens. 80

Luc. I pray thee, moralise them.

Bion. Then thus. Baptista is safe, talking with the deceiving father of a deceitful son.

Luc. And what of him?

Bion. His daughter is to be brought by you to the supper.

Luc. And then?—

Bion. The old priest at Saint Luke's Church is at your command at all hours. 90

Luc. And what of all this?

Bion. I cannot tell, except they are busied about a counterfeit assurance: take you assurance of her, *cum privilegio ad imprimendum solum.* To the church! —take the priest, clerk, and some sufficient honest witnesses. If this be not that you look for, I have no more to say, But bid Bianca farewell for ever and a day.

Luc. Hear'st thou, Biondello?

Bion. I cannot tarry: I knew a wench married in an

afternoon as she went to the garden for parsley to stuff
a rabbit; and so may you, sir; and so adieu, sir.　My
master hath appointed me to go to Saint Luke's, to bid
the priest be ready to come against you come with
your appendix.　　　　　　　　　　　　　　*[Exit.*

Luc. I may, and will, if she be so contented:
She will be pleas'd, then wherefore should I doubt?
Hap what hap may, I'll roundly go about her:
It shall go hard, if Cambio go without her.　*[Exit.*

SCENE V.—A Public Road.

Enter PETRUCHIO, KATHARINA, *and* HORTENSIO.

Pet. Come on, o' God's name: once more toward
　　　our father's.
Good Lord, how bright and goodly shines the moon!
　Kath. The moon! the sun: it is not moonlight now.
　Pet. I say, it is the moon that shines so bright.
　Kath. I know, it is the sun that shines so bright.
　Pet. Now, by my mother's son, and that's myself,
It shall be moon, or star, or what I list,
Or ere I journey to your father's house.—
Go one, and fetch our horses back again.—
Evermore cross'd, and cross'd; nothing but cross'd! 10
　Hor. Say as he says, or we shall never go.
　Kath. Forward, I pray, since we have come so far,
And be it moon, or sun, or what you please.
An if you please to call it a rush-candle,
Henceforth, I vow, it shall be so for me.
　Pet. I say, it is the moon.
　Kath.　　　　　　　I know, it is the moon.
　Pet. Nay, then you lie: it is the blessed sun.
　Kath. Then, God be bless'd, it is the blessed sun:
But sun it is not, when you say it is not,
And the moon changes, even as your mind. 20
What you will have it nam'd, even that it is;
And so it shall be so for Katharine.
　Hor. Petruchio, go thy ways: the field is won.
　Pet. Well, forward, forward! thus the bowl should
　　　run,
And not unluckily against the bias.—
But soft; what company is coming here?

Enter VINCENTIO, *in a travelling dress.*

[*To* VINCENTIO.] Good morrow, gentle mistress:
　　　where away?—
Tell me, sweet Kate, and tell me truly too,
Hast thou beheld a fresher gentlewoman?
Such war of white and red within her cheeks! 30
What stars do spangle heaven with such beauty,
As those two eyes become that heavenly face?—
Fair lovely maid, once more good day to thee.—
Sweet Kate, embrace her for her beauty's sake.
　Hor. 'A will make the man mad, to make a woman
　　　of him.
　Kath. Young budding virgin, fair, and fresh, and
　　　sweet,
Whither away, or where is thy abode?
Happy the parents of so fair a child;
Happier the man, whom favourable stars　　40
Allot thee for his lovely bedfellow!
　Pet. Why, how now, Kate? I hope thou art not
　　　mad:
This is a man, old, wrinkled, faded, wither'd,
And not a maiden, as thou say'st he is.
　Kath. Pardon, old father, my mistaking eyes,
That have been so bedazzled with the sun,
That everything I look on seemeth green:
Now I perceive thou art a reverend father;
Pardon, I pray thee, for my mad mistaking.
　Pet. Do, good old grandsire; and, withal, make
　　　known　　　　　　　　　　　　　　50
Which way thou travellest: if along with us,
We shall be joyful of thy company.

Vin. Fair sir, and you my merry mistress,
That with your strange encounter much amaz'd me,
My name is call'd Vincentio; my dwelling—Pisa;
And bound I am to Padua, there to visit
A son of mine, which long I have not seen.
　Pet. What is his name?
　Vin.　　　　　　　Lucentio, gentle sir.
　Pet. Happily met; the happier for thy son.
And now by law, as well as reverend age,　　60
I may entitle thee—my loving father:
The sister to my wife, this gentlewoman,
Thy son by this hath married.　Wonder not,

Kath. "Young budding virgin, fair, and fresh, and sweet."

Nor be not griev'd: she is of good esteem,
Her dowry wealthy, and of worthy birth;
Beside, so qualified as may beseem
The spouse of any noble gentleman.
Let me embrace with old Vincentio;
And wander we to see thy honest son,
Who will of thy arrival be full joyous.　　70
　Vin. But is this true? or is it else your pleasure,
Like pleasant travellers, to break a jest
Upon the company you overtake?
　Hor. I do assure thee, father, so it is.
　Pet. Come, go along, and see the truth hereof;
For our first merriment hath made thee jealous.
　　　　　　　　[*Exeunt* PETRUCHIO, KATHARINA, *and*
　　　　　　　　　　　　VINCENTIO.
　Hor. Well, Petruchio, this has put me in heart.
Have to my widow; and if she be froward,
Then hast thou taught Hortensio to be untoward.
　　　　　　　　　　　　　　　　　　　　[Exit.

ACT V.

SCENE I.—Padua. Before LUCENTIO'S House.

Enter on one side BIONDELLO, LUCENTIO, *and* BIANCA; GREMIO *walking on the other side.*

Biondello.

SOFTLY and swiftly, sir, for the priest is ready.

Luc. I fly, Biondello; but they may chance to need thee at home: therefore leave us.

Bion. Nay, 'faith, I 'll see the church o' your back; and then come back to my master as soon as I can.
[*Exeunt* LUCENTIO, BIANCA, *and* BIONDELLO.

Gre. I marvel Cambio comes not all this while.

Enter PETRUCHIO, KATHARINA, VINCENTIO, *and Attendants.*

Pet. Sir, here 's the door, this is Lucentio's house:
My father's bears more toward the market-place; 11
Thither must I, and here I leave you, sir.

Vin. You shall not choose but drink before you go.
I think, I shall command your welcome here,
And, by all likelihood, some cheer is toward. [*Knocks.*

Gre. They 're busy within; you were best knock louder.

Enter Pedant above, at a window.

Ped. What 's he, that knocks as he would beat down the gate?

Vin. Is Signior Lucentio within, sir? 20

Ped. He 's within, sir, but not to be spoken withal.

Vin. What, if a man bring him a hundred pound or two, to make merry withal?

Ped. Keep your hundred pounds to yourself: he shall need none, so long as I live.

Pet. Nay, I told you, your son was well beloved in Padua.—Do you hear, sir?—to leave frivolous circumstances,—I pray you, tell Signior Lucentio, that his father is come from Pisa, and is here at the door to speak with him. 30

Ped. Thou liest: his father is come from Pisa, and here looking out at the window.

Vin. Art thou his father?

Ped. Ay, sir; so his mother says, if I may believe her.

Pet. [*To* VINCENTIO.] Why, how now, gentleman!
Why, this is flat knavery, to take upon you another man's name.

Ped. Lay hands on the villain. I believe, 'a means to cozen somebody in this city under my countenance.

Re-enter BIONDELLO.

Bion. I have seen them in the church together:
God send 'em good shipping!—But who is here? mine old master, Vincentio! now we are undone, and brought to nothing.

Vin. [*Seeing* BIONDELLO.] Come hither, crack-hemp.

Bion. I hope I may choose, sir.

Vin. Come hither, you rogue. What, have you forgot me?

Bion. Forgot you? no, sir: I could not forget you, for I never saw you before in all my life. 51

Vin. What, you notorious villain, didst thou never see thy master's father, Vincentio?

Bion. What, my old, worshipful old master? yes, marry, sir; see where he looks out of the window.

Vin. Is 't so, indeed? [*Beats* BIONDELLO.

Bion. Help, help, help! here 's a madman will murder me. [*Exit.*

Ped. Help, son! help, Signior Baptista! 59
[*Exit from the window.*

Pet. Pr'ythee, Kate, let 's stand aside, and see the end of this controversy. [*They retire.*

Re-enter Pedant below; BAPTISTA, TRANIO, *and Servants.*

Tra. Sir, what are you, that offer to beat my servant?

Vin. What am I, sir? nay, what are you, sir?—O immortal gods! O fine villain! A silken doublet! a velvet hose! a scarlet cloak! and a copatain hat!—O, I am undone! I am undone! while I play the good husband at home, my son and my servant spend all at the university.

Tra. How now? what 's the matter? 70

Bap. What, is the man lunatic?

Tra. Sir, you seem a sober ancient gentleman by your habit, but your words show you a madman. Why, sir, what 'cerns it you if I wear pearl and gold? I thank my good father, I am able to maintain it.

Vin. Thy father? O villain! he is a sail-maker in Bergamo.

Bap. You mistake, sir: you mistake, sir. Pray, what do you think is his name?

Vin. His name? as if I knew not his name: I have brought him up ever since he was three years old, and his name is Tranio. 82

Ped. Away, away, mad ass! his name is Lucentio; and he is mine only son, and heir to the lands of me, Signior Vincentio.

Vin. Lucentio! O! he hath murdered his master.—Lay hold on him, I charge you, in the duke's name.—O, my son, my son!—Tell me, thou villain, where is my son Lucentio?

Tra. Call forth an officer. 90

Enter one with an Officer.

Carry this mad knave to the gaol.—Father Baptista, I charge you see him forthcoming.

Vin. Carry me to the gaol!

Gre. Stay, officer: he shall not go to prison.

Bap. Talk not, Signior Gremio. I say, he shall go to prison.

Gre. Take heed, Signior Baptista, lest you be cony-catched in this business. I dare swear this is the right Vincentio.

Ped. Swear, if thou darest. 100

Gre. Nay, I dare not swear it.

Tra. Then thou wert best say, that I am not Lucentio.

Gre. Yes, I know thee to be Signior Lucentio.

Bap. Away with the dotard! to the gaol with him!

Vin. Thus strangers may be haled and abus'd.—
O monstrous villain!

Re-enter BIONDELLO, *with* LUCENTIO *and* BIANCA.

Bion. O, we are spoiled! and yonder he is: deny him, forswear him, or else we are all undone.

Luc. Pardon, sweet father. [*Kneeling.*

Vin. Lives my sweet son? 110
[BIONDELLO, TRANIO, *and Pedant run out.*

Bian. Pardon, dear father. [*Kneeling.*
Bap. How hast thou offended?
Where is Lucentio?
Luc. Here 's Lucentio,
Right son to the right Vincentio;
That have by marriage made thy daughter mine,
While counterfeit supposes blear'd thine eyne.
Gre. Here 's packing with a witness, to deceive us
all!
Vin. Where is that damned villain, Tranio,
That fac'd and brav'd me in this matter so?
Bap. Why, tell me, is not this my Cambio? 120
Bion. Cambio is chang'd into Lucentio.
Luc. Love wrought these miracles. Bianca's love
Made me exchange my state with Tranio,
While he did bear my countenance in the town;
And happily I have arrived at the last
Unto the wished haven of my bliss.
What Tranio did, myself enforc'd him to;
Then pardon him, sweet father, for my sake.
Vin. I 'll slit the villain's nose, that would have sent
me to the gaol. 130
Bap. [*To* LUCENTIO.] But do you hear, sir? Have
you married my daughter without asking my good
will?
Vin. Fear not, Baptista; we will content you: go
to; but I will in, to be revenged for this villainy. [*Exit.*
Bap. And I, to sound the depth of this knavery.
[*Exit.*
Luc. Look not pale, Bianca; thy father will not
frown. [*Exeunt* LUCENTIO *and* BIANCA.
Gre. My cake is dough; but I 'll in among the rest,
Out of hope of all, but my share of the feast. [*Exit.*

PETRUCHIO *and* KATHARINA *advance.*

Kath. Husband, let 's follow, to see the end of this
ado. 140
Pet. First kiss me, Kate, and we will.
Kath. What, in the midst of the street?
Pet. What! art thou ashamed of me?
Kath. No, sir, God forbid; but ashamed to kiss.
Pet. Why, then let 's home again.—Come, sirrah,
let 's away.
Kath. Nay, I will give thee a kiss: now pray thee,
love, stay.
Pet. Is not this well?—Come, my sweet Kate:
Better once than never, for never too late. [*Exeunt.*

SCENE II.—A Room in LUCENTIO'S House.

A Banquet set out. Enter BAPTISTA, VINCENTIO,
GREMIO, *the Pedant,* LUCENTIO, BIANCA, PE-
TRUCHIO, KATHARINA, HORTENSIO, *and Widow;*
TRANIO, BIONDELLO, GRUMIO, *and others, attend-
ing.*

Luc. At last, though long, our jarring notes agree:
And time it is, when raging war is done,
To smile at scapes and perils overblown.—
My fair Bianca, bid my father welcome,
While I with selfsame kindness welcome thine.—
Brother Petruchio,—sister Katharina,—
And thou, Hortensio, with thy loving widow,
Feast with the best, and welcome to my house:
My banquet is to close our stomachs up,
After our great good cheer. Pray you, sit down; 10
For now we sit to chat, as well as eat.
[*They sit at table.*
Pet. Nothing but sit and sit, and eat and eat!
Bap. Padua affords this kindness, son Petruchio.
Pet. Padua affords nothing but what is kind.
Hor. For both our sakes I would that word were
true.
Pet. Now, for my life, Hortensio fears his widow.
Wid. Then never trust me, if I be afeard.
Pet. You are very sensible, and yet you miss my
sense:
I mean, Hortensio is afeard of you.
Wid. He that is giddy thinks the world turns round.
Pet. Roundly replied.
Kath. Mistress, how mean you that?

Wid. Thus I conceive by him. 22
Pet. Conceives by me!—How likes Hortensio that?
Hor. My widow says, thus she conceives her tale.
Pet. Very well mended. Kiss him for that, good
widow.
Kath. He that is giddy thinks the world turns
round:—
I pray you, tell me what you meant by that.
Wid. Your husband, being troubled with a shrew,
Measures my husband's sorrow by his woe:
And now you know my meaning. 30
Kath. A very mean meaning.
Wid. Right, I mean you.
Kath. And I am mean, indeed, respecting you.
Pet. To her, Kate!
Hor. To her, widow!
Pet. A hundred marks, my Kate does put her down.
Hor. That 's my office.
Pet. Spoke like an officer.—Ha' to thee, lad.
[*Drinks to* HORTENSIO.
Bap. How likes Gremio these quick-witted folks?
Gre. Believe me, sir, they butt together well.
Bian. Head and butt? an hasty-witted body 40
Would say, your head and butt were head and horn.
Vin. Ay, mistress bride, hath that awaken'd you?
Bian. Ay, but not frighted me; therefore, I 'll sleep
again.
• *Pet.* Nay, that you shall not; since you have begun,
Have at you for a bitter jest or two.
Bian. Am I your bird? I mean to shift my bush,
And then pursue me as you draw your bow.—
You are welcome all.
[*Exeunt* BIANCA, KATHARINA, *and Widow.*
Pet. She hath prevented me.—Here, Signior Tranio;
This bird you aim'd at, though you hit her not: 50
Therefore, a health to all that shot and miss'd.
Tra. O sir! Lucentio slipp'd me, like his greyhound,
Which runs himself, and catches for his master.
Pet. A good swift simile, but something currish.
Tra. 'T is well, sir, that you hunted for yourself:
'T is thought, your deer does hold you at a bay.
Bap. O ho, Petruchio! Tranio hits you now.
Luc. I thank thee for that gird, good Tranio.
Hor. Confess, confess, hath he not hit you here?
Pet. 'A has a little gall'd me, I confess; 60
And, as the jest did glance away from me,
'T is ten to one it maim'd you two outright.
Bap. Now, in good sadness, son Petruchio,
I think thou hast the veriest shrew of all.
Pet. Well, I say no: and therefore, for assurance,
Let 's each one send unto his wife;
And he, whose wife is most obedient
To come at first when he doth send for her,
Shall win the wager which we will propose.
Hor. Content. What is the wager?
Luc. Twenty crowns.
Pet. Twenty crowns! 71
I 'll venture so much of my hawk, or hound,
But twenty times so much upon my wife.
Luc. A hundred then.
Hor. Content.
Pet. A match! 't is done.
Hor. Who shall begin?
Luc. That will I.
Go, Biondello, bid your mistress come to me.
Bion. I go. [*Exit.*
Bap. Son, I will be your half, Bianca comes.
Luc. I 'll have no halves; I 'll bear it all myself.

Re-enter BIONDELLO.

How now! what news?
Bion. Sir, my mistress sends you word,
That she is busy, and she cannot come, 81
Pet. How! she is busy, and she cannot come!
Is that an answer?
Gre. Ay, and a kind one too:
Pray God, sir, your wife send you not a worse.
Pet. I hope, better.
Pet. Sirrah Biondello, go, and entreat my wife
To come to me forthwith. [*Exit* BIONDELLO.
Pet. O ho! entreat her!
Nay, then she must needs come.

Hor.   I am afraid, sir,
Do what you can, yours will not be entreated.

Re-enter BIONDELLO.

Now, where's my wife?   90

Hor. She will not.
Pet. The fouler fortune mine, and there an end.

Enter KATHARINA.

Bap. Now, by my holidame, here comes Katharina!

Kath. "In token of which duty, if he please, my hand is ready."

Bion. She says, you have some goodly jest in hand;
She will not come: she bids you come to her.
Pet. Worse and worse: she will not come? O vile,
Intolerable, not to be endur'd!
Sirrah Grumio, go to your mistress; say,
I command her come to me.   [*Exit* GRUMIO.
Hor.   I know her answer.
Pet. What?

Kath. What is your will, sir, that you send for me?
Pet. Where is your sister, and Hortensio's wife? 102
Kath. They sit conferring by the parlour fire.
Pet. Go, fetch them hither: if they deny to come,
Swinge me them soundly forth unto their husbands.
Away, I say, and bring them hither straight.
                              [*Exit* KATHARINA.
Luc. Here is a wonder, if you talk of a wonder.

Hor. And so it is. I wonder what it bodes.
Pet. Marry, peace it bodes, and love, and quiet life,
An awful rule, and right supremacy;   110
And, to be short, what not that's sweet and happy?
Bap. Now fair befall thee, good Petruchio!
The wager thou hast won; and I will add
Unto their losses twenty thousand crowns;
Another dowry to another daughter,
For she is chang'd, as she had never been.
Pet. Nay, I will win my wager better yet,
And show more sign of her obedience,
Her new-built virtue and obedience.
See, where she comes, and brings your froward wives
As prisoners to her womanly persuasion.—   121

Re-enter KATHARINA, *with* BIANCA *and* Widow.

Katharine, that cap of yours becomes you not:
Off with that bauble, throw it under foot.
   [KATHARINA *pulls off her cap, and throws it down.*
Wid. Lord! let me never have a cause to sigh,
Till I be brought to such a silly pass!
Bian. Fie! what a foolish duty call you this?
Luc. I would, your duty were as foolish too:
The wisdom of your duty, fair Bianca,
Hath cost me an hundred crowns since supper-time.
Bian. The more fool you for laying on my duty.   130
Pet. Katharine, I charge thee, tell these headstrong women,
What duty they do owe their lords and husbands.
Wid. Come, come, you're mocking: we will have no telling.
Pet. Come on, I say; and first begin with her.
Wid. She shall not.
Pet. I say, she shall:—and first begin with her.
Kath. Fie, fie! unknit that threatening unkind brow,
And dart not scornful glances from those eyes,
To wound thy lord, thy king, thy governor:
It blots thy beauty, as frosts do bite the meads,   140
Confounds thy fame, as whirlwinds shake fair buds,
And in no sense is meet, or amiable.
A woman mov'd is like a fountain troubled,
Muddy, ill-seeming, thick, bereft of beauty;
And, while it is so, none so dry or thirsty
Will deign to sip, or touch one drop of it.
Thy husband is thy lord, thy life, thy keeper,
Thy head, thy sovereign; one that cares for thee,
And for thy maintenance; commits his body
To painful labour, both by sea and land,   150
To watch the night in storms, the day in cold,
Whilst thou liest warm at home, secure and safe;
And craves no other tribute at thy hands,
But love, fair looks, and true obedience,
Too little payment for so great a debt.
Such duty as the subject owes the prince,
Even such a woman oweth to her husband;
And when she's froward, peevish, sullen, sour,
And not obedient to his honest will,
What is she but a foul contending rebel,   160
And graceless traitor to her loving lord?—
I am asham'd, that women are so simple
To offer war, where they should kneel for peace;
Or seek for rule, supremacy, and sway,
When they are bound to serve, love, and obey.
Why are our bodies soft, and weak, and smooth,
Unapt to toil and trouble in the world,
But that our soft conditions, and our hearts,
Should well agree with our external parts?
Come, come, you froward and unable worms,   170
My mind hath been as big as one of yours,
My heart as great, my reason, haply, more
To bandy word for word, and frown for frown;
But now I see, our lances are but straws,
Our strength as weak, our weakness past compare,—
That seeming to be most, which we indeed least are.
Then vail your stomachs, for it is no boot,
And place your hands below your husband's foot:
In token of which duty, if he please,
My hand is ready; may it do him ease.   180
Pet. Why, there's a wench!—Come on, and kiss me, Kate.
Luc. Well, go thy ways, old lad, for thou shalt ha't.
Vin. 'T is a good hearing, when children are toward.
Luc. But a harsh hearing, when women are froward.
Pet. Come, Kate, we'll to bed.—
We three are married, but you two are sped.
'T was I won the wager, though you hit the white;
And being a winner, God give you good night.
        [*Exeunt* PETRUCHIO *and* KATHARINA.
Hor. Now go thy ways, thou hast tam'd a curst shrew.
Luc. 'T is a wonder, by your leave, she will be tam'd so.   190
        [*Exeunt.*

ALL'S WELL THAT ENDS WELL.

DRAMATIS PERSONÆ.

KING OF FRANCE.
DUKE OF FLORENCE.
BERTRAM, *Count of Rousillon.*
LAFEU, *an old Lord.*
PAROLLES, *a Follower of Bertram.*
Several young French Lords, serving with Bertram.
Steward to the Countess of Rousillon.
Clown, in her Household.
A Page.

COUNTESS OF ROUSILLON, *Mother to Bertram.*
HELENA, *a Gentlewoman protected by the Countess.*
A Widow of Florence.
DIANA, *Daughter to the Widow.*
VIOLENTA, ⎫
MARIANA, ⎭ *Neighbours and Friends to the Widow.*

Lords, attending on the King; Officers, Soldiers, &c.,
French and Florentine.

SCENE—Partly in FRANCE, and partly in TUSCANY.

ACT I.

SCENE I.—Rousillon. A Room in the COUNTESS'S Palace.

Enter BERTRAM, *the* COUNTESS OF ROUSILLON, HELENA, *and* LAFEU, *all in black.*

Countess.
IN delivering my son from me, I bury a
second husband.
  Ber. And I, in going, madam, weep o'er
my father's death anew; but I must attend
his majesty's command, to whom I am now
in ward, evermore in subjection.
  Laf. You shall find of the king a husband,
madam;—you, sir, a father. He that so
generally is at all times good, must of
necessity hold his virtue to you, whose
worthiness would stir it up where it wanted,
rather than lack it where there is such
abundance.
  Count. What hope is there of his majesty's
amendment?
  Laf. He hath abandoned his physicians, madam;
under whose practices he hath persecuted time with
hope, and finds no other advantage in the process but
only the losing of hope by time.   19
  Count. This young gentlewoman had a father,—
O, that "had!" how sad a passage 't is!—whose skill
was almost as great as his honesty; had it stretched
so far, would have made nature immortal, and death
should have play for lack of work. 'Would, for the
king's sake, he were living! I think it would be the
death of the king's disease.
  Laf. How called you the man you speak of, madam?
  Count. He was famous, sir, in his profession, and
it was his great right to be so—Gerard de Narbon. 29
  Laf. He was excellent, indeed, madam: the king
very lately spoke of him, admiringly and mourn-
ingly. He was skilful enough to have lived still, if
knowledge could be set up against mortality.
  Ber. What is it, my good lord, the king languishes
of?
  Laf. A fistula, my lord.
  Ber. I heard not of it before.
  Laf. I would it were not notorious.—Was this
gentlewoman the daughter of Gerard de Narbon? 39
  Count. His sole child, my lord; and bequeathed
to my overlooking. I have those hopes of her good
that her education promises: her dispositions she
inherits, which make fair gifts fairer; for where

an unclean mind carries virtuous qualities, there
commendations go with pity; they are virtues and
traitors too: in her they are the better for their
simpleness; she derives her honesty, and achieves
her goodness.
  Laf. Your commendations, madam, get from her
tears.   50
  Count. 'T is the best brine a maiden can season her
praise in. The remembrance of her father never
approaches her heart, but the tyranny of her sorrows
takes all livelihood from her cheek.—No more of this,
Helena: go to, no more; lest it be rather thought you
affect a sorrow, than to have.
  Hel. I do affect a sorrow, indeed: but I have it too.
  Laf. Moderate lamentation is the right of the dead,
excessive grief the enemy to the living.
  Count. If the living be enemy to the grief, the
excess makes it soon mortal.   61
  Ber. Madam, I desire your holy wishes.
  Laf. How understand we that?
  Count. Be thou blest, Bertram; and succeed thy
          father
In manners, as in shape! thy blood, and virtue,
Contend for empire in thee; and thy goodness
Share with thy birthright! Love all, trust a few,
Do wrong to none: be able for thine enemy
Rather in power than use, and keep thy friend
Under thy own life's key: be check'd for silence, 70
But never tax'd for speech. What Heaven more will,
That thee may furnish, and my prayers pluck down,
Fall on thy head! Farewell.—My lord,
'T is an unseason'd courtier: good my lord,
Advise him.
  Laf.   He cannot want the best
That shall attend his love.
  Count. Heaven bless him!—Farewell, Bertram.
                                             [*Exit.*
  Ber. [*To* HELENA.] The best wishes that can be
forged in your thoughts be servants to you. Be com-
fortable to my mother, your mistress, and make much
of her.   81
  Laf. Farewell, pretty lady: you must hold the
credit of your father. [*Exeunt* BERTRAM *and* LAFEU.
  Hel. O, were that all!—I think not on my father;

And these great tears grace his remembrance more
Than those I shed for him. What was he like?
I have forgot him: my imagination
Carries no favour in 't but Bertram's.
I am undone: there is no living, none,
If Bertram be away. It were all one,   90
That I should love a bright particular star,

Count. "Heaven bless him!—Farewell, Bertram."

And think to wed it, he is so above me:
In his bright radiance and collateral light
Must I be comforted, not in his sphere.
The ambition in my love thus plagues itself:
The hind that would be mated by the lion
Must die for love. 'T was pretty, though a plague,
To see him every hour; to sit and draw
His arched brows, his hawking eye, his curls,
In our heart's table; heart too capable   100
Of every line and trick of his sweet favour:
But now he 's gone, and my idolatrous fancy
Must sanctify his relics.—Who comes here?
One that goes with him: I love him for his sake,
And yet I know him a notorious liar,
Think him a great way fool, solely a coward;
Yet these fix'd evils sit so fit in him,
That they take place, when virtue's steely bones
Look bleak in the cold wind: withal, full oft we see
Cold wisdom waiting on superfluous folly.   110

Enter Parolles.

Par. Save you, fair queen!
Hel. And you, monarch!
Par. No.
Hel. And no.
Par. Are you meditating on virginity?
Hel. Ay. You have some stain of soldier in you;
let me ask you a question. Man is enemy to virginity;
how may we barricado it against him?
Par. Keep him out.
Hel. But he assails; and our virginity, though
valiant in the defence, yet is weak. Unfold to us
some warlike resistance.   122
Par. There is none: man, sitting down before you,
will undermine you, and blow you up.
Hel. Bless our poor virginity from underminers and
blowers up!—Is there no military policy, how virgins
might blow up men?
Par. Virginity being blown down, man will quicklier
be blown up: marry, in blowing him down again, with
the breach yourselves made, you lose your city. It is
not politic in the commonwealth of nature to preserve
virginity. Loss of virginity is rational increase; and
there was never virgin got, till virginity was first lost.
That you were made of, is metal to make virgins.

Virginity, by being once lost, may be ten times found:
by being ever kept, it is ever lost. 'T is too cold a
companion: away with 't.
Hel. I will stand for 't a little, though therefore I
die a virgin.   139
Par. There 's little can be said in 't: 't is against the
rule of nature. To speak on the part of virginity is to
accuse your mothers, which is most infallible disobedience. He that hangs himself is a virgin: virginity
murders itself, and should be buried in highways, out
of all sanctified limit, as a desperate offendress against
nature. Virginity breeds mites, much like a cheese,
consumes itself to the very paring, and so dies with
feeding his own stomach. Besides, virginity is peevish,
proud, idle, made of self-love, which is the most inhibited sin in the canon. Keep it not: you cannot
choose but lose by 't. Out with 't: within the year it
will make itself two, which is a goodly increase, and
the principal itself not much the worse. Away with 't.
Hel. How might one do, sir, to lose it to her own
liking?
Par. Let me see: marry, ill, to like him that ne'er
it likes. 'T is a commodity will lose the gloss with
lying; the longer kept, the less worth: off with 't,
while 't is vendible: answer the time of request. Virginity, like an old courtier, wears her cap out of
fashion; richly suited, but unsuitable: just like the
brooch and the toothpick, which wear not now.
Your date is better in your pie and your porridge
than in your cheek: and your virginity, your old virginity, is like one of our French withered pears: it
looks ill, it eats drily: marry, 't is a withered pear; it
was formerly better; marry, yet, 't is a withered pear.
Will you anything with it?
Hel. Not my virginity yet.
There shall your master have a thousand loves,   170
A mother, and a mistress, and a friend,
A phœnix, captain, and an enemy,
A guide, a goddess, and a sovereign,
A counsellor, a traitress, and a dear;
His humble ambition, proud humility,
His jarring concord, and his discord dulcet,
His faith, his sweet disaster; with a world
Of pretty, fond, adoptious christendoms,
That blinking Cupid gossips. Now shall he—
I know not what he shall:—God send him well!—   180
The court 's a learning-place;—and he is one—
Par. What one, i' faith?
Hel. That I wish well.—'T is pity—
Par. What 's pity?
Hel. That wishing well had not a body in 't,
Which might be felt; that we, the poorer born,
Whose baser stars do shut us up in wishes,
Might with effects of them follow our friends,
And show what we alone must think; which never
Returns us thanks.   190

Enter a Page.

Page. Monsieur Parolles, my lord calls for you.
          [*Exit.*
Par. Little Helen, farewell: if I can remember
thee, I will think of thee at court.
Hel. Monsieur Parolles, you were born under a
charitable star.
Par. Under Mars, I.
Hel. I especially think, under Mars.
Par. Why under Mars?
Hel. The wars have so kept you under, that you
must needs be born under Mars.   200
Par. When he was predominant.
Hel. When he was retrograde, I think, rather.
Par. Why think you so?
Hel. You go so much backward, when you fight.
Par. That 's for advantage.
Hel. So is running away, when fear proposes the
safety. But the composition that your valour and fear
makes in you is a virtue of a good wing, and I like the
wear well.   209
Par. I am so full of businesses, I cannot answer
thee acutely. I will return perfect courtier; in the
which my instruction shall serve to naturalise thee,
so thou wilt be capable of a courtier's counsel, and

understand what advice shall thrust upon thee ; else
thou diest in thine unthankfulness, and thine ignorance makes thee away : farewell. When thou hast
leisure, say thy prayers ; when thou hast none,
remember thy friends. Get thee a good husband,
and use him as he uses thee : so farewell.   [*Exit.*

Hel. Our remedies oft in ourselves do lie,   220

Par. "I will return perfect courtier."

Which we ascribe to Heaven : the fated sky
Gives us free scope ; only, doth backward pull
Our slow designs, when we ourselves are dull.
What power is it which mounts my love so high ;
That makes me see, and cannot feed mine eye ?
The mightiest space in fortune Nature brings
To join like likes, and kiss like native things.
Impossible be strange attempts to those
That weigh their pains in sense, and do suppose,
What hath been cannot be. Who ever strove   230
To show her merit, that did miss her love ?
The king's disease—my project may deceive me,
But my intents are fix'd, and will not leave me. [*Exit.*

SCENE II.—Paris. A Room in the KING'S Palace.

Flourish of cornets. Enter the KING OF FRANCE
with letters ; Lords and others attending.

King. The Florentines and Senoys are by the ears ;
Have fought with equal fortune, and continue
A braving war.
1 Lord.   So 't is reported, sir.
King. Nay, 't is most credible : we here receive it
A certainty, vouch'd from our cousin Austria,
With caution, that the Florentine will move us
For speedy aid ; wherein our dearest friend
Prejudicates the business, and would seem
To have us make denial.
1 Lord.   His love and wisdom,
Approv'd so to your majesty, may plead   10
For amplest credence.
King.   He hath arm'd our answer,
And Florence is denied before he comes :
Yet, for our gentlemen, that mean to see
The Tuscan service, freely have they leave
To stand on either part.
2 Lord.   It may well serve
A nursery to our gentry, who are sick
For breathing and exploit.
King.   What's he comes here ?

Enter BERTRAM, LAFEU, *and* PAROLLES.

1 Lord. It is the Count Rousillon, my good lord,
Young Bertram.
King.   Youth, thou bear'st thy father's face ;
Frank nature, rather curious than in haste,   20

Hath well compos'd thee. Thy father's moral parts
May'st thou inherit too ! Welcome to Paris.
Ber. My thanks and duty are your majesty's.
King. I would I had that corporal soundness now,
As when thy father, and myself, in friendship
First tried our soldiership. He did look far
Into the service of the time, and was
DisciNed of the bravest : he lasted long
But on us both did haggish age steal on,
And wore us out of act. It much repairs me   30
To talk of your good father. In his youth
He had the wit, which I can well observe
To-day in our young lords ; but they may jest,
Till their own scorn return to them unnoted,
Ere they can hide their levity in honour.
So like a courtier, contempt nor bitterness
Were in his pride, or sharpness ; if they were,
His equal had awak'd them ; and his honour,
Clock to itself, knew the true minute when
Exception bid him speak, and at this time   40
His tongue obey'd his hand : who were below him
He us'd as creatures of another place,
And bow'd his eminent top to their low ranks,
Making them proud of his humility,
In their poor praise he humbled. Such a man
Might be a copy to these younger times,
Which, follow'd well, would demonstrate them now
But goers backward.
Ber.   His good remembrance, sir,
Lies richer in your thoughts, than on his tomb :
So in approof lives not his epitaph,   50
As in your royal speech.
King. 'Would I were with him ! He would always
    say,
(Methinks, I hear him now : his plausive words
He scatter'd not in ears, but grafted them,
To grow there, and to bear,)—"Let me not live,"—
Thus his good melancholy oft began,
On the catastrophe and heel of pastime,
When it was out,—"Let me not live," quoth he,
"After my flame lacks oil, to be the snuff
Of younger spirits, whose apprehensive senses   60
All but new things disdain ; whose judgments are
Mere fathers of their garments ; whose constancies
Expire before their fashions."—This he wish'd :
I, after him, do after him wish too,
Since I nor wax, nor honey, can bring home,
I quickly were dissolved from my hive,
To give some labourers room.
2 Lord.   You are lov'd, sir ;
They, that least lend it you, shall lack you first.
King. I fill a place, I know 't.—How long is 't, count,
Since the physician at your father's died ?   70
He was much fam'd.
Ber.   Some six months since, my lord.
King. If he were living, I would try him yet :—
Lend me an arm ;—the rest have worn me out
With several applications : nature and sickness
Debate it at their leisure. Welcome, count ;
My son 's no dearer.
Ber.   Thank your majesty. [*Exeunt.*

SCENE III.—Rousillon. A Room in the COUNTESS'S
Palace.

Enter COUNTESS, *Steward, and Clown.*

Count. I will now hear : what say you of this gentlewoman ?
Stew. Madam, the care I have had to even your
content, I wish might be found in the calendar of my
past endeavours ; for then we wound our modesty,
and make foul the clearness of our deservings, when
of ourselves we publish them.
Count. What does this knave here ? Get you gone,
sirrah : the complaints I have heard of you, I do not
all believe : 't is my slowness, that I do not ; for I
know you lack not folly to commit them, and have
ability enough to make such knaveries yours.   12
Clo. 'T is not unknown to you, madam, I am a poor
fellow.
Count. Well, sir.

Clo. No, madam; 't is not so well, that I am poor,
though many of the rich are damned. But, if I may
have your ladyship's good will to go to the world,
Isbel, the woman, and I will do as we may.

Count. Wilt thou needs be a beggar? 20

Clo. I do beg your good will in this case.

Count. In what case?

Clo. In Isbel's case, and mine own. Service is no
heritage, and, I think, I shall never have the blessing
of God, till I have issue of my body, for they say,
barnes are blessings.

Count. Tell me thy reason why thou wilt marry.

Clo. My poor body, madam, requires it: I am driven
on by the flesh, and he must needs go, that the devil
drives. 30

Count. Is this all your worship's reason?

Clo. 'Faith, madam, I have other holy reasons, such
as they are.

Count. May the world know them?

Clo. I have been, madam, a wicked creature, as
you and all flesh and blood are; and, indeed, I do
marry that I may repent.

Count. Thy marriage, sooner than thy wickedness.

Clo. I am out o' friends, madam; and I hope to have
friends for my wife's sake. 40

Count. Such friends are thine enemies, knave.

Clo. You are shallow, madam; e'en great friends;
for the knaves come to do that for me, which I am
aweary of. He that ears my land spares my team,
and gives me leave to inn the crop: if I be his cuckold, he 's my drudge. He that comforts my wife is
the cherisher of my flesh and blood; he that cherishes
my flesh and blood loves my flesh and blood; he that
loves my flesh and blood is my friend: *ergo* he that
kisses my wife is my friend. If men could be contented
to be what they are, there were no fear in marriage;
for young Charbon the Puritan, and old Poysam the
Papist, howsome'er their hearts are severed in religion, their heads are both one; they may joll horns
together, like any deer i' the herd.

Count. Wilt thou ever be a foul-mouthed and
calumnious knave?

Clo. A prophet I, madam; and I speak the truth
the next way:

> *For I the ballad will repeat,* 60
> *Which men full true shall find;*
> *Your marriage comes by destiny,*
> *Your cuckoo sings by kind.*

Count. Get you gone, sir: I 'll talk with you more
anon.

Stew. May it please you, madam, that he bid Helen
come to you: of her I am to speak.

Count. Sirrah, tell my gentlewoman, I would speak
with her; Helen I mean.

Clo. *Was this fair face the cause, quoth she,* 70
> *Why the Grecians sacked Troy?*
> *Fond done, done fond,*
> *Was this King Priam's joy?*
> *With that she sighed as she stood,*
> *With that she sighed as she stood,*
> *And gave this sentence then;*
> *Among nine bad if one be good,*
> *Among nine bad if one be good,*
> *There's yet one good in ten.*

Count. What! one good in ten? you corrupt the
song, sirrah. 81

Clo. One good woman in ten, madam, which is a
purifying o' the song. 'Would God would serve the
world so all the year! we 'd find no fault with the
tithe-woman, if I were the parson. One in ten, quoth
'a! an we might have a good woman born but for
every blazing star, or at an earthquake, 't would mend
the lottery well: a man may draw his heart out, ere
he pluck one.

Count. You 'll be gone, sir knave, and do as I command you! 91

Clo. That man should be at woman's command, and
yet no hurt done!—Though honesty be no Puritan, yet
it will do no hurt; it will wear the surplice of humility
over the black gown of a big heart.—I am going, forsooth: the business is for Helen to come hither. [*Exit.*

Count. Well, now.

Stew. I know, madam, you love your gentlewoman
entirely. 99

Count. 'Faith, I do: her father bequeathed her to
me; and she herself, without other advantage, may
lawfully make title to as much love as she finds: there
is more owing her than is paid, and more shall be
paid her than she 'll demand.

Stew. Madam, I was very late more near her than,
I think, she wished me: alone she was, and did communicate to herself, her own words to her own ears;
she thought, I dare vow for her, they touched not any
stranger sense. Her matter was, she loved your son:
Fortune, she said, was no goddess, that had put such
difference betwixt their two estates; Love, no god,
that would not extend his might, only where qualities
were level; Diana, no queen of virgins, that would
suffer her poor knight surprised, without rescue in the
first assault, or ransom afterward. This she delivered
in the most bitter touch of sorrow, that e'er I heard
virgin exclaim in; which I held my duty speedily to
acquaint you withal, sithence in the loss that may
happen, it concerns you something to know it. 119

Count. You have discharged this honestly: keep it
to yourself. Many likelihoods informed me of this
before, which hung so tottering in the balance, that
I could neither believe, nor misdoubt. Pray you,
leave me: stall this in your bosom, and I thank you
for your honest care. I will speak with you further
anon. [*Exit Steward.*

Even so it was with me, when I was young.
If ever we are nature's, these are ours; this thorn
Doth to our rose of youth rightly belong;
Our blood to us, this to our blood is born: 130
It is the show and seal of nature's truth,
Where love's strong passion is impress'd in youth:
By our remembrances of days foregone,
Such were our faults; or then we thought them none.

Enter Helena.

Her eye is sick on 't: I observe her now.

Hel. What is your pleasure, madam?

Count.   You know, Helen,
I am a mother to you.

Hel. Mine honourable mistress.

Count.   Nay, a mother.
Why not a mother? When I said, a mother,
Methought you saw a serpent: what 's in mother, 140
That you start at it? I say, I am your mother,
And put you in the catalogue of those
That were enwombed mine. 'T is often seen,
Adoption strives with nature; and choice breeds
A native slip to us from foreign seeds:
You ne'er oppress'd me with a mother's groan,
Yet I express to you a mother's care.—
God's mercy, maiden! does it curd thy blood,
To say, I am thy mother? What 's the matter,
That this distemper'd messenger of wet, 150
The many-colour'd Iris, rounds thine eye?—
Why? that you are my daughter?

Hel.   That I am not.

Count. I say, I am your mother.

Hel.   Pardon, madam;
The Count Rousillon cannot be my brother:
I am from humble, he from honour'd name;
No note upon my parents, his all noble:
My master, my dear lord he is; and I
His servant live, and will his vassal die.
He must not be my brother.

Count.   Nor I your mother?

Hel. You are my mother, madam; 'would you were
(So that my lord, your son, were not my brother) 161
Indeed my mother!—or were you both our mothers,
I care no more for, than I do for heaven,
So I were not his sister. Can't no other,
But, I your daughter, he must be my brother?

Count. Yes, Helen, you might be my daughter-in-
law.
God shield, you mean it not! daughter, and mother,
So strive upon your pulse. What, pale again?
My fear hath catch'd your fondness: now I see
The mystery of your loneliness, and find 170

Your salt tears' head. Now to all sense 't is gross,
You love my son: invention is asham'd,
Against the proclamation of thy passion,
To say, thou dost not: therefore tell me true;
But tell me then, 't is so:—for, look, thy cheeks
Confess it, the one to the other; and thine eyes
See it so grossly shown in thy behaviours,
That in their kind they speak it: only sin,
And hellish obstinacy tie thy tongue,
That truth should be suspected. Speak, is 't so? 180
If it be so, you have wound a goodly clue;
If it be not, forswear 't: howe'er, I charge thee,
As Heaven shall work in me for thine avail,
To tell me truly.
   Hel.   Good madam, pardon me.
   Count. Do you love my son?
   Hel.   Your pardon, noble mistress.
   Count. Love you my son?
   Hel.   Do not you love him, madam?
   Count. Go not about: my love hath in 't a bond,
Whereof the world takes note. Come, come, disclose
The state of your affection, for your passions
Have to the full appeach'd.
   Hel.   Then, I confess, 190
Here on my knee, before high Heaven and you,
That before you, and next unto high Heaven,
I love your son.—
My friends were poor, but honest; so 's my love:
Be not offended, for it hurts not him,
That he is lov'd of me. I follow him not
By any token of presumptuous suit;
Nor would I have him, till I do deserve him,
Yet never know how that desert should be.
I know I love in vain, strive against hope; 200
Yet, in this captious and intenible sieve,
I still pour in the waters of my love,
And lack not to lose still. Thus, Indian-like,
Religious in mine error, I adore
The sun, that looks upon his worshipper,
But knows of him no more. My dearest madam,
Let not your hate encounter with my love,
For loving where you do: but, if yourself,
Whose aged honour cites a virtuous youth,
Did ever, in so true a flame of liking, 210
Wish chastely, and love dearly, that your Dian
Was both herself and Love: O! then, give pity
To her, whose state is such, that cannot choose
But lend and give where she is sure to lose;
That seeks not to find that her search implies,

But, riddle-like, lives sweetly where she dies.
   Count. Had you not lately an intent, speak truly,
To go to Paris?
   Hel.   Madam, I had.
   Count.   Wherefore? tell true.
   Hel. I will tell truth; by grace itself I swear.
You know, my father left me some prescriptions 220
Of rare and prov'd effects, such as his reading
And manifest experience had collected
For general sovereignty: and that he will'd me
In heedfull'st reservation to bestow them,
As notes, whose faculties inclusive were,
More than they were in note. Amongst the rest,
There is a remedy approv'd, set down
To cure the desperate languishings whereof
The king is render'd lost.
   Count.   This was your motive
For Paris, was it? speak. 230
   Hel. My lord, your son, made me to think of this;
Else Paris, and the medicine, and the king,
Had, from the conversation of my thoughts,
Haply been absent then.
   Count.   But think you, Helen,
If you should tender your supposed aid,
He would receive it? He and his physicians
Are of a mind; he, that they cannot help him,
They, that they cannot help. How shall they credit
A poor unlearned virgin, when the schools,
Embowell'd of their doctrine, have left off 240
The danger to itself?
   Hel.   There 's something in 't,
More than my father's skill, which was the greatest
Of his profession, that his good receipt
Shall, for my legacy, be sanctified
By the luckiest stars in heaven: and, would your
          honour
But give me leave to try success, I 'd venture
The well-lost life of mine on his grace's cure,
By such a day and hour.
   Count.   Dost thou believe 't?
   Hel. Ay, madam, knowingly.
   Count. Why, Helen, thou shalt have my leave, and
         love, 250
Means, and attendants, and my loving greetings
To those of mine in court. I 'll stay at home,
And pray God's blessing into thy attempt.
Be gone to-morrow; and be sure of this,
What I can help thee to, thou shalt not miss.
                        [*Exeunt.*

ACT II.

SCENE I.—Paris. A Room in the KING'S Palace.

Flourish. Enter KING, *with divers young Lords taking leave for the Florentine war;* BERTRAM,
PAROLLES, *and Attendants.*

       King.
FAREWELL, young lords: these warlike
        principles
   Do not throw from you:—and you, my
        lords, farewell.—
   Share the advice betwixt you; if both
        gain, all
   The gift doth stretch itself as 't is receiv'd,
And is enough for both.
   1 Lord.   'T is our hope, sir,
After well-enter'd soldiers, to return
And find your grace in health.

   King. No, no, it cannot be; and yet my heart
Will not confess he owes the malady
That doth my life besiege. Farewell, young lords; 10
Whether I live or die, be you the sons
Of worthy Frenchmen: let higher Italy
(Those 'bated, that inherit but the fall
Of the last monarchy,) see, that you come
Not to woo honour, but to wed it: when
The bravest questant shrinks, find what you seek,
That fame may cry you loud. I say, farewell.
   2 Lord. Health, at your bidding, serve your
        majesty!

King. Those girls of Italy, take heed of them :
They say, our French lack language to deny, 20
If they demand : beware of being captives,
Before you serve.
Both. Our hearts receive your warnings.
King. Farewell.—Come hither to me.
[*The* King *retires to a couch.*
1 Lord. O my sweet lord, that you will stay behind
us !
Par. 'T is not his fault, the spark.
2 Lord. O, 't is brave wars !
Par. Most admirable : I have seen those wars.
Ber. I am commanded here, and kept a coil with,—
"Too young," and "the next year," and "'t is too
early."
Par. An thy mind stand to 't, boy, steal away
bravely.
Ber. I shall stay here the forehorse to a smock, 30
Creaking my shoes on the plain masonry,
Till honour be bought up, and no sword worn,
But one to dance with. By Heaven ! I 'll steal away.
1 Lord. There 's honour in the theft.
Par. Commit it, count.
2 Lord. I am your accessary ; and so farewell.
Ber. I grow to you, and our parting is a tortured
body.
1 Lord. Farewell, captain.
2 Lord. Sweet Monsieur Parolles ! 39
Par. Noble heroes, my sword and yours are kin.
Good sparks and lustrous, a word, good metals :
—you shall find in the regiment of the Spinii,
one Captain Spurio, with his cicatrice, an emblem of
war, here on his sinister cheek : it was this very
sword entrenched it : say to him, I live, and observe
his reports for me.
2 Lord. We shall, noble captain. [*Exeunt Lords.*
Par. Mars dote on you for his novices !—What will
you do ?
Ber. Stay ; the king— 50
Par. Use a more spacious ceremony to the noble
lords : you have restrained yourself within the list of
too cold an adieu : be more expressive to them ; for
they wear themselves in the cap of the time, there
do muster true gait, eat, speak, and move under the
influence of the most received star ; and though the
devil lead the measure, such are to be followed. After
them, and take a more dilated farewell.
Ber. And I will do so.
Par. Worthy fellows, and like to prove most sinewy
swordmen. [*Exeunt* Bertram *and* Parolles.

Enter Lafeu.

Laf. [*Kneeling.*] Pardon, my lord, for me and for
my tidings. 62
King. I 'll fee thee to stand up.
Laf. Then here 's a man stands, that has bought his
pardon.
I would, you had kneel'd, my lord, to ask me mercy,
And that, at my bidding, you could so stand up.
King. I would I had ; so I had broke thy pate,
And ask'd thee mercy for 't.
Laf. Good faith, across. But, my good lord, 't is
thus ;
Will you be cur'd of your infirmity ? 70
King. No.
Laf. O ! will you eat no grapes, my royal fox ?
Yes, but you will my noble grapes, an if
My royal fox could reach them. I have seen a medi-
cine
That 's able to breathe life into a stone,
Quicken a rock, and make you dance canary
With spritely fire and motion ; whose simple touch
Is powerful to araise King Pepin, nay,
To give great Charlemain a pen in 's hand,
And write to her a love-line.
King. What her is this ? 80
Laf. Why, doctor she. My lord, there 's one arriv'd,
If you will see her :—now, by my faith and honour,
If seriously I may convey my thoughts
In this my light deliverance, I have spoke
With one, that in her sex, her years, profession,
Wisdom, and constancy, hath amaz'd me more

Than I dare blame my weakness. Will you see her
(For that is her demand), and know her business ?
That done, laugh well at me.
King. Now, good Lafeu,
Bring in the admiration, that we with thee 90
May spend our wonder too, or take off thine,
By wond'ring how thou took'st it.
Laf. Nay, I 'll fit you,
And not be all day neither. [*Exit.*
King. Thus he his special nothing ever prologues.

Re-enter Lafeu, *with* Helena.

Laf. Nay, come your ways.
King. This haste hath wings, indeed.
Laf. Nay, come your ways.
This is his majesty, say your mind to him :
A traitor you do look like ; but such traitors
His majesty seldom fears. I am Cressid's uncle,
That dare leave two together. Fare you well. [*Exit.*
Hel. Ay, my good lord. 102
Gerard de Narbon was my father,
In what he did profess well found.
King. I knew him.
Hel. The rather will I spare my praises towards
him ;
Knowing him, is enough. On 's bed of death
Many receipts he gave me ; chiefly one,
Which, as the dearest issue of his practice,
And of his old experience the only darling,
He bade me store up, as a triple eye, 110
Safer than mine own two, more dear. I have so ;
And, hearing your high majesty is touch'd
With that malignant cause, wherein the honour
Of my dear father's gift stands chief in power,
I come to tender it and my appliance,
With all bound humbleness.
King. We thank you, maiden ;
But may not be so credulous of cure,
When our most learned doctors leave us, and
The congregated college have concluded
That labouring art can never ransom Nature 120
From her inaidable estate ; I say, we must not
So stain our judgment, or corrupt our hope,
To prostitute our past-cure malady
To empirics, or to dissever so
Our great self and our credit, to esteem
A senseless help, when help past sense we deem.
Hel. My duty then shall pay me for my pains :
I will no more enforce mine office on you ;
Humbly entreating from your royal thoughts
A modest one, to bear me back again. 130
King. I cannot give thee less, to be call'd grateful.
Thou thought'st to help me, and such thanks I give,
As one near death to those that wish him live ;
But what at full I know, thou know'st no part,
I knowing all my peril, thou no art.
Hel. What I can do, can do no hurt to try,
Since you set up your rest 'gainst remedy.
He that of greatest works is finisher,
Oft does them by the weakest minister :
So holy writ in babes hath judgment shown, 140
When judges have been babes ; great floods have
flown
From simple sources ; and great seas have dried,
When miracles have by the greatest been denied.
Oft expectation fails, and most oft there
Where most it promises ; and oft it hits,
Where hope is coldest, and despair most fits.
King. I must not hear thee : fare thee well, kind
maid.
Thy pains, not us'd, must by thyself be paid :
Proffers, not took, reap thanks for their reward.
Hel. Inspired merit so by breath is barr'd. 150
It is not so with Him that all things knows,
As 't is with us that square our guess by shows ;
But most it is presumption in us, when
The help of Heaven we count the act of men.
Dear sir, to my endeavours give consent ;
Of Heaven, not me, make an experiment.
I am not an impostor, that proclaim
Myself against the level of mine aim ;

But know I think, and think I know most sure,
My art is not past power, nor you past cure.   160
   King. Art thou so confident? Within what space
Hop'st thou my cure?
   Hel.   The great'st grace lending grace,
Ere twice the horses of the sun shall bring
Their fiery torcher his diurnal ring,
Ere twice in murk and occidental damp

King. "Give me some help here, ho!"

Moist Hesperus hath quench'd his sleepy lamp;
Or four-and-twenty times the pilot's glass
Hath told the thievish minutes how they pass,
What is infirm from your sound parts shall fly,
Health shall live free, and sickness freely die.   170
   King. Upon thy certainty and confidence,
What dar'st thou venture?
   Hel.   Tax of impudence,
A strumpet's boldness, a divulged shame,
Traduc'd by odious ballads; my maiden's name
Sear'd otherwise; ne worse of worst extended,
With vilest torture let my life be ended.
   King. Methinks, in thee some blessed spirit doth
        speak
His powerful sound, within an organ weak;
And what impossibility would slay
In common sense, sense saves another way.   180
Thy life is dear; for all, that life can rate
Worth name of life, in thee hath estimate;
Youth, beauty, wisdom, courage, all
That happiness and prime can happy call:
Thou this to hazard, needs must intimate
Skill infinite, or monstrous desperate.
Sweet practiser, thy physic I will try,
That ministers thine own death, if I die.
   Hel. If I break time, or flinch in property   190
Of what I spoke, unpitied let me die,
And well deserv'd. Not helping, death's my fee;
But, if I help, what do you promise me?
   King. Make thy demand.
   Hel.   But will you make it even?
   King. Ay, by my sceptre, and my hopes of heaven.
   Hel. Then shalt thou give me with thy kingly hand
What husband in thy power I will command:
Exempted be from me the arrogance
To choose from forth the royal blood of France,
My low and humble name to propagate
With any branch or image of thy state;   200
But such a one, thy vassal, whom I know
Is free for me to ask, thee to bestow.
   King. Here is my hand; the premises observ'd,
Thy will by my performance shall be serv'd;
So make the choice of thy own time; for I,
Thy resolv'd patient, on thee still rely.
More should I question thee, and more I must,
Though more to know could not be more to trust,
From whence thou cam'st, how tended on; but rest
Unquestion'd welcome, and undoubted blest.—   210

Give me some help here, ho!—If thou proceed
As high as word, my deed shall match thy deed.
                    [Flourish. Exeunt.

SCENE II.—Rousillon.   A Room in the COUNTESS's
Palace.

Enter COUNTESS *and Clown.*

   Count. Come on, sir: I shall now put you to the
height of your breeding.
   Clo. I will show myself highly fed, and lowly
taught. I know, my business is but to the court.
   Count. To the court! why, what place make you
special, when you put off that with such contempt?
But to the court!
   Clo. Truly, madam, if God have lent a man any
manners, he may easily put it off at court: he that
cannot make a leg, put off's cap, kiss his hand, and
say nothing, has neither leg, hands, lip, nor cap;
and, indeed, such a fellow, to say precisely, were not
for the court. But, for me, I have an answer will
serve all men.
   Count. Marry, that's a bountiful answer, that fits
all questions.
   Clo. It is like a barber's chair, that fits all buttocks;
the pin-buttock, the quatch-buttock, the brawn-but-
tock, or any buttock.   19
   Count. Will your answer serve fit to all questions?
   Clo. As fit as ten groats is for the hand of an
attorney, as your French crown for your taffeta punk,
as Tib's rush for Tom's forefinger, as a pancake for
Shrove Tuesday, a morris for Mayday, as the nail to
his hole, the cuckold to his horn, as a scolding quean
to a wrangling knave, as the nun's lip to the friar's
mouth; nay, as the pudding to his skin.
   Count. Have you, I say, an answer of such fitness
for all questions?
   Clo. From below your duke to beneath your constable, it will fit any question.   31

Clo. "Ask me, if I am a courtier."

   Count. It must be an answer of most monstrous
size, that must fit all demands.
   Clo. But a trifle neither, in good faith, if the learned
should speak truth of it. Here it is, and all that
belongs to 't: ask me, if I am a courtier; it shall do
you no harm to learn.
   Count. To be young again, if we could. I will be
a fool in question, hoping to be the wiser by your
answer. I pray you, sir, are you a courtier?   40
   Clo. O Lord, sir!—there's a simple putting off.—
More, more, a hundred of them.

Count. Sir, I am a poor friend of yours, that loves
you.

Clo. O Lord, sir!—Thick, thick, spare not me.

Count. I think, sir, you can eat none of this homely
meat.

Clo. O Lord, sir!—Nay, put me to 't, I warrant you.

Count. You were lately whipped, sir, as I think.

Clo. O Lord, sir!—Spare not me.   50

Count. Do you cry, "O Lord, sir!" at your whipping,
and "Spare not me?" Indeed, your "O Lord, sir!"
is very sequent to your whipping : you would answer
very well to a whipping, if you were but bound to 't.

Clo. I ne'er had worse luck in my life, in my—"O
Lord, sir!" I see, things may serve long, but not serve
ever.

Count. I play the noble housewife with the time,
To entertain it so merrily with a fool.

Clo. O Lord, sir!—why, there 't serves well again. 60

Count. An end, sir : to your business. Give Helen
this,
And urge her to a present answer back :
Commend me to my kinsmen, and my son.
This is not much.

Clo. Not much commendation to them.

Count. Not much employment for you : you understand me?

Clo. Most fruitfully : I am there before my legs.

Count. Haste you again.   [*Exeunt severally.*

SCENE III.—Paris. A Room in the KING'S Palace.

Enter BERTRAM, LAFEU, *and* PAROLLES.

Laf. They say, miracles are past ; and we have our
philosophical persons, to make modern and familiar,
things supernatural and causeless. Hence is it, that
we make trifles of terrors, ensconcing ourselves into
seeming knowledge, when we should submit ourselves
to an unknown fear.

Par. Why, 't is the rarest argument of wonder, that
hath shot out in our latter times.

Ber. And so 't is.

Laf. To be relinquished of the artists,—   10

Par. So I say : both of Galen and Paracelsus.

Laf. Of all the learned and authentic fellows,—

Par. Right ; so I say.

Laf. That gave him out incurable,—

Par. Why, there 't is ; so say I too.

Laf. Not to be helped,—

Par. Right ; as 't were a man assured of a—

Laf. Uncertain life, and sure death.

Par. Just, you say well ; so would I have said.

Laf. I may truly say, it is a novelty to the world. 20

Par. It is, indeed : if you will have it in showing,
you shall read it in—what do you call there?—

Laf. A showing of a heavenly effect in an earthly
actor.

Par. That 's it I would have said : the very same.

Laf. Why, your dolphin is not lustier : 'fore me, I
speak in respect—

Par. Nay, 't is strange, 't is very strange, that is
the brief and the tedious of it ; and he is of a most
facinorous spirit, that will not acknowledge it to be
the—   31

Laf. Very hand of Heaven.

Par. Ay, so I say.

Laf. In a most weak—

Par. And debile minister, great power, great tran-
scendence : which should, indeed, give us a further
use to be made, than alone the recovery of the king,
as to be—

Laf. Generally thankful.

Par. I would have said it ; you say well. Here
comes the king.   41

Enter KING, HELENA, *and Attendants.*

Laf. Lustick, as the Dutchman says : I 'll like a
maid the better, whilst I have a tooth in my head.
Why, he 's able to lead her a coranto.

Par. Mort du vinaigre! Is not this Helen?

Laf. 'Fore God, I think so.

King. Go, call before me all the lords in court.—
    [*Exit an Attendant.*
Sit, my preserver, by thy patient's side :
And with this healthful hand, whose banish'd sense
Thou hast repeal'd, a second time receive   50
The confirmation of my promis'd gift,
Which but attends thy naming.

Enter several Lords.

    Fair maid, send forth thine eye : this youthful parcel
Of noble bachelors stand at my bestowing,
O'er whom both sovereign power and father's voice
I have to use : thy frank election make.
Thou hast power to choose, and they none to forsake.

Hel. To each of you one fair and virtuous mistress
Fall, when Love please!—marry, to each, but one.

Laf. I 'd give bay curtal, and his furniture,   60
My mouth no more were broken than these boys',
And writ as little beard.

King.   Peruse them well :
Not one of those but had a noble father.

Hel. Gentlemen,
Heaven hath through me restor'd the king to health.

All. We understand it, and thank Heaven for you.

Hel. I am a simple maid ; and therein wealthiest,
That, I protest, I simply am a maid.—
Please it your majesty, I have done already :
The blushes in my cheeks thus whisper me,   70
"We blush, that thou shouldst choose ; but, be refus'd,
Let the white death sit on thy cheek for ever :
We 'll ne'er come there again."

King.   Make choice ; and see,
Who shuns thy love, shuns all his love in me.

Hel. Now, Dian, from thy altar do I fly,
And to imperial Love, that god most high,
Do my sighs stream.—Sir, will you hear my suit?

1 Lord. And grant it.

Hel.   Thanks, sir : all the rest is mute.

Laf. I had rather be in this choice, than throw
ames-ace for my life.   80

Hel. The honour, sir, that flames in your fair eyes,
Before I speak, too threateningly replies :
Love make your fortunes twenty times above
Her that so wishes, and her humble love !

2 Lord. No better, if you please.

Hel.   My wish receive,
Which great Love grant ! and so I take my leave.

Laf. Do all they deny her ? An they were sons of
mine, I 'd have them whipped, or I would send them
to the Turk to make eunuchs of.

Hel. [*To 3 Lord.*] Be not afraid that I your hand
should take ;   90
I 'll never do you wrong for your own sake :
Blessing upon your vows ! and in your bed
Find fairer fortune, if you ever wed !

Laf. These boys are boys of ice, they 'll none have
her : sure, they are bastards to the English : the French
ne'er got them.

Hel. You are too young, too happy, and too good,
To make yourself a son out of my blood.

4 Lord. Fair one, I think not so.

Laf. There 's one grape yet,—I am sure, thy father
drank wine.—But if thou be'st not an ass, I am a youth
of fourteen : I have known thee already.   102

Hel. [*To* BERTRAM.] I dare not say, I take you ; but
I give
Me, and my service, ever whilst I live,
Into your guiding power.—This is the man.

King. Why, then, young Bertram, take her ; she 's
thy wife.

Ber. My wife, my liege ! I shall beseech your high-
ness,
In such a business give me leave to use
The help of mine own eyes.

King.   Know'st thou not, Bertram,
What she has done for me?

Ber.   Yes, my good lord ;   110
But never hope to know why I should marry her.

King. Thou know'st, she has rais'd me from my
sickly bed.

Ber. But follows it, my lord, to bring me down
Must answer for your raising? I know her well :

She had her breeding at my father's charge.
A poor physician's daughter my wife!—Disdain
Rather corrupt me ever!
   King. 'T is only title thou disdain'st in her, the
     which
I can build up. Strange is it, that our bloods,
Of colour, weight, and heat, pour'd all together, 120
Would quite confound distinction, yet stand off
In differences so mighty. If she be
All that is virtuous (save what thou dislik'st,
A poor physician's daughter), thou dislik'st
Of virtue for the name ; but do not so :
From lowest place when virtuous things proceed,
The place is dignified by the doer's deed :
Where great additions swell 's, and virtue none,
It is a dropsied honour. Good alone
Is good without a name ; vileness is so :   130
The property by what it is should go,
Not by the title. She is young, wise, fair ;
In these to nature she 's immediate heir,
And these breed honour : that is honour's scorn
Which challenges itself as honour's born,
And is not like the sire : honours thrive,
When rather from our acts we them derive,
Than our foregoers. The mere word 's a slave,
Debosh'd on every tomb ; on every grave,
A lying trophy ; and as oft is dumb,   140
Where dust and damn'd oblivion is the tomb
Of honour'd bones indeed. What should be said ?
If thou canst like this creature as a maid,
I can create the rest : virtue, and she,
Is her own dower ; honour and wealth from me.
   Ber. I cannot love her, nor will strive to do 't.
   King. Thou wrong'st thyself, if thou shouldst strive
     to choose.
   Hel. That you are well restor'd, my lord, I 'm glad.
Let the rest go.
   King. My honour 's at the stake, which to defeat 150
I must produce my power. Here, take her hand,
Proud scornful boy, unworthy this good gift,
That dost in vile misprision shackle up
My love, and her desert ; that canst not dream,
We, poising us in her defective scale,
Shall weigh thee to the beam ; that wilt not know,
It is in us to plant thine honour, where
We please to have it grow. Check thy contempt :
Obey our will, which travails in thy good :
Believe not thy disdain, but presently   160
Do thine own fortunes that obedient right,
Which both thy duty owes, and our power claims ;
Or I will throw thee from my care for ever
Into the staggers and the careless lapse
Of youth and ignorance ; both my revenge and hate
Loosing upon thee, in the name of justice,
Without all terms of pity. Speak : thine answer.
   Ber. Pardon, my gracious lord, for I submit
My fancy to your eyes. When I consider
What great creation, and what dole of honour,   170
Files where you bid it, I find that she, which late
Was in my nobler thoughts most base, is now
The praised of the king ; who, so ennobled,
Is, as 't were, born so.
   King.   Take her by the hand,
And tell her, she is thine : to whom I promise
A counterpoise, if not to thy estate,
A balance more replete.
   Ber.   I take her hand.
   King. Good fortune, and the favour of the king,
Smile upon this contract ; whose ceremony
Shall seem expedient on the now-born brief,   180
And be perform'd to-night : the solemn feast
Shall more attend upon the coming space,
Expecting absent friends. As thou lov'st her,
Thy love 's to me religious, else, does err.
     [*Exeunt* KING, BERTRAM, HELENA, *Lords,*
      and Attendants.
   Laf. Do you hear, monsieur ? a word with you.
   Par. Your pleasure, sir ?
   Laf. Your lord and master did well to make his re-
cantation.
   Par. Recantation ?—My lord ? my master ?
   Laf. Ay ; is it not a language I speak ?   190

   Par. A most harsh one, and not to be understood
without bloody succeeding. My master ?
   Laf. Are you companion to the Count Rousillon ?
   Par. To any count ; to all counts ; to what is man.
   Laf. To what is count's man : count's master is of
another style.
   Par. You are too old, sir : let it satisfy you, you are
too old.
   Laf. I must tell thee, sirrah, I write man ; to which
title age cannot bring thee.   200
   Par. What I dare too well do, I dare not do.
   Laf. I did think thee, for two ordinaries, to be a
pretty wise fellow : thou didst make tolerable vent of
thy travel : it might pass ; yet the scarfs, and the ban-
nerets about thee, did manifoldly dissuade me from
believing thee a vessel of too great a burden. I have
now found thee : when I lose thee again, I care not ;

Par. "Hadst thou not the privilege of antiquity upon thee."

yet art thou good for nothing but taking up, and that
thou 'rt scarce worth.
   Par. Hadst thou not the privilege of antiquity upon
thee,—   211
   Laf. Do not plunge thyself too far in anger, lest thou
hasten thy trial ; which if—Lord have mercy on thee
for a hen ! So, my good window of lattice, fare thee
well : thy casement I need not open, for I look through
thee. Give me thy hand.
   Par. My lord, you give me most egregious indignity.
   Laf. Ay, with all my heart ; and thou art worthy of it.
   Par. I have not, my lord, deserved it.
   Laf. Yes, good faith, every drachm of it ; and I will
not bate thee a scruple.   221
   Par. Well, I shall be wiser.
   Laf. E'en as soon as thou canst, for thou hast to pull
at a smack o' the contrary. If ever thou be'st bound
in thy scarf, and beaten, thou shalt find what it is to
be proud of thy bondage. I have a desire to hold my
acquaintance with thee, or rather my knowledge,
that I may say, in the default, he is a man I know.
   Par. My lord, you do me most insupportable vexation.   230
   Laf. I would it were hell-pains for thy sake, and my
poor doing eternal : for doing I am past, as I will by
thee, in what motion age will give me leave. [*Exit.*
   Par. Well, thou hast a son shall take this disgrace
off me, scurvy, old, filthy, scurvy lord !—Well, I must
be patient ; there is no fettering of authority. I 'll
beat him, by my life, if I can meet him with any convenience, an he were double and double a lord. I 'll
have no more pity of his age, than I would have of—
I 'll beat him : an if I could but meet him again ! 240

     Re-enter LAFEU.

   Laf. Sirrah, your lord and master 's married :
there 's news for you ; you have a new mistress.

Par. I most unfeignedly beseech your lordship to make some reservation of your wrongs : he is my good lord : whom I serve above is my master.

Laf. Who ? God ?

Par. Ay, sir.

Laf. The devil it is, that's thy master. Why dost thou garter up thy arms o' this fashion ? dost make hose of thy sleeves ? do other servants so ? Thou wert best set thy lower part where thy nose stands. By mine honour, if I were but two hours younger, I'd beat thee : methinks 't, thou art a general offence, and every man should beat thee : I think, thou wast created for men to breathe themselves upon thee.

Par. This is hard and undeserved measure, my lord.

Laf. Go to, sir ; you were beaten in Italy for picking a kernel out of a pomegranate : you are a vagabond, and no true traveller. You are more saucy with lords and honourable personages, than the commission of your birth and virtue gives you heraldry. You are not worth another word, else I'd call you knave. I leave you.   [*Exit.*

Par. Good, very good ; it is so then :—good, very good. Let it be concealed awhile.

Re-enter BERTRAM.

Ber. Undone, and forfeited to cares for ever !

Par. What is the matter, sweet-heart ?

Ber. Although before the solemn priest I have sworn, I will not bed her.   270

Par. What, what, sweet-heart ?

Ber. O my Parolles, they have married me !— I'll to the Tuscan wars, and never bed her.

Par. France is a dog-hole, and it no more merits The tread of a man's foot. To the wars !

Ber. There's letters from my mother : what the import is,
I know not yet.

Par. Ay, that would be known. To the wars, my boy ! to the wars !
He wears his honour in a box, unseen,
That hugs his kicky-wicky here at home,   280
Spending his manly marrow in her arms,
Which should sustain the bound and high curvet
Of Mars's fiery steed. To other regions !
France is a stable ; we, that dwell in 't, jades ;
Therefore, to the war !

Ber. It shall be so : I'll send her to my house,
Acquaint my mother with my hate to her,
And wherefore I am fled ; write to the king
That which I durst not speak. His present gift
Shall furnish me to those Italian fields,   290
Where noble fellows strike. War is no strife
To the dark house, and the detested wife.

Par. Will this capriccio hold in thee, art sure ?

Ber. Go with me to my chamber, and advise me.
I'll send her straight away : to-morrow
I'll to the wars, she to her single sorrow.

Par. Why, these balls bound ; there's noise in it ;
't is hard.
A young man married is a man that's marr'd :
Therefore away, and leave her bravely go ;
The king has done you wrong ; but, hush ! 't is so.   300
                                        [*Exeunt.*

SCENE IV.—The Same. Another Room in the Same.

Enter HELENA *and Clown.*

Hel. My mother greets me kindly : is she well ?

Clo. She is not well ; but yet she has her health : she's very merry ; but yet she is not well : but thanks be given, she's very well, and wants nothing i' the world ; but yet she is not well.

Hel. If she be very well, what does she ail, that she's not very well ?

Clo. Truly, she's very well, indeed, but for two things.

Hel. What two things ?   10

Clo. One, that she's not in heaven, whither God send her quickly ! the other, that she's in earth, from whence God send her quickly !

Enter PAROLLES.

Par. Bless you, my fortunate lady !

Hel. I hope, sir, I have your good will to have mine own good fortunes.

Par. You had my prayers to lead them on ; and to keep them on, have them still.—O, my knave ! How does my old lady ?

Clo. So that you had her wrinkles, and I her money, I would she did as you say.   21

Par. Why, I say nothing.

Clo. Marry, you are the wiser man ; for many a man's tongue shakes out his master's undoing. To say nothing, to do nothing, to know nothing, and to have nothing, is to be a great part of your title, which is within a very little of nothing.

Par. Away ! thou 'rt a knave.

Clo. You should have said, sir, before a knave thou 'rt a knave ; that is, before me thou 'rt a knave : this had been truth, sir.   31

Par. Go to, thou art a witty fool ; I have found thee.

Clo. Did you find me in yourself, sir, or were you taught to find me ? The search, sir, was profitable ; and much fool may you find in you, even to the world's pleasure, and the increase of laughter.

Par. A good knave, i' faith, and well fed.—
Madam, my lord will go away to-night ;
A very serious business calls on him.   40
The great prerogative and rite of love,
Which, as your due, time claims, he does acknowledge,
But puts it off to a compell'd restraint ;
Whose want, and whose delay, is strew'd with sweets,
Which they distil now in the curbed time,
To make the coming hour o'erflow with joy,
And pleasure drown the brim.

Hel.   What's his will else ?

Par. That you will take your instant leave o' the king,
And make this haste as your own good proceeding,
Strengthen'd with what apology you think   50
May make it probable need.

Hel.   What more commands he ?

Par. That, having this obtain'd, you presently
Attend his further pleasure.

Hel. In everything I wait upon his will.

Par. I shall report it so.

Hel.   I pray you.—Come, sirrah. [*Exeunt.*

SCENE V.—Another Room in the Same.

Enter LAFEU *and* BERTRAM.

Laf. But, I hope, your lordship thinks not him a soldier.

Ber. Yes, my lord, and of very valiant approof.

Laf. You have it from his own deliverance.

Ber. And by other warranted testimony.

Laf. Then my dial goes not true. I took this lark for a bunting.

Ber. I do assure you, my lord, he is very great in knowledge, and accordingly valiant.   9

Laf. I have then sinned against his experience, and transgressed against his valour ; and my state that way is dangerous, since I cannot yet find in my heart to repent. Here he comes. I pray you, make us friends : I will pursue the amity.

Enter PAROLLES.

Par. [*To* BERTRAM.] These things shall be done, sir.

Laf. 'Pray you, sir, who's his tailor ?

Par. Sir ?

Laf. O ! I know him well. Ay, sir ; he, sir, is a good workman, a very good tailor.   20

Ber. [*Aside to* PAROLLES.] Is she gone to the king ?

Par. She is.

Ber. Will she away to-night ?

Par. As you'll have her.

Ber. I have writ my letters, casketed my treasure,

Given order for our horses; and to-night,
When I should take possession of the bride,
End, ere I do begin.

Laf. A good traveller is something at the latter end
of a dinner, but one that lies three thirds, and uses a

prayers. Fare you well, my lord; and believe this
of me, there can be no kernel in this light nut; the
soul of this man is his clothes: trust him not in matter
of heavy consequence; I have kept of them tame,
and know their natures.—Farewell, monsieur: I have

Hel. "I would not tell you what I would, my lord!"

known truth to pass a thousand nothings with, should
be once heard, and thrice beaten.—God save you,
captain.

Ber. Is there any unkindness between my lord and
you, monsieur?

Par. I know not how I have deserved to run into
my lord's displeasure.

Laf. You have made shift to run into 't, boots and
spurs and all, like him that leaped into the custard,
and out of it you'll run again, rather than suffer
question for your residence.   41

Ber. It may be, you have mistaken him, my lord.

Laf. And shall do so ever, though I took him at his

spoken better of you, than you have or will deserve
at my hand; but we must do good against evil. [*Exit.*

Par. An idle lord, I swear.   51

Ber. I think so.

Par. Why, do you not know him?

Ber. Yes, I do know him well; and common speech
Gives him a worthy pass.   Here comes my clog.

Enter HELENA.

Hel. I have, sir, as I was commanded from you,
Spoke with the king, and have procur'd his leave
For present parting; only he desires
Some private speech with you.

Ber.   I shall obey his will.
You must not marvel, Helen, at my course,   60
Which holds not colour with the time, nor does
The ministration and required office
On my particular : prepar'd I was not
For such a business ; therefore am I found
So much unsettled. This drives me to entreat you,
That presently you take your way for home ;
And rather muse than ask why I entreat you ;
For my respects are better than they seem,
And my appointments have in them a need
Greater than shows itself, at the first view,   70
To you that know them not. This to my mother.
                              [*Giving a letter.*
'T will be two days ere I shall see you : so,
I leave you to your wisdom.
Hel.   Sir, I can nothing say,
But that I am your most obedient servant.
Ber. Come, come, no more of that.
Hel.   And ever shall
With true observance seek to eke out that,
Wherein toward me my homely stars have fail'd
To equal my great fortune.

Ber.   Let that go :
My haste is very great. Farewell : hie home.
Hel. 'Pray, sir, your pardon.
Ber.   Well, what would you say ?
Hel. I am not worthy of the wealth I owe ;   81
Nor dare I say, 't is mine, and yet it is ;
But, like a timorous thief, most fain would steal
What law does vouch mine own.
Ber.   What would you have ?
Hel. Something, and scarce so much :—nothing, in-
          deed.—
I would not tell you what I would, my lord :—
Faith, yes ;—
Strangers and foes do sunder, and not kiss.
Ber. I pray you, stay not, but in haste to horse.
Hel. I shall not break your bidding, good my
          lord.   90
Ber. Where are my other men, monsieur ?—Fare-
          well.   [*Exit* HELENA.
Go thou toward home ; where I will never come,
Whilst I can shake my sword, or hear the drum.—
Away ! and for our flight.
Par.   Bravely, coragio. [*Exeunt.*

ACT III.

SCENE I.—Florence. A Room in the DUKE'S Palace.

Flourish. Enter the DUKE OF FLORENCE, *attended ; two French Lords, and
Soldiers.*

Duke.
SO that, from point to point, now have
          you heard
The fundamental reasons of this war,
Whose great decision hath much blood
          let forth,
And more thirsts after.
1 Lord.   Holy seems the quarrel
Upon your grace's part ; black and fearful
On the opposer.
Duke. Therefore we marvel much,
          our cousin France
Would, in so just a business shut his
          bosom
Against our borrowing prayers.
2 Lord.   Good my lord,
The reasons of our state I cannot yield,   10
But like a common and an outward man,
That the great figure of a council frames
By self-unable motion : therefore dare not
Say what I think of it, since I have found
Myself in my uncertain grounds to fail
As often as I guess'd.
Duke.   Be it his pleasure.
2 Lord. But I am sure, the younger of our nature,
That surfeit on their ease, will day by day
Come here for physic.
Duke.   Welcome shall they be,
And all the honours that can fly from us   20
Shall on them settle. You know your places well ;
When better fall, for your avails they fell.
To-morrow to the field.   [*Flourish. Exeunt.*

SCENE II.—Rousillon. A Room in the COUNTESS's
Palace.

Enter COUNTESS *and Clown.*

Count. It hath happened all as I would have had it,
save that he comes not along with her.

Clo. By my troth, I take my young lord to be a very
melancholy man.
Count. By what observance, I pray you ?
Clo. Why, he will look upon his boot, and sing :
mend the ruff, and sing ; ask questions, and sing ; pick
his teeth ; and sing. I know a man, that had this trick
of melancholy, sold a goodly manor for a song.
Count. Let me see what he writes, and when he
means to come.   11
Clo. I have no mind to Isbel, since I was at court.
Our old ling and our Isbels o' the country are nothing
like your old ling and your Isbels o' the court : the
brains of my Cupid 's knocked out, and I begin to love,
as an old man loves money, with no stomach.
Count. What have we here ?
Clo. E'en that you have there.   [*Exit.*
Count. [*Reads.*] " I have sent you a daughter-in-
law : she had recovered the king, and undone me. I
have wedded her, not bedded her ; and sworn to make
the *not* eternal. You shall hear, I am run away : know
it before the report come. If there be breadth enough
in the world, I will hold a long distance. My duty to
you.   Your unfortunate son,
                                              BERTRAM."
This is not well : rash and unbridled boy,
To fly the favours of so good a king !
To pluck his indignation on thy head,
By the misprising of a maid too virtuous   30
For the contempt of empire !

Re-enter Clown.

Clo. O madam ! yonder is heavy news within, between two soldiers and my young lady.
Count. What is the matter ?
Clo. Nay, there is some comfort in the news, some
comfort : your son will not be killed so soon as I
thought he would.
Count. Why should he be kill'd ?
Clo. So say I, madam, if he run away, as I hear he
does : the danger is in standing to 't ; that's the loss of

men, though it be the getting of children. Here they
come will tell you more ; for my part, I only hear your
son was run away.　　　　　　　　　　　　[*Exit.*

Enter HELENA *and two Gentlemen.*

1 Gent. Save you, good madam.

Hel. Madam, my lord is gone, for ever gone.

2 Gent. Do not say so.

Count. Think upon patience.—'Pray you, gentle-
men,—
I have felt so many quirks of joy and grief,
That the first face of neither, on the start,
Can woman me unto 't :—where is my son, I pray
　　you ?　　　　　　　　　　　　　　　　　50

2 Gent. Madam, he 's gone to serve the Duke of
Florence.
We met him thitherward ; for thence we came,
And, after some despatch in hand at court,
Thither we bend again.

Hel. Look on his letter, madam : here 's my passport.
[*Reads.*] " When thou canst get the ring upon my
finger, which never shall come off, and show me a
child begotten of thy body, that I am father to, then
call me husband : but in such a *then* I write a *never.*"
This is a dreadful sentence.　　　　　　　　　60

Count. Brought you this letter, gentlemen ?

1 Gent.　　　　　　　　　　　　Ay, madam ;
And, for the contents' sake, are sorry for our pains.

Count. I pr'ythee, lady, have a better cheer ;
If thou engrossest all the griefs are thine,
Thou robb'st me of a moiety. He was my son,
But I do wash his name out of my blood,
And thou art all my child.—Towards Florence is he ?

2 Gent. Ay, madam.

Count.　　　　　　　　And to be a soldier ?

2 Gent. Such is his noble purpose ; and, believe 't,
The duke will lay upon him all the honour　　70
That good convenience claims.

Count.　　　　　　　　　　Return you thither ?

1 Gent. Ay, madam, with the swiftest wing of
　　speed.

Hel. [*Reads.*] " Till I have no wife, I have nothing
in France."
'T is bitter.

Count.　　　Find you that there ?

Hel.　　　　　　　　　　　　Ay, madam.

1 Gent. 'T is but the boldness of his hand, haply,
which his heart was not consenting to.

Count. Nothing in France, until he have no wife !
There 's nothing here that is too good for him,
But only she ; and she deserves a lord,　　80
That twenty such rude boys might tend upon,
And call her hourly, mistress. Who was with him ?

1 Gent. A servant only, and a gentleman
Which I have sometime known.

Count.　　　　　　　Parolles, was it not ?

1 Gent. Ay, my good lady, he.

Count. A very tainted fellow, and full of wicked-
ness.
My son corrupts a well-derived nature
With his inducement.

1 Gent.　　　　　　　Indeed, good lady,
The fellow has a deal of that, too much,
Which holds him much to have.

Count.　　　Y' are welcome, gentlemen.
I will entreat you, when you see my son,　　91
To tell him, that his sword can never win
The honour that he loses : more I 'll entreat you
Written to bear along.

2 Gent.　　　　　We serve you, madam,
In that and all your worthiest affairs.

Count. Not so, but as we change our courtesies.
Will you draw near ?

　　　　　　[*Exeunt* COUNTESS *and Gentlemen.*

Hel. " Till I have no wife, I have nothing in France."
Nothing in France, until he has no wife !
Thou shalt have none, Rousillon, none in France ;　100
Then hast thou all again. Poor lord ! is 't I
That chase thee from thy country, and expose
Those tender limbs of thine to the event
Of the none-sparing war ? and is it I
That drive thee from the sportive court, where thou

Wast shot at with fair eyes, to be the mark
Of smoky muskets ? O you leaden messengers,
That ride upon the violent speed of fire,
Fly with false aim ; move the still-'pearing air,
That sings with piercing, do not touch my lord !　110
Whoever shoots at him, I set him there ;
Whoever charges on his forward breast,
I am the caitiff that do hold him to it ;
And, though I kill him not, I am the cause
His death was so effected. Better 't were,
I met the ravin lion when he roar'd
With sharp constraint of hunger : better 't were,
That all the miseries which nature owes
Were mine at once. No, come thou home, Rousillon,
Whence honour but of danger wins a scar,　　120
As oft it loses all : I will be gone.
My being here it is that holds thee hence :
Shall I stay here to do 't ? no, no, although
The air of paradise did fan the house,
And angels offic'd all : I will be gone,
That pitiful rumour may report my flight,
To consolate thine ear. Come, night ; end, day !
For with the dark, poor thief, I 'll steal away.　[*Exit.*

———

SCENE III.—Florence. Before the DUKE'S Palace.

Flourish. Enter the DUKE OF FLORENCE, BERTRAM,
PAROLLES, *Lords, Officers, Soldiers, and others.*

Duke. The general of our horse thou art ; and we,
Great in our hope, lay our best love and credence
Upon thy promising fortune.

Ber.　　　　　　　　Sir, it is
A charge too heavy for my strength ; but yet
We 'll strive to bear it, for your worthy sake,
To the extreme edge of hazard.

Duke.　　　　　　　　Then go thou forth,
And fortune play upon thy prosperous helm,
As thy auspicious mistress !

Ber.　　　　　　　　This very day,
Great Mars, I put myself into thy file :
Make me but like my thoughts, and I shall prove　10
A lover of thy drum, hater of love.　　　[*Exeunt.*

———

SCENE IV.—Rousillon. A Room in the COUNTESS's
Palace.

Enter COUNTESS *and her Steward.*

Count. Alas ! and would you take the letter of her ?
Might you not know, she would do as she has done,
By sending me a letter ? Read it again.

Stew. [*Reads.*] " I am Saint Jaques' pilgrim, thither
　　gone.
Ambitious love hath so in me offended,
That bare-foot plod I the cold ground upon,
With sainted vow my faults to have amended.
Write, write, that, from the bloody course of war,
My dearest master, your dear son, may hie :
Bless him at home in peace, whilst I from far　　10
His name with zealous fervour sanctify.
His taken labours bid him me forgive :
I, his despiteful Juno, sent him forth
From courtly friends, with camping foes to live,
Where death and danger dogs the heels of worth :
He is too good and fair for Death and me,
Whom I myself embrace, to set him free."

Count. Ah, what sharp stings are in her mildest
　　words !—
Rinaldo, you did never lack advice so much,
As letting her pass so : had I spoke with her,　　20
I could have well diverted her intents,
Which thus she hath prevented.

Stew.　　　　　　　　Pardon me, madam :
If I had given you this at over-night,
She might have been o'erta'en ; and yet she writes,
Pursuit would be but vain.

Count.　　　　　　　What angel shall
Bless this unworthy husband ? he cannot thrive,
Unless her prayers, whom Heaven delights to hear,

And loves to grant, reprieve him from the wrath
Of greatest justice.—Write, write, Rinaldo,
To this unworthy husband of his wife: 30
Let every word weigh heavy of her worth,
That he does weigh too light: my greatest grief,
Though little he do feel it, set down sharply.
Despatch the most convenient messenger.—
When, haply, he shall hear that she is gone,
He will return; and hope I may, that she,
Hearing so much, will speed her foot again,
Led hither by pure love. Which of them both
Is dearest to me, I have no skill in sense
To make distinction.—Provide this messenger.—   40
My heart is heavy, and mine age is weak;
Grief would have tears, and sorrow bids me speak.
                         [*Exeunt.*

SCENE V.—Without the Walls of Florence.

A tucket afar off. Enter an old Widow of Florence,
DIANA, VIOLENTA, MARIANA, *and other Citizens.*

Wid. Nay, come; for if they do approach the city,
we shall loose all the sight.
Dia. They say, the French count has done most
honourable service.
Wid. It is reported that he has taken their greatest
commander, and that with his own hand he slew the
duke's brother. We have lost our labour; they are
gone a contrary way: hark! you may know by their
trumpets.   9
Mar. Come; let's return again, and suffice ourselves with the report of it. Well, Diana, take heed
of this French earl: the honour of a maid is her
name, and no legacy is so rich as honesty.
Wid. I have told my neighbour, how you have been
solicited by a gentleman his companion.
Mar. I know that knave; hang him! one Parolles:
a filthy officer he is in those suggestions for the young
earl.—Beware of them, Diana; their promises, entice-
ments, oaths, tokens, and all these engines of lust, are
not the things they go under: many a maid hath been
seduced by them; and the misery is, example, that so
terrible shows in the wreck of maidenhood, cannot for
all that dissuade succession, but that they are limed
with the twigs that threaten them. I hope, I need not
to advise you further; but, I hope, your own grace
will keep you where you are, though there were no
further danger known, but the modesty which is so
lost.
Dia. You shall not need to fear me.
Wid. I hope so.—Look, here comes a pilgrim: I
know she will lie at my house; thither they send one
another. I'll question her.—   32

Enter HELENA, *in the dress of a pilgrim.*

God save you, pilgrim!—whither are you bound?
Hel. To Saint Jaques le Grand.
Where do the palmers lodge, I do beseech you?
Wid. At the Saint Francis, here beside the port.
Hel. Is this the way?
Wid.   Ay, marry, is 't.—Hark you!
                   [*A march afar off.*
They come this way.—If you will tarry, holy pilgrim,
But till the troops come by,
I will conduct you where you shall be lodg'd: 40
The rather, for I think I know your hostess
As ample as myself.
Hel.   Is it yourself?
Wid. If you shall please so, pilgrim.
Hel. I thank you, and will stay upon your leisure.
Wid. You came, I think, from France?
Hel.   I did so.
Wid. Here you shall see a countryman of yours,
That has done worthy service.
Hel.   His name, I pray you.
Dia. The Count Rousillon: know you such a one?
Hel. But by the ear, that hears most nobly of him;
His face I know not.
Dia.   Whatsoe'er he is,   50
He's bravely taken here. He stole from France,

As 't is reported, for the king had married him
Against his liking. Think you it is so?
Hel. Ay, surely, mere the truth: I know his lady.
Dia. There is a gentleman, that serves the count,
Reports but coarsely of her.
Hel.   What's his name?
Dia. Monsieur Parolles.
Hel.   O! I believe with him,
In argument of praise, or to the worth
Of the great count himself, she is too mean
To have her name repeated: all her deserving   60
Is a reserved honesty, and that
I have not heard examin'd.
Dia.   Alas, poor lady!
'T is a hard bondage, to become the wife
Of a detesting lord.
Wid. Ay, right; good creature, wheresoe'er she is,
Her heart weighs sadly. This young maid might do
           her
A shrewd turn, if she pleas'd.
Hel.   How do you mean?
May be, the amorous count solicits her
In the unlawful purpose.
Wid.   He does, indeed;
And brokes with all that can in such a suit   70
Corrupt the tender honour of a maid:
But she is arm'd for him, and keeps her guard
In honestest defence.
Mar.   The gods forbid else!

*Enter, with drum and colours, a party of the
Florentine army,* BERTRAM, *and* PAROLLES.

Wid. So, now they come.—
That is Antonio, the duke's eldest son;
That, Escalus.
Hel.   Which is the Frenchman?
Dia.   He;
That with the plume: 't is a most gallant fellow;
I would he lov'd his wife. If he were honester,
He were much goodlier; is 't not a handsome gentle-
           man?
Hel. I like him well.   80
Dia. 'T is pity, he is not honest. Yond's that same
           knave,
That leads him to these places: were I his lady,
I would poison that vile rascal.
Hel.   Which is he?
Dia. That jack-an-apes with scarfs. Why is he
melancholy?
Hel. Perchance he's hurt i' the battle.
Par. Lose our drum! well.
Mar. He's shrewdly vexed at something. Look, he
has spied us.
Wid. Marry, hang you!   90
Mar. And your courtesy, for a ring-carrier!
        [*Exeunt* BERTRAM, PAROLLES, *Officers,
                 and Soldiers.*
Wid. The troop is past. Come, pilgrim, I will
bring you
Where you shall host: of enjoin'd penitents
There's four or five, to Great Saint Jaques bound,
Already at my house.
Hel.   I humbly thank you.
Please it this matron, and this gentle maid,
To eat with us to-night, the charge and thanking
Shall be for me: and, to requite you further,
I will bestow some precepts of this virgin,
Worthy the note.
Both.   We'll take your offer kindly.   100
                           [*Exeunt.*

SCENE VI. Camp before Florence.

Enter BERTRAM, *and the two French Lords.*

1 Lord. Nay, good my lord, put him to 't: let him
have his way.
2 Lord. If your lordship find him not a hilding, hold
me no more in your respect.
1 Lord. On my life, my lord, a bubble.
Ber. Do you think I am so far deceived in him?
1 Lord. Believe it, my lord: in mine own direct

knowledge, without any malice, but to speak of him
as my kinsman, he's a most notable coward, an infinite and endless liar, an hourly promise-breaker, the
owner of no one good quality worthy your lordship's
entertainment.   12
  2 Lord. It were fit you knew him, lest, reposing
too far in his virtue, which he hath not, he might, at
some great and trusty business in a main danger, fail
you.
  Ber. I would I knew in what particular action to
try him.
  2 Lord. None better than to let him fetch off his
drum, which you hear him so confidently undertake
to do.   21
  1 Lord. I, with a troop of Florentines, will suddenly surprise him : such I will have, whom, I am
sure, he knows not from the enemy. We will bind
and hoodwink him so, that he shall suppose no other
but that he is carried into the leaguer of the adversaries, when we bring him to our own tents. Be but
your lordship present at his examination : if he do
not, for the promise of his life, and in the highest
compulsion of base fear, offer to betray you, and deliver all the intelligence in his power against you, and
that with the divine forfeit of his soul upon oath,
never trust my judgment in anything.
  2 Lord. O ! for the love of laughter, let him fetch
his drum : he says he has a stratagem for't. When
your lordship sees the bottom of his success in't, and
to what metal this counterfeit lump of ore will be
melted, if you give him not John Drum's entertainment, your inclining cannot be removed. Here he
comes.   40
  1 Lord. O ! for the love of laughter, hinder not the
honour of his design : let him fetch off his drum in
any hand.

Enter Parolles.

  Ber. How now, monsieur ? this drum sticks sorely
in your disposition.
  2 Lord. A pox on't ! let it go : 't is but a drum.
  Par. But a drum ! Is't but a drum ? A drum so
lost !—There was an excellent command, to charge in
with our horse upon our own wings, and to rend our
own soldiers !   50
  2 Lord. That was not to be blamed in the command
of the service : it was a disaster of war that Cæsar
himself could not have prevented, if he had been
there to command.
  Ber. Well, we cannot greatly condemn our success :
some dishonour we had in the loss of that drum ; but
it is not to be recovered.
  Par. It might have been recovered.
  Ber. It might ; but it is not now.   59
  Par. It is to be recovered. But that the merit of
service is seldom attributed to the true and exact
performer, I would have that drum or another, or *hic
jacet.*
  Ber. Why, if you have a stomach to't, monsieur, if
you think your mystery in stratagem can bring this
instrument of honour again into his native quarter,
be magnanimous in the enterprise, and go on ; I will
grace the attempt for a worthy exploit : if you speed
well in it, the duke shall both speak of it, and extend
to you what further becomes his greatness, even to
the utmost syllable of your worthiness.   71
  Par. By the hand of a soldier, I will undertake it.
  Ber. But you must not now slumber in it.
  Par. I'll about it this evening : and I will presently
pen down my dilemmas, encourage myself in my certainty, put myself into my mortal preparation, and
by midnight look to hear further from me.
  Ber. May I be bold to acquaint his grace you are
gone about it ?
  Par. I know not what the success will be, my lord ;
but the attempt I vow.   81
  Ber. I know thou art valiant, and, to the possibility
of thy soldiership, will subscribe for thee. Farewell.
  Par. I love not many words.   [*Exit.*
  1 Lord. No more than a fish loves water.—Is not
this a strange fellow, my lord, that so confidently
seems to undertake this business, which he knows is

not to be done, damns himself to do, and dares better
be damned than to do't ?   89
  2 Lord. You do not know him, my lord, as we do :
certain it is, that he will steal himself into a man's
favour, and for a week escape a great deal of discoveries ; but when you find him out, you have him
ever after.
  Ber. Why, do you think, he will make no deed at
all of this, that so seriously he does address himself
unto ?
  1 Lord. None in the world ; but return with an invention, and clap upon you two or three probable lies.
But we have almost embossed him, you shall see his
fall to-night ; for, indeed, he is not for your lordship's
respect.   102
  2 Lord. We'll make you some sport with the fox,
ere we case him. He was first smoked by the old
Lord Lafeu : when his disguise and he is parted, tell
me what a sprat you shall find him, which you shall
see this very night.
  1 Lord. I must go look my twigs : he shall be
caught.
  Ber. Your brother, he shall go along with me.
  1 Lord. As't please your lordship : I'll leave you.
                                            [*Exit.*
  Ber. Now will I lead you to the house, and show
you   111
The lass I spoke of.
  2 Lord.   But, you say, she's honest.
  Ber. That's all the fault. I spoke with her but once,
And found her wondrous cold ; but I sent to her,
By this same coxcomb that we have i' the wind,
Tokens and letters which she did re-send ;
And this is all I have done. She's a fair creature ;
Will you go see her ?
  2 Lord.   With all my heart, my lord.
                                          [*Exeunt.*

Scene VII.—Florence. A Room in the Widow's House.

Enter Helena *and* Widow.

  Hel. If you misdoubt me that I am not she,
I know not how I shall assure you further,
But I shall lose the grounds I work upon.
  Wid. Though my estate be fall'n, I was well born,
Nothing acquainted with these businesses,
And would not put my reputation now
In any staining act.
  Hel.   Nor would I wish you.
First, give me trust, the count is my husband,
And what to your sworn counsel I have spoken,
Is so, from word to word ; and then you cannot, 10
By the good aid that I of you shall borrow,
Err in bestowing it.
  Wid.   I should believe you ;
For you have show'd me that which well approves
You are great in fortune.
  Hel.   Take this purse of gold,
And let me buy your friendly help thus far,
Which I will over-pay, and pay again,
When I have found it. The count he woos your
daughter,
Lays down his wanton siege before her beauty,
Resolved to carry her : let her, in fine, consent,
As we'll direct her how't is best to bear it.   20
Now, his important blood will nought deny
That she'll demand : a ring the county wears,
That downward hath succeeded in his house
From son to son, some four or five descents
Since the first father wore it : this ring he holds
In most rich choice ; yet, in his idle fire,
To buy his will, it would not seem too dear,
Howe'er repented after.
  Wid.   Now I see
The bottom of your purpose.
  Hel. You see it lawful then. It is no more, 30
But that your daughter, ere she seems as won,
Desires this ring, appoints him an encounter,
In fine, delivers me to fill the time,
Herself most chastely absent. After this,

To marry her, I'll add three thousand crowns
To what is past already.
Wid.   I have yielded.
Instruct my daughter how she shall persever,
That time and place with this deceit so lawful
May prove coherent. Every night he comes
With musics of all sorts, and songs compos'd   40
To her unworthiness: it nothing steads us,

To chide him from our eaves, for he persists,
As if his life lay on 't.
Hel.   Why then, to-night
Let us assay our plot; which, if it speed,
Is wicked meaning in a lawful deed,
And lawful meaning in a lawful act,
Where both not sin, and yet a sinful fact.
But let 's about it.   [*Exeunt.*

ACT IV.

SCENE I.—Without the Florentine Camp.

Enter First French Lord, with five or six Soldiers in ambush.

1 *Lord.*

E can come no other way but by this hedge-corner. When you sally upon him, speak what terrible language you will: though you understand it not yourselves, no matter; for we must not seem to understand him, unless some one among us, whom we must produce for an interpreter.

1 *Sold.* Good captain, let me be the interpreter.

1 *Lord.* Art not acquainted with him? knows he not thy voice?   11

1 *Sold.* No, sir, I warrant you.

1 *Lord.* But what linsey-woolsey hast thou to speak to us again?

1 *Sold.* Even such as you speak to me.

1 *Lord.* He must think us some band of strangers i' the adversary's entertainment. Now, he hath a smack of all neighbouring languages; therefore, we must every one be a man of his own fancy, not to know what we speak one to another; so we seem to know, is to know straight our purpose: chough's language, gabble enough, and good enough. As for you, interpreter, you must seem very politic. But couch, ho! here he comes, to beguile two hours in a sleep, and then to return and swear the lies he forges.

Enter PAROLLES.

Par. Ten o'clock: within these three hours 't will be time enough to go home. What shall I say I have done? It must be a very plausive invention that carries it. They begin to smoke me, and disgraces have of late knocked too often at my door. I find, my tongue is too foolhardy; but my heart hath the fear of Mars before it, and of his creatures, not daring the reports of my tongue.

1 *Lord.* [*Aside.*] This is the first truth that e'er thine own tongue was guilty of.   38

Par. What the devil should move me to undertake the recovery of this drum, being not ignorant of the impossibility, and knowing I had no such purpose? I must give myself some hurts, and say, I got them in exploit. Yet slight ones will not carry it: they will say, "Came you off with so little?" and great ones I dare not give. Wherefore? what 's the instance? Tongue, I must put you into a butter-woman's mouth, and buy myself another of Bajazet's mule, if you prattle me into these perils.

1 *Lord.* [*Aside.*] Is it possible, he should know what he is, and be that he is?   50

Par. I would the cutting of my garments would serve the turn, or the breaking of my Spanish sword.

1 *Lord.* [*Aside.*] We cannot afford you so.

Par. Or the baring of my beard, and to say, it was in stratagem.

1 *Lord.* [*Aside.*] 'T would not do.

Par. Or to drown my clothes, and say, I was stripped.

1 *Lord.* [*Aside.*] Hardly serve.

Par. Though I swore I leaped from the window of the citadel—   61

1 *Lord.* [*Aside.*] How deep?

Par. Thirty fathom.

1 *Lord.* [*Aside.*] Three great oaths would scarce make that be believed.

Par. I would I had any drum of the enemy's: I would swear I recovered it.

1 *Lord.* [*Aside.*] You shall hear one anon.

Par. A drum now of the enemy's! [*Alarum within.*

Par. "O! ransom, ransom!—Do not hide mine eyes."

1 *Lord.* *Throca movousus, cargo, cargo, cargo.*   70
All. Cargo, cargo, villianda par corbo, cargo.
Par. O! ransom, ransom!—Do not hide mine eyes.
                    [*They seize and blindfold him.*
1 *Sold. Boskos thromuldo boskos.*
Par. I know, you are the Muskos' regiment;
And I shall lose my life for want of language.
If there be here German, or Dane, low Dutch,
Italian, or French, let him speak to me:
I will discover that which shall undo
The Florentine.
1 *Sold.*   *Boskos vauvado:—*
I understand thee, and can speak thy tongue:—   80

Kerelybonto:—Sir,
Betake thee to thy faith, for seventeen poniards
Are at thy bosom.
   Par.   O!
  1 *Sold.*   O! pray, pray, pray.—
Manka revania dulche.
  1 *Lord.*   *Oscorbi dulchos volivorco.*
  1 *Sold.* The general is content to spare thee yet,
And, hoodwink'd as thou art, will lead thee on
To gather from thee : haply, thou may'st inform
Something to save thy life.
  Par.   O! let me live,
And all the secrets of our camp I'll show,
Their force, their purposes ; nay, I'll speak that   90
Which you will wonder at.
  1 *Sold.*   But wilt thou faithfully ?
  Par. If I do not, damn me.
  1 *Sold.*   *Acordo linta.*—
Come on, thou art granted space.
            [*Exit, with* PAROLLES *guarded.*
  1 *Lord.* Go, tell the Count Rousillon, and my brother,
We have caught the woodcock, and will keep him
    muffled,
Till we do hear from them.
  2 *Sold.*   Captain, I will.
  1 *Lord.* 'A will betray us all unto ourselves.
Inform on that.
  2 *Sold.*   So I will, sir.
  1 *Lord.* Till then, I'll keep him dark, and safely
    lock'd.   [*Exeunt.*

SCENE II.—Florence. A Room in the Widow's House.

Enter BERTRAM *and* DIANA.

  Ber. They told me, that your name was Fontibell.
  Dia. No, my good lord, Diana.
  Ber.   Titled goddess,
And worth it, with addition ! But, fair soul,
In your fine frame hath love no quality ?
If the quick fire of youth light not your mind,
You are no maiden, but a monument:
When you are dead, you should be such a one
As you are now, for you are cold and stern ;
And now you should be as your mother was,
When your sweet self was got.   10
  Dia. She then was honest.
  Ber.   So should you be.
  Dia.   No :
My mother did but duty ; such, my lord,
As you owe to your wife.
  Ber.   No more o' that !
I pr'ythee, do not strive against my vows.
I was compell'd to her ; but I love thee
By love's own sweet constraint, and will for ever
Do thee all rights of service.
  Dia.   Ay, so you serve us,
Till we serve you ; but when you have our roses,
You barely leave our thorns to prick ourselves,
And mock us with our bareness.
  Ber.   How have I sworn !
  Dia. 'T is not the many oaths that make the truth, 21
But the plain single vow, that is vow'd true.
What is not holy, that we swear not by,
But take the Highest to witness : then, pray you,
    tell me,
If I should swear by Jove's great attributes,
I lov'd you dearly, would you believe my oaths,
When I did love you ill ? This has no holding,
To swear by him, whom I protest to love,
That I will work against him. Therefore, your oaths
Are words, and poor conditions, but unseal'd ;   30
At least, in my opinion.
  Ber.   Change it, change it.
Be not so holy-cruel : love is holy,
And my integrity ne'er knew the crafts
That you do charge men with. Stand no more off,
But give thyself unto my sick desires,
Who then recover : say, thou art mine, and ever
My love, as it begins, shall so persever.
  Dia. I see, that men make ropes in such a scarr,
That we'll forsake ourselves. Give me that ring.

  Ber. I'll lend it thee, my dear ; but have no power
To give it from me.
  Dia.   Will you not, my lord ?   41
  Ber. It is an honour 'longing to our house,
Bequeathed down from many ancestors,
Which were the greatest obloquy i' the world
In me to lose.
  Dia.   Mine honour's such a ring.
My chastity 's the jewel of our house,
Bequeathed down from many ancestors,
Which were the greatest obloquy i' the world
In me to lose. Thus, your own proper wisdom
Brings in the champion honour on my part   50
Against your vain assault.
  Ber.   Here, take my ring :
My house, mine honour, yea, my life, be thine,
And I'll be bid by thee.
  Dia. When midnight comes, knock at my chamber-
    window :
I'll order take, my mother shall not hear.

Ber. "Here, take my ring."

Now will I charge you in the band of truth,
When you have conquer'd my yet maiden bed,
Remain there but an hour, nor speak to me.
My reasons are most strong ; and you shall know
    them,
When back again this ring shall be deliver'd :   60
And on your finger, in the night, I'll put
Another ring, that what in time proceeds
May token to the future our past deeds.
Adieu, till then ; then, fail not. You have won
A wife of me, though there my hope be done.
  Ber. A heaven on earth I have won by wooing thee.
            [*Exit.*
  Dia. For which live long to thank both Heaven and
    me !
You may so in the end.—
My mother told me just how he would woo,
As if she sat in 's heart ; she says, all men   70
Have the like oaths. He had sworn to marry me,
When his wife 's dead ; therefore I'll lie with him,
When I am buried. Since Frenchmen are so braid,
Marry that will, I live and die a maid :
Only, in this disguise, I think 't no sin
To cozen him, that would unjustly win.   [*Exit.*

SCENE III.—The Florentine Camp.

*Enter the two French Lords, and two or three
Soldiers.*

  1 *Lord.* You have not given him his mother's letter ?
  2 *Lord.* I have delivered it an hour since : there is
something in 't that stings his nature, for on the reading
it he changed almost into another man.
  1 *Lord.* He has much worthy blame laid upon him,
for shaking off so good a wife, and so sweet a lady.
  2 *Lord.* Especially that he hath incurred the everlasting
displeasure of the king, who had even tuned his
bounty to sing happiness to him. I will tell you a
thing, but you shall let it dwell darkly within you. 10

1 Lord. When you have spoken it, 't is dead, and I am the grave of it.

2 Lord. He hath perverted a young gentlewoman, here in Florence, of a most chaste renown, and this night he fleshes his will in the spoil of her honour : he hath given her his monumental ring, and thinks himself made in the unchaste composition.

1 Lord. Now, God delay our rebellion : as we are ourselves, what things are we !   19

2 Lord. Merely our own traitors : and as in the common course of all treasons, we still see them reveal themselves, till they attain to their abhorred ends, so he that in this action contrives against his own nobility, in his proper stream o'erflows himself.

1 Lord. Is it not meant damnable in us, to be trumpeters of our unlawful intents ? We shall not then have his company to-night ?

2 Lord. Not till after midnight, for he is dieted to his hour.   29

1 Lord. That approaches apace : I would gladly have him see his company anatomised, that he might take a measure of his own judgments, wherein so curiously he had set this counterfeit.

2 Lord. We will not meddle with him till he come, for his presence must be the whip of the other.

1 Lord. In the meantime, what hear you of these wars ?

2 Lord. I hear there is an overture of peace.

1 Lord. Nay, I assure you, a peace concluded.

2 Lord. What will Count Rousillon do then ? will he travel higher, or return again into France ?   41

1 Lord. I perceive by this demand, you are not altogether of his council.

2 Lord. Let it be forbid, sir ; so should I be a great deal of his act.

1 Lord. Sir, his wife some two months since fled from his house : her pretence is a pilgrimage to Saint Jaques le Grand, which holy undertaking with most austere sanctimony she accomplished ; and, there residing, the tenderness of her nature became as a prey to her grief ; in fine, made a groan of her last breath, and now she sings in heaven.   52

2 Lord. How is this justified ?

1 Lord. The stronger part of it by her own letters ; which makes her story true, even to the point of her death : her death itself, which could not be her office to say is come, was faithfully confirmed by the rector of the place.

2 Lord. Hath the count all this intelligence ?

1 Lord. Ay, and the particular confirmations, point from point, to the full arming of the verity.   61

2 Lord. I am heartily sorry that he 'll be glad of this.

1 Lord. How mightily, sometimes, we make us comforts of our losses !

2 Lord. And how mightily, some other times, we drown our gain in tears. The great dignity, that his valour hath here acquired for him, shall at home be encountered with a shame as ample.   69

1 Lord. The web of our life is of a mingled yarn, good and ill together : our virtues would be proud, if our faults whipped them not ; and our crimes would despair, if they were not cherished by our virtues.

Enter a Servant.

How now ? where 's your master ?

Serv. He met the duke in the street, sir, of whom he hath taken a solemn leave : his lordship will next morning for France. The duke hath offered him letters of commendations to the king.

2 Lord. They shall be no more than needful there, if they were more than they can commend.

1 Lord. They cannot be too sweet for the king's tartness. Here 's his lordship now.

Enter BERTRAM.

How now, my lord ! is 't not after midnight ?

Ber. I have to-night despatched sixteen businesses, a month's length a-piece, by an abstract of success : I have conge'd with the duke, done my adieu with his nearest, buried a wife, mourned for her, writ to my lady mother I am returning, entertained my convoy ;

and between these main parcels of despatch effected many nicer needs : the last was the greatest, but that I have not ended yet.   91

2 Lord. If the business be of any difficulty, and this morning your departure hence, it requires haste of your lordship.

Ber. I mean, the business is not ended, as fearing to hear of it hereafter. But shall we have this dialogue between the fool and the soldier ? Come, bring forth this counterfeit model : he has deceived me, like a double-meaning prophesier.

2 Lord. Bring him forth. [*Exeunt Soldiers.*] He has sat i' the stocks all night, poor gallant knave.   101

Ber. No matter ; his heels have deserved it, in usurping his spurs so long. How does he carry himself ?

1 Lord. I have told your lordship already ; the stocks carry him. But, to answer you as you would be understood, he weeps, like a wench that had shed her milk. He hath confessed himself to Morgan, whom he supposes to be a friar, from the time of his remembrance to this very instant disaster of his setting i' the stocks ; and what think you he hath confessed ?   112

Ber. Nothing of me, has 'a ?

2 Lord. His confession is taken, and it shall be read to his face : if your lordship be in 't, as I believe you are, you must have the patience to hear it.

Re-enter Soldiers, with PAROLLES.

Ber. A plague upon him ! muffled ? he can say nothing of me : hush ! hush !

1 Lord. Hoodman comes !—*Porto tartarossa.*

1 Sold. He calls for the tortures : what will you say without 'em ?   121

Par. I will confess what I know without constraint : if ye pinch me like a pasty, I can say no more.

1 Sold. Bosko chimurcho.

2 Sold. Boblibindo chicurmurco.

1 Sold. You are a merciful general.—Our general bids you answer to what I shall ask you out of a note.

Par. And truly, as I hope to live.

1 Sold. "First, demand of him, how many horse the duke is strong." What say you to that ?   130

Par. Five or six thousand ; but very weak and unserviceable : the troops are all scattered, and the commanders very poor rogues, upon my reputation and credit, and as I hope to live.

1 Sold. Shall I set down your answer so ?

Par. Do : I 'll take the sacrament on 't, how and which way you will.

Ber. All 's one to him. What a past-saving slave is this !   139

1 Lord. You are deceived, my lord : this is Monsieur Parolles, the gallant militarist, (that was his own phrase) that had the whole theoric of war in the knot of his scarf, and the practice in the chape of his dagger.

2 Lord. I will never trust a man again for keeping his sword clean ; nor believe he can have every thing in him by wearing his apparel neatly.

1 Sold. Well, that 's set down.

Par. Five or six thousand horse, I said,—I will say true,—or thereabouts, set down,—for I 'll speak truth.

1 Lord. He 's very near the truth in this.   150

Ber. But I con him no thanks for 't, in the nature he delivers it.

Par. Poor rogues, I pray you, say.

1 Sold. Well, that 's set down.

Par. I humbly thank you, sir. A truth 's a truth : the rogues are marvellous poor.

1 Sold. "Demand of him, of what strength they are afoot." What say you to that ?   158

Par. By my troth, sir, if I were to live this present hour, I will tell true. Let me see : Spurio, a hundred and fifty ; Sebastian, so many ; Corambus, so many ; Jaques, so many ; Guiltian, Cosmo, Lodowick, and Gratii, two hundred fifty each ; mine own company, Chitopher, Vaumond, Bentii, two hundred fifty each : so that the muster file, rotten and sound, upon my life, amounts not to fifteen thousand poll ; half of the which dare not shake the snow from off their cassocks, lest they shake themselves to pieces.

Ber. What shall be done to him?

1 Lord. Nothing, but let him have thanks.—Demand of him my condition, and what credit I have with the duke.   172

1 Sold. Well, that's set down. "You shall demand

Par. I know him: he was a botcher's 'prentice in Paris, from whence he was whipped for getting the shrieve's fool with child; a dumb innocent, that could not say him, nay.

.[DUMAIN *lifts up his hand in anger.*

Par. "Let me live, sir, in a dungeon, i' the stocks, or anywhere, so I may live."

of him, whether one Captain Dumain be i' the camp, a Frenchman; what his reputation is with the duke; what his valour, honesty, and expertness in wars; or whether he thinks, it were not possible with well-weighing sums of gold to corrupt him to a revolt." What say you to this? what do you know of it?

Par. I beseech you, let me answer to the particular of the inter'gatories: demand them singly.   181

1 Sold. Do you know this Captain Dumain?

Ber. Nay, by your leave, hold your hands; though I know, his brains are forfeit to the next tile that falls.

1 Sold. Well, is this captain in the Duke of Florence's camp?   190

Par. Upon my knowledge he is, and lousy.

1 Lord. Nay, look not so upon me; we shall hear of your lordship anon.

1 Sold. What is his reputation with the duke?

Par. The duke knows him for no other but a poor

officer of mine, and writ to me this other day to turn him out o' the band : I think, I have his letter in my pocket.

1 Sold. Marry, we 'll search.

Par. In good sadness, I do not know : either it is there, or it is upon a file, with the duke's other letters, in my tent.   202

1 Sold. Here 't is : here 's a paper ; shall I read it to you ?

Par. I do not know if it be it, or no.

Ber. Our interpreter does it well.

1 Lord. Excellently.

1 Sold. [*Reads.*] " Dian, the count 's a fool, and full of gold,"—

Par. That is not the duke's letter, sir : that is an advertisement to a proper maid in Florence, one Diana, to take heed of the allurement of one Count Rousillon, a foolish idle boy, but, for all that, very ruttish. I pray you, sir, put it up again.

1 Sold. Nay, I 'll read it first, by your favour.

Par. My meaning in 't, I protest, was very honest in the behalf of the maid : for I knew the young count to be a dangerous and lascivious boy, who is a whale to virginity, and devours up all the fry it finds.

Ber. Damnable, both-sides rogue !

1 Sold. [*Reads.*] " When he swears oaths, bid him drop gold, and take it ;   220
After he scores, he never pays the score :
Half won is match well made ; match, and well make it :
He ne'er pays after debts ; take it before,
And say, a soldier, Dian, told thee this.
Men are to mell with, boys are not to kiss ;
For count of this, the count 's a fool, I know it,
Who pays before, but not when he does owe it.
                        Thine, as he vow'd to thee in thine ear,
                                                            PAROLLES."

Ber. He shall be whipped through the army, with this rhyme in 's forehead.   231

2 Lord. This is your devoted friend, sir ; the manifold linguist, and the armipotent soldier.

Ber. I could endure anything before but a cat, and now he 's a cat to me.

1 Sold. I perceive, sir, by our general's looks, we shall be fain to hang you.

Par. My life, sir, in any case ! not that I am afraid to die ; but that, my offences being many, I would repent out the remainder of nature. Let me live, sir, in a dungeon, i' the stocks, or anywhere, so I may live.   242

1 Sold. We 'll see what may be done, so you confess freely : therefore, once more to this Captain Dumain. You have answered to his reputation with the duke, and to his valour : what is his honesty ?

Par. He will steal, sir, an egg out of a cloister : for rapes and ravishments he parallels Nessus. He professes not keeping of oaths ; in breaking them he is stronger than Hercules. He will lie, sir, with such volubility, that you would think truth were a fool : drunkenness is his best virtue ; for he will be swine-drunk, and in his sleep he does little harm, save to his bed-clothes about him ; but they know his conditions, and lay him in straw. I have but little more to say, sir, of his honesty : he has everything that an honest man should not have ; what an honest man should have, he has nothing.

1 Lord. I begin to love him for this.

Ber. For this description of thine honesty ? A pox upon him ! for me he is more and more a cat.   261

1 Sold. What say you to his expertness in war ?

Par. 'Faith, sir, he has led the drum before the English tragedians,—to belie him, I will not,—and more of his soldiership I know not : except, in that country, he had the honour to be the officer at a place there called Mile End, to instruct for the doubling of files : I would do the man what honour I can, but of this I am not certain.

1 Lord. He hath out-villained villainy so far, that the rarity redeems him.   271

Ber. A pox on him ! he 's a cat still.

1 Sold. His qualities being at this poor price, I need not ask you, if gold will corrupt him to revolt.

Par. Sir, for a cardecue he will sell the fee-simple of his salvation, the inheritance of it ; and cut the entail from all remainders, and a perpetual succession for it perpetually.

1 Sold. What 's his brother, the other Captain Dumain ?   280

2 Lord. Why does he ask him of me ?

1 Sold. What 's he ?

Par. E'en a crow o' the same nest ; not altogether so great as the first in goodness, but greater a great deal in evil. He excels his brother for a coward, yet his brother is reputed one of the best that is. In a retreat he outruns any lackey ; marry, in coming on he has the cramp.

1 Sold. If your life be saved, will you undertake to betray the Florentine ?   290

Par. Ay, and the captain of his horse, Count Rousillon.

1 Sold. I 'll whisper with the general, and know his pleasure.

Par. [*Aside.*] I 'll no more drumming ; a plague of all drums ! Only to seem to deserve well, and to beguile the supposition of that lascivious young boy the count, have I run into this danger. Yet who would have suspected an ambush, where I was taken ?   300
There is no remedy, sir, but you must die. The general says, you, that have so traitorously discovered the secrets of your army, and made such pestiferous reports of men very nobly held, can serve the world for no honest use ; therefore you must die. Come, headsman, off with his head.

Par. O Lord, sir, let me live, or let me see my death !

1 Sold. That shall you, and take your leave of all your friends.   [*Unmuffling him.*
So, look about you : know you any here ?   311

Ber. Good morrow, noble captain.

2 Lord. God bless you, Captain Parolles.

1 Lord. God save you, noble captain.

2 Lord. Captain, what greeting will you to my Lord Lafeu ? I am for France.

1 Lord. Good captain, will you give me a copy of the sonnet you writ to Diana in behalf of the Count Rousillon ? an I were not a very coward, I 'd compel it of you ; but fare you well.   320
                        [*Exeunt* BERTRAM, *Frenchmen, &c.*

1 Sold. You are undone, captain ; all but your scarf, that has a knot on 't yet.

Par. Who cannot be crushed with a plot ?

1 Sold. If you could find out a country where but women were, that had received so much shame, you might begin an impudent nation. Fare you well, sir ; I am for France too : we shall speak of you there.
                                                            [*Exit.*

Par. Yet am I thankful : if my heart were great, 'T would burst at this. Captain I 'll be no more ;   330
But I will eat and drink, and sleep as soft
As captain shall : simply the thing I am
Shall make me live. Who knows himself a braggart,
Let him fear this ; for it will come to pass,
That every braggart shall be found an ass.
Rust, sword ! cool, blushes ! and, Parolles, live
Safest in shame ! being fool'd, by foolery thrive !
There 's place and means for every man alive !
I 'll after them.   [*Exit.*

SCENE IV.—*Florence. A Room in the Widow's House.*

Enter HELENA, *Widow, and* DIANA.

Hel. That you may well perceive I have not wrong'd you,
One of the greatest in the Christian world
Shall be my surety : 'fore whose throne, 't is needful,
Ere I can perfect mine intents, to kneel.
Time was, I did him a desired office,
Dear almost as his life ; which gratitude
Through flinty Tartar's bosom would peep forth,
And answer, thanks. I duly am inform'd,
His grace is at Marseilles ; to which place

We have convenient convoy.　You must know,　10
I am supposed dead : the army breaking,
My husband hies him home ; where, Heaven aiding,
And by the leave of my good lord the king,
We 'll be before our welcome.

Wid.　　　　　　　　　Gentle madam,
You never had a servant, to whose trust
Your business was more welcome.

Hel.　　　　　　　　　Nor you, mistress,
Ever a friend, whose thoughts more truly labour
To recompense your love.　Doubt not, but Heaven
Hath brought me up to be your daughter's dower,
As it hath fated her to be my motive,　20
And helper to a husband.　But, O strange men !
That can such sweet use make of what they hate,
When saucy trusting of the cozen'd thoughts
Defiles the pitchy night ! so lust doth play
With what it loathes, for that which is away.
But more of this hereafter.—You, Diana,
Under my poor instructions, yet must suffer
Something in my behalf.

Dia.　　　　　　Let death and honesty
Go with your impositions, I am yours
Upon your will to suffer.

Hel.　　　　　　Yet, I pray you :　30
But with the word, the time will bring on summer,
When briars shall have leaves as well as thorns,
And be as sweet as sharp.　We must away ;
Our waggon is prepar'd, and time revives us :
All 's well that ends well : still the fine 's the crown ;
Whate'er the course, the end is the renown. [*Exeunt.*

SCENE V.—Rousillon.　A Room in the COUNTESS's
Palace.

Enter COUNTESS, LAFEU, *and Clown.*

Laf. No, no, no ; your son was misled with a snipt-
taffeta fellow there, whose villainous saffron would
have made all the unbaked and doughy youth of a
nation in his colour : your daughter-in-law had been
alive at this hour, and your son here at home, more
advanced by the king, than by that red-tailed humble-
bee I speak of.

Count. I would I had not known him.　It was the
death of the most virtuous gentlewoman that ever
Nature had praise for creating : if she had partaken of
my flesh, and cost me the dearest groans of a mother,
I could not have owed her a more rooted love.　12

Laf. 'T was a good lady, 't was a good lady : we may
pick a thousand salads, ere we light on such another
herb.

Clo. Indeed, sir, she was the sweet-marjoram of the
salad, or rather the herb of grace.

Laf. They are not salad-herbs, you knave ; they are
nose-herbs.

Clo. I am no great Nebuchadnezzar, sir ; I have not
much skill in grass.　21

Laf. Whether dost thou profess thyself, a knave, or
a fool ?

Clo. A fool, sir, at a woman's service, and a knave
at a man's.

Laf. Your distinction ?

Clo. I would cozen the man of his wife, and do his
service.

Laf. So you were a knave at his service, indeed.

Clo. And I would give his wife my bauble, sir, to
do her service.　31

Laf. I will subscribe for thee, thou art both knave
and fool.

Clo. At your service.

Laf. No, no, no.

Clo. Why, sir, if I cannot serve you, I can serve as
great a prince as you are.

Laf. Who 's that ? a Frenchman ?

Clo. 'Faith, sir, 'a has an English name ; but his
phisnomy is more hotter in France, than there.　40

Laf. What prince is that ?

Clo. The black prince, sir ; *alias*, the prince of
darkness ; *alias*, the devil.

Laf. Hold thee, there 's my purse.　I give thee not
this to suggest thee from thy master thou talkest of :
serve him still.

Clo. I am a woodland fellow, sir, that always loved
a great fire ; and the master I speak of, ever keeps a
good fire.　But, sure, he is the prince of the world ;
let his nobility remain in 's court.　I am for the house
with the narrow gate, which I take to be too little for
pomp to enter : some, that humble themselves, may ;
but the many will be too chill and tender, and they 'll
be for the flowery way, that leads to the broad gate,
and the great fire.

Laf. Go thy ways, I begin to be aweary of thee ;
and I tell thee so before, because I would not fall out
with thee.　Go thy ways : let my horses be well looked
to, without any tricks.　59

Clo. If I put any tricks upon 'em, sir, they shall be
jades' tricks, which are their own right by the law of
nature.　[*Exit.*

Laf. A shrewd knave, and an unhappy.

Count. So he is.　My lord, that 's gone, made himself much sport out of him : by his authority he
remains here, which he thinks is a patent for his
sauciness ; and, indeed, he has no pace, but runs
where he will.

Laf. I like him well ; 'tis not amiss.　And I was
about to tell you, since I heard of the good lady's
death, and that my lord your son was upon his return
home, I moved the king, my master, to speak in the
behalf of my daughter ; which, in the minority of
them both, his majesty, out of a self-gracious remembrance, did first propose.　His highness hath promised
me to do it ; and to stop up the displeasure he hath
conceived against your son, there is no fitter matter.
How does your ladyship like it ?

Count. With very much content, my lord ; and I
wish it happily effected.　80

Laf. His highness comes post from Marseilles, of as
able body as when he numbered thirty : he will be
here to-morrow, or I am deceived by him that in such
intelligence hath seldom failed.

Count. It rejoices me that I hope I shall see him
ere I die.　I have letters that my son will be here to-
night : I shall beseech your lordship to remain with
me till they meet together.

Laf. Madam, I was thinking with what manners I
might safely be admitted.　90

Count. You need but plead your honourable privilege.

Laf. Lady, of that I have made a bold charter ; but,
I thank my God, it holds yet.

Re-enter Clown.

Clo. O madam ! yonder 's my lord your son with a
patch of velvet on 's face : whether there be a scar
under it, or no, the velvet knows ; but 't is a goodly
patch of velvet.　His left cheek is a cheek of two pile
and a half, but his right cheek is worn bare.

Laf. A scar nobly got, or a noble scar, is a good
livery of honour ; so, belike, is that.　100

Clo. But it is your carbonadoed face.

Laf. Let us go see your son, I pray you : I long to
talk with the young noble soldier.

Clo. 'Faith, there 's a dozen of 'em, with delicate
fine hats, and most courteous feathers, which bow the
head, and nod at every man.　[*Exeunt.*

ACT V.

SCENE I.—Marseilles. A Street.

Enter HELENA, Widow, and DIANA, with two Attendants.

Helena.

UT this exceeding posting, day and
    night,
Must wear your spirits low: we
    cannot help it;
But, since you have made the days
    and nights as one,
To wear your gentle limbs in my
    affairs,
Be bold you do so grow in my re-
    quital,
As nothing can unroot you. In
    happy time;

Enter a Gentleman.

This man may help me to his majesty's ear,
If he would spend his power.—God save you, sir.
Gent. And you.
  Hel. Sir, I have seen you in the court of France. 10
  Gent. I have been sometimes there.
  Hel. I do presume, sir, that you are not fallen
From the report that goes upon your goodness;
And therefore, goaded with most sharp occasions,
Which lay nice manners by, I put you to
The use of your own virtues, for the which
I shall continue thankful.
  Gent.   What's your will?
  Hel. That it will please you
To give this poor petition to the king,
And aid me with that store of power you have, 20
To come into his presence.
  Gent. The king's not here.
  Hel.   Nor here, sir?
  Gent.   Not, indeed:
He hence remov'd last night, and with more haste
Than is his use.
  Wid.   Lord, how we lose our pains!
  Hel. All's well that ends well yet,
Though time seem so adverse, and means unfit.—
I do beseech you, whither is he gone?
  Gent. Marry, as I take it, to Rousillon;
Whither I am going.
  Hel.   I do beseech you, sir,
Since you are like to see the king before me, 30
Commend the paper to his gracious hand;
Which, I presume, shall render you no blame,
But rather make you thank your pains for it.
I will come after you, with what good speed
Our means will make us means.
  Gent.   This I'll do for you.
  Hel. And you shall find yourself to be well thank'd,
Whate'er falls more.—We must to horse again:—
Go, go, provide.   *[Exeunt.*

SCENE II.—Rousillon. The Inner Court of the COUNTESS's Palace.

Enter Clown and PAROLLES.

Par. Good Monsieur Lavatch, give my Lord Lafeu
this letter. I have ere now, sir, been better known
to you, when I have held familiarity with fresher
clothes; but I am now, sir, muddied in Fortune's
mood, and smell somewhat strong of her strong displeasure.

Clo. Truly, Fortune's displeasure is but sluttish, if it
smell so strongly as thou speakest of: I will henceforth eat no fish of Fortune's buttering. Pr'ythee,
allow the wind.   10
  Par. Nay, you need not to stop your nose, sir: I
spake but by a metaphor.
  Clo. Indeed, sir, if your metaphor stink, I will stop
my nose; or against any man's metaphor. Pr'ythee,
get thee further.
  Par. Pray you, sir, deliver me this paper.
  Clo. Foh! pr'ythee, stand away: a paper from
Fortune's close-stool to give to a nobleman! Look,
here he comes himself.   19

Enter LAFEU.

Here is a pur of Fortune's, sir, or of Fortune's cat (but
not a musk-cat), that has fallen into the unclean fish-
pond of her displeasure, and, as he says, is muddied
withal. Pray you, sir, use the carp as you may, for
he looks like a poor, decayed, ingenious, foolish,
rascally knave. I do pity his distress in my smiles of
comfort, and leave him to your lordship.   *[Exit.*
  Par. My lord, I am a man whom Fortune hath
cruelly scratched.
  Laf. And what would you have me to do? 'Tis too
late to pare her nails now. Wherein have you played
the knave with Fortune, that she should scratch you,
who of herself is a good lady, and would not have
knaves thrive long under her? There's a cardecue
for you. Let the justices make you and Fortune
friends; I am for other business.
  Par. I beseech your honour to hear me one single
word.
  Laf. You beg a single penny more: come, you shall
ha't; save your word.   40
  Par. My name, my good lord, is Parolles.
  Laf. You beg more than one word then,—Cox my
passion! give me your hand.—How does your drum?
  Par. O my good lord! you were the first that found
me.
  Laf. Was I, in sooth? and I was the first that lost
thee.
  Par. It lies in you, my lord, to bring me in some
grace, for you did bring me out.
  Laf. Out upon thee, knave! dost thou put upon me
at once both the office of God and the devil? one
brings thee in grace, and the other brings thee out.
[Trumpets sound.] The king's coming; I know by
his trumpets.—Sirrah, inquire further after me: I had
talk of you last night. Though you are a fool and a
knave, you shall eat: go to, follow.
  Par. I praise God for you.   *[Exeunt.*

SCENE III.—The Same. A Room in the COUNTESS's Palace.

Flourish. Enter KING, COUNTESS, LAFEU, Lords, Gentlemen, Guards, &c.

King. We lost a jewel of her, and our esteem
Was made much poorer by it: but your son,
As mad in folly, lack'd the sense to know
Her estimation home.
  Count.   'Tis past, my liege;

And I beseech your majesty to make it
Natural rebellion, done i' the blaze of youth ;
When oil and fire, too strong for reason's force,
O'erbears it, and burns on.   *King.*   My honour'd lady,
I have forgiven and forgotten all,
Though my revenges were high bent upon him,   10
And watch'd the time to shoot.
 Laf.   This I must say,—
But first I beg my pardon,—the young lord
Did to his majesty, his mother, and his lady,
Offence of mighty note, but to himself
The greatest wrong of all : he lost a wife,
Whose beauty did astonish the survey
Of richest eyes ; whose words all ears took captive ;
Whose dear perfection hearts that scorn'd to serve
Humbly call'd mistress.
 King.   Praising what is lost
Makes the remembrance dear.—Well, call him hither.
We are reconcil'd, and the first view shall kill   21
All repetition.—Let him not ask our pardon :
The nature of his great offence is dead,
And deeper than oblivion we do bury
The incensing relics of it : let him approach,
A stranger, no offender ; and inform him,
So 't is our will he should.
 Gent.   I shall, my liege.   [*Exit.*
 King. What says he to your daughter ? have you
    spoke ?
 Laf. All that he is hath reference to your highness.
 King. Then shall we have a match. I have letters
    sent me,   30
That set him high in fame.

Enter BERTRAM.

 Laf.   He looks well on 't.
 King. I am not a day of season,
For thou may'st see a sunshine and a hail
In me at once ; but to the brightest beams
Distracted clouds give way : so stand thou forth ;
The time is fair again.
 Ber.   My high-repented blames,
Dear sovereign, pardon to me.
 King.   All is whole ;
Not one word more of the consumed time.
Let 's take the instant by the forward top,
For we are old, and on our quick'st decrees   40
The inaudible and noiseless foot of Time
Steals, ere we can effect them. You remember
The daughter of this lord ?
 Ber.   Admiringly, my liege.
At first I stuck my choice upon her, ere my heart
Durst make too bold a herald of my tongue :
Where the impression of mine eye infixing,
Contempt his scornful perspective did lend me,
Which warp'd the line of every other favour,
Scorn'd a fair colour, or express'd it stolen,
Extended or contracted all proportions   50
To a most hideous object. Thence it came,
That she, whom all men prais'd and whom myself,
Since I have lost, have lov'd, was in mine eye
The dust that did offend it.
 King.   Well excus'd :
That thou didst love her, strikes some scores away
From the great compt. But love, that comes too late,
Like a remorseful pardon slowly carried,
To the great sender turns a sour offence,
Crying, " That 's good that 's gone." Our rash faults
Make trivial price of serious things we have,   60
Not knowing them, until we know their grave :
Oft our displeasures, to ourselves unjust,
Destroy our friends, and after weep their dust :
Our own love, waking, cries to see what 's done,
While shameful hate sleeps out the afternoon.
Be this sweet Helen's knell, and now forget her.
Send forth your amorous token for fair Maudlin :
The main consents are had ; and here we 'll stay
To see our widower's second marriage-day.
 Count. Which better than the first, O dear Heaven,
    bless !   70
Or, ere they meet, in me, O Nature, cess !
 Laf. Come on, my son, in whom my house's name

Must be digested, give a favour from you,
To sparkle in the spirits of my daughter,
That she may quickly come. [BERTRAM *gives a ring.*]
    —By my old beard,
And every hair that 's on 't, Helen, that 's dead,
Was a sweet creature ; such a ring as this,
The last that e'er I took her leave at court,
I saw upon her finger.
 Ber.   Hers it was not.
 King. Now, 'pray you, let me see it ; for mine eye,   80
While I was speaking, oft was fasten'd to 't.—
This ring was mine ; and, when I gave it Helen,
I bade her, if her fortunes ever stood
Necessitied to help, that by this token
I would relieve her. Had you that craft to reave her
Of what should stead her most ?
 Ber.   My gracious sovereign,
Howe'er it pleases you to take it so,
The ring was never hers.
 Count.   Son, on my life,
I have seen her wear it ; and she reckon'd it
At her life's rate.
 Laf.   I am sure I saw her wear it.   90
 Ber. You are deceiv'd : my lord, she never saw it.
In Florence was it from a casement thrown me,
Wrapp'd in a paper, which contain'd the name
Of her that threw it. Noble she was, and thought
I stood ingag'd : but when I had subscrib'd
To mine own fortune, and inform'd her fully,
I could not answer in that course of honour
As she had made the overture, she ceas'd,
In heavy satisfaction, and would never
Receive the ring again.
 King.   Plutus himself,   100
That knows the tinct and multiplying medicine,
Hath not in nature's mystery more science,
Than I have in this ring : 't was mine, 't was Helen's
Whoever gave it you. Then, if you know
That you are well acquainted with yourself,
Confess 't was hers, and by what rough enforcement
You got it from her. She call'd the saints to surety,
That she would never put it from her finger,
Unless she gave it to yourself in bed,
Where you have never come, or sent it us   110
Upon her great disaster.
 Ber.   She never saw it.
 King. Thou speak'st it falsely, as I love mine honour,
And mak'st conjectural fears to come into me,
Which I would fain shut out. If it should prove
That thou art so inhuman,—'t will not prove so ;—
And yet I know not :—thou didst hate her deadly,
And she is dead ; which nothing, but to close
Her eyes myself, could win me to believe,
More than to see this ring.—Take him away.—
       [*Guards seize* BERTRAM.
My fore-past proofs, howe'er the matter fall,   120
Shall tax my fears of little vanity,
Having vainly fear'd too little.—Away with him !
We 'll sift this matter further.
 Ber.   If you shall prove
This ring was ever hers, you shall as easy
Prove that I husbanded her bed in Florence,
Where yet she never was.   [*Exit, guarded.*

Enter a Gentleman.

 King. I am wrapp'd in dismal thinkings.
 Gent.   Gracious sovereign,
Whether I have been to blame, or no, I know not :
Here 's a petition from a Florentine,
Who hath, for four or five removes, come short   130
To tender it herself. I undertook it,
Vanquish'd thereto by the fair grace and speech
Of the poor suppliant, who by this, I know,
Is here attending : her business looks in her
With an importing visage ; and she told me,
In a sweet verbal brief, it did concern
Your highness with herself.
 King. [*Reads.*] " Upon his many protestations to
marry me, when his wife was dead, I blush to say it,
he won me. Now is the Count Rousillon a widower :
his vows are forfeited to me, and my honour 's paid to
him. He stole from Florence, taking no leave, and I

follow him to his country for justice. Grant it me,
O king! in you it best lies; otherwise a seducer
flourishes, and a poor maid is undone.

          Diana Capilet."

 Laf. I will buy me a son-in-law in a fair, and toll:
for this, I'll none of him.

 King. The heavens have thought well on thee,
Lafeu,
To bring forth this discovery.—Seek these suitors:—
Go speedily, and bring again the count.   151
  [*Exeunt Gentlemen and some Attendants.*
I am afeard, the life of Helen, lady,
Was foully snatch'd.

 Count.   Now, justice on the doers!

Re-enter Bertram, guarded.

 King. I wonder, sir, sith wives are monsters to you,

Dia. "O! behold this ring.'

And that you fly them as you swear them lordship,
Yet you desire to marry.—

Re-enter Gentleman, with Widow and Diana.

       What woman's that?
 Dia. I am, my lord, a wretched Florentine,
Derived from the ancient Capilet:
My suit, as I do understand, you know,
And therefore know how far I may be pitied. 160
 Wid. I am her mother, sir, whose age and honour
Both suffer under this complaint we bring,
And both shall cease, without your remedy.
 King. Come hither, count. Do you know these
    women?
 Ber. My lord, I neither can, nor will deny
But that I know them. Do they charge me further?
 Dia. Why do you look so strange upon your wife?
 Ber. She's none of mine, my lord.
 Dia.   If you shall marry,
You give away this hand, and that is mine;
You give away Heaven's vows, and those are mine;170
You give away myself, which is known mine;
For I by vow am so embodied yours,
That she which marries you must marry me;
Either both, or none.
 Laf. [*To* Bertram.] Your reputation comes too
short for my daughter: you are no husband for her.
 Ber. My lord, this is a fond and desperate creature,
Whom sometime I have laugh'd with. Let your
   highness
Lay a more noble thought upon mine honour,
Than for to think that I would sink it here. 180
 King. Sir, for my thoughts, you have them ill to
   friend,
Till your deeds gain them: fairer prove your honour,
Than in my thought it lies.
 Dia.   Good my lord,

Ask him upon his oath, if he does think
He had not my virginity.
 King. What say'st thou to her?
 Ber.   She's impudent, my lord;
And was a common gamester to the camp.
 Dia. He does me wrong, my lord: if I were so,
He might have bought me at a common price:
Do not believe him. O! behold this ring,   190
Whose high respect, and rich validity
Did lack a parallel; yet, for all that,
He gave it to a commoner o' the camp,
If I be one.
 Count. He blushes, and 't is it:
Of six preceding ancestors, that gem
Conferr'd by testament to the sequent issue,
Hath it been ow'd and worn. This is his wife:
That ring's a thousand proofs.
 King.   Methought, you said,
  You saw one here in court could witness
    it.
 Dia. I did, my lord, but loath am to
   produce   200
So bad an instrument: his name's Pa-
   rolles.
 Laf. I saw the man to-day, if man he
   be.
 King. Find him, and bring him hither.
        [*Exit an Attendant.*
 Ber.   What of him?
He's quoted for a most perfidious slave,
With all the spots o' the world tax'd and
   debosh'd,
Whose nature sickens but to speak a
   truth.
Am I or that, or this, for what he'll utter,
That will speak anything?
 King. She hath that ring of yours.
 Ber. I think, she has: certain it is, I
   lik'd her,
And boarded her i' the wanton way of
   youth.   210
She knew her distance, and did angle
   for me,
Madding my eagerness with her re-
   straint,
As all impediments in fancy's course
Are motives of more fancy; and, in fine,
Her infinite cunning, with her modern grace,
Subdued me to her rate: she got the ring,
And I had that, which any inferior might
At market-price have bought.
 Dia.   I must be patient;
You, that have turn'd off a first so noble wife,
May justly diet me. I pray you yet,   220
(Since you lack virtue, I will lose a husband,)
Send for your ring; I will return it home,
And give me mine again.
 Ber.   I have it not.
 King. What ring was yours, I pray you?
 Dia.   Sir, much like
The same upon your finger.
 King. Know you this ring? this ring was his of late.
 Dia. And this was it I gave him, being a-bed.
 King. The story then goes false, you threw it him
Out of a casement.
 Dia.   I have spoke the truth.

Re-enter Attendant with Parolles.

 Ber. My lord, I do confess, the ring was hers. 230
 King. You boggle shrewdly, every feather starts
   you.—
Is this the man you speak of?
 Dia.   Ay, my lord.
 King. Tell me, sirrah, but tell me true, I charge you,
Not fearing the displeasure of your master
(Which, on your just proceeding, I'll keep off),
By him, and by this woman here, what know you?
 Par. So please your majesty, my master hath been
an honourable gentleman: tricks he hath had in him,
which gentlemen have.
 King. Come, come, to the purpose. Did he love this
woman?   241

Par. 'Faith, sir, he did love her ; but how ?
King. How, I pray you?
Par. He did love her, sir, as a gentleman loves a
woman.
King. How is that ?
Par. He loved her, sir, and loved her not.
King. As thou art a knave, and no knave. What
an equivocal companion is this !
Par. I am a poor man, and at your majesty's com-
mand.   251
Laf. He's a good drum, my lord, but a naughty
orator.
Dia. Do you know, he promised me marriage ?
Par. 'Faith, I know more than I 'll speak.
King. But wilt thou not speak all thou know'st ?
Par. Yes, so please your majesty. I did go between
them, as I said ; but more than that, he loved her,—
for, indeed, he was mad for her, and talked of Satan,
and of limbo, and of Furies, and I know not what : yet
I was in that credit with them at that time, that I
knew of their going to bed, and of other motions, as
promising her marriage, and things that would derive
me ill will to speak of : therefore, I will not speak
what I know.
King. Thou hast spoken all already, unless thou
canst say they are married. But thou art too fine
in thy evidence ; therefore, stand aside.—
This ring, you say, was yours ?
Dia.   Ay, my good lord.
King. Where did you buy it ? or who gave it you ?
Dia. It was not given me, nor I did not buy it.   271
King. Who lent it you ?
Dia.   It was not lent me neither.
King. Where did you find it then ?
Dia.   I found it not.
King. If it were yours by none of all these ways,
How could you give it him ?
Dia.   I never gave it him.
Laf. This woman's an easy glove, my lord : she
goes off and on at pleasure.
King. This ring was mine : I gave it his first wife.
Dia. It might be yours, or hers, for aught I know.
King. Take her away : I do not like her now.   280
To prison with her ; and away with him.—
Unless thou tell'st me where thou hadst this ring,
Thou diest within this hour.
Dia.   I 'll never tell you.
King. Take her away.
Dia.   I 'll put in bail, my liege.
King. I think thee now some common customer.
Dia. By Jove, if ever I knew man, 't was you.
King. Wherefore hast thou accus'd him all this
    while ?
Dia. Because he 's guilty, and he is not guilty.

He knows I am no maid, and he 'll swear to 't :
I 'll swear I am a maid, and he knows not.   290
Great king, I am no strumpet, by my life !
I am either maid, or else this old man's wife.
                                     [*Pointing to* LAFEU.
King. She does abuse our ears. To prison with her !
Dia. Good mother, fetch my bail. [*Exit Widow.*]—
Stay, royal sir :
The jeweller that owes the ring is sent for,
And he shall surety me. But for this lord,
Who hath abus'd me, as he knows himself,
Though yet he never harm'd me, here I quit him.
He knows himself my bed he hath defil'd,
And at that time he got his wife with child :   300
Dead though she be, she feels her young one kick.
So there 's my riddle,—one that 's dead is quick ;
And now behold the meaning.

Re-enter Widow, with HELENA.

King.   Is there no exorcist
Beguiles the truer office of mine eyes ?
Is 't real, that I see ?
Hel.   No, my good lord ;
'T is but the shadow of a wife you see ;
The name, and not the thing.
Ber.   Both, both ! O, pardon !
Hel. O my good lord, when I was like this maid,
I found you wondrous kind. There is your ring ;
And, look you, here 's your letter ; this it says :   310
" When from my finger you can get this ring,
And are by me with child," &c.—This is done.
Will you be mine, now you are doubly won ?
Ber. If she, my liege, can make me know this
    clearly,
I 'll love her dearly, ever, ever dearly.
Hel. If it appear not plain, and prove untrue,
Deadly divorce step between me and you !—
O my dear mother, do I see you living ?
Laf. Mine eyes smell onions, I shall weep anon.—
[*To* PAROLLES.] Good Tom Drum, lend me a handker-
chief : so, I thank thee. Wait on me home, I 'll make
sport with thee : let thy courtesies alone, they are
scurvy ones.   323
King. Let us from point to point this story know,
To make the even truth in pleasure flow.—
[*To* DIANA.] If thou be'st yet a fresh uncropped flower,
Choose thou thy husband, and I 'll pay thy dower ;
For I can guess, that by thy honest aid
Thou kept'st a wife herself, thyself a maid.—
Of that, and all the progress, more and less,   330
Resolvedly more leisure shall express :
All yet seems well ; and if it end so meet,
The bitter past, more welcome is the sweet.
                                          [*Flourish.*

EPILOGUE.

King. The king's a beggar now the play is done.
All is well ended, if this suit be won,
That you express content ; which we will pay,
With strife to please you, day exceeding day :
Ours be your patience then, and yours our parts ;
Your gentle hands lend us, and take our hearts.
                                          [*Exeunt.*

TWELFTH-NIGHT: OR, WHAT YOU WILL.

DRAMATIS PERSONÆ.

ORSINO, *Duke of Illyria.*
SEBASTIAN, *Brother to Viola.*
ANTONIO, *a Sea Captain, Friend to Sebastian.*
A Sea Captain, Friend to Viola.
VALENTINE, ⎱ *Gentlemen attending on the Duke.*
CURIO, ⎰
SIR TOBY BELCH, *Uncle to Olivia.*
SIR ANDREW AGUE-CHEEK.
MALVOLIO, *Steward to Olivia.*

FABIAN, ⎱ *Servants to Olivia.*
Clown, ⎰

OLIVIA, *a rich Countess.*
VIOLA, *in love with the Duke.*
MARIA, *Olivia's Woman.*

Lords, Priests, Sailors, Officers, Musicians, and other Attendants.

SCENE—A City in ILLYRIA ; and the Sea-coast near it.

ACT I.

SCENE I.—An Apartment in the DUKE'S Palace.

Enter DUKE, CURIO, *Lords ; Musicians attending.*

Duke.
F music be the food of love, play on ;
Give me excess of it, that, surfeiting,
The appetite may sicken, and so die.—
That strain again ! it had a dying fall :
O ! it came o'er my ear like the sweet sound
That breathes upon a bank of violets,
Stealing and giving odour.—Enough ! no more :
'T is not so sweet now, as it was before.
O spirit of love ! how quick and fresh art thou,
That, notwithstanding thy capacity   10
Receiveth as the sea, nought enters there,
Of what validity and pitch soe'er,
But falls into abatement and low price,
Even in a minute ! so full of shapes is fancy,
That it alone is high-fantastical.
Cur. Will you go hunt, my lord ?
Duke.   What, Curio ?
Cur.   The hart.
Duke. Why, so I do, the noblest that I have.
O ! when mine eyes did see Olivia first,
(Methought she purg'd the air of pestilence)
That instant was I turn'd into a hart,   20
And my desires, like fell and cruel hounds,
E'er since pursue me.—

Enter VALENTINE.

                How now ? what news from her ?
Val. So please my lord, I might not be admitted,
But from her handmaid do return this answer :—
The element itself, till seven years heat,
Shall not behold her face at ample view ;
But, like a cloistress, she will veiled walk,
And water once a day her chamber round
With eye-offending brine : all this, to season
A brother's dead love, which she would keep fresh 30
And lasting in her sad remembrance.
Duke. O ! she that hath a heart of that fine frame,
To pay this debt of love but to a brother,
How will she love, when the rich golden shaft
Hath kill'd the flock of all affections else
That live in her : when liver, brain, and heart,

These sovereign thrones, are all supplied, and fill'd
(Her sweet perfections) with one self king.—
Away, before me to sweet beds of flowers ;
Love-thoughts lie rich, when canopied with bowers. 40
                                        [*Exeunt.*

SCENE II.—The Sea-coast.

Enter VIOLA, *Captain, and Sailors.*

Vio. What country, friends, is this?
Cap.   This is Illyria, lady.
Vio. And what should I do in Illyria ?
My brother he is in Elysium.
Perchance, he is not drown'd :—what think you, sailors?
Cap. It is perchance that you yourself were sav'd.
Vio. O my poor brother ! and so, perchance, may he be.
Cap. True, madam : and, to comfort you with chance,
Assure yourself, after your ship did split,
When you, and those poor number saved with you,
Hung on our driving boat, I saw your brother,   10
Most provident in peril, bind himself
(Courage and hope both teaching him the practice)
To a strong mast, that lived upon the sea ;
Where, like Arion on the dolphin's back,
I saw him hold acquaintance with the waves
So long as I could see.
Vio.   For saying so there 's gold.
Mine own escape unfoldeth to my hope,
Whereto thy speech serves for authority,
The like of him. Know'st thou this country ?
Cap. Ay, madam, well ; for I was bred and born 20
Not three hours' travel from this very place.
Vio. Who governs here ?
Cap. A noble duke, in nature as in name.
Vio. What is his name ?
Cap.   Orsino.
Vio. Orsino ! I have heard my father name him :
He was a bachelor then.
Cap. And so is now, or was so very late ;
For but a month ago I went from hence,

And then 't was fresh in murmur (as, you know,
What great ones do, the less will prattle of),　30
That he did seek the love of fair Olivia.
　Vio. What's she?
　Cap. A virtuous maid, the daughter of a count
That died some twelvemonth since: then leaving her
In the protection of his son, her brother,
Who shortly also died: for whose dear love,
They say, she hath abjur'd the company
And sight of men.
　Vio.　　　O! that I serv'd that lady,
And might not be deliver'd to the world,
Till I had made mine own occasion mellow,　40
What my estate is.
　Cap.　　　That were hard to compass,
Because she will admit no kind of suit,
No, not the duke's.
　Vio. There is a fair behaviour in thee, captain;
And though that nature with a beauteous wall
Doth oft close in pollution, yet of thee
I will believe, thou hast a mind that suits
With this thy fair and outward character.
I pr'ythee (and I'll pay thee bounteously),
Conceal me what I am, and be my aid　50
For such disguise as haply shall become
The form of my intent. I'll serve this duke:
Thou shalt present me as an eunuch to him.
It may be worth thy pains; for I can sing,
And speak to him in many sorts of music,
That will allow me very worth his service.
What else may hap to time I will commit;
Only, shape thou thy silence to my wit.
　Cap. Be you his eunuch, and your mute I'll be:
When my tongue blabs, then let mine eyes not see.　60
　Vio. I thank thee. Lead me on.　[*Exeunt.*

SCENE III.—A Room in OLIVIA'S House.

Enter Sir TOBY BELCH *and* MARIA.

　Sir To. What a plague means my niece, to take the
death of her brother thus? I am sure care's an enemy
to life.
　Mar. By my troth, Sir Toby, you must come in
earlier o' nights: your cousin, my lady, takes great
exceptions to your ill hours.
　Sir To. Why, let her except before excepted.
　Mar. Ay, but you must confine yourself within the
modest limits of order.　9
　Sir To. Confine? I'll confine myself no finer than
I am. These clothes are good enough to drink in, and
so be these boots too: an they be not, let them hang
themselves in their own straps.
　Mar. That quaffing and drinking will undo you: I
heard my lady talk of it yesterday, and of a foolish
knight, that you brought in one night here, to be her
wooer.
　Sir To. Who? Sir Andrew Ague-cheek?
　Mar. Ay, he.
　Sir To. He's as tall a man as any's in Illyria.　20
　Mar. What's that to the purpose?
　Sir To. Why, he has three thousand ducats a year.
　Mar. Ay, but he'll have but a year in all these
ducats: he's a very fool, and a prodigal.
　Sir To. Fie, that you'll say so! he plays o' the viol-
de-gamboys, and speaks three or four languages word
for word without book, and hath all the good gifts of
nature.　28
　Mar. He hath, indeed,—almost natural; for, besides that he's a fool, he's a great quarreller; and, but
that he hath the gift of a coward to allay the gust he
hath in quarrelling, 'tis thought among the prudent
he would quickly have the gift of a grave.
　Sir To. By this hand, they are scoundrels, and sub-
stractors, that say so of him. Who are they?
　Mar. They that add, moreover, he's drunk nightly
in your company.
　Sir To. With drinking healths to my niece. I'll drink
to her as long as there is a passage in my throat, and
drink in Illyria. He's a coward, and a coystril, that
will not drink to my niece, till his brains turn o' the

toe like a parish-top. What, wench! *Castiliano
vulgo;* for here comes Sir Andrew Ague-face.　43

Enter Sir ANDREW AGUE-CHEEK.

　Sir And. Sir Toby Belch! how now, Sir Toby
Belch?
　Sir To. Sweet Sir Andrew.
　Sir And. Bless you, fair shrew.
　Mar. And you too, sir.
　Sir To. Accost, Sir Andrew, accost.
　Sir And. What's that?　50
　Sir To. My niece's chambermaid.
　Sir And. Good Mistress Accost, I desire better
acquaintance.
　Mar. My name is Mary, sir.
　Sir And. Good Mistress Mary Accost,—

Sir And. "Marry, but you shall have; and here's my hand."

　Sir To. You mistake, knight: accost is front her,
board her, woo her, assail her.
　Sir And. By my troth, I would not undertake her
in this company. Is that the meaning of accost?
　Mar. Fare you well, gentlemen.　60
　Sir To. An thou let part so, Sir Andrew, 'would
thou mightst never draw sword again!
　Sir And. An you part so, mistress, I would I might
never draw sword again. Fair lady, do you think you
have fools in hand?
　Mar. Sir, I have not you by the hand.
　Sir And. Marry, but you shall have; and here's
my hand.
　Mar. Now, sir, thought is free: I pray you, bring
your hand to the buttery-bar, and let it drink.　70
　Sir And. Wherefore, sweet-heart? what's your
metaphor?
　Mar. It's dry, sir.
　Sir And. Why, I think so: I am not such an ass,
but I can keep my hand dry. But what's your jest?
　Mar. A dry jest, sir.
　Sir And. Are you full of them?
　Mar. Ay, sir; I have them at my fingers' ends:
marry, now I let go your hand, I am barren.
　　　　　　　　　　　　　　　　[*Exit* MARIA.
　Sir To. O knight! thou lack'st a cup of canary.
When did I see thee so put down?　81
　Sir And. Never in your life, I think; unless you see
canary put me down. Methinks sometimes I have no
more wit than a Christian, or an ordinary man has;
but I am a great eater of beef, and, I believe, that does
harm to my wit.
　Sir To. No question.
　Sir And. An I thought that, I'd forswear it. I'll
ride home to-morrow, Sir Toby.
　Sir To. Pourquoi, my dear knight?　90
　Sir And. What is *pourquoi?* do or not do? I
would I had bestowed that time in the tongues, that I
have in fencing, dancing, and bear-baiting. O, had I
but followed the arts!
　Sir To. Then hadst thou had an excellent head of
hair!

Sir And. Why, would that have mended my hair?
Sir To. Past question; for thou seest it will not curl
by nature.   99
Sir And. But it becomes me well enough, does 't not?
Sir To. Excellent : it hangs like flax on a distaff,
and I hope to see a housewife take thee between her
legs, and spin it off.
Sir And. 'Faith, I 'll home to-morrow, Sir Toby :
your niece will not be seen; or, if she be, it 's four to
one she 'll none of me. The count himself, here hard
by, woos her.
Sir To. She 'll none o' the count; she 'll not match
above her degree, neither in estate, years, nor wit : I
have heard her swear it. Tut, there 's life in 't, man.
Sir And. I'll stay a month longer. I am a fellow o'
the strangest mind i' the world : I delight in masques
and revels sometimes altogether.
Sir To. Art thou good at these kick-shaws, knight?
Sir And. As any man in Illyria, whatsoever he be,
under the degree of my betters : and yet I will not
compare with an old man.
Sir To. What is thy excellence in a galliard, knight?
Sir And. 'Faith, I can cut a caper.
Sir To. And I can cut the mutton to 't.   120
Sir And. And, I think, I have the back-trick, simply
as strong as any man in Illyria.
Sir To. Wherefore are these things hid? wherefore
have these gifts a curtain before them? are they like
to take dust, like Mistress Mall's picture? why dost
thou not go to church in a galliard, and come home in
a coranto? My very walk should be a jig : I would not
so much as make water, but in a sink-a-pace. What
dost thou mean? is it a world to hide virtues in? I
did think, by the excellent constitution of thy leg, it
was formed under the star of a galliard.   131
Sir And. Ay, 't is strong, and it does indifferent well
in a damask-coloured stock. Shall we set about some
revels?
Sir To. What shall we do else? were we not born
under Taurus?
Sir And. Taurus? that 's sides and heart.
Sir To. No, sir, it is legs and thighs. Let me see
thee caper. Ha! higher: ha, ha!—excellent!
                  [*Exeunt.*

SCENE IV.—A Room in the DUKE's Palace.

Enter VALENTINE, *and* VIOLA *in man's attire.*

Val. If the duke continue these favours towards
you, Cesario, you are like to be much advanced : he
hath known you but three days, and already you are
no stranger.
Vio. You either fear his humour, or my negligence,
that you call in question the continuance of his love.
Is he inconstant, sir, in his favours?
Val. No, believe me.
Vio. I thank you. Here comes the count.

Enter DUKE, CURIO, *and Attendants.*

Duke. Who saw Cesario, ho?   10
Vio. On your attendance, my lord ; here.
Duke. Stand you awhile aloof.—Cesario,
Thou know'st no less but all : I have unclasp'd
To thee the book even of my secret soul :
Therefore, good youth, address thy gait unto her :
Be not denied access, stand at her doors,
And tell them, there thy fixed foot shall grow,
Till thou have audience.
Vio.   Sure, my noble lord,
If she be so abandon'd to her sorrow,
As it is spoke, she never will admit me.   20
Duke. Be clamorous, and leap all civil bounds,
Rather than make unprofited return.
Vio. Say, I do speak with her, my lord : what then?
Duke. O! then unfold the passion of my love ;
Surprise her with discourse of my dear faith :
It shall become thee well to act my woes ;
She will attend it better in thy youth,
Than in a nuncio of more grave aspect.
Vio. I think not so, my lord.
Duke.   Dear lad, believe it;

For they shall yet belie thy happy years,   30
That say thou art a man : Diana's lip
Is not more smooth and rubious ; thy small pipe
Is as the maiden's organ, shrill and sound,
And all is semblative a woman's part.
I know, thy constellation is right apt
For this affair.—Some four, or five, attend him ;
All, if you will ; for I myself am best,
When least in company.—Prosper well in this,
And thou shalt live as freely as thy lord
To call his fortunes thine.
Vio.   I 'll do my best,   40
To woo your lady : [*aside*] yet, a barful strife!
Whoe'er I woo, myself would be his wife.   [*Exeunt.*

SCENE V.—A Room in OLIVIA's House.

Enter MARIA *and Clown.*

Mar. Nay, either tell me where thou hast been, or I
will not open my lips so wide as a bristle may enter,
in way of thy excuse. My lady will hang thee for thy
absence.
Clo. Let her hang me : he that is well hanged in
this world needs to fear no colours.
Mar. Make that good.
Clo. He shall see none to fear.
Mar. A good lenten answer. I can tell thee where
that saying was born, of, I fear no colours.   10
Clo. Where, good Mistress Mary?
Mar. In the wars ; and that may you be bold to say
in your foolery.
Clo. Well, God give them wisdom that have it ; and
those that are fools, let them use their talents.
Mar. Yet you will be hanged, for being so long
absent ; or, to be turned away,—is not that so good as
a hanging to you?
Clo. Many a good hanging prevents a bad marriage ;
and for turning away, let summer bear it out.   20
Mar. You are resolute then?
Clo. Not so neither ; but I am resolved on two points.
Mar. That, if one break, the other will hold ; or, if
both break, your gaskins fall.
Clo. Apt, in good faith ; very apt. Well, go thy
way : if Sir Toby would leave drinking, thou wert as
witty a piece of Eve's flesh as any in Illyria.
Mar. Peace, you rogue, no more o' that. Here comes
my lady : make your excuse wisely, you were best.   29
                  [*Exit.*
Clo. Wit, an 't be thy will, put me into good fooling!
Those wits that think they have thee, do very oft prove
fools ; and I, that am sure I lack thee, may pass for a
wise man : for what says Quinapalus? Better a witty
fool, than a foolish wit.

Enter OLIVIA *and* MALVOLIO.

God bless thee, lady!
Oli. Take the fool away.
Clo. Do you not hear, fellows? Take away the lady.
Oli. Go to, you 're a dry fool ; I 'll no more of you :
besides, you grow dishonest.   39
Clo. Two faults, madonna, that drink and good
counsel will amend : for give the dry fool drink, then
is the fool not dry ; bid the dishonest man mend
himself : if he mend, he is no longer dishonest ; if he
cannot, let the botcher mend him. Anything that 's
mended is but patched : virtue that transgresses is
but patched with sin ; and sin that amends is but
patched with virtue. If that this simple syllogism
will serve, so ; if it will not, what remedy? As there
is no true cuckold but calamity, so beauty 's a flower.
—The lady bade take away the fool ; therefore, I say
again, take her away.   51
Oli. Sir, I bade them take away you.
Clo. Misprision in the highest degree!—Lady, *cucullus non facit monachum :* that 's as much to say as,
I wear not motley in my brain. Good madonna, give
me leave to prove you a fool.
Oli. Can you do it?
Clo. Dexteriously, good madonna.
Oli. Make your proof.

Clo. I must catechise you for it, madonna. Good
my mouse of virtue, answer me.   61
Oli. Well, sir, for want of other idleness, I 'll bide
your proof.
Clo. Good madonna, why mourn'st thou?
Oli. Good fool, for my brother's death.
Clo. I think his soul is in hell, madonna.
Oli. I know his soul is in heaven, fool.
Clo. The more fool, madonna, to mourn for your
brother's soul being in heaven.—Take away the fool,
gentlemen.   70
Oli. What think you of this fool, Malvolio? doth he
not mend?
Mal. Yes; and shall do, till the pangs of death

Clo. " The more fool, madonna, to mourn for your brother's soul
being in heaven."

shake him: infirmity, that decays the wise, doth ever
make the better fool.
Clo. God send you, sir, a speedy infirmity, for the
better increasing your folly! Sir Toby will be sworn
that I am no fox, but he will not pass his word for
twopence that you are no fool.
Oli. How say you to that, Malvolio?   80
Mal. I marvel your ladyship takes delight in such a
barren rascal: I saw him put down the other day with
an ordinary fool, that has no more brain than a stone.
Look you now, he 's out of his guard already: unless
you laugh and minister occasion to him, he is gagged.
I protest, I take these wise men, that crow so at these
set kind of fools, no better than the fools' zanies.
Oli. O! you are sick of self-love, Malvolio, and taste
with a distempered appetite. To be generous, guiltless, and of free disposition, is to take those things for
bird-bolts, that you deem cannon-bullets. There is no
slander in an allowed fool, though he do nothing but
rail; nor no railing in a known discreet man, though
he do nothing but reprove.
Clo. Now, Mercury endue thee with leasing, for
thou speakest well of fools!

Re-enter MARIA.

Mar. Madam, there is at the gate a young gentleman
much desires to speak with you.
Oli. From the Count Orsino, is it?
Mar. I know not, madam: 'tis a fair young man,
and well attended.   101
Oli. Who of my people hold him in delay?
Mar. Sir Toby, madam, your kinsman.
Oli. Fetch him off, I pray you: he speaks nothing
but madman. Fie on him! [*Exit* MARIA.] Go you,
Malvolio: if it be a suit from the count, I am sick,
or not at home; what you will, to dismiss it. [*Exit*
MALVOLIO.] Now you see, sir, how your fooling grows
old, and people dislike it.   109
Clo. Thou hast spoke for us, madonna, as if thy
eldest son should be a fool, whose skull Jove cram
with brains; for here he comes, one of thy kin, has
a most weak *pia mater.*

Enter Sir TOBY BELCH.

Oli. By mine honour, half drunk.—What is he at
the gate, cousin?
Sir To. A gentleman.
Oli. A gentleman! What gentleman?
Sir To. 'T is a gentleman here—a plague o' these
pickle-herring!—How now, sot?
Clo. Good Sir Toby!   120
Oli. Cousin, cousin, how have you come so early by
this lethargy?
Sir To. Lechery! I defy lechery. There 's one at
the gate.
Oli. Ay, marry; what is he?
Sir To. Let him be the devil, an he will, I care not:
give me faith, say I. Well, it 's all one.   [*Exit.*
Oli. What 's a drunken man like, fool?
Clo. Like a drown'd man, a fool, and a madman:
one draught above heat makes him a fool, the second
mads him, and a third drowns him.   131
Oli. Go thou and seek the coroner, and let him sit o'
my coz; for he 's in the third degree of drink, he 's
drown'd: go, look after him.
Clo. He is but mad yet, madonna; and the fool sha'l
look to the madman.   [*Exit.*

Re-enter MALVOLIO.

Mal. Madam, yond young fellow swears he will
speak with you. I told him you were sick: he takes
on him to understand so much, and therefore comes to
speak with you. I told him you were asleep: he seems
to have a foreknowledge of that too, and therefore
comes to speak with you. What is to be said to him,
lady? he 's fortified against any denial.   143
Oli. Tell him, he shall not speak with me.
Mal. Ha 's been told so; and he says, he 'll stand at
your door like a sheriff's post, and be the supporter to
a bench, but he 'll speak with you.
Oli. What kind o' man is he?
Mal. Why, of mankind.
Oli. What manner of man?   150
Mal. Of very ill manner: he 'll speak with you, will
you, or no.
Oli. Of what personage and years is he?
Mal. Not yet old enough for a man, nor young
enough for a boy; as a squash is before 't is a peascod,
or a codling when 't is almost an apple: 't is with him
in standing water, between boy and man. He is very
well-favoured, and he speaks very shrewishly: one
would think, his mother's milk were scarce out of him.
Oli. Let him approach. Call in my gentlewoman.
Mal. Gentlewoman, my lady calls.   161
            [*Exit.*

Re-enter MARIA.

Oli. Give me my veil: come, throw it o'er my face.
We 'll once more hear Orsino's embassy.

Enter VIOLA.

Vio. The honourable lady of the house, which is
she?
Oli. Speak to me; I shall answer for her. Your will?
Vio. Most radiant, exquisite, and unmatchable
beauty.—I pray you, tell me, if this be the lady of the
house, for I never saw her: I would be loath to cast
away my speech; for, besides that it is excellently
well penned, I have taken great pains to con it. Good
beauties, let me sustain no scorn; I am very comptible
even to the least sinister usage.   173
Oli. Whence came you, sir?
Vio. I can say little more than I have studied,
and that question 's out of my part. Good gentle one,
give me modest assurance if you be the lady of the
house, that I may proceed in my speech.
Oli. Are you a comedian?
Vio. No, my profound heart; and yet, by the very
fangs of malice I swear, I am not that I play. Are
you the lady of the house?   182
Oli. If I do not usurp myself, I am.
Vio. Most certain, if you are she, you do usurp
yourself; for what is yours to bestow, is not yours to
reserve. But this is from my commission. I will on
with my speech in your praise, and then show you the
heart of my message.

Oli. Come to what is important in't : I forgive you
the praise.   190
Vio. Alas! I took great pains to study it, and 't is
poetical.
Oli. It is the more like to be feigned : I pray you,
keep it in. I heard, you were saucy at my gates, and
allowed your approach, rather to wonder at you than
to hear you. If you be not mad, be gone ; if you have
reason, be brief : 't is not that time of moon with me
to make one in so skipping a dialogue.
Mar. Will you hoist sail, sir? here lies your way.
Vio. No, good swabber ; I am to hull here a little
longer.—Some mollification for your giant, sweet lady.
Oli. Tell me your mind.   202
Vio. I am a messenger.
Oli. Sure, you have some hideous matter to deliver,
when the courtesy of it is so fearful. Speak your
office.
Vio. It alone concerns your ear. I bring no over-

Oli. "Look you, sir ; such a one I was this present : is't not
well done?"

ture of war, no taxation of homage. I hold the olive
in my hand : my words are as full of peace as matter.
Oli. Yet you began rudely. What are you? what
would you?   211
Vio. The rudeness that hath appear'd in me, have I
learn'd from my entertainment. What I am, and
what I would, are as secret as maidenhead : to your
ears, divinity ; to any other's, profanation.
Oli. Give us the place alone. We will hear this
divinity. [*Exit* MARIA.] Now, sir ; what is your text?
Vio. Most sweet lady,—
Oli. A comfortable doctrine, and much may be said
of it. Where lies your text?   220
Vio. In Orsino's bosom.
Oli. In his bosom! In what chapter of his bosom?
Vio. To answer by the method, in the first of his
heart.
Oli. O! I have read it : it is heresy. Have you no
more to say?
Vio. Good madam, let me see your face.
Oli. Have you any commission from your lord to
negotiate with my face? you are now out of your
text : but we will draw the curtain, and show you the
picture. Look you, sir ; such a one I was this present :
is 't not well done?   [*Unveiling.*
Vio. Excellently done, if God did all.   233
Oli. 'T is in grain, sir : 't will endure wind and
weather.
Vio. 'T is beauty truly blent, whose red and white
Nature's own sweet and cunning hand laid on.
Lady, you are the cruell'st she alive,
If you will lead these graces to the grave,
And leave the world no copy.   240

Oli. O! sir, I will not be so hard-hearted. I will
give out divers schedules of my beauty : it shall be
inventoried, and every particle, and utensil, labelled
to my will ; as, item, two lips indifferent red ; item,
two grey eyes with lids to them ; item, one neck, one
chin, and so forth. Were you sent hither to praise
me?
Vio. I see you what you are : you are too proud ;
But, if you were the devil, you are fair.
My lord and master loves you : O! such love   250
Could be but recompens'd, though you were crown'd
The nonpareil of beauty!
Oli.   How does he love me?
Vio. With adorations, with fertile tears,
With groans that thunder love, with sighs of fire.
Oli. Your lord does know my mind ; I cannot love
him :
Yet I suppose him virtuous, know him noble,
Of great estate, of fresh and stainless youth ;
In voices well divulg'd, free, learn'd, and valiant ;
And in dimension, and the shape of nature,
A gracious person ; but yet I cannot love him.   260
He might have took his answer long ago.
Vio. If I did love you in my master's flame,
With such a suffering, such a deadly life,
In your denial I would find no sense :
I would not understand it.
Oli.   Why, what would you?
Vio. Make me a willow cabin at your gate,
And call upon my soul within the house ;
Write loyal cantons of contemned love,
And sing them loud even in the dead of night ;
Holla your name to the reverberate hills,   270
And make the babbling gossip of the air
Cry out, Olivia! O! you should not rest
Between the elements of air and earth,
But you should pity me.
Oli. You might do much. What is your parentage?
Vio. Above my fortunes, yet my state is well :
I am a gentleman.
Oli.   Get you to your lord :
I cannot love him. Let him send no more,
Unless, perchance, you come to me again,
To tell me how he takes it. Fare you well :   280
I thank you for your pains. Spend this for me.
Vio. I am no fee'd post, lady ; keep your purse :
My master, not myself, lacks recompense.
Love make his heart of flint that you shall love,
And let your fervour, like my master's, be
Plac'd in contempt! Farewell, fair cruelty. [*Exit.*
Oli. "What is your parentage?"
"Above my fortunes, yet my state is well :
I am a gentleman."—I 'll be sworn thou art :
Thy tongue, thy face, thy limbs, actions, and spirit,
Do give thee five-fold blazon.—Not too fast :—soft!
soft!   291
Unless the master were the man.—How now?
Even so quickly may one catch the plague?
Methinks, I feel this youth's perfections
With an invisible and subtle stealth
To creep in at mine eyes. Well, let it be.—
What, ho! Malvolio.—

Re-enter MALVOLIO.

Mal.   Here, madam, at your service.
Oli. Run after that same peevish messenger,
The county's man : he left this ring behind him,
Would I, or not : tell him, I 'll none of it.   300
Desire him not to flatter with his lord,
Nor hold him up with hopes : I am not for him.
If that the youth will come this way to-morrow,
I 'll give him reasons for 't. Hie thee, Malvolio.
Mal. Madam, I will.   [*Exit.*
Oli. I do I know not what, and fear to find
Mine eye too great a flatterer for my mind.
Fate, show thy force : ourselves we do not owe ;
What is decreed must be, and be this so!   [*Exit.*

ACT II.

SCENE I.—The Sea-coast.

Enter ANTONIO and SEBASTIAN.

Antonio.

WILL you stay no longer? nor will you not
 that I go with you?
 Seb. By your patience, no. My stars
shine darkly over me: the malignancy
of my fate might, perhaps, distemper
yours; therefore, I shall crave of you
your leave, that I may bear my evils
alone. It were a bad recompense for
your love, to lay any of them on you.
 Ant. Let me yet know of you, whither
you are bound.   11
 Seb. No, 'sooth, sir. My determinate voyage is
mere extravagancy. But I perceive in you so excellent a touch of modesty, that you will not extort from
me what I am willing to keep in: therefore, it charges
me in manners the rather to express myself. You
must know of me then, Antonio, my name is Sebastian,
which I called Rodorigo. My father was that Sebastian of Messaline, whom, I know, you have heard of:
he left behind him myself and a sister, both born in
an hour. If the heavens had been pleased, 'would we
had so ended! but you, sir, altered that; for some
hour before you took me from the breach of the sea
was my sister drowned.
 Ant. Alas the day!
 Seb. A lady, sir, though it was said she much resembled me, was yet of many accounted beautiful: but,
though I could not with such estimable wonder over-
far believe that, yet thus far I will boldly publish
her,—she bore a mind that envy could not but call
fair. She is drowned already, sir, with salt water,
though I seem to drown her remembrance again with
more.   33
 Ant. Pardon me, sir, your bad entertainment.
 Seb. O good Antonio! forgive me your trouble.
 Ant. If you will not murder me for my love, let me
be your servant.
 Seb. If you will not undo what you have done, that
is, kill him whom you have recovered, desire it not.
Fare ye well at once: my bosom is full of kindness;
and I am yet so near the manners of my mother, that,
upon the least occasion more, mine eyes will tell tales
of me. I am bound to the Count Orsino's court:
farewell.   [*Exit.*
 Ant. The gentleness of all the gods go with thee!
I have many enemies in Orsino's court,
Else would I very shortly see thee there;
But, come what may, I do adore thee so,
That danger shall seem sport, and I will go. [*Exit.*

SCENE II.—A Street.

Enter VIOLA; MALVOLIO *following.*

 Mal. Were not you even now with the Countess
Olivia?
 Vio. Even now, sir: on a moderate pace I have
since arrived but hither.
 Mal. She returns this ring to you, sir: you might
have saved me my pains, to have taken it away yourself. She adds, moreover, that you should put your
lord into a desperate assurance she will none of him.
And one thing more: that you be never so hardy to
come again in his affairs, unless it be to report your
lord's taking of this. Receive it so.   11
 Vio. She took the ring of me;—I'll none of it.
 Mal. Come, sir; you peevishly threw it to her, and
her will is, it should be so returned: if it be worth
stooping for, there it lies in your eye; if not, be it his
that finds it.   [*Exit.*
 Vio. I left no ring with her: what means this lady?
Fortune forbid my outside have not charm'd her!
She made good view of me; indeed, so much,
That, methought, her eyes had lost her tongue, 20
For she did speak in starts distractedly.
She loves me, sure: the cunning of her passion
Invites me in this churlish messenger.
None of my lord's ring! why, he sent her none.
I am the man:—if it be so, as 't is,
Poor lady, she were better love a dream.
Disguise, I see, thou art a wickedness,
Wherein the pregnant enemy does much.
How easy is it for the proper-false
In women's waxen hearts to set their forms! 30
Alas! our frailty is the cause, not we,
For such as we are made of, such we be.
How will this fadge? My master loves her dearly;
And I, poor monster, fond as much on him;
And she, mistaken, seems to dote on me.
What will become of this? As I am man,
My state is desperate for my master's love;
As I am woman,—now alas the day!—
What thriftless sighs shall poor Olivia breathe!
O Time! thou must untangle this, not I;   40
It is too hard a knot for me t' untie.   [*Exit.*

SCENE III.—A Room in OLIVIA's House.

Enter Sir TOBY BELCH and Sir ANDREW AGUE-CHEEK.

 Sir To. Approach, Sir Andrew: not to be a-bed
after midnight is to be up betimes; and *diluculo
surgere,* thou know'st,—
 Sir And. Nay, by my troth, I know not; but I
know, to be up late, is to be up late.
 Sir To. A false conclusion: I hate it as an unfilled
can. To be up after midnight, and to go to bed then,
is early; so that, to go to bed after midnight, is to go
to bed betimes. Does not our life consist of the four
elements?   10
 Sir And. 'Faith, so they say; but I think, it rather
consists of eating and drinking.
 Sir To. Thou art a scholar; let us therefore eat and
drink.—Marian, I say!—a stoop of wine!

Enter Clown.

 Sir And. Here comes the fool, i' faith.
 Clo. How now, my hearts? Did you never see the
picture of we three?
 Sir To. Welcome, ass. Now let's have a catch. 18
 Sir And. By my troth, the fool has an excellent
breast. I had rather than forty shillings I had such a
leg, and so sweet a breath to sing, as the fool has. In
sooth, thou wast in very gracious fooling last night,
when thou spokest of Pigrogromitus, of the Vapians
passing the equinoctial of Queubus: 't was very good,
i' faith. I sent thee sixpence for thy leman: hadst it?

Clo. I did impeticos thy gratillity, for Malvolio's nose is no whipstock : my lady has a white hand, and the Myrmidons are no bottle-ale houses.

Sir And. Excellent! Why, this is the best fooling, when all is done. Now, a song.   30

Sir To. Come on : there is sixpence for you; let's have a song.

Sir And. There's a testril of me too : if one knight give a—

Clo. Would you have a love-song, or a song of good life?

Sir To. A love-song, a love-song.

Sir And. Ay, ay; I care not for good life.

SONG.

Clo. O mistress mine! where are you roaming?
O! stay and hear; your true love's coming,   40
That can sing both high and low.
Trip no further, pretty sweeting;
Journeys end in lovers' meeting,
Every wise man's son doth know.

Sir And. Excellent good, i' faith.

Sir To. Good, good.

Clo. What is love? 'tis not hereafter;
Present mirth hath present laughter;
What's to come is still unsure:
In delay there lies no plenty;   50
Then come kiss me, sweet-and-twenty,
Youth's a stuff will not endure.

Sir And. A mellifluous voice, as I am true knight.

Sir To. A contagious breath.

Sir And. Very sweet and contagious, i' faith.

Sir To. To hear by the nose, it is dulcet in contagion. But shall we make the welkin dance indeed? Shall we rouse the night-owl in a catch, that will draw three souls out of one weaver? shall we do that?   60

Sir And. An you love me, let's do't : I am dog at a catch.

Clo. By'r lady, sir, and some dogs will catch well.

Sir And. Most certain. Let our catch be, "Thou knave."

Clo. "Hold thy peace, thou knave," knight? I shall be constrain'd in't to call thee knave, knight.

Sir And. 'T is not the first time I have constrain'd one to call me knave. Begin, fool : it begins, "Hold thy peace."   70

Clo. I shall never begin, if I hold my peace.

Sir And. Good, i' faith. Come, begin.

[*They sing a catch.*

Enter MARIA.

Mar. What a caterwauling do you keep here! If my lady have not called up her steward Malvolio and bid him turn you out of doors, never trust me.

Sir To. My lady's a Cataian ; we are politicians ; Malvolio's a Peg-a-Ramsey, and "Three merry men be we." Am not I consanguineous? am I not of her blood? Tilly-vally, lady! [*Sings.*] "There dwelt a man in Babylon, lady, lady!"   80

Clo. Beshrew me, the knight's in admirable fooling.

Sir And. Ay, he does well enough, if he be disposed, and so do I too : he does it with a better grace, but I do it more natural.

Sir To. [*Sings.*] "O! the twelfth day of December,"—

Mar. For the love o' God, peace!

Enter MALVOLIO.

Mal. My masters, are you mad? or what are you? Have you no wit, manners, nor honesty, but to gabble like tinkers at this time of night? Do ye make an alehouse of my lady's house, that ye squeak out your coziers' catches without any mitigation or remorse of voice? Is there no respect of place, persons, nor time, in you?   93

Sir To. We did keep time, sir, in our catches. Sneck up!

Mal. Sir Toby, I must be round with you. My lady bade me tell you, that, though she harbours you as her kinsman, she's nothing allied to your disorders. If you can separate yourself and your misdemeanours, you are welcome to the house ; if not, an it would

please you to take leave of her, she is very willing to bid you farewell.   102

Sir To. "Farewell, dear heart, since I must needs be gone."

Mar. Nay, good Sir Toby.

Clo. "His eyes do show, his days are almost done."

Mal. Is't even so?

Sir To. "But I will never die."

Clo. Sir Toby, there you lie.

Mal. This is much credit to you.   110

Sir To. "Shall I bid him go?"

Clo. "What an if you do?"

Sir To. "Shall I bid him go, and spare not?"

Clo. "O! no, no, no, no, you dare not."

Sir To. Out o' time? Sir, ye lie. Art any more than a steward? Dost thou think, because thou art virtuous, there shall be no more cakes and ale?

Clo. Yes, by Saint Anne ; and ginger shall be hot i' the mouth too.

Sir To. Thou'rt i' the right.—Go, sir, rub your chain with crumbs.—A stoop of wine, Maria!   121

Mal. Mistress Mary, if you prized my lady's favour at anything more than contempt, you would not give means for this uncivil rule : she shall know of it, by this hand.   [*Exit.*

Mar. Go shake your ears.

Sir And. 'T were as good a deed as to drink when a man's a-hungry, to challenge him to the field, and then to break promise with him, and make a fool of him.   130

Sir To. Do't, knight : I'll write thee a challenge, or I'll deliver thy indignation to him by word of mouth.

Mar. Sweet Sir Toby, be patient for to-night. Since the youth of the count's was to-day with my lady, she is much out of quiet. For Monsieur Malvolio, let me alone with him : if I do not gull him into a nay-word, and make him a common recreation, do not think I have wit enough to lie straight in my bed. I know, I can do it.

Sir To. Possess us, possess us : tell us something of him.   141

Mar. Marry, sir, sometimes he is a kind of Puritan.

Sir And. O! if I thought that, I'd beat him like a dog.

Sir To. What, for being a Puritan? thy exquisite reason, dear knight?

Sir And. I have no exquisite reason for't, but I have reason good enough.

Mar. The devil a Puritan that he is, or anything constantly but a time-pleaser ; an affectioned ass, that cons state without book, and utters it by great swarths : the best persuaded of himself ; so crammed, as he thinks, with excellences, that it is his ground of faith, that all that look on him love him ; and on that vice in him will my revenge find notable cause to work.

Sir To. What wilt thou do?

Mar. I will drop in his way some obscure epistles of love ; wherein, by the colour of his beard, the shape of his leg, the manner of his gait, the expressure of his eye, forehead, and complexion, he shall find himself most feelingly personated. I can write very like my lady, your niece : on a forgotten matter we can hardly make distinction of our hands.   163

Sir To. Excellent! I smell a device.

Sir And. I have't in my nose too.

Sir To. He shall think, by the letters that thou wilt drop, that they come from my niece, and that she is in love with him?

Mar. My purpose is, indeed, a horse of that colour.

Sir And. And your horse, now, would make him an ass.   171

Mar. Ass, I doubt not.

Sir And. O! 't will be admirable.

Mar. Sport royal, I warrant you : I know, my physic will work with him. I will plant you two, and let the fool make a third, where he shall find the letter : observe his construction of it. For this night, to bed and dream, on the event. Farewell.

Sir To. Good night, Penthesilea.   [*Exit* MARIA.

Sir And. Before me, she's a good wench.   180

Sir To. She's a beagle, true-bred, and one that adores me : what o' that?

Sir And. I was adored once too.

Sir To. Let's to bed, knight.—Thou hadst need send for more money.

Sir And. If I cannot recover your niece, I am a foul way out.

That old and antique song, we heard last night;
Methought, it did relieve my passion much,
More than light airs, and recollected terms,
Of these most brisk and giddy-paced times:
Come; but one verse.

Mal. "My masters, are you mad? or what are you? Have you no wit, manners, nor honesty, but to gabble like tinkers at this time of night?"

Sir To. Send for money, knight: if thou hast her not i' the end, call me cut.

Sir And. If I do not, never trust me; take it how you will.   191

Sir To. Come, come: I'll go burn some sack, 't is too late to go to bed now. Come, knight; come, knight.

                                        [Exeunt.

—

SCENE IV.—A Room in the DUKE's Palace.

Enter DUKE, VIOLA, CURIO, *and others.*

Duke. Give me some music.—Now, good morrow, friends.—

Now, good Cesario, but that piece of song,

Cur. He is not here, so please your lordship, that should sing it.

Duke. Who was it?   10

Cur. Feste, the jester, my lord; a fool, that the lady Olivia's father took much delight in. He is about the house.

Duke. Seek him out, and play the tune the while.

                         [Exit CURIO.—*Music.*

Come hither, boy: if ever thou shalt love,
In the sweet pangs of it remember me;
For such as I am all true lovers are:
Unstaid and skittish in all motions else,
Save in the constant image of the creature
That is belov'd.—How dost thou like this tune?   20

Vio. It gives a very echo to the seat
Where love is thron'd.
Duke.   Thou dost speak masterly.
My life upon 't, young though thou art, thine eye
Hath stay'd upon some favour that it loves ;
Hath it not, boy ?
Vio.   A little, by your favour.
Duke. What kind of woman is 't ?
Vio.   Of your complexion.
Duke. She is not worth thee then. What years, i' faith ?
Vio. About your years, my lord.
Duke. Too old, by Heaven. Let still the woman take   30
An elder than herself ; so wears she to him,
So sways she level in her husband's heart ;
For, boy, however we do praise ourselves,

Clo. " 'I am slain by a fair cruel maid.' "

Our fancies are more giddy and unfirm,
More longing, wavering, sooner lost and worn,
Than women's are.
Vio.   I think it well, my lord.
Duke. Then, let thy love be younger than thyself,
Or thy affection cannot hold the bent ;
For women are as roses, whose fair flower,
Being once display'd, doth fall that very hour.
Vio. And so they are : alas, that they are so ;   40
To die, even when they to perfection grow !

Re-enter CURIO *and Clown.*

Duke. O fellow ! come, the song we had last night.—
Mark it, Cesario ; it is old, and plain :
The spinsters and the knitters in the sun,
And the free maids, that weave their thread with bones,
Do use to chant it : it is silly sooth,
And dallies with the innocence of love,
Like the old age.
Clo. Are you ready, sir ?
Duke. Ay ; pr'ythee, sing.   50
        SONG.   [*Music.*

Clo. Come away, come away, death,
   And in sad cypress let me be laid ;
    Fly away, fly away, breath ;
I am slain by a fair cruel maid.
 My shroud of white, stuck all with yew,
     O ! prepare it :
My part of death, no one so true
     Did share it.

Not a flower, not a flower sweet,
On my black coffin let there be strown ;   60
Not a friend, not a friend greet
My poor corse, where my bones shall be thrown :
A thousand thousand sighs to save,
     Lay me, O ! where
Sad true lover never find my grave,
     To weep there.

Duke. There 's for thy pains.
Clo. No pains, sir : I take pleasure in singing, sir.
Duke. I 'll pay thy pleasure then.
Clo. Truly, sir, and pleasure will be paid, one time
or another.   71
Duke. Give me now leave to leave thee.
Clo. Now, the melancholy god protect thee, and the
tailor make thy doublet of changeable taffeta, for thy
mind is a very opal !—I would have men of such con-
stancy put to sea, that their business might be every-
thing, and their intent everywhere ; for that 's it, that
always makes a good voyage of nothing.—Farewell.
                                            [*Exit.*
Duke. Let all the rest give place.—
        [*Exeunt* CURIO *and Attendants.*
                Once more, Cesario,
Get thee to yond same sovereign
        cruelty :   80
Tell her, my love, more noble than
        the world,
Prizes not quantity of dirty lands :
The parts that fortune hath be-
        stow'd upon her,
Tell her, I hold as giddily as for-
        tune ;
But 't is that miracle and queen of
        gems,
That nature pranks her in, attracts
        my soul.
Vio. But, if she cannot love you,
        sir ?
Duke. I cannot be so answer'd.
Vio.   'Sooth, but you must.
Say, that some lady, as perhaps
        there is,
Hath for your love as great a pang
        of heart   90
As you have for Olivia : you can-
        not love her ;
You tell her so ; must she not then
        be answer'd ?
Duke. There is no woman's
        sides
Can bide the beating of so strong a passion
As love doth give my heart ; no woman's heart
So big to hold so much : they lack retention.
Alas ! their love may be call'd appetite,—
No motion of the liver, but the palate,—
That suffer surfeit, cloyment, and revolt ;
But mine is all as hungry as the sea,   100
And can digest as much. Make no compare
Between that love a woman can bear me,
And that I owe Olivia.
Vio.   Ay, but I know—
Duke. What dost thou know ?
Vio. Too well what love women to men may
        owe :
In faith, they are as true of heart as we.
My father had a daughter lov'd a man,
As it might be, perhaps, were I a woman,
I should your lordship.
Duke.   And what 's her history ?
Vio. A blank, my lord. She never told her
        love,—   110
But let concealment, like a worm i' the bud,
Feed on her damask cheek : she pin'd in thought :
And, with a green and yellow melancholy,
She sat like Patience on a monument,
Smiling at grief. Was not this love indeed ?
We men may say more, swear more ; but, in-
        deed,
Our shows are more than will, for still we prove
Much in our vows, but little in our love.
Duke. But died thy sister of her love, my
        boy ?
Vio. I am all the daughters of my father's
        house,   120
And all the brothers too ; and yet I know not.—
Sir, shall I to this lady ?
Duke.   Ay, that 's the theme.
To her in haste : give her this jewel ; say,
My love can give no place, bide no denay. [*Exeunt.*

SCENE V.—OLIVIA's Garden.

Enter Sir TOBY BELCH, *Sir* ANDREW AGUE-CHEEK, *and* FABIAN.

Sir To. Come thy ways, Signior Fabian.

Fab. Nay, I'll come: if I lose a scruple of this sport, let me be boiled to death with melancholy.

Sir To. Wouldst thou not be glad to have the niggardly, rascally sheep-biter come by some notable shame?

Fab. I would exult, man: you know, he brought me out o' favour with my lady about a bear-baiting here. 9

Sir To. To anger him we'll have the bear again, and we will fool him black and blue;—shall we not, Sir Andrew?

Sir And. An we do not, it is pity of our lives.

Enter MARIA.

Sir To. Here comes the little villain.—How now, my metal of India?

Mar. Get ye all three into the box-tree. Malvolio's coming down this walk: he has been yonder i' the sun, practising behaviour to his own shadow, this half-hour. Observe him, for the love of mockery; for, I know, this letter will make a contemplative idiot of him. Close, in the name of jesting! [*The men hide themselves.*] Lie thou there [*throws down a letter*]; for here comes the trout that must be caught with tickling.
[*Exit.*

Enter MALVOLIO.

Mal. 'T is but fortune; all is fortune. Maria once told me, she did affect me; and I have heard herself come thus near, that, should she fancy, it should be one of my complexion. Besides, she uses me with a more exalted respect than any one else that follows her. What should I think on 't? 31

Sir To. Here's an overweening rogue!

Fab. O, peace! Contemplation makes a rare turkey-cock of him: how he jets under his advanced plumes!

Sir And. 'Slight, I could so beat the rogue.—

Sir To. Peace! I say.

Mal. To be Count Malvolio;—

Sir To. Ah, rogue!

Sir And. Pistol him, pistol him. 40

Sir To. Peace! peace!

Mal. There is example for 't: the lady of the Strachy married the yeoman of the wardrobe.

Sir And. Fie on him, Jezebel!

Fab. O, peace! now he's deeply in; look how imagination blows him.

Mal. Having been three months married to her, sitting in my state,—

Sir To. O, for a stone-bow, to hit him in the eye!

Mal. Calling my officers about me, in my branched velvet gown; having come from a day-bed, where I have left Olivia sleeping:— 52

Sir To. Fire and brimstone!

Fab. O, peace! peace!

Mal. And then to have the humour of state: and after a demure travel of regard,—telling them, I know my place, as I would they should do theirs,—to ask for my kinsman Toby.—

Sir To. Bolts and shackles!

Fab. O, peace, peace, peace! now, now. 60

Mal. Seven of my people, with an obedient start, make out for him. I frown the while; and, perchance, wind up my watch, or play with some rich jewel. Toby approaches; court'sies there to me.

Sir To. Shall this fellow live?

Fab. Though our silence be drawn from us with cars, yet peace!

Mal. I extend my hand to him thus, quenching my familiar smile with an austere regard of control,—

Sir To. And does not Toby take you a blow o' the lips then? 71

Mal. Saying, "Cousin Toby, my fortunes, having cast me on your niece, give me this prerogative of speech,"—

Sir To. What, what?

Mal. "You must amend your drunkenness."

Sir To. Out, scab!

Fab. Nay, patience, or we break the sinews of our plot.

Mal. "Besides, you waste the treasure of your time with a foolish knight,"— 81

Sir And. That's me, I warrant you.

Mal. "One Sir Andrew,"—

Sir And. I knew 't was I; for many do call me fool.

Mal. [*Seeing the letter.*] What employment have we here?

Fab. Now is the woodcock near the gin.

Mal. " By my life, this is my lady's hand ! "

Sir To. O, peace! and the spirit of humours intimate reading aloud to him! 90

Mal. [*Taking up the letter.*] By my life, this is my lady's hand! these be her very *C*'s, her *U*'s, and her *T*'s; and thus makes she her great *P*'s. It is, in contempt of question, her hand.

Sir And. Her *C*'s, her *U*'s, and her *T*'s: why that?

Mal. [*Reads.*] "To the unknown beloved, this, and my good wishes:" her very phrases!—By your leave, wax.—Soft!—and the impressure her Lucrece, with which she uses to seal: 't is my lady. To whom should this be? 100

Fab. This wins him, liver and all.

Mal. [*Reads.*] "Jove knows, I love;
But who?
Lips, do not move:
No man must know."

"No man must know."—What follows? the numbers altered!—"No man must know:"—if this should be thee, Malvolio?

Sir To. Marry, hang thee, brock!

Mal. [*Reads.*] "I may command, where I adore; 110
But silence, like a Lucrece' knife,
With bloodless stroke my heart doth gore:
M, O, A, I, doth sway my life."

Fab. A fustian riddle.

Sir To. Excellent wench, say I.

Mal. "*M, O, A, I*, doth sway my life."—Nay, but first, let me see, let me see.

Fab. What a dish of poison has she dressed him!

Sir To. And with what wing the stannyel checks at it! 120

Mal. "I may command, where I adore." Why, she may command me: I serve her; she is my lady. Why, this is evident to any formal capacity. There is no obstruction in this.—And the end,—what should

that alphabetical position portend? if I could make
that resemble something in me,—Softly!—*M, O, A, I,*—

Sir To. O! ay, make up that. He is now at a cold
scent.

Fab. Sowter will cry upon 't, for all this, though it
be as rank as a fox. 130

Mal. M,—Malvolio:—*M,*—why, that begins my
name.

Fab. Did not I say, he would work it out? the cur
is excellent at faults.

Mal. M,—but then there is no consonancy in the
sequel; that suffers under probation: *A* should follow,
but *O* does.

Fab. And *O* shall end, I hope.

Sir To. Ay, or I 'll cudgel him, and make him cry, *O!*

Mal. And then *I* comes behind. 140

Fab. Ay, an you had an eye behind you, you might
see more detraction at your heels, than fortunes
before you.

Mal. M, O, A, I:—this simulation is not as the
former:—and yet, to crush this a little, it would bow
to me, for every one of these letters are in my name.
Soft! here follows prose.—*[Reads.]* " If this fall into
thy hand, revolve. In my stars I am above thee;
but be not afraid of greatness: some are born great,
some achieve greatness, and some have greatness
thrust upon them. Thy Fates open their hands; let
thy blood and spirit embrace them. And, to inure
thyself to what thou art like to be, cast thy humble
slough, and appear fresh. Be opposite with a kinsman, surly with servants; let thy tongue tang arguments of state; put thyself into the trick of singularity. She thus advises thee, that sighs for thee.
Remember who commended thy yellow stockings,
and wished to see thee ever cross-gartered: I say,
remember. Go to, thou art made, if thou desirest to
be so; if not, let me see thee a steward still, the
fellow of servants, and not worthy to touch Fortune's
fingers. Farewell. She that would alter services
with thee,

THE FORTUNATE-UNHAPPY."

Daylight and champian discovers not more: this is
open. I will be proud, I will read politic authors,
I will baffle Sir Toby, I will wash off gross acquaintance, I will be point-device the very man. I do not
now fool myself, to let imagination jade me, for every

reason excites to this, that my lady loves me. She
did commend my yellow stockings of late; she did
praise my leg being cross-gartered; and in this she
manifests herself to my love, and with a kind of
injunction drives me to these habits of her liking. I
thank my stars, I am happy. I will be strange, stout,
in yellow stockings, and cross-gartered, even with
the swiftness of putting on. Jove and my stars be
praised!—Here is yet a postscript. *[Reads.]* " Thou
canst not choose but know who I am. If thou en-
tertainest my love, let it appear in thy smiling: thy
smiles become thee well; therefore in my presence
still smile, dear my sweet, I pr'ythee."—Jove, I thank
thee.—I will smile: I will do everything that thou
wilt have me. *[Exit.*

Fab. I will not give my part of this sport for a
pension of thousands to be paid from the Sophy.

Sir To. I could marry this wench for this device.

Sir And. So could I too.

Sir To. And ask no other dowry with her, but such
another jest. 191

Sir And. Nor I neither.

Fab. Here comes my noble gull-catcher.

Re-enter MARIA.

Sir To. Wilt thou set thy foot o' my neck?

Sir And. Or o' mine either?

Sir To. Shall I play my freedom at tray-trip, and
become thy bond-slave?

Sir And. I' faith, or I either?

Sir To. Why, thou hast put him in such a dream,
that when the image of it leaves him, he must run
mad. 201

Mar. Nay, but say true: does it work upon him?

Sir To. Like aqua-vitæ with a midwife.

Mar. If you will then see the fruits of the sport,
mark his first approach before my lady: he will come
to her in yellow stockings, and 't is a colour she
abhors; and cross-gartered, a fashion she detests;
and he will smile upon her, which will now be so
unsuitable to her disposition, being addicted to a
melancholy as she is, that it cannot but turn him into
a notable contempt. If you will see it, follow me. 211

Sir To. To the gates of Tartar, thou most excellent
devil of wit!

Sir And. I 'll make one too. *[Exeunt.*

ACT III.

Scene I.—Olivia's Garden.

Enter Viola, *and Clown with a tabor.*

Viola.

AVE thee, friend, and thy music. Dost
thou live by thy tabor?

Clo. No, sir, I live by the church.

Vio. Art thou a churchman?

Clo. No such matter, sir: I do live by
the church; for I do live at my house,
and my house doth stand by the church.

Vio. So thou may'st say, the king lies
by a beggar, if a beggar dwell near him;
or, the church stands by thy tabor, if thy
tabor stand by the church. 11

Clo. You have said, sir.—To see this
age! A sentence is but a cheveril glove
to a good wit: how quickly the wrong
side may be turned outward!

Vio. Nay, that's certain: they, that dally nicely
with words, may quickly make them wanton.

Clo. I would therefore, my sister had had no name,
sir.

Vio. Why, man? 20

Clo. Why, sir, her name 's a word; and to dally
with that word, might make my sister wanton. But,
indeed, words are very rascals, since bonds disgraced
them.

Vio. Thy reason, man?

Clo. Troth, sir, I can yield you none without words:
and words are grown so false, I am loath to prove
reason with them.

Vio. I warrant, thou art a merry fellow, and carest
for nothing. 30

Clo. Not so, sir, I do care for something; but in my
conscience, sir, I do not care for you: if that be to
care for nothing, sir, I would it would make you
invisible.

Vio. Art not thou the Lady Olivia's fool?

Clo. No, indeed, sir ; the Lady Olivia has no folly :
she will keep no fool, sir, till she be married ; and
fools are as like husbands, as pilchards are to herrings,
the husband 's the bigger. I am, indeed, not her fool,
but her corrupter of words.   40
Vio. I saw thee late at the Count Orsino's.
Clo. Foolery, sir, does walk about the orb, like the
sun : it shines everywhere. I would be sorry, sir, but
the fool should be as oft with your master, as with my
mistress. I think I saw your wisdom there.
Vio. Nay, an thou pass upon me, I 'll no more with
thee. Hold, there 's expenses for thee.
Clo. Now Jove, in his next commodity of hair, send
thee a beard.
Vio. By my troth, I 'll tell thee : I am almost sick for
one, though I would not have it grow on my chin. Is
thy lady within ?   52
Clo. Would not a pair of these have bred, sir ?
Vio. Yes, being kept together, and put to use.
Clo. I would play Lord Pandarus of Phrygia, sir, to
bring a Cressida to this Troilus.
Vio. I understand you, sir, 't is well begg'd.
Clo. The matter, I hope, is not great, sir, begging
but a beggar : Cressida was a beggar. My lady is
within, sir. I will construe to them whence you
come ; who you are, and what you would, are out of
my welkin : I might say, element, but the word is
overworn.   [*Exit.*
Vio. This fellow 's wise enough to play the fool,
And to do that well craves a kind of wit :
He must observe their mood on whom he jests,
The quality of persons, and the time,
And, like the haggard, check at every feather
That comes before his eye. This is a practice
As full of labour as a wise man's art :   70
For folly, that he wisely shows, is fit,
But wise men, folly-fallen, quite taint their wit.

Enter Sir TOBY BELCH *and Sir* ANDREW
AGUE-CHEEK.

Sir To. 'Save you, gentleman.
Vio. And you, sir.
Sir And. Dieu vous garde, monsieur.
Vio. Et vous aussi: votre serviteur.
Sir And. I hope, sir, you are ; and I am yours.
Sir To. Will you encounter the house ? my niece is
desirous you should enter, if your trade be to her.
Vio. I am bound to your niece, sir : I mean, she is
the list of my voyage.   81
Sir To. Taste your legs, sir : put them to motion.
Vio. My legs do better understand me, sir, than I
understand what you mean by bidding me taste my
legs.
Sir To. I mean, to go, sir, to enter.
Vio. I will answer you with gait and entrance. But
we are prevented.

Enter OLIVIA *and* MARIA.

Most excellent accomplished lady, the heavens rain
odours on you !   90
Sir And. That youth 's a rare courtier. "Rain
odours !" well.
Vio. My matter hath no voice, lady, but to your own
most pregnant and vouchsafed ear.
Sir And. "Odours," "pregnant," and "vouchsafed :"
—I 'll get 'em all three all ready.
Oli. Let the garden door be shut, and leave me to
my hearing. [*Exeunt Sir* TOBY, *Sir* ANDREW, *and*
MARIA.] Give me your hand, sir.
Vio. My duty, madam, and most humble service.
Oli. What is your name ?   101
Vio. Cesario is your servant's name, fair princess.
Oli. My servant, sir ? 'T was never merry world,
Since lowly feigning was call'd compliment.
You 're servant to the Count Orsino, youth.
Vio. And he is yours, and his must needs be yours :
Your servant's servant is your servant, madam.
Oli. For him, I think not on him : for his thoughts,
'Would they were blanks, rather than fill'd with me !
Vio. Madam, I come to whet your gentle thoughts
On his behalf :—
Oli.   O ! by your leave, I pray you :   111

I bade you never speak again of him ;
But, would you undertake another suit,
I had rather hear you to solicit that,
Than music from the spheres.
Vio.   Dear lady,—
Oli. Give me leave, 'beseech you. I did send
After the last enchantment you did here,
A ring in chase of you : so did I abuse
Myself, my servant, and, I fear me, you,
Under your hard construction must I sit,   120
To force that on you, in a shameful cunning,
Which you knew none of yours : what might you
        think ?
Have you not set mine honour at the stake,
And baited it with all the unmuzzled thoughts
That tyrannous heart can think ? To one of your
        receiving
Enough is shown ; a cyprus, not a bosom,
Hides my heart. So, let me hear you speak.
Vio. I pity you.
Oli.   That 's a degree to love.
Vio. No, not a grise ; for 't is a vulgar proof,
That very oft we pity enemies.   130
Oli. Why then, methinks, 't is time to smile again.
O world, how apt the poor are to be proud !
If one should be a prey, how much the better
To fall before the lion than the wolf ! [*Clock strikes.*
The clock upbraids me with the waste of time.—
Be not afraid, good youth, I will not have you ;
And yet, when wit and youth is come to harvest,
Your wife is like to reap a proper man.
There lies your way due west.
Vio.   Then westward-ho !
Grace, and good disposition attend your ladyship !   140
You 'll nothing, madam, to my lord by me ?
Oli. Stay :
I pr'ythee, tell me what thou think'st of me.
Vio. That you do think, you are not what you are.
Oli. If I think so, I think the same of you.
Vio. Then think you right : I am not what I am.
Oli. I would, you were as I would have you be !
Vio. Would it be better, madam, than I am ?
I wish it might ; for now I am your fool.
Oli. O ! what a deal of scorn looks beautiful   150
In the contempt and anger of his lip !
A murderous guilt shows not itself more soon,
Than love that would seem hid : love's night is noon.
Cesario, by the roses of the spring,
By maidhood, honour, truth, and everything,
I love thee so, that, maugre all thy pride,
Nor wit, nor reason, can my passion hide.
Do not extort thy reasons from this clause,
For that I woo, thou therefore hast no cause ;
But rather, reason thus with reason fetter :   160
Love sought is good, but given unsought is better.
Vio. By innocence I swear, and by my youth,
I have one heart, one bosom, and one truth,
And that no woman has ; nor never none
Shall mistress be of it, save I alone.
And so adieu, good madam : never more
Will I my master's tears to you deplore.
Oli. Yet come again, for thou perhaps may'st move
That heart, which now abhors, to like his love.
                                        [*Exeunt.*

SCENE II.—*A Room in* OLIVIA'S *House.*

Enter Sir TOBY BELCH, *Sir* ANDREW AGUE-CHEEK,
and FABIAN.

Sir And. No, faith, I 'll not stay a jot longer.
Sir To. Thy reason, dear venom : give thy reason.
Fab. You must needs yield your reason, Sir Andrew.
Sir And. Marry, I saw your niece do more favours
to the count's serving-man, than ever she bestowed
upon me : I saw 't i' the orchard.
Sir To. Did she see thee the while, old boy ? tell me
that.
Sir And. As plain as I see you now.
Fab. This was a great argument of love in her
toward you.   11
Sir And. Slight ! will you make an ass o' me ?

Fab. I will prove it legitimate, sir, upon the oaths of judgment and reason.

Sir To. And they have been grand-jurymen, since before Noah was a sailor.

Fab. She did show favour to the youth in your sight only to exasperate you, to awake your dormouse valour, to put fire in your heart, and brimstone in your liver. You should then have accosted her, and with some excellent jests, fire-new from the mint, you should have banged the youth into dumbness. This was looked for at your hand, and this was balked: the double gilt of this opportunity you let time wash off, and you are now sailed into the north of my lady's opinion; where you will hang like an icicle on a Dutchman's beard, unless you do redeem it by some laudable attempt, either of valour, or policy.

Sir And. An't be any way, it must be with valour, for policy I hate: I had as lief be a Brownist as a politician.   31

Sir To. Why then, build me thy fortunes upon the basis of valour: challenge me the count's youth to fight with him; hurt him in eleven places: my niece shall take note of it; and assure thyself, there is no love-broker in the world can more prevail in man's commendation with woman, than report of valour.

Fab. There is no way but this, Sir Andrew.

Sir And. Will either of you bear me a challenge to him?   40

Sir To. Go, write it in a martial hand; be curst and brief; it is no matter how witty, so it be eloquent, and full of invention: taunt him with the license of ink: if thou thou'st him some thrice, it shall not be amiss; and as many lies as will lie in thy sheet of paper, although the sheet were big enough for the bed of Ware in England, set 'em down. Go, about it. Let there be gall enough in thy ink, though thou write with a goose-pen, no matter. About it.

Sir And. Where shall I find you?   50

Sir To. We'll call thee at the *cubiculo.* Go.

[*Exit Sir* ANDREW.

Fab. This is a dear manakin to you, Sir Toby.

Sir To. I have been dear to him, lad; some two thousand strong, or so.

Fab. We shall have a rare letter from him; but you'll not deliver it?

Sir To. Never trust me then; and by all means stir on the youth to an answer. I think, oxen and wainropes cannot hale them together. For Andrew, if he were opened, and you find so much blood in his liver as will clog the foot of a flea, I'll eat the rest of the anatomy.   62

Fab. And his opposite, the youth, bears in his visage no great presage of cruelty.

Enter MARIA.

Sir To. Look, where the youngest wren of nine comes.

Mar. If you desire the spleen, and will laugh yourselves into stitches, follow me. Yond gull Malvolio is turned heathen, a very renegado; for there is no Christian, that means to be saved by believing rightly, can ever believe such impossible passages of grossness. He's in yellow stockings.   72

Sir To. And cross-gartered?

Mar. Most villainously; like a pedant that keeps a school i' the church.—I have dogged him like his murderer. He does obey every point of the letter that I dropped to betray him: he does smile his face into more lines, than are in the new map, with the augmentation of the Indies. You have not seen such a thing as 'tis; I can hardly forbear hurling things at him. I know, my lady will strike him: if she do, he'll smile, and take't for a great favour.   82

Sir To. Come, bring us, bring us where he is.

———   [*Exeunt.*

SCENE III.—A Street.

Enter SEBASTIAN *and* ANTONIO.

Seb. I would not, by my will, have troubled you; But, since you make your pleasure of your pains, I will no further chide you.

Ant. I could not stay behind you: my desire, More sharp than filed steel, did spur me forth; And not all love to see you (though so much, As might have drawn one to a longer voyage), But jealousy what might befall your travel, Being skilless in these parts; which to a stranger, Unguided, and unfriended, often prove   10 Rough and unhospitable: my willing love, The rather by these arguments of fear, Set forth in your pursuit.

Seb.   My kind Antonio, I can no other answer make, but, thanks, And thanks, and ever thanks; and oft good turns Are shuffled off with such uncurrent pay; But, were my worth, as is my conscience, firm, You should find better dealing. What's to do? Shall we go see the reliques of this town?

Ant. To-morrow, sir: best first go see your lodging.

Seb. I am not weary, and 'tis long to night.   21 I pray you, let us satisfy our eyes With the memorials, and the things of fame, That do renown this city.

Ant.   'Would, you'd pardon me: I do not without danger walk these streets. Once, in a sea-fight 'gainst the count his galleys, I did some service; of such note, indeed, That, were I ta'en here, it would scarce be answer'd.

Seb. Belike, you slew great number of his people.

Ant. The offence is not of such a bloody nature,   30 Albeit the quality of the time, and quarrel, Might well have given us bloody argument. It might have since been answer'd in repaying What we took from them; which, for traffic's sake, Most of your city did: only myself stood out; For which, if I be lapsed in this place, I shall pay dear.

Seb.   Do not then walk too open.

Ant. It doth not fit me. Hold, sir; here's my purse. In the south suburbs, at the Elephant, Is best to lodge: I will bespeak our diet,   40 Whiles you beguile the time, and feed your knowledge, With viewing of the town: there shall you have me.

Seb. Why I your purse?

Ant. Haply your eye shall light upon some toy You have desire to purchase; and your store, I think, is not for idle markets, sir.

Seb. I'll be your purse-bearer, and leave you for an hour.

Ant. To the Elephant.—

Seb. I do remember.   ———   50

[*Exeunt.*

SCENE IV.—OLIVIA'S Garden.

Enter OLIVIA *and* MARIA.

Oli. I have sent after him: he says, he'll come; How shall I feast him? what bestow of him? For youth is bought more oft, than begg'd, or borrow'd. I speak too loud.— Where is Malvolio?—he is sad, and civil, And suits well for a servant with my fortunes.— Where is Malvolio?

Mar. He's coming, madam; but in very strange manner. He is sure possess'd, madam.

Oli. Why, what's the matter? does he rave?   10

Mar. No, madam; he does nothing but smile: your ladyship were best to have some guard about you, if he come, for sure the man is tainted in his wits.

Oli. Go call him hither.—I am as mad as he, If sad and merry madness equal be.—

Enter MALVOLIO.

How now, Malvolio?

Mal. Sweet lady, ho, ho.

Oli. Smil'st thou?

I sent for thee upon a sad occasion.   19

Mal. Sad, lady? I could be sad. This does make some obstruction in the blood, this cross-gartering; but what of that? if it please the eye of one, it is with me as the very true sonnet is, "Please one, and please all."

Oli. Why, how dost thou, man? what is the matter with thee?

Mal. Not black in my mind, though yellow in my legs. It did come to his hands, and commands shall be executed: I think we do know the sweet Roman hand. 30

Mar. Why appear you with this ridiculous boldness before my lady? 40

Mal. "Be not afraid of greatness:"—'t was well writ.

Oli. What meanest thou by that, Malvolio?

Mal. "Some are born great,"—

Oli. Ha?

Oli. " Why dost thou smile so, and kiss thy hand so oft?"

Oli. Wilt thou go to bed, Malvolio?

Mal. To bed? ay, sweet-heart, and I'll come to thee.

Oli. God comfort thee! Why dost thou smile so, and kiss thy hand so oft?

Mar. How do you, Malvolio?

Mal. At your request? Yes; nightingales answer daws.

Mal. "Some achieve greatness,"—

Oli. What say'st thou?

Mal. "And some have greatness thrust upon them."

Oli. Heaven restore thee!

Mal. "Remember, who commended thy yellow stockings,"— 50

Oli. Thy yellow stockings?

Mal. "And wished to see thee cross-gartered."

Oli. Cross-gartered?

Mal. "Go to, thou art made, if thou desirest to be so:"—

Oli. Am I made?

Mal. "If not, let me see thee a servant still."

Oli. Why, this is very midsummer madness.

Enter Servant.

Serv. Madam, the young gentleman of the Count Orsino's is returned. I could hardly entreat him back: he attends your ladyship's pleasure.

Oli. I'll come to him. [*Exit Servant.*] Good Maria, let this fellow be looked to. Where's my cousin Toby? Let some of my people have a special care of him. I would not have him miscarry for the half of my dowry.   61

[*Exeunt* OLIVIA *and* MARIA.

Mal. Oh, ho! do you come near me now? no worse man than Sir Toby to look to me? This concurs directly with the letter: she sends him on purpose, that I may appear stubborn to him; for she incites me to that in the letter. "Cast thy humble slough," says she;—"be opposite with a kinsman, surly with servants,—let thy tongue tang with arguments of state, put thyself into the trick of singularity;"—and consequently sets down the manner how; as, a sad face, a reverend carriage, a slow tongue, in the habit of some sir of note, and so forth. I have limed her; but it is Jove's doing, and Jove make me thankful! And when she went away now, "Let this fellow be looked to:" fellow! not Malvolio, nor after my degree, but fellow. Why, everything adheres together, that no drachm of a scruple, no scruple of a scruple, no obstacle, no incredulous or unsafe circumstance.—What can be said? Nothing that can be, can come between me and the full prospect of my hopes. Well, Jove, not I, is the doer of this, and he is to be thanked.

Re-enter MARIA, *with Sir* TOBY BELCH *and* FABIAN.

Sir To. Which way is he, in the name of sanctity? If all the devils of hell be drawn in little, and Legion himself possessed him, yet I'll speak to him.

Fab. Here he is, here he is.—How is't with you, sir? how is't with you, man?   90

Mal. Go off; I discard you: let me enjoy my private; go off.

Mar. Lo, how hollow the fiend speaks within him! did not I tell you?—Sir Toby, my lady prays you to have a care of him.

Mal. Ah, ha! does she so?

Sir To. Go to, go to: peace! peace! we must deal gently with him; let me alone.—How do you, Malvolio? how is't with you? What, man! defy the devil: consider, he's an enemy to mankind.   100

Mal. Do you know what you say?

Mar. La you! an you speak ill of the devil, how he takes it at heart! Pray God, he be not bewitched!

Fab. Carry his water to the wise-woman.

Mar. Marry, and it shall be done to-morrow morning, if I live. My lady would not lose him for more than I'll say.

Mal. How now, mistress?

Mar. O Lord!   109

Sir To. Pr'ythee, hold thy peace: this is not the way. Do you not see you move him? let me alone with him.

Fab. No way but gentleness; gently, gently: the fiend is rough, and will not be roughly used.

Sir To. Why, how now, my bawcock? how dost thou, chuck?

Mal. Sir!

Sir To. Ay, Biddy, come with me. What, man! 'tis not for gravity to play at cherry-pit with Satan. Hang him, foul collier!

Mar. Get him to say his prayers: good Sir Toby, get him to pray.   121

Mal. My prayers, minx!

Mar. No, I warrant you; he will not hear of godliness.

Mal. Go, hang yourselves all! you are idle shallow things: I am not of your element. You shall know more hereafter.   [*Exit.*

Sir To. Is't possible?

Fab. If this were played upon a stage now, I could condemn it as an improbable fiction.

Sir To. His very genius hath taken the infection of the device, man.   131

Mar. Nay, pursue him now, lest the device take air, and taint.

Fab. Why, we shall make him mad, indeed.

Mar. The house will be the quieter.

Sir To. Come, we'll have him in a dark room, and bound. My niece is already in the belief that he's mad: we may carry it thus, for our pleasure, and his penance, till our very pastime, tired out of breath, prompt us to have mercy on him; at which time we will bring the device to the bar, and crown thee for a finder of madmen. But see, but see.   142

Enter Sir ANDREW AGUE-CHEEK.

Fab. More matter for a May morning.

Sir And. Here's the challenge; read it: I warrant, there's vinegar and pepper in't.

Fab. Is't so saucy?

Sir And. Ay, is't, I warrant him: do but read.

Sir To. Give me. [*Reads.*] "Youth; whatsoever thou art, thou art but a scurvy fellow."

Fab. Good, and valiant.   150

Sir To. "Wonder not, nor admire not in thy mind, why I do call thee so, for I will show thee no reason for't."

Fab. A good note, that keeps you from the blow of the law.

Sir To. "Thou comest to the Lady Olivia; and in my sight she uses thee kindly: but thou liest in thy throat; that is not the matter I challenge thee for."

Fab. Very brief, and to exceeding good sense--less.

Sir To. "I will waylay thee going home; where, if it be thy chance to kill me,"—   161

Fab. Good.

Sir To. "Thou killest me like a rogue and a villain."

Fab. Still you keep o' the windy side of the law: good.

Sir To. "Fare thee well; and God have mercy upon one of our souls! He may have mercy upon mine, but my hope is better; and so look to thyself. Thy friend, as thou usest him, and thy sworn enemy, ANDREW AGUE-CHEEK."—If this letter move him not, his legs cannot. I'll give't him.   171

Mar. You may have very fit occasion for't: he is now in some commerce with my lady, and will by-and-by depart.

Sir To. Go, Sir Andrew; scout me for him at the corner of the orchard, like a bum-bailie. So soon as ever thou seest him, draw, and, as thou drawest, swear horrible; for it comes to pass oft, that a terrible oath, with a swaggering accent, sharply twanged off, gives manhood more approbation than ever proof itself would have earned him. Away!   181

Sir And. Nay, let me alone for swearing.   [*Exit.*

Sir To. Now will not I deliver his letter: for the behaviour of the young gentleman gives him out to be of good capacity and breeding: his employment between his lord and my niece confirms no less; therefore this letter, being so excellently ignorant, will breed no terror in the youth: he will find it comes from a clodpole. But, sir, I will deliver his challenge by word of mouth; set upon Ague-cheek a notable report of valour, and drive the gentleman (as, I know, his youth will aptly receive it) into a most hideous opinion of his rage, skill, fury, and impetuosity. This will so fright them both, that they will kill one another by the look, like cockatrices.

Fab. Here he comes with your niece. Give them way, till he take leave, and presently after him.

Sir To. I will meditate the while upon some horrid message for a challenge.

[*Exeunt Sir* TOBY, FABIAN, *and* MARIA.

Re-enter OLIVIA, *with* VIOLA.

Oli. I have said too much unto a heart of stone,   200
And laid mine honour too unchary out:
There's something in me that reproves my fault,
But such a headstrong potent fault it is,
That it but mocks reproof.

Vio. With the same 'haviour that your passion bears,
Goes on my master's grief.

Oli. Here; wear this jewel for me: 't is my picture.
Refuse it not, it hath no tongue to vex you;
And, I beseech you, come again to-morrow.
What shall you ask of me, that I 'll deny,   210
That honour, sav'd, may upon asking give?
  Vio. Nothing but this; your true love for my
      master.
  Oli. How with mine honour may I give him that,
Which I have given to you?
  Vio.   I will acquit you.
  Oli. Well, come again to-morrow. Fare thee well:
A fiend like thee might bear my soul to hell.   [*Exit.*

Re-enter Sir TOBY BELCH, and FABIAN.

  Sir To. Gentleman, God save thee.
  Vio. And you, sir.   218
  Sir To. That defence thou hast,
betake thee to 't: of what nature
the wrongs are thou hast done
him, I know not; but thy inter-
cepter, full of despite, bloody as the
hunter, attends thee at the orchard-
end. Dismount thy tuck; be yare
in thy preparation, for thy assailant
is quick, skilful, and deadly.
  Vio. You mistake, sir: I am sure,
no man hath any quarrel to me.
My remembrance is very free and
clear from any image of offence
done to any man.   232
  Sir To. You 'll find it otherwise,
I assure you: therefore, if you hold
your life at any price, betake you to
your guard; for your opposite hath
in him what youth, strength, skill,
and wrath, can furnish man withal.
  Vio. I pray you, sir, what is he?
  Sir To. He is knight, dubbed
with unhatch'd rapier, and on
carpet consideration; but he is a devil in private
brawl; souls and bodies hath he divorced three, and
his incensement at this moment is so implacable,
that satisfaction can be none but by pangs of death
and sepulchre. Hob, nob, is his word: give 't, or
take 't.
  Vio. I will return again into the house, and desire
some conduct of the lady: I am no fighter. I have
heard of some kind of men, that put quarrels purposely
on others to taste their valour; belike, this is a man
of that quirk.   252
  Sir To. Sir, no; his indignation derives itself out of
a very competent injury: therefore, get you on, and
give him his desire. Back you shall not to the house,
unless you undertake that with me, which with as
much safety you might answer him: therefore, on, or
strip your sword stark naked; for meddle you must,
that 's certain, or forswear to wear iron about you.
  Vio. This is as uncivil, as strange. I beseech you,
do me this courteous office, as to know of the knight
what my offence to him is: it is something of my
negligence, nothing of my purpose.   263
  Sir To. I will do so. Signior Fabian, stay you by
this gentleman till my return.   [*Exit.*
  Vio. Pray you, sir, do you know of this matter?
  Fab. I know, the knight is incensed against you,
even to a mortal arbitrement, but nothing of the
circumstance more.
  Vio. I beseech you, what manner of man is he? 270
  Fab. Nothing of that wonderful promise, to read
him by his form, as you are like to find him in the
proof of his valour. He is, indeed, sir, the most skilful,
bloody, and fatal opposite that you could possibly
have found in any part of Illyria. Will you walk
towards him? I will make your peace with him, if
I can.
  Vio. I shall be much bound to you for 't: I am one,
that would rather go with sir priest, than sir knight:
I care not who knows so much of my mettle.   280
      [*Exeunt.*

Re-enter Sir TOBY, with Sir ANDREW.

  Sir To. Why, man, he 's a very devil, I have not
seen such a firago. I had a pass with him, rapier,
scabbard, and all, and he gives me the stuck-in with
such a mortal motion, that it is inevitable; and on the
answer, he pays you as surely as your feet hit the
ground they step on. They say, he has been fencer to
the Sophy.
  Sir And. Pox on 't, I 'll not meddle with him.
  Sir To. Ay, but he will not now be pacified: Fabian
can scarce hold him yonder.   290
  Sir And. Plague on 't; an I thought he had been
valiant, and so cunning in fence, I 'd have seen him
damned ere I 'd have challenged him. Let him let the
matter slip, and I 'll give him my horse, grey Capilet.
  Sir To. I 'll make the motion. Stand here; make a
good show on 't. This shall end without the perdition

Sir To. "Come, Sir Andrew, there's no remedy."

of souls. [*Aside.*] Marry, I 'll ride your horse as well
as I ride you.

Re-enter FABIAN and VIOLA.

  [*To* FABIAN.] I have his horse to take up the quarrel.
I have persuaded him, the youth 's a devil.   300
  Fab. [*To Sir* TOBY.] He is as horribly conceited of
him; and pants, and looks pale, as if a bear were at
his heels.
  Sir To. [*To* VIOLA.] There 's no remedy, sir: he
will fight with you for 's oath sake. Marry, he hath
better bethought him of his quarrel, and he finds that
now scarce to be worth talking of: therefore draw for
the supportance of his vow: he protests, he will not
hurt you.
  Vio. [*Aside.*] Pray God defend me! A little thing
would make me tell them how much I lack of a man.
  Fab. Give ground, if you see him furious.   312
  Sir To. Come, Sir Andrew, there 's no remedy: the
gentleman will, for his honour's sake, have one bout
with you: he cannot, by the duello avoid it; but he
has promised me, as he is a gentleman and a soldier,
he will not hurt you. Come on; to 't.
  Sir And. Pray God, he keep his oath!   [*Draws.*
  Vio. I do assure you, 't is against my will.   [*Draws.*

Enter ANTONIO.

  Ant. Put up your sword.—If this young gentleman
Have done offence, I take the fault on me: 321
If you offend him, I for him defy you.   [*Drawing.*
  Sir To. You, sir? why, what are you?
  Ant. One, sir, that for his love dares yet do more,
Than you have heard him brag to you he will.
  Sir To. Nay, if you be an undertaker, I am for you.
      [*Draws.*
  Fab. O good Sir Toby, hold! here come the officers.
  Sir To. I 'll be with you anon.
  Vio. Pray, sir, put your sword up, if you please.
  Sir And. Marry, will I, sir:—and, for that I pro-
mised you, I 'll be as good as my word. He will bear
you easily, and reins well.   332

Enter two Officers.

  1 *Off.* This is the man: do thy office.

2 *Off.* Antonio, I arrest thee at the suit
Of Count Orsino.
　　Ant.　　　　　You do mistake me, sir.
1 *Off.* No, sir, no jot : I know your favour well,
Though now you have no sea-cap on your head.—
Take him away : he knows, I know him well.
　　Ant. I must obey.—[*To* VIOLA.] This comes with
　　　seeking you ;
But there 's no remedy : I shall answer it.　　340
What will you do ? Now my necessity
Makes me to ask you for my purse. It grieves me
Much more for what I cannot do for you,
Than what befalls myself. You stand amaz'd ;
But be of comfort.
　　2 *Off.* Come, sir, away.
　　Ant. I must entreat of you some of that money.
　　Vio. What money, sir ?
For the fair kindness you have show'd me here.
And part, being prompted by your present trouble, 350
Out of my lean and low ability
I 'll lend you something. My having is not much :
I 'll make division of my present with you.
Hold, there is half my coffer.
　　Ant.　　　　　Will you deny me now ?
Is 't possible, that my deserts to you
Can lack persuasion ? Do not tempt my misery,
Lest that it make me so unsound a man,
As to upbraid you with those kindnesses
That I have done for you.
　　Vio.　　　　　I know of none ;
Nor know I you by voice, or any feature.　　360
I hate ingratitude more in a man,
Than lying vainness, babbling drunkenness,
Or any taint of vice, whose strong corruption
Inhabits our frail blood.
　　Ant.　　　　　O heavens themselves !
2 *Off.* Come, sir : I pray you, go.
　　Ant. Let me speak a little. This youth, that you see
　　　here,

I snatch'd one half out of the jaws of death,
Reliev'd him with such sanctity of love,
And to his image, which, methought, did promise
Most venerable worth, did I devotion.　　370
1 *Off.* What 's that to us ? The time goes by : away !
　　Ant. But, O, how vile an idol proves this god !—
Thou hast, Sebastian, done good feature shame.
In nature there 's no blemish, but the mind ;
None can be call'd deform'd, but the unkind :
Virtue is beauty ; but the beauteous-evil
Are empty trunks, o'erflourish'd by the devil.
1 *Off.* The man grows mad : away with him !
Come, come, sir.
　　Ant. Lead me on. [*Exeunt Officers with* ANTONIO.
　　Vio. Methinks, his words do from such passion fly,
That he believes himself ; so do not I.　　382
Prove true, imagination, O, prove true,
That I, dear brother, be now ta'en for you !
　　Sir To. Come hither, knight ; come hither, Fabian :
we 'll whisper o'er a couplet or two of most sage saws.
　　Vio. He nam'd Sebastian : I my brother know
Yet living in my glass ; even such, and so,
In favour was my brother ; and he went
Still in this fashion, colour, ornament,　　390
For him I imitate. O ! if it prove,
Tempests are kind, and salt waves fresh in love !
　　　　　　　　　　　　　　　　[*Exit.*
　　Sir To. A very dishonest paltry boy, and more a
coward than a hare. His dishonesty appears in
leaving his friend here in necessity, and denying him ;
and for his cowardship, ask Fabian.
　　Fab. A coward, a most devout coward, religious
in it.
　　Sir And. 'Slid, I 'll after him again, and beat him.
　　Sir To. Do ; cuff him soundly, but never draw thy
sword.　　401
　　Sir And. An I do not,—　　　　　[*Exit.*
　　Fab. Come, let 's see the event.
　　Sir To. I dare lay any money 't will be nothing yet.
　　　　　　　　　　　　　　　　　　[*Exeunt.*

ACT IV.

SCENE I.—The Street before OLIVIA's House.

Enter SEBASTIAN *and Clown.*

　　Clown.
I LL you make me believe
that I am not sent for you ?
　　Seb. Go to, go to ; thou art a foolish
　　　fellow :
Let me be clear of thee.
　　Clo. Well held out ; i'faith ! No, I do
not know you ; nor I am not sent to
you by my lady to bid you come speak
with her ; nor your name is not Master
Cesario ; nor this is not my nose neither.
—Nothing, that is so, is so.　　10
　　Seb. I pr'ythee, vent thy folly some-
　　　where else :
Thou know'st not me.
　　Clo. Vent my folly ! He has heard that word of
some great man, and now applies it to a fool. Vent
my folly ! I am afraid this great lubber, the world,
will prove a cockney. I pr'ythee now, ungird thy
strangeness, and tell me what I shall vent to my lady.
Shall I vent to her that thou art coming ?
　　Seb. I pr'ythee, foolish Greek, depart from me.

There 's money for thee : if you tarry longer,　　20
I shall give worse payment.
　　Clo. By my troth, thou hast an open hand.—These
wise men, that give fools money, get themselves a
good report after fourteen years' purchase.

Enter Sir ANDREW.

　　Sir And. Now, sir, have I met you again ? there 's
for you.　　　　　　　　　[*Striking* SEBASTIAN.
　　Seb. Why, there 's for thee, and there, and there.
Are all the people mad ?　　[*Beating Sir* ANDREW.

Enter Sir TOBY *and* FABIAN.

　　Sir To. Hold, sir, or I 'll throw your dagger o'er the
house.　　30
　　Clo. This will I tell my lady straight. I would not
be in some of your coats for twopence.　　[*Exit.*
　　Sir To. Come on, sir : hold.
　　Sir And. Nay, let him alone ; I 'll go another way
to work with him : I 'll have an action of battery
against him, if there be any law in Illyria. Though I
struck him first, yet it 's no matter for that.

Seb. Let go thy hand.

Sir To. Come, sir, I will not let you go. Come, my young soldier, put up your iron: you are well fleshed. Come on.   41

Seb. I will be free from thee. What wouldst thou now?

If thou dar'st tempt me further, draw thy sword.

Sir To. "Come, my young soldier, put up your iron."

Sir To. What, what! Nay, then I must have an ounce or two of this malapert blood from you.
                                                         [*Draws.*

Enter OLIVIA.

Oli. Hold, Toby! on thy life I charge thee, hold!

Sir To. Madam!

Oli. Will it be ever thus? Ungracious wretch!
Fit for the mountains, and the barbarous caves,
Where manners ne'er were preach'd. Out of my sight!—   50
Be not offended, dear Cesario.—
Rudesby, be gone!

    [*Exeunt Sir* TOBY, *Sir* ANDREW, *and* FABIAN.

              I pr'ythee, gentle friend,
Let thy fair wisdom, not thy passion, sway
In this uncivil and unjust extent
Against thy peace. Go with me to my house;
And hear thou there how many fruitless pranks
This ruffian hath botch'd up, that thou thereby
May'st smile at this. Thou shalt not choose but go:
Do not deny. Beshrew his soul for me,
He started one poor heart of mine in thee.   60

Seb. What relish is in this? how runs the stream?
Or I am mad, or else this is a dream.
Let fancy still my sense in Lethe steep;
If it be thus to dream, still let me sleep.

Oli. Nay; come, I pr'ythee. 'Would thou'dst be rul'd by me!

Seb. Madam, I will.

Oli.   O! say so, and so be. [*Exeunt.*

SCENE II.—A Room in OLIVIA'S House.

Enter MARIA *and Clown.*

Mar. Nay, I pr'ythee, put on this gown, and this beard: make him believe thou art Sir Topas the curate: do it quickly; I'll call Sir Toby the whilst.
                                                         [*Exit.*

Clo. Well, I'll put it on, and I will dissemble myself in't: and I would I were the first that ever dissembled in such a gown. I am not tall enough to become the function well, nor lean enough to be thought a good student; but to be said an honest man, and a good housekeeper, goes as fairly as to say a careful man, and a great scholar. The competitors enter.   11

Enter Sir TOBY BELCH *and* MARIA.

Sir To. Jove bless thee, master parson.

Clo. *Bonos dies,* Sir Toby: for as the old hermit of Prague, that never saw pen and ink, very wittily said to a niece of King Gorboduc, "That, that is, is;" so I, being master parson, am master parson, for what is that, but that? and is, but is?

Sir To. To him, Sir Topas.

Clo. What, ho! I say.—Peace in this prison.

Sir To. The knave counterfeits well; a good knave.

Mal. [*Within.*] Who calls there?   21

Clo. Sir Topas, the curate, who comes to visit Malvolio the lunatic.

Mal. Sir Topas, Sir Topas, good Sir Topas, go to my lady.

Clo. Out, hyperbolical fiend! how vexest thou this man! Talkest thou nothing but of ladies?

Sir To. Well said, master parson.

Mal. Sir Topas, never was man thus wronged. Good Sir Topas, do not think I am mad: they have laid me here in hideous darkness.   31

Clo. Fie, thou dishonest Satan! I call thee by the most modest terms; for I am one of those gentle ones, that will use the devil himself with courtesy. Sayest thou, that house is dark?

Mal. As hell, Sir Topas.

Clo. Why, it hath bay-windows transparent as barricadoes, and the clear-stories towards the south-north are as lustrous as ebony; and yet complainest thou of obstruction?   40

Mal. I am not mad, Sir Topas. I say to you, this house is dark.

Clo. Madman, thou errest: I say, there is no darkness but ignorance, in which thou art more puzzled than the Egyptians in their fog.

Mal. I say, this house is as dark as ignorance, though ignorance were as dark as hell; and I say, there was never man thus abused. I am no more mad than you are: make the trial of it in any constant question.   50

Clo. What is the opinion of Pythagoras concerning wild-fowl?

Mal. That the soul of our grandam might haply inhabit a bird.

Clo. What thinkest thou of his opinion?

Clo. "What, ho! I say.—Peace in this prison."

Mal. I think nobly of the soul, and no way approve his opinion.

Clo. Fare thee well: remain thou still in darkness. Thou shalt hold the opinion of Pythagoras, ere I will allow of thy wits, and fear to kill a woodcock, lest thou dispossess the soul of thy grandam. Fare thee well.   62

Mal. Sir Topas! Sir Topas!—
Sir To. My most exquisite Sir Topas!
Clo. Nay, I am for all waters.
Mar. Thou mightst have done this without thy beard and gown: he sees thee not.
Sir To. To him in thine own voice, and bring me word how thou findest him: I would, we were well rid of this knavery. If he may be conveniently delivered, I would he were; for I am now so far in offence with my niece, that I cannot pursue with any safety this sport to the upshot. Come by-and-by to my chamber.   [*Exeunt Sir* TOBY *and* MARIA.
Clo. [*Singing.*] "Hey Robin, jolly Robin,
          Tell me how thy lady does.'
Mal. Fool,—
Clo. "My lady is unkind, perdy."
Mal. Fool,—
Clo. "Alas, why is she so?"   80
Mal. Fool, I say;—
Clo. "She loves another."—Who calls, ha?
Mal. Good fool, as ever thou wilt deserve well at my hand, help me to a candle, and pen, ink, and paper. As I am a gentleman, I will live to be thankful to thee for 't.
Clo. Master Malvolio!
Mal. Ay, good fool.
Clo. Alas, sir, how fell you besides your five wits?
Mal. Fool, there was never man so notoriously abused: I am as well in my wits, fool, as thou art.   91
Clo. But as well? then you are mad indeed, if you be no better in your wits than a fool.
Mal. They have here propertied me; keep me in darkness, send ministers to me, asses! and do all they can to face me out of my wits.
Clo. Advise you what you say: the minister is here. —Malvolio, Malvolio, thy wits the heavens restore! endeavour thyself to sleep, and leave thy vain bibble babble.   100
Mal. Sir Topas,—
Clo. Maintain no words with him, good fellow.— Who, I, sir? not I, sir. God b' wi' you, good Sir Topas.—Marry, Amen.—I will, sir, I will.
Mal. Fool, fool, fool, I say.
Clo. Alas, sir, be patient. What say you, sir? I am shent for speaking to you.
Mal. Good fool, help me to some light, and some paper: I tell thee, I am as well in my wits, as any man in Illyria.   110
Clo. Well-a-day, that you were, sir!
Mal. By this hand, I am. Good fool, some ink, paper, and light, and convey what I will set down to my lady: it shall advantage thee more than ever the bearing of letter did.
Clo. I will help you to 't. But tell me true, are you not mad indeed? or do you but counterfeit?
Mal. Believe me, I am not: I tell thee true.
Clo. Nay, I 'll ne'er believe a madman, till I see his brains. I will fetch you light, and paper, and ink. 120
Mal. Fool, I 'll requite it in the highest degree: I pr'ythee, be gone.

Clo.   I am gone, sir,
                    And anon, sir,
          I 'll be with you again,
                    In a trice,
                    Like to the old Vice,
          Your need to sustain;

          Who with dagger of lath,
          In his rage and his wrath,   130
               Cries, Ah, ha! to the devil:
          Like a mad lad,
          Pare thy nails, dad,
               Adieu, goodman drivel.   [*Exit.*

SCENE III.—OLIVIA'S Garden.

Enter SEBASTIAN.

Seb. This is the air; that is the glorious sun;
This pearl she gave me, I do feel 't and see 't;
And though 't is wonder that enwraps me thus,
Yet 't is not madness. Where 's Antonio then?
I could not find him at the Elephant;
Yet there he was, and there I found this credit,
That he did range the town to seek me out.
His counsel now might do me golden service:
For though my soul disputes well with my sense,
That this may be some error, but no madness,   10
Yet doth this accident and flood of fortune
So far exceed all instance, all discourse,
That I am ready to distrust mine eyes,
And wrangle with my reason, that persuades me
To any other trust but that I am mad,—
Or else the lady 's mad: yet, if 't were so,
She could not sway her house, command her fol-
          lowers,
Take and give back affairs, and their despatch,
With such a smooth, discreet, and stable bearing,
As, I perceive, she does. There 's something in 't, 20
That is deceivable. But here the lady comes.

Enter OLIVIA *and a Priest.*

Oli. Blame not this haste of mine. If you mean well,
Now go with me, and with this holy man,
Into the chantry by; there, before him,
And underneath that consecrated roof,
Plight me the full assurance of your faith;
That my most jealous and too doubtful soul
May live at peace. He shall conceal it,
Whiles you are willing it shall come to note,
What time we will our celebration keep   30
According to my birth.—What do you say?
Seb. I 'll follow this good man, and go with you,
And, having sworn truth, ever will be true.
Oli. Then lead the way, good father; and heavens so shine,
That they may fairly note this act of mine! [*Exeunt.*

ACT V.

SCENE I.—The Street before OLIVIA's House.

Enter Clown and FABIAN.

Fabian.

NOW, as thou lov'st me, let me see his letter.

Clo. Good Master Fabian, grant me another request.

Fab. Anything.

Clo. Do not desire to see this letter.

Fab. This is, to give a dog, and in recompense desire my dog again.

Enter DUKE, VIOLA, and Attendants.

Duke. Belong you to the Lady Olivia, friends?

Clo. Ay, sir; we are some of her trappings. 10

Duke. I know thee well: how dost thou, my good fellow?

Clo. Truly, sir, the better for my foes, and the worse for my friends.

Duke. Just the contrary; the better for thy friends.

Clo. No, sir, the worse.

Duke. How can that be? 17

Clo. Marry, sir, they praise me, and make an ass of me; now, my foes tell me plainly I am an ass: so that by my foes, sir, I profit in the knowledge of myself, and by my friends I am abused: so that, conclusions to be as kisses, if your four negatives make your two affirmatives, why then, the worse for my friends, and the better for my foes.

Duke. Why, this is excellent.

Clo. By my troth, sir, no; though it please you to be one of my friends.

Duke. Thou shalt not be the worse for me: there's gold.

Clo. But that it would be double-dealing, sir, I would you could make it another. 31

Duke. O, you give me ill counsel.

Clo. Put your grace in your pocket, sir, for this once; and let your flesh and blood obey it.

Duke. Well, I will be so much a sinner to be a double-dealer: there's another.

Clo. Primo, secundo, tertio, is a good play; and the old saying is, the third pays for all: the *triplex*, sir, is a good tripping measure; or the bells of Saint Bennet, sir, may put you in mind,—one, two, three. 40

Duke. You can fool no more money out of me at this throw: if you will let your lady know, I am here to speak with her, and bring her along with you, it may awake my bounty further.

Clo. Marry, sir, lullaby to your bounty, till I come again. I go, sir; but I would not have you to think, that my desire of having is the sin of covetousness: but, as you say, sir, let your bounty take a nap, I will awake it anon. *[Exit.*

Vio. Here comes the man, sir, that did rescue me.

Enter ANTONIO and Officers.

Duke. That face of his I do remember well; 51
Yet when I saw it last, it was besmear'd,
As black as Vulcan, in the smoke of war.
A bawbling vessel was he captain of,
For shallow draught and bulk unprizable,
With which such scathful grapple did he make
With the most noble bottom of our fleet,
That very envy, and the tongue of loss,
Cried fame and honour on him.—What's the matter?

1 Off. Orsino, this is that Antonio, 60
That took the Phœnix and her fraught from Candy:

And this is he, that did the Tiger board,
When your young nephew Titus lost his leg.
Here in the streets, desperate of shame and state,
In private brabble did we apprehend him.

Vio. He did me kindness, sir, drew on my side,
But, in conclusion, put strange speech upon me;
I know not what 't was but distraction.

Duke. Notable pirate, thou salt-water thief,
What foolish boldness brought thee to their mercies,
Whom thou, in terms so bloody, and so dear, 71
Hast made thine enemies?

Ant.   Orsino, noble sir,
Be pleas'd that I shake off these names you give me:
Antonio never yet was thief, or pirate,
Though, I confess, on base and ground enough,
Orsino's enemy. A witchcraft drew me hither:
That most ingrateful boy there, by your side,
From the rude sea's enrag'd and foamy mouth
Did I redeem; a wrack past hope he was:
His life I gave him, and did thereto add 80
My love, without retention, or restraint,
All his in dedication; for his sake
Did I expose myself, pure for his love,
Into the danger of this adverse town;
Drew to defend him, when he was beset:
Where being apprehended, his false cunning
(Not meaning to partake with me in danger)
Taught him to face me out of his acquaintance,
And grew a twenty-years-removed thing,
While one would wink, denied me mine own purse, 90
Which I had recommended to his use
Not half an hour before.

Vio.   How can this be?

Duke. When came he to this town?

Ant. To-day, my lord; and for three months before
(No interim, not a minute's vacancy),
Both day and night did we keep company.

Enter OLIVIA and Attendants.

Duke. Here comes the countess: now heaven walks on earth!—
But for thee, fellow; fellow, thy words are madness:
Three months this youth hath tended upon me;
But more of that anon.—Take him aside. 100

Oli. What would my lord, but that he may not have,
Wherein Olivia may seem serviceable?—
Cesario, you do not keep promise with me.

Vio. Madam?

Duke. Gracious Olivia,—

Oli. What do you say, Cesario?—Good my lord,—

Vio. My lord would speak, my duty hushes me.

Oli. If it be aught to the old tune, my lord,
It is as fat and fulsome to mine ear,
As howling after music.

Duke.   Still so cruel? 110

Oli. Still so constant, lord.

Duke. What, to perverseness? you uncivil lady,
To whose ingrate and inauspicious altars
My soul the faithfull'st offerings hath breath'd out,
That e'er devotion tender'd! What shall I do?

Oli. Even what it please my lord, that shall become him.

Duke. Why should I not, had I the heart to do it,
Like to the Egyptian thief at point of death,
Kill what I love? a savage jealousy,

That sometime savours nobly.—But hear me this : 120
Since you to non-regardance cast my faith,
And that I partly know the instrument
That screws me from my true place in your favour,
Live you, the marble-breasted tyrant, still ;
But this your minion, whom, I know, you love,
And whom, by Heaven I swear, I tender dearly,
Him will I tear out of that cruel eye,
Where he sits crowned in his master's spite.—
Come, boy, with me : my thoughts are ripe in mischief :
I 'll sacrifice the lamb that I do love,   130
To spite a raven's heart within a dove.
  Vio. And I, most jocund, apt, and willingly,
To do you rest, a thousand deaths would die.
  Oli. Where goes Cesario ?
  Vio.   After him I love,
More than I love these eyes, more than my life,
More, by all mores, than e'er I shall love wife.
If I do feign, you witnesses above,
Punish my life for tainting of my love !
  Oli. Ah me ! detested ! how am I beguil'd !
  Vio. Who does beguile you ? who does do you wrong ?
  Oli. Hast thou forgot thyself ? Is it so long ?   141
Call forth the holy father !   [*Exit an Attendant.*
  Duke. [*To* Viola.]   Come away.
  Oli. Whither, my lord ?—Cesario, husband, stay.
  Duke. Husband ?
  Oli.   Ay, husband : can he that deny ?
  Duke. Her husband, sirrah ?
  Vio.   No, my lord, not I.
  Oli. Alas ! it is the baseness of thy fear,
That makes thee strangle thy propriety.
Fear not, Cesario, take thy fortunes up ;
Be that thou know'st thou art, and then thou art
As great as that thou fear'st.

      Re-enter Attendant with the Priest.
                           O, welcome, father ! 150
Father, I charge thee, by thy reverence,
Here to unfold (though lately we intended
To keep in darkness) what occasion now
Reveals before 't is ripe) what thou dost know
Hath newly pass'd between this youth and me.
  Priest. A contract of eternal bond of love,
Confirm'd by mutual joinder of your hands,
Attested by the holy close of lips,
Strengthen'd by interchangement of your rings ;
And all the ceremony of this compact   160
Seal'd in my function, by my testimony :
Since when, my watch hath told me, toward my grave
I have travell'd but two hours.
  Duke. O thou dissembling cub ! what wilt thou be,
When time hath sow'd a grizzle on thy case ?
Or will not else thy craft so quickly grow,
That thine own trip shall be thine overthrow ?
Farewell, and take her ; but direct thy feet,
Where thou and I henceforth may never meet.
  Vio. My lord, I do protest,—
  Oli.   O ! do not swear !   170
Hold little faith, though thou hast too much fear.

        Enter Sir Andrew Ague-cheek.
  Sir And. For the love of God, a surgeon ! send one
presently to Sir Toby.
  Oli. What 's the matter ?
  Sir And. He has broke my head across, and has
given Sir Toby a bloody coxcomb too. For the love of
God, your help ! I had rather than forty pound I were
at home.
  Oli. Who has done this, Sir Andrew ?
  Sir And. The count's gentleman, one Cesario : we
took him for a coward, but he 's the very devil incar-
dinate.   182
  Duke. My gentleman, Cesario ?
  Sir And. Od's lifelings ! here he is.—You broke my
head for nothing ! and that that I did, I was set on to
do 't by Sir Toby.
  Vio. Why do you speak to me ? I never hurt you :
You drew your sword upon me, without cause ;
But I bespake you fair, and hurt you not.
  Sir And. If a bloody coxcomb be a hurt, you have
hurt me : I think you set nothing by a bloody coxcomb.

      Enter Sir Toby Belch *and Clown.*

Here comes Sir Toby halting ; you shall hear more :
but if he had not been in drink, he would have tickled
you othergates than he did.
  Duke. How now, gentleman ? how is 't with you ?
  Sir To. That 's all one : he has hurt me, and there 's
the end on 't.—Sot, didst see Dick surgeon, sot ?
  Clo. O ! he 's drunk, Sir Toby, an hour agone : his
eyes were set at eight i' the morning.
  Sir To. Then he 's a rogue, and a passy-measures
pavin. I hate a drunken rogue.   201
  Oli. Away with him ! Who hath made this havoc
with them ?
  Sir And. I 'll help you, Sir Toby, because we 'll be
dressed together.
  Sir To. Will you help ?—an ass-head, and a coxcomb,
and a knave, a thin-faced knave, a gull !
  Oli. Get him to bed ! and let his hurt be look'd to.
        [*Exeunt Clown, Sir* Toby, *and Sir* Andrew.

              Enter Sebastian.
  Seb. I am sorry, madam, I have hurt your kinsman ;
But had it been the brother of my blood,   210
I must have done no less, with wit and safety.
You throw a strange regard upon me, and by that
I do perceive it hath offended you :
Pardon me, sweet one, even for the vows
We made each other but so late ago.
  Duke. One face, one voice, one habit, and two per-
                                       sons ;
A natural perspective, that is, and is not !
  Seb. Antonio ? O my dear Antonio !
How have the hours rack'd and tortur'd me,
Since I have lost thee !   220
  Ant. Sebastian are you ?
  Seb.   Fear'st thou that, Antonio ?
  Ant. How have you made division of yourself ?—
An apple cleft in two is not more twin
Than these two creatures. Which is Sebastian ?
  Oli. Most wonderful !
  Seb. Do I stand there ? I never had a brother ;
Nor can there be that deity in my nature,
Of here and everywhere. I had a sister,
Whom the blind waves and surges have devour'd.—
[*To* Viola.] Of charity, what kin are you to me ? 230
What countryman ? what name ? what parentage ?
  Vio. Of Messaline : Sebastian was my father ;
Such a Sebastian was my brother too,
So went he suited to his watery tomb.
If spirits can assume both form and suit,
You come to fright us.
  Seb.   A spirit I am indeed ;
But am in that dimension grossly clad,
Which from the womb I did participate.
Were you a woman, as the rest goes even,
I should my tears let fall upon your cheek,   240
And say—Thrice welcome, drowned Viola !
  Vio. My father had a mole upon his brow,—
  Seb. And so had mine.
  Vio. And died that day, when Viola from her birth
Had number'd thirteen years.
  Seb. O ! that record is lively in my soul.
He finished, indeed, his mortal act
That day that made my sister thirteen years.
  Vio. If nothing lets to make us happy both,
But this my masculine usurp'd attire,   250
Do not embrace me, till each circumstance
Of place, time, fortune, do cohere, and jump,
That I am Viola : which to confirm,
I 'll bring you to a captain in this town,
Where lie my maiden weeds ; by whose gentle help
I was preserv'd, to serve this noble count.
All the occurrence of my fortune since
Hath been between this lady and this lord.
  Seb. [*To* Olivia.] So comes it, lady, you have been
                                     mistook ;
But nature to her bias drew in that.   260
You would have been contracted to a maid,
Nor are you therein, by my life, deceiv'd.
You are betroth'd both to a maid and man.
  Duke. Be not amaz'd ; right noble is his blood.—

If this be so, as yet the glass seems true,
I shall have share in this most happy wrack.
[*To* VIOLA.] Boy, thou hast said to me a thousand
     times,
Thou never shouldst love woman like to me.

Is now in durance at Malvolio's suit,
A gentleman, and follower of my lady's.
    Oli. He shall enlarge him.—Fetch Malvolio hither.—
And yet, alas, now I remember me,
They say, poor gentleman, he 's much distract.   280

Oli. " My lord, so please you, these things further thought on,
To think me as well a sister as a wife,
One day shall crown the alliance on 't, so please you,
Here at my house, and at my proper cost."

Vio. And all those sayings will I over-swear,
And all those swearings keep as true in soul,
As doth that orbed continent, the fire   270
That severs day from night.
    Duke.   Give me thy hand;
And let me see thee in thy woman's weeds.
    Vio. The captain, that did bring me first on shore,
Hath my maid's garments: he, upon some action,

A most extracting frenzy of mine own
From my remembrance clearly banish'd his.—

    Re-enter Clown, with a letter, and FABIAN.

How does he, sirrah?
    Clo. Truly, madam, he holds Belzebub at the stave's
end, as well as a man in his case may do. He has
here writ a letter to you: I should have given it you

to-day morning; but as a madman's epistles are no gospels, so it skills not much when they are delivered.

Oli. Open it, and read it. 290

Clo. Look then to be well edified, when the fool delivers the madman.—[*Reads.*] "By the Lord, madam,"—

Oli. How now! art thou mad?

Clo. No, madam, I do but read madness: an your ladyship will have it as it ought to be, you must allow *vox.*

Oli. Pr'ythee, read i' thy right wits.

Clo. So I do, madonna; but to read his right wits, is to read thus: therefore perpend, my princess, and give ear. 301

Oli. [*To* FABIAN.] Read it you, sirrah.

Fab. [*Reads.*] "By the Lord, madam, you wrong me, and the world shall know it: though you have put me into darkness, and given your drunken cousin rule over me, yet have I the benefit of my senses as well as your ladyship. I have your own letter that induced me to the semblance I put on; with the which I doubt not but to do myself much right, or you much shame. Think of me as you please. I leave my duty a little unthought of, and speak out of my injury. 312

        The madly-used MALVOLIO."

Oli. Did he write this?

Clo. Ay, madam.

Duke. This savours not much of distraction.

Oli. See him deliver'd, Fabian: bring him hither.

                    [*Exit* FABIAN.

My lord, so please you, these things further thought on,
To think me as well a sister as a wife,
One day shall crown the alliance on 't, so please you,
Here at my house, and at my proper cost. 321

Duke. Madam, I am most apt to embrace your offer.—

[*To* VIOLA.] Your master quits you; and, for your service done him,
So much against the mettle of your sex,
So far beneath your soft and tender breeding,
And since you call'd me master for so long,
Here is my hand: you shall from this time be
Your master's mistress.

Oli.   A sister!—you are she.

Re-enter FABIAN, *with* MALVOLIO.

Duke. Is this the madman?

Oli.   Ay, my lord, this same.
How now, Malvolio?

Mal.   Madam, you have done me wrong, 330
Notorious wrong.

Oli.   Have I, Malvolio? no.

Mal. Lady, you have. Pray you, peruse that letter.
You must not now deny it is your hand:
Write from it, if you can, in hand, or phrase;
Or say, 't is not your seal, nor your invention:
You can say none of this. Well, grant it then,
And tell me, in the modesty of honour,
Why you have given me such clear lights of favour,
Bade me come smiling and cross-garter'd to you,
To put on yellow stockings, and to frown 340
Upon Sir Toby, and the lighter people?
And, acting this in an obedient hope,
Why have you suffer'd me to be imprison'd,
Kept in a dark house, visited by the priest,
And made the most notorious geck and gull
That e'er invention play'd on? tell me why.

Oli. Alas! Malvolio, this is not my writing,

Though, I confess, much like the character;
But, out of question, 't is Maria's hand:
And now I do bethink me, it was she 350
First told me thou wast mad; then cam'st in smiling,
And in such forms which here were presuppos'd
Upon thee in the letter. Pr'ythee, be content:
This practice hath most shrewdly pass'd upon thee;
But when we know the grounds and authors of it,
Thou shalt be both the plaintiff and the judge
Of thine own cause.

Fab.   Good madam, hear me speak;
And let no quarrel, nor no brawl to come,
Taint the condition of this present hour,
Which I have wonder'd at. In hope it shall not, 360
Most freely I confess, myself, and Toby,
Set this device against Malvolio here,
Upon some stubborn and uncourteous parts
We had conceiv'd against him. Maria writ
The letter at Sir Toby's great importance:
In recompense whereof, he hath married her.
How with a sportful malice it was follow'd,
May rather pluck on laughter than revenge,
If that the injuries be justly weigh'd,
That have on both sides pass'd. 370

Oli. Alas, poor fool, how have they baffled thee!

Clo. Why, "some are born great, some achieve greatness, and some have greatness thrown upon them." I was one, sir, in this interlude; one Sir Topas, sir; but that's all one.—"By the Lord, fool, I am not mad."—But do you remember? "Madam, why laugh you at such a barren rascal? an you smile not, he's gagg'd:" and thus the whirligig of time brings in his revenges.

Mal. I 'll be reveng'd on the whole pack of you. 380
                      [*Exit.*

Oli. He hath been most notoriously abus'd.

Duke. Pursue him, and entreat him to a peace.
He hath not told us of the captain yet:
When that is known and golden time convents,
A solemn combination shall be made
Of our dear souls.—Meantime, sweet sister.
We will not part from hence.—Cesario, come;
For so you shall be, while you are a man;
But when in other habits you are seen,
Orsino's mistress, and his fancy's queen. 390
            [*Exeunt all, except Clown.*

          CLOWN *sings.*

When that I was and a little tiny boy,
  With hey, ho, the wind and the rain;
A foolish thing was but a toy,
  For the rain it raineth every day.

But when I came to man's estate,
  With hey, ho, the wind and the rain,
'Gainst knaves and thieves men shut their gate,
  For the rain it raineth every day.

But when I came, alas! to wive,
  With hey, ho, the wind and the rain,   400
By swaggering could I never thrive,
  For the rain it raineth every day.

But when I came unto my beds,
  With hey, ho, the wind and the rain,
With toss-pots still had drunken heads,
  For the rain it raineth every day.

A great while ago the world begun,
  With hey, ho, the wind and the rain,
But that's all one, our play is done,
  And we'll strive to please you every day.   410
                    [*Exit.*

THE WINTER'S TALE.

DRAMATIS PERSONÆ.

LEONTES, *King of Sicilia.*
MAMILLIUS, *young Prince of Sicilia.*
CAMILLO,
ANTIGONUS,
CLEOMENES, } *Lords of Sicilia.*
DION,
POLIXENES, *King of Bohemia.*
FLORIZEL, *Prince of Bohemia.*
ARCHIDAMUS, *a Lord of Bohemia.*
A Mariner.
A Gaoler.
An Old Shepherd, reputed Father of Perdita.
Clown, his Son.

AUTOLYCUS, *a Rogue.*
Time, the Chorus.

HERMIONE, *Queen to Leontes.*
PERDITA, *Daughter to Leontes and Hermione.*
PAULINA, *Wife to Antigonus.*
EMILIA, *a Lady attending the Queen.*
MOPSA,
DORCAS, } *Shepherdesses.*

*Lords, Ladies, and Gentlemen, Officers, and
Servants, Shepherds and Shepherdesses,
Guards, &c.*

SCENE—Sometimes in SICILIA, sometimes in BOHEMIA.

ACT I.

SCENE I.—Sicilia. An Ante-chamber in LEONTES' Palace.

Enter CAMILLO *and* ARCHIDAMUS.

Archidamus.

IF you shall chance, Camillo, to visit Bohemia, on the like occasion whereon my
services are now on foot, you shall see, as
I have said, great difference betwixt our
Bohemia and your Sicilia.

Cam. I think, this coming summer, the
King of Sicilia means to pay Bohemia the
visitation which he justly owes him.

Arch. Wherein our entertainment shall
shame us, we will be justified in our loves:
for, indeed,— 11

Cam. 'Beseech you,—

Arch. Verily, I speak it in the freedom of my knowledge : we cannot with such magnificence—in so rare
—I know not what to say.—We will give you sleepy
drinks, that your senses, unintelligent of our insufficiency, may, though they cannot praise us, as little
accuse us.

Cam. You pay a great deal too dear for what's
given freely. 20

Arch. Believe me, I speak as my understanding instructs me, and as mine honesty puts it to utterance.

Cam. Sicilia cannot show himself over-kind to
Bohemia. They were trained together in their
childhoods ; and there rooted betwixt them then
such an affection, which cannot choose but branch
now. Since their more mature dignities, and royal
necessities, made separation of their society, their
encounters, though not personal, have been royally
attorney'd, with interchange of gifts, letters, loving
embassies, that they have seemed to be together,
though absent, shook hands, as over a vast, and embraced, as it were, from the ends of opposed winds.
The heavens continue their loves !

Arch. I think, there is not in the world either
malice, or matter, to alter it. You have an unspeakable comfort of your young Prince Mamillius :
it is a gentleman of the greatest promise that ever
came into my note. 39

Cam. I very well agree with you in the hopes of
him. It is a gallant child ; one that, indeed, physics

the subject, makes old hearts fresh : they that went
on crutches ere he was born, desire yet their life to
see him a man.

Arch. Would they else be content to die?

Cam. Yes ; if there were no other excuse why they
should desire to live.

Arch. If the king had no son, they would desire to
live on crutches till he had one. [*Exeunt.*

SCENE II.—The Same. A Room of State in the
Palace.

Enter LEONTES, POLIXENES, HERMIONE, MAMILLIUS,
CAMILLO, *and Attendants.*

Pol. Nine changes of the watery star have been
The shepherd's note, since we have left our throne
Without a burden : time as long again
Would be fill'd up, my brother, with our thanks ;
And yet we should for perpetuity
Go hence in debt : and therefore, like a cipher,
Yet standing in rich place, I multiply
With one "We thank you" many thousands more
That go before it.

Leon.   Stay your thanks awhile,
And pay them when you part.

Pol.   Sir, that's to-morrow.
I am question'd by my fears, of what may chance, 11
Or breed upon our absence ; that may blow
No sneaping winds at home, to make us say,
"This is put forth too truly !" Besides, I have stay'd
To tire your royalty.

Leon.   We are tougher, brother,
Than you can put us to 't.

Pol.   No longer stay.

Leon. One seven-night longer.

Pol.   Very sooth, to-morrow.

Leon. We 'll part the time between 's then ; and in
                                                        that
I 'll no gainsaying.

Pol.   Press me not, 'beseech you, so.

There is no tongue that moves, none, none i' the world,
So soon as yours, could win me: so it should now, 21
Were there necessity in your request, although
'T were needful I denied it. My affairs
Do even drag me homeward ; which to hinder,
Were in your love a whip to me, my stay
To you a charge, and trouble : to save both,
Farewell, our brother.
   Leon.   Tongue-tied, our queen ? speak you.
   Her. I had thought, sir, to have held my peace,
       until
You had drawn oaths from him, not to stay. You, sir,
Charge him too coldly : tell him, you are sure 30
All in Bohemia 's well : this satisfaction
The by-gone day proclaim'd. Say this to him,
He 's beat from his best ward.
   Leon.   Well said, Hermione.
   Her. To tell he longs to see his son were strong:
But let him say so then, and let him go ;
But let him swear so, and he shall not stay
We 'll thwack him hence with distaffs.—
   [*To* Polixenes.] Yet of your royal presence I 'll ad-
      venture
The borrow of a week. When at Bohemia
You take my lord, I 'll give him my commission, 40
To let him there a month behind the gest
Prefix'd for 's parting : yet, good deed, Leontes,
I love thee not a jar o' the clock behind
What lady she her lord.—You 'll stay ?
   Pol.   No, madam.
   Her. Nay, but you will ?
   Pol.   I may not, verily.
   Her. Verily !
You put me off with limber vows ; but I,
Though you would seek to unsphere the stars with
   oaths,
Should yet say, " Sir, no going." Verily,
You shall not go : a lady's " verily" is 50
As potent as a lord's. Will you go yet ?
Force me to keep you as a prisoner,
Not like a guest ; so you shall pay your fees,
When you depart, and save your thanks. How say
   you ?
My prisoner, or my guest ? by your dread " verily,"
One of them you shall be.
   Pol.   Your guest then, madam :
To be your prisoner should import offending ;
Which is for me less easy to commit,
Than you to punish.
   Her.   Not your gaoler then,
But your kind hostess. Come, I 'll question you 60
Of my lord's tricks, and yours, when you were boys ;
You were pretty lordings then.
   Pol.   We were, fair queen,
Two lads, that thought there was no more behind,
But such a day to-morrow as to-day,
And to be boy eternal.
   Her. Was not my lord the verier wag o' the two ?
   Pol. We were as twinn'd lambs, that did frisk i' the
      sun,
And bleat the one at the other : what we chang'd,
Was innocence for innocence ; we knew not
The doctrine of ill-doing, nor dream'd 70
That any did. Had we pursu'd that life,
And our weak spirits ne'er been higher rear'd
With stronger blood, we should have answer'd heaven
Boldly, " not guilty ;" the imposition clear'd,
Hereditary ours.
   Her.   By this we gather,
You have tripp'd since.
   Pol.   O ! my most sacred lady,
Temptations have since then been born to 's ; for
In those unfledg'd days was my wife a girl :
Your precious self had then not cross'd the eyes
Of my young playfellow.
   Her.   Grace to boot ! 80
Of this make no conclusion, lest you say,
Your queen and I are devils ; yet, go on :
The offences we have made you do, we 'll answer ;
If you first sinn'd with us, and that with us
You did continue fault, and that you slipp'd not
With any but with us.

   Leon.   Is he won yet ?
   Her. He 'll stay, my lord.
   Leon.   At my request he would not.
Hermione, my dearest, thou never spok'st
To better purpose.
   Her.   Never ?
   Leon.   Never, but once.
   Her. What ? have I twice said well ? when was 't
     before ?   90
I pr'ythee, tell me. Cram 's with praise, and make 's
As fat as tame things : one good deed, dying tongue-
   less,
Slaughters a thousand waiting upon that.
Our praises are our wages : you may ride 's
With one soft kiss a thousand furlongs, ere
With spur we heat an acre. But to the goal :—
My last good deed was to entreat his stay :
What was my first ? it has an elder sister,
Or I mistake you : O, 'would her name were Grace !
But once before I spoke to the purpose : when ? 100
Nay, let me have 't ; I long.
   Leon.   Why, that was when
Three crabbed months had sour'd themselves to death,
Ere I could make thee open thy white hand,
And clap thyself my love : then didst thou utter,
" I am yours for ever."
   Her.   'T is Grace, indeed.—
Why, lo you now, I have spoke to the purpose twice :
The one for ever earn'd a royal husband,
The other for some while a friend.
             [*Giving her hand to* Polixenes.
   Leon. [*Aside.*]   Too hot, too hot !
To mingle friendship far is mingling bloods.
I have *tremor cordis* on me :—my heart dances, 110
But not for joy, not joy.—This entertainment
May a free face put on, derive a liberty
From heartiness, from bounty, fertile bosom,
And well become the agent: 't may, I grant ;
But to be paddling palms, and pinching fingers,
As now they are ; and making practis'd smiles,
As in a looking-glass ;—and then to sigh, as 't were
The mort o' the deer ; O ! that is entertainment
My bosom likes not, nor my brows.—Mamillius,
Art thou my boy ?
   Mam.   Ay, my good lord.
   Leon.   I' fecks ? 120
Why, that 's my bawcock. What ! hast smutch'd thy
   nose ?—
They say, it 's a copy out of mine. Come, captain,
We must be neat ; not neat, but cleanly, captain :
And yet the steer, the heifer, and the calf,
Are all call'd neat.—Still virginalling
Upon his palm ?—How now, you wanton calf !
Art thou my calf ?
   Mam.   Yes, if you will, my lord.
   Leon. Thou want'st a rough pash, and the shoots
     that I have,
To be full like me :—yet, they say, we are
Almost as like as eggs ; women say so, 130
That will say anything : but were they false
As o'er-dyed blacks, as wind, as waters ; false
As dice are to be wish'd, by one that fixes
No bourn 'twixt his and mine ; yet were it true
To say this boy were like me.—Come, sir page,
Look on me with your welkin eye : sweet villain !
Most dear'st ! my collop !—Can thy dam ?—may 't be ?—
Affection ! thy intention stabs the centre :
Thou dost make possible things not so held,
Communicat'st with dreams ;—(how can this be ?)—140
With what 's unreal thou co-active art,
And fellow'st nothing : Then, 't is very credent,
Thou may'st co-join with something ; and thou dost,—
And that beyond commission ; and I find it,
And that to the infection of my brains,
And hardening of my brows.
   Pol.   What means Sicilia ?
   Her. He something seems unsettled.
   Pol.   How, my lord !
What cheer ? how is 't with you, best brother ?
   Her.   You look,
As if you held a brow of much distraction :
Are you mov'd, my lord ?

Leon.   No, in good earnest.— 150
How sometimes nature will betray its folly,
Its tenderness, and make itself a pastime
To harder bosoms ! Looking on the lines
Of my boy's face, methoughts I did recoil
Twenty-three years, and saw myself unbreech'd,
In my green velvet coat ; my dagger muzzled,
Lest it should bite its master, and so prove,
As ornaments oft do, too dangerous.
How like, methought, I then was to this kernel,
This squash, this gentleman.—Mine honest friend, 160
Will you take eggs for money ?

Leon. " How like, methought, I then was to this kernel,
This squash, this gentleman."

Mam. No, my lord, I 'll fight.
Leon. You will ? why, happy man be 's dole !—My
                                                     brother,
Are you so fond of your young prince, as we
Do seem to be of ours ?
Pol.   If at home, sir,
He 's all my exercise, my mirth, my matter :
Now my sworn friend, and then mine enemy ;
My parasite, my soldier, statesman, all.
He makes a July's day short as December ;
And with his varying childness cures in me   170
Thoughts that would thick my blood.
Leon.   So stands this squire
Offic'd with me. We too will walk, my lord,
And leave you to your graver steps.—Hermione,
How thou lov'st us, show in our brother's welcome :
Let what is dear in Sicily, be cheap.
Next to thyself, and my young rover, he 's
Apparent to my heart.
Her.   If you would seek us,
We are yours i' the garden : shall 's attend you there ?
Leon. To your own bents dispose you : you 'll be
                                                     found,
Be you beneath the sky.—[*Aside.*] I am angling now,
Though you perceive me not how I give line.   181
Go to, go to !
How she holds up the neb, the bill to him ;
And arms her with the boldness of a wife
To her allowing husband !
          [*Exeunt* POLIXENES, HERMIONE, *and Attendants.*
                                        Gone already ;
Inch-thick, knee-deep, o'er head and ears a fork'd
                    one !—
Go play, boy, play ;—thy mother plays, and I
Play too, but so disgrac'd a part, whose issue
Will hiss me to my grave : contempt and clamour
Will be my knell.—Go play, boy, play.—There have
                    been,   190
Or I am much deceiv'd, cuckolds ere now ;
And many a man there is, (even at this present,
Now, while I speak this) holds his wife by the arm,
That little thinks she has been sluic'd in 's absence,
And his pond fish'd by his next neighbour, by

Sir Smile, his neighbour. Nay, there 's comfort in 't,
Whiles other men have gates, and those gates open'd,
As mine, against their will. Should all despair
That have revolted wives, the tenth of mankind
Would hang themselves. Physic for 't there is none :
It is a bawdy planet, that will strike   201
Where 't is predominant ; and 't is powerful, think it,
From east, west, north, and south : be it concluded,
No barricado for a belly : know 't ;
It will let in and out the enemy,
With bag and baggage. Many a thousand on 's
Have the disease, and feel 't not.—How now, boy ?
Mam. I am like you, they say.
Leon.   Why, that 's some comfort.—
What ! Camillo there ?
Cam. Ay, my good lord.   210
Leon. Go play, Mamillius ; thou 'rt an honest man.—
                                        [*Exit* MAMILLIUS.
Camillo, this great sir will yet stay longer.
Cam. You had much ado to make his anchor hold :
When you cast out, it still came home.
Leon.   Didst note it ?
Cam. He would not stay at your petitions ; made
His business more material.
Leon.   Didst perceive it ?—
They 're here with me already ; whispering, rounding,
" Sicilia is a—so-forth." 'T is far gone,
When I shall gust it last.—How came 't, Camillo,
That he did stay ?
Cam.   At the good queen's entreaty. 220
Leon. At the queen's, be 't : good should be pertinent ;
But so it is, it is not. Was this taken
By any understanding pate but thine ?
For thy conceit is soaking ; will draw in
More than the common blocks :—not noted, is 't,
But of the finer natures ? by some severals,
Of head-piece extraordinary ? lower messes,
Perchance, are to this business purblind : say.
Cam. Business, my lord ? I think, most understand
Bohemia stays here longer.
Leon.   Ha ?
Cam.   Stays here longer.
Leon. Ay, but why ?   231
Cam. To satisfy your highness, and the entreaties
Of our most gracious mistress.
Leon.   Satisfy ?
The entreaties of your mistress ?—satisfy ?—
Let that suffice. I have trusted thee, Camillo,
With all the nearest things to my heart, as well
My chamber-councils, wherein, priest-like, thou
Hast cleans'd my bosom : I from thee departed
Thy penitent reform'd ; but we have been
Deceiv'd in thy integrity, deceiv'd   240
In that which seems so.
Cam.   Be it forbid, my lord !
Leon. To bide upon 't,—thou art not honest ; or,
If thou inclin'st that way, thou art a coward,
Which hoxes honesty behind, restraining
From course requir'd ; or else thou must be counted
A servant grafted in my serious trust,
And therein negligent ; or else a fool,
That seest a game play'd home, the rich stake drawn,
And tak'st it all for jest.
Cam.   My gracious lord,
I may be negligent, foolish, and fearful ·   250
In every one of these no man is free,
But that his negligence, his folly, fear,
Amongst the infinite doings of the world,
Sometime puts forth. In your affairs, my lord,
If ever I were wilful-negligent,
It was my folly ; if industriously
I play'd the fool, it was my negligence,
Not weighing well the end ; if ever fearful
To do a thing, where I the issue doubted,
Whereof the execution did cry out   260
Against the non-performance, 't was a fear
Which oft infects the wisest. These, my lord,
Are such allow'd infirmities, that honesty
Is never free of : but, 'beseech your grace,
Be plainer with me : let me know my trespass
By its own visage ; if I then deny it,
'T is none of mine.

Leon.   Ha' not you seen, Camillo,
(But that's past doubt; you have: or your eye-glass
Is thicker than a cuckold's horn) or heard,
(For, to a vision so apparent, rumour   270
Cannot be mute) or thought, (for cogitation
Resides not in that man that does not think)
My wife is slippery? If thou wilt confess,
(Or else be impudently negative,
To have nor eyes, nor thought) then say
My wife's a hobbyhorse, deserves a name
As rank as any flax-wench, that puts to
Before her troth-plight : say 't, and justify 't.
   Cam. I would not be a stander-by, to hear
My sovereign mistress clouded so, without   280
My present vengeance taken. 'Shrew my heart,
You never spoke what did become you less
Than this; which to reiterate, were sin
As deep as that, though true.
   Leon.   Is whispering nothing?
Is leaning cheek to cheek? is meeting noses?
Kissing with inside lip? stopping the career
Of laughter with a sigh? (a note infallible
Of breaking honesty) horsing foot on foot?
Skulking in corners? wishing clocks more swift?
Hours, minutes? noon, midnight? and all eyes   290
Blind with the pin and web, but theirs, theirs only,
That would unseen be wicked? is this nothing?
Why, then the world, and all that is in 't, is nothing;
The covering sky is nothing; Bohemia nothing;
My wife is nothing; nor nothing have these nothings,
If this be nothing.
   Cam.   Good my lord, be cur'd
Of this diseas'd opinion, and betimes;
For 't is most dangerous.
   Leon.   Say, it be ; 't is true.
   Cam. No, no, my lord.
   Leon.   It is ; you lie, you lie :
I say, thou liest, Camillo, and I hate thee ;   300
Pronounce thee a gross lout, a mindless slave,
Or else a hovering temporiser ; that
Canst with thine eyes at once see good and evil,
Inclining to them both : were my wife's liver
Infected as her life, she would not live
The running of one glass.
   Cam.   Who does infect her?
   Leon. Why, he that wears her like her medal,
       hanging
About his neck, Bohemia: who—if I
Had servants true about me, that bare eyes
To see alike mine honour as their profits,   310
Their own particular thrifts, they would do that
Which should undo more doing : ay, and thou,
His cup-bearer,—whom I from meaner form
Have bench'd, and rear'd to worship; who may'st see
Plainly, as heaven sees earth, and earth sees heaven,
How I am galled,—might'st bespice a cup,
To give mine enemy a lasting wink ;
Which draught to me were cordial.
   Cam.   Sir, my lord,
I could do this, and that with no rash potion,
But with a lingering dram, that should not work   320
Maliciously, like poison : but I cannot
Believe this crack to be in my dread mistress,
So sovereignly being honourable.,
I have lov'd thee,—
   Leon.   Make that thy question, and go rot !
Dost think, I am so muddy, so unsettled,
To appoint myself in this vexation? sully
The purity and whiteness of my sheets,—
Which to preserve is sleep ; which, being spotted,
Is goads, thorns, nettles, tails of wasps,—
Give scandal to the blood o' the prince, my son,   330
(Who, I do think, is mine, and love as mine)
Without ripe moving to 't? Would I do this?
Could man so blench?
   Cam.   I must believe you, sir :
I do ; and will fetch off Bohemia for 't ;
Provided, that, when he 's remov'd, your highness
Will take again your queen ; as yours at first,
Even for your son's sake ; and thereby for sealing
The injury of tongues, in courts and kingdoms
Known and allied to yours.
   Leon.   Thou dost advise me,
Even so as I mine own course have set down.   340
I 'll give no blemish to her honour, none.
   Cam. My lord,
Go then ; and with a countenance as clear
As friendship wears at feasts, keep with Bohemia,
And with your queen. I am his cup-bearer ;
If from me he have wholesome beverage,
Account me not your servant.
   Leon.   This is all :
Do 't, and thou hast the one half of my heart ;
Do 't not, thou splitt'st thine own.
   Cam.   I 'll do 't, my lord.
   Leon. I will seem friendly, as thou hast advis'd me.
                           [*Exit.*   351
   Cam. O miserable lady !—But, for me,
What case stand I in? I must be the poisoner
Of good Polixenes ; and my ground to do 't
Is the obedience to a master ; one,
Who, in rebellion with himself, will have
All that are his, so too.—To do this deed,
Promotion follows. If I could find example
Of thousands that had struck anointed kings,
And flourish'd after, I 'd not do 't ; but since
Nor brass, nor stone, nor parchment, bears not one,   361
Let villainy itself forswear 't. I must
Forsake the court : to do 't, or no, is certain
To me a break-neck. Happy star, reign now !
Here comes Bohemia.

Enter POLIXENES.

   Pol.   This is strange. Methinks,
My favour here begins to warp. Not speak?—
Good day, Camillo.
   Cam.   Hail, most royal sir !
   Pol. What is the news i' the court?
   Cam.   None rare, my lord.
   Pol. The king hath on him such a countenance,
As he had lost some province, and a region
Lov'd as he loves himself : even now I met him   370
With customary compliment, when he,
Wafting his eyes to the contrary, and falling
A lip of much contempt, speeds from me, and
So leaves me to consider what is breeding,
That changes thus his manners.
   Cam. I dare not know, my lord.
   Pol. How ! dare not? do not ! Do you know, and
       dare not
Be intelligent to me? 'T is thereabouts ;
For, to yourself, what you do know, you must,
And cannot say, you dare not. Good Camillo,   380
Your chang'd complexions are to me a mirror,
Which shows me mine chang'd too ; for I must be
A party in this alteration, finding
Myself thus alter'd with 't.
   Cam.   There is a sickness
Which puts some of us in distemper ; but
I cannot name the disease, and it is caught
Of you, that yet are well.
   Pol.   How caught of me?
Make me not sighted like the basilisk :
I have look'd on thousands, who have sped the better
By my regard, but kill'd none so. Camillo,—   390
As you are certainly a gentleman ; thereto
Clerk-like experienc'd, which no less adorns
Our gentry than our parents' noble names,
In whose success we are gentle,—I beseech you,
If you know aught which does behove my knowledge
Thereof to be inform'd, imprison 't not
In ignorant concealment.
   Cam.   I may not answer.
   Pol. A sickness caught of me, and yet I well?
I must be answer'd.—Dost thou hear, Camillo,
I conjure thee, by all the parts of man   400
Which honour does acknowledge,—whereof the least
Is not this suit of mine,—that thou declare
What incidency thou dost guess of harm
Is creeping toward me ; how far off, how near ;
Which way to be prevented, if to be :
If not, how best to bear it.
   Cam.   Sir, I will tell you ;
Since I am charg'd in honour, and by him

That I think honourable.   Therefore, mark my
    counsel,
Which must be even as swiftly follow'd, as
I mean to utter it, or both yourself and me   410
Cry "lost," and so good night.
  Pol.   On, good Camillo.
  Cam. I am appointed him to murder you.
  Pol. By whom, Camillo?
  Cam.   By the king.
  Pol.   For what?
  Cam. He thinks, nay, with all confidence he swears,
As he had seen't, or been an instrument
To vice you to't,—that you have touch'd his queen
Forbiddenly.
  Pol.   O, then my best blood turn
To an infected jelly, and my name
Be yok'd with his that did betray the Best!
Turn then my freshest reputation to   420
A savour that may strike the dullest nostril
Where I arrive; and my approach be shunn'd,
Nay, hated too, worse than the great'st infection
That e'er was heard, or read!
  Cam.   Swear his thought over
By each particular star in heaven, and
By all their influences, you may as well
Forbid the sea for to obey the moon,
As, or by oath, remove, or counsel, shake,
The fabric of his folly, whose foundation
Is pil'd upon his faith, and will continue   430
The standing of his body.
  Pol.   How should this grow?
  Cam. I know not; but, I am sure, 'tis safer to
Avoid what's grown, than question how 'tis born.
If therefore you dare trust my honesty,
That lies enclosed in this trunk, which you
Shall bear along impawn'd, away to-night!
Your followers I will whisper to the business;
And will, by twos and threes, at several posterns,
Clear them o' the city.   For myself, I'll put
My fortunes to your service, which are here   440
By this discovery lost.   Be not uncertain;
For, by the honour of my parents, I
Have utter'd truth, which if you seek to prove,
I dare not stand by; nor shall you be safer
Than one condemn'd by the king's own mouth, thereon
His execution sworn.
  Pol.   I do believe thee:
I saw his heart in's face.   Give me thy hand:
Be pilot to me, and thy places shall
Still neighbour mine.   My ships are ready, and
My people did expect my hence departure   450
Two days ago.—This jealousy
Is for a precious creature: as she's rare,

Must it be great; and, as his person's mighty,
Must it be violent; and, as he does conceive
He is dishonour'd by a man which ever
Profess'd to him, why, his revenges must

  Pol.   "Give me thy hand:
Be pilot to me, and thy places shall
Still neighbour mine."

In that be made more bitter.   Fear o'ershades me:
Good expedition be my friend, and comfort
The gracious queen, part of his theme, but nothing
Of his ill-ta'en suspicion!   Come, Camillo: 460
I will respect thee as a father, if
Thou bear'st my life off hence.   Let us avoid.
  Cam. It is in mine authority to command
The keys of all the posterns.   Please your highness
To take the urgent hour.   Come, sir: away! [*Exeunt.*

ACT II.

SCENE I.—The Same.

Enter HERMIONE, MAMILLIUS, *and Ladies.*

    Hermione.
TAKE the boy to you: he so troubles me,
  'Tis past enduring.
  1 Lady.   Come, my gracious lord:
Shall I be your playfellow?
  Mam.   No, I'll none of you.
  1 Lady. Why, my sweet lord?
  Mam. You'll kiss me hard, and speak
    to me as if
I were a baby still.—I love you better.
  2 Lady. And why so, my lord?

  Mam.   Not for because
Your brows are blacker; yet black brows, they say,
Become some women best, so that there be not
Too much hair there, but in a semicircle,   10
Or a half-moon made with a pen.
  2 Lady.   Who taught ye this?
  Mam. I learn'd it out of women's faces.—Pray now,
What colour are your eyebrows?
  1 Lady.   Blue, my lord.
  Mam. Nay, that's a mock: I have seen a lady's nose
That has been blue, but not her eyebrows.

2 *Lady.*   Hark ye.
The queen, your mother, rounds apace : we shall
Present our services to a fine new prince,
One of these days ; and then you 'd wanton with us,
If we would have you. .
1 *Lady.*   She is spread of late
Into a goodly bulk : good time encounter her !   20
Her. What wisdom stirs amongst you ? Come, sir ;
                                                now
I am for you again : pray you, sit by us,
And tell 's a tale.
Mam.   Merry, or sad, shall 't be ?
Her. As merry as you will.
Mam.   A sad tale 's best for winter.
I have one of sprites and goblins.
Her.   Let 's have that, good sir.
Come on, sit down : come on, and do your best
To fright me with your sprites : you 're powerful at it.
Mam. There was a man,—
Her.   Nay, come, sit down ; then on.
Mam. Dwelt by a churchyard.—I will tell it softly ;
Yond crickets shall not hear it.
Her.   Come on then,   30
And give 't me in mine ear.

Enter LEONTES, ANTIGONUS, *Lords, and others.*

Leon. Was he met there ? his train ? Camillo with
    him ?
1 *Lord.* Behind the tuft of pines I met them : never
Saw I men scour so on their way. I ey'd them
Even to their ships.
Leon.   How blest am I
In my just censure, in my true opinion !—
Alack ! for lesser knowledge !—how accurs'd,
In being so blest !—There may be in the cup
A spider steep'd, and one may drink, depart,
And yet partake no venom, for his knowledge   40
Is not infected ; but if one present
The abhorr'd ingredient to his eye, make known
How he hath drunk, he cracks his gorge, his sides,
With violent hefts.—I have drunk, and seen the spider.
Camillo was his help in this, his pander.—
There is a plot against my life, my crown :
All 's true that is mistrusted ;—that false villain,
Whom I employ'd, was pre-employ'd by him.
He has discover'd my design, and I
Remain a pinch'd thing ; yea, a very trick   50
For them to play at will.—How came the posterns
So easily open ?
1 *Lord.*   By his great authority ;
Which often hath no less prevail'd than so,
On your command.
Leon.   I know 't too well.—
Give me the boy. [*To* HERMIONE.] I am glad, you
    did not nurse him :
Though he does bear some signs of me, yet you
Have too much blood in him.
Her.   What is this ? sport ?
Leon. Bear the boy hence ; he shall not come about
    her.
Away with him : and let her sport herself
With that she 's big with, for 't is Polixenes   60
Has made thee swell thus.
Her.   But I 'd say he had not,
And, I 'll be sworn, you would believe my saying,
Howe'er you lean to the nayward.
Leon.   You, my lords,
Look on her, mark her well ; be but about
To say, " she is a goodly lady," and
The justice of your hearts will thereto add,
" 'T is pity she 's not honest, honourable : "
Praise her but for this her without-door form
(Which, on my faith, deserves high speech), and
    straight
The shrug, the hum, or ha : these petty brands   70
That calumny doth use :—O, I am out !—
That mercy does, for calumny will sear
Virtue itself :—these shrugs, these hums, and ha's,
When you have said, " she 's goodly," come between,
Ere you can say, " she 's honest." But be 't known,
From him that has most cause to grieve it should be,
She 's an adult'ress.

Her.   Should a villain say so,
The most replenish'd villain in the world,
He were as much more villain : you, my lord,
Do but mistake.
Leon.   You have mistook, my lady,   80
Polixenes for Leontes. O thou thing,
Which I 'll not call a creature of thy place,
Lest barbarism, making me the precedent,
Should a like language use to all degrees,
And mannerly distinguishment leave out
Betwixt the prince and beggar !—I have said
She 's an adult'ress ; I have said with whom :
More, she 's a traitor ; and Camillo is
A federary with her, and one that knows
What she should shame to know herself,   90
But with her most vile principal, that she 's
A bed-swerver, even as bad as those
That vulgars give bold'st titles ; ay, and privy
To this their late escape.
Her.   No, by my life,
Privy to none of this. How will this grieve you,
When you shall come to clearer knowledge, that
You thus have publish'd me ? Gentle my lord,
You scarce can right me throughly then, to say
You did mistake.
Leon.   No ; if I mistake
In those foundations which I build upon,   100
The centre is not big enough to bear
A school-boy 's top.—Away with her ! to prison !
He, who shall speak for her, is afar off guilty,
But that he speaks.
Her.   There 's some ill planet reigns :
I must be patient, till the heavens look
With an aspect more favourable.—Good my lords,
I am not prone to weeping, as our sex
Commonly are ; the want of which vain dew,
Perchance, shall dry your pities ; but I have
That honourable grief lodg'd here, which burns   110
Worse than tears drown. 'Beseech you all, my lords,
With thoughts so qualified as your charities
Shall best instruct you, measure me ;—and so
The king's will be perform'd.
Leon.   Shall I be heard ?
Her. Who is 't, that goes with me ?—'Beseech your
    highness,
My women may be with me ; for, you see,
My plight requires it. Do not weep, good fools ;
There is no cause : when you shall know, your mis-
    tress
Has deserv'd prison, then abound in tears,
As I come out : this action, I now go on,   120
Is for my better grace.—Adieu, my lord :
I never wish'd to see you sorry ; now,
I trust, I shall.—My women, come ; you have leave.
Leon. Go, do our bidding ; hence !
                     [*Exeunt* QUEEN *and Ladies.*
1 *Lord.* 'Beseech your highness, call the queen again.
Ant. Be certain what you do, sir, lest your justice
Prove violence ; in the which three great ones suffer,
Yourself, your queen, your son.
1 *Lord.*   For her, my lord,
I dare my life lay down, and will do 't, sir,
Please you to accept it, that the queen is spotless   130
I' the eyes of heaven, and to you : I mean,
In this which you accuse her.
Ant.   If it prove
She 's otherwise, I 'll keep my stables where
I lodge my wife ; I 'll go in couples with her ;
Than when I feel, and see her, no further trust her ;
For every inch of woman in the world,
Ay, every dram of woman's flesh, is false,
If she be.
Leon.   Hold your peaces !
1 *Lord.*   Good my lord,—
Ant. It is for you we speak, not for ourselves.
You are abus'd, and by some putter-on,   140
That will be damn'd for 't ; 'would I knew the villain,
I would land-damn him. Be she honour-flaw'd,—
I have three daughters ; the eldest is eleven :
The second, and the third, nine, and some five ;
If this prove true, they 'll pay for 't : by mine honour,
I 'll geld them all : fourteen they shall not see,

To bring false generations : they are co-heirs ;
And I had rather glib myself, than they
Should not produce fair issue.
   Leon.   Cease ! no more.   150
You smell this business with a sense as cold
As is a dead man's nose ; but I do see 't, and feel 't,
As you feel doing thus, and see withal
The instruments that feel.
   Ant.   If it be so,
We need no grave to bury honesty :
There 's not a grain of it the face to sweeten
Of the whole dungy earth.

Her.   " Adieu, my lord :
I never wish'd to see you sorry ; now,
I trust, I shall."

   Leon.   What ! lack I credit ?
   1 Lord. I had rather you did lack, than I, my lord,
Upon this ground ; and more it would content me
To have her honour true, than your suspicion ;
Be blam'd for 't how you might.
   Leon.   Why, what need we
Commune with you of this, but rather follow   161
Our forcible instigation ? Our prerogative
Calls not your counsels, but our natural goodness
Imparts this ; which, if you (or stupified,
Or seeming so in skill) cannot, or will not,
Relish a truth like us, inform yourselves,
We need no more of your advice : the matter,
The loss, the gain, the ordering on 't, is all
Properly ours.
   Ant.   And I wish, my liege,
You had only in your silent judgment tried it,   170
Without more overture.
   Leon.   How could that be ?
Either thou art most ignorant by age,
Or thou wert born a fool. Camillo's flight,
Added to their familiarity
(Which was as gross as ever touch'd conjecture,
They lack'd sight only, nought for approbation,
But only seeing, all other circumstances
Made up to the deed), doth push on this proceeding :
Yet, for a greater confirmation,
(For in an act of this importance 't were   180
Most piteous to be wild) I have despatch'd in post,
To sacred Delphos, to Apollo's temple,
Cleomenes and Dion, whom you know
Of stuff'd sufficiency. Now, from the oracle
They will bring all ; whose spiritual counsel had,
Shall stop, or spur me. Have I done well ?
   1 Lord. Well done, my lord.
   Leon. Though I am satisfied, and need no more

Than what I know, yet shall the oracle
Give rest to the minds of others ; such as he,   190
Whose ignorant credulity will not
Come up to the truth. So have we thought it good,
From our free person she should be confin'd,
Lest that the treachery of the two fled hence
Be left her to perform. Come, follow us :
We are to speak in public ; for this business
Will raise us all.
   Ant. [*Aside.*] To laughter, as I take it,
If the good truth were known.   [*Exeunt.*

SCENE II.—The Same. The outer Room of a Prison.

Enter PAULINA *and Attendants.*

   Paul. The keeper of the prison, call to him :
Let him have knowledge who I am.—Good lady !
                  [*Exit an Attendant.*
No court in Europe is too good for thee ;
What dost thou then in prison ?—

Re-enter Attendant, with the Gaoler.

                  Now, good sir,
You know me, do you not ?
   Gaoler.   For a worthy lady,
And one whom much I honour.
   Paul.   Pray you then,
Conduct me to the queen.
   Gaoler. I may not, madam : to the contrary
I have express commandment.
   Paul.   Here 's ado,   10
To lock up honesty and honour from
The access of gentle visitors !—Is 't lawful,
Pray you, to see her women ? any of them ?
Emilia ?
   Gaoler. So please you, madam,
To put apart these your attendants, I
Shall bring Emilia forth.
   Paul.   I pray now, call her.—
Withdraw yourselves.   [*Exeunt Attendants.*
   Gaoler.   And, madam,
I must be present at your conference.
   Paul. Well, be 't so, pr'ythee.   [*Exit Gaoler.*
Here 's such ado to make no stain a stain,   20
As passes colouring.

Re-enter Gaoler, with EMILIA.

                  Dear gentlewoman,
How fares our gracious lady ?
   Emil. As well as one so great, and so forlorn,
May hold together. On her frights, and griefs,
(Which never tender lady hath borne greater)
She is, something before her time, deliver'd.
   Paul. A boy ?
   Emil.   A daughter ; and a goodly babe,
Lusty, and like to live : the queen receives
Much comfort in 't, says, " My poor prisoner,
I am innocent as you."
   Paul.   I dare be sworn :—   30
These dangerous, unsafe lunes i' the king, beshrew
       them !
He must be told on 't, and he shall : the office
Becomes a woman best ; I 'll take 't upon me.
If I prove honey-mouth'd, let my tongue blister,
And never to my red-look'd anger be
The trumpet any more.—Pray you, Emilia,
Commend my best obedience to the queen ;
If she dares trust me with her little babe,
I 'll show 't the king, and undertake to be
Her advocate to the loud'st. We do not know   40
How he may soften at the sight o' the child :
The silence often of pure innocence
Persuades, when speaking fails.
   Emil.   Most worthy madam,
Your honour, and your goodness, is so evident,
That your free undertaking cannot miss
A thriving issue : there is no lady living
So meet for this great errand. Please your ladyship
To visit the next room, I 'll presently
Acquaint the queen of your most noble offer,

Who, but to-day, hammer'd of this design,   50
But durst not tempt a minister of honour,
Lest she should be denied.
  Paul.   Tell her, Emilia,
I 'll use that tongue I have : if wit flow from 't,
As boldness from my bosom, let 't not be doubted
I shall do good.
  Emil.   Now, be you blest for it !
I 'll to the queen.—Please you, come something
    nearer.
  Gaoler. Madam, if 't please the queen to send the
    babe,
I know not what I shall incur to pass it,
Having no warrant.
  Paul.   You need not fear it, sir :
The child was prisoner to the womb, and is,   60
By law and process of great nature, thence
Freed and enfranchis'd ; not a party to
The anger of the king, nor guilty of,
If any be, the trespass of the queen.
  Gaoler. I do believe it.
  Paul. Do not you fear : upon mine honour, I
Will stand betwixt you and danger.   [*Exeunt.*

Scene III.—The Same. A Room in the Palace.

Enter Leontes, Antigonus, *Lords, and other*
Attendants.

  Leon. Nor night nor day, no rest. It is but weak-
    ness
To bear the matter thus, mere weakness. If
The cause were not in being,—part o' the cause,
She, the adult'ress ; for the harlot king
Is quite beyond mine arm, out of the blank
And level of my brain, plot-proof ; but she
I can hook to me :—say, that she were gone,
Given to the fire, a moiety of my rest
Might come to me again.—Who 's there ?
  1 Atten.   My lord.
  Leon. How does the boy ?
  1 Atten.   He took good rest to-night ;
'T is hop'd, his sickness is discharg'd.
  Leon.   To see his nobleness !   12
Conceiving the dishonour of his mother,
He straight declin'd, droop'd, took it deeply,
Fasten'd and fix'd the shame on 't in himself,
Threw off his spirit, his appetite, his sleep,
And downright languish'd.—Leave me solely :—go,
See how he fares. [*Exit Attendant.*]—Fie, fie ! no
    thought of him :
The very thought of my revenges that way
Recoil upon me : in himself too mighty,
And in his parties, his alliance ;—let him be,   20
Until a time may serve : for present vengeance,
Take it on her. Camillo and Polixenes
Laugh at me ; make their pastime at my sorrow :
They should not laugh, if I could reach them ; nor
Shall she, within my power.

Enter Paulina, *with a Child.*

  1 Lord.   You must not enter.
  Paul. Nay, rather, good my lords, be second to me.
Fear you his tyrannous passion more, alas,
Than the queen's life ? a gracious innocent soul,
More free than he is jealous.
  Ant.   That 's enough.
  1 Atten. Madam, he hath not slept to-night ; com-
    manded   30
None should come at him.
  Paul.   Not so hot, good sir :
I come to bring him sleep. 'T is such as you,—
That creep like shadows by him, and do sigh
At each his needless heavings,—such as you
Nourish the cause of his awaking : I
Do come with words as med'cinal as true,
Honest as either, to purge him of that humour,
That presses him from sleep.
  Leon.   What noise there, ho ?
  Paul. No noise, my lord ; but needful conference,
About some gossips for your highness.

  Leon.   How ?—   40
Away with that audacious lady. Antigonus,
I charg'd thee, that she should not come about me :
I knew she would.
  Ant.   I told her so, my lord,
On your displeasure's peril, and on mine,
She should not visit you.
  Leon.   What ! canst not rule her ?
  Paul. From all dishonesty he can : in this,
(Unless he take the course that you have done,
Commit me for committing honour) trust it,
He shall not rule me.
  Ant.   Lo you now ! you hear.
When she will take the rein, I let her run ;   50
But she 'll not stumble.
  Paul.   Good my liege, I come,—
And, I beseech you, hear me, who professes
Myself your loyal servant, your physician,
Your most obedient counsellor, yet that dares
Less appear so in comforting your evils,
Than such as most seem yours,—I say, I come
From your good queen.
  Leon.   Good queen !
  Paul. Good queen, my lord, good queen : I say,
    good queen ;
And would by combat make her good, so were I
A man, the worst about you.
  Leon.   Force her hence.   60
  Paul. Let him that makes but trifles of his eyes
First hand me. On mine own accord I 'll off,
But first I 'll do my errand.—The good queen,
For she is good, hath brought you forth a daughter :
Here 't is ; commends it to your blessing.
                    [*Laying down the Child.*
  Leon.   Out !
A mankind witch ! Hence with her, out o' door :
A most intelligencing bawd !
  Paul.   Not so :
I am as ignorant in that, as you
In so entitling me, and no less honest
Than you are mad : which is enough, I 'll warrant,   70
As this world goes, to pass for honest.
  Leon.   Traitors !
Will you not push her out ? Give her the bastard.—
[*To* Antigonus.] Thou, dotard, thou art woman-tir'd,
    unroosted
By thy dame Partlet here.—Take up the bastard :
Take 't up, I say ; give 't to thy crone.
  Paul.   For ever
Unvenerable be thy hands, if thou
Tak'st up the princess by that forced baseness
Which he has put upon 't !
  Leon.   He dreads his wife.
  Paul. So I would you did : then 't were past all
    doubt
You 'd call your children yours.
  Leon.   A nest of traitors ! 80
  Ant. I am none, by this good light.
  Paul.   Nor I ; nor any,
But one that 's here, and that 's himself ; for he
The sacred honour of himself, his queen's,
His hopeful son's, his babe's, betrays to slander,
Whose sting is sharper than the sword's, and will not
(For, as the case now stands, it is a curse
He cannot be compell'd to 't) once remove
The root of his opinion, which is rotten
As ever oak, or stone, was sound.
  Leon.   A callat,
Of boundless tongue, who late hath beat her husband,
And now baits me !—This brat is none of mine :   91
It is the issue of Polixenes.
Hence with it ; and, together with the dam,
Commit them to the fire.
  Paul.   It is yours ;
And, might we lay the old proverb to your charge,
So like you, 't is the worse.—Behold, my lords,
Although the print be little, the whole matter
And copy of the father : eye, nose, lip,
The trick of 's frown, his forehead ; nay, the valley,
The pretty dimples of his chin and cheek ; his smiles ;
The very mould and frame of hand, nail, finger.—   101
And thou, good goddess Nature, which hast made it

So like to him that got it, if thou hast
The ordering of the mind too, 'mongst all colours
No yellow in 't; lest she suspect, as he does,
Her children not her husband's.

Leon.   I 'll have thee burn'd.
  Paul.   I care not:
It is an heretic that makes the fire,
Not she which burns in 't. I 'll not call you tyrant;

Paul. "Let him that makes but trifles of his eyes
First hand me. On mine own accord I 'll off,
But first I 'll do my errand."

  Leon.   A gross hag!—
And, lozel, thou art worthy to be hang'd,
That wilt not stay her tongue.
    Ant.   Hang all the husbands
That cannot do that feat, you 'll leave yourself
Hardly one subject.
  Leon.   Once more, take her hence. 110
  Paul. A most unworthy and unnatural lord
Can do no more.

But this most cruel usage of your queen
(Not able to produce more accusation
Than your own weak-hing'd fancy) something savours
Of tyranny, and will ignoble make you,
Yea, scandalous to the world.
  Leon.   On your allegiance,
Out of the chamber with her! Were I a tyrant, 120
Where were her life? she durst not call me so,
If she did know me one. Away with her!

Paul. I pray you, do not push me ; I 'll be gone.
Look to your babe, my lord ; 't is yours : Jove send her
A better guiding spirit !—What needs these hands?—
You, that are thus so tender o'er his follies,
Will never do him good, not one of you.
So, so :—farewell ; we are gone.   *[Exit.*
  Leon. Thou, traitor, hast set on thy wife to this.—
My child? away with 't !—even thou, that hast   130
A heart so tender o'er it, take it hence,
And see it instantly consum'd with fire :
Even thou, and none but thou. Take it up straight.
Within this hour bring me word 't is done
(And by good testimony), or I 'll seize thy life,
With what thou else call'st thine. If thou refuse,
And wilt encounter with my wrath, say so ;
The bastard brains with these my proper hands
Shall I dash out. Go, take it to the fire,
For thou sett'st on thy wife.
  Ant.   I did not, sir :   140
These lords, my noble fellows, if they please,
Can clear me in 't.
  1 Lord.   We can : my royal liege,
He is not guilty of her coming hither.
  Leon. You are liars all.
  1 Lord. 'Beseech your highness, give us better
    credit.
We have always truly serv'd you, and beseech
So to esteem of us ; and on our knees we beg
(As recompense of our dear services,
Past, and to come), that you do change this purpose ; 150
Which, being so horrible, so bloody, must
Lead on to some foul issue. We all kneel.
  Leon. I am a feather for each wind that blows.—
Shall I live on, to see this bastard kneel
And call me father? Better burn it now,
Than curse it then. But, be it ; let it live :—
It shall not neither.—[*To* ANTIGONUS.] You, sir, come
    you hither ;
You, that have been so tenderly officious
With Lady Margery, your midwife, there,
To save this bastard's life,—for 't is a bastard,
So sure as this beard 's grey,—what will you adven-
    ture   160
To save this brat's life?
  Ant.   Anything, my lord,
That my ability may undergo,
And nobleness impose : at least, thus much :

I 'll pawn the little blood which I have left,
To save the innocent : anything possible.
  Leon. It shall be possible. Swear by this sword,
Thou wilt perform my bidding.
  Ant.   I will, my lord.
  Leon. Mark, and perform it, seest thou? for the fail
Of any point in 't shall not only be
Death to thyself, but to thy lewd-tongued wife,   170
Whom for this time we pardon. We enjoin thee,
As thou art liegeman to us, that thou carry
This female bastard hence ; and that thou bear it
To some remote and desert place, quite out
Of our dominions ; and that there thou leave it,
Without more mercy, to its own protection,
And favour of the climate. As by strange fortune
It came to us, I do in justice charge thee,
On thy soul's peril and thy body's torture,
That thou commend it strangely to some place,   180
Where chance may nurse, or end it. Take it up.
  Ant. I swear to do this, though a present death
Had been more merciful.—Come on, poor babe :
Some powerful spirit instruct the kites and ravens,
To be thy nurses ! Wolves, and bears, they say,
Casting their savageness aside, have done
Like offices of pity.—Sir, be prosperous
In more than this deed doth require !—And blessing
Against this cruelty fight on thy side,
Poor thing, condemn'd to loss !   [*Exit with the Child.*
  Leon.   No ; I 'll not rear 190
Another's issue.
  1 Atten.   Please your highness, posts
From those you sent to the oracle are come
An hour since : Cleomenes and Dion,
Being well arriv'd from Delphos, are both landed,
Hasting to the court.
  1 Lord.   So please you, sir, their speed
Hath been beyond account.
  Leon.   Twenty-three days
They have been absent : 't is good speed, foretells,
The great Apollo suddenly will have
The truth of this appear. Prepare you, lords :
Summon a session, that we may arraign   200
Our most disloyal lady ; for, as she hath
Been publicly accus'd, so shall she have
A just and open trial. While she lives,
My heart will be a burden to me. Leave me,
And think upon my bidding.   *[Exeunt.*

ACT III.

Scene I.—The Same. A Street in some Town.

Enter CLEOMENES *and* DION.

  Cleomenes.
THE climate 's delicate, the air most sweet,
Fertile the isle, the temple much surpassing
The common praise it bears.
  Dion.   I shall report,
For most it caught me, the celestial habits
(Methinks, I so should term them), and the
    reverence
Of the grave wearers. O, the sacrifice !
How ceremonious, solemn, and unearthly
It was i' the offering !
  Cleo.   But, of all, the burst
And the ear-deafening voice o' the oracle,
Kin to Jove's thunder, so surpris'd my sense,   10
That I was nothing.

  Dion.   If the event o' the journey
Prove as successful to the queen,—O, be 't so !—
As it hath been to us rare, pleasant, speedy,
The time is worth the use on 't.
  Cleo.   Great Apollo
Turn all to the best ! These proclamations,
So forcing faults upon Hermione,
I little like.
  Dion.   The violent carriage of it
Will clear, or end, the business : when the oracle
(Thus by Apollo's great divine seal'd up)
Shall the contents discover, something rare   20
Even then will rush to knowledge.—Go, fresh
    horses ;—
And gracious be the issue !   *[Exeunt.*

SCENE II.—The Same. A Court of Justice.

Enter LEONTES, *Lords, and Officers.*

Leon. This sessions (to our great grief we pronounce)
Even pushes 'gainst our heart: the party tried,
The daughter of a king, our wife, and one
Of us too much belov'd.—Let us be clear'd
Of being tyrannous, since we so openly
Proceed in justice, which shall have due course,
Even to the guilt, or the purgation.—
Produce the prisoner.
　Off. It is his highness' pleasure, that the queen
Appear in person here in court.—Silence!　　　10

Enter HERMIONE, *guarded ;* PAULINA *and Ladies attending.*

Leon. Read the indictment.
　Off. "Hermione, queen to the worthy Leontes, King
of Sicilia, thou art here accused and arraigned of high
treason, in committing adultery with Polixenes, King
of Bohemia, and conspiring with Camillo to take away
the life of our sovereign lord the king, thy royal
husband : the pretence whereof being by circumstances partly laid open, thou, Hermione, contrary to
the faith and allegiance of a true subject, didst counsel
and aid them, for their better safety, to fly away by
night."　　　21
　Her. Since what I am to say, must be but that
Which contradicts my accusation, and
The testimony on my part no other
But what comes from myself, it shall scarce boot me
To say, "Not guilty :" mine integrity,
Being counted falsehood, shall, as I express it,
Be so receiv'd. But thus :—if powers divine
Behold our human actions (as they do),
I doubt not then, but innocence shall make　　30
False accusation blush, and tyranny
Tremble at patience.—You, my lord, best know,
(Who least will seem to do so) my past life
Hath been as continent, as chaste, as true,
As I am now unhappy ; which is more
Than history can pattern, though devis'd
And play'd to take spectators. For behold me,
A fellow of the royal bed, which owe
A moiety of the throne, a great king's daughter,
The mother to a hopeful prince, here standing　　40
To prate and talk for life and honour 'fore
Who please to come and hear. For life, I prize it
As I weigh grief, which I would spare: for honour,
'T is a derivative from me to mine,
And only that I stand for. I appeal
To your own conscience, sir, before Polixenes
Came to your court, how I was in your grace,
How merited to be so; since he came,
With what encounter so uncurrent I
Have strain'd, to appear thus : if one jot beyond　50
The bound of honour, or, in act or will,
That way inclining, harden'd be the hearts
Of all that hear me, and my near'st of kin
Cry " Fie !" upon my grave !
　Leon. 　　　　　　　I ne'er heard yet,
That any of these bolder vices wanted
Less impudence to gainsay what they did,
Than to perform it first.
　Her. 　　　　That 's true enough ;
Though 't is a saying, sir, not due to me.
　Leon. You will not own it.
　Her. 　　　　　　More than mistress of
Which comes to me in name of fault, I must not　60
At all acknowledge. For Polixenes
(With whom I am accus'd), I do confess,
I lov'd him, as in honour he requir'd,
With such a kind of love as might become
A lady like me ; with a love, even such,
So and no other, as yourself commanded :
Which not to have done, I think, had been in me
Both disobedience and ingratitude
To you, and toward your friend, whose love had
　　spoke,
Even since it could speak from an infant, freely　70
That it was yours. Now, for conspiracy,
I know not how it tastes, though it be dish'd

For me to try how : all I know of it
Is, that Camillo was an honest man ;
And why he left your court, the gods themselves,
Wotting no more than I, are ignorant.
　Leon. You knew of his departure, as you know
What you have underta'en to do in 's absence.
　Her. Sir,
You speak a language that I understand not :　　80
My life stands in the level of your dreams,
Which I 'll lay down.
　Leon. 　　　　Your actions are my dreams :
You had a bastard by Polixenes,
And I but dream'd it.—As you were past all shame,
(Those of your fact are so) so past all truth,
Which to deny concerns more than avails ; for as
Thy brat hath been cast out, like to itself,
No father owning it (which is, indeed,
More criminal in thee than it), so thou
Shalt feel our justice, in whose easiest passage　90
Look for no less than death.
　Her. 　　　　　　Sir, spare your threats :
The bug, which you would fright me with, I seek.
To me can life be no commodity :
The crown and comfort of my life, your favour,
I do give lost ; for I do feel it gone,
But know not how it went. My second joy,
And first-fruits of my body, from his presence
I am barr'd, like one infectious. My third comfort,
Starr'd most unluckily, is from my breast,
The innocent milk in its most innocent mouth,　100
Haled out to murder : myself on every post
Proclaim'd a strumpet : with immodest hatred,
The childbed privilege denied, which 'longs
To women of all fashion : lastly, hurried
Here to this place, i' the open air, before
I have got strength of limit. Now, my liege,
Tell me what blessings I have here alive,
That I should fear to die ? Therefore, proceed.
But yet hear this ; mistake me not ;—no life,—
I prize it not a straw ; but for mine honour　　110
(Which I would free), if I shall be condemn'd
Upon surmises, all proofs sleeping else
But what your jealousies awake, I tell you,
'T is rigour, and not law.—Your honours all,
I do refer me to the oracle :
Apollo be my judge.
　1 Lord. 　　　　This your request
Is altogether just. Therefore, bring forth,
And in Apollo's name, his oracle.
　　　　　　　　　　[*Exeunt several Officers.*
　Her. The Emperor of Russia was my father :
O ! that he were alive, and here beholding　　120
His daughter's trial ; that he did but see
The flatness of my misery, yet with eyes
Of pity, not revenge !

Re-enter Officers, with CLEOMENES *and* DION.

　Off. You here shall swear upon this sword of
　　justice,
That you, Cleomenes and Dion, have
Been both at Delphos ; and from thence have brought
This seal'd-up oracle, by the hand deliver'd
Of great Apollo's priest ; and that, since then,
You have not dar'd to break the holy seal,
Nor read the secrets in 't.
　Cleo., Dion. 　　　All this we swear.　　130
　Leon. Break up the seals, and read.
　Off. [*Reads.*] "Hermione is chaste, Polixenes blame-
less, Camillo a true subject, Leontes a jealous tyrant,
his innocent babe truly begotten ; and the king shall
live without an heir, if that which is lost be not
found !"
　Lords. Now, blessed be the great Apollo !
　Her. 　　　　　　　　Praised !
　Leon. Hast thou read truth ?
　Off. 　　　　　　Ay, my lord ; even so
As it is here set down.
　Leon. There is no truth at all i' the oracle.　140
The sessions shall proceed : this is mere falsehood.

Enter a Servant, hastily.

　Serv. My lord the king, the king !

Leon.   What is the business?
Serv. O sir! I shall be hated to report it:
The prince your son, with mere conceit and fear
Of the queen's speed, is gone.
Leon.   How! gone?
Serv.   Is dead.
Leon. Apollo's angry, and the heavens themselves
Do strike at my injustice. [HERMIONE *faints.*] How
          now there!
Paul. This news is mortal to the queen.—Look
          down,
And see what death is doing.

Leon. " Apollo's angry, and the heavens themselves
Do strike at my injustice."

Leon.   Take her hence :
Her heart is but o'ercharg'd ; she will recover.— 150
I have too much believ'd mine own suspicion :—
'Beseech you, tenderly apply to her
Some remedies for life.—
          [*Exeunt* PAULINA *and Ladies, with* HERMIONE.
                    Apollo, pardon
My great profaneness 'gainst thine oracle!—
I 'll reconcile me to Polixenes,
New woo my queen, recall the good Camillo,
Whom I proclaim a man of truth, of mercy ;
For, being transported by my jealousies
To bloody thoughts and to revenge, I chose
Camillo for the minister to poison   160
My friend Polixenes : which had been done,
But that the good mind of Camillo tardied
My swift command ; though I with death and with
Reward did threaten and encourage him,
Not doing it, and being done : he, most humane,
And fill'd with honour, to my kingly guest
Unclasp'd my practice, quit his fortunes here,
Which you knew great, and to the certain hazard
Of all uncertainties himself commended,
No richer than his honour :—how he glisters   170
Thorough my rust! and how his piety
Does my deeds make the blacker!

          Re-enter PAULINA.
Paul.   Woe the while!
O, cut my lace, lest my heart, cracking it,
Break too!
1 Lord. What fit is this, good lady? '
Paul. What studied torments, tyrant, hast for me?
What wheels? racks? fires? what flaying? boiling,
In leads, or oils? what old, or newer torture
Must I receive, whose every word deserves

To taste of thy most worst? Thy tyranny,   180
Together working with thy jealousies,—
Fancies too weak for boys, too green and idle
For girls of nine,—O! think, what they have done,
And then run mad, indeed ; stark mad! for all
Thy by-gone fooleries were but spices of it.
That thou betray'dst Polixenes, 't was nothing ;
That did but show thee, of a fool, inconstant,
And damnable ingrateful : nor was 't much,
Thou wouldst have poison'd good Camillo's honour,
To have him kill a king ; poor trespasses,   190
More monstrous standing by! whereof I reckon
          The casting forth to crows thy baby
                    daughter,
To be or none, or little, though a devil
Would have shed water out of fire, ere
          done 't :
Nor is 't directly laid to thee, the death
Of the young prince, whose honourable
                    thoughts
(Thoughts high for one so tender) cleft
          the heart
That could conceive a gross and foolish
          sire
Blemish'd his gracious dam : this is
          not, no,
Laid to thy answer : but the last,—O
          lords!   200
When I have said, cry "woe!"—the
          queen, the queen,
The sweet'st, dear'st creature 's dead ;
          and vengeance for 't
Not dropp'd down yet.
1 Lord.   The higher powers
          forbid!
Paul. I say, she 's dead ; I 'll swear 't :
if word, nor oath,
Prevail not, go and see. If you can
          bring
Tincture, or lustre, in her lip, her eye,
Heat outwardly, or breath within, I 'll
          serve you
As I would do the gods.—But, O thou
          tyrant!
Do not repent these things, for they
          are heavier
Than all thy woes can stir ; therefore, betake thee 210
To nothing but despair. A thousand knees
Ten thousand years together, naked, fasting,
Upon a barren mountain, and still winter,
In storm perpetual, could not move the gods
To look that way thou wert.
Leon.   Go on, go on ;
Thou canst not speak too much : I have deserv'd
All tongues to talk their bitterest.
1 Lord.   Say no more :
Howe'er the business goes, you have made fault
I' the boldness of your speech.
Paul.   I am sorry for 't :
All faults I make, when I shall come to know them,
I do repent. Alas! I have show'd too much   221
The rashness of a woman. He is touch'd
To the noble heart.—What 's gone, and what 's past
          help,
Should be past grief : do not receive affliction
At my petition ; I beseech you rather,
Let me be punish'd, that have minded you
Of what you should forget. Now, good my liege,
Sir, royal sir, forgive a foolish woman :
The love I bore your queen,—lo, fool again!—
I 'll speak of her no more, nor of your children ;   230
I 'll not remember you of my own lord,
Who is lost too. Take your patience to you,
And I 'll say nothing.
Leon.   Thou didst speak but well,
When most the truth, which I receive much better,
Than to be pitied of thee. Pr'ythee, bring me
To the dead bodies of my queen, and son.
One grave shall be for both : upon them shall
The causes of their death appear, unto
Our shame perpetual. Once a day I 'll visit
The chapel where they lie ; and tears shed there   240

Shall be my recreation : so long as nature
Will bear up with this exercise, so long
I daily vow to use it. Come, and lead me
To these sorrows.   [*Exeunt.*

——

Scene III.—Bohemia. A Desert Country near the Sea.

Enter Antigonus, *with the Babe ; and a Mariner.*

Ant. Thou art perfect then, our ship hath touch'd
          upon
The deserts of Bohemia?
    Mar.   Ay, my lord ; and fear
We have landed in ill time : the skies look grimly,
And threaten present blusters. In my conscience,
The heavens with that we have in hand are angry,
And frown upon 's.
    Ant. Their sacred wills be done !—Go, get aboard ;
Look to thy bark : I 'll not be long, before
I call upon thee.
    Mar. Make your best haste, and go not   10
Too far i' the land : 't is like to be loud weather ;
Besides, this place is famous for the creatures
Of prey that keep upon 't.
    Ant.   Go thou away :
I 'll follow instantly.
    Mar.   I am glad at heart
To be so rid o' the business.   [*Exit.*
    Ant.   Come, poor babe :—
I have heard (but not believ'd), the spirits o' the dead
May walk again : if such thing be, thy mother
Appear'd to me last night, for ne'er was dream
So like a waking. To me comes a creature,
Sometimes her head on one side, some another ;   20
I never saw a vessel of like sorrow,
So fill'd, and so becoming : in pure white robes,
Like very sanctity, she did approach
My cabin where I lay, thrice bow'd before me,
And, gasping to begin some speech, her eyes
Became two spouts : the fury spent, anon
Did this break from her :—" Good Antigonus,
Since fate, against thy better disposition,
Hath made thy person for the thrower-out
Of my poor babe, according to thine oath,   30
Places remote enough are in Bohemia,
There weep, and leave it crying ; and, for the babe
Is counted lost for ever, Perdita,
I pr'ythee, call 't : for this ungentle business,
Put on thee by my lord, thou ne'er shalt see
Thy wife Paulina more : "—and so, with shrieks,
She melted into air. Affrighted much,
I did in time collect myself, and thought
This was so, and no slumber. Dreams are toys ;
Yet for this once, yea, superstitiously,   40
I will be squar'd by this. I do believe,
Hermione hath suffer'd death ; and that
Apollo would, this being indeed the issue
Of King Polixenes, it should here be laid,
Either for life or death, upon the earth
Of its right father.—Blossom, speed thee well !
                          [*Laying down the Babe.*
There lie ; and there thy character : there these,
                          [*Laying down a bundle.*
Which may, if fortune please, both breed thee, pretty,
And still rest thine.—The storm begins.—Poor wretch !
That for thy mother's fault art thus expos'd   50
To loss, and what may follow.—Weep I cannot,
But my heart bleeds, and most accurs'd am I,
To be by oath enjoin'd to this.—Farewell !
The day frowns more and more : thou art like to have
A lullaby too rough. I never saw
The heavens so dim by day. A savage clamour !—
Well may I get aboard !—This is the chase ;
I am gone for ever.   [*Exit, pursued by a bear.*

Enter an Old Shepherd.

Shep. I would there were no age between ten and
three-and-twenty, or that youth would sleep out the
rest ; for there is nothing in the between but getting
wenches with child, wronging the ancientry, stealing,
fighting.—Hark you now !— Would any but these
boiled-brains of nineteen, and two-and-twenty, hunt
this weather? They have scared away two of my
best sheep ; which, I fear, the wolf will sooner find
than the master : if anywhere I have them, 't is by
the sea-side, browsing of ivy. Good luck, an 't be thy
will !—What have we here ? [*Taking up the Babe.*]
Mercy on 's, a barn ; a very pretty barn ! A boy, or a
child, I wonder? A pretty one ; a very pretty one.
Sure some scape : though I am not bookish, yet I can
read waiting-gentlewoman in the scape. This has
been some stair-work, some trunk-work, some behind-
door-work : they were warmer that got this, than the
poor thing is here. I 'll take it up for pity ; yet I 'll

Shep. " Now bless thyself : thou mettest with things dying, I
with things new-born."

tarry till my son come : he hollaed but even now.—
Whoa, ho hoa !
    Clo. [*Without.*] Hilloa, loa !   79
    Shep. What ! art so near ? If thou 'lt see a thing to
talk on when thou art dead and rotten, come hither.

Enter Clown.

What ail'st thou, man ?
    Clo. I have seen two such sights, by sea, and by
land—but I am not to say it is a sea, for it is now the
sky : betwixt the firmament and it you cannot thrust
a bodkin's point.
    Shep. Why, boy, how is it ?   87
    Clo. I would you did but see how it chafes, how it
rages, how it takes up the shore ! but that 's not to the
point. O, the most piteous cry of the poor souls !
sometimes to see 'em, and not to see 'em ; now the ship
boring the moon with her mainmast, and anon swallowed with yest and froth, as you 'd thrust a cork into
a hogshead. And then for the land-service :—to see
how the bear tore out his shoulder-bone ; how he cried
to me for help, and said, his name was Antigonus, a
nobleman.—But to make an end of the ship :—to see
how the sea flap-dragoned it ;—but, first, how the poor
souls roared, and the sea mocked them ;—and how the

poor gentleman roared, and the bear mocked him,
both roaring louder than the sea or weather.   101
Shep. Name of mercy! when was this, boy?
Clo. Now, now; I have not winked since I saw
these sights: the men are not yet cold under water,
nor the bear half-dined on the gentleman: he's at it
now.
Shep. 'Would I had been by, to have helped the old
man!
Clo. I would you had been by the ship's side, to
have helped her: there your charity would have
lacked footing.   111
Shep. Heavy matters! heavy matters! but look
thee here, boy. Now bless thyself: thou mettest with
things dying, I with things new-born. Here's a sight
for thee: look thee, a bearing-cloth for a squire's
child! Look thee here: take up, take up, boy; open't.
So, let's see. It was told me, I should be rich by the
fairies: this is some changeling. — Open't: what's
within, boy?   119

Clo. You're a made old man: if the sins of your
youth are forgiven you, you're well to live. Gold!
all gold!
Shep. This is fairy gold, boy, and 't will prove so:
up with't, keep it close; home, home, the next way.
We are lucky, boy; and to be so still requires nothing
but secrecy.—Let my sheep go.—Come, good boy, the
next way home.
Clo. Go you the next way with your findings: I'll
go see if the bear be gone from the gentleman, and
how much he hath eaten: they are never curst, but
when they are hungry. If there be any of him left,
I'll bury it.   132
Shep. That's a good deed. If thou may'st discern
by that which is left of him, what he is, fetch me to
the sight of him.
Clo. Marry, will I; and you shall help to put him i'
the ground.
Shep. 'T is a lucky day, boy, and we'll do good deeds
on 't.   [*Exeunt.*

ACT IV.

Enter Time, *as Chorus.*

Time.

THAT please some, try all; both joy, and
terror,
Of good and bad; that make, and unfold
error:—
Now take upon me, in the name of Time,
To use my wings. Impute it not a crime
To me, or my swift passage, that I slide
O'er sixteen years, and leave the growth
untried
Of that wide gap; since it is in my power
To o'erthrow law, and in one-self-born hour
To plant and o'erwhelm custom. Let me
pass
The same I am, ere ancient'st order was,   10
Or what is now receiv'd: I witness to
The times that brought them in; so shall I do
To the freshest things now reigning, and make stale
The glistering of this present, as my tale
Now seems to it. Your patience this allowing,
I turn my glass, and give my scene such growing,
As you had slept between. Leontes leaving,—
The effects of his fond jealousies so grieving,
That he shuts up himself;—imagine me,
Gentle spectators, that I now may be   20
In fair Bohemia; and remember well,
I mention'd a son o' the king's, which Florizel
I now name to you; and with speed so pace
To speak of Perdita, now grown in grace
Equal with wondering: what of her ensues,
I list not prophesy; but let Time's news
Be known, when 't is brought forth:—a shepherd's
daughter,
And what to her adheres, which follows after,
Is the argument of Time. Of this allow,
If ever you have spent time worse ere now: 30
If never, yet that Time himself doth say,
He wishes earnestly you never may.   [*Exit.*

Scene I.—Bohemia. A Room in the Palace of
Polixenes.

Enter Polixenes *and* Camillo.

Pol. I pray thee, good Camillo, be no more importu-

nate: 't is a sickness denying thee anything, a death
to grant this.
Cam. It is fifteen years, since I saw my country:
though I have, for the most part, been aired abroad,
I desire to lay my bones there. Besides, the penitent
king, my master, hath sent for me; to whose feeling
sorrows I might be some allay, or I o'erween to think
so,—which is another spur to my departure.   9
Pol. As thou lovest me, Camillo, wipe not out the
rest of thy services, by leaving me now. The need I
have of thee, thine own goodness hath made: better
not to have had thee, than thus to want thee. Thou,
having made me businesses, which none without thee
can sufficiently manage, must either stay to execute
them thyself, or take away with thee the very services thou hast done; which if I have not enough
considered (as too much I cannot), to be more thankful to thee shall be my study, and my profit therein,
the heaping friendships. Of that fatal country,
Sicilia, pr'ythee speak no more, whose very naming
punishes me with the remembrance of that penitent,
as thou call'st him, and reconciled king, my brother;
whose loss of his most precious queen and children
are even now to be afresh lamented. Say to me,
when saw'st thou the Prince Florizel, my son?
Kings are no less unhappy, their issue not being
gracious, than they are in losing them when they have
approved their virtues.   29
Cam. Sir, it is three days, since I saw the prince.
What his happier affairs may be, are to me unknown;
but I have, missingly, noted, he is of late much retired from court, and is less frequent to his princely
exercises than formerly he hath appeared.
Pol. I have considered so much, Camillo, and with
some care; so far, that I have eyes under my service,
which look upon his removedness: from whom I have
this intelligence, that he is seldom from the house of a
most homely shepherd; a man, they say, that from
very nothing, and beyond the imagination of his
neighbours, is grown into an unspeakable estate.   41
Cam. I have heard, sir, of such a man, who hath a
daughter of most rare note: the report of her is
extended more that can be thought to begin from
such a cottage.
Pol. That's likewise part of my intelligence, but, I

fear, the angle that plucks our son thither. Thou shalt accompany us to the place, where we will, not appearing what we are, have some question with the shepherd; from whose simplicity I think it not uneasy to get the cause of my son's resort thither. Pr'ythee, be my present partner in this business, and lay aside the thoughts of Sicilia.   53

Cam. I willingly obey your command.

Pol. My best Camillo!—We must disguise ourselves.
     [*Exeunt.*

SCENE II.—The Same. A Road near the Shepherd's Cottage.

Enter AUTOLYCUS, *singing.*

When daffodils begin to peer,—
  With, heigh! the doxy over the dale,—
Why, then comes in the sweet o' the year;
  For the red blood reigns in the winter's pale.

The white sheet bleaching on the hedge,—
  With heigh! the sweet birds, O, how they sing!—
Doth set my pugging tooth on edge;
  For a quart of ale is a dish for a king.

The lark, that tirra-lirra chants,—
  With heigh! with heigh! the thrush and the jay,
Are summer songs for me and my aunts,   11
  While we lie tumbling in the hay.

I have served Prince Florizel, and, in my time, wore three-pile; but now I am out of service:

But shall I go mourn for that, my dear?
  The pale moon shines by night;
And when I wander here and there,
  I then do most go right.

If tinkers may have leave to live,
  And bear the sow-skin budget,   20
Then my account I well may give,
  And in the stocks avouch it.

My traffic is sheets; when the kite builds, look to lesser linen. My father named me Autolycus; who being, as I am, littered under Mercury, was likewise a snapper-up of unconsidered trifles. With die and drab, I purchased this caparison, and my revenue is the silly cheat. Gallows, and knock, are too powerful on the highway: beating, and hanging, are terrors to me: for the life to come, I sleep out the thought of it.—A prize! a prize!   31

Enter Clown.

Clo. Let me see:—every 'leven wether tods; every tod yields—pound and odd shilling: fifteen hundred shorn,—what comes the wool to?

Aut. [*Aside.*] If the springe hold, the cock's mine.

Clo. I cannot do't without counters.—Let me see; what am I to buy for our sheep-shearing feast? "Three pound of sugar; five pound of currants; rice,"—what will this sister of mine do with rice? But my father hath made her mistress of the feast, and she lays it on. She hath made me four-and-twenty nosegays for the shearers; three-man song-men all, and very good ones, but they are most of them means and bases: but one Puritan amongst them, and he sings psalms to hornpipes. I must have saffron, to colour the warden pies; mace,—dates,—none; that's out of my note: "nutmegs, seven: a race or two of ginger;" but that I may beg:—"four pound of prunes, and as many of raisins o' the sun."   50

Aut. O, that ever I was born!
     [*Grovelling on the ground.*

Clo. I' the name of me,—

Aut. O, help me, help me! pluck but off these rags, and then, death, death!

Clo. Alack, poor soul! thou hast need of more rags to lay on thee, rather than have these off.

Aut. O, sir! the loathsomeness of them offend me more than the stripes I have received, which are mighty ones, and millions.

Clo. Alas, poor man! a million of beating may come to a great matter.   61

Aut. I am robbed, sir, and beaten; my money and apparel ta'en from me, and these detestable things put upon me.

Clo. What, by a horseman, or a footman?

Aut. A footman, sweet sir, a footman.

Aut. "O, help me, help me! pluck but off these rags, and then, death, death!"

Clo. Indeed, he should be a footman, by the garments he hath left with thee: if this be a horseman's coat, it hath seen very hot service. Lend me thy hand, I'll help thee: come, lend me thy hand.   70
     [*Helping him up.*

Aut. O! good sir, tenderly, O!

Clo. Alas, poor soul!

Aut. O, good sir; softly, good sir. I fear, sir, my shoulder-blade is out.

Clo. How now? canst stand?

Aut. Softly, dear sir: [*picks his pocket*] good sir, softly. You ha' done me a charitable office.

Clo. Dost lack any money? I have a little money for thee.   79

Aut. No, good, sweet sir: no, I beseech you, sir. I have a kinsman not past three-quarters of a mile hence, unto whom I was going: I shall there have money, or anything I want. Offer me no money, I pray you! that kills my heart.

Clo. What manner of fellow was he that robbed you?

Aut. A fellow, sir, that I have known to go about with trol-my-dames: I knew him once a servant of the prince. I cannot tell, good sir, for which of his virtues it was, but he was certainly whipped out of the court.   91

Clo. His vices, you would say: there's no virtue whipped out of the court: they cherish it, to make it stay there, and yet it will no more but abide.

Aut. Vices, I would say, sir. I know this man well: he hath been since an ape-bearer; then a process-server, a bailiff; then he compassed a motion of the Prodigal Son, and married a tinker's wife within a mile where my land and living lies; and, having flown over many knavish professions, he settled only in rogue: some call him Autolycus.   101

Clo. Out upon him! Prig, for my life, prig: he haunts wakes, fairs, and bear-baitings.

Aut. Very true, sir; he, sir, he: that's the rogue,
that put me into this apparel.

Clo. Not a more cowardly rogue in all Bohemia: if
you had but looked big, and spit at him, he'd have
run.

Aut. I must confess to you, sir, I am no fighter: I
am false of heart that way, and that he knew, I
warrant him.   111

Clo. How do you now?

Aut. Sweet sir, much better than I was: I can
stand, and walk. I will even take my leave of you,
and pace softly towards my kinsman's.

Clo. Shall I bring thee on the way?

Aut. No, good-faced sir; no, sweet sir.

Clo. Then fare thee well. I must go buy spices for
our sheep-shearing.   119

Aut. Prosper you, sweet sir! [*Exit Clown.*]—Your
purse is not hot enough to purchase your spice. I'll
be with you at your sheep-shearing too. If I make
not this cheat bring out another, and the shearers
prove sheep, let me be unrolled, and my name put in
the book of virtue!

> *Jog on, jog on, the foot-path way,*
> *And merrily hent the stile-a:*
> *A merry heart goes all the day,*
> *Your sad tires in a mile-a.*   [*Exit.*

Scene III.—*The Same. A Lawn before a Shepherd's
Cottage.*

Enter Florizel *and* Perdita.

Flo. These your unusual weeds to each part of you
Do give a life: no shepherdess, but Flora
Peering in April's front. This your sheep-shearing
Is as a meeting of the petty gods,
And you the queen on't.

Per.   Sir, my gracious lord,
To chide at your extremes it not becomes me:
O! pardon, that I name them.—Your high self,
The gracious mark o' the land, you have obscur'd
With a swain's wearing, and me, poor lowly maid,
Most goddess-like prank'd up. But that our feasts 10
In every mess have folly, and the feeders
Digest it with a custom, I should blush
To see you so attired, swoon, I think,
To show myself a glass.

Flo.   I bless the time,
When my good falcon made her flight across
Thy father's ground.

Per.   Now, Jove afford you cause!
To me the difference forges dread; your greatness
Hath not bèen us'd to fear. Even now I tremble
To think, your father, by some accident,
Should pass this way, as you did. O, the Fates! 20
How would he look, to see his work, so noble,
Vilely bound up? What would he say? Or how
Should I, in these my borrow'd flaunts, behold
The sternness of his presence?

Flo.   Apprehend
Nothing but jollity. The gods themselves,
Humbling their deities to love, have taken
The shapes of beasts upon them: Jupiter
Became a bull, and bellow'd; the green Neptune
A ram, and bleated; and the fire-rob'd god,
Golden Apollo, a poor humble swain,   30
As I seem now. Their transformations
Were never for a piece of beauty rarer,
Nor in a way so chaste, since my desires
Run not before mine honour, nor my lusts
Burn hotter than my faith.

Per.   O! but, sir,
Your resolution cannot hold, when 'tis
Oppos'd, as it must be, by the power of the king.
One of these two must be necessities,
Which then will speak,—that you must change this
                                                        purpose,
Or I my life.

Flo.   Thou dearest Perdita,   40
With these forc'd thoughts, I pr'ythee, darken not

The mirth o' the feast: or I'll be thine, my fair,
Or not my father's; for I cannot be
Mine own, nor anything to any, if
I be not thine: to this I am most constant,
Though destiny say, no. Be merry, gentle;
Strangle such thoughts as these with anything
That you behold the while. Your guests are coming:
Lift up your countenance, as it were the day
Of celebration of that nuptial, which   50
We two have sworn shall come.

Per.   O Lady Fortune,
Stand you auspicious!

Flo.   See, your guests approach:
Address yourself to entertain them sprightly,
And let's be red with mirth.

Enter Shepherd, *with* Polixenes *and* Camillo, *disguised;* Clown, Mopsa, Dorcas, *and others.*

Shep. Fie, daughter! when my old wife liv'd, upon
This day she was both pantler, butler, cook;
Both dame and servant; welcom'd all, serv'd all;
Would sing her song, and dance her turn; now
                                                        here,
At upper end o' the table, now i' the middle;
On his shoulder, and his; her face o' fire   60
With labour, and the thing she took to quench it,
She would to each one sip. You are retir'd,
As if you were a feasted one, and not
The hostess of the meeting: 'pray you, bid
These unknown friends to us welcome; for it is
A way to make us better friends, more known.
Come; quench your blushes, and present yourself
That which you are, mistress o' the feast: come on,
And bid us welcome to your sheep-shearing,
As your good flock shall prosper.

Per. [*To* Polixenes.]   Sir, welcome.   70
It is my father's will, I should take on me
The hostess-ship o' the day. [*To* Camillo.] You're
                                                welcome, sir.—
Give me those flowers there, Dorcas.—Reverend sirs,
For you there's rosemary, and rue; these keep
Seeming and savour all the winter long:
Grace, and remembrance, be to you both,
And welcome to our shearing!

Pol.   Shepherdess
(A fair one are you), well you fit our ages
With flowers of winter.

Per.   Sir, the year growing ancient,—
Not yet on summer's death, nor on the birth   80
Of trembling winter,—the fairest flowers o' the season
Are our carnations, and streak'd gillyvors,
Which some call nature's bastards: of that kind
Our rustic garden's barren, and I care not
To get slips of them.

Pol.   Wherefore, gentle maiden,
Do you neglect them?

Per.   For I have heard it said,
There is an art which, in their piedness, shares
With great creating nature.

Pol.   Say, there be;
Yet nature is made better by no mean,
But nature makes that mean: so, o'er that art,   90
Which, you say, adds to nature, is an art
That nature makes. You see, sweet maid, we marry
A gentler scion to the wildest stock,
And make conceive a bark of baser kind
By bud of noble race: this is an art
Which does mend nature,—change it rather; but
The art itself is nature.

Per.   So it is.

Pol. Then make your garden rich in gillyvors,
And do not call them bastards.

Per.   I'll not put
The dibble in earth to set one slip of them: 100
No more than, were I painted, I would wish
This youth should say, 't were well, and only therefore
Desire to breed by me.—Here's flowers for you;
Hot lavender, mints, savory, marjoram;
The marigold, that goes to bed wi' the sun,
And with him rises weeping: these are flowers
Of middle summer, and, I think, they are given
To men of middle age. You are very welcome.

Cam. I should leave grazing, were I of your flock,
And only live by gazing.
     Per.   Out, alas!   110
You'd be so lean, that blasts of January

The winds of March with beauty; violets dim,   120
But sweeter than the lids of Juno's eyes,
Or Cytherea's breath; pale primroses,
That die unmarried ere they can behold

Flo.   "Thou dearest Perdita,
With these forc'd thoughts, I pr'ythee, darken not
The mirth o' the feast."

Would blow you through and through.—Now, my
     fair'st friend,
I would, I had some flowers o' the spring, that might
Become your time of day; and yours, and yours,
That wear upon your virgin branches yet
Your maidenheads growing:—O Proserpina!
For the flowers now, that, frighted, thou lett'st fall
From Dis's waggon! daffodils,
That come before the swallow dares, and take

Bright Phœbus in his strength, a malady
Most incident to maids; bold oxlips, and
The crown-imperial; lilies of all kinds,
The flower-de-luce being one. O, these I lack,
To make you garlands of, and my sweet friend,
To strew him o'er and o'er.
     Flo.   What, like a corse?
     Per. No, like a bank, for love to lie and play on, **130**
Not like a corse; or if,—not to be buried,

But quick, and in mine arms. Come, take your flowers.
Methinks, I play as I have seen them do
In Whitsun-pastorals: sure, this robe of mine
Does change my disposition.
   Flo.   What you do
Still betters what is done. When you speak, sweet,
I'd have you do it ever: when you sing,
I'd have you buy and sell so; so give alms;
Pray so; and, for the ordering your affairs,
To sing them too: when you do dance, I wish you   140
A wave o' the sea, that you might ever do
Nothing but that; move still, still so,
And own no other function: each your doing,
So singular in each particular,
Crowns what you are doing in the present deeds,
That all your acts are queens.
   Per.   O Doricles!
Your praises are too large: but that your youth,
And the true blood, which peeps fairly through it,
Do plainly give you out an unstain'd shepherd
With wisdom I might fear, my Doricles,   150
You woo'd me the false way.
   Flo.   I think, you have
As little skill to fear, as I have purpose
To put you to 't.—But, come; our dance, I pray.
Your hand, my Perdita: so turtles pair,
That never mean to part.
   Per.   I'll swear for 'em.
   Pol. This is the prettiest low-born lass, that ever
Ran on the green-sward: nothing she does, or seems,
But smacks of something greater than herself;
Too noble for this place.
   Cam.   He tells her something,
That makes her blood look out. Good sooth, she is   160
The queen of curds and cream.
   Clo.   Come on, strike up.
   Dor. Mopsa must be your mistress: marry, garlic,
To mend her kissing with!
   Mop.   Now, in good time!
   Clo. Not a word, a word: we stand upon our
manners.—
Come, strike up.   [*Music.*
   [*Here a dance of Shepherds and Shepherdesses.*
   Pol. Pray, good shepherd, what fair swain is this,
Which dances with your daughter?
   Shep. They call him Doricles, and boasts himself
To have a worthy feeding; but I have it
Upon his own report, and I believe it: 170
He looks like sooth. He says, he loves my daughter:
I think so too; for never gaz'd the moon
Upon the water, as he'll stand, and read,
As 't were, my daughter's eyes; and, to be plain,
I think, there is not half a kiss to choose,
Who loves another best.
   Pol.   She dances featly.
   Shep. So she does anything, though I report it,
That should be silent. If young Doricles
Do light upon her, she shall bring him that
Which he not dreams of.   180

               Enter a Servant.

   Serv. O master! if you did but hear the pedlar at the
door, you would never dance again after a tabor and
pipe; no, the bagpipe could not move you. He sings
several tunes faster than you'll tell money; he utters
them as he had eaten ballads, and all men's ears grew
to his tunes.
   Clo. He could never come better: he shall come in.
I love a ballad but even too well; if it be doleful
matter, merrily set down, or a very pleasant thing
indeed, and sung lamentably.   190
   Serv. He hath songs, for man, or woman, of all sizes:
no milliner can so fit his customers with gloves. He
has the prettiest love-songs for maids; so without
bawdry, which is strange; with such delicate burdens
of "dildos" and "fadings," "jump her and thump
her;" and where some stretch-mouth'd rascal would,
as it were, mean mischief, and break a foul gap into
the matter, he makes the maid to answer, "Whoop,
do me no harm, good man;" puts him off, slights him
with "Whoop, do me no harm, good man."   200
   Pol. This is a brave fellow.

   Clo. Believe me, thou talkest of an admirable-con-
ceited fellow. Has he any unbraided wares?
   Serv. He hath ribands of all the colours i' the rainbow; points, more than all the lawyers in Bohemia
can learnedly handle, though they come to him by the
gross; inkles, caddisses, cambrics, lawns: why, he
sings them over, as they were gods or goddesses. You
would think a smock were a she-angel, he so chants
to the sleeve-hand, and the work about the square
on 't.   211
   Clo. Pr'ythee, bring him in, and let him approach
singing.
   Per. Forewarn him, that he use no scurrilous words
in 's tunes.   [*Exit Servant.*
   Clo. You have of these pedlars, that have more in
them than you'd think, sister.
   Per. Ay, good brother, or go about to think.

             Enter Autolycus, *singing.*

   Lawn, as white as driven snow;
   Cyprus, black as e'er was crow;   220
   Gloves, as sweet as damask roses;
   Masks for faces, and for noses;
   Bugle-bracelet, necklace-amber,
   Perfume for a lady's chamber;
   Golden quoifs, and stomachers,
   For my lads to give their dears;
   Pins and poking-sticks of steel;
   What maids lack from head to heel:
   Come, buy of me, come; come buy, come buy;
   Buy, lads, or else your lasses cry: 230
   Come, buy.

   Clo. If I were not in love with Mopsa, thou shouldst
take no money of me; but being enthrall'd as I am, it
will also be the bondage of certain ribands and gloves.
   Mop. I was promised them against the feast, but
they come not too late now.
   Dor. He hath promised you more than that, or
there be liars.
   Mop. He hath paid you all he promised you: may
be, he has paid you more, which will shame you to
give him again.   241
   Clo. Is there no manners left among maids? will
they wear their plackets, where they should bear their
faces? Is there not milking-time, when you are going
to bed, or kiln-hole, to whistle off these secrets, but
you must be tittle-tattling before all our guests? 'T is
well they are whispering. Clamour your tongues,
and not a word more.
   Mop. I have done. Come, you promised me a
tawdry lace, and a pair of sweet gloves.   250
   Clo. Have I not told thee, how I was cozened by the
way, and lost all my money?
   Aut. And, indeed, sir, there are cozeners abroad;
therefore it behoves men to be wary.
   Clo. Fear not thou, man, thou shalt lose nothing
here.
   Aut. I hope so, sir; for I have about me many
parcels of charge.
   Clo. What hast here? ballads?
   Mop. 'Pray now, buy some: I love a ballad in print,
o' life, for then we are sure they are true.   261
   Aut. Here's one to a very doleful tune, how a
usurer's wife was brought to bed of twenty money-
bags at a burden; and how she longed to eat adders'
heads, and toads carbonadoed.
   Mop. Is it true, think you?
   Aut. Very true; and but a month old.
   Dor. Bless me from marrying a usurer!
   Aut. Here's the midwife's name to 't, one Mistress
Taleporter, and five or six honest wives' that were
present. Why should I carry lies abroad?   271
   Mop. 'Pray you now, buy it.
   Clo. Come on, lay it by: and let's first see more
ballads; we'll buy the other things anon.
   Aut. Here's another ballad, of a fish, that appeared
upon the coast, on Wednesday the forescore of April,
forty thousand fathom above water, and sung this
ballad against the hard hearts of maids: it was
thought she was a woman, and was turned into a
cold fish, for she would not exchange flesh with one
that loved her. The ballad is very pitiful, and as true.

Dor. Is it true too, think you?   282
Aut. Five justices' hands at it, and witnesses more
than my pack will hold.
Clo. Lay it by too: another.
Aut. This is a merry ballad, but a very pretty one.
Mop. Let's have some merry ones.
Aut. Why, this is a passing merry one, and goes to
the tune of "Two maids wooing a man." There's
scarce a maid westward but she sings it: 'tis in
request, I can tell you.   291
Mop. We can both sing it: if thou'lt bear a part,
thou shalt hear; 'tis in three parts.
Dor. We had the tune on't a month ago.
Aut. I can bear my part; you must know, 'tis my
occupation: have at it with you.

SONG.

Aut. Get you hence, for I must go,
    Where it fits not you to know.
Dor. Whither?
Mop. O! whither?   300
Dor. Whither?
Mop. It becomes thy oath full well,
    Thou to me thy secrets tell.
Dor. Me too: let me go thither.
Mop. Or thou go'st to the grange, or mill.
Dor. If to either, thou dost ill.
Aut. Neither.
Dor. What, neither?
Aut. Neither.
Dor. Thou hast sworn my love to be.   310
Mop. Thou hast sworn it more to me:
    Then, whither go'st? say, whither?

Clo. We'll have this song out anon by ourselves.
My father and the gentlemen are in sad talk, and we'll
not trouble them: come, bring away thy pack after
me. Wenches, I'll buy for you both. Pedlar, let's
have the first choice.—Follow me, girls.
Aut. [*Aside.*] And you shall pay well for 'em.

    Will you buy any tape,
      Or lace for your cape,   320
    My dainty duck, my dear-a?
      Any silk, any thread,
      Any toys for your head,
    Of the new'st and fin'st, fin'st wear-a?
      Come to the pedlar;
      Money's a medler,
    That doth utter all men's ware-a.   327
[*Exeunt Clown, AUTOLYCUS, DORCAS, and MOPSA.*

Re-enter Servant.

Serv. Master, there is three carters, three shepherds,
three neat-herds, three swine-herds, that have made
themselves all men of hair: they call themselves
Saltiers; and they have a dance, which the wenches
say is a gallimaufry of gambols, because they are not
in't; but they themselves are o' the mind, (if it be not
too rough for some, that know little but bowling) it
will please plentifully.
Shep. Away! we'll none on't: here has been too
much homely foolery already.—I know, sir, we weary
you.
Pol. You weary those that refresh us. Pray, let's
see these four threes of herdsmen.   340
Serv. One three of them, by their own report, sir,
hath danced before the king; and not the worst of the
three, but jumps twelve foot and a half by the squire.
Shep. Leave your prating. Since these good men
are pleased, let them come in: but quickly now.
Serv. Why, they stay at door, sir.   [*Exit.*

Re-enter Servant, with twelve Rustics habited like Satyrs. They dance, and then exeunt.

Pol. O father! you'll know more of that hereafter.—
Is it not too far gone?—'T is time to part them.—
He's simple, and tells much. How now, fair shep-
herd?
Your heart is full of something, that does take   350
Your mind from feasting. Sooth, when I was young,
And handed love as you do, I was wont
To load my she with knacks: I would have ransack'd

The pedlar's silken treasury, and have pour'd it
To her acceptance; you have let him go,
And nothing marted with him. If your lass
Interpretation should abuse, and call this
Your lack of love or bounty, you were straited
For a reply, at least, if you make a care
Of happy holding her.
Flo.   Old sir, I know   360
She prizes not such trifles as these are.
The gifts she looks from me are pack'd and lock'd
Up in my heart, which I have given already,
But not deliver'd.—O! hear me breathe my life
Before this ancient sir, who, it should seem,
Hath sometime lov'd: I take thy hand; this hand,
As soft as dove's down, and as white as it,
Or Ethiopian's tooth, or the fann'd snow
That's bolted by the northern blasts twice o'er.
Pol. What follows this?—   370
How prettily the young swain seems to wash
The hand, was fair before!—I have put you out.—
But, to your protestation: let me hear
What you profess.
Flo.   Do, and be witness to 't.
Pol. And this my neighbour too?
Flo.   And he, and more
Than he, and men; the earth, the heavens, and all;
That, were I crown'd the most imperial monarch,
Thereof most worthy, were I the fairest youth
That ever made eye swerve, had force, and knowledge
More than was ever man's, I would not prize them,
Without her love: for her, employ them all,   381
Commend them, and condemn them to her service,
Or to their own perdition.
Pol.   Fairly offer'd.
Cam. This shows a sound affection.
Shep.   But, my daughter,
Say you the like to him?
Per.   I cannot speak
So well, nothing so well; no, nor mean better:
By the pattern of mine own thoughts I cut out
The purity of his.
Shep.   Take hands; a bargain:—
And, friends unknown, you shall bear witness to 't:
I give my daughter to him, and will make   390
Her portion equal his.
Flo.   O! that must be
I' the virtue of your daughter: one being dead,
I shall have more than you can dream of yet;
Enough then for your wonder. But, come on;
Contract us 'fore these witnesses.
Shep.   Come, your hand;
And, daughter, yours.
Pol.   Soft, swain, awhile, 'beseech you.
Have you a father?
Flo.   I have; but what of him?
Pol. Knows he of this?
Flo.   He neither does, or shall.
Pol. Methinks, a father
Is at the nuptial of his son a guest   400
That best becomes the table. Pray you, once more,
Is not your father grown incapable
Of reasonable affairs? is he not stupid
With age, and altering rheums? can he speak? hear?
Know man from man? dispute his own estate?
Lies he not bed-rid? and again, does nothing,
But what he did being childish?
Flo.   No, good sir:
He has his health, and ampler strength, indeed,
Than most have of his age.
Pol.   By my white beard,   410
You offer him, if this be so, a wrong
Something unfilial. Reason, my son
Should choose himself a wife; but as good reason,
The father (all whose joy is nothing else
But fair posterity) should hold some counsel
In such a business.
Flo.   I yield all this;
But for some other reasons, my grave sir,
Which 't is not fit you know, I not acquaint
My father of this business.
Pol.   Let him know 't.
Flo. He shall not.

Pol.   Pr'ythee, let him.
Flo.   No, he must not.
Shep. Let him, my son : he shall not need to grieve
At knowing of thy choice.
Flo.   Come, come, he must not.—
Mark our contract.
Pol.   Mark your divorce, young sir, 422
                    [*Discovering himself.*
Whom son I dare not call : thou art too base
To be acknowledg'd. Thou a sceptre's heir,
That thus affects a sheep-hook !—Thou old traitor,
I am sorry, that by hanging thee I can but
Shorten thy life one week.—And thou, fresh piece
Of excellent witchcraft, who, of force, must know
The royal fool thou cop'st with,—
Shep.   O, my heart !
Pol. I 'll have thy beauty scratch'd with briers, and
made   430
More homely than thy state.—For thee, fond boy,
If I may ever know, thou dost but sigh,
That thou no more shalt see this knack (as never
I mean thou shalt), we 'll bar thee from succession ;
Not hold thee of our blood, no, not our kin,
Far than Deucalion off :—mark thou my words ;
Follow us to the court. —Thou, churl, for this time,
Though full of our displeasure, yet we free thee
From the dead blow of it.—And you, enchantment,—
Worthy enough a herdsman ; yea, him too,   440
That makes himself, but for our honour therein,
Unworthy thee,—if ever henceforth thou
These rural latches to his entrance open,
Or hoop his body more with thy embraces,
I will devise a death as cruel for thee,
As thou art tender to 't.   [*Exit.*
Per.   Even here undone !
I was not much afeard ; for once, or twice,
I was about to speak, and tell him plainly,
The selfsame sun that shines upon his court,
Hides not his visage from our cottage, but   450
Looks on alike.—[*To* Florizel.] Will 't please you,
            sir, be gone ?
I told you what would come of this. 'Beseech you,
Of your own state take care : this dream of mine,
Being now awake, I 'll queen it no inch further,
But milk my ewes, and weep.
Cam.   Why, how now, father ?
Speak, ere thou diest.
Shep.   I cannot speak, nor think,
Nor dare to know that which I know.—[*To* Florizel.]
O sir !
You have undone a man of fourscore-three,
That thought to fill his grave in quiet ; yea,   460
To die upon the bed my father died,
To lie close by his honest bones : but now
Some hangman must put on my shroud, and lay me
Where no priest shovels in dust.—[*To* Perdita.] O
cursed wretch !
That knew'st this was the prince, and wouldst adven-
            ture
To mingle faith with him.—Undone ! undone !
If I might die within this hour, I have liv'd
To die when I desire.   [*Exit.*
Flo.   Why look you so upon me ?
I am but sorry, not afear'd ; delay'd,
But nothing alter'd. What I was, I am :
More straining on, for plucking back ; not following
My leash unwillingly.
Cam.   Gracious my lord,   471
You know your father's temper : at this time
He will allow no speech (which, I do guess,
You do not purpose to him), and as hardly
Will he endure your sight as yet, I fear :
Then, till the fury of his highness settle,
Come not before him.
Flo.   I not purpose it.
I think, Camillo ?
Cam.   Even he, my lord.
Per. How often have I told you 't would be thus !
How often said, my dignity would last   480
But till 't were known !
Flo.   It cannot fail, but by
The violation of my faith ; and then,

Let nature crush the sides o' the earth together,
And mar the seeds within !—Lift up thy looks :—
From my succession wipe me, father ; I
Am heir to my affection.
Cam.   Be advis'd.
Flo. I am ; and by my fancy : if my reason
Will thereto be obedient, I have reason ;
If not, my senses, better pleas'd with madness,
Do bid it welcome.
Cam.   This is desperate, sir.   490
Flo. So call it ; but it does fulfil my vow,
I needs must think it honesty. Camillo,
Not for Bohemia, nor the pomp that may
Be thereat glean'd, for all the sun sees, or
The close earth wombs, or the profound seas hide
In unknown fathoms, will I break my oath
To this my fair belov'd. Therefore, I pray you,
As you have ever been my father's honour'd friend,
When he shall miss me (as, in faith, I mean not
To see him any more), cast your good counsels   500
Upon his passion : let myself and fortune
Tug for the time to come. This you may know,
And so deliver.—I am put to sea
With her, whom here I cannot hold on shore ;
And, most opportune to our need, I have
A vessel rides fast by, but not prepar'd
For this design. What course I mean to hold,
Shall nothing benefit your knowledge, nor
Concern me the reporting.
Cam.   O my lord !
I would your spirit were easier for advice,   510
Or stronger for your need.
Flo.   Hark, Perdita.—[*Takes her aside.*
[*To* Camillo.] I 'll hear you by-and-by.
Cam.   He 's irremovable
Resolv'd for flight. Now were I happy, if
His going I could frame to serve my turn,
Save him from danger, do him love and honour,
Purchase the sight again of dear Sicilia,
And that unhappy king, my master, whom
I so much thirst to see.
Flo.   Now, good Camillo,
I am so fraught with curious business, that   [*Going.*
I leave out ceremony.
Cam.   Sir, I think,   520
You have heard of my poor services, i' the love
That I have borne your father ?
Flo.   Very nobly
Have you deserv'd : it is my father's music,
To speak your deeds ; not little of his care,
To have them recompens'd, as thought on.
Cam.   Well, my lord,
If you may please to think I love the king,
And thorough him, what 's nearest to him, which is
Your gracious self, embrace but my direction
(If your more ponderous and settled project
May suffer alteration), on mine honour   530
I 'll point you where you shall have such receiving
As shall become your highness ; where you may
Enjoy your mistress (from the whom, I see,
There 's no disjunction to be made, but by,
As heavens forefend, your ruin) ; marry her ;
And (with my best endeavours in your absence)
Your discontenting father strive to qualify,
And bring him up to liking.
Flo.   How, Camillo,
May this, almost a miracle, be done,
That I may call thee something more than man,   540
And, after that, trust to thee.
Cam.   Have you thought on
A place whereto you 'll go ?
Flo.   Not any yet ;
But as the unthought-on accident is guilty
To what we wildly do, so we profess
Ourselves to be the slaves of chance, and flies
Of every wind that blows.
Cam.   Then list to me :
This follows :—if you will not change your purpose,
But undergo this flight, make for Sicilia,
And there present yourself, and your fair princess
(For so, I see, she must be), 'fore Leontes :   550
She shall be habited, as it becomes

The partner of your bed. Methinks, I see
Leontes, opening his free arms, and weeping
His welcomes forth ; asks thee, the son, forgiveness,
As 't were i' the father's person ; kisses the hands
Of your fresh princess ; o'er and o'er divides him
'Twixt his unkindness and his kindness: the one
He chides to hell, and bids the other grow
Faster than thought, or time.
Flo.　　　　　　Worthy Camillo,
What colour for my visitation shall I　　　　　560
Hold up before him?
Cam.　　　Sent by the king, your father,
To greet him, and to give him comforts. Sir,
The manner of your bearing towards him, with
What you, as from your father, shall deliver,
Things known betwixt us three, I 'll write you down:
The which shall point you forth at every sitting
What you must say ; that he shall not perceive,
But that you have your father's bosom there,
And speak his very heart.
Flo.　　　　　　I am bound to you.
There is some sap in this.
Cam.　　　　　A course more promising
Than a wild dedication of yourselves　　　　571
To unpath'd waters, undream'd shores ; most certain,
To miseries enough: no hope to help you,
But, as you shake off one, to take another ;
Nothing so certain as your anchors, who
Do their best office, if they can but stay you
Where you 'll be loath to be. Besides, you know,
Prosperity 's the very bond of love,
Whose fresh complexion, and whose heart together,
Affliction alters.
Per.　　　　　One of these is true :　　　580
I think affliction may subdue the cheek,
But not take in the mind.
Cam.)　　　　　Yea, say you so?
There shall not, at your father's house, these seven
　　　　　years,
Be born another such.
Flo.　　　　My good Camillo,
She is as forward of her breeding, as
She is i' the rear our birth.
Cam.　　　I cannot say, 't is pity
She lacks instructions, for she seems a mistress
To most that teach.
Per.　　　　Your pardon, sir ; for this
I 'll blush you thanks.
Flo.　　　　My prettiest Perdita !—
But, O, the thorns we stand upon !—Camillo,　　590
Preserver of my father, now of me,
The medicine of our house, how shall we do ?
We are not furnish'd like Bohemia's son,
Nor shall appear in Sicilia.
Cam.　　　　My lord,
Fear none of this. I think, you know, my fortunes
Do all lie there : it shall be so my care
To have you royally appointed, as if
The scene you play were mine. For instance, sir,
That you may know you shall not want, one word. 599
　　　　　　　　[They talk aside.

Enter AUTOLYCUS.

Aut. Ha, ha ! what a fool Honesty is ! and Trust,
his sworn brother, a very simple gentleman ! I have
sold all my trumpery : not a counterfeit stone, not
a riband, glass, pomander, brooch, table-book, ballad,
knife, tape, glove, shoe-tie, bracelet, horn-ring, to keep
my pack from fasting : they throng who should buy
first ; as if my trinkets had been hallowed, and brought
a benediction to the buyer : by which means I saw
whose purse was best in picture, and what I saw, to
my good use I remembered. My clown (who wants
but something to be a reasonable man) grew so in love
with the wenches' song, that he would not stir his
pettitoes, till he had both tune and words ; which so
drew the rest of the herd to me, that all their other
senses stuck in ears : you might have pinched a
placket, it was senseless ; 't was nothing to geld a
codpiece of a purse : I would have filed keys off, that
hung in chains : no hearing, no feeling, but my sir's
song, and admiring the nothing of it ; so that, in this

time of lethargy, I picked and cut most of their
festival purses ; and had not the old man come in
with a whoobub against his daughter and the king's
son, and scared my choughs from the chaff, I had not
left a purse alive in the whole army.
　　　　[CAMILLO, FLORIZEL, *and* PERDITA *come
　　　　　　　forward.*
Cam. Nay, but my letters, by this means being there
So soon as you arrive, shall clear that doubt.
Flo. And those that you 'll procure from King
　　　Leontes—
Cam. Shall satisfy your father.
Per.　　　　　Happy be you !
All that you speak shows fair.
Cam. [*Seeing* AUTOLYCUS.] Who have we here ?—
We 'll make an instrument of this : omit　　630
Nothing, may give us aid.
Aut. If' they have overheard me now, — why,
hanging.
Cam. How now, good fellow ? Why shakest thou so ?
Fear not, man ; here 's no harm intended to thee.
Aut. I am a poor fellow, sir.
Cam. Why, be so still ; here 's nobody will steal
that from thee : yet, for the outside of thy poverty,
we must make an exchange ; therefore, discase thee
instantly (thou must think, there 's a necessity in 't)
and change garments with this gentleman. Though
the pennyworth on his side be the worst, yet hold
thee, there 's some boot.　　　　　　　643
Aut. I am a poor fellow, sir.—[*Aside.*] I know ye
well enough.
Cam. Nay, pr'ythee, despatch : the gentleman is
half flayed already.
Aut. Are you in earnest, sir ?—[*Aside.*] I smell the
trick of it.
Flo. Despatch, I pr'ythee.　　　　　650
Aut. Indeed, I have had earnest ; but I cannot with
conscience take it.
Cam. Unbuckle, unbuckle.—
　　　　[FLORIZEL *and* AUTOLYCUS *exchange garments.*
Fortunate mistress, (let my prophecy
Come home to you !) you must retire yourself
Into some covert : take your sweet-heart's hat,
And pluck it o'er your brows ; muffle your face ;
Dismantle you, and, as you can, disliken
The truth of your own seeming, that you may
(For I do fear eyes over you) to shipboard　　660
Get undescried.
Per.　　　I see, the play so lies,
That I must bear a part.
Cam.　　　　No remedy.—
Have you done there ?
Flo.　　　Should I now meet my father
He would not call me son.
Cam.　　Nay, you shall have no hat.—
Come, lady, come.—Farewell, my friend.
Aut.　　　　　Adieu, sir.
Flo. O Perdita, what have we twain forgot !
Pray you, a word.　　　　[*They converse apart.*
Cam. What I do next shall be to tell the king
Of this escape, and whither they are bound ;
Wherein, my hope is, I shall so prevail,　　670
To force him after : in whose company
I shall review Sicilia, for whose sight
I have a woman's longing.
Flo.　　　Fortune speed us !—
Thus we set on, Camillo, to the sea-side.
Cam. The swifter speed, the better.
　　　　[*Exeunt* FLORIZEL, PERDITA, *and* CAMILLO.
Aut. I understand the business ; I hear it. To
have an open ear, a quick eye, and a nimble hand,
is necessary for a cut-purse : a good nose is requisite
also, to smell out work for the other senses. I see,
this is the time that the unjust man doth thrive.
What an exchange had this been without boot !
what a boot is here with this exchange ! Sure, the
gods do this year connive at us, and we may do
anything *extempore.* The prince himself is about a
piece of iniquity ; stealing away from his father, with
his clog at his heels. If I thought it were a piece of
honesty to acquaint the king withal, I would not do 't:
I hold it the more knavery to conceal it, and therein

am I constant to my profession. *Aside, aside:*—here is more matter for a hot brain. Every lane's end, every shop, church, session, hanging, yields a careful man work.   692

Enter Clown and Shepherd.

Clo. See, see, what a man you are now! There is no other way, but to tell the king she's a changeling, and none of your flesh and blood.

Shep. Nay, but hear me.

Clo. Nay, but hear me.

Shep. Go to, then.   698

Clo. She being none of your flesh and blood, your flesh and blood has not offended the king; and so your flesh and blood is not to be punished by him. Show those things you found about her; those secret things, all but what she has with her. This being done, let the law go whistle: I warrant you.

Shep. I will tell the king all, every word, yea, and his son's pranks too; who, I may say, is no honest man neither to his father, nor to me, to go about to make me the king's brother-in-law.   708

Clo. Indeed, brother-in-law was the furthest off you could have been to him; and then your blood had been the dearer, by I know how much an ounce.

Aut. [*Aside.*] Very wisely, puppies!

Shep. Well, let us to the king: there is that in this fardel will make him scratch his beard.

Aut. [*Aside.*] I know not what impediment this complaint may be to the flight of my master.

Clo. 'Pray heartily he be at palace.

Aut. [*Aside.*] Though I am not naturally honest, I am so sometimes by chance:—let me pocket up my pedlar's excrement. [*Takes off his false beard.*] How now, rustics? whither are you bound?   721

Shep. To the palace, an it like your worship.

Aut. Your affairs there? what? with whom? the condition of that fardel, the place of your dwelling, your names, your ages, of what having, breeding, and anything that is fitting to be known? discover.

Clo. We are but plain fellows, sir.

Aut. A lie: you are rough and hairy. Let me have no lying; it becomes none but tradesmen, and they often give us soldiers the lie; but we pay them for it with stamped coin, not stabbing steel: therefore, they do not give us the lie.   732

Clo. Your worship had like to have given us one, if you had not taken yourself with the manner.

Shep. Are you a courtier, an't like you, sir?

Aut. Whether it like me, or no, I am a courtier. Seest thou not the air of the court in these enfoldings? hath not my gait in it the measure of the court? receives not thy nose court-odour from me? reflect I not on thy baseness court-contempt? Think'st thou, for that I insinuate, or toze from thee thy business, I am therefore no courtier? I am courtier, cap-a-pè; and one that will either push on, or pluck back thy business there: whereupon I command thee to open thy affair.

Shep. My business, sir, is to the king.

Aut. What advocate hast thou to him?

Shep. I know not, an't like you.

Clo. Advocate's the court-word for a pheasant: say, you have none.   750

Shep. None, sir: I have no pheasant, cock, nor hen.

Aut. How bless'd are we that are not simple men! Yet nature might have made me as these are, Therefore I'll not disdain.

Clo. This cannot be but a great courtier.

Shep. His garments are rich, but he wears them not handsomely.

Clo. He seems to be the more noble in being fantastical: a great man, I'll warrant; I know by the picking on's teeth.   760

Aut. The fardel there? what's i' the fardel? Wherefore that box?

Shep. Sir, there lies such secrets in this fardel and box, which none must know but the king; and which he shall know within this hour, if I may come to the speech of him.

Aut. Age, thou hast lost thy labour.

Shep. Why, sir?   768

Aut. The king is not at the palace: he is gone aboard a new ship to purge melancholy, and air himself: for, if thou be'st capable of things serious, thou must know, the king is full of grief.

Shep. So 'tis said, sir; about his son, that should have married a shepherd's daughter.

Aut. If that shepherd be not in hand-fast, let him fly: the curses he shall have, the tortures he shall feel, will break the back of man, the heart of monster.

Clo. Think you so, sir?   778

Aut. Not he alone shall suffer what wit can make heavy, and vengeance bitter; but those that are germane to him, though removed fifty times, shall all come under the hangman: which, though it be great pity, yet it is necessary. An old sheep-whistling rogue, a ram-tender, to offer to have his daughter come into grace! Some say, he shall be stoned; but that death is too soft for him, say I. Draw our throne into a sheep-cote! all deaths are too few, the sharpest too easy.

Clo. Has the old man e'er a son, sir, do you hear, an't like you, sir?   790

Aut. He has a son, who shall be flayed alive; then, 'nointed over with honey, set on the head of a wasp's nest; then stand, till he be three quarters and a dram dead; then recovered again with aqua-vitæ, or some other hot infusion; then, raw as he is, and in the hottest day prognostication proclaims, shall he be set against a brick-wall, the sun looking with a southward eye upon him, where he is to behold him with flies blown to death. But what talk we of these traitorly rascals, whose miseries are to be smiled at, their offences being so capital? Tell me, (for you seem to be honest plain men) what you have to the king? being something gently considered, I'll bring you where he is aboard, tender your persons to his presence, whisper him in your behalfs; an, if it be in man, besides the king, to effect your suits, here is man shall do it.   807

Clo. He seems to be of great authority: close with him, give him gold; and though authority be a stubborn bear, yet he is oft led by the nose with gold. Show the inside of your purse to the outside of his hand, and no more ado. Remember, stoned, and flayed alive!

Shep. An't please you, sir, to undertake the business for us, here is that gold I have: I'll make it as much more, and leave this young man in pawn, till I bring it you.

Aut. After I have done what I promised?

Shep. Ay, sir.

Aut. Well, give me the moiety.—Are you a party in this business?   821

Clo. In some sort, sir: but though my case be a pitiful one, I hope I shall not be flayed out of it.

Aut. O! that's the case of the shepherd's son.—Hang him, he'll be made an example.

Clo. Comfort, good comfort! We must to the king, and show our strange sights: he must know, 'tis none of your daughter nor my sister; we are gone else. Sir, I will give you as much as this old man does, when the business is performed; and remain, as he says, your pawn, till it be brought you.   831

Aut. I will trust you. Walk before toward the sea-side: go on the right hand; I will but look upon the hedge, and follow you.

Clo. We are blessed in this man, as I may say; even blessed.

Shep. Let's before, as he bids us. He was provided to do us good. [*Exeunt Shepherd and Clown.*

Aut. If I had a mind to be honest, I see, Fortune would not suffer me: she drops booties in my mouth. I am courted now with a double occasion—gold, and a means to do the prince my master good; which, who knows how that may turn back to my advancement? I will bring these two moles, these blind ones, aboard him: if he think it fit to shore them again, and that the complaint they have to the king concerns him nothing, let him call me rogue for being so far officious; for I am proof against that title, and what shame else belongs to 't. To him will I present them: there may be matter in it.   [*Exit.*

ACT V.

Scene I.—Sicilia. A Room in the Palace of Leontes.

Enter Leontes, Cleomenes, Dion, Paulina, *and others.*

Cleomenes.
SIR, you have done enough, and have per-
form'd
A saint-like sorrow : no fault could you
make,
Which you have not redeem'd ; indeed,
paid down
More penitence than done trespass. At
the last,
Do, as the heavens have done, forget your
evil ;
With them, forgive yourself.
Leon. Whilst I remember
Her, and her virtues, I cannot forget
My blemishes in them, and so still think of
The wrong I did myself : which was so much,
That heirless it hath made my kingdom, and
Destroy'd the sweet'st companion that e'er 11
man
Bred his hopes out of.
Paul. True, too true, my lord :
If one by one you wedded all the world,
Or from the all that are took something good,
To make a perfect woman, she you kill'd
Would be unparallel'd.
Leon. I think so. Kill'd !
She I kill'd ! I did so ; but thou strik'st me
Sorely, to say I did : it is as bitter
Upon thy tongue, as in my thought. Now, good now,
Say so but seldom.
Cleo. Not at all, good lady : 20
You might have spoken a thousand things that would
Have done the time more benefit, and grac'd
Your kindness better.
Paul. You are one of those,
Would have him wed again.
Dion. If you would not so,
You pity not the state, nor the remembrance
Of his most sovereign name, consider little,
What dangers, by his highness' fail of issue,
May drop upon his kingdom, and devour
Incertain lookers-on. What were more holy
Than to rejoice the former queen is well ? 30
What holier than for royalty's repair,
For present comfort, and for future good,—
To bless the bed of majesty again
With a sweet fellow to 't ?
Paul. There is none worthy,
Respecting her that's gone. Besides, the gods
Will have fulfill'd their secret purposes ;
For has not the divine Apollo said,
Is 't not the tenor of his oracle,
That King Leontes shall not have an heir,
Till his lost child be found ? which, that it shall, 40
Is all as monstrous to our human reason,
As my Antigonus to break his grave,
And come again to me ; who, on my life,
Did perish with the infant. 'T is your counsel,
My lord should to the heavens be contrary,
Oppose against their wills.—Care not for issue ;
The crown will find an heir : great Alexander
Left his to the worthiest, so his successor
Was like to be the best.
Leon. Good Paulina,—
Who hast the memory of Hermione, 50

I know, in honour,—O, that ever I
Had squar'd me to thy counsel !—then, even now,
I might have look'd upon my queen's full eyes,
Have taken treasure from her lips,—
Paul. And left them
More rich, for what they yielded.
Leon. Thou speak'st truth.
No more such wives ; therefore, no wife : one worse,
And better us'd, would make her sainted spirit
Again possess her corse, and on this stage
(Where we offenders now) appear, soul-vex'd,
And begin, "Why to me ?"
Paul. Had she such power, 60
She had just cause.
Leon. She had ; and would incense me
To murder her I married.
Paul. I should so :
Were I the ghost that walk'd, I 'd bid you mark
Her eye, and tell me for what dull part in 't
You chose her : then I 'd shriek, that even your ears
Should rift to hear me, and the words that follow'd
Should be, " Remember mine."
Leon. Stars, stars !
And all eyes else dead coals.—Fear thou no wife ;
I 'll have no wife, Paulina.
Paul. Will you swear
Never to marry, but by my free leave ? 70
Leon. Never, Paulina ; so be bless'd my spirit !
Paul. Then, good my lords, bear witness to his oath.
Cleo. You tempt him overmuch.
Paul. Unless another,
As like Hermione as is her picture,
Affront his eye.
Cleo. Good madam,—
Paul. I have done.
Yet, if my lord will marry,—if you will, sir,
No remedy, but you will,—give me the office
To choose you a queen. She shall not be so young
As was your former ; but she shall be such
As, walk'd your first queen's ghost, it should take joy
To see her in your arms. 81
Leon. My true Paulina,
We shall not marry, till thou bidd'st us.
Paul. That
Shall be when your first queen 's again in breath :
Never till then.

Enter a Gentleman.

Gent. One that gives out himself Prince Florizel,
Son of Polixenes, with his princess (she
The fairest I have yet beheld), desires access
To your high presence.
Leon. What with him ? he comes not
Like to his father's greatness ; his approach,
So out of circumstance and sudden, tells us 90
'T is not a visitation fram'd, but forc'd
By need and accident. What train ?
Gent. But few,
And those but mean.
Leon. His princess, say you, with him ?
Gent. Ay, the most peerless piece of earth, I think,
That e'er the sun shone bright on.
Paul. O Hermione !
As every present time doth boast itself
Above a better, gone, so must thy grave

Give way to what's seen now. Sir, you yourself
Have said and writ so, but your writing now
Is colder than that theme,—"She had not been,   100
Nor was not to be equall'd;"—thus your verse
Flow'd with her beauty once: 'tis shrewdly ebb'd,
To say you have seen a better.
    Gent.   Pardon, madam:
The one I have almost forgot (your pardon);
The other, when she has obtain'd your eye,
Will have your tongue too. This is a creature,
Would she begin a sect, might quench the zeal
Of all professors else, make proselytes
Of whom she but bid follow.
    Paul.   How! not women?
    Gent. Women will love her, that she is a woman 110
More worth than any man; men, that she is
The rarest of all women.
    Leon.   Go, Cleomenes;
Yourself, assisted with your honour'd friends,
Bring them to our embracement.—Still 'tis strange,
[*Exeunt* CLEOMENES, *Lords, and Gentleman.*
He thus should steal upon us.
    Paul.   Had our prince
(Jewel of children) seen this hour, he had pair'd
Well with this lord: there was not full of month
Between their births.
    Leon. Pr'ythee, no more: cease! thou know'st,
He dies to me again, when talk'd of: sure,   120
When I shall see this gentleman, thy speeches
Will bring me to consider that which may
Unfurnish me of reason.—They are come.—

Re-enter CLEOMENES, *with* FLORIZEL, PERDITA, *and
others.*

Your mother was most true to wedlock, prince;
For she did print your royal father off,
Conceiving you. Were I but twenty-one,
Your father's image is so hit in you,
His very air, that I should call you brother,
As I did him; and speak of something, wildly
By us perform'd before. Most dearly welcome!   130
And your fair princess, goddess!—O, alas!
I lost a couple, that 'twixt heaven and earth
Might thus have stood, begetting wonder as
You, gracious couple, do. And then I lost
(All mine own folly) the society,
Amity too, of your brave father; whom,
Though bearing misery, I desire my life
Once more to look on him.
    Flo.   By his command
Have I here touch'd Sicilia; and from him
Give you all greetings, that a king, at friend,   140
Can send his brother: and, but infirmity
(Which waits upon worn times) hath something seiz'd
His wish'd ability, he had himself
The lands and waters 'twixt your throne and his
Measur'd to look upon you, whom he loves
(He bade me say so) more than all the sceptres
And those that bear them living.
    Leon.   O my brother!
Good gentleman, the wrongs I have done thee stir
Afresh within me; and these thy offices,
So rarely kind, are as interpreters   150
Of my behind-hand slackness.—Welcome hither,
As is the spring to the earth. And hath he too
Expos'd this paragon to the fearful usage
(At least ungentle) of the dreadful Neptune,
To greet a man not worth her pains, much less
The adventure of her person?
    Flo.   Good my lord,
She came from Libya.
    Leon.   Where the warlike Smalus,
That noble, honour'd lord, is fear'd and lov'd?
    Flo. Most royal sir, from thence; from him, whose
            daughter
His tears proclaim'd his, parting with her: thence 160
(A prosperous south-wind friendly) we have cross'd,
To execute the charge my father gave me,
For visiting your highness. My best train
I have from your Sicilian shores dismiss'd,
Who for Bohemia bend, to signify
Not only my success in Libya, sir,

But my arrival, and my wife's, in safety
Here, where we are.
    Leon.   The blessed gods
Purge all infection from our air, whilst you
Do climate here! You have a holy father,   170
A graceful gentleman, against whose person,
So sacred as it is, I have done sin;
For which the heavens, taking angry note,
Have left me issueless; and your father's bless'd
(As he from heaven merits it) with you,

Leon.   "O, alas!
I lost a couple, that 'twixt heaven and earth
Might thus have stood, begetting wonder as
You, gracious couple, do."

Worthy his goodness. What might I have been,
Might I a son and daughter now have look'd on,
Such goodly things as you!
    Enter a Lord.
    Lord.   Most noble sir,
That which I shall report will bear no credit,
Were not the proof so nigh. Please you, great sir, 180
Bohemia greets you from himself by me;
Desires you to attach his son, who has
(His dignity and duty both cast off)
Fled from his father, from his hopes, and with
A shepherd's daughter.
    Leon.   Where's Bohemia? speak.
    Lord. Here in your city; I now came from him:
I speak amazedly, and it becomes
My marvel, and my message. To your court
Whiles he was hastening (in the chase, it seems,
Of this fair couple), meets he on the way   190
The father of this seeming lady, and
Her brother, having both their country quitted
With this young prince.
    Flo.   Camillo has betray'd me,
Whose honour, and whose honesty, till now
Endur'd all weathers.
    Lord.   Lay 't so to his charge:
He's with the king your father.
    Leon.   Who? Camillo?
    Lord. Camillo, sir: I spake with him, who now
Has these poor men in question. Never saw I
Wretches so quake: they kneel, they kiss the earth,
Forswear themselves as often as they speak: 200
Bohemia stops his ears, and threatens them
With divers deaths in death.

Per.   O my poor father!—
The heaven sets spies upon us, will not have
Our contract celebrated.
　　Leon.   You are married?
　　Flo. We are not, sir, nor are we like to be;
The stars, I see, will kiss the valleys first:
The odds for high and low 's alike.
　　Leon.   My lord.
Is this the daughter of a king?
　　Flo.   She is,
When once she is my wife.
　　Leon. That once, I see, by your good father's speed,
Will come on very slowly. I am sorry,   211
Most sorry, you have broken from his liking,
Where you were tied in duty; and as sorry,
Your choice is not so rich in worth as beauty,
That you might well enjoy her.
　　Flo.   Dear, look up:
Though Fortune, visible an enemy,
Should chase us with my father, power no jot
Hath she to change our loves.—Beseech you, sir,
Remember since you ow'd no more to time
Than I do now; with thought of such affections,   220
Step forth mine advocate: at your request,
My father will grant precious things as trifles.
　　Leon. Would he do so, I'd beg your precious mis-
　　　　tress,
Which he counts but a trifle.
　　Paul.   Sir, my liege,
Your eye hath too much youth in 't: not a month
'Fore your queen died, she was more worth such gazes
Than what you look on now.
　　Leon.   I thought of her,
Even in these looks I made.—[*To* FLORIZEL.] But your
　　　　petition
Is yet unanswer'd. I will to your father:
Your honour not o'erthrown by your desires,   230
I am friend to them and you; upon which errand
I now go toward him. Therefore, follow me,
And mark what way I make: come, good my lord.
　　　　　　　　　　　　　　　　　　　　　[*Exeunt.*

　　　　　　　———

SCENE II.—The Same. Before the Palace.

Enter AUTOLYCUS *and a Gentleman.*

Aut. 'Beseech you, sir, were you present at this
relation?
　　1 Gent. I was by at the opening of the fardel, heard
the old shepherd deliver the manner how he found
it: whereupon, after a little amazedness, we were
all commanded out of the chamber; only this, methought, I heard the shepherd say, he found the child.
　　Aut. I would most gladly know the issue of it.   8
　　1 Gent. I make a broken delivery of the business;
but the changes I perceived in the king and Camillo,
were very notes of admiration: they seemed almost,
with staring on one another, to tear the cases of their
eyes; there was speech in their dumbness, language
in their very gesture; they looked, as they had heard
of a world ransomed, or one destroyed. A notable
passion of wonder appeared in them; but the wisest
beholder, that knew no more but seeing, could not
say, if the importance were joy or sorrow, but in the
extremity of the one it must needs be.

Enter another Gentleman.

Here comes a gentleman, that, haply, knows more.
The news, Rogero?   21
　　2 Gent. Nothing but bonfires. The oracle is fulfilled; the king's daughter is found: such a deal of
wonder is broken out within this hour, that ballad-
makers cannot be able to express it. Here comes the
Lady Paulina's steward: he can deliver you more.

Enter a third Gentleman.

How goes it now, sir? this news, which is called true,
is so like an old tale, that the verity of it is in strong
suspicion. Has the king found his heir?   29
　　3 Gent. Most true, if ever truth were pregnant by
circumstance: that which you hear you 'll swear you
see, there is such unity in the proofs. The mantle

of Queen Hermione;—her jewel about the neck of
it;—the letters of Antigonus found with it, which
they know to be his character;—the majesty of the
creature, in resemblance of the mother;—the affection
of nobleness, which nature shows above her breeding,
and many other evidences, proclaim her with all
certainty to be the king's daughter. Did you see the
meeting of the two kings?   40
　　2 Gent. No.
　　3 Gent. Then you have lost a sight, which was to be
seen, cannot be spoken of. There might you have
beheld one joy crown another; so, and in such
manner, that, it seemed, sorrow wept to take leave of
them, for their joy waded in tears. There was casting
up of eyes, holding up of hands, with countenance
of such distraction, that they were to be known by
garment, not by favour. Our king, being ready to
leap out of himself for joy of his found daughter, as
if that joy were now become a loss, cries, "O, thy
mother, thy mother!" then asks Bohemia forgiveness; then embraces his son-in-law; then again
worries he his daughter with clipping her; now he
thanks the old shepherd, which stands by like a
weather-bitten conduit of many kings' reigns. I
never heard of such another encounter, which lames
report to follow it, and undoes description to do it.
　　2 Gent. What, pray you, became of Antigonus, that
carried hence the child?   60
　　3 Gent. Like an old tale still, which will have matter
to rehearse, though credit be asleep, and not an
ear open. He was torn to pieces with a bear: this
avouches the shepherd's son, who has not only his
innocence (which seems much) to justify him, but
a handkerchief, and rings of his, that Paulina knows.
　　1 Gent. What became of his bark, and his followers?
　　3 Gent. Wracked, the same instant of their master's
death, and in the view of the shepherd: so that all
the instruments, which aided to expose the child, were
even then lost, when it was found. But, O! the noble
combat, that 'twixt joy and sorrow was fought in
Paulina! She had one eye declined for the loss of
her husband, another elevated that the oracle was
fulfilled: she lifted the princess from the earth, and
so locks her in embracing, as if she would pin her
to her heart, that she might no more be in danger
of losing.
　　1 Gent. The dignity of this act was worth the
audience of kings and princes, for by such was it
acted.   81
　　3 Gent. One of the prettiest touches of all, and that
which angled for mine eyes (caught the water, though
not the fish), was, when at the relation of the queen's
death, with the manner how she came to 't (bravely
confessed and lamented by the king), how attentive-
ness wounded his daughter; till, from one sign of
dolour to another, she did, with an alas! I would fain
say, bleed tears, for, I am sure, my heart wept blood.
Who was most marble there, changed colour; some
swooned, all sorrowed: if all the world could have
seen it, the woe had been universal.   92
　　1 Gent. Are they returned to the court?
　　3 Gent. No; the princess hearing of her mother's
statue, which is in the keeping of Paulina,—a piece
many years in doing, and now newly performed by
that rare Italian master, Julio Romano; who, had he
himself eternity and could put breath into his work,
would beguile Nature of her custom, so perfectly he is
her ape: he so near to Hermione hath done Hermione,
that, they say, one would speak to her, and stand in
hope of answer: thither, with all greediness of affection, are they gone; and there they intend to sup. 103
　　2 Gent. I thought, she had some great matter there
in hand, for she hath privately, twice or thrice a day,
ever since the death of Hermione, visited that removed
house. Shall we thither, and with our company piece
the rejoicing?
　　1 Gent. Who would be thence, that has the benefit
of access? every wink of an eye, some new grace will
be born: our absence makes us unthrifty to our knowledge. Let 's along.   [*Exeunt Gentlemen.*
　　Aut. Now, had I not the dash of my former life in
me, would preferment drop on my head. I brought

the old man and his son aboard the prince; told him
I heard them talk of a fardel, and I know not what;
but he at that time, over-fond of the shepherd's
daughter (so he then took her to be), who began to
be much sea-sick, and himself little better, extremity
of weather continuing, this mystery remained undis-
covered. But 't is all one to me; for had I been the
finder-out of this secret, it would not have relished
among my other discredits.—Here come those I have
done good to against my will, and already appearing
in the blossoms of their fortune.

Aut. " I humbly beseech you, sir, to pardon me all the faults I
have committed to your worship."

Enter Shepherd and Clown.

Shep. Come, boy: I am past more children; thy
thy sons and daughters will be all gentlemen born. 127
Clo. You are well met, sir. You denied to fight
with me this other day, because I was no gentleman
born: see you these clothes? say, you see them not,
and think me still no gentleman born: you were best
say, these robes are not gentlemen born. Give me the
lie, do, and try whether I am not now a gentleman
born.
Aut. I know, you are now, sir, a gentleman born.
Clo. Ay, and have been so any time these four hours.
Shep. And so have I, boy.   137
Clo. So you have;—but I was a gentleman born
before my father, for the king's son took me by the
hand, and called me, brother; and then the two kings
called my father, brother; and then the prince, my
brother, and the princess, my sister, called my father,
father; and so we wept; and there was the first
gentleman-like tears that ever we shed.
Shep. We may live, son, to shed many more.
Clo. Ay; or else 't were hard luck, being in so preposterous estate as we are.
Aut. I humbly beseech you, sir, to pardon me all the
faults I have committed to your worship, and to give
me your good report to the prince my master.   150
Shep. 'Pr'ythee, son, do; for we must be gentle,
now we are gentlemen.
Clo. Thou wilt amend thy life?
Aut. Ay, an it like your good worship.
Clo. Give me thy hand: I will swear to the prince,
thou art as honest a true fellow as any is in Bohemia.
Shep. You may say it, but not swear it.
Clo. Not swear it, now I am a gentleman? Let boors
and franklins say it, I 'll swear it.

Shep. How if it be false, son?   160
Clo. If it be ne'er so false, a true gentleman may
swear it in the behalf of his friend:—and I 'll swear
to the prince, thou art a tall fellow of thy hands, and
that thou wilt not be drunk; but I know, thou art no
tall fellow of thy hands, and that thou wilt be drunk:
but I 'll swear it, and I would thou wouldst be a tall
fellow of thy hands.
Aut. I will prove so, sir, to my power.   168
Clo. Ay, by any means prove a tall fellow: if I do
not wonder how thou darest venture to be drunk, not
being a tall fellow, trust me not.—Hark! the kings
and the princes, our kindred, are going to see the
queen's picture. Come, follow us: we 'll be thy good
masters.   [*Exeunt.*

SCENE III.—The Same. A Chapel in PAULINA'S House.

Enter LEONTES, POLIXENES, FLORIZEL, PERDITA,
CAMILLO, PAULINA, *Lords, and Attendants.*

Leon. O grave and good Paulina, the great comfort
That I have had of thee!
Paul.   What, sovereign sir,
I did not well, I meant well. All my services
You have paid home; but that you have vouchsaf'd
With your crown'd brother, and these your contracted
Heirs of your kingdoms, my poor house to visit,
It is a surplus of your grace, which never
My life may last to answer.
Leon.   O Paulina!
We honour you with trouble. But we came
To see the statue of our queen: your gallery   10
Have we pass'd through, not without much content
In many singularities, but we saw not
That which my daughter came to look upon,
The statue of her mother.
Paul.   As she liv'd peerless,
So her dead likeness, I do well believe,
Excels whatever yet you look'd upon,
Or hand of man hath done; therefore I keep it
Lonely, apart. But here it is: prepare
To see the life as lively mock'd, as ever
Still sleep mock'd death: behold! and say, 't is well. 20
          [PAULINA *undraws a curtain, and discovers*
                  HERMIONE *as a statue.*
I like your silence: it the more shows off
Your wonder; but yet speak:—first you, my liege.
Comes it not something near?
Leon.   Her natural posture!—
Chide me, dear stone, that I may say, indeed,
Thou art Hermione; or, rather, thou art she
In thy not chiding, for she was as tender
As infancy, and grace.—But yet, Paulina,
Hermione was not so much wrinkled; nothing
So aged, as this seems.
Pol.   O! not by much.
Paul. So much the more our carver's excellence; 30
Which lets go by some sixteen years, and makes her
As she liv'd now.
Leon.   As now she might have done,
So much to my good comfort, as it is
Now piercing to my soul. O! thus she stood,
Even with such life of majesty (warm life,
As now it coldly stands), when first I woo'd her.
I am asham'd: does not the stone rebuke me,
For being more stone than it?—O royal piece!
There 's magic in thy majesty, which has
My evils conjur'd to remembrance, and   40
From thy admiring daughter took the spirits,
Standing like stone with thee.
Per.   And give me leave,
And do not say 't is superstition, that
I kneel, and then implore her blessing.—Lady,
Dear queen, that ended when I but began,
Give me that hand of yours to kiss.
Paul.   O, patience!
The statue is but newly fix'd, the colour 's
Not dry.
Cam. My lord, your sorrow was too sore laid on,
Which sixteen winters cannot blow away,   50

So many summers dry : scarce any joy
Did ever so long live ; no sorrow,
But kill'd itself much sooner.
  Pol.   Dear my brother,
Let him that was the cause of this have power

  Leon.   Let be, let be !   61
Would I were dead, but that, methinks, already—
What was he that did make it ?—See, my lord,
Would you not deem it breath'd, and that those veins
Did verily bear blood ?

Paul. "'T is time ; descend ; be stone no more : approach ;
Strike all that look upon with marvel."

To take off so much grief from you, as he
Will piece up in himself.
  Paul.   Indeed, my lord,
If I had thought, the sight of my poor image
Would thus have wrought you (for the stone is mine),
I d not have show'd it.
  Leon.   Do not draw the curtain.
  Paul. No longer shall you gaze on 't, lest your fancy
May think anon it moves.

  Pol.   Masterly done :
The very life seems warm upon her lip.
  Leon. The fixure of her eye has motion in 't,
As we are mock'd with art.
  Paul.   I 'll draw the curtain.
My lord 's almost so far transported, that
He 'll think anon it lives.
  Leon.   O sweet Paulina !   70
Make me to think so twenty years together :

No settled senses of the world can match
The pleasure of that madness. Let 't alone.
Paul. I am sorry, sir. I have thus far stirr'd you : but
I could afflict you further.
    Leon. Do, Paulina;
For this affliction has a taste as sweet
As any cordial comfort.—Still, methinks,
There is an air comes from her : what fine chisel
Could ever yet cut breath ? Let no man mock me,
For I will kiss her.
    Paul. Good my lord, forbear.   80
The ruddiness upon her lip is wet :
You 'll mar it, if you kiss it ; stain your own
With oily painting. Shall I draw the curtain ?
    Leon. No, not these twenty years.
    Per. So long could I
Stand by, a looker-on.
    Paul. Either forbear,
Quit presently the chapel, or resolve you
For more amazement. If you can behold it,
I 'll make the statue move indeed, descend
And take you by the hand ; but then you 'll think,
(Which I protest against) I am assisted   90
By wicked powers.
    Leon. What you can make her do,
I am content to look on : what to speak,
I am content to hear ; for 't is as easy
To make her speak, as move.
    Paul. It is requir'd,
You do awake your faith. Then, all stand still ;
Or those that think it is unlawful business
I am about, let them depart.
    Leon. Proceed :
No foot shall stir.
    Paul. Music, awake her, strike !—[*Music.*
'T is time ; descend ; be stone no more : approach ;
Strike all that look upon with marvel. Come ;   100
I 'll fill your grave up : stir ; nay, come away ;
Bequeath to death your numbness, for from him
Dear life redeems you.—You perceive, she stirs.
    [HERMIONE *descends from the pedestal.*
Start not : her actions shall be holy, as
You hear my spell is lawful : do not shun her,
Until you see her die again, for then
You kill her double. Nay, present your hand :
When she was young you woo'd her ; now, in age,
Is she become the suitor !
    Leon. [*Embracing her.*] O ! she 's warm.
If this be magic, let it be an art   110
Lawful as eating.
    Pol. She embraces him.

Cam. She hangs about his neck.
If she pertain to life, let her speak too.
    Pol. Ay ; and make it manifest where she has
          liv'd,
Or, how stol'n from the dead.
    Paul. That she is living,
Were it but told you, should be hooted at
Like an old tale ; but it appears she lives,
Though yet she speak not. Mark a little while.—
Please you to interpose, fair madam : kneel,
And pray your mother's blessing.—Turn, good lady ;
Our Perdita is found. [PERDITA *kneels to* HERMIONE.
    Her. You gods, look down,   121
And from your sacred vials pour your graces
Upon my daughter's head !—Tell me, mine own,
Where hast thou been preserv'd ? where liv'd ? how
      found
Thy father's court ? for thou shalt hear, that I,
Knowing by Paulina that the oracle
Gave hope thou wast in being, have preserv'd
Myself to see the issue.
    Paul. There 's time enough for that,
Lest they desire, upon this push, to trouble
Your joys with like relation.—Go together,   130
You precious winners all : your exultation
Partake to every one. I, an old turtle,
Will wing me to some wither'd bough, and there
My mate, that 's never to be found again,
Lament till I am lost.
    Leon. O, peace, Paulina !
Thou shouldst a husband take by my consent,
As I by thine a wife : this is a match,
And made between 's by vows. Thou hast found
      mine ;
But how, is to be question'd ; for I saw her,
As I thought, dead, and have in vain said many   140
A prayer upon her grave : I 'll not seek far
(For him, I partly know his mind), to find thee
An honourable husband.—Come, Camillo,
And take her by the hand : whose worth, and honesty,
Is richly noted, and here justified
By us, a pair of kings.—Let 's from this place.—
What !—Look upon my brother :—both your pardons,
That e'er I put between your holy looks
My ill suspicion.—This' your son-in-law,
And son unto the king, whom heavens directing   150
Is troth-plight to your daughter. Good Paulina,
Lead us from hence, where we may leisurely
Each one demand, and answer to his part
Perform'd in this wide gap of time, since first
We were dissever'd : hastily lead away.   [*Exeunt.*

KING JOHN.

DRAMATIS PERSONÆ.

KING JOHN.
PRINCE HENRY, *his Son.*
ARTHUR, *Duke of Bretagne.*
WILLIAM MARESHALL, *Earl of Pembroke.*
GEFFREY FITZ-PETER, *Earl of Essex.*
WILLIAM LONGSWORD, *Earl of Salisbury.*
ROBERT BIGOT, *Earl of Norfolk.*
HUBERT DE BURGH, *Chamberlain to the King.*
ROBERT FAULCONBRIDGE.
PHILIP FAULCONBRIDGE.
JAMES GURNEY, *Servant to Lady Faulconbridge.*
PETER *of Pomfret.*
PHILIP, *King of France.*

LEWIS, *the Dauphin.*
DUKE OF AUSTRIA.
CARDINAL PANDULPH, *the Pope's Legate.*
MELUN, *a French Lord.*
CHATILLON, *Ambassador from France.*

ELINOR, *Widow of King Henry II.*
CONSTANCE, *Mother to Arthur.*
BLANCH, *Daughter to Alphonso, King of Castile.*
LADY FAULCONBRIDGE.

Lords, Ladies, Citizens of Angiers, Sheriff, Heralds,
    Officers, Soldiers, Messengers, and Attendants.

SCENE—Sometimes in ENGLAND, and sometimes in FRANCE.

ACT I.

SCENE I.—Northampton. A Room of State in the Palace.

Enter King JOHN, Queen ELINOR, PEMBROKE, ESSEX, SALISBURY, and others,
    with CHATILLON.

King John.

NOW, say, Chatillon, what would France
    with us?
Chat. Thus, after greeting, speaks the
    King of France,
In my behaviour, to the majesty,
The borrow'd majesty of England here.
Eli. A strange beginning;—borrow'd
    majesty!
K. John. Silence, good mother: hear the
    embassy.
Chat. Philip of France, in right and true
    behalf
Of thy deceased brother Geffrey's son,
Arthur Plantagenet, lays most lawful claim
To this fair island, and the territories,   10
To Ireland, Poictiers, Anjou, Touraine, Maine,
Desiring thee to lay aside the sword
Which sways usurpingly these several titles,
And put the same into young Arthur's hand,
Thy nephew and right royal sovereign.
K. John. What follows, if we disallow of this?
Chat. The proud control of fierce and bloody war,
To enforce these rights so forcibly withheld.
K. John. Here have we war for war, and blood for
    blood,
Controlment for controlment: so answer France.   20
Chat. Then take my king's defiance from my mouth,
The farthest limit of my embassy.
K. John. Bear mine to him, and so depart in peace.
Be thou as lightning in the eyes of France;
For ere thou canst report I will be there,
The thunder of my cannon shall be heard.
So, hence! Be thou the trumpet of our wrath,
And sullen presage of your own decay.—
An honourable conduct let him have:
Pembroke, look to 't. Farewell, Chatillon.   30
    [*Exeunt CHATILLON and PEMBROKE.*
Eli. What now, my son? have I not ever said,
How that ambitious Constance would not cease,

Till she had kindled France, and all the world,
Upon the right and party of her son?
This might have been prevented, and made whole,
With very easy arguments of love,
Which now the manage of two kingdoms must
With fearful bloody issue arbitrate.
K. John. Our strong possession, and our right, for
    us.
Eli. Your strong possession much more than your
    right,   40
Or else it must go wrong with you and me:
So much my conscience whispers in your ear,
Which none but Heaven, and you, and I, shall hear.

Enter the Sheriff of Northamptonshire, who
    whispers ESSEX.

Essex. My liege, here is the strangest controversy,
Come from the country to be judg'd by you,
That e'er I heard: shall I produce the men?
K. John. Let them approach.—   [*Exit Sheriff.*
Our abbeys, and our priories, shall pay
This expedition's charge.

Re-enter Sheriff, with ROBERT FAULCONBRIDGE, and
    PHILIP, his Bastard Brother.

                    What men are you?
Bast. Your faithful subject I, a gentleman   50
Born in Northamptonshire, and eldest son,
As I suppose, to Robert Faulconbridge,
A soldier, by the honour-giving hand
Of Cordelion knighted in the field.
K. John. What art thou?
Rob. The son and heir to that same Faulconbridge.
K. John. Is that the elder, and art thou the heir?
You came not of one mother then, it seems.
Bast. Most certain of one mother, mighty king;
That is well known: and, as I think, one father: 60
But, for the certain knowledge of that truth
I put you o'er to Heaven, and to my mother:
Of that I doubt, as all men's children may.

Eli. Out on thee, rude man! thou dost shame thy
    mother,
And wound her honour with this diffidence.
  Bast. I, madam? no, I have no reason for it:
That is my brother's plea and none of mine:
The which if he can prove, 'a pops me out
At least from fair five hundred pound a year.
Heaven guard my mother's honour, and my land! 70

Essex. "Shall I produce the men?"

  K. John. A good blunt fellow.—Why, being younger
    born,
Doth he lay claim to thine inheritance?
  Bast. I know not why, except to get the land.
But, once, he slander'd me with bastardy:
But whe'r I be as true-begot, or no,
That still I lay upon my mother's head;
But, that I am as well-begot, my liege,
(Fair fall the bones that took the pains for me!)
Compare our faces, and be judge yourself.
If old Sir Robert did beget us both, 80
And were our father, and this son like him;—
O old Sir Robert, father, on my knee
I give Heaven thanks, I was not like to thee!
  K. John. Why, what a madcap hath Heaven lent
    us here!
  Eli. He hath a trick of Cordelion's face;
The accent of his tongue affecteth him.
Do you not read some tokens of my son
In the large composition of this man?
  K. John. Mine eye hath well examined his parts,
And finds them perfect Richard.—Sirrah, speak: 90
What doth move you to claim your brother's land?
  Bast. Because he hath a half-face, like my father!
With half that face would he have all my land,
A half-fac'd groat four hundred pound a year!
  Rob. My gracious liege, when that my father
    liv'd,
Your brother did employ my father much,—
  Bast. Well, sir; by this you cannot get my land:
Your tale must be, how he employ'd my mother.
  Rob. And once despatch'd him in an embassy
To Germany, there, with the emperor, 100
To treat of high affairs touching that time.
The advantage of his absence took the king,
And in the mean time sojourn'd at my father's;
Where how he did prevail I shame to speak,
But truth is truth: large lengths of seas and shores
Between my father and my mother lay,
As I have heard my father speak himself,
When this same lusty gentleman was got.
Upon his death-bed he by will bequeath'd
His lands to me; and took it on his death, 110
That this, my mother's son, was none of his;
An if he were, he came into the world
Full fourteen weeks before the course of time.

Then, good my liege, let me have what is mine,
My father's land, as was my father's will.
  K. John. Sirrah, your brother is legitimate;
Your father's wife did after wedlock bear him;
And if she did play false, the fault was hers,
Which fault lies on the hazards of all husbands
That marry wives. Tell me, how if my brother, 120
Who, as you say, took pains to get this son,
Had of your father claim'd this son for his?
In sooth, good friend, your father might have kept
This calf, bred from his cow, from all the world;
In sooth, he might: then, if he were my brother's,
My brother might not claim him, nor your father,
Being none of his, refuse him. This concludes:
My mother's son did get your father's heir;
Your father's heir must have your father's land.
  Rob. Shall then my father's will be of no force 130
To dispossess that child which is not his?
  Bast. Of no more force to dispossess me, sir,
Than was his will to get me, as I think.
  Eli. Whether hadst thou rather be a Faulconbridge,
And, like thy brother, to enjoy thy land,
Or the reputed son of Cordelion,
Lord of thy presence, and no land beside?
  Bast. Madam, an if my brother had my shape,
And I had his, Sir Robert his, like him;
And if my legs were two such riding-rods, 140
My arms such eel-skins stuff'd, my face so thin,
That in mine ear I durst not stick a rose,
Lest men should say, "Look, where three-farthings
    goes;"
And, to his shape, were heir to all this land,
('Would I might never stir from off this place)
I'd give it every foot to have this face:
I would not be Sir Nob in any case.
  Eli. I like thee well. Wilt thou forsake thy fortune,
Bequeath thy land to him, and follow me?
I am a soldier, and now bound to France. 150
  Bast. Brother, take you my land, I'll take my chance.
Your face hath got five hundred pounds a year,
Yet sell your face for five pence, and 'tis dear.—
Madam, I'll follow you unto the death.
  Eli. Nay, I would have you go before me thither.
  Bast. Our country manners give our betters way.
  K. John. What is thy name?
  Bast. Philip, my liege; so is my name begun;
Philip, good old Sir Robert's wife's eldest son.
  K. John. From henceforth bear his name whose 160
    form thou bearest:
Kneel thou down Philip, but arise more great;
Arise Sir Richard, and Plantagenet.
  Bast. Brother by the mother's side, give me your
    hand:
My father gave me honour, yours gave land.—
Now blessed be the hour, by night or day
When I was got, Sir Robert was away!
  Eli. The very spirit of Plantagenet!
I am thy grandam, Richard: call me so.
  Bast. Madam, by chance, but not by truth; what
    though? 170
Something about, a little from the right,
In at the window, or else o'er the hatch:
Who dares not stir by day, must walk by night,
And have is have, however men do catch.
Near or far off, well won is still well shot,
And I am I, howe'er I was begot.
  K. John. Go, Faulconbridge: now hast thou thy
    desire;
A landless knight makes thee a landed squire.—
Come, madam, and come, Richard: we must speed
For France, for France, for it is more than need.
  Bast. Brother, adieu: good fortune come to thee,
For thou wast got i' the way of honesty.— 181
    [*Exeunt all but Bastard.*
A foot of honour better than I was,
But many a many foot of land the worse.
Well, now can I make any Joan a lady.
"Good den, Sir Richard."—"God-a-mercy, fellow;"
And if his name be George, I'll call him Peter;
For new-made honour doth forget men's names:
'Tis too respective, and too sociable,
For your conversion. Now your traveller,

He and his toothpick at my worship's mess;   190
And when my knightly stomach is suffic'd,
Why then I suck my teeth, and catechise
My picked man of countries:—"My dear sir,"
Thus leaning on mine elbow I begin,
"I shall beseech you"—that is question now;
And then comes answer like an absey-book:
"O sir," says answer, "at your best command;
At your employment; at your service, sir:"
"No, sir," says question, "I, sweet sir, at yours:"
And so, ere answer knows what question would,   200
Saving in dialogue of compliment,
And talking of the Alps, and Apennines,
The Pyrenean, and the river Po,
It draws toward supper in conclusion so.
But this is worshipful society,
And fits the mounting spirit, like myself;
For he is but a bastard to the time,
That doth not smack of observation;
(And so am I, whether I smack, or no;)
And not alone in habit and device,   210
Exterior form, outward accoutrement,
But from the inward motion to deliver
Sweet, sweet, sweet poison for the age's tooth:
Which, though I will not practise to deceive,
Yet, to avoid deceit, I mean to learn;
For it shall strew the footsteps of my rising.—
But who comes in such haste, in riding-robes?
What woman-post is this? hath she no husband,
That will take pains to blow a horn before her?

Enter Lady FAULCONBRIDGE *and* JAMES GURNEY.

O me! it is my mother.—How now, good lady?   220
What brings you here to court so hastily?
    Lady F. Where is that slave, thy brother? where
        is he,
That holds in chase mine honour up and down?
    Bast. My brother Robert? old Sir Robert's son?
Colbrand the giant, that same mighty man?
Is it Sir Robert's son, that you seek so?
    Lady F. Sir Robert's son! Ay, thou unreverent
        boy,
Sir Robert's son: why scorn'st thou at Sir Robert?
He is Sir Robert's son, and so art thou.
    Bast. James Gurney, wilt thou give us leave
        awhile?   230
    Gur. Good leave, good Philip.

    Bast.   Philip! sparrow! James,
There's toys abroad: anon I'll tell thee more.—
                                    [*Exit* GURNEY.
Madam, I was not old Sir Robert's son:
Sir Robert might have eat his part in me
Upon Good Friday, and ne'er broke his fast.
Sir Robert could do well: marry, to confess,
Could he get me? Sir Robert could not do it:
We know his handiwork.—Therefore, good mother,
To whom am I beholding for these limbs?
Sir Robert never holp to make this leg.   240
    Lady F. Hast thou conspired with thy brother too,
That for thine own gain shouldst defend mine honour?
What means this scorn, thou most untoward knave?
    Bast. Knight, knight, good mother,—Basilisco-like.
What! I am dubb'd; I have it on my shoulder.
But, mother, I am not Sir Robert's son;
I have disclaim'd Sir Robert, and my land;
Legitimation, name, and all is gone.
Then, good my mother, let me know my father:'
Some proper man, I hope; who was it, mother?   250
    Lady F. Hast thou denied thyself a Faulconbridge?
    Bast. As faithfully as I deny the devil.
    Lady F. King Richard Cordelion was thy father.
By long and vehement suit I was seduc'd
To make room for him in my husband's bed.—
Heaven lay not my transgression to my charge!—
Thou art the issue of my dear offence,
Which was so strongly urg'd, past my defence.
    Bast. Now, by this light, were I to get again,
Madam, I would not wish a better father.   260
Some sins do bear their privilege on earth,
And so doth yours; your fault was not your folly:
Needs must you lay your heart at his dispose,
Subjected tribute to commanding love,
Against whose fury and unmatched force
The awless lion could not wage the fight,
Nor keep his princely heart from Richard's hand.
He that perforce robs lions of their hearts,
May easily win a woman's. Ay, my mother,
With all my heart I thank thee for my father!   270
Who lives and dares but say thou didst not well
When I was got, I'll send his soul to hell.
Come, lady, I will show thee to my kin;
And they shall say, when Richard me begot,
If thou hadst said him nay, it had been sin:
Who says it was, he lies: I say, 't was not. [*Exeunt.*

ACT II.

SCENE I.—France. Before the Walls of Angiers.

Enter, on one side, the Duke of AUSTRIA, *and Forces; on the other,* PHILIP, *King of France, and Forces;* LEWIS, CONSTANCE, ARTHUR, *and Attendants.*

            Lewis.
BEFORE Angiers well met, brave
            Austria.—
    Arthur, that great forerunner of thy
            blood,
    Richard, that robb'd the lion of his
            heart,
    And fought the holy wars in Pales-
            tine,
    By this brave duke came early to his
            grave:
    And, for amends to his posterity,
At our importance hither is he come,
To spread his colours, boy, in thy behalf,
And to rebuke the usurpation
Of thy unnatural uncle, English John.   10
Embrace him, love him, give him welcome hither.
    Arth. God shall forgive you Cordelion's death,
The rather, that you give his offspring life,
Shadowing their right under your wings of war.
I give you welcome with a powerless hand,
But with a heart full of unstained love:
Welcome before the gates of Angiers, duke.
    Lew. A noble boy! Who would not do the right?
    Aust. Upon thy cheek lay I this zealous kiss,
As seal to this indenture of my love,   20
That to my home I will no more return,
Till Angiers, and the right thou hast in France,

'Together with that pale, that white-fac'd shore,
Whose foot spurns back the ocean's roaring tides,
And coops from other lands her islanders,
Even till that England, hedg'd in with the main,
That water-walled bulwark, still secure
And confident from foreign purposes,
Even till that utmost corner of the west
Salute thee for her king : till then, fair boy,   30
Will I not think of home, but follow arms.
  Const. O ! take his mother's thanks, a widow's
thanks,
Till your strong hand shall help to give him strength,
To make a more requital to your love.
  Aust. The peace of Heaven is theirs that lift their
swords
In such a just and charitable war.
  K. Phi. Well then, to work. Our cannon shall be
bent
Against the brows of this resisting town.
Call for our chiefest men of discipline,
To cull the plots of best advantages.   40
We 'll lay before this town our royal bones,
Wade to the market-place in Frenchmen's blood,
But we will make it subject to this boy.
  Const. Stay for an answer to your embassy,
Lest unadvis'd you stain your swords with blood.
My Lord Chatillon may from England bring
That right in peace, which here we urge in war ;
And then we shall repent each drop of blood,
That hot rash haste so indirectly shed.

Enter CHATILLON.

  K. Phi. A wonder, lady !—lo, upon thy wish,   50
Our messenger, Chatillon, is arriv'd.—
What England says, say briefly, gentle lord ;
We coldly pause for thee : Chatillon, speak.
  Chat. Then turn your forces from this paltry siege,
And stir them up against a mightier task.
England, impatient of your just demands,
Hath put himself in arms. The adverse winds,
Whose leisure I have stay'd, have given him time
To land his legions all as soon as I.
His marches are expedient to this town,   60
His forces strong, his soldiers confident.
With him along is come the mother-queen,
An Até, stirring him to blood and strife ;
With her her niece, the Lady Blanch of Spain ;
With them a bastard of the king's deceas'd :
And all the unsettled humours of the land,
Rash, inconsiderate, fiery voluntaries,
With ladies' faces, and fierce dragons' spleens,
Have sold their fortunes at their native homes,
Bearing their birthrights proudly on their backs,   70
To make a hazard of new fortunes here.
In brief, a braver choice of dauntless spirits,
Than now the English bottoms have waft o'er,
Did never float upon the swelling tide,
To do offence and scath in Christendom.   [*Drums heard within.*
The interruption of their churlish drums
Cuts off more circumstance : they are at hand,
To parley, or to fight : therefore, prepare.
  K. Phi. How much unlook'd for is this expedition !
  Aust. By how much unexpected, by so much   80
We must awake endeavour for defence,
For courage mounteth with occasion :
Let then be welcome then, we are prepar'd.

Enter King JOHN, ELINOR, BLANCH, *the Bastard,*
PEMBROKE, *and Forces.*

  K. John. Peace be to France, if France in peace
permit
Our just and lineal entrance to our own ;
If not, bleed France, and peace ascend to heaven,
Whiles we, God's wrathful agent, do correct
Their proud contempt that beat his peace to heaven.
  K. Phi. Peace be to England, if that war return   90
From France to England, there to live in peace.
England we love ; and, for that England's sake,
With burden of our armour here we sweat :
This toil of ours should be a work of thine ;
But thou from loving England art so far,

That thou hast under-wrought his lawful king,
Cut off the sequence of posterity,
Outfaced infant state, and done a rape
Upon the maiden virtue of the crown.
Look here upon thy brother Geffrey's face :
These eyes, these brows, were moulded out of his !   100
This little abstract doth contain that large
Which died in Geffrey, and the hand of time
Shall draw this brief into as huge a volume.
That Geffrey was thy elder brother born,
And this his son ; England was Geffrey's right,
And this is Geffrey's. In the name of God,
How comes it then, that thou art call'd a king,
When living blood doth in these temples beat,
Which owe the crown that thou o'ermasterest ?
  K. John. From whom hast thou this great commis-
sion, France,   110
To draw my answer from thy articles ?
  K. Phi. From that supernal Judge, that stirs good
thoughts
In any breast of strong authority,
To look into the blots and stains of right.
That Judge hath made me guardian to this boy :
Under whose warrant I impeach thy wrong,
And by whose help I mean to chastise it.   .
  K. John. Alack ! thou dost usurp authority.
  K. Phi. Excuse : it is to beat usurping down.
  Eli. Who is it, thou dost call usurper, France ?   120
  Const. Let me make answer :—thy usurping son.
  Eli. Out, insolent ! thy bastard shall be king,
That thou may'st be a queen, and check the world !
  Const. My bed was ever to thy son as true,
As thine was to thy husband, and this boy
Liker in feature to his father Geffrey,
Than thou and John, in manners being as like
As rain to water, or devil to his dam.
My boy a bastard ! By my soul, I think,
His father never was so true-begot :   130
It cannot be, an if thou wert his mother.
  Eli. There 's a good mother, boy, that blots thy
father.
  Const. There 's a good grandam, boy, that would
blot thee.
  Aust. Peace !
  Bast.   Hear the crier.
  Aust.   What the devil art thou ?
  Bast. One that will play the devil, sir, with you,
An 'a may catch your hide and you alone.
You are the hare of whom the proverb goes,
Whose valour plucks dead lions by the beard.
I 'll smoke your skin-coat, an I catch you right.
Sirrah, look to 't ; i' faith, I will, i' faith.   140
  Blanch. O ! well did he become that lion's robe,
That did disrobe the lion of that robe.
  Bast. It lies as sightly on the back of him,
As great Alcides' shows upon an ass.—
But, ass, I 'll take that burden from your back,
Or lay on that shall make your shoulders crack.
  Aust. What cracker is this same, that deafs our ears
With this abundance of superfluous breath ?—
  King,—Lewis, determine what we shall do straight.
  Lew. Women and fools, beware off your conference.—   151
King John, this is the very sum of all :
England, and Ireland, Anjou, Touraine, Maine,
In right of Arthur do I claim of thee.
Wilt thou resign them, and lay down thy arms ?
  K. John. My life as soon : I do defy thee, France.—
Arthur of Bretagne, yield thee to my hand,
And, out of my dear love, I 'll give thee more
Than e'er the coward hand of France can win.
Submit thee, boy.
  Eli.   Come to thy grandam, child.
  Const. Do, child, go to it grandam, child ;   160
Give grandam kingdom, and it grandam will
Give it a plum, a cherry, and a fig :
There 's a good grandam.
  Arth.   Good my mother, peace !
I would that I were low laid in my grave :
I am not worth this coil that 's made for me.
  Eli. His mother shames him so, poor boy, he weeps.
  Const. Now shame upon you, whe'r she does, or no !
His grandam's wrongs, and not his mother's shames,

Draw those Heaven-moving pearls from his poor eyes,
Which Heaven shall take in nature of a fee :   170
Ay, with these crystal beads Heaven shall be brib'd
To do him justice, and revenge on you.
  Eli.   Thou monstrous slanderer of Heaven and
    earth !
  Const. Thou monstrous injurer of Heaven and earth !
Call not me slanderer : thou, and thine, usurp
The dominations, royalties, and rights
Of this oppressed boy. This is thy eldest son's son,
Infortunate in nothing but in thee :
Thy sins are visited in this poor child ;
The canon of the law is laid on him,   180
Being but the second generation
Removed from thy sin-conceiving womb.
  K. John. Bedlam, have done.
  Const.   I have but this to say, —
That he is not only plagued for her sin,
But God hath made her sin and her the plague
On this removed issue, plagu'd for her,
And with her plague, her sin ; his injury
Her injury, the beadle to her sin,
All punish'd in the person of this child,
And all for her. A plague upon her !   190
  Eli. Thou unadvised scold, I can produce
A will, that bars the title of thy son.
  Const. Ay, who doubts that ? a will ! a wicked will ;
A woman's will ; a canker'd grandam's will !
  K. Phi. Peace, lady ! pause, or be more temperate.
It ill beseems this presence, to cry aim
To these ill-tuned repetitions.—
Some trumpet summon hither to the walls
These men of Angiers : let us hear them speak,
Whose title they admit, Arthur's or John's.   200

  Trumpets sound. Enter Citizens upon the walls.

  Cit. Who is it, that hath warn'd us to the walls ?
  K. Phi. 'T is France, for England.
  K. John.   England, for itself.
You men of Angiers, and my loving subjects,—
  K. Phi. You loving men of Angiers, Arthur's
    subjects,
Our trumpet call'd you to this gentle parle,—
  K. John. For our advantage, therefore, hear us
    first. —
These flags of France, that are advanced here
Before the eye and prospect of your town,
Have hither march'd to your endamagement :
The cannons have their bowels full of wrath,   210
And ready mounted are they to spit forth
Their iron indignation 'gainst your walls :
All preparation for a bloody siege
And merciless proceeding by these French,
Confront your city's eyes, your winking gates ;
And, but for our approach, those sleeping stones,
That as a waist do girdle you about,
By the compulsion of their ordnance
By this time from their fixed beds of lime
Had been dishabited, and wide havoc made   220
For bloody power to rush upon your peace.
But, on the sight of us, your lawful king,
Who painfully, with much expedient march,
Have brought a countercheck before your gates,
To save unscratch'd your city's threaten'd cheeks,
Behold, the French amaz'd vouchsafe a parle ;
And now, instead of bullets wrapp'd in fire,
To make a shaking fever in your walls,
They shoot but calm words, folded up in smoke,
To make a faithless error in your ears :   230
Which trust accordingly, kind citizens,
And let us in, your king, whose labour'd spirits,
Forwearied in this action of swift speed,
Crave harbourage within your city walls.
  K. Phi. When I have said, make answer to us both.
Lo ! in this right hand, whose protection
Is most divinely vow'd upon the right
Of him it holds, stands young Plantagenet,
Son to the elder brother of this man,
And king o'er him, and all that he enjoys.   240
For this down-trodden equity, we tread
In warlike march these greens before your town,
Being no further enemy to you,

Than the constraint of hospitable zeal,
In the relief of this oppressed child,
Religiously provokes. Be pleased then
To pay that duty which you truly owe,
To him that owes it, namely, this young prince ;
And then our arms, like to a muzzled bear,
Save in aspect, have all offence seal'd up.   250
Our cannons' malice vainly shall be spent
Against the invulnerable clouds of heaven ;
And with a blessed and unvex'd retire,
With unhack'd swords, and helmets all unbruis'd,
We will bear home that lusty blood again,
Which here we came to spout against your town,
And leave your children, wives, and you, in peace.
But if you fondly pass our proffer'd offer,
'T is not the roundure of your old-fac'd walls
Can hide you from our messengers of war,   260
Though all these English, and their discipline,
Were harbour'd in their rude circumference.
Then, tell us, shall your city call us lord,
In that behalf which we have challeng'd it,
Or shall we give the signal to our rage,
And stalk in blood to our possession ?
  Cit. In brief, we are the King of England's subjects :
For him, and in his right, we hold this town.
  K. John. Acknowledge then the king, and let me in.
  Cit. That we can not ; but he that proves the king,
To him will we prove loyal : till that time   271
Have we ramm'd up our gates against the world.
  K. John. Doth not the crown of England prove the
    king ?
And if not that, I bring you witnesses,
Twice fifteen thousand hearts of England's breed,—
  Bast. Bastards, and else.
  K. John. To verify our title with their lives.
  K. Phi. As many, and as well-born bloods as those,—
  Bast. Some bastards too.
  K. Phi. Stand in his face to contradict his claim.
  Cit. Till you compound whose right is worthiest,
We for the worthiest hold the right from both.   282
  K. John. Then God forgive the sin of all those
    souls,
That to their everlasting residence,
Before the dew of evening fall, shall fleet,
In dreadful trial of our kingdom's king !
  K. Phi. Amen, Amen.—Mount, chevaliers ! to arms !
  Bast. Saint George, that swing'd the dragon, and
    e'er since
Sits on his horseback at mine hostess' door,
Teach us some fence !—[*To* AUSTRIA.] Sirrah, were I
    at home,   290
At your den, sirrah, with your lioness,
I would set an oxhead to your lion's hide,
And make a monster of you.
  Aust.   Peace ! no more.
  Bast. O ! tremble, for you hear the lion roar.
  K. John. Up higher to the plain ; where we 'll set
    forth
In best appointment all our regiments.
  Bast. Speed then, to take advantage of the field.
  K. Phi. It shall be so ;—[*to* LEWIS] and at the
    other hill
Command the rest to stand.—God, and our right !
                        [*Exeunt.*

SCENE II.—The Same.

*Alarums and Excursions ; then a Retreat. Enter
  a French Herald, with trumpets, to the gates.*

  F. Her. You men of Angiers, open wide your gates,
And let young Arthur, Duke of Bretagne, in,
Who by the hand of France this day hath made
Much work for tears in many an English mother,
Whose sons lie scatter'd on the bleeding ground ;
Many a widow's husband grovelling lies,
Coldly embracing the discolour'd earth ;
And victory, with little loss, doth play
Upon the dancing banners of the French,
Who are at hand, triumphantly display'd,   10
To enter conquerors, and to proclaim
Arthur of Bretagne England's king, and yours.

Enter an English Herald, with trumpets.

E. Her. Rejoice, you men of Angiers, ring your
   bells :
King John, your king and England's, doth approach,
Commander of this hot malicious day.
Their armours, that march'd hence so silver-bright,
Hither return all gilt with Frenchmen's blood.
There stuck no plume in any English crest,
That is removed by a staff of France ;
Our colours do return in those same hands,   20
That did display them when we first march'd forth ;
And, like a jolly troop of huntsmen, come
Our lusty English, all with purpled hands,
Dy'd in the dying slaughter of their foes.
Open your gates, and give the victors way.
  Cit. Heralds, from off our towers we might behold,
From first to last, the onset and retire
Of both your armies ; whose equality
By our best eyes cannot be censured :
Blood hath bought blood, and blows have answer'd
   blows ;   30
Strength match'd with strength, and power confronted
   power :
Both are alike ; and both alike we like.
One must prove greatest : while they weigh so even,
We hold our town for neither, yet for both.

Enter, at one side, King JOHN, *with his Power,*
ELINOR, BLANCH, *and the Bastard ; at the other,*
King PHILIP, LEWIS, AUSTRIA, *and Forces.*

  K. John. France, hast thou yet more blood to cast
   away ?
Say, shall the current of our right roam on ?
Whose passage, vex'd with thy impediment,
Shall leave his native channel, and o'erswell
With course disturb'd even thy confining shores,
Unless thou let his silver water keep   40
A peaceful progress to the ocean.
  K. Phi. England, thou hast not sav'd one drop of
   blood,
In this hot trial, more than we of France ;
Rather, lost more : and by this hand I swear,
That sways the earth this climate overlooks,
Before we will lay down our just-borne arms,
We'll put thee down, 'gainst whom these arms we
   bear,
Or add a royal number to the dead,
Gracing the scroll, that tells of this war's loss,
With slaughter coupled to the name of kings.   50
  Bast. Ha ! majesty, how high thy glory towers,
When the rich blood of kings is set on fire !
O ! now doth Death line his dead chaps with steel
The swords of soldiers are his teeth, his fangs ;
And now he feasts, mousing the flesh of men,
In undetermin'd differences of kings.—
Why stand these royal fronts amazed thus ?
Cry, havoc, kings ! back to the stained field,
You equal-potents, fiery-kindled spirits !
Then let confusion of one part confirm   60
The other's peace ; till then, blows, blood, and death !
  K. John. Whose party do the townsmen yet admit ?
  K. Phi. Speak, citizens, for England ; who's your
   king ?
  Cit. The King of England, when we know the king.
  K. Phi. Know him in us, that here hold up his right.
  K. John. In us, that are our own great deputy,
And bear possession of our person here,
Lord of our presence, Angiers, and of you.
  Cit. A greater power than we denies all this ;
And, till it be undoubted, we do lock   70
Our former scruple in our strong-barr'd gates,
Kings, of our fear ; until our fears, resolv'd,
Be by some certain king purg'd and depos'd.
  Bast. By Heaven, these scroyles of Angiers flout
   you, kings,
And stand securely on their battlements,
As in a theatre, whence they gape and point
At your industrious scenes and acts of death.
Your royal presences be rul'd by me :
Do like the mutines of Jerusalem,
Be friends awhile, and both conjointly bend   80

Your sharpest deeds of malice on this town.
By east and west let France and England mount
Their battering cannon charged to the mouths,
Till their soul-fearing clamours have brawl'd down
The flinty ribs of this contemptuous city :
I'd play incessantly upon these jades,
Even till unfenced desolation
Leave them as naked as the vulgar air.
That done, dissever your united strengths,
And part your mingled colours once again ;   90
Turn face to face, and bloody point to point ;
Then, in a moment, Fortune shall cull forth
Out of one side her happy minion,
To whom in favour she shall give the day,
And kiss him with a glorious victory.
How like you this wild counsel, mighty states ?
Smacks it not something of the policy ?
  K. John. Now, by the sky that hangs above our
   heads,
I like it well.—France, shall we knit our powers,
And lay this Angiers even with the ground,   100
Then, after, fight who shall be king of it ?
  Bast. An if thou hast the mettle of a king,
Being wrong'd as we are by this peevish town,
Turn thou the mouth of thy artillery,
As we will ours, against these saucy walls ;
And when that we have dash'd them to the ground,
Why, then defy each other, and, pell-mell,
Make work upon ourselves, for heaven, or hell.
  K. Phi. Let it be so.—Say, where will you assault ?
  K. John. We from the west will send destruction
Into this city's bosom.   111
  Aust. I from the north.
  K. Phi.   Our thunder from the south
Shall rain their drift of bullets on this town.
  Bast. [*Aside.*] O prudent discipline ! From north
   to south,
Austria and France shoot in each other's mouth :
I'll stir them to it.—Come, away, away !
  Cit. Hear us, great kings : vouchsafe awhile to stay,
And I shall show you peace, and fair-fac'd league ;
Win you this city without stroke, or wound ;
Rescue those breathing lives to die in beds,   120
That here come sacrifices for the field.
Persever not, but hear me, mighty kings.
  K. John. Speak on, with favour : we are bent to
   hear.
  Cit. That daughter there of Spain, the Lady Blanch,
Is niece to England. Look upon the years
Of Lewis the Dauphin, and that lovely maid.
If lusty love should go in quest of beauty,
Where should he find it fairer than in Blanch ?
If zealous love should go in search of virtue,
Where should he find it purer than in Blanch ?   130
If love ambitious sought a match of birth,
Whose veins bound richer blood than Lady Blanch ?
Such as she is, in beauty, virtue, birth,
Is the young Dauphin every way complete :
If not complete of, say, he is not she ;
And she again wants nothing, to name want,
If want it be not, that she is not he ;
He is the half part of a blessed man,
Left to be finished by such as she ;—
And she a fair divided excellence,   140
Whose fulness of perfection lies in him.
O ! two such silver currents, when they join,
Do glorify the banks that bound them in ;
And two such shores to two such streams made one,
Two such controlling bounds shall you be, kings,
To these two princes, if you marry them.
This union shall do more than battery can
To our fast-closed gates ; for, at this match,
With swifter spleen than powder can enforce,
The mouth of passage shall we fling wide ope,   150
And give you entrance ; but, without this match,
The sea enraged is not half so deaf,
Lions more confident, mountains and rocks
More free from motion : no, not Death himself
In mortal fury half so peremptory,
As we to keep this city.
  Bast.   Here's a stay,
That shakes the rotten carcase of old Death

Out of his rags! Here's a large mouth, indeed,
That spits forth death, and mountains, rocks, and
　　seas,
Talks as familiarly of roaring lions,　　　　160
As maids of thirteen do of puppy-dogs.
What cannoneer begot this lusty blood?
He speaks plain cannon, fire, and smoke, and bounce;
He gives the bastinado with his tongue;
Our ears are cudgell'd: not a word of his,
But buffets better than a fist of France.
'Zounds! I was never so bethump'd with words,
Since I first call'd my brother's father, dad.
　　Eli. Son, list to this conjunction, make this match.
Give with our niece a dowry large enough;　　170
For by this knot thou shalt so surely tie
Thy now unsur'd assurance to the crown,
That yon green boy shall have no sun to ripe
The bloom that promiseth a mighty fruit.
I see a yielding in the looks of France;
Mark, how they whisper: urge them, while their souls
Are capable of this ambition,
Lest zeal, now melted, by the windy breath
Of soft petitions, pity, and remorse,
Cool and congeal again to what it was.　　　180
　　Cit. Why answer not the double majesties
This friendly treaty of our threaten'd town?
　　K. Phi. Speak England first, that hath been forward
　　　first
To speak unto this city: what say you?
　　K. John. If that the Dauphin there, thy princely
　　　son,
Can in this book of beauty read, I love,
Her dowry shall weigh equal with a queen:
For Anjou, and fair Touraine, Maine, Poictiers,
And all that we upon this side the sea
(Except this city now by us besieg'd)　　　190
Find liable to our crown and dignity,
Shall gild her bridal bed, and make her rich
In titles, honours, and promotions,
As she in beauty, education, blood,
Holds hand with any princess of the world.
　　K. Phi. What say'st thou, boy? look in the lady's
　　　face.
　　Lew. I do, my lord; and in her eye I find
A wonder, or a wondrous miracle,
The shadow of myself form'd in her eye,
Which, being but the shadow of your son,　　200
Becomes a sun, and makes your son a shadow.
I do protest, I never lov'd myself,
Till now infixed I beheld myself,
Drawn in the flattering table of her eye.
　　　　　　　　　　　　　[Whispers with BLANCH.
　　Bast. Drawn in the flattering table of her eye,
Hang'd in the frowning wrinkle of her brow,
And quarter'd in her heart, he doth espy
Himself love's traitor: this is pity now,
That hang'd, and drawn, and quarter'd, there should
　　be,
In such a love, so vile a lout as he.　　　　210
　　Blanch. My uncle's will in this respect is mine.
If he see aught in you, that makes him like,
That anything he sees, which moves his liking,
I can with ease translate it to my will;
Or if you will, to speak more properly,
I will enforce it easily to my love.
Further I will not flatter you, my lord,
That all I see in you is worthy love,
Than this,—that nothing do I see in you,
Though churlish thoughts themselves should be your
　　judge,　　　　　　　　　　　　220
That I can find should merit any hate.
　　K. John. What say these young ones? What say
　　　you, my niece?
　　Blanch. That she is bound in honour still to do
What you in wisdom still vouchsafe to say.
　　K. John. Speak then, Prince Dauphin: can you
　　love this lady?
　　Lew. Nay, ask me if I can refrain from love;
For I do love her most unfeignedly.
　　K. John. Then do I give Volquessen, Touraine,
　　　Maine,
Poictiers, and Anjou, these five provinces.

With her to thee; and this addition more,　　230
Full thirty thousand marks of English coin.—
Philip of France, if thou be pleas'd withal,
Command thy son and daughter to join hands.
　　K. Phi. It likes us well.—Young princes, close your
　　　hands.
　　Aust. And your lips too; for I am well assur'd,
That I did so, when I was first assur'd.
　　K. Phi. Now, citizens of Angiers, ope your gates,
Let in that amity which you have made;
For at Saint Mary's Chapel presently

Lew. " Nay, ask me if I can refrain from love."

The rites of marriage shall be solemnis'd.—　　240
Is not the Lady Constance in this troop?
I know, she is not; for this match, made up,
Her presence would have interrupted much.
Where is she and her son? tell me, who knows.
　　Lew. She is sad and passionate at your highness'
　　　tent.
　　K. Phi. And, by my faith, this league, that we have
　　　made,
Will give her sadness very little cure.—
Brother of England, how may we content
This widow lady? In her right we came,
Which we, God knows, have turn'd another way,　　250
To our own vantage.
　　K. John.　　　　　We will heal up all;
For we'll create young Arthur Duke of Bretagne,
And Earl of Richmond, and this rich fair town
We make him lord of.—Call the Lady Constance:
Some speedy messenger bid her repair
To our solemnity.—I trust, we shall,
If not fill up the measure of her will,
Yet in some measure satisfy her so,
That we shall stop her exclamation.
Go we, as well as haste will suffer us,　　　260
To this unlook'd-for unprepared pomp.
　　　　*[Exeunt all but the Bastard.—The Citizens
　　　　　retire from the walls.*
　　Bast. Mad world! mad kings! mad composition!
John, to stop Arthur's title in the whole,
Hath willingly departed with a part;
And France, whose armour conscience buckled on,
Whom zeal and charity brought to the field,
As God's own soldier, rounded in the ear
With that same purpose-changer, that sly devil,
That broker that still breaks the pate of faith,
That daily break-vow, he that wins of all,　　270
Of kings, of beggars, old men, young men, maids,—
Who having no external thing to lose
But the word maid, cheats the poor maid of that;—
That smooth-fac'd gentleman, tickling commodity,
Commodity, the bias of the world;
The world, who of itself is peised well,
Made to run even, upon even ground,

Till this advantage, this vile-drawing bias,
This sway of motion, this commodity,
Makes it take head from all indifferency,   280
From all direction, purpose, course, intent:
And this same bias, this commodity,
This bawd, this broker, this all-changing word,
Clapp'd on the outward eye of fickle France,
Hath drawn him from his own determin'd aid,
From a resolv'd and honourable war,
To a most base and vile-concluded peace.—
And why rail I on this commodity?

But for because he hath not woo'd me yet.
Not that I have the power to clutch my hand,   290
When his fair angels would salute my palm;
But for my hand, as unattempted yet,
Like a poor beggar, raileth on the rich.
Well, whiles I am a beggar, I will rail.
And say, there is no sin but to be rich;
And being rich, my virtue then shall be,
To say, there is no vice but beggary.
Since kings break faith upon commodity,
Gain, be my lord, for I will worship thee!   *[Exit.*

ACT III.

SCENE I.—The Same. The French King's Tent.

Enter CONSTANCE, ARTHUR, *and* SALISBURY.

Constance.
GONE to be married! gone to swear a
  peace!
False blood to false blood join'd! gone
  to be friends!
Shall Lewis have Blanch, and Blanch
  those provinces?
It is not so; thou hast misspoke, mis-
  heard;
Be well advis'd, tell o'er thy tale again:
It cannot be; thou dost but say, 't is so.
I trust, I may not trust thee, for thy
  word
Is but the vain breath of a common man:
Believe me, I do not believe thee, man:
I have a king's oath to the contrary.   10
Thou shalt be punish'd for thus frighting me;
For I am sick, and capable of fears;
Oppress'd with wrongs, and therefore full of fears;
A widow, husbandless, subject to fears;
A woman, naturally born to fears;
And though thou now confess thou didst but jest,
With my vex'd spirits I cannot take a truce,
But they will quake and tremble all this day.
What dost thou mean by shaking of thy head?
Why dost thou look so sadly on my son?   20
What means that hand upon that breast of thine?
Why holds thine eye that lamentable rheum,
Like a proud river peering o'er his bounds?
Be these sad signs confirmers of thy words?
Then speak again; not all thy former tale,
But this one word, whether thy tale be true.
  Sal. As true as, I believe, you think them false,
That give you cause to prove my saying true.
  Const. O! if thou teach me to believe this sorrow,
Teach thou this sorrow how to make me die;   30
And let belief and life encounter so,
As doth the fury of two desperate men,
Which in the very meeting fall, and die.—
Lewis marry Blanch! O boy! then where art thou?
France friend with England, what becomes of me?—
Fellow, be gone; I cannot brook thy sight:
This news hath made thee a most ugly man.
  Sal. What other harm have I, good lady, done,
But spoke the harm that is by others done?
  Const. Which harm within itself so heinous is,   40
As it makes harmful all that speak of it.
  Arth. I do beseech you, madam, be content.
  Const. If thou, that bidd'st me be content, wert
  grim,

Ugly, and slanderous to thy mother's womb,
Full of unpleasing blots and sightless stains,
Lame, foolish, crooked, swart, prodigious,
Patch'd with foul moles, and eye-offending marks,
I would not care, I then would be content;
For then I should not love thee; no, nor thou
Become thy great birth, nor deserve a crown.   50
But thou art fair; and at thy birth, dear boy,
Nature and Fortune join'd to make thee great:
Of Nature's gifts thou may'st with lilies boast,
And with the half-blown rose. But Fortune, O!
She is corrupted, chang'd, and won from thee:
She adulterates hourly with thine uncle John;
And with her golden hand hath pluck'd on France
To tread down fair respect of sovereignty,
And made his majesty the bawd to theirs.
France is a bawd to Fortune, and King John;   60
That strumpet Fortune, that usurping John!—
Tell me, thou fellow, is not France forsworn?
Envenom him with words, or get thee gone,
And leave those woes alone, which I alone
Am bound to underbear.
  Sal.   Pardon me, madam,
I may not go without you to the kings.
  Const. Thou may'st, thou shalt: I will not go with
  thee.
I will instruct my sorrows to be proud,
For grief is proud, and makes his owner stoop.
To me, and to the state of my great grief,   70
Let kings assemble; for my grief's so great,
That no supporter but the huge firm earth
Can hold it up: here I and sorrows sit;
Here is my throne, bid kings come bow to it.
  [Seats herself on the ground.

Enter King JOHN, *King* PHILIP, LEWIS, BLANCH,
  ELINOR, *Bastard,* AUSTRIA, *and Attendants.*

  K. Phi. 'T is true, fair daughter; and this blessed
  day
Ever in France shall be kept festival:
To solemnise this day, the glorious sun
Stays in his course, and plays the alchymist,
Turning, with splendour of his precious eye,
The meagre cloddy earth to glittering gold: 80
The yearly course, that brings this day about,
Shall never see it but a holiday.
  Const. [*Rising.*] A wicked day, and not a holy day!
What hath this day deserv'd? what hath it done,
That it in golden letters should be set,
Among the high tides, in the calendar?

Nay, rather, turn this day out of the week ;
This day of shame, oppression, perjury :
Or if it must stand still, let wives with child
Pray, that their burdens may not fall this day, 90
Lest that their hopes prodigiously be cross'd.
But on this day let seamen fear no wrack ;
No bargains break, that are not this day made ;
This day all things begun come to ill end ;
Yea, faith itself to hollow falsehood change !
  K. Phi. By Heaven, lady, you shall have no cause
To curse the fair proceedings of this day.
Have I not pawn'd to you my majesty ?

Const. " Here is my throne, bid kings come bow to it."

  Const. You have beguil'd me with a counterfeit,
Resembling majesty, which, being touch'd and tried,
Proves valueless. You are forsworn, forsworn ; 101
You came in arms to spill mine enemies' blood,
But now in arms you strengthen it with yours :
The grappling vigour and rough frown of war
Is cold in amity and painted peace,
And our oppression hath made up this league.—
Arm, arm, you heavens, against these perjur'd kings !
A widow cries ; be husband to me, heavens !
Let not the hours of this ungodly day
Wear out the day in peace ; but, ere sunset, 110
Set armed discord 'twixt these perjur'd kings !
Hear me, O, hear me !
  Aust.   Lady Constance, peace !
  Const. War ! war ! no peace ! peace is to me a war.
O Limoges ! O Austria ! thou dost shame
That bloody spoil : thou slave, thou wretch, thou
    coward ;
Thou little-valiant, great in villainy !
Thou ever strong upon the stronger side !
Thou Fortune's champion, that dost never fight
But when her humorous ladyship is by
To teach thee safety ! thou art perjur'd too, 120
And sooth'st up greatness. What a fool art thou,
A ramping fool, to brag, and stamp, and swear,
Upon my party ! Thou cold-blooded slave,
Hast thou not spoke like thunder on my side ?
Been sworn my soldier ? bidding me depend
Upon thy stars, thy fortune, and thy strength ?
And dost thou now fall over to my foes ?
Thou wear a lion's hide ! doff it for shame,
And hang a calf's-skin on those recreant limbs.
  Aust. O, that a man should speak those words to
    me ! 130
  Bast. And hang a calf's-skin on those recreant
    limbs.
  Aust. Thou dar'st not say so, villain, for thy life.
  Bast. And hang a calf's-skin on those recreant
    limbs.
  K. John. We like not this ; thou dost forget thyself.

Enter PANDULPH.

  K. Phi. Here comes the holy legate of the Pope.
  Pand. Hail, you anointed deputies of Heaven !—
To thee, King John, my holy errand is.
I, Pandulph, of fair Milan cardinal,
And from Pope Innocent the legate here,
Do in his name religiously demand, 140
Why thou against the Church, our holy mother,
So wilfully dost spurn ; and, force perforce,
Keep Stephen Langton, chosen archbishop
Of Canterbury, from that holy see ?
This, in our 'foresaid holy father's name,
Pope Innocent, I do demand of thee.
  K. John. What earthly name to interrogatories
Can task the free breath of a sacred king ?
Thou canst not, cardinal, devise a name
So slight, unworthy, and ridiculous, 150
To charge me to an answer, as the Pope.
Tell him this tale ; and from the mouth of England
Add thus much more,—that no Italian priest
Shall tithe or toll in our dominions ;
But as we under Heaven are supreme head,
So, under him, that great supremacy,
Where we do reign, we will alone uphold,
Without the assistance of a mortal hand :
So tell the Pope ; all reverence set apart
To him, and his usurp'd authority. 160
  K. Phi. Brother of England, you blaspheme in this.
  K. John. Though you, and all the kings of Christen-
    dom,
Are led so grossly by this meddling priest,
Dreading the curse that money may buy out,
And, by the merit of vile gold, dross, dust,
Purchase corrupted pardon of a man,
Who, in that sale, sells pardon from himself ;
Though you, and all the rest, so grossly led,
This juggling witchcraft with revenue cherish :
Yet I alone, alone do me oppose 170
Against the Pope, and count his friends my foes.
  Pand. Then, by the lawful power that I have,
Thou shalt stand curs'd, and excommunicate :
And blessed shall he be that doth revolt
From his allegiance to an heretic ;
And meritorious shall that hand be call'd,
Canonised, and worship'd as a saint,
That takes away by any secret course
Thy hateful life.
  Const.   O ! lawful let it be,
That I have room with Rome to curse awhile. 180
Good father cardinal, cry thou Amen
To my keen curses ; for, without my wrong,
There is no tongue hath power to curse him right.
  Pand. There 's law and warrant, lady, for my curse.
  Const. And for mine too : when law can do no right,
Let it be lawful that law bar no wrong.
Law cannot give my child his kingdom here,
For he that holds his kingdom holds the law :
Therefore, since law itself is perfect wrong,
How can the law forbid my tongue to curse ? 190
  Pand. Philip of France, on peril of a curse,
Let go the hand of that arch-heretic,
And raise the power of France upon his head,
Unless he do submit himself to Rome.
  Eli. Look'st thou pale, France ? do not let go thy hand.
  Const. Look to that, devil, lest that France repent,
And, by disjoining hands, hell lose a soul.
  Aust. King Philip, listen to the cardinal.
  Bast. And hang a calf's-skin on his recreant limbs.
  Aust. Well, ruffian, I must pocket up these wrongs,—
Because—
  Bast.   Your breeches best may carry them. 201
  K. John. Philip, what say'st thou to the cardinal ?
  Const. What should he say, but as the cardinal ?
  Lew. Bethink you, father ; for the difference
Is, purchase of a heavy curse from Rome,
Or the light loss of England for a friend :
Forego the easier.
  Blanch.   That 's the curse of Rome.
  Const. O Lewis, stand fast ! the devil tempts thee
    here,
In likeness of a new-uptrimmed bride.

Blanch. The Lady Constance speaks not from her
    faith,   210
But from her need.
    Const.   O! if thou grant my need,
Which only lives but by the death of faith,

K. Phi. I am perplex'd, and know not what to say.
    Pand. What canst thou say, but will perplex thee
        more,
If thou stand excommunicate, and curs'd?
    K. Phi. Good reverend father, make my person yours,

Pand. " I will denounce a curse upon his head."

That need must needs infer this principle,
That faith would live again by death of need;
O! then, tread down my need, and faith mounts up;
Keep my need up, and faith is trodden down.
    K. John. The king is mov'd, and answers not to
        this.
    Const. O! be remov'd from him, and answer well.
    Aust. Do so, King Philip: hang no more in doubt.
    Bast. Hang nothing but a calf's-skin, most sweet
        lout.   220

And tell me how you would bestow yourself.
This royal hand and mine are newly knit,
And the conjunction of our inward souls
Married in league, coupled and link'd together
With all religious strength of sacred vows;
The latest breath that gave the sound of words,   230
Was deep-sworn faith, peace, amity, true love,
Between our kingdoms, and our royal selves;
And even before this truce, but new before,
No longer than we well could wash our hands.

To clap this royal bargain up of peace,
Heaven knows, they were besmear'd and overstain'd
With slaughter's pencil; where revenge did paint
The fearful difference of incensed kings:
And shall these hands, so lately purg'd of blood,
So newly join'd in love, so strong in both,   240
Unyoke this seizure, and this kind regreet?
Play fast and loose with faith? so jest with Heaven,
Make such unconstant children of ourselves,
As now again to snatch our palm from palm,
Unswear faith sworn, and on the marriage-bed
Of smiling peace to march a bloody host,
And make a riot on the gentle brow
Of true sincerity? O! holy sir,
My reverend father, let it not be so.
Out of your grace, devise, ordain, impose   250
Some gentle order, and then we shall be bless'd
To do your pleasure, and continue friends.
    Pand. All form is formless, order orderless,
Save what is opposite to England's love.
Therefore, to arms! be champion of our Church,
Or let the Church, our mother, breathe her curse,
A mother's curse, on her revolting son.
France, thou may'st hold a serpent by the tongue,
A chafed lion by the mortal paw,
A fasting tiger safer by the tooth,   260
Than keep in peace that hand which thou dost hold.
    K. Phi. I may disjoin my hand, but not my faith.
    Pand. So mak'st thou faith an enemy to faith;
And, like a civil war, sett'st oath to oath,
Thy tongue against thy tongue. O! let thy vow,
First made to Heaven, first be to Heaven perform'd;
That is, to be the champion of our Church.
What since thou swor'st is sworn against thyself,
And may not be performed by thyself:
For that which thou hast sworn to do amiss,   270
Is not amiss when it is truly done:
And being not done, where doing tends to ill,
The truth is then most done not doing it.
The better act of purposes mistook
Is, to mistake again: though indirect,
Yet indirection thereby grows direct,
And falsehood falsehood cures; as fire cools fire,
Within the scorched veins of one new-burn'd.
It is religion that doth make vows kept;
But thou hast sworn against religion   280
By what thou swear'st, against the thing thou
    swear'st,
And mak'st an oath the surety for thy truth
Against an oath: the truth, thou art unsure
To swear, swears only not to be forsworn;
Else, what a mockery should it be to swear!
But thou dost swear only to be forsworn;
And most forsworn, to keep what thou dost swear.
Therefore, thy later vows, against thy first,
Is in thyself rebellion to thyself;
And better conquest never canst thou make,   290
Than arm thy constant and thy nobler parts
Against these giddy loose suggestions:
Upon which better part our prayers come in,
If thou vouchsafe them: but, if not, then know,
The peril of our curses light on thee
So heavy, as thou shalt not shake them off,
But in despair die under their black weight.
    Aust. Rebellion, flat rebellion!
    Bast.   Will 't not be?
Will not a calf's-skin stop that mouth of thine?
    Lew. Father, to arms!
    Blanch.   Upon thy wedding-day?
Against the blood that thou hast married?   301
What! shall our feast be kept with slaughter'd men?
Shall braying trumpets, and loud churlish drums,
Clamours of hell, be measures to our pomp?
O husband, hear me!—ah, alack! how new
Is husband in my mouth!—even for that name,
Which till this time my tongue did ne'er pronounce,
Upon my knee I beg, go not to arms
Against mine uncle.
    Const.   O! upon my knee,
Made hard with kneeling, I do pray to thee,   310
Thou virtuous Dauphin, alter not the doom
Forethought by Heaven!

    Blanch. Now shall I see thy love. What motive
    may
Be stronger with thee than the name of wife?
    Const. That which upholdeth him that thee upholds,
His honour. O! thine honour, Lewis, thine honour.
    Lew. I muse, your majesty doth seem so cold,
When such profound respects do pull you on.
    Pand. I will denounce a curse upon his head.
    K. Phi. Thou shalt not need.—England, I'll fall
    from thee.   320
    Const. O fair return of banish'd majesty!
    Eli. O foul revolt of French inconstancy!
    K. John. France, thou shalt rue this hour within
    this hour.
    Bast. Old Time the clock-setter, that bald sexton
    Time,
Is it as he will? well then, France shall rue.
    Blanch. The sun's o'ercast with blood: fair day,
    adieu!
Which is the side that I must go withal?
I am with both: each army hath a hand;
And in their rage, I having hold of both,
They whirl asunder, and dismember me.   330
Husband, I cannot pray that thou may'st win;
Uncle, I needs must pray that thou may'st lose;
Father, I may not wish the fortune thine;
Grandam, I will not wish thy wishes thrive:
Whoever wins, on that side shall I lose;
Assured loss, before the match be play'd.
    Lew. Lady, with me, with me thy fortune lies.
    Blanch. There where my fortune lives, there my life
    dies.
    K. John. Cousin, go draw our puissance together.—
                                        [*Exit Bastard.*
France, I am burn'd up with inflaming wrath;   340
A rage, whose heat hath this condition,
That nothing can allay, nothing but blood,
The blood and dearest-valu'd blood, of France.
    K. Phi. Thy rage shall burn thee up, and thou
    shalt turn
To ashes, ere our blood shall quench that fire.
Look to thyself, thou art in jeopardy.
    K. John. No more than he that threats.—To arms
    let's hie!   [*Exeunt.*

                        ───

SCENE II.—The Same. Plains near Angiers.

Alarums; Excursions. Enter the Bastard, with
AUSTRIA's *head.*

    Bast. Now, by my life, this day grows wondrous
    hot;
Some airy devil hovers in the sky,
And pours down mischief. Austria's head, lie there,
While Philip breathes.

        Enter King JOHN, ARTHUR, *and* HUBERT.

    K. John. Hubert, keep this boy.—Philip, make up!
My mother is assailed in our tent,
And ta'en, I fear.
    Bast.   My lord, I rescu'd her;
Her highness is in safety, fear you not:
But on, my liege; for very little pains
Will bring this labour to an happy end.   10 [*Exeunt.*

                        ───

SCENE III.—The Same.

Alarums; Excursions; Retreat. Enter King JOHN,
ELINOR, ARTHUR, *the Bastard,* HUBERT, *and*
Lords.

    K. John. [*To* ELINOR.] So shall it be; your grace
    shall stay behind,
So strongly guarded.—[*To* ARTHUR.] Cousin, look
    not sad:
Thy grandam loves thee, and thy uncle will
As dear be to thee as thy father was.
    Arth. O! this will make my mother die with grief.
    K. John. [*To the Bastard.*] Cousin, away for Eng-
    land: haste before;
And, ere our coming, see thou shake the bags
Of hoarding abbots; imprisoned angels

Set at liberty : the fat ribs of peace
Must by the hungry now be fed upon :   10
Use our commission in his utmost force.
Bast. Bell, book, and candle, shall not drive me
          back,
When gold and silver becks me to come on.
I leave your highness.—Grandam, I will pray
(If ever I remember to be holy)
For your fair safety : so I kiss your hand.
Eli. Farewell, gentle cousin.
K. John.   Coz, farewell. [*Exit Bastard.*
Eli. Come hither, little kinsman ; hark, a word.
                                [*She takes* ARTHUR *aside.*
K. John. Come hither, Hubert. O my gentle
          Hubert,
We owe thee much : within this wall of flesh   20

Eli. "Come, hither, little kinsman ; hark, a word."

There is a soul, counts thee her creditor,
And with advantage means to pay thy love :
And, my good friend, thy voluntary oath
Lives in this bosom, dearly cherished.
Give me thy hand. I had a thing to say,—
But I will fit it with some better tune.
By Heaven, Hubert, I am almost asham'd
To say what good respect I have of thee.
Hub. I am much bounden to your majesty.
K. John. Good friend, thou hast no cause to say so
          yet :   30
But thou shalt have : and creep time ne'er so slow,
Yet it shall come for me to do thee good.
I had a thing to say,—but let it go :
The sun is in the heaven, and the proud day,
Attended with the pleasures of the world,
Is all too wanton, and too full of gawds,
To give me audience:—if the midnight bell
Did, with his iron tongue and brazen mouth,
Sound on into the drowsy race of night;
If this same were a churchyard where we stand,   40
And thou possessed with a thousand wrongs ;
Or if that surly spirit, melancholy,
Had bak'd thy blood, and made it heavy-thick,
(Which, else, runs tickling up and down the veins,
Making that idiot, laughter, keep men's eyes,
And strain their cheeks to idle merriment,
A passion hateful to my purposes ;)
Or if that thou couldst see me without eyes,
Hear me without thine ears, and make reply
Without a tongue, using conceit alone,   50
Without eyes, ears, and harmful sound of words :
Then, in despite of brooded-watchful day,—
I would into thy bosom pour my thoughts.
But, ah ! I will not :—yet I love thee well ;
And, by my troth, I think, thou lov'st me well.
Hub. So well, that what you bid me undertake,

Though that my death were adjunct to my act,
By Heaven, I would do it.
K. John.   Do not I know, thou wouldst ?
Good Hubert ! Hubert,—Hubert, throw thine eye
On yon young boy. I 'll tell thee what, my friend, 60
He is a very serpent in my way ;
And wheresoe'er this foot of mine doth tread,
He lies before me. Dost thou understand me ?
Thou art his keeper.
Hub.   And I 'll keep him so,
That he shall not offend your majesty.
K. John. Death.
Hub. My lord.
K. John.   A grave.
Hub.   He shall not live.
K. John.   Enough.
I could be merry now. Hubert, I love thee ;
Well, I 'll not say what I intend for thee :
Remember.—Madam, fare you well :   70
I 'll send those powers o'er to your majesty.
Eli. My blessing go with thee !
K. John.   For England, cousin : go.
Hubert shall be your man, attend on you
With all true duty.—On toward Calais, ho ! [*Exeunt.*

SCENE IV.—The Same. The French King's Tent.

Enter King PHILIP, LEWIS, PANDULPH, *and
                  Attendants.*

K. Phi. So, by a roaring tempest on the flood,
A whole armado of connected sail
Is scatter'd, and disjoin'd from fellowship.
Pand. Courage and comfort ! all shall yet go well.
K. Phi. What can go well, when we have run so ill ?
Are we not beaten ? Is not Angiers lost ?
Arthur ta'en prisoner ? divers dear friends slain ?
And bloody England into England gone,
O'erbearing interruption, spite of France ?
Lew. What he hath won, that hath he fortified : 10
So hot a speed with such advice dispos'd,
Such temperate order in so fierce a cause,
Doth want example. Who hath read, or heard,
Of any kindred action like to this ?
K. Phi. Well could I bear that England had this
          praise,
So we could find some pattern of our shame.

Enter CONSTANCE.

Look, who comes here ? a grave unto a soul ;
Holding the eternal spirit, against her will,
In the vile prison of afflicted breath.—
I pr'ythee, lady, go away with me.   20
Const. Lo now, now see the issue of your peace !
K. Phi. Patience, good lady : comfort, gentle Con-
          stance !
Const. No, I defy all counsel, all redress,
But that which ends all counsel, true redress,
Death, death.—O amiable lovely death !
Thou odoriferous stench ! sound rottenness !
Arise forth from the couch of lasting night,
Thou hate and terror to prosperity,
And I will kiss thy detestable bones,
And put my eye-balls in thy vaulty brows,   30
And ring these fingers with thy household worms,
And stop this gap of breath with fulsome dust,
And be a carrion monster like thyself :
Come, grin on me ; and I will think thou smil'st,
And buss thee as thy wife ! Misery's love,
O, come to me !
K. Phi.   O fair affliction, peace !
Const. No, no, I will not, having breath to cry.—
O! that my tongue were in the thunder's mouth ;
Then with a passion would I shake the world,
And rouse from sleep that fell anatomy,   40
Which cannot hear a lady's feeble voice,
Which scorns a modern invocation.
Pand. Lady, you utter madness, and not sorrow.
Const. Thou art unholy to belie me so.
I am not mad : this hair I tear, is mine ;
My name is Constance ; I was Geffrey's **wife**

Young Arthur is my son, and he is lost !
I am not mad :—I would to Heaven, I were,
For then, 't is like I should forget myself :
O, if I could, what grief should I forget !—   50
Preach some philosophy to make me mad,

Const. "Thou art unholy to belie me so."

And thou shalt be canonis'd, cardinal ;
For, being not mad, but sensible of grief,
My reasonable part produces reason
How I may be deliver'd of these woes,
And teaches me to kill or hang myself :
If I were mad, I should forget my son,
Or madly think, a babe of clouts were he.
I am not mad : too well, too well I feel
The different plague of each calamity.   60
K. Phi. Bind up those tresses. O ! what love I note
In the fair multitude of those her hairs !
Where but by chance a silver drop hath fallen,
Even to that drop ten thousand wiry friends
Do glue themselves in sociable grief ;
Like true, inseparable, faithful loves,
Sticking together in calamity.
Const. To England, if you will.
K. Phi.   Bind up your hairs.
Const. Yes, that I will ; and wherefore will I do it ?
I tore them from their bonds, and cried aloud,   70
"O, that these hands could so redeem my son,
As they have given these hairs their liberty !"
But now I envy at their liberty,
And will again commit them to their bonds,
Because my poor child is a prisoner.—
And, father cardinal, I have heard you say,
That we shall see and know our friends in heaven.
If that be true, I shall see my boy again ;
For, since the birth of Cain, the first male child,
To him that did but yesterday suspire,   80
There was not such a gracious creature born.
But now will canker sorrow eat my bud,
And chase the native beauty from his cheek,
And he will look as hollow as a ghost,
As dim and meagre as an ague's fit,
And so he'll die ; and, rising so again,
When I shall meet him in the court of heaven,
I shall not know him : therefore, never, never
Must I behold my pretty Arthur more.
Pand. You hold too heinous a respect of grief.   90
Const. He talks to me, that never had a son.
K. Phi. You are as fond of grief as of your child.
Const. Grief fills the room up of my absent child,
Lies in his bed, walks up and down with me,
Puts on his pretty looks, repeats his words,
Remembers me of all his gracious parts,
Stuffs out his vacant garments with his form :
Then, have I reason to be fond of grief.
Fare you well : had you such a loss as I,
I could give better comfort than you do.—   100
I will not keep this form upon my head,

When there is such disorder in my wit.
O Lord ! my boy, my Arthur, my fair son !
My life, my joy, my food, my all the world !
My widow-comfort, and my sorrow's cure !   [*Exit.*
K. Phi. I fear some outrage, and I 'll follow her.
                                                     [*Exit.*
Lew. There's nothing in this world can make me
                                                          joy :
Life is as tedious as a twice-told tale,
Vexing the dull ear of a drowsy man ;
And bitter shame hath spoil'd the sweet world's taste,
That it yields nought but shame and bitterness.   111
Pand. Before the curing of a strong disease,
Even in the instant of repair and health,
The fit is strongest : evils that take leave,
On their departure most of all show evil.
What have you lost by losing of this day ?
Lew. All days of glory, joy, and happiness.
Pand. If you had won it, certainly, you had.
No, no : when Fortune means to men most good,
She looks upon them with a threatening eye.   120
'T is strange, to think how much King John hath lost
In this which he accounts so clearly won.
Are not you griev'd, that Arthur is his prisoner ?
Lew. As heartily, as he is glad he hath him.
Pand. Your mind is all as youthful as your blood.
Now hear me speak with a prophetic spirit ;
For even the breath of what I mean to speak
Shall blow each dust, each straw, each little rub,
Out of the path which shall directly lead
Thy foot to England's throne ; and therefore mark.
John hath seiz'd Arthur ; and it cannot be,   131
That whiles warm life plays in that infant's veins,
The misplac'd John should entertain an hour,
One minute, nay, one quiet breath of rest.
A sceptre, snatch'd with an unruly hand,
Must be as boisterously maintain'd as gain'd ;
And he that stands upon a slippery place,
Makes nice of no vile hold to stay him up :
That John may stand, then Arthur needs must fall ;
So be it, for it cannot be but so.   140
Lew. But what shall I gain by young Arthur's fall ?
Pand. You, in the right of Lady Blanch your wife,
May then make all the claim that Arthur did.
Lew. And lose it, life and all, as Arthur did.
Pand. How green you are, and fresh in this old
                                                          world !
John lays you plots ; the times conspire with you :
For he that steeps his safety in true blood,
Shall find but bloody safety, and untrue.
This act, so evilly borne, shall cool the hearts
Of all his people, and freeze up their zeal,   150

Pand. "How green you are."

That none so small advantage shall step forth
To check his reign, but they will cherish it :
No natural exhalation in the sky,
No scope of Nature, no distemper'd day,
No common wind, no customed event,

But they will pluck away his natural cause,
And call them meteors, prodigies, and signs,
Abortives, presages, and tongues of heaven,
Plainly denouncing vengeance upon John.

    Lew. May be, he will not touch young Arthur's life,
But hold himself safe in his prisonment.   161

    Pand. O! sir, when he shall hear of your approach,
If that young Arthur be not gone already,
Even at that news he dies; and then the hearts
Of all his people shall revolt from him,
And kiss the lips of unacquainted change,
And pick strong matter of revolt, and wrath,
Out of the bloody fingers' ends of John.
Methinks, I see this hurly all on foot:

And, O! what better matter breeds for you,   170
Than I have nam'd!—The bastard Faulconbridge
Is now in England ransacking the Church,
Offending charity: if but a dozen French
Were there in arms, they would be as a call
To train ten thousand English to their side;
Or as a little snow, tumbled about,
Anon becomes a mountain. O noble Dauphin,
Go with me to the king. 'Tis wonderful,
What may be wrought out of their discontent,
Now that their souls are topful of offence.   180
For England, go; I will whet on the king.

    Lew. Strong reasons make strong actions. Let us go:
If you say, ay, the king will not say, no.   [*Exeunt.*

ACT IV.

Scene I. Northampton. A Room in the Castle.

Enter Hubert *and two Attendants.*

    Hubert.

HEAT me these irons hot; and look thou stand
Within the arras: when I strike my foot
Upon the bosom of the ground, rush forth,
And bind the boy, which you shall find with me,
Fast to the chair: be heedful. Hence, and watch.

    1 Atten. I hope, your warrant will bear out the deed.

    Hub. Uncleanly scruples! fear not you:
look to 't.—   [*Exeunt Attendants.*
Young lad, come forth; I have to say with you.

Enter ARTHUR.

    Arth. Good morrow, Hubert.

    Hub.   Good morrow, little prince.

    Arth. As little prince (having so great a title   10
To be more prince) as may be.—You are sad.

    Hub. Indeed, I have been merrier.

    Arth.   Mercy on me!
Methinks, nobody should be sad but I:
Yet, I remember, when I was in France,
Young gentlemen would be as sad as night,
Only for wantonness. By my christendom,
So I were out of prison, and kept sheep,
I should be as merry as the day is long;
And so I would be here, but that I doubt
My uncle practises more harm to me: 20
He is afraid of me, and I of him.
Is it my fault that I was Geffrey's son?
No, indeed, is 't not; and I would to Heaven,
I were your son, so you would love me, Hubert.

    Hub. [*Aside.*] If I talk to him, with his innocent prate
He will awake my mercy, which lies dead:
Therefore I will be sudden, and despatch.

    Arth. Are you sick, Hubert? you look pale to-day.
In sooth, I would you were a little sick,
That I might sit all night, and watch with you: 30
I warrant, I love you more than you do me.

    Hub. [*Aside.*] His words do take possession of my bosom.—
Read here, young Arthur.   [*Showing a paper.*
              [*Aside.*] How now, foolish rheum!
Turning dispiteous torture out of door!
I must be brief, lest resolution drop
Out at mine eyes, in tender womanish tears.—
Can you not read it? is it not fair writ?

    Arth. Too fairly, Hubert, for so foul effect.
Must you with hot irons burn out both mine eyes?

    Hub. Young boy, I must.

    Arth.   And will you?

    Hub.   And I will.

    Arth. Have you the heart? When your head did but ache,   41
I knit my handkerchief about your brows,
(The best I had, a princess wrought it me,)
And I did never ask it you again;
And with my hand at midnight held your head,
And, like the watchful minutes to the hour,
Still and anon cheer'd up the heavy time,
Saying, "What lack you?" and, "Where lies your grief?"
Or, "What good love may I perform for you?"
Many a poor man's son would have lain still,   50
And ne'er have spoke a loving word to you;
But you at your sick-service had a prince.
Nay, you may think my love was crafty love,
And call it cunning: do, an if you will.
If Heaven be pleas'd that you will use me ill,
Why, then you must.—Will you put out mine eyes?
These eyes, that never did, nor never shall,
So much as frown on you?

    Hub.   I have sworn to do it,
And with hot irons must I burn them out.

    Arth. Ah! none but in this iron age would do it.   60
The iron of itself, though heat red-hot,
Approaching near these eyes, would drink my tears,
And quench his fiery indignation
Even in the matter of mine innocence;
Nay, after that, consume away in rust,
But for containing fire to harm mine eye.
Are you more stubborn-hard than hammer'd iron?
An if an angel should have come to me,
And told me Hubert should put out mine eyes,
I would not have believ'd him; no tongue but Hubert's.   70

    Hub. Come forth.   [*Stamps.*

Re-enter Attendants, with cords, irons, &c.

           Do as I bid you do.

    Arth. O! save me, Hubert, save me! my eyes are out,
Even with the fierce looks of these bloody men.

    Hub. Give me the iron, I say, and bind him here.

    Arth. Alas! what need you be so boisterous-rough?
I will not struggle; I will stand stone-still.

For Heaven's sake, Hubert, let me not be bound.
Nay, hear me, Hubert: drive these men away,
And I will sit as quiet as a lamb;
I will not stir, nor wince, nor speak a word,   80
Nor look upon the iron angerly.
Thrust but these men away, and I 'll forgive you,
Whatever torment you do put me to.
   Hub. Go, stand within: let me alone with him.
   1 *Atten.* I am best pleas'd to be from such a deed.
                      [*Exeunt Attendants.*
   Arth. Alas! I then have chid away my friend:
He hath a stern look, but a gentle heart.—
Let him come back, that his compassion may
Give life to yours.
   Hub.   Come, boy, prepare yourself.
   Arth. Is there no remedy?
   Hub.   None, but to lose your eyes.
   Arth. O Heaven!—that there were but a moth in
     yours,   91
A grain, a dust, a gnat, a wandering hair,
Any annoyance in that precious sense!

Arth. " O! spare mine eyes."

Then, feeling what small things are boisterous there,
Your vile intent must needs seem horrible.
   Hub. Is this your promise? go to, hold your tongue.
   Arth. Hubert, the utterance of a brace of tongues
Must needs want pleading for a pair of eyes:
Let me not hold my tongue; let me not, Hubert:
Or, Hubert, if you will, cut out my tongue,   100
So I may keep mine eyes. O! spare mine eyes;
Though to no use, but still to look on you.
Lo! by my troth, the instrument is cold,
And would not harm me.
   Hub.   I can heat it, boy.
   Arth. No, in good sooth; the fire is dead with grief,
Being create for comfort, to be us'd
In undeserv'd extremes: see else yourself;
There is no malice in this burning coal;
The breath of heaven hath blown his spirit out,
And strew'd repentant ashes on his head.   110
   Hub. But with my breath I can revive it, boy.
   Arth. An if you do, you will but make it blush,
And glow with shame of your proceedings, Hubert:
Nay, it, perchance, will sparkle in your eyes;
And like a dog that is compell'd to fight,
Snatch at his master that doth tarre him on.
All things that you should use to do me wrong,
Deny their office: only you do lack
That mercy which fierce fire and iron extends,
Creatures of note for mercy-lacking uses.   120
   Hub. Well, see to live; I will not touch thine eyes
For all the treasure that thine uncle owes:
Yet am I sworn, and I did purpose, boy,
With this same very iron to burn them out.

   Arth. O! now you look like Hubert: all this while
You were disguised.
   Hub.   Peace! no more. Adieu.
Your uncle must not know but you are dead:
I 'll fill these dogged spies with false reports.
And, pretty child, sleep doubtless, and secure,
That Hubert, for the wealth of all the world,   130
Will not offend thee.
   Arth.   O Heaven!—I thank you, Hubert.
   Hub. Silence! no more. Go closely in with me:
Much danger do I undergo for thee.   [*Exeunt.*

SCENE II.—The Same. A Room of State in the
Palace.

Enter King JOHN, *crowned;* PEMBROKE, SALISBURY,
and other Lords. The KING *takes his State.*

   K. John. Here once again we sit, once again
     crown'd,
And look'd upon, I hope, with cheerful eyes.
   Pem. This once again, but that your highness
     pleas'd,
Was once superfluous: you were crown'd before,
And that high royalty was ne'er pluck'd off,
The faiths of men ne'er stained with revolt;
Fresh expectation troubled not the land
With any long'd-for change, or better state.
   Sal. Therefore, to be possess'd with double pomp,
To guard a title that was rich before,   10
To gild refined gold, to paint the lily,
To throw a perfume on the violet,
To smooth the ice, or add another hue
Unto the rainbow, or with taper-light
To seek the beauteous eye of heaven to garnish,
Is wasteful, and ridiculous excess.
   Pem. But that your royal pleasure must be done,
This act is as an ancient tale new-told,
And in the last repeating troublesome,
Being urged at a time unseasonable.   20
   Sal. In this, the antique and well-noted face
Of plain old form is much disfigured;
And, like a shifted wind unto a sail,
It makes the course of thoughts to fetch about,
Startles and frights consideration,
Makes sound opinion sick, and truth suspected,
For putting on so new a fashion'd robe.
   Pem. When workmen strive to do better than well,
They do confound their skill in covetousness;
And, oftentimes, excusing of a fault   30
Doth make the fault the worse by the excuse:
As patches, set upon a little breach,
Discredit more in hiding of the fault,
Than did the fault before it was so patch'd.
   Sal. To this effect, before you were new-crown'd,
We breath'd our counsel: but it pleas'd your highness
To overbear it, and we are all well pleas'd;
Since all and every part of what we would,
Doth make a stand at what your highness will.
   K. John. Some reasons of this double coronation 40
I have possess'd you with, and think them strong;
And more, more strong, when lesser is my fear,
I shall indue you with: meantime, but ask
What you would have reform'd that is not well;
And well shall you perceive, how willingly
I will both hear and grant you your requests.
   Pem. Then I, as one that am the tongue of these,
To sound the purposes of all their hearts,
Both for myself and them, but, chief of all,
Your safety, for the which myself and them   50
Bend their best studies, heartily request
The enfranchisement of Arthur; whose restraint
Doth move the murmuring lips of discontent
To break into this dangerous argument:
If what in rest you have, in right you hold,
Why then your fears, which, as they say, attend
The steps of wrong, should move you to mew up
Your tender kinsman, and to choke his days
With barbarous ignorance, and deny his youth
The rich advantage of good exercise?   60
That the time's enemies may not have this

To grace occasions, let it be our suit,
That you have bid us ask his liberty ;
Which for our goods we do no further ask,
Than whereupon our weal, on you depending,
Counts it your weal, he have his liberty.

Enter HUBERT.

K. John. Let it be so : I do commit his youth
To your direction.—Hubert, what news with you?
  [HUBERT *whispers the* KING.
Pem. This is the man should do the bloody deed :
He show'd his warrant to a friend of mine. 70
The image of a wicked heinous fault
Lives in his eye : that close aspect of his
Does show the mood of a much troubled breast ;
And I do fearfully believe 't is done,
What we so fear'd he had a charge to do.
Sal. The colour of the king doth come and go,
Between his purpose and his conscience,
Like heralds 'twixt two dreadful battles set.
His passion is so ripe, it needs must break.
Pem. And when it breaks, I fear, will issue thence
The foul corruption of a sweet child's death. 81
K. John. We cannot hold mortality's strong hand.—
Good lords, although my will to give is living,
The suit which you demand is gone and dead :
He tells us, Arthur is deceas'd to-night.
Sal. Indeed, we fear'd his sickness was past cure.
Pem. Indeed, we heard how near his death he was,
Before the child himself felt he was sick.
This must be answer'd, either here, or hence.
K. John. Why do you bend such solemn brows
  on me ? 90
Think you I bear the shears of destiny?
Have I commandment on the pulse of life ?
Sal. It is apparent foul play ; and 't is shame,
That greatness should so grossly offer it.
So thrive it in your game ! and so farewell.
Pem. Stay yet, Lord Salisbury ; I'll go with thee,
And find the inheritance of this poor child,
His little kingdom of a forced grave.
That blood which ow'd the breadth of all this isle,
Three foot of it doth hold. Bad world the while ! 100
This must not be thus borne : this will break out
To all our sorrows, and ere long, I doubt.
  [*Exeunt Lords.*
K. John. They burn in indignation. I repent :
There is no sure foundation set on blood,
No certain life achiev'd by others' death.

Enter a Messenger.

A fearful eye thou hast. Where is that blood,
That I have seen inhabit in those cheeks?
So foul a sky clears not without a storm :
Pour down thy weather.—How goes all in France ?
Mess. From France to England.—Never such a
  power, 110
For any foreign preparation,
Was levied in the body of a land.
The copy of your speed is learn'd by them ;
For, when you should be told they do prepare,
The tidings come that they are all arriv'd.
K. John. O! where hath our intelligence been drunk?
Where hath it slept ? Where is my mother's care,
That such an army could be drawn in France,
And she not hear of it ?
Mess.   My liege, her ear
Is stopp'd with dust : the first of April, died 120
Your noble mother ; and, as I hear, my lord,
The Lady Constance in a frenzy died
Three days before : but this from rumour's tongue
I idly heard ; if true, or false, I know not.
K. John. Withhold thy speed, dreadful occasion !
O! make a league with me, till I have pleas'd
My discontented peers.—What ! mother dead !
How wildly then walks my estate in France !—
Under whose conduct came those powers of France,
That thou for truth giv'st out are landed here ? 130
Mess. Under the Dauphin.

Enter the Bastard, and PETER *of Pomfret.*

K. John.   Thou hast made me giddy

With these ill tidings.--Now, what says the world
To your proceedings ? do not seek to stuff
My head with more ill news, for it is full.
Bast. But, if you be afeard to hear the worst,
Then let the worst, unheard, fall on your head.
K. John. Bear with me, cousin, for I was amaz'd
Under the tide ; but now I breathe again
Aloft the flood, and can give audience
To any tongue, speak it of what it will. 140
Bast. How I have sped among the clergymen,
The sums I have collected shall express.
But as I travell'd hither through the land,
I find the people strangely fantasied,
Possess'd with rumours, full of idle dreams,
Not knowing what they fear, but full of fear.
And here 's a prophet, that I brought with me
From forth the streets of Pomfret, whom I found
With many hundreds treading on his heels ;
To whom he sung, in rude harsh-sounding rhymes,
That, ere the next Ascension-day at noon, 151
Your highness should deliver up your crown.
K. John. Thou idle dreamer, wherefore didst thou
  so ?
Peter. Foreknowing that the truth will fall out
  so.
K. John. Hubert, away with him : imprison him ;
And on that day at noon, whereon, he says,
I shall yield up my crown, let him be hang'd.
Deliver him to safety, and return,
For I must use thee. [*Exit* HUBERT *with* PETER.]—
  O my gentle cousin,
Hear'st thou the news abroad, who are arriv'd ? 160
Bast. The French, my lord ; men's mouths are full
  of it :
Besides, I met Lord Bigot, and Lord Salisbury,
With eyes as red as new-enkindled fire,
And others more, going to seek the grave
Of Arthur, whom they say is kill'd to-night
On your suggestion.
K. John.   Gentle kinsman, go,
And thrust thyself into their companies.
I have a way to win their loves again :
Bring them before me.
Bast.   I will seek them out.
K. John. Nay, but make haste ; the better foot
  before. 170
O ! let me have no subject enemies,
When adverse foreigners affright my towns
With dreadful pomp of stout invasion.
Be Mercury, set feathers to thy heels,
And fly, like thought, from them to me again.
Bast. The spirit of the time shall teach me speed.
  [*Exit.*
K. John. Spoke like a spriteful noble gentleman.—
Go after him ; for he, perhaps, shall need
Some messenger betwixt me and the peers,
And be thou he.
Mess.   With all my heart, my liege. [*Exit.*
K. John. My mother dead ! 181

Re-enter HUBERT.

Hub. My lord, they say five moons were seen to-
  night :
Four fixed ; and the fifth did whirl about
The other four in wondrous motion.
K. John. Five moons ?
Hub.   Old men, and beldams, in the streets
Do prophesy upon it dangerously.
Young Arthur's death is common in their mouths ;
And when they talk of him, they shake their heads,
And whisper one another in the ear ;
And he that speaks doth gripe the hearer's wrist, 190
Whilst he that hears makes fearful action,
With wrinkled brows, with nods, with rolling eyes.
I saw a smith stand with his hammer, thus,
The whilst his iron did on the anvil cool,
With open mouth swallowing a tailor's news ;
Who, with his shears and measure in his hand,
Standing on slippers (which his nimble haste
Had falsely thrust upon contrary feet),
Told of a many thousand warlike French,
That were embatteled and rank'd in Kent. 200

Another lean unwash'd artificer
Cuts off his tale, and talks of Arthur's death.
  K. John. Why seek'st thou to possess me with these
    fears?
Why urgest thou so oft young Arthur's death?
Thy hand hath murder'd him : I had a mighty cause
To wish him dead, but thou hadst none to kill him.
  Hub. No had, my lord! why, did you not provoke
    me?
  K. John. It is the curse of kings, to be attended
By slaves, that take their humours for a warrant
To break within the bloody house of life,   210
And, on the winking of authority,
To understand a law, to know the meaning
Of dangerous majesty, when, perchance, it frowns
More upon humour than advis'd respect.
  Hub. Here is your hand and seal for what I did.
  K. John. O! when the last account 'twixt Heaven
    and earth
Is to be made, then shall this hand and seal
Witness against us to damnation.
How oft the sight of means to do ill deeds
Makes deeds ill done! Hadst not thou been by,   220
A fellow by the hand of nature mark'd,
Quoted, and sign'd, to do a deed of shame,
This murder had not come into my mind ;
But, taking note of thy abhorr'd aspect,
Finding thee fit for bloody villainy,
Apt, liable, to be employ'd in danger,
I faintly broke with thee of Arthur's death ;
And thou, to be endeared to a king,
Made it no conscience to destroy a prince.
  Hub. My lord,—   230
  K. John. Hadst thou but shook thy head, or made
    a pause,
When I spake darkly what I purposed,
Or turn'd an eye of doubt upon my face,
As bid me tell my tale in express words,
Deep shame had struck me dumb, made me break off,
And those thy fears might have wrought fears in me :
But thou didst understand me by my signs,
And didst in signs again parley with sin ;
Yea, without stop, didst let thy heart consent,
And consequently thy rude hand to act   240
The deed which both our tongues held vile to name.
Out of my sight, and never see me more!
My nobles leave me, and my state is brav'd,
Even at my gates, with ranks of foreign powers :
Nay, in the body of this fleshly land,
This kingdom, this confine of blood and breath,
Hostility and civil tumult reigns
Between my conscience and my cousin's death.
  Hub. Arm you against your other enemies,
I'll make a peace between your soul and you.   250
Young Arthur is alive : this hand of mine
Is yet a maiden and an innocent hand,
Not painted with the crimson spots of blood.
Within this bosom never enter'd yet
The dreadful motion of a murderous thought ;
And you have slander'd nature in my form,
Which, howsoever rude exteriorly,
Is yet the cover of a fairer mind,
Than to be butcher of an innocent child.
  K. John. Doth Arthur live? O! haste thee to the
    peers,   260
Throw this report on their incensed rage,
And make them tame to their obedience.
Forgive the comment that my passion made
Upon thy feature ; for my rage was blind,
And foul imaginary eyes of blood
Presented thee more hideous than thou art.
O! answer not ; but to my closet bring
The angry lords, with all expedient haste.
I conjure thee but slowly ; run more fast.   [*Exeunt.*

SCENE III.—The Same. Before the Castle.

Enter ARTHUR, *on the walls.*

  Arth. The wall is high ; and yet will I leap down.—
Good ground, be pitiful, and hurt me not!—

There's few, or none, do know me ; if they did,
This ship-boy's semblance hath disguis'd me quite.
I am afraid ; and yet I'll venture it.
If I get down, and do not break my limbs,
I'll find a thousand shifts to get away :
As good to die and go, as die and stay. [*Leaps down.*
O me! my uncle's spirit is in these stones.—
Heaven take my soul, and England keep my bones! 10
                                    [*Dies.*

Enter PEMBROKE, SALISBURY, *and* BIGOT.

  Sal. Lords, I will meet him at Saint Edmund's
    Bury :
It is our safety, and we must embrace
This gentle offer of the perilous time.
  Pem. Who brought that letter from the cardinal?
  Sal. The Count Melun, a noble lord of France ;
Whose private with me, of the Dauphin's love,
Is much more general than these lines import.
  Big. To-morrow morning let us meet him then.
  Sal. Or rather then set forward : for 't will be
Two long days' journey, lords, or e'er we meet.   20

Enter the Bastard.

  Bast. Once more to-day well met, distemper'd
    lords.
The king by me requests your presence straight.
  Sal. The king hath dispossess'd himself of us.
We will not line his thin bestained cloak
With our pure honours, nor attend the foot
That leaves the print of blood where'er it walks.
Return, and tell him so : we know the worst.
  Bast. Whate'er you think, good words, I think,
    were best.
  Sal. Our griefs, and not our manners, reason now.
  Bast. But there is little reason in your grief :   30
Therefore, 't were reason you had manners now.
  Pem. Sir, sir, impatience hath his privilege.
  Bast. 'T is true ; to hurt his master, no man else.
  Sal. This is the prison.—[*Seeing* ARTHUR.] What is
    he lies here?
  Pem. O death, made proud with pure and princely
    beauty!
The earth had not a hole to hide this deed.
  Sal. Murder, as hating what himself hath done,
Doth lay it open to urge on revenge.
  Big. Or when he doom'd this beauty to a grave,
Found it too precious-princely for a grave.   40
  Sal. Sir Richard, what think you? Have you
    beheld,
Or have you read, or heard? or could you think?
Or do you almost think, although you see,
That you do see? could thought, without this object,
Form such another? This is the very top,
The height, the crest, or crest unto the crest,
Of murder's arms : this is the bloodiest shame,
The wildest savagery, the vildest stroke,
That ever wall-ey'd wrath, or staring rage,
Presented to the tears of soft remorse.   50
  Pem. All murders past do stand excus'd in this :
And this, so sole and so unmatchable,
Shall give a holiness, a purity,
To the yet unbegotten sin of times,
And prove a deadly bloodshed but a jest,
Exampled by this heinous spectacle.
  Bast. It is a damned and a bloody work ;
The graceless action of a heavy hand,
If that it be the work of any hand.
  Sal. If that it be the work of any hand?—   60
We had a kind of light what would ensue :
It is the shameful work of Hubert's hand ;
The practice, and the purpose, of the king :
From whose obedience I forbid my soul,
Kneeling before this ruin of sweet life,
And breathing to his breathless excellence
The incense of a vow, a holy vow,
Never to taste the pleasures of the world,
Never to be infected with delight,
Nor conversant with ease and idleness,   70
Till I have set a glory to this hand,
By giving it the worship of revenge.
  Pem., Big. Our souls religiously confirm thy words.

Enter HUBERT.

Hub. Lords, I am hot with haste in seeking you.
Arthur doth live: the king hath sent for you.
  Sal. O! he is bold, and blushes not at death.–
Avaunt, thou hateful villain! get thee gone.
  Hub. I am no villain.
  Sal.   Must I rob the law?
                     [*Drawing his sword.*
  Bast. Your sword is bright, sir: put it up again.
  Sal. Not till I sheathe it in a murderer's skin.   80

Bast. "Put up thy sword betime."

  Hub. Stand back, Lord Salisbury, stand back, I say:
By Heaven, I think, my sword's as sharp as yours.
I would not have you, lord, forget yourself,
Nor tempt the danger of my true defence;
Lest I, by marking of your rage, forget
Your worth, your greatness, and nobility.
  Big. Out, dunghill! dar'st thou brave a nobleman?
  Hub. Not for my life; but yet I dare defend
My innocent life against an emperor.
  Sal. Thou art a murderer.
  Hub.   Do not prove me so; 90
Yet, I am none. Whose tongue soe'er speaks false,
Not truly speaks; who speaks not truly, lies.
  Pem. Cut him to pieces.
  Bast.   Keep the peace, I say.
  Sal. Stand by, or I shall gall you, Faulconbridge.
  Bast. Thou wert better gall the devil, Salisbury:
If thou but frown on me, or stir thy foot,
Or teach thy hasty spleen to do me shame,
I'll strike thee dead. Put up thy sword betime,
Or I'll so maul you and your toasting-iron,
That you shall think the devil is come from hell. 100
  Big. What wilt thou do, renowned Faulconbridge?
Second a villain, and a murderer?
  Hub. Lord Bigot, I am none.
  Big.   Who kill'd this prince?

  Hub. 'T is not an hour since I left him well:
I honour'd him, I lov'd him; and will weep
My date of life out for his sweet life's loss.
  Sal. Trust not those cunning waters of his eyes.
For villainy is not without such rheum;
And he, long traded in it, makes it seem
Like rivers of remorse and innocency. 110
Away, with me, all you whose souls abhor
The uncleanly savours of a slaughter-house,
For I am stifled with this smell of sin.
  Big. Away, toward Bury: to the Dauphin there!
  Pem. There, tell the king, he may inquire us out.
                    [*Exeunt Lords.*
  Bast. Here's a good world!—Knew you of this fair
    work?
Beyond the infinite and boundless reach
Of mercy, if thou didst this deed of death,
Art thou damn'd, Hubert.
  Hub.   Do but hear me, sir.
  Bast. Ha! I'll tell thee what; 120
Thou art damn'd as black—nay, nothing is so black;
Thou art more deep damn'd than Prince Lucifer:
There is not yet so ugly a fiend of hell,
As thou shalt be, if thou didst kill this child.
  Hub. Upon my soul,—
  Bast.   If thou didst but consent
To this most cruel act, do but despair;
And if thou want'st a cord, the smallest thread,
That ever spider twisted from her womb,
Will serve to strangle thee; a rush will be a beam
To hang thee on; or wouldst thou drown thyself, 130
Put but a little water in a spoon,
And it shall be as all the ocean,
Enough to stifle such a villain up.
I do suspect thee very grievously.
  Hub. If I in act, consent, or sin of thought,
Be guilty of the stealing that sweet breath,
Which was embounded in this beauteous clay,
Let hell want pains enough to torture me.
I left him well.
  Bast.   Go, bear him in thine arms.—
I am amaz'd, methinks, and lose my way 140
Among the thorns and dangers of this world.—
How easy dost thou take all England up!
From forth this morsel of dead royalty,
The life, the right, and truth of all this realm
Is fled to heaven; and England now is left
To tug and scamble, and to part by the teeth
The unowed interest of proud-swelling state.
Now for the bare-pick'd bone of majesty
Doth dogged war bristle his angry crest,
And snarleth in the gentle eyes of peace: 150
Now powers from home, and discontents at home,
Meet in one line; and vast confusion waits,
As doth a raven on a sick-fallen beast,
The imminent decay of wrested pomp.
Now happy he whose cloak and ceinter can
Hold out this tempest.—Bear away that child,
And follow me with speed: I'll to the king.
A thousand businesses are brief in hand,
And Heaven itself doth frown upon the land. [*Exeunt.*

ACT V.

SCENE I.—The Same. A Room in the Palace.

Enter King JOHN, PANDULPH *with the crown, and Attendants.*

King John.
THUS have I yielded up into your hand
The circle of my glory.
　　Pand. [*Giving* JOHN *the crown.*] Take
　　　again
From this my hand, as holding of the
　　Pope,
Your sovereign greatness and authority.
　　K. John. Now keep your holy word : go
　　meet the French ;
And from his holiness use all your power
To stop their marches, 'fore we are in-
　　flam'd.
Our discontented counties do revolt,
Our people quarrel with obedience, 　　10
Swearing allegiance, and the love of soul,
To stranger blood, to foreign royalty.
This inundation of mistemper'd humour
Rests by you only to be qualified.
Then pause not ; for the present time 's so sick,
That present medicine must be minister'd,
Or overthrow incurable ensues.
　　Pand. It was my breath that blew this tempest up,
Upon your stubborn usage of the Pope ;
But since you are a gentle convertite,
My tongue shall hush again this storm of war, 　　20
And make fair weather in your blustering land.
On this Ascension-day, remember well,
Upon your oath of service to the Pope,
Go I to make the French lay down their arms. [*Exit.*
　　K. John. Is this Ascension-day ? Did not the
　　prophet
Say, that before Ascension-day at noon
My crown I should give off ? Even so I have.
I did suppose it should be on constraint ;
But, Heaven be thank'd, it is but voluntary ;

Enter the Bastard.

　　Bast. All Kent hath yielded ; nothing there holds
　　out 　　30
But Dover Castle : London hath receiv'd,
Like a kind host, the Dauphin and his powers.
Your nobles will not hear you, but are gone
To offer service to your enemy ;
And wild amazement hurries up and down
The little number of your doubtful friends.
　　K. John. Would not my lords return to me again,
After they heard young Arthur was alive ?
　　Bast. They found him dead, and cast into the
　　streets ;
An empty casket, where the jewel of life 　　40
By some damn'd hand was robb'd and ta'en away.
　　K. John. That villain Hubert told me he did live.
　　Bast. So, on my soul, he did, for aught he knew.
But wherefore do you droop ? why look you sad ?
Be great in act, as you have been in thought ;
Let not the world see fear, and sad distrust,
Govern the motion of a kingly eye :
Be stirring as the time ; be fire with fire ;
Threaten the threatener, and outface the brow
Of bragging horror : so shall inferior eyes, 　　50
That borrow their behaviours from the great,
Grow great by your example, and put on
The dauntless spirit of resolution.
Away ! and glister like the god of war,

When he intendeth to become the field :
Show boldness, and aspiring confidence.
What, shall they seek the lion in his den,
And fright him there ? and make him tremble there ?
O ! let it not be said.—Forage, and run
To meet displeasure further from the doors, 　　60
And grapple with him, ere he come so nigh.
　　K. John. The legate of the Pope hath been with me,
And I have made a happy peace with him ;
And he hath promis'd to dismiss the powers
Led by the Dauphin.
　　Bast. 　　　　　O inglorious league !
Shall we, upon the footing of our land,
Send fair-play orders, and make compromise,
Insinuation, parley, and base truce,
To arms invasive ? shall a beardless boy,
A cocker'd silken wanton, brave our fields, 　　70
And flesh his spirit in a warlike soil,
Mocking the air with colours idly spread,
And find no check ? Let us, my liege, to arms :
Perchance, the cardinal cannot make your peace ;
Or if he do, let it at least be said,
They saw we had a purpose of defence.
　　K. John. Have thou the ordering of this present
　　time.
　　Bast. Away then, with good courage ; yet, I know,
Our party may well meet a prouder foe. 　　[*Exeunt.*

———

SCENE II.—A Plain near Saint Edmund's Bury.

Enter in arms, LEWIS, SALISBURY, MELUN, PEMBROKE, BIGOT, *and Soldiers.*

　　Lew. My Lord Melun, let this be copied out,
And keep it safe for our remembrance.
Return the precedent to these lords again ;
That, having our fair order written down,
Both they, and we, perusing o'er these notes,
May know wherefore we took the sacrament,
And keep our faiths firm and inviolable.
　　Sal. Upon our sides it never shall be broken.
And, noble Dauphin, albeit we swear
A voluntary zeal, and unurg'd faith, 　　10
To your proceedings ; yet, believe me, prince,
I am not glad that such a sore of time
Should seek a plaster by contemn'd revolt,
And heal the inveterate canker of one wound
By making many. O ! it grieves my soul,
That I must draw this metal from my side
To be a widow-maker ; O ! and there,
Where honourable rescue, and defence,
Cries out upon the name of Salisbury.
But such is the infection of the time, 　　20
That, for the health and physic of our right,
We cannot deal but with the very hand
Of stern injustice and confused wrong.—
And is 't not pity, O my grieved friends,
That we, the sons and children of this isle,
Were born to see so sad an hour as this ;
Wherein we step after a stranger march
Upon her gentle bosom, and fill up
Her enemies' ranks, (I must withdraw, and weep
Upon the spot of this enforced cause,) 　　30
To grace the gentry of a land remote,

And follow unacquainted colours here?
What, here?—O nation, that thou couldst remove!
That Neptune's arms, who clippeth thee about,
Would bear thee from the knowledge of thyself,
And grapple thee unto a pagan shore,
Where these two Christian armies might combine
The blood of malice in a vein of league,
And not to spend it so unneighbourly!
 Lew. A noble temper dost thou show in this; 40
And great affections wrestling in thy bosom
Do make an earthquake of nobility.
O! what a noble combat hast thou fought,
Between compulsion, and a brave respect!
Let me wipe off this honourable dew,
That silverly doth progress on thy cheeks.
My heart hath melted at a lady's tears,
Being an ordinary inundation;
But this effusion of such manly drops,
This shower, blown up by tempest of the soul, 50
Startles mine eyes, and makes me more amaz'd
Than had I seen the vaulty top of heaven
Figur'd quite o'er with burning meteors.
Lift up thy brow, renowned Salisbury,
And with a great heart heave away this storm:
Commend these waters to those baby eyes,
That never saw the giant world enrag'd,
Nor met with fortune other than at feasts,
Full warm of blood, of mirth, of gossiping.
Come, come; for thou shalt thrust thy hand as deep 60
Into the purse of rich prosperity,
As Lewis himself:—so, nobles, shall you all,
That knit your sinews to the strength of mine.

Enter PANDULPH, *attended.*

And even there, methinks, an angel spake:
Look, where the holy legate comes apace,
To give us warrant from the hand of Heaven,
And on our actions set the name of right
With holy breath.
 Pand. Hail, noble Prince of France!
The next is this:—King John hath reconcil'd 70
Himself to Rome; his spirit is come in,
That so stood out against the holy Church,
The great metropolis and see of Rome.
Therefore, thy threat'ning colours now wind up,
And tame the savage spirit of wild war,
That, like a lion foster'd up at hand,
It may lie gently at the foot of peace,
And be no further harmful than in show.
 Lew. Your grace shall pardon me; I will not
  back:
I am too high-born to be propertied,
To be a secondary at control, 80
Or useful serving-man, and instrument,
To any sovereign state throughout the world.
Your breath first kindled the dead coal of wars
Between this chastis'd kingdom and myself,
And brought in matter that should feed this fire;
And now 't is far too huge to be blown out
With that same weak wind which enkindled it.
You taught me how to know the face of right,
Acquainted me with interest to this land,
Yea, thrust this enterprise into my heart; 90
And come ye now to tell me, John hath made
His peace with Rome? What is that peace to me?
I, by the honour of my marriage-bed,
After young Arthur, claim this land for mine;
And, now it is half-conquer'd, must I back,
Because that John hath made his peace with Rome?
Am I Rome's slave? What penny hath Rome
  borne,
What men provided, what munition sent,
To underprop this action? Is 't not I
That undergo this charge? who else but I, 100
And such as to my claim are liable,
Sweat in this business, and maintain this war?
Have I not heard these islanders shout out,
Vive le roy! as I have bank'd their towns?
Have I not here the best cards for the game,
To win this easy match play'd for a crown?
And shall I now give o'er the yielded set?
No, no, on my soul, it never shall be said.

 Pand. You look but on the outside of this work.
 Lew. Outside or inside, I will not return 110
Till my attempt so much be glorified,
As to my ample hope was promised
Before I drew this gallant head of war,
And cull'd these fiery spirits from the world,
To outlook conquest, and to win renown
Even in the jaws of danger and of death.—
        [Trumpet sounds.
What lusty trumpet thus doth summon us?

Enter the Bastard, attended.

 Bast. According to the fair play of the world,
Let me have audience: I am sent to speak.—
My holy Lord of Milan, from the king 120
I come, to learn how you have dealt for him;
And, as you answer, I do know the scope
And warrant limited unto my tongue.
 Pand. The Dauphin is too wilful-opposite,
And will not temporise with my entreaties:
He flatly says, he 'll not lay down his arms.
 Bast. By all the blood that ever fury breath'd,
The youth says well.—Now, hear our English king;
For thus his royalty doth speak in me.
He is prepar'd; and reason too, he should: 130
This apish and unmannerly approach,
This harness'd masque, and unadvised revel,
This unhair'd sauciness, and boyish troops,
The king doth smile at, and is well prepar'd
To whip this dwarfish war, these pigmy arms,
From out the circle of his territories.
That hand, which had the strength, even at your
  door,
To cudgel you, and make you take the hatch;
To dive, like buckets, in concealed wells;
To crouch in litter of your stable planks; 140
To lie like pawns lock'd up in chests and trunks;
To hug with swine; to seek sweet safety out
In vaults and prisons; and to thrill, and shake,
Even at the crying of your nation's crow,
Thinking this voice an armed Englishman:
Shall that victorious hand be feebled here,
That in your chambers gave you chastisement?
No! Know, the gallant monarch is in arms,
And like an eagle o'er his aiery towers,
To souse annoyance that comes near his nest.— 150
And you degenerate, you ingrate revolts,
You bloody Neroes, ripping up the womb
Of your dear mother England, blush for shame:
For your own ladies, and pale-visag'd maids,
Like Amazons, come tripping after drums;
Their thimbles into armed gauntlets change,
Their neelds to lances, and their gentle hearts
To fierce and bloody inclination.
 Lew. There end thy brave, and turn thy face in
  peace;
We grant thou canst outscold us: fare thee well; 160
We hold our time too precious to be spent
With such a brabbler.
 Pand. Give me leave to speak.
 Bast. No, I will speak.
 Lew. We will attend to neither.—
Strike up the drums! and let the tongue of war
Plead for our interest, and our being here.
 Bast. Indeed, your drums, being beaten, will cry
  out;
And so shall you, being beaten. Do but start
An echo with the clamour of thy drum,
And even at hand a drum is ready brac'd,
That shall reverberate all as loud as thine; 170
Sound but another, and another shall,
As loud as thine, rattle the welkin's ear,
And mock the deep-mouth'd thunder: for at hand
(Not trusting to this halting legate here,
Whom he hath us'd rather for sport than need)
Is warlike John; and in his forehead sits
A bare-ribb'd death, whose office is this day
To feast upon whole thousands of the French.
 Lew. Strike up our drums, to find this danger
  out.
 Bast. And thou shalt find it, Dauphin, do not doubt.
            [Exeunt.

SCENE III.—The Same. A Field of Battle.

Alarums. Enter King JOHN *and* HUBERT.

K. John. How goes the day with us? O! tell me, Hubert.

Hub. Badly, I fear. How fares your majesty?

K. John. This fever, that hath troubled me so long, Lies heavy on me: O! my heart is sick.

Enter a Messenger.

Mess. My lord, your valiant kinsman, Faulcon-bridge,
Desires your majesty to leave the field,
And send him word by me which way you go.

K. John. Tell him, toward Swinstead, to the abbey there.

Mess. Be of good comfort: for the great supply, 10
That was expected by the Dauphin here,
Are wrack'd three nights ago on Goodwin Sands.
This news was brought to Richard but even now.
The French fight coldly, and retire themselves.

K. John. Ah me! this tyrant fever burns me up,
And will not let me welcome this good news.
Set on toward Swinstead; to my litter straight:
Weakness possesseth me, and I am faint. [*Exeunt.*

SCENE IV.—The Same. Another Part of the Same.

Enter SALISBURY, PEMBROKE, BIGOT, *and others.*

Sal. I did not think the king so stor'd with friends.

Pem. Up once again; put spirit in the French:
If they miscarry, we miscarry too.

Sal. That misbegotten devil, Faulconbridge,
In spite of spite, alone upholds the day.

Pem. They say, King John, sore sick, hath left the field.

Enter MELUN *wounded, and led by Soldiers.*

Mel. Lead me to the revolts of England here.

Sal. When we were happy, we had other names.

Pem. It is the Count Melun.

Sal. Wounded to death.

Mel. Fly, noble English; you are bought and sold: 11
Unthread the rude eye of rebellion,
And welcome home again discarded faith.
Seek out King John, and fall before his feet;
For if the French be lords of this loud day,
He means to recompense the pains you take,
By cutting off your heads. Thus hath he sworn,
And I with him, and many more with me,
Upon the altar at Saint Edmund's Bury;
Even on that altar, where we swore to you
Dear amity and everlasting love. 20

Sal. May this be possible? may this be true?

Mel. Have I not hideous death within my view,
Retaining but a quantity of life,
Which bleeds away, even as a form of wax
Resolveth from his figure 'gainst the fire?
What in the world should make me now deceive,
Since I must lose the use of all deceit?
Why should I then be false, since it is true
That I must die here, and live hence by truth?
I say again, if Lewis do win the day, 30
He is forsworn, if e'er those eyes of yours
Behold another day break in the east:
But even this night, whose black contagious breath
Already smokes about the burning crest
Of the old, feeble, and day-wearied sun,
Even this ill night, your breathing shall expire,
Paying the fine of rated treachery
Even with a treacherous fine of all your lives,
If Lewis by your assistance win the day.
Commend me to one Hubert, with your king; 40
The love of him,—and this respect besides,
For that my grandsire was an Englishman,—
Awakes my conscience to confess all this.
In lieu whereof, I pray you, bear me hence
From forth the noise and rumour of the field;
Where I may think the remnant of my thoughts
In peace, and part this body and my soul
With contemplation and devout desires.

Sal. We do believe thee,—and beshrew my soul,
But I do love the favour and the form 50
Of this most fair occasion, by the which
We will untread the steps of damned flight;
And, like a bated and retired flood,
Leaving our rankness and irregular course,
Stoop low within those bounds we have o'erlook'd,
And calmly run on in obedience,
Even to our ocean, to our great King John.—
My arm shall give thee help to bear thee hence,
For I do see the cruel pangs of death
Right in thine eye.—Away, my friends! New flight;
And happy newness, that intends old right. 61
[*Exeunt, leading off* MELUN.

SCENE V.—The Same. The French Camp.

Enter LEWIS *and his Train.*

Lew. The sun of heaven, methought, was loath to set,
But stay'd, and made the western welkin blush,
When the English measur'd backward their own ground,
In faint retire. O! bravely came we off,
When with a volley of our needless shot,
After such bloody toil, we bid good night,
And wound our tattering colours clearly up,
Last in the field, and almost lords of it!

Enter a Messenger.

Mess. Where is my prince, the Dauphin?

Lew. Here.—What news?

Mess. The Count Melun is slain; the English lords, 10
By his persuasion, are again fall'n off;
And your supply, which you have wish'd so long,
Are cast away, and sunk, on Goodwin Sands.

Lew. Ah, foul shrewd news!—Beshrew thy very heart!
I did not think to be so sad to-night,
As this hath made me.—Who was he that said,
King John did fly an hour or two before
The stumbling night did part our weary powers?

Mess. Whoever spoke it, it is true, my lord.

Lew. Well; keep good quarter and good care to-night: 20
The day shall not be up so soon as I,
To try the fair adventure of to-morrow. [*Exeunt.*

SCENE VI.—An Open Place in the Neighbourhood of Swinstead Abbey.

Enter the Bastard and HUBERT, *severally.*

Hub. Who's there? speak, ho! speak quickly, or I shoot.

Bast. A friend.—What art thou?

Hub. Of the part of England.

Bast. Whither dost thou go?

Hub. What's that to thee? why may not I demand
Of thine affairs, as well as thou of mine?

Bast. Hubert, I think.

Hub. Thou hast a perfect thought:
I will, upon all hazards, well believe
Thou art my friend, that know'st my tongue so well.
Who art thou?

Bast. Who thou wilt: and, if thou please,
Thou may'st befriend me so much as to think 10
I come one way of the Plantagenets.

Hub. Unkind remembrance! thou, and endless night,
Have done me shame:—brave soldier, pardon me,
That any accent breaking from thy tongue
Should scape the true acquaintance of mine ear.

Bast. Come, come; sans compliment, what news abroad?

Hub. Why, here walk I, in the black brow of night,
To find you out.

Bast. Brief then; and what's the news?

Hub. O! my sweet sir, news fitting to the night,
Black, fearful, comfortless, and horrible.   20
  Bast. Show me the very wound of this ill news:
I am no woman; I'll not swoond at it.
  Hub. The king, I fear, is poison'd by a monk:

Hub. Why, know you not? the lords are all come back,
And brought Prince Henry in their company;
At whose request the king hath pardon'd them,
And they are all about his majesty.

Sal. " You breathe these dead news in as dead an ear."

I left him almost speechless, and broke out
To acquaint you with this evil, that you might
The better arm you to the sudden time,
Than if you had at leisure known of this.
  Bast. How did he take it? who did taste to him?
  Hub. A monk, I tell you; a resolved villain,
Whose bowels suddenly burst out: the king   30
Yet speaks, and, peradventure, may recover.
  Bast. Whom didst thou leave to tend his majesty?

Bast. Withhold thine indignation, mighty Heaven,
And tempt us not to bear above our power!
I'll tell thee, Hubert, half my power this night,
Passing these flats, are taken by the tide;   40
These Lincoln washes have devoured them:
Myself, well mounted, hardly have escap'd.
Away, before! conduct me to the king;
I doubt, he will be dead or e'er I come.   [*Exeunt.*

SCENE VII.—The Orchard of Swinstead Abbey.

Enter Prince HENRY, SALISBURY, *and* BIGOT.

P. Hen. It is too late : the life of all his blood
Is touch'd corruptibly ; and his pure brain
(Which some suppose the soul's frail dwelling-house)
Doth, by the idle comments that it makes,
Foretell the ending of mortality.

Enter PEMBROKE.

Pem. His highness yet doth speak ; and holds belief,
That being brought into the open air,
It would allay the burning quality
Of that fell poison which assaileth him.
P. Hen. Let him be brought into the orchard here.—
Doth he still rage ?   [*Exit* BIGOT.
Pem.   He is more patient   11
Than when you left him : even now he sung.
P. Hen. O vanity of sickness ! fierce extremes
In their continuance will not feel themselves.
Death, having prey'd upon the outward parts,
Leaves them, invisible ; and his siege is now
Against the mind, the which he pricks and wounds
With many legions of strange fantasies,
Which, in their throng and press to that last hold,
Confound themselves. 'T is strange that death should
sing.   20
I am the cygnet to this pale faint swan,
Who chants a doleful hymn to his own death,
And, from the organ-pipe of frailty, sings
His soul and body to their lasting rest.
Sal. Be of good comfort, prince ; for you are born
To set a form upon that indigest,
Which he hath left so shapeless and so rude.

Re-enter BIGOT *and Attendants, who bring in King*
JOHN *in a chair.*

K. John. Ay, marry, now my soul hath elbow-room ;
It would not out at windows, nor at doors.
There is so hot a summer in my bosom,   30
That all my bowels crumble up to dust :
I am a scribbled form, drawn with a pen
Upon a parchment, and against this fire
Do I shrink up.
P. Hen.   How fares your majesty ?
K. John. Poison'd,—ill fare ;—dead, forsook, cast off :
And none of you will bid the winter come,
To thrust his icy fingers in my maw ;
Nor let my kingdom's rivers take their course
Through my burn'd bosom ; nor entreat the north
To make his bleak winds kiss my parched lips,   40
And comfort me with cold.—I do not ask you much :
I beg cold comfort ; and you are so strait,
And so ingrateful, you deny me that.
P. Hen. O, that there were some virtue in my tears,
That might relieve you !
K. John.   The salt in them is hot.
Within me is a hell ; and there the poison
Is, as a fiend, confin'd to tyrannise
On unreprievable-condemned blood.

Enter the Bastard.

Bast. O ! I am scalded with my violent motion,
And spleen of speed to see your majesty.   50
K. John. O cousin ! thou art come to set mine eye :
The tackle of my heart is crack'd and burn'd ;
And all the shrouds, wherewith my life should sail,
Are turned to one thread, one little hair :

My heart hath one poor string to stay it by,
Which holds but till thy news be uttered,
And then all this thou seest is but a clod,
And module of confounded royalty.
Bast. The Dauphin is preparing hitherward,
Where Heaven he knows how we shall answer him :
For, in a night, the best part of my power,   61
As I upon advantage did remove,
Were in the washes, all unwarily,
Devoured by the unexpected flood.   [*The* KING *dies.*
Sal. You breathe these dead news in as dead an
ear.—
My liege ! my lord !—But now a king, now thus.
P. Hen. Even so must I run on, and even so stop.
What surety of the world, what hope, what stay,
When this was now a king, and now is clay ?
Bast. Art thou gone so ? I do but stay behind,   70
To do the office for thee of revenge,
And then my soul shall wait on thee to heaven,
As it on earth hath been thy servant still.—
Now, now, you stars, that move in your right spheres,
Where be your powers ? Show now your mended
faiths,
And instantly return with me again,
To push destruction, and perpetual shame,
Out of the weak door of our fainting land.
Straight let us seek, or straight we shall be sought :
The Dauphin rages at our very heels.   80
Sal. It seems you know not then so much as we.
The Cardinal Pandulph is within at rest,
Who half an hour since came from the Dauphin,
And brings from him such offers of our peace,
As we with honour and respect may take,
With purpose presently to leave this war.
Bast. He will the rather do it, when he sees
Ourselves well sinewed to our defence.
Sal. Nay, it is in a manner done already ;
For many carriages he hath despatch'd   90
To the sea-side, and put his cause and quarrel
To the disposing of the cardinal :
With whom yourself, myself, and other lords,
If you think meet, this afternoon will post
To consummate this business happily.
Bast. Let it be so.—And you, my noble prince,
With other princes that may best be spar'd,
Shall wait upon your father's funeral.
P. Hen. At Worcester must his body be interr'd ;
For so he will'd it.
Bast.   Thither shall it then.   100
And happily may your sweet self put on
The lineal state and glory of the land :
To whom, with all submission, on my knee,
I do bequeath my faithful services
And true subjection everlastingly.
Sal. And the like tender of our love we make,
To rest without a spot for evermore.
P. Hen. I have a kind soul, that would give you
thanks,
And knows not how to do it, but with tears.
Bast. O ! let us pay the time but needful woe,   110
Since it hath been beforehand with our griefs.—
This England never did, nor never shall,
Lie at the proud foot of a conqueror.
But when it first did help to wound itself.
Now these her princes are come home again,
Come the three corners of the world in arms,
And we shall shock them. Naught shall make us rue,
If England to itself do rest but true.   [*Exeunt.*

KING RICHARD II.

DRAMATIS PERSONÆ.

KING RICHARD THE SECOND.
EDMUND OF LANGLEY, *Duke of York.*
JOHN OF GAUNT, *Duke of Lancaster.*
HENRY BOLINGBROKE, *Duke of Hereford.*
DUKE OF AUMERLE, *Son to the Duke of York.*
THOMAS MOWBRAY, *Duke of Norfolk.*
DUKE OF SURREY.
EARL OF SALISBURY.
EARL BERKLEY.
BUSHY, }
BAGOT, } *Creatures to King Richard.*
GREEN, }
EARL OF NORTHUMBERLAND.
HENRY PERCY, *his Son.*
LORD ROSS.

LORD WILLOUGHBY.
LORD FITZWATER.
Bishop of Carlisle.
Abbot of Westminster.
Lord Marshal, and another Lord.
SIR PIERCE OF EXTON.
SIR STEPHEN SCROOP.
Captain of a Band of Welshmen.

Queen to King Richard.
DUCHESS OF GLOSTER.
DUCHESS OF YORK.
Lady attending on the Queen.

*Lords, Heralds, Officers, Soldiers, Gardeners, Keeper,
Messenger, Groom, and other Attendants.*

SCENE—Dispersedly in ENGLAND and WALES.

ACT I.

SCENE I.—London. A Room in the Palace.

Enter King RICHARD, *attended;* JOHN OF GAUNT, *and other Nobles, with him.*

King Richard.
OLD John of Gaunt, time - honour'd
Lancaster,
Hast thou, according to thy oath and
band,
Brought hither Henry Hereford thy
bold son,
Here to make good the boisterous late
appeal,
Which then our leisure would not let
us hear,
Against the Duke of Norfolk, Thomas
Mowbray?
Gaunt. I have, my liege.
K. Rich. Tell me, moreover, hast
thou sounded him,
If he appeal the duke on ancient
malice,
Or worthily, as a good subject should, 10
On some known ground of treachery in him?
Gaunt. As near as I could sift him on that argu-
ment,
On some apparent danger seen in him,
Aim'd at your highness,—no inveterate malice.
K. Rich. Then call them to our presence: face to face,
And frowning brow to brow, ourselves will hear
The accuser, and the accused, freely speak.—
[*Exeunt some Attendants.*
High-stomach'd are they both, and full of ire,
In rage deaf as the sea, hasty as fire.

Re-enter Attendants, with BOLINGBROKE *and*
NORFOLK.

Boling. Many years of happy days befall 20
My gracious sovereign, my most loving liege!
Nor. Each day still better other's happiness;
Until the heavens, envying earth's good hap,
Add an immortal title to your crown!

K. Rich. We thank you both: yet one but flatters
us,
As well appeareth by the cause you come:
Namely, to appeal each other of high treason.—
Cousin of Hereford, what dost thou object
Against the Duke of Norfolk, Thomas Mowbray?
Boling. First, (Heaven be the record to my speech!) 31
In the devotion of a subject's love,
Tendering the precious safety of my prince,
And free from other misbegotten hate,
Come I appellant to this princely presence.—
Now, Thomas Mowbray, do I turn to thee,
And mark my greeting well; for what I speak,
My body shall make good upon this earth,
Or my divine soul answer it in heaven.
Thou art a traitor, and a miscreant;
Too good to be so, and too bad to live; 40
Since the more fair and crystal is the sky,
The uglier seem the clouds that in it fly.
Once more, the more to aggravate the note,
With a foul traitor's name stuff I thy throat,
And wish, (so please my sovereign) ere I move,
What my tongue speaks, my right-drawn sword may
prove.
Nor. Let not my cold words here accuse my zeal.
'T is not the trial of a woman's war,
The bitter clamour of two eager tongues,
Can arbitrate this cause betwixt us twain: 50
The blood is hot that must be cool'd for this.
Yet can I not of such tame patience boast,
As to be hush'd, and nought at all to say.
First, the fair reverence of your highness curbs me
From giving reins and spurs to my free speech;
Which else would post, until it had return'd
These terms of treason doubled down his throat.
Setting aside his high blood's royalty,
And let him be no kinsman to my liege,
I do defy him, and I spit at him; 60

Call him a slanderous coward, and a villain :
Which to maintain I would allow him odds,
And meet him, were I tied to run afoot
Even to the frozen ridges of the Alps,
Or any other ground inhabitable,
Where ever Englishman durst set his foot.
Meantime, let this defend my loyalty :—
By all my hopes, most falsely doth he lie.
   Boling. Pale trembling coward, there I throw my
     gage,
Disclaiming here the kindred of the king ;   70
And lay aside my high blood's royalty,
Which fear, not reverence, makes thee to except :
If guilty dread have left thee so much strength,
As to take up mine honour's pawn, then stoop.
By that, and all the rights of knighthood else,
Will I make good against thee, arm to arm,
What I have spoke, or thou canst worse devise.
   Nor. I take it up ; and by that sword I swear,
Which gently laid my knighthood on my shoulder,
I 'll answer thee in any fair degree,   80
Or chivalrous design of knightly trial :
And, when I mount, alive may I not light,
If I be traitor, or unjustly fight !
   K. Rich. What doth our cousin lay to Mowbray's
     charge ?
It must be great, that can inherit us
So much as of a thought of ill in him.
   Boling. Look, what I said, my life shall prove it
     true :—
That Mowbray hath receiv'd eight thousand nobles,
In name of lendings for your highness' soldiers,
The which he hath detain'd for lewd employments, 90
Like a false traitor, and injurious villain.
Besides, I say, and will in battle prove,
Or here, or elsewhere, to the furthest verge
That ever was survey'd by English eye,
That all the treasons, for these eighteen years
Complotted and contrived in this land,
Fetch from false Mowbray their first head and spring.
Further I say, and further will maintain
Upon his bad life to make all this good,
That he did plot the Duke of Gloster's death,   100
Suggest his soon-believing adversaries,
And, consequently, like a traitor coward,
Sluic'd out his innocent soul through streams of
     blood :
Which blood, like sacrificing Abel's, cries,
Even from the tongueless caverns of the earth,
To me for justice and rough chastisement ;
And, by the glorious worth of my descent,
This arm shall do it, or this life be spent.
   K. Rich. How high a pitch his resolution soars !
Thomas of Norfolk, what say'st thou to this ?   110
   Nor. O ! let my sovereign turn away his face,
And bid his ears a little while be deaf,
Till I have told this slander of his blood,
How God, and good men, hate so foul a liar.
   K. Rich. Mowbray, impartial are our eyes and ears :
Were he my brother, nay, our kingdom's heir,
As he is but my father's brother's son,
Now by my sceptre's awe I make a vow,
Such neighbour nearness to our sacred blood
Should nothing privilege him, nor partialise   120
The unstooping firmness of my upright soul.
He is our subject. Mowbray ; so art thou :
Free speech and fearless I to thee allow.
   Nor. Then, Bolingbroke, as low as to thy heart,
Through the false passage of thy throat, thou liest.
Three parts of that receipt I had for Calais,
Disburs'd I duly to his highness' soldiers :
The other part reserv'd I by consent :   •
For that my sovereign liege was in my debt,
Upon remainder of a dear account,   130
Since last I went to France to fetch his queen.
Now swallow down that lie.—For Gloster's death,
I slew him not ; but to mine own disgrace
Neglected my sworn duty in that case.—
For you, my noble Lord of Lancaster,
The honourable father to my foe,
Once did I lay an ambush for your life,
A trespass that doth vex my grieved soul ;

But, ere I last receiv'd the sacrament,
I did confess it, and exactly begg'd   140
Your grace's pardon, and, I hope, I had it.
This is my fault : as for the rest appeal'd,
It issues from the rancour of a villain,
A recreant and most degenerate traitor ;
Which in myself I boldly will defend,
And interchangeably hurl down my gage
Upon this overweening traitor's foot,
To prove myself a loyal gentleman
Even in the best blood chamber'd in his bosom.
In haste whereof, most heartily I pray   150
Your highness to assign our trial day.
   K. Rich. Wrath-kindled gentlemen, be rul'd by me.
Let 's purge this choler without letting blood.
This we prescribe, though no physician ;
Deep malice makes too deep incision ;
Forget, forgive ; conclude, and be agreed.
Our doctors say, this is no month to bleed.—
Good uncle, let this end where it begun ;
We 'll calm the Duke of Norfolk, you your son.
   Gaunt. To be a make-peace shall become my age.—
Throw down, my son, the Duke of Norfolk's gage. 161
   K. Rich. And, Norfolk, throw down his.
   Gaunt.   When, Harry, when ?
Obedience bids, I should not bid again.
   K. Rich. Norfolk, throw down, we bid ; there is no
     boot.
   Nor. Myself I throw, dread sovereign, at thy foot.
My life thou shalt command, but not my shame :
The one my duty owes ; but my fair name,
Despite of death that lives upon my grave,
To dark dishonour's use thou shalt not have.
I am disgrac'd, impeach'd, and baffled here :   170
Pierc'd to the soul with slander's venom'd spear ;
The which no balm can cure, but his heart-blood
Which breath'd this poison.
   K. Rich.   Rage must be withstood.
Give me his gage :—lions make leopards tame.
   Nor. Yea, but not change his spots : take but my
     shame,
And I resign my gage. My dear, dear lord,
The purest treasure mortal times afford
Is spotless reputation ; that away,
Men are but gilded loam, or painted clay.
A jewel in a ten-times-barr'd-up chest   180
Is a bold spirit in a loyal breast.
Mine honour is my life ; both grow in one :
Take honour from me, and my life is done.
Then, dear my liege, mine honour let me try ;
In that I live, and for that will I die.
   K. Rich. Cousin, throw down your gage : do you
     begin.
   Boling. O ! God defend my soul from such deep sin !
Shall I seem crest-fall'n in my father's sight ?
Or with pale beggar-fear impeach my height
Before this outdar'd dastard ? Ere my tongue   190
Shall wound mine honour with such feeble wrong,
Or sound so base a parle, my teeth shall tear
The slavish motive of recanting fear,
And spit it bleeding in his high disgrace,
Where shame doth harbour, even in Mowbray's face.
                         [*Exit* GAUNT.
   K. Rich. We were not born to sue, but to command :
Which since we cannot do to make you friends,
Be ready, as your lives shall answer it,
At Coventry, upon Saint Lambert's day.
There shall your swords and lances arbitrate   200
The swelling difference of your settled hate.
Since we cannot atone you, we shall see
Justice design the victor's chivalry.—
Lord marshal, command our officers-at-arms
Be ready to direct these home-alarms.   [*Exeunt.*

SCENE II.—The Same. A Room in the Duke of
        LANCASTER'S Palace.

Enter GAUNT *and Duchess of* GLOSTER.

   Gaunt. Alas ! the part I had in Gloster's blood
Doth more solicit me than your exclaims,

To stir against the butchers of his life.
But since correction lieth in those hands,
Which made the fault that we cannot correct,
Put we our quarrel to the will of Heaven;
One phial full of Edward's sacred blood,
One flourishing branch of his most royal root,—
Is crack'd, and all the precious liquor spilt;
Is hack'd down, and his summer leaves all vaded, 20

Nor. "Myself I throw, dread sovereign, at thy foot."

Who, when they see the hours ripe on earth,
Will rain hot vengeance on offenders' heads.
    Duch. Finds brotherhood in thee no sharper spur?
Hath love in thy old blood no living fire? 10
Edward's seven sons, whereof thyself art one,
Were as seven phials of his sacred blood,
Or seven fair branches springing from one root:
Some of those seven are dried by nature's course,
Some of those branches by the Destinies cut;
But Thomas, my dear lord, my life, my Gloster,—

By envy's hand, and murder's bloody axe.
Ah! Gaunt, his blood was thine: that bed, that womb,
That mettle, that self mould, that fashion'd thee,
Made him a man; and though thou liv'st, and
        breath'st,
Yet art thou slain in him. Thou dost consent
In some large measure to thy father's death,
In that thou seest thy wretched brother die,
Who was the model of thy father's life.
Call it not patience, Gaunt, it is despair:

In suffering thus thy brother to be slaughter'd,   30
Thou show'st the naked pathway to thy life,
Teaching stern murder how to butcher thee.
That which in mean men we entitle patience,
Is pale cold cowardice in noble breasts.
What shall I say? to safeguard thine own life,
The best way is to venge my Gloster's death.
    Gaunt. God's is the quarrel; for God's substitute,
His deputy anointed in his sight,
Hath caus'd his death; the which, if wrongfully,
Let Heaven revenge, for I may never lift   40
An angry arm against his minister.
    Duch. Where then, alas! may I complain myself?
    Gaunt. To God, the widow's champion and defence.
    Duch. Why then, I will.—Farewell, old Gaunt.
Thou go'st to Coventry, there to behold
Our cousin Hereford and fell Mowbray fight.
O! sit my husband's wrongs on Hereford's spear,
That it may enter butcher Mowbray's breast.
Or, if misfortune miss the first career,
Be Mowbray's sins so heavy in his bosom,   50
That they may break his foaming courser's back,
And throw the rider headlong in the lists,
A caitiff recreant to my cousin Hereford.
Farewell, old Gaunt: thy sometimes brother's wife
With her companion grief must end her life.
    Gaunt. Sister, farewell: I must to Coventry.
As much good stay with thee, as go with me!
    Duch. Yet one word more.—Grief boundeth where
        it falls,
Not with the empty hollowness, but weight:
I take my leave before I have begun,   60
For sorrow ends not when it seemeth done.
Commend me to my brother, Edmund York.
Lo! this is all :—nay, yet depart not so;
Though this be all, do not so quickly go;
I shall remember more. Bid him—O! what?—
With all good speed at Plashy visit me.
Alack! and what shall good old York there see,
But empty lodgings and unfurnish'd walls,
Unpeopled offices, untrodden stones?
And what hear there for welcome, but my groans? 70
Therefore commend me; let him not come there,
To seek out sorrow that dwells everywhere.
Desolate, desolate will I hence, and die:
The last leave of thee takes my weeping eye. [*Exeunt.*

SCENE III.—Open Space near Coventry.

Lists set out, and a throne. Heralds, &c., attending.

Enter the Lord Marshal and AUMERLE.

    Mar. My Lord Aumerle, is Harry Hereford arm'd?
    Aum. Yea, at all points, and longs to enter in.
    Mar. The Duke of Norfolk, sprightfully and bold,
Stays but the summons of the appellant's trumpet.
    Aum. Why then, the champions are prepar'd, and
        stay
For nothing but his majesty's approach.

Flourish. Enter King RICHARD, *who takes his seat
on his throne;* GAUNT, BUSHY, BAGOT, GREEN,
*and others, who take their places. A trumpet is
sounded, and answered by another trumpet within.
Then enter* NORFOLK, *in armour, preceded by a
Herald.*

    K. Rich. Marshal, demand of yonder champion
The cause of his arrival here in arms:
Ask him his name, and orderly proceed
To swear him in the justice of his cause.   10
    Mar. In God's name, and the king's, say who thou
        art,
And why thou com'st thus knightly clad in arms,
Against what man thou com'st, and what thy quarrel.
Speak truly, on thy knighthood, and thine oath;
And so defend thee Heaven and thy valour!
    Nor. My name is Thomas Mowbray, Duke of
        Norfolk;
Who hither come engaged by my oath,
(Which God defend a knight should violate !)

Both to defend my loyalty and truth
To God, my king, and his succeeding issue,   20
Against the Duke of Hereford that appeals me;
And, by the grace of God and this mine arm,
To prove him, in defending of myself,
A traitor to my God, my king, and me:
And, as I truly fight, defend me Heaven!

Trumpet sounds. Enter BOLINGBROKE, *in armour,
preceded by a Herald.*

    K. Rich. Marshal, ask yonder knight in arms,
Both who he is, and why he cometh hither
Thus plated in habiliments of war;
And formally, according to our law,
Depose him in the justice of his cause.   30
    Mar. What is thy name, and wherefore com'st thou
        hither,
Before King Richard in his royal lists?
Against whom comest thou? and what's thy quarrel?
Speak like a true knight, so defend thee Heaven!
    Boling. Harry of Hereford, Lancaster, and Derby,
Am I; who ready here do stand in arms,
To prove by God's grace, and my body's valour,
In lists, on Thomas Mowbray, Duke of Norfolk,
That he's a traitor, foul and dangerous,
To God of heaven, King Richard, and to me: 40
And, as I truly fight, defend me Heaven!
    Mar. On pain of death no person be so bold,
Or daring-hardy, as to touch the lists,
Except the marshal, and such officers
Appointed to direct these fair designs.
    Boling. Lord marshal, let me kiss my sovereign's
        hand,
And bow my knee before his majesty:
For Mowbray and myself are like two men
That vow a long and weary pilgrimage;
Then let us take a ceremonious leave,   50
And loving farewell of our several friends.
    Mar. The appellant in all duty greets your highness,
And craves to kiss your hand, and take his leave.
    K. Rich. We will descend, and fold him in our arms.
Cousin of Hereford, as thy cause is right,
So be thy fortune in this royal fight.
Farewell, my blood; which if to-day thou shed,
Lament we may, but not revenge thee dead.
    Boling. O! let no noble eye profane a tear
For me, if I be gor'd with Mowbray's spear.   60
As confident as is the falcon's flight
Against a bird, do I with Mowbray fight.—
My loving lord, I take my leave of you;
Of you, my noble cousin, Lord Aumerle;—
Not sick, although I have to do with death,
But lusty, young, and cheerly drawing breath.
Lo! as at English feasts, so I regreet
The daintiest last, to make the end most sweet:
O thou, the earthly author of my blood,—
Whose youthful spirit, in me regenerate,   70
Doth with a two-fold vigour lift me up
To reach at victory above my head,
Add proof unto mine armour with thy prayers,
And with thy blessings steel my lance's point,
That it may enter Mowbray's waxen coat,
And furbish new the name of John of Gaunt,
Even in the lusty haviour of his son.
    Gaunt. God in thy good cause make thee prosperous!
Be swift like lightning in the execution;
And let thy blows, doubly redoubled,   80
Fall like amazing thunder on the casque
Of thy adverse pernicious enemy:
Rouse up thy youthful blood, be valiant and live.
    Boling. Mine innocence, and Saint George to
        thrive!
    Nor. However God, or fortune, cast my lot,
There lives or dies, true to King Richard's throne,
A loyal, just, and upright gentleman.
Never did captive with a freer heart
Cast off his chains of bondage, and embrace
His golden uncontroll'd enfranchisement,   90
More than my dancing soul doth celebrate
This feast of battle with mine adversary.—
Most mighty liege, and my companion peers,
Take from my mouth the wish of happy years.

As gentle and as jocund, as to jest,
Go I to fight. Truth hath a quiet breast.
  K. Rich. Farewell, my lord : securely I espy
Virtue with valour couched in thine eye.—
Order the trial, marshal, and begin.
  Mar. Harry of Hereford, Lancaster, and Derby, 100
Receive thy lance ; and God defend the right !
  Boling. Strong as a tower in hope, I cry, Amen.
  Mar. [*To an Officer.*] Go bear this lance to Thomas,
    Duke of Norfolk.
  1 *Her.* Harry of Hereford, Lancaster, and Derby,
Stands here for God, his sovereign, and himself,
On pain to be found false and recreant,
To prove the Duke of Norfolk, Thomas Mowbray,
A traitor to his God, his king, and him ;
And dares him to set forward to the fight.
  2 *Her.* Here standeth Thomas
    Mowbray, Duke of Norfolk,
On pain to be found false and
    recreant, 111
Both to defend himself, and to
    approve
Henry of Hereford, Lancaster, and
    Derby,
To God, his sovereign, and to him,
    disloyal ;
Courageously, and with a free
    desire,
Attending but the signal to begin.
  Mar. Sound, trumpets ; and set
    forward, combatants.
      [*A charge sounded.*
Stay, the king hath thrown his
    warder down.
  K. Rich. Let them lay by their
    helmets and their spears,
And both return back to their chairs
    again.— 120
Withdraw with us ; and let the
    trumpets sound,
While we return these dukes what
    we decree.—
      [*A long flourish.*

Draw near,
And list, what with our council we have done.
For that our kingdom's earth should not be soil'd
With that dear blood which it hath fostered ;
And for our eyes do hate the dire aspect
Of civil wounds plough'd up with neighbours' swords ;
And for we think the eagle-winged pride
Of sky-aspiring and ambitious thoughts, 130
With rival-hating envy, set on you
To wake our peace, which in our country's cradle
Draws the sweet infant breath of gentle sleep ;
Which so rous'd up with boisterous untun'd drums,
With harsh resounding trumpets' dreadful bray,
And grating shock of wrathful iron arms,
Might from our quiet confines fright fair peace,
And make us wade even in our kindred's blood :
Therefore, we banish you our territories :—
You, cousin Hereford, upon pain of life, 140
Till twice five summers have enrich'd our fields,
Shall not regreet our fair dominions,
But tread the stranger paths of banishment.
  Boling. Your will be done. This must my comfort
    be :
That sun that warms you here shall shine on me ;
And those his golden beams, to you here lent,
Shall point on me, and gild my banishment.
  K. Rich. Norfolk, for thee remains a heavier
    doom,
Which I with some unwillingness pronounce :
The sly slow hours shall not determinate 150
The dateless limit of thy dear exile.
The hopeless word of—never to return,
Breathe I against thee, upon pain of life.
  Nor. A heavy sentence, my most sovereign liege,
And all unlook'd for from your highness' mouth.
A dearer merit, not so deep a main
As to be cast forth in the common air,
Have I deserved at your highness' hands.
The language I have learn'd these forty years,

My native English, now I must forego ; 160
And now my tongue's use is to me no more
Than an unstringed viol, or a harp ;
Or like a cunning instrument cas'd up,
Or, being open, put into his hands
That knows no touch to tune the harmony.
Within my mouth you have engaol'd my tongue,
Doubly portcullis'd, with my teeth and lips ;
And dull, unfeeling, barren ignorance
Is made my gaoler to attend on me.
I am too old to fawn upon a nurse, 170
Too far in years to be a pupil now ;
What is thy sentence then but speechless death,
Which robs my tongue from breathing native breath ?
  K. Rich. It boots thee not to be compassionate :
After our sentence plaining comes too late.

Nor. "But what thou art, God, thou, and I do know."

  Nor. Then thus I turn me from my country's light,
To dwell in solemn shades of endless night. [*Retiring.*
  K. Rich. Return again, and take an oath with thee.
Lay on our royal sword your banish'd hands ;
Swear by the duty that ye owe to God, 180
(Our part therein we banish with yourselves)
To keep the oath that we administer :—
You never shall (so help you truth and God !)
Embrace each other's love in banishment ;
Nor never look upon each other's face ;
Nor never write, regreet, nor reconcile
This lowering tempest of your home-bred hate ;
Nor never by advised purpose meet,
To plot, contrive, or complot any ill,
'Gainst us, our state, our subjects, or our land. 190
  Boling. I swear.
  Nor. And I, to keep all this.
  Boling. Norfolk, so far, as to mine enemy ;
By this time, had the king permitted us,
One of our souls had wander'd in the air,
Banish'd this frail sepulchre of our flesh,
As now our flesh is banish'd from this land :
Confess thy treasons, ere thou fly the realm ;
Since thou hast far to go, bear not along
The clogging burden of a guilty soul. 200
  Nor. No, Bolingbroke ; if ever I were traitor,
My name be blotted from the book of life,
And I from heaven banish'd, as from hence.
But what thou art, God, thou, and I do know ;
And all too soon, I fear, the king shall rue.—
Farewell, my liege.—Now no way can I stray :
Save back to England, all the world's my way. [*Exit.*
  K. Rich. Uncle, even in the glasses of thine eyes
I see thy grieved heart : thy sad aspect
Hath from the number of his banish'd years 210
Pluck'd four away.—[*To* BOLINGBROKE.] Six frozen
    winters spent,
Return with welcome home from banishment.

Boling. How long a time lies in one little word !
Four lagging winters and four wanton springs
End in a word : such is the breath of kings.
  Gaunt. I thank my liege, that in regard of me
He shortens four years of my son's exile ;
But little vantage shall I reap thereby :
For, ere the six years that he hath to spend,
Can change their moons, and bring their times about,
My oil-dried lamp, and time-bewasted light,   221
Shall be extinct with age and endless night ;
My inch of taper will be burnt and done,
And blindfold death not let me see my son.
  K. Rich. Why, uncle, thou hast many years to live.
  Gaunt. But not a minute, king, that thou canst
            give :
Shorten my days thou canst with sullen sorrow,
And pluck nights from me, but not lend a morrow ;
Thou canst help Time to furrow me with age,
But stop no wrinkle in his pilgrimage ;   230
Thy word is current with him for my death ;
But, dead, thy kingdom cannot buy my breath.
  K. Rich. Thy son is banish'd upon good advice,
Whereto thy tongue a party-verdict gave.
Why at our justice seem'st thou then to lower ?
  Gaunt. Things sweet to taste prove in digestion
            sour.
You urg'd me as a judge ; but I had rather,
You would have bid me argue like a father.
O ! had it been a stranger, not my child,
To smooth his fault I should have been more mild. 240
A partial slander sought I to avoid,
And in the sentence my own life destroy'd.
Alas ! I look'd when some of you should say,
I was too strict, to make mine own away ;
But you gave leave to my unwilling tongue,
Against my will, to do myself this wrong.
  K. Rich. Cousin, farewell ;—and, uncle, bid him so ;
Six years we banish him, and he shall go.
      [*Flourish. Exeunt King RICHARD and Train.*
  Aum. Cousin, farewell : what presence must not
            know,
From where you do remain, let paper show.   250
  Mar. My lord, no leave take I ; for I will ride,
As far as land will let me, by your side.
  Gaunt. O ! to what purpose dost thou hoard thy
            words,
That thou return'st no greeting to thy friends ?
  Boling. I have too few to take my leave of you,
When the tongue's office should be prodigal
To breathe the abundant dolour of the heart.
  Gaunt. Thy grief is but thy absence for a time.
  Boling. Joy absent, grief is present for that time.
  Gaunt. What is six winters ? they are quickly gone.
  Boling. To men in joy ; but grief makes one hour
            ten.   261
  Gaunt. Call it a travel, that thou tak'st for pleasure.
  Boling. My heart will sigh when I miscall it so,
Which finds it an enforced pilgrimage.
  Gaunt. The sullen passage of thy weary steps
Esteem a foil, wherein thou art to set
The precious jewel of thy home-return.
  Boling. Nay, rather, every tedious stride I make
Will but remember me, what a deal of world
I wander from the jewels that I love.   270
Must I not serve a long apprenticehood
To foreign passages, and in the end,
Having my freedom, boast of nothing else
But that I was a journeyman to grief ?
  Gaunt. All places that the eye of Heaven visits,
Are to a wise man ports and happy havens.
Teach thy necessity to reason thus ;
There is no virtue like necessity.
Think not, the king did banish thee,
But thou the king. Woe doth the heavier sit,   280
Where it perceives it is but faintly borne.
Go, say I sent thee forth to purchase honour,
And not the king exil'd thee ; or suppose,
Devouring pestilence hangs in our air,
And thou art flying to a fresher clime.
Look, what thy soul holds dear, imagine it
To lie that way thou go'st, not whence thou com'st.
Suppose the singing birds musicians,

The grass whereon thou tread'st the presence strew'd,
The flowers fair ladies, and thy steps no more   290
Than a delightful measure, or a dance ;
For gnarling sorrow hath less power to bite
The man that mocks at it, and sets it light.
  Boling. O ! who can hold a fire in his hand
By thinking on the frosty Caucasus ?
Or cloy the hungry edge of appetite
By bare imagination of a feast ?
Or wallow naked in December snow
By thinking on fantastic summer's heat ?
O ! no : the apprehension of the good   300
Gives but the greater feeling to the worse :
Fell sorrow's tooth doth never rankle more,
Than when it bites, but lanceth not the sore.

Gaunt. " Come, come, my son, I'll bring thee on thy way."

  Gaunt. Come, come, my son, I'll bring thee on thy
            way.
Had I thy youth and cause, I would not stay.
  Boling. Then, England's ground, farewell ; sweet
            soil, adieu :
My mother, and my nurse, that bears me yet !
Where'er I wander, boast of this I can,
Though banish'd, yet a true-born Englishman.
                                      [*Exeunt.*

SCENE IV.—The Same. A Room in the King's Castle.

*Enter King RICHARD, BAGOT, and GREEN, at one
        door ; AUMERLE at another.*

  K. Rich. We did observe.—Cousin Aumerle,
How far brought you high Hereford on his way ?
  Aum. I brought high Hereford, if you call him so,
But to the next highway, and there I left him.
  K. Rich. And, say, what store of parting tears were
            shed ?
  Aum. 'Faith, none for me ; except the north-east
            wind,
Which then blew bitterly against our faces,

Awak'd the sleeping rheum, and so by chance
Did grace our hollow parting with a tear.
  K. Rich. What said our cousin, when you parted
      with him?   10
  Aum. Farewell:
And, for my heart disdained that my tongue
Should so profane the word, that taught me craft
To counterfeit oppression of such grief,
That words seem'd buried in my sorrow's grave.
Marry, would the word "farewell" have lengthen'd
    hours,
And added years to his short banishment,
He should have had a volume of farewells;
But, since it would not, he had none of me.
  K. Rich. He is our cousin, cousin; but 't is doubt, 20
When time shall call him home from banishment,
Whether our kinsman come to see his friends.
Ourself, and Bushy, Bagot here, and Green,
Observ'd his courtship to the common people,
How he did seem to dive into their hearts,
With humble and familiar courtesy;
What reverence he did throw away on slaves,
Wooing poor craftsmen with the craft of smiles,
And patient underbearing of his fortune,
As 't were to banish their affects with him.   30
Off goes his bonnet to an oyster-wench;
A brace of draymen bid—God speed him well,
And had the tribute of his supple knee,
With — "Thanks, my countrymen, my loving
    friends:"—
As were our England in reversion his,
And he our subjects' next degree in hope.

  Green. Well, he is gone; and with him go these
    thoughts.
Now for the rebels, which stand out in Ireland;—
Expedient manage must be made, my liege,
Ere further leisure yield them further means,   40
For their advantage, and your highness' loss.
  K. Rich. We will ourself in person to this war.
And, for our coffers with too great a court
And liberal largess are grown somewhat light,
We are enforc'd to farm our royal realm,
The revenue whereof shall furnish us
For our affairs in hand. If that come short,
Our substitutes at home shall have blank charters;
Whereto, when they shall know what men are rich,
They shall subscribe them for large sums of gold, 50
And send them after to supply our wants;
For we will make for Ireland presently.

           Enter BUSHY.

Bushy, what news?
  Bushy. Old John of Gaunt is grievous sick, my
    lord,
Suddenly taken, and hath sent post-haste,
To entreat your majesty to visit him.
  K. Rich. Where lies he?
  Bushy. At Ely House.
  K. Rich. Now put it, God, in his physician's mind,
To help him to his grave immediately!   60
The lining of his coffers shall make coats
To deck our soldiers for these Irish wars.—
Come, gentlemen, let 's all go to visit him:
Pray God, we may make haste, and come too late!
                      [Exeunt.

ACT II.

SCENE I.—London. An Apartment in Ely House.

GAUNT *on a couch; the Duke of* YORK *and others standing by him.*

  Gaunt. WILL the king come, that I
      may breathe my last
      In wholesome counsel to his
      unstaid youth?
  York. Vex not yourself, nor strive
      not with your breath;
For all in vain comes counsel to his
    ear.
  Gaunt. O! but they say, the tongues
    of dying men
Enforce attention like deep harmony.
Where words are scarce, they are
    seldom spent in vain,
For they breathe truth that breathe
    their words in pain
He that no more must say is listen'd more,
Than they whom youth and ease have taught to glose;
More are men's ends mark'd than their lives before. 11
The setting sun, and music at the close,
As the last taste of sweets, is sweetest last,
Writ in remembrance more than things long past.
Though Richard my life's counsel would not hear,
My death's sad tale may yet undeaf his ear.
  York. No; it is stopp'd with other flattering sounds,
As praises of his state: then there are fond
Lascivious metres, to whose venom sound
The open ear of youth doth always listen: 20
Report of fashions in proud Italy,

Whose manners still our tardy apish nation
Limps after in base imitation.
Where doth the world thrust forth a vanity,
So it be new, there 's no respect how vile,
That is not quickly buzz'd into his ears?
Then all too late comes counsel to be heard,
Where will doth mutiny with wit's regard.
Direct not him whose way himself will choose:
'T is breath thou lack'st, and that breath wilt thou
    lose.   30
  Gaunt. Methinks, I am a prophet new inspir'd,
And thus, expiring, do foretell of him.
His rash fierce blaze of riot cannot last,
For violent fires soon burn out themselves;
Small showers last long, but sudden storms are short;
He tires betimes that spurs too fast betimes;
With eager feeding food doth choke the feeder:
Light vanity, insatiate cormorant,
Consuming means, soon preys upon itself.
This royal throne of kings, this scepter'd isle,
This earth of majesty, this seat of Mars,
This other Eden, demi-paradise,
This fortress, built by Nature for herself,
Against infection, and the hand of war;
This happy breed of men, this little world,
This precious stone set in the silver sea,
Which serves it in the office of a wall,
Or as a moat defensive to a house,
Against the envy of less happier lands;

This blessed plot, this earth, this realm, this England,
This nurse, this teeming womb of royal kings,   51
Fear'd by their breed, and famous by their birth,
Renowned for their deeds as far from home
(For Christian service and true chivalry),
As is the sepulchre in stubborn Jewry
Of the world's ransom, blessed Mary's Son :
This land of such dear souls, this dear, dear land,
Dear for her reputation through the world,
Is now leas'd out, I die pronouncing it,
Like to a tenement, or pelting farm.   60
England, bound in with the triumphant sea,
Whose rocky shore beats back the envious siege
Of watery Neptune, is now bound in with shame,
With inky blots, and rotten parchment bonds :
That England, that was wont to conquer others,
Hath made a shameful conquest of itself.
Ah ! would the scandal vanish with my life,
How happy then were my ensuing death !

Enter King RICHARD *and* QUEEN ; AUMERLE,
BUSHY, GREEN, BAGOT, ROSS, *and* WILLOUGHBY.

York. The king is come : deal mildly with his youth ;
For young hot colts, being rag'd, do rage the more.   70
Queen. How fares our noble uncle, Lancaster ?
K. Rich. What comfort, man ? how is 't with aged
          Gaunt ?
Gaunt. O, how that name befits my composition !
Old Gaunt, indeed ; and gaunt in being old.
Within me grief hath kept a tedious fast ;
And who abstains from meat, that is not gaunt ?
For sleeping England long time have I watch'd ;
Watching breeds leanness, leanness is all gaunt.
The pleasure that some fathers feed upon
Is my strict fast, I mean my children's looks ;   80
And therein fasting hast thou made me gaunt.
Gaunt am I for the grave, gaunt as a grave,
Whose hollow womb inherits nought but bones.
K. Rich. Can sick men play so nicely with their
          names ?
Gaunt. No ; misery makes sport to mock itself.
Since thou dost seek to kill my name in me,
I mock my name, great king, to flatter thee.
K. Rich. Should dying men flatter with those that
          live ?
Gaunt. No, no ; men living flatter those that die.
K. Rich. Thou, now a-dying, say'st, thou flatter'st
          me.   90
Gaunt. O ! no ; thou diest, though I the sicker be.
K. Rich. I am in health, I breathe, and see thee ill.
Gaunt. Now, He that made me knows I see thee ill ;
Ill in myself to see, and in thee seeing ill.
Thy death-bed is no lesser than thy land,
Wherein thou liest in reputation sick :
And thou, too careless patient as thou art,
Committ'st thy anointed body to the cure
Of those physicians that first wounded thee.
A thousand flatterers sit within thy crown,   100
Whose compass is no bigger than thy head ;
And yet, incaged in so small a verge,
The waste is no whit lesser than thy land,
O ! had thy grandsire, with a prophet's eye,
Seen how his son's son should destroy his sons,
From forth thy reach he would have laid thy shame,
Deposing thee before thou wert possess'd,
Which art possess'd now to depose thyself.
Why, cousin, wert thou regent of the world,
It were a shame to let this land by lease ;   110
But, for thy world, enjoying but this land,
Is it not more than shame to shame it so ?
Landlord of England art thou now, not king :
Thy state of law is bondslave to the law,
And—
K. Rich. And thou a lunatic lean-witted fool,
Presuming on an ague's privilege,
Dar'st with thy frozen admonition
Make pale our cheek, chasing the royal blood
With fury from his native residence.   120
Now, by my seat's right royal majesty,
Wert thou not brother to great Edward's son,
This tongue, that runs so roundly in thy head,
Should run thy head from thy unreverent shoulders.

Gaunt. O ! spare me not, my brother Edward's son,
For that I was his father Edward's son.
That blood already, like the pelican,
Hast thou tapp'd out, and drunkenly carous'd.
My brother Gloster, plain well-meaning soul,
(Whom fair befall in heaven 'mongst happy souls !)   130
May be a precedent and witness good,
That thou respect'st not spilling Edward's blood.
Join with the present sickness that I have,
And thy unkindness be like crooked age,
To crop at once a too-long withered flower.
Live in thy shame, but die not shame with thee :
These words hereafter thy tormentors be !—
Convey me to my bed, then to my grave :
Love they to live, that love and honour have.
          [*Exit, borne out by his Attendants.*
K. Rich. And let them die, that age and sullens
          have ;   140
For both hast thou, and both become the grave.
York. I do beseech your majesty, impute his words
To wayward sickliness and age in him :
He loves you, on my life, and holds you dear
As Harry, Duke of Hereford, were he here.
K. Rich. Right, you say true : as Hereford's love,
          so his ;
As theirs so mine ; and all be as it is.

Enter NORTHUMBERLAND.

North. My liege, old Gaunt commends him to your
          majesty.
K. Rich. What says he ?
North.   Nay, nothing ; all is said.   150
His tongue is now a stringless instrument ;
Words, life, and all, old Lancaster hath spent.
York. Be York the next that must be bankrupt so !
Though death be poor, it ends a mortal woe.
K. Rich. The ripest fruit first falls, and so doth he :
His time is spent ; our pilgrimage must be.
So much for that.—Now for our Irish wars.
We must supplant those rough rug-headed kerns,
Which live like venom, where no venom else,
But only they, hath privilege to live.
And for these great affairs do ask some charge,   160
Towards our assistance we do seize to us
The plate, coin, revenues, and movables,
Whereof our uncle Gaunt did stand possess'd.
York. How long shall I be patient ? Ah ! how long
Shall tender duty make me suffer wrong ?
Not Gloster's death, nor Hereford's banishment,
Not Gaunt's rebukes, nor England's private wrongs,
Nor the prevention of poor Bolingbroke
About his marriage, nor my own disgrace,
Have ever made me sour my patient cheek,   170
Or bend one wrinkle on my sovereign's face.
I am the last of noble Edward's sons,
Of whom thy father, Prince of Wales, was first ;
In war was never lion rag'd more fierce,
In peace was never gentle lamb more mild,
Than was that young and princely gentleman.
His face thou hast, for even so look'd he,
Accomplish'd with the number of thy hours ;
But when he frown'd, it was against the French,
And not against his friends : his noble hand   180
Did win what he did spend, and spent not that
Which his triumphant father's hand had won :
His hands were guilty of no kindred blood,
But bloody with the enemies of his kin.
O Richard ! York is too far gone with grief,
Or else he never would compare between.
K. Rich. Why, uncle, what 's the matter ?
York.   O my liege,
Pardon me, if you please ; if not, I, pleas'd
Not to be pardon'd, am content withal.
Seek you to seize, and gripe into your hands,   190
The royalties and rights of banish'd Hereford ?
Is not Gaunt dead, and doth not Hereford live ?
Was not Gaunt just, and is not Harry true ?
Did not the one deserve to have an heir ?
Is not his heir a well-deserving son ?
Take Hereford's rights away, and take from time
His charters and his customary rights ;
Let not to-morrow then ensue to-day ;

Be not thyself ; for how art thou a king,
But by fair sequence and succession ?   200
Now, afore God, (God forbid, I say true !)
If you do wrongfully seize Hereford's rights,
Call in the letters-patents that he hath
By his attorneys-general to sue
His livery, and deny his offer'd homage,
You pluck a thousand dangers on your head,
You lose a thousand well-disposed hearts,
And prick my tender patience to those thoughts,
Which honour and allegiance cannot think.
K. Rich. Think what you will : we seize into our
        hands   210
His plate, his goods, his money, and his lands.
York. I 'll not be by the while. My liege, farewell :
What will ensue hereof, there 's none can tell ;
But by bad courses may be understood,
That their events can never fall out good.   [*Exit.*
K. Rich. Go, Bushy, to the Earl of Wiltshire straight :
Bid him repair to us to Ely House,
To see this business. To-morrow next
We will for Ireland ; and 't is time, I trow :
And we create, in absence of ourself,   220
Our uncle York lord governor of England,
For he is just, and always lov'd us well.—
Come on, our queen : to-morrow must we part ;
Be merry, for our time of stay is short.
        [*Flourish. Exeunt* KING, QUEEN, BUSHY,
          AUMERLE, GREEN, *and* BAGOT.
North. Well, lords, the Duke of Lancaster is dead.
Ross. And living too ; for now his son is duke.
Willo. Barely in title, not in revenue.
North. Richly in both, if justice had her right.
Ross. My heart is great ; but it must break with
        silence,
Ere 't be disburden'd with a liberal tongue.   230
North. Nay, speak thy mind ; and let him ne'er
        speak more,
That speaks thy words again to do thee harm !
Willo. Tends that thou 'dst speak to the Duke of
        Hereford ?
If it be so, out with it boldly, man :
Quick is mine ear to hear of good towards him.
Ross. No good at all that I can do for him,
Unless you call it good to pity him,
Bereft and gelded of his patrimony.
North. Now, afore God, 't is shame such wrongs
        are borne   240
In him, a royal prince, and many more
Of noble blood in this declining land.
The king is not himself, but basely led
By flatterers ; and what they will inform,
Merely in hate, 'gainst any of us all,
That will the king severely prosecute
'Gainst us, our lives, our children, and our heirs.
Ross. The commons hath he pill'd with grievous
        taxes,
And quite lost their hearts : the nobles hath he
        fin'd
For ancient quarrels, and quite lost their hearts.
Willo. And daily new exactions are devis'd ;   250
As blanks, benevolences, and I wot not what :
But what, o' God's name, doth become of this ?
North. Wars hath not wasted it, for warr'd he
        hath not,
But basely yielded upon compromise
That which his ancestors achiev'd with blows.
More hath he spent in peace than they in wars.
Ross. The Earl of Wiltshire hath the realm in farm.
Willo. The king 's grown bankrupt, like a broken
        man.
North. Reproach and dissolution hangeth over
        him.
Ross. He hath not money for these Irish wars,   260
His burdenous taxations notwithstanding,
But by the robbing of the banish'd duke.
North. His noble kinsman : most degenerate king !
But, lords, we hear this fearful tempest sing,
Yet seek no shelter to avoid the storm ;
We see the wind sit sore upon our sails,
And yet we strike not, but securely perish.
Ross. We see the very wrack that we must suffer ;

And unavoided is the danger now,
For suffering so the causes of our wrack.   270
North. Not so : even through the hollow eyes of
        death,
I spy life peering ; but I dare not say
How near the tidings of our comfort is.
Willo. Nay, let us share thy thoughts, as thou dost
        ours.
Ross. Be confident to speak, Northumberland :
We three are but thyself ; and, speaking so,
Thy words are but as thoughts : therefore, be bold.
North. Then thus :—I have from Port le Blanc, a
        bay
In Brittany, receiv'd intelligence,
That Harry Duke of Hereford, Rainold Lord Cobham,
That late broke from the Duke of Exeter,   281
His brother, Archbishop late of Canterbury,
Sir Thomas Erpingham, Sir John Ramston,
Sir John Norbery, Sir Robert Waterton, and Francis
        Quoint,
All these well furnish'd by the Duke of Bretagne,
With eight tall ships, three thousand men of war,
Are making hither with all due expedience,
And shortly mean to touch our northern shore.
Perhaps they had ere this, but that they stay
The first departing of the king for Ireland.   290
If then we shall shake off our slavish yoke,
Imp out our drooping country's broken wing,
Redeem from broking pawn the blemish'd crown,
Wipe off the dust that hides our sceptre's gilt,
And make high majesty look like itself,
Away with me in post to Ravenspurg ;
But if you faint, as fearing to do so,
Stay and be secret, and myself will go.
Ross. To horse, to horse ! urge doubts to them that
        fear.
Willo. Hold out my horse, and I will first be there.
        [*Exeunt.*

SCENE II.—*The Same. An Apartment in the Palace.*

        Enter QUEEN, BUSHY, *and* BAGOT.

Bushy. Madam, your majesty is too much sad :
You promis'd, when you parted with the king,
To lay aside life-harming heaviness,
And entertain a cheerful disposition.
Queen. To please the king, I did ; to please myself,
I cannot do it ; yet I know no cause
Why I should welcome such a guest as grief,
Save bidding farewell to so sweet a guest
As my sweet Richard. Yet, again, methinks,
Some unborn sorrow, ripe in fortune's womb,   10
Is coming towards me ; and my inward soul
With nothing trembles : at something it grieves
More than with parting from my lord the king.
Bushy. Each substance of a grief hath twenty
        shadows,
Which show like grief itself, but are not so.
For sorrow's eye, glazed with blinding tears,
Divides one thing entire to many objects ;
Like perspectives, which, rightly gaz'd upon,
Show nothing but confusion : ey'd awry,
Distinguish form : so your sweet majesty,   20
Looking awry upon your lord's departure,
Finds shapes of grief more than himself to wail ;
Which, look'd on as it is, is nought but shadows
Of what it is not. Then, thrice-gracious queen,
More than your lord's departure weep not : more 's
        not seen ;
Or if it be, 't is with false sorrow's eye,
Which for things true weeps things imaginary.
Queen. It may be so ; but yet my inward soul
Persuades me, it is otherwise : howe'er it be,
I cannot but be sad, so heavy sad,   30
As—though, in thinking, on no thought I think—
Makes me with heavy nothing faint and shrink.
Bushy. 'T is nothing but conceit, my gracious lady.
Queen. 'Tis nothing less : conceit is still deriv'd
From some forefather grief ; mine is not so,
For nothing hath begot my something grief ;
Or something hath the nothing that I grieve :

'T is in reversion that I do possess ;
But what it is, that is not yet known ; what
I cannot name : 't is nameless woe, I wot.   40

Enter GREEN.

Green. God save your majesty !—and well met,
 gentlemen.—
I hope, the king is not yet shipp'd for Ireland.
 Queen. Why hop'st thou so ? 't is better hope he is,
For his designs crave haste, his haste good hope :
Then wherefore dost thou hope he is not shipp'd ?
 Green. That he, our hope, might have retir'd his
 power,
And driven into despair an enemy's hope,
Who strongly hath set footing in this land.
The banish'd Bolingbroke repeals himself,
And with uplifted arms is safe arriv'd   50
At Ravenspurg.
 Queen.   Now, God in heaven forbid !
 Green. Ah ! madam, 't is too true : and that is
 worse,
The Lord Northumberland, his son, young Henry
 Percy,
The Lords of Ross, Beaumond, and Willoughby,
With all their powerful friends, are fled to him.
 Bushy. Why have you not proclaim'd Northumber-
 land
And the rest of the revolted faction traitors ?
 Green. We have : whereupon the Earl of Worcester
Hath broke his staff, resign'd his stewardship,
And all the household servants fled with him   60
To Bolingbroke.
 Queen. So, Green, thou art the midwife to my woe,
And Bolingbroke my sorrow's dismal heir :
Now hath my soul brought forth her prodigy,
And I, a gasping new-deliver'd mother,
Have woe to woe, sorrow to sorrow join'd.
 Bushy. Despair not, madam.
 Queen.   Who shall hinder me ?
I will despair, and be at enmity
With cozening hope : he is a flatterer,
A parasite, a keeper-back of death,   70
Who gently would dissolve the bands of life,
Which false hope lingers in extremity.

Enter YORK.

Green. Here comes the Duke of York.
 Queen. With signs of war about his aged neck.
O ! full of careful business are his looks.—
Uncle, for God's sake, speak comfortable words.
 York. Should I do so, I should belie my thoughts :
Comfort 's in heaven ; and we are on the earth,
Where nothing lives but crosses, care, and grief.
Your husband, he is gone to save far off,   80
Whilst others come to make him lose at home :
Here am I left to underprop his land,
Who, weak with age, cannot support myself.
Now comes the sick hour that his surfeit made ;
Now shall he try his friends that flatter'd him.

Enter a Servant.

Serv. My lord, your son was gone before I came.
 York. He was ?—Why, so.—Go all which way it
 will !—
The nobles they are fled, the commons they are cold,
And will, I fear, revolt on Hereford's side.—
Sirrah, get thee to Plashy, to my sister Gloster ;   90
Bid her send me presently a thousand pound.
Hold ; take my ring.
 Serv. My lord, I had forgot to tell your lordship :
To-day, as I came by, I called there ;
But I shall grieve you to report the rest.
 York. What is 't, knave ?
 Serv. An hour before I came, the duchess died.
 York. God for his mercy ! what a tide of woes
Comes rushing on this woful land at once !
I know not what to do :—I would to God,   100
(So my untruth had not provok'd him to it)
The king had cut off my head with my brother's.—
What ! are there no posts despatch'd for Ireland ?—
How shall we do for money for these wars ?—
Come, sister,—cousin, I would say : pray, pardon me.—

[To the Servant.] Go, fellow, get thee home ; provide
 some carts,
And bring away the armour that is there.—
        [Exit Servant.
Gentlemen, will you go muster men ? If I know

Queen. " Uncle, for God's sake, speak comfortable words."

How, or which way, to order these affairs,
Thus disorderly thrust into my hands,   110
Never believe me. Both are my kinsmen :
The one is my sovereign, whom both my oath
And duty bids defend ; the other again
Is my kinsman, whom the king hath wrong'd,
Whom conscience and my kindred bids to right.
Well, somewhat we must do.—Come, cousin,
I 'll dispose of you.—Gentlemen, go muster up your
 men,
And meet me presently at Berkley Castle.
I should to Plashy too,
But time will not permit.—All is uneven,   120
And everything is left at six and seven.
      [Exeunt YORK *and* QUEEN.
 Bushy. The wind sits fair for news to go to Ireland,
But none returns. For us to levy power,
Proportionable to the enemy,
Is all unpossible.
 Green. Besides, our nearness to the king in love
Is near the hate of those love not the king.
 Bagot. And that 's the wavering commons ; for their
 love
Lies in their purses, and whoso empties them,
By so much fills their hearts with deadly hate.   130
 Bushy. Wherein the king stands generally con-
 demn'd.
 Bagot. If judgment lie in them, then so do we,
Because we ever have been near the king.
 Green. Well, I 'll for refuge straight to Bristol
 Castle :
The Earl of Wiltshire is already there.
 Bushy. Thither will I with you ; for little office
Will the hateful commons perform for us,
Except like curs to tear us all to pieces.—
Will you go along with us ?

Bagot. No ; I will to Ireland to his majesty.   140
Farewell : if heart's presages be not vain,
We three here part, that ne'er shall meet again.
Bushy. That 's as York thrives to beat back Boling-
      broke.
Green. Alas, poor duke ! the task he undertakes
Is numbering sands, and drinking oceans dry :
Where one on his side fights, thousands will fly.
Farewell at once ; for once, for all, and ever.
Bushy. Well, we may meet again.
Bagot.   I fear me, never. [*Exeunt.*

SCENE III.—The Wilds in Glostershire.

Enter BOLINGBROKE *and* NORTHUMBERLAND, *with
      Forces.*

Boling. How far is it, my lord, to Berkley now ?
North. Believe me, noble lord,
I am a stranger here in Glostershire.
These high wild hills, and rough uneven ways,
Draw out our miles, and make them wearisome ;
And yet your fair discourse hath been as sugar,
Making the hard way sweet and delectable.
But, I bethink me, what a weary way
From Ravenspurg to Cotswold will be found
In Ross and Willoughby, wanting your company ;   10
Which, I protest, hath very much beguil'd
The tediousness and process of my travel :
But theirs is sweeten'd with the hope to have
The present benefit which I possess ;
And hope to joy is little less in joy
Than hope enjoy'd : by this the weary lords
Shall make their way seem short, as mine hath done
By sight of what I have, your noble company.
Boling. Of much less value is my company,
Than your good words. But who comes here ?   20

Enter HARRY PERCY.

North. It is my son, young Harry Percy,
Sent from my brother Worcester, whencesoever.—
Harry, how fares your uncle ?
Percy. I had thought, my lord, to have learn'd his
      health of you.
North. Why, is he not with the queen ?
Percy. No, my good lord : he hath forsook the
      court,
Broken his staff of office, and dispers'd
The household of the king.
North.   What was his reason ?
He was not so resolv'd, when last we spake together.
Percy. Because your lordship was proclaimed
      traitor.   30
But he, my lord, is gone to Ravenspurg,
To offer service to the Duke of Hereford,
And sent me over by Berkley, to discover
What power the Duke of York had levied there ;
Then with direction to repair to Ravenspurg.
North. Have you forgot the Duke of Hereford,
      boy ?
Percy. No, my good lord ; for that is not forgot
Which ne'er I did remember : to my knowledge,
I never in my life did look on him.
North. Then learn to know him now : this is the
      duke.   40
Percy. My gracious lord, I tender you my service,
Such as it is, being tender, raw, and young,
Which elder days shall ripen, and confirm
To more approved service and desert.
Boling. I thank thee, gentle Percy ; and be sure,
I count myself in nothing else so happy,
As in a soul remembering my good friends ;
And as my fortune ripens with thy love,
It shall be still thy true love's recompense :
My heart this covenant makes, my hand thus seals
      it.   50
North. How far is it to Berkley ? and what stir
Keeps good old York there, with his men of war ?
Percy. There stands the castle, by yond tuft of
      trees,
Mann'd with three hundred men, as I have heard ;

And in it are the Lords of York, Berkley, and Sey-
      mour ;
None else of name and noble estimate.

Enter ROSS *and* WILLOUGHBY.

North. Here come the Lords of Ross and Willoughby,
Bloody with spurring, fiery-red with haste.
Boling. Welcome, my lords. I wot, your love
      pursues
A banish'd traitor : all my treasury   60
Is yet but unfelt thanks, which, more enrich'd,
Shall be your love and labour's recompense.
Ross. Your presence makes us rich, most noble
      lord.
Willo. And far surmounts our labour to attain it.
Boling. Evermore thanks, the exchequer of the
      poor ;
Which, till my infant fortune comes to years,
Stands for my bounty. But who comes here ?

Enter BERKLEY.

North. It is my Lord of Berkley, as I guess.   70
Berk. My Lord of Hereford, my message is to you.
Boling. My lord, my answer is to Lancaster,
And I am come to seek that name in England ;
And I must find that title in your tongue,
Before I make reply to aught you say.
Berk. Mistake me not, my lord : 't is not my
      meaning
To raze one title of your honour out.
To you, my lord, I come, (what lord you will,)
From the most gracious regent of this land,
The Duke of York, to know what pricks you on
To take advantage of the absent time,
And fright our native peace with self-borne arms.   80

Enter YORK, *attended.*

Boling. I shall not need transport my words by you :
Here comes his grace in person.—My noble uncle !
                              [*Kneels.*
York. Show me thy humble heart, and not thy
      knee,
Whose duty is deceivable and false.
Boling. My gracious uncle—
York. Tut, tut !
Grace me no grace, nor uncle me no uncle :
I am no traitor's uncle ; and that word " grace,"
In an ungracious mouth, is but profane.
Why have those banish'd and forbidden legs   90
Dar'd once to touch a dust of England's ground ?
But then more why,—why have they dar'd to march
So many miles upon her peaceful bosom,
Frighting her pale-fac'd villages with war,
And ostentation of despised arms ?
Com'st thou because the anointed king is hence ?
Why, foolish boy, the king is left behind,
And in my loyal bosom lies his power.
Were I but now the lord of such hot youth,
As when brave Gaunt, thy father, and myself,   100
Rescued the Black Prince, that young Mars of men,
From forth the ranks of many thousand French,
O ! then, how quickly should this arm of mine,
Now prisoner to the palsy, chastise thee,
And minister correction to thy fault !
Boling. My gracious uncle, let me know my fault :
On what condition stands it, and wherein ?
York. Even in condition of the worst degree ;
In gross rebellion, and detested treason :
Thou art a banish'd man, and here art come   110
Before the expiration of thy time,
In braving arms against thy sovereign.
Boling. As I was banish'd, I was banish'd Hereford ;
But as I come, I come for Lancaster.
And, noble uncle, I beseech your grace,
Look on my wrongs with an indifferent eye :
You are my father, for, methinks, in you
I see old Gaunt alive : O ! then, my father,
Will you permit that I shall stand condemn'd
A wandering vagabond, my rights and royalties   120
Pluck'd from my arms perforce, and given away
To upstart unthrifts ? Wherefore was I born ?
If that my cousin king be King of England,

It must be granted I am Duke of Lancaster.
You have a son, Aumerle, my noble kinsman ;
Had you first died, and he been thus trod down,
He should have found his uncle Gaunt a father,
To rouse his wrongs, and chase them to the bay.
I am denied to sue my livery here,
And yet my letters-patents give me leave :   130
My father's goods are all distrain'd and sold ;
And these, and all, are all amiss employ'd.
What would you have me do ? I am a subject,
And challenge law. Attorneys are denied me,
And therefore personally I lay my claim
To my inheritance of free descent.
    North. The noble duke hath been too much abused.
    Ross. It stands your grace upon, to do him right.
    Willo. Base men by his endowments are made great.
    York. My lords of England, let me tell you this : 140
I have had feeling of my cousin's wrongs,
And labour'd all I could to do him right ;
But in this kind to come, in braving arms,
Be his own carver, and cut out his way,
To find out right with wrong,—it may not be ;
And you, that do abet him in this kind,
Cherish rebellion, and are rebels all.
    North. The noble duke hath sworn, his coming is
But for his own ; and for the right of that,
We all have strongly sworn to give him aid ;   150
And let him ne'er see joy that breaks that oath !
    York. Well, well, I see the issue of these arms :
I cannot mend it, I must needs confess,
Because my power is weak, and all ill left ;
But if I could, by Him that gave me life,
I would attach you all, and make you stoop
Unto the sovereign mercy of the king ;
But, since I cannot, be it known to you,
I do remain as neuter. So, fare you well ;
Unless you please to enter in the castle,   160
And there repose you for this night.
    Boling. An offer, uncle, that we will accept.
But we must win your grace to go with us

To Bristol Castle ; which, they say, is held
By Bushy, Bagot, and their complices,
The caterpillars of the commonwealth,
Which I have sworn to weed and pluck away.
    York. It may be, I will go with you ;—but yet I 'll pause,
For I am loath to break our country's laws.
Nor friends, nor foes, to me welcome you are :   170
Things past redress are now with me past care.
                            [*Exeunt.*

SCENE IV.—A Camp in Wales.

Enter SALISBURY *and a Captain.*

    Cap. My Lord of Salisbury, we have stay'd ten days,
And hardly kept our countrymen together,
And yet we hear no tidings from the king :
Therefore, we will disperse ourselves : farewell.
    Sal. Stay yet another day, thou trusty Welshman :
The king reposeth all his confidence in thee.
    Cap. 'T is thought the king is dead : we will not stay.
The bay-trees in our country are all wither'd,
And meteors fright the fixed stars of heaven ;
The pale-fac'd moon looks bloody on the earth,   10
And lean-look'd prophets whisper fearful change.
Rich men look sad, and ruffians dance and leap,
The one, in fear to lose what they enjoy,
The other to enjoy by rage and war.
These signs forerun the death or fall of kings.
Farewell : our countrymen are gone and fled,
As well assur'd Richard, their king, is dead.   [*Exit.*
    Sal. Ah, Richard ! with the eyes of heavy mind
I see thy glory, like a shooting star,
Fall to the base earth from the firmament.   20
Thy sun sets weeping in the lowly west,
Witnessing storms to come, woe, and unrest.
Thy friends are fled, to wait upon thy foes,
And crossly to thy good all fortune goes.   [*Exit.*

ACT III.

SCENE I.—BOLINGBROKE'S Camp at Bristol.

Enter BOLINGBROKE, YORK, NORTHUMBERLAND, PERCY, WILLOUGHBY, ROSS ; BUSHY *and* GREEN, *prisoners.*

    Bolingbroke.
RING forth these men.—
    Bushy, and Green, I will not vex your souls—
Since presently your souls must part your bodies—
With too much urging your pernicious lives,
For 't were no charity ; yet, to wash your blood
From off my hands, here in the view of men,
I will unfold some causes of your deaths.
    You have misled a prince, a royal king,
A happy gentleman in blood and lineaments,
By you unhappied and disfigur'd clean :   10
You have, in manner, with your sinful hours,
Made a divorce betwixt his queen and him,

Broke the possession of a royal bed,
And stain'd the beauty of a fair queen's cheeks
With tears, drawn from her eyes by your foul wrongs.
Myself, a prince by fortune of my birth,
Near to the king in blood, and near in love,
Till you did make him misinterpret me,
Have stoop'd my neck under your injuries,
And sigh'd my English breath in foreign clouds,   20
Eating the bitter bread of banishment ;
Whilst you have fed upon my signories,
Dispark'd my parks, and fell'd my forest woods,
From mine own windows torn my household coat,
Raz'd out my impress, leaving me no sign,—
Save men's opinions, and my living blood,—
To show the world I am a gentleman.
This and much more, much more than twice all this,
Condemns you to the death.—See them deliver'd over
To execution and the hand of death.   30
    Bushy. More welcome is the stroke of death to me,
Than Bolingbroke to England.—Lords, farewell.

Green. My comfort is, that Heaven will take our
souls,
And plague injustice with the pains of hell.
Boling. My Lord Northumberland, see them des-
patch'd.
      [*Exeunt* NORTHUMBERLAND *and others,*
                with BUSHY *and* GREEN.
Uncle, you say the queen is at your house :
For God's sake, fairly let her be entreated ;
Tell her, I send to her my kind commends :
Take special care my greetings be deliver'd.
  York. A gentleman of mine I have despatch'd   40
With letters of your love to her at large.
  Boling. Thanks, gentle uncle.—Come, lords, away,
To fight with Glendower and his complices :
Awhile to work, and after holiday.   [*Exeunt.*

SCENE II.—The Coast of Wales. A Castle in view.

Flourish: drums and trumpets. Enter King
RICHARD, *Bishop of* CARLISLE, AUMERLE, *and*
Soldiers.

  K. Rich. Barkloughly Castle call they this at hand ?
  Aum. Yea, my lord. How brooks your grace the
        air,
After your late tossing on the breaking seas ?
  K. Rich. Needs must I like it well : I weep for joy,
To stand upon my kingdom once again.—
Dear earth, I do salute thee with my hand,
Though rebels wound thee with their horses' hoofs :
As a long-parted mother with her child
Plays fondly with her tears and smiles in meeting,
So, weeping, smiling, greet I thee, my earth,   10
And do thee favour with my royal hands.
Feed not thy sovereign's foe, my gentle earth,
Nor with thy sweets comfort his ravenous sense ;
But let thy spiders, that suck up thy venom,
And heavy-gaited toads, lie in their way,
Doing annoyance to the treacherous feet,
Which with usurping steps do trample thee.
Yield stinging nettles to mine enemies :
And when they from thy bosom pluck a flower,
Guard it, I pray thee, with a lurking adder,   20
Whose double tongue may with a mortal touch
Throw death upon thy sovereign's enemies.—
Mock not my senseless conjuration, lords :
This earth shall have a feeling, and these stones
Prove armed soldiers, ere her native king
Shall falter under foul rebellion's arms.
  Bishop. Fear not, my lord : that Power that made
    you king,
Hath power to keep you king, in spite of all.
The means that Heaven yields must be embrac'd,
And not neglected ; else, if Heaven would,   30
And we will not, Heaven's offer we refuse,
The proffer'd means of succour and redress.
  Aum. He means, my lord, that we are too remiss ;
Whilst Bolingbroke, through our security,
Grows strong and great in substance, and in friends.
  K. Rich. Discomfortable cousin ! know'st thou not,
That when the searching eye of heaven is hid
Behind the globe, and lights the lower world,
Then thieves and robbers range abroad unseen,
In murders and in outrage bloody here ;   40
But when from under this terrestrial ball
He fires the proud tops of the eastern pines,
And darts his light through every guilty hole,
Then murders, treasons, and detested sins,
The cloak of night being pluck'd from off their backs,
Stand bare and naked, trembling at themselves ?
So when this thief, this traitor, Bolingbroke,
Who all this while hath revell'd in the night,
Whilst we were wandering with the Antipodes,
Shall see us rising in our throne, the east,   50
His treasons will sit blushing in his face,
Not able to endure the sight of day,
But, self-affrighted, tremble at his sin.
Not all the water in the rough rude sea
Can wash the balm from an anointed king ;
The breath of worldly men cannot depose

The deputy elected by the Lord.
For every man that Bolingbroke hath press'd,
To lift shrewd steel against our golden crown,
God for his Richard hath in heavenly pay   60

Bishop. " Fear not, my lord : that Power that made you king,
Hath power to keep you king, in spite of all."

A glorious angel : then, if angels fight,
Weak men must fall, for Heaven still guards the right.

        Enter SALISBURY.

Welcome, my lord. How far off lies your power ?
  Sal. Nor near, nor further off, my gracious lord,
Than this weak arm. Discomfort guides my tongue,
And bids me speak of nothing but despair.
One day too late, I fear, my noble lord,
Hath clouded all thy happy days on earth.
O ! call back yesterday, bid time return,
And thou shalt have twelve thousand fighting men :
To-day, to-day, unhappy day, too late,   71
O'erthrows thy joys, friends, fortune, and thy state ;
For all the Welshmen, hearing thou wert dead,
Are gone to Bolingbroke, dispers'd, and fled.
  Aum. Comfort, my liege ! why looks your grace so
    pale ?
  K. Rich. But now, the blood of twenty thousand
    men
Did triumph in my face, and they are fled ;
And till so much blood thither come again,
Have I not reason to look pale and dead ?
All souls that will be safe, fly from my side ;   80
For time hath set a blot upon my pride.
  Aum. Comfort, my liege ! remember who you are.
  K. Rich. I had forgot myself. Am I not king ?
Awake, thou sluggard majesty ! thou sleepest.
Is not the king's name forty thousand names ?
Arm, arm, my name ! a puny subject strikes
At thy great glory.—Look not to the ground,
Ye favourites of a king : are we not high ?
High be our thoughts. I know, my uncle York
Hath power enough to serve our turn. But who comes
    here ?   90
        Enter SCROOP.

  Scroop. More health and happiness betide my liege,
Than can my care-tun'd tongue deliver him !
  K. Rich. Mine ear is open, and my heart prepar'd :
The worst is worldly loss thou canst unfold.
Say, is my kingdom lost ? why, 't was my care ;
And what loss is it to be rid of care ?

Strives Bolingbroke to be as great as we?
Greater he shall not be: if he serve God,
We'll serve him too, and be his fellow so.
Revolt our subjects? that we cannot mend;   100
They break their faith to God, as well as us.
Cry woe, destruction, ruin, loss, decay;
The worst is death, and death will have his day.
   Scroop. Glad am I, that your highness is so arm'd
To bear the tidings of calamity.
Like an unseasonable stormy day,
Which makes the silver rivers drown their shores,
As if the world were all dissolv'd to tears;
So high above his limits swells the rage
Of Bolingbroke, covering your fearful land   110
With hard bright steel, and hearts harder than steel.
White-beards have arm'd their thin and hairless
     scalps
Against thy majesty; and boys, with women's voices,
Strive to speak big, and clap their female joints
In stiff unwieldy arms against thy crown;
Thy very beadsmen learn to bend their bows
Of double-fatal yew against thy state;
Yea, distaff-women manage rusty bills
Against thy seat: both young and old rebel,
And all goes worse than I have power to tell.   120
   K. Rich. Too well, too well thou tell'st a tale so ill.
Where is the Earl of Wiltshire? where is Bagot?
What is become of Bushy? where is Green?
That they have let the dangerous enemy
Measure our confines with such peaceful steps?
If we prevail, their heads shall pay for it.
I warrant they have made peace with Bolingbroke.
   Scroop. Peace have they made with him, indeed,
     my lord.
   K. Rich. O villains, vipers, damn'd without re-
     demption!
Dogs, easily won to fawn on any man!   130
Snakes, in my heart-blood warm'd, that sting my
     heart!
Three Judases, each one thrice worse than Judas!
Would they make peace? terrible hell make war
Upon their spotted souls for this offence!
   Scroop. Sweet love, I see, changing his property,
Turns to the sourest and most deadly hate.
Again uncurse their souls; their peace is made
With heads and not with hands: those whom you
     curse,
Have felt the worst of death's destroying wound,
And lie full low, grav'd in the hollow ground.   140
   Aum. Is Bushy, Green, and the Earl of Wiltshire,
     dead?
   Scroop. Yea, all of them at Bristol lost their heads.
   Aum. Where is the duke, my father, with his power?
   K. Rich. No matter where. Of comfort no man
     speak:
Let's talk of graves, of worms, and epitaphs;
Make dust our paper, and with rainy eyes
Write sorrow on the bosom of the earth.
Let's choose executors, and talk of wills:
And yet not so,—for what can we bequeath,
Save our deposed bodies to the ground?   150
Our lands, our lives, and all are Bolingbroke's,
And nothing can we call our own but death,
And that small model of the barren earth,
Which serves as paste and cover to our bones.
For God's sake, let us sit upon the ground,
And tell sad stories of the death of kings:—
How some have been depos'd, some slain in war,
Some haunted by the ghosts they have depos'd,
Some poison'd by their wives, some sleeping kill'd,
All murder'd:—for within the hollow crown,   160
That rounds the mortal temples of a king,
Keeps Death his court, and there the antick sits,
Scoffing his state, and grinning at his pomp;
Allowing him a breath, a little scene,
To monarchise, be fear'd, and kill with looks;
Infusing him with self and vain conceit,
As if this flesh, which walls about our life,
Were brass impregnable; and, humour'd thus,
Comes at the last, and with a little pin
Bores through his castle wall, and—farewell king!   170
Cover your heads, and mock not flesh and blood

With solemn reverence: throw away respect,
Tradition, form, and ceremonious duty,
For you have but mistook me all this while:
I live with bread like you, feel want,
Taste grief, need friends. Subjected thus,
How can you say to me, I am a king?
   Bishop. My lord, wise men ne'er wail their present
     woes,
But presently prevent the ways to wail.
To fear the foe, since fear oppresseth strength,   180
Gives, in your weakness, strength unto your foe,
And so your follies fight against yourself.
Fear, and be slain; no worse can come to fight:
And fight and die is death destroying death;
Where fearing dying pays death servile breath.
   Aum. My father hath a power, inquire of him,
And learn to make a body of a limb.
   K. Rich. Thou chid'st me well.—Proud Boling-
     broke, I come
To change blows with thee for our day of doom.
This ague-fit of fear is over-blown: 190
An easy task it is to win our own.—
Say, Scroop, where lies our uncle with his power?
Speak sweetly, man, although thy looks be sour.
   Scroop. Men judge by the complexion of the sky
The state and inclination of the day;
So may you by my dull and heavy eye,
My tongue hath but a heavier tale to say.
I play the torturer, by small and small,
To lengthen out the worst that must be spoken.
Your uncle York is join'd with Bolingbroke,   200
And all your northern castles yielded up,
And all your southern gentlemen in arms
Upon his party.
   K. Rich.   Thou hast said enough.—
Beshrew thee, cousin, which didst lead me forth
Of that sweet way I was in to despair!
What say you now? what comfort have we now?
By Heaven, I'll hate him everlastingly
That bids me be of comfort any more.
Go to Flint Castle: there I'll pine away;
A king, woe's slave, shall kingly woe obey.   210
That power I have, discharge; and let them go
To ear the land that hath some hope to grow,
For I have none.—Let no man speak again
To alter this, for counsel is but vain.
   Aum. My liege, one word.
   K. Rich.   He does me double wrong,
That wounds me with the flatteries of his tongue.
Discharge my followers: let them hence away,
From Richard's night to Bolingbroke's fair day.
                            [*Exeunt.*

SCENE III.—Wales. A Plain before Flint Castle.

Enter, with drum and colours, BOLINGBROKE *and
Forces;* YORK, NORTHUMBERLAND, *and others.*

   Boling. So that by this intelligence we learn,
The Welshmen are dispers'd, and Salisbury
Is gone to meet the king, who lately landed
With some few private friends upon this coast.
   North. The news is very fair and good, my lord:
Richard, not far from hence, hath hid his head.
   York. It would beseem the Lord Northumberland,
To say, King Richard:—alack, the heavy day,
When such a sacred king should hide his head!
   North. Your grace mistakes; only to be brief,   10
Left I his title out.
   York.   The time hath been,
Would you have been so brief with him, he would
Have been so brief with you, to shorten you,
For taking so the head, your whole head's length.
   Boling. Mistake not, uncle, further than you should.
   York. Take not, good cousin, further than you
     should,
Lest you mistake: the heavens are o'er your head.
   Boling. I know it, uncle; and oppose not myself
Against their will.—But who comes here?

             Enter PERCY.

Welcome, Harry. What, will not this castle yield?   20

Percy. The castle royally is mann'd, my lord,
Against thy entrance.
  Boling. Royally?
Why, it contains no king?
  Percy.   Yes, my good lord,
It doth contain a king : King Richard lies
Within the limits of yond lime and stone,
And with him are the Lord Aumerle, Lord Salisbury,
Sir Stephen Scroop ; besides a clergyman
Of holy reverence, who, I cannot learn.
  North. O ! belike it is the Bishop of Carlisle.   30
  Boling. [*To* Northumberland.] Noble lord,
Go to the rude ribs of that ancient castle
Through brazen trumpet send the breath of parle
Into his ruin'd ears,
And thus deliver. Henry Bolingbroke
On both his knees doth kiss King Richard's hand,
And sends allegiance, and true faith of heart,
To his most royal person ; hither come
Even at his feet to lay my arms and power,
Provided that my banishment repeal'd,   40
And lands restor'd again, be freely granted.
If not, I 'll use the advantage of my power,
And lay the summer's dust with showers of blood,
Rain'd from the wounds of slaughter'd Englishmen :
The which, how far off from the mind of Bolingbroke
It is, such crimson tempest should bedrench
The fresh green lap of fair King Richard's land,
My stooping duty tenderly shall show.
Go, signify as much, while here we march
Upon the grassy carpet of this plain.   50
Let 's march without the noise of threat'ning drum,
That from the castle's tatter'd battlements
Our fair appointments may be well perus'd.
Methinks, King Richard and myself should meet
With no less terror than the elements
Of fire and water, when their thundering shock
At meeting tears the cloudy cheeks of heaven.
Be he the fire, I 'll be the yielding water :
The rage be his, while on the earth I rain
My waters ; on the earth, and not on him.—   60
March on, and mark King Richard how he looks.

A parley sounded, and answered by a trumpet within. Flourish. Enter on the walls King Richard, *the Bishop of* Carlisle, Aumerle, Scroop, *and* Salisbury.

  Boling. See, see, King Richard doth himself appear,
As doth the blushing discontented sun
From out the fiery portal of the east,
When he perceives the envious clouds are bent
To dim his glory, and to stain the track
Of his bright passage to the occident.
  York. Yet looks he like a king : behold, his eye,
As bright as is the eagle's, lightens forth
Controlling majesty. Alack, alack, for woe,   70
That any harm should stain so fair a show !
  K. Rich. [*To* Northumberland.] We are amaz'd ;
     and thus long have we stood
To watch the fearful bending of thy knee,
Because we thought ourself thy lawful king :
And if we be, how dare thy joints forget
To pay their awful duty to our presence ?
If we be not, show us the hand of God
That hath dismiss'd us from our stewardship :
For well we know, no hand of blood and bone
Can gripe the sacred handle of our sceptre,   80
Unless he do profane, steal, or usurp.
And though you think that all, as you have done,
Have torn their souls by turning them from us,
And we are barren and bereft of friends,
Yet know, my master, God omnipotent,
Is mustering in his clouds on our behalf
Armies of pestilence ; and they shall strike
Your children yet unborn, and unbegot,
That lift your vassal hands against my head,
And threat the glory of my precious crown.   90
Tell Bolingbroke, for yond, methinks, he stands,
That every stride he makes upon my land
Is dangerous treason : he is come to ope
The purple testament of bleeding war ;
But ere the crown he looks for live in peace,

Ten thousand bloody crowns of mothers' sons
Shall ill become the flower of England's face,
Change the complexion of her maid-pale peace
To scarlet indignation, and bedew
Her pastures' grass with faithful English blood.   100
  North. The King of heaven forbid, our lord the king
Should so with civil and uncivil arms
Be rush'd upon ! Thy thrice-noble cousin,
Harry Bolingbroke, doth humbly kiss thy hand ;
And by the honourable tomb he swears,
That stands upon your royal grandsire's bones,
And by the royalties of both your bloods,
Currents that spring from one most gracious head,
And by the buried hand of warlike Gaunt,
And by the worth and honour of himself,   110
Comprising all that may be sworn or said,
His coming hither hath no further scope,
Than for his lineal royalties, and to beg
Enfranchisement immediate on his knees :
Which on thy royal party granted once,
His glittering arms he will commend to rust,
His barbed steeds to stables, and his heart
To faithful service of your majesty.
This swears he, as he is a prince, is just ;
And, as I am a gentleman, I credit him.   120
  K. Rich. Northumberland, say,—thus the king returns :—
His noble cousin is right welcome hither ;
And all the number of his fair demands
Shall be accomplish'd without contradiction.
With all the gracious utterance thou hast,
Speak to his gentle hearing kind commends.—
     [Northumberland *retires to* Bolingbroke.
[*To* Aumerle.] We do debase ourself, cousin, do we not,
To look so poorly, and to speak so fair ?
Shall we call back Northumberland, and send
Defiance to the traitor, and so die ?   130
  Aum. No, good my lord : let 's fight with gentle words,
Till time lend friends, and friends their helpful swords.
  K. Rich. O God ! O God ! that e'er this tongue of mine,
That laid the sentence of dread banishment
On yon proud man, should take it off again
With words of sooth ! O ! that I were as great
As is my grief, or lesser than my name,
Or that I could forget what I have been,
Or not remember what I must be now !
Swell'st thou, proud heart ? I 'll give thee scope to beat,
Since foes have scope to beat both thee and me.   141
  Aum. Northumberland comes back from Bolingbroke.
  K. Rich. What must the king do now ? Must he submit ?
The king shall do it. Must he be depos'd ?
The king shall be contented. Must he lose
The name of king ? o' God's name, let it go :
I 'll give my jewels for a set of beads,
My gorgeous palace for a hermitage,
My gay apparel for an alms-man's gown,
My figur'd goblets for a dish of wood,   150
My sceptre for a palmer's walking-staff,
My subjects for a pair of carved saints,
And my large kingdom for a little grave,
A little little grave, an obscure grave ;
Or I 'll be buried in the king's highway,
Some way of common trade, where subjects' feet
May hourly trample on their sovereign's head ;
For on my heart they tread, now whilst I live,
And, buried once, why not upon my head ?—
Aumerle, thou weep'st ; my tender-hearted cousin !—   161
We 'll make foul weather with despised tears ;
Our sighs and they shall lodge the summer corn,
And make a dearth in this revolting land.
Or shall we play the wantons with our woes,
And make some pretty match with shedding tears ?
As thus ;—to drop them still upon one place,
Till they have fretted us a pair of graves
Within the earth ; and, therein laid,—" There lies
Two kinsmen, digg'd their graves with weeping eyes."

Would not this ill do well?—Well, well, I see   170
I talk but idly, and you mock at me.—
Most mighty prince, my Lord Northumberland,
What says King Bolingbroke? will his majesty
Give Richard leave to live till Richard die?
You make a leg, and Bolingbroke says—ay.
    North. My lord, in the base court he doth attend
To speak with you; may 't please you to come down?
    K. Rich. Down, down, I come; like glistering
                Phaeton,
Wanting the manage of unruly jades.
            [NORTHUMBERLAND *retires again to*
                            BOLINGBROKE.

K. Rich. "Fair cousin, you debase your princely knee."

In the base court? Base court, where kings grow
            base,   180
To come at traitors' calls, and do them grace.
In the base court? Come down? Down, court!
            down, king!
For night-owls shriek, where mounting larks should
            sing.   [*Exeunt from above.*
    Boling. What says his majesty?
    North.   Sorrow and grief of heart
Makes him speak fondly, like a frantic man:
Yet he is come.

    Enter King RICHARD, *and his Attendants, below.*

    Boling. Stand all apart,
And show fair duty to his majesty.—
My gracious lord,—   [*Kneeling.*
    K. Rich. Fair cousin, you debase your princely
            knee,   190
To make the base earth proud with kissing it:
Me rather had, my heart might feel your love,
Than my unpleas'd eye see your courtesy.
Up, cousin, up: your heart is up, I know,
Thus high at least, although your knee be low.
    Boling. My gracious lord, I come but for mine own.
    K. Rich. Your own is yours; and I am yours, and all.
    Boling. So far be mine, my most redoubted lord,
As my true service shall deserve your love.
    K. Rich. Well you deserve: they well deserve *to*
            have.   200

That know the strong'st and surest way to get.—
Uncle, give me your hand: nay, dry your eyes;
Tears show their love, but want their remedies.—
Cousin, I am too young to be your father,
Though you are old enough to be my heir.
What you will have, I 'll give, and willing too;
For do we must what force will have us do.—
Set on towards London.—Cousin, is it so?
    Boling. Yea, my good lord.
    K. Rich.   Then I must not say no.
                    [*Flourish. Exeunt.*

SCENE IV.—Langley. The Duke of YORK'S Garden.

    Enter the QUEEN *and two Ladies.*

    Queen. What sport shall we devise here in this
            garden,
To drive away the heavy thought of care?
    1 *Lady.* Madam, we 'll play at bowls.
    Queen. 'T will make me think the world is full of
            rubs,
And that my fortune runs against the bias.
    1 *Lady.* Madam, we 'll dance.
    Queen. My legs can keep no measure in delight,
When my poor heart no measure keeps in grief:
Therefore, no dancing, girl; some other sport.
    1 *Lady.* Madam, we 'll tell tales.   10
    Queen. Of sorrow, or of joy?
    1 *Lady.* Of either, madam.
    Queen. Of neither, girl;
For if of joy, being altogether wanting,
It doth remember me the more of sorrow;
Or if of grief, being altogether had,
It adds more sorrow to my want of joy;
For what I have, I need not to repeat,
And what I want, it boots not to complain.
    1 *Lady.* Madam, I 'll sing.
    Queen.   'T is well that thou hast cause:
But thou shouldst please me better, wouldst thou weep.
    1 *Lady.* I could weep, madam, would it do you
            good.   22
    Queen. And I could sing, would weeping do me
            good,
And never borrow any tear of thee:
But stay, here come the gardeners.
Let 's step into the shadow of these trees.
My wretchedness unto a row of pins,
They 'll talk of state; for every one doth so
Against a change: woe is forerun with woe.
                    [QUEEN *and Ladies retire.*

    Enter a Gardener and two Servants.

    Gard. Go, bind thou up yond dangling apricocks, 36
Which, like unruly children, make their sire
Stoop with oppression of their prodigal weight:
Give some supportance to the bending twigs.—
Go thou, and like an executioner
Cut off the heads of too-fast-growing sprays,
That look too lofty in our commonwealth:
All must be even in our government.—
You thus employ'd, I will go root away
The noisome weeds, that without profit suck
The soil's fertility from wholesome flowers.   40
    1 *Serv.* Why should we, in the compass of a pale,
Keep law, and form, and due proportion,
Showing, as in a model, our firm estate,
When our sea-walled garden, the whole land,
Is full of weeds, her fairest flowers chok'd up,
Her fruit-trees all unprun'd, her hedges ruin'd,
Her knots disorder'd, and her wholesome herbs
Swarming with caterpillars?
    Gard.   Hold thy peace.
He that hath suffer'd this disorder'd spring,
Hath now himself met with the fall of leaf: 50
The weeds that his broad-spreading leaves did shelter,
That seem'd in eating him to hold him up,
Are pluck'd up, root and all, by Bolingbroke;
I mean, the Earl of Wiltshire, Bushy, Green.
    1 *Serv.* What! are they dead?
    Gard.   They are; and Bolingbroke
Hath seiz'd the wasteful king.—O! what pity is it,

That he had not so trimm'd and dress'd his land,
As we this garden! We at time of year
Do wound the bark, the skin of our fruit-trees,
Lest, being over-proud in sap and blood,   60
With too much riches it confound itself :
Had he done so to great and growing men,
They might have liv'd to bear, and he to taste
Their fruits of duty. Superfluous branches
We lop away, that bearing boughs may live :
Had he done so, himself had borne the crown,
Which waste of idle hours hath quite thrown down.
  1 Serv. What! think you then, the king shall be
    depos'd?
  Gard. Depress'd he is already ; and depos'd,
'T is doubt, he will be. Letters came last night   70
To a dear friend of the good Duke of York's,
That tell black tidings.
  Queen. O! I am press'd to death through want of
    speaking.   [*Coming forward.*
Thou, old Adam's likeness, set to dress this garden,
How dares thy harsh-rude tongue sound this unpleas-
    ing news?
What Eve, what serpent hath suggested thee
To make a second fall of cursed man?
Why dost thou say King Richard is depos'd?
Dar'st thou, thou little better thing than earth,
Divine his downfall? Say, where, when, and how 80
Cam'st thou by these ill tidings? speak, thou wretch.
  Gard. Pardon me, madam : little joy have I,
To breathe these news, yet what I say is true.
King Richard, he is in the mighty hold
Of Bolingbroke ; their fortunes both are weigh'd :
In your lord's scale is nothing but himself,
And some few vanities that make him light ;
But in the balance of great Bolingbroke,
Besides himself, are all the English peers,
And with that odds he weighs King Richard down. 90
Post you to London, and you 'll find it so ;
I speak no more than every one doth know.
  Queen. Nimble mischance, that art so light of
    foot,
Doth not thy embassage belong to me,
And am I last that knows it? O! thou think'st
To serve me last, that I may longest keep
Thy sorrow in my breast.—Come, ladies, go
To meet at London London's king in woe.—
What! was I born to this, that my sad look
Should grace the triumph of great Bolingbroke?— 100
Gardener, for telling me these news of woe,
Pray God the plants thou graft'st may never grow.
           [*Exeunt* QUEEN *and Ladies.*

  Gard. Poor queen ! so that thy state might be no
    worse,
I would my skill were subject to thy curse.—

Gard. " Pardon me, madam : little joy have I,
To breathe these news, yet what I say is true."

Here did she fall a tear ; here, in this place,
I 'll set a bank of rue, sour herb of grace ;
Rue, even for ruth, here shortly shall be seen,
In the remembrance of a weeping queen.   [*Exeunt.*

ACT IV.

SCENE I.—London. Westminster Hall.

The Lords Spiritual on the right side of the throne ; the Lords Temporal on the left ; the Commons below.

Enter BOLINGBROKE, AUMERLE, SURREY, NORTHUMBERLAND, PERCY, FITZWATER, *another Lord, the Bishop of* CARLISLE, *the Abbot of* WESTMINSTER, *and Attendants. Officers behind, with* BAGOT.

  Bolingbroke.
CALL forth Bagot.—
Now, Bagot, freely speak thy mind,
  What thou dost know of noble Gloster's
    death,
Who wrought it with the king, and who
    perform'd
  The bloody office of his timeless end.
  Bagot. Then set before my face the Lord Aumerle.

  Boling. Cousin, stand forth, and look upon that
    man.
  Bagot. My Lord Aumerle, I know your daring tongue
Scorns to unsay what once it hath deliver'd.
In that dead time when Gloster's death was plotted, 10
I heard you say,—" Is not my arm of length,
That reacheth from the restful English court
As far as Calais, to mine uncle's head ?"
Amongst much other talk, that very time,

I heard you say, that you had rather refuse
The offer of an hundred thousand crowns,
Than Bolingbroke's return to England ;
Adding withal, how blest this land would be
In this your cousin's death.
   Aum.   Princes, and noble lords,
What answer shall I make to this base man ?   20
Shall I so much dishonour my fair stars,
On equal terms to give him chastisement?
Either I must, or have mine honour soil'd
With the attainder of his slanderous lips.—
There is my gage, the manual seal of death,
That marks thee out for hell : I say, thou liest,
And will maintain, what thou hast said, is false,
In thy heart-blood, though being all too base
To stain the temper of my knightly sword.
   Boling. Bagot, forbear : thou shalt not take it up. 30
   Aum. Excepting one, I would he were the best
In all this presence, that hath mov'd me so.
   Fitz. If that thy valour stand on sympathies,
There is my gage, Aumerle, in gage to thine.
By that fair sun which shows me where thou stand'st,
I heard thee say, and vauntingly thou spak'st it,
That thou wert cause of noble Gloster's death.
If thou deny'st it twenty times, thou liest ;
And I will turn thy falsehood to thy heart,
Where it was forged, with my rapier's point.   40
   Aum. Thou dar'st not, coward, live to see that day.
   Fitz. Now, by my soul, I would it were this hour.
   Aum. Fitzwater, thou art damn'd to hell for this.
   Percy. Aumerle, thou liest ; his honour is as true
In this appeal, as thou art all unjust ;
And, that thou art so, there I throw my gage,
To prove it on thee to the extremest point
Of mortal breathing. Seize it, if thou dar'st.
   Aum. An if I do not, may my hands rot off,
And never brandish more revengeful steel   50
Over the glittering helmet of my foe !
   Lord. I task the earth to the like, forsworn Aumerle ;
And spur thee on with full as many lies
As may be holla'd in thy treacherous ear
From sun to sun. There is my honour's pawn :
Engage it to the trial, if thou dar'st.
   Aum. Who sets me else ? by Heaven, I 'll throw at all.
I have a thousand spirits in one breast,
To answer twenty thousand such as you.
   Surrey. My Lord Fitzwater, I do remember well 60
The very time Aumerle and you did talk.
   Fitz. 'T is very true : you were in presence then ;
And you can witness with me, this is true.
   Surrey. As false, by Heaven, as Heaven itself is true.
   Fitz. Surrey, thou liest.
   Surrey.   Dishonourable boy !
That lie shall lie so heavy on my sword,
That it shall render vengeance and revenge,
Till thou, the lie-giver, and that lie, do lie
In earth as quiet as thy father's skull.
In proof whereof, there is my honour's pawn :   70
Engage it to the trial, if thou dar'st.
   Fitz. How fondly dost thou spur a forward horse !
If I dare eat, or drink, or breathe, or live,
I dare meet Surrey in a wilderness,
And spit upon him, whilst I say, he lies,
And lies, and lies. There is my bond of faith,
To tie thee to my strong correction.
As I intend to thrive in this new world,
Aumerle is guilty of my true appeal.
Besides, I heard the banish'd Norfolk say,   80
That thou, Aumerle, didst send two of thy men
To execute the noble duke at Calais.
   Aum. Some honest Christian trust me with a gage.
That Norfolk lies, here do I throw down this,
If he may be repeal'd to try his honour.
   Boling. These differences shall all rest under gage,
Till Norfolk be repeal'd : repeal'd he shall be,
And, though mine enemy, restor'd again
To all his lands and signories ; when he 's return'd,
Against Aumerle we will enforce his trial.   90
   Bishop. That honourable day shall ne'er be seen.
Many a time hath banish'd Norfolk fought

For Jesu Christ in glorious Christian field,
Streaming the ensign of the Christian cross,
Against black pagans, Turks, and Saracens ;
And, toil'd with works of war, retir'd himself
To Italy, and there at Venice gave
His body to that pleasant country's earth,
And his pure soul unto his captain Christ,
Under whose colours he had fought so long.   100
   Boling. Why, bishop, is Norfolk dead ?
   Bishop. As surely as I live, my lord.
   Boling. Sweet peace conduct his sweet soul to the bosom
Of good old Abraham !—Lords appellants,
Your differences shall all rest under gage,
Till we assign you to your days of trial.

      Enter YORK, *attended.*

   York. Great Duke of Lancaster, I come to thee
From plume-pluck'd Richard, who with willing soul
Adopts thee heir, and his high sceptre yields
To the possession of thy royal hand.   110
Ascend his throne, descending now from him,
And long live Henry, of that name the fourth !
   Boling. In God's name, I 'll ascend the regal throne.
   Bishop. Marry, God forbid !—
Worst in this royal presence may I speak,
Yet best beseeming me to speak the truth.
Would God, that any in this noble presence
Were enough noble to be upright judge
Of noble Richard : then true nobless would
Learn him forbearance from so foul a wrong.   120
What subject can give sentence on his king ?
And who sits here that is not Richard's subject ?
Thieves are not judg'd, but they are by to hear,
Although apparent guilt be seen in them ;
And shall the figure of God's majesty,
His captain, steward, deputy elect,
Anointed, crowned, planted many years,
Be judg'd by subject and inferior breath,
And he himself not present ? O ! forfend it, God,
That, in a Christian climate, souls refin'd   130
Should show so heinous, black, obscene a deed !
I speak to subjects, and a subject speaks,
Stirr'd up by God thus boldly for his king.
My Lord of Hereford here, whom you call king,
Is a foul traitor to proud Hereford's king ;
And if you crown him, let me prophesy,
The blood of English shall manure the ground,
And future ages groan for this foul act ;
Peace shall go sleep with Turks and infidels,
And in this seat of peace tumultuous wars   140
Shall kin with kin, and kind with kind confound ;
Disorder, horror, fear, and mutiny,
Shall here inhabit, and this land be call'd
The field of Golgotha and dead men's skulls.
O ! if you raise this house against this house,
It will the wofullest division prove,
That ever fell upon this cursed earth.
Prevent it, resist it, let it not be so,
Lest child, child's children, cry against you— woe !
   North. Well have you argu'd, sir ; and, for your pains,   150
Of capital treason we arrest you here.
My Lord of Westminster, be it your charge
To keep him safely till his day of trial.—
May it please you, lords, to grant the commons' suit ?
   Boling. Fetch hither Richard, that in common view
He may surrender : so we shall proceed
Without suspicion.
   York.   I will be his conduct. [*Exit.*
   Boling. Lords, you that here are under our arrest,
Procure your sureties for your days of answer.—
[*To the Bishop.*] Little are we beholding to your love,
And little look'd for at your helping hands.   161

    Re-enter YORK, *with King* RICHARD, *and Officers*
       bearing the crown, &c.

   K. Rich. Alack ! why am I sent for to a king,
Before I have shook off the regal thoughts
Wherewith I reign'd ? I hardly yet have learn'd
To insinuate, flatter, bow, and bend my limbs :

Give sorrow leave awhile to tutor me
To this submission. Yet I well remember
The favours of these men : were they not mine?
Did they not sometime cry, All hail! to me?
So Judas did to Christ : but he, in twelve,   170
Found truth in all but one ; I, in twelve thousand,
  none.
God save the king!—Will no man say, Amen?
Am I both priest and clerk? well then, Amen.
God save the king! although I be not he ;
And yet, Amen, if Heaven do think him me.—
To do what service am I sent for hither?
  York. To do that office, of thine own good will,
Which tired majesty did make thee offer,
The resignation of thy state and crown
To Harry Bolingbroke.   180
  K. Rich. Give me the crown.—Here, cousin, seize
  the crown ;
Here, cousin,
On this side my hand, and on that side, thine.
Now is this golden crown like a deep well,
That owes two buckets filling one another ;
The emptier ever dancing in the air,
The other down, unseen, and full of water :
That bucket down, and full of tears, am I,
Drinking my griefs, whilst you mount up on high.
  Boling. I thought you had been willing to resign. 190
  K. Rich. My crown, I am ; but still my griefs are
  mine.
You may my glories and my state depose,
But not my griefs : still am I king of those.
  Boling. Part of your cares you give me with your
  crown.
  K. Rich. Your cares set up do not pluck my cares
  down.
My care is loss of care, by old care done :
Your care is gain of care, by new care won :
The cares I give, I have, though given away ;
They tend the crown, yet still with me they stay.
  Boling. Are you contented to resign the crown? 200
  K. Rich. Ay, no ;—no, ay ;—for I must nothing be ;
Therefore no no, for I resign to thee.
Now mark me how I will undo myself :—
I give this heavy weight from off my head,
And this unwieldy sceptre from my hand,
The pride of kingly sway from out my heart ;
With mine own tears I wash away my balm,
With mine own hands I give away my crown,
With mine own tongue deny my sacred state,
With mine own breath release all duty's rites :   210
All pomp and majesty I do forswear ;
My manors, rents, revenues, I forego ;
My acts, decrees, and statutes, I deny :
God pardon all oaths that are broke to me !
God keep all vows unbroke, that swear to thee !
Make me, that nothing have, with nothing griev'd,
And thou with all pleas'd, that hast all achiev'd !
Long may'st thou live in Richard's seat to sit,
And soon lie Richard in an earthy pit !
God save King Henry, unking'd Richard says,   220
And send him many years of sunshine days !—
What more remains?
  North. [*Offering a paper.*] No more, but that you
  read
These accusations, and these grievous crimes,
Committed by your person, and your followers,
Against the state and profit of this land ;
That, by confessing them, the souls of men
May deem that you are worthily depos'd.
  K. Rich. Must I do so? and must I ravel out
My weav'd-up follies? Gentle Northumberland,   230
If thy offences were upon record,
Would it not shame thee, in so fair a troop,
To read a lecture of them? If thou wouldst,
There shouldst thou find one heinous article,
Containing the deposing of a king.
And cracking the strong warrant of an oath,
Mark'd with a blot, damn'd in the book of Heaven.—
Nay, all of you, that stand and look upon me,
Whilst that my wretchedness doth bait myself,
Though some of you, with Pilate, wash your hands, 240
Showing an outward pity ; yet you Pilates

Have here deliver'd me to my sour cross,
And water cannot wash away your sin.
  North. My lord, despatch : read o'er these articles.
  K. Rich. Mine eyes are full of tears, I cannot see ;
And yet salt water blinds them not so much,
But they can see a sort of traitors here.
Nay, if I turn mine eyes upon myself,
I find myself a traitor with the rest ;
For I have given here my soul's consent,   250
To undeck the pompous body of a king ;
Made glory base, and sovereignty a slave,
Proud majesty a subject, state a peasant.
  North. My lord,—
  K. Rich. No lord of thine, thou haught insulting
  man,
Nor no man's lord : I have no name, no title,—
No, not that name was given me at the font,—
But 'tis usurp'd.—Alack, the heavy day !
That I have worn so many winters out,
And know not now what name to call myself.   260
O ! that I were a mockery king of snow,
Standing before the sun of Bolingbroke,
To melt myself away in water-drops !—
Good king,—great king,—and yet not greatly good,
An if my word be sterling yet in England,
Let it command a mirror hither straight,
That it may show me what a face I have,
Since it is bankrupt of his majesty.
  Boling. Go some of you, and fetch a looking-glass.
                               [*Exit an Attendant.*
  North. Read o'er this paper, while the glass doth
  come.   270
  K. Rich. Fiend ! thou torment'st me ere I come to
  hell.
  Boling. Urge it no more, my Lord Northumberland.
  North. The commons will not then be satisfied.
  K. Rich. They shall be satisfied : I 'll read enough,
When I do see the very book indeed,
Where all my sins are writ, and that 's—myself.

Re-enter Attendant, with a glass.

Give me that glass, and therein will I read.—
No deeper wrinkles yet? Hath sorrow struck
So many blows upon this face of mine,
And made no deeper wounds?—O flattering glass ! 280
Like to my followers in prosperity,
Thou dost beguile me. Was this face the face,
That every day under his household roof
Did keep ten thousand men? Was this the face,
That like the sun did make beholders wink ?
Was this the face, that fac'd so many follies,
And was at last outfac'd by Bolingbroke ?
A brittle glory shineth in this face :
As brittle as the glory is the face ;
                [*Dashes the glass against the ground.*
For there it is, crack'd in a hundred shivers.—   290
Mark, silent king, the moral of this sport,
How soon my sorrow hath destroy'd my face.
  Boling. The shadow of your sorrow hath destroy'd
The shadow of your face.
  K. Rich.   Say that again.
The shadow of my sorrow ? Ha ! let 's see :—
'Tis very true, my grief lies all within ;—
And these external manners of laments
Are merely shadows to the unseen grief,
That swells with silence in the tortur'd soul ;
There lies the substance : and I thank thee, king, 300
For thy great bounty, that not only giv'st
Me cause to wail, but teachest me the way
How to lament the cause. I 'll beg one boon,
And then be gone and trouble you no more.
Shall I obtain it?
  Boling.   Name it, fair cousin.
  K. Rich. Fair cousin ? I am greater than a king ;
For, when I was a king, my flatterers
Were then but subjects ; being now a subject,
I have a king here to my flatterer.
Being so great, I have no need to beg.   310
  Boling. Yet ask.
  K. Rich. And shall I have it?
  Boling. You shall.
  K. Rich. Why then, give me leave to go.

Boling. Whither?

K. Rich. Whither you will, so I were from your
sights.

Boling. Go, some of you; convey him to the Tower.

K. Rich. O, good! Convey?—Conveyers are you
all,
That rise thus nimbly by a true king's fall.

                  [Exeunt King RICHARD *and Guard.*

Boling. On Wednesday next we solemnly set down
Our coronation: lords, prepare yourselves.   321

          [Exeunt all but the Abbot, Bishop of CARLISLE,
          and AUMERLE.

Abbot. A woful pageant have we here beheld.

Bishop. The woe's to come: the children yet unborn
Shall feel this day as sharp to them as thorn.

Aum. You holy clergymen, is there no plot
To rid the realm of this pernicious blot?

Abbot. My lord, before I freely speak my mind
   herein,
You shall not only take the sacrament
To bury mine intents, but also to effect
Whatever I shall happen to devise.   330
I see your brows are full of discontent,
Your hearts of sorrow, and your eyes of tears:
Come home with me to supper; I will lay
A plot, shall show us all a merry day.   *[Exeunt.*

ACT V.

SCENE I.—London. A Street leading to the Tower.

Enter QUEEN *and Attendants.*

Queen.

THIS way the king will come: this is the
   way
To Julius Cæsar's ill-erected tower,
To whose flint bosom my condemned lord
Is doom'd a prisoner by proud Boling-
   broke.
Here let us rest, if this rebellious earth
Have any resting for her true king's queen.

Enter King RICHARD *and Guards.*

But soft, but see, or rather do not see,
My fair rose wither: yet look up, behold,
That you in pity may dissolve to dew,
And wash him fresh again with true-love tears.— 10
Ah! thou, the model where old Troy did stand,
Thou man of honour, thou King Richard's tomb,
And not King Richard, thou most beauteous inn,
Why should hard-favour'd grief be lodg'd in thee,
When triumph is become an ale-house guest?

K. Rich. Join not with grief, fair woman, do not so,
To make my end too sudden: learn, good soul,
To think our former state a happy dream;
From which awak'd, the truth of what we are
Shows us but this. I am sworn brother, sweet,   20
To grim necessity; and he and I
Will keep a league till death. Hie thee to France,
And cloister thee in some religious house:
Our holy lives must win a new world's crown,
Which our profane hours here have stricken down.

Queen. What! is my Richard both in shape and mind
Transform'd and weakened? Hath Bolingbroke
Depos'd thine intellect? hath he been in thy heart?
The lion, dying, thrusteth forth his paw,
And wounds the earth, if nothing else, with rage   30
To be o'erpower'd; and wilt thou, pupil-like,
Take thy correction mildly? kiss the rod,
And fawn on rage with base humility,
Which art a lion, and a king of beasts?

K. Rich. A king of beasts, indeed; if aught but
   beasts,
I had been still a happy king of men.
Good sometime queen, prepare thee hence for France:
Think I am dead, and that even here thou tak'st,
As from my death-bed, my last living leave.
In winter's tedious nights sit by the fire   40
With good old folks, and let them tell thee tales
Of woful ages, long ago betid;
And, ere thou bid good night, to quit their grief,

Tell thou the lamentable fall of me,
And send the hearers weeping to their beds

K. Rich. "I am sworn brother, sweet, to grim necessity."

For why the senseless brands will sympathise
The heavy accent of thy moving tongue,
And in compassion weep the fire out;
And some will mourn in ashes, some coal-black,
For the deposing of a rightful king.   50

Enter NORTHUMBERLAND, *attended.*

North. My lord, the mind of Bolingbroke is chang'd:

You must to Pomfret, not unto the Tower.—
And, madam, there is order ta'en for you:
With all swift speed you must away to France.
　K. Rich. Northumberland, thou ladder, wherewithal
The mounting Bolingbroke ascends my throne,
The time shall not be many hours of age
More than it is, ere foul sin gathering head
Shall break into corruption. Thou shalt think,
Though he divide the realm, and give thee half,　60
It is too little, helping him to all;
He shall think, that thou, which know'st the way
To plant unrightful kings, wilt know again,
Being ne'er so little urg'd, another way
To pluck him headlong from the usurped throne.
The love of wicked friends converts to fear;
That fear to hate; and hate turns one, or both,
To worthy danger and deserved death.
　North. My guilt be on my head, and there an end.
Take leave, and part, for you must part forthwith.　70
　K. Rich. Doubly divorc'd!—Bad men, ye violate
A two-fold marriage; 'twixt my crown and me,
And then betwixt me and my married wife.—
Let me unkiss the oath 'twixt thee and me;
And yet not so, for with a kiss 't was made.
Part us, Northumberland! I towards the north,
Where shivering cold and sickness pines the clime;
My wife to France: from whence, set forth in pomp,
She came adorned hither like sweet May,
Sent back like Hallowmas, or short'st of day.　80
　Queen. And must we be divided? must we part?
　K. Rich. Ay, hand from hand, my love, and heart
from heart.
　Queen. Banish us both, and send the king with me.
　North. That were some love, but little policy.
　Queen. Then whither he goes, thither let me go.
　K. Rich. So two, together weeping, make one woe.
Weep thou for me in France, I for thee here;
Better far off, than near, be ne'er the near'.
Go, count thy way with sighs, I mine with groans.
　Queen. So longest way shall have the longest moans.
　K. Rich. Twice for one step I'll groan, the way
being short,　91
And piece the way out with a heavy heart.
Come, come, in wooing sorrow let's be brief,
Since, wedding it, there is such length in grief.
One kiss shall stop our mouths, and dumbly part:
Thus give I mine, and thus take I thy heart. [*They kiss.*
　Queen. Give me mine own again; 't were no good
part,
To take on me to keep, and kill thy heart.
　　　　　　　　　　　　　　[*They kiss again.*
So, now I have mine own again, be gone,
That I may strive to kill it with a groan.　100
　K. Rich. We make woe wanton with this fond
delay:
Once more, adieu; the rest let sorrow say. [*Exeunt.*

SCENE II.—London. A Room in the Duke of YORK's
Palace.

Enter YORK *and the* DUCHESS.

　Duch. My lord, you told me, you would tell the rest,
When weeping made you break the story off,
Of our two cousins coming into London.
　York. Where did I leave?
　Duch.　　　　　At that sad stop, my lord,
Where rude misgovern'd hands, from windows' tops,
Threw dust and rubbish on King Richard's head.
　York. Then, as I said, the duke, great Bolingbroke,
Mounted upon a hot and fiery steed,
Which his aspiring rider seem'd to know,
With slow but stately pace kept on his course,　10
While all tongues cried—"God save thee, Boling-
broke!"
You would have thought the very windows spake,
So many greedy looks of young and old
Through casements darted their desiring eyes
Upon his visage; and that all the walls
With painted imagery had said at once,—
"Jesu preserve thee! welcome, Bolingbroke!"

Whilst he, from one side to the other turning,
Bareheaded, lower than his proud steed's neck,
Bespake them thus,—"I thank you, countrymen:"　20
And thus still doing, thus he pass'd along.
　Duch. Alas, poor Richard! where rode he the whilst?
　York. As in a theatre, the eyes of men,
After a well-grac'd actor leaves the stage,
Are idly bent on him that enters next,
Thinking his prattle to be tedious;
Even so, or with much more contempt, men's eyes
Did scowl on Richard: no man cried, God save him;
No joyful tongue gave him his welcome home;
But dust was thrown upon his sacred head,　30
Which with such gentle sorrow he shook off,
His face still combating with tears and smiles,
The badges of his grief and patience,
That had not God, for some strong purpose, steel'd
The hearts of men, they must perforce have melted,
And barbarism itself have pitied him.
But Heaven hath a hand in these events,
To whose high will we bound our calm contents.
To Bolingbroke are we sworn subjects now,
Whose state and honour I for aye allow.　40
　Duch. Here comes my son Aumerle.
　York.　　　　　Aumerle that was;
But that is lost for being Richard's friend,
And, madam, you must call him Rutland now.
I am in parliament pledge for his truth
And lasting fealty to the new-made king.

Enter AUMERLE.

　Duch. Welcome, my son. Who are the violets now,
That strew the green lap of the new-come spring?
　Aum. Madam, I know not, nor I greatly care not;
God knows, I had as lief be none, as one.
　York. Well, bear you well in this new spring of time,
Lest you be cropp'd before you come to prime.　51
What news from Oxford? hold those justs and
triumphs?
　Aum. For aught I know, my lord, they do.
　York. You will be there, I know.
　Aum. If God prevent not, I purpose so.
　York. What seal is that, that hangs without thy
bosom?
Yea, look'st thou pale? let me see the writing.
　Aum. My lord, 'tis nothing.
　York.　　　　　No matter then who sees it:
I will be satisfied, let me see the writing.
　Aum. I do beseech your grace to pardon me.　60
It is a matter of small consequence,
Which for some reasons I would not have seen.
　York. Which for some reasons, sir, I mean to see.
I fear, I fear,—
　Duch.　　　　　What should you fear?
'T is nothing but some bond that he is enter'd into
For gay apparel 'gainst the triumph day.
　York. Bound to himself? what doth he with a bond
That he is bound to? Wife, thou art a fool.—
Boy, let me see the writing.
　Aum. I do beseech you, pardon me: I may not show
it.　70
　York. I will be satisfied: let me see it, I say.
　　　　　　　　　[*Snatches it, and reads.*
Treason! foul treason!—Villain! traitor! slave!
　Duch. What is the matter, my lord?
　York. Ho! who is within there?

Enter a Servant.

　　　　　　　　　　Saddle my horse.
God for his mercy! what treachery is here!
　Duch. Why, what is it, my lord?
　York. Give me my boots, I say: saddle my horse.—
　　　　　　　　　　[*Exit Servant.*
Now, by mine honour, by my life, my troth,
I will appeach the villain.
　Duch.　　　　　What's the matter?
　York. Peace, foolish woman.　80
　Duch. I will not peace.—What is the matter,
Aumerle?
　Aum. Good mother, be content: it is no more
Than my poor life must answer.
　Duch.　　　　　Thy life answer?

York. Bring me my boots : I will unto the king.

Re-enter Servant, with boots.

Duch. Strike him, Aumerle.—Poor boy, thou art
          amaz'd.—
Hence, villain ! never more come in my sight.—
                              [*Exit Servant.*
York. Give me my boots, I say.
Duch. Why, York, what wilt thou do ?
Wilt thou not hide the trespass of thine own ?
Have we more sons, or are we like to have ?   &0
Is not my teeming date drunk up with time,
And wilt thou pluck my fair son from mine age,
And rob me of a happy mother's name ?
Is he not like thee ? is he not thine own ?
York. Thou fond, mad woman,
Wilt thou conceal this dark conspiracy ?
A dozen of them here have ta'en the sacrament,
And interchangeably set down their hands,
To kill the king at Oxford.
Duch.   He shall be none ;
We 'll keep him here : then, what is that to him ?   100
York. Away, fond woman ! were he twenty times
My son, I would appeach him.
Duch.   Hadst thou groan'd for him,
As I have done, thou wouldst be more pitiful.
But now I know thy mind : thou dost suspect,
That I have been disloyal to thy bed,
And that he is a bastard, not thy son.
Sweet York, sweet husband, be not of that mind :
He is as like thee as a man may be,
Not like to me, nor any of my kin,
And yet I love him.
York.   Make way, unruly woman ! [*Exit.*
Duch. After, Aumerle ! Mount thee upon his horse :
Spur, post, and get before him to the king,   112
And beg thy pardon ere he do accuse thee.
I 'll not be long behind ; though I be old,
I doubt not but to ride as fast as York :
And never will I rise up from the ground,
Till Bolingbroke have pardon'd thee. Away ! be gone.
                              [*Exeunt.*

SCENE III.—Windsor. A Room in the Castle.

Enter BOLINGBROKE *as King* ; PERCY, *and other
    Lords.*

Boling. Can no man tell me of my unthrifty son ?
'T is full three months, since I did see him last.
If any plague hang over us, 't is he.
I would to God, my lords, he might be found.
Inquire at London, 'mongst the taverns there,
For there, they say, he daily doth frequent,
With unrestrained loose companions,
Even such, they say, as stand in narrow lanes,
And beat our watch, and rob our passengers ;
Which he, young wanton, and effeminate boy,   10
Takes on the point of honour, to support
So dissolute a crew.
Percy.   My lord, some two days since I saw the
                  prince,
And told him of these triumphs held at Oxford.
Boling. And what said the gallant ?
Percy. His answer was,—he would unto the stews,
And from the common'st creature pluck a glove,
And wear it as a favour ; and with that
He would unhorse the lustiest challenger.
Boling. As dissolute, as desperate : yet through both
I see some sparks of better hope, which elder days   21
May happily bring forth. But who comes here ?

Enter AUMERLE.

Aum. Where is the king ?
Boling. What means our cousin, that he stares
And looks so wildly ?
Aum. God save your grace. I do beseech your
                  majesty,
To have some conference with your grace alone.
Boling. Withdraw yourselves, and leave us here
          alone.—   [*Exeunt* PERCY *and Lords.*
What is the matter with our cousin now ?

Aum. For ever may my knees grow to the earth, 30
                              [*Kneels.*
My tongue cleave to my roof within my mouth,
Unless a pardon, ere I rise, or speak.
Boling. Intended, or committed, was this fault ?
If on the first, how heinous e'er it be,
To win thy after-love, I pardon thee.
Aum. Then give me leave that I may turn the key,
That no man enter till my tale be done.
Boling. Have thy desire. [AUMERLE *locks the door.*
York. [*Within.*] My liege, beware ! look to thyself :
Thou hast a traitor in thy presence there.   40
Boling. Villain, I 'll make thee safe.   [*Drawing.*
Aum. Stay thy revengeful hand : thou hast no cause
          to fear.
York. [*Within.*] Open the door, secure, foolhardy
          king :
Shall I for love speak treason to thy face ?
Open the door, or I will break it open.
                      [BOLINGBROKE *opens the door.*

Enter YORK.

Boling. What is the matter, uncle ? speak ;
Recover breath : tell us how near is danger,
That we may arm us to encounter it.
York. Peruse this writing here, and thou shalt know 50
The treason that my haste forbids me show.
Aum. Remember, as thou read'st, thy promise past :
I do repent me ; read not my name there ;
My heart is not confederate with my hand.
York. 'T was, villain, ere thy hand did set it down.—
I tore it from the traitor's bosom, king :
Fear, and not love, begets his penitence.
Forget to pity him, lest thy pity prove
A serpent that will sting thee to the heart.
Boling. O heinous, strong, and bold conspiracy !—
O loyal father of a treacherous son !   60
Thou sheer, immaculate, and silver fountain,
From whence this stream through muddy passages
Hath held his current, and defil'd himself !
Thy overflow of good converts to bad ;
And thy abundant goodness shall excuse
This deadly blot in thy digressing son.
York. So shall my virtue be his vice's bawd,
And he shall spend mine honour with his shame,
As thriftless sons their scraping fathers' gold.
Mine honour lives when his dishonour dies,   70
Or my sham'd life in his dishonour lies :
Thou kill'st me in his life ; giving him breath,
The traitor lives, the true man 's put to death.
Duch. [*Within.*] What, ho ! my liege ! for God's
          sake, let me in.
Boling. What shrill-voic'd suppliant makes this
          eager cry ?
Duch. A woman, and thine aunt, great king ; 't is I.
Speak with me, pity me, open the door :
A beggar begs that never begg'd before.
Boling. Our scene is altered, from a serious thing,
And now chang'd to "The Beggar and the King."— 80
My dangerous cousin, let your mother in :
I know, she 's come to pray for your foul sin.
York. If thou do pardon, whosoever pray,
More sins for this forgiveness prosper may.
This fester'd joint cut off, the rest rests sound ;
This, let alone, will all the rest confound.

Enter DUCHESS.

Duch. O king ! believe not this hard-hearted man :
Love, loving not itself, none other can.
York. Thou frantic woman, what dost thou make
          here ?
Shall thy old dugs once more a traitor rear ?   90
Duch. Sweet York, be patient. Hear me, gentle
          liege.   [*Kneels.*
Boling. Rise up, good aunt.
Duch.   Not yet, I thee beseech :
For ever will I walk upon my knees,
And never see day that the happy sees,
Till thou give joy ; until thou bid me joy,
By pardoning Rutland, my transgressing boy.
Aum. Unto my mother's prayers I bend my knee.
                              [*Kneels.*

York. Against them both my true joints bended be.
[*Kneels.*
Ill may'st thou thrive, if thou grant any grace!
Duch. Pleads he in earnest? look upon his face; 100
His eyes do drop no tears, his prayers are in jest;
His words come from his mouth, ours from our
breast:
He prays but faintly, and would be denied;
We pray with heart, and soul, and all beside:
His weary joints would gladly rise, I know;
Our knees shall kneel till to the ground they grow:
His prayers are full of false hypocrisy;
Ours of true zeal and deep integrity.
Our prayers do out-pray his; then let them have
That mercy which true prayers ought to have.   110
Boling. Good aunt, stand up.
Duch.   Nay, do not say—stand up;
But, pardon first, and afterwards, stand up.
An if I were thy nurse, thy tongue to teach,
Pardon should be the first word of thy speech.
I never long'd to hear a word till now;
Say -pardon, king; let pity teach thee how:
The word is short, but not so short as sweet;
No word like pardon for kings' mouths so meet.
York. Speak it in French, king: say, *pardonnez-moi.*
Duch. Dost thou teach pardon pardon to destroy? 120
Ah! my sour husband, my hard-hearted lord,
That sett'st the word itself against the word!
Speak, pardon, as 't is current in our land!
The chopping French we do not understand.
Thine eye begins to speak, set thy tongue there,
Or in thy piteous heart plant thou thine ear,
That hearing how our plaints and prayers do pierce,
Pity may move thee pardon to rehearse.
Boling. Good aunt, stand up.
Duch.   I do not sue to stand:
Pardon is all the suit I have in hand.   130
Boling. I pardon him, as God shall pardon me.
Duch. O happy vantage of a kneeling knee!
Yet am I sick for fear: speak it again;
Twice saying pardon doth not pardon twain,
But makes one pardon strong.
Boling.   With all my heart
I pardon him.
Duch. A god on earth thou art.
Boling. But for our trusty brother-in-law, and the
abbot,
With all the rest of that consorted crew,
Destruction straight shall dog them at the heels.—
Good uncle, help to order several powers   140
To Oxford, or where'er these traitors are:
They shall not live within this world, I swear;
But I will have them, if I once know where.
Uncle, farewell,—and cousin too, adieu:
Your mother well hath pray'd, and prove you true.
Duch. Come, my old son: I pray God make thee
new.   [*Exeunt.*

SCENE IV.

Enter Sir PIERCE *of* EXTON *and a Servant.*

Exton. Didst thou not mark the king, what words
he spake?
"Have I no friend will rid me of this living fear?"
Was it not so?
Serv.   Those were his very words.
Exton. "Have I no friend?" quoth he: he spake it
twice,
And urg'd it twice together, did he not?
Serv. He did.
Exton. And, speaking it, he wistly look'd on me,
As who should say,—I would thou wert the man
That would divorce this terror from my heart,
Meaning the king at Pomfret. Come, let's go: 10
I am the king's friend, and will rid his foe. [*Exeunt.*

SCENE V.—Pomfret. The Dungeon of the Castle.

Enter King RICHARD.

K. Rich. I have been studying how I may compare
This prison, where I live, unto the world:

And for because the world is populous,
And here is not a creature but myself,
I cannot do it; yet I 'll hammer it out.
My brain I 'll prove the female to my soul;
My soul, the father: and these two beget
A generation of still-breeding thoughts,
And these same thoughts people this little world,
In humours like the people of this world,   10
For no thought is contented. The better sort,
As thoughts of things divine, are intermix'd
With scruples, and do set the word itself
Against the word:
As thus,—"Come, little ones;" and then again,—
"It is as hard to come, as for a camel
To thread the postern of a needle's eye."
Thoughts tending to ambition, they do plot
Unlikely wonders: how these vain weak nails
May tear a passage through the flinty ribs   20
Of this hard world, my ragged prison walls;
And, for they cannot, die in their own pride.
Thoughts tending to content flatter themselves,
That they are not the first of fortune's slaves,
Nor shall not be the last; like silly beggars,
Who, sitting in the stocks, refuge their shame,
That many have, and others must sit there:
And in this thought they find a kind of ease,
Bearing their own misfortune on the back
Of such as have before endur'd the like.   30
Thus play I, in one person, many people,
And none contented: sometimes am I king;
Then treason makes me wish myself a beggar,
And so I am: then, crushing penury
Persuades me I was better when a king;
Then am I king'd again: and, by-and-by,
Think that I am unking'd by Bolingbroke,
And straight am nothing.—But whate'er I am,
Nor I, nor any man, that but man is,
With nothing shall be pleas'd till he be eas'd   40
With being nothing.—[*Music.*] Music do I hear?
Ha, ha! keep time.—How sour sweet music is,
When time is broke, and no proportion kept!
So is it in the music of men's lives.
And here have I the daintiness of ear,
To check time broke in a disorder'd string;
But, for the concord of my state and time,
Had not an ear to hear my true time broke.
I wasted time, and now doth time waste me;
For now hath time made me his numbering clock: 50
My thoughts are minutes; and with sighs they jar
Their watches on unto mine eyes, the outward watch,
Whereto my finger, like a dial's point,
Is pointing still, in cleansing them from tears.
Now, sir, the sound, that tells what hour it is,
Are clamorous groans, that strike upon my heart,
Which is the bell: so sighs, and tears, and groans,
Show minutes, times, and hours; but my time
Runs posting on in Bolingbroke's proud joy,
While I stand fooling here, his Jack o' the clock.   60
This music mads me: let it sound no more;
For though it hath holp madmen to their wits,
In me, it seems, it will make wise men mad.
Yet blessing on his heart that gives it me!
For 't is a sign of love, and love to Richard
Is a strange brooch in this all-hating world.

Enter Groom.

Groom. Hail, royal prince!
K. Rich.   Thanks, noble peer;
The cheapest of us is ten groats too dear.
What art thou? and how comest thou hither,
Where no man never comes, but that sad dog   70
That brings me food to make misfortune live?
Groom. I was a poor groom of thy stable, king,
When thou wert king; who, travelling towards
York,
With much ado, at length have gotten leave
To look upon my sometimes royal master's face.
O! how it yearn'd my heart, when I beheld
In London streets that coronation day,
When Bolingbroke rode on roan Barbary!
That horse that thou so often hast bestrid,
That horse that I so carefully have dress'd!   80

K. Rich. Rode he on Barbary? Tell me, gentle friend,
How went he under him?
   Groom. So proudly, as if he disdain'd the ground.
   K. Rich. So proud that Bolingbroke was on his back!

And yet I bear a burden like an ass,
Spur-gall'd, and tir'd, by jauncing Bolingbroke.

   Enter Keeper, with a dish.

   Keep. [*To the Groom.*] Fellow, give place : here is no longer stay.

K. Rich. "That hand shall burn in never-quenching fire,
That staggers thus my person."

That jade hath eat bread from my royal hand ;
This hand hath made him proud with clapping him.
Would he not stumble? would he not fall down
(Since pride must have a fall), and break the neck
Of that proud man that did usurp his back?
Forgiveness, horse ! why do I rail on thee,   90
Since thou, created to be aw'd by man,
Wast born to bear? I was not made a horse ;

   K. Rich. If thou love me, 't is time thou wert away.
   Groom. What my tongue dares not, that my heart shall say.   [*Exit.*
   Keep. My lord, will 't please you to fall to?
   K. Rich. Taste of it first, as thou art wont to do.
   Keep. My lord, I dare not : Sir Pierce of Exton, who lately came from the king, commands the contrary.

K. Rich. The devil take Henry of Lancaster, and
    thee!   102
Patience is stale, and I am weary of it.
                  [*Strikes the Keeper.*
Keep. Help, help, help!

Enter Sir PIERCE *of* EXTON, *and Servants, armed.*

    K. Rich. How now! what means death in this rude
        assault?
Villain, thine own hand yields thy death's instrument.
        [*Snatching a weapon, and killing one.*
Go thou, and fill another room in hell.
        [*He kills another:* EXTON *strikes him down.*
That hand shall burn in never-quenching fire,
That staggers thus my person.—Exton, thy fierce
    hand
Hath with the king's blood stain'd the king's own land.
Mount, mount, my soul! thy seat is up on high,   111
Whilst my gross flesh sinks downward, here to die.
                  [*Dies.*

    Exton. As full of valour as of royal blood:
Both have I spilt; O, would the deed were good!
For now the devil, that told me I did well,
Says that this deed is chronicled in hell.
This dead king to the living king I 'll bear. —
Take hence the rest, and give them burial here.
                  [*Exeunt.*

SCENE VI.—Windsor. An Apartment in the Castle.

Flourish. Enter BOLINGBROKE *and* YORK, *with
    Lords and Attendants.*

    Boling. Kind uncle York, the latest news we hear
Is, that the rebels have consum'd with fire
Our town of Cicester in Glostershire;
But whether they be ta'en, or slain, we hear not.

Enter NORTHUMBERLAND.

Welcome, my lord. What is the news?
    North. First, to thy sacred state wish I all happi-
    ness.
The next news is,—I have to London sent
The heads of Salisbury, Spencer, Blunt, and Kent.
The manner of their taking may appear
At large discoursed in this paper here.   10
               [*Presenting a paper.*
    Boling. We thank thee, gentle Percy, for thy pains,
And to thy worth will add right worthy gains.

Enter FITZWATER.

    Fitz. My lord, I have from Oxford sent to London
The heads of Brocas and Sir Bennet Seely,
Two of the dangerous consorted traitors,
That sought at Oxford thy dire overthrow.
    Boling. Thy pains, Fitzwater, shall not be forgot;
Right noble is thy merit, well I wot.

Enter PERCY, *with the Bishop of* CARLISLE.

    Percy. The grand conspirator, Abbot of Westmin-
    ster,
With clog of conscience and sour melancholy,   20
Hath yielded up his body to the grave;
But here is Carlisle living, to abide
Thy kingly doom, and sentence of his pride.

    Boling. Carlisle, this is your doom:—
Choose out some secret place, some reverend room,
More than thou hast, and with it joy thy life;
So, as thou liv'st in peace, die free from strife:
For though mine enemy thou hast ever been,
High sparks of honour in thee have I seen.

Boling. "Exton, I thank thee not; for thou hast wrought
A deed of slander."

Enter EXTON, *with Attendants bearing a coffin.*

    Exton. Great king, within this coffin I present   30
Thy buried fear: herein all breathless lies
The mightiest of thy greatest enemies,
Richard of Bordeaux, by me hither brought.
    Boling. Exton, I thank thee not; for thou hast
    wrought
A deed of slander, with thy fatal hand,
Upon my head and all this famous land.
    Exton. From your own mouth, my lord, did I this
    deed.
    Boling. They love not poison that do poison need,
Nor do I thee: though I did wish him dead,
I hate the murderer, love him murdered.   40
The guilt of conscience take thou for thy labour,
But neither my good word, nor princely favour:
With Cain go wander through the shades of night,
And never show thy head by day nor light.—
Lords, I protest, my soul is full of woe,
That blood should sprinkle me to make me grow:
Come, mourn with me for that I do lament,
And put on sullen black, incontinent.
I 'll make a voyage to the Holy Land,
To wash this blood off from my guilty hand.   50
March sadly after; grace my mournings here,
In weeping after this untimely bier.   [*Exeunt.*

KING HENRY IV.—PART I.

DRAMATIS PERSONÆ.

King Henry the Fourth.
Henry, *Prince of Wales,* } *Sons to the King.*
Prince John of Lancaster, }
Earl of Westmoreland.
Sir Walter Blunt.
Thomas Percy, *Earl of Worcester.*
Henry Percy, *Earl of Northumberland.*
Henry Percy, *surnamed* Hotspur, *his Son.*
Edmund Mortimer, *Earl of March.*
Scroop, *Archbishop of York.*
Archibald, *Earl of Douglas.*
Owen Glendower.
Sir Richard Vernon.
Sir John Falstaff.

Sir Michael, *a Friend to the Archbishop of York.*
Poins.
Gadshill.
Peto.
Bardolph.

Lady Percy, *Wife to Hotspur, and Sister to Mortimer.*
Lady Mortimer, *Daughter to Glendower, and Wife to Mortimer.*
Mistress Quickly, *Hostess of a Tavern in Eastcheap.*

Lords, Officers, Sheriff, Vintner, Chamberlain, Drawers, Carriers, Travellers, and Attendants.

SCENE—England.

ACT I.

SCENE I.—London. An Apartment in the Palace.

Enter King Henry, Westmoreland, *Sir* Walter Blunt, *and others.*

King Henry.
So shaken as we are, so wan with care,
Find we a time for frighted peace to pant,
And breathe short-winded accents of new broils
To be commenc'd in stronds afar remote.
No more the thirsty entrance of this soil
Shall daub her lips with her own children's blood ;
No more shall trenching war channel her fields,
Nor bruise her flowerets with the armed hoofs
Of hostile paces : those opposed eyes,
Which, like the meteors of a troubled heaven,   10
All of one nature, of one substance bred,
Did lately meet in the intestine shock
And furious close of civil butchery,
Shall now, in mutual, well-beseeming ranks,
March all one way, and be no more oppos'd
Against acquaintance, kindred, and allies :
The edge of war, like an ill-sheathed knife,
No more shall cut his master. Therefore, friends,
As far as to the sepulchre of Christ,
(Whose soldier now, under whose blessed cross   20
We are impressed and engag'd to fight,)
Forthwith a power of English shall we levy,
Whose arms were moulded in their mothers' womb
To chase these pagans, in those holy fields,
Over whose acres walk'd those blessed feet,
Which, fourteen hundred years ago, were nail'd
For our advantage on the bitter cross.
But this our purpose is a twelvemonth old,
And bootless 't is to tell you, we will go :
Therefore we meet not now.—Then, let me hear   30
Of you, my gentle cousin Westmoreland,
What yesternight our council did decree,
In forwarding this dear expedience.
West : My liege, this haste was hot in question,
And many limits of the charge set down
But yesternight ; when, all athwart, there came
A post from Wales loaden with heavy news ;
Whose worst was, that the noble Mortimer,
Leading the men of Herefordshire to fight
Against the irregular and wild Glendower,   40
Was by the rude hands of that Welshman taken,
A thousand of his people butchered ;
Upon whose dead corse there was such misuse,
Such beastly, shameless transformation,
By those Welshwomen done, as may not be
Without much shame re-told or spoken of.
K. Hen. It seems then, that the tidings of this broil
Brake off our business for the Holy Land.
West. This match'd with other like, my gracious lord :
For more uneven and unwelcome news   50
Came from the north, and thus it did report :
On Holy-rood day, the gallant Hotspur there,
Young Harry Percy, and brave Archibald,
That ever-valiant and approved Scot,
At Holmedon met,
Where they did spend a sad and bloody hour,
As by discharge of their artillery,
And shape of likelihood, the news was told ;
For he that brought them, in the very heat
And pride of their contention did take horse,   60
Uncertain of the issue any way.
K. Hen. Here is a dear and true-industrious friend,
Sir Walter Blunt, new lighted from his horse,
Stain'd with the variation of each soil
Betwixt that Holmedon and this seat of ours ;
And he hath brought us smooth and welcome news.
The Earl of Douglas is discomfited ;

Ten thousand bold Scots, two-and-twenty knights,
Balk'd in their own blood, did Sir Walter see
On Holmedon's plains : of prisoners, Hotspur took   70
Mordake the Earl of Fife, and eldest son
To beaten Douglas, and the Earl of Athol,
Of Murray, Angus, and Menteith.
And is not this an honourable spoil?
A gallant prize? ha, cousin, is it not?
   West. In faith,
It is a conquest for a prince to boast of.
   K. Hen. Yea, there thou mak'st me sad, and mak'st
       me sin
In envy that my Lord Northumberland
Should be the father of so blest a son :   80
A son, who is the theme of honour's tongue ;
Amongst a grove the very straightest plant ;
Who is sweet Fortune's minion, and her pride :
Whilst I, by looking on the praise of him,
See riot and dishonour stain the brow
Of my young Harry. O! that it could be prov'd,
That some night-tripping fairy had exchang'd
In cradle-clothes our children where they lay,
And call'd mine Percy, his Plantagenet!
Then would I have his Harry, and he mine.   90
But let him from my thoughts.—What think you, coz,
Of this young Percy's pride? the prisoners,
Which he in this adventure hath surpris'd,
To his own use he keeps, and sends me word,
I shall have none but Mordake Earl of Fife.
   West. This is his uncle's teaching, this is Worcester,
Malevolent to you in all aspects ;
Which makes him prune himself, and bristle up
The crest of youth against your dignity.
   K. Hen. But I have sent for him to answer this ; 100
And, for this cause, awhile we must neglect
Our holy purpose to Jerusalem.
Cousin, on Wednesday next our council we
Will hold at Windsor : so inform the lords ;
But come yourself with speed to us again ;
For more is to be said, and to be done,
Than out of anger can be uttered.
   West. I will, my liege.   [*Exeunt.*

SCENE II.—The Same. Another Apartment in the
Palace.

Enter HENRY, *Prince of Wales, and* FALSTAFF.

   Fal. Now, Hal, what time of day is it, lad?
   P. Hen. Thou art so fat-witted, with drinking of
old sack, and unbuttoning thee after supper, and
sleeping upon benches after noon, that thou hast
forgotten to demand that truly, which thou wouldst
truly know. What a devil hast thou to do with the
time of the day? unless hours were cups of sack, and
minutes capons, and clocks the tongues of bawds, and
dials the signs of leaping-houses, and the blessed sun
himself a fair hot wench in flame-colour'd taffeta, I
see no reason why thou shouldst be so superfluous to
demand the time of the day.   12
   Fal. Indeed, you come near me, now, Hal ; for we,
that take purses, go by the moon and the seven stars,
and not by Phœbus,—he, "that wandering knight so
fair." And, I pr'ythee, sweet wag, when thou art king,
—as, God save thy grace—majesty, I should say, for
grace thou wilt have none,—
   P. Hen. What! none?
   Fal. No, by my troth ; not so much as will serve to
be prologue to an egg and butter.   21
   P. Hen. Well, how then? come roundly, roundly.
   Fal. Marry, then, sweet wag, when thou art king,
let not us, that are squires of the night's body, be
called thieves of the day's beauty : let us be Diana's
foresters, gentlemen of the shade, minions of the
moon ; and let men say, we be men of good government, being governed as the sea is, by our noble and
chaste mistress the moon, under whose countenance
we steal.   30
   P. Hen. Thou say'st well, and it holds well, too ;
for the fortune of us, that are the moon's men, doth
'ebb and flow like the sea, being governed as the sea

is, by the moon. As for proof now : a purse of gold
most resolutely snatched on Monday night, and most
dissolutely spent on Tuesday morning ; got with
swearing—lay by ; and spent with crying—bring in ;
now, in as low an ebb as the foot of the ladder, and,
by-and-by, in as high a flow as the ridge of the
gallows.   40
   Fal. By the Lord, thou say'st true, lad. And is not
my hostess of the tavern a most sweet wench?
   P. Hen. As the honey of Hybla, my old lad of the
castle. And is not a buff jerkin a most sweet robe of
durance?
   Fal. How now, how now, mad wag! what, in thy
quips, and thy quiddities? what a plague have I to do
with a buff jerkin?
   P. Hen. Why, what a pox have I to do with my
hostess of the tavern?   50
   Fal. Well, thou hast called her to a reckoning many
a time and oft.
   P. Hen. Did I ever call for thee to pay thy part?
   Fal. No ; I 'll give thee thy due, thou hast paid all
there.
   P. Hen. Yea, and elsewhere, so far as my coin
would stretch ; and, where it would not, I have used
my credit.
   Fal. Yea, and so used it, that were it not here apparent that thou art heir-apparent,—But, I pr'ythee,
sweet wag, shall there be gallows standing in England when thou art king, and resolution thus fobbed,
as it is, with the rusty curb of old father Antick the
law? Do not thou, when thou art a king, hang a
thief.
   P. Hen. No ; thou shalt.
   Fal. Shall I? O rare! By the Lord, I 'll be a brave
judge.
   P. Hen. Thou judgest false already : I mean, thou
shalt have the hanging of the thieves, and so become
a rare hangman.   71
   Fal. Well, Hal, well ; and in some sort it jumps
with my humour, as well as waiting in the court, I
can tell you.
   P. Hen. For obtaining of suits?
   Fal. Yea, for obtaining of suits, whereof the hangman hath no lean wardrobe. 'Sblood, I am as melancholy as a gib cat, or a lugged bear.
   P. Hen. Or an old lion, or a lover's lute.
   Fal. Yea, or the drone of a Lincolnshire bagpipe.
   P. Hen. What say'st thou to a hare, or the melancholy of Moor-ditch?   82
   Fal. Thou hast the most unsavoury similes, and
art, indeed, the most comparative, rascalliest,—sweet
young prince.—But, Hal, I pr'ythee, trouble me no
more with vanity. I would to God, thou and I knew
where a commodity of good names were to be bought.
An old lord of the council rated me the other day in
the street about you, sir ; but I marked him not : and
yet he talked very wisely ; but I regarded him not :
and yet he talked wisely, and in the street too. 91
   P. Hen. Thou didst well ; for wisdom cries out in
the streets, and no man regards it.
   Fal. O! thou hast damnable iteration, and art, indeed, able to corrupt a saint. Thou hast done much
harm upon me, Hal :—God forgive thee for it. Before
I knew thee, Hal, I knew nothing ; and now am I, if
a man should speak truly, little better than one of
the wicked. I must give over this life, and I will
give it over ; by the Lord, an I do not, I am a villain :
I 'll be damned for never a king's son in Christendom.
   P. Hen. Where shall we take a purse to-morrow,
Jack?   103
   Fal. 'Zounds! where thou wilt, lad, I 'll make one ;
an I do not, call me villain, and baffle me.
   P. Hen. I see a good amendment of life in thee :
from praying to purse-taking.

Enter POINS, *at a distance.*

   Fal. Why, Hal, 't is my vocation, Hal : 'tis no sin
for a man to labour in his vocation. Poins :—Now
shall we know if Gadshill have set a match.—O! if
men were to be saved by merit, what hole in hell were
hot enough for him? This is the most omnipotent
villain, that ever cried, "Stand!" to a true man.

P. Hen. Good morrow, Ned.

Poins. Good morrow, sweet Hal.—What says Monsieur Remorse? What says Sir John Sack-and-Sugar? Jack, how agrees the devil and thee about thy soul, that thou soldest him on Good Friday last, for a cup of Madeira, and a cold capon's leg?

P. Hen. Sir John stands to his word: the devil shall have his bargain, for he was never yet a breaker of proverbs; he will give the devil his due.   122

Poins. Then art thou damned for keeping thy word with the devil.

P. Hen. Else he had been damned for cozening the devil.

Poins. But, my lads, my lads, to-morrow morning, by four o'clock, early at Gadshill. There are pilgrims going to Canterbury with rich offerings, and traders riding to London with fat purses: I have visors for you all, you have horses for yourselves. Gadshill lies to-night in Rochester; I have bespoke supper to-morrow night in Eastcheap: we may do it as secure as sleep. If you will go, I will stuff your purses full of crowns; if you will not, tarry at home, and be hanged.

Fal. Hear ye, Yedward: if I tarry at home, and go not, I'll hang you for going.

Poins. You will, chops?

Fal. Hal, wilt thou make one?   140

P. Hen. Who, I rob? I a thief? not I, by my faith.

Fal. There's neither honesty, manhood, nor good fellowship in thee, nor thou cam'st not of the blood royal, if thou darest not stand for ten shillings.

P. Hen. Well then, once in my days, I'll be a madcap.

Fal. Why, that's well said.

P. Hen. Well, come what will, I'll tarry at home.

Fal. By the Lord, I'll be a traitor then, when thou art king.   150

P. Hen. I care not.

Poins. Sir John, I pr'ythee, leave the prince and me alone: I will lay him down such reasons for this adventure, that he shall go.

Fal. Well, God give thee the spirit of persuasion, and him the ears of profiting, that what thou speakest may move, and what he hears may be believed, that the true prince may (for recreation sake) prove a false thief; for the poor abuses of the time want countenance. Farewell: you shall find me in Eastcheap. 160

P. Hen. Farewell, the latter spring! Farewell, All-hallown summer!   [*Exit* FALSTAFF.

Poins. Now, my good sweet honey lord, ride with us to-morrow: I have a jest to execute, that I cannot manage alone. Falstaff, Bardolph, Peto, and Gadshill, shall rob those men that we have already waylaid: yourself and I will not be there; and when they have the booty, if you and I do not rob them, cut this head off from my shoulders.

P. Hen. But how shall we part with them in setting forth?   171

Poins. Why, we will set forth before or after them, and appoint them a place of meeting, wherein it is at our pleasure to fail; and then will they adventure upon the exploit themselves, which they shall have no sooner achieved, but we'll set upon them.

P. Hen. Yea, but 't is like that they will know us by our horses, by our habits, and by every other appointment, to be ourselves.   179

Poins. Tut! our horses they shall not see, I'll tie them in the wood; our visors we will change, after we leave them; and, sirrah, I have cases of buckram for the nonce, to immask our noted outward garments.

P. Hen. Yea, but I doubt they will be too hard for us.

Poins. Well, for two of them, I know them to be as true-bred cowards as ever turned back; and for the third, if he fight longer than he sees reason, I'll forswear arms. The virtue of this jest will be, the incomprehensible lies that this same fat rogue will tell us, when we meet at supper: how thirty at least he fought with; what wards, what blows, what extremities he endured; and in the reproof of this lies the jest.

P. Hen. Well, I'll go with thee: provide us all things necessary, and meet me to-morrow night in Eastcheap, there I'll sup. Farewell.

Poins. Farewell, my lord.   [*Exit.*

P. Hen. I know you all, and will awhile uphold
The unyok'd humour of your idleness.   200
Yet herein will I imitate the sun,
Who doth permit the base contagious clouds
To smother up his beauty from the world,
That when he please again to be himself,
Being wanted, he may be more wonder'd at,
By breaking through the foul and ugly mists
Of vapours, that did seem to strangle him.
If all the year were playing holidays,
To sport would be as tedious as to work:
But when they seldom come, they wish'd-for come, 210
And nothing pleaseth but rare accidents.
So, when this loose behaviour I throw off,
And pay the debt I never promised,
By how much better than my word I am,
By so much shall I falsify men's hopes;
And, like bright metal on a sullen ground,
My reformation, glittering o'er my fault,
Shall show more goodly, and attract more eyes
Than that which hath no foil to set it off.
I'll so offend, to make offence a skill;   220
Redeeming time, when men think least I will. [*Exit.*

SCENE III.—*The Same. Another Apartment in the Palace.*

Enter King HENRY, NORTHUMBERLAND, WORCESTER, HOTSPUR, *Sir* WALTER BLUNT, *and others.*

K. Hen. My blood hath been too cold and temperate,
Unapt to stir at these indignities,
And you have found me; for, accordingly,
You tread upon my patience: but, be sure,
I will from henceforth rather be myself,
Mighty, and to be fear'd, than my condition,
Which hath been smooth as oil, soft as young down,
And therefore lost that title of respect,
Which the proud soul ne'er pays but to the proud.

Wor. Our house, my sovereign liege, little deserves
The scourge of greatness to be used on it;   11
And that same greatness too which our own hands
Have holp to make so portly.

North. My lord,—

K. Hen. Worcester, get thee gone; for I do see
Danger and disobedience in thine eye.
O, sir, your presence is too bold and peremptory,
And majesty might never yet endure
The moody frontier of a servant brow.
You have good leave to leave us; when we need   20
Your use and counsel, we shall send for you.—
      [*Exit* WORCESTER.
[*To* NORTHUMBERLAND.] You were about to speak.

North.   Yea, my good lord.
Those prisoners in your highness' name demanded,
Which Harry Percy here at Holmedon took,
Were, as he says, not with such strength denied
As was deliver'd to your majesty:
Either envy, therefore, or misprision
Is guilty of this fault, and not my son.

Hot. My liege, I did deny no prisoners;
But, I remember, when the fight was done,   30
When I was dry with rage and extreme toil,
Breathless and faint, leaning upon my sword,
Came there a certain lord, neat and trimly dress'd,
Fresh as a bridegroom; and his chin, new reap'd,
Show'd like a stubble-land at harvest-home.
He was perfumed like a milliner,
And 'twixt his finger and his thumb he held
A pouncet-box, which ever and anon
He gave his nose, and took 't away again;
Who, therewith angry, when it next came there,   40
Took it in snuff:—and still he smil'd and talk'd;
And, as the soldiers bore dead bodies by,
He call'd them untaught knaves, unmannerly,
To bring a slovenly unhandsome corse
Betwixt the wind and his nobility.
With many holiday and lady terms

He question'd me ; among the rest, demanded
My prisoners, in your majesty's behalf.
I then, all smarting, with my wounds being cold,
To be so pester'd with a popinjay,   50
Out of my grief and my impatience
Answer'd neglectingly, I know not what,
He should, or he should not ; for he made me mad,
To see him shine so brisk, and smell so sweet,
And talk so like a waiting-gentlewoman
Of guns, and drums, and wounds, God save the mark !
And telling me, the sovereign'st thing on earth
Was parmacity for an inward bruise ;
And that it was great pity, so it was,
That villainous saltpetre should be digg'd   60
Out of the bowels of the harmless earth,
Which many a good tall fellow had destroy'd
So cowardly ; and, but for these vile guns,
He would himself have been a soldier.
This bald unjointed chat of his, my lord,
I answer'd indirectly, as I said ;
And, I beseech you, let not his report
Come current for an accusation,
Betwixt my love and your high majesty.
   Blunt. The circumstance consider'd, good my lord,
Whatever Harry Percy then had said   71
To such a person, and in such a place,
At such a time, with all the rest re-told,
May reasonably die, and never rise
To do him wrong, or any way impeach
What then he said, so he unsay it now.
   K. Hen. Why, yet he doth deny his prisoners,
But with proviso, and exception,
That we, at our own charge, shall ransom straight
His brother-in-law, the foolish Mortimer ;   80
Who, on my soul, hath wilfully betray'd
The lives of those that he did lead to fight
Against the great magician, damn'd Glendower,
Whose daughter, as we hear, the Earl of March
Hath lately married. Shall our coffers then
Be emptied to redeem a traitor home ?
Shall we buy treason, and indent with fears,
When they have lost and forfeited themselves ?
No, on the barren mountains let him starve ;
For I shall never hold that man my friend,   90
Whose tongue shall ask me for one penny cost
To ransom home revolted Mortimer.
   Hot. Revolted Mortimer !
He never did fall off, my sovereign liege,
But by the chance of war : to prove that true,
Needs no more but one tongue for all those wounds,
Those mouthed wounds, which valiantly he took,
When on the gentle Severn's sedgy bank,
In single opposition, hand to hand,
He did confound the best part of an hour   100
In changing hardiment with great Glendower.
Three times they breath'd, and three times did they
   drink,
Upon agreement, of swift Severn's flood,
Who then, affrighted with their bloody looks,
Ran fearfully among the trembling reeds,
And hid his crisp head in the hollow bank
Blood-stained with these valiant combatants.
Never did base and rotten policy
Colour her working with such deadly wounds ;
Nor never could the noble Mortimer   110
Receive so many, and all willingly :
Then let him not be slander'd with revolt.
   K. Hen. Thou dost belie him, Percy, thou dost belie
   him :
He never did encounter with Glendower.
I tell thee,
He durst as well have met the devil alone,
As Owen Glendower for an enemy.
Art thou not asham'd ? But, sirrah, henceforth
Let me not hear you speak of Mortimer.
Send me your prisoners with the speediest means, 120
Or you shall hear in such a kind from me
As will displease you.—My Lord Northumberland,
We license your departure with your son.—
Send us your prisoners, or you 'll hear of it.
   [*Exeunt King* HENRY, BLUNT, *and Train.*
   Hot. And if the devil come and roar for them,

I will not send them.—I will after straight,
And tell him so ; for I will ease my heart,
Although it be with hazard of my head.
   North. What ! drunk with choler ? stay, and pause
   awhile :
Here comes your uncle.

Hot. "Zounds ! I will speak of him."

Re-enter WORCESTER.

   Hot.   Speak of Mortimer !   130
'Zounds ! I will speak of him ; and let my soul
Want mercy, if I do not join with him :
In his behalf, I 'll empty all these veins,
And shed my dear blood drop by drop i' the dust,
But I will lift the down-trod Mortimer
As high i' the air as this unthankful king,
As this ingrate and canker'd Bolingbroke.
   North. [*To* WORCESTER.] Brother, the king hath
   made your nephew mad.
   Wor. Who struck this heat up after I was gone ?
   Hot. He will, forsooth, have all my prisoners ;   140
And when I urg'd the ransom once again
Of my wife's brother, then his cheek look'd pale,
And on my face he turn'd an eye of death,
Trembling even at the name of Mortimer.
   Wor. I cannot blame him. Was he not proclaim'd
By Richard, that dead is, the next of blood ?
   North. He was ; I heard the proclamation :
And then it was, when the unhappy king
(Whose wrongs in us God pardon !) did set forth
Upon his Irish expedition ;   150
From whence he, intercepted, did return
To be depos'd, and shortly murdered.
   Wor. And for whose death, we in the world's wide
   mouth
Live scandalis'd, and foully spoken of.
   Hot. But, soft ! I pray you, did King Richard then
Proclaim my brother Edmund Mortimer
Heir to the crown ?
   North.   He did : myself did hear it.
   Hot. Nay, then I cannot blame his cousin king,
That wish'd him on the barren mountains starve.
But shall it be that you, that set the crown   160
Upon the head of this forgetful man,
And for his sake wear the detested blot
Of murd'rous subornation, shall it be,
That you a world of curses undergo,
Being the agents, or base second means,
The cords, the ladder, or the hangman rather ?—
O ! pardon me, that I descend so low,
To show the line and the predicament,
Wherein you range under this subtle king.—
Shall it, for shame, be spoken in these days,   170
Or fill up chronicles in time to come,
That men of your nobility and power
Did gage them both in an unjust behalf
(As both of you, God pardon it ! have done),

To put down Richard, that sweet lovely rose,
And plant this thorn, this canker, Bolingbroke?
And shall it, in more shame, be further spoken,
That you are fool'd, discarded, and shook off
By him, for whom these shames ye underwent?
No! yet time serves, wherein you may redeem   180
Your banish'd honours, and restore yourselves
Into the good thoughts of the world again:
Revenge the jeering and disdain'd contempt
Of this proud king, who studies day and night
To answer all the debt he owes to you,
Even with the bloody payment of your deaths.
Therefore, I say,—
Wor.   Peace, cousin! say no more.
And now I will unclasp a secret book,
And to your quick-conceiving discontents
I 'll read you matter deep and dangerous,   190
As full of peril and adventurous spirit,
As to o'er-walk a current, roaring loud,
On the un steadfast footing of a spear.
Hot. If he fall in, good night!—or sink or swim:
Send danger from the east unto the west,
So honour cross it from the north to south,
And let them grapple:—O! the blood more stirs
To rouse a lion than to start a hare.
North. Imagination of some great exploit
Drives him beyond the bounds of patience.   200
Hot. By Heaven, methinks, it were an easy leap
To pluck bright honour from the pale-fac'd moon,
Or dive into the bottom of the deep,
Where fathom-line could never touch the ground,
And pluck up drowned honour by the locks,
So he that doth redeem her thence might wear
Without corrival all her dignities:
But out upon this half-fac'd fellowship!
Wor. He apprehends a world of figures here,
But not the form of what he should attend.—   210
Good cousin, give me audience for a while,
And list to me.
Hot.   I cry you mercy.
Wor.   Those same noble Scots,
That are your prisoners,—
Hot.   I 'll keep them all.
By God, he shall not have a Scot of them:
No, if a Scot would save his soul, he shall not.
I 'll keep them, by this hand.
Wor.   You start away,
And lend no ear unto my purposes.
Those prisoners you shall keep.
Hot.   Nay, I will: that 's flat.
He said, he would not ransom Mortimer;   220
Forbad my tongue to speak of Mortimer;
But I will find him when he lies asleep,
And in his ear I 'll holla—Mortimer!
Nay,
I 'll have a starling shall be taught to speak
Nothing but Mortimer, and give it him,
To keep his anger still in motion.
Wor. Hear you, cousin, a word.
Hot. All studies here I solemnly defy,
Save how to gall and pinch this Bolingbroke: 230
And that same sword-and-buckler Prince of Wales,
But that I think his father loves him not,
And would be glad he met with some mischance,
I would have him poison'd with a pot of ale.
Wor. Farewell, kinsman. I will talk to you,
When you are better temper'd to attend.
North. Why, what a wasp-stung and impatient fool
Art thou, to break into this woman's mood,
Tying thine ear to no tongue but thine own!

Hot. Why, look you, I am whipp'd and scourg'd
          with rods,   240
Nettled, and stung with pismires, when I hear
Of this vile politician, Bolingbroke.
In Richard's time,—what do ye call the place?—
A plague upon 't—it is in Glostershire;—
'T was where the madcap duke his uncle kept,
His uncle York,—where I first bow'd my knee
Unto this king of smiles, this Bolingbroke,
'Sblood!
When you and he came back from Ravenspurg.
North. At Berkley Castle.   250
Hot. You say true.—
Why, what a candy deal of courtesy
This fawning greyhound then did proffer me!
Look,—" when his infant fortune came to age,"
And,—" gentle Harry Percy,"—and,—" kind cousin,"—
O, the devil take such cozeners!—God forgive me!—
Good uncle, tell your tale, for I have done.
Wor. Nay, if you have not, to 't again;
We 'll stay your leisure.
Hot.   I have done, i' faith.
Wor. Then once more to your Scottish prisoners. 260
Deliver them up without their ransom straight,
And make the Douglas' son your only mean
For powers in Scotland; which, for divers reasons,
Which I shall send you written, be assur'd,
Will easily be granted.—[*To* NORTHUMBERLAND.]
          You, my lord,
Your son in Scotland being thus employ'd,
Shall secretly into the bosom creep
Of that same noble prelate well belov'd,
The archbishop.
Hot. Of York, is it not?   270
Wor. True; who bears hard
His brother's death at Bristol, the Lord Scroop.
I speak not this in estimation,
As what I think might be, but what I know
Is ruminated, plotted, and set down;
And only stays but to behold the face
Of that occasion that shall bring it on.
Hot. I smell it:
Upon my life, it will do wondrous well.
North. Before the game 's afoot, thou still lett'st slip.
Hot. Why, it cannot choose but be a noble plot.— 281
And then the power of Scotland and of York,
To join with Mortimer, ha?
Wor.   And so they shall.
Hot. In faith, it is exceedingly well aim'd.
Wor. And 't is no little reason bids us speed,
To save our heads by raising of a head;
For, bear ourselves as even as we can,
The king will always think him in our debt,
And think we think ourselves unsatisfied,
Till he hath found a time to pay us home.   290
And see already how he doth begin
To make us strangers to his looks of love.
Hot. He does, he does: we 'll be reveng'd on him.
Wor. Cousin, farewell.—No further go in this,
Than I by letters shall direct your course.
When time is ripe (which will be suddenly),
I 'll steal to Glendower, and Lord Mortimer;
Where you and Douglas, and our powers at once,
As I will fashion it, shall happily meet,
To bear our fortunes in our own strong arms,   300
Which now we hold at much uncertainty.
North. Farewell, good brother: we shall thrive, I
          trust.
Hot. Uncle, adieu.—O! let the hours be short,
Till fields and blows and groans applaud our sport.
          [*Exeunt*

ACT II.

SCENE I.—Rochester. An Inn Yard.

Enter a Carrier, with a lantern in his hand.

1 *Carrier.*

HEIGH-HO! An't be not four by the day, I'll be hanged: Charles' wain is over the new chimney, and yet our horse not packed. What, ostler!

Ostler. [*Within.*] Anon, anon.

1 *Car.* I pr'ythee, Tom, beat Cut's saddle, put a few flocks in the point; the poor jade is wrung in the withers out of all cess.

Enter another Carrier.

2 *Car.* Peas and beans are as dank here as a dog, and that is the next way to give poor jades the bots: this house is turned upside down, since Robin ostler died.

1 *Car.* Poor fellow! never joyed since the price of oats rose: it was the death of him.

2 *Car.* I think, this be the most villainous house in all London road for fleas: I am stung like a tench.

1 *Car.* Like a tench? by the mass, there is ne'er a king in Christendom could be better bit than I have been since the first cock.   21

2 *Car.* Why, they will allow us ne'er a jordan, and then we leak in your chimney; and your chamber-lie breeds fleas like a loach.

1 *Car.* What, ostler! come away and be hanged, come away.

2 *Car.* I have a gammon of bacon, and two razes of ginger, to be delivered as far as Charing Cross.

1 *Car.* 'Odsbody! the turkeys in my pannier are quite starved.—What, ostler!—A plague on thee! hast thou never an eye in thy head? canst not hear? An't were not as good a deed as drink, to break the pate of thee, I am a very villain.—Come, and be hanged:—hast no faith in thee?

Enter GADSHILL.

Gads. Good morrow, carriers. What's o'clock?

1 *Car.* I think it be two o'clock.

Gads. I pr'ythee, lend me thy lantern, to see my gelding in the stable.

1 *Car.* Nay, soft, I pray ye: I know a trick worth two of that, i' faith.   40

Gads. I pr'ythee, lend me thine.

2 *Car.* Ay, when? canst tell?—Lend me thy lantern, quoth 'a?—marry, I'll see thee hanged first.

Gads. Sirrah carrier, what time do you mean to come to London?

2 *Car.* Time enough to go to bed with a candle, I warrant thee.—Come, neighbour Mugs, we'll call up the gentlemen: they will along with company, for they have great charge.   [*Exeunt Carriers.*

Gads. What, ho! chamberlain!   50

Cham. [*Within.*] At hand, quoth pick-purse.

Gads. That's even as fair as—at hand, quoth the chamberlain; for thou variest no more from picking of purses, than giving direction doth from labouring; thou lay'st the plot how.

Enter Chamberlain.

Cham. Good morrow, Master Gadshill. It holds current that I told you yesternight: there's a franklin in the wild of Kent, hath brought three hundred marks with him in gold: I heard him tell it to one of his company, last night at supper; a kind of auditor; one that hath abundance of charge too, God knows what. They are up already, and call for eggs and butter: they will away presently.

Gads. Sirrah, if they meet not with Saint Nicholas' clerks, I'll give thee this neck.

1 *Car.* "'Odsbody! the turkeys in my pannier are quite starved."

Cham. No, I'll none of it: I pr'ythee, keep that for the hangman; for, I know, thou worshipp'st Saint Nicholas as truly as a man of falsehood may.   68

Gads. What talkest thou to me of the hangman? if I hang, I'll make a fat pair of gallows; for, if I hang, old Sir John hangs with me, and thou knowest he's no starveling. Tut! there are other Trojans that thou dreamest not of, the which, for sport sake, are content to do the profession some grace; that would, if matters should be looked into, for their own credit sake, make all whole. I am joined with no foot land-rakers, no long-staff, sixpenny strikers, none of these mad, mustachio-purple-hued malt-worms: but with nobility and tranquillity; burgomasters, and great oneyers; such as can hold in, such as will strike sooner than speak, and speak sooner than drink, and drink sooner than pray: and yet I lie; for they pray continually to their saint, the commonwealth; or, rather, not pray to her, but prey on her, for they ride up and down on her, and make her their boots.

Cham. What! the commonwealth their boots? will she hold out water in foul way?

Gads. She will, she will; justice hath liquored her.

We steal as in a castle, cock-sure; we have the receipt
of fern-seed, we walk invisible.   90
  Cham. Nay, by my faith; I think you are more
beholding to the night, than to fern-seed, for your
walking invisible.
  Gads. Give me thy hand: thou shalt have a share
in our purchase, as I am a true man.
  Cham. Nay, rather let me have it, as you are a false
thief.
  Gads. Go to; *homo* is a common name to all men.
Bid the ostler bring my gelding out of the stable.
Farewell, you muddy knave.   100
                                             [*Exeunt.*

SCENE II.—The Road by Gadshill.

Enter Prince HENRY *and* POINS; BARDOLPH *and*
PETO, *at some distance.*

  Poins. Come, shelter, shelter: I have removed
Falstaff's horse, and he frets like a gummed velvet.
  P. Hen. Stand close.

Enter FALSTAFF.

  Fal. Poins! Poins, and be hanged! Poins!
  P. Hen. Peace, ye fat-kidneyed rascal! What a
brawling dost thou keep?
  Fal. Where's Poins, Hal?
  P. Hen. He is walked up to the top of the hill: I'll
go seek him.   [*Pretends to seek* POINS.
  Fal. I am accursed to rob in that thief's company;
the rascal hath removed my horse, and tied him I
know not where. If I travel but four foot by the
squire further afoot, I shall break my wind. Well, I
doubt not but to die a fair death for all this, if I 'scape
hanging for killing that rogue. I have forsworn his
company hourly any time this two-and-twenty years,
and yet I am bewitched with the rogue's company. If
the rascal have not given me medicines to make me
love him, I'll be hanged; it could not be else: I have
drunk medicines.—Poins!—Hal!—a plague upon you
both!—Bardolph!—Peto!—I'll starve, ere I'll rob a
foot further. An 't were not as good a deed as drink,
to turn true man, and leave these rogues, I am the
veriest varlet that ever chewed with a tooth. Eight
yards of uneven ground is threescore and ten miles
afoot with me, and the stony-hearted villains know it
well enough. A plague upon 't, when thieves cannot
be true to one another! [*They whistle.*] Whew!—A
plague upon you all! Give me my horse, you rogues;
give me my horse, and be hanged.   30
  P. Hen. Peace, ye fat-guts! lie down: lay thine ear
close to the ground, and list if thou canst hear the
tread of travellers.
  Fal. Have you any levers to lift me up again, being
down? 'Sblood! I'll not bear mine own flesh so far
afoot again, for all the coin in thy father's exchequer.
What a plague mean ye to colt me thus?
  P. Hen. Thou liest: thou art not colted; thou art
uncolted.
  Fal. I pr'ythee, good Prince Hal, help me to my
horse, good king's son.   41
  P. Hen. Out, you rogue! shall I be your ostler?
  Fal. Go, hang thyself in thine own heir-apparent
garters! If I be ta'en, I'll peach for this. An I have
not ballads made on you all, and sung to filthy tunes,
let a cup of sack be my poison: when a jest is so forward, and afoot too, I hate it.

Enter GADSHILL.

  Gads. Stand.
  Fal. So I do, against my will.
  Poins. O! 't is our setter: I know his voice.   50

Enter BARDOLPH.

  Bard. What news?
  Gads. Case ye, case ye; on with your visors: there's
money of the king's coming down the hill; 't is going
to the king's exchequer.
  Fal. You lie, you rogue: 't is going to the king's
tavern.
  Gads. There's enough to make us all.

  Fal. To be hanged.
  P. Hen. Sirs, you four shall front them in the nar-
row lane; Ned Poins and I will walk lower: if they
scape from your encounter, then they light on us. 61
  Peto. How many be there of them?
  Gads. Some eight, or ten.
  Fal. 'Zounds! will they not rob us?

Fal. "Poins!—Hal!—a plague upon you both!"

  P. Hen. What, a coward, Sir John Paunch?
  Fal. Indeed, I am not John of Gaunt, your grand-
father; but yet no coward, Hal.
  P. Hen. Well, we leave that to the proof.
  Poins. Sirrah Jack, thy horse stands behind the
hedge: when thou needest him, there thou shalt find
him. Farewell, and stand fast.   71
  Fal. Now cannot I strike him, if I should be hanged.
  P. Hen. [*Aside to* POINS.] Ned, where are our dis-
guises?
  Poins. Here, hard by: stand close.
                    [*Exeunt Prince* HENRY *and* POINS.
  Fal. Now, my masters, happy man be his dole, say
I: every man to his business.

Enter Travellers.

  1 Trav. Come, neighbour: the boy shall lead our
horses down the hill; we'll walk afoot awhile, and
ease our legs.   80
  Thieves. Stand!
  Travellers. Jesu bless us!
  Fal. Strike; down with them; cut the villains'
throats. Ah! whoreson caterpillars! bacon-fed knaves!
they hate us youth: down with them; fleece them.
  Travellers. O! we are undone, both we and ours,
for ever.
  Fal. Hang ye, gorbellied knaves. Are ye undone?
No, ye fat chuffs; I would, your store were here!
On, bacons, on! What! ye knaves, young men must
live. You are grand-jurors, are ye? We'll jure ye,
i' faith.   92
     [*Exeunt* FALSTAFF, &c., *driving the Travellers out.*

Re-enter Prince HENRY *and* POINS.

P. Hen. The thieves have bound the true men. Now could thou and I rob the thieves, and go merrily to London, it would be argument for a week, laughter for a month, and a good jest for ever.

Poins. Stand close; I hear them coming.

Re-enter Thieves.

Fal. Come, my masters; let us share, and then to horse before day. An the prince and Poins be not two arrant cowards, there's no equity stirring: there's no more valour in that Poins, than in a wild duck.

P. Hen. Your money.   [*Rushing out upon them.*

Poins. Villains.

[*As they are sharing, the* PRINCE *and* POINS *set upon them. They all run away, and* FAL-STAFF, *after a blow or two, runs away too, leaving the booty behind them.*

P. Hen. Got with much ease. Now merrily to horse:
The thieves are scatter'd, and possess'd with fear
So strongly, that they dare not meet each other;
Each takes his fellow for an officer.
Away, good Ned. Falstaff sweats to death,
And lards the lean earth as he walks along:
Were 't not for laughing, I should pity him.   110

Poins. How the rogue roar'd!   [*Exeunt.*

SCENE III.—Warkworth. A Room in the Castle.

Enter HOTSPUR, *reading a letter.*

—" But, for mine own part, my lord, I could be well contented to be there, in respect of the love I bear your house."—He could be contented,—why is he not then? In respect of the love he bears our house:—he shows in this, he loves his own barn better than he loves our house. Let me see some more. " The purpose you undertake, is dangerous;"—why, that 's certain: 'tis dangerous to take a cold, to sleep, to drink; but I tell you, my lord fool, out of this nettle, danger, we pluck this flower, safety. " The purpose you undertake, is dangerous; the friends you have named, uncertain; the time itself unsorted, and your whole plot too light for the counterpoise of so great an opposition."—Say you so, say you so? I say unto you again, you are a shallow, cowardly hind, and you lie. What a lack-brain is this! By the Lord, our plot is as good a plot as ever was laid; our friends true and constant: a good plot, good friends, and full of expectation; an excellent plot, very good friends. What a frosty-spirited rogue is this! Why, my Lord of York commends the plot and the general course of the action. 'Zounds! an I were now by this rascal, I could brain him with his lady's fan. Is there not my father, my uncle, and myself? Lord Edmund Mortimer, my Lord of York, and Owen Glendower? Is there not, besides, the Douglas? Have I not all their letters, to meet me in arms by the ninth of the next month, and are they not, some of them, set forward already? What a pagan rascal is this! an infidel! Ha! you shall see now, in very sincerity of fear and cold heart, will he to the king, and lay open all our proceedings. O! I could divide myself and go to buffets, for moving such a dish of skimmed milk with so honourable an action. Hang him! let him tell the king; we are prepared. I will set forward to-night.

Enter Lady PERCY.

How now, Kate? I must leave you within these two hours.

Lady. O, my good lord! why are you thus alone?
For what offence have I this fortnight been
A banish'd woman from my Harry's bed?
Tell me, sweet lord, what is 't that takes from thee 40
Thy stomach, pleasure, and thy golden sleep?
Why dost thou bend thine eyes upon the earth,
And start so often when thou sitt'st alone?
Why hast thou lost the fresh blood in thy cheeks,
And given my treasures, and my rights of thee,
To thick-ey'd musing, and curs'd melancholy?

In thy faint slumbers I by thee hath watch'd,
And heard thee murmur tales of iron wars,
Speak terms of manage to thy bounding steed,
Cry, " Courage!—to the field!" And thou hast talk'd
Of sallies, and retires; of trenches, tents,   51
Of palisadoes, frontiers, parapets,
Of basilisks, of cannon, culverin,
Of prisoners' ransom, and of soldiers slain,
And all the currents of a heady fight.
Thy spirit within thee hath been so at war,
And thus hath so bestirr'd thee in thy sleep,
That beads of sweat have stood upon thy brow,
Like bubbles in a late-disturbed stream;

Lady. " What is it carries you away?"

And in thy face strange motions have appear'd,   60
Such as we see when men restrain their breath
On some great sudden hest. O! what portents are
    these?
Some heavy business hath my lord in hand,
And I must know it, else he loves me not.

Hot. What, ho!

Enter Servant.

         Is Gilliams with the packet gone?

Serv. He is, my lord, an hour ago.

Hot. Hath Butler brought those horses from the
    sheriff?

Serv. One horse, my lord, he brought even now.

Hot. What horse? a roan, a crop-ear, is it not?

Serv. It is, my lord.

Hot.   That roan shall be my throne. 70
Well, I will back him straight: O, *Esperance!*
Bid Butler lead him forth into the park. [*Exit Servant.*

Lady. But hear you, my lord.

Hot. What say'st thou, my lady?

Lady. What is it carries you away?

Hot. Why, my horse, my love, my horse.

Lady. Out, you mad-headed ape!
A weasel hath not such a deal of spleen,
As you are toss'd with. In faith,
I'll know your business, Harry, that I will.   80
I fear, my brother Mortimer doth stir
About his title, and hath sent for you,
To line his enterprise. But if you go—

Hot. So far afoot, I shall be weary, love.

Lady. Come, come, you paraquito, answer me
Directly unto this question that I ask.
In faith, I'll break thy little finger, Harry,
An if thou wilt not tell me all things true.

Hot. Away,
Away, you trifler!—Love!—I love thee not,   96
I care not for thee, Kate. This is no world,
To play with mammets and to tilt with lips:

We must have bloody noses and crack'd crowns,
And pass them current too.—God's me, my horse!—
What say'st thou, Kate? what wouldst thou have
    with me?
  Lady. Do you not love me? do you not, indeed?
Well, do not then; for since you love me not,
I will not love myself. Do you not love me?
Nay, tell me, if you speak in jest, or no?
  Hot. Come, wilt thou see me ride?   100
And when I am o' horseback, I will swear
I love thee infinitely. But hark you, Kate;
I must not have you henceforth question me
Whither I go, nor reason whereabout.
Whither I must, I must; and, to conclude,
This evening must I leave you, gentle Kate.
I know you wise; but yet no further wise
Than Harry Percy's wife: constant you are,
But yet a woman: and for secrecy,
No lady closer; for I well believe   110
Thou wilt not utter what thou dost not know;
And so far will I trust thee, gentle Kate.
  Lady. How! so far?
  Hot. Not an inch further. But hark you, Kate:
Whither I go, thither shall you go too;
To-day will I set forth, to-morrow you.
Will this content you, Kate?
  Lady.   It must, of force. [*Exeunt.*

SCENE IV.—Eastcheap.   A Room in the Boar's Head
                        Tavern.

Enter Prince HENRY *and* POINS.

  P. Hen. Ned, pr'ythee, come out of that fat room,
and lend me thy hand to laugh a little.
  Poins. Where hast been, Hal?
  P. Hen. With three or four loggerheads, amongst
three or four score hogsheads. I have sounded the
very base string of humility. Sirrah, I am sworn brother
to a leash of drawers, and can call them all by their
Christian names, as—Tom, Dick, and Francis. They
take it already upon their salvation, that though I be
but Prince of Wales, yet I am the king of courtesy, and
tell me flatly I am no proud Jack, like Falstaff, but a
Corinthian, a lad of mettle, a good boy, (by the Lord,
so they call me,)—and when I am King of England, I
shall command all the good lads in Eastcheap. They
call drinking deep, dying scarlet; and when you
breathe in your watering, they cry, "Hem!" and bid
you play it off. To conclude, I am so good a proficient
in one quarter of an hour, that I can drink with any
tinker in his own language during my life. I tell
thee, Ned, thou hast lost much honour, that thou wert
not with me in this action. But, sweet Ned,—to
sweeten which name of Ned, I give thee this pennyworth of sugar, clapped even now into my hand by an
under-skinker, one that never spake other English in
his life, than—"Eight shillings and sixpence," and—
"You are welcome;" with this shrill addition,--
"Anon, anon, sir! Score a pint of bastard in the
Half Moon," or so. But, Ned, to drive away the time
till Falstaff come, I pr'ythee, do thou stand in some
by-room, while I question my puny drawer to what
end he gave me the sugar; and do thou never leave
calling—Francis! that his tale to me may be nothing
but—anon. Step aside, and I'll show thee a precedent.
  Poins. Francis!
  P. Hen. Thou art perfect.
  Poins. Francis!   [*Exit.*

Enter FRANCIS.

  Fran. Anon, anon, sir.—Look down into the Pome-
granate, Ralph.
  P. Hen. Come hither, Francis.
  Fran. My lord.   40
  P. Hen. How long hast thou to serve, Francis?
  Fran. Forsooth, five years, and as much as to—
  Poins. [*Within.*] Francis!
  Fran. Anon, anon, sir.
  P. Hen. Five years! by'r lady, a long lease for the
clinking of pewter. But, Francis, darest thou be so

valiant as to play the coward with thy indenture, and
to show it a fair pair of heels, and run from it?
  Fran. O Lord, sir! I'll be sworn upon all the books
in England, I could find in my heart—   50
  Poins. [*Within.*] Francis!
  Fran. Anon, anon, sir.
  P. Hen. How old art thou, Francis?
  Fran. Let me see,—about Michaelmas next I shall
be—
  Poins. [*Within.*] Francis!
  Fran. Anon, sir.—Pray you, stay a little, my lord.
  P. Hen. Nay, but hark you, Francis. For the sugar
thou gavest me,—'t was a pennyworth, was 't not?

P. Hen. "Away, you rogue! Dost thou not hear them call?"

  Fran. O Lord, sir! I would it had been two.   60
  P. Hen. I will give thee for it a thousand pound:
ask me when thou wilt, and thou shalt have it.
  Poins. [*Within.*] Francis!
  Fran. Anon, anon.
  P. Hen. Anon, Francis? No, Francis; but to-mo-
row, Francis; or, Francis, on Thursday; or, indeed,
Francis, when thou wilt. But, Francis,—
  Fran. My lord?
  P. Hen. Wilt thou rob this leathern-jerkin, crystal-
button, nott-pated, agate-ring, puke-stocking, caddis-
garter, smooth-tongue, Spanish-pouch,—   71
  Fran. O Lord, sir, who do you mean?
  P. Hen. Why then, your brown bastard is your
only drink: for, look you, Francis, your white canvas
doublet will sully. In Barbary, sir, it cannot come to
so much.
  Fran. What, sir?
  Poins. [*Within.*] Francis!
  P. Hen. Away, you rogue! Dost thou not hear them
call? [*Here they both call him; the Drawer stands
        amazed, not knowing which way to go.*

Enter Vintner.

  Vint. What! stand'st thou still, and hear'st such a
calling? Look to the guests within. [*Exit* FRANCIS.]
My lord, old Sir John, with half a dozen more, are at
the door: shall I let them in?
  P. Hen. Let them alone awhile, and then open
the door. [*Exit Vintner.*] Poins!

Re-enter POINS.

  Poins. Anon, anon, sir.
  P. Hen. Sirrah, Falstaff and the rest of the thieves
are at the door. Shall we be merry?
  Poins. As merry as crickets, my lad. But hark ye:
what cunning match have you made with this jest of
the drawer? come, what's the issue?   92
  P. Hen. I am now of all humours, that have show'd
themselves humours, since the old days of goodman

Adam to the pupil age of this present twelve o'clock at midnight.

Re-enter FRANCIS, *with wine.*

What 's o'clock, Francis?
Fran. Anon, anon, sir.   [*Exit.*
P. Hen. That ever this fellow should have fewer words than a parrot, and yet the son of a woman! His industry is—up-stairs, and down-stairs; his eloquence, the parcel of a reckoning. I am not yet of Percy's mind, the Hotspur of the North; he that kills me some six or seven dozen of Scots at a breakfast, washes his hands, and says to his wife,—"Fie upon this quiet life! I want work." "O my sweet Harry," says she, "how many hast thou killed to-day?" "Give my roan horse a drench," says he, and answers, "Some fourteen," an hour after; "a trifle, a trifle."—I pr'ythee, call in Falstaff: I 'll play Percy, and that damned brawn shall play Dame Mortimer his wife. "Rivo!" says the drunkard. Call in ribs, call in tallow.

Enter FALSTAFF, GADSHILL, BARDOLPH, *and* PETO.

Poins. Welcome, Jack. Where hast thou been?
Fal. A plague of all cowards, I say, and a vengeance too! marry, and amen!—Give me a cup of sack, boy.—Ere I lead this life long, I 'll sew nether-stocks, and mend them, and foot them too. A plague of all cowards!— Give me a cup of sack, rogue.—Is there no virtue extant?   [*He drinks.*
P. Hen. Didst thou never see Titan kiss a dish of butter (pitiful-hearted Titan), that melted at the sweet tale of the sun? if thou didst, then behold that compound.
Fal. You rogue, here 's lime in this sack too: there is nothing but roguery to be found in villainous man: yet a coward is worse than a cup of sack with lime in it: a villainous coward.—Go thy ways, old Jack; die when thou wilt. If manhood, good manhood, be not forgot upon the face of the earth, then am I a shotten herring. There live not three good men unhanged in England, and one of them is fat, and grows old: God help the while! a bad world, I say. I would I were a weaver; I could sing psalms or anything. A plague of all cowards, I say still.   140
P. Hen. How now, wool-sack? what mutter you?
Fal. A king's son! If I do not beat thee out of thy kingdom with a dagger of lath, and drive all thy subjects afore thee like a flock of wild geese, I 'll never wear hair on my face more. You Prince of Wales!
P. Hen. Why, you whoreson round man, what 's the matter?
Fal. Are you not a coward? answer me to that; and Poins there?   151
Poins. 'Zounds! ye fat-paunch, an ye call me coward, I 'll stab thee.
Fal. I call thee coward! I 'll see thee damned ere I call thee coward; but I would give a thousand pound, I could run as fast as thou canst. You are straight enough in the shoulders; you care not who sees your back: call you that backing of your friends? A plague upon such backing! give me them that will face me. —Give me a cup of sack: I am a rogue, if I drunk to-day.   161
P. Hen. O villain! thy lips are scarce wiped since thou drunk'st last.
Fal. All 's one for that. [*He drinks.*] A plague of all cowards, still say I.
P. Hen. What 's the matter?
Fal. What 's the matter? there be four of us here have ta'en a thousand pound this day morning.
P. Hen. Where is it, Jack? where is it?
Fal. Where is it? taken from us it is: a hundred upon poor four of us.   171

P. Hen. What, a hundred, man?
Fal. I am a rogue, if I were not at half-sword with a dozen of them two hours together. I have 'scap'd by miracle. I am eight times thrust through the doublet; four through the hose; my buckler cut through and through; my sword hacked like a hand-saw: *ecce signum.* I never dealt better since I was a man: all would not do. A plague of all cowards!— Let them speak: if they speak more or less than truth, they are villains, and the sons of darkness.   181
P. Hen. Speak, sirs: how was it?

Fal. "And thus I bore my point."

Gads. We four set upon some dozen,—
Fal. Sixteen, at least, my lord.
Gads. And bound them.
Peto. No, no, they were not bound.
Fal. You rogue, they were bound, every man of them; or I am a Jew else, an Ebrew Jew.
Gads. As we were sharing, some six or seven fresh men set upon us,—   190
Fal. And unbound the rest, and then come in the other.
P. Hen. What, fought ye with them all?
Fal. All? I know not what ye call all; but if I fought not with fifty of them, I am a bunch of radish: if there were not two or three and fifty upon poor old Jack, then am I no two-legged creature.
P. Hen. Pray God, you have not murdered some of them.   199
Fal. Nay, that 's past praying for: I have peppered two of them: two, I am sure, I have paid, two rogues in buckram suits. I tell thee what, Hal,—if I tell thee a lie, spit in my face, call me horse. Thou knowest my old ward:—here I lay, and thus I bore my point. Four rogues in buckram let drive at me,—
P. Hen. What, four? thou saidst but two, even now.
Fal. Four, Hal; I told thee four.
Poins. Ay, ay, he said four.   209

Fal. These four came all a-front, and mainly thrust at me. I made me no more ado, but took all their seven points in my target, thus.

P. Hen. Seven? why, there were but four, even now.

Fal. In buckram?

Poins. Ay, four, in buckram suits.

Fal. Seven, by these hilts, or I am a villain else.

P. Hen. Pr'ythee, let him alone: we shall have more anon.

Fal. Dost thou hear me, Hal?

P. Hen. Ay, and mark thee too, Jack.   220

Fal. Do so, for it is worth the listening to. These nine in buckram, that I told thee of,—

P. Hen. So, two more already.

Fal. Their points being broken,—

Poins. Down fell their hose.

Fal. Began to give me ground; but I followed me close, came in, foot and hand, and with a thought seven of the eleven I paid.

P. Hen. O monstrous! eleven buckram men grown out of two.   230

Fal. But, as the devil would have it, three misbegotten knaves in Kendal green came at my back and let drive at me; for it was so dark, Hal, that thou couldst not see thy hand.

P. Hen. These lies are like the father that begets them; gross as a mountain, open, palpable. Why, thou clay-brained guts, thou knotty-pated fool, thou whoreson, obscene, greasy tallow-ketch,—

Fal. What! art thou mad? art thou mad? is not the truth the truth?   240

P. Hen. Why, how couldst thou know these men in Kendal green, when it was so dark thou couldst not see thy hand? come, tell us your reason: what sayest thou to this?

Poins. Come, your reason, Jack, your reason.

Fal. What, upon compulsion? No; were I at the strappado, or all the racks in the world, I would not tell you on compulsion. Give you a reason on compulsion! if reasons were as plenty as blackberries, I would give no man a reason upon compulsion, I.   250

P. Hen. I'll be no longer guilty of this sin: this sanguine coward, this bed-presser, this horse-back-breaker, this huge hill of flesh;—

Fal. Away, you starveling, you elf-skin, you dried neat's-tongue, bull's-pizzle, you stock-fish,—O, for breath to utter what is like thee!—you tailor's-yard, you sheath, you bow-case, you vile standing tuck:—

P. Hen. Well, breathe awhile, and then to it again; and when thou hast tired thyself in base comparisons, hear me speak but this.   261

Poins. Mark, Jack.

P. Hen. We two saw you four set on four, and you bound them, and were masters of their wealth.—Mark now, how a plain tale shall put you down.—Then did we two set on you four, and, with a word, outfaced you from your prize, and have it; yea, and can show it you here in the house.—And, Falstaff, you carried your guts away as nimbly, with as quick dexterity, and roared for mercy, and still ran and roared, as ever I heard bull-calf. What a slave art thou, to hack thy sword as thou hast done, and then say, it was in fight! What trick, what device, what starting-hole canst thou now find out, to hide thee from this open and apparent shame?

Poins. Come, let's hear, Jack: what trick hast thou now?

Fal. By the Lord, I knew ye, as well as he that made ye. Why, hear ye, my masters. Was it for me to kill the heir-apparent? Should I turn upon the true prince? Why, thou knowest, I am as valiant as Hercules; but beware instinct: the lion will not touch the true prince. Instinct is a great matter, I was a coward on instinct. I shall think the better of myself and thee, during my life; I for a valiant lion, and thou for a true prince. But, by the Lord, lads, I am glad you have the money.—Hostess, clap to the doors: watch to-night, pray to-morrow.—Gallants, lads, boys, hearts of gold, all the titles of good fellowship come to you! What! shall we be merry? shall we have a play extempore?   291

P. Hen. Content;—and the argument shall be, thy running away.

Fal. Ah! no more of that, Hal, an thou lovest me.

Enter Hostess.

Host. O Jesu! My lord the prince,—

P. Hen. How now, my lady the hostess? what say'st thou to me?

Host. Marry, my lord, there is a nobleman of the court at door, would speak with you: he says, he comes from your father.   300

P. Hen. Give him as much as will make him a royal man, and send him back again to my mother.

Fal. What manner of man is he?

Host. An old man.

Fal. What doth gravity out of his bed at midnight? —Shall I give him his answer?

P. Hen. Pr'ythee, do, Jack.

Fal. 'Faith, and I'll send him packing.   [*Exit.*

P. Hen. Now, sirs; by'r lady, you fought fair;—so did you, Peto;—so did you, Bardolph: you are lions, too, you ran away upon instinct, you will not touch the true prince, no;—fie!

Bard. 'Faith, I ran when I saw others run.

P. Hen. 'Faith, tell me now in earnest: how came Falstaff's sword so hacked?

Peto. Why, he hacked it with his dagger, and said, he would swear truth out of England, but he would make you believe it was done in fight; and persuaded us to do the like.   319

Bard. Yea, and to tickle our noses with spear-grass, to make them bleed; and then to beslubber our garments with it, and to swear it was the blood of true men. I did that I did not this seven years before; I blushed to hear his monstrous devices.

P. Hen. O villain! thou stolest a cup of sack eighteen years ago, and wert taken with the manner, and ever since thou hast blushed extempore. Thou hadst fire and sword on thy side, and yet thou rann'st away. What instinct hadst thou for it?

Bard. My lord, do you see these meteors? do you behold these exhalations?   331

P. Hen. I do.

Bard. What think you they portend?

P. Hen. Hot livers and cold purses.

Bard. Choler, my lord, if rightly taken.

P. Hen. No, if rightly taken, halter.

Re-enter FALSTAFF.

Here comes lean Jack, here comes bare-bone. How now, my sweet creature of bombast? How long is't ago, Jack, since thou sawest thine own knee?

Fal. My own knee? when I was about thy years, Hal, I was not an eagle's talon in the waist; I could have crept into any alderman's thumb-ring. A plague of sighing and grief! it blows a man up like a bladder. There's villainous news abroad: here was Sir John Bracy from your father: you must to the court in the morning. That same mad fellow of the north, Percy, and he of Wales, that gave Amaimon the bastinado, and made Lucifer cuckold, and swore the devil his true liegeman upon the cross of a Welsh hook,—what, a plague, call you him?—   350

Poins. O! Glendower.

Fal. Owen, Owen; the same;—and his son-in-law, Mortimer, and old Northumberland; and that sprightly Scot of Scots, Douglas, that runs o' horseback up a hill perpendicular.

P. Hen. He that rides at high speed, and with his pistol kills a sparrow flying.

Fal. You have hit it.

P. Hen. So did he never the sparrow.

Fal. Well, that rascal hath good mettle in him; he will not run.   361

P. Hen. Why, what a rascal art thou then, to praise him so for running?

Fal. O' horseback, ye cuckoo! but, afoot, he will not budge a foot.

P. Hen. Yes, Jack, upon instinct.

Fal. I grant ye, upon instinct. Well, he is there too, and one Mordake, and a thousand blue-caps more. Worcester is stolen away to-night; thy father's beard

is turned white with the news; you may buy land now
as cheap as stinking mackerel.   371

P. Hen. Why then, it is like, if there come a hot
June, and this civil buffeting hold, we shall buy
maidenheads as they buy hob-nails, by the hundreds.

Fal. By the mass, lad, thou sayest true; it is like,
we shall have good trading that way.—But, tell me,
Hal, art thou not horribly afeard? thou being heir-
apparent, could the world pick thee out three such
enemies again, as that fiend Douglas, that spirit
Percy, and that devil Glendower? Art thou not
horribly afraid? doth not thy blood thrill at it?   381

P. Hen. Not a whit, i' faith: I lack some of thy
instinct.

Fal. Well, thou wilt be horribly chid to-morrow,
when thou comest to thy father. If thou love me,
practise an answer.

P. Hen. Do thou stand for my father, and examine
me upon the particulars of my life.

Fal. Shall I? content.—This chair shall be my state,
this dagger my sceptre, and this cushion my crown.

P. Hen. Thy state is taken from a joint-stool, thy
golden sceptre for a leaden dagger, and thy precious
rich crown for a pitiful bald crown!   393

Fal. Well, an the fire of grace be not quite out of
thee, now shalt thou be moved.—Give me a cup of
sack, to make mine eyes look red, that it may be
thought I have wept: for I must speak in passion, and
I will do it in King Cambyses' vein.

P. Hen. Well, here is my leg.

Fal. And here is my speech.—Stand aside, nobility.

Host. O Jesu! This is excellent sport, i' faith.   401

Fal. Weep not, sweet queen, for trickling tears are
vain.

Host. O, the father! how he holds his countenance!

Fal. For God's sake, lords, convey my tristful
queen,
For tears do stop the flood-gates of her eyes.

Host. O Jesu! he doth it as like one of these
harlotry players as ever I see.

Fal. Peace, good pint-pot! peace, good tickle-brain!
—Harry, I do not only marvel where thou spendest
thy time, but also how thou art accompanied: for
though the camomile, the more it is trodden on, the
faster it grows, yet youth, the more it is wasted, the
sooner it wears. That thou art my son, I have partly
thy mother's word, partly my own opinion; but
chiefly, a villainous trick of thine eye, and a foolish
hanging of thy nether lip, that doth warrant me. If
then thou be son to me, here lies the point:—why,
being son to me, art thou so pointed at? Shall the
blessed sun of heaven prove a micher, and eat blackberries? a question not to be asked. Shall the son of
England prove a thief, and take purses? a question to
be asked. There is a thing, Harry, which thou hast
often heard of, and it is known to many in our land
by the name of pitch: this pitch, as ancient writers
do report, doth defile; so doth the company thou
keepest; for, Harry, now I do not speak to thee in
drink, but in tears; not in pleasure, but in passion;
not in words only, but in woes also.—And yet there is
a virtuous man, whom I have often noted in thy company, but I know not his name.   430

P. Hen. What manner of man, an it like your
majesty?

Fal. A goodly portly man, i' faith, and a corpulent;
of a cheerful look, a pleasing eye, and a most noble
carriage; and, as I think, his age some fifty, or, by'r
lady, inclining to threescore; and now I remember me,
his name is Falstaff: if that man should be lewdly
given, he deceiveth me; for, Harry, I see virtue in
his looks. If then the tree may be known by the fruit,
as the fruit by the tree, then, peremptorily I speak it,
there is virtue in that Falstaff: him keep with, the
rest banish. And tell me now, thou naughty varlet,
tell me, where hast thou been this month?   443

P. Hen. Dost thou speak like a king? Do thou
stand for me, and I'll play my father.

Fal. Depose me? if thou dost it half so gravely, so
majestically, both in word and matter, hang me up by
the heels for a rabbit-sucker, or a poulter's hare.

P. Hen. Well, here I am set.

Fal. And here I stand.—Judge, my masters.   450

P. Hen. Now, Harry! whence come you?

Fal. My noble lord, from Eastcheap.

P. Hen. The complaints I hear of thee are grievous.

Fal. 'Sblood, my lord, they are false:—nay, I'll
tickle ye for a young prince, i' faith.

P. Hen. Swearest thou, ungracious boy? henceforth ne'er look on me. Thou art violently carried
away from grace: there is a devil haunts thee, in the
likeness of a fat old man: a tun of man is thy companion. Why dost thou converse with that trunk of
humours, that bolting-hutch of beastliness, that swoln
parcel of dropsies, that huge bombard of sack, that
stuffed cloak-bag of guts, that roasted Manningtree ox
with the pudding in his belly, that reverend Vice, that
grey Iniquity, that father ruffian, that Vanity in years?
Wherein is he good, but to taste sack and drink it?
wherein neat and cleanly, but to carve a capon and
eat it? wherein cunning, but in craft? wherein crafty,
but in villainy? wherein villainous, but in all things?
wherein worthy, but in nothing?   470

Fal. I would your grace would take me with you.
Whom means your grace?

P. Hen. That villainous abominable misleader of
youth, Falstaff, that old white-bearded Satan.

Fal. My lord, the man I know.

P. Hen. I know thou dost.

Fal. But to say, I know more harm in him than in
myself, were to say more than I know. That he is
old, the more the pity, his white hairs do witness it:
but that he is, saving your reverence, a whoremaster,
that I utterly deny. If sack and sugar be a fault, God
help the wicked! If to be old and merry be a sin, then
many an old host that I know is damned: if to be fat
be to be hated, then Pharaoh's lean kine are to be
loved. No, my good lord: banish Peto, banish Bardolph, banish Poins; but for sweet Jack Falstaff, kind
Jack Falstaff, true Jack Falstaff, valiant Jack Falstaff, and therefore more valiant, being, as he is, old
Jack Falstaff, banish not him thy Harry's company:
banish plump Jack, and banish all the world.   490

P. Hen. I do, I will.   [*A knocking heard.*
[*Exeunt Hostess,* FRANCIS, *and* BARDOLPH.

Re-enter BARDOLPH, *running.*

Bard. O, my lord, my lord! the sheriff, with a most
monstrous watch, is at the door.

Fal. Out, you rogue! Play out the play: I have
much to say in the behalf of that Falstaff.

Re-enter Hostess.

Host. O Jesu! my lord, my lord!—

P. Hen. Heigh, heigh! the devil rides upon a fiddlestick. What's the matter?

Host. The sheriff and all the watch are at the door:
they are come to search the house. Shall I let them in?

Fal. Dost thou hear, Hal? never call a true piece of
gold a counterfeit: thou art essentially mad, without
seeming so.   503

P. Hen. And thou a natural coward, without
instinct.

Fal. I deny your major. If you will deny the sheriff,
so; if not, let him enter: if I become not a cart as
well as another man, a plague on my bringing up! I
hope I shall as soon be strangled with a halter as
another.   510

P. Hen. Go, hide thee behind the arras:—the rest
walk up above. Now, my masters, for a true face,
and good conscience.

Fal. Both which I have had; but their date is out,
and therefore I'll hide me.
[*Exeunt all but the* PRINCE *and* PETO.

P. Hen. Call in the sheriff.

Enter Sheriff and Carrier.

Now, master sheriff, what's your will with me?

Sher. First, pardon me, my lord. A hue and cry
Hath follow'd certain men unto this house.

P. Hen. What men?   520

Sher. One of them is well known, my gracious lord;
A gross fat man.

Car.   As fat as butter.

P. Hen. The man, I do assure you, is not here,

For I myself at this time have employ'd him.
And, sheriff, I will engage my word to thee,
That I will, by to-morrow dinner-time,
Send him to answer thee, or any man,

P. Hen. This oily rascal is known as well as Paul's.
Go, call him forth.
    Peto. Falstaff!—Fast asleep behind the arras, and
snorting like a horse.   540

Peto. "Fast asleep behind the arras, and snorting like a horse."

For anything he shall be charg'd withal:
And so, let me entreat you, leave the house.
    Sher. I will, my lord. There are two gentlemen   530
Have in this robbery lost three hundred marks.
    P. Hen. It may be so: if he have robb'd these men,
He shall be answerable; and so, farewell.
    Sher. Good night, my noble lord.
    P. Hen. I think it is good morrow, is it not?
    Sher. Indeed, my lord, I think it be two o'clock.
    [*Exeunt Sheriff and Carrier.*

P. Hen. Hark, how hard he fetches breath. Search
his pockets. [PETO *searches.*] What hast thou found.
    Peto. Nothing but papers, my lord.
    P. Hen. Let 's see what they be : read them.
    Peto. [*Reads.*] "Item, A capon . . . . . 2s. 2d.
Item, Sauce . . . . 4d.
Item, Sack, two gallons . . . . 5s. 8d.
Item, Anchovies, and sack after supper . . 2s. 6d.
Item, Bread . . . . ob."
    P. Hen. O monstrous! but one half-pennyworth of

bread to this intolerable deal of sack!—What there is else, keep close : we 'll read it at more advantage. There let him sleep till day. I 'll to the court in the morning : we must all to the wars, and thy place shall be honourable. I 'll procure this fat rogue a charge

of foot ; and, I know, his death will be a march of twelve-score. The money shall be paid back again with advantage. Be with me betimes in the morning ; and so, good morrow, Peto.

Peto. Good morrow, good my lord.   560
[*Exeunt.*

ACT III.

SCENE I.—Bangor. A Room in the Archdeacon's House.

Enter HOTSPUR, WORCESTER, MORTIMER, *and* GLENDOWER.

Mortimer.
THESE promises are fair, the parties sure,
And our induction full of prosperous hope.
    Hot. Lord Mortimer, and cousin Glen-
        dower,
Will you sit down?—
And, uncle Worcester:—a plague upon it!
I have forgot the map.
    Glend.   No, here it is.
Sit, cousin Percy ; sit, good cousin Hot-
        spur ;
For by that name as oft as Lancaster
Doth speak of you,
His cheek looks pale, and with a rising sigh   10
He wisheth you in heaven.
    Hot. And you in hell, as oft as he hears
Owen Glendower spoke of.
    Glend. I cannot blame him. At my nativity
The front of heaven was full of fiery shapes,
Of burning cressets ; and at my birth,
The frame and huge foundation of the earth
Shak'd like a coward.
    Hot. Why, so it would have done at the same
season, if your mother's cat had but kitten'd, though
yourself had never been born.   21
    Glend. I say, the earth did shake when I was born.
    Hot. And I say, the earth was not of my mind,
If you suppose as fearing you it shook.
    Glend. The heavens were all on fire, the earth did
        tremble.
    Hot. O ! then the earth shook to see the heavens on
        fire,
And not in fear of your nativity.
Diseased nature oftentimes breaks forth
In strange eruptions : oft the teeming earth
Is with a kind of colic pinch'd and vex'd   30
By the imprisoning of unruly wind
Within her womb ; which, for enlargement striving,
Shakes the old beldam earth, and topples down
Steeples, and moss-grown towers. At your birth,
Our grandam earth, having this distemperature,
In passion shook.
    Glend.   Cousin, of many men
I do not bear these crossings. Give me leave
To tell you once again,—that at my birth
The front of heaven was full of fiery shapes ;
The goats ran from the mountains, and the herds   40
Were strangely clamorous to the frighted fields.
These signs have mark'd me extraordinary,
And all the courses of my life do show,
I am not in the roll of common men.
Where is he living,—clipp'd in with the sea
That chides the banks of England, Scotland, Wales,—
Which calls me pupil, or hath read to me ?
And bring him out, that is but woman's son,
Can trace me in the tedious ways of art,
And hold me pace in deep experiments.   50

    Hot. I think, there is no man speaks better Welsh.
I 'll to dinner.
    Mort. Peace, cousin Percy ! you will make him
        mad.
    Glend. I can call spirits from the vasty deep.
    Hot. Why, so can I, or so can any man ;
But will they come, when you do call for them ?
    Glend. Why, I can teach you, cousin, to command
        the devil.
    Hot. And I can teach thee, coz, to shame the devil,
By telling truth : tell truth, and shame the devil.—
If thou have power to raise him, bring him hither,   60
And I 'll be sworn, I have power to shame him hence.
O ! while you live, tell truth, and shame the devil.
    Mort. Come, come ;
No more of this unprofitable chat.
    Glend. Three times hath Henry Bolingbroke made
        head
Against my power : thrice from the banks of Wye,
And sandy-bottom'd Severn, have I sent him
Bootless home, and weather-beaten back.
    Hot. Home without boots, and in foul weather too !
How 'scapes he agues, in the devil's name ?   70
    Glend. Come, here 's the map. Shall we divide our
        right,
According to our three-fold order ta'en ?
    Mort. The archdeacon hath divided it
Into three limits very equally.
England, from Trent and Severn hitherto,
By south and east, is to my part assign'd :
All westward, Wales, beyond the Severn shore,
And all the fertile land within that bound,
To Owen Glendower :—and, dear coz, to you
The remnant northward, lying off from Trent.   80
And our indentures tripartite are drawn,
Which being sealed interchangeably
(A business that this night may execute),
To-morrow, cousin Percy, you, and I,
And my good Lord of Worcester, will set forth,
To meet your father, and the Scottish power,
As is appointed us, at Shrewsbury.
My father Glendower is not ready yet,
Nor shall we need his help these fourteen days.—
Within that space you may have drawn together   90
Your tenants, friends, and neighbouring gentlemen.
    Glend. A shorter time shall send me to you, lords ;
And in my conduct shall your ladies come,
From whom you now must steal, and take no leave ;
For there will be a world of water shed,
Upon the parting of your wives and you.
    Hot. Methinks, my moiety, north from Burton here,
In quantity equals not one of yours.
See, how this river comes me cranking in,
And cuts me from the best of all my land   100
A huge half-moon, a monstrous cantle out.
I 'll have the current in this place damm'd up,
And here the smug and silver Trent shall run

In a new channel, fair and evenly :
It shall not wind with such a deep indent,
To rob me of so rich a bottom here.
  Glend. Not wind ? it shall, it must : you see, it doth.
  Mort. Yea, but
Mark, how he bears his course, and runs me up
With like advantage on the other side ;   110
Gelding the opposed continent as much
As on the other side it takes from you.

Hot. "See, how this river comes me cranking in."

  Wor. Yea, but a little charge will trench him here,
And on this north side win this cape of land ;
And then he runs straight and even.
  Hot. I 'll have it so ; a little charge will do it.
  Glend. I will not have it alter'd.
  Hot.   Will not you ?
  Glend. No, nor you shall not.
  Hot.   Who shall say me nay ?
  Glend. Why, that will I.
  Hot.   Let me not understand you then :
Speak it in Welsh.   120
  Glend. I can speak English, lord, as well as you,
For I was train'd up in the English court ;
Where, being but young, I framed to the harp
Many an English ditty, lovely well,
And gave the tongue a helpful ornament ;
A virtue that was never seen in you.
  Hot. Marry, and I 'm glad of it with all my heart.
I had rather be a kitten, and cry mew,
Than one of these same metre ballad-mongers ;
I had rather hear a brazen canstick turn'd,   130
Or a dry wheel grate on the axle-tree ;
And that would set my teeth nothing on edge,
Nothing so much as mincing poetry :
'T is like the forc'd gait of a shuffling nag.
  Glend. Come, you shall have Trent turn'd.
  Hot. I do not care : I 'll give thrice so much land
To any well-deserving friend ;
But in the way of bargain, mark ye me,
I 'll cavil on the ninth part of a hair.
Are the indentures drawn ? shall we be gone ?   140
  Glend. The moon shines fair, you may away by
         night :
I 'll haste the writer, and, withal,
Break with your wives of your departure hence.
I am afraid my daughter will run mad,
So much she doteth on her Mortimer.   [*Exit.*
  Mort. Fie, cousin Percy ! how you cross my father !
  Hot. I cannot choose : sometime he angers me
With telling me of the moldwarp and the ant,
Of the dreamer Merlin and his prophecies,
And of a dragon, and a finless fish,   150
A clip-wing'd griffin, and a moulten raven,
A couching lion, and a ramping cat,
And such a deal of skimble-skamble stuff

As puts me from my faith. I tell you what,—
He held me, last night, at least nine hours,
In reckoning up the several devils' names,
That were his lackeys : I cried, "Humph," and "Well,
     go to,"
But mark'd him not a word. O ! he 's as tedious
As a tired horse, a railing wife ;
Worse than a smoky house. I had rather live   160
With cheese and garlic in a windmill, far,
Than feed on cates, and have him talk to me
In any summer-house in Christendom.
  Mort. In faith, he is a worthy gentleman,
Exceedingly well read, and profited
In strange concealments, valiant as a lion,
And wondrous affable, and as bountiful
As mines of India. Shall I tell you, cousin ?
He holds your temper in a high respect,
And curbs himself even of his natural scope,   170
When you do cross his humour ; 'faith, he does.
I warrant you, that man is not alive,
Might so have tempted him as you have done,
Without the taste of danger and reproof :
But do not use it oft, let me entreat you.
  Wor. In faith, my lord, you are too wilful-blame ;
And since your coming hither, have done enough
To put him quite beside his patience.
You must needs learn, lord, to amend this fault :
Though sometimes it show greatness, courage, blood,
(And that 's the dearest grace it renders you,)   181
Yet oftentimes it doth present harsh rage,
Defect of manners, want of government,
Pride, haughtiness, opinion, and disdain :
The least of which, haunting a nobleman,
Loseth men's hearts, and leaves behind a stain
Upon the beauty of all parts besides,
Beguiling them of commendation.
  Hot. Well, I am school'd ; good manners be your
     speed !
Here come our wives, and let us take our leave.   190

Re-enter GLENDOWER, *with the Ladies.*

  Mort. This is the deadly spite that angers me,
My wife can speak no English, I no Welsh.
  Glend. My daughter weeps ; she will not part with
     you :
She 'll be a soldier too ; she 'll to the wars.
  Mort. Good father, tell her, that she, and my aunt
     Percy,
Shall follow in your conduct speedily.
     [GLENDOWER *speaks to her in Welsh, and she*
         answers him in the same.
  Glend. She 's desperate here ; a peevish self-will'd
     harlotry,
One that no persuasion can do good upon.
     [*She speaks to* MORTIMER *in Welsh.*
  Mort. I understand thy looks : that pretty Welsh
Which thou pourest down from these swelling heavens,
I am too perfect in : and, but for shame,   201
In such a parley should I answer thee.
     [*She speaks again.*
I understand thy kisses, and thou mine,
And that 's a feeling disputation :
But I will never be a truant, love,
Till I have learn'd thy language ; for thy tongue
Makes Welsh as sweet as ditties highly penn'd,
Sung by a fair queen in a summer's bower,
With ravishing division, to her lute.
  Glend. Nay, if you melt, then will she run mad.   210
     [*She speaks again.*
  Mort. O ! I am ignorance itself in this.
  Glend. She bids you on the wanton rushes lay you
     down,
And rest your gentle head upon her lap,
And she will sing the song that pleaseth you,
And on your eyelids crown the god of sleep,
Charming your blood with pleasing heaviness,
Making such difference 'twixt wake and sleep,
As is the difference betwixt day and night,
The hour before the heavenly-harness'd team
Begins his golden progress in the east.   220
  Mort. With all my heart I 'll sit, and hear her sing :
By that time will our book, I think, be drawn.

Glend. Do so;
And those musicians that shall play to you,
Hang in the air a thousand leagues from hence ;
And straight they shall be here. Sit, and attend.
  Hot. Come, Kate, thou art perfect in lying down :
come, quick, quick ; that I may lay my head in thy lap.
  Lady P. Go, ye giddy goose.   [*The music plays.*
  Hot. Now I perceive, the devil understands Welsh ;
And 't is no marvel, he is so humorous.   231
By 'r lady, he 's a good musician.
  Lady P. Then should you be nothing but musical,
for you are altogether governed by humours. Lie still,
ye thief, and hear the lady sing in Welsh.
  Hot. I had rather hear Lady, my brach, howl in
Irish.
  Lady P. Wouldst have thy head broken ?
  Hot. No.
  Lady P. Then be still.   240
  Hot. Neither ; 't is a woman's fault.
  Lady P. Now, God help thee !
  Hot. To the Welsh lady's bed.
  Lady P. What 's that ?
  Hot. Peace ! she sings.
          [*A Welsh song sung by Lady* MORTIMER.
  Hot. Come, Kate, I 'll have your song too.
  Lady P. Not mine, in good sooth.
  Hot. Not yours, in good sooth ! 'Heart ! you swear
like a comfit-maker's wife. "Not you, in good sooth ;"
and, "As true as I live ;" and, "As God shall mend
me ;" and, "As sure as day :"   251
And giv'st such sarcenet surety for thy oaths,
As if thou never walk'dst further than Finsbury.
Swear me, Kate, like a lady as thou art,
A good mouth-filling oath ; and leave "in sooth,"
And such protest of pepper-gingerbread,
To velvet-guards, and Sunday-citizens.
Come, sing.
  Lady P. I will not sing.
  Hot. 'T is the next way to turn tailor, or be red-
breast teacher. An the indentures be drawn, I 'll away
within these two hours ; and so come in when ye will.
          [*Exit.*
  Glend. Come, come, Lord Mortimer ; you are as slow
As hot Lord Percy is on fire to go.
By this our book is drawn : we will but seal,
And then to horse immediately.
  Mort. With all my heart.   [*Exeunt.*

SCENE II.—London. A Room in the Palace.

Enter King HENRY, *Prince of* WALES, *and Lords.*

  K. Hen. Lords, give us leave.   The Prince of Wales
and I
Must have some private conference : but be near at
hand,
For we shall presently have need of you.—
          [*Exeunt Lords.*
I know not whether God will have it so,
For some displeasing service I have done,
That, in his secret doom, out of my blood
He 'll breed revengement and a scourge for me ;
But thou dost, in thy passages of life,
Make me believe, that thou art only mark'd
For the hot vengeance and the rod of Heaven,   10
To punish my mistreadings. Tell me else,
Could such inordinate and low desires,
Such poor, such bare, such lewd, such mean attempts,
Such barren pleasures, rude society,
As thou art match'd withal, and grafted to,
Accompany the greatness of thy blood,
And hold their level with thy princely heart?
  P. Hen. So please your majesty, I would I could
Quit all offences with as clear excuse,
As well as, I am doubtless, I can purge   20
Myself of many I am charg'd withal :
Yet such extenuation let me beg,
As, in reproof of many tales devis'd
(Which oft the ear of greatness needs must hear)
By smiling pick-thanks and base newsmongers,
I may, for some things true, wherein my youth

Hath faulty wander'd and irregular,
Find pardon on my true submission.
  K. Hen. God pardon thee !—yet let me wonder,
Harry,
At thy affections, which do hold a wing   30
Quite from the flight of all thy ancestors.
Thy place in council thou hast rudely lost,
Which by thy younger brother is supplied ;
And art almost an alien to the hearts
Of all the court, and princes of my blood.
The hope and expectation of thy time
Is ruin'd, and the soul of every man
Prophetically does forethink thy fall.
Had I so lavish of my presence been,
So common-hackney'd in the eyes of men,   40
So stale and cheap to vulgar company,
Opinion, that did help me to the crown,
Had still kept loyal to possession,
And left me in reputeless banishment,
A fellow of no mark, nor likelihood.
By being seldom seen, I could not stir,
But like a comet I was wonder'd at ;
That men would tell their children, "This is he ;"
Others would say,—"Where ? which is Bolingbroke ?"
And then I stole all courtesy from Heaven,   50
And dress'd myself in such humility,
That I did pluck allegiance from men's hearts,
Loud shouts and salutations from their mouths,
Even in the presence of the crowned king.
Thus did I keep my person fresh, and new ;
My presence, like a robe pontifical,
Ne'er seen but wonder'd at : and so my state,
Seldom, but sumptuous, showed like a feast,
And won by rareness such solemnity.
The skipping king, he ambled up and down   60
With shallow jesters, and rash bavin wits,
Soon kindled, and soon burn'd ; carded his state,
Mingled his royalty with carping fools,
Had his great name profaned with their scorns,
And gave his countenance, against his name,
To laugh at gibing boys, and stand the push
Of every beardless vain comparative ;
Grew a companion to the common streets,
Enfeoff'd himself to popularity,
That, being daily swallow'd by men's eyes,   70
They surfeited with honey, and began
To loathe the taste of sweetness, whereof a little
More than a little is by much too much.
So, when he had occasion to be seen,
He was but as the cuckoo is in June,
Heard, not regarded ; seen, but with such eyes,
As, sick and blunted with community,
Afford no extraordinary gaze,
Such as is bent on sun-like majesty,
When it shines seldom in admiring eyes ;   80
But rather drows'd, and hung their eyelids down,
Slept in his face, and render'd such aspect
As cloudy men use to their adversaries,
Being with his presence glutted, gorg'd, and full.
And in that very line, Harry, stand'st thou ;
For thou hast lost thy princely privilege
With vile participation. Not an eye
But is aweary of thy common sight,
Save mine, which hath desir'd to see thee more ;
Which now doth that I would not have it do,   90
Make blind itself with foolish tenderness.
  P. Hen. I shall hereafter, my thrice-gracious lord,
Be more myself.
  K. Hen.   For all the world,
As thou art to this hour, was Richard then,
When I from France set foot at Ravenspurg ;
And even as I was then, is Percy now.
Now, by my sceptre, and my soul to boot,
He hath more worthy interest to the state,
Than thou the shadow of succession :
For, of no right, nor colour like to right,   100
He doth fill fields with harness in the realm,
Turns head against the lion's armed jaws,
And, being no more in debt to years than thou,
Leads ancient lords and reverend bishops on
To bloody battles, and to bruising arms.
What never-dying honour hath he got

Against renowned Douglas, whose high deeds,
Whose hot incursions, and great name in arms,
Holds from all soldiers chief majority,
And military title capital, 110
Through all the kingdoms that acknowledge Christ.
Thrice hath this Hotspur, Mars in swathing-clothes,
This infant warrior, in his enterprises
Discomfited great Douglas: ta'en him once,
Enlarged him, and made a friend of him,
To fill the mouth of deep defiance up,
And shake the peace and safety of our throne.
And what say you to this? Percy, Northumberland,
The Archbishop's Grace of York, Douglas, Mortimer,
Capitulate against us, and are up. 120

P. Hen. "This, in the name of God, I promise here."

But wherefore do I tell these news to thee?
Why, Harry, do I tell thee of my foes,
Which art my near'st and dearest enemy?
Thou that art like enough, through vassal fear,
Base inclination, and the start of spleen,
To fight against me under Percy's pay,
To dog his heels, and curtsy at his frowns,
To show how much thou art degenerate.
P. Hen. Do not think so; you shall not find it so:
And God forgive them that so much have sway'd 130
Your majesty's good thoughts away from me!
I will redeem all this on Percy's head,
And, in the closing of some glorious day,
Be bold to tell you that I am your son;
When I will wear a garment all of blood,
And stain my favours in a bloody mask,
Which, wash'd away, shall scour my shame with it:
And that shall be the day, whene'er it lights,
That this same child of honour and renown,
This gallant Hotspur, this all-praised knight, 140
And your unthought-of Harry, chance to meet.
For every honour sitting on his helm,
'Would they were multitudes; and on my head
My shames redoubled! for the time will come,
That I shall make this northern youth exchange
His glorious deeds for my indignities.
Percy is but my factor, good my lord,
To engross up glorious deeds on my behalf;
And I will call him to so strict account,
That he shall render every glory up, 150
Yea, even the slightest worship of his time,
Or I will tear the reckoning from his heart.
This, in the name of God, I promise here:
The which, if he be pleas'd I shall perform,
I do beseech your majesty, may salve
The long-grown wounds of my intemperance:
If not, the end of life cancels all bands,
And I will die a hundred thousand deaths,
E'er break the smallest parcel of this vow.

K. Hen. A hundred thousand rebels die in this: 160
Thou shalt have charge and sovereign trust herein.

Enter BLUNT.

How now, good Blunt? thy looks are full of speed.
Blunt. So hath the business that I come to speak of.
Lord Mortimer of Scotland hath sent word,
That Douglas and the English rebels met,
The eleventh of this month, at Shrewsbury.
A mighty and a fearful head they are,
If promises be kept on every hand,
As ever offer'd foul play in a state.
K. Hen. The Earl of Westmoreland set forth to-day,
With him my son, Lord John of Lancaster; 171
For this advertisement is five days old.—
On Wednesday next, Harry, you shall set forward;
On Thursday we ourselves will march:
Our meeting is Bridgnorth; and, Harry, you
Shall march through Glostershire; by which account,
Our business valued, some twelve days hence
Our general forces at Bridgnorth shall meet.
Our hands are full of business: let 's away;
Advantage feeds him fat, while men delay. 180
[*Exeunt.*

SCENE III.—Eastcheap.   A Room in the Boar's Head
Tavern.

Enter FALSTAFF *and* BARDOLPH.

Fal. Bardolph, am I not fallen away vilely since
this last action? do I not bate? do I not dwindle? Why,
my skin hangs about me like an old lady's loose gown:
I am wither'd like an old apple-John. Well, I'll repent, and that suddenly, while I am in some liking;
I shall be out of heart shortly, and then I shall have
no strength to repent.   An I have not forgotten what
the inside of a church is made of, I am a pepper-corn,
a brewer's horse.   The inside of a church!   Company,
villainous company, hath been the spoil of me. 10
Bard. Sir John, you are so fretful, you cannot live
long.
Fal. Why, there is it.—Come, sing me a bawdy
song; make me merry.   I was as virtuously given as
a gentleman need to be; virtuous enough: swore
little; diced not above seven times a week; went to a
bawdy-house not above once in a quarter—of an hour;
paid money that I borrowed three or four times; lived
well, and in good compass; and now I live out of all
order, out of all compass. 20
Bard. Why, you are so fat, Sir John, that you must
needs be out of all compass, out of all reasonable
compass, Sir John.
Fal. Do thou amend thy face, and I'll amend my
life.   Thou art our admiral, thou bearest the lantern
in the poop,—but 't is in the nose of thee: thou art the
Knight of the Burning Lamp.
Bard. Why, Sir John, my face does you no harm.
Fal. No; I'll be sworn, I make as good use of it as
many a man doth of a death's-head, or a *memento mori.*
I never see thy face but I think upon hell-fire, and
Dives that lived in purple; for there he is in his robes,
burning, burning.   If thou wert any way given to
virtue, I would swear by thy face; my oath should be,
"By this fire, that 's God's angel."   But thou art altogether given over, and wert indeed, but for the light
in thy face, the sun of utter darkness.   When thou
rann'st up Gadshill in the night to catch my horse, if
I did not think thou hadst been an *ignis fatuus*, or
a ball of wildfire, there 's no purchase in money.   O!
thou art a perpetual triumph, an everlasting bonfire-
light.   Thou hast saved me a thousand marks in links
and torches, walking with thee in the night betwixt
tavern and tavern: but the sack that thou hast drunk
me, would have bought me lights as good cheap, at
the dearest chandler's in Europe.   I have maintained
that salamander of yours with fire any time this two
and-thirty years: God reward me for it!
Bard. 'Sblood! I would my face were in your
belly. 50
Fal. God-a-mercy! so should I be sure to be heart-
burned.

Enter Hostess.

How now, Dame Partlet the hen? have you inquired yet who picked my pocket?

Host. Why, Sir John, what do you think, Sir John? Do you think I keep thieves in my house? I have searched, I have inquired, so has my husband, man by man, boy by boy, servant by servant: the tithe of a hair was never lost in my house before.

Fal. You lie, hostess; Bardolph was shaved, and lost many a hair; and I'll be sworn, my pocket was picked. Go to, you are a woman; go.   62

Host. Who, I? No. I defy thee: God's light! I was never called so in mine own house before.

Fal. Go to, I know you well enough.

Host. No, Sir John; you do not know me, Sir John: I know you, Sir John: you owe me money, Sir John, and now you pick a quarrel to beguile me of it. I bought you a dozen of shirts to your back.   70

Fal. Dowlas, filthy dowlas: I have given them away to bakers' wives, and they have made bolters of them.

Host. Now, as I am a true woman, holland of eight shillings an ell. You owe money here besides, Sir John, for your diet, and by-drinkings, and money lent you, four-and-twenty pound.

Fal. He had his part of it: let him pay.

Host. He? alas! he is poor: he hath nothing.

Fal. How! poor? look upon his face; what call you rich? let them coin his nose, let them coin his cheeks. I'll not pay a denier. What, will you make a younker of me? shall I not take mine ease in mine inn, but I shall have my pocket picked? I have lost a seal-ring of my grandfather's, worth forty mark.

Host. O Jesu! I have heard the prince tell him, I know not how oft, that that ring was copper.

Fal. How! the prince is a Jack, a sneak-cup; 'sblood! an he were here, I would cudgel him like a dog, if he would say so.   92

Enter Prince HENRY *and* POINS, *marching.* FAL-STAFF *meets the* PRINCE, *playing on his truncheon, like a fife.*

Fal. How now, lad? is the wind in that door, i' faith? must we all march?

Bard. Yea, two and two, Newgate-fashion.

Host. My lord, I pray you, hear me.

P. Hen. What sayest thou, Mistress Quickly? How does thy husband? I love him well, he is an honest man.

Host. Good my lord, hear me.   100

Fal. Pr'ythee, let her alone, and list to me.

P. Hen. What sayest thou, Jack?

Fal. The other night I fell asleep, here, behind the arras, and had my pocket picked: this house is turned bawdy-house; they pick pockets.

P. Hen. What didst thou lose, Jack?

Fal. Wilt thou believe me, Hal? three or four bonds of forty pound a-piece, and a seal-ring of my grand-father's.

P. Hen. A trifle; some eight-penny matter.   110

Host. So I told him, my lord; and I said I heard your grace say so: and, my lord, he speaks most vilely of you, like a foul-mouthed man as he is, and said he would cudgel you.

P. Hen. What! he did not?

Host. There's neither faith, truth, nor womanhood in me else.

Fal. There's no more faith in thee than in a stewed prune; nor no more truth in thee than in a drawn fox; and for womanhood, Maid Marian may be the deputy's wife of the ward to thee. Go, you thing, go.   122

Host. Say, what thing? what thing?

Fal. What thing? why, a thing to thank God on.

Host. I am no thing to thank God on, I would thou shouldst know it; I am an honest man's wife; and, setting thy knighthood aside, thou art a knave to call me so.

Fal. Setting thy womanhood aside, thou art a beast to say otherwise.   130

Host. Say, what beast, thou knave, thou?

Fal. What beast? why, an otter.

P. Hen. An otter, Sir John! why an otter?

Fal. Why? she's neither fish nor flesh; a man knows not where to have her.

Host. Thou art an unjust man in saying so: thou or any man knows where to have me, thou knave thou!

P. Hen. Thou sayest true, hostess; and he slanders thee most grossly.   140

Host. "Thou art a knave to call me so."

Host. So he doth you, my lord; and said this other day, you ought him a thousand pound.

P. Hen. Sirrah! do I owe you a thousand pound?

Fal. A thousand pound, Hal! a million: thy love is worth a million; thou owest me thy love.

Host. Nay, my lord, he called you Jack, and said he would cudgel you.

Fal. Did I, Bardolph?

Bard. Indeed, Sir John, you said so.

Fal. Yea; if he said my ring was copper.   150

P. Hen. I say, 't is copper; darest thou be as good as thy word now?

Fal. Why, Hal, thou knowest, as thou art but a man, I dare; but as thou art a prince, I fear thee, as I fear the roaring of the lion's whelp.

P. Hen. And why not as the lion?

Fal. The king himself is to be feared as the lion. Dost thou think, I'll fear thee as I fear thy father? nay, an I do, I pray God, my girdle break!   159

P. Hen. O! if it should, how would thy guts fall about thy knees! But, sirrah, there's no room for faith, truth, nor honesty, in this bosom of thine; it is filled up with guts and midriff. Charge an honest woman with picking thy pocket! Why, thou whore-son, impudent, embossed rascal, if there were any-thing in thy pocket but tavern-reckonings, memoran-dums of bawdy-houses, and one poor pennyworth of sugar-candy to make thee long-winded; if thy pocket were enriched with any other injuries but these, I am a villain. And yet you will stand to it, you will not pocket up wrong. Art thou not ashamed?   171

Fal. Dost thou hear, Hal? thou knowest, in the state of innocency, Adam fell; and what should poor Jack Falstaff do, in the days of villainy? Thou seest I have more flesh than another man, and therefore more frailty. You confess then, you picked my pocket?

P. Hen. It appears so by the story.

Fal. Hostess, I forgive thee. Go, make ready breakfast; love thy husband, look to thy servants, cherish thy guests: thou shalt find me tractable to any honest reason: thou seest I am pacified.—Still?—

Nay, pr'ythee, be gone. [*Exit Hostess.*] Now, Hal, to
the news at court: for the robbery, lad,—how is that
answered?
P. Hen. O! my sweet beef, I must still be good
angel to thee.—The money is paid back again.
Fal. O! I do not like that paying back; 'tis a
double labour.
P. Hen. I am good friends with my father, and may
do anything.   191
Fal. Rob me the exchequer the first thing thou
dost, and do it with unwashed hands too.
Bard. Do, my lord.
P. Hen. I have procured thee, Jack, a charge of foot.
Fal. I would it had been of horse. Where shall
I find one that can steal well? O, for a fine thief, of
the age of two-and-twenty, or thereabouts! I am
heinously unprovided. Well, God be thanked for
these rebels; they offend none but the virtuous: I
laud them, I praise them.   201

P. Hen. Bardolph!
Bard. My lord.
P. Hen. Go bear this letter to Lord John of Lan-
caster,
To my brother John; this to my Lord of Westmore-
land.—
Go, Poins, to horse, to horse! for thou and I
Have thirty miles to ride yet ere dinner-time.—
Jack, meet me to-morrow in the Temple Hall
At two o'clock in the afternoon:
There shalt thou know thy charge, and there re-
ceive   210
Money, and order for their furniture.
The land is burning, Percy stands on high,
And either they, or we, must lower lie.
            [*Exeunt* PRINCE, POINS, *and* BARDOLPH.
Fal. Rare words! brave world!—Hostess, my
breakfast; come.—
O! I could wish, this tavern were my drum.   [*Exit.*

ACT IV.

SCENE I.—The Rebel Camp near Shrewsbury.

Enter HOTSPUR, WORCESTER, *and* DOUGLAS.

Hotspur.
WELL said, my noble Scot. If speaking
truth
In this fine age were not thought flattery,
Such attribution should the Douglas
have,
As not a soldier of this season's stamp
Should go so general current through
the world.
By God, I cannot flatter: I defy
The tongues of soothers; but a braver
place
In my heart's love hath no man than yourself.
Nay, task me to my word; approve me, lord.
Doug. Thou art the king of honour: 10
No man so potent breathes upon the ground,
But I will beard him.
Hot.   Do so, and 't is well.—

Enter a Messenger, with letters.

What letters hast thou there?—I can but thank you.
Mess. These letters come from your father,—
Hot. Letters from him! why comes he not himself?
Mess. He cannot come, my lord: he's grievous sick.
Hot. 'Zounds! how has he the leisure to be sick
In such a justling time? Who leads his power?
Under whose government come they along?
Mess. His letters bear his mind, not I, my lord.   20
Wor. I pr'ythee, tell me, doth he keep his bed?
Mess. He did, my lord, four days ere I set forth;
And at the time of my departure thence,
He was much fear'd by his physicians.
Wor. I would the state of time had first been whole,
Ere he by sickness had been visited:
His health was never better worth than now.
Hot. Sick now! droop now! this sickness doth infect
The very life-blood of our enterprise.
'T is catching hither, even to our camp.   30
He writes me here,—that inward sickness—
And that his friends by deputation could not
So soon be drawn; nor did he think it meet,
To lay so dangerous and dear a trust
On any soul remov'd, but on his own.

Yet doth he give us bold advertisement,
That with our small conjunction we should on,
To see how fortune is dispos'd to us;
For, as he writes, there is no quailing now,
Because the king is certainly possess'd   40
Of all our purposes. What say you to it?
Wor. Your father's sickness is a maim to us.
Hot. A perilous gash, a very limb lopp'd off:—
And yet, in faith, 't is not; his present want
Seems more than we shall find it.—Were it good,
To set the exact wealth of all our states
All at one cast? to set so rich a main
On the nice hazard of one doubtful hour?
It were not good; for therein should we read
The very bottom and the soul of hope,   50
The very list, the very utmost bound
Of all our fortunes.
Doug.   'Faith, and so we should;
Where now remains a sweet reversion:
We may boldly spend upon the hope of what
Is to come in:
A comfort of retirement lives in this.
Hot. A rendezvous, a home to fly unto,
If that the devil and mischance look big
Upon the maidenhead of our affairs.
Wor. But yet, I would your father had been here.
The quality and hair of our attempt   61
Brooks no division. It will be thought
By some, that know not why he is away,
That wisdom, loyalty, and mere dislike
Of our proceedings, kept the earl from hence.
And think, how such an apprehension
May turn the tide of fearful faction,
And breed a kind of question in our cause:
For, well you know, we of the offering side
Must keep aloof from strict arbitrement,   70
And stop all sight-holes, every loop, from whence
The eye of reason may pry in upon us.
This absence of your father's draws a curtain,
That shows the ignorant a kind of fear
Before not dreamt of.
Hot.   You strain too far.
I, rather, of his absence make this use:—

It lends a lustre, and more great opinion,
A larger dare to our great enterprise,
Than if the earl were here : for men must think,
If we, without his help, can make a head   80
To push against the kingdom, with his help,
We shall o'erturn it topsy-turvy down.—
Yet all goes well, yet all our joints are whole.
Doug. As heart can think : there is not such a word
Spoke of in Scotland as this term of fear.

Enter Sir RICHARD VERNON.

Hot. My cousin Vernon! welcome, by my soul.
Ver. Pray God, my news be worth a welcome, lord.
The Earl of Westmoreland, seven thousand strong,
Is marching hitherwards ; with him, Prince John.
Hot. No harm : what more ?
Ver.   And further, I have learn'd,
The king himself in person is set forth,   91
Or hitherwards intended speedily,
With strong and mighty preparation.
Hot. He shall be welcome too. Where is his son,
The nimble-footed madcap Prince of Wales,
And his comrades, that daff'd the world aside,
And bid it pass?
Ver.   All furnish'd, all in arms,
All plum'd like estridges, that with the wind
Bated,—like eagles having lately bath'd ;
Glittering in golden coats, like images ;   100
As full of spirit as the month of May,
And gorgeous as the sun at midsummer ;
Wanton as youthful goats, wild as young bulls.
I saw young Harry, with his beaver on,
His cuisses on his thighs, gallantly arm'd,
Rise from the ground like feather'd Mercury,
And vaulted with such ease into his seat,
As if an angel dropp'd down from the clouds,
To turn and wind a fiery Pegasus,
And witch the world with noble horsemanship.   110
Hot. No more, no more : worse than the sun in
                March,
This praise doth nourish agues. Let them come ;
They come like sacrifices in their trim,
And to the fire-ey'd maid of smoky war,
All hot, and bleeding, will we offer them :
The mailed Mars shall on his altar sit,
Up to the ears in blood. I am on fire,
To hear this rich reprisal is so nigh,
And yet not ours.—Come, let me taste my horse,
Who is to bear me, like a thunderbolt,   120
Against the bosom of the Prince of Wales :
Harry to Harry shall, hot horse to horse,
Meet, and ne'er part, till one drop down a corse.—
O, that Glendower were come!
Ver.   There is more news :
I learn'd in Worcester, as I rode along,
He cannot draw his power this fourteen days.
Doug. That 's the worst tidings that I hear of yet.
Wor. Ay, by my faith, that bears a frosty sound.
Hot. What may the king's whole battle reach unto ?
Ver. To thirty thousand.
Hot.   Forty let it be :   130
My father and Glendower being both away,
The powers of us may serve so great a day.
Come, let us take a muster speedily :
Doomsday is near ; die all, die merrily.
Doug. Talk not of dying : I am out of fear
Of death, or death's hand, for this one half year.
                                        [*Exeunt.*

SCENE II.—A Public Road near Coventry.

Enter FALSTAFF and BARDOLPH.

Fal. Bardolph, get thee before to Coventry : fill me
a bottle of sack. Our soldiers shall march through ;
we 'll to Sutton Co'fil' to-night.
Bard. Will you give me money, captain ?
Fal. Lay out, lay out.
Bard. This bottle makes an angel.
Fal. An if it do, take it for thy labour ; and if it
make twenty, take them all, I 'll answer the coinage.
Bid my lieutenant Peto meet me at the town's end. 9
Bard. I will, captain : farewell.   [*Exit.*

Fal. If I be not ashamed of my soldiers, I am a
soused gurnet. I have misused the king's press dam-
nably. I have got, in exchange of a hundred and
fifty soldiers, three hundred and odd pounds. I press
me none but good householders, yeomen's sons ;
inquire me out contracted bachelors, such as had been
asked twice on the banns ; such a commodity of warm
slaves, as had as lief hear the devil as a drum ; such
as fear the report of a caliver worse than a struck
fowl, or a hurt wild-duck. I pressed me none but
such toasts-and-butter, with hearts in their bellies
no bigger than pins' heads, and they have bought
out their services ; and now my whole charge consists
of ancients, corporals, lieutenants, gentlemen of companies, slaves as ragged as Lazarus in the painted cloth,
where the glutton's dogs licked his sores ; and such
as, indeed, were never soldiers, but discarded unjust
serving-men, younger sons to younger brothers, revolted tapsters, and ostlers trade-fallen ; the cankers of
a calm world, and a long peace ; ten times more dishonourable ragged than an old faced ancient : and
such have I, to fill up the rooms of them that have
bought out their services, that you would think that
I had a hundred and fifty tattered prodigals, lately
come from swine-keeping, from eating draff and
husks. A mad fellow met me on the way, and told
me I had unloaded all the gibbets, and pressed the
dead bodies. No eye hath seen such scarecrows.
I 'll not march through Coventry with them, that 's
flat :—nay, and the villains march wide betwixt the
legs, as if they had gyves on ; for, indeed, I had the
most of them out of prison, There 's not a shirt and
a half in all my company : and the half-shirt is two
napkins, tacked together, and thrown over the
shoulders like a herald's coat without sleeves ; and
the shirt, to say the truth, stolen from my host at
Saint Albans, or the red-nose innkeeper of Daventry.
But that 's all one ; they 'll find linen enough on every
hedge.

Enter Prince HENRY and WESTMORELAND.

P. Hen. How now, blown Jack ? how now, quilt? 50
Fal. What, Hal ! How now, mad wag? what a devil
dost thou in Warwickshire ?—My good Lord of Westmoreland, I cry you mercy : I thought your honour
had already been at Shrewsbury.
West. 'Faith, Sir John, 'tis more than time that I
were there, and you too ; but my powers are there
already. The king, I can tell you, looks for us all : we
must away all night.
Fal. Tut, never fear me : I am as vigilant as a cat
to steal cream.   60
P. Hen. I think, to steal cream indeed ; for thy
theft hath already made thee butter. But tell me,
Jack ; whose fellows are these that come after ?
Fal. Mine, Hal, mine.
P. Hen. I did never see such pitiful rascals.
Fal. Tut, tut ! good enough to toss ; food for
powder, food for powder ; they 'll fill a pit, as well as
better : tush, man, mortal men, mortal men.
West. Ay, but, Sir John, methinks they are exceed-
ing poor and bare ; too beggarly.   70
Fal. 'Faith, for their poverty, I know not where
they had that ; and for their bareness, I am sure, they
never learned that of me.
P. Hen. No, I 'll be sworn ; unless you call three
fingers on the ribs, bare. But, sirrah, make haste :
Percy is already in the field.
Fal. What, is the king encamped ?
West. He is, Sir John : I fear we shall stay too long.
Fal. Well,
To the latter end of a fray, and the beginning of a
                feast,   80
Fits a dull fighter, and a keen guest.   [*Exeunt.*

SCENE III.—The Rebel Camp near Shrewsbury.

Enter HOTSPUR, WORCESTER, DOUGLAS, and
VERNON.

Hot. We 'll fight with him to-night.
Wor.   It may not be.

Doug. You give him then advantage.
Ver.   Not a whit.
Hot. Why say you so? looks he not for supply?
Ver. So do we.
Hot.   His is certain, ours is doubtful.
Wor. Good cousin, be advis'd: stir not to-night.
Ver. Do not, my lord.
Doug.   You do not counsel well.
You speak it out of fear and cold heart.
Ver. Do me no slander, Douglas: by my life,
And I dare well maintain it with my life,
If well-respected honour bid me on,   10
I hold as little counsel with weak fear,
As you, my lord, or any Scot that this day lives:
Let it be seen to-morrow in the battle,
Which of us fears.
Doug.   Yea, or to-night.
Ver.   Content.
Hot. To-night, say I.
Ver. Come, come, it may not be. I wonder much,
Being men of such great leading as you are,
That you foresee not what impediments
Drag back our expedition: certain horse   20
Of my cousin Vernon's are not yet come up;
Your uncle Worcester's horse came but to-day;
And now their pride and mettle is asleep,
Their courage with hard labour tame and dull,
That not a horse is half the half of himself.
Hot. So are the horses of the enemy
In general, journey-bated, and brought low;
The better part of ours are full of rest.
Wor. The number of the king exceedeth ours:
For God's sake, cousin, stay till all come in.
        [*The trumpet sounds a parley.*

Enter Sir WALTER BLUNT.

Blunt. I come with gracious offers from the king, 30
If you vouchsafe me hearing and respect.
Hot. Welcome, Sir Walter Blunt; and 'would to God
You were of our determination!
Some of us love you well: and even those some
Envy your great deservings and good name,
Because you are not of our quality,
But stand against us like an enemy.
Blunt. And God defend but still I should stand so,
So long as, out of limit and true rule,
You stand against anointed majesty.   40
But, to my charge.—The king hath sent to know
The nature of your griefs, and whereupon
You conjure from the breast of civil peace
Such bold hostility, teaching his duteous land
Audacious cruelty? If that the king
Have any way your good deserts forgot,
Which he confesseth to be manifold,
He bids you name your griefs, and, with all speed,
You shall have your desires with interest,
And pardon absolute for yourself, and these,   50
Herein misled by your suggestion.
Hot. The king is kind; and, well we know, the king
Knows at what time to promise, when to pay.
My father, and my uncle, and myself,
Did give him that same royalty he wears:
And, when he was not six-and-twenty strong,
Sick in the world's regard, wretched and low,
A poor unminded outlaw sneaking home,
My father gave him welcome to the shore;
And, when he heard him swear, and vow to God,   60
He came but to be Duke of Lancaster,
To sue his livery, and beg his peace,
With tears of innocency, and terms of zeal,
My father, in kind heart and pity mov'd,
Swore him assistance, and perform'd it too.
Now, when the lords and barons of the realm
Perceiv'd Northumberland did lean to him,
The more and less came in with cap and knee;
Met him in boroughs, cities, villages,
Attended him on bridges, stood in lanes,   70
Laid gifts before him, proffer'd him their oaths,
Gave him their heirs as pages: follow'd him,
Even at the heels, in golden multitudes.
He presently, as greatness knows itself,

Steps me a little higher than his vow
Made to my father, while his blood was poor,
Upon the naked shore at Ravenspurg;
And now, forsooth, takes on him to reform
Some certain edicts, and some strait decrees,
That lie too heavy on the commonwealth;   80
Cries out upon abuses, seems to weep
Over his country's wrongs; and, by this face,
This seeming brow of justice, did he win
The hearts of all that he did angle for;
Proceeded further; cut me off the heads
Of all the favourites, that the absent king

Arch.   "I must go write again
To other friends; and so farewell, Sir Michael."

In deputation left behind him here,
When he was personal in the Irish war.
Blunt. Tut! I came not to hear this.
Hot.   Then, to the point.
In short time after he depos'd the king;   90
Soon after that, depriv'd him of his life;
And, in the neck of that, task'd the whole state;
To make that worse, suffer'd his kinsman March
(Who is, if every owner were well plac'd,
Indeed his king) to be engag'd in Wales,
There without ransom to lie forfeited;
Disgrac'd me in my happy victories;
Sought to entrap me by intelligence;
Rated my uncle from the council-board;
In rage dismiss'd my father from the court;   100
Broke oath on oath, committed wrong on wrong,
And, in conclusion, drove us to seek out
This head of safety, and, withal, to pry
Into his title, the which we find
Too indirect for long continuance.
Blunt. Shall I return this answer to the king?
Hot. Not so, Sir Walter: we'll withdraw awhile.
Go to the king, and let there be impawn'd
Some surety for a safe return again,
And in the morning early shall mine uncle   110
Bring him our purposes; and so farewell.
Blunt. I would you would accept of grace and love.
Hot. And, may be, so we shall.
Blunt.   'Pray God, you do!
                        ————   [*Exeunt.*

SCENE IV.—York. A Room in the Archbishop's
                        House.

Enter the Archbishop of YORK *and Sir* MICHAEL.

Arch. Hie, good Sir Michael; bear this sealed brief
With winged haste to the lord marshal;
This to my cousin Scroop; and all the rest
To whom they are directed. If you knew
How much they do import, you would make haste.

Sir M. My good lord,
I guess their tenor.
Arch. Like enough, you do.
To-morrow, good Sir Michael, is a day,
Wherein the fortune of ten thousand men
Must bide the touch. For, sir, at Shrewsbury, 10
As I am truly given to understand,
The king, with mighty and quick-raised power,
Meets with Lord Harry : and, I fear, Sir Michael,
What with the sickness of Northumberland,
Whose power was in the first proportion,
And what with Owen Glendower's absence thence,
Who with them was a rated sinew too,
And comes not in, o'er-rul'd by prophecies,
I fear, the power of Percy is too weak
To wage an instant trial with the king. 20
Sir M. Why, my good lord, you need not fear :
There is Douglas, and Lord Mortimer.
Arch. No, Mortimer is not there.

Sir M. But there is Mordake, Vernon, Lord Harry
Percy,
And there's my Lord of Worcester, and a head
Of gallant warriors, noble gentlemen.
Arch. And so there is ; but yet the king hath drawn
The special head of all the land together :
The Prince of Wales, Lord John of Lancaster,
The noble Westmoreland, and warlike Blunt, 30
And many more corrivals, and dear men
Of estimation and command in arms.
Sir M. Doubt not, my lord, they shall be well oppos'd.
Arch. I hope no less, yet needful 't is to fear ;
And, to prevent the worst, Sir Michael, speed :
For, if Lord Percy thrive not, ere the king
Dismiss his power, he means to visit us,
For he hath heard of our confederacy,
And 't is but wisdom to make strong against him :
Therefore, make haste. I must go write again 40
To other friends ; and so farewell, Sir Michael.
[*Exeunt.*

ACT V.

SCENE I.—The King's Camp near Shrewsbury.

Enter King HENRY, *Prince* HENRY, *Prince* JOHN *of* LANCASTER, *Sir* WALTER BLUNT, *and Sir* JOHN FALSTAFF.

King Henry.
OW bloodily the sun begins to peer
Above yon busky hill : the day looks pale
At his distemperature.
P. Hen. The southern wind
Doth play the trumpet to his purposes ;
And by his hollow whistling in the leaves
Foretells a tempest, and a blustering day.
K. Hen. Then with the losers let it sym-
pathise,
For nothing can seem foul to those that
win.— [*Trumpet sounds.*

Enter WORCESTER *and* VERNON.

How now, my Lord of Worcester? 't is not well,
That you and I should meet upon such terms 10
As now we meet. You have deceiv'd our trust,
And made us doff our easy robes of peace,
To crush our old limbs in ungentle steel :
This is not well, my lord ; this is not well.
What say you to it ? will you again unknit
This churlish knot of all-abhorred war,
And move in that obedient orb again,
Where you did give a fair and natural light ;
And be no more an exhal'd meteor,
A prodigy of fear, and a portent 20
Of broached mischief to the unborn times?
Wor. Hear me, my liege.
For mine own part, I could be well content
To entertain the lag-end of my life
With quiet hours ; for, I do protest,
I have not sought the day of this dislike.
K. Hen. You have not sought it! how comes it
then?
Fal. Rebellion lay in his way, and he found it.
P. Hen. Peace, chewet, peace !
Wor. It pleas'd your majesty, to turn your looks 30
Of favour from myself, and all our house ;
And yet I must remember you, my lord,
We were the first and dearest of your friends.
For you my staff of office did I break

In Richard's time ; and posted day and night
To meet you on the way, and kiss your hand,
When yet you were in place and in account
Nothing so strong and fortunate as I.
It was myself, my brother, and his son,
That brought you home, and boldly did outdare 40
The dangers of the time. You swore to us,
And you did swear that oath at Doncaster,
That you did nothing purpose 'gainst the state,
Nor claim no further than your new-fall'n right,
The seat of Gaunt, dukedom of Lancaster.
To this we swore our aid : but, in short space,
It rain'd down fortune showering on your head,
And such a flood of greatness fell on you,
What with our help, what with the absent king,
What with the injuries of a wanton time, 50
The seeming sufferances that you had borne,
And the contrarious winds, that held the king
So long in his unlucky Irish wars,
That all in England did repute him dead :
And, from this swarm of fair advantages,
You took occasion to be quickly woo'd
To gripe the general sway into your hand ;
Forgot your oath to us at Doncaster,
And, being fed by us, you us'd us so
As that ungentle gull, the cuckoo's bird, 60
Useth the sparrow : did oppress our nest,
Grew by our feeding to so great a bulk,
That even our love durst not come near your sight,
For fear of swallowing ; but with nimble wing
We were enforc'd, for safety sake, to fly
Out of your sight, and raise this present head ;
Whereby we stand opposed by such means
As you yourself have forg'd against yourself,
By unkind usage, dangerous countenance,
And violation of all faith and troth 70
Sworn to us in your younger enterprise.
K. Hen. These things, indeed, you have articulate,
Proclaim'd at market-crosses, read in churches,
To face the garment of rebellion
With some fine colour, that may please the eye

Of fickle changelings and poor discontents,
Which gape, and rub the elbow, at the news
Of hurly-burly innovation:
And never yet did insurrection want
Such water-colours, to impaint his cause;   80
Nor moody beggars, starving for a time
Of pell-mell havoc and confusion.
P. Hen. In both our armies there is many a soul
Shall pay full dearly for this encounter,
If once they join in trial. Tell your nephew,
The Prince of Wales doth join with all the world
In praise of Henry Percy: by my hopes,
This present enterprise set off his head,
I do not think, a braver gentleman,
More active-valiant, or more valiant-young,   90
More daring, or more bold, is now alive

Fal. "What is that word honour?"

To grace this latter age with noble deeds.
For my part, I may speak it to my shame,
I have a truant been to chivalry,
And so, I hear, he doth account me too;
Yet this before my father's majesty:
I am content, that he shall take the odds
Of his great name and estimation,
And will, to save the blood on either side,
Try fortune with him in a single fight.   100
K. Hen. And, Prince of Wales, so dare we venture thee,
Albeit considerations infinite
Do make against it.—No, good Worcester, no,
We love our people well; even those we love,
That are misled upon your cousin's part,
And, will they take the offer of our grace,
Both he, and they, and you, yea, every man,
Shall be my friend again, and I'll be his.
So tell your cousin, and bring me word
What he will do; but if he will not yield,   110
Rebuke and dread correction wait on us,
And they shall do their office. So, be gone.
We will not now be troubled with reply:
We offer fair, take it advisedly.
            [*Exeunt* WORCESTER *and* VERNON.
P. Hen. It will not be accepted, on my life.
The Douglas and the Hotspur both together
Are confident against the world in arms.
K. Hen. Hence, therefore, every leader to his charge;
For, on their answer, will we set on them;   120
And God befriend us, as our cause is just!
            [*Exeunt* KING, BLUNT, *and Prince* JOHN.
Fal. Hal, if thou see me down in the battle, and bestride me, so; 't is a point of friendship.
P. Hen. Nothing but a colossus can do thee that friendship. Say thy prayers, and farewell.
Fal. I would it were bed-time, Hal, and all well.

P. Hen. Why, thou owest God a death.   [*Exit.*
Fal. 'T is not due yet: I would be loath to pay him before his day. What need I be so forward with him that calls not on me? Well, 't is no matter; honour pricks me on. Yea, but how if honour prick me off when I come on? how then? Can honour set to a leg? No. Or an arm? No. Or take away the grief of a wound? No. Honour hath no skill in surgery then? No. What is honour? A word. What is that word honour? Air. A trim reckoning!—Who hath it? He that died o' Wednesday. Doth he feel it? No. Doth he hear it? No. Is it insensible then? Yea, to the dead. But will it not live with the living? No. Why? Detraction will not suffer it.—Therefore, I'll none of it: honour is a mere scutcheon; and so ends my catechism.   [*Exit.*

SCENE II.—The Rebel Camp.

Enter WORCESTER *and* VERNON.

Wor. O, no! my nephew must not know, Sir Richard,
The liberal kind offer of the king.
Ver. 'T were best, he did.
Wor.   Then are we all undone.
It is not possible, it cannot be,
The king should keep his word in loving us;
He will suspect us still, and find a time
To punish this offence in other faults:
Suspicion all our lives shall be stuck full of eyes;
For treason is but trusted like the fox,
Who, ne'er so tame, so cherish'd, and lock'd up,   10
Will have a wild trick of his ancestors.
Look how we can, or sad, or merrily,
Interpretation will misquote our looks;
And we shall feed like oxen at a stall,
The better cherish'd, still the nearer death.
My nephew's trespass may be well forgot,
It hath the excuse of youth, and heat of blood;
And an adopted name of privilege,
A hare-brain'd Hotspur, govern'd by a spleen.
All his offences live upon my head,   20
And on his father's: we did train him on;
And, his corruption being ta'en from us,
We, as the spring of all, shall pay for all.
Therefore, good cousin, let not Harry know
In any case the offer of the king.
Ver. Deliver what you will, I'll say 't is so.
Here comes your cousin.

Enter HOTSPUR *and* DOUGLAS; *Officers and Soldiers, behind.*

Hot. My uncle is return'd:—deliver up
My Lord of Westmoreland.—Uncle, what news?
Wor. The king will bid you battle presently.   30
Doug. Defy him by the Lord of Westmoreland.
Hot. Lord Douglas, go you and tell him so.
Doug. Marry, and shall, and very willingly. [*Exit.*
Wor. There is no seeming mercy in the king.
Hot. Did you beg any? God forbid!
Wor. I told him gently of our grievances,
Of his oath-breaking; which he mended thus,
By now forswearing that he is forsworn:
He calls us rebels, traitors; and will scourge
With haughty arms this hateful name in us.   40

Re-enter DOUGLAS.

Doug. Arm, gentlemen! to arms! for I have thrown
A brave defiance in King Henry's teeth,
And Westmoreland, that was engag'd, did bear it;
Which cannot choose but bring him quickly on.
Wor. The Prince of Wales stepp'd forth before the king,
And, nephew, challeng'd you to single fight.
Hot. O! 'would the quarrel lay upon our heads,
And that no man might draw short breath to-day,
But I and Harry Monmouth! Tell me, tell me,
How show'd his tasking? seem'd it in contempt?   50
Ver. No, by my soul! I never in my life
Did hear a challenge urg'd more modestly,
Unless a brother should a brother dare

To gentle exercise and proof of arms.
He gave you all the duties of a man,
Trimm'd up your praises with a princely tongue,
Spoke your deservings like a chronicle,
Making you ever better than his praise,
By still dispraising praise, valu'd with you;
And, which became him like a prince indeed,   60
He made a blushing cital of himself,
And chid his truant youth with such a grace,
As if he master'd there a double spirit,
Of teaching, and of learning, instantly.
There did he pause. But let me tell the world,—
If he outlive the envy of this day,
England did never owe so sweet a hope,
So much misconstru'd in his wantonness.
    Hot. Cousin, I think thou art enamoured
On his follies: never did I hear   70
Of any prince so wild a libertine.
But, be he as he will, yet once ere night
I will embrace him with a soldier's arm,
That he shall shrink under my courtesy.
Arm, arm, with speed!—And, fellows, soldiers, friends,
Better consider what you have to do,
Than I, that have not well the gift of tongue,
Can lift your blood up with persuasion.

Enter a Messenger.

    Mess. My lord, here are letters for you.
    Hot. I cannot read them now.—   80
O gentlemen! the time of life is short;
To spend that shortness basely, were too long,
If life did ride upon a dial's point,
Still ending at the arrival of an hour.
An if we live, we live to tread on kings;
If die, brave death, when princes die with us.
Now, for our consciences, the arms are fair,
When the intent of bearing them is just.

Enter another Messenger.

    Mess. My lord, prepare; the king comes on apace.
    Hot. I thank him, that he cuts me from my tale,   90
For I profess not talking. Only this,—
Let each man do his best: and here draw I
A sword, whose temper I intend to stain
With the best blood that I can meet withal
In the adventure of this perilous day.
Now,—*Esperance!*—Percy!—and set on!—
Sound all the lofty instruments of war,
And by that music let us all embrace;
For, heaven to earth, some of us never shall
A second time do such a courtesy.   100
    [*The trumpets sound. They embrace, and exeunt.*

SCENE III.—Plain near Shrewsbury.

*Excursions, and Parties fighting. Alarum to the
battle. Then enter* DOUGLAS *and* BLUNT, *meeting.*

    Blunt. What is thy name, that in the battle thus
Thou crossest me? what honour dost thou seek
Upon my head?
    Doug.   Know then, my name is Douglas;
And I do haunt thee in the battle thus,
Because some tell me that thou art a king.
    Blunt. They tell thee true.
    Doug. The Lord of Stafford dear to-day hath bought
Thy likeness; for, instead of thee, King Harry,
This sword hath ended him: so shall it thee,
Unless thou yield thee as my prisoner.   10
    Blunt. I was not born a yielder, thou proud Scot;
And thou shalt find a king that will revenge
Lord Stafford's death. [*They fight, and* BLUNT *is slain.*

Enter HOTSPUR.

    Hot. O Douglas! hadst thou fought at Holmedon
        thus,
I never had triumph'd upon a Scot.
    Doug. All's done, all's won: here breathless lies the
        king.
    Hot. Where?
    Doug. Here.

    Hot. This, Douglas? no; I know this face full well:
A gallant knight he was, his name was Blunt,   20
Semblably furnish'd like the king himself.
    Doug. A fool go with thy soul, whither it goes!
A borrow'd title hast thou bought too dear:
Why didst thou tell me that thou wert a king?
    Hot. The king hath many marching in his coats.
    Doug. Now, by my sword, I will kill all his coats;
I'll murder all his wardrobe, piece by piece,
Until I meet the king.
    Hot.   Up, and away!
Our soldiers stand full fairly for the day. [*Exeunt.*

Alarums. Enter FALSTAFF.

    Fal. Though I could 'scape shot-free at London, I
fear the shot here; here's no scoring, but upon the
pate.—Soft! who art thou? Sir Walter Blunt:—there's
honour for you; here's no vanity.—I am as hot as
molten lead, and as heavy too: God keep lead out of
me! I need no more weight than mine own bowels.—
I have led my ragamuffins where they are peppered:
there's not three of my hundred and fifty left alive,
and they are for the town's end, to beg during life.
But who comes here?

Enter Prince HENRY.

    P. Hen. What! stand'st thou idle here? lend me thy
        sword: 40
Many a nobleman lies stark and stiff
Under the hoofs of vaunting enemies,
Whose deaths are unreveng'd: pr'ythee, lend me thy
        sword.
    Fal. O Hal! I pr'ythee, give me leave to breathe
awhile.—Turk Gregory never did such deeds in arms,
as I have done this day. I have paid Percy, I have
made him sure.
    P. Hen. He is, indeed; and living to kill thee. I
pr'ythee, lend me thy sword.
    Fal. Nay, before God, Hal, if Percy be alive, thou
gett'st not my sword; but take my pistol, if thou wilt.
    P. Hen. Give it me. What, is it in the case?   52
    Fal. Ay, Hal; 'tis hot, 'tis hot: there's that will
sack a city. [*The* PRINCE *draws out a bottle of sack.*
    P. Hen. What! is't a time to jest and dally now?
                    [*Throws it at him, and exit.*
    Fal. Well, if Percy be alive, I'll pierce him. If he
do come in my way, so: if he do not, if I come in his
willingly, let him make a carbonado of me. I like not
such grinning honour as Sir Walter hath: give me
life; which if I can save, so; if not, honour comes   60
unlooked for, and there's an end.
                    [*Exit.*

SCENE IV.—Another Part of the Field.

Alarums. Excursions. Enter the KING, *Prince*
HENRY, *Prince* JOHN, *and* WESTMORELAND.

    K. Hen. I pr'ythee,
Harry, withdraw thyself; thou bleed'st too much.—
Lord John of Lancaster, go you with him.
    P. John. Not I, my lord, unless I did bleed too.
    P. Hen. I beseech your majesty, make up,
Lest your retirement do amaze your friends.
    K. Hen. I will do so.—
My Lord of Westmoreland, lead him to his tent.
    West. Come, my lord, I'll lead you to your tent.
    P. Hen. Lead me, my lord? I do not need your
        help: 10
And Heaven forbid, a shallow scratch should drive
The Prince of Wales from such a field as this,
Where stain'd nobility lies trodden on,
And rebels' arms triumph in massacres!
    P. John. We breathe too long.—Come, cousin West-
        moreland,
Our duty this way lies: for God's sake, come.
            [*Exeunt Prince* JOHN *and* WESTMORELAND.
    P. Hen. By God, thou hast deceiv'd me, Lancaster,
I did not think thee fond of such a spirit:
Before, I lov'd thee as a brother, John;
But now, I do respect thee as my soul.   20
    K. Hen. I saw him hold Lord Percy at the point,

With lustier maintenance than I did look for
Of such an ungrown warrior.
P. Hen.   O ! this boy
Lends mettle to us all.   [*Exit.*

Alarums. Enter DOUGLAS.

Doug. Another king ! they grow like Hydra's heads.
I am the Douglas, fatal to all those
That wear those colours on them.—What art thou,
That counterfeit'st the person of a king ?
K. Hen. The king himself ; who, Douglas, grieves
            at heart,
So many of his shadows thou hast met,   30
And not the very king. I have two boys
Seek Percy, and thyself, about the field :
But, seeing thou fall'st on me so luckily,
I will assay thee ; and defend thyself.
Doug. I fear thou art another counterfeit,
And yet, in faith, thou bear'st thee like a king :
But mine I am sure thou art, whoe'er thou be,
And thus I win thee.
            [*They fight : the* KING *being in danger, re-enter
                Prince* HENRY.
P. Hen. Hold up thy head, vile Scot, or thou art like
Never to hold it up again ! the spirits   40
Of valiant Shirley, Stafford, Blunt, are in my arms :
It is the Prince of Wales, that threatens thee,
Who never promiseth, but he means to pay.—
                [*They fight :* DOUGLAS *flies.*
Cheerly, my lord : how fares your grace ?—
Sir Nicholas Gawsey hath for succour sent,
And so hath Clifton : I 'll to Clifton straight.
K. Hen. Stay, and breathe awhile.
Thou hast redeem'd thy lost opinion ;
And show'd thou mak'st some tender of my life,
In this fair rescue thou hast brought to me.   50
P. Hen. O God! they did me too much injury,
That ever said I hearken'd for your death.
If it were so, I might have let alone
The insulting hand of Douglas over you ;
Which would have been as speedy in your end,
As all the poisonous potions in the world,
And sav'd the treacherous labour of your son.
K. Hen. Make up to Clifton : I 'll to Sir Nicholas
Gawsey.   [*Exit.*

Enter HOTSPUR.

Hot. If I mistake not, thou art Harry Monmouth.
P. Hen. Thou speak'st as if I would deny my name.
Hot. My name is Harry Percy.
P. Hen.   Why, then I see 61
A very valiant rebel of that name.
I am the Prince of Wales ; and think not, Percy,
To share with me in glory any more :
Two stars keep not their motion in one sphere ;
Nor can one England brook a double reign,
Of Harry Percy, and the Prince of Wales.
Hot. Nor shall it, Harry, for the hour is come
To end the one of us ; and 'would to God,
Thy name in arms were now as great as mine !   70
P. Hen. I 'll make it greater, ere I part from thee ;
And all the budding honours on thy crest
I 'll crop, to make a garland for my head.
Hot. I can no longer brook thy vanities. [*They fight.*

Enter FALSTAFF.

Fal. Well said, Hal! to it, Hal !—Nay, you shall
find no boy's play here, I can tell you.
Re-enter DOUGLAS; *he fights with* FALSTAFF, *who
falls down as if he were dead, and exit* DOUGLAS.
HOTSPUR *is wounded, and falls.*

Hot. O Harry ! thou hast robb'd me of my youth.
I better brook the loss of brittle life,
Than those proud titles thou hast won of me ;
They wound my thoughts worse than thy sword my
            flesh :—   80
But thought 's the slave of life, and life time 's fool ;
And time, that takes survey of all the world,
Must have a stop. O! I could prophesy,
But that the earthy and cold hand of death
Lies on my tongue.—No, Percy, thou art dust,
And food for—   [*Dies.*

P. Hen. For worms, brave Percy.   Fare thee well,
            great heart !—
Ill-weav'd ambition, how much art thou shrunk !
When that this body did contain a spirit,
A kingdom for it was too small a bound ;   90
But now, two paces of the vilest earth
Is room enough :—this earth, that bears thee dead,
Bears not alive so stout a gentleman.
If thou wert sensible of courtesy,
I should not make so dear a show of zeal :—
But let my favours hide thy mangled face,
And, even in thy behalf, I 'll make myself
For doing these fair rites of tenderness.
Adieu, and take thy praise with thee to heaven !
Thy ignomy sleep with thee in the grave,   100
But not remember'd in thy epitaph !—
                        [*He spieth* FALSTAFF *on the ground.*
What ! old acquaintance ! could not all this flesh
Keep in a little life ? Poor Jack, farewell !
I could have better spar'd a better man.
O! I should have a heavy miss of thee,
If I were much in love with vanity.
Death hath not struck so fat a deer to-day,
Though many dearer, in this bloody fray.—
Embowell'd will I see thee by-and-by ;
Till then, in blood by noble Percy lie.   [*Exit.*
Fal. [*Rising.*] Embowelled ! if thou embowel me
to-day, I 'll give you leave to powder me, and eat me
too, to-morrow. 'Sblood ! 't was time to counterfeit,
or that hot termagant Scot had paid me scot and lot
too. Counterfeit ? I lie ; I am no counterfeit : to die,
is to be a counterfeit ; for he is but the counterfeit of
a man, who hath not the life of a man ; but to counterfeit dying, when a man thereby liveth, is to be no
counterfeit, but the true and perfect image of life
indeed. The better part of valour is discretion ; in the
which better part I have saved my life. 'Zounds !
I am afraid of this gunpowder Percy, though he be
dead. How, if he should counterfeit too, and rise ?
By my faith, I am afraid he would prove the better
counterfeit. Therefore I 'll make him sure ; yea, and
I 'll swear I killed him. Why may not he rise, as well
as I ? Nothing confutes me but eyes, and nobody sees
me : therefore, sirrah, [*stabbing him*] with a new
wound in your thigh come you along with me.
                        [*He takes* HOTSPUR *on his back.*

Re-enter Prince HENRY *and Prince* JOHN.

P. Hen. Come, brother John ; full bravely hast thou
            flesh'd   130
Thy maiden sword.
P. John.   But, soft ! whom have we here ?
Did you not tell me this fat man was dead ?
P. Hen. I did ; I saw him dead,
Breathless and bleeding on the ground.—
Art thou alive ? or is it phantasy
That plays upon our eyesight ? I pr'ythee, speak ;
We will not trust our eyes without our ears.
Thou art not what thou seem'st.
Fal. No, that 's certain : I am not a double man ;
but if I be not Jack Falstaff, then am I Jack. There
is Percy : if your father will do me any honour, so ; if
not, let him kill the next Percy himself. I look to be
either earl or duke, I can assure you.   143
P. Hen. Why, Percy I killed myself, and saw thee
            dead.
Fal. Didst thou?—Lord, Lord, how this world is
given to lying !—I grant you I was down, and out of
breath, and so was he ; but we rose both at an instant,
and fought a long hour by Shrewsbury clock. If I
may be believed, so : if not, let them that should
reward valour bear the sin upon their own heads.
I 'll take it upon my death, I gave him this wound in
the thigh : if the man were alive, and would deny it,
'zounds ! I would make him eat a piece of my sword.
P. John. This is the strangest tale that e'er I heard.
P. Hen. This is the strangest fellow, brother John.—
Come, bring your luggage nobly on your back :
For my part, if a lie may do thee grace,
I 'll gild it with the happiest terms I have.
                                [*A retreat is sounded.*
The trumpet sounds retreat ; the day is ours.

Come, brother, let us to the highest of the field,   160
To see what friends are living, who are dead.
                    [*Exeunt Prince* Henry *and Prince* John.

Ill-spirited Worcester, did we not send grace,
Pardon, and terms of love to all of you?
And wouldst thou turn our offers contrary?

Hot. "O Harry! thou hast robb'd me of my youth."

Fal. I'll follow, as they say, for reward. He that
rewards me, God reward him! If I do grow great, I'll
grow less; for I'll purge, and leave sack, and live
cleanly, as a nobleman should do.   [*Exit, bearing off
                                        the body.*

SCENE V.—*Another Part of the Field.*
The trumpets sound. Enter King Henry, *Prince*
Henry, *Prince* John, Westmoreland, *and others,
with* Worcester, *and* Vernon, *prisoners.*
K. Hen. Thus ever did rebellion find rebuke.—

Misuse the tenor of thy kinsman's trust?
Three knights upon our party slain to-day,
A noble earl, and many a creature else,
Had been alive this hour,
If, like a Christian, thou hadst truly borne
Betwixt our armies true intelligence.   10
    Wor. What I have done, my safety urg'd me
                                               to,
And I embrace this fortune patiently,
Since not to be avoided it falls on me.
    K. Hen. Bear Worcester to the death, and Vernon
                                               too:

Other offenders we will pause upon.—
    [*Exeunt* WORCESTER *and* VERNON, *guarded.*
How goes the field?
  P. Hen. The noble Scot, Lord Douglas, when he saw
The fortune of the day quite turn'd from him,
The noble Percy slain, and all his men
Upon the foot of fear, fled with the rest: 20
And falling from a hill he was so bruis'd,
That the pursuers took him. At my tent
The Douglas is, and I beseech your grace,
I may dispose of him.
  K. Hen.   With all my heart.
  P. Hen. Then, brother John of Lancaster, to you
This honourable bounty shall belong.
Go to the Douglas, and deliver him
Up to his pleasure, ransomless, and free:
His valour, shown upon our crests to-day,

Hath taught us how to cherish such high deeds,   30
Even in the bosom of our adversaries.
  P. John. I thank your grace for this high courtesy,
Which I shall give away immediately.
  K. Hen. Then this remains,—that we divide our
         power.—
You, son John, and my cousin Westmoreland,
Towards York shall bend you, with your dearest
         speed,
To meet Northumberland, and the prelate Scroop,
Who, as we hear, are busily in arms:
Myself, and you, son Harry, will towards Wales,
To fight with Glendower and the Earl of March.   40
Rebellion in this land shall lose his sway,
Meeting the check of such another day:
And since this business so fair is done,
Let us not leave till all our own be won.   [*Exeunt.*

KING HENRY IV.—PART II.

DRAMATIS PERSONÆ.

KING HENRY THE FOURTH.
HENRY, *Prince of Wales,*
THOMAS, *Duke of Clarence,*
PRINCE JOHN OF LANCASTER, } *His Sons.*
PRINCE HUMPHREY OF GLOSTER,
EARL OF WARWICK,
EARL OF WESTMORELAND,
EARL OF SURREY, } *Of the King's Party.*
GOWER,
HARCOURT,
Lord Chief Justice of the King's Bench.
A Gentleman attending on the Chief Justice.
EARL OF NORTHUMBERLAND,
SCROOP, *Archbishop of York,*
LORD MOWBRAY, } *Opposites to the*
LORD HASTINGS, *King.*
LORD BARDOLPH,
SIR JOHN COLEVILLE,

TRAVERS *and* MORTON, *Retainers of Northumberland.*
FALSTAFF, BARDOLPH, PISTOL, *and a Page.*
POINS *and* PETO.
SHALLOW *and* SILENCE, *Country Justices.*
DAVY, *Servant to Shallow.*
MOULDY, SHADOW, WART, FEEBLE, *and* BULL-CALF, *Recruits.*
FANG *and* SNARE, *Sheriff's Officers.*
RUMOUR, *the Presenter.*
A Porter. A Dancer, Speaker of the Epilogue.

LADY NORTHUMBERLAND.
LADY PERCY.
Hostess QUICKLY.
DOLL TEAR-SHEET.

Lords, and Attendants; Officers, Soldiers, Messenger, Drawers, Beadles, Grooms, &c.

SCENE—ENGLAND.

INDUCTION.

Warkworth. Before NORTHUMBERLAND's Castle.

Enter RUMOUR, *painted full of tongues.*

Rumour.

PEN your ears; for which of you will
stop
The vent of hearing, when loud Rumour
speaks?
I, from the orient to the drooping west,
Making the wind my post-horse, still unfold
The acts commenced on this ball of earth:
Upon my tongues continual slanders ride,
The which in every language I pronounce,
Stuffing the ears of men with false reports.
I speak of peace, while covert enmity,
Under the smile of safety, wounds the
world: 10
And who but Rumour, who but only I,
Make fearful musters, and prepar'd defence,
Whilst the big year, swoln with some other grief,
Is thought with child by the stern tyrant war,
And no such matter? Rumour is a pipe
Blown by surmises, jealousies, conjectures,
And of so easy and so plain a stop,
That the blunt monster with uncounted heads,
The still-discordant wavering multitude,

Can play upon it. But what need I thus 20
My well-known body to anatomise
Among my household? Why is Rumour here?
I run before King Harry's victory;
Who in a bloody field by Shrewsbury
Hath beaten down young Hotspur, and his troops,
Quenching the flame of bold rebellion
Even with the rebels' blood. But what mean I
To speak so true at first? my office is
To noise abroad, that Harry Monmouth fell
Under the wrath of noble Hotspur's sword, 30
And that the king before the Douglas' rage
Stoop'd his anointed head as low as death.
This have I rumour'd through the peasant towns
Between that royal field of Shrewsbury
And this worm-eaten hold of ragged stone,
Where Hotspur's father, old Northumberland,
Lies crafty sick. The posts come tiring on,
And not a man of them brings other news
Than they have learn'd of me: from Rumour's
tongues
They bring smooth comforts false, worse than true
wrongs. 40
[*Exit.*

ACT. I.

SCENE I.—The Same.

Enter Lord BARDOLPH.

Lord Bardolph.
HO keeps the gate here? ho!

The Porter opens the gate.

Port. What shall I say you are?
L. Bard.   Tell thou the earl,
That the Lord Bardolph doth attend
    him here.
Port. His lordship is walk'd forth
    into the orchard:
Please it your honour, knock but at the
    gate,
And he himself will answer.

Enter NORTHUMBERLAND.

L. Bard.   Here comes the earl.
North. What news, Lord Bardolph? every minute now
Should be the father of some stratagem.
The times are wild: contention, like a
    horse
Full of high feeding, madly hath broke
    loose,   10
And bears down all before him.
L. Bard.   Noble earl,
I bring you certain news from Shrewsbury.
North. Good, an God will!
L. Bard.   As good as heart can wish.
The king is almost wounded to the death,
And, in the fortune of my lord your son,
Prince Harry slain outright; and both the
    Blunts
Kill'd by the hand of Douglas; young
    Prince John,
And Westmoreland, and Stafford, fled the
    field;
And Harry Monmouth's brawn, the hulk
    Sir John,
Is prisoner to your son. O! such a day, 20
So fought, so follow'd, and so fairly won,
Came not till now to dignify the times,
Since Cæsar's fortunes.
North.   How is this deriv'd?
Saw you the field? came you from Shrews-
    bury?
L. Bard. I spake with one, my lord, that
    came from thence;
A gentleman well bred, and of good name,
That freely render'd me these news for true.
North. Here comes my servant, Travers, whom I sent
On Tuesday last to listen after news.
L. Bard. My lord, I over-rode him on the way; 30
And he is furnish'd with no certainties,
More than he haply may retail from me.

Enter TRAVERS.

North. Now, Travers, what good tidings come with
    you?
Tra. My lord, Sir John Umfrevile turn'd me back
With joyful tidings; and, being better hors'd,
Out-rode me. After him came spurring hard
A gentleman, almost forspent with speed,
That stopp'd by me to breathe his bloodied horse.
He ask'd the way to Chester; and of him

I did demand, what news from Shrewsbury.   40
He told me that rebellion had ill luck,
And that young Harry Percy's spur was cold.
With that he gave his able horse the head,
And, bending forward, struck his armed heels
Against the panting sides of his poor jade
Up to the rowel-head; and starting so,
He seem'd in running to devour the way,
Staying no longer question.
North.   Ha!—Again.
Said he, young Harry Percy's spur was cold?
Of Hotspur, Coldspur? that rebellion   50
Had met ill luck?
L. Bard.   My lord, I'll tell you what:
If my young lord your son have not the day,
Upon mine honour, for a silken point
I'll give my barony: never talk of it.

Mor. "I ran from Shrewsbury, my noble lord."

North. Why should that gentleman, that rode by
    Travers,
Give then such instances of loss?
L. Bard.   Who, he?
He was some hilding fellow, that had stolen
The horse he rode on, and, upon my life,
Spoke at a venture. Look, here comes more news.

Enter MORTON.

North. Yea, this man's brow, like to a title-
    leaf,   60
Foretells the nature of a tragic volume:
So looks the strond, whereon the imperious flood
Hath left a witness'd usurpation.
Say, Morton, didst thou come from Shrewsbury?
Mor. I ran from Shrewsbury, my noble lord,

Where hateful death put on his ugliest mask,
To fright our party.
  North. How doth my son, and brother?
Thou tremblest, and the whiteness in thy cheek
Is apter than thy tongue to tell thy errand.
Even such a man, so faint, so spiritless,   70
So dull, so dead in look, so woe-begone,
Drew Priam's curtain in the dead of night,
And would have told him, half his Troy was burn'd:
But Priam found the fire, ere he is tongue,
And I my Percy's death, ere thou report'st it.
This thou wouldst say,—Your son did thus, and
  thus;
Your brother, thus; so fought the noble Douglas;
Stopping my greedy ear with their bold deeds:
But in the end, to stop mine ear indeed,
Thou hast a sigh to blow away this praise, 80
Ending with—brother, son, and all are dead.
  Mor. Douglas is living, and your brother, yet;
But for my lord your son,—
  North. Why, he is dead.—
See, what a ready tongue suspicion hath!
He that but fears the thing he would not know,
Hath, by instinct, knowledge from others' eyes,
That what he fear'd is chanced. Yet speak, Morton;
Tell thou thy earl his divination lies,
And I will take it as a sweet disgrace,
And make thee rich for doing me such wrong. 90
  Mor. You are too great to be by me gainsaid:
Your spirit is too true, your fears too certain.
  North. Yet, for all this, say not that Percy's dead.—
I see a strange confession in thine eye:
Thou shak'st thy head, and hold'st it fear, or sin,
To speak a truth. If he be slain, say so:
The tongue offends not that reports his death;
And he doth sin that doth belie the dead,
Not he which says the dead is not alive.
Yet the first bringer of unwelcome news 100
Hath but a losing office, and his tongue
Sounds ever after as a sullen bell,
Remember'd knolling a departing friend.
  L. Bard. I cannot think, my lord, your son is dead.
  Mor. I am sorry I should force you to believe
That which I would to Heaven I had not seen;
But these mine eyes saw him in bloody state,
Rendering faint quittance, wearied and outbreath'd,
To Harry Monmouth; whose swift wrath beat down
The never-daunted Percy to the earth, 110
From whence with life he never more sprung up.
In few, his death, whose spirit lent a fire
Even to the dullest peasant in his camp,
Being bruited once, took fire and heat away
From the best-temper'd courage in his troops:
For from his metal was his party steel'd;
Which once in him abated, all the rest
Turn'd on themselves, like dull and heavy lead.
And as the thing that's heavy in itself,
Upon enforcement flies with greatest speed, 120
So did our men, heavy in Hotspur's loss,
Lend to this weight such lightness with their fear,
That arrows fled not swifter toward their aim,
Than did our soldiers, aiming at their safety,
Fly from the field. Then was that noble Worcester
Too soon ta'en prisoner; and that furious Scot,
The bloody Douglas, whose well-labouring sword
Had three times slain the appearance of the king,
'Gan vail his stomach, and did grace the shame
Of those that turn'd their backs; and in his flight, 130
Stumbling in fear, was took. The sum of all
Is, that the king hath won, and hath sent out
A speedy power, to encounter you, my lord,
Under the conduct of young Lancaster,
And Westmoreland. This is the news at full.
  North. For this I shall have time enough to mourn.
In poison there is physic; and these news,
Having been well, that would have made me sick,
Being sick, have in some measure made me well:
And as the wretch, whose fever-weaken'd joints, 140
Like strengthless hinges, buckle under life,
Impatient of his fit, breaks like a fire
Out of his keeper's arms, even so my limbs,
Weaken'd with grief, being now enrag'd with grief,

Are thrice themselves. Hence, therefore, thou nice
  crutch!
A scaly gauntlet now, with joints of steel,
Must glove this hand: and hence, thou sickly quoif!
Thou art a guard too wanton for the head,
Which princes, flesh'd with conquest, aim to hit.
Now bind my brows with iron; and approach 150
The ragged'st hour that time and spite dare bring,
To frown upon the enrag'd Northumberland!
Let heaven kiss earth! now, let not Nature's hand
Keep the wild flood confin'd! let order die!
And let this world no longer be a stage,
To feed contention in a lingering act;
But let one spirit of the first-born Cain
Reign in all bosoms, that, each heart being set
On bloody courses, the rude scene may end,
And darkness be the burier of the dead! 160
  Tra. This strained passion doth you wrong, my lord.
  L. Bard. Sweet earl, divorce not wisdom from your
  honour.
  Mor. The lives of all your loving complices
Lean on your health; the which, if you give o'er
To stormy passion, must perforce decay.
You cast the event of war, my noble lord,
And summ'd the account of chance, before you said,—
Let us make head. It was your presurmise,
That in the dole of blows your son might drop:
You knew, he walk'd o'er perils, on an edge, 170
More likely to fall in than to get o'er:
You were advis'd, his flesh was capable
Of wounds and scars, and that his forward spirit
Would lift him where most trade of danger rang'd;
Yet did you say,—Go forth; and none of this,
Though strongly apprehended, could restrain
The stiff-borne action: what hath then befallen,
Or what hath this bold enterprise brought forth,
More than that being which was like to be?
  L. Bar. We all, that are engaged to this loss, 180
Knew that we ventur'd on such dangerous seas,
That, if we wrought out life, 't was ten to one;
And yet we ventur'd, for the gain propos'd
Chok'd the respect of likely peril fear'd,
And, since we are o'erset, venture again.
Come, we will all put forth, body, and goods.
  Mor. 'T is more than time: and, my most noble lord,
I hear for certain, and do speak the truth,
The gentle Archbishop of York is up,
With well-appointed powers: he is a man, 190
Who with a double surety binds his followers.
My lord your son had only but the corse,
But shadows, and the shows of men, to fight;
For that same word, rebellion, did divide
The action of their bodies from their souls,
And they did fight with queasiness, constrain'd,
As men drink potions, that their weapons only
Seem'd on our side: but, for their spirits and souls,
This word, rebellion, it had froze them up,
As fish are in a pond. But now the bishop 200
Turns insurrection to religion:
Suppos'd sincere and holy in his thoughts,
He's follow'd both with body and with mind,
And doth enlarge his rising with the blood
Of fair King Richard, scrap'd from Pomfret stones;
Derives from Heaven his quarrel, and his cause;
Tells them, he doth bestride a bleeding land,
Gasping for life under great Bolingbroke;
And more, and less, do flock to follow him.
  North. I knew of this before; but, to speak truth,
This present grief had wip'd it from my mind. 211
Go in with me; and counsel every man
The aptest way for safety, and revenge:
Get posts and letters, and make friends with speed:
Never so few, nor never yet more need. [*Exeunt.*

SCENE II.—London. A Street.

Enter Sir JOHN FALSTAFF, *with his Page bearing his
sword and buckler.*

  Fal. Sirrah, you giant, what says the doctor to my
water?

Page. He said, sir, the water itself was a good healthy water; but for the party that owed it, he might have more diseases than he knew for.

Fal. Men of all sorts take a pride to gird at me: the brain of this foolish-compounded clay, man, is not able to invent anything that tends to laughter, more than I invent, or is invented on me: I am not only witty in myself, but the cause that wit is in other men. I do here walk before thee, like a sow that hath overwhelmed all her litter but one. If the prince put thee into my service for any other reason than to set me off, why then, I have no judgment. Thou whoreson mandrake, thou art fitter to be worn in my cap, than to wait at my heels. I was never manned with an agate till now: but I will set you neither in gold nor silver, but in vile apparel, and send you back again to your master, for a jewel; the juvenal, the prince your master, whose chin is not yet fledged. I will sooner have a beard grow in the palm of my hand, than he shall get one on his cheek; and yet he will not stick to say, his face is a face-royal. God may finish it when he will, it is not a hair amiss yet: he may keep it still as a face-royal, for a barber shall never earn sixpence out of it; and yet he will be crowing, as if he had writ man ever since his father was a bachelor. He may keep his own grace, but he is almost out of mine, I can assure him.—What said Master Dombledon about the satin for my short cloak, and my slops?

Page. He said, sir, you should procure him better assurance than Bardolph; he would not take his bond and yours: he liked not the security.   33

Fal. Let him be damned like the glutton! pray God his tongue be hotter!—A whoreson Achitophel! a rascally yea-forsooth knave, to bear a gentleman in hand, and then stand upon security!—The whoreson smooth-pates do now wear nothing but high shoes, and bunches of keys at their girdles; and if a man is thorough with them in honest taking up, then must they stand upon security. I had as lief they would put ratsbane in my mouth, as offer to stop it with security. I looked he should have sent me two-and-twenty yards of satin, as I am a true knight, and he sends me security. Well, he may sleep in security; for he hath the horn of abundance, and the lightness of his wife shines through it: and yet cannot he see, though he have his own lantern to light him.—Where's Bardolph?

Page. He's gone into Smithfield to buy your worship a horse.   51

Fal. I bought him in Paul's, and he'll buy me a horse in Smithfield: an I could get me but a wife in the stews, I were manned, horsed, and wived.

Enter the Lord Chief Justice and an Attendant.

Page. Sir, here comes the nobleman that committed the prince for striking him about Bardolph.

Fal. Wait close; I will not see him.

Ch. Just. What's he that goes there?

Atten. Falstaff, an't please your lordship.

Ch. Just. He that was in question for the robbery?

Atten. He, my lord; but he hath since done good service at Shrewsbury, and, as I hear, is now going with some charge to the Lord John of Lancaster.   63

Ch. Just. What, to York? Call him back again.

Atten. Sir John Falstaff!

Fal. Boy, tell him I am deaf.

Page. You must speak louder, my master is deaf.

Ch. Just. I am sure he is, to the hearing of anything good.—Go, pluck him by the elbow; I must speak with him.   70

Atten. Sir John,—

Fal. What! a young knave, and beg? Is there not wars? is there not employment? doth not the king lack subjects? do not the rebels want soldiers? Though it be a shame to be on any side but one, it is worse shame to beg than to be on the worst side, were it worse than the name of rebellion can tell how to make it.

Atten. You mistake me, sir.

Fal. Why, sir, did I say you were an honest man? setting my knighthood and my soldiership aside, I had lied in my throat if I had said so.   82

Atten. I pray you, sir, then set your knighthood and your soldiership aside, and give me leave to tell you, you lie in your throat, if you say I am any other than an honest man.

Fal. I give thee leave to tell me so? I lay aside that which grows to me? If thou gett'st any leave of me, hang me: if thou takest leave, thou wert better be hanged. You hunt-counter, hence! avaunt!   90

Atten. Sir, my lord would speak with you.

Ch. Just. Sir John Falstaff, a word with you.

Fal. My good lord!—God give your lordship good time of day. I am glad to see your lordship abroad; I heard say, your lordship was sick: I hope, your lordship goes abroad by advice. Your lordship, though not clean past your youth, hath yet some smack of age in you, some relish of the saltness of time, and I most humbly beseech your lordship to have a reverent care of your health.   100

Ch. Just. Sir John, I sent for you before your expedition to Shrewsbury.

Fal. An't please your lordship, I hear his majesty is returned with some discomfort from Wales.

Ch. Just. I talk not of his majesty.—You would not come when I sent for you.

Fal. And I hear, moreover, his highness is fallen into this same whoreson apoplexy.

Ch. Just. Well, God mend him!—I pray you, let me speak with you.   110

Fal. This apoplexy is, as I take it, a kind of lethargy, an't please your lordship; a kind of sleeping in the blood, a whoreson tingling.

Ch. Just. What tell you me of it? be it as it is.

Fal. It hath its original from much grief; from study, and perturbation of the brain. I have read the cause of his effects in Galen: it is a kind of deafness.

Ch. Just. I think you are fallen into the disease, for you hear not what I say to you.

Fal. Very well, my lord, very well: rather, an't please you, it is the disease of not listening, the malady of not marking, that I am troubled withal.   122

Ch. Just. To punish you by the heels would amend the attention of your ears; and I care not, if I do become your physician.

Fal. I am as poor as Job, my lord, but not so patient: your lordship may minister the potion of imprisonment to me, in respect of poverty; but how I should be your patient to follow your prescriptions, the wise may make some dram of a scruple, or, indeed, a scruple itself.

Ch. Just. I sent for you, when there were matters against you for your life, to come speak with me.   132

Fal. As I was then advised by my learned counsel in the laws of this land-service, I did not come.

Ch. Just. Well, the truth is, Sir John, you live in great infamy.

Fal. He that buckles him in my belt cannot live in less.

Ch. Just. Your means are very slender, and your waste is great.   140

Fal. I would it were otherwise: I would my means were greater, and my waist slenderer.

Ch. Just. You have misled the youthful prince.

Fal. The young prince hath misled me: I am the fellow with the great belly, and he my dog.

Ch. Just. Well, I am loath to gall a new-healed wound. Your day's service at Shrewsbury hath a little gilded over your night's exploit on Gadshill: you may thank the unquiet time for your quiet o'er-posting that action.   150

Fal. My lord,—

Ch. Just. But since all is well, keep it so: wake not a sleeping wolf.

Fal. To wake a wolf, is as bad as to smell a fox.

Ch. Just. What! you are as a candle, the better part burnt out.

Fal. A wassail candle, my lord; all tallow: if I did say of wax, my growth would approve the truth.

Ch. Just. There is not a white hair on your face, but should have his effect of gravity.   160

Fal. His effect of gravy, gravy, gravy.

Ch. Just. You follow the young prince up and down, like his ill angel.

Fal. Not so, my lord; your ill angel is light, but, I

hope, he that looks upon me will take me without
weighing: and yet, in some respects, I grant, I cannot
go, I cannot tell. Virtue is of so little regard in these
costermonger times, that true valour is turned bear-
herd. Pregnancy is made a tapster, and hath his
quick wit wasted in giving reckonings: all the other
gifts appertinent to man, as the malice of this age
shapes them, are not worth a gooseberry. You, that
are old, consider not the capacities of us that are
young: you measure the heat of our livers with the
bitterness of your galls; and we that are in the vaward
of our youth, I must confess, are wags too.

Ch. Just. Do you set down your name in the scroll
of youth, that are written down old with all the
characters of age? Have you not a moist eye, a dry
hand, a yellow cheek, a white beard, a decreasing leg,
an increasing belly? Is not your voice broken, your
wind short, your chin double, your wit single, and
every part about you blasted with antiquity, and will
you yet call yourself young? Fie, fie, fie, Sir John!

Fal. My lord, I was born about three of the clock in
the afternoon, with a white head, and something a
round belly. For my voice, I have lost it with hollaing, and singing of anthems. To approve my youth
further, I will not: the truth is, I am only old in judgment and understanding; and he that will caper with
me for a thousand marks, let him lend me the money,
and have at him. For the box o' the ear that the
prince gave you, he gave it like a rude prince, and you
took it like a sensible lord. I have checked him for
it, and the young lion repents; marry, not in ashes and
sackcloth, but in new silk and old sack.

Ch. Just. Well, God send the prince a better companion!

Fal. God send the companion a better prince! I
cannot rid my hands of him.   200

Ch. Just. Well, the king hath severed you and Prince
Harry. I hear, you are going with Lord John of
Lancaster against the archbishop, and the Earl of
Northumberland.

Fal. Yea; I thank your pretty sweet wit for it. But
look you pray, all you that kiss my lady Peace at
home, that our armies join not in a hot day; for, by
the Lord, I take but two shirts out with me, and I
mean not to sweat extraordinarily: if it be a hot day,
and I brandish anything but my bottle, I would I
might never spit white again. There is not a dangerous action can peep out his head, but I am thrust
upon it. Well, I cannot last ever. But it was always
yet the trick of our English nation, if they have a
good thing, to make it too common. If you will needs
say I am an old man, you should give me rest. I would
to God, my name were not so terrible to the enemy as
it is: I were better to be eaten to death with rust,
than to be scoured to nothing with perpetual motion.

Ch. Just. Well, be honest, be honest; and God bless
your expedition.   221

Fal. Will your lordship lend me a thousand pound
to furnish me forth?

Ch. Just. Not a penny, not a penny: you are too
impatient to bear crosses. Fare you well: commend
me to my cousin Westmoreland.
           [*Exeunt Chief Justice and Attendant.*

Fal. If I do, fillip me with a three-man beetle. A
man can no more separate age and covetousness, than
he can part young limbs and lechery; but the gout
galls the one, and the pox pinches the other, and so
both the degrees prevent my curses.—Boy!   231

Page. Sir?

Fal. What money is in my purse?

Page. Seven groats and twopence.

Fal. I can get no remedy against this consumption
of the purse: borrowing only lingers and lingers it
out, but the disease is incurable.—Go bear this letter
to my Lord of Lancaster; this to the prince; this to
the Earl of Westmoreland; and this to old Mistress
Ursula, whom I have weekly sworn to marry since
I perceived the first white hair on my chin. About it:
you know where to find me. [*Exit Page.*] A pox of
this gout! or, a gout of this pox! for the one, or the
other, plays the rogue with my great toe. 'T is no
matter, if I do halt; I have the wars for my colour,

and my pension shall seem the more reasonable. A
good wit will make use of anything; I will turn
diseases to commodity.   [*Exit.*

SCENE III.—York. A Room in the Archbishop's
                    Palace.

Enter the Archbishop of YORK, *the Lords* HASTINGS,
           MOWBRAY, *and* BARDOLPH.

Arch. Thus have you heard our cause, and known
                    our means;
And, my most noble friends, I pray you all,
Speak plainly your opinions of our hopes:—
And first, lord marshal, what say you to it?

Mowb. I well allow the occasion of our arms;
But gladly would be better satisfied,
How, in our means, we should advance ourselves
To look with forehead bold and big enough
Upon the power and puissance of the king.

Hast. Our present musters grow upon the file   10
To five-and-twenty thousand men of choice;
And our supplies live largely in the hope
Of great Northumberland, whose bosom burns
With an incensed fire of injuries.

L. Bard. The question then, Lord Hastings,
                    standeth thus:—
Whether our present five-and-twenty thousand
May hold up head without Northumberland.

Hast. With him, we may.

L. Bard.   Ay, marry, there 's the point:
But if without him we be thought too feeble,
My judgment is, we should not step too far,   20
Till we had his assistance by the hand;
For in a theme so bloody-fac'd as this,
Conjecture, expectation, and surmise
Of aids incertain, should not be admitted.

Arch. 'T is very true, Lord Bardolph; for, indeed,
It was young Hotspur's case at Shrewsbury.

L. Bard. It was, my lord; who lin'd himself with
                    hope,
Eating the air on promise of supply,
Flattering himself with project of a power
Much smaller than the smallest of his thoughts;   30
And so, with great imagination,
Proper to madmen, led his powers to death,
And winking leap'd into destruction.

Hast. But, by your leave, it never yet did hurt,
To lay down likelihoods, and forms of hope.

L. Bard. Yes, if this present quality of war,
Indeed the instant action, a cause on foot,
Lives so in hope, as in an early spring
We see the appearing buds; which, to prove fruit,
Hope gives not so much warrant, as despair   40
That frosts will bite them. When we mean to build,
We first survey the plot, then draw the model,
And, when we see the figure of the house,
Then must we rate the cost of the erection;
Which if we find outweighs ability,
What do we then, but draw anew the model
In fewer offices, or, at least, desist
To build at all? Much more, in this great work
(Which is, almost, to pluck a kingdom down,
And set another up) should we survey   50
The plot of situation, and the model;
Consent upon a sure foundation;
Question surveyors, know our own estate,
How able such a work to undergo,
To weigh against his opposite; or else,
We fortify in paper, and in figures,
Using the names of men, instead of men:
Like one that draws the model of a house,
Beyond his power to build it; who, half through,
Gives o'er, and leaves his part-created cost   60
A naked subject to the weeping clouds,
And waste for churlish winter's tyranny.

Hast. Grant, that our hopes, yet likely of fair birth,
Should be still-born, and that we now possess'd
The utmost man of expectation,
I think we are a body strong enough,
Even as we are, to equal with the king.

L. Bard. What! is the king but five-and-twenty
    thousand?
Hast. To us no more; nay, not so much, Lord Bar-
    dolph.
For his divisions, as the times do brawl,   70
Are in three heads: one power against the French,
And one against Glendower; perforce, a third
Must take up us. So is the unfirm king
In three divided, and his coffers sound
With hollow poverty and emptiness.
    Arch. That he should draw his several strengths
    together,
And come against us in full puissance,
Need not be dreaded.
    Hast.   If he should do so,
He leaves his back unarm'd, the French and Welsh
Baying him at the heels: never fear that.   80
    L. Bard. Who is it like should lead his forces
    hither?
    Hast. The Duke of Lancaster, and Westmoreland;
Against the Welsh, himself and Harry Monmouth;
But who is substituted 'gainst the French,
I have no certain notice.
    Arch.   Let us on,
And publish the occasion of our arms.

The commonwealth is sick of their own choice,
Their over-greedy love hath surfeited.—
An habitation giddy and unsure
Hath he that buildeth on the vulgar heart.   90
O thou fond many! with what loud applause
Didst thou beat heaven with blessing Bolingbroke,
Before he was what thou wouldst have him be:
And being now trimm'd in thine own desires,
Thou, beastly feeder, art so full of him,
That thou provok'st thyself to cast him up.
So, so, thou common dog, didst thou disgorge
Thy glutton bosom of the royal Richard,
And now thou wouldst eat thy dead vomit up,
And howl'st to find it.　What trust is in these times?
They that, when Richard liv'd, would have him die,
Are now become enamour'd on his grave: 102
Thou, that threw'st dust upon his goodly head,
When through proud London he came sighing on
After the admired heels of Bolingbroke,
Cry'st now, "O earth, yield us that king again,
And take thou this!" O thoughts of men accurst!
Past, and to come, seems best; things present, worst.
    Mowb. Shall we go draw our numbers, and set on?
    Hast. We are time's subjects, and time bids be gone.
                               [*Exeunt.*

ACT II.

SCENE I.—London.　A Street.

Enter Hostess, FANG, *and his Boy, with her; and* SNARE *following.*

    Hostess.
MASTER Fang, have you entered
the action?
    Fang. It is entered.
    Host. Where's your yeoman? Is't a
lusty yeoman? will he stand to't?
    Fang. Sirrah, where's Snare?
    Host. O Lord! ay: good Master Snare.
    Snare. Here, here.
    Fang. Snare, we must arrest Sir John
Falstaff.   10
    Host. Yea, good Master Snare; I have
entered him and all.
    Snare. It may chance cost some of us
our lives, for he will stab.
    Host. Alas the day! take heed of him: he stabbed
me in mine own house, and that most beastly. In
good faith, he cares not what mischief he doth, if his
weapon be out: he will foin like any devil; he will
spare neither man, woman, nor child.
    Fang. If I can close with him, I care not for his thrust.
    Host. No, nor I neither: I'll be at your elbow.   21
    Fang. An I but fist him once; an he come but
within my vice,—
    Host. I am undone with his going; I warrant you,
he's an infinitive thing upon my score.—Good Master
Fang, hold him sure:—good Master Snare, let him
not 'scape. 'A comes continuantly to Pie Corner,
(saving your manhoods,) to buy a saddle; and he's
indited to dinner to the Lubbar's Head in Lumbert
Street, to Master Smooth's the silkman: I pray ye,
since my exion is entered, and my case so openly
known to the world, let him be brought in to his
answer.　A hundred mark is a long one for a poor
lone woman to bear; and I have borne, and borne,
and borne; and have been fubbed off, and fubbed off,
from this day to that day, that it is a shame to be

thought on.　There is no honesty in such dealing,
unless a woman should be made an ass, and a beast,
to bear every knave's wrong.—   39

Enter Sir JOHN FALSTAFF, *Page, and* BARDOLPH.

Yonder he comes; and that arrant malmsey-nose,
Bardolph, with him.　Do your offices, do your offices,
Master Fang, and Master Snare: do me, do me, do me
your offices.
    Fal. How now? whose mare's dead? what's the
matter?
    Fang. Sir John, I arrest you at the suit of Mistress
Quickly.
    Fal. Away, varlets!—Draw, Bardolph: cut me off
the villain's head; throw the quean in the channel. 49
    Host. Throw me in the channel? I'll throw thee
there.　Wilt thou? wilt thou? thou bastardly rogue!
—Murder, murder! O, thou honey-suckle villain!
wilt thou kill God's officers, and the king's? O, thou
honey-seed rogue! thou art a honey-seed; a man-
queller, and a woman-queller.
    Fal. Keep them off, Bardolph.
    Fang. A rescue! a rescue!
    Host. Good people, bring a rescue or two.—Thou
wilt not? thou wilt not? do, do, thou rogue! do, thou
hemp-seed!   60
    Fal. Away, you scullion! you rampallian! you fus-
tilarian! I'll tickle your catastrophe.

Enter the Lord Chief Justice, attended.

    Ch. Just. What is the matter? keep the peace here,
ho!
    Host. Good my lord, be good to me! I beseech you,
stand to me!
    Ch. Just. How now, Sir John! what, are you
    brawling here?
Doth this become your place, your time, and business?

You should have been well on your way to York.— 69
Stand from him, fellow: wherefore hang'st upon him?
  Host. O my most worshipful lord, an't please your
grace, I am a poor widow of Eastcheap, and he is
arrested at my suit.
  Ch. Just. For what sum?
  Host. It is more than for some, my lord; it is for all,
all I have. He hath eaten me out of house and home:
he hath put all my substance into that fat belly of his;
but I will have some of it out again, or I will ride thee
o' nights, like the mare.
  Fal. I think, I am as like to ride the mare, if I have
any vantage of ground to get up.   81
  Ch. Just. How comes this, Sir John? Fie! what
man of good temper would endure this tempest of
exclamation? Are you 'not ashamed to enforce a
poor widow to so rough a course to come by her own?
  Fal. What is the gross sum that I owe thee?
  Host. Marry, if thou wert an honest man, thyself,
and the money too. Thou didst swear to me upon a
parcel-gilt goblet, sitting in my Dolphin-chamber, at
the round table, by a sea-coal fire, upon Wednesday
in Wheeson week, when the prince broke thy head
for liking his father to a singing-man of Windsor;
thou didst swear to me then, as I was washing thy
wound, to marry me, and make me my lady thy wife.
Canst thou deny it? Did not goodwife Keech, the
butcher's wife, come in then, and call me gossip
Quickly? coming in to borrow a mess of vinegar;
telling us, she had a good dish of prawns, whereby
thou didst desire to eat some, whereby I told thee,
they were ill for a green wound? And didst thou not,
when she was gone down-stairs, desire me to be no
more so familiarity with such poor people; saying,
that ere long they should call me madam? And didst
thou not kiss me, and bid me fetch thee thirty
shillings? I put thee now to thy book-oath: deny it,
if thou canst.
  Fal. My lord, this is a poor mad soul; and she says,
up and down the town, that her eldest son is like you.
She hath been in good case, and the truth is, poverty
hath distracted her. But for these foolish officers, I
beseech you, I may have redress against them.   111
  Ch. Just. Sir John, Sir John, I am well acquainted
with your manner of wrenching the true cause the
false way. It is not a confident brow, nor the throng
of words that come with such more than impudent
sauciness from you, can thrust me from a level consideration; you have, as it appears to me, practised
upon the easy-yielding spirit of this woman, and made
her serve your uses both in purse and person.
  Host. Yes, in troth, my lord.   120
  Ch. Just. Pr'ythee, peace.—Pay her the debt you
owe her, and unpay the villainy you have done with
her: the one you may do with sterling money, and the
other with current repentance.
  Fal. My lord, I will not undergo this sneap without
reply. You call honourable boldness, impudent sauciness: if a man will court'sy, and say nothing, he is
virtuous. No, my lord, my humble duty remember'd,
I will not be your suitor: I say to you, I do desire
deliverance from these officers, being upon hasty
employment in the king's affairs.   131
  Ch. Just. You speak as having power to do wrong:
but answer in the effect of your reputation, and satisfy
the poor woman.
  Fal. Come hither, hostess.   [*Taking her aside.*

Enter GOWER.

  Ch. Just. Now, Master Gower! what news?
  Gow. The king, my lord, and Henry Prince of Wales
Are near at hand: the rest the paper tells.
  Fal. As I am a gentleman;—
  Host. Nay, you said so before   140
  Fal. As I am a gentleman;—Come, no more words
of it.
  Host. By this heavenly ground I tread on, I must be
fain to pawn both my plate, and the tapestry of my
dining-chambers.
  Fal. Glasses, glasses, is the only drinking: and for
thy walls,—a pretty slight drollery, or the story of the
Prodigal, or the German hunting in water-work, is

worth a thousand of these bed-hangings, and these fly-
bitten tapestries. Let it be ten pound, if thou canst.
Come, an it were not for thy humours, there is not a
better wench in England. Go, wash thy face, and
draw thy action. Come, thou must not be in this
humour with me. Dost not know me? Come, come,
I know thou wast set on to this.
  Host. Pr'ythee, Sir John, let it be but twenty nobles:
i' faith, I am loath to pawn my plate, in good earnest, la.
  Fal. Let it alone; I'll make other shift: you'll be a
fool still.
  Host. Well, you shall have it, though I pawn my
gown. I hope, you'll come to supper. You'll pay me
all together?   162
  Fal. Will I live?—Go, with her, with her; hook on,
hook on.
  Host. Will you have Doll Tear-sheet meet you at
supper?
  Fal. No more words: let's have her.
          [*Exeunt Hostess, BARDOLPH, Officers, and Page.*
  Ch. Just. I have heard better news.
  Fal. What's the news, my good lord?
  Ch. Just. Where lay the king last night?   170
  Gow. At Basingstoke, my lord.
  Fal. I hope, my lord, all's well: what is the news,
my lord?
  Ch. Just. Come all his forces back?
  Gow. No; fifteen hundred foot, five hundred horse,
Are march'd up to my Lord of Lancaster,
Against Northumberland, and the archbishop.
  Fal. Comes the king back from Wales, my noble
lord?
  Ch. Just. You shall have letters of me presently.
Come, go along with me, good Master Gower.   181
  Fal. My lord!
  Ch. Just. What's the matter?
  Fal. Master Gower, shall I entreat you with me to
dinner?
  Gow. I must wait upon my good lord here: I thank
you, good Sir John.
  Ch. Just. Sir John, you loiter here too long, being
you are to take soldiers up in counties as you go.
  Fal. Will you sup with me, Master Gower?   190
  Ch. Just. What foolish master taught you these
manners, Sir John?
  Fal. Master Gower, if they become me not, he was
a fool that taught them me.—This is the right fencing
grace, my lord; tap for tap, and so part fair.
  Ch. Just. Now, the Lord lighten thee! thou art a
great fool.   [*Exeunt.*

SCENE II.—The Same. Another Street.

Enter Prince HENRY and POINS.

  P. Hen. Trust me, I am exceeding weary.
  Poins. Is it come to that? I had thought, weariness
durst not have attached one of so high blood.
  P. Hen. 'Faith, it does me, though it discolours the
complexion of my greatness to acknowledge it. Doth
it not show vilely in me, to desire small beer?
  Poins. Why, a prince should not be so loosely
studied, as to remember so weak a composition.
  P. Hen. Belike then, my appetite was not princely
got; for, by my troth, I do now remember the poor
creature, small beer. But, indeed, these humble considerations make me out of love with my greatness.
What a disgrace is it to me, to remember thy name?
or to know thy face to-morrow? or to take note how
many pair of silk stockings thou hast; viz. these, and
those that were thy peach-colour'd ones? or to bear
the inventory of thy shirts; as, one for superfluity,
and one other for use?—but that the tennis-court-
keeper knows better than I, for it is a low ebb of linen
with thee, when thou keepest not racket there, as
thou hast not done a great while, because the rest of
thy low-countries have made a shift to eat up thy
holland: and God knows, whether those that bawl
out the ruins of thy linen shall inherit his kingdom;
but the midwives say, the children are not in the
fault, whereupon the world increases, and kindreds
are mightily strengthened.

Poins. How ill it follows, after you have laboured so hard, you should talk so idly! Tell me, how many good young princes would do so, their fathers being so sick as yours at this time is? 31

P. Hen. Shall I tell thee one thing, Poins?

Poins. Yes, faith, and let it be an excellent good thing.

P. Hen. It shall serve among wits of no higher breeding than thine.

Poins. Go to; I stand the push of your one thing that you will tell.

P. Hen. Marry, I tell thee,—it is not meet that I should be sad, now my father is sick: albeit I could tell to thee (as to one it pleases me, for fault of a better, to call my friend), I could be sad, and sad indeed too.

Poins. Very hardly upon such a subject.

P. Hen. By this hand, thou think'st me as far in the devil's book, as thou and Falstaff, for obduracy and persistency: let the end try the man. But I tell thee, my heart bleeds inwardly, that my father is so sick: and keeping such vile company as thou art, hath in reason taken from me all ostentation of sorrow. 50

Poins. The reason?

P. Hen. What wouldst thou think of me, if I should weep?

Poins. I would think thee a most princely hypocrite.

P. Hen. It would be every man's thought; and thou art a blessed fellow to think as every man thinks: never a man's thought in the world keeps the road-way better than thine: every man would think me an hypocrite indeed. And what accites your most worshipful thought to think so? 60

Poins. Why, because you have been so lewd, and so much engraffed to Falstaff.

P. Hen. And to thee.

Poins. By this light, I am well spoken of; I can hear it with mine own ears: the worst that they can say of me is, that I am a second brother, and that I am a proper fellow of my hands; and those two things, I confess, I cannot help. By the mass, here comes Bardolph.

Enter BARDOLPH *and Page.*

P. Hen. And the boy that I gave Falstaff: he had him from me Christian; and look, if the fat villain have not transformed him ape. 72

Bard. God save your grace.

P. Hen. And yours, most noble Bardolph.

Bard. [*To the Page.*] Come, you virtuous ass, you bashful fool, must you be blushing? wherefore blush you now? What a maidenly man-at-arms are you become? Is it such a matter to get a pottle-pot's maidenhead?

Page. He called me even now, my lord, through a red lattice, and I could discern no part of his face from the window: at last, I spied his eyes; and, methought, he had made two holes in the ale-wife's new petticoat, and peeped through.

P. Hen. Hath not the boy profited?

Bard. Away, you whoreson upright rabbit, away!

Page. Away, you rascally Althea's dream, away!

P. Hen. Instruct us, boy: what dream, boy?

Page. Marry, my lord, Althea dreamed she was delivered of a fire-brand; and therefore I call him her dream. 91

P. Hen. A crown's worth of good interpretation.—There it is, boy.				[*Gives him money.*

Poins. O, that this good blossom could be kept from cankers!—Well, there is sixpence to preserve thee.

Bard. An you do not make him be hanged among you, the gallows shall have wrong.

P. Hen. And how doth thy master, Bardolph?

Bard. Well, my good lord. He heard of your grace's coming to town: there's a letter for you. 100

Poins. Delivered with good respect.—And how doth the martlemas, your master?

Bard. In bodily health, sir.

Poins. Marry, the immortal part needs a physician; but that moves not him: though that be sick, it dies not.

P. Hen. I do allow this wen to be as familiar with me as my dog; and he holds his place, for look you how he writes. 109

Poins. [*Reads.*] "John Falstaff, knight,"- every man must know that, as oft as he has occasion to name himself; even like those that are kin to the king, for they never prick their finger, but they say, "There is some of the king's blood spilt:" "How comes that?" says he, that takes upon him not to conceive: the answer is as ready as a borrower's cap; "I am the king's poor cousin, sir."

P. Hen. Nay, they will be kin to us, or they will fetch it from Japhet. But to the letter:—

Poins. "Sir John Falstaff, knight, to the son of the king, nearest his father, Harry Prince of Wales, greeting."—Why, this is a certificate. 122

P. Hen. Peace!

Poins. "My lord, I will steep this letter in sack, and make him eat it."

Poins. "I will imitate the honourable Romans in brevity:"—he sure means brevity in breath, short-winded.—"I commend me to thee, I commend thee, and I leave thee. Be not too familiar with Poins; for he misuses thy favours so much, that he swears, thou art to marry his sister Nell. Repent at idle times as thou may'st, and so farewell. 130

 Thine, by yea and no, (which is as much as to say, as thou usest him,) JACK FALSTAFF, with my familiars; JOHN, with my brothers and sisters; and SIR JOHN with all Europe."

My lord, I will steep this letter in sack, and make him eat it.

P. Hen. That's to make him eat twenty of his words. But do you use me thus, Ned? must I marry your sister?

Poins. God send the wench no worse fortune! but I never said so. 141

P. Hen. Well, thus we play the fools with the time, and the spirits of the wise sit in the clouds, and mock us.—Is your master here in London?

Bard. Yes, my lord.

P. Hen. Where sups he? doth the old boar feed in the old frank?

Bard. At the old place, my lord, in Eastcheap.

P. Hen. What company?

Page. Ephesians, my lord; of the old church. 150

P. Hen. Sup any women with him?

Page. None, my lord, but old Mistress Quickly, and Mistress Doll Tear-sheet.

P. Hen. What pagan may that be?

Page. A proper gentlewoman, sir, and a kins-woman of my master's.

P. Hen. Even such kin as the parish-heifers are to the town-bull.—Shall we steal upon them, Ned, at supper?

Poins. I am your shadow, my lord; I'll follow you.

P. Hen. Sirrah, you boy,—and Bardolph;—no word to your master that I am yet come to town: there's for your silence. 163

Bard. I have no tongue, sir.

Page. And for mine, sir, I will govern it.
P. Hen. Fare ye well ; go. [*Exeunt* Bardolph *and*
Page.]—This Doll Tear-sheet should be some road.
Poins. I warrant you, as common as the way
between St. Albans and London.
P. Hen. How might we see Falstaff bestow himself
to-night in his true colours, and not ourselves be seen ?
Poins. Put on two leathern jerkins, and aprons, and
wait upon him at his table as drawers.   173
P. Hen. From a god to a bull ? a heavy declen-
sion ! it was Jove's case. From a prince to a prentice ?
a low transformation ! that shall be mine ; for in
everything the purpose must weigh with the folly.
Follow me, Ned.   [*Exeunt.*

Scene III.—Warkworth. Before the Castle.

Enter Northumberland, *Lady* Northumberland,
and Lady Percy.

North. I pray thee, loving wife and gentle daughter,
Give even way unto my rough affairs :
Put not you on the visage of the times,
And be like them to Percy troublesome.
Lady N. I have given over, I will speak no more.
Do what you will ; your wisdom be your guide.
North. Alas, sweet wife, my honour is at pawn,
And, but my going, nothing can redeem it.
Lady P. O, yet, for God's sake, go not to these
wars !
The time was, father, that you broke your word,   10
When you were more endear'd to it than now ;
When your own Percy, when my heart's dear Harry,
Threw many a northward look, to see his father
Bring up his powers ; but he did long in vain.
Who then persuaded you to stay at home ?
There were two honours lost, yours, and your son's :
For yours,—may heavenly glory brighten it !
For his,—it stuck upon him, as the sun
In the grey vault of heaven : and, by his light,
Did all the chivalry of England move   20
To do brave acts ; he was, indeed, the glass
Wherein the noble youth did dress themselves.
He had no legs, that practised not his gait ;
And speaking thick, which nature made his blemish,
Became the accents of the valiant ;
For those that could speak low, and tardily,
Would turn their own perfection to abuse,
To seem like him : so that, in speech, in gait,
In diet, in affections of delight,
In military rules, humours of blood,   30
He was the mark and glass, copy and book,
That fashion'd others. And him,—O wondrous him !
O miracle of men !—him did you leave,
(Second to none, unseconded by you,)
To look upon the hideous god of war
In disadvantage ; to abide a field,
Where nothing but the sound of Hotspur's name
Did seem defensible :—so you left him.
Never, O ! never, do his ghost the wrong,
To hold your honour more precise and nice   40
With others, than with him : let them alone.
The marshal, and the archbishop, are strong :
Had my sweet Harry had but half their numbers,
To-day might I, hanging on Hotspur's neck,
Have talk'd of Monmouth's grave.
North.   Beshrew your heart,
Fair daughter ! you do draw my spirits from me,
With new lamenting ancient oversights.
But I must go, and meet with danger there,
Or it will seek me in another place,
And find me worse provided.
Lady N.   O ! fly to Scotland, 50
Till that the nobles, and the armed commons,
Have of their puissance made a little taste.
Lady P. If they get ground and vantage of the king,
Then join you with them, like a rib of steel,
To make strength stronger ; but, for all our loves,
First let them try themselves. So did your son :
He was so suffer'd ; so came I a widow,
And never shall have length of life enough,

To rain upon remembrance with mine eyes,
That it may grow and sprout as high as heaven,   60
For recordation to my noble husband.
North. Come, come, go in with me. 'T is with my
mind,
As with the tide swell'd up unto its height,
That makes a still-stand, running neither way :
Fain would I go to meet the archbishop,
But many thousand reasons hold me back.—
I will resolve for Scotland : there am I,
Till time and vantage crave my company.   [*Exeunt.*

Scene IV.—London. A Room in the Boar's Head
Tavern, in Eastcheap.

Enter two Drawers.

1 *Draw.* What the devil hast thou brought there ?
apple-Johns ? thou know'st Sir John cannot endure an
apple-John.
2 *Draw.* Mass, thou sayest true. The prince once
set a dish of apple-Johns before him, and told him,
there were five more Sir Johns ; and, putting off his
hat, said, " I will now take my leave of these six dry,
round, old, withered knights." It angered him to the
heart, but he hath forgot that.   9
1 *Draw.* Why then, cover, and set them down : and
see if thou canst find out Sneak's noise ; Mistress
Tear-sheet would fain have some music. Despatch :—
the room where they supped is too hot ; they 'll come
in straight.
2 *Draw.* Sirrah, here will be the prince, and Master
Poins anon ; and they will put on two of our jerkins
and aprons, and Sir John must not know of it : Bardolph hath brought word.
1 *Draw.* By the mass, here will be old utis : it will
be an excellent stratagem.   20
2 *Draw.* I 'll see if I can find out Sneak.   [*Exit.*

Enter Hostess *and* Doll Tear-sheet.

Host. I' faith, sweet-heart, methinks now, you are
in an excellent good temperality : your pulsidge beats
as extraordinarily as heart would desire, and your
colour, I warrant you, is as red as any rose ; but, i'
faith, you have drunk too much canaries, and that 's
a marvellous searching wine, and it perfumes the
blood ere one can say,—What 's this ? How do you now ?
Doll. Better than I was. Hem.
Host. Why, that 's well said ; a good heart 's worth
gold. Lo ! here comes Sir John.   31

Enter Falstaff, *singing.*

Fal. " When Arthur first in court "—Empty the
jordan.—" And was a worthy king." [*Exit Drawer.*]
How now, Mistress Doll ?
Host. Sick of a calm : yea, good sooth.
Fal. So is all her sect ; an they be once in a calm,
they are sick.
Doll. You muddy rascal, is that all the comfort you
give me ?
Fal. You make fat rascals, Mistress Doll.   40
Doll. I make them ! gluttony and diseases make
them ; I make them not.
Fal. If the cook help to make the gluttony, you
help to make the diseases, Doll : we catch of you,
Doll, we catch of you ; grant that, my poor virtue,
grant that.
Doll. Ay, marry ; our chains, and our jewels.
Fal. " Your brooches, pearls, and owches :"—for to
serve bravely, is to come halting off, you know : to
come off the breach with his pike bent bravely, and
to surgery bravely ; to venture upon the charged
chambers bravely :—   52
Doll. Hang yourself, you muddy conger, hang yourself !
Host. By my troth, this is the old fashion : you two
never meet, but you fall to some discord. You are
both, in good troth, as rheumatic as two dry toasts ;
you cannot one bear with another's confirmities.
What the good-year ! one must bear, and that must
be you : you are the weaker vessel, as they say, the
emptier vessel.   61

Doll. Can a weak empty vessel bear such a huge full hogshead? there's a whole merchant's venture of Bourdeaux stuff in him: you have not seen a hulk better stuffed in the hold.—Come, I'll be friends with thee, Jack: thou art going to the wars; and whether

no swaggerers. I am in good name and fame with the very best.—Shut the door;—there comes no swaggerers here: I have not lived all this while, to have swaggering now.—Shut the door, I pray you.

Fal. Dost thou hear, hostess?   80

Doll. "Come, I'll be friends with thee, Jack."

I shall ever see thee again, or no, there is nobody cares.

Re-enter Drawer.

Draw. Sir, Ancient Pistol's below, and would speak with you.   70

Doll. Hang him, swaggering rascal! let him not come hither: it is the foul-mouthed'st rogue in England.

Host. If he swagger, let him not come here: no, by my faith; I must live amongst my neighbours; I'll

Host. Pray you, pacify yourself, Sir John: there comes no swaggerers here.

Fal. Dost thou hear? it is mine ancient.

Host. Tilly-fally, Sir John, never tell me: your ancient swaggerer comes not in my doors. I was before Master Tisick, the deputy, the other day; and, as he said to me,—it was no longer ago than Wednesday last,—"Neighbour Quickly," says he;—Master Dumb, our minister, was by then;—"Neighbour Quickly," says he, "receive those that are civil; for," said he, "you are in an ill name:"—now 'a said so, I can tell whereupon; "for," says he, "you are an honest woman, and well thought on; therefore take heed what guests you receive: receive," says he, "no swaggering companions."—There comes none here: —you would bless you to hear what he said.—No, I 'll no swaggerers.

Fal. He 's no swaggerer, hostess; a tame cheater, i' faith; you may stroke him as gently as a puppy greyhound: he will not swagger with a Barbary hen, if her feathers turn back in any show of resistance.— Call him up, drawer.   102

Host. Cheater, call you him? I will bar no honest man my house, nor no cheater; but I do not love swaggering: by my troth, I am the worse, when one says—swagger. Feel, masters, how I shake; look you, I warrant you.

Doll. So you do, hostess,

Host. Do i? yea, in very truth do I, an 't were an aspen-leaf. I cannot abide swaggerers.   110

Enter Pistol, Bardolph, and Page.

Pist. God save you, Sir John !

Fal. Welcome, Ancient Pistol. Here, Pistol, I charge you with a cup of sack: do you discharge upon mine hostess.

Pist. I will discharge upon her, Sir John, with two bullets.

Fal. She is pistol-proof, sir; you shall hardly offend her.

Host. Come, I 'll drink no proofs, nor no bullets. I 'll drink no more than will do me good, for no man's pleasure, I.   121

Pist. Then to you, Mistress Dorothy: I will charge you.

Doll. Charge me? I scorn you, scurvy companion. What! you poor, base, rascally, cheating, lack-linen mate! Away, you mouldy rogue, away! I am meat for your master.

Pist. I know you, Mistress Dorothy.

Doll. Away, you cut-purse rascal! you filthy bung, away! By this wine, I 'll thrust my knife in your mouldy chaps, an you play the saucy cuttle with me. Away, you bottle-ale rascal! you basket-hilt stale juggler, you!—Since when, I pray you, sir?—God's light! with two points on your shoulder? much!

Pist. I will murder your ruff for this.

Fal. No more, Pistol: I would not have you go off here. Discharge yourself of our company, Pistol.

Host. No, good Captain Pistol; not here, sweet captain.   139

Doll. Captain! thou abominable damned cheater, art thou not ashamed to be called captain? An captains were of my mind, they would truncheon you out, for taking their names upon you before you have earned them. You a captain, you slave! for what? for tearing a poor whore's ruff in a bawdy-house?— He a captain! hang him, rogue! he lives upon mouldy stewed prunes, and dried cakes. A captain! these villains will make the word captain as odious as the word occupy, which was an excellent good word before it was ill-sorted: therefore captains had need look to 't.   151

Bard. Pray thee, go down, good ancient.

Fal. Hark thee hither, Mistress Doll.

Pist. Not I: I tell thee what, Corporal Bardolph; I could tear her.—I 'll be revenged on her.

Page. Pray thee, go down.

Pist. I 'll see her damned first ;—to Pluto's damned lake, to the infernal deep, with Erebus and tortures vile also. Hold hook and line, say I. Down! down, dogs! down, fates! Have we not Hiren here?   160

Host. Good Captain Peesel, be quiet; it is very late, i' faith. I beseek you now, aggravate your choler.

Pist. These be good humours, indeed! Shall packhorses,
And hollow pamper'd jades of Asia,
Which cannot go but thirty miles a day,
Compare with Cæsars, and with Cannibals,
And Trojan Greeks? nay, rather damn them with
King Cerberus, and let the welkin roar.
Shall we fall foul for toys?   170

Host. By my troth, captain, these are very bitter words.

Bard. Be gone, good ancient: this will grow to a brawl anon.

Pist. Die men like dogs; give crowns like pins. Have we not Hiren here?

Host. On my word, captain, there 's none such here. What the good-year! do you think I would deny her? for God's sake, be quiet.

Pist. Then feed, and be fat, my fair Calipolis.   180
Come, give 's some sack.
Si fortune me tormente, sperato me contente.—
Fear we broadsides? no, let the fiend give fire:
Give me some sack; and, sweet-heart, lie thou there.
                                  [*Laying down his sword.*
Come we to full points here, and are *et ceteras*
      nothing?

Fal. Pistol, I would be quiet.

Pist. Sweet knight, I kiss thy neif. What! we have seen the seven stars.

Doll. For God's sake, thrust him down-stairs! I cannot endure such a fustian rascal.   190

Pist. Thrust him down-stairs! know we not Galloway nags?

Fal. Quoit him down, Bardolph, like a shove-groat shilling: nay, an he do nothing but speak nothing, he shall be nothing here.

Bard. Come, get you down-stairs.

Pist. What! shall we have incision? shall we imbrue?—   [*Snatching up his sword.*
Then, death, rock me asleep, abridge my doleful days!
Why then, let grievous, ghastly, gaping wounds
Untwine the Sisters Three! Come, Atropos, I say! 201

Host. Here 's goodly stuff toward!

Fal. Give me my rapier, boy.

Doll. I pray thee, Jack, I pray thee, do not draw.

Fal. Get you down-stairs.   [*Drawing.*

Host. Here 's a goodly tumult! I 'll forswear keeping house, afore I 'll be in these tirrits and frights. So; murder, I warrant now.—Alas, alas! put up your naked weapons; put up your naked weapons.
                          [*Exeunt Bardolph and Pistol.*

Doll. I pray thee, Jack, be quiet; the rascal is gone. Ah! you whoreson little valiant villain, you.   210

Host. Are you not hurt i' the groin? methought, he made a shrewd thrust at your belly.

Re-enter Bardolph.

Fal. Have you turned him out o' doors?

Bard. Yes, sir: the rascal's drunk. You have hurt him, sir, in the shoulder.

Fal. A rascal, to brave me!

Doll. Ah, you sweet little rogue, you! Alas, poor ape, how thou sweat'st! Come, let me wipe thy face; —come on, you whoreson chops.—Ah, rogue! i' faith, I love thee. Thou art as valorous as Hector of Troy, worth five of Agamemnon, and ten times better than the Nine Worthies. Ah, villain!   222

Fal. A rascally slave! I will toss the rogue in a blanket.

Doll. Do, if thou darest for thy heart: if thou dost, I 'll canvass thee between a pair of sheets.

Enter Music.

Page. The music is come, sir.

Fal. Let them play.—Play, sirs.—Sit on my knee, Doll.—A rascal bragging slave! the rogue fled from me like quicksilver.   230

Doll. I' faith, and thou followedst him like a church. Thou whoreson little tidy Bartholomew boar-pig, when wilt thou leave fighting o' days, and foining o' nights, and begin to patch up thine old body for heaven?

Enter behind, Prince Henry and Poins, disguised like Drawers.

Fal. Peace, good Doll! do not speak like a death's-head: do not bid me remember mine end.

Doll. Sirrah, what humour is the prince of?

Fal. A good shallow young fellow: he would have made a good pantler, he would have chipped bread well.   241

Doll. They say, Poins has a good wit.

Fal. He a good wit? hang him, baboon! his wit is as thick as Tewksbury mustard : there is no more conceit in him, than is in a mallet.

Doll. Why does the prince love him so, then?

Fal. Because their legs are both of a bigness; and he plays at quoits well; and eats conger and fennel; and drinks off candles' ends for flap-dragons; and rides the wild mare with the boys; and jumps upon joint-stools; and swears with a good grace; and wears his boot very smooth, like unto the sign of the leg; and breeds no bate with telling of discreet stories; and such other gambol faculties he has, that show a weak mind and an able body, for the which the prince admits him : for the prince himself is such another; the weight of a hair will turn the scales between their avoirdupois.

P. Hen. Would not this nave of a wheel have his ears cut off?   260

Poins. Let's beat him before his whore.

P. Hen. Look, whether the withered elder hath not his poll clawed like a parrot.

Poins. Is it not strange, that desire should so many years outlive performance?

Fal. Kiss me, Doll.

P. Hen. Saturn and Venus this year in conjunction! what says the almanac to that?

Poins. And, look, whether the fiery Trigon, his man, be not lisping to his master's old tables, his note-book, his counsel-keeper.   271

Fal. Thou dost give me flattering busses.

Doll. Nay, truly; I kiss thee with a most constant heart.

Fal. I am old, I am old.

Doll. I love thee better than I love e'er a scurvy young boy of them all.

Fal. What stuff wilt thou have a kirtle of? I shall receive money on Thursday; thou shalt have a cap to-morrow. A merry song! come : it grows late; we'll to bed. Thou'lt forget me, when I am gone. 281

Doll. By my troth, thou'lt set me a-weeping, an thou say'st so : prove that ever I dress myself handsome till thy return.—Well, hearken the end.

Fal. Some sack, Francis!

P. Hen., Poins. Anon, anon, sir.   [*Advancing.*

Fal. Ha! a bastard son of the king's.—And art not thou Poins his brother?

P. Hen. Why, thou globe of sinful continents, what a life dost thou lead!   290

Fal. A better than thou : I am a gentleman; thou art a drawer.

P. Hen. Very true, sir; and I come to draw you out by the ears.

Host. O, the Lord preserve thy good grace! by my troth, welcome to London.—Now, the Lord bless that sweet face of thine! O Jesu! are you come from Wales?

Fal. Thou whoreson mad compound of majesty,—by this light flesh and corrupt blood, thou art welcome.   [*Placing his hand upon* DOLL.

Doll. How, you fat fool? I scorn you.   302

Poins. My lord, he will drive you out of your revenge, and turn all to a merriment, if you take not the heat.

P. Hen. You whoreson candle-mine, you, how vilely did you speak of me even now, before this honest, virtuous, civil gentlewoman?

Host. God's blessing of your good heart! and so she is, by my troth.   310

Fal. Didst thou hear me?

P. Hen. Yes; and you knew me, as you did, when you ran away by Gadshill : you knew I was at your back, and spoke it on purpose to try my patience.

Fal. No, no, no; not so; I did not think thou wast within hearing.

P. Hen. I shall drive you, then, to confess the wilful abuse; and then I know how to handle you.

Fal. No abuse, Hal, on mine honour; no abuse.

P. Hen. Not! to dispraise me, and call me pantler, and bread-chipper, and I know not what?   321

Fal. No abuse, Hal.

Poins. No abuse!

Fal. No abuse, Ned, i' the world : honest Ned, none. I dispraised him before the wicked, that the wicked might not fall in love with him;—in which doing, I have done the part of a careful friend, and a true subject, and thy father is to give me thanks for it. No abuse, Hal;—none, Ned, none;—no, 'faith, boys, none.   330

P. Hen. See now, whether pure fear, and entire cowardice, doth not make thee wrong this virtuous gentlewoman to close with us? Is she of the wicked? Is thine hostess here of the wicked? Or is the boy of the wicked? Or honest Bardolph, whose zeal burns in his nose, of the wicked?

Poins. Answer, thou dead elm, answer.

Fal. The fiend hath pricked down Bardolph irrecoverable; and his face is Lucifer's privy-kitchen, where he doth nothing but roast maltworms. For the boy,—there is a good angel about him, but the devil outbids him too.   342

P. Hen. For the women?

Fal. For one of them, she is in hell already, and burns poor souls. For the other, I owe her money, and whether she be damned for that, I know not.

Host. No, I warrant you.

Fal. No, I think thou art not; I think, thou art quit for that. Marry, there is another indictment upon thee, for suffering flesh to be eaten in thy house, contrary to the law; for the which, I think, thou wilt howl.   352

Host. All victuallers do so : what's a joint of mutton or two in a whole Lent?

P. Hen. You, gentlewoman,—

Doll. What says your grace?

Fal. His grace says that which his flesh rebels against.   [*Knocking heard.*

Host. Who knocks so loud at door? look to the door there, Francis.   360

Enter PETO.

P. Hen. Peto, how now? what news?

Peto. The king your father is at Westminster;
And there are twenty weak and wearied posts
Come from the north : and, as I came along,
I met, and overtook, a dozen captains,
Bare-headed, sweating, knocking at the taverns,
And asking every one for Sir John Falstaff.

P. Hen. By Heaven, Poins, I feel me much to blame,
So idly to profane the precious time,
When tempest of commotion, like the south,   370
Borne with black vapour, doth begin to melt,
And drop upon our bare unarmed heads.
Give me my sword and cloak.—Falstaff, good night.
              [*Exeunt Prince* HENRY, POINS, PETO, *and*
                                          BARDOLPH.

Fal. Now comes in the sweetest morsel of the night, and we must hence, and leave it unpicked. [*Knocking heard.*] More knocking at the door!

Re-enter BARDOLPH.

How now? what's the matter?

Bard. You must away to court, sir, presently;
A dozen captains stay at door for you.   379

Fal. [*To the Page.*] Pay the musicians, sirrah.—
Farewell, hostess;—farewell, Doll. You see, my good wenches, how men of merit are sought after : the undeserver may sleep, when the man of action is called on. Farewell, good wenches. If I be not sent away post, I will see you again ere I go.

Doll. I cannot speak;—if my heart be not ready to burst,—well, sweet Jack, have a care of thyself.

Fal. Farewell, farewell.

              [*Exeunt* FALSTAFF *and* BARDOLPH.

Host. Well, fare thee well : I have known thee these twenty-nine years, come peascod-time; but an honester, and truer-hearted man,—well, fare thee well.

Bard. [*Within.*] Mistress Tear-sheet,—   392

Host. What's the matter?

Bard. [*Within.*] Bid Mistress Tear-sheet come to my master.

Host. O! run, Doll, run; run, good Doll. [*Exeunt.*

ACT III.

SCENE I.—A Room in the Palace.

Enter King HENRY in his night-gown, with a Page.

King Henry.
O, call the Earls of Surrey and of
    Warwick;
But, ere they come, bid them o'er-
    read these letters,
And well consider of them. Make
    good speed. [*Exit Page.*
How many thousand of my poorest
    subjects
Are at this hour asleep!—O sleep!
    O gentle sleep!
Nature's soft nurse, how have I frighted thee,
That thou no more wilt weigh my eyelids down,
And steep my senses in forgetfulness?
Why rather, sleep, liest thou in smoky cribs,   10
Upon uneasy pallets stretching thee,
And hush'd with buzzing night-flies to thy
    slumber,
Than in the perfum'd chambers of the great,
Under the canopies of costly state,
And lull'd with sounds of sweetest melody?
O thou dull god! why liest thou with the vile,
In loathsome beds, and leav'st the kingly couch,
A watch-case, or a common 'larum bell?
Wilt thou upon the high and giddy mast
Seal up the ship-boy's eyes, and rock his brains   20
In cradle of the rude imperious surge,
And in the visitation of the winds,
Who take the ruffian billows by the top,
Curling their monstrous heads, and hanging them
With deaf'ning clamours in the slippery clouds,
That with the hurly death itself awakes?
Canst thou, O partial sleep! give thy repose
To the wet sea-boy in an hour so rude;
And in the calmest and most stillest night,
With all appliances and means to boot,
Deny it to a king? Then, happy low, lie down!   30
Uneasy lies the head that wears a crown.

Enter WARWICK and SURREY.

War. Many good morrows to your majesty!
K. Hen. Is it good morrow, lords?
War. 'T is one o'clock, and past.
K. Hen. Why then, good morrow to you all, my
    lords.
Have you read o'er the letters that I sent you?
War. We have, my liege.
K. Hen. Then you perceive, the body of our king-
    dom
How foul it is; what rank diseases grow,
And with what danger, near the heart of it.   40
War. It is but as a body yet distemper'd,
Which to his former strength may be restor'd,
With good advice, and little medicine.
My Lord Northumberland will soon be cool'd.
K. Hen. O God! that one might read the book of
    fate,
And see the revolution of the times
Make mountains level, and the continent,
Weary of solid firmness, melt itself
Into the sea! and, other times, to see
The beachy girdle of the ocean   50
Too wide for Neptune's hips; how chances mock,
And changes fill the cup of alteration
With divers liquors! O, if this were seen,

The happiest youth, viewing his progress through,
What perils past, what crosses to ensue,
Would shut the book, and sit him down and die.
'T is not ten years gone,
Since Richard and Northumberland, great friends,
Did feast together, and in two years after
Were they at wars: it is but eight years, since   60
This Percy was the man nearest my soul;
Who like a brother toil'd in my affairs,
And laid his love and life under my foot:
Yea, for my sake, even to the eyes of Richard,
Gave him defiance. But which of you was by,

War. "Your majesty hath been this fortnight ill."

[*To* WARWICK.] (You, cousin Nevil, as I may re-
    member,)
When Richard, with his eye brimful of tears,
Then check'd and rated by Northumberland,
Did speak these words, now prov'd a prophecy?
"Northumberland, thou ladder, by the which   70
My cousin Bolingbroke ascends my throne;"—
Though then, God knows, I had no such intent,
But that necessity so bow'd the state,
That I and greatness were compell'd to kiss.
"The time shall come," thus did he follow it,
"The time will come, that foul sin, gathering head,
Shall break into corruption:"—so went on,
Foretelling this same time's condition,
And the division of our amity.
War. There is a history in all men's lives,   80
Figuring the nature of the times deceas'd;
The which observ'd, a man may prophesy,
With a near aim, of the main chance of things
As yet not come to life, which in their seeds,
And weak beginnings, lie intreasured.
Such things become the hatch and brood of time;
And, by the necessary form of this,
King Richard might create a perfect guess,
That great Northumberland, then false to him,
Would, of that seed, grow to a greater falseness,   90
Which should not find a ground to root upon,
Unless on you.
K. Hen.   Are these things then necessities?

Then let us meet them like necessities;
And that same word even now cries out on us.
They say, the bishop and Northumberland
Are fifty thousand strong.

War.   It cannot be, my lord:
Rumour doth double, like the voice and echo,
The numbers of the fear'd.—Please it your grace
To go to bed; upon my life, my lord,
The powers that you already have sent forth,   100
Shall bring this prize in very easily.
To comfort you the more, I have receiv'd
A certain instance that Glendower is dead.
Your majesty hath been this fortnight ill,
And these unseason'd hours, perforce, must add
Unto your sickness.

K. Hen.   I will take your counsel:
And were these inward wars once out of hand,
We would, dear lords, unto the Holy Land. [*Exeunt.*

SCENE II.—Court before Justice SHALLOW's House
in Glostershire.

Enter SHALLOW *and* SILENCE, *meeting;* MOULDY,
SHADOW, WART, FEEBLE, BULL-CALF, *and Servants, behind.*

Shal. Come on, come on, come on, sir; give me your
hand, sir, give me your hand, sir: an early stirrer, by
the rood. And how doth my good cousin Silence?
Sil. Good morrow, good cousin Shallow.
Shal. And how doth my cousin, your bedfellow?
and your fairest daughter, and mine, my god-
daughter Ellen?
Sil. Alas! a black ousel, cousin Shallow.
Shal. By yea and nay, sir, I dare say, my cousin
William is become a good scholar. He is at Oxford,
still, is he not?   11
Sil. Indeed, sir; to my cost.
Shal. He must then to the inns of court shortly. I
was once of Clement's Inn; where, I think, they will
talk of mad Shallow yet.
Sil. You were called lusty Shallow then, cousin.
Shal. By the mass, I was called anything; and I
would have done anything, indeed, and roundly too.
There was I, and little John Doit of Staffordshire, and
black George Bare, and Francis Pickbone, and Will
Squele, a Cotswold man; you had not four such
swinge-bucklers in all the inns of court again: and, I
may say to you, we knew where the bona-robas were,
and had the best of them all at commandment. Then
was Jack Falstaff, now Sir John, a boy, and page to
Thomas Mowbray, Duke of Norfolk.
Sil. This Sir John, cousin, that comes hither anon
about soldiers?   28
Shal. The same Sir John, the very same. I saw him
break Skogan's head at the court gate, when he was
a crack, not thus high: and the very same day did I
fight with one Sampson Stockfish, a fruiterer, behind
Gray's Inn. Jesu! Jesu! the mad days that I have
spent! and to see how many of mine old acquaintance
are dead!
Sil. We shall all follow, cousin.
Shal. Certain, 'tis certain; very sure, very sure:
death, as the Psalmist saith, is certain to all; all shall
die. How a good yoke of bullocks at Stamford fair?
Sil. Truly, cousin, I was not there.   40
Shal. Death is certain.—Is old Double of your town
living yet?
Sil. Dead, sir.
Shal. Jesu! Jesu! dead!—he drew a good bow;—
and dead!—he shot a fine shoot:—John of Gaunt loved
him well, and betted much money on his head. Dead!
—he would have clapped in the clout at twelve score;
and carried you a forehand shaft a fourteen and fourteen and a half, that it would have done a man's
heart good to see.—How a score of ewes now?   50
Sil. Thereafter as they be; a score of good ewes
may be worth ten pounds.
Shal. And is old Double dead?
Sil. Here come two of Sir John Falstaff's men, as I
think.

Enter BARDOLPH, *and one with him.*

Bard. Good morrow, honest gentlemen. I beseech
you, which is Justice Shallow?
Shal. I am Robert Shallow, sir; a poor esquire of
this county, and one of the king's justices of the peace.
What is your good pleasure with me?   60
Bard. My captain, sir, commends him to you; my
captain, Sir John Falstaff: a tall gentleman, by
Heaven, and a most gallant leader.
Shal. He greets me well, sir: I knew him a good
backsword man. How doth the good knight? may I
ask, how my lady his wife doth?
Bard. Sir, pardon; a soldier is better accommodated than with a wife.
Shal. It is well said, in faith, sir; and it is well said
indeed too. Better accommodated!—it is good; yea,
indeed, is it: good phrases are surely, and ever were,
very commendable. Accommodated! it comes of
accommodo: very good; a good phrase.
Bard. Pardon me, sir; I have heard the word.
Phrase, call you it? By this good day, I know not the
phrase: but I will maintain the word with my sword
to be a soldier-like word, and a word of exceeding
good command, by Heaven. Accommodated; that is,
when a man is, as they say, accommodated; or, when
a man is,—being,—whereby,—he may be thought to
be accommodated, which is an excellent thing.   81

Enter FALSTAFF.

Shal. It is very just.—Look, here comes good Sir
John.—Give me your good hand, give me your wor-
ship's good hand. By my troth, you like well, and
bear your years very well: welcome, good Sir John.
Fal. I am glad to see you well, good Master Robert
Shallow.—Master Sure-card, as I think.
Shal. No, Sir John; it is my cousin Silence, in com-
mission with me.
Fal. Good Master Silence, it well befits you should
be of the peace.   91
Sil. Your good worship is welcome.
Fal. Fie! this is hot weather.—Gentlemen, have
you provided me here half a dozen sufficient men?
Shal. Marry, have we, sir. Will you sit?
Fal. Let me see them, I beseech you.
Shal. Where's the roll? where's the roll? where's
the roll?—Let me see, let me see, let me see: so, so,
so, so. Yea, marry, sir:—Ralph Mouldy!—let them
appear as I call; let them do so, let them do so.—Let
me see; where is Mouldy?   101
Moul. Here, an it please you.
Shal. What think you, Sir John? a good-limbed
fellow; young, strong, and of good friends.
Fal. Is thy name Mouldy?
Moul. Yea, an it please you.
Fal. 'T is the more time thou wert used.
Shal. Ha, ha, ha! most excellent, i' faith! things
that are mouldy lack use: very singular good!—In
faith, well said, Sir John: very well said.   110
Fal. [*To* SHALLOW.] Prick him.
Moul. I was pricked well enough before, an you
could have let me alone: my old dame will be undone
now, for one to do her husbandry, and her drudgery.
You need not to have pricked me; there are other
men fitter to go out than I.
Fal. Go to; peace, Mouldy! you shall go. Mouldy,
it is time you were spent.
Moul. Spent!
Shal. Peace, fellow, peace! stand aside: know you
where you are?—For the other, Sir John:—let me see.
—Simon Shadow!   122
Fal. Yea, marry, let me have him to sit under: he's
like to be a cold soldier.
Shal. Where's Shadow?
Shad. Here, sir.
Fal. Shadow, whose son art thou?
Shad. My mother's son, sir.
Fal. Thy mother's son! like enough; and thy
father's shadow: so the son of the female is the
shadow of the male: it is often so, indeed; but not
of the father's substance.   132
Shal. Do you like him, Sir John?

Fal. Shadow will serve for summer,—prick him; for we have a number of shadows to fill up the muster-book.

Shal. Thomas Wart!

Fal. Where's he?

Wart. Here, sir.

Fal. Is thy name Wart? 140

Wart. Yea, sir.

Fal. Thou art a very ragged wart.

Shal. Shall I prick him, Sir John?

Fal. It were superfluous, for his apparel is built upon his back, and the whole frame stands upon pins: prick him no more.

Shal. Ha, ha, ha!—you can do it, sir; you can do it: I commend you well.—Francis Feeble!

Fal. "'Fore God, a likely fellow!"

Fee. Here, sir.

Fal. What trade art thou, Feeble. 150

Fee. A woman's tailor, sir. ·

Shal. Shall I prick him, sir?

Fal. You may; but if he had been a man's tailor, he would have pricked you.—Wilt thou make as many holes in an enemy's battle, as thou hast done in a woman's petticoat?

Fee. I will do my good will, sir: you can have no more.

Fal. Well said, good woman's tailor! well said, courageous Feeble! Thou wilt be as valiant as the wrathful dove, or most magnanimous mouse.—Prick the woman's tailor. Well, Master Shallow, deep Master Shallow.

Fee. I would Wart might have gone, sir.

Fal. I would thou wert a man's tailor, that thou mightst mend him, and make him fit to go. I cannot put him to a private soldier, that is the leader of so many thousands: let that suffice, most forcible Feeble.

Fee. It shall suffice, sir.

Fal. I am bound to thee, reverend Feeble.—Who is next? 171

Shal. Peter Bull-calf of the green!

Fal. Yea, marry, let us see Bull-calf.

Bull. Here, sir.

Fal. 'Fore God, a likely fellow!—Come, prick me Bull-calf till he roar again.

Bull. O Lord! good my lord captain,—

Fal. What, dost thou roar before thou art pricked?

Bull. O Lord! sir, I am a diseased man.

Fal. What disease hast thou? 180

Bull. A whoreson cold, sir; a cough, sir; which I caught with ringing in the king's affairs, upon his coronation-day, sir.

Fal. Come, thou shalt go to the wars in a gown; we will have away thy cold; and I will take such order, that thy friends shall ring for thee.—Is here all?

Shal. Here is two more called than your number; you must have but four here, sir:—and so, I pray you, go in with me to dinner.

Fal. Come, I will go drink with you, but I cannot tarry dinner. I am glad to see you, by my troth, Master Shallow. 192

Shal. O, Sir John, do you remember since we lay all night in the windmill in Saint George's fields?

Fal. No more of that, good Master Shallow, no more of that.

Shal. Ha, it was a merry night. And is Jane Night-work alive?

Fal. She lives, Master Shallow.

Shal. She never could away with me. 200

Fal. Never, never: she would always say, she could not abide Master Shallow.

Shal. By the mass, I could anger her to the heart. She was then a bona-roba. Doth she hold her own well?

Fal. Old, old, Master Shallow.

Shal. Nay, she must be old; she cannot choose but be old; certain she's old, and had Robin Night-work by old Night-work, before I came to Clement's Inn. 210

Sil. That's fifty-five years ago.

Shal. Ha, cousin Silence, that thou hadst seen that that this knight and I have seen!—Ha, Sir John, said I well?

Fal. We have heard the chimes at midnight, Master Shallow.

Shal. That we have, that we have, that we have; in faith, Sir John, we have. Our watchword was, "Hem, boys!"—Come, let's to dinner; come, let's to dinner.—O, the days that we have seen!—Come, come. 222

[*Exeunt* FALSTAFF, SHALLOW, *and* SILENCE.

Bull. Good Master corporate Bardolph, stand my friend, and here is four Harry ten shillings in French crowns for you. In very truth, sir, I had as lief be hanged, sir, as go: and yet, for mine own part, sir, I do not care; but rather, because I am unwilling, and, for mine own part, have a desire to stay with my friends: else, sir, I did not care, for mine own part, so much. 231

Bard. Go to; stand aside.

Moul. And good master corporal captain, for my old dame's sake, stand my friend: she has nobody to do anything about her, when I am gone; and she is old, and cannot help herself. You shall have forty, sir.

Bard. Go to; stand aside.

Fee. By my troth, I care not; a man can die but once;—we owe God a death. I'll ne'er bear a base mind:—an't be my destiny, so; an't be not, so. No man's too good to serve his prince; and let it go which way it will, he that dies this year is quit for the next.

Bard. Well said; thou art a good fellow.

Fee. 'Faith, I'll bear no base mind.

Re-enter FALSTAFF *and Justices.*

Fal. Come, sir, which men shall I have?

Shal. Four, of which you please.

Bard. Sir, a word with you.—I have three pound to free Mouldy and Bull-calf.

Fal. Go to; well. 250

Shal. Come, Sir John, which four will you have?

Fal. Do you choose for me.

Shal. Marry then,—Mouldy, Bull-calf, Feeble, and Shadow.

Fal. Mouldy, and Bull-calf:—for you, Mouldy, stay at home till you are past service:—and, for your part, Bull-calf, grow till you come unto it: I will none of you.

Shal. Sir John, Sir John, do not yourself wrong. They are your likeliest men, and I would have you served with the best. 261

Fal. Will you tell me, Master Shallow, how to choose a man? Care I for the limb, the thewes, the stature, bulk, and big assemblance of a man?

Give me the spirit, Master Shallow.—Here's Wart;—you see what a ragged appearance it is: he shall charge you, and discharge you, with the motion of a pewterer's hammer; come off, and on, swifter than he that gibbets-on the brewer's bucket. And this same half-faced fellow, Shadow,—give me this man: he presents no mark to the enemy; the foeman may with as great aim level at the edge of a penknife. And, for a retreat,—how swiftly will this Feeble, the woman's tailor, run off! O, give me the spare men, and spare me the great ones.—Put me a caliver into Wart's hand, Bardolph.

Bard. Hold, Wart, traverse; thus, thus, thus.

Fal. Come, manage me your caliver. So:—very well:—go to:—very good:—exceeding good.—O, give me always a little, lean, old, chapped, bald shot.—Well said, i' faith, Wart: thou 'rt a good scab; hold, there's a tester for thee.   282

Shal. He is not his craft's master, he doth not do it right. I remember at Mile End Green, (when I lay at Clement's Inn,) I was then Sir Dagonet in Arthur's show, there was a little quiver fellow, and he would manage you his piece thus: and he would about, and about, and come you in: "rah, tah, tah," would he say; "bounce," would he say; and away again would he go, and again would he come.—I shall never see such a fellow.   291

Fal. These fellows will do well, Master Shallow.—God keep you, Master Silence: I will not use many words with you.—Fare you well, gentlemen both: I thank you: I must a dozen mile to-night.—Bardolph, give the soldiers coats.

Shal. Sir John, the Lord bless you, and God prosper your affairs, and send us peace! As you return, visit my house. Let our old acquaintance be renewed: peradventure, I will with you to the court.   300

Fal. 'Fore God, I would you would.

Shal. Go to; I have spoke at a word. Fare you well.

Fal. Fare you well, gentle gentlemen. [*Exeunt* SHALLOW *and* SILENCE.] On, Bardolph; lead the men away. [*Exeunt* BARDOLPH, *Recruits, &c.*] As I return, I will fetch off these justices: I do see the bottom of Justice Shallow. Lord, Lord, how subject we old men are to this vice of lying! This same starved justice hath done nothing but prate to me of the wildness of his youth, and the feats he hath done about Turnbull Street; and every third word a lie, duer paid to the hearer than the Turk's tribute. I do remember him at Clement's Inn, like a man made after supper of a cheese-paring: when he was naked, he was, for all the world, like a forked radish, with a head fantastically carved upon it with a knife: he was so forlorn, that his dimensions to any thick sight were invincible: he was the very genius of famine; yet lecherous as a monkey, and the whores called him—mandrake. He came ever in the rearward of the fashion, and sung those tunes to the overscutched huswives that he heard the carmen whistle, and sware—they were his fancies, or his good-nights. And now is this Vice's dagger become a squire, and talks as familiarly of John of Gaunt, as if he had been sworn brother to him; and I 'll be sworn he never saw him but once in the Tilt-yard, and then he burst his head, for crowding among the marshal's men. I saw it, and told John of Gaunt, he beat his own name; for you might have truss'd him, and all his apparel, into an eel-skin: the case of a treble hautboy was a mansion for him, a court; and now has he land and beeves. Well, I will be acquainted with him, if I return; and it shall go hard, but I will make him a philosopher's two stones to me. If the young dace be a bait for the old pike, I see no reason in the law of nature, but I may snap at him. Let time shape, and there an end.   [*Exit.*

ACT IV.

SCENE I.—A Forest in Yorkshire.

Enter the Archbishop of YORK, MOWBRAY, HASTINGS, *and others.*

Archbishop.
HAT is this forest call'd?

Hast. 'T is Gualtree Forest, an 't shall please your grace.

Arch. Here stand, my lords, and send discoverers forth,
To know the numbers of our enemies.

Hast. We have sent forth already.

Arch.   'T is well done.—
My friends and brethren in these great affairs,
I must acquaint you, that I have receiv'd
New-dated letters from Northumberland;
Their cold intent, tenor and substance, thus:—
Here doth he wish his person, with such powers   10
As might hold sortance with his quality;
The which he could not levy; whereupon
He is retir'd, to ripe his growing fortunes,
To Scotland; and concludes in hearty prayers,
That your attempts may overlive the hazard
And fearful meeting of their opposite.

Mowb. Thus do the hopes we have in him touch ground,
And dash themselves to pieces.

Enter a Messenger.

Hast.   Now, what news?

Mess. West of this forest, scarcely off a mile,
In goodly form comes on the enemy: 20
And, by the ground they hide, I judge their number
Upon, or near, the rate of thirty thousand.

Mowb. The just proportion that we gave them out.
Let us sway on, and face them in the field.

Enter WESTMORELAND.

Arch. What well-appointed leader fronts us here?

Mowb. I think it is my Lord of Westmoreland.

West. Health and fair greeting from our general,
The prince, Lord John and Duke of Lancaster.

Arch. Say on, my Lord of Westmoreland, in peace,
What doth concern your coming?

West.   Then, my lord,   30
Unto your grace do I in chief address
The substance of my speech. If that rebellion
Came like itself, in base and abject routs,
Led on by bloody youth, guarded with rage,
And countenanc'd by boys, and beggary;
I say, if damn'd commotion so appear'd,
In his true, native, and most proper shape,

You, reverend father, and these noble lords,
Had not been here, to dress the ugly form
Of base and bloody insurrection   40
With your fair honours. You, lord archbishop,
Whose see is by a civil peace maintain'd ;
Whose beard the silver hand of peace hath touch'd ;
Whose learning and good letters peace hath tutor'd ;
Whose white investments figure innocence,
The dove and very blessed spirit of peace :
Wherefore do you so ill translate yourself,
Out of the speech of peace, that bears such grace,
Into the harsh and boisterous tongue of war ?
Turning your books to graves, your ink to blood,   50
Your pens to lances, and your tongue divine
To a loud trumpet, and a point of war ?
    Arch. Wherefore do I this ?—so the question stands.
Briefly to this end :—we are all diseas'd ;
And, with our surfeiting, and wanton hours,
Have brought ourselves into a burning fever,
And we must bleed for it : of which disease
Our late king, Richard, being infected, died.
But, my most noble Lord of Westmoreland,
I take not on me here as a physician,   60
Nor do I, as an enemy to peace,
Troop in the throngs of military men ;
But, rather, show awhile like fearful war,
To diet rank minds, sick of happiness,
And purge the obstructions, which begin to stop
Our very veins of life. Hear me more plainly.
I have in equal balance justly weigh'd
What wrongs our arms may do, what wrongs we suffer,
And find our griefs heavier than our offences.
We see which way the stream of time doth run,   70
And are enforc'd from our most quiet sphere
By the rough torrent of occasion ;
And have the summary of all our griefs,
When time shall serve, to show in articles,
Which, long ere this, we offer'd to the king,
And might by no suit gain our audience :
When we are wrong'd, and would unfold our griefs,
We are denied access unto his person,
Even by those men that most have done us wrong.
The dangers of the days but newly gone,   80
Whose memory is written on the earth
With yet-appearing blood, and the examples
Of every minute's instance, present now,
Have put us in these ill-beseeming arms ;
Not to break peace, or any branch of it,
But to establish here a peace indeed,
Concurring both in name and quality.
    West. When ever yet was your appeal denied ?
Wherein have you been galled by the king ?
What peer hath been suborn'd to grate on you,   90
That you should seal this lawless bloody book
Of forg'd rebellion with a seal divine,
And consecrate commotion's bitter edge ?
    Arch. My brother general, the commonwealth,
To brother born an household cruelty,
I make my quarrel in particular.
    West. There is no need of any such redress ;
Or, if there were, it not belongs to you.
    Mowb. Why not to him, in part, and to us all,
That feel the bruises of the days before,   100
And suffer the condition of these times
To lay a heavy and unequal hand
Upon our honours ?
    West.   O ! my good Lord Mowbray,
Construe the times to their necessities,
And you shall say indeed, it is the time,
And not the king, that doth you injuries.
Yet, for your part, it not appears to me,
Either from the king, or in the present time,
That you should have an inch of any ground
To build a grief on. Were you not restor'd   110
To all the Duke of Norfolk's signiories,
Your noble and right-well-remember'd father's ?
    Mowb. What thing, in honour, had my father lost,
That need to be reviv'd, and breath'd in me ?
The king, that lov'd him, as the state stood then,
Was, force perforce, compell'd to banish him :
And then that Harry Bolingbroke, and he,
Being mounted, and both roused in their seats,

Their neighing coursers daring of the spur,
Their armed staves in charge, their beavers down, 120
Their eyes of fire sparkling through sights of steel,
And the loud trumpet blowing them together ;
Then, then, when there was nothing could have stay'd
My father from the breast of Bolingbroke,
O ! when the king did throw his warder down,
His own life hung upon the staff he threw :
Then threw he down himself, and all their lives,
That, by indictment, and by dint of sword,
Have since miscarried under Bolingbroke.
    West. You speak, Lord Mowbray, now you know
             not what.   130
The Earl of Hereford was reputed then
In England the most valiant gentleman :
Who knows, on whom fortune would then have
             smil'd ?
But if your father had been victor there,
He ne'er had borne it out of Coventry ;
For all the country, in a general voice,
Cried hate upon him ; and all their prayers, and love,
Were set on Hereford, whom they doted on,
And bless'd, and grac'd indeed, more than the king.
But this is mere digression from my purpose.   140
Here come I from our princely general,
To know your griefs ; to tell you from his grace,
That he will give you audience ; and wherein
It shall appear that your demands are just,
You shall enjoy them ; everything set off,
That might so much as think you enemies.
    Mowb. But he hath forc'd us to compel this offer,
And it proceeds from policy, not love.
    West. Mowbray, you overween, to take it so.
This offer comes from mercy, not from fear ;   150
For, lo ! within a ken our army lies,
Upon mine honour, all too confident
To give admittance to a thought of fear.
Our battle is more full of names than yours,
Our men more perfect in the use of arms,
Our armour all as strong, our cause the best ;
Then, reason wills, our hearts should be as good :
Say you not then, our offer is compell'd.
    Mowb. Well, by my will, we shall admit no parley.
    West. That argues but the shame of your offence :
A rotten case abides no handling.   161
    Hast. Hath the Prince John a full commission,
In very ample virtue of his father,
To hear, and absolutely to determine
Of what conditions we shall stand upon ?
    West. That is intended in the general's name.
I muse you make so slight a question.
    Arch. Then take, my Lord of Westmoreland, this
             schedule,
For this contains our general grievances :
Each several article herein redress'd ;   170
All members of our cause, both here and hence,
That are insinew'd to this action,
Acquitted by a true substantial form ;
And present execution of our wills
To us, and to our purposes, consign'd ;
We come within our awful banks again,
And knit our powers to the arm of peace.
    West. This will I show the general. Please you,
             lords,
In sight of both our battles we may meet :
And either end in peace, which God so frame,   180
Or to the place of difference call the swords
Which must decide it.
    Arch.   My lord, we will do so.
                         [*Exit* WESTMORELAND.
    Mowb. There is a thing within my bosom tells me,
That no conditions of our peace can stand.
    Hast. Fear you not that : if we can make our peace
Upon such large terms, and so absolute,
As our conditions shall consist upon,
Our peace shall stand as firm as rocky mountains.
    Mowb. Ay, but our valuation shall be such,
That every slight and false-derived cause,   190
Yea, every idle, nice, and wanton reason,
Shall to the king taste of this action :
That, were our royal faiths martyrs in love,
We shall be winnow'd with so rough a wind,

That even our corn shall seem as light as chaff,
And good from bad find no partition.
  Arch. No, no, my lord. Note this,—the king is
weary
Of dainty and such picking grievances:
For he hath found, to end one doubt by death,
Revives two greater in the heirs of life.   200
And therefore will he wipe his tables clean,
And keep no tell-tale to his memory,
That may repeat and history his loss
To new remembrance. For full well he knows,
He cannot so precisely weed this land,
As his misdoubts present occasion:
His foes are so enrooted with his friends,
That, plucking to unfix an enemy,
He doth unfasten so, and shake a friend.
So that this land, like an offensive wife,   210
That hath enrag'd him on to offer strokes,
As he is striking, holds his infant up,
And hangs resolv'd correction in the arm
That was uprear'd to execution.
  Hast. Besides, the king hath wasted all his rods
On late offenders, that he now doth lack
The very instruments of chastisement;
So that his power, like to a fangless lion,
May offer, but not hold.
  Arch.   'Tis very true:
And therefore be assur'd, my good lord marshal, 220
If we do now make our atonement well,
Our peace will, like a broken limb united,
Grow stronger for the breaking.
  Mowb.   Be it so.
Here is return'd my Lord of Westmoreland.

Re-enter WESTMORELAND.

  West. The prince is here at hand. Pleaseth your
lordship,
To meet his grace just distance 'tween our armies?
  Mowb. Your grace of York, in God's name then, set
forward.
  Arch. Before, and greet his grace, my lord: we come.
                                  [*Exeunt.*

SCENE II.—Another Part of the Forest.

Enter, from one side, MOWBRAY, *the Archbishop,*
HASTINGS, *and others: from the other side, Prince*
JOHN *of* LANCASTER, WESTMORELAND, *Officers, and*
Attendants.

  P. John. You are well encounter'd here, my cousin
Mowbray.—
Good day to you, gentle lord archbishop:
And so to you, Lord Hastings,—and to all.—
My Lord of York, it better show'd with you,
When that your flock, assembled by the bell,
Encircled you, to hear with reverence
Your exposition on the holy text,
Than now to see you here an iron man,
Cheering a rout of rebels with your drum,
Turning the word to sword, and life to death.   10
That man, that sits within a monarch's heart,
And ripens in the sunshine of his favour,
Would he abuse the countenance of the king,
Alack! what mischiefs might he set abroach,
In shadow of such greatness. With you, lord bishop,
It is even so. Who hath not heard it spoken,
How deep you were within the books of God?
To us, the speaker in his parliament;
To us, the imagin'd voice of God himself;
The very opener and intelligencer,   20
Between the grace, the sanctities of heaven,
And our dull workings: O! who shall believe,
But you misuse the reverence of your place,
Employ the countenance and grace of Heaven,
As a false favourite doth his prince's name,
In deeds dishonourable? You have taken up,
Under the counterfeited zeal of God,
The subjects of his substitute, my father;
And, both against the peace of Heaven and him,
Have here up-swarm'd them.
  Arch.   Good my Lord of Lancaster,

I am not here against your father's peace;   31
But, as I told my Lord of Westmoreland,
The time misorder'd doth, in common sense,
Crowd us, and crush us to this monstrous form,
To hold our safety up. I sent your grace
The parcels and particulars of our grief,
(The which hath been with scorn shov'd from the
court,)
Whereon this Hydra son of war is born;
Whose dangerous eyes may well be charm'd asleep,
With grant of our most just and right desires,   40
And true obedience, of this madness cur'd,
Stoop tamely to the foot of majesty.
  Mowb. If not, we ready are to try our fortunes
To the last man.
  Hast.   And though we here fall down,
We have supplies to second our attempt;
If they miscarry, theirs shall second them;
And so success of mischief shall be born,
And heir from heir shall hold this quarrel up,
Whiles England shall have generation.
  P. John. You are too shallow, Hastings, much too
shallow,   50
To sound the bottom of the after-times.
  West. Pleaseth your grace, to answer them directly,
How far-forth you do like their articles?
  P. John. I like them all, and do allow them well:
And swear here by the honour of my blood,
My father's purposes have been mistook;
And some about him have too lavishly
Wrested his meaning and authority.—
My lord, these griefs shall be with speed redress'd;
Upon my soul, they shall. If this may please you, 60
Discharge your powers unto their several counties,
As we will ours; and here, between the armies,
Let's drink together friendly, and embrace,
That all their eyes may bear those tokens home,
Of our restored love and amity.
  Arch. I take your princely word for these redresses.
  P. John. I give it you, and will maintain my
word:
And thereupon I drink unto your grace.
  Hast. [*To an Officer.*] Go, captain, and deliver to
the army
This news of peace: let them have pay, and part. 70
I know, it will well please them: hie thee, captain.
                             [*Exit Officer.*
  Arch. To you, my noble Lord of Westmoreland.
  West. I pledge your grace: an if you knew what
pains
I have bestow'd to breed this present peace,
You would drink freely; but my love to you
Shall show itself more openly hereafter.
  Arch. I do not doubt you.
  West.   I am glad of it.—
Health to my lord, and gentle cousin Mowbray.
  Mowb. You wish me health in very happy season;
For I am, on the sudden, something ill.   80
  Arch. Against all chances men are ever merry,
But heaviness foreruns the good event.
  West. Therefore be merry, coz; since sudden
sorrow
Serves to say thus,—Some good thing comes to-
morrow.
  Arch. Believe me, I am passing light in spirit.
  Mowb. So much the worse, if your own rule be true.
                           [*Shouts within.*
  P. John. The word of peace is render'd: hark, how
they shout!
  Mowb. This had been cheerful after victory.
  Arch. A peace is of the nature of a conquest;   90
For then both parties nobly are subdued,
And neither party loser.
  P. John.   Go, my lord,
And let our army be discharged too.—
                    [*Exit* WESTMORELAND.
And, good my lord, so please you, let our trains
March by us, that we may peruse the men
We should have cop'd withal.
  Arch.   Go, good Lord Hastings,
And, ere they be dismiss'd, let them march by.
                         [*Exit* HASTINGS.

P. John. I trust, lords, we shall lie to-night together.—

Re-enter WESTMORELAND.

Now, cousin, wherefore stands our army still?
West. The leaders, having charge from you to stand,
Will not go off until they hear you speak.   100
P. John. They know their duties.

Re-enter HASTINGS.

Hast. My lord, our army is dispers'd already.
Like youthful steers unyok'd, they take their courses
East, west, north, south; or, like a school broke up,
Each hurries toward his home, and sporting-place.
West. Good tidings, my Lord Hastings; for the
    which
I do arrest thee, traitor, of high treason :—

West. "I do arrest thee, traitor, of high treason."

And you, lord archbishop,—and you, Lord Mowbray,
Of capital treason I attach you both.
Mowb. Is this proceeding just and honourable? 110
West. Is your assembly so?
Arch. Will you thus break your faith?
P. John.   I pawn'd thee none.
I promis'd you redress of these same grievances,
Whereof you did complain; which, by mine honour,
I will perform with a most Christian care.
But, for you, rebels, look to taste the due
Meet for rebellion, and such acts as yours.
Most shallowly did you these summons commence,
Fondly brought here, and foolishly sent hence.—
Strike up our drums! pursue the scatter'd stray; 120
God, and not we, hath safely fought to-day.—
Some guard these traitors to the block of death;
Treason's true bed, and yielder up of breath. [*Exeunt.*

SCENE III.—Another Part of the Forest.

Alarums: Excursions. Enter FALSTAFF *and*
    COLEVILLE, *meeting.*

Fal. What's your name, sir? of what condition are
you, and of what place, I pray?
Cole. I am a knight, sir; and my name is Coleville of
the dale.
Fal. Well then, Coleville is your name, a knight is
your degree, and your place, the dale: Coleville shall
still be your name, a traitor your degree, and the
dungeon your place,—a place deep enough; so shall
you be still Coleville of the dale.
Cole. Are not you Sir John Falstaff?   10
Fal. As good a man as he, sir, whoe'er I am. Do ye
yield, sir, or shall I sweat for you? If I do sweat, they
are the drops of thy lovers, and they weep for thy
death: therefore, rouse up fear and trembling, and do
observance to my mercy.

Cole. I think, you are Sir John Falstaff, and in that
thought yield me.
Fal. I have a whole school of tongues in this belly
of mine, and not a tongue of them all speaks any
other word but my name. An I had but a belly of any
indifferency, I were simply the most active fellow in
Europe: my womb, my womb, my womb undoes
me.—Here comes our general.

Enter Prince JOHN *of* LANCASTER, WESTMORELAND.
    and others.

P. John. The heat is past, follow no further
    now.—
Call in the powers, good cousin Westmoreland.—
           [*Exit* WESTMORELAND.
Now, Falstaff, where have you been all this while?
When everything is ended, then you come:
   These tardy tricks of yours will, on my life,
   One time or other break some gallows' back. 29
Fal. I would be sorry, my lord, but it should
be thus: I never knew yet but rebuke and
check was the reward of valour. Do you think
me a swallow, an arrow, or a bullet? have I,
in my poor and old motion, the expedition of
thought? I have speeded hither with the
very extremest inch of possibility: I have
foundered nine-score and odd posts, and here,
travel-tainted as I am, have, in my pure and
immaculate valour, taken Sir John Coleville
of the dale, a most furious knight, and valorous
enemy. But what of that? he saw me,
and yielded; that I may justly say with the
hook-nosed fellow of Rome, I came, saw, and
overcame.
P. John. It was more of his courtesy than
your deserving.
Fal. I know not: here he is, and here I yield
him, and I beseech your grace, let it be booked
with the rest of this day's deeds; or, by the
Lord, I will have it in a particular ballad else,
with mine own picture on the top of it, Coleville kissing my foot. To the which course if
I be enforced, if you do not all show like gilt
twopences to me, and I, in the clear sky of fame,
o'ershine you as much as the full moon doth the
cinders of the element, which show like pins' heads
to her, believe not the word of the noble. Therefore
let me have right, and let desert mount.
P. John. Thine's too heavy to mount.
Fal. Let it shine then.   60
P. John. Thine's too thick to shine.
Fal. Let it do something, my good lord, that may do
me good, and call it what you will.
P. John. Is thy name Coleville?
Cole.   It is, my lord.
P. John. A famous rebel art thou, Coleville.
Fal. And a famous true subject took him.
Cole. I am, my lord, but as my betters are,
That led me hither: had they been rul'd by me,
You should have won them dearer than you have.
Fal. I know not how they sold themselves: but
thou, like a kind fellow, gavest thyself away gratis,
and I thank thee for thee.   72

Re-enter WESTMORELAND.

P. John. Now, have you left pursuit?
West. Retreat is made, and execution stay'd.
P. John. Send Coleville, with his confederates,
To York, to present execution.
Blunt, lead him hence, and see you guard him sure.
           [*Exit* COLEVILLE, *guarded.*
And now despatch we toward the court, my lords.
I hear, the king my father is sore sick:
Our news shall go before us to his majesty,   80
Which, cousin, you shall bear,—to comfort him;
And we with sober speed will follow you.
Fal. My lord, I beseech you, give me leave to go
through Glostershire; and, when you come to court,
stand my good lord, 'pray, in your good report.
P. John. Fare you well, Falstaff: I, in my condition,
Shall better speak of you than you deserve.   [*Exit.*
Fal. I would, you had but the wit: 't were better

than your dukedom.—Good faith, this same young sober-blooded boy doth not love me, nor a man cannot make him laugh; but that's no marvel, he drinks no wine. There's never any of these demure boys come to any proof; for thin drink doth so over-cool their blood, and making many fish-meals, that they fall into a kind of male green-sickness; and then, when they marry, they get wenches. They are generally fools and cowards, which some of us should be too, but for inflammation. A good sherris-sack hath a two-fold operation in it. It ascends me into the brain; dries me there all the foolish, and dull, and crudy vapours which environ it; makes it apprehensive, quick, forgetive, full of nimble, fiery, and delectable shapes; which, deliver'd o'er to the voice, the tongue, which is the birth, becomes excellent wit. The second property of your excellent sherris is, the warming of the blood; which, before cold and settled, left the liver white and pale, which is the badge of pusillanimity and cowardice: but the sherris warms it, and makes it course from the inwards to the parts extreme. It illumineth the face, which, as a beacon, gives warning to all the rest of this little kingdom, man, to arm; and then the vital commoners, and inland petty spirits, muster me all to their captain, the heart, who, great, and puffed up with this retinue, doth any deed of courage; and this valour comes of sherris. So that skill in the weapon is nothing without sack, for that sets it a-work; and learning, a mere hoard of gold kept by a devil, till sack commences it, and sets it in act and use. Hereof comes it, that Prince Harry is valiant: for the cold blood he did naturally inherit of his father, he hath, like lean, steril, and bare land, manured, husbanded, and tilled, with excellent endeavour of drinking good, and good store of fertile sherris, that he is become very hot and valiant. If I had a thousand sons, the first human principle I would teach them should be, to forswear thin potations, and to addict themselves to sack.

Enter BARDOLPH.

How now, Bardolph?

Bard. The army is discharged all, and gone.   129

Fal. Let them go. I'll through Glostershire; and there will I visit Master Robert Shallow, esquire: I have him already tempering between my finger and my thumb, and shortly will I seal with him. Come away.   [*Exeunt.*

SCENE IV.—Westminster. The Jerusalem Chamber.

Enter King HENRY, CLARENCE, *Prince* HUMPHREY, WARWICK, *and others.*

K. Hen. Now, lords, if God doth give successful end
To this debate that bleedeth at our doors,
We will our youth lead on to higher fields,
And draw no swords but what are sanctified.
Our navy is address'd, our power collected,
Our substitutes in absence well invested,
And everything lies level to our wish:
Only, we want a little personal strength,
And pause us, till these rebels, now afoot,
Come underneath the yoke of government.   10

War. Both which we doubt not but your majesty
Shall soon enjoy.

K. Hen.   Humphrey, my son of Gloster,
Where is the prince your brother?

P. Humph. I think, he's gone to hunt, my lord, at Windsor.

K. Hen. And how accompanied?

P. Humph.   I do not know, my lord.

K. Hen. Is not his brother, Thomas of Clarence, with him?

P. Humph. No, my good lord; he is in presence here.

Clar. What would my lord and father?

K. Hen. Nothing but well to thee, Thomas of Clarence.
How chance thou art not with the prince thy brother?
He loves thee, and thou dost neglect him, Thomas. 21
Thou hast a better place in his affection,

Than all thy brothers: cherish it, my boy,
And noble offices thou may'st effect
Of mediation, after I am dead,
Between his greatness and thy other brethren:
Therefore, omit him not; blunt not his love,
Nor lose the good advantage of his grace,
By seeming cold, or careless of his will;
For he is gracious, if he be observ'd: 30
He hath a tear for pity, and a hand
Open as day for melting charity;
Yet, notwithstanding, being incens'd, he's flint,
As humorous as winter, and as sudden
As flaws congealed in the spring of day.
His temper, therefore, must be well observ'd:
Chide him for faults, and do it reverently,
When you perceive his blood inclin'd to mirth;
But, being moody, give him line and scope,
Till that his passions, like a whale on ground, 40
Confound themselves with working. Learn this, Thomas,
And thou shalt prove a shelter to thy friends,
A hoop of gold to bind thy brothers in,
That the united vessel of their blood,
Mingled with venom of suggestion
(As, force perforce, the age will pour it in),
Shall never leak, though it do work as strong
As aconitum, or rash gunpowder.

Clar. I shall observe him with all care and love.

K. Hen. Why art thou not at Windsor with him, Thomas?   50

Clar. He is not there to-day: he dines in London.

K. Hen. And how accompanied? canst thou tell that?

Clar. With Poins, and other his continual followers.

K. Hen. Most subject is the fattest soil to weeds;
And he, the noble image of my youth,
Is overspread with them: therefore, my grief
Stretches itself beyond the hour of death.
The blood weeps from my heart, when I do shape,
In forms imaginary, the unguided days,
And rotten times, that you shall look upon   60
When I am sleeping with my ancestors.
For when his headstrong riot hath no curb,
When rage and hot blood are his counsellors,
When means and lavish manners meet together,
O, with what wings shall his affections fly
Towards fronting peril and oppos'd decay!

War. My gracious lord, you look beyond him quite.
The prince but studies his companions,
Like a strange tongue: wherein, to gain the language,
'T is needful, that the most immodest word   70
Be look'd upon and learn'd; which once attain'd,
Your highness knows, comes to no further use,
But to be known and hated. So, like gross terms,
The prince will, in the perfectness of time,
Cast off his followers; and their memory
Shall as a pattern or a measure live,
By which his grace must mete the lives of others,
Turning past evils to advantages.

K. Hen. 'T is seldom when the bee doth leave her comb
In the dead carrion.

Enter WESTMORELAND.

                Who's here? Westmoreland? 80

West. Health to my sovereign, and new happiness
Added to that I am to deliver!
Prince John, your son, doth kiss your grace's hand:
Mowbray, the Bishop Scroop, Hastings, and all,
Are brought to the correction of your law.
There is not now a rebel's sword unsheath'd,
But Peace puts forth her olive everywhere.
The manner how this action hath been borne,
Here at more leisure may your highness read,
With every course in his particular.   90

K. Hen. O Westmoreland! thou art a summer bird,
Which ever in the haunch of winter sings
The lifting up of day.

Enter HARCOURT.

                Look! here's more news.

Har. From enemies Heaven keep your majesty;

And, when they stand against you, may they fall
As those that I am come to tell you of.
The Earl Northumberland, and the Lord Bardolph,
With a great power of English, and of Scots,
Are by the sheriff of Yorkshire overthrown.
The manner and true order of the fight,   100
This packet, please it you, contains at large.
  K. Hen. And wherefore should these good news
      make me sick?
Will Fortune never come with both hands full,
But write her fair words still in foulest letters?
She either gives a stomach, and no food,—
Such are the poor, in health ; or else a feast,
And takes away the stomach,—such are the rich,
That have abundance, and enjoy it not.
I should rejoice now at this happy news,
And now my sight fails, and my brain is giddy.— 110
O me! come near me, now I am much ill. [*Swoons.*
  P. Humph. Comfort, your majesty!
  Clar.   O my royal father!
  West. My sovereign lord, cheer up yourself: look up!
  War. Be patient, princes : you do know, these fits
Are with his highness very ordinary.
Stand from him, give him air ; he'll straight be well.
  Clar. No, no ; he cannot long hold out these pangs.
The incessant care and labour of his mind
Hath wrought the mure, that should confine it in,
So thin, that life looks through, and will break out. 120
  P. Humph. The people fear me ; for they do observe
Unfather'd heirs, and loathly births of nature :
The seasons change their manners, as the year
Had found some months asleep, and leap'd them over.
  Clar. The river hath thrice flow'd, no ebb between ;
And the old folk, time's doting chronicles,
Say, it did so, a little time before
That our great-grandsire, Edward, sick'd and died.
  War. Speak lower, princes, for the king recovers.
  P. Humph. This apoplexy will, certain, be his end.
  K. Hen. I pray you, take me up, and bear me hence
Into some other chamber : softly, pray.   132
    [*They place the* King *on a bed in an inner
      part of the room.*
Let there be no noise made, my gentle friends ;
Unless some dull and favourable hand
Will whisper music to my wearied spirit.
  War. Call for the music in the other room.
  K. Hen. Set me the crown upon my pillow here.
  Clar. His eye is hollow, and he changes much.
  War. Less noise, less noise!

Enter Prince HENRY.

  P. Hen.   Who saw the Duke of Clarence?
  Clar. I am here, brother, full of heaviness.   140
  P. Hen. How now! rain within doors, and none
    abroad!
How doth the king?
  P. Humph.   Exceeding ill.
  P. Hen.   Heard he the good news yet?
Tell it him.
  P. Humph. He alter'd much upon the hearing it.
  P. Hen. If he be sick with joy,
He will recover without physic.
  War. Not so much noise, my lords.—Sweet prince,
    speak low ;
The king your father is dispos'd to sleep.
  Clar. Let us withdraw into the other room.
  War. Will't please your grace to go along with us?
  P. Hen. No ; I will sit and watch here by the king.
    [*Exeunt all but Prince* HENRY.
Why doth the crown lie there, upon his pillow,   152
Being so troublesome a bedfellow?
O polish'd perturbation! golden care!
That keep'st the ports of slumber open wide
To many a watchful night!—sleep with it now!
Yet not so sound, and half so deeply sweet,
As he, whose brow with homely biggen bound,
Snores out the watch of night. O majesty!
When thou dost pinch thy bearer, thou dost sit   160
Like a rich armour worn in heat of day,
That scalds with safety. By his gates of breath
There lies a downy feather, which stirs not :
Did he suspire, that light and weightless down

Perforce must move.—My gracious lord! my father!—
This sleep is sound indeed ; this is a sleep,
That from this golden rigol hath divorc'd
So many English kings. Thy due from me
Is tears and heavy sorrows of the blood,
Which nature, love, and filial tenderness,   170
Shall, O dear father! pay thee plenteously :
My due from thee is this imperial crown,
Which, as immediate from thy place and blood,
Derives itself to me. Lo! here it sits,
      [*Putting it on his head.*
Which Heaven shall guard ; and put the world's whole
    strength
Into one giant arm, it shall not force
This lineal honour from me. This from thee
Will I to mine leave, as 't is left to me.   [*Exit.*
  K. Hen. Warwick! Gloster! Clarence!

Re-enter WARWICK *and the rest.*

  Clar.   Doth the king call?
  War. What would your majesty? How fares your
    grace?   180
  K. Hen. Why did you leave me here alone, my
    lords?
  Clar. We left the prince, my brother, here, my
    liege,
Who undertook to sit and watch by you.
  K. Hen. The Prince of Wales? Where is he? let
    me see him :
He is not here.
  War. This door is open ; he is gone this way.
  P. Humph. He came not through the chamber
    where we stay'd.
  K. Hen. Where is the crown? who took it from my
    pillow?
  War. When we withdrew, my liege, we left it here.
  K. Hen. The prince hath ta'en it hence :—go, seek
    him out.   190
Is he so hasty, that he doth suppose
My sleep my death?—
Find him, my Lord of Warwick, chide him hither.
      [*Exit* WARWICK.
This part of his conjoins with my disease,
And helps to end me.—See, sons, what things you are!
How quickly Nature falls into revolt,
When gold becomes her object!
For this the foolish over-careful fathers
Have broke their sleeps with thoughts,
Their brains with care, their bones with industry ; 200
For this they have engrossed and pil'd up
The canker'd heaps of strange-achieved gold ;
For this they have been thoughtful to invest
Their sons with arts, and martial exercises :
When, like the bee, culling from every flower
The virtuous sweets,
Our thighs packed with wax, our mouths with honey,
We bring it to the hive, and, like the bees,
Are murder'd for our pains. This bitter taste
Yield his engrossments to the ending father.—   210

Re-enter WARWICK.

Now, where is he that will not stay so long,
Till his friend sickness hath determin'd me?
  War. My lord, I found the prince in the next room,
Washing with kindly tears his gentle cheeks ;
With such a deep demeanour in great sorrow,
That tyranny, which never quaff'd but blood,
Would, by beholding him, have wash'd his knife
With gentle eye-drops. He is coming hither.
  K. Hen. But wherefore did he take away the crown?

Re-enter Prince HENRY.

Lo, where he comes.—Come hither to me, Harry.— 220
Depart the chamber, leave us here alone.
    [*Exeunt* CLARENCE, *Prince* HUMPHREY,
      Lords, &c.
  P. Hen. I never thought to hear you speak again.
  K. Hen. Thy wish was father, Harry, to that
    thought :
I stay too long by thee, I weary thee.
Dost thou so hunger for mine empty chair,
That thou wilt needs invest thee with mine honours

Before thy hour be ripe? O foolish youth!
Thou seek'st the greatness that will overwhelm thee.
Stay but a little; for my cloud of dignity
Is held from falling with so weak a wind,   230
That it will quickly drop: my day is dim.

To stab at half an hour of my life.
What! canst thou not forbear me half an hour?   240
Then get thee gone, and dig my grave thyself,
And bid the merry bells ring to thine ear
That thou art crowned, not that I am dead.

P. Hen. "Lo! here it sits, which Heaven shall guard."

Thou hast stol'n that, which, after some few hours,
Were thine without offence; and at my death
Thou hast seal'd up my expectation:
Thy life did manifest thou lov'dst me not,
And thou wilt have me die assur'd of it.
Thou hid'st a thousand daggers in thy thoughts,
Which thou hast whetted on thy stony heart,

Let all the tears that should bedew my hearse,
Be drops of balm, to sanctify thy head;
Only compound me with forgotten dust:
Give that which gave thee life unto the worms.
Pluck down my officers, break my decrees;
For now a time is come to mock at form.
Harry the Fifth is crown'd!—Up, vanity!   250

Down, royal state ! all you sage counsellors, hence !
And to the English court assemble now,
From every region, apes of idleness !
Now, neighbour confines, purge you of your scum :
Have you a ruffian that will swear, drink, dance,
Revel the night, rob, murder, and commit
The oldest sins the newest kind of ways ?
Be happy, he will trouble you no more :
England shall double gild his treble guilt,
England shall give him office, honour, might ;　260
For the fifth Harry from curb'd license plucks
The muzzle of restraint, and the wild dog
Shall flesh his tooth in every innocent.
O my poor kingdom, sick with civil blows !
When that my care could not withhold thy riots,
What wilt thou do when riot is thy care ?
O ! thou wilt be a wilderness again,
Peopled with wolves, thy old inhabitants.
　　P. Hen. [*Kneeling.*] O, pardon me, my liege ! but
　　　　for my tears,
The moist impediments unto my speech,　　270
I had forestall'd this dear and deep rebuke,
Ere you with grief had spoke, and I had heard
The course of it so far.　There is your crown :
And that wears the crown immortally,
Long guard it yours !　If I affect it more
Than as your honour and as your renown,
Let me no more from this obedience rise,
Which my most true and inward duteous spirit
Teacheth, this prostrate and exterior bending.
God witness with me, when I here came in,　280
And found no course of breath within your majesty,
How cold it struck my heart ! if I do feign,
O ! let me in my present wildness die,
And never live to show the incredulous world
The noble change that I have purposed !
Coming to look on you, thinking you dead,
And dead almost, my liege, to think you were,
I spake unto the crown as having sense,
And thus upbraided it : "The care on thee depending
Hath fed upon the body of my father ;　　290
Therefore, thou, best of gold, art worst of gold.
Other, less fine in carat, is more precious,
Preserving life in medicine potable :
But thou, most fine, most honour'd, most renown'd,
Hast eat thy bearer up."　Thus, my most royal
　　　　liege,
Accusing it, I put it on my head ;
To try with it, as with an enemy
That had before my face murder'd my father,
The quarrel of a true inheritor.
But if it did infect my blood with joy,　　300
Or swell my thoughts to any strain of pride ;
If any rebel or vain spirit of mine
Did, with the least affection of a welcome,
Give entertainment to the might of it,
Let God for ever keep it from my head,
And make me as the poorest vassal is,
That doth with awe and terror kneel to it !
　　K. Hen. O my son !
God put it in thy mind to take it hence,
That thou mightst·win the more thy father's love, 310
Pleading so wisely in excuse of it.
Come hither, Harry : sit thou by my bed,
And hear, I think, the very latest counsel
That ever I shall breathe.　God knows, my son,

By what by-paths, and indirect crook'd ways,
I met this crown ; and I myself know well
How troublesome it sat upon my head :
To thee it shall descend with better quiet,
Better opinion, better confirmation ;
For all the soil of the achievement goes　　320
With me into the earth.　It seem'd in me
But as an honour snatch'd with boisterous hand,
And I had many living to upbraid
My gain of it by their assistances ;
Which daily grew to quarrel, and to bloodshed,
Wounding supposed peace.　All these bold fears,
Thou seest, with peril I have answered ;
For all my reign hath been but as a scene
Acting that argument, and now my death
Changes the mode : for what in me was purchas'd, 330
Falls upon thee in a more fairer sort ;
So thou the garland wear'st successively.
Yet, though thou stand'st more sure than I could do,
Thou art not firm enough ; since griefs are green,
And all thy friends, which thou must make thy
　　　　friends,
Have but their stings and teeth newly ta'en out ;
By whose fell working I was first advanc'd,
And by whose power I well might lodge a fear
To be again displac'd : which to avoid,
I cut them off ; and had a purpose now　　340
To lead out many to the Holy Land,
Lest rest, and lying still, might make them look
Too near unto my state.　Therefore, my Harry,
Be it thy course, to busy giddy minds
With foreign quarrels ; that action, hence borne out,
May waste the memory of the former days.
More would I, but my lungs are wasted so,
That strength of speech is utterly denied me.
How I came by the crown, O God forgive ;
And grant it may with thee in true peace live !　350
　　P. Hen. My gracious liege,
You won it, wore it, kept it, gave it me ;
Then plain and right must my possession be :
Which I with more than with a common pain
'Gainst all the world will rightfully maintain.

Enter Prince John *of* Lancaster, Warwick, *Lords,
　　and others.*

　　K. Hen. Look, look, here comes my John of Lan-
　　　　caster.
　　P. John. Health, peace, and happiness to my royal
　　　　father !
　　K. Hen. Thou bring'st me happiness, and peace, son
　　　　John ;
But health, alack, with youthful wings is flown
From this bare, wither'd trunk : upon thy sight,　360
My worldly business makes a period.
Where is my Lord of Warwick ?
　　P. Hen.　　　　　My Lord of Warwick !
　　K. Hen. Doth any name particular belong
Unto the lodging where I first did swoon ?
　　War. 'T is call'd Jerusalem, my noble lord.
　　K. Hen. Laud be to God !—even there my life must
　　　　end.
It hath been prophesied to me many years,
I should not die but in Jerusalem,
Which vainly I suppos'd the Holy Land.—
But, bear me to that chamber ; there I 'll lie :　370
In that Jerusalem shall Harry die.　　　　[*Exeunt.*

ACT V.

Scene I.—Glostershire. A Hall in Shallow's House.

Enter Shallow, Falstaff, Bardolph, *and* Page.

Shallow. BY cock and pie, sir, you shall not away to-night.—What, Davy, I say!

Fal. You must excuse me, Master Robert Shallow.

Shal. I will not excuse you; you shall not be excused; excuses shall not be admitted; there is no excuse shall serve; you shall not be excused.—Why, Davy!

Enter Davy.

Davy. Here, sir.   10

Shal. Davy, Davy, Davy,—let me see, Davy; let me see:—yea, marry, William cook, bid him come hither.—Sir John, you shall not be excused.

Davy. Marry, sir, thus; those precepts cannot be served: and, again, sir,—shall we sow the headland with wheat?

Shal. With red wheat, Davy. But for William cook:—are there no young pigeons?

Davy. Yes, sir.—Here is now the smith's note for shoeing, and plough-irons.   21

Shal. Let it be cast, and paid.—Sir John, you shall not be excused.

Davy. Now, sir, a new link to the bucket must needs be had:—and, sir, do you mean to stop any of William's wages, about the sack he lost the other day at Hinckley fair?

Shal. 'A shall answer it.—Some pigeons, Davy; a couple of short-legged hens, a joint of mutton, and any pretty little tiny kick-shaws, tell William cook.   30

Davy. Doth the man of war stay all night, sir?

Shal. Yea, Davy. I will use him well. A friend i' the court is better than a penny in purse. Use his men well, Davy, for they are arrant knaves, and will backbite.

Davy. No worse than they are backbitten, sir; for they have marvellous foul linen.

Shal. Well conceited, Davy. About thy business, Davy.

Davy. I beseech you, sir, to countenance William Visor of Wincot against Clement Perkes of the hill.   41

Shal. There are many complaints, Davy, against that Visor: that Visor is an arrant knave, on my knowledge.

Davy. I grant your worship that he is a knave, sir; but yet, God forbid, sir, but a knave should have some countenance at his friend's request. An honest man, sir, is able to speak for himself, when a knave is not. I have served your worship truly, sir, these eight years; and if I cannot once or twice in a quarter bear out a knave against an honest man, I have but a very little credit with your worship. The knave is mine honest friend, sir; therefore, I beseech your worship, let him be countenanced.

Shal. Go to; I say, he shall have no wrong. Look about, Davy. [*Exit* Davy.] Where are you, Sir John? Come, come, come; off with your boots.—Give me your hand, Master Bardolph.

Bard. I am glad to see your worship.

Shal. I thank thee with all my heart, kind Master Bardolph:—[*to the* Page.] and welcome, my tall fellow. Come, Sir John.   62

Fal. I'll follow you, good Master Robert Shallow. [*Exit* Shallow.] Bardolph, look to our horses. [*Exeunt* Bardolph *and* Page.] If I were sawed into quantities, I should make four dozen of such bearded hermit's staves as Master Shallow. It is a wonderful thing, to see the semblable coherence of his men's spirits and his: they, by observing of him, do bear themselves like foolish justices; he, by conversing with them, is turned into a justice-like serving-man. Their spirits are so married in conjunction with the participation of society, that they flock together in consent, like so many wild-geese. If I had a suit to Master Shallow, I would humour his men with the imputation of being near their master: if to his men, I would curry with Master Shallow, that no man could better command his servants. It is certain, that either wise bearing, or ignorant carriage, is caught, as men take diseases, one of another: therefore, let men take heed of their company. I will devise matter enough out of this Shallow, to keep Prince Harry in continual laughter the wearing-out of six fashions, which is four terms, or two actions, and he shall laugh without *intervallums.* O! it is much, that a lie with a slight oath, and a jest with a sad brow, will do with a fellow that never had the ache in his shoulders. O! you shall see him laugh, till his face be like a wet cloak ill laid up.

Shal. [*Within.*] Sir John!

Fal. I come, Master Shallow: I come, Master Shallow.   90

——   [*Exit.*

Scene II.—Westminster. An Apartment in the Palace.

Enter Warwick *and the Lord Chief Justice.*

War. How now, my lord chief justice? whither away?

Ch. Just. How doth the king?

War. Exceeding well: his cares are now all ended.

Ch. Just. I hope, not dead.

War.   He's walk'd the way of nature,
And to our purposes he lives no more.

Ch. Just. I would, his majesty had call'd me with him:
The service that I truly did his life,
Hath left me open to all injuries.

War. Indeed, I think the young king loves you not.

Ch. Just. I know he doth not, and do arm myself,   10
To welcome the condition of the time;
Which cannot look more hideously upon me
Than I have drawn it in my fantasy.

Enter Prince John, *Prince* Humphrey, Clarence, Westmoreland, *and others.*

War. Here come the heavy issue of dead Harry:
O! that the living Harry had the temper
Of him, the worst of these three gentlemen!
How many nobles then should hold their places,
That must strike sail to spirits of vile sort!

Ch. Just. O God! I fear, all will be overturn'd.

P. John. Good morrow, cousin Warwick, good morrow.   20

P. Humph., Clar. Good morrow, cousin.

P. John. We meet like men that had forgot to speak.

War. We do remember; but our argument
Is all too heavy to admit much talk.
P. John. Well, peace be with him that hath made
  us heavy!
Ch. Just. Peace be with us, lest we be heavier!
P. Humph. O! good my lord, you have lost a friend,
  indeed;
And I dare swear, you borrow not that face
Of seeming sorrow: it is, sure, your own.
P. John. Though no man be assur'd what grace to
  find,   30
You stand in coldest expectation.
I am the sorrier; 'would, 't were otherwise.
Clar. Well, you must now speak Sir John Falstaff
  fair,
Which swims against your stream of quality.
Ch. Just. Sweet princes, what I did, I did in honour,
Led by the impartial conduct of my soul;
And never shall you see, that I will beg
A ragged and forestall'd remission.
If truth and upright innocency fail me,
I'll to the king, my master, that is dead,   40
And tell him who hath sent me after him.
War. Here comes the prince.

        Enter King HENRY *the Fifth, attended.*

Ch. Just. Good morrow, and God save your majesty!
King. This new and gorgeous garment, majesty,
Sits not so easy on me as you think.—
Brothers, you mix your sadness with some fear:
This is the English, not the Turkish court:
Not Amurath an Amurath succeeds,
But Harry Harry. Yet be sad, good brothers,
For, to speak truth, it very well becomes you: 50
Sorrow so royally in you appears,
That I will deeply put the fashion on,
And wear it in my heart. Why then, be sad;
But entertain no more of it, good brothers,
Than a joint burden laid upon us all.
For me, by Heaven, I bid you be assur'd,
I'll be your father and your brother too;
Let me but bear your love, I'll bear your cares:
Yet weep, that Harry's dead, and so will I;
But Harry lives, that shall convert those tears,   60
By number, into hours of happiness.
P. John, &c. We hope no other from your majesty.
King. You all look strangely on me:—[*to the Chief
        Justice*] and you most;
You are, I think, assur'd I love you not.
Ch. Just. I am assur'd if I be measur'd rightly,
Your majesty hath no just cause to hate me.
King. No!
How might a prince of my great hopes forget
So great indignities you laid upon me?
What! rate, rebuke, and roughly send to prison   70
The immediate heir of England! Was this easy?
May this be wash'd in Lethe, and forgotten?
Ch. Just. I then did use the person of your father;
The image of his power lay then in me:
And, in the administration of his law,
Whiles I was busy for the commonwealth,
Your highness pleased to forget my place,
The majesty and power of law and justice,
The image of the king whom I presented,
And struck me in my very seat of judgment;   80
Whereon, as an offender to your father,
I gave bold way to my authority,
And did commit you. If the deed were ill,
Be you contented, wearing now the garland,
To have a son set your decrees at nought;
To pluck down justice from your awful bench;
To trip the course of law, and blunt the sword
That guards the peace and safety of your person;
Nay, more; to spurn at your most royal image,
And mock your workings in a second body.   90
Question your royal thoughts, make the case yours,
Be now the father, and propose a son:
Hear your own dignity so much profan'd,
See your most dreadful laws so loosely slighted,
Behold yourself so by a son disdain'd,
And then imagine me taking your part,
And, in your power, soft silencing your son:

After this cold considerance, sentence me;
And, as you are a king, speak in your state,
What I have done, that misbecame my place,   100
My person, or my liege's sovereignty.
King. You are right, justice; and you weigh this
  well;
Therefore still bear the balance and the sword:
And I do wish your honours may increase,
Till you do live to see a son of mine
Offend you, and obey you, as I did.
So shall I live to speak my father's words:—

King.   " I do commit into your hand
The unstained sword that you have used to bear."

" Happy am I, that have a man so bold,
That dares do justice on my proper son;
And not less happy, having such a son,   110
That would deliver up his greatness so
Into the hands of justice."—You did commit me:
For which, I do commit into your hand
The unstained sword that you have used to bear;
With this remembrance,—that you use the same
With the like bold, just, and impartial spirit,
As you have done 'gainst me. There is my hand;
You shall be as a father to my youth:
My voice shall sound as you do prompt mine ear,
And I will stoop and humble my intents   120
To your well-practis'd, wise directions.—
And, princes all, believe me, I beseech you;
My father is gone wild into his grave,
For in his tomb lie my affections;
And with his spirit sadly I survive,
To mock the expectation of the world,
To frustrate prophecies, and to raze out
Rotten opinion, who hath writ me down
After my seeming. The tide of blood in me
Hath proudly flow'd in vanity till now: 130
Now doth it turn, and ebb back to the sea,
Where it shall mingle with the state of floods,
And flow henceforth in formal majesty.
Now call we our high court of parliament,
And let us choose such limbs of noble counsel,
That the great body of our state may go
In equal rank with the best govern'd nation;
That war, or peace, or both at once, may be
As things acquainted and familiar to us;
[*To the Lord Chief Justice.*] In which you, father,
  shall have foremost hand.—   140
Our coronation done, we will accite,
As I before remember'd, all our state:
And (God consigning to my good intents)
No prince, nor peer, shall have just cause to say,
God shorten Harry's happy life one day. [*Exeunt.*

Scene III.—Glostershire. The Garden of SHALLOW'S
          House.

Enter FALSTAFF, SHALLOW, SILENCE, BARDOLPH,
          the Page, and DAVY.

Shal. Nay, you shall see mine orchard, where, in an

arbour, we will eat a last year's pippin of my own
graffing, with a dish of caraways, and so forth;—
come, cousin Silence;—and then to bed.

Fal. 'Fore God, you have here a goodly dwelling,
and a rich.

Shal. Barren, barren, barren; beggars all, beggars
all, Sir John:—marry, good air.—Spread, Davy;
spread, Davy; well said, Davy.

Fal. This Davy serves you for good uses: he is your serving-man, and your husband. 11

Shal. A good varlet, a good varlet, a very
good varlet, Sir John :—by the mass, I have
drunk too much sack at supper:—a good
varlet. Now sit down, now sit down.—
Come, cousin.

Sil. Ah, sirrah! quoth-a,—we shall
[*Singing.*] *Do nothing but eat, and make good
     cheer,*
And praise Heaven for the merry year;
When flesh is cheap and females dear, 20
And lusty lads roam here and there,
     So merrily,
And ever among so merrily.

Fal. There's a merry heart!—Good Master
Silence, I'll give you a health for that anon.

Shal. Give Master Bardolph some wine,
Davy.

Davy. Sweet sir, sit; I'll be with you anon :
—most sweet sir, sit.—Master page, good
master page, sit: proface! What you want
in meat, we'll have in drink. But you must
bear: the heart's all.   [*Exit.*

Shal. Be merry, Master Bardolph;—and
my little soldier there, be merry.

Sil. [*Singing.*] *Be merry, be merry, my wife has all;*
For women are shrews, both short and tall:
'T is merry in hall, when beards wag all,
     And welcome merry shrove-tide.
Be merry, be merry, &c.

Fal. I did not think Master Silence had been a man
of this metal. 41

Sil. Who, I? I have been merry twice and once,
ere now.

Re-enter DAVY.

Davy. There is a dish of leather-coats for you.
         [*Setting them before* BARDOLPH.

Shal. Davy,—

Davy. Your worship?—I'll be with you straight.—
A cup of wine, sir?

Sil. [*Singing.*] *A cup of wine, that's brisk and fine,*
And drink unto the leman mine;
     And a merry heart lives long-a. 50

Fal. Well said, Master Silence.

Sil. If we shall be merry, now comes in the sweet
of the night.

Fal. Health and long life to you, Master Silence.

Sil. [*Singing.*] *Fill the cup, and let it come;*
     I'll pledge you a mile to the bottom.

Shal. Honest Bardolph, welcome: if thou wantest
anything, and wilt not call, beshrew thy heart.—Welcome, my little tiny thief; and welcome, indeed, too.—
I'll drink to Master Bardolph, and to all the cavale-
roes about London. 61

Davy. I hope to see London once ere I die.

Bard. If I might see you there, Davy,—

Shal. By the mass, you'll crack a quart together:
ha! will you not, Master Bardolph?

Bard. Yea, sir, in a pottle-pot.

Shal. By God's liggens, I thank thee.—The knave
will stick by thee, I can assure thee that: he will not
out; he is true bred.

Bard. And I'll stick by him, sir. 70

Shal. Why, there spoke a king. Lack nothing: be
merry. [*Knocking heard.*] Look, who's at door there.
Ho! who knocks?   [*Exit* DAVY.

Fal. [*To* SILENCE, *who drinks a bumper.*] Why, now
you have done me right.

Sil. [*Singing.*] *Do me right,*
     And dub me knight:
         Samingo.
Is 't not so?

Fal. 'T is so. 80

Sil. Is 't so? Why, then say, an old man can do
somewhat.

Re-enter DAVY.

Davy. If it please your worship, there's one Pistol
come from the court with news.

Fal. From the court? let him come in.

Pist. "And helter-skelter have I rode to thee."

Enter PISTOL.

How now, Pistol?

Pist. Sir John, God save you, sir.

Fal. What wind blew you hither, Pistol?

Pist. Not the ill wind which blows no man to good.
—Sweet knight, thou art now one of the greatest men
in the realm. 91

Sil. By 'r lady, I think he be, but goodman Puff of
Barson.

Pist. Puff?
Puff in thy teeth, most recreant coward base!—
Sir John, I am thy Pistol, and thy friend,
And helter-skelter have I rode to thee;
And tidings do I bring, and lucky joys,
And golden times, and happy news of price.

Fal. I pr'ythee now, deliver them like a man of this
world. 101

Pist. A foutre for the world, and worldlings base!
I speak of Africa, and golden joys.

Fal. O base Assyrian knight, what is thy news?
Let King Cophetua know the truth thereof.

Sil. [*Sings.*] *And Robin Hood, Scarlet, and John.*

Pist. Shall Dunghill curs confront the Helicons?
And shall good news be baffled?
Then, Pistol, lay thy head in Furies' lap.

Shal. Honest gentleman, I know not your breeding.

Pist. Why then, lament therefore. 111

Shal. Give me pardon, sir:—if, sir, you come with
news from the court, I take it, there is but two ways:
either to utter them, or to conceal them. I am, sir,
under the king, in some authority.

Pist. Under which king, Bezonian? speak, or die.

Shal. Under King Harry.

Pist.   Harry the Fourth? or Fifth?

Shal. Harry the Fourth.

Pist.   A foutre for thine office!—
Sir John, thy tender lambkin now is king;
Harry the Fifth's the man. I speak the truth: 120
When Pistol lies, do this; and fig me, like
The bragging Spaniard.

Fal. What! is the old king dead?

Pist. As nail in door: the things I speak are just.

Fal. Away, Bardolph! saddle my horse.—Master
Robert Shallow, choose what office thou wilt in the
land, 't is thine.—Pistol, I will double-charge thee with
dignities.

Bard. O joyful day!—I would not take a knighthood for my fortune. 130

Pist. What! I do bring good news?
Fal. Carry Master Silence to bed.—Master Shallow, my Lord Shallow, be what thou wilt, I am fortune's steward. Get on thy boots: we 'll ride all night.—O sweet Pistol!—Away, Bardolph. [*Exit* BARDOLPH.]—Come, Pistol, utter more to me; and, withal, devise something to do thyself good.—Boot, boot, Master Shallow: I know, the young king is sick for me. Let us take any man's horses; the laws of England are at my commandment. Happy are they which have been my friends, and woe unto my lord chief justice!   141
Pist. Let vultures vile seize on his lungs also!
"Where is the life that late I led," say they;
Why, here it is: welcome these pleasant days!
                        [*Exeunt.*

SCENE IV.—London. A Street.

Enter Beadles, dragging in Hostess QUICKLY *and* DOLL TEAR-SHEET.

Host. No, thou arrant knave: I would to God I might die, that I might have thee hanged; thou hast drawn my shoulder out of joint.
1 Bead. The constables have delivered her over to me, and she shall have whipping-cheer enough, I warrant her. There hath been a man or two lately killed about her.
Doll. Nuthook, nuthook, you lie. Come on: I 'll tell thee what, thou damned tripe-visaged rascal. An the child I now go with do miscarry, thou hadst better thou hadst struck thy mother, thou paper-faced villain.   12
Host. O the Lord, that Sir John were come! he would make this a bloody day to somebody. But I pray God the fruit of her womb miscarry!
1 Bead. If it do, you shall have a dozen of cushions again; you have but eleven now. Come, I charge you both go with me; for the man is dead, that you and Pistol beat among you.   21
Doll. I 'll tell thee what, thou thin man in a censer, I will have you as soundly swinged for this,—you blue-bottle rogue! you filthy famished correctioner! if you be not swinged, I 'll forswear half-kirtles.
1 Bead. Come, come, you she knight-errant, come.
Host. O God, that right should thus overcome might! Well, of sufferance comes ease.   30
Doll. Come, you rogue, come: bring me to a justice.
Host. Ay; come, you starved blood-hound.
Doll. Goodman death! goodman bones!
Host. Thou atomy, thou!
Doll. Come, you thin thing; come, you rascal!
1 Bead. Very well.   [*Exeunt.*

SCENE V.—A Public Place near Westminster Abbey.

Enter two Grooms, strewing rushes.

1 Groom. More rushes, more rushes!
2 Groom. The trumpets have sounded twice.
1 Groom. It will be two o'clock ere they come from the coronation. Despatch, despatch. [*Exeunt Grooms.*

Enter FALSTAFF, SHALLOW, PISTOL, BARDOLPH, *and the Page.*

Fal. Stand here by me, Master Robert Shallow; I will make the king do you grace. I will leer upon him, as he comes by, and do but mark the countenance that he will give me.
Pist. God bless thy lungs, good knight.   9
Fal. Come here, Pistol; stand behind me.—[*To* SHALLOW.] O! if I had had time to have made new liveries, I would have bestowed the thousand pound I borrowed of you. But 't is no matter; this poor show doth better: this doth infer the zeal I had to see him.
Shal. It doth so.
Fal. It shows my earnestness of affection.
Shal. It doth so.

Fal. My devotion.
Shal. It doth, it doth, it doth.
Fal. As it were, to ride day and night; and not to deliberate, not to remember, not to have patience to shift me.   22
Shal. It is most certain.
Fal. But to stand stained with travel, and sweating with desire to see him: thinking of nothing else; putting all affairs else in oblivion, as if there were nothing else to be done but to see him.
Pist. 'T is *semper idem,* for *absque hoc nihil est.* 'T is all in every part.
Shal. 'T is so, indeed.   30
Pist. My knight, I will inflame thy noble liver, And make thee rage.
Thy Doll, and Helen of thy noble thoughts, Is in base durance, and contagious prison; Haul'd thither
By most mechanical and dirty hand :—
Rouse up revenge from ebon den with fell Alecto's snake,
For Doll is in; Pistol speaks nought but truth.

King. "My lord chief justice, speak to that vain man."

Fal. I will deliver her.
         [*Shouts within, and trumpets sound.*
Pist. There roar'd the sea, and trumpet-clangor sounds.   40

Enter KING *and his Train, including the Chief Justice.*

Fal. God save thy grace, King Hal! my royal Hal!
Pist. The heavens thee guard and keep, most royal imp of fame!
Fal. God save thee, my sweet boy!
King. My lord chief justice, speak to that vain man.
Ch. Just. Have you your wits? know you what 't is you speak?
Fal. My king! my Jove! I speak to thee, my heart!
King. I know thee not, old man: fall to thy prayers; How ill white hairs become a fool and jester! I have long dream'd of such a kind of man, So surfeit-swell'd, so old, and so profane;   50
But, being awake, I do despise my dream. Make less thy body, hence, and more thy grace; Leave gormandising; know, the grave doth gape For thee thrice wider than for other men. Reply not to me with a fool-born jest; Presume not that I am the thing I was; For God doth know, so shall the world perceive, That I have turn'd away my former self; So will I those that kept me company. When thou dost hear I am as I have been,   60
Approach me, and thou shalt be as thou wast, The tutor and the feeder of my riots: Till then, I banish thee, on pain of death, As I have done the rest of my misleaders,

Not to come near our person by ten mile.
For competence of life I will allow you,
That lack of means enforce you not to evil :
And as we hear you do reform yourselves,
We will, according to your strength and qualities,
Give you advancement.—Be it your charge, my
      lord,   70
To see perform'd the tenor of our word.—
Set on.   [*Exeunt* KING *and his Train.*
  Fal. Master Shallow, I owe you a thousand pound.
  Shal. Ay, marry, Sir John ; which I beseech you to
let me have home with me.
  Fal. That can hardly be, Master Shallow. Do not
you grieve at this : I shall be sent for in private to
him. Look you, he must seem thus to the world.
Fear not your advancement ; I will be the man yet
that shall make you great.   80
  Shal. I cannot perceive how, unless you should give
me your doublet, and stuff me out with straw. I
beseech you, good Sir John, let me have five hundred
of my thousand.
  Fal. Sir, I will be as good as my word : this that you
heard was but a colour.
  Shal. A colour, I fear, that you will die in, Sir
John.
  Fal. Fear no colours : go with me to dinner. Come,

Lieutenant Pistol ;—come, Bardolph :—I shall be sent
for soon at night.   91
  Re-enter Prince JOHN, *the Chief Justice, Officers, &c.*
  Ch. Just. Go, carry Sir John Falstaff to the Fleet ;
Take all his company along with him.
  Fal. My lord, my lord !—
  Ch. Just. I cannot now speak : I will hear you soon.
Take them away.
  Pist. Si fortune me tormente, sperato me contente.
      [*Exeunt* FALSTAFF, SHALLOW, PISTOL, BAR-
        DOLPH, *Page, and Officers.*
  P. John. I like this fair proceeding of the king's.
He hath intent, his wonted followers
Shall all be very well provided for ;
But all are banish'd, till their conversations   100
Appear more wise and modest to the world.
  Ch. Just. And so they are.
  P. John. The king hath call'd his parliament, my
      lord.
  Ch. Just. He hath.
  P. John. I will lay odds, that, ere this year expire,
We bear our civil swords, and native fire,
As far as France. I heard a bird so sing,
Whose music, to my thinking, pleas'd the king.
Come, will you hence ?   [*Exeunt.*

EPILOGUE.

FIRST my fear, then my courtesy, last my speech.
My fear is your displeasure, my courtesy my duty,
and my speech to beg your pardons. If you look for
a good speech now, you undo me ; for what I have to
say, is of mine own making ; and what indeed I
should say, will, I doubt, prove mine own marring.
But to the purpose, and so to the venture.—Be it
known to you (as it is very well), I was lately here in
the end of a displeasing play, to pray your patience
for it, and to promise you a better. I did mean,
indeed, to pay you with this ; which, if, like an ill
venture, it come unluckily home, I break, and you,
my gentle creditors, lose. Here, I promised you, I
would be, and here I commit my body to your mercies :
bate me some, and I will pay you some ; and, as most
debtors do, promise you infinitely.
  If my tongue cannot entreat you to acquit me, will

you command me to use my legs ? and yet that were
but light payment, to dance out of your debt. But a
good conscience will make any possible satisfaction,
and so will I. All the gentlewomen here have forgiven me : if the gentlemen will not, then the gentlemen do not agree with the gentlewomen, which was
never seen before in such an assembly.
  One word more, I beseech you. If you be not too
much cloyed with fat meat, our humble author will
continue the story, with Sir John in it, and make you
merry with fair Katharine of France : where, for
anything I know, Falstaff shall die of a sweat, unless
already he be killed with your hard opinions ; for
Oldcastle died a martyr, and this is not the man. My
tongue is weary ; when my legs are too, I will bid you
good night : and so kneel down before you ; but,
indeed, to pray for the queen.

KING HENRY V.

DRAMATIS PERSONÆ.

KING HENRY THE FIFTH.
DUKE OF GLOSTER, ⎫ *Brothers to the King.*
DUKE OF BEDFORD, ⎰
DUKE OF EXETER, *Uncle to the King.*
DUKE OF YORK, *Cousin to the King.*
EARLS OF SALISBURY, WESTMORELAND, *and* WARWICK.
ARCHBISHOP OF CANTERBURY.
BISHOP OF ELY.
EARL OF CAMBRIDGE, ⎫
LORD SCROOP, ⎬ *Conspirators.*
SIR THOMAS GREY, ⎭
SIR THOMAS ERPINGHAM, GOWER, FLUELLEN, MACMORRIS, JAMY, *Officers in King Henry's Army.*
BATES, COURT, WILLIAMS, *Soldiers.*
PISTOL, NYM, BARDOLPH.
BOY, *Servant to them. A Herald.*

CHARLES THE SIXTH, *King of France.*
LEWIS, *the Dauphin.*
DUKES OF BURGUNDY, ORLEANS, *and* BOURBON.
The Constable of France.
RAMBURES *and* GRANDPRÉ, *French Lords.*
MONTJOY, *a French Herald.*
Governor of Harfleur.
Ambassadors to England.

ISABEL, *Queen of France.*
KATHARINE, *Daughter of Charles and Isabel.*
ALICE, *a Lady attending on the Princess.*
MISTRESS QUICKLY, *a Hostess.*

Chorus.

Lords, Ladies, Officers, French and English Soldiers, Messengers, and Attendants.

SCENE—In ENGLAND and in FRANCE.

ACT I.

Enter Chorus.

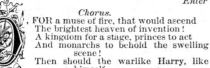

Chorus.

FOR a muse of fire, that would ascend
The brightest heaven of invention!
A kingdom for a stage, princes to act
And monarchs to behold the swelling scene!
Then should the warlike Harry, like himself,
Assume the port of Mars; and at his heels,
Leash'd in like hounds, should famine, sword, and fire,
Crouch for employment. But pardon, gentles all,
The flat unraised spirits that have dar'd
On this unworthy scaffold to bring forth   10
So great an object: can this cockpit hold
The vasty fields of France? or may we cram
Within this wooden O the very casques,
That did affright the air at Agincourt?

O, pardon! since a crooked figure may
Attest in little place a million;
And let us, ciphers to this great accompt,
On your imaginary forces work.
Suppose, within the girdle of these walls
Are now confin'd two mighty monarchies,   20
Whose high upreared and abutting fronts
The perilous, narrow ocean parts asunder.
Piece out our imperfections with your thoughts;
Into a thousand parts divide one man,
And make imaginary puissance:
Think, when we talk of horses, that you see them
Printing their proud hoofs i' the receiving earth;
For 'tis your thoughts that now must deck our kings,
Carry them here and there, jumping o'er times,
Turning the accomplishment of many years   30
Into an hour-glass: for the which supply,
Admit me Chorus to this history;
Who, prologue-like, your humble patience pray,
Gently to hear, kindly to judge, our play.   *[Exit.*

SCENE I.—London. An Ante-Chamber in the KING's Palace.

Enter the Archbishop of CANTERBURY *and Bishop of* ELY.

Canterbury.

MY lord, I'll tell you, that self bill is
      urg'd,
Which in the eleventh year of
      the last king's reign
Was like, and had indeed against us pass'd,
But that the scambling and unquiet time
Did push it out of further question.
    Ely. But how, my lord, shall we resist
      it now?
    Cant. It must be thought on. If it pass
      against us,
We lose the better half of our possession:
For all the temporal lands, which men
      devout
By testament have given to the Church,   10
Would they strip from us; being valued thus,—
As much as would maintain, to the king's honour,
Full fifteen earls, and fifteen hundred knights,
Six thousand and two hundred good esquires;
And, to relief of lazars, and weak age,
Of indigent faint souls, past corporal toil,
A hundred almshouses, right well supplied;
And to the coffers of the king beside,
A thousand pounds by the year. Thus runs the bill.
    Ely. This would drink deep.
    Cant.   'T would drink the cup and all.
    Ely. But what prevention?   21
    Cant. The king is full of grace, and fair regard.
    Ely. And a true lover of the holy church.
    Cant. The courses of his youth promis'd it not.
The breath no sooner left his father's body,
But that his wildness, mortified in him,
Seem'd to die too: yea, at that very moment,
Consideration like an angel came,
And whipp'd the offending Adam out of him,
Leaving his body as a paradise,   30
To envelop and contain celestial spirits.
Never was such a sudden scholar made;
Never came reformation in a flood,
With such a heady currance, scouring faults:
Nor never Hydra-headed wilfulness
So soon did lose his seat and all at once
As in this king.
    Ely.   We are blessed in the change.
    Cant. Hear him but reason in divinity,
And, all-admiring, with an inward wish
You would desire the king were made a prelate: 40
Hear him debate of commonwealth affairs,
You would say, it hath been all-in-all his study:
List his discourse of war, and you shall hear
A fearful battle render'd you in music:
Turn him to any cause of policy,
The Gordian knot of it he will unloose,
Familiar as his garter; that, when he speaks,
The air, a charter'd libertine, is still,
And the mute wonder lurketh in men's ears,
To steal his sweet and honey'd sentences;   50
So that the art and practic part of life
Must be the mistress to this theoric:
Which is a wonder, how his grace should glean it,
Since his addiction was to courses vain;
His companies unletter'd, rude, and shallow;
His hours fill'd up with riots, banquets, sports;
And never noted in him any study,
Any retirement, any sequestration
From open haunts and popularity.

    Ely. The strawberry grows underneath the nettle,
And wholesome berries thrive and ripen best,   61
Neighbour'd by fruit of baser quality:
And so the prince obscur'd his contemplation
Under the veil of wildness; which, no doubt,
Grew like the summer grass, fastest by night,
Unseen, yet crescive in his faculty.
    Cant. It must be so; for miracles are ceas'd;
And therefore we must needs admit the means,
How things are perfected.
    Ely.   But, my good lord,
How now for mitigation of this bill
Urg'd by the commons? Doth his majesty
Incline to it, or no?
    Cant.   He seems indifferent,
Or, rather, swaying more upon our part,
Than cherishing the exhibiters against us;
For I have made an offer to his majesty,—
Upon our spiritual convocation,
And in regard of causes now in hand,
Which I have open'd to his grace at large,
As touching France,—to give a greater sum
Than ever at one time the clergy yet   80
Did to his predecessors part withal.
    Ely. How did this offer seem receiv'd, my lord?
    Cant. With good acceptance of his majesty;
Save, that there was not time enough to hear
(As, I perceiv'd, his grace would fain have done)
The severals, and unhidden passages
Of his true titles to some certain dukedoms,
And, generally, to the crown and seat of France,
Deriv'd from Edward, his great-grandfather.
    Ely. What was the impediment that broke this off?
    Cant. The French ambassador upon that instant   91
Crav'd audience; and the hour, I think, is come,
To give him hearing. Is it four o'clock?
    Ely. It is.
    Cant. Then go we in, to know his embassy,
Which I could with a ready guess declare,
Before the Frenchman speak a word of it.
    Ely. I'll wait upon you, and I long to hear it.
                              [*Exeunt.*

———

SCENE II.—The Same. A Room of State in the Same.

Enter King HENRY, GLOSTER, BEDFORD, EXETER,
WARWICK, WESTMORELAND, *and Attendants.*

    K. Hen. Where is my gracious Lord of Canterbury?
    Exe. Not here in presence.
    K. Hen.   Send for him, good uncle.
    West. Shall we call in the ambassador, my liege?
    K. Hen. Not yet, my cousin: we would be resolv'd,
Before we hear him, of some things of weight,
That task our thoughts, concerning us and France.

Enter the Archbishop of CANTERBURY *and Bishop*
of ELY.

    Cant. God and his angels guard your sacred throne,
And make you long become it!
    K. Hen.   Sure, we thank you.
My learned lord, we pray you to proceed,
And justly and religiously unfold,   10
Why the law Salique, that they have in France,
Or should, or should not, bar us in our claim.
And God forbid, my dear and faithful lord,

That you should fashion, wrest, or bow your reading,
Or nicely charge your understanding soul.
With opening titles miscreate, whose right
Suits not in native colours with the truth ;
For God doth know, how many, now in health,
Shall drop their blood in approbation
Of what your reverence shall incite us to.   20
Therefore, take heed how you impawn our person,
How you awake our sleeping sword of war :
We charge you in the name of God, take heed ;
For never two such kingdoms did contend
Without much fall of blood ; whose guiltless drops
Are every one a woe, a sore complaint,
'Gainst him whose wrongs give edge unto the swords
That make such waste in brief mortality.
Under this conjuration, speak, my lord,
And we will hear, note, and believe in heart,   30
That what you speak is in your conscience wash'd,
As pure as sin with baptism.
    Cant. Then hear me, gracious sovereign, and you
          peers,
That owe yourselves, your lives, and services,
To this imperial throne.—There is no bar
To make against your highness' claim to France.
But this, which they produce from Pharamond, —
In terram Salicam mulieres ne succedant,
" No woman shall succeed in Salique land :"
Which Salique land the French unjustly gloze   40
To be the realm of France, and Pharamond
The founder of this law, and female bar.
Yet their own authors faithfully affirm,
That the land Salique is in Germany,
Between the floods of Sala and of Elbe ;
Where Charles the Great, having subdued the Saxons,
There left behind and settled certain French ;
Who, holding in disdain the German women,
For some dishonest manners of their life,
Establish'd then this law,—to wit, no female   50
Should be inheritrix in Salique land :
Which Salique, as I said, 'twixt Elbe and Sala,
Is at this day in Germany call'd Meisen.
Then doth it well appear, the Salique law
Was not devised for the realm of France ;
Nor did the French possess the Salique land
Until four hundred one-and-twenty years
After defunction of King Pharamond,
Idly suppos'd the founder of this law ;
Who died within the year of our redemption   60
Four hundred twenty-six ; and Charles the Great
Subdued the Saxons, and did seat the French
Beyond the river Sala in the year
Eight hundred five. Besides, their writers say,
King Pepin, which deposed Childeric,
Did, as heir general, being descended
Of Blithild, which was daughter to King Clothair,
Make claim and title to the crown of France.
Hugh Capet also,—who usurp'd the crown
Of Charles the Duke of Lorain, sole heir male   70
Of the true line and stock of Charles the Great,—
To find his title with some shows of truth,
Though, in pure truth, it was corrupt and naught,
Convey'd himself as the heir to the Lady Lingare,
Daughter to Charlemain, who was the son
To Lewis the emperor, and Lewis the son
Of Charles the Great. Also King Lewis the Tenth,
Who was sole heir to the usurper Capet,
Could not keep quiet in his conscience,
Wearing the crown of France, till satisfied   80
That fair Queen Isabel, his grandmother,
Was lineal of the Lady Ermengare,
Daughter to Charles the foresaid Duke of Lorain :
By the which marriage the line of Charles the
          Great
Was re-united to the crown of France.
So that, as clear as is the summer's sun,
King Pepin's title, and Hugh Capet's claim,
King Lewis his satisfaction, all appear
To hold in right and title of the female.
So do the Kings of France unto this day ;   90
Howbeit they would hold up this Salique law,
To bar your highness' claiming from the female ;
And rather choose to hide them in a net,

Than amply to imbare their crooked titles
Usurp'd from you and your progenitors.
    K. Hen. May I with right and conscience make this
          claim ?
    Cant. The sin upon my head, dread sovereign !
For in the Book of Numbers is it writ,—
When the man dies, let the inheritance
Descend unto the daughter. Gracious lord,   100
Stand for your own ; unwind your bloody flag ;
Look back into your mighty ancestors :
Go, my dread lord, to your great-grandsire's tomb,
From whom you claim : invoke his warlike spirit,
And your great uncle's, Edward the Black Prince,
Who on the French ground play'd a tragedy,
Making defeat on the full power of France ;
Whiles his most mighty father on a hill
Stood smiling, to behold his lion's whelp
Forage in blood of French nobility.   110
O noble English ! that could entertain
With half their forces the full pride of France,
And let another half stand laughing by,
All out of work, and cold for action.
    Ely. Awake remembrance of these valiant dead,
And with your puissant arm renew their feats.
You are their heir, you sit upon their throne ;
The blood and courage, that renowned them,
Runs in your veins ; and my thrice-puissant liege
Is in the very May-morn of his youth,   120
Ripe for exploits and mighty enterprises.
    Exe. Your brother kings and monarchs of the
          earth
Do all expect that you should rouse yourself,
As did the former lions of your blood.
    West. They know, your grace hath cause, and
          means, and might :—
So hath your highness—never King of England
Had nobles richer, and more loyal subjects,
Whose hearts have left their bodies here in England,
And lie pavilion'd in the fields of France.
    Cant. O ! let their bodies follow, my dear liege,   130
With blood, and sword, and fire, to win your right :
In aid whereof, we of the spiritualty
Will raise your highness such a mighty sum,
As never did the clergy at one time
Bring in to any of your ancestors.
    K. Hen. We must not only arm to invade the
          French,
But lay down our proportions to defend
Against the Scot, who will make road upon us
With all advantages.
    Cant. They of those marches, gracious sovereign, 140
Shall be a wall sufficient to defend
Our inland from the pilfering borderers.
    K. Hen. We do not mean the coursing snatchers
          only,
But fear the main intendment of the Scot,
Who hath been still a giddy neighbour to us :
For you shall read, that my great-grandfather
Never went with his forces into France,
But that the Scot on his unfurnish'd kingdom
Came pouring, like the tide into a breach,
With ample and brim fulness of his force,   150
Galling the gleaned land with hot essays,
Girding with grievous siege castles and towns ;
That England, being empty of defence,
Hath shook and trembled at the ill neighbourhood.
    Cant. She hath been then more fear'd than harm'd,
          my liege ;
For hear her but exampled by herself :
When all her chivalry hath been in France,
And she a mourning widow of her nobles,
She hath herself not only well defended,
But taken, and impounded as a stray,   160
The King of Scots ; whom she did send to France,
To fill King Edward's fame with prisoner kings,
And make her chronicle as rich with praise,
As is the ooze and bottom of the sea
With sunken wrack and sumless treasuries.
    West. There 's a saying, very old and true,—
          " If that you will France win,
          Then with Scotland first begin :"
For once the eagle England being in prey,

To her unguarded nest the weasel Scot   170
Comes sneaking, and so sucks her princely eggs;
Playing the mouse in absence of the cat,
To tear and havoc more than she can eat.
    Exe. It follows then, the cat must stay at home:
Yet that is but a crush'd necessity;
Since we have locks to safeguard necessaries,
And pretty traps to catch the petty thieves,
While that the armed hand doth fight abroad,
The advised head defends itself at home:
For government, though high, and low, and lower, 180
Put into parts, doth keep in one concent,
Congreeing in a full and natural close,
Like music.
    Cant.   Therefore doth Heaven divide
The state of man in divers functions,
Seting endeavour in continual motion;
To which is fixed, as an aim or butt,
Obedience: for so work the honey-bees,
Creatures, that by a rule in nature teach
The act of order to a peopled kingdom:
They have a king, and officers of sorts;   190
Where some, like magistrates, correct at home,
Others, like merchants, venture trade abroad,
Others, like soldiers, armed in their stings,
Make boot upon the summer's velvet buds;
Which pillage they with merry march bring home
To the tent-royal of their emperor:
Who, busied in his majesty, surveys
The singing masons building roofs of gold,
The civil citizens kneading up the honey,
The poor mechanic porters crowding in   200
Their heavy burdens at his narrow gate,
The sad-ey'd justice, with his surly hum,
Delivering o'er to executors pale
The lazy yawning drone. I this infer,—
That many things, having full reference
To one concent, may work contrariously;
As many arrows, loosed several ways,
Come to one mark; as many ways meet in one town;
As many fresh streams meet in one salt sea;
As many lines close in the dial's centre;   210
So may a thousand actions, once afoot,
End in one purpose, and be all well borne
Without defeat. Therefore to France, my liege.
Divide your happy England into four;
Whereof take you one quarter into France,
And you withal shall make all Gallia shake.
If we, with thrice such powers left at home,
Cannot defend our own doors from the dog,
Let us be worried, and our nation lose
The name of hardiness, and policy.   220
    K. Hen. Call in the messengers sent from the
         Dauphin.   [*Exit an Attendant.*
Now are we well resolv'd: and by God's help,
And yours, the noble sinews of our power,
France being ours, we'll bend it to our awe,
Or break it all to pieces: or there we'll sit,
Ruling in large and ample empery
O'er France, and all her almost kingly dukedoms,
Or lay these bones in an unworthy urn,
Tombless, with no remembrance over them:
Either our history shall with full mouth   230
Speak freely of our acts; or else our grave,
Like Turkish mute, shall have a tongueless mouth,
Not worshipp'd with a waxen epitaph.

       Enter Ambassadors of France.

Now are we well prepar'd to know the pleasure
Of our fair cousin Dauphin; for, we hear,
Your greeting is from him, not from the king.
    1 *Amb.* May't please your majesty, to give us leave
Freely to render what we have in charge;
Or shall we sparingly show you far off
The Dauphin's meaning, and our embassy?   240
    K. Hen. We are no tyrant, but a Christian king,
Unto whose grace our passion is as subject,
As are our wretches fetter'd in our prisons:
Therefore with frank and with uncurbed plainness,
Tell us the Dauphin's mind.
    1 *Amb.*   Thus then, in few.
Your highness, lately sending into France,

Did claim some certain dukedoms, in the right
Of your great predecessor, King Edward the Third.
In answer of which claim, the prince our master
Says, that you savour too much of your youth,   250
And bids you be advis'd, there's naught in France
That can be with a nimble galliard won:
You cannot revel into dukedoms there.
He therefore sends you, meeter for your spirit,
This tun of treasure; and, in lieu of this,
Desires you, let the dukedoms, that you claim,
Hear no more of you. This the Dauphin speaks.
    K. Hen. What treasure, uncle?
    Exe.   Tennis-balls, my liege.
    K. Hen. We are glad the Dauphin is so pleasant
         with us.
His present, and your pains, we thank you for: 260
When we have match'd our rackets to these balls,

K. Hen. "His present, and your pains, we thank you for."

We will in France, by God's grace, play a set,
Shall strike his father's crown into the hazard.
Tell him, he hath made a match with such a wrangler,
That all the courts of France will be disturb'd
With chases. And we understand him well,
How he comes o'er us with our wilder days,
Not measuring what use we made of them.
We never valu'd this poor seat of England;
And therefore, living hence, did give ourself   270
To barbarous license; as 'tis ever common,
That men are merriest when they are from home.
But tell the Dauphin,—I will keep my state;
Be like a king, and show my sail of greatness,
When I do rouse me in my throne of France:
For that I have laid by my majesty,
And plodded like a man for working-days;
But I will rise there with so full a glory,
That I will dazzle all the eyes of France,
Yea, strike the Dauphin blind to look on us.   280
And tell the pleasant prince, this mock of his
Hath turn'd his balls to gun-stones; and his soul
Shall stand sore charged for the wasteful vengeance
That shall fly with them: for many a thousand
         widows
Shall this his mock mock out of their dear husbands;
Mock mothers from their sons, mock castles down;
And some are yet ungotten and unborn,
That shall have cause to curse the Dauphin's scorn.
But this lies all within the will of God,
To whom I do appeal; and in whose name,   299
Tell you the Dauphin, I am coming on,
To venge me as I may, and to put forth

My rightful hand in a well-hallow'd cause.
So, get you hence in peace ; and tell the Dauphin,
His jest will savour but of shallow wit,
When thousands weep, more than did laugh at it.—
Convey them with safe conduct.—Fare you well.
                       [*Exeunt Ambassadors.*
Exe. This was a merry message.
K. Hen. We hope to make the sender blush at it.
Therefore, my lords, omit no happy hour,   300
That may give furtherance to our expedition ;

For we have now no thought in us but France,
Save those to God, that run before our business.
Therefore, let our proportions for these wars
Be soon collected, and all things thought upon,
That may with reasonable swiftness add
More feathers to our wings ; for, God before,
We 'll chide this Dauphin at his father's door.
Therefore, let every man now task his thought,
That this fair action may on foot be brought.   310
                         [*Exeunt.*

ACT II.

Enter Chorus..

Chorus.

OW all the youth of England are on fire,
And silken dalliance in the wardrobe
     lies :
Now thrive the armourers, and honour's
     thought
Reigns solely in the breast of every man.
They sell the pasture now to buy the
     horse ;
Following the mirror of all Christian
     kings,
With winged heels, as English Mer-
     curies.
For now sits Expectation in the air ;
And hides a sword, from hilts unto the
     point,
With crowns imperial, crowns, and
     coronets,   10
Promis'd to Harry and his followers.
The French, advis'd by good intelligence
Of this most dreadful preparation,
Shake in their fear, and with pale policy
Seek to divert the English purposes.
O England ! model to thy inward greatness,
Like little body with a mighty heart,
What mightst thou do, that honour would thee do,
Were all thy children kind and natural !
But see thy fault ! France hath in thee found out   20
A nest of hollow bosoms, which he fills
With treacherous crowns ; and three corrupted men,
One, Richard Earl of Cambridge, and the second,
Henry Lord Scroop of Masham, and the third,
Sir Thomas Grey, knight of Northumberland,
Have, for the gilt of France (O guilt, indeed !),
Confirm'd conspiracy with fearful France ;
And by their hands this grace of kings must die,
If hell and treason hold their promises,
Ere he take ship for France, and in Southampton.   30
Linger your patience on : and we 'll digest
The abuse of distance ; force a play.
The sum is paid ; the traitors are agreed ;
The king is set from London ; and the scene
Is now transported, gentles, to Southampton :
There is the playhouse now, there must you sit,
And thence to France shall we convey you safe,
And bring you back, charming the narrow seas
To give you gentle pass ; for, if we may,
We 'll not offend one stomach with our play.   40
But, till the king come forth, and not till then,
Unto Southampton do we shift our scene.   [*Exit.*

SCENE I.—London. Eastcheap.

Enter NYM *and* BARDOLPH.

Bard. Well met, Corporal Nym.

Nym. Good morrow, Lieutenant Bardolph.
Bard. What, are Ancient Pistol and you friends
yet ?
Nym. For my part, I care not : I say little ; but
when time shall serve, there shall be smiles :—but
that shall be as it may. I dare not fight ; but I will
wink, and hold out mine iron. It is a simple one ;
but what though ? it will toast cheese, and it will
endure cold as another man's sword will ; and there 's
an end.   11
Bard. I will bestow a breakfast to make you
friends, and we 'll be all three sworn brothers to
France : let it be so, good Corporal Nym.
Nym. 'Faith, I will live so long as I may, that 's the
certain of it ; and when I cannot live any longer, I
will do as I may : that is my rest, that is the rendezvous of it.
Bard. It is certain, corporal, that he is married to
Nell Quickly ; and, certainly, she did you wrong, for
you were troth-plight to her.   21
Nym. I cannot tell ; things must be as they may :
men may sleep, and they may have their throats about
them at that time ; and some say, knives have edges.
It must be as it may : though patience be a tired mare,
yet she will plod. There must be conclusions. Well,
I cannot tell.

Enter PISTOL *and Mistress* QUICKLY.

Bard. Here comes Ancient Pistol, and his wife.—
Good corporal, be patient here.—How now, mine host
Pistol ?   30
Pist. Base tike, call'st thou me host ?
Now, by this hand I swear, I scorn the term ;
Nor shall my Nell keep lodgers.
Quick. No, by my troth, not long : for we cannot
lodge and board a dozen or fourteen gentlewomen,
that live honestly by the prick of their needles, but it
will be thought we keep a bawdy-house straight.
[NYM *draws his sword.*] O well-a-day, Lady ! if he be
not drawn !—Now we shall see wilful adultery and
murder committed.   40
Bard. Good lieutenant,—good corporal, offer no-
thing here.
Nym. Pish !
Pist. Pish for thee, Iceland dog ! thou prick-ear'd
cur of Iceland !
Quick. Good Corporal Nym, show thy valour, and
put up your sword.
Nym. Will you shog off ? I would have you *solus.*
                           [*Sheathing his sword.*
Pist. Solus, egregious dog ? O viper vile !
The *solus* in thy most marvellous face ;
The *solus* in thy teeth, and in thy throat,   50
And in thy hateful lungs, yea, in thy maw, perdy ;
And, which is worse, within thy nasty mouth !
I do retort the *solus* in thy bowels :

For I can take, and Pistol's cock is up,
And flashing fire will follow.
   Nym. I am not Barbason ; you cannot conjure me.
I have an humour to knock you indifferently well. If
you grow foul with me, Pistol, I will scour you with
my rapier, as I may, in fair terms : if you would walk
off, I would prick your guts a little, in good terms, as
I may ; and that 's the humour of it.   61
   Pist. O braggart vile, and damned furious wight !
The grave doth gape, and doting death is near ;
Therefore exhale.   [PISTOL *and* NYM *draw.*
   Bard. Hear me, hear me what I say :—he that
strikes the first stroke, I 'll run him up to the hilts, as
I am a soldier.   [*Draws.*
   Pist. An oath of mickle might, and fury shall abate.
Give me thy fist, thy fore-foot to me give ;
Thy spirits are most tall.
   Nym. I will cut thy throat, one time or other, in fair
terms ; that is the humour of it.   70
   Pist, Coupe le gorge !
That is the word. I thee defy again.
O hound of Crete, think'st thou my spouse to get ?
No ; to the spital go,
And from the powdering-tub of infamy
Fetch forth the lazar kite of Cressid's kind,
Doll Tear-sheet she by name, and her espouse :
I have, and I will hold, the *quondam* Quickly   80
For the only she ; and—*pauca*, there 's enough. Go to.

Enter the Boy.

   Boy, Mine host Pistol, you must come to my
master, and your hostess.—He is very sick, and would
to bed.—Good Bardolph, put thy face between his
sheets, and do the office of a warming-pan : 'faith,
he 's very ill.
   Bard. Away, you rogue !
   Quick. By my troth, he 'll yield the crow a pudding
one of these days : the king has killed his heart.—
Good husband, come home presently.   90
     [*Exeunt Mistress* QUICKLY *and Boy.*
   Bard. Come, shall I make you two friends ? We
must to France together. Why, the devil, should we
keep knives to cut one another's throats ?
   Pist. Let floods o'erswell, and fiends for food howl on !
   Nym. You 'll pay me the eight shillings I won of
you at betting ?
   Pist. Base is the slave that pays.
   Nym. That now I will have ; that 's the humour
of it.
   Pist. As manhood shall compound. Push home.
      [*Draws.*
   Bard. By this sword, he that makes the first thrust,
I 'll kill him ; by this sword, I will.   102
   Pist. Sword is an oath, and oaths must have their
course.
   Bard. Corporal Nym, an thou wilt be friends, be
friends : an thou wilt not, why, then be enemies with
me too. Pr'ythee, put up.
   Nym. I shall have my eight shillings I won of you
at betting ?
   Pist. A noble shalt thou have, and present pay ;
And liquor likewise will I give to thee,   110
And friendship shall combine, and brotherhood :
I 'll live by Nym, and Nym shall live by me.
Is not this just ? for I shall sutler be
Unto the camp, and profits will accrue.
Give me thy hand.
   Nym. I shall have my noble ?
   Pist. In cash most justly paid.
   Nym. Well then, that 's the humour of it.

Re-enter Mistress QUICKLY.

   Quick. As ever you came of women, come in quickly
to Sir John. Ah, poor heart ! he is so shaked of a
burning quotidian tertian, that it is most lamentable
to behold. Sweet men, come to him.   122
   Nym. The king hath run bad humours on the knight,
that 's the even of it.
   Pist. Nym, thou hast spoke the right ;
His heart is fracted, and corroborate.
   Nym. The king is a good king ; but it must be as it
may : he passes some humours, and careers.

   Pist. Let us condole the knight ; for, lambkins, we
     will live.   ———   [*Exeunt.*

SCENE II.—Southampton. A Council-Chamber.

Enter EXETER, BEDFORD, *and* WESTMORELAND.

   Bed. 'Fore God, his grace is bold to trust these
     traitors.
   Exe. They shall be apprehended by-and-by.
   West. How smooth and even they do bear them-
     selves,
As if allegiance in their bosom sat,
Crowned with faith, and constant loyalty.
   Bed. The king hath note of all that they intend,
By interception which they dream not of.
   Exe. Nay, but the man that was his bedfellow,
Whom he hath dull'd and cloy'd with gracious favours,
That he should, for a foreign purse, so sell   10
His sovereign's life to death and treachery !

Trumpets sound. *Enter King* HENRY, SCROOP,
  CAMBRIDGE, GREY, *Lords, and Attendants.*

   K. Hen. Now sits the wind fair, and we will aboard.
My Lord of Cambridge,—and my kind Lord of
    Masham,—
And you, my gentle knight, give me your thoughts.
Think you not, that the powers we bear with us
Will cut their passage through the force of France,
Doing the execution, and the act,
For which we have in head assembled them ?
   Scroop. No doubt, my liege, if each man do his best.
   K. Hen. I doubt not that : since we are well per-
    suaded,   20
We carry not a heart with us from hence,
That grows not in a fair concent with ours ;
Nor leave not one behind, that doth not wish
Success and conquest to attend on us.
   Cam. Never was monarch better fear'd and lov'd
Than is your majesty : there 's not, I think, a subject,
That sits in heart-grief and uneasiness
Under the sweet shade of your government.
   Grey. True : those that were your father's enemies
Have steep'd their galls in honey, and do serve you 30
With hearts create of duty and of zeal.
   K. Hen. We therefore have great cause of thank-
    fulness,
And shall forget the office of our hand,
Sooner than quittance of desert and merit,
According to the weight and worthiness.
   Scroop. So service shall with steeled sinews toil,
And labour shall refresh itself with hope,
To do your grace incessant services.
   K. Hen. We judge no less.—Uncle of Exeter,
Enlarge the man committed yesterday,   40
That rail'd against our person : we consider,
It was excess of wine that set him on ;
And, on his more advice, we pardon him.
   Scroop. That 's mercy, but too much security :
Let him be punish'd, sovereign ; lest example
Breed, by his sufferance, more of such a kind.
   K. Hen. O ! let us yet be merciful.
   Cam. So may your highness, and yet punish too.
   Grey. Sir, you show great mercy, if you give him life
After the taste of much correction.   50
   K. Hen. Alas ! your too much love and care of me
Are heavy orisons 'gainst this poor wretch.
If little faults, proceeding on distemper,
Shall not be wink'd at, how shall we stretch our eye,
When capital crimes, chew'd, swallow'd, and digested,
Appear before us ?—We 'll yet enlarge that man,
Though Cambridge, Scroop, and Grey, in their dear
    care
And tender preservation of our person,
Would have him punish'd. And now to our French
    causes :
Who are the late commissioners ?   60
   Cam. I one, my lord :
Your highness bade me ask for it to-day.
   Scroop. So did you me, my liege.
   Grey. And I, my royal sovereign.
   K. Hen. Then, Richard Earl of Cambridge, there
    is yours ;—

There yours, Lord Scroop of Masham ;—and, sir
　　knight,
Grey of Northumberland, this same is yours :—
Read them ; and know, I know your worthiness.—
My Lord of Westmoreland, and uncle Exeter,
We will aboard to-night.—Why, how now, gentlemen?
What see you in those papers, that you lose　　71
So much complexion ?—Look ye, how they change :
Their cheeks are paper.—Why, what read you there,
That hath so cowarded and chas'd your blood
Out of appearance ?
　　Cam.　　　　I do confess my fault,
And do submit me to your highness' mercy.
　　Grey, Scroop. To which we all appeal.
　　K. Hen. The mercy that was quick in us but
　　late
By your own counsel is suppress'd and kill'd :
You must not dare, for shame, to talk of mercy ;　80
For your own reasons turn into your bosoms,
As dogs upon their masters, worrying you.
See you, my princes, and my noble peers.
These English monsters! My Lord of Cambridge
　　here,—
You know how apt our love was, to accord
To furnish him with all appertinents
Belonging to his honour ; and this man
Hath, for a few light crowns, lightly conspir'd,
And sworn unto the practices of France,
To kill us here in Hampton : to the which,　　90
This knight, no less for bounty bound to us
Than Cambridge is, hath likewise sworn.—But O !
What shall I say to thee, Lord Scroop? thou cruel,
Ingrateful, savage, and inhuman creature !
Thou, that didst bear the key of all my counsels,
That knew'st the very bottom of my soul,
That almost mightst have coin'd me into gold,
Wouldst thou have practis'd on me for thy use !
May it be possible, that foreign hire
Could out of thee extract one spark of evil,　100
That might annoy my finger ? 'tis so strange,
That, though the truth of it stands off as gross
As black and white, my eye will scarcely see it.
Treason and murder ever kept together,
As two yoke-devils sworn to either's purpose,
Working so grossly in a natural cause,
That admiration did not whoop at them :
But thou, 'gainst all proportion, didst bring in
Wonder to wait on treason, and on murder :
And whatsoever cunning fiend it was,　　110
That wrought upon thee so preposterously,
Hath got the voice in hell for excellence :
And other devils, that suggest by treasons,
Do botch and bungle up damnation
With patches, colours, and with forms, being fetch'd
From glistering semblances of piety ;
But he that temper'd thee bade thee stand up,
Gave thee no instance why thou shouldst do treason,
Unless to dub thee with the name of traitor.
If that same demon, that hath gull'd thee thus,　120
Should with his lion gait walk the whole world,
He might return to vasty Tartar back,
And tell the legions,—I can never win
A soul so easy as that Englishman's.
O, how hast thou with jealousy infected
The sweetness of affiance! Show men dutiful?
Why, so didst thou : seem they grave and learned ?
Why, so didst thou : come they of noble family ?
Why, so didst thou : seem they religious ?
Why, so didst thou : or are they spare in diet;　130
Free from gross passion, or of mirth, or anger ;
Constant in spirit, not swerving with the blood ;
Garnish'd and deck'd in modest complement ;
Not working with the eye without the ear,
And but in purged judgment trusting neither ?
Such, and so finely bolted, didst thou seem ;
And thus thy fall hath left a kind of blot,
To mark the full-fraught man, and best indued,
With some suspicion.　I will weep for thee ;
For this revolt of thine, methinks, is like　140
Another fall of man.—Their faults are open :
Arrest them to the answer of the law,
And God acquit them of their practices !

Exe. I arrest thee of high treason, by the name of
Richard Earl of Cambridge.
　　I arrest thee of high treason, by the name of Henry
Lord Scroop of Masham.
　　I arrest thee of high treason, by the name of Thomas
Grey, knight of Northumberland.

K. Hen.　　"Their faults are open :
Arrest them to the answer of the law."

Scroop. Our purposes God justly hath discover'd,150
And I repent my fault more than my death ;
Which I beseech your highness to forgive,
Although my body pay the price of it.
　　Cam. For me,—the gold of France did not seduce,
Although I did admit it as a motive,
The sooner to effect what I intended.
But God be thanked for prevention ;
Which I in sufferance heartily will rejoice,
Beseeching God and you to pardon me.
　　Grey. Never did faithful subject more rejoice　160
At the discovery of most dangerous treason,
Than I do at this hour joy o'er myself,
Prevented from a damned enterprise.
My fault, but not my body, pardon, sovereign.
　　K. Hen. God quit you in his mercy! Hear your
　　sentence.
You have conspir'd against our royal person,
Join'd with an enemy proclaim'd, and from his coffers
Receiv'd the golden earnest of our death ;
Wherein you would have sold your king to slaughter,
His princes and his peers to servitude,　　170
His subjects to oppression and contempt,
And his whole kingdom into desolation.
Touching our person, seek we no revenge ;
But we our kingdom's safety must so tender,
Whose ruin you have sought, that to her laws
We do deliver you.　Get you therefore hence,
Poor miserable wretches, to your death ;
The taste whereof, God, of his mercy, give you
Patience to endure, and true repentance
Of all your dear offences.—Bear them hence.　180
　　　　　[*Exeunt* CAMBRIDGE, SCROOP, *and* GREY,
　　　　　　　guarded.
Now, lords, for France ; the enterprise whereof
Shall be to you, as us, like glorious.
We doubt not of a fair and lucky war,

Since God so graciously hath brought to light
This dangerous treason, lurking in our way
To hinder our beginnings : we doubt not now,
But every rub is smoothed on our way.
Then forth, dear countrymen : let us deliver
Our puissance into the hand of God,
Putting it straight in expedition.   190
Cheerly to sea ; the signs of war advance :
No King of England, if not King of France. [*Exeunt.*

Scene III.—London. Mistress QUICKLY'S House in
Eastcheap.

Enter PISTOL, *Mistress* QUICKLY, NYM, BARDOLPH,
and Boy.

Quick. Pr'ythee, honey-sweet husband, let me bring
thee to Staines.

Pist. No ; for my manly heart doth yearn.—
Bardolph, be blithe ; Nym, rouse thy vaunting veins ;
Boy, bristle thy courage up ; for Falstaff he is dead,
And we must yearn therefore.

Bard. 'Would I were with him, wheresome'er he is,
either in heaven, or in hell.

Quick. Nay, sure, he 's not in hell : he 's in Arthur's
bosom, if ever man went to Arthur's bosom. 'A made
a finer end, and went away, an it had been any
christom child ; 'a parted even just between twelve
and one, even at the turning o' the tide : for after I
saw him fumble with the sheets, and play with
flowers, and smile upon his fingers' ends, I knew
there was but one way ; for his nose was as sharp
as a pen, and a table of green fields. "How now, Sir
John ?" quoth I : "what, man ! be of good cheer."
So 'a cried out—"God, God, God !" three or four times :
now I, to comfort him, bid him, 'a should not think of
God ; I hoped, there was no need to trouble himself
with any such thoughts yet. So, 'a bade me lay more
clothes on his feet : I put my hand into the bed, and
felt them, and they were as cold as any stone ; then I
felt to his knees, and so upward, and upward, and all
was as cold as any stone.

Nym. They say, he cried out of sack.

Quick. Ay, that 'a did.

Bard. And of women.

Quick. Nay, that 'a did not.   30

Boy. Yes, that 'a did ; and said, they were devils
incarnate.

Quick. 'A could never abide carnation ; 't was a
colour he never liked.

Boy. 'A said once, the devil would have him about
women.

Quick. 'A did in some sort, indeed, handle women ;
but then he was rheumatic, and talked of the whore
of Babylon.

Boy. Do you not remember, 'a saw a flea stick upon
Bardolph's nose, and 'a said it was a black soul burning
in hell ?   42

Bard. Well, the fuel is gone that maintained that
fire : that 's all the riches I got in his service.

Nym. Shall we shog ? the king will be gone from
Southampton.

Pist. Come, let 's away.—My love, give me thy lips.
Look to my chattels, and my movables :
Let senses rule, the word is, "Pitch and pay ;"
Trust none ;   50
For oaths are straws, men's faiths are wafer-cakes,
And hold-fast is the only dog, my duck :
Therefore, *caveto* be thy counsellor.
Go, clear thy crystals.—Yoke-fellows in arms,
Let us to France : like horse-leeches, my boys,
To suck, to suck, the very blood to suck !

Boy. And that is but unwholesome food, they say.

Pist. Touch her soft mouth, and march.

Bard. Farewell, hostess.   [*Kissing her.*

Nym. I cannot kiss, that is the humour of it ; but
adieu.   61

Pist. Let housewifery appear : keep close, I thee
command.

Quick. Farewell ; adieu.   [*Exeunt.*

Scene IV.—France. A Room in the French KING'S
Palace.

Flourish. Enter the French KING, *attended ; the*
DAUPHIN, *the Duke of* BURGUNDY, *the Constable,
and others.*

Fr. King. Thus come the English with full power
upon us ;
And more than carefully it us concerns,
To answer royally in our defences.
Therefore the Dukes of Berry, and of Bretagne,
Of Brabant, and of Orleans, shall make forth,
And you, Prince Dauphin, with all swift despatch,
To line and new-repair our towns of war
With men of courage, and with means defendant :
For England his approaches makes as fierce
As waters to the sucking of a gulf.   10
It fits us then to be as provident
As fear may teach us, out of late examples
Left by the fatal and neglected English
Upon our fields.

Dau.   My most redoubted father,
It is most meet we arm us 'gainst the foe :
For peace itself should not so dull a kingdom,
(Though war, nor no known quarrel, were in question,)
But that defences, musters, preparations,
Should be maintain'd, assembled, and collected,
As were a war in expectation.   20
Therefore, I say, 't is meet we all go forth,
To view the sick and feeble parts of France :
And let us do it with no show of fear ;
No, with no more, than if we heard that England
Were busied with a Whitsun morris-dance :
For, my good liege, she is so idly king'd,
Her sceptre so fantastically borne
By a vain, giddy, shallow, humorous youth,
That fear attends her not.

Con.   O peace, Prince Dauphin !
You are too much mistaken in this king.   30
Question your grace the late ambassadors,
With what great state he heard their embassy,
How well supplied with noble counsellors,
How modest in exception, and, withal,
How terrible in constant resolution,
And you shall find, his vanities forespent
Were but the outside of the Roman Brutus,
Covering discretion with a coat of folly ;
As gardeners do with ordure hide those roots
That shall first spring, and be most delicate.   40

Dau. Well, 't is not so, my lord high constable ;
But though we think it so, it is no matter :
In cases of defence, 't is best to weigh
The enemy more mighty than he seems :
So the proportions of defence are fill'd ;
Which, of a weak and niggardly projection,
Doth like a miser spoil his coat with scanting
A little cloth.

Fr. King.   Think we King Harry strong ;
And, princes, look you strongly arm to meet him.
The kindred of him hath been flesh'd upon us,   50
And he is bred out of that bloody strain,
That haunted us in our familiar paths :
Witness our too much memorable shame,
When Cressy battle fatally was struck,
And all our princes captiv'd, by the hand
Of that black name, Edward Black Prince of Wales ;
Whiles that his mountain-sire,—on mountain standing,
Up in the air, crown'd with the golden sun,—
Saw his heroical seed, and smil'd to see him
Mangle the work of nature, and deface   60
The patterns that by God and by French fathers
Had twenty years been made. This is a stem
Of that victorious stock ; and let us fear
The native mightiness and fate of him.

Enter a Messenger.

Mess. Ambassadors from Harry King of England
Do crave admittance to your majesty.

Fr. King. We 'll give them present audience : Go,
and bring them.
      [*Exeunt Messenger and certain Lords.*
You see, this chase is hotly follow'd, friends.

Dau. Turn head, and stop pursuit; for coward dogs
Most spend their mouths, when what they seem to
    threaten   70
Runs far before them. Good my sovereign,
Take up the English short, and let them know
Of what a monarchy you are the head :
Self-love, my liege, is not so vile a sin
As self-neglecting.

    Re-enter Lords, with EXETER *and Train.*

Fr. King. From our brother England ?
Exe. From him ; and thus he greets your majesty.
He wills you, in the name of God Almighty,
That you divest yourself, and lay apart
The borrow'd glories, that by gift of Heaven,   80
By law of nature, and of nations, 'long
To him, and to his heirs ; namely, the crown,
And all wide-stretched honours that pertain,
By custom and the ordinance of times,
Unto the crown of France. That you may know,
'T is no sinister, nor no awkward claim,
Pick'd from the worm-holes of long-vanish'd days,
Nor from the dust of old oblivion rak'd,
He sends you this most memorable line,
                   [*Gives a pedigree.*
In every branch truly demonstrative ;   90
Willing you overlook this pedigree,
And when you find him evenly deriv'd
From his most fam'd of famous ancestors,
Edward the Third, he bids you then resign
Your crown and kingdom, indirectly held
From him, the native and true challenger.
Fr. King. Or else what follows ?
Exe. Bloody constraint ; for if you hide the crown
Even in your hearts, there will he rake for it :
Therefore in fierce tempest is he coming,   100
In thunder, and in earthquake, like a Jove,
That, if requiring fail, he will compel ;
And bids you, in the bowels of the Lord,
Deliver up the crown, and to take mercy
On the poor souls, for whom this hungry war
Opens his vasty jaws ; and on your head
Turning the widows' tears, the orphans' cries,

The dead men's blood, the pining maidens' groans,
For husbands, fathers, and betrothed lovers,
That shall be swallow'd in this controversy.   110
This is his claim, his threat'ning, and my message ;
Unless the Dauphin be in presence here,
To whom expressly I bring greeting too.
Fr. King. For us, we will consider of this further :
To-morrow shall you bear our full intent
Back to our brother England.
    Dau.   For the Dauphin,
I stand here for him : what to him from England ?
Exe. Scorn and defiance, slight regard, contempt,
And anything that may not misbecome
The mighty sender, doth he prize you at.   120
Thus says my king : an if your father's highness,
Do not, in grant of all demands at large,
Sweeten the bitter mock you sent his majesty,
He 'll call you to so hot an answer of it,
That caves and womby vaultages of France
Shall chide your trespass, and return your mock
In second accent of his ordinance.
Dau. Say, if my father render fair return,
It is against my will : for I desire
Nothing but odds with England : to that end,   130
As matching to his youth and vanity,
I did present him with the Paris balls.
Exe. He 'll make your Paris Louvre shake for it,
Were it the mistress court of mighty Europe :
And, be assur'd, you 'll find a difference,
As we, his subjects, have in wonder found,
Between the promise of his greener days,
And these he masters now. Now he weighs time,
Even to the utmost grain ; that you shall read
In your own losses, if he stay in France.   140
Fr. King. To-morrow shall you know our mind at
    full.
Exe. Despatch us with all speed, lest that our king
Come here himself to question our delay ;
For he is footed in this land already.
Fr. King. You shall be soon despatch'd with fair
    conditions.
A night is but small breath, and little pause,
To answer matters of this consequence.   [*Exeunt.*

ACT III.

Enter Chorus.

Chorus.
THUS with imagin'd wing our swift scene
    flies,
In motion of no less celerity
Than that of thought. Suppose, that you
    have seen
The well-appointed king at Hampton pier
Embark his royalty ; and his brave fleet
With silken streamers the young Phœbus
    fanning.
Play with your fancies, and in them
    behold
Upon the hempen tackle ship-boys climb-
    ing ;
Hear the shrill whistle, which doth order give
To sounds confus'd ; behold the threaden sails,   10
Borne with the invisible and creeping wind,
Draw the huge bottoms through the furrow'd sea,
Breasting the lofty surge. O ! do but think,
You stand upon the rivage, and behold
A city on the inconstant billows dancing ;

For so appears this fleet majestical,
Holding due course to Harfleur. Follow, follow !
Grapple your minds to sternage of this navy,
And leave your England, as dead midnight still,
Guarded with grandsires, babies, and old women,   20
Either past, or not arriv'd to, pith and puissance :
For who is he, whose chin is but enrich'd
With one appearing hair, that will not follow
These cull'd and choice-drawn cavaliers to France ?
Work, work your thoughts, and therein see a siege :
Behold the ordnance on their carriages,
With fatal mouths gaping on girded Harfleur.
Suppose, the ambassador from the French comes back ;
Tells Harry that the king doth offer him
Katharine his daughter ; and with her, to dowry,   30
Some petty and unprofitable dukedoms.
The offer likes not ; and the nimble gunner
With linstock now the devilish cannon touches,
            [*Alarum, and chambers go off.*
And down goes all before them. Still be kind,
And eke out our performance with your mind. [*Exit.*

SCENE I.—France.   Before Harfleur.

Alarums.   Enter King HENRY, EXETER, BEDFORD,
GLOSTER, *and Soldiers, with scaling-ladders.*

K. Hen. Once more unto the breach, dear friends,
        once more ;
Or close the wall up with our English dead !
In peace, there 's nothing so becomes a man,
As modest stillness and humility :
But when the blast of war blows in our ears,
Then imitate the action of the tiger ;

K. Hen. " Cry—God for Harry ! England and Saint George ! "

Stiffen the sinews, summon up the blood,
Disguise fair nature with hard-favour'd rage ;
Then lend the eye a terrible aspect ;
Let it pry through the portage of the head,   10
Like the brass cannon ; let the brow o'erwhelm it,
As fearfully as doth a galled rock
O'erhang and jutty his confounded base,
Swill'd with the wild and wasteful ocean.
Now set the teeth, and stretch the nostril wide ;
Hold hard the breath, and bend up every spirit
To his full height !—On, on, you noblest English !
Whose blood is fet from fathers of war-proof,
Fathers, that, like so many Alexanders,
Have in these parts from morn till even fought,   20
And sheath'd their swords for lack of argument.
Dishonour not your mothers : now attest,
That those, whom you call'd fathers, did beget you.
Be copy now to men of grosser blood,
And teach them how to war.—And you, good yeomen,
Whose limbs were made in England, show us here
The mettle of your pasture ; let us swear
That you are worth your breeding : which I doubt not ;
For there is none of you so mean and base,
That hath not noble lustre in your eyes.   30
I see you stand like greyhounds in the slips,
Straining upon the start.   The game 's afoot :
Follow your spirit ; and upon this charge,
Cry—God for Harry ! England and Saint George !
        [*Exeunt.   Alarum, and chambers go off.*

SCENE II.—The Same.

Enter NYM, BARDOLPH, PISTOL, *and Boy.*

Bard. On, on, on, on, on ! to the breach, to the
breach !

Nym. Pray thee, corporal, stay : the knocks are too
hot ; and for mine own part, I have not a case of
lives : the humour of it is too hot, that is the very
plain-song of it.

Pist. The plain-song is most just, for humours do
        abound ;
Knocks go and come, God's vassals drop and die ;
                And sword and shield,
                    In bloody field,   10
                Doth win immortal fame.

Boy. 'Would I were in an ale-house in London ! I
would give all my fame for a pot of ale, and safety.

Pist. And I :
        If wishes would prevail with me,
        My purpose should not fail with me,
                But thither would I hie.

Boy.   As duly,
                But not as truly,
                As bird doth sing on bough.   20

Enter FLUELLEN.

Flu. Up to the breach, you dogs ! avaunt, you
cullions !   [*Driving them forward.*

Pist. Be merciful, great duke, to men of mould !
Abate thy rage, abate thy manly rage ;
Abate thy rage, great duke !
Good bawcock, bate thy rage ; use lenity, sweet chuck !

Nym. These be good humours !—your honour wins
bad humours.   [*Exeunt* NYM, PISTOL, *and* BARDOLPH,
                    followed by FLUELLEN.

Boy. As young as I am, I have observed these three
swashers.   I am boy to them all three, but all they
three, though they would serve me, could not be man
to me ; for, indeed, three such anticks do not amount
to a man.   For Bardolph, he is white-livered, and
red-faced ; by the means whereof, 'a faces it out, but
fights not.   For Pistol, he hath a killing tongue, and
a quiet sword ; by the means whereof 'a breaks words,
and keeps whole weapons.   For Nym, he hath heard,
that men of few words are the best men ; and therefore he scorns to say his prayers, lest 'a should be
thought a coward : but his few bad words are match'd
with as few good deeds ; for 'a never broke any man's
head but his own, and that was against a post when
he was drunk.   They will steal anything, and call it
purchase.   Bardolph stole a lute-case, bore it twelve
leagues, and sold it for three half-pence.   Nym and
Bardolph are sworn brothers in filching, and in Calais
they stole a fire-shovel ; I knew, by that piece of service, the men would carry coals.   They would have
me as familiar with men's pockets, as their gloves or
their handkerchiefs : which makes much against my
manhood, if I should take from another's pocket, to
put into mine ; for it is plain pocketing up of wrongs.
I must leave them, and seek some better service :
their villainy goes against my weak stomach, and
therefore I must cast it up.   [*Exit.*

Re-enter FLUELLEN, GOWER *following.*

Gow. Captain Fluellen, you must come presently to
the mines : the Duke of Gloster would speak with you.

Flu. To the mines ! tell you the duke, it is not so
good to come to the mines.   For, look you, the mines
is not according to the disciplines of the war ; the
concavities of it is not sufficient ; for, look you,
th' athversary (you may discuss unto the duke, look
you) is digt himself four yard under the countermines.
By Cheshu, I think, 'a will plow up all ; if there is
not better directions.

Gow. The Duke of Gloster, to whom the order of the
siege is given, is altogether directed by an Irishman ;
a very valiant gentleman, i' faith.

Flu. It is Captain Macmorris, is it not ?

Gow. I think it be.   70

Flu. By Cheshu, he is an ass, as in the world.   I
will verify as much in his peard : he has no more
directions in the true disciplines of the wars, look
you, of the Roman disciplines, than is a puppy-dog.

Enter MACMORRIS *and* JAMY, *at a distance.*

Gow. Here 'a comes ; and the Scots captain, Captain
Jamy, with him.

Flu. Captain Jamy is a marvellous falorous gentleman, that is certain; and of great expedition, and
knowledge in the ancient wars, upon my particular
knowledge of his directions: by Cheshu, he will
maintain his argument as well as any military man
in the world, in the disciplines of the pristine wars of
the Romans.   83
   Jamy. I say, gud day, Captain Fluellen.
   Flu. God-den to your worship, good Captain James.
   Gow. How now, Captain Macmorris! have you quit
the mines? have the pioners given o'er?
   Mac. By Chrish la, tish ill done: the work ish give
over, the trumpet sound the retreat. By my hand, I
swear, and my father's soul, the work ish ill done; it
ish give over: I would have blowed up the town, so
Chrish save me, la, in an hour. O! tish ill done, tish
ill done; by my hand, tish ill done.
   Flu. Captain Macmorris, I beseech you now, will
you vouchsafe me, look you, a few disputations with
you, as partly touching or concerning the disciplines
of the war; the Roman wars, in the way of argument,
look you, and friendly communication; partly to
satisfy my opinion, and partly for the satisfaction,
look you, of my mind, as touching the direction of the
military discipline: that is the point.   101
   Jamy. It sall be very gud, gud feith, gud captains
bath: and I sall quit you with gud leve, as I may pick
occasion; that sall I, marry.
   Mac. It is no time to discourse, so Chrish save me.
The day is hot, and the weather, and the wars, and
the king, and the dukes: it is no time to discourse.
The town is beseeched, and the trumpet call us to the
breach, and we talk, and, be Chrish, do nothing: 'tis
shame for us all; so God sa' me, 'tis shame to stand
still; it is shame, by my hand; and there is throats to
be cut, and works to be done, and there ish nothing
done, so Chrish sa' me, la.
   Jamy. By the mess, ere theise eyes of mine take
themselves to slomber, aile de gud service, or aile lig
i' the grund for it; ay, or go to death; and aile pay it
as valorously as I may, that sal I surely do, that is the
breff and the long. Marry, I wad full fain heard some
question 'tween you tway.   119
   Flu. Captain Macmorris, I think, look you, under
your correction, there is not many of your nation—
   Mac. Of my nation! What ish my nation? Ish a
villain, and a bastard, and a knave, and a rascal.
What ish my nation? Who talks of my nation?
   Flu. Look you, if you take the matter otherwise
than is meant, Captain Macmorris, peradventure, I
shall think you do not use me with that affability as
in discretion you ought to use me, look you; being
as good a man as yourself, both in the disciplines of
wars, and in the derivation of my birth, and in other
particularities.   131
   Mac. I do not know you so good a man as myself:
so Chrish save me, I will cut off your head.
   Gow. Gentlemen both, you will mistake each other.
   Jamy. Au! that's a foul fault. [*A parley sounded.*
   Gow. The town sounds a parley.
   Flu. Captain Macmorris, when there is more better
opportunity to be required, look you, I will be so bold
as to tell you, I know the disciplines of wars; and
there is an end.   [*Exeunt.*

SCENE III.— The Same. Before the Gates of Harfleur.

*The Governor and some Citizens on the walls; the
English Forces below. Enter King* HENRY *and
his Train.*

   K. Hen. How yet resolves the governor of the town?
This is the latest parle we will admit:
Therefore, to our best mercy give yourselves;
Or, like to men proud of destruction,
Defy us to our worst: for, as I am a soldier,
A name that in my thoughts becomes me best,
If I begin the battery once again,
I will not leave the half-achieved Harfleur,
Till in her ashes she lie buried.
The gates of mercy shall be all shut up;   10
And the flesh'd soldier, rough and hard of heart,

In liberty of bloody hand shall range
With conscience wide as hell, mowing like grass
Your fresh-fair virgins, and your flowering infants.
What is it then to me, if impious war,
Array'd in flames like to the prince of fiends,
Do, with his smirch'd complexion, all fell feats
Enlink'd to waste and desolation?
What is 't to me, when you yourselves are cause,
If your pure maidens fall into the hand   20
Of hot and forcing violation?
What rein can hold licentious wickedness,
When down the hill he holds his fierce career?
We may as bootless spend our vain command
Upon the enraged soldiers in their spoil,
As send precepts to the leviathan
To come ashore. Therefore, you men of Harfleur,
Take pity of your town, and of your people,
Whiles yet my soldiers are in my command;
Whiles yet the cool and temperate wind of grace   30
O'erblows the filthy and contagious clouds
Of heady murder, spoil, and villainy.
If not, why, in a moment look to see
The blind and bloody soldier with foul hand
Defile the locks of your shrill-shrieking daughters;
Your fathers taken by the silver beards,
And their most reverend heads dash'd to the walls;
Your naked infants spitted upon pikes,
Whiles the mad mothers with their howls confus'd
Do break the clouds, as did the wives of Jewry   40
At Herod's bloody-hunting slaughtermen.
What say you? will you yield, and this avoid?
Or, guilty in defence, be thus destroy'd?
   Gov. Our expectation hath this day an end.
The Dauphin, whom of succour we entreated,
Returns us, that his powers are yet not ready
To raise so great a siege. Therefore, great king,
We yield our town and lives to thy soft mercy.
Enter our gates; dispose of us and ours;
For we no longer are defensible.   50
   K. Hen. Open your gates!—Come, uncle Exeter,
Go you and enter Harfleur; there remain,
And fortify it strongly 'gainst the French:
Use mercy to them all. For us, dear uncle,
The winter coming on, and sickness growing
Upon our soldiers, we will retire to Calais.
To-night in Harfleur will we be your guest;
To-morrow for the march are we address.
         [*Flourish. The* KING, *&c., enter the town.*

SCENE IV.—Rouen. A Room in the Palace.

Enter KATHARINE *and* ALICE.

   Kate. Alice, tu as esté en Angleterre, et tu bien
parles le langage.
   Alice. Un peu, madame.
   Kath. Je te prie, m'enseigniez; il faut que je
apprend à parler. Comment appellez vous le main
en Anglois?
   Alice. Le main? il est appellé, de hand.
   Kath. De hand. Et les doigts?
   Alice. Les doigts? ma foy, je oublie les doigts;
mais je me souviendray. Les doigts? je pense, qu'ils
sont appellé de fingres; ouy, de fingres.   11
   Kath. Le main, de hand; les doigts, de fingres. Je
pense, que je suis le bon escolier. J'ai gagné deux
mots d'Anglois vistement. Comment appellez vous
les ongles?
   Alice. Les ongles? les appellons, de nails.
   Kath. De nails. Escoutez; dites moy, si je parle
bien: de hand, de fingres, et de nails.
   Alice. C'est bien dict, madame; il est fort bon
Anglois.   20
   Kath. Dites moy l'Anglois pour le bras.
   Alice. De arm, madame.
   Kath. Et le coude?
   Alice. De elbow.
   Kath. De elbow. Je m'en faitz la repetition de tous
les mots, que vous m'avez apprins dès à present.
   Alice. Il est trop difficile, madame, comme je
pense.

Kath. Excuse moy, Alice; escoute: de hand, de
fingre. de nails, de arm, de bilbow.   30
Alice. De elbow. *madame.*
Kath. O Seigneur Dieu! je m'en oublie; de elbow.
Comment appellez vous le col?
Alice. De nick, *madame.*
Kath. De nick. *Et le menton?*
Alice. De chin.
Kath. De sin. *Le col,* de nick; *le menton,* de sin.
*Alice. Ouy. Sauf vostre honneur, en verité, vous
prononcez les mots aussi droict que les natifs
d'Angleterre.*   40
*Kath. Je ne doute point d'apprendre par la grace
de Dieu, et en peu de temps.*

Kath. "Je reciterai une autre fois ma leçon ensemble."

*Alice. N'avez vous deja oublié ce que je vous ay
enseigné?*
Kath. Non, je reciteray à vous promptement. De
hand, de fingre, de mails, —
Alice. De nails, *madame.*
Kath. De nails, de arme, de ilbow.
Alice. Sauf vostre honneur, de elbow.
Kath. Ainsi dis je; de elbow, de nick, *et* de sin.
Comment appellez vous le pied et la robe?   51
Alice. De foot, *madame; et* de coun.
Kath. De foot, *et* de coun? *O Seigneur Dieu! ils
sont les mots de son mauvais, corruptible, grosse, et
impudique, et non pour les dames de honneur d'user.
Je ne voudrois prononcer ces mots devant les Seig-
neurs de France, pour tout le monde. Il faut* de foot,
et de coun, *neant-moins. Je reciterai une autre fois
ma leçon ensemble:* de hand, de fingre, de nails,
de arm, de elbow, de nick, de sin, de foot, de coun. 60
Alice. Excellent, madame.
*Kath. C'est assez pour une fois: allons nous à
disner.*   [*Exeunt.*

SCENE V.—The Same. Another Room in the Same.

Enter the French KING, *the* DAUPHIN, *Duke of*
BOURBON, *the Constable of France, and others.*
Fr. King. 'T is certain, he hath pass'd the river
Somme.
Con. And if he be not fought withal, my lord,
Let us not live in France; let us quit all,
And give our vineyards to a barbarous people.
Dau. O Dieu vivant! shall a few sprays of us,
The emptying of our fathers' luxury,
Our scions, put in wild and savage stock,

Spirt up so suddenly into the clouds,
And overlook their grafters?
Bour. Normans, but bastard Normans, Norman
bastards.   19
Mort de ma vie! if they march along
Unfought withal, but I will sell my dukedom,
To buy a slobbery and a dirty farm
In that nook-shotten isle of Albion.
Con. Dieu de battailes! where have they this
mettle?
Is not their climate foggy, raw, and dull,
On whom, as in despite, the sun looks pale,
Killing their fruit with frowns? Can sodden water,
A drench for su;-rein'd jades, their barley-broth,
Decoct their cold blood to such valiant heat?   20
And shall our quick blood, spirited with wine,
Seem frosty? O! for honour of our land,
Let us not hang like roping icicles
Upon our houses' thatch, whiles a more frosty people
Sweat drops of gallant youth in our rich fields;
Poor we may call them in their native lords.
Dau. By faith and honour,
Our madams mock at us, and plainly say,
Our mettle is bred out; and they will give
Their bodies to the lust of English youth,   30
To new-store France with bastard warriors.
Bour. They bid us to the English dancing-schools,
And teach lavoltas high, and swift corantos;
Saying, our grace is only in our heels,
And that we are most lofty runaways.
Fr. King. Where is Montjoy, the herald? speed him
hence:
Let him greet England with our sharp defiance.—
Up, princes! and, with spirit of honour edg'd
More sharper than your swords, hie to the field:
Charles Delabreth, high constable of France;   40
You Dukes of Orleans, Bourbon, and of Berry,
Alençon, Brabant, Bar, and Burgundy;
Jaques Chatillon, Rambures, Vaudemont,
Beaumont, Grandpré, Roussi, and Fauconberg,
Foix, Lestrale, Bouciqualt, and Charolois;
High dukes, great princes, barons, lords, and knights,
For your great seats, now quit you of great shames,
Bar Harry England, that sweeps through our land
With pennons painted in the blood of Harfleur:
Rush on his host, as doth the melted snow   56
Upon the valleys, whose low vassal seat
The Alps doth spit and void his rheum upon:
Go, down upon him,—you have power enough,—
And in a captive chariot into Roan
Bring him our prisoner.
Con.   This becomes the great.
Sorry am I, his numbers are so few,
His soldiers sick, and famish'd in their march;
For, I am sure, when he shall see our army,
He 'll drop his heart into the sink of fear,
And, for achievement, offer us his ransom.   60
Fr. King. Therefore, lord constable, haste on Mont-
joy,
And let him say to England, that we send
To know what willing ransom he will give.—
Prince Dauphin, you shall stay with us in Roan.
Dau. Not so. I do beseech your majesty.
Fr. King. Be patient, for you shall remain with
us.—
Now, forth, lord constable, and princes all,
And quickly bring us word of England's fall. [*Exeunt.*

SCENE VI.—The English Camp in Picardy.

Enter GOWER *and* FLUELLEN.

Gow. How now, Captain Fluellen? come you from
the bridge?
Flu. I assure you, there is very excellent services
committed at the pridge.
Gow. Is the Duke of Exeter safe?
Flu. The Duke of Exeter is as magnanimous as
Agamemnon; and a man that I love and honour with
my soul, and my heart, and my duty, and my life,
and my living, and my uttermost power: he is not

(God be praised and blessed !) any hurt in the world,
but keeps the pridge most valiantly, with excellent
discipline. There is an aunchient lieutenant there at
the pridge,—I think, in my very conscience, he is as
valiant a man as Mark Antony ; and he is a man of
no estimation in the world : but I did see him do as
gallant service.
Gow. What do you call him ?
Flu. He is called Aunchient Pistol.
Gow. I know him not.

            Enter PISTOL.

Flu. Here is the man.   20
Pist. Captain, I thee beseech to do me favours :
The Duke of Exeter doth love thee well.
Flu. Ay, I praise God ; and I have merited some
love at his hands.
Pist. Bardolph, a soldier firm and sound of heart,
And of buxom valour, hath, by cruel fate
And giddy Fortune's furious fickle wheel,
That goddess blind,
That stands upon the rolling restless stone,—   29
Flu. By your patience, Aunchient Pistol. Fortune
is painted blind, with a muffler afore his eyes, to signify
to you that Fortune is blind. And she is painted also
with a wheel, to signify to you, which is the moral of
it, that she is turning, and inconstant, and mutability,
and variation : and her foot, look you, is fixed upon a
spherical stone, which rolls, and rolls, and rolls. In
good truth, the poet makes a most excellent description
of it : Fortune is an excellent moral.
Pist. Fortune is Bardolph's foe, and frowns on him :
For he hath stol'n a pax, and hanged must 'a be.   40
A damned death !
Let gallows gape for dog, let man go free,
And let not hemp his wind-pipe suffocate.
But Exeter hath given the doom of death,
For pax of little price.
Therefore, go speak, the duke will hear thy voice,
And let not Bardolph's vital thread be cut
With edge of penny cord, and vile reproach :
Speak, captain, for his life, and I will thee requite.
Flu. Aunchient Pistol, I do partly understand your
meaning.   51
Pist. Why then, rejoice therefore.
Flu. Certainly, aunchient, it is not a thing to rejoice
at ; for if, look you, he were my brother, I would
desire the duke to use his good pleasure, and put him
to execution ; for discipline ought to be used.
Pist. Die and be damn'd ; and figo for thy friendship !
Flu. It is well.
Pist. The fig of Spain !   [*Exit.*
Flu. Very good.   60
Gow. Why, this is an arrant counterfeit rascal : I
remember him now ; a bawd, a cutpurse.
Flu. I'll assure you, 'a utter'd as prave words at the
pridge, as you shall see in a summer's day. But it is
very well ; what he has spoke to me, that is well, I
warrant you, when time is serve.
Gow. Why, 'tis a gull, a fool, a rogue : that now and
then goes to the wars, to grace himself at his return
into London under the form of a soldier. And such
fellows are perfect in the great commanders' names,
and they will learn you by rote where services were
done ;—at such and such a sconce, at such a breach, at
such a convoy ; who came off bravely, who was shot,
who disgraced, what terms the enemy stood on ; and
this they con perfectly in the phrase of war, which
they trick up with new-tuned oaths : and what a beard
of the general's cut, and a horrid suit of the camp, will
do among foaming bottles, and ale-washed wits, is
wonderful to be thought on. But you must learn to
know such slanders of the age, or else you may be
marvellously mistook.   81
Flu. I tell you what, Captain Gower ; I do perceive,
he is not the man that he would gladly make show to
the world he is : if I find a hole in his coat, I will tell
him my mind. [*Drum heard.*] Hark you, the king is
coming, and I must speak with him from the pridge.

    Enter King HENRY, GLOSTER, *and Soldiers.*

Flu. God pless your majesty !

K. Hen. How now, Fluellen ? cam'st thou from the
bridge ?   88
Flu. Ay, so please your majesty. The Duke of
Exeter has very gallantly maintained the pridge : the
French is gone off, look you, and there is gallant and
most prave passages. Marry, th' athversary was have
possession of the pridge, but he is enforced to retire,
and the Duke of Exeter is master of the pridge. I can
tell your majesty, the duke is a prave man.
K. Hen. What men have you lost, Fluellen ?
Flu. The perdition of th' athversary hath been very
great, reasonable great : marry, for my part, I think the
duke hath lost never a man, but one that is like to be
executed for robbing a church ; one Bardolph, if your
majesty know the man : his face is all bubukles, and
whelks, and knobs, and flames of fire ; and his lips
blows at his nose, and it is like a coal of fire, sometimes plue, and sometimes red ; but his nose is executed,
and his fire's out.
K. Hen. We would have all such offenders so cut
off : and we give express charge, that in our marches
through the country none compelled from
the villages, nothing taken but paid for ; none of the
French upbraided, or abused in disdainful language ;
for when lenity and cruelty play for a kingdom, the
gentler gamester is the soonest winner.   112

        Tucket. Enter MONTJOY.

Mont. You know me by my habit.
K. Hen. Well then, I know thee : what shall I know
of thee ?
Mont. My master's mind.
K. Hen. Unfold it.
Mont. Thus says my king :—Say thou to Harry of
England, though we seemed dead, we did but sleep ;
advantage is a better soldier than rashness. Tell him,
we could have rebuked him at Harfleur ; but that we
thought not good to bruise an injury, till it were full
ripe : now we speak upon our cue, and our voice is
imperial. England shall repent his folly, see his
weakness, and admire our sufferance. Bid him, therefore, consider of his ransom ; which must proportion
the losses we have borne, the subjects we have lost,
the disgrace we have digested ; which, in weight to
re-answer, his pettiness would bow under. For our
losses, his exchequer is too poor : for the effusion of
our blood, the muster of his kingdom too faint a
number ; and for our disgrace, his own person, kneeling at our feet, but a weak and worthless satisfaction.
To this add defiance ; and tell him, for conclusion, he
hath betrayed his followers, whose condemnation is
pronounced. So far my king and master, so much my
office.
K. Hen. What is thy name ? I know thy quality.
Mont. Montjoy.
K. Hen. Thou dost thy office fairly. Turn thee
back,
And tell thy king,—I do not seek him now,   140
But could be willing to march on to Calais
Without impeachment ; for, to say the sooth,
Though 't is no wisdom to confess so much
Unto an enemy of craft and vantage,
My people are with sickness much enfeebled,
My numbers lessen'd, and those few I have
Almost no better than so many French :
Who, when they were in health, I tell thee, herald,
I thought upon one pair of English legs
Did march three Frenchmen.—Yet, forgive me, God,
That I do brag thus !—this your air of France   151
Hath blown that vice in me : I must repent.
Go therefore, tell thy master, here I am :
My ransom is this frail and worthless trunk,
My army but a weak and sickly guard ;
Yet, God before, tell him we will come on,
Though France himself, and such another neighbour,
Stand in our way. There's for thy labour, Montjoy.
Go, bid thy master well advise himself :
If we may pass, we will ; if we be hinder'd,   160
We shall your tawny ground with your red blood
Discolour : and so, Montjoy, fare you well.
The sum of all our answer is but this :
We would not seek a battle, as we are ;

Nor, as we are, we say, we will not shun it:
So tell your master.

Mont. I shall deliver so.   Thanks to your highness.
          [*Exit.*

Glo. I hope they will not come upon us now.

K. Hen. We are in God's hand, brother, not in
theirs.
March to the bridge : it now draws toward night : 170
Beyond the river we 'll encamp ourselves,
And on to-morrow bid them march away.   [*Exeunt.*

———

Scene VII.—The French Camp, near Agincourt.

Enter the Constable of France, the Lord Rambures,
the Duke of Orleans, *the* Dauphin, *and others.*

Con. Tut! I have the best armour of the world.
'Would it were day!

Orl. You have an excellent armour; but let my
horse have his due.

Dau. " It is a theme as fluent as the sea."

Con. It is the best horse of Europe.

Orl. Will it never be morning?

Dau. My Lord of Orleans, and my lord high constable, you talk of horse and armour—

Orl. You are as well provided of both as any prince
in the world.   10

Dau. What a long night is this!—I will not change
my horse with any that treads but on four pasterns.
Ça, ha! He bounds from the earth, as if his entrails
were hairs; *le cheval volant,* the Pegasus, *qui a les
narines de feu!* When I bestride him, I soar, I am
a hawk: he trots the air; the earth sings when he
touches it; the basest horn of his hoof is more musical
than the pipe of Hermes.

Orl. He 's of the colour of the nutmeg.   19

Dau. And of the heat of the ginger. It is a beast
for Perseus: he is pure air and fire; and the dull
elements of earth and water never appear in him,
but only in patient stillness, while his rider mounts
him: he is, indeed, a horse; and all other jades you
may call beasts.

Con. Indeed, my lord, it is a most absolute and
excellent horse.

Dau. It is the prince of palfreys: his neigh is like
the bidding of a monarch, and his countenance enforces homage.   30

Orl. No more, cousin.

Dau. Nay, the man hath no wit that cannot, from
the rising of the lark to the lodging of the lamb, vary
deserved praise on my palfrey: it is a theme as fluent
as the sea; turn the sands into eloquent tongues, and

my horse is argument for them all. 'Tis a subject for
a sovereign to reason on, and for a sovereign's sovereign to ride on; and for the world (familiar to us, and
unknown) to lay apart their particular functions, and
wonder at him. I once writ a sonnet in his praise,
and began thus: " Wonder of nature!"—   41

Orl. I have heard a sonnet begin so to one's mistress.

Dau. Then did they imitate that which I composed
to my courser : for my horse is my mistress.

Orl. Your mistress bears well.

Dau. Me well; which is the prescript praise and
perfection of a good and particular mistress.

Con. Nay, for methought yesterday, your mistress
shrewdly shook your back.

Dau. So, perhaps, did yours.   50

Con. Mine was not bridled.

Dau. O! then, belike, she was old and gentle; and
you rode, like a kern of Ireland, your French hose off,
and in your strait strossers.

Con. You have good judgment in horsemanship.

Dau. Be warned by me, then : they that ride so,
and ride not warily, fall into foul bogs. I had rather
have my horse to my mistress.

Con. I had as lief have my mistress a jade.

Dau. I tell thee, constable, my mistress wears his
own hair.   61

Con. I could make as true a boast as that, if I had a
sow to my mistress.

*Dau. Le chien est retourné à son propre vomisse-
ment, et la truie lavée au bourbier:* thou makest use
of anything.

Con. Yet do I not use my horse for my mistress; or
any such proverb, so little kin to the purpose.

Ram. My lord constable, the armour, that I saw in
your tent to-night, are those stars, or suns, upon it ? 70

Con. Stars, my lord.

Dau. Some of them will fall to-morrow, I hope.

Con. And yet my sky shall not want.

Dau. That may be; for you bear a many super-
fluously, and 't were more honour some were away.

Con. Even as your horse bears your praises : who
would trot as well, were some of your brags dismounted.   78

Dau. 'Would I were able to load him with his
desert! Will it never be day? I will trot to-morrow
a mile, and my way shall be paved with English faces.

Con. I will not say so, for fear I should be faced out
of my way. But I would it were morning, for I would
fain be about the ears of the English.

Ram. Who will go to hazard with me for twenty
prisoners?

Con. You must first go yourself to hazard, ere you
have them.

Dau. 'T is midnight: I 'll go arm myself.   [*Exit.*

Orl. The Dauphin longs for morning.   90

Ram. He longs to eat the English.

Con. I think he will eat all he kills.

Orl. By the white hand of my lady, he 's a gallant
prince.

Con. Swear by her foot, that she may tread out the
oath.

Orl. He is simply the most active gentleman of
France.

Con. Doing is activity, and he will still be doing.

Orl. He never did harm, that I heard of.   100

Con. Nor will do none to-morrow: he will keep that
good name still.

Orl. I know him to be valiant.

Con. I was told that, by one that knows him better
than you.

Orl. What 's he?

Con. Marry, he told me so himself; and he said, he
cared not who knew it.

Orl. He needs not; it is no hidden virtue in him.

Con. By my faith, sir, but it is; never anybody saw
it, but his lackey: 't is a hooded valour; and when it
appears, it will bate.   112

Orl. Ill will never said well.

Con. I will cap that proverb with—There is flattery
in friendship.

Orl. And I will take up that with—Give the devil
his due.

Con. Well placed : there stands your friend for the
devil : have at the very eye of that proverb, with—A
pox of the devil.   120
Orl. You are the better at proverbs, by how much—
A fool's bolt is soon shot.
Con. You have shot over.
Orl. 'T is not the first time you were overshot.

Enter a Messenger.

Mess. My lord high constable, the English lie within
fifteen hundred paces of your tents.
Con. Who hath measured the ground ?
Mess. The Lord Grandpré.
Con. A valiant and most expert gentleman.—'Would
it were day !—Alas, poor Harry of England !—he longs
not for the dawning, as we do.   131
Orl. What a wretched and peevish fellow is this
King of England, to mope with his fat-brained
followers so far out of his knowledge.
Con. If the English had any apprehension, they
would run away.

Orl. That they lack ; for if their heads had any
intellectual armour, they could never wear such
heavy head-pieces.
Ram. That island of England breeds very valiant
creatures : their mastiffs are of unmatchable courage.
Orl. Foolish curs ! that run winking into the mouth
of a Russian bear, and have their heads crushed like
rotten apples. You may as well say, that 's a valiant
flea, that dare eat his breakfast on the lip of a lion.
Con. Just, just ; and the men do sympathise with
the mastiffs in robustious and rough coming on,
leaving their wits with their wives : and then give
them great meals of beef, and iron and steel, they
will eat like wolves, and fight like devils.   150
Orl. Ay, but these English are shrewdly out of
beef.
Con. Then shall we find to-morrow, they have only
stomachs to eat, and none to fight. Now is it time to
arm ; come, shall we about it ?
Orl. It is now two o'clock : but, let me see, by ten,
We shall have each a hundred Englishmen. [*Exeunt.*

ACT IV.

Enter Chorus.

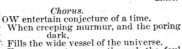

Chorus.

NOW entertain conjecture of a time,
When creeping murmur, and the poring
  dark,
Fills the wide vessel of the universe.
From camp to camp, through the foul
  womb of night,
The hum of either army stilly sounds,
That the fix'd sentinels almost receive
The secret whispers of each other's
  watch :
Fire answers fire, and through their paly
  flames
Each battle sees the other's umber'd face :
Steed threatens steed, in high and boast-
  ful neighs   10
Piercing the night's dull ear ; and from
  the tents,
The armourers, accomplishing the knights,
With busy hammers closing rivets up,
Give dreadful note of preparation.
The country cocks do crow, the clocks do toll,
And the third hour of drowsy morning name.
Proud of their numbers, and secure in soul,
The confident and over-lusty French
Do the low-rated English play at dice ;
And chide the cripple, tardy-gaited night,   20
Who, like a foul and ugly witch, doth limp
So tediously away. The poor condemned English,
Like sacrifices, by their watchful fires
Sit patiently, and inly ruminate
The morning's danger ; and their gesture sad,
Investing lank-lean cheeks, and war-worn coats,
Presenteth them unto the gazing moon
So many horrid ghosts. O ! now, who will behold
The royal captain of this ruin'd band,
Walking from watch to watch, from tent to tent,   30
Let him cry—Praise and glory on his head !
For forth he goes, and visits all his host,
Bids them good-morrow with a modest smile,
And calls them brothers, friends, and countrymen.
Upon his royal face there is no note,

How dread an army hath enrounded him ;
Nor doth he dedicate one jot of colour
Unto the weary and all-watched night :
But freshly looks, and overbears attaint
With cheerful semblance, and sweet majesty ;   40
That every wretch, pining and pale before,
Beholding him, plucks comfort from his looks.
A largess universal, like the sun,
His liberal eye doth give to every one,
Thawing cold fear, that mean and gentle all,
Behold, as may unworthiness define,
A little touch of Harry in the night.
And so our scene must to the battle fly ;
Where, O for pity ! we shall much disgrace—
With four or five most vile and ragged foils,   50
Right ill dispos'd in brawl ridiculous—
The name of Agincourt. Yet, sit and see ;
Minding true things by what their mockeries be.
                      [*Exit.*

SCENE I.—The English Camp at Agincourt.

Enter King HENRY, BEDFORD, *and* GLOSTER.

K. Hen. Gloster, 't is true that we are in great
    danger ;
The greater therefore should our courage be.—
Good morrow, brother Bedford.—God Almighty !
There is some soul of goodness in things evil,
Would men observingly distil it out ;
For our bad neighbour makes us early stirrers,
Which is both healthful and good husbandry :
Besides, they are our outward consciences,
And preachers to us all ; admonishing,
That we should dress us fairly for our end.   10
Thus may we gather honey from the weed,
And make a moral of the devil himself.

Enter ERPINGHAM.

Good morrow, old Sir Thomas Erpingham :
A good soft pillow for that good white head
Were better than a churlish turf of France.

Erp. Not so, my liege: this lodging likes me
    better,
Since I may say, now lie I like a king.
K. Hen. 'Tis good for men to love their present
    pains
Upon example ; so the spirit is eased :
And when the mind is quicken'd, out of doubt,   20
The organs, though defunct and dead before,
Break up their drowsy grave, and newly move
With casted slough and fresh legerity.
Lend me thy cloak, Sir Thomas.—Brothers both,
Commend me to the princes in our camp ;
Do my good-morrow to them ; and, anon,
Desire them all to my pavilion.
Glo. We shall, my liege.
            [Exeunt GLOSTER *and* BEDFORD.
Erp. Shall I attend your grace ?
K. Hen.   No, my good knight ;
Go with my brothers to my lords of England :   30
I and my bosom must debate awhile,
And then I would no other company.
Erp. The Lord in heaven bless thee, noble Harry !
                      [Exit.
K. Hen. God-a-mercy, old heart ! thou speak'st
    cheerfully.

Enter PISTOL.

Pist. Qui va là ?
K. Hen. A friend.
Pist. Discuss unto me ; art thou officer ?
Or art thou base, common, and popular ?
K. Hen. I am a gentleman of a company.
Pist. Trail'st thou the puissant pike ?   40
K. Hen. Even so.   What are you ?
Pist. As good a gentleman as the emperor.
K. Hen. Then you are a better than the king.
Pist. The king's a bawcock, and a heart of gold,
A lad of life, an imp of fame ;
Of parents good, of fist most valiant :
I kiss his dirty shoe, and from heartstring
I love the lovely bully. What's thy name ?
K. Hen. Harry *le Roy.*
Pist. Le Roy ! a Cornish name : art thou of Cornish
    crew ?   50
K. Hen. No, I am a Welshman.
Pist. Know'st thou Fluellen ?
K. Hen. Yes.
Pist. Tell him, I'll knock his leek about his
    pate,
Upon Saint Davy's day.
K. Hen. Do not you wear your dagger in your cap
that day, lest he knock that about yours.
Pist. Art thou his friend ?
K. Hen. And his kinsman too.
Pist. The figo for thee then !   60
K. Hen. I thank you. God be with you !
Pist. My name is Pistol called.   *[Exit.*
K. Hen. It sorts well with your fierceness.

Enter FLUELLEN *and* GOWER, *severally.*

Gow. Captain Fluellen !
Flu. So, in the name of Cheshu Christ, speak lower.
It is the greatest admiration in the universal world,
when the true and aunchient prerogatifes and laws of
the wars is not kept. If you would take the pains but
to examine the wars of Pompey the Great, you shall
find, I warrant you, that there is no tiddle taddle, nor
pibble pabble, in Pompey's camp ; I warrant you, you
shall find the ceremonies of the wars, and the cares of
it, and the forms of it, and the sobriety of it, and the
modesty of it, to be otherwise.
Gow. Why, the enemy is loud ; you hear him all
night.
Flu. If the enemy is an ass and a fool, and a prating
coxcomb, is it meet, think you, that we should also,
look you, be an ass, and a fool, and a prating coxcomb ? in your own conscience now ?   80
Gow. I will speak lower.
Flu. I pray you, and beseech you, that you will.
           [Exeunt GOWER *and* FLUELLEN.
K. Hen. Though it appear a little out of fashion,
There is much care and valour in this Welshman.

Enter BATES, COURT, *and* WILLIAMS.

Court. Brother John Bates, is not that the morning
which breaks yonder ?
Bates. I think it be ; but we have no great cause to
desire the approach of day.
Will. We see yonder the beginning of the day, but
I think we shall never see the end of it.—Who goes
there ?   91
K. Hen. A friend.
Will. Under what captain serve you ?
K. Hen. Under Sir Thomas Erpingham.
Will. A good old commander, and a most kind
gentleman : I pray you, what thinks he of our estate ?
K. Hen. Even as men wracked upon a sand, that
look to be washed off the next tide.
Bates. He hath not told his thought to the king ?
K. Hen. No ; nor it is not meet he should. For,
though I speak it to you, I think the king is but a man,
as I am : the violet smells to hi.n, as it doth to me ;
the element shows to him, as it doth to me ; all his
senses have but human conditions : his ceremonies
laid by, in his nakedness he appears but a man, and
though his affections are higher mounted than ours,
yet, when they stoop, they stoop with the like wing.
Therefore, when he sees reason of fears, as we do,
his fears, out of doubt, be of the same relish as ours
are : yet, in reason, no man should possess him with
any appearance of fear, lest he, by showing it, should
dishearten his army.   112
Bates. He may show what outward courage he will ;
but, I believe, as cold a night as 'tis, he could wish
himself in Thames up to the neck : and I by him, at
all adventures, so we were quit here.
K. Hen. By my troth, I will speak my conscience of
the king : I think, he would not wish himself any
where but where he is.
Bates. Then I would he were here alone ; so should
he be sure to be ransomed, and a many poor men's
lives saved.   122
K. Hen. I dare say, you love him not so ill, to wish
him here alone, howsoever you speak this, to feel
other men's minds. Methinks, I could not die anywhere so contented as in the king's company, his
cause being just, and his quarrel honourable.
Will. That's more than we know.
Bates. Ay, or more than we should seek after ; for
we know enough, if we know we are the king's subjects. If his cause be wrong, our obedience to the
king wipes the crime of it out of us.   132
Will. But if the cause be not good, the king himself hath a heavy reckoning to make : when all those
legs, and arms, and heads, chopped off in a battle,
shall join together at the latter day, and cry all—"We
died at such a place ;" some swearing, some crying
for a surgeon, some upon their wives left poor behind
them, some upon the debts they owe, some upon their
children rawly left. I am afeard there are few die
well, that die in a battle ; for how can they charitably
dispose of anything, when blood is their argument ?
Now, if these men do not die well, it will be a black
matter for the king that led them to it, whom to disobey were against all proportion of subjection.
K. Hen. So, if a son, that is by his father sent
about merchandise, do sinfully miscarry upon the sea,
the imputation of his wickedness, by your rule, should
be imposed upon his father that sent him : or if a
servant, under his master's command, transporting
a sum of money, be assailed by robbers, and die in
many irreconciled iniquities, you may call the business of the master the author of the servant's damnation. But this is not so : the king is not bound to
answer the particular endings of his soldiers, the
father of his son, nor the master of his servant ; for
they purpose not their death, when they purpose their
services. Besides, there is no king, be his cause
never so spotless, if it come to the arbitrement of
swords, can try it out with all unspotted soldiers.
Some, peradventure, have on them the guilt of premeditated and contrived murder ; some, of beguiling
virgins with the broken seals of perjury ; some, making
the wars their bulwark, that have before gored the

gentle bosom of peace with pillage and robbery. Now, if these men have defeated the law, and outrun native punishment, though they can outstrip men, they have no wings to fly from God : war is his beadle, war is his vengeance ; so that here men are punished, for before-breach of the king's laws, in now the king's quarrel : where they feared the death, they have borne life away, and where they would be safe, they perish. Then, if they die unprovided, no more is the king guilty of their damnation, than he was before guilty of those impieties for the which they are now visited. Every subject's duty is the king's ; but every subject's soul is his own. Therefore should every soldier in the wars do as every sick man in his bed, wash every moth out of his conscience ; and dying so, death is to him advantage ; or not dying, the time was blessedly lost, wherein such preparation was gained : and in him that escapes, it were not sin to think, that making God so free an offer, he let him outlive that day to see his greatness, and to teach others how they should prepare.

Will. 'T is certain, every man that dies ill, the ill upon his own head : the king is not to answer it.

Bates. I do not desire he should answer for me ; and yet I determine to fight lustily for him.

K. Hen. I myself heard the king say, he would not be ransomed. 191

Will. Ay, he said so, to make us fight cheerfully ; but when our throats are cut, he may be ransomed, and we ne'er the wiser.

K. Hen. If I live to see it, I will never trust his word after.

Will. You pay him then ! That 's a perilous shot out of an elder gun, that a poor and a private displeasure can do against a monarch. You may as well go about to turn the sun to ice with fanning in his face with a peacock's feather. You 'll never trust his word after ! come, 't is a foolish saying. 202

K. Hen. Your reproof is something too round : I should be angry with you, if the time were convenient.

Will. Let it be a quarrel between us, if you live.

K. Hen. I embrace it.

Will. How shall I know thee again ?

K. Hen. Give me any gage of thine, and I will wear in my bonnet : then, if ever thou darest acknowledge it, I will make it my quarrel. 210

Will. Here 's my glove : give me another of thine.

K. Hen. There.

Will. This will I also wear in my cap : if ever thou come to me and say, after to-morrow, "This is my glove," by this hand, I will take thee a box on the ear.

K. Hen. If ever I live to see it, I will challenge it.

Will. Thou darest as well be hanged.

K. Hen. Well, I will do it, though I take thee in the king's company.

Will. Keep thy word : fare thee well. 220

Bates. Be friends, you English fools, be friends : we have French quarrels enow, if you could tell how to reckon.

K. Hen. Indeed, the French may lay twenty French crowns to one, they will beat us ; for they bear them on their shoulders : but it is no English treason to cut French crowns, and to-morrow the king himself will be a clipper. [*Exeunt Soldiers.*

Upon the king ! let us our lives, our souls, Our debts, our careful wives, 230
Our children, and our sins, lay on the king !—
We must bear all. O hard condition,
Twin-born with greatness, subject to the breath.
Of every fool, whose sense no more can feel
But his own wringing ! What infinite heart's ease
Must kings neglect, that private men enjoy !
And what have kings, that privates have not too,
Save ceremony, save general ceremony ?
And what art thou, thou idol ceremony ?
What kind of god art thou, that suffer'st more 240
Of mortal griefs, than do thy worshippers ?
What are thy rents ? what are thy comings-in ?
O ceremony, show me but thy worth !
What is thy soul of adoration ?
Art thou aught else but place, degree, and form,
Creating awe and fear in other men ?

Wherein thou art less happy, being fear'd,
Than they in fearing.
What drink'st thou oft, instead of homage sweet,
But poison'd flattery ? O ! be sick, great greatness, 250
And bid thy ceremony give thee cure.
Think'st thou, the fiery fever will go out
With titles blown from adulation ?
Will it give place to flexure and low bending ?

K. Hen. " What infinite heart's ease
Must kings neglect, that private men enjoy ! "

Canst thou, when thou command'st the beggar's knee,
Command the health of it ? No, thou proud dream,
That play'st so subtly with a king's repose :
I am a king, that find thee ; and I know,
'T is not the balm, the sceptre, and the ball,
The sword, the mace, the crown imperial, 260
The inter-tissued robe of gold and pearl,
The farced title running 'fore the king,
The throne he sits on, nor the tide of pomp
That beats upon the high shore of this world ;
No, not all these, thrice-gorgeous ceremony,
Not all these, laid in bed majestical,
Can sleep so soundly as the wretched slave,
Who, with a body fill'd, and vacant mind,
Gets him to rest, cramm'd with distressful bread,
Never sees horrid night, the child of hell, 270
But, like a lackey, from the rise to set,
Sweats in the eye of Phœbus, and all night
Sleeps in Elysium ; next day, after dawn,
Doth rise and help Hyperion to his horse ;
And follows so the ever-running year
With profitable labour to his grave :
And, but for ceremony, such a wretch,
Winding up days with toil, and nights with sleep,
Had the forehand and vantage of a king.
The slave, a member of the country's peace, 280
Enjoys it ; but in gross brain little wots,
What watch the king keeps to maintain the peace,
Whose hours the peasant best advantages.

Enter ERPINGHAM.

Erp. My lord, your nobles, jealous of your absence,
Seek through your camp to find you.
K. Hen. Good old knight,
Collect them all together at my tent :
I 'll be before thee.
Erp. I shall do 't, my lord. [*Exit.*
K. Hen. O God of battles ! steel my soldiers' hearts ;
Possess them not with fear ; take from them now
The sense of reckoning, if the opposed numbers 290
Pluck their hearts from them !—Not to-day, O Lord !
O ! not to-day, think not upon the fault
My father made in compassing the crown.
I Richard's body have interred new,
And on it have bestow'd more contrite tears
Than from it issued forced drops of blood.
Five hundred poor I have in yearly pay,

Who twice a day their wither'd hands hold up
Toward heaven, to pardon blood ; and I have built
Two chantries, where the sad and solemn priests   300
Sing still for Richard's soul.   More will I do ;
Though all that I can do is nothing worth,
Since that my penitence comes after all,
Imploring pardon.

Enter GLOSTER.

Glo. My liege !
K. Hen.   My brother Gloster's voice ?—Ay ;
I know thy errand, I will go with thee :—
The day, my friends, and all things stay for me.
                                        [*Exeunt.*

SCENE II.—The French Camp.

Enter DAUPHIN, ORLEANS, RAMBURES, *and others.*

Orl. The sun doth gild our armour : up, my lords !
Dau. Montez à cheval !—My horse ! *valet ! lacquay !*
   ha !
Orl. O brave spirit !
Dau. Via !—les eaux et la terre !
Orl. Rien puis ? l'air et le feu !
Dau. Ciel ? cousin Orleans.

Enter CONSTABLE.

Now, my lord constable !
Con. Hark, how our steeds for present service neigh.
Dau. Mount them, and make incision in their hides,
That their hot blood may spin in English eyes,   10
And dout them with superfluous courage : ha !
Ram. What, will you have them weep our horses'
          blood ?
How shall we then behold their natural tears ?

Enter a Messenger.

Mess. The English are embattled, you French peers.
Con. To horse, you gallant princes ! straight to
          horse !
Do but behold yon poor and starved band,
And your fair show shall suck away their souls,
Leaving them but the shales and husks of men.
There is not work enough for all our hands ;
Scarce blood enough in all their sickly veins,   20
To give each naked curtle-axe a stain,
That our French gallants shall to-day draw out,
And sheathe for lack of sport : let us but blow on them,
The vapour of our valour will o'erturn them.
'T is positive 'gainst all exceptions, lords,
That our superfluous lackeys, and our peasants,
Who, in unnecessary action, swarm
About our squares of battle, were enow
To purge this field of such a hilding foe,
Though we upon this mountain's basis by   30
Took stand for idle speculation :
But that our honours must not.   What's to say ?
A very little little let us do,
And all is done.   Then, let the trumpets sound
The tucket-sonance, and the note to mount :
For our approach shall so much dare the field,
That England shall couch down in fear, and yield.

Enter GRANDPRÉ.

Grand. Why do you stay so long, my lords of France ?
Yon island carrions, desperate of their bones,
Ill-favour'dly become the morning field :   40
Their ragged curtains poorly are let loose,
And our air shakes them passing scornfully.
Big Mars seems bankrupt in their beggar'd host,
And faintly through a rusty beaver peeps.
The horsemen sit like fixed candlesticks,
With torch-staves in their hand ; and their poor jades
Lob down their heads, dropping the hides and hips,
The gum down-roping from their pale-dead eyes,
And in their pale dull mouths the gimmal'd bit
Lies foul with chew'd grass, still and motionless ;   50
And their executors, the knavish crows,
Fly o'er them all, impatient for their hour.
Description cannot suit itself in words,
To demonstrate the life of such a battle,
In life so lifeless as it shows itself.

Con. They have said their prayers, and they stay for
          death.
Dau. Shall we go send them dinners, and fresh suits,
And give their fasting horses provender,
And after fight with them ?
Con. I stay but for my guard.   On, to the field !   60
I will the banner from a trumpet take,
And use it for my haste.   Come, come, away !
The sun is high, and we outwear the day.   [*Exeunt.*

SCENE III.—The English Camp.

Enter the English Host ; GLOSTER, BEDFORD,
     EXETER, SALISBURY, *and* WESTMORELAND.

Glo. Where is the king ?
Bed. The king himself is rode to view their battle.
West. Of fighting men they have full threescore
          thousand.
Exe. There's five to one ; besides, they all are
          fresh.
Sal. God's arm strike with us ! 't is a fearful odds.
God be wi' you, princes all ; I 'll to my charge :
If we no more meet, till we meet in heaven,
Then, joyfully,—my noble Lord of Bedford,—
My dear Lord Gloster,—and my good Lord Exeter,—
And my kind kinsman,—warriors all, adieu !   10
Bed. Farewell, good Salisbury ; and good luck go
          with thee !
Exe. Farewell, kind lord.   Fight valiantly to-day :
And yet I do thee wrong, to mind thee of it,
For thou art fram'd of the firm truth of valour.
                                        [*Exit* SALISBURY.
Bed. He is as full of valour as of kindness ;
Princely in both.

Enter King HENRY.

West.   O ! that we now had here
But one ten thousand of those men in England,
That do no work to-day !
K. Hen.   What's he, that wishes so ?
My cousin Westmoreland ?—No, my fair cousin :
If we are mark'd to die, we are enow   20
To do our country loss ; and if to live,
The fewer men, the greater share of honour.
God's will ! I pray thee, wish not one man more.
By Jove, I am not covetous for gold ;
Nor care I who doth feed upon my cost ;
It yearns me not if men my garments wear ;
Such outward things dwell not in my desires :
But, if it be a sin to covet honour,
I am the most offending soul alive.
No, 'faith, my coz, wish not a man from England :   30
God's peace ! I would not lose so great an honour,
As one man more, methinks, would share from me,
For the best hope I have.   O ! do not wish one more :
Rather proclaim it, Westmoreland, through my host,
That he, which hath no stomach to this fight,
Let him depart, his passport shall be made,
And crowns for convoy put into his purse :
We would not die in that man's company,
That fears his fellowship to die with us.
This day is call'd the feast of Crispian :   40
He that outlives this day, and comes safe home,
Will stand a tip-toe when this day is nam'd,
And rouse him at the name of Crispian.
He that shall live this day, and see old age,
Will yearly on the vigil feast his neighbours,
And say,—To-morrow is Saint Crispian :
Then will he strip his sleeve, and show his scars.
Old men forget ; yet all shall be forgot,
But he 'll remember with advantages,
What feats he did that day.   Then shall our names,   50
Familiar in his mouth as household words,—
Harry the king, Bedford and Exeter,
Warwick and Talbot, Salisbury and Gloster,—
Be in their flowing cups freshly remember'd.
This story shall the good man teach his son,
And Crispin Crispian shall ne'er go by,
From this day to the ending of the world,
But we in it shall be remember'd ;

We few, we happy few, we band of brothers :
For he to-day that sheds his blood with me   60
Shall be my brother ; be he ne'er so vile,
This day shall gentle his condition :
And gentlemen in England, now a-bed,
Shall think themselves accurs'd, they were not here,
And hold their manhoods cheap, whiles any speaks
That fought with us upon Saint Crispin's day.

Enter SALISBURY.

Sal. My sovereign lord, bestow yourself with speed:
The French are bravely in their battles set,
And will with all expedience charge on us.
K. Hen. All things are ready, if our minds be so. 70
West. Perish the man whose mind is backward
    now !
K. Hen. Thou dost not wish more help from Eng-
    land, cousin ?
West. God's will! my liege, 'would you and I
    alone,
Without more help, could fight this royal battle !
K. Hen. Why, now thou hast unwish'd five thou-
    sand men ;
Which likes me better than to wish us one.—
You know your places : God be with you all !

Tucket. Enter MONTJOY.

Mont. Once more I come to know of thee, King
    Harry,
If for thy ransom thou wilt now compound,
Before thy most assured overthrow :   80
For, certainly, thou art so near the gulf,
Thou needs must be englutted. Besides, in mercy,
The constable desires thee, thou wilt mind
Thy followers of repentance ; that their souls
May make a peaceful and a sweet retire
From off these fields, where, wretches, their poor
    bodies
Must lie and fester.
    K. Hen.   Who hath sent thee now ?
Mont. The constable of France.
K. Hen. I pray thee, bear my former answer back :
Bid them achieve me, and then sell my bones. 90
Good God ! why should they mock poor fellows thus ?
The man, that once did sell the lion's skin
While the beast liv'd, was kill'd with hunting him.
A many of our bodies shall, no doubt,
Find native graves ; upon the which, I trust,
Shall witness live in brass of this day's work;
And those that leave their valiant bones in France,
Dying like men, though buried in your dunghills,
They shall be fam'd : for there the sun shall greet
    them,
And draw their honours reeking up to heaven, 100
Leaving their earthly parts to choke your clime,
The smell whereof shall breed a plague in France.
Mark then abounding valour in our English ;
That, being dead, like to the bullet's grazing,
Break out into a second course of mischief,
Killing in relapse of mortality.
Let me speak proudly :—tell the constable,
We are but warriors for the working-day;
Our gayness and our gilt are all besmirch'd
With rainy marching in the painful field ; 110
There 's not a piece of feather in our host
(Good argument, I hope, we will not fly),
And time hath worn us into slovenry :
But, by the mass, our hearts are in the trim ;
And my poor soldiers tell me, yet ere night
They 'll be in fresher robes, or they will pluck
The gay new coats o'er the French soldiers' heads,
And turn them out of service. If they do this
(As, if God please, they shall), my ransom then
Will soon be levied. Herald, save thou thy labour ;
Come thou no more for ransom, gentle herald : 121
They shall have none, I swear, but these my joints ;
Which, if they have as I will leave 'em them,
Shall yield them little, tell the constable.
Mont. I shall, King Harry. And so fare thee well :
Thou never shalt hear herald any more.   [*Exit.*
K. Hen. I fear, thou 'lt once more come again for
    ransom.

Enter the Duke of YORK.

York. My lord, most humbly on my knee I beg
The leading of the vaward.
K. Hen. Take it, brave York.—Now, soldiers, march
    away :   130
And how thou pleasest, God, dispose the day !
            [*Exeunt.*

SCENE IV.—The Field of Battle.

Alarums ; Excursions. Enter French Soldier,
    PISTOL, *and Boy.*

Pist. Yield, cur !

Pist. " Yield, cur ! "

    *Fr. Sold. Je pense, que vous estes le gentilhomme de
bonne qualité.*
    Pist. Quality ? *Callino, castore me !* Art thou a
    gentleman ?
What is thy name ? discuss.
    Fr. Sold. O Seigneur Dieu !
    Pist. O, Signieur Dew should be a gentleman.
Perpend my words, O Signieur Dew, and mark :—
O Signieur Dew, thou diest on point of fox,
Except, O signieur, thou do give to me   10
Egregious ransom.
    *Fr. Sold. O, prenez misericorde ! ayez pitié de
moy !*
    Pist. Moy shall not serve, I will have forty moys ;
For I will fetch thy rim out at thy throat,
In drops of crimson blood.
    *Fr. Sold. Est il impossible d'eschapper la force de
ton bras ?*
    Pist. Brass, cur ?
Thou damned and luxurious mountain goat,   20
Offer'st me brass ?
    Fr. Sold. O pardonne moy !
    Pist. Say'st thou me so ? is that a ton of moys ?
Come hither, boy : ask me this slave in French,
What is his name.
    Boy. Escoutez : comment estes vous appellé ?
    Fr. Sold. Monsieur le Fer.
    Boy. He says, his name is Master Fer.
    Pist. Master Fer ! I 'll fer him, and firk him, and
ferret him.—Discuss the same in French unto him. 30
    Boy. I do not know the French for fer, and ferret,
and firk.
    Pist. Bid him prepare, for I will cut his throat.
    Fr. Sold. Que dit-il, monsieur ?
    *Boy. Il me commande à vous dire que vous faites
vous prest ; car ce soldat icy est disposé tout à cette
heure de couper vostre gorge.*
    Pist. Ouy, couper le gorge, par ma foy, peasant,

Unless thou give me crowns, brave crowns;
Or mangled shalt thou be by this my sword.   40
   Fr. Sold. *O, je vous supplie pour l'amour de Dieu,
me pardonner! Je suis le gentilhomme de bonne
maison: gardez ma vie, et je vous donneray deux
cents escus.*
   Pist. What are his words?
   Boy. He prays you to save his life: he is a gentleman of a good house; and, for his ransom, he will
give you two hundred crowns.
   Pist. Tell him,—my fury shall abate, and I the
     crowns will take.
   Fr. Sold. *Petit monsieur, que dit-il?*   50
   Boy. *Encore qu'il est contre son jurement, de pardonner aucun prisonier; neantmoins, pour les escus
que vous l'avez promis, il est content à vous donner
la liberté, le franchisement.*
   Fr. Sold. *Sur mes genoux, je vous donne mille
remerciemens; et je m'estime heureux que je suis
tombé entre les mains d'un chevalier, je pense, le plus
brave, valiant, et très-distingué seigneur d'Angleterre.*
   Pist. Expound unto me, boy.   59
   Boy. He gives you, upon his knees, a thousand
thanks; and he esteems himself happy that he hath
fallen into the hands of one (as he thinks) the most
brave, valorous, and thrice-worthy signieur of England.
   Pist. As I suck blood, I will some mercy show.
Follow me!   [*Exit.*
   Boy. *Suivez vous le grand capitain*. [*Exit French
Soldier.*] I did never know so full a voice issue from
so empty a heart: but the saying is true,—the empty
vessel makes the greatest sound. Bardolph and Nym
had ten times more valour than this roaring devil i'
the old play, that every one may pare his nails with a
wooden dagger; and they are both hanged; and so
would this be, if he durst steal anything adventu-
rously. I must stay with the lackeys, with the luggage
of our camp: the French might have a good prey of
us, if he knew of it; for there is none to guard it, but
boys.   [*Exit.*

SCENE V.—Another Part of the Field of Battle.

Alarums. Enter DAUPHIN, ORLEANS, BOURBON,
     Constable, RAMBURES, *and others.*

   Con. O diable!
   Orl. *O seigneur!—le jour est perdu! tout est perdu!*
   Dau. *Mort de ma vie!* all is confounded, all!
Reproach and everlasting shame
Sit mocking in our plumes.—*O meschante fortune!*
Do not run away.   [*A short alarum.*
   Con.   Why, all our ranks are broke.
   Dau. O perdurable shame!—let's stab ourselves.
Be these the wretches that we play'd at dice for?
   Orl. Is this the king we sent to for his ransom?
   Bour. Shame, and eternal shame, nothing but
     shame!   10
Let us die in honour!—Once more back again;
And he that will not follow Bourbon now,
Let him go hence, and, with his cap in hand,
Like a base pander, hold the chamber-door,
Whilst by a slave, no gentler than my dog,
His fairest daughter is contaminated.
   Con. Disorder, that hath spoil'd us, friend us now!
Let us, in heaps, go offer up our lives.
   Orl. We are enough, yet living in the field,
To smother up the English in our throngs,   20
If any order might be thought upon.
   Bour. The devil take order now! I'll to the throng:
Let life be short, else shame will be too long. [*Exeunt.*

SCENE VI.—Another Part of the Field.

Alarums. Enter King HENRY *and Forces;* EXETER,
     and others.

   K. Hen. Well have we done, thrice-valiant country-
     men:
But all's not done; yet keep the French the field.

   Exe. The Duke of York commends him to your
     majesty.
   K. Hen. Lives he, good uncle? thrice within this
     hour
I saw him down, thrice up again, and fighting;
From helmet to the spur all blood he was.
   Exe. In which array, brave soldier, doth he lie,
Larding the plain; and by his bloody side
(Yoke-fellow to his honour-owing wounds)
The noble Earl of Suffolk also lies.   10
Suffolk first died; and York, all haggled over,
Comes to him, where in gore he lay insteep'd,
And takes him by the beard, kisses the gashes,
That bloodily did yawn upon his face;
He cries aloud.—"Tarry, dear cousin Suffolk!
My soul shall thine keep company to heaven:
Tarry, sweet soul, for mine; then fly abreast,
As in this glorious and well-foughten field
We kept together in our chivalry!"
Upon these words I came and cheer'd him up: 20
He smil'd me in the face, raught me his hand,
And, with a feeble gripe, says, "Dear my lord,
Commend my service to my sovereign."
So did he turn, and over Suffolk's neck
He threw his wounded arm, and kiss'd his lips;
And so, espous'd to death, with blood he seal'd
A testament of noble-ending love.
The pretty and sweet manner of it forc'd
Those waters from me, which I would have stopp'd;
But I had not so much of man in me,   30
And all my mother came into mine eyes,
And gave me up to tears.
   K. Hen.   I blame you not;
For, hearing this, I must perforce compound
With mistful eyes, or they will issue too.—[*Alarum.*
But, hark! what new alarum is this same?—
The French have reinforc'd their scatter'd men:—
Then, every soldier kill his prisoners!
Give the word through.   [*Exeunt.*

SCENE VII.—Another Part of the Field.

Alarums. Enter FLUELLEN *and* GOWER.

   Flu. Kill thé poys and the luggage! 'tis expressly
against the law of arms: 'tis as arrant a piece of
knavery, mark you now, as can be offer't; in your
conscience now, is it not?
   Gow. 'T is certain, there's not a boy left alive; and
the cowardly rascals, that ran from the battle, have
done this slaughter: besides, they have burned and
carried away all that was in the king's tent; wherefore the king most worthily hath caused every soldier
to cut his prisoner's throat. O! 'tis a gallant king. 10
   Flu. Ay, he was porn at Monmouth, Captain Gower.
What call you the town's name, where Alexander the
Pig was born?
   Gow. Alexander the Great.
   Flu. Why, I pray you, is not pig, great? The pig,
or the great, or the mighty, or the huge, or the magnanimous, are all one reckonings, save the phrase is a
little variations.
   Gow. I think, Alexander the Great was born in
Macedon: his father was called Philip of Macedon, as
I take it.   21
   Flu. I think, it is in Macedon, where Alexander is
porn. I tell you, captain,—if you look in the maps of
the 'orld, I warrant, you shall find, in the comparisons
between Macedon and Monmouth, that the situations,
look you, is both alike. There is a river in Macedon,
and there is also moreover a river at Monmouth: it is
called Wye, at Monmouth; but it is out of my prains,
what is the name of the other river; but 'tis all one,
'tis alike as my fingers is to my fingers, and there is
salmons in both. If you mark Alexander's life well,
Harry of Monmouth's life is come after it indifferent
well; for there is figures in all things. Alexander,
(God knows, and you know,) in his rages, and his
furies, and his wraths, and his cholers, and his moods,
and his displeasures, and his indignations, and also
being a little intoxicates in his prains, did, in his ales
and his angers, look you, kill his pest friend, Cleitus.

Gow. Our king is not like him in that : he never
killed any of his friends.   40
Flu. It is not well done, mark you now, to take the
tales out of my mouth, ere it is made and finished. I
speak but in the figures and comparisons of it : as
Alexander killed his friend Cleitus, being in his ales
and his cups, so also Harry Monmouth, being in his
right wits and his good judgments, turned away the
fat knight with the great belly-doublet : he was full of
jests, and gipes, and knaveries, and mocks ; I have
forgot his name.
Gow. Sir John Falstaff.   50
Flu. That is he. I 'll tell you, there is good men porn
at Monmouth.
Gow. Here comes his majesty.

Alarum. Enter King HENRY, *with a part of the
English Forces ;* WARWICK, GLOSTER, EXETER,
and others.
K. Hen. I was not angry since I came to France
Until this instant.—Take a trumpet, herald ;
Ride thou unto the horsemen on yon hill :
If they will fight with us, bid them come down,
Or void the field ; they do offend our sight.
If they 'll do neither, we will come to them,
And make them skirr away, as swift as stones   60
Enforced from the old Assyrian slings.
Besides, we 'll cut the throats of those we have
And not a man of them, that we shall take,
Shall taste our mercy.—Go, and tell them so.

Enter MONTJOY.
Exe. Here comes the herald of the French, my liege.
Glo. His eyes are humbler than they us'd to be.
K. Hen. How now ! what means this, herald ?
know'st thou not,
That I have fin'd these bones of mine for ransom ?
Com'st thou again for ransom ?
Mont.   No, great king :   70
I come to thee for charitable license,
That we may wander o'er this bloody field,
To book our dead, and then to bury them ;
To sort our nobles from our common men ;
For many of our princes, woe the while !
Lie drown'd and soak'd in mercenary blood
(So do our vulgar drench their peasant limbs
In blood of princes) ; and their wounded steeds
Fret fetlock deep in gore, and with wild rage
Yerk out their armed heels at their dead masters,
Killing them twice. O ! give us leave, great king, 80
To view the field in safety, and dispose
Of their dead bodies.
K. Hen.   I tell thee truly, herald,
I know not if the day be ours, or no ;
For yet a many of your horsemen peer,
And gallop o'er the field.
Mont.   The day is yours.
K. Hen. Praised be God, and not our strength, for
it !—
What is this castle call'd, that stands hard by ?
Mont. They call it Agincourt.
K. Hen. Then call we this the field of Agincourt,
Fought on the day of Crispin Crispianus.   90
Flu. Your grandfather of famous memory, an 't
please your majesty, and your great-uncle Edward
the Plack Prince of Wales, as I have read in the
chronicles, fought a most prave pattle here in France.
K. Hen. They did, Fluellen.
Flu. Your majesty says very true. If your majesties is remembered of it, the Welshmen did good
service in a garden where leeks did grow, wearing
leeks in their Monmouth caps ; which, your majesty
know, to this hour is an honourable badge of the
service ; and, I do believe, your majesty takes no
scorn to wear the leek upon Saint Tavy's day.   102
K. Hen. I wear it for a memorable honour :
For I am Welsh, you know, good countryman.
Flu. All the water in Wye cannot wash your
majesty's Welsh plood out of your pody, I can tell you
that ; Got pless it, and preserve it, as long as it pleases
his grace, and his majesty too !
K. Hen. Thanks, good my countryman.

Flu. By Jeshu, I am your majesty's countryman, I
care not who know it ; I will confess it to all the 'orld :
I need not to be ashamed of your majesty, praised be
God, so long as your majesty is an honest man.
K. Hen. God keep me so !—Our heralds go with him :
Bring me just notice of the numbers dead,
On both our parts.—Call yonder fellow hither.
      [*Points to* WILLIAMS. *Exeunt* MONTJOY *and
            others.*
Exe. Soldier, you must come to the king.
K. Hen. Soldier, why wear'st thou that glove in thy
cap ?
Will. An 't please your majesty, 't is the gage of one
that I should fight withal, if he be alive.   121
K. Hen. An Englishman ?
Will. An 't please your majesty, a rascal that swag-
gered with me last night ; who, if 'a live and ever dare
to challenge this glove, I have sworn to take him a box
o' the ear : or, if I can see my glove in his cap (which
he swore, as he was a soldier, he would wear, if alive),
I will strike it out soundly.
K. Hen. What think you, Captain Fluellen ? is it fit
this soldier keep his oath.   130
Flu. He is a craven and a villain else, an 't please
your majesty, in my conscience.
K. Hen. It may be, his enemy is a gentleman of
great sort, quite from the answer of his degree.
Flu. Though he be as good a gentleman as the devil
is, as Lucifer and Belzebub himself, it is necessary,
look your grace, that he keep his vow and his oath.
If he be perjured, see you now, his reputation is as
arrant a villain, and a Jack-sauce, as ever his black
shoe trod upon God's ground and his earth, in my
conscience, la.   141
K. Hen. Then keep thy vow, sirrah, when thou
meet'st the fellow.
Will. So I will, my liege, as I live.
K. Hen. Who servest thou under ?
Will. Under Captain Gower, my liege.
Flu. Gower is a good captain, and is good knowe-
ledge, and literatured in the wars.   149
K. Hen. Call him hither to me, soldier.
Will. I will, my liege.   [*Exit.*
K. Hen. Here, Fluellen ; wear thou this favour for
me, and stick it in thy cap. When Alençon and myself were down together, I plucked this glove from his
helm : if any man challenge this, he is a friend to
Alençon, and an enemy to our person ; if thou encounter any such, apprehend him, an thou dost me
love.
Flu. Your grace does me as great honours as can be
desired in the hearts of his subjects : I would fain see
the man, that has but two legs, that shall find himself
aggriefed at this glove, that is all ; but I would fain see
it once, and please God of his grace, that I might see.
K. Hen. Knowest thou Gower ?   163
Flu. He is my dear friend, an 't please you.
K. Hen. Pray thee, go seek him, and bring him to
my tent.
Flu. I will fetch him.   [*Exit.*
K. Hen. My Lord of Warwick, and my brother
      Gloster,
Follow Fluellen closely at the heels.
The glove, which I have given him for a favour, 170
May haply purchase him a box o' the ear :
It is the soldier's ; I, by bargain, should
Wear it myself. Follow, good cousin Warwick :
If that the soldier strike him (as, I judge
By his bold bearing, he will keep his word),
Some sudden mischief may arise of it ;
For I do know Fluellen valiant,
And, touch'd with choler, hot as gunpowder,
And quickly will return an injury :
Follow, and see there be no harm between them.— 180
Go you with me, uncle of Exeter.   [*Exeunt.*

SCENE VIII.—Before King HENRY's Pavilion.

Enter GOWER *and* WILLIAMS.

Will. I warrant it is to knight you, captain.

Enter FLUELLEN.

Flu. God's will and his pleasure, captain, I beseech you now, come apace to the king: there is more good toward you, peradventure, than is in your knowledge to dream of.

Gow. How now, sir! you villain!

Will. Do you think I'll be forsworn?

Flu. Stand away, Captain Gower: I will give treason his payment into plows, I warrant you.

Will. I am no traitor.

Flu. That's a lie in thy throat.—I charge you in his

K. Hen.   "O God! thy arm was here,
And not to us, but to thy arm alone,
Ascribe we all."

Will. Sir, know you this glove?

Flu. Know the glove? I know, the glove is a glove.

Will. I know this, and thus I challenge it.
                                        [*Strikes him.*

Flu. 'Sblood! an arrant traitor, as any's in the universal 'orld, or in France, or in England.   110

majesty's name, apprehend him: he is a friend of the Duke Alençon's.

Enter WARWICK *and* GLOSTER.

War. How now, how now! what's the matter? 119

Flu. My Lord of Warwick, here is (praised be God

for it !) a most contagious treason come to light, look you, as you shall desire in a summer's day. Here is his majesty.

Enter King HENRY *and* EXETER.

K. Hen. How now ! what 's the matter?
Flu. My liege, here is a villain, and a traitor, that, look your grace, has struck the glove which your majesty is take out of the helmet of Alençon.
Will. My liege, this was my glove ; here is the fellow of it ; and he that I gave it to in change promised to wear it in his cap : I promised to strike him if he did. I met this man with my glove in his cap, and I have been as good as my word.   132
Flu. Your majesty hear now, saving your majesty's manhood, what an arrant, rascally, beggarly, lousy knave it is. I hope, your majesty is pear me testimony, and witness, and will avouchment, that this is the glove of Alençon, that your majesty is give me, in your conscience now.
K. Hen. Give me thy glove, soldier : look, here is the fellow of it.   140
'T was I, indeed, thou promisedst to strike ;
And thou hast given me most bitter terms.
Flu. An 't please your majesty, let his neck answer for it, if there is any martial law in the 'orld.
K. Hen. How canst thou make me satisfaction?
Will. All offences, my lord, come from the heart : never came any from mine, that might offend your majesty.
K. Hen. It was ourself thou didst abuse.   149
Will. Your majesty came not like yourself : you appeared to me but as a common man ; witness the night, your garments, your lowliness ; and what your highness suffered under that shape, I beseech you, take it for your own fault, and not mine : for had you been as I took you for, I made no offence ; therefore, I beseech your highness, pardon me.
K. Hen. Here, uncle Exeter, fill this glove with
            crowns,
And give it to this fellow.—Keep it, fellow,
And wear it for an honour in thy cap,
Till I do challenge it.—Give him the crowns.—   160
And, captain, you must needs be friends with him.
Flu. By this day and this light, the fellow has mettle enough in his belly.—Hold, there is twelve pence for you, and I pray you to serve God, and keep you out of prawls, and prabbles, and quarrels, and dissensions ; and, I warrant you, it is the better for you.
Will. I will none of your money.
Flu. It is with a good will ; I can tell you, it will serve you to mend your shoes : come, wherefore should you be so pashful? your shoes is not so good : 't is a good silling, I warrant you, or I will change it.

Enter an English Herald.

K. Hen. Now, herald, are the dead number'd?   172
Her. Here is the number of the slaughter'd French.
            [*Delivers a paper.*

K. Hen. What prisoners of good sort are taken,
            uncle?
Exe. Charles Duke of Orleans, nephew to the king ;
John Duke of Bourbon, and Lord Bouciqualt :
Of other lords, and barons, knights, and squires,
Full fifteen hundred, besides common men.
K. Hen. This note doth tell me of ten thousand
            French,
That in the field lie slain : of princes, in this number,
And nobles bearing banners, there lie dead   181
One hundred twenty-six : added to these,
Of knights, esquires, and gallant gentlemen,
Eight thousand and four hundred ; of the which,
Five hundred were but yesterday dubb'd knights :
So that, in these ten thousand they have lost,
There are but sixteen hundred mercenaries ;
The rest are princes, barons, lords, knights, squires,
And gentlemen of blood and quality.
The names of those their nobles that lie dead,—   190
Charles Delabreth, high constable of France ;
Jaques of Chatillon, admiral of France ;
The master of the cross-bows, Lord Rambures ;
Great-master of France, the brave Sir Guischard
            Dauphin ;
John Duke of Alençon ; Antony Duke of Brabant,
The brother to the Duke of Burgundy ;
And Edward Duke of Bar : of lusty earls,
Grandpré, and Roussi, Fauconberg, and Foix,
Beaumont, and Marle, Vaudemont, and Lestrale.
Here was a royal fellowship of death !—   200
Where is the number of our English dead?
            [*Herald presents another paper.*
Edward the Duke of York, the Earl of Suffolk,
Sir Richard Ketly, Davy Gam, esquire :
None else of name ; and of all other men,
But five-and-twenty. O God ! thy arm was here,
And not to us, but to thy arm alone,
Ascribe we all.—When, without stratagem,
But in plain shock and even play of battle,
Was ever known so great and little loss,
On one part and on the other?—Take it, God,   210
For it is none but thine !
Exe.   'T is wonderful !
K. Hen. Come, go we in procession to the village :
And be it death proclaimed through our host,
To boast of this, or take that praise from God,
Which is his only.
Flu. Is it not lawful, an 't please your majesty, to tell how many is killed?
K. Hen. Yes, captain ; but with this acknowledg-
            ment,
That God fought for us.
Flu. Yes, my conscience, he did us great good.   220
K. Hen. Do we all holy rites :
Let there be sung *Non nobis,* and *Te Deum,*
The dead with charity enclos'd in clay.
And then to Calais ; and to England then,
Where ne'er from France arriv'd more happy men.
            [*Exeunt.*

ACT V.

Enter Chorus.

Chorus.

VOUCHSAFE to those that have not read the story,
That I may prompt them: and of such as have,
I humbly pray them to admit the excuse
Of time, of numbers, and due course of things,
Which cannot in their huge and proper life
Be here presented. Now, we bear the king
Toward Calais: grant him there; there seen,
Heave him away upon your winged thoughts,
Athwart the sea. Behold, the English beach
Pales in the flood with men, with wives, and boys, 10
Whose shouts and claps out-voice the deep-mouth'd sea,
Which, like a mighty whiffler 'fore the king,
Seems to prepare his way. So, let him land,
And, solemnly, see him set on to London.
So swift a pace hath thought, that even now
You may imagine him upon Blackheath;
Where that his lords desire him to have borne
His bruised helmet, and his bended sword,
Before him, through the city: he forbids it,
Being free from vainness and self-glorious pride; 20
Giving full trophy, signal, and ostent,
Quite from himself, to God. But now behold,
In the quick forge and working-house of thought,
How London doth pour out her citizens.
The mayor, and all his brethren, in best sort,
Like to the senators of the antique Rome,
With the plebeians swarming at their heels,
Go forth, and fetch their conquering Cæsar in:
As, by a lower but loving likelihood,
Were now the general of our gracious empress 30
(As, in good time, he may) from Ireland coming,
Bringing rebellion broached on his sword,
How many would the peaceful city quit,
To welcome him! much more (and much more cause)
Did they this Harry. Now, in London place him;
As yet the lamentation of the French
Invites the King of England's stay at home
(The emperor coming in behalf of France,
To order peace between them)); and omit
All the occurrences, whatever chanc'd, 40
Till Harry's back-return again to France:
There must we bring him; and myself have play'd
The interim, by remembering you 't is past.
Then brook abridgment, and your eyes advance,
After your thoughts, straight back again to France.
[Exit.

SCENE I.—France. An English Court of Guard.

Enter FLUELLEN and GOWER.

Gow. Nay, that 's right; but why wear you your leek to-day? Saint Davy's day is past.

Flu. There is occasions, and causes, why and wherefore, in all things: I will tell you, as my friend, Captain Gower. The rascally, scald, beggarly, lousy, pragging knave, Pistol, which you and yourself, and all the 'orld, know to be no petter than a fellow, look you now, of no merits, he is come to me, and prings me pread and salt yesterday, look you, and bid me eat my leek. It was in a place where I could not breed no contention with him; but I will be so bold as to wear it in my cap till I see him once again, and then I will tell him a little piece of my desires.

Gow. Why, here he comes, swelling like a turkey-cock.

Enter PISTOL.

Flu. 'T is no matter for his swellings, nor his turkey-cocks.—God pless you, Aunchient Pistol! you scurvy, lousy knave, God pless you!

Pist. Ha! art thou Bedlam? dost thou thirst, base Trojan,
To have me fold up Parca's fatal web? 20
Hence! I am qualmish at the smell of leek.

Flu. I peseech you heartily, scurvy lousy knave, at my desires, and my requests, and my petitions, to eat, look you, this leek; because, look you, you do not love it, nor your affections, and your appetites, and your digestions, does not agree with it, I would desire you to eat it.

Pist. Not for Cadwallader, and all his goats.

Flu. There is one goat for you. [*Strikes him.*] Will you be so good, scald knave, as eat it? 30

Pist. Base Trojan, thou shalt die.

Flu. You say very true, scald knave, when God's will is. I will desire you to live in the meantime, and eat your victuals: come, there is sauce for it. [*Striking him again.*] You called me yesterday mountain-squire, but I will make you to-day a squire of low degree. I pray you, fall to: if you can mock a leek, you can eat a leek.

Gow. Enough, captain: you have astonished him. 39

Flu. I say, I will make him eat some part of my leek, or I will peat his pate four days.—Bite, I pray you; it is good for your green wound, and your ploody coxcomb.

Pist. Must I bite?

Flu. Yes, certainly, and out of doubt, and out of question too, and ambiguities.

Pist. By this leek, I will most horribly revenge. I eat, and eat I swear—

Flu. Eat, I pray you. Will you have some more sauce to your leek? there is not enough leek to swear by. 51

Pist. Quiet thy cudgel: thou dost see, I eat.

Flu. Much good do you, scald knave, heartily. Nay, pray you, throw none away; the skin is good for your broken coxcomb. When you take occasions to see leeks hereafter, I pray you, mock at 'em; that is all.

Pist. Good.

Flu. Ay, leeks is good.—Hold you, there is a groat to heal your pate. 60

Pist. Me a groat!

Flu. Yes, verily, and in truth, you shall take it, or I have another leek in my pocket, which you shall eat.

Pist. I take thy groat, in earnest of revenge.

Flu. If I owe you anything, I will pay you in cudgels : you shall be a woodmonger, and buy nothing of me but cudgels. God be wi' you, and keep you, and heal your pate.   [*Exit.*
Pist. All hell shall stir for this.   70
Gow. Go, go ; you are a counterfeit cowardly knave. Will you mock at an ancient tradition, begun upon an honourable respect, and worn as a memorable trophy of predeceased valour, and dare not avouch in your deeds any of your words? I have seen you gleeking and galling at this gentleman twice or

Flu. "Will you have some more sauce to your leek?"

thrice. You thought, because he could not speak English in the native garb, he could not therefore handle an English cudgel: you find it otherwise; and, henceforth, let a Welsh correction teach you a good English condition. Fare ye well.   [*Exit.*
Pist. Doth Fortune play the huswife with me now? News have I, that my Nell is dead i' the spital Of malady of France ;
And there my rendezvous is quite cut off.
Old I do wax, and from my weary limbs
Honour is cudgelled. Well, bawd I'll turn,
And something lean to cutpurse of quick hand.
To England will I steal, and there I'll steal :
And patches will I get unto these cudgell'd scars, 90
And swear, I got them in the Gallia wars.   [*Exit.*

SCENE II.—Troyes in Champagne. An Apartment in the French KING'S Palace.

Enter, at one door, King HENRY, BEDFORD, GLOSTER, EXETER, WARWICK, WESTMORELAND, *and other Lords; at another, the French* KING, *Queen* ISABEL, *the Princess* KATHARINE, *Lords, Ladies, &c., the Duke of* BURGUNDY, *and his Train.*

K. Hen. Peace to this meeting, wherefore we are met !
Unto our brother France, and to our sister,
Health and fair time of day ;—joy and good wishes
To our most fair and princely cousin Katharine ;—
And, as a branch and member of this royalty,
By whom this great assembly is contriv'd,
We do salute you, Duke of Burgundy :—
And, princes French, and peers, health to you all !
Fr. King. Right joyous are we to behold your face,
Most worthy brother England ; fairly met :—   10
So are you, princes English, every one.

Q. Isa. So happy be the issue, brother England,
Of this good day, and of this gracious meeting,
As we are now glad to behold your eyes ;
Your eyes, which hitherto have borne in them
Against the French, that met them in their bent,
The fatal balls of murdering basilisks :
The venom of such looks, we fairly hope,
Have lost their quality, and that this day
Shall change all griefs and quarrels into love.   20
K. Hen. To cry Amen to that, thus we appear.
Q. Isa. You English princes all, I do salute you.
Bur. My duty to you both, on equal love.
Great Kings of France and England, that I have labour'd
With all my wits, my pains, and strong endeavours,
To bring your most imperial majesties
Unto this bar and royal interview,
Your mightiness on both parts best can witness.
Since then my office hath so far prevail'd,
That face to face, and royal eye to eye,   30
You have congreeted, let it not disgrace me,
If I demand before this royal view,
What rub, or what impediment, there is,
Why that the naked, poor, and mangled Peace,
Dear nurse of arts, plenties, and joyful births,
Should not in this best garden of the world,
Our fertile France, put up her lovely visage?
Alas ! she hath from France too long been chas'd,
And all her husbandry doth lie on heaps,
Corrupting in its own fertility.   40
Her vine, the merry cheerer of the heart,
Unpruned dies ; her edges even-pleached,
Like prisoners wildly overgrown with hair,
Put forth disorder'd twigs ; her fallow leas
The darnel, hemlock, and rank fumitory,
Doth root upon, while that the coulter rusts,
That should deracinate such savagery ;
The even mead, that erst brought sweetly forth
The freckled cowslip, burnet, and green clover,
Wanting the scythe, all uncorrected, rank,   50
Conceives by idleness, and nothing teems,
But hateful docks, rough thistles, kecksies, burs,
Losing both beauty and utility ;
And as our vineyards, fallows, meads, and hedges,
Defective in their natures, grow to wildness ;
Even so our houses, and ourselves, and children,
Have lost, or do not learn, for want of time,
The sciences that should become our country,
But grow, like savages,—as soldiers will,
That nothing do but meditate on blood,—   60
To swearing, and stern looks, diffus'd attire,
And everything that seems unnatural.
Which to reduce into our former favour,
You are assembled ; and my speech entreats,
That I may know the let, why gentle Peace
Should not expel these inconveniencies,
And bless us with her former qualities.
K. Hen. If, Duke of Burgundy, you would the peace,
Whose want gives growth to the imperfections
Which you have cited, you must buy that peace   70
With full accord to all our just demands ;
Whose tenors and particular effects
You have, enschedul'd briefly, in your hands.
Bur. The king hath heard them ; to the which, as yet,
There is no answer made.
K. Hen.   Well then, the peace
Which you before so urg'd, lies in his answer.
Fr. King. I have but with a cursorary eye
O'erglanc'd the articles : pleaseth your grace
To appoint some of your council presently
To sit with us once more, with better heed   80
To re-survey them, we will suddenly
Pass our accept, and peremptory answer.
K. Hen. Brother, we shall.—Go, uncle Exeter,—
And brother Clarence,—and you, brother Gloster,—
Warwick,—and Huntington,—go with the king ;
And take with you free power to ratify,
Augment, or alter, as your wisdoms best
Shall see advantageable for our dignity,
Anything in, or out of, our demands,

And we 'll consign thereto.—Will you, fair sister,   90
Go with the princes, or stay here with us?

Q. Isa. Our gracious brother, I will go with them.
Haply a woman's voice may do some good,
When articles, too nicely urg'd, be stood on.

K. Hen. Yet leave our cousin Katharine here with
     us:
She is our capital demand, compris'd
Within the fore-rank of our articles.

Q. Isa. She hath good leave.

     [*Exeunt all but King* HENRY, KATHARINE,
     and her Gentlewoman.

K. Hen.   Fair Katharine, and most fair!
Will you vouchsafe to teach a soldier terms,
Such as will enter at a lady's ear,   100
And plead his love-suit to her gentle heart?

Kath. Your majesty shall mock at me; I cannot
speak your England.

K. Hen. O fair Katharine! if you will love me
soundly with your French heart, I will be glad to
hear you confess it brokenly with your English
tongue. Do you like me, Kate?

Kath. *Pardonnez-moy,* I cannot tell vat is—like
me.

K. Hen. An angel is like you, Kate; and you are
like an angel.   111

Kath. *Que dit-il? que je suis semblable à les anges?*

Alice. *Ouy, vrayment, sauf vostre grace, ainsi
dit-il.*

K. Hen. I said so, dear Katharine, and I must not
blush to affirm it.

Kath. *O bon Dieu! les langues des hommes sont
pleines de tromperies.*

K. Hen. What says she, fair one? that the tongues
of men are full of deceits?   120

Alice. *Ouy;* dat de tongues of de mans is be full of
deceits: dat is de princess.

K. Hen. The princess is the better Englishwoman.
I' faith, Kate, my wooing is fit for thy understanding:
I am glad, thou canst speak no better English; for,
if thou couldst, thou wouldst find me such a plain
king, that thou wouldst think, I had sold my farm to
buy my crown. I know no ways to mince it in love,
but directly to say—I love you: then, if you urge me
further than to say—Do you in faith? I wear out my
suit. Give me your answer; i' faith, do, and so clap
hands and a bargain. How say you, lady?   132

Kath. *Sauf vostre honneur,* me understand well.

K. Hen. Marry, if you would put me to verses, or
to dance for your sake, Kate, why you undid me:
for the one, I have neither words nor measure; and
for the other, I have no strength in measure, yet a
reasonable measure in strength. If I could win a
lady at leap-frog, or by vaulting into my saddle with
my armour on my back, under the correction of
bragging be it spoken, I should quickly leap into a
wife. Or if I might buffet for my love, or bound my
horse for her favours, I could lay on like a butcher,
and sit like a jack-an-apes, never off; but, before
God, Kate, I cannot look greenly, nor gasp out my
eloquence, nor I have no cunning in protestation;
only downright oaths, which I never use till urged,
nor never break for urging. If thou canst love a
fellow of this temper, Kate, whose face is not worth
sun-burning, that never looks in his glass for love of
anything he sees there, let thine eye be thy cook.
I speak to thee plain soldier: if thou canst love me
for this, take me; if not, to say to thee, that I shall
die, is true; but for thy love, by the Lord, no; yet
I love thee too. And while thou livest, dear Kate,
take a fellow of plain and uncoined constancy, for he
perforce must do thee right, because he hath not
the gift to woo in other places; for these fellows
of infinite tongue, that can rhyme themselves into
ladies' favours, they do always reason themselves out
again. What! a speaker is but a prater; a rhyme
is but a ballad. A good leg will fall, a straight back
will stoop, a black beard will turn white, a curled
pate will grow bald, a fair face will wither, a full eye
will wax hollow; but a good heart, Kate, is the sun
and the moon; or, rather, the sun, and not the moon,
for it shines bright, and never changes, but keeps his

course truly. If thou would have such a one, take
me; and take me, take a soldier; take a soldier, take
a king. And what sayest thou then to my love?
speak, my fair, and fairly, I pray thee.   171

Kath. Is it possible dat I sould love de enemy of
Fraunce?

K. Hen. No; it is not possible you should love
the enemy of France, Kate; but, in loving me, you
should love the friend of France, for I love France so
well, that I will not part with a village of it; I will
have it all mine: and, Kate, when France is mine
and I am yours, then yours is France, and you are
mine.   180

Kath. I cannot tell vat is dat.

K. Hen. No, Kate? I will tell thee in French, which
I am sure will hang upon my tongue like a new-
married wife about her husband's neck, hardly to be
shook off.—*Quand j'ay le possession de France, et
quand vous avez le possession de moy,* (let me see,
what then? Saint Dennis be my speed!)—*donc vostre
est France, et vous estes mienne.* It is as easy for me,
Kate, to conquer the kingdom, as to speak so much
more French. I shall never move thee in French,
unless it be to laugh at me.   191

Kath. *Sauf vostre honneur, le François que vous
parlez est meilleur que l'Anglois lequel je parle.*

K. Hen. No, 'faith, is 't not, Kate; but thy speaking
of my tongue, and I thine, most truly falsely, must
needs be granted to be much at one. But, Kate, dost
thou understand thus much English? Canst thou
love me?

Kath. I cannot tell.   199

K. Hen. Can any of your neighbours tell, Kate?
I'll ask them. Come, I know, thou lovest me: and
at night when you come into your closet, you 'll
question this gentlewoman about me; and I know,
Kate, you will, to her, dispraise those parts in me,
that you love with your heart: but, good Kate, mock
me mercifully; the rather, gentle princess, because I
love thee cruelly. If ever thou be'st mine, Kate, (as I
have a saving faith within me tells me thou shalt) I
get thee with scambling, and thou must therefore
needs prove a good soldier-breeder. Shall not thou
and I, between Saint Dennis and Saint George, compound a boy, half French, half English, that shall go
to Constantinople, and take the Turk by the beard?
shall we not? what sayest thou, my fair flower-de-
luce?

Kath. I do not know dat.

K. Hen. No; 'tis hereafter to know, but now to
promise: do but now promise, Kate, you will endeavour for your French part of such a boy, and for
my English moiety take the word of a king and a
bachelor. How answer you, *la plus belle Katharine
du monde, mon très cher et divin déesse?*   222

Kath. Your *majesté* have *fausse* French enough to
deceive de most *sage damoiselle* dat is *en France.*

K. Hen. Now, fie upon my false French! By mine
honour, in true English, I love thee, Kate: by which
honour I dare not swear thou lovest me; yet my blood
begins to flatter me that thou dost, notwithstanding
the poor and untempering effect of my visage. Now
beshrew my father's ambition! he was thinking of
civil wars when he got me: therefore was I created
with a stubborn outside, with an aspect of iron, that,
when I come to woo ladies, I fright them. But, in
faith, Kate, the elder I wax, the better I shall appear:
my comfort is, that old age, that ill layer-up of beauty,
can do no more spoil upon my face: thou hast me, if
thou hast me, at the worst; and thou shalt wear me,
if thou wear me, better and better. And therefore
tell me, most fair Katharine, will you have me? Put
off your maiden blushes; avouch the thoughts of your
heart with the looks of an empress; take me by the
hand, and say—Harry of England, I am thine: which
word thou shalt no sooner bless mine ear withal, but
I will tell thee aloud—England is thine, Ireland is
thine, France is thine, and Henry Plantagenet is
thine; who, though I speak it before his face, if he
be not fellow with the best king, thou shalt find the
best king of good fellows. Come, your answer in
broken music: for thy voice is music, and thy English

broken ; therefore, queen of all, Katharine, break thy
mind to me in broken English : wilt thou have me ?
   Kath. Dat is, as it shall please de *roy mon père.* 252
   K. Hen. Nay, it will please him well, Kate : it shall
please him, Kate.

   K. Hen. Then I will kiss your lips, Kate.
   *Kath. Les dames, et damoiselles, pour estre
baisées devant leur nopces, il n'est pas le costume de
France.*
   K. Hen. Madam my interpreter, what says she ?

K. Hen. "O Kate! nice customs curtesy to great kings."

   Kath. Den it sall also content me.
   K. Hen. Upon that I kiss your hand, and I call you
my queen.
   *Kath. Laissez, mon seigneur, laissez, laissez !
Ma foy, je ne veux point que vous abbaissez vostre
grandeur, en baisant le main d'une vostre indigne
serviteur : excusez moy, je vous supplie, mon très
puissant seigneur.*   262

   Alice. Dat it is not be de fashion *pour les* ladies of
France,—I cannot tell what is *baiser* in English.
   K. Hen. To kiss.   270
   Alice. Your majesty *entendre* bettre *que moy.*
   K. Hen. It is not a fashion for the maids in France
to kiss before they are married, would she say ?
   Alice. Ouy, vraiment.
   K. Hen. O Kate ! nice customs curtesy to great

kings. Dear Kate, you and I cannot be confined within the weak list of a country's fashion : we are the makers of manners, Kate ; and the liberty that follows our places stops the mouths of all find-faults, as I will do yours, for upholding the nice fashion of your country in denying me a kiss : therefore, patiently, and yielding. [*Kissing her.*] You have witchcraft in your lips, Kate : there is more eloquence in a sugar touch of them, than in the tongues of the French council ; and they should sooner persuade Harry of England, than a general petition of monarchs. Here comes your father.

Enter the French KING *and* QUEEN, BURGUNDY, BEDFORD, GLOSTER, EXETER, WESTMORELAND, *and other French and English Lords.*

Bur. God save your majesty ! My royal cousin, Teach you our princess English ?

K. Hen. I would have her learn, my fair cousin, how perfectly I love her ; and that is good English.

Bur. Is she not apt ?   292

K. Hen. Our tongue is rough, coz, and my condition is not smooth ; so that, having neither the voice nor the heart of flattery about me, I cannot so conjure up the spirit of love in her, that he will appear in his true likeness.

Bur. Pardon the frankness of my mirth, if I answer you for that. If you would conjure in her, you must make a circle ; if conjure up love in her in his true likeness, he must appear naked, and blind. Can you blame her, then, being a maid yet rosed over with the virgin crimson of modesty, if she deny the appearance of a naked blind boy in her naked seeing self ? It were, my lord, a hard condition for a maid to consign to.

K. Hen. Yet they do wink, and yield, as love is blind, and enforces.

Bur. They are then excused, my lord, when they see not what they do.   310

K. Hen. Then, good my lord, teach your cousin to consent winking.

Bur. I will wink on her to consent, my lord, if you will teach her to know my meaning : for maids, well summered and warm kept, are like flies at Bartholomew-tide, blind, though they have their eyes ; and then they will endure handling, which before would not abide looking on.

K. Hen. This moral ties me over to time, and a hot summer ; and so I shall catch the fly, your cousin, in the latter end, and she must be blind too.   321

Bur. As love is, my lord, before it loves.

K. Hen. It is so : and you may, some of you, thank love for my blindness, who cannot see many a fair French city, for one fair French maid that stands in my way.

Fr. King. Yes, my lord, you see them perspectively : the cities turned into a maid ; for they are all girdled with maiden walls, that war hath never entered.

K. Hen. Shall Kate be my wife ?   330

Fr. King. So please you.

K. Hen. I am content ; so the maiden cities you talk of, may wait on her : so the maid, that stood in the way for my wish, shall show me the way to my will.

Fr. King. We have consented to all terms of reason.

K. Hen. Is 't so, my lords of England ?

West. The king hath granted every article : His daughter, first ; and then, in sequel, all, According to their firm proposed natures.   340

Exe. Only, he hath not yet subscribed this :— Where your majesty demands,—that the King of France, having any occasion to write for matter of grant, shall name your highness in this form, and with this addition, in French,—*Notre très cher filz Henry roy d' Angleterre, heretier de France ;* and thus in Latin,—*Præclarissimus filius noster Henricus, rex Angliæ, et hæres Franciæ.*

Fr. King. Nor this I have not, brother, so denied, But your request shall make me let it pass.   350

K. Hen. I pray you then, in love and dear alliance, Let that one article rank with the rest ; And, thereupon, give me your daughter.

Fr. King. Take her, fair son ; and from her blood raise up Issue to me, that the contending kingdoms Of France and England, whose very shores look pale With envy of each other's happiness, May cease their hatred ; and this dear conjunction Plant neighbourhood and Christian-like accord In their sweet bosoms, that never war advance   360 His bleeding sword 'twixt England and fair France.

All. Amen !

K. Hen. Now welcome, Kate :—and bear me witness all, That here I kiss her as my sovereign queen.
                                            [*Flourish.*

Q. Isa. God, the best maker of all marriages, Combine your hearts in one, your realms in one ! As man and wife, being two, are one in love, So be there 'twixt your kingdoms such a spousal, That never may ill office, or fell jealousy, Which troubles oft the bed of blessed marriage,   370 Thrust in between the paction of these kingdoms, To make divorce of their incorporate league ; That English may as French, French Englishmen, Receive each other !—God speak this Amen !

All. Amen !

K. Hen. Prepare we for our marriage :—on which day, My Lord of Burgundy, we 'll take your oath, And all the peers', for surety of our leagues. Then shall I swear to Kate, and you to me ; And may our oaths well kept and prosperous be !   380
                                            [*Exeunt.*

Enter Chorus.

Chor. Thus far, with rough and all-unable pen, Our bending author hath pursu'd the story ; In little room confining mighty men, Mangling by starts the full course of their glory. Small time, but in that small most greatly liv'd This star of England. Fortune made his sword, By which the world's best garden he achiev'd, And of it left his son imperial lord. Henry the Sixth, in infant bands crown'd king Of France and England, did this king succeed ;   10 Whose state so many had the managing, That they lost France, and made his England bleed : Which oft our stage hath shown ; and, for their sake, In your fair minds let this acceptance take.   [*Exit.*

KING HENRY VI.—PART I.

DRAMATIS PERSONÆ.

KING HENRY THE SIXTH.
DUKE OF GLOSTER, *Uncle to the King, and Pro-
tector.*
DUKE OF BEDFORD, *Uncle to the King, Regent of
France.*
THOMAS BEAUFORT, *Duke of Exeter, Great-uncle to
the King.*
HENRY BEAUFORT, *Bishop of Winchester.*
JOHN BEAUFORT, *Earl of Somerset.*
RICHARD PLANTAGENET, *Duke of York.*
EARL OF WARWICK.
EARL OF SALISBURY.
EARL OF SUFFOLK.
TALBOT, *afterwards Earl of Shrewsbury.*
JOHN TALBOT, *his Son.*
EDMUND MORTIMER, *Earl of March.*
Mortimer's Keeper, and a Lawyer.
SIR JOHN FASTOLFE, SIR WILLIAM LUCY, SIR
WILLIAM GLANSDALE, SIR THOMAS GARGRAVE.
WOODVILLE, *Lieutenant of the Tower.*
Mayor of London.

VERNON, *of the White-Rose or York Faction.*
BASSET, *of the Red-Rose or Lancaster Faction.*

CHARLES, *Dauphin, and afterwards King of France.*
REIGNIER, *Duke of Anjou, and titular King of
Naples.*
DUKE OF BURGUNDY, DUKE OF ALENÇON.
BASTARD OF ORLEANS.
Governor of Paris.
Master-Gunner of Orleans, and his Son.
General of the French Forces in Bordeaux.
A French Sergeant. A Porter.
An old Shepherd, Father to Joan la Pucelle.

MARGARET, *Daughter to Reignier.*
COUNTESS OF AUVERGNE.
JOAN LA PUCELLE, *commonly called Joan of Arc.*

*Fiends appearing to La Pucelle, Lords, Warders
of the Tower, Heralds, Officers, Soldiers, Messengers, and several Attendants both on the
English and French.*

SCENE—Partly in England, and partly in France.

ACT I.

SCENE I.—Westminster Abbey.

Dead March. The Corse of King HENRY *the Fifth is discovered, lying in state; attended on by the
Dukes of* BEDFORD, GLOSTER, *and* EXETER; *the Earl of* WARWICK, *the Bishop of* WINCHESTER,
Heralds, &c.

Bedford.

HUNG be the heavens with black, yield day
to night!
Comets, importing change of times and
states,
Brandish your crystal tresses in the sky,
And with them scourge the bad revolting
stars,
That have consented unto Henry's death!
King Henry the Fifth, too famous to live
long!
England ne'er lost a king of so much worth.
Glo. England ne'er had a king, until his time.
Virtue he had, deserving to command:
His brandish'd sword did blind men with his beams:
His arms spread wider than a dragon's wings;   11
His sparkling eyes, replete with wrathful fire,
More dazzled and drove back his enemies,
Than mid-day sun, fierce bent against their faces.
What should I say? his deeds exceed all speech:
He ne'er lift up his hand, but conquered.
Exe. We mourn in black: why mourn we not in
blood?
Henry is dead, and never shall revive.
Upon a wooden coffin we attend;
And death's dishonourable victory   20
We with our stately presence glorify,
Like captives bound to a triumphant car.
What! shall we curse the planets of mishap,
That plotted thus our glory's overthrow?
Or shall we think the subtle-witted French

Conjurers and sorcerers, that, afraid of him,
By magic verses have contriv'd his end?
Win. He was a king, bless'd of the King of kings.
Unto the French the dreadful judgment-day
So dreadful will not be, as was his sight.   30
The battles of the Lord of hosts he fought:
The Church's prayers made him so prosperous.
Glo. The Church! where is it? Had not Church-
men pray'd,
His thread of life had not so soon decay'd:
None do you like but an effeminate prince,
Whom, like a school-boy, you may over-awe.
Win. Gloster, whate'er we like, thou art protector,
And lookest to command the prince and realm.
Thy wife is proud; she holdeth thee in awe,
More than God or religious Churchmen may.   40
Glo. Name not religion, for thou lov'st the flesh;
And ne'er throughout the year to church thou go'st,
Except it be to pray against thy foes.
Bed. Cease, cease these jars, and rest your minds in
peace!
Let's to the altar:—heralds, wait on us.—
Instead of gold, we'll offer up our arms,
Since arms avail not, now that Henry's dead.
Posterity, await for wretched years,
When at their mothers' moist eyes babes shall suck,
Our isle be made a marish of salt tears,   50
And none but women left to wail the dead.—
Henry the Fifth! thy ghost I invocate:
Prosper this realm, keep it from civil broils!
Combat with adverse planets in the heavens!

A far more glorious star thy soul will make,
Than Julius Cæsar, or bright—

Enter a Messenger.

Mess. My honourable lords, health to you all.
Sad tidings bring I to you out of France,
Of loss, of slaughter, and discomfiture:
Guienne, Champaigne, Rheims, Orleans,   60
Paris, Guysors, Poictiers, are all quite lost.
Bed. What say'st thou, man! before dead Henry's
        corse
Speak softly, or the loss of those great towns
Will make him burst his lead, and rise from death.
Glo. Is Paris lost? is Roan yielded up?
If Henry were recall'd to life again,
These news would cause him once more yield the
        ghost.
Exe. How were they lost? what treachery was us'd?
Mess. No treachery; but want of men and money.
Among the soldiers this is muttered,—   70
That here you maintain several factions;
And, whilst a field should be despatch'd and fought,
You are disputing of your generals.
One would have lingering wars with little cost;
Another would fly swift, but wanteth wings;
A third man thinks, without expense at all,
By guileful fair words peace may be obtain'd.
Awake, awake, English nobility!
Let not sloth dim your honours new-begot:
Cropp'd are the flower-de-luces in your arms;   80
Of England's coat one half is cut away.
Exe. Were our tears wanting to this funeral,
These tidings would call forth their flowing tides.
Bed. Me they concern; regent I am of France.—
Give me my steeled coat! I'll fight for France.—
Away with these disgraceful wailing robes!
Wounds will I lend the French, instead of eyes,
To weep their intermissive miseries.

Enter another Messenger.

2 Mess. Lords, view these letters, full of bad mis-
        chance.
France is revolted from the English quite,   90
Except some petty towns of no import:
The Dauphin Charles is crowned king in Rheims;
The Bastard of Orleans with him is join'd;
Reignier, Duke of Anjou, doth take his part;
The Duke of Alençon flieth to his side.
Exe. The Dauphin crowned king! all fly to him!
O! whither shall we fly from this reproach?
Glo. We will not fly, but to our enemies' throats.—
Bedford, if thou be slack, I'll fight it out.
Bed. Gloster, why doubt'st thou of my forward-
        ness?   100
An army have I muster'd in my thoughts,
Wherewith already France is overrun.

Enter a third Messenger.

3 Mess. My gracious lords, to add to your laments,
Wherewith you now bedew King Henry's hearse,
I must inform you of a dismal fight
Betwixt the stout Lord Talbot and the French.
Win. What! wherein Talbot overcame? is't so?
3 Mess. O, no! wherein Lord Talbot was o'er-
        thrown:
The circumstance I'll tell you more at large.
The tenth of August last, this dreadful lord,   110
Retiring from the siege of Orleans,
Having full scarce six thousand in his troop,
By three-and-twenty thousand of the French
Was round encompassed and set upon.
No leisure had he to enrank his men;
He wanted pikes to set before his archers;
Instead whereof, sharp stakes, pluck'd out of hedges,
They pitched in the ground confusedly,
To keep the horsemen off from breaking in.
More than three hours the fight continued: 120
Where valiant Talbot, above human thought,
Enacted wonders with his sword and lance.
Hundreds he sent to hell, and none durst stand
        him:
Here, there, and everywhere, enrag'd he flew.

The French exclaim'd, the devil was in arms;
All the whole army stood agaz'd on him.
His soldiers, spying his undaunted spirit,
A Talbot! a Talbot! cried out amain,
And rush'd into the bowels of the battle.
Here had the conquest fully been seal'd up,   130
If Sir John Fastolfe had not play'd the coward.
He, being in the vaward, plac'd behind
With purpose to relieve and follow them,
Cowardly fled, not having struck one stroke.
Hence grew the general wrack and massacre:
Enclosed were they with their enemies.
A base Walloon, to win the Dauphin's grace,
Thrust Talbot with a spear into the back;
Whom all France, with their chief assembled strength,
Durst not presume to look once in the face.   140
Bed. Is Talbot slain? then I will slay myself,
For living idly here in pomp and ease,
Whilst such a worthy leader, wanting aid,
Unto his bastard foemen is betray'd.
3 Mess. O, no! he lives; but is took prisoner,
And Lord Scales with him, and Lord Hungerford:
Most of the rest slaughter'd, or took, likewise.
Bed. His ransom there is none but I shall pay.
I'll hale the Dauphin headlong from his throne;
His crown shall be the ransom of my friend;   150
Four of their lords I'll change for one of ours.—
Farewell, my masters; to my task will I.
Bonfires in France forthwith I am to make,
To keep our great Saint George's feast withal:
Ten thousand soldiers with me I will take,
Whose bloody deeds shall make all Europe quake.
3 Mess. So you had need; for Orleans is besieg'd:
The English army is grown weak and faint;
The Earl of Salisbury craveth supply,
And hardly keeps his men from mutiny,   160
Since they, so few, watch such a multitude.
Exe. Remember, lords, your oaths to Henry sworn,
Either to quell the Dauphin utterly,
Or bring him in obedience to your yoke.
Bed. I do remember it; and here take my leave,
To go about my preparation.   [*Exit.*
Glo. I'll to the Tower, with all the haste I can,
To view the artillery and munition;
And then I will proclaim young Henry king. [*Exit.*
Exe. To Eltham will I, where the young king is, 170
Being ordain'd his special governor;
And for his safety there I'll best devise. [*Exit.*
Win. Each hath his place and function to attend:
I am left out; for me nothing remains.
But long I will not be Jack-out-of-office.
The king from Eltham I intend to steal,
And sit at chiefest stern of public weal.   [*Exeunt.*

SCENE II.—France. Before Orleans.

Flourish. Enter CHARLES, *with his Forces;*
ALENÇON, REIGNIER, *and others.*

Char. Mars his true moving, even as in the
        heavens,
So in the earth, to this day is not known.
Late did he shine upon the English side;
Now we are victors, upon us he smiles.
What towns of any moment but we have?
At pleasure here we lie near Orleans;
Otherwhiles, the famish'd English, like pale ghosts,
Faintly besiege us one hour in a month.
Alen. They want their porridge, and their fat bull-
        beeves:
Either they must be dieted like mules,   10
And have their provender tied to their mouths,
Or piteous they will look like drowned mice.
Reig. Let's raise the siege. Why live we idly here?
Talbot is taken, whom we wont to fear:
Remaineth none but mad-brain'd Salisbury,
And he may well in fretting spend his gall;
Nor men nor money hath he to make war.
Char. Sound, sound alarum! we will rush on
        them.
Now for the honour of the forlorn French!

Him I forgive my death, that killeth me, 20
When he sees me go back one foot, or fly. [*Exeunt.*

*Alarums; Excursions; afterwards a Retreat. Re-
enter* CHARLES, ALENÇON, REIGNIER, *and others.*

Char. Who ever saw the like? what men have
I!—
Dogs! cowards! dastards!—I would ne'er have fled,
But that they left me 'midst my enemies.
Reig. Salisbury is a desperate homicide;
He fighteth as one weary of his life:
The other lords, like lions wanting food,
Do rush upon us as their hungry prey.
Alen. Froissart, a countryman of ours, records,
England all Olivers and Rowlands bred 30
During the time Edward the Third did reign.
More truly now may this be verified;
For none but Samsons, and Goliases,
It sendeth forth to skirmish. One to ten!
Lean raw-bon'd rascals! who would e'er suppose
They had such courage and audacity?
Char. Let's leave this town; for they are hare-
brain'd slaves,
And hunger will enforce them to be more eager:
Of old I know them; rather with their teeth
The walls they'll tear down than forsake the siege. 40
Reig. I think, by some odd gimmors, or device,
Their arms are set like clocks still to strike on;
Else ne'er could they hold out so, as they do.
By my consent, we'll e'en let them alone.
Alen. Be it so.

Enter the BASTARD *of Orleans.*

Bast. Where's the Prince Dauphin? I have news
for him.
Char. Bastard of Orleans, thrice welcome to us.
Bast. Methinks, your looks are sad, your cheer
appall'd:
Hath the late overthrow wrought this offence?
Be not dismay'd, for succour is at hand: 50
A holy maid hither with me I bring,
Which, by a vision sent to her from heaven,
Ordained is to raise this tedious siege,
And drive the English forth the bounds of France.
The spirit of deep prophecy she hath,
Exceeding the nine sibyls of old Rome;
What's past and what's to come, she can descry.
Speak, shall I call her in? Believe my words,
For they are certain and unfallible.
Char. Go, call her in. [*Exit* BASTARD.] But first,
to try her skill, 60
Reignier, stand thou as Dauphin in my place:
Question her proudly, let thy looks be stern:
By this means shall we sound what skill she hath.
[*Retires.*

Enter LA PUCELLE, BASTARD *of Orleans, and
others.*

Reig. Fair maid, is't thou wilt do these wondrous
feats?
Puc. Reignier, is't thou that thinkest to beguile
me?
Where is the Dauphin?—Come, come from behind;
I know thee well, though never seen before.
Be not amaz'd, there's nothing hid from me:
In private will I talk with thee apart.—
Stand back, you lords, and give us leave awhile. 70
Reig. She takes upon her bravely at first dash.
Puc. Dauphin, I am by birth a shepherd's daughter,
My wit untrain'd in any kind of art.
Heaven and our Lady gracious hath it pleas'd
To shine on my contemptible estate:
Lo! whilst I waited on my tender lambs,
And to sun's parching heat display'd my cheeks,
God's mother deigned to appear to me;
And, in a vision full of majesty,
Will'd me to leave my base vocation, 80
And free my country from calamity.
Her aid she promis'd, and assur'd success:
In complete glory she reveal'd herself;
And, whereas I was black and swart before,
With those clear rays which she infus'd on me,

That beauty am I bless'd with, which you see.
Ask me what question thou canst possible,
And I will answer unpremeditated:
My courage try by combat, if thou dar'st,
And thou shalt find that I exceed my sex. 90
Resolve on this,—thou shalt be fortunate,
If thou receive me for thy warlike mate.
Char. Thou hast astonish'd me with thy high
terms.
Only this proof I'll of thy valour make:
In single combat thou shalt buckle with me,
And, if thou vanquishest, thy words are true;
Otherwise, I renounce all confidence.
Puc. I am prepar'd. Here is my keen-edg'd sword,
Deck'd with five flower-de-luces on each side;
The which at Touraine, in Saint Katharine's church-
yard,
Out of a great deal of old iron I chose for'h. 100

Puc. "Stand back, you lords, and give us leave awhile."

Char. Then come, o' God's name: I fear no
woman.
Puc. And, while I live, I'll ne'er fly from a man.
[*They fight.*
Char. Stay, stay thy hands! thou art an Amazon,
And fightest with the sword of Deborah.
Puc. Christ's mother helps me, else I were too
weak.
Char. Whoe'er helps thee, 't is thou that must help
me.
Impatiently I burn with thy desire;
My heart and hands thou hast at once subdued.
Excellent Pucelle, if thy name be so, 110
Let me thy servant, and not sovereign, be:
'Tis the French Dauphin sueth to thee thus.
Puc. I must not yield to any rites of love,
For my profession's sacred from above:
When I have chased all thy foes from hence,
Then will I think upon a recompense.
Char. Meantime look gracious on thy prostrate
thrall.
Reig. My lord, methinks, is very long in talk.
Alen. Doubtless he shrives this woman to her
smock;
Else ne'er could he so long protract his speech. 120
Reig. Shall we disturb him, since he keeps no
mean?
Alen. He may mean more than we poor men
do know:
These women are shrewd tempters with their tongues.
Reig. My lord, where are you? what devise you on?
Shall we give over Orleans, or no?
Puc. Why, no, I say: distrustful recreants!
Fight till the last gasp; I will be your guard.
Char. What she says, I'll confirm: we'll fight it
out.

Puc. Assign'd am I to be the English scourge.
This night the siege assuredly I 'll raise :   130
Expect Saint Martin's summer, halcyon days,
Since I have entered into these wars.
Glory is like a circle in the water,
Which never ceaseth to enlarge itself,
Till, by broad spreading, it disperse to nought.
With Henry's death the English circle ends ;
Dispersed are the glories it included.
Now am I like that proud insulting ship,
Which Cæsar and his fortune bare at once.
   Char. Was Mahomet inspired with a dove ?   140
Thou with an eagle art inspired then.
Helen, the mother of great Constantine,
Nor yet Saint Philip's daughters were like thee.
Bright star of Venus, fall'n down on the earth,
How may I reverently worship thee enough ?
   Alen. Leave off delays, and let us raise the siege.
   Reig. Woman, do what thou canst to save our
honours.
Drive them from Orleans, and be immortalis'd.
   Char. Presently we 'll try.—Come, let 's away about
it :
No prophet will I trust, if she prove false.   150
                            [*Exeunt.*

SCENE III.—London. Tower Hill.

Enter, at the gates, the Duke of GLOSTER, *with his
Serving-men, in blue coats.*

   Glo. I am come to survey the Tower this day ;
Since Henry's death, I fear, there is conveyance.
Where be these warders, that they wait not here ?
Open the gates ! 'Tis Gloster that calls.
                        [*Servants knock.*
   1 *Ward.* [*Within.*] Who 's there, that knocks so
imperiously ?
   1 *Serv.* It is the noble Duke of Gloster.
   2 *Ward.* [*Within.*] Whoe'er he be, you may not be
let in.
   1 *Serv.* Villains, answer you so the lord protector ?
   1 *Ward.* [*Within.*] The Lord protect him ! so we
answer him :
We do no otherwise than we are will'd.   10
   Glo. Who willed you ? or whose will stands but
mine ?
There 's none protector of the realm but I.—
Break up the gates, I 'll be your warrantise.
Shall I be flouted thus by dunghill grooms ?

GLOSTER'S *Men rush at the Tower gates. Enter to
the gates,* WOODVILLE, *the Lieutenant.*

   Wood. [*Within.*] What noise is this ? what traitors
have we here ?
   Glo. Lieutenant, is it you whose voice I hear ?
Open the gates ! here 's Gloster that would enter.
   Wood. [*Within.*] Have patience, noble duke ; I
may not open ;
The Cardinal of Winchester forbids :
From him I have express commandement,   20
That thou, nor none of thine, shall be let in.
   Glo. Faint-hearted Woodville, prizest him 'fore me ?
Arrogant Winchester, that haughty prelate,
Whom Henry, our late sovereign, ne'er could brook ?
Thou art no friend to God, or to the king :
Open the gates, or I 'll shut thee out shortly.
   1 *Serv.* Open the gates unto the lord protector,
Or we 'll burst them open, if that you come not
quickly.

Enter WINCHESTER, *attended by Servants in tawny
coats.*

   Win. How now, ambitious Humphrey ? what means
this ?
   Glo. Peel'd priest, dost thou command me to be
shu' out ?   30
   Win. I do, thou most usurping rroditor,
And not protector, of the king or realm.
   Glo. Stand back, thou manifest conspirator,
Thou that contriv'dst to murder our dead lord ;
Thou that giv'st whores indulgences to sin.

I 'll canvass thee in thy broad cardinal's hat,
If thou proceed in this thy insolence.
   Win. Nay, stand thou back ; I will not budge a
foot :
This be Damascus, be thou cursed Cain,
To slay thy brother Abel, if thou wilt.   40
   Glo. I will not slay thee, but I 'll drive thee back.
Thy scarlet robes as a child's bearing-cloth
I 'll use to carry thee out of this place.
   Win. Do what thou dar'st ; I 'll beard thee to thy
face.
   Glo. What ! am I dar'd, and bearded to my face ?—
Draw, men, for all this privileged place ;
Blue-coats to tawny-coats. Priest, beware your beard ;
        [GLOSTER *and his Men attack the Bishop.*
I mean to tug it, and to cuff you soundly.
Under my feet I stamp thy cardinal's hat,
In spite of pope or dignities of Church ;   50
Here by the cheeks I 'll drag thee up and down.
   Win. Gloster, thou 'lt answer this before the pope.
   Glo. Winchester goose ! I cry—a rope ! a rope !—
Now beat them hence : why do you let them stay ?—
Thee I 'll chase hence, thou wolf in sheep's array.—
Out, tawny-coats !—out, scarlet hypocrite !

Here GLOSTER'S *Men beat out the Cardinal's Men,
and enter in the hurly-burly the Mayor of London
and his Officers.*

   May. Fie, lords ! that you, being supreme magis-
trates,
Thus contumeliously should break the peace !
   Glo. Peace, mayor ! thou know'st little of my
wrongs.
Here 's Beaufort, that regards nor God nor king,   60
Hath here distrain'd the Tower to his use.
   Win. Here 's Gloster, a foe to citizens ;
One that still motions war, and never peace,
O'ercharging your free purses with large fines ;
That seeks to overthrow religion,
Because he is protector of the realm ;
And would have armour here out of the Tower,
To crown himself king, and suppress the prince.
   Glo. I will not answer thee with words, but blows.
                [*Here they skirmish again.*
   May. Nought rests for me, in this tumultuous strife,
But to make open proclamation.—   71
Come, officer : as loud as e'er thou canst :
Cry.
   Off. All manner of men, assembled here in arms
this day, against God's peace, and the king's, we
charge and command you, in his highness' name, to
repair to your several dwelling-places ; and not to
wear, handle, or use, any sword, weapon, or dagger,
henceforward, upon pain of death.
   Glo. Cardinal, I 'll be no breaker of the law ;   80
But we shall meet, and break our minds at large.
   Win. Gloster, we will meet ; to thy cost, be sure :
Thy heart-blood I will have for this day's work.
   May. I 'll call for clubs, if you will not away.—
This cardinal 's more haughty than the devil.
   Glo. Mayor, farewell : thou dost but what thou
may'st.
   Win. Abominable Gloster ! guard thy head ;
For I intend to have it, ere long.   [*Exeunt.*
   May. See the coast clear'd, and then we will
depart.—
Good God ! these nobles should such stomachs bear !
I myself fight not once in forty year.   91
                            [*Exeunt.*

SCENE IV.—France. Before Orleans.

Enter, on the walls, the Master-Gunner and his Son.

   M. Gun. Sirrah, thou know'st how Orleans is
besieg'd,
And how the English have the suburbs won.
   Son. Father, I know ; and oft have shot at them,
Howe'er, unfortunate, I miss'd my aim.
   M. Gun. But now thou shalt not. Be thou rul'd by
me :
Chief master-gunner am I of this town ;

Something I must do to procure me grace.
The prince's espials have informed me,
How the English, in the suburbs close intrench'd,
Wont, through a secret grate of iron bars   10
In yonder tower, to overpeer the city ;
And thence discover, how, with most advantage,
They may vex us with shot, or with assault.
To intercept this inconvenience,
A piece of ordnance 'gainst it I have plac'd ;
And fully even these three days have I watch'd,
If I could see them. Now, boy, do thou watch,
For I can stay no longer.
If thou spy'st any, run and bring me word ;
And thou shalt find me at the governor's.   [*Exit.*
   Son. Father, I warrant you ; take you no care :   21
I 'll never trouble you, if I may spy them.

Enter, in an upper chamber of a tower, the Lords
Salisbury *and* Talbot ; *Sir* William Glansdale,
Sir Thomas Gargrave, *and others.*

   Sal. Talbot, my life, my joy ! again return'd ?
How wert thou handled, being prisoner,
Or by what means got'st thou to be releas'd ?
Discourse, I pr'ythee, on this turret's top.
   Tal. The Duke of Bedford had a prisoner,
Called the brave Lord Ponton de Santrailles ;
For him I was exchang'd and ransomed.
But with a baser man of arms by far,   30
Once, in contempt, they would have barter'd me :
Which I, disdaining, scorn'd ; and craved death,
Rather than I would be so vile-esteem'd.
In fine, redeem'd I was as I desir'd.
But, O ! the treacherous Fastolfe wounds my heart :
Whom with my bare fists I would execute,
If I now had him brought into my power.
   Sal. Yet tell'st thou not, how thou wert entertain'd.
   Tal. With scoffs, and scorns, and contumelious
     taunts.
In open market-place produc'd they me,   40
To be a public spectacle to all :
Here, said they, is the terror of the French,
The scarecrow that affrights our children so.
Then broke I from the officers that led me,
And with my nails digg'd stones out of the ground,
To hurl at the beholders of my shame.
My grisly countenance made others fly ;
None durst come near, for fear of sudden death.
In iron walls they deem'd me not secure ;
So great fear of my name 'mongst them was spread,   51
That they suppos'd I could rend bars of steel,
And spurn in pieces posts of adamant :
Wherefore a guard of chosen shot I had,
That walk'd about me every minute-while ;
And if I did but stir out of my bed,
Ready they were to shoot me to the heart.
   Sal. I grieve to hear what torments you endur'd ;
But we will be reveng'd sufficiently.
Now, it is supper-time in Orleans :
Here, through this grate, I count each one,   60
And view the Frenchmen how they fortify.
Let us look in ; the sight will much delight thee.
Sir Thomas Gargrave, and Sir William Glansdale,
Let me have your express opinions,
Where is best place to make our battery next.
   Gar. I think, at the north gate ; for there stand lords.
   Glan. And I, here, at the bulwark of the bridge.
   Tal. For aught I see, this city must be famish'd,
Or with light skirmishes enfeebled.
     [*Shot from the town.* Salisbury *and Sir*
     Thomas Gargrave *fall.*
   Sal. O Lord ! have mercy on us, wretched sinners !
   Gar. O Lord ! have mercy on me, woful man !   71
   Tal. What chance is this, that suddenly hath cross'd
     us ?—
Speak, Salisbury ; at least, if thou canst speak :
How far'st thou, mirror of all martial men ?
One of thy eyes, and thy cheek's side struck off !—
Accursed tower ! accursed fatal hand,
That hath contriv'd this woful tragedy !
In thirteen battles Salisbury o'ercame :
Henry the Fifth he first train'd to the wars ;
Whilst any trump did sound, or drum struck up,   80

His sword did ne'er leave striking in the field.—
Yet liv'st thou, Salisbury ? though thy speech doth fail,
One eye thou hast to look to heaven for grace :
The sun with one eye vieweth all the world.—
Heaven, be thou gracious to none alive,
If Salisbury wants mercy at thy hands !—
Bear hence his body, I will help to bury it.
Sir Thomas Gargrave, hast thou any life ?
Speak unto Talbot ; nay, look up to him.
Salisbury, cheer thy spirit with this comfort ;   90
Thou shalt not die, whiles—
He beckons with his hand, and smiles on me,
As who should say, " When I am dead and gone,
Remember to avenge me on the French."—
Plantagenet, I will ; and like thee, Nero,

Tal. "What chance is this, that suddenly hath cross'd us ?"

Play on the lute, beholding the towns burn :
Wretched shall France be only in my name.
     [*An alarum ; it thunders and lightens.*
What stir is this ? what tumult 's in the heavens ?
Whence cometh this alarum, and the noise ?

Enter a Messenger.

   Mess. My lord, my lord ! the French have gather'd
     head :   100
The Dauphin, with one Joan la Pucelle join'd,—
A holy prophetess, new risen up,—
Is come with a great power to raise the siege.
     [Salisbury *groans.*
   Tal. Hear, hear, how dying Salisbury doth groan !
It irks his heart he cannot be reveng'd.—
Frenchmen, I 'll be a Salisbury to you,
Pucelle or puzzel, dolphin or dogfish,
Your hearts I 'll stamp out with my horse's heels,
And make a quagmire of your mingled brains.—
Convey me Salisbury into his tent,   110
And then we 'll try what these dastard Frenchmen
     dare.   [*Exeunt, bearing out the bodies.*

SCENE V.—The Same. Before one of the Gates.

Alarum. Skirmishings. Talbot *pursues the* Dauphin, *drives him in and exit : then enter* Joan la
Pucelle, *driving Englishmen before her, and exit
after them. Then re-enter* Talbot.

   Tal. Where is my strength, my valour, and my
     force ?
Our English troops retire, I cannot stay them ;
A woman clad in armour chaseth them.

Re-enter La Pucelle.

Here, here she comes.—I 'll have a bout with thee ;
Devil, or devil's dam, I 'll conjure thee :

Blood will I draw on thee, thou art a witch,
And straightway give thy soul to him thou serv'st.
  Puc. Come, come; 'tis only I that must disgrace
    thee.   [*They fight.*
  Tal. Heavens, can you suffer hell so to prevail?
My breast I'll burst with straining of my courage,   10
And from my shoulders crack my arms asunder,
But I will chastise this high-minded strumpet.
  Puc. Talbot, farewell; thy hour is not yet come:
I must go victual Orleans forthwith.
O'ertake me, if thou canst; I scorn thy strength.
Go, go, cheer up thy hunger-starved men;
Help Salisbury to make his testament:
This day is ours, as many more shall be.
       [PUCELLE *enters the town, with Soldiers.*
  Tal. My thoughts are whirled like a potter's wheel;
I know not where I am, nor what I do.   20
A witch, by fear, not force, like Hannibal,
Drives back our troops, and conquers as she lists:
So bees with smoke, and doves with noisome stench,
Are from their hives and houses driven away.
They call'd us for our fierceness English dogs;
Now, like to whelps, we crying run away.
               [*A short alarum.*
Hark, countrymen! either renew the fight,
Or tear the lions out of England's coat;
Renounce your soil, give sheep in lions' stead:
Sheep run not half so treacherous from the wolf,   30
Or horse, or oxen, from the leopard,
As you fly from your oft-subdued slaves.
         [*Alarum. Another skirmish.*
It will not be.—Retire into your trenches:
You all consented unto Salisbury's death,
For none would strike a stroke in his revenge.—
Pucelle is enter'd into Orleans
In spite of us, or aught that we could do.
O, 'would I were to die with Salisbury!
The shame hereof will make me hide my head.
   [*Alarum; Retreat. Exeunt* TALBOT *and his Forces.*

SCENE VI.—The Same.

Flourish. Enter, on the walls, PUCELLE, CHARLES,
       REIGNIER, ALENÇON, *and Soldiers.*

  Puc. Advance our waving colours on the walls!
Rescu'd is Orleans from the English.
Thus Joan la Pucelle hath perform'd her word.
  Char. Divinest creature, Astræa's daughter,
How shall I honour thee for this success?
Thy promises are like Adonis' gardens,
That one day bloom'd, and fruitful were the next.—
France, triumph in thy glorious prophetess!—
Recover'd is the town of Orleans:
More blessed hap did ne'er befall our state.   10
  Reig. Why ring not out the bells aloud throughout
    the town?
Dauphin, command the citizens make bonfires,
And feast and banquet in the open streets,
To celebrate the joy that God hath given us.
  Alen. All France will be replete with mirth and
    joy.
When they shall hear how we have play'd the
    men.
  Char. 'T is Joan, not we, by whom the day is
    won;
For which I will divide my crown with her;
And all the priests and friars in my realm
Shall in procession sing her endless praise.   20
A statelier pyramis to her I'll rear,
Than Rhodope's, or Memphis', ever was:
In memory of her, when she is dead,
Her ashes, in an urn more precious
Than the rich-jewell'd coffer of Darius,
Transported shall be at high festivals
Before the kings and queens of France.
No longer on Saint Dennis will we cry,
But Joan la Pucelle shall be France's saint.
Come in; and let us banquet royally,   30
After this golden day of victory. [*Flourish. Exeunt.*

ACT II.

SCENE I.—The Same.

Enter to the gates, a French Sergeant, and two Sentinels.

        Sergeant.
IRS, take your places, and be vigilant.
  If any noise, or soldier, you perceive
  Near to the walls, by some apparent sign
Let us have knowledge at the court of guard.
  1 Sent. Sergeant, you shall. [*Exit Sergeant.*]
    Thus are poor servitors
(When others sleep upon their quiet beds)
Constrain'd to watch in darkness, rain, and
    cold.

Enter TALBOT, BEDFORD, BURGUNDY, *and*
  Forces, with scaling-ladders; their drums
  beating a dead march.

  Tal. Lord regent, and redoubted Burgundy,
By whose approach the regions of Artois,
Walloon, and Picardy, are friends to us,   10
This happy night the Frenchmen are secure,
Having all day carous'd and banqueted:
Embrace we then this opportunity,
As fitting best to quittance their deceit,
Contriv'd by art, and baleful sorcery.

  Bed. Coward of France!—how much he wrongs his
    fame,
Despairing of his own arm's fortitude,
To join with witches, and the help of hell!
  Bur. Traitors have never other company.
But what's that Pucelle, whom they term so pure? 20
  Tal. A maid, they say.
  Bed.   A maid, and be so martial!
  Bur. Pray God, she prove not masculine ere long;
If underneath the standard of the French
She carry armour, as she hath begun.
  Tal. Well, let them practise and converse with
    spirits:
God is our fortress, in whose conquering name
Let us resolve to scale their flinty bulwarks.
  Bed. Ascend, brave Talbot; we will follow thee.
  Tal. Not all together: better far, I guess,   30
That we do make our entrance several ways,
That if it chance the one of us do fail,
The other yet may rise against their force.
  Bed. Agreed. I'll to yond corner.
  Bur.   And I to this.

Tal. And here will Talbot mount, or make his
     grave.—
Now, Salisbury, for thee, and for the right
Of English Henry, shall this night appear
How much in duty I am bound to both.
    [*The English scale the walls, crying :* "*Saint*
      George ! A Talbot !" and all enter the town.
Sent. [*Within.*] Arm, arm ! the enemy doth make
    assault !

*The French leap over the walls in their shirts.
Enter, several ways,* BASTARD, ALENÇON, REIGNIER,
half ready, and half unready.
Alen. How now, my lords ? what, all unready so ?
Bast. Unready ? ay, and glad we 'scap'd so well. 40
Reig. 'T was time, I trow, to wake and leave our beds,
Hearing alarums at our chamber-doors.
Alen. Of all exploits, since first I follow'd arms,
Ne'er heard I of a warlike enterprise
More venturous, or desperate, than this.
Bast. I think, this Talbot be a fiend of hell.
Reig. If not of hell, the heavens sure favour him.

But weakly guarded, where the breach was made.
And now there rests no other shift but this,—
To gather our soldiers, scatter'd and dispers'd,
And lay new platforms to endamage them.

Alarum. Enter an English Soldier, crying : "*A
Talbot ! A Talbot !*" *They fly, leaving their
clothes behind.*
    Sold. I 'll be so bold to take what they have left.
The cry of Talbot serves me for a sword ;
For I have loaden me with many spoils,   80
Using no other weapon but his name.   [*Exit.*

SCENE II.—Orleans. Within the Town.

Enter TALBOT, BEDFORD, BURGUNDY, *a Captain,
and others.*

Bed. The day begins to break, and night is fled,
Whose pitchy mantle over-veil'd the earth.
Here sound retreat, and cease our hot pursuit.
    [*Retreat sounded.*

Sent. "Arm, arm ! the enemy doth make assault !"

Alen. Here cometh Charles : I marvel how he sped.
Bast. Tut ! holy Joan was his defensive guard.

    Enter CHARLES *and* LA PUCELLE.

Char. Is this thy cunning, thou deceitful dame ? 50
Didst thou at first, to flatter us withal,
Make us partakers of a little gain,
That now our loss might be ten times so much ?
Puc. Wherefore is Charles impatient with his friend ?
At all times will you have my power alike ?
Sleeping or waking, must I still prevail,
Or will you blame, and lay the fault on me ?—
Improvident soldiers ! had your watch been good,
This sudden mischief never could have fallen.
Char. Duke of Alençon, this was your default, 60
That, being captain of the watch to-night,
Did look no better to that weighty charge.
Alen. Had all your quarters been as safely kept,
As that whereof I had the government,
We had not been thus shamefully surpris'd.
Bast. Mine was secure.
Reig.   And so was mine, my lord.
Char. And for myself, most part of all this night,
Within her quarter, and mine own precinct,
I was employ'd in passing to and fro,
About relieving of the sentinels :   70
Then how, or which way, should they first break in ?
Puc. Question, my lords, no further of the case,
How, or which way : 't is sure, they found some place

Tal. Bring forth the body of old Salisbury ;
And here advance it in the market-place,
The middle centre of this cursed town.—
Now have I paid my vow unto his soul ;
For every drop of blood was drawn from him,
There hath at least five Frenchmen died to-night.
And that hereafter ages may behold   10
What ruin happen'd in revenge of him,
Within their chiefest temple I 'll erect
A tomb, wherein his corse shall be interr'd :
Upon the which, that every one may read,
Shall be engrav'd the sack of Orleans,
The treacherous manner of his mournful death,
And what a terror he had been to France.
But, lords, in all our bloody massacre,
I muse, we met not with the Dauphin's grace,
His new-come champion, virtuous Joan of Arc,   20
Nor any of his false confederates.
Bed. 'T is thought, Lord Talbot, when the fight
    began,
Rous'd on the sudden from their drowsy beds,
They did, amongst the troops of armed men,
Leap o'er the walls for refuge in the field.
Bur. Myself, as far as I could well discern,
For smoke, and dusky vapours of the night,
Am sure I scar'd the Dauphin, and his trull ;
When arm in arm they both came swiftly running,
Like to a pair of loving turtle-doves,   30
That could not live asunder, day or night.

After that things are set in order here,
We 'll follow them with all the power we have.

Enter a Messenger.

Mess. All hail, my lords! Which of this princely
　　train
Call ye the warlike Talbot, for his acts
So much applauded through the realm of France?
Tal. Here is the Talbot; who would speak with him?
Mess. The virtuous lady, Countess of Auvergne,
With modesty admiring thy renown,
By me entreats, great lord, thou wouldst vouchsafe 40
To visit her poor castle where she lies;
That she may boast she hath beheld the man
Whose glory fills the world with loud report.
Bur. Is it even so? Nay, then, I see, our wars
Will turn unto a peaceful comic sport,
When ladies crave to be encounter'd with.—
You may not, my lord, despise her gentle suit.
Tal. Ne'er trust me then; for when a world of men
Could not prevail with all their oratory,
Yet hath a woman's kindness over-rul'd.— 50
And therefore tell her, I return great thanks,
And in submission will attend on her.—
Will not your honours bear me company?
Bed. No, truly, it is more than manners will;
And I have heard it said, unbidden guests
Are often welcomest when they are gone.
Tal. Well then, alone, since there 's no remedy,
I mean to prove this lady's courtesy.
Come hither, captain. [*Whispers.*]—You perceive my
　　mind.
Capt. I do, my lord, and mean accordingly. 60
　　　　　　　　　　　　　　　　　[*Exeunt.*

Scene III.—Auvergne. Court of the Castle.

Enter the Countess *and her Porter.*

Count. Porter, remember what I gave in charge;
And when you have done so, bring the keys to me.
Port. Madam, I will. [*Exit.*
Count. The plot is laid: if all things fall out right,
I shall as famous be by this exploit,
As Scythian Tomyris by Cyrus' death.
Great is the rumour of this dreadful knight,
And his achievements of no less account:
Fain would mine eyes be witness with mine ears,
To give their censure of these rare reports. 10

Enter Messenger and Talbot.

Mess. Madam, according as your ladyship desir'd,
By message crav'd, so is Lord Talbot come.
Count. And he is welcome. What! is this the man?
Mess. Madam, it is.
Count. 　　　　　Is this the scourge of France?
Is this the Talbot, so much fear'd abroad,
That with his name the mothers still their babes?
I see, report is fabulous and false:
I thought, I should have seen some Hercules,
A second Hector, for his grim aspect,
And large proportion of his strong-knit limbs. 20
Alas! this is a child, a silly dwarf:
It cannot be, this weak and writhled shrimp
Should strike such terror to his enemies.
Tal. Madam, I have been bold to trouble you;
But, since your ladyship is not at leisure,
I 'll sort some other time to visit you.
Count. What means he now?—Go ask him, whither
　　he goes.
Mess. Stay, my Lord Talbot; for my lady craves
To know the cause of your abrupt departure.
Tal. Marry, for that she 's in a wrong belief, 30
I go to certify her, Talbot 's here.

Re-enter Porter, with keys.

Count. If thou be he, then art thou prisoner.
Tal. Prisoner! to whom?
Count. 　　　　　To me, blood-thirsty lord;
And for that cause I train'd thee to my house.
Long time thy shadow hath been thrall to me,
For in my gallery thy picture hangs:

But now the substance shall endure the like,
And I will chain these legs and arms of thine,
That hast by tyranny, these many years,
Wasted our country, slain our citizens, 40
And sent our sons and husbands captivate.
Tal. Ha, ha, ha!
Count. Laughest thou, wretch? thy mirth shall
　　turn to moan.
Tal. I laugh to see your ladyship so fond,
To think that you have aught but Talbot's shadow,
Whereon to practise your severity.
Count. Why, art not thou the man?
Tal. 　　　　　　　　I am, indeed.
Count. Then have I substance too.
Tal. No, no, I am but shadow of myself:
You are deceiv'd, my substance is not here; 50
For what you see, is but the smallest part
And least proportion of humanity.
I tell you, madam, were the whole frame here,
It is of such a spacious lofty pitch,
Your roof were not sufficient to contain it.
Count. This is a riddling merchant for the nonce;
He will be here, and yet he is not here:
How can these contrarieties agree?
Tal. That will I show you presently.

*He winds his horn. Drums strike up; a peal of
　　ordnance. The gates being forced, enter Soldiers.*

How say you, madam? are you now persuaded, 60
That Talbot is but shadow of himself?
These are his substance, sinews, arms, and strength,
With which he yoketh your rebellious necks,
Razeth your cities, and subverts your towns,
And in a moment makes them desolate.
Count. Victorious Talbot, pardon my abuse:
I find, thou art no less than fame hath bruited,
And more than may be gather'd by thy shape.
Let my presumption not provoke thy wrath;
For I am sorry, that with reverence 70
I did not entertain thee as thou art.
Tal. Be not dismay'd, fair lady; nor misconster
The mind of Talbot, as you did mistake
The outward composition of his body.
What you have done hath not offended me:
No other satisfaction do I crave,
But only, with your patience, that we may
Taste of your wine, and see what cates you have;
For soldiers' stomachs always serve them well.
Count. With all my heart; and think me honoured
To feast so great a warrior in my house. 81
　　　　　　　　　　　　　　　　　[*Exeunt.*

Scene IV.—London. The Temple Garden.

Enter the Earls of Somerset, Suffolk, *and* Warwick; Richard Plantagenet, Vernon, *and a
Lawyer.*

Plan. Great lords, and gentlemen, what means this
　　silence?
Dare no man answer in a case of truth?
Suf. Within the Temple Hall we were too loud:
The garden here is more convenient.
Plan. Then say at once, if I maintain'd the truth,
Or, else, was wrangling Somerset in the error?
Suf. 'Faith, I have been a truant in the law,
And never yet could frame my will to it;
And, therefore, frame the law unto my will.
Som. Judge you, my Lord of Warwick, then between
　　us. 10
War. Between two hawks, which flies the higher
　　pitch,
Between two dogs, which hath the deeper mouth,
Between two blades, which bears the better temper,
Between two horses, which doth bear him best,
Between two girls, which hath the merriest eye,
I have, perhaps, some shallow spirit of judgment;
But in these nice sharp quillets of the law,
Good faith, I am no wiser than a daw.
Plan. Tut, tut! here is a mannerly forbearance:
The truth appears so naked on my side, 20
That any purblind eye may find it out.

Som. And on my side it is so well apparell'd,
So clear, so shining, and so evident,
That it will glimmer through a blind man's eye.
   Plan. Since you are tongue-tied, and so loath to
      speak,
In dumb significants proclaim your thoughts:
Let him that is a true-born gentleman,

Till you conclude that he, upon whose side   40
The fewest roses are cropp'd from the tree,
Shall yield the other in the right opinion.
   Som. Good Master Vernon, it is well objected:
If I have fewest, I subscribe in silence.
   Plan. And I.
   Ver. Then, for the truth and plainness of the case,

War. "I pluck this white rose with Plantagenet."

And stands upon the honour of his birth,
If he suppose that I have pleaded truth,
From off this brier pluck a white rose with me.   30
   Som. Let him that is no coward, nor no flatterer,
But dare maintain the party of the truth,
Pluck a red rose from off this thorn with me.
   War. I love no colours; and, without all colour
Of base insinuating flattery,
I pluck this white rose with Plantagenet.
   Suf. I pluck this red rose with young Somerset;
And say withal, I think he held the right.
   Ver. Stay, lords and gentlemen, and pluck no more,

I pluck this pale and maiden blossom here,
Giving my verdict on the white rose side.
   Som. Prick not your finger as you pluck it off,
Lest, bleeding, you do paint the white rose red,   50
And fall on my side so, against your will.
   Ver. If I, my lord, for my opinion bleed,
Opinion shall be surgeon to my hurt,
And keep me on the side where still I am.
   Som. Well, well, come on: who else?
   Law. Unless my study and my books be false,
The argument you held was wrong in you;
In sign whereof, I pluck a white rose too.

Plan. Now, Somerset, where is your argument?
Som. Here, in my scabbard; meditating that,　60
Shall dye your white rose in a bloody red.
Plan. Meantime, your cheeks do counterfeit our
　roses;
For pale they look with fear, as witnessing
The truth on our side.
Som.　No, Plantagenet,
'T is not for fear, but anger, that thy cheeks
Blush for pure shame, to counterfeit our roses,
And yet thy tongue will not confess thy error.
Plan. Hath not thy rose a canker, Somerset?
Som. Hath not thy rose a thorn, Plantagenet?
Plan. Ay, sharp and piercing, to maintain his truth,
Whiles thy consuming canker eats his falsehood.　71
Som. Well, I 'll find friends to wear my bleeding
　roses,
That shall maintain what I have said is true,
Where false Plantagenet dare not be seen.
Plan. Now, by this maiden blossom in my hand,
I scorn thee and thy faction, peevish boy.
Suf. Turn not thy scorns this way, Plantagenet.
Plan. Proud Poole, I will; and scorn both him and
　thee.
Suf. I 'll turn my part thereof into thy throat.
Som. Away, away, good William de la Poole:　80
We grace the yeoman by conversing with him.
War. Now, by God's will, thou wrong'st him,
　Somerset:
His grandfather was Lionel, Duke of Clarence,
Third son to the third Edward, King of England.
Spring crestless yeomen from so deep a root?
Plan. He bears him on the place's privilege,
Or durst not, for his craven heart, say thus.
Som. By Him that made me, I 'll maintain my
　words
On any plot of ground in Christendom.
Was not thy father, Richard, Earl of Cambridge,　90
For treason executed in our late king's days?
And by his treason stand'st not thou attainted,
Corrupted, and exempt from ancient gentry?
His trespass yet lives guilty in thy blood;
And, till thou be restor'd, thou art a yeoman.
Plan. My father was attached, not attainted,
Condemn'd to die for treason, but no traitor;
And that I 'll prove on better men than Somerset,
Were growing time once ripen'd to my will.
For your partaker Poole, and you yourself,　100
I 'll note you in my book of memory,
To scourge you for this apprehension:
Look to it well, and say you are well warn'd.
Som. Ay, thou shalt find us ready for thee still,
And know us by these colours for thy foes;
For these my friends, in spite of thee, shall wear.
Plan. And, by my soul, this pale and angry rose,
As cognisance of my blood-drinking hate,
Will I for ever, and my faction, wear,
Until it wither with me to my grave,　110
Or flourish to the height of my degree.
Suf. Go forward, and be chok'd with thy ambition:
And so farewell, until I meet thee next.　[*Exit.*
Som. Have with thee, Poole.—Farewell, ambitious
　Richard.　[*Exit.*
Plan. How I am brav'd, and must perforce endure
　it!
War. This blot, that they object against your house,
Shall be wip'd out in the next parliament,
Call'd for the truce of Winchester and Gloster;
And if thou be not then created York,
I will not live to be accounted Warwick.　120
Meantime, in signal of my love to thee,
Against proud Somerset, and William Poole,
Will I upon thy party wear this rose.
And here I prophesy:—this brawl to-day,
Grown to this faction in the Temple Garden,
Shall send, between the red rose and the white,
A thousand souls to death and deadly night.
Plan. Good Master Vernon, I am bound to you,
That you on my behalf would pluck a flower.
Ver. In your behalf still will I wear the same.　130
Law. And so will I.
Plan. Thanks, gentle sir.

Come, let us four to dinner: I dare say,
This quarrel will drink blood another day.　[*Exeunt.*

SCENE V.—The Same.　A Room in the Tower.

Enter Mortimer, *brought in a chair by two
Keepers.*

Mor. Kind keepers of my weak decaying age,
Let dying Mortimer here rest himself.—
Even like a man new haled from the rack,
So fare my limbs with long imprisonment;
And these grey locks, the pursuivants of death,
Nestor-like aged, in an age of care,
Argue the end of Edmund Mortimer.
These eyes, like lamps whose wasting oil is spent,
Wax dim, as drawing to their exigent;
Weak shoulders, overborne with burdening grief,　10
And pithless arms, like to a wither'd vine
That droops his sapless branches to the ground:
Yet are these feet,—whose strengthless stay is numb,
Unable to support this lump of clay,—
Swift-winged with desire to get a grave,
As witting I no other comfort have.—
But tell me, keeper, will my nephew come?
1 Keep. Richard Plantagenet, my lord, will come:
We sent unto the Temple, unto his chamber,
And answer was return'd that he will come.　20
Mor. Enough; my soul shall then be satisfied.—
Poor gentleman! his wrong doth equal mine.
Since Henry Monmouth first began to reign,
Before whose glory I was great in arms,
This loathsome sequestration have I had;
And even since then hath Richard been obscur'd,
Depriv'd of honour and inheritance:
But now, the arbitrator of despairs,
Just death, kind umpire of men's miseries,
With sweet enlargement doth dismiss me hence.　30
I would his troubles likewise were expir'd,
That so he might recover what was lost.

Enter Richard Plantagenet.

1 Keep. My lord, your loving nephew now is come.
Mor. Richard Plantagenet, my friend, is he come?
Plan. Ay, noble uncle, thus ignobly us'd,
Your nephew, late despised Richard, comes.
Mor. Direct mine arms, I may embrace his neck,
And in his bosom spend my latter gasp.
O! tell me, when my lips do touch his cheeks,
That I may kindly give one fainting kiss.—　40
And now declare, sweet stem from York's great stock,
Why didst thou say, of late thou wert despis'd?
Plan. First, lean thine aged back against mine
　arm,
And in that ease I 'll tell thee my disease.
This day, in argument upon a case,
Some words there grew 'twixt Somerset and me;
Among which terms he us'd his lavish tongue,
And did upbraid me with my father's death:
Which obloquy set bars before my tongue,
Else with the like I had requited him.　50
Therefore, good uncle, for my father's sake,
In honour of a true Plantagenet,
And for alliance sake, declare the cause
My father, Earl of Cambridge, lost his head.
Mor. That cause, fair nephew, that imprison'd me,
And hath detain'd me all my flow'ring youth
Within a loathsome dungeon, there to pine,
Was cursed instrument of his disease.
Plan. Discover more at large what cause that
　was;
For I am ignorant, and cannot guess.　60
Mor. I will, if that my fading breath permit,
And death approach not ere my tale be done.
Henry the Fourth, grandfather to this king,
Depos'd his nephew Richard, Edward's son,
The first-begotten, and the lawful heir
Of Edward king, the third of that descent:
During whose reign the Percies of the north,
Finding his usurpation most unjust,
Endeavour'd my advancement to the throne.

The reason mov'd these warlike lords to this,   70
Was, for that (young King Richard thus remov'd,
Leaving no heir begotten of his body)
I was the next by birth and parentage ;
For by my mother I derived am
From Lionel, Duke of Clarence, the third son
To King Edward the Third ; whereas he
From John of Gaunt doth bring his pedigree,
Being but fourth of that heroic line.
But mark : as, in this haughty great attempt
They laboured to plant the rightful heir,   80
I lost my liberty, and they their lives.
Long after this, when Henry the Fifth
(Succeeding his father Bolingbroke) did reign,
Thy father, Earl of Cambridge, then deriv'd
From famous Edmund Langley, Duke of York,
Marrying my sister, that thy mother was,
Again, in pity of my hard distress,
Levied an army, weening to redeem
And have install'd me in the diadem ;
But, as the rest, so fell that noble earl,   90
And was beheaded. Thus the Mortimers,
In whom the title rested, were suppress'd.
Plan. Of which, my lord, your honour is the
      last.
Mor. True ; and thou seest, that I no issue have,
And thou my fainting words do warrant death.
Thou art my heir : the rest, I wish thee gather ;
But yet be wary in thy studious care.
Plan. Thy grave admonishments prevail with
      me.
But yet, methinks, my father's execution
Was nothing less than bloody tyranny.   100

Mor. With silence, nephew, be thou politic :
Strong-fixed is the house of Lancaster,
And, like a mountain, not to be remov'd.
But now thy uncle is removing hence,
As princes do their courts, when they are cloy'd
With long continuance in a settled place.
Plan. O, uncle ! 'would some part of my young
      years
Might but redeem the passage of your age !
Mor. Thou dost then wrong me ; as the slaughterer
      doth,
Which giveth many wounds, when one will kill.   110
Mourn not, except thou sorrow for my good ;
Only, give order for my funeral :
And so farewell ; and fair be all thy hopes,
And prosperous be thy life, in peace, and war ! [*Dies.*
Plan. And peace, no war, befall thy parting soul !
In prison hast thou spent a pilgrimage,
And like a hermit overpass'd thy days.—
Well, I will lock his counsel in my breast ;
And what I do imagine, let that rest.—
Keepers, convey him hence ; and I myself   120
Will see his burial better than his life.—
    [*Exeunt Keepers, bearing out the body of*
           Mortimer.
Here lies the dusky torch of Mortimer,
Chok'd with ambition of the meaner sort :
And, for those wrongs, those bitter injuries,
Which Somerset hath offer'd to my house,
I doubt not but with honour to redress ;
And therefore haste I to the parliament,
Either to be restored to my blood,
Or make my ill the advantage of my good.   [*Exit.*

ACT III.

Scene I.—The Same. The Parliament-House.

Flourish. Enter King Henry, Exeter, Gloster, Warwick, Somerset, *and* Suffolk ; *the Bishop of*
Winchester, Richard Plantagenet, *and others.* Gloster *offers to put up a bill;* Winchester
snatches it, and tears it.

       Winchester.
COM'ST thou with deep-premeditated
      lines,
With written pamphlets studiously
      devis'd,
Humphrey of Gloster ? If thou canst
      accuse,
Or aught intend'st to lay unto my
      charge,
Do it without invention suddenly ;
As I with sudden and extemporal speech
Purpose to answer what thou canst object.
Glo. Presumptuous priest ! this place commands
      my patience,
Or thou shouldst find thou hast dishonour'd me.
Think not, although in writing I preferr'd   10
The manner of thy vile outrageous crimes,
That therefore I have forg'd, or am not able
Verbatim to rehearse the method of my pen :
No, prelate ; such is thy audacious wickedness,
Thy lewd, pestiferous, and dissentious pranks,
As very infants prattle of thy pride.
Thou art a most pernicious usurer,
Froward by nature, enemy to peace :
Lascivious, wanton, more than well beseems
A man of thy profession and degree :   20
And for thy treachery, what 's more manifest ?

In that thou laidst a trap to take my life,
As well at London Bridge, as at the Tower.
Beside, I fear me, if thy thoughts were sifted,
The king, thy sovereign, is not quite exempt
From envious malice of thy swelling heart.
  Win. Gloster, I do defy thee. — Lords, vouch-
      safe
To give me hearing what I shall reply.
If I were covetous, ambitious, or perverse,
As he will have me, how am I so poor ?   30
Or how haps it, I seek not to advance
Or raise myself, but keep my wonted calling ?
And for dissension, who preferreth peace
More than I do, except I be provok'd ?
No, my good lords, it is not that offends ;
It is not that that hath incens'd the duke :
It is, because no one should sway but me ;
No one but he should be about the king ;
And that engenders thunder in his breast,
And makes him roar these accusations forth.   40
But he shall know, I am as good—
  Glo.   As good !
Thou bastard of my grandfather !—
  Win. Ay, lordly sir ; for what are you, I pray,
But one imperious in another's throne ?
  Glo. Am I not protector, saucy priest ?
  Win. And am not I a prelate of the church ?

Glo. Yes, as an outlaw in a castle keeps,
And useth it to patronage his theft.
Win. Unreverent Gloster !
Glo.   Thou art reverent,
Touching thy spiritual function, not thy life.   50
Win. Rome shall remedy this.
War.   Roam thither then.
Som. My lord, it were your duty to forbear.
War. Ay, see the bishop be not overborne.
Som. Methinks, my lord should be religious,
And know the office that belongs to such.
War. Methinks, his lordship should be humbler ;
It fitteth not a prelate so to plead.
Som. Yes, when his holy state is touch'd so near.
War. State holy, or unhallow'd, what of that ?
Is not his grace protector to the king ?   60
Plan. [*Aside.*] Plantagenet, I see, must hold his
          tongue,
Lest it be said, " Speak, sirrah, when you should ;
Must your bold verdict enter talk with lords ? "
Else would I have a fling at Winchester.

Glo. " Presumptuous priest ! this place commands my patience."

K. Hen. Uncles of Gloster, and of Winchester,
The special watchmen of our English weal,
I would prevail, if prayers might prevail,
To join your hearts in love and amity.
O ! what a scandal is it to our crown,
That two such noble peers as ye should jar.   70
Believe me, lords, my tender years can tell,
Civil dissension is a viperous worm,
That gnaws the bowels of the commonwealth.—
          [*A noise within :* " *Down with the tawny-coats !* "
What tumult 's this ?
War.   An uproar, I dare warrant,
Begun through malice of the bishop's men.
          [*A noise again :* " *Stones ! stones !* "

Enter the Mayor of London, attended.

May. O, my good lords, and virtuous Henry,
Pity the city of London, pity us !
The bishop and the Duke of Gloster's men,
Forbidden late to carry any weapon,
Have fill'd their pockets full of pebble-stones ;   80
And banding themselves in contrary parts,
Do pelt so fast at one another's pate,
That many have their giddy brains knock'd out.
Our windows are broke down in every street,
And we, for fear, compell'd to shut our shops.

Enter, skirmishing, the Retainers of GLOSTER *and*
WINCHESTER, *with bloody pates.*

K. Hen. We charge you, on allegiance to ourself,

To hold your slaught'ring hands, and keep the
          peace.
Pray, uncle Gloster, mitigate this strife.
1 Serv. Nay, if we be
Forbidden stones, we 'll fall to it with our teeth.   90
2 Serv. Do what ye dare ; we are as resolute.
          [*Skirmish again.*
Glo. You of my household, leave this peevish
          broil,
And set this unaccustom'd fight aside.
1 Serv. My lord, we know your grace to be a
          man
Just and upright, and, for your royal birth,
Inferior to none but to his majesty ;
And ere that we will suffer such a prince,
So kind a father of the commonweal,
To be disgraced by an inkhorn mate,
We, and our wives, and children, all will fight,   100
And have our bodies slaughter'd by thy foes.
3 Serv. Ay, and the very parings of our nails
Shall pitch a field, when we are dead.
          [*Skirmish again.*
Glo.   Stay, stay, I say !
And, if you love me, as you say you do,
Let me persuade you to forbear awhile.
K. Hen. O, how this discord doth afflict my soul !—
Can you, my Lord of Winchester, behold
My sighs and tears, and will not once relent ?
Who should be pitiful, if you be not ?
Or who should study to prefer a peace,   110
If holy churchmen take delight in broils ?
War. Yield, my lord protector ;—yield, Winchester ;
Except you mean, with obstinate repulse,
To slay your sovereign, and destroy the realm.
You see what mischief, and what murder too,
Hath been enacted through your enmity :
Then, be at peace, except ye thirst for blood.
Win. He shall submit, or I will never yield.
Glo. Compassion on the king commands me stoop ;
Or I would see his heart out, ere the priest   120
Should ever get that privilege of mine.
War. Behold, my Lord of Winchester, the duke
Hath banish'd moody discontented fury,
As by his smoothed brows it doth appear :
Why look you still so stern, and tragical ?
Glo. Here, Winchester, I offer thee my hand.
K. Hen. Fie, uncle Beaufort ! I have heard you
          preach,
That malice was a great and grievous sin ;
And will not you maintain the thing you teach,
But prove a chief offender in the same ?   130
War. Sweet king !—the bishop hath a kindly gird.—
For shame, my Lord of Winchester, relent :
What, shall a child instruct you what to do ?
Win. Well, Duke of Gloster, I will yield to thee ;
Love for thy love, and hand for hand I give.
Glo. [*Aside.*] Ay ; but, I fear me, with a hollow
          heart.—
See here, my friends, and loving countrymen,
This token serveth for a flag of truce
Betwixt ourselves and all our followers.
So help me God, as I dissemble not !   140
Win. [*Aside.*] So help me God, as I intend it
          not !
K. Hen. O loving uncle, kind Duke of Gloster,
How joyful am I made by this contract !—
Away, my masters : trouble us no more ;
But join in friendship, as your lords have done.
1 Serv. Content : I 'll to the surgeon's.
2 Serv.   And so will I.
3 Serv. And I will see what physic the tavern
          affords.
          [*Exeunt Mayor, Servants, &c.*
War. Accept this scroll, most gracious sovereign,
Which in the right of Richard Plantagenet
We do exhibit to your majesty.   150
Glo. Well urg'd, my Lord of Warwick :—for, sweet
          prince,
An if your grace mark every circumstance,
You have great reason to do Richard right ;
Especially for those occasions
At Eltham Place I told your majesty.

K. Hen. And those occasions, uncle, were of
　　force :
Therefore, my loving lords, our pleasure is,
That Richard be restored to his blood.
　　War. Let Richard be restored to his blood ;
So shall his father's wrongs be recompens'd.　160
　　Win. As will the rest, so willeth Winchester.
　　K. Hen. If Richard will be true, not that alone,
But all the whole inheritance I give,
That doth belong unto the house of York,
From whence you spring by lineal descent.
　　Plan. Thy humble servant vows obedience,
And humble service, till the point of death.
　　K. Hen. Stoop then, and set your knee against my
　　foot ;
And, in reguerdon of that duty done,
I girt thee with the valiant sword of York.　170
Rise, Richard, like a true Plantagenet,
And rise created princely Duke of York.
　　Plan. And so thrive Richard as thy foes may fall !
And as my duty springs, so perish they
That grudge one thought against your majesty !
　　All. Welcome, high prince, the mighty Duke of
　　York !
　　Som. [Aside.] Perish, base prince, ignoble Duke of
　　York !
　　Glo. Now will it best avail your majesty,
To cross the seas, and to be crown'd in France.
The presence of a king engenders love　　180
Amongst his subjects, and his loyal friends,
As it disanimates his enemies.
　　K. Hen. When Gloster says the word, King Henry
　　goes ;
For friendly counsel cuts off many foes.
　　Glo. Your ships already are in readiness.
　　　　　　　[Flourish. Exeunt all but EXETER.
　　Exe. Ay, we may march in England, or in France,
Not seeing what is likely to ensue.
This late dissension, grown betwixt the peers,
Burns under feigned ashes of forg'd love,
And will at last break out into a flame :　　190
As fester'd members rot but by degree,
Till bones, and flesh, and sinews, fall away,
So will this base and envious discord breed.
And now I fear that fatal prophecy,
Which, in the time of Henry nam'd the Fifth,
Was in the mouth of every sucking babe,—
That Henry born at Monmouth should win all,
And Henry born at Windsor should lose all :
Which is so plain, that Exeter doth wish
His days may finish ere that hapless time.　200
　　　　　　　　　　　　　　　　　[Exit.

────────

SCENE II.—France. Before Rouen.

Enter LA PUCELLE, disguised, and Soldiers dressed
　　like countrymen, with sacks upon their backs.

　　Puc. These are the city gates, the gates of Roan,
Through which our policy must make a breach.
Take heed, be wary how you place your words ;
Talk like the vulgar sort of market-men,
That come to gather money for their corn.
If we have entrance (as I hope we shall),
And that we find the slothful watch but weak,
I 'll by a sign give notice to our friends,
That Charles the Dauphin may encounter them.
　　1 Sold. Our sacks shall be a mean to sack the city,
And we be lords and rulers over Roan ;　　11
Therefore we 'll knock.　　　　　　[Knocks.
　　Guard. [Within.] Qui est là ?
　　Puc. Paisans, pauvres gens de France :
Poor market-folks, that come to sell their corn.
　　Guard. [Opens the gates.] Enter, go in : the market-
　　bell is rung.
　　Puc. Now, Roan, I 'll shake thy bulwarks to the
　　ground.　　　　[PUCELLE, &c., enter the city.

Enter CHARLES, BASTARD of Orleans, ALENÇON,
　　and Forces.

　　Char. Saint Dennis bless this happy stratagem,
And once again we 'll sleep secure in Roan.

　　Bast. Here enter'd Pucelle, and her practisants ;　20
Now she is there, how will she specify
Where is the best and safest passage in ?
　　Alen. By thrusting out a torch from yonder tower ;
Which, once discern'd, shows that her meaning is,—
No way to that, for weakness, which she enter'd.

Enter LA PUCELLE on a battlement, holding out a
　　torch burning.

　　Puc. Behold ! this is the happy wedding torch,
That joineth Roan unto her countrymen,
But burning fatal to the Talbotites.
　　Bast. See, noble Charles, the beacon of our friend,
The burning torch in yonder turret stands.　　30
　　Char. Now shine it like a comet of revenge,
A prophet to the fall of all our foes !
　　Alen. Defer no time ; delays have dangerous ends :
Enter, and cry, " The Dauphin !" presently,
And then do execution on the watch.　[They enter.

Alarums. Enter TALBOT and English Soldiers.

　　Tal. France, thou shalt rue this treason with thy
　　tears,
If Talbot but survive thy treachery.
Pucelle, that witch, that damned sorceress,
Hath wrought this hellish mischief unawares,
That hardly we escap'd the pride of France.　40
　　　　　　　　　　　　　[Exeunt to the town.

Alarum : Excursions. Enter, from the town, BED-
　　FORD, brought in sick in a chair, with TALBOT,
　　BURGUNDY, and the English Forces. Then, enter
　　on the walls, LA PUCELLE, CHARLES, BASTARD,
　　ALENÇON, REIGNIER, and others.

　　Puc. Good morrow, gallants. Want ye corn for
　　bread ?
I think, the Duke of Burgundy will fast,
Before he 'll buy again at such a rate.
'T was full of darnel : do you like the taste?
　　Bur. Scoff on, vile fiend, and shameless courtesan !
I trust, ere long, to choke thee with thine own,
And make thee curse the harvest of that corn.
　　Char. Your grace may starve, perhaps, before that
　　time.
　　Bed. O ! let no words, but deeds, revenge this
　　treason.
　　Puc. What will you do, good grey-beard ? break a
　　lance,　　　　　　　　　　　　　　50
And run a tilt at death within a chair ?
　　Tal. Foul fiend of France, and hag of all despite,
Encompass'd with thy lustful paramours,
Becomes it thee to taunt his valiant age,
And twit with cowardice a man half dead ?
Damsel, I 'll have a bout with you again,
Or else let Talbot perish with this shame.
　　Puc. Are you so hot, sir ?—Yet, Pucelle, hold thy
　　peace :
If Talbot do but thunder, rain will follow.—
　　　　　　[TALBOT, and the rest, consult together.
God speed the parliament ! who shall be the speaker ?
　　Tal. Dare you come forth, and meet us in the
　　field ?　　　　　　　　　　　　　61
　　Puc. Belike, your lordship takes us then for fools,
To try if that our own be ours, or no.
　　Tal. I speak not to that railing Hecate,
But unto thee, Alençon, and the rest.
Will ye, like soldiers, come and fight it out ?
　　Alen. Signior, no.
　　Tal. Signior, hang !—base muleters of France !
Like peasant footboys do they keep the walls,
And dare not take up arms like gentlemen.　70
　　Puc. Away, captains ! let 's get us from the
　　walls,
For Talbot means no goodness by his looks.—
God bu wi' you, my lord : we came but to tell you
That we are here.
　　　　　　[Exeunt LA PUCELLE, &c., from the walls.
　　Tal. And there will we be too, ere it be long,
Or else reproach be Talbot's greatest fame.
Vow, Burgundy, by honour of thy house,
Prick'd on by public wrongs, sustain'd in France,
Either to get the town again, or die ;

And I, as sure as English Henry lives,
And as his father here was conqueror,   80
As sure as in this late-betrayed town
Great Cordelion's heart was buried,
So sure I swear, to get the town, or die.
  Bur. My vows are equal partners with thy vows.

Came to the field, and vanquished his foes.
Methinks, I should revive the soldiers' hearts,
Because I ever found them as myself.
  Tal. Undaunted spirit in a dying breast !—
Then, be it so :—heavens keep old Bedford safe !—   100
And now no more ado, brave Burgundy,

Tal. " Damsel, I 'll have a bout with you again."

  Tal. But ere we go, regard this dying prince,
The valiant Duke of Bedford.—Come, my lord,
We will bestow you in some better place,
Fitter for sickness, and for crazy age.
  Bed. Lord Talbot, do not so dishonour me ;   90
Here will I sit before the walls of Roan,
And will be partner of your weal or woe.
  Bur. Courageous Bedford, let us now persuade you.
  Bed. Not to be gone from hence ; for once I read,
That stout Pendragon, in his litter, sick,

But gather we our forces out of hand,
And set upon our boasting enemy.
  [*Exeunt* BURGUNDY, TALBOT, *and Forces, leaving*
    BEDFORD *and others.*

Alarum : Excursions. Enter Sir JOHN FASTOLFE
    and a Captain.

  Cap. Whither away, Sir John Fastolfe, in such haste ?
  Fast. Whither away ? to save myself by flight :
We are like to have the overthrow again.

Cap. What! will you fly, and leave Lord Talbot?
Fast.   Ay,
All the Talbots in the world, to save my life.   [*Exit.*
Cap. Cowardly knight! ill fortune follow thee!
                                                 [*Exit.*

Retreat: Excursions. Enter, from the town, LA PU-
CELLE, ALENÇON, CHARLES, *&c., and exeunt, flying.*
Bed. Now, quiet soul, depart when Heaven please,
For I have seen our enemies' overthrow.   111
What is the trust or strength of foolish man?
They, that of late were daring with their scoffs,
Are glad and fain by flight to save themselves.
                 [*Dies, and is carried off in his chair.*

Alarum. Enter TALBOT, BURGUNDY, *and others.*
Tal. Lost, and recover'd in a day again!
This is a double honour, Burgundy;
Yet heavens have glory for this victory!
Bur. Warlike and martial Talbot, Burgundy
Enshrines thee in his heart, and there erects
Thy noble deeds, as valour's monument.   120
Tal. Thanks, gentle duke. But where is Pucelle
now?
I think her old familiar is asleep:
Now where's the Bastard's braves, and Charles his
gleeks?
What, all a-mort? Roan hangs her head for grief,
That such a valiant company are fled.
Now will we take some order in the town,
Placing therein some expert officers,
And then depart to Paris to the king;
For there young Henry with his nobles lie.
Bur. What wills Lord Talbot pleaseth Burgundy.130
Tal. But yet, before we go, let's not forget
The noble Duke of Bedford, late deceas'd,
But see his exequies fulfill'd in Roan.
A braver soldier never couched lance,
A gentler heart did never sway in court;
But kings, and mightiest potentates, must die;
For that's the end of human misery.   [*Exeunt.*

SCENE III.—The Same. The Plains near the City.

Enter CHARLES, *the* BASTARD, ALENÇON, LA
PUCELLE, *and Forces.*

Puc. Dismay not, princes, at this accident,
Nor grieve that Roan is so recovered:
Care is no cure, but rather corrosive,
For things that are not to be remedied.
Let frantic Talbot triumph for a while,
And like a peacock sweep along his tail;
We'll pull his plumes, and take away his train,
If Dauphin and the rest will be but rul'd.
Char. We have been guided by thee hitherto,
And of thy cunning had no diffidence: 10
One sudden foil shall never breed distrust.
Bast. Search out thy wit for secret policies,
And we will make thee famous through the world.
Alen. We'll set thy statue in some holy place,
And have thee reverenc'd like a blessed saint:
Employ thee then, sweet virgin, for our good.
Puc. Then thus it must be; this doth Joan
devise:
By fair persuasions, mix'd with sugar'd words,
We will entice the Duke of Burgundy
To leave the Talbot, and to follow us.   20
Char. Ay, marry, sweeting, if we could do that,
France were no place for Henry's warriors;
Nor should that nation boast it so with us,
But be extirped from our provinces.
Alen. For ever should they be expuls'd from
France,
And not have title of an earldom here.
Puc. Your honours shall perceive how I will
work,
To bring this matter to the wished end.
                 [*Drums heard afar off.*
Hark! by the sound of drum you may perceive
Their powers are marching unto Paris-ward.   30

An English march. Enter, and pass over, TALBOT
and his Forces.
There goes the Talbot, with his colours spread,
And all the troops of English after him.

A French march. Enter the Duke of BURGUNDY
and Forces.
Now, in the rearward comes the duke, and his:
Fortune in favour makes him lag behind.
Summon a parley; we will talk with him.
                 [*Trumpets sound a parley.*
Char. A parley with the Duke of Burgundy.
Bur. Who craves a parley with the Burgundy?
Puc. The princely Charles of France, thy country-
man.
Bur. What say'st thou, Charles? for I am marching
hence.
Char. Speak, Pucelle, and enchant him with thy
words.   40
Puc. Brave Burgundy, undoubted hope of France,
Stay, let thy humble handmaid speak to thee.
Bur. Speak on; but be not over-tedious.
Puc. Look on thy country, look on fertile France,
And see the cities and the towns defac'd
By wasting ruin of the cruel foe.
As looks the mother on her lowly babe,
When death doth close his tender dying eyes,
See, see the pining malady of France;
Behold the wounds, the most unnatural wounds,   50
Which thou thyself hast given her woful breast.
O! turn thy edged sword another way;
Strike those that hurt, and hurt not those that help.
One drop of blood, drawn from thy country's bosom,
Should grieve thee more than streams of foreign gore:
Return thee, therefore, with a flood of tears,
And wash away thy country's stained spots.
Bur. Either she hath bewitch'd me with her words,
Or nature makes me suddenly relent.
Puc. Besides, all French and France exclaims on
thee,   60
Doubting thy birth and lawful progeny.
Who join'st thou with, but with a lordly nation,
That will not trust thee but for profit's sake?
When Talbot hath set footing once in France,
And fashion'd thee that instrument of ill,
Who then but English Henry will be lord,
And thou be thrust out like a fugitive?
Call we to mind, and mark but this for proof,
Was not the Duke of Orleans thy foe,
And was he not in England prisoner?   70
But, when they heard he was thine enemy,
They set him free, without his ransom paid,
In spite of Burgundy, and all his friends.
See then, thou fight'st against thy countrymen,
And join'st with them will be thy slaughter-men.
Come, come, return; return, thou wand'ring lord;
Charles and the rest will take thee in their arms.
Bur. I am vanquished: these haughty words of hers
Have batter'd me like roaring cannon-shot,
And made me almost yield upon my knees.—   80
Forgive me, country, and sweet countrymen!
And, lords, accept this hearty kind embrace:
My forces and my power of men are yours.—
So, farewell, Talbot; I'll no longer trust thee.
Puc. [*Aside.*] Done like a Frenchman: turn, and
turn again!
Char. Welcome, brave duke! thy friendship makes
us fresh.
Bast. And doth beget new courage in our breasts.
Alen. Pucelle hath bravely play'd her part in this,
And doth deserve a coronet of gold.
Char. Now let us on, my lords, and join our powers,
And seek how we may prejudice the foe.   [*Exeunt.*

SCENE IV.—Paris. A Room in the Palace.

Enter King HENRY, GLOSTER, *and other Lords;*
VERNON. BASSET, *&c. To them* TALBOT *and some*
of his Officers.

Tal. My gracious prince, and honourable peers,

Hearing of your arrival in this realm,
I have awhile given truce unto my wars,
To do my duty to my sovereign :
In sign whereof, this arm—that hath reclaim'd
To your obedience fifty fortresses,
Twelve cities, and seven walled towns of strength,
Beside five hundred prisoners of esteem—
Lets fall his sword before your highness' feet ;
                        [*Kneeling.*
And, with submissive loyalty of heart,   10
Ascribes the glory of his conquest got
First to my God, and next unto your grace.
  K. Hen. Is this the Lord Talbot, uncle Gloster,
That hath so long been resident in France ?
  Glo. Yes, if it please your majesty, my liege.
  K. Hen. Welcome, brave captain, and victorious
      lord.
When I was young (as yet I am not old),
I do remember how my father said,
A stouter champion never handled sword.
Long since we were resolved of your truth,   20
Your faithful service, and your toil in war ;
Yet never have you tasted our reward,
Or been reguerdon'd with so much as thanks,
Because till now we never saw your face :

Therefore, stand up ; and, for these good deserts,
We here create you Earl of Shrewsbury ;
And in our coronation take your place.
      [*Flourish. Exeunt King* HENRY, GLOSTER,
               TALBOT, *and Nobles.*
  Ver. Now, sir, to you, that were so hot at sea,
Disgracing of these colours, that I wear
In honour of my noble Lord of York,   30
Dar'st thou maintain the former words thou spak'st ?
  Bas. Yes, sir ; as well as you dare patronage
The envious barking of your saucy tongue
Against my lord, the Duke of Somerset.
  Ver. Sirrah, thy lord I honour as he is.
  Bas. Why, what is he ? as good a man as York.
  Ver. Hark ye ; not so : in witness, take ye that.
                    [*Striking him.*
  Bas. Villain. thou know'st, the law of arms is such,
That, whoso draws a sword, 't is present death,
Or else this blow should broach thy dearest blood. 40
But I 'll unto his majesty, and crave
I may have liberty to venge this wrong ;
When thou shalt see, I 'll meet thee to thy cost.
  Ver. Well, miscreant, I 'll be there as soon as you ;
And, after, meet you sooner than you would. [*Exeunt.*

ACT IV.

SCENE I.—The Same. A Room of State.

Enter King HENRY, GLOSTER, EXETER, YORK, SUFFOLK, SOMERSET, WINCHESTER,
WARWICK, TALBOT, *the Governor of Paris, and others.*

  Gloucester.
ORD bishop, set the crown upon his
     head.
  Win. God save King Henry, of
     that name the sixth !
  Glo. Now, governor of Paris, take
     your oath,—
         [*Governor kneels.*
That you elect no other king but him,
Esteem none friends, but such as are
     his friends,
And none your foes, but such as
     shall pretend
Malicious practices against his state :
This shall ye do, so help you
     righteous God !
      [*Exeunt Governor and his Train.*

Enter Sir JOHN FASTOLFE.

  Fast. My gracious sovereign, as I rode from Calais,
To haste unto your coronation,   10
A letter was deliver'd to my hands,
Writ to your grace from the Duke of Burgundy.
  Tal. Shame to the Duke of Burgundy, and thee !
I vow'd, base knight, when I did meet thee next,
To tear the garter from thy craven's leg ;
             [*Plucking it off.*
Which I have done, because unworthily
Thou wast installed in that high degree.—
Pardon me. princely Henry, and the rest.
This dastard, at the battle of Patay,
When but in all I was six thousand strong,   20
And that the French were almost ten to one,
Before we met, or that a stroke was given,
Like to a trusty squire, did run away :

In which assault we lost twelve hundred men ;
Myself, and divers gentlemen beside,
Were there surpris'd, and taken prisoners.
Then judge, great lords, if I have done amiss ;
Or whether that such cowards ought to wear
This ornament of knighthood, yea, or no.
  Glo. To say the truth, this fact was infamous,   30
And ill beseeming any common man,
Much more a knight, a captain, and a leader.
  Tal. When first this order was ordain'd, my lords,
Knights of the garter were of noble birth,
Valiant and virtuous, full of haughty courage,
Such as were grown to credit by the wars ;
Not fearing death, nor shrinking for distress,
But always resolute in most extremes.
He then, that is not furnish'd in this sort,
Doth but usurp the sacred name of knight,   40
Profaning this most honourable order,
And should (if I were worthy to be judge)
Be quite degraded, like a hedge-born swain
That doth presume to boast of gentle blood.
  K. Hen. Stain to thy countrymen ! thou hear'st thy
     doom.
Be packing therefore, thou that wast a knight.
Henceforth we banish thee on pain of death.—
              [*Exit* FASTOLFE.
And now, my lord protector, view the letter
Sent from our uncle Duke of Burgundy.
  Glo. What means his grace, that he hath chang'd
     his style ?   50
No more but, plain and bluntly,—" To the king !"
Hath he forgot, he is his sovereign ?
Or doth this churlish superscription
Pretend some alteration in good will ?
What 's here ? [*Reads.*] " I have upon especial cause,

Mov'd with compassion of my country's wrack,
Together with the pitiful complaints
Of such as your oppression feeds upon,
Forsaken your pernicious faction,
And join'd with Charles, the rightful King of France."
O monstrous treachery ! Can this be so,   61
That in alliance, amity, and oaths,
There should be found such false dissembling guile?
K. Hen. What! doth my uncle Burgundy revolt?
Glo. He doth, my lord, and is become your foe.
K. Hen. Is that the worst this letter doth contain?
Glo. It is the worst, and all, my lord, he writes.
K. Hen. Why then, Lord Talbot there shall talk
          with him,
And give him chastisement for this abuse.—
How say you, my lord? are you not content?   70
Tal. Content, my liege? Yes: but that I am pre-
          vented,
I should have begg'd I might have been employ'd.
K. Hen. Then gather strength, and march unto him
          straight.
Let him perceive, how ill we brook his treason ;
And what offence it is, to flout his friends.
Tal. I go, my lord ; in heart desiring still,
You may behold confusion of your foes.   [*Exit.*

          Enter VERNON *and* BASSET.

Ver. Grant me the combat, gracious sovereign !
Bas. And me, my lord ; grant me the combat too !
York. This is my servant : hear him, noble prince !
Som. And this is mine : sweet Henry, favour him !
K. Hen. Be patient, lords ; and give them leave to
          speak.—   82
Say, gentlemen, what makes you thus exclaim ?
And wherefore crave you combat? or with whom ?
Ver. With him, my lord ; for he hath done me wrong.
Bas. And I with him ; for he hath done me wrong.
K. Hen. What is that wrong whereof you both
          complain ?
First let me know, and then I 'll answer you.
Bas. Crossing the sea from England into France,
This fellow here, with envious carping tongue,   90
Upbraided me about the rose I wear ;
Saying, the sanguine colour of the leaves
Did represent my master's blushing cheeks,
When stubbornly he did repugn the truth,
About a certain question in the law,
Argu'd betwixt the Duke of York and him ;
With other vile and ignominious terms :
In confutation of which rude reproach,
And in defence of my lord's worthiness,
I crave the benefit of law of arms.   100
Ver. And that is my petition, noble lord :
For though he seem, with forged quaint conceit,
To set a gloss upon his bold intent,
Yet know, my lord, I was provok'd by him,
And he first took exceptions at this badge,
Pronouncing, that the paleness of this flower
Bewray'd the faintness of my master's heart.
York. Will not this malice, Somerset, be left ?
Som. Your private grudge, my Lord of York, will
          out,
Though ne'er so cunningly you smother it.   110
K. Hen. Good Lord ! what madness rules in brain-
          sick men,
When, for so slight and frivolous a cause,
Such factious emulations shall arise !—
Good cousins both, of York and Somerset,
Quiet yourselves, I pray, and be at peace.
York. Let this dissension first be tried by fight,
And then your highness shall command a peace.
Som. The quarrel toucheth none but us alone ;
Betwixt ourselves let us decide it then.
York. There is my pledge ; accept it, Somerset.   120
Ver. Nay, let it rest where it began at first.
Bas. Confirm it so, mine honourable lord.
Glo. Confirm it so ? Confounded be your strife !
And perish ye, with your audacious prate !
Presumptuous vassals ! are you not asham'd,
With this immodest clamorous outrage
To trouble and disturb the king and us ?
And you, my lords, methinks you do not well,

To bear with their perverse objections ;
Much less, to take occasion from their mouths   130
To raise a mutiny betwixt yourselves :
Let me persuade you, take a better course.
Exe. It grieves his highness :—good my lords, be
          friends.
K. Hen. Come hither, you that would be com-
          batants.
Henceforth I charge you, as you love our favour,
Quite to forget this quarrel, and the cause.—
And you, my lords, remember where we are ;
In France, amongst a fickle wavering nation.
If they perceive dissension in our looks,
And that within ourselves we disagree,   140
How will their grudging stomachs be provok'd
To wilful disobedience, and rebel !
Beside, what infamy will there arise,
When foreign princes shall be certified,
That for a toy, a thing of no regard,
King Henry's peers, and chief nobility,
Destroy'd themselves, and lost the realm of France !
O ! think upon the conquest of my father,
My tender years ; and let us not forego
That for a trifle that was bought with blood.   150
Let me be umpire in this doubtful strife.
          [*Putting on a red rose.*
I see no reason, if I wear this rose,
That any one should therefore be suspicious
I more incline to Somerset than York :
Both are my kinsmen, and I love them both.
As well they may upbraid me with my crown,
Because, forsooth, the King of Scots is crown'd.
But your discretions better can persuade,
Than I am able to instruct or teach :
And therefore, as we hither came in peace,   160
So let us still continue peace and love.—
Cousin of York, we institute your grace
To be our regent in these parts of France :
And, good my Lord of Somerset, unite
Your troops of horsemen with his bands of foot ;
And, like true subjects, sons of your progenitors,
Go cheerfully together, and digest
Your angry choler on your enemies.
Ourself, my lord protector, and the rest,
After some respite, will return to Calais ;   170
From thence to England, where I hope ere long
To be presented, by your victories,
With Charles, Alençon, and that traitorous rout.
          [*Flourish. Exeunt King* HENRY, GLOSTER,
               SOMERSET, WINCHESTER, SUFFOLK,
               and BASSET.
War. My Lord of York, I promise you, the king
Prettily, methought, did play the orator.
York. And so he did : but yet I like it not,
In that he wears the badge of Somerset.
War. Tush ! that was but his fancy, blame him not ;
I dare presume, sweet prince, he thought no harm.
York. An if I wist, he did,—but let it rest ;   180
Other affairs must now be managed.
          [*Exeunt* YORK, WARWICK, *and* VERNON.
Exe. Well didst thou, Richard, to suppress thy
          voice ;
For, had the passions of thy heart burst out,
I fear, we should have seen decipher'd there
More rancorous spite, more furious raging broils,
Than yet can be imagin'd or suppos'd.
But howsoe'er, no simple man that sees
This jarring discord of nobility,
This shouldering of each other in the court,
This factious bandying of their favourites,   190
But that it doth presage some ill event.
'Tis much, when sceptres are in children's hands,
But more, when envy breeds unkind division :
There comes the ruin, there begins confusion.   [*Exit.*

          ————

          SCENE II.—France. Before Bourdeaux.

          Enter TALBOT, *with his Forces.*

Tal. Go to the gates of Bourdeaux, trumpeter :
Summon their general unto the wall.

Trumpet sounds a parley. Enter, on the walls, the
General of the French Forces, and others.
English John Talbot, captains, calls you forth,
Servant in arms to Harry King of England ;
And thus he would.—Open your city gates,
Be humble to us, call my sovereign yours,
And do him homage as obedient subjects,
And I 'll withdraw me and my bloody power ;
But, if you frown upon this proffer'd peace,
You tempt the fury of my three attendants,   10
Lean famine, quartering steel, and climbing fire ;
Who, in a moment, even with the earth
Shall lay your stately and air-braving towers,
If you forsake the offer of their love.
Gen. Thou ominous and fearful owl of death,

York. "There is my pledge ; accept it, Somerset."

Our nation's terror, and their bloody scourge !
The period of thy tyranny approacheth.
On us thou canst not enter but by death ;
For, I protest, we are well fortified,
And strong enough to issue out and fight :   20
If thou retire, the Dauphin, well appointed,
Stands with the snares of war to tangle thee :
On either hand thee there are squadrons pitch'd,
To wall thee from the liberty of flight ;
And no way canst thou turn thee for redress,
But death doth front thee with apparent spoil,
And pale destruction meets thee in the face.
Ten thousand French have ta'en the sacrament,
To rive their dangerous artillery
Upon no Christian soul but English Talbot.   30
Lo ! there thou stand'st, a breathing valiant man,
Of an invincible unconquer'd spirit :
This is the latest glory of thy praise,
That I, thy enemy, 'due thee withal ;
For ere the glass, that now begins to run,
Finish the process of his sandy hour,
These eyes, that see thee now well coloured,
Shall see thee wither'd, bloody, pale, and dead.
                              [*Drum afar off.*
Hark ! hark ! the Dauphin's drum, a warning bell,
Sings heavy music to thy timorous soul,   40
And mine shall ring thy dire departure out.
           [*Exeunt General, &c., from the walls.*
Tal. He fables not, I hear the enemy.—
Out, some light horsemen, and peruse their wings.—
O, negligent and heedless discipline !
How are we park'd, and bounded in a pale !
A little herd of England's timorous deer,
Maz'd with a yelping kennel of French curs !
If we be English deer, be then in blood ;
Not rascal-like, to fall down with a pinch,

But rather moody-mad and desperate stags,   50
Turn on the bloody hounds with heads of steel,
And make the cowards stand aloof at bay :
Sell every man his life as dear as mine,
And they shall find dear deer of us, my friends.—
God, and Saint George, Talbot, and England's right,
Prosper our colours in this dangerous fight ! [*Exeunt.*

SCENE III.—Plains in Gascony.

Enter YORK, *with Forces ; to him, a Messenger.*

York. Are not the speedy scouts return'd again,
That dogg'd the mighty army of the Dauphin ?
      Mess. They are return'd, my lord ; and
                       give it out,
      That he is march'd to Bourdeaux with
                       his power,
      To fight with Talbot. As he march'd
                       along,
      By your espials were discovered
      Two mightier troops than that the
                       Dauphin led,
      Which join'd with him, and made their
                       march for Bourdeaux.
      York. A plague upon that villain
                       Somerset,
      That thus delays my promised supply   10
Of horsemen, that were levied for this
                       siege !
Renowned Talbot doth expect my aid,
And I am lowted by a traitor villain,
And cannot help the noble chevalier.
God comfort him in this necessity !
If he miscarry, farewell wars in France.

Enter Sir WILLIAM LUCY.

      Lucy. Thou princely leader of our
                       English strength,
Never so needful on the earth of France,
Spur to the rescue of the noble Talbot,
Who now is girdled with a waist of
                       iron,   20
And hemm'd about with grim destruc-
                       tion.
To Bourdeaux, warlike duke ! to Bourdeaux, York !
Else, farewell Talbot, France, and England's honour.
      York. O God ! that Somerset, who in proud heart
Doth stop my cornets, were in Talbot's place !
So should we save a valiant gentleman,
By forfeiting a traitor and a coward.
Mad ire, and wrathful fury, make me weep,
That thus we die, while remiss traitors sleep.
      Lucy. O, send some succour to the distress'd lord !
      York. He dies, we lose ; I break my warlike
                       word ;   31
We mourn, France smiles ; we lose, they daily get ;
All 'long of this vile traitor Somerset.
      Lucy. Then, God take mercy on brave Talbot's
                       soul ;
And on his son, young John, whom two hours
                       since
I met in travel toward his warlike father.
This seven years did not Talbot see his son,
And now they meet where both their lives are done.
      York. Alas ! what joy shall noble Talbot have,
To bid his young son welcome to his grave ?   40
Away ! vexation almost stops my breath,
That sunder'd friends greet in the hour of death.—
Lucy, farewell : no more my fortune can,
But curse the cause I cannot aid the man.—
Maine, Blois, Poictiers, and Tours, are won away,
'Long all of Somerset, and his delay.
                       [*Exit, with his Forces.*
      Lucy. Thus, while the vulture of sedition
Feeds in the bosom of such great commanders,
Sleeping neglection doth betray to loss
The conquest of our scarce-cold conqueror,   50
That ever-living man of memory,
Henry the Fifth : whiles they each other cross,
Lives, honours, lands, and all, hurry to loss. [*Exit.*

SCENE IV.—Other Plains of Gascony.

Enter SOMERSET, *with his Army; an Officer of* TALBOT'S *with him.*

Som. It is too late ; I cannot send them now.
This expedition was by York and Talbot
Too rashly plotted : all our general force
Might with a sally of the very town
Be buckled with. The over-daring Talbot
Hath sullied all his gloss of former honour
By this unheedful, desperate, wild adventure.
York set him on to fight and die in shame,
That, Talbot dead, great York might bear the name.
Off. Here is Sir William Lucy, who with me   10
Set from our o'ermatch'd forces forth for aid.

Enter Sir WILLIAM LUCY.

Som. How now, Sir William ? whither were you
      sent ?
Lucy. Whither, my lord ? from bought and sold
Lord Talbot ;
Who, ring'd about with bold adversity,
Cries out for noble York and Somerset,
To beat assailing death from his weak legions.
And whiles the honourable captain there
Drops bloody sweat from his war-wearied limbs,
And, in advantage lingering, looks for rescue,
You, his false hopes, the trust of England's honour,
Keep off aloof with worthless emulation.   21
Let not your private discord keep away
The levied succours that should lend him aid,
While he, renowned noble gentleman,
Yields up his life unto a world of odds.
Orleans the Bastard, Charles, Burgundy,
Alençon, Reignier, compass him about,
And Talbot perisheth by your default.
Som. York set him on, York should have sent him
      aid.
Lucy. And York as fast upon your grace exclaims ;
Swearing that you withhold his levied horse,   31
Collected for this expedition.
Som. York lies : he might have sent and had the
      horse.
I owe him little duty, and less love,
And take foul scorn to fawn on him by sending.
Lucy. The fraud of England, not the force of
      France,
Hath now entrapp'd the noble-minded Talbot.
Never to England shall he bear his life,
But dies, betray'd to fortune by your strife.
Som. Come, go ; I will despatch the horsemen
      straight :   40
Within six hours they will be at his aid.
Lucy. Too late comes rescue : he is ta'en, or slain ;
For fly he could not, if he would have fled :
And fly would Talbot never, though he might.
Som. If he be dead, brave Talbot, then adieu !
Lucy. His fame lives in the world, his shame in
      you.   [*Exeunt.*

SCENE V.—The English Camp near Bordeaux.

Enter TALBOT *and* JOHN *his son.*

Tal. O young John Talbot ! I did send for thee,
To tutor thee in stratagems of war,
That Talbot's name might be in thee reviv'd,
When sapless age, and weak unable limbs,
Should bring thy father to his drooping-chair.
But,—O malignant and ill-boding stars !—
Now thou art come unto a feast of death,
A terrible and unavoided danger :
Therefore, dear boy, mount on my swiftest horse,
And I 'll direct thee how thou shalt escape   10
By sudden flight : come, dally not, be gone.
John. Is my name Talbot ? and am I your son ?
And shall I fly ? O ! if you love my mother,
Dishonour not her honourable name,
To make a bastard, and a slave of me :
The world will say, he is not Talbot's blood,
That basely fled, when noble Talbot stood.
Tal. Fly, to revenge my death, if I be slain.

John. He that flies so will ne'er return again.
Tal. If we both stay, we both are sure to die.   20
John. Then let me stay ; and, father, do you fly :
Your loss is great, so your regard should be ;
My worth unknown, no loss is known in me.
Upon my death the French can little boast ;
In yours they will, in you all hopes are lost.
Flight cannot stain the honour you have won ;
But mine it will, that no exploit have done :
You fled for vantage, every one will swear ;
But if I bow, they 'll say, it was for fear.
There is no hope that ever I will stay,   30
If the first hour I shrink, and run away.
Here, on my knee, I beg mortality,
Rather than life preserv'd with infamy.
Tal. Shall all thy mother's hopes lie in one tomb ?
John. Ay, rather than I 'll shame my mother's
      womb.
Tal. Upon my blessing I command thee go.
John. To fight I will, but not to fly the foe.
Tal. Part of thy father may be sav'd in thee.
John. No part of him but will be shame in me.
Tal. Thou never hadst renown, nor canst not lose it.
John. Yes, your renowned name : shall flight abuse
      it ?   41
Tal. Thy father's charge shall clear thee from that
      stain.
John. You cannot witness for me, being slain.
If death be so apparent, then both fly.
Tal. And leave my followers here, to fight and
      die ?
My age was never tainted with such shame.
John. And shall my youth be guilty of such blame ?
No more can I be sever'd from your side,
Than can yourself yourself in twain divide.
Stay, go, do what you will, the like do I ;   50
For live I will not, if my father die.
Tal. Then here I take my leave of thee, fair son,
Born to eclipse thy life this afternoon.
Come, side by side together live and die,
And soul with soul from France to heaven fly.
      [*Exeunt.*

SCENE VI.—A Field of Battle.

Alarum : Excursions, wherein TALBOT'S *Son is hemmed about, and* TALBOT *rescues him.*

Tal. Saint George and victory ! fight, soldiers, fight !
The regent hath with Talbot broke his word,
And left us to the rage of France his sword.
Where is John Talbot ?—pause, and take thy breath :
I gave thee life, and rescu'd thee from death.
John. O, twice my father ! twice am I thy son :
The life thou gav'st me first was lost and done ;
Till with thy warlike sword, despite of fate,
To my determin'd time thou gav'st new date.
Tal. When from the Dauphin's crest thy sword
      struck fire,   10
It warm'd thy father's heart with proud desire
Of bold-fac'd victory. Then leaden age,
Quicken'd with youthful spleen and warlike rage,
Beat down Alençon, Orleans, Burgundy,
And from the pride of Gallia rescu'd thee.
The ireful Bastard Orleans, that drew blood
From thee, my boy, and had the maidenhood
Of thy first fight, I soon encountered,
And, interchanging blows, I quickly shed
Some of his bastard blood ; and, in disgrace,   20
Bespoke him thus : " Contaminated, base,
And misbegotten blood I spill of thine,
Mean and right poor ; for that pure blood of mine,
Which thou didst force from Talbot, my brave boy :"—
Here, purposing the Bastard to destroy,
Came in strong rescue. Speak, thy father's care,
Art thou not weary, John ? How dost thou fare ?
Wilt thou yet leave the battle, boy, and fly,
Now thou art seal'd the son of chivalry ?
Fly to revenge my death, if I am dead ;   30
The help of one stands me in little stead.
O ! too much folly is it, well I wot,
To hazard all our lives in one small boat.

If I to-day die not with Frenchmen's rage,
To-morrow I shall die with mickle age :
By me they nothing gain, and if I stay,
'Tis but the short'ning of my life one day.
In thee thy mother dies, our household's name,
My death's revenge, thy youth, and England's
   fame.
All these, and more, we hazard by thy stay ;   40
All these are sav'd, if thou wilt fly away.
   John. The sword of Orleans hath not made me
   smart ;
These words of yours draw life-blood from my
   heart.
On that advantage, bought with such a shame,
To save a paltry life, and slay bright fame,
Before young Talbot from old Talbot fly,
The coward horse that bears me fall and die !
And like me to the peasant boys of France,
To be shame's scorn, and subject of mischance !
Surely, by all the glory you have won,   50
An if I fly, I am not Talbot's son :
Then talk no more of flight, it is no boot ;
If son to Talbot, die at Talbot's foot.
   Tal. Then follow thou thy desperate sire of Crete,
Thou Icarus. Thy life to me is sweet :
If thou wilt fight, fight by thy father's side,
And, commendable prov'd, let 's die in pride. [*Exeunt.*

SCENE VII.—Another Part of the Same.

Alarums : Excursions. Enter TALBOT, *wounded,
supported by a Servant.*

   Tal. Where is my other life ?—mine own is gone :
O, where 's young Talbot ? where is valiant John ?—
Triumphant death, smear'd with captivity,
Young Talbot's valour makes me smile at thee.—
When he perceiv'd me shrink, and on my knee,

Tal. " His bloody sword he brandish'd over me."

His bloody sword he brandish'd over me,
And like a hungry lion did commence
Rough deeds of rage, and stern impatience ;
But when my angry guardant stood alone,
Tend'ring my ruin, and assail'd of none,   10
Dizzy-ey'd fury, and great rage of heart,
Suddenly made him from my side to start
Into the clust'ring battle of the French :
And in that sea of blood my boy did drench
His overmounting spirit ; and there died
My Icarus, my blossom, in his pride.

Enter Soldiers, bearing the body of JOHN TALBOT.

   Serv. O my dear lord ! lo, where your son is borne !
   Tal. Thou antick death, which laugh'st us here to
   scorn,
Anon, from thy insulting tyranny,
Coupled in bonds of perpetuity,   20
Two Talbots, winged through the lither sky,
In thy despite shall 'scape mortality.—
O ! thou whose wounds become hard-favour'd death,
Speak to thy father, ere thou yield thy breath :
Brave death by speaking, whether he will or no ;
Imagine like a Frenchman, and thy foe.—
Poor boy ! he smiles, methinks, as who should say,
Had death been French, then death had died to-day.
Come, come, and lay him in his father's arms ;
My spirit can no longer bear these harms.   30
Soldiers, adieu ! I have what I would have,
Now my old arms are young John Talbot's grave.
                         [*Dies.*

*Alarums. Exeunt Soldiers and Servant, leaving the
two bodies. Enter* CHARLES, ALENÇON, BURGUNDY,
BASTARD, LA PUCELLE, *and Forces.*

   Char. Had York and Somerset brought rescue in,
We should have found a bloody day of this.
   Bast. How the young whelp of Talbot's, raging-
   wood,
Did flesh his puny sword in Frenchmen's blood !
   Puc. Once I encounter'd him, and thus I said :
" Thou maiden youth, be vanquish'd by a maid ;"
But, with a proud majestical high scorn,
He answered thus : " Young Talbot was not born   40
To be the pillage of a giglot wench."
So, rushing in the bowels of the French,
He left me proudly, as unworthy fight.
   Bur. Doubtless, he would have made a noble knight ;
See, where he lies inhearsed in the arms
Of the most bloody nurser of his harms.
   Bast. Hew them to pieces, hack their bones asunder,
Whose life was England's glory, Gallia's wonder.
   Char. O, no ! forbear ; for that which we have
   fled
During the life, let us not wrong it dead.   50

Enter Sir WILLIAM LUCY, *attended ; a French
Herald preceding.*

   Lucy. Herald, conduct me to the Dauphin's tent,
To know who hath obtain'd the glory of the day.
   Char. On what submissive message art thou sent ?
   Lucy. Submission, Dauphin ! 'tis a mere French
   word ;
We English warriors wot not what it means.
I come to know what prisoners thou hast ta'en,
And to survey the bodies of the dead.
   Char. For prisoners ask'st thou ? hell our prison is.
But tell me whom thou seek'st ?
   Lucy. But where 's the great Alcides of the field,   60
Valiant Lord Talbot, Earl of Shrewsbury,
Created, for his rare success in arms,
Great Earl of Washford, Waterford, and Valence ;
Lord Talbot of Goodrig and Urchinfield,
Lord Strange of Blackmere, Lord Verdun of Alton,
Lord Cromwell of Wingfield, Lord Furnival of Shef-
   field,
The thrice victorious Lord of Falconbridge,
Knight of the noble order of Saint George,
Worthy Saint Michael, and the Golden Fleece,
Great Mareshal to Henry the Sixth   70
Of all his wars within the realm of France ?
   Puc. Here is a silly stately style indeed !
The Turk, that two-and-fifty kingdoms hath,
Writes not so tedious a style as this.—
Him, that thou magnifiest with all these titles,
Stinking, and fly-blown, lies here at our feet.
   Lucy. Is Talbot slain, the Frenchmen's only scourge,
Your kingdom's terror and black Nemesis ?
O ! were mine eyeballs into bullets turn'd,
That I in rage might shoot them at your faces !   80
O, that I could but call these dead to life !
It were enough to fright the realm of France.
Were but his picture left among you here,

It would amaze the proudest of you all.
Give me their bodies, that I may bear them hence,
And give them burial as beseems their worth.
Puc. I think, this upstart is old Talbot's ghost,
He speaks with such a proud-commanding spirit.
For God's sake, let him have 'em ; to keep them here,
They would but stink, and putrefy the air.   90

Char. Go, take their bodies hence.
Lucy.   I 'll bear them hence :
But from their ashes shall be rear'd
A phœnix that shall make all France afeard.
Char. So we be rid of them, do with 'em what thou wilt.
And now to Paris, in this conquering vein :
All will be ours, now bloody Talbot 's slain. [*Exeunt.*

ACT V.

SCENE I.—London.   A Room in the Palace.

Enter King HENRY, GLOSTER, *and* EXETER.

King Henry.
HAVE you perus'd the letters from the pope,
The emperor, and the Earl of Armagnac?
Glo. I have, my lord ; and their intent is this :—
They humbly sue unto your excellence,
To have a godly peace concluded of
Between the realms of England and of France.
K. Hen. How doth your grace affect their motion?
Glo. Well, my good lord ; and as the only means
To stop effusion of our Christian blood,
And 'stablish quietness on every side.   10
K. Hen. Ay, marry, uncle ; for I always thought,
It was both impious and unnatural,
That such immanity and bloody strife
Should reign among professors of one faith.
Glo. Beside, my lord, the sooner to effect,
And surer bind, this knot of amity,
The Earl of Armagnac, near knit to Charles,
A man of great authority in France,
Proffers his only daughter to your grace
In marriage, with a large and sumptuous dowry. 20
K. Hen. Marriage, uncle ! alas ! my years are young,
And fitter is my study and my books
Than wanton dalliance with a paramour.
Yet, call the ambassadors ; and, as you please,
So let them have their answers every one :
I shall be well content with any choice
Tends to God's glory and my country's weal.

Enter a Legate and two Ambassadors, with
WINCHESTER *in a cardinal's habit.*

Exe. What ! is my Lord of Winchester install'd,
And call'd unto a cardinal's degree?
Then, I perceive, that will be verified,   30
Henry the Fifth did sometime prophesy,—
" If once he come to be a cardinal,
He 'll make his cap co-equal with the crown."
K. Hen. My lords ambassadors, your several suits
Have been consider'd and debated on.
Your purpose is both good and reasonable ;
And, therefore, are we certainly resolv'd
To draw conditions of a friendly peace ;
Which, by my Lord of Winchester, we mean
Shall be transported presently to France.   40
Glo. And for the proffer of my lord your master,
I have inform'd his highness so at large,
As—liking of the lady's virtuous gifts,

Her beauty, and the value of her dower—
He doth intend she shall be England's queen.
K. Hen. In argument and proof of which contract,
Bear her this jewel, pledge of my affection.—
And so, my lord protector, see them guarded,
And safely brought to Dover ; where, inshipp'd,
Commit them to the fortune of the sea.   50
[*Exeunt King* HENRY *and Train ;* GLOSTER,
EXETER, *and Ambassadors.*
Win. Stay, my lord legate : you shall first receive
The sum of money, which I promised
Should be deliver'd to his holiness
For clothing me in these grave ornaments.
Leg. I will attend upon your lordship's leisure.
Win. Now, Winchester will not submit, I trow,
Or be inferior to the proudest peer.
Humphrey of Gloster, thou shalt well perceive,
That, neither in birth, or for authority,
The bishop will be overborne by thee :   60
I 'll either make thee stoop, and bend thy knee,
Or sack this country with a mutiny.   [*Exeunt.*

SCENE II.—France.   Plains in Anjou.

Enter CHARLES, BURGUNDY, ALENÇON, LA PUCELLE,
and Forces, marching.

Char. These news, my lords, may cheer our drooping spirits.
'T is said, the stout Parisians do revolt,
And turn again unto the warlike French.
Alen. Then march to Paris, royal Charles of France,
And keep not back your powers in dalliance.
Puc. Peace be amongst them, if they turn to us ;
Else, ruin combat with their palaces !

Enter a Scout.

Scout. Success unto our valiant general,
And happiness to his accomplices !
Char. What tidings send our scouts ? I pr'ythee, speak.   10
Scout. The English army, that divided was
Into two parties, is now conjoin'd in one,
And means to give you battle presently.
Char. Somewhat too sudden, sirs, the warning is ;
But we will presently provide for them.
Bur. I trust, the ghost of Talbot is not there :
Now he is gone, my lord, you need not fear.
Puc. Of all base passions fear is most accurs'd.—
Command the conquest, Charles, it shall be thine ;
Let Henry fret, and all the world repine.   20
Char. Then on, my lords ; and France be fortunate !
[*Exeunt.*

SCENE III.—The Same. Before Angiers.

Alarums: Excursions. Enter LA PUCELLE.

Puc. The regent conquers, and the Frenchmen fly.—
Now help, ye charming spells, and periapts ;
And ye choice spirits that admonish me,
And give me signs of future accidents :   [*Thunder.*
You speedy helpers, that are substitutes
Under the lordly monarch of the north,
Appear, and aid me in this enterprise !

Enter Fiends.

This speedy and quick appearance argues proof
Of your accustom'd diligence to me.
Now, ye familiar spirits, that are cull'd   10
Out of the powerful legions under earth,
Help me this once, that France may get the field.
               [*They walk, and speak not.*
O! hold me not with silence over-long.
Where I was wont to feed you with my blood,
I 'll lop a member off, and give it you,
In earnest of a further benefit,
So you do condescend to help me now.—
               [*They hang their heads.*
No hope to have redress ?—My body shall
Pay recompense, if you will grant my suit.
               [*They shake their heads.*
Cannot my body, nor blood-sacrifice,   20
Entreat you to your wonted furtherance ?
Then take my soul ; my body, soul, and all,
Before that England give the French the foil.
               [*They depart.*
See ! they forsake me. Now the time is come,
That France must vail her lofty-plumed crest,
And let her head fall into England's lap.
My ancient incantations are too weak,
And hell too strong for me to buckle with :
Now, France, thy glory droopeth to the dust.   [*Exit.*

Alarums. Enter French and English, fighting ;
LA PUCELLE *and* YORK *fight hand to hand.*
LA PUCELLE *is taken. The French fly.*

York. Damsel of France, I think, I have you fast:30
Unchain your spirits now with spelling charms,
And try if they can gain your liberty.—
A goodly prize, fit for the devil's grace !
See, how the ugly witch doth bend her brows,
As if, with Circe, she would change my shape.
Puc. Chang'd to a worser shape thou canst not be.
York. O ! Charles the Dauphin is a proper man :
No shape but his can please your dainty eye.
Puc. A plaguing mischief light on Charles, and
    thee !
And may ye both be suddenly surpris'd   40
By bloody hands, in sleeping on your beds !
York. Fell banning hag, enchantress, hold thy
    tongue !
Puc. I pr'ythee, give me leave to curse awhile.
York. Curse, miscreant, when thou cdmest to the
    stake.   [*Exeunt.*

Alarums. Enter SUFFOLK, *leading in Lady*
MARGARET.

Suf. Be what thou wilt, thou art my prisoner.
                    [*Gazes on her.*
O, fairest beauty ! do not fear, nor fly,
For I will touch thee but with reverent hands.
I kiss these fingers for eternal peace,
And lay them gently on thy tender side.
Who art thou ? say, that I may honour thee.   50
Mar. Margaret my name, and daughter to a king,
The King of Naples, whosoe'er thou art.
Suf. An earl I am, and Suffolk am I call'd.
Be not offended, nature's miracle,
Thou art allotted to be ta'en by me :
So doth the swan her downy cygnets save,
Keeping them prisoner underneath her wings.
Yet, if this servile usage once offend,
Go, and be free again, as Suffolk's friend.
                    [*She turns away as going.*
O, stay !—I have no power to let her pass ;   60
My hand would free her, but my heart says—no.

As plays the sun upon the glassy streams,
Twinkling another counterfeited beam,
So seems this gorgeous beauty to mine eyes.
Fain would I woo her, yet I dare not speak :
I 'll call for pen and ink, and write my mind.
Fie, de la Poole ! disable not thyself ;
Hast not a tongue ? is she not here thy prisoner ?
Wilt thou be daunted at a woman's sight ?
Ay ; beauty's princely majesty is such,   70
Confounds the tongue, and makes the senses rough.
Mar. Say, Earl of Suffolk, if thy name be so,
What ransom must I pay before I pass ?
For, I perceive, I am thy prisoner.

York. " Damsel of France, I think, I have you fast."

Suf. [*Aside.*] How canst thou tell she will deny thy
    suit,
Before thou make a trial of her love ?
Mar. Why speak'st thou not ? what ransom must I
    pay ?
Suf. [*Aside.*] She 's beautiful, and therefore to be
    woo'd ;
She is a woman, therefore to be won.
Mar. Wilt thou accept of ransom, yea, or no ?   80
Suf. [*Aside.*] Fond man ! remember, that thou hast
    a wife ;
Then, how can Margaret be thy paramour ?
Mar. I were best to leave him, for he will not hear.
Suf. [*Aside.*] There all is marr'd ; there lies a cool-
    ing card.
Mar. He talks at random : sure, the man is mad.
Suf. [*Aside.*] And yet a dispensation may be had.
Mar. And yet I would that you would answer me.
Suf. [*Aside.*] I 'll win this Lady Margaret. For
    whom ?
Why, for my king : tush ! that 's a wooden thing.
Mar. He talks of wood : it is some carpenter.   90
Suf. [*Aside.*] Yet so my fancy may be satisfied,
And peace established between these realms.
But there remains a scruple in that too ;
For though her father be the King of Naples,
Duke of Anjou and Maine, yet is he poor,
And our nobility will scorn the match.
Mar. Hear ye, captain ? Are you not at leisure ?
Suf. [*Aside.*] It shall be so, disdain they ne'er so
    much :
Henry is youthful, and will quickly yield.—
Madam, I have a secret to reveal.   100
Mar. [*Aside.*] What though I be enthrall'd ? he
    seems a knight,
And will not any way dishonour me.

Suf. Lady, vouchsafe to listen what I say.
Mar. [*Aside.*] Perhaps, I shall be rescu'd by the
 French ;
And then I need not crave his courtesy.
Suf. Sweet madam, give me hearing in a cause—
Mar. [*Aside.*] Tush ! women have been captivate
 ere now.
Suf. Lady, wherefore talk you so ?
Mar. I cry you mercy, 't is but *quid* for *quo.*
Suf. Say, gentle princess, would you not suppose 110
Your bondage happy, to be made a queen ?
Mar. To be a queen in bondage is more vile,
Than is a slave in base servility ;
For princes should be free.
Suf.   And so shall you,
If happy England's royal king be free.
Mar. Why, what concerns his freedom unto me ?
Suf. I 'll undertake to make thee Henry's queen,
To put a golden sceptre in thy hand,
And set a precious crown upon thy head,
If thou wilt condescend to be my—
Mar.   What ?   120
Suf. His love.
Mar. I am unworthy to be Henry's wife.
Suf. No, gentle madam ; I unworthy am
To woo so fair a dame to be his wife,
And have no portion in the choice myself.
How say you, madam, are you so content ?
Mar. An if my father please, I am content.
Suf. Then call our captains, and our colours, forth !
And, madam, at your father's castle walls
We 'll crave a parley, to confer with him.   130
                          [*Troops come forward.*

A parley sounded. Enter REIGNIER, *on the walls.*

Suf. See, Reignier, see thy daughter prisoner.
Reig. To whom ?
Suf.   To me.
Reig.   Suffolk, what remedy ?
I am a soldier, and unapt to weep,
Or to exclaim on fortune's fickleness.
Suf. Yes, there is remedy enough, my lord :
Consent, and for thy honour give consent,
Thy daughter shall be wedded to my king ;
Whom I with pain have woo'd and won thereto,
And this her easy-held imprisonment
Hath gain'd thy daughter princely liberty.   140
Reig. Speaks Suffolk as he thinks ?
Suf.   Fair Margaret knows,
That Suffolk doth not flatter, face, or feign.
Reig. Upon thy princely warrant, I descend,
To give thee answer of thy just demand.
                        [*Exit from the walls.*

Trumpets sounded. Enter REIGNIER, *below.*

Reig. Welcome, brave earl, into our territories :
Command in Anjou what your honour pleases.
Suf. Thanks, Reignier, happy for so sweet a child,
Fit to be made companion with a king.
What answer makes your grace unto my suit ?   150
Reig. Since thou dost deign to woo her little
 worth,
To be the princely bride of such a lord,
Upon condition I may quietly
Enjoy mine own, the counties Maine and Anjou,
Free from oppression or the stroke of war,
My daughter shall be Henry's, if he please.
Suf. That is her ransom, I deliver her ;
And those two counties I will undertake,
Your grace shall well and quietly enjoy.
Reig. And I again in Henry's royal name,   160
As deputy unto that gracious king,
Give thee her hand, for sign of plighted faith.
Suf. Reignier of France, I give thee kingly thanks,
Because this is in traffic of a king :
[*Aside.*] And yet, methinks, I could be well content
To be mine own attorney in this case.—
I 'll over then to England with this news,
And make this marriage to be solemnis'd.
So, farewell, Reignier. Set this diamond safe
In golden palaces, as it becomes.   170

Reig. I do embrace thee, as I would embrace
The Christian prince, King Henry, were he here.
Mar. Farewell, my lord. Good wishes, praise, and
 prayers,
Shall Suffolk ever have of Márgaret.   [*Going.*
Suf. Farewell, sweet madam ! But hark you, Mar-
 garet :
No princely commendations to my king ?
Mar. Such commendations as become a maid,
A virgin, and his servant, say to him.
Suf. Words sweetly plac'd, and modestly directed.
But, madam, I must trouble you again,—   180
No loving token to his majesty ?
Mar. Yes, my good lord ; a pure unspotted heart,
Never yet taint with love, I send the king.
Suf. And this withal.   [*Kisses her.*
Mar. That for thyself : I will not so presume,
To send such peevish tokens to a king.
            [*Exeunt* REIGNIER *and* MARGARET.
Suf. O, wert thou for myself !—But, Suffolk, stay ;
Thou may'st not wander in that labyrinth :
There Minotaurs, and ugly treasons, lurk.
Solicit Henry with her wondrous praise :   190
Bethink thee on her virtues that surmount,
And natural graces that extinguish art ;
Repeat their semblance often on the seas,
That, when thou com'st to kneel at Henry's feet,
Thou may'st bereave him of his wits with wonder.
                                            [*Exit.*

――――

SCENE IV.—*Camp of the Duke of York, in Anjou.*

Enter YORK, WARWICK, *and others.*

York. Bring forth that sorceress, condemn'd to
 burn.

Enter LA PUCELLE, *guarded ; and a Shepherd.*

Shep. Ah, Joan ! this kills thy father's heart out-
 right.
Have I sought every country far and near,
And, now it is my chance to find thee out,
Must I behold thy timeless cruel death ?
Ah, Joan ! sweet daughter Joan, I 'll die with thee.
Puc. Decrepit miser ! base ignoble wretch !
I am descended of a gentler blood :
Thou art no father, nor no friend, of mine.
Shep. Out, out !—My lords, an please you, 't is not so : 11
I did beget her, all the parish knows :
Her mother liveth yet, can testify
She was the first fruit of my bachelorship.
War. Graceless ! wilt thou deny thy parentage ?
York. This argues what her kind of life hath been :
Wicked and vile ; and so her death concludes.
Shep. Fie, Joan, that thou wilt be so obstacle !
God knows, thou art a collop of my flesh,
And for thy sake have I shed many a tear :
Deny me not, I pr'ythee, gentle Joan.   20
Puc. Peasant, avaunt ! — You have suborn'd this
 man,
Of purpose to obscure my noble birth.
Shep. 'T is true, I gave a noble to the priest,
The morn that I was wedded to her mother.―
Kneel down, and take my blessing, good my girl.—
Wilt thou not stoop ? Now cursed be the time
Of thy nativity ! I would, the milk
Thy mother gave thee, when thou suck'dst her breast,
Had been a little ratsbane for thy sake !
Or else, when thou didst keep my lambs a-field,   30
I wish some ravenous wolf had eaten thee !
Dost thou deny thy father, cursed drab ?
O ! burn her, burn her : hanging is too good.   [*Exit.*
York. Take her away ; for she hath lived too long,
To fill the world with vicious qualities.
Puc. First, let me tell you whom you have con-
 demn'd ;
Not me begotten of a shepherd swain,
But issu'd from the progeny of kings ;
Virtuous, and holy ; chosen from above,
By inspiration of celestial grace,   40
To work exceeding miracles on earth.
I never had to do with wicked spirits :

But you,—that are polluted with your lusts,
Stain'd with the guiltless blood of innocents,
Corrupt and tainted with a thousand vices,—
Because you want the grace that others have,
You judge it straight a thing impossible
To compass wonders, but by help of devils.
No, misconceived! Joan of Arc hath been　　　　　50
A virgin from her tender infancy,
Chaste and immaculate in very thought;
Whose maiden blood, thus rigorously effus'd,
Will cry for vengeance at the gates of heaven.
　York. Ay, ay.—Away with her to execution!
　War. And hark ye, sirs; because she is a maid,
Spare for no fagots, let there be enow:
Place barrels of pitch upon the fatal stake,
That so her torture may be shortened.

Shep. "Deny me not, I pr'ythee, gentle Joan."

　Puc. Will nothing turn your unrelenting hearts?—
Then, Joan, discover thine infirmity,　　　　　60
That warranteth by law to be thy privilege.—
I am with child, ye bloody homicides:
Murder not then the fruit within my womb,
Although ye hale me to a violent death.
　York. Now, heaven forfend! the holy maid with
child?
　War. The greatest miracle that e'er ye wrought!
Is all your strict preciseness come to this?
　York. She and the Dauphin have been juggling:
I did imagine what would be her refuge.
　War. Well, go to: we will have no bastards live;　70
Especially, since Charles must father it.
　Puc. You are deceiv'd; my child is none of his:
It was Alençon, that enjoy'd my love.
　York. Alençon, that notorious Machiavel!
It dies, an if it had a thousand lives.
　Puc. O! give me leave; I have deluded you:
'T was neither Charles, nor yet the duke I nam'd,
But Reignier, King of Naples, that prevail'd.
　War. A married man: that's most intolerable.
　York. Why, here's a girl! I think, she knows not
well,　　　　　80
There were so many, whom she may accuse.
　War. It's sign she hath been liberal and free.
　York. And yet, forsooth, she is a virgin pure.—
Strumpet, thy words condemn thy brat, and thee:
Use no entreaty, for it is in vain.
　Puc. Then lead me hence;—with whom I leave my
curse.
May never glorious sun reflex his beams
Upon the country where you make abode;
But darkness and the gloomy shade of death
Environ you, till mischief, and despair,　　　　　90
Drive you to break your necks, or hang yourselves!
　　　　　[*Exit, guarded.*

　York. Break thou in pieces, and consume to ashes,
Thou foul accursed minister of hell!

　　Enter Cardinal BEAUFORT, *attended.*
　Car. Lord regent, I do greet your excellence
With letters of commission from the king.
For know, my lords, the states of Christendom,
Mov'd with remorse of these outrageous broils,
Have earnestly implor'd a general peace
Betwixt our nation and the aspiring French;
And here at hand the Dauphin, and his train,　　100
Approacheth to confer about some matter.
　York. Is all our travail turn'd to this effect?
After the slaughter of so many peers,
So many captains, gentlemen, and soldiers,
That in this quarrel have been overthrown,
And sold their bodies for their country's benefit,
Shall we at last conclude effeminate peace?
Have we not lost most part of all the towns,
By treason, falsehood, and by treachery,
Our great progenitors had conquer'd?—　　　　110
O, Warwick, Warwick! I foresee with grief
The utter loss of all the realm of France.
　War. Be patient, York! if we conclude a peace,
It shall be with such strict and severe covenants
As little shall the Frenchmen gain thereby.

　　Enter CHARLES, *attended;* ALENÇON, BASTARD,
　　　　　REIGNIER, *and others.*
　Char. Since, lords of England, it is thus agreed,
That peaceful truce shall be proclaim'd in France,
We come to be informed by yourselves
What the conditions of that league must be.
　York. Speak, Winchester; for boiling choler chokes
The hollow passage of my poison'd voice,　　　121
By sight of these our baleful enemies.
　Win. Charles, and the rest, it is enacted thus:—
That, in regard King Henry gives consent,
Of mere compassion and of lenity,
To ease your country of distressful war,
And suffer you to breathe in fruitful peace,
You shall become true liegemen to his crown.
And, Charles, upon condition thou wilt swear
To pay him tribute, and submit thyself,　　　　130
Thou shalt be plac'd as viceroy under him,
And still enjoy thy regal dignity.
　Alen. Must he be then as shadow of himself?
Adorn his temples with a coronet,
And yet, in substance and authority,
Retain but privilege of a private man?
This proffer is absurd and reasonless.
　Char. 'T is known already that I am possess'd
With more than half the Gallian territories,
And therein reverenc'd for their lawful king:　　140
Shall I, for lucre of the rest unvanquish'd,
Detract so much from that prerogative,
As to be call'd but viceroy of the whole?
No, lord ambassador; I'll rather keep
That which I have, than, coveting for more,
Be cast from possibility of all.
　York. Insulting Charles! hast thou by secret
means
Us'd intercession to obtain a league,
And, now the matter grows to compromise,
Stand'st thou aloof upon comparison?　　　　150
Either accept the title thou usurp'st,
Of benefit proceeding from our king,
And not of any challenge of desert,
Or we will plague thee with incessant wars.
　Reig. My lord, you do not well in obstinacy
To cavil in the course of this contract:
If once it be neglected, ten to one,
We shall not find like opportunity.
　Alen. [*Aside to* CHARLES.] To say the truth, it is
your policy
To save your subjects from such massacre,　　　160
And ruthless slaughters, as are daily seen
By our proceeding in hostility;
And therefore take this compact of a truce,
Although you break it when your pleasure serves.
　War. How say'st thou, Charles? shall our condition
stand?

Char. It shall;
Only reserv'd, you claim no interest
In any of our towns of garrison.
　York. Then swear allegiance to his majesty;
As thou art knight, never to disobey,　　　　　170
Nor be rebellious to the crown of England,
Thou, nor thy nobles, to the crown of England.—
　[CHARLES, *and his Nobles, give tokens of fealty.*
So; now dismiss your army when ye please:
Hang up your ensigns, let your drums be still,
For here we entertain a solemn peace.　　[*Exeunt.*

SCENE V.—London. A Room in the Palace.

Enter King HENRY, *in conference with* SUFFOLK;
GLOSTER *and* EXETER *following.*

　K. Hen. Your wondrous rare description, noble earl,
Of beauteous Margaret hath astonish'd me:
Her virtues, graced with external gifts,
Do breed love's settled passions in my heart;
And like as rigour of tempestuous gusts
Provokes the mightiest hulk against the tide,
So am I driven, by breath of her renown,
Either to suffer shipwrack, or arrive
Where I may have fruition of her love.
　Suf. Tush! my good lord, this superficial tale　10
Is but a preface of her worthy praise:
The chief perfections of that lovely dame
(Had I sufficient skill to utter them)
Would make a volume of enticing lines,
Able to ravish any dull conceit,
And, which is more, she is not so divine,
So full replete with choice of all delights,
But, with as humble lowliness of mind,
She is content to be at your command;
Command, I mean, of virtuous chaste intents,　20
To love and honour Henry as her lord.
　K. Hen. And otherwise will Henry ne'er presume.
Therefore, my lord protector, give consent,
That Margaret may be England's royal queen.
　Glo. So should I give consent to flatter sin.
You know, my lord, your highness is betroth'd
Unto another lady of esteem;
How shall we then dispense with that contract,
And not deface your honour with reproach?
　Suf. As doth a ruler with unlawful oaths;　30
Or one that, at a triumph having vow'd
To try his strength, forsaketh yet the lists
By reason of his adversary's odds.
A poor earl's daughter is unequal odds,
And therefore may be broke without offence.
　Glo. Why, what, I pray, is Margaret more than that?
Her father is no better than an earl,
Although in glorious titles he excel.
　Suf. Yes, my good lord, her father is a king,
The King of Naples and Jerusalem;　　40
And of such great authority in France,
As his alliance will confirm our peace,
And keep the Frenchmen in allegiance.
　Glo. And so the Earl of Armagnac may do,
Because he is near kinsman unto Charles.
　Exe. Beside, his wealth doth warrant a liberal
　　dower,
Where Reignier sooner will receive than give.

　Suf. A dower, my lords! disgrace not so your
　　king,
That he should be so abject, base, and poor,
To choose for wealth, and not for perfect love.　50
Henry is able to enrich his queen,
And not to seek a queen to make him rich.
So worthless peasants bargain for their wives,
As market-men for oxen, sheep, or horse.
Marriage is a matter of more worth
Than to be dealt in by attorneyship:
Not whom we will, but whom his grace affects,
Must be companion of his nuptial bed;
And therefore, lords, since he affects her most,
It most of all these reasons bindeth us,　60
In our opinions she should be preferr'd.
For what is wedlock forced, but a hell,
An age of discord and continual strife?
Whereas the contrary bringeth bliss,
And is a pattern of celestial peace.
Whom should we match with Henry, being a
　　king,
But Margaret, that is daughter to a king?
Her peerless feature, joined with her birth,
Approves her fit for none but for a king:
Her valiant courage, and undaunted spirit,　70
(More than in women commonly is seen,)
Will answer our hope in issue of a king;
For Henry, son unto a conqueror,
Is likely to beget more conquerors,
If with a lady of so high resolve,
As is fair Margaret, he be link'd in love.
Then yield, my lords; and here conclude with me.
That Margaret shall be queen, and none but she.
　K. Hen. Whether it be through force of your re-
　　port,
My noble Lord of Suffolk, or for that　　80
My tender youth was never yet attaint
With any passion of inflaming love,
I cannot tell; but this I am assur'd,
I feel such sharp dissension in my breast,
Such fierce alarums both of hope and fear,
As I am sick with working of my thoughts.
Take, therefore, shipping; post, my lord, to France;
Agree to any covenants, and procure
That Lady Margaret do vouchsafe to come
To cross the seas to England, and be crown'd　90
King Henry's faithful and anointed queen.
For your expenses and sufficient charge,
Among the people gather up a tenth.
Be gone, I say; for till you do return,
I rest perplexed with a thousand cares.—
And you, good uncle, banish all offence:
If you do censure me by what you were,
Not what you are, I know it will excuse
This sudden execution of my will.
And so conduct me, where from company　100
I may revolve and ruminate my grief.　[*Exit.*
　Glo. Ay, grief, I fear me, both at first and last.
　　　　　[*Exeunt* GLOSTER *and* EXETER.
　Suf. Thus Suffolk hath prevail'd; and thus he
　　goes,
As did the youthful Paris once to Greece;
With hope to find the like event in love,
But prosper better than the Trojan did.
Margaret shall now be queen, and rule the king;
But I will rule both her, the king, and realm.　[*Exit.*

KING HENRY VI.—PART II.

DRAMATIS PERSONÆ.

KING HENRY THE SIXTH.
HUMPHREY, *Duke of Gloster, his Uncle.*
CARDINAL BEAUFORT, *Bishop of Winchester.*
RICHARD PLANTAGENET, *Duke of York.*
EDWARD *and* RICHARD, *his Sons.*
DUKE OF SOMERSET,
DUKE OF SUFFOLK, } *Of the King's*
DUKE OF BUCKINGHAM, } *Party.*
LORD CLIFFORD, *and his Son,*
EARL OF SALISBURY, } *Of the York Faction.*
EARL OF WARWICK, }
LORD SCALES, *Governor of the Tower.*
LORD SAY.
SIR HUMPHREY STAFFORD, *and his Brother.*
SIR JOHN STANLEY.
WALTER WHITMORE.
A Sea Captain, Master, and Master's-Mate.
Two Gentlemen, Prisoners with Suffolk.
VAUX,

HUME *and* SOUTHWELL, *Priests.*
BOLINGBROKE, *a Conjurer. A Spirit raised by him.*
THOMAS HORNER, *an Armourer.*
PETER, *his Man.*
Clerk of Chatham. Mayor of Saint Albans.
SIMPCOX, *an Impostor. Two Murderers.*
JACK CADE.
GEORGE, JOHN, DICK, SMITH *the Weaver,* MICHAEL,
&c., Cade's Followers.
ALEXANDER IDEN, *a Kentish Gentleman.*

MARGARET, *Queen to King Henry.*
ELEANOR, *Duchess of Gloster.*
MARGERY JOURDAIN, *a Witch. Wife to Simpcox.*

*Lords, Ladies, and Attendants; Herald; Petition-
ers, Aldermen, a Beadle, Sheriff, and Officers;
Citizens, Prentices, Falconers, Guards, Soldiers,
Messengers, &c.*

SCENE—In various parts of ENGLAND.

ACT I.

SCENE I.—London. A Room of State in the Palace.

Flourish of trumpets: then hautboys. Enter, on one side, King HENRY, Duke of GLOSTER, SALISBURY, WARWICK, and Cardinal BEAUFORT; on the other, Queen MARGARET, led in by SUFFOLK; YORK, SOMERSET, BUCKINGHAM, and others, following.

Suffolk.
AS by your high imperial majesty
I had in charge at my depart for
France,
As procurator to your excellence,
To marry Princess Margaret for your
grace ;
So, in the famous ancient city, Tours,
In presence of the Kings of France and
Sicil,
The Dukes of Orleans, Calaber, Bretagne,
and Alençon,
Seven earls, twelve barons, and twenty
reverend bishops,
I have perform'd my task, and was espous'd :
And humbly now upon my bended knee,   10
In sight of England and her lordly peers,
Deliver up my title in the queen
To your most gracious hands, that are the substance
Of that great shadow I did represent ;
The happiest gift that ever marquess gave,
The fairest queen that ever king receiv'd.
  K. Hen. Suffolk, arise.—Welcome, Queen Margaret :
I can express no kinder sign of love,
Than this kind kiss.—O Lord ! that lends me life,
Lend me a heart replete with thankfulness !   20
For thou hast given me, in this beauteous face,
A world of earthly blessings to my soul,
If sympathy of love unite our thoughts.
  Q. Mar. Great King of England, and my gracious
lord,
The mutual conference that my mind hath had
By day, by night, waking, and in my dreams,
In courtly company, or at my beads,

With you mine alderliefest sovereign,
Makes me the bolder to salute my king
With ruder terms, such as my wit affords,   30
And over-joy of heart doth minister.
  K. Hen. Her sight did ravish, but her grace in
speech,
Her words y-clad with wisdom's majesty,
Makes me from wondering fall to weeping joys ;
Such is the fulness of my heart's content.
Lords, with one cheerful voice welcome my love.
  All. Long live Queen Margaret, England's happi-
ness !
  Q. Mar. We thank you all.   [*Flourish.*
  Suf. My lord protector, so it please your grace,
Here are the articles of contracted peace,   40
Between our sovereign, and the French king Charles,
For eighteen months concluded by consent.
  Glo. [*Reads.*] "Imprimis, It is agreed between the
French king, Charles, and William de la Poole, Mar-
quess of Suffolk, ambassador for Henry King of
England, that the said Henry shall espouse the Lady
Margaret, daughter unto Reignier King of Naples,
Sicilia, and Jerusalem ; and crown her Queen of
England ere the thirtieth of May next ensuing.—
Item,—That the duchy of Anjou and the county of
Maine shall be released and delivered to the king her
father"—   52
  K. Hen. Uncle, how now?
  Glo.   Pardon me, gracious lord ;
Some sudden qualm hath struck me at the heart,
And dimm'd mine eyes, that I can read no further.
  K. Hen. Uncle of Winchester, I pray, read on.
  Win. "Item,—It is further agreed between them,—
that the duchies of Anjou and Maine shall be released

and delivered over to the king her father ; and she
sent over of the King of England's own proper cost
and charges, without having any dowry."   61
K. Hen. They please us well.—Lord marquess, kneel
        down :
We here create thee the first Duke of Suffolk,
And girt thee with the sword.—Cousin of York,
We here discharge your grace from being regent
I' the parts of France, till term of eighteen months
Be full expir'd.—Thanks, uncle Winchester,
Gloster, York, Buckingham, Somerset,
Salisbury, and Warwick ;
We thank you all for this great favour done,   70
In entertainment to my princely queen.
Come, let us in ; and with all speed provide
To see her coronation be perform'd.
                        [*Exeunt* KING, QUEEN, *and* SUFFOLK.
    Glo. Brave peers of England, pillars of the state,
To you Duke Humphrey must unload his grief,
Your grief, the common grief of all the land.
What ! did my brother Henry spend his youth,
His valour, coin, and people, in the wars ?
Did he so often lodge in open field,
In winter's cold, and summer's parching heat,   80
To conquer France, his true inheritance ?
And did my brother Bedford toil his wits,
To keep by policy what Henry got ?
Have you ourselves, Somerset, Buckingham,
Brave York, Salisbury, and victorious Warwick,
Receiv'd deep scars in France and Normandy ?
Or hath mine uncle Beaufort, and myself,
With all the learned council of the realm,
Studied so long, sat in the council-house
Early and late, debating to and fro   90
How France and Frenchmen might be kept in awe ?
And hath his highness in his infancy
Been crown'd in Paris, in despite of foes ?
And shall these labours, and these honours, die ?
Shall Henry's conquest, Bedford's vigilance,
Your deeds of war, and all our counsel, die ?
O peers of England ! shameful is this league ;
Fatal this marriage ; cancelling your fame,
Blotting your names from books of memory,
Razing the characters of your renown,   100
Defacing monuments of conquer'd France,
Undoing all, as all had never been !
    Car. Nephew, what means this passionate discourse,
This peroration with such circumstance ?
For France, 'tis ours ; and we will keep it still.
    Glo. Ay, uncle ; we will keep it, if we can ;
But now it is impossible we should.
Suffolk, the new-made duke that rules the roast,
Hath given the duchy of Anjou, and Maine,
Unto the poor King Reignier, whose large style   110
Agrees not with the leanness of his purse.
    Sal. Now, by the death of Him that died for all
These counties were the keys of Normandy.—
But wherefore weeps Warwick, my valiant son ?
    War. For grief, that they are past recovery ;
For, were there hope to conquer them again,
My sword should shed hot blood, mine eyes no tears.
Anjou and Maine ! myself did win them both ;
Those provinces these arms of mine did conquer :
And are the cities, that I got with wounds,   120
Deliver'd up again with peaceful words ?
Mort Dieu !
    York. For Suffolk's duke, may he be suffocate,
That dims the honour of this warlike isle !
France should have torn and rent my very heart,
Before I would have yielded to this league.
I never read but England's kings have had
Large sums of gold, and dowries, with their wives ;
And our King Henry gives away his own,
To match with her that brings no vantages.   130
    Glo. A proper jest, and never heard before,
That Suffolk should demand a whole fifteenth,
For costs and charges in transporting her !
She should have stay'd in France, and starv'd in
        France,
Before—
    Car. My Lord of Gloster, now you grow too hot.
It was the pleasure of my lord the king.

    Glo. My Lord of Winchester, I know your mind :
'T is not my speeches that you do mislike,
But 't is my presence that doth trouble ye.   140
Rancour will out : proud prelate, in thy face
I see thy fury. If I longer stay,
We shall begin our ancient bickerings.—
Lordings, farewell ; and say, when I am gone,
I prophesied, France will be lost ere long.   [*Exit.*
    Car. So, there goes our protector in a rage.
'T is known to you he is mine enemy ;
Nay, more, an enemy unto you all,
And no great friend, I fear me, to the king.
Consider, lords, he is the next of blood,   150
And heir-apparent to the English crown :
Had Henry got an empire by his marriage,
And all the wealthy kingdoms of the west,
There 's reason he should be displeas'd at it.
Look to it, lords : let not his smoothing words
Bewitch your hearts ; be wise, and circumspect.
What though the common people favour him,
Calling him " Humphrey, the good Duke of Gloster ;"
Clapping their hands, and crying with loud voice—
" Jesu maintain your royal excellence ! "   160
With—" God preserve the good Duke Humphrey ! "
I fear me, lords, for all this flattering gloss,
He will be found a dangerous protector.
    Buck. Why should he then protect our sovereign
He being of age to govern of himself ?—
Cousin of Somerset, join you with me,
And all together, with the Duke of Suffolk,
We 'll quickly hoise Duke Humphrey from his seat.
    Car. This weighty business will not brook delay ;
I 'll to the Duke of Suffolk presently.   [*Exit.*
    Som. Cousin of Buckingham, though Humphrey's
        pride,   171
And greatness of his place, be grief to us,
Yet let us watch the haughty cardinal :
His insolence is more intolerable
Than all the princes' in the land beside :
If Gloster be displac'd, he 'll be protector.
    Buck. Or thou, or I, Somerset, will be protector,
Despite Duke Humphrey, or the cardinal.
                    [*Exeunt* BUCKINGHAM *and* SOMERSET.
    Sal. Pride went before, ambition follows him.
While these do labour for their own preferment,   180
Behoves it us to labour for the realm.
I never saw but Humphrey, Duke of Gloster,
Did bear him like a noble gentleman.
Oft have I seen the haughty cardinal,
More like a soldier, than a man o' the church,
As stout and proud, as he were lord of all,
Swear like a ruffian, and demean himself
Unlike the ruler of a commonweal.—
Warwick, my son, the comfort of my age,
Thy deeds, thy plainness, and thy housekeeping,   190
Hath won the greatest favour of the commons,
Excepting none but good Duke Humphrey ;
And, brother York, thy acts in Ireland,
In bringing them to civil discipline,
Thy late exploits, done in the heart of France,
When thou wert regent for our sovereign,
Have made thee fear'd and honour'd of the people.—
Join we together, for the public good,
In what we can, to bridle and suppress
The pride of Suffolk, and the cardinal,   200
With Somerset's and Buckingham's ambition ;
And, as we may, cherish Duke Humphrey's deeds,
While they do tend the profit of the land.
    War. So God help Warwick, as he loves the land,
And common profit of his country.
    York. [*Aside.*] And so says York, for he hath
        greatest cause.
    Sal. Then let 's make haste away, and look unto
        the main.
    War. Unto the main ! O father, Maine is lost ;
That Maine, which by main force Warwick did win,
And would have kept, so long as breath did last : 210
Main chance, father, you meant : but I meant Maine,
Which I will win from France, or else be slain.
                    [*Exeunt* WARWICK *and* SALISBURY.
    York. Anjou and Maine are given to the French ;
Paris is lost : the state of Normandy

Stands on a tickle point, now they are gone.
Suffolk concluded on the articles,
The peers agreed, and Henry was well pleas'd,
To change two dukedoms for a duke's fair daughter.
I cannot blame them all : what is 't to them ?
'T is thine they give away, and not their own.   220
Pirates may make cheap pennyworths of their pillage,
And purchase friends, and give to courtesans,
Still revelling, like lords, till all be gone;
Whileas the silly owner of the goods
Weeps over them, and wrings his hapless hands,
And shakes his head, and trembling stands aloof,
While all is shar'd, and all is borne away,
Ready to starve, and dare not touch his own :
So York must sit, and fret, and bite his tongue,
While his own lands are bargain'd for, and sold.   230
Methinks, the realms of England, France, and
      Ireland,
Bear that proportion to my flesh and blood,
As did the fatal brand Althæa burn'd,
Unto the prince's heart of Calydon.
Anjou and Maine, both given unto the French !
Cold news for me ; for I had hope of France,
Even as I have of fertile England's soil.
A day will come when York shall claim his own ;
And therefore I will take the Nevils' parts,
And make a show of love to proud Duke Humphrey,
And, when I spy advantage, claim the crown,   241
For that 's the golden mark I seek to hit.
Nor shall proud Lancaster usurp my right,
Nor hold the sceptre in his childish fist,
Nor wear the diadem upon his head,
Whose church-like humours fit not for a crown.
Then, York, be still awhile, till time do serve :
Watch thou, and wake, when others be asleep,
To pry into the secrets of the state,
Till Henry, surfeiting in joys of love,   250
With his new bride, and England's dear-bought
      queen,
And Humphrey with the peers be fall'n at jars :
Then will I raise aloft the milk-white rose,
With whose sweet smell the air shall be perfum'd,
And in my standard bear the arms of York,
To grapple with the house of Lancaster ;
And, force perforce, I 'll make him yield the crown,
Whose bookish rule hath pull'd fair England down.
                                                  [Exit.

SCENE II.—The Same. A Room in the Duke of
            GLOSTER'S House.

Enter GLOSTER and the DUCHESS.

Duch. Why droops my lord, like over-ripen'd corn,
Hanging the head at Ceres' plenteous load ?
Why doth the great Duke Humphrey knit his brows,
As frowning at the favours of the world ?
Why are thine eyes fix'd to the sullen earth,
Gazing on that which seems to dim thy sight ?
What seest thou there ? King Henry's diadem,
Enchas'd with all the honours of the world ?
If so, gaze on, and grovel on thy face,
Until thy head be circled with the same.   10
Put forth thy hand ; reach at the glorious gold.—
What, is 't too short ? I 'll lengthen it with mine ;
And, having both together heav'd it up,
We 'll both together lift our heads to heaven,
And never more abase our sight so low,
As to vouchsafe one glance unto the ground.
  Glo. O Nell, sweet Nell, if thou dost love thy lord,
Banish the canker of ambitious thoughts :
And may that thought, when I imagine ill
Against my king and nephew, virtuous Henry,   20
Be my last breathing in this mortal world.
My troublous dream this night doth make me sad.
  Duch. What dream'd my lord ? tell me, and I 'll re-
      quite it
With sweet rehearsal of my morning's dream.
  Glo. Methought, this staff, mine office-badge in
      court,
Was broke in twain : by whom, I have forgot,
But, as I think, it was by the cardinal ;

And on the pieces of the broken wand
Were plac'd the heads of Edmund Duke of Somerset,
And William de la Poole, first Duke of Suffolk.   30
This was my dream : what it doth bode, God knows.
  Duch. Tut ! this was nothing but an argument,
That he that breaks a stick of Gloster's grove,
Shall lose his head for his presumption.
But list to me, my Humphrey, my sweet duke :
Methought, I sat in seat of majesty,
In the cathedral church of Westminster,
And in that chair where kings and queens are
      crown'd ;
Where Henry, and Dame Margaret, kneel'd to me,
And on my head did set the diadem.   40
  Glo. Nay, Eleanor, then must I chide outright.
Presumptuous dame ! ill-nurtur'd Eleanor !
Art thou not second woman in the realm,
And the protector's wife, belov'd of him ?
Hast thou not worldly pleasure at command,
Above the reach or compass of thy thought ?
And wilt thou still be hammering treachery,
To tumble down thy husband, and thyself,
From top of honour to disgrace's feet ?
Away from me, and let me hear no more.   50
  Duch. What, what, my lord ! are you so choleric
With Eleanor, for telling but her dream ?
Next time I 'll keep my dreams unto myself,
And not be check'd.
  Glo. Nay, be not angry, I am pleas'd again.

Enter a Messenger.

  Mess. My lord protector, 't is his highness' pleasure,
You do prepare to ride unto Saint Albans.
Whereas the king and queen do mean to hawk.
  Glo. I go.—Come, Nell ; thou wilt ride with us ?
  Duch. Yes, my good lord, I 'll follow presently.   60
                    [Exeunt GLOSTER and Messenger.
Follow I must ; I cannot go before,
While Gloster bears this base and humble mind.
Were I a man, a duke, and next of blood,
I would remove these tedious stumbling-blocks,
And smooth my way upon their headless necks :
And, being a woman, I will not be slack
To play my part in Fortune's pageant.
Where are you there ? Sir John ! nay, fear not, man,
We are alone : here 's none but thee, and I.

Enter HUME.

  Hume. Jesus preserve your royal majesty .   70
  Duch. What say'st thou ? majesty ! I am but grace.
  Hume. But, by the grace of God, and Hume's
      advice,
Your grace's title shall be multiplied.
  Duch. What say'st thou, man ? hast thou as yet
      conferr'd
With Margery Jourdain, the cunning witch
And Roger Bolingbroke, the conjurer ?
And will they undertake to do me good ?
  Hume. This they have promised, — to show your
      highness
A spirit rais'd from depth of under-ground,
That shall make answer to such questions,   80
As by your grace shall be propounded him.
  Duch. It is enough ; I 'll think upon the questions.
When from Saint Albans we do make return,
We 'll see these things effected to the full.
Here, Hume, take this reward ; make merry, man,
With thy confederates in this weighty cause.   [Exit.
  Hume. Hume must make merry with the duchess'
      gold ;
Marry, and shall. But how now, Sir John Hume ?
Seal up your lips, and give no words but—mum :
The business asketh silent secrecy.   90
Dame Eleanor gives gold to bring the witch :
Gold cannot come amiss, were she a devil.
Yet have I gold, flies from another coast :
I dare not say, from the rich cardinal,
And from the great and new-made Duke of Suffolk ;
Yet I do find it so : for, to be plain,
They, knowing Dame Eleanor's aspiring humour,
Have hired me to undermine the duchess,
And buz these conjurations in her brain.

They say, a crafty knave does need no broker ;   100
Yet am I Suffolk and the cardinal's broker.
Hume, if you take not heed, you shall go near
To call them both a pair of crafty knaves.
Well, so it stands ; and thus, I fear, at last,
Hume's knavery will be the duchess' wrack,
And her attainture will be Humphrey's fall.
Sort how it will, I shall have gold for all.   [*Exit.*

SCENE III.—The Same. A Room in the Palace.

Enter PETER, *and others, with petitions.*

1 *Pet.* My masters, let 's stand close : my lord protector will come this way by-and-by, and then we
may deliver our supplications in the quill.
2 *Pet.* Marry, the Lord protect him, for he 's a good
man ! Jesu bless him !

Enter SUFFOLK *and Queen* MARGARET.

1 *Pet.* Here 'a comes, methinks, and the queen with
him. I 'll be the first, sure.
2 *Pet.* Come back, fool ! this is the Duke of Suffolk,
and not my lord protector.
Suf. How now, fellow ? wouldst anything with me ?
1 *Pet.* I pray, my lord, pardon me : I took ye for my
lord protector.   12
Q. Mar. " To my lord protector ! " are your supplications to his lordship ? Let me see them. What is
thine ?
1 *Pet.* Mine is, an 't please your grace, against John
Goodman, my lord cardinal's man, for keeping my
house, and lands, and wife, and all, from me.
Suf. Thy wife too ? that is some wrong indeed.—
What 's yours ?—What 's here ? [*Reads.*]   " Against
the Duke of Suffolk, for enclosing the commons of
Melford."—How now, sir knave ?   22
2 *Pet.* Alas ! sir, I am but a poor petitioner of our
whole township.
Peter. [*Presenting his petition.*] Against my master,
Thomas Horner, for saying, that the Duke of York
was rightful heir to the crown.
Q. Mar. What say'st thou ? did the Duke of York
say, he was rightful heir to the crown ?
Pet. That my master was ? No, forsooth : my
master said, that he was ; and that the king was an
usurper.   32
Suf. Who is there ?

Enter Servants.

Take this fellow in, and send for his master with
a pursuivant presently.—We 'll hear more of your
matter before the king.
                    [*Exeunt Servants with* PETER.
Q. Mar. And as for you, that love to be protected
Under the wings of our protector's grace,
Begin your suits anew, and sue to him.
                                  [*Tears the petition.*
Away, base cullions !—Suffolk, let them go.   40
All. Come, let 's be gone.   [*Exeunt Petitioners.*
Q. Mar. My Lord of Suffolk, say, is this the guise,
Is this the fashion in the court of England ?
Is this the government of Britain's isle,
And this the royalty of Albion's king ?
What ! shall King Henry be a pupil still,
Under the surly Gloster's governance ?
Am I a queen in title and in style,
And must be made a subject to a duke ?
I tell thee, Poole, when in the city Tours   50
Thou rann'st a tilt in honour of my love,
And stol'st away the ladies' hearts of France,
I thought King Henry had resembled thee,
In courage, courtship, and proportion :
But all his mind is bent to holiness,
To number *Ave-Maries* on his beads ;
His champions are the prophets and apostles
His weapons, holy saws of sacred writ ;
His study is his tilt-yard, and his loves
Are brazen images of canonis'd saints.   60
I would, the college of the cardinals
Would choose him pope, and carry him to Rome,

And set the triple crown upon his head :
That were a state fit for his holiness.
Suf. Madam, be patient ; as I was cause
Your highness came to England, so will I
In England work your grace's full content.
Q. Mar. Beside the haughty protector, have we
Beaufort,
The imperious churchman, Somerset, Buckingham.
And grumbling York : and not the least of these, 70
But can do more in England than the king.
Suf. And he of these that can do most of all,
Cannot do more in England than the Nevils :
Salisbury and Warwick are no simple peers.
Q. Mar. Not all these lords do vex me half so much,
As that proud dame, the lord protector's wife :
She sweeps it through the court with troops of ladies,
More like an empress than Duke Humphrey's wife.
Strangers in court do take her for the queen :
She bears a duke's revenues on her back,   80
And in her heart she scorns our poverty.
Shall I not live to be aveng'd on her ?
Contemptuous base-born callat as she is,
She vaunted 'mongst her minions t' other day,
The very train of her worst wearing-gown
Was better worth than all my father's lands,
Till Suffolk gave two dukedoms for his daughter.
Suf. Madam, myself have lim'd a bush for her ;
And plac'd a quire of such enticing birds,
That she will light to listen to the lays,   90
And never mount to trouble you again.
So, let her rest, and, madam, list to me ;
For I am bold to counsel you in this.
Although we fancy not the cardinal,
Yet must we join with him, and with the lords,
Till we have brought Duke Humphrey in disgrace.
As for the Duke of York, this late complaint
Will make but little for his benefit :
So, one by one, we 'll weed them all at last,
And you yourself shall steer the happy helm.   100

Enter King HENRY, YORK, *and* SOMERSET ; *Duke
and Duchess of* GLOSTER, *Cardinal* BEAUFORT,
BUCKINGHAM, SALISBURY, *and* WARWICK.

K. Hen. For my part, noble lords, I care not
which ;
Or Somerset, or York, all 's one to me.
York. If York have ill demean'd himself in France,
Then let him be denay'd the regentship.
Som. If Somerset be unworthy of the place,
Let York be regent ; I will yield to him.
War. Whether your grace be worthy, yea, or no,
Dispute not that : York is the worthier.
Car. Ambitious Warwick, let thy betters speak.
War. The cardinal 's not my better in the field. 110
Buck. All in this presence are thy betters, Warwick.
War. Warwick may live to be the best of all.
Sal. Peace, son !—and show some reason, Bucking-
ham,
Why Somerset should be preferr'd in this.
Q. Mar. Because the king, forsooth, will have it so.
Glo. Madam, the king is old enough himself
To give his censure. These are no women's matters.
Q. Mar. If he be old enough, what needs your grace
To be protector of his excellence ?
Glo. Madam, I am protector of the realm,   120
And at his pleasure will resign my place.
Suf. Resign it then, and leave thine insolence.
Since thou wert king, (as who is king but thou ?)
The commonwealth hath daily run to wrack ;
The Dauphin hath prevail'd beyond the seas ;
And all the peers and nobles of the realm
Have been as bondmen to thy sovereignty.
Car. The commons hast thou rack'd ; the clergy's
bags
Are lank and lean with thy extortions.
Som. Thy sumptuous buildings, and thy wife's
attire,   130
Have cost a mass of public treasury.
Buck. Thy cruelty in execution
Upon offenders hath exceeded law,
And left thee to the mercy of the law.
Q. Mar. Thy sale of offices, and towns in France,

If they were known, as the suspect is great,
Would make thee quickly hop without thy head.
　　　　[*Exit* GLOSTER. *The* QUEEN *drops her fan.*
Give me my fan : what, minion ! can you not ?
　　　　　　　[*Giving the* DUCHESS *a box on the ear.*
I cry you mercy, madam : was it you ?
　　Duch. Was 't I ? yea, I it was, proud Frenchwoman :
Could I come near your beauty with my nails, 141
I 'd set my ten commandments in your face.
　　K. Hen. Sweet aunt, be quiet : 't was against her
will.
　　Duch. Against her will ! Good king, look to 't in
time ;
She 'll hamper thee, and dandle thee like a baby :
Though in this place most master wear no breeches,
She shall not strike Dame Eleanor unreveng'd. [*Exit.*

Duch. " Was't I ? yea, I it was, proud Frenchwoman."

　　Buck. Lord cardinal, I will follow Eleanor,
And listen after Humphrey, how he proceeds :.
She 's tickled now ; her fume needs no spurs, 150
She 'll gallop far enough to her destruction.　[*Exit.*

Re-enter GLOSTER.

　　Glo. Now, lords, my choler being over-blown
With walking once about the quadrangle,
I come to talk of commonwealth affairs.
As for your spiteful false objections,
Prove them, and I lie open to the law ;
But God in mercy so deal with my soul,
As I in duty love my king and country.
But, to the matter that we have in hand.—
I say, my sovereign, York is meetest man 160
To be your regent in the realm of France.
　　Suf. Before we make election, give me leave
To show some reason, of no little force,
That York is most unmeet of any man.
　　York. I 'll tell thee, Suffolk, why I am unmeet :
First, for I cannot flatter thee in pride ;
Next, if I be appointed for the place,
My Lord of Somerset will keep me here,
Without discharge, money, or furniture,
Till France be won into the Dauphin's hands. 170
Last time I danc'd attendance on his will,
Till Paris was besieg'd, famish'd, and lost.
　　War. That can I witness : and a fouler fact
Did never traitor in the land commit.
　　Suf. Peace, headstrong Warwick !
　　War. Image of pride, why should I hold my peace ?

Enter Servants of SUFFOLK, *bringing in* HORNER
and PETER.

　　Suf. Because here is a man accus'd of treason :
Pray God, the Duke of York excuse himself !
　　York. Doth any one accuse York for a traitor ?

　　K. Hen. What mean'st thou, Suffolk ? Tell me,
　　　　what are these ?　　　　　　　　　180
　　Suf. Please it your majesty, this is the man
That doth accuse his master of high treason.
His words were these :—that Richard, Duke of York,
Was rightful heir unto the English crown,
And that your majesty was an usurper.
　　K. Hen. Say, man, were these thy words ?
　　Hor. An 't shall please your majesty, I never said
nor thought any such matter. God is my witness, I
am falsely accused by the villain.
　　Pet. By these ten bones, my lords, he did speak them
to me in the garret one night, as we were scouring his
Lord of York's armour.　　　　　　　　192
　　York. Base dunghill villain, and mechanical,
I 'll have thy head for this thy traitor's speech.—
I do beseech your royal majesty,
Let him have all the rigour of the law.
　　Hor. Alas ! my lord, hang me, if ever I spake the
words. My accuser is my prentice ; and when I did
correct him for his fault the other day, he did vow
upon his knees, he would be even with me. I have
good witness of this : therefore, I beseech your
majesty, do not cast away an honest man for a
villain's accusation.　　　　　　　　　203
　　K. Hen. Uncle, what shall we say to this in law ?
　　Glo. This doom, my lord, if I may judge :
Let Somerset be regent o'er the French,
Because in York this breeds suspicion ;
And let these have a day appointed them
For single combat in convenient place ;
For he hath witness of his servant's malice. 210
This is the law, and this Duke Humphrey's doom.
　　Som. I humbly thank your royal majesty.
　　Hor. And I accept the combat willingly.
　　Pet. Alas ! my lord, I cannot fight : for God's sake,
pity my case ! the spite of man prevaileth against me.
O Lord, have mercy upon me ! I shall never be able to
fight a blow. O Lord, my heart !
　　Glo. Sirrah, or you must fight or else be hang'd.
　　K. Hen. Away with them to prison ; and the day
Of combat shall be the last of the next month.— 220
Come, Somerset, we 'll see thee sent away.　[*Exeunt.*

SCENE IV.—*The Same. The Duke of* GLOSTER'S
Garden.

Enter MARGERY JOURDAIN, HUME, SOUTHWELL,
and BOLINGBROKE.

　　Hume. Come, my masters ; the duchess, I tell you,
expects performance of your promises.
　　Boling. Master Hume, we are therefore provided.
Will her ladyship behold and hear our exorcisms ?
　　Hume. Ay ; what else ? fear you not her courage.
　　Boling. I have heard her reported to be a woman of
an invincible spirit : but it shall be convenient, Master
Hume, that you be by her aloft, while we be busy
below ; and so, I pray you, go in God's name, and
leave us. [*Exit* HUME.] Mother Jourdain, be you
prostrate, and grovel on the earth :—John Southwell,
read you, and let us to our work.　　　　　12

Enter DUCHESS *above.*

　　Duch. Well said, my masters, and welcome all. To
this gear ; the sooner, the better.
　　Boling. Patience, good lady ; wizards know their
times.
Deep night, dark night, the silent of the night,
The time of night when Troy was set on fire ;
The time when screech-owls cry, and ban-dogs howl,
And spirits walk, and ghosts break up their graves,
That time best fits the work we have in hand. 20
Madam, sit you, and fear not : whom we raise,
We will make fast within a hallow'd verge.
　　　　[*Here they perform the ceremonies belonging,
　　　　and make the circle ;* BOLINGBROKE, *or*
　　　　SOUTHWELL, *reads,* Conjuro te, &c. *It
　　　　thunders and lightens terribly ; then the
　　　　Spirit riseth.*
　　Spir. Adsum.

M. Jourd. Asmath !
By the eternal God, whose name and power
Thou tremblest at, answer that I shall ask ;
For till thou speak, thou shalt not pass from hence.
Spir. Ask what thou wilt.—That I had said and
    done !

Than where castles mounted stand.
Have done, for more I hardly can endure.
Boling. Descend to darkness and the burning
    lake :
False fiend, avoid !   40
    [*Thunder and lightning. Spirit descends.*

Spir. "Have done, for more I hardly can endure."

Boling. First, of the king. What shall of him be-
    come ?
Spir. The duke yet lives, that Henry shall depose ;
But him outlive, and die a violent death.   31
    [*As the Spirit speaks,* SOUTHWELL *writes
    the answer.*
Boling. What fates await the Duke of Suffolk ?
Spir. By water shall he die, and take his end.
Boling. What shall befall the Duke of Somerset ?
Spir. Let him shun castles :
Safer shall he be upon the sandy plains,

Enter YORK *and* BUCKINGHAM, *hastily, with
    their Guards.*

York. Lay hands upon these traitors, and their
    trash.
Beldam, I think, we watch'd you at an inch.
What ! madam, are you there ? the king and com-
    monweal
Are deeply indebted for this piece of pains :
My lord protector will, I doubt it not,
See you well guerdon'd for these good deserts.

Duch. Not half so bad as thine to England's king,
Injurious duke, that threat'st where is no cause.
　Buck. True, madam, none at all.　What call you
　　　this?　　　　　　　*[Showing her the papers.*
Away with them! let them be clapp'd up close,　　50
And kept asunder.—You, madam, shall with us:
Stafford, take her to thee.—
　　　　　　　　[Exit DUCHESS *from above.*
We 'll see your trinkets here all forthcoming;
All, away!
　　　[Exeunt Guards, with SOUTHWELL, BOLING-
　　　　　　BROKE, *&c.*
　York. Lord Buckingham, methinks, you watch'd
　　her well:
A pretty plot, well chosen to build upon!
Now, pray, my lord, let 's see the devil's writ.
What have we here?
[Reads.] " The duke yet lives, that Henry shall de-
　pose;
But him outlive, and die a violent death."　　60
Why, this is just,
Aio te, Æacida, Romanos vincere posse.
Well, to the rest:

" Tell me, what fate awaits the Duke of Suffolk?—
By water shall he die, and take his end.—
What shall betide the Duke of Somerset?—
Let him shun castles:
Safer shall he be upon the sandy plains,
Than where castles mounted stand."
Come, come, my lords;　　　　　　　　　　　70
These oracles are hardly attain'd,
And hardly understood.
The king is now in progress towards Saint Albans;
With him the husband of this lovely lady:
Thither go these news, as fast as horse can carry
　them;
A sorry breakfast for my lord protector.
　Buck. Your grace shall give me leave, my Lord of
　　York,
To be the post, in hope of his reward.
　York. At your pleasure, my good lord. — Who 's
　　within there, ho!

　　　　　　　　Enter a Servant.

Invite my Lords of Salisbury and Warwick,　　80
To sup with me to-morrow night.—Away! *[Exeunt.*

ACT II.

SCENE I.—Saint Albans.

Enter King HENRY, *Queen* MARGARET, GLOSTER, *Cardinal, and* SUFFOLK,
with Falconers hollaing.

Queen Margaret.
BELIEVE me, lords, for flying at the
　　brook,
I saw not better sport these seven
　years' day:
Yet, by your leave, the wind was
　very high,
And, ten to one, old Joan had not
　gone out.
　K. Hen. But what a point, my
　lord, your falcon made,
And what a pitch she flew above the
　rest!—
To see how God in all his creatures
　works!
Yes, man and birds are fain of climb-
　ing high.
　Suf. No marvel, an it like your majesty,
My lord protector's hawks do tower so well:　　10
They know their master loves to be aloft,
And bears his thoughts above his falcon's pitch.
　Glo. My lord, 't is but a base ignoble mind,
That mounts no higher than a bird can soar.
　Car. I thought as much: he 'd be above the
　　clouds.
　Glo. Ay, my lord cardinal: how think you by
　that?
Were it not good your grace could fly to heaven?
　K. Hen. The treasury of everlasting joy.
　Car. Thy heaven is on earth; thine eyes and
　thoughts
Beat on a crown, the treasure of thy heart:　　20
Pernicious protector, dangerous peer,
That smooth'st it so with king and commonweal.
　Glo. What, cardinal, is your priesthood grown
　peremptory?
Tantæne animis cælestibus iræ?

Churchmen so hot? good uncle, hide such malice;
With such holiness can you do it?
　Suf. No malice, sir; no more than well becomes
So good a quarrel, and so bad a peer.
　Glo. As who, my lord?
　Suf.　　　　　　Why, as you, my lord;
An 't like your lordly lord-protectorship.　　30
　Glo. Why, Suffolk, England knows thine insolence.
　Q. Mar. And thy ambition, Gloster.
　K. Hen.　　　　　I pr'ythee, peace,
Good queen; and whet not on these furious peers,
For blessed are the peacemakers on earth.
　Car. Let me be blessed for the peace I make
Against this proud protector with my sword.
　Glo. [Aside to the Cardinal.] 'Faith, holy uncle,
　'would 't were come to that!
　Car. [Aside.] Marry, when thou dar'st.
　Glo. [Aside.] Make up no factious numbers for the
　matter;
In thine own person answer thy abuse.　　40
　Car. [Aside.] Ay, where thou dar'st not peep: an if
　thou dar'st,
This evening on the east side of the grove.
　K. Hen. How now, my lords!
　Car.　　　　　　Believe me, cousin Gloster,
Had not your man put up the fowl so suddenly,
We had had more sport.—*[Aside to* GLOSTER.*]* Come
　with thy two-hand sword.
　Glo. True, uncle.
　Car. [Aside.] Are you advis'd?—the east side of the
　grove.
　Glo. [Aside.] Cardinal, I am with you.
　K. Hen.　　　　Why, how now, uncle Gloster!
　Glo. Talking of hawking; nothing else, my lord.—
[Aside.] Now, by God's mother, priest, I 'll shave your
　crown　　50
For this, or all my fence shall fail.

Car. [*Aside.*] *Medice, teipsum—*
Protector, see to 't well, protect yourself.
K. Hen. The winds grow high ; so do your stomachs,
  lords.
How irksome is this music to my heart !
When such strings jar, what hope of harmony ?
I pray, my lords, let me compound this strife.

    Enter One, crying, " A miracle ! "

Glo. What means this noise ?
Fellow, what miracle dost thou proclaim ?
One. A miracle ! a miracle !   60
Suf. Come to the king, and tell him what miracle.
One. Forsooth, a blind man, at Saint Alban's
  shrine,
Within this half hour hath receiv'd his sight ;
A man that ne'er saw in his life before.
K. Hen. Now, God be prais'd, that to believing souls
Gives light in darkness, comfort in despair !

*Enter the Mayor of Saint Albans and his Brethren ;
and* SIMPCOX, *borne between two persons in a
chair ; his Wife and a great multitude following.*

Car. Here come the townsmen on procession,
To present your highness with the man.
K. Hen. Great is his comfort in this earthly vale,
Although by his sight his sin be multiplied.   70
Glo. Stand by, my masters ; bring him near the
  king :
His highness' pleasure is to talk with him.
K. Hen. Good fellow, tell us here the circumstance,
That we for thee may glorify the Lord.
What ! hast thou been long blind, and now restor'd ?
Simp. Born blind, an 't please your grace.
Wife. Ay, indeed, was he.
Suf. What woman is this ?
Wife. His wife, an 't like your worship.
Glo. Hadst thou been his mother, thou couldst have
  better told.   80
K. Hen. Where wert thou born ?
Simp. At Berwick in the north, an 't like your grace.
K. Hen. Poor soul ! God's goodness hath been great
  to thee :
Let never day nor night unhallow'd pass,
But still remember what the Lord hath done.
Q. Mar. Tell me, good fellow, cam'st thou here by
  chance,
Or of devotion, to this holy shrine ?
Simp. God knows, of pure devotion ; being call'd
A hundred times, and oft'ner, in my sleep,
By good Saint Alban ; who said,—" Simpcox, come ;
Come, offer at my shrine, and I will help thee."   91
Wife. Most true, forsooth ; and many time and oft
Myself have heard a voice to call him so.
Car. What ! art thou lame ?
Simp.   Ay, God Almighty help me !
Suf. How cam'st thou so ?
Simp.   A fall off a tree.
Wife. A plum-tree, master.
Glo.   How long hast thou been blind ?
Simp. O ! born so, master.
Glo.   What ! and wouldst climb a tree ?
Simp. But that in all my life, when I was a youth.
Wife. Too true ; and bought his climbing very dear.
Glo. 'Mass, thou lov'dst plums well, that wouldst
  venture so.   100
Simp. Alas, master, my wife desir'd some damsons,
And made me climb with danger of my life.
Glo. A subtle knave ; but yet it shall not serve.—
Let me see thine eyes : — wink now ; — now open
  them.—
In my opinion yet thou seest not well.
Simp. Yes, master, clear as day ; I thank God, and
Saint Alban.
Glo. Say'st thou me so ? What colour is this cloak
  of ?
Simp. Red, master ; red as blood.
Glo. Why, that 's well said. What colour is my
  gown of ?
Simp. Black, forsooth ; coal-black as jet.   110
K. Hen. Why then, thou know'st what colour jet is
  of ?

Suf. And yet, I think, jet did he never see.
Glo. But cloaks, and gowns, before this day a many.
Wife. Never, before this day, in all his life.
Glo. Tell me, sirrah, what 's my name ?
Simp. Alas ! master, I know not.
Glo. What 's his name ?
Simp. I know not.
Glo. Nor his ?
Simp. No, indeed, master.   120
Glo. What 's thine own name ?
Simp. Saunder Simpcox, an if it please you, master.
Glo. Then, Saunder, sit there, the lyingest knave in
Christendom. If thou hadst been born blind, thou
mightst as well have known all our names, as thus to
name the several colours we do wear. Sight may
distinguish of colours ; but suddenly to nominate them
all, it is impossible.—My lords, Saint Alban here hath
done a miracle ; and would ye not think his cunning
to be great, that could restore this cripple to his legs
again ?   131
Simp. O master, that you could !
Glo. My masters of Saint Albans, have you not
beadles in your town, and things called whips ?
May. Yes, my lord, if it please your grace.
Glo. Then send for one presently.
May. Sirrah, go fetch the beadle hither straight.
                  [*Exit an Attendant.*
Glo. Now fetch me a stool hither by-and-by. [*A
stool brought out.*] Now, sirrah, if you mean to save
yourself from whipping, leap me over this stool, and
run away.   141
Simp. Alas ! master, I am not able to stand alone :
You go about to torture me in vain.

    Re-enter Attendant, and a Beadle with a whip.

Glo. Well, sir, we must have you find your legs.
Sirrah beadle, whip him till he leap over that same-
stool.
Bead. I will, my lord.—Come on, sirrah ; off with
your doublet quickly.
Simp. Alas ! master, what shall I do ? I am not able
to stand.   15)
    [*After the Beadle hath hit him once, he leaps
      over the stool, and runs away ; and the
      People follow and cry, " A miracle ! "*
K. Hen. O God ! seest thou this, and bearest so
  long ?
Q. Mar. It made me laugh to see the villain run.
Glo. Follow the knave, and take this drab away.
Wife. Alas ! sir, we did it for pure need.
Glo. Let them be whipp'd through every market-
town, till they come to Berwick, from whence they
came.   [*Exeunt Mayor, Beadle, Wife, &c.*
Car. Duke Humphrey has done a miracle to-day.
Suf. True ; made the lame to leap, and fly away.
Glo. But you have done more miracles than I ;   160
You made in a day, whole towns to fly.

      Enter BUCKINGHAM.

K. Hen. What tidings with our cousin Buckingham ?
Buck. Such as my heart doth tremble to unfold.
A sort of naughty persons, lewdly bent,
Under the countenance and confederacy
Of Lady Eleanor, the protector's wife,
The ringleader and head of all this rout,
Have practis'd dangerously against your state,
Dealing with witches, and with conjurers :
Whom we have apprehended in the fact ;   170
Raising up wicked spirits from under-ground,
Demanding of King Henry's life and death,
And other of your highness' privy council,
As more at large your grace shall understand.
Car. And so, my lord protector, by this means
Your lady is forthcoming yet at London.
This news, I think, hath turn'd your weapon's edge
'T is like, my lord, you will not keep your hour.
Glo. Ambitious churchman, leave to afflict my heart.
Sorrow and grief have vanquish'd all my powers ; 180
And, vanquish'd as I am, I yield to thee,
Or to the meanest groom.
K. Hen. O God ! what mischiefs work the wicked
  ones ;
Heaping confusion on their own heads thereby.

Q. Mar. Gloster, see here the tainture of thy nest;
And look thyself be faultless, thou wert best.
Glo. Madam, for myself, to Heaven I do appeal,
How I have lov'd my king, and commonweal;
And, for my wife, I know not how it stands.
Sorry I am to hear what I have heard ;   190
Noble she is, but if she have forgot
Honour, and virtue, and convers'd with such
As, like to pitch, defile nobility,
I banish her my bed and company,
And give her, as a prey, to law, and shame,
That hath dishonour'd Gloster's honest name.
K. Hen. Well, for this night, we will repose us here:
To-morrow toward London, back again,
To look into this business thoroughly,
And call these foul offenders to their answers ;   200
And poise the cause in justice' equal scales,
Whose beam stands sure, whose rightful cause pre-
        vails.   [*Flourish. Exeunt.*

SCENE II.—London.   The Duke of YORK'S Garden.

Enter YORK, SALISBURY, *and* WARWICK.

York. Now, my good Lords of Salisbury and War-
        wick,
Our simple supper ended, give me leave,
In this close walk, to satisfy myself,
In craving your opinion of my title,
Which is infallible, to England's crown.
Sal. My lord, I long to hear it at full.
War. Sweet York, begin ; and if thy claim be good,
The Nevils are thy subjects to command.
York. Then thus :—
Edward the Third, my lords, had seven sons :   10
The first, Edward the Black Prince, Prince of Wales;
The second, William of Hatfield ; and the third,
Lionel, Duke of Clarence ; next to whom
Was John of Gaunt, the Duke of Lancaster.
The fifth was Edmund Langley, Duke of York ;
The sixth was Thomas of Woodstock, Duke of Gloster;
William of Windsor was the seventh, and last.
Edward, the Black Prince, died before his father,
And left behind him Richard, his only son ;
Who, after Edward the Third's death, reign'd as
        king.   20
Till Henry Bolingbroke, Duke of Lancaster,
The eldest son and heir of John of Gaunt,
Crown'd by the name of Henry the Fourth,
Seized on the realm ; depos'd the rightful king ;
Sent his poor queen to France, from whence she
        came,
And him to Pomfret ; where, as all you know,
Harmless Richard was murder'd traitorously.
War. Father, the duke hath told the truth ;
Thus got the house of Lancaster the crown.
York. Which now they hold by force, and not by
        right;   30
For Richard, the first son's heir, being dead,
The issue of the next son should have reign'd.
Sal. But William of Hatfield died without an heir.
York. The third son, Duke of Clarence, from whose
        line
I claim the crown, had issue—Philippe, a daughter,
Who married Edmund Mortimer, Earl of March ;
Edmund had issue—Roger, Earl of March ;
Roger had issue—Edmund, Anne, and Eleanor.
Sal. This Edmund, in the reign of Bolingbroke,
As I have read, laid claim unto the crown;   40
And, but for Owen Glendower, had been king,
Who kept him in captivity till he died.
But to the rest.
York.   His eldest sister, Anne,
My mother, being heir unto the crown,
Married Richard, Earl of Cambridge, who was son
To Edmund Langley, Edward the Third's fifth son.
By her I claim the kingdom : she was heir
To Roger, Earl of March, who was the son
Of Edmund Mortimer, who married Philippe,
Sole daughter unto Lionel, Duke of Clarence :   50
So, if the issue of the elder son
Succeed before the younger, I am king.

War. What plain proceeding is more plain than
        this ?
Henry doth claim the crown from John of Gaunt,
The fourth son ; York claims it from the third.
Till Lionel's issue fails, his should not reign :
It fails not yet, but flourishes in thee,
And in thy sons, fair slips of such a stock.
Then, father Salisbury, kneel we together
And, in this private plot, be we the first,   60
That shall salute our rightful sovereign
With honour of his birthright to the crown.
Both. Long live our sovereign Richard, England's
        king !
York. We thank you, lords ! But I am not your
        king,
Till I be crown'd, and that my sword be stain'd
With heart-blood of the house of Lancaster ;
And that 's not suddenly to be perform'd,
But with advice, and silent secrecy.
Do you, as I do, in these dangerous days,
Wink at the Duke of Suffolk's insolence,   70
At Beaufort's pride, at Somerset's ambition,
At Buckingham, and all the crew of them,
Till they have snar'd the shepherd of the flock,
That virtuous prince, the good Duke Humphrey.
'T is that they seek : and they, in seeking that,
Shall find their deaths, if York can prophesy.
Sal. My lord, break we off : we know your mind at
        full.
War. My heart assures me, that the Earl of War-
        wick
Shall one day make the Duke of York a king.
York. And, Nevil, this I do assure myself :   80
Richard shall live to make the Earl of Warwick
The greatest man in England but the king. [*Exeunt.*

SCENE III.—The Same.   A Hall of Justice.

Trumpets sounded.   Enter King HENRY, *Queen*
MARGARET, GLOSTER, YORK, SUFFOLK, *and* SALIS-
BURY ; *the Duchess of* GLOSTER, MARGERY JOUR-
DAIN, SOUTHWELL, HUME, *and* BOLINGBROKE,
under guard.

K. Hen. Stand forth, Dame Eleanor Cobham, Glos-
        ter's wife.
In sight of God, and us, your guilt is great :
Receive the sentence of the law, for sins
Such as by God's book are adjudg'd to death.—
[*To* JOURDAIN, *&c.*] You four, from hence to prison
        back again ;
From thence, unto the place of execution :
The witch in Smithfield shall be burn'd to ashes,
And you three shall be strangled on the gallows.—
You, madam, for you are more nobly born,
Despoiled of your honour in your life,   10
Shall, after three days' open penance done,
Live in your country here in banishment,
With Sir John Stanley in the Isle of Man.
Duch. Welcome is banishment ; welcome were my
        death.
Glo. Eleanor, the law, thou seest, hath judged thee :
I cannot justify whom the law condemns.—
        [*Exeunt the* DUCHESS *and the other Prisoners,*
                guarded.
Mine eyes are full of tears, my heart of grief.
Ah, Humphrey ! this dishonour in thine age
Will bring thy head with sorrow to the ground.—
I beseech your majesty, give me leave to go ;   20
Sorrow would solace, and mine age would ease.
K. Hen. Stay, Humphrey, Duke of Gloster.   Ere
        thou go,
Give up thy staff : Henry will to himself
Protector be ; and God shall be my hope,
My stay, my guide, and lantern to my feet.
And go in peace, Humphrey ; no less belov'd,
Than when thou wert protector to thy king.
Q. Mar. I see no reason why a king of years
Should be to be protected like a child.—
God and King Henry govern England's helm !—   30
Give up your staff, sir, and the king his realm.

Glo. My staff?—here, noble Henry, is my staff:
As willingly do I the same resign,
As e'er thy father Henry made it mine;
And even as willingly at thy feet I leave it,
As others would ambitiously receive it.
Farewell, good king: when I am dead and gone,
May honourable peace attend thy throne.   [Exit.
Q. Mar. Why, now is Henry king, and Margaret
    queen;
And Humphrey, Duke of Gloster, scarce himself,   40
That bears so shrewd a maim: two pulls at once,—
His lady banish'd, and a limb lopp'd off;
This staff of honour raught:—there let it stand,
Where it best fits to be, in Henry's hand.

Glo. "Here, noble Henry, is my staff."

Suf. Thus droops this lofty pine, and hangs his
    sprays;
Thus Eleanor's pride dies in her youngest days.
York. Lords, let him go.—Please it your majesty,
This is the day appointed for the combat;
And ready are the appellant and defendant,
The armourer and his man, to enter the lists,   50
So please your highness to behold the fight.
Q. Mar. Ay, good my lord; for purposely therefore
Left I the court, to see this quarrel tried.
K. Hen. O' God's name, see the lists and all things
    fit:
Here let them end it, and God defend the right!
York. I never saw a fellow worse bested,
Or more afraid to fight, than is the appellant,
The servant of this armourer, my lords.

Enter, on one side, HORNER, and his Neighbours,
    drinking to him so much that he is drunk; and he
    enters bearing his staff with a sand-bag fastened
    to it; a drum before him: at the other side, PETER,
    with a drum and a similar staff; accompanied by
    Prentices drinking to him.

1 Neigh. Here, neighbour Horner, I drink to you in
a cup of sack. And fear not, neighbour, you shall do
well enough.   61
2 Neigh. And here, neighbour, here's a cup of
charneco.
3 Neigh. And here's a pot of good double beer,
neighbour: drink, and fear not your man.
Hor. Let it come, i'faith, and I'll pledge you all;
and a fig for Peter!
1 Pren. Here, Peter, I drink to thee; and be not
afraid.

2 Pren. Be merry, Peter, and fear not thy master:
fight for credit of the prentices.
Peter. I thank you all: drink, and pray for me, I   71
pray you; for, I think, I have taken my last draught
in this world.—Here, Robin, an if I die, I give thee
my apron; and, Will, thou shalt have my hammer:
—and here, Tom, take all the money that I have.—
O Lord, bless me! I pray God, for I am never able to
deal with my master, he hath learnt so much fence
already.
Sal. Come, leave your drinking, and fall to blows.—
Sirrah, what's thy name?   81
Peter. Peter, forsooth.
Sal. Peter! what more?
Peter. Thump.
Sal. Thump! then see thou thump thy master well.
Hor. Masters, I am come hither, as it were, upon
my man's instigation, to prove him a knave, and my-
self an honest man: and touching the Duke of York,
I will take my death, I never meant him any ill, nor
the queen: and therefore, Peter, have at thee with a
downright blow.   91
York. Despatch: this knave's tongue begins to
double. Sound, trumpets, alarum to the combatants.
    [Alarum. They fight, and PETER strikes down
        his Master.
Hor. Hold, Peter, hold! I confess, I confess treason.
                                                    [Dies.
York. Take away his weapon.—Fellow, thank God,
and the good wine in thy master's way.
Peter. O God! have I overcome mine enemies in
this presence? O Peter! thou hast prevailed in right.
K. Hen. Go, take hence that traitor from our sight;
For, by his death, we do perceive his guilt.   100
And God in justice hath reveal'd to us
The truth and innocence of this poor fellow,
Which he had thought to have murder'd wrongfully.—
Come, fellow; follow us for thy reward.   [Exeunt.

SCENE IV.—The Same. A Street.

Enter GLOSTER and Servants, in mourning cloaks.

Glo. Thus, sometimes hath the brightest day a cloud;
And after summer evermore succeeds
Barren winter, with his wrathful nipping cold:
So cares and joys abound, as seasons fleet.—
Sirs, what's o'clock?
Serv.   Ten, my lord.
Glo. Ten is the hour that was appointed me
To watch the coming of my punish'd duchess:
Uneath may she endure the flinty streets,
To tread them with her tender-feeling feet.
Sweet Nell, ill can thy noble mind abrook   10
The abject people, gazing on thy face,
With envious looks, laughing at thy shame,
That erst did follow thy proud chariot wheels,
When thou didst ride in triumph through the streets.
But soft! I think, she comes; and I'll prepare
My tear-stain'd eyes to see her miseries.

Enter the Duchess of GLOSTER, in a white sheet, with
    papers pinned upon her back, her feet bare, and a
    taper burning in her hand; Sir JOHN STANLEY, a
    Sheriff, and Officers.

Serv. So please your grace, we'll take her from the
    sheriff.
Glo. No, stir not, for your lives: let her pass by.
Duch. Come you, my lord, to see my open shame?
Now thou dost penance too. Look, how they gaze!   21
See, how the giddy multitude do point,
And nod their heads, and throw their eyes on thee.
Ah, Gloster, hide thee from their hateful looks,
And, in thy closet pent up, rue my shame,
And ban thine enemies, both mine and thine.
Glo. Be patient, gentle Nell: forget this grief.
Duch. Ah, Gloster! teach me to forget myself;
For, whilst I think I am thy married wife,
And thou a prince, protector of this land,
Methinks, I should not thus be led along,   30
Mail'd up in shame, with papers on my back,

And follow'd with a rabble, that rejoice
To see my tears, and hear my deep-fet groans.
The ruthless flint doth cut my tender feet ;
And when I start, the envious people laugh,
And bid me be advised how I tread.
Ah, Humphrey ! can I bear this shameful yoke ?
Trow'st thou, that e'er I 'll look upon the world,
Or count them happy that enjoy the sun ?
No ; dark shall be my light, and night my day :　40
To think upon my pomp, shall be my hell.
Sometime I 'll say, I am Duke Humphrey's wife,
And he a prince, and ruler of the land ;

Duch. " Come you, my lord, to see my open shame ? "

Yet so he rul'd, and such a prince he was,
As he stood by, whilst I, his forlorn duchess,
Was made a wonder, and a pointing-stock,
To every idle rascal follower.
But be thou mild, and blush not at my shame ;
Nor stir at nothing, till the axe of death
Hang over thee, as, sure, it shortly will :　50
For Suffolk,—he that can do all in all
With her that hateth thee, and hates us all,—
And York, and impious Beaufort, that false priest,
Have all lim'd bushes to betray thy wings ;
And, fly thou how thou canst, they 'll tangle thee.
But fear not thou, until thy foot be snar'd,
Nor never seek prevention of thy foes.
　　Glo. Ah, Nell ! forbear : thou aimest all awry ;

I must offend before I be attainted ;
And had I twenty times so many foes,　60
And each of them had twenty times their power,
All these could not procure me any scath,
So long as I am loyal, true, and crimeless.
Wouldst have me rescue thee from this reproach ?
Why, yet thy scandal were not wip'd away,
But I in danger for the breach of law.
Thy greatest help is quiet, gentle Nell ;
I pray thee, sort thy heart to patience :
These few days' wonder will be quickly worn.

Enter a Herald.

　　Her. I summon your grace to his majesty's parlia-
ment, holden at Bury the first of this next month.　71
　　Glo. And my consent ne'er ask'd herein before ?
This is close dealing.—Well, I will be there.
　　　　　　　　　　　　　　　　[*Exit Herald.*
My Nell, I take my leave :—and, master sheriff,
Let not her penance exceed the king's commission.
　　Sher. An 't please your grace, here my commission
　　　　stays,
And Sir John Stanley is appointed now
To take her with him to the Isle of Man.
　　Glo. Must you, Sir John, protect my lady here ?
　　Stan. So am I given in charge, may 't please your
　　　　grace.　80
　　Glo. Entreat her not the worse, in that I pray
You use her well.　The world may laugh again ;
And I may live to do you kindness, if
You do it her : and so, Sir John, farewell.
　　Duch. What ! gone, my lord, and bid me not fare-
　　　　well ?
　　Glo. Witness my tears, I cannot stay to speak.
　　　　　　　　[*Exeunt* GLOSTER *and Servants.*
　　Duch. Art thou gone too ?　All comfort go with thee,
For none abides with me : my joy is death,—
Death, at whose name I oft have been afear'd,
Because I wish'd this world's eternity.—　90
Stanley, I pr'ythee, go, and take me hence ;
I care not whither, for I beg no favour,
Only convey me where thou art commanded.
　　Stan. Why, madam, that is to the Isle of Man ;
There to be us'd according to your state.
　　Duch. That 's bad enough, for I am but reproach :
And shall I then be us'd reproachfully ?
　　Stan. Like to a duchess, and Duke Humphrey's
　　　　lady :
According to that state you shall be used.
　　Duch. Sheriff, farewell, and better than I fare,　100
Although thou hast been conduct of my shame.
　　Sher. It is my office ; and, madam, pardon me.
　　Duch. Ay, ay, farewell : thy office is discharg'd.—
Come, Stanley, shall we go ?
　　Stan. Madam, your penance done, throw off this
　　　　sheet,
And go we to attire you for our journey.
　　Duch. My shame will not be shifted with my sheet :
No ; it will hang upon my richest robes,
And show itself, attire me how I can.
Go, lead the way : I long to see my prison.　110
　　　　　　　　　　　　　　　　　　　　[*Exeunt.*

ACT III.

SCENE I.—The Abbey at Bury.

A Sennet. Enter to the Parliament, *King* HENRY, *Queen* MARGARET, *Cardinal* BEAUFORT, SUFFOLK, YORK, BUCKINGHAM, *and others.*

King Henry.
MUSE, my Lord of Gloster is not come :
"T is not his wont to be the hindmost man,
Whate'er occasion keeps him from us now.
Q. Mar. Can you not see ? or will you not
    observe
The strangeness of his alter'd countenance ?
With what a majesty he bears himself ;
How insolent of late he is become,
How proud, how peremptory, and unlike
    himself ?
We know the time, since he was mild and
    affable ;
And if we did but glance a far-off look,   10
Immediately he was upon his knee,
That all the court admir'd him for submission :
But meet him now, and, be it in the morn,
When every one will give the time of day,
He knits his brow, and shows an angry eye,
And passeth by with stiff unbowed knee,
Disdaining duty that to us belongs.
Small curs are not regarded when they grin,
But great men tremble when the lion roars ;
And Humphrey is no little man in England.   20
First, note, that he is near you in descent,
And should you fall, he is the next will mount.
Me seemeth then, it is no policy,
Respecting what a rancorous mind he bears,
And his advantage following your decease,
That he should come about your royal person,
Or be admitted to your highness' council.
By flattery hath he won the commons' hearts,
And, when he please to make commotion,
'T is to be fear'd they all will follow him.   30
Now 't is the spring, and weeds are shallow-rooted ;
Suffer them now, and they 'll o'ergrow the garden,
And choke the herbs for want of husbandry.
The reverent care I bear unto my lord
Made me collect these dangers in the duke.
If it be fond, call it a woman's fear ;
Which fear if better reasons can supplant,
I will subscribe and say, I wrong'd the duke.
My Lord of Suffolk,—Buckingham, and York,—
Reprove my allegation, if you can,   40
Or else conclude my words effectual.
Suf. Well hath your highness seen into this duke ;
And had I first been put to speak my mind,
I think, I should have told your grace's tale.
The duchess, by his subornation,
Upon my life, began her devilish practices :
Or if were not privy to those faults,
Yet, by reputing of his high descent,
(As next the king he was successive heir,)
And such high vaunts of his nobility,   50
Did instigate the bedlam brain-sick duchess
By wicked means to frame our sovereign's fall.
Smooth runs the water where the brook is deep,
And in his simple show he harbours treason.
The fox barks not when he would steal the lamb :
No, no, my sovereign ; Gloster is a man
Unsounded yet, and full of deep deceit.
Car. Did he not, contrary to form of law,
Devise strange deaths for small offences done ?

York. And did he not, in his protectorship,   60
Levy great sums of money through the realm
For soldiers' pay in France, and never sent it ?
By means whereof the towns each day revolted.
Buck. Tut ! these are petty faults to faults unknown,
Which time will bring to light in smooth Duke Hum-
    phrey.
K. Hen. My lords, at once : the care you have of us,
To mow down thorns that would annoy our foot,
Is worthy praise ; but shall I speak my conscience ?
Our kinsman Gloster is as innocent
From meaning treason to our royal person,   70
As is the sucking lamb, or harmless dove.
The duke is virtuous, mild, and too well given,
To dream on evil, or to work my downfall.
Q. Mar. Ah ! what 's more dangerous than this fond
    affiance ?
Seems he a dove ? his feathers are but borrow'd,
For he 's disposed as the hateful raven.
Is he a lamb ? his skin is surely lent him,
For he 's inclin'd as is the ravenous wolf.
Who cannot steal a shape, that means deceit ?
Take heed, my lord ; the welfare of us all   80
Hangs on the cutting short that fraudful man.

Enter SOMERSET.

Som. All health unto my gracious sovereign !
K. Hen. Welcome, Lord Somerset. What news
    from France ?
Som. That all your interest in those territories
Is utterly bereft you : all is lost.
K. Hen. Cold news, Lord Somerset ; but God's will
    be done.
York. [*Aside.*] Cold news for me ; for I had hope of
    France,
As firmly as I hope for fertile England.
Thus are my blossoms blasted in the bud,
And caterpillars eat my leaves away ;   90
But I will remedy this gear ere long,
Or sell my title for a glorious grave.

Enter GLOSTER.

Glo. All happiness unto my lord the king !
Pardon, my liege, that I have stay'd so long.
Suf. Nay, Gloster, know, that thou art come too
    soon,
Unless thou wert more loyal than thou art.
I do arrest thee of high treason here.
Glo. Well, Suffolk's duke, thou shalt not see me
    blush,
Nor change my countenance for this arrest :
A heart unspotted is not easily daunted.   100
The purest spring is not so free from mud,
As I am clear from treason to my sovereign.
Who can accuse me ? wherein am I guilty ?
York. 'T is thought, my lord, that you took bribes of
    France,
And, being protector, stay'd the soldiers' pay ;
By means whereof his highness hath lost France.
Glo. Is it but thought so ? What are they that think
    it ?
I never robb'd the soldiers of their pay,
Nor ever had one penny bribe from France.

So help me God, as I have watch'd the night,   110
Ay, night by night, in studying good for England!
That doit that e er I wrested from the king,
Or any groat I hoarded to my use,
Be brought against me at my trial-day!
No; many a pound of mine own proper store,
Because I would not tax the needy commons,
Have I dispursed to the garrisons,
And never ask'd for restitution.
  Car. It serves you well, my lord, to say so much.
  Glo. I say no more than truth, so help me God!   120
  York. In your protectorship you did devise
Strange tortures for offenders, never heard of,
That England was defam'd by tyranny.
  Glo. Why, 't is well known, that whiles I was pro-
     tector,
Pity was all the fault that was in me ;
For I should melt at an offender's tears,
And lowly words were ransom for their fault.
Unless it were a bloody murderer,
Or foul felonious thief that fleec'd poor passengers,
I never gave them condign punishment.   130
Murder, indeed, that bloody sin, I tortur'd
Above the felon, or what trespass else.
  Suf. My lord, these faults are easy, quickly an-
     swer'd ;
But mightier crimes are laid unto your charge,
Whereof you cannot easily purge yourself.
I do arrest you in his highness' name ;
And here commit you to my lord cardinal
To keep, until your further time of trial.
  K. Hen. My Lord of Gloster, 't is my special hope,
That you will clear yourself from all suspect ;   140
My conscience tells me you are innocent.
  Glo. Ah, gracious lord! these days are dangerous.
Virtue is chok'd with foul ambition,
And charity chas'd hence by rancour's hand ;
Foul subornation is predominant,
And equity exil'd your highness' land.
I know, their complot is to have my life ;
And if my death might make this island happy,
And prove the period of their tyranny,
I would expend it with all willingness ;   150
But mine is made the prologue to their play ;
For thousands more, that yet suspect no peril,
Will not conclude their plotted tragedy.
Beaufort's red sparkling eyes blab his heart's malice,
And Suffolk's cloudy brow his stormy hate ;
Sharp Buckingham unburdens with his tongue
The envious load that lies upon his heart ;
And dogged York, that reaches at the moon,
Whose overweening arm I have pluck'd back,
By false accuse doth level at my life :   160
And you, my sovereign lady, with the rest,
Causeless have laid disgraces on my head,
And with your best endeavour have stirr'd up
My liefest liege to be mine enemy.
Ay, all of you have laid your heads together ;
Myself had notice of your conventicles,
And all to make away my guiltless life.
I shall not want false witness to condemn me,
Nor store of treasons to augment my guilt ;
The ancient proverb will be well effected,—   170
A staff is quickly found to beat a dog.
  Car. My liege, his railing is intolerable.
If those that care to keep your royal person
From treason's secret knife, and traitors' rage,
Be thus upbraided, chid, and rated at,
And the offender granted scope of speech,
'T will make them cool in zeal unto your grace.
  Suf. Hath he not twit our sovereign lady here,
With ignominious words, though clerkly couch'd,
As if she had suborned some to swear   180
False allegations to o'erthrow his state?
  Q. Mar. But I can give the loser leave to chide.
  Glo. Far truer spoke, than meant : I lose, indeed ;
Beshrew the winners, for they play'd me false !
And well such losers may have leave to speak.
  Buck. He 'll wrest the sense, and hold us here all
     day.—
Lord cardinal, he is your prisoner.
  Car. Sirs, take away the duke, and guard him sure.

  Glo. Ah, thus King Henry throws away his crutch,
Before his legs be firm to bear his body :   190
Thus is the shepherd beaten from thy side,
And wolves are gnarling who shall gnaw thee first.
Ah, that my fear were false ! ah, that it were !
For, good King Henry, thy decay I fear.
                 [*Exeunt Attendants with* GLOSTER.
  K. Hen. My lords, what to your wisdoms seemeth
     best,
Do, or undo, as if ourself were here.
  Q. Mar. What ! will your highness leave the parlia-
     ment ?
  K. Hen. Ay, Margaret, my heart is drown'd with
     grief,
Whose flood begins to flow within mine eyes ;
My body round engirt with misery,   200
For what 's more miserable than discontent?—
Ah, uncle Humphrey ! in thy face I see
The map of honour, truth, and loyalty ;
And yet, good Humphrey, is the hour to come,
That e'er I prov'd thee false, or fear'd thy faith.
What low'ring star now envies thy estate,
That these great lords, and Margaret our queen,
Do seek subversion of thy harmless life ?
Thou never didst them wrong, nor no man wrong ;
And as the butcher takes away the calf,   210
And binds the wretch, and beats it when it strays,
Bearing it to the bloody slaughter-house ;
Even so, remorseless, have they borne him hence ;
And as the dam runs lowing up and down,
Looking the way her harmless young one went,
And can do nought but wail her darling's loss ;
Even so myself bewails good Gloster's case,
With sad unhelpful tears ; and with dimm'd eyes
Look after him, and cannot do him good ;
So mighty are his vowed enemies.   220
His fortunes I will weep ; and, 'twixt each groan,
Say—" Who 's a traitor ? Gloster he is none."   [*Exit.*
  Q. Mar. Fair lords, cold snow melts with the sun's
     hot beams.
Henry my lord is cold in great affairs,
Too full of foolish pity ; and Gloster's show
Beguiles him, as the mournful crocodile
With sorrow snares relenting passengers ;
Or as the snake, roll'd in a flowering bank,
With shining checker'd slough, doth sting a child,
That for the beauty thinks it excellent.   230
Believe me, lords, were none more wise than I
(And yet herein I judge mine own wit good),
This Gloster should be quickly rid the world,
To rid us from the fear we have of him.
  Car. That he should die is worthy policy,
But yet we want a colour for his death.
'T is meet he be condemn'd by course of law.
  Suf. But, in my mind that were no policy :
The king will labour still to save his life ;
The commons haply rise to save his life ;   240
And yet we have but trivial argument,
More than distrust, that shows him worthy death.
  York. So that, by this, you would not have him die.
  Suf. Ah ! York, no man alive so fain as I.
  York. 'T is York that hath more reason for his
     death.
But, my lord cardinal, and you, my Lord of Suffolk,
Say, as you think, and speak it from your souls,
Were 't not all one, an empty eagle were set
To guard the chicken from a hungry kite,
As place Duke Humphrey for the king's protector?
  Q. Mar. So the poor chicken should be sure of
     death.   251
  Suf. Madam, 't is true : and were 't not madness
     then,
To make the fox surveyor of the fold ?
Who, being accus'd a crafty murderer,
His guilt should be but idly posted over,
Because his purpose is not executed.
No ; let him die, in that he is a fox,
By nature prov'd an enemy to the flock,
Before his chaps be stain'd with crimson blood,
As Humphrey prov'd by reasons to my liege.   260
And do not stand on quillets, how to slay him :
Be it by gins, by snares, by subtilty,

Sleeping, or waking, 't is no matter how,
So he be dead ; for that is good deceit
Which mates him first, that first intends deceit.
Q. Mar. Thrice-noble Suffolk, 't is resolutely spoke.
Suf. Not resolute, except so much were done,
For things are often spoke, and seldom meant ;
But, that my heart accordeth with my tongue,—
Seeing the deed is meritorious,   270
And to preserve my sovereign from his foe,—
Say but the word, and I will be his priest.
Car. But I would have him dead, my Lord of
        Suffolk,
Ere you can take due orders for a priest.
Say, you consent, and censure well the deed,
And I 'll provide his executioner ;
I tender so the safety of my liege.
Suf. Here is my hand ; the deed is worthy doing.
Q. Mar. And so say I.

Suf. " Here is my hand ; the deed is worthy doing."

York. And I ; and now we three have spoke it,   280
It skills not greatly who impugns our doom.

Enter a Messenger.

Mess. Great lords, from Ireland am I come amain,
To signify that rebels there are up,
And put the Englishmen unto the sword.
Send succours, lords, and stop the rage betime,
Before the wound do grow incurable ;
For, being green, there is great hope of help.
Car. A breach that craves a quick expedient stop !
What counsel give you in this weighty cause ?
York. That Somerset be sent as regent thither.   290
'T is meet, that lucky ruler be employ'd ;
Witness the fortune he hath had in France.
Som. If York, with all his far-fet policy,
Had been the regent there instead of me,
He never would have stay'd in France so long.
York. No, not to lose it all, as thou hast done.
I rather would have lost my life betimes,
Than bring a burden of dishonour home,
By staying there so long, till all were lost.
Show me one scar character'd on thy skin :   300
Men's flesh preserv'd so whole do seldom win.
Q. Mar. Nay then, this spark will prove a raging
        fire,
If wind and fuel be brought to feed it with.—
No more, good York ;—sweet Somerset, be still :—
Thy fortune, York, hadst thou been regent there,
Might happily have prov'd far worse than his.
York. What, worse than nought ? nay, then a shame
        take all !
Som. And, in the number, thee, that wishest shame.
Car. My Lord of York, try what your fortune is.
The uncivil kerns of Ireland are in arms,   310
And temper clay with blood of Englishmen :

To Ireland will you lead a band of men,
Collected choicely, from each county some,
And try your hap against the Irishmen ?
York. I will, my lord, so please his majesty.
Suf. Why, our authority is his consent,
And what we do establish, he confirms :
Then, noble York, take thou this task in hand.
York. I am content. Provide me soldiers, lords,
Whiles I take order for mine own affairs.   320
Suf. A charge, Lord York, that I will see perform'd.
But now return we to the false Duke Humphrey.
Car. No more of him ; for I will deal with him,
That henceforth he shall trouble us no more :
And so break off ; the day is almost spent.
Lord Suffolk, you and I must talk of that event.
York. My Lord of Suffolk, within fourteen days,
At Bristol I expect my soldiers ;
For there I 'll ship them all for Ireland.
Suf. I 'll see it truly done, my Lord of York.
                    [*Exeunt all but* York.
York. Now, York, or never, steel thy fearful
        thoughts,   231
And change misdoubt to resolution :
Be that thou hop'st to be, or what thou art
Resign to death ; it is not worth the enjoy-
        ing.
Let pale-fac'd fear keep with the mean-born
        man,
And find no harbour in a royal heart.
Faster than spring-time showers comes
        thought on thought,
And not a thought but thinks on dignity.
My brain, more busy than the labouring
        spider,
Weaves tedious snares to trap mine enemies.
Well, nobles, well ; 't is politicly done,   341
To send me packing with an host of men :
I fear me, you but warm the starved
        snake,
Who, cherish'd in your breasts, will sting
        your hearts.
'T was men I lack'd, and you will give them
        me :
I take it kindly ; yet, be well assur'd,
You put sharp weapons in a madman's
        hands.
Whiles I in Ireland nourish a mighty band,
I will stir up in England some black storm,
Shall blow ten thousand souls to heaven, or hell ;   350
And this fell tempest shall not cease to rage,
Until the golden circuit on my head,
Like to the glorious sun's transparent beams,
Do calm the fury of this mad-bred flaw.
And, for a minister of my intent,
I have seduc'd a headstrong Kentishman,
John Cade of Ashford,
To make commotion, as full well he can,
Under the title of John Mortimer.
In Ireland have I seen this stubborn Cade   360
Oppose himself against a troop of kerns ;
And fought so long, till that his thighs with darts
Were almost like a sharp-quill'd porpentine :
And, in the end being rescu'd, I have seen
Him caper upright, like a wild Morisco,
Shaking the bloody darts, as he his bells.
Full often, like a shag-hair'd crafty kern,
Hath he conversed with the enemy,
And undiscover'd come to me again,
And given me notice of their villainies.   370
This devil here shall be my substitute ;
For that John Mortimer, which now is dead,
In face, in gait, in speech, he doth resemble :
By this I shall perceive the commons' mind,
How they affect the house and claim of York.
Say, he be taken, rack'd, and tortured,
I know, no pain they can inflict upon him
Will make him say, I mov'd him to those arms.
Say, that he thrive, as 't is great like he will,
Why, then from Ireland come I with my strength,   380
And reap the harvest which that rascal sow'd ;
For, Humphrey being dead, as he shall be,
And Henry put apart, the next for me.   [*Exit.*

SCENE II.—Bury. A Room in the Palace.

Enter certain Murderers, hastily.

1 Mur. Run to my Lord of Suffolk ; let him know,
We have despatch'd the duke, as he commanded.
2 Mur. O, that it were to do !—What have we done ?
Didst ever hear a man so penitent ?
1 Mur. Here comes my lord.

Enter SUFFOLK.

Suf. Now, sirs, have you despatch'd this thing ?
1 Mur. Ay, my good lord, he 's dead.
Suf. Why, that 's well said. Go, get you to my
     house ;
I will reward you for this venturous deed.
The king and all the peers are here at hand.   10
Have you laid fair the bed ? Is all things well,
According as I gave directions ?
1 Mur. 'T is, my good lord.
Suf. Away, be gone.   [*Exeunt Murderers.*

Sound trumpets. Enter King HENRY, *Queen* MAR-
GARET, *Cardinal* BEAUFORT, SOMERSET, *Lords,
and others.*

K. Hen. Go, call our uncle to our presence straight :
Say, we intend to try his grace to-day,
If he be guilty, as 't is published.
Suf. I 'll call him presently, my noble lord.   [*Exit.*
K. Hen. Lords, take your places ; and, I pray you all,
Proceed no straiter 'gainst our uncle Gloster,   20
Than from true evidence, of good esteem,
He be approv'd in practice culpable.
Q. Mar. God forbid any malice should prevail,
That faultless may condemn a nobleman !
Pray God, he may acquit him of suspicion !
K. Hen. I thank thee, Nell ; these words content
     me much.

Re-enter SUFFOLK.

How now ? why look'st thou pale ? why tremblest
     thou ?
Where is our uncle ? what 's the matter, Suffolk ?
Suf. Dead in his bed, my lord ; Gloster is dead.
Q. Mar. Marry, God forfend !   ·   30
Car. God's secret judgment !—I did dream to-night,
The duke was dumb, and could not speak a word.
     [*The* KING *swoons.*
Q. Mar. How fares my lord ?—Help, lords ! the king
     is dead.
Som. Rear up his body : wring him by the nose.
Q. Mar. Run, go, help, help !—O Henry, ope thine
     eyes !
Suf. He doth revive again.—Madam, be patient.
K. Hen. O heavenly God !
Q. Mar.   How fares my gracious lord ?
Suf. Comfort, my sovereign ! gracious Henry, com-
     fort !
K. Hen. What ! doth my Lord of Suffolk comfort
     me ?
Came he right now to sing a raven's note,   40
Whose dismal tune bereft my vital powers,
And thinks he, that the chirping of a wren,
By crying comfort from a hollow breast,
Can chase away the first-conceived sound ?
Hide not thy poison with such sugar'd words ;
Lay not thy hands on me ; forbear, I say :
Their touch affrights me as a serpent's sting.
Thou baleful messenger, out of my sight !
Upon thy eye-balls murderous tyranny
Sits in grim majesty to fright the world.   50
Look not upon me, for thine eyes are wounding.
Yet do not go away :—come, basilisk,
And kill the innocent gazer with thy sight ;
For in the shade of death I shall find joy,
In life but double death, now Gloster 's dead.
Q. Mar. Why do you rate my Lord of Suffolk thus ?
Although the duke was enemy to him,
Yet he, most Christian-like, laments his death :
And for myself, foe as he was to me,
Might liquid tears, or heart-offending groans   60

Or blood-consuming sighs, recall his life,
I would be blind with weeping, sick with groans,
Look pale as primrose with blood-drinking sighs,
And all to have the noble duke alive.
What know I how the world may deem of me ?
For it is known, we were but hollow friends ;
It may be judg'd, I made the duke away :
So shall my name with slander's tongue be wounded,
And princes' courts be fill'd with my reproach.
This get I by his death. Ah me, unhappy !   70
To be a queen, and crown'd with infamy !
K. Hen. Ah, woe is me for Gloster, wretched man !
Q. Mar. Be woe for me, more wretched than he is.
What, dost thou turn away, and hide thy face ?
I am no loathsome leper ; look on me.
What, art thou, like the adder, waxen deaf ?
Be poisonous too, and kill thy forlorn queen.
Is all thy comfort shut in Gloster's tomb ?
Why, then Dame Margaret was ne'er thy joy :
Erect his statua, and worship it,   80
And make my image but an ale-house sign.
Was I for this nigh wrack'd upon the sea,
And twice by awkward wind from England's bank
Drove back again unto my native clime ?
What boded this, but well-forewarning wind
Did seem to say,—Seek not a scorpion's nest,
Nor set no footing on this unkind shore ?
What did I then, but curs'd the gentle gusts,
And he that loos'd them from their brazen caves ;
And bid them blow towards England's blessed shore,
Or turn our stern upon a dreadful rock.   91
Yet Æolus would not be a murderer,
But left that hateful office unto thee :
The pretty-vaulting sea refus'd to drown me,
Knowing that thou wouldst have me drown'd on
     shore,
With tears as salt as sea through thy unkindness :
The splitting rocks cower'd in the sinking sands,
And would not dash me with their ragged sides,
Because thy flinty heart, more hard than they,
Might in thy palace perish Margaret.   100
As far as I could ken thy chalky cliffs,
When from the shore the tempest beat us back,
I stood upon the hatches in the storm ;
And when the dusky sky began to rob
My earnest-gaping sight of thy land's view,
I took a costly jewel from my neck,—
A heart it was, bound in with diamonds,—
And threw it towards thy land. The sea receiv'd it,
And so I wish'd thy body might my heart :
And even with this I lost fair England's view,   110
And bid mine eyes be packing with my heart,
And call'd them blind and dusky spectacles,
For losing ken of Albion's wished coast.
How often have I tempted Suffolk's tongue
(The agent of thy foul inconstancy),
To sit and witch me, as Ascanius did,
When he to madding Dido would unfold
His father's acts, commenc'd in burning Troy !
Am I not witch'd like her ? or thou not false like him ?
Ah me ! I can no more. Die, Margaret,   120
For Henry weeps that thou dost live so long.

Noise within. Enter WARWICK *and* SALISBURY.
The Commons press to the door.

War. It is reported, mighty sovereign,
That good Duke Humphrey traitorously is murder'd
By Suffolk and the Cardinal Beaufort's means.
The commons, like an angry hive of bees,
That want their leader, scatter up and down,
And care not who they sting in his revenge.
Myself have calm'd their spleenful mutiny,
Until they hear the order of his death.
K. Hen. That he is dead, good Warwick, 't is too
     true ;   130
But how he died, God knows, not Henry.
Enter his chamber, view his breathless corse,
And comment then upon his sudden death.
War. That I shall do, my liege.—Stay, Salisbury,
With the rude multitude, till I return.
     [WARWICK *goes into an inner room, and*
     SALISBURY *retires.*

K. Hen. O Thou that judgest all things, stay my
    thoughts !
My thoughts that labour to persuade my soul,
Some violent hands were laid on Humphrey's life.
If my suspect be false, forgive me, God,
For judgment only doth belong to Thee.   140

The doors of an inner chamber are thrown open, and
    Gloster *is discovered dead in his bed ;* Warwick
    and others standing by it.

War. Come hither, gracious sovereign, view this
    body.

Suf. "Dead in his bed, my lord ; Gloster is dead."

Fain would I go to chafe his paly lips
With twenty thousand kisses, and to drain
Upon his face an ocean of salt tears,
To tell my love unto his dumb deaf trunk,
And with my fingers feel his hand unfeeling ;
But all in vain are these mean obsequies,
And to survey his dead and earthy image,
What were it but to make my sorrow greater ?

K. Hen. That is to see how deep my grave is made ;
For with his soul fled all my worldly solace,   151
For seeing him, I see my life in death.
    War. As surely as my soul intends to live
With that dread King, that took our state upon Him
To free us from His Father's wrathful curse,
I do believe that violent hands were laid
Upon the life of this thrice-famed duke.

Suf. A dreadful oath, sworn with a solemn tongue!
What instance gives Lord Warwick for his vow?
War. See, how the blood is settled in his face. 160
Oft have I seen a timely-parted ghost,
Of ashy semblance, meagre, pale, and bloodless,
Being all descended to the labouring heart;
Who, in the conflict that it holds with death,
Attracts the same for aidance 'gainst the enemy;
Which with the heart there cools, and ne'er returneth
To blush and beautify the cheek again.
But see, his face is black, and full of blood;
His eye-balls further out than when he liv'd,
Staring full ghastly like a strangled man: 170
His hair uprear'd, his nostrils stretch'd with struggling;
His hands abroad display'd, as one that grasp'd
And tugg'd for life, and was by strength subdued.
Look, on the sheets, his hair, you see, is sticking;
His well-proportion'd beard made rough and rugged,
Like to the summer's corn by tempest lodg'd.
It cannot be but he was murder'd here;
The least of all these signs were probable.
Suf. Why, Warwick, who should do the duke to
        death?
Myself and Beaufort had him in protection, 180
And we, I hope, sir, are no murderers.
War. But both of you were vow'd Duke Humphrey's
        foes,
And you, forsooth, had the good duke to keep:
'T is like you would not feast him like a friend,
And 't is well seen he found an enemy.
Q. Mar. Then you, belike, suspect these noblemen
As guilty of Duke Humphrey's timeless death.
War. Who finds the heifer dead, and bleeding fresh,
And sees fast by a butcher with an axe,
But will suspect 't was he that made the slaughter? 191
Who finds the partridge in the puttock's nest,
But may imagine how the bird was dead,
Although the kite soar with unbloodied beak?
Even so suspicious is this tragedy.
Q. Mar. Are you the butcher, Suffolk? where 's
        your knife?
Is Beaufort term'd a kite? where are his talons?
Suf. I wear no knife, to slaughter sleeping men;
But here 's a vengeful sword, rusted with ease,
That shall be scoured in his rancorous heart, 200
That slanders me with murder's crimson badge.—
Say, if thou dar'st, proud Lord of Warwickshire,
That I am faulty in Duke Humphrey's death.
        [*Exeunt Cardinal,* SOMERSET, *and others.*
War. What dares not Warwick, if false Suffolk
        dare him?
Q. Mar. He dares not calm his contumelious spirit,
Nor cease to be an arrogant controller,
Though Suffolk dare him twenty thousand times.
War. Madam, be still, with reverence may I say;
For every word you speak in his behalf
Is slander to your royal dignity.
Suf. Blunt-witted lord, ignoble in demeanour, 210
If ever lady wrong'd her lord so much,
Thy mother took into her blameful bed
Some stern untutor'd churl, and noble stock
Was graft with crab-tree slip; whose fruit thou art,
And never of the Nevils' noble race.
War. But that the guilt of murder bucklers thee,
And I should rob the deathsman of his fee,
Quitting thee thereby of ten thousand shames,
And that my sovereign's presence makes me mild,
I would, false murderous coward, on thy knee 220
Make thee beg pardon for thy passed speech,
And say, it was thy mother that thou meant'st;
That thou thyself wast born in bastardy:
And, after all this fearful homage done,
Give thee thy hire, and send thy soul to hell,
Pernicious bloodsucker of sleeping men.
Suf. Thou shalt be waking while I shed thy blood,
If from this presence thou dar'st go with me.
War. Away even now, or I will drag thee hence.
Unworthy though thou art, I 'll cope with thee, 230
And do some service to Duke Humphrey's ghost.
        [*Exeunt* SUFFOLK *and* WARWICK.
K. Hen. What stronger breastplate than a heart
        untainted?

Thrice is he arm'd that hath his quarrel just;
And he but naked, though lock'd up in steel,
Whose conscience with injustice is corrupted.
                        [*A noise within.*
Q. Mar. What noise is this?

Re-enter SUFFOLK *and* WARWICK, *with their
        weapons drawn.*

K. Hen. Why, how now, lords? your wrathful
        weapons drawn
Here in our presence? dare you be so bold?—
Why, what tumultuous clamour have we here?
Suf. The traitorous Warwick, with the men of
        Bury, 240
Set all upon me, mighty sovereign.

Noise of a crowd within.   Re-enter SALISBURY.

Sal. [*Speaking to those within.*] Sirs, stand apart;
        the king shall know your mind.—
Dread lord, the commons send you word by me,
Unless false Suffolk straight be done to death,
Or banished fair England's territories,
They will by violence tear him from your palace,
And torture him with grievous lingering death.
They say, by him the good Duke Humphrey died;
They say, in him they fear your highness' death;
And mere instinct of love, and loyalty, 250
Free from a stubborn opposite intent,
As being thought to contradict your liking,
Makes them thus forward in his banishment.
They say, in care of your most royal person,
That, if your highness should intend to sleep,
And charge, that no man should disturb your rest,
In pain of your dislike, or pain of death,
Yet, notwithstanding such a strait edict,
Were there a serpent seen, with forked tongue,
That slily glided towards your majesty, 260
It were but necessary, you were wak'd;
Lest, being suffer'd in that harmful slumber,
The mortal worm might make the sleep eternal:
And therefore do they cry, though you forbid,
That they will guard you, whe'r you will or no,
From such fell serpents as false Suffolk is;
With whose envenomed and fatal sting,
Your loving uncle, twenty times his worth,
They say, is shamefully bereft of life.
Commons. [*Within.*] An answer from the king, my
        Lord of Salisbury! 270
Suf. 'T is like, the commons, rude unpolish'd hinds,
Could send such message to their sovereign;
But you, my lord, were glad to be employ'd,
To show how quaint an orator you are:
But all the honour Salisbury hath won,
Is, that he was the lord ambassador,
Sent from a sort of tinkers to the king.
Commons. [*Within.*] An answer from the king, or
        we will all break in!
K. Hen. Go, Salisbury, and tell them all from me,
I thank them for their tender loving care; 280
And had I not been cited so by them,
Yet did I purpose as they do entreat;
For sure, my thoughts do hourly prophesy
Mischance unto my state by Suffolk's means:
And therefore, by His Majesty I swear,
Whose far unworthy deputy I am,
He shall not breathe infection in this air
But three days longer, on the pain of death.
                        [*Exit* SALISBURY.
Q. Mar. O Henry! let me plead for gentle Suffolk.
K. Hen. Ungentle queen, to call him gentle Suffolk.
No more, I say; if thou dost plead for him, 291
Thou wilt but add increase unto my wrath.
Had I but said, I would have kept my word,
But when I swear, it is irrevocable.—
If after three days' space thou here be'st found
On any ground that I am ruler of,
The world shall not be ransom for thy life.—
Come, Warwick, come, good Warwick, go with me;
I have great matters to impart to thee.
                [*Exeunt King* HENRY, WARWICK, *Lords, &c.*
Q. Mar. Mischance and sorrow go along with you!
Heart's discontent, and sour affliction, 301

Be playfellows to keep you company!
There's two of you; the devil make a third,
And threefold vengeance tend upon your steps!
  Suf. Cease, gentle queen, these execrations,
And let thy Suffolk take his heavy leave.
  Q. Mar. Fie, coward woman, and soft-hearted
      wretch!
Hast thou not spirit to curse thine enemy?
  Suf. A plague upon them! wherefore should I
      curse them?
Would curses kill, as doth the mandrake's groan, 310
I would invent as bitter-searching terms,
As curst, as harsh, and horrible to hear,
Deliver'd strongly through my fixed teeth,
With full as many signs of deadly hate,
As lean-fac'd Envy in her loathsome cave.
My tongue should stumble in mine earnest words;
Mine eyes should sparkle like the beaten flint;
My hair be fix'd on end, as one distract;
Ay, every joint should seem to curse and ban:
And even now my burden'd heart would break, 320
Should I not curse them. Poison be their drink!
Gall, worse than gall, the daintiest that they taste!
Their sweetest shade a grove of cypress trees!
Their chiefest prospect murdering basilisks!
Their softest touch as smart as lizards' stings!
Their music frightful as the serpent's hiss,
And boding screech-owls make the concert full!
All the foul terrors in dark-seated hell—
  Q. Mar. Enough, sweet Suffolk: thou torment'st
      thyself;
And these dread curses, like the sun 'gainst glass, 330
Or like an overcharged gun, recoil,
And turn the force of them upon thyself.
  Suf. You bade me ban, and will you bid me leave?
Now, by the ground that I am banish'd from,
Well could I curse away a winter's night,
Though standing naked on a mountain top,
Where biting cold would never let grass grow,
And think it but a minute spent in sport.
  Q. Mar. O! let me entreat thee, cease. Give me thy
      hand,
That I may dew it with my mournful tears; 340
Nor let the rain of heaven wet this place,
To wash away my woful monuments.
O! could this kiss be printed in thy hand,
That thou mightst think upon these by the seal,
Through whom a thousand sighs are breath'd for thee.
So, get thee gone, that I may know my grief;
'T is but surmis'd whilst thou art standing by,
As one that surfeits, thinking on a want.
I will repeal thee, or, be well assur'd,
Adventure to be banished myself; 350
And banished I am, if but from thee.
Go, speak not to me; even now be gone.—
O! go not yet.—Even thus two friends condemn'd
Embrace, and kiss, and take ten thousand leaves,
Loather a hundred times to part than die.
Yet now farewell; and farewell life with thee!
  Suf. Thus is poor Suffolk ten times banished,
Once by the king, and three times thrice by thee.
'T is not the land I care for, wert thou thence;
A wilderness is populous enough, 360
So Suffolk had thy heavenly company:
For where thou art, there is the world itself,
With every several pleasure in the world,
And where thou art not, desolation.
I can no more.—Live thou to joy thy life;
Myself no joy in nought, but that thou liv'st.

Enter VAUX.

  Q. Mar. Whither goes Vaux so fast? what news,
      pr'ythee?
  Vaux. To signify unto his majesty,
That Cardinal Beaufort is at point of death;
For suddenly a grievous sickness took him, 370
That makes him gasp, and stare, and catch the air,
Blaspheming God, and cursing men on earth.
Sometime he talks as if Duke Humphrey's ghost
Were by his side; sometime he calls the king,
And whispers to his pillow, as to him,
The secrets of his overcharged soul:

And I am sent to tell his majesty,
That even now he cries aloud for him.
  Q. Mar. Go, tell this heavy message to the king.
                     [*Exit* VAUX.
Ah me! what is this world? what news are these? 380
But wherefore grieve I at an hour's poor loss,
Omitting Suffolk's exile, my soul's treasure?
Why only, Suffolk, mourn I not for thee,
And with the southern clouds contend in tears?
Theirs for the earth's increase, mine for my sorrows.

Car. "O! torture me no more, I will confess."

Now, get thee hence: the king, thou know'st, is
      coming;
If thou be found by me, thou art but dead.
  Suf. If I depart from thee, I cannot live;
And in thy sight to die, what were it else,
But like a pleasant slumber in thy lap? 390
Here could I breathe my soul into the air,
As mild and gentle as the cradle-babe,
Dying with mother's dug between its lips;
Where, from thy sight, I should be raging mad,
And cry out for thee to close up mine eyes,
To have thee with thy lips to stop my mouth:
So shouldst thou either turn my flying soul,
Or I should breathe it so into thy body,
And then it liv'd in sweet Elysium.
To die by thee, were but to die in jest; 400
From thee to die, were torture more than death.
O! let me stay, befall what may befall.
  Q. Mar. Away! though parting be a fretful corsive,
It is applied to a deathful wound.
To France, sweet Suffolk: let me hear from thee;
For wheresoe'er thou art in this world's globe,
I'll have an Iris that shall find thee out.
  Suf. I go.
  Q. Mar.   And take my heart with thee.
  Suf. A jewel, lock'd into the wofull'st cask
That ever did contain a thing of worth. 410
Even as a splitted bark, so sunder we:
This way fall I to death.
  Q. Mar.   This way for me.
                   [*Exeunt severally.*

SCENE III.—London. Cardinal BEAUFORT'S Bedchamber.

Enter King HENRY, SALISBURY, WARWICK, *and
others. The Cardinal in bed; Attendants with him.*

  K. Hen. How fares my lord? speak, Beaufort, to
      thy sovereign.
  Car. If thou be'st death, I'll give thee England's
      treasure,
Enough to purchase such another island,
So thou wilt let me live, and feel no pain.

K. Hen. Ah, what a sign it is of evil life,
Where death's approach is seen so terrible!
War. Beaufort, it is thy sovereign speaks to thee.
Car. Bring me unto my trial when you will.
Died he not in his bed? where should he die?
Can I make men live, whe r they will or no?— 10
O! torture me no more, I will confess.—
Alive again? then show me where he is:
I 'll give a thousand pound to look upon him.—
He hath no eyes, the dust hath blinded them.—
Comb down his hair: look! look! it stands upright,
Like lime-twigs set to catch my winged soul.—
Give me some drink; and bid the apothecary
Bring the strong poison that I bought of him.
    K. Hen. O Thou eternal Mover of the heavens,

Look with a gentle eye upon this wretch! 20
O! beat away the busy meddling fiend,
That lays strong siege unto this wretch's soul,
And from his bosom purge this black despair.
    War. See, how the pangs of death do make him grin.
    Sal. Disturb him not, let him pass peaceably.
    K. Hen. Peace to his soul, if God's good pleasure be.
Lord cardinal, if thou think'st on heaven's bliss,
Hold up thy hand, make signal of thy hope.—
He dies, and makes no sign. O God, forgive him!
    War. So bad a death argues a monstrous life. 30
    K. Hen. Forbear to judge, for we are sinners all.—
Close up his eyes, and draw the curtain close,
And let us all to meditation.   [*Exeunt.*

ACT IV.

SCENE I.—Kent. The Sea-shore near Dover.

Firing heard at sea. Then enter from a boat, a Captain, a Master, a Master's Mate, WALTER WHITMORE, and others; with them SUFFOLK, disguised, and other Gentlemen, prisoners.

    Captain.
THE gaudy, blabbing, and remorseful day
   Is crept into the bosom of the sea,
   And now loud-howling wolves arouse
       the jades
   That drag the tragic melancholy night;
   Who with their drowsy, slow, and flag-
       ging wings
   Clip dead men's graves, and from their
       misty jaws
   Breathe foul contagious darkness in the
       air.
   Therefore, bring forth the soldiers of our
       prize;
For, whilst our pinnace anchors in the Downs,
Here shall they make their ransom on the sand, 10
Or with their blood stain this discolour'd shore.—
Master, this prisoner freely give I thee;—
And thou that art his mate, make boot of this:—
The other [*pointing to* SUFFOLK], Walter Whitmore,
is thy share.
    1 *Gent.* What is my ransom, master? let me know.
    Mast. A thousand crowns, or else lay down your
       head.
    Mate. And so much shall you give, or off goes
       yours.
    Cap. What! think you much to pay two thousand
       crowns,
And bear the name and port of gentlemen?
Cut both the villains' throats!—for die you shall: 20
The lives of those which we have lost in fight,
Be counterpois'd with such a petty sum!
    1 *Gent.* I 'll give it, sir; and therefore spare my
       life.
    2 *Gent.* And so will I, and write home for it straight.
    Whit. I lost mine eye in laying the prize aboard,
[*To* SUFFOLK] And, therefore, to revenge it shalt
       thou die;
And so should these, if I might have my will.
    Cap. Be not so rash: take ransom; let him live.
    Suf. Look on my George: I am a gentleman.
Rate me at what thou wilt, thou shalt be paid. 30
    Whit. And so am I; my name is Walter Whitmore.
How now? why start'st thou? what! doth death
       affright?
    Suf. Thy name affrights me, in whose sound is death.

A cunning man did calculate my birth,
And told me that by *Water* I should die:
Yet let not this make thee be bloody-minded;
Thy name is *Gaultier*, being rightly sounded.
    Whit. Gaultier, or *Walter,* which it is, I care not;
Never yet did base dishonour blur our name,
But with our sword we wip'd away the blot: 40
Therefore, when merchant-like I sell revenge,
Broke be my sword, my arms torn and defac'd,
And I proclaim'd a coward through the world!
          [*Lays hold on* SUFFOLK.
    Suf. Stay, Whitmore; for thy prisoner is a prince,
The Duke of Suffolk, William de la Poole.
    Whit. The Duke of Suffolk muffled up in rags!
    Suf. Ay, but these rags are no part of the duke:
[*Jove sometime went disguis'd, and why not I?*]
    Cap. But Jove was never slain, as thou shalt be.
    Suf. Obscure and lowly swain, King Henry's blood,
The honourable blood of Lancaster, 51
Must not be shed by such a jaded groom.
Hast thou not kiss'd thy hand, and held my stirrup?
Bare-headed plodded by my foot-cloth mule,
And thought thee happy when I shook my head?
How often hast thou waited at my cup,
Fed from my trencher, kneel'd down at the board,
When I have feasted with Queen Margaret?
Remember it, and let it make thee crest-fall'n;
Ay, and allay this thy abortive pride. 60
How in our voiding lobby hast thou stood,
And duly waited for my coming forth?
This hand of mine hath writ in thy behalf,
And therefore shall it charm thy riotous tongue.
    Whit. Speak, captain, shall I stab the forlorn swain?
    Cap. First let my words stab him, as he hath me.
    Suf. Base slave, thy words are blunt, and so art
       thou.
    Cap. Convey him hence, and on our long-boat's
       side
Strike off his head.
    Suf.   Thou dar'st not for thy own.
    Cap. [Yes, Poole.
    Suf.   Poole?]
    Cap.   Poole? Sir Poole? lord?
Ay, kennel, puddle, sink; whose filth and dirt 71
Troubles the silver spring where England drinks.
Now will I dam up this thy yawning mouth,

For swallowing the treasure of the realm :
Thy lips, that kiss'd the queen, shall sweep the ground ;
And thou, that smil'dst at good Duke Humphrey's death,
Against the senseless winds shalt grin in vain,
Who in contempt shall hiss at thee again :
And wedded be thou to the hags of hell,
For daring to affy a mighty lord   80
Unto the daughter of a worthless king,
Having neither subject, wealth, nor diadem.
By devilish policy art thou grown great,
And, like ambitious Sylla, overgorg'd
With gobbets of thy mother's bleeding heart.
By thee Anjou and Maine were sold to France ;
The false revolting Normans thorough thee
Disdain to call us lord ; and Picardy
Hath slain their governors, surpris'd our forts,
And sent the ragged soldiers wounded home.   90
The princely Warwick, and the Nevils all,
Whose dreadful swords were never drawn in vain,
As hating thee, are rising up in arms :
And now the house of York—thrust from the crown,
By shameful murder of a guiltless king,
And lofty proud encroaching tyranny—
Burns with revenging fire ; whose hopeful colours
Advance our half-fac'd sun, striving to shine,
Under the which is writ—Invitis nubibus.
The commons, here in Kent, are up in arms ;   100
And, to conclude, reproach and beggary
Is crept into the palace of our king,
And all by thee.—Away !—Convey him hence.
  Suf. O, that I were a god, to shoot forth thunder
Upon these paltry, servile, abject drudges !
Small things make base men proud : this villain here,
Being captain of a pinnace, threatens more
Than Bargulus the strong Illyrian pirate.
Drones suck not eagles' blood, but rob bee-hives.
It is impossible, that I should die   110
By such a lowly vassal as thyself.
Thy words move rage, and not remorse, in me :
I go of message from the queen to France ;
I charge thee, waft me safely cross the Channel.
  Cap. Walter !—
  Whit. Come, Suffolk ; I must waft thee to thy death.
  Suf. Gelidus timor occupat artus : ·it is thee I fear.
  Whit. Thou shalt have cause to fear, before I leave thee.
What ! are ye daunted now ? now will ye stoop ?
1 Gent. My gracious lord, entreat him, speak him fair.   120
  Suf. Suffolk's imperial tongue is stern and rough,
Us'd to command, untaught to plead for favour.
Far be it we should honour such as these
With humble suit : no, rather let my head
Stoop to the block than these knees bow to any,
Save to the God of heaven, and to my king :
And sooner dance upon a bloody pole,
Than stand uncover'd to the vulgar groom.
True nobility is exempt from fear :
More can I bear, than you dare execute.   130
  Cap. Hale him away, and let him talk no more.
  Suf. Come, soldiers, show what cruelty ye can,
That this my death may never be forgot.—
Great men oft die by vile Bezonians.
A Roman sworder and banditto slave
Murder'd sweet Tully ; Brutus' bastard hand
Stabb'd Julius Cæsar ; savage islanders
Pompey the Great ; and Suffolk dies by pirates.
        [Exit Suffolk, with Whitmore and others.
  Cap. And as for these whose ransom we have set,
It is our pleasure one of them depart :   140
Therefore, come you with us, and let him go.
        [Exeunt all but the First Gentleman.

Re-enter Whitmore, with Suffolk's body.

  Whit. There let his head and lifeless body lie,
Until the queen, his mistress, bury it.   [Exit.
1 Gent. O barbarous and bloody spectacle !
His body will I bear unto the king ;
If he revenge it not, yet will his friends ;
So will the queen, that living held him dear.
        [Exit, with the body.

Scene II.—Blackheath.

Enter George Bevis and John Holland.

  Geo. Come, and get thee a sword, though made of a lath : they have been up these two days.
  John. They have the more need to sleep now then.
  Geo. I tell thee, Jack Cade the clothier means to dress the commonwealth, and turn it, and set a new nap upon it.
  John. So he had need, for 't is threadbare. Well, I say, it was never merry world in England, since gentlemen came up.
  Geo. O miserable age ! Virtue is not regarded in handicraftsmen.   11
  John. The nobility think scorn to go in leather aprons.
  Geo. Nay, more ; the king's council are no good workmen.
  John. True ; and yet it is said, Labour in thy vocation : which is as much to say as,—let the magistrates be labouring men ; and therefore should we be magistrates.
  Geo. Thou hast hit it ; for there's no better sign of a brave mind than a hard hand.   21
  John. I see them ! I see them ! There's Best's son, the tanner of Wingham,—
  Geo. He shall have the skins of our enemies to make dog's-leather of.
  John. And Dick the butcher,—
  Geo. Then is sin struck down like an ox, and iniquity's throat cut like a calf.
  John. And Smith the weaver,—
  Geo. Argo, their thread of life is spun.   30
  John. Come, come ; let 's fall in with them.

Drum. Enter Cade, Dick the Butcher, Smith the Weaver, and others in great number.

  Cade. We John Cade, so termed of our supposed father,—
  Dick. [Aside.] Or rather, of stealing a cade of herrings.
  Cade. For our enemies shall fall before us, inspired with the spirit of putting down kings and princes,—Command silence.
  Dick. Silence !
  Cade. My father was a Mortimer,—   40
  Dick. [Aside.] He was an honest man, and a good bricklayer.
  Cade. My mother a Plantagenet,—
  Dick. [Aside.] I knew her well ; she was a midwife.
  Cade. My wife descended of the Lacies,—
  Dick. [Aside.] She was, indeed, a pedlar's daughter, and sold many laces.
  Smith. [Aside.] But, now of late, not able to travel with her furred pack, she washes bucks here at home.
  Cade. Therefore am I of an honourable house.   50
  Dick. [Aside.] Ay, by my faith, the field is honourable, and there was he born, under a hedge ; for his father had never a house, but the cage.
  Cade. Valiant I am.
  Smith. [Aside.] 'A must needs ; for beggary is valiant.
  Cade. I am able to endure much.
  Dick. [Aside.] No question of that, for I have seen him whipped three market-days together.
  Cade. I fear neither sword nor fire.   60
  Smith. [Aside.] He need not fear the sword, for his coat is of proof.
  Dick. [Aside.] But, methinks, he should stand in fear of fire, being burnt i' the hand for stealing of sheep.
  Cade. Be brave then ; for your captain is brave, and vows reformation. There shall be in England seven halfpenny loaves sold for a penny ; the three-hooped pot shall have ten hoops ; and I will make it felony to drink small beer. All the realm shall be in common, and in Cheapside shall my palfrey go to grass. And, when I am king (as king I will be),—   72
  All. God save your majesty !
  Cade. I thank you, good people :—there shall be no money ; all shall eat and drink on my score ; and I

will apparel them all in one livery, that they may agree like brothers, and worship me their lord.

Dick. The first thing we do, let's kill all the lawyers.

Cade. Nay, that I mean to do. Is not this a lamentable thing, that of the skin of an innocent lamb should be made parchment? that parchment, being scribbled o'er, should undo a man? Some say, the bee stings; but I say, 'tis the bee's wax, for I did but seal once to a thing, and I was never mine own man since. How now? who's there?

Enter some, bringing in the Clerk of Chatham.

Smith. The clerk of Chatham: he can write and read, and cast accompt.

Cade. O monstrous!

Smith. We took him setting of boy's copies. 90

Cade. Here's a villain!

Smith. H'as a book in his pocket, with red letters in't.

Cade. Nay, then he is a conjurer.

Dick. Nay, he can make obligations, and write court-hand.

Cade. I am sorry for't: the man is a proper man, of mine honour; unless I find him guilty, he shall not die.—Come hither, sirrah, I must examine thee. What is thy name? 100

Clerk. Emmanuel.

Dick. They use to write it on the top of letters.— 'T will go hard with you.

Cade. Let me alone.—Dost thou use to write thy name, or hast thou a mark to thyself, like an honest plain-dealing man?

Clerk. Sir, I thank God, I have been so well brought up, that I can write my name.

All. He hath confessed: away with him! he's a villain and a traitor. 110

Cade. Away with him, I say: hang him with his pen and ink-horn about his neck.

　　　　　　　　　　　　　[*Exeunt some with the Clerk.*

Enter MICHAEL.

Mich. Where's our general?

Cade. Here I am, thou particular fellow.

Mich. Fly, fly, fly! Sir Humphrey Stafford and his brother are hard by, with the king's forces.

Cade. Stand, villain, stand, or I'll fell thee down. He shall be encountered with a man as good as himself: he is but a knight, is 'a?

Mich. No. 120

Cade. To equal him, I will make myself a knight presently. [*Kneels.*]—Rise up Sir John Mortimer. Now have at him.

Enter Sir HUMPHREY STAFFORD, *and* WILLIAM *his Brother, with drum and Forces.*

Staf. Rebellious hinds, the filth and scum of Kent, Mark'd for the gallows, lay your weapons down: Home to your cottages, forsake this groom. The king is merciful, if you revolt.

W. Staf. But angry, wrathful, and inclin'd to blood, If you go forward: therefore yield, or die.

Cade. As for these silken-coated slaves, I pass not: 130 It is to you, good people, that I speak, O'er whom in time to come I hope to reign; For I am rightful heir unto the crown.

Staf. Villain! thy father was a plasterer; And thou thyself a shearman, art thou not?

Cade. And Adam was a gardener.

W. Staf. And what of that?

Cade. Marry, this:—Edmund Mortimer, Earl of March, Married the Duke of Clarence' daughter, did he not?

Staf. Ay, sir. 140

Cade. By her he had two children at one birth.

W. Staf. That's false.

Cade. Ay, there's the question; but I say, 'tis true.

The elder of them, being put to nurse, ~Was by a beggar-woman stol'n away;

And, ignorant of his birth and parentage, Became a bricklayer when he came to age. His son am I: deny it, if you can.

Dick. Nay, 'tis too true; therefore, he shall be king. 150

Smith. Sir, he made a chimney in my father's house, and the bricks are alive at this day to testify it: therefore, deny it not.

Staf. And will you credit this base drudge's words, That speaks he knows not what?

All. Ay, marry, will we; therefore get ye gone.

W. Staf. Jack Cade, the Duke of York hath taught you this.

Cade. [*Aside.*] He lies, for I invented it myself.—

Cade. "His son am I: deny it, if you can."

Go to, sirrah: tell the king from me, that for his father's sake, Henry the Fifth, in whose time boys went to span-counter for French crowns, I am content he shall reign; but I'll be protector over him. 162

Dick. And, furthermore, we'll have the Lord Say's head, for selling the dukedom of Maine.

Cade. And good reason; for thereby is England mained, and fain to go with a staff, but that my puissance holds it up. Fellow kings, I tell you that that Lord Say hath gelded the commonwealth, and made it an eunuch; and more than that, he can speak French, and therefore he is a traitor. 170

Staf. O gross and miserable ignorance!

Cade. Nay, answer, if you can: the Frenchmen are our enemies; go to then, I ask but this: can he that speaks with the tongue of an enemy be a good counsellor, or no?

All. No, no; and therefore we'll have his head.

W. Staf. Well, seeing gentle words will not prevail, Assail them with the army of the king.

Staf. Herald, away; and, throughout every town, Proclaim them traitors that are up with Cade; 180 That those which fly before the battle ends, May, even in their wives' and children's sight, Be hang'd up for example at their doors.— And you, that be the king's friends, follow me.

　　　　　　　　[*Exeunt the two* STAFFORDS *and Forces.*

Cade. And you, that love the commons, follow me.—

Now show yourselves men: 'tis for liberty. We will not leave one lord, one gentleman: Spare none but such as go in clouted shoon, For they are thrifty honest men, and such As would (but that they dare not) take our parts. 190

Dick. They are all in order, and march toward us.

Cade. But then are we in order, when we are most out of order. Come: march! forward! [*Exeunt.*

SCENE III.—Another Part of Blackheath.

Alarums. The two parties enter, and fight, and
both the STAFFORDS *are slain.*

Cade. Where 's Dick, the butcher of Ashford ?
Dick. Here, sir.
Cade. They fell before thee like sheep and oxen,
and thou behavedst thyself as if thou hadst been in
thine own slaughter-house : therefore thus will I
reward thee,—the Lent shall be as long again as it is ;
and thou shalt have a license to kill for a hundred
lacking one.   9
Dick. I desire no more.
Cade. And, to speak truth, thou deservest no less.
This monument of the victory will I bear ; and the
bodies shall be dragged at my horse' heels, till I do
come to London, where we will have the mayor's
sword borne before us.
Dick. If we mean to thrive and do good, break open
the gaols, and let out the prisoners.
Cade. Fear not that, I warrant thee. Come ; let 's
march towards London.   [*Exeunt.*

SCENE IV.—London. A Room in the Palace.

Enter King HENRY, *reading a supplication ; the*
Duke of BUCKINGHAM, *and Lord* SAY, *with him :*
at a distance, Queen MARGARET, *mourning over*
SUFFOLK'S *head.*

Q. Mar. Oft have I heard that grief softens the
     mind,
And makes it fearful and degenerate ;
Think therefore on revenge, and cease to weep.
But who can cease to weep, and look on this ?
Here may his head lie on my throbbing breast ;
But where 's the body that I should embrace ?
Buck. What answer makes your grace to the rebels'
     supplication ?
K. Hen. I 'll send some holy bishop to entreat ;
For God forbid, so many simple souls   10
Should perish by the sword ! And I myself,
Rather than bloody war shall cut them short,
Will parley with Jack Cade, their general.—
But stay, I 'll read it over once again.
Q. Mar. Ah, barbarous villains ! hath this lovely
     face
Rul'd like a wandering planet over me,
And could it not enforce them to relent,
That were unworthy to behold the same ?
K. Hen. Lord Say, Jack Cade hath sworn to have
     thy head.
Say. Ay, but I hope, your highness shall have his.
K. Hen. How now, madam ?   21
Still lamenting, and mourning for Suffolk's death ?
I fear me, love, if that I had been dead,
Thou wouldest not have mourn'd so much for me.
Q. Mar. No, my love ; I should not mourn, but die
     for thee.

Enter a Messenger.

K. Hen. How now ! what news ? why com'st thou
     in such haste ?
Mess. The rebels are in Southwark. Fly, my lord !
Jack Cade proclaims himself Lord Mortimer,
Descended from the Duke of Clarence' house,
And calls your grace usurper openly,   30
And vows to crown himself in Westminster.
His army is a ragged multitude
Of hinds and peasants, rude and merciless :
Sir Humphrey Stafford and his brother's death
Hath given them heart and courage to proceed.
All scholars, lawyers, courtiers, gentlemen,
They call false caterpillars, and intend their death.
K. Hen. O graceless men ! they know not what
     they do.
Buck. My gracious lord, retire to Killingworth,
Until a power be rais'd to put them down.   40
Q. Mar. Ah ! were the Duke of Suffolk now alive,
These Kentish rebels would be soon appeas'd.

K. Hen. Lord Say, the traitors hate thee,
Therefore away with us to Killingworth.
Say. So might your grace's person be in danger.
The sight of me is odious in their eyes ;
And therefore in this city will I stay,
And live alone as secret as I may.

Enter another Messenger.

2 Mess. Jack Cade hath gotten London Bridge ;
The citizens fly and forsake their houses ;   50
The rascal people, thirsting after prey,
Join with the traitor ; and they jointly swear,
To spoil the city, and your royal court.
Buck. Then linger not, my lord : away, take horse.
K. Hen. Come, Margaret : God, our hope, will suc-
     cour us.
Q. Mar. My hope is gone, now Suffolk is deceas'd.
K. Hen. [*To Lord* SAY.] Farewell, my lord : trust
     not the Kentish rebels.
Buck. Trust nobody, for fear you be betray'd.
Say. The trust I have is in mine innocence,
And therefore am I bold and resolute.   60
                           [*Exeunt.*

SCENE V.—The Same. The Tower.

Enter Lord SCALES, *and others, walking on the*
walls. Then enter certain Citizens, below.

Scales. How now ! is Jack Cade slain ?
1 Cit. No, my lord, nor likely to be slain ; for they
have won the bridge, killing all those that withstand
them. The lord mayor craves aid of your honour
from the Tower, to defend the city from the rebels.
Scales. Such aid as I can spare, you shall command ;
But I am troubled here with them myself :
The rebels have essay'd to win the Tower.
But get you to Smithfield, and gather head,
And thither I will send you Matthew Goffe.   10
Fight for your king, your country, and your lives ;
And so farewell, for I must hence again.   [*Exeunt.*

SCENE VI.—The Same. Cannon Street.

Enter JACK CADE *and his Followers. He strikes his*
staff on London Stone.

Cade. Now is Mortimer lord of this city. And
here, sitting upon London Stone, I charge and command, that, of the city's cost, the pissing-conduit run
nothing but claret wine this first year of our reign.
And now, henceforward, it shall be treason for any
that calls me other than Lord Mortimer.

Enter a Soldier, running.

Sold. Jack Cade ! Jack Cade !
Cade. Knock him down there.   [*They kill him.*
Smith. If this fellow be wise, he 'll never call you
Jack Cade more : I think, he hath a very fair warning.
Dick. My lord, there 's an army gathered together
in Smithfield.   12
Cade. Come then, let 's go fight with them. But
first, go and set London Bridge on fire, and, if you
can, burn down the Tower too. Come, let 's away.
                              [*Exeunt.*

SCENE VII.—The Same. Smithfield.

Alarum. Enter, on one side, CADE *and his Com-*
pany ; on the other, the Citizens, and the King's
Forces, headed by MATTHEW GOUGH. *They fight ;*
the Citizens are routed, and MATTHEW GOUGH *is*
slain.

Cade. So, sirs.—Now go some and pull down the
Savoy ; others to the inns of court : down with
them all.
Dick. I have a suit unto your lordship.
Cade. Be it a lordship, thou shalt have it for that
word.

Dick. Only, that the laws of England may come
out of your mouth.

John. [*Aside.*] Mass, 't will be sore law then ; for
he was thrust in the mouth with a spear, and 't is not
whole yet.   11

Smith. [*Aside.*] Nay, John, it will be stinking law ;
for his breath stinks with eating toasted cheese.

Cade. I have thought upon it ; it shall be so.
Away ! burn all the records of the realm : my mouth
shall be the parliament of England.

John. [*Aside.*] Then we are like to have biting
statutes, unless his teeth be pulled out.

Cade. And henceforward all things shall be in
common.   20

Enter a Messenger.

Mess. My lord, a prize, a prize ! here 's the Lord
Say, which sold the towns in France ; he that made
us pay one-and-twenty fifteens, and one shilling to
the pound, the last subsidy.

Enter GEORGE BEVIS, *with the Lord* SAY.

Cade. Well, he shall be beheaded for it ten times.—
Ah, thou say, thou serge, nay, thou buckram lord !
now art thou within point-blank of our jurisdiction
regal. What canst thou answer to my majesty, for
giving up of Normandy unto Monsieur Basimecu, the
dauphin of France ? Be it known unto thee by these
presence, even the presence of Lord Mortimer, that I
am the besom that must sweep the court clean of
such filth as thou art. Thou hast most traitorously
corrupted the youth of the realm in erecting a gram-
mar-school : and whereas, before, our forefathers had
no other books but the score and the tally, thou hast
caused printing to be used ; and, contrary to the king,
his crown, and dignity, thou hast built a paper-mill.
It will be proved to thy face, that thou hast men
about thee, that usually talk of a noun, and a verb,
and such abominable words, as no Christian ear can
endure to hear. Thou hast appointed justices of
peace, to call poor men before them about matters
they were not able to answer. Moreover, thou hast
put them in prison ; and because they could not read,
thou hast hanged them ; when, indeed, only for that
cause they have been most worthy to live. Thou dost
ride in a foot-cloth, dost thou not ?

Say. What of that ?

Cade. Marry, thou oughtest not to let thy horse
wear a cloak, when honester men than thou go in
their hose and doublets.   52

Dick. And work in their shirt too ; as myself, for
example, that am a butcher.

Say. You men of Kent,—

Dick. What say you of Kent ?

Say. Nothing but this : 't is *bona terra, mala gens.*

Cade. Away with him ! away with him ! he speaks
Latin.

Say. Hear me but speak, and bear me where you
will.   60
Kent, in the Commentaries Cæsar writ,
Is term'd the civil'st place of all this isle :
Sweet is the country, because full of riches ;
The people liberal, valiant, active, wealthy ;
Which makes me hope you are not void of pity.
I sold not Maine, I lost not Normandy ;
Yet, to recover them, would lose my life.
Justice with favour have I always done ;
Prayers and tears have mov'd me, gifts could never.
When have I aught exacted at your hands,   70
But to maintain the king, the realm, and you ?
Large gifts have I bestow'd on learned clerks,
Because my book preferr'd me to the king,
And seeing ignorance is the curse of God,
Knowledge the wing wherewith we fly to heaven.
Unless you be possess'd with devilish spirits,
You cannot but forbear to murder me.
This tongue hath parley'd unto foreign kings
For your behoof,—

Cade. Tut ! when struck'st thou one blow in the
field ?   81

Say. Great men have reaching hands : oft have I
struck
Those that I never saw, and struck them dead.

Geo. O monstrous coward ! what, to come behind
folks ?

Say. These cheeks are pale for watching for your
good.

Cade. Give him a box o' the ear, and that will make
'em red again.

Say. Long sitting, to determine poor men's causes,
Hath made me full of sickness and diseases.   90

Cade. Ye shall have a hempen caudle then, and the
help of hatchet.

Dick. Why dost thou quiver, man ?

Say. The palsy, and not fear, provokes me.

Cade. Nay, he nods at us ; as who should say, I 'll
be even with you. I 'll see if his head will stand
steadier on a pole, or no. Take him away, and be-
head him.

Say. Tell me, wherein have I offended most ?
Have I affected wealth, or honour ? speak.   100
Are my chests fill'd up with extorted gold ?
Is my apparel sumptuous to behold ?
Whom have I injur'd, that ye seek my death ?
These hands are free from guiltless blood-shedding,
This breast from harbouring foul deceitful thoughts.
O, let me live !

Cade. I feel remorse in myself with his words ; but
I 'll bridle it : he shall die, an it be but for pleading so
well for his life. Away with him ! he has a familiar
under his tongue : he speaks not o' God's name. Go,
take him away, I say, and strike off his head presently ; and then break into his son-in-law's house,
Sir James Cromer, and strike off his head, and bring
them both upon two poles hither.   114

All. It shall be done.

Say. Ah, countrymen ! if when you make your
prayers,
God should be so obdurate as yourselves,
How would it fare with your departed souls ?
And therefore yet relent, and save my life.

Cade. Away with him, and do as I command ye. 120
[*Exeunt some, with Lord* SAY.
The proudest peer in the realm shall not wear a head
on his shoulders, unless he pay me tribute : there shall
not a maid be married, but she shall pay to me her
maidenhead, ere they have it. Men shall hold of me
in capite ; and we charge and command, that their
wives be as free as heart can wish, or tongue can tell.

Dick. My lord, when shall we go to Cheapside, and
take up commodities upon our bills ?

Cade. Marry, presently.

All. O, brave !   130

Re-enter Rebels, with the heads of Lord SAY *and his
Son-in-law.*

Cade. But is not this braver ?—Let them kiss one
another, for they loved well, when they were alive.
Now part them again, lest they consult about the
giving up of some more towns in France. Soldiers,
defer the spoil of the city until night ; for with these
borne before us, instead of maces, will we ride through
the streets ; and at every corner have them kiss.—
Away !   [*Exeunt.*

SCENE VIII.—Southwark.

Alarum. Enter CADE *and all his Rabblement.*

Cade. Up Fish Street ! down Saint Magnus' Corner !
kill and knock down ! throw them into Thames !—[*A
parley sounded, then a retreat.*] What noise is this I
hear ? Dare any be so bold to sound retreat or parley,
when I command them kill ?

Enter BUCKINGHAM, *and Old* CLIFFORD, *with
Forces.*

Buck. Ay, here they be that dare and will disturb
thee.
Know, Cade, we come ambassadors from the king
Unto the commons whom thou hast misled ;
And here pronounce free pardon to them all
That will forsake thee, and go home in peace.   10

Clif. What say ye, countrymen ? will ye relent,
And yield to mercy, whilst 't is offer'd you,

Or let a rabble lead you to your deaths?
Who loves the king, and will embrace his pardon,
Fling up his cap, and say—God save his majesty!
Who hateth him, and honours not his father,
Henry the Fifth, that made all France to quake,
Shake he his weapon at us, and pass by.
All. God save the king! God save the king!   19

Cade. " But is not this braver?"

Cade. What! Buckingham, and Clifford, are ye so
brave?—And you, base peasants, do ye believe him?
will you needs be hanged with your pardons about
your necks? Hath my sword therefore broke through
London gates, that you should leave me at the White
Hart in Southwark? I thought, ye would never have
given out these arms, till you had recovered your
ancient freedom; but you are all recreants, and dastards, and delight to live in slavery to the nobility.
Let them break your backs with burdens, take your
houses over your heads, ravish your wives and
daughters before your faces: for me,—I will make
shift for one, and so,—God's curse light upon you all!
All. We 'll follow Cade, we 'll follow Cade.   33
Clif. Is Cade the son of Henry the Fifth,
That thus you do exclaim, you 'll go with him?
Will he conduct you through the heart of France
And make the meanest of you earls and dukes?
Alas, he hath no home, no place to fly to;
Nor knows he how to live, but by the spoil,
Unless by robbing of your friends, and us.   40
Were 't not a shame, that whilst you live at jar,
The fearful French, whom you late vanquished,
Should make a start o'er seas, and vanquish you?
Methinks, already, in this civil broil,
I see them lording it in London streets,
Crying—" Villiago!" unto all they meet.
Better ten thousand base-born Cades miscarry,
Than you should stoop unto a Frenchman's mercy.
To France, to France! and get what you have lost.
Spare England, for it is your native coast.   50
Henry hath money, you are strong and manly:
God on our side, doubt not of victory.
All. A Clifford! a Clifford! we 'll follow the king,
and Clifford.
Cade. Was ever feather so lightly blown to and fro,
as this multitude? The name of Henry the Fifth hales
them to an hundred mischiefs, and makes them leave
me desolate. I see them lay their heads together to
surprise me: my sword make way for me, for here is

no staying.—In despite of the devils and hell, have
through the very midst of you; and heavens and
honour be witness, that no want of resolution in me,
but only my followers' base and ignominious treasons,
makes me betake me to my heels.   *[Exit.*
Buck. What! is he fled? go some, and follow him;
And he, that brings his head unto the king,
Shall have a thousand crowns for his reward.—
    [Exeunt some of them.
Follow me, soldiers: we 'll devise a mean
To reconcile you all unto the king.   *[Exeunt.*

SCENE IX.—Kenilworth Castle.

Sound trumpets. Enter King HENRY, *Queen* MAR-
GARET, *and* SOMERSET, *on the Terrace of the Castle.*

K. Hen. Was ever king that joy'd an earthly
        throne,
And could command no more content than I?
No sooner was I crept out of my cradle,
But I was made a king, at nine months old:
Was never subject long'd to be a king,
As I do long and wish to be a subject.

Enter BUCKINGHAM *and* CLIFFORD.

Buck. Health, and glad tidings, to your majesty!
K. Hen. Why, Buckingham, is the traitor, Cade,
        surpris'd?
Or is he but retir'd to make him strong?

Enter, below, a number of CADE's *Followers, with
halters about their necks.*

Clif. He 's fled, my lord, and all his powers do yield,
And humbly thus, with halters on their necks,   11
Expect your highness' doom, of life, or death.
K. Hen. Then, heaven, set ope thy everlasting
        gates,
To entertain my vows of thanks and praise!—
Soldiers, this day have you redeem'd your lives,
And show'd how well you love your prince and
        country:
Continue still in this so good a mind,
And Henry, though he be infortunate,
Assure yourselves, will never be unkind:
And so, with thanks and pardon to you all,   20
I do dismiss you to your several countries.
All. God save the king! God save the king!

Enter a Messenger.

Mess. Please it your grace to be advertised,
The Duke of York is newly come from Ireland,
And with a puissant and a mighty power
Of Gallowglasses and stout Kernes,
Is marching hitherward in proud array;
And still proclaimeth, as he comes along,
His arms are only to remove from thee
The Duke of Somerset, whom he terms a traitor.   30
K. Hen. Thus stands my state, 'twixt Cade and
        York distress'd,
Like to a ship, that, having scap'd a tempest,
Is straightway calm'd and boarded with a pirate.
But now is Cade driven back, his men dispers'd,
And now is York in arms to second him.—
I pray thee, Buckingham, go and meet him,
And ask him, what 's the reason of these arms.
Tell him, I 'll send Duke Edmund to the Tower;—
And, Somerset, we will commit thee thither,
Until his army be dismiss'd from him.   40
Som. My lord,
I 'll yield myself to prison willingly,
Or unto death, to do my country good.
K. Hen. In any case, be not too rough in terms,
For he is fierce, and cannot brook hard language.
Buck. I will, my lord; and doubt not so to deal,
As all things shall redound unto your good.
K. Hen. Come, wife, let 's in, and learn to govern
        better;
For yet may England curse my wretched reign.
    [Exeunt.

SCENE X.—Kent. IDEN's Garden.

Enter CADE.

Cade. Fie on ambition! fie on myself, that have a sword, and yet am ready to famish! These five days have I hid me in these woods, and durst not peep out, for all the country is laid for me; but now am I so hungry, that if I might have a lease of my life for a thousand years, I could stay no longer. Wherefore, on a brick wall have I climbed into this garden, to see if I can eat grass, or pick a sallet another while, which is not amiss to cool a man's stomach this hot weather. And I think this word sallet was born to do me good: for many a time, but for a sallet, my brain-pan had been cleft with a brown bill; and many a time, when I have been dry and bravely marching, it hath served me instead of a quart-pot to drink in; and now the word sallet must serve me to feed on.

Enter IDEN, *with Servants, behind.*

Iden. Lord! who would live turmoiled in the court, And may enjoy such quiet walks as these?
This small inheritance, my father left me,
Contenteth me, and worth a monarchy.
I seek not to wax great by others' waning;   20
Or gather wealth I care not with what envy:
Sufficeth that I have maintains my state,
And sends the poor well pleased from my gate.
Cade. Here's the lord of the soil come to seize me for a stray, for entering his fee-simple without leave. Ah, villain, thou wilt betray me, and get a thousand crowns of the king by carrying my head to him; but I'll have thee eat iron like an ostrich, and swallow my sword like a great pin, ere thou and I part.
Iden. Why, rude companion, whatsoe'er thou be, 30 I know thee not; why then should I betray thee?
Is't not enough, to break into my garden,
And like a thief to come to rob my grounds,
Climbing my walls in spite of me, the owner,
But thou wilt brave me with these saucy terms?
Cade. Brave thee? ay, by the best blood that ever was broached, and beard thee too. Look on me well: I have eat no meat these five days; yet, come thou and thy five men; and if I do not leave you all as dead as a door-nail, I pray God I may never eat grass more. 40
Iden. Nay, it shall ne'er be said, while England stands,

That Alexander Iden, an esquire of Kent,
Took odds to combat a poor famish'd man.
Oppose thy steadfast-gazing eyes to mine,
See if thou canst outface me with thy looks:
Set limb to limb, and thou art far the lesser;
Thy hand is but a finger to my fist;
Thy leg a stick, compared with this truncheon;
My foot shall fight with all the strength thou hast; And if mine arm be heaved in the air,   50
Thy grave is digg'd already in the earth.
As for words, whose greatness answers words,
Let this my sword report what speech forbears.
Cade. By my valour, the most complete champion that ever I heard.—Steel, if thou turn the edge, or cut not out the burly-boned clown in chines of beef ere thou sleep in thy sheath, I beseech Jove on my knees, thou mayest be turned to hobnails. [*They fight.* CADE *falls.*] O! I am slain. Famine, and no other, hath slain me: let ten thousand devils come against me, and give me but the ten meals I have lost, and I'd defy them all. Wither, garden; and be henceforth a burying-place to all that do dwell in this house, because the unconquered soul of Cade is fled.   61
Iden. Is't Cade that I have slain, that monstrous traitor?
Sword, I will hallow thee for this thy deed,
And hang thee o'er my tomb, when I am dead:
Ne'er shall this blood be wiped from thy point,
But thou shalt wear it as a herald's coat,
To emblaze the honour that thy master got.   70
Cade. Iden, farewell; and be proud of thy victory. Tell Kent from me, she hath lost her best man, and exhort all the world to be cowards; for I, that never feared any, am vanquished by famine, not by valour.
[*Dies.*
Iden. How much thou wrong'st me, Heaven be my judge.
Die, damned wretch, the curse of her that bare thee! And as I thrust thy body in with my sword,
So wish I, I might thrust thy soul to hell.
Hence will I drag thee headlong by the heels
Unto a dunghill, which shall be thy grave,   80
And there cut off thy most ungracious head;
Which I will bear in triumph to the king,
Leaving thy trunk for crows to feed upon.
[*Exeunt* IDEN, *dragging out the body, and Servants.*

ACT V.

SCENE I.—The Same.   Fields between Dartford and Blackheath.

The King's Camp on one side.   On the other, enter YORK *attended, with drum and colours; his Forces at some distance.*

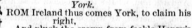

York.

FROM Ireland thus comes York, to claim his right,
And pluck the crown from feeble Henry's head:
Ring, bells, aloud; burn, bonfires, clear and bright,
To entertain great England's lawful king.
Ah, *sancta majestas!* who would not buy thee dear?
Let them obey, that know not how to rule;
This hand was made to handle nought but gold:
I cannot give due action to my words,
Except a sword, or sceptre, balance it.

A sceptre shall it have, have I a soul,   10
On which I'll toss the flower-de-luce of France.

Enter BUCKINGHAM.

Whom have we here? Buckingham, to disturb me? The king hath sent him, sure: I must dissemble.
Buck. York, if thou meanest well, I greet thee well.
York. Humphrey of Buckingham, I accept thy greeting.
Art thou a messenger, or come of pleasure?
Buck. A messenger from Henry, our dread liege, To know the reason of these arms in peace;
Or why thou,—being a subject as I am,—
Against thy oath and true allegiance sworn,   20

Shouldst raise so great a power without his leave,
Or dare to bring thy force so near the court.
   York. [*Aside.*] Scarce can I speak, my choler is so
     great.
O! I could hew up rocks, and fight with flint,
I am so angry at these abject terms;
And now, like Ajax Telamonius,
On sheep or oxen could I spend my fury.
I am far better born than is the king,
More like a king, more kingly in my thoughts;
But I must make fair weather yet awhile.   30
Till Henry be more weak, and I more strong.—
O Buckingham, I pr'ythee, pardon me,
That I have given no answer all this while:
My mind was troubled with deep melancholy.
The cause why I have brought this army hither,
Is, to remove proud Somerset from the king,
Seditious to his grace, and to the state.
   Buck. That is too much presumption on thy part;
But if thy arms be to no other end,
The king hath yielded unto thy demand: 40
The Duke of Somerset is in the Tower.
   York. Upon thine honour, is he prisoner?
   Buck. Upon mine honour, he is prisoner.
   York. Then, Buckingham, I do dismiss my powers.—
Soldiers, I thank you all; disperse yourselves:
Meet me to-morrow in Saint George's field,
You shall have pay, and everything you wish.
And let my sovereign, virtuous Henry,
Command my eldest son,—nay, all my sons,
As pledges of my fealty and love;   50
I'll send them all, as willing as I live:
Lands, goods, horse, armour, anything I have
Is his to use, so Somerset may die.
   Buck. York, I commend this kind submission:
We twain will go into his highness' tent.

     Enter King HENRY, *attended.*

   K. Hen. Buckingham, doth York intend no harm
     to us,
That thus he marcheth with thee arm in arm?
   York. In all submission and humility.
York doth present himself unto your highness.
   K. Hen. Then what intend these forces thou dost
     bring?   60
   York. To heave the traitor Somerset from hence;
And fight against that monstrous rebel, Cade,
Who since I heard to be discomfited.

     Enter IDEN, *with* CADE'S *head.*

   Iden. If one so rude, and of so mean condition,
May pass into the presence of a king,
Lo! I present your grace a traitor's head,
The head of Cade, whom I in combat slew.
   K. Hen. The head of Cade?—Great God, how just
     art Thou!—
O! let me view his visage being dead,
That living wrought me such exceeding trouble.   70
Tell me, my friend, art thou the man that slew him?
   Iden. I was, an 't like your majesty.
   K. Hen. How art thou call'd, and what is thy
     degree?
   Iden. Alexander Iden, that 's my name:
A poor esquire of Kent, that loves his king.
   Buck. So please it you, my lord, 't were not amiss,
He were created knight for his good service.
   K. Hen. Iden, kneel down. [*He kneels.*] Rise up a
     knight.
We give thee for reward a thousand marks;
And will, that thou henceforth attend on us.   80
   Iden. May Iden live to merit such a bounty,
And never live but true unto his liege.
   K. Hen. See, Buckingham! Somerset comes with
     the queen:
Go, bid her hide him quickly from the duke.

     Enter Queen MARGARET *and* SOMERSET.

   Q. Mar. For thousand Yorks he shall not hide his
     head,
But boldly stand, and front him to his face.
   York. How now! is Somerset at liberty?
Then, York, unloose thy long-imprison'd thoughts,

And let thy tongue be equal with thy heart.
Shall I endure the sight of Somerset?—   90
False king, why hast thou broken faith with me,
Knowing how hardly I can brook abuse?
King did I call thee? no, thou art not king;
Not fit to govern and rule multitudes,
Which dar'st not, no, nor canst not rule a traitor.
That head of thine doth not become a crown;
Thy hand is made to grasp a palmer's staff,
And not to grace an awful princely sceptre.
That gold must round engirt these brows of mine;
Whose smile and frown, like to Achilles' spear,   100
Is able with the change to kill and cure.
Here is a hand to hold a sceptre up,
And with the same to act controlling laws.
Give place: by Heaven, thou shalt rule no more
O'er him whom Heaven created for thy ruler.
   Som. O monstrous traitor!—I arrest thee, York,
Of capital treason 'gainst the king and crown.
Obey, audacious traitor: kneel for grace.
   York. Wouldst have me kneel? first let me ask of
     these,
If they can brook I bow a knee to man?   110
Sirrah, call in my sons to be my bail;
                 [*Exit an Attendant.*
I know, ere they will have me go to ward,
They'll pawn their swords for my enfranchisement.
   Q. Mar. Call hither Clifford; bid him come amain,
To say, if that the bastard boys of York
Shall be the surety for their traitor father.
                 [*Exit* BUCKINGHAM.
   York. O blood-bespotted Neapolitan,
Outcast of Naples, England's bloody scourge,
The sons of York, thy betters in their birth,
Shall be their father's bail; and bane to those   120
That for my surety will refuse the boys.

     Enter EDWARD *and* RICHARD PLANTAGENET, *with*
     Forces, at one side; at the other, with Forces also,
     Old CLIFFORD *and his Son.*

See, where they come: I'll warrant they'll make it
     good.
   Q. Mar. And here comes Clifford, to deny their
     bail.
   Clif. Health and all happiness to my lord the king!
                    [*Kneels.*
   York. I thank thee, Clifford: say, what news with
     thee?
Nay, do not fright us with an angry look:
We are thy sovereign, Clifford, kneel again;
For thy mistaking so, we pardon thee.
   Clif. This is my king, York: I do not mistake;
But thou mistak'st me much, to think I do.—
To Bedlam with him! is the man grown mad?   130
   K. Hen. Ay, Clifford; a bedlam and ambitious
     humour
Makes him oppose himself against his king.
   Clif. He is a traitor: let him to the Tower,
And chop away that factious pate of his.
   Q. Mar. He is arrested, but will not obey:
His sons, he says, shall give their words for him.
   York. Will you not, sons?
   Edw. Ay, noble father, if our words will serve.
   Rich. And if words will not, then our weapons
     shall.
   Clif. Why, what a brood of traitors have we here!
   York. Look in a glass, and call thy image so;   141
I am thy king, and thou a false-heart traitor.—
Call hither to the stake my two brave bears,
That with the very shaking of their chains
They may astonish these fell-lurking curs:
Bid Salisbury and Warwick, come to me.

     Drums. Enter WARWICK *and* SALISBURY, *with*
     Forces.

   Clif. Are these thy bears? we'll bait thy bears to
     death,
And manacle the bear-ward in their chains,
If thou dar'st bring them to the baiting-place.
   Rich. Oft have I seen a hot o'erweening cur   150
Run back and bite, because he was withheld;
Who, being suffer'd with the bear's fell paw,

Hath clapp'd his tail between his legs, and cry'd:
And such a piece of service will you do,
If you oppose yourselves to match Lord Warwick.
  Clif. Hence, heap of wrath, foul indigested lump,
As crooked in thy manners as thy shape!
  York. Nay, we shall heat you thoroughly anon.
  Clif. Take heed, lest by your heat you burn your-
selves.
  K. Hen. Why, Warwick, hath thy knee forgot to
    bow?—   160
Old Salisbury,—shame to thy silver hair,
Thou mad misleader of thy brain-sick son!—
What, wilt thou on thy death-bed play the ruffian,
And seek for sorrow with thy spectacles?
O! where is faith? O! where is loyalty?
If it be banish'd from the frosty head,
Where shall it find a harbour in the earth?—
Wilt thou go dig a grave to find out war,
And shame thine honourable age with blood?
Why art thou old, and want'st experience?   170
Or wherefore dost abuse it, if thou hast it?
For shame! in duty bend thy knee to me,
That bows unto the grave with mickle age.
  Sal. My lord, I have consider'd with myself
The title of this most renowned duke;
And in my conscience do repute his grace
The rightful heir to England's royal seat.
  K. Hen. Hast thou not sworn allegiance unto me?
  Sal. I have.
  K. Hen. Canst thou dispense with heaven for such
    an oath?   180
  Sal. It is great sin to swear unto a sin,
But greater sin to keep a sinful oath.
Who can be bound by any solemn vow
To do a murderous deed, to rob a man,
To force a spotless virgin's chastity,
To reave the orphan of his patrimony,
To wring the widow from her custom'd right,
And have no other reason for this wrong,
But that he was bound by a solemn oath?
  Q. Mar. A subtle traitor needs no sophister. 190
  K. Hen. Call Buckingham, and bid him arm him-
self.
  York. Call Buckingham, and all the friends thou
hast,
I am resolv'd for death, or dignity.
  Clif. The first I warrant thee, if dreams prove true.
  War. You were best to go to bed, and dream again,
To keep thee from the tempest of the field.
  Clif. I am resolv'd to bear a greater storm,
Than any thou canst conjure up to-day;
And that I'll write upon thy burgonet,
Might I but know thee by thy household badge. 200
  War. Now, by my father's badge, old Nevil's crest,
The rampant bear chain'd to the ragged staff,
This day I'll wear aloft my burgonet,
(As on a mountain-top the cedar shows,
That keeps his leaves in spite of any storm,)
Even to affright thee with the view thereof.
  Clif. And from thy burgonet I'll rend thy bear,
And tread it under foot with all contempt,
Despite the bear-ward that protects the bear.
  Y. Clif. And so to arms, victorious father, 210
To quell the rebels, and their complices.
  Rich. Fie! charity! for shame! speak not in spite,
For you shall sup not with Jesu Christ to-night.
  Y. Clif. Foul stigmatic, that's more than thou canst
tell.
  Rich. If not in heaven, you'll surely sup in hell.
                          [Exeunt severally.

SCENE II.—Saint Albans.

Alarums: Excursions. Enter WARWICK.

  War. Clifford of Cumberland, 't is Warwick calls:
And if thou dost not hide thee from the bear,
Now, when the angry trumpet sounds alarm,
And dead men's cries do fill the empty air,
Clifford, I say, come forth and fight with me!
Proud northern lord, Clifford of Cumberland,
Warwick is hoarse with calling thee to arms.

Enter YORK.

How now, my noble lord? what, all afoot?
  York. The deadly-handed Clifford slew my steed;
But match to match I have encounter'd him, 10
And made a prey for carrion kites and crows
Even of the bonny beast he lov'd so well.

Enter CLIFFORD.

  War. Of one or both of us the time is come.
  York. Hold, Warwick! seek thee out some other
chase,
For I myself must hunt this deer to death.
  War. Then, nobly, York; 't is for a crown thou
fight'st.—
As I intend, Clifford, to thrive to-day,
It grieves my soul to leave thee unassail'd.   *[Exit.*
  Clif. What seest thou in me, York? why dost thou
pause?
  York. With thy brave bearing should I be in love,
But that thou art so fast mine enemy. 21

York. "A dreadful lay! Address thee instantly."

  Clif. Nor should thy prowess want praise and
    esteem,
But that 't is shown ignobly, and in treason.
  York. So let it help me now against thy sword,
As I in justice and true right express it.
  Clif. My soul and body on the action both!—
  York. A dreadful lay! Address thee instantly.
  Clif. La fin couronne les œuvres.
        [They fight, and CLIFFORD *falls and dies.*
  York. Thus war hath given thee peace, for thou art
still.
Peace with his soul, Heaven, if it be thy will! 30
                             [Exit.

Enter Young CLIFFORD.

  Y. Clif. Shame and confusion! all is on the rout:
Fear frames disorder, and disorder wounds
Where it should guard. O war! thou son of hell,
Whom angry heavens do make their minister,
Throw in the frozen bosoms of our part
Hot coals of vengeance!—Let no soldier fly:
He that is truly dedicate to war
Hath no self-love; nor he that loves himself
Hath not essentially, but by circumstance,
The name of valour.—[*Seeing his father's body.*]
          O! let the vile world end, 40
And the premised flames of the last day
Knit earth and heaven together!
Now let the general trumpet blow his blast,
Particularities and petty sounds
To cease!—Wast thou ordain'd, dear father,
To lose thy youth in peace, and to achieve
The silver livery of advised age,
And, in thy reverence, and thy chair-days, thus
To die in ruffian battle?—Even at this sight,
My heart is turn'd to stone: and while 't is mine, 50

It shall be stony. York not our old men spares;
No more will I their babes: tears virginal
Shall be to me even as the dew to fire;
And beauty, that the tyrant oft reclaims,
Shall to my flaming wrath be oil and flax.
Henceforth I will not have to do with pity:
Meet I an infant of the house of York,
Into as many gobbets will I cut it,
As wild Medea young Absyrtus did:
In cruelty will I seek out my fame.   60
Come, thou new ruin of old Clifford's house:
                        [*Taking up the body.*
As did Æneas old Anchises bear,
So bear I thee upon my manly shoulders;
But then Æneas bare a living load,
Nothing so heavy as these woes of mine.   [*Exit.*

    Enter RICHARD PLANTAGENET *and* SOMERSET,
        fighting. SOMERSET *is killed.*

Rich. So, lie thou there;—
For, underneath an ale-house' paltry sign,
The Castle in Saint Albans, Somerset
Hath made the wizard famous in his death.
Sword, hold thy temper; heart, be wrathful still: 70
Priests pray for enemies, but princes kill.   [*Exit.*

Alarums: Excursions. Enter King HENRY, *Queen*
    MARGARET, *and others, retreating.*
Q. Mar. Away, my lord! you are slow: for shame,
        away!
K. Hen. Can we outrun the heavens? good Margaret,
        stay.
Q. Mar. What are you made of? you'll nor fight,
        nor fly;
Now is it manhood, wisdom, and defence,
To give the enemy way, and to secure us
By what we can, which can no more but fly.
                        [*Alarum afar off.*
If you be ta'en, we then should see the bottom
Of all our fortunes: but if we haply scape   80
(As well we may, if not through your neglect),
We shall to London get, where you are lov'd,
And where this breach, now in our fortunes made,
May readily be stopp'd.

        Enter Young CLIFFORD.

Y. Clif. But that my heart's on future mischief set,
I would speak blasphemy ere bid you fly;
But fly you must: uncurable discomfit

Reigns in the hearts of all our present parts.
Away, for your relief! and we will live
To see their day, and them our fortune give.
Away, my lord, away!   90
                        [*Exeunt.*

            ──────

    SCENE III.—Fields near Saint Albans.

Alarum: Retreat. Flourish; then enter YORK,
    RICHARD PLANTAGENET, WARWICK, *and Soldiers,
    with drum and colours.*
York. Of Salisbury, who can report of him?
That winter lion, who in rage forgets
Aged contusions and all brush of time,
And, like a gallant in the brow of youth,
Repairs him to his feeble body.
But, noble as he is, look where he comes.
Rich.   My noble father,
Three times to-day I holp him to his horse,
Three times bestrid him; thrice I led him off,
Persuaded him from any further act: 10
But still, where danger was, still there I met him;
And like rich hangings in a homely house,
So was his will in his old feeble body.
But, noble as he is, look where he comes.

        Enter SALISBURY.

Sal. Now, by my sword, well hast thou fought to-
        day;
By the mass, so did we all.—I thank you, Richard:
God knows how long it is I have to live;
And it hath pleas'd Him, that three times to-day
You have defended me from imminent death.—
Well, lords, we have not got that which we have: 20
'T is not enough our foes are this time fled,
Being opposites of such repairing nature.
York. I know, our safety is to follow them;
For, as I hear, the king is fled to London,
To call a present court of parliament:
Let us pursue him, ere the writs go forth.—
What says Lord Warwick? shall we after them?
War. After them? nay, before them, if we can.
Now, by my faith, lords, 't was a glorious day:
Saint Alban's battle, won by famous York,   30
Shall be eternis'd in all age to come.—
Sound, drums and trumpets!—and to London all:
And more such days as these to us befall!   [*Exeunt.*

KING HENRY VI.—PART III.

DRAMATIS PERSONÆ.

King Henry the Sixth.
Edward, *Prince of Wales, his Son.*
Lewis XI., *King of France.*
Duke of Somerset,
Duke of Exeter,
Earl of Oxford, } *On King Henry's*
Earl of Northumberland, } *Side.*
Earl of Westmoreland,
Lord Clifford,
Richard Plantagenet, *Duke of York.*
Edward, *Earl of March, afterwards*
  King Edward IV.,
Edmund, *Earl of Rutland,* } *His Sons.*
George, *afterwards Duke of Clarence,*
Richard, *afterwards Duke of Gloster,*
Duke of Norfolk,
Marquess of Montague,
Earl of Warwick, } *Of the Duke of York's*
Earl of Pembroke, } *Party.*
Lord Hastings,
Lord Stafford,

Sir John Mortimer, } *Uncles to the Duke of*
Sir Hugh Mortimer, } *York.*
Henry, *Earl of Richmond, a Youth.*
Lord Rivers, *Brother to Lady Grey.*
Sir William Stanley.
Sir John Montgomery.
Sir John Somerville.
Tutor to Rutland.
Mayor of York.
Lieutenant of the Tower.
A Nobleman.
Two Keepers.
A Huntsman.
A Son that has killed his Father.
A Father that has killed his Son.

Queen Margaret.
Lady Grey, *afterwards Queen to Edward IV.*
Bona, *Sister to the French Queen.*

Soldiers, and other Attendants on King Henry and
  King Edward, Messengers, Watchmen, &c.

SCENE—During part of the Third Act, in France; during the rest of the Play, in England.

ACT I.

Scene I.—London. The Parliament-House.

Drums. Some Soldiers of York's *party break in. Then enter the Duke of* York, Edward, Richard, Norfolk, Montague, Warwick, *and others, with white roses in their hats.*

Warwick.
WONDER how the king escap'd
    our hands.
  York. While we pursu'd the
    horsemen of the north,
He slily stole away, and left his men:
Whereat the great Lord of Northumber-
    land,
Whose warlike ears could never brook
    retreat,
Cheer'd up the drooping army; and
    himself,
Lord Clifford, and Lord Stafford, all
    abreast,
Charg'd our main battle's front, and, breaking in,
Were by the swords of common soldiers slain.
  Edw. Lord Stafford's father, Duke of Buckingham,
Is either slain or wounded dangerous: 11
I cleft his beaver with a downright blow;
That this is true, father, behold his blood.
    [*Showing his bloody sword.*
  Mont. [*To* York, *showing his.*] And, brother,
    here's the Earl of Wiltshire's blood,
Whom I encounter'd as the battles join'd.
  Rich. Speak thou for me, and tell them what I did.
    [*Throwing down the Duke of* Somerset's *head.*
  York. Richard hath best deserv'd of all my sons.—
But, is your grace dead, my Lord of Somerset?
  Norf. Such hope have all the line of John of Gaunt!
  Rich. Thus do I hope to shake King Henry's head.
  War. And so do I.—Victorious Prince of York,   21

Before I see thee seated in that throne,
Which now the house of Lancaster usurps,
I vow by Heaven these eyes shall never close.
This is the palace of the fearful king,
And this the regal seat: possess it, York;
For this is thine, and not King Henry's heirs'.
  York. Assist me then, sweet Warwick, and I
    will;
For hither we have broken in by force.
  Norf. We'll all assist you; he that flies shall die.   30
  York. Thanks, gentle Norfolk.—Stay by me, my
    lords:—
And, soldiers, stay, and lodge by me this night.
  War. And when the king comes, offer him no
    violence,
Unless he seek to thrust you out perforce.
    [*The Soldiers retire.*
  York. The queen this day here holds her parlia-
    ment,
But little thinks we shall be of her council.
By words or blows here let us win our right.
  Rich. Arm'd as we are, let's stay within this house.
  War. The bloody parliament shall this be call'd,
Unless Plantagenet, Duke of York, be king,   40
And bashful Henry depos'd, whose cowardice
Hath made us by-words to our enemies.
  York. Then leave me not, my lords; be resolute;
I mean to take possession of my right.
  War. Neither the king, nor he that loves him best,
The proudest he that holds up Lancaster,
Dares stir a wing, if Warwick shake his bells.

I 'll plant Plantagenet, root him up who dares.—
Resolve thee, Richard : claim the English crown.
    [Warwick *leads* York *to the throne, who
    seats himself.*

Flourish. Enter King Henry, Clifford, North-
umberland, Westmoreland, Exeter, *and others,
with red roses in their hats.*
K. Hen. My lords, look where the sturdy rebel sits,
Even in the chair of state! belike, he means,   51
Back'd by the power of Warwick, that false peer,
To aspire unto the crown, and reign as king.—
Earl of Northumberland, he slew thy father,—
And thine, Lord Clifford ; and you both have vow'd
    revenge
On him, his sons, his favourites, and his friends.
North. If I be not, heavens be reveng'd on me !
Clif. The hope thereof makes Clifford mourn in
    steel.
West. What ! shall we suffer this ? let 's pluck him
    down :
My heart for anger burns, I cannot brook it.   60
K. Hen. Be patient, gentle Earl of Westmoreland.
Clif. Patience is for poltroons, such as he :
He durst not sit there, had your father liv'd.
My gracious lord, here in the parliament
Let us assail the family of York.
North. Well hast thou spoken, cousin : be it so.
K. Hen. Ah ! know you no, the city favours them,
And they have troops of soldiers at their beck ?
Exe. But when the duke is slain, they 'll quickly
    fly.
K. Hen. Far be the thought of this from Henry's
    heart,   70
To make a shambles of the parliament-house !
Cousin of Exeter, frowns, words, and threats,
Shall be the war that Henry means to use.
    [*They advance to the* Duke.
Thou factious Duke of York, descend my throne,
And kneel for grace and mercy at my feet ;
I am thy sovereign.
York.   I am thine.
Exe. For shame ! come down : he made thee Duke
    of York.
York. 'T was my inheritance, as the earldom was.
Exe. Thy father was a traitor to the crown.
War. Exeter, thou art a traitor to the crown,   80
In following this usurping Henry.
Clif. Whom should he follow but his natural king ?
War. True, Clifford ; and that 's Richard, Duke of
    York.
K. Hen. And shall I stand, and thou sit in my
    throne ?
York. It must and shall be so. Content thyself.
War. Be Duke of Lancaster : let him be king.
West. He is both king and Duke of Lancaster ;
And that the Lord of Westmoreland shall maintain.
War. And Warwick shall disprove it. You forget,
That we are those which chas'd you from the field,   90
And slew your fathers, and with colours spread
March'd through the city to the palace gates.
North. Yes, Warwick, I remember it to my grief ;
And, by his soul, thou and thy house shall rue it.
West. Plantagenet, of thee, and these thy sons,
Thy kinsmen, and thy friends, I 'll have more lives,
Than drops of blood were in my father's veins.
Clif. Urge it no more ; lest that instead of words
I send thee, Warwick, such a messenger,
As shall revenge his death before I stir.   100
War. Poor Clifford ! how I scorn his worthless
    threats.
York. Will you, we show our title to the crown ?
If not, our swords shall plead it in the field.
K. Hen. What title hast thou, traitor, to the crown ?
Thy father was, as thou art, Duke of York ;
Thy grandfather, Roger Mortimer, Earl of March.
I am the son of Henry the Fifth,
Who made the Dauphin and the French to stoop,
And seiz'd upon their towns and provinces.
War. Talk not of France, sith thou hast lost it all.
K. Hen. The lord protector lost it, and not I :   111
When I was crown'd, I was but nine months old.

Rich. You are old enough now, and yet, methinks,
    you lose.
Father, tear the crown from the usurper's head.
Edw. Sweet father, do so : set it on your head.
Mont. [*To* York.] Good brother, as thou lov'st and
    honour'st arms,
Let 's fight it out, and not stand cavilling thus.
Rich. Sound drums and trumpets, and the king will
    fly.
York. Sons, peace !
K. Hen. Peace thou, and give King Henry leave to
    speak.   120
War. Plantagenet shall speak first : hear him,
    lords ;
And be you silent and attentive too,
For he that interrupts him shall not live.
K. Hen. Think'st thou, that I will leave my kingly
    throne,
Wherein my grandsire and my father sat ?
No : first shall war unpeople this my realm ;
Ay, and their colours—often borne in France,
And now in England, to our heart's great sorrow,—
Shall be my winding-sheet.—Why faint you, lords ?
My title 's good, and better far than his.   130
War. Prove it, Henry, and thou shalt be king.
K. Hen. Henry the Fourth by conquest got the
    crown.
York. 'T was by rebellion against his king.
K. Hen. [*Aside.*] I know not what to say : my
    title 's weak.—
Tell me, may not a king adopt an heir ?
York. What then ?
K. Hen. An if he may, then am I lawful king ;
For Richard, in the view of many lords,
Resign'd the crown to Henry the Fourth,
Whose heir my father was, and I am his.   140
York. He rose against him, being his sovereign,
And made him to resign his crown perforce.
War. Suppose, my lords, he did it unconstrain'd,
Think you, 't were prejudicial to his crown ?
Exe. No ; for he could not so resign his crown,
But that the next heir should succeed and reign.
K. Hen. Art thou against us, Duke of Exeter ?
Exe. His is the right, and therefore pardon me.
York. Why whisper you, my lords, and answer not ?
Exe. My conscience tells me he is lawful king.   150
K. Hen. All will revolt from me, and turn to him.
North. Plantagenet, for all the claim thou lay'st,
Think not, that Henry shall be so depos'd.
War. Depos'd he shall be in despite of all.
North. Thou art deceiv'd : 'tis not thy southern
    power,
Of Essex, Norfolk, Suffolk, nor of Kent,—
Which makes thee thus presumptuous and proud,—
Can set the duke up in despite of me.
Clif. King Henry, be thy title right or wrong,
Lord Clifford vows to fight in thy defence :   160
May that ground gape, and swallow me alive,
Where I shall kneel to him that slew my father !
K. Hen. O Clifford, how thy words revive my
    heart !
York. Henry of Lancaster, resign thy crown.
What mutter you, or what conspire you, lords ?
War. Do right unto this princely Duke of York,
Or I will fill the house with armed men,
And o'er the chair of state, where now he sits,
Write up his title with usurping blood.
    [*He stamps with his foot, and the Soldiers
    show themselves.*
K. Hen. My Lord of Warwick, hear me but one
    word.   170
Let me for this my life-time reign as king.
York. Confirm the crown to me, and to mine heirs,
And thou shalt reign in quiet while thou liv'st.
K. Hen. I am content : Richard Plantagenet,
Enjoy the kingdom after my decease.
Clif. What wrong is this unto the prince your son !
War. What good is this to England, and himself !
West. Base, fearful, and despairing Henry !
Clif. How hast thou injur'd both thyself and us !
West. I cannot stay to hear these articles.   180
North. Nor I.

Clif. Come, cousin, let us tell the queen these news.
West. Farewell, faint-hearted and degenerate king,
In whose cold blood no spark of honour bides.
North. Be thou a prey unto the house of York,
And die in bands for this unmanly deed!
Clif. In dreadful war may'st thou be overcome,
Or live in peace, abandon'd, and despis'd!
        [*Exeunt* NORTHUMBERLAND, CLIFFORD, *and*
                WESTMORELAND.
War. Turn this way, Henry, and regard them not.
Exe. They seek revenge, and therefore will not
        yield.   190
K. Hen. Ah, Exeter!
War.   Why should you sigh, my lord?
K. Hen. Not for myself, Lord Warwick, but my son,
Whom I unnaturally shall disinherit.
But be it as it may, I here entail
The crown to thee, and to thine heirs for ever ;
Conditionally, that here thou take an oath
To cease this civil war, and, whilst I live,

York. "Farewell, my gracious lord : I'll to my castle."

To honour me as thy king and sovereign ;
And neither by treason, nor hostility,
To seek to put me down, and reign thyself.   200
York. This oath I willingly take, and will perform.
                        [*Coming from the throne.*
War. Long live King Henry!—Plantagenet, em-
        brace him.
K. Hen. And long live thou, and these thy forward
        sons!
York. Now York and Lancaster are reconcil'd.
Exe. Accurs'd be he that seeks to make them foes!
                [*Sennet. The Lords come forward.*
York. Farewell, my gracious lord : I'll to my castle.
War. And I'll keep London with my soldiers.
Norf. And I to Norfolk with my followers.
Mont. And I unto the sea from whence I came.
        [*Exeunt* YORK *and his Sons,* WARWICK, NOR-
        FOLK, MONTAGUE, *Soldiers, and Attendants.*
K. Hen. And I, with grief and sorrow, to the court.

Enter Queen MARGARET *and the Prince of* WALES.

Exe. Here comes the queen, whose looks bewray
        her anger :   211
I'll steal away.
K. Hen.   Exeter, so will I.
Q. Mar. Nay, go not from me ; I will follow thee.
K. Hen. Be patient, gentle queen, and I will stay.
Q. Mar. Who can be patient in such extremes?
Ah, wretched man! 'would I had died a maid,
And never seen thee, never borne thee son,
Seeing thou hast prov'd so unnatural a father!
Hath he deserv'd to lose his birthright thus?
Hadst thou but lov'd him half so well as I,   220

Or felt that pain which I did for him once,
Or nourish'd him, as I did with my blood,
Thou wouldst have left thy dearest heart-blood there,
Rather than have made that savage duke thine heir,
And disinherited thine only son.
Prince. Father, you cannot disinherit me.
If you be king, why should not I succeed?
K. Hen. Pardon me, Margaret ;—pardon me, sweet
        son :—
The Earl of Warwick and the duke enforc'd me.
Q. Mar. Enforc'd thee! art thou king, and wilt be
        forc'd?   230
I shame to hear thee speak.   Ah, timorous wretch!
Thou hast undone thyself, thy son, and me,
And given unto the house of York such head,
As thou shalt reign but by their sufferance.
To entail him and his heirs unto the crown,
What is it, but to make thy sepulchre,
And creep into it far before thy time?
Warwick is chancellor, and the Lord of Calais ;
        Stern Faulconbridge commands the narrow
                seas ;
The duke is made protector of the realm ;
And yet shalt thou be safe? such safety
        finds   241
The trembling lamb, environed with
        wolves.
Had I been there, which am a silly woman,
The soldiers should have toss'd me on their
        pikes,
Before I would have granted to that act ;
But thou preferr'st thy life before thine
        honour :
And seeing thou dost, I here divorce
        myself,
Both from thy table, Henry, and thy bed,
Until that act of parliament be repeal'd,
Whereby my son is disinherited.   250
The northern lords, that have forsworn
        thy colours,
Will follow mine, if once they see them
        spread ;
And spread they shall be, to thy foul
        disgrace,
And utter ruin of the house of York.
Thus do I leave thee.—Come, son, let's
        away :
Our army is ready ; come, we'll after
        them.
K. Hen. Stay, gentle Margaret, and hear me speak.
Q. Mar. Thou hast spoke too much already : get
        thee gone.
K. Hen. Gentle son Edward, thou wilt stay with
        me?
Q. Mar. Ay, to be murder'd by his enemies.   260
Prince. When I return with victory from the field,
I'll see your grace ; till then, I'll follow her.
Q. Mar. Come, son, away! we may not linger thus.
        [*Exeunt Queen* MARGARET *and the* PRINCE.
K. Hen. Poor queen! how love to me, and to her
        son,
Hath made her break out into terms of rage!
Reveng'd may she be on that hateful duke,
Whose haughty spirit, winged with desire,
Will cost my crown, and, like an empty eagle,
Tire on the flesh of me and of my son!
The loss of those three lords torments my heart : 270
I'll write unto them, and entreat them fair.—
Come, cousin ; you shall be the messenger.
Exe. And I, I hope, shall reconcile them all.
                                            [*Exeunt.*

SCENE II.—A Room in Sandal Castle, near Wakefield.

Enter EDWARD, RICHARD, *and* MONTAGUE.

Rich. Brother, though I be youngest, give me leave.
Edw. No, I can better play the orator.
Mont. But I have reasons strong and forcible.

Enter YORK.

York. Why, how now, sons and brother, at a strife?
What is your quarrel? how began it first?

Edw. No quarrel, but a slight contention.
York. About what?
Rich. About that which concerns your grace, and us;
The crown of England, father, which is yours.
York. Mine, boy? not till King Henry be dead.   10
Rich. Your right depends not on his life, or death.
Edw. Now you are heir, therefore enjoy it now:
By giving the house of Lancaster leave to breathe,
It will outrun you, father, in the end.
York. I took an oath that he should quietly reign.
Edw. But for a kingdom any oath may be broken:
I would break a thousand oaths to reign one year.
Rich. No; God forbid, your grace should be for-
          sworn.
York. I shall be, if I claim by open war.
Rich. I 'll prove the contrary, if you 'll hear me
          speak.   20
York. Thou canst not, son: it is impossible.
Rich. An oath is of no moment, being not took
Before a true and lawful magistrate,
That hath authority over him that swears:
Henry had none, but did usurp the place;
Then, seeing 't was he that made you to depose,
Your oath, my lord, is vain and frivolous.
Therefore, to arms. And, father, do but think,
How sweet a thing it is to wear a crown,
Within whose circuit is Elysium,   30
And all that poets feign of bliss and joy.
Why do we linger thus? I cannot rest,
Until the white rose, that I wear, be dyed
Even in the lukewarm blood of Henry's heart.
York. Richard, enough: I will be king, or die.—
Brother, thou shalt to London presently,
And whet on Warwick to this enterprise.—
Thou, Richard, shalt to the Duke of Norfolk
And tell him privily of our intent.—
You, Edward, shall unto my Lord Cobham,   40
With whom the Kentishmen will willingly rise:
In them I trust; for they are soldiers,
Witty, courteous, liberal, full of spirit.—
While you are thus employ'd, what resteth more
But I seek occasion how to rise,
And yet the king not privy to my drift,
Nor any of the house of Lancaster?

              Enter a Messenger.

But, stay.—What news? Why com'st thou in such
          post?
Mess. The queen with all the northern earls and
          lords
Intend here to besiege you in your castle.   50
She is hard by with twenty thousand men,
And therefore fortify your hold, my lord.
York. Ay, with my sword. What! think'st thou,
          that we fear then?—
Edward and Richard, you shall stay with me;
My brother Montague shall post to London:
Let noble Warwick, Cobham, and the rest,
Whom we have left protectors of the king,
With powerful policy strengthen themselves,
And trust not simple Henry, nor his oaths.
Mont. Brother, I go; I 'll win them, fear it not: 60
And thus most humbly I do take my leave.   [*Exit.*

      Enter Sir JOHN *and Sir* HUGH MORTIMER.

York. Sir John, and Sir Hugh Mortimer, mine
          uncles,
You are come to Sandal in a happy hour;
The army of the queen mean to besiege us.
Sir John. She shall not need, we 'll meet her in the
          field.
York. What, with five thousand men?
Rich. Ay, with five hundred, father, for a need.
A woman's general; what should we fear?
                            [*A march afar off.*
Edw. I hear their drums: let 's set our men in
          order,
And issue forth, and bid them battle straight.   70
York. Five men to twenty!—though the odds be
          great,
I doubt not, uncle, of our victory.
Many a battle have I won in France,

Whenas the enemy hath been ten to one:
Why should I not now have the like success?
                            [*Alarum.   Exeunt.*

          SCENE III.—Plains near Sandal Castle.

Alarums: Excursions.   Enter RUTLAND *and his
                    Tutor.*

Rut. Ah! whither shall I fly to 'scape their hands?
Ah, tutor! look, where bloody Clifford comes.

          Enter CLIFFORD *and Soldiers.*

Clif. Chaplain, away: thy priesthood saves thy life.
As for the brat of this accursed duke,
Whose father slew my father, he shall die.
Tut. And I, my lord, will bear him company.
Clif. Soldiers, away with him.
Tut. Ah, Clifford! murder not this innocent child,
Lest thou be hated both of God and man.
                    [*Exit, forced off by Soldiers.*
Clif. How now! is he dead already? Or is it fear
That makes him close his eyes? I 'll open them.   11
Rut. So looks the pent-up lion o'er the wretch
That trembles under his devouring paws;
And so he walks, insulting o'er his prey,
And so he comes to rend his limbs asunder.—
Ah, gentle Clifford! kill me with thy sword,
And not with such a cruel threatening look.
Sweet Clifford! hear me speak before I die:
I am too mean a subject for thy wrath;
Be thou reveng'd on men, and let me live.   20
Clif. In vain thou speak'st, poor boy: my father's
          blood
Hath stopp'd the passage where thy words should
          enter.
Rut. Then let my father's blood open it again:
He is a man, and, Clifford, cope with him.
Clif. Had I thy brethren here, their lives and thine
Were not revenge sufficient for me.
No, if I digg'd up thy forefathers' graves,
And hung their rotten coffins up in chains,
It could not slake mine ire, nor ease my heart.
The sight of any of the house of York   30
Is as a fury to torment my soul;
And till I root out their accursed line,
And leave not one alive, I live in hell.
Therefore—
Rut. O! let me pray before I take my death.—
To thee I pray: sweet Clifford, pity me!
Clif. Such pity as my rapier's point affords.
Rut. I never did thee harm: why wilt thou slay me?
Clif. Thy father hath.
Rut.   But 't was ere I was born.
Thou hast one son, for his sake pity me,   40
Lest, in revenge thereof, sith God is just,
He be as miserably slain as I.
Ah! let me live in prison all my days;
And when I give occasion of offence,
Then let me die, for now thou hast no cause.
Clif. No cause?
Thy father slew my father: therefore, die. [*Stabs him.*
Rut. Di faciant, laudis summa sit ista tuæ! [*Dies.*
Clif. Plantagenet! I come, Plantagenet!
And this thy son's blood, cleaving to my blade,   50
Shall rust upon my weapon, till thy blood,
Congeal'd with this, do make me wipe off both. [*Exit.*

          SCENE IV.—The Same.

          Alarum.   Enter YORK.

York. The army of the queen hath got the field:
My uncles both are slain in rescuing me;
And all my followers to the eager foe
Turn back, and fly like ships before the wind,
Or lambs pursu'd by hunger-starved wolves.
My sons—God knows, what hath bechanced them:
But this I know, they have demean'd themselves
Like men born to renown, by life, or death.
Three times did Richard make a lane to me,

And thrice cried,—" Courage, father ! fight it out !" 10
And full as oft came Edward to my side,
With purple faulchion, painted to the hilt
In blood of those that had encounter'd him :
And when the hardiest warriors did retire,
Richard cried,—" Charge ! and give no foot of
    ground ! "
And cried,—" A crown, or else a glorious tomb !
A sceptre, or an earthly sepulchre ! "
With this, we charg'd again ; but, out, alas !
We bodg'd again : as I have seen a swan
With bootless labour swim against the tide,   20
And spend her strength with over-matching waves.
        [*A short alarum within.*
Ah, hark ! the fatal followers do pursue ;
And I am faint, and cannot fly their fury ;
And were I strong, I would not shun their
    fury.
The sands are number'd, that make up my
    life ;
Here must I stay, and here my life must
    end.

Enter Queen MARGARET, CLIFFORD,
  NORTHUMBERLAND, *the young* PRINCE,
  and Soldiers.

Come, bloody Clifford,—rough Northum-
    berland,—
I dare your quenchless fury to more rage.
I am your butt, and I abide your shot.
  North. Yield to our mercy, proud Planta-
    genet.   30
  Clif. Ay, to such mercy, as his ruthless
    arm
With downright payment show'd unto my
    father.
Now Phaëthon hath tumbled from his car,
And made an evening at the noontide prick.
  York. My ashes, as the phœnix, may
    bring forth
A bird that will revenge upon you all ;
And in that hope I throw mine eyes to
    heaven,
Scorning whate'er you can afflict me with.
Why come you not ?—what ! multitudes, and fear ?
  Clif. So cowards fight, when they can fly no further ;
So doves do peck the falcon's piercing talons ;   41
So desperate thieves, all hopeless of their lives,
Breathe out invectives 'gainst the officers.
  York. O Clifford ! but bethink thee once again,
And in thy thought o'errun my former time ;
And, if thou canst for blushing, view this face,
And bite thy tongue, that slanders him with cowardice,
Whose frown hath made thee faint and fly ere this.
  Clif. I will not bandy with thee word for word,
But buckle with thee blows, twice two for one.   50
                [*Draws.*
  Q. Mar. Hold, valiant Clifford ! for a thousand
    causes
I would prolong awhile the traitor's life.—
Wrath makes him deaf : speak thou, Northumberland.
  North. Hold, Clifford ! do not honour him so much
To prick thy finger, though to wound his heart.
What valour were it, when a cur doth grin,
For one to thrust his hand between his teeth,
When he might spurn him with his foot away ?
It is war's prize to take all vantages,
And ten to one is no impeach of valour.   60
    [*They lay hands on* YORK, *who struggles.*
  Clif. Ay, ay : so strives the woodcock with the gin.
  North. So doth the cony struggle in the net.
           [YORK *is taken prisoner.*
  York. So triumph thieves upon their conquer'd
    booty ;
So true men yield, with robbers so o'ermatch'd.
  North. What would your grace have done unto him
    now ?
  Q. Mar. Brave warriors, Clifford and Northumber-
    land,
Come, make him stand upon this molehill here,
That raught at mountains with outstretched arms,
Yet parted but the shadow with his hand.—

What ! was it you, that would be England's king ?   70
Was 't you that revell'd in our parliament,
And made a preachment of your high descent ?
Where are your mess of sons to back you now ?
The wanton Edward, and the lusty George ?
And where 's that valiant crook-back prodigy,
Dicky your boy, that, with his grumbling voice,
Was wont to cheer his dad in mutinies ?
Or, with the rest, where is your darling Rutland ?
Look, York : I stain'd this napkin with the blood
That valiant Clifford with his rapier's point   80
Made issue from the bosom of the boy ;
And if thine eyes can water for his death,
I give thee this to dry thy cheeks withal.

Q. Mar. " Ay, marry, sir, now looks he like a king."

Alas, poor York ! but that I hate thee deadly,
I should lament thy miserable state.
I pr'ythee, grieve, to make me merry, York :
What, hath thy fiery heart so parch'd thine entrails,
That not a tear can fall for Rutland's death ?
Why art thou patient, man ? thou shouldst be mad ;
And I, to make thee mad, do mock thee thus.   90
Stamp, rave, and fret, that I may sing and dance.
Thou wouldst be fee'd, I see, to make me sport ;
York cannot speak, unless he wear a crown.—
A crown for York !—and, lords, bow low to him.—
Hold you his hands, whilst I do set it on.—
         [*Putting a paper crown on his head.*
Ay, marry, sir, now looks he like a king.
Ay, this is he that took King Henry's chair
And this is he was his adopted heir.—
But how is it, that great Plantagenet
Is crown'd so soon, and broke his solemn oath ?   100
As I bethink me, you should not be king,
Till our King Henry had shook hands with death.
And will you pale your head in Henry's glory,
And rob his temples of the diadem,
Now in his life, against your holy oath ?
O ! 'tis a fault too too unpardonable.—
Off with the crown ; and, with the crown, his head !
And, whilst we breathe, take time to do him dead.
  Clif. That is my office, for my father's sake.
  Q. Mar. Nay, stay ; let 's hear the orisons he
    makes.   110
  York. She-wolf of France, but worse than wolves of
    France ;
Whose tongue more poisons than the adder's tooth !
How ill-beseeming is it in thy sex,
To triumph, like an Amazonian trull,
Upon their woes whom fortune captivates !
But that thy face is, visor-like, unchanging,
Made impudent with use of evil deeds,
I would assay, proud queen, to make thee blush :
To tell thee whence thou cam'st, of whom deriv'd,

Were shame enough to shame thee, wert thou not
　　shameless.　　　　　　　　　　　　　　　120
Thy father bears the type of King of Naples,
Of both the Sicils, and Jerusalem,
Yet not so wealthy as an English yeoman.
Hath that poor monarch taught thee to insult?
It needs not, nor it boots thee not, proud queen;
Unless the adage must be verified,
That beggars, mounted, run their horse to death.
'T is beauty that doth oft make women proud;
But, God he knows, thy share thereof is small.
'T is virtue that doth make them most admir'd;　130
The contrary doth make thee wonder'd at.
'T is government that makes them seem divine;
The want thereof makes thee abominable.
Thou art as opposite to every good,
As the Antipodes are unto us,
Or as the south to the septentrion.
O tiger's heart, wrapp'd in a woman's hide!
How couldst thou drain the life-blood of the child,
To bid the father wipe his eyes withal;
And yet be seen to bear a woman's face?　　　140
Women are soft, mild, pitiful, and flexible;
Thou stern, obdurate, flinty, rough, remorseless.
Bidd'st thou me rage? why, now thou hast thy wish:
Wouldst have me weep? why, now thou hast thy will.
For raging wind blows up incessant showers,
And when the rage allays, the rain begins.
These tears are my sweet Rutland's obsequies,
And every drop cries vengeance for his death,
'Gainst thee, fell Clifford, and thee, false French-
　　woman.
　North. Beshrew me, but his passions move me so,
That hardly can I check my eyes from tears.　151
　York. That face of his the hungry cannibals

Would not have touch'd, would not have stain'd with
　　blood;
But you are more inhuman, more inexorable,
O, ten times more, than tigers of Hyrcania.
See, ruthless queen, a hapless father's tears!
This cloth thou dipp'dst in blood of my sweet boy,
And I with tears do wash the blood away.
Keep thou the napkin, and go boast of this;
And if thou tell'st the heavy story right,　　　160
Upon my soul, the hearers will shed tears;
Yea, even my foes will shed fast-falling tears,
And say,—"Alas! it was a piteous deed."—
There, take the crown, and with the crown my curse,
And in thy need such comfort come to thee,
As now I reap at thy too cruel hand!—
Hard-hearted Clifford, take me from the world;
My soul to heaven, my blood upon your heads!
　North. Had he been slaughter-man to all my kin,
I should not, for my life, but weep with him,　170
To see how inly sorrow gripes his soul.
　Q. Mar. What! weeping-ripe, my Lord Northumber-
　　land?
Think but upon the wrong he did us all,
And that will quickly dry thy melting tears.
　Clif. Here's for my oath; here's for my father's
　　death.　　　　　　　　　　　　　[*Stabbing him.*
　Q. Mar. And here's to right our gentle-hearted
　　king.　　　　　　　　　　　　　[*Stabbing him.*
　York. Open thy gate of mercy, gracious God!
My soul flies through these wounds to seek out thee.
　　　　　　　　　　　　　　　　　　　　[*Dies.*
　Q. Mar. Off with his head, and set it on York
　　gates:
So York may overlook the town of York.　　　180
　　　　　　　　　　　　　　　[*Flourish. Exeunt.*

ACT II.

Scene I.—A Plain near Mortimer's Cross in Herefordshire.

A March.　Enter Edward *and* Richard, *with their Power.*

　Edward.
WONDER, how our princely father 'scap'd;
Or whether he be 'scap'd away, or no,
From Clifford's and Northumberland's
　　pursuit.
Had he been ta'en, we should have heard
　　the news;
Had he been slain, we should have heard
　　the news;
Or had he 'scap'd, methinks we should
　　have heard
The happy tidings of his good escape.—
How fares my brother? why is he so sad?
　Rich. I cannot joy, until I be resolv'd
Where our right valiant father is become.
　　I saw him in the battle range about,　11
And watch'd him how he singled Clifford forth
Methought, he bore him in the thickest troop,
As doth a lion in a herd of neat:
Or as a bear, encompass'd round with dogs;
Who having pinch'd a few, and made them cry,
The rest stand all aloof, and bark at him.
So far'd our father with his enemies;
So fled his enemies my warlike father:
Methinks, 't is prize enough to be his son.　20

See, how the morning opes her golden gates,
And takes her farewell of the glorious sun:
How well resembles it the prime of youth,
Trimm'd like a younker, prancing to his love!
　Edw. Dazzle mine eyes, or do I see three suns?
　Rich. Three glorious suns, each one a perfect
　　sun,
Not separated with the racking clouds,
But sever'd in a pale clear-shining sky.
See, see! they join, embrace, and seem to kiss,
As if they vow'd some league inviolable:　　　30
Now are they but one lamp, one light, one sun!
In this the heaven figures some event.
　Edw. 'Tis wondrous strange, the like yet never
　　heard of.
I think, it cites us, brother, to the field,
That we, the sons of brave Plantagenet,
Each one already blazing by our meeds,
Should, notwithstanding, join our lights together,
And over-shine the earth, as this the world.
Whate'er it bodes, henceforward will I bear
Upon my target three fair-shining suns.　　　40
　Rich. Nay, bear three daughters: by your leave I
　　speak it,
You love the breeder better than the male.

Enter a Messenger.

But what art thou, whose heavy looks foretell
Some dreadful story hanging on thy tongue?
  Mess. Ah! one that was a woful looker-on,
Whenas the noble Duke of York was slain,
Your princely father, and my loving lord.
  Edw. O, speak no more! for I have heard too
      much.
  Rich. Say, how he died, for I will hear it all.
  Mess. Environed he was with many foes;   50
And stood against them, as the hope of Troy
Against the Greeks, that would have enter'd Troy.
But Hercules himself must yield to odds;
And many strokes, though with a little axe,
Hew down and fell the hardest-timber'd oak.
By many hands your father was subdu'd;
But only slaughter'd by the ireful arm
Of unrelenting Clifford, and the queen,
Who crown'd the gracious duke in high despite;
Laugh'd in his face; and, when with grief he wept,
The ruthless queen gave him, to dry his cheeks,   61
A napkin steeped in the harmless blood
Of sweet young Rutland, by rough Clifford slain:
And, after many scorns, many foul taunts,
They took his head, and on the gates of York
They set the same; and there it doth remain,
The saddest spectacle that e'er I view'd.
  Edw. Sweet Duke of York! our prop to lean upon,
Now thou art gone, we have no staff, no stay.
O Clifford! boisterous Clifford! thou hast slain   70
The flower of Europe for his chivalry;
And treacherously hast thou vanquish'd him,
For, hand to hand, he would have vanquish'd thee.
Now, my soul's palace is become a prison:
Ah! would she break from hence, that this my body
Might in the ground be closed up in rest!
For never henceforth shall I joy again,
Never, O! never, shall I see more joy.
  Rich. I cannot weep, for all my body's moisture 79
Scarce serves to quench my furnace-burning heart:
Nor can my tongue unload my heart's great burden;
For selfsame wind, that I should speak withal,
Is kindling coals that fire all my breast,
And burn me up with flames that tears would
      quench.
To weep is to make less the depth of grief:
Tears, then, for babes; blows and revenge for me!—
Richard, I bear thy name, I'll venge thy death,
Or die renowned by attempting it.
  Edw. His name that valiant duke hath left with
      thee;
His dukedom and his chair with me is left.   90
  Rich. Nay, if thou be that princely eagle's bird,
Show thy descent by gazing 'gainst the sun:
For chair and dukedom, throne and kingdom say;
Either that is thine, or else thou wert not his.

March. Enter WARWICK *and* MONTAGUE, *with their
Army.*

  War. How now, fair lords? What fare? what news
      abroad?
  Rich. Great Lord of Warwick, if we should recount
Our baleful news, and at each word's deliverance
Stab poniards in our flesh till all were told,
The words would add more anguish than the wounds.
O valiant lord! the Duke of York is slain.   100
  Edw. O Warwick! Warwick! that Plantagenet,
Which held thee dearly as his soul's redemption,
Is by the stern Lord Clifford done to death.
  War. Ten days ago I drown'd these news in tears,
And now, to add more measure to your woes,
I come to tell you things sith then befallen.
After the bloody fray at Wakefield fought,
Where your brave father breath'd his latest gasp,
Tidings, as swiftly as the posts could run,
Were brought me of your loss, and his depart.   110
I, then in London, keeper of the king,
Muster'd my soldiers, gather'd flocks of friends,
And very well appointed, as I thought,
March'd towards Saint Albans to intercept the
      queen,

Bearing the king in my behalf along;
For by my scouts I was advertised,
That she was coming with a full intent
To dash our late decree in parliament,
Touching King Henry's oath and your succession.
Short tale to make,—we at Saint Albans met,   120
Our battles join'd, and both sides fiercely fought;
But, whether 't was the coldness of the king,
Who look'd full gently on his warlike queen,
That robb'd my soldiers of their heated spleen,
Or whether 't was report of her success,
Or more than common fear of Clifford's rigour,
Who thunders to his captives blood and death,
I cannot judge: but, to conclude with truth,
Their weapons like to lightning came and went;
Our soldiers'—like the night-owl's lazy flight,   130
Or like an idle thresher with a flail,—
Fell gently down, as if they struck their friends.
I cheer'd them up with justice of our cause,
With promise of high pay and great rewards:
But all in vain; they had no heart to fight,
And we, in them, no hope to win the day;
So that we fled: the king unto the queen;
Lord George your brother, Norfolk, and myself,
In haste, post-haste, are come to join with you;
For in the marches here, we heard, you were,   140
Making another head to fight again.
  Edw. Where is the Duke of Norfolk, gentle War-
      wick?
And when came George from Burgundy to England?
  War. Some six miles off the duke is with the
      soldiers;
And for your brother, he was lately sent
From your kind aunt, Duchess of Burgundy,
With aid of soldiers to this needful war.
  Rich. 'T was odds, belike, when valiant Warwick
      fled:
Oft have I heard his praises in pursuit,
But ne'er, till now, his scandal of retire.   150
  War. Nor now my scandal, Richard, dost thou
      hear;
For thou shalt know, this strong right hand of mine
Can pluck the diadem from faint Henry's head,
And wring the awful sceptre from his fist,
Were he as famous, and as bold in war,
As he is fam'd for mildness, peace, and prayer.
  Rich. I know it well, Lord Warwick; blame me
      not:
'T is love I bear thy glories makes me speak.
But in this troublous time, what 's to be done?
Shall we go throw away our coats of steel,   160
And wrap our bodies in black mourning gowns,
Numbering our Ave-Maries with our beads?
Or shall we on the helmets of our foes
Tell our devotion with revengeful arms?
If for the last, say—Ay, and to it, lords.
  War. Why, therefore Warwick came to seek you
      out,
And therefore comes my brother Montague.
Attend me, lords. The proud insulting queen,
With Clifford, and the haught Northumberland,
And of their feather many more proud birds,   170
Have wrought the easy-melting king like wax.
He swore consent to your succession,
His oath enrolled in the parliament;
And now to London all the crew are gone,
To frustrate both his oath, and what beside
May make against the house of Lancaster:
Their power, I think, is thirty thousand strong.
Now, if the help of Norfolk, and myself,
With all the friends that thou, brave Earl of March,
Amongst the loving Welshmen canst procure,   180
Will but amount to five-and-twenty thousand,
Why, *Via!* to London will we march amain,
And once again bestride our foaming steeds,
And once again cry—Charge! upon our foes!
But never once again turn back, and fly.
  Rich. Ay, now, methinks, I hear great Warwick
      speak.
Ne'er may he live to see a sunshine day,
That cries—Retire, if Warwick bid him stay.
  Edw. Lord Warwick, on thy shoulder will I lean;

And when thou fail'st, (as God forbid the hour!)   190
Must Edward fall, which peril Heaven forfend!
  War. No longer Earl of March, but Duke of York:
The next degree is England's royal throne;
For King of England shalt thou be proclaim'd
In every borough as we pass along;
And he that throws not up his cap for joy,
Shall for the fault make forfeit of his head.
King Edward,—valiant Richard,—Montague,—
Stay we no longer dreaming of renown,
But sound the trumpets, and about our task.   200
  Rich. Then, Clifford, were thy heart as hard as
      steel,
As thou hast shown it flinty by thy deeds,
I come to pierce it, or to give thee mine.
  Edw. Then strike up, drums!—God and Saint
      George for us!

Enter a Messenger.

  War. How now? what news?
  Mess. The Duke of Norfolk sends you word by me,
The queen is coming with a puissant host;
And craves your company for speedy counsel.
  War. Why then it sorts: brave warriors, let's
      away.   [*Exeunt.*

___

Scene II.—Before York.

Flourish. Enter King Henry, *Queen* Margaret,
  the Prince of Wales, Clifford, *and* Northumberland, *with drums and trumpets.*

  Q. Mar. Welcome, my lord, to this brave town of
      York.
Yonder's the head of that arch-enemy,
That sought to be encompass'd with your crown:
Doth not the object cheer your heart, my lord?
  K. Hen. Ay, as the rocks cheer them that fear their
      wrack:
To see this sight, it irks my very soul.—
Withhold revenge, dear God! 'tis not my fault,
Nor wittingly have I infring'd my vow.
  Clif. My gracious liege, this too much lenity,
And harmful pity, must be laid aside.   10
To whom do lions cast their gentle looks?
Not to the beast that would usurp their den.
Whose hand is that the forest bear doth lick?
Not his that spoils her young before her face.
Who 'scapes the lurking serpent's mortal sting?
Not he that sets his foot upon her back.
The smallest worm will turn, being trodden on;
And doves will peck in safeguard of their brood.
Ambitious York did level at thy crown;
Thou smiling, while he knit his angry brows: 20
He, but a duke, would have his son a king,
And raise his issue like a loving sire;
Thou, being a king, bless'd with a goodly son,
Didst yield consent to disinherit him,
Which argu'd thee a most unloving father.
Unreasonable creatures feed their young;
And though man's face be fearful to their eyes,
Yet, in protection of their tender ones,
Who hath not seen them, even with those wings
Which sometime they have us'd with fearful flight,
Make war with him that climb'd unto their nest, 31
Offering their own lives in their young's defence?
For shame, my liege! make them your precedent.
Were it not pity, that this goodly boy
Should lose his birthright by his father's fault,
And long hereafter say unto his child,—
" What my great-grandfather and grandsire got,
My careless father fondly gave away."
Ah! what a shame were this! Look on the boy;
And let his manly face, which promiseth   40
Successful fortune, steel thy melting heart
To hold thine own, and leave thine own with him.
  K. Hen. Full well hath Clifford play'd the orator,
Inferring arguments of mighty force.
But, Clifford, tell me, didst thou never hear,
That things ill got had ever bad success?
And happy always was it for that son,
Whose father for his hoarding went to hell?

I'll leave my son my virtuous deeds behind;
And 'would my father had left me no more;   50
For all the rest is held at such a rate
As brings a thousand-fold more care to keep,
Than in possession any jot of pleasure.
Ah, cousin York! 'would thy best friends did know
How it doth grieve me that thy head is here!
  Q. Mar. My lord, cheer up your spirits: our foes
      are nigh,
And this soft courage makes your followers faint.
You promis'd knighthood to our forward son;
Unsheathe your sword, and dub him presently.—
Edward, kneel down.   60
  K. Hen. Edward Plantagenet, arise a knight;
And learn this lesson,—Draw thy sword in right.
  Prince. My gracious father, by your kingly leave,
I'll draw it as apparent to the crown,
And in that quarrel use it to the death.
  Clif. Why, that is spoken like a toward prince.

Enter a Messenger.

  Mess. Royal commanders, be in readiness:
For, with a band of thirty thousand men,
Comes Warwick, backing of the Duke of York;
And in the towns, as they do march along,   70
Proclaims him king, and many fly to him.
Darraign your battle, for they are at hand.
  Clif. I would, your highness would depart the field:
The queen hath best success when you are absent.
  Q. Mar. Ay, good my lord, and leave us to our
      fortune.
  K. Hen. Why, that's my fortune too; therefore I'll
      stay.
  North. Be it with resolution then to fight.
  Prince. My royal father, cheer these noble lords,
And hearten those that fight in your defence.
Unsheathe your sword, good father: cry, "Saint
      George!"   80

March. Enter Edward, George, Richard, Warwick, Norfolk, Montague, *and Soldiers.*

  Edw. Now, perjur'd Henry, wilt thou kneel for
      grace,
And set thy diadem upon my head,
Or bide the mortal fortune of the field?
  Q. Mar. Go, rate thy minions, proud insulting boy!
Becomes it thee to be thus bold in terms,
Before thy sovereign, and thy lawful king?
  Edw. I am his king, and he should bow his knee;
I was adopted heir by his consent;
Since when, his oath is broke: for, as I hear,
You, that are king, though he do wear the crown, 90
Have caus'd him, by new act of parliament,
To blot out me, and put his own son in.
  Clif. And reason too:
Who should succeed the father but the son?
  Rich. Are you there, butcher?—O! I cannot speak.
  Clif. Ay, crook-back; here I stand, to answer thee,
Or any he the proudest of thy sort.
  Rich. 'T was you that kill'd young Rutland, was it
      not?
  Clif. Ay, and old York, and yet not satisfied.
  Rich. For God's sake, lords, give signal to the fight.
  War. What say'st thou, Henry, wilt thou yield the
      crown?   101
  Q. Mar. Why, how now, long-tongu'd Warwick!
      dare you speak?
When you and I met at Saint Albans last,
Your legs did better service than your hands.
  War. Then 't was my turn to fly, and now 't is thine.
  Clif. You said so much before, and yet you fled.
  War. 'T was not your valour, Clifford, drove me
      thence.
  North. No, nor your manhood, that durst make you
      stay.
  Rich. Northumberland, I hold thee reverently.
Break off the parley; for scarce I can refrain   110
The execution of my big-swoln heart
Upon that Clifford, that cruel child-killer.
  Clif. I slew thy father: call'st thou him a child?
  Rich. Ay, like a dastard, and a treacherous coward,

As thou didst kill our tender brother Rutland;
But ere sunset I'll make thee curse the deed.
K. Hen. Have done with words, my lords, and hear
  me speak.
Q. Mar. Defy them then, or else hold close thy lips.
K. Hen. I pr'ythee, give no limits to my tongue:
I am a king, and privileg'd to speak.   120
Clif. My liege, the wound, that bred this meeting
  here,
Cannot be cur'd by words; therefore be still.
Rich. Then, executioner, unsheathe thy sword.
By Him that made us all, I am resolv'd
That Clifford's manhood lies upon his tongue.
Edw. Say, Henry, shall I have my right, or no?
A thousand men have broke their fasts to-day,
That ne'er shall dine, unless thou yield the crown.
War. If thou deny, their blood upon thy head;
For York in justice puts his armour on.   130
Prince. If that be right, which Warwick says is right,
There is no wrong, but everything is right.
Rich. Whoever got thee, there thy mother stands;
For, well I wot, thou hast thy mother's tongue.
Q. Mar. But thou art neither like thy sire, nor dam;
But like a foul misshapen stigmatic,
Mark'd by the destinies to be avoided,
As venom toads, or lizards' dreadful stings.
Rich. Iron of Naples, hid with English gilt,
Whose father bears the title of a king,   140
(As if a channel should be call'd the sea,)
Sham'st thou not, knowing whence thou art extraught,
To let thy tongue detect thy base-born heart?
Edw. A wisp of straw were worth a thousand
  crowns,
To make this shameless callat know herself.
Helen of Greece was fairer far than thou,
Although thy husband may be Menelaus;
And ne'er was Agamemnon's brother wrong'd
By that false woman, as this king by thee.
His father revell'd in the heart of France,   150
And tam'd the king, and made the Dauphin stoop;
And had he match'd according to his state,
He might have kept that glory to this day;
But when he took a beggar to his bed,
And grac'd thy poor sire with his bridal-day,
Even then that sunshine brew'd a shower for him,
That wash'd his father's fortunes forth of France,
And heap'd sedition on his crown at home.
For what hath broach'd this tumult, but thy pride?
Hadst thou been meek, our title still had slept,   160
And we, in pity of the gentle king,
Had slipp'd our claim until another age.
Geo. But when we saw our sunshine made thy
  spring,
And that thy summer bred us no increase,
We set the axe to thy usurping root:
And though the edge hath something hit ourselves,
Yet, know thou, since we have begun to strike,
We'll never leave, till we have hewn thee down,
Or bath'd thy growing with our heated bloods.
Edw. And in this resolution I defy thee;   170
Not willing any longer conference,
Since thou deniest the gentle king to speak.—
Sound trumpets!—let our bloody colours wave!
And either victory, or else a grave.
Q. Mar. Stay, Edward.
Edw. No, wrangling woman; we'll no longer stay:
These words will cost ten thousand lives this day.
                            [*Exeunt.*

SCENE III.—A Field of Battle near Towton.

Alarums: Excursions. Enter WARWICK.

War. Forspent with toil, as runners with a race,
I lay me down a little while to breathe;
For strokes receiv'd, and many blows repaid,
Have robb'd my strong-knit sinews of their strength,
And, spite of spite, needs must I rest awhile.

Enter EDWARD, *running.*

Edw. Smile, gentle Heaven, or strike, ungentle
  death!
Fo this world frowns, and Edward's sun is clouded.

War. How now, my lord? what hap? what hope of
  good?

Enter GEORGE.

Geo. Our hap is lost, our hope but sad despair:
Our ranks are broke, and ruin follows us.   10
What counsel give you? whither shall we fly?
Edw. Bootless is flight; they follow us with wings;
And weak we are, and cannot shun pursuit.

Enter RICHARD.

Rich. Ah, Warwick! why hast thou withdrawn
  thyself?
Thy brother's blood the thirsty earth hath drunk,
Broach'd with the steely point of Clifford's lance;
And in the very pangs of death he cried,
Like to a dismal clangor heard from far,
"Warwick, revenge! brother, revenge my death!"
So, underneath the belly of their steeds,   20
That stain'd their fetlocks in his smoking blood,
The noble gentleman gave up the ghost.
War. Then let the earth be drunken with our blood:
I'll kill my horse, because I will not fly.
Why stand we like soft-hearted women here,
Wailing our losses, whiles the foe doth rage;
And look upon, as if the tragedy
Were play'd in jest by counterfeiting actors?
Here on my knee I vow to God above,
I'll never pause again, never stand still,   30
Till either death hath clos'd these eyes of mine,
Or fortune given me measure of revenge.
Edw. O Warwick! I do bend my knee with thine;
And, in this vow, do chain my soul to thine.—
And, ere my knee rise from the earth's cold face,
I throw my hands, mine eyes, my heart to thee,
Thou setter-up and plucker-down of kings,
Beseeching thee,—if with thy will it stands,
That to my foes this body must be prey,—
Yet that thy brazen gates of heaven may ope,   40
And give sweet passage to my sinful soul.—
Now, lords, take leave until we meet again,
Where'er it be, in heaven, or in earth.
Rich. Brother, give me thy hand;—and, gentle
  Warwick,
Let me embrace thee in my weary arms.
I, that did never weep, now melt with woe,
That winter should cut off our spring-time so.
War. Away, away! Once more, sweet lords, fare-
  well.
Geo. Yet let us all together to our troops,
And give them leave to fly that will not stay,   50
And call them pillars that will stand to us;
And if we thrive promise them such rewards
As victors wear at the Olympian games.
This may plant courage in their quailing breasts;
For yet is hope of life, and victory.—
Forslow no longer; make we hence amain. [*Exeunt.*

SCENE IV.—The Same. Another Part of the Field.

Excursions. Enter RICHARD *and* CLIFFORD.

Rich. Now, Clifford, I have singled thee alone.
Suppose, this arm is for the Duke of York,
And this for Rutland; both bound to revenge,
Wert thou environ'd with a brazen wall.
Clif. Now, Richard, I am with thee here alone.
This is the hand that stabb'd thy father York,
And this the hand that slew thy brother Rutland;
And there's the heart that triumphs in their death,
And cheers these hands, that slew thy sire and
  brother,
And so, have at thee!   10
    [*They fight.* WARWICK *comes;* CLIFFORD *flies.*
Rich. Nay, Warwick, single out some other chase;
For I myself will hunt this wolf to death. [*Exeunt.*

SCENE V.—Another Part of the Field.

Alarum. Enter King HENRY.

K. Hen. This battle fares like to the morning's war,
When dying clouds contend with growing light;

What time the shepherd, blowing of his nails,
Can neither call it perfect day, nor night.
Now sways it this way, like a mighty sea,
Forc'd by the tide to combat with the wind :
Now sways it that way, like the selfsame sea,
Forc'd to retire by fury of the wind :

Rich. " Now, Clifford, I have singled thee alone."

Sometime, the flood prevails ; and then, the wind ;
Now, one the better, then, another best ;   10
Both tugging to be victors, breast to breast,
Yet neither conqueror, nor conquered :
So is the equal poise of this fell war.
Here, on this molehill, will I sit me down.
To whom God will, there be the victory ;
For Margaret my queen, and Clifford too,
Have chid me from the battle ; swearing both,
They prosper best of all when I am thence.
'Would I were dead ! if God's good will were so ;
For what is in this world but grief and woe ?   20
O God ! methinks, it were a happy life,
To be no better than a homely swain ;
To sit upon a hill, as I do now,
To carve out dials quaintly, point by point,
Thereby to see the minutes how they run,
How many make the hour full complete ;
How many hours bring about the day ;
How many days will finish up the year ;
How many years a mortal man may live.
When this is known, then to divide the times :   30
So many hours must I tend my flock ;
So many hours must I take my rest ;
So many hours must I contemplate ;
So many hours must I sport myself ;
So many days my ewes have been with young ;
So many weeks ere the poor fools will ean ;
So many years ere I shall shear the fleece :
So minutes, hours, days, months, and years,
Pass'd over to the end they were created,
Would bring white hairs unto a quiet grave.   40
Ah, what a life were this ! how sweet ! how lovely !
Gives not the hawthorn-bush a sweeter shade
To shepherds looking on their silly sheep,
Than doth a rich-embroider'd canopy
To kings that fear their subjects' treachery ?
O ! yes, it doth ; a thousand-fold it doth.
And to conclude,—the shepherd's homely curds,
His cold thin drink out of his leather bottle,
His wonted sleep under a fresh tree's shade,
All which secure and sweetly he enjoys,   50
Is far beyond a prince's delicates,
His viands sparkling in a golden cup,

His body couched in a curious bed,
When care, mistrust, and treason waits on him.

*Alarum. Enter a Son that hath killed his Father,
with the dead body.*

Son. Ill blows the wind that profits nobody.
    This man, whom hand to hand I slew in
        fight,
May be possessed with some store of crowns :
And I, that haply take them from him now,
May yet ere night yield both my life and
        them
To some man else, as this dead man doth
        me.   60
Who 's this ?—O God ! it is my father's face,
Whom in this conflict I unawares have
        kill'd.
O heavy times, begetting such events !
From London by the king was I press'd
        forth :
My father, being the Earl of Warwick's
        man,
Came on the part of York, press'd by his
        master ;
And I, who at his hands receiv'd my life,
Have by my hands of life bereaved him.—
Pardon me, God, I knew not what I did ;—
And pardon, father, for I knew not thee.—
My tears shall wipe away these bloody
        marks ;   71
And no more words, till they have flow'd
        their fill.
    K. Hen. O piteous spectacle ! O bloody
        times !
While lions war, and battle for their dens,
Poor harmless lambs abide their enmity.
Weep, wretched man, I 'll aid thee, tear for
        tear ;
And let our hearts, and eyes, like civil war,
Be blind with tears, and break o'ercharg'd with grief.

*Enter a Father, who has killed his Son, with the
body in his arms.*

Fath. Thou that so stoutly hast resisted me,
Give me thy gold, if thou hast any gold,   80
For I have bought it with an hundred blows.—
But let me see :—is this our foeman's face ?
Ah, no, no, no ! it is mine only son !—
Ah, boy ! if any life be left in thee,
Throw up thine eye : see, see, what showers arise,
Blown with the windy tempest of my heart,
Upon thy wounds, that kill mine eye and heart !—
O, pity, God, this miserable age !
What stratagems, how fell, how butcherly,
Erroneous, mutinous, and unnatural,   90
This deadly quarrel daily doth beget !—
O boy ! thy father gave thee life too soon,
And hath bereft thee of thy life too late.
    K. Hen. Woe above woe ! grief more than common
        grief !
O, that my death would stay these ruthful deeds !
O, pity, pity ! gentle Heaven, pity !—
The red rose and the white are on his face,
The fatal colours of our striving houses :
The one his purple blood right well resembles ;
The other his pale cheeks, methinks, presenteth ;   100
Wither one rose, and let the other flourish !
If you contend, a thousand lives must wither.
    Son. How will my mother, for a father's death,
Take on with me, and ne'er be satisfied !
    Fath. How will my wife, for slaughter of my son,
Shed seas of tears, and ne'er be satisfied !
    K. Hen. How will the country, for these woful
        chances,
Misthink the king, and not be satisfied !
    Son. Was ever son so rued a father's death ?
    Fath. Was ever father so bemoan'd his son ?   110
    K. Hen. Was ever king so griev'd for subjects' woe ?
Much is your sorrow ; mine, ten times so much.
    Son. I 'll bear thee hence, where I may weep my fill.
                  [*Exit, with the body.*
    Fath. These arms of mine shall be thy winding-sheet ;

My heart, sweet boy, shall be thy sepulchre,
For from my heart thine image ne'er shall go.
My sighing breast shall be thy funeral bell;
And so obsequious will thy father be,
Son, for the loss of thee, having no more,

And Warwick rages like a chafed bull.
Away! for death doth hold us in pursuit.
  Q. Mar. Mount you, my lord: towards Berwick
        post amain.
Edward and Richard, like a brace of greyhounds,

Q. Mar. " Mount you, my lord: towards Berwick post amain."

As Priam was for all his valiant sons.   120
I 'll bear thee hence; and let them fight that will,
For I have murder'd where I should not kill.
        [*Exit, with the body.*
  K. Hen. Sad-hearted men, much overgone with
        care,
Here sits a king more woful than you are.

  Alarum: Excursions.   Enter Queen MARGARET,
        Prince of WALES, *and* EXETER.

  Prince. Fly, father, fly! for all your friends are
        fled,

Having the fearful flying hare in sight,   130
With fiery eyes, sparkling for very wrath,
And bloody steel grasp'd in their ireful hands,
Are at our backs; and therefore hence amain.
  Exe. Away! for vengeance comes along with them.
Nay, stay not to expostulate; make speed,
Or else come after: I 'll away before.
  K. Hen. Nay, take me with thee, good sweet
        Exeter:
Not that I fear to stay, but love to go
Whither the queen intends. Forward! away!
        [*Exeunt.*

SCENE VI.—The Same.

A loud Alarum. Enter CLIFFORD, *wounded.*

Clif. Here burns my candle out ; ay, here it dies,
Which, while it lasted, gave King Henry light.
O Lancaster ! I fear thy overthrow,
More than my body's parting with my soul.
My love, and fear, glued many friends to thee ;
And, now I fall, thy tough commixture melts,
Impairing Henry, strengthening misproud York ;
And whither fly the gnats, but to the sun ?
And who shines now but Henry's enemies ?
O Phœbus ! hadst thou never given consent	10
That Phaëthon should check thy fiery steeds,
Thy burning car never had scorch'd the earth ;
And, Henry, hadst thou sway'd as kings should do,
Or as thy father, and his father, did,
Giving no ground unto the house of York,
They never then had sprung like summer-flies ;
I, and ten thousand in this luckless realm,
Had left no mourning widows for our death,
And thou this day hadst kept thy chair in peace.
For what doth cherish weeds but gentle air ?	20
And what makes robbers bold but too much lenity ?
Bootless are plaints, and cureless are my wounds ;
No way to fly, nor strength to hold out flight :
The foe is merciless, and will not pity ;
For at their hands I have deserv'd no pity.
The air hath got into my deadly wounds,
And much effuse of blood doth make me faint.—
Come, York, and Richard, Warwick, and the rest ;
I stabb'd your fathers' bosoms, split my breast.
[*He faints.*

Alarum and Retreat. Enter EDWARD, GEORGE,
RICHARD, MONTAGUE, WARWICK, *and Soldiers.*

Edw. Now breathe we, lords : good fortune bids us
pause,	30
And smooth the frowns of war with peaceful looks.—
Some troops pursue the bloody-minded queen,
That led calm Henry, though he were a king,
As doth a sail, fill'd with a fretting gust,
Command an argosy to stem the waves.
But think you, lords, that Clifford fled with them?
War. No, 'tis impossible he should escape ;
For, though before his face I speak the words,
Your brother Richard mark'd him for the grave ;
And wheresoe'er he is, he 's surely dead.	40
[CLIFFORD *groans and dies.*
Edw. Whose soul is that which takes her heavy
leave ?
Rich. A deadly groan, like life and death's departing.
Edw. See who it is : and, now the battle 's ended,
If friend, or foe, let him be gently us'd.
Rich. Revoke that doom of mercy, for 'tis Clifford ;
Who not contented that he lopp'd the branch
In hewing Rutland when his leaves put forth,
But set his murdering knife unto the root
From whence that tender spray did sweetly spring,—	50
I mean, our princely father, Duke of York.
War. From off the gates of York fetch down the
head,
Your father's head, which Clifford placed there ;

Instead whereof, let this supply the room :
Measure for measure must be answered.
Edw. Bring forth that fatal screech-owl to our
house,
That nothing sung but death to us and ours :
Now death shall stop his dismal threatening sound,
And his ill-boding tongue no more shall speak.
[*Attendants bring the body forward.*
War. I think, his understanding is bereft.—
Speak, Clifford, dost thou know who speaks to thee?—
Dark cloudy death o'ershades his beams of life,	61
And he nor sees, nor hears us what we say.
Rich. O, 'would he did ! and so, perhaps, he doth :
'Tis but his policy to counterfeit,
Because he would avoid such bitter taunts
Which in the time of death he gave our father.
Geo. If so thou think'st, vex him with eager words.
Rich. Ask mercy, and obtain no grace.
Edw. Clifford ! repent in bootless penitence.
War. Clifford ! devise excuses for thy faults.	70
Geo. While we devise fell tortures for thy faults.
Rich. Thou didst love York, and I am son to York.
Edw. Thou pitiedst Rutland, I will pity thee.
Geo. Where 's Captain Margaret, to fence you now ?
War. They mock thee, Clifford : swear as thou
wast wont.
Rich. What ! not an oath ? nay, then the world goes
hard,
When Clifford cannot spare his friends an oath.—
I know by that, he 's dead ; and, by my soul,
If this right hand would buy two hours' life,
That I in all despite might rail at him,	80
This hand should chop it off ; and with the issuing
blood
Stifle the villain, whose unstaunched thirst
York and young Rutland could not satisfy.
War. Ay, but he 's dead. Off with the traitor's
head,
And rear it in the place your father's stands.
And now to London with triumphant march,
There to be crowned England's royal king.
From whence shall Warwick cut the sea to France,
And ask the Lady Bona for thy queen.
So shalt thou sinew both these lands together ;	90
And, having France thy friend, thou shalt not dread
The scatter'd foe that hopes to rise again ;
For though they cannot greatly sting to hurt,
Yet look to have them buz, to offend thine ears.
First will I see the coronation,
And then to Brittany I 'll cross the sea,
To effect this marriage, so it please my lord.
Edw. Even as thou wilt, sweet Warwick, let it be ;
For in thy shoulder do I build my seat,
And never will I undertake the thing,	100
Wherein thy counsel and consent is wanting.—
Richard, I will create thee Duke of Gloster ;—
And George, of Clarence ;—Warwick, as ourself,
Shall do, and undo, as him pleaseth best.
Rich. Let me be Duke of Clarence, George of Gloster,
For Gloster's dukedom is too ominous.
War. Tut ! that 's a foolish observation :
Richard, be Duke of Gloster. Now to London,
To see these honours in possession.	[*Exeunt.*

ACT III.

SCENE I.—A Chase in the North of England.

Enter two Keepers, with cross-bows in their hands.

1 Keeper.

UNDER this thick-grown brake we 'll
    shroud ourselves ;
For through this laund anon the deer
    will come ;
And in this covert will we make our
    stand,
Culling the principal of all the deer.
    2 *Keep.* I 'll stay above the hill, so
      both may shoot.
    1 *Keep.* That cannot be ; the noise of
      thy cross-bow
Will scare the herd, and so my shoot is
    lost.
    Here stand we both, and aim we at the
    best :
And, for the time shall not seem tedious,
I 'll tell thee what befell me on a day,   10
In this self place where now we mean to stand.
    2 *Keep.* Here comes a man, let 's stay till he be past.

Enter King HENRY, *disguised, with a prayer-book.*

    K. Hen. From Scotland am I stol'n, even of pure
      love,
To greet mine own land with my wishful sight.
No, Harry, Harry, 't is no land of thine ;
Thy place is fill'd, thy sceptre wrung from thee,
Thy balm wash'd off wherewith thou wast anointed :
No bending knee will call thee Cæsar now,
No humble suitors press to speak for right,
No, not a man comes for redress of thee,   20
For how can I help them, and not myself ?
    1 *Keep.* Ay, here 's a deer whose skin 's a keeper's
    fee :
This is the *quondam* king ; let 's seize upon him.
    K. Hen. Let me embrace the sour adversities ;
For wise men say, it is the wisest course.
    2 *Keep.* Why linger we ? let us lay hands upon him.
    1 *Keep.* Forbear awhile ; we 'll hear a little more.
    K. Hen. My queen and son are gone to France for
      aid ;
And, as I hear, the great commanding Warwick
Is thither gone, to crave the French king's sister   30
To wife for Edward. If this news be true,
Poor queen and son, your labour is but lost :
For Warwick is a subtle orator,
And Lewis a prince soon won with moving words.
By this account then, Margaret may win him,
For she 's a woman to be pitied much :
Her sighs will make a battery in his breast,
Her tears will pierce into a marble heart ;
The tiger will be mild whiles she doth mourn,
And Nero will be tainted with remorse,   40
To hear and see her plaints, her brinish tears.
Ay, but she 's come to beg ; Warwick, to give :
She on his left side craving aid for Henry,
He on his right asking a wife for Edward.
She weeps, and says—her Henry is depos'd :
He smiles, and says—his Edward is install'd ;
That she, poor wretch, for grief can speak no more :
Whiles Warwick tells his title, smooths the wrong,
Inferreth arguments of mighty strength,
And, in conclusion, wins the king from her,   50
With promise of his sister, and what else,
To strengthen and support King Edward's place.

O Margaret ! thus 't will be ; and thou, poor soul,
Art then forsaken, as thou went'st forlorn.
    2 *Keep.* Say, what art thou that talk'st of kings
      and queens ?
    K. Hen. More than I seem, and less than I was
      born to :
A man at least, for less I should not be ;
And men may talk of kings, and why not I ?   58
    2 *Keep.* Ay, but thou talk'st as if thou wert a king.
    K. Hen. Why, so I am, in mind ; and that 's enough.
    2 *Keep.* But, if thou be a king, where is thy crown ?
    K. Hen. My crown is in my heart, not on my head ;
Not deck'd with diamonds, and Indian stones,
Nor to be seen : my crown is call'd, content ;
A crown it is, that seldom kings enjoy.
    2 *Keep.* Well, if you be a king crown'd with content,
Your crown content, and you, must be contented
To go along with us ; for, as we think,
You are the king, King Edward hath depos'd ;
And we his subjects, sworn in all allegiance,   70
Will apprehend you as his enemy.
    K. Hen. But did you never swear, and break an
      oath ?
    2 *Keep.* No, never such an oath ; nor will not now.
    K. Hen. Where did you dwell, when I was King of
      England ?
    2 *Keep.* Here in this country, where we now remain.
    K. Hen. I was anointed king at nine months old ;
My father and my grandfather were kings ;
And you were sworn true subjects unto me :
And tell me then, have you not broke your oaths ?
    1 *Keep.* No ;   80
For we were subjects but while you were king.
    K. Hen. Why am I dead ? do I not breathe a man ?
Ah, simple men ! you know not what you swear.
Look, as I blow this feather from my face,
And as the air blows it to me again,
Obeying with my wind when I do blow,
And yielding to another when it blows,
Commanded always by the greater gust :
Such is the lightness of you common men.
But do not break your oaths ; for of that sin   90
My mild entreaty shall not make you guilty.
Go where you will, the king shall be commanded ;
And be you kings : command, and I 'll obey.
    1 *Keep.* We are true subjects to the king, King
      Edward.
    K. Hen. So would you be again to Henry,
If he were seated as King Edward is.
    1 *Keep.* We charge you, in God's name, and the
      king's,
To go with us unto the officers.
    K. Hen. In God's name, lead ; your king's name be
      obey'd :
And what God will, that let your king perform ;   100
And what he will, I humbly yield unto.   *[Exeunt.*

SCENE II.—London. A Room in the Palace.

Enter King EDWARD, GLOSTER, CLARENCE, *and*
Lady GREY.

    K. Edw. Brother of Gloster, at Saint Albans field
This lady's husband, Sir Richard Grey, was slain,

His lands then seiz'd on by the conqueror:
Her suit is now, to repossess those lands;
Which we in justice cannot well deny,
Because in quarrel of the house of York
The worthy gentleman did lose his life.
  Glo. Your highness shall do well, to grant her suit;
It were dishonour, to deny it her.
  K. Edw. It were no less; but yet I'll make a pause.
  Glo. [*Aside to* Clarence.] Yea; is it so? 11
I see, the lady hath a thing to grant,
Before the king will grant her humble suit.
  Clar. [*Aside to* Gloster.] He knows the game:
    how true he keeps the wind!
  Glo. [*Aside to* Clarence.] Silence!
  K. Edw. Widow, we will consider of your suit,
And come some other time to know our mind.
  L. Grey. Right gracious lord, I cannot brook delay:
May it please your highness to resolve me now,
And what your pleasure is shall satisfy me. 20
  Glo. [*Aside to* Clarence.] Ay, widow? then I'll
    warrant you all your lands,
An if what pleases him shall pleasure you.
Fight closer, or, good faith, you'll catch a blow.
  Clar. [*Aside to* Gloster.] I fear her not, unless she
    chance to fall.
  Glo. [*Aside to* Clarence.] God forbid that, for
    he'll take vantages.
  K. Edw. How many children hast thou, widow?
    tell me.
  Clar. [*Aside to* Gloster.] I think, he means to beg
    a child of her.
  Glo. [*Aside to* Clarence.] Nay, whip me then;
    he'll rather give her two.
  L. Grey. Three, my most gracious lord.
  Glo. [*Aside to* Clarence.] You shall have four, if
    you'll be rul'd by him. 30
  K. Edw. 'T were pity, they should lose their father's
    lands.
  L. Grey. Be pitiful, dread lord, and grant it then.
  K. Edw. Lords, give us leave: I'll try this widow's
    wit.
  Glo. [*Aside to* Clarence.] Ay, good leave have you;
    for you will have leave,
Till youth take leave, and leave you to the crutch.
  [Gloster *and* Clarence *stand apart.*
  K. Edw. Now tell me, madam, do you love your
    children?
  L. Grey. Ay, full as dearly as I love myself.
  K. Edw. And would you not do much, to do them
    good?
  L. Grey. To do them good I would sustain some
    harm.
  K. Edw. Then get your husband's lands, to do them
    good. 40
  L. Grey. Therefore I came unto your majesty.
  K. Edw. I'll tell you how these lands are to be got.
  L. Grey. So shall you bind me to your highness'
    service.
  K. Edw. What service wilt thou do me, if I give
    them?
  L. Grey. What you command, that rests in me to do.
  K. Edw. But you will take exceptions to my boon.
  L. Grey. No, gracious lord, except I cannot do it.
  K. Edw. Ay, but thou canst do what I mean to
    ask.
  L. Grey. Why then, I will do what your grace com-
    mands.
  Glo. [*Aside to* Clarence.] He plies her hard; and
    much rain wears the marble. 50
  Clar. [*Aside to* Gloster.] As red as fire! nay, then
    her wax must melt.
  L. Grey. Why stops my lord? shall I not hear my
    task?
  K. Edw. An easy task: 't is but to love a king.
  L. Grey. That's soon perform'd, because I am a
    subject.
  K. Edw. Why then, thy husband's lands I freely
    give thee.
  L. Grey. I take my leave with many thousand
    thanks.
  Glo. [*Aside to* Clarence.] The match is made: she
    seals it with a curtsy.

  K. Edw. But stay thee; 't is the fruits of love I
    mean.
  L. Grey. The fruits of love I mean, my loving liege.
  K. Edw. Ay, but, I fear me, in another sense. 60
What love think'st thou I sue so much to get?
  L. Grey. My love till death, my humble thanks, my
    prayers:
That love which virtue begs, and virtue grants.
  K. Edw. No, by my troth, I did not mean such love.
  L. Grey. Why, then you mean not as I thought you
    did.
  K. Edw. But now you partly may perceive my mind.
  L. Grey. My mind will never grant what I perceive
Your highness aims at, if I aim aright.
  K. Edw. To tell thee plain, I aim to lie with thee.
  L. Grey. To tell you plain, I had rather lie in prison.
  K. Edw. Why, then thou shalt not have thy hus-
    band's lands. 71
  L. Grey. Why, then mine honesty shall be my
    dower;
For by that loss I will not purchase them.
  K. Edw. Therein thou wrong'st thy children
    mightily.
  L. Grey. Herein your highness wrongs both them
    and me.
But, mighty lord, this merry inclination
Accords not with the sadness of my suit;
Please you dismiss me, either with ay, or no.
  K. Edw. Ay, if thou wilt say ay to my request;
No, if thou dost say no to my demand. 80
  L. Grey. Then, no, my lord. My suit is at an end.
  Glo. [*Aside to* Clarence.] The widow likes him
    not, she knits her brows.
  Clar. [*Aside to* Gloster.] He is the bluntest wooer
    in Christendom.
  K. Edw. [*Aside.*] Her looks do argue her replete
    with modesty;
Her words do show her wit incomparable;
All her perfections challenge sovereignty:
One way, or other, she is for a king,
And she shall be my love, or else my queen.—
Say, that King Edward take thee for his queen?

K. Edw. "Say, that King Edward take thee for his queen?"

  L. Grey. 'T is better said than done, my gracious
    lord; 90
I am a subject fit to jest withal,
But far unfit to be a sovereign.
  K. Edw. Sweet widow, by my state I swear to thee,
I speak no more than what my soul intends;
And that is, to enjoy thee for my love.
  L. Grey. And that is more than I will yield unto.
I know, I am too mean to be your queen,
And yet too good to be your concubine.
  K. Edw. You cavil, widow: I did mean, my queen.
  L. Grey. 'T will grieve your grace, my sons should
    call you father. 100

K. Edw. No more than when my daughters call
 thee mother.
Thou art a widow, and thou hast some children ;
And, by God's mother, I, being but a bachelor,
Have other some : why, 't is a happy thing
To be the father unto many sons.
Answer no more, for thou shalt be my queen.
 Glo. [*Aside to* CLARENCE.] The ghostly father now
  hath done his shrift.
 Clar. [*Aside to* GLOSTER.] When he was made a
  shriver, 't was for shift.
 K. Edw. Brothers, you muse what chat we two
  have had.
 Glo. The widow likes it not, for she looks very sad.
 K. Edw. You 'd think it strange if I should marry
  her.   111
 Clar. To whom, my lord?
 K. Edw.   Why, Clarence, to myself.
 Glo. That would be ten days' wonder at the least.
 Clar. That 's a day longer than a wonder lasts.
 Glo. By so much is the wonder in extremes.
 K. Edw. Well, jest on, brothers : I can tell you
  both,
Her suit is granted for her husband's lands.

Enter a Nobleman.

 Nob. My gracious lord, Henry your foe is taken,
And brought your prisoner to your palace gate.
 K. Edw. See that he be convey'd unto the Tower :—
And go we, brothers, to the man that took him, 121
To question of his apprehension.—
Widow, go you along.—Lords, use her honourably.
  [*Exeunt King* EDWARD, *Lady* GREY,
       CLARENCE, *and Lord.*
 Glo. Ay, Edward will use women honourably.
'Would he were wasted, marrow, bones, and all,
That from his loins no hopeful branch may spring,
To cross me from the golden time I look for !
And yet, between my soul's desire, and me,—
The lustful Edward's title buried,—
Is Clarence, Henry, and his son young Edward, 130
And all the unlook'd-for issue of their bodies,
To take their rooms, ere I can place myself :
A cold premeditation for my purpose !
Why then, I do but dream on sovereignty ;
Like one that stands upon a promontory,
And spies a far-off shore where he would tread,
Wishing his foot were equal with his eye ;
And chides the sea that sunders him from thence,
Saying—he 'll lade it dry to have his way :
So do I wish the crown, being so far off, 140
And so I chide the means that keep me from it ;
And so I say—I 'll cut the causes off,
Flattering me with impossibilities.—
My eye's too quick, my heart o'erweens too much,
Unless my hand and strength could equal them.
Well, say there is no kingdom then for Richard,
What other pleasure can the world afford ?
I 'll make my heaven in a lady's lap,
And deck my body in gay ornaments,
And witch sweet ladies with my words and looks. 150
O miserable thought ! and more unlikely,
Than to accomplish twenty golden crowns.
Why, love forswore me in my mother's womb :
And, for I should not deal in her soft laws,
She did corrupt frail nature with some bribe,
To shrink mine arm up like a wither'd shrub ;
To make an envious mountain on my back,
Where sits deformity to mock my body ;
To shape my legs of an unequal size ;
To disproportion me in every part ;   160
Like to a chaos, or an unlick'd bear-whelp,
That carries no impression like the dam.
And am I then a man to be belov'd ?
O monstrous fault, to harbour such a thought !
Then, since this earth affords no joy to me
But to command, to check, to o'erbear such
As are of better person than myself,
I 'll make my heaven to dream upon the crown ;
And, whiles I live, to account this world but hell,
Until my misshap'd trunk, that bears this head, 170
Be round impaled with a glorious crown.

And yet I know not how to get the crown,
For many lives stand between me and home :
And I,—like one lost in a thorny wood,
That rents the thorns, and is rent with the thorns,
Seeking a way, and straying from the way,
Not knowing how to find the open air,
But toiling desperately to find it out,—
Torment myself to catch the English crown :
And from that torment I will free myself, 180
Or hew my way out with a bloody axe.
Why, I can smile, and murder while I smile,
And cry, content, to that which grieves my heart,
And wet my cheeks with artificial tears,
And frame my face to all occasions.
I 'll drown more sailors than the mermaid shall,
I 'll slay more gazers than the basilisk ;
I 'll play the orator as well as Nestor,
Deceive more slily than Ulysses could,
And, like a Sinon, take another Troy.   190
I can add colours to the chameleon,
Change shapes with Proteus, for advantages,
And set the murd'rous Machiavel to school.
Can I do this, and cannot get a crown ?
Tut ! were it further off, I 'll pluck it down. [*Exit.*

———

SCENE III.—France. A Room in the Palace.

Flourish. Enter LEWIS *the French King, and Lady*
BONA, *attended : the King takes his state. Then
enter Queen* MARGARET, *Prince* EDWARD, *and the
Earl of* OXFORD.

 K. Lew. [*Rising.*] Fair Queen of England, worthy
  Margaret,
Sit down with us : it ill befits thy state
And birth, that thou shouldst stand, while Lewis doth
  sit.
 Q. Mar. No, mighty King of France ; now Margaret
Must strike her sail, and learn awhile to serve,
Where kings command. I was, I must confess,
Great Albion's queen in former golden days ;
But now mischance hath trod my title down,
And with dishonour laid me on the ground,
Where I must take like seat unto my fortune, 10
And to my humble seat conform myself.
 K. Lew. Why, say, fair queen, whence springs this
  deep despair ?
 Q. Mar. From such a cause as fills mine eyes with
  tears,
And stops my tongue, while heart is drown'd in
  cares.
 K. Lew. Whate'er it be, be thou still like thyself,
And sit thee by our side : [*seats her by him*] yield not
  thy neck
To fortune's yoke, but let thy dauntless mind
Still ride in triumph over all mischance.
Be plain, Queen Margaret, and tell thy grief ;
It shall be eas'd, if France can yield relief. 20
 Q. Mar. Those gracious words revive my drooping
  thoughts,
And give my tongue-tied sorrows leave to speak.
Now, therefore, be it known to noble Lewis,
That Henry, sole possessor of my love,
Is of a king become a banish'd man,
And forc'd to live in Scotland, a forlorn ;
While proud ambitious Edward, Duke of York,
Usurps the regal title, and the seat
Of England's true-anointed lawful king.
This is the cause, that I, poor Margaret, 30
With this my son, Prince Edward, Henry's heir,
Am come to crave thy just and lawful aid ;
And if thou fail us, all our hope is done.
Scotland hath will to help, but cannot help ;
Our people and our peers are both misled,
Our treasure seiz'd, our soldiers put to flight,
And, as thou seest, ourselves in heavy plight.
 K. Lew. Renowned queen, with patience calm the
  storm,
While we bethink a means to break it off.
 Q. Mar. The more we stay, the stronger grows our
  foe.   40

K. Lew. The more I stay, the more I 'll succour
thee.
Q. Mar. O ! but impatience waiteth on true sorrow :
And see where comes the breeder of my sorrow.

Enter WARWICK, *attended.*

K. Lew. What 's he, approacheth boldly to our pre-
sence ?
Q. Mar. Our Earl of Warwick, Edward's greatest
friend.
K. Lew. Welcome, brave Warwick. What brings
thee to France ?
　　　　　　　[Descending from his state. Queen
　　　　　　　MARGARET *rises.*
Q. Mar. Ay, now begins a second storm to rise ;
For this is he that moves both wind and tide.
War. From worthy Edward, King of Albion,
My lord and sovereign, and thy vowed friend,　50
I come, in kindness, and unfeigned love,

War. " I come, in kindness, and unfeigned love."

First, to do greetings to thy royal person ;
And then, to crave a league of amity ;
And lastly, to confirm that amity
With nuptial knot, if thou vouchsafe to grant
That virtuous Lady Bona, thy fair sister,
To England's king in lawful marriage.
Q. Mar. If that go forward, Henry's hope is done.
War. [*To* BONA.] And, gracious madam, in our
　　　　　king's behalf,
I am commanded, with your leave and favour,　60
Humbly to kiss your hand, and with my tongue
To tell the passion of my sovereign's heart ;
Where fame, late entering at his heedful ears,
Hath plac'd thy beauty's image, and thy virtue.
Q. Mar. King Lewis, and Lady Bona, hear me
　　　　　speak,
Before you answer Warwick. His demand
Springs not from Edward's well-meant honest love,
But from deceit, bred by necessity ;
For how can tyrants safely govern home,
Unless abroad they purchase great alliance ?　70
To prove him tyrant, this reason may suffice,
That Henry liveth still ; but were he dead,
Yet here Prince Edward stands, King Henry's son.
Look, therefore, Lewis, that by this league and
　　　　　marriage
Thou draw not on thy danger and dishonour ;
For though usurpers sway the rule awhile,
Yet heavens are just, and time suppresseth wrongs.

War. Injurious Margaret !
Prince.　　　　　　　　　And why not queen ?
War. Because thy father Henry did usurp,
And thou no more art prince, than she is queen.　80
Oxf. Then Warwick disannuls great John of Gaunt,
Which did subdue the greatest part of Spain ;
And, after John of Gaunt, Henry the Fourth,
Whose wisdom was a mirror to the wisest ;
And after that wise prince, Henry the Fifth,
Who by his prowess conquered all France :
From these our Henry lineally descends.
War. Oxford, how haps it, in this smooth discourse,
You told not, how Henry the Sixth hath lost
All that which Henry the Fifth had gotten ?　90
Methinks, these peers of France should smile at
　　　　　that.
But for the rest,—you tell a pedigree
Of threescore and two years ; a silly time
To make prescription for a kingdom's worth.
Oxf. Why, Warwick, canst thou speak
　　　　　against thy liege,
Whom thou obeyedst thirty and six years,
And not bewray thy treason with a blush ?
War. Can Oxford, that did ever fence
　　　　　the right,
Now buckler falsehood with a pedigree ?
For shame ! leave Henry, and call Edward
　　　　　king.　　　　　　　　　　100
Oxf. Call him my king, by whose injurious
　　　　　doom
My elder brother, the Lord Aubrey Vere,
Was done to death ? and more than so, my
　　　　　father,
Even in the downfall of his mellow'd years,
When nature brought him to the door of
　　　　　death ?
No, Warwick, no ; while life upholds this
　　　　　arm,
This arm upholds the house of Lancaster.
War. And I the house of York.
K. Lew. Queen Margaret, Prince Edward,
　　　　　and Oxford,
Vouchsafe at our request to stand aside, 110
While I use further conference with War-
　　　　　wick.
Q. Mar. Heavens grant, that Warwick's
　　　　　words bewitch him not !
　　　　[*Retiring with the* PRINCE *and* OXFORD.
K. Lew. Now, Warwick, tell me, even
　　　　　upon thy conscience,
Is Edward your true king ? for I were loath,
To link with him that were not lawful
　　　　　chosen.
War. Thereon I pawn my credit, and mine honour.
K. Lew. But is he gracious in the people's eye ?
War. The more, that Henry was unfortunate.
K. Lew. Then further, all dissembling set aside,
Tell me for truth the measure of his love 120
Unto our sister Bona.
War.　　　　　　　　　Such it seems,
As may beseem a monarch like himself.
Myself have often heard him say, and swear,
That this his love was an eternal plant,
Whereof the root was fix'd in virtue's ground,
The leaves and fruit maintain'd with beauty's sun,
Exempt from envy, but not from disdain,
Unless the Lady Bona quit his pain.
K. Lew. Now, sister, let us hear your firm resolve.
Bona. Your grant, or your denial, shall be mine.—
　　　　[*To* WARWICK.] Yet I confess, that often ere this
　　　　　day,　　　　　　　　　　131
When I have heard your king's desert recounted,
Mine ear hath tempted judgment to desire.
K. Lew. Then, Warwick, thus :—our sister shall be
　　　　　Edward's ;
And now forthwith shall articles be drawn
Touching the jointure that your king must make,
Which with her dowry shall be counterpois'd.—
Draw near, Queen Margaret, and be a witness,
That Bona shall be wife to the English king.
Prince. To Edward, but not to the English king. 140
Q. Mar. Deceitful Warwick ! it was thy device,

By this alliance to make void my suit :
Before thy coming, Lewis was Henry's friend.
  K. Lew. And still is friend to him and Margaret
But if your title to the crown be weak,
As may appear by Edward's good success,
Then 't is but reason, that I be releas'd
From giving aid which late I promised.
Yet shall you have all kindness at my hand,
That your estate requires, and mine can yield. 150
  War. Henry now lives in Scotland, at his ease,
Where having nothing, nothing can he lose.
And as for you yourself, our *quondam* queen,
You have a father able to maintain you,
And better 't were you troubled him than France.
  Q. Mar. Peace ! impudent and shameless Warwick,
    peace,
Proud setter-up and puller-down of kings ;
I will not hence, till with my talk and tears,
Both full of truth, I make King Lewis behold
Thy sly conveyance, and thy lord's false love ; 160
For both of you are birds of selfsame feather.
                 [A horn sounded within.
  K. Lew. Warwick, this is some post to us, or thee.

          Enter a Messenger.

  Mess. My lord ambassador, these letters are for you,
Sent from your brother, Marquess Montague ;—
These from our king unto your majesty ;—
And, madam, these for you ; from whom, I know not.
              [They all read their letters.
  Oxf. I like it well, that our fair queen and mistress
Smiles at her news, while Warwick frowns at his.
  Prince. Nay, mark how Lewis stamps as he were
    nettled :
I hope all 's for the best. 170
  K. Lew. Warwick, what are thy news ? and yours,
    fair queen ?
  Q. Mar. Mine, such as fill my heart with unhop'd
    joys.
  War. Mine, full of sorrow and heart's discontent.
  K. Lew. What ! has your king married the Lady
    Grey,
And now, to sooth your forgery and his,
Sends me a paper to persuade me patience ?
Is this the alliance that he seeks with France ?
Dare he presume to scorn us in this manner ?
  Q. Mar. I told your majesty as much before :
This proveth Edward's love, and Warwick's honesty.
  War. King Lewis, I here protest, in sight of heaven,
And by the hope I have of heavenly bliss, 182
That I am clear from this misdeed of Edward's ;
No more my king, for he dishonours me ;
But most himself, if he could see his shame.
Did I forget, that by the house of York
My father came untimely to his death ?
Did I let pass the abuse done to my niece ?
Did I impale him with the regal crown ?
Did I put Henry from his native right ? 190
And am I guerdon'd at the last with shame ?
Shame on himself, for my desert is honour :
And to repair my honour lost for him,
I here renounce him, and return to Henry.
My noble queen, let former grudges pass,
And henceforth I am thy true servitor.
I will revenge his wrong to Lady Bona,
And replant Henry in his former state.
  Q. Mar. Warwick, these words have turn'd my
    hate to love ;
And I forgive and quite forget old faults, 200
And joy that thou becom'st King Henry's friend.
  War. So much his friend, ay, his unfeigned friend,
That if King Lewis vouchsafe to furnish us

With some few bands of chosen soldiers,
I 'll undertake to land them on our coast,
And force the tyrant from his seat by war.
'T is not his new-made bride shall succour him :
And as for Clarence, as my letters tell me,
He 's very likely now to fall from him,
For matching more for wanton lust than honour, 210
Or than for strength and safety of our country.
  Bona. Dear brother, how shall Bona be reveng'd,
But by thy help to this distressed queen ?
  Q. Mar. Renowned prince, how shall poor Henry
    live,
Unless thou rescue him from foul despair ?
  Bona. My quarrel, and this English queen's, are
    one.
  War. And mine, fair Lady Bona, joins with yours.
  K. Lew. And mine, with hers, and thine, and
    Margaret's.
Therefore, at last, I firmly am resolv'd,
You shall have aid. 220
  Q. Mar. Let me give humble thanks for all at once.
  K. Lew. Then, England's messenger, return in post ;
And tell false Edward, thy supposed king,
That Lewis of France is sending over masquers,
To revel it with him and his new bride.
Thou seest what 's past ; go fear thy king withal.
  Bona. Tell him, in hope he 'll prove a widower
    shortly,
I 'll wear the willow garland for his sake.
  Q. Mar. Tell him, my mourning weeds are laid
    aside,
And I am ready to put armour on. 230
  War. Tell him from me, that he hath done me
    wrong,
And therefore I 'll uncrown him ere 't be long.
There 's thy reward : be gone. *[Exit Messenger.*
  K. Lew. But, Warwick, thou,
And Oxford, with five thousand men,
Shall cross the seas, and bid false Edward battle :
And, as occasion serves, this noble queen
And prince shall follow with a fresh supply.
Yet, ere thou go, but answer me one doubt :
What pledge have we of thy firm loyalty ?
  War. This shall assure my constant loyalty :— 240
That if our queen and this young prince agree,
I 'll join mine eldest daughter, and my joy,
To him forthwith in holy wedlock bands.
  Q. Mar. Yes, I agree, and thank you for your
    motion.
Son Edward, she is fair and virtuous,
Therefore delay not, give thy hand to Warwick ;
And with thy hand thy faith irrevocable,
That only Warwick's daughter shall be thine.
  Prince. Yes, I accept her, for she well deserves it ;
And here, to pledge my vow, I give my hand. 250
           [He gives his hand to Warwick.
  K. Lew. Why stay we now ? These soldiers shall
    be levied,
And thou, Lord Bourbon, our high admiral,
Shalt waft them over with our royal fleet.—
I long till Edward fall by war's mischance,
For mocking marriage with a dame of France.
           [Exeunt all but Warwick.
  War. I came from Edward as ambassador,
But I return his sworn and mortal foe :
Matter of marriage was the charge he gave me,
But dreadful war shall answer his demand.
Had he none else to make a stale but me ? 260
Then none but I shall turn his jest to sorrow.
I was the chief that rais'd him to the crown,
And I 'll be chief to bring him down again :
Not that I pity Henry's misery,
But seek revenge on Edward's mockery. *[Exit.*

ACT IV.

SCENE I.—London. A Room in the Palace.

Enter GLOSTER, CLARENCE, SOMERSET, *and* MONTAGUE.

Gloster. NOW tell me, brother Clarence, what think you
Of this new marriage with the Lady Grey?
Hath not our brother made a worthy choice?

Clar. Alas! you know, 't is far from hence to France:
How could he stay till Warwick made return?

Som. My lords, forbear this talk: here comes the king.

Glo. And his well-chosen bride.

Clar. I mind to tell him plainly what I think.

Flourish. Enter King EDWARD, *attended; Lady* GREY, *as Queen;* PEMBROKE, STAFFORD, *and* HASTINGS.

K. Edw. Now, brother of Clarence, how like you our choice,
That you stand pensive as half malcontent?   10

Clar. As well as Lewis of France, or the Earl of Warwick;
Which are so weak of courage, and in judgment,
That they 'll take no offence at our abuse.

K. Edw. Suppose they take offence without a cause,
They are but Lewis and Warwick: I am Edward,
Your king and Warwick's, and must have my will.

Glo. And you shall have your will, because our king;
Yet hasty marriage seldom proveth well.

K. Edw. Yea, brother Richard, are you offended too?

Glo. Not I: 20
No, God forbid, that I should wish them sever'd
Whom God hath join'd together; ay, and 't were pity,
To sunder them that yoke so well together.

K. Edw. Setting your scorns, and your mislike, aside,
Tell me some reason why the Lady Grey
Should not become my wife, and England's queen.—
And you too, Somerset, and Montague,
Speak freely what you think.

Clar. Then this is mine opinion,—that King Lewis
Becomes your enemy, for mocking him   30
About the marriage of the Lady Bona.

Glo. And Warwick, doing what you gave in charge,
Is now dishonour'd by this new marriage.

K. Edw. What, if both Lewis and Warwick be appeas'd
By such invention as I can devise?

Mont. Yet to have join'd with France in such alliance,
Would more have strengthen'd this our common-wealth
'Gainst foreign storms, than any home-bred marriage.

Hast. Why, knows not Montague, that of itself
England is safe, if true within itself?   40

Mont. Yes; but the safer, when 't is back'd with France.

Hast. 'T is better using France, than trusting France.
Let us be back'd with God, and with the seas,
Which he hath given for fence impregnable,
And with their helps only defend ourselves:
In them and in ourselves our safety lies.

Clar. For this one speech Lord Hastings well deserves
To have the heir of the Lord Hungerford.

K. Edw. Ay, what of that? it was my will, and grant;
And for this once my will shall stand for law.   50

Glo. And yet, methinks, your grace hath not done well,
To give the heir and daughter of Lord Scales
Unto the brother of your loving bride:
She better would have fitted me, or Clarence;
But in your bride you bury brotherhood.

Clar. Or else you would not have bestow'd the heir
Of the Lord Bonville on your new wife's son,
And leave your brothers to go speed elsewhere.

K. Edw. Alas, poor Clarence! is it for a wife,
That thou art malcontent? I will provide thee.   60

Clar. In choosing for yourself you show'd your judgment;
Which being shallow, you shall give me leave
To play the broker in mine own behalf;
And to that end I shortly mind to leave you.

K. Edw. Leave me, or tarry, Edward will be king,
And not be tied unto his brother's will.

Q. Eliz. My lords, before it pleas'd his majesty
To raise my state to title of a queen,
Do me but right, and you must all confess
That I was not ignoble of descent: 70
And meaner than myself have had like fortune.
But as this title honours me and mine,
So your dislikes, to whom I would be pleasing,
Do cloud my joys with danger and with sorrow.

K. Edw. My love, forbear to fawn upon their frowns.
What danger, or what sorrow can befall thee,
So long as Edward is thy constant friend,
And their true sovereign, whom they must obey?
Nay, whom they shall obey, and love thee too,
Unless they seek for hatred at my hands;   80
Which if they do, yet will I keep thee safe,
And they shall feel the vengeance of my wrath.

Glo. [*Aside.*] I hear, yet say not much, but think the more.

Enter a Messenger.

K. Edw. Now, messenger, what letters, or what news,
From France?

Mess. My sovereign liege, no letters, and few words;
But such as I, without your special pardon,
Dare not relate.

K. Edw. Go to, we pardon thee: therefore, in brief,
Tell me their words as near as thou canst guess them.
What answer makes King Lewis unto our letters?   91

Mess. At my depart these were his very words:—
" Go tell false Edward, thy supposed king,
That Lewis of France is sending over masquers,
To revel it with him and his new bride."

K. Edw. Is Lewis so brave? belike, he thinks me Henry.
But what said Lady Bona to my marriage?

Mess. These were her words, utter'd with mild disdain:

"Tell him, in hope he 'll prove a widower shortly,
I 'll wear the willow garland for his sake." 100
K. Edw. I blame not her, she could say little less ;
She had the wrong : but what said Henry's queen ?
For I have heard, that she was there in place.
Mess. "Tell him," quoth she, "any mourning weeds
are done,
And I am ready to put armour on."
K. Edw. Belike, she minds to play the Amazon.
But what said Warwick to these injuries ?
Mess. He, more incens'd against your majesty
Than all the rest, discharg'd me with these words :—
"Tell him from me, that he hath done me wrong, 110
And therefore I 'll uncrown him ere 't be long."
K. Edw. Ha ! durst the traitor breathe out so proud
words ?
Well, I will arm me, being thus forewarn'd :
They shall have wars, and pay for their presumption.
But say, is Warwick friends with Margaret ?
Mess. Ay, gracious sovereign : they are so link'd in
friendship,
That young Prince Edward marries Warwick's
daughter.
Clar. Belike, the elder ; Clarence will have the
younger.
Now, brother king, farewell, and sit you fast,
For I will hence to Warwick's other daughter ; 120
That, though I want a kingdom, yet in marriage
I may not prove inferior to yourself.—
You, that love me and Warwick, follow me.
[*Exit* CLARENCE, *and* SOMERSET *follows.*
Glo. [*Aside.*] Not I :
My thoughts aim at a further matter ; I
Stay not for the love of Edward, but the crown.
K. Edw. Clarence and Somerset both gone to War-
wick !
Yet am I arm'd against the worst can happen,
And haste is needful in this desperate case.—
Pembroke, and Stafford, you in our behalf 130
Go levy men, and make prepare for war ;
They are already, or quickly will be landed
Myself in person will straight follow you.
[*Exeunt* PEMBROKE *and* STAFFORD.
But, ere I go, Hastings, and Montague,
Resolve my doubt. You twain, of all the rest,
Are near to Warwick by blood, and by alliance :
Tell me if you love Warwick more than me ?
If it be so, then both depart to him :
I rather wish you foes, than hollow friends :
But, if you mind to hold your true obedience, 140
Give me assurance with some friendly vow,
That I may never have you in suspect.
Mont. So God help Montague, as he proves true !
Hast. And Hastings, as he favours Edward's cause !
K. Edw. Now, brother Richard, will you stand by us ?
Glo. Ay, in despite of all that shall withstand you.
K. Edw. Why so ; then am I sure of victory.
Now therefore let us hence ; and lose no hour,
Till we meet Warwick with his foreign power.
[*Exeunt.*

SCENE II.—A Plain in Warwickshire.

Enter WARWICK *and* OXFORD *with French and
other Forces.*

War. Trust me, my lord, all hitherto goes well :
The common people by numbers swarm to us.

Enter CLARENCE *and* SOMERSET.

But see, where Somerset and Clarence come !
Speak suddenly, my lords, are we all friends ?
Clar. Fear not that, my lord.
War. Then, gentle Clarence, welcome unto War-
wick :
And welcome, Somerset.—I hold it cowardice,
To rest mistrustful where a noble heart
Hath pawn'd an open hand in sign of love :
Else might I think, that Clarence, Edward's brother,
Were but a feigned friend to our proceedings : 11
But welcome, sweet Clarence ; my daughter shall be
thine.

And now what rests, but in night's coverture,
Thy brother being carelessly encamp'd,
His soldiers lurking in the towns about,
And but attended by a simple guard,
We may surprise and take him at our pleasure ?
Our scouts have found the adventure very easy :
That as Ulysses, and stout Diomede,
With sleight and manhood stole to Rhesus' tents, 20
And brought from thence the Thracian fatal steeds ;
So we, well cover'd with the night's black mantle,
At unawares may beat down Edward's guard,
And seize himself ; I say not, slaughter him,
For I intend but only to surprise him.—
You, that will follow me to this attempt,
Applaud the name of Henry with your leader.
[*They all cry,* "*Henry !*"
Why, then, let 's on our way in silent sort.
For Warwick and his friends, God and Saint George !
[*Exeunt.*

SCENE III.—EDWARD'S Camp near Warwick.

Enter certain Watchmen, to guard the KING'S *Tent.*

1 Watch. Come on, my masters, each man take his
stand :
The king by this is set him down to sleep.
2 Watch. What, will he not to bed ?
1 Watch. Why, no ; for he hath made a solemn vow,
Never to lie and take his natural rest,
Till Warwick or himself be quite suppress'd.
2 Watch. To-morrow then, belike, shall be the day,
If Warwick be so near as men report.
3 Watch. But say, I pray, what nobleman is that,
That with the king here resteth in his tent ? 10
1 Watch. 'T is the Lord Hastings, the king's chiefest
friend.
3 Watch. O ! is it so ? But why commands the king,
That his chief followers lodge in towns about him,
While he himself keeps in the cold field ?
2 Watch. 'T is the more honour, because more
dangerous.
3 Watch. Ay, but give me worship and quietness ;
I like it better than a dangerous honour.
If Warwick knew in what estate he stands,
'T is to be doubted, he would waken him.
1 Watch. Unless our halberds did shut up his
passage. 20
2 Watch. Ay ; wherefore else guard we his royal tent,
But to defend his person from night-foes ?

Enter WARWICK, CLARENCE, OXFORD, SOMERSET,
and Forces.

War. This is his tent ; and see, where stand his
guard.
Courage, my masters ! honour now, or never !
But follow me, and Edward shall be ours.
1 Watch. Who goes there ?
2 Watch. Stay, or thou diest.
[WARWICK, *and the rest, cry all—*"*Warwick !
Warwick !*" *and set upon the Guard ; who
fly, crying—*"*Arm ! Arm !*" WARWICK, *and
the rest, following them.*

Drums beating, and trumpets sounding, re-enter
WARWICK, *and the rest, bringing the* KING *out
in his gown, sitting in a chair ;* GLOSTER *and*
HASTINGS *fly over the stage.*

Som. What are they that fly there ?
War. Richard, and Hastings : let them go ; here 's
the duke.
K. Edw. The duke ! why, Warwick, when we
parted last,
Thou call'dst me king !
War. Ay, but the case is alter'd : 30
When you disgrac'd me in my embassade,
Then I degraded you from being king,
And come now to create you Duke of York.
Alas ! how should you govern any kingdom,
That know not how to use ambassadors,
Nor how to be contented with one wife,
Nor how to use your brothers brotherly,

Nor how to study for the people's welfare,
Nor how to shroud yourself from enemies?
K. Edw. Yea, brother of Clarence, art thou here
    too?   40
Nay, then I see that Edward needs must down.—
Yet, Warwick, in despite of all mischance,
Of thee thyself, and all thy complices,
Edward will always bear himself as king:
Though fortune's malice overthrow my state,
My mind exceeds the compass of her wheel.
  War. Then, for his mind, be Edward England's
    king: [*Takes off his crown.*
But Henry now shall wear the English crown,

War. " But Henry now shall wear the English crown."

And be true king indeed; thou but the shadow.—
My Lord of Somerset, at my request,   50
See that forthwith Duke Edward be convey'd
Unto my brother, Archbishop of York.
When I have fought with Pembroke and his fellows,
I 'll follow you, and tell what answer
Lewis, and the Lady Bona, send to him :—
Now, for a while, farewell, good Duke of York.
  K. Edw. What fates impose, that men must needs
    abide :
It boots not to resist both wind and tide.
        [*Exit King* EDWARD, *led out ;* SOMERSET
          with him.
  Oxf. What now remains, my lords, for us to do,
But march to London with our soldiers?   60
  War. Ay, that 's the first thing that we have to do ;
To free King Henry from imprisonment,
And see him seated in the regal throne.   [*Exeunt.*

SCENE IV.—London.   A Room in the Palace.

Enter Queen ELIZABETH *and* RIVERS.

  Riv. Madam, what makes you in this sudden
    change?
  Q. Eliz. Why, brother Rivers, are you yet to learn,
What late misfortune is befall'n King Edward?
  Riv. What! loss of some pitch'd battle against
    Warwick?
  Q. Eliz. No, but the loss of his own royal person.
  Riv. Then is my sovereign slain?
  Q. Eliz. Ay, almost slain, for he is taken prisoner ;
Either betray'd by falsehood of his guard,
Or by his foe surpris'd at unawares :
And, as I further have to understand,   10
Is new committed to the Bishop of York,
F.ll Warwick's brother, and by that our foe.
  Riv. These news, I must confess, are full of grief ;
Yet, gracious madam, bear it as you may :
Warwick may lose, that now hath won the day.

  Q. Eliz. Till then, fair hope must hinder life's decay ;
And I the rather wean me from despair,
For love of Edward's offspring in my womb :
This is it that makes me bridle passion.
And bear with mildness my misfortune's cross :   20
Ay, ay, for this I draw in many a tear,
And stop the rising of blood-sucking sighs,
Lest with my sighs or tears I blast or drown
King Edward's fruit, true heir to the English crown.
  Riv. But, madam, where is Warwick then become?
  Q. Eliz. I am informed, that he comes towards
    London,
To set the crown once more on Henry's head.
    Guess thou the rest ; King Edward's friends
      must down :
But to prevent the tyrant's violence,
(For trust not him that hath once broken
    faith,)   30
I 'll hence forthwith unto the sanctuary,
To save at least the heir of Edward's right :
There shall I rest secure from force, and fraud.
Come therefore ; let us fly while we may fly :
If Warwick take us, we are sure to die.
                      [*Exeunt.*

SCENE V.—A Park near Middleham Castle
in Yorkshire.

Enter GLOSTER, HASTINGS, *Sir* WILLIAM
STANLEY, *and others.*

  Glo. Now, my Lord Hastings, and Sir
    William Stanley,
Leave off to wonder why I drew you hither,
Into this chiefest thicket of the park.
Thus stands the case. You know, our king,
    my brother,
Is prisoner to the bishop here, at whose hands
He hath good usage and great liberty,
And often, but attended with weak guard,
Comes hunting this way to disport himself.
I have advertis'd him by secret means,
That if about this hour he make this way,   10
Under the colour of his usual game,
He shall here find his friends, with horse and men,
To set him free from his captivity.

Enter King EDWARD *and a Huntsman.*

  Hunt. This way, my lord, for this way lies the game.
  K. Edw. Nay, this way, man : see, where the hunts-
    men stand.—
Now, brother of Gloster, Lord Hastings, and the rest,
Stand you thus close, to steal the bishop's deer?
  Glo. Brother, the time and case requireth haste.
Your horse stands ready at the park-corner.
  K. Edw. But whither shall we then ?   20
  Hast. To Lynn, my lord ; and ship from thence to
    Flanders.
  Glo. Well guess'd, believe me ; for that was my
    meaning.
  K. Edw. Stanley, I will requite thy forwardness.
  Glo. But wherefore stay we ? 'tis no time to talk.
  K. Edw. Huntsman, what say'st thou ? wilt thou go
    along ?
  Hunt. Better do so, than tarry and be hang'd.
  Glo. Come then ; away ! let 's have no more ado.
  K. Edw. Bishop, farewell : shield thee from War-
    wick's frown,
And pray that I may repossess the crown.   [*Exeunt.*

SCENE VI.—A Room in the Tower.

Enter King HENRY, CLARENCE, WARWICK, SOMER-
SET, *young* RICHMOND, OXFORD, MONTAGUE,
Lieutenant of the Tower, and Attendants.

  K. Hen. Master lieutenant, now that God and
    friends
Have shaken Edward from the regal seat,
And turn'd my captive state to liberty,
My fear to hope, my sorrows unto joys,
At our enlargement what are thy due fees ?

Lieu. Subjects may challenge nothing of their
    sovereigns;
But if an humble prayer may prevail,
I then crave pardon of your majesty.
  K. Hen. For what, lieutenant? for well using me?
Nay, be thou sure, I'll well requite thy kindness, 10
For that it made my imprisonment a pleasure:
Ay, such a pleasure as incaged birds
Conceive, when, after many moody thoughts,
At last by notes of household harmony
They quite forget their loss of liberty.—
But, Warwick, after God, thou set'st me free,
And chiefly therefore I thank God, and thee;
He was the author, thou the instrument.
Therefore, that I may conquer fortune's spite,
By living low, where fortune cannot hurt me, 20
And that the people of this blessed land
May not be punish'd with my thwarting stars,
Warwick, although my head still wear the
    crown,
I here resign my government to thee,
For thou art fortunate in all thy deeds.
  War. Your grace hath still been fam'd for
    virtuous,
And now may seem as wise as virtuous,
By spying, and avoiding, fortune's malice;
For few men rightly temper with the stars:
Yet in this one thing let me blame your grace, 30
For choosing me when Clarence is in place.
  Clar. No, Warwick, thou art worthy of the
    sway,
To whom the heavens in thy nativity
Adjudg'd an olive branch, and laurel crown,
As likely to be blest in peace, and war;
And, therefore, I yield thee my free consent.
  War. And I choose Clarence only for pro-
    tector.
  K. Hen. Warwick, and Clarence, give me both your
    hands.
Now join your hands, and with your hands your
    hearts,
That no dissension hinder government: 40
I make you both protectors of this land,
While I myself will lead a private life,
And in devotion spend my latter days,
To sin's rebuke, and my Creator's praise.
  War. What answers Clarence to his sovereign's
    will?
  Clar. That he consents, if Warwick yield consent;
For on thy fortune I repose myself.
  War. Why then, though loath, yet must I be
    content.
We'll yoke together, like a double shadow
To Henry's body, and supply his place; 50
I mean, in bearing weight of government,
While he enjoys the honour, and his ease.
And, Clarence, now then, it is more than needful,
Forthwith that Edward be pronounc'd a traitor,
And all his lands and goods be confiscate.
  Clar. What else? and that succession be determin'd.
  War. Ay, therein Clarence shall not want his
    part.
  K. Hen. But, with the first of all your chief affairs,
Let me entreat (for I command no more),
That Margaret your queen, and my son Edward, 60
Be sent for to return from France with speed;
For, till I see them here, by doubtful fear
My joy of liberty is half eclips'd.
  Clar. It shall be done, my sovereign, with all speed.
  K. Hen. My Lord of Somerset, what youth is that,
Of whom you seem to have so tender care?
  Som. My liege, it is young Henry, Earl of Richmond.
  K. Hen. Come hither, England's hope. [*Lays his
    hand on his head.*] If secret powers
Suggest but truth to my divining thoughts,
This pretty lad will prove our country's bliss. 70
His looks are full of peaceful majesty;
His head by nature fram'd to wear a crown,
His hand to wield a sceptre; and himself
Likely in time to bless a regal throne.
Make much of him, my lords; for this is he,
Must help you more than you are hurt by me,

Enter a Messenger.

  War. What news, my friend?
  Mess. That Edward is escaped from your brother,
And fled, as he hears since, to Burgundy. 79
  War. Unsavoury news! but how made he escape?
  Mess. He was convey'd by Richard Duke of Gloster,

K. Hen. "This pretty lad will prove our country's bliss."

And the Lord Hastings, who attended him
In secret ambush on the forest side,
And from the bishop's huntsmen rescu'd him;
For hunting was his daily exercise.
  War. My brother was too careless of his charge.—
But let us hence, my sovereign, to provide
A salve for any sore that may betide.
         [*Exeunt all but* SOMERSET, RICHMOND,
         and OXFORD.
  Som. My lord, I like not of this flight of Edward's;
For, doubtless, Burgundy will yield him help, 90
And we shall have more wars, before 't be long.
As Henry's late presaging prophecy
Did glad my heart with hope of this young Richmond,
So doth my heart misgive me, in these conflicts
What may befall him, to his harm and ours:
Therefore, Lord Oxford, to prevent the worst,
Forthwith we'll send him hence to Brittany,
Till storms be past of civil enmity.
  Oxf. Ay, for if Edward repossess the crown,
'T is like that Richmond with the rest shall down. 100
  Som. It shall be so; he shall to Brittany.
Come therefore; let's about it speedily. [*Exeunt.*

        SCENE VII.—Before York.

Enter King EDWARD, GLOSTER, HASTINGS, *and
    Forces.*

  K. Edw. Now, brother Richard, Lord Hastings, and
    the rest,
Yet thus far fortune maketh us amends,
And says that once more I shall interchange
My waned state for Henry's regal crown.
Well have we pass'd, and now repass'd the seas,
And brought desired help from Burgundy:
What then remains, we being thus arriv'd
From Ravenspurg haven before the gates of York,
But that we enter, as into our dukedom?
  Glo. The gates made fast!—Brother, I like not this;
For many men, that stumble at the threshold, 11
Are well foretold that danger lurks within.
  K. Edw. Tush, man! abodements must not now
    affright us:

By fair or foul means we must enter in,
For hither will our friends repair to us.
Hast. My liege, I 'll knock once more to summon
them.

*Enter, on the walls, the Mayor of York, and his
Brethren.*

May. My lords, we were forewarned of your coming,
And shut the gates for safety of ourselves ;
For now we owe allegiance unto Henry.
    K. Edw. But, master mayor, if Henry be your king,
Yet Edward, at the least, is Duke of York.   21
    May. True, my good lord ; I know you for no less.
    K. Edw. Why, and I challenge nothing but my
dukedom,
As being well content with that alone.
    Glo. [*Aside.*] But when the fox hath once got in his
nose,
He 'll soon find means to make the body follow.
    Hast. Why, master mayor, why stand you in a
doubt ?
Open the gates : we are King Henry's friends.
    May. Ay, say you so ? the gates shall then be open'd.
                              [*Exeunt from above.*
    Glo. A wise stout captain, and soon persuaded !   30
    Hast. The good old man would fain that all were
well,
So 't were not 'long of him ; but, being enter'd,
I doubt not, I, but we shall soon persuade
Both him and all his brothers unto reason.

Re-enter the Mayor, and two Aldermen, below.

    K. Edw. So, master mayor : these gates must not
be shut,
But in the night, or in the time of war.
What ! fear not, man, but yield me up the keys,
                              [*Takes his keys.*
For Edward will defend the town, and thee,
And all those friends that deign to follow me.

March. Enter MONTGOMERY *and Forces.*

    Glo. Brother, this is Sir John Montgomery,   40
Our trusty friend, unless I be deceiv'd.
    K. Edw. Welcome, Sir John ; but why come you
in arms ?
    Mont. To help King Edward in his time of storm,
As every loyal subject ought to do.
    K. Edw. Thanks, good Montgomery ; but we now
forget
Our title to the crown, and only claim
Our dukedom, till God please to send the rest.
    Mont. Then fare you well, for I will hence again :
I came to serve a king, and not a duke.—
Drummer, strike up, and let us march away.   50
                              [*A march begun.*
    K. Edw. Nay, stay, Sir John, awhile ; and we 'll
debate,
By what safe means the crown may be recover'd.
    Mont. What talk you of debating ? in few words,
If you 'll not here proclaim yourself our king,
I 'll leave you to your fortune, and be gone
To keep them back that come to succour you.
Why shall we fight, if you pretend no title ?
    Glo. Why, brother, wherefore stand you on nice
points ?
    K. Edw. When we grow stronger, then we 'll make
our claim.
Till then, 't is wisdom to conceal our meaning.   60
    Hast. Away with scrupulous wit ! now arms must
rule.
    Glo. And fearless minds climb soonest unto crowns.
Brother, we will proclaim you out of hand :
The bruit thereof will bring you many friends.
    K. Edw. Then be it as you will ; for 't is my right,
And Henry but usurps the diadem.
    Mont. Ay, now my sovereign speaketh like himself,
And now will I be Edward's champion.
    Hast. Sound, trumpet ! Edward shall be here pro-
claim'd.—
Come, fellow-soldier, make thou proclamation.   70
                              [*Gives him a paper. Flourish.*

Sold. [*Reads.*] " Edward the Fourth, by the grace
of God, King of England and France, and Lord of
Ireland, &c."
    Mont. And whoso'er gainsays King Edward's right,
By this I challenge him to single fight.
                              [*Throws down his gauntlet.*
    All. Long live Edward the Fourth !
    K. Edw. Thanks, brave Montgomery, and thanks
unto you all :
If fortune serve me, I 'll requite this kindness.
Now, for this night, let 's harbour here in York,
And when the morning sun shall raise his car   80
Above the border of this horizon,
We 'll forward towards Warwick, and his mates ;
For, well I wot, that Henry is no soldier.—
Ah, froward Clarence ! how evil it beseems thee,
To flatter Henry, and forsake thy brother !
Yet, as we may, we 'll meet both thee and War-
wick.—
Come on, brave soldiers : doubt not of the day ;
And, that once gotten, doubt not of large pay.
                              [*Exeunt.*

SCENE VIII.—London. A Room in the Palace.

Flourish. Enter King HENRY, WARWICK, CLARENCE,
MONTAGUE, EXETER, *and* OXFORD.

    War. What counsel, lords ? Edward from Belgia,
With hasty Germans, and blunt Hollanders,
Hath pass'd in safety through the narrow seas,
And with his troops doth march amain to London ;
And many giddy people flock to him.
    K. Hen. Let 's levy men, and beat him back again.
    Clar. A little fire is quickly trodden out,
Which, being suffer'd, rivers cannot quench.
    War. In Warwickshire I have true-hearted friends,
Not mutinous in peace, yet bold in war ;   10
Those will I muster up :—and thou, son Clarence,
Shalt stir up in Suffolk, Norfolk, and in Kent,
The knights and gentlemen to come with thee :—
Thou, brother Montague, in Buckingham,
Northampton, and in Leicestershire, shalt find
Men well inclin'd to hear what thou command'st :—
And thou, brave Oxford, wondrous well belov'd
In Oxfordshire, shalt muster up thy friends.—
My sovereign, with the loving citizens,
Like to his island girt in with the ocean,   20
Or modest Dian circled with her nymphs,
Shall rest in London, till we come to him.—
Fair lords, take leave, and stand not to reply.—
Farewell, my sovereign.
    K. Hen. Farewell, my Hector, and my Troy's true
hope.
    Clar. In sign of truth, I kiss your highness' hand.
    K. Hen. Well-minded Clarence, be thou fortunate.
    Mont. Comfort, my lord ;—and so I take my leave.
    Oxf. [*Kissing* HENRY'S *hand.*] And thus I seal my
truth, and bid adieu.
    K. Hen. Sweet Oxford, and my loving Montague,   30
And all at once, once more a happy farewell.
    War. Farewell, sweet lords : let 's meet at Coventry.
                              [*Exeunt* WARWICK, CLARENCE, OXFORD
                              and MONTAGUE.
    K. Hen. Here at the palace will I rest awhile.
Cousin of Exeter, what thinks your lordship ?
Methinks, the power, that Edward hath in field,
Should not be able to encounter mine.
    Exe. The doubt is, that he will seduce the rest.
    K. Hen. That 's not my fear ; my meed hath got me
fame.
I have not stopp'd mine ears to their demands,
Nor posted off their suits with slow delays ;   40
My pity hath been balm to heal their wounds,
My mildness hath allay'd their swelling griefs,
My mercy dry'd their water-flowing tears ;
I have not been desirous of their wealth,
Nor much oppress'd them with great subsidies,
Nor forward of revenge, though they much err'd.
Then, why should they love Edward more than me ?
No, Exeter, these graces challenge grace :

And, when the lion fawns upon the lamb,
The lamb will never cease to follow him.   50
　　[*Shout within:* " *A Lancaster! A Lancaster!*"
Exc. Hark, hark, my lord! what shouts are these?

　　Enter King EDWARD, GLOSTER, *and Soldiers.*

K. Edw. Seize on the shame-fac'd Henry! bear him
　　hence,
And once again proclaim us King of England.—
You are the fount that makes small brooks to flow:
Now stops thy spring; my sea shall suck them dry,

And swell so much the higher by their ebb.
Hence with him to the Tower! let him not speak.
　　　　　　　　　　　[*Exeunt some with King* HENRY.
And, lords, towards Coventry bend we our course,
Where peremptory Warwick now remains.
The sun shines hot, and, if we use delay,   60
Cold biting winter mars our hop'd-for hay.
Glo. Away betimes, before his forces join,
And take the great-grown traitor unawares:
Brave warriors, march amain towards Coventry.
　　　　　　　　　　　　　　　　　[*Exeunt.*

ACT V.

SCENE I.—Coventry.

Enter, upon the walls, WARWICK, *the Mayor of Coventry, two Messengers, and others.*

Warwick.
THERE is the post that came from valiant
　　Oxford?
How far hence is thy lord, mine honest
　　fellow?
1 *Mess.* By this at Dunsmore, marching
　　hitherward.
　　War. How far off is our brother Mon-
　　　　tague?—
Where is the post that came from Mon-
　　tague?
2 *Mess.* By this at Daintry, with a puissant troop.

　　Enter Sir JOHN SOMERVILLE.

War. Say, Somerville, what says my loving son?
And, by thy guess, how nigh is Clarence now?
Som. At Southam I did leave him with his forces,
And do expect him here some two hours hence.   10
　　　　　　　　　　　　　　[*Drum heard.*
War. Then Clarence is at hand, I hear his drum.
Som. It is not his, my lord; here Southam lies:
The drum your honour hears marcheth from Warwick.
War. Who should that be? belike, unlook'd-for
　　friends.
Som. They are at hand, and you shall quickly
　　know.

　　March. Flourish. Enter King EDWARD, GLOSTER,
　　　　　and Forces.

K. Edw. Go, trumpet, to the walls, and sound a
　　parle.
Glo. See, how the surly Warwick mans the wall.
War. O unbid spite! is sportful Edward come?
Where slept our scouts, or how are they seduc'd,
That we could hear no news of his repair?   20
K. Edw. Now, Warwick, wilt thou ope the city
　　gates?
Speak gentle words, and humbly bend thy knee,
Call Edward king, and at his hands beg mercy,
And he shall pardon thee these outrages.
War. Nay, rather, wilt thou draw thy forces hence,
Confess who set thee up and pluck'd thee down?
Call Warwick patron, and be penitent,
And thou shalt still remain the Duke of York.
Glo. I thought, at least, he would have said—the
　　king,
Or did he make the jest against his will?   30
War. Is not a dukedom, sir, a goodly gift?
Glo. Ay, by my faith, for a poor earl to give:
I'll do thee service for so good a gift.
War. 'T was I, that gave the kingdom to thy
　　brother.

K. Edw. Why then, 't is mine, if but by Warwick's
　　gift.
War. Thou art no Atlas for so great a weight:
And, weakling, Warwick takes his gift again;
And Henry is my king, Warwick his subject.
K. Edw. But Warwick's king is Edward's prisoner:
And, gallant Warwick, do but answer this: 40
What is the body, when the head is off?
Glo. Alas! that Warwick had no more forecast,
But, whiles he thought to steal the single ten,
The king was slily finger'd from the deck!
You left poor Henry at the bishop's palace,
And, ten to one, you'll meet him in the Tower.
K. Edw. 'T is even so: yet you are Warwick still.
Glo. Come, Warwick, take the time; kneel down,
　　kneel down.
Nay, when? strike now, or else the iron cools.
War. I had rather chop this hand off at a blow,   50
And with the other fling it at thy face,
Than bear so low a sail to strike to thee.
K. Edw. Sail how thou canst, have wind and tide
　　thy friend,
This hand, fast wound about thy coal-black hair,
Shall, whiles thy head is warm, and new cut off,
Write in the dust this sentence with thy blood,—
"Wind-changing Warwick now can change no more."

　　Enter OXFORD, *with drum and colours.*

War. O cheerful colours! see, where Oxford comes.
Oxf. Oxford, Oxford, for Lancaster!
　　　　　　　　[OXFORD *and his Forces enter the city.*
Glo. The gates are open, let us enter too.   60
K. Edw. So other foes may set upon our backs.
Stand we in good array; for they, no doubt,
Will issue out again, and bid us battle:
If not, the city being but of small defence,
We'll quickly rouse the traitors in the same.
War. O! welcome, Oxford, for we want thy help.

　　Enter MONTAGUE, *with drum and colours.*

Mont. Montague, Montague, for Lancaster!
　　　　　　　　[*He and his Forces enter the city.*
Glo. Thou and thy brother both shall buy this
　　treason,
Even with the dearest blood your bodies bear.
K. Edw. The harder match'd, the greater victory:
My mind presageth happy gain, and conquest.   71

　　Enter SOMERSET, *with drum and colours.*

Som. Somerset, Somerset, for Lancaster!
　　　　　　　　[*He and his Forces enter the city.*
Glo. Two of thy name, both Dukes of Somerset,

Have sold their lives unto the house of York ;
And thou shalt be the third, if this sword hold.

Enter CLARENCE, *with drum and colours.*

War. And lo ! where George of Clarence sweeps
 along,
Of force enough to bid his brother battle :
With whom an upright zeal to right prevails,
More than the nature of a brother's love.—
     [GLOSTER *and* CLARENCE *whisper.*
Come, Clarence, come ; thou wilt, if Warwick calls.
Clar. Father of Warwick, know you what this
 means ? [*Taking the red rose out of his hat.*
Look here, I throw my infamy at thee : 82
I will not ruinate my father's house,
Who gave his blood to lime the stones together,
And set up Lancaster. Why, trow'st thou, Warwick,
That Clarence is so harsh, so blunt-unnatural,
To bend the fatal instruments of war
Against his brother, and his lawful king ?
Perhaps, thou wilt object my holy oath : 90
Than Jephtha's, when he sacrific'd his daughter.
I am so sorry for my trespass made,
That to deserve well at my brother's hands,
I here proclaim myself thy mortal foe ;
With resolution, wheresoe'er I meet thee,
(As I will meet thee, if thou stir abroad,)
To plague thee for thy foul misleading me.
And so, proud-hearted Warwick, I defy thee,
And to my brother turn my blushing cheeks.—
Pardon me, Edward, I will make amends : 100
And, Richard, do not frown upon my faults,
For I will henceforth be no more unconstant.
 K. Edw. Now welcome more, and ten times more
 belov'd,
Than if thou never hadst deserv'd our hate.
 Glo. Welcome, good Clarence : this is brother-like.
 War. O passing traitor, perjur'd, and unjust !
 K. Edw. What, Warwick, wilt thou leave the
 town, and fight,
Or shall we beat the stones about thine ears ?
 War. Alas ! I am not coop'd here for defence :
I will away towards Barnet presently, 110
And bid thee battle, Edward, if thou dar'st.
 K. Edw. Yes, Warwick, Edward dares, and leads
 the way.—
Lords, to the field ! Saint George, and victory !
         [*March. Exeunt.*

SCENE II.—A Field of Battle near Barnet.

Alarums and Excursions. Enter King EDWARD,
 bringing in WARWICK *wounded.*

K. Edw. So, lie thou there : die thou, and die our
 fear ;
For Warwick was a bug, that fear'd us all.—
Now, Montague, sit fast : I seek for thee,
That Warwick's bones may keep thine company.
            [*Exit.*
 War. Ah ! who is nigh ? come to me, friend or foe,
And tell me, who is victor, York, or Warwick ?
Why ask I that ? my mangled body shows,
My blood, my want of strength, my sick heart shows,
That I must yield my body to the earth,
And, by my fall, the conquest to my foe. 10
Thus yields the cedar to the axe's edge,
Whose arms gave shelter to the princely eagle,
Under whose shade the ramping lion slept ;
Whose top-branch overpeer'd Jove's spreading tree,
And kept low shrubs from winter's powerful wind.
These eyes, that now are dimm'd with death's black
 veil,
Have been as piercing as the mid-day sun,
To search the secret treasons of the world :
The wrinkles in my brows, now fill'd with blood,
Were liken'd oft to kingly sepulchres ; 20
For who liv'd king, but I could dig his grave ?
And who durst smile when Warwick bent his brow ?
Lo, now my glory smear'd in dust and blood !
My parks, my walks, my manors that I had,

Even now forsake me ; and, of all my lands,
Is nothing left me, but my body's length.
Why, what is pomp, rule, reign, but earth and dust ?
And, live we how we can, yet die we must.

Enter OXFORD *and* SOMERSET.

Som. Ah, Warwick, Warwick ! wert thou as we
 are,
We might recover all our loss again. 30
The queen from France hath brought a puissant
 power ;
Even now we heard the news. Ah, couldst thou fly !
 War. Why, then I would not fly.—Ah, Montague !
If thou be there, sweet brother, take my hand,
And with thy lips keep in my soul awhile.
Thou lov'st me not ; for, brother, if thou didst,
Thy tears would wash this cold congealed blood,
That glues my lips, and will not let me speak.
Come quickly, Montague, or I am dead.
 Som. Ah, Warwick ! Montague hath breath'd his
 last ; 40
And to the latest gasp cried out for Warwick,
And said—"Commend me to my valiant brother."
And more he would have said ; and more he spoke,
Which sounded like a cannon in a vault,
That mought not be distinguish'd : but, at last,
I well might hear, deliver'd with a groan,—
"O, farewell, Warwick !"
 War. Sweet rest his soul !—Fly, lords, and save
 yourselves ;
For Warwick bids you all farewell, to meet in heaven.
             [*Dies.*
 Oxf. Away, away, to meet the queen's great power !
   [*Exeunt, bearing off* WARWICK'S *body.*

SCENE III.—Another Part of the Field.

Flourish. Enter King EDWARD *in triumph ; with*
 CLARENCE, GLOSTER, *and the rest.*

K. Edw. Thus far our fortune keeps an upward
 course,
And we are grac'd with wreaths of victory.
But, in the midst of this bright-shining day,
I spy a black, suspicious, threat'ning cloud,
That will encounter with our glorious sun,
Ere he attain his easeful western bed :
I mean, my lords, those powers, that the queen
Hath rais'd in Gallia, have arriv'd our coast,
And, as we hear, march on to fight with us.
 Clar. A little gale will soon disperse that cloud, 10
And blow it to the source from whence it came :
Thy very beams will dry those vapours up,
For every cloud engenders not a storm.
 Glo. The queen is valu'd thirty thousand strong,
And Somerset, with Oxford, fled to her ;
If she have time to breathe, be well assur'd,
Her faction will be full as strong as ours.
 K. Edw. We are advertis'd by our loving friends,
That they do hold their course toward Tewksbury.
We, having now the best at Barnet field, 20
Will thither straight, for willingness rids way ;
And, as we march, our strength will be augmented
In every county as we go along.—
Strike up the drum ! cry—Courage ! and away.
         [*Flourish. Exeunt.*

SCENE IV.—Plains near Tewksbury.

March. Enter Queen MARGARET, *Prince* EDWARD,
 SOMERSET, OXFORD, *and Soldiers.*

Q. Mar. Great lords, wise men ne'er sit and wail
 their loss,
But cheerly seek how to redress their harms.
What though the mast be now blown overboard,
The cable broke, the holding-anchor lost,
And half our sailors swallow'd in the flood ;
Yet lives our pilot still : is't meet that he
Should leave the helm, and, like a fearful lad,
With tearful eyes add water to the sea,

And give more strength to that which hath too much;
Whiles in his moan the ship splits on the rock,   10
Which industry and courage might have sav'd?
Ah, what a shame! ah, what a fault were this!
Say, Warwick was our anchor; what of that?
And Montague our topmast; what of him?
Our slaughter'd friends the tackles; what of these?
Why, is not Oxford here another anchor,
And Somerset another goodly mast?
The friends of France our shrouds and tacklings?
And, though unskilful, why not Ned and I
For once allow'd the skilful pilot's charge?   20
We will not from the helm, to sit and weep,
But keep our course, though the rough wind say no,
From shelves and rocks that threaten us with wrack.
As good to chide the waves, as speak them fair.
And what is Edward but a ruthless sea?
What Clarence but a quicksand of deceit?
And Richard but a ragged fatal rock?
All these the enemies to our poor bark.
Say, you can swim; alas! 'tis but a while:
Tread on the sand; why, there you quickly sink: 30
Bestride the rock; the tide will wash you off,
Or else you famish; that's a threefold death.
This speak I, lords, to let you understand,
In case some one of you would fly from us,
That there's no hop'd-for mercy with the brothers,
More than with ruthless waves, with sands, and rocks.
Why, courage, then! what cannot be avoided,
'T were childish weakness to lament, or fear.
  Prince. Methinks, a woman of this valiant spirit
Should, if a coward heard her speak these words,   40
Infuse his breast with magnanimity,
And make him, naked, foil a man at arms.
I speak not this as doubting any here;
For, did I but suspect a fearful man,
He should have leave to go away betimes,
Lest, in our need, he might infect another,
And make him of like spirit to himself.
If any such be here,—as God forbid!—
Let him depart before we need his help.
  Oxf. Women and children of so high a courage,   50
And warriors faint! why, 't were perpetual shame.—
O brave young prince! thy famous grandfather
Doth live again in thee: long may'st thou live,
To bear his image, and renew his glories!
  Som. And he, that will not fight for such a hope
Go home to bed, and, like the owl by day,
If he arise, be mock'd and wonder'd at.
  Q. Mar. Thanks, gentle Somerset:—sweet Oxford,
    thanks.
  Prince. And take his thanks, that yet hath nothing
    else.

     Enter a Messenger.

  Mess. Prepare you, lords, for Edward is at hand,   60
Ready to fight: therefore, be resolute.
  Oxf. I thought no less: it is his policy
To haste thus fast, to find us unprovided.
  Som. But he's deceiv'd: we are in readiness.
  Q. Mar. This cheers my heart to see your for-
    wardness.
  Oxf. Here pitch our battle; hence we will not budge.

    Flourish and march. Enter King EDWARD,
      CLARENCE, GLOSTER, *and Forces.*

  K. Edw. Brave followers, yonder stands the thorny
    wood,
Which, by the heavens' assistance and your strength,
Must by the roots be hewn up yet ere night.
I need not add more fuel to your fire,   70
For, well I wot, ye blaze to burn them out.
Give signal to the fight, and to it, lords!
  Q. Mar. Lords, knights, and gentlemen, what I
    should say,
My tears gainsay; for every word I speak,
Ye see, I drink the water of mine eyes.
Therefore, no more but this:—Henry, your sovereign,
Is prisoner to the foe; his state usurp'd,
His realm a slaughter-house, his subjects slain,
His statutes cancell'd, and his treasure spent;

And yonder is the wolf that makes this spoil.   80
You fight in justice: then, in God's name, lords,
Be valiant, and give signal to the fight.
                [*Exeunt both Armies.*

    SCENE V.—*Another Part of the Same.*

  Alarums: Excursions: and afterwards a Retreat.
   Then enter King EDWARD, CLARENCE, GLOSTER,
   and Forces; with Queen MARGARET, OXFORD,
   and SOMERSET, *prisoners.*

  K. Edw. Now, here a period of tumultuous broils.
Away with Oxford to Ham's Castle straight:
For Somerset, off with his guilty head.
Go, bear them hence: I will not hear them speak.
  Oxf. For my part, I'll not trouble thee with words.
  Som. Nor I; but stoop with patience to my fortune.
       [*Exeunt* OXFORD *and* SOMERSET, *guarded.*
  Q. Mar. So part we sadly in this troublous world,
To meet with joy in sweet Jerusalem.
  K. Edw. Is proclamation made, that who finds
    Edward
Shall have a high reward, and he his life?   10
  Glo. It is: and lo, where youthful Edward comes!

   Enter Soldiers, with Prince EDWARD.

  K. Edw. Bring forth the gallant: let us hear him
    speak.
What! can so young a thorn begin to prick?
Edward, what satisfaction canst thou make,
For bearing arms, for stirring up my subjects,
And all the trouble thou hast turn'd me to?
  Prince. Speak like a subject, proud ambitious York.
Suppose, that I am now my father's mouth:
Resign thy chair, and where I stand kneel thou,
Whilst I propose the selfsame words to thee,   20
Which, traitor, thou wouldst have me answer to.
  Q. Mar. Ah, that thy father had been so resolv'd!
  Glo. That you might still have worn the petticoat,
And ne'er have stol'n the breech from Lancaster.
  Prince. Let Æsop fable in a winter's night;
His currish riddles sort not with this place.
  Glo. By Heaven, brat, I'll plague you for that word.
  Q. Mar. Ay, thou wast born to be a plague to men.
  Glo. For God's sake, take away this captive scold.
  Prince. Nay, take away this scolding crook-back,
    rather.   30
  K. Edw. Peace, wilful boy, or I will charm your
    tongue.
  Clar. Untutor'd lad, thou art too malapert.
  Prince. I know my duty: you are all undutiful.
Lascivious Edward,—and thou perjur'd George,—
And thou misshapen Dick,—I tell ye all,
I am your better, traitors as ye are;
And thou usurp'st my father's right and mine.
  K. Edw. Take that, the likeness of this railer here.
                [*Stabs him.*
  Glo. Sprawl'st thou? take that, to end thy agony.
                [*Stabs him.*
  Clar. And there's for twitting me with perjury.   40
                [*Stabs him.*
  Q. Mar. O, kill me too!
  Glo. Marry, and shall.   [*Offers to kill her.*
  K. Edw. Hold, Richard, hold! for we have done
    too much.
  Glo. Why should she live, to fill the world with
    words?
  K. Edw. What! doth she swoon? use means for
    her recovery.
  Glo. Clarence, excuse me to the king, my brother.
I'll hence to London on a serious matter:
Ere ye come there, be sure to hear some news.
  Clar. What? what?
  Glo. The Tower! the Tower!   [*Exit.*
  Q. Mar. O Ned! sweet Ned! speak to thy mother,
    boy!   51
Canst thou not speak?—O traitors! murderers!
They that stabb'd Cæsar shed no blood at all,
Did not offend, nor were not worthy blame,
If this foul deed were by to equal it:
He was a man; this, in respect, a child;

And men ne'er spend their fury on a child.
What's worse than murderer, that I may name it?
No, no; my heart will burst, an if I speak;
And I will speak, that so my heart may burst.— 60
Butchers and villains! bloody cannibals!
How sweet a plant have you untimely cropp'd

Q. Mar. "O. kill me too!"

You have no children, butchers! if you had,
The thought of them would have stirr'd up remorse:
But, if you ever chance to have a child,
Look in his youth to have him so cut off,
As, deathsmen, you have rid this sweet young prince!
  K. Edw. Away with her! go, bear her hence perforce.
  Q. Mar. Nay, never bear me hence, despatch me here:
Here sheathe thy sword, I'll pardon thee my death. 70
What! wilt thou not?—then, Clarence, do it thou.
  Clar. By Heaven, I will not do thee so much case.
  Q. Mar. Good Clarence, do; sweet Clarence, do thou do it.
  Clar. Didst thou not hear me swear I would not do it?
  Q. Mar. Ay, but thou usest to forswear thyself:
'T was sin before, but now 't is charity.
What! wilt thou not? Where is that devil's butcher,
Hard-favour'd Richard? Richard, where art thou?
Thou art not here: murder is thy alms-deed;
Petitioners for blood thou ne'er putt'st back. 80
  K. Edw. Away, I say! I charge ye, bear her hence.
  Q. Mar. So come to you, and yours, as to this prince!   [*Exit.*
  K. Edw. Where's Richard gone?
  Clar. To London, all in post; and, as I guess,
To make a bloody supper in the Tower.
  K. Edw. He's sudden, if a thing comes in his head.
Now march we hence: discharge the common sort
With pay and thanks, and let's away to London,
And see our gentle queen how well she fares:
By this, I hope, she hath a son for me. 90
                     [*Exeunt.*

SCENE VI.—London. A Room in the Tower.

King HENRY *is discovered sitting with a book in his hand, the Lieutenant attending. Enter* GLOSTER.

  Glo. Good day, my lord. What! at your book so hard?
  K. Hen. Ay, my good lord: my lord, I should say rather:

'T is sin to flatter; good was little better:
Good Gloster, and good devil, were alike,
And both preposterous; therefore, not good lord.
  Glo. Sirrah, leave us to ourselves: we must confer.
              [*Exit Lieutenant.*
  K. Hen. So flies the reckless shepherd from the wolf:
So first the harmless sheep doth yield his fleece,
And next his throat unto the butcher's knife.—
What scene of death hath Roscius now to act? 10
  Glo. Suspicion always haunts the guilty mind:
The thief doth fear each bush an officer.
  K. Hen. The bird, that hath been limed in a bush,
With trembling wings misdoubteth every bush;
And I, the hapless male to one sweet bird,
Have now the fatal object in my eye,
Where my poor young was lim'd, was caught, and kill'd.
  Glo. Why, what a peevish fool was that of Crete,
That taught his son the office of a fowl?
And yet, for all his wings, the fool was drown'd. 20
  K. Hen. I, Dædalus; my poor boy, Icarus;
Thy father, Minos, that denied our course;
The sun, that sear'd the wings of my sweet boy,
Thy brother Edward; and thyself, the sea,
Whose envious gulf did swallow up his life.
Ah! kill me with thy weapon, not with words.
My breast can better brook thy dagger's point,
Than can my ears that tragic history.
But wherefore dost thou come? is 't for my life?
  Glo. Think'st thou I am an executioner? 30
  K. Hen. A persecutor, I am sure, thou art:
If murdering innocents be executing,
Why, then thou art an executioner.
  Glo. Thy son I kill'd for his presumption.
  K. Hen. Hadst thou been kill'd, when first thou didst presume,
Thou hadst not liv'd to kill a son of mine.
And thus I prophesy,—that many a thousand,
Which now mistrust no parcel of my fear;
And many an old man's sigh, and many a widow's,
And many an orphan's water-standing eye,— 40
Men for their sons', wives for their husbands',
Orphans for their parents' timeless death,—
Shall rue the hour that ever thou wast born.
The owl shriek'd at thy birth, an evil sign;
The night-crow cried, aboding luckless time;
Dogs howl'd, and hideous tempest shook down trees;
The raven rook'd her on the chimney's top,
And chattering pies in dismal discords sung.
Thy mother felt more than a mother's pain,
And yet brought forth less than a mother's hope; 50
To wit,—an indigested and deformed lump,
Not like the fruit of such a goodly tree.
Teeth hadst thou in thy head, when thou wast born,
To signify, thou cam'st to bite the world;
And, if the rest be true which I have heard,
Thou cam'st—
  Glo. I'll hear no more;—die, prophet, in thy speech: [*Stabs him.*
For this, amongst the rest, was I ordain'd.
  K. Hen. Ay, and for much more slaughter after this.
O! God forgive my sins, and pardon thee.   [*Dies.*
  Glo. What! will the aspiring blood of Lancaster 61
Sink in the ground? I thought it would have mounted.

See, how my sword weeps for the poor king's death!
O, may such purple tears be always shed
From those that wish the downfall of our house!—
If any spark of life be yet remaining,
Down, down to hell; and say I sent thee thither:

               [Stabs him again.

Then, since the heavens have shap'd my body so,
Let hell make crook'd my mind to answer it.
I have no brother, I am like no brother;   89
And this word love, which greybeards call divine,
Be resident in men like one another,
And not in me: I am myself alone.—
Clarence, beware: thou keep'st me from the light;

Glo. "See, how my sword weeps for the poor king's death!"

I, that have neither pity, love nor fear.
Indeed, 't is true, that Henry told me of;
For I have often heard my mother say,   70
I came into the world with my legs forward.
Had I not reason, think ye, to make haste,
And seek their ruin that usurp'd our right?
The midwife wonder'd; and the women cried,
"O, Jesus bless us, he is born with teeth!"
And so I was; which plainly signified
That I should snarl, and bite, and play the dog.

But I will sort a pitchy day for thee:
For I will buz abroad such prophecies,
That Edward shall be fearful of his life;
And then, to purge his fear, I'll be thy death.
King Henry, and the prince his son, are gone:
Clarence, thy turn is next, and then the rest;   90
Counting myself but bad, till I be best.—
I'll throw thy body in another room,
And triumph, Henry, in thy day of doom.

             [Exit, with the body.

SCENE VII.— The Same. A Room in the Palace.

King EDWARD *is discovered sitting on his throne;*
Queen ELIZABETH *with the infant Prince,* CLAR-
ENCE, GLOSTER, HASTINGS, *and others, near*
him.

K. Edw. Once more we sit in England's royal
    throne,
Re-purchas'd with the blood of enemies.
What valiant foemen, like to autumn's corn,
Have we mow'd down, in tops of all their pride!
Three Dukes of Somerset, threefold renown'd
For hardy and undoubted champions;
Two Cliffords, as the father and the son;
And two Northumberlands: two braver men
Ne'er spurr'd their coursers at the trumpet's sound;
With them, the two brave bears, Warwick and
    Montague,   10
That in their chains fetter'd the kingly lion,
And made the forest tremble when they roar'd.
Thus have we swept suspicion from our seat,
And made our footstool of security.—
Come hither, Bess, and let me kiss my boy.—
Young Ned, for thee, thine uncles, and myself,
Have in our armours watch'd the winter's night
Went all a-foot in summer's scalding heat,
That thou might'st repossess the crown in peace;
And of our labours thou shalt reap the gain.   20
    Glo. [*Aside.*] I 'll blast his harvest, if your head
        were laid;

For yet I am not look'd on in the world.
This shoulder was ordain'd so thick, to heave;
And heave it shall some weight, or break my back. —
Work thou the way,—and thou shalt execute.
    K. Edw. Clarence, and Gloster, love my lovely
        queen,
And kiss your princely nephew, brothers both.
    Clar. The duty, that I owe unto your majesty,
I seal upon the lips of this sweet babe.
    Q. Eliz. Thanks, noble Clarence; worthy brother,
        thanks.   30
    Glo. And, that I love the tree from whence thou
        sprang'st,
Witness the loving kiss I give the fruit.—
[*Aside.*] To say the truth, so Judas kiss'd his master,
And cried—All hail! when as he meant—all harm.
    K. Edw. Now am I seated as my soul delights,
Having my country's peace, and brothers' loves.
    Clar. What will your grace have done with Mar-
        garet?
Reignier, her father, to the King of France
Hath pawn'd the Sicils and Jerusalem,
And hither have they sent it for her ransom.   40
    K. Edw. Away with her, and waft her hence to
        France.—
And now what rests, but that we spend the time
With stately triumphs, mirthful comic shows,
Such as befits the pleasure of the court?
Sound, drums and trumpets!—farewell, sour annoy!
For here, I hope, begins our lasting joy.   [*Exeunt.*

KING RICHARD III.

DRAMATIS PERSONÆ.

KING EDWARD THE FOURTH.
EDWARD, *Prince of Wales,* } *Sons to the King.*
RICHARD, *Duke of York,* }
GEORGE, *Duke of Clarence,* } *Brothers to the King.*
RICHARD, *Duke of Gloster,* }
A young Son of Clarence.
HENRY, *Earl of Richmond.*
CARDINAL BOURCHIER, *Archbishop of Canterbury.*
THOMAS ROTHERHAM, *Archbishop of York.*
JOHN MORTON, *Bishop of Ely.*
DUKE OF BUCKINGHAM.
DUKE OF NORFOLK.
EARL OF SURREY, *his Son.*
EARL RIVERS, *Brother to King Edward's Queen.*
MARQUESS OF DORSET, *and* LORD GREY, *her Sons.*
EARL OF OXFORD.
LORD HASTINGS.
LORD STANLEY.
LORD LOVEL.
SIR THOMAS VAUGHAN.

SIR RICHARD RATCLIFF.
SIR WILLIAM CATESBY.
SIR JAMES TYRREL.
SIR JAMES BLOUNT.
SIR WALTER HERBERT.
SIR ROBERT BRAKENBURY, *Lieutenant of the Tower.*
CHRISTOPHER URSWICK, *a Priest. Another Priest.*
Lord Mayor of London. Sheriff of Wiltshire.

ELIZABETH, *Queen of King Edward IV.*
MARGARET, *Widow of King Henry VI.*
DUCHESS OF YORK, *Mother to King Edward IV., Clarence, and Gloster.*
LADY ANNE, *Widow of Edward Prince of Wales.*
A young Daughter of Clarence.

Lords, and other Attendants; two Gentlemen, a Pursuivant, Scrivener, Citizens, Murderers, Messengers, Ghosts, Soldiers, &c.

SCENE—ENGLAND.

ACT I.

SCENE I.—London. A Street.

Enter GLOSTER.

Gloster.

NOW is the winter of our discontent
Made glorious summer by this sun of York;
And all the clouds that lour'd upon our house
In the deep bosom of the ocean buried.
Now are our brows bound with victorious wreaths;
Our bruised arms hung up for monuments;
Our stern alarums chang'd to merry meetings,
Our dreadful marches to delightful measures.
Grim-visag'd war hath smooth'd his wrinkled front;   10
And now, instead of mounting barbed steeds,
To fright the souls of fearful adversaries,
He capers nimbly in a lady's chamber,
To the lascivious pleasing of a lute.
But I, that am not shap'd for sportive tricks,
Nor made to court an amorous looking-glass;
I, that am rudely stamp'd, and want love's majesty,
To strut before a wanton ambling nymph;
I, that am curtail'd of this fair proportion,
Cheated of feature by dissembling Nature,
Deform'd, unfinish'd, sent before my time   20
Into this breathing world, scarce half made up,
And that so lamely and unfashionable,
That dogs bark at me as I halt by them ;—

Why I, in this weak piping time of peace,
Have no delight to pass away the time,
Unless to see my shadow in the sun,
And descant on mine own deformity:
And therefore, since I cannot prove a lover,
To entertain these fair well-spoken days,
I am determined to prove a villain,   30
And hate the idle pleasures of these days.
Plots have I laid, inductions dangerous,
By drunken prophecies, libels, and dreams,
To set my brother Clarence and the king
In deadly hate the one against the other:
And if King Edward be as true and just,
As I am subtle, false, and treacherous,
This day should Clarence closely be mew'd up,
About a prophecy, which says—that G
Of Edward's heirs the murderer shall be.   40
Dive, thoughts, down to my soul: here Clarence comes.

Enter CLARENCE, *guarded, and* BRAKENBURY.

Brother, good day. What means this armed guard,
That waits upon your grace?
Clar.   His majesty,
Tendering my person's safety, hath appointed
This conduct to convey me to the Tower.
Glo. Upon what cause?
Clar.   Because my name is George.
Glo. Alack! my lord, that fault is none of yours;
He should, for that, commit your godfathers.

O ! belike, his majesty hath some intent,
That you should be new-christen'd in the Tower. 50
But what's the matter, Clarence ? may I know ?
  Clar. Yea, Richard, when I know ; but I protest,
As yet I do not : but, as I can learn,
He hearkens after prophecies and dreams ;
And from the cross-row plucks the letter G,
And says, a wizard told him, that by G
His issue disinherited should be ;
And, for my name of George begins with G,
It follows in his thought that I am he.
These, as I learn, and such like toys as these, 60
Have mov'd his highness to commit me now.
  Glo. Why, this it is, when men are rul'd by women !
'T is not the king, that sends you to the Tower :
My Lady Grey, his wife, Clarence, 't is she
That tempers him to this extremity.
Was it not she, and that good man of worship,
Antony Woodville, her brother there,
That made him send Lord Hastings to the Tower,
From whence this present day he is deliver'd ?
We are not safe, Clarence ; we are not safe. 70
  Clar. By Heaven, I think, there is no man secure
But the queen's kindred, and night-walking heralds
That trudge betwixt the king and Mistress Shore.
Heard you not, what an humble suppliant
Lord Hastings was to her for his delivery ?
  Glo. Humbly complaining to her deity
Got my lord chamberlain his liberty.
I 'll tell you what ; I think, it is our way,
If we will keep in favour with the king,
To be her men, and wear her livery : 80
The jealous o'erworn widow, and herself,
Since that our brother dubb'd them gentlewomen,
Are mighty gossips in our monarchy.
  Brak. I beseech your graces both to pardon me :
His majesty hath straitly given in charge,
That no man shall have private conference,
Of what degree soever, with his brother.
  Glo. Even so ; an 't please your worship, Braken-
       bury,
You may partake of anything we say.
We speak no treason, man : we say, the king 90
Is wise and virtuous, and his noble queen
Well struck in years, fair, and not jealous :—
We say that Shore's wife hath a pretty foot,
A cherry lip, a bonny eye, a passing pleasing tongue ;
And that the queen's kindred are made gentlefolks.
How say you, sir ? can you deny all this ?
  Brak. With this, my lord, myself have nought to do.
  Glo. Naught to do with Mistress Shore ? I tell thee,
       fellow,
He that doth naught with her, excepting one,
Were best to do it secretly, alone. 100
  Brak. What one, my lord ?
  Glo. Her husband, knave. Wouldst thou betray me ?
  Brak. I beseech your grace to pardon me ; and
       withal,
Forbear your conference with the noble duke.
  Clar. We know thy charge, Brakenbury, and will
       obey.
  Glo. We are the queen's abjects, and must obey. —
Brother, farewell : I will unto the king ;
And whatsoe'er you will employ me in,
Were it to call King Edward's widow sister,
I will perform it to enfranchise you. 110
Meantime, this deep disgrace in brotherhood
Touches me deeper than you can imagine.
  Clar. I know, it pleaseth neither of us well.
  Glo. Well, your imprisonment shall not be long ;
I will deliver you, or else lie for you :
Meantime, have patience.
  Clar.   I must perforce : farewell.
    [*Exeunt* CLARENCE, BRAKENBURY, *and Guard.*
  Glo. Go, tread the path that thou shalt ne'er return,
Simple, plain Clarence !—I do love thee so,
That I will shortly send thy soul to heaven,
If Heaven will take the present at our hands. 120
But who comes here ? the new-deliver'd Hastings ?

Enter HASTINGS.

  Hast. Good time of day unto my gracious lord.

  Glo. As much unto my good lord chamberlain.
Well are you welcome to this open air.
How hath your lordship brook'd imprisonment ?
  Hast. With patience, noble lord, as prisoners must ;
But I shall live, my lord, to give them thanks,
That were the cause of my imprisonment.
  Glo. No doubt, no doubt, and so shall Clarence too ;
For they that were your enemies are his, 130
And have prevail'd as much on him as you.
  Hast. More pity that the eagle should be mew'd,
While kites and buzzards prey at liberty.
  Glo. What news abroad ?
  Hast. No news so bad abroad as this at home :—
The king is sickly, weak, and melancholy,
And his physicians fear him mightily.
  Glo. Now, by Saint Paul, that news is bad indeed.
O ! he hath kept an evil diet long,
And overmuch consum'd his royal person : 140
'T is very grievous to be thought upon.
What, is he in his bed ?
  Hast. He is.
  Glo. Go you before, and I will follow you.
                  [*Exit* HASTINGS.
He cannot live, I hope ; and must not die,
Till George be pack'd with posthorse up to heaven.
I 'll in, to urge his hatred more to Clarence,
With lies well steel'd with weighty arguments ;
And, if I fail not in my deep intent,
Clarence hath not another day to live : 150
Which done, God take King Edward to his mercy,
And leave the world for me to bustle in :
For then I 'll marry Warwick's youngest daughter :
What though I kill'd her husband, and her father ?
The readiest way to make the wench amends,
Is to become her husband and her father :
The which will I ; not all so much for love
As for another secret close intent,
By marrying her which I must reach unto.
But yet I run before my horse to market : 160
Clarence still breathes ; Edward still lives and reigns ;
When they are gone, then must I count my gains.
                      [*Exit.*

SCENE II.—The Same. Another Street.

Enter the corse of King HENRY *the Sixth, borne in
an open coffin, Gentlemen bearing halberds, to
guard it ; and Lady* ANNE *as mourner.*

  Anne. Set down, set down your honourable load—
If honour may be shrouded in a hearse—
Whilst I awhile obsequiously lament
The untimely fall of virtuous Lancaster.—
Poor key-cold figure of a holy king !
Pale ashes of the house of Lancaster !
Thou bloodless remnant of that royal blood !
Be it lawful that I invocate thy ghost,
To hear the lamentations of poor Anne,
Wife to thy Edward, to thy slaughter'd son, 10
Stabb'd by the selfsame hand that made these wounds !
Lo, in these windows, that let forth thy life,
I pour the helpless balm of my poor eyes :—
O, cursed be the hand that made these holes !
Cursed the heart that had the heart to do it !
Cursed the blood that let this blood from hence !
More direful hap betide that hated wretch,
That makes us wretched by the death of thee,
Than I can wish to adders, spiders, toads,
Or any creeping venom'd thing that lives ! 20
If ever he have child, abortive be it,
Prodigious, and untimely brought to light,
Whose ugly and unnatural aspect
May fright the hopeful mother at the view ;
And that be heir to his unhappiness !
If ever he have wife, let her be made
More miserable by the death of him,
Than I am made by my young lord, and thee !—
Come, now towards Chertsey with your holy load,
Taken from Paul's to be interred there ; 30
And still, as you are weary of this weight,
Rest you, whiles I lament King Henry's corse.
       [*The Bearers take up the corse and advance.*

Enter GLOSTER.

Glo. Stay you, that bear the corse, and set it down.

Anne. What black magician conjures up this fiend,
To stop devoted charitable deeds?

Glo. Villains! set down the corse; or, by Saint Paul,
I'll make a corse of him that disobeys.

1 Gent. My lord, stand back, and let the coffin pass.

Glo. Unmanner'd dog! stand thou when I command:
Advance thy halberd higher than my breast,   40
Or, by Saint Paul, I'll strike thee to my foot,
And spurn upon thee, beggar, for thy boldness.

[*The Bearers set down the coffin.*

Anne. What! do you tremble? are you all afraid?
Alas! I blame you not; for you are mortal,
And mortal eyes cannot endure the devil.—
Avaunt, thou dreadful minister of hell!
Thou hadst but power over his mortal body,
His soul thou canst not have: therefore, be gone.

Glo. Sweet saint, for charity, be not so curst.

Anne. Foul devil, for God's sake, hence, and trouble
us not;   50
For thou hast made the happy earth thy hell,
Fill'd it with cursing cries, and deep exclaims.
If thou delight to view thy heinous deeds,
Behold this pattern of thy butcheries.—
O, gentlemen! see, see! dead Henry's wounds
Open their congeal'd mouths and bleed afresh!—
Blush, blush, thou lump of foul deformity,
For 't is thy presence that exhales this blood
From cold and empty veins, where no blood dwells:
Thy deed, inhuman and unnatural,   60
Provokes this deluge most unnatural.—
O God, which this blood mad'st, revenge his death!
O earth, which this blood drink'st, revenge his death!
Either, heaven, with lightning strike the murderer
dead,
Or, earth, gape open wide, and eat him quick,
As thou dost swallow up this good king's blood,
Which his hell-govern'd arm hath butchered!

Glo. Lady, you know no rules of charity,
Which renders good for bad, blessings for curses.

Anne. Villain, thou know'st no law of God nor
man: 70
No beast so fierce but knows some touch of pity.

Glo. But I know none, and therefore am no beast.

Anne. O wonderful, when devils tell the truth!

Glo. More wonderful, when angels are so angry.—
Vouchsafe, divine perfection of a woman,
Of these supposed evils, to give me leave,
By circumstance, but to acquit myself.

Anne. Vouchsafe, diffus'd infection of a man,
For these known evils but to give me leave,
By circumstance, to curse thy cursed self.   80

Glo. Fairer than tongue can name thee, let me have
Some patient leisure to excuse myself.

Anne. Fouler than heart can think thee, thou canst
make
No excuse current, but to hang thyself.

Glo. By such despair, I should accuse myself.

Anne. And by despairing shalt thou stand excus'd;
For doing worthy vengeance on thyself,
That didst unworthy slaughter upon others.

Glo. Say, that I slew them not.

Anne.   Then say they were not slain:
But dead they are, and, devilish slave, by thee.   90

Glo. I did not kill your husband.

Anne.   Why, then he is alive.

Glo. Nay, he is dead; and slain by Edward's hand.

Anne. In thy foul throat thou liest: Queen Margaret
saw
Thy murderous falchion smoking in his blood;
The which thou once didst bend against her breast,
But that thy brothers beat aside the point.

Glo. I was provoked by her sland'rous tongue,
That laid their guilt upon my guiltless shoulders.

Anne. Thou wast provoked by thy bloody mind,
That never dreamt on aught but butcheries.
Didst thou not kill this king?

Glo.   I grant ye.

Anne. Dost grant me, hedgehog? then, God grant
me too,

Thou may'st be damned for that wicked deed!
O! he was gentle, mild, and virtuous.

Glo. The better for the King of heaven that hath
him.

Anne. He is in heaven, where thou shalt never
come.

Glo. Let him thank me, that holp to send him
thither;
For he was fitter for that place than earth.

Anne. And thou unfit for any place but hell.

Glo. Yes, one place else, if you will hear me name it.

Anne. Some dungeon.

Glo.   Your bed-chamber.   111

Anne. Ill rest betide the chamber where thou liest!

Glo. So will it, madam, till I lie with you.

Anne. I hope so.

Glo.   I know so.—But, gentle Lady Anne,—
To leave this keen encounter of our wits,
And fall somewhat into a slower method,
Is not the causer of the timeless deaths
Of these Plantagenets, Henry and Edward,
As blameful as the executioner?

Anne. Thou wast the cause, and most accurs'd
effect.   120

Glo. Your beauty was the cause of that effect;
Your beauty, that did haunt me in my sleep,
To undertake the death of all the world,
So I might live one hour in your sweet bosom.

Anne. If I thought that, I tell thee, homicide,
These nails should rend that beauty from my cheeks.

Glo. These eyes could not endure that beauty's
wrack;
You should not blemish it, if I stood by:
As all the world is cheered by the sun,
So I by that; it is my day, my life.   130

Anne. Black night o'ershade thy day, and death thy
life!

Glo. Curse not thyself, fair creature; thou art both.

Anne. I would I were, to be reveng'd on thee.

Glo. It is a quarrel most unnatural,
To be reveng'd on him that loveth thee.

Anne. It is a quarrel just and reasonable,
To be reveng'd on him that kill'd my husband.

Glo. He that bereft thee, lady, of thy husband,
Did it to help thee to a better husband.   139

Anne. His better doth not breathe upon the earth.

Glo. He lives that loves you better than he could.

Anne. Name him.

Glo.   Plantagenet.

Anne.   Why, that was he.

Glo. The selfsame name, but one of better nature.

Anne. Where is he?

Glo.   Here. [*She spitteth at him.*]
Why dost thou spit at me?

Anne. 'Would it were mortal poison, for thy sake!

Glo. Never came poison from so sweet a place.

Anne. Never hung poison on a fouler toad.
Out of my sight! thou dost infect mine eyes.

Glo. Thine eyes, sweet lady, have infected mine.

Anne. 'Would they were basilisks, to strike thee
dead!   150

Glo. I would they were, that I might die at once;
For now they kill me with a living death.
Those eyes of thine from mine have drawn salt tears,
Sham'd their aspects with store of childish drops:
These eyes, which never shed remorseful tear;
No, when my father York and Edward wept
To hear the piteous moan that Rutland made,
When black-fac'd Clifford shook his sword at him;
Nor when thy warlike father, like a child,
Told the sad story of my father's death,   160
And twenty times made pause to sob and weep,
That all the standers-by had wet their cheeks,
Like trees bedash'd with rain: in that sad time
My manly eyes did scorn an humble tear;
And what these sorrows could not thence exhale,
Thy beauty hath, and made them blind with weeping.
I never sued to friend, nor enemy;
My tongue could never learn sweet smoothing word;
But now thy beauty is propos'd my fee,
My proud heart sues, and prompts my tongue to speak.

[*She looks scornfully at him.*

Teach not thy lip such scorn ; for it was made   171
For kissing, lady, not for such contempt.
If thy revengeful heart cannot forgive,
Lo ! here I lend thee this sharp-pointed sword ;
Which if thou please to hide in this true breast,

But 't was thy heavenly face that set me on.
                                        [*She lets fall the sword.*
Take up the sword again, or take up me.
    Anne. Arise, dissembler : though I wish thy death,
I will not be thy executioner.

Glo. " And humbly beg the death upon my knee."

And let the soul forth that adoreth thee,
I lay it naked to the deadly stroke,
And humbly beg the death upon my knee.
        [*He lays his breast open : she offers at it with
            his sword.*
Nay, do not pause ; for I did kill King Henry ;—
But 't was thy beauty that provoked me.   180
Nay, now despatch ; 't was I that stabb'd young
        Edward :—

Glo. Then bid me kill myself, and I will do it.
Anne. I have already.
Glo.   That was in thy rage :
Speak it again, and even with the word,
This hand, which, for thy love, did kill thy love,
Shall, for thy love, kill a far truer love :   190
To both their deaths shalt thou be accessary.
Anne. I would, I knew thy heart.
Glo. 'T is figur'd in my tongue.

Anne. I fear me, both are false.
Glo. Then never man was true.
Anne. Well, well, put up your sword.
Glo. Say, then, my peace is made.
Anne. That shalt thou know hereafter.
Glo. But shall I live in hope?
Anne. All men, I hope, live so.   200
Glo. Vouchsafe to wear this ring.
Anne. To take is not to give. [*She puts on the ring.*
Glo. Look, how my ring encompasseth thy finger,
Even so thy breast encloseth my poor heart;
Wear both of them, for both of them are thine.
And if thy poor devoted servant may
But beg one favour at thy gracious hand,
Thou dost confirm his happiness for ever.
Anne. What is it?
Glo. That it may please you leave these sad designs
To him that hath more cause to be a mourner,   211
And presently repair to Crosby Place;
Where, after I have solemnly interr'd,
At Chertsey monastery, this noble king,
And wet his grave with my repentant tears,
I will with all expedient duty see you:
For divers unknown reasons, I beseech you,
Grant me this boon.
Anne. With all my heart; and much it joys me too,
To see you are become so penitent.—   220
Tressel, and Berkley, go along with me.
Glo. Bid me farewell.
Anne.   'T is more than you deserve;
But since you teach me how to flatter you,
Imagine I have said farewell already.
     [*Exeunt Lady* ANNE, TRESSEL, *and* BERKLEY.
Glo. Sirs, take up the corse.
Gent. Towards Chertsey, noble lord?
Glo. No, to White Friars; there attend my coming.
         [*Exeunt the rest, with the corse.*
Was ever woman in this humour woo'd?
Was ever woman in this humour won?
I 'll have her, but I will not keep her long.   230
What! I, that kill'd her husband, and his father,
To take her in her heart's extremest hate;
With curses in her mouth, tears in her eyes,
The bleeding witness of her hatred by;
Having God, her conscience, and these bars against me,
And I no friends to back my suit withal,
But the plain devil, and dissembling looks,
And yet to win her,—all the world to nothing!
Ha!
Hath she forgot already that brave prince,   240
Edward, her lord, whom I, some three months since,
Stabb'd in my angry mood at Tewksbury?
A sweeter and a lovelier gentleman,—
Fram'd in the prodigality of nature,
Young, valiant, wise, and, no doubt, right royal,—
The spacious world cannot again afford:
And will she yet abase her eyes on me,
That cropp'd the golden prime of this sweet prince,
And made her widow to a woful bed?
On me, whose all not equals Edward's moiety?   250
On me, that halt, and am misshapen thus?
My dukedom to a beggarly denier,
I do mistake my person all this while:
Upon my life, she finds, although I cannot,
Myself to be a marvellous proper man.
I 'll be at charges for a looking-glass;
And entertain a score or two of tailors,
To study fashions to adorn my body:
Since I am crept in favour with myself,
I will maintain it with some little cost.   260
But, first, I 'll turn yon fellow in his grave,
And then return lamenting to my love.—
Shine out, fair sun, till I have bought a glass,
That I may see my shadow as I pass.   [*Exit.*

SCENE III.—The Same. A Room in the Palace.
Enter Queen ELIZABETH, *Lord* RIVERS, *and Lord*
GREY.

Riv. Have patience, madam: there 's no doubt, his
     majesty
Will soon recover his accustom'd health.

Grey. In that you brook it ill, it makes him worse:
Therefore, for God's sake, entertain good comfort,
And cheer his grace with quick and merry words.
Q. Eliz. If he were dead, what would betide on
     me?
Grey. No other harm, but loss of such a lord.
Q. Eliz. The loss of such a lord includes all harms.
Grey. The heavens have bless'd you with a goodly
     son,   10
To be your comforter when he is gone.
Q. Eliz. Ah! he is young; and his minority
Is put unto the trust of Richard Gloster,
A man that loves not me, nor none of you.
Riv. Is it concluded, he shall be protector?
Q. Eliz. It is determin'd, not concluded yet:
But so it must be, if the king miscarry.

Enter BUCKINGHAM *and* STANLEY.

Grey. Here come the Lords of Buckingham and
     Stanley.
Buck. Good time of day unto your royal grace.
Stan. God make your majesty joyful as you have
     been!
Q. Eliz. The Countess Richmond, good my Lord of
     Stanley,   20
To your good prayer will scarcely say Amen.
Yet, Stanley, notwithstanding she 's your wife,
And loves not me, be you, good lord, assur'd,
I hate not you for her proud arrogance.
Stan. I do beseech you, either not believe
The envious slanders of his false accusers;
Or, if she be accus'd on true report,
Bear with her weakness, which, I think, proceeds
From wayward sickness, and no grounded malice.
Q. Eliz. Saw you the king to-day, my Lord of
     Stanley?   30
Stan. But now, the Duke of Buckingham and I
Are come from visiting his majesty.
Q. Eliz. What likelihood of his amendment, lords?
Buck. Madam, good hope: his grace speaks cheer-
     fully.
Q. Eliz. God grant him health! Did you confer
     with him?
Buck. Ay, madam: he desires to make atonement
Between the Duke of Gloster and your brothers,
And between them and my lord chamberlain;
And sent to warn them to his royal presence.
Q. Eliz. 'Would all were well!—But that will never
     be.   40
I fear, our happiness is at the height.

Enter GLOSTER, HASTINGS, *and* DORSET.

Glo. They do me wrong, and I will not endure it.—
Who are they that complain unto the king,
That I, forsooth, am stern and love them not?
By holy Paul, they love his grace but lightly
That fill his ears with such dissentious rumours.
Because I cannot flatter, and speak fair,
Smile in men's faces, smooth, deceive, and cog,
Duck with French nods and apish courtesy,
I must be held a rancorous enemy.   50
Cannot a plain man live, and think no harm,
But thus his simple truth must be abus'd
With silken, sly, insinuating Jacks?
Grey. To whom in all this presence speaks your
     grace?
Glo. To thee, that hast nor honesty nor grace.
When have I injur'd thee? when done thee wrong?—
Or thee?—or thee?—or any of your faction?
A plague upon you all! His royal person
(Whom God preserve better than you would wish!)
Cannot be quiet scarce a breathing-while,   60
But you must trouble him with lewd complaints.
Q. Eliz. Brother of Gloster, you mistake the matter.
The king, on his own royal disposition,
And not provok'd by any suitor else,
Aiming, belike, at your interior hatred,
That in your outward action shows itself
Against my children, brothers, and myself,
Makes him to send; that thereby he may gather
The ground of your ill-will, and so remove it.
Glo. I cannot tell;—the world is grown so bad,   70

That wrens make prey where eagles dare not perch :
Since every Jack became a gentleman,
There 's many a gentle person made a Jack.
  Q. Eliz. Come, come, we know your meaning,
    brother Gloster :
You envy my advancement, and my friends'.
God grant, we never may have need of you !
  Glo. Meantime, God grants that we have need of
    you :
Our brother is imprison'd by your means,
Myself disgrac'd, and the nobility
Held in contempt ; while great promotions   80
Are daily given, to ennoble those
That scarce, some two days since, were worth a noble.
  Q. Eliz. By Him that rais'd me to this careful
    height
From that contented hap which I enjoy'd,
I never did incense his majesty
Against the Duke of Clarence, but have been
An earnest advocate to plead for him.—
My lord, you do me shameful injury,
Falsely to draw me in these vile suspects.
  Glo. You may deny, that you were not the mean 90
Of my Lord Hastings' late imprisonment.
  Riv. She may, my lord ; for—
  Glo. She may, Lord Rivers,—why, who knows not
    so ?
She may do more, sir, than denying that :
She may help you to many fair preferments,
And then deny her aiding hand therein,
And lay those honours on your high desert.
What may she not ? She may,—ay, marry, may she,—
  Riv. What, marry, may she ?
  Glo. What, marry, may she ? marry with a king,
A bachelor, and a handsome stripling too.   101
I wis, your grandam had a worser match.
  Q. Eliz. My Lord of Gloster, I have too long borne
Your blunt upbraidings and your bitter scoffs ;
By Heaven, I will acquaint his majesty
Of those gross taunts that oft I have endur'd.
I had rather be a country serving-maid,
Than a great queen, with this condition,
To be so baited, scorn'd, and stormed at :
Small joy have I in being England's queen.   110

    Enter Queen Margaret, *behind.*

  Q. Mar. And lessen'd be that small, God, I beseech
    him !
Thy honour, state, and seat, is due to me.
  Glo. What ! threat you me with telling of the king ?
Tell him, and spare not : look, what I have said
I will avouch in presence of the king :
I dare adventure to be sent to the Tower.
'T is time to speak ; my pains are quite forgot.
  Q. Mar. Out, devil ! I do remember them too well :
Thou kill'dst my husband Henry in the Tower,
And Edward, my poor son, at Tewksbury.   120
  Glo. Ere you were queen, ay, or your husband
    king,
I was a pack-horse in his great affairs ;
A weeder-out of his proud adversaries,
A liberal rewarder of his friends :
To royalise his blood, I spent mine own.
  Q. Mar. Ay, and much better blood than his, or
    thine.
  Glo. In all which time, you, and your husband
    Grey,
Were factious for the house of Lancaster ;—
And, Rivers, so were you.—Was not your husband
In Margaret's battle at Saint Albans slain ?   130
Let me put in your minds, if you forget,
What you have been ere this, and what you are ;
Withal, what I have been, and what I am.
  Q. Mar. A murd'rous villain, and so still thou art.
  Glo. Poor Clarence did forsake his father Warwick,
Ay, and forswore himself,—which Jesu pardon !
  Q. Mar. Which God revenge !
  Glo. To fight on Edward's party, for the crown ;
And, for his meed, poor lord, he is mew'd up.
I would to God, my heart were flint, like Edward's,
Or Edward's soft and pitiful, like mine :   141
I am too childish-foolish for this world.

  Q. Mar. Hie thee to hell for shame, and leave this
    world,
Thou cacodemon ! there thy kingdom is.
  Riv. My Lord of Gloster, in those busy days,
Which here you urge to prove us enemies,
We follow'd then our lord, our sovereign king ;
So should we you, if you should be our king.
  Glo. If I should be !—I had rather be a pedlar.
Far be it from my heart, the thought thereof !   150
  Q. Eliz. As little joy, my lord, as you suppose
You should enjoy, were you this country's king,
As little joy you may suppose in me
That I enjoy, being the queen thereof.
  Q. Mar. A little joy enjoys the queen thereof ;
For I am she, and altogether joyless.
I can no longer hold me patient.—   [*Advancing.*
Hear me, you wrangling pirates, that fall out
In sharing that which you have pill'd from me !
Which of you trembles not, that looks on me ?   160
If not, that, I being queen, you bow like subjects,
Yet that, by you depos'd, you quake like rebels ?—
Ah ! gentle villain, do not turn away.
  Glo. Foul wrinkled witch, what mak'st thou in my
    sight ?
  Q. Mar. But repetition of what thou hast marr'd ;
That will I make, before I let thee go.
  Glo. Wert thou not banished on pain of death ?
  Q. Mar. I was ; but I do find more pain in banish-
    ment
Than death can yield me here by my abode.
A husband, and a son, thou ow'st to me,—   170
And thou, a kingdom ;—all of you, allegiance :
This sorrow that I have, by right is yours,
And all the pleasures you usurp are mine.
  Glo. The curse my noble father laid on thee,
When thou didst crown his warlike brows with paper,
And with thy scorns drew'st rivers from his eyes ;
And then, to dry them, gav'st the duke a clout,
Steep'd in the faultless blood of pretty Rutland ;—
His curses, then from bitterness of soul
Denounc'd against thee, are all fallen upon thee ; 180
And God, not we, hath plagu'd thy bloody deed.
  Q. Eliz. So just is God, to right the innocent.
  Hast. O ! 't was the foulest deed to slay that babe,
And the most merciless, that e'er was heard of.
  Riv. Tyrants themselves wept when it was reported.
  Dor. No man but prophesied revenge for it.
  Buck. Northumberland, then present, wept to see it.
  Q. Mar. What ! were you snarling all, before I
    came,
Ready to catch each other by the throat,
And turn you all your hatred now on me ?   190
Did York's dread curse prevail so much with Heaven,
That Henry's death, my lovely Edward's death,
Their kingdom's loss, my woful banishment,
Should all but answer for that peevish brat ?
Can curses pierce the clouds, and enter heaven ?—
Why, then give way, dull clouds, to my quick
    curses !—
Though not by war, by surfeit die your king,
As ours by murder, to make him a king !
Edward, thy son, that now is Prince of Wales,
For Edward, my son, that was Prince of Wales, 200
Die in his youth by like untimely violence !
Thyself a queen, for me that was a queen,
Outlive thy glory, like my wretched self !
Long may'st thou live, to wail thy children's loss,
And see another, as I see thee now,
Deck'd in thy rights, as thou art stall'd in mine !
Long die thy happy days before thy death ;
And, after many lengthen'd hours of grief,
Die neither mother, wife, nor England's queen !
Rivers, and Dorset, you were standers-by,   210
And so wast thou, Lord Hastings, when my son
Was stabb'd with bloody daggers : God, I pray him,
That none of you may live his natural age,
But by some unlook'd accident cut off !
  Glo. Have done thy charm, thou hateful wither'd
    hag.
  Q. Mar. And leave out thee ? stay, dog, for thou
    shalt hear me.
If Heaven have any grievous plague in store,

Exceeding those that I can wish upon thee,
O! let them keep it, till thy sins be ripe,
And then hurl down their indignation   220
On thee, the troubler of the poor world's peace!
The worm of conscience still begnaw thy soul!
Thy friends suspect for traitors while thou liv'st,
And take deep traitors for thy dearest friends!
No sleep close up that deadly eye of thine,
Unless it be while some tormenting dream
Affrights thee with a hell of ugly devils!
Thou elvish-mark'd, abortive, rooting hog!
Thou that wast seal'd in thy nativity
The slave of nature, and the son of hell!   230
Thou slander of thy heavy mother's womb!
Thou loathed issue of thy father's loins!
Thou rag of honour! thou detested—

Q. Mar. " Thou rag of honour! thou detested "—

Glo. Margaret.
Q. Mar.   Richard!
Glo.   Ha?
Q. Mar.   I call thee not.
Glo. I cry thee mercy then; for I did think,
That thou hadst call'd me all these bitter names.
Q. Mar. Why, so I did; but look'd for no reply.
O! let me make the period to my curse.
Glo. 'T is done by me, and ends in—Margaret.
Q. Eliz. Thus have you breath'd your curse against
     yourself.   210
Q. Mar. Poor painted queen, vain flourish of my
     fortune!
Why strew'st thou sugar on that bottled spider,
Whose deadly web ensnareth thee about?
Fool, fool! thou whett'st a knife to kill thyself.
The day will come that thou shalt wish for me
To help thee curse this pois'nous bunch-back'd toad.
Hast. False-boding woman, end thy frantic curse,
Lest to thy harm thou move our patience.
Q. Mar. Foul shame upon you! you have all mov'd
     mine.
Riv. Were you well serv'd, you would be taught
     your duty.   250
Q. Mar. To serve me well, you all should do me
     duty,
Teach me to be your queen, and you my subjects.
O! serve me well, and teach yourselves that duty.
Dor. Dispute not with her, she is lunatic.
Q. Mar. Peace, master marquess; you are malapert:
Your fire-new stamp of honour is scarce current.
O! that your young nobility could judge,
What 't were to lose it, and be miserable!
They that stand high have many blasts to shake them,
And if they fall, they dash themselves to pieces. 260

Glo. Good counsel, marry:—learn it, learn it, mar-
     quess.
Dor. It touches you, my lord, as much as me.
Glo. Ay, and much more; but I was born so high,
Our aery buildeth in the cedar's top,
And dallies with the wind, and scorns the sun.
Q. Mar. And turns the sun to shade,—alas! alas!—
Witness my son, now in the shade of death;
Whose bright out-shining beams thy cloudy wrath
Hath in eternal darkness folded up.
Your aery buildeth in our aery's nest.—   270
O God! that seest it, do not suffer it:
As it was won with blood, lost be it so!
Buck. Peace, peace! for shame, if not for charity.
Q. Mar. Urge neither charity nor shame to me:
Uncharitably with me have you dealt,
     And shamefully my hopes by you
          are butcher'd.
My charity is outrage, life my
     shame,
And in that shame still live my
     sorrow's rage!
Buck. Have done, have done.
Q. Mar. O princely Buckingham!
     I 'll kiss thy hand,   280
In sign of league and amity with
     thee:
Now fair befall thee and thy noble
     house!
Thy garments are not spotted with
     our blood,
Nor thou within the compass of my
     curse.
Buck. Nor no one here; for curses
     never pass
The lips of those that breathe them
     in the air.
Q. Mar. I will not think but they
     ascend the sky,
And there awake God's gentle-
     sleeping peace.
O Buckingham! take heed of yon-
     der dog:
Look, when he fawns, he bites;
     and, when he bites,   290
His venom tooth will rankle to
     the death:
Have not to do with him, beware of him;
Sin, death, and hell, have set their marks on him,
And all their ministers attend on him.
Glo. What doth she say, my Lord of Buckingham?
Buck. Nothing that I respect, my gracious lord.
Q. Mar. What! dost thou scorn me for my gentle
     counsel,
And soothe the devil that I warn thee from?
O! but remember this another day,
When he shall split thy very heart with sorrow,   300
And say, poor Margaret was a prophetess.—
Live each of you the subjects to his hate,
And he to yours, and all of you to God's!   [*Exit.*
Hast. My hair doth stand on end to hear her
     curses.
Riv. And so doth mine. I muse, why she's at
     liberty.
Glo. I cannot blame her: by God's holy mother,
She hath had too much wrong, and I repent
My part thereof, that I have done to her.
Q. Eliz. I never did her any, to my knowledge.
Glo. Yet you have all the vantage of her wrong. 310
I was too hot to do somebody good,
That is too cold in thinking of it now.
Marry, as for Clarence, he is well repaid;
He is frank'd up to fatting for his pains;—
God pardon them that are the cause thereof!
Riv. A virtuous and a Christian-like conclusion,
To pray for them that have done scath to us.
Glo. So do I ever, [*aside*] being well advis'd;
For had I curs'd now, I had curs'd myself.

Enter CATESBY.

Cates. Madam, his majesty doth call for you;   320
And for your grace; and you, my noble lords.

Q. Eliz. Catesby, I come.—Lords, will you go with me?
Riv. We wait upon your grace.
       [*Exeunt all but* Gloster.
Glo. I do the wrong, and first begin to brawl.
The secret mischiefs that I set abroach,
I lay unto the grievous charge of others.
Clarence, whom I, indeed, have cast in darkness,
I do beweep to many simple gulls;
Namely, to Stanley, Hastings, Buckingham;
And tell them, 't is the queen and her allies   330
That stir the king against the duke my brother.
Now they believe it; and withal whet me
To be reveng'd on Rivers, Vaughan, Grey:
But then I sigh, and, with a piece of Scripture,
Tell them, that God bids us do good for evil:
And thus I clothe my naked villainy
With old odd ends stol'n forth of holy writ,
And seem a saint, when most I play the devil.

    Enter two Murderers.

But soft! here come my executioners.—
How now, my hardy, stout, resolved mates!   340
Are you now going to despatch this thing?
1 Murd. We are, my lord; and come to have the warrant,
That we may be admitted where he is.
Glo. Well thought upon; I have it here about me.
       [*Gives the warrant.*
When you have done, repair to Crosby Place.
But, sirs, be sudden in the execution,
Withal obdurate: do not hear him plead,
For Clarence is well-spoken, and, perhaps,
May move your hearts to pity, if you mark him.
1 Murd. Tut, tut! my lord, we will not stand to prate;   350
Talkers are no good doers: be assur'd,
We go to use our hands, and not our tongues.
Glo. Your eyes drop millstones, when fools' eyes fall tears:
I like you, lads;—about your business straight;
Go, go, despatch.
1 Murd.   We will, my noble lord. [*Exeunt.*

Scene IV.—London. A Room in the Tower.

   Enter Clarence *and* Brakenbury.

Brak. Why looks your grace so heavily to-day?
Clar. O! I have pass'd a miserable night,
So full of fearful dreams, of ugly sights,
That, as I am a Christian faithful man,
I would not spend another such a night,
Though 't were to buy a world of happy days;
So full of dismal terror was the time.
Brak. What was your dream, my lord? I pray you, tell me.
Clar. Methought that I had broken from the Tower,
And was embark'd to cross to Burgundy;   10
And in my company my brother Gloster,
Who from my cabin tempted me to walk
Upon the hatches: thence we look'd toward England,
And cited up a thousand heavy times,
During the wars of York and Lancaster
That had befall'n us. As we pac'd along
Upon the giddy footing of the hatches,
Methought that Gloster stumbled; and, in falling,
Struck me (that thought to stay him) overboard,
Into the tumbling billows of the main.   20
O Lord! methought, what pain it was to drown!
What dreadful noise of water in mine ears!
What sights of ugly death within mine eyes!
Methought I saw a thousand fearful wracks;
A thousand men that fishes gnaw'd upon;
Wedges of gold, great anchors, heaps of pearl,
Inestimable stones, unvalued jewels,
All scatter'd in the bottom of the sea.
Some lay in dead men's skulls; and in those holes
Where eyes did once inhabit, there were crept   30
(As 't were in scorn of eyes) reflecting gems,

That woo'd the slimy bottom of the deep,
And mock'd the dead bones that lay scatter'd by.
Brak. Had you such leisure in the time of death,
To gaze upon these secrets of the deep?
Clar. Methought I had, and often did I strive
To yield the ghost; but still the envious flood
Stopt in my soul, and would not let it forth
To find the empty, vast, and wandering air;
But smother'd it within my panting bulk,   40
Which almost burst to belch it in the sea.
Brak. Awak'd you not in this sore agony?
Clar. No, no, my dream was lengthen'd after life;
O! then began the tempest to my soul!
I pass'd, methought, the melancholy flood,
With that sour ferryman which poets write of,
Unto the kingdom of perpetual night.
The first that there did greet my stranger soul,
Was my great father-in-law, renowned Warwick;
Who spake aloud,—" What scourge for perjury   50
Can this dark monarchy afford false Clarence?"
And so he vanish'd. Then came wandering by
A shadow like an angel, with bright hair
Dabbled in blood; and he shriek'd out aloud,—
"Clarence is come,—false, fleeting, perjur'd Clarence,—
That stabb'd me in the field by Tewksbury;—
Seize on him, Furies! take him unto torment!"
With that, methought, a legion of foul fiends
Environ'd me, and howled in mine ears
Such hideous cries, that, with the very noise,   60
I trembling wak'd, and, for a season after,
Could not believe but that I was in hell;
Such terrible impression made my dream.
Brak. No marvel, lord, though it affrighted you;
I am afraid, methinks, to hear you tell it.
Clar. Ah, keeper, keeper! I have done these things,
That now give evidence against my soul,
For Edward's sake; and see how he requites me!—
O God! if my deep prayers cannot appease thee,
But thou wilt be aveng'd on my misdeeds,   70
Yet execute thy wrath in me alone:
O, spare my guiltless wife and my poor children!—
Keeper, I pr'ythee, sit by me awhile;
My soul is heavy, and I fain would sleep.
Brak. I will, my lord: God give your grace good rest.—   [Clarence *sleeps.*
Sorrow breaks seasons and reposing hours,
Makes the night morning, and the noon-tide night.
Princes have but their titles for their glories,
An outward honour for an inward toil;
And, for unfelt imaginations,   80
They often feel a world of restless cares:
So that, between their titles, and low name,
There's nothing differs but the outward fame.

    Enter the two Murderers.

1 Murd. Ho! who's here?
Brak. What wouldst thou, fellow? and how cam'st thou hither?
1 Murd. I would speak with Clarence, and I came hither on my legs.
Brak. What! so brief?
2 Murd. 'T is better, sir, than to be tedious.—
Let him see our commission, and talk no more.—   90
  [*A paper delivered to* Brakenbury, *who reads it.*
Brak. I am, in this, commanded to deliver
The noble Duke of Clarence to your hands:—
I will not reason what is meant hereby,
Because I will be guiltless from the meaning.
There lies the duke asleep, and there the keys.
I'll to the king, and signify to him,
That thus I have resign'd to you my charge.
1 Murd. You may, sir; 't is a point of wisdom: fare you well.   [*Exit* Brakenbury.
2 Murd. What, shall we stab him as he sleeps?   100
1 Murd. No; he'll say, 't was done cowardly, when he wakes.
2 Murd. Why, he shall never wake until the great judgment-day.
1 Murd. Why, then he'll say, we stabb'd him sleeping.
2 Murd. The urging of that word, judgment, hath bred a kind of remorse in me.

1 Murd. What! art thou afraid?
2 Murd. Not to kill him, having a warrant; but to be damn'd for killing him, from the which no warrant can defend me.   112
1 Murd. I thought, thou hadst been resolute.
2 Murd. So I am, to let him live.
1 Murd. I 'll back to the Duke of Gloster, and tell him so.
2 Murd. Nay, I pr'ythee, stay a little: I hope, this passionate humour of mine will change; it was wont to hold me but while one tells twenty.
1 Murd. How dost thou feel thyself now?   120
2 Murd. Some certain dregs of conscience are yet within me.
1 Murd. Remember our reward, when the deed's done.
2 Murd. 'Zounds! he dies: I had forgot the reward.
1 Murd. Where's thy conscience now?
2 Murd. O! in the Duke of Gloster's purse.
1 Murd. When he opens his purse to give us our reward, thy conscience flies out.
2 Murd. 'T is no matter; let it go: there 's few or none will entertain it.   131
1 Murd. What, if it come to thee again?
2 Murd. I 'll not meddle with it; it makes a man a coward; a man cannot steal, but it accuseth him; a man cannot swear, but it checks him; a man cannot lie with his neighbour's wife, but it detects him: 't is a blushing shame-faced spirit, that mutinies in a man's bosom; it fills a man full of obstacles: it made me once restore a purse of gold, that by chance I found; it beggars any man that keeps it: it is turned out of all towns and cities for a dangerous thing; and every man, that means to live well, endeavours to trust to himself, and live without it.   143
1 Murd. 'Zounds! it is even now at my elbow, persuading me not to kill the duke.
2 Murd. Take the devil in thy mind, and believe him not: he would insinuate with thee, but to make thee sigh.
1 Murd. I am strong-fram'd; he cannot prevail with me.   150
2 Murd. Spoke like a tall man that respects his reputation. Come, shall we fall to work?
1 Murd. Take him on the costard with the hilts of thy sword, and then throw him into the malmsey-butt in the next room.
2 Murd. O excellent device! and make a sop of him.
1 Murd. Soft! he wakes.
2 Murd. Strike.
1 Murd. No; we 'll reason with him.
Clar. [*Waking.*] Where art thou, keeper? give me a cup of wine.   160
1 Murd. You shall have wine enough, my lord, anon.
Clar. In God's name, what art thou?
1 Murd. A man, as you are.
Clar. But not, as I am, royal.
1 Murd. Nor you, as we are, loyal.
Clar. Thy voice is thunder, but thy looks are humble.
1 Murd. My voice is now the king's, my looks mine own.
Clar. How darkly, and how deadly dost thou speak!
Your eyes do menace me: why look you pale?
Who sent you hither? Wherefore do you come?   170
Both Murd. To, to, to—
Clar. To murder me?
Both Murd. Ay, ay.
Clar. You scarcely have the hearts to tell me so,
And therefore cannot have the hearts to do it.
Wherein, my friends, have I offended you?
1 Murd. Offended you have not, but the king.
Clar. I shall be reconcil'd to him again.
2 Murd. Never, my lord; therefore prepare to die.
Clar. Are you drawn forth among a world of men,   180
To slay the innocent? What is my offence?
Where are the evidence that do accuse me?
What lawful quest have given their verdict up

Unto the frowning judge? or who pronounc'd
The bitter sentence of poor Clarence' death?
Before I be convict by course of law,
To threaten me with death is most unlawful.
I charge you, as you hope to have redemption
By Christ's dear blood shed for our grievous sins,
That you depart, and lay no hands on me;   190
The deed you undertake is damnable.
1 Murd. What we will do, we do upon command.
2 Murd. And he that hath commanded is our king.
Clar. Erroneous vassals! the great King of kings
Hath in the table of his law commanded,
That thou shalt do no murder: will you then
Spurn at his edict, and fulfil a man's?
Take heed; for he holds vengeance in his hand,
To hurl upon their heads that break his law.
2 Murd. And that same vengeance doth he hurl on thee,   200
For false forswearing, and for murder too.
Thou didst receive the sacrament, to fight
In quarrel of the house of Lancaster.
1 Murd. And, like a traitor to the name of God,
Didst break that vow, and with thy treacherous blade
Unripp'dst the bowels of thy sovereign's son.
2 Murd. Whom thou wast sworn to cherish and defend.
1 Murd. How canst thou urge God's dreadful law to us,
When thou hast broke it in such dear degree?
Clar. Alas! for whose sake did I that ill deed?   210
For Edward, for my brother, for his sake;
He sends you not to murder me for this;
For in that sin he is as deep as I.
If God will be avenged for the deed,
O! know you yet, he doth it publicly;
Take not the quarrel from his powerful arm:
He needs no indirect or lawless course,
To cut off those that have offended him.
1 Murd. Who made thee then a bloody minister,
When gallant-springing, brave Plantagenet,   220
That princely novice, was struck dead by thee?
Clar. My brother's love, the devil, and my rage.
1 Murd. Thy brother's love, our duty, and thy faults,
Provoke us hither now to slaughter thee.
Clar. If you do love my brother, hate not me;
I am his brother, and I love him well.
If you are hir'd for meed, go back again,
And I will send you to my brother Gloster;
Who shall reward you better for my life
Than Edward will for tidings of my death.   230
2 Murd. You are deceiv'd; your brother Gloster hates you.
Clar. O! no; he loves me, and he holds me dear.
Go you to him from me.
Both Murd.   Ay, so we will.
Clar. Tell him, when that our princely father York
Bless'd his three sons with his victorious arm,
And charg'd us from his soul to love each other,
He little thought of this divided friendship:
Bid Gloster think on this, and he will weep.
1 Murd. Ay, millstones; as he lesson'd us to weep.
Clar. O! do not slander him, for he is kind.   240
1 Murd. Right; as snow in harvest.—Come, you deceive yourself;
'T is he that sends us to destroy you here.
Clar. It cannot be; for he bewept my fortune,
And hugg'd me in his arms, and swore, with sobs,
That he would labour my delivery.
1 Murd. Why, so he doth, when he delivers you
From this earth's thraldom to the joys of heaven.
2 Murd. Make peace with God, for you must die, my lord.
Clar. Have you that holy feeling in your souls,
To counsel me to make my peace with God,   250
And are you yet to your own souls so blind,
That you will war with God by murdering me?
O! sirs, consider, they that set you on
To do this deed, will hate you for the deed.
2 Murd. What shall we do?

Clar.   Relent, and save your souls.
1 Murd. Relent! no: 't is cowardly, and womanish.

Clar. " My friend, I spy some pity in thy looks."

Clar. Not to relent, is beastly, savage, devilish.—
Which of you, if you were a prince's son,

Being pent from liberty, as I am now,
If two such murderers as yourselves came to you,   260
Would not entreat for life?—
My friend, I spy some pity in thy looks;
O! if thine eye be not a flatterer,
Come thou on my side, and entreat for me,
As you would beg, were you in my distress.
A begging prince what beggar pities not?
2 Murd. Look behind you, my lord.
1 Murd. Take that, and that: [*stabs him*] if all this
          will not do,
I 'll drown you in the malmsey-butt within.
                              [*Exit, with the body.*
2 Murd. A bloody deed, and desperately despatch'd!
How fain, like Pilate, would I wash my hands   271
Of this most grievous murder.

Re-enter First Murderer.

1 Murd. How now! what mean'st thou, that thou
          help'st me not?
By Heaven, the duke shall know how slack you have
          been.
2 Murd. I would he knew that I had sav'd his
          brother!
Take thou the fee, and tell him what I say,
For I repent me that the duke is slain.   [*Exit.*
1 Murd. So do not I: go, coward, as thou art.
Well, I 'll go hide the body in some hole,
Till that the duke give order for his burial: 280
And when I have my meed, I will away;
For this will out, and then I must not stay.   [*Exit.*

ACT II.

Scene I.—London. A Room in the Palace.

Enter King Edward, *led in sick, Queen* Elizabeth, Dorset, Rivers, Hastings, Buckingham, Grey,
and others.

            King Edward.
HY, so:—now have I done a good day's
          work.—
You peers, continue this united league:
I every day expect an embassage
From my Redeemer to redeem me hence;
And more in peace my soul shall part to
          heaven,
Since I have made my friends at peace
          on earth.
Rivers and Hastings, take each other's
          hand;
Dissemble not your hatred, swear your love.
Riv. By Heaven, my soul is purg'd from grudging
          hate:
And with my hand I seal my true heart's love.   10
Hast. So thrive I, as I truly swear the like!
K. Edw. Take heed, you dally not before your king;
Lest he that is the supreme King of kings
Confound your hidden falsehood, and award
Either of you to be the other's end.
Hast. So prosper I, as I swear perfect love!
Riv. And I, as I love Hastings with my heart!
K. Edw. Madam, yourself are not exempt from
          this,—
Nor you, son Dorset,—Buckingham, nor you;—
You have been factious one against the other.   20
Wife, love Lord Hastings, let him kiss your hand;
And what you do, do it unfeignedly.

Q. Eliz. There, Hastings:—I will never more re-
          member
Our former hatred, so thrive I, and mine!
K. Edw. Dorset, embrace him;—Hastings, love
          lord marquess.
Dor. This interchange of love, I here protest,
Upon my part shall be inviolable.
Hast. And so swear I, my lord.   [*They embrace.*
K. Edw. Now, princely Buckingham, seal thou this
          league
With thy embracements to my wife's allies,   30
And make me happy in your unity.
Buck. Whenever Buckingham doth turn his hate
Upon your grace [*to the* Queen], but with all duteous
          love
Doth cherish you and yours, God punish me
With hate in those where I expect most love!
When I have most need to employ a friend,
And most assured that he is a friend,
Deep, hollow, treacherous, and full of guile,
Be he unto me. This do I beg of Heaven,
When I am cold in love to you or yours.   40
                              [*They embrace.*
K. Edw. A pleasing cordial, princely Buckingham,
Is this thy vow unto my sickly heart.
There wanteth now our brother Gloster here,
To make the blessed period of this peace.
Buck. And, in good time, here comes the noble
          duke.

Enter GLOSTER.

Glo. Good morrow to my sovereign king, and queen;
And, princely peers, a happy time of day!
K. Edw. Happy, indeed, as we have spent the day.—
Gloster, we have done deeds of charity;
Made peace of enmity, fair love of hate,　　　50
Between these swelling wrong-incensed peers.
Glo. A blessed labour, my most sovereign lord.—
Among this princely heap, if any here,
By false intelligence, or wrong surmise,
Hold me a foe;
If I unwittingly, or in my rage,
Have aught committed that is hardly borne
By any in this presence, I desire
To reconcile me to his friendly peace:
'T is death to me to be at enmity;　　　60
I hate it, and desire all good men's love.—
First, madam, I entreat true peace of you,
Which I will purchase with my duteous service;
Of you, my noble cousin Buckingham,
If ever any grudge were lodg'd between us;
Of you, and you, Lord Rivers, and of Dorset,
That all without desert have frown'd on me;
Of you, Lord Woodville, and, Lord Scales, of you,
Dukes, earls, lords, gentlemen; indeed, of all.
I do not know that Englishman alive　　　70
With whom my soul is any jot at odds,
More than the infant that is born to-night:
I thank my God for my humility.
Q. Eliz. A holy day shall this be kept hereafter:—
I would to God, all strifes were well compounded.—
My sovereign lord, I do beseech your highness
To take our brother Clarence to your grace.
Glo. Why, madam, have I offer'd love for this,
To be so flouted in this royal presence?
Who knows not, that the gentle duke is dead?　　　80
　　　　　　　　　[*They all start.*
You do him injury to scorn his corse.
K. Edw. Who knows not, he is dead! who knows
　　　he is?
Q. Eliz. All-seeing Heaven, what a world is this!
Buck. Look I so pale, Lord Dorset, as the rest?
Dor. Ay, my good lord; and no man in the presence,
But his red colour hath forsook his cheeks.
K. Edw. Is Clarence dead? the order was revers'd.
Glo. But he, poor man, by your first order died,
And that a winged Mercury did bear;
Some tardy cripple bare the countermand,　　　90
That came too lag to see him buried.
God grant that some, less noble and less loyal,
Nearer in bloody thoughts, and not in blood,
Deserve not worse than wretched Clarence did,
And yet go current from suspicion.

Enter STANLEY.

Stan. A boon, my sovereign, for my service done!
K. Edw. I pr'ythee, peace: my soul is full of sorrow.
Stan. I will not rise, unless your highness hear me.
K. Edw. Then say at once, what is it thou re-
　　　quest'st.
Stan. The forfeit, sovereign, of my servant's life;　　　101
Who slew to-day a riotous gentleman,
Lately attendant on the Duke of Norfolk.
K. Edw. Have I a tongue to doom my brother's
　　　death,
And shall that tongue give pardon to a slave?
My brother kill'd no man, his fault was thought,
And yet his punishment was bitter death.
Who sued to me for him? who, in my wrath,
Kneel'd at my feet, and bade me be advis'd?
Who spoke of brotherhood? who spoke of love?
Who told me, how the poor soul did forsake　　　110
The mighty Warwick, and did fight for me?
Who told me, in the field at Tewksbury,
When Oxford had me down, he rescu'd me,
And said, " Dear brother, live, and be a king?"
Who told me, when we both lay in the field,
Frozen almost to death, how he did lap me
Even in his garments; and did give himself,
All thin and naked, to the numb-cold night?
All this from my remembrance brutish wrath
Sinfully pluck'd, and not a man of you　　　120

Had so much grace to put it in my mind.
But when your carters, or your waiting-vassals,
Have done a drunken slaughter, and defac'd
The precious image of our dear Redeemer,
You straight are on your knees for pardon, pardon;
And I, unjustly too, must grant it you.
But for my brother not a man would speak,
Nor I, ungracious, speak unto myself
For him, poor soul.—The proudest of you all
Have been beholding to him in his life,　　　130
Yet none of you would once beg for his life.—
O God! I fear, thy justice will take hold
On me, and you, and mine, and yours, for this.—
Come, Hastings, help me to my closet. Ah, poor
　　　Clarence!
　　　[*Exeunt* KING, QUEEN, HASTINGS, RIVERS,
　　　　　　　DORSET, *and* GREY.
Glo. This is the fruit of rashness.—Mark'd you not,
How that the guilty kindred of the queen
Look'd pale, when they did hear of Clarence' death?
O! they did urge it still unto the king:
God will revenge it. Come, lords; will you go,
To comfort Edward with our company?　　　140
Buck. We wait upon your grace.　　　[*Exeunt.*

SCENE II.—London.　A Room in the Palace.

Enter the Duchess of YORK, *with a Son and
Daughter of* CLARENCE.

Son. Good grandam, tell us, is our father dead?
Duch. No, boy.
Daugh. Why do you weep so oft? and beat your
　　　breast;
And cry—" O Clarence, my unhappy son!"

Son. " Good grandam, tell us, is our father dead?"

Son. Why do you look on us, and shake your
　　　head,
And call us orphans, wretches, castaways,
If that our noble father were alive?
Duch. My pretty cousins, you mistake me both;
I do lament the sickness of the king,
As loath to lose him, not your father's death.　　　10
It were lost sorrow to wail one that 's lost.
Son. Then you conclude, my grandam, he is dead?
The king mine uncle is to blame for it:
God will revenge it; whom I will importune
With earnest prayers all to that eff·ct.
Daugh. And so will I.
Duch. Peace, children, peace! the king doth love
　　　you well:
Incapable and shallow innocents,
You cannot guess who caus'd your father's death.
Son. Grandam, we can; for my good uncle Gloster　　　21
Told me, the king, provok'd to it by the queen,
Devis'd impeachments to imprison him:
And when my uncle told me so, he wept,
And pitied me, and kindly kiss'd my cheek;
Bade me rely on him as on my father,
And he would love me dearly as his child.

Duch. Ah! that deceit should steal such gentle shape,
And with a virtuous visor hide deep vice!
He is my son, ay, and therein my shame,
Yet from my dugs he drew not this deceit.   30
Son. Think you, my uncle did dissemble, grandam?
Duch. Ay, boy.
Son. I cannot think it.   Hark! what noise is this?

Enter Queen ELIZABETH, *distractedly;* RIVERS
and DORSET *following her.*

Q. Eliz. Ah! who shall hinder me to wail and weep,
To chide my fortune, and torment myself?
I'll join with black despair against my soul,
And to myself become an enemy.
Duch. What means this scene of rude impatience?
Q. Eliz. To make an act of tragic violence:—
Edward, my lord, thy son, our king, is dead!—   40
Why grow the branches, when the root is gone?
Why wither not the leaves, that want their sap?—
If you will live, lament; if die, be brief;
That our swift-winged souls may catch the king's;
Or, like obedient subjects, follow him
To his new kingdom of ne'er changing night.
Duch. Ah! so much interest have I in thy sorrow,
As I had title in thy noble husband.
I have bewept a worthy husband's death,
And liv'd with looking on his images;   50
But now, two mirrors of his princely semblance
Are crack'd in pieces by malignant death,
And I for comfort have but one false glass,
That grieves me when I see my shame in him.
Thou art a widow: yet thou art a mother,
And hast the comfort of thy children left:
But death hath snatch'd my husband from mine arms,
And pluck'd two crutches from my feeble hands,
Clarence and Edward.   O! what cause have I
(Thine being but a moiety of my moan),   60
To over-go thy woes, and drown thy cries!
Son. Ah, aunt! you wept not for our father's death;
How can we aid you with our kindred tears?
Daugh. Our fatherless distress was left unmoan'd;
Your widow-dolour likewise be unwept.
Q. Eliz. Give me no help in lamentation;
I am not barren to bring forth complaints.
All springs reduce their currents to mine eyes,
That I, being govern'd by the watery moon,
May send forth plenteous tears to drown the world!
Ah, for my husband, for my dear lord Edward!   71
Chil. Ah, for our father, for our dear lord Clarence!
Duch. Alas, for both! both mine, Edward and Clarence.
Q. Eliz. What stay had I but Edward? and he's gone.
Chil. What stay had we but Clarence? and he's gone.
Duch. What stays had I but they? and they are gone.
Q. Eliz. Was never widow had so dear a loss.
Chil. Were never orphans had so dear a loss.
Duch. Was never mother had so dear a loss.
Alas! I am the mother of these griefs: 80
Their woes are parcell'd, mine are general.
She for an Edward weeps, and so do I;
I for a Clarence weep, so doth not she:
These babes for Clarence weep, and so do I;
I for an Edward weep, so do not they:—
Alas! you three on me, threefold distress'd,
Pour all your tears, I am your sorrow's nurse,
And I will pamper'it with lamentation.
Dor. Comfort, dear mother: God is much displeas'd,
That you take with unthankfulness his doing.   90
In common worldly things 't is call'd ungrateful,
With dull unwillingness to repay a debt,
Which with a bounteous hand was kindly lent;
Much more to be thus opposite with Heaven,
For it requires the royal debt it lent you.
Riv. Madam, bethink you, like a careful mother,
Of the young prince your son: send straight for him;
Let him be crown'd; in him your comfort lives.
Drown desperate sorrow in dead Edward's grave,
And plant your joys in living Edward's throne.   100

Enter GLOSTER, BUCKINGHAM, STANLEY, HASTINGS,
RATCLIFF, *and others.*

Glo. Sister, have comfort: all of us have cause
To wail the dimming of our shining star;
But none can cure their harms by wailing them.—
Madam, my mother, I do cry you mercy;
I did not see your grace.—Humbly on my knee
I crave your blessing.
Duch. God bless thee, and put meekness in thy breast,
Love, charity, obedience, and true duty.
Glo. Amen; [*aside*] and make me die a good old man!—
That is the butt-end of a mother's blessing;   110
I marvel, that her grace did leave it out.
Buck. You cloudy princes, and heart-sorrowing peers,
That bear this heavy mutual load of moan,
Now cheer each other in each other's love:
Though we have spent our harvest of this king,
We are to reap the harvest of his son.
The broken rancour of your high-swoln hearts,
But lately splinter'd, knit, and join'd together,
Must gently be preserv'd, cherish'd, and kept:
Me seemeth good, that, with some little train,   120
Forthwith from Ludlow the young prince be fet
Hither to London, to be crown'd our king.
Riv. Why with some little train, my Lord of Buckingham?
Buck. Marry, my lord, lest, by a multitude,
The new-heal'd wound of malice should break out;
Which would be so much the more dangerous,
By how much the estate is green, and yet ungovern'd:
Where every horse bears his commanding rein,
And may direct his course as please himself,
As well the fear of harm, as harm apparent,   130
In my opinion, ought to be prevented.
Glo. I hope the king made peace with all of us;
And the compact is firm and true in me.
Riv. And so in me; and so, I think, in all:
Yet, since it is but green, it should be put
To no apparent likelihood of breach,
Which, haply, by much company might be urg'd:
Therefore, I say with noble Buckingham,
That it is meet so few should fetch the prince.
Hast. And so say I.   140
Glo. Then be it so; and go we to determine
Who they shall be that straight shall post to Ludlow.
Madam,—and you, my sister,—will you go
To give your censures in this business?
[*Exeunt all but* BUCKINGHAM *and* GLOSTER.
Buck. My lord, whoever journeys to the prince,
For God's sake, let not us two stay at home:
For by the way I'll sort occasion,
As index to the story we late talk'd of,
To part the queen's proud kindred from the prince.
Glo. My other self, my counsel's consistory,   150
My oracle, my prophet!—My dear cousin,
I, as a child, will go by thy direction.
Towards Ludlow then, for we'll not stay behind.
[*Exeunt.*

SCENE III.—The Same.   A Street.

Enter two Citizens, meeting.

1 *Cit.* Good morrow, neighbour: whither away so fast?
2 *Cit.* I promise you, I scarcely know myself.
Hear you the news abroad?
1 *Cit.*   Yes; that the king is dead.
2 *Cit.* Ill news, by 'r lady; seldom comes the better:
I fear, I fear, 't will prove a giddy world.

Enter another Citizen.

3 *Cit.* Neighbours, God speed!
1 *Cit.*   Give you good morrow, sir.
3 *Cit.* Doth the news hold of good King Edward's death?
2 *Cit.* Ay, sir, it is too true; God help, the while!
3 *Cit.* Then, masters, look to see a troublous world.

1 *Cit.* No, no; by God's good grace, his son shall
    reign.   10
3 *Cit.* Woe to that land that's govern'd by a child!
2 *Cit.* In him there is a hope of government;
That, in his nonage, council under him,
And, in his full and ripen'd years, himself,
No doubt, shall then, and till then, govern well.
1 *Cit.* So stood the state, when Henry the Sixth
Was crown'd in Paris but at nine months old.
3 *Cit.* Stood the state so? no, no, good friends, God
    wot;
For then this land was famously enrich'd
With politic grave counsel: then the king   20
Had virtuous uncles to protect his grace.
1 *Cit.* Why, so hath this, both by his father and
    mother.
3 *Cit.* Better it were, they all came by his father,
Or by his father there were none at all;
For emulation, who shall now be nearest,
Will touch us all too near, if God prevent not.
O! full of danger is the Duke of Gloster;
And the queen's sons and brothers haught and proud:
And were they to be rul'd, and not to rule,
This sickly land might solace as before.   30
1 *Cit.* Come, come; we fear the worst; all will be
    well.
3 *Cit.* When clouds are seen, wise men put on their
    cloaks;
When great leaves fall, then winter is at hand;
When the sun sets, who doth not look for night?
Untimely storms make men expect a dearth.
All may be well; but, if God sort it so,
'T is more than we deserve, or I expect.
2 *Cit.* Truly, the hearts of men are full of fear:
You cannot reason almost with a man
That looks not heavily and full of dread.   40
3 *Cit.* Before the days of change, still is it so.
By a divine instinct, men's minds mistrust
Ensuing danger; as by proof we see
The water swell before a boisterous storm.
But leave it all to God. Whither away?
2 *Cit.* Marry, we were sent for to the justices.
3 *Cit.* And so was I: I'll bear you company.
                    [*Exeunt.*

SCENE IV.—London. A Room in the Palace.

Enter the Archbishop of YORK, *the young Duke of*
YORK, *Queen* ELIZABETH, *and the Duchess of*
YORK.

Arch. Last night, I heard, they lay at Stony Strat-
    ford,
And at Northampton they do rest to-night:
To-morrow, or next day, they will be here.
Duch. I long with all my heart to see the prince.
I hope, he is much grown since last I saw him.
Q. Eliz. But I hear, no: they say, my son of York
Hath almost overta'en him in his growth.
York. Ay, mother, but I would not have it so.
Duch. Why, my young cousin, it is good to grow.
York. Grandam, one night, as we did sit at supper,
My uncle Rivers talk'd how I did grow   11
More than my brother: "Ay," quoth my uncle Gloster,
"Small herbs have grace, great weeds do grow
    apace:"
And since, methinks, I would not grow so fast,
Because sweet flowers are slow, and weeds make
    haste.

Duch. 'Good faith, 'good faith, the saying did not hold
In him that did object the same to thee:
He was the wretched'st thing when he was young,
So long a-growing, and so leisurely,
That, if his rule were true, he should be gracious.   20
Arch. And so, no doubt, he is, my gracious madam.
Duch. I hope, he is; but yet let mothers doubt.
York. Now, by my troth, if I had been remember'd,
I could have given my uncle's grace a flout,
To touch his growth nearer than he touch'd mine.
Duch. How, my young York? I pr'ythee, let me
    hear it.
York. Marry, they say, my uncle grew so fast,
That he could gnaw a crust at two hours old:
'T was full two years ere I could get a tooth.
Grandam, this would have been a biting jest.   30
Duch. I pr'ythee, pretty York, who told thee this?
York. Grandam, his nurse.
Duch. His nurse! why, she was dead ere thou wast
    born.
York. If 't were not she, I cannot tell who told me.
Q. Eliz. A parlous boy. Go to, you are too shrewd.
Arch. Good madam, be not angry with the child.
Q. Eliz. Pitchers have ears.

Enter a Messenger.

Arch. Here comes a messenger: what news?
Mess. Such news, my lord, as grieves me to report.
Q. Eliz. How doth the prince?
Mess.   Well, madam, and in health.
Duch. What is thy news?   41
Mess. Lord Rivers and Lord Grey are sent to Pom-
    fret,
And with them Sir Thomas Vaughan, prisoners.
Duch. Who hath committed them?
Mess.   The mighty dukes,
Gloster and Buckingham.
Arch.   For what offence?
Mess. The sum of all I can, I have disclos'd:
Why, or for what, the nobles were committed,
Is all unknown to me, my gracious lord.
Q. Eliz. Ah me! I see the ruin of my house.
The tiger now hath seiz'd the gentle hind;   50
Insulting tyranny begins to jet
Upon the innocent and awless throne:
Welcome, destruction, blood, and massacre!
I see, as in a map, the end of all.
Duch. Accursed and unquiet wrangling days,
How many of you have mine eyes beheld!
My husband lost his life to get the crown,
And often up and down my sons were toss'd,
For me to joy, and weep, their gain and loss:
And being seated, and domestic broils   60
Clean over-blown, themselves, the conquerors,
Make war upon themselves; brother to brother,
Blood to blood, self against self:—O! preposterous
And frantic outrage, end thy damned spleen,
Or let me die, to look on death no more.
Q. Eliz. Come, come, my boy; we will to sanc-
    tuary.—
Madam, farewell.
Duch.   Stay, I will go with you.
Q. Eliz. You have no cause.
Arch. [*To the* QUEEN.]   My gracious lady, go,
And thither bear your treasure and your goods.
For my part, I'll resign unto your grace   70
The seal I keep: and so betide to me,
As well I tender you, and all of yours.
Go; I'll conduct you to the sanctuary.   [*Exeunt.*

ACT III.

SCENE I.—London. A Street.

The Trumpets sound. Enter the Prince of WALES, GLOSTER, BUCKINGHAM, *Cardinal* BOURCHIER, *and others.*

Buckingham.
WELCOME, sweet prince, to
   London, to your
   chamber.
Glo. Welcome, dear cousin, my
   thoughts' sovereign:
The weary way hath made you me-
   lancholy.
Prince. No, uncle; but our crosses
   on the way
Have made it tedious, wearisome
   and heavy:
I want more uncles here to welcome
   me.
Glo. Sweet prince, the untainted
   virtue of your years
Hath not yet div'd into the world's deceit:
No more can you distinguish of a man
Than of his outward show; which, God he knows, 10
Seldom or never jumpeth with the heart.
Those uncles which you want were dangerous;
Your grace attended to their sugar'd words,
But look'd not on the poison of their hearts:
God keep you from them, and from such false friends!
Prince. God keep me from false friends! but they
   were none.
Glo. My lord, the mayor of London comes to greet you.

Enter the Lord Mayor, and his Train.

May. God bless your grace with health and happy
   days!
Prince. I thank you, good my lord; and thank you
   all.—   *[Exeunt Mayor, &c.*
I thought my mother and my brother York   20
Would long ere this have met us on the way:
Fie! what a slug is Hastings, that he comes not
To tell us whether they will come or no.

Enter HASTINGS.

Buck. And in good time here comes the sweating
   lord.
Prince. Welcome, my lord. What! will our mother
   come?
Hast. On what occasion, God he knows, not I,
The queen your mother, and your brother York,
Have taken sanctuary: the tender prince
Would fain have come with me to meet your grace,
But by his mother was perforce withheld.   30
Buck. Fie! what an indirect and peevish course
Is this of hers.—Lord cardinal, will your grace
Persuade the queen to send the Duke of York
Unto his princely brother presently?
If she deny, Lord Hastings, go with him,
And from her jealous arms pluck him perforce.
Card. My Lord of Buckingham, if my weak oratory
Can from his mother win the Duke of York,
Anon expect him here: but if she be obdurate
To mild entreaties, God in heaven forbid   40
We should infringe the holy privilege
Of blessed sanctuary! not for all this land
Would I be guilty of so great a sin.
Buck. You are too senseless-obstinate, my lord,
Too ceremonious and traditional:
Weigh it but with the grossness of this age,
You break not sanctuary in seizing him.

The benefit thereof is always granted
To those whose dealings have deserv'd the place,
And those who have the wit to claim the place: 50
This prince hath neither claim'd it, nor deserv'd it;
And therefore, in mine opinion, cannot have it:
Then, taking him from thence that is not there,
You break no privilege nor charter there.
Oft have I heard of sanctuary men,
But sanctuary children, ne'er till now.
Card. My lord, you shall o'er-rule my mind for
   once.—
Come on, Lord Hastings, will you go with me?
Hast. I go, my lord.
Prince. Good lords, make all the speedy haste you
   may.--   *[Exeunt Cardinal and* HASTINGS.
Say, uncle Gloster, if our brother come,   61
Where shall we sojourn till our coronation?
Glo. Where it seems best unto your royal self.
If I may counsel you, some day or two
Your highness shall repose you at the Tower:
Then, where you please, and shall be thought most fit
For your best health and recreation.
Prince. I do not like the Tower, of any place.—-
Did Julius Cæsar build that place, my lord?
Buck. He did, my gracious lord, begin that place,
Which, since, succeeding ages have re-edified.   71
Prince. Is it upon record, or else reported
Successively from age to age, he built it?
Buck. Upon record, my gracious lord.
Prince. But say, my lord, it were not register'd,
Methinks, the truth should live from age to age,
As 't were retail'd to all posterity,
Even to the general all-ending day.
Glo. [*Aside.*] So wise so young, they say, do never
   live long.
Prince. What say you, uncle?   80
Glo. I say, without characters, fame lives long.
[*Aside.*] Thus, like the formal Vice, Iniquity,
I moralise two meanings in one word.
Prince. That Julius Cæsar was a famous man:
With what his valour did enrich his wit,
His wit set down to make his valour live:
Death makes no conquest of this conqueror,
For now he lives in fame, though not in life.—
I 'll tell you what, my cousin Buckingham,—
Buck. What, my gracious lord?   90
Prince. An if I live until I be a man,
I 'll win our ancient right in France again,
Or die a soldier, as I liv'd a king.
Glo. [*Aside.*] Short summers lightly have a forward
   spring.

Enter YORK, HASTINGS, *and the Cardinal.*

Buck. Now, in good time, here comes the Duke of
   York.
Prince. Richard of York! how fares our noble
   brother?
York. Well, my dread lord; so must I call you now.
Prince. Ay, brother, to our grief, as it is yours.
Too late he died, that might have kept that title,   100
Which by his death hath lost much majesty.
Glo. How fares our cousin, noble Lord of York?
York. I thank you, gentle uncle. O! my lord,
You said, that idle weeds are fast in growth:
The prince my brother hath outgrown me far.

Glo. He hath, my lord.
York.   And therefore is he idle?
Glo. O! my fair cousin, I must not say so.
York. Then he is more beholding to you, than I.
Glo. He may command me as my sovereign,
But you have power in me as in a kinsman.
York. I pray you, uncle, give me this dagger.   110
Glo. My dagger, little cousin? with all my heart.
Prince. A beggar, brother?
York. Of my kind uncle, that I know will give;
And being but a toy, which is no grief to give.
Glo. A greater gift than that I 'll give my cousin.
York. A greater gift? O! that 's the sword to it.
Glo. Ay, gentle cousin, were it light enough.
York. O! then, I see, you 'll part but with light
        gifts:
In weightier things you 'll say a beggar, nay.
Glo. It is too weighty for your grace to wear.   120
York. I weigh it lightly, were it heavier.
Glo. What! would you have my weapon, little lord?
York. I would, that I might thank you as you call
        me.
Glo. How?
York. Little.
Prince. My Lord of York will still be cross in talk.—
Uncle, your grace knows how to bear with him.
York. You mean, to bear me, not to bear with me.
Uncle, my brother mocks both you and me.
Because that I am little, like an ape,   130
He thinks that you should bear me on your shoulders.
Buck. With what a sharp-provided wit he reasons!
To mitigate the scorn he gives his uncle,
He prettily and aptly taunts himself.
So cunning, and so young, is wonderful.
Glo. My lord, will 't please you pass along?
Myself, and my good cousin Buckingham,
Will to your mother, to entreat of her
To meet you at the Tower, and welcome you.
York. What! will you go unto the Tower, my lord?
Prince. My lord protector needs will have it so.   141
York. I shall not sleep in quiet at the Tower.
Glo. Why, what should you fear?
York. Marry, my uncle Clarence' angry ghost:
My grandam told me, he was murder'd there.
Prince. I fear no uncles dead.
Glo. Nor none that live, I hope.
Prince. An if they live, I hope, I need not fear.
But come, my lord; and, with a heavy heart,
Thinking on them, go I unto the Tower.   150
        [*A Sennet. Exeunt* PRINCE, YORK, HAST.,
            Card., and Attendants.
Buck. Think you, my lord, this little prating York
Was not incensed by his subtle mother
To taunt and scorn you thus opprobriously?
Glo. No doubt, no doubt. O! 't is a parlous boy;
Bold, quick, ingenious, forward, capable:
He 's all the mother's, from the top to toe.
Buck. Well, let them rest.—Come hither, Catesby;
        thou art sworn
As deeply to effect what we intend,
As closely to conceal what we impart.
Thou know'st our reasons urg'd upon the way:—   160
What think'st thou? is it not an easy matter
To make William Lord Hastings of our mind,
For the instalment of this noble duke
In the seat royal of this famous isle?
Cates. He for his father's sake so loves the prince,
That he will not be won to aught against him.
Buck. What think'st thou then of Stanley? will not
        he?
Cates. He will do all in all as Hastings doth.
Buck. Well then, no more but this. Go, gentle
        Catesby,
And, as it were far off, sound thou Lord Hastings, 170
How he doth stand affected to our purpose;
And summon him to-morrow to the Tower,
To sit about the coronation.
If thou dost find him tractable to us,
Encourage him, and tell him all our reasons:
If he be leaden, icy, cold, unwilling,
Be thou so too, and so break off the talk,
And give us notice of his inclination;

For we to-morrow hold divided councils,
Wherein thyself shalt highly be employ'd.   180
Glo. Commend me to Lord William: tell him,
        Catesby,
His ancient knot of dangerous adversaries
To-morrow are let blood at Pomfret Castle;
And bid my lord, for joy of this good news,
Give Mistress Shore one gentle kiss the more.
Buck. Good Catesby, go, effect this business soundly.
Cates. My good lords both, with all the heed I can.
Glo. Shall we hear from you, Catesby, ere we sleep?
Cates. You shall, my lord.
Glo. At Crosby Place, there shall you find us both.
                                    [*Exit* CATESBY.
Buck. Now, my lord, what shall we do, if we per-
        ceive   191
Lord Hastings will not yield to our complots?
Glo. Chop off his head;—something we will deter-
        mine:—
And, look, when I am king, claim thou of me
The earldom of Hereford, and all the movables
Whereof the king, my brother, was possess'd.
Buck. I 'll claim that promise at your grace's hand.
Glo. And look to have it yielded with all kindness.
Come, let us sup betimes, that afterwards
We may digest our complots in some form.   200
                                          [*Exeunt.*

——

SCENE II.—Before Lord HASTINGS' House.

Enter a Messenger.

Mess. My lord, my lord!—   [*Knocking.*
Hast. [*Within.*] Who knocks?
Mess. One from the Lord Stanley.
Hast. [*Within.*] What is 't o'clock?
Mess. Upon the stroke of four.

Enter HASTINGS.

Hast. Cannot my Lord Stanley sleep these tedious
        nights?
Mess. So it appears by that I have to say.
First, he commends him to your noble self.
Hast. What then?
Mess. Then certifies your lordship, that this night 10
He dreamt the boar had rased off his helm:
Besides, he says, there are two councils held;
And that may be determin'd at the one,
Which may make you and him to rue at th'other.
Therefore, he sends to know your lordship's pleasure,—
If you will presently take horse with him,
And with all speed post with him toward the north,
To shun the danger that his soul divines.
Hast. Go, fellow, go: return unto thy lord;
Bid him not fear the separated councils: 20
His honour and myself are at the one,
And at the other is my good friend Catesby;
Where nothing can proceed that toucheth us,
Whereof I shall not have intelligence.
Tell him, his fears are shallow, without instance:
And for his dreams—I wonder he 's so simple
To trust the mockery of unquiet slumbers.
To fly the boar, before the boar pursues,
Were to incense the boar to follow us,
And make pursuit, where he did mean no chase.   30
Go, bid thy master rise and come to me;
And we will both together to the Tower,
Where, he shall see, the boar will use us kindly.
Mess. I 'll go, my lord, and tell him what you say.
                                          [*Exit.*

Enter CATESBY.

Cates. Many good morrows to my noble lord!
Hast. Good morrow, Catesby: you are early stir-
        ring.
What news, what news, in this our tottering state?
Cates. It is a reeling world, indeed, my lord;
And, I believe, will never stand upright,
Till Richard wear the garland of the realm.   40
Hast. How! wear the garland! dost thou mean the
        crown?
Cates. Ay, my good lord.

Hast. I 'll have this crown of mine cut from my
    shoulders,
Before I 'll see the crown so foul misplac'd.
But canst thou guess that he doth aim at it?
  Cates. Ay, on my life; and hopes to find you
    forward
Upon his party, for the gain thereof:
And thereupon he sends you this good news,—
That this same very day your enemies,
The kindred of the queen, must die at Pomfret.   50
  Hast. Indeed, I am no mourner for that news,
Because they have been still my adversaries;
But, that I 'll give my voice on Richard's side,
To bar my master's heirs in true descent,
God knows, I will not do it, to the death.
  Cates. God keep your lordship in that gracious mind.
  Hast. But I shall laugh at this a twelvemonth hence,
That they which brought me in my master's hate,
I live to look upon their tragedy.
Well, Catesby, ere a fortnight make me older,   60
I 'll send some packing that yet think not on 't.
  Cates. 'T is a vile thing to die, my gracious lord,
When men are unprepar'd, and look not for it.
  Hast. O monstrous, monstrous! and so falls it out
With Rivers, Vaughan, Grey; and so 't will do
With some men else, who think themselves as safe
As thou and I; who, as thou know'st, are dear
To princely Richard, and to Buckingham.
  Cates. The princes both make high account of you;
  [*Aside.*] For they account his head upon the bridge. 70
  Hast. I know they do, and I have well deserv'd it.

           Enter STANLEY.

Come on, come on; where is your boar-spear, man?
Fear you the boar, and go so unprovided?
  Stan. My lord, good morrow:—good morrow,
    Catesby.—
You may jest on, but, by the holy rood,
I do not like these several councils, I.
  Hast. My lord, I hold my life as dear as yours;
And never, in my days, I do protest,
Was it so precious to me as 't is now.
Think you, but that I know our state secure,   80
I would be so triumphant as I am?
  Stan. The lords at Pomfret, when they rode from
    London,
Were jocund, and suppos'd their states were sure,
And they, indeed, had no cause to mistrust;
But yet, you see, how soon the day o'ercast:
This sudden stab of rancour I misdoubt.
Pray God, I say, I prove a needless coward!
What, shall we toward the Tower? the day is spent.
  Hast. Come, come, have with you.—Wot you what,
    my lord?
To-day, the lords you talk of are beheaded.   90
  Stan. They, for their truth, might better wear their
    heads,
Than some that have accus'd them wear their hats.
But come, my lord, let 's away.

        Enter a Pursuivant.

  Hast. Go on before; I 'll talk with this good fellow.
       [*Exeunt* STANLEY *and* CATESBY.
How now, sirrah? how goes the world with thee?
  Purs. The better, that your lordship please to ask.
  Hast. I tell thee, man, 't is better with me now,
Than when thou mett'st me last, where now we meet:
Then was I going prisoner to the Tower,
By the suggestion of the queen's allies;   100
But now, I tell thee (keep it to thyself),
This day those enemies are put to death,
And I in better state than e'er I was.
  Purs. God hold it, to your honour's good content.
  Hast. Gramercy, fellow. There, drink that for me.
          [*Throwing him his purse.*
  Purs. I thank your honour.   [*Exit.*

         Enter a Priest.

  Priest. Well met, my lord; I am glad to see your
    honour.
  Hast. I thank thee, good Sir John, with all my
    heart.

I am in your debt for your last exercise;
Come the next Sabbath, and I will content you.   110

       Enter BUCKINGHAM.

  Buck. What, talking with a priest, lord chamber-
    lain!
Your friends at Pomfret, they do need the priest:
Your honour hath no shriving work in hand.
  Hast. 'Good faith, and when I met this holy man,
The men you talk of came into my mind.
What, go you toward the Tower?
  Buck. I do, my lord; but long I cannot stay there:
I shall return before your lordship thence.
  Hast. Nay, like enough, for I stay dinner there.
  Buck. [*Aside.*] And supper too, although thou
    know'st it not.   120
Come, will you go?
  Hast.   I 'll wait upon your lordship. [*Exeunt.*

SCENE III.—Pomfret. Before the Castle.

Enter RATCLIFF, *with a Guard, conducting* RIVERS,
  GREY, *and* VAUGHAN *to execution.*

  Riv. Sir Richard Ratcliff, let me tell thee this:—
To-day shalt thou behold a subject die
For truth, for duty, and for loyalty.
  Grey. God bless the prince from all the pack of
    you!
A knot you are of damned blood-suckers.
  Vaugh. You live, that shall cry woe for this here-
    after.
  Rat. Despatch: the limit of your lives is out.
  Riv. O Pomfret, Pomfret! O thou bloody prison,
Fatal and ominous to noble peers!
Within the guilty closure of thy walls   10
Richard the Second here was hack'd to death:
And, for more slander to thy dismal seat,
We give to thee our guiltless blood to drink.
  Grey. Now Margaret's curse is fallen upon our
    heads,
When she exclaim'd on Hastings, you, and I,
For standing by when Richard stabb'd her son.
  Riv. Then curs'd she Richard, then curs'd she
    Buckingham,
Then curs'd she Hastings:—O, remember, God,
To hear her prayer for them, as now for us!
And for my sister, and her princely sons,   20
Be satisfied, dear God, with our true blood,
Which, as thou know'st, unjustly must be spilt!
  Rat. Make haste: the hour of death is expiate.
  Riv. Come, Grey,—come, Vaughan;—let us here
    embrace:
Farewell, until we meet again in heaven.   [*Exeunt.*

SCENE IV.—London. A Room in the Tower.

BUCKINGHAM, STANLEY, HASTINGS, *the Bishop of*
  ELY, CATESBY, LOVEL, *and others, sitting at a*
  table: Officers of the Council attending.

  Hast. Now, noble peers, the cause why we are met
Is, to determine of the coronation:
In God's name, speak, when is the royal day?
  Buck. Are all things ready for the royal time?
  Stan. They are; and wants but nomination.
  Ely. To-morrow then I judge a happy day.
  Buck. Who knows the lord protector's mind herein?
Who is most inward with the noble duke?
  Ely. Your grace, we think, should soonest know his
    mind.
  Buck. We know each other's faces; for our hearts,
He knows no more of mine than I of yours;   11
Nor I of his, my lord, than you of mine.
Lord Hastings, you and he are near in love.
  Hast. I thank his grace, I know he loves me well;
But, for his purpose in the coronation,
I have not sounded him, nor he deliver'd
His gracious pleasure any way therein:
But you, my honourable lords, may name the time;

And in the duke's behalf I 'll give my voice,
Which, I presume, he 'll take in gentle part.　　　20

　　　　　　　Enter GLOSTER.

Ely. In happy time, here comes the duke himself.
Glo. My noble lords and cousins, all, good morrow.
I have been long a sleeper; but, I trust,
My absence doth neglect no great design,
Which by my presence might have been concluded.
Buck. Had you not come upon your cue, my lord,
William Lord Hastings had pronounc'd your part,
I mean, your voice, for crowning of the king.
Glo. Than my Lord Hastings, no man might be
　　bolder:
His lordship knows me well, and loves me well.　30
My Lord of Ely, when I was last in Holborn,
I saw good strawberries in your garden there;
I do beseech you, send for some of them.
Ely. Marry, and will, my lord, with all my heart.
　　　　　　　　　　　　　　　　　　　[*Exit.*
Glo. Cousin of Buckingham, a word with you.
　　　　　　　　　　　　　　　[*Takes him aside.*
Catesby hath sounded Hastings in our business,
And finds the testy gentleman so hot,

Glo. " Look how I am bewitch'd."

That he will lose his head, ere give consent,
His master's child, as worshipfully he terms it,
Shall lose the royalty of England's throne.　　40
Buck. Withdraw yourself awhile; I 'll go with you.
　　　　　　[*Exeunt* GLOSTER *and* BUCKINGHAM.
Stan. We have not yet set down this day of triumph.
To-morrow, in my judgment, is too sudden;
For I myself am not so well provided,
As else I would be, were the day prolong'd.

　　　　Re-enter Bishop of ELY.

Ely. Where is my lord, the Duke of Gloster?
I have sent for these strawberries.
Hast. His grace looks cheerfully and smooth this
　　morning:
There 's some conceit or other likes him well,
When that he bids good morrow with such spirit.　50
I think, there 's never a man in Christendom
Can lesser hide his love or hate than he;
For by his face straight shall you know his heart.
Stan. What of his heart perceive you in his face,
By any livelihood he show'd to-day?
Hast. Marry, that with no man here he is offended;
For, were he, he had shown it in his looks.

　　　Re-enter GLOSTER *and* BUCKINGHAM.

Glo. I pray you all, tell me what they deserve,
That do conspire my death with devilish plots
Of damned witchcraft, and that have prevail'd　60
Upon my body with their hellish charms?
Hast. The tender love I bear your grace, my lord,

Makes me most forward in this princely presence
To doom the offenders: whosoe'er they be,
I say, my lord, they have deserved death.
Glo. Then be your eyes the witness of their evil.
Look how I am bewitch'd; behold mine arm
Is, like a blasted sapling, wither'd up:
And this is Edward's wife, that monstrous witch,
Consorted with that harlot strumpet Shore,　　70
That by their witchcraft thus have marked me.
Hast. If they have done this deed, my noble lord, -
Glo. If! thou protector of this damned strumpet,
Talk'st thou to me of ifs?—Thou art a traitor:
Off with his head!—now, by Saint Paul I swear,
I will not dine until I see the same.—
Lovel and Ratcliff, look that it be done;
The rest that love me, rise, and follow me.
　　　　　　[*Exeunt Council, with* GLOSTER *and*
　　　　　　　　　　　　　　　BUCKINGHAM.
Hast. Woe, woe, for England! not a whit for me:
For I, too fond, might have prevented this.　　80
Stanley did dream, the boar did rase his helm;
And I did scorn it, and disdain'd to fly.
Three times to-day my foot-cloth horse did stumble,
And started when he look'd upon the Tower,
　　　As loath to bear me to the slaughter-
　　　　　house.
　　　O! now I need the priest that spake to
　　　　　me:
　　　I now repent I told the pursuivant,
　　　As too triumphing, how mine enemies
　　　To-day at Pomfret bloodily were
　　　　　butcher'd,
　　　And I myself secure in grace and
　　　　　favour.　　　　　　　　　90
　　　O Margaret, Margaret! now thy heavy
　　　　　curse
　　　Is lighted on poor Hastings' wretched
　　　　　head.
　　　Rat. Come, come, despatch; the
　　　　　duke would be at dinner:
　　　Make a short shrift, he longs to see
　　　　　your head.
　　　Hast. O momentary grace of mortal
　　　　　men!
　　　Which we more hunt for than the
　　　　　grace of God.
　　　Who builds his hope in air of your
　　　　　good looks,
　　　Lives like a drunken sailor on a mast;
　　　Ready with every nod to tumble down
　　　Into the fatal bowels of the deep.　　100
Lov. Come, come, despatch; 't is bootless to exclaim.
Hast. O bloody Richard!—miserable England!
I prophesy the fearfull'st time to thee,
That ever wretched age hath look'd upon.
Come, lead me to the block, bear him my head;
They smile at me, who shortly shall be dead. [*Exeunt.*

　　　SCENE V.—The Same.　The Tower Walls.

Enter GLOSTER *and* BUCKINGHAM, *in rotten armour,*
　　　marvellous ill-favoured.

Glo. Come, cousin, canst thou quake, and change
　　thy colour,
Murder thy breath in middle of a word,
And then again begin, and stop again,
As if thou wert distraught and mad with terror?
Buck. Tut! I can counterfeit the deep tragedian;
Speak, and look back, and pry on every side,
Tremble and start at wagging of a straw,
Intending deep suspicion: ghastly looks
Are at my service, like enforced smiles;
And both are ready in their offices,　　　　10
At any time to grace my stratagems.
But what! is Catesby gone?
Glo. He is; and, see, he brings the mayor along.

　　　Enter the Lord Mayor and CATESBY.

Buck. Lord mayor,—
Glo. Look to the drawbridge there!

Buck.   Hark ! a drum.
Glo. Catesby, o'erlook the walls.
Buck. Lord mayor, the reason we have sent—

That breath'd upon the earth a Christian;
Made him my book, wherein my soul recorded
The history of all her secret thoughts:

Glo. "Now will I go, to take some privy order.
To draw the brats of Clarence out of sight."

Glo. Look back, defend thee: here are enemies.
Buck. God and our innocency defend and guard us!

Enter LOVEL *and* RATCLIFF, *with* HASTINGS' *head.*
Glo. Be patient, they are friends; Ratcliff and
        Lovel.   20
Lov. Here is the head of that ignoble traitor,
The dangerous and unsuspected Hastings.
Glo. So dear I lov'd the man, that I must weep.
I took him for the plainest harmless creature

So smooth he daub'd his vice with show of virtue,
That, his apparent open guilt omitted,
I mean his conversation with Shore's wife,   30
He liv'd from all attainder of suspect.
Buck. Well, well, he was the covert'st shelter'd
        traitor
That ever liv'd.—
Would you imagine, or almost believe
(Were 't not that by great preservation
We live to tell it), that the subtle traitor

This day had plotted, in the council-house,
To murder me, and my good Lord of Gloster?
  May. Had he done so?
  Glo. What! think you we are Turks, or infidels? 40
Or that we would, against the form of law,
Proceed thus rashly in the villain's death,
But that the extreme peril of the case,
The peace of England, and our persons' safety,
Enforc'd us to this execution?
  May. Now, fair befall you! he deserv'd his death;
And your good graces both have well proceeded,
To warn false traitors from the like attempts.
  Buck. I never look'd for better at his hands,
After he once fell in with Mistress Shore; 50
Yet had we not determin'd he should die,
Until your lordship came to see his end;
Which now the loving haste of these our friends,
Something against our meanings, have prevented:
Because, my lord, I would have had you heard
The traitor speak, and timorously confess
The manner and the purpose of his treasons;
That you might well have signified the same
Unto the citizens, who haply, may
Misconster us in him, and wail his death. 60
  May. But, my good lord, your grace's words shall serve,
As well as I had seen, and heard him speak:
And do not doubt, right noble princes both,
But I'll acquaint our duteous citizens
With all your just proceedings in this case.
  Glo. And to that end we wish'd your lordship here,
To avoid the censures of the carping world.
  Buck. But since you come too late of our intent,
Yet witness what you hear we did intend:
And so, my good lord mayor, we bid farewell. 70
                  [Exit Lord Mayor.
  Glo. Go after, after, cousin Buckingham.
The mayor towards Guildhall hies him in all post
There, at your meetest vantage of the time,
Infer the bastardy of Edward's children:
Tell them, how Edward put to death a citizen,
Only for saying he would make his son
Heir to the crown; meaning, indeed, his house,
Which by the sign thereof was termed so.
Moreover, urge his hateful luxury,
And bestial appetite in change of lust; 80
Which stretch'd unto their servants, daughters, wives,
Even where his raging eye, or savage heart,
Without control lusted to make a prey.
Nay, for a need, thus far come near my person:
Tell them, when that my mother went with child
Of that insatiate Edward, noble York,
My princely father then had wars in France;
And by true computation of the time,
Found that the issue was not his begot;
Which well appeared in his lineaments, 90
Being nothing like the noble duke my father.
Yet touch this sparingly, as 't were far off;
Because, my lord, you know, my mother lives.
  Buck. Doubt not, my lord, I'll play the orator,
As if the golden fee, for which I plead,
Were for myself: and so, my lord, adieu.
  Glo. If you thrive well, bring them to Baynard's Castle;
Where you shall find me well accompanied
With reverend fathers, and well-learned bishops.
  Buck. I go; and, towards three or four o'clock, 100
Look for the news that the Guildhall affords. *[Exit.*
  Glo. Go, Lovel, with all speed to Doctor Shaw,—
Go thou *[to* CATES.] to Friar Penker:—bid them both
Meet me within this hour at Baynard's Castle.
             [Exeunt LOVEL *and* CATESBY.
Now will I go, to take some privy order,
To draw the brats of Clarence out of sight;
And to give notice, that no manner person
Have any time recourse unto the princes. *[Exit.*

    SCENE VI.—The Same. A Street.
      Enter a Scrivener.
  Scriv. Here is the indictment of the good Lord Hastings;

Which in a set hand fairly is engross'd,
That it may be to-day read o'er in Paul's:
And mark how well the sequel hangs together.
Eleven hours I have spent to write it over,
For yesternight by Catesby was it sent me.
The precedent was full as long a-doing;
And yet within these five hours Hastings liv'd,
Untainted, unexamin'd, free, at liberty.
Here's a good world the while!—Who is so gross, 10
That cannot see this palpable device?
Yet who so bold but says he sees it not?
Bad is the world; and all will come to naught,
When such ill dealing must be seen in thought. *[Exit.*

    SCENE VII.—The Same. The Court of Baynard's Castle.

  Enter GLOSTER *at one door, and* BUCKINGHAM *at another.*

  Glo. How now, how now? what say the citizens?
  Buck. Now by the holy mother of our Lord,
The citizens are mum, say not a word.
  Glo. Touch'd you the bastardy of Edward's children?
  Buck. I did; with his contract with Lady Lucy,
And his contract by deputy in France;
The insatiate greediness of his desires,
And his enforcement of the city wives;
His tyranny for trifles; his own bastardy,
As being got, your father then in France; 10
And his resemblance, being not like the duke.
Withal I did infer your lineaments,
Being the right idea of your father,
Both in your form and nobleness of mind;
Laid open all your victories in Scotland,
Your discipline in war, wisdom in peace,
Your bounty, virtue, fair humility;
Indeed, left nothing fitting for your purpose
Untouch'd, or slightly handled in discourse;
And, when my oratory drew toward end, 20
I bade them that did love their country's good,
Cry—"God save Richard, England's royal king!"
  Glo. And did they so?
  Buck. No, so God help me, they spake not a word:
But, like dumb statuas, or breathing stones,
Star'd each on other, and look'd deadly pale.
Which when I saw, I reprehended them,
And ask'd the mayor, what meant this wilful silence:
His answer was, the people were not us'd
To be spoke to but by the recorder. 30
Then he was urg'd to tell my tale again:—
"Thus saith the duke, thus hath the duke inferr'd;"
But nothing spoke in warrant from himself.
When he had done, some followers of mine own,
At lower end of the hall, hurl'd up their caps,
And some ten voices cried, "God save King Richard!"
And thus I took the vantage of those few,—
"Thanks, gentle citizens, and friends," quoth I;
"This general applause and cheerful shout
Argues your wisdom, and your love to Richard:" 40
And even here brake off, and came away.
  Glo. What tongueless blocks were they! would they not speak?
Will not the mayor then and his brethren come?
  Buck. The mayor is here at hand. Intend some fear;
Be not you spoke with but by mighty suit:
And look you get a prayer-book in your hand,
And stand between two churchmen, good my lord:
For on that ground I'll make a holy descant:
And be not easily won to our requests:
Play the maid's part, still answer nay, and take it. 50
  Glo. I go; and if you plead as well for them
As I can say nay to thee for myself,
No doubt we bring it to a happy issue.
  Buck. Go, go, up to the leads! the lord mayor knocks. *[Exit* GLOSTER.

  Enter the Lord Mayor, Aldermen, and Citizens.

Welcome, my lord: I dance attendance here;
I think the duke will not be spoke withal.—

Enter, from the Castle, Catesby.

Now, Catesby! what says your lord to my request?
  Cates. He doth entreat your grace, my noble lord,
To visit him to-morrow, or next day.
He is within, with two right reverend fathers,   60
Divinely bent to meditation;
And in no worldly suits would he be mov'd,
To draw him from his holy exercise.
  Buck. Return, good Catesby, to the gracious duke:
Tell him, myself, the mayor and aldermen,
In deep designs, in matter of great moment,
No less importing than our general good,
Are come to have some conference with his grace.
  Cates. I 'll signify so much unto him straight. [*Exit.*
  Buck. Ah, ha! my lord, this prince is not an
      Edward;   70
He is not lolling on a lewd day-bed,
But on his knees at meditation;
Not dallying with a brace of courtesans,
But meditating with two deep divines;
Not sleeping, to engross his idle body,
But praying, to enrich his watchful soul.
Happy were England, would this virtuous prince
Take on his grace the sovereignty thereof;
But, sure, I fear, we shall not win him to it.
  May. Marry, God defend his grace should say us
      nay!   80
  Buck. I fear, he will. Here Catesby comes again.—

Re-enter Catesby.

Now, Catesby, what says his grace?
  Cates. He wonders to what end you have assembled
Such troops of citizens to come to him:
His grace not being warn'd thereof before,
He fears, my lord, you mean no good to him:
  Buck. Sorry I am, my noble cousin should
Suspect me, that I mean no good to him:
By Heaven, we come to him in perfect love;
And so once more return, and tell his grace.   90
                                    [*Exit* Catesby.
When holy and devout religious men
Are at their beads, 't is much to draw them thence;
So sweet is zealous contemplation.

Enter Gloster, *in a gallery above, between two
    Bishops.* Catesby *returns.*

  May. See, where his grace stands 'tween two
      clergymen!
  Buck. Two props of virtue for a Christian prince,
To stay him from the fall of vanity;
And, see, a book of prayer in his hand,
True ornament to know a holy man.—
Famous Plantagenet, most gracious prince,
Lend favourable ear to our requests,   100
And pardon us the interruption
Of thy devotion, and right Christian zeal.
  Glo. My lord, there needs no such apology;
I do beseech your grace to pardon me,
Who, earnest in the service of my God,
Deferr'd the visitation of my friends.
But, leaving this, what is your grace's pleasure?
  Buck. Even that, I hope, which pleaseth God above,
And all good men of this ungovern'd isle.
  Glo. I do suspect, I have done some offence,   110
That seems disgracious in the city's eye;
And that you come to reprehend my ignorance.
  Buck. You have, my lord: 'would it might please
      your grace,
On our entreaties to amend your fault.
  Glo. Else wherefore breathe I in a Christian land?
  Buck. Know then, it is your fault that you resign
The supreme seat, the throne majestical,
The scepter'd office of your ancestors,
Your state of fortune, and your due of birth,
The lineal glory of your royal house,   120
To the corruption of a blemish'd stock;
Whiles, in the mildness of your sleepy thoughts,
Which here we waken to our country's good,
This noble isle doth want her proper limbs;
Her face defac'd with scars of infamy,
Her royal stock graft with ignoble plants,

And almost shoulder'd in the swallowing gulf
Of dark forgetfulness and deep oblivion.
Which to recure we heartily solicit
Your gracious self to take on you the charge   130
And kingly government of this your land:
Not as protector, steward, substitute,
Or lowly factor for another's gain;
But as successively from blood to blood,
Your right of birth, your empery, your own.
For this, consorted with the citizens,
Your very worshipful and loving friends,
And by their vehement instigation,
In this just cause come I to move your grace.
  Glo. I cannot tell, if to depart in silence,   140
Or bitterly to speak in your reproof,
Best fitteth my degree, or your condition:
If not to answer,—you might haply think,
Tongue-tied ambition, not replying, yielded
To bear the golden yoke of sovereignty,
Which fondly you would here impose on me;
If to reprove you for this suit of yours,
So season'd with your faithful love to me,
Then, on the other side, I check'd my friends.
Therefore, to speak, and to avoid the first,   150
And then, in speaking, not to incur the last,
Definitely thus I answer you.
Your love deserves my thanks; but my desert
Unmeritable shuns your high request.
First, if all obstacles were cut away,
And that my path were even to the crown,
As the ripe revenue and due of birth,
Yet so much is my poverty of spirit,
So mighty, and so many, my defects,
That I would rather hide me from my greatness,   160
Being a bark to brook no mighty sea,
Than in my greatness covet to be hid,
And in the vapour of my glory smother'd.
But, God be thank'd, there is no need of me;
And much I need to help you, were there need;
The royal tree hath left us royal fruit,
Which, mellow'd by the stealing hours of time,
Will well become the seat of majesty,
And make, no doubt, us happy by his reign.
On him I lay that you would lay on me,   170
The right and fortune of his happy stars;
Which God defend that I should wring from him!
  Buck. My lord, this argues conscience in your
      grace;
But the respects thereof are nice and trivial,
All circumstances well considered.
You say, that Edward is your brother's son:
So say we too, but not by Edward's wife;
For first was he contract to Lady Lucy—
Your mother lives a witness to his vow—
And afterward by substitute betroth'd   180
To Bona, sister to the King of France.
These both put off, a poor petitioner,
A care-craz'd mother to a many sons,
A beauty-waning and distressed widow,
Even in the afternoon of her best days,
Made prize and purchase of his wanton eye,
Seduc'd the pitch and height of his degree
To base declension and loath'd bigamy.
By her, in his unlawful bed, he got
This Edward, whom our manners call the prince. 190
More bitterly could I expostulate,
Save that, for reverence to some alive,
I give a sparing limit to my tongue.
Then, good my lord, take to your royal self
This proffer'd benefit of dignity;
If not to bless us and the land withal,
Yet to draw forth your noble ancestry
From the corruption of abusing times,
Unto a lineal true-derived course.   199
  May. Do, good my lord; your citizens entreat you.
  Buck. Refuse not, mighty lord, this proffer'd love.
  Cates. O! make them joyful: grant their lawful suit.
  Glo. Alas! why would you heap this care on me?
I am unfit for state and majesty;
I do beseech you, take it not amiss;
I cannot, nor I will not, yield to you.
  Buck. If you refuse it,—as in love and zeal.

Loath to depose the child, your brother's son ;
As well we know your tenderness of heart,
And gentle, kind, effeminate remorse,   210
Which we have noted in you to your kindred,
And equally, indeed, to all estates,—
Yet know, whe'r you accept our suit or no,
Your brother's son shall never reign our king ;
But we will plant some other in the throne,
To the disgrace and downfall of your house :
And in this resolution here we leave you.—
Come, citizens, we will entreat no more.
          [*Exeunt* BUCKINGHAM *and Citizens.*
  Cates. Call him again, sweet prince ; accept their
          suit :
If you deny them, all the land will rue it.   220
  Glo. Will you enforce me to a world of cares ?
Call them again : I am not made of stone,
But penetrable to your kind entreaties,
                              [*Exit* CATESBY.
Albeit against my conscience and my soul.—

          Re-enter BUCKINGHAM, *and the rest.*

Cousin of Buckingham, and sage, grave men,

Since you will buckle fortune on my back,
To bear her burden, whe'r I will, or no,
I must have patience to endure the load :
But if black scandal, or foul-fac'd reproach,
Attend the sequel of your imposition,   230
Your mere enforcement shall acquittance me
From all the impure blots and stains thereof ;
For God doth know, and you may partly see,
How far I am from the desire of this.
  May. God bless your grace ! we see it, and will
          say it.
  Glo. In saying so, you shall but say the truth.
  Buck. Then I salute you with this royal title,—
" Long live King Richard, England's worthy king ! "
  All. Amen.   239
  Buck. To-morrow may it please you to be crown'd ?
  Glo. Even when you please, for you will have it so.
  Buck. To-morrow then we will attend your grace :
And so most joyfully we take our leave.
  Glo. [*To the Bishops.*] Come, let us to our holy
          work again.—
Farewell, my cousin :—farewell, gentle friends.
                                    [*Exeunt.*

ACT IV.

SCENE I.—Before the Tower.

Enter, on one side, Queen ELIZABETH, *Duchess of* YORK, *and Marquess of* DORSET; *on the other,* ANNE,
Duchess of GLOSTER, *leading Lady* MARGARET PLANTAGENET, CLARENCE'S *young daughter.*

Duchess.

WHO meets us here?—my niece Plantagenet,
Led in the hand of her kind aunt of
          Gloster !
Now, for my life, she's wand'ring to the
          Tower,
On pure heart's love, to greet the tender
          princes.—
Daughter, well met.
          Anne.   God give your graces both
A happy and a joyful time of day.
  Q. Eliz. As much to you, good sister : whither
          away ?
  Anne. No further than the Tower ; and, as I guess,
Upon the like devotion as yourselves,
To gratulate the gentle princes there.   10
  Q. Eliz. Kind sister, thanks : we 'll enter all to-
          gether.

          Enter BRAKENBURY.

And, in good time, here the lieutenant comes.—
Master lieutenant, pray you, by your leave,
How doth the prince, and my young son of York ?
  Brak. Right well, dear madam. By your patience,
I may not suffer you to visit them :
The king hath strictly charg'd the contrary.
  Q. Eliz. The king ! who's that ?
  Brak.   I mean the lord protector.
  Q. Eliz. The Lord protect him from that kingly
          title !
Hath he set bounds between their love and me ?   20
I am their mother ; who shall bar me from them ?
  Duch. I am their father's mother ; I will see them.
  Anne. Their aunt I am in law, in love their mother ;
Then bring me to their sights ; I 'll bear thy blame,
And take thy office from thee, on my peril.

  Brak. No, madam, no ; I may not leave it so :
I am bound by oath, and therefore pardon me. [*Exit.*

          Enter STANLEY.

  Stan. Let me but meet you, ladies, one hour hence,
And I 'll salute your grace of York as mother,
And reverend looker-on of two fair queens.—   30
[*To* ANNE.] Come, madam, you must straight to West-
          minster,
There to be crowned Richard's royal queen.
  Q. Eliz. Ah ! cut my lace asunder,
That my pent heart may have some scope to beat,
Or else I swoon with this dead-killing news.
  Anne. Despiteful tidings ! O, unpleasing news !
  Dor. Be of good cheer :—mother, how fares your
          grace ?
  Q. Eliz. O Dorset ! speak not to me, get thee gone ;
Death and destruction dog thee at thy heels :
Thy mother's name is ominous to children.   40
If thou wilt outstrip death, go cross the seas,
And live with Richmond, from the reach of hell.
Go, hie thee, hie thee, from this slaughter-house,
Lest thou increase the number of the dead,
And make me die the thrall of Margaret's curse,—
Nor mother, wife, nor England's 'counted queen.
  Stan. Full of wise care is this your counsel,
          madam.—
Take all the swift advantage of the hours ;
You shall have letters from me to my son
In your behalf, to meet you on the way :   50
Be not ta'en tardy by unwise delay.
  Duch. O ill-dispersing wind of misery !—
O, my accursed womb ! the bed of death,
A cockatrice hast thou hatch'd to the world,
Whose unavoided eye is murderous !
  Stan. Come, madam, come : I in all haste was sent.

Anne. And I with all unwillingness will go.—
O! 'would to God, that the inclusive verge
Of golden metal, that must round my brow,
Were red-hot steel to sear me to the brain!   60
Anointed let me be with deadly venom;
And die, ere men can say—God save the queen!
Q. Eliz. Go, go, poor soul, I envy not thy glory;
To feed my humour, wish thyself no harm.
Anne. No! why?—When he, that is my husband
    now,
Came to me, as I follow'd Henry's corse;
When scarce the blood was well wash'd from his
    hands,
Which issu'd from my other angel husband,
And that dear saint which then I weeping follow'd;
O! when, I say, I look'd on Richard's face,   70
This was my wish,—" Be thou," quoth I, " accurs'd,
For making me, so young, so old a widow!
And, when thou wedd'st, let sorrow haunt thy bed;
And be thy wife (if any be so mad)
More miserable by the life of thee,
Than thou hast made me by my dear lord's death!"
Lo! ere I can repeat this curse again,
Within so small a time, my woman's heart
Grossly grew captive to his honey words,
And prov'd the subject of mine own soul's curse: 80
Which hitherto hath held mine eyes from rest;
For never yet one hour in his bed
Did I enjoy the golden dew of sleep,
But with his timorous dreams was still awak'd.
Besides, he hates me for my father Warwick,
And will, no doubt, shortly be rid of me.
Q. Eliz. Poor heart, adieu; I pity thy complaining.
Anne. No more than with my soul I mourn for
    yours.
Dor. Farewell, thou woful welcomer of glory.
Anne. Adieu, poor soul, that tak'st thy leave of it.   90
Duch. [*To* DOR.] Go thou to Richmond, and good
    fortune guide thee!—
[*To* ANNE.] Go thou to Richard, and good angels tend
    thee!—
[*To* Q. ELIZ.] Go thou to sanctuary, and good thoughts
    possess thee!—
I to my grave, where peace and rest lie with me!
Eighty odd years of sorrow have I seen,
And each hour's joy wrack'd with a week of teen.
Q. Eliz. Stay yet; look back with me unto the
    Tower.
Pity, you ancient stones, those tender babes,
Whom envy hath immur'd within your walls;
Rough cradle for such little pretty ones!   100
Rude ragged nurse, old sullen playfellow
For tender princes, use my babies well!
So foolish sorrow bids your stones farewell. [*Exeunt.*

SCENE II.—A Room of State in the Palace.

Flourish of Trumpets. RICHARD, *crowned;* BUCK-
    INGHAM, CATESBY, *a Page, and others.*

K. Rich. Stand all apart.—Cousin of Buckingham,—
Buck. My gracious sovereign!
K. Rich. Give me thy hand. [RICH. *ascends the
    throne.*] Thus high, by thy advice,
And thy assistance, is King Richard seated:—
But shall we wear these glories for a day,
Or shall they last, and we rejoice in them?
Buck. Still live they, and for ever let them last!
K. Rich. Ah! Buckingham, now do I play the touch,
To try if thou be current gold indeed.—
Young Edward lives.—Think now what I would
    speak.   10
Buck. Say on, my loving lord.
K. Rich. Why, Buckingham, I say, I would be king.
Buck. Why, so you are, my thrice-renowned lord.
K. Rich. Ha! am I king? 'Tis so; but Edward lives.
Buck. True, noble prince.
K. Rich.   O bitter consequence,
That Edward still should live!—" True, noble
    prince."—
Cousin, thou wast not wont to be so dull:—

Shall I be plain?—I wish the bastards dead;
And I would have it suddenly perform'd.
What say'st thou now? speak suddenly, be brief.   20
Buck. Your grace may do your pleasure.
K. Rich. Tut, tut! thou art all ice, thy kindness
    freezes.
Say, have I thy consent that they shall die?
Buck. Give me some little breath, some pause, dear
    lord,
Before I positively speak in this:
I will resolve you herein presently.   [*Exit.*
Cates. [*Aside.*] The king is angry: see, he gnaws
    his lip.
K. Rich. [*Descends from his throne.*] I will converse
    with iron-witted fools,
And unrespective boys: none are for me
That look into me with considerate eye.   30
High-reaching Buckingham grows circumspect.
Boy!—
Page. My lord.
K. Rich. Know'st thou not any, whom corrupting
    gold
Will tempt unto a close exploit of death?
Page. I know a discontented gentleman,
Whose humble means match not his haughty spirit:
Gold were as good as twenty orators,
And will, no doubt, tempt him to anything.   39
K. Rich. What is his name?
Page.   His name, my lord, is Tyrrel.
K. Rich. I partly know the man: go, call him
    hither, boy.--   [*Exit Page.*
The deep-revolving witty Buckingham
No more shall be the neighbour to my counsels.
Hath he so long held out with me untir'd,
And stops he now for breath?—well, be it so.—

Enter STANLEY.

How now, Lord Stanley? what's the news?
Stan. Know, my loving lord,
The Marquess Dorset, as I hear, is fled
To Richmond, in the parts where he abides.
K. Rich. Come hither, Catesby: rumour it abroad,
That Anne, my wife, is very grievous sick;   51
I will take order for her keeping close.
Inquire me out some mean poor gentleman,
Whom I will marry straight to Clarence' daughter:—
The boy is foolish, and I fear not him.—
Look, how thou dream'st!—I say again, give out,
That Anne, my queen, is sick, and like to die:
About it; for it stands me much upon,
To stop all hopes whose growth may damage me.—
    [*Exit* CATESBY.
I must be married to my brother's daughter,   60
Or else my kingdom stands on brittle glass.—
Murder her brothers, and then marry her?
Uncertain way of gain! But I am in
So far in blood, that sin will pluck on sin.
Tear-falling pity dwells not in this eye.—

Re-enter Page, with TYRREL.

Is thy name Tyrrel?
Tyr. James Tyrrel, and your most obedient subject.
K. Rich. Art thou, indeed?
Tyr.   Prove me, my gracious lord.
K. Rich. Dar'st thou resolve to kill a friend of mine?
Tyr. Please you; but I had rather kill two enemies.
K. Rich. Why, then thou hast it: two deep enemies,
Foes to my rest, and my sweet sleep's disturbers,   72
Are they that I would have thee deal upon.
Tyrrel, I mean those bastards in the Tower.
Tyr. Let me have open means to come to them,
And soon I'll rid you from the fear of them.
K. Rich. Thou sing'st sweet music. Hark, come
    hither, Tyrrel:
Go, by this token.—Rise, and lend thine ear.
    [*Whispers.*
There is no more but so:—say, it is done,
And I will love thee, and prefer thee for it.   80
Tyr. I will despatch it straight.   [*Exit.*

Re-enter BUCKINGHAM.

Buck. My lord, I have consider'd in my mind
The late request that you did sound me in.

K. Rich. Well, let that rest. Dorset is fled to Richmond.
Buck. I hear the news, my lord.
K. Rich. Stanley, he is your wife's son :—well look unto it.
Buck. My lord, I claim the gift, my due by promise,
For which your honour and your faith is pawn'd ;
The earldom of Hereford, and the movables,
Which you have promised I shall possess.   90

K. Rich. "Rise, and lend thine ear."

K. Rich. Stanley, look to your wife: if she convey
Letters to Richmond, you shall answer it.
Buck. What says your highness to my just request?
K. Rich. I do remember me,—Henry the Sixth
Did prophesy, that Richmond should be king,
When Richmond was a little peevish boy.
A king !—perhaps—
Buck. My lord,—
K. Rich. How chance, the prophet could not at that time   100
Have told me, I being by, that I should kill him ?
Buck. My lord, your promise for the earldom,—
K. Rich. Richmond !—When last I was at Exeter,
The mayor in courtesy show'd me the castle,
And call'd it—Rougemont: at which name I started,
Because a bard of Ireland told me once,
I should not live long after I saw Richmond.
Buck. My lord,—
K. Rich. Ay ; what's o'clock?
Buck. I am thus bold to put your grace in mind
Of what you promis'd me.   110
K. Rich. Well, but what's o'clock ?
Buck.   Upon the stroke of ten.
K. Rich. Well, let it strike.
Buck.   Why, let it strike ?
K. Rich. Because that, like a Jack, thou keep'st the stroke
Betwixt thy begging and my meditation.
I am not in the giving vein to-day.
Buck. Why, then resolve me whether you will, or no.
K. Rich. Thou troublest me : I am not in the vein.
    [*Exeunt King* RICHARD *and Train.*
Buck. And is it thus ? repays he my deep service
With such contempt ? made I him king for this?
O ! let me think on Hastings, and be gone   120
To Brecknock, while my fearful head is on.   [*Exit.*

SCENE III.—The Same.

Enter TYRREL.

Tyr. The tyrannous and bloody act is done ;
The most arch deed of piteous massacre,
That ever yet this land was guilty of.
Dighton and Forrest, whom I did suborn
To do this piece of ruthless butchery,
Albeit they were flesh'd villains, bloody dogs,
Melted with tenderness and mild compassion,
Wept like to children in their death's sad story.

"Oh ! thus," quoth Dighton, "lay the gentle babes,"—
"Thus, thus," quoth Forrest, "girdling one another   10
Within their alabaster innocent arms :
Their lips were four red roses on a stalk,
And, in their summer beauty, kiss'd each other.
A book of prayers on their pillow lay ;
Which once," quoth Forrest, "almost chang'd my mind ;
But, O ! the devil"—there the villain stopp'd ;
When Dighton thus told on,—"We smothered
The most replenished sweet work of nature,
That, from the prime creation, e'er she fram'd."   20
Hence both are gone with conscience and remorse :
They could not speak ; and so I left them both,
To bear this tidings to the bloody king.

Enter King RICHARD.

And here he comes.—All health, my sovereign lord !
K. Rich. Kind Tyrrel, am I happy in thy news?
Tyr. If to have done the thing you gave in charge
Beget your happiness, be happy then,
For it is done.
K. Rich.   But didst thou see them dead ?
Tyr. I did, my lord.
K. Rich.   And buried, gentle Tyrrel ?
Tyr. The chaplain of the Tower hath buried them ;
But where, to say the truth, I do not know.   30
K. Rich. Come to me, Tyrrel, soon, at after-supper,
When thou shalt tell the process of their death.
Meantime, but think how I may do thee good,
And be inheritor of thy desire.
Farewell till then.
Tyr.   I humbly take my leave.   [*Exit.*
K. Rich. The son of Clarence have I pent up close ;
His daughter meanly have I match'd in marriage ;
The sons of Edward sleep in Abraham's bosom,
And Anne, my wife, hath bid this world good night.
Now, for I know the Bretagne Richmond aims   40

Tyr. "'Thus, thus,' quoth Forrest, 'girdling one another Within their alabaster innocent arms.'"

At young Elizabeth, my brother's daughter,
And, by that knot, looks proudly on the crown,
To her go I, a jolly thriving wooer.

Enter CATESBY.

Cates. My lord !—
K. Rich. Good or bad news, that thou com'st in so bluntly?
Cates. Bad news, my lord : Morton is fled to Richmond ;
And Buckingham, back'd with the hardy Welshmen,
Is in the field, and still his power increaseth.
K. Rich. Ely with Richmond troubles me more near,
Than Buckingham and his rash-levied strength.   50
Come : I have learn'd, that fearful commenting
Is leaden servitor to dull delay :
Delay leads impotent and snail-pac'd beggary :

Then fiery expedition be my wing,
Jove's Mercury, and herald for a king.
Go, muster men : my counsel is my shield ;
We must be brief, when traitors brave the field.
                                        [*Exeunt.*

———

SCENE IV.—Before the Palace.

Enter Queen MARGARET.

Q. Mar. So, now prosperity begins to mellow,
And drop into the rotten mouth of death.
Here in these confines slily have I lurk'd,
To watch the waning of mine enemies.
A dire induction am I witness to,
And will to France ; hoping, the consequence
Will prove as bitter, black, and tragical.
Withdraw thee, wretched Margaret: who comes
        here ?   [*Retiring.*

Enter Queen ELIZABETH *and the Duchess of* YORK.

Q. Eliz. Ah, my poor princes ! ah, my tender babes !
My unblown flowers, new-appearing sweets !   10
If yet your gentle souls fly in the air,
And be not fix'd in doom perpetual,
Hover about me with your airy wings,
And hear your mother's lamentation.
Q. Mar. Hover about her ; say, that right for right
Hath dimm'd your infant morn to aged night.
Duch. So many miseries have craz'd my voice,
That my woe-wearied tongue is still and mute.—
Edward Plantagenet, why art thou dead ?
Q. Mar. Plantagenet doth quit Plantagenet ;   20
Edward for Edward pays a dying debt.
Q. Eliz. Wilt thou, O God ! fly from such gentle
        lambs,
And throw them in the entrails of the wolf ?
When didst thou sleep, when such a dead was done ?
Q. Mar. When holy Harry died, and my sweet son.
Duch. Dead life, blind sight, poor mortal living
        ghost,
Woe's scene, world's shame, grave's due by life
        usurp'd,
Brief abstract and record of tedious days,
Rest thy unrest on England's lawful earth,
                                [*Sitting down.*
Unlawfully made drunk with innocent blood !   30
Q. Eliz. Ah ! that thou wouldst as soon afford a
        grave,
As thou canst yield a melancholy seat :
Then would I hide my bones, not rest them here !
Ah ! who hath any cause to mourn but we ?
                        [*Sitting down by her.*
Q. Mar. [*Coming forward.*] If ancient sorrow be
        most reverend,
Give mine the benefit of seniory,
And let my griefs frown on the upper hand.
If sorrow can admit society, [*Sitting down with them.*
Tell o'er your woes again by viewing mine :—
I had an Edward, till a Richard kill'd him ;   40
I had a Henry, till a Richard kill'd him ;
Thou hadst an Edward, till a Richard kill'd him ;
Thou hadst a Richard, till a Richard kill'd him.
Duch. I had a Richard too, and thou didst kill him ;
I had a Rutland too ; thou holp'st to kill him.
Q. Mar. Thou hadst a Clarence too, and Richard
        kill'd him.
From forth the kennel of thy womb hath crept
A hell-hound, that doth hunt us all to death ;
That dog, that had his teeth before his eyes,
To worry lambs, and lap their gentle blood :   50
That foul defacer of God's handy-work,
That excellent grand-tyrant of the earth,
That reigns in galled eyes of weeping souls,
Thy womb let loose, to chase us to our graves.—
O ! upright, just, and true-disposing God,
How do I thank thee, that this carnal cur
Preys on the issue of his mother's body,
And makes her pew-fellow with others' moan !
Duch. O, Harry's wife ! triumph not in my woes :
God witness with me, I have wept for thine.   60
Q. Mar. Bear with me : I am hungry for revenge,

And now I cloy me with beholding it.
Thy Edward he is dead, that kill'd my Edward ;
Thy other Edward dead, to quit my Edward ;
Young York he is but boot, because both they
Match not the high perfection of my loss.
Thy Clarence he is dead, that stabb'd my Edward ;
And the beholders of this frantic play,
The adulterate Hastings, Rivers, Vaughan, Grey,
Untimely smother'd in their dusky graves.   70
Richard yet lives, hell's black intelligencer,
Only reserv'd their factor, to buy souls,
And send them thither ; but at hand, at hand,
Ensues his piteous and unpitied end :
Earth gapes, hell burns, fiends roar, saints pray,
To have him suddenly convey'd from hence.—
Cancel his bond of life, dear God ! I pray,
That I may live and say, the dog is dead.
Q. Eliz. O ! thou didst prophesy, the time would
        come,
That I should wish for thee to help me curse   80
That bottled spider, that foul bunch-back'd toad.
Q. Mar. I call'd thee then vain flourish of my
        fortune ;
I call'd thee then poor shadow, painted queen ;
The presentation of but what I was ;
The flattering index of a direful pageant ;
One heav'd o' high, to be hurl'd down below ;
A mother only mock'd with two fair babes ;
A dream of what thou wast ; a garish flag,
To be the aim of every dangerous shot ;
A sign of dignity, a breath, a bubble ;   90
A queen in jest, only to fill the scene.
Where is thy husband now ? where be thy brothers ?
Where be thy two sons ? wherein dost thou joy ?
Who sues, and kneels, and says—God save the
        queen ?
Where be the bending peers that flatter'd thee ?
Where be the thronging troops that follow'd thee ?
Decline all this, and see what now thou art.
For happy wife, a most distressed widow ;
For joyful mother, one that wails the name ;
For one being sued to, one that humbly sues ;   100
For queen, a very caitiff crown'd with care ;
For she that scorn'd at me, now scorn'd of me ;
For she being fear'd of all, now fearing one ;
For she commanding all, obey'd of none.
Thus hath the course of justice whirl'd about,
And left thee but a very prey to time ;
Having no more but thought of what thou wast,
To torture thee the more, being what thou art.
Thou didst usurp my place, and dost thou not
Usurp the just proportion of my sorrow ?   110
Now thy proud neck bears half my burden'd yoke ;
From which, even here, I slip my wearied head,
And leave the burden of it all on thee.
Farewell, York's wife, and queen of sad mischance :
These English woes shall make me smile in France.
Q. Eliz. O thou ! well skill'd in curses, stay awhile,
And teach me how to curse mine enemies.
Q. Mar. Forbear to sleep the night, and fast the
        day ;
Compare dead happiness with living woe :
Think that thy babes were fairer than they were, 120
And he that slew them fouler than he is :
Bettering thy loss makes the bad-causer worse :
Revolving this will teach thee how to curse.
Q. Eliz. My words are dull ; O ! quicken them with
        thine.
Q. Mar. Thy woes will make them sharp, and
        pierce like mine.   [*Exit.*
Duch. Why should calamity be full of words ?
Q. Eliz. Windy attorneys to their client woes,
Airy succeeders of intestate joys,
Poor breathing orators of miseries !
Let them have scope : though what they do impart
Help nothing else, yet do they ease the heart. 131
Duch. If so, then be not tongue-tied : go with
        me,
And in the breath of bitter words let 's smother
My damned son, that thy two sweet sons smother'd.
                                [*A Trumpet heard.*
The trumpet sounds : be copious in exclaims.

Enter King RICHARD, *and his Train, marching.*

K. Rich. Who intercepts me in my expedition?
Duch. O! she that might have intercepted thee,
By strangling thee in her accursed womb,
From all the slaughters, wretch, that thou hast done.
Q. Eliz. Hid'st thou that forehead with a golden
      crown,   140
Where should be branded, if that right were right,
The slaughter of the prince that ow'd that crown,
And the dire death of my poor sons and brothers?
Tell me, thou villain-slave, where are my children?
Duch. Thou toad, thou toad, where is thy brother
      Clarence,
And little Ned Plantagenet, his son?
Q. Eliz. Where is the gentle Rivers, Vaughan,
      Grey?
Duch. Where is kind Hastings?

K. Rich. " Who intercepts me in my expedition?"

K. Rich. A flourish, trumpets!—strike alarum,
      drums!   150
Let not the heavens hear these tell-tale women
Rail on the Lord's anointed. Strike, I say!—
                 [*Flourish. Alarums.*
Either be patient, and entreat me fair,
Or with the clamorous report of war
Thus will I drown your exclamations.
Duch. Art thou my son?
K. Rich. Ay; I thank God, my father, and yourself.
Duch. Then patiently hear my impatience.
K. Rich. Madam, I have a touch of your condition,
That cannot brook the accent of reproof.
Duch. O! let me speak.
K. Rich.   Do, then; but I'll not hear.
Duch. I will be mild and gentle in my words.   161
K. Rich. And brief, good mother; for I am in haste.
Duch. Art thou so hasty? I have stay'd for thee,
God knows, in torment and in agony.
K. Rich. And came I not at last to comfort you?
Duch. No, by the holy rood, thou know'st it well,
Thou cam'st on earth to make the earth my hell.
A grievous burden was thy birth to me;
Tetchy and wayward was thy infancy;
Thy school-days frightful, desperate, wild and furious;
Thy prime of manhood daring, bold and venturous;
Thy age confirm'd, proud, subtle, sly, and bloody, 172
More mild, but yet more harmful, kind in hatred:
What comfortable hour canst thou name,
That ever grac'd me with thy company?
    K. Rich. 'Faith, none, but Humphrey Hour, that
      call'd your grace
To breakfast once, forth of my company.

If I be so disgracious in your eye,
Let me march on, and not offend you, madam.—
Strike up the drum!
Duch.   I pr'ythee, hear me speak.   180
K. Rich. You speak too bitterly.
Duch.   Hear me a word;
For I shall never speak to thee again.
K. Rich. So.
Duch. Either thou wilt die by God's just ordinance,
Ere from this war thou turn a conqueror;
Or I with grief and extreme age shall perish,
And never more behold thy face again.
Therefore, take with thee my most grievous curse;
Which, in the day of battle, tire thee more
Than all the complete armour that thou wear'st! 190
My prayers on the adverse party fight;
And there the little souls of Edward's children
Whisper the spirits of thine enemies,
      And promise them success and
           victory.
Bloody thou art, bloody will be thy
           end;
Shame serves thy life, and doth thy
           death attend.   [*Exit.*
    Q. Eliz. Though far more cause,
           yet much less spirit to
           curse
Abides in me; I say Amen to her.
                 [*Going.*
    K. Rich. Stay, madam, I must
           talk a word with you.
    Q. Eliz. I have no more sons of
           the royal blood   200
For thee to slaughter: for my
           daughters, Richard,
They shall be praying nuns, not
           weeping queens;
And therefore level not to hit their
           lives.
    K. Rich. You have a daughter
           call'd Elizabeth,
Virtuous and fair, royal and
           gracious.
    Q. Eliz. And must she die for
           this? O! let her live,
And I'll corrupt her manners, stain
           her beauty;
Slander myself as false to Edward's
           bed;
Throw over her the veil of infamy:
So she may live unscarr'd of bleeding slaughter, 210
I will confess she was not Edward's daughter.
    K. Rich. Wrong not her birth; she is a royal
      princess.
Q. Eliz. To save her life, I'll say she is not so.
K. Rich. Her life is safest only in her birth.
Q. Eliz. And only in that safety died her brothers.
K. Rich. Lo! at their birth good stars were opposite.
Q. Eliz. No, to their lives ill friends were contrary.
K. Rich. All unavoided is the doom of destiny.
Q. Eliz. True, when avoided grace makes destiny.
My babes were destin'd to a fairer death,   220
If grace had bless'd thee with a fairer life.
K. Rich. You speak, as if that I had slain my cousins.
Q. Eliz. Cousins, indeed; and by their uncle
      cozen'd
Of comfort, kingdom, kindred, freedom, life.
Whose hands soever lanc'd their tender hearts,
Thy head, all indirectly, gave direction:
No doubt the murderous knife was dull and blunt,
Till it was whetted on thy stone-hard heart,
To revel in the entrails of my lambs.
But that still use of grief makes wild grief tame, 230
My tongue should to thy ears not name my boys,
Till thy nails were anchor'd in thine eyes;
And I, in such a desperate bay of death,
Like a poor bark, of sails and tackling reft,
Rush all to pieces on thy rocky bosom.
    K. Rich. Madam, so thrive I in my enterprise,
And dangerous success of bloody wars,
As I intend more good to you and yours,
Than ever you or yours by me were harm'd!

Q. Eliz. What good is cover'd with the face of
   heaven,   240
To be discover'd, that can do me good?
K. Rich. The advancement of your children, gentle
   lady.
Q. Eliz. Up to some scaffold, there to lose their
   heads?
K. Rich. Unto the dignity and height of fortune,
The high imperial type of this earth's glory.
Q. Eliz. Flatter my sorrow with report of it :
Tell me, what state, what dignity, what honour,
Canst thou demise to any child of mine ?
K. Rich. Even all I have ; ay, and myself and all,
Will I withal endow a child of thine ;   250
So in the Lethe of thy angry soul
Thou drown the sad remembrance of those wrongs,
Which thou supposest I have done to thee.
Q. Eliz. Be brief, lest that the process of thy kind-
   ness
Last longer telling than thy kindness' date.
K. Rich. Then know, that from my soul I love thy
   daughter.
Q. Eliz. My daughter's mother thinks it with her
   soul.
K. Rich. What do you think ?
Q. Eliz. That thou dost love my daughter from thy
   soul.
So, from thy soul's love, didst thou love her brothers ;
And from my heart's love I do thank thee for it. 261
K. Rich. Be not so hasty to confound my meaning.
I mean, that with my soul I love thy daughter,
And do intend to make her Queen of England.
Q. Eliz. Well then, who dost thou mean shall be
   her king?
K. Rich. Even he that makes her queen : who else
   should be?
Q. Eliz. What ! thou ?
K. Rich. Even so : how think you of it ?
Q. Eliz. How canst thou woo her?
K. Rich.   That I would learn of you,
As one being best acquainted with her humour. 270
Q. Eliz. And wilt thou learn of me ?
K. Rich.   Madam, with all my heart.
Q. Eliz. Send to her, by the man that slew her
   brothers,
A pair of bleeding hearts ; thereon engrave
Edward and York ; then, haply, will she weep :
Therefore present to her—as sometime Margaret
Did to thy father, steep'd in Rutland's blood,—
A handkerchief, which, say to her, did drain
The purple sap from her sweet brothers' body,
And bid her wipe her weeping eyes withal.
If this inducement move her not to love, 280
Send her a letter of thy noble deeds ;
Tell her, thou mad'st away her uncle Clarence,
Her uncle Rivers ; ay, and, for her sake,
Mad'st quick conveyance with her good aunt Anne.
K. Rich. You mock me, madam ; this is not the way
To win your daughter.
Q. Eliz.   There is no other way,
Unless thou couldst put on some other shape,
And not be Richard that hath done all this.
K. Rich. Say, that I did all this for love of her ?
Q. Eliz. Nay, then indeed, she cannot choose but
   hate thee, 290
Having bought love with such a bloody spoil.
K. Rich. Look, what is done cannot be now
   amended :
Men shall deal unadvisedly sometimes,
Which after-hours give leisure to repent :
If I did take the kingdom from your sons,
To make amends I 'll give it to your daughter.
If I have kill'd the issue of your womb,
To quicken your increase, I will beget
Mine issue of your blood upon your daughter.
A grandam's name is little less in love 300
Than is the doting title of a mother :
They are as children but one step below,
Even of your mettle, of your very blood :
Of all one pain—save for a night of groans
Endur'd of her, for whom you bid like sorrow.
Your children were vexation to your youth ;

But mine shall be a comfort to your age.
The loss you have is but a son being king,
And by that loss your daughter is made queen.
I cannot make you what amends I would, 310
Therefore accept such kindness as I can.
Dorset, your son, that with a fearful soul
Leads discontented steps in foreign soil,
This fair alliance quickly shall call home
To high promotions and great dignity :
The king, that calls your beauteous daughter wife,
Familiarly shall call thy Dorset brother ;
Again shall you be mother to a king,
And all the ruins of distressful times
Repair'd with double riches of content. 320
What ! we have many goodly days to see :
The liquid drops of tears that you have shed,
Shall come again transform'd to orient pearl,
Advantaging their loan with interest
Of ten times double gain of happiness.
Go then, my mother ; to thy daughter go :
Make bold her bashful years with your experience ;
Prepare her ears to hear a wooer's tale ;
Put in her tender heart the aspiring flame
Of golden sovereignty ; acquaint the princess 330
With the sweet silent hours of marriage joys :
And when this arm of mine hath chastised
The petty rebel, dull-brain'd Buckingham,
Bound with triumphant garlands will I come,
And lead thy daughter to a conqueror's bed ;
To whom I will retail my conquest won,
And she shall be sole victress, Cæsar's Cæsar.
Q. Eliz. What were I best to say ? her father's
   brother
Would be her lord ? or shall I say, her uncle ?
Or he that slew her brothers and her uncles ? 340
Under what title shall I woo for thee,
That God, the law, my honour, and her love,
Can make seem pleasing to her tender years ?
K. Rich. Infer fair England's peace by this alliance.
Q. Eliz. Which she shall purchase with still lasting
   war.
K. Rich. Tell her, the king, that may command,
   entreats.
Q. Eliz. That at her hands, which the kings' King
   forbids.
K. Rich. Say, she shall be a high and mighty queen.
Q. Eliz. To wail the title, as her mother doth.
K. Rich. Say, I will love her everlastingly. 350
Q. Eliz. But how long shall that title, ever, last ?
K. Rich. Sweetly in force unto her fair life's end.
Q. Eliz. But how long fairly shall her sweet life
   last ?
K. Rich. As long as Heaven, and nature, lengthens
   it.
Q. Eliz. As long as hell, and Richard, likes of it.
K. Rich. Say, I, her sovereign, am her subject low.
Q. Eliz. But she, your subject, loathes such sove-
   reignty.
'K. Rich. Be eloquent in my behalf to her.
Q. Eliz. An honest tale speeds best, being plainly
   told. 359
K. Rich. Then plainly to her tell my loving tale.
Q. Eliz. Plain, and not honest, is too harsh a style.
K. Rich. Your reasons are too shallow and too quick.
Q. Eliz. O, no, my reasons are too deep and dead ;—
Too deep and dead, poor infants, in their graves.
K. Rich. Harp not on that string, madam ; that is
   past.
Q. Eliz. Harp on it still shall I, till heartstrings
   break.
K. Rich. Now, by my George, my garter, and my
   crown,—
Q. Eliz. Profan'd, dishonour'd, and the third usurp'd.
K. Rich. I swear—
Q. Eliz.   By nothing ; for this is no oath.
Thy George, profan'd, hath lost his holy honour ; 370
Thy garter, blemish'd, pawn'd his knightly virtue ;
Thy crown, usurp'd, disgrac'd his kingly glory.
If something thou wouldst swear to be believ'd,
Swear then by something that thou hast not wrong'd.
K. Rich. Now, by the world,—
Q. Eliz.   'T is full of thy foul wrongs.

K. Rich. My father's death,—
Q. Eliz. Thy life hath it dishonour'd.
K. Rich. Then, by myself,—
Q. Eliz. Thyself is self-misus'd.
K. Rich. Why then, by God,—
Q. Eliz. God's wrong is most of all.
If thou hadst fear'd to break an oath by Him,
The unity, the king my husband made,　　　　380
Thou hadst not broken, nor my brothers died.
If thou hadst fear'd to break an oath by Him,
The imperial metal, circling now thy head,
Had grac'd the tender temples of my child ;
And both the princes had been breathing here,
Which now, two tender bedfellows for dust,
Thy broken faith hath made the prey for worms.
What canst thou swear by now ?
K. Rich. The time to come.
Q. Eliz. That thou hast wronged in the time o'er-
　past ;
For I myself have many tears to wash　　　　390
Hereafter time, for time past, wrong'd by thee.
The children live, whose fathers thou hast slaughter'd,
Ungovern'd youth, to wail it in their age :
The parents live, whose children thou hast butcher'd,
Old barren plants, to wail it with their age.
Swear not by time to come ; for that thou hast
Misus'd ere us'd, by times ill-us'd o'erpast.
K. Rich. As I intend to prosper, and repent,
So thrive I in my dangerous affairs
Of hostile arms ! myself myself confound !　　400
Heaven and fortune bar me happy hours !
Day, yield me not thy light, nor, night, thy rest !
Be opposite all planets of good luck
To my proceeding, if, with dear heart's love,
Immaculate devotion, holy thoughts,
I tender not thy beauteous princely daughter !
In her consists my happiness and thine :
Without her, follows to myself, and thee,
Herself, the land, and many a Christian soul,
Death, desolation, ruin, and decay :　　　　410
It cannot be avoided but by this ;
It will not be avoided but by this.
Therefore, dear mother (I must call you so),
Be the attorney of my love to her.
Plead what I will be, not what I have been ;
Not my deserts, but what I will deserve :
Urge the necessity and state of times,
And be not peevish-fond in great designs.
Q. Eliz. Shall I be tempted of the devil thus ?
K. Rich. Ay, if the devil tempt thee to do good.　420
Q. Eliz. Shall I forget myself to be myself ?
K. Rich. Ay, if yourself's remembrance wrong
　yourself.
Q. Eliz. Yet thou didst kill my children.
K. Rich. But in your daughter's womb I bury
　them :
Where, in that nest of spicery, they will breed
Selves of themselves to your recomforture.
Q. Eliz. Shall I go win my daughter to thy will ?
K. Rich. And be a happy mother by the deed.
Q. Eliz. I go.—Write to me very shortly,
And you shall understand from me her mind.　　430
K. Rich. Bear her my true love's kiss, and so fare-
well.　　[*Kissing her. Exit* Q. ELIZABETH.
Relenting fool, and shallow, changing woman !
How now ? what news ?

Enter RATCLIFF ; CATESBY *following.*

Rat. Most mighty sovereign, on the western coast
Rideth a puissant navy ; to our shores
Throng many doubtful hollow-hearted friends,
Unarm'd, and unresolv'd to beat them back.
'T is thought that Richmond is their admiral ;
And there they hull, expecting but the aid
Of Buckingham to welcome them ashore.　　440
K. Rich. Some light-foot friend post to the Duke of
　　Norfolk :—
Ratcliff, thyself,—or Catesby ; where is he ?
Cates. Here, my good lord.
K. Rich. Catesby, fly to the duke.
Cates. I will, my lord, with all convenient haste.
K. Rich. Ratcliff, come hither. Post to Salisbury :

When thou com'st thither,—[*To* CATES.] Dull, un-
　mindful villain,
Why stay'st thou here, and go'st not to the duke ?
Cates. First, mighty liege, tell me your highness'
　pleasure,
What from your grace I shall deliver to him.
K. Rich. O ! true, good Catesby.—Bid him levy
　straight　　　　450
The greatest strength and power he can make,
And meet me suddenly at Salisbury.
Cates. I go.　　　　[*Exit.*
Rat. What, may it please you, shall I do at
　Salisbury ?
K. Rich. Why, what wouldst thou do there, before
　I go ?
Rat. Your highness told me, I should post before.

Enter STANLEY.

K. Rich. My mind is chang'd.—Stanley, what news
　with you ?
Stan. None good, my liege, to please you with the
　hearing ;
Nor none so bad, but well may be reported.
K. Rich. Heyday, a riddle ! neither good nor bad ?
What need'st thou run so many miles about,　　461
When thou may'st tell thy tale the nearest way ?
Once more, what news ?
Stan. Richmond is on the seas.
K. Rich. There let him sink, and·be the seas on him !
White-liver'd runagate ! what doth he there ?
Stan. I know not, mighty sovereign, but by guess.
K. Rich. Well, as you guess ?
Stan. Stirr'd up by Dorset, Buckingham, and
　Morton,
He makes for England, here to claim the crown.
K. Rich. Is the chair empty ? is the sword unsway'd ?
Is the king dead ? the empire unpossess'd ?　　471
What heir of York is there alive, but we ?
And who is England's king, but great York's heir ?
Then, tell me, what makes he upon the seas ?
Stan. Unless for that, my liege, I cannot guess.
K. Rich. Unless for that he comes to be your liege,
You cannot guess wherefore the Welshman comes.
Thou wilt revolt, and fly to him, I fear.
Stan. No, my good lord ; therefore mistrust me not.
K. Rich. Where is thy power then to beat him back ?
Where be thy tenants, and thy followers ?　　481
Are they not now upon the western shore,
Safe-conducting the rebels from their ships ?
Stan. No, my good lord, my friends are in the north.
K. Rich. Cold friends to me : what do they in the
　north,
When they should serve their sovereign in the west ?
Stan. They have not been commanded, mighty king.
Pleaseth your majesty to give me leave,
I 'll muster up my friends, and meet your grace,
Where, and what time, your majesty shall please.
K. Rich. Ay, ay, thou wouldst be gone to join with
　Richmond :　　　　491
But I 'll not trust thee.
Stan. Most mighty sovereign,
You have no cause to hold my friendship doubtful.
I never was, nor never will be false.
K. Rich. Go then, and muster men : but leave behind
Your son, George Stanley. Look your heart be firm,
Or else his head's assurance is but frail.
Stan. So deal with him, as I prove true to you.
　　　　　　　　　　　　　[*Exit.*

Enter a Messenger.

Mess. My gracious sovereign, now in Devonshire,
As I by friends am well advertised,　　　　500
Sir Edward Courtney, and the haughty prelate,
Bishop of Exeter, his elder brother,
With many more confederates, are in arms.

Enter another Messenger.

2 Mess. In Kent, my liege, the Guildfords are in
　arms ;
And every hour more competitors
Flock to the rebels, and their power grows strong.

Enter a third Messenger.

3 Mess. My lord, the army of great Buckingham—

K. Rich. Out on ye, owls! nothing but songs of
  death?   [*He strikes him.*
There, take thou that, till thou bring better news.
3 *Mess.* The news I have to tell your majesty 510
Is, that by sudden floods and fall of waters,
Buckingham's army is dispers'd and scatter'd ;
And he himself wander'd away alone,
No man knows whither.
 K. Rich.   I cry thee mercy :
There is my purse, to cure that blow of thine.
Hath any well-advised friend proclaim'd
Reward to him that brings the traitor in ?
3 *Mess.* Such proclamation hath been made, my
  lord.

   Enter a fourth Messenger.

4 *Mess.* Sir Thomas Lovel, and Lord Marquess
  Dorset,
'T is said, my liege, in Yorkshire are in arms : 520
But this good comfort bring I to your highness,—
The Bretagne navy is dispers'd by tempest.
Richmond, in Dorsetshire, sent out a boat
Unto the shore, to ask those on the banks,
If they were his assistants, yea, or no ;
Who answer'd him, they came from Buckingham
Upon his party : he, mistrusting them,
Hois'd sail, and made his course again for Bretagne.
 K. Rich. March on, march on, since we are up in
  arms ;
If not to fight with foreign enemies, 530
Yet to beat down these rebels here at home.

   Enter CATESBY.

 Cates. My liege, the Duke of Buckingham is taken ;
That is the best news. That the Earl of Richmond

Is with a mighty power landed at Milford,
Is colder news, but yet they must be told.
 K. Rich. Away towards Salisbury! while we reason
  here,
A royal battle might be won and lost.—
Some one take order, Buckingham be brought
To Salisbury : the rest march on with me. [*Exeunt.*

   SCENE V.—A Room in Lord STANLEY's House.

   Enter STANLEY *and* Sir CHRISTOPHER URSWICK.

 Stan. Sir Christopher, tell Richmond this from
  me :—
That, in the sty of the most bloody boar,
My son George Stanley is frank'd up in hold :
If I revolt, off goes young George's head ;
The fear of that holds off my present aid.
So, get thee gone : commend me to thy lord.
Withal, say, that the queen hath heartily consented,
He should espouse Elizabeth her daughter.
But, tell me, where is princely Richmond now ?
 Chris. At Pembroke, or at Ha'rford-west, in Wales.
 Stan. What men of name resort to him ? 11
 Chris. Sir Walter Herbert, a renowned soldier,
Sir Gilbert Talbot, Sir William Stanley ;
Oxford, redoubted Pembroke, Sir James Blunt,
And Rice ap Thomas, with a valiant crew ;
And many other of great name and worth :
And towards London do they bend their power,
If by the way they be not fought withal.
 Stan. Well, hie thee to thy lord ; I kiss his hand ;
My letter will resolve him of my mind. 20
Farewell. [*Giving papers to* Sir CHRISTOPHER.
              [*Exeunt.*

ACT V.

SCENE I.—Salisbury. An Open Place.

Enter the Sheriff, and Guard, with BUCKINGHAM, *led to execution.*

 Buckingham.
WILL not King Richard let me speak with
  him?
 Sher. No, my good lord ; therefore be
  patient.
 Buck. Hastings, and Edward's chil-
  dren, Grey, and Rivers,
Holy King Henry, and thy fair son
  Edward,
Vaughan, and all that have miscarried
By underhand corrupted foul injustice,
If that your moody discontented souls
Do through the clouds behold this
  present hour,
Even for revenge mock my destruction !—
This is All-Souls' day, fellow, is it not ? 10
 Sher. It is.
 Buck. Why, then All-Souls' day is my body's dooms-
  day.
This is the day, which, in King Edward's time,
I wish'd might fall on me, when I was found
False to his children, or his wife's allies :
This is the day, wherein I wish'd to fall
By the false faith of him whom most I trusted ;
This, this All-Souls' day to my fearful soul

Is the determin'd respite of my wrongs.
That high All-Seer, which I dallied with, 20
Hath turn'd my feigned prayer on my head,
And given in earnest what I begg'd in jest.
Thus doth he force the swords of wicked men
To turn their own points in their masters' bosoms :
Thus Margaret's curse falls heavy on my neck :—
" When he," quoth she, " shall split thy heart with
  sorrow,
Remember, Margaret was a prophetess."—
Come, lead me, officers, to the block of shame ;
Wrong hath but wrong, and blame the due of blame.
   [*Exeunt* BUCKINGHAM *and Officers.*

   SCENE II.—A Plain near Tamworth.

Enter, with drum and colours, RICHMOND, OXFORD,
 Sir JAMES BLUNT, Sir WALTER HERBERT, *and
 others, with Forces, marching.*

 Richm. Fellows in arms, and my most loving friends,
Bruis'd underneath the yoke of tyranny,
Thus far into the bowels of the land
Have we march'd on without impediment :
And here receive we from our father Stanley

Lines of fair comfort and encouragement.
The wretched, bloody, and usurping boar,
That spoil'd your summer fields and fruitful vines,
Swills your warm blood like wash, and makes his
    trough
In your embowell'd bosoms, this foul swine   10
Lies now even in the centre of this isle,
Near to the town of Leicester, as we learn :
From Tamworth thither is but one day's march.
In God's name, cheerly on, courageous friends,
To reap the harvest of perpetual peace
By this one bloody trial of sharp war.
   Oxf. Every man's conscience is a thousand men,
To fight against this guilty homicide.
   Herb. I doubt not, but his friends will turn to us.
   Blunt. He hath no friends, but what are friends for
    fear,   20
Which in his dearest need will fly from him.
   Richm. All for our vantage : then, in God's name,
    march.
True hope is swift, and flies with swallow's wings ;
Kings it makes gods, and meaner creatures kings.
                           [*Exeunt.*

SCENE III.—Bosworth Field.

Enter King RICHARD, *and Forces ; the Duke of*
   NORFOLK, *Earl of* SURREY, *and others.*

   K. Rich. Here pitch our tents, even here in Bos-
    worth Field.—
My Lord of Surrey, why look you so sad ?
   Sur. My heart is ten times lighter than my looks.
   K. Rich. My Lord of Norfolk, —
   Nor.   Here, most gracious liege.
   K. Rich. Norfolk, we must have knocks ; ha ! must
    we not ?
   Nor. We must both give and take, my loving lord.
   K. Rich. Up with my tent ! here will I lie to-night ;
But where to-morrow ?—Well, all 's one for that.—
Who hath descried the number of the traitors ?
   Nor. Six or seven thousand is their utmost power. 10
   K. Rich. Why, our battalia trebles that account :
Besides, the king's name is a tower of strength,
Which they upon the adverse faction want.
Up with the tent !—Come, noble gentlemen,
Let us survey the vantage of the ground.—
Call for some men of sound direction.—
Let 's lack no discipline, make no delay,
For, lords, to-morrow is a busy day.   [*Exeunt.*

Enter, on the other side of the field, RICHMOND, Sir
   WILLIAM BRANDON, OXFORD, *and other Officers.*
   Some of the Soldiers pitch RICHMOND'S *Tent.*

   Richm. The weary sun hath made a golden set,
And, by the bright track of his fiery car,   20
Gives token of a goodly day to-morrow.—
Sir William Brandon, you shall bear my standard.—
Give me some ink and paper in my tent :
I 'll draw the form and model of our battle,
Limit each leader to his several charge,
And part in just proportion our small power.
My Lord of Oxford,—you, Sir William Brandon,—
And you, Sir Walter Herbert, stay with me.
The Earl of Pembroke keeps his regiment :
Good Captain Blunt, bear my good night to him,   30
And by the second hour in the morning
Desire the earl to see me in my tent.—
Yet one thing more, good captain, do for me :
Where is Lord Stanley quarter'd, do you know ?
   Blunt. Unless I have mista'en his colours much
(Which, well I am assur'd, I have not done),
His regiment lies half a mile, at least,
South from the mighty power of the king.
   Richm. If without peril it be possible,
Sweet Blunt, make some good means to speak with
    him,   40
And give him from me this most needful note.
   Blunt. Upon my life, my lord, I 'll undertake it :
And so, God give you quiet rest to-night !
   Richm. Good night, good Captain Blunt. Come,
    gentlemen,

Let us consult upon to-morrow's business ;
In to my tent ; the dew is raw and cold.
                [*They withdraw into the Tent.*

Enter, to his Tent, King RICHARD, NORFOLK,
   RATCLIFF, *and* CATESBY.

   K. Rich. What is 't o'clock ?
   Cates. It 's supper-time, my lord ; it 's nine o'clock.
   K. Rich. I will not sup to-night.—
Give me some ink and paper.—   50
What, is my beaver easier than it was,
And all my armour laid into my tent ?
   Cates. It is, my liege ; and all things are in readi-
    ness.
   K. Rich. Good Norfolk, hie thee to thy charge.
Use careful watch ; choose trusty sentinels.
   Nor. I go, my lord.
   K. Rich. Stir with the lark to-morrow, gentle Nor-
    folk.
   Nor. I warrant you, my lord.   [*Exit.*
   K. Rich. Ratcliff !
   Rat. My lord ?
   K. Rich.   Send out a pursuivant-at-arms   60
To Stanley's regiment : bid him bring his power
Before sun-rising, lest his son George fall
Into the blind cave of eternal night.—
Fill me a bowl of wine. Give me a watch.—
Saddle white Surrey for the field to-morrow.
Look that my staves be sound, and not too heavy.
Ratcliff !—
   Rat. My lord ?
   K. Rich. Saw'st thou the melancholy Lord North-
    umberland ?
   Rat. Thomas the Earl of Surrey, and himself,   70
Much about cock-shut time, from troop to troop
Went through the army, cheering up the soldiers.
   K. Rich. So : I am satisfied. Give me a bowl of
    wine :
I have not that alacrity of spirit,
Nor cheer of mind, that I was wont to have.—
Set it down.—Is ink and paper ready ?
   Rat. It is, my lord.
   K. Rich. Bid my guard watch. Leave me.
Ratcliff, about the mid of night come to my tent,
And help to arm me.—Leave me, I say.   80
           [*King* RICHARD *retires into his Tent.*
              Exeunt RATCLIFF *and* CATESBY.

RICHMOND'S *Tent opens, and discovers him and his*
   Officers, &c.

Enter STANLEY.

   Stan. Fortune and victory sit on thy helm !
   Richm. All comfort that the dark night can afford,
Be to thy person, noble father-in-law !
Tell me, how fares our loving mother ?
   Stan. I, by attorney, bless thee from thy mother,
Who prays continually for Richmond's good.
So much for that.—The silent hours steal on,
And flaky darkness breaks within the east.
In brief, for so the season bids us be,
Prepare thy battle early in the morning ;   90
And put thy fortune to the arbitrement
Of bloody strokes, and mortal-staring war.
I, as I may (that which I would I cannot),
With best advantage will deceive the time,
And aid thee in this doubtful shock of arms :
But on thy side I may not be too forward,
Lest, being seen, thy brother, tender George,
Be executed in his father's sight.
Farewell. The leisure and the fearful time
Cuts off the ceremonious vows of love,   100
And ample interchange of sweet discourse,
Which so long sunder'd friends should dwell upon.
God give us leisure for these rites of love !
Once more, adieu.—Be valiant, and speed well !
   Richm. Good lords, conduct him to his regiment.
I 'll strive, with troubled thoughts, to take a nap :
Lest leaden slumber peise me down to-morrow,
When I should mount with wings of victory.
Once more, good night, kind lords, and gentlemen.
            [*Exeunt Lords, &c., with* STANLEY.

O ! Thou, whose captain I account myself,   110
Look on my forces with a gracious eye ;
Put in their hands thy bruising irons of wrath,
That they may crush down with a heavy fall

Think, how thou stabb'dst me in my prime of youth
At Tewksbury : despair, therefore, and die.—
[*To* Richm.] Be cheerful, Richmond ; for the wronged
    souls

Ghost. "Dream on, dream on, of bloody deeds and death."

The usurping helmets of our adversaries !
Make us thy ministers of chastisement,
That we may praise thee in thy victory !
To thee I do commend my watchful soul,
Ere I let fall the windows of mine eyes :
Sleeping, and waking, O ! defend me still !   [*Sleeps.*

The Ghost of Prince EDWARD, *Son to* HENRY *the
    Sixth, rises between the two Tents.*

Ghost. [*To* K. Rich.] Let me sit heavy on thy soul
    to-morrow !   120

Of butcher'd princes fight in thy behalf :
King Henry's issue, Richmond, comforts thee.

The Ghost of King HENRY *the Sixth rises.*

Ghost. [*To* K. Rich.] When I was mortal, my anointed
    body
By thee was punched full of deadly holes.
Think on the Tower, and me : despair, and die ;
Harry the Sixth bids thee despair, and die !—
[*To* Richm.] Virtuous and holy, be thou conqueror !

Harry that prophesy'd thou shouldst be king,   131
Doth comfort thee in sleep: live, and flourish!

The Ghost of CLARENCE *rises.*

Ghost. [*To K.* RICH.] Let me sit heavy on thy soul
  to-morrow!
I, that was wash'd to death with fulsome wine,
Poor Clarence, by thy guile betray'd to death!
To-morrow in the battle think on me,
And fall thy edgeless sword. Despair, and die!
[*To* RICHM.] Thou offspring of the house of Lancaster,
The wronged heirs of York do pray for thee;
Good angels guard thy battle! Live, and flourish! 140

The Ghosts of RIVERS, GREY, *and* VAUGHAN, *rise.*

Ghost of Riv. [*To K.* RICH.] Let me sit heavy on
  thy soul to-morrow!
Rivers, that died at Pomfret. Despair, and die!
Ghost of Grey. [*To K.* RICH.] Think upon Grey, and
  let thy soul despair.
Ghost of Vaugh. [*To K.* RICH.] Think upon Vaughan,
  and with guilty fear
Let fall thy lance. Despair, and die!—
All. [*To* RICHM.] Awake, and think, our wrongs in
  Richard's bosom
Will conquer him.—Awake, and win the day!

The Ghost of HASTINGS *rises.*

Ghost. [*To K.* RICH.] Bloody and guilty, guiltily
  awake;
And in a bloody battle end thy days.
Think on Lord Hastings. Despair, and die!—   150
[*To* RICHM.] Quiet untroubled soul, awake, awake!
Arm, fight, and conquer, for fair England's sake.

The Ghosts of the two young Princes rise.

Ghosts. [*To K.* RICH.] Dream on thy cousins
  smother'd in the Tower:
Let us be lead within thy bosom, Richard,
And weigh thee down to ruin, shame, and death.
Thy nephews' souls bid thee despair, and die!—
[*To* RICHM.] Sleep, Richmond, sleep in peace, and
  wake in joy;
Good angels guard thee from the boar's annoy!
Live, and beget a happy race of kings.
Edward's unhappy sons do bid thee flourish.   160

The Ghost of Queen ANNE *rises.*

Ghost. [*To K.* RICH.] Richard, thy wife, that
  wretched Anne thy wife,
That never slept a quiet hour with thee,
Now fills thy sleep with perturbations:
To-morrow in the battle think on me,
And fall thy edgeless sword. Despair, and die!—
[*To* RICHM.] Thou, quiet soul, sleep thou a quiet sleep;
Dream of success and happy victory:
Thy adversary's wife doth pray for thee.

The Ghost of BUCKINGHAM *rises.*

Ghost. [*To K.* RICH.] The first was I that help'd thee
  to the crown;
The last was I that felt thy tyranny.   170
O! in the battle think on Buckingham,
And die in terror of thy guiltiness.
Dream on, dream on, of bloody deeds and death:
Fainting, despair; despairing, yield thy breath!—
[*To* RICHM.] I died for hope ere I could lend thee aid:
But cheer thy heart, and be thou not dismay'd:
God and good angels fight on Richmond's side;
And Richard falls in height of all his pride.
    [*The Ghosts vanish.* King RICHARD *starts
      out of his dream.*
K. Rich. Give me another horse!—bind up my
  wounds!—
Have mercy, Jesu!—Soft! I did but dream.—   180
O, coward conscience, how dost thou afflict me!—
The lights burn blue.—It is now dead midnight.
Cold fearful drops stand on my trembling flesh.
What, do I fear myself? there's none else by:
Richard loves Richard; that is, I am I.
Is there a murderer here? No;—yes; I am:
Then fly,—what, from myself? Great reason, why:

Lest I revenge. What, myself upon myself?
Alack! I love myself. Wherefore? for any good
That I myself have done unto myself?   190
O! no: alas! I rather hate myself,
For hateful deeds committed by myself.
I am a villain. Yet I lie; I am not.
Fool, of thyself speak well:—fool, do not flatter
My conscience hath a thousand several tongues,
And every tongue brings in a several tale,
And every tale condemns me for a villain.
Perjury, perjury, in the high'st degree;
Murder, stern murder, in the dir'st degree;
All several sins, all us'd in each degree,   200
Throng to the bar, crying all,—Guilty! guilty!
I shall despair.—There is no creature loves me;
And if I die, no soul shall pity me:—
Nay, wherefore should they? since that I myself
Find in myself no pity to myself.
Methought, the souls of all that I had murder'd
Came to my tent; and every one did threat
To-morrow's vengeance on the head of Richard.

Enter RATCLIFF.

Rat. My lord,—
K. Rich. Who's there?   210
Rat. Ratcliff, my lord; 'tis I. The early village cock
Hath twice done salutation to the morn:
Your friends are up, and buckle on their armour.
K. Rich. O Ratcliff! I have dream'd a fearful
  dream.—
What thinkest thou? will our friends prove all true?
Rat. No doubt, my lord.
K. Rich.   O Ratcliff! I fear, I fear,—
Rat. Nay, good my lord, be not afraid of shadows.
K. Rich. By the Apostle Paul, shadows to-night
Have struck more terror to the soul of Richard,
Than can the substance of ten thousand soldiers,   220
Armed in proof, and led by shallow Richmond.
It is not yet near day. Come, go with me:
Under our tents I'll play the eaves-dropper,
To hear if any mean to shrink from me.   [*Exeunt.*

RICHMOND *wakes. Enter* OXFORD *and others.*

Lords. Good morrow, Richmond.
Richm. Cry mercy, lords, and watchful gentlemen,
That you have ta'en a tardy sluggard here.
Lords. How have you slept, my lord?
Richm. The sweetest sleep, and fairest-boding
  dreams,
That ever enter'd in a drowsy head,   230
Have I since your departure had, my lords.
Methought, their souls, whose bodies Richard
  murder'd,
Came to my tent, and cried on victory:
I promise you, my heart is very jocund
In the remembrance of so fair a dream.
How far into the morning is it, lords?
Lords. Upon the stroke of four.
Richm. Why, then 'tis time to arm, and give direc-
  tion.—   [*He advances to the Troops.*
More than I have said, loving countrymen,
The leisure and enforcement of the time   240
Forbids to dwell on: yet remember this,—
God and our good cause fight upon our side;
The prayers of holy saints, and wronged souls,
Like high-rear'd bulwarks, stand before our faces.
Richard except, those whom we fight against
Had rather have us win, than him they follow.
For what is he they follow? truly, gentlemen,
A bloody tyrant, and a homicide;
One rais'd in blood, and one in blood establish'd;
One that made means to come by what he hath,   250
And slaughter'd those that were the means to help
  him;
A base foul stone, made precious by the foil
Of England's chair, where he is falsely set:
One that hath ever been God's enemy.
Then, if you fight against God's enemy,
God will, in justice, ward you as his soldiers;
If you do sweat to put a tyrant down,
You sleep in peace, the tyrant being slain;
If you do fight against your country's foes,

Your country's fat shall pay your pains the hire; 260
If you do fight in safeguard of your wives,
Your wives shall welcome home the conquerors;
If you do free your children from the sword,
Your children's children quit it in your age.
Then, in the name of God, and all these rights,
Advance your standards, draw your willing swords.
For me, the ransom of my bold attempt
Shall be this cold corse on the earth's cold face;
But if I thrive, the gain of my attempt,
The least of you shall share his part thereof.   270
Sound, drums and trumpets, boldly and cheerfully;
God and Saint George! Richmond and victory!
                                   [*Exeunt.*

Re-enter King RICHARD; RATCLIFF, *Attendants, and
      Forces.*

K. Rich. What said Northumberland, as touching
      Richmond?
Rat. That he was never trained up in arms.
K. Rich. He said the truth: and what said Surrey
      then?
Rat. He smil'd and said, the better for our purpose.
K. Rich. He was i' the right; and so, indeed it is.
                                   [*Clock strikes.*
Tell the clock there.—Give me a calendar.—
Who saw the sun to-day?
Rat.   Not I, my lord.
K. Rich. Then he disdains to shine! for, by the book,
He should have brav'd the east an hour ago: 281
A black day will it be to somebody. —
Ratcliff,—
Rat. My lord?
K. Rich.   The sun will not be seen to-day:
The sky doth frown and lour upon our army.
I would, these dewy tears were from the ground.
Not shine to-day! Why, what is that to me
More than to Richmond? for the selfsame heaven,
That frowns on me, looks sadly upon him.

                Enter NORFOLK.

Nor. Arm, arm, my lord! the foe vaunts in the
      field.   290
K. Rich. Come, bustle, bustle. Caparison my horse.
Call up Lord Stanley, bid him bring his power.
I will lead forth my soldiers to the plain,
And thus my battle shall be ordered.
My forward shall be drawn out all in length,
Consisting equally of horse and foot:
Our archers shall be placed in the midst.
John Duke of Norfolk, Thomas Earl of Surrey,
Shall have the leading of the foot and horse.
They thus directed, we will follow   300
In the main battle; whose puissance on either side
Shall be well winged with our chiefest horse.
This, and Saint George to boot!—What think'st thou,
      Norfolk?
Nor. A good direction, warlike sovereign.—
This found I on my tent this morning.
                                   [*Giving a scroll.*
K. Rich. [*Reads.*] " Jocky of Norfolk, be not too bold,
For Dickon thy master is bought and sold."
A thing devised by the enemy.—
Go, gentlemen; every man to his charge.
Let not our babbling dreams affright our souls; 310
Conscience is but a word that cowards use,
Devis'd at first to keep the strong in awe:
Our strong arm be our conscience, swords our law.
March on, join bravely, let us to 't pell-mell;
If not to heaven, then hand in hand to hell.—
What shall I say more than I have inferr'd?
Remember whom you are to cope withal;—
A sort of vagabonds, rascals, and runaways,
A scum of Bretagnes, and base lackey peasants,
Whom their o'er-cloyed country vomits forth   320
To desperate adventures and assur'd destruction.
You sleeping safe, they bring to you unrest;
You having lands, and bless'd with beauteous wives,
They would restrain the one, distain the other.
And who doth lead them, but a paltry fellow,
Long kept in Bretagne at our mother's cost?
A milksop, one that never in his life

Felt so much cold as over shoes in snow?
Let 's whip these stragglers o'er the seas again;
Lash hence these overweening rags of France,   330
These famish'd beggars, weary of their lives;
Who, but for dreaming on this fond exploit,
For want of means, poor rats, had hang'd themselves.
If we be conquer'd, let men conquer us.
And not these bastard Bretagnes, whom our fathers
Have in their own land beaten, bobb'd, and thump'd,
And, on record, left them the heirs of shame.
Shall these enjoy our lands? lie with our wives?
Ravish our daughters?—[*Drum afar off.*] Hark; I
      hear their drum.
Fight, gentlemen of England! fight, bold yeomen! 340
Draw, archers, draw your arrows to the head!
Spur your proud horses hard, and ride in blood:
Amaze the welkin with your broken staves!

                Enter a Messenger.

What says Lord Stanley? will he bring his power?
Mess. My lord, he doth deny to come.
K. Rich. Off with his son George's head!
Nor. My lord, the enemy is pass'd the marsh:
After the battle let George Stanley die.
K. Rich. A thousand hearts are great within my
      bosom.
Advance our standards! set upon our foes!   350
Our ancient word of courage, fair Saint George,
Inspire us with the spleen of fiery dragons!
Upon them! Victory sits on our helms. [*Exeunt.*

          SCENE IV.—Another Part of the Field.

Alarum: Excursions. Enter NORFOLK, *and Forces;
      to him* CATESBY.

Cates. Rescue, my Lord of Norfolk! rescue, rescue!
The king enacts more wonders than a man,
Daring an opposite to every danger.
His horse is slain, and all on foot he fights,
Seeking for Richmond in the throat of death.
Rescue, fair lord, or else the day is lost!

          Alarum. Enter King RICHARD.

K. Rich. A horse! a horse! my kingdom for a
      horse!
Cates. Withdraw, my lord; I 'll help you to a horse.
K. Rich. Slave! I have set my life upon a cast,
And I will stand the hazard of the die.   10
I think there be six Richmonds in the field;
Five have I slain to-day, instead of him.—
A horse! a horse! my kingdom for a horse! [*Exeunt.*

Alarums. Enter King RICHARD *and* RICHMOND;
      *and exeunt fighting. Retreat and flourish. Then
      enter* RICHMOND, STANLEY *bearing the crown, with
      divers other Lords, and Forces.*

Richm. God, and your arms, be prais'd, victorious
      friends,
The day is ours, the bloody dog is dead.
Stan. Courageous Richmond, well hast thou acquit
      thee.
Lo! here, this long-usurped royalty
From the dead temples of this bloody wretch
Have I pluck'd off, to grace thy brows withal:
Wear it, enjoy it, and make much of it.   20
Richm. Great God of heaven, say Amen to all!—
But, tell me, is young George Stanley living?
Stan. He is, my lord, and safe in Leicester town,
Whither, if you please, we may withdraw us.
Richm. What men of name are slain on either side?
Stan. John Duke of Norfolk, Walter Lord Ferrers,
Sir Robert Brakenbury, and Sir William Brandon.
Richm. Inter their bodies as becomes their births.
Proclaim a pardon to the soldiers fled
That in submission will return to us;   30
And then, as we have ta'en the sacrament,
We will unite the white rose and the red:—
Smile Heaven upon this fair conjunction,
That long hath frown'd upon their enmity!—
What traitor hears me, and says not Amen?

England hath long been mad, and scarr'd herself ;
The brother blindly shed the brother's blood,
The father rashly slaughter'd his own son,
The son, compell'd, been butcher to the sire ;
All this divided York and Lancaster 40
Divided in their dire division.—
O ! now, let Richmond and Elizabeth,
The true succeeders of each royal house,
By God's fair ordinance conjoin together !
And let their heirs (God, if thy will be so)
Enrich the time to come with smooth-fac'd peace,
With smiling plenty, and fair prosperous days !
Abate the edge of traitors, gracious Lord,
That would reduce these bloody days again,
And make poor England weep in streams of blood ! 50
Let them not live to taste this land's increase,
That would with treason wound this fair land's
    peace !
Now civil wounds are stopp'd, peace lives again :
That she may long live here, God say Amen ! [*Exeunt.*

KING HENRY VIII.

DRAMATIS PERSONÆ.

KING HENRY THE EIGHTH.
CARDINAL WOLSEY.
CARDINAL CAMPEIUS.
CAPUCIUS, *Ambassador from Charles V.*
CRANMER, *Archbishop of Canterbury.*
DUKE OF NORFOLK.
DUKE OF SUFFOLK.
DUKE OF BUCKINGHAM.
EARL OF SURREY.
Lord Chamberlain.
Lord Chancellor.
GARDINER, *Bishop of Winchester.*
BISHOP OF LINCOLN.
LORD ABERGAVENNY.
LORD SANDS.
SIR HENRY GUILDFORD.
SIR THOMAS LOVELL.
SIR ANTHONY DENNY.
SIR NICHOLAS VAUX.
Secretaries to Wolsey.

CROMWELL, *Servant to Wolsey.*
GRIFFITH, *Gentleman-Usher to Queen Katharine.*
Three other Gentlemen.
Garter King-at-Arms.
DOCTOR BUTTS, *Physician to the King.*
Surveyor to the Duke of Buckingham.
BRANDON, *and a Sergeant-at-Arms.*
Door-keeper of the Council-chamber.
Porter, and his Man.
Page to Gardiner. A Crier.

QUEEN KATHARINE, *Wife to King Henry.*
ANNE BULLEN, *her Maid of Honour.*
An Old Lady, Friend to Anne Bullen.
PATIENCE, *Woman to Queen Katharine.*

Several Lords and Ladies in the Dumb-shows;
Women attending upon the Queen; Spirits,
which appear to her; Scribes, Officers, Guards,
and other Attendants.

SCENE—Chiefly in LONDON and WESTMINSTER; once, at KIMBOLTON.

PROLOGUE.

COME no more to make you laugh : things
  now,
That bear a weighty and a serious brow,
Sad, high, and working, full of state and
  woe,
Such noble scenes as draw the eye to flow,
We now present. Those that can pity,
  here
May, if they think it well, let fall a tear ;
The subject will deserve it. Such as give
Their money out of hope they may believe,
May here find truth too. Those that come
  to see
Only a show or two, and so agree   10
The play may pass, if they be still and willing,
I 'll undertake, may see away their shilling
Richly in two short hours. Only they
That come to hear a merry, bawdy play,
A noise of targets, or to see a fellow
In a long motley coat, guarded with yellow,
Will be deceiv'd ; for, gentle hearers, know,
To rank our chosen truth with such a show
As fool and fight is, beside forfeiting
Our own brains, and the opinion that we bring,   20
To make that only true we now intend,
Will leave us never an understanding friend.
Therefore, for goodness' sake, and as you are known
The first and happiest hearers of the town,
Be sad, as we would make ye : think, ye see
The very persons of our noble story,
As they were living ; think, you see them great,
And follow'd with the general throng, and sweat
Of thousand friends ; then, in a moment, see
How soon this mightiness meets misery :   30
And if you can be merry then, I 'll say,
A man may weep upon his wedding-day.

ACT I.

SCENE I.—London. An Ante-chamber in the Palace.

Enter the Duke of NORFOLK, *at one door; at the other, the Duke of* BUCKINGHAM, *and the Lord* ABERGAVENNY.

Buckingham.
GOOD morrow, and well met. How have
    you done,
Since last we saw in France?
    Nor.   I thank your grace,
Healthful; and ever since a fresh admirer
Of what I saw there.
    Buck.   An untimely ague
Stay'd me a prisoner in my chamber, when
Those suns of glory, those two lights of men,
Met in the vale of Andren.
Nor.   'Twixt Guynes and Arde:
I was then present, saw them salute on horseback;
Beheld them, when they lighted, how they clung
In their embracement, as they grew together;   10
Which had they, what four thron'd ones could have
    weigh'd
Such a compounded one?
    Buck.   All the whole time
I was my chamber's prisoner.
    Nor.   Then you lost
The view of earthly glory: men might say,
Till this time pomp was single, but now married
To one above itself. Each following day
Became the next day's master, till the last
Made former wonders its. To-day the French
All clinquant, all in gold, like heathen gods,
Shone down the English; and to-morrow they   20
Made Britain, India: every man that stood
Show'd like a mine. Their dwarfish pages were
As cherubins, all gilt: the madams too,
Not us'd to toil, did almost swear to bear
The pride upon them, that their very labour
Was to them as a painting. Now this masque
Was cried incomparable; and the ensuing night
Made it a fool, and beggar. The two kings,
Equal in lustre, were now best, now worst,
As presence did present them; him in eye,   30
Still him in praise; and, being present both,
'T was said, they saw but one, and no discerner
Durst wag his tongue in censure. When these suns
(For so they phrase them) by their heralds challeng'd
The noble spirits to arms, they did perform
Beyond thought's compass; that former fabulous
    story,
Being now seen possible enough, got credit,
That Bevis was believ'd.
    Buck.   O! you go far.
Nor. As I belong to worship, and affect
In honour honesty, the tract of everything   40
Would by a good discourser lose some life,
Which action's self was tongue to. All was royal:
To the disposing of it nought rebell'd;
Order gave each thing view, the office did
Distinctly his full function.
    Buck.   Who did guide,
I mean, who set the body and the limbs
Of this great sport together, as you guess?
Nor. One, certes, that promises no element
In such a business.
    Buck.   I pray you, who, my lord?
Nor. All this was order'd by the good discretion   50
Of the right reverend Cardinal of York.

Buck. The devil speed him! no man's pie is freed
From his ambitious finger. What had he
To do in these fierce vanities? I wonder,
That such a keech can with his very bulk
Take up the rays o' the beneficial sun,
And keep it from the earth.
    Nor.   Surely, sir,
There's in him stuff that puts him to these ends;
For, being not propp'd by ancestry, whose grace
Chalks successors their way, nor call'd upon   60
For high feats done to the crown; neither allied
To eminent assistants; but, spider-like,
Out of his self-drawing web, he gives us note,
The force of his own merit makes his way;
A gift that Heaven gives for him, which buys
A place next to the king.
    Aber.   I cannot tell
What Heaven hath given him: let some graver eye
Pierce into that; but I can see his pride
Peep through each part of him: whence has he that?
If not from hell, the devil is a niggard,   70
Or has given all before, and he begins
A new hell in himself.
    Buck.   Why the devil,
Upon this French going-out, took he upon him,
Without the privity o' the king, t' appoint
Who should attend on him? He makes up the file
Of all the gentry; for the most part such
To whom as great a charge as little honour
He meant to lay upon: and his own letter,
The honourable board of council out,
Must fetch him in he papers.
    Aber.   I do know   80
Kinsmen of mine, three at the least, that have
By this so sicken'd their estates, that never
They shall abound as formerly.
    Buck.   O, many
Have broke their backs with laying manors on them
For this great journey. What did this vanity,
But minister communication of
A most poor issue?
    Nor.   Grievingly I think,
The peace between the French and us not values
The cost that did conclude it.
    Buck.   Every man,
After the hideous storm that follow'd, was   90
A thing inspir'd; and, not consulting, broke
Into a general prophecy,—that this tempest,
Dashing the garment of this peace, aboded
The sudden breach on 't.
    Nor.   Which is budded out:
For France hath flaw'd the league, and hath attach'd
Our merchants' goods at Bourdeaux.
    Aber.   Is it therefore
The ambassador is silenc'd?
    Nor.   Marry, is 't.
Aber. A proper title of a peace, and purchas'd
At a superfluous rate.
    Buck.   Why, all this business
Our reverend cardinal carried.
    Nor.   Like it your grace,
The state takes notice of the private difference   101
Betwixt you and the cardinal. I advise you,
(And take it from a heart that wishes towards you
Honour and plenteous safety,) that you read

The cardinal's malice and his potency
Together : to consider further, that
What his high hatred would effect wants not
A minister in his power. You know his nature,
That he 's revengeful ; and, I know, his sword
Hath a sharp edge : it 's long, and 't may be said,   110
It reaches far ; and where 't will not extend,
Thither he darts it. Bosom up my counsel,
You 'll find it wholesome. Lo, where comes that rock,
That I advise your shunning.

Enter Cardinal WOLSEY, *(the purse borne before
him,) certain of the Guard, and two Secretaries
with papers. The Cardinal in his passage fixeth
his eye on* BUCKINGHAM, *and* BUCKINGHAM *on
him, both full of disdain.*

Wol. The Duke of Buckingham's surveyor ? ha !
Where 's his examination ?

CARDINAL WOLSEY AND THE DUKE OF BUCKINGHAM.

1 *Secr.*   Here, so please you.
Wol. Is he in person ready ?
1 *Secr.*   Ay, please your grace.
Wol. Well, we shall then know more ; and Buck-
ingham
Shall lessen this big look.
                    [*Exeunt* WOLSEY *and Train.*
Buck. This butcher's cur is venom-mouth'd, and I
Have not the power to muzzle him ; therefore, best   121
Not wake him in his slumber. A beggar's book
Outworths a noble's blood.
Nor.   What ! are you chaf'd ?
Ask God for temperance ; that 's the appliance only,
Which your disease requires.
Buck.   I read in 's looks
Matter against me ; and his eye revil'd
Me, as his abject object : at this instant
He bores me with some trick. He 's gone to the
king ;
I 'll follow, and outstare him.
Nor.   Stay, my lord,
And let your reason with your choler question   130
What 't is you go about. To climb steep hills
Requires slow pace at first : anger is like
A full-hot horse, who being allow'd his way,
Self-mettle tires him. Not a man in England
Can advise me like you : be to yourself
As you would to your friend.
Buck.   I 'll to the king ;
And from a mouth of honour quite cry down
This Ipswich fellow's insolence, or proclaim
There 's difference in no persons.
Nor.   Be advis'd ;
Heat not a furnace for your foe so hot   140
That it do singe yourself. We may outrun
By violent swiftness that which we run at,
And lose by over-running. Know you not,
The fire that mounts the liquor till 't run o'er,
In seeming to augment it, wastes it ? Be advis'd :
I say again, there is no English soul
More stronger to direct you than yourself,

If with the sap of reason you would quench,
Or but allay, the fire of passion.
Buck.   Sir,
I am thankful to you, and I 'll go along   150
By your prescription ; but this top-proud fellow,
Whom from the flow of gall I name not, but
From sincere motions, by intelligence,
And proofs as clear as founts in July, when
We see each grain of gravel, I do know
To be corrupt and treasonous.
Nor.   Say not, treasonous.
Buck. To the king I 'll say 't, and make my vouch as
strong
As shore of rock. Attend. This holy fox,
Or wolf, or both (for he is equal ravenous,
As he is subtle, and as prone to mischief,   160
As able to perform 't, his mind and place
Infecting one another, yea, reciprocally),
Only to show his pomp as well in France
As here at home, suggests the king, our master,
To this last costly treaty, the interview,
That swallow'd so much treasure, and like a
glass
Did break i' the rinsing.
Nor.   'Faith, and so it did.
Buck. Pray, give me favour, sir. This
cunning cardinal
The articles o' the combination drew
As himself pleas'd ; and they were ratified,   170
As he cried, " Thus let be," to as much end,
As give a crutch to the dead. But our count-
cardinal
Has done this, and 't is well ; for worthy Wolsey,
Who cannot err, he did it. Now this follows,
(Which, as I take it, is a kind of puppy
To the old dam, treason,) Charles the emperor,
Under pretence to see the queen, his aunt,
(For 't was, indeed, his colour, but he came
To whisper Wolsey,) here makes visitation :
His fears were, that the interview betwixt   180
England and France might, through their amity,
Breed him some prejudice ; for from this league
Peep'd harms that menac'd him. He privily
Deals with our cardinal, and, as I trow,—
Which I do well ; for, I am sure, the emperor
Paid ere he promis'd, whereby his suit was granted,
Ere it was ask'd : but when the way was made,
And pav'd with gold, the emperor thus desir'd :—
That he would please to alter the king's course,
And break the foresaid peace. Let the king
know   190
(As soon as he shall by me), that thus the cardinal
Does buy and sell his honour as he pleases,
And for his own advantage.
Nor.   I am sorry
To hear this of him ; and could wish he were
Something mistaken in 't.
Buck.   No, not a syllable :
I do pronounce him in that very shape,
He shall appear in proof.

Enter BRANDON ; *a Sergeant-at-Arms before him,
and two or three of the Guard.*

Bran. Your office, sergeant : execute it.
Serg.   Sir,
My lord the Duke of Buckingham, and Earl
Of Hereford, Stafford, and Northampton, I   200
Arrest thee of high treason, in the name
Of our most sovereign king.
Buck.   Lo you, my lord,
The net has fall'n upon me : I shall perish
Under device and practice.
Bran.   I am sorry
To see you ta'en from liberty, to look on
The business, present. 'T is his highness' pleasure,
You shall to the Tower.
Buck.   It will help me nothing,
To plead mine innocence ; for that die is on me,
Which makes my whitest part black. The will of
Heaven
Be done in this and all things.—I obey.—   210
O ! my Lord Aberga'ny, fare you well.

Bran. Nay, he must bear you company. —[*To*
　　ABERGAVENNY.] The king
Is pleas'd you shall to the Tower, till you know
How he determines further.
　Aber.　　　　　　As the duke said,
The will of Heaven be done, and the king's pleasure
By me obey'd.
　Bran.　　　　Here is a warrant from
The king to attach Lord Montacute; and the bodies
Of the duke's confessor, John de la Car,
One Gilbert Peck, his chancellor,—
　Buck.　　　　　　　　So, so;
These are the limbs o' the plot. No more, I hope. 220
　Bran. A monk o' the Chartreux.
　Buck.　　　　　O! Nicholas Hopkins?
　Bran.　　　　　　　　　　　He.
　Buck. My surveyor is false: the o'er-great cardinal
Hath show'd him gold. My life is spann'd already:
I am the shadow of poor Buckingham,
Whose figure even this instant cloud puts on,
By darkening my clear sun.—My lord, farewell.
　　　　　　　　　　　　　　　[*Exeunt.*

SCENE II.—The Council-chamber.

Cornets. Enter King HENRY, *Cardinal* WOLSEY,
the Lords of the Council, Sir THOMAS LOVELL,
Officers, and Attendants. The KING *enters leaning
on the Cardinal's shoulder.*

K. Hen. My life itself, and the best heart of it,
Thanks you for this great care. I stood i' the level
Of a full-charg'd confederacy, and give thanks
To you that chok'd it.—Let be call'd before us
That gentleman of Buckingham's: in person
I'll hear him his confessions justify,
And point by point the treasons of his master
He shall again relate.

*A noise within, crying "Room for the Queen!" Enter
the* QUEEN, *ushered by the Dukes of* NORFOLK *and*
SUFFOLK: *she kneels. The* KING *riseth from his
state, takes her up, kisses, and placeth her by him.*

　Q. Kath. Nay, we must longer kneel: I am a suitor.
　K. Hen. Arise, and take place by us.—Half your
　　suit　　　　　　　　　　　　　　　　　　10
Never name to us; you have half our power:
The other moiety, ere you ask, is given;
Repeat your will, and take it.
　Q. Kath.　　　　　　Thank your majesty.
That you would love yourself, and in that love
Not unconsider'd leave your honour, nor
The dignity of your office, is the point
Of my petition.
　K. Hen.　　　Lady mine, proceed.
　Q. Kath. I am solicited, not by a few,
And those of true condition, that your subjects
Are in great grievance. There have been commis-
　　sions　　　　　　　　　　　　　　　　　20
Sent down among them, which hath flaw'd the heart
Of all their loyalties: wherein, although,
My good lord cardinal, they vent reproaches
Most bitterly on you, as putter-on
Of these exactions, yet the king our master,
Whose honour Heaven shield from soil! even he
　　escapes not
Language unmannerly; yea, such which breaks
The side of loyalty, and almost appears
In loud rebellion.
　Nor.　　　Not almost appears,
It doth appear; for upon these taxations, 　　30
The clothiers all, not able to maintain
The many to them 'longing, have put off
The spinsters, carders, fullers, weavers, who,
Unfit for other life, compell'd by hunger
And lack of other means, in desperate manner
Daring the event to the teeth, are all in uproar,
And danger serves among them.
　K. Hen.　　　　　　　Taxation!
Wherein? and what taxation?—My lord cardinal,
You that are blam'd for it alike with us,
Know you of this taxation?

　Wol.　　　　　Please you, sir,　　40
I know but of a single part, in aught
Pertains to the state; and front but in that file
Where others tell steps with me.
　Q. Kath.　　　　No, my lord,
You know no more than others; but you frame
Things, that are known alike, which are not wholesome
To those which would not know them, and yet must
Perforce be their acquaintance. These exactions,
Whereof my sovereign would have note, they are
Most pestilent to the hearing; and to bear them,
The back is sacrifice to the load. They say,　　50
They are devis'd by you, or else you suffer
Too hard an exclamation.
　K. Hen.　　　　Still exaction!
The nature of it? In what kind, let's know,
Is this exaction?
　Q. Kath.　　I am much too venturous
In tempting of your patience; but am bolden'd
Under your promis'd pardon. The subjects' grief
Comes through commissions, which compel from each
The sixth part of his substance, to be levied
Without delay; and the pretence for this
Is nam'd, your wars in France. This makes bold
　　mouths:　　　　　　　　　　　　　　　60
Tongues spit their duties out, and cold hearts freeze
Allegiance in them: their curses now
Live where their prayers did; and it's come to pass,
This tractable obedience is a slave
To each incensed will. I would, your highness
Would give it quick consideration, for
There is no primer business.
　K. Hen.　　　　　By my life,
This is against our pleasure.
　Wol.　　　　　And for me,
I have no further gone in this, than by
A single voice, and that not pass'd me but　　70
By learned approbation of the judges. If I am
Traduc'd by ignorant tongues, which neither know
My faculties, nor person, yet will be
The chronicles of my doing, let me say,
'T is but the fate of place, and the rough brake
That virtue must go through. We must not stint
Our necessary actions, in the fear
To cope malicious censurers; which ever,
As ravenous fishes, do a vessel follow
That is new-trimm'd, but benefit no further　　80
Than vainly longing. What we oft do best,
By sick interpreters (once weak ones) is
Not ours, or not allow'd; what worst, as oft,
Hitting a grosser quality, is cried up
For our best act. If we shall stand still,
In fear our motion will be mock'd or carp'd at,
We should take root here, where we sit, or sit
State-statues only.
　K. Hen.　　　　Things done well,
And with a care, exempt themselves from fear;
Things done without example, in their issue　　90
Are to be fear'd. Have you a precedent
Of this commission? I believe, not any.
We must not rend our subjects from our laws,
And stick them in our will. Sixth part of each?
A trembling contribution! Why, we take
From every tree, lop, bark, and part o' the timber;
And, though we leave it with a root, thus hack'd,
The air will drink the sap. To every county,
Where this is question'd, send our letters, with
Free pardon to each man that has denied　　100
The force of this commission. Pray, look to't;
I put it to your care.
　Wol. [*To the Secretary.*] A word with you.
Let there be letters writ to every shire,
Of the king's grace and pardon. The griev'd commons
Hardly conceive of me; let it be nois'd,
That through our intercession this revokement
And pardon comes. I shall anon advise you
Further in the proceeding.　　[*Exit Secretary.*

Enter Surveyor.

　Q. Kath. I am sorry that the Duke of Buckingham
Is run in your displeasure.
　K. Hen.　　　　It grieves many:　　110

The gentleman is learn'd, and a most rare speaker,
To nature none more bound; his training such
That he may furnish and instruct great teachers,
And never seek for aid out of himself. Yet see,

(This was his gentleman in trust) of him
Things to strike honour sad.—Bid him recount
The fore-recited practices; whereof
We cannot feel too little, hear too much.

Q. Kath. "Nay, we must longer kneel: I am a suitor."

When these so noble benefits shall prove
Not well dispos'd, the mind growing once corrupt,
They turn to vicious forms, ten times more ugly
Than ever they were fair. This man so complete,
Who was enroll'd 'mongst wonders, and when we,
Almost with ravish'd list'ning, could not find   120
His hour of speech a minute, he, my lady,
Hath into monstrous habits put the graces
That once were his, and is become as black
As if besmear'd in hell. Sit by us; you shall hear

Wol. Stand forth; and with bold spirit relate what
     you,
Most like a careful subject, have collected   130
Out of the Duke of Buckingham.
     K. Hen.   Speak freely.
     Surv. First, it was usual with him, every day
It would infect his speech, that if the king
Should without issue die, he'll carry it so
To make the sceptre his. These very words
I've heard him utter to his son-in-law,

Lord Aberga'ny, to whom by oath he menac'd
Revenge upon the cardinal.
Wol. Please your highness, note
This dangerous conception in this point.
Not friended by his wish, to your high person 140
His will is most malignant; and it stretches
Beyond you, to your friends.
Q. Kath. My learn'd lord cardinal,
Deliver all with charity.
K. Hen. Speak on.
How grounded he his title to the crown,
Upon our fail? to this point hast thou heard him
At any time speak aught?
Surv. He was brought to this
By a vain prophecy of Nicholas Hopkins.
K. Hen. What was that Hopkins?
Surv. Sir, a Chartreux friar,
His confessor: who fed him every minute
With words of sovereignty.
K. Hen. How know'st thou this?
Surv. Not long before your highness sped to France,
The duke being at the Rose, within the parish 152
Saint Lawrence Poultney, did of me demand
What was the speech among the Londoners
Concerning the French journey? I replied,
Men fear'd the French would prove perfidious,
To the king's danger. Presently the duke
Said, 't was the fear, indeed; and that he doubted,
'T would prove the verity of certain words
Spoke by a holy monk: "that oft," says he, 160
"Hath sent to me, wishing me to permit
John de la Car, my chaplain, a choice hour
To hear from him a matter of some moment:
Whom after, under the confession's seal,
He solemnly had sworn, that, what he spoke,
My chaplain to no creature living, but
To me, should utter, with demure confidence
This pausingly ensu'd, —Neither the king, nor his
heirs,
(Tell you the duke) shall prosper: bid him strive
To gain the love of the commonalty: the duke 170
Shall govern England."
Q. Kath. If I know you well,
You were the duke's surveyor, and lost your office
On the complaint o' the tenants: take good heed,
You charge not in your spleen a noble person,
And spoil your nobler soul. I say, take heed;
Yes, heartily beseech you.
K. Hen. Let him on.—
Go forward.
Surv. On my soul, I'll speak but truth.
I told my lord the duke, by the devil's illusions
The monk might be deceiv'd; and that 't was
dangerous for him
To ruminate on this so far, until 180
It forg'd him some design, which, being believ'd,
It was much like to do. He answer'd, "Tush!
It can do me no damage:" adding further,
That had the king in his last sickness fail'd,
The cardinal's and Sir Thomas Lovell's heads
Should have gone off.
K. Hen. Ha! what, so rank? Ah ha!
There's mischief in this man.—Canst thou say
further?
Surv. I can, my liege.
K. Hen. Proceed.
Surv. Being at Greenwich,
After your highness had reprov'd the duke
About Sir William Blomer,—
K. Hen. I remember 190
Of such a time: being my sworn servant,
The duke retain'd him his.—But on: what hence?
Surv. "If," quoth he, "I for this had been com-
mitted,
As, to the Tower, I thought, I would have play'd
The part my father meant to act upon
The usurper Richard; who, being at Salisbury,
Made suit to come in his presence; which if
granted,
As he made semblance of his duty, would
Have put his knife into him,"
K. Hen. A giant traitor!

Wol. Now, madam, may his highness live in
freedom, 200
And this man out of prison?
Q. Kath. God mend all!
K. Hen. There's something more would out of
thee: what say'st?
Surv. After "the duke his father," with "the
knife,"
He stretch'd him, and, with one hand on his dagger,
Another spread on his breast, mounting his eyes,
He did discharge a horrible oath; whose tenor
Was,—were he evil us'd, he would outgo
His father, by as much as a performance
Does an irresolute purpose.
K. Hen. There's his period,
To sheathe his knife in us. He is attach'd; 210
Call him to present trial: if he may
Find mercy in the law, 't is his; if none,
Let him not seek 't of us. By day and night!
He's traitor to the height. [*Exeunt.*

SCENE III.—A Room in the Palace.

Enter the Lord Chamberlain and Lord SANDS.

Cham. Is 't possible, the spells of France should
juggle
Men into such strange mysteries?
Sands. New customs,
Though they be never so ridiculous,
Nay, let 'em be unmanly, yet are follow'd.
Cham. As far as I see, all the good our English
Have got by the late voyage is but merely
A fit or two o' the face; but they are shrewd ones,
For when they hold 'em, you would swear directly,
Their very noses had been counsellors
To Pepin or Clotharius, they keep state so. 10
Sands. They have all new legs, and lame ones: one
would take it,
That never saw 'em pace before, the spavin
And springhalt reign'd among 'em.
Cham. Death! my lord,
Their clothes are after such a pagan cut too,
That, sure, they've worn out Christendom.

Enter Sir THOMAS LOVELL.

How now?
What news, Sir Thomas Lovell?
Lov. 'Faith, my lord,
I hear of none, but the new proclamation
That 's clapp'd upon the court-gate.
Cham. What is 't for?
Lov. The reformation of our travell'd gallants,
That fill the court with quarrels, talk, and tailors. 20
Cham. I am glad 't is there: now, I would pray our
monsieurs
To think an English courtier may be wise,
And never see the Louvre.
Lov. They must either
(For so run the conditions) leave those remnants
Of fool, and feather, that they got in France,
With all their honourable points of ignorance
Pertaining thereunto, as fights and fireworks;
Abusing better men than they can be,
Out of a foreign wisdom: renouncing clean
The faith they have in tennis and tall stockings, 30
Short blister'd breeches, and those types of travel,
And understand again like honest men;
Or pack to their old playfellows: there, I take it,
They may, *cum privilegio,* wear away
The lag end of their lewdness, and be laugh'd at.
Sands. 'T is time to give 'em physic, their diseases
Are grown so catching.
Cham. What a loss our ladies
Will have of these trim vanities!
Lov. Ay, marry,
There will be woe indeed, lords: the sly whoresons
Have got a speeding trick to lay down ladies; 40
A French song, and a fiddle, has no fellow.
Sands. The devil fiddle 'em! I am glad they're
going,

For, sure, there 's no converting of 'em : now,
An honest country lord, as I am, beaten
A long time out of play, may bring his plain-song,
And have an hour of hearing ; and, by 'r lady,
Held current music too.
Cham. Well said, Lord Sands :
Your colt's tooth is not cast yet.
Sands. No, my lord ;
Nor shall not, while I have a stump.
Cham. Sir Thomas,
Whither were you a-going ?
Lov. To the cardinal's. 50
Your lordship is a guest too.
Cham. O! 't is true :
This night he makes a supper, and a great one,
To many lords and ladies ; there will be
The beauty of this kingdom, I 'll assure you.
Lov. That churchman bears a bounteous mind
        indeed,
A hand as fruitful as the land that feeds us :
His dews fall everywhere.
Cham. No doubt, he 's noble ;
He had a black mouth that said other of him.
Sands. He may, my lord ; has wherewithal : in him,
Sparing would show a worse sin than ill doctrine : 60
Men of his way should be most liberal ;
They are set here for examples.
Cham. True, they are so ;
But few now give so great ones. My barge stays ;
Your lordship shall along.—Come, good Sir Thomas,
We shall be late else ; which I would not be,
For I was spoke to, with Sir Henry Guildford,
This night to be comptrollers.
Sands. I am your lordship's.
        [*Exeunt.*

SCENE IV.—The Presence-chamber in York Place.

*Hautboys. A small table under a state for the Car-
dinal, a longer table for the guests ; then enter
ANNE BULLEN, and divers Lords, Ladies, and
Gentlewomen, as guests, at one door ; at another
door, enter Sir HENRY GUILDFORD.*

Guild. Ladies, a general welcome from his grace
Salutes ye all : this night he dedicates
To fair content, and you. None here, he hopes,
In all this noble bevy, has brought with her
One care abroad : he would have all as merry
As, first, good company, good wine, good welcome
Can make good people.

*Enter Lord Chamberlain, Lord SANDS, and Sir
THOMAS LOVELL.*

        O, my lord ! you are tardy ;
The very thought of this fair company
Clapp'd wings to me.
Cham. You are young, Sir Harry Guildford.
Sands. Sir Thomas Lovell, had the cardinal 10
But half my lay-thoughts in him, some of these
Should find a running banquet ere they rested,
I think would better please 'em : by my life,
They are a sweet society of fair ones.
Lov. O ! that your lordship were but now confessor
To one or two of these.
Sands. I would, I were ;
They should find easy penance.
Lov. 'Faith, how easy?
Sands. As easy as a down-bed would afford it.
Cham. Sweet ladies, will it please you sit ? Sir
        Harry,
Place you that side, I 'll take the charge of this : 20
His grace is entering.—Nay, you must not freeze ;
Two women plac'd together makes cold weather :—
My Lord Sands, you are one will keep 'em waking ;
Pray, sit between these ladies.
Sands. By my faith,
And thank your lordship.—By your leave, sweet
        ladies :
        [*Seats himself between ANNE BULLEN and
        another Lady.*

If I chance to talk a little wild, forgive me ;
I had it from my father.
Anne. Was he mad, sir ?
Sands. O ! very mad, exceeding mad ; in love
        too ;
But he would bite none : just as I do now,
He would kiss you twenty with a breath. [*Kisses her.*
Cham. Well said, my lord.—
So, now you are fairly seated.—Gentlemen, 31
The penance lies on you, if these fair ladies
Pass away frowning.
Sands. For my little cure,
Let me alone.

*Hautboys. Enter Cardinal WOLSEY, attended, and
        takes his state.*

Wol. You are welcome, my fair guests : that noble
        lady,
Or gentleman, that is not freely merry,
Is not my friend. This, to confirm my welcome ;
And to you all good health. [*Drinks.*
Sands. Your grace is noble :
Let me have such a bowl may hold my thanks,
And save me so much talking.
Wol. My Lord Sands, 40
I am beholding to you : cheer your neighbours.—
Ladies, you are not merry :—gentlemen,
Whose fault is this ?
Sands. The red wine first must rise
In their fair cheeks, my lord ; then, we shall have 'em
Talk us to silence.
Anne. You are a merry gamester,
My Lord Sands.
Sands. Yes, if I make my play.
Here 's to your lordship ; and pledge it, madam,
For 't is to such a thing,—
Anne. You cannot show me.
Sands. I told your grace, they would talk anon.
        [*Drum and trumpets within ; chambers
        discharged.*
Wol. What 's that ?
Cham. Look out there, some of you.
        [*Exit a Servant.*
Wol. What warlike voice,
And to what end is this ?—Nay, ladies, fear not ; 51
By all the laws of war you are privileg'd.

Re-enter Servant.

Cham. How now ? what is 't ?
Serv. A noble troop of strangers ;
For so they seem : they 've left their barge, and
        landed ;
And hither make, as great ambassadors
From foreign princes.
Wol. Good lord chamberlain,
Go, give them welcome ; you can speak the French
        tongue ;
And, pray, receive 'em nobly, and conduct 'em
Into our presence, where this heaven of beauty
Shall shine at full upon them.—Some attend him.— 60
        [*Exit Chamberlain, attended. All arise, and
        tables removed.*
You have now a broken banquet ; but we 'll mend
        it.
A good digestion to you all ; and, once more,
I shower a welcome on ye.—Welcome all.

*Hautboys. Enter the KING, and others, as Masquers,
habited like shepherds, ushered by the Lord Chamberlain. They pass directly before the Cardinal,
and gracefully salute him.*

A noble company ! what are their pleasures ?
Cham. Because they speak no English, thus they
        pray'd
To tell your grace :—that, having heard by fame
Of this so noble and so fair assembly
This night to meet here, they could do no less,
Out of the great respect they bear to beauty,
But leave their flocks ; and, under your fair conduct,
Crave leave to view these ladies, and entreat 71
An hour of revels with 'em.
Wol. Say, lord chamberlain

They have done my poor house grace; for which I
     pay 'em
A thousand thanks, and pray 'em take their pleasures.
     [Ladies chosen for the dance. The KING
       takes ANNE BULLEN.

If I but knew him, with my love and duty   80
I would surrender it.
  Cham.   I will, my lord.
       [Goes to the Masquers, and returns.
  Wol. What say they?

KING HENRY DANCING WITH ANNE BULLEN.

  K. Hen. The fairest hand I ever touch'd. O beauty!
Till now I never knew thee.   *[Music. Dance.*
  Wol. My lord!
  Cham.   Your grace?
  Wol.   Pray, tell them thus much from me:
There should be one amongst them, by his person,
More worthy this place than myself; to whom,

  Cham.   Such a one, they all confess,
There is, indeed; which they would have your grace
Find out, and he will take it.
  Wol.   Let me see then.—
       [Comes from his state.
By all your good leaves, gentlemen, here I'll make
My royal choice.

K. Hen. [*Unmasking.*] Ye have found him, cardinal.
You hold a fair assembly ; you dó well, lord :
You are a churchman, or, I 'll tell you, cardinal,
I should judge now unhappily.
Wol.   I am glad,
Your grace is grown so pleasant.
K. Hen.   My lord chamberlain,
Pr'ythee, come hither. What fair lady 's that?   91
Cham. An 't please your grace, Sir Thomas Bullen's
     daughter,
The Viscount Rochford, one of her highness' women.
K. Hen. By Heaven, she is a dainty one.—Sweet-
     heart,
I were unmannerly to take you out,
And not to kiss you.—A health, gentlemen !
Let it go round.

Wol.   Sir Thomas Lovell, is the banquet ready
I' the privy chamber ?
Lov.   Yes, my lord.
Wol.   Your grace,
I fear, with dancing is a little heated.
K. Hen. I fear, too much.
Wol.   There 's fresher air, my lord,
In the next chamber.   101
K. Hen. Lead in your ladies, every one.—Sweet
     partner,
I must not yet forsake you.—Let 's be merry,
Good my lord cardinal : I have half a dozen healths
To drink to these fair ladies, and a measure
To lead 'em once again ; and then let 's dream
Who 's best in favour.—Let the music knock it.
          [*Exeunt, with trumpets.*

ACT II.

SCENE I.—A Street.

Enter two Gentlemen, meeting.

1 *Gentleman.*
HITHER away so fast?
2 *Gent.*   O !—God
          save you.
E'en to the hall, to hear what shall
     become
Of the great Duke of Buckingham.
1 *Gent.*   I 'll save you
That labour, sir. All 's now done, but
     the ceremony
Of bringing back the prisoner.
2 *Gent.*   Were you there ?
1 *Gent.* Yes, indeed, was I.
2 *Gent.*   Pray, speak what has
     happen'd.
1 *Gent.* You may guess quickly what.
2 *Gent.*   Is he found guilty ?
1 *Gent.* Yes, truly is he, and condemn'd upon it.
2 *Gent.* I am sorry for 't.
1 *Gent.*   So are a number more.
2 *Gent.* But, pray, how pass'd it?   10
1 *Gent.* I 'll tell you in a little. The great duke
Came to the bar ; where to his accusations
He pleaded still not guilty, and alleg'd
Many sharp reasons to defeat the law.
The king's attorney, on the contrary,
Urg'd on the examinations, proofs, confessions
Of divers witnesses, which the duke desir'd
To have brought, *vivâ voce*, to his face :
At which appeared against him, his surveyor ;
Sir Gilbert Peck his chancellor ; and John Car,   20
Confessor to him ; with that devil-monk,
Hopkins, that made this mischief.
2 *Gent.*   That was he
That fed him with his prophecies?
1 *Gent.*   The same.
All these accus'd him strongly ; which he fain
Would have flung from him, but, indeed, he could not :
And so his peers, upon this evidence,
Have found him guilty of high treason. Much
He spoke, and learnedly, for life ; but all
Was either pitied in him, or forgotten.
2 *Gent.* After all this, how did he bear himself?   30
1 *Gent.* When he was brought again to the bar, to hear
His knell rung out, his judgment, he was stirr'd
With such an agony, he sweat extremely,
And something spoke in choler, ill, and hasty :

But he fell to himself again, and sweetly
In all the rest show'd a most noble patience.
2 *Gent.* I do not think, he fears death.
1 *Gent.*   Sure, he does not ;
He was never so womanish ; the cause
He may a little grieve at.
2 *Gent.*   Certainly,
The cardinal is the end of this.
1 *Gent.*   'T is likely,   40
By all conjectures : first, Kildare's attainder,
Then deputy of Ireland ; who remov'd,
Earl Surrey was sent thither, and in haste too,
Lest he should help his father.
2 *Gent.*   That trick of state
Was a deep envious one.
1 *Gent.*   At his return,
No doubt, he will requite it. This is noted,
And generally ; whoever the king favours,
The cardinal instantly will find employment,
And far enough from court too.
2 *Gent.*   All the commons   50
Hate him perniciously, and, o' my conscience,
Wish him ten fathom deep : this duke as much
They love and dote on ; call him bounteous Bucking-
     ham,
The mirror of all courtesy—
1 *Gent.*   Stay there, sir,
And see the noble ruin'd man you speak of.

Enter BUCKINGHAM *from his arraignment ; tipstaves
     before him ; the axe with the edge towards him ;
     halberds on each side ; accompanied with Sir*
     THOMAS LOVELL, *Sir* NICHOLAS VAUX, *Sir* WILLIAM
     SANDS, *and common people.*

2 *Gent.* Let 's stand close, and behold him.
Buck.   All good people,
You that thus far have come to pity me,
Hear what I say, and then go home and lose me.
I have this day receiv'd a traitor's judgment,
And by that name must die : yet, Heaven bear witness,
And if I have a conscience, let it sink me,   60
Even as the axe falls, if I be not faithful.
The law I bear no malice for my death,
It has done upon the premises but justice :
But those that sought it I could wish more Christians:
Be what they will, I heartily forgive them.
Yet let them look they glory not in mischief,

Nor build their evils on the graves of great men;
For then my guiltless blood must cry against them.
For further life in this world I ne'er hope,
Nor will I sue, although the king have mercies　　70
More than I dare make faults.　You few that lov'd me,
And dare be bold to weep for Buckingham,
His noble friends and fellows, whom to leave
Is only bitter to him, only dying,
Go with me, like good angels, to my end;
And, as the long divorce of steel falls on me,
Make of your prayers one sweet sacrifice,
And lift my soul to heaven.—Lead on, o' God's name.
　Lov. I do beseech your grace for charity,

Buck. "Sir Thomas Lovell, I as free forgive you,
As I would be forgiven."

If ever any malice in your heart　　　　　　80
Were hid against me, now to forgive me frankly.
　Buck. Sir Thomas Lovell, I as free forgive you,
As I would be forgiven: I forgive all.
There cannot be those numberless offences
'Gainst me, that I cannot take peace with: no black
　　　envy
Shall make my grave.　Commend me to his grace;
And, if he speak of Buckingham, pray, tell him,
You met him half in heaven.　My vows and prayers
Yet are the king's; and, till my soul forsake,
Shall cry for blessings on him.　May he live　　90
Longer than I have time to tell his years!
Ever belov'd, and loving, may his rule be!
And when old time shall lead him to his end,
Goodness and he fill up one monument!
　Lov. To the water side I must conduct your grace;
Then, give my charge up to Sir Nicholas Vaux,
Who undertakes you to your end.
　Vaux.　　　　　　　　Prepare there
The duke is coming: see the barge be ready,
And fit it with such furniture, as suits
The greatness of his person.
　Buck.　　　　　Nay, Sir Nicholas,　100
Let it alone: my state now will but mock me.
When I came hither, I was lord high constable,
And Duke of Buckingham; now, poor Edward Bohun:
Yet I am richer than my base accusers,
That never knew what truth meant.　I now seal it;
And with that blood will make them one day groan
　　　for 't.
My noble father, Henry of Buckingham,
Who first rais'd head against usurping Richard,
Flying for succour to his servant Banister,
Being distress'd, was by that wretch betray'd,　110

And without trial fell: God's peace be with him!
Henry the Seventh succeeding, truly pitying
My father's loss, like a most royal prince,
Restor'd me to my honours, and, out of ruins,
Made my name once more noble.　Now, his son,
Henry the Eighth, life, honour, name, and all
That made me happy, at one stroke has taken
For ever from the world.　I had my trial,
And, must needs say, a noble one; which makes me
A little happier than my wretched father:　120
Yet thus far we are one in fortunes,—both
Fell by our servants, by those men we lov'd most:
A most unnatural and faithless service!
　　　Heaven has an end in all; yet, you
　　　　　that hear me,
This from a dying man receive as
　　　　　certain:
Where you are liberal of your loves
　　　　　and counsels,
Be sure you be not loose; for those
　　　　　you make friends,
And give your hearts to, when they
　　　　　once perceive
The least rub in your fortunes, fall
　　　　　away
Like water from ye, never found
　　　　　again　　　　　130
But where they mean to sink ye.
　　　　　All good people,
Pray for me!　I must now forsake
　　　　　ye: the last hour
Of my long weary life is come upon
　　　　　me.
　　　　　Farewell!
And when you would say something
　　　　　that is sad,
Speak how I fell.—I have done; and
　　　　　God forgive me!
　　　　　　　[*Exeunt* BUCKINGHAM *and*
　　　　　　　　　Train.
　1 *Gent.* O! this is full of pity.—
　　　　　Sir, it calls,
I fear, too many curses on their
　　　　　heads
That were the authors.
　2 *Gent.*　　　　　If the duke
　　　　　be guiltless,
'T is full of woe; yet I can give you inkling　140
Of an ensuing evil, if it fall,
Greater than this.
　1 *Gent.*　　　Good angels keep it from us!
What may it be?　You do not doubt my faith, sir?
　2 *Gent.* This secret is so weighty, 't will require
A strong faith to conceal it.
　1 *Gent.*　　　　　Let me have it:
I do not talk much.
　2 *Gent.*　　　I am confident:
You shall, sir.　Did you not of late days hear
A buzzing of a separation
Between the king and Katharine?
　1 *Gent.*　　　　Yes, but it held not;　150
For when the king once heard it, out of anger
He sent command to the lord mayor straight
To stop the rumour, and allay those tongues
That durst disperse it.
　2 *Gent.*　　　But that slander, sir,
Is found a truth now; for it grows again
Fresher than e'er it was; and held for certain,
The king will venture at it.　Either the cardinal,
Or some about him near, have, out of malice
To the good queen, possess'd him with a scruple,
That will undo her: to confirm this too,　
Cardinal Campeius is arriv'd, and lately,　160
As all think, for this business.
　1 *Gent.*　　　　'T is the cardinal;
And merely to revenge him on the emperor,
For not bestowing on him, at his asking,
The archbishoprick of Toledo, this is purpos'd.
　2 *Gent.* I think, you have hit the mark: but is it not
　　　cruel,
That she should feel the smart of this?　The cardinal
Will have his will, and she must fall.

1 Gent.   'T is woful.
We are too open here to argue this ;
Let 's think in private more.   [*Exeunt.*

Scene II.—*An Ante-chamber in the Palace.*

Enter the Lord Chamberlain, reading a letter.

Cham. "My lord,—The horses your lordship sent
for, with all the care I had, I saw well chosen, ridden,
and furnished. They were young, and handsome, and
of the best breed in the north. When they were ready
to set out for London, a man of my lord cardinal's, by
commission and main power, took them from me ;
with this reason,—his master would be served before
a subject, if not before the king ; which stopped our
mouths, sir."
I fear, he will, indeed. Well, let him have them :   10
He will have all, I think.

Enter the Dukes of Norfolk *and* Suffolk.

Nor. Well met, my lord chamberlain.
Cham. Good day to both your graces.
Suf. How is the king employ'd ?
Cham.   I left him private,
Full of sad thoughts and troubles.
Nor.   What 's the cause ?
Cham. It seems, the marriage with his brother's
    wife
Has crept too near his conscience.
Suf.   No ; his conscience
Has crept too near another lady.
Nor.   'T is so.
This is the cardinal's doing, the king-cardinal :
That blind priest, like the eldest son of fortune,   20
Turns what he list. The king will know him one
    day.
Suf. 'Pray God, he do : he 'll never know himself
    else.
Nor. How holily he works in all his business,
And with what zeal! for now he has crack'd the
    league
Between us and the emperor, the queen's great
    nephew,
He dives into the king's soul ; and there scatters
Dangers, doubts, wringing of the conscience,
Fears, and despairs, and all these for his marriage :
And out of all these to restore the king,
He counsels a divorce ; a loss of her,   30
That like a jewel has hung twenty years
About his neck, yet never lost her lustre ;
Of her, that loves him with that excellence
That angels love good men with ; even of her,
That, when the greatest stroke of fortune falls,
Will bless the king : and is not this course pious?
Cham. Heaven keep me from such counsel ! 'T is
    most true,
These news are everywhere ; every tongue speaks
    them,
And every true heart weeps for 't. All, that dare
Look into these affairs, see this main end,—   40
The French king's sister. Heaven will one day open
The king's eyes, that so long have slept upon
This bold bad man.
Suf.   And free us from his slavery.
Nor. We had need pray,
And heartily, for our deliverance,
Or this imperious man will work us all
From princes into pages. All men's honours
Lie like one lump before him, to be fashion'd
Into what pitch he please.
Suf.   For me, my lords,
I love him not, nor fear him ; there 's my creed.   50
As I am made without him, so I 'll stand,
If the king please : his curses and his blessings
Touch me alike, they 're breath I not believe in.
I knew him, and I know him ; so I leave him
To him that made him proud, the Pope.
Nor.   Let 's in ;
And with some other business put the king

From these sad thoughts, that work too much upon
    him.—
My lord, you 'll bear us company ?
Cham.   Excuse me ;
The king hath sent me otherwhere : besides,
You 'll find a most unfit time to disturb him.   60
Health to your lordships.
Nor.   Thanks, my good lord chamberlain.
          [*Exit Lord Chamberlain.*

Norfolk *opens a folding-door. The* King *is discovered sitting, and reading pensively.*

Suf. How sad he looks : sure, he is much afflicted.
K. Hen. Who is there ? ha !
Nor.   'Pray God, he be not angry.
K. Hen. Who 's there, I say ? How dare you thrust
    yourselves
Into my private meditations?
Who am I ? ha !
Nor. A gracious king, that pardons all offences,
Malice ne'er meant : our breach of duty this way
Is business of estate ; in which we come
To know your royal pleasure.
K. Hen.   Ye are too bold.   70
Go to ; I 'll make ye know your times of business :
Is this an hour for temporal affairs? ha !—

Enter Wolsey *and* Campeius.

Who 's there ? my good lord cardinal ?—O ! my Wolsey,
The quiet of my wounded conscience ;
Thou art a cure fit for a king.—[*To* Campeius.] You 're
    welcome,
Most learned reverend sir, into our kingdom :
Use us, and it.—[*To* Wolsey.] My good lord, have
    great care
I be not found a talker.
Wol.   Sir, you cannot.
I would, your grace would give us but an hour
Of private conference.
K. Hen. [*To* Norfolk *and* Suffolk.] We are
    busy ; go.   80
Nor. [*Aside to* Suffolk.] This priest has no pride
    in him !
Suf. [*Aside to* Norfolk.] Not to speak of ;
I would not be so sick though for his place :
But this cannot continue.
Nor. [*Aside to* Suffolk.] If it do,
I 'll venture one have-at-him.
Suf. [*Aside to* Norfolk.]   I another.
          [*Exeunt* Norfolk *and* Suffolk.
Wol. Your grace has given a precedent of wisdom
Above all princes, in committing freely
Your scruple to the voice of Christendom.
Who can be angry now ? what envy reach you?
The Spaniard, tied by blood and favour to her,
Must now confess, if they have any goodness,   90
The trial just and noble. All the clerks,
I mean the learned ones, in Christian kingdoms,
Have their free voices : Rome, the nurse of judgment,
Invited by your noble self, hath sent
One general tongue unto us, this good man,
This just and learned priest, Cardinal Campeius,
Whom once more I present unto your highness.
K. Hen. And once more in mine arms I bid him
    welcome,
And thank the holy conclave for their loves :
They have sent me such a man I would have wish'd
    for.   100
Cam. Your grace must needs deserve all strangers'
    loves,
You are so noble. To your highness' hand
I tender my commission, by whose virtue
(The court of Rome commanding) you, my lord
Cardinal of York, are join'd with me, their servant,
In the unpartial judging of this business.
K. Hen. Two equal men. The queen shall be ac-
    quainted
Forthwith for what you come.—Where 's Gardiner ?
Wol. I know, your majesty has always lov'd her
So dear in heart, not to deny her that   110
A woman of less place might ask by law,
Scholars allow'd freely to argue for her.

K. Hen. Ay, and the best she shall have; and my
favour
To him that does best : God forbid else. Cardinal,
Pr'ythee, call Gardiner to me, my new secretary :
I find him a fit fellow. [*Exit* Wolsey.

Re-enter Wolsey, *with* Gardiner.

Wol. Give me your hand ; much joy and favour to
you :
You are the king's now.
Gard. But to be commanded
For ever by your grace, whose hand has rais'd me.
K. Hen. Come hither, Gardiner. 120
[*They converse apart.*
Cam. My Lord of York, was not one Doctor Pace
In this man's place before him ?
Wol. Yes, he was.
Cam. Was he not held a learned man ?
Wol. Yes, surely.
Cam. Believe me, there 's an ill opinion spread then
Even of yourself, lord cardinal.
Wol. How ! of me ?
Cam. They will not stick to say, you envied him,
And, fearing he would rise, he was so virtuous,
Kept him a foreign man still ; which so griev'd him,
That he ran mad, and died.
Wol. Heaven's peace be with him !
That is Christian care enough : for living murmurers
There 's places of rebuke. He was a fool, 131
For he would needs be virtuous : that good fellow,
If I command him, follows my appointment :
I will have none so near else. Learn this, brother,
We live not to be grip'd by meaner persons.
K. Hen. Deliver this with modesty to the queen.
[*Exit* Gardiner.
The most convenient place that I can think of,
For such receipt of learning, is Blackfriars :
There ye shall meet about this weighty business.—
My Wolsey, see it furnish'd :—O my lord ! 140
Would it not grieve an able man, to leave
So sweet a bedfellow ? But, conscience, conscience,—
O ! 't is a tender place, and I must leave her. [*Exeunt.*

Scene III.—An Ante-chamber in the Queen's
Apartments.

Enter Anne Bullen *and an Old Lady.*

Anne. Not for that neither :—here 's the pang that
pinches :
His highness having liv'd so long with her, and she
So good a lady, that no tongue could ever
Pronounce dishonour of her,—by my life,
She never knew harm-doing,—O ! now, after
So many courses of the sun enthron'd,
Still growing in a majesty and pomp, the which
To leave a thousand-fold more bitter than
'T is sweet at first to acquire,—after this process,
To give her the avaunt ! it is a pity 10
Would move a monster.
Old L. Hearts of most hard temper
Melt and lament for her.
Anne. O, God's will ! much better,
She ne'er had known pomp : though it be temporal,
Yet, if that quarrel, fortune, do divorce
It from the bearer, 't is a sufferance, panging
As soul and body's severing.
Old L. Alas, poor lady !
She 's a stranger now again.
Anne. So much the more
Must pity drop upon her. Verily,
I swear, 'tis better to be lowly born,
And range with humble livers in content, 20
Than to be perk'd up in a glistering grief,
And wear a golden sorrow.
Old L. Our content
Is our best having.
Anne. By my troth and maidenhead,
I would not be a queen.
Old L. Beshrew me, I would,
And venture maidenhead for 't ; and so would you,

For all this spice of your hypocrisy.
You, that have so fair parts of woman on you,
Have too a woman's heart ; which ever yet
Affected eminence, wealth, sovereignty :
Which, to say sooth, are blessings, and which gifts 30
(Saving your mincing) the capacity
Of your soft cheveril conscience would receive,
If you might please to stretch it.
Anne. Nay, good troth,—
Old L. Yes, troth, and troth.—You would not be a
queen ?
Anne. No, not for all the riches under heaven.
Old L. 'T is strange : a three-pence bow'd would
hire me,
Old as I am, to queen it. But, I pray you,
What think you of a duchess ? have you limbs
To bear that load of title ?
Anne. No, in truth.
Old L. Then you are weakly made. Pluck off a
little : 40
I would not be a young count in your way,
For more than blushing comes to. If your back
Cannot vouchsafe this burden, 't is too weak
Ever to get a boy.
Anne. How you do talk !
I swear again, I would not be a queen
For all the world.
Old L. In faith, for little England
You 'd venture an emballing : I myself
Would for Carnarvonshire, although there 'long'd
No more to the crown but that. Lo ! who comes here?

Enter the Lord Chamberlain.

Cham. Good morrow, ladies. What were it worth
to know 50
The secret of your conference ?
Anne. My good lord,
Not your demand : it values not your asking.
Our mistress' sorrows we were pitying.
Cham. It was a gentle business, and becoming
The action of good women : there is hope
All will be well.
Anne. Now, I pray God, Amen !
Cham. You bear a gentle mind, and heavenly
blessings
Follow such creatures. That you may, fair lady,
Perceive I speak sincerely, and high note 's
Ta'en of your many virtues, the king's majesty 60
Commends his good opinion of you to you, and
Does purpose honour to you no less flowing
Than Marchioness of Pembroke ; to wh'ch title
A thousand pound a year, annual support,
Out of his grace he adds.
Anne. I do not know,
What kind of my obedience I should tender :
More than my all is nothing, nor my prayers
Are not words duly hallow'd, nor my wishes
More worth than empty vanities : yet prayers, and
wishes,
Are all I can return. 'Beseech your lordship, 70
Vouchsafe to speak my thanks, and my obedience,
As from a blushing handmaid, to his highness ;
Whose health and royalty I pray for.
Cham. Lady,
I shall not fail to approve the fair conceit,
The king hath of you.—[*Aside.*] I have perus'd her
well :
Beauty and honour in her are so mingled,
That they have caught the king : and who knows yet,
But from this lady may proceed a gem
To lighten all this isle?—[*To her.*] I'll to the king,
And say, I spoke with you.
Anne. My honour'd lord. 80
[*Exit Lord Chamberlain.*
Old L. Why, this it is ; see, see!
I have been begging sixteen years in court,
(Am yet a courtier beggarly,) nor could
Come pat betwixt too early and too late,
For any suit of pounds ; and you, O fate !
A very fresh-fish here, (fie, fie, fie upon
This compell'd fortune !) have your mouth fill'd up,
Before you open it.

Anne.   This is strange to me.
Old L. How tastes it? is it bitter? forty pence, no.
There was a lady once, ('t is an old story,)   90
That would not be a queen, that would she not,
For all the mud in Egypt:—have you heard it?
Anne. Come, you are pleasant.
Old L.   With your theme, I could
O'ermount the lark. The Marchioness of Pembroke!
A thousand pounds a year, for pure respect!
No other obligation. By my life,
That promises more thousands : honour's train
Is longer than his foreskirt. By this time,
I know, your back will bear a duchess.—Say,
Are you not stronger than you were?
Anne.   Good lady, 100
Make yourself mirth with your particular fancy,
And leave me out on 't. 'Would I had no being,
If this salute my blood a jot : it faints me,
To think what follows.
The queen is comfortless, and we forgetful
In our long absence. Pray, do not deliver
What here you 've heard, to her.
Old L.   What do you think me?
                                [*Exeunt.*

SCENE IV.—A Hall in Blackfriars.

Trumpets, sennet, and cornets. Enter two Vergers,
with short silver wands; next them, two Scribes,
in the habit of doctors ; after them, the Archbishop
of CANTERBURY *alone ; after him, the Bishops of*
LINCOLN, ELY, ROCHESTER, *and* SAINT ASAPH ;
next them, with some small distance, follows a
Gentleman bearing the purse, with the great seal,
and a cardinal's hat ; then two Priests, bearing
each a silver cross; then a Gentleman-Usher bare-
headed, accompanied with a Sergeant-at-Arms,
bearing a silver mace ; then two Gentlemen bear-
ing two great silver pillars ; after them, side by
side, the two Cardinals WOLSEY *and* CAMPEIUS ;
two Noblemen with the sword and mace. Then
enter the KING *and* QUEEN *and their Trains. The*
KING *takes place under the cloth of state ; the two*
Cardinals sit under him as judges. The QUEEN
takes place at some distance from the KING. *The*
Bishops place themselves on each side the court, in
manner of a consistory ; below them, the Scribes.
The Lords sit next the Bishops. The rest of the
Attendants stand in convenient order about the
stage.

Wol. Whilst our commission from Rome is read,
Let silence be commanded.
K. Hen.   What 's the need?
It hath already publicly been read,
And on all sides the authority allow'd ;
You may then spare that time.
Wol.   Be 't so.—Proceed.
Scribe. Say, Henry King of England, come into the
court.
Crier. Henry King of England, &c.
K. Hen. Here.
Scribe. Say, Katharine Queen of England, come
into the court.   11
Crier. Katharine Queen of England, &c.
   [*The* QUEEN *makes no answer, rises out of*
   her chair, goes about the court, comes to
   the KING, *and kneels at his feet ; then*
   speaks.
Q. Kath. Sir, I desire you, do me right and justice,
And to bestow your pity on me ; for
I am a most poor woman, and a stranger,
Born out of your dominions ; having here
No judge indifferent, nor no more assurance
Of equal friendship and proceeding. Alas! sir,
In what have I offended you? what cause
Hath my behaviour given to your displeasure,   20
That thus you should proceed to put me off,
And take your good grace from me? Heaven witness,
I have been to you a true and humble wife,
At all times to your will conformable :
Even in fear to kindle your dislike,

Yea, subject to your countenance ; glad, or sorry,
As I saw it inclin'd. When was the hour
I ever contradicted your desire,
Or made it not mine too? Or which of your friends
Have I not strove to love, although I knew   30
He were mine enemy? What friend of mine,
That had to him deriv'd your anger, did I
Continue in my liking? nay, gave notice
He was from thence discharg'd. Sir, call to mind
That I have been your wife, in this obedience,
Upward of twenty years, and have been blest
With many children by you : if, in the course
And process of this time, you can report,
And prove it too, against mine honour aught,
My bond to wedlock, or my love and duty,   40
Against your sacred person, in God's name,
Turn me away ; and let the foul'st contempt
Shut door upon me, and so give me up
To the sharpest kind of justice. Please you, sir,
The king, your father, was reputed for
A prince most prudent, of an excellent
And unmatch'd wit and judgment: Ferdinand,
My father, King of Spain, was reckon'd one
The wisest prince, that there had reign'd by many
A year before : it is not to be question'd   50
That they had gather'd a wise council to them
Of every realm, that did debate this business,
Who deem'd our marriage lawful. Wherefore I
                                          humbly
Beseech you, sir, to spare me, till I may
Be by my friends in Spain advis'd, whose counsel
I will implore : if not, i' the name of God,
Your pleasure be fulfill'd !
Wol.   You have here, lady,
(And of your choice) these reverend fathers ; men
Of singular integrity and learning,
Yea, the elect of the land, who are assembled   60
To plead your cause. It shall be therefore bootless,
That longer you desire the court, as well
For your own quiet, as to rectify
What is unsettled in the king.
Cam.   His grace
Hath spoken well, and justly: therefore, madam,
It 's fit this royal session do proceed,
And that, without delay, their arguments
Be now produc'd and heard.
Q. Kath.   Lord cardinal,
To you I speak.
Wol.   Your pleasure, madam?
Q. Kath.   Sir,
I am about to weep ; but, thinking that   70
We are a queen, (or long have dream'd so,) certain,
The daughter of a king, my drops of tears
I 'll turn to sparks of fire.
Wol.   Be patient yet.
Q. Kath. I will, when you are humble ; nay, before,
Or God will punish me. I do believe,
Induc'd by potent circumstances, that
You are mine enemy ; and make my challenge
You shall not be my judge ; for it is you
Have blown this coal betwixt my lord and me,
Which God's dew quench.—Therefore, I say again, 80
I utterly abhor, yea, from my soul,
Refuse you for my judge ; whom, yet once more,
I hold my most malicious foe, and think not
At all a friend to truth.
Wol.   I do profess,
You speak not like yourself ; who ever yet
Have stood to charity, and display'd the effects
Of disposition gentle, and of wisdom
O'ertopping woman's power. Madam, you do me
                                          wrong :
I have no spleen against you ; nor injustice
For you, or any : how far I have proceeded,   90
Or how far further shall, is warranted
By a commission from the consistory,
Yea, the whole consistory of Rome. You charge me,
That I have blown this coal : I do deny it.
The king is present : if it be known to him,
That I gainsay my deed, how may he wound,
And worthily, my falsehood ; yea, as much
As you have done my truth. If he know

That I am free of your report, he knows,
I am not of your wrong. Therefore in him 100
It lies to cure me ; and the cure is, to
Remove these thoughts from you : the which before
His highness shall speak in, I do beseech
You, gracious madam, to unthink your speaking,
And to say so no more.
 Q. Kath.   My lord, my lord,
I am a simple woman, much too weak
To oppose your cunning. You are meek, and humble-
 mouth'd ;
You sign your place and calling, in full seeming,
With meekness and humility ; but your heart
Is cramm'd with arrogancy, spleen, and pride. 110
You have, by fortune and his highness' favours,
Gone slightly o'er low steps, and now are mounted
Where powers are your retainers, and your words,
Domestics to you, serve your will, as 't please
Yourself pronounce their office. I must tell you,
You tender more your person's honour, than
Your high profession spiritual ; that again
I do refuse you for my judge, and here,
Before you all, appeal unto the Pope,
To bring my whole cause 'fore his holiness, 120
And to be judg'd by him.
  [*She curtsies to the* KING, *and offers to depart.*
 Cam.   The queen is obstinate,
Stubborn to justice, apt to accuse it, and
Disdainful to be tried by it : 't is not well.
She 's going away.
 K. Hen.   Call her again.
 Crier. Katharine, Queen of England, come into the
court.
 Griffith. Madam, you are call'd back.
 Q. Kath. What need you note it ? pray you, keep
   your way :
When you are call'd, return.—Now the Lord help !
They vex me past my patience.—Pray you, pass on :
I will not tarry ; no, nor ever more, 131
Upon this business, my appearance make
In any of their courts.
   [*Exeunt* QUEEN *and her Attendants.*
 K. Hen.   Go thy ways, Kate :
That man i' the world who shall report he has
A better wife, let him in nought be trusted,
For speaking false in that. Thou art, alone,
(If thy rare qualities, sweet gentleness,
Thy meekness saint-like, wife-like government,
Obeying in commanding, and thy parts
Sovereign and pious else, could speak thee out,) 140
The queen of earthly queens.—She 's noble born ;
And, like her true nobility, she has
Carried herself towards me.
 Wol.   Most gracious sir,
In humblest manner I require your highness,
That it shall please you to declare, in hearing
Of all these ears, (for where I am robb'd and bound,
There must I be unloos'd, although not there
At once and fully satisfied,) whether ever I
Did broach this business to your highness, or
Laid any scruple in your way, which might 150
Induce you to the question on 't ? or ever
Have to you, but with thanks to God for such
A royal lady, spake one the least word, that might
Be to the prejudice of her present state,
Or touch of her good person ?
 K. Hen.   My lord cardinal,
I do excuse you ; yea, upon mine honour,
I free you from 't. You are not to be taught
That you have many enemies, that know not
Why they are so, but, like to village curs,
Bark when their fellows do : by some of these 160
The queen is put in anger. You are excus'd :
But will you be more justified ? you ever
Have wish'd the sleeping of this business ; never
Desir'd it to be stirr'd ; but oft have hinder'd, oft,
The passages made toward it.—On my honour,
I speak my good lord cardinal to this point,
And thus far clear him. Now, what mov'd me to 't :
I will be bold with time, and your attention :—
Then, mark the inducement. Thus it came ;—give
 heed to 't.

My conscience first receiv'd a tenderness, 170
Scruple, and prick, on certain speeches utter'd
By the Bishop of Bayonne, then French ambassador,
Who had been hither sent on the debating
A marriage 'twixt the Duke of Orleans and
Our daughter Mary. I' the progress of this business,
Ere a determinate resolution, he
(I mean, the bishop) did require a respite,
Wherein he might the king his lord advertise
Whether our daughter were legitimate,
Respecting this our marriage with the dowager, 180
Sometimes our brother's wife. This respite shook

  Q. Kath. "Now the Lord help !
  They vex me past my patience."

The bosom of my conscience, enter'd me,
Yea, with a splitting power, and made to tremble
The region of my breast ; which forc'd such way,
That many maz'd considerings did throng,
And press'd in with this caution. First, methought,
I stood not in the smile of Heaven, who had
Commanded nature, that my lady's womb,
If it conceiv'd a male child by me, should
Do no more offices of life to 't, than 190
The grave does to the dead ; for her male issue
Or died where they were made, or shortly after
This world had air'd them. Hence I took a thought,
This was a judgment on me ; that my kingdom,
Well worthy the best heir o' the world, should not
Be gladded in 't by me. Then follows, that
I weigh'd the danger which my realms stood in
By this my issue's fail ; and that gave to me
Many a groaning throe. Thus hulling in
The wild sea of my conscience, I did steer 200
Toward this remedy, whereupon we are
Now present here together ; that 's to say,
I meant to rectify my conscience,—which
I then did feel full sick, and yet not well,—
By all the reverend fathers of the land,
And doctors learn'd. First, I began in private
With you, my Lord of Lincoln ; you remember
How under my oppression I did reek,
When I first mov'd you.
 Lin.   Very well, my liege.
 K. Hen. I have spoke long : be pleas'd yourself to
   say 210
How far you satisfied me.
 Lin.   So please your highness,
The question did at first so stagger me,—
Bearing a state of mighty moment in 't,
And consequence of dread,—that I committed
The daring'st counsel which I had, to doubt,
And did entreat your highness to this course,
Which you are running here.
 K. Hen.   I then mov'd you,
My Lord of Canterbury, and got your leave
To make this present summons.—Unsolicited
I left no reverend person in this court ; 220
But by particular consent proceeded,

Under your hands and seals : therefore, go on ;
For no dislike i' the world against the person
Of the good queen, but the sharp thorny points
Of my alleged reasons drive this forward.
Prove but our marriage lawful, by my life,
And kingly dignity, we are contented
To wear our mortal state to come with her,
Katharine our queen, before the primest creature
That 's paragon'd o' the world.
   Cam.   So please your highness,
The queen being absent, 't is a needful fitness 231

That we adjourn this court till further day :
Meanwhile must be an earnest motion
Made to the queen, to call back her appeal
She intends unto his holiness.
   K. Hen. [*Aside.*]   I may perceive,
These cardinals trifle with me : I abhor
This dilatory sloth, and tricks of Rome.
My learn'd and well-beloved servant, Cranmer!
Pr'ythee, return : with thy approach, I know,
My comfort comes along.—Break up the court : 210
I say, set on.   [*Exeunt, in manner as they entered.*

ACT III.

Scene I.—The Palace at Bridewell. A Room in the Queen's Apartment.

The Queen, *and her Women, at work.*

   Queen Katharine.
AKE thy lute, wench : my soul grows sad
    with troubles ;
Sing, and disperse them, if thou canst.
  Leave working.

        Song.

Orpheus with his lute made trees,
And the mountain-tops that freeze,
  Bow themselves, when he did sing :
To his music, plants, and flowers
Ever sprung ; as sun and showers
  There had made a lasting spring.

Everything that heard him play,
Even the billows of the sea, 10
  Hung their heads, and then lay by.
In sweet music is such art :
Killing care and grief of heart
  Fall asleep, or, hearing, die.

   Enter a Gentleman.
   Q. Kath. How now?
   Gent. An 't please your grace, the two great
    cardinals
Wait in the presence.
   Q. Kath.   Would they speak with me?
   Gent. They will'd me say so, madam.
   Q. Kath.   Pray their graces
To come near. [*Exit Gentleman.*] What can be their
    business
With me, a poor weak woman, fall'n from favour? 20
I do not like their coming, now I think on 't.
They should be good men, their affairs as righteous ;
But all hoods make not monks.

   Enter Wolsey *and* Campeius.
   Wol.   Peace to your highness !
   Q. Kath. Your graces find me here part of a house-
    wife ;
I would be all, against the worst may happen.
What are your pleasures with me, reverend lords?
   Wol. May it please you, noble madam, to withdraw
Into your private chamber, we shall give you
The full cause of our coming.
   Q. Kath.   Speak it here.
There 's nothing I have done yet, o' my conscience, 30
Deserves a corner : 'would all other women
Could speak this with as free a soul as I do !
My lords, I care not, (so much I am happy
Above a number,) if my actions
Were tried by every tongue, every eye saw them,

Envy and base opinion set against them,
I know my life so even. If your business
Seek me out, and that way I am wife in,
Out with it boldly : truth loves open dealing.
   Wol. Tanta est erga te mentis integritas, regina
   serenissima,—   41
   Q. Kath. O, good my lord, no Latin :
I am not such a truant since my coming,
As not to know the language I have liv'd in :
A strange tongue makes my cause more strange,
    suspicious ;
Pray, speak in English. Here are some will thank
    you,
If you speak truth, for their poor mistress' sake :
Believe me, she has had much wrong. Lord cardinal,
The willing'st sin I ever yet committed
May be absolv'd in English.
   Wol.   Noble lady, 50
I am sorry, my integrity should breed
(And service to his majesty and you)
So deep suspicion, where all faith was meant.
We come not by the way of accusation,
To taint that honour every good tongue blesses,
Nor to betray you any way to sorrow ;
You have too much, good lady ; but to know
How you stand minded in the weighty difference
Between the king and you, and to deliver,
Like free and honest men, our just opinions, 60
And comforts to your cause.
   Cam.   Most honour'd madam,
My Lord of York,—out of his noble nature,
Zeal and obedience he still bore your grace,
Forgetting, like a good man, your late censure
Both of his truth and him (which was too far),—
Offers, as I do, in a sign of peace,
His service and his counsel.
   Q. Kath. [*Aside.*]   To betray me.—
My lords, I thank you both for your good wills,
Ye speak like honest men ; (pray God, ye prove
    so !)
But how to make you suddenly an answer, 70
In such a point of weight, so near mine honour,
(More near my life, I fear,) with my weak wit,
And to such men of gravity and learning,
In truth, I know not. I was set at work
Among my maids ; full little, God knows, looking
Either for such men, or such business.
For her sake that I have been, for I feel
The last fit of my greatness, good your graces,
Let me have time and counsel for my cause.
Alas ! I am a woman, friendless, hopeless. 80

Wol. Madam, you wrong the king's love with these
      fears:
Your hopes and friends are infinite.
   Q. Kath.   In England
But little for my profit. Can you think, lords,

Cam.   I would, your grace
Would leave your griefs, and take my counsel.
   Q. Kath.   How, sir?
   Cam. Put your main cause into the king's protection;
He 's loving, and most gracious : 't will be much

   Q. Kath. "Your graces find me here part of a housewife;
     I would be all, against the worst may happen."

That any Englishman dare give me counsel?
Or be a known friend, 'gainst his highness' pleasure,
(Though he be grown so desperate to be honest,)
And live a subject? Nay, forsooth, my friends,
They that must weigh out my afflictions,
They that my trust must grow to, live not here:
They are, as all my other comforts, far hence,   90
In mine own country, lords.

Both for your honour better, and your cause;
For if the trial of the law o'ertake you,
You 'll part away disgrac'd.
   Wol.   He tells you rightly.
   Q. Kath. Ye tell me what ye wish for both,—my ruin.
Is this your Christian counsel? out upon ye!
Heaven is above all yet: there sits a Judge   100
That no king can corrupt.

Cam.   Your rage mistakes us.
Q. Kath. The more shame for ye! holy men I
    thought ye,
Upon my soul, two reverend cardinal virtues ;
But cardinal sins, and hollow hearts, I fear ye.
Mend them, for shame, my lords. Is this your com-
    fort ?
The cordial that ye bring a wretched lady ?
A woman lost among ye, laugh'd at, scorn'd ?
I will not wish ye half my miseries,
I have more charity ; but say, I warn'd ye :
Take heed, for Heaven's sake, take heed, lest at once
The burden of my sorrows fall upon ye.   111
    Wol. Madam, this is a mere distraction ;
You turn the good we offer into envy.
Q. Kath. Ye turn me into nothing. Woe upon ye,
And all such false professors ! Would ye have me
(If ye have any justice, any pity,
If ye be anything but churchmen's habits)
Put my sick cause into his hands that hates me ?
Alas ! has banish'd me his bed already ;
His love, too long ago : I am old, my lords,   120
And all the fellowship I hold now with him
Is only my obedience. What can happen
To me, above this wretchedness ? all your studies
Make me a curse like this.
    Cam.   Your fears are worse.
Q. Kath. Have I liv'd thus long—(let me speak
    myself,
Since virtue finds no friends)—a wife, a true one ?
A woman (I dare say, without vain-glory)
Never yet branded with suspicion ?
Have I with all my full affections
Still met the king ? lov'd him next Heaven ? obey'd
    him ?   130
Been, out of fondness, superstitious to him ?
Almost forgot my prayers to content him ?
And am I thus rewarded ? 't is not well, lords.
Bring me a constant woman to her husband,
One that ne'er dream'd a joy beyond his pleasure,
And to that woman, when she has done most,
Yet will I add an honour,—a great patience.
    Wol. Madam, you wander from the good we aim at.
Q. Kath. My lord, I dare not make myself so guilty,
To give up willingly that noble title   140
Your master wed me to : nothing but death
Shall e'er divorce my dignities.
    Wol.   'Pray, hear me.
Q. Kath. 'Would I had never trod this English earth,
Or felt the flatteries that grow upon it !
Ye have angels' faces, but Heaven knows your hearts.
What will become of me now, wretched lady ?
I am the most unhappy woman living.—
[*To her Women.*] Alas ! poor wenches, where are now
    your fortunes ?
Shipwrack'd upon a kingdom, where no pity,
No friends, no hope, no kindred weep for me,   150
Almost no grave allow'd me.—Like the lily,
That once was mistress of the field and flourish'd,
I 'll hang my head, and perish.
    Wol.   If your grace
Could but be brought to know our ends are honest,
You 'd feel more comfort. Why should we, good lady,
Upon what cause, wrong you ? alas ! our places,
The way of our profession is against it :
We are to cure such sorrows, not to sow them.
For goodness' sake, consider what you do ;
How you may hurt yourself, ay, utterly   160
Grow from the king's acquaintance by this carriage.
The hearts of princes kiss obedience,
So much they love it ; but to stubborn spirits,
They swell, and grow as terrible as storms.
I know, you have a gentle, noble temper,
A soul as even as a calm : pray, think us
Those we profess, peace-makers, friends, and servants.
    Cam. Madam, you 'll find it so. You wrong your
    virtues
With these weak women's fears : a noble spirit,
As yours was put into you, ever casts   170
Such doubts, as false coin, from it. The king loves
    you ;
Beware, you lose it not : for us, if you please

To trust us in your business, we are ready
To use our utmost studies in your service.
Q. Kath. Do what ye will, my lords : and, pray,
    forgive me,
If I have us'd myself unmannerly.
You know, I am a woman, lacking wit
To make a seemly answer to such persons.
Pray, do my service to his majesty :
He has my heart yet, and shall have my prayers.   180
While I shall have my life. Come, reverend fathers ;
Bestow your counsels on me ; she now begs,
That little thought, when she set footing here,
She should have bought her dignities so dear.
                                        [*Exeunt.*

SCENE II.—Ante-chamber to the KING's Apartment.

Enter the Duke of NORFOLK, *the Duke of* SUFFOLK,
    the Earl of SURREY, *and the Lord Chamberlain.*

    Nor. If you will now unite in your complaints,
And force them with a constancy, the cardinal
Cannot stand under them : if you omit
The offer of this time, I cannot promise,
But that you shall sustain more new disgraces,
With these you bear already.
    Sur.   I am joyful
To meet the least occasion, that may give me
Remembrance of my father-in-law, the duke,
To be reveng'd on him.
    Suf.   Which of the peers
Have uncontemn'd gone by him, or at least   10
Strangely neglected ? when did he regard
The stamp of nobleness in any person,
Out of himself ?
    Cham.   My lords, you speak your pleasures.
What he deserves of you and me, I know ;
What we can do to him, (though now the time
Gives way to us,) I much fear. If you cannot
Bar his access to the king, never attempt
Anything on him, for he hath a witchcraft
Over the king in his tongue.
    Nor.   O ! fear him not ;
His spell in that is out : the king hath found   20
Matter against him, that for ever mars
The honey of his language. No, he 's settled,
Not to come off, in his displeasure.
    Sur.   Sir,
I should be glad to hear such news as this
Once every hour.
    Nor.   Believe it, this is true.
In the divorce, his contrary proceedings
Are all unfolded ; wherein he appears,
As I would wish mine enemy.
    Sur.   How came
His practices to light ?
    Suf.   Most strangely.
    Sur.   O ! how ? how ?
Suf. The cardinal's letter to the Pope miscarried, 30
And came to the eye o' the king ; wherein was read,
How that the cardinal did entreat his holiness
To stay the judgment o' the divorce ; for if
It did take place, " I do," quoth he, " perceive,
My king is tangled in affection to
A creature of the queen's, Lady Anne Bullen."
    Sur. Has the king this ?
    Suf.   Believe it.
    Sur.   Will this work ?
Cham. The king in this perceives him, how he
    coasts,
And hedges, his own way. But in this point
All his tricks founder, and he brings his physic   40
After his patient's death : the king already
Hath married the fair lady.
    Sur.   'Would he had !
Suf. May you be happy in your wish, my lord ;
For, I profess, you have it.
    Sur.   Now all my joy
Trace the conjunction !
    Suf.   My Amen to 't !
    Nor.   All men's
Suf. There 's order given for her coronation :

Marry, this is yet but young, and may be left
To some ears unrecounted.—But, my lords,
She is a gallant creature, and complete
In mind and feature : I persuade me, from her   50
Will fall some blessing to this land, which shall
In it be memoris'd.
   Sur.   But, will the king
Digest this letter of the cardinal's?
The Lord forbid !
   Nor.   Marry, Amen !
   Suf.   No, no :
There be moe wasps that buz about his nose,
Will make this sting the sooner.   Cardinal Campeius
Is stol'n away to Rome ; hath ta'en no leave ;
Has left the cause o' the king unhandled, and
Is posted, as the agent of our cardinal,
To second all his plot.   I do assure you,   60
The king cried, ha ! at this.
   Cham.   Now, God incense him,
And let him cry, ha ! louder !
   Nor.   But, my lord,
When returns Cranmer?
   Suf. He is return'd, in his opinions ; which
Have satisfied the king for his divorce,
Together with all famous colleges
Almost in Christendom.   Shortly, I believe,
His second marriage shall be publish'd, and
Her coronation.   Katharine no more
Shall be call'd queen, but princess dowager,   70
And widow to Prince Arthur.
   Nor.   This same Cranmer's
A worthy fellow, and hath ta'en much pain
In the king's business.
   Suf.   He has ; and we shall see him
For it an archbishop.
   Nor.   So I hear.
   Suf.   'T is so.
The cardinal—

   Enter WOLSEY *and* CROMWELL.

   Nor.   Observe, observe ; he's moody.
   Wol. The packet, Cromwell,
Gave't you the king?
   Crom.   To his own hand, in his bedchamber.
   Wol. Look'd he o' th' inside of the paper?
   Crom.   Presently
He did unseal them, and the first he view'd,
He did it with a serious mind ; a heed   80
Was in his countenance. You he bade
Attend him here this morning.
   Wol.   Is he ready
To come abroad?
   Crom.   I think, by this he is.
   Wol. Leave me awhile.—   [*Exit* CROMWELL.
It shall be to the Duchess of Alençon,
The French king's sister : he shall marry her.—
Anne Bullen? No ; I'll no Anne Bullen for him :
There's more in't than fair visage.—Bullen !
No, we'll no Bullens.—Speedily I wish
To hear from Rome.—The Marchioness of Pem-
      broke!   90
   Nor. He's discontented.
   Suf.   May be, he hears the king
Does whet his anger to him.
   Sur.   Sharp enough,
Lord, for thy justice !
   Wol. The late queen's gentlewoman, a knight's
      daughter,
To be her mistress' mistress ! the queen's queen !—
This candle burns not clear : 'tis I must snuff it ;
Then, out it goes.—What though I know her virtuous,
And well deserving? yet I know her for
A spleeny Lutheran ; and not wholesome to
Our cause, that she should lie i' the bosom of   100
Our hard-rul'd king.   Again, there is sprung up
An heretic, an arch one, Cranmer ; one
Hath crawl'd into the favour of the king,
And is his oracle.
   Nor.   He is vex'd at something.
   Suf. I would, 't were something that would fret the
      string,
The master-cord of his heart !

   Enter the KING, *reading a schedule ; and* LOVELL.

   Suf.   The king, the king.
   K. Hen. What piles of wealth hath he accumulated
To his own portion ! and what expense by the hour
Seems to flow from him !   How, i' the name of thrift,
Does he rake this together?—Now, my lords,   110
Saw you the cardinal?
   Nor.   My lord, we have
Stood here observing him.   Some strange commotion
Is in his brain : he bites his lip, and starts ;
Stops on a sudden, looks upon the ground,
Then lays his finger on his temple ; straight,
Springs out into fast gait ; then, stops again
Strikes his breast hard ; and anon, he casts
His eye against the moon.   In most strange postures
We have seen him set himself.
   K. Hen.   It may well be :
There is a mutiny in his mind.   This morning   120
Papers of state he sent me to peruse,
As I requir'd ; and wot you what I found
There, on my conscience, put unwittingly?
Forsooth an inventory, thus importing,—
The several parcels of his plate, his treasure,
Rich stuffs, and ornaments of household, which
I find at such proud rate, that it outspeaks
Possession of a subject.
   Nor.   It's Heaven's will :
Some spirit put this paper in the packet,
To bless your eye withal.
   K. Hen.   If we did think   130
His contemplation were above the earth,
And fix'd on spiritual object, he should still
Dwell in his musings : but, I am afraid,
His thinkings are below the moon, not worth
His serious considering.
         [*He takes his seat, and whispers* LOVELL,
          who goes to WOLSEY.
   Wol.   Heaven forgive me !
Ever God bless your highness !
   K. Hen.   Good my lord,
You are full of heavenly stuff, and bear the inventory
Of your best graces in your mind, the which
You were now running o'er : you have scarce time
To steal from spiritual leisure a brief span,   140
To keep your earthly audit.   Sure, in that
I deem you an ill husband, and am glad
To have you therein my companion.
   Wol.   Sir,
For holy offices I have a time ; a time
To think upon the part of business, which
I bear i' the state ; and nature does require
Her times of preservation, which, perforce,
I, her frail son, amongst my brethren mortal,
Must give my tendance to.
   K. Hen.   You have said well.
   Wol. And ever may your highness yoke together,
As I will lend you cause, my doing well   151
With my well-saying !
   K. Hen.   'T is well said again ;
And 't is a kind of good deed, to say well :
And yet words are no deeds.   My father lov'd you ;
He said he did, and with his deed did crown
His word upon you : since I had my office,
I have kept you next my heart ; have not alone
Employ'd you where high profits might come home,
But par'd my present havings, to bestow
My bounties upon you.
   Wol.   What should this mean?   160
   Sur. [*Aside.*] The Lord increase this business !
   K. Hen.   Have I not made you
The prime man of the state?   I pray you, tell me,
If what I now pronounce you have found true ;
And, if you may confess it, say withal,
If you are bound to us, or no.   What say you?
   Wol. My sovereign, I confess, your royal graces,
Shower'd on me daily, have been more than could
My studied purposes requite ; which went
Beyond all man's endeavours : my endeavours
Have ever come too short of my desires,   170
Yet fil'd with my abilities.   Mine own ends
Have been mine so, that evermore they pointed

To the good of your most sacred person, and
The profit of the state. For your great graces
Heap'd upon me, poor undeserver, I
Can nothing render but allegiant thanks,
My prayers to Heaven for you, my loyalty,
Which ever has, and ever shall be growing,
Till death, that winter, kill it.
  K. Hen.   Fairly answer'd :
A loyal and obedient subject is   180
Therein illustrated. The honour of it
Does pay the act of it, as, i' the contrary,
The foulness is the punishment. I presume,
That, as my hand has open'd bounty to you,

K. Hen.   "Read o'er this :
And, after, this ; and then to breakfast, with
What appetite you have."

My heart dropp'd love, my power rain'd honour,
  more
On you than any ; so your hand, and heart,
Your brain, and every function of your power,
Should, notwithstanding that your bond of duty,
As 't were in love's particular, be more
To me, your friend, than any.
  Wol.   I do profess,   190
That for your highness' good I ever labour'd
More than mine own : that am, have, and will be—
(Though all the world should crack their duty to you,
And throw it from their soul ; though perils did
Abound, as thick as thought could make them, and
Appear in forms more horrid) yet my duty,
As doth a rock against the chiding flood,
Should the approach of this wild river break,
And stand unshaken yours.
  K. Hen.   'T is nobly spoken.
Take notice, lords, he has a loyal breast,   200
For you have seen him open 't.—Read o'er this :
                [*Giving him papers.*
And, after, this ; and then to breakfast, with
What appetite you have.
  [*Exit* KING, *frowning upon Cardinal* WOLSEY :
    *the Nobles throng after him, smiling, and
    whispering.*
  Wol.   What should this mean ?
What sudden anger 's this ? how have I reap'd it ?
He parted frowning from me, as if ruin
Leap'd from his eyes : so looks the chafed lion
Upon the daring huntsman that has gall'd him,
Then makes him nothing. I must read this paper ;
I fear, the story of his anger.—'T is so :
This paper has undone me !—'T is the account 210
Of all that world of wealth I have drawn together
For mine own ends ; indeed, to gain the Popedom,
And fee my friends in Rome. O negligence !
Fit for a fool to fall by. What cross devil
Made me put this main secret in the packet
I sent the king ? Is there no way to cure this ?
No new device to beat this from his brains ?
I know 't will stir him strongly : yet I know

A way, if it take right, in spite of fortune
Will bring me off again. What 's this ?—"To the
  Pope !"   220
The letter, as I live, with all the business
I writ to his holiness. Nay then, farewell !
I have touch'd the highest point of all my greatness ;
And, from that full meridian of my glory,
I haste now to my setting : I shall fall
Like a bright exhalation in the evening,
And no man see me more.

  Re-enter the Dukes of NORFOLK *and* SUFFOLK, *the
    Earl of* SURREY, *and the Lord Chamberlain.*

  Nor. Hear the king's pleasure, cardinal ; who com-
    mands you
To render up the great seal presently
Into our hands, and to confine yourself   230
To Asher House, my Lord of Winchester's,
Till your hear further from his highness.
  Wol.   Stay :
Where 's your commission, lords ? words cannot carry
Authority so weighty.
  Suf.   Who dare cross them,
Bearing the king's will from his mouth expressly ?
  Wol. Till I find more than will, or words, to do it,
(I mean your malice,) know, officious lords,
I dare, and must deny it. Now I feel
Of what coarse metal ye are moulded,—envy.
How eagerly ye follow my disgraces,   240
As if it fed ye ! and how sleek and wanton
Ye appear in everything may bring my ruin !
Follow your envious courses, men of malice ;
You have Christian warrant for them, and, no doubt,
In time will find their fit rewards. That seal,
You ask with such a violence, the king
(Mine, and your master) with his own hand gave me ;
Bade me enjoy it, with the place and honours,
During my life ; and, to confirm his goodness,
Tied it by letters-patents. Now, who 'll take it ? 250
  Sur. The king that gave it.
  Wol.   It must be himself then.
  Sur. Thou art a proud traitor, priest.
  Wol.   Proud lord, thou liest :
Within these forty hours Surrey durst better
Have burnt that tongue than said so.
  Sur.   Thy ambition,
Thou scarlet sin, robb'd this bewailing land
Of noble Buckingham, my father-in-law :
The heads of all thy brother cardinals
(With thee, and all thy best parts bound together)
Weigh'd not a hair of his. Plague of your policy !
You sent me deputy for Ireland,   260
Far from his succour, from the king, from all
That might have mercy on the fault thou gav'st him ;
Whilst your great goodness, out of holy pity,
Absolv'd him with an axe.
  Wol.   This, and all else
This talking lord can lay upon my credit,
I answer, is most false. The duke by law
Found his deserts : how innocent I was
From any private malice in his end,
His noble jury and foul cause can witness.
If I lov'd many words, lords, I should tell you, 270
You have as little honesty as honour,
That in the way of loyalty and truth
Toward the king, my ever royal master,
Dare mate a sounder man than Surrey can be,
And all that love his follies.
  Sur.   By my soul,
Your long coat, priest, protects you : thou shouldst
My sword i' the life-blood of thee else.—My lords,
Can ye endure to hear this arrogance ?
And from this fellow ? If we live thus tamely,
To be thus jaded by a piece of scarlet,   280
Farewell nobility ; let his grace go forward,
And dare us with his cap, like larks.
  Wol.   All goodness
Is poison to thy stomach.
  Sur.   Yes, that goodness
Of gleaning all the land's wealth into one,
Into your own hands, cardinal, by extortion ;

The goodness of your intercepted packets,
You writ to the Pope, against the king ; your good-
    ness,
Since you provoke me, shall be most notorious.—
My Lord of Norfolk,—as you are truly noble,
As you respect the common good, the state   290
Of our despis'd nobility, our issues
(Who, if he live, will scarce be gentlemen),
Produce the grand sum of his sins, the articles
Collected from his life :—I 'll startle you
Worse than the sacring bell, when the brown wench
Lay kissing in your arms, lord cardinal.
   Wol. How much, methinks, I could despise this
    man,
But that I am bound in charity against it.
   Nor. Those articles, my lord, are in the king's hand ;
But, thus much, they are foul ones.
   Wol.   So much fairer
And spotless shall mine innocence arise,   301
When the king knows my truth.
   Sur.   This cannot save you :
I thank my memory, I yet remember
Some of these articles ; and out they shall.
Now, if you can blush, and cry guilty, cardinal,
You 'll show a little honesty.
   Wol.   Speak on, sir ;
I dare your worst objections : if I blush,
It is to see a nobleman want manners.
   Sur. I had rather want those, than my head. Have
    at you.
First, that without the king's assent or knowledge 310
You wrought to be a legate ; by which power
You maim'd the jurisdiction of all bishops.
   Nor. Then, that in all you writ to Rome, or else
To foreign princes, *Ego et Rex meus*
Was still inscrib'd ; in which you brought the king
To be your servant.
   Suf.   Then, that without the knowledge
Either of king or council, when you went
Ambassador to the emperor, you made bold
To carry into Flanders the great seal.
   Sur. Item, you sent a large commission   320
To Gregory de Cassado, to conclude,
Without the king's will or the state's allowance,
A league between his highness and Ferrara.
   Suf. That, out of mere ambition, you have caus'd
Your holy hat to be stamp'd on the king's coin.
   Sur. Then, that you have sent innumerable sub-
    stance,
(By what means got, I leave to your own conscience,)
To furnish Rome, and to prepare the ways
You have for dignities ; to the mere undoing
Of all the kingdom. Many more there are ;   330
Which, since they are of you, and odious,
I will not taint my mouth with.
   Cham.   O my lord!
Press not a falling man too far ; 't is virtue :
His faults lie open to the laws ; let them,
Not you, correct him. My heart weeps to see him
So little of his great self.
   Sur.   I forgive him.
   Suf. Lord cardinal, the king's further pleasure is,—
Because all those things, you have done of late
By your power legatine within this kingdom,
Fall into the compass of a *præmunire*,—   340
That therefore such a writ be sued against you ;
To forfeit all your goods, lands, tenements,
Chattels, and whatsoever, and to be
Out of the king's protection.—This is my charge.
   Nor. And so we 'll leave you to your meditations,
How to live better. For your stubborn answer,
About the giving back the great seal to us,
The king shall know it, and, no doubt, shall thank
    you.
So, fare you well, my little good lord cardinal.
              [*Exeunt all but* WOLSEY.
   Wol. So, farewell to the little good you bear me. 350
Farewell ! a long farewell, to all my greatness !
This is the state of man : to-day he puts forth
The tender leaves of hope, to-morrow blossoms,
And bears his blushing honours thick upon him :
The third day comes a frost, a killing frost ;

And,—when he thinks, good easy man, full surely
His greatness is a-ripening,—nips his root,
And then he falls, as I do. I have ventur'd,
Like little wanton boys that swim on bladders,
This many summers in a sea of glory,   360
But far beyond my depth : my high-blown pride
At length broke under me, and now has left me
Weary, and old with service, to the mercy
Of a rude stream, that must for ever hide me.
Vain pomp and glory of this world, I hate ye :
I feel my heart new open'd. O, how wretched
Is that poor man, that hangs on princes' favours !
There is, betwixt that smile we would aspire to,
That sweet aspect of princes, and their ruin,
More pangs and fears than wars or women have ; 370
And when he falls, he falls like Lucifer,
Never to hope again.—

         Enter CROMWELL, *and stands amazed.*
                 Why, how now, Cromwell ?
   Crom. I have no power to speak, sir.
   Wol.   What ! amaz'd
At my misfortunes ? can thy spirit wonder,
A great man should decline ? Nay, an you weep,
I am fall'n indeed.
   Crom.   How does your grace ?
   Wol.   Why, well :
Never so truly happy, my good Cromwell.
I know myself now ; and I feel within me
A peace above all earthly dignities,
A still and quiet conscience. The king has cur'd
    me,   380
I humbly thank his grace, and from these shoulders,
These ruin'd pillars, out of pity, taken
A load would sink a navy,—too much honour.
O ! 't is a burden, Cromwell, 't is a burden,
Too heavy for a man that hopes for heaven.
   Crom. I am glad your grace has made that right
    use of it.
   Wol. I hope I have : I am able now, methinks,
(Out of a fortitude of soul I feel)
To endure more miseries, and greater far,
Than my weak-hearted enemies dare offer.   390
What news abroad ?
   Crom.   The heaviest, and the worst,
Is your displeasure with the king.
   Wol.   God bless him !
   Crom. The next is, that Sir Thomas More is chosen
Lord chancellor in your place.
   Wol.   That 's somewhat sudden ;
But he 's a learned man. May he continue
Long in his highness' favour, and do justice
For truth's sake, and his conscience ; that his bones,
When he has run his course and sleeps in blessings,
May have a tomb of orphans' tears wept on 'em !
What more ?
   Crom.   That Cranmer is return'd with welcome,
Installed Lord Archbishop of Canterbury.   401
   Wol. That 's news indeed !
   Crom.   Last, that the Lady Anne,
Whom the king hath in secrecy long married,
This day was view'd in open, as his queen,
Going to chapel ; and the voice is now
Only about her coronation.
   Wol. There was the weight that pull'd me down.
    O Cromwell !
The king has gone beyond me : all my glories
In that one woman I have lost for ever.
No sun shall ever usher forth mine honours,   410
Or gild again the noble troops that waited
Upon my smiles. Go, get thee from me, Cromwell ;
I am a poor fall'n man, unworthy now
To be thy lord and master. Seek the king ;
(That sun, I pray, may never set !) I have told him
What and how true thou art : he will advance thee.
Some little memory of me will stir him,
(I know his noble nature,) not to let
Thy hopeful service perish too. Good Cromwell,
Neglect him not ; make use now, and provide   420
For thine own future safety.
   Crom.   O my lord !
Must I then leave you ? must I needs forego

So good, so noble, and so true a master?
Bear witness all that have not hearts of iron,
With what a sorrow Cromwell leaves his lord.—
The king shall have my service; but my prayers,
For ever and for ever, shall be yours.
    Wol. Cromwell, I did not think to shed a tear
In all my miseries; but thou hast forc'd me,
Out of thy honest truth, to play the woman.   430
Let's dry our eyes; and thus far hear me, Cromwell:
And,—when I am forgotten, as I shall be,
And sleep in dull cold marble, where no mention
Of me more must be heard of,—say, I taught thee,
Say, Wolsey, that once trod the ways of glory,
And sounded all the depths and shoals of honour,
Found thee a way, out of his wrack, to rise in;
A sure and safe one, though thy master miss'd it.
Mark but my fall, and that that ruin'd me.
Cromwell, I charge thee, fling away ambition: 440
By that sin fell the angels; how can man then,
The image of his Maker, hope to win by 't?
Love thyself last: cherish those hearts that hate thee;
Corruption wins not more than honesty.
Still in thy right hand carry gentle peace,
To silence envious tongues: be just, and fear not.
Let all the ends thou aim'st at be thy country's,
Thy God's, and truth's: then, if thou fall'st, O
                                        Cromwell,
Thou fall'st a blessed martyr. Serve the king;
And—Pry'thee, lead me in: 450
There take an inventory of all I have,
To the last peñny; 't is the king's: my robe,
And my integrity to Heaven, is all
I dare now call my own. O Cromwell, Cromwell!
Had I but serv'd my God with half the zeal
I serv'd my king, he would not in mine age
Have left me naked to mine enemies.

Crom. Good sir, have patience.

Wol.   "O Cromwell, Cromwell!
Had I but serv'd my God with half the zeal
I serv'd my king, he would not in mine age
Have left me naked to mine enemies."

Wol.   So I have. Farewell
The hopes of court: my hopes in heaven do dwell.
                                        [*Exeunt.*

ACT IV.

Scene I.—A Street in Westminster.

Enter two Gentlemen, meeting.

    1 Gentleman.
Y OU 'RE well met once again.
    2 Gent.   So are you.
    1 Gent. You come to take your stand
        here, and behold
The Lady Anne pass from her coronation?
    2 Gent. 'T is all my business. At our last
        encounter,
The Duke of Buckingham came from his
        trial.
    1 Gent. 'T is very true: but that time offer'd
        sorrow;
This, general joy.
    2 Gent.   'T is well: the citizens,
I am sure, have shown at full their royal minds,
As, let 'em have their rights, they are ever forward
In celebration of this day with shows,   10
Pageants, and sights of honour.
    1 Gent.   Never greater;
Nor, I 'll assure you, better taken, sir.
    2 Gent. May I be bold to ask what that contains,
That paper in your hand?
    1 Gent.   Yes; 't is the list
Of those that claim their offices this day,
By custom of the coronation.
The Duke of Suffolk is the first, and claims

To be high-steward; next, the Duke of Norfolk,
He to be earl marshal. You may read the rest.
    2 Gent. I thank you, sir: had I not known those
        customs,   20
I should have been beholding to your paper.
But, I beseech you, what's become of Katharine,
The princess dowager? how goes her business?
    1 Gent. That I can tell you too. The Archbishop
Of Canterbury, accompanied with other
Learned and reverend fathers of his order,
Held a late court at Dunstable, six miles off
From Ampthill, where the princess lay; to which
She was often cited by them, but appear'd not:
And, to be short, for not-appearance, and   30
The king's late scruple, by the main assent
Of all these learned men she was divorc'd,
And the late marriage made of none effect:
Since which she was remov'd to Kimbolton,
Where she remains now, sick.
    2 Gent.   Alas, good lady!—[*Trumpets.*
The trumpets sound: stand close, the queen is coming.
                                        [*Hautboys.*

THE ORDER OF THE CORONATION.

A lively flourish of trumpets.

1. *Two Judges.*

2. *Lord Chancellor, with purse and mace before him.*
3. *Choristers, singing.*   [*Music.*
4. *Mayor of London, bearing the mace. Then, Garter in his coat of arms, and on his head a gilt copper crown.*
5. *Marquess* DORSET, *bearing a sceptre of gold; on his head a demi-coronal of gold. With him, the Earl of* SURREY, *bearing the rod of silver with the dove, crowned with an earl's coronet. Collars of SS.*
6. *Duke of* SUFFOLK, *in his robe of estate, his coronet on his head, bearing a long white wand, as high-steward. With him, the Duke of* NORFOLK, *with the rod of marshalship, a coronet on his head. Collars of SS.*
7. *A canopy born by four of the Cinque-ports; under it, the* QUEEN *in her robe; in her hair richly adorned with pearl, crowned. On each side of her, the Bishops of* LONDON *and* WIN-CHESTER.
8. *The old Duchess of* NORFOLK, *in a coronal of gold, wrought with flowers, bearing the* QUEEN'S *train.*
9. *Certain Ladies or Countesses, with plain circlets of gold without flowers.*

2 Gent. A royal train, believe me.—These I
    know;—
Who's that, that bears the sceptre?
  1 Gent.   Marquess Dorset:
And that the Earl of Surrey, with the rod.
  2 Gent. A bold brave gentleman. That
    should be   40
The Duke of Suffolk.
  1 Gent.   'T is the same; high-steward.
  2 Gent. And that my Lord of Norfolk?
  1 Gent.   Yes.
  2 Gent.   Heaven bless thee!
        [*Looking on the* QUEEN.
Thou hast the sweetest face I ever look'd on.—
Sir, as I have a soul, she is an angel;
Our king has all the Indies in his arms,
And more, and richer, when he strains that lady:
I cannot blame his conscience.
  1 Gent.   They, that bear
The cloth of honour over her, are four barons,
Of the Cinque-ports.
  2 Gent. Those men are happy; and so are all, are
    near her.   50
I take it, she that carries up the train
Is that old noble lady, Duchess of Norfolk.
  1 Gent. It is; and all the rest are countesses.
  2 Gent. Their coronets say so. These are stars,
    indeed;
And sometimes falling ones.
  1 Gent.   No more of that.
    [*Exit Procession, with a great flourish of
    trumpets.*

      Enter a third Gentleman.

God save you, sir! Where have you been broiling?
  3 Gent. Among the crowd i' the abbey; where a
    finger
Could not be wedg'd in more: I am stifled
With the mere rankness of their joy.
  2 Gent. You saw the ceremony?   60
  3 Gent. That I did.
  1 Gent. How was it?
  3 Gent. Well worth the seeing.
  2 Gent. Good sir, speak it to us.
  3 Gent. As well as I am able. The rich stream
Of lords, and ladies, having brought the queen
To a prepar'd place in the choir, fell off
A distance from her; while her grace sat down
To rest awhile, some half an hour or so,
In a rich chair of state, opposing freely   70
The beauty of her person to the people.
Believe me, sir, she is the goodliest woman
That ever lay by man: which when the people

Had the full view of, such a noise arose
As the shrouds make at sea in a stiff tempest,
As loud, and to as many tunes: hats, cloaks,
Doublets, I think, flew up; and had their faces
Been loose, this day they had been lost. Such joy
I never saw before. Great-bellied women,
That had not half a week to go, like rams   80
In the old time of war, would shake the press,
And make them reel before them. No man living
Could say, "This is my wife," there; all were woven
So strangely in one piece.
  2 Gent. But, what follow'd?

THE QUEEN IN THE CORONATION PROCESSION.

  3 Gent. At length her grace rose, and with modest
    paces
Came to the altar; where she kneel'd, and saint-like
Cast her fair eyes to heaven, and pray'd devoutly.
Then rose again, and bow'd her to the people:
When by the Archbishop of Canterbury   90
She had all the royal makings of a queen;
As holy oil, Edward Confessor's crown,
The rod, and bird of peace, and all such emblems
Laid nobly on her: which perform'd, the choir,
With all the choicest music of the kingdom,
Together sung *Te Deum.* So she parted,
And with the same full state pac'd back again
To York Place, where the feast is held.
  1 Gent.   Sir,
You must no more call it York Place, that is past;
For, since the cardinal fell, that title 's lost: 100
'T is now the king's, and call'd Whitehall.
  3 Gent.   I know it;
But 't is so lately alter'd, that the old name
Is fresh about me.
  2 Gent.   What two reverend bishops
Were those that went on each side of the queen?
  3 Gent. Stokesly and Gardiner; the one, of Win-
    chester,
Newly preferr'd from the king's secretary;
The other, London.
  2 Gent.   He of Winchester
Is held no great good lover of the archbishop's,
The virtuous Cranmer.
  3 Gent.   All the land knows that: 109
However, yet there 's no great breach; when it comes,
Cranmer will find a friend will not shrink from him.
  2 Gent. Who may that be, I pray you?
  3 Gent.   Thomas Cromwell;
A man in much esteem with the king, and truly
A worthy friend.—The king
Has made him master of the jewel-house,
And one, already, of the privy-council.
  2 Gent. He will deserve more.

3 Gent.   Yes, without all doubt.
Come, gentlemen, ye shall go my way, which
Is to the court, and there ye shall be my guests :
Something I can command. As I walk thither, 120
I 'll tell ye more.
  Both.   You may command us, sir. [*Exeunt.*

SCENE II.—Kimbolton.

Enter KATHARINE, *Dowager, sick ; led between*
GRIFFITH *and* PATIENCE.

Grif. How does your grace ?
  Kath.   O Griffith ! sick to death :
My legs, like loaden branches, bow to the earth,
Willing to leave their burden. Reach a chair :—
So,—now, methinks, I feel a little ease.
Didst thou not tell me, Griffith, as thou ledd'st me,
That the great child of honour, Cardinal Wolsey,
Was dead ?
  Grif.   Yes, madam ; but, I think, your grace,
Out of the pain you suffer'd, gave no ear to 't.
  Kath. Pr'ythee, good Griffith, tell me how he died :
If well, he stepp'd before me, happily, 10
For my example.
  Grif.   Well, the voice goes, madam :
For after the stout Earl Northumberland
Arrested him at York, and brought him forward,
As a man sorely tainted, to his answer,
He fell sick suddenly, and grew so ill,
He could not sit his mule.
  Kath.   Alas, poor man !
  Grif. At last, with easy roads, he came to Leicester ;
Lodg'd in the abbey, where the reverend abbot,
With all his covent, honourably receiv'd him :
To whom he gave these words,—" O father abbot, 20
An old man, broken with the storms of state,
Is come to lay his weary bones among ye ;
Give him a little earth for charity ! "
So went to bed, where eagerly his sickness
Pursu'd him still ; and three nights after this,
About the hour of eight, which he himself
Foretold should be his last, full of repentance,
Continual meditations, tears, and sorrows,
He gave his honours to the world again,
His blessed part to heaven, and slept in peace. 30
  Kath. So may he rest : his faults lie gently on him !
Yet thus far, Griffith, give me leave to speak him,
And yet with charity.—He was a man
Of an unbounded stomach, ever ranking
Himself with princes ; one, that by suggestion
Tied all the kingdom : simony was fair-play ;
His own opinion was his law : i' the presence
He would say untruths, and be ever double,
Both in his words and meaning. He was never,
But where he meant to ruin, pitiful : 40
His promises were, as he then was, mighty ;
But his performance, as he is now, nothing.
Of his own body he was ill, and gave
The clergy ill example.
  Grif.   Noble madam,
Men's evil manners live in brass ; their virtues
We write in water. May it please your highness
To hear me speak his good now ?
  Kath.   Yes, good Griffith ;
I were malicious else.
  Grif.   This cardinal,
Though from an humble stock, undoubtedly
Was fashion'd to much honour from his cradle. 50
He was a scholar, and a ripe and good one ;
Exceeding wise, fair-spoken, and persuading :
Lofty and sour to them that lov'd him not ;
But, to those men that sought him, sweet as summer :
And though he were unsatisfied in getting,
(Which was a sin,) yet in bestowing, madam,
He was most princely. Ever witness for him
Those twins of learning, that he rais'd in you,
Ipswich, and Oxford ! one of which fell with him,
Unwilling to outlive the good that did it ; 60
The other, though unfinish'd, yet so famous,
So excellent in art, and still so rising,

That Christendom shall ever speak his virtue.
His overthrow heap'd happiness upon him ;
For then, and not till then, he felt himself,
And found the blessedness of being little :
And, to add greater honours to his age
Than man could give him, he died fearing God.
  Kath. After my death I wish no other herald,
No other speaker of my living actions, 70
To keep mine honour from corruption,
But such an honest chronicler as Griffith.
Whom I most hated living, thou hast made me,
With thy religious truth and modesty,
Now in his ashes honour. Peace be with him !—
Patience, be near me still, and set me lower :
I have not long to trouble thee.—Good Griffith,
Cause the musicians play me that sad note
I nam'd my knell, whilst I sit meditating
On that celestial harmony I go to. 80
                       [*Sad and solemn music.*
  Grif. She is asleep. Good wench, let 's sit down
        quiet,
For fear we wake her :—softly, gentle Patience.

Grif. " She is asleep. Good wench, let 's sit down quiet,
For fear we wake her."

*The Vision. Enter, solemnly tripping one after
another, six Personages, clad in white robes, wearing on their heads garlands of bays, and golden
visards on their faces ; branches of bays, or palm,
in their hands. They first congee unto her, then
dance ; and, at certain changes, the first two hold
a spare garland over her head ; at which the other
four make reverent curtsies : then, the two that held
the garland deliver the same to the other next two,
who observe the same order in their changes, and
holding the garland over her head. Which done,
they deliver the same garland to the last two, who
likewise observe the same order : at which, (as it
were by inspiration,) she makes in her sleep signs
of rejoicing, and holdeth up her hands to heaven.
And so in their dancing they vanish, carrying the
garland with them. The music continues.*
  Kath. Spirits of peace, where are ye ? are ye all
        gone,
And leave me here in wretchedness behind ye ?
  Grif. Madam, we are here.
  Kath.   It is not you I call for.
Saw ye none enter, since I slept ?
  Grif.   None, madam.
  Kath. No ? Saw you not, even now, a blessed troop
Invite me to a banquet ; whose bright faces
Cast thousand beams upon me, like the sun ?
They promis'd me eternal happiness, 90
And brought me garlands, Griffith, which I feel
I am not worthy yet to wear : I shall, assuredly.
  Grif. I am most joyful, madam, such good dreams
Possess your fancy.

Kath.   Bid the music leave,
They are harsh and heavy to me.   [*Music ceases.*
Pat.   Do you note,
How much her grace is alter'd on the sudden?
How long her face is drawn? how pale she looks,
And of an earthy cold? Mark her eyes!
  Grif. She is going, wench. Pray, pray.
  Pat.   Heaven comfort her!

Enter a Messenger.

  Mess. An't like your grace,—
  Kath.   You are a saucy fellow:
Deserve we no more reverence?
  Grif.   You are to blame, 101
Knowing she will not lose her wonted greatness,
To use so rude behaviour: go to; kneel.
  Mess. I humbly do entreat your highness' pardon;
My haste made me unmannerly. There is staying
A gentleman, sent from the king to see you.
  Kath. Admit him entrance, Griffith: but this fellow
Let me ne'er see again.
         [*Exeunt* GRIFFITH *and Messenger.*

Re-enter GRIFFITH, *with* CAPUCIUS.

           If my sight fail not,
You should be lord ambassador from the emperor,
My royal nephew, and your name Capucius.   110
  Cap. Madam, the same, your servant.
  Kath.   O my lord!
The times, and titles, now are alter'd strangely
With me, since first you knew me. But, I pray you,
What is your pleasure with me?
  Cap.   Noble lady,
First, mine own service to your grace; the next,
The king's request that I would visit you;
Who grieves much for your weakness, and by me
Sends you his princely commendations,
And heartily entreats you take good comfort.
  Kath. O! my good lord, that comfort comes too late;   120
'T is like a pardon after execution.
That gentle physic, given in time, had cur'd me;
But now I am past all comforts here, but prayers.
How does his highness?
  Cap.   Madam, in good health.
  Kath. So may he ever do; and ever flourish,
When I shall dwell with worms, and my poor name
Banish'd the kingdom.—Patience, is that letter,
I caus'd you write, yet sent away?

  Pat.   No, madam.
         [*Giving it to* KATHARINE.
  Kath. Sir, I most humbly pray you to deliver
This to my lord the king.
  Cap.   Most willing, madam. 130
  Kath. In which I have commended to his goodness
The model of our chaste loves, his young daughter:—
The dews of heaven fall thick in blessings on her!
Beseeching him to give her virtuous breeding,—
She is young, and of a noble modest nature;
I hope, she will deserve well,—and a little
To love her for her mother's sake, that lov'd him,
Heaven knows how dearly. My next poor petition
Is, that his noble grace would have some pity
Upon my wretched women, that so long   140
Have follow'd both my fortunes faithfully:
Of which there is not one, I dare avow
(And now I should not lie), but will deserve,
For virtue, and true beauty of the soul,
For honesty, and decent carriage,
A right good husband, let him be a noble;
And, sure, those men are happy that shall have them.
The last is, for my men:—they are the poorest,
But poverty could never draw them from me;—
That they may have their wages duly paid them,   150
And something over to remember me by:
If Heaven had pleas'd to have given me longer life,
And able means, we had not parted thus.
These are the whole contents:—and, good my lord,
By that you love the dearest in this world,
As you wish Christian peace to souls departed,
Stand these poor people's friend, and urge the king
To do me this last right.
  Cap.   By Heaven, I will,
Or let me lose the fashion of a man!
  Kath. I thank you, honest lord. Remember me 160
In all humility unto his highness:
Say, his long trouble now is passing
Out of this world; tell him, in death I bless'd him,
For so I will.—Mine eyes grow dim.—Farewell,
My lord.—Griffith, farewell.—Nay, Patience,
You must not leave me yet: I must to bed;
Call in more women.—When I am dead, good wench,
Let me be us'd with honour: strew me over
With maiden flowers, that all the world may know
I was a chaste wife to my grave. Embalm me,   170
Then lay me forth: although unqueen'd, yet like
A queen, and daughter to a king, inter me.
I can no more.—   [*Exeunt, leading* KATHARINE.

ACT V.

SCENE I.—A Gallery in the Palace.

Enter GARDINER, *Bishop of* WINCHESTER, *a Page with a torch before him, met by*
Sir THOMAS LOVELL.

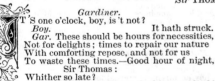

        Gardiner.
I T'S one o'clock, boy, is 't not?
  Boy.   It hath struck.
  Gar. These should be hours for necessities,
Not for delights; times to repair our nature
With comforting repose, and not for us
To waste these times.—Good hour of night,
         Sir Thomas:—
Whither so late?
  Lov. Came you from the king, my lord?
  Gar. I did, Sir Thomas; and left him at primero
With the Duke of Suffolk.

  Lov.   I must to him too,
Before he go to bed. I 'll take my leave.
  Gar. Not yet, Sir Thomas Lovell. What 's the matter?   10
It seems you are in haste: an if there be
No great offence belongs to 't, give your friend
Some touch of your late business. Affairs that walk
(As, they say, spirits do) at midnight, have
In them a wilder nature, than the business
That seeks despatch by day.
  Lov.   My lord, I love you,
And durst commend a secret to your ear
Much weightier than this work. The queen's in labour,

They say, in great extremity ; and fear'd,
She 'll with the labour end.
    Gar.   The fruit she goes with
I pray for heartily, that it may find   21
Good time, and live : but for the stock, Sir Thomas,
I wish it grubb'd up now.
    Lov.   Methinks, I could
Cry the Amen ; and yet my conscience says
She 's a good creature, and, sweet lady, does
Deserve our better wishes.
    Gar.   But, sir, sir,—
Hear me, Sir Thomas : you are a gentleman
Of mine own way ; I know you wise, religious ;
And, let me tell you, it will ne'er be well,
'T will not, Sir Thomas Lovell, take 't of me,   30
Till Cranmer, Cromwell, her two hands, and she,
Sleep in their graves.
    Lov.   Now, sir, you speak of two
The most remark'd i' the kingdom. As for Cromwell,—
Beside that of the jewel-house, is made master
O' the rolls, and the king's secretary ; further, sir,
Stands in the gap and trade of more preferments,
With which the time will load him. The archbishop
Is the king's hand and tongue ; and who dare speak
One syllable against him ?
    Gar.   Yes, yes, Sir Thomas,
There are that dare ; and I myself have ventur'd 40
To speak my mind of him : and, indeed, this day,
Sir, (I may tell it you,) I think, I have
Incens'd the lords o' the council, that he is
(For so I know he is, they know he is)
A most arch heretic, a pestilence
That does infect the land : with which they moved
Have broken with the king ; who hath so far
Given ear to our complaint, (of his great grace
And princely care, foreseeing those fell mischiefs
Our reasons laid before him,) hath commanded, 50
To-morrow morning to the council-board
He be convented. He 's a rank weed, Sir Thomas,
And we must root him out. From your affairs
I hinder you too long : good night, Sir Thomas.
    Lov. Many good nights, my lord. I rest your servant.
                [*Exeunt* GARDINER *and Page.*

As LOVELL *is going out, enter the* KING *and the*
           Duke of SUFFOLK.

    K. Hen. Charles, I will play no more to-night :
My mind 's not on 't ; you are too hard for me.
    Suf. Sir, I did never win of you before.
    K. Hen. But little, Charles ;
Nor shall not when my fancy 's on my play. 60
Now, Lovell, from the queen what is the news ?
    Lov. I could not personally deliver to her
What you commanded me, but by her woman
I sent your message ; who return'd her thanks
In the greatest humbleness, and desir'd your highness
Most heartily to pray for her.
    K. Hen.   What say'st thou ? ha !
To pray for her ? what ! is she crying out ?
    Lov. So said her woman ; and that her sufferance
      made
Almost each pang a death.
    K. Hen.   Alas, good lady !
    Suf. God safely quit her of her burden, and 70
With gentle travail, to the gladding of
Your highness with an heir !
    K. Hen.   'T is midnight, Charles :
Pr'ythee, to bed ; and in thy prayers remember
The estate of my poor queen. Leave me alone ;
For I must think of that, which company
Would not be friendly to.
    Suf.   I wish your highness
A quiet night, and my good mistress will
Remember in my prayers.
    K. Hen.   Charles, good night.—
                  [*Exit* SUFFOLK.

    Enter Sir ANTHONY DENNY.

Well, sir, what follows ?
    Den. Sir, I have brought my lord the archbishop, 80
As you commanded me.
    K. Hen.   Ha ! Canterbury ?

    Den. Ay, my good lord.
    K. Hen.   'T is true : where is he, Denny ?
    Den. He attends your highness' pleasure.
    K. Hen.   Bring him to us. [*Exit* DENNY.
    Lov. [*Aside.*] This is about that which the bishop
      spake :
I am happily come hither.

    Re-enter DENNY, *with* CRANMER.

    K. Hen.   Avoid the gallery.
             [LOVELL *seems to stay.*
Ha !—I have said.—Be gone.
What !—   [*Exeunt* LOVELL *and* DENNY.
    Cran. I am fearful.—Wherefore frowns he thus ?
'T is his aspect of terror : all 's not well.
    K. Hen. How now, my lord ? You do desire to know
Wherefore I sent for you.
    Cran.   It is my duty 91
To attend your highness' pleasure.
    K. Hen.   'Pray you, arise,
My good and gracious Lord of Canterbury.
Come, you and I must walk a turn together ;
I have news to tell you. Come, come, give me your
    hand.
Ah, my good lord, I grieve at what I speak,
And am right sorry to repeat what follows.
I have, and most unwillingly, of late
Heard many grievous, I do say, my lord,
Grievous complaints of you ; which, being consider'd,
Have mov'd us and our council, that you shall 101
This morning come before us : where, I know,
You cannot with such freedom purge yourself,
But that, till further trial in those charges
Which will require your answer, you must take
Your patience to you, and be well contented
To make your house our Tower : you a brother of us,
It fits we thus proceed, or else no witness
Would come against you.
    Cran.   I humbly thank your highness,
And am right glad to catch this good occasion 110
Most throughly to be winnow'd, where my chaff
And corn shall fly asunder ; for, I know,
There 's none stands under more calumnious tongues,
Than I myself, poor man.
    K. Hen.   Stand up, good Canterbury :
Thy truth, and thy integrity, is rooted
In us, thy friend. Give me thy hand, stand up :
Pr'ythee, let 's walk. Now, by my holidame,
What manner of man are you ? My lord, I look'd
You would have given me your petition, that
I should have ta'en some pains to bring together 120
Yourself and your accusers ; and to have heard you,
Without indurance, further.
    Cran.   Most dread liege,
The good I stand on, is my truth and honesty :
If they shall fail, I, with mine enemies,
Will triumph o'er my person, which I weigh not,
Being of those virtues vacant. I fear nothing
What can be said against me.
    K. Hen.   Know you not
How your state stands i' the world, with the whole
    world ?
Your enemies are many, and not small ; their
    practices
Must bear the same proportion : and not ever 120
The justice and the truth o' the question carries
The due o' the verdict with it. At what ease
Might corrupt minds procure knaves as corrupt
To swear against you ? such things have been done.
You are potently oppos'd, and with a malice
Of as great size. Ween you of better luck,
I mean in perjur'd witness, than your master,
Whose minister you are, whiles here he liv'd
Upon this naughty earth ? Go to, go to ;
You take a precipice for no leap of danger, 140
And woo your own destruction.
    Cran.   God, and your majesty,
Protect mine innocence, or I fall into
The trap is laid for me !
    K. Hen.   Be of good cheer ;
They shall no more prevail than we give way to.
Keep comfort to you ; and this morning, see

You do appear before them. If they shall chance,
In charging you with matters, to commit you,
The best persuasions to the contrary
Fail not to use, and with what vehemency
The occasion shall instruct you : if entreaties   150
Will render you no remedy, this ring
Deliver them, and your appeal to us
There make before them.—Look, the good man weeps :
He 's honest, on mine honour. God's blest mother !
I swear, he is true-hearted ; and a soul
None better in my kingdom.—Get you gone,
And do as I have bid you. [*Exit* CRANMER.]—He has
        strangled
His language in his tears.

       Enter an Old Lady.

Gent. [*Within.*]   Come back : what mean you?
Old L. I 'll not come back ; the tidings that I bring
Will make my boldness manners.—Now, good angels
Fly o'er thy royal head, and shade thy person   161
Under their blessed wings !
K. Hen.   Now, by thy looks
I guess thy message. Is the queen deliver'd ?
Say, ay ; and of a boy.
Old L.   Ay, ay, my liege ;
And of a lovely boy : the God of heaven
Both now and ever bless her !—'t is a girl,
Promises boys hereafter. Sir, your queen
Desires your visitation, and to be
Acquainted with this stranger : 't is as like you,
As cherry is to cherry.
K. Hen.   Lovell !

      Re-enter LOVELL.

Lov.   Sir.   170
K. Hen. Give her an hundred marks. I 'll to the
        queen.   [*Exit.*
Old L. An hundred marks ! By this light, I 'll ha'
        more.
An ordinary groom is for such payment :
I will have more, or scold it out of him.
Said I for this, the girl was like to him?
I will have more, or else unsay 't ; and now,
While it is hot, I 'll put it to the issue.   [*Exeunt.*

SCENE II.—The Lobby before the Council-chamber.

  Enter CRANMER; *Servants, Door-keeper, &c.,*
        attending.

Cran. I hope, I am not too late ; and yet the gentle-
        man,
That was sent to me from the council, pray'd me
To make great haste. All fast? what means this?
        Hoa !
Who waits there?—Sure, you know me ?
D. Keep.   Yes, my lord ;
But yet I cannot help you.
Cran.   Why?
D. Keep. Your grace must wait, till you be call'd
        for.

      Enter Doctor BUTTS.

Cran.   So.
Butts. This is a piece of malice. I am glad,
I came this way so happily : the king
Shall understand it presently.   [*Exit.*
Cran. [*Aside.*]   'T is Butts,
The king's physician. As he pass'd along,   10
How earnestly he cast his eyes upon me.
'Pray Heaven, he sound not my disgrace ! For certain,
This is of purpose laid by some that hate me,
(God turn their hearts ! I never sought their malice,)
To quench mine honour : they would shame to make
        me
Wait else at door, a fellow-counsellor,
'Mong boys, grooms, and lackeys. But their pleasures
Must be fulfill'd, and I attend with patience.

  Enter the KING *and* BUTTS, *at a window above.*

Butts. I 'll show your grace the strangest sight,—
K. Hen.   What 's that, Butts?

Butts. I think, your highness saw this many a day.
K. Hen. Body o' me, where is it?
Butts.   There, my lord :
The high promotion of his grace of Canterbury ;   22
Who holds his state at door, 'mongst pursuivants,
Pages, and footboys.
K. Hen.   Ha ! 'T is he, indeed.
Is this the honour they do one another ?
'T is well, there 's one above them yet. I had thought,
They had parted so much honesty among them
(At least good manners), as not thus to suffer
A man of his place, and so near our favour,
To dance attendance on their lordship's pleasures,   30
And at the door too, like a post with packets.
By holy Mary, Butts, there 's knavery :
Let 'em alone, and draw the curtain close ;
We shall hear more anon.   [*Exeunt.*

D. Keep. " Your grace may enter now."

The Council-chamber.

Enter the Lord Chancellor, the Duke of SUFFOLK,
Earl of SURREY, *Lord Chamberlain,* GARDINER,
and CROMWELL. *The Chancellor places himself at
the upper end of the table on the left hand ; a seat
being left void above him, as for the Archbishop of*
CANTERBURY. *The rest seat themselves in order
on each side.* CROMWELL *at the lower end, as
secretary.*

Chan. Speak to the business, master secretary :
Why are we met in council ?
Crom.   Please your honours,
The chief cause concerns his grace of Canterbury.
Gar. Has he had knowledge of it ?
Crom.   Yes.
Nor.   Who waits there ?
D. Keep. Without, my noble lords ?
Gar.   Yes.
D. Keep.   My lord archbishop ;
And has done half an hour, to know your pleasures. 40
Chan. Let him come in.
D. Keep.   Your grace may enter now.
      [CRANMER *approaches the council-table.*
Chan. My good lord archbishop, I am very sorry
To sit here at this present, and behold
That chair stand empty : but we all are men,
In our own natures frail, and capable
Of our flesh ; few are angels : out of which frailty,
And want of wisdom, you, that best should teach us,
Have misdemean'd yourself, and not a little,
Toward the king first, then his laws, in filling
The whole realm, by your teaching, and your
        chaplains,   50
(For so we are inform'd,) with new opinions,
Divers and dangerous ; which are heresies,
And, not reform'd, may prove pernicious.
Gar. Which reformation must be sudden too,
My noble lords ; for those that tame wild horses
Pace them not in their hands to make them gentle,
But stop their mouths with stubborn bits, and spur
        them,
Till they obey the manage. If we suffer,

Out of our easiness and childish pity
To one man's honour, this contagious sickness,   60
Farewell all physic : and what follows then ?
Commotions, uproars, with a general taint
Of the whole state : as, of late days, our neighbours,
The upper Germany, can dearly witness,
Yet freshly pitied in our memories.
    Cran. My good lords, hitherto, in all the progress
Both of my life and office, I have labour'd,
And with no little study, that my teaching,
And the strong course of my authority,
Might go one way, and safely, and the end   70
Was ever to do well : nor is there living
(I speak it with a single heart, my lords)
A man, that more detests, more stirs against,
Both in his private conscience and his place,
Defacers of a public peace, than I do.
'Pray Heaven, the king may never find a heart
With less allegiance in it ! Men, that make
Envy and crooked malice nourishment,
Dare bite the best. I do beseech your lordships,
That in this case of justice, my accusers,   80
Be what they will, may stand forth face to face,
And freely urge against me.
    Suf.   Nay, my lord,
That cannot be : you are a counsellor,
And by that virtue no man dare accuse you.
    Gar. My lord, because we have business of more
                                          moment,
We will be short with you. 'T is his highness'
                                          pleasure,
And our consent, for better trial of you,
From hence you be committed to the Tower ;
Where, being but a private man again,
You shall know many dare accuse you boldly,   90
More than, I fear, you are provided for.
    Cran. Ah ! my good Lord of Winchester, I thank you ;
You are always my good friend : if your will pass,
I shall both find your lordship judge and juror,
You are so merciful. I see your end :
'T is my undoing. Love and meekness, lord,
Become a churchman better than ambition ;
Win straying souls with modesty again,
Cast none away. That I shall clear myself,
Lay all the weight ye can upon my patience,   100
I make as little doubt, as you do conscience,
In doing daily wrongs. I could say more,
But reverence to your calling makes me modest.
    Gar. My lord, my lord, you are a sectary ;
That 's the plain truth : your painted gloss discovers,
To men that understand you, words and weakness.
    Crom. My Lord of Winchester, you are a little,
By your good favour, too sharp ; men so noble,
However faulty, yet should find respect
For what they have been : 't is a cruelty,   110
To load a falling man.
    Gar.   Good master secretary,
I cry your honour mercy : you may, worst
Of all this table, say so.
    Crom.   Why, my lord ?
    Gar. Do not I know you for a favourer
Of this new sect ? ye are not sound.
    Crom.   Not sound ?
    Gar. Not sound, I say.
    Crom.   'Would you were half so honest ;
Men's prayers then would seek you, not their fears.
    Gar. I shall remember this bold language.
    Crom.   Do.
Remember your bold life too.
    Chan.   This is too much ;
Forbear, for shame, my lords.
    Gar.   I have done.
    Crom.   And I.
    Chan. Then thus for you, my lord :—it stands
                                          agreed,   121
I take it, by all voices, that forthwith
You be convey'd to the Tower a prisoner,
There to remain, till the king's further pleasure
Be known unto us. Are you all agreed, lords ?
    All. We are.
    Cran.   Is there no other way of mercy,
But I must needs to the Tower, my lords ?

    Gar.   What other
Would you expect ? You are strangely troublesome.
Let some o' the guard be ready there.

                     Enter Guard.

    Cran.   For me ?
Must I go like a traitor thither ?
    Gar.   Receive him,   130
And see him safe i' the Tower.
    Cran.   Stay, good my lords ;
I have a little yet to say.—Look there, my lords :
By virtue of that ring I take my cause
Out of the gripes of cruel men, and give it
To a most noble judge, the king my master.
    Chan. This is the king's ring.
    Sur.   'T is no counterfeit.
    Suf. 'T is the right ring, by Heaven ! I told ye all,
When we first put this dangerous stone a-rolling,
'T would fall upon ourselves.
    Nor.   Do you think, my lords,
The king will suffer but the little finger   140
Of this man to be vex'd ?
    Chan.   'T is now too certain :
How much more is his life in value with him ?
'Would I were fairly out on 't !
    Crom.   My mind gave me,
In seeking tales and informations
Against this man, whose honesty the devil
And his disciples only envy at,
Ye blew the fire that burns ye. Now have at ye !

    Enter the KING, *frowning on them; he takes his seat.*

    Gar. Dread sovereign, how much are we bound to
                                          Heaven
In daily thanks, that gave us such a prince ;
Not only good and wise, but most religious :   150
One that in all obedience makes the church
The chief aim of his honour ; and, to strengthen
That holy duty, out of dear respect,
His royal self in judgment comes to hear
The cause betwixt her and this great offender.
    K. Hen. You were ever good at sudden commenda-
                                          tions,
Bishop of Winchester ; but know, I come not
To hear such flattery now, and in my presence :
They are too thin and bare to hide offences.
To me you cannot reach. You play the spaniel,   160
And think with wagging of your tongue to win me ;
But, whatsoe'er thou tak'st me for, I 'm sure,
Thou hast a cruel nature, and a bloody.—
[*To* CRANMER.] Good man, sit down. Now let me
                      see the proudest
He, that dares most, but wag his finger at thee :
By all that 's holy, he had better starve,
Than but once think this place becomes thee not.
    Sur. May it please your grace,—
    K. Hen.   No, sir, it does not please me.
I had thought, I had had men of some understanding
And wisdom of my council ; but I find none.   170
Was it discretion, lords, to let this man,
This good man (few of you deserve that title),
This honest man, wait like a lousy footboy
At chamber-door ? and one as great as you are ?
Why, what a shame was this ! Did my commission
Bid ye so far forget yourselves ? I gave ye
Power, as he was a counsellor to try him,
Not as a groom. There 's some of ye, I see,
More out of malice than integrity,
Would try him to the utmost, had ye mean ;   180
Which ye shall never have while I live.
    Chan.   Thus far,
My most dread sovereign, may it like your grace
To let my tongue excuse all. What was purpos'd
Concerning his imprisonment, was rather
(If there be faith in men) meant for his trial,
And fair purgation to the world, than malice,
I 'm sure, in me.
    K. Hen.   Well, well, my lords, respect him ;
Take him, and use him well ; he 's worthy of it.
I will say thus much for him : if a prince
May be beholding to a subject, I   190
Am, for his love and service, so to him.

Make me no more ado, but all embrace him :
Be friends, for shame, my lords !—My Lord of Canter-
    bury,
I have a suit which you must not deny me;
That is, a fair young maid that yet wants baptism,
You must be godfather, and answer for her.
  Cran. The greatest monarch now alive may glory
In such an honour : how may I deserve it,
That am a poor and humble subject to you?
  K. Hen. Come, come, my lord, you'd spare your
    spoons. You shall have   200
Two noble partners with you ; the old Duchess of
    Norfolk,
And Lady Marquess Dorset : will these please you?
Once more, my Lord of Winchester, I charge you,
Embrace, and love this man.
  Gar.   With a true heart,
And brother-love, I do it.
  Cran.   And let Heaven
Witness, how dear I hold this confirmation.
  K. Hen. Good man ! those joyful tears show thy
    true heart.
The common voice, I see, is verified
Of thee, which says thus, " Do my Lord of Canterbury
A shrewd turn, and he is your friend for ever."— 210
Come, lords, we trifle time away ; I long
To have this young one made a Christian.
As I have made ye one, lords, one remain ;
So I grow stronger, you more honour gain. [*Exeunt.*

SCENE III.—The Palace Yard.

*Noise and tumult within. Enter Porter and his
    Man.*

  Port. You'll leave your noise anon, ye rascals. Do
you take the court for Paris-garden? ye rude slaves,
leave your gaping.
  [*Within.*] Good master porter, I belong to the larder.
  Port. Belong to the gallows, and be hanged, you
rogue !—Is this a place to roar in?—Fetch me a dozen
crab-tree staves, and strong ones : these are but
switches to them.—I'll scratch your heads : you must
be seeing christenings? Do you look for ale and
cakes here, you rude rascals?   10
  Man. Pray, sir, be patient: 'tis as much impossible,
Unless we sweep them from the door with cannons,
To scatter them, as 'tis to make them sleep
On May-day morning ; which will never be.
We may as well push against Paul's, as stir them.
  Port. How got they in, and be hang'd?
  Man. Alas, I know not: how gets the tide in?
As much as one sound cudgel of four foot
(You see the poor remainder) could distribute,
I made no spare, sir.
  Port.   You did nothing, sir.   20
  Man. I am not Samson, nor Sir Guy, nor Colbrand,
To mow them down before me; but if I spared any,
That had a head to hit, either young or old,
He or she, cuckold or cuckold-maker,
Let me ne'er hope to see a chine again ;
And that I would not for a cow, God save her.
  [*Within.*] Do you hear, master porter?
  Port. I shall be with you presently, good master
puppy.—Keep the door close, sirrah.
  Man. What would you have me do?   30
  Port. What should you do, but knock 'em down by
the dozens? Is this Moorfields to muster in? or have
we some strange Indian with the great tool come to
court, the women so besiege us? Bless me, what a fry
of fornication is at door ! On my Christian conscience,
this one christening will beget a thousand : here will
be father, godfather, and all together.   37
  Man. The spoons will be the bigger, sir. There is a
fellow somewhat near the door, he should be a brazier
by his face, for, o' my conscience, twenty of the dog-
days now reign in 's nose: all that stand about him are
under the line, they need no other penance. That fire-
drake did I hit three times on the head, and three
times was his nose discharged against me : he stands
there, like a mortar-piece, to blow us. There was a

haberdasher's wife of small wit near him, that railed
upon me till her pink'd porringer fell off her head, for
kindling such a combustion in the state. I miss'd the
meteor once, and hit that woman, who cried out:
Clubs! when I might see from far some forty trun-
cheoners draw to her succour, which were the hope o'
the Strand, where she was quartered. They fell on;
I made good my place ; at length they came to the
broomstaff to me : I defied 'em still ; when suddenly
a file of boys behind 'em, loose shot, delivered such
a shower of pebbles, that I was fain to draw mine
honour in, and let 'em win the work. The devil was
amongst 'em, I think, surely.   58
  Port. These are the youths that thunder at a playhouse, and fight for bitten apples ; that no audience,
but the Tribulation of Tower Hill, or the Limbs of
Limehouse, their dear brothers, are able to endure.
I have some of 'em in *Limbo Patrum*, and there they
are like to dance these three days, besides the running
banquet of two beadles, that is to come.

Enter the Lord Chamberlain.

  Cham. Mercy o' me, what a multitude are here!
They grow still too, from all parts they are coming,
As if we kept a fair here ! Where are these porters,
These lazy knaves?—Ye have made a fine hand,
    fellows :   70
There is a trim rabble let in. Are all these
Your faithful friends o' the suburbs? We shall have
Great store of room, no doubt, left for the ladies,
When they pass back from the christening.
  Port.   An't please your honour,
We are but men ; and what so many may do,
Not being torn a-pieces, we have done :
An army cannot rule 'em.
  Cham.   As I live,
If the king blame me for 't, I'll lay ye all
By the heels, and suddenly ; and on your heads
Clap round fines for neglect. You are lazy knaves;
And here ye lie baiting of bombards, when   80
Ye should do service. Hark ! the trumpets sound ;
They're come already from the christening.
Go, break among the press, and find a way out
To let the troop pass fairly, or I'll find
A Marshalsea, shall hold you play these two months.
  Port. Make way there for the princess.
  Man.   You great fellow,
Stand close up, or I'll make your head ache.
  Port. You i' the camlet, get up o' the rail ;
I'll pick you o'er the pales else.   [*Exeunt.*

SCENE IV.—The Palace.

*Enter Trumpets, sounding; then two Aldermen,
    Lord Mayor, Garter, CRANMER, Duke of* NORFOLK,
    with his marshal's staff, Duke of SUFFOLK, *two
    Noblemen bearing great standing-bowls for the
    christening-gifts; then, four Noblemen bearing a
    canopy, under which the Duchess of* NORFOLK, *god-
    mother, bearing the child richly habited in a mantle,
    &c. Train borne by a Lady: then follows the
    Marchioness of* DORSET, *the other godmother, and
    Ladies. The troop pass once about the stage, and
    Garter speaks.*

  Gart. Heaven, from thy endless goodness, send
prosperous life, long, and ever happy, to the high and
mighty princess of England, Elizabeth !

Flourish. Enter KING *and Train.*

  Cran. [*Kneeling.*] And to your royal grace, and the
    good queen,
My noble partners, and myself, thus pray :
All comfort, joy, in this most gracious lady,
Heaven ever laid up to make parents happy,
May hourly fall upon ye !
  K. Hen.   Thank you, good lord archbishop;
What is her name?
  Cran.   Elizabeth.
  K. Hen.   Stand up, lord.—
                             [*The* KING *kisses the Child.*

With this kiss take my blessing: God protect thee! 10
Into whose hand I give thy life.
Cran.   Amen.
K. Hen. My noble gossips, ye have been too prodigal.

(But few now living can behold that goodness)
A pattern to all princes living with her,
And all that shall succeed: Saba was never
More covetous of wisdom, and fair virtue,

K. Hen. " With this kiss take my blessing: God protect thee!
Into whose hand I give thy life."

I thank ye heartily: so shall this lady,
When she has so much English.
Cran.   Let me speak, sir,
For Heaven now bids me; and the words I utter
Let none think flattery, for they 'll find them truth.
This royal infant,—Heaven still move about her!—
Though in her cradle, yet now promises
Upon this land a thousand thousand blessings,
Which time shall bring to ripeness. She shall be   20

Than this pure soul shall be : all princely graces,
That mould up such a mighty piece as this is,
With all the virtues that attend the good,
Shall still be doubled on her : truth shall nurse her;
Holy and heavenly thoughts still counsel her :
She shall be lov'd, and fear'd : her own shall bless her;
Her foes shake like a field of beaten corn,   31
And hang their heads with sorrow : good grows with
   her.

In her days, every man shall eat in safety
Under his own vine what he plants; and sing
The merry songs of peace to all his neighbours.
God shall be truly known; and those about her
From her shall read the perfect ways of honour,
And by those claim their greatness, not by blood.
Nor shall this peace sleep with her: but as when
The bird of wonder dies, the maiden phœnix,　40
Her ashes new create another heir,
As great in admiration as herself:
So shall she leave her blessedness to one,
(When Heaven shall call her from this cloud of dark-
　　　　ness,)
Who, from the sacred ashes of her honour,
Shall star-like rise, as great in fame as she was,
And so stand fix'd. Peace, plenty, love, truth, terror,
That were the servants to this chosen infant,
Shall then be his, and like a vine grow to him:
Wherever the bright sun of heaven shall shine,　50
His honour and the greatness of his name
Shall be, and make new nations: he shall flourish,
And, like a mountain cedar, reach his branches
To all the plains about him. Our children's children
Shall see this, and bless Heaven.

K. Hen.　　　　　　　Thou speakest wonders.
Cran. She shall be, to the happiness of England,
An aged princess; many days shall see her,
And yet no day without a deed to crown it.
'Would I had known no more! but she must die—
She must, the saints must have her—yet a virgin;　60
A most unspotted lily shall she pass
To the ground, and all the world shall mourn her.
K. Hen. O lord archbishop!
Thou hast made me now a man: never, before
This happy child, did I get anything.
This oracle of comfort has so pleas'd me,
That, when I am in heaven, I shall desire
To see what this child does, and praise my Maker.—
I thank ye all.—To you, my good lord mayor,
And your good brethren, I am much beholding:　70
I have receiv'd much honour by your presence,
And ye shall find me thankful.—Lead the way,
　　　　lords:
Ye must all see the queen, and she must thank
　　　　ye;
She will be sick else. This day, no man think
H'as business at his house, for all shall stay:
This little one shall make it holiday.　　[*Exeunt.*

EPILOGUE.

'T is ten to one, this play can never please
All that are here. Some come to take their ease,
And sleep an act or two; but those, we fear,
We have frighted with our trumpets; so, 't is clear,
They 'll say, 't is naught: others, to hear the city
Abus'd extremely, and to cry,—"That's witty!"
Which we have not done neither: that, I fear,

All the expected good we 're like to hear
For this play, at this time, is only in
The merciful construction of good women;　10
For such a one we show'd them. If they smile,
And say, 't will do, I know, within a while
All the best men are ours; for 't is ill hap,
If they hold, when their ladies bid them clap.

TROILUS AND CRESSIDA.

DRAMATIS PERSONÆ.

PRIAM, *King of Troy.*
HECTOR, ⎫
TROILUS, ⎪
PARIS, ⎬ *His Sons.*
DEIPHOBUS, ⎪
HELENUS, ⎭
ÆNEAS, ⎫ *Trojan Commanders.*
ANTENOR, ⎭
CALCHAS, *a Trojan Priest, taking part with the Greeks.*
PANDARUS, *Uncle to Cressida.*
MARGARELON, *a Bastard Son of Priam.*
AGAMEMNON, *the Grecian General.*
MENELAUS, *his Brother.*
ACHILLES, ⎫ *Grecian Commanders.*
AJAX, ⎭

ULYSSES, ⎫
NESTOR, ⎪
DIOMEDES, ⎬ *Grecian Commanders.*
PATROCLUS, ⎭
THERSITES, *a deformed and scurrilous Grecian.*
ALEXANDER, *Servant to Cressida.*
Servant to Troilus; Servant to Paris; Servant to Diomedes.

HELEN, *Wife to Menelaus.*
ANDROMACHE, *Wife to Hector.*
CASSANDRA, *Daughter to Priam, a Prophetess.*
CRESSIDA, *Daughter to Calchas.*

Trojan and Greek Soldiers, and Attendants.

SCENE—TROY, and the Grecian Camp.

PROLOGUE.

IN Troy there lies the scene. From isles of Greece
The princes orgulous, their high blood chaf'd,
Have to the port of Athens sent their ships,
Fraught with the ministers and instruments
Of cruel war: sixty and nine, that wore
Their crownets regal, from the Athenian bay
Put forth toward Phrygia; and their vow is made,
To ransack Troy, within whose strong immures
The ravish'd Helen, Menelaus' queen,
With wanton Paris sleeps;—and that's the quarrel. 10
To Tenedos they come,
And the deep-drawing barks do there disgorge
Their warlike fraughtage: now on Dardan plains
The fresh and yet unbruised Greeks do pitch
Their brave pavilions: Priam's six-gated city,
Dardan, and Tymbria, Helias, Chetas, Trojan,
And Antenorides, with massy staples
And corresponsive and fulfilling bolts,
Sperr up the sons of Troy.
Now expectation, tickling skittish spirits 20
On one and other side, Trojan and Greek,
Sets all on hazard.—And hither am I come
A prologue arm'd, but not in confidence
Of author's pen, or actor's voice, but suited
In like conditions as our argument,—
To tell you, fair beholders, that our play
Leaps o'er the vaunt and firstlings of those broils,
Beginning in the middle; starting thence away
To what may be digested in a play.
Like, or find fault; do as your pleasures are: 30
Now good, or bad, 't is but the chance of war.

ACT I.

SCENE I.—Troy. Before PRIAM'S Palace.

Enter TROILUS *armed, and* PANDARUS.

Troilus.
CALL here my varlet, I 'll unarm again:
Why should I war without the walls
    of Troy,
That find such cruel battle here
    within?
Each Trojan that is master of his
    heart,
Let him to field; Troilus, alas! hath
    none.
Pan. Will this gear ne'er be mended?
Tro. The Greeks are strong, and skilful to their
    strength,
Fierce to their skill, and to their fierceness valiant;
But I am weaker than a woman's tear,
Tamer than sleep, fonder than ignorance,   10
Less valiant than the virgin in the night,
And skilless as unpractis'd infancy.
Pan. Well, I have told you enough of this: for my
part, I 'll not meddle nor make no further. He that
will have a cake out of the wheat, must needs tarry
the grinding.
Tro. Have I not tarried?
Pan. Ay, the grinding; but you must tarry the
bolting.
Tro. Have I not tarried?   20
Pan. Ay, the bolting; but you must tarry the
leavening.
Tro. Still have I tarried.
Pan. Ay, to the leavening; but here 's yet in the
word hereafter, the kneading, the making of the cake,
the heating of the oven, and the baking; nay, you
must stay the cooling too, or you may chance to burn
your lips.
Tro. Patience herself, what goddess e'er she be,
Doth lesser blench at sufferance than I do.   30
At Priam's royal table do I sit;
And when fair Cressid comes into my thoughts,—
So, traitor!—when she comes!—When is she thence?
Pan. Well, she looked yesternight fairer than ever I
saw her look, or any woman else.
Tro. I was about to tell thee:—when my heart,
As wedged with a sigh, would rive in twain,
Lest Hector or my father should perceive me,
I have (as when the sun doth light a storm)
Buried this sigh in wrinkle of a smile;   40
But sorrow, that is couch'd in seeming gladness,
Is like that mirth fate turns to sudden sadness.
Pan. An her hair were not somewhat darker than
Helen's, (well, go to,) there were no more comparison
between the women;—but, for my part, she is my kins-
woman: I would not, as they term it, praise her;—
but I would somebody had heard her talk yesterday,
as I did: I will not dispraise your sister Cassandra's
wit, but—
Tro. O Pandarus! I tell thee, Pandarus,—   50
When I do tell thee, there my hopes lie drown'd,
Reply not in how many fathoms deep
They lie indrench'd. I tell thee, I am mad
In Cressid's love: thou answer'st, she is fair;
Pour'st in the open ulcer of my heart
Her eyes, her hair, her cheek, her gait, her voice;
Handlest in thy discourse, O! that her hand,
In whose comparison all whites are ink,
Writing their own reproach; to whose soft seizure
The cygnet's down is harsh, and spirit of sense   60
Hard as the palm of ploughman: this thou tell'st me,
As true thou tell'st me, when I say I love her;
But, saying thus, instead of oil and balm,
Thou lay'st in every gash that love hath given me
The knife that made it.
Pan. I speak no more than truth.
Tro. Thou dost not speak so much.
Pan. 'Faith, I 'll not meddle in 't. Let her be as she
is: if she be fair, 'tis the better for her; and she be
not, she has the mends in her own hands.   70
Tro. Good Pandarus! How now, Pandarus?
Pan. I have had my labour for my travail; ill-
thought on of her, and ill-thought on of you: gone
between, and between, but small thanks for my
labour.
Tro. What, art thou angry, Pandarus? what, with
me?
Pan. Because she 's kin to me, therefore she 's not
so fair as Helen: an she were not kin to me, she
would be as fair on Friday, as Helen is on Sunday.
But what care I? I care not, an she were a black-a-
moor; 'tis all one to me.   81
Tro. Say I, she is not fair?
Pan. I do not care whether you do or no. She 's a
fool to stay behind her father: let her to the Greeks,
and so I 'll tell her the next time I see her. For my
part, I 'll meddle nor make no more i' the matter.
Tro. Pandarus,—
Pan. Not I.
Tro. Sweet Pandarus,—
Pan. Pray you, speak no more to me! I will leave
all as I found it, and there an end.   91
                    [Exit PANDARUS. *An alarum.*
Tro. Peace, you ungracious clamours! peace, rude
    sounds!
Fools on both sides! Helen must needs be fair,
When with your blood you daily paint her thus.
I cannot fight upon this argument;
It is too starv'd a subject for my sword.
But Pandarus—O gods, how do you plague me!
I cannot come to Cressid, but by Pandar;
And he 's as tetchy to be woo'd to woo,
As she is stubborn-chaste against all suit.   100
Tell me, Apollo, for thy Daphne's love,
What Cressid is, what Pandar, and what we?
Her bed is India; there she lies, a pearl:
Between our Ilium and where she resides,
Let it be call'd the wild and wandering flood;
Ourself the merchant, and this sailing Pandar
Our doubtful hope, our convoy, and our bark.

Alarum. Enter ÆNEAS.

Æne. How now, Prince Troilus? wherefore not
    afield?
Tro. Because not there: this woman's answer
    sorts,
For womanish it is to be from thence.   110
What news, Æneas, from the field to-day?
Æne. That Paris is returned home, and hurt.
Tro. By whom, Æneas?
Æne.   Troilus, by Menelaus.
Tro. Let Paris bleed: 'tis but a scar to scorn;
Paris is gor'd with Menelaus' horn.   *[Alarum.*
Æne. Hark, what good sport is out of town to-day!

Tro. Better at home, if "'would I might" were
"may."—
But to the sport abroad :—are you bound thither?
Æne. In all swift haste.
Tro.   Come, go we then together.
                                    [*Exeunt.*

Scene II.—The Same. A Street.

Enter CRESSIDA *and* ALEXANDER.

Cres. Who were those went by?
Alex.   Queen Hecuba, and Helen.
Cres. And whither go they?
Alex.   Up to the eastern tower,
Whose height commands as subject all the vale,
To see the battle. Hector, whose patience
Is, as a virtue, fix'd, to-day was mov'd :
He chid Andromache, and struck his armourer ;
And, like as there were husbandry in war,
Before the sun rose, he was harness'd light,
And to the field goes he ; where every flower
Did, as a prophet, weep what it foresaw   10
In Hector's wrath.
Cres.   What was his cause of anger?
Alex. The noise goes, this : there is among the Greeks
A lord of Trojan blood, nephew to Hector ;
They call him Ajax.
Cres.   Good ; and what of him?
Alex. They say he is a very man *per se*,
And stands alone.
Cres. So do all men ; unless they are drunk, sick,
or have no legs.   18
Alex. This man, lady, hath robbed many beasts of
their particular additions : he is as valiant as the lion,
churlish as the bear, slow as the elephant ; a man into
whom nature hath so crowded humours, that his
valour is crushed into folly, his folly sauced with
discretion : there is no man hath a virtue that he hath
not a glimpse of, nor any man an attaint but he carries
some stain of it. He is melancholy without cause,
and merry against the hair : he hath the joints of
everything ; but everything so out of joint, that he
is a gouty Briareus, many hands and no use ; or pur-
blinded Argus, all eyes and no sight.   30
Cres. But how should this man, that makes me
smile, make Hector angry?
Alex. They say, he yesterday coped Hector in the
battle, and struck him down ; the disdain and shame
whereof hath ever since kept Hector fasting and
waking.

Enter PANDARUS.

Cres. Who comes here?
Alex. Madam, your uncle Pandarus.
Cres. Hector's a gallant man.
Alex. As may be in the world, lady.   40
Pan. What's that? what's that?
Cres. Good morrow, uncle Pandarus.
Pan. Good morrow, cousin Cressid. What do you
talk of?—Good' morrow, Alexander.—How do you,
cousin? When were you at Ilium?
Cres. This morning, uncle.
Pan. What were you talking of, when I came?
Was Hector armed, and gone, ere ye came to Ilium?
Helen was not up, was she?
Cres. Hector was gone ; but Helen was not up. 50
Pan. E'en so : Hector was stirring early.
Cres. That were we talking of, and of his anger.
Pan. Was he angry?
Cres. So he says here.
Pan. True, he was so ; I know the cause too : he'll
lay about him to-day, I can tell them that : and there's
Troilus will not come far behind him ; let them take
heed of Troilus, I can tell them that too.
Cres. What, is he angry too?
Pan. Who? Troilus? Troilus is the better man of
the two.   61
Cres. O Jupiter ! there's no comparison.
Pan. What, not between Troilus and Hector? Do
you know a man if you see him?
Cres. Ay ; if I ever saw him before, and knew him.

Pan. Well, I say, Troilus is Troilus.
Cres. Then you say as I say ; for I am sure he is not
Hector.
Pan. No, nor Hector is not Troilus, in some degrees.
Cres. 'T is just to each of them ; he is himself.   70
Pan. Himself? Alas, poor Troilus ! I would he were.
Cres. So he is.
Pan. Condition, I had gone bare-foot to India.
Cres. He is not Hector.
Pan. Himself? no, he's not himself.—'Would 'a were
himself ! Well, the gods are above ; time must friend,
or end. Well, Troilus, well,—I would, my heart were
in her body !—No, Hector is not a better man than
Troilus.
Cres. Excuse me.   80
Pan. He is elder.
Cres. Pardon me, pardon me.
Pan. The other's not come to 't ; you shall tell me
another tale, when the other's come to 't. Hector
shall not have his wit this year.
Cres. He shall not need it, if he have his own.
Pan. Nor his qualities.
Cres. No matter.
Pan. Nor his beauty.
Cres. 'T would not become him ; his own's better. 90
Pan. You have no judgment, niece. Helen herself
swore the other day, that Troilus, for a brown favour
(for so 't is, I must confess)—not brown neither—
Cres. No, but brown.
Pan. 'Faith, to say truth, brown and not brown.
Cres. To say the truth, true and not true.
Pan. She prais'd his complexion above Paris.
Cres. Why, Paris hath colour enough.
Pan. So he has.   99
Cres. Then Troilus should have too much : if she
praised him above, his complexion is higher than his :
he having colour enough, and the other higher, is too
flaming a praise for a good complexion. I had as lief
Helen's golden tongue had commended Troilus for a
copper nose.
Pan. I swear to you, I think Helen loves him better
than Paris.
Cres. Then she's a merry Greek, indeed.   108
Pan. Nay, I am sure she does. She came to him
the other day into the compassed window ;—and, you
know, he has not past three or four hairs on his chin,—
Cres. Indeed, a tapster's arithmetic may soon bring
his particulars therein to a total.
Pan. Why, he is very young ; and yet will he,
within three pound, lift as much as his brother Hector.
Cres. Is he so young a man, and so old a lifter?
Pan. But, to prove to you that Helen loves him :—
she came, and puts me her white hand to his cloven
chin,—
Cres. Juno have mercy !—How came it cloven? 120
Pan. Why, you know, 't is dimpled. I think his
smiling becomes him better than any man in all
Phrygia.'
Cres. O ! he smiles valiantly.
Pan. Does he not?
Cres. O ! yes, an 't were a cloud in autumn.
Pan. Why, go to then.—But to prove to you that
Helen loves Troilus,—
Cres. Troilus will stand to the proof, if you'll prove
it so.   130
Pan. Troilus? why, he esteems her no more than I
esteem an addle egg.
Cres. If you love an addle egg as well as you love
an idle head, you would eat chickens i' the shell.
Pan. I cannot choose but laugh, to think how she
tickled his chin :—indeed, she has a marvellous white
hand, I must needs confess,—
Cres. Without the rack.
Pan. And she takes upon her to spy a white hair on
his chin.   140
Cres. Alas, poor chin ! many a wart is richer.
Pan. But there was such laughing : Queen Hecuba
laughed, that her eyes ran o'er.
Cres. With millstones.
Pan. And Cassandra laughed.
Cres. But there was more temperate fire under the
pot of her eyes :—did her eyes run o'er too?

Pan. And Hector laughed.

Cres. At what was all this laughing?

Pan. Marry, at the white hair that Helen spied on Troilus' chin. 151

Cres. An 't had been a green hair, I should have laughed too.

Pan. They laughed not so much at the hair, as at his pretty answer.

Cres. What was his answer?

Pan. Quoth she, "Here 's but two-and-fifty hairs on your chin, and one of them is white."

Cres. This is her question. 159

Pan. That 's true; make no question of that. "Two-and-fifty hairs," quoth he, "and one white: that white hair is my father, and all the rest are his sons."— "Jupiter!" quoth she, "which of these hairs is Paris, my husband?"—"The forked one," quoth he; "pluck 't out, and give it him." But there was such laughing, and Helen so blushed, and Paris so chafed, and all the rest so laughed, that it passed.

Cres. So let it now, for it has been a great while going by.

Pan. Well, cousin, I told you a thing yesterday, think on 't. 171

Cres. So I do.

Pan. I 'll be sworn, 't is true: he will weep you, an 't were a man born in April.

Cres. And I 'll spring up in his tears, an 't were a nettle against May.   [*A retreat sounded.*

Pan. Hark! they are coming from the field. Shall we stand up here, and see them, as they pass toward Ilium? good niece, do; sweet niece Cressida.

Cres. At your pleasure. 180

Pan. Here, here; here 's an excellent place: here we may see most bravely. I 'll tell you them all by their names, as they pass by, but mark Troilus above the rest.

Cres. Speak not so loud.

ÆNEAS passes over the stage.

Pan. That 's Æneas. Is not that a brave man? he 's one of the flowers of Troy, I can tell you: but mark Troilus; you shall see anon.

Cres. Who 's that? 189

ANTENOR passes over.

Pan. That 's Antenor; he has a shrewd wit, I can tell you; and he 's a man good enough: he 's one o' the soundest judgments in Troy, whosoever, and a proper man of person.—When comes Troilus?—I 'll show you Troilus anon: if he see me, you shall see him nod at me.

Cres. Will he give you the nod?

Pan. You shall see.

Cres. If he do, the rich shall have more. 198

HECTOR passes over.

Pan. That 's Hector, that, that, look you, that, there 's a fellow!—Go thy way, Hector.—There 's a brave man, niece.—O brave Hector!—Look how he looks; there 's a countenance. Is 't not a brave man?

Cres. O! a brave man.

Pan. Is 'a not? It does a man's heart good. Look you what hacks are on his helmet! look you yonder, do you see? look you there. There 's no jesting: there 's laying on; take 't off who will, as they say: there be hacks!

Cres. Be those with swords? 209

PARIS passes over.

Pan. Swords? anything, he cares not; an the devil come to him, it 's all one: by God's lid, it does one's heart good.—Yonder comes Paris; yonder comes Paris: look ye yonder, niece: is 't not a gallant man too, is 't not?—Why, this is brave now.—Who said he came hurt home to-day? he 's not hurt: why, this will do Helen's heart good now. Ha! 'would I could see Troilus now.—You shall see Troilus anon.

Cres. Who 's that?

HELENUS passes over.

Pan. That 's Helenus.—I marvel, where Troilus is.—

That 's Helenus.—I think he went not forth to-day.— That 's Helenus. 221

Cres. Can Helenus fight, uncle?

Pan. Helenus? no;—yes, he 'll fight indifferent well.—I marvel, where Troilus is.—Hark! do you not hear the people cry, Troilus?—Helenus is a priest.

Cres. What sneaking fellow comes yonder?

TROILUS passes over.

Pan. Where? yonder? that 's Deiphobus.—'T is Troilus! there 's a man, niece!—Hem!—Brave Troilus, the prince of chivalry!

Cres. Peace! for shame; peace! 230

Pan. Mark him; note him.—O brave Troilus!—look well upon him, niece: look you, how his sword is

Pan. "Mark him; note him.—O brave Troilus!—look well upon him, niece."

bloodied, and his helm more hack'd than Hector's; and how he looks, and how he goes!—O admirable youth! he ne'er saw three-and-twenty. Go thy way, Troilus, go thy way: had I a sister were a grace, or a daughter a goddess, he should take his choice. O admirable man! Paris?—Paris is dirt to him; and, I warrant, Helen, to change, would give an eye to boot.

Soldiers pass over the stage.

Cres. Here come more. 240

Pan. Asses, fools, dolts, chaff and bran, chaff and bran: porridge after meat. I could live and die i' the eyes of Troilus. Ne'er look, ne'er look: the eagles are gone; crows and daws, crows and daws. I had rather be such a man as Troilus, than Agamemnon and all Greece.

Cres. There is among the Greeks Achilles, a better man than Troilus.

Pan. Achilles? a drayman, a porter, a very camel.

Cres. Well, well. 250

Pan. Well, well?—Why, have you any discretion? have you any eyes? Do you know what a man is? Is not birth, beauty, good shape, discourse, manhood, learning, gentleness, virtue, youth, liberality, and so forth, the spice and salt that season a man?

Cres. Ay, a minced man: and then to be baked with no date in the pie,—for then the man's date 's out.

Pan. You are such a woman! one knows not a' what ward you lie. 259

Cres. Upon my back, to defend my belly; upon my wit, to defend my wiles; upon my secrecy, to defend mine honesty; my mask, to defend my beauty; and you, to defend all these: and at all these wards I lie, at a thousand watches.

Pan. Say one of your watches.

Cres. Nay, I 'll watch you for that; and that 's one of the chiefest of them too: if I cannot ward what I would not have hit I can watch you for telling how I

took the blow, unless it swell past hiding, and then
it 's past watching.   270
Pan. You are such another!

Enter Troilus' *Boy.*

Boy. Sir, my lord would instantly speak with you.
Pan. Where?
Boy. At your own house, there he unarms him.
Pan. Good boy, tell him I come.   [*Exit Boy.*
I doubt he be hurt. Fare ye well, good niece.
Cres. Adieu, uncle.
Pan. I 'll be with you, niece, by-and-by.
Cres. To bring, uncle?
Pan. Ay, a token from Troilus.   280
Cres..By the same token, you are a bawd.—
                                        [*Exit* Pandarus.
Words, vows, gifts, tears, and love's full sacrifice,
He offers in another's enterprise ;
But more in Troilus thousand-fold I see,
Than in the glass of Pandar's praise may be.
Yet hold I off. Women are angels, wooing:
Things won are done, joy's soul lies in the doing :
That she belov'd knows nought, that knows not this,—
Men prize the thing ungain'd more than it is :
That she was never yet, that ever knew   290
Love got so sweet as when desire did sue.
Therefore, this maxim out of love I teach,—
Achievement is command ; ungain'd, beseech :
Then though my heart's content firm love doth bear,
Nothing of that shall from mine eyes appear.   [*Exit.*

———

Scene III.—The Grecian Camp.   Before
            Agamemnon's Tent.

Sennet.   Enter Agamemnon, Nestor, Ulysses,
            Menelaus, *and others.*

Agam. Princes,
What grief hath set the jaundice on your cheeks?
The ample proposition, that hope makes
In all designs begun on earth below,
Fails in the promis'd largeness : checks and disasters
Grow in the veins of actions highest rear'd ;
As knots, by the conflux of meeting sap,
Infect the sound pine, and divert his grain
Tortive and errant from his course of growth.
Nor, princes, is it matter new to us,   10
That we come short of our suppose so far,
That, after seven years' siege, yet Troy walls stand ;
Sith every action that hath gone before,
Whereof we have record, trial did draw
Bias and thwart, not answering the aim,
And that unbodied figure of the thought
That gave 't surmised shape. Why then, you princes,
Do you with cheeks abash'd behold our works,
And think them shames, which are, indeed, nought
                                                  else
But the protractive trials of great Jove,   20
To find persistive constancy in men?
The fineness of which metal is not found
In fortune's love ; for then, the bold and coward,
The wise and fool, the artist and unread,
The hard and soft, seem all affin'd and kin :
But, in the wind and tempest of her frown,
Distinction, with a broad and powerful fan,
Puffing at all, winnows the light away :
And what hath mass, or matter, by itself
Lies rich in virtue, and unmingled.   30
Nest. With due observance of thy godlike seat,
Great Agamemnon, Nestor shall apply
Thy latest words. In the reproof of chance
Lies the true proof of men : the sea being smooth,
How many shallow bauble boats dare sail
Upon her patient breast, making their way
With those of nobler bulk?
But let the ruffian Boreas once enrage
The gentle Thetis, and, anon, behold
The strong-ribb'd bark through liquid mountains cut, 41
Bounding between the two moist elements,
Like Perseus' horse : where 's then the saucy boat,
Whose weak untimber'd sides but even now

Co-rivall'd greatness? either to harbour fled,
Or made a toast for Neptune. Even so
Doth valour's show, and valour's worth, divide
In storms of fortune : for, in her ray and brightness,
The herd hath more annoyance by the breese
Than by the tiger ; but when the splitting wind
Makes flexible the knees of knotted oaks,   50
And flies fled under shade, why then, the thing of
                                                  courage,
As rous'd with rage, with rage doth sympathise,
And with an accent tun'd in selfsame key,
Retorts to chiding fortune.
    Ulyss.   Agamemnon,
Thou great commander, nerve and bone of Greece,
Heart of our numbers, soul and only spirit,
In whom the tempers and the minds of all
Should be shut up, hear what Ulysses speaks.
Besides the applause and approbation
The which,—[*to* Agamemnon] most mighty for thy
                    place and sway,—   60
[*To* Nestor] And thou most reverend for thy
                    stretch'd-out life,—
I give to both your speeches, which were such,
As Agamemnon and the hand of Greece
Should hold up high in brass ; and such again,
As venerable Nestor, hatch'd in silver,
Should with a bond of air (strong as the axletree
On which heaven rides) knit all the Greekish ears
To his experienc'd tongue,—yet let it please both,—
Thou great,—and wise,—to hear Ulysses speak.
    Agam. Speak, Prince of Ithaca ; and be 't of less
        expect   70
That matter needless, of importless burden,
Divide thy lips, than we are confident,
When rank Thersites opes his mastiff jaws,
We shall hear music, wit, and oracle.
    Ulyss. Troy, yet upon his basis, had been down,
And the great Hector's sword had lack'd a master,
But for these instances.
The specialty of rule hath been neglected :
And, look, how many Grecian tents do stand
Hollow upon this plain, so many hollow factions. 80
When that the general is not like the hive,
To whom the foragers shall all repair,
What honey is expected? Degree being visarded,
The unworthiest shows as fairly in the mask.
Observe degree, priority, and place,
Insisture, course, proportion, season, form,
Office, and custom, in all line of order :
And therefore is the glorious planet, Sol,
In noble eminence enthron'd and spher'd   90
Amidst the other ; whose med'cinable eye
Corrects the ill aspects of planets evil,
And posts, like the commandment of a king,
Sans check, to good and bad : but when the planets,
In evil mixture, to disorder wander,
What plagues, and what portents, what mutiny,
What raging of the sea, shaking of earth,
Commotion in the winds, frights, changes, horrors,
Divert and crack, rend and deracinate
The unity and married calm of states   100
Quite from their fixture ! O ! when degree is shak'd,
Which is the ladder to all high designs,
The enterprise is sick. How could communities,
Degrees in schools, and brotherhoods in cities,
Peaceful commerce from dividable shores,
The primogenitive and due of birth,
Prerogative of age, crowns, sceptres, laurels,
But by degree, stand in authentic place?
Take but degree away, untune that string,
And, hark, what discord follows! each thing meets 110
In mere oppugnancy : the bounded waters
Should lift their bosoms higher than the shores,
And make a sop of all this solid globe :
Strength should be lord of imbecility,
And the rude son should strike his father dead :
Force should be right ; or, rather, right and wrong
(Between whose endless jar justice resides)
Should lose their names, and so should justice too.
Then everything includes itself in power,
Power into will, will into appetite ;   120

And appetite, an universal wolf,
So doubly seconded with will and power,
Must make perforce an universal prey,
And last eat up himself.   Great Agamemnon,
This chaos, when degree is suffocate,
Follows the choking.
And this neglection of degree it is,
That by a pace goes backward, in a purpose
It hath to climb.   The general's disdain'd
By him one step below ; he, by the next ;   130
That next, by him beneath : so, every step,
Exampled by the first pace that is sick
Of his superior, grows to an envious fever
Of pale and bloodless emulation :
And 't is this fever that keeps Troy on foot,
Not her own sinews.   To end a tale of length,
Troy in our weakness lives, not in her strength.
    Nest. Most wisely hath Ulysses here discover'd
The fever whereof all our power is sick.
    Agam. The nature of this sickness found, Ulysses,
What is the remedy ?   141
    Ulyss. The great Achilles, whom opinion crowns
The sinew and the forehand of our host,
Having his ear full of his airy fame,
Grows dainty of his worth, and in his tent
Lies mocking our designs.   With him, Patroclus,
Upon a lazy bed, the livelong day
Breaks scurril jests ;
And with ridiculous and awkward action
(Which, slanderer, he imitation calls)   150
He pageants us.   Sometime, great Agamemnon,
Thy topless deputation he puts on ;
And, like a strutting player,—whose conceit
Lies in his hamstring, and doth think it rich
To hear the wooden dialogue and sound
'Twixt his stretch'd footing and the scaffoldage,—
Such to-be-pitied and o'er-wrested seeming
He acts thy greatness in : and when he speaks,
'T is like a chime a-mending ; with terms unsquar'd,
Which, from the tongue of roaring Typhon dropp'd,
Would seem hyperboles.   At this fusty stuff,   161
The large Achilles, on his press'd bed lolling,
From his deep chest laughs out a loud applause ;
Cries—" Excellent !—'t is Agamemnon just.—
Now play me Nestor ;—hem, and stroke thy beard,
As he, being dress'd to some oration."
That 's done ;—as near as the extremest ends
Of parallels,—as like as Vulcan and his wife :
Yet good Achilles still cries, " Excellent !
'T is Nestor right !   Now play him me, Patroclus,   170
Arming to answer in a night alarm."
And then, forsooth, the faint defects of age
Must be the scene of mirth ; to cough, and spit,
And with a palsy, fumbling on his gorget,
Shake in and out the rivet :—and at this sport,
Sir Valour dies ; cries, " O !—enough, Patroclus ;
Or give me ribs of steel !   I shall split all
In pleasure of my spleen."   And in this fashion,
All our abilities, gifts, natures, shapes,
Severals and generals of grace exact,   180
Achievements, plots, orders, preventions,
Excitements to the field, or speech for truce,
Success, or loss, what is, or is not, serves
As stuff for these two to make paradoxes.
    Nest. And in the imitation of these twain
(Who, as Ulysses says, opinion crowns
With an imperial voice) many are infect.
Ajax is grown self-will'd ; and bears his head
In such a rein, in full as proud a place
As broad Achilles ; keeps his tent like him ;   190
Makes factious feasts ; rails on our state of war,
Bold as an oracle, and sets Thersites
(A slave whose gall coin slanders like a mint)
To match us in comparisons with dirt :
To weaken and discredit our exposure,
How rank soever rounded in with danger.
    Ulyss. They tax our policy, and call it cowardice ;
Count wisdom as no member of the war ;
Forestall prescience, and esteem no act
But that of hand : the still and mental parts,—   200
That do contrive how many hands shall strike,
When fitness calls them on, and know, by measure

Of their observant toil, the enemies' weight,—
Why, this hath not a finger's dignity.
They call this bed-work, mappery, closet-war :
So that the ram, that batters down the wall,
For the great swing and rudeness of his poise,
They place before his hand that made the engine,
Or those that with the fineness of their souls
By reason guide his execution.   210
    Nest. Let this be granted, and Achilles' horse
Makes many Thetis' sons.   [*A tucket.*
    Agam.   What trumpet ? look, Menelaus.
    Men. From Troy.

Enter ÆNEAS.

    Agam. What would you 'fore our tent ?
    Æne. Is this great Agamemnon's tent, I pray you ?
    Agam. Even this.
    Æne. May one, that is a herald and a prince,
Do a fair message to his kingly ears ?
    Agam. With surety stronger than Achilles' arm
'Fore all the Greekish heads, which with one voice 220
Call Agamemnon head and general.
    Æne. Fair leave, and large security.   How may
A stranger to those most imperial looks
Know them from eyes of other mortals ?
    Agam.   How !
    Æne. Ay ;
I ask, that I might waken reverence,
And bid the cheek be ready with a blush,
Modest as morning when she coldly eyes
The youthful Phœbus.
Which is that god in office, guiding men ?   230
Which is the high and mighty Agamemnon ?
    Agam. This Trojan scorns us, or the men of Troy
Are ceremonious courtiers.
    Æne. Courtiers as free, as debonair, unarm'd,
As bending angels : that 's their fame in peace ;
But when they would seem soldiers, they have galls,
Good arms, strong joints, true swords ; and, Jove's
        accord,
Nothing so full of heart.   But peace, Æneas,
Peace, Trojan ! lay thy finger on thy lips.
The worthiness of praise distains his worth,   240
If that the prais'd himself bring the praise forth ;
But what the repining enemy commends,
That breath fame blows ; that praise, sole pure,
        transcends.
    Agam. Sir, you of Troy, call you yourself Æneas ?
    Æne. Ay, Greek, that is my name.
    Agam. What 's your affair, I pray you ?
    Æne. Sir, pardon : 't is for Agamemnon's ears.
    Agam. He hears nought privately that comes from
        Troy.
    Æne. Nor I from Troy came not to whisper him :
I bring a trumpet to awake his ear ;   250
To set his sense on the attentive bend,
And then to speak.
    Agam.   Speak frankly as the wind.
It is not Agamemnon's sleeping hour :
That thou shalt know, Trojan, he is awake,
He tells thee so himself.
    Æne.   Trumpet, blow loud,
Send thy brass voice through all these lazy tents ;
And every Greek of mettle, let him know,
What Troy means fairly shall be spoke aloud.
        [*Trumpet sounds.*
We have, great Agamemnon, here in Troy
A prince call'd Hector (Priam is his father,)   260
Who in this dull and long-continued truce
Is rusty grown : he bade me take a trumpet,
And to this purpose speak.—Kings, princes, lords !
If there be one among the fair'st of Greece,
That holds his honour higher than his ease ;
That seeks his praise more than he fears his peril ;
That knows his valour, and knows not his fear ;
That loves his mistress more than in confession
(With truant vows to her own lips he loves),
And dare avow her beauty and her worth   270
In other arms than hers,—to him this challenge.
Hector, in view of Trojans and of Greeks,
Shall make it good, or do his best to do it,
He hath a lady, wiser, fairer, truer,

Than ever Greek did compass in his arms ;
And will to-morrow with his trumpet call,
Midway between your tents and walls of Troy,
To rouse a Grecian that is true in love :
If any come, Hector shall honour him ;
If none, he 'll say in Troy, when he retires,   280
The Grecian dames are sun-burnt, and not worth
The splinter of a lance.   Even so much.
    Agam. This shall be told our lovers, Lord Æneas ;
If none of them have soul in such a kind,
We left them all at home : but we are soldiers ;
And may that soldier a mere recreant prove,
That means not, hath not, or is not in love !
If then one is, or hath, or means to be,
That one meets Hector ; if none else, I am he.
    Nest. Tell him of Nestor, one that was a man   290
When Hector's grandsire suck'd : he is old now ;
But if there be not in our Grecian host
One noble man, that hath one spark of fire
To answer for his love, tell him from me,
I 'll hide my silver beard in a gold beaver,
And in my vantbrace put this wither'd brawn ;
And, meeting him, will tell him, that my lady
Was fairer than his grandam, and as chaste
As may be in the world.   His youth in flood,
I 'll pawn this truth with my three drops of blood. 300
    Æne. Now heavens forbid such scarcity of youth !
    Ulyss. Amen.
    Agam. Fair Lord Æneas, let me touch your hand ;
To our pavilion shall I lead you first.
Achilles shall have word of this intent ;
So shall each lord of Greece, from tent to tent ;
Yourself shall feast with us before you go,
And find the welcome of a noble foe.
        [*Exeunt all but* Ulysses *and* Nestor.
    Ulyss. Nestor,—
    Nest. What says Ulysses?   310
    Ulyss. I have a young conception in my brain ;
Be you my time to bring it to some shape.
    Nest. What is 't ?
    Ulyss. This 't is :
Blunt wedges rive hard knots : the seeded pride,
That hath to this maturity blown up
In rank Achilles, must or now be cropp'd,
Or, shedding, breed a nursery of like evil,
To overbulk us all.
    Nest.   Well, and how?
    Ulyss. This challenge that the gallant Hector sends,
However it is spread in general name,   321
Relates in purpose only to Achilles.
    Nest. The purpose is perspicuous even as substance,
Whose grossness little characters sum up :
And, in the publication, make no strain,
But that Achilles, were his brain as barren
As banks of Libya, (though, Apollo knows,
'T is dry enough,) will, with great speed of judgment,
Ay, with celerity, find Hector's purpose
Pointing on him.   330
    Ulyss. And wake him to the answer, think you?
    Nest. Yes, 'tis most meet : who may you else
        oppose,

That can from Hector bring his honour off,
If not Achilles?   Though 't be a sportful combat.
Yet in the trial much opinion dwells ;
For here the Trojans taste our dear'st repute
With their fin'st palate : and trust to me, Ulysses,
Our imputation shall be oddly pois'd
In this wild action ; for the success,
Although particular, shall give a scantling   340
Of good or bad unto the general ;
And in such indexes (although small pricks
To their subsequent volumes) there is seen
The baby figure of the giant mass
Of things to come at large.   It is suppos'd,
He, that meets Hector, issues from our choice :
And choice, being mutual act of all our souls,
Makes merit her election, and doth boil,
As 't were from forth us all, a man distill'd
Out of our virtues ; who miscarrying,   350
What heart receives from hence the conquering part,
To steel a strong opinion to themselves ?
Which entertain'd, limbs are his instruments,
In no less working, than are swords and bows
Directive by the limbs.
    Ulyss. Give pardon to my speech :—
Therefore 't is meet, Achilles meet not Hector.
Let us like merchants show our foulest wares,
And think, perchance, they 'll sell ; if not,
The lustre of the better yet to show   360
Shall show the better.   Do not consent,
That ever Hector and Achilles meet ;
For both our honour and our shame, in this,
Are dogg'd with two strange followers.
    Nest. I see them not with my old eyes : what are
        they ?
    Ulyss. What glory our Achilles shares from Hector,
Were he not proud, we all should wear with him :
But he already is too insolent ;
And we were better parch in Afric sun,
Than in the pride and salt scorn of his eyes,   370
Should he 'scape Hector fair : if he were foil'd,
Why, then we did our main opinion crush
In taint of our best man.   No ; make a lottery,
And by device let blockish Ajax draw
The sort to fight with Hector : among ourselves,
Give him allowance as the worthier man,
For that will physic the great Myrmidon,
Who broils in loud applause ; and make him fall
His crest, that prouder than blue Iris bends.
If the dull brainless Ajax come safe off,   380
We 'll dress him up in voices : if he fail,
Yet go we under our opinion still,
That we have better men.   But, hit or miss,
Our project's life this shape of sense assumes,—
Ajax employ'd plucks down Achilles' plumes.
    Nest. Ulysses,
Now I begin to relish thy advice ;
And I will give a taste of it forthwith
To Agamemnon : go we to him straight.
Two curs shall tame each other : pride alone   390
Must tarre the mastiffs on, as 't were their bone.
                                        [*Exeunt.*

ACT II.

Scene I.—Another Part of the Grecian Camp.

Enter Ajax *and* Thersites.

Ajax.

THERSITES!

Ther. Agamemnon—how if he had biles? full, all over, generally?

Ajax. Thersites!

Ther. And those biles did run?—Say so, —did not the general run then? were not that a botchy core?

Ajax. Dog!

Ther. Then would come some matter from him: I see none now. 10

Ajax. Thou bitch-wolf's son, canst thou not hear? Feel then. [*Strikes him.*

Ther. The plague of Greece upon thee, thou mongrel beef-witted lord!

Ajax. Speak then, thou vinnewedst leaven, speak: I will beat thee into handsomeness.

Ther. I shall sooner rail thee into wit and holiness: but, I think, thy horse will sooner con an oration, than thou learn a prayer without book. Thou canst strike, canst thou? a red murrain o' thy jade's tricks!

Ajax. Toadstool, learn me the proclamation. 21

Ther. Dost thou think I have no sense, thou strik'st me thus?

Ajax. The proclamation!

Ther. Thou art proclaimed a fool, I think.

Ajax. Do not, porpentine, do not: my fingers itch.

Ther. I would, thou didst itch from head to foot, and I had the scratching of thee; I would make thee the loathsomest scab in Greece. When thou art forth in the incursions, thou strikest as slow as another. 31

Ajax. I say, the proclamation!

Ther. Thou grumblest and railest every hour on Achilles; and thou art as full of envy at his greatness, as Cerberus is at Proserpina's beauty, ay, that thou barkest at him.

Ajax. Mistress Thersites!

Ther. Thou shouldst strike him.

Ajax. Cobloaf!

Ther. He would pun thee into shivers with his fist, as a sailor breaks a biscuit. 41

Ajax. You whoreson cur! [*Beating him.*

Ther. Do, do.

Ajax. Thou stool for a witch!

Ther. Ay, do, do; thou sodden-witted lord! thou hast no more brain than I have in mine elbows; an assinego may tutor thee: thou scurvy-valiant ass! thou art here but to thrash Trojans; and thou art bought and sold among those of any wit, like a barbarian slave. If thou use to beat me, I will begin at thy heel, and tell what thou art by inches, thou thing of no bowels, thou! 52

Ajax. You dog!

Ther. You scurvy lord!

Ajax. You cur! [*Beating him.*

Ther. Mars his idiot; do, rudeness; do, camel; do, do.

Enter Achilles *and* Patroclus.

Achil. Why, how now, Ajax? wherefore do you this?

How now, Thersites? what's the matter, man?

Ther. You see him there, do you? 60

Achil. Ay; what's the matter?

Ther. Nay, look upon him.

Achil. So I do: what's the matter?

Ther. Nay, but regard him well.

Achil. Well! why, so I do.

Ther. But yet you look not well upon him; for, whosoever you take him to be, he is Ajax.

Achil. I know that, fool.

Ther. Ay, but that fool knows not himself.

Ajax. Therefore I beat thee. 70

Ther. "Ay, do, do; thou sodden-witted lord!"

Ther. Lo, lo, lo, lo, what modicums of wit he utters! his evasions have ears thus long. I have bobbed his brain more than he has beat my bones: I will buy nine sparrows for a penny, and his *pia mater* is not worth the ninth part of a sparrow. This lord, Achilles, Ajax, who wears his wit in his belly, and his guts in his head, I'll tell you what I say of him.

Achil. What?

Ther. I say, this Ajax—

[Ajax *offers to strike him,* Achilles *interposes.*

Achil. Nay, good Ajax. 80

Ther. Has not so much wit—

Achil. Nay, I must hold you.

Ther. As will stop the eye of Helen's needle, for whom he comes to fight.

Achil. Peace, fool!

Ther. I would have peace and quietness, but the fool will not: he there; that he, look you there.

Ajax. O thou damned cur! I shall—

Achil. Will you set your wit to a fool's?

Ther. No, I warrant you; for a fool's will shame it.

Patr. Good words, Thersites. 91

Achil. What's the quarrel?

Ajax. I bade the vile owl go learn me the tenor of the proclamation, and he rails upon me.

Ther. I serve thee not.

Ajax. Well, go to, go to.

Ther. I serve here voluntary.

Achil. Your last service was sufferance, 't was not

voluntary ; no man is beaten voluntary : Ajax was
here the voluntary, and you as under an impress. 100
  Ther. E'en so ;—a great deal of your wit too lies in
your sinews, or else there be liars. Hector shall have
a great catch, if he knock out either of your brains : 'a
were as good crack a fusty nut with no kernel.
  Achil. What, with me too, Thersites?
  Ther. There 's Ulysses, and old Nestor,—whose wit
was mouldy ere your grandsires had nails on their
toes,—yoke you like draught-oxen, and make you
plough up the wars.
  Achil. What? what?
  Ther. Yes, good sooth : to, Achilles! to, Ajax! to!
  Ajax. I shall cut out your tongue.
  Ther. 'T is no matter ; I shall speak as much as
thou, afterwards.
  Patr. No more words, Thersites, peace!
  Ther. I will hold my peace when Achilles' brach
bids me, shall I?
  Achil. There 's for you, Patroclus.
  Ther. I will see you hanged, like clotpoles, ere I
come any more to your tents : I will keep where there
is wit stirring, and leave the faction of fools. [*Exit.*
  Patr. A good riddance.   122
  Achil. Marry, this, sir, is proclaim'd through all
    our host :—
That Hector, by the fifth hour of the sun,
Will, with a trumpet, 'twixt our tents and Troy,
To-morrow morning call some knight to arms,
That hath a stomach ; and such a one, that dare
Maintain—I know not what : 'tis trash. Farewell.
  Ajax. Farewell. Who shall answer him?
  Achil. I know not : it is put to lottery ; otherwise,
He knew his man.   131
  Ajax. O! meaning you.—I will go learn more of it.
                                              [*Exeunt.*

SCENE II.—Troy. A Room in PRIAM'S Palace.

Enter PRIAM, HECTOR, TROILUS, PARIS, *and*
    HELENUS.

  Pri. After so many hours, lives, speeches spent,
Thus once again says Nestor from the Greeks :
" Deliver Helen, and all damage else—
As honour, loss of time, travail, expense,
Wounds, friends, and what else dear that is consum d
In hot digestion of this cormorant war—
Shall be struck off."—Hector, what say you to 't?
  Hect. Though no man lesser fears the Greeks than I,
As far as toucheth my particular, yet,
Dread Priam,   10
There is no lady of more softer bowels,
More spungy to suck in the sense of fear,
More ready to cry out—" Who knows what follows?"
Than Hector is. The wound of peace is surety,
Surety secure ; but modest doubt is call'd
The beacon of the wise, the tent that searches
To the bottom of the worst. Let Helen go :
Since the first sword was drawn about this question,
Every tithe soul, 'mongst many thousand dismes,
Hath been as dear as Helen : I mean, of ours :   20
If we have lost so many tenths of ours,
To guard a thing not ours, nor worth to us,
Had it our name, the value of one ten ;
What merit 's in that reason, which denies
The yielding of her up?
  Tro.   Fie, fie! my brother!
Weigh you the worth and honour of a king,
So great as our dread father, in a scale
Of common ounces? will you with counters sum
The past-proportion of his infinite?
And buckle in a waist most fathomless   30
With spans and inches so diminutive
As fears and reasons? fie, for godly shame!
  Hel. No marvel, though you bite so sharp at
    reasons,
You are so empty of them. Should not our father
Bear the great sway of his affairs with reasons,
Because your speech hath none, that tells him so?
  Tro. You are for dreams and slumbers, brother
    priest ;

You fur your gloves with reason.   Here are your
    reasons :
You know, an enemy intends you harm ;
You know, a sword employ'd is perilous,   40
And reason flies the object of all harm.
Who marvels then, when Helenus beholds
A Grecian and his sword, if he do set
The very wings of reason to his heels,
And fly like chidden Mercury from Jove,
Or like a star disorb'd?—Nay, if we talk of reason,
Let 's shut our gates, and sleep : manhood and honour
Should have hare-hearts, would they but fat their
    thoughts
With this cramm'd reason : reason and respect
Make livers pale, and lustihood deject.   50
  Hect. Brother, she is not worth what she doth cost
The holding.
  Tro.   What is aught but as 't is valued?
  Hect. But value dwells not in particular will ;
It holds his estimate and dignity
As well wherein 't is precious of itself,
As in the prizer. 'T is mad idolatry,
To make the service greater than the god ;
And the will dotes, that is inclinable
To what infectiously itself affects,
Without some image of the affected merit.   60
  Tro. I take to-day a wife, and my election
Is led on in the conduct of my will :
My will enkindled by mine eyes and ears,
Two traded pilots 'twixt the dangerous shores
Of will and judgment. How may I avoid,
Although my will distaste what it elected,
The wife I chose? there can be no evasion
To blench from this, and to stand firm by honour.
We turn not back the silks upon the merchant,
When we have soil'd them ; nor the remainder viands
We do not throw in unrespective sink,   71
Because we now are full. It was thought meet,
Paris should do some vengeance on the Greeks :
Your breath of full consent bellied his sails ;
The seas and winds (old wranglers) took a truce,
And did him service : he touch'd the ports desir'd ;
And, for an old aunt, whom the Greeks held captive,
He brought a Grecian queen, whose youth and fresh-
    ness
Wrinkles Apollo's, and makes stale the morning.
Why keep we her? the Grecians keep our aunt.   80
Is she worth keeping? why, she is a pearl,
Whose price hath launch'd above a thousand ships,
And turned crown'd kings to merchants.
If you 'll avouch 't was wisdom Paris went
(As you must needs, for you all cried—" Go, go "),
If you 'll confess he brought home noble prize
(As you must needs, for you all clapp'd your hands,
And cried—" Inestimable ! "), why do you now
The issue of your proper wisdoms rate,
And do a deed that Fortune never did,   90
Beggar the estimation which you priz'd
Richer than sea and land? O theft most base,
That we have stol'n what we do fear to keep !
But thieves unworthy of a thing so stol'n,
That in their country did them that disgrace,
We fear to warrant in our native place !
  Cas. [*Within.*] Cry, Trojans, cry !
  Pri.   What noise? what shriek is this?
  Tro. 'T is our mad sister, I do know her voice.
  Cas. [*Within.*] Cry, Trojans !
  Hect. It is Cassandra.   100

Enter CASSANDRA, *raving*.

  Cas. Cry, Trojans, cry ! lend me ten thousand eyes,
And I will fill them with prophetic tears.
  Hect. Peace, sister, peace !
  Cas. Virgins and boys, mid-age and wrinkled old,
Soft infancy, that nothing canst but cry,
Add to my clamours ! let us pay betimes
A moiety of that mass of moan to come.
Cry, Trojans, cry ! practise your eyes with tears !
Troy must not be, nor goodly Ilion stand ;
Our firebrand brother, Paris, burns us all.   110
Cry, Trojans, cry ! a Helen, and a woe !
Cry, cry ! Troy burns, or else let Helen go.   [*Exit,*

Hect. Now, youthful Troilus, do not these high
     strains
Of divination in our sister work
Some touches of remorse? or is your blood
So madly hot, that no discourse of reason,
Nor fear of bad success in a bad cause,
Can qualify the same?
    Tro.   Why, brother Hector,
We may not think the justness of each act
Such and no other than event doth form it;   120
Nor once deject the courage of our minds,
Because Cassandra's mad : her brain-sick raptures
Cannot distaste the goodness of a quarrel,
Which hath our several honours all engag'd
To make it gracious. For my private part,
I am no more touch'd than all Priam's sons ;
And Jove forbid, there should be done amongst us
Such things as might offend the weakest spleen
To fight for, and maintain.
    Par. Else might the world convince of levity 130
As well my undertakings as your counsels ;
But, I attest the gods, your full consent
Gave wings to my propension, and cut off
All fears attending on so dire a project :
For what, alas ! can these my single arms?
What propugnation is in one man's valour,
To stand the push and enmity of those
This quarrel would excite? Yet, I protest,
Were I alone to pass the difficulties,
And had as ample power as I have will,   140
Paris should ne'er retract what he hath done,
Nor faint in the pursuit.
    Pri.   Paris, you speak
Like one besotted on your sweet delights :
You have the honey still, but these the gall ;
So to be valiant is no praise at all.
    Par. Sir, I propose not merely to myself
The pleasures such a beauty brings with it ;
But I would have the soil of her fair rape
Wip'd off in honourable keeping her.
What treason were it to the ransack'd queen, 150
Disgrace to your great worths, and shame to me,
Now to deliver her possession up,
On terms of base compulsion? Can it be,
That so degenerate a strain as this
Should once set footing in your generous bosoms?
There's not the meanest spirit on our party,
Without a heart to dare, or sword to draw,
When Helen is defended ; nor none so noble,
Whose life were ill bestow'd, or death unfam'd,
Where Helen is the subject : then, I say,   160
Well may we fight for her, whom, we know well,
The world's large spaces cannot parallel.
    Hect. Paris, and Troilus, you have both said well ;
And on the cause and question now in hand
Have gloz'd,—but superficially ; not much
Unlike young men, whom Aristotle thought
Unfit to hear moral philosophy.
The reasons you allege do more conduce
To the hot passion of distemper'd blood,
Than to make up a free determination   170
'Twixt right and wrong ; for pleasure, and revenge,
Have ears more deaf than adders to the voice
Of any true decision. Nature craves,
All dues be render'd to their owners : now,
What nearer debt in all humanity
Than wife is to the husband? If this law
Of nature be corrupted through affection,
And that great minds, of partial indulgence
To their benumbed wills, resist the same,
There is a law in each well-order'd nation, 180
To curb those raging appetites that are
Most disobedient and refractory.
If Helen then be wife to Sparta's king,
As it is known she is, these moral laws
Of nature, and of nation, speak aloud
To have her back return'd : thus to persist
In doing wrong extenuates not wrong,
But makes it much more heavy. Hector's opinion
Is this, in way of truth : yet, ne'ertheless,
My spritely brethren, I propend to you   190
In resolution to keep Helen still ;

For 't is a cause that hath no mean dependance
Upon our joint and several dignities.
    Tro. Why, there you touch'd the life of our design :
Were it not glory that we more affected
Than the performance of our heaving spleens,
I would not wish a drop of Trojan blood
Spent more in her defence. But, worthy Hector,
She is a theme of honour and renown,
A spur to valiant and magnanimous deeds, 200
Whose present courage may beat down our foes,
And fame, in time to come, canonise us :
For, I presume, brave Hector would not lose
So rich advantage of a promis'd glory,
As smiles upon the forehead of this action,
For the wide world's revenue.
    Hect.   I am yours,
You valiant offspring of great Priamus.—
I have a roisting challenge sent amongst
The dull and factious nobles of the Greeks,
Will strike amazement to their drowsy spirits. 210
I was advertis'd, their great general slept,
Whilst emulation in the army crept :
This, I presume, will wake him.   *[Exeunt.*

SCENE III.—The Grecian Camp. Before ACHILLES'
              Tent.

Enter THERSITES.

    Ther. How now, Thersites? what ! lost in the laby-
rinth of thy fury? Shall the elephant Ajax carry it
thus? he beats me, and I rail at him : O worthy satisfaction ! 'would, it were otherwise, that I could beat
him, whilst he railed at me. 'Sfoot, I 'll learn to conjure and raise devils, but I 'll see some issue of my
spiteful execrations. Then, there 's Achilles,—a rare
enginer. If Troy be not taken till these two undermine it, the walls will stand till they fall of themselves. O thou great thunder-darter of Olympus !
forget that thou art Jove the king of gods, and,
Mercury, lose all the serpentine craft of thy caduceus,
if ye take not that little, little, less-than-little wit from
them that they have ; which short-armed ignorance
itself knows is so abundant scarce, it will not in
circumvention deliver a fly from a spider, without
drawing the massy irons and cutting the web. After
this, the vengeance on the whole camp ! or rather,
the Neapolitan bone-ache ; for that, methinks, is the
curse dependant on those that war for a placket. I
have said my prayers, and devil Envy, say Amen.
What, ho ! my Lord Achilles !   22

Enter PATROCLUS.

    Patr. Who's there? Thersites? Good Thersites,
come in and rail.
    Ther. If I could have remembered a gilt counter-
feit, thou wouldst not have slipped out of my contemplation ; but it is no matter : thyself upon thyself !
The common curse of mankind, folly and ignorance,
be thine in great revenue ! heaven bless thee from a
tutor, and discipline come not near thee ! Let thy
blood be thy direction till thy death ! then, if she, that
lays thee out, says thou art a fair corse, I 'll be sworn
and sworn upon 't, she never shrouded any but lazars.
Amen. Where's Achilles?
    Patr. What ! art thou devout? wast thou in prayer?
    Ther. Ay ; the heavens hear me !

Enter ACHILLES.

    Achil. Who's there?
    Patr. Thersites, my lord.
    Achil. Where, where?—Art thou come? Why, my
cheese, my digestion, why hast thou not served thyself in to my table so many meals? Come, what 's
Agamemnon?   42
    Ther. Thy commander, Achilles. Then tell me,
Patroclus, what 's Achilles?
    Patr. Thy lord, Thersites. Then tell me, I pray
thee, what 's thyself?
    Ther. Thy knower, Patroclus. Then tell me, Patro-
clus, what art thou?

Patr. Thou may'st tell, that knowest.
Achil. O! tell, tell.   50
Ther. I'll decline the whole question. Agamemnon
commands Achilles; Achilles is my lord; I am Pa-
troclus' knower; and Patroclus is a fool.
Patr. You rascal!
Ther. Peace, fool! I have not done.
Achil. He is a privileged man.—Proceed, Thersites.
Ther. Agamemnon is a fool; Achilles is a fool;
Thersites is a fool; and, as aforesaid, Patroclus is a
fool.
Achil. Derive this, come.   60
Ther. Agamemnon is a fool to offer to command
Achilles; Achilles is a fool to be commanded of
Agamemnon; Thersites is a fool to serve such a fool;
and Patroclus is a fool positive.
Patr. Why am I a fool?
Ther. Make that demand to the Creator. It suffices
me thou art. Look you, who comes here?   67

Enter AGAMEMNON, ULYSSES, NESTOR, DIOMEDES,
and AJAX.

Achil. Patroclus, I'll speak with nobody.—Come in
with me, Thersites.   [*Exit.*
Ther. Here is such patchery, such juggling, and
such knavery! all the argument is, a cuckold and a
whore; a good quarrel, to draw emulous factions, and
bleed to death upon. Now, the dry serpigo on the
subject, and war and lechery confound all! [*Exit.*
Agam. Where is Achilles?
Patr. Within his tent; but ill-dispos'd, my lord.
Agam. Let it be known to him that we are here.
He shent our messengers; and we lay by
Our appertainments, visiting of him:
Let him be told so; lest, perchance, he think   80
We dare not move the question of our place,
Or know not what we are.
Patr.   I shall say so to him. [*Exit.*
Ulyss. We saw him at the opening of his tent:
He is not sick.
Ajax. Yes, lion-sick, sick of proud heart: you may
call it melancholy, if you will favour the man; but,
by my head, 't is pride: but why? why? let him show
us a cause.—A word, my lord.
                              [*Taking* AGAMEMNON *aside.*
Nest. What moves Ajax thus to bay at him?
Ulyss. Achilles hath inveigled his fool from him.
Nest. Who? Thersites?   91
Ulyss. He.
Nest. Then will Ajax lack matter, if he have lost
his argument.
Ulyss. No, you see, he is his argument that has his
argument, Achilles.
Nest. All the better; their fraction is more our wish
than their faction: but it was a strong counsel, a fool
could disunite.
Ulyss. The amity that wisdom knits not, folly may
easily untie. Here comes Patroclus.   101
Nest. No Achilles with him?

Re-enter PATROCLUS.

Ulyss. The elephant hath joints, but none for cour-
tesy: his legs are legs for necessity, not for flexure.
Patr. Achilles bids me say, he is much sorry,
If anything more than your sport and pleasure
Did move your greatness, and this noble state,
To call upon him; he hopes, it is no other
But, for your health and your digestion sake,
An after-dinner's breath.
Agam.   Hear you, Patroclus.   110
We are too well acquainted with these answers;
But his evasion, wing'd thus swift with scorn,
Cannot outfly our apprehensions.
Much attribute he hath, and much the reason
Why we ascribe it to him; yet all his virtues,
Not virtuously on his own part beheld,
Do in our eyes begin to lose their gloss;
Yea, like fair fruit in an unwholesome dish,
Are like to rot untasted. Go and tell him,
We come to speak with him; and you shall not sin,
If you do say, we think him over-proud,   121
And under-honest; in self-assumption greater

Than in the note of judgment; and worthier than
  himself
Here tend the savage strangeness he puts on,
Disguise the holy strength of their command,
And underwrite in an observing kind
His humorous predominance; yea, watch
His pettish lunes, his ebbs, his flows, as if
The passage and whole carriage of this action
Rode on his tide. Go, tell him this; and add,   130
That, if he overhold his price so much,
We'll none of him; but let him, like an engine
Not portable, lie under this report:—
Bring action hither, this cannot go to war;
A stirring dwarf we do allowance give
Before a sleeping giant:—tell him so.
Patr. I shall; and bring his answer presently.
                                                  [*Exit.*
Agam. In second voice we'll not be satisfied;
We come to speak with him.—Ulysses, enter you.
                                         [*Exit* ULYSSES.
Ajax. What is he more than another?   140
Agam. No more than what he thinks he is.
Ajax. Is he so much? Do you not think, he thinks
himself a better man than I am?
Agam. No question.
Ajax. Will you subscribe his thought, and say he is?
Agam. No, noble ·Ajax; you are as strong, as
valiant, as wise, no less noble, much more gentle, and
altogether more tractable.
Ajax. Why should a man be proud? How doth
pride grow? I know not what pride is.   150
Agam. Your mind is the clearer, Ajax, and your
virtues the fairer. He that is proud eats up himself:
pride is his own glass, his own trumpet, his own
chronicle; and whatever praises itself but in the
deed, devours the deed in the praise.
Ajax. I do hate a proud man, as I hate the engen-
dering of toads.
Nest. [*Aside.*] Yet he loves himself: is 't not strange?

Re-enter ULYSSES.

Ulyss. Achilles will not to the field to-morrow.
Agam. What's his excuse?
Ulyss.   He doth rely on none:
But carries on the stream of his dispose   161
Without observance or respect of any,
In will peculiar and in self-admission.
Agam. Why, will he not, upon our fair request,
Untent his person, and share the air with us?
Ulyss. Things small as nothing, for request's sake
  only,
He makes important. Possess'd he is with greatness;
And speaks not to himself, but with a pride
That quarrels at self-breath: imagin'd worth
Holds in his blood such swoln and hot discourse,   170
That, 'twixt his mental and his active parts,
Kingdom'd Achilles in commotion rages,
And batters 'gainst itself: what should I say?
He is so plaguy proud, that the death-tokens of it
Cry—"No recovery."
Agam.   Let Ajax go to him.—
Dear lord, go you and greet him in his tent:
'T is said, he holds you well; and will be led,
At your request, a little from himself.
Ulyss. O Agamemnon! let it not be so.
We'll consecrate the steps that Ajax makes   180
When they go from Achilles: shall the proud lord,
That bates his arrogance with his own seam,
And never suffers matter of the world
Enter his thoughts,—save such as do revolve
And ruminate himself,—shall he be worshipp'd
Of that we hold an idol more than he?
No, this thrice-worthy and right valiant lord
Must not so stale his palm, nobly acquir'd;
Nor, by my will, assubjugate his merit,
As amply titled as Achilles is,   190
By going to Achilles:
That were to inlard his fat-already pride;
And add more coals to Cancer, when he burns
With entertaining great Hyperion.
This lord go to him! Jupiter forbid,
And say in thunder—"Achilles, go to him."

Nest. [*Aside.*] O! this is well; he rubs the vein of him.

Dio. [*Aside.*] And how his silence drinks up this applause!

Ajax. If I go to him, with my armed fist I 'll pash him o'er the face.   200

Agam. O, no! you shall not go.

Ajax. An 'a be proud with me, I 'll pheese his pride. Let me go to him.

Ulyss. Not for the worth that hangs upon our quarrel.

Ajax. A paltry, insolent fellow!

Nest. [*Aside.*] How he describes himself!

Ajax. Can he not be sociable?

Ulyss. [*Aside.*] The raven chides blackness.

Ajax. I 'll let his humours blood.

Agam. [*Aside.*] He will be the physician, that should be the patient.   211

Ajax. An all men were o' my mind,—

Ulyss. [*Aside.*] Wit would be out of fashion.

Ajax. 'A should not bear it so, 'a should eat swords first: shall pride carry it?

Nest. [*Aside.*] An 't would, you 'd carry half.

Ulyss. [*Aside.*] 'A would have ten shares.

Ajax. I will knead him; I will make him supple.

Nest. [*Aside.*] He 's not yet thorough warm: force him with praises. Pour in, pour in; his ambition is dry.   221

Ulyss. [*To* AGAMEMNON.] My lord, you feed too much on this dislike.

Nest. Our noble general, do not do so.

Dio. You must prepare to fight without Achilles.

Ulyss. Why, 't is this naming of him does him harm.

Here is a man—But 't is before his face; I will be silent.

Nest.   Wherefore should you so? He is not emulous, as Achilles is.

Ulyss. Know the whole world, he is as valiant.

Ajax. A whoreson dog, that shall palter thus with us!   230 'Would, he were a Trojan!

Nest. What a vice were it in Ajax now,—

Ulyss. If he were proud,—

Dio.   Or covetous of praise,—

Ulyss. Ay, or surly borne,—

Dio.   Or strange, or self-affected!

Ulyss. Thank the heavens, lord, thou art of sweet composure;

Praise him that got thee, she that gave thee suck:

Fam'd be thy tutor, and thy parts of nature

Thrice-fam'd, beyond all erudition:

But he that disciplin'd thine arms to fight,

Let Mars divide eternity in twain,   240

And give him half: and, for thy vigour,

Bull-bearing Milo his addition yield

To sinewy Ajax. I will not praise thy wisdom,

Which, like a bourn, a pale, a shore, confines

Thy spacious and dilated parts: here 's Nestor;

Instructed by the antiquary times,

He must, he is, he cannot but be wise:

But pardon, father Nestor, were your days

As green as Ajax', and your brain so temper'd,

You should not have the eminence of him,   250

But be as Ajax.

Ajax.   Shall I call you father?

Nest. Ay, my good son.

Dio.   Be rul'd by him, Lord Ajax.

Ulyss. There is no tarrying here: the hart Achilles

Keeps thicket. Please it our great general

To call together all his state of war;

Fresh kings are come to Troy: to-morrow,

We must with all our main of power stand fast:

And here 's a lord,—come knights from east to west,

And cull their flower, Ajax shall cope the best.

Agam. Go we to council. Let Achilles sleep: 260

Light boats sail swift, though greater hulks draw deep.   [*Exeunt.*

ACT III.

SCENE I.—Troy. A Room in PRIAM'S Palace.

Enter PANDARUS *and a Servant.*

Pandarus.

FRIEND! you! pray you, a word. Do not you follow the young Lord Paris?

Serv. Ay, sir, when he goes before me.

Pan. You depend upon him, I mean.

Serv. Sir, I do depend upon the lord.

Pan. You depend upon a noble gentleman: I must needs praise him.

Serv. The lord be praised!

Pan. You know me, do you not?

Serv. 'Faith, sir, superficially.   10

Pan. Friend, know me better. I am the Lord Pandarus.

Serv. I hope, I shall know your honour better.

Pan. I do desire it.

Serv. You are in the state of grace.

Pan. Grace! not so, friend; honour and lordship are my titles.—[*Music within.*] What music is this?

Serv. I do but partly know, sir: it is music in parts.   21

Pan. Know you the musicians?

Serv. Wholly, sir.

Pan. Who play they to?

Serv. To the hearers, sir.

Pan. At whose pleasure, friend?

Serv. At mine, sir, and theirs that love music.

Pan. Command, I mean, friend.

Serv. Who shall I command, sir?   29

Pan. Friend, we understand not one another: I am too courtly, and thou art too cunning. At whose request do these men play?

Serv. That 's to 't, indeed, sir. Marry, sir, at the request of Paris, my lord, who is there in person; with him the mortal Venus, the heart-blood of beauty, love's invisible soul.

Pan. Who, my cousin Cressida?

Serv. No, sir, Helen: could you not find out that by her attributes?   39

Pan. It should seem, fellow, that thou hast not seen the Lady Cressida. I come to speak with Paris from the Prince Troilus: I will make a complimental assault upon him, for my business seethes.

Serv. Sodden business: there 's a steward phrase, indeed.

Enter Paris *and* Helen, *attended.*

Pan. Fair be to you, my lord, and to all this fair company! fair desires, in all fair measure, fairly guide them! especially to you, fair queen! fair thoughts be your fair pillow!

Helen. Dear lord, you are full of fair words.   50

Pan. You speak your fair pleasure, sweet queen.— Fair prince, here is good broken music.

Par. You have broke it, cousin; and, by my life, you shall make it whole again: you shall piece it out with a piece of your performance.—Nell, he is full of harmony.

Pan. Truly, lady, no.

Helen. O, sir!—

Pan. Rude, in sooth; in good sooth, very rude.   59

Par. Well said, my lord! Well, you say so in fits.

Pan. I have business to my lord, dear queen.—My lord, will you vouchsafe me a word?

Helen. Nay, this shall not hedge us out: we'll hear you sing, certainly.

Helen. "Nay, this shall not hedge us out: we'll hear you sing, certainly."

Pan. Well, sweet queen, you are pleasant with me. But, marry, thus, my lord.—My dear lord, and most esteemed friend, your brother Troilus,—

Helen. My Lord Pandarus; honey-sweet lord,—

Pan. Go to, sweet queen, go to:—commends himself most affectionately to you.   70

Helen. You shall not bob us out of our melody: if you do, our melancholy upon your head!

Pan. Sweet queen, sweet queen; that's a sweet queen,—i' faith,—

Helen. And to make a sweet lady sad is a sour offence.

Pan. Nay, that shall not serve your turn; that shall it not, in truth, la! Nay, I care not for such words; no, no.—And, my lord, he desires you, that if the king call for him at supper, you will make his excuse.   80

Helen. My Lord Pandarus,—

Pan. What says my sweet queen,—my very very sweet queen?

Par. What exploit's in hand? where sups he to-night?

Helen. Nay, but, my lord,—

Pan. What says my sweet queen? My cousin will fall out with you.—You must not know where he sups.

Par. I'll lay my life, with my disposer Cressida.

Pan. No, no; no such matter, you are wide. Come, your disposer is sick.   91

Par. Well, I'll make excuse.

Pan. Ay, good my lord. Why should you say Cressida? no, your poor disposer's sick.

Par. I spy.

Pan. You spy! what do you spy?—Come, give me an instrument.—Now, sweet queen.

Helen. Why, this is kindly done.

Pan. My niece is horribly in love with a thing you have, sweet queen.   100

Helen. She shall have it, my lord, if it be not my Lord Paris.

Pan. He! no, she'll none of him; they two are twain.

Helen. Falling in, after falling out, may make them three.

Pan. Come, come, I'll hear no more of this. I'll sing you a song now.

Helen. Ay, ay, pr'ythee now. By my troth, sweet lord, thou hast a fine forehead.   110

Pan. Ay, you may, you may.

Helen. Let thy song be love: this love will undo us all. O Cupid, Cupid, Cupid!

Pan. Love! ay, that it shall, i' faith.

Par. Ay, good now, love, love, nothing but love.

Pan. In good troth, it begins so.   [*Sings.*

> *Love, love, nothing but love, still more!*
>   *For, oh! love's bow*
>   *Shoots buck and doe:*
>   *The shaft confounds,*   120
>   *Not that it wounds,*
> *But tickles still the sore.*

> *These lovers cry—Oh! oh! they die!*
>   *Yet that which seems the wound to kill,*
> *Doth turn oh! oh! to ha! ha! he!*
>   *So dying love lives still:*
>   *Oh! oh! a while, but ha! ha! ha!*
>   *Oh! oh! groans out for ha! ha! ha!*

Heigh-ho!   129

Helen. In love, i' faith, to the very tip of the nose.

Par. He eats nothing but doves, love; and that breeds hot blood, and hot blood begets hot thoughts, and hot thoughts beget hot deeds, and hot deeds is love.

Pan. Is this the generation of love? hot blood, hot thoughts, and hot deeds? Why, they are vipers: is love a generation of vipers? Sweet lord, who's afield to-day?

Par. Hector, Deiphobus, Helenus, Antenor, and all the gallantry of Troy: I would fain have armed to-day, but my Nell would not have it so. How chance my brother Troilus went not?   142

Helen. He hangs the lip at something:—you know all, Lord Pandarus.

Pan. Not I, honey-sweet queen.—I long to hear how they sped to-day. — You'll remember your brother's excuse?

Par. To a hair.

Pan. Farewell, sweet queen.

Helen. Commend me to your niece.   150

Pan. I will, sweet queen.   [*Exit.*

                                        [*A retreat sounded.*

Par. They're come from field: let us to Priam's hall, To greet the warriors. Sweet Helen, I must woo you To help unarm our Hector: his stubborn buckles, With these your white enchanting fingers touch'd, Shall more obey than to the edge of steel, Or force of Greekish sinews: you shall do more Than all the island kings,—disarm great Hector.

Helen. 'T will make us proud to be his servant, Paris: 160
Yea, what he shall receive of us in duty,
Gives us more palm in beauty than we have,
Yea, overshines ourself.

Par. Sweet, above thought I love thee.   [*Exeunt.*

Scene II.—*The Same.* Pandarus' *Orchard.*

Enter Pandarus *and a Servant, meeting.*

Pan. How now? where's thy master? at my cousin Cressida's?

Serv. No, sir; he stays for you to conduct him thither.

Enter Troilus.

Pan. O! here he comes.—How now, how now?

Tro. Sirrah, walk off.   [*Exit Servant.*
Pan. Have you seen my cousin?
Tro. No, Pandarus: I stalk about her door,
Like a strange soul upon the Stygian banks
Staying for waftage. O! be thou my Charon;   10
And give me swift transportation to those fields,
Where I may wallow in the lily-beds
Propos'd for the deserver. O gentle Pandarus!
From Cupid's shoulder pluck his painted wings,
And fly with me to Cressid.
Pan. Walk here i' the orchard. I'll bring her
straight.   [*Exit.*
Tro. I am giddy: expectation whirls me round.
The imaginary relish is so sweet

Pan. "Come, draw this curtain, and let's see your picture."

That it enchants my sense. What will it be,   20
When that the watery palate tastes indeed
Love's thrice-reputed nectar? death, I fear me;
Swounding destruction; or some joy too fine,
Too subtle-potent, and too sharp in sweetness,
For the capacity of my ruder powers.
I fear it much; and I do fear besides,
That I shall lose distinction in my joys;
As doth a battle, when they charge on heaps
The enemy flying.   29

Re-enter PANDARUS.

Pan. She's making her ready; she'll come straight:
you must be witty now. She does so blush, and
fetches her wind so short, as if she were frayed with
a sprite: I'll fetch her. It is the prettiest villain:
she fetches her breath so short as a new-ta'en sparrow.
                                              [*Exit.*
Tro. Even such a passion doth embrace my bosom:
My heart beats thicker than a feverous pulse,
And all my powers do their bestowing lose,
Like vassalage at unawares encountering
The eye of majesty.   39

Enter PANDARUS and CRESSIDA.

Pan. Come, come, what need you blush? shame's
a baby.—Here she is now: swear the oaths now to
her, that you have sworn to me.—What! are you gone
again? you must be watched ere you be made tame,
must you? Come your ways, come your ways; an
you draw backward, we'll put you i' the fills.—Why
do you not speak to her?—Come, draw this curtain,
and let's see your picture.—Alas the day, how loath
you are to offend daylight! an 't were dark, you'd
close sooner. So, so; rub on, and kiss the mistress.
How now! a kiss in fee-farm! build there, carpenter;
the air is sweet. Nay, you shall fight your hearts out,
ere I part you. The falcon as the tercel, for all the
ducks i' the river: go to, go to.

Tro. You have bereft me of all words, lady.
Pan. Words pay no debts, give her deeds; but
she'll bereave you of the deeds too, if she call your
activity in question. What! billing again? Here's—
"In witness whereof the parties interchangeably"—
Come in, come in: I'll go get a fire.   [*Exit.*
Cres. Will you walk in, my lord?   60
Tro. O Cressida! how often have I wished me thus!
Cres. Wished, my lord?—The gods grant.—O my
lord!
Tro. What should they grant? what makes this
pretty abruption? What too curious dreg espies my
sweet lady in the fountain of our love?
Cres. More dregs than water, if my fears have eyes.
Tro. Fears make devils of cherubins; they never
see truly.
Cres. Blind fear, that seeing reason leads, finds safer
footing than blind reason, stumbling without fear: to
fear the worst oft cures the worse.   72
Tro. O! let my lady apprehend no fear: in all
Cupid's pageant there is presented no monster.
Cres. Nor nothing monstrous neither?
Tro. Nothing, but our undertakings; when we vow
to weep seas, live in fire, eat rocks, tame tigers;
thinking it harder for our mistress to devise imposition enough, than for us to undergo any difficulty
imposed. This is the monstruosity in love, lady,—
that the will is infinite, and the execution confined;
that the desire is boundless, and the act a slave to limit.
Cres. They say, all lovers swear more performance
than they are able, and yet reserve an ability that
they never perform; vowing more than the perfection
of ten, and discharging less than the tenth part of one.
They that have the voice of lions, and the act of hares,
are they not monsters?   88
Tro. Are there such? such are not we. Praise us
as we are tasted; allow us as we prove; our head
shall go bare, till merit crown it. No perfection in
reversion shall have a praise in present: we will not
name desert, before his birth, and, being born, his
addition shall be humble. Few words to fair faith:
Troilus shall be such to Cressid, as what envy can say
worst, shall be a mock for his truth; and what truth
can speak truest, not truer than Troilus.
Cres. Will you walk in, my lord?

Re-enter PANDARUS.

Pan. What! blushing still? have you not done
talking yet?   100
Cres. Well, uncle, what folly I commit, I dedicate
to you.
Pan. I thank you for that: if my lord get a boy of
you, you'll give him me. Be true to my lord; if he
flinch, chide me for it.
Tro. You know now your hostages; your uncle's
word, and my firm faith.
Pan. Nay, I'll give my word for her too. Our
kindred, though they be long ere they be wooed,
they are constant, being won: they are burs, I can
tell you; they'll stick where they are thrown.   111
Cres. Boldness comes to me now, and brings me
heart.—
Prince Troilus, I have lov'd you night and day,
For many weary months.
Tro. Why was my Cressid then so hard to win?
Cres. Hard to seem won; but I was won, my lord,
With the first glance that ever—Pardon me :—
If I confess much, you will play the tyrant.
I love you now; but not, till now, so much
But I might master it.—In faith, I lie: 120
My thoughts were like unbridled children, grown
Too headstrong for their mother. See, we fools!
Why have I blabb'd? who shall be true to us,
When we are so unsecret to ourselves?—
But, though I lov'd you well, I woo'd you not;
And yet, good faith, I wish'd myself a man,
Or that we women had men's privilege
Of speaking first. Sweet, bid me hold my tongue:
For, in this rapture, I shall surely speak
The thing I shall repent. See, see! your silence, 130
Cunning in dumbness, from my weakness draws
My very soul of counsel. Stop my mouth.

Tro. And shall, albeit sweet music issues thence.
Pan. Pretty, i' faith.
Cres. My lord, I do beseech you, pardon me ;
'T was not my purpose, thus to beg a kiss :
I am asham'd :—O heavens ! what have I done ?—
For this time will I take my leave, my lord.
Tro. Your leave, sweet Cressid ?
Pan. Leave ! an you take leave till to-morrow
morning,—   141
Cres. Pray you, content you.
Tro.   What offends you, lady ?
Cres. Sir, mine own company.
Tro. You cannot shun yourself.
Cres. Let me go and try.
I have a kind of self resides with you ;
But an unkind self, that itself will leave,
To be another's fool.—Where is my wit ?
I would be gone.—I speak I know not what.
Tro. Well know they what they speak, that speak
so wisely.   150
Cres. Perchance, my lord, I show more craft than
love,
And fell so roundly to a large confession,
To angle for your thoughts : but you are wise,
Or else you love not, for to be wise, and love,
Exceeds man's might ; that dwells with gods above.
Tro. O ! that I thought it could be in a woman,
(As, if it can, I will presume in you,)
To feed for aye her lamp and flames of love ;
To keep her constancy in plight and youth,
Outliving beauty's outward, with a mind   160
That doth renew swifter than blood decays :
Or, that persuasion could but thus convince me,
That my integrity and truth to you
Might be affronted with the match and weight
Of such a winnow'd purity in love ;
How were I then uplifted ! but, alas !
I am as true as truth's simplicity,
And simpler than the infancy of truth.
Cres. In that I 'll war with you.
Tro.   O virtuous fight !
When right with right wars who shall be most right.
True swains in love shall, in the world to come,   171
Approve their truths by Troilus : when their rhymes,
Full of protest, of oath, and big compare,
Want similes, truth tir'd with iteration,—
As true as steel, as plantage to the moon,
As sun to day, as turtle to her mate,
As iron to adamant, as earth to the centre,
Yet, after all comparisons of truth,
As truth's authentic author to be cited,
As true as Troilus shall crown up the verse,   180
And sanctify the numbers.
Cres.   Prophet may you be !
If I be false, or swerve a hair from truth,
When time is old and hath forgot itself,
When waterdrops have worn the stones of Troy,
And blind oblivion swallow'd cities up,
And mighty states characterless are grated
To dusty nothing ; yet let memory,
From false to false, among false maids in love,
Upbraid my falsehood ! when they have said, as
false
As air, as water, wind, or sandy earth,   190
As fox to lamb, as wolf to heifer's calf,
Pard to the hind, or stepdame to her son ;
Yea, let them say, to stick the heart of falsehood,
As false as Cressid.
Pan. Go to, a bargain made ; seal it, seal it : I 'll
be the witness.—Here I hold your hand ; here, my
cousin's. If ever you prove false one to another, since
I have taken such pains to bring you together, let all
pitiful goers-between be called to the world's end after
my name, call them all Pandars ; let all constant men
be Troiluses, all false women Cressids, and all brokers
between Pandars ! say, Amen.   202
Tro. Amen.
Cres. Amen.
Pan. Amen. Whereupon I will show you a
chamber with a bed ; which bed, because it shall
not speak of your pretty encounters, press it to death :
away !

And Cupid grant all tongue-tied maidens here
Bed, chamber, Pandar to provide this gear !   210
                                                [Exeunt.

SCENE III.—The Grecian Camp.

Enter AGAMEMNON, ULYSSES, DIOMEDES, NESTOR,
AJAX, MENELAUS, *and* CALCHAS.

Cal. Now, princes, for the service I have done you,
The advantage of the time prompts me aloud
To call for recompense. Appear it to your mind,
That, through the sight I bear in things to come,
I have abandon'd Troy, left my possession,
Incurr'd a traitor's name ; expos'd myself,
From certain and possess'd conveniences,
To doubtful fortunes, sequestering from me all
That time, acquaintance, custom, and condition,
Made tame and most familiar to my nature ;   10
And here, to do you service, am become
As new into the world, strange, unacquainted :
I do beseech you, as in way of taste,
To give me now a little benefit,
Out of those many register'd in promise,
Which, you say, live to come in my behalf.
Agam. What wouldst thou of us, Trojan ? make
demand.
Cal. You have a Trojan prisoner, call'd Antenor,
Yesterday took : Troy holds him very dear.
Oft have you (often have you thanks therefore)   20
Desir'd my Cressid in right great exchange,
Whom Troy hath still denied ; but this Antenor,
I know, is such a wrest in their affairs,
That their negotiations all must slack,
Wanting his manage ; and they will almost
Give us a prince of blood, a son of Priam,
In change of him : let him be sent, great princes,
And he shall buy my daughter ; and her presence
Shall quite strike off all service I have done,
In most accepted pain.
Agam.   Let Diomedes bear him,   30
And bring us Cressid hither : Calchas shall have
What he requests of us.—Good Diomed,
Furnish you fairly for this interchange :
Withal, bring word, if Hector will to-morrow
Be answer'd in his challenge : Ajax is ready.
Dio. This shall I undertake ; and 'tis a burden
Which I am proud to bear.
                    [Exeunt DIOMEDES *and* CALCHAS.

Enter ACHILLES *and* PATROCLUS, *before their Tent.*

Ulyss. Achilles stands i' the entrance of his tent :
Please it our general to pass strangely by him,
As if he were forgot ; and, princes all,   40
Lay negligent and loose regard upon him :
I will come last. 'T is like, he 'll question me,
Why such unplausive eyes are bent on him :
If so, I have derision medicinable,
To use between your strangeness and his pride,
Which his own will shall have desire to drink.
It may do good : pride hath no other glass
To show itself, but pride ; for supple knees
Feed arrogance, and are the proud man's fees.
Agam. We 'll execute your purpose, and put on   50
A form of strangeness as we pass along :—
So do each lord ; and either greet him not,
Or else disdainfully, which shall shake him more
Than if not look'd on. I will lead the way.
Achil. What ! comes the general to speak with me ?
You know my mind : I 'll fight no more 'gainst Troy.
Agam. What says Achilles ? would he aught with
us ?
Nest. Would you, my lord, aught with the general ?
Achil. No.
Nest. Nothing, my lord.
Agam. The better.   60
                    [Exeunt AGAMEMNON *and* NESTOR.
Achil. Good day, good day.
Men. How do you ? how do you ?   *[Exit.*
Achil. What ! does the cuckold scorn me ?
Ajax. How now, Patroclus ?
Achil. Good morrow, Ajax.

Ajax. Ha?
Achil. Good morrow.
Ajax. Ay, and good next day too.   [*Exit.*
Achil. What mean these fellows? Know they not
  Achilles?   70
Patr. They pass by strangely: they were us'd to bend,
To send their smiles before them to Achilles;
To come as humbly as they us'd to creep
To holy altars.
Achil.   What! am I poor of late?
'T is certain, greatness, once fall'n out with fortune,
Must fall out with men too: what the declin'd is,
He shall as soon read in the eyes of others,
As feel in his own fall; for men, like butterflies,
Show not their mealy wings but to the summer,
And not a man, for being simply man,   80
Hath any honour; but honour for those honours
That are without him, as place, riches, and favour,
Prizes of accident as oft as merit:
Which, when they fall, as being slippery standers,
The love that lean'd on them as slippery too,
Doth one pluck down another, and together
Die in the fall. But 't is not so with me:
Fortune and I are friends: I do enjoy
At ample point all that I did possess,
Save these men's looks; who do, methinks, find out 90
Something not worth in me such rich beholding
As they have often given. Here is Ulysses:
I'll interrupt his reading.—
How now, Ulysses?
Ulyss.   Now, great Thetis' son!
Achil. What are you reading?
Ulyss.   A strange fellow here
Writes me: That man, how dearly ever parted,
How much in having, or without, or In,
Cannot make boast to have that which he hath,
Nor feels not what he owes, but by reflection;
As when his virtues shining upon others   100
Heat them, and they retort that heat again
To the first giver.
Achil.   This is not strange, Ulysses.
The beauty that is borne here in the face
The bearer knows not, but commends itself
To others' eyes: nor doth the eye itself,
That most pure spirit of sense, behold itself,
Not going from itself; but eye to eye oppos'd
Salutes each other with each other's form:
For speculation turns not to itself
Till it hath travell'd, and is married there   110
Where it may see itself. This is not strange at all.
Ulyss. I do not strain at the position,
It is familiar, but at the author's drift;
Who in his circumstance expressly proves,
That no man is the lord of anything,
(Though in and of him there be much consisting,
Till he communicate his parts to others:
Nor doth he of himself know them for aught
Till he behold them form'd in the applause
Where they're extended; who, like an arch, rever-   120
  berates
The voice again; or, like a gate of steel
Fronting the sun, receives and renders back
His figure and his heat. I was much rapt in this;
And apprehended here immediately
The unknown Ajax.
Heavens, what a man is there! a very horse;
That has he knows not what. Nature, what things
  there are,
Most abject in regard, and dear in use!
What things, again, most dear in the esteem,
And poor in worth! Now shall we see to-morrow—
An act that very chance doth throw upon him—   131
Ajax renown'd. O heavens, what some men do,
While some men leave to do!
How some men creep in skittish Fortune's hall,
Whiles others play the idiots in her eyes!
How one man eats into another's pride,
While pride is feasting in his wantonness!
To see these Grecian lords!—why, even already
They clap the lubber Ajax on the shoulder,
As if his foot were on brave Hector's breast,   140
And great Troy shrinking.

Achil. I do believe it; for they pass'd by me,
As misers do by beggars, neither gave to me
Good word nor look. What! are my deeds forgot?
Ulyss. Time hath, my lord, a wallet at his back,
Wherein he puts alms for oblivion;
A great-siz'd monster of ingratitudes:
Those scraps are good deeds past; which are devour'd
As fast as they are made, forgot as soon
As done: perseverance, dear my lord,   150
Keeps honour bright: to have done, is to hang
Quite out of fashion, like a rusty mail
In monumental mockery. Take the instant way;
For honour travels in a strait so narrow,
Where one but goes abreast: keep then the path;
For emulation hath a thousand sons,
That one by one pursue: if you give way,
Or hedge aside from the direct forthright,
Like to an enter'd tide, they all rush by,
And leave you hindmost;   160
Or, like a gallant horse fall'n in fl st rank,
Lie there for pavement to the abject rear,
O'er-run and tramp ed on: then what they do in present,
Though less than yours in past, must o'er-top yours;
For time is like a fashionable host,
That slightly shakes his parting guest by the hand,
And with his arms outstretch'd, as he would fly,
Grasps-in the comer: welcome ever smiles,
And farewell goes out sighing. O, let not virtue seek
Remuneration for the thing it was;   170
For beauty, wit,
High birth, vigour of bone, desert in service,
Love, friendship, charity, are subjects all
To envious and calumniating time.
One touch of nature makes the whole world kin,
That all, with one consent, praise new-born gawds,
Though they are made and moulded of things past,
And give to dust, that is a little gilt,
More laud than gilt o'er-dusted.
The present eye praises the present object: 180
Then marvel not, thou great and complete man,
That all the Greeks begin to worship Ajax;
Since things in motion sooner catch the eye,
Than what not stirs. The cry went once on thee,
And still it might, and yet it may again,
If thou wouldst not entomb thyself alive,
And case thy reputation in thy tent;
Whose glorious deeds, but in these fields of late,
Made emulous missions 'mongst the gods themselves,
And drave great Mars to faction.
Achil.   Of this my privacy
I have strong reasons.
Ulyss.   But 'gainst your privacy   191
The reasons are more potent and heroical.
'T is known, Achilles, that you are in love
With one of Priam's daughters.
Achil. Ha! known?
Ulyss. Is that a wonder?
The providence that's in a watchful state,
Knows almost every grain of Plutus' gold,
Finds bottom in the uncomprehensive deeps,
Keeps place with thought, and almost, like the gods,
Does thoughts unveil in their dumb cradles.   201
There is a mystery (with whom relation
Durst never meddle) in the soul of state,
Which hath an operation more divine,
Than breath, or pen, can give expressure to.
All the commerce that you have had with Troy,
As perfectly is ours, as yours, my lord;
And better would it fit Achilles much
To throw down Hector, than Polyxena;
But it must grieve young Pyrrhus, now at home,   210
When fame shall in our islands sound her trump,
And all the Greekish girls shall tripping sing,—
"Great Hector's sister did Achilles win,
But our great Ajax bravely beat down him."
Farewell, my lord: I as your lover speak;
The fool slides o'er the ice that you should break.
          [*Exit.*
Patr. To this effect, Achilles, have I mov'd you.
A woman impudent and mannish grown
Is not more loath'd, than an effeminate man
In time of action. I stand condemn'd for this: 220

They think, my little stomach to the war,
And your great love to me, restrains you thus.
Sweet, rouse yourself; and the weak wanton Cupid
Shall from your neck unloose his amorous fold,
And, like a dew-drop from the lion's mane,
Be shook to air.

Achil. Go call Thersites hither, sweet Patroclus.
I'll send the fool to Ajax, and desire him
To invite the Trojan lords, after the combat,
To see us here unarm'd. I have a woman's longing,
An appetite that I am sick withal,
To see great Hector in his weeds of peace;   240

Ther. "Let Patroclus make his demands to me, you shall see the pageant of Ajax."

Achil.   Shall Ajax fight with Hector?
Patr. Ay; and, perhaps, receive much honour by him.
Achil. I see, my reputation is at stake;
My fame is shrewdly gor'd.
Patr.   O! then beware:
Those wounds heal ill that men do give themselves:
Omission to do what is necessary   231
Seals a commission to a blank of danger;
And danger, like an ague, subtly taints
Even then when we sit idly in the sun.

To talk with him, and to behold his visage,
Even to my full of view.—A labour sav'd!

                    Enter THERSITES.

Ther. A wonder!
Achil. What?
Ther. Ajax goes up and down the field, asking for himself.
Achil. How so?
Ther. He must fight singly to-morrow with Hector;

and is so prophetically proud of an heroical cudgelling, that he raves in saying nothing.   250
Achil. How can that be?
Ther. Why, he stalks up and down like a peacock; a stride, and a stand: ruminates like an hostess that hath no arithmetic but her brain to set down her reckoning: bites his lip with a politic regard, as who should say, there were wit in his head, an 't would out: and so there is; but it lies as coldly in him as fire in a flint, which will not show without knocking. The man's undone for ever; for if Hector break not his neck i' the combat, he 'll break 't himself in vainglory. He knows not me: I said, "Good morrow, Ajax;" and he replies, "Thanks, Agamemnon." What think you of this man, that takes me for the general? He's grown a very land-fish, languageless, a monster. A plague of opinion! a man may wear it on both sides, like a leather jerkin.
Achil. Thou must be my ambassador to him, Thersites.   268
Ther. Who, I? why, he 'll answer nobody; he professes not answering: speaking is for beggars; he wears his tongue in his arms. I will put on his presence: let Patroclus make his demands to me, you shall see the pageant of Ajax.
Achil. To him, Patroclus: tell him, I humbly desire the valiant Ajax to invite the most valorous Hector to come unarmed to my tent; and to procure safe-conduct for his person of the magnanimous, and most illustrious, six-or-seven-times-honoured captain-general of the Grecian army, Agamemnon, et cætera. Do this.
Patr. Jove bless great Ajax!   280
Ther. Humph!
Patr. I come from the worthy Achilles,—
Ther. Ha?
Patr. Who most humbly desires you to invite Hector to his tent,—
Ther. Humph!
Patr. And to procure safe-conduct from Agamemnon.
Ther. Agamemnon?
Patr. Ay, my lord.   290
Ther. Ha?
Patr. What say you to 't?
Ther. God be wi' you, with all my heart.
Patr. Your answer, sir.
Ther. If to-morrow be a fair day, by eleven o'clock it will go one way or other; howsoever, he shall pay for me ere he has me.
Patr. Your answer, sir.
Ther. Fare you well, with all my heart.
Achil. Why, but he is not in this tune, is he?   300

Ther. "I had rather be a tick in a sheep, than such a valiant ignorance."

Ther. No, but he 's out o' tune thus. What music will be in him when Hector has knocked out his brains, I know not; but, I am sure, none, unless the fiddler Apollo get his sinews to make catlings on.
Achil. Come, thou shalt bear a letter to him straight.
Ther. Let me bear another to his horse, for that 's the more capable creature.
Achil. My mind is troubled, like a fountain stirr'd;
And I myself see not the bottom of it.   309
[*Exeunt* ACHILLES *and* PATROCLUS.
Ther. 'Would the fountain of your mind were clear again, that I might water an ass at it. I had rather be a tick in a sheep, than such a valiant ignorance.
[*Exit.*

ACT IV.

SCENE I.—Troy. A Street.

Enter, at one side, ÆNEAS, *and Servant, with a torch; at the other,* PARIS, DEIPHOBUS, ANTENOR, DIOMEDES, *and others, with torches.*

Paris.
EE ho! who is that there?
Dei.   It is the Lord Æneas.
Æne. Is the prince there in person?—
Had I so good occasion to lie long,
As you, Prince Paris, nothing but heavenly business
Should rob my bed-mate of my company.
Dio. That 's my mind too.—Good morrow, Lord Æneas.
Par. A valiant Greek, Æneas; take his hand:
Witness the process of your speech, wherein
You told how Diomed, a whole week by days,
Did haunt you in the field.
Æne.   Health to you, valiant sir,   10
During all question of the gentle truce;
But when I meet you arm'd, as black defiance,
As heart can think, or courage execute.
Dio. The one and other Diomed embraces.
Our bloods are now in calm, and, so long, health:
But when contention and occasion meet,
By Jove, I 'll play the hunter for thy life,
With all my force, pursuit, and policy.
Æne. And thou shalt hunt a lion, that will fly
With his face backward.—In humane gentleness,   20
Welcome to Troy: now, by Anchises' life,
Welcome, indeed. By Venus' hand I swear,
No man alive can love, in such a sort,
The thing he means to kill, more excellently.
Dio. We sympathise.—Jove, let Æneas live,

If to my sword his fate be not the glory,
A thousand complete courses of the sun!
But, in mine emulous honour, let him die,
With every joint a wound, and that to-morrow!
Æne. We know each other well.   30
Dio. We do; and long to know each other worse.
Par. This is the most despiteful gentle greeting,
The noblest hateful love, that e'er I heard of.—
What business, lord, so early?
Æne. I was sent for to the king; but why, I know
          not.
Par. His purpose meets you: 't was to bring this
          Greek
To Calchas' house; and there to render him,
For the enfreed Antenor, the fair Cressid.
Let 's have your company; or, if you please,
Haste there before us. I constantly do think,   40
(Or, rather, call my thought a certain knowledge,)
My brother Troilus lodges there to-night:
Rouse him, and give him note of our approach,
With the whole quality wherefore: I fear,
We shall be much unwelcome.
Æne.   That I assure you:
Troilus had rather Troy were borne to Greece,
Than Cressid borne from Troy.
Par.   There is no help;
The bitter disposition of the time
Will have it so. On, lord; we 'll follow you.
Æne. Good morrow, all.   [*Exit.*
Par. And tell me, noble Diomed; 'faith, tell me
          true,   51
Even in the soul of sound good-fellowship,—
Who, in your thoughts, merits fair Helen most,
Myself, or Menelaus?
Dio.   Both alike:
He merits well to have her, that doth seek her,
Not making any scruple of her soilure,
With such a hell of pain, and world of charge;
And you as well to keep her, that defend her,
Not palating the taste of her dishonour,
With such a costly loss of wealth and friends: 60
He, like a puling cuckold, would drink up
The lees and dregs of a flat tamed piece;
You, like a lecher, out of whorish loins
Are pleas'd to breed out your inheritors:
Both merits pois'd, each weighs nor less nor more;
But he as he, the heavier for a whore.
Par. You are too bitter to your countrywoman.
Dio. She 's bitter to her country. Hear me, Paris:—
For every false drop in her bawdy veins
A Grecian's life hath sunk; for every scruple   70
Of her contaminated carrion weight
A Trojan hath been slain. Since she could speak,
She hath not given so many good words breath,
As for her Greeks and Trojans suffer'd death.
Par. Fair Diomed, you do as chapmen do,
Dispraise the thing that you desire to buy;
But we in silence hold this virtue well,—
We 'll not commend what we intend to sell.
Here lies our way.   [*Exeunt.*

Scene II.—The Same. A Court before the House of
          Pandarus.

Enter Troilus *and* Cressida.

Tro. Dear, trouble not yourself: the morn is cold.
Cres. Then, sweet my lord, I 'll call mine uncle
          down;
He shall unbolt the gates.
Tro.   Trouble him not;
To bed, to bed: sleep kill those pretty eyes,
And give as soft attachment to thy senses,
As infants' empty of all thought!
Cres.   Good morrow then.
Tro. Pr'ythee now, to bed.
Cres.   Are you aweary of me?
Tro. O Cressida! but that the busy day,
Wak'd by the lark, hath rous'd the ribald crows,
And dreaming night will hide our joys no longer,   10
I would not from thee.
Cres.   Night hath been too brief.

Tro. Beshrew the witch! with venomous wights
          she stays,
As tediously as hell; but flies the grasps of love,
With wings more momentary-swift than thought.
You will catch cold, and curse me.
Cres.   Pr'ythee, tarry.—
You men will never tarry.
O foolish Cressid!—I might have still held off,
And then you would have tarried. Hark! there 's
          one up.
Pan. [*Within.*] What! are all the doors open here?
Tro. It is your uncle.   20
Cres. A pestilence on him! now will he be mocking:
I shall have such a life.—

Enter Pandarus.

Pan. How now, how now? how go maidenheads?—
Here, you maid! where 's my cousin Cressid?
Cres. Go hang yourself, you naughty mocking uncle!
You bring me to do,—and then you flout me too.
Pan. To do what? to do what?—let her say what:
—what have I brought you to do?
Cres. Come, come; beshrew your heart! you 'll ne'er
          be good,
Nor suffer others.   30
Pan. Ha, ha! Alas, poor wretch! a poor capocchia!
—hast not slept to-night? a bugbear take him!
man, let it sleep? a bugbear take him!   [*Knocking.*
Cres. Did not I tell you?—'would he were knock'd
          o' the head!—
Who 's that at door? good uncle, go and see.—
My lord, come you again into my chamber:
You smile, and mock me, as if I meant naughtily.
Tro. Ha, ha!
Cres. Come, you are deceiv'd; I think of no such
          thing.—   [*Knocking.*
How earnestly they knock!—Pray you, come in: 40
I would not for half Troy have you seen here.
                    [*Exeunt* Troilus *and* Cressida.
Pan. [*Going to the door.*] Who 's there? what 's the
matter? will you beat down the door? How now?
what 's the matter?

Enter Æneas.

Æne. Good morrow, lord, good morrow.
Pan. Who 's there? my lord Æneas! By my troth,
I knew you not: what news with you so early?
Æne. Is not Prince Troilus here?
Pan. Here! what should he do here?
Æne. Come, he is here, my lord; do not deny him:
It doth import him much to speak with me.   51
Pan. Is he here, say you? 't is more than I know,
I 'll be sworn:—for my own part, I came in late.
Who should he do here?
Æne. Who!—nay, then:—come, come, you 'll do
him wrong ere you are 'ware. You 'll be so true to
him, to be false to him. Do not you know of him; but
yet go fetch him hither: go.

Re-enter Troilus.

Tro. How now? what 's the matter?
Æne. My lord, I scarce have leisure to salute you,
My matter is so rash. There is at hand   61
Paris your brother, and Deiphobus,
The Grecian Diomed, and our Antenor
Deliver'd to us; and for him forthwith,
Ere the first sacrifice, within this hour,
We must give up to Diomedes' hand
The Lady Cressida.
Tro.   Is it concluded so?
Æne. By Priam, and the general state of Troy:
They are at hand, and ready to effect it.
Tro. How my achievements mock me!   70
I will go meet them:—and, my Lord Æneas,
We met by chance; you did not find me here.
Æne. Good, good, my lord; the secrets of nature
Have not more gift in taciturnity.
                    [*Exeunt* Troilus *and* Æneas.
Pan. Is 't possible? no sooner got but lost? The
devil take Antenor! the young prince will go mad.
A plague upon Antenor! I would, they had broke 's
neck!

Re-enter CRESSIDA.

Cres. How now? what is the matter? Who was here?
Pan. Ah! ah!   80

Pan. Thou must be gone, wench; thou must be gone: thou art changed for Antenor. Thou must to thy father, and be gone from Troilus: 't will be his death; 't will be his bane; he cannot bear it.
Cres. O you immortal gods!—I will not go.

Cres. "Who's that at door? good uncle, go and see."

Cres. Why sigh you so profoundly? where's my lord? gone?
Tell me, sweet uncle, what's the matter?
Pan. 'Would I were as deep under the earth as I am above!
Cres. O the gods!—what's the matter?
Pan. Pr'ythee, get thee in. 'Would thou hadst ne'er been born! I knew, thou wouldst be his death.—O poor gentleman!—A plague upon Antenor.
Cres. Good uncle, I beseech you, on my knees   90
I beseech you, what's the matter?

Pan. Thou must.
Cres. I will not, uncle: I have forgot my father;
I know no touch of consanguinity;
No kin, no love, no blood, no soul so near me,   100
As the sweet Troilus.—O you gods divine!
Make Cressid's name the very crown of falsehood,
If ever she leave Troilus! Time, force, and death,
Do to this body what extremes you can,
But the strong base and building of my love
Is as the very centre of the earth,
Drawing all things to it.—I'll go in, and weep,—
Pan. Do, do.

Cres. Tear my bright hair, and scratch my praised
   cheeks;
Crack my clear voice with sobs, and break my heart
With sounding Troilus. I will not go from Troy. 111
                                   [*Exeunt.*

SCENE III.—The Same. Before PANDARUS' House.

Enter PARIS, TROILUS, ÆNEAS, DEIPHOBUS,
   ANTENOR, *and* DIOMEDES.

Par. It is great morning, and the hour prefix'd
Of her delivery to this valiant Greek

Pan. "'Would I were as deep under the earth as I am above."

Comes fast upon.—Good my brother Troilus,
Tell you the lady what she is to do,
And haste her to the purpose.
  Tro.   Walk into her house;
I'll bring her to the Grecian presently;
And to his hand when I deliver her,
Think it an altar, and thy brother Troilus
A priest, there offering to it his own heart.   [*Exit.*
  Par. I know what 'tis to love;   10
And 'would, as I shall pity, I could help!—
Please you, walk in, my lords.   [*Exeunt.*

SCENE IV.—The Same. A Room in PANDARUS' House.

Enter PANDARUS *and* CRESSIDA.

Pan. Be moderate, be moderate.
Cres. Why tell you me of moderation?
The grief is fine, full, perfect, that I taste,
And violenteth in a sense as strong
As that which causeth it: how can I moderate it?
If I could temporise with my affection,
Or brew it to a weak and colder palate,
The like allayment could I give my grief:
My love admits no qualifying dross;
No more my grief, it is a precious loss.   10

Enter TROILUS.

Pan. Here, here, here he comes.—Ah, sweet ducks!
Cres. O Troilus! Troilus!   [*Embracing him.*
Pan. What a pair of spectacles is here! Let me
embrace too: O *heart,*—as the goodly saying is,—

   —O *heart, heavy heart,*
    Why sigh'st thou without breaking?

where he answers again,

   Because thou canst not ease thy smart,
    By friendship nor by speaking.

There was never a truer rhyme. Let us cast away

nothing, for we may live to have need of such a verse:
we see it, we see it.—How now, lambs?   22
  Tro. Cressid, I love thee in so strain'd a purity,
That the bless'd gods—as angry with my fancy,
More bright in zeal than the devotion which
Cold lips blow to their deities—take thee from me.
  Cres. Have the gods envy?
  Pan. Ay, ay, ay, ay: 'tis too plain a case.
  Cres. And is it true, that I must go from Troy?
  Tro. A hateful truth.
  Cres.   What! and from Troilus too?
  Tro. From Troy, and Troilus.
  Cres.   Is it possible?   31
  Tro. And suddenly; where injury of chance
Puts back leave-taking, justles roughly by
All time of pause, rudely beguiles our lips
Of all rejoindure, forcibly prevents
Our lock'd embrasures, strangles our dear vows
Even in the birth of our own labouring breath.
We two, that with so many thousand sighs
Did buy each other, must poorly sell ourselves
With the rude brevity and discharge of one.   40
Injurious time now, with a robber's haste,
Crams his rich thievery up, he knows not how:
As many farewells as be stars in heaven,
With distinct breath and consign'd kisses to them,
He fumbles up into a loose adieu;
And scants us with a single famish'd kiss,
Distasting with the salt of broken tears.
  Æne. [*Within.*] My lord, is the lady ready?
  Tro. Hark! you are call'd: some say, the Genius so
Cries "Come!" to him that instantly must die.   50
Bid them have patience; she shall come anon.
  Pan. Where are my tears? rain, to lay this wind, or
my heart will be blown up by the root!   [*Exit.*
  Cres. I must then to the Grecians?
  Tro.   No remedy.
  Cres. A woful Cressid 'mongst the merry Greeks!
When shall we see again?
  Tro. Hear me, my love. Be thou but true of heart,—
  Cres. I true! how now? what wicked deem is this?
  Tro. Nay, we must use expostulation kindly,
For it is parting from us: 60
I speak not, "be thou true," as fearing thee;
For I will throw my glove to Death himself,

Pan. "What a pair of spectacles is here!"

That there's no maculation in thy heart;
But, "be thou true," say I, to fashion in
My sequent protestation; be thou true,
And I will see thee.
  Cres. O! you shall be expos'd, my lord, to dangers
As infinite as imminent! but I'll be true.
  Tro. And I'll grow friend with danger. Wear this
    sleeve.

Cres. And you this glove. When shall I see you? 70
Tro. I will corrupt the Grecian sentinels,
To give thee nightly visitation.
But yet, be true.
    Cres.	O heavens!—be true, again?
Tro. Hear why I speak it, love :
The Grecian youths are full of quality ;
Their loving well compos'd with gift of nature,
Flowing and swelling o'er with arts and exercise :
How novelties may move, and parts with person,
Alas, a kind of godly jealousy
(Which, I beseech you, call a virtuous sin)	80
Makes me afraid.
    Cres.	O heavens! you love me not.
Tro. Die I a villain then !
In this I do not call your faith in question,
So mainly as my merit : I cannot sing,
Nor heel the high lavolt, nor sweeten talk,
Nor play at subtle games ; fair virtues all,
To which the Grecians are most prompt and pregnant:
But I can tell, that in each grace of these
There lurks a still and dumb-discoursive devil
That tempts most cunningly. But be not tempted. 90
  Cres. Do you think I will?
  Tro.	No.
But something may be done that we will not :
And sometimes we are devils to ourselves,
When we will tempt the frailty of our powers,
Presuming on their changeful potency.
  Æne. [*Within.*] Nay, good my lord,—
  Tro.	Come, kiss ; and let us part.
  Par. [*Within.*] Brother Troilus !
  Tro.	Good brother, come you hither ;
And bring Æneas and the Grecian with you.
  Cres. My lord, will you be true ?	100
  Tro. Who, I ? alas, it is my vice, my fault :
Whiles others fish with craft for great opinion,
I with great truth catch mere simplicity ;
Whilst some with cunning gild their copper crowns,
With truth and plainness I do wear mine bare.
Fear not my truth ; the moral of my wit
Is—plain, and true,—there's all the reach of it.

Enter ÆNEAS, PARIS, ANTENOR, DEIPHOBUS, *and*
DIOMEDES.

Welcome, Sir Diomed. Here is the lady,
Which for Antenor we deliver you :
At the port, lord, I'll give her to thy hand,	110
And by the way possess thee what she is.
Entreat her fair ; and, by my soul, fair Greek,
If e'er thou stand at mercy of my sword,
Name Cressid, and thy life shall be as safe,
As Priam is in Ilion.
  Dio.	Fair Lady Cressid,
So please you, save the thanks this prince expects :
The lustre in your eye, heaven in your cheek,
Pleads your fair usage ; and to Diomed
You shall be mistress, and command him wholly.
  Tro. Grecian, thou dost not use me courteously, 120
To shame the seal of my petition to thee,
In praising her. I tell thee, lord of Greece,
She is as far high-soaring o'er thy praises,
As thou unworthy to be call'd her servant.
I charge thee, use her well, even for my charge ;
For, by the dreadful Pluto, if thou dost not,
Though the great bulk Achilles be thy guard,
I'll cut thy throat.
  Dio.	O ! be not mov'd, Prince Troilus.
Let me be privileg'd by my place and message,
To be a speaker free : when I am hence,	130
I'll answer to my lust ; and know you, lord,
I'll nothing do on charge. To her own worth
She shall be priz'd ; but that you say—be't so,
I'll speak it in my spirit and honour,—no.
  Tro. Come, to the port.—I'll tell thee, Diomed,
This brave touch off make thee to hide thy head.—
Lady, give me your hand ; and, as we walk,
To our own selves bend we our needful talk.
    [*Exeunt* TROILUS, CRESSIDA, *and* DIOMEDES.
            [*Trumpet sounded.*
  Par. Hark ! Hector's trumpet.
  Æne.	How have we spent this morning !

The prince must think me tardy and remiss,	140
That swore to ride before him to the field.
  Par. 'T is Troilus' fault. Come, come, to field with
    him.
  Dei. Let us make ready straight.
  Æne. Yea, with a bridegroom's fresh alacrity,
Let us address to tend on Hector's heels.
The glory of our Troy doth this day lie
On his fair worth, and single chivalry.	[*Exeunt.*

SCENE V.—The Grecian Camp. Lists set out.

Enter AJAX, *armed ;* AGAMEMNON, ACHILLES, PA-
TROCLUS, MENELAUS, ULYSSES, NESTOR, *and
others.*

  Agam. Here art thou in appointment fresh and fair,
Anticipating time with starting courage.
Give with thy trumpet a loud note to Troy,
Thou dreadful Ajax ; that the appalled air
May pierce the head of the great combatant,
And hale him hither.
  Ajax.	Thou, trumpet, there's my purse.
Now crack thy lungs, and split thy brazen pipe :
Blow, villain, till thy sphered bias cheek
Outswell the colic of puff'd Aquilon.	9
Come, stretch thy chest, and let thy eyes spout blood ;
Thou blow'st for Hector.	[*Trumpet sounds.*
  Ulyss. No trumpet answers.
  Achil.	'T is but early days.
  Agam. Is not yond Diomed with Calchas' daughter?
  Ulyss. 'T is he, I ken the manner of his gait ;
He rises on the toe : that spirit of his
In aspiration lifts him from the earth.

Enter DIOMEDES, *with* CRESSIDA.

  Agam. Is this the Lady Cressid ?
  Dio.	Even she.
  Agam. Most dearly welcome to the Greeks, sweet
    lady.
  Nest. Our general doth salute you with a kiss.
  Ulyss. Yet is the kindness but particular ;	20
'T were better she were kiss'd in general.
  Nest. And very courtly counsel : I'll begin.—
So much for Nestor.
  Achil. I'll take that winter from your lips, fair lady :
Achilles bids you welcome.
  Men. I had good argument for kissing once.
  Patr. But that's no argument for kissing now :
For thus popp'd Paris in his hardiment,
And parted thus you and your argument.
  Ulyss. O deadly gall, and theme of all our scorns !
For which we lose our heads, to gild his horns.	31
  Patr. The first was Menelaus' kiss ;—this, mine :
Patroclus kisses you.
  Men.	O ! this is trim.
  Patr. Paris, and I, kiss evermore for him.
  Men. I'll have my kiss, sir.—Lady, by your leave.
  Cres. In kissing do you render or receive ?
  Patr. Both take and give.
  Cres.	I'll make my match to live,
The kiss you take is better than you give ;
Therefore no kiss.	39
  Men. I'll give you boot ; I'll give you three for one.
  Cres. You're an odd man : give even, or give none.
  Men. An odd man, lady ? every man is odd.
  Cres. No, Paris is not ; for, you know, 't is true,
That you are odd, and he is even with you.
  Men. You fillip me o' the head.
  Cres.	No, I'll be sworn.
  Ulyss. It were no match, your nail against his
    horn.—
May I, sweet lady, beg a kiss of you ?
  Cres. You may.
  Ulyss.	I do desire it.
  Cres.	Why, beg then.
  Ulyss. Why then, for Venus' sake, give me a kiss,
When Helen is a maid again, and his.	50
  Cres. I am your debtor ; claim it when 't is due.
  Ulyss. Never's my day, and then a kiss of you.
  Dio. Lady, a word :—I'll bring you to your father.
      [DIOMEDES *leads out* CRESSIDA.

Nest. A woman of quick sense.
Ulyss. Fie, fie upon her!
There's language in her eye, her cheek, her lip,
Nay, her foot speaks; her wanton spirits look out
At every joint and motive of her body.
O! these encounterers, so glib of tongue,
That give a coasting welcome ere it comes,
And wide unclasp the tables of their thoughts   60
To every tickling reader, set them down
For sluttish spoils of opportunity,
And daughters of the game.   [*Trumpet within.*
All. The Trojans' trumpet.
Agam.   Yonder comes the troop.

Enter HECTOR, *armed;* ÆNEAS, TROILUS, *and other*
    Trojans, with Attendants.

Æne. Hail, all you state of Greece! what shall be
  done
To him that victory commands? Or do you purpose,
A victor shall be known? will you, the knights
Shall to the edge of all extremity
Pursue each other, or shall be divided
By any voice or order of the field?   70
Hector bade ask.
Agam.   Which way would Hector have it?
Æne. He cares not: he'll obey conditions.
Achil. 'T is done like Hector; but securely done,
A little proudly, and great deal disprising
The knight oppos'd.
Æne.   If not Achilles, sir,
What is your name?'
Achil.   If not Achilles, nothing.
Æne. Therefore Achilles; but, whate'er, know
  this:—
In the extremity of great and little,
Valour and pride excel themselves in Hector;
The one almost as infinite as all,   80
The other blank as nothing. Weigh him well,
And that which looks like pride is courtesy.
This Ajax is half made of Hector's blood:
In love whereof half Hector stays at home;
Half heart, half hand, half Hector comes to seek
This blended knight, half Trojan, and half Greek.
Achil. A maiden battle then?—O! I perceive you.

Re-enter DIOMEDES.

Agam. Here is Sir Diomed.—Go, gentle knight,
Stand by our Ajax: as you and Lord Æneas
Consent upon the order of their fight,   90
So be it; either to the uttermost,
Or else a breath: the combatants being kin,
Half stints their strife before their strokes begin.
    [AJAX *and* HECTOR *enter the lists.*
Ulyss. They are oppos'd already.
Agam. What Trojan is that same that looks so
  heavy?
Ulyss. The youngest son of Priam, a true knight;
Not yet mature, yet matchless; firm of word,
Speaking in deeds, and deedless in his tongue;
Not soon provok'd, nor, being provok'd, soon calm'd:
His heart and hand both open, and both free;   100
For what he has, he gives; what thinks, he shows;
Yet gives he not till judgment guide his bounty,
Nor dignifies an impure thought with breath.
Manly as Hector, but more dangerous;
For Hector, in his blaze of wrath, subscribes
To tender objects; but he, in heat of action,
Is more vindicative than jealous love.
They call him Troilus; and on him erect
A second hope, as fairly built as Hector.
Thus says Æneas; one that knows the youth,   110
Even to his inches, and with private soul
Did in great Ilion thus translate him to me.
    [*Alarum.* HECTOR *and* AJAX *fight.*
Agam. They are in action.
Nest. Now, Ajax, hold thine own!
Tro. Hector, thou sleep'st: awake thee!
Agam. His blows are well dispos'd:—there, Ajax!
Dio. You must no more.   [*Trumpets cease.*
Æne.   Princes, enough, so please you.
Ajax. I am not warm yet: let us fight again.
Dio. As Hector pleases.

Hect.   Why, then will I no more.—
Thou art, great lord, my father's sister's son,   120
A cousin-german to great Priam's seed;
The obligation of our blood forbids
A gory emulation 'twixt us twain.
Were thy commixtion Greek and Trojan so,
That thou couldst say—"This hand is Grecian all,
And this is Trojan; the sinews of this leg
All Greek, and this all Troy; my mother's blood
Runs on the dexter cheek, and this sinister
Bounds-in my father's;" by Jove multipotent,
Thou shouldst not bear from me a Greekish member
Wherein my sword had not impressure made   131
Of our rank feud. But the just gods gainsay,
That any drop thou borrow'dst from thy mother,
My sacred aunt, should by my mortal sword
Be drain'd! Let me embrace thee, Ajax.—
By him that thunders, thou hast lusty arms;
Hector would have them fall upon him thus:
Cousin, all honour to thee!
Ajax.   I thank thee, Hector:
Thou art too gentle, and too free a man.
I came to kill thee, cousin, and bear hence   140
A great addition earned in thy death.
Hect. Not Neoptolemus so mirable
(On whose bright crest Fame with her loudest *Oyez*
Cries, "This is he!") could promise to himself
A thought of added honour torn from Hector.
Æne. There is expectance here from both the sides,
What further you will do.
Hect.   We'll answer it;
The issue is embracement.—Ajax, farewell.
Ajax. If I might in entreaties find success,
As seld I have the chance, I would desire   150
My famous cousin to our Grecian tents.
Dio. 'T is Agamemnon's wish; and great Achilles
Doth long to see unarm'd the valiant Hector.
Hect. Æneas, call my brother Troilus to me:
And signify this loving interview
To the expecters of our Trojan part;
Desire them home.—Give me thy hand, my cousin;
I will go eat with thee, and see your knights.
Ajax. Great Agamemnon comes to meet us here.
Hect. The worthiest of them tell me name by name;   161
But for Achilles, mine own searching eyes
Shall find him by his large and portly size.
Agam. Worthy of arms! as welcome as to one
That would be rid of such an enemy;
But that's no welcome: understand more clear,
What's past, and what's to come, is strew'd with
  husks
And formless ruin of oblivion;
But in this extant moment, faith and troth,
Strain'd purely from all hollow bias-drawing,
Bids thee, with most divine integrity,   170
From heart of very heart, great Hector, welcome.
Hect. I thank thee, most imperious Agamemnon.
Agam. [*To* TROILUS.] My well-fam'd lord of Troy,
  no less to you.
Men. Let me confirm my princely brother's greet-
  ing:
You brace of warlike brothers, welcome hither.
Hect. Who must we answer?
Æne.   The noble Menelaus.
Hect. O! you, my lord? by Mars his gauntlet,
  thanks.
Mock not, that I affect the untraded oath:
Your *quondam* wife swears still by Venus' glove;
She's well, but bade me not commend her to you.   180
Men. Name her not now, sir; she's a deadly theme.
Hect. O! pardon; I offend.
Nest. I have, thou gallant Trojan, seen thee oft,
Labouring for destiny, make cruel way
Through ranks of Greekish youth: and I have seen
  thee,
As hot as Perseus, spur thy Phrygian steed,
And seen thee scorning forfeits and subduements,
When thou hast hung thy advanced sword i' th' air,
Not letting it decline on the declin'd;
That I have said unto my standers-by,   190
"Lo, Jupiter is yonder, dealing life!"
And I have seen thee pause, and take thy breath,

When that a ring of Greeks have hemm'd thee in,
Like an Olympian wrestling: this have I seen;
But this thy countenance, still lock'd in steel,
I never saw till now. I knew thy grandsire;
And once fought with him: he was a soldier good;
But, by great Mars, the captain of us all,
Never like thee. Let an old man embrace thee;
And, worthy warrior, welcome to our tents. 200
  Æne. 'T is the old Nestor.
  Hect. Let me embrace thee, good old chronicle,
That hast so long walk'd hand in hand with time.—
Most reverend Nestor, I am glad to clasp thee.
  Nest. I would, my arms could match thee in con-
                tention,
As they contend with thee in courtesy.
  Hect. I would they could.
  Nest. Ha!
By this white beard, I 'd fight with thee to-morrow.
Well, welcome, welcome! I have seen the time— 210
  Ulyss. I wonder now how yonder city stands,
When we have here her base and pillar by us.
  Hect. I know your favour, Lord Ulysses, well.
Ah, sir, there 's many a Greek and Trojan dead,
Since first I saw yourself and Diomed
In Ilion, on your Greekish embassy.
  Ulyss. Sir, I foretold you then what would ensue:
My prophecy is but half his journey yet;
For yonder walls, that pertly front your town,
Yond towers, whose wanton tops do buss the clouds,
Must kiss their own feet.
  Hect.   I must not believe you: 221
There they stand yet; and modestly I think,
The fall of every Phrygian stone will cost
A drop of Grecian blood: the end crowns all;
And that old common arbitrator, Time,
Will one day end it.
  Ulyss.   So to him we leave it.
Most gentle, and most valiant Hector, welcome.
After the general, I beseech you next
To feast with me, and see me at my tent.
  Achil. I shall forestall thee, Lord Ulysses, thou!—
Now, Hector, I have fed mine eyes on thee: 231
I have with exact view perus'd thee, Hector,
And quoted joint by joint.
  Hect.   Is this Achilles?
  Achil. I am Achilles.
  Hect. Stand fair, I pray thee: let me look on thee.
  Achil. Behold thy fill.
  Hect.   Nay, I have done already.
  Achil. Thou art too brief: I will the second time,
As I would buy thee, view thee limb by limb.
  Hect. O! like a book of sport thou 'lt read me o'er;
But there 's more in me than thou understand'st. 240
Why dost thou so oppress me with thine eye?
  Achil. Tell me, you heavens, in which part of his
                body
Shall I destroy him, whether there, or there, or there?

That I may give the local wound a name,
And make distinct the very breach, whereout
Hector's great spirit flew. Answer me, heavens!
  Hect. It would discredit the bless'd gods, proud
                man,
To answer such a question. Stand again:
Think'st thou to catch my life so pleasantly,
As to prenominate in nice conjecture, 250
Where thou wilt hit me dead?
  Achil.   I tell thee, yea.
  Hect. Wert thou the oracle to tell me so,
I 'd not believe thee. Henceforth guard thee well,
For I 'll not kill thee there, nor there, nor there;
But, by the forge that stithied Mars his helm,
I 'll kill thee everywhere, yea, o'er and o'er.—
You, wisest Grecians, pardon me this brag:
His insolence draws folly from my lips;
But I 'll endeavour deeds to match these words,
Or may I never—
  Ajax.   Do not chafe thee, cousin;— 260
And you, Achilles, let these threats alone,
Till accident, or purpose, bring you to 't:
You may have every day enough of Hector,
If you have stomach. The general state, I fear,
Can scarce entreat you to be odd with him.
  Hect. I pray you, let us see you in the field;
We have had pelting wars, since you refus'd
The Grecians' cause.
  Achil.   Dost thou entreat me, Hector?
To-morrow do I meet thee, fell as death;
To-night, all friends.
  Hect.   Thy hand upon that match. 270
  Agam. First, all you peers of Greece, go to my tent;
There in the full convive we: afterwards,
As Hector's leisure and your bounties shall
Concur together, severally entreat him.—
Beat loud the tabourines, let the trumpets blow,
That this great soldier may his welcome know.
            [*Exeunt all but* TROILUS *and* ULYSSES.
  Tro. My Lord Ulysses, tell me, I beseech you,
In what place of the field doth Calchas keep?
  Ulyss. At Menelaus' tent, most princely Troilus:
There Diomed doth feast with him to-night; 280
Who neither looks on heaven, nor on earth,
But gives all gaze and bent of amorous view
On the fair Cressid.
  Tro. Shall I, sweet lord, be bound to you so much,
After we part from Agamemnon's tent,
To bring me thither?
  Ulyss.   You shall command me, sir.
As gentle tell me, of what honour was
This Cressida in Troy? Had she no lover there,
That wails her absence?
  Tro. O, sir! to such as boasting show their scars, 290
A mock is due. Will you walk on, my lord?
She was belov'd, she lov'd; she is, and doth:
But, still, sweet love is food for fortune's tooth.
                        [*Exeunt.*

ACT V.

SCENE I.—The Grecian Camp. Before ACHILLES' Tent.

Enter ACHILLES *and* PATROCLUS.

Achilles.

'LL heat his blood with Greekish wine
  to-night,
Which with my scimitar I'll cool to-
  morrow.—
Patroclus, let us feast him to the height.
Patr. Here comes Thersites.

Enter THERSITES.

Achil. How now, thou core of envy?
Thou crusty batch of nature, what's the
  news?
Ther. Why, thou picture of what thou
seemest, and idol of idiot-worshippers,
here's a letter for thee.
Achil. From whence, fragment?
Ther. Why, thou full dish of fool,
from Troy. 11
Patr. Who keeps the tent now?
Ther. The surgeon's box, or the patient's wound.
Patr. Well said, Adversity! and what need these
tricks?
Ther. Pr'ythee, be silent, boy; I profit not by thy
talk: thou art thought to be Achilles' male varlet.
Patr. Male varlet, you rogue! what's that? 18
Ther. Why, his masculine whore. Now the rotten
diseases of the south, the guts-griping, ruptures,
catarrhs, loads o'gravel i'the back, lethargies, cold
palsies, raw eyes, dirt-rotten livers, wheezing lungs,
bladders full of imposthume, sciaticas, lime-kilns i'
the palm, incurable bone-ache, and the rivelled fee-
simple of the tetter, take and take again such preposterous discoveries!
Patr. Why, thou damnable box of envy, thou, what
meanest thou to curse thus?
Ther. Do I curse thee?
Patr. Why, no, you ruinous butt; you whoreson
indistinguishable cur, no. 31
Ther. No? why art thou then exasperate, thou idle
immaterial skein of sleave silk, thou green sarcenet
flap for a sore eye, thou tassel of a prodigal's purse,
thou? Ah, how the poor world is pestered with such
water-flies, diminutives of nature!
Patr. Out, gall!
Ther. Finch-egg!
Achil. My sweet Patroclus, I am thwarted quite
From my great purpose in to-morrow's battle. 40
Here is a letter from Queen Hecuba;
A token from her daughter, my fair love;
Both taxing me, and gaging me to keep
An oath that I have sworn. I will not break it:
Fall, Greeks; fail, fame; honour, or go, or stay;
My major vow lies here, this I'll obey.—
Come, come, Thersites, help to trim my tent;
This night in banqueting must all be spent.—
Away, Patroclus. 49
      [*Exeunt* ACHILLES *and* PATROCLUS.
Ther. With too much blood, and too little brain,
these two may run mad; but if with too much brain
and too little blood they do, I'll be a curer of madmen.
Here's Agamemnon,—an honest fellow enough, and
one that loves quails, but he has not so much brain
as ear-wax: and the goodly transformation of Jupiter
there, his brother, the bull, the primitive statue, and
oblique memorial of cuckolds; a thrifty shoeing-horn

in a chain, hanging at his brother's leg,—to what
form, but that he is, should wit larded with malice,
and malice forced with wit, turn him to? To an ass
were nothing: he is both ass and ox; to an ox were
nothing: he is both ox and ass. To be a dog, a mule,
a cat, a fitchew, a toad, a lizard, an owl, a puttock, or
a herring without a roe, I would not care; but to be
Menelaus,—I would conspire against destiny. Ask
me not what I would be, if I were not Thersites, for
I care not to be the louse of a lazar, so I were not
Menelaus.—Hey-day! spirits and fires!

Enter HECTOR, TROILUS, AJAX, AGAMEMNON,
ULYSSES, NESTOR, MENELAUS, *and* DIOMEDES,
with lights.

Agam. We go wrong; we go wrong.
Ajax. No, yonder 'tis; there, where we see the
  lights. 70
Hect. I trouble you.
Ajax. No, not a whit.
Ulyss.   Here comes himself to guide you.

Enter ACHILLES.

Achil. Welcome, brave Hector: welcome, princes
  all.
Agam. So now, fair prince of Troy, I bid good
  night.
Ajax commands the guard to tend on you.
Hect. Thanks, and good night, to the Greeks'
  general.
Men. Good night, my lord.
Hect.   Good night, sweet Lord Menelaus.
Ther. Sweet draught: sweet, quoth 'a! sweet sink,
sweet sewer.
Achil. Good night, and welcome, both at once to
  those 80
That go, or tarry.
Agam. Good night.
      [*Exeunt* AGAMEMNON *and* MENELAUS.
Achil. Old Nestor tarries; and you too, Diomed,
Keep Hector company an hour or two.
Dio. I cannot, lord; I have important business,
The tide whereof is now.—Good night, great Hector.
Hect. Give me your hand.
Ulyss. [*Aside to* TROILUS.] Follow his torch, he
      goes to Calchas' tent.
I'll keep you company.
Tro. Sweet sir, you honour me.
Hect.   And so, good night.
      [*Exit* DIOMEDES; ULYSSES *and* TROILUS
      following.
Achil. Come, come; enter my tent. 91
      [*Exeunt* ACHILLES, HECTOR, AJAX, *and*
      NESTOR.
Ther. That same Diomed's a false-hearted rogue, a
most unjust knave: I will no more trust him when he
leers, than I will a serpent when he hisses. He will
spend his mouth, and promise, like Brabbler the
hound; but when he performs, astronomers foretell
it: it is prodigious, there will come some change:
the sun borrows of the moon, when Diomed keeps
his word. I will rather leave to see Hector, than not
to dog him: they say, he keeps a Trojan drab, and
uses the traitor Calchas' tent. I'll after.—Nothing
but lechery! all incontinent varlets!   [*Exit.*

Scene II.—The Same. Before Calchas' Tent.

Enter Diomedes.

Dio. What, are you up here, ho? speak.
Cal. [*Within.*] Who calls?
Dio. Diomed.—Calchas, I think.—Where 's your
   daughter?
Cal. [*Within.*] She comes to you.

Enter Troilus *and* Ulysses, *at a distance; after*
   them, Thersites.

Ulyss. Stand where the torch may not discover us.

Enter Cressida.

Tro. Cressid comes forth to him.
Dio.   How now, my charge?
Cres. Now, my sweet guardian.—Hark! a word
   with you.   [*Whispers.*
Tro. Yea, so familiar!
Ulyss. She will sing any man at first sight.
Ther. And any man may sing her, if he can take
her cliff; she 's noted.   11
Dio. Will you remember?
Cres. Remember? yes.
Dio. Nay, but do then;
And let your mind be coupled with your words.
Tro. What should she remember?
Ulyss. List!
Cres. Sweet honey Greek, tempt me no more to
   folly.
Ther. Roguery!
Dio. Nay, then,—   20
Cres. I 'll tell you what,—
Dio. Pho! pho! come, tell a pin: you are forsworn.
Cres. In faith, I cannot. What would you have me
do?
Ther. A juggling trick,—to be secretly open.
Dio. What did you swear you would bestow on me?
Cres. I pr'ythee, do not hold me to mine oath;
Bid me do anything but that, sweet Greek.
Dio. Good night.
Tro.   Hold, patience!
Ulyss.   How now, Trojan?
Cres.   Diomed,—
Dio. No, no; good night: I 'll be your fool no more.
Tro. Thy better must.
Cres.   Hark! one word in your ear.
Tro. O plague and madness!   31
Ulyss. You are mov'd, prince: let us depart, I pray
   you,
Lest your displeasure should enlarge itself
To wrathful terms. This place is dangerous;
The time right deadly: I beseech you, go.
Tro. Behold, I pray you!
Ulyss.   Nay, good my lord, go off:
You flow to great distraction; come, my lord.
Tro. I pr'ythee, stay.
Ulyss.   You have not patience; come.
Tro. I pray you, stay. By hell, and all hell's tor-
   ments,
I will not speak a word.
Dio.   And so, good night.   40
Cres. Nay, but you part in anger.
Tro.   Doth that grieve thee?
O wither'd truth!
Ulyss.   Why, how now, lord?
Tro.   By Jove,
I will be patient.
Cres.   Guardian!—why, Greek!
Dio. Pho, pho! adieu, you palter.
Cres. In faith, I do not: come hither once again.
Ulyss. You shake, my lord, at something: will you
   go?
You will break out.
Tro.   She strokes his cheek!
Ulyss.   Come, come.
Tro. Nay, stay; by Jove, I will not speak a word:
There is between my will and all offences
A guard of patience:—stay a little while.   50
Ther. How the devil Luxury, with his fat rump
and potato-finger, tickles these together! Fry, lechery,
fry!

Dio. But will you then?
Cres. In faith, I will, la: never trust me else.
Dio. Give me some token for the surety of it.
Cres. I 'll fetch you one.   [*Exit.*
Ulyss. You have sworn patience.
Tro.   Fear me not, sweet lord;
I will not be myself, nor have cognition
Of what I feel: I am all patience.   60

Re-enter Cressida.

Ther. Now the pledge! now, now, now!
Cres. Here, Diomed, keep this sleeve.
Tro. O beauty! where is thy faith?
Ulyss.   My lord,—
Tro. I will be patient; outwardly I will.
Cres. You look upon that sleeve; behold it well.—
He lov'd me—O false wench!—Give 't me again.
Dio. Whose was 't?
Cres. It is no matter, now I have 't again:
I will not meet with you: to-morrow night.
I pr'ythee, Diomed, visit me no more.   70
Ther. Now she sharpens.—Well said, whetstone!
Dio. I shall have it.
Cres.   What, this?
Dio.   Ay, that.
Cres. O, all you gods!—O pretty, pretty pledge!
Thy master now lies thinking on his bed
Of thee, and me; and sighs, and takes my glove,
And gives memorial dainty kisses to it,
As I kiss thee.—Nay, do not snatch it from me;
He that takes that doth take my heart withal.
Dio. I had your heart before; this follows it.
Tro. I did swear patience.   80
Cres. You shall not have it, Diomed; 'faith, you
   shall not.
I 'll give you something else.
Dio. I will have this. Whose was it?
Cres.   'T is no matter.
Dio. Come, tell me whose it was.
Cres. 'T was one's that lov'd me better than you
   will.
But, now you have it, take it.
Dio.   Whose was it?
Cres. By all Diana's waiting-women, yond,
And by herself, I will not tell you whose.
Dio. To-morrow will I wear it on my helm,
And grieve his spirit that dares not challenge it. 90
Tro. Wert thou the devil, and wor'st it on thy horn,
It should be challeng'd.
Cres. Well, well, 't is done, 't is past;—and yet it is
   not:
I will not keep my word.
Dio.   Why then, farewell;
Thou never shalt mock Diomed again.
Cres. You shall not go.—One cannot speak a word,
But it straight starts you.
Dio.   I do not like this fooling.
Ther. Nor I, by Pluto: but that that likes not me,
Pleases me best.
Dio. What! shall I come? the hour?
Cres.   Ay, come:—O Jove!—
Do come:—I shall be plagu'd.
Dio.   Farewell till then.   101
Cres. Good night: I pr'ythee, come.—
                                   [*Exit* Diomedes.
Troilus, farewell! one eye yet looks on thee,
But with my heart the other eye doth see.
Ah, poor our sex! this fault in us I find,
The error of our eye directs our mind.
What error leads, must err. O! then conclude,
Minds, sway'd by eyes, are full of turpitude. [*Exit.*
Ther. A proof of strength she could not publish
   more,
Unless she said, "My mind is now turn'd whore." 110
Ulyss. All 's done, my lord.
Tro.   It is.
Ulyss.   Why stay we then?
Tro. To make a recordation to my soul
Of every syllable that here was spoke.
But if I tell how these two did co-act,
Shall I not lie in publishing a truth?
Sith yet there is a credence in my heart,

An esperance so obstinately strong,
That doth invert the attest of eyes and ears,
As if those organs had deceptious functions,
Created only to calumniate.   120
Was Cressid here?
Ulyss.   I cannot conjure, Trojan.
Tro. She was not, sure.
Ulyss.   Most sure she was.
Tro. Why, my negation hath no taste of madness.
Ulyss. Nor mine, my lord: Cressid was here but
    now.
Tro. Let it not be believ'd for womanhood!
Think we had mothers: do not give advantage
To stubborn critics,—apt, without a theme,
For depravation,—to square the general sex
By Cressid's rule: rather think this not Cressid.
Ulyss. What hath she done, prince, that can soil
    our mothers?   130
Tro. Nothing at all, unless that this were she.
Ther. Will he swagger himself out on 's own eyes?
Tro. This she? no; this is Diomed's Cressida.
If beauty have a soul, this is not she:
If souls guide vows, if vows be sanctimony,
If sanctimony be the gods' delight,
If there be rule in unity itself,
This is not she. O madness of discourse,
That cause sets up with and against thyself!
Bi-fold authority! where reason can revolt   140
Without perdition, and loss assume all reason
Without revolt: this is, and is not, Cressid!
Within my soul there doth conduce a fight
Of this strange nature, that a thing inseparate
Divides more wider than the sky and earth;
And yet the spacious breadth of this division
Admits no orifice for a point, as subtle
As Ariachne's broken woof, to enter.
Instance, O instance! strong as Pluto's gates;
Cressid is mine, tied with the bonds of heaven: 150
Instance, O instance! strong as heaven itself;
The bonds of heaven are slipp'd, dissolv'd, and loos'd;
And with another knot, five-finger-tied,
The fractions of her faith, orts of her love,
The fragments, scraps, the bits, and greasy reliques
Of her o'er-eaten faith, are bound to Diomed.
Ulyss. May worthy Troilus be half attach'd
With that which here his passion doth express?
Tro. Ay, Greek; and that shall be divulged well
In characters as red as Mars his heart   160
Inflam'd with Venus: never did young man fancy
With so eternal and so fix'd a soul.
Hark, Greek :—as much as I do Cressid love,
So much by weight hate I her Diomed;
That sleeve is mine that he 'll bear in his helm:
Were it a casque compos'd by Vulcan's skill,
My sword should bite it. Not the dreadful spout,
Which shipmen do the hurricane call,
Constring'd in mass by the almighty sun,
Shall dizzy with more clamour Neptune's ear   170
In his descent, than shall my prompted sword
Falling on Diomed.
Ther. He 'll tickle it for his concupy.
Tro. O Cressid! O false Cressid! false, false, false!
Let all untruths stand by thy slandered name,
And they 'll seem glorious.
Ulyss.   O! contain yourself;
Your passion draws ears hither.

Enter ÆNEAS.

Æne. I have been seeking you this hour, my lord.
Hector, by this, is arming him in Troy:
Ajax, your guard, stays to conduct you home.   180
Tro. Have with you, prince.—My courteous lord,
    adieu.—
Farewell, revolted fair!—and, Diomed,
Stand fast, and wear a castle on thy head!
Ulyss. I 'll bring you to the gates.
Tro. Accept distracted thanks.
        [*Exeunt* TROILUS, ÆNEAS, *and* ULYSSES.
Ther. [*Coming forward.*] 'Would, I could meet that
rogue Diomed. I would croak like a raven; I would
bode, I would bode. Patroclus will give me anything
for the intelligence of this whore: the parrot will not

do more for an almond, than he for a commodious
drab. Lechery, lechery; still, wars and lechery:
nothing else holds fashion. A burning devil take
them!   [*Exit.*

SCENE III.—Troy. Before PRIAM'S Palace.

Enter HECTOR *and* ANDROMACHE.

And. When was my lord so much ungently
    temper'd,
To stop his ears against admonishment?
Unarm, unarm, and do not fight to-day.
Hect. You train me to offend you; get you gone:
By the everlasting gods, I 'll go.
And. My dreams will, sure, prove ominous to the day.
Hect. No more, I say.

Enter CASSANDRA.

Cas.   Where is my brother Hector?
And. Here, sister; arm'd, and bloody in intent.
Consort with me in loud and dear petition:
Pursue we him on knees; for I have dream'd   10
Of bloody turbulence, and this whole night
Hath nothing been but shapes and forms of slaughter.
Cas. O! 't is true.
Hect.   Ho! bid my trumpet sound!
Cas. No notes of sally, for the heavens, sweet
    brother.
Hect. Be gone, I say: the gods have heard me swear.
Cas. The gods are deaf to hot and peevish vows:
They are polluted offerings, more abhorr'd
Than spotted livers in the sacrifice.
And. O! be persuaded: do not count it holy
To hurt thy being just: it is as lawful,   20
— — — — — — — — — — — —
For we would give as much to violent thefts,
And rob in the behalf of charity.
Cas. It is the purpose that makes strong the vow;
But vows to every purpose must not hold.
Unarm, sweet Hector.
Hect.   Hold you still, I say;
Mine honour keeps the weather of my fate:
Life every man holds dear; but the dear man
Holds honour far more precious-dear than life.--

Enter TROILUS.

How now, young man? mean'st thou to fight to-day?
And. Cassandra, call my father to persuade.   30
                            [*Exit* CASSANDRA.
Hect. No, 'faith, young Troilus; doff thy harness,
    youth;
I am to-day i' the vein of chivalry.
Let grow thy sinews till their knots be strong,
And tempt not yet the brushes of the war,
Unarm thee, go; and doubt thou not, brave boy,
I 'll stand to-day for thee, and me, and Troy.
Tro. Brother, you have a vice of mercy in you,
Which better fits a lion than a man.
Hect. What vice is that, good Troilus? chide me
    for it.
Tro. When many times the captive Grecian falls, 40
Even in the fan and wind of your fair sword,
You bid them rise, and live.
Hect. O! 't is fair play.
Tro.   Fool's play, by heaven, Hector.
Hect. How now? how now?
Tro.   For the love of all the gods,
Let 's leave the hermit pity with our mothers,
And when we have our armours buckled on,
The venom'd vengeance ride upon our swords:
Spur them to ruthful work, rein them from ruth.
Hect. Fie, savage, fie!
Tro.   Hector, then 't is wars.
Hect. Troilus, I would not have you fight to-day. 50
Tro. Who should withhold me?
Not fate, obedience, nor the hand of Mars
Beckoning with fiery truncheon my retire;
Not Priamus and Hecuba on knees,
Their eyes o'ergalled with recourse of tears;
Nor you, my brother, with your true sword drawn,
Oppos'd to hinder me, should stop my way,
But by my ruin.

Re-enter CASSANDRA, *with* PRIAM.

Cas. Lay hold upon him, Priam, hold him fast:
He is thy crutch; now, if thou lose thy stay,   60
Thou on him leaning, and all Troy on thee,
Fall all together.
Pri.   Come, Hector, come; go back:
Thy wife hath dream'd; thy mother hath had visions;
Cassandra doth foresee; and I myself
Am like a prophet suddenly enrapt,
To tell thee that this day is ominous:
Therefore, come back.
Hect.   Æneas is afield;
And I do stand engag'd to many Greeks,
Even in the faith of valour, to appear
This morning to them.
Pri.   Ay, but thou shalt not go.   70
Hect. I must not break my faith.
You know me dutiful; therefore, dear sir,
Let me not shame respect, but give me leave
To take that course by your consent and voice,
Which you do here forbid me, royal Priam.
Cas. O Priam! yield not to him.
And.   Do not, dear father.
Hect. Andromache, I am offended with you:
Upon the love you bear me, get you in.
                        [*Exit* ANDROMACHE.
Tro. This foolish, dreaming, superstitious girl
Makes all these bodements.
Cas.   O farewell, dear Hector!
Look, how thou diest! look, how thy eye turns pale!
Look, how thy wounds do bleed at many vents!   82
Hark, how Troy roars! how Hecuba cries out!
How poor Andromache shrills her dolour forth!
Behold, distraction, frenzy, and amazement,
Like witless anticks, one another meet,
And all cry—Hector! Hector's dead! O Hector!
Tro. Away! away!
Cas. Farewell.—Yet, soft!—Hector, I take my
                                leave:
Thou dost thyself and all our Troy deceive.   [*Exit.*
Hect. You are amaz'd, my liege, at her exclaim.   91
Go in, and cheer the town: we'll forth, and fight,
Do deeds worth praise, and tell you them at night.
Pri. Farewell: the gods with safety stand about
thee!   [*Exeunt severally* PRIAM *and*
                        HECTOR. *Alarums.*
Tro. They are at it; hark!—Proud Diomed, believe,
I come to lose my arm, or win my sleeve.   [*Going.*

Enter PANDARUS.

Pan. Do you hear, my lord? do you hear?
Tro. What now?
Pan. Here's a letter come from yond poor girl.
Tro. Let me read.   100
Pan. A whoreson tisick, a whoreson rascally tisick
so troubles me, and the foolish fortune of this girl; and
what one thing, what another, that I shall leave you
one o' these days: and I have a rheum in mine eyes
too; and such an ache in my bones, that, unless a man
were cursed, I cannot tell what to think on't.—What
says she there?
Tro. Words, words, mere words, no matter from the
heart;   [*Tearing the letter.*
The effect doth operate another way.—
Go, wind to wind, there turn and change together.—
My love with words and errors still she feeds,   111
But edifies another with her deeds. [*Exeunt severally.*

SCENE IV.—Between Troy and the Grecian Camp.

Alarums: Excursions. Enter THERSITES.

Ther. Now they are clapper-clawing one another:
I'll go look on. That dissembling abominable varlet,
Diomed, has got that same scurvy doting foolish young
knave's sleeve of Troy there, in his helm: I would
fain see them meet; that that same young Trojan ass,
that loves the whore there, might send that Greekish
whoremasterly villain, with the sleeve, back to the
dissembling luxurious drab of a sleeveless errand.

O' the other side, the policy of those crafty swearing
rascals,—that stale old mouse-eaten dry cheese, Nestor,
and that same dog-fox, Ulysses,—is not proved worth
a blackberry:—they set me up, in policy, that mongrel
cur, Ajax, against that dog of as bad a kind, Achilles;
and now is the cur Ajax prouder than the cur Achilles,
and will not arm to-day: whereupon the Grecians
begin to proclaim barbarism, and policy grows into
an ill opinion. Soft! here comes sleeve, and t' other.

Enter DIOMEDES, TROILUS *following.*

Tro. Fly not; for shouldst thou take the river Styx,
I would swim after.

Ther. "No, no;—I am a rascal; a scurvy railing knave; a very filthy rogue."

Dio.   Thou dost miscall retire:
I do not fly, but advantageous care   20
Withdrew me from the odds of multitude.
Have at thee!
Ther. Hold thy whore, Grecian!—now for thy
whore, Trojan!—now the sleeve! now the sleeve!
                [*Exeunt* TROILUS *and* DIOMEDES, *fighting.*

Enter HECTOR.

Hect. What art thou, Greek? art thou for Hector's
match?
Art thou of blood and honour?
Ther. No, no;—I am a rascal; a scurvy railing
knave; a very filthy rogue.   28
Hect. I do believe thee:—live.   [*Exit.*
Ther. God-a-mercy, that thou wilt believe me; but
a plague break thy neck, for frighting me! What's
become of the wenching rogues? I think, they have
swallowed one another: I would laugh at that
miracle; yet, in a sort, lechery eats itself. I'll seek
them.   [*Exit.*

SCENE V.—The Same.

Enter DIOMEDES *and a Servant.*

Dio. Go, go, my servant, take thou Troilus' horse;
Present the fair steed to my Lady Cressid.
Fellow, commend my service to her beauty:
Tell her, I have chastis'd the amorous Trojan,
And am her knight by proof.
Serv.   I go, my lord.   [*Exit.*

Enter AGAMEMNON.

Agam. Renew, renew! The fierce Polydamas
Hath beat down Menon: bastard Margarelon
Hath Doreus prisoner,

And stands colossus-wise, waving his beam,
Upon the pashed corses of the kings　　　　10
Epistrophus and Cedius : Polixenes is slain :
Amphimachus, and Thoas, deadly hurt :
Patroclus ta'en, or slain ; and Palamedes
Sore hurt and bruis'd : the dreadful Sagittary
Appals our numbers.　Haste we, Diomed,
To reinforcement, or we perish all.

Enter NESTOR.

Nest. Go, bear Patroclus' body to Achilles ;
And bid the snail-pac'd Ajax arm for shame.—
There is a thousand Hectors in the field :
Now, here he fights on Galathe his horse,　　20
And there lacks work ; anon, he 's there afoot,
And there they fly, or die, like scaled sculls
Before the belching whale ; then is he yonder,
And there the strawy Greeks, ripe for his edge,
Fall down before him, like the mower's swath :
Here, there, and everywhere, he leaves, and takes ;
Dexterity so obeying appetite,
That what he will, he does ; and does so much,
That proof is call'd impossibility.

Enter ULYSSES.

Ulyss. O, courage, courage, princes ! great Achilles
Is arming, weeping, cursing, vowing vengeance :　31
Patroclus' wounds have rous'd his drowsy blood,
Together with his mangled Myrmidons,
That noseless, handless, hack'd and chipp'd, come to
　him,
Crying on Hector.　Ajax hath lost a friend,
And foams at mouth, and he is arm'd, and at it,
Roaring for Troilus ; who hath done to-day
Mad and fantastic execution,
Engaging and redeeming of himself,
With such a careless force, and forceless care,　40
As if that luck, in very spite of cunning,
Bade him win all.

Enter AJAX.

Ajax. Troilus ! thou coward Troilus !　　　*[Exit.*
Dio.　　　　　　　　　Ay, there, there.
Nest. So, so, we draw together.

Enter ACHILLES.

Achil.　　　　　　　Where is this Hector ?
Come, come, thou boy-queller, show thy face ;
Know what it is to meet Achilles angry.
Hector ! where 's Hector ?　I will none but Hector.
　　　　　　　　　　　　　　　[Exeunt.

———

SCENE VI.—Another Part of the Field.

Enter AJAX.

Ajax. Troilus, thou coward Troilus, show thy head !

Enter DIOMEDES.

Dio. Troilus, I say ! where 's Troilus ?
Ajax.　　　　　　　What wouldst thou ?
Dio. I would correct him.
Ajax. Were I the general, thou shouldst have my
　office
Ere that correction.—Troilus, I say ! what, Troilus !

Enter TROILUS.

Tro. O traitor Diomed !—turn thy false face, thou
　traitor,
And pay thy life thou ow'st me for my horse !
Dio. Ha ! art thou there ?
Ajax. I 'll fight with him alone ; stand, Diomed.
Dio. He is my prize ; I will not look upon.　　10
Tro. Come both, you cogging Greeks, have at you
　both.　　　　　　　*[Exeunt, fighting.*

Enter HECTOR.

Hect. Yea, Troilus ?　O, well fought, my youngest
　brother !

Enter ACHILLES.

Achil. Now do I see thee.　Ha !—Have at thee,
　Hector.
Hect. Pause, if thou wilt.

Achil. I do disdain thy courtesy, proud Trojan.
Be happy that my arms are out of use :
My rest and negligence befriend thee now,
But thou anon shalt hear of me again ;
Till when, go seek thy fortune.　　　　*[Exit.*
Hect.　　　　　　　Fare thee well.—
I would have been much more a fresher man,　20
Had I expected thee.—How now, my brother ?

Re-enter TROILUS.

Tro. Ajax hath ta'en Æneas : shall it be ?
No, by the flame of yonder glorious heaven,
He shall not carry him : I 'll be taken too,
Or bring him off.—Fate, hear me what I say !
I reck not though thou end my life to-day.　　*[Exit.*

Enter one in sumptuous armour.

Hect. Stand, stand, thou Greek : thou art a goodly
　　mark.—
No ? wilt thou not ?—I like thy armour well ;
I 'll frush it, and unlock the rivets all,
But I 'll be master of it.—Wilt thou not, beast, abide ?
Why then, fly on, I 'll hunt thee for thy hide.　31
　　　　　　　　　　　　　　[Exeunt.

———

SCENE VII.—The Same.

Enter ACHILLES, *with* MYRMIDONS.

Achil. Come here about me, you my Myrmidons ;
Mark what I say.—Attend me where I wheel :
Strike not a stroke, but keep yourselves in breath ;
And when I have the bloody Hector found,
Empale him with your weapons round about ;
In fellest manner execute your arms.
Follow me, sirs, and my proceedings eye.—
It is decreed—Hector the great must die.　　*[Exeunt.*

———

SCENE VIII.—The Same.

Enter MENELAUS *and* PARIS, *fighting : then,*
　　　　　　　　THERSITES.

Ther. The cuckold and the cuckold-maker are at
it.　Now, bull ! now, dog ! 'Loo, Paris, 'loo ! now, my
double-henned sparrow ! 'loo, Paris, 'loo ! The bull
has the game :—'ware horns, ho !
　　　　　　[Exeunt PARIS *and* MENELAUS.

Enter MARGARELON.

Mar. Turn, slave, and fight.
Ther. What art thou ?
Mar. A bastard son of Priam's.　　　　　7
Ther. I am a bastard too.　I love bastards ; I am a
bastard begot, bastard instructed, bastard in mind,
bastard in valour, in everything illegitimate.　One
bear will not bite another, and wherefore should one
bastard ?　Take heed, the quarrel's most ominous to
us : if the son of a whore fight for a whore, he tempts
judgment.　Farewell, bastard.
Mar. The devil take thee, coward !　　*[Exeunt.*

———

SCENE IX.—Another Part of the Field.

Enter HECTOR.

Hect. Most putrefied core, so fair without,
Thy goodly armour thus hath cost thy life.
Now is my day's work done ; I 'll take good breath :
Rest, sword ; thou hast thy fill of blood and death !
　　　[Puts off his helmet, and lays his sword aside.

Enter ACHILLES *and* MYRMIDONS.

Achil. Look, Hector, how the sun begins to set
How ugly night comes breathing at his heels :
Even with the vail and darking of the sun,
To close the day up, Hector's life is done.
Hect. I am unarm'd ; forego this vantage, Greek.
Achil. Strike, fellows, strike ! this is the man I seek.
　　　　　　　　　　　　　　*[*HECTOR *falls.*

So, Ilion, fall thou next! now, Troy, sink down!   11
Here lies thy heart, thy sinews, and thy bone.
On, Myrmidons; and cry you all amain,
Achilles hath the mighty Hector slain.
                    [*A retreat sounded.*
Hark! a retreat upon our Grecian part.
  Myr. The Trojan trumpets sound the like, my lord.
  Achil. The dragon wing of night o'erspreads the
       earth,
And, stickler-like, the armies separates.
My half-supp'd sword, that frankly would have fed,
Pleas'd with this dainty bit, thus goes to bed.—   20
                    [*Sheathes his sword.*
Come, tie his body to my horse's tail:
Along the field I will the Trojan trail.   [*Exeunt.*

SCENE X.—The Same.

Enter AGAMEMNON, AJAX, MENELAUS, NESTOR,
DIOMEDES, *and others, marching. Shouts within.*

  Agam. Hark! hark! what shout is that?
  Nest.   Peace, drums!
  [*Within.*] Achilles! Achilles! Hector's slain!
     Achilles!
  Dio. The bruit is, Hector's slain, and by Achilles.
  Ajax. If it be so, yet bragless let it be:
Great Hector was a man as good as he.
  Agam. March patiently along.—Let one be sent
To pray Achilles see us at our tent.—
If in his death the gods have us befriended,
Great Troy is ours, and our sharp wars are ended.
                    [*Exeunt, marching.*

SCENE XI.—Another Part of the Field.

Enter ÆNEAS *and Trojan Forces.*

  Æne. Stand, ho! yet are we masters of the field.
Never go home: here starve we out the night.

Enter TROILUS.

  Tro. Hector is slain.
  All.   Hector?—The gods forbid!
  Tro. He's dead; and at the murderer's horse's tail,
In beastly sort, dragg'd through the shameful field.—
Frown on, you heavens, effect your rage with speed!
Sit, gods, upon your thrones, and smile at Troy!
I say, at once let your brief plagues be mercy,
And linger not our sure destructions on!
  Æne. My lord, you do discomfort all the host.   10

  Tro. You understand me not, that tell me so.
I do not speak of flight, of fear, of death;
But dare all imminence that gods and men
Address their dangers in. Hector is gone!
Who shall tell Priam so, or Hecuba?
Let him that will a screech-owl aye be call'd
Go in to Troy, and say there—Hector's dead:
There is a word will Priam turn to stone,
Make wells and Niobes of the maids and wives,
Cold statues of the youth; and, in a word,   20
Hector is dead; there is no more to say.
Stay yet.—You vile abominable tents,
Thus proudly pight upon our Phrygian plains,
Let Titan rise as early as he dare,
I'll through and through you!—And thou, great-siz'd
     coward,
No space of earth shall sunder our two hates:
I'll haunt thee like a wicked conscience still,
That mouldeth goblins swift as frenzy thoughts.—
Strike a free march to Troy!—with comfort go: 30
Hope of revenge shall hide our inward woe.
               [*Exeunt* ÆNEAS *and Trojan Forces.*

As TROILUS *is going out, enter, from the other side,*
              PANDARUS.

  Pan. But hear you, hear you!
  Tro. Hence, broker-lackey! ignomy and shame
Pursue thy life, and live aye with thy name!   [*Exit.*
  Pan. A goodly medicine for mine aching bones!—O
world! world! world! thus is the poor agent despised.
O traitors and bawds, how earnestly are you set a-work,
and how ill requited! why should our endeavour be so
desired, and the performance so loathed? what verse
for it? what instance for it?—Let me see.—   40
     Full merrily the humble-bee doth sing,
     Till he hath lost his honey, and his sting;
     And being once subdued in armed tail,
     Sweet honey and sweet notes together fail.—
Good traders in the flesh, set this in your painted
cloths.
As many as be here of pander's hall,
Your eyes, half out, weep out at Pandar's fall;
Or, if you cannot weep, yet give some groans,
Though not for me, yet for your aching bones.   50
Brethren, and sisters, of the hold-door trade,
Some two months hence my will shall here be made:
It should be now, but that my fear is this,—
Some galled goose of Winchester would hiss.
Till then I'll sweat, and seek about for eases;
And at that time bequeath you my diseases.   [*Exit.*

CORIOLANUS.

DRAMATIS PERSONÆ.

CAIUS MARCIUS, *afterwards* CAIUS MARCIUS
CORIOLANUS, *a noble Roman.*
TITUS LARTIUS, } *Generals against the Volscians.*
COMINIUS,
MENENIUS AGRIPPA, *Friend to Coriolanus.*
SICINIUS VELUTUS, } *Tribunes of the People.*
JUNIUS BRUTUS,
Young MARCIUS, *Son to Coriolanus.*
A Roman Herald.
TULLUS AUFIDIUS, *General of the Volscians.*
Lieutenant to Aufidius.

Conspirators with Aufidius.
A Citizen of Antium.
Two Volscian Guards.
VOLUMNIA, *Mother to Coriolanus.*
VIRGILIA, *Wife to Coriolanus.*
VALERIA, *Friend to Virgilia.*
Gentlewoman, attending on Virgilia.

*Roman and Volscian Senators, Patricians, Ædiles,
Lictors, Soldiers, Citizens, Messengers, Servants
to Aufidius, and other Attendants.*

SCENE—Partly in ROME ; and partly in the Territories of the Volscians and Antiates.

ACT I.

SCENE I.—Rome. A Street.

Enter a company of mutinous Citizens, with staves, clubs, and other weapons.

1 *Citizen.* EFORE we proceed any further, hear me speak.

All. Speak, speak.

1 *Cit.* You are all resolved rather to die than to famish?

All. Resolved, resolved.

1 *Cit.* First, you know, Caius Marcius is chief enemy to the people.

All. We know 't, we know 't.

1 *Cit.* Let us kill him, and we 'll have corn at our own price. Is 't a verdict? 11

All. No more talking on 't ; let it be done. Away, away !

2 *Cit.* One word, good citizens.

1 *Cit.* We are accounted poor citizens, the patricians good. What authority surfeits on would relieve us. If they would yield us but the superfluity, while it were wholesome, we might guess they relieved us humanely ; but they think, we are too dear : the leanness that afflicts us, the object of our misery, is as an inventory to particularise their abundance ; our sufferance is a gain to them.—Let us revenge this with our pikes, ere we become rakes : for the gods know, I speak this in hunger for bread, not in thirst for revenge.

2 *Cit.* Would you proceed especially against Caius Marcius?

All. Against him first : he 's a very dog to the commonalty.

2 *Cit.* Consider you what services he has done for his country? 31

1 *Cit.* Very well ; and could be content to give him good report for 't, but that he pays himself with being proud.

2 *Cit.* Nay, but speak not maliciously.

1 *Cit.* I say unto you, what he hath done famously, he did it to that end : though soft-conscienced men can be content to say it was for his country, he did it to please his mother, and to be partly proud ; which he is, even to the altitude of his virtue. 40

2 *Cit.* What he cannot help in his nature, you account a vice in him. You must in no way say he is covetous.

1 *Cit.* If I must not, I need not be barren of accusations : he hath faults, with surplus, to tire in repetition. [*Shouts within.*] What shouts are these ? The other side o' the city is risen : why stay we prating here ? to the Capitol !

All. Come, come.

1 *Cit.* Soft ! who comes here ? 50

Enter MENENIUS AGRIPPA.

2 *Cit.* Worthy Menenius Agrippa ; one that hath always loved the people.

1 *Cit.* He 's one honest enough : 'would, all the rest were so !

Men. What work 's, my countrymen, in hand ? Where go you
With bats and clubs ? The matter ? Speak, I pray you.

1 *Cit.* Our business is not unknown to the senate : they have had inkling, this fortnight, what we intend to do, which now we 'll show 'em in deeds. They say, poor suitors have strong breaths : they shall know, we have strong arms too. 61

Men. Why, masters, my good friends, mine honest
                                        neighbours,
Will you undo yourselves ?
1 *Cit.* We cannot, sir ; we are undone already.
Men. I tell you, friends, most charitable care
Have the patricians of you. For your wants,
Your suffering in this dearth, you may as well
Strike at the heaven with your staves, as lift them
Against the Roman state, whose course will on
The way it takes, cracking ten thousand curbs   70
Of more strong link asunder than can ever
Appear in your impediment. For the dearth,
The gods, not the patricians, make it ; and
Your knees to them, not arms, must help. Alack !

Men. " There was a time, when all the body's members
Rebell'd against the belly."

You are transported by calamity
Thither where more attends you ; and you slander
The helms o' the state, who care for you like fathers,
When you curse them as enemies.   78
1 *Cit.* Care for us !—True, indeed !—They ne'er cared
for us yet. Suffer us to famish, and their store-houses
crammed with grain ; make edicts for usury, to support usurers ; repeal daily any wholesome act established against the rich, and provide more piercing
statutes daily to chain up and restrain the poor. If
the wars eat us not up, they will ; and there 's all the
love they bear us.
Men. Either you must
Confess yourselves wondrous malicious,
Or be accus'd of folly. I shall tell you
A pretty tale : it may be, you have heard it ;   90
But, since it serves my purpose, I will venture
To stale 't a little more.
1 *Cit.* Well, I 'll hear it, sir : yet you must not think
to fob off our disgrace with a tale ; but, an 't please
you, deliver.
Men. There was a time, when all the body's mem-
                                        bers
Rebell'd against the belly ; thus accus'd it :—
That only like a gulf it did remain
I' the midst o' the body, idle and unactive,
Still cupboarding the viand, never bearing   100
Like labour with the rest ; where the other instru-
                                        ments
Did see and hear, devise, instruct, walk, feel,
And, mutually participate, did minister
Unto the appetite and affection common
Of the whole body. The belly answered,—
1 *Cit.* Well, sir, what answer made the belly ?
Men. Sir, I shall tell you.—With a kind of smile,
Which ne'er came from the lungs, but even thus,
(For, look you, I may make the belly smile,

As well as speak,) it tauntingly replied   110
To the discontented members, the mutinous parts
That envied his receipt ; even so most fitly
As you malign our senators, for that
They are not such as you.
1 *Cit.*   Your belly's answer ? What !
The kingly-crowned head, the vigilant eye,
The counsellor heart, the arm our soldier,
Our steed the leg, the tongue our trumpeter,
With other muniments and petty helps
In this our fabric, if that they—
Men.   What then ?—
'Fore me, this fellow speaks !—What then ? what
                                        then ?   120
1 *Cit.* Should by the cormorant belly be
                                        restrain'd,
Who is the sink o' the body,—
Men.   Well, what then ?
1 *Cit.* The former agents, if they did
                                        complain,
What could the belly answer ?
Men.   I will tell you :
If you 'll bestow a small (of what you have
                                        little)
Patience awhile, you 'll hear the belly's
                                        answer.
1 *Cit.* Ye 're long about it.
Men.   Note me this, good friend ;
Your most grave belly was deliberate,
Not rash like his accusers, and thus an-
                                        swer'd :—
" True is it, my incorporate friends," quoth
                                        he,   130
" That I receive the general food at first,
Which you do live upon ; and fit it is,
Because I am the store-house, and the shop
Of the whole body : but, if you do remember,
I send it through the rivers of your blood,
Even to the court, the heart, to the seat o' the
                                        brain ;
And, through the cranks and offices of
                                        man,
The strongest nerves, and small inferior
                                        veins,
From me receive that natural competency
Whereby they live. And though that all at once,   140
You, my good friends,"—this says the belly, mark
                                        me,—
1 *Cit.* Ay, sir ; well, well.
Men.   " Though all at once cannot
See what I do deliver out to each,
Yet I can make my audit up, that all
From me do back receive the flour of all,
And leave me but the bran." What say you to 't ?
1 *Cit.* It was an answer. How apply you this ?
Men. The senators of Rome are this good belly,
And you the mutinous members : for examine
Their counsels and their cares ; digest things rightly,
Touching the weal o' the common ; you shall find, 151
No public benefit which you receive,
But it proceeds, or comes, from them to you,
And no way from yourselves.—What do you think,
You, the great toe of this assembly ?
1 *Cit.* I the great toe ? Why the great toe ?
Men. For that, being one o' the lowest, basest,
                                        poorest,
Of this most wise rebellion, thou go'st foremost :
Thou rascal, that art worst in blood to run,
Lead'st first to win some vantage.—   160
But make you ready your stiff bats and clubs :
Rome and her rats are at the point of battle ;
The one side must have bale.—Hail, noble Marcius !

Enter CAIUS MARCIUS.

Mar. Thanks.—What 's the matter, you dissentious
                                        rogues,
That, rubbing the poor itch of your opinion,
Make yourselves scabs ?
1 *Cit.*   We have ever your good word.
Mar. He that will give good words to thee, will
                                        flatter
Beneath abhorring.—What would you have, you curs,

That like nor peace, nor war? the one affrights you,
The other makes you proud. He that trusts to you,
Where he should find you lions, finds you hares; 171
Where foxes, geese: you are no surer, no,
Than is the coal of fire upon the ice,
Or hailstone in the sun. Your virtue is
To make him worthy whose offence subdues him,
And curse that justice did it.—Who deserves great-
ness,
Deserves your hate; and your affections are
A sick man's appetite, who desires most that
Which would increase his evil. He that depends
Upon your favours, swims with fins of lead, 180
And hews down oaks with rushes. Hang ye! Trust
ye?
With every minute you do change a mind,
And call him noble that was now your hate,
Him vile that was your garland. What's the matter,
That in these several places of the city
You cry against the noble senate, who,
Under the gods, keep you in awe, which else
Would feed on one another?—What's their seeking?
Men. For corn at their own rates: whereof, they
say,
The city is well stor'd.
  Mar.   Hang 'em! They say! 190
They'll sit by the fire, and presume to know
What's done i' the Capitol; who's like to rise,
Who thrives, and who declines; side factions, and
give out
Conjectural marriages; making parties strong,
And feebling such as stand not in their liking,
Below their cobbled shoes. They say, there's grain
enough!
Would the nobility lay aside their ruth,
And let me use my sword, I'd make a quarry
With thousands of these quarter'd slaves, as high
As I could pick my lance.   200
Men. Nay, these are almost thoroughly persuaded;
For though abundantly they lack discretion,
Yet are they passing cowardly. But, I beseech you,
What says the other troop?
  Mar.   They are dissolved. Hang 'em!
They said, they were an-hungry; sigh'd forth pro-
verbs:
That hunger broke stone walls; that dogs must eat;
That meat was made for mouths; that the gods sent
not
Corn for the rich men only.—With these shreds
They vented their complainings; which being an-
swer'd,
And a petition granted them, a strange one,   210
(To break the heart of generosity,
And make bold power look pale,) they threw their
caps
As they would hang them on the horns o' the moon,
Shouting their emulation.
  Men.   What is granted them?
Mar. Five tribunes, to defend their vulgar wisdoms,
Of their own choice: one's Junius Brutus,
Sicinius Velutus, and I know not—'Sdeath!
The rabble should have first unroof'd the city,
Ere so prevail'd with me; it will in time
Win upon power, and throw forth greater themes 220
For insurrection's arguing.
  Men.   This is strange.
Mar. Go; get you home, you fragments!

Enter a Messenger, hastily.

Mess. Where's Caius Marcius?
  Mar.   Here. What is the matter?
Mess. The news is, sir, the Volsces are in arms.
Mar. I am glad on't; then we shall ha' means to
vent
Our musty superfluity.—See, our best elders.

Enter Cominius, Titus Lartius, *and other Senators;*
Junius Brutus *and* Sicinius Velutus.

1 Sen. Marcius, 'tis true that you have lately told us;
The Volsces are in arms.
  Mar.   They have a leader,
Tullus Aufidius, that will put you to't.

I sin in envying his nobility;   230
And were I anything but what I am,
I would wish me only he.
  Com.   You have fought together.
Mar. Were half to half the world by the ears, and
he
Upon my party, I'd revolt, to make
Only my wars with him: he is a lion
That I am proud to hunt.
  1 Sen.   Then, worthy Marcius,
Attend upon Cominius to these wars.
  Com. It is your former promise.
  Mar.   Sir, it is;
And I am constant.—Titus Lartius, thou
Shalt see me once more strike at Tullus' face. 240
What! art thou stiff? stand'st out?
  Tit.   No, Caius Marcius;
I'll lean upon one crutch, and fight with the other,
Ere stay behind this business.
  Men.   O, true-bred!
1 Sen. Your company to the Capitol; where, I know,
Our greatest friends attend us.
  Tit. [*To* Cominius.]   Lead you on:
[*To* Marcius.] Follow Cominius; we must follow you;
Right worthy you priority.
  Com.   Noble Marcius!
1 Sen. [*To the Citizens.*] Hence! To your homes!
be gone.
  Mar.   Nay, let them follow:
The Volsces have much corn; take these rats thither,
To gnaw their garners.—Worshipful mutiners, 250
Your valour puts well forth; pray, follow.
    [*Exeunt Senators,* Cominius, Marcius, Titus,
        and Menenius. *Citizens steal away.*
Sic. Was ever man so proud as is this Marcius?
Bru. He has no equal.
Sic. When we were chosen tribunes for the people,—
Bru. Mark'd you his lip and eyes?
Sic.   Nay, but his taunts.
Bru. Being mov'd, he will not spare to gird the
gods.
Sic. Bemock the modest moon,
Bru. The present wars devour him! he is grown
Too proud to be so valiant.
  Sic.   Such a nature,
Tickled with good success, disdains the shadow 260
Which he treads on at noon. But I do wonder,
His insolence can brook to be commanded
Under Cominius.
  Bru.   Fame, at the which he aims,
In whom already he's well grac'd, cannot
Better be held, nor more attain'd, than by
A place below the first; for what miscarries
Shall be the general's fault, though he perform
To the utmost of a man; and giddy censure
Will then cry out of Marcius, "O, if he
Had borne the business!"
  Sic.   Besides, if things go well,
Opinion, that so sticks on Marcius, shall 271
Of his demerits rob Cominius.
  Bru.   Come:
Half all Cominius' honours are to Marcius,
Though Marcius earn'd them not; and all his faults
To Marcius shall be honours, though, indeed,
In aught he merit not.
  Sic.   Let's hence and hear
How the despatch is made; and in what fashion,
More than his singularity, he goes
Upon his present action.
  Bru.   Let's along.   [*Exeunt.*

SCENE II.—Corioli. The Senate-house.

Enter Tullus Aufidius *and Senators.*

1 Sen. So, your opinion is, Aufidius,
That they of Rome are enter'd in our counsels,
And know how we proceed.
  Auf.   Is it not yours?
Whatever have been thought on in this state,
That could be brought to bodily act ere Rome

Had circumvention? 'T is not four days gone,
Since I heard thence; these are the words: I think,
I have the letter here; yes, here it is :—
[*Reads.*] "They have press'd a power, but it is not
    known
Whether for east, or west. The dearth is great;   10
The people mutinous; and it is rumour'd,
Cominius, Marcius your old enemy
(Who is of Rome worse hated than of you),
And Titus Lartius, a most valiant Roman,
These three lead on this preparation
Whither 't is bent : most likely, 't is for you.
Consider of it."
  1 Sen.   Our army 's in the field :
We never yet made doubt but Rome was ready
To answer us.
  Auf.   Nor did you think it folly,
To keep your great pretences veil'd till when   20
They needs must show themselves; which in the
    hatching,
It seem'd, appear'd to Rome. By the discovery
We shall be shorten'd in our aim; which was,
To take in many towns, ere, almost, Rome
Should know we were afoot.
  2 Sen.   Noble Aufidius,
Take your commission; hie you to your bands;
Let us alone to guard Corioli :
If they set down before 's, for the remove
Bring up your army; but, I think, you 'll find
They 've not prepar'd for us.
  Auf.   O! doubt not that;   30
I speak from certainties. Nay, more;
Some parcels of their power are forth already,
And only hitherward. I leave your honours.
If we and Caius Marcius chance to meet,
'T is sworn between us, we shall ever strike
Till one can do no more.
  All.   The gods assist you!
  Auf. And keep your honours safe!
  1 Sen.   Farewell.
  2 Sen.   Farewell.
  All. Farewell.   [*Exeunt.*

SCENE III.—Rome.   An Apartment in MARCIUS'
House.

Enter VOLUMNIA *and* VIRGILIA. *They sit down on
two low stools, and sew.*

Vol. I pray you, daughter, sing; or express yourself
in a more comfortable sort. If my son were my husband, I should freelier rejoice in that absence wherein
he won honour, than in the embracements of his bed,
where he would show most love. When yet he was
but tender-bodied, and the only son of my womb;
when youth with comeliness pluck'd all gaze his way;
when, for a day of kings' entreaties, a mother should
not sell him an hour from her beholding; I,—considering how honour would become such a person;
that it was no better than picture-like to hang by the
wall, if renown made it not stir,—was pleased to let
him seek danger where he was like to find fame. To
a cruel war I sent him; from whence he returned, his
brows bound with oak. I tell thee, daughter, I sprang
not more in joy at first hearing he was a man-child,
than now in first seeing he had proved himself a man.
  Vir. But had he died in the business, madam? how
then?   19
  Vol. Then his good report should have been my son:
I therein would have found issue. Hear me profess
sincerely :—had I a dozen sons,—each in my love alike,
and none less dear than thine and my good Marcius,—
I had rather had eleven die nobly for their country,
than one voluptuously surfeit out of action.

Enter a Gentlewoman.

  Gent. Madam, the Lady Valeria is come to visit you.
  Vir. 'Beseech you, give me leave to retire myself.
  Vol. Indeed, you shall not.
Methinks, I hear hither your husband's drum,
See him pluck Aufidius down by the hair;   30
As children from a bear, the Volsces shunning him:

Methinks, I see him stamp thus, and call thus,—
"Come on, you cowards! you were got in fear,
Though you were born in Rome." His bloody brow
With his mail'd hand then wiping, forth he goes,
Like to a harvest-man, that 's task'd to mow
Or all, or lose his hire.
  Vir. His bloody brow! O Jupiter, no blood!
  Vol. Away, you fool! it more becomes a man,
Than gilt his trophy : the breasts of Hecuba,   40
When she did suckle Hector, look'd not lovelier
Than Hector's forehead, when it spit forth blood
At Grecian swords, contemning.—Tell Valeria,
We are fit to bid her welcome.   [*Exit Gentlewoman.*
  Vir. Heavens bless my lord from fell Aufidius!
  Vol. He 'll beat Aufidius' head below his knee,
And tread upon his neck.

Re-enter Gentlewoman, with VALERIA *and an Usher.*

  Val. My ladies both, good day to you.
  Vol. Sweet madam.
  Vir. I am glad to see your ladyship.   50
  Val. How do you both? you are manifest house-
keepers. What are you sewing here? A fine spot, in
good faith.—How does your little son?
  Vir. I thank your ladyship; well, good madam.
  Vol. He had rather see the swords, and hear a drum,
than look upon his schoolmaster.
  Val. O' my word, the father's son; I 'll swear, 't is
a very pretty boy. O' my troth, I looked upon him o'
Wednesday half an hour together: he has such a con-
firmed countenance. I saw him run after a gilded
butterfly; and when he caught it, he let it go again;
and after it again; and over and over he comes, and
up again, catched it again : or whether his fall enraged
him, or how 't was, he did so set his teeth, and tear it;
O! I warrant, how he mammocked it!
  Vol. One of his father's moods.
  Val. Indeed, la, 't is a noble child.
  Vir. A crack, madam.
  Val. Come, lay aside your stitchery; I must have
you play the idle huswife with me this afternoon.   70
  Vir. No, good madam; I will not out of doors.
  Val. Not out of doors!
  Vol. She shall, she shall.
  Vir. Indeed, no, by your patience : I 'll not over the
threshold, till my lord return from the wars.
  Val. Fie! you confine yourself most unreasonably.
Come; you must go visit the good lady that lies in.
  Vir. I will wish her speedy strength, and visit her
with my prayers; but I cannot go thither.
  Vol. Why, I pray you?   80
  Vir. 'T is not to save labour, nor that I want love.
  Val. You would be another Penelope; yet, they say,
all the yarn she spun in Ulysses' absence did but fill
Ithaca full of moths. Come; I would, your cambric
were sensible as your finger, that you might leave
pricking it for pity. Come, you shall go with us.
  Vir. No, good madam, pardon me; indeed, I will
not forth.
  Val. In truth, la, go with me; and I 'll tell you
excellent news of your husband.   90
  Vir. O, good madam, there can be none yet.
  Val. Verily, I do not jest with you : there came
news from him last night.
  Vir. Indeed, madam?
  Val. In earnest, it 's true; I heard a senator speak
it. Thus it is :—the Volsces have an army forth,
against whom Cominius the general is gone, with one
part of our Roman power; your lord, and Titus
Lartius, are set down before their city Corioli; they
nothing doubt prevailing, and to make it brief wars.
This is true, on mine honour; and so, I pray, go with us.
  Vir. Give me excuse, good madam; I will obey you
in everything hereafter.   103
  Vol. Let her alone, lady: as she is now, she will
but disease our better mirth.
  Val. In troth, I think she would.—Fare you well
then.—Come, good sweet lady.—Pr'ythee, Virgilia,
turn thy solemness out o' door, and go along with us.
  Vir. No, at a word, madam; indeed, I must not. I
wish you much mirth.   109
  Val. Well then, farewell.   [*Exeunt.*

SCENE IV.—Before Corioli.

Enter, with drum and colours, MARCIUS, TITUS
LARTIUS, *Officers, and Soldiers. To them a Messenger.*

Mar. Yonder comes news :—a wager, they have
    met.
Lart. My horse to yours, no.
Mar.   'T is done.
Lart.   Agreed.
Mar. Say, has our general met the enemy?
Mess. They lie in view, but have not spoke as yet.
Lart. So, the good horse is mine.
Mar.   I 'll buy him of you.
Lart. No, I 'll nor sell nor give him : lend you him
    I will,
For half a hundred years.—Summon the town.
Mar. How far off lie these armies?
Mess.   Within this mile and half.
Mar. Then shall we hear their 'larum, and they ours.
Now, Mars, I pr'ythee, make us quick in work,   10
That we with smoking swords may march from hence,
To help our fielded friends!—Come, blow thy blast.

*A parley sounded. Enter, on the walls, two
Senators, and others.*

Tullus Aufidius, is he within your walls?
1 Sen. No, nor a man that fears you less than he.
That 's lesser than a little. [*Drums afar off.*] Hark, our
    drums
Are bringing forth our youth : we 'll break our walls,
Rather than they shall pound us up. Our gates,
Which yet seem shut, we have but pinn'd with rushes ;
They 'll open of themselves. [*Alarum afar off.*] Hark
    you, far off !
There is Aufidius : list, what work he makes   20
Amongst your cloven army.
Mar.   O ! they are at it.
Lart. Their noise be our instruction.—Ladders, ho !

The Volsces enter, and pass over the stage.

Mar. They fear us not, but issue forth their city.
Now put your shields before your hearts, and fight
With hearts more proof than shields.—Advance,
    brave Titus :
They do disdain us much beyond our thoughts,
Which makes me sweat with wrath.—Come on, my
    fellows :
He that retires, I 'll take him for a Volsce,
And he shall feel mine edge.

*Alarum, and exeunt Romans and Volsces, fighting.
The Romans are beaten back to their trenches.
Re-enter* MARCIUS.

Mar. All the contagion of the south light on you, 30
You shames of Rome ! you herd of—Biles and plagues
Plaster you o'er, that you may be abhorr'd
Further than seen, and one infect another
Against the wind a mile ! You souls of geese,
That bear the shapes of men, how have you run
From slaves that apes would beat ! Pluto and hell !
All hurt behind ; backs red, and faces pale
With flight and agued fear ! Mend, and charge home,
Or, by the fires of heaven, I 'll leave the foe,
And make my wars on you ; look to 't : come on ;   40
If you 'll stand fast, we 'll beat them to their wives,
As they us to our trenches followed.

*Another alarum. The Volsces and Romans re-enter,
and the fight is renewed. The Volsces retire into
Corioli, and* MARCIUS *follows them to the gates.*

So, now the gates are ope :—now prove good seconds.
'T is for the followers fortune widens them,
Not for the fliers : mark me, and do the like.
    [*He enters the gates, and is shut in.*
1 Sol. Fool-hardiness ! not I.
2 Sol.   Nor I.
3 Sol. See, they have shut him in.
    [*Alarum continues.*
All.   To the pot, I warrant him.

Enter TITUS LARTIUS.

Lart. What is become of Marcius?

All.   Slain, sir, doubtless.
1 Sol. Following the fliers at the very heels,
With them he enters ; who, upon the sudden,   50
Clapp'd-to their gates : he is himself alone,
To answer all the city.
Lart.   O noble fellow !
Who sensibly outdares his senseless sword,
And, when it bows, stands up. Thou art left, Marcius :
A carbuncle entire, as big as thou art,
Were not so rich a jewel. Thou wast a soldier
Even to Cato's wish, not fierce and terrible
Only in strokes ; but, with thy grim looks, and
The thunder-like percussion of thy sounds,
Thou mad'st thine enemies shake, as if the world   60
Were feverous and did tremble.

Re-enter MARCIUS, *bleeding, assaulted by the enemy.*

1 Sol.   Look, sir !
Lart.   O, 't is Marcius !
Let 's fetch him off, or make remain alike.
    [*They fight, and all enter the city.*

SCENE V.—Within Corioli. A Street.

Enter certain Romans, with spoils.

1 Rom. This will I carry to Rome.
2 Rom. And I this.
3 Rom. A murrain on 't ! I took this for silver.
    [*Alarum continues still afar off.*

Enter MARCIUS *and* TITUS LARTIUS, *with a trumpet.*

Mar. See here these movers, that do prize their
    hours
At a crack'd drachm ! Cushions, leaden spoons,
Irons of a doit, doublets that hangmen would
Bury with those that wore them, these base slaves,
Ere yet the fight be done, pack up.—Down with
    them !—
And hark, what noise the general makes !—To him !
There is the man of my soul's hate, Aufidius,   10
Piercing our Romans : then, valiant Titus, take
Convenient numbers to make good the city,
Whilst I, with those that have the spirit, will haste
To help Cominius.
Lart.   Worthy sir, thou bleed'st ;
Thy exercise hath been too violent
For a second course of fight.
Mar.   Sir, praise me not :
My work hath yet not warm'd me. Fare you well.
The blood I drop is rather physical
Than dangerous to me. To Aufidius thus
I will appear, and fight.
Lart.   Now the fair goddess, Fortune,
Fall deep in love with thee ; and her great charms   21
Misguide thy opposers' swords ! Bold gentleman,
Prosperity be thy page !
Mar.   Thy friend no less
Than those she placeth highest ! So, farewell.
Lart. Thou worthiest Marcius !—   [*Exit* MARCIUS.
Go, sound thy trumpet in the market-place ;
Call thither all the officers of the town,
Where they shall know our mind. Away ! [*Exeunt.*

SCENE VI.—Near the Camp of COMINIUS.

Enter COMINIUS *and Forces, as in retreat.*

Com. Breathe you, my friends : well fought ; we are
    come off
Like Romans, neither foolish in our stands,
Nor cowardly in retire : believe me, sirs,
We shall be charg'd again. Whiles we have struck,
By interims and conveying gusts we have heard
The charges of our friends.—Ye Roman gods,
Lead their successes as we wish our own,
That both our powers, with smiling fronts encoun-
    tering,
May give you thankful sacrifice !—

Enter a Messenger.
           Thy news?
Mess. The citizens of Corioli have issued,   10
And given to Lartius and to Marcius battle :
I saw our party to their trenches driven,
And then I came away.
Com.   Though thou speak'st truth,
Methinks, thou speak'st not well. How long is 't
since?
Mess. Above an hour, my lord.
Com. 'T is not a mile; briefly we heard their drums:
How couldst thou in a mile confound an hour,
And bring thy news so late?
Mess.   Spies of the Volsces
Held me in chase, that I was forc'd to wheel
Three or four miles about ; else had I, sir,   20
Half an hour since brought my report.

Enter MARCIUS.
Com.   Who 's yonder,
That does appear as he were flay'd? O gods !
He has the stamp of Marcius, and I have
Before-time seen him thus.
Mar.   Come I too late?
Com. The shepherd knows not thunder from a
tabor,
More than I know the sound of Marcius' tongue
From every meaner man.
Mar.   Come I too late ?
Com. Ay, if you come not in the blood of others,
But mantled in your own.
Mar.   O! let me clip you
In arms as sound as when I woo'd ; in heart   30
As merry as when our nuptial day was done,
And tapers burn'd to bedward.
Com.   Flower of warriors,
How is 't with Titus Lartius ?
Mar. As with a man busied about decrees :
Condemning some to death, and some to exile ;
Ransoming him, or pitying, threat'ning the other ;
Holding Corioli in the name of Rome,
Even like a fawning greyhound in the leash,
To let him slip at will.
Com.   Where is that slave,
Which told me they had beat you to your trenches ? 40
Where is he ? Call him hither.
Mar.   Let him alone ;
He did inform the truth : but for our gentlemen,
The common file, (a plague !—tribunes for them !)
The mouse ne'er shunn'd the cat, as they did budge
From rascals worse than they.
Com.   But how prevail'd you ?
Mar. Will the time serve to tell ? I do not think :
Where is the enemy ? are you lords o' the field ?
If not, why cease you till you are so ?
Com. Marcius, we have at disadvantage fought,
And did retire to win our purpose.   50
Mar. How lies their battle ? know you on which
side
They have plac'd their men of trust ?
Com.   As I guess, Marcius,
Their bands i' the vaward are the Antiates,
Of their best trust ; o'er them Aufidius,
Their very heart of hope.
Mar.   I do beseech you,
By all the battles wherein we have fought,
By the blood we have shed together, by the vows
We have made to endure friends, that you directly
Set me against Aufidius, and his Antiates ;
And that you not delay the present, but,   60
Filling the air with swords advanc'd and darts,
We prove this very hour.
Com.   Though I could wish
You were conducted to a gentle bath,
And balms applied to you, yet dare I never
Deny your asking. Take your choice of those
That best can aid your action.
Mar.   Those are they
That most are willing.—If any such be here,
(As it were sin to doubt,) that love this painting
Wherein you see me smear'd ; if any fear
Lesser his person than an ill report ;   70

If any think, brave death outweighs bad life,
And that his country 's dearer than himself ;
Let him, alone, or so many so minded,
Wave thus, to express his disposition,
And follow Marcius.
     [*They all shout, and wave their swords ; take
       him up in their arms, and cast up their
       caps.*
O me, alone ! Make you a sword of me ?
If these shows be not outward, which of you
But is four Volsces ? None of you but is
Able to bear against the great Aufidius
A shield as hard as his. A certain number,   80
Though thanks to all, must I select from all : the rest
Shall bear the business in some other fight,
As cause will be obey'd. Please you to march ;
And four shall quickly draw out my command,
Which men are best inclin'd.
Com.   March on, my fellows :
Make good this ostentation, and you shall
Divide in all with us.   [*Exeunt.*

SCENE VII.—The Gates of Corioli.

TITUS LARTIUS, *having set a guard upon Corioli, going
with a drum and trumpet toward* COMINIUS *and*
CAIUS MARCIUS, *enters with a Lieutenant, a party
of Soldiers, and a Scout.*

Lart. So ; let the ports be guarded : keep your
duties,
As I have set them down. If I do send, despatch
Those centuries to our aid ; the rest will serve
For a short holding : if we lose the field,
We cannot keep the town.
Lieu.   Fear not our care, sir.
Lart. Hence, and shut your gates upon us.—
Our guider, come ; to the Roman camp conduct us.
       [*Exeunt.*

SCENE VIII.—A Field of Battle between the Roman
and the Volscian Camps.

Alarum. Enter MARCIUS *and* AUFIDIUS.

Mar. I 'll fight with none but thee ; for I do hate thee
Worse than a promise-breaker.
Auf.   We hate alike :
Not Afric owns a serpent, I abhor
More than thy fame and envy. Fix thy foot.
Mar. Let the first budger die the other's slave,
And the gods doom him after !
Auf.   If I fly, Marcius,
Halloo me like a hare.
Mar.   Within these three hours, Tullus,
Alone I fought in your Corioli walls,
And made what work I pleas'd ; 't is not my blood,
Wherein thou seest me mask'd : for thy revenge   10
Wrench up thy power to the highest.
Auf.   Wert thou the Hector,
That was the whip of your bragg'd progeny,
Thou shouldst not scape me here.—
     [*They fight, and certain Volsces come to the
       aid of* AUFIDIUS.
Officious, and not valiant,—you have sham'd me
In your condemned seconds.
     [*Exeunt fighting, all driven by* MARCIUS.

SCENE IX.—The Roman Camp.

*Alarum. A retreat sounded. Flourish. Enter, at
one side,* COMINIUS *and Romans; at the other side,*
MARCIUS, *with his arm in a scarf, and other
Romans.*

Com. If I should tell thee o'er this thy day's work,
Thou 'lt not believe thy deeds : but I 'll report it,
Where senators shall mingle tears with smiles ;
Where great patricians shall attend, and shrug,
I' the end admire ; where ladies shall be frighted,
And, gladly quak'd, hear more ; where the dull
tribunes.

That, with the fusty plebeians, hate thine honours,
Shall say, against their hearts,—
" We thank the gods, our Rome hath such a soldier!"—
Yet cam'st thou to a morsel of this feast,   10
Having fully din'd before.

The grave of your deserving: Rome must know   20
The value of her own: 't were a concealment
Worse than a theft, no less than a traducement,
To hide your doings ; and to silence that,
Which, to the spire and top of praises vouch'd,

THE FIGHT BETWEEN MARCIUS AND AUFIDIUS.

Enter TITUS LARTIUS, *with his Power, from the
pursuit.*

Lart.   O general,
Here is the steed, we the caparison :
Hadst thou beheld—
Mar.   Pray now, no more : my mother,
Who has a charter to extol her blood,
When she does praise me, grieves me.   I have done
As you have done ; that 's what I can ; induc'd
As you have been ; that 's for my country :
He that has but effected his good will
Hath overta'en mine act.
Com.   You shall not be

Would seem but modest.   Therefore, I beseech you,
(In sign of what you are, not to reward
What you have done,) before our army hear me.
Mar.   I have some wounds upon me, and they smart
To hear themselves remember'd.
Com.   Should they not,
Well might they fester 'gainst ingratitude,   30
And tent themselves with death.   Of all the horses
(Whereof we have ta'en good, and good store), of all
The treasure, in this field achiev'd and city,
We render you the tenth ; to be ta'en forth,
Before the common distribution,
At your only choice.
Mar.   I thank you, general;

But cannot make my heart consent to take
A bribe to pay my sword : I do refuse it ;
And stand upon my common part with those
That have beheld the doing.   40
   [*A long flourish. They all cry, "*MARCIUS*!
     MARCIUS!" cast up their caps and lances :*
     COMINIUS *and* LARTIUS *stand bare.*
  Mar. May these same instruments, which you pro-
    fane,
Never sound more ! When drums and trumpets shall
I' the field prove flatterers, let courts and cities be
Made all of false-fac'd soothing !
When steel grows soft as the parasite's silk,
Let him be made a coverture for the wars !
No more, I say. For that I have not wash'd
My nose that bled, or foil'd some debile wretch,
Which, without note, here's many else have done,
You shout me forth   50
In acclamations hyperbolical ;
As if I loved my little should be dieted
In praises sauc'd with lies.
  Com.   Too modest are you,
More cruel to your good report, than grateful
To us that give you truly. By your patience,
If 'gainst yourself you be incens'd, we'll put you
(Like one that means his proper harm) in manacles,
Then reason safely with you.—Therefore, be it known,
As to us, to all the world, that Caius Marcius
Wears this war's garland : in token of the which 60
My noble steed, known to the camp, I give him,
With all his trim belonging ; and, from this time,
For what he did before Corioli, call him,
With all the applause and clamour of the host,
CAIUS MARCIUS CORIOLANUS.—
Bear the addition nobly ever !
  All. Caius Marcius Coriolanus !
    [*Flourish. Trumpets sound, and drums.*
  Cor. I will go wash ;
And when my face is fair, you shall perceive
Whether I blush, or no : howbeit, I thank you.— 70
I mean to stride your steed ; and, at all times,
To undercrest your good addition
To the fairness of my power.
  Com.   So, to our tent ;
Where, ere we do repose us, we will write
To Rome of our success.—You, Titus Lartius,
Must to Corioli back : send us to Rome
The best, with whom we may articulate,
For their own good, and ours.
  Lart.   I shall, my lord.
  Cor. The gods begin to mock me. I, that now
Refus'd most princely gifts, am bound to beg   80
Of my lord general.
  Com.   Take it : 't is yours.—What is 't ?
  Cor. I sometime lay, here in Corioli,
At a poor man's house ; he us'd me kindly :
He cried to me ; I saw him prisoner ;
But then Aufidius was within my view,
And wrath o'erwhelm'd my pity. I request you
To give my poor host freedom.
  Com.   O, well begg'd !
Were he the butcher of my son, he should
Be free as is the wind. Deliver him, Titus.
  Lart. Marcius, his name ?
  Cor.   By Jupiter, forgot !— 90
I am weary ; yea, my memory is tir'd.—
Have we no wine here ?
  Com.   Go we to our tent.
The blood upon your visage dries ; 't is time
It should be look'd to. Come.   [*Exeunt.*

SCENE X.—The Camp of the Volsces.

A Flourish. Cornets. Enter TULLUS AUFIDIUS,
  bloody, with two or three Soldiers.
  Auf. The town is ta'en !
  1 Sold. 'T will be deliver'd back on good condition.
  Auf. Condition !—
I would I were a Roman ; for I cannot,
Being a Volsce, be that I am.—Condition !
What good condition can a treaty find
I' the part that is at mercy ?—Five times, Marcius,
I have fought with thee : so often hast thou beat me ;

  Auf. "I would I were a Roman ; for I cannot.
  Being a Volsce, be that I am."

And wouldst do so, I think, should we encounter
As often as we eat.—By the elements,   10
If e'er again I meet him beard to beard,
He is mine, or I am his. Mine emulation
Hath not that honour in 't, it had ; for where
I thought to crush him in an equal force,
True sword to sword, I'll potch at him some way,
Or wrath, or craft, may get him.
  1 Sold.   He's the devil.
  Auf. Bolder, though not so subtle. My valour's
    poison'd,
With only suffering stain by him ; for him
Shall fly out of itself. Nor sleep, nor sanctuary,
Being naked, sick ; nor fane, nor Capitol,   20
The prayers of priests, nor times of sacrifice,
Embarquements all of fury, shall lift up
Their rotten privilege and custom 'gainst
My hate to Marcius. Where I find him, were it
At home, upon my brother's guard, even there,
Against the hospitable canon, would I
Wash my fierce hand in his heart. Go you to the city :
Learn, how 't is held, and what they are, that must
Be hostages for Rome.
  1 Sold.   Will not you go ?
  Auf. I am attended at the cypress grove : I pray you,
('T is south the city mills,) bring me word thither 31
How the world goes, that to the pace of it
I may spur on my journey.
  1 Sold.   I shall, sir.   [*Exeunt.*

ACT II.

SCENE I.—Rome. A Public Place.

Enter MENENIUS, SICINIUS, *and* BRUTUS.

Menenius.

THE augurer tells me, we shall have news to-night.

Bru. Good, or bad?

Men. Not according to the prayer of the people, for they love not Marcius.

Sic. Nature teaches beasts to know their friends.

Men. Pray you, who does the wolf love?

Sic. The lamb.

Men. Ay, to devour him: as the hungry plebeians would the noble Marcius.   11

Bru. He's a lamb, indeed, that baes like a bear.

Men. He's a bear, indeed, that lives like a lamb. You two are old men: tell me one thing that I shall ask you.

Both Trib. Well, sir.

Men. In what enormity is Marcius poor in, that you two have not in abundance?

Bru. He's poor in no one fault, but stored with all.   21

Sic. Especially in pride.

Bru. And topping all others in boasting.

Men. This is strange now. Do you two know how you are censured here in the city, I mean of us o' the right-hand file? Do you?

Both Trib. Why, how are we censured?

Men. Because you talk of pride now,—will you not be angry?

Both Trib. Well, well, sir; well.

Men. Why, 'tis no great matter; for a very little   30 thief of occasion will rob you of a great deal of patience: give your dispositions the reins, and be angry at your pleasures; at the least, if you take it as a pleasure to you, in being so. You blame Marcius for being proud?

Bru. We do it not alone, sir.

Men. I know, you can do very little alone; for your helps are many, or else your actions would grow wondrous single: your abilities are too infant-like for doing much alone. You talk of pride: O! that you could turn your eyes toward the napes of your necks, and make but an interior survey of your good selves! O, that you could!

Bru. What then, sir?

Men. Why, then you should discover a brace of unmeriting, proud, violent, testy magistrates, (alias, fools,) as any in Rome.

Sic. Menenius, you are known well enough too.   49

Men. I am known to be a humorous patrician, and one that loves a cup of hot wine, with not a drop of allaying Tiber in 't; said to be something imperfect, in favouring the first complaint: hasty, and tinder-like, upon too trivial motion; one that converses more with the buttock of the night, than with the forehead of the morning. What I think, I utter, and spend my malice in my breath. Meeting two such weals-men as you are (I cannot call you Lycur-guses), if the drink you give me touch my palate adversely, I make a crooked face at it. I can't say, your worships have delivered the matter well, when I find the ass in compound with the major part of your syllables; and though I must be content to bear with those that say you are reverend grave men, yet they lie deadly that tell you have good faces. If you see this in the map of my microcosm, follows it, that I am known well enough too? What harm can your bisson conspectuities glean out of this character, if I be known well enough too?

Bru. Come, sir, come, we know you well enough.   70

Men. You know neither me, yourselves, nor anything. You are ambitious for poor knaves' caps and legs: you wear out a good wholesome forenoon in hearing a cause between an orange-wife and a fosset-seller; and then rejourn the controversy of three-pence to a second day of audience.—When you are hearing a matter between party and party, if you chance to be pinched with the colic, you make faces like mummers, set up the bloody flag against all patience, and, in roaring for a chamber-pot, dismiss the controversy bleeding, the more entangled by your hearing: all the peace you make in their cause is, calling both the parties knaves. You are a pair of strange ones.

Bru. Come, come, you are well understood to be a perfecter giber for the table, than a necessary bencher in the Capitol.   87

Men. Our very priests must become mockers, if they shall encounter such ridiculous subjects as you are. When you speak best unto the purpose, it is not worth the wagging of your beards; and your beards deserve not so honourable a grave as to stuff a botcher's cushion, or to be entombed in an ass's pack-saddle. Yet you must be saying, Marcius is proud; who, in a cheap estimation, is worth all your pre-decessors since Deucalion, though, peradventure, some of the best of 'em were hereditary hangmen. Good den to your worships: more of your conversation would infect my brain, being the herdsmen of the beastly plebeians; I will be bold to take my leave of you.   101

[BRUTUS *and* SICINIUS *retire to the back of the scene.*

Enter VOLUMNIA, VIRGILIA, *and* VALERIA, &c.

How now, my, as fair as noble ladies, (and the moon, were she earthly, no nobler,) whither do you follow your eyes so fast?

Vol. Honourable Menenius, my boy Marcius ap-proaches; for the love of Juno, let's go.

Men. Ha! Marcius coming home?

Vol. Ay, worthy Menenius, and with most pros-perous approbation.

Men. Take my cap, Jupiter, and I thank thee.—Ho! Marcius coming home?   111

Two Ladies. Nay, 'tis true.

Vol. Look, here's a letter from him: the state hath

another, his wife another; and, I think, there's one
at home for you.

Men. I will make my very house reel to-night.—A
letter for me!   117

Vir. Yes, certain, there's a letter for you; I saw it.

Men. A letter for me! It gives me an estate of
seven years' health; in which time I will make a 'n
at the physician: the most sovereign prescription in
Galen is but empirictic, and, to this preservative, of
no better report than a horse-drench. Is he not
wounded? he was wont to come home wounded.

Vir. O! no, no, no.

Vol. O! he is wounded; I thank the gods for 't.

Men. So do I too, if it be not too much.
—Brings 'a victory in his pocket?—The
wounds become him.

Vol. On 's brows, Menenius: he comes
the third time home with the oaken
garland.   132

Men. Has he disciplined Aufidius
soundly?

Vol. Titus Lartius writes, they fought
together, but Aufidius got off.

Men. And 't was time for him too, I 'll
warrant him that: an he had stay'd by
him, I would not have been so fidiused
for all the chests in Corioli, and the gold
that 's in them. Is the senate possessed
of this?   142

Vol. Good ladies, let 's go.—Yes, yes,
yes: the senate has letters from the
general, wherein he gives my son the
whole name of the war. He hath in this
action outdone his former deeds doubly.

Val. In troth, there 's wondrous things
spoke of him.

Men. Wondrous: ay, I warrant you,
and not without his true purchasing. 151

Vir. The gods grant them true!

Vol. True! pow, wow.

Men. True! I 'll be sworn they are
true.—Where is he wounded?—[*To the
Tribunes, who come forward.*] God save
your good worships! Marcius is coming
home: he has more cause to be proud.—Where is he
wounded?   159

Vol. I' the shoulder, and i' the left arm: there will
be large cicatrices to show the people, when he shall
stand for his place. He received in the repulse of
Tarquin seven hurts i' the body.

Men. One i' the neck, and two i' the thigh,—there 's
nine that I know.

Vol. He had, before this last expedition, twenty-five
wounds upon him.

Men. Now it 's twenty-seven: every gash was an
enemy's grave. [*A shout and flourish.*] Hark! the
trumpets.   170

Vol. These are the ushers of Marcius: before him
he carries noise, and behind him he leaves tears;
Death, that dark spirit, in 's nervy arm doth lie;
Which, being advanc'd, declines, and then men die.

A sennet. Trumpets sound. Enter COMINIUS *and*
TITUS LARTIUS; *between them,* CORIOLANUS,
*crowned with an oaken garland; with Captains,
Soldiers, and a Herald.*

Her. Know, Rome, that all alone Marcius did
fight:
Within Corioli gates: where he hath won,
With fame, a name to Caius Marcius; these
In honour follows Coriolanus:—
Welcome to Rome, renowned Coriolanus! [*Flourish.*

All. Welcome to Rome, renowned Coriolanus! 180

Cor. No more of this; it does offend my heart:
Pray now, no more.

Com.   Look, sir, your mother!

Cor.   O!
You have, I know, petition'd all the gods
For my prosperity.   [*Kneels.*

Vol.   Nay, my good soldier, up;
My gentle Marcius, worthy Caius, and
By deed-achieving honour newly nam'd,—

What is it?—Coriolanus must I call thee?—
But, O! thy wife—

Cor.   My gracious silence, hail!
Wouldst thou have laugh'd, had I come coffin'd home,
That weep'st to see me triumph? Ah! my dear, 190
Such eyes the widows in Corioli wear,
And mothers that lack sons.

Men.   Now the gods crown thee!

Cor. And live you yet?—[*To* VALERIA.] O my sweet
lady, pardon.

Vol. I know not where to turn:—O! welcome home;
And welcome, general;—and you are welcome all.

Men. A hundred thousand welcomes: I could weep.

THE RETURN OF CORIOLANUS TO ROME.

And I could laugh; I am light, and heavy. Welcome!
A curse begin at very root of his heart,
That is not glad to see thee!—You are three,
That Rome should dote on; yet, by the faith of men,
We have some old crab-trees here at home, that will
not   201
Be grafted to your relish. Yet welcome, warriors!
We call a nettle but a nettle, and
The faults of fools but folly.

Com.   Ever right.

Cor. Menenius, ever, ever.

Her. Give way there, and go on!

Cor. [*To his Wife and Mother.*] Your hand,—and
yours:
Ere in our own house I do shade my head,
The good patricians must be visited;
From whom I have received not only greetings, 210
But with them change of honours.

Vol.   I have liv'd
To see inherited my very wishes,
And the buildings of my fancy: only
There 's one thing wanting, which I doubt not but
Our Rome will cast upon thee.

Cor.   Know, good mother,
I had rather be their servant in my way,
Than sway with them in theirs.

Com.   On, to the Capitol!
[*Flourish. Cornets. Exeunt in state, as
before. The Tribunes remain.*

Bru. All tongues speak of him, and the bleared
sights
Are spectacled to see him. Your prattling nurse 220
Into a rapture lets her baby cry
While she chats him: the kitchen malkin pins
Her richest lockram 'bout her reechy neck,
Clambering the walls to eye him: stalls, bulks, win-
dows,
Are smother'd up, leads fill'd, and ridges hors'd

With variable complexions, all agreeing
In earnestness to see him : seld-shown flamens
Do press among the popular throngs, and puff
To win a vulgar station : our veil'd dames
Commit the war of white and damask, in
Their nicely-gawded cheeks, to the wanton spoil   230
Of Phœbus' burning kisses : such a pother
As if that whatsoever god, who leads him,
Were slily crept into his human powers,
And gave him graceful posture.
Sic.   On the sudden,
I warrant him consul.
Bru.   Then our office may,
During his power, go sleep.
Sic. He cannot temperately transport his honours
From where he should begin, and end ; but will   241
Lose those he hath won.
Bru.   In that there 's comfort.
Sic. Doubt not the commoners, for whom we stand,
But they, upon their ancient malice, will
Forget, with the least cause, these his new honours ;
Which that he 'll give them, make I as little question
As he is proud to do 't.
Bru.   I heard him swear,
Were he to stand for consul, never would he
Appear i' the market-place, nor on him put
The napless vesture of humility ;
Nor, showing (as the manner is) his wounds
To the people, beg their stinking breaths.
Sic.   'T is right.
Bru. It was his word. O ! he would miss it, rather
Than carry it, but by the suit o' the gentry   251
To him, and the desire of the nobles.
Sic.   I wish no better
Than have him hold that purpose, and to put it
In execution.
Bru.   'T is most like, he will.
Sic. It shall be to him then, as our good wills,
A sure destruction.
Bru.   So it must fall out
To him, or our authorities. For an end,
We must suggest the people, in what hatred
He still hath held them ; that to 's power he would
Have made them mules, silenc'd their pleaders, and
Dispropertied their freedoms ; holding them,   261
In human action and capacity,
Of no more soul, nor fitness for the world,
Than camels in their war ; who have their provand
Only for bearing burdens, and sore blows
For sinking under them.
Sic.   This, as you say, suggested
At some time when his soaring insolence
Shall reach the people, (which time shall not want,
If he be put upon 't : and that 's as easy
As to set dogs on sheep,) will be his fire   270
To kindle their dry stubble ; and their blaze
Shall darken him for ever.

Enter a Messenger.

Bru.   What 's the matter ?
Mess. You are sent for to the Capitol. 'T is thought,
That Marcius shall be consul. I have seen
The dumb men throng to see him, and the blind
To hear him speak : matrons flung gloves,
Ladies and maids their scarfs and handkerchers,
Upon him as he pass'd ; the nobles bended,
As to Jove's statue, and the commons made
A shower and thunder, with their caps and shouts :
I never saw the like.
Bru.   Let 's to the Capitol ;   281
And carry with us ears and eyes for the time,
But hearts for the event.
Sic.   Have with you. [*Exeunt.*

Scene II.—The Same. The Capitol.

Enter Two Officers, to lay cushions.

1 *Off.* Come, come ; they are almost here. How
many stand for consulships ?

2 *Off.* Three, they say ; but 't is thought of every
one Coriolanus will carry it.
1 *Off.* That 's a brave fellow ; but he 's vengeance
proud, and loves not the common people.
2 *Off.* Faith, there have been many great men that
have flattered the people, who ne'er loved them ; and
there be many that they have loved, they know not
wherefore : so that, if they love they know not why,
they hate upon no better a ground. Therefore, for
Coriolanus neither to care whether they love or hate
him, manifests the true knowledge he has in their
disposition ; and, out of his noble carelessness, lets
them plainly see 't.
1 *Off.* If he did not care whether he had their
love or no, he waved indifferently 'twixt doing them
neither good nor harm ; but he seeks their hate with
greater devotion than they can render it him, and
leaves nothing undone that may fully discover him
their opposite. Now, to seem to affect the malice and
displeasure of the people, is as bad as that which he
dislikes, to flatter them for their love.   23
2 *Off.* He hath deserved worthily of his country ;
and his ascent is not by such easy degrees as those
who, having been supple and courteous to the people,
bonneted, without any further deed to have them at
all, into their estimation and report ; but he hath so
planted his honours in their eyes, and his actions in
their hearts, that for their tongues to be silent, and
not confess so much, were a kind of ingrateful injury ;
to report otherwise were a malice, that, giving itself
the lie, would pluck reproof and rebuke from every
ear that heard it.
1 *Off.* No more of him : he is a worthy man. Make
way, they are coming.

A sennet. Enter, with Lictors before them, Cominius
the Consul, Menenius, Coriolanus, *many other
Senators,* Sicinius *and* Brutus. *The Senators
take their places ; the Tribunes take theirs also by
themselves.*

Men. Having determin'd of the Volsces, and
To send for Titus Lartius, it remains,
As the main point of this our after-meeting,
To gratify his noble service, that   40
Hath thus stood for his country. Therefore, please you,
Most reverend and grave elders, to desire
The present consul, and last general
In our well-found successes, to report
A little of that worthy work perform'd
By Caius Marcius Coriolanus ; whom
We met here, both to thank, and to remember
With honours like himself.
1 *Sen.*   Speak, good Cominius :
Leave nothing out for length, and make us think,
Rather our state 's defective for requital,   50
Than we to stretch it out. Masters o' the people,
We do request your kindest ears ; and, after,
Your loving motion toward the common body,
To yield what passes here.
Sic.   We are convented
Upon a pleasing treaty ; and have hearts
Inclinable to honour and advance
The theme of our assembly.
Bru.   Which the rather
We shall be bless'd to do, if he remember
A kinder value of the people than
He hath hereto priz'd them at.
Men.   That 's off, that 's off :
I would you rather had been silent. Please you   61
To hear Cominius speak ?
Bru.   Most willingly ;
But yet my caution was more pertinent
Than the rebuke you give it.
Men.   He loves your people :
But tie him not to be their bedfellow.—
Worthy Cominius, speak.—Nay, keep your place.
[Coriolanus *rises, and offers to go away.*
1 *Sen.* Sit, Coriolanus : never shame to hear
What you have nobly done.
Cor.   Your honours' pardon :
I had rather have my wounds to heal again,
Than hear say how I got them.

Bru. Sir, I hope, 70
My words dis-bench'd you not.
Cor. No. sir : yet oft,
When blows have made me stay, I fled from words.
You sooth'd not, therefore hurt not. But, your people,
I love them as they weigh.
Men. Pray now, sit down.
Cor. I had rather have one scratch my head i' the
sun,
When the alarum were struck, than idly sit
To hear my nothings monster'd. [*Exit.*
Men. Masters o' the people,
Your multiplying spawn how can he flatter,
(That 's thousand to one good one,) when you now
see,
He had rather venture all his limbs for honour, 80
Than one of his ears to hear it ?—Proceed, Cominius.
Com. I shall lack voice : the deeds of Coriolanus
Should not be utter'd feebly.—It is held,
That valour is the chiefest virtue, and
Most dignifies the haver : if it be,
The man I speak of cannot in the world
Be singly counterpois'd. At sixteen years,
When Tarquin made a head for Rome, he fought
Beyond the mark of others ; our then dictator,
Whom with all praise I point at, saw him fight, 90
When with his Amazonian chin he drove
The bristled lips before him. He bestrid
An o'er-press'd Roman, and i' the consul's view
Slew three opposers : Tarquin's self he met,
And struck him on his knee : in that day's feats,
When he might act the woman in the scene,
He prov'd best man i' the field, and for his meed
Was brow-bound with the oak. His pupil age
Man-enter'd thus, he waxed like a sea ;
And, in the brunt of seventeen battles since, 100
He lurch'd all swords of the garland. For this last,
Before and in Corioli, let me say,
I cannot speak him home : he stopp'd the fliers,
And by his rare example made the coward
Turn terror into sport. As weeds before
A vessel under sail, so men obey'd,
And fell below his stem : his sword, death's stamp,
Where it did mark, it took ; from face to foot
He was a thing of blood, whose every motion
Was tim'd with dying cries. Alone he enter'd 110
The mortal gate of the city, which he painted
With shunless destiny ; aidless came off,
And with a sudden reinforcement struck
Corioli like a planet. Now all 's his ;
When by-and-by the din of war 'gan pierce
His ready sense : then straight his doubled spirit
Re-quicken'd what in flesh was fatigate,
And to the battle came he ; where he did
Run reeking o'er the lives of men, as if
'T were a perpetual spoil ; and, till we call'd 120
Both field and city ours, he never stood
To ease his breast with panting.
Men. Worthy man !
1 Sen. He cannot but with measure fit the honours
Which we devise him.
Com. Our spoils he kick'd at ;
And look'd upon things precious, as they were
The common muck o' the world : he covets less
Than misery itself would give, rewards
His deeds with doing them, and is content
To spend the time, to end it.
Men. He 's right noble
Let him be call'd for.
1 Sen. Call Coriolanus. 130
Off. He doth appear.

Re-enter CORIOLANUS.

Men. The senate, Coriolanus, are well pleas'd
To make thee consul.
Cor. I do owe them still
My life and services.
Men. It then remains,
That you do speak to the people.
Cor. I do beseech you,
Let me o'erleap that custom ; for I cannot
Put on the gown, stand naked, and entreat them,

For my wounds' sake, to give their suffrage : please
you,
That I may pass this doing.
Sic. Sir, the people
Must have their voices : neither will they bate 140
One jot of ceremony.
Men. Put them not to 't :
Pray yóu, go fit you to the custom, and
Take to you, as your predecessors have,
Your honour with your form.
Cor. It is a part
That I shall blush in acting, and might well
Be taken from the people.
Bru. Mark you that ?
Cor. To brag unto them,—Thus I did, and thus ;—
Show them the unaching scars which I should hide,
As if I had receiv'd them for the hire
Of their breath only !
Men. Do not stand upon 't.— 150
We recommend to you, tribunes of the people,
Our purpose to them ;—and to our noble consul
Wish we all joy and honour.
Sen. To Coriolanus come all joy and honour !
[*Flourish. Exeunt all but* SICINIUS *and* BRUTUS.
Bru. You see how he intends to use the people.
Sic. May they perceive his intent ! He will require
them,
As if he did contemn what he requested
Should be in them to give.
Bru. Come ; we 'll inform them
Of our proceedings here : on the market-place
I know they do attend us. 160
[*Exeunt.*

SCENE III.—The Same. The Forum.

Enter several Citizens.

1 Cit. Once, if he do require our voices, we ought
not to deny him.
2 Cit. We may, sir, if we will.
3 Cit. We have power in ourselves to do it, but it is
a power that we have no power to do : for if he show
us his wounds, and tell us his deeds, we are to put
our tongues into those wounds, and speak for them ;
so, if he tell us his noble deeds, we must also tell
him our noble acceptance of them. Ingratitude is
monstrous, and for the multitude to be ingrateful
were to make a monster of the multitude ; of the
which we being members, should bring ourselves to
be monstrous members.
1 Cit. And to make us no better thought of, a little
help will serve : for once we stood up about the corn,
he himself stuck not to call us the many-headed
multitude. 17
3 Cit. We have been called so of many ; not that our
heads are some brown, some black, some auburn,
some bald, but that our wits are so diversely coloured :
and truly, I think, if all our wits were to issue out of
one skull, they would fly east, west, north, south ; and
their consent of one direct way should be at once to
all the points o' the compass.
2 Cit. Think you so ? Which way do you judge my
wit would fly ?
3 Cit. Nay, your wit will not so soon out as another
man's will : 't is strongly wedged up in a block-head ;
but if it were at liberty, 't would, sure, southward.
2 Cit. Why that way ? 30
3 Cit. To lose itself in a fog ; where, being three
parts melted away with rotten dews, the fourth would
return, for conscience sake, to help to get thee a wife.
2 Cit. You are never without your tricks :—you
may, you may.
3 Cit. Are you all resolved to give your voices ?
But that 's no matter ; the greater part carries it. I
say, if he would incline to the people, there was never
a worthier man. 39

Enter CORIOLANUS *and* MENENIUS.

Here he comes, and in the gown of humility : mark
his behaviour. We are not to stay all together, but
to come by him where he stands, by ones, by twos,

and by threes. He 's to make his requests by particulars; wherein every one of us has a single honour, in giving him our own voices with our own tongues: therefore, follow me, and I 'll direct you how you shall go by him.

All. Content, content. [*Exeunt.*

Men. O sir, you are not right: have you not known The worthiest men have done 't?

Cor. What must I say?
I pray, sir,—Plague upon 't! I cannot bring 51
My tongue to such a pace.—Look, sir :—my wounds;—
I got them in my country's service, when
Some certain of your brethren roar'd, and ran
From the noise of our own drums.

Men. O me, the gods!
You must not speak of that: you must desire them
To think upon you.

Cor. Think upon me? Hang 'em!
I would they would forget me, like the virtues
Which our divines lose by 'em.

Men. You 'll mar all:
I 'll leave you. Pray you, speak to them, I pray you,
In wholesome manner. [*Exit.*

Enter two Citizens.

Cor. Bid them wash their faces, 61
And keep their teeth clean.—So, here comes a brace.
You know the cause, sir, of my standing here.

1 Cit. We do, sir: tell us what hath brought you to 't.

Cor. Mine own desert.

2 Cit. Your own desert?

Cor. Ay, not mine own desire.

1 Cit. How ! not your own desire?

Cor. No, sir : 't was never my desire yet, to trouble the poor with begging. 71

1 Cit. You must think, if we give you anything, we hope to gain by you.

Cor. Well then, I pray, your price o' the consulship?

1 Cit. The price is, to ask it kindly.

Cor. Kindly! Sir, I pray, let me ha't : I have wounds to show you, which shall be yours in private.—Your good voice, sir ; what say you?

2 Cit. You shall ha't, worthy sir.

Cor. A match, sir.—There is in all two worthy voices begg'd.—I have your alms : adieu. 81

1 Cit. But this is something odd.

2 Cit. An 't were to give again,—but 't is no matter. [*Exeunt the two Citizens.*

Enter two other Citizens.

Cor. Pray you now, if it may stand with the tune of your voices that I may be consul, I have here the customary gown.

3 Cit. You have deserved nobly of your country, and you have not deserved nobly.

Cor. Your enigma? 89

3 Cit. You have been a scourge to her enemies, you have been a rod to her friends ; you have not, indeed, loved the common people.

Cor. You should account me the more virtuous, that I have not been common in my love. I will, sir, flatter my sworn brother the people, to earn a dearer estimation of them : 't is a condition they account gentle ; and since the wisdom of their choice is rather to have my hat than my heart, I will practise the insinuating nod, and be off to them most counterfeitly : that is, sir, I will counterfeit the bewitchment of some popular man, and give it bountifully to the desirers. Therefore, beseech you, I may be consul. 102

4 Cit. We hope to find you our friend, and therefore give you our voices heartily.

3 Cit. You have received many wounds for your country.

Cor. I will not seal your knowledge with showing them. I will make much of your voices, and so trouble you no further.

Both Cit. The gods give you joy, sir, heartily! 110 [*Exeunt.*

Cor. Most sweet voices !—
Better it is to die, better to starve,
Than crave the hire which first we do deserve.

Why in this wolvish toge should I stand here,
To beg of Hob and Dick, that do appear,
Their needless vouches? Custom calls me to 't :—
What custom wills, in all things should we do 't,
The dust on antique time would lie unswept,
And mountainous error be too highly heap'd
For truth to o'er-peer.—Rather than fool it so, 120
Let the high office and the honour go
To one that would do thus.—I am half through :
The one part suffer'd, the other will I do.

Enter three other Citizens.

Here come more voices.—
Your voices : for your voices I have fought ;
Watch'd for your voices ; for your voices bear
Of wounds two dozen odd ; battles thrice six
I have seen and heard of ; for your voices have
Done many things, some less, some more. Your voices :
Indeed, I would be consul. 130

5 Cit. He has done nobly, and cannot go without any honest man's voice.

6 Cit. Therefore, let him be consul. The gods give him joy, and make him good friend to the people!

All. Amen, amen.—
God save thee, noble consul ! [*Exeunt Citizens.*

Cor. Worthy voices!

Re-enter Menenius, *with* Brutus *and* Sicinius.

Men. You have stood your limitation ; and the tribunes
Endue you with the people's voice : remains
That, in the official marks invested, you
Anon do meet the senate.

Cor. Is this done? 140

Sic. The custom of request you have discharg'd :
The people do admit you ; and are summon'd
To meet anon, upon your approbation.

Cor. Where? at the senate-house?

Sic. There, Coriolanus.

Cor. May I change these garments?

Sic. You may, sir.

Cor. That I 'll straight do ; and, knowing myself again,
Repair to the senate-house.

Men. I 'll keep you company.—Will you along?

Bru. We stay here for the people.

Sic. Fare you well. [*Exeunt* Coriolanus *and* Menenius.

He has it now ; and by his looks, methinks, 151
'T is warm at his heart.

Bru. With a proud heart he wore
His humble weeds. Will you dismiss the people?

Re-enter Citizens.

Sic. How now, my masters? have you chose this man?

1 Cit. He has our voices, sir.

Bru. We pray the gods he may deserve your loves.

2 Cit. Amen, sir. To my poor unworthy notice, He mock'd us when he begg'd our voices.

3 Cit. Certainly,
He flouted us downright.

1 Cit. No, 't is his kind of speech ; he did not mock us. 160

2 Cit. Not one amongst us, save yourself, but says, He us'd us scornfully : he should have show'd us His marks of merit, wounds receiv'd for his country.

Sic. Why, so he did, I am sure.

All. No, no ; no man saw 'em.

3 Cit. He said, he had wounds, which he could show in private ;
And with his hat, thus waving it in scorn,
" I would be consul," says he : " aged custom,
But by your voices, will not so permit me ;
Your voices therefore." When we granted that,
Here was,—" I thank you for your voices,—thank you,— 170
Your most sweet voices :—now you have left your voices,
I have no further with you."—Was not this mockery?

Sic. Why, either, were you ignorant to see 't,

Or, seeing it, of such childish friendliness
To yield your voices?
  Bru.   Could you not have told him,
As you were lesson'd,—when he had no power,
But was a petty servant to the state,
He was your enemy : ever spake against
Your liberties, and the charters that you bear
I' the body of the weal : and now, arriving   180
A place of potency, and sway o' the state,
If he should still malignantly remain
Fast foe to the plebeii, your voices might
Be curses to yourselves? You should have said,
That, as his worthy deeds did claim no less
Than what he stood for, so his gracious nature
Would think upon you for your voices, and
Translate his malice towards you into love,
Standing your friendly lord.
  Sic.   Thus to have said,
As you were fore-advis'd, had touch'd his spirit,   190
And tried his inclination ; from him pluck'd
Either his gracious promise, which you might,
As cause had call'd you up, have held him to ;
Or else it would have gall'd his surly nature,
Which easily endures not article
Tying him to aught ; so, putting him to rage,
You should have ta'en the advantage of his choler,
And pass'd him unelected.
  Bru.   Did you perceive,
He did solicit you in free contempt,
When he did need your loves ; and do you think,   200
That his contempt shall not be bruising to you,
When he hath power to crush? Why, had your bodies
No heart among you? or had you tongues to cry
Against the rectorship of judgment?
  Sic.   Have you,
Ere now, denied the asker? and, now again,
Of him that did not ask, but mock, bestow
Your sued-for tongues?
  3 *Cit.* He 's not confirm'd ; we may deny him yet.
  2 *Cit.* And will deny him :
I 'll have five hundred voices of that sound.   210
  1 *Cit.* I twice five hundred, and their friends to
    piece 'em.
  Bru. Get you hence instantly ; and tell those friends,
They have chose a consul that will from them take
Their liberties ; make them of no more voice
Than dogs, that are as often beat for barking
As therefore kept to do so.
  Sic.   Let them assemble ;
And, on a safer judgment, all revoke
Your ignorant election. Enforce his pride,

And his old hate unto you : besides, forget not
With what contempt he wore the humble weed; 220
How in his suit he scorn'd you : but your loves,
Thinking upon his services, took from you
The apprehension of his present portance,
Which most gibingly, ungravely, he did fashion
After the inveterate hate he bears you.
  Bru.   Lay
A fault on us, your tribunes, that we labour'd
(No impediment between) but that you must
Cast your election on him.
  Sic.   Say, you chose him
More after our commandment, than as guided
By your own true affections ; and that your minds, 230
Pre-occupied with what you rather must do
Than what you should, made you against the grain
To voice him consul. Lay the fault on us.
  Bru. Ay, spare us not. Say, we read lectures to you,
How youngly he began to serve his country,
How long continued, and what stock he springs of,
The noble house o' the Marcians ; from whence came
That Ancus Marcius, Numa's daughter's son,
Who, after great Hostilius, here was king ;
Of the same house Publius and Quintus were, 240
That our best water brought by conduits hither ;
[And Censorinus that was so surnam'd,]
And nobly named so, twice being censor,
Was his great ancestor.
  Sic.   One thus descended,
That hath beside well in his person wrought
To be set high in place, we did commend
To your remembrances : but you have found,
Scaling his present bearing with his past,
That he 's your fixed enemy, and revoke
Your sudden approbation.
  Bru.   Say, you ne'er had done 't,
(Harp on that still,) but by our putting on ; 251
And presently, when you have drawn your number,
Repair to the Capitol.
  All.   We will so : almost all
Repent in their election.   *[Exeunt Citizens.*
  Bru.   Let them go on :
This mutiny were better put in hazard,
Than stay, past doubt, for greater.
If, as his nature is, he fall in rage
With their refusal, both observe and answer
The vantage of his anger.
  Sic.   To the Capitol :
Come, we 'll be there before the stream o' the people ;
And this shall seem, as partly 't is, their own, 261
Which we have goaded onward.   *[Exeunt.*

ACT III.

SCENE I.—The Same. A Street.

Cornets. Enter CORIOLANUS, MENENIUS, COMINIUS, TITUS LARTIUS, *Senators, and Patricians.*

Coriolanus.
ULLUS Aufidius then had made new head?
Lart. He had, my lord; and that it was,
 which caus'd
Our swifter composition.
 Cor. So then, the Volsces stand but as at
 first;
Ready, when time shall prompt them, to
 make road
Upon us again.
 Com.   They are worn, lord consul, so,
That we shall hardly in our ages see
Their banners wave again.
 Cor.   Saw you Aufidius?
Lart. On safe-guard he came to me; and did curse
Against the Volsces, for they had so vildly   10
Yielded the town: he is retir'd to Antium.
 Cor. Spoke he of me?
 Lart.   He did, my lord.
 Cor.   How? what?
Lart. How often he had met you, sword to sword;
That of all things upon the earth he hated
Your person most; that he would pawn his fortunes
To hopeless restitution, so he might
Be call'd your vanquisher.
 Cor.   At Antium lives he?
 Lart. At Antium.
 Cor. I wish I had a cause to seek him there,
To oppose his hatred fuily. Welcome home.   20

Enter SICINIUS *and* BRUTUS.

Behold! these are the tribunes of the people,
The tongues o' the common mouth. I do despise them;
For they do prank them in authority,
Against all noble sufferance.
 Sic.   Pass no further.
 Cor. Ha! what is that?
 Bru. It will be dangerous to go on: no further.
 Cor. What makes this change?
 Men.   The matter?
 Com. Hath he not pass'd the noble, and the
 common?
 Bru. Cominius, no.
 Cor.   Have I had children's voices?
1 *Sen.* Tribunes, give way: he shall to the market-
 place.   30

Bru. The people are incens'd against him.
 Sic.   Stop,
Or all will fall in broil.
 Cor.   Are these your herd?—
Must these have voices, that can yield them now,
And straight disclaim their tongues?—What are your
 offices?
You being their mouths, why rule you not their
 teeth?
Have you not set them on?
 Men.   Be calm, be calm.
 Cor. It is a purpos'd thing, and grows by plot,
To curb the will of the nobility:
Suffer 't, and live with such as cannot rule,
Nor ever will be rul'd.
 Bru.   Call 't not a plot: 40
The people cry, you mock'd them; and, of late,
When corn was given them gratis, you repin'd;
Scandal'd the suppliants for the people, call'd them
Time-pleasers, flatterers, foes to nobleness.
 Cor. Why, this was known before.
 Bru.   Not to them all.
 Cor. Have you inform'd them sithence?
 Bru.   How! I inform them!
 Com. You are like to do such business.
 Bru.   Not unlike,
Each way, to better yours.
 Cor. Why then should I be consul? By yond clouds,
Let me deserve so ill as you, and make me   50
Your fellow tribune.
 Sic.   You show too much of that
For which the people stir. If you will pass
To where you are bound, you must inquire your way,
Which you are out of, with a gentler spirit;
Or never be so noble as a consul,
Nor yoke with him for tribune.
 Men.   Let 's be calm.
 Com. The people are abus'd.—Set on.—This palter-
 ing
Becomes not Rome; nor has Coriolanus
Deserv'd this so dishonour'd rub, laid falsely
I' the plain way of his merit.
 Cor.   Tell me of corn!   60
This was my speech, and I will speak 't again—
 Men. Not now, not now.
 1 *Sen.*   Not in this heat, sir, now.

Cor. Now, as I live, I will.—My nobler friends,
I crave their pardons :—
For the mutable, rank-scented many, let them
Regard me as I do not flatter, and
Therein behold themselves. I say again,
In soothing them we nourish 'gainst our senate
The cockle of rebellion, insolence, sedition,
Which we ourselves have plough'd for, sow'd and
    scatter'd, 70
By mingling them with us, the honour'd number ;
Who lack not virtue, no, nor power, but that
Which they have given to beggars.
  Men. Well, no more.
  1 Sen. No more words, we beseech you.
  Cor. How ! no more?
As for my country I have shed my blood,
Not fearing outward force, so shall my lungs
Coin words till they decay, against those meazels,
Which we disdain should tetter us, yet sought
The very way to catch them.
  Bru. You speak o' the people,
As if you were a god to punish, not 80
A man of their infirmity.
  Sic. 'T were well,
We let the people know 't.
  Men. What, what? his choler?
  Cor. Choler !
Were I as patient as the midnight sleep,
By Jove, 't would be my mind.
  Sic. It is a mind,
That shall remain a poison where it is,
Not poison any further.
  Cor. Shall remain !—
Hear you this Triton of the minnows? mark you
His absolute "shall?"
  Com. 'T was from the canon.
  Cor. "Shall !"
O good, but most unwise patricians ! why, 90
You grave, but reckless senators, have you thus
Given Hydra here to choose an officer,
That with his peremptory "shall," being but
The horn and noise o' the monster's, wants not spirit
To say, he'll turn your current in a ditch,
And make your channel his ? If he have power,
Then vail your ignorance : if none, awake
Your dangerous lenity. If you are learned,
Be not as common fools : if you are not,
Let them have cushions by you. You are plebeians,
If they be senators : and they are no less, 101
When, both your voices blended, the greatest taste
Most palates theirs. They choose their magistrate ;
And such a one as he, who puts his "shall,"
His popular "shall," against a graver bench
Than ever frown'd in Greece. By Jove himself,
It makes the consuls base ; and my soul aches,
To know, when two authorities are up,
Neither supreme, how soon confusion
May enter 'twixt the gap of both, and take 110
The one by the other.
  Com. Well,—on to the market-place.
  Cor. Whoever gave that counsel, to give forth
The corn o' the store-house gratis, as 't was us'd
Sometime in Greece,—
  Men. Well, well ; no more of that.
  Cor. Though there the people had more absolute
    power,
I say, they nourish'd disobedience, fed
The ruin of the state.
  Bru. Why, shall the people give
One that speaks thus, their voice ?
  Cor. I'll give my reasons,
More worthier than their voices. They know, the corn
Was not our recompense, resting well assur'd 120
They ne'er did service for 't. Being press'd to the war,
Even when the navel of the state was touch'd,
They would not thread the gates : this kind of service
Did not deserve corn gratis. Being i' the war,
Their mutinies and revolts, wherein they show'd
Most valour, spoke not for them. The accusation
Which they have often made against the senate,
All cause unborn, could never be the native
Of our so frank donation. Well, what then ?

How shall this bosom multiplied digest 130
The senate's courtesy ? Let deeds express
What 's like to be their words :—" We did request it ;
We are the greater poll, and in true fear
They gave us our demands."—Thus we debase
The nature of our seats, and make the rabble
Call our cares, fears ; which will in time break ope
The locks o' the senate, and bring in the crows
To peck the eagles.—
  Men. Come, enough.
  Bru. Enough, with over-measure.
  Cor. No, take more :
What may be sworn by, both divine and human, 140
Seal what I end withal !—This double worship,—
Where one part does disdain with cause, the other
Insult without all reason ; where gentry, title, wisdom,
Cannot conclude, but by the yea and no
Of general ignorance,—it must omit
Real necessities, and give way the while
To unstable slightness : purpose so barr'd, it follows,
Nothing is done to purpose. Therefore, beseech
    you,—
You that will be less fearful than discreet,
That love the fundamental part of state 150
More than you doubt the change of 't, that prefer
A noble life before a long, and wish
To jump a body with a dangerous physic
That 's sure of death without it,—at once pluck out
The multitudinous tongue : let them not lick
The sweet which is their poison. Your dishonour
Mangles true judgment, and bereaves the state
Of that integrity which should become it,
Not having the power to do the good it would,
For the ill which doth control 't.
  Bru. H'as said enough.
  Sic. H'as spoken like a traitor, and shall answer 161
As traitors do.
  Cor. Thou wretch ! despite o'erwhelm thee !—
What should the people do with these bald tribunes ?
On whom depending, their obedience fails
To the greater bench. In a rebellion,
When what 's not meet, but what must be, was law,
Then were they chosen : in a better hour,
Let what is meet be said, it must be meet,
And throw their power i' the dust. 170
  Bru. Manifest treason !
  Sic. This a consul ? no.
  Bru. The Ædiles, ho !—Let him be apprehended.

Enter an Ædile.

  Sic. Go, call the people ; [*Exit Ædile*] in whose
    name myself
Attach thee as a traitorous innovator,
A foe to the public weal. Obey, I charge thee,
And follow to thine answer.
  Cor. Hence, old goat !
  Sen. We'll surety him.
  Com. Aged sir, hands off.
  Cor. Hence, rotten thing, or I shall shake thy bones
Out of thy garments.
  Sic. Help, ye citizens !

*Re-enter the Ædile, with others, and a rabble of
Citizens.*

  Men. On both sides more respect. 180
  Sic. Here 's he that would take from you all your
    power.
  Bru. Seize him, Ædiles.
  Cit. Down with him ! down with him !
    [*Several speak.*
  2 Sen. Weapons ! weapons ! weapons !
    [*They all bustle about* CORIOLANUS.
Tribunes, patricians, citizens !—what, ho !—
Sicinius, Brutus, Coriolanus, citizens !
  Cit. Peace, peace, peace ! stay, hold, peace !
  Men. What is about to be ?—I am out of breath ;
Confusion 's near : I cannot speak.—You, tribunes,
To the people,—Coriolanus, patience :— 190
Speak, good Sicinius.
  Sic. Hear me, people ; peace !
  Cit. Let 's hear our tribune :—peace ! Speak, speak,
    speak.

Sic. You are at point to lose your liberties:
Marcius would have all from you; Marcius,
Whom late you have nam'd for consul.
Men.   Fie, fie, fie!
This is the way to kindle, not to quench.
1 Sen. To unbuild the city, and to lay all flat.
Sic. What is the city, but the people?
Cit.   True,
The people are the city.
Bru. By the consent of all, we were establish'd 200
The people's magistrates.
Cit.   You so remain.
Men. And so are like to do.
Com. That is the way to lay the city flat;

Cor.   "No; I'll die here.
There's some among you have beheld me fighting:
Come, try upon yourselves what you have seen me."

To bring the roof to the foundation,
And bury all, which yet distinctly ranges,
In heaps and piles of ruin.
Sic.   This deserves death.
Bru. Or let us stand to our authority,
Or let us lose it.—We do here pronounce,
Upon the part o' the people, in whose power
We were elected theirs, Marcius is worthy 210
Of present death.
Sic.   Therefore lay hold of him;
Bear him to the rock Tarpeian, and from thence
Into destruction cast him.
Bru.   Ædiles, seize him.
Cit. Yield, Marcius, yield.
Men.   Hear me one word;
Beseech you, tribunes, hear me but a word.
Æd. Peace, peace!
Men. Be that you seem, truly your country's friend,
And temperately proceed to what you would
Thus violently redress.
Bru.   Sir, those cold ways,
That seem like prudent helps, are very poisonous 220
Where the disease is violent. — Lay hands upon
        him,
And bear him to the rock.
Cor.   No; I'll die here.
                    [*Drawing his sword.*
There's some among you have beheld me fighting:
Come, try upon yourselves what you have seen me.
Men. Down with that sword!—Tribunes, withdraw
        awhile.
Bru. Lay hands upon him.
Men.   Help Marcius, help,
You that be noble; help him, young and old!

Cit. Down with him! down with him!
    [*In this mutiny, the Tribunes, the Ædiles,
        and the People, are beat in.*
Men. Go, get you to your house: be gone, away!
All will be naught else.
2 Sen.   Get you gone.
Com.   Stand fast:
We have as many friends as enemies.   231
Men. Shall it be put to that?
1 Sen.   The gods forbid!
I pr'ythee, noble friend, home to thy house;
Leave us to cure this cause.
Men.   For 't is a sore upon us
You cannot tent yourself: be gone, 'beseech you.
Com. Come, sir, along with us.
Cor.   I would they were bar-
        barians, as they are,
Though in Rome litter'd, not
        Romans, as they are not,
Though calv'd i' the porch o' the
        Capitol,—
Men.   Be gone;
Put not your worthy rage into
        your tongue;   240
One time will owe another.
Cor.   On fair ground
I could beat forty of them.
Men.   I could myself take up a
brace of the best of them; yea, the
        two tribunes.
Com. But now 't is odds beyond
        arithmetic;
And manhood is call'd foolery,
        when it stands
Against a falling fabric.—Will you
        hence,
Before the tag return? whose rage
        doth rend
Like interrupted waters, and o'er-
        bear   250
What they are us'd to bear.
Men.   Pray you, be gone.
I'll try whether my old wit be in
        request
With those that have but little:
        this must be patch'd
With cloth of any colour.
Com.   Nay, come away.
    [*Exeunt* CORIOLANUS, COMINIUS, *and others.*
1 Pat. This man has marr'd his fortune.
Men. His nature is too noble for the world:
He would not flatter Neptune for his trident,
Or Jove for his power to thunder. His heart's his
        mouth:
What his breast forges, that his tongue must vent;
And, being angry, does forget that ever   260
He heard the name of death.   [*A noise within.*
Here's goodly work!
2 Pat.   I would they were a-bed!
Men. I would they were in Tiber!—What, the
        vengeance,
Could he not speak 'em fair?

Re-enter BRUTUS *and* SICINIUS, *with the rabble.*
Sic.   Where is this viper,
That would depopulate the city, and
Be every man himself?
Men.   You worthy tribunes,—
Sic. He shall be thrown down the Tarpeian rock
With rigorous hands: he hath resisted law,
And therefore law shall scorn him further trial
Than the severity of the public power,   270
Which he so sets at nought.
1 Cit.   He shall well know,
The noble tribunes are the people's mouths,
And we their hands.
Cit.   He shall, sure on 't.
Men.   Sir, sir,—
Sic. Peace!
Men. Do not cry havoc, where you should but
        hunt
With modest warrant.

Sic.   Sir, how comes 't, that you
Have holp to make this rescue?
Men.   Hear me speak.—
As I do know the consul's worthiness,
So can I name his faults.—
Sic.   Consul!—what consul?
Men. The consul Coriolanus.
Bru.   He a consul!   280
Cit. No, no, no, no, no.
Men. If, by the tribunes' leave, and yours, good
          people,
I may be heard, I would crave a word or two,
The which shall turn you to no further harm
Than so much loss of time.
Sic.   Speak briefly then;
For we are peremptory to despatch
This viperous traitor. To eject him hence,
Were but one danger; and to keep him here,
Our certain death: therefore, it is decreed
He dies to-night.
Men.   New the good gods forbid,   290
That our renowned Rome, whose gratitude
Towards her deserved children is enroll'd
In Jove's own book, like an unnatural dam
Should now eat up her own!
Sic. He 's a disease, that must be cut away.
Men. O! he 's a limb, that has but a disease;
Mortal, to cut it off; to cure it, easy.
What has he done to Rome that 's worthy death?
Killing our enemies? The blood he hath lost,
(Which, I dare vouch, is more than that he hath,   300
By many an ounce,) he dropp'd it for his country:
And what is left, to lose it by his country,
Were to us all, that do 't, and suffer it,
A brand to th' end o' the world.
Sic.   This is clean kam.
Bru. Merely awry. When he did love his country,
It honour'd him.
Men.   The service of the foot,
Being once gangren'd, is not then respected
For what before it was—
Bru.   We 'll hear no more.—
Pursue him to his house, and pluck him thence,
Lest his infection, being of catching nature,   310
Spread further.
Men.   One word more, one word.
This tiger-footed rage, when it shall find
The harm of unscann'd swiftness, will, too late,
Tie leaden pounds to his heels. Proceed by pro-
          cess;
Lest parties (as he is belov'd) break out,
And sack great Rome with Romans.
Bru.   If it were so,—
Sic. What do ye talk?
Have we not had a taste of his obedience?
Our Ædiles smote? ourselves resisted?—Come!—
Men. Consider this:—he has been bred i' the
          wars   320
Since he could draw a sword, and is ill school'd
In bolted language; meal and bran together
He throws without distinction. Give me leave,
I 'll go to him, and undertake to bring him
Where he shall answer, by a lawful form,
In peace, to his utmost peril.
1 Sen.   Noble tribunes,
It is the humane way: the other course
Will prove too bloody, and the end of it
Unknown to the beginning.
Sic.   Noble Menenius,
Be you then as the people's officer.—   330
Masters, lay down your weapons.
Bru.   Go not home.
Sic. Meet on the market-place.—We 'll attend you
          there:
Where, if you bring not Marcius, we 'll proceed
In our first way.
Men.   I 'll bring him to you.
[*To the Senators.*] Let me desire your company. He
          must come,
Or what is worst will follow.
1 Sen.   Pray you, let 's to him.
                                          [*Exeunt.*

SCENE II.—A Room in CORIOLANUS' House.

Enter CORIOLANUS *and Patricians.*

Cor. Let them pull all about mine ears; present me
Death on the wheel, or at wild horses' heels;
Or pile ten hills on the Tarpeian rock,
That the precipitation might down stretch
Below the beam of sight: yet will I still
Be thus to them.
1 Pat.   You do the nobler.
Cor. I muse, my mother
Does not approve me further, who was wont
To call them woollen vassals; things created
To buy and sell with groats; to show bare heads   10
In congregations, to yawn, be still, and wonder,
When one but of my ordinance stood up
To speak of peace or war.

Enter VOLUMNIA.

                        I talk of you:
Why did you wish me milder? Would you have me
False to my nature? Rather say, I play
The man I am.
Vol.   O, sir, sir, sir!
I would have had you put your power well on,
Before you had worn it out.
Cor.   Let go.
Vol. You might have been enough the man you are,
With striving less to be so: lesser had been   20
The thwartings of your dispositions, if
You had not show'd them how you were dispos'd,
Ere they lack'd power to cross you.
Cor.   Let them hang.
Vol. Ay, and burn too.

Enter MENENIUS *and Senators.*

Men. Come, come; you have been too rough, some-
          thing too rough:
You must return, and mend it.
1 Sen.   There 's no remedy;
Unless, by not so doing, our good city
Cleave in the midst, and perish.
Vol.   Pray, be counsell'd.
I have a heart as little apt as yours,
But yet a brain that leads my use of anger   30
To better vantage.
Men.   Well said, noble woman!
Before he should thus stoop to the herd, but that
The violent fit o' the time craves it as physic
For the whole state, I would put mine armour on,
Which I can scarcely bear.
Cor.   What must I do?
Men. Return to the tribunes.
Cor.   Well, what then? what then?
Men. Repent what you have spoke.
Cor. For them?—I cannot do it to the gods;
Must I then do 't to them?
Vol.   You are too absolute;
Though therein you can never be too noble;   40
But when extremities speak—I have heard you say,
Honour and policy, like unsever'd friends,
I' the war do grow together: grant that, and tell me,
In peace, what each of them by the other lose,
That they combine not there?
Cor.   Tush, tush!
Men.   A good demand.
Vol. If it be honour, in your wars, to seem
The same you are not, (which, for your best ends,
You adopt your policy,) how is it less, or worse,
That it shall hold companionship in peace
With honour, as in war, since that to both   50
It stands in like request?
Cor.   Why force you this?
Vol. Because that now it lies you on to speak
To the people; not by your own instruction,
Nor by the matter which your heart prompts you,
But with such words that are but roted in
Your tongue, though but bastards, and syllables
Of no allowance, to your bosom's truth.
Now, this no more dishonours you at all,
Than to take in a town with gentle words,
Which else would put you to your fortune, and   60

The hazard of much blood.—
I would dissemble with my nature, where
My fortunes and my friends at stake requir'd
I should do so in honour : I am in this,
Your wife, your son, these senators, the nobles ;
And you will rather show our general louts
How you can frown, than spend a fawn upon 'em,
For the inheritance of their loves, and safeguard
Of what that want might ruin.
Men.   Noble lady !—
Come, go with us : speak fair ; you may salve so,   70
Not what is dangerous present, but the loss
Of what is past.
Vol.   I pr'ythee now, my son,
Go to them, with this bonnet in thy hand ;
And thus far having stretch'd it, (here be with them,)
Thy knee bussing the stones, (for in such business
Action is eloquence, and the eyes of the ignorant
More learned than the ears,) waving thy head,
Which often, thus, correcting thy stout heart,
Now humble as the ripest mulberry
That will not hold the handling : or say to them,   80
Thou art their soldier, and, being bred in broils,
Hast not the soft way, which, thou dost confess,
Were fit for thee to use, as they to claim,
In asking their good loves ; but thou wilt frame
Thyself, forsooth, hereafter theirs, so far
As thou hast power, and person.
Men.   This but done,
Even as she speaks, why, their hearts were yours ;
For they have pardons, being ask'd, as free
As words to little purpose.
Vol.   Pr'ythee now,
Go, and be rul'd ; although, I know, thou hadst rather   91
Follow thine enemy in a fiery gulf,
Than flatter him in a bower. Here is Cominius.

Enter COMINIUS.

Com. I have been i' the market-place ; and, sir, 't is
fit
You make strong party, or defend yourself
By calmness, or by absence : all 's in anger.
Men. Only fair speech.
Com.   I think, 't will serve, if he
Can thereto frame his spirit.
Vol.   He must, and will.—
Pr'ythee now, say you will, and go about it.
Cor. Must I go show them my unbarbed sconce ?
Must I with my base tongue give to my noble heart
A lie, that it must bear ? Well, I will do 't :   101
Yet were there but this single plot to lose,
This mould of Marcius, they to dust should grind it,
And throw 't against the wind.—To the market-place !
You have put me now to such a part, which never
I shall discharge to the life.
Com.   Come, come, we 'll prompt you.
Vol. I pr'ythee now, sweet son : as thou hast said,
My praises made thee first a soldier, so,
To have my praise for this, perform a part
Thou hast not done before.
Cor.   Well, I must do 't.   110
Away, my disposition, and possess me
Some harlot's spirit ! My throat of war be turn'd,
Which quired with my drum, into a pipe
Small as an eunuch, or the virgin voice
That babies lulls asleep ! The smiles of knaves
Tent in my cheeks ; and school-boys' tears take up
The glasses of my sight ! A beggar's tongue
Make motion through my lips ; and my arm'd knees,
Who bow'd but in my stirrup, bend like his
That hath receiv'd an alms !—I will not do 't ;   120
Lest I surcease to honour mine own truth,
And by my body's action teach my mind
A most inherent baseness.
Vol.   At thy choice then :
To beg of thee, it is my more dishonour,
Than thou of them. Come all to ruin : let
Thy mother rather feel thy pride, than fear
Thy dangerous stoutness ; for I mock at death
With as big heart as thou. Do as thou list.
Thy valiantness was mine, thou suck'dst it from me,
But owe thy pride thyself.

Cor.   Pray, be content :   130
Mother, I am going to the market-place ;
Chide me no more. I 'll mountebank their loves,
Cog their hearts from them, and come home belov'd
Of all the trades in Rome, Look, I am going.
Commend me to my wife. I 'll return consul,
Or never trust to what my tongue can do
I' the way of flattery further.
Vol.   Do your will.   [*Exit.*
Com. Away ! the tribunes do attend you : arm your
self
To answer mildly ; for they are prepar'd
With accusations, as I hear, more strong   140
Than are upon you yet.
Cor. The word is, mildly.—Pray you, let us go :
Let them accuse me by invention, I
Will answer in mine honour.
Men.   Ay, but mildly.
Cor. Well, mildly be it then ; mildly.   [*Exeunt.*

_____

SCENE III.—*The Same. The Forum.*

Enter SICINIUS *and* BRUTUS.

Bru. In this point charge him home, that he affects
Tyrannical power : if he evade us there,
Enforce him with his envy to the people ;
And that the spoil, got on the Antiates,
Was ne'er distributed.—

Enter an ÆDILE.

What, will he come ?
Æd.   He 's coming.
Bru.   How accompanied ?
Æd. With old Menenius, and those senators
That always favour'd him.
Sic.   Have you a catalogue
Of all the voices that we have procur'd,
Set down by the poll ?
Æd.   I have ; 't is ready.   10
Sic. Have you collected them by tribes ?
Æd.   I have.
Sic. Assemble presently the people hither :
And when they hear me say, " It shall be so
I' the right and strength o' the commons," be it either
For death, for fine, or banishment, then let them,
If I say fine, cry " fine ; " if death, cry " death ; "
Insisting on the old prerogative
And power i' the truth o' the cause.
Æd.   I shall inform them.
Bru. And when such time they have begun to cry,
Let them not cease, but with a din confus'd   20
Enforce the present execution
Of what we chance to sentence.
Æd.   Very well.
Sic. Make them be strong, and ready for this hint,
When we shall hap to give 't them.
Bru.   Go ; about it.—[*Exit Ædile.*
Put him to choler straight. He hath been us'd
Ever to conquer, and to have his worth
Of contradiction : being once chaf'd, he cannot
Be rein'd again to temperance ; then he speaks
What 's in his heart ; and that is there, which looks
With us to break his neck.   30

Enter CORIOLANUS, MENENIUS, COMINIUS, *Senators,*
and Patricians.

Sic. Well, here he comes.
Men.   Calmly, I do beseech you.
Cor. Ay, as an ostler, that for the poorest piece
Will bear the knave by the volume.—The honour'd
gods
Keep Rome in safety, and the chairs of justice
Supplied with worthy men ! plant love among us !
Throng our large temples with the shows of peace,
And not our streets with war !
1 Sen.   Amen, amen.
Men. A noble wish.

Re-enter ÆDILE, with Citizens.

Sic. Draw near, ye people.   39

Æd. List to your tribunes. Audience: peace! I say.
Cor. First, hear me speak.
Both Tri.   Well, say.—Peace, ho!
Cor. Shall I be charg'd no further than this present?
Must all determine here?
Sic.   I do demand,
If you submit you to the people's voices,
Allow their officers, and are content
To suffer lawful censure for such faults
As shall be prov'd upon you?
Cor.   I am content.
Men. Lo, citizens! he says, he is content:
The warlike service he has done, consider; think
Upon the wounds his body bears, which show   50
Like graves i' the holy churchyard.
Cor.   Scratches with briers;
Scars to move laughter only.
Men.   Consider further,
That when he speaks not like a citizen,
You find him like a soldier. Do not take
His rougher accents for malicious sounds,
But, as I say, such as become a soldier,
Rather than envy you.
Com.   Well, well; no more.
Cor. What is the matter,
That, being pass'd for consul with full voice,
I am so dishonour'd, that the very hour   60
You take it off again?
Sic.   Answer to us.
Cor. Say then: 't is true, I ought so.
Sic. We charge you, that you have contriv'd to take
From Rome all season'd office, and to wind
Yourself into a power tyrannical;
For which you are a traitor to the people.
Cor. How! traitor!
Men.   Nay, temperately; your promise.
Cor. The fires i' the lowest hell fold in the people!
Call me their traitor!—Thou injurious tribune,
Within thine eyes sat twenty thousand deaths,   70
In thy hands clutch'd as many millions, in
Thy lying tongue both numbers, I would say,
Thou liest, unto thee, with a voice as free
As I do pray the gods.
Sic.   Mark you this, people?
Cit. To the rock! to the rock with him!
Sic.   Peace!
We need not put new matter to his charge:
What you have seen him do, and heard him speak,
Beating your officers, cursing yourselves,
Opposing laws with strokes, and here defying
Those whose great power must try him; even this,   80
So criminal, and in such capital kind,
Deserves the extremest death.
Bru.   But since he hath
Serv'd well for Rome,—
Cor.   What do you prate of service?
Bru. I talk of that, that know it.
Cor.   You?
Men. Is this the promise that you made your mother?
Com. Know, I pray you,—
Cor.   I 'll know no further.
Let them pronounce the steep Tarpeian death,
Vagabond exile, flaying, pent to linger

But with a grain a day; I would not buy
Their mercy at the price of one fair word,   90
Nor check my courage for what they can give,
To have 't with saying, Good morrow.
Sic.   For that he has
(As much as in him lies) from time to time
Envied against the people, seeking means
To pluck away their power; as now at last
Given hostile strokes, and that not in the presence
Of dreaded justice, but on the ministers
That do distribute it: in the name o' the people,
And in the power of us, the tribunes, we,
Even from this instant, banish him our city,   100
In peril of precipitation
From off the rock Tarpeian, never more
To enter our Rome gates. I' the people's name,
I say, it shall be so.
Cit. It shall be so, it shall be so; let him away:
He 's banish'd, and it shall be so.
Com. Hear me, my masters, and my common
          friends:—
Sic. He 's sentenc'd: no more hearing.
Com.   Let me speak:
I have been consul, and can show for Rome
Her enemies' marks upon me. I do love   110
My country's good, with a respect more tender,
More holy and profound, than mine own life,
My dear wife's estimate, her womb's increase,
And treasure of my loins; then if I would
Speak that—
Sic.   We know your drift: speak what?
Bru. There 's no more to be said, but he is banish'd,
As enemy to the people and his country:
It shall be so.
Cit.   It shall be so, let it be so.
Cor. You common cry of curs! whose breath I hate
As reek o' the rotten fens, whose loves I prize   120
As the dead carcasses of unburied men
That do corrupt my air, I banish you;
And here remain with your uncertainty!
Let every feeble rumour shake your hearts!
Your enemies, with nodding of their plumes,
Fan you into despair! Have the power still
To banish your defenders; till, at length,
Your ignorance (which finds not, till it feels),
Making not reservation of yourselves
(Still your own foes), deliver you,   130
As most abated captives, to some nation
That won you without blows! Despising,
For you, the city, thus I turn my back:
There is a world elsewhere.
          [*Exeunt* CORIOLANUS, COMINIUS, MENENIUS,
                     Senators, and Patricians.
Æd. The people's enemy is gone, is gone!
Cit. Our enemy is banish'd! he is gone! Hoo! hoo!
          [*They all shout, and throw up their caps.*
Sic. Go, see him out at gates; and follow him,
As he hath follow'd you, with all despite;
Give him deserv'd vexation. Let a guard
Attend us through the city.   140
Cit. Come, come; let us see him out at gates:
          come.—
The gods preserve our noble tribunes!—Come.
                              [*Exeunt.*

ACT IV.

SCENE I.—The Same.   Before a Gate of the City.

Enter CORIOLANUS, VOLUMNIA, VIRGILIA, MENENIUS, COMINIUS, *and several young Patricians.*

Coriolanus.

OME, leave your tears : a brief fare-
well.—The beast
With many heads butts me away.—
    Nay, mother,
Where is your ancient courage?
    you were us'd
To say, extremities was the trier of
    spirits ;
That common chances common
    men could bear ;
That, when the sea was calm, all boats alike
Show'd mastership in floating ; fortune's blows,
When most struck home, being gentle wounded, craves
A noble cunning : you were us'd to load me
With precepts, that would make invincible   10
The heart that conn'd them.
    Vir. O heavens! O heavens!
    Cor.   Nay, I pr'ythee, woman,—
    Vol. Now, the red pestilence strike all trades in
    Rome,
And occupations perish !
    Cor.   What, what, what!
I shall be lov'd when I am lack'd. Nay, mother,
Resume that spirit, when you were wont to say,
If you had been the wife of Hercules,
Six of his labours you'd have done, and sav'd
Your husband so much sweat.—Cominius,
Droop not ; adieu.—Farewell, my wife! my mother! 20
I 'll do well yet.—Thou old and true Menenius,
Thy tears are salter than a younger man's,
And venomous to thine eyes.—My sometime general,
I have seen thee stern, and thou hast oft beheld
Heart-hardening spectacles ; tell these sad women,
'T is fond to wail inevitable strokes,
As 't is to laugh at 'em.—My mother, you wot well,
My hazards still have been your solace ; and
Believe 't not lightly, (though I go alone,
Like to a lonely dragon, that his fen   30
Makes fear'd, and talk'd of more than seen,) your son
Will or exceed the common, or be caught
With cautelous baits and practice.
    Vol.   My first son,
Whither wilt thou go? Take good Cominius
With thee awhile : determine on some course,
More than a wild exposure to each chance
That starts i' the way before thee.
    Cor.   O the gods !
    Com. I 'll follow thee a month ; devise with thee
Where thou shalt rest, that thou may'st hear of us,
And we of thee : so, if the time thrust forth   40
A cause for thy repeal, we shall not send
O'er the vast world to seek a single man,
And lose advantage, which doth ever cool
I' the absence of the needer.
    Cor.   Fare ye well :

Thou hast years upon thee ; and thou art too full
Of the war's surfeits, to go rove with one
That 's yet unbruis'd : bring me but out at gate.—
Come, my sweet wife, my dearest mother, and
My friends of noble touch, when I am forth,
Bid me farewell, and smile.   I pray you, come.   50
While I remain above the ground, you shall
Hear from me still ; and never of me aught
But what is like me formerly.
    Men.   That 's worthily
As any ear can hear.—Come : let 's not weep.—
If I could shake off but one seven years
From these old arms and legs, by the good gods,
I 'd with thee every foot.
    Cor.   Give me thy hand.—
Come.   [*Exeunt.*

———

SCENE II.—The Same.   A Street near the Gate.

Enter SICINIUS, BRUTUS, *and an Ædile.*

Sic. Bid them all home : he 's gone, and we 'll no
    further.—
The nobility are vex'd, whom we see have sided
In his behalf.
    Bru.   Now we have shown our power,
Let us seem humbler after it is done,
Than when it was a-doing.
    Sic.   Bid them home :
Say, their great enemy is gone, and they
Stand in their ancient strength.
    Bru.   Dismiss them home. [*Exit Ædile.*

Enter VOLUMNIA, VIRGILIA, *and* MENENIUS.

Here comes his mother.
    Sic.   Let 's not meet her.
    Bru.   Why ?
    Sic. They say, she 's mad.
    Bru. They have ta'en note of us : keep on your way.
    Vol. O ! you 're well met.   The hoarded plague o'
    the gods   11
Requite your love !
    Men.   Peace, peace ! be not so loud.
    Vol. If that I could for weeping, you should hear,—
Nay, and you shall hear some.—[*To* BRUTUS.] Will
    you be gone ?
    Vir. [*To* SICINIUS.] You shall stay too. I would I
    had the power
To say so to my husband.
    Sic.   Are you mankind ?
    Vol. Ay, fool ; is that a shame?—Note but this
    fool.—
Was not a man my father ?   Hadst thou foxship
To banish him that struck more blows for Rome
Than thou hast spoken words ?
    Sic.   O blessed heavens ! 20

Vol. More noble blows, than ever thou wise words ;
And for Rome's good.—I 'll tell thee what :—yet go :—
Nay, but thou shalt stay too.—I would my son
Were in Arabia, and thy tribe before him,
His good sword in his hand.
Sic.   What then?
Vir.   What then!
He 'd make an end of thy posterity.
Vol. Bastards, and all.—
Good man, the wounds that he does bear for Rome!
Men. Come, come : peace!
Sic. I would he had continu'd to his country,   30
As he began ; and not unknit himself
The noble knot he made.
Bru. I would he had.
Vol. I would he had! 'T was you incens'd the
        rabble :
Cats, that can judge as fitly of his worth,
As I can of those mysteries which heaven
Will not have earth to know.
Bru.   Pray, let us go.
Vol. Now, pray, sir, get you gone :
You have done a brave deed. Ere you go, hear this :—
As far as doth the Capitol exceed   40
The meanest house in Rome, so far my son,—
This lady's husband here, this, do you see?—
Whom you have banish'd, does exceed you all.
Bru. Well, well ; we 'll leave you.
Sic.   Why stay we to be baited
With one that wants her wits?
Vol.   Take my prayers with you.—
                                    [*Exeunt Tribunes.*
I would the gods had nothing else to do,
But to confirm my curses. Could I meet 'em
But once a day, it would unclog my heart
Of what lies heavy to 't.
Men.   You have told them home.
And, by my troth, you have cause. You 'll sup with
        me?   50
Vol. Anger 's my meat : I sup upon myself,
And so shall starve with feeding.—Come, let 's go.
Leave this faint puling, and lament as I do,
In anger, Juno-like. Come, come, come.
Men. Fie, fie, fie!   [*Exeunt.*

SCENE III.—A Highway between Rome and Antium.

Enter a Roman and a Volsce, meeting.

Rom. I know you well, sir, and you know me.
Your name, I think, is Adrian.
Vols. It is so, sir : truly, I have forgot you.
Rom. I am a Roman ; and my services are, as you
are, against 'em. Know you me yet?
Vols. Nicanor? No.
Rom. The same, sir.
Vols. You had more beard, when I last saw you ;
but your favour is well appeared by your tongue.
What 's the news in Rome? I have a note from the
Volscian state, to find you out there : you have well
saved me a day's journey.   12
Rom. There hath been in Rome strange insurrec-
tions : the people against the senators, patricians, and
nobles.
Vols. Hath been! Is it ended then? Our state
thinks not so ; they are in a most warlike preparation, and hope to come upon them in the heat of their
division.   19
Rom. The main blaze of it is past, but a small
thing would make it flame again. For the nobles
receive so to heart the banishment of that worthy
Coriolanus, that they are in a ripe aptness to take all
power from the people, and to pluck from them their
tribunes for ever. This lies glowing, I can tell you,
and is almost mature for the violent breaking out.
Vols. Coriolanus banished!
Rom. Banished, sir.
Vols. You will be welcome with this intelligence,
Nicanor.   30
Rom. The day serves well for them now. I have
heard it said, the fittest time to corrupt a man's wife is
when she 's fallen out with her husband. Your noble

Tullus Aufidius will appear well in these wars, his
great opposer, Coriolanus, being now in no request of
his country.
Vols. He cannot choose. I am most fortunate, thus
accidentally to encounter you : you have ended my
business, and I will merrily accompany you home.   39
Rom. I shall, between this and supper, tell you
most strange things from Rome, all tending to the
good of their adversaries. Have you an army ready,
say you?
Vols. A most royal one : the centurions and their
charges distinctly billeted, already in the entertainment, and to be on foot at an hour's warning.
Rom. I am joyful to hear of their readiness, and am
the man, I think, that shall set them in present action.
So, sir, heartily well met, and most glad of your company.   50
Vols. You take my part from me, sir : I have the
most cause to be glad of yours.
Rom. Well, let us go together.   [*Exeunt.*

SCENE IV.—Antium. Before AUFIDIUS'S House.

Enter CORIOLANUS, *in mean apparel, disguised and
muffled.*

Cor. A goodly city is this Antium.—City,
'T is I that made thy widows : many an heir
Of these fair edifices 'fore my wars
Have I heard groan, and drop : then, know me not,
Lest that thy wives with spits, and boys with stones,
In puny battle slay me.

Enter a Citizen.

                                        Save you, sir.
Cit. And you.
Cor.   Direct me, if it be your will,
Where great Aufidius lies. Is he in Antium?
Cit. He is, and feasts the nobles of the state   9
At his house this night.
Cor.   Which is his house, beseech you?
Cit. This, here before you.
Cor.   Thank you, sir. Farewell.
                                        [*Exit Citizen.*
O world, thy slippery turns! Friends now fast sworn,
Whose double bosoms seem to wear one heart,
Whose hours, whose bed, whose meal and exercise,
Are still together, who twin, as 't were, in love
Unseparable, shall within this hour,
On dissension of a doit, break out
To bitterest enmity : so, fellest foes,
Whose passions and whose plots have broke their
        sleep
To take the one the other, by some chance,   20
Some trick not worth an egg, shall grow dear friends,
And interjoin their issues. So with me :—
My birth-place hate I, and my love 's upon
This enemy town.—I 'll enter : if he slay me,
He does fair justice ; if he give me way,
I 'll do his country service.   [*Exit.*

SCENE V.—The Same. A Hall in AUFIDIUS'S House.

Music within. Enter a Servant.

1 *Serv.* Wine, wine, wine! What service is here! I
think our fellows are asleep.   [*Exit.*

Enter a second Servant.

2 *Serv.* Where 's Cotus? my master calls for him.—
Cotus!   [*Exit.*

Enter CORIOLANUS.

Cor. A goodly house : the feast smells well ; but I
Appear not like a guest.

Re-enter the first Servant.

1 *Serv.* What would you have, friend? Whence are
you? Here 's no place for you : pray, go to the door.
Cor. I have deserv'd no better entertainment,
In being Coriolanus.   10

Re-enter second Servant.

2 Ser. Whence are you, sir? Has the porter his eyes in his head, that he gives entrance to such companions? Pray, get you out.

Cor. Away!

2 Serv. Away? Get you away.

Cor. Now thou art troublesome.

2 Serv. Are you so brave? I 'll have you talked with anon.

Enter a third Servant. The first meets him.

3 Serv. What fellow 's this?

1 Serv. A strange one as ever I looked on : I cannot get him out o' the house : pr'ythee, call my master to him.   22

3 Serv. What have you to do here, fellow? Pray you avoid the house.

Cor. Let me but stand ; I will not hurt your hearth.

3 Serv. What are you?

Cor. A gentleman.

3 Serv. A marvellous poor one.

Cor. True, so I am.

3 Serv. Pray you, poor gentleman, take up some other station : here 's no place for you. Pray you, avoid : come.   32

Cor. Follow your function ; go, and batten on cold bits.   [*Pushes him away.*

3 Serv. What, will you not? Pr'ythee, tell my master what a strange guest he has here.

2 Serv. And I shall.   [*Exit.*

3 Serv. Where dwell'st thou?

Cor. Under the canopy.

3 Serv. Under the canopy?   40

Cor. Ay.

3 Serv. Where 's that?

Cor. I' the city of kites and crows.

3 Serv. I' the city of kites and crows!—What an ass it is!—Then thou dwellest with daws too?

Cor. No : I serve not thy master.

3 Serv. How, sir! Do you meddle with my master?

Cor. Ay ; 't is an honester service than to meddle with thy mistress.

Thou prat'st, and prat'st : serve with thy trencher. Hence!   [*Beats him away.*

Enter Aufidius *and the second Servant.*

Auf. Where is this fellow?   51

2 Serv. Here, sir. I 'd have beaten him like a dog, but for disturbing the lords within.

Auf. Whence com'st thou? what wouldst thou? thy name? Why speak'st not? speak, man : what 's thy name?

Cor. [*Unmuffling.*] If, Tullus, not yet thou know'st me, and, seeing me, dost not think me for the man I am, necessity commands me name myself.

Auf. What is thy name?   [*Servants retire.*

Cor. A name unmusical to the Volscians' ears,   61 And harsh in sound to thine.

Auf.   Say, what 's thy name? Thou hast a grim appearance, and thy face Bears a command in 't : though thy tackle 's torn, Thou show'st a noble vessel. What 's thy name?

Cor. Prepare thy brow to frown. Know'st thou me yet?

Auf. I know thee not.—Thy name?

Cor. My name is Caius Marcius, who hath done To thee particularly, and to all the Volsces, Great hurt and mischief! thereto witness may   70 My surname, Coriolanus. The painful service, The extreme dangers, and the drops of blood Shed for my thankless country, are requited But with that surname ; a good memory, And witness of the malice and displeasure Which thou should'st bear me. Only that name remains :

The cruelty and envy of the people, Permitted by our dastard nobles, who Have all forsook me, hath devour'd the rest ; And suffer'd me by the voice of slaves to be   80 Whoop'd out of Rome. Now, this extremity Hath brought me to thy hearth : not out of hope— Mistake me not—to save my life ; for if

I had fear'd death, of all the men i' the world I would have 'voided thee ; but in mere spite, To be full quit of those my banishers, Stand I before thee here. Then, if thou hast A heart of wreak in thee, that will revenge Thine own particular wrongs, and stop those maims Of shame seen through thy country, speed thee straight,   90 And make my misery serve thy turn : so use it,

Cor. " Prepare thy brow to frown. Know'st thou me yet?"

That my revengeful services may prove As benefits to thee ; for I will fight Against my canker'd country with the spleen Of all the under fiends. But if so be Thou dar'st not this, and that to prove more fortunes Thou 'rt tir'd, then, in a word, I also am Longer to live most weary, and present My throat to thee, and to thy ancient malice ; Which not to cut would show thee but a fool,   100 Since I have ever follow'd thee with hate, Drawn tuns of blood out of thy country's breast, And cannot live but to thy shame, unless It be to do thee service.

Auf.   O Marcius, Marcius! Each word thou hast spoke hath weeded from my heart A root of ancient envy. If Jupiter Should from yond cloud speak divine things, And say " 'T is true," I 'd not believe them more Than thee, all noble Marcius.—Let me twine Mine arms about that body, where against   110 My grained ash an hundred times hath broke, And scarr'd the moon with splinters ! Here I clip The anvil of my sword, and do contest As hotly and as nobly with thy love, As ever in ambitious strength I did Contend against thy valour. Know thou first, I lov'd the maid I married : never man Sigh'd truer breath ; but that I see thee here, Thou noble thing, more dances my rapt heart, Than when I first my wedded mistress saw   120 Bestride my threshold. Why, thou Mars, I tell thee. We have a power on foot ; and I had purpose Once more to hew thy target from thy brawn, Or lose mine arm for 't. Thou hast beat me out Twelve several times, and I have nightly since Dreamt of encounters 'twixt thyself and me : We have been down together in my sleep, Unbuckling helms, fisting each other's throat, And wak'd half dead with nothing. Worthy Marcius, Had we no other quarrel else to Rome, but that   130 Thou art thence banish'd, we would muster all From twelve to seventy : and, pouring war Into the bowels of ungrateful Rome, Like a bold flood o'er-bear. O! come ; go in, And take our friendly senators by the hands,

Who now are here, taking their leaves of me,
Who am prepar'd against your territories,
Though not for Rome itself.
  Cor.   You bless me, gods!
  Auf. Therefore, most absolute sir, if thou wilt have
The leading of thine own revenges, take   140
The one half of my commission ; and set down—
As best thou art experienc'd, since thou know'st
Thy country's strength and weakness—thine own
          ways ;
Whether to knock against the gates of Rome,
Or rudely visit them in parts remote,
To fright them, ere destroy. But come in :
Let me commend thee first to those, that shall
Say yea to thy desires. A thousand welcomes !
And more a friend than e'er an enemy ;   149
Yet, Marcius, that was much. Your hand : most wel-
    come ! [*Exeunt* CORIOLANUS *and* AUFIDIUS.
  1 Serv. [*Advancing.*] Here 's a strange alteration !
  2 Serv. By my hand, I had thought to have strucken
him with a cudgel; and yet my mind gave me, his
clothes made a false report of him.
  1 Serv. What an arm he has ! He turned me about
with his finger and his thumb, as one would set up a
top.
  2 Serv. Nay, I knew by his face that there was
something in him : he had, sir, a kind of face, methought,—I cannot tell how to term it.   160
  1 Serv. He had so ; looking as it were,—'would I
were hanged, but I thought there was more in him
than I could think.
  2 Serv. So did I, I 'll be sworn. He is simply the
rarest man i' the world.
  1 Serv. I think he is ; but a greater soldier than he,
you wot one.
  2 Serv. Who ? my master ?
  1 Serv. Nay, it 's no matter for that.
  2 Serv. Worth six on him.   170
  1 Serv. Nay, not so neither ; but I take him to be the
greater soldier.
  2 Serv. 'Faith, look you, one cannot tell how to say
that : for the defence of a town, our general is excellent.
  1 Serv. Ay, and for an assault too.

Re-enter third Servant.

  3 Serv. O slaves, I can tell you news ; news, you
rascals.
  1 & 2 Serv. What, what, what ? let 's partake.
  3 Serv. I would not be a Roman, of all nations ; I
had as lieve be a condemned man.   181
  1 & 2 Serv. Wherefore ? wherefore ?
  3 Serv. Why, here 's he that was wont to thwack
our general,—Caius Marcius.
  1 Serv. Why do you say thwack our general ?
  3 Serv. I do not say, thwack our general ; but he
was always good enough for him.
  2 Serv. Come, we are fellows, and friends : he was
ever too hard for him ; I have heard him say so himself.   190
  1 Serv. He was too hard for him directly, to say the
truth on 't : before Corioli he scotched him and notched
him like a carbonado.
  2 Serv. An he had been cannibally given, he might
have broiled and eaten him too.
  1 Serv. But, more of thy news ?
  3 Serv. Why, he is so made on here within, as if he
were son and heir to Mars : set at upper end o' the
table ; no question asked him by any of the senators,
but they stand bald before him. Our general himself
makes a mistress of him ; sanctifies himself with 's
hand, and turns up the white o' the eye to his discourse. But the bottom of the news is, our general is
cut i' the middle, and but one half of what he was
yesterday, for the other has half, by the entreaty and
grant of the whole table. He 'll go, he says, and sowl
the porter of Rome gates by the ears. He will mow
down all before him, and leave his passage polled.
  2 Serv. And he 's as like to do 't, as any man I can
imagine.   200
  3 Serv. Do 't ! he will do 't : for, look you, sir, he
has as many friends as enemies ; which friends, sir,

(as it were) durst not (look you, sir) show themselves
(as we term it) his friends, whilst he 's in directitude.
  1 Serv. Directitude ! what 's that ?
  3 Serv. But when they shall see, sir, his crest up
again, and the man in blood, they will out of their
burrows, like conies after rain, and revel all with him.
  1 Serv. But when goes this forward ?   219
  3 Serv. To-morrow ; to-day ; presently. You shall
have the drum struck up this afternoon : 'tis, as it
were, a parcel of their feast, and to be executed ere
they wipe their lips.
  2 Serv. Why, then we shall have a stirring world
again. This peace is nothing, but to rust iron, increase
tailors, and breed ballad-makers.
  1 Serv. Let me have war, say I : it exceeds peace as
far as day does night ; it 's spritely, waking, audible,
and full of vent. Peace is a very apoplexy, lethargy ;
mulled, deaf, sleepy, insensible ; a getter of more
bastard children than war 's a destroyer of men. 231
  2 Serv. 'T is so : and as war, in some sort, may be
said to be a ravisher, so it cannot be denied but peace
is a great maker of cuckolds.
  1 Serv. Ay, and it makes men hate one another.
  3 Serv. Reason : because they then less need one
another. The wars, for my money. I hope to see
Romans as cheap as Volscians.—They are rising, they
are rising.
  All. In, in, in, in !   240
                                  [*Exeunt.*

SCENE VI.—Rome. A Public Place.

Enter SICINIUS *and* BRUTUS.

  Sic. We hear not of him, neither need we fear him;
His remedies are tame i' the present peace
And quietness o' the people, which before
Were in wild hurry. Here do we make his friends
Blush that the world goes well ; who rather had,
Though they themselves did suffer by 't, behold
Dissentious numbers pestering streets, than see
Our tradesmen singing in their shops, and going
About their functions friendly.

Enter MENENIUS.

  Bru. We stood to 't in good time. Is this Menenius?
  Sic. 'T is he, 't is he. O ! he is grown most kind 11
Of late.—Hail, sir !
  Men.   Hail to you both !
  Sic. Your Coriolanus is not much miss'd
But with his friends : the commonwealth doth stand,
And so would do, were he more angry at it.
  Men. All 's well ; and might have been much better,
      if
He could have temporis'd.
  Sic.   Where is he, hear you?
  Men. Nay, I hear nothing : his mother and his wife
Hear nothing from him.

Enter three or four Citizens.

  Cit. The gods preserve you both !
  Sic.   Good e'en, our neighbours.
  Bru. Good e'en to you all, good e'en to you all. 21
  1 Cit. Ourselves, our wives, and children, on our
      knees,
Are bound to pray for you both.
  Sic.   Live, and thrive!
  Bru. Farewell, kind neighbours. We wish'd Corio-
      lanus
Had lov'd you as we did.
  Cit.   Now the gods keep you !
  Both Tri. Farewell, farewell. [*Exeunt Citizens.*
  Sic. This is a happier and more comely time,
Than when these fellows ran about the streets,
Crying confusion.
  Bru.   Caius Marcius was
A worthy officer i' the war ; but insolent,   30
O'ercome with pride, ambitious past all thinking,
Self-loving,—
  Sic.   And affecting one sole throne,
Without assistance.
  Men.   I think not so.

Sic. We should by this, to all our lamentation,
If he had gone forth consul, found 't so.
Bru. The gods have well prevented it, and Rome
Sits safe and still without him.

Enter an Ædile.

Æd. Worthy tribunes,
There is a slave, whom we have put in prison,
Reports, the Volsces with two several powers
Are enter'd in the Roman territories, 40
And with the deepest malice of the war
Destroy what lies before 'em.
Men. 'T is Aufidius,
Who, hearing of our Marcius' banishment,
Thrusts forth his horns again into the world ;
Which were inshell'd when Marcius stood for Rome,
And durst not once peep out.
Sic. Come, what talk you of Marcius?
Bru. Go see this rumourer whipp'd.—It cannot be
The Volsces dare break with us.
Men. Cannot be !
We have record that very well it can ; 50
And three examples of the like have been
Within my age. But reason with the fellow,
Before you punish him, where he heard this ;
Lest you shall chance to whip your information,
And beat the messenger who bids beware
Of what is to be dreaded.
Sic. Tell not me :
I know, this cannot be.
Bru. Not possible.

Enter a Messenger.

Mess. The nobles in great earnestness are going
All to the senate-house : some news is come,
That turns their countenances.
Sic. 'T is this slave. 60
Go whip him 'fore the people's eyes :—his raising !
Nothing but his report !
Mess. Yes, worthy sir,
The slave's report is seconded ; and more,
More fearful, is deliver'd.
Sic. What more fearful?
Mess. It is spoke freely out of many mouths,
How probable I do not know, that Marcius,
Join'd with Aufidius, leads a power 'gainst Rome,
And vows revenge as spacious as between
The young'st and oldest thing.
Sic. This is most likely !
Bru. Rais'd only, that the weaker sort may wish 70
Good Marcius home again.
Sic. The very trick on 't.
Men. This is unlikely :
He and Aufidius can no more atone,
Than violentest contrariety.

Enter another Messenger.

Mess. You are sent for to the senate :
A fearful army, led by Caius Marcius,
Associated with Aufidius, rages
Upon our territories ; and have already
O'erborne their way, consum'd with fire, and took
What lay before them. 80

Enter COMINIUS.

Com. O ! you have made good work.
Men. What news? what news?
Com. You have holp to ravish your own daughters,
and
To melt the city leads upon your pates ;
To see your wives dishonour'd to your noses ;—
Men. What 's the news? what 's the news?
Com. Your temples burned in their cement ; and
Your franchises, whereon you stood, confin'd
Into an auger's bore.
Men. Pray now, your news ?—
You have made fair work, I fear me.—Pray, your
news ?—
If Marcius should be join'd with Volscians,—
Com. If ! 90
He is their god : he leads them like a thing
Made by some other deity than nature,
That shapes man better ; and they follow him

Against us brats, with no less confidence
Than boys pursuing summer butterflies,
Or butchers killing flies.
Men. You have made good work,
You, and your apron-men ; you that stood so much
Upon the voice of occupation and
The breath of garlic-eaters !
Com. He will shake
Your Rome about your ears.
Men. As Hercules 100
Did shake down mellow fruit. You have made fair
work.
Bru. But is this true, sir?
Com. Ay ; and you 'll look pale
Before you find it other. All the regions
Do smilingly revolt ; and, who resist,
Are mock'd for valiant ignorance,
And perish constant fools. Who is 't can blame him?
Your enemies, and his, find something in him.
Men. We are all undone, unless
The noble man have mercy.
Com. Who shall ask it?
The tribunes cannot do 't for shame ; the people 110
Deserve such pity of him, as the wolf
Does of the shepherds : for his best friends, if they
Should say, " Be good to Rome," they charg'd him
even
As those should do that had deserv'd his hate,
And therein show'd like enemies.
Men. 'T is true.
If he were putting to my house the brand
That should consume it, I have not the face
To say, " Beseech you, cease."—You have made fair
hands,
You and your crafts ; you have crafted fair.
Com. You have brought
A trembling upon Rome, such as was never 120
So incapable of help.
Tri. Say not, we brought it.
Men. How ! Was it we ? We lov'd him ; but, like
beasts,
And cowardly nobles, gave way unto your clusters,
Who did hoot him out o' the city.
Com. But, I fear,
They 'll roar him in again. Tullus Aufidius,
The second name of men, obeys his points
As if he were his officer. Desperation
Is all the policy, strength, and defence,
That Rome can make against them.

Enter a troop of Citizens.

Men. Here come the clusters.—
And is Aufidius with him?—You are they 130
That made the air unwholesome, when you cast
Your stinking, greasy caps, in hooting at
Coriolanus' exile. Now he 's coming ;
And not a hair upon a soldier's head
Which will not prove a whip : as many coxcombs
As you threw caps up, will he tumble down,
And pay you for your voices. 'T is no matter
If he could burn us all into one coal,
We have deserv'd it.
Cit. 'Faith, we hear fearful news.
1 *Cit.* For mine own part,
When I said, banish him, I said, 't was pity. 141
2 *Cit.* And so did I.
3 *Cit.* And so did I ; and, to say the truth, so did
very many of us. That we did, we did for the best ;
and though we willingly consented to his banishment,
yet it was against our will.
Com. Ye 're goodly things, you voices !
Men. You have made
Good work, you and your cry !—Shall 's to the Capitol?
Com. O ! ay ; what else ?
[*Exeunt* COMINIUS *and* MENENIUS.
Sic. Go, masters, get you home ; be not dismay'd : 151
These are a side that would be glad to have
This true, which they so seem to fear. Go home,
And show no sign of fear.
1 *Cit.* The gods be good to us ! Come, masters, let 's
home. I ever said, we were i' the wrong, when we
banished him.

2 Cit. So did we all. But come, let's home.
　　　　　　　　　　　　　　[Exeunt Citizens.
Bru. I do not like this news.
Sic. Nor I.
Bru. Let's to the Capitol.—'Would, half my wealth
Would buy this for a lie!
Sic.　　　　　　Pray, let us go.　　　　161
　　　　　　　　　　　　　　　[Exeunt.

SCENE VII.—A Camp, at a small distance from Rome.

Enter AUFIDIUS *and his Lieutenant.*

Auf. Do they still fly to the Roman?
Lieu. I do not know what witchcraft's in him; but
Your soldiers use him as the grace 'fore meat,
Their talk at table, and their thanks at end;
And you are darken'd in this action, sir,
Even by your own.
Auf.　　　　　I cannot help it now,
Unless, by using means, I lame the foot
Of our design. He bears himself more proudlier,
Even to my person, than I thought he would
When first I did embrace him; yet his nature 10
In that's no changeling, and I must excuse
What cannot be amended.
Lieu.　　　　　Yet I wish, sir,
(I mean, for your particular,) you had not
Join'd in commission with him; but either
Had borne the action of yourself, or else
To him had left it solely.
Auf. I understand thee well; and be thou sure,
When he shall come to his account, he knows not
What I can urge against him. Although it seems,
And so he thinks, and is no less apparent　　20
To the vulgar eye, that he bears all things fairly,
And shows good husbandry for the Volscian state,

Fights dragon-like, and does achieve as soon
As draw his sword; yet he hath left undone
That which shall break his neck, or hazard mine,
Whene'er we come to our account.
Lieu. Sir, I beseech you, think you he'll carry
　　Rome?
Auf. All places yield to him ere he sits down;
And the nobility of Rome are his:
The senators and patricians love him too:　　30
The tribunes are no soldiers; and their people
Will be as rash in the repeal, as hasty
To expel him thence. I think, he'll be to Rome,
As is the osprey to the fish, who takes it
By sovereignty of nature. First he was
A noble servant to them, but he could not
Carry his honours even: whether 'twas pride,
Which out of daily fortune ever taints
The happy man; whether defect of judgment,
To fail in the disposing of those chances　　40
Which he was lord of; or whether nature,
Not to be other than one thing, not moving
From the casque to the cushion, but commanding
　　peace
Even with the same austerity and garb
As he controll'd the war; but one of these
(As he hath spices of them all, not all,
For I dare so far free him) made him fear'd,
So hated, and so banish'd: but he has a merit,
To choke it in the utterance. So our virtues
Lie in the interpretation of the time;　　50
And power, unto itself most commendable,
Hath not a tomb so evident as a chair
To extol what it hath done.
One fire drives out one fire; one nail, one nail;
Rights by rights falter, strengths by strengths do fail.
Come, let's away. When, Caius, Rome is thine,
Thou art poor'st of all; then, shortly art thou mine.
　　　　　　　　　　　　　　　[Exeunt.

ACT V.

SCENE I.—Rome. A Public Place.

Enter MENENIUS, COMINIUS, SICINIUS, BRUTUS, *and others.*

Menenius.
O, I'll not go: you hear what he hath said,
Which was sometime his general; who
　　lov'd him
In a most dear particular. He call'd me
　　father:
But what o' that? Go, you that banish'd
　　him;
A mile before his tent fall down, and knee

The way into his mercy. Nay, if he coy'd
To hear Cominius speak, I'll keep at home.
Com. He would not seem to know me.
Men.　　　　　　　　Do you hear?
Com. Yet one time he did call me by my name:
I urg'd our old acquaintance, and the drops 10
That we have bled together. Coriolanus
He would not answer to, forbad all names;
He was a kind of nothing, titleless,

Till he had forg'd himself a name o'.the fire
Of burning Rome.
Men.   Why, so ; you have made good work :
A pair of tribunes that have rack'd for Rome,
To make coals cheap : a noble memory !
Com. I minded him, how royal 't was to pardon
When it was less expected : he replied,
It was a bare petition of a state   20
To one whom they had punish'd.
Men. Very well : could he say less?
Com. I offer'd to awaken his regard
For 's private friends : his answer to me was,
He could not stay to pick them in a pile
Of noisome, musty chaff. He said, 't was folly,
For one poor grain or two to leave unburnt,
And still to nose the offence.
Men.   For one poor grain or two?
I am one of those ; his mother, wife, his child,
And this brave fellow too, we are the grains :   30
You are the musty chaff, and you are smelt
Above the moon. We must be burnt for you.
Sic. Nay, pray, be patient : if you refuse your aid
In this so never-needed help, yet do not
Upbraid 's with our distress. But, sure, if you
Would be your country's pleader, your good tongue,
More than the instant army we can make,
Might stop our countryman.
Men.   No ; I 'll not meddle.
Sic. Pray you, go to him.
Men.   What should I do?
Bru. Only make trial what your love can do   40
For Rome, towards Marcius.
Men.   Well ; and say that Marcius
Return me, as Cominius is return'd,
Unheard ; what then?—
But as a discontented friend, grief-shot
With his unkindness? say 't be so?
Sic.   Yet your good will
Must have that thanks from Rome, after the measure
As you intended well.
Men.   I 'll undertake it :
I think, he 'll hear me. Yet to bite his lip,
And hum at good Cominius, much unhearts me.
He was not taken well ; he had not din'd :   50
The veins unfill'd, our blood is cold, and then
We pout upon the morning, are unapt
To give or to forgive ; but when we have stuff'd
These pipes and these conveyances of our blood
With wine and feeding, we have supper souls
Than in our priest-like fasts : therefore, I 'll watch him
Till he be dieted to my request,
And then I 'll set upon him.
Bru. You know the very road into his kindness,
And cannot lose your way.
Men.   Good faith, I 'll prove him.
Speed how it will, I shall ere long have knowledge 61
Of my success.   [*Exit.*
Com.   He 'll never hear him.
Sic.   Not?
Com. I tell you, he does sit in gold, his eye
Red as 't would burn Rome, and his injury
The gaoler to his pity. I kneel'd before him ;
'T was very faintly he said, " Rise ;" dismiss'd me
Thus, with his speechless hand : what he would do,
He sent in writing after me,—what he would not ;
Bound with an oath to yield to his conditions :
So that all hope is vain,   70
Unless his noble mother, and his wife,
Who, as I hear, mean to solicit him
For mercy to his country. Therefore, let 's hence,
And with our fair entreaties haste them on. [*Exeunt.*

SCENE II.—*The Volscian Camp before Rome. The Guards at their stations.*

Enter to them MENENIUS.

1 G. Stay ! Whence are you?
2 G.   Stand, and go back.
Men. You guard like men : 't is well ; but, by your leave,

I am an officer of state, and come
To speak with Coriolanus.
1 G.   From whence?
Men.   From Rome.
1 G. You may not pass ; you must return : our general
Will no more hear from thence.
2 G. You 'll see your Rome embrac'd with fire, before
You 'll speak with Coriolanus.
Men.   Good my friends,
If you have heard your general talk of Rome,
And of his friends there, it is lots to blanks,   10
My name hath touch'd your ears : it is Menenius.
1 G. Be it so ; go back : the virtue of your name
Is not here passable.
Men.   I tell thee, fellow,
Thy general is my lover : I have been
The book of his good acts, whence men have read
His fame unparallel'd, haply amplified ;
For I have ever verified my friends
(Of whom he 's chief) with all the size that verity
Would without lapsing suffer : nay, sometimes,
Like to a bowl upon a subtle ground,   20
I have tumbled past the throw, and in his praise
Have almost stamp'd the leasing. Therefore, fellow,
I must have leave to pass.
1 G. 'Faith, sir, if you had told as many lies in his
behalf, as you have uttered words in your own, you
should not pass here ; no, though it were as virtuous
to lie as to live chastely. Therefore, go back.
Men. Pr'ythee, fellow, remember my name is
Menenius, always factionary on the party of your
general.   30
2 G. Howsoever you have been his liar, as you say
you have, I am one that, telling true under him, must
say, you cannot pass. Therefore, go back.
Men. Has he dined, canst thou tell? for I would
not speak with him till after dinner.
1 G. You are a Roman, are you?
Men. I am, as thy general is.   37
1 G. Then you should hate Rome, as he does. Can
you, when you have pushed out your gates the very
defender of them, and, in a violent popular ignorance,
given your enemy your shield, think to front his
revenges with the easy groans of old women, the
virginal palms of your daughters, or with the palsied
intercession of such a decayed dotant as you seem to
be? Can you think to blow out the intended fire your
city is ready to flame in, with such weak breath as
this? No, you are deceived ; therefore, back to
Rome, and prepare for your execution. You are
condemned, our general has sworn you out of reprieve
and pardon.   50
Men. Sirrah, if thy captain knew I were here, he
would use me with estimation.
2 G. Come, my captain knows you not.
Men. I mean, thy general.
1 G. My general cares not for you. Back, I say :
go, lest I let forth your half-pint of blood ;—back,—
that 's the utmost of your having :—back.
Men. Nay, but, fellow, fellow,—

Enter CORIOLANUS *and* AUFIDIUS.

Cor. What 's the matter?   59
Men. Now, you companion, I 'll say an errand for
you : you shall know now that I am in estimation ;
you shall perceive that a Jack-guardant cannot office
me from my son Coriolanus : guess, but by my entertainment with him, if thou stand'st not i' the state of
hanging, or of some death more long in spectatorship,
and crueller in suffering : behold now presently, and
swoond for what 's to come upon thee.—The glorious
gods sit in hourly synod about thy particular prosperity, and love thee no worse than thy old father
Menenius does ! O my son ! my son ! thou art preparing fire for us ; look thee, here 's water to quench
it. I was hardly moved to come to thee ; but being
assured, none but myself could move thee, I have
been blown out of your gates with sighs, and conjure
thee to pardon Rome, and thy petitionary countrymen. The good gods assuage thy wrath, and turn the

dregs of it upon this varlet here; this, who, like a
block, hath denied my access to thee.
Cor. Away!
Men. How! away! 80
Cor. Wife, mother, child, I know not. My affairs
Are servanted to others : though I owe
My revenge properly, my remission lies
In Volscian breasts. That we have been familiar,
Ingrate forgetfulness shall poiso·, rather
Than pity note how much.—Therefore, be gone :
Mine ears against your suits are stronger than
Your gates against my force. Yet, for I lov'd thee,
Take this along ; I writ it for thy sake, [*Gives a paper.*
And would have sent it. Another word, Menenius,
I will not hear thee speak.—This man, Aufidius, 91
Was my belov'd in Rome ; yet thou behold'st—
Auf. You keep a constant temper.
[*Exeunt* CORIOLANUS *and* AUFIDIUS.
1 G. Now, sir, is your name Menenius?
2 G. 'T is a spell, you see, of much power. You
know the way home again.
1 G. Do you hear how we are shent for keeping
your greatness back? 98
2 G. What cause, do you think, I have to swoond?
Men. I neither care for the world, nor your general :
for such things as you, I can scarce think there 's any,
you are so slight. He that hath a will to die by himself, fears it not from another. Let your general do
his worst. For you, be that you are, long ; and your
misery increase with your age. I say to you, as I was
said to, Away! [*Exit.*
1 G. A noble fellow, I warrant him.
2 G. The worthy fellow is our general : he is the
rock, the oak not to be wind-shaken. [*Exeunt.*

SCENE III.—The Tent of CORIOLANUS.

Enter CORIOLANUS, AUFIDIUS, *and others.*

Cor. We will before the walls of Rome to-morrow
Set down our host.—My partner in this action,
You must report to the Volscian lords, how plainly
I have borne this business.
Auf. Only their ends
You have respected ; stopp'd your ears against
The general suit of Rome ; never admitted
A private whisper, no, not with such friends
That thought them sure of you.
Cor. This last old man,
Whom with a crack'd heart I have sent to Rome,
Lov'd me above the measure of a father ; 10
Nay, godded me, indeed. Their latest refuge
Was to send him ; for whose old love I have
(Though I show'd sourly to him) once more offer'd
The first conditions, which they did refuse,
And cannot now accept, to grace him only
That thought he could do more. A very little
I have yielded to : fresh embassies, and suits,
Nor from the state, nor private friends, hereafter
Will I lend ear to.—[*Shout within.*] Ha! what shout
is this?
Shall I be tempted to infringe my vow 20
In the same time 't is made? I will not.—

Enter, in mourning habits, VIRGILIA, VOLUMNIA,
leading Young MARCIUS, VALERIA, *and Attend-*
ants.

My wife comes foremost ; then the honour'd mould
Wherein this trunk was fram'd, and in her hand
The grandchild to her blood. But out, affection !
All bond and privilege of nature, break !
Let it be virtuous to be obstinate.—
What is that curt'sy worth? or those doves' eyes,
Which can make gods forsworn?—I melt, and am not
Of stronger earth than others.—My mother bows,
As if Olympus to a molehill should 30
In supplication nod ; and my young boy
Hath an aspect of intercession, which
Great nature cries, " Deny not."—Let the Volsces
Plough Rome, and harrow Italy ; I 'll never
Be such a gosling to obey instinct, but stand,

As if a man were author of himself,
And knew no other kin.
Vir. My lord and husband !
Cor. These eyes are not the same I wore in Rome.
Vir. The sorrow that delivers us thus chang'd,
Makes you think so.
Cor. Like a dull actor now, 40
I have forgot my part, and I am out,
Even to a full disgrace. Best of my flesh,
Forgive my tyranny ; but do not say
For that, " Forgive our Romans."—O ! a kiss
Long as my exile, sweet as my revenge !
Now, by the jealous queen of heaven, that kiss
I carried from thee, dear[and my true lip
Hath virgin'd it e'er since.—You gods ! I prate,
And the most noble mother of the world
Leave insaluted. Sink, my knee, i' the earth ; [*Kneels.*
Of thy deep duty more impression show 51
Than that of common sons.
Vol. O, stand up bless'd !
Whilst, with no softer cushion than the flint,
I kneel before thee, and unproperly
Show duty, as mistaken all this while
Between the child and parent. [*Kneels.*
Cor. What is this?
Your knees to me? to your corrected son?
Then let the pebbles on the hungry beach
Fillip the stars ; then let the mutinous winds
Strike the proud cedars 'gainst the fiery sun, 60
Murd'ring impossibility, to make
What cannot be, slight work.
Vol. Thou art my warrior ;
I holp to frame thee. Do you know this lady?
Cor. The noble sister of Publicola,
The moon of Rome ; chaste as the icicle,
That 's curdied by the frost from purest snow,
And hangs on Dian's temple : dear Valeria !
Vol. This is a poor epitome of yours,
Which, by the interpretation of full time,
May show like all yourself.
Cor. The god of soldiers, 70
With the consent of supreme Jove, inform
Thy thoughts with nobleness ; that thou may'st prove
To shame unvulnerable, and stick i' the wars
Like a great sea-mark, standing every flaw,
And saving those that eye thee !
Vol. Your knee, sirrah.
Cor. That 's my brave boy !
Vol. Even he, your wife, this lady, and myself,
Are suitors to you.
Cor. I beseech you, peace ;
Or, if you 'd ask, remember this before :
The things I have forsworn to grant may never 80
Be held by your denials. Do not bid me
Dismiss my soldiers, or capitulate
Again with Rome's mechanics : tell me not
Wherein I seem unnatural : desire not
To allay my rages and revenges with
Your colder reasons.
Vol. O ! no more, no more !
You have said, you will not grant us anything :
For we have nothing else to ask but that
Which you deny already : yet we will ask ;
That, if you fail in our request, the blame 90
May hang upon your hardness. Therefore, hear us.
Cor. Aufidius, and you Volsces, mark ; for we 'll
Hear nought from Rome in private.—Your request?
Vol. Should we be silent and not speak, our raiment
And state of bodies would bewray what life
We have led since thy exile. Think with thyself,
How more unfortunate than all living women
Are we come hither : since that thy sight, which
should
Make our eyes flow with joy, hearts dance with
comforts,
Constrains them weep, and shake with fear and
sorrow ; 100
Making the mother, wife, and child, to see
The son, the husband, and the father, tearing
His country's bowels out. And to poor we
Thine enmity 's most capital : thou barr'st us
Our prayers to the gods, which is a comfort

That all but we enjoy; for how can we,
Alas! how can we for our country pray,
Whereto we are bound, together with thy victory,
Whereto we are bound? Alack! or we must lose
The country, our dear nurse; or else thy person, 110

Rather to show a noble grace to both parts,
Than seek the end of one, thou shalt no sooner
March to assault thy country than to tread
(Trust to 't, thou shalt not) on thy mother's womb.
That brought thee to this world.

Vol.   "Why dost not speak?
Think'st thou it honourable for a noble man
Still to remember wrongs?"

Our comfort in the country. We must find
An evident calamity, though we had
Our wish, which side should win; for either thou
Must, as a foreign recreant, be led
With manacles through our streets, or else
Triumphantly tread on thy country's ruin,
And bear the palm, for having bravely shed
Thy wife and children's blood. For myself, son,
I purpose not to wait on fortune, till
These wars determine: if I cannot persuade thee 120

Vir.   Ay, and mine,
That brought you forth this boy, to keep your name
Living to time.
   Boy.   'A shall not tread on me:
I 'll run away till I am bigger, but then I 'll fight.
   Cor. Not of a woman's tenderness to be,
Requires nor child nor woman's face to see. 130
I have sat too long.   [*Rising.*
   Vol.   Nay, go not from us thus.
If it were so, that our request did tend

To save the Romans, thereby to destroy
The Volsces whom you serve, you might condemn us,
As poisonous of your honour : no ; our suit
Is, that you reconcile them : while the Volsces
May say, " This mercy we have show'd ; " the Romans,
" This we receiv'd ; " and each in either side
Give the all-hail to thee, and cry, " Be bless'd
For making up this peace ! "   Thou know'st, great
     son,   140
The end of war 's uncertain : but this certain,
That, if thou conquer Rome, the benefit
Which thou shalt thereby reap is such a name,
Whose repetition will be dogg'd with curses ;
Whose chronicle thus writ,—" The man was noble,
But with his last attempt he wip'd it out,
Destroy'd his country, and his name remains
To the ensuing age abhorr'd."   Speak to me, son !
Thou hast affected the fine strains of honour,
To imitate the graces of the gods ;   150
To tear with thunder the wide cheeks o' the air,
And yet to charge thy sulphur with a bolt
That should but rive an oak.   Why dost not speak ?
Think'st thou it honourable for a noble man
Still to remember wrongs ?—Daughter, speak you :
He cares not for your weeping.—Speak thou, boy :
Perhaps thy childishness will move him more
Than can our reasons.—There is no man in the world
More bound to 's mother ; yet here he lets me prate,
Like one i' the stocks.—Thou hast never in thy life 160
Show'd thy dear mother any courtesy ;
When she, (poor hen !) fond of no second brood,
Has cluck'd thee to the wars, and safely home,
Loaden with honour. Say, my request 's unjust,
And spurn me back ; but, if it be not so,
Thou art not honest, and the gods will plague thee,
That thou restrain'st from me the duty which
To a mother's part belongs.—He turns away :
Down, ladies ; let us shame him with our knees.
To his surname Coriolanus 'longs more pride,   170
Than pity to our prayers. Down : an end ;
This is the last :—so we will home to Rome,
And die among our neighbours.—Nay, behold 's.
This boy, that cannot tell what he would have,
But kneels and holds up hands for fellowship,
Does reason our petition with more strength
Than thou hast to deny 't.—Come, let us go.
This fellow had a Volscian to his mother ;
His wife is in Corioli, and his child
Like him by chance.—Yet give us our despatch :   180
I am hush'd until our city be a-fire
And then I 'll speak a little.

       [*He holds* VOLUMNIA *by the hands, silent.*
Cor.   O mother, mother !
What have you done ? Behold ! the heavens do ope,
The gods look down, and this unnatural scene
They laugh at. O my mother ! mother ! O !
You have won a happy victory to Rome ;
But, for your son,—believe it, O ! believe it,—
Most dangerously you have with him prevail'd,
If not most mortal to him. But let it come.—
Aufidius, though I cannot make true wars,   190
I 'll frame convenient peace. Now, good Aufidius,
Were you in my stead, would you have heard
A mother less, or granted less, Aufidius ?
Auf. I was mov'd withal.
Cor.   I dare be sworn, you were :
And, sir, it is no little thing to make
Mine eyes to sweat compassion. But, good sir,
What peace you 'll make, advise me. For my part,
I 'll not to Rome, I 'll back with you ; and pray you,
Stand to me in this cause.—O mother ! wife !
Auf. [*Aside.*] I am glad thou hast set thy mercy and
     thy honour   200
At difference in thee : out of that I 'll work
Myself a former fortune.

        [*The Ladies make signs to* CORIOLANUS.
Cor. [*To* VOLUMNIA, VIRGILIA, *&c.*] Ay, by-and-by ;
But we will drink together ; and you shall bear
A better witness back than words, which we,
On like conditions, will have counter-seal'd.
Come, enter with us. Ladies, you deserve
To have a temple built you : all the swords

In Italy, and her confederate arms,
Could not have made this peace.   [*Exeunt.*

SCENE IV.—Rome.   A Public Place.

Enter MENENIUS *and* SICINIUS.

Men. See you yond coign o' the Capitol, yond corner-
stone ?
Sic. Why, what of that ?
Men. If it be possible for you to displace it with your
little finger, there is some hope the ladies of Rome,
especially his mother, may prevail with him. But I
say, there is no hope in 't. Our throats are sentenced,
and stay upon execution.
Sic. Is 't possible, that so short a time can alter the
condition of a man ?   10
Men. There is differency between a grub and a
butterfly ; yet your butterfly was a grub. This Marcius
is grown from man to dragon : he has wings ; he 's
more than a creeping thing.
Sic. He loved his mother dearly.
Men. So did he me ; and he no more remembers his
mother now, than an eight-year-old horse. The tartness of his face sours ripe grapes. When he walks, he
moves like an engine, and the ground shrinks before
his treading. He is able to pierce a corslet with his
eye ; talks like a knell, and his hum is a battery. He
sits in his state, as a thing made for Alexander. What
he bids be done, is finished with his bidding. He
wants nothing of a god but eternity, and a heaven to
throne in.
Sic. Yes, mercy, if you report him truly.
Men. I paint him in the character. Mark what
mercy his mother shall bring from him : there is no
more mercy in him, than there is milk in a male tiger ;
that shall our poor city find : and all this is 'long of you.
Sic. The gods be good unto us !   31
Men. No, in such a case the gods will not be good
unto us. When we banished him, we respected not
them ; and, he returning to break our necks, they
respect not us.

Enter a Messenger.

Mess. Sir, if you 'd save your life, fly to your house.
The plebeians have got your fellow-tribune,
And hale him up and down ; all swearing, if
The Roman ladies bring not comfort home,
They 'll give him death by inches.

Enter another Messenger.

Sic.   What 's the news ?
Mess. Good news, good news !—The ladies have
     prevail'd,   41
The Volscians are dislodg'd, and Marcius gone.
A merrier day did never yet greet Rome,
No, not the expulsion of the Tarquins.
Sic.   Friend,
Art thou certain this is true ? is it most certain ?
Mess. As certain as I know the sun is fire.
Where have you lurk'd, that you make doubt of it ?
Ne'er through an arch so hurried the blown tide,
As the comforted through the gates. Why, hark you !
     [*Trumpets and hautboys sounded, and drums
        beaten, all together. Shouting also within.*
The trumpets, sackbuts, psalteries, and fifes,   50
Tabors, and cymbals, and the shouting Romans,
Make the sun dance. Hark you !   [*Shouting again.*
Men.   This is good news.
I will go meet the ladies. This Volumnia
Is worth of consuls, senators, patricians,
A city full ; of tribunes, such as you,
A sea and land full. You have pray'd well to-day :
This morning for ten thousand of your throats
I 'd not have given a doit. Hark, how they joy !
                   [*Shouting and music.*
Sic. First, the gods bless you for their tidings ;
     next,
Accept my thankfulness.
Mess.   Sir, we have all   60
Great cause to give great thanks.

Sic.   They are near the city?
Mess. Almost at point to enter.
Sic.   We will meet them,
And help the joy.   [*Going.*

Scene V.—Antium.   A Public Place.

Enter Tullus Aufidius, *with Attendants.*

Auf. Go tell the lords of the city, I am here:

THE RETURN OF VOLUMNIA.

Enter the Ladies, accompanied by Senators, Patri-
cians, and People.   They pass over the stage.

1 *Sen.* Behold our patroness, the life of Rome!
Call all your tribes together, praise the gods,
And make triumphant fires; strew flowers before
   them:
Unshout the noise that banish'd Marcius;
Repeal him with the welcome of his mother;
Cry,—Welcome, ladies, welcome!—
   All. Welcome, ladies, welcome!   70
   [*A flourish with drums and trumpets.   Exeunt.*

Deliver them this paper: having read it,
Bid them repair to the market-place; where I,
Even in theirs and in the commons' ears,
Will vouch the truth of it.   Him I accuse
The city ports by this hath enter'd, and
Intends to appear before the people, hoping
To purge himself with words.   Despatch.
                    [*Exeunt Attendants.*

Enter three or four Conspirators of Aufidius'
                    faction.
Most welcome!

1 *Con.* How is it with our general?
  Auf.   Even so   10
As with a man by his own alms empoison'd,
And with his charity slain.

He water'd his new plants with dews of flattery,
Seducing so my friends ; and, to this end,
He bow'd his nature, never known before
But to be rough, unswayable, and free.

All. " Welcome, ladies, welcome!"

  2 *Con.*   Most noble sir,
If you do hold the same intent, wherein
You wish'd us parties, we 'll deliver you
Of your great danger.
  Auf.   Sir, I cannot tell :
We must proceed, as we do find the people.
  3 *Con.* The people will remain uncertain, whilst
'Twixt you there 's difference ; but the fall of either
Makes the survivor heir of all.
  Auf.   I know it ;
And my pretext to strike at him admits   20
A good construction. I rais'd him, and I pawn'd
Mine honour for his truth : who being so heighten'd,

  3 *Con.* Sir, his stoutness,
When he did stand for consul, which he lost
By lack of stooping,—
  Auf.   That I would have spoke of.
Being banish'd for 't, he came unto my hearth ;   30
Presented to my knife his throat : I took him ;
Made him joint-servant with me ; gave him way
In all his own desires ; nay, let him choose
Out of my files, his projects to accomplish,
My best and freshest men ; serv'd his designments
In mine own person ; holp to reap the fame,
Which he did end all his ; and took some pride
To do myself this wrong : till, at the last,

I seem'd his follower, not partner ; and
He wag'd me with his countenance, as if   40
I had been mercenary.
  1 Con.   So he did, my lord:
The army marvell'd at it ; and, in the last,
When he had carried Rome, and that we look'd
For no less spoil than glory,—
  Auf.   There was it ;
For which my sinews shall be stretch'd upon him.
At a few drops of women's rheum, which are
As cheap as lies, he sold the blood and labour
Of our great action : therefore shall he die,
And I 'll renew me in his fall. But, hark !
      [*Drums and trumpets sound, with great
             shouts of the People.*
  1 Con. Your native town you enter'd like a post, 50
And had no welcomes home ; but he returns,
Splitting the air with noise.
  2 Con.   And patient fools,
Whose children he hath slain, their base throats tear
With giving him glory.
  3 Con.   Therefore, at your vantage,
Ere he express himself, or move the people
With what he would say, let him feel your sword,
Which we will second. When he lies along,
After your way his tale pronounc'd shall bury
His reasons with his body.
  Auf.   Say no more :
Here come the lords.   60

    Enter the Lords of the City.

  Lords. You are most welcome home.
  Auf.   I have not deserv'd it.
But, worthy lords, have you with heed perus'd
What I have written to you ?
  Lords.   We have.
  1 Lord.   And grieve to hear 't.
What faults he made before the last, I think,
Might have found easy fines ; but there to end,
Where he was to begin, and give away
The benefit of our levies, answering us
With our own charge, making a treaty where
There was a yielding,—this admits no excuse.
  Auf. He approaches : you shall hear him.   70

  Enter CORIOLANUS, *with drums and colours ; a
     crowd of Citizens with him.*

  Cor. Hail, lords ! I am return'd your soldier ;
No more infected with my country's love
Than when I parted hence, but still subsisting
Under your great command. You are to know,
That prosperously I have attempted, and
With bloody passage led your wars even to
The gates of Rome. Our spoils we have brought
     home
Do more than counterpoise, a full third part,
The charges of the action. We have made peace,
With no less honour to the Antiates,   80
Than shame to the Romans ; and we here deliver,
Subscribed by the consuls and patricians,
Together with the seal o' the senate, what
We have compounded on.
  Auf.   Read it not, noble lords ;
But tell the traitor in the highest degree
He hath abus'd your powers.
  Cor. Traitor !—How now !—
  Auf.   Ay, traitor, Marcius.
  Cor.   Marcius !
  Auf. Ay, Marcius, Caius Marcius. Dost thou think
I 'll grace thee with that robbery, thy stol'n name
Coriolanus in Corioli ?—   90
You lords and heads of the state, perfidiously
He has betray'd your business, and given up,
For certain drops of salt, your city Rome,
(I say, your city,) to his wife and mother ;
Breaking his oath and resolution, like

A twist of rotten silk ; never admitting
Counsel o' the war, but at his nurse's tears
He whin'd and roar'd away your victory,
That pages blush'd at him, and men of heart
Look'd wondering each at other.
  Cor.   Hear'st thou, Mars ?
  Auf. Name not the god, thou boy of tears.
  Cor.   Ha ! 101
  Auf. No more.
  Cor. Measureless liar, thou hast made my heart
Too great for what contains it. Boy ! O slave !—
Pardon me, lords, 't is the first time that ever
I was forc'd to scold. Your judgments, my grave lords,
Must give this cur the lie : and his own notion
(Who wears my stripes impress'd upon him, that
Must bear my beating to his grave) shall join
To thrust the lie unto him.
  1 Lord.   Peace, both, and hear me speak.
  Cor. Cut me to pieces, Volsces ; men and lads, 111
Stain all your edges on me.—Boy ! False hound !
If you have writ your annals true, 't is there,
That, like an eagle in a dove-cote, I
Flutter'd your Volscians in Corioli :
Alone I did it.—Boy !
  Auf.   Why, noble lords,
Will you be put in mind of his blind fortune,
Which was your shame, by this unholy braggart,
'Fore your own eyes and ears ?
  All Con.   Let him die for 't.
  All People. Tear him to pieces : do it presently. He
killed my son ;—my daughter ; he killed my cousin
Marcus ;—he killed my father.—   122
  2 Lord. Peace, ho !—no outrage :—peace !
The man is noble, and his fame folds in
This orb o' the earth. His last offences to us
Shall have judicious hearing.—Stand, Aufidius,
And trouble not the peace.
  Cor.   O ! that I had him,
With six Aufidiuses, or more, his tribe,
To use my lawful sword !
  Auf.   Insolent villain !
  All Con. Kill, kill, kill, kill, kill him !
    [AUFIDIUS *and the Conspirators draw, and kill*
     CORIOLANUS, *who falls :* AUFIDIUS *stands
     on his body.*
  Lords.   Hold, hold, hold, hold !
  Auf. My noble masters, hear me speak.
  1 Lord.   O Tullus !—
  2 Lord. Thou hast done a deed whereat valour will
     weep.   132
  3 Lord. Tread not upon him.—Masters all, be quiet.—
Put up your swords.
  Auf. My lords, when you shall know (as in this rage,
Provok'd by him, you cannot) the great danger
Which this man's life did owe you, you 'll rejoice
That he is thus cut off. Please it your honours
To call me to your senate, I 'll deliver
Myself your loyal servant, or endure   140
Your heaviest censure.
  1 Lord.   Bear from hence his body,
And mourn you for him. Let him be regarded
As the most noble corse that ever herald
Did follow to his urn.
  2 Lord.   His own impatience
Takes from Aufidius a great part of blame.
Let 's make the best of it.
  Auf.   My rage is gone,
And I am struck with sorrow.—Take him up :—
Help, three o' the chiefest soldiers ; I 'll be one.—
Beat thou the drum, that it speak mournfully ;
Trail your steel pikes.—Though in this city he   150
Hath widow'd and unchilded many a one,
Which to this hour bewail the injury,
Yet he shall have a noble memory.—
  Assist.   [*Exeunt, bearing the body of* CORIOLANUS.
            A dead march sounded.

TITUS ANDRONICUS.

DRAMATIS PERSONÆ.

SATURNINUS, *Son to the late Emperor of Rome.*
BASSIANUS, *Brother to Saturninus.*
TITUS ANDRONICUS, *a noble Roman.*
MARCUS ANDRONICUS, *Brother to Titus.*
LUCIUS,
QUINTUS,
MARTIUS, } *Sons to Titus Andronicus.*
MUTIUS,
Young LUCIUS, *a Boy, Son to Lucius.*
PUBLIUS, *Son to Marcus Andronicus.*
ÆMILIUS, *a noble Roman.*
ALARBUS,
DEMETRIUS, } *Sons to Tamora.*
CHIRON,

AARON, *a Moor.*
A Captain, Tribune, Messenger, *and* Clown,
  Romans.
Goths and Romans.

TAMORA, *Queen of the Goths.*
LAVINIA, *Daughter to Titus Andronicus.*
A Nurse, *and a black Child.*

Kinsmen *of Titus, Senators, Tribunes, Officers,*
  Soldiers, and Attendants.

SCENE—ROME, and the Country near it.

ACT I.

SCENE I.—Rome.

Flourish. **Enter the Tribunes and Senators aloft; and then enter** SATURNINUS **and his Followers at one
door, and** BASSIANUS **and his Followers at the other, with drum and colours.**

Saturninus.

NOBLE patricians, patrons of my right,
Defend the justice of my cause with
      arms;
And, countrymen, my loving followers,
Plead my successive title with your
      swords.
I am his first-born son, that was the last
That wore the imperial diadem of Rome:
Then let my father's honours live in me,
Nor wrong mine age with this indignity.
   Bass. Romans, friends, followers, fa-
      vourers of my right,
If ever Bassianus, Cæsar's son,   10
Were gracious in the eyes of royal Rome,
Keep then this passage to the Capitol;
And suffer not dishonour to approach
The imperial seat, to virtue consecrate,
To justice, continence, and nobility:
But let desert in pure election shine;
And, Romans, fight for freedom in your choice.

Enter MARCUS ANDRONICUS, *aloft, with the crown.*

   Marc. Princes, that strive by factions and by
      friends
Ambitiously for rule and empery,
Know, that the people of Rome, for whom we stand
A special party, have by common voice,   21
In election for the Roman empery,
Chosen Andronicus, surnamed Pius,
For many good and great deserts to Rome:
A nobler man, a braver warrior,
Lives not this day within the city walls.
He by the senate is accited home,
From weary wars against the barbarous Goths;
That, with his sons, a terror to our foes,
Hath yok'd a nation strong, train'd up in arms.   30
Ten years are spent since first he undertook
This cause of Rome, and chastised with arms
Our enemies' pride: five times he hath return'd
Bleeding to Rome, bearing his valiant sons

In coffins from the field;
And now at last, laden with honour's spoils,
Returns the good Andronicus to Rome,
Renowned Titus, flourishing in arms.
Let us entreat,—by honour of his name,
Whom worthily you would have now succeed,   40
And in the Capitol and senate's right,
Whom you pretend to honour and adore,—
That you withdraw you, and abate your strength.
Dismiss your followers, and, as suitors should,
Plead your deserts in peace and humbleness.
   Sat. How fair the tribune speaks to calm my
      thoughts!
   Bass. Marcus Andronicus, so I do affy
In thy uprightness and integrity,
And so I love and honour thee and thine,
Thy noble brother Titus and his sons,   50
And her to whom my thoughts are humbled all,
Gracious Lavinia, Rome's rich ornament,
That I will here dismiss my loving friends:
And to my fortune's and the people's favour
Commit my cause in balance to be weigh'd.
            [*Exeunt the Followers of* BASSIANUS.
   Sat. Friends, that have been thus forward in my
      right,
I thank you all, and here dismiss you all;
And to the love and favour of my country
Commit myself, my person, and the cause.
            [*Exeunt the Followers of* SATURNINUS.
Rome, be as just and gracious unto me,   60
As I am confident and kind to thee.—
Open the gates, and let me in.
   Bass. Tribunes, and me, a poor competitor.
            [*They go up into the Senate-house.*

SCENE II.—The Same.

Enter a Captain, and others.

   Cap. Romans, make way! The good Andronicus,
Patron of virtue, Rome's best champion,

Successful in the battles that he fights,
With honour and with fortune is return'd
From where he circumscribed with his sword,
And brought to yoke, the enemies of Rome.

Sound drums and trumpets, and then enter two of
    Titus's *Sons. After them two Men bearing a coffin*

To re-salute his country with his tears,
Tears of true joy for his return to Rome.
Thou great defender of this Capitol,
Stand gracious to the rites that we intend !
Romans, of five-and-twenty valiant sons,
Half of the number that King Priam had,
Behold the poor remains, alive, and dead !

Tit. " Stand gracious to the rites that we intend ! "

covered with black ; then two other Sons. After
them Titus Andronicus ; *and then* Tamora, *with*
Alarbus, Chiron, Demetrius, Aaron, *and other*
Goths, *prisoners ; Soldiers and People following.*
They set down the coffin, and Titus *speaks.*

Tit. Hail, Rome, victorious in thy mourning weeds!
Lo ! as the bark, that hath discharg'd her fraught,
Returns with precious lading to the bay,
From whence at first she weigh'd her anchorage,   10
Cometh Andronicus, bound with laurel boughs,

These, that survive, let Rome reward with love ;
These, that I bring unto their latest home,   20
With burial amongst their ancestors.
Here Goths have given me leave to sheath my sword.
Titus, unkind, and careless of thine own,
Why suffer'st thou thy sons, unburied yet,
To hover on the dreadful shore of Styx ?—
Make way to lay them by their brethren.
                            [*The tomb is opened.*
There greet in silence, as the dead are wont,
And sleep in peace, slain in your country's wars !

O sacred receptacle of my joys,
Sweet cell of virtue and nobility,   30
How many sons of mine hast thou in store,
That thou wilt never render to me more !
  Luc. Give us the proudest prisoner of the Goths,
That we may hew his limbs, and on a pile
Ad manes fratrum sacrifice his flesh,
Before this earthy prison of their bones ;
That so the shadows be not unappeas'd,
Nor we disturb'd with prodigies on earth.
  Tit. I give him you, the noblest that survives,
The eldest son of this distressed queen.   40
  Tam. Stay, Roman brethren !—Gracious conqueror,
Victorious Titus, rue the tears I shed,
A mother's tears in passion for her son :
And if thy sons were ever dear to thee,
O, think my son to be as dear to me.
Sufficeth not, that we are brought to Rome,
To beautify thy triumphs and return,
Captive to thee, and to thy Roman yoke ;
But must my sons be slaughter'd in the streets,
For valiant doings in their country's cause ?   50
O ! if to fight for king and commonweal
Were piety in thine, it is in these.
Andronicus, stain not thy tomb with blood :
Wilt thou draw near the nature of the gods ?
Draw near them then in being merciful :
Sweet mercy is nobility's true badge ;
Thrice-noble Titus, spare my first-born son.
  Tit. Patient yourself, madam, and pardon me.
These are their brethren, whom you Goths beheld
Alive, and dead ; and for their brethren slain   60
Religiously they ask a sacrifice :
To this your son is mark'd, and die he must,
To appease their groaning shadows that are gone.
  Luc. Away with him ! and make a fire straight ;
And with our swords, upon a pile of wood,
Let's hew his limbs, till they be clean consum'd.
    [*Exeunt* LUCIUS, QUINTUS, MARTIUS, *and*
      MUTIUS, *with* ALARBUS.
  Tam. O cruel, irreligious piety !
  Chi. Was ever Scythia half so barbarous ?
  Dem. Oppose not Scythia to ambitious Rome.
Alarbus goes to rest, and we survive   70
To tremble under Titus' threatening look.
Then, madam, stand resolv'd ; but hope withal,
The self-same gods that arm'd the Queen of Troy
With opportunity of sharp revenge
Upon the Thracian tyrant in his tent,
May favour Tamora, the Queen of Goths
(When Goths were Goths, and Tamora was queen),
To quit the bloody wrongs upon her foes.

  Re-enter LUCIUS, QUINTUS, MARTIUS, *and* MUTIUS,
    with their swords bloody.
  Luc. See, lord and father, how we have perform'd
Our Roman rites. Alarbus' limbs are lopp'd,   80
And entrails feed the sacrificing fire,
Whose smoke, like incense, doth perfume the sky.
Remaineth nought, but to inter our brethren,
And with loud 'larums welcome them to Rome.
  Tit. Let it be so ; and let Andronicus
Make this his latest farewell to their souls.
    [*Trumpets sounded, and the coffins laid in
      the tomb.*
In peace and honour rest you here, my sons ;
Rome's readiest champions, repose you here in rest,
Secure from worldly chances and mishaps !
Here lurks no treason, here no envy swells ;   90
Here grow no damned drugs ; here are no storms,
No noise, but silence and eternal sleep.
In peace and honour rest you here, my sons !

        Enter LAVINIA.
  Lav. In peace and honour live Lord Titus long ;
My noble lord and father, live in fame.
Lo ! at this tomb my tributary tears
I render for my brethren's obsequies :
And at thy feet I kneel, with tears of joy
Shed on the earth for thy return to Rome.
O ! bless me here with thy victorious hand,   100
Whose fortune Rome's best citizens applaud.

  Tit. Kind Rome, that hast thus lovingly reserv'd
The cordial of mine age to glad my heart !—
Lavinia, live ; outlive thy father's days,
And fame's eternal date, for virtue's praise !

   Enter MARCUS ANDRONICUS, SATURNINUS, BAS-
      SIANUS, *and others.*
  Marc. Long live Lord Titus, my beloved brother,
Gracious triumpher in the eyes of Rome !
  Tit. Thanks, gentle tribune, noble brother Marcus.
  Marc. And welcome, nephews, from successful
    wars,
You that survive, and you that sleep in fame.   110
Fair lords, your fortunes are alike in all,
That in your country's service drew your swords ;
But safer triumph is this funeral pomp,
That hath aspir'd to Solon's happiness,
And triumphs over chance in honour's bed.—
Titus Andronicus, the people of Rome,
Whose friend in justice thou hast ever been,
Send thee by me, their tribune and their trust,
This palliament of white and spotless hue,
And name thee in election for the empire,   120
With these our late-deceased emperor's sons.
Be *candidatus* then, and put it on,
And help to set a head on headless Rome.
  Tit. A better head her glorious body fits,
Than his that shakes for age and feebleness.
What should I don this robe, and trouble you ?
Be chosen with proclamations to-day,
To-morrow yield up rule, resign my life,
And set abroad new business for you all ?
Rome, I have been thy soldier forty years,   130
And led my country's strength successfully,
And buried one-and-twenty valiant sons,
Knighted in field, slain manfully in arms,
In right and service of their noble country.
Give me a staff of honour for mine age,
But not a sceptre to control the world :
Upright he held it, lords, that held it last.
  Marc. Titus, thou shalt obtain and ask the empery.
  Sat. Proud and ambitious tribune, canst thou tell ?
  Tit. Patience, Prince Saturninus.
  Sat.   Romans, do me right.—
Patricians, draw your swords, and sheathe them not
Till Saturninus be Rome's emperor.—   142
Andronicus, 'would thou wert shipp'd to hell,
Rather than rob me of the people's hearts.
  Luc. Proud Saturnine, interrupter of the good
That noble-minded Titus means to thee !
  Tit. Content thee, prince : I will restore to thee
The people's hearts, and wean them from themselves.
  Bass. Andronicus, I do not flatter thee,
But honour thee, and will do till I die :   150
My faction if thou strengthen with thy friends,
I will most thankful be ; and thanks to men
Of noble minds is honourable meed.
  Tit. People of Rome, and noble tribunes here,
I ask your voices and your suffrages :
Will you bestow them friendly on Andronicus ?
  Trib. To gratify the good Andronicus,
And gratulate his safe return to Rome,
The people will accept whom he admits.
  Tit. Tribunes, I thank you ; and this suit I make,
That you create your emperor's eldest son,   161
Lord Saturnine, whose virtues will, I hope,
Reflect on Rome as Titan's rays on earth,
And ripen justice in this commonweal :
Then, if you will elect by my advice,
Crown him, and say,—" Long live our emperor ! "
  Marc. With voices and applause of every sort,
Patricians, and plebeians, we create
Lord Saturninus Rome's great emperor,
And say,—" Long live our Emperor Saturnine ! "   170
                [*A long flourish.*
  Sat. Titus Andronicus, for thy favours done
To us in our election this day,
I give thee thanks in part of thy deserts,
And will with deeds requite thy gentleness :
And for an onset, Titus, to advance
Thy name and honourable family,
Lavinia will I make my empress,

Rome's royal mistress, mistress of my heart,
And in the sacred Pantheon her espouse.
Tell me, Andronicus, doth this motion please thee?
  Tit. It doth, my worthy lord ; and in this match 181
I hold me highly honour'd of your grace :
And here, in sight of Rome, to Saturnine,
King and commander of our commonweal,
The wide world's emperor, do I consecrate
My sword, my chariot, and my prisoners;
Presents well worthy Rome's imperious lord :
Receive them then, the tribute that I owe,
Mine honour's ensigns humbled at thy feet.
  Sat. Thanks, noble Titus, father of my life ! 190
How proud I am of thee, and of thy gifts,
Rome shall record ; and when I do forget
The least of these unspeakable deserts,
Romans, forget your fealty to me.
  Tit. [*To* TAMORA.] Now, madam, are you prisoner
          to an emperor ;
To him that, for your honour and your state,
Will use you nobly, and your followers.
  Sat. A goodly lady, trust me, of the hue
That I would choose, were I to choose anew.—
Clear up, fair queen, that cloudy countenance : 200
Though chance of war hath wrought this change of
          cheer,
Thou com'st not to be made a scorn in Rome :
Princely shall be thy usage every way.
Rest on my word, and let not discontent
Daunt all your hopes : madam, he comforts you.
Can make you greater than the Queen of Goths.—
Lavinia, you are not displeas'd with this ?
  Lav. Not I, my lord ; sith true nobility
Warrants these words in princely courtesy.
  Sat. Thanks, sweet Lavinia.—Romans, let us go.
Ransomless here we set our prisoners free : 211
Proclaim our honours, lords, with trump and drum.
  Bass. Lord Titus, by your leave, this maid is mine.
                  [*Seizing* LAVINIA.
  Tit. How, sir ? Are you in earnest then, my lord ?
  Bass. Ay, noble Titus ; and resolv'd withal,
To do myself this reason and this right.
  Marc. *Suum cuique* is our Roman justice :
This prince in justice seizeth but his own.
  Luc. And that he will, and shall, if Lucius live.
  Tit. Traitors, avaunt ! Where is the emperor's
       guard ? 220
Treason, my lord ! Lavinia is surpris'd.
  Sat. Surpris'd ! by whom ?
  Bass.   By him that justly may
Bear his betroth'd from all the world away.
  [*Exeunt* MARCUS *and* BASSIANUS, *with* LAVINIA.
  Mut. Brothers, help to convey her hence away,
And with my sword I 'll keep this door safe.
      [*Exeunt* LUCIUS, QUINTUS, *and* MARTIUS.
  Tit Follow, my lord, and I 'll soon bring her back.
  Mut. My lord, you pass not here.
  Tit.   What, villain boy !
Barr'st me my way in Rome ?   [*Kills* MUTIUS.
  Mut.   Help, Lucius, help !

         Re-enter LUCIUS.

  Luc. My lord, you are unjust, and more than so :
In wrongful quarrel you have slain your son. 230
  Tit. Nor thou, nor he, are any sons of mine :
My sons would never so dishonour me.
Traitor, restore Lavinia to the emperor.
  Luc. Dead, if you will ; but not to be his wife,
That is another's lawful promis'd love.   [*Exit.*
  Sat. No, Titus, no ; the emperor needs her not,
Nor her, nor thee, nor any of thy stock :
I 'll trust, by leisure, him that mocks me once ;
Thee never, nor thy traitorous haughty sons,
Confederates all thus to dishonour me. 240
Was there none else in Rome to make a stale,
But Saturnine ? Full well, Andronicus,
Agree these deeds with that proud brag of thine,
That saidst, I begg'd the empire at thy hands.
  Tit. O monstrous ! what reproachful words are these?
  Sat. But go thy ways ; go, give that changing piece
To him that flourish'd for her with his sword.
A valiant son-in-law thou shalt enjoy ;

One fit to bandy with thy lawless sons,
To ruffle in the commonwealth of Rome. 250
  Tit. These words are razors to my wounded heart.
  Sat. And therefore, lovely Tamora, Queen of Goths,
That, like the stately Phœbe 'mongst her nymphs,
Dost overshine the gallant'st dames of Rome,
If thou be pleas'd with this my sudden choice,
Behold, I choose thee, Tamora, for my bride,
And will create thee Empress of Rome.
Speak, Queen of Goths, dost thou applaud my choice?
And here I swear by all the Roman gods,—
Sith priest and holy water are so near, 260
And tapers burn so bright, and every thing
In readiness for Hymenæus stand,—
I will not re-salute the streets of Rome,
Or climb my palace, till from forth this place
I lead espous'd my bride along with me.
  Tam. And here, in sight of heaven, to Rome I
          swear,
If Saturnine advance the Queen of Goths,
She will a handmaid be to his desires,
A loving nurse, a mother to his youth.
  Sat. Ascend, fair queen, Pantheon.—Lords, accom-
      pany 270
Your noble emperor, and his lovely bride,
Sent by the heavens for Prince Saturnine,
Whose wisdom hath her fortune conquered.
There shall we consummate our spousal rites.
      [*Exeunt* SATURNINUS *and his Followers;*
      TAMORA *and her Sons;* AARON *and*
      Goths.
  Tit. I am not bid to wait upon this bride.
Titus, when wert thou wont to walk alone,
Dishonour'd thus, and challenged of wrongs?

  Re-enter MARCUS, LUCIUS, QUINTUS, *and* MARTIUS.

  Marc. O Titus, see ! O, see what thou hast done !
In a bad quarrel slain a virtuous son.
  Tit. No, foolish tribune, no ; no son of mine, 280
Nor thou, nor these, confederates in the deed
That hath dishonour'd all our family :
Unworthy brother, and unworthy sons !
  Luc. But let us give him burial, as becomes :
Give Mutius burial with our brethren.
  Tit. Traitors, away ! he rests not in this tomb.
This monument five hundred years hath stood,
Which I have sumptuously re-edified :
Here none but soldiers, and Rome's servitors,
Repose in fame ; none basely slain in brawls. 290
Bury him where you can ; he comes not here.
  Marc. My lord, this is impiety in you.
My nephew Mutius' deeds do plead for him :
He must be buried with his brethren.
  Quint., Mart. And shall, or him we will accom-
      pany.
  Tit. And shall ! What villain was it spake that
      word?
  Quint. He that would vouch it in any place but
      here.
  Tit. What ! would you bury him in my despite ?
  Marc. No, noble Titus ; but entreat of thee
To pardon Mutius, and to bury him. 300
  Tit. Marcus, even thou hast struck upon my crest,
And with these boys mine honour thou hast wounded :
My foes I do repute you every one ;
So, trouble me no more, but get you gone.
  Mart. He is not with himself ! let us withdraw.
  Quint. Not I, till Mutius' bones be buried.
      [MARCUS *and the Sons of* TITUS *kneel.*
  Marc. Brother, for in that name doth nature plead,—
  Quint. Father, and in that name doth nature
      speak,—
  Tit. Speak thou no more, if all the rest will speed.
  Marc. Renowned Titus, more than half my soul,—
  Luc. Dear father, soul and substance of us all,—
  Marc. Suffer thy brother Marcus to inter 312
His noble nephew here in virtue's nest,
That died in honour and Lavinia's cause.
Thou art a Roman ; be not barbarous :
The Greeks upon advice did bury Ajax,
That slew himself ; and wise Laertes' son
Did graciously plead for his funerals.

Let not young Mutius then, that was thy joy,
Be barr'd his entrance here.
   Tit.   Rise, Marcus, rise.— 320
The dismall'st day is this that e'er I saw,
To be dishonour'd by my sons in Rome !—
Well, bury him, and bury me the next.
              [MUTIUS *is put into the tomb.*
   Luc. There lie thy bones, sweet Mutius, with thy
       friends,
Till we with trophies do adorn thy tomb.
   All. No man shed tears for noble Mutius ;
He lives in fame that died in virtue's cause.
   Marc. My lord, — to step out of these dreary
       dumps,—
How comes it that the subtle Queen of Goths
Is of a sudden thus advanc'd in Rome ? 330
   Tit. I know not, Marcus, but I know it is ;
Whether by device or no, the heavens can tell.
Is she not then beholding to the man
That brought her for this high good turn so far ?
Yes, and will nobly him remunerate.

Flourish. Re-enter, at one door, SATURNINUS, *attended ;* TAMORA, DEMETRIUS, CHIRON, *and*
AARON ; *at the other door,* BASSIANUS, LAVINIA,
and others.

   Sat. So, Bassianus, you have play'd your prize :
God give you joy, sir, of your gallant bride !
   Bass. And you of yours, my lord ! I say no
       more,
Nor wish no less ; and so I take my leave.
   Sat. Traitor, if Rome have law, or we have power,
Thou and thy faction shall repent this rape. 341
   Bass. Rape call you it, my lord, to seize my own,
My true-betrothed love, and now my wife?
But let the laws of Rome determine all ;
Meanwhile, I am possess'd of that is mine.
   Sat. 'T is good, sir : you are very short with us ;
But, if we live, we 'll be as sharp with you.
   Bass. My lord, what I have done, as best I may,
Answer I must, and shall do with my life.
Only thus much I give your grace to know : 350
By all the duties that I owe to Rome,
This noble gentleman, Lord Titus here,
Is in opinion and in honour wrong'd ;
That, in the rescue of Lavinia,
With his own hand did slay his youngest son,
In zeal to you, and highly mov'd to wrath,
To be controll'd in that he frankly gave.
Receive him then to favour, Saturnine,
That hath express'd himself, in all his deeds,
A father, and a friend to thee and Rome. 360
   Tit. Prince Bassianus, leave to plead my deeds :
'T is thou, and those, that have dishonour'd me.
Rome and the righteous heavens be my judge,
How I have lov'd and honour'd Saturnine.
   Tam. My worthy lord, if ever Tamora
Were gracious in those princely eyes of thine,
Then hear me speak indifferently for all ;
And at my suit, sweet, pardon what is past.
   Sat. What, madam ! be dishonour'd openly,
And basely put it up without revenge ? 370
   Tam. Not so, my lord : the gods of Rome forfend,
I should be author to dishonour you !

But on mine honour dare I undertake
For good Lord Titus' innocence in all,
Whose fury not dissembled speaks his griefs.
Then, at my suit, look graciously on him ;
Lose not so noble a friend on vain suppose,
Nor with sour looks afflict his gentle heart.—
   [*Aside to* SATURNINUS.] My lord, be rul'd by me, be
       won at last ;
Dissemble all your griefs and discontents : 380
You are but newly planted in your throne ;
Lest then the people, and patricians too,
Upon a just survey, take Titus' part,
And so supplant you for ingratitude,
Which Rome reputes to be a heinous sin.
Yield at entreats, and then let me alone.
I 'll find a day to massacre them all,
And raze their faction and their family,
The cruel father, and his traitorous sons,
To whom I sued for my dear son's life ; 390
And make them know what 't is to let a queen
Kneel in the streets, and beg for grace in vain.—
   [*Aloud.*] Come, come, sweet emperor ;—come, Andro-
       nicus ;—
Take up this good old man, and cheer the heart
That dies in tempest of thy angry frown.
   Sat. Rise, Titus, rise : my empress hath prevail'd.
   Tit. I thank your majesty, and her, my lord.
These words, these looks, infuse new life in me.
   Tam. Titus, I am incorporate in Rome,
A Roman now adopted happily, 400
And must advise the emperor for his good.
This day all quarrels die, Andronicus ;—
And let it be mine honour, good my lord,
That I have reconcil'd your friends and you.—
For you, Prince Bassianus, I have pass'd
My word and promise to the emperor,
That you will be more mild and tractable.—
And fear not, lords,—and you, Lavinia ;—
By my advice, all humbled on your knees,
You shall ask pardon of his majesty. 410
   Luc. We do ; and vow to heaven, and to his highness,
That what we did was mildly, as we might,
Tend'ring our sister's honour, and our own.
   Marc. That on mine honour here I do protest.
   Sat. Away, and talk not : trouble us no more.—
   Tam. Nay, nay, sweet emperor, we must all be
       friends :
The tribune and his nephews kneel for grace ;
I will not be denied : sweet heart, look back.
   Sat. Marcus, for thy sake, and thy brother's here,
And at my lovely Tamora's entreats, 420
I do remit these young men's heinous faults.
Stand up.
Lavinia, though you left me like a churl,
I found a friend ; and sure as death I swore,
I would not part a bachelor from the priest.
Come ; if the emperor's court can feast two brides,
You are my guest, Lavinia, and your friends.—
This day shall be a love-day, Tamora.
   Tit. To-morrow, an it please your majesty,
To hunt the panther and the hart with me, 430
With horn and hound we 'll give your grace *bon jour.*
   Sat. Be it so, Titus, and gramercy too.
              [*Trumpets. Exeunt.*

ACT II.

SCENE I.—The Same. Before the Palace.

Enter AARON.

Aaron.

NOW climbeth Tamora Olympus' top,
Safe out of fortune's shot ; and sits aloft,
Secure of thunder's crack, or lightning flash,
Advanc'd above pale envy's threat'ning reach.
As when the golden sun salutes the morn,
And, having gilt the ocean with his beams,
Gallops the zodiac in his glistering coach,
And overlooks the highest-peering hills ;
So Tamora.
Upon her wit doth earthly honour wait,   10
And virtue stoops and trembles at her frown.
Then, Aaron, arm thy heart, and fit thy thoughts,
To mount aloft with thy imperial mistress,
And mount her pitch, whom thou in triumph long
Hast prisoner held, fetter'd in amorous chains,
And faster bound to Aaron's charming eyes,
Than is Prometheus tied to Caucasus.
Away with slavish weeds and servile thoughts !
I will be bright, and shine in pearl and gold,
To wait upon this new-made empress.   20
To wait, said I ? to wanton with this queen,
This goddess, this Semiramis, this nymph,
This siren, that will charm Rome's Saturnine,
And see his shipwrack, and his commonweal's.
Holla ! what storm is this ?

Enter DEMETRIUS *and* CHIRON, *braving.*

Dem. Chiron, thy years want wit, thy wit wants edge,
And manners, to intrude where I am grac'd,
And may, for aught thou know'st, affected be.
Chi. Demetrius, thou dost overween in all,
And so in this, to bear me down with braves.   30
'T is not the difference of a year, or two,
Makes me less gracious, or thee more fortunate :
I am as able, and as fit, as thou,
To serve, and to deserve my mistress' grace ;
And that my sword upon thee shall approve,
And plead my passions for Lavinia's love.
Aar. Clubs, clubs ! these lovers will not keep the peace.
Dem. Why, boy, although our mother, unadvis'd,
Gave you a dancing-rapier by your side,
Are you so desperate grown, to threat your friends? 40
Go to ; have your lath glued within your sheath,
Till you know better how to handle it.
Chi. Meanwhile, sir, with the little skill I have,
Full well shalt thou perceive how much I dare.
Dem. Ay, boy, grow ye so brave ?   [*They draw.*
Aar.   Why, how now, lords ?
So near the emperor's palace dare you draw,
And maintain such a quarrel openly ?
Full well I wot the ground of all this grudge :
I would not for a million of gold
The cause were known to them it most concerns ;   50
Nor would your noble mother, for much more,
Be so dishonour'd in the court of Rome.
For shame, put up.
Dem.   Not I, till I have sheath'd
My rapier in his bosom, and, withal,
Thrust those reproachful speeches down his throat,
That he hath breath'd in my dishonour here.

Chi. For that I am prepar d and full resolv'd,
Foul-spoken coward, that thunder'st with thy tongue,
And with thy weapon nothing dar'st perform.
Aar. Away, I say !   60
Now, by the gods that warlike Goths adore,
This petty brabble will undo us all.—
Why, lords,—and think you not how dangerous
It is to jet upon a prince's right ?
What ! is Lavinia then become so loose,
Or Bassianus so degenerate,
That for her love such quarrels may be broach'd,
Without controlment, justice, or revenge ?
Young lords, beware !—an should the empress know
This discord's ground, the music would not please. 70

Dem. "Ay, boy, grow ye so brave ?"

Chi. I care not, I, knew she and all the world :
I love Lavinia more than all the world.
Dem. Youngling, learn thou to make some meaner choice :
Lavinia is thine elder brother's hope.
Aar. Why, are ye mad ? or know ye not, in Rome
How furious and impatient they be,
And cannot brook competitors in love ?
I tell you, lords, you do but plot your deaths
By this device.
Chi.   Aaron, a thousand deaths
Would I propose, to achieve her whom I love.   80
Aar. To achieve her, how ?
Dem.   Why mak'st thou it so strange ?
She is a woman, therefore may be woo'd ;
She is a woman, therefore may be won ;
She is Lavinia, therefore must be lov'd.
What, man ! more water glideth by the mill
Than wots the miller of : and easy it is
Of a cut loaf to steal a shive, we know :
Though Bassianus be the emperor's brother,
Better than he have worn Vulcan's badge.
Aar. [*Aside.*] Ay, and as good as Saturninus may.
Dem. Then, why should he despair that knows to court it

91

With words, fair looks, and liberality?
What! hast thou not full often struck a doe,
And borne her cleanly by the keeper's nose?
Aar. Why, then, it seems, some certain snatch or so
Would serve your turns.
Chi. Ay, so the turn were serv'd.
Dem. Aaron, thou hast hit it.
Aar. 'Would you had hit it too;
Then should not we be tir'd with this ado.
Why, hark ye, hark ye,—and are you such fools,
To square for this? would it offend you then, 100
That both should speed?
Chi. Faith, not me.
Dem. Nor me, so I were one.
Aar. For shame, be friends, and join for that you jar.
'T is policy and stratagem must do
That you affect; and so must you resolve,
That what you cannot as you would achieve,
You must perforce accomplish as you may.
Take this of me: Lucrece was not more chaste
Than this Lavinia, Bassianus' love.
A speedier course than lingering languishment 110
Must we pursue, and I have found the path.
My lords, a solemn hunting is in hand;
There will the lovely Roman ladies troop:
The forest walks are wide and spacious,
And many unfrequented plots there are,
Fitted by kind for rape and villainy.
Single you thither then this dainty doe,
And strike her home by force, if not by words:
This way, or not at all, stand you in hope.
Come, come; our empress, with her sacred wit, 120
To villainy and vengeance consecrate,
Will we acquaint with all that we intend;
And she shall file our engines with advice,
That will not suffer you to square yourselves,
But to your wishes' height advance you both.
The emperor's court is like the house of Fame,
The palace full of tongues, of eyes, of ears:
The woods are ruthless, dreadful, deaf, and dull;
There speak, and strike, brave boys, and take your
turns;
There serve your lust, shadow'd from heaven's eye, 131
And revel in Lavinia's treasury.
Chi. Thy counsel, lad, smells of no cowardice.
Dem. *Sit fas aut nefas,* till I find the stream
To cool this heat, a charm to calm these fits,
Per Styga, per manes vehor. [*Exeunt.*

Scene II.—A Forest.

Horns and cry of hounds heard.

Enter Titus Andronicus, *with Hunters, &c.,*
Marcus, Lucius, Quintus, *and* Martius.

Tit. The hunt is up, the morn is bright and grey,
The fields are fragrant, and the woods are green.
Uncouple here, and let us make a bay,
And wake the emperor and his lovely bride,
And rouse the prince, and ring a hunter's peal,
That all the court may echo with the noise.
Sons, let it be your charge, as it is ours,
To attend the emperor's person carefully:
I have been troubled in my sleep this night,
But dawning day new comfort hath inspir'd. 10
[*Horns wind a peal.*

Enter Saturninus, Tamora, Bassianus, Lavinia,
Demetrius, Chiron, *and Attendants.*

Tit. Many good morrows to your majesty;
Madam, to you as many and as good.—
I promised your grace a hunter's peal.
Sat. And you have rung it lustily, my lords,
Somewhat too early for new-married ladies.
Bass. Lavinia, how say you?
Lav. I say, no;
I have been broad awake two hours and more.
Sat. Come on then, horse and chariots let us have,
And to our sport. [*To* Tamora.] Madam, now shall
ye see
Our Roman hunting.

Marc. I have dogs, my lord, 20
Will rouse the proudest panther in the chase,
And climb the highest promontory top.
Tit. And I have horse will follow where the game
Makes way, and run like swallows o'er the plain.
Dem. Chiron, we hunt not, we, with horse nor
hound;
But hope to pluck a dainty doe to ground. [*Exeunt.*

Scene III.—A desert Part of the Forest.

Enter Aaron, *with a bag of gold.*

Aar. He that had wit would think that I had none,
To bury so much gold under a tree,
And never after to inherit it.
Let him that thinks of me so abjectly
Know that this gold must coin a stratagem,
Which, cunningly effected, will beget
A very excellent piece of villainy:
And so repose, sweet gold, for their unrest,
[*Hides the gold.*
That have their alms out of the empress' chest.

Enter Tamora.

Tam. My lovely Aaron, wherefore look'st thou sad,
When every thing doth make a gleeful boast? 11

Aar. "And so repose, sweet gold, for their unrest."

The birds chaunt melody on every bush;
The snake lies rolled in the cheerful sun;
The green leaves quiver with the cooling wind,
And make a chequer'd shadow on the ground.
Under their sweet shade, Aaron, let us sit,
And, whilst the babbling echo mocks the hounds,
Replying shrilly to the well-tun'd horns,
As if a double hunt were heard at once,
Let us sit down and mark their yelping noise: 20
And—after conflict, such as was suppos'd
The wandering prince and Dido once enjoy'd,
When with a happy storm they were surpris'd,
And curtain'd with a counsel-keeping cave—
We may, each wreathed in the other's arms,
Our pastimes done, possess a golden slumber;
Whiles hounds, and horns, and sweet melodious birds,
Be unto us as is a nurse's song
Of lullaby, to bring her babe asleep.
Aar. Madam, though Venus govern your desires,
Saturn is dominator over mine. 31
What signifies my deadly-standing eye,
My silence, and my cloudy melancholy:
My fleece of woolly hair, that now uncurls
Even as an adder, when she doth unroll
To do some fatal execution?
No, madam, these are no venereal signs:

Vengeance is in my heart, death in my hand,
Blood and revenge are hammering in my head.
Hark, Tamora, the empress of my soul,   40
Which never hopes more heaven than rests in thee,
This is the day of doom for Bassianus :
His Philomel must lose her tongue to-day :
Thy sons make pillage of her chastity,
And wash their hands in Bassianus' blood.
Seest thou this letter? take it up, I pray thee,
And give the king this fatal-plotted scroll.—
Now question me no more ; we are espied :
Here comes a parcel of our hopeful brood,
Which dreads not yet their lives' destruction.   50
    Tam. Ah, my sweet Moor, sweeter to me than life !
    Aar. No more, great empress. Bassianus comes :
Be cross with him ; and I 'll go fetch thy sons
To back thy quarrels, whatsoe'er they be.   [*Exit.*

            Enter BASSIANUS *and* LAVINIA.

    Bass. Whom have we here? Rome's royal empress,
Unfurnish'd of her well-beseeming troop?
Or is it Dian, habited like her,
Who hath abandoned her holy groves,
To see the general hunting in this forest?
    Tam. Saucy controller of my private steps !   60
Had I the power that some say Dian had,
Thy temples should be planted presently
With horns as was Actæon's, and the hounds
Should drive upon thy new-transformed limbs,
Unmannerly intruder as thou art !
    Lav. Under your patience, gentle empress,
'T is thought you have a goodly gift in horning ;
And to be doubted that your Moor and you
Are singled forth to try experiments.
Jove shield your husband from his hounds to-day ;   70
'T is pity they should take him for a stag.
    Bass. Believe me, queen, your swarth Cimmerian
Doth make your honour of his body's hue,
Spotted, detested, and abominable.
Why are you sequester'd from all your train,
Dismounted from your snow-white goodly steed,
And wander'd hither to an obscure plot,
Accompanied but with a barbarous Moor,
If foul desire had not conducted you?
    Lav. And being intercepted in your sport,   80
Great reason that my noble lord be rated
For sauciness !—I pray you, let us hence,
And let her joy her raven-colour'd love ;
This valley fits the purpose passing well.
    Bass. The king, my brother, shall have note of
    this.
    Lav. Ay, for these slips have made him noted
    long :
Good king, to be so mightily abus'd !
    Tam. Why have I patience to endure all this?

          Enter DEMETRIUS *and* CHIRON.

    Dem. How now, dear sovereign, and our gracious
    mother,
Why doth your highness look so pale and wan?   90
    Tam. Have I not reason, think you, to look pale ?
These two have tic'd me hither to this place :
A barren detested vale, you see, it is ;
The trees, though summer, yet forlorn and lean,
O'ercome with moss and baleful mistletoe :
Here never shines the sun ; here nothing breeds,
Unless the nightly owl or fatal raven.
And when they show'd me this abhorred pit,
They told me, here, at dead time of the night,
A thousand fiends, a thousand hissing snakes,   100
Ten thousand swelling toads, as many urchins,
Would make such fearful and confused cries,
As any mortal body, hearing it,
Should straight fall mad, or else die suddenly.
No sooner had they told this hellish tale,
But straight they told me, they would bind me here
Unto the body of a dismal yew,
And leave me to this miserable death :
And then they call'd me foul adulteress,
Lascivious Goth, and all the bitterest terms   110
That ever ear did hear to such effect :
And, had you not by wondrous fortune come,

This vengeance on me had they executed.
Revenge it, as you love your mother's life,
Or be ye not henceforth call'd my children.
    Dem. This is a witness that I am thy son.
                              [*Stabs* BASSIANUS.
    Chi. And this for me, struck home to show my
        strength.   [*Stabbing him likewise.*
    Lav. Ay, come, Semiramis,—nay, barbarous Tamora ;
For no name fits thy nature but thy own.
    Tam. Give me thy poniard : you shall know, my
        boys,   120
Your mother's hand shall right your mother's wrong.
    Dem. Stay, madam, here is more belongs to her :
First thrash the corn, then after burn the straw.
This minion stood upon her chastity,
Upon her nuptial vow, her loyalty,
And, with that painted hope, braves your mightiness :
And shall she carry this unto her grave?
    Chi. An if she do, I would I were an eunuch.
Drag hence her husband to some secret hole,
And make his dead trunk pillow to our lust.   130
    Tam. But when ye have the honey ye desire,
Let not this wasp outlive, us both to sting.
    Chi. I warrant you, madam, we will make that
        sure.—
Come, mistress, now perforce we will enjoy
That nice-preserved honesty of yours.
    Lav. O Tamora ! thou bear'st a woman's face,—
    Tam. I will not hear her speak ; away with her !
    Lav. Sweet lords, entreat her hear me but a word.
    Dem. Listen, fair madam : let it be your glory
To see her tears ; but be your heart to them   140
As unrelenting flint to drops of rain.
    Lav. When did the tiger's young ones teach the
        dam?
O ! do not learn her wrath ; she taught it thee ;
The milk thou suck'dst from her did turn to marble ;
Even at thy teat thou hadst thy tyranny.
Yet every mother breeds not sons alike :
[*To* CHIRON.] Do thou entreat her show a woman
        pity.
    Chi. What ! wouldst have me prove myself a
        bastard ?
    Lav. 'T is true, the raven doth not hatch a lark :
Yet have I heard,—O, could I find it now !—   150
The lion mov'd with pity did endure
To have his princely paws par'd all away.
Some say that ravens foster forlorn children,
The whilst their own birds famish in their nests :
O ! be to me, though thy hard heart say no,
Nothing so kind, but something pitiful.
    Tam. I know not what it means ; away with her !
    Lav. O ! let me teach thee : for my father's sake,
That gave thee life, when well he might have slain
        thee,
Be not obdurate, open thy deaf ears.   160
    Tam. Hadst thou in person ne'er offended me,
Even for his sake am I pitiless.—
Remember, boys, I pour'd forth tears in vain,
To save your brother from the sacrifice ;
But fierce Andronicus would not relent.
Therefore, away with her, and use her as you will :
The worse to her, the better lov'd of me.
    Lav. O Tamora ! be call'd a gentle queen,
And with thine own hands kill me in this place ;
For 't is not life that I have begg'd so long :   170
Poor I was slain when Bassianus died.
    Tam. What begg'st thou then? fond woman, let
        me go.
    Lav. 'T is present death I beg ; and one thing more,
That womanhood denies my tongue to tell.
O ! keep me from their worse than killing lust,
And tumble me into some loathsome pit,
Where never man's eye may behold my body :
Do this, and be a charitable murderer.
    Tam. So should I rob my sweet sons of their fee :
No, let them satisfy their lust on thee.   180
    Dem. Away ! thou hast stay'd us here too long.
    Lav. No grace? no womanhood? Ah, beastly
        creature !
The blot and enemy to our general name !
Confusion fall—

Chi. Nay, then I 'll stop your mouth.—Bring thou
    her husband :   [*Dragging off* LAVINIA.
This is the hole where Aaron bid us hide him.
        [*Exeunt* CHIRON *and* DEMETRIUS.
Tam. Farewell, my sons : see, that you make her
    sure.
Ne'er let my heart know merry cheer indeed,
Till all the Andronici be made away.
Now will I hence to seek my lovely Moor,   190
And let my spleenful sons this trull deflour. [*Exit.*

_____

SCENE IV. -The Same.

Enter AARON, *with* QUINTUS *and* MARTIUS.

Aar. Come on, my lords, the better foot before :
Straight will I bring you to the loathsome pit,
Where I espied the panther fast asleep.
  Quint. My sight is very dull, whate'er it bodes.
  Mart. And mine, I promise you : were 't not for
    shame,
Well could I leave our sport to sleep awhile.
        [*Falls into the pit.*
  Quint. What ! art thou fall'n ?—What subtle hole is
    this,
Whose mouth is cover'd with rude-growing briers,
Upon whose leaves are drops of new-shed blood,
As fresh as morning's dew distill'd on flowers ?   10
A very fatal place it seems to me.
Speak, brother, hast thou hurt thee with the fall ?
  Mart. O brother ! with the dismall'st object hurt,
That ever eye with sight made heart lament.
  Aar. [*Aside.*] Now will I fetch the king to find
    them here,
That he thereby may give a likely guess,
How these were they that made away his brother.
        [*Exit.*
  Mart. Why dost not comfort me, and help me out
From this unhallow'd and blood-stained hole ?
  Quint. I am surprised with an uncouth fear ;   20
A chilling sweat o'erruns my trembling joints :
My heart suspects more than mine eye can see.
  Mart. To prove thou hast a true-divining heart,
Aaron and thou look down into this den,
And see a fearful sight of blood and death.
  Quint. Aaron is gone ; and my compassionate heart
Will not permit mine eyes once to behold
The thing whereat it trembles by surmise.
O ! tell me how it is ; for ne'er till now
Was I a child, to fear I know not what.   30
  Mart. Lord Bassianus lies embrewed here,
All on a heap, like to a slaughter'd lamb,
In this detested, dark, blood-drinking pit.
  Quint. If it be dark, how dost thou know 'tis he ?
  Mart. Upon his bloody finger he doth wear
A precious ring, that lightens all the hole,
Which, like a taper in some monument,
Doth shine upon the dead man's earthy cheeks,
And shows the ragged entrails of this pit :
So pale did shine the moon on Pyramus,   40
When he by night lay bath'd in maiden blood.
O brother ! help me with thy fainting hand—
If fear hath made thee faint, as me it hath—
Out of this fell devouring receptacle,
As hateful as Cocytus' misty mouth.
  Quint. Reach me thy hand, that I may help thee
    out ;
Or, wanting strength to do thee so much good,
I may be pluck'd into the swallowing womb
Of this deep pit, poor Bassianus' grave.
I have no strength to pluck thee to the brink. 50
  Mart. Nor I no strength to climb without thy help.
  Quint. Thy hand once more ; I will not loose
    again,
Till thou art here aloft, or I below.
Thou canst not come to me ; I come to thee. [*Falls in.*

Enter SATURNINUS *and* AARON.

Sat. Along with me :—I 'll see what hole is here,
And what he is that now is leap'd into it.
Say, who art thou, that lately didst descend
Into this gaping hollow of the earth ?

Mart. The unhappy son of old Andronicus,
Brought hither in a most unlucky hour,   60
To find thy brother Bassianus dead.
  Sat. My brother dead ! I know, thou dost but
    jest :
He and his lady both are at the lodge,
Upon the north side of this pleasant chase ;
'T is not an hour since I left him there.
  Mart. We know not where you left him all alive,
But, out, alas ! here have we found him dead.

Enter TAMORA, *with Attendants ;* TITUS
ANDRONICUS, *and* LUCIUS.

Tam. Where is my lord the king ?
  Sat. Here, Tamora ; though griev'd with killing
    grief.
  Tam. Where is thy brother Bassianus ?   70
  Sat. Now to the bottom dost thou search my
    wound :
Poor Bassianus here lies murdered.
  Tam. Then all too late I bring this fatal writ,
        [*Giving a letter.*
The complot of this timeless tragedy ;
And wonder greatly that man's face can fold
In pleasing smiles such murderous tyranny.
  Sat. [*Reads.*] " An if we miss to meet him hand-
    somely,—
Sweet huntsman, Bassianus 't is, we mean,—
Do thou so much as dig the grave for him.
Thou know'st our meaning : look for thy reward 80
Among the nettles at the elder-tree,
Which overshades the mouth of that same pit,
Where we decreed to bury Bassianus.
Do this, and purchase us thy lasting friends."
O Tamora ! was ever heard the like ?
This is the pit, and this the elder-tree.
Look, sirs, if you can find the huntsman out,
That should have murder'd Bassianus here.
  Aar. My gracious lord, here is the bag of gold.
        [*Showing it.*
  Sat. [*To* TITUS.] Two of thy whelps, fell curs of
    bloody kind,   90
Have here bereft my brother of his life.—
Sirs, drag them from the pit unto the prison :
There let them bide, until we have devis'd
Some never-heard-of torturing pain for them.
  Tam. What ! are they in this pit ? O wondrous
    thing !
How easily murder is discovered !
  Tit. High emperor, upon my feeble knee
I beg this boon with tears not lightly shed ;
That this fell fault of my accursed sons,
Accursed, if the fault be prov'd in them,—   100
  Sat. If it be prov'd ! you see, it is apparent.—
Who found this letter ? Tamora, was it you ?
  Tam. Andronicus himself did take it up.
  Tit. I did, my lord : yet let me be their bail ;
For, by my fathers' reverend tomb, I vow,
They shall be ready at your highness' will,
To answer their suspicion with their lives.
  Sat. Thou shalt not bail them : see, thou follow
    me.
Some bring the murder'd body, some the mur-
    derers :
Let them not speak a word, the guilt is plain ; 110
For, by my soul, were there worse end than death,
That end upon them should be executed.
  Tam. Andronicus, I will entreat the king :
Fear not thy sons, they shall do well enough.
  Tit. Come, Lucius, come ; stay not to talk with
    them.   [*Exeunt severally.*

_____

SCENE V.—The Same.

Enter DEMETRIUS *and* CHIRON, *with* LAVINIA,
*ravished ; her hands cut off, and her tongue cut
out.*

Dem. So, now go tell, an if thy tongue can speak,
Who 't was that cut thy tongue, and ravish'd thee.
  Chi. Write down thy mind, bewray thy meaning
    so ;
An if thy stumps will let thee, play the scribe.

Dem. See, how with signs and tokens she can
　　scrawl.
Chi. Go home, call for sweet water, wash thy
　　hands.
Dem. She hath no tongue to call, nor hands to
　　wash ;
And so let 's leave her to her silent walks.
Chi. An 't were my case, I should go hang my-
　　self.
Dem. If thou hadst hands to help thee knit the cord,
　　　　　[*Exeunt* DEMETRIUS *and* CHIRON.

　　Enter MARCUS, *from hunting.*
Marc. Who 's this?—my niece, that flies away so
　　fast ? 11
Cousin, a word : where is your husband ?—
If I do dream, 'would all my wealth would wake
　　me !
If I do wake, some planet strike me down,
That I may slumber in eternal sleep !—
Speak, gentle niece, what stern ungentle hands
Have lopp'd and hew'd, and made thy body bare
Of her two branches, those sweet ornaments,
Whose circling shadows kings have sought to sleep
　　in,
And might not gain so great a happiness 20
As have thy love ? Why dost not speak to me ?—
Alas ! a crimson river of warm blood,
Like to a bubbling fountain stirr'd with wind,
Doth rise and fall between thy rosed lips,
Coming and going with thy honey breath.
But, sure, some Tereus hath defloured thee,

And, lest thou shouldst detect him, cut thy tongue.
Ah ! now thou turn'st away thy face for shame ;
And, notwithstanding all this loss of blood,
As from a conduit with three issuing spouts, 30
Yet do thy cheeks look red as Titan's face
Blushing to be encounter'd with a cloud.
Shall I speak for thee ? shall I say, 't is so ?
O, that I knew thy heart ; and knew the beast,
That I might rail at him, to ease my mind !
Sorrow concealed, like an oven stopp'd,
Doth burn the heart to cinders where it is.
Fair Philomela, she but lost her tongue,
And in a tedious sampler sew'd her mind :
But, lovely niece, that mean is cut from thee ; 40
A craftier Tereus hast thou met withal,
And he hath cut those pretty fingers off,
That could have better sew'd than Philomel.
O ! had the monster seen those lily hands
Tremble like aspen-leaves upon a lute,
And make the silken strings delight to kiss them,
He would not then have touch'd them for his life ;
Or had he heard the heavenly harmony,
Which that sweet tongue hath made,
He would have dropp'd his knife, and fell asleep, 50
As Cerberus at the Thracian poet's feet.
Come, let us go, and make thy father blind ;
For such a sight will blind a father's eye :
One hour's storm will drown the fragrant meads ;
What will whole months of tears thy father's
　　eyes ?
Do not draw back, for we will mourn with thee :
O, could our mourning ease thy misery ! [*Exeunt.*

ACT III.

SCENE I.—Rome. A Street.

Enter Senators, Tribunes, and Officers of Justice, with MARTIUS *and* QUINTUS, *bound,
passing on to the place of execution;* TITUS *going before, pleading.*

Titus.
EAR me, grave fathers ! noble tribunes,
　　stay !
For pity of mine age, whose youth was
　　spent
In dangerous wars, whilst you securely
　　slept ;
For all my blood in Rome's great quarrel
　　shed ;
For all the frosty nights that I have
　　watch'd ;
And for these bitter tears, which now
　　you see
Filling the aged wrinkles in my cheeks ;
Be pitiful to my condemned sons,
Whose souls are not corrupted as 't is
　　thought.
For two-and-twenty sons I never wept, 10
Because they died in honour's lofty bed :
For these, tribunes, in the dust I write
　　　　　[*Throwing himself on the ground.*
My heart's deep languor, and my soul's sad tears.
Let my tears stanch the earth's dry appetite ;
My sons' sweet blood will make it shame and blush.
　　　　　[*Exeunt Senators, Tribunes, &c., with the
　　　　　Prisoners.*
O earth ! I will befriend thee more with rain,
That shall distil from these two ancient urns,
Than youthful April shall with all his showers :

In summer's drought, I 'll drop upon thee still ;
In winter, with warm tears I 'll melt the snow, 20
And keep eternal spring-time on thy face,
So thou refuse to drink my dear son's blood.

　　Enter LUCIUS, *with his weapon drawn.*

O reverend tribunes ! O gentle-aged men !
Unbind my sons, reverse the doom of death ;
And let me say, that never wept before,
My tears are now prevailing orators. ,
Luc. O noble father, you lament in vain :
The tribunes hear you not, no man is by,
And you recount your sorrows to a stone.
Tit. Ah, Lucius, for thy brothers let me plead.— 30
Grave tribunes, once more I entreat of you,—
Luc. My gracious lord, no tribune hears you
　　speak.
Tit. Why, 't is no matter, man : if they did hear,
They would not mark me, or if they did mark,
They would not pity me, yet plead I must,
And bootless unto them.
Therefore I tell my sorrows to the stones,
Who, though they cannot answer my distress,
Yet in some sort they are better than the tribunes,
For that they will not intercept my tale. 40
When I do weep, they, humbly at my feet,
Receive my tears, and seem to weep with me ;
And were they but attired in grave weeds,
Rome could afford no tribune like to these.

A stone is soft as wax, tribunes more hard than
  stones;
A stone is silent, and offendeth not,
And tribunes with their tongues doom men to
  death.   [*Rises.*
But wherefore stand'st thou with thy weapon drawn?

Tit. "In the dust I write my heart's deep languor."

Luc. To rescue my two brothers from their death;
For which attempt the judges have pronounc'd   50
My everlasting doom of banishment.
  Tit. O happy man! they have befriended thee.
Why, foolish Lucius, dost thou not perceive,
That Rome is but a wilderness of tigers?
Tigers must prey; and Rome affords no prey,
But me and mine: how happy art thou then,
From these devourers to be banished!
But who comes with our brother Marcus here?

        Enter MARCUS *and* LAVINIA.

  Marc. Titus, prepare thy aged eyes to weep;
Or, if not so, thy noble heart to break: 60
I bring consuming sorrow to thine age.
  Tit. Will it consume me? let me see it then.
  Marc. This was thy daughter.
  Tit.   Why, Marcus, so she is.
  Luc. Ah me! this object kills me.
  Tit. Faint-hearted boy, arise, and look upon her.—
Speak, Lavinia, what accursed hand
Hath made thee handless in thy father's sight?
What fool hath added water to the sea,
Or brought a faggot to bright-burning Troy?
My grief was at the height before thou cam'st,   70
And now, like Nilus, it disdaineth bounds.—
Give me a sword, I'll chop off my hands too;
For they have fought for Rome, and all in vain;
And they have nurs'd this woe, in feeding life;
In bootless prayer have they been held up,
And they have serv'd me to effectless use:
Now all the service I require of them
Is that the one will help to cut the other.—
'T is well, Lavinia, that thou hast no hands,
For hands, to do Rome service, are but vain.   80
  Luc. Speak, gentle sister, who hath martyr'd thee?
  Marc. O! that delightful engine of her thoughts,
That blabb'd them with such pleasing eloquence,
Is torn from forth that pretty hollow cage,
Where, like a sweet melodious bird, it sung
Sweet varied notes, enchanting every ear.
  Luc. O! say thou for her, who hath done this deed?
  Marc. O! thus I found her, straying in the park,
Seeking to hide herself, as doth the deer,
That hath receiv'd some unrecuring wound.   90
  Tit. It was my deer; and he that wounded her
Hath hurt me more, than had he kill'd me dead:

For now I stand as one upon a rock,
Environ'd with a wilderness of sea,
Who marks the waxing tide grow wave by wave,
Expecting ever when some envious surge
Will in his brinish bowels swallow him.
This way to death my wretched sons are gone;
Here stands my other son, a banish'd man,
And here my brother, weeping at my woes;   100
But that which gives my soul the greatest spurn,
Is dear Lavinia, dearer than my soul.—
Had I but seen thy picture in this plight,
It would have madded me: what shall I do
Now I behold thy lively body so?
Thou hast no hands to wipe away thy tears,
Nor tongue to tell me who hath martyr'd thee:
Thy husband he is dead, and for his death
Thy brothers are condemn'd and dead by this.
Look, Marcus; ah! son Lucius, look on her: 110
When I did name her brothers, then fresh tears
Stood on her cheeks, as doth the honey-dew
Upon a gather'd lily almost wither'd.
  Marc. Perchance, she weeps because they kill'd her
  husband;
Perchance, because she knows them innocent.
  Tit. If they did kill thy husband, then be joyful,
Because the law hath ta'en revenge on them.—
No, no, they would not do so foul a deed;
Witness the sorrow that their sister makes.—
Gentle Lavinia, let me kiss thy lips,   120
Or make some sign how I may do thee ease.
Shall thy good uncle, and thy brother Lucius,
And thou, and I, sit round about some fountain,
Looking all downwards, to behold our cheeks
How they are stain'd, like meadows yet not dry,
With miry slime left on them by a flood?
And in the fountain shall we gaze so long,
Till the fresh taste be taken from that clearness,
And made a brine-pit with our bitter tears?
Or shall we cut away our hands, like thine?   130
Or shall we bite our tongues, and in dumb shows
Pass the remainder of our hateful days?
What shall we do? let us, that have our tongues,
Plot some device of further misery,
To make us wonder'd at in time to come.
  Luc. Sweet father, cease your tears; for at your
  grief,
See, how my wretched sister sobs and weeps.
  Marc. Patience, dear niece.—Good Titus, dry thine
  eyes.
  Tit. Ah, Marcus, Marcus! brother, well I wot,
Thy napkin cannot drink a tear of mine,   140
For thou, poor man, hast drown'd it with thine own.
  Luc. Ah, my Lavinia! I will wipe thy cheeks.
  Tit. Mark, Marcus, mark! I understand her signs.
Had she a tongue to speak, now would she say
That to her brother which I said to thee:
His napkin, with his true tears all bewet,
Can do no service on her sorrowful cheeks.
O! what a sympathy of woe is this;
As far from help as limbo is from bliss!

          Enter AARON.

  Aar. Titus Andronicus, my lord the emperor   150
Sends thee this word,—that, if thou love thy sons,
Let Marcus, Lucius, or thyself, old Titus,
Or any one of you, chop off your hand,
And send it to the king: he, for the same,
Will send thee hither both thy sons alive,
And that shall be the ransom for their fault.
  Tit. O gracious emperor! O gentle Aaron!
Did ever raven sing so like a lark,
That gives sweet tidings of the sun's uprise?
With all my heart, I'll send the emperor my hand. 160
Good Aaron, wilt thou help to chop it off?
  Luc. Stay, father! for that noble hand of thine,
That hath thrown down so many enemies,
Shall not be sent: my hand will serve the turn.
My youth can better spare my blood than you,
And therefore mine shall save my brothers' lives.
  Marc. Which of your hands hath not defended
  Rome,
And rear'd aloft the bloody battle-axe,

Writing destruction on the enemy's castle?
O! none of both but are of high desert.   170
My hand hath been but idle; let it serve
To ransom my two nephews from their death:
Then have I kept it to a worthy end.

  Aar. Nay, come, agree, whose hand shall go along,
For fear they die before their pardon come.

  Luc. Then I'll go fetch an axe.
  Marc. But I will use the axe.
                [*Exeunt* Lucius *and* Marcus.
  Tit. Come hither, Aaron; I'll deceive them both:
Lend me thy hand, and I will give thee mine.
  Aar. [*Aside.*] If that be call'd deceit, I will be honest,
And never, whilst I live, deceive men so:—

Tit. "Faint-hearted boy, arise, and look upon her."

  Marc. My hand shall go.
  Luc.   By heaven, it shall not go!
  Tit. Sirs, strive no more: such wither'd herbs as
    these
Are meet for plucking up, and therefore mine.
  Luc. Sweet father, if I shall be thought thy son,
Let me redeem my brothers both from death.   180
  Marc. And for our father's sake, and mother's
    care,
Now let me show a brother's love to thee.
  Tit. Agree between you; I will spare my hand.

But I'll deceive you in another sort,   190
And that you'll say, ere half an hour pass.
                 [*Cuts off* Titus's *hand.*

     Re-enter Lucius *and* Marcus.

  Tit. Now, stay your strife; what shall be, is de-
    spatch'd.—
Good Aaron, give his majesty my hand:
Tell him, it was a hand that warded him
From thousand dangers; bid him bury it:
More hath it merited; that let it have.

As for my sons, say, I account of them
As jewels purchas'd at an easy price ;
And yet dear too, because I bought mine own.

Tit. " Lend me thy hand, and I will give thee mine."

Aar. I go, Andronicus ; and, for thy hand,   200
Look by and by to have thy sons with thee.
[*Aside.*] Their heads, I mean.—O, how this villainy
Doth fat me with the very thoughts of it !
Let fools do good, and fair men call for grace,
Aaron will have his soul black like his face.   [*Exit.*
  Tit. O ! here I lift this one hand up to heaven,
And bow this feeble ruin to the earth :
If any power pities wretched tears,
To that I call.—[*To* LAVINIA.] What ! wilt thou kneel
  with me ?
Do then, dear heart ; for heaven shall hear our
  prayers,   210
Or with our sighs we 'll breathe the welkin dim,
And stain the sun with fog, as sometime clouds,
When they do hug him in their melting bosoms.
  Marc. O ! brother, speak with possibilities,
And do not break into these deep extremes.
  Tit. Is not my sorrow deep, having no bottom ?
Then be my passions bottomless with them.
  Marc. But yet let reason govern thy lament.
  Tit. If there were reason for these miseries,
Then into limits could I bind my woes.   220
When heaven doth weep, doth not the earth o'er-
  flow ?
If the winds rage, doth not the sea wax mad,
Threat'ning the welkin with his big-swoln face ?
And wilt thou have a reason for this coil ?
I am the sea ; hark, how her sighs do blow !
She is the weeping welkin, I the earth :
Then must my sea be moved with her sighs ;
Then must my earth with her continual tears
Become a deluge, overflow'd and drown'd :   230
For why my bowels cannot hide her woes,
But like a drunkard must I vomit them.
Then give me leave, for losers will have leave
To ease their stomachs with their bitter tongues.

Enter a Messenger, with two heads and a hand.

  Mess. Worthy Andronicus, ill art thou repaid
For that good hand thou sentst the emperor.
Here are the heads of thy two noble sons,
And here 's thy hand, in scorn to thee sent back :
Thy griefs their sports, thy resolution mock'd ;
That woe is me to think upon thy woes,
More than remembrance of my father's death. [*Exit.*   241
  Marc. Now let hot Ætna cool in Sicily,
And be my heart an ever-burning hell !
These miseries are more than may be borne.
To weep with them that weep doth ease some deal,
But sorrow flouted at is double death.

  Luc. Ah, that this sight should make so deep a
  wound,
And yet detested life not shrink thereat !
That ever death should let life bear his name,
Where life hath no more interest but to breathe !
                            [LAVINIA *kisses* TITUS.
  Marc. Alas, poor heart ! that kiss is comfortless,   250
As frozen water to a starved snake.
  Tit. When will this fearful slumber have an end ?
  Marc. Now farewell, flattery : die, Andronicus.
Thou dost not slumber : see thy two sons' heads,
Thy warlike hand, thy mangled daughter here ;
Thy other banish'd son with this dear sight
Struck pale and bloodless ; and thy brother, I,
Even like a stony image, cold and numb.
Ah ! now no more will I control thy griefs.
Rent off thy silver hair, thy other hand   260
Gnawing with thy teeth ; and be this dismal sight
The closing up of our most wretched eyes !
Now is a time to storm ; why art thou still ?
  Tit. Ha, ha, ha !
  Marc. Why dost thou laugh ? it fits not with this
  hour.
  Tit. Why, I have not another tear to shed :
Besides, this sorrow is an enemy,
And would usurp upon my watery eyes,
And make them blind with tributary tears ;
Then, which way shall I find Revenge's cave ?   270
For these two heads do seem to speak to me,
And threat me, I shall never come to bliss,
Till all these mischiefs be return'd again,
Even in their throats that have committed them.

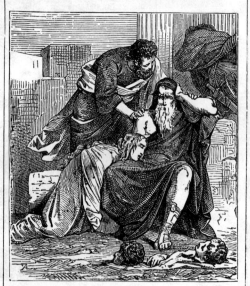

Tit. " When will this fearful slumber have an end ?"

Come, let me see what task I have to do.—
You heavy people, circle me about,
That I may turn me to each one of you,
And swear unto my soul to write your wrongs.—
The vow is made.—Come, brother, take a head ;
And in this hand the other will I bear.   280
Lavinia, thou shalt be employed in these things :
Bear thou my hand, sweet wench, between thy
  teeth.
As for thee, boy, go, get thee from my sight ;
Thou art an exile, and thou must not stay :

Hie to the Goths, and raise an army there ;
And if you love me, as I think you do,
Let's kiss and part, for we have much to do.
    [*Exeunt* Titus, Marcus, *and* Lavinia.
  Luc. Farewell, Andronicus, my noble father ;
The wofull'st man that ever liv'd in Rome.
Farewell, proud Rome : till Lucius come again,   290
He leaves his pledges dearer than his life.
Farewell, Lavinia, my noble sister ;
O, 'would thou wert as thou tofore hast been !
But now nor Lucius, nor Lavinia lives,
But in oblivion, and hateful griefs.
If Lucius live, he will requite your wrongs,
And make proud Saturnine and his empress
Beg at the gates like Tarquin and his queen.
Now will I to the Goths, and raise a power,
To be reveng'd on Rome and Saturnine. [*Exit.* 300

Scene II.—A Room in Titus's House. A Banquet
    set out.

Enter Titus, Marcus, Lavinia, *and young* Lucius,
    a boy.

  Tit. So, so ; now sit ; and look, you eat no more
Than will preserve just so much strength in us
As will revenge these bitter woes of ours.
Marcus, unknit that sorrow-wreathen knot :
Thy niece and I, poor creatures, want our hands,
And cannot passionate our ten-fold grief
With folded arms. This poor right hand of mine
Is left to tyrannise upon my breast ;
And when my heart, all mad with misery,
Beats in this hollow prison of my flesh,   10
Then thus I thump it down.—
[*To* Lavinia.] Thou map of woe, that thus dost talk
    in signs,
When thy poor heart beats with outrageous beating
Thou canst not strike it thus to make it still.
Wound it with sighing, girl, kill it with groans ;
Or get some little knife between thy teeth,
And just against thy heart make thou a hole ;
That all the tears that thy poor eyes let fall
May run into that sink, and, soaking in,
Drown the lamenting fool in sea-salt tears.   20
  Marc. Fie, brother, fie ! teach her not thus to lay
Such violent hands upon her tender life.
  Tit. How now ! has sorrow made thee dote already ?
Why, Marcus, no man should be mad but I.
What violent hands can she lay on her life ?
Ah ! wherefore dost thou urge the name of hands ;
To bid Æneas tell the tale twice o'er,
How Troy was burnt, and he made miserable ?
O ! handle not the theme, to talk of hands,
Lest we remember still that we have none.   30
Fie, fie ! how franticly I square my talk,
As if we should forget we had no hands,
If Marcus did not name the word of hands !—
Come, let's fall to ; and, gentle girl, eat this.—

Here is no drink. Hark, Marcus, what she says ;
I can interpret all her martyr'd signs.
She says she drinks no other drink but tears,
Brew'd with her sorrow, mash'd upon her cheeks.
Speechless complainer, I will learn thy thought ;
In thy dumb action will I be as perfect,   40
As begging hermits in their holy prayers :
Thou shalt not sigh, nor hold thy stumps to heaven,
Nor wink, nor nod, nor kneel, nor make a sign,
But I, of these, will wrest an alphabet,
And, by still practice, learn to know thy meaning.
  Boy. Good grandsire, leave these bitter deep
    laments :
Make my aunt merry with some pleasing tale.
  Marc. At that that I have kill'd, my lord,—a fly.
Doth weep to see his grandsire's heaviness.
  Tit. Peace, tender sapling ; thou art made of
    tears,   50
And tears will quickly melt thy life away.—
    [Marcus *strikes the dish with a knife.*
What dost thou strike at, Marcus, with thy knife ?
  Marc. At that that I have kill'd, my lord,—a fly.
  Tit. Out on thee, murderer ! thou kill'st my
    heart ;
Mine eyes are cloy'd with view of tyranny :
A deed of death, done on the innocent,
Becomes not Titus' brother. Get thee gone ;
I see, thou art not for my company.
  Marc. Alas ! my lord, I have but kill'd a fly. 60
  Tit. But how, if that fly had a father and mother,
How would he hang his slender gilded wings,
And buzz lamenting doings in the air ?
Poor harmless fly,
That, with his pretty buzzing melody,
Came here to make us merry ! and thou hast kill'd
    him.
  Marc. Pardon me, sir : it was a black ill-favour'd
    fly,
Like to the empress' Moor ; therefore I kill'd him.
  Tit. O, O, O !
Then pardon me for reprehending thee,
For thou hast done a charitable deed.   70
Give me thy knife, I will insult on him ;
Flattering myself, as if it were the Moor,
Come hither purposely to poison me.—
There's for thyself, and that's for Tamora.
Ah, sirrah !—
Yet I think we are not brought so low,
But that between us we can kill a fly,
That comes in likeness of a coal-black Moor.
  Marc. Alas, poor man ! grief has so wrought on
    him,
He takes false shadows for true substances. 80
  Tit. Come, take away.—Lavinia, go with me :
I'll to thy closet ; and go read with thee
Sad stories, chanced in the times of old.—
Come, boy, and go with me : thy sight is young,
And thou shalt read, when mine begins to dazzle.
    [*Exeunt.*

ACT IV.

SCENE I.—The Same. Before TITUS's House.

Enter TITUS and MARCUS. Then enter young LUCIUS, LAVINIA running after him.

Boy.
HELP, grandsire, help! my aunt Lavinia
Follows me every where, I know not
   why.—
Good uncle Marcus, see, how swift she
   comes!
Alas! sweet aunt, I know not what you
   mean.
  Marc. Stand by me, Lucius; do not
   fear thine aunt.
  Tit. She loves thee, boy, too well to
   do thee harm.
  Boy. Ay, when my father was in
   Rome, she did.
  Marc. What means my niece Lavinia
   by these signs?
  Tit. Fear her not, Lucius: — some-
   what doth she mean.
See, Lucius, see, how much she makes of thee: 10
Somewhither would she have thee go with her.
Ah, boy! Cornelia never with more care
Read to her sons, than she hath read to thee,
Sweet poetry, and Tully's Orator.
  Marc. Canst thou not guess wherefore she plies
   thee thus?
  Boy. My lord, I know not, I, nor can I guess,
Unless some fit or frenzy do possess her;
For I have heard my grandsire say full oft,
Extremity of griefs would make men mad;
And I have read that Hecuba of Troy 20
Ran mad through sorrow: that made me to fear;
Although, my lord, I know, my noble aunt
Loves me as dear as e'er my mother did,
And would not, but in fury, fright my youth;
Which made me down to throw my books, and fly,
Causeless, perhaps. But pardon me, sweet aunt;
And, madam, if my uncle Marcus go,
I will most willingly attend your ladyship.
  Marc. Lucius, I will.
    [LAVINIA *turns over the books which* LUCIUS
    had let fall.
  Tit. How now, Lavinia? — Marcus, what means
   this? 30
Some book there is that she desires to see.—
Which is it, girl, of these?—Open them, boy.·
But thou art deeper read, and better skill'd;
Come, and take choice of all my library,
And so beguile thy sorrow, till the heavens
Reveal the damn'd contriver of this deed.—
What book?
Why lifts she up her arms in sequence thus?
  Marc. I think, she means that there was more than
   one
Confederate in the fact:—ay, more there was; 40
Or else to heaven she heaves them for revenge.
  Tit. Lucius, what book is that she tosseth so?
  Boy. Grandsire, 't is Ovid's Metamorphoses:
My mother gave it me.
  Marc.   For love of her that 's gone,
Perhaps, she cull'd it from among the rest.
  Tit. Soft! so busily she turns the leaves!
Help her:
What would she find?—Lavinia, shall I read?

This is the tragic tale of Philomel,
And treats of Tereus' treason and his rape; 50
And rape, I fear, was root of thine annoy.
  Marc. See, brother, see! note, how she quotes the
   leaves.
  Tit. Lavinia, wert thou thus surpris'd, sweet girl,
Ravish'd and wrong'd, as Philomela was,
Forc'd in the ruthless, vast, and gloomy woods?—
See, see!—
Ay, such a place there is, where we did hunt,
(O, had we never, never hunted there!)
Pattern'd by that the poet here describes,
By nature made for murders, and for rapes. 60
  Marc. O! why should nature build so foul a den,
Unless the gods delight in tragedies?
  Tit. Give signs, sweet girl, for here are none but
   friends,
What Roman lord it was durst do the deed:
Or slunk not Saturnine, as Tarquin erst,
That left the camp to sin in Lucrece' bed?
  Marc. Sit down, sweet niece :—brother, sit down by
   me.—
Apollo, Pallas, Jove, or Mercury,
Inspire me, that I may this treason find!—
My lord, look here;—look here, Lavinia : 70
This sandy plot is plain; guide, if thou canst,
This after me.
    [*He writes his name with his staff, and guides
    it with feet and mouth.*
        I have writ my name
Without the help of any hand at all.
Curs'd be that heart that forc'd us to this shift!—
Write thou, good niece, and here display at last
What God will have discover'd for revenge.
Heaven guide thy pen to print thy sorrows plain,
That we may know the traitors and the truth!
    [*She takes the staff in her mouth, and guides
    it with her stumps, and writes.*
  Tit. O! do you read, my lord, what she hath
   writ?
Stuprum—Chiron—Demetrius. 80
  Marc. What, what!—the lustful sons of Tamora
Performers of this heinous, bloody deed?
  *Tit. Magni dominator poli,
Tam lentus audis scelera? tam lentus vides?*
  Marc. O! calm thee, gentle lord; although I know
There is enough written upon this earth,
To stir a mutiny in the mildest thoughts,
And arm the minds of infants to exclaims.
My lord, kneel down with me; Lavinia, kneel;
And kneel, sweet boy, the Roman Hector's hope; 90
And swear with me,—as with the woful fere,
And father, of that chaste dishonour'd dame,
Lord Junius Brutus sware for Lucrece' rape,—
That we will prosecute, by good advice,
Mortal revenge upon these traitorous Goths,
And see their blood, or die with this reproach.
  Tit. 'T is sure enough, an you knew how;
But if you hunt these bear-whelps, then beware:
The dam will wake, an if she wind you once:
She 's with the lion deeply still in league, 100
And lulls him whilst she playeth on her back;
And when he sleeps will she do what she list.

You 're a young huntsman : Marcus, let alone ;
And, come, I will go get a leaf of brass,
And with a gad of steel will write these words,
And lay it by. The angry northern wind
Will blow these sands like Sibyl's leaves abroad,
And where 's your lesson then ?—Boy, what say you ?
  Boy. I say, my lord, that if I were a man,
Their mother's bedchamber should not be safe   110
For these bad bondmen to the yoke of Rome.
  Marc. Ay, that 's my boy ! thy father hath full oft
For his ungrateful country done the like.
  Boy. And, uncle, so will I, an if I live.
  Tit. Come, go with me into mine armoury :
Lucius, I 'll fit thee ; and withal my boy
Shall carry from me to the empress' sons
Presents, that I intend to send them both.
Come, come ; thou 'lt do thy message, wilt thou
   not ?
  Boy. Ay, with my dagger in their bosoms, grand-
   sire.   120
  Tit. No, boy, not so ; I 'll teach thee another course.
Lavinia, come.—Marcus, look to my house :
Lucius and I 'll go brave it at the court ;
Ay, marry, will we, sir ; and we 'll be waited on.
       [*Exeunt* Titus, Lavinia, *and Boy.*
  Marc. O heavens! can you hear a good man
   groan,
And not relent, or not compassion him ?
Marcus, attend him in his ecstacy,
That hath more scars of sorrow in his heart,
Than foemen's marks upon his batter'd shield ;
But yet so just, that he will not revenge.—   130
Revenge the heavens for old Andronicus !   [*Exit.*

Scene II.—The Same. A Room in the Palace.

Enter Aaron, Demetrius, *and* Chiron, *at one door;
at another door, young* Lucius, *and an Attendant,
with a bundle of weapons, and verses writ upon
them.*

  Chi. Demetrius, here 's the son of Lucius ;
He hath some message to deliver us.
  Aar. Ay, some mad message from his mad grand-
   father.
  Boy. My lords, with all the humbleness I may,
I greet your honours from Andronicus ;—
[*Aside.*] And pray the Roman gods confound you
   both.
  Dem. Gramercy, lovely Lucius. What 's the news?
  Boy. [*Aside.*] That you are both decipher'd, that 's
   the news,
For villains mark'd with rape. [*To them.*] May it
   please you,
My grandsire, well advis'd, hath sent by me   10
The goodliest weapons of his armoury,
To gratify your honourable youth,
The hope of Rome ; for so he bade me say,
And so I do, and with his gifts present
Your lordships, that, whenever you have need,
You may be armed and appointed well.
And so I leave you both, [*aside*] like bloody villains.
       [*Exeunt Boy and Attendant.*
  Dem. What 's here ? A scroll ; and written round
   about ?
Let 's see :
  Integer vitæ, scelerisque purus,   20
  Non eget Mauri jaculis, nec arcu.
  Chi. O ! 'tis a verse in Horace ; I know it well :
I read it in the grammar long ago.
  Aar. Ay, just!—a verse in Horace ;—right, you
   have it.
[*Aside.*] Now, what a thing it is to be an ass !
Here 's no sound jest ! the old man hath found their
   guilt,
And sends them weapons wrapp'd about with lines,
That wound, beyond their feeling, to the quick ;
But were our witty empress well afoot,
She would applaud Andronicus' conceit :   30
But let her rest in her unrest awhile.—
[*To them.*] And now, young lords, was 't not a happy
   star

Led us to Rome, strangers, and more than so,
Captives, to be advanced to this height ?
It did me good, before the palace gate
To brave the tribune in his brother's hearing.
  Dem. But me more good, to see so great a lord
Basely insinuate, and send us gifts.
  Aar. Had he not reason, Lord Demetrius ?
Did you not use his daughter very friendly ?   40
  Dem. I would we had a thousand Roman dames
At such a bay, by turn to serve our lust.
  Chi. A charitable wish, and full of love.
  Aar. Here lacks but your mother for to say amen.
  Chi. And that would she for twenty thousand
   more.
  Dem. Come, let us go, and pray to all the gods
For our beloved mother in her pains.
  Aar. [*Aside.*] Pray to the devils ; the gods have
   given us over.   [*Trumpets sound.*
  Dem. Why do the emperor's trumpets flourish thus ?
  Chi. Belike, for joy the emperor hath a son.   50
  Dem. Soft ! who comes here ?

    Enter a Nurse, with a blackamoor Child.

  Nur. Good morrow, lords. O ! tell me, did you see
Aaron the Moor ?
  Aar. Well, more, or less, or ne'er a whit at all,
Here Aaron is ; and what with Aaron now ?
  Nur. O gentle Aaron ! we are all undone.
Now help, or woe betide thee evermore !
  Aar. Why, what a caterwauling dost thou keep !
What dost thou wrap and fumble in thine arms ?
  Nur. O ! that which I would hide from heaven's
   eye,   60
Our empress' shame, and stately Rome's disgrace.—
She is deliver'd, lords, she is deliver'd.
  Aar. To whom?
  Nur.   I mean she 's brought a-bed.
  Aar. Well, God give her good rest ! What hath he
   sent her ?
  Nur. A devil.
  Aar.   Why, then she is the devil's dam :
A joyful issue.
  Nur. A joyless, dismal, black, and sorrowful issue.
Here is the babe, as loathsome as a toad
Amongst the fairest breeders of our clime.
The empress sends it thee, thy stamp, thy seal,   70
And bids thee christen it with thy dagger's point.
  Aar. Out, you whore ! is black so base a hue ?—
Sweet blowse, you are a beauteous blossom, sure.
  Dem. Villain, what hast thou done ?
  Aar. That which thou canst not undo.
  Chi. Thou hast undone our mother.
  Aar. Villain, I have done thy mother.
  Dem. And therein, hellish dog, thou hast undone
   her.
Woe to her chance, and damn'd her loathed choice !
Accurs'd the offspring of so foul a fiend !   80
  Chi. It shall not live.
  Aar. It shall not die.
  Nur. Aaron, it must : the mother wills it so.
  Aar. What ! must it, nurse ? then let no man but I
Do execution on my flesh and blood.
  Dem. I 'll broach the tadpole on my rapier's point :
Nurse, give it me ; my sword shall soon despatch it.
  Aar. Sooner this sword shall plough thy bowels up.
    [*Takes the Child from the Nurse, and draws.*
Stay, murderous villains ! will you kill your brother?
Now, by the burning tapers of the sky,   90
That shone so brightly when this boy was got,
He dies upon my scimitar's sharp point
That touches this my first-born son and heir.
I tell you, younglings, not Enceladus,
With all his threatening band of Typhon's brood,
Nor great Alcides, nor the god of war,
Shall seize this prey out of his father's hands.
What, what, ye sanguine, shallow-hearted boys !
Ye white-lim'd walls ! ye ale-house painted signs !
Coal-black is better than another hue,   100
In that it scorns to bear another hue ;
For all the water in the ocean
Can never turn the swan's black legs to white,
Although she lave them hourly in the flood.

Tell the empress from me, I am of age
To keep mine own ; excuse it how she can.
Dem. Wilt thou betray thy noble mistress thus?
Aar. My mistress is my mistress ; this, myself ;
The vigour, and the picture of my youth :
This before all the world do I prefer ;   110
This, maugre all the world, will I keep safe,
Or some of you shall smoke for it in Rome.

Aar. "Stay, murderous villains!"

Dem. By this our mother is for ever shamed.
Chi. Rome will despise her for this foul escape.
Nur. The emperor in his rage will doom her death.
Chi. I blush to think upon this ignomy.
Aar. Why, there's the privilege your beauty
    bears.
Fie, treacherous hue! that will betray with blushing
The close enacts and counsels of the heart :
Here's a young lad fram'd of another leer.   120
Look, how the black slave smiles upon the father,
As who should say, "Old lad, I am thine own."
He is your brother, lords, sensibly fed
Of that self blood that first gave life to you ;
And from that womb, where you imprison'd were,
He is enfranchised and come to light :
Nay, he is your brother by the surer side,
Although my seal be stamped in his face.
Nur. Aaron, what shall I say unto the empress?
Dem. Advise thee, Aaron, what is to be done,   130
And we will all subscribe to thy advice :
Save thou the child, so we may all be safe.
Aar. Then sit we down, and let us all consult.
My son and I will have the wind of you ;
Keep there : now talk at pleasure of your safety.
                                            [*They sit.*
Dem. How many women saw this child of his?
Aar. Why, so, brave lords : when we join in
    league,
I am a lamb ; but if you brave the Moor,
The chafed boar, the mountain lioness,
The ocean swells not so as Aaron storms.—   140
But say again, how many saw the child?
Nur. Cornelia the midwife, and myself,
And no one else but the deliver'd empress.
Aar. The empress, the midwife, and yourself :
Two may keep counsel, when the third's away.
Go to the empress ; tell her this I said :
                                        [*Stabbing her.*
Weke, weke!—so cries a pig prepared to the spit.
Dem. What mean'st thou, Aaron? wherefore didst
    thou this?
Aar. O Lord, sir, 'tis a deed of policy.
Shall she live to betray this guilt of ours,   150
A long-tongu'd babbling gossip? no, lords, no.
And now be it known to you my full intent.
Not far, one Muliteus, my countryman ;
His wife but yesternight was brought to bed.

His child is like to her, fair as you are :
Go pack with him, and give the mother gold,
And tell them both the circumstance of all,
And how by this their child shall be advanc'd,
And be received for the emperor's heir,
And substituted in the place of mine,   160
To calm this tempest whirling in the court ;
And let the emperor dandle him for his own.
Hark ye, lords ; you see, I have given her physic.
                                    [*Pointing to the Nurse.*
And you must needs bestow her funeral ;
The fields are near, and you are gallant grooms.
This done, see that you take no longer days,
But send the midwife presently to me.
The midwife and the nurse well made away,
Then let the ladies tattle what they please.
Chi. Aaron, I see thou wilt not trust the air   170
With secrets.
Dem.   For this care of Tamora,
Herself and hers are highly bound to thee.
    [*Exeunt* DEMETRIUS *and* CHIRON, *bearing off the
        dead Nurse.*
Aar. Now to the Goths, as swift as swallow flies ;
There to dispose this treasure in mine arms,
And secretly to greet the empress' friends.—
Come on, you thick-lipp'd slave, I'll bear you hence ;
For it is you that puts us to our shifts :
I'll make you feed on berries and on roots,
And feed on curds and whey, and suck the goat,
And cabin in a cave, and bring you up   180
To be a warrior, and command a camp.
                                    [*Exit, with the Child.*

SCENE III.—The Same.   A public Place.

Enter TITUS, *bearing arrows, with letters on the ends
    of them ; with him* MARCUS, *young* LUCIUS, *and
    other Gentlemen, with bows.*

Tit. Come, Marcus, come ;—kinsmen, this is the
    way.—
Sir boy, now let me see your archery :
Look ye draw home enough, and 'tis there straight.
Terras Astræa reliquit :
Be you remember'd, Marcus, she's gone, she's fled.
Sirs, take you to your tools.   You, cousins, shall

Tit. "Sirs, take you to your tools."

Go sound the ocean, and cast your nets ;
Happily you may find her in the sea ;
Yet there's as little justice as at land.—
No ; Publius and Sempronius, you must do it ;   10
'Tis you must dig with mattock, and with spade,

And pierce the inmost centre of the earth :
Then, when you come to Pluto's region,
I pray you, deliver him this petition ;
Tell him, it is for justice and for aid,
And that it comes from old Andronicus,
Shaken with sorrows in ungrateful Rome.—
Ah, Rome !—Well, well ; I made thee miserable,
What time I threw the people's suffrages
On him that thus doth tyrannise o'er me.—   20
Go, get you gone ; and pray be careful all,
And leave you not a man-of-war unsearch'd :
This wicked emperor may have shipp'd her hence ;
And, kinsmen, then we may go pipe for justice.
    Marc. O Publius ! is not this a heavy case,
To see thy noble uncle thus distract ?
    Pub. Therefore, my lord, it highly us concerns,
By day and night to attend him carefully ;
And feed his humour kindly as we may,
Till time beget some careful remedy.   30
    Marc. Kinsmen, his sorrows are past remedy.
Join with the Goths, and with revengeful war
Take wreak on Rome for this ingratitude,
And vengeance on the traitor Saturnine.
    Tit. Publius, how now ? how now, my masters ?
What, have you met with her ?
    Pub. No, my good lord ; but Pluto sends you word,
If you will have Revenge from hell, you shall :
Marry, for Justice, she is so employ'd,
He thinks, with Jove in heaven, or somewhere else, 40
So that perforce you must needs stay a time.
    Tit. He doth me wrong to feed me with delays.
I 'll dive into the burning lake below,
And pull her out of Acheron by the heels.—
Marcus, we are but shrubs, no cedars we ;
No big-bon'd men, fram'd of the Cyclops' size,
But metal, Marcus, steel to the very back ;
Yet wrung with wrongs, more than our backs can bear :
And sith there is no justice in earth nor hell,
We will solicit heaven, and move the gods,   50
To send down Justice for to wreak our wrongs.
Come, to this gear. You are a good archer, Marcus.
           [*He gives them the arrows.*
Ad Jovem, that 's for you :—here, *ad Apollinem* :—
Ad Martem, that 's for myself :—
Here, boy, to Pallas :—here, to Mercury :
To Saturn, Caius, not to Saturnine ;
You were as good to shoot against the wind.—
To it, boy ; Marcus, loose when I bid.
Of my word, I have written to effect ;
There 's not a god left unsolicited.   60
    Marc. Kinsmen, shoot all your shafts into the court :
We will afflict the emperor in his pride.
    Tit. Now, masters, draw. [*They shoot.*] O, well said, Lucius !
Good boy, in Virgo's lap : give it Pallas.
    Marc. My lord, I aim a mile beyond the moon :
Your letter is with Jupiter by this.
    Tit. Ha ! Publius, Publius, what hast thou done ?
See, see ! thou hast shot off one of Taurus' horns.
    Marc. This was the sport, my lord : when Publius shot,
The Bull, being gall'd, gave Aries such a knock,   70
That down fell both the Ram's horns in the court ;
And who should find them but the empress' villain ?
She laugh'd, and told the Moor he should not choose
But give them to his master for a present.
    Tit. Why, there it goes : God give his lordship joy !

   Enter the Clown, with a basket and two pigeons in it.
News ! news from heaven ! Marcus, the post is come.
Sirrah, what tidings ? have you any letters ?
Shall I have justice ? what says Jupiter ?
    Clo. Ho ! the gibbet-maker ? he says that he hath taken them down again, for the man must not be hanged till the next week.   81
    Tit. But what says Jupiter, I ask thee ?
    Clo. Alas, sir ! I know not Jupiter : I never drank with him in all my life.

    Tit. Why, villain, art not thou the carrier ?
    Clo. Ay, of my pigeons, sir ; nothing else.
    Tit. Why, didst thou not come from heaven ?
    Clo. From heaven ? alas, sir ! I never came there. God forbid, I should be so bold to press to heaven in my young days. Why, I am going with my pigeons to the tribunal plebs, to take up a matter of brawl betwixt my uncle and one of the emperial's men.   92
    Marc. Why, sir, that is as fit as can be, to serve for your oration ; and let him deliver the pigeons to the emperor from you.
    Tit. Tell me, can you deliver an oration to the emperor with a grace ?
    Clo. Nay, truly, sir, I could never say grace in all my life.
    Tit. Sirrah, come hither. Make no more ado,   100
But give your pigeons to the emperor :
By me thou shalt have justice at his hands.
Hold, hold meanwhile, here 's money for thy charges.
Give me pen and ink.—
Sirrah, can you with a grace deliver a supplication ?
    Clo. Ay, sir.
    Tit. Then here is a supplication for you. And when you come to him, at the first approach you must kneel ; then kiss his foot ; then deliver up your pigeons ; and then look for your reward. I 'll be at hand, sir ; see you do it bravely.   111
    Clo. I warrant you, sir ; let me alone.
    Tit. Sirrah, hast thou a knife ? Come, let me see it.—
Here, Marcus, fold it in the oration ;
For thou hast made it like an humble suppliant :—
And when thou hast given it to the emperor,
Knock at my door, and tell me what he says.
    Clo. God be with you, sir ; I will.
    Tit. Come, Marcus, let us go.—Publius, follow me.
                                [*Exeunt.*

        SCENE IV.—The Same. Before the Palace.

Enter SATURNINUS, TAMORA, DEMETRIUS, CHIRON, *Lords, and others :* SATURNINUS *with the arrows in his hand that* TITUS *shot.*
    Sat. Why, lords, what wrongs are these ? Was ever seen
An emperor in Rome thus overborne,
Troubled, confronted thus ; and, for the extent
Of egal justice, us'd in such contempt ?
My lords, you know, as do the mightful gods,
(However these disturbers of our peace
Buz in the people's ears) there nought hath pass'd,
But even with law, against the wilful sons
Of old Andronicus. And what an if
His sorrows have so overwhelm'd his wits,   10
Shall we be thus afflicted in his wreaks,
His fits, his frenzy, and his bitterness ?
And now he writes to heaven for his redress :
See, here 's to Jove, and this to Mercury ;
This to Apollo ; this to the god of war ;
Sweet scrolls to fly about the streets of Rome !
What 's this but libelling against the senate,
And blazoning our injustice every where ?
A goodly humour, is it not, my lords ?
As who would say, in Rome no justice were.   20
But if I live, his feigned ecstacies
Shall be no shelter to these outrages ;
But he and his shall know, that justice lives
In Saturninus' health ; whom, if he sleep,
He 'll so awake, as he in fury shall
Cut off the proud'st conspirator that lives.
    Tam. My gracious lord, my lovely Saturnine,
Lord of my life, commander of my thoughts,
Calm thee, and bear the faults of Titus' age,
The effects of sorrow for his valiant sons,   30
Whose loss hath pierc'd him deep, and scarr'd his heart ;
And rather comfort his distressed plight,
Than prosecute the meanest, or the best,
For these contempts. [*Aside.*] Why, thus it shall become
High-witted Tamora to gloze with all :
But, Titus, I have touch'd thee to the quick,

Thy life-blood out. If Aaron now be wise,
Then is all safe, the anchor's in the port.—

Enter Clown.

How now, good fellow! wouldst thou speak with us?
  Clo. Yes, forsooth, an your mistership be imperial. 40
  Tam. Empress I am, but yonder sits the emperor.
  Clo. 'T is he.—God and Saint Stephen give you good
den. I have brought you a letter, and a couple of
pigeons here.   [SATURNINUS *reads the letter.*
  Sat. Go, take him away, and hang him presently.
  Clo. How much money must I have?
  Tam. Come, sirrah; you must be hang'd.
  Clo. Hang'd! By 'r lady, then I have brought up a
neck to a fair end.   [*Exit, guarded.*
  Sat. Despiteful and intolerable wrongs!   50
Shall I endure this monstrous villainy?
I know from whence this same device proceeds.
May this be borne?—As if his traitorous sons,
That died by law for murder of our brother,
Have by my means been butcher'd wrongfully!—
Go, drag the villain hither by the hair:
Nor age, nor honour, shall shape privilege.—
For this proud mock I 'll be thy slaughterman;
Sly frantic wretch, that holpst to make me great,
In hope thyself should govern Rome and me.   60

Enter ÆMILIUS.

What news with thee, Æmilius?
  Æmil. Arm, my lords! Rome never had more
cause.
The Goths have gather'd head, and with a power
Of high-resolved men, bent to the spoil,
They hither march amain, under conduct
Of Lucius, son to old Andronicus:
Who threats, in course of this revenge, to do
As much as ever Coriolanus did.
  Sat. Is warlike Lucius general of the Goths?
These tidings nip me; and I hang the head   70
As flowers with frost, or grass beat down with storms.
Ay, now begin our sorrows to approach.
'T is he the common people love so much:

Myself hath often heard them say,
When I have walked like a private man,
That Lucius' banishment was wrongfully,
And they have wish'd that Lucius were their emperor.
  Tam. Why should you fear? is not our city strong?
  Sat. Ay, but the citizens favour Lucius,
And will revolt from me to succour him.   80
  Tam. King, be thy thoughts imperious, like thy
name.
Is the sun dimm'd, that gnats do fly in it?
The eagle suffers little birds to sing,
And is not careful what they mean thereby;
Knowing that with the shadow of his wings
He can at pleasure stint their melody.
Even so may'st thou the giddy men of Rome.
Then cheer thy spirit; for know, thou emperor,
I will enchant the old Andronicus,
With words more sweet, and yet more dangerous,   90
Than baits to fish, or honey-stalks to sheep,
Whenas the one is wounded with the bait,
The other rotted with delicious feed.
  Sat. But he will not entreat his son for us.
  Tam. If Tamora entreat him, then he will;
For I can smooth and fill his aged ear
With golden promises, that, were his heart
Almost impregnable, his old ears deaf,
Yet should both ear and heart obey my tongue.—
[*To* ÆMILIUS.] Go thou before, be our ambassador: 100
Say that the emperor requests a parley
Of warlike Lucius, and appoint the meeting,
Even at his father's house, the old Andronicus.
  Sat. Æmilius, do this message honourably:
And if he stand on hostage for his safety,
Bid him demand what pledge will please him best.
  Æmil. Your bidding shall I do effectually.   [*Exit.*
  Tam. Now will I to that old Andronicus,
And temper him with all the art I have,
To pluck proud Lucius from the warlike Goths.   110
And now, sweet emperor, be blithe again,
And bury all thy fear in my devices.
  Sat. Then go successantly, and plead to him.
    [*Exeunt.*

ACT V.

SCENE I.—Plains near Rome.

Enter LUCIUS, *and an army of Goths, with drum and colours.*

  Lucius.
APPROVED warriors, and my faithful
    friends,
I have received letters from great
    Rome,
Which signify what hate they bear
    their emperor,
And how desirous of our sight they are.
Therefore, great lords, be, as your
    titles witness,
Imperious, and impatient of your
    wrongs;
And wherein Rome hath done you any
    scath,
Let them make treble satisfaction.
  1 Goth. Brave slip, sprung from the
    great Andronicus,
Whose name was once our terror, now
    our comfort;   10
Whose high exploits, and honourable deeds,
Ingrateful Rome requites with foul contempt,

Be bold in us: we 'll follow where thou lead'st,
Like stinging bees in hottest summer's day,
Led by their master to the flower'd fields,
And be aveng'd on cursed Tamora.
  Goths. And, as he saith, so say we all with him.
  Luc. I humbly thank him, and I thank you all.
But who comes here, led by a lusty Goth?

Enter a Goth, leading AARON, *with his Child in
his arms.*

  2 Goth. Renowned Lucius, from our troops I
    stray'd,   20
To gaze upon a ruinous monastery;
And as I earnestly did fix mine eye
Upon the wasted building, suddenly
I heard a child cry underneath a wall.
I made unto the noise; when soon I heard
The crying babe controll'd with this discourse:—
"Peace, tawny slave, half me, and half thy dam!
Did not thy hue bewray whose brat thou art,
Had nature lent thee but thy mother's look,

Villain, thou mightst have been an emperor : 30
But where the bull and cow are both milk-white,
They never do beget a coal-black calf.
Peace, villain, peace!" — even thus he rates the
    babe,—
"For I must bear thee to a trusty Goth ;
Who, when he knows thou art the empress' babe,
Will hold thee dearly for thy mother's sake."
With this, my weapon drawn, I rush'd upon him,
Surpris'd him suddenly, and brought him hither,
To use as you think needful of the man.
 Luc. O worthy Goth, this is the incarnate devil, 40
That robb'd Andronicus of his good hand :
This is the pearl that pleas'd your empress' eye,
And here 's the base fruit of his burning lust.—
Say, wall-ey'd slave, whither wouldst thou convey
This growing image of thy fiend-like face?
Why dost not speak ? What ! deaf ? not a word ?
A halter, soldiers ! hang him on this tree,
And by his side his fruit of bastardy.

2 *Goth.* " With this, my weapon drawn, I rush'd upon him."

 Aar. Touch not the boy ; he is of royal blood.
 Luc. Too like the sire for ever being good.— 50
First hang the child, that he may see it sprawl ;
A sight to vex the father's soul withal.
Get me a ladder ! [*A ladder brought, which* AARON
    is made to ascend.
 Aar. Lucius, save the child ;
And bear it from me to the empress.
If thou do this, I 'll show thee wondrous things,
That highly may advantage thee to hear :
If thou wilt not, befall what may befall,
I 'll speak no more ; but vengeance rot you all !
 Luc. Say on ; an if it please me which thou
    speak'st,
Thy child shall live, and I will see it nourish'd. 60
 Aar. An if it please thee? why, assure thee,
    Lucius,
'T will vex thy soul to hear what I shall speak :
For I must talk of murders, rapes, and massacres,
Acts of black night, abominable deeds,
Complots of mischief, treason, villainies
Ruthful to hear, yet piteously perform'd :
And this shall all be buried in my death,
Unless thou swear to me, my child shall live.
 Luc. Tell on thy mind : I say, thy child shall live.
 Aar. Swear that he shall, and then I will begin. 70
 Luc. Who should I swear by ? thou believ'st no
    god :
That granted, how canst thou believe an oath ?

 Aar. What if I do not ? as, indeed, I do not ;
Yet, for I know thou art religious,
And hast a thing within thee, called conscience,
With twenty popish tricks and ceremonies,
Which I have seen thee careful to observe,
Therefore I urge thy oath :—for that I know
An idiot holds his bauble for a god,
And keeps the oath which by that god he swears, 80
To that I 'll urge him :—therefore, thou shalt vow
By that same god, what god soe'er it be,
That thou ador'st and hast in reverence,
To save my boy, to nourish, and bring him up ;
Or else I will discover nought to thee.
 Luc. Even by my god I swear to thee I will.
 Aar. First know thou, I begot him on the empress.
 Luc. O most insatiate and luxurious woman !
 Aar. Tut! Lucius, this was but a deed of charity,
To that which thou shalt hear of me anon. 90
'T was her two sons that murder'd Bassianus :
They cut thy sister's tongue, and ravish'd her,
And cut her hands, and trimm'd her as thou saw'st.
 Luc. O detestable villain ! call'st thou that trimming?
 Aar. Why, she was wash'd, and cut, and trimm'd,
    and 't was
Trim sport for them that had the doing of it.
 Luc. O barbarous, beastly villains, like thyself !
 Aar. Indeed, I was their tutor to instruct them.
That codding spirit had they from their mother,
As sure a card as ever won the set ; 100
That bloody mind, I think, they learn'd of me,
As true a dog as ever fought at head.
Well, let my deeds be witness of my worth.
I train'd thy brethren to that guileful hole,
Where the dead corse of Bassianus lay ;
I wrote the letter that thy father found,
And hid the gold within the letter mention'd,
Confederate with the queen and her two sons ;
And what not done, that thou hast cause to rue,
Wherein I had no stroke of mischief in it ? 110
I play'd the cheater for thy father's hand,
And, when I had it, drew myself apart,
And almost broke my heart with extreme laughter.
I pry'd me through the crevice of a wall,
When, for his hand, he had his two sons' heads ;
Beheld his tears, and laugh'd so heartily,
That both mine eyes were rainy like to his :
And when I told the empress of this sport,
She swounded almost at my pleasing tale,
And for my tidings gave me twenty kisses. 120
 Goth. What! canst thou say all this, and never
    blush?
 Aar. Ay, like a black dog, as the saying is.
 Luc. Art thou not sorry for these heinous deeds ?
 Aar. Ay, that I had not done a thousand more.
Even now I curse the day (and yet, I think,
Few come within the compass of my curse),
Wherein I did not some notorious ill :
As kill a man, or else devise his death ;
Ravish a maid, or plot the way to do it ;
Accuse some innocent, and forswear myself ; 130
Set deadly enmity between two friends ;
Make poor men's cattle break their necks ;
Set fire on barns and hay-stacks in the night,
And bid the owners quench them with their tears.
Oft have I digg'd up dead men from their graves,
And set them upright at their dear friends' doors,
Even when their sorrows almost were forgot ;
And on their skins, as on the bark of trees,
Have with my knife carved in Roman letters,
"Let not your sorrow die, though I am dead." 140
Tut ! I have done a thousand dreadful things,
As willingly as one would kill a fly ;
And nothing grieves me heartily indeed,
But that I cannot do ten thousand more.
 Luc. Bring down the devil, for he must not die
So sweet a death as hanging presently.
 Aar. If there be devils, 'would I were a devil,
To live and burn in everlasting fire ;
So I might have your company in hell,
But to torment you with my bitter tongue ! 150
 Luc. Sirs, stop his mouth, and let him speak no
    more.

Enter a Goth.

Goth. My lord, there is a messenger from Rome,
Desires to be admitted to your presence.
Luc. Let him come near.

Enter ÆMILIUS.

Welcome, Æmilius! what's the news from Rome?
Æmil. Lord Lucius, and you princes of the Goths,
The Roman emperor greets you all by me:
And, for he understands you are in arms,
He craves a parley at your father's house,
Willing you to demand your hostages,   160
And they shall be immediately deliver'd.
1 *Goth.* What says our general?
Luc. Æmilius, let the emperor give his pledges
Unto my father and my uncle Marcus,
And we will come.—March away.   [*Exeunt.*

SCENE II.—Rome.   Before TITUS'S House.

Enter TAMORA, DEMETRIUS, *and* CHIRON, *disguised.*

Tam. Thus in this strange and sad habiliment
I will encounter with Andronicus,
And say I am Revenge, sent from below,
To join with him and right his heinous wrongs.—
Knock at his study, where they say he keeps,
To ruminate strange plots of dire revenge:
Tell him, Revenge is come to join with him,
And work confusion on his enemies.   [*They knock.*

TITUS *opens his study door.*

Tit. Who doth molest my contemplation?
Is it your trick, to make me ope the door,   10
That so my sad decrees may fly away,
And all my study be to no effect?
You are deceiv'd: for what I mean to do,
See here, in bloody lines I have set down;
And what is written shall be executed.
Tam. Titus, I am come to talk with thee.
Tit. No, not a word: how can I grace my talk,
Wanting a hand to give it action?
Thou hast the odds of me, therefore no more.
Tam. If thou didst know me, thou wouldst talk
   with me.   20
Tit. I am not mad; I know thee well enough:
Witness this wretched stump, witness these crimson
   lines;
Witness these trenches made by grief and care;
Witness the tiring day and heavy night;
Witness all sorrow, that I know thee well
For our proud empress, mighty Tamora.
Is not thy coming for my other hand?
Tam. Know, thou sad man, I am not Tamora:
She is thy enemy, and I thy friend.
I am Revenge, sent from the infernal kingdom,   30
To ease the gnawing vulture of thy mind,
By working wreakful vengeance on thy foes.
Come down, and welcome me to this world's light;
Confer with me of murder and of death.
There's not a hollow cave or lurking-place,
No vast obscurity or misty vale,
Where bloody murder, or detested rape,
Can couch for fear, but I will find them out;
And in their ears tell them my dreadful name,
Revenge, which makes the foul offender quake.   40
Tit. Art thou Revenge? and art thou sent to me,
To be a torment to mine enemies?
Tam. I am; therefore come down, and welcome me.
Tit. Do me some service, ere I come to thee.
Lo, by thy side where Rape, and Murder, stands;
Now give some 'surance that thou art Revenge,
Stab them, or tear them on thy chariot-wheels,
And then I'll come and be thy waggoner,
And whirl along with thee about the globes.
Provide thee two proper palfreys, black as jet,   50
To hale thy vengeful waggon swift away,
And find out murderers in their guilty caves:
And when thy car is loaden with their heads,
I will dismount, and by the waggon-wheel
Trot like a servile footman all day long,
Even from Hyperion's rising in the east

Until his very downfall in the sea:
And day by day I'll do this heavy task,
So thou destroy Rapine and Murder there.
Tam. These are my ministers, and come with me.   60
Tit. Are these thy ministers? what are they call'd?
Tam. Rapine and Murder; therefore called so,
'Cause they take vengeance of such kind of men.
Tit. Good Lord, how like the empress' sons they are,
And you the empress! but we worldly men
Have miserable, mad-mistaking eyes.
O sweet Revenge! now do I come to thee;
And, if one arm's embracement will content thee,
I will embrace thee in it by and by.   [*Exit.*
Tam. This closing with him fits his lunacy.   70
Whate'er I forge to feed his brain-sick fits,
Do you uphold and maintain in your speeches,
For now he firmly takes me for Revenge;
And, being credulous in this mad thought,
I'll make him send for Lucius, his son;
And, whilst I at a banquet hold him sure,
I'll find some cunning practice out of hand
To scatter and disperse the giddy Goths,
Or, at the least, make them his enemies.
See, here he comes, and I must ply my theme.   80

Enter TITUS.

Tit. Long have I been forlorn, and all for thee.
Welcome, dread Fury, to my woful house.—
Rapine and Murder, you are welcome too.—
How like the empress and her sons you are!
Well are you fitted, had you but a Moor:—
Could not all hell afford you such a devil?
For, well I wot, the empress never wags,
But in her company there is a Moor;
And would you represent our queen aright,
It were convenient you had such a devil.   90
But welcome as you are. What shall we do?
Tam. What wouldst thou have us do, Andronicus?
Dem. Show me a murderer, I'll deal with him.
Chi. Show me a villain that hath done a rape,
And I am sent to be reveng'd on him.
Tam. Show me a thousand that have done thee
   wrong,
And I will be revenged on them all.
Tit. Look round about the wicked streets of Rome,
And when thou find'st a man that's like thyself,
Good Murder, stab him: he's a murderer.—   100
Go thou with him; and when it is thy hap
To find another that is like to thee,
Good Rapine, stab him: he's a ravisher.—
Go thou with them; and in the emperor's court
There is a queen attended by a Moor:
Well may'st thou know her by thine own proportion,
For up and down she doth resemble thee.
I pray thee, do on them some violent death;
They have been violent to me and mine.
Tam. Well hast thou lesson'd us: this shall we do.
But would it please thee, good Andronicus,   111
To send for Lucius, thy thrice-valiant son,
Who leads towards Rome a band of warlike Goths,
And bid him come and banquet at thy house:
When he is here, even at thy solemn feast,
I will bring in the empress and her sons,
The emperor himself, and all thy foes,
And at thy mercy shall they stoop and kneel,
And on them shalt thou ease thy angry heart.   120
What says Andronicus to this device?
Tit. Marcus, my brother!—'t is sad Titus calls.

Enter MARCUS.

Go, gentle Marcus, to thy nephew Lucius;
Thou shalt inquire him out among the Goths:
Bid him repair to me, and bring with him
Some of the chiefest princes of the Goths;
Bid him encamp his soldiers where they are.
Tell him, the emperor, and the empress too,
Feast at my house, and he shall feast with them.
This do thou for my love, and so let him,
As he regards his aged father's life.   130
Marc. This will I do, and soon return again. [*Exit.*
Tam. Now will I hence about thy business,
And take my ministers along with me.

Tit. Nay, nay, let Rape and Murder stay with me,
Or else I 'll call my brother back again,
And cleave to no revenge but Lucius.
Tam. [*Aside to them.*] What say you, boys? will you
    abide with him,
Whiles I go tell my lord the emperor,
How I have govern'd our determin'd jest?
Yield to his humour, smooth and speak him fair, 140
And tarry with him, till I turn again.
Tit. [*Aside.*] I know them all, though they suppose
    me mad,
And will o'erreach them in their own devices,
A pair of cursed hell-hounds, and their dam.
Dem. Madam, depart at pleasure; leave us here.
Tam. Farewell, Andronicus: Revenge now goes
To lay a complot to betray thy foes.
Tit. I know thou dost; and, sweet Revenge, fare-
well.   [*Exit* TAMORA.
Chi. Tell us, old man, how shall we be employ'd?
Tit. Tut! I have work enough for you to do.— 150
Publius, come hither, Caius, and Valentine!

    Enter PUBLIUS, *and others.*

Pub. What is your will?
Tit. Know you these two?
Pub. The empress' sons
I take them, Chiron and Demetrius.
Tit. Fie, Publius, fie! thou art too much deceiv'd;
The one is Murder, Rape is the other's name;
And therefore bind them, gentle Publius;
Caius, and Valentine, lay hands on them.
Oft have you heard me wish for such an hour, 160
And now I find it: therefore, bind them sure,
And stop their mouths, let them begin to cry.
    [*Exit* TITUS.—PUBLIUS, *&c.*, seize CHIRON and
    DEMETRIUS.
Chi. Villains, forbear! we are the empress' sons.
Pub. And therefore do we what we are com-
manded.—
Stop close their mouths, let them not speak a word.
Is he sure bound? look that you bind them fast.

    Re-enter TITUS ANDRONICUS, *with* LAVINIA; *she
        bearing a basin, and he a knife.*

Tit. Come, come, Lavinia; look, thy foes are
bound.—
Sirs, stop their mouths; let them not speak to me,
But let them hear what fearful words I utter.—
O villains, Chiron and Demetrius! 170
Here stands the spring whom you have stain'd with
    mud;
This goodly summer with your winter mix'd.
You kill'd her husband, and for that vild fault
Two of her brothers were condemn'd to death,
My hand cut off, and made a merry jest:
Both her sweet hands, her tongue, and that more dear
Than hands or tongue, her spotless chastity,
Inhuman traitors, you constrain'd and forc'd.
What would you say, if I should let you speak?
Villains, for shame you could not beg for grace. 180
Hark, wretches, how I mean to martyr you.
This one hand yet is left to cut your throats,
Whilst that Lavinia 'tween her stumps doth hold
The basin that receives your guilty blood.
You know, your mother means to feast with me,
And calls herself Revenge, and thinks me mad.—
Hark, villains! I will grind your bones to dust,
And with your blood and it I 'll make a paste;
And of the paste a coffin I will rear,
And make two pasties of your shameful heads; 190
And bid that strumpet, your unhallow'd dam,
Like to the earth, swallow her own increase.
This is the feast that I have bid her to,
And this the banquet she shall surfeit on;
For worse than Philomel you us'd my daughter,
And worse than Progne I will be reveng'd.
And now prepare your throats.—Lavinia, come,
                        [*He cuts their throats.*
Receive the blood: and when that they are dead,
Let me go grind their bones to powder small,
And with this hateful liquor temper it; 200
And in that paste let their vild heads be bak'd.—

Come, come, be every one officious
To make this banquet, which I wish may prove
More stern and bloody than the Centaurs' feast.
So, now bring them in, for I will play the cook,
And see them ready 'gainst their mother comes.
            [*Exeunt, bearing the dead bodies.*

        SCENE III.—The Same. A Pavilion.

    Enter LUCIUS, MARCUS, *and Goths; with* AARON,
        prisoner.

Luc. Uncle Marcus, since 't is my father's mind,
That I repair to Rome, I am content.
1 Goth. And ours, with thine; befall what fortune
    will.
Luc. Good uncle, take you in this barbarous Moor,
This ravenous tiger, this accursed devil.
Let him receive no sustenance; fetter him,
Till he be brought unto the empress' face,
For testimony of her foul proceedings.
And see the ambush of our friends be strong:
I fear the emperor means no good to us. 10
Aar. Some devil whisper curses in mine ear,
And prompt me, that my tongue may utter forth
The venomous malice of my swelling heart!
Luc. Away, inhuman dog! unhallow'd slave!—
Sirs, help you uncle to convey him in.—
    [*Exeunt Goths, with* AARON. *Trumpets sound.*
The trumpets show the emperor is at hand.

    Enter SATURNINUS *and* TAMORA, *with Tribunes,
        and others.*

Sat. What! hath the firmament more suns than
    one?
Luc. What boots it thee to call thyself a sun?
Marc. Rome's emperor, and nephew, break the
    parle;
These quarrels must be quietly debated. 20
The feast is ready, which the careful Titus
Hath ordain'd to an honourable end,
For peace, for love, for league, and good to Rome:
Please you, therefore, draw nigh, and take your
    places.
Sat. Marcus, we will. [*Hautboys sound.*

Enter TITUS, *dressed like a cook,* LAVINIA, *veiled,
    young* LUCIUS, *and others.* TITUS *places the dishes
    on the table.*

Tit. Welcome, my gracious lord; welcome, dread
    queen;
Welcome, ye warlike Goths; welcome, Lucius;
And welcome, all. Although the cheer be poor,
'T will fill your stomachs; please you eat of it.
Sat. Why art thou thus attir'd, Andronicus? 30
Tit. Because I would be sure to have all well,
To entertain your highness, and your empress.
Tam. We are beholding to you, good Andronicus.
Tit. An if your highness knew my heart, you were.
My lord the emperor, resolve me this:
Was it well done of rash Virginius,
To slay his daughter with his own right hand,
Because she was enforc'd, stain'd, and deflour'd?
Sat. It was, Andronicus.
Tit. Your reason, mighty lord? 40
Sat. Because the girl should not survive her shame,
And by her presence still renew his sorrows.
Tit. A reason mighty, strong, and effectual;
A pattern, precedent, and lively warrant,
For me, most wretched, to perform the like.—
Die, die, Lavinia, and thy shame with thee;
And with thy shame thy father's sorrow die!
                        [*Kills* LAVINIA.
Sat. What hast thou done, unnatural and unkind?
Tit. Kill'd her, for whom my tears have made me
    blind.
I am as woful as Virginius was, 50
And have a thousand times more cause than he
To do this outrage:—and it is now done.
Sat. What, was she ravish'd? tell, who did the deed?
Tit. Will 't please you eat? will 't please your high-
ness feed?

Tam. Why hast thou slain thine only daughter thus?
Tit. Not I ; 't was Chiron, and Demetrius :
They ravish'd her, and cut away her tongue,
And they, 't was they, that did her all this wrong.
Sat. Go, fetch them hither to us presently.
Tit. Why, there they are both, baked in that pie ;   60
Whereof their mother daintily hath fed,
Eating the flesh that she herself hath bred.
'T is true, 't is true ; witness my knife's sharp point.
                                    [*Killing* TAMORA.
Sat. Die, frantic wretch, for this accursed deed !
                                    [*Killing* TITUS.
Luc. Can the son's eye behold his father bleed ?
There 's meed for meed, death for a deadly deed.
[*Killing* SATURNINUS. *A great tumult. The people
  in confusion disperse.* MARCUS, LUCIUS, *and
  their partisans, go up into the balcony.*
Marc. You sad-fac'd men, people and sons of Rome,
By uproar sever'd, like a flight of fowl
Scatter'd by winds and high tempestuous gusts,
O ! let me teach you how to knit again   70
This scatter'd corn into one mutual sheaf,
These broken limbs again into one body,
Lest Rome herself be bane unto herself ;
And she whom mighty kingdoms curtsy to,
Like a forlorn and desperate castaway,
Do shameful execution on herself.
But if my frosty signs and chaps of age,
Grave witnesses of true experience,
Cannot induce you to attend my words,—
[*To* LUCIUS.] Speak, Rome's dear friend, as erst our
                                    ancestor,   80
When with his solemn tongue he did discourse
To love-sick Dido's sad-attending ear
The story of that baleful burning night,
When subtle Greeks surpris'd King Priam's Troy,
Tell us, what Sinon hath bewitch'd our ears,
Or who hath brought the fatal engine in,
That gives our Troy, our Rome, the civil wound.—
My heart is not compact of flint nor steel,
Nor can I utter all our bitter grief ;
But floods of tears will drown my oratory,   90
And break my very utterance, even in the time
When it should move you to attend me most,
Lending your kind commiseration.
Here is a captain, let him tell the tale ;
Your hearts will throb and weep to hear him speak.
Luc. Then, noble auditory, be it known to you,
That cursed Chiron and Demetrius
Were they that murdered our emperor's brother ;
And they it was that ravished our sister.
For their fell faults our brothers were beheaded, 100
Our father's tears despis'd and basely cozen'd
Of that true hand that fought Rome's quarrel out,
And sent her enemies unto the grave :
Lastly, myself unkindly banished,
The gates shut on me, and turn'd weeping out,
To beg relief among Rome's enemies ;
Who drown'd their enmity in my tears,
And op'd their arms to embrace me as a friend :
I am the turn'd-forth, be it known to you,
That have preserv'd her welfare in my blood,   110
And from her bosom took the enemy's point,
Sheathing the steel in my adventurous body.
Alas ! you know, I am no vaunter, I ;
My scars can witness, dumb although they are,
That my report is just and full of truth.
But soft, methinks I do digress too much,
Citing my worthless praise. O ! pardon me ;
For, when no friends are by, men praise themselves.
Marc. Now is my turn to speak. Behold this child ;
Of this was Tamora delivered,   120
The issue of an irreligious Moor,
Chief architect and plotter of these woes.
The villain is alive in Titus' house,
Damn'd as he is, to witness this is true.
Now judge, what cause had Titus to revenge
These wrongs, unspeakable, past patience,
Or more than any living man could bear.
Now you have heard the truth, what say you,
                                    Romans ?
Have we done aught amiss ? Show us wherein,

And, from the place where you behold us now,   130
The poor remainder of Andronici
Will hand in hand all headlong cast us down,
And on the ragged stones beat forth our brains,
And make a mutual closure of our house.
Speak, Romans, speak ! and if you say we shall,
Lo ! hand in hand, Lucius and I will fall.
Æmil. Come, come, thou reverend man of Rome,
And bring our emperor gently in thy hand,
Lucius our emperor ; for well I know,
The common voice do cry, it shall be so.   140
Marc. Lucius, all hail ! Rome's royal emperor !—
[*To Attendants.*] Go, go into old Titus' sorrowful
                                    house,
And hither hale that misbelieving Moor,
To be adjudg'd some direful slaughtering death,
As punishment for his most wicked life.—

LUCIUS, &c., *descend.*

Lucius, all hail ! Rome's gracious governor !
Luc. Thanks, gentle Romans : may I govern so,
To heal Rome's harms, and wipe away her woe !
But, gentle people, give me aim a while,—
For nature puts me to a heavy task.—   150
Stand all aloof ;—but, uncle, draw you near,
To shed obsequious tears upon this trunk.—
O ! take this warm kiss on thy pale cold lips,
                                    [*Kisses* TITUS.
These sorrowful drops upon thy blood-stain'd face,
The last true duties of thy noble son !
Marc. Tear for tear, and loving kiss for kiss,
Thy brother Marcus tenders on thy lips :
O ! were the sum of these that I should pay
Countless and infinite, yet would I pay them.
Luc. Come hither, boy : come, come, and learn of us
To melt in showers. Thy grandsire lov'd thee well ;
Many a time he danc'd thee on his knee,   162
Sung thee asleep, his loving breast thy pillow ;
Many a matter hath he told to thee,
Meet and agreeing with thine infancy :
In that respect, then, like a loving child,
Shed yet some small drops from thy tender spring,
Because kind nature doth require it so :
Friends should associate friends in grief and woe.
Bid him farewell, commit him to the grave ;   170
Do him that kindness, and take leave of him.
Boy. O grandsire, grandsire ! even with all my
                                    heart
'Would I were dead, so you did live again.—
O Lord ! I cannot speak to him for weeping ;
My tears will choke me, if I ope my mouth.

Enter Attendants, with AARON.

1 *Rom.* You sad Andronici, have done with woes !
Give sentence on this execrable wretch,
That hath been breeder of these dire events.
Luc. Set him breast-deep in earth, and famish him ;
There let him stand, and rave, and cry for food : 180
If any one relieves or pities him,
For the offence he dies. This is our doom ;
Some stay to see him fasten'd in the earth.
Aar. O ! why should wrath be mute, and fury dumb ?
I am no baby, I, that with base prayers
I should repent the evils I have done.
Ten thousand worse than ever yet I did
Would I perform, if I might have my will :
If one good deed in all my life I did,
I do repent it from my very soul.   190
Luc. Some loving friends convey the emperor hence,
And give him burial in his father's grave.
My father, and Lavinia, shall forthwith
Be closed in our household's monument.
As for that heinous tiger, Tamora,
No funeral rite, nor man in mournful weeds,
No mournful bell shall ring her burial ;
But throw her forth to beasts, and birds of prey :
Her life was beast-like, and devoid of pity,
And, being so, shall have like want of pity.   200
See justice done on Aaron, that damn'd Moor,
By whom our heavy haps had their beginning :
Then, afterwards, to order well the state,
That like events may ne'er it ruinate.   [*Exeunt.*

ROMEO AND JULIET.

DRAMATIS PERSONÆ.

ESCALUS, *Prince of Verona.*
PARIS, *a young Nobleman, Kinsman to the Prince.*
MONTAGUE, } *Heads of two Houses, at variance*
CAPULET, } *with each other.*
Uncle to Capulet.
ROMEO, *Son to Montague.*
MERCUTIO, *Kinsman to the Prince, and Friend to Romeo.*
BENVOLIO, *Nephew to Montague, and Friend to Romeo.*
TYBALT, *Nephew to Lady Capulet.*
FRIAR LAURENCE, *a Franciscan.*
FRIAR JOHN, *of the same Order.*
BALTHASAR, *Servant to Romeo.*
SAMPSON, } *Servants to Capulet.*
GREGORY, }

PETER, *another Servant to Capulet.*
ABRAM, *Servant to Montague.*
An Apothecary.
Three Musicians.
Chorus.
Boy ; Page to Paris; an Officer.

LADY MONTAGUE, *Wife to Montague.*
LADY CAPULET, *Wife to Capulet.*
JULIET, *Daughter to Capulet.*
Nurse to Juliet.

Citizens of Verona ; male and female Relations to both Houses; Maskers, Guards, Watchmen, and Attendants.

SCENE—During the greater part of the Play, in VERONA : once, in the Fifth Act, at MANTUA.

PROLOGUE.

Enter Chorus.

Two households, both alike in dignity,
 In fair Verona, where we lay our scene,
From ancient grudge break to new mutiny,
 Where civil blood makes civil hands unclean.
From forth the fatal loins of these two foes
 A pair of star-cross'd lovers take their life ;
Whose misadventur'd piteous overthrows
Do with their death bury their parents' strife.
The fearful passage of their death-mark'd love,
 And the continuance of their parents' rage,   10
Which, but their children's end, nought could remove,
 Is now the two hours' traffic of our stage ;
The which if you with patient ears attend,
What here shall miss, our toil shall strive to mend.
[*Exit.*

ACT I.

SCENE I.—A Public Place.

Enter SAMPSON *and* GREGORY, *armed with swords and bucklers.*

Sampson.
GREGORY, on my word, we'll not carry coals.
 Gre. No, for then we should be colliers.
 Sam. I mean, an we be in choler, we'll draw.
 Gre. Ay, while you live, draw your neck out o' the collar.
 Sam. I strike quickly, being moved.
 Gre. But thou art not quickly moved to strike.   10
 Sam. A dog of the house of Montague moves me.
 Gre. To move is to stir, and to be valiant is to stand ; therefore, if thou art moved, thou runn'st away.
 Sam. A dog of that house shall move me to stand. I will take the wall of any man or maid of Montague's.
 Gre. That shows thee a weak slave ; for the weakest goes to the wall.   20
 Sam. 'T is true ; and therefore women, being the weaker vessels, are ever thrust to the wall :—there-fore I will push Montague's men from the wall, and thrust his maids to the wall.
 Gre. The quarrel is between our masters, and us their men.
 Sam. 'T is all one, I will show myself a tyrant : when I have fought with the men, I will be cruel with the maids ; I will cut off their heads.
 Gre. The heads of the maids ?   30
 Sam. Ay, the heads of the maids, or their maiden-heads ; take it in what sense thou wilt.
 Gre. They must take it in sense, that feel it.
 Sam. Me they shall feel, while I am able to stand ; and, 't is known, I am a pretty piece of flesh.
 Gre. 'T is well, thou art not fish ; if thou hadst, thou hadst been poor John.   Draw thy tool ; here comes of the house of the Montagues.

Enter ABRAM *and* BALTHASAR.

 Sam. My naked weapon is out : quarrel, I will back thee.   40
 Gre. How ! turn thy back, and run ?
 Sam. Fear me not.
 Gre. No, marry : I fear thee !

Sam. Let us take the law of our sides : let them begin.

Gre. I will frown as I pass by, and let them take it as they list.

Sam. Nay, as they dare. I will bite my thumb at them ; which is a disgrace to them, if they bear it.

Abr. Do you bite your thumb at us, sir ?　　　50

Sam. I do bite my thumb, sir.

Abr. Do you bite your thumb at us, sir ?

Sam. Is the law of our side, if I say ay ?

Gre. No.

Sam. No, sir, I do not bite my thumb at you, sir ; but I bite my thumb, sir.

Sam.　My naked weapon is out : quarrel, I will back thee."

Gre. Do you quarrel, sir ?

Abr. Quarrel, sir ? no, sir.

Sam. If you do, sir, I am for you : I serve as good a man as you.　　　60

Abr. No better.

Sam. Well, sir.

Enter BENVOLIO, *at a distance.*

Gre. Say—better : here comes one of my master's kinsmen.

Sam. Yes, better, sir.

Abr. You lie.

Sam. Draw, if you be men.—Gregory, remember thy swashing blow.　　　[*They fight.*

Ben. Part, fools ! put up your swords ; you know not what you do.　　　70

[*Beats down their swords.*

Enter TYBALT.

Tyb. What ! art thou drawn among these heartless hinds ?

Turn thee, Benvolio ; look upon thy death.

Ben. I do but keep the peace : put up thy sword, Or manage it to part these men with me.

Tyb. What ! drawn, and talk of peace ? I hate the word,

As I hate hell, all Montagues, and thee.

Have at thee, coward.　　　[*They fight.*

Enter several persons of both Houses, who join the fray ; then enter Citizens, with clubs.

1 *Cit.* Clubs, bills, and partisans ! strike ! beat them down !

Down with the Capulets ! down with the Montagues !

Enter CAPULET, *in his gown ; and Lady* CAPULET.

Cap. What noise is this ?—Give me my long sword, ho !　　　80

La. Cap. A crutch, a crutch !—Why call you for a sword ?

Cap. My sword, I say !—Old Montague is come, And flourishes his blade in spite of me.

Enter MONTAGUE *and Lady* MONTAGUE.

Mon. Thou villain Capulet !—Hold me not ; let me go.

La. Mon. Thou shalt not stir a foot to seek a foe.

Enter PRINCE, *with his Train.*

Prin. Rebellious subjects, enemies to peace, Profaners of this neighbour-stained steel,— Will they not hear ?—what ho ! you men, you beasts, That quench the fire of your pernicious rage With purple fountains issuing from your veins,—　90 On pain of torture, from those bloody hands Throw your mistemper'd weapons to the ground, And hear the sentence of your moved prince.— Three civil brawls, bred of an airy word, By thee, old Capulet, and Montague, Have thrice disturb'd the quiet of our streets ; And made Verona's ancient citizens Cast by their grave beseeming ornaments, To wield old partisans, in hands as old, Canker'd with peace, to part your canker'd hate.　100 If ever you disturb our streets again, Your lives shall pay the forfeit of the peace. For this time, all the rest depart away : You, Capulet, shall go along with me ; And, Montague, come you this afternoon, To know our further pleasure in this case, To old Free-town, our common judgment-place. One more, on pain of death, all men depart.

[*Exeunt* PRINCE, *and Attendants ;* CAPULET, *Lady* CAPULET, TYBALT, *Citizens, and Servants.*

Mon. Who set this ancient quarrel new abroach ?— Speak, nephew, were you by, when it began ?　110

Ben. Here were the servants of your adversary, And yours, close fighting ere I did approach. I drew to part them ; in the instant came The fiery Tybalt, with his sword prepar'd ; Which, as he breath'd defiance to my ears, He swung about his head, and cut the winds, Who, nothing hurt withal, hiss'd him in scorn. While we were interchanging thrusts and blows, Came more and more, and fought on part and part, Till the prince came, who parted either part.　120

La. Mon. O ! where is Romeo ? saw you him to-day ? Right glad I am he was not at this fray.

Ben. Madam, an hour before the worshipp'd sun Peer'd forth the golden window of the east, A troubled mind drave me to walk abroad ; Where, underneath the grove of sycamore, That westward rooteth from the city's side, So early walking did I see your son. Towards him I made ; but he was 'ware of me, And stole into the covert of the wood :　130 I, measuring his affections by my own, Which then most sought, where most might not be found,

Being one too many by my weary self, Pursu'd my humour, not pursuing his, And gladly shunn'd who gladly fled from me.

Mon. Many a morning hath he there been seen, With tears augmenting the fresh morning's dew, Adding to clouds more clouds with his deep sighs : But all so soon as the all-cheering sun Should in the farthest east begin to draw　140

The shady curtains from Aurora's bed,
Away from light steals home my heavy son,
And private in his chamber pens himself;
Shuts up his windows, locks fair daylight out,
And makes himself an artificial night.
Black and portentous must this humour prove,
Unless good counsel may the cause remove.
  Ben. My noble uncle, do you know the cause?
  Mon. I neither know it, nor can learn of him.
  Ben. Have you importun'd him by any means? 150
  Mon. Both by myself, and many other friends:
But he, his own affections' counsellor,
Is to himself—I will not say, how true—
But to himself so secret and so close,
So far from sounding and discovery,
As is the bud bit with an envious worm,
Ere he can spread his sweet leaves to the air,
Or dedicate his beauty to the sun.
Could we but learn from whence his sorrows grow,
We would as willingly give cure, as know.   160

          Enter ROMEO, *at a distance.*

  Ben. See, where he comes: so please you, step
          aside;
I'll know his grievance, or be much denied.
  Mon. I would thou wert so happy by thy stay,
To hear true shrift.—Come, madam, let's away.
          [*Exeunt* MONTAGUE *and Lady.*
  Ben. Good morrow, cousin.
  Rom.   Is the day so young?
  Ben. But new struck nine.
  Rom.   Ah me! sad hours seem long.
Was that my father that went hence so fast?
  Ben. It was. What sadness lengthens Romeo's
          hours?
  Rom. Not having that, which, having, makes them
          short.
  Ben. In love?   170
  Rom. Out—
  Ben. Of love?
  Rom. Out of her favour, where I am in love.
  Ben. Alas, that love, so gentle in his view,
Should be so tyrannous and rough in proof!
  Rom. Alas, that love, whose view is muffled still,
Should without eyes see pathways to his will!
Where shall we dine?—O me!—What fray was here?
Yet tell me not, for I have heard it all.
Here's much to do with hate, but more with love:—
Why then, O brawling love! O loving hate!   181
O anything, of nothing first created!
O heavy lightness! serious vanity!
Misshapen chaos of well-seeming forms!
Feather of lead, bright smoke, cold fire, sick health!
Still-waking sleep, that is not what it is!
This love feel I, that feel no love in this.
Dost thou not laugh?
  Ben.   No, coz, I rather weep.
  Rom. Good heart, at what?
  Ben.   At thy good heart's oppression.
  Rom. Why, such is love's transgression.—   190
Griefs of mine own lie heavy in my breast;
Which thou wilt propagate, to have it press'd
With more of thine: this love, that thou hast shown,
Doth add more grief to too-much of mine own.
Love is a smoke made with the fume of sighs;
Being purg'd, a fire sparkling in lovers' eyes;
Being vex'd, a sea nourish'd with lovers' tears:
What is it else? a madness most discreet,
A choking gall, and a preserving sweet.
Farewell, my coz.   [*Going.*
  Ben.   Soft, I will go along;   200
An if you leave me so, you do me wrong.
  Rom. Tut! I have lost myself; I am not here;
This is not Romeo, he's some other where.
  Ben. Tell me in sadness, who is that you love.
  Rom. What! shall I groan, and tell thee?
  Ben.   Groan? why, no;
But sadly tell me, who.
  Rom. Bid a sick man in sadness make his will;
A word ill urg'd to one that is so ill.—
In sadness, cousin, I do love a woman.
  Ben. I aim'd so near, when I suppos'd you lov'd. 210

  Rom. A right good mark-man!—And she's fair I
          love.
  Ben. A right fair mark, fair coz, is soonest hit.
  Rom. Well, in that hit you miss: she'll not be hit
With Cupid's arrow,—she hath Dian's wit;
And, in strong proof of chastity well arm'd,
From love's weak childish bow she lives unharm'd.
She will not stay the siege of loving terms,
Nor bide the encounter of assailing eyes,
Nor ope her lap to saint-seducing gold:
O! she is rich in beauty; only poor,   220
That, when she dies, with beauty dies her store.
  Ben. Then she hath sworn, that she will still live
          chaste?
  Rom. She hath, and in that sparing makes huge
          waste;
For beauty, starv'd with her severity,
Cuts beauty off from all posterity.
She is too fair, too wise; wisely too fair,
To merit bliss by making me despair:
She hath forsworn to love, and in that vow
Do I live dead, that live to tell it now.
  Ben. Be rul'd by me; forget to think of her.   230
  Rom. O! teach me how I should forget to think.
  Ben. By giving liberty unto thine eyes:
Examine other beauties.
  Rom.   'T is the way
To call hers, exquisite, in question more.
These happy masks, that kiss fair ladies' brows,
Being black, put us in mind they hide the fair:
He that is strucken blind, cannot forget
The precious treasure of his eyesight lost.
Show me a mistress that is passing fair,
What doth her beauty serve, but as a note   240
Where I may read who pass'd that passing fair?
Farewell: thou canst not teach me to forget.
  Ben. I'll pay that doctrine, or else die in debt.
                                        [*Exeunt.*

             SCENE II.—*A Street.*

        Enter CAPULET, PARIS, *and Servant.*

  Cap. And Montague is bound as well as I,
In penalty alike; and 't is not hard, I think,
For men so old as we to keep the peace.
  Par. Of honourable reckoning are you both;
And pity 't is, you liv'd at odds so long.
But now, my lord, what say you to my suit?
  Cap. But saying o'er what I have said before:
My child is yet a stranger in the world,
She hath not seen the change of fourteen years;
Let two more summers wither in their pride,   10
Ere we may think her ripe to be a bride.
  Par. Younger than she are happy mothers made.
  Cap. And too soon marr'd are those so early made.
The earth hath swallow'd all my hopes but she,
She is the hopeful lady of my earth:
But woo her, gentle Paris, get her heart,
My will to her consent is but a part;
An she agree, within her scope of choice
Lies my consent and fair according voice.
This night I hold an old-accustom'd feast,   20
Whereto I have invited many a guest,
Such as I love; and you, among the store,
One more, most welcome, makes my number more.
At my poor house look to behold this night
Earth-treading stars, that make dark heaven light.
Such comfort, as do lusty young men feel,
When well-apparell'd April on the heel
Of limping winter treads, even such delight
Among fresh female buds shall you this night
Inherit at my house; hear all, all see,   30
And like her most, whose merit most shall be:
Which, on more view of many, mine, being one,
May stand in number, though in reckoning none.
Come, go with me.—Go, sirrah, trudge about
Through fair Verona; find those persons out,
Whose names are written there [*giving a paper*], and
          to them say,
My house and welcome on their pleasure stay.
                  [*Exeunt* CAPULET *and* PARIS

Serv. Find them out, whose names are written here?
It is written, that the shoemaker should meddle with
his yard, and the tailor with his last, the fisher with
his pencil, and the painter with his nets; but I am
sent to find those persons, whose names are here writ,
and can never find what names the writing person
hath here writ. I must to the learned.—In good time.

Enter BENVOLIO *and* ROMEO.

Ben. Tut, man! one fire burns out another's burn-
　　ing,
One pain is lessen'd by another's anguish;
Turn giddy, and be holp by backward turning;
One desperate grief cures with another's languish:
Take thou some new infection to thy eye,
And the rank poison of the old will die.　　　　50
Rom. Your plantain-leaf is excellent for that.
Ben. For what, I pray thee?
Rom.　　　　　　　　For your broken shin.
Ben. Why, Romeo, art thou mad?

Rom. "Stay, fellow; I can read."

Rom. Not mad, but bound more than a madman is:
Shut up in prison, kept without my food,
Whipp'd, and tormented, and—Good den, good fellow.
Serv. God gi' good den.—I pray, sir, can you read?
Rom. Ay, mine own fortune in my misery.
Serv. Perhaps you have learn'd it without book:
but, I pray, can you read anything you see?　　　60
Rom. Ay, if I know the letters, and the language.
Serv. Ye say honestly; rest you merry.
Rom. Stay, fellow; I can read.　　　　　[*Reads.*
"Signior Martino, and his wife, and daughters;
County Anselme, and his beauteous sisters; the lady
widow of Vitruvio; Signior Placentio, and his lovely
nieces; Mercutio, and his brother Valentine; mine
uncle Capulet, his wife, and daughters; my fair niece
Rosaline; Livia; Signior Valentio, and his cousin
Tybalt; Lucio, and the lively Helena."　　　70
A fair assembly; whither should they come?
Serv. Up.
Rom. Whither to supper?
Serv. To our house.
Rom. Whose house?
Serv. My master's.
Rom. Indeed, I should have asked you that before.
Serv. Now I'll tell you without asking. My master
is the great rich Capulet; and if you be not of the
house of Montagues, I pray, come and crush a cup of
wine. Rest you merry.　　　　81
　　　　　　　　　　　　[*Exit.*
Ben. At this same ancient feast of Capulet's
Sups the fair Rosaline, whom thou so lov'st,

With all the admired beauties of Verona:
Go thither; and, with unattainted eye,
Compare her face with some that I shall show,
And I will make thee think thy swan a crow.
Rom. When the devout religion of mine eye
Maintains such falsehood, then turn tears to fires;
And these, who, often drown'd, could never die,　90
Transparent heretics, be burnt for liars.
One fairer than my love! the all-seeing sun
Ne'er saw her match, since first the world begun.
Ben. Tut! you saw her fair, none else being by
Herself pois'd with herself in either eye;
But in that crystal scales, let there be weigh'd
Your lady's love against some other maid,
That I will show you shining at this feast,
And she shall scant show well, that now shows best.
Rom. I'll go along, no such sight to be shown,　100
But to rejoice in splendour of mine own.　[*Exeunt.*

SCENE III.—A Room in CAPULET'S House.

Enter Lady CAPULET *and Nurse.*

La. Cap. Nurse, where's my daughter? call her
　　forth to me.
Nurse. Now, by my maidenhead,—at twelve year
　　old,—
I bade her come.—What, lamb! what, lady-bird!—
God forbid!—where's this girl?—what, Juliet!

Enter JULIET.

Jul. How now! who calls?
Nurse.　　　　　　　Your mother.
Jul.　　　　　　　　Madam, I am here.
What is your will?
La. Cap. This is the matter.—Nurse, give leave
　　awhile,
We must talk in secret.—Nurse, come back again:
I have remember'd me, thou's hear our counsel.
Thou know'st, my daughter's of a pretty age.　　10
Nurse. 'Faith, I can tell her age unto an hour.
La. Cap. She's not fourteen.
Nurse.　　　　　　I'll lay fourteen of my teeth,—
And yet, to my teen be it spoken, I have but four,—
She is not fourteen. How long is it now
To Lammas-tide?
La. Cap.　　　A fortnight, and odd days.
Nurse. Even or odd, of all days in the year,
Come Lammas-eve at night shall she be fourteen.
Susan and she—God rest all Christian souls!—
Were of an age.—Well, Susan is with God;
She was too good for me. But, as I said,　　20
On Lammas-eve at night shall she be fourteen;
That shall she, marry: I remember it well.
'Tis since the earthquake now eleven years;
And she was wean'd,—I never shall forget it,—
Of all the days of the year, upon that day;
For I had then laid wormwood to my dug,
Sitting in the sun under the dove-house wall:
My lord and you were then at Mantua.—
Nay, I do bear a brain:—but, as I said,
When it did taste the wormwood on the nipple　30
Of my dug, and felt it bitter, pretty fool!
To see it tetchy, and fall out with the dug!
Shake, quoth the dove-house: 'twas no need, I trow,
To bid me trudge.
And since that time it is eleven years;
For then she could stand alone, nay, by the rood,
She could have run and waddled all about;
For even the day before she broke her brow:
And then my husband—God be with his soul!
'A was a merry man—took up the child:　　40
"Yea," quoth he, "dost thou fall upon thy face?
Thou wilt fall backward, when thou hast more wit;
Wilt thou not, Jule?" and, by my holy-dam,
The pretty wretch left crying, and said—"Ay."
To see now, how a jest shall come about!
I warrant, an I should live a thousand years,
I never should forget it: "Wilt thou not, Jule?"
　　quoth he;
And, pretty fool, it stinted, and said—"Ay."

La. Cap. Enough of this; I pray thee, hold thy
  peace.
Nurse. Yes, madam. Yet I cannot choose but laugh,
To think it should leave crying, and say—"Ay:" 51
And yet, I warrant, it had upon its brow
A bump as big as a young cockrel's stone;
A perilous knock; and it cried bitterly.
"Yea," quoth my husband, "fall'st upon thy face?
Thou wilt fall backward, when thou com'st to age;
Wilt thou not, Jule?" it stinted, and said—"Ay."
Jul. And stint thou too, I pray thee, nurse, say I.
Nurse. Peace, I have done. God mark thee to his
  grace!
Thou wast the prettiest babe that e'er I nurs'd: 60
An I might live to see thee married once,
I have my wish.
La. Cap. Marry, that marry is the very theme
I come to talk of.—Tell me, daughter Juliet,
How stands your disposition to be married?
Jul. It is an honour that I dream not of.
Nurse. An honour! were not I thine only nurse,
I would say, thou hadst suck'd wisdom from thy teat.
La. Cap. Well, think of marriage now; younger
  than you,
Here in Verona, ladies of esteem, 70
Are made already mothers: by my count,
I was your mother, much upon these years
That you are now a maid. Thus then, in brief,—
The valiant Paris seeks you for his love.
Nurse. A man, young lady! lady, such a man,
As all the world—why, he 's a man of wax.
La. Cap. Verona's summer hath not such a flower.
Nurse. Nay, he 's a flower; in faith, a very flower.
La. Cap. What say you? can you love the gentleman?
This night you shall behold him at our feast: 80
Read o'er the volume of young Paris' face,
And find delight writ there with beauty's pen;
Examine every several lineament,
And see how one another lends content;
And what obscur'd in this fair volume lies,
Find written in the margent of his eyes.
This precious book of love, this unbound lover,
To beautify him, only lacks a cover:
The fish lives in the sea; and 't is much pride,
For fair without the fair within to hide. 90
That book in many's eyes doth share the glory,
That in gold clasps locks in the golden story:
So shall you share all that he doth possess,
By having him, making yourself no less.
Nurse. No less? nay, bigger: women grow by men.
La. Cap. Speak briefly, can you like of Paris' love?
Jul. I 'll look to like, if looking liking move;
But no more deep will I endart mine eye,
Than your consent gives strength to make it fly. 99

Enter a Servant.

Serv. Madam, the guests are come, supper served
up, you called, my young lady asked for, the nurse
cursed in the pantry, and everything in extremity.
I must hence to wait; I beseech you, follow straight.
La. Cap. We follow thee. Juliet, the county stays.
Nurse. Go, girl, seek happy nights to happy days.
                                             [Exeunt.

Scene IV.—A Street.

Enter Romeo, Mercutio, Benvolio, *with five or
six Maskers, Torch-bearers, and others.*

Rom. What, shall this speech be spoke for our
  excuse,
Or shall we on without apology?
Ben. The date is out of such prolixity:
We 'll have no Cupid hoodwink'd with a scarf,
Bearing a Tartar's painted bow of lath,
Scaring the ladies like a crow-keeper;
(Nor no without-book prologue, faintly spoke
After the prompter, for our entrance:)
But, let them measure us by what they will,
We 'll measure them a measure, and be gone. 10
Rom. Give me a torch: I am not for this ambling;
Being but heavy, I will bear the light.

Mer. Nay, gentle Romeo, we must have you dance.
Rom. Not I, believe me. You have dancing shoes,
With nimble soles; I have a soul of lead,
So stakes me to the ground, I cannot move.
Mer. You are a lover: borrow Cupid's wings,
And soar with them above a common bound.
Rom. I am too sore enpierced with his shaft,
To soar with his light feathers; and so bound, 20
I cannot bound a pitch above dull woe:
Under love's heavy burden do I sink.
Mer. And, to sink in it, should you burden love;
Too great oppression for a tender thing.
Rom. Is love a tender thing? it is too rough,
Too rude, too boisterous; and it pricks like thorn.
Mer. If love be rough with you, be rough with
  love:
Prick love for pricking, and you beat love down.—
Give me a case to put my visage in:
                      [Putting on a mask.
A visor for a visor!—what care I, 30

Rom. "And we mean well in going to this mask."

What curious eye doth quote deformities?
Here are the beetle-brows shall blush for me.
Ben. Come, knock, and enter; and no sooner in,
But every man betake him to his legs.
Rom. A torch for me: let wantons, light of heart,
Tickle the senseless rushes with their heels;
For I am proverb'd with a grandsire phrase,—
I 'll be a candle-holder, and look on:
The game was ne'er so fair, and I am done.
Mer. Tut! dun 's the mouse, the constable's own
  word. 40
If thou art dun, we 'll draw thee from the mire
Of this, save reverence, love, wherein thou stick'st
Up to the ears.—Come, we burn daylight, ho.
Rom. Nay, that 's not so.
Mer.   I mean, sir, in delay
We waste our lights in vain, like lamps by day.
Take our good meaning, for our judgment sits
Five times in that, ere once in our five wits.
Rom. And we mean well in going to this mask;
But 't is no wit to go.
Mer.   Why, may one ask?
Rom. I dreamt a dream to-night.
Mer.   And so did I. 50
Rom. Well, what was yours?
Mer.   That dreamers often lie.
Rom. In bed asleep, while they do dream things
  true.
Mer. O! then, I see, Queen Mab hath been with you.

She is the fairies' midwife ; and she comes
In shape no bigger than an agate-stone
On the forefinger of an alderman,
Drawn with a team of little atomies
Over men's noses as they lie asleep :
Her waggon-spokes made of long spinners' legs ;
The cover, of the wings of grasshoppers ;   60
The traces, of the smallest spider's web ;
The collars, of the moonshine's watery beams ;
Her whip, of cricket's bone ; the lash, of film ;
Her waggoner, a small grey-coated gnat,
Not half so big as a round little worm
Prick'd from the lazy finger of a maid.
Her chariot is an empty hazel-nut,
Made by the joiner squirrel, or old grub,
Time out of mind the fairies' coach-makers.
And in this state she gallops night by night   70
Through lovers' brains, and then they dream of love :
O'er courtiers' knees, that dream on court'sies straight:
O'er lawyers' fingers, who straight dream on fees :
O'er ladies' lips, who straight on kisses dream ;
Which oft the angry Mab with blisters plagues,
Because their breaths with sweetmeats tainted are.
Sometime she gallops o'er a courtier's nose,
And then dreams he of smelling out a suit :
And sometime comes she with a tithe-pig's tail,
Tickling a parson's nose as 'a lies asleep,   80
Then dreams he of another benefice.
Sometime she driveth o'er a soldier's neck,
And then dreams he of cutting foreign throats,
Of breaches, ambuscadoes, Spanish blades,
Of healths five fathom deep ; and then anon
Drums in his ear, at which he starts, and wakes ;
And, being thus frighted, swears a prayer or two,
And sleeps again.   This is that very Mab,
That plats the manes of horses in the night ;
And bakes the elf-locks in foul sluttish hairs,   90
Which, once untangled, much misfortune bodes.
This is the hag, when maids lie on their backs,
That presses them, and learns them first to bear,
Making them women of good carriage.
This is she—
     Rom.   Peace, peace ! Mercutio, peace !
Thou talk'st of nothing.
     Mer.   True, I talk of dreams,
Which are the children of an idle brain,
Begot of nothing but vain fantasy ;
Which is as thin of substance as the air ;
And more inconstant than the wind, who woos   100
Even now the frozen bosom of the north,
And, being anger'd, puffs away from thence,
Turning his face to the dew-dropping south.
     Ben. This wind, you talk of, blows us from our-
         selves ;
Supper is done, and we shall come too late.
     Rom. I fear, too early ; for my mind misgives,
Some consequence, yet hanging in the stars,
Shall bitterly begin his fearful date
With this night's revels ; and expire the term
Of a despised life, clos'd in my breast,   110
By some vile forfeit of untimely death :
But He, that hath the steerage of my course,
Direct my sail.—On, lusty gentlemen.
     Ben. Strike, drum.   [*Exeunt.*

SCENE V.—A Hall in CAPULET'S House.

Musicians waiting. Enter Servants.

1 *Serv.* Where's Potpan, that he helps not to take
away ? he shift-a-trencher ! he scrape-a-trencher !
     2 *Serv.* When good manners shall lie all in one or
two men's hands, and they unwashed too, 't is a foul
thing.
     1 *Serv.* Away with the joint-stools, remove the
court-cupboard, look to the plate.—Good thou, save
me a piece of marchpane ; and, as thou lovest me, let
the porter let in Susan Grindstone, and Nell.—Antony !
and Potpan !   10
     2 *Serv.* Ay, boy ; ready.
     1 *Serv.* You are looked for, and called for, asked for,
and sought for, in the great chamber.

     2 *Serv.* We cannot be here and there too.—Cheerly,
boys : be brisk awhile, and the longer liver take all.
                            [*They retire behind.*

Enter CAPULET, *&c., with the Guests, and the
Maskers.*

     Cap. Welcome, gentlemen ! ladies, that have their
         toes
Unplagu'd with corns, will have a bout with you :—
Ah ha, my mistresses ! which of you all
Will now deny to dance ? she that makes dainty, she,
I 'll swear, hath corns.   Am I come near you now ?   20
Welcome, gentlemen !   I have seen the day,
That I have worn a visor, and could tell
A whispering tale in a fair lady's ear,
Such as would please ; 't is gone, 't is gone, 't is gone.
You are welcome, gentlemen ! — Come, musicians,
         play.
A hall ! a hall ! give room, and foot it, girls.
                     [*Music plays, and they dance.*
More light, ye knaves ! and turn the tables up,
And quench the fire, the room is grown too hot.—
Ah ! sirrah, this unlook'd-for sport comes well.
Nay, sit, nay, sit, good cousin Capulet,   30
For you and I are past our dancing days ;
How long is 't now, since last yourself and I
Were in a mask ?
     2 *Cap.*   By 'r lady, thirty years.
     Cap. What, man ! 't is not so much, 't is not so
         much.
'T is since the nuptial of Lucentio,
Come Pentecost as quickly as it will,
Some five-and-twenty years ; and then we mask'd.
     2 *Cap.* 'T is more, 't is more : his son is elder, sir ;
His son is thirty.
     Cap.   Will you tell me that ?
His son was but a ward two years ago.   40
     Rom. What lady 's that, which doth enrich the
         hand
Of yonder knight ?
     Serv. I know not, sir.
     Rom. O ! she doth teach the torches to burn bright.
It seems she hangs upon the cheek of night
Like a rich jewel in an Ethiop's ear ;
Beauty too rich for use, for earth too dear !
So shows a snowy dove trooping with crows,
As yonder lady o'er her fellows shows.
The measure done, I 'll watch her place of stand,   50
And, touching hers, make blessed my rude hand.
Did my heart love till now ? forswear it, sight !
For I ne'er saw true beauty till this night.
     Tyb. This, by his voice, should be a Montague.—
Fetch me my rapier, boy.—What ! dares the slave
Come hither, cover'd with an antick face,
To fleer and scorn at our solemnity ?
Now, by the stock and honour of my kin,
To strike him dead I hold it not a sin.
     Cap. Why, how now, kinsman ? wherefore storm
         you so ?   60
     Tyb. Uncle, this is a Montague, our foe ;
A villain, that is hither come in spite,
To scorn at our solemnity this night.
     Cap. Young Romeo is 't ?
     Tyb.   'T is he, that villain Romeo.
     Cap. Content thee, gentle coz, let him alone :
He bears him like a portly gentleman ;
And, to say truth, Verona brags of him,
To be a virtuous and well-govern'd youth.
I would not for the wealth of all this town,
Here, in my house, do him disparagement ;   70
Therefore be patient, take no note of him :
It is my will ; the which if thou respect,
Show a fair presence, and put off these frowns,
An ill-beseeming semblance for a feast.
     Tyb. It fits, when such a villain is a guest.
I 'll not endure him.
     Cap.   He shall be endur'd :
What ! goodman boy !—I say, he shall ;—go to ;—
Am I the master here, or you ? go to.
You 'll not endure him !—God shall mend my soul—
You 'll make a mutiny among my guests.   80
You will set cock-a-hoop ! you 'll be the man !

Tyb. Why, uncle, 'tis a shame.
Cap.   Go to, go to ;
You are a saucy boy.—Is 't so, indeed ?—
This trick may chance to scathe you ;—I know what.
You must contrary me ! marry, 't is time.—
Well said, my hearts !—You are a princox ; go :—
Be quiet, or—More light, more light !—For shame !
I 'll make you quiet. What !—cheerly, my hearts !
Tyb. Patience perforce with wilful choler meeting
Makes my flesh tremble in their different greeting. 90
I will withdraw : but this intrusion shall,
Now seeming sweet, convert to bitter gall.   [*Exit.*
Rom. [*To* JULIET.] If I profane with my unwor-
        thiest hand
This holy shrine, the gentle sin is this ;
My lips, two blushing pilgrims, ready stand
To smooth that rough touch with a tender kiss.
Jul. Good pilgrim, you do wrong your hand too
        much,
Which mannerly devotion shows in this ;
For saints have hands that pilgrims' hands do touch,
And palm to palm is holy palmers' kiss.   100
Rom. Have not saints lips, and holy palmers too ?
Jul. Ay, pilgrim, lips that they must use in prayer.
Rom. O, then, dear saint, let lips do what hands do ;
They pray, grant thou, lest faith turn to despair.
Jul. Saints do not move, though grant for prayers'
        sake.
Rom. Then move not, while my prayer's effect
        I take.
Thus from my lips, by thine, my sin is purg'd.
                              [*Kissing her.*
Jul. Then have my lips the sin that they have took.
Rom. Sin from my lips ? O trespass sweetly urg'd !
Give me my sin again.
Jul.   You kiss by the book.   110
Nurse. Madam, your mother craves a word with
        you.
Rom. What is her mother ?
Nurse.   Marry, bachelor,
Her mother is the lady of the house,
And a good lady, and a wise, and virtuous.
I nurs'd her daughter, that you talk'd withal ;
I tell you—he that can lay hold of her
Shall have the chinks.
Rom.   Is she a Capulet ?
O dear account ! my life is my foe's debt.
Ben. Away, be gone : the sport is at the best.

Rom. Ay, so I fear ; the more is my unrest.   120
Cap. Nay, gentlemen, prepare not to be gone :
We have a trifling foolish banquet towards.—
Is it e'en so ? Why then, I thank you all ;
I thank you, honest gentlemen ; good night :—
More torches here !—Come on, then let 's to bed.
Ah, sirrah, by my fay, it waxes late ;
I 'll to my rest.   [*Exeunt all but* JULIET *and Nurse.*
Jul. Come hither, nurse. What is yond gentle-
        man ?
Nurse. The son and heir of old Tiberio.
Jul. What 's he, that now is going out of door ? 130
Nurse. Marry, that, I think, be young Petruchio.
Jul. What 's he, that follows there, that would not
        dance ?
Nurse. I know not.
Jul. Go, ask his name.—If he be married,
My grave is like to be my wedding bed.
Nurse. His name is Romeo, and a Montague ;
The only son of your great enemy.
Jul. My only love sprung from my only hate !
Too early seen unknown, and known too late !
Prodigious birth of love it is to me,   140
That I must love a loathed enemy.
Nurse. What 's this ? what 's this ?
Jul.   A rhyme I learn'd even now
Of one I danc'd withal.   [*One calls within,* "*Juliet.*"
Nurse.   Anon, anon :—
Come, let 's away ; the strangers all are gone.
                                          [*Exeunt.*

Enter Chorus.

Now old desire doth in his death-bed lie,
And young affection gapes to be his heir :
That fair, for which love groan'd for, and would die,
With tender Juliet match'd, is now not fair.
Now Romeo is belov'd, and loves again,
Alike bewitched by the charm of looks ;
But to his foe suppos'd he must complain,
And she steal love's sweet bait from fearful hooks :
Being held a foe, he may not have access
To breathe such vows as lovers use to swear ;
And she as much in love, her means much less
To meet her new-beloved anywhere :
But passion lends them power, time means to meet,
Tempering extremities with extremes sweet.   [*Exit.*

ACT II.

SCENE I.—An Open Place, adjoining CAPULET's Garden.

Enter ROMEO.

Romeo.
C AN I go forward, when my heart is
        here ?
Turn back, dull earth, and find thy
        centre out.
        [*He climbs the wall, and leaps
            down within it.*

Enter BENVOLIO *and* MERCUTIO.

Ben. Romeo ! my cousin Romeo !
        Romeo !
Mer.   He is wise ;
And, on my life, hath stol'n him home to bed.

Ben. He ran this way, and leap'd this orchard wall.
Call, good Mercutio.
Mer.   Nay, I'll conjure too.—
Romeo, humours, madman, passion, lover !
Appear thou in the likeness of a sigh :
Speak but one rhyme, and I am satisfied ;
Cry but—Ah me ! pronounce but—love and dove ; 10
Speak to my gossip Venus one fair word,
One nickname for her purblind son and heir,
Young Adam Cupid, he that shot so trim,
When King Cophetua lov'd the beggar-maid.—
He heareth not, he stirreth not, he moveth not ;
The ape is dead, and I must conjure him.—

I conjure thee by Rosaline's bright eyes,
By her high forehead, and her scarlet lip,
By her fine foot, straight leg, and quivering thigh,
And the demesnes that there adjacent lie,　　20
That in thy likeness thou appear to us.
　Ben. An if he hear thee, thou wilt anger him.
　Mer. This cannot anger him : 't would anger him
To raise a spirit in his mistress' circle
Of some strange nature, letting it there stand
Till she had laid it, and conjur'd it down ;
That were some spite : my invocation
Is fair and honest, and, in his mistress' name,
I conjure only but to raise up him.
　Ben. Come, he hath hid himself among these trees,
To be consorted with the humorous night :　　31
Blind is his love, and best befits the dark.
　Mer. If love be blind, love cannot hit the mark.
Now will he sit under a medlar-tree,
And wish his mistress were that kind of fruit,

Rom. "Can I go forward, when my heart is here?"

As maids call medlars, when they laugh alone.—
O Romeo! that she were, O! that she were
An open *et cætera*, thou a poprin pear!
Romeo, good night :—I 'll to my truckle-bed ;
This field-bed is too cold for me to sleep.　　40
Come, shall we go?
　Ben.　　　　　　Go, then ; for 't is in vain
To seek him here, that means not to be found.
　　　　　　　　　　　　　　　　　[Exeunt.

SCENE II.

Enter ROMEO.

　Rom. He jests at scars, that never felt a wound.—
　　　　　[JULIET *appears above, at a window.*
But, soft! what light through yonder window breaks?
It is the east, and Juliet is the sun!—
Arise, fair sun, and kill the envious moon,
Who is already sick and pale with grief,
That thou, her maid, art far more fair than she :
Be not her maid, since she is envious ;
Her vestal livery is but sick and green,
And none but fools do wear it ; cast it off.—
It is my lady ; O! it is my love :　　10
O, that she knew she were!—
She speaks, yet she says nothing : what of that?
Her eye discourses, I will answer it.—
I am too bold, 't is not to me she speaks :
Two of the fairest stars in all the heaven,
Having some business, do entreat her eyes

To twinkle in their spheres till they return.
What if her eyes were there, they in her head?
The brightness of her cheek would shame those stars,
As daylight doth a lamp : her eye in heaven　　20
Would through the airy region stream so bright,
That birds would sing, and think it were not night.
See, how she leans her cheek upon her hand!
O! that I were a glove upon that hand,
That I might touch that cheek!
　Jul.　　　　　　　　　Ah me!
　Rom.　　　　　　　　　　She speaks :—
O, speak again, bright angel! for thou art
As glorious to this night, being o'er my head,
As is a winged messenger of heaven
Unto the white-upturned wond'ring eyes
Of mortals, that fall back to gaze on him,　　30
When he bestrides the lazy-pacing clouds,
And sails upon the bosom of the air.
　Jul. O Romeo, Romeo! wherefore art thou Romeo?
Deny thy father, and refuse thy name :
Or, if thou wilt not, be but sworn my love,
And I 'll no longer be a Capulet.
　Rom. [*Aside.*] Shall I hear more, or shall I speak at
　　　　this?
　Jul. 'T is but thy name, that is my enemy :
Thou art thyself though, not a Montague.
What 's Montague? it is nor hand, nor foot,　　40
Nor arm, nor face, nor any other part
Belonging to a man.　O! be some other name.
What 's in a name? that which we call a rose,
By any other word would smell as sweet :
So Romeo would, were he not Romeo call'd,
Retain that dear perfection which he owes,
Without that title.—Romeo, doff thy name ;
And for thy name, which is no part of thee,
Take all myself!
　Rom.　　　　　I take thee at thy word.
Call me but love, and I 'll be new baptis'd ;　　50
Henceforth I never will be Romeo.
　Jul. What man art thou, that, thus bescreen'd in
　　　　night,
So stumblest on my counsel?
　Rom.　　　　　　　By a name
I know not how to tell thee who I am :
My name, dear saint, is hateful to myself,
Because it is an enemy to thee :
Had I it written, I would tear the word.
　Jul. My ears have yet not drunk a hundred words
Of that tongue's utterance, yet I know the sound.
Art thou not Romeo, and a Montague?　　60
　Rom. Neither, fair maid, if either thee dislike.
　Jul. How cam'st thou hither, tell me, and where-
　　　　fore?
The orchard walls are high, and hard to climb ;
And the place death, considering who thou art,
If any of my kinsmen find thee here.
　Rom. With love's light wings did I o'erperch these
　　　　walls ;
For stony limits cannot hold love out :
And what love can do, that dares love attempt ;
Therefore, thy kinsmen are no stop to me.
　Jul. If they do see thee, they will murder thee.　　70
　Rom. Alack! there lies more peril in thine eye,
Than twenty of their swords : look thou but sweet,
And I am proof against their enmity.
　Jul. I would not for the world they saw thee here.
　Rom. I have night's cloak to hide me from their
　　　　eyes ;
And, but thou love me, let them find me here :
My life were better ended by their hate,
Than death prorogued, wanting of thy love.
　Jul. By whose direction found'st thou out this place?
　Rom. By Love, that first did prompt me to inquire ;
He lent me counsel, and I lent him eyes.　　81
I am no pilot ; yet, wert thou as far
As that vast shore wash'd with the farthest sea,
I would adventure for such merchandise.
　Jul. Thou know'st the mask of night is on my face ;
Else would a maiden blush bepaint my cheek,
For that which thou hast heard me speak to-night.
Fain would I dwell on form, fain, fain deny
What I have spoke : but farewell compliment!

Dost thou love me? I know thou wilt say—Ay;   90
And I will take thy word; yet, if thou swear'st,
Thou may'st prove false: at lovers' perjuries,
They say, Jove laughs. O gentle Romeo!
If thou dost love, pronounce it faithfully:
Or if thou think'st I am too quickly won,
I 'll frown, and be perverse, and say thee nay,
So thou wilt woo; but, else, not for the world.
In truth, fair Montague, I am too fond;
And therefore thou may'st think my haviour light:
But trust me, gentleman, I 'll prove more true   100
Than those that have more cunning to be strange.
I should have been more strange, I must confess,
But that thou overheard'st, ere I was ware,
My true love's passion: therefore, pardon me;
And not impute this yielding to light love,
Which the dark night hath so discovered.
    Rom. Lady, by yonder blessed moon I swear,
That tips with silver all these fruit-tree tops,—

Jul. "O, swear not by the moon."

Jul. O, swear not by the moon, the inconstant moon,
That monthly changes in her circled orb,   110
Lest that thy love prove likewise variable.
    Rom. What shall I swear by?
    Jul.   Do not swear at all;
Or, if thou wilt, swear by thy gracious self,
Which is the god of my idolatry,
And I 'll believe thee.
    Rom.   If my heart's dear love—
    Jul. Well, do not swear. Although I joy in thee,
I have no joy of this contract to-night:
It is too rash, too unadvis'd, too sudden;
Too like the lightning, which doth cease to be,
Ere one can say, it lightens. Sweet, good night!   120
This bud of love, by summer's ripening breath,
May prove a beauteous flower when next we meet.
Good night, good night! as sweet repose and rest
Come to thy heart, as that within my breast!
    Rom. O! wilt thou leave me so unsatisfied?
    Jul. What satisfaction canst thou have to-night?
    Rom. The exchange of thy love's faithful vow for
            mine.
    Jul. I gave thee mine before thou didst request it;
And yet I would it were to give again.
    Rom. Wouldst thou withdraw it? for what purpose,
            love?   130
    Jul. But to be frank, and give it thee again.
And yet I wish but for the thing I have.
My bounty is as boundless as the sea,
My love as deep; the more I give to thee,
The more I have, for both are infinite.
                        [*Nurse calls within.*

I hear some noise within: dear love, adieu!—
Anon, good nurse!—Sweet Montague, be true.
Stay but a little, I will come again.   [*Exit.*
    Rom. O blessed, blessed night! I am afeard,
Being in night, all this is but a dream,   140
Too flattering-sweet to be substantial.

            Re-enter JULIET, *above.*

    Jul. Three words, dear Romeo, and good night,
            indeed.
If that thy bent of love be honourable,
Thy purpose marriage, send me word to-morrow,
By one that I 'll procure to come to thee,
Where, and what time, thou wilt perform the rite;
And all my fortunes at thy foot I 'll lay,
And follow thee my lord throughout the world.
    Nurse. [*Within.*] Madam!
    Jul. I come, anon.—But if thou mean'st not well,   150
I do beseech thee—
    Nurse. [*Within.*] Madam!
    Jul.   By-and-by; I come.—
To cease thy suit, and leave me to my grief:
To-morrow will I send.
    Rom.   So thrive my soul,—
    Jul. A thousand times good night!   [*Exit.*
    Rom. A thousand times the worse, to want thy
            light.—
Love goes toward love, as school-boys from their
            books;
But love from love, toward school with heavy looks.
                            [*Retiring.*

            Re-enter JULIET, *above.*

    Jul. Hist! Romeo, hist!—O, for a falconer's voice,
To lure this tassel-gentle back again!   160
Bondage is hoarse, and may not speak aloud;
Else would I tear the cave where Echo lies,
And make her airy tongue more hoarse than mine
With repetition of my Romeo's name.
    Rom. It is my soul, that calls upon my name:
How silver-sweet sound lovers' tongues by night,
Like softest music to attending ears!
    Jul. Romeo!
    Rom.   My dear?
    Jul.   What o'clock to-morrow
Shall I send to thee?
    Rom.   By the hour of nine.
    Jul. I will not fail: 't is twenty years till then.   170
I have forgot why I did call thee back.
    Rom. Let me stand here, till thou remember it.
    Jul. I shall forget, to have thee still stand there,
Remembering how I love thy company.
    Rom. And I 'll still stay, to have thee still forget,
Forgetting any other home but this.
    Jul. 'T is almost morning; I would have thee gone:
And yet no further than a wanton's bird,
Who lets it hop a little from her hand,
Like a poor prisoner in his twisted gyves,
And with a silk thread plucks it back again,   180
So loving-jealous of his liberty.
    Rom. I would, I were thy bird.
    Jul.   Sweet, so would I:
Yet I should kill thee with much cherishing.
Good night, good night: parting is such sweet sorrow,
That I shall say good night, till it be morrow.   [*Exit.*
    Rom. Sleep dwell upon thine eyes, peace in thy
            breast!—
'Would I were sleep and peace, so sweet to rest!
Hence will I to my ghostly father's cell,
His help to crave, and my dear hap to tell.   [*Exit.*

———

            SCENE III.—Friar LAURENCE'S Cell.

            Enter Friar LAURENCE, *with a basket.*

    Fri. The grey-ey'd morn smiles on the frowning
            night,
Chequering the eastern clouds with streaks of light;
And flecked darkness like a drunkard reels
From forth day's path and Titan's fiery wheels:
Now, ere the sun advance his burning eye

The day to cheer, and night's dank dew to dry,
I must up-fill this osier cage of ours
With baleful weeds, and precious-juiced flowers.
The earth, that 's nature's mother, is her tomb ;
What is her burying grave, that is her womb ;　　10
And from her womb children of divers kind
We sucking on her natural bosom find :
Many for many virtues excellent,
None but for some, and yet all different.
O ! mickle is the powerful grace that lies
In herbs, plants, stones, and their true qualities :
For nought so vile that on the earth doth live,
But to the earth some special good doth give ;
Nor aught so good, but, strain'd from that fair use,
Revolts from true birth, stumbling on abuse :　　20
Virtue itself turns vice, being misapplied,
And vice sometime 's by action dignified.
Within the infant rind of this weak flower
Poison hath residence, and medicine power :
For this, being smelt, with that part cheers each
　　　　　part ;
Being tasted, slays all senses with the heart.
Two such opposed kings encamp them still
In man as well as herbs,—grace, and rude will ;
And where the worser is predominant,
Full soon the canker death eats up that plant.　　30

Enter ROMEO.

Rom. Good morrow, father !
Fri. 　　　　　　　*Benedicite !*
What early tongue so sweet saluteth me ?
Young son, it argues a distemper'd head,
So soon to bid good morrow to thy bed :
Care keeps his watch in every old man's eye,
And where care lodges, sleep will never lie ;
But where unbruised youth with unstuff'd brain
Doth couch his limbs, there golden sleep doth reign.
Therefore, thy earliness doth me assure,
Thou art up-rous'd by some distemperature :　　40
Or if not so, than here I hit it right,—
Our Romeo hath not been in bed to-night.
Rom. That last is true ; the sweeter rest was mine.
Fri. God pardon sin ! wast thou with Rosaline ?
Rom. With Rosaline, my ghostly father ? no ;
ᵀ have forgot that name, and that name's woe.
Fri. That 's my good son : but where hast thou
　　　　been, then ?
Rom. I 'll tell thee, ere thou ask it me again.
I have been feasting with mine enemy ;
Where, on a sudden, one hath wounded me,　　50
That 's by me wounded : both our remedies
Within thy help and holy physic lies :
I bear no hatred, blessed man ; for, lo !
My intercession likewise steads my foe.
Fri. Be plain, good son, and homely in thy drift ;
Riddling confession finds but riddling shrift.
Rom. Then plainly know, my heart's dear love is
　　　　set
On the fair daughter of rich Capulet :
As mine on hers, so hers is set on mine ;
And all combin'd, save what thou must combine　　60
By holy marriage. When, and where, and how,
We met, we woo'd, and made exchange of vow,
I 'll tell thee as we pass ; but this I pray,
That thou consent to marry us to-day.
Fri. Holy Saint Francis ! what a change is here !
Is Rosaline, whom thou didst love so dear,
So soon forsaken ? young men's love, then, lies
Not truly in their hearts, but in their eyes.
Jesu Maria ! what a deal of brine
Hath wash'd thy sallow cheeks for Rosaline !　　70
How much salt water thrown away in waste,
To season love, that of it doth not taste !
The sun not yet thy sighs from heaven clears,
Thy old groans ring yet in my ancient ears ;
Lo ! here upon thy cheek the stain doth sit
Of an old tear that is not wash'd off yet.
If e'er thou wast thyself, and these woes thine,
Thou and these woes were all for Rosaline :
And art thou chang'd ? pronounce this sentence,
　　　　then,—
Women may fall, when there 's no strength in men. 80

Rom. Thou chidd'st me oft for loving Rosaline.
Fri. For doting, not for loving, pupil mine.
Rom. And bad'st me bury love.
Fri. 　　　　　　　Not in a grave,
To lay one in, another out to have.
Rom. I pray thee, chide me not : her I love now
Doth grace for grace, and love for love allow :
The other did not so.
Fri. 　　　　　O ! she knew well,
Thy love did read by rote, and could not spell.
But come, young waverer, come, go with me,
In one respect I 'll thy assistant be ;　　90
For this alliance may so happy prove,
To turn your households' rancour to pure love.
Rom. O ! let us hence ; I stand on sudden haste.
Fri. Wisely, and slow : they stumble that run fast.
　　　　　　　　　　　　　　[*Exeunt.*

───────

SCENE IV.—A Street.

Enter BENVOLIO *and* MERCUTIO.

Mer. Where the devil should this Romeo be ?—
Came he not home to-night ?
Ben. Not to his father's : I spoke with his man.
Mer. Why, that same pale hard-hearted wench,
　　　　that Rosaline,
Torments him so, that he will sure run mad.
Ben. Tybalt, the kinsman to old Capulet,
Hath sent a letter to his father's house.
Mer. A challenge, on my life.
Ben. Romeo will answer it.
Mer. Any man, that can write, may answer a
letter.　　11
Ben. Nay, he will answer the letter's master, how
he dares, being dared.
Mer. Alas, poor Romeo ! he is already dead ; stabbed
with a white wench's black eye ; run thorough the ear
with a love-song ; the very pin of his heart cleft with
the blind bow-boy's butt-shaft ; and is he a man to
encounter Tybalt ?
Ben. Why, what is Tybalt ?　　19
Mer. More than prince of cats, I can tell you. O !
he is the courageous captain of complements. He
fights as you sing prick-song, keeps time, distance,
and proportion ; rests me his minim rest, one, two, and
the third in your bosom : the very butcher of a silk
button, a duellist, a duellist ; a gentleman of the very
first house, of the first and second cause. Ah, the
immortal passado ! the punto reverso ! the hay !—
Ben. The what ?　　28
Mer. The pox of such antick, lisping, affecting fan-
tasticoes, these new tuners of accents !—"By Jesu, a
very good blade !—a very tall man !—a very good
whore !"—Why, is not this a lamentable thing, grandsire, that we should be thus afflicted with these strange
flies, these fashion-mongers, these *pardonnez-mois,*
who stand so much on the new form, that they cannot sit at ease on the old bench ? O, their *bons,* their
bons !

Enter ROMEO.

Ben. Here comes Romeo, here comes Romeo.　　38
Mer. Without his roe, like a dried herring.—O flesh,
flesh, how art thou fish'fied !—Now is he for the
numbers that Petrarch flowed in : Laura, to his lady,
was a kitchen-wench ; marry, she had a better love to
be-rhyme her ; Dido, a dowdy ; Cleopatra, a gipsy ;
Helen and Hero, hildings and harlots : Thisbe, a grey
eye or so, but not to the purpose.—Signior Romeo,
bon jour ! there 's a French salutation to your French
slop. You gave us the counterfeit fairly last night.
Rom. Good morrow to you both. What counterfeit
did I give you ?
Mer. The slip, sir, the slip : can you not conceive ? 50
Rom. Pardon, good Mercutio, my business was
great ; and in such a case as mine, a man may strain
courtesy.
Mer. That 's as much as to say—such a case as
yours constrains a man to bow in the hams.
Rom. Meaning—to court'sy.

Mer. Thou hast most kindly hit it.
Rom. A most courteous exposition.
Mer. Nay, I am the very pink of courtesy.
Rom. Pink for flower. 60
Mer. Right.
Rom. Why, then is my pump well flowered.
Mer. Sure wit : follow me this jest now, till thou hast worn out thy pump ; that, when the single sole of it is worn, the jest may remain, after the wearing, solely singular.
Rom. O single-soled jest ! solely singular for the singleness.
Mer. Come between us, good Benvolio ; my wit faints.
Rom. Switch and spurs, switch and spurs ; or I 'll cry a match. 70
Mer. Nay, if our wits run the wild-goose chase, I am done ; for thou hast more of the wild-goose in one of thy wits, than, I am sure, I have in my whole five. Was I with you there for the goose ?
Rom. Thou wast never with me for anything, when thou wast not there for the goose.
Mer. I will bite thee by the ear for that jest.
Rom. Nay, good goose, bite not. 80
Mer. Thy wit is a very bitter-sweeting ; it is a most sharp sauce.
Rom. And is it not well served in to a sweet goose ?
Mer. O ! here 's a wit of cheveril, that stretches from an inch narrow to an ell broad.
Rom. I stretch it out for that word—broad : which added to the goose, proves thee far and wide a broad goose. 88
Mer. Why, is not this better now than groaning for love ? now art thou sociable, now art thou Romeo ; now art thou what thou art, by art as well as by nature : for this drivelling love is like a great natural, that runs lolling up and down to hide his bauble in a hole.
Ben. Stop there, stop there.
Mer. Thou desirest me to stop in my tale against the hair.
Ben. Thou wouldst else have made thy tale large.
Mer. O, thou art deceived ! I would have made it short ; for I was come to the whole depth of my tale and meant, indeed, to occupy the argument no longer. 102
Rom. Here 's goodly gear !

Enter Nurse and PETER.

Mer. A sail, a sail !
Ben. Two, two ; a shirt, and a smock.
Nurse. Peter !
Peter. Anon?
Nurse. My fan, Peter.
Mer. Good Peter, to hide her face ; for her fan 's the fairer face. 110
Nurse. God ye good morrow, gentlemen.
Mer. God ye good den, fair gentlewoman.
Nurse. Is it good den ?
Mer. 'T is no less, I tell you ; for the bawdy hand of the dial is now upon the prick of noon.
Nurse. Out upon you ! what a man are you ?
Rom. One, gentlewoman, that God hath made himself to mar.
Nurse. By my troth, it is well said :—for himself to mar, quoth 'a ?—Gentlemen, can any of you tell me where I may find the young Romeo ? 121
Rom. I can tell you ; but young Romeo will be older when you have found him, than he was when you sought him. I am the youngest of that name, for fault of a worse.
Nurse. You say well.
Mer. Yea ! is the worst well ? very well took, i' faith ; wisely, wisely.
Nurse. If you be he, sir, I desire some confidence with you. 130
Ben. She will indite him to some supper.
Mer. A bawd, a bawd, a bawd ! So ho !
Rom. What hast thou found ?
Mer. No hare, sir ; unless a hare, sir, in a lenten pie, that is something stale and hoar ere it be spent.

An old hare hoar, and an old hare hoar,
  Is very good meat in Lent :
But a hare that is hoar, is too much for a score,
  When it hoars ere it be spent.—

Romeo, will you come to your father's ? we 'll to dinner thither. 141
Rom. I will follow you.
Mer. Farewell, ancient lady ; farewell, lady, lady, lady. [*Exeunt* MERCUTIO *and* BENVOLIO.
Nurse. Marry, farewell !—I pray you, sir, what saucy merchant was this, that was so full of his ropery ?
Rom. A gentleman, nurse, that loves to hear himself talk ; and will speak more in a minute, than he will stand to in a month. 150
Nurse. An 'a speak anything against me, I 'll take him down, an 'a were lustier than he is, and twenty such Jacks ; and if I cannot, I 'll find those that shall. Scurvy knave ! I am none of his flirt-gills ; I am none of his skains-mates.—And thou must stand by too, and suffer every knave to use me at his pleasure ?
Peter. I saw no man use you at his pleasure ; if I had, my weapon should quickly have been out, I warrant you. I dare draw as soon as another man, if I see occasion in a good quarrel, and the law on my side. 162
Nurse. Now, afore God, I am so vexed, that every part about me quivers.—Scurvy knave !—Pray you, sir, a word ; and as I told you, my young lady bade me inquire you out : what she bid me say, I will keep to myself ; but first let me tell ye, if ye should lead her in a fool's paradise, as they say, it were a very gross kind of behaviour, as they say : for the gentlewoman is young ; and, therefore, if you should deal double with her, truly, it were an ill thing to be offered to any gentlewoman, and very weak dealing.
Rom. Nurse, commend me to thy lady and mistress. I protest unto thee,—
Nurse. Good heart ! and, i' faith, I will tell her as much. Lord, Lord ! she will be a joyful woman.
Rom. What wilt thou tell her, nurse ? thou dost not mark me.
Nurse. I will tell her, sir,—that you do protest ; which, as I take it, is a gentlemanlike offer. 180
Rom. Bid her devise
Some means to come to shrift this afternoon ;
And there she shall at Friar Laurence' cell
Be shriv'd, and married. Here is for thy pains.
Nurse. No, truly, sir ; not a penny.
Rom. Go to ; I say, you shall.
Nurse. This afternoon, sir ? well, she shall be there.
Rom. And stay, good nurse, behind the abbey-wall : Within this hour my man shall be with thee. 190
And bring thee cords made like a tackled stair ;
Which to the high top-gallant of my joy
Must be my convoy in the secret night.
Farewell !—Be trusty, and I 'll quite thy pains.
Farewell !—Commend me to thy mistress.
Nurse. Now God in heaven bless thee !—Hark you, sir.
Rom. What say'st thou, my dear nurse ?
Nurse. Is your man secret ? Did you ne'er hear say, Two may keep counsel, putting one away ? 200
Rom. I warrant thee ; my man 's as true as steel.
Nurse. Well, sir ; my mistress is the sweetest lady —Lord, Lord !—when 't was a little prating thing,— O !—There 's a nobleman in town, one Paris, that would fain lay knife aboard ; but she, good soul, had as lief see a toad, a very toad, as see him. I anger her sometimes, and tell her that Paris is the properer man ; but, I 'll warrant you, when I say so, she looks as pale as any clout in the versal world. Doth not rosemary and Romeo begin both with a letter ? 210
Rom. Ay, nurse ; what of that ? both with an R.
Nurse. Ah, mocker ! that 's the dog's name. R is for the—— No : I know it begins with some other letter ; and she hath the prettiest sententious of it, of you and rosemary, that it would do you good to hear it.

Rom. Commend me to thy lady.
Nurse. Ay, a thousand times. [*Exit* ROMEO.] Peter!
Peter. Anon?
Nurse. Before, and apace. [*Exeunt.*

SCENE V.—CAPULET'S Garden.

Enter JULIET.

Jul. The clock struck nine, when I did send the
    nurse;
In half an hour she promis'd to return.
Perchance, she cannot meet him :—that 's not so.—
Oh! she is lame : love's heralds should be thoughts,
Which ten times faster glide than the sun's beams
Driving back shadows over louring hills :
Therefore do nimble-pinion'd doves draw love,
And therefore hath the wind-swift Cupid wings.
Now is the sun upon the highmost hill
Of this day's journey; and from nine till twelve   10

Jul. " Now, good sweet nurse,—O Lord! why look'st thou sad?"

Is three long hours,—yet she is not come.
Had she affections, and warm youthful blood,
She 'd be as swift in motion as a ball;
My words would bandy her to my sweet love,
And his to me:
But old folks, many feign as they were dead;
Unwieldy, slow, heavy and pale as lead.

Enter Nurse and PETER.

O God! she comes.—O honey nurse! what news?
Hast thou met with him? Send thy man away.
Nurse. Peter, stay at the gate.   [*Exit* PETER.
Jul. Now, good sweet nurse,—O Lord! why look'st
    thou sad?   21
Though news be sad, yet tell them merrily;
If good, thou sham'st the music of sweet news
By playing it to me with so sour a face.
Nurse. I am aweary, give me leave awhile.—
Fie, how my bones ache! What a jaunt have I had!
Jul. I would, thou hadst my bones, and I thy
    news:
Nay, come, I pray thee, speak:—good, good nurse,
    speak.
Nurse. Jesu, what haste! can you not stay awhile?
Do you not see, that I am out of breath?   30
Jul. How art thou out of breath, when thou hast
    breath
To say to me—that thou art out of breath?

The excuse that thou dost make in this delay
Is longer than the tale thou dost excuse.
Is thy news good, or bad? answer to that;
Say either, and I 'll stay the circumstance.
Let me be satisfied, is 't good or bad?
  Nurse. Well, you have made a simple choice; you
know not how to choose a man : Romeo! no, not he;
though his face be better than any man's, yet his leg
excels all men's; and for a hand. and a foot, and a
body,—though they be not to be talked on, yet they
are past compare. He is not the flower of courtesy,—
but, I 'll warrant him, as gentle as a lamb.—Go thy
ways, wench; serve God.—What, have you dined at
home?
  Jul. No, no : but all this did I know before.
What says he of our marriage? what of that?
  Nurse. Lord, how my head aches! what a head
    have I!
It beats as it would fall in twenty pieces.   50
My back o' t' other side.—O, my back, my back!—
Beshrew your heart, for sending me about,
To catch my death with jaunting up and down!
  Jul. I' faith, I am sorry that thou art not well.
Sweet, sweet, sweet nurse, tell me, what says my
    love?
  Nurse. Your love says like an honest gentleman,
And a courteous, and a kind, and a handsome,
And, I warrant, a virtuous :—Where is your mother?
  Jul. Where is my mother?—why, she is within;
Where should she be? How oddly thou repliest :   60
" Your love says like an honest gentleman,—
Where is your mother?"
  Nurse.   O, God's lady dear!
Are you so hot? Marry, come up, I trow;
Is this the poultice for my aching bones?
Henceforward do your messages yourself.
  Jul. Here 's such a coil;—come, what says Romeo?
  Nurse. Have you got leave to go to shrift to-day?
  Jul. I have.
  Nurse. Then hie you hence to Friar Laurence' cell;
There stays a husband to make you a wife: 70
Now comes the wanton blood up in your cheeks,
They 'll be in scarlet straight at any news.
Hie you to church; I must another way,
To fetch a ladder, by the which your love
Must climb a bird's nest soon, when it is dark;
I am the drudge, and toil in your delight,
But you shall bear the burden soon at night.
Go; I 'll to dinner : hie you to the cell.
  Jul. Hie to high fortune!—Honest nurse, farewell.
    [*Exeunt.*

SCENE VI.— Friar LAURENCE'S Cell.

Enter Friar LAURENCE *and* ROMEO.

Fri. So smile the heavens upon this holy act,
That after-hours with sorrow chide us not!
Rom. Amen, Amen! but come what sorrow can,
It cannot countervail the exchange of joy
That one short minute gives me in her sight:
Do thou but close our hands with holy words,
Then love-devouring death do what he dare;
It is enough I may but call her mine.
  Fri. These violent delights have violent ends,
And in their triumph die : like fire and powder,   10
Which, as they kiss, consume. The sweetest honey
Is loathsome in his own deliciousness,
And in the taste confounds the appetite :
Therefore, love moderately; long love doth so;
Too swift arrives as tardy as too slow.

Enter JULIET.

Here comes the lady.—O! so light a foot
Will ne'er wear out the everlasting flint:
A lover may bestride the gossamer
That idles in the wanton summer air,
And yet not fall; so light is vanity.   20
  Jul. Good even to my ghostly confessor.
  Fri. Romeo shall thank thee, daughter, for us both.
  Jul. As much to him, else is his thanks too much.
  Rom. Ah, Juliet! if the measure of thy joy

Be heap'd like mine, and that thy skill be more
To blazon it, then sweeten with thy breath
This neighbour air, and let rich music's tongue
Unfold the imagin'd happiness, that both
Receive in either by this dear encounter.
Jul. Conceit, more rich in matter than in words, 30
Brags of his substance, not of ornament :

They are but beggars that can count their worth ;
But my true love is grown to such excess,
I cannot sum up half my sum of wealth.
Fri. Come, come with me, and we will make short
    work ;
For, by your leaves, you shall not stay alone,
Till holy church incorporate two in one.   [*Exeunt.*

ACT III.

SCENE I.—A Public Place.

Enter MERCUTIO, BENVOLIO, *Page, and Servants.*

Benvolio.

PRAY thee, good Mercutio, let 's retire.:
  The day is hot, the Capulets abroad,
And, if we meet, we shall not 'scape a
  brawl ;
For now, these hot days, is the mad
  blood stirring.
Mer. Thou art like one of those fellows
that, when he enters the confines of a
tavern, claps me his sword upon the
table and says, "God send me no need
of thee !" and, by the operation of the
second cup, draws it on the drawer,
when, indeed, there is no need.   11
Ben. Am I like such a fellow?
Mer. Come, come, thou art as hot a
Jack in thy mood, as any in Italy ; and
as soon moved to be moody, and as soon
moody to be moved.
Ben. And what too?
Mer. Nay, an there were two such, we should have
none shortly, for one would kill the other. Thou !
why, thou wilt quarrel with a man that hath a hair
more, or a hair less, in his beard, than thou hast.
Thou wilt quarrel with a man for cracking nuts,
having no other reason, but because thou hast hazel
eyes. What eye, but such an eye, would spy out such
a quarrel? Thy head is as full of quarrels, as an egg
is full of meat ; and yet thy head hath been beaten as
addle as an egg for quarrelling. Thou hast quarrelled
with a man for coughing in the street, because he
hath wakened thy dog that hath lain asleep in the
sun. Didst thou not fall out with a tailor for wearing
his new doublet before Easter? with another, for
tying his new shoes with old riband? and yet thou
wilt tutor me from quarrelling !   33
Ben. An I were so apt to quarrel as thou art, any
man should buy the fee-simple of my life for an hour
and a quarter.
Mer. The fee-simple? O simple !
Ben. By my head, here come the Capulets.
Mer. By my heel, I care not.

Enter TYBALT *and others.*

Tyb. Follow me close, for I will speak to them.— 40
Gentlemen, good den ! a word with one of you.
Mer. And but one word with one of us ? Couple it
with something : make it a word and a blow.
Tyb. You shall find me apt enough to that, sir, an
you will give me occasion.
Mer. Could you not take some occasion without
giving?
Tyb. Mercutio, thou consort'st with Romeo,—
Mer. Consort ! what ! dost thou make us minstrels ?
an thou make minstrels of us, look to hear nothing

but discords : here 's my fiddlestick ; here 's that shall
make you dance. 'Zounds, consort !   52
Ben. We talk here in the public haunt of men :
Either withdraw unto some private place,
And reason coldly of your grievances ;
Or else depart ; here all eyes gaze on us.
Mer. Men's eyes were made to look, and let them gaze :
I will not budge for no man's pleasure, I.

Enter ROMEO.

Tyb. Well, peace be with you, sir. Here comes my
  man.
Mer. But I 'll be hang'd, sir, if he wear your livery :
Marry, go before to field, he'll be your follower ;   61
Your worship, in that sense, may call him—man.
Tyb. Romeo, the love I bear thee can afford
No better term than this,—thou art a villain.
Rom. Tybalt, the reason that I have to love thee
Doth much excuse the appertaining rage
To such a greeting :—villain am I none ;
Therefore farewell ; I see, thou know'st me not.
Tyb. Boy, this shall not excuse the injuries
That thou hast done me ; therefore turn, and draw. 70
Rom. I do protest, I never injur'd thee ;
But love thee better than thou canst devise,
Till thou shalt know the reason of my love :
And so, good Capulet, which name I tender
As dearly as mine own,—be satisfied.
Mer. O calm, dishonourable, vile submission !
Alla stoccata carries it away.   [*Draws.*
Tybalt, you rat-catcher, will you walk ?
Tyb. What wouldst thou have with me ?   79
Mer. Good king of cats, nothing but one of your
nine lives ; that I mean to make bold withal, and, as
you shall use me hereafter, dry-beat the rest of the
eight. Will you pluck your sword out of his pilcher
by the ears ? make haste, lest mine be about your ears
ere it be out.
Tyb. I am for you.   [*Drawing.*
Rom. Gentle Mercutio, put thy rapier up.
Mer. Come, sir, your *passado.*   [*They fight.*
Rom. Draw, Benvolio ; beat down their weapons.—
Gentlemen, for shame, forbear this outrage !—   90
Tybalt,—Mercutio,—the prince expressly hath
Forbidden bandying in Verona streets.—
Hold, Tybalt !—good Mercutio !
    [*Exeunt* TYBALT *and his Partisans.*
Mer.   I am hurt.—
A plague o' both the houses !—I am sped :—
Is he gone, and hath nothing ?
Ben.   What ! art thou hurt?
Mer. Ay, ay, a scratch, a scratch ; marry, 'tis
  enough.—
Where is my page ?—Go, villain, fetch a surgeon.
    [*Exit Page.*

Rom. Courage, man; the hurt cannot be much.

Mer. No, 'tis not so deep as a well, nor so wide as a church-door; but 'tis enough, 'twill serve: ask for me to-morrow, and you shall find me a grave man. I am peppered, I warrant, for this world.—A plague o' both your houses!—'Zounds! a dog, a rat, a mouse, a cat, to scratch a man to death! a braggart, a rogue, a villain, that fights by the book of arithmetic!—Why the devil came you between us? I was hurt under your arm.

Rom. I thought all for the best.

Mer. Help me into some house, Benvolio, Or I shall faint.—A plague o' both your houses!   110

Rom. "This shall determine that."

They have made worms' meat of me: I have it, And soundly too:—your houses!
     [*Exeunt* MERCUTIO *and* BENVOLIO.

Rom. This gentleman, the prince's near ally, My very friend, hath got this mortal hurt In my behalf; my reputation stain'd With Tybalt's slander, Tybalt, that an hour Hath been my cousin.—O sweet Juliet! Thy beauty hath made me effeminate, And in my temper soften'd valour's steel.

Re-enter BENVOLIO.

Ben. O Romeo, Romeo! brave Mercutio's dead; 120 That gallant spirit hath aspir'd the clouds, Which too untimely here did scorn the earth.

Rom. This day's black fate on more days doth depend; This but begins the woe, others must end.

Re-enter TYBALT.

Ben. Here comes the furious Tybalt back again.

Rom. Alive! in triumph! and Mercutio slain! Away to heaven, respective lenity, And fire-ey'd fury be my conduct now!— Now, Tybalt, take the villain back again, That late thou gav'st me; for Mercutio's soul 130 Is but a little way above our heads, Staying for thine to keep him company: Either thou, or I, or both, must go with him.

Tyb. Thou, wretched boy, that didst consort him here, Shalt with him hence.

Rom.   This shall determine that.
     [*They fight;* TYBALT *falls.*

Ben. Romeo, away! be gone! The citizens are up, and Tybalt slain:— Stand not amaz'd:—the prince will doom thee death, If thou art taken:—hence!—be gone!—away!

Rom. O, I am fortune's fool!

Ben.   Why dost thou stay? 140
     [*Exit* ROMEO.

Enter Citizens, &c.

1 Cit. Which way ran he, that kill'd Mercutio? Tybalt, that murderer, which way ran he?

Ben. There lies that Tybalt.

1 Cit.   Up, sir:—go with me; I charge thee in the prince's name, obey.

Enter PRINCE, attended; MONTAGUE, CAPULET, their Wives, and others.

Prin. Where are the vile beginners of this fray?

Ben. O noble prince! I can discover all The unlucky manage of this fatal brawl: There lies the man, slain by young Romeo, That slew thy kinsman, brave Mercutio.

La. Cap. Tybalt, my cousin!—O my brother's child!   150 O prince! O cousin! husband! O, the blood is spill'd Of my dear kinsman!—Prince, as thou art true, For blood of ours, shed blood of Montague.— O cousin, cousin!

Prin. Benvolio, who began this bloody fray?

Ben. Tybalt, here slain, whom Romeo's hand did slay: Romeo, that spoke him fair, bade him bethink How nice the quarrel was; and urg'd withal Your high displeasure:—all this, uttered With gentle breath, calm look, knees humbly bow'd,   160 Could not take truce with the unruly spleen Of Tybalt, deaf to peace, but that he tilts With piercing steel at bold Mercutio's breast; Who, all as hot, turns deadly point to point, And, with a martial scorn, with one hand beats Cold death aside, and with the other sends It back to Tybalt, whose dexterity Retorts it. Romeo he cries aloud, "Hold, friends! friends, part!" and, swifter than his tongue, His agile arm beats down their fatal points,   170 And 'twixt them rushes; underneath whose arm An envious thrust from Tybalt hit the life Of stout Mercutio, and then Tybalt fled; But by-and-by comes back to Romeo, Who had but newly entertain'd revenge, And to't they go like lightning; for ere I Could draw to part them, was stout Tybalt slain; And as he fell, did Romeo turn and fly. This is the truth, or let Benvolio die.

La. Cap. He is a kinsman to the Montague;   180 Affection makes him false, he speaks not true: Some twenty of them fought in this black strife, And all those twenty could but kill one life. I beg for justice, which thou, prince, must give: Romeo slew Tybalt, Romeo must not live.

Prin. Romeo slew him, he slew Mercutio; Who now the price of his dear blood doth owe?

Mon. Not Romeo, prince, he was Mercutio's friend; His fault concludes but what the law should end, The life of Tybalt.

Prin.   And for that offence,   190 Immediately we do exile him hence: I have an interest in your hate's proceeding, My blood for your rude brawls doth lie a-bleeding; But I'll amerce you with so strong a fine, That you shall all repent the loss of mine. I will be deaf to pleading and excuses;

Nor tears, nor prayers, shall purchase out abuses;
Therefore use none : let Romeo hence in haste,
Else, when he's found, that hour is his last.
Bear hence this body, and attend our will :   200
Mercy but murders, pardoning those that kill.
                                        [*Exeunt.*

SCENE II.—A Room in CAPULET'S House.

Enter JULIET.

Jul. Gallop apace, you fiery-footed steeds,
Towards Phœbus' lodging ; such a waggoner
As Phaethon would whip you to the west,
And bring in cloudy night immediately.—
Spread thy close curtain, love-performing night!
That runaways' eyes may wink, and Romeo
Leap to these arms, untalk'd-of, and unseen !—
Lovers can see to do their amorous rites
By their own beauties ; or, if love be blind,
It best agrees with night.—Come, civil night,   10
Thou sober-suited matron, all in black,
And learn me how to lose a winning match,
Play'd for a pair of stainless maidenhoods :
Hood my unmann'd blood, bating in my cheeks,
With thy black mantle ; till strange love, grown bold,
Think true love acted simple modesty.
Come, night ! come, Romeo ! come, thou day in night !
For thou wilt lie upon the wings of night
Whiter than new snow upon a raven's back.—
Come, gentle night ; come, loving, black-brow'd night,
Give me my Romeo : and, when he shall die,   21
Take him and cut him out in little stars,
And he will make the face of heaven so fine,
That all the world will be in love with night,
And pay no worship to the garish sun.—
O, I have bought the mansion of a love,
But not possess'd it ; and though I am sold,
Not yet enjoy'd. So tedious is this day,
As is the night before some festival
To an impatient child that hath new robes,   30
And may not wear them. O ! here comes my nurse,
And she brings news ; and every tongue, that speaks
But Romeo's name, speaks heavenly eloquence.

Enter Nurse, with cords.

Now, nurse, what news ? What hast thou there ? the
          cords
That Romeo bid thee fetch ?
    Nurse.   Ay, ay, the cords.
                              [*Throws them down.*
Jul. Ah me ! what news ? why dost thou wring thy
          hands ?
Nurse. Ah, well-a-day ! he's dead, he's dead, he's
          dead !
We are undone, lady, we are undone !—
Alack the day !—he's gone, he's killed, he's dead !
Jul. Can Heaven be so envious ?
Nurse.   Romeo can,   40
Though Heaven cannot.—O, Romeo, Romeo—
Who ever would have thought it ?—Romeo—
Jul. What devil art thou, that dost torment me
          thus ?
This torture should be roar'd in dismal hell.
Hath Romeo slain himself ? say thou but *I*,
And that bare vowel, *I*, shall poison more
Than the death-darting eye of cockatrice :
I am not I, if there be such an *I*;
Or those eyes shut, that make thee answer, *I*.
If he be slain, say—*I* ; or if not,—no :   50
Brief sounds determine of my weal or woe.
Nurse. I saw the wound, I saw it with mine eyes,—
God save the mark !—here on his manly breast :
A piteous corse, a bloody piteous corse ;
Pale, pale as ashes, all bedaub'd in blood,
All in gore blood ;—I swounded at the sight.
Jul. O, break, my heart !—poor bankrout, break at
          once !
To prison, eyes ; ne'er look on liberty !
Vile earth, to earth resign ; end motion here,
And thou, and Romeo, press one heavy bier !   60

Nurse. O Tybalt, Tybalt ! the best friend I had :
O courteous Tybalt ! honest gentleman !
That ever I should live to see thee dead !
Jul. What storm is this, that blows so contrary ?
Is Romeo slaughter'd ? and is Tybalt dead ?
My dearest cousin, and my dearer lord ?—
Then, dreadful trumpet, sound the general doom
For who is living, if those two are gone ?
Nurse. Tybalt is gone, and Romeo banished ;
Romeo, that kill'd him, he is banished.   70
Jul. O God !—did Romeo's hand shed Tybalt's
          blood ?
Nurse. It did, it did : alas the day ! it did.
Jul. O serpent heart, hid with a flowering face !
Did ever dragon keep so fair a cave ?
Beautiful tyrant ! fiend angelical !
Dove-feather'd raven ! wolvish-ravening lamb !
Despised substance of divinest show !
Just opposite to what thou justly seem'st ;
A damned saint, an honourable villain !—
O nature ! what hadst thou to do in hell,   80
When thou didst bower the spirit of a fiend
In mortal paradise of such sweet flesh ?—
Was ever book containing such vile matter
So fairly bound ? O, that deceit should dwell
In such a gorgeous palace !
    Nurse.   There's no trust,
No faith, no honesty in men ; all perjur'd,
All forsworn, all naught, all dissemblers.—
Ah ! where's my man ? give me some *aqua vitæ :—*
These griefs, these woes, these sorrows make me old.
Shame come to Romeo !
    Jul.   Blister'd be thy tongue   90
For such a wish ! he was not born to shame :
Upon his brow shame is asham'd to sit ;
For 't is a throne where honour may be crown'd
Sole monarch of the universal earth.
O, what a beast was I to chide at him !
Nurse. Will you speak well of him that kill'd your
          cousin ?
Jul. Shall I speak ill of him that is my husband ?
Ah, poor my lord, what tongue shall smooth thy
          name,
When I, thy three-hours' wife, have mangled it ?—
But, wherefore, villain, didst thou kill my cousin ?   100
That villain cousin would have kill'd my husband :
Back, foolish tears, back to your native spring ;
Your tributary drops belong to woe,
Which you, mistaking, offer up to joy.
My husband lives, that Tybalt would have slain ;
And Tybalt's dead, that would have slain my hus-
          band.
All this is comfort ; wherefore weep I then ?
Some word there was, worser than Tybalt's death,
That murder'd me. I would forget it fain ;
But, O ! it presses to my memory,   110
Like damned guilty deeds to sinners' minds.
" Tybalt is dead, and Romeo banished !"
That " banished," that one word " banished,"
Hath slain ten thousand Tybalts. Tybalt's death
Was woe enough, if it had ended there :
Or,—if sour woe delights in fellowship,
And needly will be rank'd with other griefs,—
Why follow'd not, when she said—Tybalt's dead,
Thy father, or thy mother, nay, or both,
Which modern lamentation might have mov'd ?   120
But, with a rearward following Tybalt's death,
" Romeo is banished !"—to speak that word,
Is father, mother, Tybalt, Romeo, Juliet,
All slain, all dead :—" Romeo is banished !"—
There is no end, no limit, measure, bound,
In that word's death ; no words can that woe sound.—
Where is my father, and my mother, nurse ?
Nurse. Weeping and wailing over Tybalt's corse :
Will you go to them ? I will bring you thither.
Jul. Wash they his wounds with tears : mine shall
          be spent,   130
When theirs are dry, for Romeo's banishment.
Take up those cords.—Poor ropes, you are beguil'd,
Both you and I, for Romeo is exil'd :
He made you for a highway to my bed,
But I, a maid, die maiden-widowed.

Come, cords; come, nurse; I'll to my wedding-bed;
And death, not Romeo, take my maidenhead!
Nurse. Hie to your chamber; I'll find Romeo
To comfort you:—I wot well where he is.
Hark ye, your Romeo will be here at night :   140
I'll to him; he is hid at Laurence' cell.
Jul. O, find him! give this ring to my true knight,
And bid him come to take his last farewell. [*Exeunt.*

SCENE III.—Friar LAURENCE'S Cell.

Enter Friar LAURENCE *and* ROMEO.

Fri. Romeo, come forth; come forth, thou fearful
          man :
Affliction is enamour'd of thy parts,
And thou art wedded to calamity.
Rom. Father, what news? what is the prince's
          doom?
What sorrow craves acquaintance at my hand,
That I yet know not?
Fri.   Too familiar
Is my dear son with such sour company :
I bring thee tidings of the prince's doom.
Rom. What less than doomsday is the prince's
          doom?
Fri. A gentler judgment vanish'd from his lips,   10
Not body's death, but body's banishment.
Rom. Ha! banishment? be merciful, say—death;
For exile hath more terror in his look,
Much more than death : do not say—banishment.
Fri. Here from Verona art thou banished.
Be patient, for the world is broad and wide.
Rom. There is no world without Verona walls;
But purgatory, torture, hell itself.
Hence banished is banish'd from the world,
And world's exile is death ;—then " banished "   20
Is death mis-term'd. Calling death—" banished,"
Thou cutt'st my head off with a golden axe,
And smil'st upon the stroke that murders me.
Fri. O deadly sin! O rude unthankfulness!
Thy fault our law calls death; but the kind prince,
Taking thy part, hath rush'd aside the law,
And turn'd that black word death to banishment :
This is dear mercy, and thou seest it not.
Rom. 'T is torture, and not mercy; heaven is here,
Where Juliet lives; and every cat, and dog,   30
And little mouse, every unworthy thing,
Live here in heaven, and may look on her;
But Romeo may not.—More validity,
More honourable state, more courtship lives
In carrion flies, than Romeo : they may seize
On the white wonder of dear Juliet's hand,
And steal immortal blessing from her lips;
Who, even in pure and vestal modesty,
Still blush, as thinking their own kisses sin;
But Romeo may not; he is banished.   40
Flies may do this, but I from this must fly :
They are free men, but I am banished.
And say'st thou yet, that exile is not death?
Hadst thou no poison mix'd, no sharp-ground knife,
No sudden mean of death, though ne'er so mean,
But—" banished "—to kill me? " Banished?"
O friar! the damned use that word in hell;
Howling attends it : how hast thou the heart,
Being a divine, a ghostly confessor,
A sin-absolver, and my friend profess'd,   50
To mangle me with that word—" banished?"
Fri. Thou fond mad man, hear me a little speak.
Rom. O! thou wilt speak again of banishment.
Fri. I'll give thee armour to keep off that word;
Adversity's sweet milk, philosophy,
To comfort thee, though thou art banished.
Rom. Yet " banished?"—Hang up philosophy!
Unless philosophy can make a Juliet,
Displant a town, reverse a prince's doom,
It helps not, it prevails not : talk no more.   60
Fri. O! then I see that madmen have no ears.
Rom. How should they, when that wise men have
          no eyes?
Fri. Let me dispute with thee of thy estate.

Rom. Thou canst not speak of that thou dost not
          feel.
Wert thou as young as I, Juliet thy love,
An hour but married, Tybalt murdered,
Doting like me, and like me banished,
Then mightst thou speak, then mightst thou tear thy
          hair,
And fall upon the ground, as I do now,
Taking the measure of an unmade grave.   70
          [*Knocking within.*
Fri. Arise; one knocks : good Romeo, hide thyself.
Rom. Not I; unless the breath of heart-sick groans,
Mist-like, infold me from the search of eyes.
          [*Knocking.*
Fri. Hark, how they knock! — Who's there?—
          Romeo, arise;

Fri. " There on the ground, with his own tears made drunk."

Thou wilt be taken.—Stay awhile.—Stand up;
          [*Knocking.*
Run to my study.—By-and-by.—God's will!
What simpleness is this!—I come, I come.
          [*Knocking.*
Who knocks so hard? whence come you? what's
          your will?
Nurse. [*Within.*] Let me come in, and you shall
          know my errand :
I come from Lady Juliet.
Fri.   Welcome then.   80

Enter Nurse.

Nurse. O holy friar, O, tell me, holy friar,
Where is my lady's lord? where's Romeo?
Fri. There on the ground, with his own tears made
          drunk.
Nurse. O! he is even in my mistress' case,
Just in her case. O woful sympathy!
Piteous predicament! Even so lies she,
Blubbering and weeping, weeping and blubbering.—
Stand up, stand up; stand, an you be a man :
For Juliet's sake, for her sake, rise and stand;
Why should you fall into so deep an O?   90
Rom. Nurse!
Nurse. Ah sir! ah sir!—Well, death's the end
          of all.

Rom. Spak'st thou of Juliet? how is it with her?
Doth she not think me an old murderer,
Now I have stain'd the childhood of our joy
With blood remov'd but little from her own?
Where is she? and how doth she? and what says
My conceal'd lady to our cancell'd love?
  Nurse. O, she says nothing, sir, but weeps and
      weeps;
And now falls on her bed; and then starts up;   100
And Tybalt calls; and then on Romeo cries,
And then down falls again.
  Rom.   As if that name,
Shot from the deadly level of a gun,
Did murder her; as that name's cursed hand
Murder'd her kinsman.—O, tell me, friar, tell me,
In what vile part of this anatomy
Doth my name lodge? tell me, that I may sack
The hateful mansion.   [*Drawing his sword.*
  Fri.   Hold thy desperate hand:
Art thou a man? thy form cries out, thou art;
Thy tears are womanish; thy wild acts denote   110
The unreasonable fury of a beast:
Unseemly woman, in a seeming man;
And ill-beseeming beast, in seeming both!
Thou hast amaz'd me: by my holy order,
I thought thy disposition better temper'd.
Hast thou slain Tybalt? wilt thou slay thyself?
And slay thy lady, that in thy life lives,
By doing damned hate upon thyself?
Why rail'st thou on thy birth, the heaven, and earth?
Since birth, and heaven, and earth, all three do meet
In thee at once, which thou at once wouldst lose. 121
Fie, fie! thou sham'st thy shape, thy love, thy wit;
Which, like an usurer, abound'st in all,
And usest none in that true use indeed
Which should bedeck thy shape, thy love, thy wit.
Thy noble shape is but a form of wax,
Digressing from the valour of a man;
Thy dear love sworn, but hollow perjury,
Killing that love which thou hast vow'd to cherish;
Thy wit, that ornament to shape and love,   130
Misshapen in the conduct of them both,
Like powder in a skilless soldier's flask,
Is set a-fire by thine own ignorance,
And thou dismember'd with thine own defence.
What! rouse thee, man; thy Juliet is alive,
For whose dear sake thou wast but lately dead;
There art thou happy: Tybalt would kill thee,
But thou slew'st Tybalt: there art thou happy too:
The law, that threaten'd death, becomes thy friend,
And turns it to exile: there art thou happy: 140
A pack of blessings light upon thy back;
Happiness courts thee in her best array;
But, like a misbehav'd and sullen wench,
Thou pout'st upon thy fortune and thy love.
Take heed, take heed, for such die miserable.
Go, get thee to thy love, as was decreed,
Ascend her chamber, hence, and comfort her;
But, look, thou stay not till the watch be set,
For then thou canst not pass to Mantua;
Where thou shalt live, till we can find a time 150
To blaze your marriage, reconcile your friends,
Beg pardon of the prince, and call thee back,
With twenty hundred thousand times more joy
Than thou went'st forth in lamentation.—
Go before, nurse: commend me to thy lady;
And bid her hasten all the house to bed,
Which heavy sorrow makes them apt unto:
Romeo is coming.
  Nurse. O Lord! I could have stay'd here all the
      night,
To hear good counsel: O, what learning is!— 160
My lord, I'll tell my lady you will come.
  Rom. Do so, and bid my sweet prepare to chide.
  Nurse. Here, sir, a ring she bid me give you, sir.
Hie you, make haste, for it grows very late.   [*Exit.*
  Rom. How well my comfort is reviv'd by this!
  Fri. Go hence. Good night; and here stands all
      your state:—
Either be gone before the watch be set,
Or by the break of day disguis'd from hence.
Sojourn in Mantua: I'll find out your man,

And he shall signify from time to time   170
Every good hap to you that chances here.
Give me thy hand; 't is late: farewell; good night.
  Rom. But that a joy past joy calls out on me,
It were a grief, so brief to part with thee:
Farewell.   [*Exeunt.*

SCENE IV.—A Room in CAPULET's House.

Enter CAPULET, *Lady* CAPULET, *and* PARIS.

  Cap. Things have fall'n out, sir, so unluckily,
That we have had no time to move our daughter.
Look you, she lov'd her kinsman Tybalt dearly,
And so did I:—well, we were born to die.—
'T is very late, she'll not come down to-night:
I promise you, but for your company,
I would have been a-bed an hour ago.
  Par. These times of woe afford no time to woo.—
Madam, good night: commend me to your daughter.
  La. Cap. I will, and know her mind early to-
      morrow;   10
To-night she's mew'd up to her heaviness.
  Cap. Sir Paris, I will make a desperate tender
Of my child's love: I think, she will be rul'd
In all respects by me; nay, more, I doubt it not.
Wife, go you to her ere you go to bed;
Acquaint her here of my son Paris' love,
And bid her, mark you me, on Wednesday next—
But, soft: what day is this?
  Par.   Monday, my lord.
  Cap. Monday? ha! ha! Well, Wednesday is too
      soon;
O' Thursday let it be:—o' Thursday, tell her, 20
She shall be married to this noble earl.—
Will you be ready? do you like this haste?
We'll keep no great ado:—a friend, or two;—
For, hark you, Tybalt being slain so late,
It may be thought we held him carelessly,
Being our kinsman, if we revel much.
Therefore, we'll have some half a dozen friends,
And there an end. But what say you to Thursday?
  Par. My lord, I would that Thursday were to-
      morrow.
  Cap. Well, get you gone:—o' Thursday be it
      then.—   30
Go you to Juliet ere you go to bed,
Prepare her, wife, against this wedding-day.—
Farewell, my lord.—Light to my chamber, ho!
Afore me! it is so very late, that we
May call it early by-and-by.—Good night.   [*Exeunt.*

SCENE V.—JULIET's Chamber.

Enter ROMEO *and* JULIET.

  Jul. Wilt thou be gone? it is not yet near day:
It was the nightingale, and not the lark,
That pierc'd the fearful hollow of thine ear;
Nightly she sings on yon pomegranate-tree:
Believe me, love, it was the nightingale.
  Rom. It was the lark, the herald of the morn,
No nightingale: look, love, what envious streaks
Do lace the severing clouds in yonder east.
Night's candles are burnt out, and jocund day
Stands tiptoe on the misty mountain tops: 10
I must be gone and live, or stay and die.
  Jul. Yon light is not daylight, I know it, I:
It is some meteor that the sun exhales,
To be to thee this night a torch-bearer,
And light thee on thy way to Mantua:
Therefore stay yet; thou need'st not to be gone.
  Rom. Let me be ta'en; let me be put to death;
I am content, so thou wilt have it so.
I'll say, yon grey is not the morning's eye,
'T is but the pale reflex of Cynthia's brow; 20
Nor that is not the lark, whose notes do beat
The vaulty heaven so high above our heads:
I have more care to stay than will to go:—

Come, death, and welcome ! Juliet wills it so.—
How is 't, my soul ? let 's talk, it is not day.
   Jul. It is, it is ; hie hence, be gone, away !
It is the lark that sings so out of tune,
Straining harsh discords, and unpleasing sharps.

   Rom. More light and light : more dark and dark
    our woes.
              Enter Nurse.
   Nurse. Madam !
   Jul. Nurse ?

Rom. " Farewell, farewell ! one kiss, and I 'll descend."

Some say, the lark makes sweet division ;
This doth not so, for she divideth us :   30
Some say, the lark and loathed toad change eyes ;
O ! now I would they had chang'd voices too,
Since arm from arm that voice doth us affray,
Hunting thee hence with hunts-up to the day.
O ! now be gone : more light and light it grows.

   Nurse. Your lady mother 's coming to your
    chamber :
The day is broke ; be wary, look about.   40
                            [Exit.
   Jul. Then, window, let day in, and let life out.
   Rom. Farewell, farewell ! one kiss, and I 'll descend.
                           [Descends.

Jul. Art thou gone so? love! lord! ay, husband,
    friend!
I must hear from thee every day in the hour,
For in a minute there are many days:
O! by this count I shall be much in years,
Ere I again behold my Romeo.
    Rom. Farewell! I will omit no opportunity
That may convey my greetings, love, to thee.
    Jul. O! think'st thou, we shall ever meet again? 50
    Rom. I doubt it not; and all these woes shall serve
For sweet discourses in our time to come.
    Jul. O God! I have an ill-divining soul:
Methinks, I see thee, now thou art so low,
As one dead in the bottom of a tomb:
Either my eyesight fails, or thou look'st pale.
    Rom. And trust me, love, in my eye so do you:
Dry sorrow drinks our blood. Adieu! adieu! [*Exit.*
    Jul. O fortune, fortune! all men call thee fickle:
If thou art fickle, what dost thou with him   60
That is renown'd for faith? Be fickle, fortune;
For then, I hope, thou wilt not keep him long,
But send him back.
    La. Cap. [*Within.*] Ho, daughter! are you up?
    Jul. Who is't that calls? is it my lady mother?
Is she not down so late, or up so early?
What unaccustom'd cause procures her hither?

        Enter Lady CAPULET.

    La. Cap. Why, how now, Juliet?
    Jul.   Madam, I am not well.
    La. Cap. Evermore weeping for your cousin's death?
What! wilt thou wash him from his grave with tears?
An if thou couldst, thou couldst not make him live :70
Therefore, have done. Some grief shows much of love;
But much of grief shows still some want of wit.
    Jul. Yet let me weep for such a feeling loss.
    La. Cap. So shall you feel the loss, but not the friend
Which you weep for.
    Jul.   Feeling so the loss,
I cannot choose but ever weep the friend.
    La. Cap. Well, girl, thou weep'st not so much for
    his death,
As that the villain lives which slaughter'd him.
    Jul. What villain, madam?
    La. Cap.   That same villain, Romeo.
    Jul. Villain and he are many miles asunder.   80
God pardon him! I do, with all my heart;
And yet no man like he doth grieve my heart.
    La. Cap. That is, because the traitor murderer lives.
    Jul. Ay, madam, from the reach of these my hands.
'Would, none but I might venge my cousin's death!
    La. Cap. We will have vengeance for it, fear thou
    not:
Then weep no more. I'll send to one in Mantua,—
Where that same banish'd runagate doth live,—
Shall give him such an unaccustom'd dram,
That he shall soon keep Tybalt company: 90
And then, I hope, thou wilt be satisfied.
    Jul. Indeed, I never shall be satisfied
With Romeo, till I behold him—dead—
Is my poor heart, so for a kinsman vex'd.—
Madam, if you could find out but a man
To bear a poison, I would temper it,
That Romeo should, upon receipt thereof,
Soon sleep in quiet.—O! how my heart abhors
To hear him nam'd,—and cannot come to him,—
To wreak the love I bore my cousin Tybalt   100
Upon his body that hath slaughter'd him!
    La. Cap. Find thou the means, and I'll find such a
    man.
But now I'll tell thee joyful tidings, girl.
    Jul. And joy comes well in such a needy time.
What are they, I beseech your ladyship?
    La. Cap. Well, well, thou hast a careful father,
    child;
One who, to put thee from thy heaviness,
Hath sorted out a sudden day of joy,
That thou expect'st not, nor I look'd not for.
    Jul. Madam, in happy time, what day is that? 110
    La. Cap. Marry, my child, early next Thursday
    morn,
The gallant, young, and noble gentleman,

The County Paris, at Saint Peter's Church,
Shall happily make thee there a joyful bride.
    Jul. Now, by Saint Peter's Church, and Peter too,
He shall not make me there a joyful bride.
I wonder at this haste; that I must wed
Ere he, that should be husband, comes to woo.
I pray you, tell my lord and father, madam,
I will not marry yet; and, when I do, I swear,   120
It shall be Romeo, whom you know I hate,
Rather than Paris.—These are news indeed!
    La. Cap. Here comes your father; tell him so your-
    self,
And see how he will take it at your hands.

        Enter CAPULET *and Nurse.*

    Cap. When the sun sets, the earth doth drizzle dew;
But for the sunset of my brother's son,
It rains downright.—
How now? a conduit, girl? what! still in tears?
Evermore showering? In one little body
Thou counterfeit'st a bark, a sea, a wind: 130
For still thy eyes, which I may call the sea,
Do ebb and flow with tears; the bark thy body is,
Sailing in this salt flood; the winds, thy sighs:
Who, raging with thy tears, and they with them,
Without a sudden calm, will overset
Thy tempest-tossed body.—How now, wife?
Have you deliver'd to her our decree?
    La. Cap. Ay, sir; but she will none, she gives you
    thanks.
I would, the fool were married to her grave!
    Cap. Soft, take me with you, take me with you, wife.
How! will she none? doth she not give us thanks?141
Is she not proud? doth she not count her bless'd,
Unworthy as she is, that we have wrought
So worthy a gentleman to be her bridegroom?
    Jul. Not proud, you have; but thankful, that you
    have:
Proud can I never be of what I hate;
But thankful even for hate, that is meant love.
    Cap. How now! how now, chop-logic! What is
    this?
"Proud,"—and "I thank you,"—and "I thank you
    not;"—
And yet "not proud;"—mistress minion, you,   150
Thank me no thankings, nor proud me no prouds,
But fettle your fine joints 'gainst Thursday next,
To go with Paris to Saint Peter's Church,
Or I will drag thee on a hurdle thither.
Out, you green-sickness carrion! out, you baggage!
You tallow-face!
    La. Cap.   Fie, fie! what, are you mad?
    Jul. Good father, I beseech you on my knees,
Hear me with patience but to speak a word.
    Cap. Hang thee, young baggage! disobedient
    wretch!
I tell thee what,—get thee to church o' Thursday, 160
Or never after look me in the face.
Speak not, reply not, do not answer me;
My fingers itch.—Wife, we scarce thought us bless'd,
That God had lent us but this only child;
But now I see this one is one too much,
And that we have a curse in having her.
Out on her, hilding!
    Nurse.   God in heaven bless her!—
You are to blame, my lord, to rate her so.
    Cap. And why, my lady wisdom? hold your tongue,
Good prudence: smatter with your gossips; go.   170
    Nurse. I speak no treason.
    Cap.   O! God ye good den.
    Nurse. May not one speak?
    Cap.   Peace, you mumbling fool!
Utter your gravity o'er a gossip's bowl,
For here we need it not.
    La. Cap.   You are too hot.
    Cap. God's bread! it makes me mad.
Day, night, hour, tide, time, work, play,
Alone, in company, still my care hath been
To have her match'd; and having now provided
A gentleman of noble parentage,
Of fair demesnes, youthful, and nobly train'd,   180
Stuff'd (as they say) with honourable parts,

Proportion'd as one's thought would wish a man,—
And then to have a wretched puling fool,
A whining mammet, in her fortune's tender,
To answer—"I'll not wed,"—"I cannot love,"—

Jul. "Good father, I beseech you on my knees."

"I am too young,"—"I pray you, pardon me;"—
But, an you will not wed, I'll pardon you;
Graze where you will, you shall not house with me:
Look to 't, think on 't, I do not use to jest.
Thursday is near; lay hand on heart, advise.		190
An you be mine, I'll give you to my friend;
An you be not, hang, beg, starve, die i' the streets,
For, by my soul, I'll ne'er acknowledge thee,

Nor what is mine shall never do thee good.
Trust to 't, bethink you, I'll not be forsworn.	[*Exit.*
	Jul. Is there no pity sitting in the clouds,
That sees into the bottom of my grief?—
O, sweet my mother, cast me not away!
Delay this marriage for a month, a week;
Or, if you do not, make the bridal bed		200
In that dim monument where Tybalt lies.
	La. Cap. Talk not to me, for I'll not speak a word.
Do as thou wilt, for I have done with thee.	[*Exit.*
	Jul. O God!—O nurse! how shall this be prevented?
My husband is on earth, my faith in heaven;
How shall that faith return again to earth,
Unless that husband send it me from heaven
By leaving earth?—comfort me, counsel me.—
Alack, alack! that Heaven should practise stratagems
Upon so soft a subject as myself!—		210
What say'st thou? hast thou not a word of joy?
Some comfort, nurse.
	Nurse.			Faith, here it is.
Romeo is banished; and all the world to nothing,
That he dares ne'er come back to challenge you;
Or, if he do, it needs must be by stealth.
Then, since the case so stands as now it doth,
I think it best you married with the county.
O! he's a lovely gentleman;
Romeo's a dishclout to him: an eagle, madam,
Hath not so green, so quick, so fair an eye,		220
As Paris hath. Beshrew my very heart,
I think you are happy in this second match,
For it excels your first: or if it did not,
Your first is dead; or 't were as good he were,
As living here and you no use of him.
	Jul. Speakest thou from thy heart?
	Nurse. And from my soul too; else beshrew them
		both.
	Jul. Amen!
	Nurse. What?
	Jul. Well, thou hast comforted me marvellous
		much.		230
Go in; and tell my lady I am gone,
Having displeas'd my father, to Laurence' cell
To make confession, and to be absolv'd.
	Nurse. Marry, I will; and this is wisely done. [*Exit.*
	Jul. Ancient damnation! O most wicked fiend!
Is it more sin to wish me thus forsworn,
Or to dispraise my lord with that same tongue
Which she hath prais'd him with above compare
So many thousand times?—Go, counsellor;
Thou and my bosom henceforth shall be twain.— 240
I'll to the friar, to know his remedy:
If all else fail, myself have power to die.		[*Exit.*

ACT IV.

Scene I.—Friar Laurence's Cell.

Enter Friar Laurence *and* Paris.

	Friar.
		N Thursday, sir? the time is very short.
	Par. My father Capulet will have it so;
And I am nothing slow, to slack his
	haste.
	Fri. You say, you do not know the
	lady's mind:
Uneven is the course, I like it not.
	Par. Immoderately she weeps for Tybalt's
		death,
And therefore have I little talk'd of love;

For Venus smiles not in a house of tears.
Now, sir, her father counts it dangerous,
That she doth give her sorrow so much sway		10
And in his wisdom hastes our marriage,
To stop the inundation of her tears;
Which, too much minded by herself alone,
May be put from her by society.
Now do you know the reason of this haste.
	Fri. [*Aside.*] I would I knew not why it should be
		slow'd.
Look, sir, here comes the lady towards my cell.

Enter JULIET.

Par. Happily met, my lady, and my wife!
Jul. That may be, sir, when I may be a wife.
Par. That may be, must be, love, on Thursday
    next.   20
Jul. What must be shall be.
Fri.   That 's a certain text.
Par. Come you to make confession to this father?
Jul. To answer that, I should confess to you.
Par. Do not deny to him, that you love me.
Jul. I will confess to you, that I love him.
Par. So will ye, I am sure, that you love me.
Jul. If I do so, it will be of more price,
Being spoke behind your back, than to your face.
Par. Poor soul, thy face is much abus'd with tears.
Jul. The tears have got small victory by that; 30
For it was bad enough before their spite.
Par. Thou wrong'st it, more than tears, with that
    report.
Jul. That is no slander, sir, which is a truth;
And what I spake, I spake it to my face.
Par. Thy face is mine, and thou hast slander'd it.
Jul. It may be so, for it is not mine own.—
Are you at leisure, holy father, now,
Or shall I come to you at evening mass?
Fri. My leisure serves me, pensive daughter, now.—
My lord, we must entreat the time alone. 40
Par. God shield, I should disturb devotion!—
Juliet, on Thursday early will I rouse you:
Till then, adieu; and keep this holy kiss.   [*Exit.*
Jul. O! shut the door; and when thou hast done
    so,
Come weep with me; past hope, past cure, past help!
Fri. Ah, Juliet! I already know thy grief;
It strains me past the compass of my wits:
I hear thou must, and nothing may prorogue it,
On Thursday next be married to this county.
Jul. Tell me not, friar, that thou hear'st of this, 50
Unless thou tell me how I may prevent it:
If in thy wisdom thou canst give no help,
Do thou but call my resolution wise,
And with this knife I 'll help it presently.
God join'd my heart and Romeo's, thou our hands;
And ere this hand, by thee to Romeo seal'd,
Shall be the label to another deed,
Or my true heart with treacherous revolt
Turn to another, this shall slay them both.
Therefore, out of thy long experienc'd time, 60
Give me some present counsel; or, behold,
'Twixt my extremes and me this bloody knife
Shall play the umpire; arbitrating that
Which the commission of thy years and art
Could to no issue of true honour bring.
Be not so long to speak; I long to die,
If what thou speak'st speak not of remedy.
Fri. Hold, daughter; I do spy a kind of hope,
Which craves as desperate an execution
As that is desperate which we would prevent. 70
If, rather than to marry County Paris,
Thou hast the strength of will to slay thyself,
Then is it likely thou wilt undertake
A thing like death to chide away this shame,
Thou cop'st with death himself to 'scape from it;
And, if thou dar'st, I 'll give thee remedy.
Jul. O! bid me leap, rather than marry Paris,
From off the battlements of yonder tower;
Or walk in thievish ways; or bid me lurk
Where serpents are; chain me with roaring bears; 80
Or shut me nightly in a charnel-house,
O'er-cover'd quite with dead men's rattling bones,
With reeky shanks, and yellow chapless skulls;
Or bid me go into a new-made grave
And hide me with a dead man in his shroud;
Things that, to hear them told, have made me
    tremble;
And I will do it without fear or doubt,
To live an unstain'd wife to my sweet love.
Fri. Hold, then: go home, be merry, give consent
To marry Paris. Wednesday is to-morrow; 90
To-morrow night look that thou lie alone,
Let not thy nurse lie with thee in thy chamber:

Take thou this vial, being then in bed,
And this distilled liquor drink thou off;
When, presently, through all thy veins shall run
A cold and drowsy humour; for no pulse
Shall keep his native progress, but surcease:
No warmth, no breath, shall testify thou livest;
The roses in thy lips and cheeks shall fade
To paly ashes; thy eyes' windows fall, 100
Like death, when he shuts up the day of life;
Each part, depriv'd of supple government,
Shall, stiff and stark and cold, appear like death:
And in this borrow'd likeness of shrunk death
Thou shalt continue two and forty hours,
And then awake as from a pleasant sleep.
Now, when the bridegroom in the morning comes
To rouse thee from thy bed, there art thou dead:
Then, as the manner of our country is,
In thy best robes uncover'd on the bier, 110
Thou shalt be borne to that same ancient vault,
Where all the kindred of the Capulets lie.

Jul. "Farewell, dear father."

In the meantime, against thou shalt awake,
Shall Romeo by my letters know our drift;
And hither shall he come, and he and I
Will watch thy waking, and that very night
Shall Romeo bear thee hence to Mantua.
And this shall free thee from this present shame,
If no unconstant toy, nor womanish fear,
Abate thy valour in the acting it. 120
Jul. Give me, give me! O! tell not me of fear.
Fri. Hold; get you gone: be strong and prosperous
In this resolve. I 'll send a friar with speed
To Mantua, with my letters to thy lord.
Jul. Love, give me strength! and strength shall
    help afford.
Farewell, dear father.   [*Exeunt.*

SCENE II.—A Room in CAPULET'S House.

Enter CAPULET, *Lady* CAPULET, *Nurse, and*
Servants.

Cap. So many guests invite as here are writ.—
                    [*Exit Servant.*
Sirrah, go hire me twenty cunning cooks.
2 Serv. You shall have none ill, sir; for I 'll try if
they can lick their fingers.
Cap. How canst thou try them so?
2 Serv. Marry, sir, 'tis an ill cook that cannot lick

his own fingers : therefore, he that cannot lick his
fingers goes not with me.
  Cap. Go, be gone.—   [*Exit Servant.*
We shall be much unfurnish'd for this time.—   10
What, is my daughter gone to Friar Laurence ?
  Nurse. Ay, forsooth.
  Cap. Well, he may chance to do some good on her :
A peevish self-will'd harlotry it is.

           Enter JULIET.

  Nurse. See, where she comes from shrift with merry
    look.
  Cap. How now, my headstrong? where have you
    been gadding?
  Jul. Where I have learn'd me to repent the sin
Of disobedient opposition
To you, and your behests ; and am enjoin'd
By holy Laurence to fall prostrate here,   20
To beg your pardon.—Pardon, I beseech you :
Henceforward I am ever rul'd by you.
  Cap. Send for the county : go tell him of this ;
I 'll have this knot knit up to-morrow morning.
  Jul. I met the youthful lord at Laurence' cell ;
And gave him what becomed love I might,
Not stepping o'er the bounds of modesty.
  Cap. Why, I am glad on 't ; this is well,—stand up :
This is as 't should be.—Let me see the county :
Ay, marry, go, I say, and fetch him hither.— 30
Now, afore God, this reverend holy friar,
All our whole city is much bound to him.
  Jul. Nurse, will you go with me into my closet,
To help me sort such needful ornaments
As you think fit to furnish me to-morrow?
  La. Cap. No, not till Thursday : there is time
    enough.
  Cap. Go, nurse, go with her.—We 'll to church to-
    morrow.   [*Exeunt* JULIET *and Nurse.*
  La. Cap. We shall be short in our provision :
'T is now near night.
  Cap.   Tush ! I will stir about,
And all things shall be well, I warrant thee, wife. 40
Go thou to Juliet ; help to deck up her :
I 'll not to bed to-night ;—let me alone ;
I 'll play the housewife for this once.—What, ho !—
They are all forth : well, I will walk myself
To County Paris, to prepare him up
Against to-morrow. My heart is wondrous light,
Since this same wayward girl is so reclaim'd.
                         [*Exeunt.*

SCENE III.—JULIET'S Chamber.

      Enter JULIET *and Nurse.*

  Jul. Ay, those attires are best :—but, gentle nurse,
I pray thee, leave me to myself to-night ;
For I have need of many orisons
To move the heavens to smile upon my state,
Which, well thou know'st, is cross and full of sin.

     Enter Lady CAPULET.

  La. Cap. What, are you busy, ho? need you my
    help?
  Jul. No, madam ; we have cull'd such necessaries
As are behoveful for our state to-morrow :
So please you, let me now be left alone,
And let the nurse this night sit up with you ; 10
For, I am sure, you have your hands full all
In this so sudden business.
  La. Cap.   Good night :
Get thee to bed, and rest ; for thou hast need.
          [*Exeunt Lady* CAPULET *and Nurse.*
  Jul. Farewell !—God knows when we shall meet
    again.
I have a faint cold fear thrills through my veins,
That almost freezes up the heat of life :
I 'll call them back again to comfort me.—
Nurse !—What should she do here ?
My dismal scene I needs must act alone.
Come, vial.—   20
What if this mixture do not work at all ?
Shall I be married then to-morrow morning ?—

No, no ;—this shall forbid it :—lie thou there.
                 [*Laying down a dagger.*
What if it be a poison, which the friar
Subtly hath minister'd to have me dead,
Lest in this marriage he should be dishonour'd,
Because he married me before to Romeo ?
I fear, it is ; and yet, methinks, it should not,
For he hath still been tried a holy man.—
How if, when I am laid into the tomb,   30
I wake before the time that Romeo
Come to redeem me ? there 's a fearful point !
Shall I not then be stifled in the vault,
To whose foul mouth no healthsome air breathes in,
And there die strangled ere my Romeo comes ?
Or, if I live, is it not like, that I,
The horrible conceit of death and night,
Together with the terror of the place,—
As in a vault, an ancient receptacle,
Where, for this many hundred years, the bones 40
Of all my buried ancestors are pack'd ;
Where bloody Tybalt, yet but green in earth,
Lies fest'ring in his shroud ; where, as they say,
At some hours in the night spirits resort :—
Alack, alack ! is it not like, that I,
So early waking,—what with loathsome smells,
And shrieks like mandrakes' torn out of the earth,
That living mortals, hearing them, run mad ;—
O ! if I wake, shall I not be distraught,
Environed with all these hideous fears,   50
And madly play with my forefathers' joints,
And pluck the mangled Tybalt from his shroud ?
And, in this rage, with some great kinsman's bone,
As with a club, dash out my desperate brains ?
O, look ! methinks, I see my cousin's ghost
Seeking out Romeo, that did spit his body
Upon a rapier's point.—Stay, Tybalt, stay !—
Romeo, I come ! this do I drink to thee.
              [*She throws herself on the bed.*

SCENE IV.—CAPULET'S Hall.

    Enter Lady CAPULET *and Nurse.*

  La. Cap. Hold, take these keys, and fetch more
    spices, nurse.
  Nurse. They call for dates and quinces in the pastry.

        Enter CAPULET.

  Cap. Come, stir, stir, stir ! the second cock hath
    crow'd,
The curfew bell hath rung, 't is three o'clock :—
Look to the bak'd meats, good Angelica :
Spare not for cost.
  Nurse.   Go, go, you cot-quean, go ;
Get you to bed : 'faith, you 'll be sick to-morrow
For this night's watching.
  Cap. No, not a whit. What ! I have watch'd ere now
All night for lesser cause, and ne'er been sick.   10
  La. Cap. Ay, you have been a mouse-hunt in your
    time ;
But I will watch you from such watching now.
         [*Exeunt Lady* CAPULET *and Nurse.*
  Cap. A jealous-hood, a jealous-hood !—Now, fellow,
What 's there ?

   Enter Servants, with spits, logs, and baskets.

  1 *Serv.* Things for the cook, sir ; but I know not
    what.
  Cap. Make haste, make haste. [*Exit* 1 *Serv.*]—
    Sirrah, fetch drier logs :
Call Peter, he will show thee where they are.
  2 *Serv.* I have a head, sir, that will find out logs,
And never trouble Peter for the matter.   [*Exit.*
  Cap. 'Mass, and well said ; a merry whoreson, ha !
Thou shalt be logger-head.—Good faith ! 't is day : 21
The county will be here with music straight,
For so he said he would.—[*Music within.*] I hear him
    near.—
Nurse !—Wife !—What, ho !—What, nurse, I say !

         Enter Nurse.

Go, waken Juliet ; go, and trim her up :

I 'll go and chat with Paris.—Hie, make haste,
Make haste ; the bridegroom he is come already :
Make haste, I say.

SCENE V.—JULIET'S Chamber ; JULIET on the bed.

Enter Nurse.

Nurse. Mistress !—what, mistress !—Juliet !—fast, I
　　warrant her, she :—
Why, lamb !—why, lady !—fie, you slug-a-bed !—
Why, love, I say !—madam ! sweet-heart !—why,
　　bride !—
What ! not a word ?—you take your pennyworths now :
Sleep for a week ; for the next night, I warrant,
The County Paris hath set up his rest,
That you shall rest but little.—God forgive me,
Marry, and amen, how sound is she asleep !
I needs must wake her. Madam, madam, madam !
Ay, let the county take you in your bed :　　　10
He 'll fright you up, i' faith.—Will it not be ?
What, dress'd ! and in your clothes ! and down again !
I must needs wake you. Lady ! lady ! lady !—
Alas ! alas !—Help ! help ! my lady 's dead !—
O, well-a-day, that ever I was born !—
Some *aqua vitœ*, ho !—my lord, my lady !—

Enter Lady CAPULET.

La. Cap. What noise is here ?
Nurse.　　　　　　　　　　O lamentable day !
La. Cap. What is the matter ?
Nurse.　　　　　　Look, look ! O heavy day !
La. Cap. O me ! O me !—my child, my only life,
Revive, look up, or I will die with thee !—　　　20
Help, help !—Call help.

Enter CAPULET.

Cap. For shame ! bring Juliet forth ; her lord is
　　come.
Nurse. She 's dead, deceas'd, she 's dead ; alack the
　　day !
La. Cap. Alack the day ! she 's dead, she 's dead,
　　she 's dead.
Cap. Ha ! let me see her.—Out, alas ! she 's cold ;
Her blood is settled, and her joints are stiff ;
Life and these lips have long been separated
Death lies on her, like an untimely frost
Upon the sweetest flower of all the field.
Nurse. O lamentable day !
La. Cap.　　　　　　　　O woful time !　　　30
Cap. Death, that hath ta'en her hence to make me
　　wail,
Ties up my tongue, and will not let me speak.

Enter Friar LAURENCE *and* PARIS, *with Musicians.*

Fri. Come, is the bride ready to go to church ?
Cap. Ready to go, but never to return.—
O son ! the night before thy wedding-day
Hath Death lain with thy wife.—There she lies,
Flower as she was, deflowered by him.
Death is my son-in-law, Death is my heir ;
My daughter he hath wedded. I will die,
And leave him all ; life, living, all is Death's !　　40
Par. Have I thought long to see this morning's face,
And doth it give me such a sight as this ?
La. Cap. Accurs'd, happy, wretched, hateful day !
Most miserable hour, that e'er time saw
In lasting labour of his pilgrimage !
But one, poor one, one poor and loving child,
But one thing to rejoice and solace in,
And cruel death hath catch'd it from my sight !
Nurse. O woe ! O woful, woful, woful day !
Most lamentable day, most woful day,
That ever, ever, I did yet behold !
O day ! O day ! O day ! O hateful day !
Never was seen so black a day as this
O woful day, O woful day !
Par. Beguil'd, divorced, wronged, spited, slain !
Most detestable death, by thee beguil'd,
By cruel cruel thee quite overthrown !—
O love ! O life !—not life, but love in death !
Cap. Despis'd, distressed, hated, martyr'd, kill'd !

Uncomfortable time, why cam'st thou now　　　60
To murder, murder our solemnity ?—
O child ! O child !—my soul, and not my child !—
Dead art thou !—alack ! my child is dead ;
And with my child my joys are buried.
Fri. Peace, ho ! for shame ! confusion's cure lives
　　not
In these confusions. Heaven and yourself
Had part in this fair maid ; now Heaven hath all,
And all the better is it for the maid :
Your part in her you could not keep from death,
But Heaven keeps his part in eternal life.　　　70
The most you sought was her promotion,
For 't was your heaven, she should be advanc'd :
And weep ye now, seeing she is advanc'd
Above the clouds, as high as heaven itself ?
O ! in this love, you love your child so ill,

Cap. "There she lies, flower as she was."

That you run mad, seeing that she is well :
She 's not well married that lives married long ;
But she 's best married that dies married young.
Dry up your tears, and stick your rosemary
On this fair corse ; and, as the custom is,　　　80
In all her best array bear her to church :
For though fond nature bids us all lament,
Yet nature's tears are reason's merriment.
Cap. All things, that we ordained festival,
Turn from their office to black funeral :
Our instruments to melancholy bells ;
Our wedding cheer to a sad burial feast ;
Our solemn hymns to sullen dirges change ;
Our bridal flowers serve for a buried corse,
And all things change them to the contrary.　　　90
Fri. Sir, go you in ;—and, madam, go with him ;—
And go, Sir Paris :—every one prepare
To follow this fair corse unto her grave.
The heavens do lour upon you, for some ill ;
Move them no more, by crossing their high will.
　　[*Exeunt* CAPULET, *Lady* CAPULET, PARIS, *and*
　　　　　　　　Friar.
1 *Mus.* 'Faith, we may put up our pipes, and be
　　gone.
Nurse. Honest good fellows, ah ! put up, put up ;
For, well you know, this is a pitiful case.　　　[*Exit.*
1 *Mus.* Ay, by my troth, the case may be amended.

Enter PETER.

Peter. Musicians, O, musicians ! "Heart's ease,
Heart's ease :" O ! an you will have me live, play
"Heart's ease."　　　　　　　　　　　　102

1 *Mus.* Why "Heart's ease?"
Peter. O, musicians, because my heart itself plays
—" My heart is full of woe." O! play me some merry
dump, to comfort me.
2 *Mus.* Not a dump we: 'tis no time to play
now.
Peter. You will not then?
Mus. No.   110
Peter. I will then give it you soundly.
1 *Mus.* What will you give us?
Peter. No money, on my faith; but the gleek: I
will give you the minstrel.
1 *Mus.* Then will I give you the serving-creature.
Peter. Then will I lay the serving-creature's dagger
on your pate. I will carry no crotchets: I 'll *re* you,
I 'll *fa* you. Do you note me?
1 *Mus.* An you *re* us, and *fa* us, you note us.
2 *Mus.* Pray you, put up your dagger, and put out
your wit.   121
Peter. Then have at you with my wit. I will dry-
beat you with an iron wit, and put up my iron dagger.
—Answer me like men:

When griping grief the heart doth wound,
 And doleful dumps the mind oppress,
Then music with her silver sound—

Why "silver sound?" why "music with her silver
sound?" What say you, Simon Catling?
1 *Mus.* Marry, sir, because silver hath a sweet
sound.   131
Peter. Pretty!—What say you, Hugh Rebeck?
2 *Mus.* I say—" silver sound," because musicians
sound for silver.
Peter. Pretty too!—what say you, James Soundpost?
3 *Mus.* 'Faith, I know not what to say.
Peter. O! I cry you mercy; you are the singer: I
will say for you. It is—"music with her silver sound,"
because musicians have no gold for sounding:—

Then music with her silver sound 140
 With speedy help doth lend redress. [*Exit.*

1 *Mus.* What a pestilent knave is this same!
2 *Mus.* Hang him, Jack! Come, we 'll in here;
tarry for the mourners, and stay dinner. [*Exeunt.*

ACT V.

SCENE I.—Mantua. A Street.

Enter ROMEO.

   Romeo.
F I may trust the flattering truth of
  sleep,
My dreams presage some joyful news
  at hand.
My bosom's lord sits lightly in his
  throne;
And, all this day, an unaccustom'd
  spirit
Lifts me above the ground with cheer-
  ful thoughts.
I dreamt, my lady came and found me
  dead;
(Strange dream, that gives a dead man
  leave to think!)
And breath'd such life with kisses in
  my lips,
That I reviv'd, and was an emperor.
Ah me! how sweet is love itself pos-
  sess'd,   10
When but love's shadows are so rich in joy!

Enter BALTHASAR.

News from Verona!—How now, Balthasar?
Dost thou not bring me letters from the friar?
How doth my lady? Is my father well?
How doth my Lady Juliet? that I ask again;
For nothing can be ill if she be well.
 Bal. Then she is well, and nothing can be ill.
Her body sleeps in Capels' monument,
And her immortal part with angels lives.
I saw her laid low in her kindred's vault, 20
And presently took post to tell it you.
O, pardon me for bringing these ill news,
Since you did leave it for my office, sir.
 Rom. Is it e'en so? then, I deny you, stars!
Thou know'st my lodging: get me ink and paper,
And hire post-horses; I will hence to-night.
 Bal. I do beseech you, sir, have patience:
Your looks are pale and wild, and do import
Some misadventure.

 Rom.   Tush! thou art deceiv'd:
Leave me, and do the thing I bid thee do. 30
Hast thou no letters to me from the friar?
 Bal. No, my good lord.
 Rom.   No matter; get thee gone,
And hire those horses: I 'll be with thee straight.—
      [*Exit* BALTHASAR.
Well, Juliet, I will lie with thee to-night.
Let 's see for means:—O mischief! thou art swift
To enter in the thoughts of desperate men!
I do remember an apothecary,
And hereabouts 'a dwells, which late I noted
In tatter'd weeds, with overwhelming brows,
Culling of simples; meagre were his looks, 40
Sharp misery had worn him to the bones:
And in his needy shop a tortoise hung,
An alligator stuff'd, and other skins
Of ill-shap'd fishes; and about his shelves
A beggarly account of empty boxes,
Green earthen pots, bladders, and musty seeds,
Remnants of packthread, and old cakes of roses,
Were thinly scatter'd to make up a show.
Noting this penury, to myself I said—
An if a man did need a poison now, 50
Whose sale is present death in Mantua,
Here lives a caitiff wretch would sell it him.
O! this same thought did but forerun my need,
And this same needy man must sell it me.
As I remember, this should be the house:
Being holiday, the beggar's shop is shut.—
What, ho! apothecary!

   Enter Apothecary.

 Ap.   Who calls so loud?
 Rom. Come hither, man.—I see, that thou art
  poor;
Hold, there is forty ducats: let me have
A dram of poison; such soon-speeding gear 60
As will disperse itself through all the veins,
That the life-weary taker may fall dead;
And that the trunk may be discharg'd of breath

As violently, as hasty powder fir'd
Doth hurry from the fatal cannon's womb.
  Ap. Such mortal drugs I have ; but Mantua's law
Is death to any he that utters them.
  Rom. Art thou so bare, and full of wretchedness,
And fear'st to die ? famine is in thy cheeks,
Need and oppression starveth in thy eyes,   70
Contempt and beggary hang upon thy back ;
The world is not thy friend, nor the world's law :
The world affords no law to make thee rich ;
Then be not poor, but break it, and take this.
  Ap. My poverty, but not my will, consents.
  Rom. I pay thy poverty, and not thy will.
  Ap. Put this in any liquid thing you will,
And drink it off; and, if you had the strength
Of twenty men, it would despatch you straight.
  Rom. There is thy gold ; worse poison to men's
    souls,   80
Doing more murder in this loathsome world,
Than these poor compounds that thou may'st not sell :
I sell thee poison, thou hast sold me none.
Farewell ; buy food, and get thyself in flesh.—
Come, cordial, and not poison, go with me
To Juliet's grave, for there must I use thee. [*Exeunt.*

SCENE II.—Friar LAURENCE'S Cell.

Enter Friar JOHN.

  John. Holy Franciscan friar ! brother ! ho !

Enter Friar LAURENCE.

  Lau. This same should be the voice of Friar John.—
Welcome from Mantua : what says Romeo ?
Or, if his mind be writ, give me his letter.
  John. Going to find a bare-foot brother out,
One of our order, to associate me,
Here in this city visiting the sick,
And finding him, the searchers of the town,
Suspecting that we both were in a house
Where the infectious pestilence did reign,   10
Seal'd up the doors, and would not let us forth ;
So that my speed to Mantua there was stay'd.
  Lau. Who bare my letter then to Romeo ?
  John. I could not send it,—here it is again,—
Nor get a messenger to bring it thee,
So fearful were they of infection.
  Lau. Unhappy fortune ! by my brotherhood,
The letter was not nice, but full of charge,
Of dear import ; and the neglecting it
May do much danger. Friar John, go hence ;   20
Get me an iron crow, and bring it straight
Unto my cell.
  John. Brother, I 'll go and bring it thee. [*Exit.*
  Lau. Now must I to the monument alone ;
Within this three hours will fair Juliet wake :
She will beshrew me much, that Romeo
Hath had no notice of these accidents ;
But I will write again to Mantua,
And keep her at my cell till Romeo come :
Poor living corse, clos'd in a dead man's tomb !   30
              [*Exit.*

SCENE III.—A Churchyard ; in it a Monument
belonging to the CAPULETS.

Enter PARIS, *and his Page, bearing flowers and a
torch.*

  Par. Give me thy torch, boy : hence, and stand
    aloof ;—
Yet put it out, for I would not be seen.
Under yond yew-trees lay thee all along,
Holding thine ear close to the hollow ground :
So shall no foot upon the churchyard tread,
Being loose, unfirm with digging up of graves,
But thou shalt hear it : whistle then to me,
As signal that thou hear'st something approach.
Give me those flowers. Do as I bid thee ; go.
  Page. I am almost afraid to stand alone   10
Here in the churchyard ; yet I will adventure. [*Retires.*

  Par. Sweet flower, with flowers thy bridal bed I
    strew,
(O woe ! thy canopy is dust and stones !)
Which with sweet water nightly I will dew,
Or, wanting that, with tears distill'd by moans :
The obsequies that I for thee will keep,
Nightly shall be, to strew thy grave and weep!—
              [*The Boy whistles.*
The boy gives warning something doth approach.
What cursed foot wanders this way to-night,
To cross my obsequies, and true love's rite ?   20
What ! with a torch?—muffle me, night, awhile.
              [*Retires.*

Enter ROMEO *and* BALTHASAR, *with a torch,
mattock, &c.*

  Rom. Give me that mattock, and the wrenching
    iron.
Hold, take this letter : early in the morning
See thou deliver it to my lord and father.
Give me the light. Upon thy life I charge thee,
Whate'er thou hear'st or seest, stand all aloof,
And do not interrupt me in my course.
Why I descend into this bed of death,
Is, partly, to behold my lady's face ;
But, chiefly, to take thence from her dead finger   30
A precious ring, a ring that I must use
In dear employment. Therefore hence, be gone :
But if thou, jealous, dost return to pry
In what I further shall intend to do,
By Heaven, I will tear thee joint by joint,
And strew this hungry churchyard with thy limbs.
The time and my intents are savage-wild,
More fierce, and more inexorable far,
Than empty tigers, or the roaring sea.
  Bal. I will be gone, sir, and not trouble you.   40
  Rom. So shalt thou show me friendship.—Take
    thou that :
Live, and be prosperous ; and farewell, good fellow.
  Bal. For all this same, I 'll hide me hereabout :
His looks I fear, and his intents I doubt. [*Retires.*
  Rom. Thou detestable maw, thou womb of death,
Gorg'd with the dearest morsel of the earth,
Thus I enforce thy rotten jaws to open,
        [*Breaking open the door of the monument.*
And, in despite, I 'll cram thee with more food !
  Par. This is that banish'd haughty Montague,
That murder'd my love's cousin,—with which grief, 50
It is supposed, the fair creature died,—
And here is come to do some villainous shame
To the dead bodies : I will apprehend him.
              [*Advancing.*
Stop thy unhallow'd toil, vile Montague.
Can vengeance be pursu'd further than death ?
Condemned villain, I do apprehend thee :
Obey, and go with me ; for thou must die.
  Rom. I must, indeed ; and therefore came I hither.—
Good gentle youth, tempt not a desperate man ;
Fly hence, and leave me :—think upon these gone ;   60
Let them affright thee.—I beseech thee, youth,
Put not another sin upon my head,
By urging me to fury :—O, be gone !
By Heaven, I love thee better than myself,
For I come hither arm'd against myself :
Stay not, be gone ;—live, and hereafter say—
A madman's mercy bade thee run away.
  Par. I do defy thy conjurations,
And apprehend thee for a felon here.
  Rom. Wilt thou provoke me ? then, have at thee,
    boy.   70
              [*They fight.*
  Page. O Lord ! they fight : I will go call the watch.
              [*Exit.*
  Par. O ! I am slain. [*Falls.*]—If thou be merciful,
Open the tomb, lay me with Juliet. [*Dies.*
  Rom. In faith, I will.—Let me peruse this face :—
Mercutio's kinsman, noble County Paris !—
What said my man, when my betossed soul
Did not attend him as we rode ? I think,
He told me, Paris should have married Juliet :
Said he not so ? or did I dream it so ?
Or am I mad, hearing him talk of Juliet,   80

To think it was so?—O! give me thy hand,
One writ with me in sour misfortune's book!
I'll bury thee in a triumphant grave.—
A grave? O, no! a lantern, slaughter'd youth,
For here lies Juliet, and her beauty makes
This vault a feasting presence full of light.
Death, lie thou there, by a dead man interr'd.
        [*Laying* PARIS *in the monument.*
How oft, when men are at the point of death,
Have they been merry! which their keepers call
A lightning before death: O! how may I   90
Call this a lightning? O my love! my wife!
Death, that hath suck'd the honey of thy breath
Hath had no power yet upon thy beauty:
Thou art not conquer'd; beauty's ensign yet
Is crimson in thy lips, and in thy cheeks,
And death's pale flag is not advanced there.—
Tybalt, liest thou there in thy bloody sheet?
O! what more favour can I do to thee,
Than with that hand that cut thy youth in twain
To sunder his that was thine enemy?   100
Forgive me, cousin!—Ah! dear Juliet,
Why art thou yet so fair? Shall I believe
That unsubstantial death is amorous;
And that the lean abhorred monster keeps
Thee here in dark to be his paramour?
For fear of that I still will stay with thee,
And never from this palace of dim night
Depart again: here, here will I remain
With worms that are thy chambermaids; O! here
Will I set up my everlasting rest,   110
And shake the yoke of inauspicious stars
From this world-wearied flesh.—Eyes, look your last!
Arms, take your last embrace! and, lips, O you,
The doors of breath, seal with a righteous kiss
A dateless bargain to engrossing death!
Come, bitter conduct, come, unsavoury guide!
Thou desperate pilot, now at once run on
The dashing rocks thy sea-sick weary bark!
Here's to my love! [*Drinks.*]—O true apothecary!
Thy drugs are quick.—Thus with a kiss I die.   120
        [*Dies.*

Enter, at the other end of the Churchyard, Friar
LAURENCE, *with a lantern, crow, and spade.*

Fri. Saint Francis be my speed! how oft to-night
Have my old feet stumbled at graves!—Who's there?
Bal. Here's one, a friend, and one that knows you
        well.
Fri. Bliss be upon you! Tell me, good my friend,
What torch is yond, that vainly lends his light
To grubs and eyeless sculls? as I discern,
It burneth in the Capels' monument.
Bal. It doth so, holy sir; and there's my master,
One that you love.
Fri.   Who is it?
Bal.   Romeo.
Fri. How long hath he been there?
Bal.   Full half an hour.
Fri. Go with me to the vault.
Bal.   I dare not, sir.   131
My master knows not but I am gone hence;
And fearfully did menace me with death,
If I did stay to look on his intents.
Fri. Stay then, I'll go alone.—Fear comes upon me;
O! much I fear some ill unlucky thing.
Bal. As I did sleep under this yew-tree here,
I dreamt my master and another fought,
And that my master slew him.
Fri.   Romeo!—[*Advancing.*
Alack, alack! what blood is this, which stains   140
The stony entrance of this sepulchre?—
What mean these masterless and gory swords
To lie discolour'd by this place of peace?
        [*Enters the tomb.*
Romeo! O, pale!—Who else? what! Paris too?
And steep'd in blood?—Ah! what an unkind hour
Is guilty of this lamentable chance!—
The lady stirs.   [JULIET *wakes.*
Jul. O comfortable friar! where is my lord?
I do remember well where I should be,
And there I am.—Where is my Romeo? [*Noise within.*

Fri. I hear some noise.—Lady, come from that nest
Of death, contagion, and unnatural sleep: 152
A greater Power than we can contradict
Hath thwarted our intents: come, come away.
Thy husband in thy bosom there lies dead;
And Paris too: come, I'll dispose of thee
Among a sisterhood of holy nuns.
Stay not to question, for the watch is coming;
Come, go, good Juliet.—[*Noise again.*] I dare no
        longer stay.
Jul. Go, get thee hence, for I will not away.—   160
        [*Exit Friar* LAURENCE.
What's here? a cup clos'd in my true love's hand?

Fri. " Go with me to the vault."

Poison, I see, hath been his timeless end.
O churl! drunk all, and left no friendly drop,
To help me after?—I will kiss thy lips;
Haply, some poison yet doth hang on them,
To make me die with a restorative.   [*Kisses him.*
Thy lips are warm!
1 Watch. [*Within.*] Lead, boy:—which way?
Jul. Yea, noise?—then I'll be brief.—O happy
        dagger!   [*Snatching* ROMEO's *dagger.*
This is thy sheath; [*stabs herself*] there rust, and let
        me die.   170
        [*Dies.*

Enter Watch, with the Page of PARIS.

Page. This is the place; there, where the torch
        doth burn.
1 Watch. The ground is bloody: search about the
        churchyard.
Go, some of you; whoe'er you find, attach.
        [*Exeunt some.*
Pitiful sight! here lies the county slain;—
And Juliet bleeding; warm, and newly dead,
Who here hath lain this two days buried.—
Go, tell the prince,—run to the Capulets,—
Raise up the Montagues,—some others search:—
        [*Exeunt other Watchmen.*
We see the ground whereon these woes do lie;
But the true ground of all these piteous woes   180
We cannot without circumstance descry.

Enter some of the Watch, with BALTHASAR.

2 Watch. Here's Romeo's man; we found him in
        the churchyard.
1 Watch. Hold him in safety, till the prince come
        hither.

Enter another Watchman, with Friar Laurence.

3 *Watch.* Here is a friar, that trembles, sighs, and weeps :
We took this mattock and this spade from him,

La. Cap. The people in the street cry—Romeo, 191
Some—Juliet, and some—Paris ; and all run
With open outcry toward our monument.
Prince. What fear is this, which startles in our ears ?

Jul. "O churl ! drunk all, and left no friendly drop."

As he was coming from this churchyard side.
1 *Watch.* A great suspicion ; stay the friar too.

Enter the Prince *and Attendants.*

Prince. What misadventure is so early up,
That calls our person from our morning's rest ?

Enter Capulet, *Lady* Capulet, *and others.*

Cap. What should it be, that they so shriek abroad ?

1 *Watch.* Sovereign, here lies the County Paris slain ;
And Romeo dead ; and Juliet, dead before,
Warm and new kill'd.
Prince. Search, seek, and know how this foul murder comes.
1 *Watch.* Here is a friar, and slaughter'd Romeo's man,
With instruments upon them, fit to open   200
These dead men's tombs.

Cap. O Heaven !—O wife ! look how our daughter
  bleeds !
This dagger hath mista'en,—for, lo ! his house
Is empty on the back of Montague,—
And is mis-sheathed in my daughter's bosom.
  La. Cap. O me ! this sight of death is as a bell,
That warns my old age to a sepulchre.

Enter MONTAGUE and others.

Prince. Come, Montague ; for thou art early up,
To see thy son and heir more early down.
  Mon. Alas, my liege, my wife is dead to-night ; 210
Grief of my son's exile hath stopp'd her breath.
What further woe conspires against mine age ?
  Prince. Look, and thou shalt see.
  Mon. O thou untaught ! what manners is in this,
To press before thy father to a grave ?
  Prince. Seal up the mouth of outrage for a while,
Till we can clear these ambiguities,
And know their spring, their head, their true descent ;
And then will I be general of your woes,
And lead you even to death. Meantime forbear, 220
And let mischance be slave to patience.—
Bring forth the parties of suspicion.
  Fri. I am the greatest, able to do least,
Yet most suspected, as the time and place
Doth make against me, of this direful murder ;
And here I stand, both to impeach and purge
Myself condemned and myself excus'd.
  Prince. Then say at once what thou dost know in
  this.
  Fri. I will be brief, for my short date of breath
Is not so long as is a tedious tale. 230
Romeo, there dead, was husband to that Juliet ;
And she, there dead, that Romeo's faithful wife :
I married them ; and their stolen marriage-day
Was Tybalt's doomsday, whose untimely death
Banish'd the new-made bridegroom from this city
For whom, and not for Tybalt, Juliet pin'd.
You, to remove that siege of grief from her,
Betroth'd, and would have married her perforce,
To County Paris :—then comes she to me,
And, with wild looks, bid me devise some means 240
To rid her from this second marriage,
Or in my cell there would she kill herself.
Then gave I her (so tutor'd by my art)
A sleeping potion ; which so took effect
As I intended, for it wrought on her
The form of death : meantime, I writ to Romeo,
That he should hither come as this dire night,
To help to take her from her borrow'd grave,
Being the time the potion's force should cease.
But he which bore my letter, Friar John, 250
Was stay'd by accident, and yesternight
Return'd my letter back. Then, all alone,
Came I to take her from her kindred's vault,
Meaning to keep her closely at my cell,
Till I conveniently could send to Romeo :

But when I came (some minute ere the time
Of her awakening), here untimely lay
The noble Paris, and true Romeo, dead.
She wakes ; and I entreated her come forth, 260
And bear this work of Heaven with patience :
But then a noise did scare me from the tomb,
And she, too desperate, would not go with me,
But (as it seems) did violence on herself.
All this I know ; and to the marriage
Her nurse is privy ; and, if aught in this
Miscarried by my fault, let my old life
Be sacrific'd, some hour before his time,
Unto the rigour of severest law.
  Prince. We still have known thee for a holy man.—
Where 's Romeo's man ? what can he say to this ? 271
  Bal. I brought my master news of Juliet's death ;
And then in post he came from Mantua,
To this same place, to this same monument.
This letter he early bid me give his father ;
And threaten'd me with death, going in the vault,
If I departed not, and left him there.
  Prince. Give me the letter, I will look on it.—
Where is the county's page, that rais'd the watch ?—
Sirrah, what made your master in this place ? 280
  Page. He came with flowers to strew his lady's
  grave,
And bid me stand aloof, and so I did :
Anon comes one with light to ope the tomb,
And, by-and-by, my master drew on him ;
And then I ran away to call the watch.
  Prince. This letter doth make good the friar's
  words,
Their course of love, the tidings of her death :
And here he writes, that he did buy a poison
Of a poor 'pothecary, and therewithal
Came to this vault to die, and lie with Juliet.— 290
Where be these enemies ? Capulet ! Montague !
See, what a scourge is laid upon your hate,
That Heaven finds means to kill your joys with love ;
And I, for winking at your discords too,
Have lost a brace of kinsmen :—all are punish'd.
  Cap. O brother Montague ! give me thy hand :
This is my daughter's jointure ; for no more
Can I demand.
  Mon.   But I can give thee more :
For I will raise her statue in pure gold ;
That, while Verona by that name is known, 300
There shall no figure at such rate be set,
As that of true and faithful Juliet.
  Cap. As rich shall Romeo by his lady lie ;
Poor sacrifices of our enmity !
  Prince. A glooming peace this morning with it
  brings ;
The sun for sorrow will not show his head.
Go hence, to have more talk of these sad things ;
Some shall be pardon'd, and some punished :
For never was a story of more woe,
Than this of Juliet and her Romeo. 310
                                        [*Exeunt.*

TIMON OF ATHENS.

DRAMATIS PERSONÆ.

TIMON, *a noble Athenian.*
LUCIUS,
LUCULLUS, } *Three flattering Lords.*
SEMPRONIUS,
VENTIDIUS, *one of Timon's false Friends.*
APEMANTUS, *a churlish Philosopher.*
ALCIBIADES, *an Athenian Captain.*
FLAVIUS, *Steward to Timon.*
FLAMINIUS,
LUCILIUS, } *Servants to Timon.*
SERVILIUS,
CAPHIS, PHILOTUS, TITUS, LUCIUS, HORTENSIUS, *Servants to Timon's Creditors.*

Servants of Varro, and Isidore, two of Timon's Creditors.
Cupid and Maskers.
Three Strangers.
Poet, Painter, Jeweller, and Merchant.
An Old Athenian.
A Page.
A Fool.
PHRYNIA, } *Mistresses to Alcibiades.*
TIMANDRA,
Lords, Senators, Officers, Soldiers, Thieves, and Attendants.

SCENE—ATHENS; and the Woods adjoining.

ACT I.

SCENE I.—Athens. A Hall in TIMON'S House.

Enter Poet, Painter, Jeweller, Merchant, and others, at several doors.

Poet.
OOD day, sir.
  Pain. I am glad you are well.
Poet. I have not seen you long.
  How goes the world?
  Pain. It wears, sir, as it grows.
  Poet. Ay, that 's well known;
But what particular rarity? what
  strange,
Which manifold record not
  matches? See,
Magic of bounty! all these spirits thy power
Hath conjur'd to attend. I know the merchant.
  Pain. I know them both: th' other 's a
  jeweller.
Mer. O! 't is a worthy lord!
Jew. Nay, that 's most fix'd.
Mer. A most incomparable man; breath'd,
  as it were, 10
To an untirable and continuate goodness:
He passes.
Jew. I have a jewel here—
Mer. O, pray, let 's see 't: for the Lord Timon, sir?
Jew. If he will touch the estimate: but, for that—
Poet. When we for recompense have prais'd the
  vile,
It stains the glory in that happy verse
Which aptly sings the good.
Mer. 'T is a good form.
Jew. And rich: here is a water, look ye.
Pain. You are rapt, sir, in some work, some dedi-
  cation 20
To the great lord.
Poet. A thing slipp'd idly from me.
Our poesy is as a gum, which oozes
From whence 't is nourish'd: the fire i' the flint
Shows not, till it be struck; our gentle flame
Provokes itself, and, like the current, flies
Each bound it chafes. What have you there?
Pain. A picture, sir.—When comes your book forth?

Poet. Upon the heels of my presentment, sir.
Let 's see your piece.
Pain. 'T is a good piece. 30
Poet. So 't is: this comes off well and excellent.
Pain. Indifferent.
Poet. Admirable! How this grace
Speaks his own standing! what a mental power
This eye shoots forth! how big imagination
Moves in this lip! to the dumbness of the gesture
One might interpret.
Pain. It is a pretty mocking of the life.
Here is a touch; is 't good?
Poet. I 'll say of it,
It tutors nature: artificial strife
Lives in these touches, livelier than life. 40

Enter certain Senators, who pass over the stage.

Pain. How this lord is follow'd!
Poet. The senators of Athens:—happy men!
Pain. Look, more!
Poet. You see this confluence, this great flood of
  visitors.
I have, in this rough work, shap'd out a man,
Whom this beneath-world doth embrace and hug
With amplest entertainment: my free drift
Halts not particularly, but moves itself
In a wide sea of wax: no levell'd malice
Infects one comma in the course I hold; 50
But flies an eagle flight, bold, and forth on,
Leaving no tract behind.
Pain. How shall I understand you?
Poet. I will unbolt to you.
You see how all conditions, how all minds,
(As well of glib and slippery creatures, as
Of grave and austere quality,) tender down
Their services to Lord Timon: his large fortune,
Upon his good and gracious nature hanging,
Subdues and properties to his love and tendance 60
All sorts of hearts; yea, from the glass-fac'd flatterer
To Apemantus, that few things loves better

Than to abhor himself: even he drops down
The knee before him, and returns in peace
Most rich in Timon's nod.
Pain.   I saw them speak together.
Poet. Sir, I have upon a high and pleasant hill
Feign'd Fortune to be thron'd: the base o' the mount
Is rank'd with all deserts, all kinds of natures,
That labour on the bosom of this sphere
To propagate their states: amongst them all,   70
Whose eyes are on this sovereign lady fix'd,

Poet.   "Artificial strife
Lives in these touches, livelier than life."

One do I personate of Lord Timon's frame,
Whom Fortune with her ivory hand wafts to her;
Whose present grace to present slaves and servants
Translates his rivals.
Pain.   'T is conceiv'd to scope.
This throne, this Fortune, and this hill, methinks,
With one man beckon'd from the rest below,
Bowing his head against the steepy mount
To climb his happiness, would be well express'd
In our condition.
Poet.   Nay, sir, but hear me on.   80
All those which were his fellows but of late
(Some better than his value), on the moment
Follow his strides, his lobbies filled with tendance,
R010n sacrificial whisperings in his ear,
Make sacred even his stirrup, and through him
Drink the free air.
Pain.   Ay, marry, what of these?
Poet. When Fortune, in her shift and change of mood,
Spurns down her late belov'd, all his dependants,
Which labour'd after him to the mountain's top,
Even on their knees and hands, let him slip down,   90
Not one accompanying his declining foot.
Pain. 'T is common:
A thousand moral paintings I can show,
That shall demonstrate these quick blows of Fortune's
More pregnantly than words. Yet you do well,
To show Lord Timon, that mean eyes have seen
The foot above the head.

Trumpets sound. Enter TIMON, *attended; the
Servant of* VENTIDIUS *talking with him.*

Tim.   Imprison'd is he, say you?
Ven. Serv. Ay, my good lord: five talents is his
debt,
His means most short, his creditors most strait:
Your honourable letter he desires   100
To those have shut him up; which failing
Periods his comfort.
Tim.   Noble Ventidius! Well;
I am not of that feather, to shake off
My friend when he must need me. I do know him
A gentleman that well deserves a help,
Which he shall have: I 'll pay the debt, and free him.
Ven. Serv. Your lordship ever binds him.

Tim. Commend me to him: I will send his ransom;
And, being enfranchis'd, bid him come to me.—
'T is not enough to help the feeble up,   110
But to support him after.—Fare you well.
Ven. Serv. All happiness to your honour!   [*Exit.*

Enter an Old Athenian.

Old Ath. Lord Timon, hear me speak.
Tim.   Freely, good father.
Old Ath. Thou hast a servant nam'd Lucilius.
Tim. I have so: what of him?
Old Ath. Most noble Timon, call the man before thee.
Tim. Attends he here, or no?—Lucilius!

Enter LUCILIUS.

Luc. Here, at your lordship's service.
Old Ath. This fellow here, Lord Timon, this thy
creature,
By night frequents my house. I am a man   120
That from my first have been inclin'd to thrift,
And my estate deserves an heir more rais'd
Than one which holds a trencher.
Tim.   Well; what further?
Old Ath. One only daughter have I, no kin else,
On whom I may confer what I have got:
The maid is fair, o' the youngest for a bride,
And I have bred her at my dearest cost,
In qualities of the best. This man of thine
Attempts her love: I pr'ythee, noble lord,
Join with me to forbid him her resort;   130
Myself have spoke in vain.
Tim.   The man is honest.
Old Ath. Therefore he will be, Timon:
His honesty rewards him in itself,
It must not bear my daughter.
Tim.   Does she love him?
Old Ath. She is young, and apt:
Our own precedent passions do instruct us
What levity 's in youth.
Tim. [To LUCILIUS.] Love you the maid?
Luc. Ay, my good lord; and she accepts of it.
Old Ath. If in her marriage my consent be missing,
I call the gods to witness, I will choose   140
Mine heir from forth the beggars of the world,
And dispossess her all.
Tim.   How shall she be endow'd,
If she be mated with an equal husband?
Old Ath. Three talents on the present; in future, all.
Tim. This gentleman of mine hath serv'd me long:
To build his fortune, I will strain a little,
For 't is a bond in men. Give him thy daughter;
What you bestow, in him I 'll counterpoise,
And make him weigh with her.
Old Ath.   Most noble lord,
Pawn me to this your honour, she is his.   150
Tim. My hand to thee: mine honour on my promise.
Luc. Humbly I thank your lordship. Never may
That state or fortune fall into my keeping,
Which is not ow'd to you!
                    [*Exeunt* LUCILIUS *and Old Athenian.*
Poet. Vouchsafe my labour, and long live your
lordship!
Tim. I thank you; you shall hear from me anon:
Go not away.—What have you there, my friend?
Pain. A piece of painting, which I do beseech
Your lordship to accept.
Tim.   Painting is welcome.
The painting is almost the natural man;   160
For since dishonour traffics with man's nature,
He is but outside: these pencill'd figures are
Even such as they give out. I like your work;
And you shall find I like it: wait attendance
Till you hear further from me.
Pain.   The gods preserve you!
Tim. Well fare you, gentleman: give me your
hand;
We must needs dine together.—Sir, your jewel
Hath suffer'd under praise.
Jew.   What, my lord! dispraise?
Tim. A mere satiety of commendations.
If I should pay you for 't as 't is extoll'd,   170
It would unclew me quite.

Jew.   My lord, 't is rated
As those which sell would give: but you well know,
Things of like value, differing in the owners,
Are prized by their masters. Believe 't, dear lord,
You mend the jewel by the wearing it.
Tim. Well mock'd.
Mer. No, my good lord; he speaks the common
                                tongue,
Which all men speak with him.
Tim. Look, who comes here. Will you be chid?

                Enter APEMANTUS.

Jew. We will bear, with your lordship.
Mer.   He 'll spare none.
Tim. Good morrow to thee, gentle Apemantus! 181
Apem. Till I be gentle, stay thou for thy good
                                morrow ;
When thou art Timon's dog, and these knaves honest.
Tim. Why dost thou call them knaves? thou know'st
                                them not.
Apem. Are they not Athenians?
Tim. Yes.
Apem. Then I repent not.
Jew. You know me, Apemantus?
Apem. Thou know'st I do ; I call'd thee by thy name.
Tim. Thou art proud, Apemantus.   190
Apem. Of nothing so much as that I am not like
                                Timon.
Tim. Whither art going?
Apem. To knock out an honest Athenian's brains.
Tim. That 's a deed thou 'lt die for.
Apem. Right, if doing nothing be death by the law.
Tim. How likest thou this picture, Apemantus?
Apem. The best, for the innocence.
Tim. Wrought he not well that painted it?
Apem. He wrought better that made the painter;
and yet he 's but a filthy piece of work.   200
Pain. You are a dog.
Apem. Thy mother 's of my generation : what 's she,
if I be a dog?
Tim. Wilt dine with me, Apemantus?
Apem. No ; I eat not lords.
Tim. An thou shouldst, thou 'dst anger ladies.
Apem. O! they eat lords ; so they come by great
bellies.
Tim. That 's a lascivious apprehension.   209
Apem. So thou apprehend'st it, take it for thy labour.
Tim. How dost thou like this jewel, Apemantus?
Apem. Not so well as plain-dealing, which will not
cost a man a doit.
Tim. What dost thou think 't is worth?
Apem. Not worth my thinking.—How now, poet?
Poet. How now, philosopher?
Apem. Thou liest.
Poet. Art not one?
Apem. Yes.
Poet. Then I lie not.   220
Apem. Art not a poet?
Poet. Yes.
Apem. Then thou liest: look in thy last work,
where thou hast feign'd him a worthy fellow.
Poet. That 's not feign'd ; he is so.
Apem. Yes, he is worthy of thee, and to pay thee
for thy labour : he that loves to be flattered is worthy
o' the flatterer. Heavens, that I were a lord !
Tim. What wouldst do then, Apemantus?
Apem. Even as Apemantus does now, hate a lord
with my heart.   231
Tim. What, thyself?
Apem. Ay.
Tim. Wherefore?
Apem. That I had no angry wit, to be a lord.—Art
not thou a merchant?
Mer. Ay, Apemantus.
Apem. Traffic confound thee, if the gods will not !
Mer. If traffic do it, the gods do it.
Apem. Traffic 's thy god, and thy god confound thee!

        Trumpets sound. Enter a Servant.

Tim. What trumpet 's that?   241
Serv. 'T is Alcibiades, and some twenty horse,
All of companionship.

Tim. Pray, entertain them ; give them guide to
        us.—   [*Exeunt some Attendants.*
You must needs dine with me.—Go not you hence,
Till I have thank'd you ; and, when dinner 's done,
Show me this piece.—I am joyful of your sights.—

        Enter ALCIBIADES, *with his Company.*

Most welcome, sir !
Apem.   So, so ; there !—
Aches contract and starve your supple joints !—
That there should be small love 'mongst these sweet
        knaves,   250
And all this courtesy ! The strain of man 's bred out
Into baboon and monkey.
Alcib. Sir, you have sav'd my longing, and I feed
Most hungerly on your sight.
Tim.   Right welcome, sir :
Ere we depart, we 'll share a bounteous time
In different pleasures. Pray you, let us in.
                        [*Exeunt all but* APEMANTUS.

                Enter two Lords.

1 Lord. What time a day is 't, Apemantus?
Apem. Time to be honest.
1 Lord. That time serves still.
Apem. The most accursed thou, that still omitt'st it.
2 Lord. Thou art going to Lord Timon's feast.   261
Apem. Ay ; to see meat fill knaves, and wine heat
        fools.
2 Lord. Fare thee well, fare thee well.
Apem. Thou art a fool to bid me farewell twice.
2 Lord. Why, Apemantus?
Apem. Shouldst have kept one to thyself, for I mean
to give thee none.
1 Lord. Hang thyself.
Apem. No, I will do nothing at thy bidding : make
thy requests to thy friend.   270
2 Lord. Away, unpeaceable dog ! or I 'll spurn thee
hence.
Apem. I will fly, like a dog, the heels o' the ass.
                                        [*Exit.*
1 Lord. He 's opposite to humanity. Come, shall
        we in,
And taste Lord Timon's bounty? he outgoes
The very heart of kindness.
2 Lord. He pours it out ; Plutus, the god of gold,
Is but his steward : no meed, but he repays
Seven-fold above itself ; no gift to him,
But breeds the giver a return exceeding   280
All use of quittance.
1 Lord.   The noblest mind he carries,
That ever govern'd man.
2 Lord. Long may he live in fortunes ! Shall we in?
1 Lord. I 'll keep you company.   [*Exeunt.*

        ———

SCENE II.—*The Same. A Room of State in* TIMON'S
                House.

*Hautboys playing loud music. A great banquet
served in ;* FLAVIUS *and others attending : then
enter* TIMON, ALCIBIADES, LUCIUS, LUCULLUS,
SEMPRONIUS, *and other Athenian Senators, with*
VENTIDIUS, *and Attendants. Then comes, dropping after all,* APEMANTUS, *discontentedly, like
himself.*

Ven. Most honour'd Timon,
It hath pleas'd the gods to remember my father's age,
And call him to long peace.
He is gone happy, and has left me rich :
Then, as in grateful virtue I am bound
To your free heart, I do return those talents,
Doubled, with thanks and service, from whose help
I deriv'd liberty.
Tim.   O ! by no means,
Honest Ventidius : you mistake my love ;
I gave it freely ever ; and there 's none   10
Can truly say, he gives, if he receives :
If our betters play at that game, we must not dare
To imitate them : faults that are rich are fair.
Ven. A noble spirit !

Tim.   Nay, my lords,
Ceremony was but devis'd at first,
To set a gloss on faint deeds, hollow welcomes,
Recanting goodness, sorry ere 't is shown ;
But where there is true friendship, there needs none.
Pray, sit : more welcome are ye to my fortunes,
Than my fortunes to me.   [*They sit.*
1 Lord. My lord, we always have confess'd it—   21
Apem. Ho, ho, confess'd it ! hang'd it, have you
      not?
Tim. O, Apemantus!—you are welcome.
Apem. No, you shall not make me welcome :
I come to have thee thrust me out of doors.
Tim. Fie ! thou art a churl : ye've got a humour
      there
Does not become a man, 't is much to blame.—
They say, my lords, *Ira furor brevis est*,
But yond man is ever angry.
Go, let him have a table by himself ;   30
For he does neither affect company,
Nor is he fit for it, indeed.
Apem. Let me stay at thine apperil, Timon :
I come to observe ; I give thee warning on 't.
Tim. I take no heed of thee ; thou art an Athenian ;
therefore, welcome. I myself would have no power ;
pr'ythee, let my meat make thee silent.
Apem. I scorn thy meat ; 't would choke me, for I
      should
Ne'er flatter thee.—O you gods ! what a number
Of men eat Timon, and he sees 'em not !   40
It grieves me to see so many dip their meat
In one man's blood ; and all the madness is,
He cheers them up too.
I wonder, men dare trust themselves with men :
Methinks, they should invite them without knives ;
Good for their meat, and safer for their lives.
There 's much example for 't ; the fellow, that
Sits next him now, parts bread with him, and pledges
The breath of him in a divided draught,
Is the readiest man to kill him : it has been proved. 50
If I were a huge man, I should fear to drink at meals,
Lest they should spy my wind-pipe's dangerous notes :
Great men should drink with harness on their throats.
Tim. My lord, in heart; and let the health go round.
2 Lord. Let it flow this way, my good lord.
Apem. Flow this way ! A brave fellow !—he keeps
his tides well. Those healths will make thee and thy
state look ill, Timon.
Here 's that, which is too weak to be a sinner,
Honest water, which ne'er left man i' the mire :   60
This and my food are equals, there 's no odds.
Feasts are too proud to give thanks to the gods.
      Immortal gods, I crave no pelf ;
      I pray for no man, but myself.
      Grant I may never prove so fond,
      To trust man on his oath or bond ;
      Or a harlot for her weeping ;
      Or a dog that seems a-sleeping ;
      Or a keeper with my freedom ;
      Or my friends, if I should need 'em.   70
      Amen. So fall to 't :
      Rich men sin, and I eat root.
                          [*Eats and drinks.*
Much good dich thy good heart, Apemantus !
Tim. Captain Alcibiades, your heart 's in the field
now.
Alcib. My heart is ever at your service, my lord.
Tim. You had rather be at a breakfast of enemies,
than a dinner of friends.
Alcib. So they were bleeding-new, my lord, there 's
no meat like 'em : I could wish my best friend at such
a feast.   81
Apem. 'Would all those flatterers were thine enemies
then, that then thou mightst kill 'em, and bid me to
'em.
1 Lord. Might we but have that happiness, my lord,
that you would once use our hearts, whereby we might
express some part of our zeals, we should think ourselves for ever perfect.   88
Tim. O ! no doubt, my good friends, but the gods
themselves have provided that I shall have much help
from you : how had you been my friends else ? why

have you that charitable title from thousands, did you
not chiefly belong to my heart ? I have told more of
you to myself, than you can with modesty speak in
your own behalf ; and thus far I confirm you. O you
gods ! think I, what need we have any friends, if we
should ne'er have need of 'em ? they were the most
needless creatures living, should we ne'er have use
for 'em ; and would most resemble sweet instruments
hung up in cases, that keep their sounds to themselves. Why, I have often wished myself poorer, that
I might come nearer to you. We are born to do
benefits ; and what better or properer can we call our
own, than the riches of our friends ? O, what a
precious comfort 't is, to have so many, like brothers,
commanding one another's fortunes ! O joy, e'en
made away ere 't can be born ! Mine eyes cannot hold
out water, methinks : to forget their faults, I drink to
you.
Apem. Thou weep'st to make them drink, Timon.
2 Lord. Joy had the like conception in our eyes, 111
And, at that instant, like a babe, sprung up.
Apem. Ho, ho ! I laugh to think that babe a bastard.
3 Lord. I promise you, my lord, you mov'd me
      much.
Apem. Much !   [*Tucket sounded.*
Tim. What means that trump?

              Enter a Servant.
                              How now?
Serv. Please you, my lord, there are certain ladies
most desirous of admittance.
Tim. Ladies ! What are their wills?
Serv. There comes with them a forerunner, my
lord, which bears that office to signify their pleasures.
Tim. I pray, let them be admitted.   122

              Enter CUPID.

Cup. Hail to thee, worthy Timon ; and to all
That of his bounties taste !—The five best senses
Acknowledge thee their patron ; and come freely
To gratulate thy plenteous bosom.
Th' ear, taste, touch, smell, pleas'd from thy table rise ;
They only now come but to feast thine eyes.
Tim. They 're welcome all : let 'em have kind ad-
      mittance :
Music, make their welcome !   [*Exit* CUPID.
1 Lord. You see, my lord, how ample you 're be-
      lov'd.   131

Music. Re-enter CUPID, *with a masque of Ladies as
Amazons, with lutes in their hands, dancing and
playing.*

Apem. Hoy-day, what a sweep of vanity comes this
      way !
They dance ! they are mad women.
Like madness is the glory of this life,
As this pomp shows to a little oil and root.
We make ourselves fools, to disport ourselves ;
And spend our flatteries, to drink those men,
Upon whose age we void it up again
With poisonous spite and envy.
Who lives, that 's not depraved, or depraves?   140
Who dies, that bears not one spurn to their graves
Of their friends' gift ?
I should fear, those that dance before me now
Would one day stamp upon me : 't has been done ;
Men shut their doors against a setting sun.

The Lords rise from table, with much adoring of
TIMON ; *and, to show their loves, each singles out
an Amazon, and all dance, men with women, a
lofty strain or two to the hautboys, and cease.*

Tim. You have done our pleasures much grace, fair
      ladies,
Set a fair fashion on our entertainment,
Which was not half so beautiful and kind :
You have added worth unto 't, and lively lustre,
And entertain'd me with mine own device ;   150
I am to thank you for it.
1 Lady. My lord, you take us even at the best.
Apem. 'Faith, for the worst is filthy ; and would not
hold taking, I doubt me.

Tim. Ladies, there is an idle banquet
Attends you : please you to dispose yourselves.
All Lad. Most thankfully, my lord.
[*Exeunt* Cupid *and Ladies.*
Tim. Flavius!
Flav. My lord.
Tim.   The little casket bring me hither.
Flav. Yes, my lord. [*Aside.*] More jewels yet ! 160
There is no crossing him in 's humour ;
Else I should tell him well, i' faith, I should,
When all 's spent, he 'd be cross'd then, an he could.
'T is pity bounty had not eyes behind,
That man might ne'ᵉr be wretched for his mind. [*Exit.*
1 Lord. Where be our men ?
Serv. Here, my lord, in readiness.
2 Lord. Our horses !

Re-enter Flavius, *with the casket.*

Tim. O my friends, I have one word to say to you.
Look you, my good lord,   170
I must entreat you, honour me so much,
As to advance this jewel ; accept it, and wear it,
Kind my lord.
1 Lord. I am so far already in your gifts.
All. So are we all.

Enter a Servant.

Serv. My lord, there are certain nobles of the senate
Newly alighted, and come to visit you.
Tim. They are fairly welcome.
Flav.   I beseech your honour,
Vouchsafe me a word : it does concern you near.
Tim. Near ? why, then another time I 'll hear thee.
I pr'ythee, let 's be provided to show them entertain-
ment.   181
Flav. [*Aside.*] I scarce know how.

Enter another Servant.

2 Serv. May it please your honour, Lord Lucius,
Out of his free love, hath presented to you
Four milk-white horses, trapp'd in silver.
Tim. I shall accept them fairly : let the presents
Be worthily entertain'd.

Enter a third Servant.

                    How now, what news ?
3 Serv. Please you, my lord, that honourable gentle-
man, Lord Lucullus, entreats your company to-
morrow to hunt with him ; and has sent your
honour two brace of greyhounds.   191
Tim. I 'll hunt with him ; and let them be receiv'd,
Not without fair reward.
Flav. [*Aside.*]   What will this come to ?
He commands us to provide, and give great gifts,
And all out of an empty coffer :
Nor will he know his purse ; or yield me this,
To show him what a beggar his heart is,
Being of no power to make his wishes good.
His promises fly so beyond his state,
That what he speaks is all in debt, he owes 200
For every word : he is so kind, that he now
Pays interest for 't ; his land 's put to their books.
Well, 'would I were gently put out of office,
Before I were forc'd out !
Happier is he that has no friend to feed
Than such as do even enemies exceed.
I bleed inwardly for my lord.   [*Exit.*
Tim.   You do yourselves
Much wrong : you bate too much of your own merits.
Here, my lord, a trifle of our love.
2 Lord. With more than common thanks I will
receive it.   210
3 Lord. O ! he 's the very soul of bounty.
Tim. And now I remember, my lord, you gave

Good words the other day of a bay courser
I rode on : it is yours, because you lik'd it.
3 Lord. O ! I beseech you, pardon me, my lord, in
that.
Tim. You may take my word, my lord ; I know, no
man
Can justly praise, but what he does affect :
I weigh my friend's affection with mine own ;
I 'll tell you true, I 'll call to you.

Apem. "So thou wilt not hear me now,
Thou shalt not then."

All Lords.   O ! none so welcome.
Tim. I take all and your several visitations   220
So kind to heart, 't is not enough to give :
Methinks, I could deal kingdoms to my friends,
And ne'er be weary.—Alcibiades,
Thou art a soldier, therefore seldom rich :
It comes in charity to thee ; for all thy living
Is 'mongst the dead, and all the lands thou hast
Lie in a pitch'd field.
Alcib.   Ay, defil'd land, my lord.
1 Lord. We are so virtuously bound—
Tim. And so am I to you.
2 Lord. So infinitely endear'd—   230
Tim. All to you.—Lights, more lights !
1 Lord.   The best of happiness,
Honour and fortunes, keep with you, Lord Timon !
Tim. Ready for his friends.
[*Exeunt* Alcibiades, *Lords, &c.*
Apem.   What a coil 's here !
Serving of becks, and jutting-out of bums !
I doubt whether their legs be worth the sums
That are given for 'em.—Friendship 's full of dregs :
Methinks, false hearts should never have sound legs.
Thus honest fools lay out their wealth on court'sies.
Tim. Now, Apemantus, if thou wert not sullen,
I would be good to thee.   240
Apem. No, I 'll nothing ; for if I should be brib'd too,
there would be none left to rail upon thee ; and then
thou wouldst sin the faster. Thou giv'st so long,
Timon, I fear me, thou wilt give away thyself in
paper shortly : what need these feasts, pomps, and
vain-glories ?
Tim. Nay, an you begin to rail on society once, I am
sworn not to give regard to you. Farewell ; and come
with better music.   [*Exit.*
Apem. So thou wilt not hear me now,   250
Thou shalt not then ; I 'll lock thy heaven from thee.
O, that men's ears should be
To counsel deaf, but not to flattery !   [*Exit.*

ACT II.

SCENE I.—The Same. A Room in a Senator's House.

Enter a Senator, with papers in his hand.

Senator.
AND late, five thousand : to Varro and
    to Isidore
He owes nine thousand ; besides my
    former sum,
Which makes it five-and-twenty.—
    Still in motion
Of raging waste? It cannot hold ;
    it will not.
If I want gold, steal but a beggar's
    dog,
And give it Timon, why, the dog coins
    gold ;
If I would sell my horse, and buy twenty
    more
Better than he, why, give my horse to Timon,
Ask nothing, give it him, it foals me, straight,
And able horses. No porter at his gate ;   10
But rather one that smiles, and still invites
All that pass by. It cannot hold ; no reason
Can sound his state in safety. Caphis, ho!
Caphis, I say!

Enter CAPHIS.

Caph.   Here, sir : what is your pleasure?
Sen. Get on your cloak, and haste you to Lord Timon ;
Importune him for my moneys ; be not ceas'd
With slight denial ; nor then silenc'd, when—
"Commend me to your master"—and the cap
Plays in the right hand, thus ;—but tell him,
My uses cry to me : I must serve my turn   20
Out of mine own ; his days and times are past,
And my reliances on his fracted dates
Have smit my credit : I love, and honour him ;
But must not break my back to heal his finger :
Immediate are my needs ; and my relief
Must not be toss'd and turn'd to me in words,
But find supply immediate. Get you gone :
Put on a most importunate aspect,
A visage of demand ; for, I do fear,
When every feather sticks in his own wing,   30
Lord Timon will be left a naked gull,
Which flashes now a phœnix. Get you gone.
Caph. I go, sir.
Sen. I go, sir? Take the bonds along with you,
And have the dates in compt.
Caph.   I will, sir.
Sen.   Go.
    [*Exeunt.*

SCENE II.—The Same. A Hall in TIMON'S House.

Enter FLAVIUS, *with many bills in his hand.*

Flav. No care, no stop! so senseless of expense,
That he will neither know how to maintain it,
Nor cease his flow of riot : takes no account
How things go from him, nor resumes no care
Of what is to continue. Never mind
Was to be so unwise, to be so kind.
What shall be done? He will not hear, till feel.
I must be round with him, now he comes from hunting.
Fie, fie, fie, fie!

Enter CAPHIS, *and the Servants of* ISIDORE *and* VARRO.

Caph.   Good even, Varro. What,
You come for money?

Var. Serv.   Is 't not your business too?   10
Caph. It is ;—and yours too, Isidore?
Isid. Serv.   It is so.
Caph. 'Would we were all discharg'd!
Var. Serv.   I fear it.
Caph. Here comes the lord.

Enter TIMON, ALCIBIADES, *and Lords, &c.*

Tim. So soon as dinner's done, we 'll forth again,
My Alcibiades.—With me? what is your will?

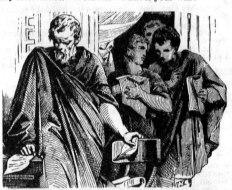

Flav. "I must be round with him, now he comes from hunting."

Caph. My lord, here is a note of certain dues.
Tim. Dues! Whence are you?
Caph.   Of Athens here, my lord.
Tim. Go to my steward.
Caph. Please it your lordship, he hath put me off
To the succession of new days this month ·   20
My master is awak'd by great occasion,
To call upon his own ; and humbly prays you,
That with your other noble parts you 'll suit,
In giving him his right.
Tim.   Mine honest friend,
I pr'ythee, but repair to me next morning.
Caph. Nay, good my lord,—
Tim.   Contain thyself, good friend.
Var. Serv. One Varro's servant, my good lord,—
Isid. Serv.   From Isidore ;
He humbly prays your speedy payment,—
Caph. If you did know, my lord, my master's
    wants,—
Var. Serv. 'T was due on forfeiture, my lord, six
    weeks,   30
And past,—
Isid. Serv. Your steward puts me off, my lord ;
And I am sent expressly to your lordship.
Tim. Give me breath.
I do beseech you, good my lords, keep on ;
I 'll wait upon you instantly.—
    [*Exeunt* ALCIBIADES *and Lords.*
[*To* FLAVIUS.]   Come hither : pray you,
How goes the world, that I am thus encounter'd

With clamorous demands of broken bonds,
And the detention of long-since-due debts,
Against my honour?
  Flav.   Please you, gentlemen,
The time is unagreeable to this business: 40
Your importunacy cease till after dinner,
That I may make his lordship understand
Wherefore you are not paid.
  Tim.   Do so, my friends.—
See them well entertained.   [*Exit.*
  Flav.   Pray, draw near. [*Exit.*

      Enter APEMANTUS *and Fool.*

  Caph. Stay, stay; here comes the fool with Ape-
mantus: let 's have some sport with 'em.
  Var. Serv. Hang him, he 'll abuse us.
  Isid. Serv. A plague upon him, dog!
  Var. Serv. How dost, fool?
  Apem. Dost dialogue with thy shadow?   50
  Var. Serv. I speak not to thee.
  Apem. No; 'tis to thyself.—[*To the Fool.*] Come
away.
  Isid. Serv. [*To* VAR. *Serv.*] There 's the fool hangs
on your back already.
  Apem. No, thou stand'st single; thou 'rt not on him
yet.
  Caph. Where 's the fool now?
  Apem. He last asked the question.—Poor rogues,
and usurer's men! bawds between gold and want! 60
  All Serv. What are we, Apemantus?
  Apem. Asses.
  All Serv. Why?
  Apem. That you ask me what you are, and do not
know yourselves.—Speak to 'em, fool.
  Fool. How do you, gentlemen?
  All Serv. Gramercies, good fool. How does your
mistress?
  Fool. She 's e'en setting on water to scald such
chickens as you are. 'Would, we could see you at
Corinth!   71
  Apem. Good! gramercy.

      Enter Page.

  Fool. Look you, here comes my mistress' page.
  Page. [*To the Fool.*] Why, how now, captain? what
do you in this wise company?—How dost thou, Ape-
mantus?
  Apem. 'Would I had a rod in my mouth, that I might
answer thee profitably.
  Page. Pr'ythee, Apemantus, read me the super-
scription of these letters: I know not which is which.
  Apem. Canst not read?   81
  Page. No.
  Apem. There will little learning die then, that day
thou art hanged. This is to Lord Timon; this to
Alcibiades. Go; thou wast born a bastard, and
thou 'lt die a bawd.
  Page. Thou wast whelped a dog, and thou shalt
famish a dog's death. Answer not; I am gone. [*Exit.*
  Apem. Even so thou outrunn'st grace. Fool, I will
go with you to Lord Timon's.   90
  Fool. Will you leave me there?
  Apem. If Timon stay at home.—You three serve
three usurers?
  All Serv. Ay, fool.
  Fool. So would I,—as good a trick as ever hangman served thief.
  Fool. Are you three usurers' men?
  All Serv. Ay, fool.   99
  Fool. I think, no usurer but has a fool to his servant: my mistress is one, and I am her fool. When
men come to borrow of your masters, they approach
sadly, and go away merry; but they enter my mis-
tress' house merrily, and go away sadly. The reason
of this?
  Var. Serv. I could render one.
  Apem. Do it then, that we may account thee a
whoremaster, and a knave; which notwithstanding,
thou shalt be no less esteemed.
  Var. Serv. What is a whoremaster, fool?   109
  Fool. A fool in good clothes, and something like
thee. 'T is a spirit: sometime it appears like a lord;

sometime like a lawyer; sometime like a philosopher,
with two stones more than 's artificial one. He is very
often like a knight; and generally in all shapes, that
man goes up and down in, from fourscore to thirteen,
this spirit walks in.
  Var. Serv. Thou art not altogether a fool.
  Fool. Nor thou altogether a wise man : as much
foolery as I have, so much wit thou lackest.
  Apem. That answer might have become Apemantus.
  All Serv. Aside, aside: here comes Lord Timon. 121

      Re-enter TIMON *and* FLAVIUS.

  Apem. Come with me, fool, come.

    Tim. " You make me marvel: wherefore, ere this time,
    Had you not fully laid my state before me?"

  Fool. I do not always follow lover, elder brother,
and woman; sometime, the philosopher.
             [*Exeunt* APEMANTUS *and Fool.*
  Flav. Pray you, walk near: I 'll speak with you
anon.   [*Exeunt Servants.*
  Tim. You make me marvel: wherefore, ere this
      time,
Had you not fully laid my state before me;
That I might so have rated my expense,
As I had leave of means?
  Flav.   You would not hear me, 130
At many leisures I propos'd.
  Tim.   Go to:
Perchance, some single vantages you took,
When my indisposition put you back;
And that unaptness made your minister,
Thus to excuse yourself.
  Flav.   O my good lord!
At many times I brought in my accounts,
Laid them before you: you would throw them off,
And say, you found them in mine honesty.
When for some trifling present you have bid me
Return so much, I have shook my head, and wept; 140
Yea, 'gainst the authority of manners, pray'd you
To hold your hand more close: I did endure
Not seldom, nor so slight checks, when I have
Prompted you, in the ebb of your estate
And your great flow of debts. My loved lord,
Though you hear now, (too late!) yet now 's a time,
The greatest of your having lacks a half
To pay your present debts.
  Tim.   Let all my land be sold.
  Flav. 'T is all engag'd, some forfeited and gone;
And what remains will hardly stop the mouth   150
Of present dues : the future comes apace;
What shall defend the interim? and at length
How goes our reckoning?
  Tim. To Lacedæmon did my land extend.

Flav. O my good lord! the world is but a word;
Were it all yours to give it in a breath,
How quickly were it gone!
Tim.　　　　　　You tell me true.
Flav. If you suspect my husbandry, or falsehood,
Call me before the exactest auditors,
And set me on the proof. So the gods bless me, 160
When all our offices have been oppress'd
With riotous feeders, when our vaults have wept
With drunken spilth of wine, when every room
Hath blaz'd with lights, and bray'd with minstrelsy,
I have retir'd me to a wasteful cock,
And set mine eyes at flow.
Tim.　　　　　　Pr'ythee no more.
Flav. Heavens, have I said, the bounty of this lord!
How many prodigal bits have slaves, and peasants,
This night englutted! Who is not Timon's?
What heart, head, sword, force, means, but is Lord 170
Timon's?
Great Timon, noble, worthy, royal Timon!
Ah! when the means are gone that buy this praise,
The breath is gone whereof this praise is made:
Feast-won, fast-lost; one cloud of winter showers,
These flies are couch'd.
Tim.　　　　　Come, sermon me no further:
No villainous bounty yet hath pass'd my heart;
Unwisely, not ignobly, have I given.
Why dost thou weep? Canst thou the conscience lack,
To think I shall lack friends? Secure thy heart;
If I would broach the vessels of my love, 180
And try the argument of hearts by borrowing,
Men, and men's fortunes, could I frankly use,
As I can bid thee speak.
Flav.　　　　　Assurance bless your thoughts!
Tim. And, in some sort, these wants of mine are
crown'd,
That I account them blessings; for by these
Shall I try friends. You shall perceive, how you
Mistake my fortunes; I am wealthy in my friends.—
Within there! Flaminius! Servilius!

Enter FLAMINIUS, SERVILIUS, *and other Servants.*
Servants. My lord? my lord? 189
Tim. I will despatch you severally.—You, to Lord
Lucius;—to Lord Lucullus you; I hunted with his
honour to-day;—you, to Sempronius. Commend me
to their loves; and, I am proud, say, that my occasions

have found time to use them toward a supply of
money: let the request be fifty talents.
Flam. As you have said, my lord.
Flav. [*Aside.*] Lord Lucius and Lucullus? humph!
Tim. [*To another Servant.*] Go you, sir, to the
senators,
(Of whom, even to the state's best health, I have
Deserv'd this hearing), bid 'em send o' the instant 200
A thousand talents to me.
Flav.　　　　　I have been bold,
(For that I knew it the most general way,)
To them to use your signet, and your name;
But they do shake their heads, and I am here
No richer in return.
Tim.　　　　　Is 't true? can 't be?
Flav. They answer, in a joint and corporate voice,
That now they are at fall, want treasure, cannot
Do what they would; are sorry—you are honourable,—
But yet they could have wish'd—they know not—
Something hath been amiss—a noble nature 210
May catch a wrench—would all were well—'t is pity;—
And so, intending other serious matters,
After distasteful looks, and these hard fractions,
With certain half-caps, and cold-moving nods,
They froze me into silence.
Tim.　　　　　You gods, reward them!—
Pr'ythee, man, look cheerly. These old fellows
Have their ingratitude in them hereditary:
Their blood is cak'd, 't is cold, it seldom flows;
'T is lack of kindly warmth, they are not kind;
And nature, as it grows again toward earth, 220
Is fashion'd for the journey, dull, and heavy.
Go to Ventidius.—'Pr'ythee, be not sad;
Thou art true, and honest: ingenuously I speak;
No blame belongs to thee.—Ventidius lately
Buried his father; by whose death he 's stepp'd
Into a great estate: when he was poor,
Imprison'd, and in scarcity of friends,
I clear'd him with five talents: greet him from me;
Bid him suppose, some good necessity 229
Touches his friend, which craves to be remember'd
With those five talents: that had, give it these fellows
To whom 't is instant due. Ne'er speak, or think,
That Timon's fortunes 'mong his friends can sink.
Flav. I would, I could not think it: that thought is
bounty's foe;
Being free itself, it thinks all others so. [*Exeunt.*

ACT III.

SCENE I.—The Same. A Room in LUCULLUS's House.
FLAMINIUS *waiting. Enter a Servant to him.*

Servant.
HAVE told my lord of you; he is
coming down to you.
Flam. I thank you, sir.

Enter LUCULLUS.
Serv. Here 's my lord.
Lucul. [*Aside.*] One of Lord Timon's
men? a gift, I warrant. Why, this hits
right; I dreamt of a silver basin and ewer
to-night. Flaminius, honest Flaminius,
you are very respectively welcome, sir.—
Fill me some wine. [*Exit Servant.*]—And
how does that honourable, complete, free-
hearted gentleman of Athens, thy very bountiful good
lord and master? 13

Flam. His health is well, sir.
Lucul. I am right glad that his health is well, sir.
And what hast thou there under thy cloak, pretty
Flaminius?
Flam. 'Faith, nothing but an empty box, sir, which,
in my lord's behalf, I come to entreat your honour to
supply; who, having great and instant occasion to use
fifty talents, hath sent to your lordship to furnish him,
nothing doubting your present assistance therein. 22
Lucul. La, la, la, la,—nothing doubting, says he?
alas, good lord! a noble gentleman 't is, if he would
not keep so good a house. Many a time and often I
have dined with him, and told him on 't; and come
again to supper to him, of purpose to have him spend
less: and yet he would embrace no counsel, take no
warning by my coming. Every man has his fault,

and honesty is his: I have told him on 't, but I could
ne'er get him from it.   31
        Re-enter Servant, with wine.
Serv. Please your lordship, here is the wine.
Lucul. Flaminius, I have noted thee always wise.
Here 's to thee.
Flam. Your lordship speaks your pleasure.
Lucul. I have observed thee always for a towardly
prompt spirit,—give thee thy due,—and one that
knows what belongs to reason; and canst use the
time well, if the time use thee well: good parts in
thee.—[*To the Servant.*] Get you gone, sirrah. [*Exit*

Flam. "'Faith, nothing but an empty box, sir, which, in my
lord's behalf, I come to entreat your honour to supply."

Servant.]—Draw nearer, honest Flaminius. Thy
lord 's a bountiful gentleman; but thou art wise, and
thou knowest well enough, although thou comest to
me, that this is no time to lend money, especially
upon bare friendship, without security. Here 's three
solidares for thee: good boy, wink at me, and say,
thou saw'st me not. Fare thee well.
Flam. Is 't possible, the world should so much
differ,
And we alive that liv'd? Fly, damned baseness,
To him that worships thee!   50
                    [*Throwing the money away.*
Lucul. Ha! now I see thou art a fool, and fit for thy
master.   [*Exit.*
Flam. May these add to the number that may scald
thee!
Let molten coin be thy damnation,
Thou disease of a friend, and not himself!
Has friendship such a faint and milky heart,
It turns in less than two nights? O you gods!
I feel my master's passion. This slave unto his
honour
Has my lord's meat in him:
Why should it thrive, and turn to nutriment,   60
When he is turn'd to poison?
O, may diseases only work upon 't!
And, when he 's sick to death, let not that part of
nature,
Which my lord paid for, be of any power
To expel sickness, but prolong his hour!   [*Exit.*

                    SCENE II.—The Same. A Public Place.

                    Enter Lucius, *with three Strangers.*
Luc. Who? the Lord Timon? he is my very good
friend, and an honourable gentleman.
1 *Stran.* We know him for no less, though we are
but strangers to him. But I can tell you one thing,
my lord, and which I hear from common rumours:

now Lord Timon's happy hours are done and past,
and his estate shrinks from him.
Luc. Fie, no, do not believe it; he cannot want for
money.   9
2 *Stran.* But believe you this, my lord, that, not
long ago, one of his men was with the Lord Lucullus,
to borrow so many talents; nay, urged extremely
for 't, and showed what necessity belonged to 't, and
yet was denied.
Luc. How?
2 *Stran.* I tell you, denied, my lord.
Luc. What a strange case was that! now, before
the gods, I am ashamed on 't. Denied that honourable man? there was very little honour shown in 't.
For my own part, I must needs confess, I have received some small kindnesses from him, as money,
plate, jewels, and such like trifles, nothing comparing
to his; yet, had he mistook him, and sent to me, I
should ne'er have denied his occasion so many talents.

                    Enter Servilius.
Ser. See, by good hap, yonder 's my lord; I have
sweat to see his honour.—[*To* Lucius.] My honoured
lord,—
Luc. Servilius! you are kindly met, sir. Fare thee
well: commend me to thy honourable-virtuous lord,
my very exquisite friend.   30
Ser. May it please your honour, my lord hath sent—
Luc. Ha! what has he sent? I am so much en-
deared to that lord; he 's ever sending: how shall I
thank him, thinkest thou? And what has he sent
now?
Ser. He has only sent his present occasion, now, my
lord: requesting your lordship to supply his instant
use with so many talents.   40
Luc. I know, his lordship is but merry with me:
He cannot want fifty-five hundred talents.
Ser. But in the meantime he wants less, my lord.
If his occasion were not virtuous,
I should not urge it half so faithfully.
Luc. Dost thou speak seriously, Servilius?
Ser. Upon my soul, 't is true, sir.
Luc. What a wicked beast was I, to disfurnish myself against such a good time, when I might have
shown myself honourable! how unluckily it happened,
that I should purchase the day before for a little part,
and undo a great deal of honour!—Servilius, now,
before the gods, I am not able to do; the more beast,
I say.—I was sending to use Lord Timon myself, these
gentlemen can witness; but I would not, for the
wealth of Athens, I had done it now. Commend me
bountifully to his good lordship; and I hope, his
honour will conceive the fairest of me, because I have
no power to be kind:—and tell him this from me, I
count it one of my greatest afflictions, say, that I
cannot pleasure such an honourable gentleman.
Good Servilius, will you befriend me so far, as to use
mine own words to him?   61
Ser. Yes, sir, I shall.
Luc. I 'll look you out a good turn, Servilius.—
                    [*Exit* Servilius.
True, as you said, Timon is shrunk, indeed;
And he that 's once denied will hardly speed.   [*Exit.*
1 *Stran.* Do you observe this, Hostilius?
2 *Stran.* Ay, too well.
1 *Stran.* Why, this is the world's soul; and just of
the same piece
Is every flatterer's sport. Who can call him his friend,
That dips in the same dish? for, in my knowing,   70
Timon has been this lord's father,
And kept his credit with his purse,
Supported his estate; nay, Timon's money
Has paid his men their wages: he ne'er drinks,
But Timon's silver treads upon his lip;
And yet (O, see the monstrousness of man,
When he looks out in an ungrateful shape!)
He does deny him, in respect of his,
What charitable men afford to beggars.
3 *Stran.* Religion groans at it.
1 *Stran.*   For mine own part, 80
I never tasted Timon in my life,
Nor came any of his bounties over me,

To mark me for his friend; yet, I protest,
For his right noble mind, illustrious virtue,
And honourable carriage,
Had his necessity made use of me,
I would have put my wealth into donation,
And the best half should have return'd to him,
So much I love his heart. But, I perceive,
Men must learn now with pity to dispense:　　90
For policy sits above conscience.　　　　[*Exeunt.*

SCENE III.—The Same.　A Room in SEMPRONIUS's
House.

Enter SEMPRONIUS, *and a Servant of* TIMON's.

Sem. Must he needs trouble me in 't? Humph!
　　'bove all others!
He might have tried Lord Lucius, or Lucullus;
And now Ventidius is wealthy too,
Whom he redeem'd from prison: all these
Owe their estates unto him.
Serv.　　　　　　　My lord,
They have all been touch'd, and found base metal;
For they have all denied him.
Sem.　　　　How! have they denied him?
Has Ventidius and Lucullus denied him?
And does he send to me? Three? humph!
It shows but little love or judgment in him:　10
Must I be his last refuge? His friends, like physi-
　　cians,
Thrice give him over! must I take the cure upon
　　me?
He has much disgrac'd me in 't: I am angry at him,
That might have known my place. I see no sense
　　for 't,
But his occasions might have woo'd me first;
For, in my conscience, I was the first man
That e'er received gift from him:
And does he think so backwardly of me now,
That I 'll requite it last? No:
So it may prove an argument of laughter　20
To the rest, and I 'mongst lords be thought a fool.
I had rather than the worth of thrice the sum,
He had sent to me first, but for my mind's sake:
I had such a courage to do him good. But now
　　return,
And with their faint reply this answer join:
Who bates mine honour, shall not know my coin.
　　　　　　　　　　　　　　　　[*Exit.*
Serv. Excellent! Your lordship 's a goodly villain.
The devil knew not what he did, when he made man
politic; he crossed himself by 't: and I cannot think,
but, in the end, the villainies of man will set him clear.
How fairly this lord strives to appear foul! takes
virtuous copies to be wicked; like those that, under
hot ardent zeal, would set whole realms on fire. Of
such a nature is his politic love.　　　34
This was my lord's best hope; now all are fled,
Save only the gods. Now his friends are dead,
Doors, that were ne'er acquainted with their wards
Many a bounteous year, must be employ'd
Now to guard sure their master:
And this is all a liberal course allows;　　40
Who cannot keep his wealth must keep his house.
　　　　　　　　　　　　　　　　[*Exit.*

SCENE IV.—The Same.　A Hall in TIMON's House.

Enter two Servants of VARRO, *and the Servant of*
LUCIUS, *meeting* TITUS, HORTENSIUS, *and other*
Servants to TIMON's *Creditors, waiting his coming*
out.

1 Var. Serv. Well met; good morrow, Titus and
　　Hortensius.
Tit. The like to you, kind Varro.
Hor.　　　　　　　　　　　　Lucius!
What, do we meet together?
Luc. Serv.　　　　　　Ay, and I think,

One business does command us all; for mine
Is money.
Tit.　　　So is theirs and ours.

Enter PHILOTUS.

Luc. Serv.　　　　　　And Sir Philotus too!
Phi. Good day at once.
Luc. Serv.　　　　　Welcome, good brother.
What do you think the hour?
Phi.　　　　　　Labouring for nine.
Luc. Serv. So much?
Phi.　　　　Is not my lord seen yet?
Luc. Serv.　　　　　　　　Not yet.
Phi. I wonder on 't: he was wont to shine at seven.
Luc. Serv. Ay, but the days are wax'd shorter with
　　him:　　　　　　　　　　　　　　　10
You must consider, that a prodigal course
Is like the sun's; but not, like his, recoverable.
I fear,
'T is deepest winter in Lord Timon's purse;
That is, one may reach deep enough, and yet
Find little.
Phi.　　　I am of your fear for that.
Tit. I 'll show you how to observe a strange event.
Your lord sends now for money.
Hor.　　　　　　Most true, he does.
Tit. And he wears jewels now of Timon's gift,
For which I wait for money.　　　　　　　20
Hor.　　　　It is against my heart.
Luc. Serv.　　　Mark, how strange it shows.
Timon in this should pay more than he owes:
And e'en as if your lord should wear rich jewels,
And send for money for 'em.
Hor. I 'm weary of this charge, the gods can
　　witness:
I know, my lord hath spent of Timon's wealth,
And now ingratitude makes it worse than stealth.
1 Var. Serv. Yes, mine 's three thousand crowns;
　　what 's yours?
Luc. Serv. Five thousand mine.
1 Var. Serv. 'T is much deep: and it should seem
　　by the sum,　　　　　　　　　　　　30
Your master's confidence was above mine;
Else, surely, his had equall'd.

Enter FLAMINIUS.

Tit. One of Lord Timon's men.
Luc. Serv. Flaminius! Sir, a word. Pray, is my lord
ready to come forth?
Flam. No, indeed, he is not.
Tit. We attend his lordship: pray, signify so much.
Flam. I need not tell him that; he knows you are
too diligent.　　　　　　　　　　　　[*Exit.*

Enter FLAVIUS *in a cloak, muffled.*

Luc. Serv. Ha! is not that his steward muffled so?
He goes along in a cloud: call him, call him.　41
Tit. Do you hear, sir?
1 Var. Serv. By your leave, sir,—
Flav. What do you ask of me, my friend?
Tit. We wait for certain money here, sir.
Flav.　　　　　　　　　　　　Ay,
If money were as certain as your waiting,
'T were sure enough.
Why then preferr'd you not your sums and bills,
When your false masters eat of my lord's meat?
Then they could smile, and fawn upon his debts,　50
And take down the interest into their gluttonous
　　maws.
You do yourselves but wrong, to stir me up;
Let me pass quietly:
Believe 't, my lord and I have made an end;
I have no more to reckon, he to spend.
Luc. Serv. Ay, but this answer will not serve.
Flav. If 't will not serve, 't is not so base as you;
For you serve knaves.　　　　　　　　[*Exit.*
1 Var. Serv. How! what does his cashier'd worship
mutter?　　　　　　　　　　　　　60
2 Var. Serv. No matter what: he 's poor, and that 's
revenge enough. Who can speak broader than he
that has no house to put his head in? such may rail
against great buildings.

Enter SERVILIUS.

Tit. O! here's Servilius; now we shall know some answer.

Ser. If I might beseech you, gentlemen, to repair some other hour, I should derive much from it; for, take it on my soul, my lord leans wondrously to discontent. His comfortable temper has forsook him: he's much out of health, and keeps his chamber.

Luc. Serv. Many do keep their chambers, are not sick: 72
And if it be so far beyond his health,
Methinks, he should the sooner pay his debts,
And make a clear way to the gods.

Ser.   Good gods!

Tit. We cannot take this for answer, sir.

Flam. [*Within.*] Servilius, help!—my lord! my lord!

Enter TIMON, *in a rage;* FLAMINIUS *following.*

Tim. What! are my doors oppos'd against my passage?
Have I been ever free, and must my house
Be my retentive enemy, my gaol?   80
The place which I have feasted, does it now,
Like all mankind, show me an iron heart?

Luc. Serv. Put in now, Titus.

Tit. My lord, here is my bill.

Luc. Serv. Here's mine.

Hor. And mine, my lord.

Both Var. Serv. And ours, my lord.

Phi. All our bills.

Tim. Knock me down with 'em: cleave me to the girdle.

Luc. Serv. Alas! my lord,—   90

Tim. Cut my heart in sums.

Tit. Mine, fifty talents.

Tim. Tell out my blood.

Luc. Serv. Five thousand crowns, my lord.

Tim. Five thousand drops pays that.—What yours? —and yours?

1 *Var. Serv.* My lord,—

2 *Var. Serv.* My lord,—

Tim. Tear me, take me; and the gods fall upon you!   [*Exit.*

Hor. 'Faith, I perceive our masters may throw their caps at their money: these debts may well be called desperate ones, for a madman owes 'em.   101
                                              [*Exeunt.*

Re-enter TIMON *and* FLAVIUS.

Tim. They have e'en put my breath from me, the slaves:
Creditors?—devils!

Flav. My dear lord,—

Tim. What if it should be so?

Flav. My lord,—

Tim. I'll have it so.—My steward!

Flav. Here, my lord.

Tim. So fitly? Go, bid all my friends again,
Lucius, Lucullus, and Sempronius; all: 110
I'll once more feast the rascals.

Flav.   O my lord!
You only speak from your distracted soul:
There is not so much left to furnish out
A moderate table.

Tim.   Be 't not in thy care: go,
I charge thee; invite them all: let in the tide
Of knaves once more; my cook and I'll provide.
                                              [*Exeunt.*

SCENE V.—*The Same.   The Senate-House.*

The Senate sitting.

1 *Sen.* My lord, you have my voice to 't: the fault's bloody:
'T is necessary he should die:
Nothing emboldens sin so much as mercy.

2 *Sen.* Most true; the law shall bruise him.

Enter ALCIBIADES, *attended.*

Alcib. Honour, health, and compassion to the senate!

1 *Sen.* Now, captain?

Alcib. I am an humble suitor to your virtues;
For pity is the virtue of the law,
And none but tyrants use it cruelly.
It pleases time and fortune to lie heavy   10
Upon a friend of mine; who, in hot blood,
Hath stepp'd into the law, which is past depth
To those that without heed do plunge into 't.
He is a man, setting his fate aside,
Of comely virtues:
Nor did he soil the fact with cowardice
(An honour in him, which buys out his fault);
But, with a noble fury, and fair spirit,
Seeing his reputation touch'd to death,
He did oppose his foe: 20
And with such sober and unnoted passion
He did behave his anger, ere 't was spent,
As if he had but prov'd an argument.

1 *Sen.* You undergo too strict a paradox,
Striving to make an ugly deed look fair:
Your words have took such pains, as if they labour'd
To bring manslaughter into form, and set quarrelling
Upon the head of valour; which, indeed,
Is valour misbegot, and came into the world
When sects and factions were newly born.   30
He's truly valiant that can wisely suffer
The worst that man can breathe;
And make his wrongs his outsides,
To wear them like his raiment, carelessly;
And ne'er prefer his injuries to his heart,
To bring it into danger.
If wrongs be evils, and enforce us kill,
What folly 't is to hazard life for ill!

Alcib. My lord,—

1 *Sen.*   You cannot make gross sins look clear:
To revenge is no valour, but to bear.   40

Alcib. My lords, then, under favour, pardon me,
Why do fond men expose themselves to battle,
And not endure all threats? sleep upon 't,
And let the foes quietly cut their throats,
Without repugnancy? If there be
Such valour in the bearing, what make we
Abroad? why then, women are more valiant,
That stay at home, if bearing carry it;
And the ass more captain than the lion; the felon 50
Loaden with irons wiser than the judge,
If wisdom be in suffering. O my lords!
As you are great, be pitifully good:
Who cannot condemn rashness in cold blood?
To kill, I grant, is sin's extremest gust;
But in defence, by mercy! 't is most just.
To be in anger, is impiety;
But who is man that is not angry?
Weigh but the crime with this.

2 *Sen.* You breathe in vain.

Alcib.   In vain? his service done 61
At Lacedæmon, and Byzantium,
Were a sufficient briber for his life.

1 *Sen.* What's that?

Alcib. Why, I say, my lords, h'as done fair service,
And slain in fight many of your enemies.
How full of valour did he bear himself
In the last conflict, and made plenteous wounds!

2 *Sen.* He has made too much plenty with 'em;
He's a sworn rioter: he has a sin, that often   70
Drowns him, and takes his valour prisoner:
If there were no foes, that were enough
To overcome him: in that beastly fury
He has been known to commit outrages
And cherish factions. 'T is inferr'd to us,
His days are foul, and his drink dangerous.

1 *Sen.* He dies.

Alcib.   Hard fate! he might have died in war.
My lords, if not for any parts in him,—
Though his right arm might purchase his own time,
And be in debt to none,—yet, more to move you,   80
Take my deserts to his, and join 'em both:
And, for I know, your reverend ages love
Security, I'll pawn my victories, all
My honour to you, upon his good returns.
If by this crime he owes the law his life,

Why, let the war receive 't in valiant gore;
For law is strict, and war is nothing more.
   1 *Sen.* We are for law: he dies; urge it no more,
On height of our displeasure. Friend, or brother,
He forfeits his own blood that spills another.

'T is in few words, but spacious in effect:
We banish thee for ever.
   Alcib.   Banish me?
Banish your dotage; banish usury,   100
That makes the senate ugly.

Tim.   "What, dost thou go?
Soft, take thy physic first,—thou too,—and thou."

   Alcib. Must it be so? it must not be. My lords, 90
I do beseech you, know me.
   2 *Sen.* How!
   Alcib. Call me to your remembrances.
   3 *Sen.*   What!
   Alcib. I cannot think, but your age has forgot
    me:
It could not else be I should prove so base,
To sue, and be denied such common grace.
My wounds ache at you.
   1 *Sen.*   Do you dare our anger?

   1 *Sen.* If, after two days' shine, Athens contain thee,
Attend our weightier judgment. And, not to swell
    our spirit,
He shall be executed presently.   *[Exeunt Senators.*
   Alcib. Now the gods keep you old enough; that you
    may live
Only in bone, that none may look on you!
I am worse than mad: I have kept back their foes,
While they have told their money, and let out
Their coin upon large interest; I myself,
Rich only in large hurts:—all those, for this? 110

Is this the balsam, that the usuring senate
Pours into captains' wounds? Banishment?
It comes not ill; I hate not to be banish'd:
It is a cause worthy my spleen and fury,
That I may strike at Athens. I'll cheer up
My discontented troops, and lay for hearts.
'T is honour, with most lands to be at odds;
Soldiers should brook as little wrongs as gods. [*Exit.*

Scene VI.—A Banquet-hall in Timon's House.

*Music. Tables set out: Servants attending. Enter
divers Lords, at several doors.*

1 *Lord.* The good time of day to you, sir.
2 *Lord.* I also wish it to you. I think, this honourable lord did but try us this other day.
1 *Lord.* Upon that were my thoughts tiring, when
we encountered. I hope, it is not so low with him, as
he made it seem in the trial of his several friends.
2 *Lord.* It should not be, by the persuasion of his
new feasting.
1 *Lord.* I should think so. He hath sent me an
earnest inviting, which many my near occasions did
urge me to put off; but he hath conjured me beyond
them, and I must needs appear.
2 *Lord.* In like manner was I in debt to my importunate business, but he would not hear my excuse. I
am sorry, when he sent to borrow of me, that my
provision was out.
1 *Lord.* I am sick of that grief too, as I understand
how all things go.
2 *Lord.* Every man here's so. What would he have
borrowed of you?   20
1 *Lord.* A thousand pieces.
2 *Lord.* A thousand pieces!
1 *Lord.* What of you?
3 *Lord.* He sent to me, sir,—Here he comes.

Enter Timon and Attendants.

Tim. With all my heart, gentlemen both:—and how
fare you?
1 *Lord.* Ever at the best, hearing well of your
lordship.
2 *Lord.* The swallow follows not summer more
willing than we your lordship.   30
Tim. [*Aside.*] Nor more willingly leaves winter;
such summer-birds are men. –[*To them.*] Gentlemen,
our dinner will not recompense this long stay: feast
your ears with the music awhile, if they will fare so
harshly on the trumpet's sound; we shall to't presently.
1 *Lord.* I hope, it remains not unkindly with your
lordship, that I returned you an empty messenger.
Tim. O, sir! let it not trouble you.
2 *Lord.* My noble lord,—   40
Tim. Ah! my good friend, what cheer?
                         [*The banquet brought in.*
2 *Lord.* My most honourable lord, I am e'en sick of
shame, that, when your lordship this other day sent
to me, I was so unfortunate a beggar.
Tim. Think not on 't, sir.
2 *Lord.* If you had sent but two hours before,—
Tim. Let it not cumber your better remembrance.
– Come, bring in all together.
2 *Lord.* All covered dishes!
1 *Lord.* Royal cheer, I warrant you.   50
3 *Lord.* Doubt not that, if money, and the season,
can yield it.
1 *Lord.* How do you? What's the news?
3 *Lord.* Alcibiades is banished: hear you of it?
1 *& 2 Lord.* Alcibiades banished!
3 *Lord.* 'T is so, be sure of it.

1 *Lord.* How? how?
2 *Lord.* I pray you, upon what?
Tim. My worthy friends, will you draw near?
3 *Lord.* I'll tell you more anon. Here's a noble
feast toward.   61
2 *Lord.* This is the old man still.
3 *Lord.* Will't hold? will't hold?
2 *Lord.* It does; but time will—and so—
3 *Lord.* I do conceive.
Tim. Each man to his stool, with that spur as he
would to the lip of his mistress: your diet shall be in
all places alike. Make not a city feast of it, to let the
meat cool ere we can agree upon the first place: sit,
sit. The gods require our thanks.   70
You great benefactors, sprinkle our society with
thankfulness. For your own gifts make yourselves
praised: but reserve still to give, lest your deities be
despised. Lend to each man enough, that one need
not lend to another: for, were your godheads to
borrow of men, men would forsake the gods. Make
the meat be beloved, more than the man that gives
it. Let no assembly of twenty be without a score of
villains: if there sit twelve women at the table, let a
dozen of them be—as they are.—The rest of your fees,
O gods!—the senators of Athens, together with the
common lag of people,—what is amiss in them, you
gods, make suitable for destruction. For these, my
present friends,--as they are to me nothing, so in
nothing bless them, and to nothing are they welcome.
Uncover, dogs, and lap.
                 [*The dishes are uncovered and seem
                         to be full of warm water.*
Some speak. What does his lordship mean?
Some other. I know not.
Tim. May you a better feast never behold,
You knot of mouth-friends! smoke, and luke-warm
                  water,   90
Is your perfection. This is Timon's last;
Who, stuck and spangled with your flatteries,
Washes it off, and sprinkles in your faces
                 [*Throwing water in their faces.*
Your reeking villainy. Live loath'd, and long,
Most smiling, smooth, detested parasites,
Courteous destroyers, affable wolves, meek bears,
You fools of fortune, trencher-friends, time's flies,
Cap-and-knee slaves, vapours, and minute-jacks!
Of man, and beast, the infinite malady
Crust you quite o'er!—What, dost thou go?   100
Soft, take thy physic first,—thou too,—and thou :--
                 [*Throws the dishes at them.*
Stay, I will lend thee money, borrow none.—
What, all in motion? Henceforth be no feast,
Whereat a villain's not a welcome guest.
Burn, house! sink, Athens! henceforth hated be
Of Timon man and all humanity!   [*Exit.*

Re-enter the Lords, with other Lords, and Senators.

1 *Lord.* How now, my lords?
2 *Lord.* Know you the quality of Lord Timon's fury?
3 *Lord.* Push! did you see my cap?
4 *Lord.* I have lost my gown.   110
3 *Lord.* He's but a mad lord, and nought but humour
sways him. He gave me a jewel the other day, and
now he has beat it out of my hat:—did you see my
jewel?
4 *Lord.* Did you see my cap?
2 *Lord.* Here 't is.
4 *Lord.* Here lies my gown.
1 *Lord.* Let's make no stay.
2 *Lord.* Lord Timon's mad.
3 *Lord.*   I feel 't upon my bones.
4 *Lord.* One day he gives us diamonds, next day
                  stones.   120
                                               [*Exeunt.*

ACT IV.

Scene I.—Without the Walls of Athens.

Enter Timon.

Timon.

ET me look back upon thee. O thou wall,
That girdlest in those wolves, dive in the earth,
And fence not Athens! Matrons, turn incontinent!
Obedience fail in children! Slaves, and fools,
Pluck the grave wrinkled · senate from the bench,
And minister in their steads! To general filths
Convert o' the instant, green virginity!
Do 't in your parents' eyes! Bankrupts, hold fast;
Rather than render back, out with your knives,
And cut your trusters' throats! Bound servants, steal!
Large-handed robbers your grave masters are,   11
And pill by law. Maid, to thy master's bed;
Thy mistress is o' the brothel! Son of sixteen,
Pluck the lin'd crutch from thy old limping sire,
With it beat out his brains! Piety, and fear,
Religion to the gods, peace, justice, truth,
Domestic awe, night-rest, and neighbourhood,
Instruction, manners, mysteries, and trades,
Degrees, observances, customs, and laws,
Decline to your confounding contraries,   20
And yet confusion live! Plagues, incident to men,
Your potent and infectious fevers heap
On Athens, ripe for stroke! Thou cold sciatica,
Cripple our senators, that their limbs may halt
As lamely as their manners! Lust and liberty,
Creep in the minds and marrows of our youth,
That 'gainst the stream of virtue they may strive,
And drown themselves in riot! Itches, blains,
Sow all the Athenian bosoms, and their crop
Be general leprosy! Breath infect breath,   30
That their society, as their friendship, may
Be merely poison! Nothing I 'll bear from thee,
But nakedness, thou detestable town!
Take thou that too, with multiplying bans!
Timon will to the woods; where he shall find
The unkindest beast more kinder than mankind.
The gods confound (hear me, you good gods all)
The Athenians both within and out that wall!
And grant, as Timon grows, his hate may grow
To the whole race of mankind, high and low!   40
Amen.   [*Exit.*

Scene II.—Athens. A Room in Timon's House.

Enter Flavius, *with two or three Servants.*

1 Serv. Hear you, master steward! where 's our master?
Are we undone? cast off? nothing remaining?
Flav. Alack! my fellows, what should I say to you?
Let me be recorded by the righteous gods,
I am as poor as you.
1 Serv.   Such a house broke!
So noble a master fallen! All gone, and not
One friend to take his fortune by the arm,
And go along with him!

2 Serv.   As we do turn our backs
From our companion thrown into his grave,
So his familiars to his buried fortunes   10
Slink all away; leave their false vows with him,
Like empty purses pick'd; and his poor self,
A dedicated beggar to the air,
With his disease of all-shunn'd poverty,
Walks, like contempt, alone.—More of our fellows.

Enter other Servants.

Flav. All broken implements of a ruin'd house.
3 Serv. Yet do our hearts wear Timon's livery,
That see I by our faces; we are fellows still,
Serving alike in sorrow. Leak'd is our bark;
And we, poor mates, stand on the dying deck,   20
Hearing the surges threat: we must all part
Into the sea of air.
Flav.   Good fellows all,
The latest of my wealth I 'll share amongst you.
Wherever we shall meet, for Timon's sake,
Let 's yet be fellows; let 's shake our heads, and say,
As 't were a knell unto our master's fortunes,
" We have seen better days." Let each take some;
        [*Giving them money.*
Nay, put out all your hands. Not one word more :
Thus part we rich in sorrow, parting poor.
        [*They embrace, and part several ways.*
O, the fierce wretchedness that glory brings us!   30
Who would not wish to be from wealth exempt,
Since riches point to misery and contempt?
Who 'd be so mock'd with glory? or so live
But in a dream of friendship?
To have his pomp, and all what state compounds,
But only painted, like his varnish'd friends?
Poor honest lord! brought low by his own heart,
Undone by goodness. Strange, unusual blood,
When man's worst sin is, he does too much good!
Who then dares to be half so kind again?   40
For bounty, that makes gods, does still mar men.
My dearest lord,—bless'd, to be most accurs'd,
Rich, only to be wretched,—thy great fortunes
Are made thy chief afflictions. Alas, kind lord!
He 's flung in rage from this ingrateful seat
Of monstrous friends;
Nor has he with him to supply his life,
Or that which can command it.
I 'll follow, and inquire him out:
I 'll ever serve his mind with my best will;   50
Whilst I have gold, I 'll be his steward still.   [*Exit.*

Scene III.—The Woods.

Enter Timon.

Tim. O blessed-breeding sun! draw from the earth
Rotten humidity; below thy sister's orb
Infect the air! Twinn'd brothers of one womb,
Whose procreation, residence, and birth,
Scarce is dividant, touch them with several fortunes;
The greater scorns the lesser: not nature
(To whom all sores lay siege) can bear great fortune,
But by contempt of nature.
Raise me this beggar, and deny 't that lord;
The senator shall bear contempt hereditary,   10

The beggar native honour.
It is the pasture lards the brother's sides,
The want that makes him lean.   Who dares, who
    dares,
In purity of manhood stand upright,
And say " This man 's a flatterer ?" if one be,
So are they all ; for every grise of fortune
Is smooth'd by that below : the learned pate
Ducks to the golden fool. All is oblique ;
There 's nothing level in our cursed natures,
But direct villainy. Therefore, be abhorr'd   20
All feasts, societies, and throngs of men !
His semblable, yea, himself, Timon disdains :

Tim.   " Therefore, be abhorr'd
    All feasts, societies, and throngs of men !"

Destruction fang mankind !—Earth, yield me roots !
                                    [*Digging.*
Who seeks for better of thee, sauce his palate
With thy most operant poison !—What is here ?
Gold ? yellow, glittering, precious gold ? No, gods,
I am no idle votarist. Roots, you clear heavens !
Thus much of this will make black, white ; foul,
    fair ;
Wrong, right ; base, noble ; old, young ; coward,
    valiant.
Ha ! you gods, why this ? What this, you gods ?   30
Why, this
Will lug your priests and servants from your sides,
Pluck stout men's pillows from below their heads.
This yellow slave
Will knit and break religions ; bless the accurs'd ;
Make the hoar leprosy ador'd ; place thieves,
And give them title, knee, and approbation,
With senators on the bench : this is it,
That makes the wappen'd widow wed again ;
She, whom the spital-house and ulcerous sores   40
Would cast the gorge at, this embalms and spices
To the April day again. Come, damned earth,
Thou common whore of mankind, that putt'st odds
Among the rout of nations, I will make thee
Do thy right nature.—[*March afar off.*] Ha ! a drum !
    —Thou 'rt quick,
But yet I 'll bury thee : thou 'lt go, strong thief,
When gouty keepers of thee cannot stand :—
Nay, stay thou out for earnest. [*Reserving some gold.*

Enter ALCIBIADES, *with drum and fife, in warlike
    manner ; and* PHRYNIA *and* TIMANDRA.
Alcib.   What art thou there ? speak.

Tim. A beast, as thou art. The canker gnaw thy
    heart,
For showing me again the eyes of man !
Alcib. What is thy name ? Is man so hateful to
    thee,   50
That art thyself a man ?
    Tim. I am *Misanthropos*, and hate mankind.
For thy part, I do wish thou wert a dog,
That I might love thee something.
    Alcib.   I know thee well ;
But in thy fortunes am unlearn'd and strange.
    Tim. I know thee too ; and more, than that I know
    thee,
I not desire to know. Follow thy drum :
With man's blood paint the ground, gules, gules :
Religious canons, civil laws are cruel ;
Then what should war be ? This fell whore of thine
Hath in her more destruction than thy sword,   61
For all her cherubin look.
    Phry.   Thy lips rot off !
    Tim. I will not kiss thee ; then the rot returns
To thine own lips again.
    Alcib. How came the noble Timon to this change ?
    Tim. As the moon does, by wanting light to give :
But then, renew I could not, like the moon ;
There were no suns to borrow of.
    Alcib. Noble Timon, what friendship may I do thee ?
    Tim. None, but to maintain my opinion.   70
    Alcib. What is it, Timon ?
    Tim. Promise me friendship, but perform none : if
thou wilt not promise, the gods plague thee, for thou
art a man ! if thou dost perform, confound thee, for
thou art a man !
    Alcib. I have heard in some sort of thy miseries.
    Tim. Thou saw'st them, when I had prosperity.
    Alcib. I see them now ; then was a blessed time.
    Tim. As thine is now, held with a brace of harlots.
    Timan. Is this the Athenian minion, whom the world
Voic'd so regardfully ?
    Tim.   Art thou Timandra ?
    Timan.   Yes.   81
    Tim. Be a whore still ! they love thee not that use
    thee :
Give them diseases, leaving with thee their lust.
Make use of thy salt hours ; season the slaves
For tubs and baths ; bring down rose-cheeked youth
To the tub-fast and the diet.
    Timan.   Hang thee, monster !
    Alcib. Pardon him, sweet Timandra, for his wits
Are drown'd and lost in his calamities.—
I have but little gold of late, brave Timon,
The want whereof doth daily make revolt   90
In my penurious band : I have heard and griev'd,
How cursed Athens, mindless of thy worth,
Forgetting thy great deeds, when neighbour states,
But for thy sword and fortune, trod upon them,—
    Tim. I pr'ythee, beat thy drum, and get thee gone.
    Alcib. I am thy friend, and pity thee, dear Timon.
    Tim. How dost thou pity him, whom thou dost
    trouble ?
I had rather be alone.
    Alcib.   Why, fare thee well :   98
Here is some gold for thee.
    Tim.   Keep it, I cannot eat it.
    Alcib. When I have laid proud Athens on a heap,—
    Tim. Warr'st thou 'gainst Athens ?
    Alcib.   Ay, Timon, and have cause.
    Tim. The gods confound them all in thy conquest ;
And thee after, when thou hast conquered !
    Alcib. Why me, Timon ?
    Tim.   That, by killing of villains,
Thou wast born to conquer my country.
Put up thy gold : go on,—here 's gold,—go on ;
Be as a planetary plague, when Jove
Will o'er some high-vic'd city hang his poison
In the sick air : let not thy sword skip one.
Pity not honour'd age for his white beard ;   110
He is an usurer. Strike me the counterfeit matron ;
It is her habit only that is honest,
Herself 's a bawd. Let not the virgin's cheek
Make soft thy trenchant sword ; for those milk-paps,
That through the window-bars bore at men's eyes,

Are not within the leaf of pity writ,
But set them down horrible traitors. Spare not the
      babe,
Whose dimpled smiles from fools exhaust their mercy:
Think it a bastard, whom the oracle
Hath doubtfully pronounc'd thy throat shall cut,   120
And mince it sans remorse. Swear against objects;
Put armour on thine ears, and on thine eyes,
Whose proof, nor yells of mothers, maids, nor babes,
Nor sight of priests in holy vestments bleeding,
Shall pierce a jot. There's gold to pay thy soldiers:
Make large confusion; and, thy fury spent,
Confounded be thyself! Speak not, be gone.
      Alcib. Hast thou gold yet? I'll take the gold thou
            giv'st me,
Not all thy counsel.
      Tim. Dost thou, or dost thou not, heaven's curse
            upon thee!   130
      Phr. & Timan. Give us some gold, good Timon:
            hast thou more?
      Tim. Enough to make a whore forswear her trade,
And to make whores, a bawd. Hold up, you sluts,
Your aprons mountant: you are not oathable,—
Although, I know, you'll swear, terribly swear,
Into strong shudders, and to heavenly agues,
The immortal gods that hear you,—spare your oaths,
I'll trust to your conditions: be whores still;
And he whose pious breath seeks to convert you,
Be strong in whore, allure him, burn him up;   140
Let your close fire predominate his smoke,
And be no turncoats. Yet may your pains, six
      months,
Be quite contrary: and thatch your poor thin roofs
With burdens of the dead:—some that were hang'd,
No matter:—wear them, betray with them: whore
      still;
Paint till a horse may mire upon your face:
A pox of wrinkles!
      Phr. & Timan. Well, more gold.—What then?--
Believe't, that we'll do anything for gold.
      Tim. Consumptions sow   150
In hollow bones of man! strike their sharp shins,
And mar men's spurring. Crack the lawyer's voice,
That he may never more false title plead,
Nor sound his quillets shrilly: hoar the flamen,
That scolds against the quality of flesh,
And not believes himself: down with the nose,
Down with it flat; take the bridge quite away
Of him, that, his particular to foresee,
Smells from the general weal: make curl'd-pate
            ruffians bald;
And let the unscarr'd braggarts of the war   160
Derive some pain from you. Plague all,
That your activity may defeat and quell
The source of all erection:—There's more gold:
Do you damn others, and let this damn you,
And ditches grave you all!
      Phr. & Timan. More counsel with more money,
bounteous Timon.
      Tim. More whore, more mischief first; I have given
            you earnest.
      Alcib. Strike up the drum towards Athens! Fare-
            well, Timon:
If I thrive well, I'll visit thee again.
      Tim. If I hope well, I'll never see thee more.   170
      Alcib. I never did thee harm.
      Tim. Yes, thou spok'st well of me.
      Alcib.   Call'st thou that harm?
      Tim. Men daily find it.
Get thee away, and take thy beagles with thee.
      Alcib. We but offend him.—Strike!
            [*Drum beats. Exeunt* ALCIBIADES,
                  PHRYNIA, *and* TIMANDRA.
      Tim. That nature, being sick of man's unkindness,
Should yet be hungry!—Common mother, thou,
                                          [*Digging.*
Whose womb unmeasurable, and infinite breast,
Teems, and feeds all; whose selfsame mettle,
Whereof thy proud child, arrogant man, is puff'd,   180
Engenders the black toad, and adder blue,
The gilded newt, and eyeless venom'd worm,
With all the abhorred births below crisp heaven

Whereon Hyperion's quickening fire doth shine;
Yield him, who all thy human sons doth hate,
From forth thy plenteous bosom, one poor root!
Ensear thy fertile and conceptious womb,
Let it no more bring out ingrateful man!
Go great with tigers, dragons, wolves, and bears;
Teem with new monsters, whom thy upward face 190
Hath to the marbled mansion all above
Never presented!—O! a root,—dear thanks!—
Dry up thy marrows, vines, and plough-torn leas;
Whereof ingrateful man, with liquorish draughts,
And morsels unctuous, greases his pure mind,
That from it all consideration slips!

Enter APEMANTUS.

More man? Plague! plague!
      Apem. I was directed hither: men report,
Thou dost affect my manners, and dost use them.
      Tim. 'Tis, then, because thou dost not keep a dog,
Whom I would imitate. Consumption catch thee! 201
      Apem. This is in thee a nature but infected;
A poor unmanly melancholy, sprung
From change of fortune. Why this spade? this place?
This slave-like habit? and these looks of care?
Thy flatterers yet wear silk, drink wine, lie soft,
Hug their diseas'd perfumes, and have forgot
That ever Timon was. Shame not these woods,
By putting on the cunning of a carper.
Be thou a flatterer now, and seek to thrive   210
By that which has undone thee: hinge thy knee,
And let his very breath, whom thou'lt observe,
Blow off thy cap; praise his most vicious strain,
And call it excellent. Thou wast told thus;
Thou gav'st thine ear, like tapsters that bid welcome,
To knaves, and all approachers: 'tis most just,
That thou turn rascal; hadst thou wealth again,
Rascals should have't. Do not assume my likeness.
      Tim. Were I like thee, I'd throw away myself.
      Apem. Thou hast cast away thyself, being like
            thyself;   220
A madman so long, now a fool. What! think'st
That the bleak air, thy boisterous chamberlain,
Will put thy shirt on warm? Will these moss'd
            trees,
That have outliv'd the eagle, page thy heels,
And skip when thou point'st out? Will the cold
            brook,
Candied with ice, caudle thy morning taste,
To cure thy o'er-night's surfeit? Call the creatures,—
Whose naked natures live in all the spite
Of wreakful heaven, whose bare unhoused trunks,
To the conflicting elements expos'd,   230
Answer mere nature,—bid them flatter thee;
O! thou shalt find—
      Tim.   A fool of thee. Depart.
      Apem. I love thee better now than e'er I did.
      Tim. I hate thee worse.
      Apem.   Why?
      Tim.   Thou flatter'st misery.
      Apem. I flatter not, but say thou art a caitiff.
      Tim. Why dost thou seek me out?
      Apem.   To vex thee.
      Tim. Always a villain's office, or a fool's.
Dost please thyself in't?
      Apem.   Ay.
      Tim.   What! a knave too?
      Apem. If thou didst put this sour-cold habit on
To castigate thy pride, 'twere well; but thou   240
Dost it enforcedly: thou'dst courtier be again,
Wert thou not beggar. Willing misery
Outlives incertain pomp, is crown'd before;
The one is filling still, never complete;
The other, at high wish: best state, contentless,
Hath a distracted and most wretched being,
Worse than the worst, content.
Thou shouldst desire to die, being miserable.
      Tim. Not by his breath that is more miserable.
Thou art a slave, whom Fortune's tender arm   250
With favour never clasp'd, but bred a dog.
Hadst thou, like us, from our first swath, proceeded
The sweet degrees that this brief world affords
To such as may the passive drudges of it

Freely command, thou wouldst have plung'd thyself
In general riot; melted down thy youth
In different beds of lust; and never learn'd
The icy precepts of respect, but follow'd
The sugar'd game before thee. But myself,
Who had the world as my confectionary;   260
The mouths, the tongues, the eyes, and hearts of men
At duty, more than I could frame employment;
That numberless upon me stuck, as leaves
Do on the oak, have with one winter's brush
Fell from their boughs, and left me open, bare
For every storm that blows;—I, to bear this,
That never knew but better, is some burden:
Thy nature did commence in sufferance, time
Hath made thee hard in 't. Why shouldst thou hate
    men?
They never flatter'd thee: what hast thou given? 270
If thou wilt curse, thy father, that poor rag,
Must be thy subject; who, in spite, put stuff
To some she beggar, and compounded thee
Poor rogue hereditary. Hence! be gone!—
If thou hadst not been born the worst of men,
Thou hadst been a knave, and flatterer.
  Apem. Art thou proud yet?
  Tim.   Ay, that I am not thee.
  Apem. I, that I was no prodigal.
  Tim.   I, that I am one now:
Were all the wealth I have, shut up in thee,
I 'd give thee leave to hang it. Get thee gone.—   280
That the whole life of Athens were in this!
Thus would I eat it.   [*Eating a root.*
  Apem.   Here ; I will mend thy feast.
                [*Offering him something.*
  Tim. First mend my company, take away thyself.
  Apem. So I shall mend mine own, by the lack of
thine.
  Tim. 'T is not well mended so, it is but botch'd ;
If not, I would it were.
  Apem. What wouldst thou have to Athens?
  Tim. Thee thither in a whirlwind. If thou wilt,
Tell them there I have gold : look, so I have.
  Apem. Here is no use for gold.
  Tim.   The best and truest;
For here it sleeps, and does no hired harm.   291
  Apem. Where liest o' nights, Timon?
  Tim.   Under that 's above me.
Where feed'st thou o' days, Apemantus?
  Apem. Where my stomach finds meat ; or, rather,
where I eat it.
  Tim. 'Would poison were obedient, and knew my
mind!
  Apem. Where wouldst thou send it?
  Tim. To sauce thy dishes.   299
  Apem. The middle of humanity thou never knewest,
but the extremity of both ends. When thou wast in
thy gilt, and thy perfume, they mocked thee for too
much curiosity ; in thy rags thou knowest none, but
art despised for the contrary. There 's a medlar for
thee ; eat it.
  Tim. On what I hate I feed not.
  Apem. Dost hate a medlar?
  Tim. Ay, though it look like thee.
  Apem. An thou hadst hated meddlers sooner, thou
shouldst have loved thyself better now. What man
didst thou ever know unthrift that was beloved after
his means?   312
  Tim. Who, without those means thou talkest of,
didst thou ever know beloved?
  Apem. Myself.
  Tim. I understand thee : thou hadst some means to
keep a dog.
  Apem. What things in the world canst thou nearest
compare to thy flatterers?
  Tim. Women nearest ; but men, men are the things
themselves. What wouldst thou do with the world,
Apemantus, if it lay in thy power?   322
  Apem. Give it the beasts, to be rid of the men.
  Tim. Wouldst thou have thyself fall in the con-
fusion of men, and remain a beast with the beasts?
  Apem. Ay, Timon.
  Tim. A beastly ambition, which the gods grant
thee to attain to. If thou wert the lion, the fox would

beguile thee : if thou wert the lamb, the fox would eat
thee : if thou wert the fox, the lion would suspect
thee, when, peradventure, thou wert accused by the
ass : if thou wert the ass, thy dulness would torment
thee, and still thou livedst but as a breakfast to the
wolf : if thou wert the wolf, thy greediness would
afflict thee, and oft thou shouldst hazard thy life for
thy dinner : wert thou the unicorn, pride and wrath
would confound thee, and make thine own self the
conquest of thy fury : wert thou a bear, thou wouldst
be killed by the horse : wert thou a horse, thou wouldst
be seized by the leopard : wert thou a leopard, thou
wert german to the lion, and the spots of thy kindred
were jurors on thy life ; all thy safety were remotion,
and thy defence, absence. What beast couldst thou be,
that were not subject to a beast? and what a beast art
thou already, that seest not thy loss in transformation!
  Apem. If thou couldst please me with speaking to
me, thou mightst have hit upon it here : the commonwealth of Athens is become a forest of beasts.
  Tim. How has the ass broke the wall, that thou art
out of the city?   350
  Apem. Yonder comes a poet, and a painter. The
plague of company light upon thee! I will fear to
catch it, and give way. When I know not what else
to do, I 'll see thee again.
  Tim. When there is nothing living but thee, thou
shalt be welcome. I had rather be a beggar's dog,
than Apemantus.
  Apem. Thou art the cap of all the fools alive.
  Tim. 'Would thou wert clean enough to spit upon.
  Apem. A plague on thee, thou art too bad to curse.
  Tim. All villains that do stand by thee are pure. 361
  Apem. There is no leprosy but what thou speak'st.
  Tim. If I name thee.—
I 'll beat thee,—but I should infect my hands.
  Apem. I would my tongue could rot them off!
  Tim. Away, thou issue of a mangy dog!
Choler does kill me, that thou art alive ;
I swoon to see thee.
  Apem. 'Would thou wouldst burst!
  Tim.   Away, thou tedious rogue!
I am sorry I shall lose a stone by thee.   370
               [*Throws a stone at him.*
  Apem. Beast!
  Tim. Slave!
  Apem. Toad!
  Tim. Rogue, rogue, rogue!
    [*Apemantus retreats backward, as going.*
I am sick of this false world, and will love nought
But even the mere necessities upon 't.
Then, Timon, presently prepare thy grave :
Lie where the light foam of the sea may beat
Thy grave-stone daily : make thine epitaph,
That death in me at others' lives may laugh.   380
[*Looking on the gold.*] O thou sweet king-killer, and
  dear divorce
'Twixt natural son and sire! thou bright defiler
Of Hymen's purest bed! thou valiant Mars!
Thou ever young, fresh, lov'd, and delicate wooer,
Whose blush doth thaw the consecrated snow
That lies on Dian's lap! thou visible god,
That solder'st close impossibilities,
And mak'st them kiss! that speak'st with every
    tongue,
To every purpose! O thou touch of hearts!
Think, thy slave man rebels ; and by thy virtue   390
Set them into confounding odds, that beasts
May have the world in empire!
  Apem.   'Would 't were so ;
But not till I am dead!—I 'll say, thou 'st gold:
Thou wilt be throng'd to shortly.
  Tim.   Throng'd to?
  Apem.   Ay.
  Tim. Thy back, I pr'ythee.
  Apem.   Live, and love thy misery!
  Tim. Long live so, and so die!—I am quit.—
                  [*Exit Apemantus.*
More things like men?—Eat, Timon, and abhor them.

Enter Thieves.

  1 Thief. Where should he have this gold? It is

some fragment, some slender ort of his remainder.
The mere want of gold, and the falling-from of his
friends, drove him into this melancholy.   401
  2 Thief. It is noised he hath a mass of treasure.
  3 Thief. Let us make the assay upon him : if he
care not for 't, he will supply us easily ; if he covetously
reserve it, how shall 's get it ?
  2 Thief. True ; for he bears it not about him, 't is
hid.
  1 Thief. Is not this he ?
  All. Where ?
  2 Thief. 'T is his description.   410
  3 Thief. He ; I know him.

3 Thief. "Let us make the assay upon him."

  All. Save thee, Timon.
  Tim. Now, thieves?
  All. Soldiers, not thieves.
  Tim. Both too ; and women's sons.
  All. We are not thieves, but men that much do
        want.
  Tim. Your greatest want is, you want much of
        meat.
Why should you want? Behold, the earth hath roots ;
Within this mile break forth a hundred springs ;
The oaks bear mast, the briers scarlet hips ;   420
The bounteous housewife, Nature, on each bush
Lays her full mess before you. Want ! why want ?
  1 Thief. We cannot live on grass, on berries, water,
As beasts, and birds, and fishes.
  Tim. Nor on the beasts themselves, the birds, and
        fishes ;
You must eat men. Yet thanks I must you con,
That you are thieves profess'd, that you work not
In holier shape ; for there is boundless theft
In limited professions. Rascal thieves,
Here 's gold. Go, suck the subtle blood o' the grape,
Till the high fever seethe your blood to froth,   431
And so 'scape hanging. Trust not the physician ;
His antidotes are poison, and he slays
More than you rob. Take wealth and lives together ;
Do villainy, do, since you protest to do 't,
Like workmen. I 'll example you with thievery :
The sun 's a thief, and with his great attraction
Robs the vast sea ; the moon 's an arrant thief,
And her pale fire she snatches from the sun ;
The sea 's a thief, whose liquid surge resolves   440
The moon into salt tears ; the earth 's a thief,
That feeds and breeds by a composture stolen
From general excrement ; each thing 's a thief ;
The laws, your curb and whip, in their rough power
Have uncheck'd theft. Love not yourselves ; away !
Rob one another. There 's more gold : cut throats ;
All that you meet are thieves. To Athens, go :
Break open shops ; nothing can you steal,
But thieves do lose it. Steal not less, for this
I give you ;   450
And gold confound you howsoe'er ! Amen.
                        [*Retires to his cave.*

  3 Thief. He has almost charmed me from my profession, by persuading me to it.
  1 Thief. 'T is in the malice of mankind, that he
thus advises us ; not to have us thrive in our mystery.
  2 Thief. I 'll believe him as an enemy, and give
over my trade.
  1 Thief. Let us first see peace in Athens ; there is
no time so miserable, but a man may be true.
                        [*Exeunt Thieves.*

                Enter FLAVIUS.

  Flav. O you gods !   460
Is yond despis'd and ruinous man my lord ?
Full of decay and failing ? O monument
And wonder of good deeds evilly bestow'd !
What an alteration of honour
Has desperate want made !
What vilder thing upon the earth, than friends,
Who can bring noblest minds to basest ends ?
How rarely does it meet with this time's guise,
When man was wish'd to love his enemies !
Grant, I may ever love, and rather woo   470
Those that would mischief me, than those that do !
He has caught me in his eye : I will present
My honest grief unto him ; and, as my lord,
Still serve him with my life.—My dearest master !

         TIMON *comes forward from his cave.*

  Tim. Away ! what art thou ?
  Flav.   Have you forgot me, sir ?
  Tim. Why dost ask that ? I have forgot all men ;
Then, if thou grant'st thou 'rt a man, I have forgot
        thee.
  Flav. An honest poor servant of yours.
  Tim.   Then I know thee not :
I never had honest man about me ; ay, all
I kept were knaves, to serve in meat to villains. 480
  Flav. The gods are witness,
Ne'er did poor steward wear a truer grief
For his undone lord, than mine eyes for you.
  Tim. What ! dost thou weep ?—Come nearer : then,
        I love thee,
Because thou art a woman, and disclaim'st
Flinty mankind ; whose eyes do never give,
But thorough lust and laughter. Pity 's sleeping :
Strange times, that weep with laughing, not with
        weeping !
  Flav. I beg of you to know me, good my lord,
To accept my grief, and, whilst this poor wealth
        lasts,   490
To entertain me as your steward still.
  Tim. Had I a steward
So true, so just, and now so comfortable ?
It almost turns my dangerous nature wild.
Let me behold thy face. Surely, this man
Was born of woman.—
Forgive my general and exceptless rashness,
You perpetual-sober gods ! I do proclaim
One honest man,—mistake me not,—but one ;
No more, I pray,—and he 's a steward.—   500
How fain would I have hated all mankind,
And thou redeem'st thyself : but all, save thee,
I fell with curses.
Methinks, thou art more honest now than wise ;
For, by oppressing and betraying me,
Thou mightst have sooner got another service :
For many so arrive at second masters,
Upon their first lord's neck. But tell me true,
(For I must ever doubt, though ne'er so sure,)
Is not thy kindness subtle, covetous,   510
If not a usuring kindness ; and as rich men deal gifts,
Expecting in return twenty for one ?
  Flav. No, my most worthy master ; in whose breast
Doubt and suspect, alas ! are plac'd too late.
You should have fear'd false times, when you did
        feast :
Suspect still comes where an estate is least.
That which I show, heaven knows, is merely love,
Duty and zeal to your unmatched mind,
Care of your food and living : and, believe it,
My most honour'd lord,   520
For any benefit that points to me,

Either in hope, or present, I'd exchange
For this one wish,—that you had power and wealth
To requite me by making rich yourself.
    Tim. Look thee, 't is so.—Thou singly honest man,

Debts wither 'em to nothing; be men like blasted
        woods,
And may diseases lick up their false bloods !
And so, farewell, and thrive.

Flav. " The gods are witness,
Ne'er did poor steward wear a truer grief
For his undone lord, than mine eyes for you."

Here, take :—the gods out of my misery
Have sent thee treasure.   Go, live rich, and happy ;
But thus condition'd : thou shalt build from men ;
Hate all, curse all ; show charity to none,
But let the famish'd flesh slide from the bone,   530
Ere thou relieve the beggar ; give to dogs
What thou deniest to men ; let prisons swallow 'em,

    Flav.   O ! let me stay,
And comfort you, my master.
    Tim.   If thou hat'st
Curses, stay not ; fly, whilst thou art bless'd and
        free :
Ne'er see thou man, and let me ne'er see thee.
                                [*Exeunt severally.*

ACT V.

SCENE I.—The Same. Before TIMON's Cave.

Enter Poet and Painter.

Painter.

AS I took note of the place, it cannot be
far where he abides.

Poet. What's to be thought of him?
Does the rumour hold for true, that he
is so full of gold?

Pain. Certain: Alcibiades reports it;
Phrynia and Timandra had gold of
him: he likewise enriched poor straggling soldiers with great quantity. 'T is
said he gave unto his steward a mighty
sum.   11

Poet. Then this breaking of his has
been but a try for his friends.

Pain. Nothing else; you shall see
him a palm in Athens again, and
flourish with the highest. Therefore,
't is not amiss, we tender our loves to
him, in this supposed distress of his: it will show
honestly in us, and is very likely to load our purposes
with what they travel for, if it be a just and true
report that goes of his having.   21

Poet. What have you now to present unto him?

Pain. Nothing at this time but my visitation; only
I will promise him an excellent piece.

Poet. I must serve him so too; tell him of an intent
that's coming toward him.

Pain. Good as the best. Promising is the very air
o' the time: it opens the eyes of expectation: performance is ever the duller for his act; and, but in
the plainer and simpler kind of people, the deed of
saying is quite out of use. To promise is most courtly
and fashionable: performance is a kind of will, or
testament, which argues a great sickness in his judgment that makes it.

Enter TIMON, from his cave.

Tim. [*Aside.*] Excellent workman! Thou canst
not paint a man so bad as is thyself.

Poet. I am thinking, what I shall say I have provided for him. It must be a personating of himself:
a satire against the softness of prosperity, with a
discovery of the infinite flatteries that follow youth
and opulency.   41

Tim. [*Aside.*] Must thou needs stand for a villain in
thine own work? Wilt thou whip thine own faults in
other men? Do so; I have gold for thee.

Poet. Nay, let's seek him:
Then do we sin against our own estate,
When we may profit meet, and come too late.

Pain. True:
When the day serves, before black-corner'd night,
Find what thou want'st by free and offer'd light.   50
Come.

Tim. [*Aside.*] I'll meet you at the turn. What a
          god's gold,
That he is worshipp'd in a baser temple,
Than where swine feed!
'T is thou that rigg'st the bark, and plough'st the foam;
Settlest admired reverence in a slave:
To thee be worship; and thy saints for aye
Be crown'd with plagues, that thee alone obey!
Fit I meet them.   [*Advancing.*

Poet. Hail, worthy Timon!

Pain.   Our late noble master.

Tim. Have I once liv'd to see two honest men?   61

Poet. Sir,
Having often of your open bounty tasted,
Hearing you were retir'd, your friends fall'n off,
Whose thankless natures—O abhorred spirits!
Not all the whips of heaven are large enough—
What! to you,
Whose star-like nobleness gave life and influence
To their whole being! I am rapt, and cannot cover
The monstrous bulk of this ingratitude   70
With any size of words.

Tim. Let it go naked, men may see 't the better:
You, that are honest, by being what you are,
Make them best seen, and known.

Pain.   He, and myself,
Have travell'd in the great shower of your gifts,
And sweetly felt it.

Tim. Ay, you are honest men.

Pain. We are hither come to offer you our service.

Tim. Most honest men! Why, how shall I require
          you?
Can you eat roots, and drink cold water? no.

Both. What we can do, we'll do, to do you service.

Tim. You are honest men. You have heard that I
          have gold;   81
I am sure you have: speak truth; you are honest
          men.

Pain. So it is said, my noble lord; but therefore
Came not my friend, nor I.

Tim. Good honest men!—Thou draw'st a counterfeit
Best in all Athens: thou art, indeed, the best;
Thou counterfeit'st most lively.

Pain.   So, so, my lord.

Tim. Even so, sir, as I say.—And, for thy fiction,
Why, thy verse swells with stuff so fine and smooth,
That thou art even natural in thine art.—   90
But, for all this, my honest-natur'd friends,
I must needs say, you have a little fault:
Marry, 't is not monstrous in you; neither wish I,
You take much pains to mend.

Both.   Beseech your honour,
To make it known to us.

Tim.   You'll take it ill.

Both. Most thankfully, my lord.

Tim.   Will you, indeed?

Both. Doubt it not, worthy lord.

Tim. There's never a one of you but trusts a knave,
That mightily deceives you.

Both.   Do we, my lord?

Tim. Ay, and you hear him cog, see him dissemble,
Know his gross patchery, love him, feed him,   101
Keep in your bosom; yet remain assur'd,
That he's a made-up villain.

Pain. I know none such, my lord.

Poet.   Nor I.

Tim. Look you, I love you well; I'll give you gold,
Rid me these villains from your companies:
Hang them, or stab them, drown them in a draught,
Confound them by some course, and come to me,
I'll give you gold enough.

Both. Name them, my lord; let's know them.   110

Tim. You that way, and you this, but two in com-
          pany:—
Each man apart, all single and alone,
Yet an arch-villain keeps him company.
[*To the Painter.*] If, where thou art, two villains
          shall not be,

Come not near him.—[*To the Poet.*] If thou wouldst
      not reside
But where one villain is, then him abandon.—
Hence! pack! there's gold; ye came for gold, ye
      slaves:
You have work for me, there's payment: hence!
You are an alchymist, make gold of that.
Out, rascal dogs!   120
            [*Exit, beating and driving them out.*

Scene II.—The Same.

Enter Flavius *and two Senators.*

Flav. It is in vain that you would speak with
      Timon;
For he is set so only to himself,
That nothing but himself, which looks like man,
Is friendly with him.
   1 Sen.   Bring us to his cave:
It is our part, and promise to the Athenians,
To speak with Timon.
   2 Sen.   At all times alike
Men are not still the same. 'T was time, and griefs,
That fram'd him thus: time, with his fairer hand,
Offering the fortunes of his former days,
The former man may make him. Bring us to him, 10
And chance it as it may.
   Flav.   Here is his cave.—
Peace and content be here! Lord Timon! Timon!
Look out, and speak to friends. The Athenians,
By two of their most reverend senate, greet thee:
Speak to them, noble Timon.

Enter Timon.

Tim. Thou sun, that comfort'st, burn!—Speak, and
      be hang'd:
For each true word, a blister; and each false
Be as a cauterising to the root o' the tongue,
Consuming it with speaking!
   1 Sen.   Worthy Timon,—
Tim. Of none but such as you, and you of Timon. 20
2 Sen. The senators of Athens greet thee, Timon.
Tim. I thank them; and would send them back the
      plague,
Could I but catch it for them.
   1 Sen.   O! forget
What we are sorry for ourselves in thee.
The senators, with one consent of love,
Entreat thee back to Athens; who have thought
On special dignities, which vacant lie
For thy best use and wearing.
   2 Sen.   They confess
Toward thee forgetfulness too general, gross;
Which now the public body,—which doth seldom 30
Play the recanter,—feeling in itself
A lack of Timon's aid, hath sense withal
Of its own fall, restraining aid to Timon;
And send forth us, to make their sorrowed render,
Together with a recompense more fruitful
Than their offence can weigh down by the dram;
Ay, even such heaps and sums of love and wealth,
As shall to thee blot out what wrongs were theirs,
And write in thee the figures of their love,
Ever to read them thine.
   Tim.   You witch me in it; 40
Surprise me to the very brink of tears:
Lend me a fool's heart, and a woman's eyes,
And I'll beweep these comforts, worthy senators.
   1 Sen. Therefore, so please thee to return with us,
And of our Athens, thine and ours, to take
The captainship, thou shalt be met with thanks,
Allow'd with absolute power, and thy good name
Live with authority:—so soon we shall drive back
Of Alcibiades the approaches wild;
Who, like a boar too savage, doth root up   50
His country's peace.
   2 Sen.   And shakes his threat'ning sword
Against the walls of Athens.
   1 Sen.   Therefore, Timon,—
Tim. Well, sir, I will; therefore, I will, sir, thus:—

If Alcibiades kill my countrymen,
Let Alcibiades know this of Timon,
That Timon cares not. But if he sack fair Athens,
And take our goodly aged men by the beards,
Giving our holy virgins to the stain
Of contumelious, beastly, mad-brain'd war,
Then, let him know,—and tell him, Timon speaks
      it,—   60
In pity of our aged, and our youth,
I cannot choose but tell him, that I care not,
And let him take 't at worst; for their knives care
      not,
While you have throats to answer; for myself,
There's not a whittle in the unruly camp,
But I do prize it at my love, before
The reverend'st throat in Athens. So I leave you
To the protection of the prosperous gods,
As thieves to keepers.
   Flav.   Stay not: all 's in vain.
   Tim. Why, I was writing of my epitaph;   70
It will be seen to-morrow. My long sickness
Of health, and living, now begins to mend,
And nothing brings me all things. Go; live still:
Be Alcibiades your plague, you his,
And last so long enough!
   1 Sen.   We speak in vain.
   Tim. But yet I love my country, and am not
One that rejoices in the common wrack,
As common bruit doth put it.
   1 Sen.   That 's well spoke.
   Tim. Commend me to my loving countrymen,—
   1 Sen. These words become your lips as they pass
      through them.   80
   2 Sen. And enter in our ears like great triumphers
In their applauding gates.
   Tim.   Commend me to them;
And tell them, that, to ease them of their griefs,
Their fears of hostile strokes, their aches, losses,
Their pangs of love, with other incident throes
That nature's fragile vessel doth sustain
In life's uncertain voyage, I will some kindness do
      them:
I'll teach them to prevent wild Alcibiades' wrath.
   2 Sen. I like this well; he will return again.
   Tim. I have a tree which grows here in my close, 90
That mine own use invites me to cut down,
And shortly must I fell it; tell my friends,
Tell Athens, in the sequence of degree,
From high to low throughout, that whoso please
To stop affliction, let him take his haste,
Come hither, ere my tree hath felt the axe,
And hang himself.—I pray you, do my greeting.
   Flav. Trouble him no further; thus you still shall
      find him.
   Tim. Come not to me again; but say to Athens,
Timon hath made his everlasting mansion   100
Upon the beached verge of the salt flood;
Whom once a day with his embossed froth
The turbulent surge shall cover: thither come,
And let my grave-stone be your oracle.—
Lips, let sour words go by, and language end:
What is amiss, plague and infection mend!
Graves only be men's works, and death their gain!
Sun, hide thy beams! Timon hath done his reign.
                                             [*Exit.*
   1 Sen. His discontents are unremovably
Coupled to nature.   110
   2 Sen. Our hope in him is dead. Let us return,
And strain what other means is left unto us
In our dear peril.
   1 Sen.   It requires swift foot. [*Exeunt.*

Scene III.—The Walls of Athens.

Enter two Senators and a Messenger.

   1 Sen. Thou hast painfully discover'd: are his files
As full as thy report?
   Mess.   I have spoke the least;
Besides, his expedition promises
Present approach.

2 Sen. We stand much hazard, if they bring not
   Timon.
Mess. I met a courier, one mine ancient friend,
Whom, though in general part we were oppos'd,
Yet our old love made a particular force,
And made us speak like friends :—this man was riding
From Alcibiades to Timon's cave,   10
With letters of entreaty, which imported
His fellowship i' the cause against your city,
In part for his sake mov'd.

    Enter the Senators from TIMON.

1 Sen.   Here come our brothers.
3 Sen. No talk of Timon ; nothing of him expect.—

Sold.   " What's on this tomb
I cannot read ; the character I 'll take with wax."

The enemy's drum is heard, and fearful scouring
Doth choke the air with dust. In, and prepare :
Ours is the fall, I fear ; our foes the snare.   *[Exeunt.*

SCENE IV.—The Woods. TIMON'S Cave, and a
    Tomb-stone seen.

    Enter a Soldier, seeking TIMON.

Sold. By all description this should be the place.
Who 's here ? speak, ho !—No answer ?—What is this ?
Timon is dead, who hath outstretch'd his span :
Some beast made this ; there does not live a man.
Dead, sure ; and this his grave.—What 's on this tomb
I cannot read ; the character I 'll take with wax :
Our captain hath in every figure skill ;
An ag'd interpreter, though young in days.
Before proud Athens he 's set down by this,
Whose fall the mark of his ambition is.   10
                     [Exit.

SCENE V.—Before the Walls of Athens.

Trumpets sound. Enter ALCIBIADES *and Forces.*
Alcib. Sound to this coward and lascivious town
Our terrible approach.   *[A parley sounded.*

    Enter Senators on the walls.

Till now you have gone on, and fill'd the time
With all licentious measure, making your wills
The scope of justice : till now, myself, and such
As slept within the shadow of your power,
Have wander'd with our travers'd arms, and breath'd
Our sufferance vainly. Now the time is flush,
When crouching marrow, in the bearer strong,

Cries of itself, " No more :" now breathless wrong 10
Shall sit and pant in your great chairs of ease ;
And pursy insolence shall break his wind
With fear, and horrid flight.
1 Sen.   Noble, and young,
When thy first griefs were but a mere conceit,
Ere thou hadst power, or we had cause of fear,
We sent to thee ; to give thy rages balm,
To wipe out our ingratitude with loves
Above their quantity.
2 Sen.   So did we woo
Transformed Timon to our city's love,
By humble message, and by promis'd means :   20
We were not all unkind, nor all deserve
The common stroke of war.
1 Sen.   These walls of ours
Were not erected by their hands, from whom
You have receiv'd your grief ; nor are they such,
That these great towers, trophies, and schools, should
    fall
For private faults in them.
2 Sen.   Nor are they living,
Who were the motives that you first went out ;
Shame, that they wanted cunning in excess,
Hath broke their hearts. March, noble lord,
Into our city with thy banners spread :   30
By decimation, and a tithed death,
(If thy revenges hunger for that food
Which nature loathes,) take thou the destin'd tenth ;
And, by the hazard of the spotted die,
Let die the spotted.
1 Sen.   All have not offended ;
For those that were, it is not square to take,
On those that are, revenge : crimes, like lands,
Are not inherited. Then, dear countryman,
Bring in thy ranks, but leave without thy rage :
Spare thy Athenian cradle, and those kin,   40
Which, in the bluster of thy wrath, must fall
With those that have offended. Like a shepherd,
Approach the fold, and cull the infected forth,
But kill not all together.
2 Sen.   What thou wilt,
Thou rather shalt enforce it with thy smile,
Than hew to 't with thy sword.
1 Sen.   Set but thy foot
Against our rampir'd gates, and they shall ope,
So thou wilt send thy gentle heart before,
To say, thou 'lt enter friendly.
2 Sen.   Throw thy glove,
Or any token of thine honour else,   50
That thou wilt use the wars as thy redress,
And not as our confusion, all thy powers
Shall make their harbour in our town, till we
Have seal'd thy full desire.
Alcib.   Then, there 's my glove :
Descend, and open your uncharged ports.
Those enemies of Timon's, and mine own,
Whom you yourselves shall set out for reproof,
Fall, and no more ; and,—to atone your fears
With my more noble meaning,—not a man
Shall pass his quarter, or offend the stream   60
Of regular justice in your city's bounds,
But shall be render'd to your public laws
At heaviest answer.
Both.   'T is most nobly spoken.
Alcib. Descend, and keep your words.
    [The Senators descend, and open the gates.

    Enter a Soldier.

Sold. My noble general, Timon is dead ;
Entomb'd upon the very hem o' the sea :
And on his grave-stone this insculpture, which
With wax I brought away, whose soft impression
Interprets for my poor ignorance.
Alcib. [*Reads.*] " Here lies a wretched corse, of
    wretched soul bereft :   70
Seek not my name : a plague consume you wicked
    caitiffs left !
Here lie I, Timon ; who, alive, all living men did
    hate :
Pass by, and curse thy fill ; but pass, and stay not here
    thy gait."

These well express in thee thy latter spirits:
Though thou abhorr'dst in us our human griefs,
Scorn'dst our brain's flow, and those our droplet
    which
From niggard nature fall, yet rich conceit
Taught thee to make vast Neptune weep for aye
On thy low grave, on faults forgiven. Dead

Is noble Timon; of whose memory   80
Hereafter more.—Bring me into your city,
And I will use the olive with my sword:
Make war breed peace; make peace stint war; make
    each
Prescribe to other, as each other's leech.—
Let our drums strike.   [*Exeunt.*

JULIUS CÆSAR.

DRAMATIS PERSONÆ.

JULIUS CÆSAR.
OCTAVIUS CÆSAR, ⎫
MARCUS ANTONIUS, ⎬ *Triumvirs after the death of*
M. ÆMIL. LEPIDUS, ⎭ *Julius Cæsar.*
CICERO, ⎫
PUBLIUS, ⎬ *Senators.*
POPILIUS LENA, ⎭
MARCUS BRUTUS, ⎫
CASSIUS, ⎪
CASCA, ⎪
TREBONIUS, ⎬ *Conspirators against Julius*
LIGARIUS, ⎪ *Cæsar.*
DECIUS BRUTUS, ⎪
METELLUS CIMBER, ⎪
CINNA, ⎭

FLAVIUS *and* MARULLUS, *Tribunes.*
ARTEMIDORUS, *a Sophist of Cnidos.*
A Soothsayer.
CINNA, *a Poet. Another Poet.*
LUCILIUS, TITINIUS, MESSALA, *Young* CATO, *and*
VOLUMNIUS, *Friends to Brutus and Cassius.*
VARRO, CLITUS, CLAUDIUS, STRATO, LUCIUS, DAR-
DANIUS, *Servants to Brutus.*
PINDARUS, *Servant to Cassius.*

CALPHURNIA, *Wife to Cæsar.*
PORTIA, *Wife to Brutus.*

Senators, Citizens, Guards, Attendants, &c.

SCENE—During a great part of the Play, at ROME: afterwards at SARDIS, and near PHILIPPI.

ACT I.

SCENE I.—Rome. A Street.

Enter FLAVIUS, MARULLUS, *and a rabble of Citizens.*

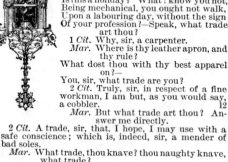

Flavius.

ENCE! home, you idle creatures, get you
home.
Is this a holiday? What! know you not,
Being mechanical, you ought not walk,
Upon a labouring day, without the sign
Of your profession?—Speak, what trade
art thou?
1 Cit. Why, sir, a carpenter.
Mar. Where is thy leather apron, and
thy rule?
What dost thou with thy best apparel
on?—
You, sir, what trade are you?
2 Cit. Truly, sir, in respect of a fine
workman, I am but, as you would say,
a cobbler. 12
Mar. But what trade art thou? Answer me directly.
2 Cit. A trade, sir, that, I hope, I may use with a
safe conscience; which is, indeed, sir, a mender of
bad soles.
Mar. What trade, thou knave? thou naughty knave,
what trade?
2 Cit. Nay, I beseech you, sir, be not out with me:
yet, if you be out, sir, I can mend you.
Mar. What mean'st thou by that? Mend me, thou
saucy fellow? 21
2 Cit. Why, sir, cobble you.
Flav. Thou art a cobbler, art thou?
2 Cit. Truly, sir, all that I live by is with the awl:
I meddle with no tradesman's matters, nor women's
matters, but with all. I am, indeed, sir, a surgeon
to old shoes; when they are in great danger, I re-cover

them. As proper men as ever trod upon neat's-leather,
have gone upon my handiwork.
Flav. But wherefore art not in thy shop to-day? 30
Why dost thou lead these men about the streets?
2 Cit. Truly, sir, to wear out their shoes, to get
myself into more work. But, indeed, sir, we make
holiday, to see Cæsar, and to rejoice in his triumph.
Mar. Wherefore rejoice? What conquest brings
he home?
What tributaries follow him to Rome,
To grace in captive bonds his chariot wheels?
You blocks, you stones, you worse than senseless
things!
O you hard hearts, you cruel men of Rome,
Knew you not Pompey? Many a time and oft 40
Have you climb'd up to walls and battlements,
To towers and windows, yea, to chimney-tops,
Your infants in your arms, and there have sat
The livelong day, with patient expectation,
To see great Pompey pass the streets of Rome:
And when you saw his chariot but appear,
Have you not made an universal shout,
That Tiber trembled underneath her banks,
To hear the replication of your sounds
Made in her concave shores? 50
And do you now put on your best attire?
And do you now cull out a holiday?
And do you now strew flowers in his way,
That comes in triumph over Pompey's blood?
Be gone!
Run to your houses, fall upon your knees,
Pray to the gods to intermit the plague
That needs must light on this ingratitude.
Flav. Go, go, good countrymen, and for this fault

Assemble all the poor men of your sort: 60
Draw them to Tiber banks, and weep your tears
Into the channel, till the lowest stream
Do kiss the most exalted shores of all.
       [*Exeunt Citizens.*
See, whe'r their basest metal be not mov'd ;
They vanish tongue-tied in their guiltiness.
Go you down that way towards the Capitol :
This way will I. Disrobe the images,
If you do find them deck'd with ceremonies.
 Mar. May we do so?
 Flav. It is no matter ; let no images 70
Be hung with Cæsar's trophies. I'll about,
And drive away the vulgar from the streets :
So do you too, where you perceive them thick.
These growing feathers pluck'd from Cæsar's wing
Will make him fly an ordinary pitch ;
Who else would soar above the view of men,
And keep us all in servile fearfulness. [*Exeunt.*

SCENE II.—The Same. A Public Place.

Enter, in procession, with music, CÆSAR ; ANTONY,
for the course ; CALPHURNIA, PORTIA, DECIUS,
CICERO, BRUTUS, CASSIUS, *and* CASCA ; *a great
Crowd following, among them a Soothsayer.*

Cæs. Calphurnia !
Casca.   Peace, ho ! Cæsar speaks.
       [*Music ceases.*
Cæs.   Calphurnia !
Cal. Here, my lord.
Cæs. Stand you directly in Antonius' way,
When he doth run his course.—Antonius !
 Ant. Cæsar, my lord.
 Cæs. Forget not, in your speed, Antonius,
To touch Calphurnia ; for our elders say,
The barren, touched in this holy chase,
Shake off their steril curse.
 Ant.   I shall remember ·
When Cæsar says, "Do this," it is perform'd. 10
 Cæs. Set on ; and leave no ceremony out. [*Music.*
 Sooth. Cæsar !
 Cæs. Ha ! Who calls?
 Casca. Bid every noise be still :—peace yet again !
       [*Music ceases.*
 Cæs. Who is it in the press that calls on me?
I hear a tongue, shriller than all the music,
Cry, Cæsar !—Speak : Cæsar is turn'd to hear.
 Sooth. Beware the ides of March.
 Cæs.   What man is that?
 Bru. A soothsayer, bids you beware the ides of
  March.
 Cæs. Set him before me ; let me see his face. 20
 Cas. Fellow, come from the throng : look upon
  Cæsar.
 Cæs. What say'st thou to me now? Speak once
  again.
 Sooth. Beware the ides of March.
 Cæs. He is a dreamer ; let us leave him :—pass.
  [*Sennet. Exeunt all but* BRUTUS *and* CASSIUS.
 Cas. Will you go see the order of the course?
 Bru. Not I.
 Cas. I pray you, do.
 Bru. I am not gamesome : I do lack some part
Of that quick spirit that is in Antony.
Let me not hinder, Cassius, your desires ; 30
I'll leave you.
 Cas. Brutus, I do observe you now of late :
I have not from your eyes that gentleness,
And show of love, as I was wont to have :
You bear too stubborn and too strange a hand
Over your friend that loves you.
 Bru.   Cassius,
Be not deceiv'd : if I have veil'd my look,
I turn the trouble of my countenance
Merely upon myself. Vexed I am,
Of late, with passions of some difference, 40
Conceptions only proper to myself,
Which give some soil, perhaps, to my behaviours ;

But let not therefore my good friends be griev'd,
(Among which number, Cassius, be you one,)
Nor construe any further my neglect,
Than that poor Brutus, with himself at war,
Forgets the shows of love to other men.
 Cas. Then, Brutus, I have much mistook your
  passion ;
By means whereof, this breast of mine hath buried
Thoughts of great value, worthy cogitations. 50
Tell me, good Brutus, can you see your face ?
 Bru. No, Cassius ; for the eye sees not itself,
But by reflection, by some other things.
 Cas. 'T is just :
And it is very much lamented, Brutus,
That you have no such mirrors as will turn
Your hidden worthiness into your eye,
That you might see your shadow. I have heard,
Where many of the best respect in Rome
(Except immortal Cæsar), speaking of Brutus, 60
And groaning underneath this age's yoke,
Have wish'd that noble Brutus had his eyes.
 Bru. Into what dangers would you lead me, Cassius,
That you would have me seek into myself
For that which is not in me?
 Cas. Therefore, good Brutus, be prepar'd to hear :
And, since you know you cannot see yourself
So well as by reflection, I, your glass,
Will modestly discover to yourself
That of yourself which you yet know not of. 70
And be not jealous on me, gentle Brutus :
Were I a common laugher, or did use
To stale with ordinary oaths my love
To every new protester ; if you know
That I do fawn on men, and hug them hard,
And after scandal them ; or if you know
That I profess myself in banqueting
To all the rout, then hold me dangerous.
      [*Flourish, and shout.*
 Bru. What means this shouting? I do fear, the
  people
Choose Cæsar for their king.
 Cas.   Ay, do you fear it ? 80
Then must I think you would not have it so.
 Bru. I would not, Cassius ; yet I love him well :—
But wherefore do you hold me here so long?
What is it that you would impart to me ?
If it be aught toward the general good,
Set honour in one eye, and death i' the other,
And I will look on both indifferently :
For, let the gods so speed me, as I love
The name of honour more than I fear death.
 Cas. I know that virtue to be in you, Brutus, 90
As well as I do know your outward favour.
Well, honour is the subject of my story.—
I cannot tell what you and other men
Think of this life ; but for my single self,
I had as lief not be, as live to be
In awe of such a thing as I myself.
I was born free as Cæsar ; so were you :
We both have fed as well, and we can both
Endure the winter's cold as well as he :
For once, upon a raw and gusty day, 100
The troubled Tiber chafing with her shores,
Cæsar said to me, " Dar'st thou, Cassius, now
Leap in with me into this angry flood,
And swim to yonder point ? "—Upon the word,
Accoutred as I was, I plunged in,
And bad him follow : so, indeed, he did.
The torrent roar'd, and we did buffet it
With lusty sinews, throwing it aside,
And stemming it with hearts of controversy ;
But ere we could arrive the point propos'd, 110
Cæsar cried, " Help me, Cassius, or I sink."
I, as Æneas, our great ancestor,
Did from the flames of Troy upon his shoulder
The old Anchises bear, so from the waves of Tiber
Did I the tired Cæsar. And this man
Is now become a god ; and Cassius is
A wretched creature, and must bend his body,
If Cæsar carelessly but nod on him.
He had a fever when he was in Spain,
And when the fit was on him, I did mark 120

How he did shake : 't is true, this god did shake :
His coward lips did from their colour fly ;
And that same eye, whose bend doth awe the world,
Did lose his lustre. I did hear him groan ;
Ay, and that tongue of his, that bad the Romans
Mark him, and write his speeches in their books,
Alas ! it cried, " Give me some drink, Titinius,"
As a sick girl. Ye gods, it doth amaze me,
A man of such a feeble temper should
So get the start of the majestic world,   130
And bear the palm alone.   [*Shout. Flourish.*
  Bru.   Another general shout !
I do believe that these applauses are
For some new honours that are heap'd on Cæsar.
  Cas. Why, man, he doth bestride the narrow world,
Like a colossus ; and we petty men
Walk under his huge legs, and peep about
To find ourselves dishonourable graves.
Men at some time are masters of their fates :
The fault, dear Brutus, is not in our stars,
But in ourselves, that we are underlings.   140
Brutus, and Cæsar : what should be in that Cæsar ?
Why should that name be sounded more than yours ?
Write them together, yours is as fair a name ;
Sound them, it doth become the mouth as well ;
Weigh them, it is as heavy ; conjure with 'em,
Brutus will start a spirit as soon as Cæsar.
Now, in the names of all the gods at once,
Upon what meat doth this our Cæsar feed,
That he is grown so great ? Age, thou art sham'd !
Rome, thou hast lost the breed of noble bloods !   150
When went there by an age, since the great flood,
But it was fam'd with more than with one man ?
When could they say, till now, that talk'd of Rome,
That her wide walks encompass'd but one man ?
Now is it Rome indeed, and room enough,
When there is in it but one only man.
O ! you and I have heard our fathers say,
There was a Brutus once, that would have brook'd
The eternal devil to keep his state in Rome,
As easily as a king.   160
  Bru. That you do love me, I am nothing jealous ;
What you would work me to, I have some aim ;
How I have thought of this, and of these times,
I shall recount hereafter : for this present,
I would not, so with love I might entreat you,
Be any further mov'd. What you have said,
I will consider ; what you have to say,
I will with patience hear, and find a time
Both meet to hear and answer such high things.
Till then, my noble friend, chew upon this :   170
Brutus had rather be a villager,
Than to repute himself a son of Rome
Under these hard conditions, as this time
Is like to lay upon us.
  Cas. I am glad, that my weak words
Have struck but thus much show of fire from Brutus.
  Bru. The games are done, and Cæsar is returning.
  Cas. As they pass by, pluck Casca by the sleeve,
And he will, after his sour fashion, tell you
What hath proceeded worthy note to-day.   180

        Re-enter CÆSAR *and his Train.*

  Bru. I will do so.—But, look you, Cassius,
The angry spot doth glow on Cæsar's brow,
And all the rest look like a chidden train,
Calphurnia's cheek is pale ; and Cicero
Looks with such ferret and such fiery eyes,
As we have seen him in the Capitol,
Being cross'd in conference by some senators.
  Cas. Casca will tell us what the matter is.
  Cæs. Antonius !
  Ant. Cæsar.   190
  Cæs. Let me have men about me that are fat ;
Sleek-headed men, and such as sleep o' nights.
Yond Cassius has a lean and hungry look ;
He thinks too much : such men are dangerous.
  Ant. Fear him not, Cæsar, he 's not dangerous :
He is a noble Roman, and well given.
  Cæs. 'Would he were fatter ! But I fear him not :
Yet if my name were liable to fear,
I do not know the man I should avoid

So soon as that spare Cassius. He reads much ;   20C
He is a great observer, and he looks
Quite through the deeds of men ; he loves no plays,
As thou dost, Antony ; he hears no music ;
Seldom he smiles, and smiles in such a sort,
As if he mock'd himself, and scorn'd his spirit
That could be mov'd to smile at anything.
Such men as he be never at heart's ease,
Whiles they behold a greater than themselves ;
And therefore are they very dangerous.
I rather tell thee what is to be fear'd,   210
Than what I fear, for always I am Cæsar.
Come on my right hand, for this ear is deaf,
And tell me truly what thou think'st of him.
          [*Exeunt* CÆSAR *and his Train.* CASCA
                                stays behind.
  Casca. You pull'd me by the cloak : would you speak
with me ?
  Bru. Ay, Casca ; tell us what hath chanc'd to-day,
That Cæsar looks so sad.
  Casca. Why, you were with him, were you not ?
  Bru. I should not then ask Casca what hath chanc'd.
  Casca. Why, there was a crown offered him ; and,
being offered him, he put it by with the back of his
hand, thus ; and then the people fell a-shouting.   221
  Bru. What was the second noise for ?
  Casca. Why, for that too.
  Cas. They shouted thrice : what was the last cry
for ?
  Casca. Why, for that too.
  Bru. Was the crown offer'd him thrice ?
  Casca. Ay, marry, was 't, and he put it by thrice,
every time gentler than other ; and at every putting-
by, mine honest neighbours shouted.
  Cas. Who offered him the crown ?   230
  Casca. Why, Antony.
  Bru. Tell us the manner of it, gentle Casca.
  Casca. I can as well be hanged as tell the manner
of it : it was mere foolery ; I did not mark it. I saw
Mark Antony offer him a crown :—yet 't was not a
crown neither, 't was one of these coronets ;—and, as
I told you, he put it by once : but, for all that, to my
thinking, he would fain have had it. Then he offered
it to him again ; then he put it by again : but, to my
thinking, he was very loath to lay his fingers off it.
And then he offered it the third time ; he put it
the third time by : and still as he refused it, the rabblement hooted, and clapped their chopped hands, and
threw up their sweaty night-caps, and uttered such a
deal of stinking breath, because Cæsar refused the
crown, that it had almost choked Cæsar ; for he
swooned, and fell down at it. And for mine own part,
I durst not laugh, for fear of opening my lips, and
receiving the bad air.   24)
  Cas. But, soft, I pray you : what, did Cæsar swoond ?
  Casca. He fell down in the market-place, and
foamed at mouth, and was speechless.
  Bru. 'T is very like : he hath the falling-sickness.
  Cas. No, Cæsar hath it not ; but you, and I,
And honest Casca, we have the falling-sickness.
  Casca. I know not what you mean by that ; but, I
am sure, Cæsar fell down. If the tag-rag people did
not clap him, and hiss him, according as he pleased
and displeased them, as they use to do the players in
the theatre, I am no true man.   260
  Bru. What said he, when he came unto himself ?
  Casca. Marry, before he fell down, when he perceived the common herd was glad he refused the
crown, he plucked me ope his doubtlet, and offered
them his throat to cut.—An I had been a man of any
occupation, if I would not have taken him at a word,
I would I might go to hell among the rogues.—And so
he fell. When he came to himself again, he said, If
he had done or said anything amiss, he desired their
worships to think it was his infirmity. Three or four
wenches, where I stood, cried, " Alas, good soul !"—
and forgave him with all their hearts ; but there 's no
heed to be taken of them : if Cæsar had stabbed their
mothers, they would have done no less.
  Bru. And after that, he came, thus sad, away ?
  Casca. Ay.
  Cas. Did Cicero say anything ?

Casca. Ay, he spoke Greek.
Cas. To what effect? 279
Casca. Nay, an I tell you that, I 'll ne'er look you i'
the face again: but those that understood him smiled
at one another, and shook their heads; but, for mine
own part, it was Greek to me. I could tell you more
news too: Marullus and Flavius, for pulling scarfs
off Cæsar's images, are put to silence. Fare you
well. There was more foolery yet, if I could remember it.
Cas. Will you sup with me to-night, Casca?

For who so firm that cannot be seduc'd?
Cæsar doth bear me hard; but he loves Brutus:
If I were Brutus now, and he were Cassius,
He should not humour me. I will this night,
In several hands, in at his windows throw,
As if they came from several citizens,
Writings, all tending to the great opinion
That Rome holds of his name; wherein obscurely
Cæsar's ambition shall be glanced at: 320
And, after this, let Cæsar seat him sure;
For we will shake him, or worse days endure. [Exit.

CÆSAR REFUSING THE CROWN.

Casca. No, I am promised forth.
Cas. Will you dine with me to-morrow? 290
Casca. Ay, if I be alive, and your mind hold, and
your dinner worth the eating.
Cas. Good; I will expect you.
Casca. Do so. Farewell, both. [Exit.
Bru. What a blunt fellow is this grown to be!
He was quick metal when he went to school.
Cas. So is he now, in execution
Of any bold or noble enterprise,
However he puts on this tardy form.
This rudeness is a sauce to his good wit, 300
Which gives men stomach to digest his words
With better appetite.
Bru. And so it is. For this time I will leave you:
To-morrow, if you please to speak with me,
I will come home to you; or, if you will,
Come home to me, and I will wait for you.
Cas. I will do so:—till then, think of the world.—
[Exit BRUTUS.
Well, Brutus, thou art noble; yet, I see,
Thy honourable metal may be wrought
From that it is dispos'd: therefore, 't is meet 310
That noble minds keep ever with their likes;

SCENE III.—The Same. A Street.

Thunder and lightning. Enter, from opposite sides,
CASCA, with his sword drawn, and CICERO.

Cic. Good even, Casca. Brought you Cæsar home?
Why are you breathless, and why stare you so?
Casca. Are not you mov'd, when all the sway of
earth
Shakes like a thing unfirm? O Cicero!
I have seen tempests, when the scolding winds
Have riv'd the knotty oaks; and I have seen
The ambitious ocean swell, and rage, and foam,
To be exalted with the threat'ning clouds:
But never till to-night, never till now,
Did I go through a tempest dropping fire. 10
Either there is a civil strife in heaven,
Or else the world, too saucy with the gods,
Incenses them to send destruction.
Cic. Why, saw you anything more wonderful?
Casca. A common slave (you know him well by sight)
Held up his left hand, which did flame, and burn
Like twenty torches join'd; and yet his hand,
Not sensible of fire, remain'd unscorch'd.
Besides, (I have not since put up my sword,)

Against the Capitol I met a lion,   20
Who glar'd upon me, and went surly by,
Without annoying me: and there were drawn
Upon a heap a hundred ghastly women,
Transformed with their fear, who swore they saw

Cic. "Why are you breathless, and why stare you so?"

Men, all in fire, walk up and down the streets.
And yesterday the bird of night did sit,
Even at noon-day, upon the market-place,
Hooting, and shrieking. When these prodigies
Do so conjointly meet, let not men say,
"These are their reasons,—they are natural;"   30
For, I believe, they are portentous things
Unto the climate that they point upon.
    Cic. Indeed, it is a strange-disposed time:
But men may construe things after their fashion,
Clean from the purpose of the things themselves.
Comes Cæsar to the Capitol to-morrow?
    Casca. He doth; for he did bid Antonius
Send word to you, he would be there to-morrow.
    Cic. Good night then, Casca: this disturbed sky   39
Is not to walk in.
    Casca.   Farewell, Cicero.   [*Exit* CICERO.

            Enter CASSIUS.

    Cas. Who's there?
    Casca.   A Roman.
    Cas.   Casca, by your voice.
    Casca. Your ear is good. Cassius, what night is this!
    Cas. A very pleasing night to honest men.
    Casca. Who ever knew the heavens menace so?
    Cas. Those that have known the earth so full of
            faults.
For my part, I have walk'd about the streets,
Submitting me unto the perilous night;
And, thus unbraced, Casca, as you see,
Have bar'd my bosom to the thunder-stone:
And, when the cross blue lightning seem'd to open 50
The breast of heaven, I did present myself
Even in the aim and very flash of it.
    Casca. But wherefore did you so much tempt the
            heavens?
It is the part of men to fear and tremble,
When the most mighty gods, by tokens, send
Such dreadful heralds to astonish us.
    Cas. You are dull, Casca; and those sparks of life,
That should be in a Roman, you do want,
Or else you use not. You look pale, and gaze,
And put on fear, and cast yourself in wonder,   60
To see the strange impatience of the heavens;
But if you would consider the true cause,
Why all these fires, why all these gliding ghosts,
Why birds, and beasts, from quality and kind;

Why old men, fools, and children, calculate;
Why all these things change from their ordinance,
Their natures, and performed faculties,
To monstrous quality,—why, you shall find,
That heaven hath infus'd them with these spirits,
To make them instruments of fear and warning   70
Unto some monstrous state.
Now could I, Casca, name to thee a man
Most like this dreadful night;
That thunders, lightens, opens graves, and roars
As doth the lion in the Capitol:—
A man no mightier than thyself, or me,
In personal action; yet prodigious grown,
And fearful, as these strange eruptions are.
    Casca. 'T is Cæsar that you mean; is it not, Cassius?
    Cas. Let it be who it is: for Romans now   80
Have thews and limbs like to their ancestors;
But, woe the while! our fathers' minds are dead,
And we are govern'd with our mothers' spirits;
Our yoke and sufferance show us womanish.
    Casca. Indeed, they say the senators to-morrow
Mean to establish Cæsar as a king:
And he shall wear his crown by sea and land,
In every place, save here in Italy.
    Cas. I know where I will wear this dagger then;
Cassius from bondage will deliver Cassius: 90
Therein, ye gods, you make the weak most strong;
Therein, ye gods, you tyrants do defeat:
Nor stony tower, nor walls of beaten brass,
Nor airless dungeon, nor strong links of iron,
Can be retentive to the strength of spirit;
But life, being weary of these worldly bars,
Never lacks power to dismiss itself.
If I know this, know all the world besides,
That part of tyranny, that I do bear,
I can shake off at pleasure.   [*Thunder still.*
    Casca.   So can I: 100
So every bondman in his own hand bears
The power to cancel his captivity.
    Cas. And why should Cæsar be a tyrant then?
Poor man! I know, he would not be a wolf,
But that he sees the Romans are but sheep;
He were no lion, were not Romans hinds.
Those that with haste will make a mighty fire,
Begin with weak straws: what trash is Rome,
What rubbish, and what offal, when it serves
For the base matter to illuminate   110
So vile a thing as Cæsar! But, O grief!
Where hast thou led me? I, perhaps, speak this
Before a willing bondman: then I know
My answer must be made; but I am arm'd,
And dangers are to me indifferent.
    Casca. You speak to Casca; and to such a man
That is no fleering tell-tale. Hold, my hand:
Be factious for redress of all these griefs,
And I will set this foot of mine as far
As who goes farthest.
    Cas.   There's a bargain made.   120
Now know you, Casca, I have mov'd already
Some certain of the noblest-minded Romans,
To undergo with me an enterprise
Of honourable-dangerous consequence;
And I do know, by this they stay for me
In Pompey's porch: for now, this fearful night,
There is no stir or walking in the streets;
And the complexion of the element
In favour's like the work we have in hand,
Most bloody, fiery, and most terrible.   130
    Casca. Stand close awhile, for here comes one in
            haste.
    Cas. 'T is Cinna; I do know him by his gait:
He is a friend.

            Enter CINNA.

                Cinna, where haste you so?
    Cin. To find out you. Who's that? Metellus
            Cimber?
    Cas. No, it is Casca; one incorporate
To our attempts. Am I not stay'd for, Cinna?
    Cin. I am glad on 't. What a fearful night is this!
There's two or three of us have seen strange sights.
    Cas. Am I not stay'd for? Tell me.

Cin.   Yes, you are.
O Cassius! if you could   140
But win the noble Brutus to our party—
Cas. Be you content. Good Cinna, take this paper,
And look you lay it in the prætor's chair,
Where Brutus may but find it ; and throw this
In at his window : set this up with wax
Upon old Brutus' statue : all this done,
Repair to Pompey's porch, where you shall find
    us.
Is Decius Brutus, and Trebonius, there ?
Cin. All but Metellus Cimber, and he 's gone
To seek you at your house. Well, I will hie,   150
And so bestow these papers as you bad me.

Cas. That done, repair to Pompey's theatre.
                              [*Exit* CINNA.
Come, Casca, you and I will yet, ere day,
See Brutus at his house : three parts of him
Is ours already ; and the man entire,
Upon the next encounter, yields him ours.
Casca. O ! he sits high in all the people's hearts :
And that which would appear offence in us,
His countenance, like richest alchymy,
Will change to virtue and to worthiness.   160
Cas. Him, and his worth, and our great need of him.
You have right well conceited. Let us go,
For it is after midnight ; and, ere day,
We will awake him, and be sure of him.   [*Exeunt.*

ACT II.

SCENE I.—The Same. BRUTUS's Orchard.

Enter BRUTUS.

Brutus.
HAT, Lucius! ho!—
I cannot, by the progress of the stars,
Give guess how near to day.—Lucius, I
    say !—
I would it were my fault to sleep so
    soundly.—
When, Lucius, when! Awake, I say!
    What, Lucius!

Enter LUCIUS.

Luc. Call'd you, my lord?
Bru. Get me a taper in my study, Lucius :
When it is lighted, come and call me here.
Luc. I will, my lord.   [*Exit.*
Bru. It must be by his death : and, for my part,   10
I know no personal cause to spurn at him,
But for the general. He would be crown'd :—
How that might change his nature, there 's the ques-
    tion.
It is the bright day that brings forth the adder ;
And that craves wary walking. Crown him!—that !
And then, I grant, we put a sting in him,
That at his will he may do danger with.
The abuse of greatness is, when it disjoins
Remorse from power : and, to speak truth of Cæsar,
I have not known when his affections sway'd   20
More than his reason. But 't is a common proof,
That lowliness is young ambition's ladder,
Whereto the climber-upward turns his face ;
But when he once attains the upmost round,
He then unto the ladder turns his back,
Looks in the clouds, scorning the base degrees
By which he did ascend. So Cæsar may :
Then, lest he may, prevent. And, since the quarrel
Will bear no colour for the thing he is,
Fashion it thus ; that what he is, augmented,   30
Would run to these and these extremities ;
And therefore think him as a serpent's egg,
Which, hatch'd, would as his kind grow mischievous ;
And kill him in the shell.

Re-enter LUCIUS.

Luc. The taper burneth in your closet, sir.
Searching the window for a flint, I found
                         [*Giving him a letter.*

This paper, thus seal'd up ; and, I am sure,
It did not lie there when I went to bed.
Bru. Get you to bed again ; it is not day.
Is not to-morrow, boy, the first of March ?   40
Luc. I know not, sir.
Bru. Look in the calendar, and bring me word.
Luc. I will, sir.   [*Exit.*
Bru. The exhalations, whizzing in the air,
Give so much light that I may read by them.
                    [*Opens the letter, and reads.*
" Brutus, thou sleep'st : awake, and see thyself.
Shall Rome, &c. Speak, strike, redress !
Brutus, thou sleep'st : awake !"—
Such instigations have been often dropp'd
Where I have took them up.   50
" Shall Rome, &c." Thus must I piece it out :
Shall Rome stand under one man's awe ? What
    Rome ?
My ancestors did from the streets of Rome
The Tarquin drive, when he was call'd a king.
" Speak, strike, redress !"—Am I entreated
To speak, and strike ? O Rome ! I make thee promise,
If the redress will follow, thou receiv'st
Thy full petition at the hand of Brutus !

Re-enter LUCIUS.

Luc. Sir, March is wasted fifteen days.
                         [*Knocking within.*
Bru. 'T is good. Go to the gate ; somebody knocks.
                         [*Exit* LUCIUS.
Since Cassius first did whet me against Cæsar,   61
I have not slept.
Between the acting of a dreadful thing
And the first motion, all the interim is
Like a phantasma, or a hideous dream :
The genius and the mortal instruments
Are then in council ; and the state of a man,
Like to a little kingdom, suffers then
The nature of an insurrection.

Re-enter LUCIUS.

Luc. Sir, 't is your brother Cassius at the door,   70
Who doth desire to see you.
Bru.   Is he alone ?
Luc. No, sir, there are more with him.
Bru.   Do you know them ?

Luc. No, sir ; their hats are pluck'd about their ears,
And half their faces buried in their cloaks,
That by no means I may discover them
By any mark of favour.
Bru. 　　　　　　　　 Let 'em enter. [*Exit* LUCIUS.
They are the faction. O Conspiracy !
Sham'st thou to show thy dangerous brow by night,

Bru. "Am I entreated to speak, and strike?"

When evils are most free? O! then, by day
Where wilt thou find a cavern dark enough　　80
To mask thy monstrous visage? Seek none, Conspiracy ;
Hide it in smiles and affability :
For if thou path, thy native semblance on,
Not Erebus itself were dim enough
To hide thee from prevention.
Enter CASSIUS, CASCA, DECIUS, CINNA, METELLUS
　　CIMBER, *and* TREBONIUS.
Cas. I think we are too bold upon your rest :
Good morrow, Brutus ; do we trouble you?
Bru. I have been up this hour ; awake all night.
Know I these men that come along with you?
Cas. Yes, every man of them ; and no man here　90
But honours you : and every one doth wish,
You had but that opinion of yourself,
Which every noble Roman bears of you.
This is Trebonius.
Bru. 　　　　　　　　 He is welcome hither.
Cas. This, Decius Brutus.
Bru. 　　　　　　　　 He is welcome too.
Cas. This, Casca ; this, Cinna ; and this, Metellus
　　Cimber.
Bru. They are all welcome.
What watchful cares do interpose themselves
Betwixt your eyes and night?
Cas. I entreat a word? 　　　 [*They whisper.*
Dec. Here lies the east : doth not the day break
　　here? 　　　　　　　　　　　　　　101
Casca. No.
Cin. O! pardon, sir, it doth ; and yon grey lines,
That fret the clouds, are messengers of day.
Casca. You shall confess that you are both deceiv'd,
Here, as I point my sword, the sun arises ;
Which is a great way growing on the south,
Weighing the youthful season of the year.
Some two months hence, up higher toward the north
He first presents his fire ; and the high east　110
Stands, as the Capitol, directly here.
Bru. Give me your hands all over, one by one.
Cas. And let us swear our resolution.
Bru. No, not an oath : if not the face of men,
The sufferance of our souls, the time's abuse,—

If these be motives weak, break off betimes,
And every man hence to his idle bed ;
So let high-sighted tyranny range on,
Till each man drop by lottery. But if these,
As I am sure they do, bear fire enough　　120
To kindle cowards, and to steel with valour
The melting spirits of women, then, countrymen,
What need we any spur but our own cause,
To prick us to redress? what other bond,
Than secret Romans, that have spoke the word,
And will not palter? and what other oath,
Than honesty to honesty engag'd,
That this shall be, or we will fall for it?
Swear priests, and cowards, and men cautelous,
Old feeble carrions, and such suffering souls　130
That welcome wrongs ; unto bad causes swear
Such creatures as men doubt ; but do not stain
The even virtue of our enterprise,
Nor the insuppressive mettle of our spirits,
To think that, or our cause, or our performance,
Did need an oath ; when every drop of blood,
That every Roman bears, and nobly bears,
Is guilty of a several bastardy,
If he do break the smallest particle
Of any promise that hath pass'd from him.　140
Cas. But what of Cicero? Shall we sound him?
I think he will stand very strong with us.
Casca. Let us not leave him out.
Cin. 　　　　　　　　 No, by no means.
Met. O! let us have him : for his silver hairs
Will purchase us a good opinion,
And buy men's voices to commend our deeds :
It shall be said, his judgment rul'd our hands ;
Our youths, and wildness, shall no whit appear,
But all be buried in his gravity.
Bru. O! name him not ; let us not break with him ;
For he will never follow anything　　　　151
That other men begin.
Cas. 　　　　　　　　 Then leave him out.
Casca. Indeed, he is not fit.
Dec. Shall no man else be touch'd, but only Cæsar?
Cas. Decius, well urg'd.—I think it is not meet,
Mark Antony, so well belov'd of Cæsar,
Should outlive Cæsar : we shall find of him
A shrewd contriver ; and, you know, his means,
If he improve them, may well stretch so far
As to annoy us all ; which to prevent,　　160
Let Antony and Cæsar fall together.
Bru. Our course will seem too bloody, Caius Cassius,
To cut the head off, and then hack the limbs ;
Like wrath in death, and envy afterwards :
For Antony is but a limb of Cæsar.
Let us be sacrificers, but not butchers, Caius.
We all stand up against the spirit of Cæsar ;
And in the spirit of men there is no blood :
O, that we then could come by Cæsar's spirit,
And not dismember Cæsar! But, alas!　　170
Cæsar must bleed for it. And, gentle friends,
Let 's kill him boldly, but not wrathfully ;
Let 's carve him as a dish fit for the gods,
Not hew him as a carcass fit for hounds :
And let our hearts, as subtle masters do,
Stir up their servants to an act of rage,
And after seem to chide 'em. This shall make
Our purpose necessary, and not envious ;
Which so appearing to the common eyes,
We shall be call'd purgers, not murderers.　180
And for Mark Antony, think not of him ;
For he can do no more than Cæsar's arm,
When Cæsar's head is off.
Cas. 　　　　　　　　 Yet I fear him :
For in the ingrafted love he bears to Cæsar,—
Bru. Alas! good Cassius, do not think of him.
If he love Cæsar, all that he can do
Is to himself,—take thought, and die for Cæsar :
And that were much he should ; for he is given
To sports, to wildness, and much company.
Treb. There is no fear in him ; let him not die ;　190
For he will live, and laugh at this hereafter.
　　　　　　　　　　　　　　 [*Clock strikes.*
Bru. Peace ! count the clock.
Cas. 　　　　　　　 The clock hath stricken three.

Treb. 'T is time to part.
Cas.   But it is doubtful yet,
Whether Cæsar will come forth to-day, or no : ·
For he is superstitious grown of late ;
Quite from the main opinion he held once
Of fantasy, of dreams, and ceremonies.

He says, he does, being then most flattered.
Let me work ;
For I can give his humour the true bent,   210
And I will bring him to the Capitol.
    Cas. Nay, we will all of us be there to fetch him.
    Bru. By the eighth hour : is that the uttermost?

BRUTUS AND THE CONSPIRATORS.

It may be, these apparent prodigies,
The unaccustom'd terror of this night,
And the persuasion of his augurers,   200
May hold him from the Capitol to-day.
    Dec. Never fear that : if he be so resolv'd,
I can o'ersway him ; for he loves to hear,
That unicorns may be betray'd with trees,
And bears with glasses, elephants with holes,
Lions with toils, and men with flatterers ;
But, when I tell him, he hates flatterers,

    Cin. Be that the uttermost, and fail not then.
    Met. Caius Ligarius doth bear Cæsar hard,
Who rated him for speaking well of Pompey :
I wonder, none of you have thought of him.
    Bru. Now, good Metellus, go along by him :
He loves me well, and I have given him reasons ;
Send him but hither, and I 'll fashion him.   220
    Cas. The morning comes upon us : we 'll leave you,
                Brutus.—
And, friends, disperse yourselves ; but all remember

What you have said, and show yourselves true
    Romans.
  Bru. Good gentlemen, look fresh and merrily ;
Let not our looks put on our purposes ;
But bear it as our Roman actors do,
With untir'd spirits and formal constancy :
And so, good morrow to you every one.
                 [Exeunt all but BRUTUS.
Boy ! Lucius !—Fast asleep ? It is no matter ;
Enjoy the honey-heavy dew of slumber :   230
Thou hast no figures, nor no fantasies,
Which busy care draws in the brains of men ;
Therefore, thou sleep'st so sound.

             Enter PORTIA.

  Por.   Brutus, my lord !
  Bru. Portia, what mean you ? Wherefore rise you
    now ?
It is not for your health thus to commit
Your weak condition to the raw-cold morning.

      Bru. " Portia, what mean you ? Wherefore rise you now ?"

  Por. Nor for yours neither. You have ungently,
    Brutus,
Stole from my bed : and yesternight, at supper,
You suddenly arose, and walk'd about,
Musing and sighing, with your arms across ;   240
And when I ask'd you what the matter was,
You star'd upon me with ungentle looks.
I urg'd you further ; then you scratch'd your head,
And too impatiently stamp'd with your foot :
Yet I insisted, yet you answer'd not :
But, with an angry wafture of your hand,
Gave sign for me to leave you. So I did ;
Fearing to strengthen that impatience,
Which seem'd too much enkindled ; and, withal,
Hoping it was but an effect of humour,   250
Which sometime hath his hour with every man.
It will not let you eat, nor talk, nor sleep ;
And, could it work so much upon your shape,
As it hath much prevail'd on your condition,
I should not know you, Brutus. Dear my lord,
Make me acquainted with your cause of grief.
  Bru. I am not well in health, and that is all.
  Por. Brutus is wise, and, were he not in health,
He would embrace the means to come by it.
  Bru. Why, so I do.—Good Portia, go to bed.   260
  Por. Is Brutus sick, and is it physical
To walk unbraced, and suck up the humours
Of the dank morning ? What ! is Brutus sick,
And will he steal out of his wholesome bed,
To dare the vile contagion of the night,
And tempt the rheumy and unpurged air
To add unto his sickness ? No, my Brutus ;
You have some sick offence within your mind,
Which, by the right and virtue of my place,
I ought to know of : and upon my knees   270

I charm you, by my once commended beauty,
By all your vows of love, and that great vow
Which did incorporate and make us one,
That you unfold to me, your self, your half,
Why you are heavy, and what men to-night
Have had resort to you ; for here have been
Some six or seven, who did hide their faces
Even from darkness.
  Bru.   Kneel not, gentle Portia.
  Por. I should not need, if you were gentle Brutus.
Within the bond of marriage, tell me, Brutus,   280
Is it excepted, I should know no secrets
That appertain to you ? Am I yourself
But, as it were, in sort, or limitation ;
To keep with you at meals, comfort your bed,
And talk to you sometimes ? Dwell I but in the
    suburbs
Of your good pleasure ? If it be no more,
Portia is Brutus' harlot, not his wife.
  Bru. You are my true and honourable wife ;
As dear to me as are the ruddy drops
That visit my sad heart.   290
  Por. If this were true, then should I
    know this secret.
I grant, I am a woman ; but, withal,
A woman that Lord Brutus took to wife :
I grant, I am a woman ; but, withal,
A woman well-reputed,—Cato's daughter.
Think you I am no stronger than my sex,
Being so father'd, and so husbanded ?
Tell me your counsels, I will not disclose
    them.
I have made strong proof of my constancy,
Giving myself a voluntary wound   300
Here, in the thigh : can I bear that with
    patience,
And not my husband's secrets ?
  Bru.   O ye gods,
Render me worthy of this noble wife !
               [Knocking within.
Hark, hark ! one knocks. Portia, go in
    awhile ;
And by-and-by thy bosom shall partake
The secrets of my heart.
All my engagements I will construe to
    thee,
All the charactery of my sad brows.
Leave me with haste.   *[Exit* PORTIA.

      Enter LUCIUS *and* LIGARIUS.
           Lucius, who 's that knocks ?
  Luc. Here is a sick man, that would speak with
    you.   310
  Bru. Caius Ligarius, that Metellus spake of.—
Boy, stand aside.—Caius Ligarius ! how ?
  Lig. Vouchsafe good morrow from a feeble tongue.
  Bru. O, what a time have you chose out, brave
    Caius,
To wear a kerchief ! 'Would you were not sick !
  Lig. I am not sick, if Brutus have in hand
Any exploit worthy the name of honour.
  Bru. Such an exploit have I in hand, Ligarius,
Had you a healthful ear to hear of it.
  Lig. By all the gods that Romans bow before,   320
I here discard my sickness. Soul of Rome !
Brave son, deriv'd from honourable loins !
Thou, like an exorcist, hast conjur'd up
My mortified spirit. Now bid me run,
And I will strive with things impossible ;
Yea, get the better of them. What 's to do ?
  Bru. A piece of work that will make sick men
    whole.
  Lig. But are not some whole that we must make
    sick ?
  Bru. That must we also. What it is, my Caius,
I shall unfold to thee, as we are going   330
To whom it must be done.
  Lig.   Set on your foot,
And with a heart new-fir'd I follow you,
To do I know not what ; but it sufficeth,
That Brutus leads me on.
  Bru.   Follow me then. *[Exeunt.*

SCENE II.—The Same.　A Room in CÆSAR'S Palace.

Thunder and lightning.　Enter CÆSAR, *in his*
night-gown.

Cæs. Nor heaven, nor earth, have been at peace
　　to-night:
Thrice hath Calphurnia in her sleep cried out,
"Help, ho! They murder Cæsar!"—Who's within?

Enter a Servant.

Serv. My lord.
Cæs. Go bid the priests do present sacrifice,
And bring me their opinions of success.
Serv. I will, my lord.　　　　　　　　　*[Exit.*

Enter CALPHURNIA.

Cal. What mean you, Cæsar?　Think you to walk
　　forth?
You shall not stir out of your house to-day.
Cæs. Cæsar shall forth: the things that threaten'd
　　me　　　　　　　　　　　　　　　10
Ne'er look'd but on my back; when they shall see
The face of Cæsar, they are vanished.
Cal. Cæsar, I never stood on ceremonies,
Yet now they fright me.　There is one within,
Besides the things that we have heard and seen,
Recounts most horrid sights seen by the watch.
A lioness hath whelped in the streets;
And graves have yawn'd, and yielded up their
　　dead;
Fierce fiery warriors fight upon the clouds,
In ranks and squadrons, and right form of war,　20
Which drizzled blood upon the Capitol;
The noise of battle hurtled in the air,
Horses do neigh, and dying men did groan,
And ghosts did shriek, and squeal about the streets.
O Cæsar! these things are beyond all use,
And I do fear them.
Cæs.　　　　　　　What can be avoided,
Whose end is purpos'd by the mighty gods?
Yet Cæsar shall go forth; for these predictions
Are to the world in general, as to Cæsar.
Cal. When beggars die, there are no comets seen; 30
The heavens themselves blaze forth the death of
　　princes.
Cæs. Cowards die many times before their deaths;
The valiant never taste of death but once.
Of all the wonders that I yet have heard,
It seems to me most strange that men should fear;
Seeing that death, a necessary end,
Will come, when it will come.

Re-enter Servant.

　　　　　　　What say the augurers?
Serv. They would not have you to stir forth to-day.
Plucking the entrails of an offering forth,
They could not find a heart within the beast.　40
Cæs. The gods do this in shame of cowardice:
Cæsar should be a beast without a heart,
If he should stay at home to-day for fear.
No, Cæsar shall not: danger knows full well,
That Cæsar is more dangerous than he.
We are two lions litter'd in one day,
And I the elder and more terrible;—
And Cæsar shall go forth.
Cal.　　　　　　　　Alas! my lord,
Your wisdom is consum'd in confidence.
Do not go forth to-day: call it my fear,　50
That keeps you in the house, and not your own.
We'll send Mark Antony to the senate-house,
And he shall say, you are not well to-day:
Let me, upon my knee, prevail in this.
Cæs. Mark Antony shall say, I am not well;
And, for thy humour, I will stay at home.

Enter DECIUS.

Here's Decius Brutus, he shall tell them so.
Dec. Cæsar, all hail!　Good morrow, worthy Cæsar:
I come to fetch you to the senate-house.
Cæs. And you are come in very happy time,　60
To bear my greeting to the senators,

And tell them that I will not come to-day:
Cannot, is false; and that I dare not, falser;
I will not come to-day,—tell them so, Decius.
Cal. Say, he is sick.
Cæs.　　　　　　Shall Cæsar send a lie?
Have I in conquest stretch'd mine arm so far,
To be afeard to tell grey-beards the truth?
Decius, go tell them, Cæsar will not come.
Dec. Most mighty Cæsar, let me know some cause,
Lest I be laugh'd at, when I tell them so.　　70
Cæs. The cause is in my will; I will not come:
That is enough to satisfy the senate;
But, for your private satisfaction,
Because I love you, I will let you know.
Calphurnia here, my wife, stays me at home:
She dream'd to-night she saw my statua,
Which, like a fountain with a hundred spouts,
Did run pure blood; and many lusty Romans
Came smiling, and did bathe their hands in it.
And these does she apply for warnings and portents, 80
And evils imminent; and on her knee
Hath begg'd, that I will stay at home to-day.
Dec. This dream is all amiss interpreted:
It was a vision, fair and fortunate.
Your statue spouting blood in many pipes,
In which so many smiling Romans bath'd,
Signifies that from you great Rome shall suck
Reviving blood; and that great men shall press
For tinctures, stains, relics, and cognisance.
This by Calphurnia's dream is signified.　　90
Cæs. And this way have you well expounded it.
Dec. I have, when you have heard what I can
　　say:
And know it now.　The senate have concluded
To give, this day, a crown to mighty Cæsar:
If you shall send them word, you will not come,
Their minds may change.　Besides, it were a mock
Apt to be render'd, for some one to say,
"Break up the senate till another time,
When Cæsar's wife shall meet with better dreams."
If Cæsar hide himself, shall they not whisper,　100
"Lo! Cæsar is afraid?"
Pardon me, Cæsar; for my dear, dear love
To your proceeding bids me tell you this,
And reason to my love is liable.
Cæs. How foolish do your fears seem now, Cal-
　　phurnia!
I am ashamed I did yield to them.—
Give me my robe, for I will go:—

Enter PUBLIUS, BRUTUS, LIGARIUS, METELLUS,
　　CASCA, TREBONIUS, *and* CINNA.

And look where Publius is come to fetch me.
Pub. Good morrow, Cæsar.
Cæs.　　　　　　　Welcome, Publius.—
What, Brutus, are you stirr'd so early too?—　110
Good morrow, Casca.—Caius Ligarius,
Cæsar was ne'er so much your enemy,
As that same ague which hath made you lean.—
What is't o'clock?
Bru.　　　　　Cæsar, 't is strucken eight.
Cæs. I thank you for your pains and courtesy.

Enter ANTONY.

See! Antony, that revels long o' nights,
Is notwithstanding up.—Good morrow, Antony.
Ant. So to most noble Cæsar.
Cæs.　　　　　　Bid them prepare within:
I am to blame to be thus waited for.—
Now, Cinna:—now, Metellus:—what, Trebonius! 120
I have an hour's talk in store for you.
Remember that you call on me to-day:
Be near me, that I may remember you.
Treb. Cæsar, I will:—[*aside*] and so near will
　　I be,
That your best friends shall wish I had been further.
Cæs. Good friends, go in, and taste some wine with
　　me;
And we, like friends, will straightway go together.
Bru. [*Aside.*] That every like is not the same, O
　　Cæsar,
The heart of Brutus yearns to think upon! [*Exeunt.*

SCENE III.—The Same. A Street near the Capitol.

Enter ARTEMIDORUS, *reading a paper.*

Art. "Cæsar, beware of Brutus; take heed of Cassius; come not near Casca; have an eye to Cinna; trust not Trebonius; mark well Metellus Cimber; Decius Brutus loves thee not; thou hast wronged Caius Ligarius. There is but one mind in all these men, and it is bent against Cæsar. If thou be'st not immortal, look about you; security gives way to conspiracy. The mighty gods defend thee! Thy lover,

ARTEMIDORUS." 10

Here will I stand till Cæsar pass along,
And as a suitor will I give him this.
My heart laments that virtue cannot live
Out of the teeth of emulation.
If thou read this, O Cæsar! thou may'st live:
If not, the Fates with traitors do contrive. [*Exit.*

SCENE IV.—The Same. Another Part of the same Street, before the House of BRUTUS.

Enter PORTIA *and* LUCIUS.

Por. I pr'ythee, boy, run to the senate-house:
Stay not to answer me, but get thee gone.
Why dost thou stay?
Luc.   To know my errand, madam.
Por. I would have had thee there, and here again,
Ere I can tell thee what thou shouldst do there.—
O constancy, be strong upon my side!
Set a hugh mountain 'tween my heart and tongue!
I have a man's mind, but a woman's might.
How hard it is for women to keep counsel!—
Art thou here yet?
Luc.   Madam, what should I do? 10
Run to the Capitol, and nothing else?
And so return to you, and nothing else?
Por. Yes, bring me word, boy, if thy lord look well,

For he went sickly forth: and take good note,
What Cæsar doth, what suitors press to him.
Hark, boy! what noise is that?
Luc. I hear none, madam.
Por.   Pr'ythee, listen well;
I heard a bustling rumour, like a fray,
And the wind brings it from the Capitol.
Luc. Sooth, madam, I hear nothing. 20

Enter the Soothsayer.

Por. Come hither, fellow: which way hast thou been?
Sooth. At mine own house, good lady.
Por. What is 't o'clock?
Sooth.   About the ninth hour, lady.
Por. Is Cæsar yet gone to the Capitol?
Sooth. Madam, not yet: I go to take my stand,
To see him pass on to the Capitol.
Por. Thou hast some suit to Cæsar, hast thou not?
Sooth. That I have, lady: if it will please Cæsar
To be so good to Cæsar as to hear me,
I shall beseech him to befriend himself. 30
Por. Why, know'st thou any harm's intended towards him?
Sooth. None that I know will be, much that I fear may chance.
Good morrow to you. Here the street is narrow:
The throng that follows Cæsar at the heels,
Of senators, or prætors, common suitors,
Will crowd a feeble man almost to death:
I 'll get me to a place more void, and there
Speak to great Cæsar as he comes along. [*Exit.*
Por. I must go in.—Ah me! how weak a thing
The heart of woman is! O Brutus! 40
The heavens speed thee in thine enterprise!
Sure, the boy heard me:—Brutus hath a suit,
That Cæsar will not grant.—O! I grow faint.—
Run, Lucius, and commend me to my lord;
Say, I am merry: come to me again,
And bring me word what he doth say to thee.
[*Exeunt severally.*

ACT III.

SCENE I.—The Same. The Capitol; the Senate sitting.

A crowd of People in the street leading to the Capitol; among them ARTEMIDORUS *and the Soothsayer. Flourish. Enter* CÆSAR, BRUTUS, CASSIUS, CASCA, DECIUS, METELLUS, TREBONIUS, CINNA, ANTONY, LEPIDUS, POPILIUS, PUBLIUS, *and others.*

Cæsar.
HE ides of March are come.
Sooth. Ay, Cæsar; but not gone.
Art. Hail, Cæsar! Read this schedule.
Dec. Trebonius doth desire you to o'er-read,
At your best leisure, this his humble suit.
Art. O Cæsar! read mine first; for mine 's a suit
That touches Cæsar nearer. Read it, great Cæsar.
Cæs. What touches us ourself shall be last serv'd.
Art. Delay not, Cæsar; read it instantly. 9
Cæs. What! is the fellow mad?
Pub.   Sirrah, give place.
Cas. What! urge you your petitions in the street?
Come to the Capitol.

CÆSAR *enters the Capitol, the rest following.*
All the Senators rise.

Pop. I wish, your enterprise to-day may thrive.
Cas. What enterprise, Popilius?
Pop.   Fare you well.
[*Advances to* CÆSAR.
Bru. What said Popilius Lena?
Cas. He wish'd, to-day our enterprise might thrive.
I fear, our purpose is discovered.
Bru. Look, how he makes to Cæsar: mark him.
Cas. Casca, be sudden, for we fear prevention.—
Brutus, what shall be done? If this be known, 20
Cassius or Cæsar never shall turn back,
For I will slay myself.
Bru.   Cassius, be constant:
Popilius Lena speaks not of our purposes;
For, look, he smiles, and Cæsar doth not change.

Cas. Trebonius knows his time; for, look you,
    Brutus,
He draws Mark Antony out of the way.
    [*Exeunt* ANTONY *and* TREBONIUS. CÆSAR
    and the Senators take their seats.
Dec. Where is Metellus Cimber? Let him go.
And presently prefer his suit to Cæsar.
Bru. He is address'd : press near, and second him.
Cin. Casca, you are the first that rears your hand. 30
Cæs. Are we all ready? What is now amiss,
That Cæsar and his senate must redress?

Art. " Hail, Cæsar! Read this schedule."

Met. Most high, most mighty, and most puissant
    Cæsar,
Metellus Cimber throws before thy seat
An humble heart :—   [*Kneeling.*
Cæs.   I must prevent thee, Cimber.
These couchings, and these lowly courtesies,
Might fire the blood of ordinary men,
And turn pre-ordinance, and first decree,
Into the law of children. Be not fond,
To think that Cæsar bears such rebel blood,   40
That will be thaw'd from the true quality
With that which melteth fools ; I mean sweet words,
Low-crooked curtsies, and base spaniel fawning.
Thy brother by decree is banished :
If thou dost bend, and pray, and fawn, for him,
I spurn thee, like a cur, out of my way.
Know, Cæsar doth not wrong ; nor without cause
Will he be satisfied.
Met. Is there no voice more worthy than my own,
To sound more sweetly in great Cæsar's ear,   50
For the repealing of my banish'd brother?
Bru. I kiss thy hand, but not in flattery, Cæsar ;
Desiring thee, that Publius Cimber may
Have an immediate freedom of repeal.
Cæs. What, Brutus!
Cas.   Pardon, Cæsar ; Cæsar, pardon :
As low as to thy foot doth·Cassius fall,
To beg enfranchisement for Publius Cimber.
Cæs. I could be well mov'd, if I were as you ;
If I could pray to move, prayers would move me ;
But I am constant as the northern star,   60
Of whose true-fix'd and resting quality
There is no fellow in the firmament.
The skies are painted with unnumber'd sparks,
They are all fire, and every one doth shine ;
But there 's but one in all doth hold his place :
So, in the world ;—'t is furnish'd well with men,
And men are flesh and blood, and apprehensive ;
Yet in the number, I do know but one
That unassailable holds on his rank,
Unshak'd of motion : and, that I am he,   70
Let me a little show it, even in this,

That I was constant Cimber should be banish'd,
And constant do remain to keep him so.
Cin. O Cæsar,—
Cæs.   Hence! Wilt thou lift up Olympus?
Dec. Great Cæsar,—
Cæs.   Doth not Brutus bootless kneel?
Casca. Speak, hands, for me.
    [CASCA *stabs* CÆSAR *in the neck.* CÆSAR *catches
    hold of his arm. He is then stabbed by
    several other Conspirators, and last by*
    MARCUS BRUTUS.
Cæs. Et tu,Brute?—Then fall,Cæsar!
    [*Dies. The Senators and People
    retire in confusion.*
Cin. Liberty! Freedom! Tyranny is
    dead!—
Run hence, proclaim, cry it about the
    streets.
Cas. Some to the common pulpits,
    and cry out,   80
"Liberty, freedom, and enfranchise-
    ment!"
Bru. People, and senators! be not
    affrighted ;
Fly not ; stand still :—ambition's debt
    is paid.
Casca. Go to the pulpit, Brutus.
Dec.   And Cassius too.
Bru. Where 's Publius?
Cin. Here, quite confounded with
    this mutiny.
Met. Stand fast together, lest some
    friend of Cæsar's
Should chance—
Bru. Talk not of standing.—Publius,
    good cheer :
There is no harm intended to your
    person,   90
Nor to no Roman else, so tell them,
    Publius.
Cas. And leave us, Publius ; lest that the people,
Rushing on us, should do your age some mischief.
Bru. Do so :—and let no man abide this deed,
But we, the doers.

        Re-enter TREBONIUS.

Cas. Where's Antony?
Tre.   Fled to his house amaz'd.
Men, wives, and children, stare, cry out, and run,
As it were doomsday.
Bru.   Fates, we will know your pleasures.—
That we shall die, we know ; 't is but the time,
And drawing days out, that men stand upon.   100
Cas. Why, he that cuts off twenty years of life,
Cuts off so many years of fearing death.
Bru. Grant that, and then is death a benefit :
So are we Cæsar's friends, that have abridg'd
His time of fearing death.—Stoop, Romans, stoop,
And let us bathe our hands in Cæsar's blood
Up to the elbows, and besmear our swords :
Then walk we forth, even to the market-place ;
And, waving our red weapons o'er our heads,
Let 's all cry, " Peace, freedom, and liberty !" 110
Cas. Stoop then, and wash.—How many ages hence
Shall this our lofty scene be acted over,
In states unborn, and accents yet unknown !
Bru. How many times shall Cæsar bleed in sport,
That now on Pompey's basis lies along,
No worthier than the dust!
Cas.   So oft as that shall be,
So often shall the knot of us be call'd
The men that gave their country liberty.
Dec. What! shall we forth?
Cas.   Ay, every man away :
Brutus shall lead ; and we will grace his heels 120
With the most boldest and best hearts of Rome.

        Enter a Servant.

Bru. Soft! who comes here? A friend of Antony's.
Serv. Thus, Brutus, did my master bid me kneel ;
Thus did Mark Antony bid me fall down,
And, being prostrate, thus he bad me say :

Brutus is noble, wise, valiant, and honest;
Cæsar was mighty, bold, royal, and loving:
Say, I love Brutus, and I honour him;
Say, I fear'd Cæsar, honour'd him, and lov'd him.
If Brutus will vouchsafe that Antony   130
May safely come to him, and be resolv'd
How Cæsar hath deserv'd to lie in death,
Mark Antony shall not love Cæsar dead
So well as Brutus living; but will follow
The fortunes and affairs of noble Brutus,
Thorough the hazards of this untrod state,
With all true faith. So says my master Antony.

THE SLAIN CÆSAR.

Bru. Thy master is a wise and valiant Roman;
I never thought him worse.
Tell him, so please him come unto this place,   140
He shall be satisfied; and, by my honour,
Depart untouch'd.
Serv.   I'll fetch him presently.   [*Exit.*
Bru. I know that we shall have him well to friend.
Cas. I wish we may: but yet have I a mind,
That fears him much; and my misgiving still
Falls shrewdly to the purpose.

Re-enter ANTONY.

Bru. But here comes Antony.—Welcome, Mark
Antony.
Ant. O mighty Cæsar! dost thou lie so low?
Are all thy conquests, glories, triumphs, spoils,
Shrunk to this little measure?—Fare thee well.— 150
I know not, gentlemen, what you intend,
Who else must be let blood, who else is rank:
If I myself, there is no hour so fit
As Cæsar's death's hour; nor no instrument
Of half that worth as those your swords, made rich
With the most noble blood of all this world.
I do beseech ye, if you bear me hard,
Now, whilst your purpled hands do reek and smoke,
Fulfil your pleasure. Live a thousand years,
I shall not find myself so apt to die: 160
No place will please me so, no mean of death,
As here by Cæsar, and by you cut off,
The choice and master spirits of this age.
Bru. O Antony! beg not your death of us.
Though now we must appear bloody and cruel,
As, by our hands, and this our present act,
You see we do, yet see you but our hands,
And this the bleeding business they have done:
Our hearts you see not; they are pitiful;
And pity to the general wrong of Rome   170
(As fire drives out fire, so pity pity)
Hath done this deed on Cæsar. For your part,
To you our swords have leaden points, Mark Antony:
Our arms, in strength of malice, and our hearts,
Of brothers' temper, do receive you in
With all kind love, good thoughts, and reverence.
Cas. Your voice shall be as strong as any man's
In the disposing of new dignities.

Bru. Only be patient, till we have appeas'd
The multitude, beside themselves with fear,   180
And then we will deliver you the cause,
Why I, that did love Cæsar when I struck him,
Have thus proceeded.
Ant.   I doubt not of your wisdom.
Let each man render me his bloody hand;
First, Marcus Brutus, will I shake with you;
Next, Caius Cassius, do I take your hand;
Now, Decius Brutus, yours; now yours, Metellus;
Yours, Cinna; and, my valiant Casca, yours;
Though last, not least in love, yours, good Trebonius.
Gentlemen all,—alas! what shall I
        say?   190
My credit now stands on such slippery
        ground,
That one of two bad ways you must
        conceit me,
Either a coward, or a flatterer.—
That I did love thee, Cæsar, O! 'tis
        true:
If then thy spir't look upon us now,
Shall it not grieve thee, dearer than
        thy death,
To see thy Antony making his peace,
Shaking the bloody fingers of thy
        foes,
Most noble! in the presence of thy
        corse?
Had I as many eyes as thou hast
        wounds,   200
Weeping as fast as they stream forth
        thy blood,
It would become me better than to
        close
In terms of friendship with thine
        enemies.
Pardon me, Julius!—Here wast thou bay'd, brave hart;
Here didst thou fall; and here thy hunters stand,
Sign'd in thy spoil, and crimson'd in thy lethe.
O world! thou wast the forest to this hart;
And this, indeed, O world! the heart of thee.—
How like a deer, strucken by many princes,
Dost thou here lie!   210
Cas. Mark Antony,—
Ant.   Pardon me, Caius Cassius:
The enemies of Cæsar shall say this;
Then, in a friend, it is cold modesty.
Cas. I blame you not for praising Cæsar so:
But what compact mean you to have with us?
Will you be prick'd in number of our friends,
Or shall we on, and not depend on you?
Ant. Therefore I took your hands; but was, indeed,
Sway'd from the point by looking down on Cæsar.
Friends am I with you all, and love you all,   220
Upon this hope, that you shall give me reasons,
Why and wherein Cæsar was dangerous.
Bru. Or else were this a savage spectacle.
Our reasons are so full of good regard,
That were you, Antony, the son of Cæsar,
You should be satisfied.
Ant.   That's all I seek:
And am moreover suitor, that I may
Produce his body to the market-place;
And in the pulpit, as becomes a friend,
Speak in the order of his funeral.   230
Bru. You shall, Mark Antony.
Cas.   Brutus, a word with you.—
[*Aside to Brutus.*] You know not what you do; do
        not consent,
That Antony speak in his funeral.
Know you how much the people may be mov'd
By that which he will utter?
Bru.   By your pardon;
I will myself into the pulpit first,
And show the reason of our Cæsar's death:
What Antony shall speak, I will protest
He speaks by leave and by permission;
And that we are contented, Cæsar shall   240
Have all true rites, and lawful ceremonies.
It shall advantage more than do us wrong.
Cas. I know not what may fall: I like it not.

Bru. Mark Antony, here, take you Cæsar's body.
You shall not in your funeral speech blame us,
But speak all good you can devise of Cæsar ;
And say, you do 't by our permission :
Else shall you not have any hand at all
About his funeral. And you shall speak
In the same pulpit whereto I am going,   250
After my speech is ended.
    Ant.   Be it so ;
I do desire no more.
    Bru. Prepare the body then, and follow us.
                          [*Exeunt all but* ANTONY.
    Ant. O, pardon me, thou bleeding piece of earth,
That I am meek and gentle with these butchers !
Thou art the ruins of the noblest man
That ever lived in the tide of times.
Woe to the hand that shed this costly blood !
Over thy wounds now do I prophesy,
(Which, like dumb mouths, do ope their ruby lips, 260
To beg the voice and utterance of my tongue),
A curse shall light upon the limbs of men ;
Domestic fury, and fierce civil strife,
Shall cumber all the parts of Italy ;
Blood and destruction shall be so in use,
And dreadful objects so familiar,
That mothers shall but smile, when they behold
Their infants quarter'd with the hands of war ;
All pity chok'd with custom of fell deeds :
And Cæsar's spirit, ranging for revenge,   270
With Até by his side, come hot from hell,
Shall in these confines, with a monarch's voice,
Cry "Havoc !" and let slip the dogs of war,
That this foul deed shall smell above the earth
With carrion men, groaning for burial.

            Enter a Servant.

You serve Octavius Cæsar, do you not ?
    Serv. I do, Mark Antony.
    Ant. Cæsar did write for him to come to Rome.
    Serv. He did receive his letters, and is coming ;
And bid me say to you by word of mouth,—   280
O Cæsar !   [*Seeing the body.*
    Ant. Thy heart is big, get thee apart and weep.
Passion, I see, is catching ; for mine eyes,
Seeing those beads of sorrow stand in thine,
Began to water. Is thy master coming ?
    Serv. He lies to-night within seven leagues of Rome.
    Ant. Post back with speed, and tell him what hath
chanc'd :
Here is a mourning Rome, a dangerous Rome,
No Rome of safety for Octavius yet ;
Hie hence, and tell him so. Yet stay awhile ;   290
Thou shalt not back, till I have borne this corse
Into the market-place : there shall I try,
In my oration, how the people take
The cruel issue of these bloody men ;
According to the which thou shalt discourse
To young Octavius of the state of things.
Lend me your hand.   [*Exeunt, with* CÆSAR'S *body.*

            SCENE II.—The Same. The Forum.

        Enter BRUTUS *and* CASSIUS, *and a throng of
                      Citizens.*

    Cit. We will be satisfied : let us be satisfied.
    Bru. Then follow me, and give me audience,
friends.—
Cassius, go you into the other street,
And part the numbers.—
Those that will hear me speak, let them stay here ;
Those that will follow Cassius, go with him ;
And public reasons shall be rendered
Of Cæsar's death.
    1 *Cit.*   I will hear Brutus speak.
    2 *Cit.* I will hear Cassius ; and compare their
reasons,
When severally we hear them render'd.   10
        [*Exit* CASSIUS, *with some of the Citizens.*
            BRUTUS *goes into the pulpit.*
    3 *Cit.* The noble Brutus is ascended. Silence !

    Bru. Be patient till the last.
Romans, countrymen, and lovers ! hear me for my
cause, and be silent, that you may hear : believe me
for mine honour, and have respect to mine honour,
that you may believe : censure me in your wisdom,
and awake your senses, that you may the better judge.
If there be any in this assembly, any dear friend of
Cæsar's, to him I say, that Brutus' love to Cæsar was
no less than his. If then that friend demand, why
Brutus rose against Cæsar, this is my answer :—Not
that I loved Cæsar less, but that I loved Rome more.
Had you rather Cæsar were living, and die all slaves,
than that Cæsar were dead, to live all free men ? As
Cæsar loved me, I weep for him ; as he was fortunate,
I rejoice at it ; as he was valiant, I honour him : but,
as he was ambitious, I slew him. There is tears for
his love ; joy for his fortune ; honour for his valour ;
and death for his ambition. Who is here so base, that
would be a bondman ? If any, speak ; for him have I
offended. Who is here so rude, that would not be a
Roman ? If any, speak ; for him have I offended.
Who is here so vile, that will not love his country ?
If any, speak ; for him have I offended. I pause for
a reply.
    All. None, Brutus, none.
    Bru. Then none have I offended. I have done no
more to Cæsar than you shall do to Brutus. The
question of his death is enrolled in the Capitol : his
glory not extenuated, wherein he was worthy, nor his
offences enforced, for which he suffered death.   41

    Enter ANTONY *and others, with* CÆSAR'S *body.*

Here comes his body, mourned by Mark Antony : who,
though he had no hand in his death, shall receive the
benefit of his dying, a place in the commonwealth ;
as which of you shall not ? With this I depart : that,
as I slew my best lover for the good of Rome, I have
the same dagger for myself, when it shall please my
country to need my death.
    All. Live, Brutus ! live ! live !
    1 *Cit.* Bring him with triumph home unto his house.
    2 *Cit.* Give him a statue with his ancestors.   51
    3 *Cit.* Let him be Cæsar.
    4 *Cit.*   Cæsar's better parts
Shall be crown'd in Brutus.
    1 *Cit.* We 'll bring him to his house with shouts and
clamours.
    Bru. My countrymen,—
    2 *Cit.*   Peace ! silence ! Brutus speaks.
    1 *Cit.* Peace, ho !
    Bru. Good countrymen, let me depart alone,
And, for my sake, stay here with Antony.
Do grace to Cæsar's corse, and grace his speech
Tending to Cæsar's glories, which Mark Antony,   60
By our permission, is allow'd to make.
I do entreat you, not a man depart,
Save I alone, till Antony have spoke.   [*Exit.*
    1 *Cit.* Stay, ho ! and let us hear Mark Antony.
    3 *Cit.* Let him go up into the public chair ;
We 'll hear him.—Noble Antony, go up.
    Ant. For Brutus' sake, I am beholding to you.
    4 *Cit.* What does he say of Brutus ?
    3 *Cit.*   He says, for Brutus' sake,
He finds himself beholding to us all.   69
    4 *Cit.* 'T were best he speak no harm of Brutus here.
    1 *Cit.* This Cæsar was a tyrant.
    3 *Cit.*   Nay, that 's certain :
We are bless'd that Rome is rid of him.
    2 *Cit.* Peace ! let us hear what Antony can say.
    Ant. You gentle Romans,—
    Cit.   Peace, ho ! let us hear him.
    Ant. Friends, Romans, countrymen, lend me your
ears :
I come to bury Cæsar, not to praise him.
The evil that men do lives after them,
The good is oft interred with their bones ;
So let it be with Cæsar. The noble Brutus
Hath told you, Cæsar was ambitious :   80
If it were so, it was a grievous fault,
And grievously hath Cæsar answer'd it.
Here, under leave of Brutus and the rest,
(For Brutus is an honourable man,

So are they all, all honourable men,)
Come I to speak in Cæsar's funeral.
He was my friend, faithful and just to me:
But Brutus says, he was ambitious;
And Brutus is an honourable man.
He hath brought many captives home to Rome,   90
Whose ransoms did the general coffers fill:
Did this in Cæsar seem ambitious?
When that the poor have cried, Cæsar hath wept;
Ambition should be made of sterner stuff:
Yet Brutus says, he was ambitious;
And Brutus is an honourable man.
You all did see, that on the Lupercal
I thrice presented him a kingly crown,
Which he did thrice refuse: was this ambition?
Yet Brutus says, he was ambitious;   100
And, sure, he is an honourable man.
I speak not to disprove what Brutus spoke,
But here I am to speak what I do know.
You all did love him once, not without cause:
What cause withholds you then to mourn for him?
O judgment! thou art fled to brutish beasts,
And men have lost their reason!—Bear with me;
My heart is in the coffin there with Cæsar,
And I must pause till it come back to me.
1 Cit. Methinks, there is much reason in his sayings.
2 Cit. If thou consider rightly of the matter,   111
Cæsar has had great wrong.
3 Cit.   Has he, masters?
I fear, there will a worse come in his place.
4 Cit. Mark'd ye his words? He would not take the
crown:
Therefore, 't is certain, he was not ambitious.
1 Cit. If it be found so, some will dear abide it.
2 Cit. Poor soul! his eyes are red as fire with
weeping.
3 Cit. There 's not a nobler man in Rome than
Antony.
4 Cit. Now mark him; he begins again to speak.
Ant. But yesterday the word of Cæsar might   120
Have stood against the world: now lies he there,
And none so poor to do him reverence.
O masters! if I were dispos'd to stir
Your hearts and minds to mutiny and rage,
I should do Brutus wrong, and Cassius wrong,
Who, you all know, are honourable men.
I will not do them wrong: I rather choose
To wrong the dead, to wrong myself, and you,
Than I will wrong such honourable men.
But here's a parchment, with the seal of Cæsar;   130
I found it in his closet, 't is his will.
Let but the commons hear this testament,
(Which, pardon me, I do not mean to read,)
And they would go and kiss dead Cæsar's wounds,
And dip their napkins in his sacred blood,
Yea, beg a hair of him for memory,
And, dying, mention it within their wills,
Bequeathing it, as a rich legacy,
Unto their issue.
4 Cit. We 'll hear the will: read it, Mark Antony. 140
All. The will, the will! we will hear Cæsar's
will.
Ant. Have patience, gentle friends; I must not
read it:
It is not meet you know how Cæsar lov'd you.
You are not wood, you are not stones, but men;
And, being men, hearing the will of Cæsar,
It will enflame you, it will make you mad.
'T is good you know not that you are his heirs;
For if you should, O, what would come of it!
4 Cit. Read the will! we 'll hear it, Antony;
You shall read us the will, Cæsar's will.   150
Ant. Will you be patient? will you stay awhile?
I have o'ershot myself to tell you of it.
I fear, I wrong the honourable men,
Whose daggers have stabb'd Cæsar: I do fear it.
4 Cit. They were traitors:—honourable men!
All. The will! the testament!
2 Cit. They were villains, murderers. The will!
read the will!
Ant. You will compel me then to read the will?
Then make a ring about the corse of Cæsar,   160

And let me show you him that made the will.
Shall I descend? and will you give me leave?
All. Come down.
2 Cit. Descend.   [*He comes down from the pulpit.*
3 Cit. You shall have leave.
4 Cit. A ring; stand round.
1 Cit. Stand from the hearse; stand from the
body.
2 Cit. Room for Antony; most noble Antony.
Ant. Nay, press not so upon me; stand far off.
All. Stand back! room! bear back!   170
Ant. If you have tears, prepare to shed them
now.
You all do know this mantle! I remember
The first time ever Cæsar put it on:
'T was on a summer's evening, in his tent,
That day he overcame the Nervii.
Look! in this place ran Cassius' dagger through:
See, what a rent the envious Casca made:
Through this, the well-beloved Brutus stabb'd;
And, as he pluck'd his cursed steel away,
Mark how the blood of Cæsar follow'd it,   180
As rushing out of doors, to be resolv'd
If Brutus so unkindly knock'd, or no;
For Brutus, as you know, was Cæsar's angel:
Judge, O you gods, how dearly Cæsar lov'd him!
This was the most unkindest cut of all;
For when the noble Cæsar saw him stab,
Ingratitude, more strong than traitors' arms,
Quite vanquish'd him: then burst his mighty heart;
And, in his mantle muffling up his face,
Even at the base of Pompey's statua,   190
Which all the while ran blood, great Cæsar fell.
O, what a fall was there, my countrymen!
Then I, and you, and all of us fell down,
Whilst bloody treason flourish'd over us.
O! now you weep; and, I perceive, you feel
The dint of pity: these are gracious drops.
Kind souls! what, weep you, when you but behold
Our Cæsar's vesture wounded? Look you here,
Here is himself, marr'd, as you see, with traitors.
1 Cit. O piteous spectacle!   200
2 Cit. O noble Cæsar!
3 Cit. O woful day!
4 Cit. O traitors! villains!
1 Cit. O most bloody sight!
2 Cit. We will be revenged: revenge! about,—seek,—
burn,—fire,—kill,—slay!—let not a traitor live.
Ant. Stay, countrymen.
1 Cit. Peace there! Hear the noble Antony.
2 Cit. We 'll hear him, we 'll follow him, we 'll die
with him.   210
Ant. Good friends, sweet friends, let me not stir
you up
To such a sudden flood of mutiny.
They that have done this deed are honourable:
What private griefs they have, alas! I know not,
That made them do it; they are wise and honourable,
And will, no doubt, with reasons answer you.
I come not, friends, to steal away your hearts:
I am no orator, as Brutus is;
But, as you know me all, a plain blunt man,
That love my friend; and that they know full
well   220
That gave me public leave to speak of him.
For I have neither wit, nor words, nor worth,
Action, nor utterance, nor the power of speech,
To stir men's blood: I only speak right on;
I tell you that which you yourselves do know,
Show you sweet Cæsar's wounds, poor poor dumb
mouths,
And bid them speak for me: but were I Brutus,
And Brutus Antony, there were an Antony
Would ruffle up your spirits, and put a tongue
In every wound of Cæsar, that should move   230
The stones of Rome to rise and mutiny.
All. We 'll mutiny.
1 Cit.   We 'll burn the house of Brutus.
3 Cit. Away then! come, seek the conspirators.
Ant. Yet hear me, countrymen; yet hear me
speak.
All. Peace, ho! Hear Antony; most noble Antony.

Ant. Why, friends, you go to do you know not
   what.
Wherein hath Cæsar thus deserv'd your loves?
Alas! you know not:—I must tell you then.
You have forgot the will I told you of.
All. Most true;—the will: let's stay, and hear the
   will.   240
Ant. Here is the will, and under Cæsar's seal.
To every Roman citizen he gives,
To every several man, seventy-five drachmas.
2 Cit. Most noble Cæsar!—we 'll revenge his death.
3 Cit. O royal Cæsar!
Ant. Hear me with patience.
All. Peace, ho!
Ant. Moreover, he hath left you all his walks,
His private arbours, and new-planted orchards,
On this side Tiber: he hath left them you,   250
And to your heirs for ever; common pleasures,
To walk abroad, and recreate yourselves.
Here was a Cæsar! when comes such another?
1 Cit. Never, never!—Come, away, away!
We 'll burn his body in the holy place,
And with the brands fire the traitors' houses.
Take up the body.
2 Cit. Go, fetch fire.
3 Cit. Pluck down benches.
4 Cit. Pluck down forms, windows, anything.   260
    [*Exeunt Citizens, with the body.*
Ant. Now let it work. Mischief, thou art afoot,
Take thou what course thou wilt!

Enter a Servant.

            How now, fellow?
Serv. Sir, Octavius is already come to Rome.
Ant. Where is he?
Serv. He and Lepidus are at Cæsar's house.
Ant. And thither will I straight to visit him.
He comes upon a wish: Fortune is merry,
And in this mood will give us anything.
Serv. I heard him say, Brutus and Cassius
Are rid like madmen through the gates of Rome.   270
Ant. Belike, they had some notice of the people,
How I had mov'd them. Bring me to Octavius.
          [*Exeunt.*

Scene III.—The Same. A Street.

Enter Cinna, *the Poet.*

Cin. I dreamt to-night, that I did feast with Cæsar,
And things unlucky charge my fantasy.
I have no will to wander forth of doors,
Yet something leads me forth.

Enter Citizens.

1 Cit. What is your name?
2 Cit. Whither are you going?
3 Cit. Where do you dwell?
4 Cit. Are you a married man, or a bachelor?
2 Cit. Answer every man directly.
1 Cit. Ay, and briefly.   10
4 Cit. Ay, and wisely.
3 Cit. Ay, and truly; you were best.
Cin. What is my name? Whither am I going?
Where do I dwell? Am I a married man, or a
bachelor? Then, to answer every man directly, and
briefly, wisely, and truly: wisely I say, I am a
bachelor.
2 Cit. That 's as much as to say, they are fools that
marry:—you 'll bear me a bang for that, I fear. Proceed; directly.   20
Cin. Directly, I am going to Cæsar's funeral.
1 Cit. As a friend, or an enemy?
Cin. As a friend.
2 Cit. That matter is answered directly.
4 Cit. For your dwelling,—briefly.
Cin. Briefly, I dwell by the Capitol.
3 Cit. Your name, sir, truly.
Cin. Truly, my name is Cinna.
1 Cit. Tear him to pieces, he 's a conspirator.
Cin. I am Cinna the poet; I am Cinna the poet.   30
4 Cit. Tear him for his bad verses; tear him for his
bad verses.
Cin. I am not Cinna the conspirator.
2 Cit. It is no matter; his name 's Cinna: pluck but
his name out of his heart, and turn him going.
3 Cit. Tear him, tear him! Come, brands, ho! fire-
brands! To Brutus, to Cassius; burn all. Some to
Decius' house, and some to Casca's; some to Ligarius'.
Away! go!   [*Exeunt.*

ACT IV.

Scene I.—The Same. A Room in Antony's House.

Antony, Octavius, *and* Lepidus, *seated at a table.*

Antony.
THESE many then shall die; their names
   are prick'd.
Oct. Your brother too must die: con-
   sent you, Lepidus?
Lep. I do consent,—
Oct.   Prick him down, Antony.
Lep. Upon condition Publius shall not
   live,
Who is your sister's son, Mark Antony.
Ant. He shall not live; look, with a spot I damn
   him.

But, Lepidus, go you to Cæsar's house;
Fetch the will hither, and we shall determine
How to cut off some charge in legacies.
Lep. What, shall I find you here?   10
Oct. Or here, or at the Capitol.   [*Exit* Lepidus.
Ant. This is a slight unmeritable man,
Meet to be sent on errands: is it fit,
The three-fold world divided, he should stand
One of the three to share it?
Oct.   So you thought him;
And took his voice who should be prick'd to die,
In our black sentence and proscription.

Ant. Octavius, I have seen more days than you:
And though we lay these honours on this man,
To ease ourselves of divers slanderous loads, 20
He shall but bear them as the ass bears gold,
To groan and sweat under the business,
Either led or driven, as we point the way;
And having brought our treasure where we will,
Then take we down his load, and turn him off,
Like to the empty ass, to shake his ears,
And graze in commons.
Oct. You may do your will;
But he's a tried and valiant soldier.

Ant. " He shall not live; look, with a spot I damn him."

Ant. So is my horse, Octavius; and for that
I do appoint him store of provender. 30
It is a creature that I teach to fight,
To wind, to stop, to run directly on,
His corporal motion govern'd by my spirit.
And, in some taste, is Lepidus but so;
He must be taught, and train'd, and bid go forth:
A barren-spirited fellow; one that feeds
On abject orts, and imitations,
Which, out of use and stal'd by other men,
Begin his fashion: do not talk of him,
But as a property. And now, Octavius, 40
Listen great things:—Brutus and Cassius
Are levying powers: we must straight make head:
Therefore, let our alliance be combin'd,
Our best friends made, and our best means stretch'd out;
And let us presently go sit in council,
How covert matters may be best disclos'd,
And open perils surest answered.
Oct. Let us do so: for we are at the stake,
And bay'd about with many enemies;
And some, that smile, have in their hearts, I fear, 50
Millions of mischiefs. [*Exeunt.*

SCENE II.—Before BRUTUS's Tent, in the Camp near
Sardis.

Drum. Enter BRUTUS, LUCILIUS, LUCIUS, *and
Soldiers:* TITINIUS *and* PINDARUS *meet them.*
Bru. Stand, ho!
Lucil. Give the word, ho! and stand.
Bru. What now, Lucilius? is Cassius near?
Lucil. He is at hand; and Pindarus is come
To do you salutation from his master.
Bru. He greets me well.—Your master, Pindarus,
In his own change, or by ill officers,
Hath given me some worthy cause to wish
Things done, undone; but, if he be at hand,
I shall be satisfied.
Pin. I do not doubt, 10
But that my noble master will appear
Such as he is, full of regard and honour.

Bru. He is not doubted.—A word, Lucilius:
How he receiv'd you, let me be resolv'd.
Lucil. With courtesy, and with respect enough;
But not with such familiar instances,
Nor with such free and friendly conference,
As he hath us'd of old.
Bru. Thou hast describ'd
A hot friend cooling. Ever note, Lucilius,
When love begins to sicken and decay, 20
It useth an enforced ceremony.
There are no tricks in plain and simple faith;
But hollow men, like horses hot at hand,
Make gallant show and promise of their
mettle;
But when they should endure the bloody
spur,
They fall their crests, and, like deceitful
jades,
Sink in the trial. Comes his army on?
Lucil. They mean this night in Sardis to
be quarter'd:
The greater part, the horse in general, 29
Are come with Cassius. [*March within.*
Bru. Hark! he is arriv'd.—
March gently on to meet him.

Enter CASSIUS *and Soldiers.*

Cas. Stand, ho!
Bru. Stand, ho! Speak the word along.
1 *Sold.* Stand!
2 *Sold.* Stand!
3 *Sold.* Stand!
Cas. Most noble brother, you have done
me wrong.
Bru. Judge me, you gods! wrong I mine
enemies?
And, if not so, how should I wrong a brother?
Cas. Brutus, this sober form of yours
hides wrongs; 40
And when you do them—
Bru. Cassius, be content,
Speak your griefs softly: I do know you well.
Before the eyes of both our armies here,
Which should perceive nothing but love from us,
Let us not wrangle: bid them move away;
Then in my tent, Cassius, enlarge your griefs,
And I will give you audience.
Cas. Pindarus,
Bid our commanders lead their charges off
A little from this ground.
Bru. Lucilius, do you the like; and let no man 50
Come to our tent, till we have done our conference.
Let Lucius and Titinius guard our door. [*Exeunt.*

SCENE III.—Within the Tent of BRUTUS.

Enter BRUTUS *and* CASSIUS.

Cas. That you have wrong'd me, doth appear in
this:
You have condemn'd and noted Lucius Pella
For taking bribes here of the Sardians;
Wherein my letters, praying on his side,
Because I knew the man, were slighted off.
Bru. You wrong'd yourself to write in such a case.
Cas. In such a time as this, it is not meet
That every ncie offence should bear his comment.
Bru. Let me tell you, Cassius, you yourself
Are much condemn'd to have an itching palm; 10
To sell and mart your offices for gold
To undeservers.
Cas. I an itching palm?
You know, that you are Brutus that speak this,
Or, by the gods, this speech were else your last.
Bru. The name of Cassius honours this corruption,
And chastisement does therefore hide his head.
Cas. Chastisement!
Bru. Remember March, the ides of March remem-
ber:
Did not great Julius bleed for justice' sake?
What villain touch'd his body, that did stab, 20

And not for justice? What! shall one of us,
That struck the foremost man of all this world,
But for supporting robbers, shall we now
Contaminate our fingers with base bribes,
And sell the mighty space of our large honours
For so much trash as may be grasped thus?
I had rather be a dog, and bay the moon,
Than such a Roman.
   Cas.   Brutus, bay not me,
I 'll not endure it : you forget yourself,
To hedge me in. I am a soldier, I,   30
Older in practice, abler than yourself
To make conditions.
   Bru.   Go to ; you are not, Cassius.
   Cas. I am.
   Bru. I say, you are not.
   Cas. Urge me no more, I shall forget myself :
Have mind upon your health ; tempt me no further.
   Bru. Away, slight man !
   Cas. Is 't possible?
   Bru.   Hear me, for I will speak.
Must I give way and room to your rash choler?
Shall I be frighted, when a madman stares?   40
   Cas. O ye gods! ye gods! Must I endure all this?
   Bru. All this? ay, more : fret, till your proud heart
     break ;
Go, show your slaves how choleric you are,
And make your bondmen tremble. Must I budge?
Must I observe you? Must I stand and crouch
Under your testy humour? By the gods,
You shall digest the venom of your spleen,
Though it do split you ; for from this day forth,
I 'll use you for my mirth, yea, for my laughter,
When you are waspish.
   Cas.   Is it come to this?   50
   Bru. You say, you are a better soldier :
Let it appear so ; make your vaunting true,
And it shall please me well. For mine own part,
I shall be glad to learn of noble men.
   Cas. You wrong me every way ; you wrong me,
     Brutus ;
I said, an elder soldier, not a better :
Did I say, better?
   Bru.   If you did, I care not.
   Cas. When Cæsar liv'd, he durst not thus have
     mov'd me.
   Bru. Peace, peace! you durst not so have tempted
     him.
   Cas. I durst not?   60
   Bru. No.
   Cas. What! durst not tempt him?
   Bru.   For your life you durst not.
   Cas. Do not presume too much upon my love ;
I may do that I shall be sorry for.
   Bru. You have done that you should be sorry for.
There is no terror, Cassius, in your threats ;
For I am arm'd so strong in honesty,
That they pass by me as the idle wind,
Which I respect not. I did send to you
For certain sums of gold, which you denied me ;— 70
For I can raise no money by vile means :
By heaven, I had rather coin my heart,
And drop my blood for drachmas, than to wring
From the hard hands of peasants their vile trash
By any indirection. I did send
To you for gold to pay my legions,
Which you denied me : was that done like Cassius?
Should I have answer'd Caius Cassius so?
When Marcus Brutus grows so covetous,
To lock such rascal counters from his friends,   80
Be ready, gods, with all your thunderbolts ;
Dash him to pieces!
   Cas.   I denied you not.
   Bru. You did.
   Cas.   I did not : he was but a fool
That brought my answer back.—Brutus hath riv'd my
     heart :
A friend should bear his friend's infirmities,
But Brutus makes mine greater than they are.
   Bru. I do not, till you practise them on me.
   Cas. You love me not.
   Bru.   I do not like your faults.

   Cas. A friendly eye could never see such faults.   89
   Bru. A flatterer's would not, though they do appear
As huge as high Olympus.
   Cas. Come, Antony, and young Octavius, come,
Revenge yourselves alone on Cassius,
For Cassius is aweary of the world :
Hated by one he loves ; brav'd by his brother ;
Check'd like a bondman ; all his faults observ'd,
Set in a note-book, learn'd, and conn'd by rote,
To cast into my teeth. O! I could weep
My spirit from mine eyes.—There is my dagger,
And here my naked breast ; within, a heart   100
Dearer than Plutus' mine, richer than gold :
If that thou be'st a Roman, take it forth ;
I, that denied thee gold, will give my heart :
Strike, as thou didst at Cæsar ; for, I know,
When thou didst hate him worst, thou lov'dst him
     better
Than ever thou lov'dst Cassius.
   Bru.   Sheathe your dagger :
Be angry when you will, it shall have scope ;
Do what you will, dishonour shall be humour.
O Cassius! you are yoked with a lamb,
That carries anger, as the flint bears fire ;   110
Who, much enforced, shows a hasty spark,
And straight is cold again.
   Cas.   Hath Cassius liv'd
To be but mirth and laughter to his Brutus,
When grief, and blood ill-temper'd, vexeth him?
   Bru. When I spoke that, I was ill-temper'd too.
   Cas. Do you confess so much? Give me your hand.
   Bru. And my heart too.
   Cas.   O Brutus!
   Bru.   What 's the matter?
   Cas. Have you not love enough to bear with me,
When that rash humour, which my mother gave me,
Makes me forgetful?
   Bru.   Yes, Cassius ; and, from henceforth,
When you are over-earnest with your Brutus,   121
He 'll think your mother chides, and leave you so.
                       [Noise within.
   Poet. [*Within.*] Let me go in to see the generals :
There is some grudge between 'em ; 't is not meet
They be alone.
   Lucil. [*Within.*] You shall not come to them.
   Poet. [*Within.*] Nothing but death shall stay me.

Enter Poet, followed by LUCILIUS, TITINIUS, *and*
     LUCIUS.

   Cas. How now? What 's the matter?
   Poet. For shame, you generals! What do you
     mean?
Love, and be friends, as two such men should be ; 130
For I have seen more years, I am sure, than ye.
   Cas. Ha, ha! how vilely doth this cynic rhyme!
   Bru. Get you hence, sirrah : saucy fellow, hence !
   Cas. Bear with him, Brutus ; 't is his fashion.
   Bru. I 'll know his humour, when he knows his
     time :
What should the wars do with these jigging fools?—
Companion, hence !
   Cas.   Away, away! be gone.
                          [Exit Poet.
   Bru. Lucilius and Titinius, bid the commanders
Prepare to lodge their companies to-night.
   Cas. And come yourselves, and bring Messala with
     you,   140
Immediately to us. [*Exeunt* LUCILIUS *and* TITINIUS.
   Bru.   Lucius, a bowl of wine. [*Exit* LUCIUS.
   Cas. I did not think, you could have been so angry.
   Bru. O Cassius! I am sick of many griefs.
   Cas. Of your philosophy you make no use,
If you give place to accidental evils.
   Bru. No man bears sorrow better : Portia is dead.
   Cas. Ha! Portia?
   Bru. She is dead.
   Cas. How 'scap'd I killing, when I cross'd you so?— 150
O insupportable and touching loss!—
Upon what sickness?
   Bru.   Impatient of my absence ;
And grief, that young Octavius with Mark Antony
Have made themselves so strong : for with her death

That tidings came ;—with this she fell distract,
And, her attendants absent, swallow'd fire.
  Cas. And died so?
  Bru.   Even so.
  Cas.   O ye immortal gods!

    Re-enter LUCIUS, *with wine and tapers.*

  Bru. Speak no more of her.—Give me a bowl of
    wine :—
In this I bury all unkindness, Cassius.   [*Drinks.*
  Cas. My heart is thirsty for that noble pledge.—
Fill, Lucius, till the wine o'erswell the cup;   160
I cannot drink too much of Brutus' love.   [*Drinks.*
  Bru. Come in, Titinius.   [*Exit* LUCIUS.

Bru. "In this I bury all unkindness, Cassius."

    Re-enter TITINIUS, *with* MESSALA.

               Welcome, good Messala.—
Now sit we close about this taper here,
And call in question our necessities.
  Cas. Portia, art thou gone?
  Bru.   No more, I pray you.—
Messala, I have here received letters,
That young Octavius and Mark Antony
Come down upon us with a mighty power,
Bending their expedition toward Philippi.
  Mes. Myself have letters of the selfsame tenor. 170
  Bru. With what addition?
  Mes. That by proscription, and bills of outlawry,
Octavius, Antony, and Lepidus,
Have put to death an hundred senators.
  Bru. Therein our letters do not well agree:
Mine speak of seventy senators, that died
By their proscriptions, Cicero being one.
  Cas. Cicero one?
  Mes.   Cicero is dead,
And by that order of proscription.—
Had you your letters from your wife, my lord? 180
  Bru. No, Messala.
  Mes. Nor nothing in your letters writ of her?
  Bru. Nothing, Messala.
  Mes.   That, methinks, is strange.
  Bru. Why ask you? Hear you aught of her in yours?
  Mes. No, my lord.
  Bru. Now, as you are a Roman, tell me true.
  Mes. Then like a Roman bear the truth I tell :
For certain she is dead, and by strange manner.
  Bru. Why, farewell, Portia.—We must die, Messala:
With meditating that she must die once, 190
I have the patience to endure it now.
  Mes. Even so great men great losses should endure.
  Cas. I have as much of this in art as you,
But yet my nature could not bear it so.
  Bru. Well, to our work alive.—What do you think
Of marching to Philippi presently?
  Cas. I do not think it good.

  Bru.   Your reason?
  Cas.   This it is.
'T is better that the enemy seek us :
So shall he waste his means, weary his soldiers,
Doing himself offence ; whilst we, lying still, 200
Are full of rest, defence, and nimbleness.
  Bru. Good reasons must, of force, give place to
    better.
The people, 'twixt Philippi and this ground,
Do stand but in a forc'd affection ;
For they have grudg'd us contribution :
The enemy, marching along by them,
By them shall make a fuller number up,
Come on refresh'd, new-added, and encourag'd :
From which advantage shall we cut him
    off,
If at Philippi we do face him there, 210
These people at our back.
  Cas. Hear me, good brother.
  Bru. Under your pardon.—You must
    note beside,
That we have tried the utmost of our
    friends,
Our legions are brim-full, our cause is
    ripe :
The enemy increaseth every day ;
We, at the height, are ready to decline.
There is a tide in the affairs of men,
Which, taken at the flood, leads on to
    fortune ;
Omitted, all the voyage of their life 220
Is bound in shallows and in miseries.
On such a full sea are we now afloat ;
And we must take the current when it
    serves,
Or lose our ventures.
  Cas.   Then, with your will, go on :
We 'll along ourselves, and meet them at
    Philippi.
  Bru. The deep of night is crept upon
    our talk,
And nature must obey necessity ;
Which we will niggard with a little rest.
There is no more to say ?
  Cas.   No more. Good night :
Early to-morrow will we rise, and hence. 230
  Bru. Lucius! [*Re-enter* LUCIUS.] My gown. [*Exit*
    LUCIUS.]—Farewell, good Messala :—
Good night, Titinius.—Noble, noble Cassius,
Good night, and good repose.
  Cas.   O my dear brother !
This was an ill beginning of the night.
Never come such division 'tween our souls !
Let it not, Brutus.
  Bru.   Everything is well.
  Cas. Good night, my lord.
  Bru.   Good night, good brother.
  Tit., Mes. Good night, Lord Brutus.
  Bru. Farewell, every one.
    [*Exeunt* CASSIUS, TITINIUS, *and* MESSALA.

    Re-enter LUCIUS, *with the gown.*

Give me the gown. Where is thy instrument? 240
  Luc. Here in the tent.
  Bru.   What ! thou speak'st drowsily ?
Poor knave, I blame thee not ; thou art o'er-watch'd.
Call Claudius, and some other of my men ;
I 'll have them sleep on cushions in my tent.
  Luc. Varro, and Claudius !

    Enter VARRO *and* CLAUDIUS.

  Var. Calls my lord ?
  Bru. I pray you, sirs, lie in my tent, and sleep :
It may be, I shall raise you by-and-by
On business to my brother Cassius.
  Var. So please you, we will stand, and watch your
    pleasure. 250
  Bru. I will not have it so ; lie down, good sirs :
It may be, I shall otherwise bethink me.
Look, Lucius, here 's the book I sought for so ;
I put it in the pocket of my gown.
    [VARRO *and* CLAUDIUS *lie down.*

Luc. I was sure, your lordship did not give it me.
Bru. Bear with me, good boy, I am much forgetful.
Canst thou hold up thy heavy eyes awhile,
And touch thy instrument a strain or two?

That plays thee music?—Gentle knave, good night;
I will not do thee so much wrong to wake thee. 271
If thou dost nod, thou break'st thy instrument:
I'll take it from thee; and, good boy, good night.—

Bru. "Art thou some god, some angel, or some devil,
That mak'st my blood cold, and my hair to stare?"

Luc. Ay, my lord, an 't please you.
Bru.   It does, my boy.
I trouble thee too much, but thou art willing.   260
Luc. It is my duty, sir.
Bru. I should not urge thy duty past thy might:
I know, young bloods look for a time of rest.
Luc. I have slept, my lord, already.
Bru. It was well done, and thou shalt sleep again;
I will not hold thee long: if I do live,
I will be good to thee.   [*Music, and a Song.*
This is a sleepy tune:—O murderous slumber!
Lay'st thou thy leaden mace upon my boy,

Let me see, let me see:—is not the leaf turn'd down,
Where I left reading? Here it is, I think.
[*He sits down.*

Enter the Ghost of CÆSAR.

How ill this taper burns!—Ha! who comes here?
I think, it is the weakness of mine eyes
That shapes this monstrous apparition.
It comes upon me.—Art thou anything?
Art thou some god, some angel, or some devil,   280
That mak'st my blood cold, and my hair to stare?
Speak to me, what thou art.

Ghost. Thy evil spirit, Brutus.
Bru.   Why com'st thou?
Ghost. To tell thee, thou shalt see me at Philippi.
Bru. Well; then I shall see thee again?
Ghost. Ay, at Philippi.
Bru. Why, I will see thee at Philippi then.—
                              [*Ghost vanishes.*
Now I have taken heart, thou vanishest:
Ill spirit, I would hold more talk with thee.—
Boy! Lucius!—Varro! Claudius! sirs, awake!—   290
Claudius!
Luc. The strings, my lord, are false.
Bru. He thinks he still is at his instrument.—
Lucius, awake!
Luc. My lord?
Bru. Didst thou dream, Lucius, that thou so criedst
    out?

Luc. My lord, I do not know that I did cry.
Bru. Yes, that thou didst. Didst thou see any-
    thing?
Luc. Nothing, my lord.
Bru. Sleep again, Lucius.—Sirrah, Claudius!   300
[*To* VARRO.] Fellow thou! awake!
Var. My lord?
Clau. My lord?
Bru. Why did you so cry out, sirs, in your sleep?
Var., Clau. Did we, my lord?
Bru.   Ay: saw you anything?
Var. No, my lord, I saw nothing.
Clau.   Nor I, my lord.
Bru. Go, and commend me to my brother Cassius:
Bid him set on his powers betimes before,
And we will follow.
Var., Clau.   It shall be done, my lord. [*Exeunt.*

ACT V.

SCENE I.—The Plains of Philippi.

Enter OCTAVIUS, ANTONY, *and their Army.*

Octavius.
NOW, Antony, our hopes are answered:
    You said, the enemy would not come down,
    But keep the hills and upper regions;
    It proves not so: their battles are at hand;
    They mean to warn us at Philippi here,
    Answering before we do demand of them.
Ant. Tut! I am in their bosoms, and I know
    Wherefore they do it: they could be content
    To visit other places; and come down
    With fearful bravery, thinking by this face
    To fasten in our thoughts that they have
        courage;   11
But 't is not so.

Enter a Messenger.

Mess.   Prepare you, generals:
The enemy comes on in gallant show;
Their bloody sign of battle is hung out,
And something to be done immediately.
Ant. Octavius, lead your battle softly on,
Upon the left hand of the even field.
Oct. Upon the right hand I; keep thou the left.
Ant. Why do you cross me in this exigent?
Oct. I do not cross you; but I will do so.   [*March.*

Drum. Enter BRUTUS, CASSIUS, *and their Army;*
LUCILIUS, TITINIUS, MESSALA, *and others.*
Bru. They stand, and would have parley.   21
Cas. Stand fast, Titinius: we must out and talk.
Oct. Mark Antony, shall we give sign of battle?
Ant. No, Cæsar, we will answer on their charge.
Make forth; the generals would have some words.
Oct. Stir not until the signal.
Bru. Words before blows: is it so, countrymen?
Oct. Not that we love words better, as you do.
Bru. Good words are better than bad strokes,
    Octavius.

Ant. In your bad strokes, Brutus, you give good
        words: 30
Witness the hole you made in Cæsar's heart,
Crying, "Long live! hail, Cæsar!"
Cas.   Antony,
The posture of your blows are yet unknown;
But for your words, they rob the Hybla bees,
And leave them honeyless.
Ant.   Not stingless too.
Bru. O! yes, and soundless too;
For you have stol'n their buzzing, Antony,
And very wisely threat before you sting.
Ant. Villains! you did not so, when your vile daggers
Hack'd one another in the sides of Cæsar: 40
You show'd your teeth like apes, and fawn'd like
        hounds,
And bow'd like bondmen, kissing Cæsar's feet;
Whilst damned Casca, like a cur, behind,
Struck Cæsar on the neck. O you flatterers!
Cas. Flatterers!—Now, Brutus, thank yourself:
This tongue had not offended so to-day,
If Cassius might have rul'd.
Oct. Come, come, the cause: if arguing make us
        sweat,
The proof of it will turn to redder drops.
Look;   50
I draw a sword against conspirators:
When think you that the sword goes up again?—
Never, till Cæsar's three-and-thirty wounds
Be well aveng'd; or till another Cæsar
Have added slaughter to the sword of traitors.
Bru. Cæsar, thou canst not die by traitors' hands,
Unless thou bring'st them with thee.
Oct.   So I hope,
I was not born to die on Brutus' sword.
Bru. O! if thou wert the noblest of thy strain,
Young man, thou couldst not die more honourable. 60
Cas. A peevish school-boy, worthless of such honour,
Join'd with a masker and a reveller.

Ant. Old Cassius still!
Oct.   Come, Antony; away!—
Defiance, traitors, hurl we in your teeth.
If you dare fight to-day, come to the field;
If not, when you have stomachs.
    [*Exeunt* Octavius, Antony, *and their Army.*
Cas. Why now, blow, wind; swell, billow; and
     swim, bark!
The storm is up, and all is on the hazard.
Bru. Ho!
Lucilius, hark, a word with you.
Lucil.   My lord?   70
    [Brutus *and* Lucilius *talk apart.*
Cas. Messala,—
Mes.   What says my general?
Cas.   Messala,
This is my birth-day; as this very day
Was Cassius born. Give me thy hand,
     Messala:
Be thou my witness, that against my
     will,
As Pompey was, am I compell'd to set
Upon one battle all our liberties.
You know, that I held Epicurus strong,
And his opinion: now, I change my
     mind,
And partly credit things that do pre-
     sage.
Coming from Sardis, on our former
     ensign   80
Two mighty eagles fell; and there they
     perch'd,
Gorging and feeding from our soldiers'
     hands;
Who to Philippi here consorted us:
This morning are they fled away, and
     gone,
And in their steads do ravens, crows,
     and kites,
Fly o'er our heads, and downward look
     on us,
As we were sickly prey: their shadows
     seem
A canopy most fatal, under which
Our army lies, ready to give up the ghost.
Mes. Believe not so.
Cas.   I but believe it partly,   90
For I am fresh of spirit, and resolv'd
To meet all perils very constantly.
Bru. Even so, Lucilius.
Cas.   Now, most noble Brutus,
The gods to-day stand friendly, that we may,
Lovers in peace, lead on our days to age!
But since the affairs of men rest still incertain,
Let's reason with the worst that may befall.
If we do lose this battle, then is this
The very last time we shall speak together:
What are you then determined to do?   100
Bru. Even by the rule of that philosophy,
By which I did blame Cato for the death
Which he did give himself:—I know not how,
But I do find it cowardly and vile,
For fear of what might fall, so to prevent
The time of life:—arming myself with patience,
To stay the providence of some high powers,
That govern us below.
Cas.   Then, if we lose this battle,
You are contented to be led in triumph
Thorough the streets of Rome?   110
Bru. No, Cassius, no: think not, thou noble Roman,
That ever Brutus will go bound to Rome;
He bears too great a mind: but this same day
Must end that work the ides of March begun;
And, whether we shall meet again, I know not.
Therefore, our everlasting farewell take:—
For ever, and for ever, farewell, Cassius!
If we do meet again, why, we shall smile;
If not, why then, this parting was well made.
Cas. For ever, and for ever, farewell, Brutus!   120
If we do meet again, we'll smile indeed;
If not, 'tis true, this parting was well made.
Bru. Why then, lead on.—O, that a man might know

The end of this day's business, ere it come!
But it sufficeth, that the day will end,
And then the end is known.—Come, ho! away!
                          [*Exeunt.*

Scene II.—The Same. The Field of Battle.

Alarum. Enter Brutus *and* Messala.

Bru. Ride, ride, Messala, ride, and give these bills
Unto the legions on the other side.   [*Loud alarum*
Let them set on at once; for I perceive
But cold demeanour in Octavius' wing,

Pin. [*Above.*] "Titinius is enclosed round about
With horsemen, that make to him on the spur."

And sudden push gives them the overthrow.
Ride, ride, Messala: let them all come down. [*Exeunt.*

Scene III.—The Same. Another Part of the Field.

Alarum. Enter Cassius *and* Titinius.

Cas. O, look, Titinius, look, the villains fly!
Myself have to mine own turn'd enemy:
This ensign here of mine was turning back;
I slew the coward, and did take it from him.
Tit. O Cassius! Brutus gave the word too early;
Who, having some advantage on Octavius,
Took it too eagerly: his soldiers fell to spoil,
Whilst we by Antony are all enclos'd.

Enter Pindarus.

Pin. Fly further off, my lord, fly further off;
Mark Antony is in your tents, my lord!
Fly, therefore, noble Cassius, fly far off.
Cas. This hill is far enough. Look, look, Titinius;
Are those my tents where I perceive the fire?
Tit. They are, my lord.
Cas.   Titinius, if thou lov'st me,
Mount thou my horse, and hide thy spurs in him,
Till he have brought thee up to yonder troops,
And here again; that I may rest assur'd,
Whether yond troops are friend or enemy.
Tit. I will be here again, even with a thought. [*Exit.*
Cas. Go, Pindarus, get higher on that hill: 20
My sight was ever thick; regard Titinius,
And tell me what thou not'st about the field.—
                          [*Exit* Pindarus.
This day I breathed first: time is come round,
And where I did begin, there shall I end;
My life is run his compass.—Sirrah, what news?
Pin. [*Above.*] O my lord!
Cas. What news?
Pin. Titinius is enclosed round about

With horsemen, that make to him on the spur ;
Yet he spurs on :—now they are almost on him.   30
Now, Titinius!—now some light :—O ! he lights too:—
He's ta'en : [*Shout.*] and, hark ! they shout for joy.
  Cas. Come down ; behold no more.—
O, coward that I am, to live so long,
To see my best friend ta'en before my face !

Re-enter PINDARUS.

Come hither, sirrah.
In Parthia did I take thee prisoner ;
And then I swore thee, saving of thy life,
That whatsoever I did bid thee do,
Thou shouldst attempt it. Come now, keep thine
        oath :   40
Now be a freeman ; and with this good sword,
That ran through Cæsar's bowels, search this bosom.
Stand not to answer : here, take thou the hilts ; ·
And, when my face is cover'd, as 'tis now,
Guide thou the sword.—Cæsar, thou art reveng'd,
Even with the sword that kill'd thee.   [*Dies.*
  Pin. So, I am free ; yet would not so have been,
Durst I have done my will. O Cassius !
Far from this country Pindarus shall run,
Where never Roman shall take note of him.   50
                                              [*Exit.*

Re-enter TITINIUS, *with* MESSALA.

  Mes. It is but change, Titinius ; for Octavius
Is overthrown by noble Brutus' power,
As Cassius' legions are by Antony.
  Tit. These tidings will well comfort Cassius.
  Mes. Where did you leave him ?
  Tit.   All disconsolate,
With Pindarus, his bondman, on this hill.
  Mes. Is not that he, that lies upon the ground ?
  Tit. He lies not like the living. O my heart !
  Mes. Is not that he ?
  Tit.   No, this was he, Messala,
But Cassius is no more.—O setting sun !   60
As in thy red rays thou dost sink to night,
So in his red blood Cassius' day is set :
The sun of Rome is set. Our day is gone ;
Clouds, dews, and dangers come ; our deeds are done.
Mistrust of my success hath done this deed.
  Mes. Mistrust of good success hath done this deed.
O hateful error, melancholy's child !
Why dost thou show to the apt thoughts of men
The things that are not ? O error ! soon conceiv'd,
Thou never com'st unto a happy birth,   70
But kill'st the mother that engender'd thee.
  Tit. What, Pindarus ! Where art thou, Pindarus ?
  Mes. Seek him, Titinius, whilst I go to meet
The noble Brutus, thrusting this report
Into his ears : I may say, thrusting it ;
For piercing steel, and darts envenomed,
Shall be as welcome to the ears of Brutus,
As tidings of this sight.
  Tit.   Hie you, Messala,
And I will seek for Pindarus the while.
                                    [*Exit* MESSALA.
Why didst thou send me forth, brave Cassius ?   80
Did I not meet thy friends ? and did not they
Put on my brows this wreath of victory,
And bid me give it thee ? Didst thou not hear their
        shouts ?
Alas ! thou hast misconstrued everything.
But hold thee, take this garland on thy brow :
Thy Brutus bid me give it thee, and I
Will do his bidding.—Brutus, come apace,
And see how I regarded Caius Cassius.—
By your leave, gods :—this is a Roman's part :
Come, Cassius' sword, and find Titinius' heart. [*Dies.*

Alarum. *Re-enter* MESSALA, *with* BRUTUS, *Young*
        CATO, STRATO, VOLUMNIUS, *and* LUCILIUS.

  Bru. Where, where, Messala, doth his body lie ? 91
  Mes. Lo, yonder ; and Titinius mourning it.
  Bru. Titinius' face is upward.
  Cato.   He is slain.
  Bru. O Julius Cæsar ! thou art mighty yet :
Thy spirit walks abroad, and turns our swords
In our own proper entrails.   [*Low alarums.*

  Cato.   Brave Titinius !
Look, whe'r he have not crown'd dead Cassius !
  Bru. Are yet two Romans living such as these ?—
The last of all the Romans, fare thee well !
It is impossible that ever Rome   100
Should breed thy fellow.—Friends, I owe more tears
To this dead man than you shall see me pay.—
I shall find time, Cassius, I shall find time.—
Come, therefore, and to Thassos send his body :
His funerals shall not be in our camp,
Lest it discomfort us.—Lucilius, come :—
And come, young Cato ; let us to the field.—
Labeo, and Flavius, set our battles on :—
'T is three o'clock ; and, Romans, yet ere night
We shall try fortune in a second fight.   110
                                        [*Exeunt.*

─────────

SCENE IV.—Another Part of the Field.

*Alarum. Enter, fighting, Soldiers of both Armies ;
    then* BRUTUS, CATO, LUCILIUS, *and others.*

  Bru. Yet, countrymen, O ! yet hold up your heads.
  Cato. What bastard doth not ? Who will go with
        me ?
I will proclaim my name about the field :—
I am the son of Marcus Cato, ho !
A foe to tyrants, and my country's friend ;
I am the son of Marcus Cato, ho !
                          [*Charges the enemy.*
  Bru. And I am Brutus, Marcus Brutus, I ;
Brutus, my country's friend : know me for Brutus.
      [*Exit, charging the enemy.* CATO *is
        overpower'd, and falls.*
  Lucil. O young and noble Cato ! art thou down ?
Why, now thou diest as bravely as Titinius,   10
And may'st be honour'd, being Cato's son.
  1 Sold. Yield, or thou diest.
  Lucil.   Only I yield to die :
There is so much that thou wilt kill me straight.
                              [*Offering money.*
Kill Brutus, and be honour'd in his death.
  1 Sold. We must not.—A noble prisoner !
  2 Sold. Room, ho ! Tell Antony, Brutus is ta'en.
  1 Sold. I 'll tell the news.—Here comes the general.—

Enter ANTONY.

Brutus is ta'en, Brutus is ta'en, my lord.
  Ant. Where is he ?
  Lucil. Safe, Antony ; Brutus is safe enough.   20
I dare assure thee, that no enemy
Shall ever take alive the noble Brutus :
The gods defend him from so great a shame !
When you do find him, or alive, or dead,
He will be found like Brutus, like himself.
  Ant. This is not Brutus, friend ; but, I assure you,
A prize no less in worth. Keep this man safe ;
Give him all kindness : I had rather have
Such men my friends, than enemies. Go on,
And see whe'r Brutus be alive, or dead ;   30
And bring us word, unto Octavius' tent,
How everything is chanc'd.   [*Exeunt.*

─────────

SCENE V.—Another Part of the Field.

Enter BRUTUS, DARDANIUS, CLITUS, STRATO, *and*
        VOLUMNIUS.

  Bru. Come, poor remains of friends, rest on this
        rock.
  Cli. Statilius show'd the torch-light ; but, my lord,
He came not back : he is or ta'en, or slain.
  Bru. Sit thee down, Clitus : slaying is the word ;
It is a deed in fashion. Hark thee, Clitus.
                                  [*Whispering.*
  Cli. What ! I, my lord ? No, not for all the world.
  Bru.' Peace then ! no words.
  Cli.   I 'll rather kill myself.
  Bru. Hark thee, Dardanius.—   [*Whispers him.*
  Dar.   Shall I do such a deed ?
  Cli. O Dardanius !

Dar. O Clitus!   10
Cli. What ill request did Brutus make to thee?
Dar. To kill him, Clitus. Look, he meditates.
Cli. Now is that noble vessel full of grief,
That it runs over even at his eyes.
Bru. Come hither, good Volumnius: list a word.
Vol. What says my lord?
Bru.   Why, this, Volumnius:
The ghost of Cæsar hath appear'd to me
Two several times by night: at Sardis
    once;
And, this last night, here in Philippi
    fields.
I know my hour is come.
Vol.   Not so, my lord.
Bru. Nay, I am sure it is, Volumnius.
Thou seest the world, Volumnius, how it
    goes;   22
Our enemies have beat us to the pit:
                          [*Low alarums.*
It is more worthy to leap in ourselves,
Than tarry till they push us. Good
    Volumnius,
Thou know'st, that we two went to school
    together;
Even for that our love of old, I pray thee,
Hold thou my sword-hilts, whilst I run
    on it.
Vol. That 's not an office for a friend,
    my lord.   [*Alarum still.*
Cli. Fly, fly, my lord! there is no
    tarrying here.   30
Bru. Farewell to you;—and you;—and
    you, Volumnius.—
Strato, thou hast been all this while asleep;
Farewell to thee too, Strato.—Countrymen,
My heart doth joy, that yet in all my life
I found no man, but he was true to me.
I shall have glory by this losing day,
More than Octavius and Mark Antony
By this vile conquest shall attain unto.
So, fare you well at once; for Brutus' tongue
Hath almost ended his life's history.   40
Night hangs upon mine eyes; my bones would
    rest,
That have but labour'd to attain this hour.
          [*Alarum. Cry within, "Fly, fly, fly!"*
Cli. Fly, my lord, fly!
Bru.   Hence! I will follow.
          [*Exeunt* CLITUS, DARDANIUS, *and*
                    VOLUMNIUS.
I pr'ythee, Strato, stay thou by thy lord.
Thou art a fellow of a good respect;
Thy life hath had some smatch of honour in it:
Hold then my sword, and turn away thy face,
While I do run upon it. Wilt thou, Strato?
Stra. Give me your hand first: fare you well, my
    lord.
Bru. Farewell, good Strato.—Cæsar, now be
    still: 50
I kill'd not thee with half so good a will.
          [*He runs on his sword, and dies.*

Alarum: Retreat. Enter OCTAVIUS, ANTONY,
    MESSALA, LUCILIUS, *and their Army.*

Oct. What man is that?
Mes. My master's man.—Strato, where is thy master?
Stra. Free from the bondage you are in, Messala;

Ant. "This was the noblest Roman of them all."

The conquerors can but make a fire of him;
For Brutus only overcame himself,
And no man else hath honour by his death.
Lucil. So Brutus should be found.—I thank thee,
    Brutus,
That thou hast prov'd Lucilius' saying true.
Oct. All that serv'd Brutus, I will entertain them. 60
Fellow, wilt thou bestow thy time with me?
Stra. Ay; if Messala will prefer me to you.
Oct. Do so, good Messala.
Mes. How died my master, Strato?
Stra. I held the sword, and he did run on it.
Mes. Octavius, then take him to follow thee,
That did the latest service to my master.
Ant. This was the noblest Roman of them all:
All the conspirators, save only he,
Did that they did in envy of great Cæsar;   70
He only, in a general honest thought
And common good to all, made one of them.
His life was gentle; and the elements
So mix'd in him that Nature might stand up,
And say to all the world, "This was a man!"
Oct. According to his virtue let us use him,
With all respect, and rites of burial.
Within my tent his bones to-night shall lie,
Most like a soldier, order'd honourably.—
So, call the field to rest; and let 's away,   80
To part the glories of this happy day.   [*Exeunt.*

MACBETH.

DRAMATIS PERSONÆ.

DUNCAN, *King of Scotland.*
MALCOLM, } *His Sons.*
DONALBAIN, }
MACBETH, } *Generals of the King's Army.*
BANQUO, }
MACDUFF,
LENOX,
ROSSE,
MENTETH, } *Noblemen of Scotland.*
ANGUS,
CATHNESS,
FLEANCE, *Son to Banquo.*
SIWARD, *Earl of Northumberland, General of the English Forces.*
Young SIWARD, *his Son.*
SEYTON, *an Officer attending on Macbeth.*

Boy, Son to Macduff.
An English Doctor.
A Scotch Doctor.
A Soldier.
A Porter.
An Old Man.

LADY MACBETH.
LADY MACDUFF.
Gentlewoman attending on Lady Macbeth.
HECATE, *and Three Witches.*

Lords, Gentlemen, Officers, Soldiers, Murderers, Attendants, and Messengers.

The Ghost of Banquo, and other Apparitions.

SCENE—In the end of the Fourth Act, in ENGLAND; through the rest of the Play, in SCOTLAND.

ACT I.

SCENE I.--An Open Place.

Thunder and lightning. Enter three Witches.

1 *Witch.* WHEN shall we three meet
    again,
In thunder, lightning, or in
    rain?
2 *Witch.* When the hurlyburly 's done,
When the battle 's lost and won.
3 *Witch.* That will be ere the set of
    sun.
1 *Witch.* Where the place?
2 *Witch.*   Upon the heath.
3 *Witch.* There to meet with Macbeth.
1 *Witch.* I come, Graymalkin!
    All. Paddock calls.—Anon!—
Fair is foul, and foul is fair: 10
Hover through the fog and filthy air.
                  [*Exeunt.*

SCENE II.—A Camp near Fores.

Alarum within. Enter King DUNCAN, MALCOLM, DONALBAIN, LENOX, *with Attendants, meeting a bleeding Captain.*

Dun. What bloody man is that? He can report,
As seemeth by his plight, of the revolt
The newest state.

Mal.   This is the sergeant,
Who, like a good and hardy soldier, fought
'Gainst my captivity.—Hail, brave friend!
Say to the king the knowledge of the broil,
As thou didst leave it.

Cap.   Doubtful it stood;
As two spent swimmers, that do cling together
And choke their art. The merciless Macdonwald
(Worthy to be a rebel, for to that   10
The multiplying villanies of nature
Do swarm upon him) from the western isles
Of Kernes and Gallowglasses is supplied;
And fortune, on his damned quarrel smiling,
Show'd like a rebel's whore: but all 's too weak:
For brave Macbeth (well he deserves that name),
Disdaining fortune, with his brandish'd steel,
Which smok'd with bloody execution,
Like valour's minion, carv'd out his passage,
Till he fac'd the slave;   20
Which ne'er shook hands, nor bade farewell to him,
Till he unseam'd him from the nave to the chaps,
And fix'd his head upon our battlements.
Dun. O valiant cousin! worthy gentleman!
Cap. As whence the sun 'gins his reflection
Shipwracking storms and direful thunders break,
So from that spring, whence comfort seem'd to come,
Discomfort swells. Mark, King of Scotland, mark:

No sooner justice had, with valour arm'd,
Compell'd these skipping Kernes to trust their heels,
But the Norweyan lord, surveying vantage,   31
With furbish'd arms, and new supplies of men,
Began a fresh assault.
    Dun.   Dismay'd not this
Our captains, Macbeth and Banquo?
    Cap.   Yes;
As sparrows eagles, or the hare the lion.
If I say sooth, I must report they were
As cannons overcharg'd with double cracks;
So they
Doubly redoubled strokes upon the foe:
Except they meant to bathe in reeking wounds,   40
Or memorise another Golgatha,
I cannot tell--
But I am faint, my gashes cry for help.
    Dun. So well thy words become thee, as thy wounds:
They smack of honour both.—Go, get him surgeons.
                  [*Exit Captain, attended.*
Who comes here?
               Enter ROSSE.
    Mal.   The worthy thane of Rosse.
    Len. What a haste looks through his eyes!
So should he look that seems to speak things strange.
    Rosse. God save the king!
    Dun.   Whence cam'st thou, worthy thane?
    Rosse. From Fife, great king,   50
Where the Norweyan banners flout the sky
And fan our people cold.
Norway himself, with terrible numbers,
Assisted by that most disloyal traitor,
The thane of Cawdor, began a dismal conflict;
Till that Bellona's bridegroom, lapp'd in proof,
Confronted him with self-comparisons,
Point against point, rebellious arm 'gainst arm,
Curbing his lavish spirit: and, to conclude,
The victory fell on us;—
    Dun.   Great happiness!   60
    Rosse. That now
Sweno, the Norways' king, craves composition;
Nor would we deign him burial of his men
Till he disbursed at Saint Colme's Inch
Ten thousand dollars to our general use.
    Dun. No more that thane of Cawdor shall deceive
Our bosom interest.—Go, pronounce his present death,
And with his former title greet Macbeth.
    Rosse. I 'll see it done.
    Dun. What he hath lost, noble Macbeth hath won.
                       [*Exeunt.*

         SCENE III.—A Heath.

   • *Thunder. Enter the three Witches.*

    1 *Witch.* Where hast thou been, sister?
    2 *Witch.* Killing swine.
    3 *Witch.* Sister, where thou?
    1 *Witch.* A sailor's wife had chestnuts in her lap,
And mounch'd, and mounch'd, and mounch'd: "Give
me," quoth I: -
"Aroint thee, witch!" the rump-fed ronyon cries.
Her husband 's to Aleppo gone, master o' the Tiger:
But in a sieve I 'll thither sail,
And like a rat without a tail;
I 'll do, I 'll do, and I 'll do.   10
    2 *Witch.* I 'll give thee a wind.
    1 *Witch.* Th' art kind.
    3 *Witch.* And I another.
    1 *Witch.* I myself have all the other;
And the very ports they blow,
All the quarters that they know
I' the shipman's card.
I 'll drain him dry as hay:
Sleep shall neither night nor day
Hang upon his penthouse lid;   20
He shall live a man forbid.
Weary sev'n-nights, nine times nine,
Shall he dwindle, peak, and pine:
Though his bark cannot be lost,
Yet it shall be tempest-tost.
Look what I have.

    2 *Witch.* Show me, show me.
    1 *Witch.* Here I have a pilot's thumb,
Wrack'd, as homeward he did come.   [*Drum within.*
    3 *Witch.* A drum! a drum!   30
Macbeth doth come.
    All. The weird sisters, hand in hand,
Posters of the sea and land,
Thus do go about, about:
Thrice to thine, and thrice to mine,
And thrice again, to make up nine.
Peace!—the charm 's wound up.

       Enter MACBETH *and* BANQUO.

    Macb. So foul and fair a day I have not seen.
    Ban. How far is 't call'd to Fores?—What are these,
So wither'd and so wild in their attire,   40
That look not like th' inhabitants o' the earth,
And yet are on 't? Live you? or are you aught
That man may question? You seem to understand me,
By each at once her choppy finger laying
Upon her skinny lips:—you should be women,
And yet your beards forbid me to interpret
That you are so.
    Macb.   Speak, if you can:—what are you?
    1 *Witch.* All hail, Macbeth! hail to thee, thane of
         Glamis!
    2 *Witch.* All hail, Macbeth! hail to thee, thane of
         Cawdor!
    3 *Witch.* All hail, Macbeth! that shalt be king
         hereafter.   50
    Ban. Good sir, why do you start, and seem to fear
Things that do sound so fair?—I' the name of truth,
Are ye fantastical, or that indeed
Which outwardly ye show? My noble partner
You greet with present grace, and great prediction
Of noble having, and of royal hope,
That he seems rapt withal: to me you speak not.
If you can look into the seeds of time,
And say which grain will grow, and which will not,
Speak then to me, who neither beg, nor fear,   60
Your favours nor your hate.
    1 *Witch.* Hail!
    2 *Witch.* Hail!
    3 *Witch.* Hail!
    1 *Witch.* Lesser than Macbeth, and greater.
    2 *Witch.* Not so happy, yet much happier.
    3 *Witch.* Thou shalt get kings, though thou be
         none:
So, all hail, Macbeth and Banquo!
    1 *Witch.* Banquo and Macbeth, all hail!
    Macb. Stay, you imperfect speakers, tell me more. 70
By Sinel's death, I know, I am thane of Glamis;
But how of Cawdor? the thane of Cawdor lives,
A prosperous gentleman; and to be king
Stands not within the prospect of belief,
No more than to be Cawdor. Say, from whence
You owe this strange intelligence? or why
Upon this blasted heath you stop our way
With such prophetic greeting?—Speak, I charge you.
                   [*Witches vanish.*
    Ban. The earth hath bubbles, as the water has,
And these are of them.—Whither are they vanish'd? 80
    Macb. Into the air; and what seem'd corporal,
melted
As breath into the wind.—'Would they had stay'd!
    Ban. Were such things here, as we do speak about,
Or have we eaten on the insane root,
That takes the reason prisoner?
    Macb. Your children shall be kings.
    Ban.   You shall be king.
    Macb. And thane of Cawdor too; went it not so?
    Ban. To the selfsame tune, and words. Who 's
here?

       Enter ROSSE *and* ANGUS.

    Rosse. The king hath happily receiv'd, Macbeth,
The news of thy success; and when he reads   90
Thy personal venture in the rebel's fight,
His wonders and his praises do contend,
Which should be thine, or his. Silenc'd with that,
In viewing o'er the rest o' the selfsame day,
He finds thee in the stout Norweyan ranks,

Nothing afeard of what thyself didst make,
Strange images of death. As thick as hail,
Came post with post ; and every one did bear
Thy praises in his kingdom's great defence,
And pour'd them down before him.

Ban.   What ! can the devil speak true ?
Macb. The thane of Cawdor lives : why do you dress me
In borrow'd robes ?
Ang.   Who was the thane, lives yet ;

3 *Witch.* "All hail, Macbeth ! that shalt be king hereafter."

Ang.   We are sent, 100
To give thee from our royal master thanks ;
Only to herald thee into his sight,
Not pay thee.
  Rosse. And, for an earnest of a greater honour,
He bade me, from him, call thee thane of Cawdor :
In which addition, hail, most worthy thane,
For it is thine.

But under heavy judgment bears that life   110
Which he deserves to lose. Whether he was com-
          bin'd
With those of Norway, or did line the rebel
With hidden help and vantage, or that with both
He labour'd in his country's wrack, I know not ;
But treasons capital, confess'd and prov'd,
Have overthrown him.

Macb.   Glamis, and thane of Cawdor :
The greatest is behind.—Thanks for your pains.—
Do you not hope your children shall be kings,
When those that gave the thane of Cawdor to me
Promis'd no less to them ?
Ban.   That, trusted home,   120
Might yet enkindle you unto the crown,
Besides the thane of Cawdor. But 't is strange :
And oftentimes, to win us to our harm,
The instruments of darkness tell us truths ;
Win us with honest trifles, to betray 's
In deepest consequence.—
Cousins, a word, I pray you.
Macb. [*Aside.*]   Two truths are told,
As happy prologues to the swelling act
Of the imperial theme.—I thank you, gentlemen.—
[*Aside.*] This supernatural soliciting   130
Cannot be ill ; cannot be good :—if ill,
Why hath it given me earnest of success,
Commencing in a truth? I am thane of Cawdor :
If good, why do I yield to that suggestion
Whose horrid image doth unfix my hair,
And make my seated heart knock at my ribs,
Against the use of nature? Present fears
Are less than horrible imaginings.
My thought, whose murder yet is but fantastical,
Shakes so my single state of man, that function 140
Is smother'd in surmise, and nothing is,
But what is not.
Ban.   Look, how our partner's rapt.
Macb. [*Aside.*] If chance will have me king, why,
        chance may crown me,
Without my stir.
Ban.   New honours come upon him,
Like our strange garments, cleave not to their mould,
But with the aid of use.
Macb. [*Aside.*]   Come what come may,
Time and the hour runs through the roughest day.
Ban. Worthy Macbeth, we stay upon your leisure.
Macb. Give me your favour : my dull brain was
        wrought
With things forgotten. Kind gentlemen, your pains
Are register'd where every day I turn   151
The leaf to read them.—Let us toward the king.—
Think upon what hath chanc'd ; and at more time,
The interim having weigh'd it, let us speak
Our free hearts each to other.
Ban.   Very gladly.
Macb. Till then, enough.—Come, friends. [*Exeunt.*

SCENE IV.—Fores. A Room in the Palace.

Flourish. Enter DUNCAN, MALCOLM, DONALBAIN,
      LENOX, *and Attendants.*

Dun. Is execution done on Cawdor? Are not
Those in commission yet return'd ?
Mal.   My liege,
They are not yet come back ; but I have spoke
With one that saw him die : who did report,
That very frankly he confess'd his treasons,
Implor'd your highness' pardon, and set forth
A deep repentance. Nothing in his life
Became him like the leaving it : he died
As one that had been studied in his death,
To throw away the dearest thing he ow'd,   10
As 't were a careless trifle.
Dun.   There's no art
To find the mind's construction in the face :
He was a gentleman on whom I built
An absolute trust—

Enter MACBETH, BANQUO, ROSSE, *and* ANGUS.

                O worthiest cousin !
The sin of my ingratitude even now
Was heavy on me. Thou art so far before,
That swiftest wing of recompense is slow
To overtake thee : 'would thou hadst less deserv'd,
That the proportion both of thanks and payment
Might have been mine ! only I have left to say,   20
More is thy due than more than all can pay.

Macb. The service and the loyalty I owe,
In doing it, pays itself. Your highness' part
Is to receive our duties : and our duties
Are to your throne and state, children and servants ;
Which do but what they should, by doing everything
Safe toward your love and honour.
Dun.   Welcome hither :
I have begun to plant thee, and will labour
To make thee full of growing.—Noble Banquo,
That hast no less deserv'd, nor must be known   30
No less to have done so, let me infold thee,
And hold thee to my heart.
Ban.   There if I grow,
The harvest is your own.
Dun.   My plenteous joys,
Wanton in fulness, seek to hide themselves
In drops of sorrow.—Sons, kinsmen, thanes,
And you whose places are the nearest, know,
We will establish our estate upon
Our eldest, Malcolm ; whom we name hereafter
The Prince of Cumberland : which honour must
Not, unaccompanied, invest him only,   40
But signs of nobleness, like stars, shall shine
On all deservers.—From hence to Inverness,
And bind us further to you.
Macb. The rest is labour, which is not us'd for you :
I'll be myself the harbinger, and make joyful
The hearing of my wife with your approach ;
So, humbly take my leave.
Dun.   My worthy Cawdor !
Macb. [*Aside.*] The Prince of Cumberland !—That
                is a step,
On which I must fall down, or else o'erleap,
For in my way it lies. Stars, hide your fires !   50
Let not light see my black and deep desires ;
The eye wink at the hand ; yet let that be,
Which the eye fears, when it is done, to see.   [*Exit.*
Dun. True, worthy Banquo : he is full so valiant.
And in his commendations I am fed ;
It is a banquet to me. Let us after him,
Whose care is gone before to bid us welcome :
It is a peerless kinsman.   [*Flourish. Exeunt.*

SCENE V.—Inverness. A Room in MACBETH'S Castle.

Enter Lady MACBETH, *reading a letter.*

Lady M. " They met me in the day of success ; and
I have learned by the perfectest report, they have
more in them than mortal knowledge. When I
burned in desire to question them further, they made
themselves air, into which they vanished. Whiles I
stood rapt in the wonder of it, came missives from
the king, who all-hailed me, 'Thane of Cawdor ;' by
which title, before, these weird sisters saluted me,
and referred me to the coming on of time, with 'Hail,
king that shalt be !' This have I thought good to
deliver thee, my dearest partner of greatness, that
thou mightest not lose the dues of rejoicing, by being
ignorant of what greatness is promised thee. Lay it
to thy heart, and farewell."
Glamis thou art, and Cawdor ; and shalt be
What thou art promis'd.—Yet do I fear thy nature :
It is too full o' the milk of human kindness,
To catch the nearest way. Thou wouldst be great ;
Art not without ambition, but without
The illness should attend it : what thou wouldst
        highly,   20
That wouldst thou holily ; wouldst not play false,
And yet wouldst wrongly win ; thou'dst have, great
        Glamis,
That which cries, " Thus thou must do, if thou have
        it ; "
And that which rather thou dost fear to do,
Than wishest should be undone. Hie thee hither,
That I may pour my spirits in thine ear,
And chastise with the valour of my tongue
All that impedes thee from the golden round,
Which fate and metaphysical aid doth seem
To have thee crown'd withal.—

Enter a Messenger.

What is your tidings? 30
Mess. The king comes here to-night.
Lady M. Thou 'rt mad to say it.
Is not thy master with him? who, were 't so,
Would have inform'd for preparation.
Mess. So please you, it is true : our thane is coming ;
One of my fellows had the speed of him,
Who, almost dead for breath, had scarcely more
Than would make up his message.
Lady M. Give him tending :
He brings great news. [*Exit Messenger.*] The raven
himself is hoarse,
That croaks the fatal entrance of Duncan
Under my battlements. Come, you spirits 40
That tend on mortal thoughts, unsex me here,
And fill me, from the crown to the toe, top-full
Of direst cruelty ! make thick my blood,
Stop up th' access and passage to remorse ;
That no compunctious visitings of nature
Shake my fell purpose, nor keep peace between
Th' effect and it ! Come to my woman's breasts,
And take my milk for gall, you murdering ministers,
Wherever in your sightless substances
You wait on nature's mischief ! Come, thick night, 50
And pall thee in the dunnest smoke of hell,
That my keen knife see not the wound it makes,
Nor heaven peep through the blanket of the dark,
To cry, " Hold, hold ! "—

Enter MACBETH.

Great Glamis ! worthy Cawdor !
Greater than both, by the all-hail hereafter !
Thy letters have transported me beyond
This ignorant present, and I feel now
The future in the instant.
Macb. My dearest love,
Duncan comes here to-night.
Lady.M. And when goes he hence?
Macb. To-morrow, as he proposes.
Lady M. O ! never 60
Shall sun that morrow see !
Your face, my thane, is as a book, where men
May read strange matters. To beguile the time,
Look like the time ; bear welcome in your eye,
Your hand, your tongue : look like the innocent
flower,
But be the serpent under 't. He that 's coming
Must be provided for ; and you shall put
This night's great business into my despatch ;
Which shall to all our nights and days to come
Give solely sovereign sway and masterdom. 70
Macb. We will speak further.
Lady M. Only look up clear ;
To alter favour ever is to fear.
Leave all the rest to me. [*Exeunt.*

SCENE VI.—The Same. Before the Castle.

Hautboys and torches. Enter DUNCAN, MALCOLM,
DONALBAIN, BANQUO, LENOX, MACDUFF, ROSSE,
ANGUS, *and Attendants.*

Dun. This castle hath a pleasant seat ; the air
Nimbly and sweetly recommends itself
Unto our gentle senses.
Ban. This guest of summer,
The temple-haunting martlet, does approve,
By his lov'd mansionry, that the heaven's breath
Smells wooingly here : no jutty, frieze,
Buttress, nor coign of vantage, but this bird
Hath made his pendent bed, and procreant cradle :
Where they most breed and haunt, I have observ'd,
The air is delicate.

Enter Lady MACBETH.

Dun. See, see ! our honour'd hostess.—
The love that follows us sometime is our trouble, 11
Which still we thank as love. Herein I teach you,
How you shall bid God yield us for your pains,
And thank us for your trouble.

Lady M. All our service,
In every point twice done, and then done double,
Were poor and single business, to contend
Against those honours deep and broad, wherewith
Your majesty loads our house : for those of old,
And the late dignities heap'd up to them,
We rest your hermits.
Dun. Where 's the thane of Cawdor?
We cours'd him at the heels, and had a purpose 21
To be his purveyor : but he rides well ;
And his great love, sharp as his spur, hath holp him
To his home before us. Fair and noble hostess,
We are your guest to-night.
Lady M. Your servants ever
Have theirs, themselves, and what is theirs, in compt,
To make their audit at your highness' pleasure,
Still to return your own.
Dun. Give me your hand ;
Conduct me to mine host : we love him highly,
And shall continue our graces towards him. 30
By your leave, hostess. [*Exeunt.*

SCENE VII.—The Same. A Room in the Castle.

*Hautboys and torches. Enter, and pass over the
stage, a Sewer, and divers Servants with dishes
and service. Then enter* MACBETH.

Macb. If it were done, when 't is done, then 't were
well
It were done quickly : if the assassination
Could trammel up the consequence, and catch
With his surcease success ; that but this blow
Might be the be-all and the end-all here,
But here, upon this bank and shoal of time,—
We 'd jump the life to come.—But in these cases,
We still have judgment here ; that we but teach
Bloody instructions, which, being taught, return
To plague th' inventor : this even-handed justice 10
Commends th' ingredients of our poison'd chalice
To our own lips. He 's here in double trust :
First, as I am his kinsman and his subject,
Strong both against the deed ; then, as his host,
Who should against his murderer shut the door,
Not bear the knife myself. Besides, this Duncan
Hath borne his faculties so meek, hath been
So clear in his great office, that his virtues
Will plead like angels, trumpet-tongued, against
The deep damnation of his taking off ; 20
And pity, like a naked new-born babe,
Striding the blast, or heaven's cherubin, hors'd
Upon the sightless couriers of the air,
Shall blow the horrid deed in every eye,
That tears shall drown the wind.—I have no spur
To prick the sides of my intent, but only
Vaulting ambition, which o'erleaps itself,
And falls on the other—

Enter Lady MACBETH.

How now ! what news?
Lady M. He has almost supp'd. Why have you
left the chamber?
Macb. Hath he ask'd for me?
Lady M. Know you not, he has? 30
Macb. We will proceed no further in this business :
He hath honour'd me of late ; and I have bought
Golden opinions from all sorts of people,
Which would be worn now in their newest gloss,
Not cast aside so soon.
Lady M. Was the hope drunk,
Wherein you dress'd yourself? hath it slept since,
And wakes it now, to look so green and pale
At what it did so freely? From this time,
Such I account thy love. Art thou afeard
To be the same in thine own act and valour, 40
As thou art in desire? Wouldst thou have that
Which thou esteem'st the ornament of life,
And live a coward in thine own esteem,
Letting " I dare not " wait upon " I would,"
Like the poor cat i' the adage?
Macb. Pr'ythee, peace.

I dare do all that may become a man ;
Who dares do more, is none.
   Lady M.   What beast was 't then,
That made you break this enterprise to me ?
When you durst do it, then you were a man ;
And, to be more than what you were, you would   50
Be so much more the man. Nor time, nor place,
Did then adhere, and yet you would make both :
They have made themselves, and that their fitness now
Does unmake you. I have given suck, and know
How tender 't is to love the babe that milks me :
I would, while it was smiling in my face,
Have pluck'd my nipple from his boneless gums,
And dash'd the brains out, had I so sworn as you
Have done to this.
   Macb.   If we should fail,—
   Lady M.   We fail !
But screw your courage to the sticking-place,   60
And we 'll not fail. When Duncan is asleep
(Whereto the rather shall his day's hard journey
Soundly invite him), his two chamberlains
Will I with wine and wassail so convince,
That memory, the warder of the brain,
Shall be a fume, and the receipt of reason
A limbeck only : when in swinish sleep
Their drenched natures lie, as in a death,
What cannot you and I perform upon
Th' unguarded Duncan ? what not put upon   70
His spongy officers, who shall bear the guilt
Of our great quell ?
   Macb.   Bring forth men-children only !
For thy undaunted mettle should compose
Nothing but males. Will it not be receiv'd,
When we have mark'd with blood those sleepy two
Of his own chamber, and us'd their very daggers,
That they have done 't ?
   Lady M.   Who dares receive it other,
As we shall make our griefs and clamour roar
Upon his death ?

   Macb.   I am settled, and bend up
Each corporal agent to this terrible feat.   80

Lady M.   " We fail !
But screw your courage to the sticking-place,
And we 'll not fail."

Away, and mock the time with fairest show :
False face must hide what the false heart doth know.
                       [Exeunt.

ACT II.

Scene I.—The Same.   Court within the Castle.

Enter Banquo, *and* Fleance, *with a torch before him.*

   Banquo.
OW goes the night, boy ?
   Fle. The moon is down ; I have not
      heard the clock.
   Ban. And she goes down at twelve.
   Fle.   I take 't, 't is later, sir.
   Ban. Hold, take my sword.—There 's
      husbandry in heaven ;
Their candles are all out.—Take thee
      that too.
A heavy summons lies like lead upon
      me,
And yet I would not sleep : merciful
      powers !
Restrain in me the cursed thoughts that
      nature
Gives way to in repose !—Give me my
      sword.

   Enter Macbeth, *and a Servant with a torch.*
Who 's there ?   10
   Macb. A friend.
   Ban. What, sir ! not yet at rest ? The king 's a-bed :
He hath been in unusual pleasure, and

Sent forth great largess to your offices.
This diamond he greets your wife withal,
By the name of most kind hostess, and shut up
In measureless content.
   Macb.   Being unprepar'd,
Our will became the servant to defect,
Which else should free have wrought.
   Ban.   All 's well.
I dreamt last night of the three weird sisters :   20
To you they have show'd some truth.
   Macb.   I think not of them :
Yet, when we can entreat an hour to serve,
We would spend it in some words upon that business,
If you would grant the time.
   Ban.   At your kind'st leisure.
   Macb. If you shall cleave to my consent, when 't is,
It shall make honour for you.
   Ban.   So I lose none
In seeking to augment it, but still keep
My bosom franchis'd, and allegiance clear,
I shall be counsell'd.
   Macb.   Good repose, the while !
   Ban. Thanks, sir : the like to you.   30
         [Exeunt Banquo *and* Fleance.

Macb. Go, bid thy mistress, when my drink is ready,
She strike upon the bell. Get thee to bed.—
                              [*Exit Servant.*
Is this a dagger, which I see before me,
The handle toward my hand? Come, let me clutch
              thee :—
I have thee not, and yet I see thee still.
Art thou not, fatal vision, sensible
To feeling, as to sight? or art thou but
A dagger of the mind, a false creation,
Proceeding from the heat-oppressed brain?
I see thee yet, in form as palpable   40
As this which now I draw.
Thou marshall'st me the way that I was going ;
And such an instrument I was to use.—
Mine eyes are made the fools o' the other senses,
Or else worth all the rest : I see thee still ;
And on thy blade, and dudgeon, gouts of blood,
Which was not so before.—There 's no such thing.
It is the bloody business which informs
Thus to mine eyes.—Now o'er the one half-world
Nature seems dead, and wicked dreams abuse   50
The curtain'd sleep : witchcraft celebrates
Pale Hecate's offerings ; and wither'd murder,
Alarum'd by his sentinel, the wolf,
Whose howl 's his watch, thus with his stealthy pace,
With Tarquin's ravishing strides, towards his design
Moves like a ghost.—Thou sure and firm-set earth,
Hear not my steps, which way they walk, for fear
Thy very stones prate of my where-about,
And take the present horror from the time,
Which now suits with it.—Whiles I threat, he lives :
Words to the heat of deeds too cold breath gives.   61
                              [*A bell rings.*
I go, and it is done : the bell invites me.
Hear it not, Duncan ; for it is a knell
That summons thee to heaven, or to hell.   [*Exit.*

SCENE II.—The Same.

Enter Lady MACBETH.

Lady M. That which hath made them drunk hath
              made me bold :
What hath quench'd them hath given me fire.—Hark!
              —Peace !
It was the owl that shriek'd, the fatal bellman,
Which gives the stern'st good-night. He is about it.
The doors are open ; and the surfeited grooms
Do mock their charge with snores : I have drugg'd
              their possets,
That death and nature do contend about them,
Whether they live, or die.
Macb. [*Within.*]   Who 's there?—what, ho !
Lady M. Alack ! I am afraid they have awak'd,
And 't is not done :—the attempt and not the deed   10
Confounds us.—Hark !—I laid their daggers ready ;
He could not miss them.—Had he not resembled
My father as he slept, I had done 't.—My husband !

Enter MACBETH.

Macb. I have done the deed.—Didst thou not hear
              a noise ?
Lady M. I heard the owl scream, and the crickets
              cry.
Did not you speak ?
Macb.   When ?
Lady M.   Now.
Macb.   As I descended ?
Lady M. Ay.
Macb. Hark !
Who lies i' the second chamber ?
Lady M.   Donalbain.
Macb. This is a sorry sight.   20
Lady M. A foolish thought to say a sorry sight.
Macb. There 's one did laugh in 's sleep, and one
              cried, " Murder !"
That they did wake each other : I stood and heard
              them ;
But they did say their prayers, and address'd them
Again to sleep.

Lady M.   There are two lodg'd together.
Macb. One cried, " God bless us !" and, "Amen," the
              other,
As they had seen me with these hangman's hands.
Listening their fear, I could not say, "Amen,"
When they did say, " God bless us."
Lady M.   Consider it not so deeply.
Macb. But wherefore could not I pronounce
              "Amen?"   30
I had most need of blessing, and "Amen"
Stuck in my throat.
Lady M.   These deeds must not be thought
After these ways : so, it will make us mad.
Macb. Methought, I heard a voice cry, " Sleep no
              more !
Macbeth does murder sleep,"—the innocent sleep ;
Sleep, that knits up the ravell'd sleave of care,
The death of each day's life, sore labour's bath,
Balm of hurt minds, great nature's second course,
Chief nourisher in life's feast ;—
Lady M.   What do you mean ?
Macb. Still it cried, " Sleep no more !" to all the
              house :   40
Glamis hath murder'd sleep, and therefore Cawdor
Shall sleep no more, Macbeth shall sleep no more !
Lady M. Who was it that thus cried ? Why, worthy
              thane,
You do unbend your noble strength, to think
So brainsickly of things. Go, get some water,
And wash this filthy witness from your hand.—
Why did you bring these daggers from the place ?
They must lie there : go, carry them, and smear
The sleepy grooms with blood.
Macb.   I 'll go no more :
I am afraid to think what I have done ;   50
Look on 't again I dare not.
Lady M.   Infirm of purpose !
Give me the daggers. The sleeping, and the dead,
Are but as pictures ; 't is the eye of childhood
That fears a painted devil. If he do bleed,
I 'll gild the faces of the grooms withal,
For it must seem their guilt.
                              [*Exit.—Knocking within.*
Macb.   Whence is that knocking?—
How is 't with me, when every noise appals me?
What hands are here? Ha! they pluck out mine
              eyes.
Will all great Neptune's ocean wash this blood
Clean from my hand? No, this my hand will rather
The multitudinous seas incarnadine,   61
Making the green one red.

Re-enter Lady MACBETH.

Lady M. My hands are of your colour ; but I shame
To wear a heart so white. [*Knock.*] I hear a knocking
At the south entry :—retire we to our chamber.
A little water clears us of this deed :
How easy is it then ! Your constancy
Hath left you unattended.—[*Knock.*] Hark ! more
              knocking.
Get on your night-gown, lest occasion call us,
And show us to be watchers.—Be not lost   70
So poorly in your thoughts.
Macb. To know my deed, 't were best not know
              myself.   [*Knock.*
Wake Duncan with thy knocking: I would thou
              couldst !   [*Exeunt.*

SCENE III.—The Same.

Enter a Porter.

                              [*Knocking within.*
Porter. Here 's a knocking, indeed! If a man were
porter of hell-gate, he should have old turning the
key. [*Knocking.*] Knock, knock, knock. Who 's
there, i' the name of Belzebub?—Here's a farmer, that
hanged himself on the expectation of plenty : come in
time ; have napkins enough about you ; here you 'll
sweat for 't. [*Knocking.*] Knock, knock. Who 's
there, i' the other devil's name?—'Faith, here 's an

equivocator, that could swear in both the scales against either scale ; who committed treason enough for God's sake, yet could not equivocate to heaven : O ! come in, equivocator. [*Knocking.*] Knock, knock, knock. Who's there?—'Faith, here 's an English tailor come hither for stealing out of a French hose : come in, tailor ; here you may roast your goose. [*Knocking.*] Knock, knock. Never at quiet ! What are you ?—But this place is too cold for hell. I 'll devil-porter it no further : I had thought to have let in some of all professions, that go the primrose way to the everlasting bonfire. [*Knocking.*] Anon, anon : I pray you, remember the porter.   21
[*Opens the gate.*

Enter MACDUFF and LENOX.

Macd. Was it so late, friend, ere you went to bed, That you do lie so late ?

Port. 'Faith, sir, we were carousing till the second cock ;
And drink, sir, is a great provoker of three things.

Macd. What three things does drink especially provoke ?

Port. Marry, sir, nose-painting, sleep, and urine. Lechery, sir, it provokes, and unprovokes : it provokes the desire, but it takes away the performance. There-fore, much drink may be said to be an equivocator with lechery : it makes him, and it mars him ; it sets him on, and it takes him off ; it persuades him, and disheartens him ; makes him stand to, and not stand to : in conclusion, equivocates him in a sleep, and, giving him the lie, leaves him.

Macd. I believe, drink gave thee the lie last night.

Port. That it did, sir, i' the very throat o' me : but I requited him for his lie ; and, I think, being too strong for him, though he took up my legs sometime, yet I made a shift to cast him.   41

Macd. Is thy master stirring ?

Enter MACBETH.

Our knocking has awak'd him ; here he comes.

Len. Good morrow, noble sir !

Macb.   Good morrow, both !

Macd. Is the king stirring, worthy thane ?

Macb.   Not yet.

Macd. He did command me to call timely on him : I have almost slipp'd the hour.

Macb.   I 'll bring you to him.

Macd. I know, this is a joyful trouble to you ; But yet 'tis one.

Macb. The labour we delight in physics pain.   50 This is the door.

Macd.   I 'll make so bold to call, For 'tis my limited service.   [*Exit.*

Len. Goes the king hence to-day ?

Macb.   He does :—he did appoint so.

Len. The night has been unruly : where we lay, Our chimneys were blown down ; and, as they say, Lamentings heard i' the air ; strange screams of death, And prophesying with accents terrible Of dire combustion, and confus'd events, New hatch'd to the woful time. The obscure bird clamour'd the livelong night :   60 Some say, the earth was feverous, and did shake.

Macb. 'T was a rough night.

Len. My young remembrance cannot parallel A fellow to it.

Re-enter MACDUFF.

Macd. O horror ! horror ! horror ! Tongue, nor heart, Cannot conceive, nor name thee !

Macb., Len.   What 's the matter ?

Macd. Confusion now hath made his master-piece ! Most sacrilegious murder hath broke ope The Lord's anointed temple, and stole thence The life o' the building.

Macb.   What is 't you say ? the life ? 70

Len. Mean you his majesty ?

Macd. Approach the chamber, and destroy your sight With a new Gorgon.—Do not bid me speak :

See, and then speak yourselves.—
[*Exeunt* MACBETH *and* LENOX.
                   Awake ! awake !—
Ring the alarum-bell.—Murder, and treason ! Banquo, and Donalbain ! Malcolm ! awake ! Shake off this downy sleep, death's counterfeit, And look on death itself !—up, up, and see The great doom's image !—Malcolm ! Banquo ! As from your graves rise up, and walk like sprites, 80 To countenance this horror ! Ring the bell.
[*Bell rings.*

Enter Lady MACBETH.

Lady M. What 's the business, That such a hideous trumpet calls to parley The sleepers of the house ? speak, speak !

Macd.   O gentle lady, 'T is not for you to hear what I can speak : The repetition, in a woman's ear, Would murder as it fell.

Enter BANQUO.

                   O Banquo ! Banquo ! Our royal master 's murder'd !

Lady M.   Woe, alas ! What ! in our house ?

Ban.   Too cruel, anywhere. Dear Duff, I pr'ythee, contradict thyself,   90 And say, it is not so.

Re-enter MACBETH and LENOX.

Macb. Had I but died an hour before this chance, I have liv'd a blessed time ; for, from this instant, There 's nothing serious in mortality : All is but toys : renown, and grace, is dead ; The wine of life is drawn, and the mere lees Is left this vault to brag of.

Enter MALCOLM and DONALBAIN.

Don. What is amiss ?

Macb.   You are, and do not know 't : The spring, the head, the fountain of your blood Is stopp'd ; the very source of it is stopp'd.   100

Macd. Your royal father 's murder'd.

Mal.   O ! by whom ?

Len. Those of his chamber, as it seem'd, had done 't : Their hands and faces were all badg'd with blood ; So were their daggers, which, unwip'd, we found Upon their pillows : They star'd, and were distracted ; no man's life Was to be trusted with them.

Macb. O ! yet I do repent me of my fury, That I did kill them.

Macd.   Wherefore did you so ?

Macb. Who can be wise, amaz'd, temperate and furious,   110 Loyal and neutral, in a moment ? No man : The expedition of my violent love Outrun the pauser reason.—Here lay Duncan, His silver skin lac'd with his golden blood ; And his gash'd stabs look'd like a breach in nature For ruin's wasteful entrance : there, the murderers, Steep'd in the colours of their trade, their daggers Unmannerly breech'd with gore. Who could refrain, That had a heart to love, and in that heart Courage, to make 's love known ?

Lady M.   Help me hence, ho !

Macd. Look to the lady.

Mal.   Why do we hold our tongues, That most may claim this argument for ours ?   122

Don. What should be spoken Here, where our fate, hid in an auger-hole, May rush, and seize us ? Let 's away : our tears Are not yet brew'd.

Mal.   Nor our strong sorrow Upon the foot of motion.

Ban.   Look to the lady :—
[*Lady* MACBETH *is carried out.*
And when we have our naked frailties hid, That suffer in exposure, let us meet, And question this most bloody piece of work,   130 To know it further. Fears and scruples shake us : In the great hand of God I stand ; and, thence,

Against the undivulg'd pretence I fight
Of treasonous malice.
Macd.　　　　　　And so do I.
All.　　　　　　　　So all.
Macd. Let's briefly put on manly readiness,
And meet i' the hall together.
All.　　　　　　　Well contented.
　　　　[*Exeunt all but* MALCOLM *and* DONALBAIN.
Mal. What will you do? Let's not consort with them:
To show an unfelt sorrow is an office
Which the false man does easy. I'll to England.
Don. To Ireland, I: our separated fortune　140
Shall keep us both the safer; where we are,
There's daggers in men's smiles: the near' in blood,
The nearer bloody.
Mal.　　　This murderous shaft that's shot
Hath not yet lighted, and our safest way
Is to avoid the aim: therefore, to horse;
And let us not be dainty of leave-taking,
But shift away. There's warrant in that theft
Which steals itself, when there's no mercy left.
　　　　　　　　　　　　　　[*Exeunt.*

　　　　　　　　―――

SCENE IV.—Without the Castle.

Enter ROSSE *and an Old Man.*

Old M. Threescore and ten I can remember well;
Within the volume of which time I have seen
Hours dreadful, and things strange, but this sore night
Hath trifled former knowings.
Rosse.　　　　　Ah! good father,
Thou seest, the heavens, as troubled with man's act,
Threaten his bloody stage: by the clock 't is day,
And yet dark night strangles the travelling lamp.
Is 't night's predominance, or the day's shame,
That darkness does the face of earth entomb,
When living light should kiss it?
Old M.　　　　'T is unnatural,　10
Even like the deed that's done. On Tuesday last,
A falcon, towering in her pride of place,
Was by a mousing owl hawk'd at, and kill'd.

Rosse. And Duncan's horses (a thing most strange
　　　　　　　　and certain),
Beauteous and swift, the minions of their race,
Turn'd wild in nature, broke their stalls, flung out,
Contending 'gainst obedience, as they would make
War with mankind.
Old M.　　　　'T is said, they eat each other.
Rosse. They did so; to th' amazement of mine eyes,
That look'd upon 't. Here comes the good Macduff.—

Enter MACDUFF.

How goes the world, sir, now?
Macd.　　　　　Why, see you not?　21
Rosse. Is 't known, who did this more than bloody
　　　　deed?
Macd. Those that Macbeth hath slain.
Rosse.　　　　　　Alas, the day!
What good could they pretend?
Macd.　　　　　They were suborn'd.
Malcolm, and Donalbain, the king's two sons,
Are stol'n away and fled; which puts upon them
Suspicion of the deed.
Rosse.　　　　'Gainst nature still:
Thriftless ambition, that wilt ravin up
Thine own life's means!—Then 't is most like
The sovereignty will fall upon Macbeth.　30
Macd. He is already nam'd, and gone to Scone
To be invested.
Rosse.　　Where is Duncan's body?
Macd. Carried to Colme-kill,
The sacred storehouse of his predecessors,
And guardian of their bones.
Rosse.　　　　Will you to Scone?
Macd. No, cousin: I'll to Fife.
Rosse.　　　　　Well, I will thither.
Macd. Well, may you see things well done there:—
　　　　adieu!—
Lest our old robes sit easier than our new!
Rosse. Farewell, father.
Old M. God's benison go with you; and with
　　　　those　　　　　　　　　　　　40
That would make good of bad, and friends of foes!
　　　　　　　　　　　　　　[*Exeunt.*

ACT III.

SCENE I.—Fores. A Room in the Palace.

Enter BANQUO.

Banquo.
THOU hast it now, king, Cawdor, Glamis, all,
As the weird woman promis'd; and, I fear,
Thou play'dst most foully for 't; yet it was
　　said,
It should not stand in thy posterity;
But that myself should be the root and
　　father
Of many kings. If there come truth from
　　them,
(As upon thee, Macbeth, their speeches
　　shine,)
Why, by the verities on thee made good,
May they not be my oracles as well,
And set me up in hope? But, hush; no more.　10

Sennet sounded. Enter MACBETH, *as King; Lady*
MACBETH, *as Queen;* LENOX, ROSSE, *Lords and*
Attendants.

Macb. Here's our chief guest.
Lady M.　　　　If he had been forgotten,

It had been as a gap in our great feast,
And all-thing unbecoming.
Macb. To-night we hold a solemn supper, sir,
And I'll request your presence.
Ban.　　　　　Let your highness
Command upon me, to the which my duties
Are with a most indissoluble tie
For ever knit.
Macb. Ride you this afternoon?
Ban.　　　　　Ay, my good lord.
Macb. We should have else desir'd your good advice
(Which still hath been both grave and prosperous)　21
In this day's council; but we'll take to-morrow.
Is 't far you ride?
Ban. As far, my lord, as will fill up the time
'Twixt this and supper: go not my horse the better,
I must become a borrower of the night,
For a dark hour, or twain.
Macb.　　　　Fail not our feast.
Ban. My lord, I will not.
Macb. We hear, our bloody cousins are bestow'd

In England, and in Ireland; not confessing 30
Their cruel parricide, filling their hearers
With strange invention. But of that to-morrow,
When, therewithal, we shall have cause of state,
Craving us jointly. Hie you to horse: adieu,
Till you return at night. Goes Fleance with you?
Ban. Ay, my good lord: our time does call upon 's.
Macb. I wish your horses swift, and sure of foot;
And so I do commend you to their backs.
Farewell.— [*Exit* BANQUO.
Let every man be master of his time 40
Till seven at night, to make society
The sweeter welcome: we will keep ourself
Till supper-time alone: while then, God be with you.
[*Exeunt Lady* MACBETH, *Lords, &c.*
Sirrah, a word with you. Attend those men
Our pleasure?
Atten. They are, my lord, without the palace gate.
Macb. Bring them before us. [*Exit Attendant.*]—
To be thus is nothing,
But to be safely thus.—Our fears in Banquo
Stick deep, and in his royalty of nature
Reigns that which would be fear'd: 'tis much he
dares; 50
And, to that dauntless temper of his mind,
He hath a wisdom that doth guide his valour
To act in safety. There is none but he
Whose being I do fear: and under him
My genius is rebuk'd; as, it is said,
Mark Antony's was by Cæsar. He chid the sisters,
When first they put the name of king upon me,
And bade them speak to him; then, prophet-like,
They hail'd him father to a line of kings.
Upon my head they plac'd a fruitless crown, 60
And put a barren sceptre in my gripe,
Thence to be wrench'd with an unlineal hand,
No son of mine succeeding. If 't be so,
For Banquo's issue have I fil'd my mind;
For them the gracious Duncan have I murder'd;
Put rancours in the vessel of my peace,
Only for them; and mine eternal jewel
Given to the common enemy of man,
To make them kings, the seed of Banquo kings!
Rather than so, come, fate, into the list, 70
And champion me to the utterance!—Who's there?—

Re-enter Attendant, with two Murderers.

Now, go to the door, and stay there till we call.
[*Exit Attendant.*
Was it not yesterday we spoke together?
1 *Mur.* It was, so please your highness.
Macb. Well then, now
Have you consider'd of my speeches? Know,
That it was he, in the times past, which held you
So under fortune, which, you thought, had been
Our innocent self. This I made good to you
In our last conference; pass'd in probation with you,
How you were borne in hand; how cross'd; the
instruments; 80
Who wrought with them; and all things else, that
might,
To half a soul, and to a notion craz'd,
Say, "Thus did Banquo."
1 *Mur.* You made it known to us.
Macb. I did so; and went further, which is now
Our point of second meeting. Do you find
Your patience so predominant in your nature,
That you can let this go? Are you so gospell'd,
To pray for this good man, and for his issue,
Whose heavy hand hath bow'd you to the grave,
And beggar'd yours for ever?
1 *Mur.* We are men, my liege.
Macb. Ay, in the catalogue ye go for men; 91
As hounds and greyhounds, mongrels, spaniels, curs,
Shoughs, water-rugs, and demi-wolves, are clept
All by the name of dogs: the valu'd file
Distinguishes the swift, the slow, the subtle,
The housekeeper, the hunter, every one
According to the gift which bounteous nature
Hath in him clos'd; whereby he does receive
Particular addition, from the bill
That writes them all alike; and so of men. 100

Now, if you have a station in the file,
Not i' the worst rank of manhood, say it;
And I will put that business in your bosoms,
Whose execution takes your enemy off,
Grapples you to the heart and love of us,
Who wear our health but sickly in his life,
Which in his death were perfect.
2 *Mur.* I am one, my liege,
Whom the vile blows and buffets of the world
Have so incens'd, that I am reckless what
I do, to spite the world.
1 *Mur.* And I another, 110
So weary with disasters, tugg'd with fortune,
That I would set my life on any chance,
To mend it, or be rid on 't.
Macb. Both of you
Know, Banquo was your enemy.
2 *Mur.* True, my lord.
Macb. So is he mine; and in such bloody distance,
That every minute of his being thrusts
Against my near'st of life: and though I could
With bare-fac'd power sweep him from my sight,
And bid my will avouch it, yet I must not,
For certain friends that are both mine and mine, 120
Whose loves I may not drop, but wail his fall
Who I myself struck down: and thence it is
That I to your assistance do make love,
Masking the business from the common eye,
For sundry weighty reasons.
2 *Mur.* We shall, my lord,
Perform what you command us.
1 *Mur.* Though our lives—
Macb. Your spirits shine through you. Within this
hour, at most,
I will advise you where to plant yourselves,
Acquaint you with the perfect spy o' the time,
The moment on 't; for 't must be done to-night, 130
And something from the palace; always thought,
That I require a clearness: and with him,
(To leave no rubs, nor botches, in the work,)
Fleance his son, that keeps him company,
Whose absence is no less material to me
Than is his father's, must embrace the fate
Of that dark hour. Resolve yourselves apart;
I 'll come to you anon.
2 *Mur.* We are resolv'd, my lord.
Macb. I 'll call upon you straight: abide within.—
[*Exeunt Murderers.*
It is concluded: Banquo, thy soul's flight, 140
If it find heaven, must find it out to-night. [*Exit.*

SCENE II.—*The Same. Another Room.*

Enter Lady MACBETH *and a Servant.*

Lady M. Is Banquo gone from court?
Serv. Ay, madam, but returns again to-night.
Lady M. Say to the king, I would attend his leisure
For a few words.
Serv. Madam, I will. [*Exit.*
Lady M. Nought's had, all's spent,
Where our desire is got without content:
'T is safer to be that which we destroy,
Than by destruction dwell in doubtful joy.

Enter MACBETH.

How now, my lord? why do you keep alone,
Of sorriest fancies your companions making, 9
Using those thoughts, which should indeed have died
With them they think on? Things without all remedy
Should be without regard: what's done is done.
Macb. We have scotch'd the snake, not kill'd it:
She 'll close, and be herself; whilst our poor malice
Remains in danger of her former tooth.
But let the frame of things disjoint, both the worlds
suffer,
Ere we will eat our meal in fear, and sleep
In the affliction of these terrible dreams,
That shake us nightly. Better be with the dead,
Whom we, to gain our peace, have sent to peace, 20
Than on the torture of the mind to lie

In restless ecstacy. Duncan is in his grave;
After life's fitful fever he sleeps well;
Treason has done his worst: nor steel, nor poison,
Malice domestic, foreign levy, nothing
Can touch him further!
    Lady M.   Come on:
Gentle my lord, sleek o'er your rugged looks;
Be bright and jovial among your guests to-night.
    Macb. So shall I, love; and so, I pray, be you.
Let your remembrance apply to Banquo: 30
Present him eminence, both with eye and tongue:
Unsafe the while, that we
Must lave our honours in these flattering streams,
And make our faces visards to our hearts,
Disguising what they are.
    Lady M.   You must leave this.
    Macb. O! full of scorpions is my mind, dear wife!
Thou know'st that Banquo, and his Fleance, lives.
    Lady M. But in them nature's copy's not eterne.
    Macb. There's comfort yet; they are assailable:
Then be thou jocund. Ere the bat hath flown   40
His cloister'd flight; ere to black Hecate's summons
The shard-borne beetle, with his drowsy hums,
Hath rung night's yawning peal,
There shall be done a deed of dreadful note.
    Lady M. What's to be done?
    Macb. Be innocent of the knowledge, dearest chuck,
Till thou applaud the deed. Come, seeling night,
Scarf up the tender eye of pitiful day,
And, with thy bloody and invisible hand,
Cancel, and tear to pieces, that great bond   50
Which keeps me pale!—Light thickens; and the crow
Makes wing to the rooky wood;
Good things of day begin to droop and drowse,
Whiles night's black agents to their preys do rouse.
Thou marvell'st at my words: but hold thee still;
Things bad begun make strong themselves by ill.
So, pr'ythee, go with me.   [*Exeunt.*

SCENE III.—The Same. A Park, with a Road leading
to the Palace.

Enter three Murderers.

    1 *Mur.* But who did bid thee join with us?
    3 *Mur.*   Macbeth.
    2 *Mur.* He needs not our mistrust; since he delivers
Our offices, and what we have to do,
To the direction just.
    1 *Mur.*   Then stand with us.
The west yet glimmers with some streaks of day:
Now spurs the lated traveller apace,
To gain the timely inn; and near approaches
The subject of our watch.
    3 *Mur.*   Hark! I hear horses.
    Ban. [*Within.*] Give us a light there, ho!
    2 *Mur.*   Then it is he: the rest
That are within the note of expectation,   10
Already are i' the court.
    1 *Mur.*   His horses go about.
    3 *Mur.* Almost a mile; but he does usually,
So all men do, from hence to the palace gate
Make it their walk.

Enter BANQUO, *and* FLEANCE, *with a torch.*

    2 *Mur.* A light, a light!
    3 *Mur.*   'T is he.
    1 *Mur.* Stand to 't.
    Ban. It will be rain to-night.
    1 *Mur.*   Let it come down.
              [*Assaults* BANQUO.
    Ban. O, treachery! Fly, good Fleance, fly, fly, fly!
Thou may'st revenge—O slave!
          [*Dies.* FLEANCE *escapes.*
    3 *Mur.* Who did strike out the light?
    1 *Mur.*   Was 't not the way?
    3 *Mur.* There's but one down: the son is fled.
    2 *Mur.*   We have lost
Best half of our affair.   22
    1 *Mur.* Well, let's away, and say how much is done.
                    [*Exeunt.*

SCENE IV.—A Room of State in the Palace.

A Banquet prepared. Enter MACBETH, *Lady* MAC-
BETH, ROSSE, LENOX, *Lords, and Attendants.*

    Macb. You know your own degrees, sit down: at
        first and last,
The hearty welcome.
    Lords.   Thanks to your majesty.
    Macb. Ourself will mingle with society,
And play the humble host.
Our hostess keeps her state; but, in best time,
We will require her welcome.

    1 *Mur.*   "And near approaches
The subject of our watch."

    Lady M. Pronounce it for me, sir, to all our friends;
For my heart speaks, they are welcome.

Enter first Murderer, to the door.

    Macb. See, they encounter thee with their hearts'
        thanks.
Both sides are even: here I'll sit i' the midst.   10
Be large in mirth; anon, we'll drink a measure
The table round.—There's blood upon thy face.
    Mur. 'T is Banquo's then.
    Macb. 'T is better thee without, than he within.
Is he despatch'd?
    Mur. My lord, his throat is cut; that I did for him.
    Macb. Thou art the best o' the cut-throats; yet he's
      good.
That did the like for Fleance: if thou didst it,
Thou art the nonpareil.
    Mur.   Most royal sir,
Fleance is 'scap'd.   20
    Macb. Then comes my fit again: I had else been
        perfect;
Whole as the marble, founded as the rock,
As broad and general as the casing air:
But now, I am cabin'd, cribb'd, confin'd, bound in
To saucy doubts and fears.—But Banquo's safe?
    Mur. Ay, my good lord, safe in a ditch he bides,
With twenty trenched gashes on his head;
The least a death to nature.
    Macb.   Thanks for that.—
There the grown serpent lies: the worm, that's fled,
Hath nature that in time will venom breed,   30
No teeth for the present.—Get thee gone; to-morrow
We'll hear ourselves again.   [*Exit Murderer.*
    Lady M.   My royal lord,
You do not give the cheer: the feast is sold,
That is not often vouch'd, while 'tis a-making,
'T is given with welcome. To feed were best at home;
From thence, the sauce to meat is ceremony;
Meeting were bare without it.
    Macb.   Sweet remembrancer!—
Now, good digestion wait on appetite,
And health on both!

Len. May it please your highness sit?

The Ghost of BANQUO *enters, and sits in* MACBETH'S
place.

Macb. Here had we now our country's honour
roof'd, 40
Were the grac'd person of our Banquo present;
Who may I rather challenge for unkindness,
Than pity for mischance!
Rosse. His absence, sir,
Lays blame upon his promise. Please it your high-
ness
To grace us with your royal company?
Macb. The table's full.
Len. Here is a place reserv'd, sir.
Macb. Where?
Len. Here, my good lord. What is 't that moves
your highness?
Macb. Which of you have done this?
Lords. What, my good lord?
Macb. Thou canst not say, I did it : never shake 50
Thy gory locks at me.
Rosse. Gentlemen, rise ; his highness is not well.
Lady M. Sit, worthy friends. My lord is often
thus,
And hath been from his youth : pray you, keep seat;
The fit is momentary ; upon a thought
He will again be well. If much you note him,
You shall offend him, and extend his passion ;
Feed, and regard him not.—Are you a man?
Macb. Ay, and a bold one, that dare look on that
Which might appal the devil.
Lady M. O proper stuff! 60
This is the very painting of your fear:
This is the air-drawn dagger, which, you said,
Led you to Duncan. O! these flaws, and starts,
(Impostors to true fear,) would well become
A woman's story at a winter's fire,
Authoris'd by her grandam. Shame itself!
Why do you make such faces? When all 's done,
You look but on a stool.
Macb. Pr'ythee, see there! behold! look! lo! how
say you?—
Why, what care I? If thou canst nod, speak too.— 70
If charnel-houses, and our graves, must send
Those that we bury, back, our monuments
Shall be the maws of kites. [*Ghost disappears.*
Lady M. What! quite unmann'd in folly?
Macb. If I stand here, I saw him.
Lady M. Fie! for shame!
Macb. Blood hath been shed ere now, i' th' olden
time,
Ere human statute purg'd the gentle weal;
Ay, and since too, murders have been perform'd
Too terrible for the ear : the time has been,
That, when the brains were out, the man would die,
And there an end ; but now, they rise again, 80
With twenty mortal murders on their crowns,
And push us from our stools. This is more strange
Than such a murder is.
Lady M. My worthy lord,·
Your noble friends do lack you.
Macb. I do forget.—
Do not muse at me, my most worthy friends;
I have a strange infirmity, which is nothing
To those that know me. Come, love and health to all;
Then, I 'll sit down.—Give me some wine : fill full :—
I drink to the general joy of the whole table,
And to our dear friend Banquo, whom we miss ; 90
'Would he were here! to all, and him, we thirst,
And all to all.
Lords. Our duties, and the pledge.

Re-enter Ghost.

Macb. Avaunt! and quit my sight! Let the earth
hide thee!
Thy bones are marrowless, thy blood is cold ;
Thou hast no speculation in those eyes,
Which thou dost glare with.
Lady M. Think of this, good peers,
But as a thing of custom : 't is no other ;
Only it spoils the pleasure of the time.

Macb. What man dare, I dare:
Approach thou like the rugged Russian bear, 100
The arm'd rhinoceros, or the Hyrcan tiger ;
Take any shape but that, and my firm nerves
Shall never tremble : or, be alive again,
And dare me to the desert with thy sword ;
If trembling I inhabit then, protest me
The baby of a girl. Hence, horrible shadow!
Unreal mockery, hence! [*Ghost disappears.*]—Why,
so ;—being gone,
I am a man again.—Pray you, sit still.
Lady M. You have displaced the mirth, broke the
good meeting,
With most admir'd disorder.
Macb. Can such things be, 110
And overcome us like a summer's cloud,
Without our special wonder? You make me strange
Even to the disposition that I owe,
When now I think you can behold such sights,
And keep the natural ruby of your cheeks,
When mine is blanch'd with fear.
Rosse. What sights, my lord?
Lady M. I pray you, speak not : he grows worse
and worse ;
Question enrages him. At once, good night :—
Stand not upon the order of your going,
But go at once.
Len. Good night, and better health 120
Attend his majesty!
Lady M. A kind good night to all!
[*Exeunt Lords and Attendants.*
Macb. It will have blood, they say ; blood will have
blood :
Stones have been known to move, and trees to speak;
Augurs, and understood relations, have
By magot-pies, and choughs, and rooks, brought forth
The secret'st man of blood.—What is the night?
Lady M. Almost at odds with morning, which is
which.
Macb. How say'st thou, that Macduff denies his
person,
At our great bidding?
Lady M. Did you send to him, sir?
Macb. I hear it by the way ; but I will send. 130
There 's not a one of them, but in his house
I keep a servant fee'd. I will to-morrow
(And betimes I will) to the weird sisters :
More shall they speak ; for now I am bent to know,
By the worst means, the worst. For mine own good,
All causes shall give way : I am in blood
Stepp'd in so far, that, should I wade no more,
Returning were as tedious as go o'er.
Strange things I have in head, that will to hand,
Which must be acted, ere they may be scann'd. 140
Lady M. You lack the season of all natures, sleep.
Macb. Come, we 'll to sleep. My strange and self-
abuse
Is the initiate fear, that wants hard use :
We are yet but young in deed. [*Exeunt.*

SCENE V.—The Heath.

Thunder. Enter the three Witches, meeting HECATE.

1 *Witch.* Why, how now, Hecate? you look angerly.
Hec. Have I not reason, beldams as you are,
Saucy, and overbold? How did you dare
To trade and traffic with Macbeth,
In riddles, and affairs of death ;
And I, the mistress of your charms,
The close contriver of all harms,
Was never call'd to bear my part,
Or show the glory of our art?
And, which is worse, all you have done 10
Hath been but for a wayward son,
Spiteful, and wrathful ; who, as others do,
Loves for his own ends, not for you.
But make amends now : get you gone,
And at the pit of Acheron
Meet me i' the morning : thither he
Will come to know his destiny.

Your vessels, and your spells, provide,
Your charms, and everything beside.
I am for the air; this night I 'll spend   20
Unto a dismal and a fatal end:

His hopes 'bove wisdom, grace, and fear;
And you all know, security
Is mortals' chiefest enemy.
   [*Song, within:* "*Come away, come away,*" &c.

Macb. "Avaunt! and quit my sight! Let the earth hide thee!
Thy bones are marrowless, thy blood is cold;
Thou hast no speculation in those eyes,
Which thou dost glare with."

Great business must be wrought ere noon.
Upon the corner of the moon
There hangs a vaporous drop profound;
I 'll catch it ere it come to ground:
And that, distill'd by magic sleights,
Shall raise such artificial sprites,
As, by the strength of their illusion,
Shall draw him on to his confusion.
He shall spurn fate, scorn death, and bear   30

Hark! I am call'd: my little spirit, see,
Sits in a foggy cloud, and stays for me.   [*Exit.*
1 *Witch.* Come, let 's make haste: she 'll soon be
    back again.   ———   [*Exeunt.*

SCENE VI.—Fores. A Room in the Palace.

Enter LENOX *and another Lord.*

Len. My former speeches have but hit your thoughts,

Which can interpret further : only, I say,
Things have been strangely borne.   The gracious
     Duncan
Was pitied of Macbeth :—marry, he was dead :—
And the right-valiant Banquo walk'd too late ;
Whom, you may say, if 't please you, Fleance kill'd,
For Fleance fled.   Men must not walk too late.
Who cannot want the thought, how monstrous
It was for Malcolm, and for Donalbain,
To kill their gracious father ? damned fact !   10
How it did grieve Macbeth ! did he not straight,
In pious rage, the two delinquents tear,
That were the slaves of drink, and thralls of sleep ?
Was not that nobly done ? Ay, and wisely too ;
For 't would have anger'd any heart alive
To hear the men deny it. So that, I say,
He has borne all things well : and I do think,
That, had he Duncan's sons under his key,
(As, an 't please Heaven, he shall not,) they should
     find
What 't were to kill a father ; so should Fleance.   20
But, peace !—for from broad words, and 'cause he
     fail'd
His presence at the tyrant's feast, I hear,
Macduff lives in disgrace. Sir, can you tell
Where he bestows himself ?
     Lord.   The son of Duncan,
From whom this tyrant holds the due of birth,

Lives in the English court ; and is receiv'd
Of the most pious Edward with such grace,
That the malevolence of fortune nothing
Takes from his high respect.   Thither Macduff
Is gone to pray the holy king, upon his aid   30
To wake Northumberland, and warlike Siward ;
That, by the help of these, (with Him above
To ratify the work,) we may again
Give to our tables meat, sleep to our nights,
Free from our feasts and banquets bloody knives,
Do faithful homage, and receive free honours,
All which we pine for now.   And this report
Hath so exasperate the king, that he
Prepares for some attempt of war.
     Len.   Sent he to Macduff ?
     Lord. He did : and with an absolute " Sir, not I," 40
The cloudy messenger turns me his back,
And hums, as who should say, " You 'll rue the
     time
That clogs me with this answer."
     Len.   And that well might
Advise him to a caution, to hold what distance
His wisdom can provide. Some holy angel
Fly to the court of England, and unfold
His message ere he come, that a swift blessing
May soon return to this our suffering country
Under a hand accurs'd !
     Lord.   I 'll send my prayers with him.
                                          [Exeunt.

ACT IV.

Scene I.—A Dark Cave.   In the middle, a boiling Cauldron.

Thunder.   Enter the three Witches.

      1 *Witch.*
THRICE the brinded cat hath mew'd.
     2 *Witch.* Thrice and once the hedge-pig
whin'd.
     3 *Witch.* Harpier cries :—'T is time, 't is
time.
     1 *Witch.* Round about the cauldron go ;
In the poison'd entrails throw.—
Toad, that under cold stone
Days and nights has thirty-one
Swelter'd venom, sleeping got,
Boil thou first i' the charmed pot.
     All. Double, double toil and trouble : 10
Fire, burn ; and, cauldron, bubble.
     2 *Witch.* Fillet of a fenny snake,
In the cauldron boil and bake ;
Eye of newt, and toe of frog,
Wool of bat, and tongue of dog,
Adder's fork, and blind-worm's sting,
Lizard's leg, and howlet's wing,
For a charm of powerful trouble,
Like a hell-broth boil and bubble.
     All. Double, double toil and trouble :   20
Fire, burn ; and, cauldron, bubble.
     3 *Witch.* Scale of dragon, tooth of wolf ;
Witches' mummy ; maw, and gulf,
Of the ravin'd salt-sea shark ;
Root of hemlock, digg'd i' the dark ;
Liver of blaspheming Jew ;
Gall of goat, and slips of yew,
Sliver'd in the moon's eclipse ;
Nose of Turk, and Tartar's lips ;
Finger of birth-strangled babe,   30
Ditch-deliver'd by a drab,
Make the gruel thick and slab :

Add thereto a tiger's chaudron,
For the ingredients of our cauldron.
     All. Double, double toil and trouble :
Fire, burn ; and, cauldron, bubble.
     2 *Witch.* Cool it with a baboon's blood ;
Then the charm is firm and good.

Enter Hecate.

     Hec. O, well done ! I commend your pains,
And every one shall share i' the gains.   40
     And now about the cauldron sing,
Like elves and fairies in a ring,
Enchanting all that you put in.
          [*Music and a Song, "Black spirits," &c.*
     2 *Witch.* By the pricking of my thumbs,
Something wicked this way comes.—   [*Knocking.*
Open, locks,
Whoever knocks.

Enter Macbeth.

     Macb. How now, you secret, black, and midnight
     hags !
What is 't you do ?
     All.   A deed without a name.
     Macb. I conjure you, by that which you profess,   50
Howe'er you come to know it, answer me :
Though you untie the winds, and let them fight
Against the churches ; though the yesty waves
Confound and swallow navigation up ;
Though bladed corn be lodg'd, and trees blown down ;
Though castles topple on their warders' heads ;
Though palaces, and pyramids, do slope
Their heads to their foundations ; though the treasure
Of nature's germen tumble all together,
Even till destruction sicken, answer me   60
To what I ask you.

1 *Witch.*   Speak.
2 *Witch.*   Demand.
3 *Witch.*   We 'll answer.
1 *Witch.* Say, if thou 'dst rather hear it from our
    mouths,
Or from our masters?
  Macb.   Call 'em; let me see 'em.
    1 *Witch.* Pour in sow's blood, that hath eaten
Her nine farrow; grease, that 's sweaten
From the murderer's gibbet, throw
Into the flame.
  All.   Come, high, or low;
Thyself, and office, deftly show.

Thunder. First Apparition, an armed Head.

Macb. Tell me, thou unknown power,—
  1 *Witch.*   He knows thy thought:
Hear his speech, but say thou nought.   70
  1 *App.* Macbeth! Macbeth! Macbeth! beware
    Macduff;
Beware the thane of Fife.—Dismiss me.—Enough.
                              [*Descends.*
Macb. Whate'er thou art, for thy good caution,
    thanks:
Thou hast harp'd my fear aright.—But one word
    more:—
  1 *Witch.* He will not be commanded. Here 's
    another,
More potent than the first.

Thunder. Second Apparition, a bloody Child.

2 *App.* Macbeth! Macbeth! Macbeth!—
Macb. Had I three ears, I 'd hear thee.
  2 *App.* Be bloody, bold, and resolute: laugh to scorn
The power of man, for none of woman born   80
Shall harm Macbeth.   [*Descends.*
Macb. Then live, Macduff: what need I fear of thee?
But yet I 'll make assurance double sure,
And take a bond of fate: thou shalt not live;
That I may tell pale-hearted fear it lies,
And sleep in spite of thunder.—

*Thunder. Third Apparition, a Child crowned,
    with a tree in his hand.*

                    What is this,
That rises like the issue of a king;
And wears upon his baby brow the round
And top of sovereignty?
  All.   Listen, but speak not to 't.
  3 *App.* Be lion-mettled, proud, and take no care 90
Who chafes, who frets, or where conspirers are:
Macbeth shall never vanquish'd be, until
Great Birnam wood to high Dunsinane hill
Shall come against him.   [*Descends.*
Macb.   That will never be:
Who can impress the forest; bid the tree
Unfix his earth-bound root? Sweet bodements!
    good!
Rebellious head, rise never, till the wood
Of Birnam rise; and our high-plac'd Macbeth
Shall live the lease of nature, pay his breath
To time, and mortal custom.—Yet my heart   100
Throbs to know one thing: tell me (if your art
Can tell so much), shall Banquo's issue ever
Reign in this kingdom?
  All.   Seek to know no more.
Macb. I will be satisfied: deny me this,
And an eternal curse fall on you! Let me know.—
Why sinks that cauldron? and what noise is this?
                              [*Hautboys.*
1 *Witch.* Show!
2 *Witch.* Show!
3 *Witch.* Show!
All. Show his eyes, and grieve his heart;   110
Come like shadows, so depart.

*A show of eight Kings, the last with a glass in his
    hand; BANQUO following.*

Macb. Thou art too like the spirit of Banquo: down!
Thy crown does sear mine eye-balls:—and thy hair,
Thou other gold-bound brow, is like the first:—
A third is like the former:—filthy hags!

Why do you show me this?—A fourth?—Start, eyes!
What! will the line stretch out to the crack of doom?
Another yet?—A seventh?—I 'll see no more:—
And yet the eighth appears, who bears a glass,
Which shows me many more; and some I see,   120
That two-fold balls and treble scepters carry.
Horrible sight!—Now, I see, 't is true;
For the blood-bolter'd Banquo smiles upon me,
And points at them for his.—What! is this so?
  1 *Witch.* Ay, sir, all this is so:—but why
Stands Macbeth thus amazedly?—
Come, sisters, cheer we up his sprites,
And show the best of our delights.
I 'll charm the air to give a sound,
While you perform your antick round;   130
That this great king may kindly say,
Our duties did his welcome pay.
          [*Music. The Witches dance, and vanish.*
Macb. Where are they? Gone?—Let this pernicious
    hour
Stand aye accursed in the calendar!—
Come in, without there!

Enter LENOX.

  Len.   What 's your grace's will?
Macb. Saw you the weird sisters?
  Len.   No, my lord.
Macb. Came they not by you?
  Len.   No, indeed, my lord.
Macb. Infected be the air whereon they ride,
And damn'd all those that trust them!—I did hear
The galloping of horse: who was 't came by?   140
  Len. 'T is two or three, my lord, that bring you
    word,
Macduff is fled to England.
  Macb.   Fled to England?
  Len. Ay, my good lord.
  Macb. Time, thou anticipat'st my dread exploits:
The flighty purpose never is o'ertook,
Unless the deed go with it. From this moment,
The very firstlings of my heart shall be
The firstlings of my hand. And even now,
To crown my thoughts with acts, be it thought and
    done:
The castle of Macduff I will surprise;   150
Seize upon Fife; give to the edge o' the sword
His wife, his babes, and all unfortunate souls
That trace him in his line. No boasting like a fool;
This deed I 'll do, before this purpose cool:
But no more sights!—Where are these gentlemen?
Come, bring me where they are.   [*Exeunt.*

SCENE II.—Fife. A Room in MACDUFF's Castle.

Enter Lady MACDUFF, her Son, and ROSSE.

L. Macd. What had he done, to make him fly the
    land?
Rosse. You must have patience, madam.
L. Macd.   He had none:
His flight was madness: when our actions do not,
Our fears do make us traitors.
  Rosse.   You know not,
Whether it was his wisdom, or his fear.
L. Macd. Wisdom! to leave his wife, to leave his
    babes,
His mansion, and his titles, in a place
From whence himself does fly? He loves us not:
He wants the natural touch; for the poor wren,
The most diminutive of birds, will fight,   10
Her young ones in her nest, against the owl.
All is the fear, and nothing is the love;
As little is the wisdom, where the flight
So runs against all reason.
  Rosse.   My dearest coz,
I pray you, school yourself: but, for your husband,
He is noble, wise, judicious, and best knows
The fits o' the season. I dare not speak much further:
But cruel are the times, when we are traitors,
And do not know ourselves; when we hold rumour
From what we fear, yet know not what we fear,   20

But float upon a wild and violent sea,
Each way, and move.—I take my leave of you:
Shall not be long but I'll be here again.
Things at the worst will cease, or else climb upward
To what they were before.—My pretty cousin,
Blessing upon you!
   L. Macd. Father'd he is, and yet he's fatherless.
   Rosse. I am so much a fool, should I stay longer,
It would be my disgrace, and your discomfort:
I take my leave at once.   [*Exit.*
   L. Macd.   Sirrah, your father's dead : 30
And what will you do now? How will you live?
   Son. As birds do, mother.
   L. Macd.   What, with worms and flies?
   Son. With what I get, I mean; and so do they.

Son. "Was my father a traitor, mother?"

   L. Macd. Poor bird! thou'dst never fear the net,
nor lime,
The pit-fall, nor the gin.
   Son. Why should I, mother? Poor birds they are
not set for.
My father is not dead, for all your saying.
   L. Macd. Yes, he is dead : how wilt thou do for a
father?
   Son. Nay, how will you do for a husband?
   L. Macd. Why, I can buy me twenty at any market.
   Son. Then you'll buy 'em to sell again.   41
   L. Macd. Thou speak'st with all thy wit;
And yet, i' faith, with wit enough for thee.
   Son. Was my father a traitor, mother?
   L. Macd. Ay, that he was.
   Son. What is a traitor?
   L. Macd. Why, one that swears and lies.
   Son. And be all traitors that do so?
   L. Macd. Every one that does so is a traitor, and
must be hanged.   50
   Son. And must they all be hanged that swear and
lie?
   L. Macd. Every one.
   Son. Who must hang them?
   L. Macd. Why, the honest men.
   Son. Then the liars and swearers are fools; for
there are liars and swearers enough to beat the
honest men, and hang up them.
   L. Macd. Now God help thee, poor monkey! But
how wilt thou do for a father?   60
   Son. If he were dead, you'd weep for him : if you
would not, it were a good sign that I should quickly
have a new father.
   L. Macd. Poor prattler, how thou talk'st!

Enter a Messenger.

   Mess. Bless you, fair dame! I am not to you known,

Though in your state of honour I am perfect.
I doubt, some danger does approach you nearly:
If you will take a homely man's advice,
Be not found here ; hence, with your little ones.
To fright you thus, methinks, I am too savage ;   70
To do worse to you were fell cruelty,
Which is too nigh your person. Heaven preserve you!
I dare abide no longer.   [*Exit.*
   L. Macd. Whither should I fly?
I have done no harm. But I remember now
I am in this earthly world, where, to do harm,
Is often laudable ; to do good, sometime,
Accounted dangerous folly : why then, alas!
Do I put up that womanly defence,
To say, I have done no harm? What are these faces?

            Enter Murderers.

   Mur. Where is your husband?   80
   L. Macd. I hope, in no place so unsanctified,
Where such as thou may'st find him.
   Mur.   He's a traitor.
   Son. Thou liest, thou shag-hair'd villain!
   Mur.   What, you egg! [*Stabbing him.*
Young fry of treachery!
   Son. He has kill'd me, mother ; run away, I pray
you.   [*Dies.*
   [*Exit Lady* Macduff, *crying "Murder!"*
   and pursued by the Murderers.

Scene III.—England. A Room in the King's Palace.

         Enter Malcolm *and* Macduff.

   Mal. Let us seek out some desolate shade, and
there
Weep our sad bosoms empty.
   Macd.   Let us rather
Hold fast the mortal sword, and like good men
Bestride our down-fall'n birthdom. Each new morn,
New widows howl, new orphans cry ; new sorrows
Strike heaven on the face, that it resounds
As if it felt with Scotland, and yell'd out
Like syllable of dolour.
   Mal.   What I believe, I'll wail ;
What know, believe ; and what I can redress,
As I shall find the time to friend, I will.   10
What you have spoke, it may be so, perchance.
This tyrant, whose sole name blisters our tongues,
Was once thought honest : you have lov'd him well ;
He hath not touch'd you yet. I am young ; but some-
thing
You may deserve of him through me, and wisdom
To offer up a weak, poor, innocent lamb,
To appease an angry God.
   Macd. I am not treacherous.
   Mal.   But Macbeth is.
A good and virtuous nature may recoil,
In an imperial charge. But I shall crave your pardon :
That which you are my thoughts cannot transpose ; 21
Angels are bright still, though the brightest fell :
Though all things foul would wear the brows of
grace,
Yet grace must still look so.
   Macd.   I have lost my hopes.
   Mal. Perchance even there where I did find my
doubts.
Why in that rawness left you wife and child,
(Those precious motives, those strong knots of love,)
Without leave-taking?—I pray you,
Let not my jealousies be your dishonours,
But mine own safeties : you may be rightly just, 30
Whatever I shall think.
   Macd.   Bleed, bleed, poor country!
Great tyranny, lay thou thy basis sure,
For goodness dare not check thee! wear thou thy
wrongs ;
The title is affeer'd!—Fare thee well, lord :
I would not be the villain that thou think'st
For the whole space that's in the tyrant's grasp,
And the rich East to boot.
   Mal.   Be not offended :

I speak not as in absolute fear of you.
I think our country sinks beneath the yoke ;
It weeps, it bleeds ; and each new day a gash   40
Is added to her wounds : I think, withal,
There would be hands uplifted in my right ;
And here, from gracious England, have I offer
Of goodly thousands : but, for all this,
When I shall tread upon the tyrant's head,
Or wear it on my sword, yet my poor country
Shall have more vices than it had before,
More suffer, and more sundry ways than ever,
By him that shall succeed.
     Macd.   What should he be ?
     Mal. It is myself I mean ; in whom I know   50
All the particulars of vice so grafted,
That, when they shall be open'd, black Macbeth
Will seem as pure as snow ; and the poor state
Esteem him as a lamb, being compar'd
With my confineless harms.
     Macd.   Not in the legions
Of horrid hell can come a devil more damn'd
In evils, to top Macbeth.
     Mal.   I grant him bloody,
Luxurious, avaricious, false, deceitful,
Sudden, malicious, smacking of every sin
That has a name ; but there 's no bottom, none,   60
In my voluptuousness : your wives, your daughters,
Your matrons, and your maids, could not fill up
The cistern of my lust ; and my desire
All continent impediments would o'erbear,
That did oppose my will : better Macbeth,
Than such a one to reign.
     Macd.   Boundless intemperance
In nature is a tyranny ; it hath been
The untimely emptying of the happy throne,
And fall of many kings. But fear not yet
To take upon you what is yours : you may   70
Convey your pleasures in a spacious plenty,
And yet seem cold, the time you may so hoodwink.
We have willing dames enough ; there cannot be
That vulture in you, to devour so many
As will to greatness dedicate themselves,
Finding it so inclin'd.
     Mal.   With this, there grows
In my most ill-compos'd affection such
A stanchless avarice, that, were I king,
I should cut off the nobles for their lands ;
Desire his jewels, and this other's house :   80
And my more-having would be as a sauce
To make me hunger more ; that I should forge
Quarrels unjust against the good and loyal,
Destroying them for wealth.
     Macd.   This avarice
Sticks deeper, grows with more pernicious root
Than summer-seeming lust ; and it hath been
The sword of our slain kings : yet do not fear ;
Scotland hath foisons to fill up your will,
Of your mere own. All these are portable,
With other graces weigh'd.   90
     Mal. But I have none : the king-becoming graces,
As justice, verity, temperance, stableness,
Bounty, perseverance, mercy, lowliness,
Devotion, patience, courage, fortitude,
I have no relish of them ; but abound
In the division of each several crime,
Acting it many ways. Nay, had I power, I should
Pour the sweet milk of concord into hell,
Uproar the universal peace, confound
All unity on earth.
     Macd.   O Scotland, Scotland !   100
     Mal. If such a one be fit to govern, speak :
I am as I have spoken.
     Macd.   Fit to govern !
No, not to live.—O nation miserable,
With an untitled tyrant bloody-scepter'd,
When shalt thou see thy wholesome days again,
Since that the truest issue of thy throne
By his own interdiction stands accurs'd,
And does blaspheme his breed ? Thy royal father
Was a most sainted king : the queen, that bore thee,
Oft'ner upon her knees than on her feet,   110
Died every day she liv'd. Fare thee well !

These evils thou repeat'st upon thyself
Have banish'd me from Scotland.—O my breast,
Thy hope ends here !
     Mal.   Macduff, this noble passion,
Child of integrity, hath from my soul
Wip'd the black scruples, reconcil'd my thoughts
To thy good truth and honour. Devilish Macbeth
By many of these trains hath sought to win me
Into his power, and modest wisdom plucks me
From over-credulous haste : but God above   120
Deal between thee and me ! for even now
I put myself to thy direction, and
Unspeak mine own detraction ; here abjure
The taints and blames I laid upon myself,
For strangers to my nature. I am yet
Unknown to woman ; never was forsworn ;
Scarcely have coveted what was mine own ;
At no time broke my faith : would not betray
The devil to his fellow ; and delight
No less in truth, than life : my first false speaking 130
Was this upon myself. What I am truly,
Is thine, and my poor country's, to command :
Whither, indeed, before thy here-approach,
Old Siward, with ten thousand warlike men,
Already at a point, was setting forth.
Now, we 'll together, and the chance of goodness
Be like our warranted quarrel. Why are you silent ?
     Macd. Such welcome and unwelcome things at
            once,
'T is hard to reconcile.

           Enter a Doctor.

     Mal. Well ; more anon.—Comes the king forth, I
       pray you ?   140
     Doct. Ay, sir ; there are a crew of wretched souls,
That stay his cure : their malady convinces
The great assay of art ; but at his touch,
Such sanctity hath Heaven given his hand,
They presently amend.
     Mal.   I thank you, doctor. [*Exit Doctor.*
     Macd. What 's the disease he means ?
     Mal.   'T is call'd the evil :
A most miraculous work in this good king,
Which often, since my here-remain in England,
I have seen him do. How he solicits Heaven,
Himself best knows ; but strangely-visited people, 150
All swoln and ulcerous, pitiful to the eye,
The mere despair of surgery, he cures ;
Hanging a golden stamp about their necks,
Put on with holy prayers ; and 't is spoken,
To the succeeding royalty he leaves
The healing benediction. With this strange virtue,
He hath a heavenly gift of prophecy ;
And sundry blessings hang about his throne,
That speak him full of grace.

           Enter ROSSE.

     Macd.   See, who comes here ?
     Mal. My countryman ; but yet I know him not. 160
     Macd. My ever-gentle cousin, welcome hither.
     Mal. I know him now. Good God, betimes remove
The means that makes us strangers !
     Rosse.   Sir, Amen.
     Macd. Stands Scotland where it did ?
     Rosse.   Alas, poor country !
Almost afraid to know itself. It cannot
Be call'd our mother, but our grave ; where nothing,
But who knows nothing, is once seen to smile ;
Where sighs, and groans, and shrieks that rent the
            air,
Are made, not mark'd ; where violent sorrow seems
A modern ecstacy : the dead man's knell   170
Is there scarce ask'd for who ; and good men's lives
Expire before the flowers in their caps,
Dying or ere they sicken.
     Macd.   O relation,
Too nice, and yet too true !
     Mal.   What is the newest grief ?
     Rosse. That of an hour's age doth hiss the speaker ;
Each minute teems a new one.
     Macd. How does my wife ?
     Rosse.   Why, well.

Macd. And all my children?
Rosse. Well too.
Macd. The tyrant has not batter'd at their peace?
Rosse. No ; they were well at peace, when I did
leave them. 180
Macd. Be not a niggard of your speech : how goes it?
Rosse. When I came hither to transport the tidings,
Which I have heavily borne, there ran a rumour
Of many worthy fellows that were out ;
Which was to my belief witness'd the rather,
For that I saw the tyrant's power afoot.
Now is the time of help. Your eye in Scotland
Would create soldiers, make our women fight,
To doff their dire distresses.
Mal. Be 't their comfort,
We are coming thither. Gracious England hath 190
Lent us good Siward, and ten thousand men ;
An older, and a better soldier, none
That Christendom gives out.
Rosse. 'Would I could answer
This comfort with the like ! But I have words,
That would be howl'd out in the desert air,
Where hearing should not latch them.
Macd. What concern they?
The general cause? or is it a fee-grief,
Due to some single breast?
Rosse. No mind that 's honest
But in it shares some woe, though the main part
Pertains to you alone.
Macd. If it be mine, 200
Keep it not from me ; quickly let me have it.
Rosse. Let not your ears despise my tongue for ever,
Which shall possess them with the heaviest sound,
That ever yet they heard.
Macd. Humph ! I guess at it.
Rosse. Your castle is surpris'd ; your wife, and babes,
Savagely slaughter'd : to relate the manner,
Were, on the quarry of these murder'd deer,
To add the death of you.
Mal. Merciful Heaven !—

What, man ! ne'er pull your hat upon your brows :
Give sorrow words ; the grief, that does not speak, 210
Whispers the o'er-fraught heart, and bids it break.
Macd. My children too?
Rosse. Wife, children, servants, all
That could be found.
Macd. And I must be from thence !
My wife kill'd too?
Rosse. I have said.
Mal. Be comforted :
Let 's make us medicines of our great revenge,
To cure this deadly grief.
Macd. He has no children.—All my pretty ones?
Did you say, all?—O hell-kite !—All?
What, all my pretty chickens, and their dam,
At one fell swoop? 220
Mal. Dispute it like a man.
Macd. I shall do so ;
But I must also feel it as a man :
I cannot but remember such things were,
That were most precious to me.—Did Heaven look on,
And would not take their part? Sinful Macduff !
They were all struck for thee. Naught that I am,
Not for their own demerits, but for mine,
Fell slaughter on their souls. Heaven rest them now !
Mal. Be this the whetstone of your sword : let grief
Convert to anger ; blunt not the heart, enrage it. 230
Macd. O ! I could play the woman with mine eyes,
And braggart with my tongue.—But, gentle heavens,
Cut short all intermission ; front to front,
Bring thou this fiend of Scotland, and myself ;
Within my sword's length set him ; if he 'scape,
Heaven forgive him too !
Mal. This tune goes manly.
Come, go we to the king : our power is ready ;
Our lack is nothing but our leave. Macbeth
Is ripe for shaking, and the powers above
Put on their instruments. Receive what cheer you
may ; 240
The night is long that never finds the day. [*Exeunt.*

ACT V.

Scene I.—Dunsinane. A Room in the Castle.

Enter a Doctor of Physic and a waiting Gentlewoman.

Doctor.
HAVE two nights watched with you, but
can perceive no truth in your report. When
was it she last walked?
Gent. Since his majesty went into the
field, I have seen her rise from her bed,
throw her night-gown upon her, unlock
her closet, take forth paper, fold it, write
upon it, read it, afterwards seal it, and
again return to bed ; yet all this while in a
most fast sleep. 10
Doct. A great perturbation in nature, to
receive at once the benefit of sleep, and do
the effects of watching. In this slumbery
agitation, besides her walking and other
actual performances, what, at any time,
have you heard her say?
Gent. That, sir, which I will not report after her.
Doct. You may, to me ; and 't is most meet you
should.
Gent. Neither to you, nor any one ; having no
witness to confirm my speech. 21

Enter Lady MACBETH, *with a taper.*

Lo you ! here she comes. This is her very guise ; and,
upon my life, fast asleep. Observe her : stand close.
Doct. How came she by that light?
Gent. Why, it stood by her : she has light by her
continually ; 't is her command.
Doct. You see, her eyes are open.
Gent. Ay, but their sense' are shut.
Doct. What is it she does now? Look, how she rubs
her hands. 30
Gent. It is an accustomed action with her, to seem
thus washing her hands. I have known her continue
in this a quarter of an hour.
Lady M. Yet here 's a spot.
Doct. Hark ! she speaks. I will set down what
comes from her, to satisfy my remembrance the more
strongly.
Lady M. Out, damned spot ! out, I say !—One ; two :
why, then 't is time to do 't.—Hell is murky !—Fie, my
lord, fie ! a soldier, and afeard?—What need we fear
who knows it, when none can call our power to

account?—Yet who would have thought the old man
to have had so much blood in him?   43
  Doct. Do you mark that?
  Lady M. The thane of Fife had a wife: where is
she now?—What, will these hands ne'er be clean?—No
more o' that, my lord, no more o' that: you mar all
with this starting.
  Doct. Go to, go to: you have known what you
should not.   50
  Gent. She has spoke what she should not, I am sure
of that: Heaven knows what she has known.
  Lady M. Here's the smell of the blood still: all the
perfumes of Arabia will not sweeten this little hand.
Oh! oh! oh!
  Doct. What a sigh is there! The heart is sorely
charged.
  Gent. I would not have such a heart in my bosom,
for the dignity of the whole body.
  Doct. Well, well, well.   60
  Gent. 'Pray God, it be, sir.
  Doct. This disease is beyond my practice: yet I have
known those which have walked in their sleep, who
have died holily in their beds.
  Lady M. Wash your hands, put on your night-
gown; look not so pale.—I tell you yet again, Banquo's
buried: he cannot come out on's grave.
  Doct. Even so?   68
  Lady M. To bed, to bed: there's knocking at the
gate. Come, come, come, come, give me your hand.
What's done cannot be undone. To bed, to bed, to
bed.   [*Exit.*
  Doct. Will she go now to bed?
  Gent. Directly.
  Doct. Foul whisperings are abroad. Unnatural
                                                    deeds
Do breed unnatural troubles: infected minds
To their deaf pillows will discharge their secrets.
More needs she the divine than the physician.—
God, God, forgive us all! Look after her;
Remove from her the means of all annoyance,   80
And still keep eyes upon her.—So, good night:
My mind she has mated, and amaz'd my sight.
I think, but dare not speak.
  Gent.   Good night, good doctor. [*Exeunt.*

SCENE II.—The Country near Dunsinane.

Enter, with drum and colours, MENTETH, CATHNESS,
             ANGUS, LENOX, *and Soldiers.*

  Ment. The English power is near, led on by Malcolm,
His uncle Siward, and the good Macduff.
Revenges burn in them; for their dear causes
Would, to the bleeding and the grim alarm,
Excite the mortified man.
  Ang.   Near Birnam wood
Shall we well meet them: that way are they coming.
  Cath. Who knows if Donalbain be with his brother?
  Len. For certain, sir, he is not. I have a file
Of all the gentry: there is Siward's son,
And many unrough youths, that even now   10
Protest their first of manhood.
  Ment.   What does the tyrant?
  Cath. Great Dunsinane he strongly fortifies.
Some say he's mad; others, that lesser hate him,
Do call it valiant fury: but, for certain,
He cannot buckle his distemper'd cause
Within the belt of rule.
  Ang.   Now does he feel
His secret murders sticking on his hands;
Now minutely revolts upbraid his faith-breach:
Those he commands move only in command,
Nothing in love: now does he feel his title   20
Hang loose about him, like a giant's robe
Upon a dwarfish thief.
  Ment.   Who then shall blame
His pester'd senses to recoil and start,
When all that is within him does condemn
Itself, for being there?
  Cath.   Well; march we on,
To give obedience where 't is truly ow'd:

Meet we the medicine of the sickly weal;
And with him pour we, in our country's purge,
Each drop of us.
  Len.   Or so much as it needs
To dew the sovereign flower, and drown the weeds. 30
Make we our march towards Birnam.
                                   [*Exeunt, marching.*

SCENE III.—Dunsinane. A Room in the Castle.

  Enter MACBETH, *Doctor, and Attendants.*

  Macb. Bring me no more reports; let them fly all:
Till Birnam wood remove to Dunsinane,
I cannot taint with fear. What's the boy Malcolm?
Was he not born of woman? The spirits that know
All mortal consequences have pronounc'd me thus:
"Fear not, Macbeth; no man that's born of woman
Shall e'er have power upon thee."—Then fly, false
                                                 thanes,
And mingle with the English epicures:
The mind I sway by, and the heart I bear,
Shall never sag with doubt, nor shake with fear.   10

              Enter a Servant.

The devil damn thee black, thou cream-fac'd loon!
Where gott'st thou that goose look?
  Serv. There is ten thousand—
  Macb.   Geese, villain?
  Serv.   Soldiers, sir.
  Macb. Go, prick thy face, and over-red thy fear,
Thou lily-liver'd boy. What soldiers, patch?
Death of thy soul! those linen cheeks of thine
Are counsellors to fear. What soldiers, whey-face?
  Serv. The English force, so please you.
  Macb. Take thy face hence. [*Exit Servant.*]—Sey-
ton!—I am sick at heart,
When I behold—Seyton, I say!—This push   20
Will cheer me ever, or disseat me now.
I have liv'd long enough: my way of life
Is fall'n into the sere, the yellow leaf;
And that which should accompany old age,
As honour, love, obedience, troops of friends,
I must not look to have; but, in their stead,
Curses, not loud, but deep, mouth-honour, breath,
Which the poor heart would fain deny, and dare not.
Seyton!—   29

              Enter SEYTON.

  Sey. What is your gracious pleasure?
  Macb.   What news more?
  Sey. All is confirm'd, my lord, which was reported.
  Macb. I'll fight, till from my bones my flesh be
                                            hack'd.
Give me my armour.
  Sey.   'T is not needed yet.
  Macb. I'll put it on.
Send out moe horses, skir the country round;
Hang those that talk of fear. Give me mine armour.—
How does your patient, doctor?
  Doct.   Not so sick, my lord,
As she is troubled with thick-coming fancies,
That keep her from her rest.
  Macb.   Cure her of that:
Canst thou not minister to a mind diseas'd,   40
Pluck from the memory a rooted sorrow,
Raze out the written troubles of the brain,
And with some sweet oblivious antidote
Cleanse the stuff'd bosom of that perilous stuff,
Which weighs upon the heart?
  Doct.   Therein the patient
Must minister to himself.
  Macb. Throw physic to the dogs; I'll none of it.—
Come, put mine armour on; give me my staff.—
Seyton, send out—Doctor, the thanes fly from me.—
Come, sir, despatch.—If thou couldst, doctor, cast 50
The water of my land, find her disease,
And purge it to a sound and pristine health,
I would applaud thee to the very echo,
That should applaud again.—Pull 't off, I say.—
What rhubarb, senna, or what purgative drug,
Would scour these English hence?—Hear'st thou of
                                          them?

Doct. Ay, my good lord : your royal preparation
Makes us hear something.
Macb. Bring it after me.—
I will not be afraid of death and bane,   59
Till Birnam forest come to Dunsinane.   [*Exit.*
Doct. [*Aside.*] Were I from Dunsinane away and
  clear.
Profit again should hardly draw me here.   [*Exeunt.*

Siw. " What wood is this before us ? "

SCENE IV.—Country near Dunsinane. A Wood in
view.

Enter, with drum and colours, MALCOLM, *Old*
SIWARD *and his Son,* MACDUFF, MENTETH,
CATHNESS, ANGUS, LENOX, ROSSE, *and Soldiers,*
marching.

Mal. Cousins, I hope the days are near at hand,
That chambers will be safe.
Ment.   We doubt it nothing.
Siw. What wood is this before us ?
Ment.   The wood of Birnam.
Mal. Let every soldier hew him down a bough,
And bear 't before him : thereby shall we shadow
The numbers of our host, and make discovery
Err in report of us.
Sold.   It shall be done.
Siw. We learn no other, but the confident tyrant
Keeps still in Dunsinane, and will endure
Our setting down before 't.
Mal.   'T is his main hope ;   10
For where there is advantage to be given,
Both more and less have given him the revolt,
And none serve with him but constrained things,
Whose hearts are absent too.
Macd.   Let our just censures
Attend the true event, and put we on
Industrious soldiership.
Siw.   The time approaches,
That will with due decision make us know
What we shall say we have, and what we owe.
Thoughts speculative their unsure hopes relate,
But certain issue strokes must arbitrate ;   20
Towards which advance the war. [*Exeunt, marching.*

SCENE V.—Dunsinane. Within the Castle.

Enter, with drum and colours, MACBETH, SEYTON,
and Soldiers.

Macb. Hang out our banners on the outward walls ;
The cry is still, "They come !" Our castle's strength
Will laugh a siege to scorn : here let them lie,
Till famine and the ague eat them up.

Were they not forc'd with those that should be ours,
We might have met them dareful, beard to beard,
And beat them backward home. What is that noise ?
       [*A cry within, of Women.*
Sey. It is the cry of women, my good lord. [*Exit.*
Macb. I have almost forgot the taste of fears.
The time has been, my senses would have cool'd 10
To hear a night-shriek ; and my fell of hair
Would at a dismal treatise rouse,
          and stir,
As life were in 't. I have supp'd
          full with horrors :
Direness, familiar to my slaugh-
          terous thoughts,
Cannot once start me.

Re-enter SEYTON.
          Wherefore was that cry ?
Sey. The queen, my lord, is dead.
Macb. She should have died
          hereafter :
There would have been a time for
          such a word.—
To-morrow, and to-morrow, and
          to-morrow,
Creeps in this petty pace from day
          to day,   20
To the last syllable of recorded
          time ;
And all our yesterdays have
          lighted fools
The way to dusty death. Out, out,
          brief candle !
Life 's but a walking shadow ; a
          poor player,
That struts and frets his hour upon
          the stage,
And then is heard no more : it is a tale
Told by an idiot, full of sound and fury,
Signifying nothing.

Enter a Messenger.

Thou com'st to use thy tongue ; thy story quickly.
Mess. Gracious my lord,   30
I should report that which I say I saw,
But know not how to do it.
Macb.   Well, say, sir.
Mess. As I did stand my watch upon the hill,
I look'd toward Birnam, and anon, methought,
The wood began to move.
Macb.   Liar, and slave !
Mess. Let me endure your wrath, if 't be not so.
Within this three mile may you see it coming ;
I say, a moving grove.
Macb.   If thou speak'st false,
Upon the next tree shalt thou hang alive,
Till famine cling thee : if thy speech be sooth,   40
I care not if thou dost for me as much.—
I pull in resolution ; and begin
To doubt the equivocation of the fiend,
That lies like truth : " Fear not, till Birnam wood
Do come to Dunsinane ;"—and now a wood
Comes toward Dunsinane.—Arm, arm, and out !—
If this which he avouches does appear,
There is nor flying hence, nor tarrying here.
I 'gin to be aweary of the sun,
And wish the estate o' the world were now undone.—
Ring the alarum-bell !—Blow, wind ! come, wrack ! 51
At least we 'll die with harness on our back. [*Exeunt.*

SCENE VI.—The Same. A Plain before the Castle.

Enter, with drum and colours, MALCOLM, *Old*
SIWARD, MACDUFF, &c., *and their Army, with*
boughs.

Mal. Now, near enough : your leavy screens throw
          down,
And show like those you are.—You, worthy uncle,
Shall, with my cousin, your right-noble son,
Lead our first battle : worthy Macduff, and we,

Shall take upon's what else remains to do,
According to our order.
  Siw.   Fare you well.—
Do we but find the tyrant's power to-night,
Let us be beaten, if we cannot fight.

That was not born of woman? Such a **one**
Am I to fear, or none.

            Enter Young Siward.
  Yo. Siw. What is thy name?

Macb. " Of all men else I have avoided thee:
But get thee back, my soul is too much charg'd
With blood of thine already."

  Macd. Make all our trumpets speak ; give them all
      breath,
Those clamorous harbingers of blood and death.   10
          [*Exeunt. Alarums continued.*

Scene VII.—The Same. Another Part of the Plain.

        Enter Macbeth.
  Macb. They have tied me to a stake : I cannot fly,
But, bear-like, I must fight the course.—What 's he,

  Macb.   Thou 'lt be afraid to hear it.
  Yo. Siw. No ; though thou call'st thyself a hotter
      name
Than any is in hell.
  Macb.   My name 's Macbeth.
  Yo. Siw. The devil himself could not pronounce a title
More hateful to mine ear.
  Macb.   No, nor more fearful.   9
  Yo. Siw. Thou liest, abhorred tyrant : with my sword
I 'll prove the lie thou speak'st.
          [*They fight, and Young* Siward *is slain.*

Macb.   Thou wast born of woman :—
But swords I smile at, weapons laugh to scorn,
Brandish'd by man that 's of a woman born.   [*Exit.*

    Alarums. Enter MACDUFF.
Macd. That way the noise is.—Tyrant, show thy face:
If thou be'st slain, and with no stroke of mine,
My wife and children's ghosts will haunt me still.
I cannot strike at wretched Kernes, whose arms
Are hir'd to bear their staves : either thou, Macbeth,
Or else my sword, with an unbatter'd edge,
I sheathe again undeeded. There thou shouldst be ; 20

I bear a charmed life ; which must not yield
To one of woman born.
    Macd.   Despair thy charm ;
And let the angel, whom thou still hast serv'd,
Tell thee, Macduff was from his mother's womb
Untimely ripp'd.
    Macb. Accursed be that tongue that tells me so,
For it hath cow'd my better part of man :
And be these juggling fiends no more believ'd,
That palter with us in a double sense ;
That keep the word of promise to our ear,   50
And break it to our hope.—I 'll not fight with thee.

Macd. "Hail, king! for so thou art. Behold, where stands
The usurper's cursed head."

By this great clatter, one of greatest note
Seems bruited. Let me find him, fortune!
And more I beg not.   [*Exit. Alarum.*

    Enter MALCOLM *and Old* SIWARD.
Siw. This way, my lord ;—the castle 's gently ren-
    der'd :
The tyrant's people on both sides do fight ;
The noble thanes do bravely in the war.
The day almost itself professes yours,
And little is to do.
    Mal.   We have met with foes
That strike beside us.
    Siw.   Enter, sir, the castle.
                        [*Exeunt. Alarum.*

    Re-enter MACBETH.
Macb. Why should I play the Roman fool, and die
On mine own sword ? whiles I see lives, the gashes 31
Do better upon them.

    Re-enter MACDUFF.
Macd.   Turn, hell-hound, turn !
Macb. Of all men else I have avoided thee :
But get thee back, my soul is too much charg'd
With blood of thine already.
    Macd.   I have no words ;
My voice is in my sword : thou bloodier villain
Than terms can give thee out !   [*They fight.*
    Macb.   Thou losest labour :
As easy may'st thou the intrenchant air
With thy keen sword impress, as make me bleed :
Let fall thy blade on vulnerable crests ;   40

Macd. Then yield thee, coward,
And live to be the show and gaze o' the time :
We 'll have thee, as our rarer monsters are,
Painted upon a pole, and underwrit,
" Here may you see the tyrant."
    Macb.   I will not yield,
To kiss the ground before young Malcolm's feet,
And to be baited with the rabble's curse.   '
Though Birnam wood be come to Dunsinane,
And thou oppos'd, being of no woman born,   60
Yet I will try the last : before my body
I throw my warlike shield : lay on, Macduff ;
And damn'd be him that first cries, " Hold, enough !"
                        [*Exeunt, fighting.*

Retreat. Flourish. Re-enter, with drum and colours,
    MALCOLM, *Old* SIWARD, ROSSE, *Thanes, and*
    Soldiers.
Mal. I would the friends we miss were safe arriv'd.
Siw. Some must go off ; and yet, by these I see,
So great a day as this is cheaply bought.
    Mal. Macduff is missing, and your noble son.
    Rosse. Your son, my lord, has paid a soldier's debt :
He only liv'd but till he was a man ;
The which no sooner had his prowess confirm'd,   70
In the unshrinking station where he fought,
But like a man he died.
    Siw.   Then he is dead ?
Rosse. Ay, and brought off the field. Your cause of
                        sorrow
Must not be measur'd by his worth, for then
It hath no end.
    Siw.   Had he his hurts before ?

Rosse. Ay, on the front.
Siw.   Why then, God's soldier be he !
Had I as many sons as I have hairs,
I would not wish them to a fairer death :
And so, his knell is knoll'd.
  Mal.   He 's worth more sorrow,
And that I 'll spend for him.
  Siw.   He 's worth no more ; 80
They say, he parted well, and paid his score :
And so, God be with him !—Here comes newer comfort.

    Re-enter MACDUFF, *with* MACBETH'S *head.*

  Macd. Hail, king ! for so thou art. Behold, where
        stands
The usurper's cursed head : the time is free.
I see thee compass'd with thy kingdom's pearl,
That speak my salutation in their minds ;
Whose voices I desire aloud with mine,—
Hail, King of Scotland !

  All.   Hail, King of Scotland !
                        [*Flourish.*
  Mal. We shall not spend a large expense of time,
Before we reckon with your several loves,   90
And make us even with you. My thanes and kinsmen,
Henceforth be earls ; the first that ever Scotland
In such an honour nam'd. What 's more to do,
Which would be planted newly with the time,—
As calling home our exil'd friends abroad,
That fled the snares of watchful tyranny ;
Producing forth the cruel ministers
Of this dead butcher, and this fiend-like queen,
Who, as 't is thought, by self and violent hands
Took off her life ;—this, and what needful else 100
That calls upon us, by the grace of Grace
We will perform in measure, time, and place.
So thanks to all at once, and to each one,
Whom we invite to see us crown'd at Scone.
                  [*Flourish. Exeunt.*

HAMLET, PRINCE OF DENMARK.

DRAMATIS PERSONÆ.

CLAUDIUS, *King of Denmark.*
HAMLET, *Son to the former, and Nephew to the present King.*
HORATIO, *Friend to Hamlet.*
POLONIUS, *Lord Chamberlain.*
LAERTES, *his Son.*
VOLTIMAND, ⎫
CORNELIUS, ⎪
ROSENCRANTZ, ⎬ *Courtiers.*
GUILDENSTERN, ⎪
OSRICK, ⎪
A Gentleman, ⎭
A Priest.
MARCELLUS, ⎫ *Officers.*
BERNARDO, ⎬

FRANCISCO, *a Soldier.*
REYNALDO, *Servant to Polonius.*
A Captain.
English Ambassadors.
Ghost of Hamlet's Father.
FORTINBRAS, *Prince of Norway.*
Players.
Two Clowns, Grave-diggers.

GERTRUDE, *Queen of Denmark, and Mother to Hamlet.*
OPHELIA, *Daughter to Polonius.*

Lords, Ladies, Officers, Soldiers, Sailors, Messengers, and Attendants.

SCENE—DENMARK.

ACT I.

SCENE I.—Elsinore. A Platform before the Castle.

FRANCISCO *on his post.* *Enter to him* BERNARDO.

Bernardo.
WHO's there?
Fran. Nay, answer me: stand, and unfold yourself.
Ber. Long live the king!
Fran. Bernardo?
Ber. He.
Fran. You come most carefully upon your hour.
Ber. 'T is now struck twelve: get thee to bed, Francisco.
Fran. For this relief much thanks: 't is bitter cold,
And I am sick at heart.
Ber. Have you had quiet guard?
Fran. Not a mouse stirring. 10
Ber. Well, good night.
If you do meet Horatio and Marcellus,
The rivals of my watch, bid them make haste.
Fran. I think I hear them.—Stand! Who's there?

Enter HORATIO *and* MARCELLUS.

Hor. Friends to this ground.
Mar. And liegemen to the Dane.
Fran. Give you good night.
Mar. O! farewell, honest soldier:
Who hath reliev'd you?
Fran. Bernardo has my place.
Give you good night. [*Exit.*
Mar. Holla! Bernardo!
Ber. Say.
What! is Horatio there?
Hor. A piece of him.
Ber. Welcome, Horatio: welcome, good Marcellus.
Mar. What, has this thing appear'd again to-night?
Ber. I have seen nothing. 22
Mar. Horatio says, 't is but our fantasy,
And will not let belief take hold of him,

Touching this dreaded sight twice seen of us.
Therefore, I have entreated him along
With us to watch the minutes of this night,
That, if again this apparition come,
He may approve our eyes, and speak to it.
Hor. Tush, tush! 't will not appear.
Ber. Sit down awhile, 30
And let us once again assail your ears,
That are so fortified against our story,
What we two nights have seen.
Hor. Well, sit we down,
And let us hear Bernardo speak of this.
Ber. Last night of all,
When yond same star, that's westward from the pole,
Had made his course to illume that part of heaven
Where now it burns, Marcellus, and myself,
The bell then beating one,—
Mar. Peace! break thee off: look, where it comes again! 40

Enter Ghost.

Ber. In the same figure, like the king that's dead.
Mar. Thou art a scholar; speak to it, Horatio.
Ber. Looks it not like the king? mark it, Horatio.
Hor. Most like:—it harrows me with fear and wonder.
Ber. It would be spoke to.
Mar. Question it, Horatio.
Hor. What art thou, that usurp'st this time of night,
Together with that fair and warlike form,
In which the majesty of buried Denmark
Did sometimes march? by Heaven, I charge thee, speak!
Mar. It is offended.
Ber. See! it stalks away. 50
Hor. Stay! speak: speak, I charge thee, speak!
[*Exit Ghost.*

Mar. 'T is gone, and will not answer.
Ber. How now, Horatio? you tremble, and look pale :
Is not this something more than fantasy?
What think you on 't?
Hor. Before my God, I might not this believe,
Without the sensible and true avouch
Of mine own eyes.
Mar.   Is it not like the king?
Hor. As thou art to thyself.
Such was the very armour he had on,   69
When he the ambitious Norway combated.
So frown'd he once, when, in an angry parle,
He smote the sledded Polacks on the ice.
'T is strange.
Mar. Thus, twice before, and just at this dead hour,
With martial stalk hath he gone by our watch.
Hor. In what particular thought to work, I know
not;
But in the gross and scope of my opinion,
This bodes some strange eruption to our state.
Mar. Good now, sit down, and tell me, he that
knows,   70
Why this same strict and most observant watch
So nightly toils the subject of the land?
And why such daily cast of brazen cannon,
And foreign mart for implements of war?
Why such impress of shipwrights, whose sore task
Does not divide the Sunday from the week?
What might be toward, that this sweaty haste
Doth make the night joint-labourer with the day,
Who is 't, that can inform me?
Hor.   That can I ;
At least, the whisper goes so. Our last king,   80
Whose image even but now appear'd to us,
Was, as you know, by Fortinbras of Norway,
Thereto prick'd on by a most emulate pride,
Dar'd to the combat ; in which our valiant Hamlet
(For so this side of our known esteem'd him)
Did slay this Fortinbras ; who, by a seal'd compact,
Well ratified by law and heraldry,
Did forfeit with his life all those his lands,
Which he stood seiz'd of, to the conqueror :
Against the which, a moiety competent   90
Was gaged by our king ; which had return'd
To the inheritance of Fortinbras,
Had he been vanquisher ; as, by the same cov'nant,
And carriage of the article design'd,
His fell to Hamlet. Now, sir, young Fortinbras,
Of unimproved mettle hot and full,
Hath in the skirts of Norway, here and there,
Shark'd up a list of landless resolutes,
For food and diet, to some enterprise
That hath a stomach in 't : which is no other   100
(As it doth well appear unto our state)
But to recover of us, by strong hand
And terms compulsative, those 'foresaid lands.
So by his father lost. And this, I take it,
Is the main motive of our preparations,
The source of this our watch, and the chief head
Of this post-haste and romage in the land.
Ber. I think, it be no other, but e'en so :
Well may it sort, that this portentous figure
Comes armed through our watch, so like the king   110
That was, and is, the question of these wars.
Hor. A moth it is to trouble the mind's eye.
In the most high and palmy state of Rome,
A little ere the mightiest Julius fell,
The graves stood tenantless, and the sheeted dead
Did squeak and gibber in the Roman streets :
As stars with trains of fire and dews of blood,
Disasters in the sun ; and the moist star,
Upon whose influence Neptune's empire stands,
Was sick almost to doomsday with eclipse :   120
And even the like precurse of fierce events—
As harbingers preceding still the fates,
And prologue to the omen coming on—
Have heaven and earth together demonstrated
Unto our climatures and countrymen.—
But, soft ! behold ! lo, where it comes again !

Re-enter Ghost.

I 'll cross it, though it blast me.—Stay, illusion !

If thou hast any sound, or use of voice,
Speak to me :
If there be any good thing to be done,   130
That may to thee do ease, and grace to me,
Speak to me :
If thou art privy to thy country's fate,
Which happily foreknowing may avoid,
O, speak !
Or if thou hast uphoarded in thy life

Hor.   "Stay, illusion !
If thou hast any sound, or use of voice,
Speak to me."

Extorted treasure in the womb of earth,
For which, they say, you spirits oft walk in death,
[*Cock crows.*
Speak of it :—stay, and speak !—Stop it, Marcellus.
Mar. Shall I strike at it with my partisan?   140
Hor. Do, if it will not stand.
Ber.   'T is here !
Hor.   'T is here !
Mar. 'T is gone !   [*Exit Ghost.*
We do it wrong, being so majestical,
To offer it the show of violence ;
For it is, as the air, invulnerable,
And our vain blows malicious mockery.
Ber. It was about to speak, when the cock crew.
Hor. And then it started, like a guilty thing
Upon a fearful summons. I have heard,
The cock, that is the trumpet to the morn,   150
Doth with his lofty and shrill-sounding throat
Awake the god of day ; and, at his warning,
Whether in sea or fire, in earth or air,
The extravagant and erring spirit hies
To his confine ; and of the truth herein
This present object made probation.
Mar. It faded on the crowing of the cock.
Some say, that ever 'gainst that season comes
Wherein our Saviour's birth is celebrated,
The bird of dawning singeth all night long :   160
And then, they say, no spirit can walk abroad ;
The nights are wholesome ; then no planets strike,
No fairy takes, nor witch hath power to charm,
So hallow'd and so gracious is the time.
Hor. So have I heard, and do in part believe it.
But, look, the morn, in russet mantle clad,
Walks o'er the dew of yon high eastern hill.
Break we our watch up ; and, by my advice,

Let us impart what we have seen to-night
Unto young Hamlet ; for, upon my life, 170
This spirit, dumb to us, will speak to him.
Do you consent we shall acquaint him with it,
As needful in our loves, fitting our duty ?
  Mar. Let's do't, I pray ; and I this morning know
Where we shall find him most conveniently. [*Exeunt.*

SCENE II.—The Same. A Room of State.

Enter the KING, QUEEN, HAMLET, POLONIUS,
LAERTES, VOLTIMAND, CORNELIUS, *Lords, and
Attendants.*
  King. Though yet of Hamlet our dear brother's
      death
The memory be green, and that it us befitted
To bear our hearts in grief, and our whole kingdom
To be contracted in one brow of woe ;
Yet so far hath discretion fought with nature,
That we with wisest sorrow think on him,
Together with remembrance of ourselves.
Therefore, our sometime sister, now our queen,
The imperial jointress of this warlike state,
Have we, as 't were, with a defeated joy,— 10
With one auspicious, and one dropping eye,
With mirth in funeral, and with dirge in marriage,
In equal scale weighing delight and dole,—
Taken to wife : nor have we herein barr'd
Your better wisdoms, which have freely gone
With this affair along : for all, our thanks.
Now follows, that you know, young Fortinbras,
Holding a weak supposal of our worth,
Or thinking, by our late dear brother's death,
Our state to be disjoint and out of frame, 20
Colleagued with the dream of his advantage,
He hath not fail'd to pester us with message,
Importing the surrender of those lands
Lost by his father, with all bonds of law,
To our most valiant brother.—So much for him.
Now for ourself, and for this time of meeting.
Thus much the business is. We have here writ
To Norway, uncle of young Fortinbras,—
Who, impotent and bed-rid, scarcely hears
Of this his nephew's purpose,—to suppress 30
His further gait herein, in that the levies,
The lists, and full proportions, are all made
Out of his subject : and we here despatch
You, good Cornelius, and you, Voltimand,
For bearers of this greeting to old Norway ;
Giving to you no further personal power
To business with the king, more than the scope
Of these dilated articles allow.
Farewell ; and let your haste commend your duty.
  Cor., Vol. In that, and all things, will we show our
      duty. 40
  King. We doubt it nothing : heartily farewell.
            [*Exeunt* VOLTIMAND *and* CORNELIUS.
And now, Laertes, what's the news with you ?
You told us of some suit ; what is 't, Laertes ?
You cannot speak of reason to the Dane,
And lose your voice : what wouldst thou beg, Laertes,
That shall not be my offer, not thy asking ?
The head is not more native to the heart,
The hand more instrumental to the mouth,
Than is the throne of Denmark to thy father.
What wouldst thou have, Laertes ?
  Laer.   Dread my lord, 50
Your leave and favour to return to France ;
From whence though willingly I came to Denmark,
To show my duty in your coronation,
Yet now, I must confess, that duty done,
My thoughts and wishes bend again toward France,
And bow them to your gracious leave and pardon.
  King. Have you your father's leave ? What says
      Polonius ?
  Pol. He hath, my lord, wrung from me my slow
      leave,
By laboursome petition ; and, at last,
Upon his will I seal'd my hard consent : 60
I do beseech you, give him leave to go.

  King. Take thy fair hour, Laertes ; time be thine,
And thy best graces spend it at thy will.—
But now, my cousin Hamlet, and my son,—
  Ham. [*Aside.*] A little more than kin, and less than
      kind.
  King. How is it that the clouds still hang on you ?
  Ham. Not so, my lord ; I am too much i' the sun.
  Queen. Good Hamlet, cast thy nighted colour off,
And let thine eye look like a friend on Denmark.
Do not, for ever, with thy vailed lids 70
Seek for thy noble father in the dust :
Thou know'st, 't is common ; all that lives must die,
Passing through nature to eternity.
  Ham. Ay, madam, it is common.
  Queen.   If it be,
Why seems it so particular with thee ?
  Ham. Seems, madam ! nay, it is ; I know not seems.
'T is not alone my inky cloak, good mother,
Nor customary suits of solemn black,
Nor windy suspiration of forc'd breath,
No, nor the fruitful river in the eye, 80
Nor the dejected haviour of the visage,
Together with all forms, modes, shows of grief,
That can denote me truly : these, indeed, seem,
For they are actions that a man might play ;
But I have that within, which passeth show ;
These but the trappings and the suits of woe.
  King. 'T is sweet and commendable in your nature,
      Hamlet,
To give these mourning duties to your father :
But, you must know, your father lost a father ;
That father lost, lost his ; and the survivor bound 90
In filial obligation, for some term,
To do obsequious sorrow : but to persever
In obstinate condolement, is a course
Of impious stubbornness ; 't is unmanly grief ;
It shows a will most incorrect to Heaven,
A heart unfortified, a mind impatient,
An understanding simple and unschool'd :
For what, we know, must be, and is as common
As any the most vulgar thing to sense,
Why should we, in our peevish opposition, 100
Take it to heart ? Fie ! 't is a fault to Heaven,
A fault against the dead, a fault to nature,
To reason most absurd, whose common theme
Is death of fathers, and who still hath cried,
From the first corse till he that died to-day,
" This must be so." We pray you, throw to earth
This unprevailing woe, and think of us
As of a father ; for let the world take note,
You are the most immediate to our throne ;
And, with no less nobility of love, 110
Than that which dearest father bears his son,
Do I impart toward you. For your intent
In going back to school in Wittenberg,
It is most retrograde to our desire :
And we beseech you, bend you to remain
Here, in the cheer and comfort of our eye,
Our chiefest courtier, cousin, and our son.
  Queen. Let not thy mother lose her prayers, Ham-
      let :
I pray thee, stay with us ; go not to Wittenberg.
  Ham. I shall in all my best obey you, madam. 120
  King. Why, 'tis a loving and a fair reply :
Be as ourself in Denmark.—Madam, come ;
This gentle and unforc'd accord of Hamlet
Sits smiling to my heart : in grace whereof,
No jocund health that Denmark drinks to-day,
But the great cannon to the clouds shall tell,
And the king's rouse the heavens shall bruit again,
Re-speaking earthly thunder. Come away.
      [*Flourish. Exeunt* KING, QUEEN, *Lords, &c.,*
            POLONIUS, *and* LAERTES.
  Ham. O ! that this too too solid flesh would melt,
Thaw, and resolve itself into a dew ! 130
Or that the Everlasting had not fix'd
His canon 'gainst self-slaughter ! O God ! O God !
How weary, stale, flat, and unprofitable,
Seem to me all the uses of this world !
Fie on 't ! O fie ! 't is an unweeded garden,
That grows to seed ; things rank and gross in nature,
Possess it merely. That it should come to this !

But two months dead !—nay, not so much, not two :
So excellent a king ; that was, to this,
Hyperion to a satyr ; so loving to my mother,   140
That he might not beteem the winds of heaven
Visit her face too roughly.   Heaven and earth !
Must I remember ? why, she would hang on him,
As if increase of appetite had grown
By what it fed on ; and yet, within a month,—
Let me not think on 't :— Frailty, thy name is
          woman !—
A little month ; or ere those shoes were old,
With which she follow'd my poor father's body,
Like Niobe, all tears ;—why she, even she,
(O God ! a beast, that wants discourse of reason,   150
Would have mourn'd longer,)—married with my
          uncle,
My father's brother, but no more like my father
Than I to Hercules : within a month ;
Ere yet the salt of most unrighteous tears
Had left the flushing in her galled eyes,
She married.—O most wicked speed, to post
With such dexterity to incestuous sheets !
It is not, nor it cannot come to, good ;
But break, my heart, for I must hold my tongue !

    Enter HORATIO, BERNARDO, *and* MARCELLUS.
  Hor. Hail to your lordship !
  Ham.   I am glad to see you well :
Horatio,—or I do forget myself.   161
  Hor. The same, my lord, and your poor servant ever.
  Ham. Sir, my good friend ; I 'll change that name
          with you.
And what make you from Wittenberg, Horatio ?—
Marcellus ?
  Mar. My good lord,—
  Ham. I am very glad to see you.—Good even, sir.—
But what, in faith, make you from Wittenberg ?
  Hor. A truant disposition, good my lord.
  Ham. I would not hear your enemy say so ;   170
Nor shall you do mine ear that violence,
To make it truster of your own report
Against yourself : I know, you are no truant,
But what is your affair in Elsinore ?
We 'll teach you to drink deep, ere you depart.
  Hor. My lord, I came to see your father's funeral.
  Ham. I pray thee, do not mock me, fellow-student ;
I think, it was to see my mother's wedding.
  Hor. Indeed, my lord, it follow'd hard upon.
  Ham. Thrift, thrift, Horatio ! the funeral bak'd
          meats   180
Did coldly furnish forth the marriage tables.
'Would I had met my dearest foe in heaven
Ere I had ever seen that day, Horatio !—
My father,—methinks, I see my father.
  Hor. O ! where, my lord ?
  Ham.   In my mind's eye, Horatio.
  Hor. I saw him once : he was a goodly king.
  Ham. He was a man, take him for all in all,
I shall not look upon his like again.
  Hor. My lord, I think I saw him yesternight.
  Ham. Saw who ?   190
  Hor. My lord, the king your father.
  Ham.   The king my father !
  Hor. Season your admiration for a while
With an attent ear, till I may deliver,
Upon the witness of these gentlemen,
This marvel to you.
  Ham.   For God's love, let me hear.
  Hor. Two nights together had these gentlemen,
Marcellus and Bernardo, on their watch,
In the dead waste and middle of the night,
Been thus encounter'd : a figure like your father,
Arm'd at point, exactly, cap-a-pe,   200
Appears before them, and with solemn march
Goes slow and stately by them : thrice he walk'd,
By their oppress'd and fear-surprised eyes,
Within his truncheon's length ; whilst they, distill'd
Almost to jelly with the act of fear,
Stand dumb, and speak not to him.   This to me
In dreadful secrecy impart they did,
And I with them the third night kept the watch ;
Where, as they had deliver'd, both in time,

Form of the thing, each word made true and good, 210
The apparition comes.   I knew your father :
These hands are not more like.
  Ham.   But where was this ?
  Mar. My lord, upon the platform where we watch'd.
  Ham. Did you not speak to it ?
  Hor.   My lord, I did ;
But answer made it none : yet once, methought,
It lifted up its head, and did address
Itself to motion, like as it would speak ;
But, even then, the morning cock crew loud,
And at the sound it shrunk in haste away,
And vanish'd from our sight.
  Ham.   'T is very strange.   220
  Hor. As I do live, my honour'd lord, 't is true ;
And we did think it writ down in our duty,
To let you know of it.
  Ham. Indeed, indeed, sirs, but this troubles me.
Hold you the watch to-night ?
  Mar., Ber.   We do, my lord.
  Ham. Arm'd, say you ?
  Mar., Ber.   Arm'd, my lord.
  Ham.   From top to toe ?
  Mar., Ber. My lord, from head to foot.
  Ham.   Then, saw you not his face ?
  Hor. O ! yes, my lord ; he wore his beaver up.
  Ham. What, look'd he frowningly ?
  Hor. A countenance more in sorrow than in anger.
  Ham. Pale, or red ?   231
  Hor. Nay, very pale.
  Ham.   And fix'd his eyes upon you ?
  Hor. Most constantly.
  Ham.   I would I had been there.
  Hor. It would have much amaz'd you.
  Ham. Very like, very like.   Stay'd it long ?
  Hor. While one with moderate haste might tell a
          hundred.
  Mar., Ber. Longer, longer.
  Hor. Not when I saw 't.
  Ham.   His beard was grizzled ? no ?
  Hor. It was, as I have seen it in his life,
A sable silver'd.
  Ham.   I will watch to-night :   240
Perchance, 't will walk again.
  Hor.   I warrant it will.
  Ham. If it assume my noble father's person,
I 'll speak to it, though hell itself should gape,
And bid me hold my peace.   I pray you all,
If you have hitherto conceal'd this sight,
Let it be tenable in your silence still ;
And whatsoever else shall hap to-night,
Give it an understanding, but no tongue :
I will requite your loves.   So, fare you well.
Upon the platform, 'twixt eleven and twelve,   250
I 'll visit you.
  All.   Our duty to your honour.
  Ham. Your loves, as mine to you.   Farewell.
          [*Exeunt* HORATIO, MARCELLUS, *and* BERNARDO.
My father's spirit in arms ! all is not well ;
I doubt some foul play : 'would, the night were come !
Till then sit still, my soul.   Foul deeds will rise,
Though all the earth o'erwhelm them, to men's eyes.
                                            [*Exit.*

    SCENE III.—A Room in POLONIUS' House.

        Enter LAERTES *and* OPHELIA.

  Laer. My necessaries are embark'd : farewell ;
And, sister, as the winds give benefit,
And convoy is assistant, do not sleep,
But let me hear from you.
  Oph.   Do you doubt that ?
  Laer. For Hamlet, and the trifling of his favour,
Hold it a fashion, and a toy in blood ;
A violet in the youth of primy nature,
Forward, not permanent, sweet, not lasting,
The perfume and suppliance of a minute ;
No more.
  Oph.   No more but so ?
  Laer.   Think it no more :   10
For nature, crescent, does not grow alone

In thews, and bulk ; but, as this temple waxes,
The inward service of the mind and soul
Grows wide withal. Perhaps, he loves you now ;
And now no soil, nor cautel, doth besmirch
The virtue of his will : but you must fear,
His greatness weigh'd, his will is not his own,
For he himself is subject to his birth :
He may not, as unvalu'd persons do,
Carve for himself ; for on his choice depends   20
The safety and the health of the whole state ;
And therefore must his choice be circumscrib'd
Unto the voice and yielding of that body,
Whereof he is the head. Then, if he says he loves you,
It fits your wisdom so far to believe it,
As he in his particular act and place
May give his saying deed ; which is no further,
Than the main voice of Denmark goes withal.
Then weigh what loss your honour may sustain,
If with too credent ear you list his songs,   30
Or lose your heart, or your chaste treasure open
To his unmaster'd importunity.
Fear it, Ophelia, fear it, my dear sister ;
And keep within the rear of your affection,
Out of the shot and danger of desire.
The chariest maid is prodigal enough,
If she unmask her beauty to the moon.
Virtue itself 'scapes not calumnious strokes :
The canker galls the infants of the spring,
Too oft before their buttons be disclos'd ;   40
And in the morn and liquid dew of youth
Contagious blastments are most imminent.
Be wary then ; best safety lies in fear :
Youth to itself rebels, though none else near.
  Oph. I shall the effect of this good lesson keep,
As watchman to my heart. But, good my brother,
Do not, as some ungracious pastors do,
Show me the steep and thorny way to heaven,
Whilst like a puff'd and reckless libertine,
Himself the primrose path of dalliance treads,   50
And recks not his own read.
  Laer.   O ! fear me not.
I stay too long ;—but here my father comes.

Enter POLONIUS.

A double blessing is a double grace ;
Occasion smiles upon a second leave.
  Pol. Yet here, Laertes ? aboard, aboard, for shame !
The wind sits in the shoulder of your sail,
And you are stay'd for. There,—my blessing with
    you ; [*Laying his hand on* LAERTES' *head.*
And these few precepts in thy memory
See thou character. Give thy thoughts no tongue,   60
Nor any unproportion'd thought his act.
Be thou familiar, but by no means vulgar :
The friends thou hast, and their adoption tried,
Grapple them to thy soul with hoops of steel ;
But do not dull thy palm with entertainment
Of each new-hatch'd, unfledg'd comrade. Beware
Of entrance to a quarrel ; but, being in,
Bear 't, that the opposed may beware of thee.
Give every man thine ear, but few thy voice ;
Take each man's censure, but reserve thy judgment.
Costly thy habit as thy purse can buy,   70
But not express'd in fancy ; rich, not gaudy :
For the apparel oft proclaims the man ;
And they in France, of the best rank and station,
Are most select and generous, chief in that.
Neither a borrower, nor a lender be ;
For loan oft loses both itself and friend,
And borrowing dulls the edge of husbandry.
This above all,—to thine own self be true ;
And it must follow, as the night the day,
Thou canst not then be false to any man.   80
Farewell ; my blessing season this in thee !
  Laer. Most humbly do I take my leave, my lord.
  Pol. The time invites you : go, your servants tend.
  Laer. Farewell, Ophelia, and remember well
What I have said to you.
  Oph.   'T is in my memory lock'd,
And you yourself shall keep the key of it.
  Laer. Farewell.   [*Exit.*
  Pol. What is 't, Ophelia, he hath said to you ?

  Oph. So please you, something touching the Lord
    Hamlet.
  Pol. Marry, well bethought :   90
'T is told me, he hath very oft of late
Given private time to you ; and you yourself
Have of your audience been most free and bounteous.
If it be so, (as so 't is put on me,
And that in way of caution,) I must tell you,
You do not understand yourself so clearly,
As it behoves my daughter, and your honour.
What is between you ? give me up the truth.
  Oph. He hath, my lord, of late made many tenders
Of his affection to me.   100
  Pol. Affection ? pooh ! you speak like a green girl,
Unsifted in such perilous circumstance.
Do you believe his tenders, as you call them ?
  Oph. I do not know, my lord, what I should think.
  Pol. Marry, I 'll teach you : think yourself a baby ;
That you have ta'en these tenders for true pay,
Which are not sterling. Tender yourself more dearly ;
Or, not to crack the wind of the poor phrase,
Running it thus, you 'll tender me a fool.
  Oph. My lord, he hath importun'd me with love, 110
In honourable fashion.
  Pol. Ay, fashion you may call it ; go to, go to.
  Oph. And hath given countenance to his speech,
    my lord,
With almost all the holy vows of heaven.
  Pol. Ay, springes to catch woodcocks. I do know,
When the blood burns, how prodigal the soul
Lends the tongue vows : these blazes, daughter,
Giving more light than heat,—extinct in both,
Even in their promise, as it is a-making,—
You must not take for fire. From this time,   120
Be somewhat scanter of your maiden presence :
Set your entreatments at a higher rate,
Than a command to parley. For Lord Hamlet,
Believe so much in him, that he is young ;
And with a larger tether may he walk,
Than may be given you. In few, Ophelia,
Do not believe his vows, for they are brokers
Not of that dye which their investments show,
But mere implorators of unholy suits,
Breathing like sanctified and pious bawds,   130
The better to beguile. This is for all,—
I would not, in plain terms, from this time forth,
Have you so slander any moment leisure,
As to give words or talk with the Lord Hamlet.
Look to 't, I charge you ; come your ways.
  Oph. I shall obey, my lord.   [*Exeunt.*

Scene IV.—The Platform.

Enter HAMLET, HORATIO, *and* MARCELLUS.

  Ham. The air bites shrewdly ; it is very cold.
  Hor. It is a nipping and an eager air.
  Ham. What hour now ?
  Hor.   I think, it lacks of twelve.
  Mar. No, it is struck.
  Hor. Indeed ? I heard it not : it then draws near
    the season,
Wherein the spirit held his wont to walk.
    [*A flourish of trumpets, and ordnance
        shot off, within.*
What does this mean, my lord ?
  Ham. The king doth wake to-night, and takes his
    rouse,
Keeps wassail, and the swaggering up-spring reels ;
And as he drains his draughts of Rhenish down,   10
The kettle-drum and trumpet thus bray out
The triumph of his pledge.
  Hor.   Is it a custom ?
  Ham. Ay, marry, is 't :
But to my mind,—though I am native here,
And to the manner born,—it is a custom
More honour'd in the breach than the observance.
This heavy-headed revel, east and west,
Makes us traduc'd and tax'd of other nations :
They clepe us drunkards, and with swinish phrase
Soil our addition ; and, indeed, it takes   20

From our achievements, though perform'd at height,
The pith and marrow of our attribute.
So, oft it chances in particular men,
That for some vicious mole of nature in them,
As, in their birth, (wherein they are not guilty,
Since nature cannot choose his origin,)
By their o'ergrowth of some complexion,
Oft breaking down the pales and forts of reason ;
Or by some habit, that too much o'er-leavens
The form of plausive manners ;—that these men,— 30
Carrying, I say, the stamp of one defect,
Being nature's livery, or fortune's star,—
Their virtues else, be they as pure as grace,
As infinite as man may undergo,
Shall in the general censure take corruption
From that particular fault : the dram of bale
Doth all the noble substance off and out
To his own scandal.

Enter Ghost.

Hor. Look, my lord ! it comes.
Ham. Angels and ministers of grace defend us !
Be thou a spirit of health, or goblin damn'd, 40
Bring with thee airs from heaven, or blasts from hell,
Be thy intents wicked, or charitable,
Thou com'st in such a questionable shape,
That I will speak to thee. I 'll call thee Hamlet,
King, father, royal Dane : O ! answer me :
Let me not burst in ignorance ; but tell,
Why thy canonis'd bones, hearsed in death,
Have burst their cerements ; why the sepulchre,
Wherein we saw thee quietly in-urn'd,
Hath op'd his ponderous and marble jaws, 50
To cast thee up again. What may this mean,
That thou, dead corse, again, in complete steel,
Revisit'st thus the glimpses of the moon,
Making night hideous ; and we fools of nature,
So horridly to shake our disposition,
With thoughts beyond the reaches of our souls ?
Say, why is this ? wherefore ? what should we do ?
                                    [*The Ghost beckons* HAMLET.
Hor. It beckons you to go away with it,
As if it some impartment did desire
To you alone.
Mar.   Look, with what courteous action 60
It waves you to a more removed ground :
But do not go with it.
Hor.   No, by no means.
Ham. It will not speak ; then will I follow it.
Hor. Do not, my lord.
Ham.   Why, what should be the fear ?
I do not set my life at a pin's fee ;
And, for my soul, what can it do to that,
Being a thing immortal as itself ?
It waves me forth again :—I 'll follow it.
Hor. What, if it tempt you toward the flood, my
                lord,
Or to the dreadful summit of the cliff, 70
That beetles o'er his base into the sea,
And there assume some other horrible form,
Which might deprive your sovereignty of reason
And draw you into madness ? think of it :
The very place puts toys of desperation,
Without more motive, into every brain
That looks so many fathoms to the sea,
And hears it roar beneath.
Ham. It waves me still :—go on, I 'll follow thee.
Mar. You shall not go, my lord.
Ham.   Hold off your hands.
Hor. Be rul'd : you shall not go.
Ham.   My fate cries out, 81
And makes each petty artery in this body
As hardy as the Nemean lion's nerve.—
                                    [*Ghost beckons.*
Still am I call'd.—Unhand me, gentlemen,—
                                [*Breaking from them.*
By Heaven, I 'll make a ghost of him that lets me :—
I say, away !—Go on, I 'll follow thee.
                            [*Exeunt Ghost and* HAMLET.
Hor. He waxes desperate with imagination.
Mar. Let 's follow ; 't is not fit thus to obey him.
Hor. Have after.—To what issue will this come ? 89

Mar. Something is rotten in the state of Denmark.
Hor. Heaven will direct it.
Mar.   Nay, let 's follow him. [*Exeunt.*

SCENE V.—A more remote Part of the Platform.

Enter Ghost and HAMLET.

Ham. Where wilt thou lead me ? speak, I 'll go no
        further.
Ghost. Mark me.
Ham.   I will.
Ghost.   My hour is almost come,
When I to sulphurous and tormenting flames
Must render up myself.
Ham.   Alas, poor ghost !
Ghost. Pity me not ; but lend thy serious hearing
To what I shall unfold.
Ham.   Speak, I am bound to hear.
Ghost. So art thou to revenge, when thou shalt
        hear.
Ham. What ?
Ghost. I am thy father's spirit ;
Doom'd for a certain term to walk the night, 10
And for the day confin'd to fast in fires,
Till the foul crimes, done in my days of nature,
Are burnt and purg'd away. But that I am forbid
To tell the secrets of my prison-house,
I could a tale unfold, whose lightest word
Would harrow up thy soul, freeze thy young blood,
Make thy two eyes, like stars, start from their spheres,
Thy knotted and combined locks to part,
And each particular hair to stand an-end,
Like quills upon the fretful porpentine ; 20
But this eternal blazon must not be
To ears of flesh and blood.—List, Hamlet, O list !—
If thou didst ever thy dear father love,—
Ham. O God !
Ghost. Revenge his foul and most unnatural murder.
Ham. Murder ?
Ghost. Murder most foul, as in the best it is ;
But this most foul, strange, and unnatural.
Ham. Haste me to know 't, that I, with wings as
        swift
As meditation, or the thoughts of love, 30
May sweep to my revenge.
Ghost.   I find thee apt ;
And duller shouldst thou be than the fat weed
That rots itself in ease on Lethe wharf,
Wouldst thou not stir in this. Now, Hamlet, hear.
'T is given out, that, sleeping in mine orchard,
A serpent stung me ; so the whole ear of Denmark
Is by a forged process of my death
Rankly abus'd ; but know, thou noble youth,
The serpent that did sting thy father's life
Now wears his crown.
Ham.   O my prophetic soul ! 40
Mine uncle !
Ghost. Ay, that incestuous, that adulterate beast,
With witchcraft of his wit, with traitorous gifts,
(O wicked wit, and gifts, that have the power
So to seduce !) won to his shameful lust
The will of my most seeming-virtuous queen.
O Hamlet, what a falling-off was there !
From me, whose love was of that dignity,
That it went hand in hand even with the vow
I made to her in marriage ; and to decline 50
Upon a wretch, whose natural gifts were poor
To those of mine !
But virtue, as it never will be mov'd,
Though lewdness court it in a shape of heaven,
So lust, though to a radiant angel link'd,
Will sate itself in a celestial bed,
And prey on garbage.
But, soft ! methinks, I scent the morning air :
Brief let me be.—Sleeping within mine orchard,
My custom always in the afternoon, 60
Upon my secure hour thy uncle stole,
With juice of cursed hebenon in a vial,
And in the porches of mine ears did pour
The leperous distilment ; whose effect

Holds such an enmity with blood of man,
That, swift as quicksilver, it courses through
The natural gates and alleys of the body ;
And with a sudden vigour it doth posset
And curd, like eager droppings into milk,
The thin and wholesome blood : so did it mine ; 70
And a most instant tetter bark'd about,
Most lazar-like, with vile and loathsome crust,
All my smooth body.
Thus was I, sleeping, by a brother's hand,
Of life, of crown, and queen, at once despatch'd ;
Cut off even in the blossoms of my sin,
Unhousel'd, disappointed, unanel'd ;
No reckoning made, but sent to my account
With all my imperfections on my head :
O, horrible ! O, horrible ! most horrible ! 80
If thou hast nature in thee, bear it not ;
Let not the royal bed of Denmark be
A couch for luxury and damned incest.
But, howsoever thou pursu'st this act,
Taint not thy mind, nor let thy soul contrive
Against thy mother aught : leave her to Heaven,
And to those thorns that in her bosom lodge,
To prick and sting her. Fare thee well at once.
The glow-worm shows the matin to be near,
And 'gins to pale his uneffectual fire : 90
Adieu, adieu ! Hamlet, remember me. [*Exit.*
   Ham. O all you host of heaven ! O earth ! What
      else ?
And shall I couple hell ? O fie !—Hold, hold, my heart ;
And you, my sinews, grow not instant old,
But bear me stiffly up !—Remember thee !
Ay, thou poor ghost, while memory holds a seat
In this distracted globe. Remember thee !
Yea, from the table of my memory
I 'll wipe away all trivial fond records,
All saws of books, all forms, all pressures past, 100
That youth and observation copied there ;
And thy commandment all alone shall live
Within the book and volume of my brain,
Unmix'd with baser matter : yes, by Heaven !
O most pernicious woman !
O villain, villain, smiling, damned villain !
My tables,—meet it is, I set it down,
That one may smile, and smile, and be a· villain ;
At least, I am sure, it may be so in Denmark :
                                                   [*Writing.*
So, uncle, there you are. Now to my word ; 110
It is, " Adieu, adieu ! remember me."
I have sworn 't.
   Hor. [*Within.*] My lord ! my lord !
   Mar. [*Within.*]   Lord Hamlet !
   Hor. [*Within.*]   Heaven secure him !
   Mar. [*Within.*] So be it !
   Hor. [*Within.*] Illo, ho, ho, my lord !
   Ham. Hillo, ho, ho, boy ! come, bird, come.

           Enter Horatio *and* Marcellus.

   Mar. How is 't, my noble lord ?
   Hor.   What news, my·lord ?
   Ham. O, wonderful !
   Hor. Good my lord, tell it.
   Ham.   No ; you will reveal it.
   Hor. Not I, my lord, by Heaven.
   Mar.   Nor I, my lord. 120
   Ham. How say you, then ; would heart of man once
      think it ?—
But you 'll be secret ?
   Hor., *Mar.*   Ay, by Heaven, my lord.
   Ham. There 's ne'er a villain dwelling in all Den-
      mark,
But he 's an arrant knave.
   Hor. There needs no ghost, my lord, come from the
      grave,
To tell us this.
   Ham.   Why, right ; you are i' the right ;
And so, without more circumstance at all,
I hold it fit that we shake hands, and part :
You, as your business and desire shall point you,
For every man hath business and desire, 130
Such as it is ; and, for mine own poor part,
Look you, I 'll go pray.

   Hor. These are but wild and whirling words, my
      lord.
   Ham. I am sorry they offend you, heartily ; yes,
'Faith, heartily.
   Hor.   There 's no offence, my lord.
   Ham. Yes, by Saint Patrick, but there is, Horatio,
And much offence too. Touching this vision here,
It is an honest ghost, that let me tell you :
For your desire to know what is between us,
O'ermaster 't as you may. And now, good friends, 140
As you are friends, scholars, and soldiers,
Give me one poor request.
   Hor. What is 't, my lord ? we will.
   Ham. Never make known what you have seen to-
      night.
   Hor., *Mar.* My lord, we will not.
   Ham.   Nay, but swear 't.
   Hor.   In faith,
My lord, not I.
   Mar.   Nor I, my lord, in faith.
   Ham. Upon my sword.
   Mar.   We have sworn, my lord, already.
   Ham. Indeed, upon my sword, indeed.
   Ghost. [*Beneath.*] Swear.
   Ham. Ha, ha, boy ! say'st thou so ? art thou there,
      true-penny ? 150

Ham. " Ha, ha, boy ! say'st thou so ? art thou there, true-penny ? "

Come on,—you hear this fellow in the cellarage,—
Consent to swear.
   Hor.   Propose the oath, my lord.
   Ham. Never to speak of this that you have seen,
Swear by my sword.
   Ghost. [*Beneath.*] Swear.
   Ham. *Hic et ubique ?* then, we 'll shift our ground.—
Come hither, gentlemen,
And lay your hands again upon my sword :
Never to speak of this that you have heard,
Swear by my sword. 160
   Ghost. [*Beneath.*] Swear.
   Ham. Well said, old mole ! canst work i' the earth
      so fast ?
A worthy pioner !—Once more remove, good friends.
   Hor. O day and night, but this is wondrous strange !
   Ham. And therefore as a stranger give it welcome.
There are more things in heaven and earth, Horatio,
Than are dreamt of in your philosophy.
But come ;—
Here, as before, never, so help you mercy,
How strange or odd soe'er I bear myself,— 170
As I, perchance, hereafter shall think meet
To put an antick disposition on,—
That you, at such times seeing me, never shall,
With arms encumber'd thus, or this head-shake,
Or by pronouncing of some doubtful phrase,

As, "Well, well, we know;"—or, "We could, an if we
　　would;"—
Or, "If we list to speak;"—or, "There be, an if they
　　might;"—
Or such ambiguous giving out, to note
That you know aught of me:—this not to do,
So grace and mercy at your most need help you,　180
Swear.
　　Ghost. [*Beneath.*] Swear.

　　Ham. Rest, rest, perturbed spirit!—So, gentlemen,
With all my love I do commend me to you:
And what so poor a man as Hamlet is
May do, to express his love and friending to you,
God willing, shall not lack. Let us go in together;
And still your fingers on your lips, I pray.
The time is out of joint:—O cursed spite,
That ever I was born to set it right!　　　190
Nay, come; let 's go together.　　　[*Exeunt.*

ACT II.

SCENE I.—A Room in POLONIUS' House.

Enter POLONIUS *and* REYNALDO.

　　Polonius.
GIVE him this money, and these
　　　notes, Reynaldo.
　　Rey. I will, my lord.
　　Pol. You shall do marvellous
　　　wisely, good Reynaldo,
　　Before you visit him, to make
　　　inquiry
　　Of his behaviour.
　　Rey.　　My lord, I did intend it.
　　Pol. Marry, well said: very well said. Look
　　　you, sir,
Inquire me first what Danskers are in Paris;
And how, and who, what means, and where
　　they keep,
What company, at what expense; and finding,
By this encompassment and drift of question, 10
That they do know my son, come you more
　　nearer
Than your particular demands will touch it:
Take you, as 't were, some distant knowledge
　　of him;
As thus,—"I know his father, and his friends,
And, in part, him:"—do you mark this, Reynaldo?
　　Rey. Ay, very well, my lord.
　　Pol. "And, in part, him; but," you may say, "not
　　well:
But if 't be he I mean, he 's very wild,
Addicted so and so;"—and there put on him
What forgeries you please; marry, none so rank　20
As may dishonour him: take heed of that;
But, sir, such wanton, wild, and usual slips,
As are companions noted and most known
To youth and liberty.
　　Rey.　　　As gaming, my lord.
　　Pol. Ay, or drinking, fencing, swearing, quarrelling,
Drabbing: you may go so far.
　　Rey. My lord, that would dishonour him.
　　Pol. 'Faith, no; as you may season it in the charge.
You must not put another scandal on him,
That he is open to incontinency:　　　30
That 's not my meaning; but breathe his faults so
　　quaintly,
That they may seem the taints of liberty;
The flash and outbreak of a fiery mind;
A savageness in unreclaimed blood,
Of general assault.
　　Rey.　　　But, my good lord,—
　　Pol. Wherefore should you do this?
　　Rey.　　　　　　Ay, my lord,
I would know that.
　　Pol.　　Marry, sir, here 's my drift;

And, I believe, it is a fetch of warrant:
You laying these slight sullies on my son,
As 't were a thing a little soil'd i' the working,　40
Mark you,
Your party in converse, him you would sound,
Having ever seen in the prenominate crimes
The youth you breathe of guilty, be assur'd,
He closes with you in this consequence:
"Good sir," or so; or "friend," or "gentleman,"—
According to the phrase, or the addition,
Of man, and country.
　　Rey.　　　Very good, my lord.
　　Pol. And then, sir, does he this,—he does—
What was I about to say?—By the mass, I was　50
About to say something:—where did I leave?
　　Rey. At "closes in the consequence,"
At "friend or so," and "gentleman."
　　Pol. At, closes in the consequence,—ay, marry:
He closes with you thus:—"I know the gentleman;
I saw him yesterday, or t' other day,
Or then, or then; with such, or such; and, as you
　　say,
There was he gaming; there o'ertook in 's rouse;
There falling out at tennis;" or, perchance,
"I saw him enter such a house of sale,"　　60
Videlicet, a brothel, or so forth.—
See you now;
Your bait of falsehood takes this carp of truth:
And thus do we of wisdom and of reach,
With windlaces, and with assays of bias,
By indirections find directions out:
So, by my former lecture and advice,
Shall you my son. You have me, have you not?
　　Rey. My lord, I have.
　　Pol.　　　　God be wi' you; fare you well.
　　Rey. Good my lord!　　　　　　70
　　Pol. Observe his inclination in yourself.
　　Rey. I shall, my lord.
　　Pol. And let him ply his music.
　　Rey.　　　　　Well, my lord.
　　Pol. Farewell!　　　　[*Exit* REYNALDO.

Enter OPHELIA.

　　　　　How now, Ophelia? what 's the matter?
　　Oph. Alas, my lord, I have been so affrighted!
　　Pol. With what, in the name of God?
　　Oph. My lord, as I was sewing in my chamber,
Lord Hamlet,—with his doublet all unbrac'd;
No hat upon his head; his stockings foul'd,
Ungarter'd, and down-gyved to his ancle;　　80
Pale as his shirt; his knees knocking each other;
And with a look so piteous in purport,

As if he had been loosed out of hell,
To speak of horrors,—he comes before me.
　Pol. Mad for thy love?
　Oph. 　　　　　　My lord, I do not know ;
But, truly, I do fear it.
　Pol. 　　　　　What said he?
　Oph. He took me by the wrist, and held me hard ;
Then goes he to the length of all his arm,
And, with his other hand thus o'er his brow,
He falls to such perusal of my face,　　　　90
As he would draw it.　Long stay'd he so :
At last,—a little shaking of mine arm,
And thrice his head thus waving up and down,—
He rais'd a sigh so piteous and profound,
That it did seem to shatter all his bulk,
And end his being.　That done, he lets me go,
And, with his head over his shoulder turn'd,
He seem'd to find his way without his eyes ;
For out o' doors he went without their help,
And to the last bended their light on me.　　100
　Pol. Come, go with me : I will go seek the king.
This is the very ecstacy of love,
Whose violent property fordoes itself,
And leads the will to desperate undertakings,
As oft as any passion under heaven,
That does afflict our natures.　I am sorry—
What! have you given him any hard words of late?
　Oph. No, my good lord ; but, as you did command,
I did repel his letters, and denied
His access to me.
　Pol. 　　　　That hath made him mad.　110
I am sorry that with better heed and judgment
I had not quoted him : I fear'd he did but trifle,
And meant to wrack thee ; but, beshrew my jealousy !
It seems, it is as proper to our age
To cast beyond ourselves in our opinions,
As it is common for the younger sort
To lack discretion.　Come, go we to the king :
This must be known ; which, being kept close, might
　　move
More grief to hide, than hate to utter love.
Come.　　　　　　　　　　　　　　　120
　　　　　　———　　　　　　　　[*Exeunt.*

SCENE II.—A Room in the Castle.

Enter KING, QUEEN, ROSENCRANTZ, GUILDENSTERN,
and Attendants.

　King. Welcome, dear Rosencrantz, and Guilden-
　　stern !
Moreover that we much did long to see you,
The need we have to use you did provoke
Our hasty sending.　Something have you heard
Of Hamlet's transformation ; so I call it,
Since not the exterior nor the inward man
Resembles that it was.　What it should be,
More than his father's death, that thus hath put him
So much from the understanding of himself,
I cannot dream of : I entreat you both,　　10
That, being of so young days brought up with him,
And since so neighbour'd to his youth and humour,
That you vouchsafe your rest here in our court
Some little time ; so by your companies
To draw him on to pleasures, and to gather,
So much as from occasions you may glean,
Whether aught, to us unknown, afflicts him thus,
That, open'd, lies within our remedy.
　Queen. Good gentlemen, he hath much talk'd of
　　you ;
And, sure I am, two men there are not living,　　20
To whom he more adheres.　If it will please you
To show us so much gentry, and good will,
As to expend your time with us awhile,
For the supply and profit of our hope,
Your visitation shall receive such thanks
As fits a king's remembrance.
　Ros. 　　　　　Both your majesties
Might, by the sovereign power you have of us,
Put your dread pleasures more into command
Than to entreaty.
　Guil. 　　　　We both obey ;
And here give up ourselves, in the full bent,　　30

To lay our services freely at your feet,
To be commanded.
　King. Thanks, Rosencrantz, and gentle Guilden-
　　stern.
　Queen. Thanks, Guildenstern, and gentle Rosen-
　　crantz :
And I beseech you instantly to visit
My too much changed son.—Go, some of you,
And bring these gentlemen where Hamlet is.
　Guil. Heavens make our presence, and our prac-
　　tices,
Pleasant and helpful to him !
　Queen. 　　　　　　Ay, Amen !
　　　　[*Exeunt* ROSENCRANTZ, GUILDENSTERN, *and*
　　　　　　some Attendants.

Enter POLONIUS.

　Pol. The ambassadors from Norway, my good lord,
Are joyfully return'd.　　　　　　　41
　King. Thou still hast been the father of good news.
　Pol. Have I, my lord ? Assure you, my good liege,
I hold my duty, as I hold my soul,
Both to my God, and to my gracious king :
And I do think (or else this brain of mine
Hunts not the trail of policy so sure
As it hath us'd to do), that I have found
The very cause of Hamlet's lunacy.
　King. O! speak of that ; that do I long to hear.　50
　Pol. Give first admittance to the ambassadors ;
My news shall be the fruit to that great feast.
　King. Thyself do grace to them, and bring them
　　in.—　　　　　　　　　[*Exit* POLONIUS.
He tells me, my sweet queen, that he hath found
The head and source of all your son's distemper.
　Queen. I doubt, it is no other but the main ;
His father's death, and our o'erhasty marriage.
　King. Well, we shall sift him.—

Re-enter POLONIUS, *with* VOLTIMAND, *and*
　　　　　　CORNELIUS.
　　　　　　　　Welcome, my good friends.
Say, Voltimand, what from our brother Norway ?
　Volt. Most fair return of greetings and desires.　60
Upon our first, he sent out to suppress
His nephew's levies ; which to him appear'd
To be a preparation 'gainst the Polack :
But, better look'd into, he truly found
It was against your highness : whereat griev'd,—
That so his sickness, age, and impotence,
Was falsely borne in hand,—sends out arrests
On Fortinbras ; which he, in brief, obeys,
Receives rebuke from Norway, and, in fine,
Makes vow before his uncle, never more　　70
To give the assay of arms against your majesty.
Whereon old Norway, overcome with joy,
Gives him three thousand crowns in annual fee,
And his commission to employ those soldiers,
So levied as before, against the Polack ;
With an entreaty, herein further shown.
　　　　　　　　　　　[*Giving a paper.*
That it might please you to give quiet pass
Through your dominions for this enterprise ;
On such regards of safety, and allowance,
As therein are set down.
　King. 　　　　It likes us well ;　80
And, at our more consider'd time, we 'll read,
Answer, and think upon this business :
Meantime, we thank you for your well-took labour.
Go to your rest ; at night we 'll feast together :
Most welcome home !
　　　　　　[*Exeunt* VOLTIMAND *and* CORNELIUS.
　Pol. 　　　　This business is well ended.
My liege, and madam, to expostulate
What majesty should be, what duty is,
Why day is day, night, night, and time is time,
Were nothing but to waste night, day, and time.
Therefore, since brevity is the soul of wit,　　90
And tediousness the limbs and outward flourishes,
I will be brief.　Your noble son is mad :
Mad call I it ; for, to define true madness,
What is 't, but to be nothing else but mad ?
But let that go.

Queen.   More matter, with less art.
Pol. Madam, I swear, I use no art at all.
That he is mad, 't is true : 't is true 't is pity ;
And pity 't is 't is true : a foolish figure ;
But farewell it, for I will use no art.
Mad let us grant him, then ; and now remains,   100
That we find out the cause of this effect ;
Or rather say, the cause of this defect,
For this effect defective comes by cause :
Thus it remains, and the remainder thus.
Perpend.
I have a daughter ; have, whilst she is mine ;
Who, in her duty and obedience, mark,
Hath given me this. Now gather, and surmise.
—"To the celestial, and my soul's idol, the most beau-
tified Ophelia,"—   110
That 's an ill phrase, a vile phrase : "beautified" is a
vile phrase ; but you shall hear.—Thus :
   " In her excellent-white bosom, these," &c.—
Queen. Came this from Hamlet to her?
Pol. Good madam, stay awhile ; I will be faithful.—
[*Reads.*]   "Doubt thou, the stars are fire ;
                Doubt, that the sun doth move ;
                Doubt truth to be a liar ;
                But never doubt, I love.
"O dear Ophelia! I am ill at these numbers : I have
not art to reckon my groans ; but that I love thee best,
O most best ! believe it. Adieu.   122
      " Thine evermore, most dear lady, whilst this
                machine is to him,   HAMLET."
This in obedience hath my daughter show'd me ;
And more above, hath his solicitings,
As they fell out by time, by means, and place,
All given to mine ear.
King.   But how hath she
Receiv'd his love ?
Pol.   What do you think of me ?
King. As of a man faithful and honourable.   130
Pol. I would fain prove so. But what might you
      think,
When I had seen this hot love on the wing,
(As I perceiv'd it, I must tell you that,
Before my daughter told me,) what might you,
Or my dear majesty, your queen here, think,
If I had play'd the desk, or table-book ;
Or given my heart a winking, mute and dumb ;
Or look'd upon this love with idle sight :
What might you think ? No, I went round to work,
And my young mistress thus I did bespeak :   140
"Lord Hamlet is a prince, out of thy star ;
This must not be :" and then I precepts gave her,
That she should lock herself from his resort,
Admit no messengers, receive no tokens.
Which done, she took the fruits of my advice ;
And he, repulsed,—a short tale to make,—
Fell into a sadness ; then into a fast ;
Thence to a watch ; thence into a weakness ;
Thence to a lightness ; and, by this declension,
Into the madness wherein now he raves,   150
And all we wail for.
King.   Do you think 't is this ?
Queen. It may be, very likely.
Pol. Hath there been such a time, I 'd fain know
      that,
That I have positively said, "'T is so,"
When it prov'd otherwise ?
King.   Not that I know.
Pol. Take this from this, if this be otherwise.
If circumstances lead me, I will find
Where truth is hid, though it were hid indeed
Within the centre.
King.   How may we try it further ?
Pol. You know, sometimes he walks four hours to-
      gether,
Here in the lobby.   160
Queen.   So he does, indeed.
Pol. At such a time I 'll loose my daughter to him :
Be you and I behind an arras then ;
Mark the encounter : if he love her not,
And he not from his reason fall'n thereon,
Let me be no assistant for a state,
But keep a farm, and carters.

King.   We will try it.
Queen. But, look, where sadly the poor wretch comes
      reading.
Pol. Away ! I do beseech you, both away.
I 'll board him presently :—O ! give me leave.—   170
      [*Exeunt* KING, QUEEN, *and Attendants.*

Enter HAMLET, *reading.*

How does my good Lord Hamlet ?
Ham. Well, God-a-mercy.
Pol. Do you know me, my lord ?
Ham. Excellent well ; you are a fishmonger.
Pol. Not I, my lord.
Ham. Then I would you were so honest a man.
Pol. Honest, my lord ?
Ham. Ay, sir : to be honest, as this world goes, is to
be one man picked out of ten thousand.
Pol. That 's very true, my lord.   180
Ham. For if the sun breed maggots in a dead dog,
being a god kissing carrion,—Have you a daughter ?
Pol. I have, my lord.
Ham. Let her not walk i' the sun : conception is a
blessing ; but not as your daughter may conceive.—
Friend, look to 't.
Pol. How say you by that ?—[*Aside.*] Still harping
on my daughter :—yet he knew me not at first ; he
said, I was a fishmonger. He is far gone, far gone :
and truly in my youth I suffered much extremity for
love ; very near this. I 'll speak to him again.—What
do you read, my lord ?   192
Ham. Words, words, words.
Pol. What is the matter, my lord ?
Ham. Between who ?
Pol. I mean, the matter that you read, my lord.
Ham. Slanders, sir : for the satirical slave says
here, that old men have grey beards ; that their faces
are wrinkled ; their eyes purging thick amber and
plum-tree gum ; and that they have a plentiful lack of
wit, together with most weak hams : all of which, sir,
though I most powerfully and potently believe, yet
I hold it not honesty to have it thus set down ; for
you yourself, sir, should be old as I am, if like a crab
you could go backward.
Pol. [*Aside.*] Though this be madness, yet there is
method in 't.—Will you walk out of the air, my lord ?
Ham. Into my grave ?   208
Pol. Indeed, that is out o' the air.—[*Aside.*] How
pregnant sometimes his replies are ! a happiness that
often madness hits on, which reason and sanity could
not so prosperously be delivered of. I will leave him,
and suddenly contrive the means of meeting between
him and my daughter.—My honourable lord, I will
most humbly take my leave of you.
Ham. You cannot, sir, take from me anything that
I will more willingly part withal ; except my life,
except my life, except my life.
Pol. Fare you well, my lord.
Ham. These tedious old fools !   220

Enter ROSENCRANTZ *and* GUILDENSTERN.

Pol. You go to seek the Lord Hamlet ; there he is.
Ros. [*To* POLONIUS.] God save you, sir !
      [*Exit* POLONIUS.
Guil. Mine honour'd lord !—
Ros. My most dear lord !
Ham. My excellent good friends ! How dost thou,
Guildenstern ? Ah, Rosencrantz ! Good lads, how
do ye both ?
Ros. As the indifferent children of the earth.
Guild. Happy, in that we are not overhappy ;
On Fortune's cap we are not the very button.   230
Ham. Nor the soles of her shoe ?
Ros. Neither, my lord.
Ham. Then you live about her waist, or in the
middle of her favours ?
Guil. 'Faith, her privates we.
Ham. In the secret parts of Fortune ? O! most
true ; she is a strumpet. What news ?
Ros. None, my lord, but that the world 's grown
honest.   239
Ham. Then is doomsday near ; but your news is not
true. Let me question more in particular : what have

you, my good friends, deserved at the hands of For-
tune, that she sends you to prison hither?
Guil. Prison, my lord?
Ham. Denmark's a prison.
Ros. Then is the world one.
Ham. A goodly one; in which there are many
confines, wards, and dungeons, Denmark being one
of the worst.
Ros. We think not so, my lord.   250
Ham. Why, then 'tis none to you: for there is
nothing either good or bad, but thinking makes it
so: to me it is a prison.
Ros. Why, then your ambition makes it one: 'tis
too narrow for your mind.
Ham. O God! I could be bounded in a nut-shell,
and count myself a king of infinite space, were it not
that I have bad dreams.
Guil. Which dreams, indeed, are ambition; for the
very substance of the ambitious is merely the shadow
of a dream.   261
Ham. A dream itself is but a shadow.
Ros. Truly, and I hold ambition of so airy and light
a quality, that it is but a shadow's shadow.
Ham. Then are our beggars bodies, and our
monarchs, and outstretched heroes, the beggars'
shadows. Shall we to the court? for, by my fay, I
cannot reason.
Ros., Guil. We 'll wait upon you.   269
Ham. No such matter: I will not sort you with the
rest of my servants; for, to speak to you like an honest
man, I am most dreadfully attended. But, in the
beaten way of friendship, what make you at Elsinore?
Ros. To visit you, my lord; no other occasion.
Ham. Beggar that I am, I am even poor in thanks;
but I thank you: and sure, dear friends, my thanks
are too dear, a halfpenny. Were you not sent for? Is
it your own inclining? Is it a free visitation? Come,
come; deal justly with me: come, come; nay, speak.
Guil. What should we say, my lord?   280
Ham. Why, anything,—but to the purpose. You
were sent for; and there is a kind of confession in
your looks, which your modesties have not craft
enough to colour; I know, the good king and queen
have sent for you.
Ros. To what end, my lord?
Ham. That you must teach me. But let me conjure
you, by the rights of our fellowship, by the consonancy of our youth, by the obligation of our ever-
preserved love, and by what more dear a better
proposer could charge you withal, be even and
direct with me, whether you were sent for, or no. 292
Ros. What say you?
Ham. Nay, then I have an eye of you.—If you love
me, hold not off.
Guil. My lord, we were sent for.
Ham. I will tell you why; so shall my anticipation
prevent your discovery, and your secrecy to the king
and queen moult no feather. I have of late (but
wherefore I know not) lost all my mirth, forgone all
custom of exercises; and, indeed, it goes so heavily
with my disposition, that this goodly frame, the earth,
seems to me a steril promontory; this most excellent
canopy, the air, look you, this brave o'erhanging
firmament, this majestical roof fretted with golden
fire, why, it appeareth no other thing to me than a
foul and pestilent congregation of vapours. What a
piece of work is a man! how noble in reason! how
infinite in faculty! in form and moving, how express
and admirable! in action, how like an angel! in
apprehension, how like a god! the beauty of the
world! the paragon of animals! And yet, to me,
what is this quintessence of dust? man delights not
me; no, nor woman neither, though by your smiling
you seem to say so.
Ros. My lord, there was no such stuff in my
thoughts.
Ham. Why did you laugh then, when I said, man
delights not me?   319
Ros. To think, my lord, if you delight not in man,
what lenten entertainment the players shall receive
from you: we coted them on the way, and hither are
they coming to offer you service.

Ham. He that plays the king shall be welcome; his
majesty shall have tribute of me: the adventurous
knight shall use his foil and target: the lover shall
not sigh gratis: the humorous man shall end his part
in peace: the clown shall make those laugh, whose
lungs are tickled o' the sere: and the lady shall say
her mind freely, or the blank verse shall halt for 't.
What players are they?   331
Ros. Even those you were wont to take such delight
in, the tragedians of the city.
Ham. How chances it they travel? their residence,
both in reputation and profit, was better both ways.
Ros. I think, their inhibition comes by the means
of the late innovation.
Ham. Do they hold the same estimation they did
when I was in the city? Are they so followed?
Ros. No, indeed, they are not.   340
Ham. How comes it? Do they grow rusty?
Ros. Nay, their endeavour keeps in the wonted
pace: but there is, sir, an aery of children, little
eyases, that cry out on the top of question, and are
most tyrannically clapped for 't: these are now the
fashion; and so berattle the common stages (so they
call them), that many wearing rapiers are afraid of
goose-quills, and dare scarce come thither.   348
Ham. What! are they children? who maintains
them? how are they escoted? Will they pursue the
quality no longer than they can sing? will they not
say afterwards, if they should grow themselves to
common players, (as it is most like, if their means are
not better,) their writers do them wrong, to make
them exclaim against their own succession?
Ros. 'Faith, there has been much to do on both
sides; and the nation holds it no sin, to tarre them to
controversy: there was, for a while, no money bid for
argument, unless the poet and the player went to cuffs
in the question.   360
Ham. Is it possible?
Guil. O! there has been much throwing about of
brains.
Ham. Do the boys carry it away?
Ros. Ay, that they do, my lord; Hercules, and his
load too.
Ham. It is not strange; for my uncle is King of
Denmark, and those that would make mows at him
while my father lived, give twenty, forty, fifty, an
hundred ducats a-piece, for his picture in little.
'Sblood, there is something in this more than natural,
if philosophy could find it out.   372
                    [*Flourish of trumpets within.*
Guil. There are the players.
Ham. Gentlemen, you are welcome to Elsinore.
Your hands. Come, then; the appurtenance of welcome is fashion and ceremony: let me comply with
you in this garb, lest my extent to the players (which,
I tell you, must show fairly outward) should more
appear like entertainment than yours. You are
welcome; but my uncle-father, and aunt-mother,
are deceived.   381
Guil. In what, my dear lord?
Ham. I am but mad north-north-west: when the
wind is southerly, I know a hawk from a handsaw.

Re-enter POLONIUS.

Pol. Well be with you, gentlemen!
Ham. Mark you, Guildenstern;—and you too;—at
each ear a hearer: that great baby, you see there, is
not yet out of his swathing-clouts.
Ros. Happily he 's the second time come to them:
for, they say, an old man is twice a child.   390
Ham. I will prophesy, he comes to tell me of the
players; mark it.—You say right, sir: for o' Monday
morning: 'twas so indeed.
Pol. My lord, I have news to tell you.
Ham. My lord, I have news to tell you. When
Roscius was an actor in Rome,—
Pol. The actors are come hither, my lord.
Ham. Buz, buz!
Pol. Upon my honour,—
Ham. Then came each actor on his ass,—   400
Pol. The best actors in the world, either for
tragedy, comedy, history, pastoral, pastoral-comical,

historical-pastoral, tragical-historical, tragical-comi-cal-historical-pastoral, scene individable, or poem unlimited : Seneca cannot be too heavy, nor Plautus too light. For the law of writ, and the liberty, these are the only men.

Ham. "O Jephthah, judge of Israel," what a treasure hadst thou!

Pol. What a treasure had he, my lord?   410

Ham. Why,
    "One fair daughter, and no more,
        The which he loved passing well."

Pol. [*Aside.*] Still on my daughter.

Ham. Am I not i' the right, old Jephthah?

Pol. If you call me Jephthah, my lord, I have a daughter that I love passing well.

Ham. Nay, that follows not.

Pol. What follows then, my lord?

Ham. Why,   420
    "As by lot, God wot,"
and then, you know,
    "It came to pass, as most like it was,"—
the first row of the pious chanson will show you more ; for look, where my abridgment comes.

Enter four or five Players.

You are welcome, masters ; welcome, all.—I am glad to see thee well :—welcome, good friends.—O, my old friend ! Why, thy face is valanced since I saw thee last : com'st thou to beard me in Denmark?—What ! my young lady and mistress ! By 'r lady, your lady-ship is nearer to heaven, than when I saw you last, by the altitude of a chopine. Pray God, your voice, like a piece of uncurrent gold, be not cracked within the ring. Masters, you are all welcome. We 'll e'en to 't like French falconers, fly at anything we see : we 'll have a speech straight. Come, give us a taste of your quality ; come, a passionate speech.

1 Play. What speech, my good lord?   438

Ham. I heard thee speak me a speech once,—but it was never acted ; or, if it was, not above once ; for the play, I remember, pleased not the million ; 't was caviare to the general : but it was (as I received it, and others, whose judgments in such matters cried in the top of mine) an excellent play, well digested in the scenes, set down with as much modesty as cunning. I remember, one said, there were no sallets in the lines to make the matter savoury, nor no matter in the phrase that might indite the author of affecta-tion, but called it an honest method, as wholesome as sweet, and by very much more handsome than fine. One speech in it I chiefly loved : 't was Æneas' tale to Dido ; and thereabout of it especially, where he speaks of Priam's slaughter. If it live in your memory, begin at this line : — let me see, let me see :—
    "The rugged Pyrrhus, like the Hyrcanian beast,"
—'t is not so ; it begins with Pyrrhus :—
    "The rugged Pyrrhus,—he, whose sable arms,
    Black as his purpose, did the night resemble
    When he lay couched in the ominous horse,   460
    Hath now this dread and black complexion smear'd
    With heraldry more dismal ; head to foot
    Now is he total gules ; horridly trick'd
    With blood of fathers, mothers, daughters, sons ;
    Bak'd and impasted with the parching streets,
    That lend a tyrannous and a damned light
    To their vile murders : roasted in wrath and fire,
    And thus o'er-sized with coagulate gore,
    With eyes like carbuncles, the hellish Pyrrhus
    Old grandsire Priam seeks."—   470
So, proceed you.

Pol. 'Fore God, my lord, well spoken ; with good accent, and good discretion.

1 Play. "Anon he finds him
    Striking too short at Greeks : his antique sword,
    Rebellious to his arm, lies where it falls,
    Repugnant to command. Unequal match'd,
    Pyrrhus at Priam drives ; in rage, strikes wide ;
    But with the whiff and wind of his fell sword
    The unnerved father falls. Then senseless Ilium,
    Seeming to feel this blow, with flaming top   481

Stoops to his base ; and with a hideous crash
    Takes prisoner Pyrrhus' ear : for, lo ! his sword,
    Which was declining on the milky head
    Of reverend Priam, seem'd i' the air to stick :
    So, as a painted tyrant, Pyrrhus stood ;
    And, like a neutral to his will and matter,
    Did nothing.
    But, as we often see, against some storm,
    A silence in the heavens, the rack stand still,   490
    The bold winds speechless, and the orb below
    As hush as death, anon the dreadful thunder
    Doth rend the region : so, after Pyrrhus' pause,
    Aroused vengeance sets him new a-work ;
    And never did the Cyclops' hammers fall
    On Mars his armour, forg'd for proof eterne,
    With less remorse than Pyrrhus' bleeding sword
    Now falls on Priam.—
    Out, out, thou strumpet, Fortune ! All you gods,
    In general synod, take away her power ;   500
    Break all the spokes and fellies from her wheel,
    And bowl the round nave down the hill of heaven,
    As low as to the fiends !"

Pol. This is too long.

Ham. It shall to the barber's, with your beard.—Pr'ythee, say on :—he 's for a jig, or a tale of bawdry, or he sleeps.—Say on : come to Hecuba.

1 Play. "But who, O ! who had seen the mobled queen "—

Ham. The mobled queen?

Pol. That 's good ; mobled queen is good.   510

1 Play. "Run barefoot up and down, threat'ning the flames
    With bisson rheum ; a clout upon that head,
    Where late the diadem stood ; and, for a robe,
    About her lank and all o'er-teemed loins,
    A blanket, in the alarm of fear caught up ;
    Who this had seen, with tongue in venom steep'd,
    'Gainst Fortune's state would treason have pro-nounc'd :
    But if the gods themselves did see her then,
    When she saw Pyrrhus make malicious sport
    In mincing with his sword her husband's limbs,   520
    The instant burst of clamour that she made,
    (Unless things mortal move them not at all,)
    Would have made milch the burning eyes of heaven,
    And passion in the gods."

Pol. Look, where'er he has not turned his colour, and has tears in 's eyes!—Pr'ythee, no more.

Ham. 'T is well ; I 'll have thee speak out the rest of this soon.—Good my lord, will you see the players well bestowed? Do you hear, let them be well used ; for they are the abstracts, and brief chronicles, of the time : after your death you were better have a bad epitaph, than their ill report while you lived.   532

Pol. My lord, I will use them according to their desert.

Ham. God's bodikin, man, much better : use every man after his desert, and who should 'scape whipping? Use them after your own honour and dignity : the less they deserve, the more merit is in your bounty. Take them in.

Pol. Come, sirs.   540

Ham. Follow him, friends : we 'll hear a play to-morrow. [*Exit* POLONIUS, *with all the Players ex-cept the First.*] Dost thou hear me, old friend? can you play the Murder of Gonzago?

1 Play. Ay, my lord.

Ham. We 'll have it to-morrow night. You could, for a need, study a speech of some dozen or sixteen lines, which I would set down and insert in 't, could you not?

1 Play. Ay, my lord.   550

Ham. Very well.—Follow that lord ; and look you mock him not. [*Exit First Player.*] My good friends [*to* ROS. *and* GUIL.], I 'll leave you till night : you are welcome to Elsinore.

Ros. Good my lord !

Ham. Ay, so, God be wi' ye.—
            [*Exeunt* ROSENCRANTZ *and* GUILDENSTERN.
                Now I am alone.
O, what a rogue and peasant slave am I !

Is it not monstrous, that this player here,
But in a fiction, in a dream of passion,
Could force his soul so to his whole conceit, 560
That, from her working, all his visage wann'd;
Tears in his eyes, distraction in 's aspect,
A broken voice, and his whole function suiting
With forms to his conceit? and all for nothing!
For Hecuba!
What's Hecuba to him, or he to Hecuba,
That he should weep for her? What would he do,
Had he the motive and the cue for passion,
That I have? He would drown the stage with tears,
And cleave the general ear with horrid speech; 570
Make mad the guilty, and appal the free,
Confound the ignorant; and amaze, indeed,
The very faculties of eyes and ears.
Yet I,
A dull and muddy-mettled rascal, peak,
Like John-a-dreams, unpregnant of my cause,
And can say nothing; no, not for a king,
Upon whose property, and most dear life,
A damn'd defeat was made. Am I a coward?
Who calls me villain? breaks my pate across? 580
Plucks off my beard, and blows it in my face?
Tweaks me by the nose? gives me the lie i' the throat,
As deep as to the lungs? Who does me this?
Ha!
'Swounds! I should take it; for it cannot be,
But I am pigeon-liver'd, and lack gall

To make oppression bitter, or, ere this,
I should have fatted all the region kites
With this slave's offal. Bloody, bawdy villain!
Remorseless, treacherous, lecherous, kindless villain!
O, vengeance! 591
Why, what an ass am I! Ay, sure, this is most brave;
That I, the son of a dear father murder'd,
Prompted to my revenge by heaven and hell,
Must, like a whore, unpack my heart with words,
And fall a-cursing, like a very drab,
A scullion!
Fie upon 't! foh! About, my brain!—I have heard,
That guilty creatures, sitting at a play,
Have by the very cunning of the scene 600
Been struck so to the soul, that presently
They have proclaim'd their malefactions;
For murder, though it have no tongue, will speak
With most miraculous organ. I 'll have these players
Play something like the murder of my father,
Before mine uncle: I 'll observe his looks;
I 'll tent him to the quick: if he but blench,
I know my course. The spirit that I have seen
May be the devil: and the devil hath power
To assume a pleasing shape; yea, and, perhaps, 610
Out of my weakness, and my melancholy,
As he is very potent with such spirits,
Abuses me to damn me. I 'll have grounds
More relative than this:—the play 's the thing,
Wherein I 'll catch the conscience of the king. [Exit.

ACT III.

SCENE I.—A Room in the Castle.

Enter KING, QUEEN, POLONIUS, OPHELIA, ROSENCRANTZ, *and* GUILDENSTERN.

King.
AND can you, by no drift of circumstance,
Get from him, why he puts on this confusion,
Grating so harshly all his days of quiet
With turbulent and dangerous lunacy?
Ros. He does confess, he feels himself
    distracted;
But from what cause he will by no means
    speak.
Guil. Nor do we find him forward to be
    sounded,
But, with a crafty madness, keeps aloof,
When we would bring him on to some confession
Of his true state.
Queen.   Did he receive you well? 10
Ros. Most like a gentleman.
Guil. But with much forcing of his disposition.
Ros. Niggard of question; but, of our demands,
Most free in his reply.
Queen.   Did you assay him
To any pastime?
Ros. Madam, it so fell out, that certain players
We o'er-raught on the way: of these we told him;
And there did seem in him a kind of joy
To hear of it. They are about the court;
And, as I think, they have already order 20
This night to play before him.
Pol.   'T is most true:
And he beseech'd me to entreat your majesties,
To hear and see the matter.
King. With all my heart; and it doth much content
    me

To hear him so inclin'd.
Good gentlemen, give him a further edge,
And drive his purpose on to these delights.
Ros. We shall, my lord.
          [*Exeunt* ROSENCRANTZ *and* GUILDENSTERN.
King.   Sweet Gertrude, leave us too;
For we have closely sent for Hamlet hither,
That he, as 't were by accident, may here 30
Affront Ophelia.
Her father, and myself, (lawful espials,)
Will so bestow ourselves, that, seeing, unseen,
We may of their encounter frankly judge;
And gather by him, as he is behav'd,
If 't be the affliction of his love, or no,
That thus he suffers for.
Queen.   I shall obey you.—
And, for your part, Ophelia, I do wish,
That your good beauties be the happy cause
Of Hamlet's wildness; so shall I hope, your virtues 40
Will bring him to his wonted way again,
To both your honours.
Oph.   Madam, I wish it may.
          [*Exit* QUEEN.
Pol. Ophelia, walk you here.—Gracious, so please
    you,
We will bestow ourselves.—[*To* OPHELIA.] Read on
    this book;
That show of such an exercise may colour
Your loneliness.—We are oft to blame in this,—
'T is too much prov'd, that, with devotion's visage,
And pious action, we do sugar o'er
The devil himself.

King. [*Aside.*] O! 't is too true!
How smart a lash that speech doth give my conscience!
The harlot's cheek, beautied with plastering art,   51
Is not more ugly to the thing that helps it,
Than is my deed to my most painted word.
O heavy burden!
Pol. I hear him coming: let 's withdraw, my lord.
                    [*Exeunt* KING *and* POLONIUS.

Enter HAMLET.

Ham. To be, or not to be, that is the question:—
Whether 't is nobler in the mind, to suffer

Ham. "To be, or not to be, that is the question."

The slings and arrows of outrageous fortune;
Or to take arms against a sea of troubles,
And by opposing end them?—To die,—to sleep,   60
No more;—and, by a sleep, to say we end
The heart-ache, and the thousand natural shocks
That flesh is heir to,—'t is a consummation
Devoutly to be wish'd. To die,—to sleep:—
To sleep! perchance to dream:—ay, there 's the rub;
For in that sleep of death what dreams may come,
When we have shuffled off this mortal coil,
Must give us pause. There 's the respect,
That makes calamity of so long life:
For who would bear the whips and scorns of time,   70
The oppressor's wrong, the proud man's contumely,
The pangs of despis'd love, the law's delay,
The insolence of office, and the spurns
That patient merit of the unworthy takes,
When he himself might his quietus make
With a bare bodkin? who would these fardels bear,
To grunt and sweat under a weary life,
But that the dread of something after death,—
The undiscover'd country, from whose bourn
No traveller returns,—puzzles the will,   80
And makes us rather bear those ills we have,
Than fly to others that we know not of?
Thus conscience does make cowards of us all;
And thus the native hue of resolution
Is sicklied o'er with the pale cast of thought;
And enterprises of great pith and moment
With this regard their currents turn awry,
And lose the name of action.—Soft you, now!
The fair Ophelia.—Nymph, in thy orisons
Be all my sins remember'd.
Oph.   Good my lord,   90
How does your honour for this many a day?
Ham. I humbly thank you; well, well, well.
Oph. My lord, I have remembrances of yours,
That I have longed long to re-deliver;
I pray you, now receive them.
Ham.   No, not I;
I never gave you aught.
Oph. My honour'd lord, you know right well you
               did;
And, with them, words of so sweet breath compos'd,
As made the things more rich: their perfume lost,
Take these again; for, to the noble mind,   100
Rich gifts wax poor when givers prove unkind.
There, my lord.
Ham. Ha, ha! are you honest?
Oph. My lord!

Ham. Are you fair?
Oph. What means your lordship?
Ham. That if you be honest, and fair, your honesty
should admit no discourse to your beauty.
Oph. Could beauty, my lord, have better commerce
than with honesty?   110
Ham. Ay, truly; for the power of beauty will
sooner transform honesty from what it is to a bawd,
than the force of honesty can translate beauty into
his likeness: this was sometime a paradox, but now
the time gives it proof. I did love you once.
Oph. Indeed, my lord, you made me believe so.
Ham. You should not have believed
me; for virtue cannot so inoculate our
old stock, but we shall relish of it. I
loved you not.   120
Oph. I was the more deceived.
Ham. Get thee to a nunnery: why
wouldst thou be a breeder of sinners?
I am myself indifferent honest; but yet
I could accuse me of such things, that it
were better, my mother had not borne
me. I am very proud, revengeful, ambitious; with more offences at my beck,
than I have thoughts to put them in,
imagination to give them shape, or time
to act them in. What should such
fellows as I do crawling between
heaven and earth? We are arrant
knaves, all; believe none of us. Go
thy ways to a nunnery. Where 's your
father?
Oph. At home, my lord.
Ham. Let the doors be shut upon him, that he may
play the fool nowhere but in 's own house. Farewell.
Oph. O! help him, you sweet heavens!   140
Ham. If thou dost marry, I 'll give thee this plague
for thy dowry: be thou as chaste as ice, as pure as
snow, thou shalt not escape calumny. Get thee to a
nunnery; go, farewell. Or, if thou wilt needs marry,
marry a fool; for wise men know well enough what
monsters you make of them. To a nunnery, go; and
quickly too. Farewell.
Oph. O heavenly powers, restore him!   148
Ham. I have heard of your paintings too, well
enough: God hath given you one face, and you make
yourselves another: you jig, you amble, and you lisp,
and nickname God's creatures, and make your wantonness your ignorance. Go to; I 'll no more on 't: it
hath made me mad. I say, we will have no more
marriages: those that are married already, all but
one, shall live; the rest shall keep as they are. To a
nunnery, go.   [*Exit.*
Oph. O, what a noble mind is here o'erthrown!
The courtier's, soldier's, scholar's, eye, tongue, sword;
The expectancy and rose of the fair state,   160
The glass of fashion, and the mould of form,
The observ'd of all observers, quite, quite down!
And I, of ladies most deject and wretched,
That suck'd the honey of his music vows,
Now see that noble and most sovereign reason,
Like sweet bells jangled, out of tune and harsh;
That unmatch'd form and feature of blown youth
Blasted with ecstasy. O, woe is me,
To have seen what I have seen, see what I see!

Re-enter KING *and* POLONIUS.

King. Love! his affections do not that way tend; 170
Nor what he spake, though it lack'd form a little,
Was not like madness. There 's something in his
               soul,
O'er which his melancholy sits on brood;
And, I do doubt, the hatch, and the disclose,
Will be some danger: which for to prevent,
I have, in quick determination,
Thus set it down. He shall with speed to England,
For the demand of our neglected tribute:
Haply, the seas, and countries different,
With variable objects, shall expel   180
This something-settled matter in his heart;
Whereon his brains still beating puts him thus
From fashion of himself. What think you on 't?

Pol. It shall do well : but yet do I believe,
The origin and commencement of his grief
Sprung from neglected love.—How now, Ophelia !
You need not tell us what Lord Hamlet said ;
We heard it all.—My lord, do as you please ;
But, if you hold it fit, after the play,
Let his queen mother all alone entreat him   190
To show his griefs : let her be round with him ;
And I 'll be plac'd, so please you, in the ear
Of all their conference. If she find him not,
To England send him ; or confine him, where
Your wisdom best shall think.
     King.   It shall be so :
Madness in great ones must not unwatch'd go.
                                          [*Exeunt.*

SCENE II.—*A Hall in the Same.*

Enter HAMLET *and certain Players.*

Ham. Speak the speech, I pray you, as I pronounced
it to you, trippingly on the tongue ; but if you mouth
it, as many of your players do, I had as lief the town-
crier spoke my lines. Nor do not saw the air too
much with your hand, thus ; but use all gently : for
in the very torrent, tempest, and (as I may say) the
whirlwind of passion, you must acquire and beget
a temperance, that may give it smoothness. O! it
offends me to the soul, to hear a robustious periwig-
pated fellow tear a passion to tatters, to very rags, to
split the ears of the groundlings; who, for the most
part, are capable of nothing but inexplicable dumb-
shows, and noise : I would have such a fellow whipped
for o'erdoing Termagant ; it out-herods Herod : pray
you, avoid it.
1 Play. I warrant your honour.   16
Ham. Be not too tame neither, but let your own
discretion be your tutor : suit the action to the word,
the word to the action, with this special observance,
that you o'erstep not the modesty of nature ; for anything so overdone is from the purpose of playing,
whose end, both at the first, and now, was, and is,
to hold, as 't were, the mirror up to nature ; to show
virtue her own feature, scorn her own image, and the
very age and body of the time, his form and pressure.
Now, this overdone, or come tardy off, though it make
the unskilful laugh, cannot but make the judicious
grieve ; the censure of the which one must, in your
allowance, o'erweigh a whole theatre of others. O!
there be players, that I have seen play,—and heard
others praise, and that highly,—not to speak it pro-
fanely, that, neither having the accent of Christians,
nor the gait of Christian, pagan, nor man, have so
strutted, and bellowed, that I have thought some of
nature's journeymen had made men, and not made
them well, they imitated humanity so abominably.
1 Play. I hope, we have reformed that indifferently
with us.   38
Ham. O! reform it altogether. And let those that
play your clowns speak no more than is set down for
them : for there be of them, that will themselves
laugh, to set on some quantity of barren spectators to
laugh too ; though, in the meantime, some necessary
question of the play be then to be considered : that 's
villanous, and shows a most pitiful ambition in the
rool that uses it. Go, make you ready.—
                              [*Exeunt Players.*

Enter POLONIUS, ROSENCRANTZ, *and* GUILDENSTERN.

How now, my lord ? will the king hear this piece of
     work ?
Pol. And the queen too, and that presently.
Ham. Bid the players make haste.—
                              [*Exit* POLONIUS.
Will you two help to hasten them ?   50
Ros., Guil. We will, my lord.
     [*Exeunt* ROSENCRANTZ *and* GUILDENSTERN.
Ham. What, ho ! Horatio !

Enter HORATIO.

Hor. Here, sweet lord, at your service.

Ham. Horatio, thou art e'en as just a man
As e'er my conversation cop'd withal.
Hor. O! my dear lord,—
Ham.   Nay, do not think I flatter ;
For what advancement may I hope from thee,
That no revenue hast but thy good spirits,
To feed and clothe thee ? Why should the poor be
                                   flatter'd ?
No ; let the candied tongue lick absurd pomp,   60
And crook the pregnant hinges of the knee,
Where thrift may follow fawning. Dost thou hear ?
Since my dear soul was mistress of her choice,
And could of men distinguish, her election
Hath seal'd thee for herself : for thou hast been
As one, in suffering all, that suffers nothing
A man, that Fortune's buffets and rewards
Hast ta'en with equal thanks : and bless'd are those,
Whose blood and judgment are so well co-mingled,
That they are not a pipe for Fortune's finger   70
To sound what stop she please. Give me that man
That is not passion's slave, and I will wear him
In my heart's core, ay, in my heart of heart,
As I do thee.—Something too much of this.—
There is a play to-night before the king ;
One scene of it comes near the circumstance,
Which I have told thee, of my father's death :
I pr'ythee, when thou seest that act afoot,
Even with the very comment of thy soul
Observe mine uncle : if his occulted guilt   80
Do not itself unkennel in one speech,
It is a damned ghost that we have seen,
And my imaginations are as foul
As Vulcan's stithy. Give him heedful note :
For I mine eyes will rivet to his face ;
And, after, we will both our judgments join
In censure of his seeming.
Hor.   Well, my lord :
If he steal aught, the whilst this play is playing,
And 'scape detecting, I will pay the theft.
Ham. They are coming to the play : I must be
                                   idle ;   90
Get you a place.

Danish march. A flourish. Enter KING, QUEEN,
POLONIUS, OPHELIA, ROSENCRANTZ, GUILDEN-
STERN, *and others.*

King. How fares our cousin Hamlet ?
Ham. Excellent, i' faith ; of the chameleon's dish :
I eat the air, promise-crammed. You cannot feed
capons so.
King. I have nothing with this answer, Hamlet :
these words are not mine.
Ham. No, nor mine now.—[*To* POLONIUS.] My
lord, you played once in the university, you say ?
Pol. That did I, my lord ; and was accounted a good
actor.   101
Ham. And what did you enact ?
Pol. I did enact Julius Cæsar : I was killed i' the
Capitol ; Brutus killed me.
Ham. It was a brute part of him to kill so capital a
calf there.—Be the players ready ?
Ros. Ay, my lord ; they stay upon your patience.
Queen. Come hither, my good Hamlet, sit by me.
Ham. No, good mother, here 's metal more attrac-
tive.   110
Pol. O ho ! do you mark that ?
Ham. Lady, shall I lie in your lap ?
          [*Lying down at* OPHELIA'S *feet.*
Oph. No, my lord.
Ham. I mean, my head upon your lap ?
Oph. Ay, my lord.
Ham. Do you think, I meant country matters ?
Oph. I think nothing, my lord.
Ham. That 's a fair thought to lie between maids'
legs.
Oph. What is, my lord ?   120
Ham. Nothing.
Oph. You are merry, my lord.
Ham. Who, I ?
Oph. Ay, my lord.
Ham. O God ! your only jig-maker. What should a
man do, but be merry ? for, look you, how cheerfully

my mother looks, and my father died within 's two
hours.
Oph. Nay, 't is twice two months, my lord.   129
Ham. So long? Nay then, let the devil wear black,
for I 'll have a suit of sables. O heavens! die two
months ago, and not forgotten yet? Then there 's
hope, a great man's memory may outlive his life half
a year; but, by 'r lady, he must build churches then,
or else shall he suffer not thinking on, with the hobby-
horse; whose epitaph is, "For, O! for, O! the hobby-
horse is forgot."

Hautboys play.   The dumb-show enters.

*Enter a King and a Queen, very lovingly; the Queen
embracing him, and he her.   She kneels, and makes
show of protestation unto him.   He takes her up,
and declines his head upon her neck; lays him
down upon a bank of flowers; she, seeing him
asleep, leaves him.   Anon comes in a fellow, takes
off his crown, kisses it, and pours poison in the
King's ears, and exit.   The Queen returns, finds the
King dead, and makes passionate action.   The
Poisoner, with some two or three Mutes, comes in
again, seeming to lament with her.   The dead body
is carried away.   The Poisoner woos the Queen
with gifts: she seems loath and unwilling awhile;
but in the end accepts his love.   [Exeunt.*

Oph. What means this, my lord?
Ham. Marry, this is miching mallecho; it means
mischief.   140
Oph. Belike, this show imports the argument of the
play.

Enter Prologue.

Ham. We shall know by this fellow: the players
cannot keep counsel; they 'll tell all.
Oph. Will he tell us what this show meant?
Ham. Ay, or any show that you will show him: be
not you ashamed to show, he 'll not shame to tell you
what it means.
Oph. You are naught, you are naught. I 'll mark
the play.   150
Pro. For us, and for our tragedy,
Here stooping to your clemency,
We beg your hearing patiently.   [Exit.*
Ham. Is this a prologue, or the posy of a ring?
Oph. 'T is brief, my lord.
Ham. As woman's love.

Enter a King and a Queen.

P. King. Full thirty times hath Phœbus' cart gone
round
Neptune's salt wash, and Tellus' orbed ground;
And thirty dozen moons, with borrow'd sheen,
About the world have times twelve thirties been; 160
Since love our hearts, and Hymen did our hands,
Unite commutual in most sacred bands.
P. Queen. So many journeys may the sun and moon
Make us again count o'er, ere love be done.
But, woe is me! you are so sick of late,
So far from cheer, and from your former state,
That I distrust you. Yet, though I distrust,
Discomfort you, my lord, it nothing must;
For women's fear and love holds quantity,
In neither aught, or in extremity.   170
Now, what my love is, proof hath made you know;
And as my love is siz'd, my fear is so.
Where love is great, the littlest doubts are fear;
Where little fears grow great, great love grows there.
P. King. 'Faith, I must leave thee, love, and shortly
too;
My operant powers their functions leave to do:
And thou shalt live in this fair world behind,
Honour'd, belov'd; and, haply, one as kind
For husband shalt thou—
P. Queen.   O, confound the rest!
Such love must needs be treason in my breast: 180
In second husband let me be accurst;
None wed the second, but who kill'd the first.
Ham. [*Aside.*] Wormwood, wormwood.
P. Queen. The instances, that second marriage
move,
Are base respects of thrift, but none of love:

A second time I kill my husband dead,
When second husband kisses me in bed.
P. King. I do believe you think what now you
speak;
But what we do determine oft we break.
Purpose is but the slave to memory,   190
Of violent birth, but poor validity;
Which now, like fruit unripe, sticks on the tree,
But fall unshaken, when they mellow be.
Most necessary 't is, that we forget
To pay ourselves what to ourselves is debt:
What to ourselves in passion we propose,
The passion ending, doth the purpose lose.
The violence of either grief or joy
Their own enactures with themselves destroy:
Where joy most revels, grief doth most lament; 200
Grief joys, joy grieves, on slender accident.
This world is not for aye; nor 't is not strange,
That even our loves should with our fortunes change:
For 't is a question left us yet to prove,
Whether love lead fortune, or else fortune love.
The great man down, you mark, his favourite flies;
The poor advanc'd makes friends of enemies.
And hitherto doth love on fortune tend:
For who not needs shall never lack a friend;
And who in want a hollow friend doth try,   210
Directly seasons him his enemy.
But, orderly to end where I begun,
Our wills and fates do so contrary run,
That our devices still are overthrown;
Our thoughts are ours, their ends none of our own:
So think thou wilt no second husband wed;
But die thy thoughts, when thy first lord is dead.
P. Queen. Nor earth to me give food, nor heaven
light!
Sport and repose lock from me, day and night!
To desperation turn my trust and hope!   220
An anchor's cheer in prison be my scope!
Each opposite, that blanks the face of joy,
Meet what I would have well, and it destroy!
Both here, and hence, pursue me lasting strife,
If, once a widow, ever I be wife!
Ham. If she should break it now?
P. King. 'T is deeply sworn. Sweet, leave me here
awhile:
My spirits grow dull, and fain I would beguile
The tedious day with sleep.   [*Sleeps.*
P. Queen.   Sleep rock thy brain;
And never come mischance between us twain! [*Exit.*
Ham. Madam, how like you this play?   231
Queen. The lady protests too much, methinks.
Ham. O! but she 'll keep her word.
King. Have you heard the argument? Is there no
offence in 't?
Ham. No, no; they do but jest, poison in jest: no
offence i' the world.
King. What do you call the play?   238
Ham. The Mouse-trap. Marry, how? Tropically.
This play is the image of a murder done in Vienna:
Gonzago is the duke's name; his wife, Baptista. You
shall see anon; 't is a knavish piece of work: but what
of that? your majesty, and we, that have free souls,
it touches us not: let the galled jade wince, our
withers are unwrung.

Enter LUCIANUS.

This is one Lucianus, nephew to the king.
Oph. You are a good chorus, my lord.
Ham. I could interpret between you and your love,
if I could see the puppets dallying.
Oph. You are keen, my lord, you are keen.   250
Ham. It would cost you a groaning to take off my
edge.
Oph. Still better, and worse.
Ham. So you must take your husbands.—Begin,
murderer: pox, leave thy damnable faces, and begin.
Come:—the croaking raven doth bellow for revenge.
Luc. Thoughts black, hands apt, drugs fit, and time
agreeing;
Confederate season, else no creature seeing;
Thou mixture rank, of midnight weeds collected,
With Hecate's ban thrice blasted, thrice infected, 260

Thy natural magic and dire property,
On wholesome life usurp immediately.
　　　　[*Pours the poison into the Sleeper's ears.*
　Ham. He poisons him i' the garden for 's estate.
His name 's Gonzago: the story is extant, and writ in

　Ham. Why, let the strucken deer go weep,
　　　　The hart ungalled play;
　　For some must watch, while some must sleep:
　　　　Thus runs the world away.
Would not this, sir, and a forest of feathers, (if the

Ham. "Marry, this is miching mallecho; it means mischief."

choice Italian. You shall see anon, how the murderer gets the love of Gonzago's wife.
　Oph. The king rises.
　Ham. What! frighted with false fire?
　Queen. How fares my lord?
　Pol. Give o'er the play.　　　　　　　　　　270
　King. Give me some light!—away!
　All. Lights, lights, lights!
　　　　[*Exeunt all but* HAMLET *and* HORATIO.

rest of my fortunes turn Turk with me,) with two Provincial roses on my razed shoes, get me a fellowship in a cry of players, sir?　　　　　　　　　　280
　Hor. Half a share.
　Ham.　　A whole one, I.
　　　　For thou dost know, O Damon dear,
　　　　　This realm dismantled was
　　　　Of Jove himself; and now reigns here
　　　　　A very, very—pajock.

Hor. You might have rhymed.
Ham. O good Horatio! I'll take the ghost's word
for a thousand pound. Didst perceive?
  Hor. Very well, my lord.   290
  Ham. Upon the talk of the poisoning,—
  Hor. I did very well note him.
  Ham. Ah, ha!—Come, some music! come, the re-
corders!
For if the king like not the comedy,
Why then, belike,—he likes it not, perdy.—
Come, some music!

    Enter ROSENCRANTZ *and* GUILDENSTERN.

  Guil. Good my lord, vouchsafe me a word with you.
  Ham. Sir, a whole history.
  Guil. The king, sir,—
  Ham. Ay, sir, what of him?   300
  Guil. Is, in his retirement, marvellous distem-
pered.
  Ham. With drink, sir?
  Guil. No, my lord, rather with choler.
  Ham. Your wisdom should show itself more richer,
to signify this to his doctor; for, for me to put him to
his purgation, would, perhaps, plunge him into far
more choler.
  Guil. Good my lord, put your discourse into some
frame, and start not so wildly from my affair.   310
  Ham. I am tame, sir;—pronounce.
  Guil. The queen, your mother, in most great affliction of spirit, hath sent me to you.
  Ham. You are welcome.
  Guil. Nay, good my lord, this courtesy is not of the
right breed. If it shall please you to make me a
wholesome answer, I will do your mother's commandment; if not, your pardon and my return shall be the
end of my business.
  Ham. Sir, I cannot.   320
  Guil. What, my lord?
  Ham. Make you a wholesome answer; my wit's
diseased; but, sir, such answer as I can make, you
shall command; or, rather, as you say, my mother:
therefore no more, but to the matter. My mother, you
say,—
  Ros. Then, thus she says. Your behaviour hath
struck her into amazement and admiration.
  Ham. O wonderful son, that can so astonish a
mother!—But is there no sequel at the heels of this
mother's admiration? impart.   331
  Ros. She desires to speak with you in her closet,
ere you go to bed.
  Ham. We shall obey, were she ten times our mother.
Have you any further trade with us?
  Ros. My lord, you once did love me.
  Ham. And do still, by these pickers and stealers.
  Ros. Good my lord, what is your cause of dis-
temper? you do freely bar the door of your own
liberty, if you deny your griefs to your friend.   340
  Ham. Sir, I lack advancement.
  Ros. How can that be, when you have the voice
of the king himself for your succession in Denmark?
  Ham. Ay, sir, but " While the grass grows;"—the
proverb is something musty.

    Enter Players with recorders.

O! the recorders: let me see one.—To withdraw with
you.—Why do you go about to recover the wind of
me, as if you would drive me into a toil?
  Guil. O, my lord, if my duty be too bold, my love is
too unmannerly.   350
  Ham. I do not well understand that. Will you play
upon this pipe?
  Guil. My lord, I cannot.
  Ham. I pray you.
  Guil. Believe me, I cannot.
  Ham. I do beseech you.
  Guil. I know no touch of it, my lord.
  Ham. It is as easy as lying: govern these ventages
with your finger and thumb, give it breath with your
mouth, and it will discourse most eloquent music.
Look you, these are the stops.   361
  Guil. But these cannot I command to any utterance
of harmony: I have not the skill.

  Ham. Why, look you now, how unworthy a thing
you make of me. You would play upon me; you
would seem to know my stops; you would pluck out
the heart of my mystery; you would sound me from
my lowest note to the top of my compass; and there
is much music, excellent voice, in this little organ, yet
cannot you make it speak. 'Sblood! do you think
I am easier to be played on than a pipe? Call me
what instrument you will, though you can fret me,
you cannot play upon me.   373

    Enter POLONIUS.

God bless you, sir!
  Pol. My lord, the queen would speak with you, and
presently.
  Ham. Do you see yonder cloud, that's almost in
shape of a camel?
  Pol. By the mass, and 'tis like a camel, indeed.
  Ham. Methinks, it is like a weasel.   380
  Pol. It is backed like a weasel.
  Ham. Or, like a whale?
  Pol. Very like a whale.
  Ham. Then will I come to my mother by-and-by.—
They fool me to the top of my bent.—I will come by-
and-by.
  Pol. I will say so.   *[Exit.*
  Ham. By-and-by is easily said.—Leave me, friends.
    [*Exeunt* ROSENCRANTZ, GUILDENSTERN,
      HORATIO, *&c.*
'T is now the very witching time of night,
When churchyards yawn, and hell itself breathes out
Contagion to this world: now could I drink hot blood,
And do such bitter business as the day   392
Would quake to look on. Soft! now to my mother.—
O heart! lose not thy nature; let not ever
The soul of Nero enter this firm bosom:
Let me be cruel, not unnatural:
I will speak daggers to her, but use none;
My tongue and soul in this be hypocrites:
How in my words soever she be shent,
To give them seals never, my soul, consent!   400
    [*Exit.*

     SCENE III.—A Room in the Same.

  Enter KING, ROSENCRANTZ, *and* GUILDENSTERN.

  King. I like him not; nor stands it safe with us,
To let his madness range. Therefore, prepare you:
I your commission will forthwith despatch,
And he to England shall along with you.
The terms of our estate may not endure
Hazard so dangerous, as doth hourly grow
Out of his lunacies.
  Guil.   We will ourselves provide.
Most holy and religious fear it is,
To keep those many many bodies safe,
That live and feed upon your majesty.   10
  Ros. The single and peculiar life is bound,
With all the strength and armour of the mind,
To keep itself from noyance; but much more
That spirit, upon whose weal depends and rests
The lives of many. The cease of majesty
Dies not alone; but, like a gulf, doth draw
What's near it with it: it is a massy wheel,
Fix'd on the summit of the highest mount,
To whose huge spokes ten thousand lesser things
Are mortis'd and adjoin'd; which, when it falls,   20
Each small annexment, petty consequence,
Attends the boisterous ruin. Never alone
Did the king sigh, but with a general groan.
  King. Arm you, I pray you, to this speedy voyage;
For we will fetters put upon this fear,
Which now goes too free-footed.
  Ros., Guil.   We will haste us.
    [*Exeunt* ROSENCRANTZ *and* GUILDENSTERN.

     Enter POLONIUS.

  Pol. My lord, he's going to his mother's closet.
Behind the arras I'll convey myself,
To hear the process: I'll warrant, she'll tax him home;
And, as you said, and wisely was it said,   30

'T is meet that some more audience than a mother,
Since nature makes them partial, should o'erhear
The speech, of vantage. Fare you well, my liege:
I 'll call upon you ere you go to bed,
And tell you what I know.
    King.   Thanks, dear my lord.
                                 [Exit Polonius.
O ! my offence is rank, it smells to heaven ;
It hath the primal eldest curse upon 't,
A brother's murder !—Pray can I not,
Though inclination be as sharp as will :
My stronger guilt defeats my strong intent ;   40
And, like a man to double business bound,
I stand in pause where I shall first begin,
And both neglect. What if this cursed hand
Were thicker than itself with brother's blood,
Is there not rain enough in the sweet heavens,
To wash it white as snow? Whereto serves mercy,
But to confront the visage of offence?
And what 's in prayer, but this two-fold force,—
To be forestalled, ere we come to fall,
Or pardon'd, being down? Then, I 'll look up :   50
My fault is past. But, O ! what form of prayer
Can serve my turn? Forgive me my foul murder !—
That cannot be ; since I am still possess'd
Of those effects for which I did the murder,
My crown, mine own ambition, and my queen.
May one be pardon'd, and retain the offence?
In the corrupted currents of this world,
Offence's gilded hand may shove by justice ;
And oft 't is seen, the wicked prize itself
Buys out the law : but 't is not so above ;   60
There is no shuffling, there the action lies
In his true nature ; and we ourselves compell'd,
Even to the teeth and forehead of our faults,
To give in evidence. What then? what rests?
Try what repentance can : what can it not?
Yet what can it, when one can not repent?
O wretched state ! O bosom, black as death !
O limed soul, that, struggling to be free,
Art more engaged ! Help, angels ! make assay :
Bow, stubborn knees ; and, heart, with strings of steel,
Be soft as sinews of the new-born babe.   71
All may be well.   *[Retires and kneels.*

             Enter Hamlet.

  Ham. Now might I do it, pat, now he is praying ;
And now I 'll do 't :—and so he goes to heaven ;
And so am I reveng'd ? That would be scann'd :
A villain kills my father ; and, for that,
I, his sole son, do this same villain send
To heaven.
Why, this is hire and salary, not revenge.
He took my father grossly, full of bread ;   80
With all his crimes broad blown, as flush as May ;
And how his audit stands, who knows, save Heaven?
But, in our circumstance and course of thought,
'T is heavy with him. And am I then reveng'd,
To take him in the purging of his soul,
When he is fit and season'd for his passage?
No.
Up, sword ; and know thou a more horrid hent :
When he is drunk, asleep, or in his rage ;
Or in the incestuous pleasures of his bed ;   90
At gaming, swearing ; or about some act,
That has no relish of salvation in 't ;
Then trip him, that his heels may kick at heaven,
And that his soul may be as damn'd, and black,
As hell, whereto it goes. My mother stays :
This physic but prolongs thy sickly days.   '[Exit.

     The King *rises and advances.*

  King. My words fly up, my thoughts remain below :
Words without thoughts never to heaven go. *[Exit.*

          SCENE IV.—A Room in the Same.

        Enter Queen *and* Polonius.

  Pol. He will come straight. Look, you lay home
    to him ;

Tell him, his pranks have been too broad to bear with,
And that your grace hath screen'd and stood between
Much heat and him. I 'll silence me e'en here.
Pray you, be round with him.
  Ham. *[Within.]* Mother, mother, mother !
  Queen. I 'll warrant you ; fear me not :
Withdraw, I hear him coming.
        *[*Polonius *hides himself behind the arras.*

      Ham. " Now might I do it, pat, now he is praying."

             Enter Hamlet.

  Ham. Now, mother, what 's the matter?
  Queen. Hamlet, thou hast thy father much offended.
  Ham. Mother, you have my father much offended.
  Queen. Come, come ; you answer with an idle
    tongue.   12
  Ham. Go, go ; you question with a wicked tongue.
  Queen. Why, how now, Hamlet?
  Ham.   What 's the matter now?
  Queen. Have you forgot me?
  Ham.   No, by the rood, not so :
You are the queen, your husband's brother's wife ;
But—'would you were not so !—you are my mother.
  Queen. Nay then, I 'll set those to you that can
    speak.
  Ham. Come, come, and sit you down ; you shall not
    budge :
You go not, till I set you up a glass   20
Where you may see the inmost part of you.
  Queen. What wilt thou do? thou wilt not murder
    me?
Help, help, ho !
  Pol. *[Behind.]* What, ho ! help, help, help !
  Ham. How now ! a rat? *[Draws.]* Dead ! for a ducat,
    dead !   *[Makes a pass through the arras.*
  Pol. *[Behind.]* O ! I am slain.   *[Falls, and dies.*
  Queen. O me ! what hast thou done?
  Ham.   Nay, I know not :
Is it the king?
  Queen. O, what a rash and bloody deed is this !
  Ham. A bloody deed ; almost as bad, good mother,
As kill a king, and marry with his brother.   30
  Queen. As kill a king !
  Ham.   Ay, lady, 't was my word.
    [Lifts up the arras, and draws forth Polonius.
Thou wretched, rash, intruding fool, farewell !
I took thee for thy better ; take thy fortune :

Thou find'st, to be too busy is some danger.—
Leave wringing of your hands. Peace! sit you down,
And let me wring your heart : for so I shall,
If it be made of penetrable stuff;
If damned custom have not braz'd it so,
That it is proof and bulwark against sense.

   Queen. What have I done, that thou dar'st wag thy
      tongue   40
In noise so rude against me?
   Ham.   Such an act,
That blurs the grace and blush of modesty;
Calls virtue, hypocrite ; takes off the rose
From the fair forehead of an innocent love,
And sets a blister there ; makes marriage vows
As false as dicers' oaths : O! such a deed,
As from the body of contraction plucks
The very soul ; and sweet religion makes
A rhapsody of words : heaven's face doth glow;
Yea, this solidity and compound mass,   50
With tristful visage, as against the doom,
Is thought-sick at the act.

Ham. "Look here, upon this picture, and on this."

   Queen.   Ah me! what act,
That roars so loud, and thunders in the index?
   Ham. Look here, upon this picture, and on this ;
The counterfeit presentment of two brothers.
See, what a grace was seated on this brow;
Hyperion's curls ; the front of Jove himself ;
An eye like Mars, to threaten and command ;
A station like the herald Mercury,
New-lighted on a heaven-kissing hill ;   60
A combination, and a form, indeed,
Where every god did seem to set his seal,
To give the world assurance of a man.
This was your husband : look you now, what follows.
Here is your husband ; like a mildew'd ear,
Blasting his wholesome brother. Have you eyes?
Could you on this fair mountain leave to feed,
And batten on this moor ? Ha ! have you eyes?
You cannot call it love ; for, at your age,
The hey-day in the blood is tame, it 's humble,   70
And waits upon the judgment ; and what judgment
Would step from this to this ? Sense, sure, you have,
Else could you not have motion ; but, sure, that sense
Is apoplex'd ; for madness would not err,
Nor sense to ecstacy was ne'er so thrall'd,
But it reserv'd some quantity of choice,
To serve in such a difference. What devil was 't,
That thus hath cozen'd you at hoodman-blind?
Eyes without feeling, feeling without sight,
Ears without hands or eyes, smelling sans all,   80
Or but a sickly part of one true sense
Could not so mope.

O shame ! where is thy blush ? Rebellious hell,
If thou canst mutine in a matron's bones,
To flaming youth let virtue be as wax,
And melt in her own fire : proclaim no shame,
When the compulsive ardour gives the charge ;
Since frost itself as actively doth burn,
And reason panders will.
   Queen.   O Hamlet ! speak no more ! 90
Thou turn'st mine eyes into my very soul ;
And there I see such black and grained spots,
As will not leave their tinct.
   Ham.   Nay, but to live
In the rank sweat of an enseamed bed ;
Stew'd in corruption ; honeying, and making love
Over the nasty sty ;—
   Queen.   O, speak to me no more !
These words like daggers enter in mine ears :
No more, sweet Hamlet !
   Ham.   A murderer, and a villain ;
A slave, that is not twentieth part the tithe
Of your precedent lord :—a Vice of kings ;
   A cutpurse of the empire and the rule,   100
   That from a shelf the precious diadem stole,
And put it in his pocket !
   Queen.   No more !
   Ham. A king of shreds and patches.—

                Enter Ghost.

Save me, and hover o'er me with your wings,
You heavenly guards !—What would your gracious
    figure ?
   Queen. Alas ! he 's mad.
   Ham. Do you not come your tardy son to chide,
That, laps'd in time and passion, lets go by
The important acting of your dread command?
O, say !   110
   Ghost. Do not forget. This visitation
Is but to whet thy almost blunted purpose.
But, look ! amazement on thy mother sits ;
O, step between her and her fighting soul ;
Conceit in weakest bodies strongest works :
Speak to her, Hamlet.
   Ham.   How is it with you, lady ?
   Queen. Alas ! how is 't with you,
That you do bend your eye on vacancy,
And with the incorporal air do hold discourse?
Forth at your eyes your spirits wildly peep ; 120
And, as the sleeping soldiers in the alarm,
Your bedded hair, like life in excrements,
Starts up, and stands on end. O gentle son !
Upon the heat and flame of thy distemper
Sprinkle cool patience. Whereon do you look?
   Ham. On him, on him !—Look you, how pale he
    glares !
His form and cause conjoin'd, preaching to stones,
Would make them capable.—Do not look upon me ;
Lest with this piteous action you convert
My stern effects : then, what I have to do   130
Will want true colour ; tears, perchance, for blood.
   Queen. To whom do you speak this?
   Ham.   Do you see nothing there?
   Queen. Nothing at all ; yet all, that is, I see.
   Ham. Nor did you nothing hear?
   Queen.   No, nothing but ourselves.
   Ham. Why, look you there ! look, how it steals
    away !
My father, in his habit as he liv'd !
Look, where he goes, even now, out at the portal !
                         [*Exit Ghost.*
   Queen. This is the very coinage of your brain :
This bodiless creation ecstacy
Is very cunning in.
   Ham.   Ecstacy !   140
My pulse, as yours, doth temperately keep time,
And makes as healthful music. It is not madness
That I have utter'd : bring me to the test,
And I the matter will re-word ; which madness
Would gambol from. Mother, for love of grace,
Lay not that flattering unction to your soul,
That not your trespass, but my madness speaks :
It will but skin and film the ulcerous place ;
Whilst rank corruption, mining all within,

Infects unseen. Confess yourself to Heaven; 150
Repent what 's past; avoid what is to come;
And do not spread the compost on the weeds,
To make them ranker. Forgive me this my virtue;
For, in the fatness of these pursy times,
Virtue itself of vice must pardon beg,
Yea, curb and woo, for leave to do him good.
  Queen. O Hamlet! thou hast cleft my heart in
    twain.
  Ham. O, throw away the worser part of it,
And live the purer with the other half.
Good night; but go not to mine uncle's bed: 160
Assume a virtue, if you have it not.
That monster, custom, who all sense doth eat,
Of habits' devil, is angel yet in this,
That to the use of actions fair and good
He likewise gives a frock, or livery,
That aptly is put on. Refrain to-night;
And that shall lend a kind of easiness
To the next abstinence: the next more easy;
For use almost can change the stamp of nature,
And master the devil, or throw him out 170
With wondrous potency. Once more, good night:
And when you are desirous to be bless'd,
I 'll blessing beg of you.—For this same lord,
            [*Pointing to* Polonius.
I do repent: but Heaven hath pleas'd it so,—
To punish me with this, and this with me,—
That I must be their scourge and minister.
I will bestow him, and will answer well
The death I gave him. So, again, good night.—
I must be cruel, only to be kind:
Thus bad begins, and worse remains behind.— 180
One word more, good lady.
  Queen.   What shall I do?
  Ham. Not this, by no means, that I bid you do:
Let the bloat king tempt you again to bed;
Pinch wanton on your cheek; call you his mouse;

And let him, for a pair of reechy kisses,
Or paddling in your neck with his damn'd fingers,
Make you to ravel all this matter out,
That I essentially am not in madness,
But mad in craft. 'T were good, you let him know;
For who, that 's but a queen, fair, sober, wise, 190
Would from a paddock, from a bat, a gib,
Such dear concernings hide? who would do so?
No, in despite of sense, and secrecy,
Unpeg the basket on the house's top,
Let the birds fly, and, like the famous ape,
To try conclusions, in the basket creep,
And break your own neck down.
  Queen. Be thou assur'd, if words be made of breath,
And breath of life, I have no life to breathe
What thou hast said to me. 200
  Ham. I must to England; you know that.
  Queen.   Alack!
I had forgot: 't is so concluded on.
  Ham. There 's letters seal'd: and my two school-
    fellows,—
Whom I will trust, as I will adders fang'd,—
They bear the mandate; they must sweep my way,
And marshal me to knavery. Let it work;
For 't is the sport, to have the enginer
Hoist with his own petar: and 't shall go hard,
But I will delve one yard below their mines,
And blow them at the moon. O! 't is most sweet, 210
When in one line two crafts directly meet. —
This man shall set me packing:
I 'll lug the guts into the neighbour room.—
Mother, good night.—Indeed, this counsellor
Is now most still, most secret, and most grave,
Who was in life a foolish prating knave.
Come, sir, to draw toward an end with you.
Good night, mother.
        [*Exeunt severally;* Hamlet *dragging in*
          Polonius.

ACT IV.

Scene I.—The Same.

Enter King, Queen, Rosencrantz, *and* Guildenstern.

  King.
THERE 'S matter in these sighs: these pro-
      found heaves
You must translate; 't is fit we understand
    them.
Where is your son?
  Queen. Bestow this place on us a little
    while.—
        [*Exeunt* Rosencrantz *and*
          Guildenstern.
Ah, my good lord, what have I seen
    to-night!
  King. What, Gertrude? How does
    Hamlet?
  Queen. Mad as the sea, and wind, when both con-
    tend
Which is the mightier. In his lawless fit,
Behind the arras hearing something stir,
He whips his rapier out, and cries, "A rat! a rat!" 10
And, in this brainish apprehension, kills
The unseen good old man.
  King.   O heavy deed!
It had been so with us, had we been there.
His liberty is full of threats to all;

To you yourself, to us, to every one.
Alas! how shall this bloody deed be answer'd
It will be laid to us, whose providence
Should have kept short, restrain'd, and out of haunt,
This mad young man; but so much was our love,
We would not understand what was most fit; 20
But, like the owner of a foul disease,
To keep it from divulging, let it feed
Even on the pith of life. Where is he gone?
  Queen. To draw apart the body he hath kill'd;
O'er whom his very madness, like some ore
Among a mineral of metals base,
Shows itself pure: he weeps for what is done.
  King. O Gertrude! come away.
The sun no sooner shall the mountains touch,
But we will ship him hence; and this vile deed 30
We must, with all our majesty and skill,
Both countenance and excuse.—Ho! Guildenstern!

Re-enter Rosencrantz *and* Guildenstern.

Friends both, go join you with some further aid.
Hamlet in madness hath Polonius slain,
And from his mother's closet hath he dragg'd him:
Go, seek him out; speak fair, and bring the body

Into the chapel. I pray you, haste in this.
　　　[*Exeunt* ROSENCRANTZ *and* GUILDENSTERN.
Come, Gertrude, we'll call up our wisest friends;
And let them know, both what we mean to do,
And what's untimely done: so, haply, slander— 40
Whose whisper o'er the world's diameter,
As level as the cannon to his blank,
Transports his poison'd shot—may miss our name,
And hit the woundless air. O, come away!
My soul is full of discord, and dismay. [*Exeunt.*

SCENE II.—Another Room in the Same.

Enter HAMLET.

Ham. Safely stowed.
Ros., Guil. [*Within.*] Hamlet! Lord Hamlet!
Ham. What noise? who calls on Hamlet? O! here
they come.

Enter ROSENCRANTZ *and* GUILDENSTERN.

Ros. What have you done, my lord, with the dead
　　　body?
Ham. Compounded it with dust, whereto 't is kin.
Ros. Tell us where 't is; that we may take it thence,
And bear it to the chapel.
Ham. Do not believe it.
Ros. Believe what? 10
Ham. That I can keep your counsel, and not mine
own. Besides, to be demanded of a sponge, what
replication should be made by the son of a king?
Ros. Take you me for a sponge, my lord?
Ham. Ay, sir; that soaks up the king's countenance,
his rewards, his authorities. But such officers do the
king best service in the end: he keeps them, like an
ape, in the corner of his jaw; first mouthed, to be last
swallowed: when he needs what you have gleaned, it
is but squeezing you, and, sponge, you shall be dry
again. 21
Ros. I understand you not, my lord.
Ham. I am glad of it: a knavish speech sleeps in a
foolish ear.
Ros. My lord, you must tell us where the body is,
and go with us to the king.
Ham. The body is with the king, but the king is not
with the body. The king is a thing—
Guil. A thing, my lord!
Ham. Of nothing: bring me to him. Hide fox, and
all after. [*Exeunt.*

SCENE III.—Another Room in the Same.

Enter KING, *attended.*

King. I have sent to seek him, and to find the body.
How dangerous is it, that this man goes loose!
Yet must not we put the strong law on him:
He's lov'd of the distracted multitude,
Who like not in their judgment, but their eyes;
And where 't is so, the offender's scourge is weigh'd,
But never the offence. To bear all smooth and even,
This sudden sending him away must seem
Deliberate pause: diseases, desperate grown,
By desperate appliance are reliev'd, 10
Or not at all.—

Enter ROSENCRANTZ.

　　　　How now! what hath befallen?
Ros. Where the dead body is bestow'd, my lord,
We cannot get from him.
King. 　　　But where is he?
Ros. Without, my lord; guarded, to know your
　　　pleasure.
King. Bring him before us.
Ros. Ho, Guildenstern! bring in my lord.

Enter HAMLET *and* GUILDENSTERN.

King. Now, Hamlet, where's Polonius?
Ham. At supper.
King. At supper! Where? 19
Ham. Not where he eats, but where he is eaten: a

certain convocation of politic worms are e'en at him.
Your worm is your only emperor for diet: we fat
all creatures else, to fat us, and we fat ourselves for
maggots: your fat king, and your lean beggar, is but
variable service; two dishes, but to one table: that's
the end.
King. Alas, alas!
Ham. A man may fish with the worm that hath eat
of a king; and eat of the fish that hath fed of that
worm. 30
King. What dost thou mean by this?
Ham. Nothing, but to show you how a king may go
a progress through the guts of a beggar.
King. Where is Polonius?
Ham. In heaven: send thither to see; if your mes-
senger find him not there, seek him i' the other place
yourself. But, indeed, if you find him not within this
month, you shall nose him as you go up the stairs into
the lobby.
King. [*To some Attendants.*] Go seek him there. 40
Ham. He will stay till you come.
　　　　　　　　　　[*Exeunt Attendants.*
King. Hamlet, this deed, for thine especial safety,—
Which we do tender, as we dearly grieve
For that which thou hast done,—must send thee hence
With fiery quickness; therefore, prepare thyself.
The bark is ready, and the wind at help,
The associates tend, and everything is bent
For England.
Ham. 　　　For England?
King. 　　　　　　　Ay, Hamlet.
Ham. 　　　　　　　　　　　Good.
King. So is it, if thou knew'st our purposes.
Ham. I see a cherub that sees them.—But, come;
for England!—Farewell, dear mother. 51
King. Thy loving father, Hamlet.
Ham. My mother: father and mother is man and
wife, man and wife is one flesh; and so, my mother.
Come, for England! [*Exit.*
King. Follow him at foot; tempt him with speed
　　　aboard:
Delay it not, I 'll have him hence to-night.
Away, for everything is seal'd and done,
That else leans on the affair: pray you, make haste.
　　　　[*Exeunt* ROSENCRANTZ *and* GUILDENSTERN.
And, England, if my love thou hold'st at aught, 60
(As my great power thereof may give thee sense,
Since yet thy cicatrice looks raw and red
After the Danish sword, and thy free awe
Pays homage to us,) thou may'st not coldly set
Our sovereign process, which imports at full,
By letters conjuring to that effect,
The present death of Hamlet. Do it, England;
For like the hectic in my blood he rages,
And thou must cure me. Till I know 't is done,
Howe'er my haps, my joys were ne'er begun. 70
　　　　　　　　　　　　　[*Exit.*

SCENE IV.—A Plain in Denmark.

Enter FORTINBRAS, *a Captain, and Soldiers,
marching.*

For. Go, captain; from me greet the Danish king;
Tell him, that, by his license, Fortinbras
Claims the conveyance of a promis'd march
Over his kingdom. You know the rendezvous.
If that his majesty would aught with us,
We shall express our duty in his eye,
And let him know so.
Cap. 　　　　I will do 't, my lord.
For. Go softly on.
　　　　　　[*Exeunt* FORTINBRAS *and Soldiers.*

Enter HAMLET, ROSENCRANTZ, GUILDENSTERN, *&c.*

Ham. Good sir, whose powers are these?
Cap. They are of Norway, sir. 10
Ham. How purpos'd, sir, I pray you?
Cap. Against some part of Poland.
Ham. Who commands them, sir?
Cap. The nephew to old Norway, Fortinbras.
Ham. Goes it against the main of Poland, sir,
Or for some frontier?

Cap. Truly to speak, sir, and with no addition,
We go to gain a little patch of ground,
That hath in it no profit but the name.
To pay five ducats, five, I would not farm it ;   20
Nor will it yield to Norway, or the Pole,
A ranker rate, should it be sold in fee.
Ham. Why, then the Polack never will defend it.
Cap. Yes, 't is already garrison'd.
Ham. Two thousand souls, and twenty thousand
     ducats,
Will not debate the question of this straw :
This is the imposthume of much wealth and peace,
That inward breaks, and shows no cause without
Why the man dies.—I humbly thank you, sir.
Cap. God be wi' you, sir.   [*Exit.*
Ros.   Will 't please you go, my lord ?
Ham. I 'll be with you straight. Go a little before.
     [*Exeunt* ROSENCRANTZ, GUILDENSTERN, &c.
How all occasions do inform against me,   32
And spur my dull revenge ! What is a man,
If his chief good, and market of his time,
Be but to sleep, and feed ? a beast, no more.
Sure, He, that made us with such large discourse,
Looking before and after, gave us not
That capability and godlike reason
To fust in us unus'd. Now, whether it be
Bestial oblivion, or some craven scruple   40
Of thinking too precisely on the event,—
A thought, which, ,quarter'd, hath but one part
     wisdom,
And ever three parts coward,—I do not know
Why yet I live to say, "This thing 's to do ;"
Sith I have cause, and will, and strength, and means,
To do 't. Examples, gross as earth, exhort me :
Witness this army, of such mass and charge,
Led by a delicate and tender prince,
Whose spirit, with divine ambition puff'd,
Makes mouths at the invisible event ;   50
Exposing what is mortal, and unsure,
To all that fortune, death, and danger, dare,
Even for an egg-shell. Rightly to be great
Is not to stir without great argument,
But greatly to find quarrel in a straw,
When honour 's at the stake. How stand I then,
That have a father kill'd, a mother stain'd,
Excitements of my reason, and my blood,
And let all sleep ? while, to my shame, I see
The imminent death of twenty thousand men,   60
That, for a fantasy and trick of fame,
Go to their graves like beds ; fight for a plot
Whereon the numbers cannot try the cause ;
Which is not tomb enough, and continent,
To hide the slain ?—O ! from this time forth,
My thoughts be bloody, or be nothing worth ! [*Exit.*

SCENE V.—Elsinore. A Room in the Castle.

Enter QUEEN *and* HORATIO.

Queen. I will not speak with her.
Hor. She is importunate ; indeed, distract :
Her mood will needs be pitied.
Queen.   What would she have ?
Hor. She speaks much of her father ; says, she
     hears,
There 's tricks i' the world ; and hems, and beats her
     heart ;
Spurns enviously at straws ; speaks things in doubt,
That carry but half sense : her speech is nothing,
Yet the unshaped use of it doth move
The hearers to collection ; they aim at it,
And botch the words up fit to their own thoughts ;
Which, as her winks, and nods, and gestures yield
     them,
Indeed would make one think, there might be thought,
Though nothing sure, yet much unhappily.
'T were good she were spoken with, for she may strew
Dangerous conjectures in ill-breeding minds.
Queen. Let her come in.   [*Exit* HORATIO.
To my sick soul, as sin's true nature is,
Each toy seems prologue to some great amiss :

So full of artless jealousy is guilt,
It spills itself in fearing to be spilt.   20

Re-enter HORATIO, *with* OPHELIA.

Oph. Where is the beauteous majesty of Denmark ?
Queen. How now, Ophelia ?
Oph. [*Sings.*] *How should I your true love know
     From another one ?
     By his cockle hat and staff,
     And his sandal shoon.*

Queen. Alas, sweet lady, what imports this song?
Oph. Say you ? nay, pray you, mark.
     *He is dead and gone, lady,
     He is dead and gone ;   30
     At his head a grass-green turf,
     At his heels a stone.*
O, ho !
Queen. Nay, but, Ophelia,—
Oph.   Pray you, mark.
     White his shroud as the mountain snow,—

Enter KING.

Queen. Alas ! look here, my lord.
Oph.   *Larded with sweet flowers ;
     Which bewept to the grave did go,
     With true-love showers.*

King. How do you, pretty lady ?   40
Oph. Well, God 'ield you ! They say, the owl was a
baker's daughter. Lord ! we know what we are, but
know not what we may be. God be at your table !
King. Conceit upon her father.
Oph. Pray you, let 's have no words of this ; but
when they ask you what it means, say you this :
     *To-morrow is Saint Valentine's day,
     All in the morning betime,
     And I a maid at your window,
     To be your Valentine :   50
     Then up he rose, and donn'd his clothes,
     And dupp'd the chamber door ;
     Let in the maid, that out a maid
     Never departed more.*

King. Pretty Ophelia !
Oph. Indeed, la ! without an oath, I 'll make an end
on 't :
     *By Gis, and by Saint Charity,
     Alack, and fie for shame !
     Young men will do 't, if they come to 't ;   60
     By cock, they are to blame.
     Quoth she, before you tumbled me,
     You promis'd me to wed :
     So would I ha' done, by yonder sun,
     An thou hadst not come to my bed.*

King. How long hath she been thus ?
Oph. I hope, all will be well. We must be patient :
but I cannot choose but weep, to think, they should
lay him i' the cold ground. My brother shall know of
it, and so I thank you for your good counsel. Come,
my coach ! Good night, ladies ; good night, sweet
ladies ; good night, good night.   [*Exit.*
King. Follow her close ; give her good watch, I
     pray you.   [*Exit* HORATIO.
O ! this is the poison of deep grief ; it springs
All from her father's death. And now, behold,
O Gertrude, Gertrude !
When sorrows come, they come not single spies,
But in battalions. First, her father slain :
Next, your son gone ; and he most violent author
Of his own just remove : the people muddied,   80
Thick and unwholesome in their thoughts and whis-
     pers,
For good Polonius' death ; and we have done but
     greenly,
In hugger-mugger to inter him : poor Ophelia
Divided from herself, and her fair judgment,
Without the which we are pictures, or mere beasts :
Last, and as much containing as all these,
Her brother is in secret come from France,
Feeds on his wonder, keeps himself in clouds,
And wants not buzzers to infect his ear

With pestilent speeches of his father's death ;   90
Wherein necessity, of matter beggar'd,
Will nothing stick our person to arraign
In ear and ear. O my dear Gertrude! this,
Like to a murdering-piece, in many places
Gives me superfluous death.   [*A noise within.*
    Queen.   Alack! what noise is this?

Enter a Gentleman.

King. Where are my Switzers? Let them guard
    the door.
What is the matter?
    Gent.   Save yourself, my lord ;
The ocean, overpeering of his list,
Eats not the flats with more impetuous haste,
Than young Laertes, in a riotous head,   100
O'erbears your officers. The rabble call him lord ;
And, as the world were now but to begin,
Antiquity forgot, custom not known,
The ratifiers and props of every word,
They cry, "Choose we ; Laertes shall be king!"
Caps, hands, and tongues, applaud it to the clouds,
"Laertes shall be king, Laertes king!"
    Queen. How cheerfully on the false trail they cry!
O! this is counter, you false Danish dogs.
    King. The doors are broke.   [*Noise within.*

Enter LAERTES, *armed ; Danes following.*

Laer. Where is this king?—Sirs, stand you all
    without.   111
Dan. No, let's come in.
Laer.   I pray you, give me leave.
Dan. We will, we will.
              [*They retire without the door.*
Laer. I thank you : keep the door.—O thou vile
    king,
Give me my father.
Queen.   Calmly, good Laertes.
Laer. That drop of blood that's calm proclaims me
    bastard ;
Cries, cuckold, to my father ; brands the harlot
Even here, between the chaste unsmirched brow
Of my true mother.
    King.   What is the cause, Laertes,
That thy rebellion looks so giant-like?—   120
Let him go, Gertrude ; do not fear our person ·
There's such divinity doth hedge a king,
That treason can but peep to what it would,
Acts little of his will.—Tell me, Laertes,
Why thou art thus incens'd.—Let him go, Gertrude.—
Speak, man.
Laer. Where is my father?
King.   Dead.
Queen.   But not by him.
King. Let him demand his fill.
Laer. How came he dead? I'll not be juggled
    with.
To hell, allegiance! vows, to the blackest devil !   130
Conscience, and grace, to the profoundest pit !
I dare damnation. To this point I stand,
That both the worlds I give to negligence ;
Let come what comes, only I'll be reveng'd
Most throughly for my father.
King.   Who shall stay you?
Laer. My will, not all the world :
And, for my means, I'll husband them so well,
They shall go far with little.
King.   Good Laertes,
If you desire to know the certainty
Of your dear father's death, is't writ in your revenge,
That, swoopstake, you will draw both friend and foe,
Winner and loser?   142
Laer. None but his enemies.
King.   Will you know them then?
Laer. To his good friends thus wide I'll ope my
    arms ;
And, like the kind life-rendering pelican,
Repast them with my blood.
King.   Why, now you speak
Like a good child, and a true gentleman.
That I am guiltless of your father's death,
And am most sensibly in grief for it.

It shall as level to your judgment pierce,   150
As day does to your eye.
    Danes. [*Within.*]   Let her come in.
Laer. How now! what noise is that?

Re-enter OPHELIA.

O heat, dry up my brains ! tears seven times salt,
Burn out the sense and virtue of mine eye !—
By Heaven, thy madness shall be paid by weight,
Till our scale turn the beam. O rose of May !
Dear maid, kind sister, sweet Ophelia !
O heavens ! is't possible, a young maid's wits
Should be as mortal as an old man's life ?
Nature is fine in love ; and, where 't is fine,   160
It sends some precious instance of itself
After the thing it loves.
    Oph. *They bore him barefac'd on the bier ;*
        Hey non nonny, nonny, hey nonny :
        And in his grave rain'd many a tear ;—
Fare you well, my dove !
    Laer. Hadst thou thy wits, and didst persuade
    revenge,
It could not move thus.
    Oph. You must sing, *Down a-down, an you call him
    a-down-a.* O, how the wheel becomes it ! It is the
false steward, that stole his master's daughter.   171
    Laer. This nothing's more than matter.
    Oph. There's rosemary, that's for remembrance ;
pray you, love, remember : and there is pansies, that's
for thoughts.
    Laer. A document in madness ; thoughts and re-
membrance fitted.
    Oph. There's fennel for you, and columbines ;—
there's rue for you : and here's some for me : we may
call it herb-grace o' Sundays :—O, you must wear your
rue with a difference.—There's a daisy : I would give
you some violets ; but they withered all when my
father died.—They say, he made a good end,—   183
    For bonny sweet Robin is all my joy,—
    Laer. Thought and affliction, passion, hell itself,
She turns to favour, and to prettiness.
    Oph.   *And will he not come again ?*
        And will he not come again ?
        No, no, he is dead :
        Go to thy death-bed :   190
        He never will come again.

        His beard as white as snow,
        All flaxen was his poll ;
        He is gone, he is gone,
        And we cast away moan :
        God ha' mercy on his soul !
And of all Christian souls, I pray God. God be wi' you !
              [*Exit.*
    Laer. Do you see this? O God !
    King. Laertes, I must commune with your grief,
Or you deny me right. Go but apart,   200
Make choice of whom your wisest friends you will,
And they shall hear and judge 'twixt you and me.
If by direct, or by collateral hand
They find us touch'd, we will our kingdom give,
Our crown, our life, and all that we call ours,
To you in satisfaction ; but if not,
Be you content to lend your patience to us,
And we shall jointly labour with your soul
To give it due content.
    Laer.   Let this be so :
His means of death, his obscure burial,—   210
No trophy, sword, nor hatchment, o'er his bones,
No noble rite, nor formal ostentation,—
Cry to be heard, as 't were from heaven to earth,
That I must call't in question.
    King.   So you shall ;
And, where the offence is, let the great axe fall.
I pray you, go with me.   [*Exeunt.*

SCENE VI.—*Another Room in the Same.*

Enter HORATIO *and a Servant.*

Hor. What are they, that would speak with me ?

Serv. Sailors, sir: they say, they have letters for you.
Hor. Let them come in.— [Exit Servant.
I do not know from what part of the world
I should be greeted, if not from Lord Hamlet.

king: they have letters for him. Ere we were two
days old at sea, a pirate of very warlike appointment
gave us chase. Finding ourselves too slow of sail, we
put on a compelled valour; in the grapple I boarded

Oph. "There's fennel for you, and columbines;—there's rue for you; and here's some for me."

Enter Sailors.

1 Sail. God bless you, sir.
Hor. Let him bless thee too.
1 Sail. He shall, sir, an't please him. There's a
letter for you, sir: it comes from the ambassador that
was bound for England, if your name be Horatio, as
I am let to know it is.   11
, Hor. [Reads.] "Horatio, when thou shalt have over-
looked this, give these fellows some means to the

them: on the instant they got clear of our ship, so I
alone became their prisoner. They have dealt with
me like thieves of mercy; but they knew what they
did; I am to do a good turn for them. Let the king
have the letters I have sent; and repair thou to me
with as much haste as thou wouldst fly death. I have
words to speak in thine ear, will make thee dumb;
yet are they much too light for the bore of the matter.
These good fellows will bring thee where I am.
Rosencrantz and Guildenstern hold their course for

England : of them I have much to tell thee. Farewell.
    He that thou knowest thine,   HAMLET."
Come, I will give you way for these your letters; 30
And do 't the speedier, that you may direct me
To him from whom you brought them.   [*Exeunt.*

SCENE VII.—Another Room in the Same.

Enter KING *and* LAERTES.

King. Now must your conscience my acquittance
    seal,
And you must put me in your heart for friend,
Sith you have heard, and with a knowing ear,
That he, which hath your noble father slain,
Pursu'd my life.
    Laer.   It well appears : but tell me
Why you proceeded not against these feats,
So crimeful and so capital in nature,
As by your safety, wisdom, all things else,
You mainly were stirr'd up.
    King.   O ! for two special reasons;
Which may to you, perhaps, seem much unsinew'd, 10
And yet to me they are strong. The queen, his mother,
Lives almost by his looks ; and for myself,
(My virtue, or my plague, be it either which,)
She 's so conjunctive to my life and soul,
That, as the star moves not but in his sphere,
I could not but by her. The other motive,
Why to a public count I might not go,
Is the great love the general gender bear him ;
Who, dipping all his faults in their affection,
Would, like the spring that turneth wood to stone, 20
Convert his gyves to graces ; so that my arrows,
Too slightly timber'd for so loud a wind,
Would have reverted to my bow again,
And not where I had aim'd them.
    Laer. And so have I a noble father lost ;
A sister driven into desperate terms ;
Whose worth, if praises may go back again,
Stood challenger on mount of all the age
For her perfections. But my revenge will come.
    King. Break not your sleeps for that ; you must not
    think,   30
That we are made of stuff so flat and dull,
That we can let our beard be shook with danger,
And think it pastime. You shortly shall hear more :
I lov'd your father, and we love ourself ;
And that, I hope, will teach you to imagine,—

Enter a Messenger.

How now ! what news ?
    Mess.   Letters, my lord, from Hamlet.
This to your majesty : this to the queen.
    King. From Hamlet ! who brought them ?
    Mess. Sailors, my lord, they say ; I saw them not :
They were given me by Claudio, he receiv'd them 40
Of him that brought them.
    King.   Laertes, you shall hear them.—
Leave us.   [*Exit Messenger.*
[*Reads.*] "High and mighty, you shall know, I am
set naked on your kingdom. To-morrow shall I beg
leave to see your kingly eyes ; when I shall, first
asking your pardon thereunto, recount the occasions
of my sudden and more strange return. HAMLET."
What should this mean ? Are all the rest come back ?
Or is it some abuse, and no such thing ?
    Laer. Know you the hand ?
    King.   'T is Hamlet's character. "Naked,"—
And, in a postscript here, he says, "alone." 51
Can you advise me ?
    Laer. I 'm lost in it, my lord. But let him come :
It warms the very sickness in my heart,
That I shall live and tell him to his teeth,
"Thus diddest thou."
    King.   If it be so, Laertes,
(As how should it be so ? how otherwise ?)
Will you be ruled by me ?
    Laer.   Ay, my lord ;
So you will not o'er-rule me to a peace.
    King. To thine own peace. If he be now return'd,—

As checking at his voyage, and that he means 61
No more to undertake it,—I will work him
To an exploit, now ripe in my device,
Under the which he shall not choose but fall ;
And for his death no wind of blame shall breathe,
But even his mother shall uncharge the practice,
And call it accident.
    Laer.   My lord, I will be rul'd ;
The rather, if you could devise it so,
That I might be the organ.
    King.   It falls right.
You have been talk'd of since your travel much, 70
And that in Hamlet's hearing, for a quality
Wherein, they say, you shine : your sum of parts
Did not together pluck such envy from him,
As did that one ; and that, in my regard,
Of the unworthiest siege.
    Laer.   What part is that, my lord ?
    King. A very riband in the cap of youth,
Yet needful too ; for youth no less becomes
The light and careless livery that it wears,
Than settled age his sables, and his weeds,
Importing health and graveness.—Two months since,
Here was a gentleman of Normandy :— 81
I have seen myself, and serv'd against, the French,
And they can well on horseback ; but this gallant
Had witchcraft in 't ; he grew unto his seat ;
And to such wondrous doing brought his horse,
As he had been incorps'd and demi-natur'd
With the brave beast : so far he topp'd my thought,
That I, in forgery of shapes and tricks,
Come short of what he did.
    Laer.   A Norman, was 't ?
    King. A Norman. 90
    Laer. Upon my life, Lamord.
    King.   The very same.
    Laer. I know him well : he is the brooch, indeed,
And gem of all the nation.
    King. He made confession of you ;
And gave you such a masterly report,
For art and exercise in your defence,
And for your rapier most especially,
That he cried out, 't would be a sight indeed,
If one could match you : the scrimers of their nation,
He swore, had neither motion, guard, nor eye, 100
If you oppos'd them. Sir, this report of his
Did Hamlet so envenom with his envy,
That he could nothing do, but wish and beg
Your sudden coming o'er, to play with him.
Now, out of this,—
    Laer.   What out of this, my lord ?
    King. Laertes, was your father dear to you ?
Or are you like the painting of a sorrow,
A face without a heart ?
    Laer.   Why ask you this ?
    King. Not that I think you did not love your father ;
But that I know love is begun by time ; 110
And that I see, in passages of proof,
Time qualifies the spark and fire of it.
There lives within the very flame of love
A kind of wick, or snuff, that will abate it ;
And nothing is at a like goodness still ;
For goodness, growing to a plurisy,
Dies in his own too-much. That we would do,
We should do when we would ; for this "would'
    changes,
And hath abatements and delays as many,
As there are tongues, are hands, are accidents , 120
And then this "should " is like a spendthrift sigh,
That hurts by easing. But, to the quick o' the ulcer :
Hamlet comes back : what would you undertake,
To show yourself your father's son in deed,
More than in words ?
    Laer.   To cut his throat i' the church.
    King. No place, indeed, should murder sanctuarise ;
Revenge should have no bounds. But, good Laertes,
Will you do this, keep close within your chamber.
Hamlet, return'd, shall know you are come home :
We 'll put on those shall praise your excellence, 130
And set a double varnish on the fame
The Frenchman gave you ; bring you, in fine, together,
And wager on your heads : he, being remiss,

Most generous, and free from all contriving,
Will not peruse the foils; so that with ease,
Or with a little shuffling, you may choose
A sword unbated, and, in a pass of practice,
Requite him for your father.

With this contagion, that, if I gall him slightly,
It may be death.
  King.   Let's further think of this;
Weigh, what convenience, both of time and means,
May fit us to our shape. If this should fail,

OPHELIA ON THE WILLOW.

 Laer.   I will do 't;
And, for that purpose, I 'll anoint my sword.
I bought an unction of a mountebank, 140
So mortal, that but dip a knife in it,
Where it draws blood, no cataplasm so rare,
Collected from all simples that have virtue
Under the moon, can save the thing from death,
That is but scratch'd withal: I 'll touch my point

And that our drift look through our bad performance,
'T were better not assay'd: therefore, this project 151
Should have a back, or second, that might hold,
If this should blast in proof. Soft!—let me see:—
We 'll make a solemn wager on your cunnings,—
I ha 't:
When in your motion you are hot and dry,
(As make your bouts more violent to that end,)

And that he calls for drink, I'll have prepar'd him
A chalice for the nonce; whereon but sipping,
If he by chance escape your venom'd stuck,   160
Our purpose may hold there. But stay! what noise?

Enter QUEEN.

How now, sweet queen?
  Queen. One woe doth tread upon another's heel,
So fast they follow.—Your sister's drown'd, Laertes.
  Laer. Drown'd!—O, where?
  Queen. There is a willow grows aslant a brook,
That shows his hoar leaves in the glassy stream;
There with fantastic garlands did she come,
Of crow-flowers, nettles, daisies, and long purples,
That liberal shepherds give a grosser name,   170
But our cold maids do dead men's fingers call them:
There, on the pendant boughs her coronet weeds
Clambering to hang, an envious sliver broke,
When down her weedy trophies, and herself,
Fell in the weeping brook. Her clothes spread
     wide,

And, mermaid-like, awhile they bore her up:
Which time, she chanted snatches of old tunes,
As one incapable of her own distress,
Or like a creature native and indu'd
Unto that element: but long it could not be,   180
Till that her garments, heavy with their drink,
Pull'd the poor wretch from her melodious lay
To muddy death.
  Laer.   Alas! then, is she drown'd?
  Queen. Drown'd, drown'd.
  Laer. Too much of water hast thou, poor Ophelia,
And therefore I forbid my tears: but yet
It is our trick; nature her custom holds,
Let shame say what it will: when these are gone,
The woman will be out.—Adieu, my lord!
I have a speech of fire, that fain would blaze,   190
But that this folly douts it.   [*Exit.*
  King.   Let's follow, Gertrude.
How much I had to do to calm his rage!
Now fear I, this will give it start again;
Therefore, let's follow.   *Exeunt.*

ACT V.

SCENE I.—A Churchyard.

Enter two Clowns, with spades and mattocks.

  1 Clown.
IS she to be buried in Christian burial, that
wilfully seeks her own salvation?
  2 Clo. I tell thee, she is; and therefore
make her grave straight: the crowner hath
sat on her, and finds it Christian burial.
  1 Clo. How can that be, unless she drowned
herself in her own defence?
  2 Clo. Why, 't is found so.   8
  1 Clo. It must be *se offendendo;* it cannot
be else. For here lies the point: if I drown
myself wittingly, it argues an act, and an
act hath three branches; it is, to act, to do,
and to perform: argal, she drowned herself wittingly.
  2 Clo. Nay, but hear you, goodman delver.—
  1 Clo. Give me leave. Here lies the water; good:
here stands the man; good: if the man go to this
water, and drown himself, it is, will he, nill he, he
goes; mark you that: but if the water come to him,
and drown him, he drowns not himself: argal, he
that is not guilty of his own death shortens not his
own life.   21
  2 Clo. But is this law?
  1 Clo. Ay, marry, is 't, crowner's quest-law.
  2 Clo. Will you ha' the truth on 't? If this had not
been a gentlewoman, she should have been buried out
of Christian burial.
  1 Clo. Why, there thou say'st; and the more pity,
that great folk shall have countenance in this world
to drown or hang themselves, more than their even-
Christian. Come, my spade. There is no ancient
gentlemen but gardeners, ditchers, and grave-makers:
they hold up Adam's profession.   32
  2 Clo. Was he a gentleman?
  1 Clo. He was the first that ever bore arms.
  2 Clo. Why, he had none.
  1 Clo. What, art a heathen? How dost thou understand the Scripture? The Scripture says, Adam
digged: could he dig without arms? I'll put another
question to thee: if thou answerest me not to the
purpose, confess thyself—   40

  2 Clo. Go to.
  1 Clo. What is he, that builds stronger than either
the mason, the shipwright, or the carpenter?
  2 Clo. The gallows-maker; for that frame outlives a
thousand tenants.
  1 Clo. I like thy wit well, in good faith: the gallows
does well; but how does it well? it does well to those
that do ill: now, thou dost ill to say the gallows is
built stronger than the church: argal, the gallows
may do well to thee. To 't again; come.   50
  2 Clo. Who builds stronger than a mason, a shipwright, or a carpenter?
  1 Clo. Ay, tell me that, and unyoke.
  2 Clo. Marry, now I can tell.
  1 Clo. To 't.
  2 Clo. Mass, I cannot tell.

Enter HAMLET and HORATIO, at a distance.

  1 Clo. Cudgel thy brains no more about it, for your
dull ass will not mend his pace with beating; and,
when you are asked this question next, say, a grave-
maker: the houses that he makes last till doomsday.
Go, get thee to Yaughan; fetch me a stoop of liquor.
       [*Exit 2 Clown.*

  1 Clown digs, and sings.
  In youth, when I did love, did love,   62
    Methought it was very sweet,
  To contract, O! the time, for-a! my behove,
    O, methought, there was nothing-a meet.

  Ham. Hath this fellow no feeling of his business,
that he sings at grave-making?
  Hor. Custom hath made it in him a property of
easiness.
  Ham. 'T is e'en so: the hand of little employment
hath the daintier sense.   71
  1 Clo. But age, with his stealing steps,
    Hath claw'd me in his clutch,
    And hath shipped me intil the land,
    As if I had never been such.
       [*Throws up a skull.*

Ham. That skull had a tongue in it, and could sing once : how the knave jowls it to the ground, as if it were Cain's jaw-bone, that did the first murder! This might be the pate of a politician, which this ass now o'er-offices, one that would circumvent God, might it not? 81

Hor. It might, my lord.

Ham. Or of a courtier, which could say, "Good morrow, sweet lord! How dost thou, good lord?" This might be my Lord Such-a-one, that praised my Lord Such-a-one's horse, when he meant to beg it, might it not?

Hor. Ay, my lord. 88

Ham. Why, e'en so, and now my Lady Worm's; chapless, and knocked about the mazzard with a sexton's spade. Here's fine revolution, an we had the trick to see't. Did these bones cost no more the breeding, but to play at loggats with 'em? mine ache to think on 't.

1 Clo. *A pick-axe, and a spade, a spade,*
 For and a shrouding sheet :
 O! a pit of clay for to be made
 For such a guest is meet. 99
   [*Throws up another skull.*

Ham. There's another : why may not that be the skull of a lawyer? Where be his quiddits now, his quillets, his cases, his tenures, and his tricks? why does he suffer this rude knave now to knock him about the sconce with a dirty shovel, and will not tell him of his action of battery? Humph! This fellow might be in's time a great buyer of land, with his statutes, his recognisances, his fines, his double vouchers, his recoveries : is this the fine of his fines, and the recovery of his recoveries, to have his fine pate full of fine dirt? will his vouchers vouch him no more of his purchases, and double ones too, than the length and breadth of a pair of indentures? The very conveyances of his lands will hardly lie in this box, and must the inheritor himself have no more? ha?

Hor. Not a jot more, my lord.

Ham. Is not parchment made of sheep-skins?

Hor. Ay, my lord, and of calf-skins too.

Ham. They are sheep, and calves, which seek out assurance in that. I will speak to this fellow.—Whose grave 's this, sir? 122

1 Clo. Mine, sir.—

 O! a pit of clay for to be made
 For such a guest is meet.

Ham. I think it be thine, indeed ; for thou liest in 't.

1 Clo. You lie out on 't, sir, and therefore it is not yours ; for my part, I do not lie in 't, and yet it is mine.

Ham. Thou dost lie in 't, to be in 't, and say it is thine ; 'tis for the dead, not for the quick ; therefore, thou liest. 132

1 Clo. 'T is a quick lie, sir ; 't will away again, from me to you.

Ham. What man dost thou dig it for?

1 Clo. For no man, sir.

Ham. What woman, then?

1 Clo. For none, neither.

Ham. Who is to be buried in 't?

1 Clo. One, that was a woman, sir; but, rest her soul, she 's dead. 141

Ham. How absolute the knave is! we must speak by the card, or equivocation will undo us. By the Lord, Horatio, this three years I have taken note of it ; the age is grown so picked, that the toe of the peasant comes so near the heel of the courtier, he galls his kibe.—How long hast thou been a grave-maker?

1 Clo. Of all the days i' the year, I came to 't that day that our last King Hamlet o'ercame Fortinbras.

Ham. How long is that since? 151

1 Clo. Cannot you tell that? every fool can tell that. It was the very day that young Hamlet was born ; he that is mad, and sent into England.

Ham. Ay, marry ; why was he sent into England?

1 Clo. Why, because he was mad : he shall recover his wits there ; or, if he do not, 't is no great matter there.

Ham. Why?

1 Clo. 'T will not be seen in him there ; there the men are as mad as he. 161

Ham. How came he mad?

1 Clo. Very strangely, they say.

Ham. How strangely?

1 Clo. 'Faith, e'en with losing his wits.

Ham. "Alas, poor Yorick!"

Ham. Upon what ground?

1 Clo. Why, here in Denmark : I have been sexton here, man, and boy, thirty years.

Ham. How long will a man lie i' the earth ere he rot? 170

1 Clo. 'Faith, if he be not rotten before he die, (as we have many pocky corses now-a-days, that will scarce hold the laying in,) he will last you some eight year, or nine year : a tanner will last you nine year.

Ham. Why he more than another?

1 Clo. Why, sir, his hide is so tanned with his trade, that he will keep out water a great while ; and your water is a sore decayer of your whoreson dead body. Here 's a skull now ; this skull hath lain i' the earth three-and-twenty years. 180

Ham. Whose was it?

1 Clo. A whoreson mad fellow's it was : whose do you think it was?

Ham. Nay, I know not.

1 Clo. A pestilence on him for a mad rogue! 'a poured a flagon of Rhenish on my head once. This same skull, sir, this same skull, sir, was Yorick's skull, the king's jester.

Ham. This?

1 Clo. E'en that. 190

Ham. Let me see. [*Takes the skull.*] Alas, poor Yorick!—I knew him, Horatio : a fellow of infinite jest, of most excellent fancy : he hath borne me on his back a thousand times ; and now, how abhorred my imagination is! my gorge rises at it. Here hung those lips, that I have kissed I know not how oft. Where be your gibes now? your gambols? your songs? your flashes of merriment, that were wont to set the table on a roar? Not one now, to mock your own grinning? quite chap-fallen? Now, get you to my lady's chamber, and tell her, let her paint an inch thick, to this favour she must come ; make her laugh at that.—Pr'ythee, Horatio, tell me one thing. 203

Hor. What 's that, my lord?

Ham. Dost thou think, Alexander looked o' this fashion i' the earth?

Hor. E'en so.

Ham. And smelt so? pah!   [*Puts down the skull.*
Hor. E'en so, my lord.
Ham. To what base uses we may return, Horatio!
Why may not imagination trace the noble dust of
Alexander, till he find it stopping a bung-hole?   212
Hor. 'T were to consider too curiously, to con-
sider so.
Ham. No, faith, not a jot; but to follow him thither
with modesty enough, and likelihood to lead it: as
thus: Alexander died, Alexander was buried, Alexan-
der returneth into dust; the dust is earth; of earth
we make loam; and why of that loam, whereto he
was converted, might they not stop a beer-barrel? 220
Imperious Cæsar, dead, and turn'd to clay,
Might stop a hole to keep the wind away:
O! that that earth, which kept the world in awe,
Should patch a wall to expel the winter's flaw!
But soft! but soft! aside:—here comes the king,

Enter Priests, &c., in procession; the Corse of
   OPHELIA, LAERTES *and Mourners following;*
   KING, QUEEN, *their Trains, &c.*
The queen, the courtiers. Who is that they follow,
And with such maimed rites? This doth betoken,
The corse they follow did with desperate hand
Fordo its own life; 't was of some estate.
Couch we awhile, and mark.   230
                [*Retiring with* HORATIO.
Laer. What ceremony else?
Ham.   That is Laertes,
A very noble youth: mark.
Laer. What ceremony else?
Priest. Her obsequies have been as far enlarg'd
As we have warrantise: her death was doubtful;
And, but that great command o'ersways the order,
She should in ground unsanctified have lodg'd,
Till the last trumpet; for charitable prayers,
Shards, flints, and pebbles, should be thrown on her;
Yet here she is allow'd her virgin crants,   240
Her maiden strewments, and the bringing home
Of bell and burial.
Laer. Must there no more be done?
Priest.   No more be done:
We should profane the service of the dead,
To sing a requiem, and such rest to her,
As to peace-parted souls.
Laer.   Lay her i' the earth;
And from her fair and unpolluted flesh
May violets spring!—I tell thee, churlish priest,
A ministering angel shall my sister be,
When thou liest howling.
Ham.   What! the fair Ophelia? 250
Queen. Sweets to the sweet: farewell.
               [*Scattering flowers.*
I hop'd thou shouldst have been my Hamlet's wife:
I thought thy bride-bed to have deck'd, sweet maid,
And not have strew'd thy grave.
Laer.   O! treble woe
Fall ten times treble on that cursed head,
Whose wicked deed thy most ingenious sense
Depriv'd thee of!—Hold off the earth awhile,
Till I have caught her once more in mine arms.
               [*Leaping into the grave.*
Now pile your dust upon the quick and dead,
Till of this flat a mountain you have made,   260
To o'er-top old Pelion, or the skyish head
Of blue Olympus.
Ham. [*Advancing.*] What is he, whose grief
Bears such an emphasis? whose phrase of sorrow
Conjures the wandering stars, and makes them stand,
Like wonder-wounded hearers? This is I,
Hamlet the Dane.   [*Leaping into the grave.*
Laer.   The devil take thy soul!
                 [*Grappling with him.*
Ham. Thou pray'st not well.
I pr'ythee, take thy fingers from my throat;
For though I am not splenitive and rash,   270
Yet have I something in me dangerous,
Which let thy wiseness fear. Away thy hand!
King. Pluck them asunder.
Queen.   Hamlet! Hamlet!
All. Gentlemen,—

Hor.   Good my lord, be quiet.
   [*The Attendants part them, and they come*
         out of the grave.
Ham. Why, I will fight with him upon this theme,
Until my eyelids will no longer wag.
Queen. O my son! what theme?
Ham. I lov'd Ophelia: forty thousand brothers
Could not, with all their quantity of love,
Make up my sum.—What wilt thou do for her?   280
King. O! he is mad, Laertes.
Queen. For love of God, forbear him.
Ham. 'Swounds! show me what thou 'lt do:
Woo't weep? woo't fight? woo't fast? woo't tear thy-
    self?
Woo't drink up Esill? eat a crocodile?
I 'll do 't.—Dost thou come here to whine?
To outface me with leaping in her grave?
Be buried quick with her, and so will I:
And, if thou prate of mountains, let them throw
Millions of acres on us, till our ground,   290
Singeing his pate against the burning zone,
Make Ossa like a wart! Nay, an thou 'lt mouth,
I 'll rant as well as thou.
Queen.   This is mere madness:
And thus awhile the fit will work on him;
Anon, as patient as the female dove,
When that her golden couplet are disclos'd,
His silence will sit drooping.
Ham.   Hear you, sir:
What is the reason that you use me thus?
I lov'd you ever: but it is no matter;
Let Hercules himself do what he may,   300
The cat will mew, and dog will have his day.   [*Exit.*
King. I pray you, good Horatio, wait upon him.
                  [*Exit* HORATIO.
[*To* LAERTES.] Strengthen your patience in our last
      night's speech;
We 'll put the matter to the present push.—
Good Gertrude, set some watch over your son.
This grave shall have a living monument:
An hour of quiet shortly shall we see;
Till then, in patience our proceeding be.   [*Exeunt.*

SCENE II.—A Hall in the Castle.

Enter HAMLET *and* HORATIO.

Ham. So much for this, sir: now let me see the
     other;—
You do remember all the circumstance?
Hor. Remember it, my lord!
Ham. Sir, in my heart there was a kind of fighting,
That would not let me sleep: methought, I lay
Worse than the mutines in the bilboes. Rashly,—
And prais'd be rashness for it,—let us know,
Our indiscretion sometimes serves us well,
When our dear plots do pall; and that should teach
     us,
There 's a divinity that shapes our ends,   10
Rough-hew them how we will,—
Hor.   That is most certain.
Ham. Up from my cabin,
My sea-gown scarf'd about me, in the dark
Grop'd I to find out them; had my desire;
Finger'd their packet; and, in fine, withdrew
To mine own room again: making so bold,
My fears forgetting manners, to unseal
Their grand commission; where I found, Horatio,
O royal knavery! an exact command,—
Larded with many several sorts of reasons,   20
Importing Denmark's health, and England's too,
With, ho! such bugs and goblins in my life,—
That, on the supervise, no leisure bated,
No, not to stay the grinding of the axe,
My head should be struck off.
Hor.   Is 't possible?
Ham. Here 's the commission: read it at more
     leisure.
But wilt thou hear me how I did proceed?
Hor. Ay, 'beseech you.
Ham. Being thus benetted round with villainies,—

Ere I could make a prologue to my brains,   30
They had begun the play,—I sat me down,
Devis'd a new commission; wrote it fair:
I once did hold it, as our statists do,
A baseness to write fair, and labour'd much
How to forget that learning; but, sir, now
It did me yeoman's service. Wilt thou know
The effect of what I wrote?
  Hor.   Ay, good my lord.
  Ham. An earnest conjuration from the king,—
As England was his faithful tributary,
As love between them as the palm should flourish, 40
As peace should still her wheaten garland wear,
And stand a comma 'tween their amities,
And many such-like as's of great charge,—
That, on the view and know of these contents,
Without debatement further, more or less,
He should the bearers put to sudden death,
Not shriving-time allow'd.
  Hor.   How was this seal'd?
  Ham. Why, even in that was Heaven ordinant.
I had my father's signet in my purse,
Which was the model of that Danish seal;   50
Folded the writ up in form of the other;
Subscrib'd it; gave 't the impression; plac'd it safely,
The changeling never known. Now, the next day
Was our sea-fight; and what to this was sequent
Thou know'st already.
  Hor. So Guildenstern and Rosencrantz go to 't.
  Ham. Why, man, they did make love to this
          employment:
They are not near my conscience: their defeat
Does by their own insinuation grow.
'T is dangerous, when the baser nature comes   60
Between the pass and fell-incensed points
Of mighty opposites.
  Hor.   Why, what a king is this!
  Ham. Does it not, thinks 't thee, stand me now
          upon—
He that hath kill'd my king, and whor'd my mother;
Popp'd in between the election and my hopes;
Thrown out his angle for my proper life,
And with such cozenage—is 't not perfect conscience,
To quit him with this arm? and is 't not to be damn'd.
To let this canker of our nature come
In further evil?   70
  Hor. It must be shortly known to him from Eng-
          land,
What is the issue of the business there.
  Ham. It will be short: the interim is mine;
And a man's life no more than to say, one.
But I am very sorry, good Horatio,
That to Laertes I forgot myself;
For, by the image of my cause, I see
The portraiture of his: I 'll court his favours:
But, sure, the bravery of his grief did put me
Into a towering passion.
  Hor.   Peace! who comes here? 80

Enter OSRICK.

  Osr. Your lordship is right welcome back to Denmark.
  Ham. I humbly thank you, sir.—Dost know this
water-fly?
  Hor. No, my good lord.
  Ham. Thy state is the more gracious; for 't is a
vice to know him. He hath much land, and fertile:
let a beast be lord of beasts, and his crib shall stand
at the king's mess: 't is a chough; but, as I say,
spacious in the possession of dirt.   90
  Osr. Sweet lord, if your lordship were at leisure, I
should impart a thing to you from his majesty.
  Ham. I will receive it, sir, with all diligence of
spirit. Your bonnet to his right use; 't is for the
head.
  Osr. I thank your lordship, 't is very hot.
  Ham. No, believe me, 't is very cold; the wind is
northerly.
  Osr. It is indifferent cold, my lord, indeed.
  Ham. But yet, methinks, it is very sultry and hot,
for my complexion.   101
  Osr. Exceedingly, my lord; it is very sultry,—as

't were,—I cannot tell how.—But, my lord, his majesty
bade me signify to you, that he has laid a great wager
on your head. Sir, this is the matter,—
  Ham. I beseech you, remember—
          [HAMLET *moves him to put on his hat.*
  Osr. Nay, in good faith; for mine ease, in good
faith. Sir, here is newly come to court, Laertes;
believe me, an absolute gentleman, full of most excellent differences, of very soft society, and great showing: indeed, to speak feelingly of him, he is the card
or calendar of gentry, for you shall find in him the
continent of what part a gentleman would see.   113
  Ham. Sir, his definement suffers no perdition in
you; though, I know, to divide him inventorially,
would dizzy the arithmetic of memory, and it but yaw
neither, in respect of his quick sail. But, in the
verity of extolment, I take him to be a soul of great
article; and his infusion of such dearth and rareness,
as, to make true diction of him, his semblable is his
mirror; and who else would trace him, his umbrage,
nothing more.   122
  Osr. Your lordship speaks most infallibly of him.
  Ham. The concernancy, sir? why do we wrap the
gentleman in our more rawer breath?
  Osr. Sir?
  Hor. Is 't not possible to understand in another
tongue? You will do 't, sir, really.
  Ham. What imports the nomination of this gentle-
man?   130
  Osr. Of Laertes?
  Hor. His purse is empty already; all 's golden words
are spent.
  Ham. Of him, sir.
  Osr. I know, you are not ignorant—
  Ham. I would, you did, sir; yet, in faith, if you did,
it would not much approve me.—Well, sir.
  Osr. You are not ignorant of what excellence
Laertes is—   139
  Ham. I dare not confess that, lest I should compare
with him in excellence; but, to know a man well,
were to know himself.
  Osr. I mean, sir, for his weapon; but in the imputation laid on him by them, in his meed he 's un-
fellowed.
  Ham. What 's his weapon?
  Osr. Rapier and dagger.
  Ham. That 's two of his weapons: but, well.   148
  Osr. The king, sir, hath wagered with him six Barbary horses: against the which he has imponed, as I
take it, six French rapiers and poniards, with their
assigns, as girdle, hangers, and so. Three of the carriages, in faith, are very dear to fancy, very responsive
to the hilts, most delicate carriages, and of very liberal
conceit.
  Ham. What call you the carriages?
  Hor. I knew, you must be edified by the margent
ere you had done.
  Osr. The carriages, sir, are the hangers.   159
  Ham. The phrase would be more german to the
matter, if we could carry cannon by our sides: I
would it might be hangers till then. But, on: six
Barbary horses against six French swords, their
assigns, and three liberal-conceited carriages; that 's
the French bet against the Danish. Why is this
imponed, as you call it?
  Osr. The king, sir, hath laid, sir, that in a dozen
passes between yourself and him, he shall not exceed
you three hits: he hath laid on twelve for nine; and
that would come to immediate trial, if your lordship
would vouchsafe the answer.   171
  Ham. How, if I answer no?
  Osr. I mean, my lord, the opposition of your person
in trial.
  Ham. Sir, I will walk here in the hall: if it please
his majesty, it is the breathing time of day with me;
let the foils be brought, the gentleman willing, and
the king hold his purpose, I will win for him, if I can;
if not, I will gain nothing but my shame, and the odd
hits.   180
  Osr. Shall I re-deliver you e'en so?
  Ham. To this effect, sir; after what flourish your
nature will.

Osr. I commend my duty to your lordship.

Ham. Yours, yours. [*Exit* OSRICK.]—He does well to commend it himself; there are no tongues else for 's turn.

Hor. This lapwing runs away with the shell on his head.   189

Ham. He did comply with his dug before he sucked it. Thus has he (and many more of the same bevy, that, I know, the drossy age dotes on) only got the tune of the time, and outward habit of encounter, a kind of yesty collection, which carries them through and through the most fond and winnowed opinions; and do but blow them to their trial, the bubbles are out.

Enter a Lord.

Lord. My lord, his majesty commended him to you by young Osrick, who brings back to him, that you attend him in the hall: he sends to know, if your pleasure hold to play with Laertes, or that you will take longer time.   203

Ham. I am constant to my purposes; they follow the king's pleasure: if his fitness speaks, mine is ready; now, or whensoever, provided I be so able as now.

Lord. The king, and queen, and all are coming down.

Ham. In happy time.   210

Lord. The queen desires you to use some gentle entertainment to Laertes, before you fall to play.

Ham. She well instructs me. [*Exit Lord.*

Hor. You will lose this wager, my lord.

Ham. I do not think so: since he went into France, I have been in continual practice; I shall win at the odds. Thou wouldst not think, how ill all 's here about my heart; but it is no matter.   220

Hor. Nay, good my lord,—

Ham. It is but foolery; but it is such a kind of gain-giving, as would, perhaps, trouble a woman.

Hor. If your mind dislike anything, obey it: I will forestall their repair hither, and say, you are not fit.

Ham. Not a whit, we defy augury: there is a special providence in the fall of a sparrow. If it be now, 't is not to come; if it be not to come, it will be now; if it be not now, yet it will come: the readiness is all. Since no man has aught of what he leaves, what is 't to leave betimes? Let be.   232

Enter KING, QUEEN, LAERTES, *Lords,* OSRICK, *and Attendants with foils, &c.*

King. Come, Hamlet, come, and take this hand from me.

[*The* KING *puts the hand of* LAERTES *into that of* HAMLET.

Ham. Give me your pardon, sir: I 've done you wrong;
But pardon 't, as you are a gentleman.
This presence knows,
And you must needs have heard, how I am punish'd
With sore distraction. What I have done,
That might your nature, honour, and exception,
Roughly awake, I here proclaim was madness.   240
Was 't Hamlet wrong'd Laertes? Never Hamlet:
If Hamlet from himself be ta'en away,
And, when he 's not himself, does wrong Laertes,
Then Hamlet does it not; Hamlet denies it.
Who does it then? His madness. If 't be so,
Hamlet is of the faction that is wrong'd;
His madness is poor Hamlet's enemy.
Sir, in this audience,
Let my disclaiming from a purpos'd evil
Free me so far in your most generous thoughts,   250
That I have shot mine arrow o'er the house,
And hurt my brother.

Laer.   I am satisfied in nature,
Whose motive, in this case, should stir me most
To my revenge: but in my terms of honour,
I stand aloof, and will no reconcilement,

Till by some elder masters, of known honour,
I have a voice and precedent of peace,
To keep my name ungor'd. But till that time,
I do receive your offer'd love like love,
And will not wrong it.

Ham.   I embrace it freely;   260
And will this brother's wager frankly play.—
Give us the foils.—Come on.

Laer.   Come, one for me.

Ham. I 'll be your foil, Laertes: in mine ignorance,

King. "Stay; give me drink. Hamlet, this pearl is thine;
Here 's to thy health."

Your skill shall, like a star i' the darkest night,
Stick fiery off indeed.

Laer.   You mock me, sir.

Ham. No, by this hand.

King. Give them the foils, young Osrick.—Cousin Hamlet,
You know the wager?

Ham.   Very well, my lord;
Your grace hath laid the odds o' the weaker side.

King. I do not fear it: I have seen you both;   270
But since he 's better'd, we have therefore odds.

Laer. This is too heavy; let me see another.

Ham. This likes me well. These foils have all a length?   [*They prepare to play.*

Osr. Ay, my good lord.

King. Set me the stoops of wine upon that table.—
If Hamlet give the first or second hit,
Or quit in answer of the third exchange,
Let all the battlements their ordnance fire;
The king shall drink to Hamlet's better breath:
And in the cup an union shall he throw,   280
Richer than that which four successive kings
In Denmark's crown have worn. Give me the cups;
And let the kettle to the trumpet speak,
The trumpet to the cannoneer without,
The cannons to the heavens, the heavens to earth,
"Now the king drinks to Hamlet!"—Come, begin;—
And you, the judges, bear a wary eye.

Ham. Come on, sir.

Laer.   Come, my lord. [*They play.*

Ham.   One.

Laer.   No.

Ham.   Judgment.

Osr. A hit, a very palpable hit.

Laer.   Well :—again.

King. Stay; give me drink. Hamlet, this pearl is thine;   290
Here 's to thy health.—Give him the cup,

[*Trumpets sound; and cannon shot off within.*

Ham. I 'll play this bout first : set it by awhile.
Come.—[*They play.*] Another hit ; what say you ?
Laer. A touch, a touch, I do confess.
King. Our son shall win.
Queen.   He 's fat, and scant of breath.—
Here, Hamlet, take my napkin, rub thy brows :
The queen carouses to thy fortune, Hamlet.
Ham. Good madam !
King.   Gertrude, do not drink.
Queen. I will, my lord : I pray you, pardon me.   299
King. [*Aside.*] It is the poison'd cup ! it is too late.
Ham. I dare not drink yet, madam ; by-and-by.
Queen. Come, let me wipe thy face.
Laer. My lord, I 'll hit him now.
King.   I do not think it.
Laer. [*Aside.*] And yet it is almost against my
          conscience.
Ham. Come, for the third, Laertes.   You but dally :
I pray you, pass with your best violence.
I am afeard, you make a wanton of me.
Laer. Say you so ? come on.   [*They play.*
Osr. Nothing, neither way.   309
Laer. Have at you now.
          [LAERTES *wounds* HAMLET ; *then, in scuffling,
          they change rapiers, and* HAMLET *wounds*
          LAERTES.
King.   Part them ! they are incens'd.
Ham. Nay, come again.   [*The* QUEEN *falls.*
Osr.   Look to the queen there.—Ho !
Hor. They bleed on both sides.—How is it, my lord ?
Osr. How is 't, Laertes ?
Laer. Why, as a woodcock to mine own springe,
          Osrick ;
I am justly kill'd with mine own treachery.
Ham. How does the queen ?
King.   She swoonds to see them bleed.
Queen. No, no, the drink, the drink,—O my dear
          Hamlet !
The drink, the drink : I am poison'd.   [*Dies.*
Ham. O villainy !—Ho ! let the door be lock'd :
Treachery ! seek it out.   [LAERTES *falls.*
Laer. It is here, Hamlet.   Hamlet, thou art slain ;
No medicine in the world can do thee good ;   322
In thee there is not half an hour of life ;
The treacherous instrument is in thy hand,
Unbated and envenom'd.   The foul practice
Hath turn'd itself on me : lo ! here I lie,
Never to rise again.   Thy mother 's poison'd.
I can no more.   The king, the king 's to blame.
Ham. The point—envenom'd too !
Then, venom, to thy work.   [*Stabs the* KING.
All. Treason ! treason !   331
King. O ! yet defend me, friends, I am but hurt.
Ham. Here, thou incestuous, murderous, damned
          Dane,
Drink off this potion :—is thy union here ?
Follow my mother.   [KING *dies.*
Laer.   He is justly serv'd ;
It is a poison temper'd by himself.—
Exchange forgiveness with me, noble Hamlet ;
Mine and my father's death come not upon thee,
Nor thine on me !   [*Dies.*
Ham. Heaven make thee free of it !   I follow thee.
I am dead, Horatio.—Wretched queen, adieu !—   341
You that look pale and tremble at this chance,
That are but mutes or audience to this act,
Had I but time, (as this fell sergeant, death,
Is strict in his arrest,) O ! I could tell you,—
But let it be.—Horatio, I am dead ;
Thou liv'st : report me and my cause aright
To the unsatisfied.
Hor.   Never believe it :
I am more an antique Roman than a Dane :
Here 's yet some liquor left.
Ham.   As thou 'rt a man,   350

Give me the cup : let go ; by Heaven, I 'll have it.--
O good Horatio, what a wounded name,
Things standing thus unknown, shall live behind me !
If thou didst ever hold me in thy heart,
Absent thee from felicity awhile,
And in this harsh world draw thy breath in pain,
To tell my story.   [*March afar off, and shot within.*
          What warlike noise is this ?
Osr. Young Fortinbras, with conquest come from
          Poland,
To the ambassadors of England gives
This warlike volley.
Ham.   O ! I die, Horatio ;   360
The potent poison quite o'er-crows my spirit :
I cannot live to hear the news from England ;
But I do prophesy the election lights
On Fortinbras : he has my dying voice ;
So tell him, with the occurrents, more and less,
Which have solicited.—The rest is silence.   [*Dies.*
Hor. Now cracks a noble heart.—Good night, sweet
          prince ;
And flights of angels sing thee to thy rest !—
Why does the drum come hither ?   [*March within.*

Enter FORTINBRAS, *the English Ambassadors, and
          others.*

For. Where is this sight ?
Hor.   What is it ye would see ?
If aught of woe, or wonder, cease your search.   371
For. This quarry cries on havock.—O proud death !
What feast is toward in thine eternal cell,
That thou so many princes at a shot
So bloodily hast struck ?
1 Amb.   The sight is dismal,
And our affairs from England come too late :
The ears are senseless that should give us hearing,
To tell him his commandment is fulfill'd,
That Rosencrantz and Guildenstern are dead.
Where should we have our thanks ?
Hor.   Not from his mouth,
Had it the ability of life to thank you :   381
He never gave commandment for their death.
But since, so jump upon this bloody question,
You from the Polack wars, and you from England,
Are here arriv'd, give order that these bodies
High on a stage be placed to the view ;
And let me speak to the yet unknowing world,
How these things came about : so shall you hear
Of carnal, bloody, and unnatural acts,
Of accidental judgments, casual slaughters,   390
Of deaths put on by cunning, and forc'd cause,
And, in this upshot, purposes mistook
Fall'n on the inventors' heads : all this can I
Truly deliver.
For.   Let us haste to hear it,
And call the noblest to the audience.
For me, with sorrow I embrace my fortune :
I have some rights of memory in this kingdom,
Which now to claim my vantage doth invite me.
Hor. Of that I shall have also cause to speak,
And from his mouth whose voice will draw on more :
But let this same be presently perform'd,   401
Even while men's minds are wild, lest more mischance,
On plots and errors, happen.
For.   Let four captains
Bear Hamlet, like a soldier, to the stage ;
For he was likely, had he been put on,
To have prov'd most royally : and for his passage,
The soldiers' music, and the rites of war,
Speak loudly for him.
Take up the bodies :—such a sight as this
Becomes the field, but here shows much amiss.   410
Go, bid the soldiers shoot.
          [*Exeunt, bearing off the bodies ; after which,
          a peal of ordnance is shot off.*

KING LEAR.

DRAMATIS PERSONÆ.

LEAR, *King of Britain.*
KING OF FRANCE.
DUKE OF BURGUNDY.
DUKE OF CORNWALL.
DUKE OF ALBANY.
EARL OF KENT.
EARL OF GLOSTER.
EDGAR, *Son to Gloster.*
EDMUND, *Bastard Son to Gloster.*
CURAN, *a Courtier.*
OSWALD, *Steward to Goneril.*
Old Man, *Tenant to Gloster.*

Physician.
Fool.
An Officer, *employed by Edmund.*
Gentleman, *Attendant on Cordelia.*
A Herald.
Servants to Cornwall.

GONERIL, ⎫
REGAN, ⎬ *Daughters to Lear.*
CORDELIA, ⎭

Knights of Lear's Train, Officers, Messengers,
    Soldiers, and Attendants.

SCENE—BRITAIN.

ACT I.

SCENE I.—A Room of State in King LEAR's Palace.

Enter KENT, GLOSTER, *and* EDMUND.

Kent.
THOUGHT, the king had more affected
the Duke of Albany, than Cornwall.
  Glo. It did always seem so to us: but
now, in the division of the kingdom,
it appears not which of the dukes he
values most; for equalities are so
weighed, that curiosity in neither can
make choice of either's moiety.
  Kent. Is not this your son, my lord? 9
  Glo. His breeding, sir, hath been at
my charge: I have so often blushed to
acknowledge him, that now I am brazed
to it.
  Kent. I cannot conceive you.
  Glo. Sir, this young fellow's mother
could; whereupon she grew round-
wombed, and had, indeed, sir, a son for
her cradle, ere she had a husband for
her bed. Do you smell a fault?
  Kent. I cannot wish the fault undone, the issue of it
being so proper. 21
  Glo. But I have a son, sir, by order of law, some
year elder than this, who yet is no dearer in my
account: though this knave came somewhat saucily
into the world, before he was sent for, yet was his
mother fair; there was good sport at his making, and
the whoreson must be acknowledged.—Do you know
this noble gentleman, Edmund?
  Edm. No, my lord.
  Glo. My Lord of Kent: remember him hereafter as
my honourable friend. 31
  Edm. My services to your lordship.
  Kent. I must love you, and sue to know you better.
  Edm. Sir, I shall study deserving.
  Glo. He hath been out nine years, and away he
shall again.—The king is coming.   [*Sennet within.*

Enter LEAR, CORNWALL, ALBANY, GONERIL, REGAN,
    CORDELIA, *and Attendants.*

  Lear. Attend the Lords of France and Burgundy,
Gloster.

  Glo. I shall, my liege.
          [*Exeunt* GLOSTER *and* EDMUND.
  Lear. Meantime we shall express our darker pur-
    pose.
Give me the map there.—Know, that we have divided,
In three, our kingdom; and 't is our fast intent   41
To shake all cares and business from our age,
Conferring them on younger strengths, while we
Unburden'd crawl toward death.—Our son of Corn-
    wall,
And you, our no less loving son of Albany,
We have this hour a constant will to publish
Our daughters' several dowers, that future strife
May be prevented now. The princes, France and
    Burgundy,
Great rivals in our youngest daughter's love,
Long in our court have made their amorous sojourn,
And here are to be answer'd.—Tell me, my daughters,
(Since we will divest us, both of rule,   52
Interest of territory, cares of state,)
Which of you, shall we say, doth love us most?
That we our largest bounty may extend
Where nature doth with merit challenge.—Goneril,
Our eldest-born, speak first.
  Gon. Sir, I love you more than words can wield the
    matter;
Dearer than eye-sight, space, and liberty;
Beyond what can be valued, rich or rare;   60
No less than life, with grace, health, beauty, honour;
As much as child e'er lov'd, or father found;
A love that makes breath poor, and speech unable;
Beyond all manner of so much I love you.
  Cor. [*Aside.*] What shall Cordelia do? Love, and
    be silent.
  Lear. Of all these bounds, even from this line to
    this,
With shadowy forests and with champains rich'd,
With plenteous rivers and wide-skirted meads,
We make thee lady: to thine and Albany's issue
Be this perpetual.—What says our second daughter,
Our dearest Regan, wife to Cornwall? Speak.   71
  Reg. I am made of that self metal as my sister,

And prize me at her worth. In my true heart
I find, she names my very deed of love ;
Only she comes too short,—that I profess
Myself an enemy to all other joys,
Which the most precious square of sense possesses,
And find, I am alone felicitate
In your dear highness' love.
    Cor. [*Aside.*]   Then, poor Cordelia !
And yet not so ; since, I am sure, my love 's   80
More ponderous than my tongue.
    Lear. To thee, and thine, hereditary ever,
Remain this ample third of our fair kingdom ;
No less in space, validity, and pleasure,
Than that conferr'd on Goneril.—Now, our joy,
Although our last, not least ; to whose young love
The vines of France, and milk of Burgundy,
Strive to be interess'd ; what can you say, to draw
A third more opulent than your sisters? Speak.
    Cor. Nothing, my lord.   90
    Lear. Nothing ?
    Cor. Nothing.
    Lear. Nothing will come of nothing : speak again.
    Cor. Unhappy that I am, I cannot heave
My heart into my mouth : I love your majesty
According to my bond ; nor more, nor less.
    Lear. How, how, Cordelia ! mend your speech a
    little,
Lest you may mar your fortunes.
    Cor.   Good my lord,
You have begot me, bred me, lov'd me : I   100
Return those duties back as are right fit,
Obey you, love you, and most honour you.
Why have my sisters husbands, if they say,
They love you all ? Haply, when I shall wed,
That lord, whose hand must take my plight, shall
    carry
Half my love with him, half my care, and duty :
Sure, I shall never marry like my sisters,
To love my father all.
    Lear. But goes thy heart with this ?
    Cor.   Ay, my good lord.
    Lear. So young, and so untender?
    Cor. So young, my lord, and true.   110
    Lear. Let it be so : thy truth then be thy dower ;
For, by the sacred radiance of the sun,
The mysteries of Hecate, and the night,
By all the operation of the orbs,
From whom we do exist, and cease to be,
Here I disclaim all my paternal care,
Propinquity and property of blood,
And as a stranger to my heart and me
Hold thee, from this, for ever. The barbarous
Scythian,   120
Or he that makes his generation messes
To gorge his appetite, shall to my bosom
Be as well neighbour'd, pitied, and reliev'd,
As thou my sometime daughter.
    Kent.   Good my liege,—
    Lear. Peace, Kent !
Come not between the dragon and his wrath.
I lov'd her most, and thought to set my rest
On her kind nursery.—Hence, and avoid my sight !—
So be my grave my peace, as here I give
Her father's heart from her !—Call France.—Who
    stirs ?—
Call Burgundy.—Cornwall, and Albany,   130
With my two daughters' dowers digest the third :
Let pride, which she calls plainness, marry her.
I do invest you jointly with my power,
Pre-eminence, and all the large effects
That troop with majesty.—Ourself, by monthly course,
With reservation of an hundred knights,
By you to be sustain'd, shall our abode
Make with you by due turn. Only, we shall retain
The name, and all the additions to a king ;
The sway, revenue, execution of the rest,   140
Beloved sons, be yours : which to confirm,
This coronet part between you.
    Kent.   Royal Lear,
Whom I have ever honour'd as my king,
Lov'd as my father, as my master follow'd,
As my great patron thought on in my prayers,—

    Lear. The bow is bent and drawn ; make from the
    shaft.
    Kent. Let it fall rather, though the fork invade
The region of my heart : be Kent unmannerly,
When Lear is mad.—What wouldst thou do, old
    man ?
Think'st thou, that duty shall have dread to speak, 150
When power to flattery bows ? To plainness honour 's
    bound,
When majesty falls to folly. Reserve thy state ;
And, in thy best consideration, check
This hideous rashness : answer my life my judgment,
Thy youngest daughter does not love thee least ;
Nor are those empty-hearted, whose low sound
Reverbs no hollowness.
    Lear.   Kent, on thy life, no more.
    Kent. My life I never held but as a pawn
To wage against thine enemies ; ne'er fear to lose it,
Thy safety being the motive.
    Lear.   Out of my sight !   160
    Kent. See better, Lear ; and let me still remain
The true blank of thine eye.
    Lear. Now, by Apollo,—
    Kent.   Now, by Apollo, king,
Thou swear'st thy gods in vain.
    Lear.   O, vassal ! miscreant !
        [*Laying his hand upon his sword.*
    Alb., *Corn.* Dear sir, forbear.
    Kent. Do ;
Kill thy physician, and the fee bestow
Upon the foul disease. Revoke thy gift ;
Or, whilst I can vent clamour from my throat,
I 'll tell thee, thou dost evil.
    Lear.   Hear me, recreant !   170
On thine allegiance, hear me !
Since thou hast sought to make us break our vow
(Which we durst never yet), and, with strain'd pride,
To come betwixt our sentence and our power
(Which nor our nature nor our place can bear),
Our potency made good, take thy reward.
Five days we do allot thee for provision
To shield thee from disasters of the world ;
And on the sixth to turn thy hated back
Upon our kingdom : if, on the tenth day following, 180
Thy banish'd trunk be found in our dominions,
The moment is thy death. Away ! By Jupiter,
This shall not be revok'd.
    Kent. Fare thee well, king : since thus thou wilt
    appear,
Freedom lives hence, and banishment is here.—
[*To* CORDELIA.] The gods to their dear shelter take
    thee, maid,
That justly think'st, and hast most rightly said !—
[*To* REGAN *and* GONERIL.] And your large speeches
    may your deeds approve,
That good effects may spring from words of love.—
Thus Kent, O princes ! bids you all adieu ;   190
He 'll shape his old course in a country new. [*Exit.*

    Flourish. Re-enter GLOSTER ; *with* FRANCE,
    BURGUNDY, *and Attendants.*

    Glo. Here 's France and Burgundy, my noble lord.
    Lear. My Lord of Burgundy,
We first address toward you, who with this king
Hath rivall'd for our daughter. What, in the least,
Will you require in present dower with her,
Or cease your quest of love ?
    Bur.   Most royal majesty,
I crave no more than hath your highness offer'd,
Nor will you tender less.
    Lear.   Right noble Burgundy,
When she was dear to us, we did hold her so ;   200
But now her price is fall'n. Sir, there she stands :
If aught within that little seeming substance,
Or all of it, with our displeasure piec'd,
And nothing more, may fitly like your grace,
She 's there, and she is yours.
    Bur.   I know no answer.
    Lear. Will you, with those infirmities she owes,
Unfriended, new-adopted to our hate,
Dower'd with our curse, and stranger'd with our oath,
Take her, or leave her ?

Bur.   Pardon me, royal sir;
Election makes not up on such conditions.   210
   Lear. Then leave her, sir; for, by the power that
         made me,

Most best, most dearest, should in this trice of time 220
Commit a thing so monstrous, to dismantle
So many folds of favour.   Sure, her offence
Must be of such unnatural degree,

Lear. " Peace, Kent!
Come not between the dragon and his wrath."

I tell you all her wealth.—[*To* FRANCE.] For you,
       great king,
I would not from your love make such a stray,
To match you where I hate : therefore, beseech you
To avert your liking a more worthier way,
Than on a wretch whom Nature is asham'd
Almost to acknowledge hers.
   France.   This is most strange,
That she, who even but now was your best object,
The argument of your praise, balm of your age,

That monsters it, or your fore-vouch'd affection
Fall into taint : which to believe of her,
Must be a faith that reason without miracle
Could never plant in me.
   Cor.   I yet beseech your majesty
(If for I want that glib and oily art,
To speak and purpose not ; since what I well intend,
I 'll do 't before I speak) that you make known   230
It is no vicious blot, murder, or foulness,
No unchaste action, or dishonour'd step,

That hath depriv'd me of your grace and favour;
But even for want of that for which I am richer,
A still-soliciting eye, and such a tongue
That I am glad I have not, though not to have it
Hath lost me in your liking.
 Lear.   Better thou
Hadst not been born, than not to have pleas'd me
 better.
 France. Is it but this? a tardiness in nature,
Which often leaves the history unspoke, 240
That it intends to do?—My Lord of Burgundy,
What say you to the lady? Love's not love,
When it is mingled with regards, that stand
Aloof from the entire point. Will you have her?
She is herself a dowry.
 Bur.   Royal king,
Give but that portion which yourself propos'd,
And here I take Cordelia by the hand,
Duchess of Burgundy.
 Lear. Nothing: I have sworn; I am firm.
 Bur. I am sorry, then, you have so lost a father, 250
That you must lose a husband.
 Cor.   Peace be with Burgundy!
Since that respects of fortune are his love,
I shall not be his wife.
 France. Fairest Cordelia, that art most rich, being
 poor;
Most choice, forsaken; and most lov'd, despis'd;
Thee and thy virtues here I seize upon:
Be it lawful, I take up what's cast away.
Gods, gods! 't is strange, that from their cold'st neglect
My love should kindle to inflam'd respect.—
Thy dowerless daughter, king, thrown to my chance,
Is queen of us, of ours, and our fair France: 261
Not all the dukes of waterish Burgundy
Shall buy this unpriz'd precious maid of me.—
Bid them farewell, Cordelia, though unkind:
Thou losest here, a better where to find.
 Lear. Thou hast her, France: let her be thine; for
 we
Have no such daughter, nor shall ever see
That face of hers again :—therefore, be gone
Without our grace, our love, our benison.—
Come, noble Burgundy.   270
 [*Flourish. Exeunt* LEAR, BURGUNDY, CORN-
 WALL, ALBANY, GLOSTER, *and Attendants.*
 France. Bid farewell to your sisters.
 Cor. The jewels of our father, with wash'd eyes
Cordelia leaves you: I know you what you are;
And, like a sister, am most loath to call
Your faults as they are nam'd. Love well our father:
To your professed bosoms I commit him;
But yet, alas! stood I within his grace,
I would prefer him to a better place.
So farewell to you both.
 Reg. Prescribe not us our duty.
 Gon.   Let your study 280
Be, to content your lord, who hath receiv'd you
At fortune's alms: you have obedience scanted,
And well are worth the want that you have wanted.
 Cor. Time shall unfold what plighted cunning
 hides;
Who cover faults, at last shame them derides.
Well may you prosper!
 France.   Come, my fair Cordelia.
 [*Exeunt* FRANCE *and* CORDELIA.
 Gon. Sister, it is not little I have to say of what
most nearly appertains to us both. I think, our father
will hence to-night.
 Reg. That's most certain, and with you; next month
with us. 291
 Gon. You see how full of changes his age is; the
observation we have made of it hath not been little:
he always loved our sister most; and with what poor
judgment he hath now cast her off, appears too grossly.
 Reg. 'T is the infirmity of his age; yet he hath ever
but slenderly known himself.
 Gon. The best and soundest of his time hath been
but rash; then must we look to receive from his age,
not alone the imperfections of long-engraffed condition, but, therewithal, the unruly waywardness that
infirm and choleric years bring with them. 302

 Reg. Such unconstant starts are we like to have
from him, as this of Kent's banishment.
 Gon. There is further compliment of leave-taking
between France and him. Pray you, let us hit
together: if our father carry authority with such
disposition as he bears, this last surrender of his
will but offend us.
 Reg. We shall further think of it. 310
 Gon. We must do something, and i' the heat.
         [*Exeunt.*

SCENE II.—A Hall in the Earl of GLOSTER's Castle.

Enter EDMUND, *with a letter.*

 Edm. Thou, Nature, art my goddess; to thy law
My services are bound. Wherefore should I
Stand in the plague of custom, and permit
The curiosity of nations to deprive me,
For that I am some twelve or fourteen moonshines
Lag of a brother? Why bastard? wherefore base?
When my dimensions are as well compact,
My mind as generous, and my shape as true,
As honest madam's issue? Why brand they us
With base? with baseness? bastardy? base, base? 10
Who in the lusty stealth of nature take
More composition and fierce quality,
Than doth, within a dull, stale, tired bed,
Go to the creating a whole tribe of fops,
Got 'tween asleep and wake?—Well then,
Legitimate Edgar, I must have your land:
Our father's love is to the bastard Edmund,
As to the legitimate. Fine word,—legitimate!
Well, my legitimate, if this letter speed,
And my invention thrive, Edmund the base 20
Shall to the legitimate :—I grow, I prosper;—
Now, gods, stand up for bastards!

Enter GLOSTER.

 Glo. Kent banish'd thus! And France in choler
 parted!
And the king gone to-night! subscrib'd his power!
Confin'd to exhibition! All this done
Upon the gad!—Edmund! How now! what news?
 Edm. So please your lordship, none.
       [*Putting up the letter.*
 Glo. Why so earnestly seek you to put up that
letter?
 Edm. I know no news, my lord. 30
 Glo. What paper were you reading?
 Edm. Nothing, my lord.
 Glo. No? What needed then that terrible despatch
of it into your pocket? the quality of nothing hath not
such need to hide itself. Let's see; come; if it be
nothing, I shall not need spectacles.
 Edm. I beseech you, sir, pardon me : it is a letter
from my brother, that I have not all o'er-read: and for
so much as I have perused, I find it not fit for your
o'erlooking. 40
 Glo. Give me the letter, sir.
 Edm. I shall offend, either to detain or give it. The
contents, as in part I understand them, are to blame.
 Glo. Let's see, let's see.
 Edm. I hope, for my brother's justification, he wrote
this but as an essay or taste of my virtue.
 Glo. [*Reads.*] "This policy, and reverence of age,
makes the world bitter to the best of our times; keeps
our fortunes from us, till our oldness cannot relish
them. I begin to find an idle and fond bondage in the
oppression of aged tyranny, who sways, not as it hath
power, but as it is suffered. Come to me, that of this
I may speak more. If our father would sleep till I
waked him, you should enjoy half his revenue for
ever, and live the beloved of your brother, EDGAR."—
Humph!—Conspiracy!—"Sleep till I waked him,—you
should enjoy half his revenue."—My son Edgar! Had
he a hand to write this? a heart and brain to breed it
in?—When came this to you? Who brought it? 59
 Edm. It was not brought me, my lord; there's the
cunning of it: I found it thrown in at the casement of
my closet.
 Glo. You know the character to be your brother's?

Edm. If the matter were good, my lord, I durst swear it were his; but, in respect of that, I would fain think it were not.

Glo. It is his.

Edm. It is his hand, my lord; but, I hope, his heart is not in the contents.

Glo. Has he never before sounded you in this business? 71

Edm. Never, my lord: but I have often heard him maintain it to be fit, that, sons at perfect age, and fathers declined, the father should be as ward to the son, and the son manage his revenue.

Edm. "It is his hand, my lord; but, I hope, his heart is not in the contents."

Glo. O villain, villain!—His very opinion in the letter!—Abhorred villain! Unnatural, detested, brutish villain! worse than brutish!—Go, sirrah, seek him; I'll apprehend him.—Abominable villain!—Where is he? 80

Edm. I do not well know, my lord. If it shall please you to suspend your indignation against my brother, till you can derive from him better testimony of his intent, you shall run a certain course; where, if you violently proceed against him, mistaking his purpose, it would make a great gap in your own honour, and shake in pieces the heart of his obedience. I dare pawn down my life for him, that he hath writ this to feel my affection to your honour, and to no other pretence of danger. 90

Glo. Think you so?

Edm. If your honour judge it meet, I will place you where you shall hear us confer of this, and by an auricular assurance have your satisfaction; and that without any further delay than this very evening.

Glo. He cannot be such a monster—

Edm. Nor is not, sure.

Glo. To his father, that so tenderly and entirely loves him.—Heaven and earth!—Edmund, seek him out; wind me into him, I pray you: frame the business after your own wisdom. I would unstate myself to be in a due resolution. 102

Edm. I will seek him, sir, presently; convey the business as I shall find means, and acquaint you withal.

Glo. These late eclipses in the sun and moon portend no good to us: though the wisdom of nature can reason it thus and thus, yet nature finds itself scourged by the sequent effects. Love cools, friendship falls off, brothers divide: in cities, mutinies; in countries, discord; in palaces, treason; and the bond cracked

between son and father. This villain of mine comes under the prediction; there's son against father: the king falls from bias of nature; there's father against child. We have seen the best of our time: machinations, hollowness, treachery, and all ruinous disorders, follow us disquietly to our graves.—Find out this villain, Edmund; it shall lose thee nothing: do it carefully.—And the noble and true-hearted Kent banished! his offence, honesty!—'T is strange. [*Exit.*

Edm. This is the excellent foppery of the world, that, when we are sick in fortune (often the surfeit of our own behaviour), we make guilty of our disasters the sun, the moon, and the stars: as if we were villains by necessity; fools by heavenly compulsion; knaves, thieves, and treachers, by spherical predominance; drunkards, liars, and adulterers, by an enforced obedience of planetary influence; and all that we are evil in, by a divine thrusting on. An admirable evasion of whoremaster man, to lay his goatish disposition on the charge of a star! My father compounded with my mother under the dragon's tail; and my nativity was under *ursa major:* so that it follows, I am rough and lecherous.—Tut! I should have been that I am, had the maidenliest star in the firmament twinkled on my bastardising.

Enter EDGAR.

Pat: he comes, like the catastrophe of the old comedy: my cue is villainous melancholy, with a sigh like Tom o' Bedlam.—O! these eclipses do portend these divisions. Fa, sol, la, mi. 140

Edg. How now, brother Edmund! What serious contemplation are you in?

Edm. I am thinking, brother, of a prediction I read this other day, what should follow these eclipses.

Edg. Do you busy yourself with that?

Edm. I promise you, the effects he writes of succeed unhappily: as of unnaturalness between the child and the parent; death, dearth, dissolutions of ancient amities; divisions in state; menaces and maledictions against king and nobles; needless diffidences, banishment of friends, dissipation of cohorts, nuptial breaches, and I know not what. 153

Edg. How long have you been a sectary astronomical?

Edm. Come, come; when saw you my father last?

Edg. The night gone by.

Edm. Spake you with him?

Edg. Ay, two hours together. 160

Edm. Parted you in good terms? Found you no displeasure in him, by word, or countenance?

Edg. None at all.

Edm. Bethink yourself, wherein you may have offended him: and at my entreaty forbear his presence, till some little time hath qualified the heat of his displeasure, which at this instant so rageth in him, that with the mischief of your person it would scarcely allay.

Edg. Some villain hath done me wrong. 170

Edm. That's my fear. I pray you, have a continent forbearance, till the speed of his rage goes slower; and, as I say, retire with me to my lodging, from whence I will fitly bring you to hear my lord speak. Pray you, go: there's my key.—If you do stir abroad, go armed.

Edg. Armed, brother?

Edm. Brother, I advise you to the best; I am no honest man, if there be any good meaning towards you: I have told you what I have seen and heard, but faintly; nothing like the image and horror of it. Pray you, away. 182

Edg. Shall I hear from you anon?

Edm. I do serve you in this business.—

[*Exit* EDGAR.

A credulous father, and a brother noble,
Whose nature is so far from doing harms,
That he suspects none; on whose foolish honesty
My practices ride easy!—I see the business.—
Let me, if not by birth, have lands by wit:
All with me's meet, that I can fashion fit. [*Exit.*

SCENE III.—A Room in the Duke of ALBANY'S Palace.

Enter GONERIL, *and* OSWALD, *her Steward.*

Gon. Did my father strike my gentleman for chiding of his fool?

Osw. Ay, madam.

Gon. By day and night he wrongs me : every hour
He flashes into one gross crime or other,
That sets us all at odds : I 'll not endure it.
His knights grow riotous, and himself upbraids us
On every trifle.—When he returns from hunting,
I will not speak with him ; say, I am sick :
If you come slack of former services,   10
You shall do well ; the fault of it I 'll answer.

Osw. He 's coming, madam ; I hear him.
                       [*Horns within.*

Gon. Put on what weary negligence you please,
You and your fellows ; I 'd have it come to question :
If he distaste it, let him to my sister,
Whose mind and mine, I know, in that are one,
Not to be over-rul'd. Idle old man,
That still would manage those authorities
That he hath given away !—Now, by my life,
Old fools are babes again ; and must be us'd   20
With checks, as flatteries, when they are seen abus'd.
Remember what I have said.

Osw.   Well, madam.

Gon. And let his knights have colder looks among you ;
What grows of it, no matter ; advise your fellows so :
I would breed from hence occasions, and I shall,
That I may speak :—I 'll write straight to my sister,
To hold my course.—Prepare for dinner.   [*Exeunt.*

SCENE IV.—A Hall in the Same.

Enter KENT, *disguised.*

Kent. If but as well I other accents borrow,
That can my speech diffuse, my good intent
May carry through itself to that full issue
For which I raz'd my likeness.—Now, banish'd Kent,
If thou canst serve where thou dost stand condemn'd,
(So may it come !) thy master, whom thou lov'st,
Shall find thee full of labours.

Horns within. Enter LEAR, *Knights, and Attendants.*

Lear. Let me not stay a jot for dinner : go, get it
ready. [*Exit an Attendant.*] How now ! what art thou ?   10

Kent. A man, sir.

Lear. What dost thou profess ? What wouldst thou with us ?

Kent. I do profess to be no less than I seem ; to
serve him truly that will put me in trust ; to love
him that is honest ; to converse with him that is
wise, and says little ; to fear judgment ; to fight when
I cannot choose ; and to eat no fish.

Lear. What art thou ?

Kent. A very honest-hearted fellow, and as poor as
the king.   21

Lear. If thou be as poor for a subject, as he is for a
king, thou art poor enough. What wouldst thou ?

Kent. Service.

Lear. Whom wouldst thou serve ?

Kent. You.

Lear. Dost thou know me, fellow ?

Kent. No, sir ; but you have that in your countenance, which I would fain call master.   30

Lear. What 's that ?

Kent. Authority.

Lear. What services canst thou do ?

Kent. I can keep honest counsel, ride, run, mar a
curious tale in telling it, and deliver a plain message
bluntly : that which ordinary men are fit for, I am
qualified in ; and the best of me is diligence.

Lear. How old art thou ?

Kent. Not so young, sir, to love a woman for singing ; nor so old, to dote on her for anything : I have
years on my back forty-eight.   40

Lear. Follow me ; thou shalt serve me : if I like
thee no worse after dinner, I will not part from thee
yet.—Dinner, ho ! dinner !—Where 's my knave ? my
fool ? Go you, and call my fool hither.
                       [*Exit an Attendant.*

Enter OSWALD.

You, you, sirrah, where 's my daughter ?

Osw. So please you,—   [*Exit.*

Lear. What says the fellow there ? Call the clotpoll
back. [*Exit a Knight.*]—Where 's my fool, ho ?—I
think the world 's asleep.

Re-enter Knight.

How now ! where 's that mongrel ?   50

Knight. He says, my lord, your daughter is not well.

Lear. Why came not the slave back to me, when I
called him ?

Knight. Sir, he answered me in the roundest
manner, he would not.

Lear. He would not !

Knight. My lord, I know not what the matter is ;
but, to my judgment, your highness is not entertained
with that ceremonious affection as you were wont :
there 's a great abatement of kindness appears, as
well in the general dependants, as in the duke himself
also, and your daughter.   62

Lear. Ha ! sayest thou so ?

Knight. I beseech you, pardon me, my lord, if I be
mistaken ; for my duty cannot be silent, when I think
your highness wronged.

Lear. Thou but rememberest me of mine own conception. I have perceived a most faint neglect of
late ; which I have rather blamed as mine own jealous
curiosity, than as a very pretence and purpose of
unkindness : I will look further into 't.—But where 's
my fool ? I have not seen him this two days.   72

Knight. Since my young lady 's going into France,
sir, the fool hath much pined away.

Lear. No more of that ; I have noted it well.—Go
you, and tell my daughter I would speak with her.
[*Exit an Attendant.*]—Go you, call hither my fool.
                       [*Exit an Attendant.*

Re-enter OSWALD.

O ! you sir, you, come you hither, sir. Who am I, sir ?

Osw. My lady 's father.   80

Lear. My lady 's father ! my lord 's knave : you
whoreson dog ! you slave ! you cur !

Osw. I am none of these, my lord ; I beseech your
pardon.

Lear. Do you bandy looks with me, you rascal ?
                       [*Striking him.*

Osw. I 'll not be struck, my lord.

Kent. Nor tripped neither, you base foot-ball player.
                       [*Tripping up his heels.*

Lear. I thank thee, fellow ; thou servest me, and
I 'll love thee.   89

Kent. Come, sir, arise, away ! I 'll teach you differences : away, away ! If you will measure your
lubber 's length again, tarry ; but away ! Go to : have
you wisdom ? so.   [*Pushes* OSWALD *out.*

Lear. Now, my friendly knave, I thank thee :
there 's earnest of thy service. [*Giving* KENT *money.*

Enter Fool.

Fool. Let me hire him too :—here 's my coxcomb.
                       [*Giving* KENT *his cap.*

Lear. How now, my pretty knave ! how dost thou ?

Fool. Sirrah, you were best take my coxcomb.

Kent. Why, fool ?   99

Fool. Why, for taking one 's part that 's out of
favour.—Nay, an thou canst not smile as the wind
sits, thou 'lt catch cold shortly : there, take my coxcomb. Why, this fellow has banished two on 's
daughters, and did the third a blessing against his
will : if thou follow him, thou must needs wear
my coxcomb.—How now, nuncle ? 'Would I had two
coxcombs, and two daughters !

Lear. Why, my boy?

Fool. If I gave them all my living, I'd keep my coxcombs myself. There's mine; beg another of thy daughters.   111

Lear. Take heed, sirrah,—the whip.

Fool. Truth's a dog must to kennel; he must be whipped out, when the lady brach may stand by the fire and stink.

Lear. A pestilent gall to me!

Fool. Sirrah, I'll teach thee a speech.

Lear. Do.

Fool. Mark it, nuncle:—

> Have more than thou showest,   120
> Speak less than thou knowest,
> Lend less than thou owest,
> Ride more than thou goest,
> Learn more than thou trowest,
> Set less than thou throwest;
> Leave thy drink and thy whore,
> And keep in-a-door,
> And thou shalt have more
> Than two tens to a score.

Kent. This is nothing, fool.   130

Fool. Then 't is like the breath of an unfee'd lawyer; you gave me nothing for 't.—Can you make no use of nothing, nuncle?

Lear. Why, no, boy; nothing can be made out of nothing.

Fool. [*To* KENT.] Pr'ythee, tell him, so much the rent of his land comes to: he will not believe a fool.

Lear. A bitter fool!

Fool. Dost thou know the difference, my boy, between a bitter fool and a sweet one?   140

Lear. No, lad; teach me.

Fool.
> That lord, that counsell'd thee
> To give away thy land,
> Come place him here by me;
> Do thou for him stand:
> The sweet and bitter fool
> Will presently appear;
> The one in motley here,
> The other found out there.

Lear. Dost thou call me fool, boy?   150

Fool. All thy other titles thou hast given away; that thou wast born with.

Kent. This is not altogether fool, my lord.

Fool. No, 'faith; lords and great men will not let me: if I had a monopoly out, they would have part on 't; and ladies too: they will not let me have all fool to myself; they 'll be snatching.—Nuncle, give me an egg, and I 'll give thee two crowns.

Lear. What two crowns shall they be?   159

Fool. Why, after I have cut the egg i' the middle, and eat up the meat, the two crowns of the egg. When thou clovest thy crown i' the middle, and gavest away both parts, thou borest thine ass on thy back o'er the dirt: thou hadst little wit in thy bald crown, when thou gavest thy golden one away. If I speak like myself in this, let him be whipped that first finds it so.   [*Singing.*

> Fools had ne'er less grace in a year;
> For wise men are grown foppish,
> And know not how their wits to wear,   170
> Their manners are so apish.

Lear. When were you wont to be so full of songs, sirrah?

Fool. I have used it, nuncle, ever since thou madest thy daughters thy mothers: for when thou gavest them the rod and putt'st down thine own breeches,
[*Singing.*

> Then they for sudden joy did weep,
> And I for sorrow sung,
> That such a king should play bo-peep,
> And go the fools among.   180

Pr'ythee, nuncle, keep a schoolmaster that can teach thy fool to lie: I would fain learn to lie.

Lear. An you lie, sirrah, we 'll have you whipped.

Fool. I marvel, what kin thou and thy daughters are: they'll have me whipped for speaking true, thou 'lt have me whipped for lying; and sometimes I am whipped for holding my peace. I had rather be any kind o' thing than a fool; and yet I would not be thee, nuncle: thou hast pared thy wit o' both sides, and left nothing i' the middle. Here comes one o' the parings.   191

Enter GONERIL.

Lear. How now, daughter? what makes that frontlet on?

Methinks, you are too much of late i' the frown.

Fool. Thou wast a pretty fellow, when thou hadst no need to care for her frowning; now thou art an O without a figure. I am better than thou art now: I am a fool, thou art nothing.—Yes, forsooth, I will hold my tongue; so your face [*to* GONERIL] bids me, though you say nothing.

> Mum, mum: 200
> He that keeps nor crust nor crum,
> Weary of all, shall want some.

That's a sheal'd peascod.

Gon. Not only, sir, this your all-licens'd fool,
But other of your insolent retinue
Do hourly carp and quarrel; breaking forth
In rank and not-to-be-endured riots. Sir,
I had thought, by making this well known unto you,
To have found a safe redress; but now grow fearful,
By what yourself too late have spoke and done,   210
That you protect this course, and put it on
By your allowance; which if you should, the fault
Would not 'scape censure, nor the redresses sleep,
Which, in the tender of a wholesome weal,
Might in their working do you that offence,
Which else were shame, that then necessity
Will call discreet proceeding.

Fool. For you know, nuncle,
> The hedge-sparrow fed the cuckoo so long,
> That it had it head bit off by it young.   220
So, out went the candle, and we were left darkling.

Lear. Are you our daughter?

Gon. I would you would make use of your good wisdom,
Whereof I know you are fraught, and put away
These dispositions, which of late transport you
From what you rightly are.

Fool. May not an ass know when the cart draws the horse?—Whoop, Jug! I love thee.

Lear. Does any here know me? This is not Lear:
Does Lear walk thus? speak thus? Where are his eyes?   230
Either his notion weakens, his discernings
Are lethargied.—Ha! waking? 't is not so.—
Who is it that can tell me who I am?—

Fool. Lear's shadow.

Lear. I would learn that; for by the marks of sovereignty, knowledge, and reason, I should be false persuaded I had daughters.

Fool. Which they will make an obedient father.

Lear. Your name, fair gentlewoman?

Gon. This admiration, sir, is much o' the savour   240
Of other your new pranks. I do beseech you
To understand my purposes aright:
As you are old and reverend, should be wise.
Here do you keep a hundred knights and squires;
Men so disorder'd, so debosh'd, and bold,
That this our court, infected with their manners,
Shows like a riotous inn: epicurism and lust
Make it more like a tavern, or a brothel,
Than a grac'd palace. The shame itself doth speak
For instant remedy: be then desir'd   250
By her, that else will take the thing she begs,
A little to disquantity your train;
And the remainder, that shall still depend,
To be such men as may besort your age,
Which know themselves and you.

Lear.   Darkness and devils!—
Saddle my horses; call my train together.—
Degenerate bastard! I 'll not trouble thee:
Yet have I left a daughter.

Gon. You strike my people; and your disorder'd rabble
Make servants of their betters.   260

Enter Albany.

Lear. Woe, that too late repents,—[*To* Albany.]
O, sir, are you come?
Is it your will? Speak, sir.—Prepare my horses.
Ingratitude, thou marble-hearted fiend,
More hideous, when thou show'st thee in a child,
Than the sea-monster!
Alb.   Pray, sir, be patient.
Lear. [*To* Goneril.] Detested kite! thou liest:
My train are men of choice and rarest parts,
That all particulars of duty know,
And in the most exact regard support
The worships of their name.—O most small fault, 270
How ugly didst thou in Cordelia show!
Which, like an engine, wrench'd my frame of nature
From the fix'd place, drew from my heart all love,
And added to the gall. O Lear, Lear, Lear!
Beat at this gate, that let thy folly in,
                              [*Striking his head.*
And thy dear judgment out!—Go, go, my people.
Alb. My lord, I am guiltless, as I am ignorant
Of what hath mov'd you.
Lear.   It may be so, my lord.—
Hear, Nature, hear! dear goddess, hear!
Suspend thy purpose, if thou didst intend   280
To make this creature fruitful!
Into her womb convey sterility!
Dry up in her the organs of increase,
And from her derogate body never spring
A babe to honour her! If she must teem,
Create her child of spleen; that it may live,
And be a thwart disnatur'd torment to her!
Let it stamp wrinkles in her brow of youth;
With cadent tears fret channels in her cheeks;
Turn all her mother's pains, and benefits,   290
To laughter and contempt; that she may feel
How sharper than a serpent's tooth it is
To have a thankless child!—Away, away!   [*Exit.*
Alb. Now, gods, that we adore, whereof comes
this?
Gon. Never afflict yourself to know more of it;
But let his disposition have that scope
As dotage gives it.
Re-enter Lear.

Lear. What, fifty of my followers at a clap!
Within a fortnight?
Alb.   What's the matter, sir?
Lear. I'll tell thee:—Life and death! [*To* Goneril.]
I am ashamed,   300
That thou hast power to shake my manhood thus;
That these hot tears, which break from me perforce,
Should make thee worth them. Blasts and fogs
upon thee!
The untented woundings of a father's curse
Pierce every sense about thee!—Old fond eyes,
Beweep this cause again, I'll pluck you out,
And cast you, with the waters that you lose,
To temper clay.—Yea, is it come to this?
Let it be so:—yet have I left a daughter,
Who, I am sure, is kind and comfortable: 310
When she shall hear this of thee, with her nails
She'll flay thy wolfish visage. Thou shalt find,
That I'll resume the shape which thou dost think
I have cast off for ever.
          [*Exeunt* Lear, Kent, *and Attendants.*
Gon. Do you mark this?
Alb. I cannot be so partial, Goneril,
To the great love I bear you,—
Gon. Pray you, content.—What, Oswald, ho!—
[*To the Fool.*] You, sir, more knave than fool, after
your master.
Fool. Nuncle Lear, nuncle Lear! tarry, and take
the fool with thee.   321
     A fox, when one has caught her,
     And such a daughter,
     Should sure to the slaughter,
     If my cap would buy a halter;
     So the fool follows after.   [*Exit.*
Gon. This man hath had good counsel.—A hundred
knights!
'T is politic, and safe, to let him keep

At point a hundred knights: yes, that on every
dream,
Each buz, each fancy, each complaint, dislike,   330
He may enguard his dotage with their powers,
And hold our lives in mercy.—Oswald, I say!—
Alb. Well, you may fear too far.
Gon.   Safer than trust too far.
Let me still take away the harms I fear,
Not fear still to be taken: I know his heart.
What he hath utter'd, I have writ my sister:
If she sustain him and his hundred knights,
When I have show'd the unfitness,—

Re-enter Oswald.

                              How now, Oswald!
What, have you writ that letter to my sister?
Osw. Ay, madam.   340
Gon. Take you some company, and away to horse:
Inform her full of my particular fear;
And thereto add such reasons of your own,
As may compact it more. Get you gone,
And hasten your return. [*Exit* Oswald.] No, no, my
lord,
This milky gentleness and course of yours
Though I condemn not, yet, under pardon,
You are much more attask'd for want of wisdom,
Than prais'd for harmful mildness.
Alb. How far your eyes may pierce, I cannot tell:
Striving to better, oft we mar what's well.   351
Gon. Nay, then—
Alb. Well, well; the event.   [*Exeunt.*

Scene V.—Court before the Same.

Enter Lear, Kent, *and* Fool.

Lear. Go you before to Gloster with these letters.
Acquaint my daughter no further with anything you
know, than comes from her demand out of the letter.
If your diligence be not speedy, I shall be there before
you.
Kent. I will not sleep, my lord, till I have delivered
your letter.   [*Exit.*
Fool. If a man's brains were in his heels, were't not
in danger of kibes?
Lear. Ay, boy.   10
Fool. Then, I pr'ythee, be merry; thy wit shall not
go slip-shod.
Lear. Ha, ha, ha!
Fool. Shalt see, thy other daughter will use thee
kindly; for though she's as like this as a crab is like
an apple, yet I can tell what I can tell.
Lear. What canst tell, boy?
Fool. She will taste as like this as a crab does to a
crab. Thou canst tell why one's nose stands i' the
middle on's face?   20
Lear. No.
Fool. Why, to keep one's eyes of either side's nose;
that what a man cannot smell out, he may spy into.
Lear. I did her wrong:—
Fool. Canst tell how an oyster makes his shell?
Lear. No.
Fool. Nor I neither; but I can tell why a snail has
a house.   29
Lear. Why?
Fool. Why, to put his head in; not to give it away
to his daughters, and leave his horns without a case.
Lear. I will forget my nature.—So kind a father!—
Be my horses ready?
Fool. Thy asses are gone about 'em. The reason
why the seven stars are no more than seven is a
pretty reason.
Lear. Because they are not eight?
Fool. Yes, indeed. Thou wouldst make a good fool.
Lear. To take it again perforce!—Monster ingrati-
tude!   40
Fool. If thou wert my fool, nuncle, I'd have thee
beaten for being old before thy time.
Lear. How's that?
Fool. Thou shouldst not have been old till thou
hadst been wise.

Lear. O, let me not be mad, not mad, sweet heaven !
Keep me in temper : I would not be mad !—

Enter Gentleman.

How now ! Are the horses ready?

Gent. Ready, my lord.
Lear. Come, boy.   50
Fool. She that 's a maid now, and laughs at my
    departure,
Shall not be a maid long, unless things be cut shorter.
                                      [*Exeunt.*

ACT II.

SCENE I.—A Court within the Castle of the Earl of GLOSTER.

Enter EDMUND *and* CURAN, *meeting.*

Edmund.

SAVE thee, Curan.
Cur. And you, sir. I have been with your
  father, and given him notice, that the Duke
  of Cornwall, and Regan his duchess, will be
  here with him to-night.
    Edm. How comes that?
    Cur. Nay, I know not. You have heard of
  the news abroad ? I mean, the whispered
  ones, for they are yet but ear-kissing arguments.   10
    Edm. Not I: pray you, what are they?
Cur. Have you heard of no likely wars toward,
'twixt the Dukes of Cornwall and Albany?
    Edm. Not a word.
    Cur. You may do then, in time. Fare you well, sir.
                                      [*Exit.*
    Edm. The duke be here to-night? The better! best!
This weaves itself perforce into my business.
My father hath set guard to take my brother;
And I have one thing, of a queasy question,
Which I must act.—Briefness, and fortune, work!— 20
Brother, a word ;—descend :—brother, I say!

Enter EDGAR.

My father watches.—O sir ! fly this place ;
Intelligence is given where you are hid :
You have now the good advantage of the night.—
Have you not spoken 'gainst the Duke of Cornwall?
He 's coming hither ; now, i' the night, i' the haste,
And Regan with him : have you nothing said
Upon his party 'gainst the Duke of Albany?
Advise yourself.
    Edg.   I am sure on 't, not a word.
    Edm. I hear my father coming.—Pardon me . 30
In cunning, I must draw my sword upon you :
Draw : seem to defend yourself. Now quit you well.
Yield :—come before my father.—Light, ho ! here !—
Fly, brother.—Torches ! torches !—So, farewell.—
                            [*Exit* EDGAR.
Some blood drawn on me would beget opinion
                [*Wounds his arm.*
Of my more fierce endeavour: I have seen drunkards
Do more than this in sport.—Father ! father !
Stop, stop ! No help ?

Enter GLOSTER, *and Servants with torches.*

    Glo. Now, Edmund, where 's the villain ?
    Edm. Here stood he in the dark, his sharp sword
    out,
Mumbling of wicked charms, conjuring the moon 40
To stand auspicious mistress,—
    Glo.   But where is he ?
    Edm. Look, sir, I bleed.
    Glo.   Where is the villain, Edmund ?
    Edm. Fled this way, sir. When by no means he
    could—

    Glo. Pursue him, ho !—Go after. [*Exit Servant.*]—
    By no means,—what ?
    Edm. Persuade me to the murder of your lordship;
But that I told him, the revenging gods
'Gainst parricides did all their thunders bend ;
Spoke, with how manifold and strong a bond
The child was bound to the father :—sir, in fine,
Seeing how loath'y opposite I stood   50
To his unnatural purpose, in fell motion,
With his prepared sword he charges home
My unprovided body, lanc'd mine arm :
But when he saw my best alarum'd spirits,
Bold in the quarrel's right, rous'd to the encounter,
Or whether ghasted by the noise I made,
Full suddenly he fled.
    Glo.   Let him fly far :
Not in this land shall he remain uncaught ;
And found—despatch.—The noble duke my master,
My worthy arch and patron, comes to-night :   60
By his authority I will proclaim it,
That he which finds him shall deserve our thanks,
Bringing the murderous coward to the stake ;
He that conceals him, death.
    Edm. When I dissuaded him from his intent,
And found him pight to do it, with curst speech
I threaten'd to discover him : he replied,
" Thou unpossessing bastard ! dost thou think,
If I would stand against thee, would the reposal
Of any trust, virtue, or worth, in thee   70
Make thy words faith'd ? No : what I should deny,
(As this I would ; ay, though thou didst produce
My very character,) I 'd turn it all
To thy suggestion, plot, and damned practice :
And thou must make a dullard of the world,
If they not thought the profits of my death
Were very pregnant and potential spurs
To make thee seek it."
    Glo.   Strong and fasten'd villain !
Would he deny his letter ?—I never got him.
                      [*Tucket within.*
Hark ! the duke's trumpets. I know not why he
    comes.   80
All ports I 'll bar ; the villain shall not 'scape ;
The duke must grant me that : besides, his picture
I will send far and near, that all the kingdom
May have due note of him ; and of my land,
Loyal and natural boy, I 'll work the means
To make thee capable.

Enter CORNWALL, REGAN, *and Attendants.*

    Corn. How now, my noble friend ! since I came
    hither
(Which I can call but now), I have heard strange
    news.
    Reg. If it be true, all vengeance comes too short, 89
Which can pursue the offender. How dost, my lord?

Glo. O, madam, my old heart is crack'd, it 's crack'd!
Reg. What! did my father's godson seek your life?
He whom my father nam'd? your Edgar?
Glo. O, lady, lady! shame would have it hid.
Reg. Was he not companion with the riotous knights
That tend upon my father?
Glo. I know not, madam, 't is too bad, too bad.
Edm. Yes, madam, he was of that consort.
Reg. No marvel then, though he were ill affected:
'T is they have put him on the old man's death,   100
To have the expense and waste of his revenues.
I have this present evening from my sister
Been well inform'd of them; and with such cautions,
That if they come to sojourn at my house,
I 'll not be there.
Corn.   Nor I, assure thee, Regan.—
Edmund, I hear that you have shown your father
A child-like office.
Edm.   'T was my duty, sir.
Glo. He did bewray his practice; and receiv'd
This hurt you see, striving to apprehend him.
Corn. Is he pursued?
Glo.   Ay, my good lord.   110
Corn. If he be taken, he shall never more
Be fear'd of doing harm: make your own purpose,
How in my strength you please.—For you, Edmund,
Whose virtue and obedience doth this instant
So much commend itself, you shall be ours:
Natures of such deep trust we shall much need;
You we first seize on.
Edm.   I shall serve you, sir,
Truly, however else.
Glo.   For him I thank your grace.
Corn. You know not why we came to visit you,—
Reg. Thus out of season, threading dark-ey'd night.   121
Occasions, noble Gloster, of some poise,
Wherein we must have use of your advice.
Our father he hath writ, so hath our sister,
Of differences, which I best thought it fit
To answer from our home: the several messengers
From hence attend despatch. Our good old friend,
Lay comforts to your bosom, and bestow
Your needful counsel to our businesses,
Which crave the instant use.
Glo.   I serve you, madam.   130
Your graces are right welcome.
                              [*Exeunt.*

SCENE II.—Before GLOSTER'S Castle.

Enter KENT *and* OSWALD, *severally.*

Osw. Good dawning to thee, friend: art of this
house?
Kent. Ay.
Osw. Where may we set our horses?
Kent. I' the mire.
Osw. Pr'ythee, if thou lov'st me, tell me.
Kent. I love thee not.
Osw. Why, then I care not for thee.
Kent. If I had thee in Lipsbury pinfold, I would
make thee care for me.   10
Osw. Why dost thou use me thus? I know thee not.
Kent. Fellow, I know thee.
Osw. What dost thou know me for?
Kent. A knave, a rascal, an eater of broken meats;
a base, proud, shallow, beggarly, three-suited, hun-
dred-pound, filthy, worsted-stocking knave; a lily-
liver'd, action-taking knave; a whoreson, glass-
gazing, super-serviceable, finical rogue; one-trunk-
inheriting slave; one that wouldst be a bawd, in
way of good service, and art nothing but the
composition of a knave, beggar, coward, pander,
and the son and heir of a mongrel bitch: one whom
I will beat into clamorous whining, if thou deniest
the least syllable of thy addition.
Osw. Why, what a monstrous fellow art thou, thus
to rail on one, that is neither known of thee, nor knows
thee!
Kent. What a brazen-faced varlet art thou, to deny
thou knowest me! Is it two days since I tripped up
thy heels, and beat thee, before the king? Draw, you

rogue; for though it be night, yet the moon shines:
I 'll make a sop o' the moonshine of you. [*Drawing
his sword.*] Draw, you whoreson cullionly barber-
monger, draw.
Osw. Away! I have nothing to do with thee.
Kent. Draw, you rascal: you come with letters
against the king, and take Vanity the puppet's part,
against the royalty of her father. Draw, you rogue,
or I 'll so carbonado your shanks:—draw, you rascal;
come your ways.   40
Osw. Help, ho! murder! help!
Kent. Strike, you slave: stand, rogue, stand; you
neat slave, strike.   [*Beating him.*

Kent. "Strike, you slave: stand, rogue, stand; you neat slave, strike."

Osw. Help, ho! murder! murder!

Enter EDMUND.

Edm. How now! What 's the matter?
Kent. With you, goodman boy, if you please: come,
I 'll flesh you, come on, young master.

Enter CORNWALL, REGAN, GLOSTER, *and Servants.*

Glo. Weapons! arms! What 's the matter here?
Corn. Keep peace, upon your lives:
He dies that strikes again. What is the matter?   50
Reg. The messengers from our sister and the king.
Corn. What is your difference? speak.
Osw. I am scarce in breath, my lord.
Kent. No marvel, you have so bestirred your valour.
You cowardly rascal, nature disclaims in thee: a tailor
made thee.
Corn. Thou art a strange fellow: a tailor make a
man?
Kent. Ay, a tailor, sir: a stone-cutter, or a painter,
could not have made him so ill, though they had been
but two hours o' the trade.   61
Corn. Speak yet, how grew your quarrel?
Osw. This ancient ruffian, sir, whose life I have
spar'd,
At suit of his grey beard,—
Kent. Thou whoreson zed! thou unnecessary letter!
—My lord, if you will give me leave, I will tread this
unbolted villain into mortar, and daub the wall of a
jakes with him.—Spare my grey beard, you wag-tail?
Corn. Peace, sirrah!
You beastly knave, know you no reverence?   70
Kent. Yes, sir; but anger hath a privilege.
Corn. Why art thou angry?
Kent. That such a slave as this should wear a sword,
Who wears no honesty. Such smiling rogues as these,
Like rats, oft bite the holy cords a-twain

Which are too intrinse t' unloose; smooth every
    passion
That in the natures of their lords rebel;
Bring oil to fire, snow to their colder moods;
Renege, affirm, and turn their halcyon beaks
With every gale and vary of their masters,   8)
Knowing nought, like dogs, but following.—
A plague upon your epileptic visage!
Smile you my speeches, as I were a fool?
Goose, if I had you upon Sarum plain,
I 'd drive ye cackling home to Camelot.
  Corn. What! art thou mad, old fellow?
  Glo. How fell you out? say that.
  Kent. No contraries hold more antipathy,
Than I and such a knave.
  Corn. Why dost thou call him knave? What is his
    fault?   90
  Kent. His countenance likes me not.
  Corn. No more, perchance, does mine, nor his, nor
    hers.
  Kent. Sir, 't is my occupation to be plain:
I h ive seen better faces in my time,
Than stands on any shoulder that I see
Before me at this instant.
  Corn. This is some fellow,
Who, having been prais'd for bluntness, doth affect
A saucy roughness, and constrains the garb,
Quite from his nature: he cannot flatter, he;
An honest mind and plain,—he must speak truth: 100
An they will take it, so; if not, he 's plain.
These kind of knaves I know, which in this plainness
Harbour more craft, and more corrupter ends,
Than twenty silly ducking observants,
That stretch their duties nicely.
  Kent. Sir, in good sooth, in sincere verity,
Under the allowance of your great aspect,
Whose influence, like the wreath of radiant fire   108
On flickering Phœbus' front,—
  Corn. What mean'st by this?
  Kent. To go out of my dialect, which you discom-
mend so much. I know, sir, I am no flatterer: he
that beguiled you in a plain accent, was a plain
knave; which, for my part, I will not be, though I
should win your displeasure to entreat me to 't.
  Corn. What was the offence you gave him?
  Osw. I never gave him any:
It pleas'd the king, his master, very late,
To strike at me, upon his misconstruction;
When he, compact, and flattering his displeasure,
Tripp'd me behind; being down, insulted, rail'd, 120
And put upon him such a deal of man,
That worthied him, got praises of the king
For him attempting who was self-subdu'd;
And, in the fleshment of this dread exploit,
Drew on me here again.
  Kent. None of these rogues, and cowards,
But Ajax is their fool.
  Corn. Fetch forth the stocks!
You stubborn ancient knave, you reverend braggart,
We 'll teach you.
  Kent. Sir, I am too old to learn.
Call not your stocks for me; I serve the king,
On whose employment I was sent to you: 130
You shall do small respect, show too bold malice
Against the grace and person of my master,
Stocking his messenger.
  Corn. Fetch forth the stocks!
As I have life and honour, there shall he sit till noon.
  Reg. Till noon! till night, my lord; and all night
    too.
  Kent. Why, madam, if I were your father's dog,
You should not use me so.
  Reg. Sir, being his knave, I will.
  Corn. This is a fellow of the selfsame colour
Our sister speaks of.—Come, bring away the stocks.
                              [Stocks brought out.
  Glo. Let me beseech your grace not to do so.   140
His fault is much, and the good king his master
Will check him for 't: your purpos'd low correction
Is such as basest and contemned'st wretches,
For pilferings and most common trespasses,
Are punish'd with. The king must take it ill,

That he, so slightly valued in his messenger,
Should have him thus restrain'd.
  Corn. I 'll answer that.
  Reg. My sister may receive it much more worse,
To have her gentleman abus'd, assaulted,
For following her affairs.—Put in his legs.—   150
                  [KENT is put in the stocks.
Come, my lord, away.
            [Exeunt all but GLOSTER *and* KENT.
  Glo. I am sorry for thee, friend; 't is the duke's
    pleasure,
Whose disposition, all the world well knows,
Will not be rubb'd, nor stopp'd: I 'll entreat for thee.
  Kent. Pray, do not, sir. I have watch'd, and
    travell'd hard;
Some time I shall sleep out, the rest I 'll whistle.
A good man's fortune may grow out at heels:
Give you good morrow!
  Glo. The duke 's to blame in this: 't will be ill taken.
                                  [Exit.
  Kent. Good king, that must approve the common
    saw: 160
Thou out of heaven's benediction com'st
To the warm sun.
Approach, thou beacon to this under globe,
That by thy comfortable beams I may
Peruse this letter.—Nothing almost sees miracles,
But misery:—I know, 't is from Cordelia;
Who hath most fortunately been inform'd
Of my obscured course; and shall find time
From this enormous state,—seeking to give
Losses their remedies.—All weary and o'er-watch'd, 171
Take vantage, heavy eyes, not to behold
This shameful lodging.
Fortune, good night; smile once more; turn thy
    wheel!   *[He sleeps.*
            ————

      SCENE III.—A Part of the Heath.

           Enter EDGAR.

  Edg. I heard myself proclaim'd;
And, by the happy hollow of a tree,
Escap'd the hunt. No port is free; no place,
That guard, and most unusual vigilance,
Does not attend my taking. While I may 'scape,
I will preserve myself; and am bethought
To take the basest and most poorest shape,
That ever penury, in contempt of man,
Brought near to beast; my face I 'll grime with filth,
Blanket my loins, elf all my hair in knots,   10
And with presented nakedness outface
The winds and persecutions of the sky.
The country gives me proof and precedent
Of Bedlam beggars, who, with roaring voices,
Strike in their numb'd and mortified bare arms
Pins, wooden pricks, nails, sprigs of rosemary;
And with this horrible object, from low farms,
Poor pelting villages, sheep-cotes, and mills,
Sometime with lunatic bans, sometime with prayers,
Enforce their charity.—Poor Turlygood! poor Tom! 20
That 's something yet:—Edgar I nothing am.   *[Exit.*

            ————

  SCENE IV.—Before GLOSTER'S Castle. KENT in
             the Stocks.

    Enter LEAR, *Fool, and Gentleman.*

  Lear. 'T is strange that they should so depart from
    home,
And not send back my messenger.
  Gent. As I learn'd,
'The night before there was no purpose in them
Of this remove.
  Kent. Hail to thee, noble master!
  Lear. Ha!
Mak'st thou this shame thy pastime?
  Kent. No, my lord.
  Fool. Ha, ha! look; he wears cruel garters. Horses
are tied by the head, dogs and bears by the neck,
monkeys by the loins, and men by the legs: when a

man's over-lusty at legs, then he wears wooden
nether-stocks.   11
   Lear. What's he that hath so much thy place
         mistook,
To set thee here?
   Kent.   It is both he and she,
Your son and daughter.
   Lear. No.
   Kent. Yes.
   Lear. No, I say.
   Kent. I say, yea.
   Lear. No, no; they would not.
   Kent. Yes, they have.   20
   Lear. By Jupiter, I swear, no.
   Kent. By Juno, I swear, ay.
   Lear.   They durst not do't;
They could not, would not do't: 'tis worse than
         murder,
To do upon respect such violent outrage.
Resolve me, with all modest haste, which way
Thou mightst deserve, or they impose, this usage,
Coming from us.
   Kent.   My lord, when at their home
I did commend your highness' letters to them,
Ere I was risen from the place that show'd
My duty kneeling, came there a reeking post,   30
Stew'd in his haste, half breathless, panting forth
From Goneril, his mistress, salutations;
Deliver'd letters, spite of intermission,
Which presently they read: on whose contents
They summon'd up their meiny, straight took horse;
Commanded me to follow, and attend
The leisure of their answer; gave me cold looks:
And meeting here the other messenger,
Whose welcome, I perceiv'd, had poison'd mine,
(Being the very fellow which of late   40
Display'd so saucily against your highness,)
Having more man than wit about me, drew:
He rais'd the house with loud and coward cries.
Your son and daughter found this trespass worth
The shame which here it suffers.
   Fool. Winter's not gone yet, if the wild-geese fly
that way.

         Fathers, that wear rags,
           Do make their children blind;
         But fathers, that bear bags,   50
           Shall see their children kind.
         Fortune, that arrant whore,
           Ne'er turns the key to the poor.—
But, for all this, thou shalt have as many dolours for
thy daughters, as thou canst tell in a year.
   Lear. O, how this mother swells up toward my heart!
Hysterica passio! down, thou climbing sorrow!
Thy element's below.—Where is this daughter?
   Kent. With the earl; here, within.
   Lear. Follow me not; stay here.   [*Exit.*
   Gent. Made you no more offence than what you
         speak of?   61
   Kent. None.
How chance the king comes with so small a number?
   Fool. An thou hadst been set i' the stocks for that
question, thou hadst well deserved it.
   Kent. Why, fool?
   Fool. We'll set thee to school to an ant, to teach
thee there's no labouring i' the winter. All that
follow their noses are led by their eyes, but blind
men; and there's not a nose among twenty but can
smell him that's stinking. Let go thy hold, when a
great wheel runs down a hill, lest it break thy neck
with following it; but the great one that goes up the
hill, let him draw thee after. When a wise man
gives thee better counsel, give me mine again: I
would have none but knaves follow it, since a fool
gives it.

         That sir, which serves and seeks for gain,
           And follows but for form,
         Will pack when it begins to rain,   80
           And leave thee in the storm.
         But I will tarry; the fool will stay,
           And let the wise man fly:
         The knave turns fool that runs away;
           The fool no knave, perdy.

   Kent. Where learn'd you this, fool?
   Fool. Not i' the stocks, fool.

        Re-enter LEAR, *with* GLOSTER.

   Lear. Deny to speak with me? They are sick? they
         are weary?
They have travell'd all the night? Mere fetches,
The images of revolt and flying off!   90
Fetch me a better answer.
   Glo.   My dear lord,
You know the fiery quality of the duke;
How unremovable and fix'd he is
In his own course.
   Lear. Vengeance! plague! death! confusion!
Fiery? what quality? Why, Gloster, Gloster,
I'd speak with the Duke of Cornwall and his wife.
   Glo. Well, my good lord, I have inform'd them so.
   Lear. Inform'd them! Dost thou understand me,
         man?
   Glo. Ay, my good lord.   100
   Lear. The king would speak with Cornwall; the
         dear father
Would with his daughter speak, commands her
         service:
Are they inform'd of this? My breath and blood!—
Fiery? the fiery duke?—Tell the hot duke, that—
No, but not yet;—may be, he is not well:
Infirmity doth still neglect all office,
Whereto our health is bound; we are not ourselves,
When nature, being oppress'd, commands the mind
To suffer with the body. I'll forbear;
And am fall'n out with my more headier will,   110
To take the indispos'd and sickly fit
For the sound man.—Death on my state! wherefore
            [*Looking on* KENT.
Should he sit here? This act persuades me,
That this remotion of the duke and her
Is practice only. Give me my servant forth.
Go, tell the duke and's wife, I'd speak with them,
Now, presently: bid them come forth and hear me,
Or at their chamber-door I'll beat the drum,
Till it cry—"Sleep to death."
   Glo. I would have all well betwixt you.   [*Exit.*
   Lear. O me! my heart, my rising heart!—but,
         down.   121
   Fool. Cry to it, nuncle, as the cockney did to the
eels, when she put them i' the paste alive; she knapp'd
'em o' the coxcombs with a stick, and cried, "Down,
wantons, down!" 'Twas her brother that, in pure
kindness to his horse, buttered his hay.

   Enter CORNWALL, REGAN, GLOSTER, *and Servants.*

   Lear. Good morrow to you both.
   Corn.   Hail to your grace!
            [KENT *is set at liberty.*
   Reg. I am glad to see your highness.
   Lear. Regan, I think you are; I know what reason
I have to think so: if thou shouldst not be glad,   130
I would divorce me from thy mother's tomb,
Sepulchring an adult'ress.—[*To* KENT.] O! are you
         free?
Some other time for that.—Beloved Regan,
Thy sister's naught: O Regan! she hath tied
Sharp-tooth'd unkindness, like a vulture, here.—
            [*Points to his heart.*
I can scarce speak to thee: thou'lt not believe,
With how deprav'd a quality—O Regan!
   Reg. I pray you, sir, take patience. I have hope,
You less know how to value her desert,
Than she to scant her duty.
   Lear.   Say, how is that?   140
   Reg. I cannot think my sister in the least
Would fail her obligation: if, sir, perchance,
She have restrain'd the riots of your followers,
'Tis on such ground, and to such wholesome end,
As clears her from all blame.
   Lear. My curses on her!
   Reg.   O, sir! you are old;
Nature in you stands on the very verge
Of her confine: you should be rul'd and led
By some discretion, that discerns your state
Better than you yourself. Therefore, I pray you,   150

That to our sister you do make return:
Say, you have wrong'd her, sir.
 Lear.   Ask her forgiveness?
Do you but mark how this becomes the house:
" Dear daughter, I confess that I am old ;
Age is unnecessary : on my knees I beg, [*Kneeling.*
That you 'll vouchsafe me raiment, bed, and food."
 Reg. Good sir, no more : these are unsightly tricks.
Return you to my sister.
 Lear. [*Rising.*]   Never, Regan.
She hath abated me of half my train ;
Look'd black upon me ; struck me with her tongue,
Most serpent-like, upon the very heart.— 161
All the stor'd vengeances of heaven fall
On her ungrateful top ! Strike her young bones,
You taking airs, with lameness !
 Corn.   Fie, sir, fie !
 Lear. You nimble lightnings, dart your blinding
  flames
Into her scornful eyes ! Infect her beauty,
You fen-suck'd fogs, drawn by the powerful sun,
To fall and blast her pride !
 Reg. O the blest gods ! so will you wish on me,
When the rash mood is on.   170
 Lear. No, Regan ; thou shalt never have my curse :
Thy tender-hefted nature shall not give
Thee o'er to harshness : her eyes are fierce ; but thine
Do comfort, and not burn. 'T is not in thee
To grudge my pleasures, to cut off my train,
To bandy hasty words, to scant my sizes,
And, in conclusion, to oppose the bolt
Against my coming in : thou better know'st
The offices of nature, bond of childhood,
Effects of courtesy, dues of gratitude ; 180
Thy half o' the kingdom hast thou not forgot,
Wherein I thee endow'd.
 Reg.   Good sir, to the purpose.
 Lear. Who put my man i' the stocks?
       [*Tucket within.*
 Corn.   What trumpet 's that?
 Reg. I know 't, my sister's : this approves her letter,
That she would soon be here.—

   Enter OSWALD.
       Is your lady come?
 Lear. This is a slave, whose easy-borrow'd pride
Dwells in the fickle grace of her he follows.—
Out, varlet, from my sight !
 Corn.   What means your grace ?
 Lear. Who stock'd my servant ? Regan, I have good
  hope
Thou didst not know on 't.—Who comes here? O
  heavens,   190
   Enter GONERIL.
If you do love old men, if your sweet sway
Allow obedience, if yourselves are old,
Make it your cause ; send down, and take my part !—
[*To* GONERIL.] Art not asham'd to look upon this
  beard?—
O Regan ! wilt thou take her by the hand ?
 Gon. Why not by the hand, sir? How have I
  offended?
All 's not offence that indiscretion finds,
And dotage terms so.
 Lear.   O sides ! you are too tough :
Will you yet hold?—How came my man i' the stocks?
 Corn. I set him there, sir ; but his own disorders 200
Deserv'd much less advancement.
 Lear.   You ! did you ?
 Reg. I pray you, father, being weak, seem so.
If, till the expiration of your month,
You will return and sojourn with my sister,
Dismissing half your train, come then to me :
I am now from home, and out of that provision
Which shall be needful for your entertainment.
 Lear. Return to her? and fifty men dismiss'd?
No, rather I abjure all roofs, and choose
To wage against the enmity o' the air ; 210
To be a comrade with the wolf and owl,—
Necessity's sharp pinch !—Return with her ?
Why, the hot-blooded France, that dowerless took
Our youngest-born, I could as well be brought

To knee his throne, and, squire-like, pension beg
To keep base life afoot.—Return with her ?
Persuade me rather to be slave and sumpter
To this detested groom. [*Pointing at* OSWALD.
 Gon.   At your choice, sir.
 Lear. I pr'ythee, daughter, do not make me mad :
I will not trouble thee, my child ; farewell. 220
We 'll no more meet, no more see one another ;
But yet thou art my flesh, my blood, my daughter ;
Or, rather, a disease that 's in my flesh,
Which I must needs call mine : thou art a bile,
A plague-sore, an embossed carbuncle,
In my corrupted blood. But I 'll not chide thee ;
Let shame come when it will, I do not call it :
I do not bid the thunder-bearer shoot,
Nor tell tales of thee to high-judging Jove.
Mend, when thou canst ; be better, at thy leisure : 230
I can be patient ; I can stay with Regan,
I, and my hundred knights.
 Reg.   Not altogether so :
I look'd not for you yet, nor am provided
For your fit welcome. Give ear, sir, to my sister ;
For those that mingle reason with your passion,
Must be content to think you old, and so—
But she knows what she does.
 Lear.   Is this well spoken?
 Reg. I dare avouch it, sir. What ! fifty followers?
Is it not well ? What should you need of more ?
Yea, or so many, sith that both charge and danger 240
Speak 'gainst so great a number ? How, in one house,
Should many people, under two commands,
Hold amity ? 'T is hard ; almost impossible.
 Gon. Why might not you, my lord, receive atten-
  dance
From those that she calls servants, or from mine ?
 Reg. Why not, my lord ? If then they chanc'd to
  slack you,
We could control them. If you will come to me
(For now I spy a danger), I entreat you
To bring but five-and-twenty : to no more
Will I give place, or notice.   250
 Lear. I gave you all—
 Reg.   And in good time you gave it.
 Lear. Made you my guardians, my depositaries ;
But kept a reservation to be follow'd
With such a number. What ! must I come to you
With five-and-twenty ? Regan, said you so ?
 Reg. And speak 't again, my lord ; no more with me.
 Lear. Those wicked creatures yet do look well-
  favour'd !
When others are more wicked, not being the worst
Stands in some rank of praise.—[*To* GONERIL.] I 'll
  go with thee :
Thy fifty yet doth double five-and-twenty, 260
And thou art twice her love.
 Gon.   Hear me, my lord.
What need you five-and-twenty, ten, or five,
To follow in a house, where twice so many
Have a command to tend you ?
 Reg.   What need one ?
 Lear. O ! reason not the need ; our basest beggars
Are in the poorest thing superfluous :
Allow not nature more than nature needs,
Man's life is cheap as beast's. Thou art a lady ;
If only to go warm were gorgeous,
Why, nature needs not what thou gorgeous wear'st,
Which scarcely keeps thee warm. But, for true
  need,—   271
You heavens, give me that patience, patience I need !
You see me here, you gods, a poor old man,
As full of grief as age ; wretched in both :
If it be you that stir these daughters' hearts
Against their father, fool me not so much
To bear it tamely ; touch me with noble anger.
O ! let not women's weapons, water-drops,
Stain my man's cheeks.—No, you unnatural hags,
I will have such revenges on you both, 280
That all the world shall—I will do such things,—
What they are, yet I know not ; but they shall be
The terrors of the earth. You think, I 'll weep ;
No, I 'll not weep :—
I have full cause of weeping ; but this heart

Shall break into a hundred thousand flaws,
Or ere I 'll weep.—O fool, I shall go mad!
            [*Exeunt* LEAR, GLOSTER, KENT, *and* Fool.
    Corn. Let us withdraw, 't will be a storm.
            [*Storm heard at a distance.*

Re-enter GLOSTER.

    Corn. Follow'd the old man forth.—He is return'd.
    Glo. The king is in high rage.
    Corn.   Whither is he going?

Lear. "O fool, I shall go mad!"

    Reg. This house is little: the old man and his
        people
Cannot be well bestow'd.   290
    Gon. 'T is his own blame; hath put himself from
        rest,
And must needs taste his folly.
    Reg. For his particular, I 'll receive him gladly,
But not one follower.
    Gon.   So am I purpos'd.
Where is my Lord of Gloster?

    Glo. He calls to horse; but will I know not whither.
    Corn. 'T is best to give him way; he leads himself.
    Gon. My lord, entreat him by no means to stay. 300
    Glo. Alack! the night comes on, and the high
        winds
Do sorely ruffle; for many miles about
There 's scarce a bush.
    Reg.   O, sir, to wilful men,
The injuries that they themselves procure
Must be their schoolmasters. Shut up your doors:

He is attended with a desperate train;
And what they may incense him to, being apt
To have his ear abus'd, wisdom bids fear.

Corn. Shut up your doors, my lord; 'tis a wild
 night:
My Regan counsels well.   Come out o' the storm. 310
                                        [*Exeunt.*

ACT III.

Scene I.—A Heath.

A storm, with thunder and lightning.   Enter Kent *and a Gentleman, meeting.*

Kent.
WHO 'S there, beside foul weather?
     Gent. One minded like the weather,
          most unquietly.
     Kent. I know you. Where 's the king?
     Gent. Contending with the fretful
          elements;
Bids the wind blow the earth into the
          sea,
Or swell the curled waters 'bove the
          main,
That things might change or cease; tears his white
          hair,
Which the impetuous blasts, with eyeless rage,
Catch in their fury, and make nothing of:
Strives in his little world of man to out-scorn   10
The to-and-fro conflicting wind and rain.
This night, wherein the cub-drawn bear would couch,
The lion and the belly-pinched wolf
Keep their fur dry, unbonneted he runs,
And bids what will take all.
     Kent.   But who is with him?
     Gent. None but the fool, who labours to out-jest
His heart-struck injuries.
     Kent.   Sir, I do know you;
And dare, upon the warrant of my note,
Commend a dear thing to you. There is division,
Although as yet the face of it be cover'd   20
With mutual cunning, 'twixt Albany and Cornwall;
Who have (as they have not, that their great stars
Thron'd and set high?) servants; who seem no less,
Which are to France the spies and speculations
Intelligent of our state; what hath been seen,
Either in snuffs and packings of the dukes,
Or the hard rein which both of them have borne
Against the old kind king; or something deeper,
Whereof, perchance, these are but furnishings;—
(But, true it is, from France there comes a power   30
Into this scatter'd kingdom; who already,
Wise in our negligence, have secret feet
In some of our best ports, and are at point
To show their open banner.—Now to you:
If on my credit you dare build so far
To make your speed to Dover, you shall find
Some that w'll thank you, making just report
Of how unnatural and bemadding sorrow
The king hath cause to plain.
I am a gentleman of blood and breeding,   40
And from some knowledge and assurance offer
This office to you.)
     Gent. I will talk further with you.
     Kent.   No, do not.
For confirmation that I am much more
Than my out-wall, open this purse, and take
What it contains. If you shall see Cordelia
(As fear not but you shall), show her this ring,
And she will tell you who your fellow is
That yet you do not know. Fie on this storm!
I will go seek the king.   50

Gent. Give me your hand. Have you no more to say?
     Kent. Few words, but, to effect, more than all yet;
That, when we have found the king, (in which your
          pain
That way, I 'll this,) he that first lights on him,
Holla the other.   [*Exeunt severally.*

Scene II.—Another Part of the Heath.   Storm continues.

Enter Lear *and* Fool.

Lear. Blow, winds, and crack your cheeks! rage!
          blow!
You cataracts and hurricanoes, spout
Till you have drench'd our steeples, drown'd the cocks!
You sulphurous and thought-executing fires,
Vaunt-couriers of oak-cleaving thunderbolts,
Singe my white head! And thou, all-shaking thunder,
Strike flat the thick rotundity o' the world!
Crack nature's moulds, all germens spill at once,
That make ingrateful man!   9
     Fool. O nuncle, court holy-water in a dry house is
better than this rain-water out o' door. Good nuncle,
in; ask thy daughters' blessing: here 's a night pities
neither wise men nor fools.
     Lear. Rumble thy bellyful! spit, fire! spout, rain!
Nor rain, wind, thunder, fire, are my daughters:
I tax not you, you elements, with unkindness;
I never gave you kingdom, call'd you children,
You owe me no subscription: then, let fall
Your horrible pleasure; here I stand, your slave,
A poor, infirm, weak, and despis'd old man.   20
But yet I call you servile ministers,
That will with two pernicious daughters join
Your high-engender'd battles 'gainst a head
So old and white as this. O! O! 'tis foul!
     Fool. He that has a house to put 's head in, has a
good head-piece.
               The cod-piece that will house,
                    Before the head has any,
               The head and he shall louse:—
                    So beggars marry many.   30
               The man that makes his toe
                    What he his heart should make,
               Shall of a corn cry woe,
                    And turn his sleep to wake.
For there was never yet fair woman but she made
mouths in a glass.
     Lear. No, I will be the pattern of all patience;
I will say nothing.

Enter Kent.

     Kent. Who 's there?
     Fool. Marry, here 's grace, and a cod-piece; that 's
a wise man, and a fool.   41
     Kent. Alas, sir! are you here? things that love
          night,
Love not such nights as these; the wrathful skies

Gallow the very wanderers of the dark,
And make them keep their caves. Since I was man,
Such sheets of fire, such bursts of horrid thunder,
Such groans of roaring wind and rain, I never
Remember to have heard : man's nature cannot carry
The affliction, nor the fear.
 Lear.   Let the great gods,
That keep this dreadful pother o'er our heads, 50
Find out their enemies now. Tremble, thou wretch,
That hast within the undivulged crimes,
Unwhipp'd of justice : hide thee, thou bloody hand ;
Thou perjur'd, and thou similar of virtue
That art incestuous : caitiff, to pieces shake,
That under covert and convenient seeming
Hast practis'd on man's life : close pent-up guilts,
Rive your concealing continents, and cry
These dreadful summoners grace. I am a man
More sinn'd against than sinning.
 Kent.   Alack, bare-headed !
Gracious my lord, hard by here is a hovel ; 61
Some friendship will it lend you 'gainst the tempest :
Repose you there, while I to this hard house
(More harder than the stones whereof 't is rais'd,
Which even but now, demanding after you,
Denied me to come in) return, and force
Their scanted courtesy.
 Lear.   My wits begin to turn.—
Come on, my boy. How dost, my boy ? Art cold ?
I am cold myself.—Where is this straw, my fellow ?
The art of our necessities is strange, 70
That can make vile things precious. Come, your
   hovel.
Poor fool and knave, I have one part in my heart
That 's sorry yet for thee.
 Fool. [*Sings.*] *He that has a little tiny wit,—*
  With heigh, ho, the wind and the rain,-
  Must make content with his fortunes fit,
  Though the rain it raineth every day.
 Lear. True, my good boy.—Come, bring us to this
  hovel.   [*Exeunt* LEAR *and* KENT.
 Fool. This is a brave night to cool a courtesan.—
I 'll speak a prophecy ere I go : 80
 When priests are more in word than matter ;
 When brewers mar their malt with water ;
 When nobles are their tailor's tutors ;
 No heretics burn'd, but wenches' suitors ;
 When every case in law is right ;
 No squire in debt, nor no poor knight ;
 When slanders do not live in tongues ;
 Nor cutpurses come not to throngs ;
 When usurers tell their gold i' the field ;
 And bawds and whores do churches build ; 90
 Then shall the realm of Albion
 Come to great confusion :
 Then comes the time, who lives to see 't,
 That going shall be us'd with feet.
This prophecy Merlin shall make ; for I live before
his time.   [*Exit.*

SCENE III.—A Room in GLOSTER'S Castle.

Enter GLOSTER *and* EDMUND.

 Glo. Alack, alack ! Edmund, I like not this unnatural dealing. When I desired their leave that I
might pity him, they took from me the use of mine
own house, charged me, on pain of perpetual displeasure, neither to speak of him, entreat for him,
nor any way sustain him.
 Edm. Most savage and unnatural ! 7
 Glo. Go to ; say you nothing. There is division
between the dukes, and a worse matter than that.
I have received a letter this night ;—'t is dangerous to
be spoken :—I have locked the letter in my closet.
These injuries the king now bears will be revenged
home ; there is part of a power already footed : we
must incline to the king. I will look him, and privily
relieve him : go you, and maintain talk with the duke,
that my charity be not of him perceived. If he ask
for me, I am ill, and gone to bed. If I die for it, as no
less is threatened me, the king, my old master, must

be relieved. There is some strange thing toward,
Edmund ; pray you, be careful.   [*Exit.*
 Edm. This courtesy, forbid thee, shall the duke 21
Instantly know ; and of that letter too.
This seems a fair deserving, and must draw me
That which my father loses : no less than all :
The younger rises, when the old doth fall. [*Exit.*

SCENE IV.—A Part of the Heath, with a Hovel.

Enter LEAR, KENT, *and* FOOL.

 Kent. Here is the place, my lord ; good my lord,
  enter :
The tyranny of the open night 's too rough
For nature to endure.   [*Storm still.*
 Lear.   Let me alone.
 Kent. Good my lord, enter here.
 Lear.   Wilt break my heart ?
 Kent. I 'd rather break mine own. Good my lord,
  enter.
 Lear. Thou think'st 't is much, that this contentious
  storm
Invades us to the skin : so 't is to thee ;
But where the greater malady is fix'd,
The lesser is scarce felt. Thou 'dst shun a bear ;
But if thy flight lay toward the roaring sea, 10
Thou 'dst meet the bear i' the mouth. When the
  mind 's free,
The body 's delicate : the tempest in my mind
Doth from my senses take all feeling else,
Save what beats there : filial ingratitude.
Is it not as this mouth should tear this hand,
For lifting food to 't ?—But I will punish home :—
No, I will weep no more.—In such a night
To shut me out !—Pour on ; I will endure.—
In such a night as this ! O Regan, Goneril !—
Your old kind father, whose frank heart gave all,— 20
O ! that way madness lies ; let me shun that ;
No more of that.
 Kent.   Good my lord, enter here.
 Lear. Pr'ythee, go in thyself ; seek thine own ease :
This tempest will not give me leave to ponder
On things would hurt me more.—But I 'll go in.
[*To the Fool.*] In, boy ; go first. You houseless
  poverty,—
Nay, get thee in. I 'll pray, and then I 'll sleep.—
         [*Fool goes in.*
Poor naked wretches, wheresoe'er you are,
That bide the pelting of this pitiless storm,
How shall your houseless heads, and unfed sides, 30
Your loop'd and window'd raggedness, defend you
From seasons such as these ? O ! I have ta'en
Too little care of this. Take physic, pomp ;
Expose thyself to feel what wretches feel,
That thou may'st shake the superflux to them,
And show the heavens more just.
 Edg. [*Within.*] Fathom and half, fathom and half !
Poor Tom !   [*The Fool runs out from the hovel.*
 Fool. Come not in here, nuncle ; here 's a spirit.
Help me ! help me ! 40
 Kent. Give me thy hand.—Who 's there ?
 Fool. A spirit, a spirit : he says his name 's poor
Tom.
 Kent. What art thou that dost grumble there i' the
  straw ?
Come forth.

Enter EDGAR, *disguised as a madman.*

 Edg. Away ! the foul fiend follows me !—
Through the sharp hawthorn blow the winds.—
Humph ! go to thy bed, and warm thee.
 Lear. Didst thou give all to thy daughters ?
And art thou come to this ? 50
 Edg. Who gives anything to poor Tom ? whom the
foul fiend hath led through fire and through flame,
through ford and whirlpool, over bog and quagmire ;
that hath laid knives under his pillow, and halters
in his pew ; set ratsbane by his porridge ; made him
proud of heart, to ride on a bay trotting-horse over
four-inched bridges, to course his own shadow for a

traitor.—Bless thy five wits! Tom's a-cold.—O! do
de, do de, do de.—Bless thee from whirlwinds, star-
blasting, and taking! Do poor Tom some charity,
whom the foul fiend vexes.—There could I have him
now,—and there,—and there,—and there again, and
there. [*Storm continues.*

Lear. What! have his daughters brought him to
this pass?—
Couldst thou save nothing? Didst thou give them
all?

Fool. Nay, he reserved a blanket, else we had been
all shamed.

Lear. Now, all the plagues that in the pendulous
air
Hang fated o'er men's faults, light on thy daughters!

Kent. He hath no daughters, sir. 70

Lear. Death, traitor! nothing could have subdued
nature
To such a lowness, but his unkind daughters.—
Is it the fashion, that discarded fathers
Should have thus little mercy on their flesh?
Judicious punishment! 't was this flesh begot
Those pelican daughters.

Edg. Pillicock sat on Pillicock-hill:—
Halloo, halloo, loo, loo!

Fool. This cold night will turn us all to fools and
madmen. 80

Edg. Take heed o' the foul fiend: obey thy parents;
keep thy word justly; swear not; commit not with
man's sworn spouse; set not thy sweet heart on proud
array. Tom's a-cold.

Lear. What hast thou been?

Edg. A serving-man, proud in heart and mind;
that curled my hair, wore gloves in my cap, served
the lust of my mistress's heart, and did the act of
darkness with her; swore as many oaths as I spake
words, and broke them in the sweet face of heaven:
one, that slept in the contriving of lust, and waked to
do it. Wine loved I deeply; dice dearly; and in
woman, out-paramoured the Turk: false of heart,
light of ear, bloody of hand; hog in sloth, fox in
stealth, wolf in greediness, dog in madness, lion in
prey. Let not the creaking of shoes, nor the rustling
of silks, betray thy poor heart to woman: keep thy
foot out of brothels, thy hand out of plackets, thy pen
from lenders' books, and defy the foul fiend.—Still
through the hawthorn blows the cold wind, says
suum, mun, ha no nonny. Dolphin my boy, my boy;
sessa! let him trot by. [*Storm still continues.*

Lear. Why, thou wert better in thy grave, than to
answer with thy uncovered body this extremity of the
skies.—Is man no more than this? Consider him well.
Thou owest the worm no silk, the beast no hide, the
sheep no wool, the cat no perfume.—Ha! here's
three on 's are sophisticated: thou art the thing itself:
unaccommodated man is no more but such a poor,
bare, forked animal as thou art.—Off, off, you lendings.—Come; unbutton here.— 111
[*Tearing off his clothes.*

Fool. Pry'thee, nuncle, be contented; 't is a naughty
night to swim in.—Now, a little fire in a wild field
were like an old lecher's heart; a small spark, all the
rest on 's body cold.—Look! here comes a walking fire.

Edg. This is the foul fiend Flibbertigibbet: he
begins at curfew, and walks till the first cock; he
gives the web and the pin, squints the eye, and makes
the hare-lip; mildews the white wheat, and hurts the
poor creature of earth. 120

> *Swithold footed thrice the wold;*
> *He met the night-mare, and her nine-fold*
>   *Bid her alight,*
>   *And her troth plight,*
> *And, aroint thee, witch, aroint thee!*

Kent. How fares your grace?

Enter GLOSTER, *with a torch.*

Lear. What's he?

Kent. Who's there? What is 't you seek?

Glo. What are you there? Your names? 129

Edg. Poor Tom; that eats the swimming frog, the
toad, the tadpole, the wall-newt, and the water; that

in the fury of his heart, when the foul fiend rages, eats
cow-dung for sallets; swallows the old rat, and the
ditch-dog; drinks the green mantle of the standing
pool; who is whipped from tithing to tithing, and
stocked, punished, and imprisoned; who hath had
three suits to his back, six shirts to his body, horse to
ride, and weapon to wear,—

> *But mice, and rats, and such small deer,*
> *Have been Tom's food for seven long year.* 140

Beware my follower.—Peace, Smulkin! peace, thou
fiend!

Glo. What! hath your grace no better company?

Glo. "What! hath your grace no better company?"

Edg. The prince of darkness is a gentleman;
Modo he's call'd, and Mahu.

Glo. Our flesh and blood, my lord, is grown so vile,
That it doth hate what gets it.

Edg. Poor Tom's a-cold.

Glo. Go in with me. My duty cannot suffer
To obey in all your daughters' hard commands: 150
Though their injunction be to bar my doors,
And let this tyrannous night take hold upon you,
Yet have I ventur'd to come seek you out,
And bring you where both fire and food is ready.

Lear. First let me talk with this philosopher.—
What is the cause of thunder?

Kent. Good my lord, take his offer: go into the
house.

Lear. I'll talk a word with this same learned
Theban.
What is your study?

Edg. How to prevent the fiend, and to kill vermin.

Lear. Let me ask you one word in private. 161

Kent. Importune him once more to go, my lord;
His wits begin to unsettle.

Glo. Canst thou blame him?
His daughters seek his death.—Ah, that good Kent!—
He said it would be thus, poor banish'd man!—
Thou say'st, the king grows mad: I'll tell thee, friend,
I am almost mad myself. I had a son,
Now outlaw'd from my blood; he sought my life,
But lately, very late: I lov'd him, friend,—
No father his son dearer: true to tell thee, 170
The grief hath craz'd my wits. What a night's this!
[*Storm continues.*
I do beseech your grace,—

Lear.   O! cry you mercy, sir.—
Noble philosopher, your company.
Edg. Tom 's a-cold.
Glo. In, fellow, there, into the hovel : keep thee
     warm.
Lear. Come, let 's in all.
Kent.   This way, my lord.
Lear.   With him :
I will keep still with my philosopher.
Kent. Good my lord, soothe him ; let him take the
     fellow.
Glo. Take him you on.
Kent. Sirrah, come on ; go along with us.   180
Lear. Come, good Athenian.
Glo. No words, no words : hush.

Edg. *Child Rowland to the dark tower came,*
     His word was still,—Fie, foh, and fum,
     I smell the blood of a British man.   [*Exeunt.*

SCENE V.—A Room in GLOSTER'S Castle.

Enter CORNWALL *and* EDMUND.

Corn. I will have my revenge, ere I depart his
house.
Edm. How, my lord, I may be censured, that nature
thus gives way to loyalty, something fears me to
think of.
Corn. I now perceive, it was not altogether your
brother's evil disposition made him seek his death ;
but a provoking merit, set a-work by a reprovable
badness in himself.   9
Edm. How malicious is my fortune, that I must
repent to be just ! This is the letter which he spoke
of, which approves him an intelligent part to the
advantages of France. O heavens ! that this treason
were not, or not I the detector !
Corn. Go with me to the duchess.
Edm. If the matter of this paper be certain, you
have mighty business in hand.
Corn. True, or false, it hath made thee Earl of
Gloster. Seek out where thy father is, that he may be
ready for our apprehension.   20
Edm. [*Aside.*] If I find him comforting the king,
it will stuff his suspicion more fully.—I will persever
in my course of loyalty, though the conflict be sore
between that and my blood.
Corn. I will lay trust upon thee, and thou shalt find
a dearer father in my love.   [*Exeunt.*

SCENE VI.—A Chamber in a Farm-house, adjoining
the Castle.

Enter GLOSTER, LEAR, KENT, *Fool, and* EDGAR.

Glo. Here is better than the open air ; take it thank-
fully. I will piece out the comfort with what addition
I can : I will not be long from you.
Kent. All the power of his wits have given way to
his impatience.—The gods reward your kindness !
                    [*Exit* GLOSTER.
Edg. Frateretto calls me, and tells me, Nero is an
angler in the lake of darkness. Pray, innocent, and
beware the foul fiend.
Fool. Pr'ythee, nuncle, tell me, whether a madman
be a gentleman, or a yeoman ?   10
Lear. A king, a king !
Fool. No : he 's a yeoman, that has a gentleman to
his son ; for he 's a mad yeoman, that sees his on a
gentleman before him.
Lear. To have a thousand with red-burning spits
Come hissing in upon them :—
Edg. The foul fiend bites my back.
Fool. He 's mad, that trusts in the tameness of a
wolf, a horse's health, a boy's love, or a whore's oath.
Lear. It shall be done ; I will arraign them
straight.—   20
[*To* EDGAR.] Come, sit thou here, most learned jus-
ticer :—

[*To the Fool.*] Thou, sapient sir, sit here.—Now, you
     she-foxes !—
Edg. Look, where he stands and glares !—
Wantest thou eyes at trial, madam ?
     Come o'er the bourn, Bessy, to me :—
Fool.   *Her boat hath a leak,*
       And she must not speak
     Why she dares not come over to thee.
Edg. The foul fiend haunts poor Tom in the voice of
a nightingale. Hopdance cries in Tom's belly for two
white herring. Croak not, black angel ; I have no
food for thee.   32
Kent. How do you, sir ? Stand you not so amaz'd :
Will you lie down and rest upon the cushions ?
Lear. I 'll see their trial first.—Bring in the evi-
dence.—
[*To* EDGAR.] Thou robed man of justice, take thy
     place ;—
[*To the Fool.*] And thou, his yoke-fellow of equity,
Bench by his side :—
[*To* KENT.] You are o' the commission, sit you too.
Edg. Let us deal justly.   40
     Sleepest, or wakest thou, jolly shepherd ?
       Thy sheep be in the corn ;
     And for one blast of thy minikin mouth,
       Thy sheep shall take no harm.
Pur ! the cat is grey.
Lear. Arraign her first ; 'tis Goneril. I here take
my oath before this honourable assembly, she kicked
the poor king her father.
Fool. Come hither, mistress. Is your name Goneril ?
Lear. She cannot deny it.   50
Fool. Cry you mercy, I took you for a joint-stool.
Lear. And here 's another, whose warp'd looks pro-
claim
What store her heart is made of.—Stop her there !
Arms, arms, sword, fire !—corruption in the place !
False justicer, why hast thou let her 'scape ?
Edg. Bless thy five wits !
Kent. O pity !—Sir, where is the patience now,
That you so oft have boasted to retain ?
Edg. [*Aside.*] My tears begin to take his part so
     much,
They 'll mar my counterfeiting.   60
Lear. The little dogs and all,
Tray, Blanch, and Sweet-heart, see, they bark at me.
Edg. Tom will throw his head at them.—Avaunt,
you curs !
     Be thy mouth or black or white,
     Tooth that poisons if it bite ;
     Mastiff, greyhound, mongrel, grim,
     Hound or spaniel, brach or lym ;
     Or bobtail tike, or trundle-tail :
     Tom will make them weep and wail ;   70
     For, with throwing thus my head,
     Dogs leap the hatch, and all are fled.
Do, de, de, de. Sessa ! Come, march to wakes and
fairs, and market-towns.—Poor Tom, thy horn is dry.
Lear. Then let them anatomise Regan, see what
breeds about her heart. Is there any cause in nature,
that makes these hard hearts ?—[*To* EDGAR.] You, sir,
I entertain you for one of my hundred ; only, I do not
like the fashion of your garments : you will say, they
are Persian ; but let them be changed.   80
Kent. Now, good my lord, lie here, and rest awhile.
Lear. Make no noise, make no noise ; draw the curtains : so, so, so. We 'll go to supper i' the morning :
so, so, so.
Fool. And I 'll go to bed at noon.

Re-enter GLOSTER.

Glo. Come hither, friend : where is the king my
     master ?
Kent. Here, sir ; but trouble him not, his wits are
     gone.
Glo. Good friend, I pr'ythee, take him in thy arms ;
I have o'erheard a plot of death upon him.
There is a litter ready ; lay him in 't,   90
And drive toward Dover, friend, where thou shalt
     meet
Both welcome and protection. Take up thy master :

If thou shouldst dally half an hour, his life,
With thine, and all that offer to defend him,
Stand in assured loss.   Take up, take up;
And follow me, that will to some provision
Give thee quick conduct.
    Kent.   Oppressed nature sleeps :—
This rest might yet have balm'd thy broken sinews,
Which, if convenience will not allow,
Stand in hard cure.—[*To the Fool.*] Come, help to bear
    thy master;   100
Thou must not stay behind.
    Glo.   Come, come, away.
          [*Exeunt* KENT, GLOSTER, *and the Fool,
                  bearing off the* KING.
    Edg. When we our betters see bearing our woes,
We scarcely think our miseries our foes.
Who alone suffers, suffers most i' the mind,
Leaving free things, and happy shows, behind ;
But then the mind much sufferance doth o'erskip,
When grief hath mates, and bearing-fellowship.
How light and portable my pain seems now,
When that which makes me bend, makes the king
    bow :
He childed, as I father'd !—Tom, away !   110
Mark the high noises, and thyself bewray,
When false opinion, whose wrong thought defiles thee,
In thy just proof, repeals and reconciles thee.
What will hap more to-night, safe 'scape the king !
Lurk, lurk.   [*Exit.*

- - -

SCENE VII.—*A Room in* GLOSTER's *Castle.*

Enter CORNWALL, REGAN, GONERIL, EDMUND, *and
                  Servants.*

    Corn. Post speedily to my lord your husband ; show
him this letter :—the army of France is landed.—
Seek out the traitor Gloster.
                  [*Exeunt some of the Servants.*
    Reg. Hang him instantly.
    Gon. Pluck out his eyes.
    Corn. Leave him to my displeasure.—Edmund, keep
you our sister company : the revenges we are bound
to take upon your traitorous father are not fit for your
beholding.   Advise the duke, where you are going,
to a most festinate preparation : we are bound to the
like.   Our posts shall be swift and intelligent betwixt
us.   Farewell, dear sister :—farewell, my Lord of
Gloster.   13
              Enter OSWALD.
How now ! Where 's the king ?
    Osw. My Lord of Gloster hath convey'd him hence :
Some five or six and thirty of his knights,
Hot questrists after him, met him at gate ;
Who, with some other of the lord's dependants,
Are gone with him towards Dover, where they boast
To have well-armed friends.
    Corn.   Get horses for your mistress.
    Gon. Farewell, sweet lord, and sister.   21
          [*Exeunt* GONERIL, EDMUND, *and* OSWALD.
    Corn. Edmund, farewell.—Go, seek the traitor
    Gloster,
Pinion him like a thief, bring him before us.
                  [*Exeunt other Servants.*
Though well we may not pass upon his life
Without the form of justice, yet our power
Shall do a courtesy to our wrath, which men
May blame, but not control.   Who 's there ?   The
    traitor ?
          Re-enter Servants, with GLOSTER.
    Reg. Ingrateful fox ! 't is he.
    Corn. Bind fast his corky arms.
    Glo. What mean your graces?—Good my friends,
    consider   30
You are my guests : do me no foul play, friends.
    Corn. Bind him, I say.   [*Servants bind him.*
    Reg.   Hard, hard.—O filthy traitor !
    Glo. Unmerciful lady as you are, I 'm none.
    Corn. To this chair bind him.—Villain, thou shalt
    find—   [REGAN *plucks his beard.*

    Glo. By the kind gods, 't is most ignobly done
To pluck me by the beard.
    Reg. So white, and such a traitor !
    Glo.   Naughty lady,
These hairs, which thou dost ravish from my chin,
Will quicken, and accuse thee.   I am your host :
With robbers' hands my hospitable favours   40
You should not ruffle thus.   What will you do ?
    Corn. Come, sir, what letters had you late from
    France ?
    Reg. Be simple-answer'd, for we know the truth.
    Corn. And what confederacy have you with the
    traitors
Late footed in the kingdom ?

Glo. "By the kind gods, 't is most ignobly done
To pluck me by the beard."

    Reg. To whose hands have you sent the lunatic
king ? Speak.
    Glo. I have a letter guessingly set down,
Which came from one that 's of a neutral heart,
And not from one oppos'd.
    Corn.   Cunning.
    Reg.   And false.   50
    Corn. Where hast thou sent the king ?
    Glo.   To Dover.
    Reg. Wherefore to Dover ? Wast thou not charg'd
    at peril—
    Corn. Wherefore to Dover ? Let him answer that.
    Glo. I am tied to the stake, and I must stand the
    course.
    Reg. Wherefore to Dover ?
    Glo. Because I would not see thy cruel nails
Pluck out his poor old eyes ; nor thy fierce sister
In his anointed flesh stick boarish fangs.
The sea, with such a storm as his bare head
In hell-black night endur'd, would have buoy'd up,   60
And quench'd the stelled fires ;
Yet, poor old heart, he holp the heavens to rain.
If wolves had at thy gate howl'd that stern time,
Thou shouldst have said, "Good porter, turn the
    key,"
All cruels else subscrib'd :—but I shall see
The winged vengeance overtake such children.
    Corn. See 't shalt thou never.—Fellows, hold the
    chair.—
Upon these eyes of thine I 'll set my foot.
    Glo. He, that will think to live till he be old,
Give me some help !—O cruel !—O ye gods !   70
    Reg. One side will mock another ; the other too.

Corn. If you see vengeance,—
1 Serv.   Hold your hand, my lord.
I have serv'd you ever since I was a child ;
But better service have I never done you,
Than now to bid you hold.
Reg.   How now, you dog !
1 Serv. If you did wear a beard upon your chin,
I'd shake it on this quarrel. What do you mean ?   77
Corn. My villain !   [*Draws and runs at him.*
1 Serv. Nay then, come on, and take the chance of
    anger.   [*Draws.* CORNWALL *is wounded.*
Reg. Give me thy sword. A peasant stand up thus !
1 Serv. O, I am slain !—My lord, you have one eye left
To see some mischief on him.—O !   [*Dies.*
Corn. Lest it see more, prevent it.—Out, vile jelly !
Where is thy lustre now ?
Glo. All dark and comfortless.—Where's my son
    Edmund ?
Edmund, enkindle all the sparks of nature,
To quit this horrid act.
Reg.   Out, treacherous vil'ain !
Thou call'st on him that hates thee : it was he
That made the overture of thy treasons to us,
Who is too good to pity thee.

Glo.   O my follies !   90
Then Edgar was abus'd.—
Kind gods, forgive me that, and prosper him !
Reg. Go, thrust him out at gates, and let him smell
His way to Dover.—How is 't, my lord ? How look
    you ?
Corn. I have receiv'd a hurt.—Follow me, lady.
Turn out that eyeless villain ;—throw this slave
Upon the dunghill.—Regan, I bleed apace :
Untimely comes this hurt. Give me your arm.
    [*Exit* CORNWALL, *led by* REGAN ;—*Servants
        unbind* GLOSTER, *and lead him out.*
2 Serv. I'll never care what wickedness I do,
If this man come to good.
3 Serv.   If she live long,   100
And in the end meet the old course of death,
Women will all turn monsters.
2 Serv. Let's follow the old earl, and get the Bedlam
To lead him where he would : his roguish madness
Allows itself to anything.
3 Serv. Go thou ; I'll fetch some flax, and whites of
    eggs,
To apply to his bleeding face. Now, heaven help
    him !   [*Exeunt severally.*

ACT IV.

SCENE I.—The Heath.

Enter EDGAR.

Edgar.
ET better thus, and known to be con-
    temn'd,
Than still contemn'd and flatter'd. To
    be worst,
The lowest and most dejected thing of
    fortune,
Stands still in esperance, lives not in
    fear :
The lamentable change is from the
    best ;
The worst returns to laughter. Welcome,
    then,
Thou unsubstantial air, that I embrace :
The wretch, that thou hast blown unto the
    worst,
Owes nothing to thy blasts.—But who comes
    here ?—

Enter GLOSTER, *led by an Old Man.*

My father, poorly led ?—World, world, O world !   10
But that thy strange mutations make us hate thee,
Life would not yield to age.
Old Man. O my good lord ! I have been your tenant,
and your father's tenant, these fourscore years.
Glo. Away, get thee away ; good friend, be gone :
Thy comforts can do me no good at all ;
Thee they may hurt.
Old Man.   You cannot see your way.
Glo. I have no way, and therefore want no eyes :
I stumbled when I saw. Full oft 't is seen,
Our means secure us, and our mere defects   20
Prove our commodities.—Ah ! dear son Edgar,
The food of thy abused father's wrath !
Might I but live to see thee in my touch,
I'd say I had eyes again !
Old Man.   How now ! Who's there ?

Edg. [*Aside.*] O gods ! Who is 't can say "I am at
    the worst ?"
I am worse than e'er I was.
Old Man.   'T is poor mad Tom.
Edg. [*Aside.*] And worse I may be yet : the worst
    is not
So long as we can say, "This is the worst."
Old Man. Fellow, where goest ?
Glo.   Is it a beggar-man ?
Old Man. Madman and beggar too.   30
Glo. He has some reason, else he could not beg.
I' the last night's storm I such a fellow saw,
Which made me think a man a worm : my son
Came then into my mind ; and yet my mind
Was then scarce friends with him : I have heard
    more since.
As flies to wanton boys, are we to the gods ;
They kill us for their sport.
Edg. [*Aside.*]   How should this be ?—
Bad is the trade that must play fool to sorrow,
Angering itself and others.—Bless thee, master !
Glo. Is that the naked fellow ?
Old Man.   Ay, my lord.   40
Glo. Get thee away. If, for my sake,
Thou wilt o'ertake us, hence a mile or twain,
I' the way toward Dover, do it for ancient love ;
And bring some covering for this naked soul,
Which I'll entreat to lead me.
Old Man.   Alack, sir ! he is mad.
Glo. 'T is the times' plague, when madmen lead the
    blind.
Do as I bid thee, or rather do thy pleasure ;
Above the rest, be gone.
Old Man. I'll bring him the best 'parel that I
    have,
Come on 't what will.   [*Exit.*
Glo. Sirrah, naked fellow,   51

Edg. Poor Tom's a-cold.—[*Aside.*] I cannot daub it
further.
Glo. Come hither, fellow.
Edg. [*Aside.*] And yet I must.—Bless thy sweet
eyes, they bleed.
Glo. Know'st thou the way to Dover?
Edg. Both stile and gate, horse-way and foot-path.
Poor Tom hath been scared out of his good wits: bless
thee, good man's son, from the foul fiend! Five fiends
have been in poor Tom at once; of lust, as Obidicut;
Hobbididance, prince of dumbness; Mahu, of stealing;
Modo, of murder; Flibbertigibbet, of mopping and
mowing; who since possesses chambermaids and
waiting-women. So, bless thee, master!   63
Glo. Here, take this purse, thou whom the heaven's
plagues
Have humbled to all strokes: that I am wretched,
Makes thee the happier:—heavens, deal so still!
Let the superfluous and lust-dieted man,
That slaves your ordinance, that will not see
Because he doth not feel, feel your power quickly;
So distribution should undo excess,   70
And each man have enough.—Dost thou know Dover?
Edg. Ay, master.
Glo. There is a cliff, whose high and bending head
Looks fearfully in the confined deep:
Bring me but to the very brim of it,
And I'll repair the misery thou dost bear
With something rich about me: from that place
I shall no leading need.
    Edg.   Give me thy arm:
Poor Tom shall lead thee.   [*Exeunt.*

SCENE II.—Before the Duke of ALBANY's Palace.

Enter GONERIL *and* EDMUND; OSWALD *meeting
them.*

Gon. Welcome, my lord: I marvel, our mild hus-
band
Not met us on the way.—Now, where's your master?
Osw. Madam, within; but never man so chang'd.
I told him of the army that was landed;
He smil'd at it: I told him, you were coming;
His answer was, "The worse:" of Gloster's treachery,
And of the loyal service of his son,
When I inform'd him, then he call'd me sot,
And told me, I had turn'd the wrong side out.
What most he should dislike, seems pleasant to him;
What like, offensive.   11
Gon. [*To* EDMUND.] Then shall you go no further.
It is the cowish terror of his spirit,
That dares not undertake: he'll not feel wrongs
Which tie him to an answer. Our wishes on the way
May prove effects. Back, Edmund, to my brother;
Hasten his musters, and conduct his powers:
I must change arms at home, and give the distaff
Into my husband's hands. This trusty servant
Shall pass between us: ere long you are like to hear,
If you dare venture in your own behalf,   20
A mistress's command. Wear this; spare speech;
                     [*Giving a favour.*
Decline your head: this kiss, if it durst speak,
Would stretch thy spirits up into the air.—
Conceive, and fare thee well.
    Edm. Yours in the ranks of death.
    Gon.   My most dear Gloster!
                     [*Exit* EDMUND.
O, the difference of man and man!
To thee a woman's services are due:
My fool usurps my body.
    Osw.   Madam, here comes my lord.
                     [*Exit.*

Enter ALBANY.

Gon. I have been worth the whistle.
Alb.   O Goneril! 30
You are not worth the dust which the rude wind
Blows in your face.—I fear your disposition:
That nature, which contemns its origin,
Cannot be border'd certain in itself;

She that herself will sliver and disbranch
From her material sap, perforce must wither,
And come to deadly use.
Gon. No more: the text is foolish.
Alb. Wisdom and goodness to the vile seem vile;
Filths savour but themselves. What have you done?
Tigers, not daughters, what have you perform'd?   41
A father, and a gracious aged man,
Whose reverence the head-lugg'd bear would lick,
Most barbarous, most degenerate! have you madded.

      Gon.   "This kiss, if it durst speak,
Would stretch thy spirits up into the air.'

Could my good brother suffer you to do it?
A man, a prince, by him so benefited!
If that the heavens do not their visible spirits
Send quickly down to tame these vile offences,
It will come,
Humanity must perforce prey on itself,   50
Like monsters of the deep.
Gon.   Milk-liver'd man!
That bear'st a cheek for blows, a head for wrongs;
Who hast not in thy brows an eye discerning
Thine honour from thy suffering; that not know'st,
Fools do those villains pity, who are punish'd
Ere they have done their mischief. Where's thy
drum?
France spreads his banners in our noiseless land;
With plumed helm thy slayer begins threats;
Whilst thou, a moral fool, sitt'st still, and criest,
"Alack! why does he so?"
Alb.   See thyself, devil!   60
Proper deformity seems not in the fiend
So horrid, as in woman.
Gon.   O vain fool!
Alb. Thou changed and self-cover'd thing, for
shame,
Be-monster not thy feature. Were it my fitness
To let these hands obey my blood,
They are apt enough to dislocate and tear
Thy flesh and bones:—howe'er thou art a fiend,
A woman's shape doth shield thee.
Gon. Marry, your manhood now!—

Enter a Messenger.

Alb. What news?   70
Mess. O, my good lord, the Duke of Cornwall's
dead;
Slain by his servant, going to put out
The other eye of Gloster.

Alb.   Gloster's eyes!
Mess. A servant that he bred, thrill'd with remorse,
Oppos'd against the act, bending his sword
To this great master ; who, thereat enrag'd,
Flew on him, and amongst them fell'd him dead ;
But not without that harmful stroke, which since
Hath pluck'd him after.
Alb.   This shows you are above,
You justicers, that these our nether crimes   80
So speedily can venge !—But, O poor Gloster !
Lost he his other eye ?
Mess.   Both, both, my lord.—
This letter, madam, craves a speedy answer ;
'T is from your sister.
Gon. [*Aside.*]   One way I like this well ;
But being widow, and my Gloster with her,
May all the building in my fancy pluck
Upon my hateful life. Another way,
The news is not so tart.—I 'll read, and answer. [*Exit.*
Alb. Where was his son, when they did take his
    eyes ?
Mess. Come with my lady hither.
Alb.   He is not here.   90
Mess. No, my good lord ; I met him back again.
Alb. Knows he the wickedness ?
Mess. Ay, my good lord ; 't was he inform'd against
    him,
And quit the house on purpose, that their punishment
Might have the freer course.
Alb.   Gloster, I live
To thank thee for the love thou show'dst the king,
And to revenge thine eyes.—Come hither, friend :
Tell me what more thou knowest.   [*Exeunt.*

SCENE III.—The French Camp near Dover.

Enter KENT *and a Gentleman.*

Kent. Why the King of France is so suddenly gone
back, know you the reason ?
Gent. Something he left imperfect in the state,
which since his coming forth is thought of ; which
imports to the kingdom so much fear and danger,
that his personal return was most required, and
necessary.
Kent. Who hath he left behind him general ?
Gent. The Marshal of France, Monsieur La Far.
Kent. Did your letters pierce the queen to any
demonstration of grief ?   11
Gent. Ay, sir ; she took them, read them in my
presence ;
And now and then an ample tear trill'd down
Her delicate cheek : it seem'd, she was a queen
Over her passion, who, most rebel-like,
Sought to be king o'er her.
Kent.   O ! then it mov'd her.
Gent. Not to a rage : patience and sorrow strove
Who should express her goodliest. You have seen
Sunshine and rain at once ; her smiles and tears
Were like a better way : those happy smilets,   20
That play'd on her ripe lip, seem'd not to know
What guest were in her eyes ; which parted thence,
As pearls from diamonds dropp'd.—In brief,
Sorrow would be a rarity most belov'd,
If all could so become it.
Kent.   Made she no verbal question ?
Gent. 'Faith, once, or twice, she heav'd the name of
    "father"
Pantingly forth, as if it press'd her heart ;
Cried, "Sisters ! sisters ! Shame of ladies ! sisters !
Kent ! father ! sisters ! What ? i' the storm ? i' the
night ?
Let pity not be believed !"—There she shook   30
The holy water from her heavenly eyes,
And clamour moisten'd : then away she started
To deal with grief alone.
Kent.   It is the stars,
The stars above us, govern our conditions ;
Else one self mate and mate could not beget
Such different issues. You spoke not with her since ?
Gent. No.

Kent. Was this before the king return'd ?
Gent.   No, since.
Kent. Well, sir ; the poor distress'd Lear 's i' the
    town ;
Who sometime, in his better tune, remembers   40
What we are come about, and by no means
Will yield to see his daughter.
Gent.   Why, good sir ?
Kent. A sovereign shame so elbows him : his own
unkindness,
That stripp'd her from his benediction, turn'd her
To foreign casualties ; gave her dear rights
To his dog-hearted daughters : these things sting
His mind so venomously, that burning shame
Detains him from Cordelia.
Gent.   Alack, poor gentleman !
Kent. Of Albany's and Cornwall's powers you heard
    not ?
Gent. 'T is so, they are afoot.   50
Kent. Well, sir, I'll bring you to our master Lear,
And leave you to attend him. Some dear cause
Will in concealment wrap me up awhile :
When I am known aright, you shall not grieve
Lending me this acquaintance.
I pray you, go along with me.   [*Exeunt.*

SCENE IV.—The Same. A Camp.

Enter CORDELIA, *Physician, and Soldiers.*

Cor. Alack ! 'tis he : why, he was met even now
As mad as the vex'd sea : singing aloud ;
Crown'd with rank fumiter, and furrow-weeds,
With hoar-docks, hemlock, nettles, cuckoo-flowers,
Darnel, and all the idle weeds that grow
In our sustaining corn.—A century send forth ;
Search every acre in the high-grown field,
And bring him to our eye. [*Exit an Officer.*]—What
    can man's wisdom
In the restoring his bereaved sense ?
He that helps him, take all my outward worth.   10
Phy. There is means, madam ;
Our foster-nurse of nature is repose,
The which he lacks ; that to provoke in him,
Are many simples operative, whose power
Will close the eye of anguish.
Cor.   All bless'd secrets,
All you unpublish'd virtues of the earth,
Spring with my tears ! be aidant, and remediate,
In the good man's distress !—Seek, seek for him ;
Lest his ungovern'd rage dissolve the life
That wants the means to lead it.

Enter a Messenger.

Mess.   News, madam : 20
The British powers are marching hitherward.
Cor. 'T is known before : our preparation stands
In expectation of them.—O dear father,
It is thy business that I go about ;
Therefore great France
My mourning, and important tears, hath pitied.
No blown ambition doth our arms incite,
But love, dear love, and our ag'd father's right.
Soon may I hear and see him !   [*Exeunt.*

SCENE V.—A Room in GLOSTER'S Castle.

Enter REGAN *and* OSWALD.

Reg. But are my brother's powers set forth ?
Osw.   Ay, madam.
Reg. Himself in person there ?
Osw.   Madam, with much ado :
Your sister is the better soldier.
Reg. Lord Edmund spake not with your lord at
    home ?
Osw. No, madam.
Reg. What might import my sister's letter to him ?
Osw. I know not, lady.
Reg. 'Faith, he is posted hence on serious matter.

It was great ignorance, Gloster's eyes being out,
To let him live : where he arrives, he moves　10
All hearts against us. Edmund, I think, is gone,
In pity on his misery, to despatch
His nighted life ; moreover, to descry
The strength o' the enemy.
　Osw.　I must needs after him, madam, with my
　　letter.
　Reg. Our troops set forth to-morrow : stay with us ;
The ways are dangerous.
　Osw.　　　　　I may not, madam ;
My lady charg'd my duty in this business.
　Reg. Why should she write to Edmund? Might
　　not you
Transport her purposes by word? Belike,　20
Something—I know not what.—I 'll love thee much,
Let me unseal the letter.
　Osw.　　　　　Madam, I had rather—
　Reg. I know your lady does not love her husband ;
I am sure of that : and, at her late being here,
She gave strange eyliads, and most speaking looks
To noble Edmund. I know, you are of her bosom.
　Osw. I, madam?
　Reg. I speak in understanding ; you are, I know 't :
Therefore, I do advise you, take this note :
My lord is dead ; Edmund and I have talk'd ;　30
And more convenient is he for my hand,
Than for your lady's.—You may gather more.
If you do find him, pray you, give him this ;
And when your mistress hears thus much from you,
I pray, desire her call her wisdom to her :
So, fare you well.
If you do chance to hear of that blind traitor,
Preferment falls on him that cuts him off.
　Osw. 'Would I could meet him, madam : I would
　　show
What party I do follow.
　Reg.　　　　　Fare thee well.　40
　　　　　　　　　　　　　[*Exeunt.*

SCENE VI.—The Country near Dover.

Enter GLOSTER, *and* EDGAR *dressed like a peasant.*
　Glo. When shall I come to the top of that same hill?
　Edg. You do climb up it now : look, how we labour.
　Glo. Methinks, the ground is even.
　Edg.　　　　　Horrible steep :
Hark ! do you hear the sea?
　Glo.　　　　　No, truly.
　Edg. Why, then your other senses grow imperfect
By your eyes' anguish.
　Glo.　　　　　So may it be, indeed.
Methinks, thy voice is alter'd ; and thou speak'st
In better phrase, and matter, than thou didst.
　Edg. You 're much deceiv'd : in nothing am I
　　chang'd,
But in my garments.
　Glo.　　　　　Methinks, you 're better spoken.
　Edg. Come on, sir ; here 's the place : stand still.—
How fearful　11
And dizzy 't is, to cast one's eyes so low !
The crows and choughs, that wing the midway air,
Show scarce so gross as beetles : half way down
Hangs one that gathers samphire ; dreadful trade !
Methinks, he seems no bigger than his head.
The fishermen, that walk upon the beach,
Appear like mice ; and yond tall anchoring bark,
Diminish'd to her cock ; her cock, a buoy
Almost too small for sight. The murmuring surge, 20
That on the unnumber'd idle pebbles chafes,
Cannot be heard so high.—I 'll look no more ;
Lest my brain turn, and the deficient sight
Topple down headlong.
　Glo.　　　　　Set me where you stand.
　Edg. Give me your hand ; you are now within a foot
Of the extreme verge : for all beneath the moon
Would I not leap upright.
　Glo.　　　　　Let go my hand.
Here, friend, 's another purse ; in it, a jewel
Well worth a poor man's taking : fairies, and gods,

Prosper it with thee ! Go thou further off ;　30
Bid me farewell, and let me hear thee going.
　Edg. Now fare you well, good sir.
　Glo.　　　　　With all my heart.
　Edg. Why I do trifle thus with his despair,
Is done to cure it.
　Glo.　　　　　O you mighty gods !
This world I do renounce, and in your sights
Shake patiently my great affliction off ;
If I could bear it longer, and not fall
To quarrel with your great opposeless wills,
My snuff, and loathed part of nature, should
Burn itself out. If Edgar live, O, bless him !—　40
Now, fellow, fare thee well.
　Edg.　　　　　Gone, sir : farewell.—
And yet I know not how conceit may rob
The treasury of life, when life itself
Yields to the theft : had he been where he thought,
By this had thought been past.—Alive, or dead?
Ho, you sir ! friend !—Hear you, sir?—speak !-
Thus might he pass indeed,—yet he revives.—
What are you, sir?
　Glo.　　　　　Away, and let me die.
　Edg. Hadst thou been aught but gossamer, feather,
　　air,
So many fathom down precipitating,　50
Thou 'dst shiver'd like an egg : but thou dost breathe ;
Hast heavy substance ; bleed'st not ; speak'st ; art
　　sound.
Ten masts at each make not the altitude
Which thou hast perpendicularly fell :
Thy life 's a miracle. Speak yet again.
　Glo. But have I fallen, or no?
　Edg. From the dread summit of this chalky bourn.
Look up a-height ; the shrill-gorg'd lark so far
Cannot be seen or heard : do but look up.
　Glo. Alack ! I have no eyes.—　60
Is wretchedness depriv'd that benefit,
To end itself by death? 'T was yet some comfort,
When misery could beguile the tyrant's rage,
And frustrate his proud will.
　Edg.　　　　　Give me your arm :
Up :—so ;—how is 't? Feel you your legs? You stand.
　Glo. Too well, too well.
　Edg.　　　　　This is above all strangeness.
Upon the crown o' the cliff, what thing was that
Which parted from you?
　Glo.　　　　　A poor unfortunate beggar.
　Edg. As I stood here below, methought, his eyes
Were two full moons ; he had a thousand noses,　70
Horns whelk'd and wav'd like the enridged sea :
It was some fiend ; therefore, thou happy father,
Think that the clearest gods, who make them honours
Of men's impossibilities, have preserv'd thee.
　Glo. I do remember now : henceforth I 'll bear
Affliction, till it do cry out itself
"Enough, enough," and "die." That thing you speak
　　of,
I took it for a man ; often 't would say,
"The fiend, the fiend :" he led me to that place.
　Edg. Bear free and patient thoughts.—But who
comes here?　80

Enter LEAR, *fantastically dressed with wild flowers.*
The safer sense will ne'er accommodate
His master thus.
　Lear. No, they cannot touch me for coining ; I am
the king himself.
　Edg. O thou side-piercing sight !
　Lear. Nature 's above art in that respect.—There 's
your press-money. That fellow handles his bow like a
crow-keeper : draw me a clothier's yard.—Look, look !
a mouse. Peace, peace !—this piece of toasted cheese
will do 't.—There 's my gauntlet, I 'll prove it on a
giant.—Bring up the brown-bills.—O, well flown,
bird !—i' the clout, i' the clout : hewgh !—Give the word.
　Edg. Sweet marjoram.　93
　Lear. Pass.
　Glo. I know that voice.
　Lear. Ha ! Goneril !—with a white beard !—They
flatter'd me like a dog ; and told me, I had white hairs
in my beard, ere the black ones were there. To say

"ay" and "no" to everything I said!—"Ay" and "no"
too was no good divinity. When the rain came to wet
me once, and the wind to make me chatter; when the
thunder would not peace at my bidding: there I found
'em, there I smelt 'em out. Go to, they are not men o'
their words: they told me I was everything; 'tis a lie,
I am not ague-proof.

Glo. The trick of that voice I do well remember:
Is 't not the king?

Lear.   Ay, every inch a king:
When I do stare, see, how the subject quakes.
I pardon that man's life. What was thy cause?—
Adultery?—   110
Thou shalt not die: die for adultery! No:
The wren goes to 't, and the small gilded fly
Does lecher in my sight.
Let copulation thrive; for Gloster's bastard son
Was kinder to his father, than my daughters
Got 'tween the lawful sheets.
To 't, luxury, pell-mell! for I lack soldiers.—
Behold yond simpering dame,
Whose face between her forks presageth snow;
That minces virtue, and does shake the head   120
To hear of pleasure's name;
The fitchew, nor the soiled horse, goes to 't
With a more riotous appetite.
Down from the waist they are centaurs,
Though women all above:
But to the girdle do the gods inherit,
Beneath is all the fiend's: there 's hell, there 's dark-
ness, there is the sulphurous pit, burning, scalding,
stench, consumption;—fie, fie, fie! pah, pah! Give
me an ounce of civet, good apothecary, to sweeten my
imagination: there 's money for thee.   131

Glo. O, let me kiss that hand!

Lear. Let me wipe it first; it smells of mortality.

Glo. O ruin'd piece of nature! This great world
Shall so wear out to nought.—Dost thou know me?

Lear. I remember thine eyes well enough. Dost
thou squiny at me? No, do thy worst, blind Cupid;
I 'll not love.—Read thou this challenge: mark but
the penning of it.

Glo. Were all thy letters suns, I could not see.   140

Edg. I would not take this from report; it is,
And my heart breaks at it.

Lear. Read.

Glo. What! with the case of eyes?

Lear. O, ho! are you there with me? No eyes in
your head, nor no money in your purse? Your eyes
are in a heavy case, your purse in a light: yet you see
how this world goes.

Glo. I see it feelingly.   149

Lear. What, art mad? A man may see how this
world goes, with no eyes. Look with thine ears: see
how yond justice rails upon yond simple thief. Hark,
in thine ear: change places; and, handy-dandy, which
is the justice, which is the thief?—Thou hast seen a
farmer's dog bark at a beggar?

Glo. Ay, sir.

Lear. And the creature run from the cur? There
thou mightst behold the great image of authority: a
dog 's obey'd in office.—
Thou rascal beadle, hold thy bloody hand!   160
Why dost thou lash that whore? Strip thine own
back;
Thou hotly lust'st to use her in that kind
For which thou whipp'st her. The usurer hangs the
cozener.
Through tatter'd clothes small vices do appear;
Robes and furr'd gowns hide all. Plate sin with gold,
And the strong lance of justice hurtless breaks;
Arm it in rags, a pigmy's straw does pierce it.
None does offend, none, I say, none; I 'll able 'em:
Take that of me, my friend, who have the power
To seal the accuser's lips. Get thee glass eyes;   170
And, like a scurvy politician, seem
To see the things thou dost not.—Now, now, now,
now,
Pull off my boots:—harder, harder;—so.

Edg. O, matter and impertinency mix'd!
Reason in madness!

Lear. If thou wilt weep my fortunes, take my eyes.

I know thee well enough; thy name is Gloster:
Thou must be patient. We came crying hither:
Thou know'st, the first time that we smell the air,
We wawl, and cry. I will preach to thee: mark me.

Glo. Alack, alack the day!   181

Lear. When we are born, we cry that we are come
To this great stage of fools.—This a good block!—
It were a delicate stratagem, to shoe
A troop of horse with felt: I 'll put 't in proof;
And when I have stol'n upon these sons-in-law,
Then, kill, kill, kill, kill, kill, kill!

Enter a Gentleman, with Attendants.

Gent. O! here he is: lay hand upon him.—Sir,
Your most dear daughter—

Lear. No rescue? What! a prisoner? I am even
The natural fool of fortune.—Use me well;   191
You shall have ransom. Let me have surgeons;
I am cut to the brains.

Gent.   You shall have anything.

Lear. No seconds? All myself?
Why, this would make a man a man of salt,
To use his eyes for garden water-pots,
Ay, and laying autumn's dust.

Gent.   Good sir,—

Lear. I will die bravely, like a smug bridegroom.
What!
I will be jovial; come, come; I am a king,
My masters, know you that?   200

Gent. You are a royal one, and we obey you.

Lear. Then there 's life in it. Nay, an you get it,
you shall get it by running. Sa, sa, sa, sa.
                   [*Exit; Attendants follow.*

Gent. A sight most pitiful in the meanest wretch,
Past speaking of in a king!—Thou hast one daughter,
Who redeems nature from the general curse
Which twain have brought her to.

Edg. Hail, gentle sir!

Gent.   Sir, speed you: what 's your will?

Edg. Do you hear aught, sir, of a battle toward?

Gent. Most sure, and vulgar: every one hears that,
Which can distinguish sound.

Edg.   But, by your favour,
How near 's the other army?   212

Gent. Near, and on speedy foot; the main descry
Stands on the hourly thought.

Edg.   I thank you, sir: that 's all.

Gent. Though that the queen on special cause is
here,
Her army is mov'd on.

Edg.   I thank you, sir. [*Exit Gentleman.*

Glo. You ever-gentle gods, take my breath from me:
Let not my worser spirit tempt me again
To die before you please!

Edg.   Well pray you, father.

Glo. Now, good sir, what are you?   220

Edg. A most poor man, made tame to fortune's
blows;
Who, by the art of known and feeling sorrows,
Am pregnant to good pity. Give me your hand,
I 'll lead you to some biding.

Glo.   Hearty thanks:
The bounty and the benison of heaven
To boot, and boot!

Enter OSWALD.

Osw.   A proclaim'd prize! Most happy!
That eyeless head of thine was first fram'd flesh
To raise my fortunes.—Thou old unhappy traitor,
Briefly thyself remember:—the sword is out
That must destroy thee.

Glo.   Now let thy friendly hand
Put strength enough to it.   [EDGAR *interposes.*

Osw.   Wherefore, bold peasant,
Dar'st thou support a publish'd traitor? Hence;   232
Lest that the infection of his fortune take
Like hold on thee. Let go his arm.

Edg. Ch'ill not let go, zir, without vurther 'casion.

Osw. Let go, slave, or thou diest.

Edg. Good gentleman, go your gait, and let poor
volk pass. An ch'ud ha' been zwagger'd out of my
life, 't would not ha' been zo long as 't is by a vortnight

Nay, come not near the old man: keep out, che vor'ye,
or ise try whether your costard or my ballow be the
harder. Ch'ill be plain with you.   242
  Osw. Out, dunghill!
  Edg. Ch'ill pick your teeth, zir. Come; no matter
vor your foins.
     [*Th·y fight, and* EDGAR *knocks him down.*
  Osw. Slave, thou hast slain me.—Villain, take my
      purse.
If ever thou wilt thrive, bury my body;
And give the letters, which thou find'st about me,
To Edmund Earl of Gloster: seek him out
Upon the English party;—O, untimely death! [*Dies.*
  Edg. I know thee well: a serviceable villain;   251
As duteous to the vices of thy mistress,
As badness would desire.

Edg.   "Give me your hand,
I'll lead you to some biding.'

  Glo.   What! is he dead?
  Edg. Sit you down, father; rest you.—
Let's see these pockets: the letters, that he speaks of,
May be my friends.—He's dead: I am only sorry
He had no other death's-man.—Let us see:—
Leave, gentle wax; and, manners, blame us not:
To know our enemies' minds, we rip their hearts;
Their papers is more lawful.   260
  [*Reads.*] "Let our reciprocal vows be remembered.
You have many opportunities to cut him off; if your
will want not, time and place will be fruitfully offered.
There is nothing done, if he return the conqueror;
then am I the prisoner, and his bed my gaol; from
the loathed warmth whereof deliver me, and supply
the place for your labour.
      Your (wife, so I would say)
           affectionate servant,
               GONERIL."
O undistinguish'd space of woman's will!   271
A plot upon her virtuous husband's life;
And the exchange, my brother!—Here, in the sands,
Thee I'll rake up, the post unsanctified
Of murderous lechers; and, in the mature time,
With this ungracious paper strike the sight
Of the death-practis'd duke. For him 'tis well,
That of thy death and business I can tell.
  Glo. The king is mad: how stiff is my vile sense,
That I stand up, and have ingenious feeling   280
Of my huge sorrows! Better I were distract:
So should my thoughts be sever'd from my griefs;

And woes, by wrong imaginations, lose
The knowledge of themselves.   [*Drum afar off.*
  Edg.   Give me your hand:
Far off, methinks, I hear the beaten drum.
Come, father; I'll bestow you with a friend. [*Exeunt.*

SCENE VII.—A Tent in the French Camp.

Enter CORDELIA, KENT, *Doctor, and Gentleman.*

  Cor. O thou good Kent! 'how shall I live and work,
To match thy goodness? My life will be too short,
And every measure fail me.
  Kent. To be acknowledg'd, madam, is o'er-paid.
All my reports go with the modest truth;
Nor more, nor clipp'd, but so.
  Cor.   Be better suited:
These weeds are memories of those worser hours:
I pr'ythee, put them off.
  Kent.   Pardon me, dear madam;
Yet to be known shortens my made intent:
My boon I make it, that you know me not,   10
Till time and I think meet.
  Cor. Then be't so, my good lord.—[*To the Doctor.*]
      How does the king?
  Doct. Madam, sleeps still.
  Cor. O you kind gods,
Cure this great breach in his abused nature!
The untun'd and jarring senses, O, wind up
Of this child-changed father!
  Doct.   So please your majesty,
That we may wake the king? he hath slept long.
  Cor. Be govern'd by your knowledge, and proceed
I' the sway of your own will. Is he array'd?   20

Enter LEAR *in a chair carried by Servants.*

  Doct. Ay, madam; in the heaviness of sleep,
We put fresh garments on him.
  Kent. Be by, good madam, when we do awake him;
I doubt not of his temperance.
  Cor.   Very well. [*Music.*
  Doct. Please you, draw near.—Louder the music
      there!
  Cor. O my dear father! Restoration hang
Thy medicine on my lips, and let this kiss
Repair those violent harms, that my two sisters
Have in thy reverence made!
  Kent.   Kind and dear princess!
  Cor. Had you not been their father, these white
      flakes   30
Had challeng'd pity of them. Was this a face
To be oppos'd against the warring winds?
To stand against the deep dread-bolted thunder?
In the most terrible and nimble stroke
Of quick cross lightning? to watch (poor perdu!)
With this thin helm? Mine enemy's dog,
Though he had bit me, should have stood that night
Against my fire. And wast thou fain, poor father,
To hovel thee with swine, and rogues forlorn,
In short and musty straw? Alack, alack!   40
'Tis wonder, that thy life and wits at once
Had not concluded all.—He wakes; speak to him.
  Doct. Madam, do you; 'tis fittest.
  Cor. How does my royal lord? How fares your
      majesty?
  Lear. You do me wrong, to take me out o' the
      grave.—
Thou art a soul in bliss; but I am bound
Upon a wheel of fire, that mine own tears
Do scald like molten lead.
  Cor.   Sir, do you know me?
  Lear. You are a spirit, I know. When did you die?
  Cor. Still, still, far wide.   50
  Doct. He's scarce awake: let him alone awhile.
  Lear. Where have I been? Where am I?—Fair
      daylight?—
I am mightily abus'd.—I should even die with pity,
To see another thus.—I know not what to say.—
I will not swear, these are my hands:—let's see;
I feel this pin prick. 'Would I were assur'd
Of my condition!

Cor.   O! look upon me, sir,
And hold your hands in benediction o'er me.—
No, sir, you must not kneel.
    Lear.   Pray, do not mock me:
I am a very foolish fond old man,   60
Fourscore and upward, not an hour more, nor less;
And, to deal plainly,
I fear, I am not in my perfect mind.
Methinks, I should know you, and know this man;
Yet I am doubtful, for I am mainly ignorant
What place is this; and all the skill I have
Remembers not these garments; nor I know not
Where I did lodge last night. Do not laugh at
    me;
For, as I am a man, I think this lady
To be my child Cordelia.
    Cor.   And so I am, I am.   70
    Lear. Be your tears wet? Yes, 'faith. I pray, weep
    not:
If you have poison for me, I will drink it.
I know, you do not love me; for your sisters
Have, as I do remember, done me wrong:
You have some cause, they have not.
    Cor.   No cause, no cause.
    Lear. Am I in France?
    Kent.   In your own kindom, sir.
    Lear. Do not abuse me.
    Doct. Be comforted, good madam: the great rage,
You see, is kill'd in him; and yet it is danger
To make him even o'er the time he has lost.   80
Desire him to go in; trouble him no more,
Till further settling.
    Cor. Will 't please your highness walk?
    Lear.   You must bear with me.
Pray you now, forget and forgive: I am old and
    foolish.
            [*Exeunt* LEAR, CORDELIA, *Doctor, and
                        Attendants.*
    Gent. Holds it true, sir, that the Duke of Cornwall
was so slain?

Kent. Most certain, sir.
    Gent. Who is conductor of his people?
    Kent. As 't is said, the bastard son of Gloster.
    Gent. They say, Edgar, his banished son, is with
the Earl of Kent in Germany.   91

Lear. "For, as I am a man, I think this lady
To be my child Cordelia."

Kent. Report is changeable. 'T is time to look
about; the powers of the kingdom approach apace.
    Gent. The arbitrement is like to be bloody. Fare
you well, sir.   [*Exit.*
    Kent. My point and period will be throughly
    wrought,
Or well, or ill, as this day's battle's fought.   [*Exit.*

ACT V.

SCENE I.—The Camp of the British Forces, near Dover.

Enter, with drums and colours, EDMUND, REGAN, *Officers, Soldiers, and others.*

            Edmund.
NOW of the duke, if his last purpose
    hold;
Or whether, since, he is advis'd by aught
To change the course. He's full of
    alteration,
And self-reproving:—bring his constant
    pleasure.
            [*To an Officer, who goes out.*
    Reg. Our sister's man is certainly
    miscarried.
    Edm. 'T is to be doubted, madam.
    Reg.   Now, sweet lord,
You know the goodness I intend upon
    you:
Tell me,—but truly,—but then speak the
    truth,
Do you not love my sister?
    Edm.   In honour'd love.
    Reg. But have you never found my brother's way 10
To the forfended place?
    Edm.   That thought abuses you.

    Reg. I am doubtful that you have been conjunct
And bosom'd with her, as far as we call hers.
    Edm. No, by mine honour, madam.
    Reg. I never shall endure her. Dear my lord,
Be not familiar with her.
    Edm.   Fear me not.—
She, and the duke her husband!

        Enter ALBANY, GONERIL, *and Soldiers.*

    Gon. [*Aside.*] I had rather lose the battle, than that
        sister
Should loosen him and me.
    Alb. Our very loving sister, well be-met.—   20
Sir, this I heard,—the king is come to his daughter,
With others, whom the rigour of our state
Forc'd to cry out. Where I could not be honest,
I never yet was valiant: for this business,
It toucheth us, as France invades our land,
Not bolds the king, with others, whom, I fear,
Most just and heavy causes make oppose.
    Edm. Sir, you speak nobly.
    Reg.   Why is this reason'd?

Gon. Combine together 'gainst the enemy;
For these domestic and particular broils   30
Are not the question here.
  Alb.   Let us then determine
With the ancient of war on our proceeding.
  Edm. I shall attend you presently at your tent.
  Reg. Sister, you'll go with us?
  Gon. No.
  Reg. 'T is most convenient; pray you, go with
    us.
  Gon. [*Aside.*] O, ho! I know the riddle.—I will go.

Enter EDGAR, *disguised.*

  Edg. If e'er your grace had speech with man so
    poor,
Hear me one word.
  Alb.   I'll overtake you.—Speak.
  [*Exeunt* EDMUND, REGAN, GONERIL, *Officers,
    Soldiers, and Attendants.*
  Edg. Before you fight the battle, ope this letter.   40
If you have victory, let the trumpet sound
For him that brought it: wretched though I seem,
I can produce a champion, that will prove
What is avouched there. If you miscarry,
Your business of the world hath so an end,
And machination ceases. Fortune love you!
  Alb. Stay till I have read the letter.
  Edg.   I was forbid it.
When time shall serve, let but the herald cry,
And I'll appear again.
  Alb. Why, fare thee well: I will o'erlook thy paper.
                                [*Exit* EDGAR.

Re-enter EDMUND.

  Edm. The enemy's in view; draw up your powers.
Here is the guess of their true strength and forces   52
By diligent discovery; but your haste
Is now urg'd on you.
  Alb.   We will greet the time. [*Exit.*
  Edm. To both these sisters have I sworn my
    love;
Each jealous of the other, as the stung
Are of the adder. Which of them shall I take?
Both? one? or neither? Neither can be enjoy'd,
If both remain alive: to take the widow,
Exasperates, makes mad, her sister Goneril;   60
And hardly shall I carry out my side,
Her husband being alive. Now then, we'll use
His countenance for the battle; which being done,
Let her who would be rid of him devise
His speedy taking-off. As for the mercy
Which he intends to Lear and to Cordelia,—
The battle done, and they within our power,
Shall never see his pardon; for my state
Stands on me to defend, not to debate.   [*Exit.*

SCENE II.—A Field between the two Camps.

Alarum within. Enter, with drum and colours,
LEAR, CORDELIA, *and their Forces; and exeunt.*

Enter EDGAR and GLOSTER.

  Edg. Here, father, take the shadow of this tree
For your good host; pray that the right may thrive.
If ever I return to you again,
I'll bring you comfort.
  Glo.   Grace go with you, sir!
                                [*Exit* EDGAR.

Alarum; afterwards a Retreat. Re-enter EDGAR.

  Edg. Away, old man! give me thy hand: away!
King Lear hath lost, he and his daughter ta'en.
Give me thy hand; come on.
  Glo. No further, sir; a man may rot even here.
  Edg. What! in ill thoughts again? Men must
    endure
Their going hence, even as their coming hither: 10
Ripeness is all. Come on.
  Glo.   And that's true too. [*Exeunt.*

SCENE III.—The British Camp near Dover.

Enter, in conquest, with drum and colours, EDMUND;
LEAR, *and* CORDELIA, *as prisoners; Captain,
Officers, Soldiers, &c.*

  Edm. Some officers take them away: good guard,
Until their greater pleasures first be known,
That are to censure them.
  Cor.   We are not the first,
Who, with best meaning, have incurr'd the worst.
For thee, oppressed king, am I cast down;
Myself could else out-frown false fortune's frown.
Shall we not see these daughters, and these sisters?
  Lear. No, no, no, no! Come, let's away to prison;
We two alone will sing like birds i' the cage:
When thou dost ask me blessing, I'll kneel down,   10
And ask of thee forgiveness. So we'll live,
And pray, and sing, and tell old tales, and laugh
At gilded butterflies, and hear poor rogues
Talk of court news; and we'll talk with them too,
Who loses, and who wins; who's in, who's out;
And take upon's the mystery of things,
As if we were God's spies: and we'll wear out,
In a wall'd prison, packs and sects of great ones,
That ebb and flow by the moon.
  Edm.   Take them away.
  Lear. Upon such sacrifices, my Cordelia,   20
The gods themselves throw incense. Have I caught
    thee?
He that parts us shall bring a brand from heaven,
And fire us hence like foxes. Wipe thine eyes;
The goujeers shall devour them, flesh and fell,
Ere they shall make us weep: we'll see 'em starve
    first.
Come.   [*Exeunt* LEAR *and* CORDELIA, *guarded.*
  Edm. Come hither, captain; hark.
Take thou this note [*giving a paper*]; go, follow
    them to prison.
One step I have advanc'd thee; if thou dost
As this instructs thee, thou dost make thy way
To noble fortunes. Know thou this, that men   30
Are as the time is: to be tender-minded
Does not become a sword. Thy great employment
Will not bear question: either say, thou'lt do't,
Or thrive by other means.
  Capt.   I'll do't, my lord.
  Edm. About it; and write happy, when thou hast
    done.
Mark,—I say, instantly; and carry it so,
As I have set it down.
  Capt. I cannot draw a cart, nor eat dried oats:
If it be man's work, I will do it.   [*Exit.*

Flourish. Enter ALBANY, GONERIL, REGAN, *Officers,
and Attendants.*

  Alb. Sir, you have show'd to-day your valiant
    strain,   40
And fortune led you well. You have the captives
Who were the opposites of this day's strife:
We do require them of you, so to use them,
As we shall find their merits and our safety
May equally determine.
  Edm.   Sir, I thought it fit
To send the old and miserable king
To some retention, and appointed guard;
Whose age has charms in it, whose title more,
To pluck the common bosom on his side,
And turn our impress'd lances in our eyes,   50
Which do command them. With him I sent the
    queen;
My reason all the same; and they are ready
To-morrow, or at further space, to appear
Where you shall hold your session. At this time
We sweat and bleed: the friend hath lost his friend;
And the best quarrels, in the heat, are curs'd
By those that feel their sharpness.—
The question of Cordelia and her father
Requires a fitter place.
  Alb.   Sir, by your patience,
I hold you but a subject of this war,   60
Not as a brother.
  Reg.   That's as we list to grace him:

Methinks, our pleasure might have been demanded,
Ere you had spoke so far. He led our powers,
Bore the commission of my place and person ;
The which immediacy may well stand up,
And call itself your brother.
  Gon.   Not so hot :
In his own grace he doth exalt himself,
More than in your addition.
  Reg.   In my rights,
By me invested, he compeers the best.
  Alb. That were the most, if he should husband you.
  Reg. Jesters do oft prove prophets.
  Gon.   Holla, holla ! 71
That eye that told you so look'd but a-squint.
  Reg. Lady, I am not well ; else I should answer
From a full-flowing stomach.—General,
Take thou my soldiers, prisoners, patrimony :
Dispose of them, of me ; the walls are thine.
Witness the world, that I create thee here
My lord and master.
  Gon.   Mean you to enjoy him ?
  Alb. The let-alone lies not in your good will.
  Edm. Nor in thine, lord.
  Alb.   Half-blooded fellow, yes.
  Reg. [*To* EDMUND.] Let the drum strike, and prove
      my title thine. 81
  Alb. Stay yet ; hear reason.—Edmund, I arrest thee
On capital treason ; and, in thy arrest,
This gilded serpent [*pointing to* GONERIL].—For your
    claim, fair sister,
I bar it in the interest of my wife ;
'T is she is sub-contracted to this lord,
And I, her husband, contradict your bans.
If you will marry, make your loves to me,
My lady is bespoke.
  Gon.   An interlude !
  Alb. Thou art arm'd, Gloster : — let the trumpet
    sound : 90
If none appear to prove upon thy person
Thy heinous, manifest, and many treasons,
There is my pledge [*throwing down a glove*] ; I 'll
    make it on thy heart,
Ere I taste bread, thou art in nothing less
Than I have here proclaim'd thee.
  Reg.   Sick ! O, sick !
  Gon. [*Aside.*] If not, I 'll ne'er trust medicine.
  Edm. There 's my exchange [*throwing down a
    glove*] : what in the world he is
That names me traitor, villain-like he lies.
Call by thy trumpet : he that dares approach,
On him, on you,—who not?—I will maintain 100
My truth and honour firmly.
  Alb. A herald, ho !
  Edm.   A herald, ho ! a herald !
  Alb. Trust to thy single virtue ; for thy soldiers,
All levied in my name, have in my name
Took their discharge.
  Reg.   My sickness grows upon me.
  Alb. She is not well ; convey her to my tent.
                [*Exit* REGAN, *led.*
         Enter a Herald.
Come hither, herald.—Let the trumpet sound,
And read out this. 108
  Capt. Sound, trumpet !   [*A trumpet sounds.*
         Herald reads.
  " If any man of quality, or degree, within the lists
of the army, will maintain upon Edmund, supposed
Earl of Gloster, that he is a manifold traitor, let him
appear by the third sound of the trumpet. He is bold
in his defence."
  Edm. Sound !   [1 *trumpet.*
  Her. Again !   [2 *trumpet.*
  Her. Again !   [3 *trumpet.*
          [*Trumpet answers within.*
  Enter EDGAR, *armed, preceded by a trumpet.*
  Alb. Ask him his purposes, why he appears
Upon this call o' the trumpet.
  Her.   What are you ?
Your name? your quality ? and why you answer 120
This present summons?

  Edg.   Know, my name is lost ;
By treason's tooth bare-gnawn, and canker-bit :
Yet am I noble, as the adversary
I come to cope.
  Alb.   Which is that adversary?
  Edg. What 's he, that speaks for Edmund Earl of
    Gloster ?
  Edm. Himself : what say'st thou to him ?
  Edg.   Draw thy sword,
That, if my speech offend a noble heart,
Thy arm may do thee justice ; here is mine :
Behold, it is the privilege of mine honours,
My oath, and my profession : I protest, 130
Maugre thy strength, youth, place, and eminence,

Alb. "No tearing, lady ; I perceive you know it."

Despite thy victor sword, and fire-new fortune,
Thy valour, and thy heart, thou art a traitor :
False to thy gods, thy brother, and thy father ;
Conspirant 'gainst this high illustrious prince ;
And, from the extremest upward of thy head,
To the descent and dust below thy foot,
A most toad-spotted traitor. Say thou, " No,"
This sword, this arm, and my best spirits, are bent
To prove upon thy heart, whereto I speak, 140
Thou liest.
  Edm.   In wisdom, I should ask thy name ;
But, since thy outside looks so fair and warlike,
And that thy tongue some say of breeding breathes,
What safe and nicely I might well delay
By rule of knighthood, I disdain and spurn.
Back do I toss these treasons to thy head ;
With the hell-hated lie o'erwhelm thy heart ;
Which, for they yet glance by, and scarcely bruise,
This sword of mine shall give them instant way,
Where they shall rest for ever.—Trumpets, speak. 150
        [*Alarums. They fight.* EDMUND *falls.*
  Alb. Save him ! save him !
  Gon.   This is practice, Gloster :
By the law of arms, thou wast not bound to answer :
An unknown opposite ; thou art not vanquish'd,
But cozen'd and beguil'd.
  Alb.   Shut your mouth, dame ;
Or with this paper shall I stop it?—Hold, sir ;
Thou worse than any name, read thine own evil :—
No tearing, lady ; I perceive, you know it.
        [*Gives the letter to* EDMUND.
  Gon. Say, if I do, the laws are mine, not thine :
Who can arraign me for 't ?
  Alb. Most monstrous ! know'st thou this paper ? 160

Gon. Ask me not what I know.   [*Exit.*
Alb. Go after her: she's desperate; govern her.
                                   [*Exit an Officer.*
Edm. What you have charg'd me with, that have I
        done,
And more, much more; the time will bring it out:
'T is past, and so am I. But what art thou,
That hast this fortune on me? If thou art noble,
I do forgive thee.
Edg.   Let's exchange charity.
I am no less in blood than thou art, Edmund;
If more, the more thou hast wrong'd me.
My name is Edgar, and thy father's son.   170
The gods are just, and of our pleasant vices
Make instruments to plague us:
The dark and vicious place where thee he got,
Cost him his eyes.
Edm.   Thou hast spoken right, 't is true.
The wheel is come full circle: I am here.
Alb. Methought, thy very gait did prophesy
A royal nobleness. I must embrace thee:
Let sorrow split my heart, if ever I
Did hate thee, or thy father.
Edg.   Worthy prince, I know 't.
Alb. Where have you hid yourself?   180
How have you known the miseries of your father?
Edg. By nursing them, my lord.—List a brief
        tale;
And when 't is told, O, that my heart would burst!—
The bloody proclamation to escape,
That follow'd me so near, (O, our lives' sweetness!
That we the pain of death would hourly die,
Rather than die at once!) taught me to shift
Into a madman's rags, to assume a semblance
That very dogs disdain'd: and in this habit
Met I my father with his bleeding rings,   190
Their precious stones new lost; became his guide,
Led him, begg'd for him, sav'd him from despair;
Never (O fault!) reveal'd myself unto him,
Until some half-hour past, when I was arm'd;
Not sure, though hoping, of this good success,
I ask'd his blessing, and from first to last
Told him my pilgrimage: but his flaw'd heart,—
Alack! too weak the conflict to support!—
'Twixt two extremes of passion, joy and grief,
Burst smilingly.
Edm.   This speech of yours hath mov'd me,
And shall, perchance, do good; but speak you on: 201
You look as you had something more to say.
Alb. If there be more, more woful, hold it in;
For I am almost ready to dissolve,
Hearing of this.
Edg.   This would have seem'd a period
To such as love not sorrow; but another,
To amplify too-much, would make much more,
And top extremity.
Whilst I was big in clamour, came there a man,
Who, having seen me in my worst estate,   210
Shunn'd my abhorr'd society; but then, finding
Who 't was that so endur'd, with his strong arms
He fasten'd on my neck, and bellow'd out
As he 'd burst heaven; threw him on my father;
Told the most piteous tale of Lear and him,
That ever ear receiv'd; which in recounting,
His grief grew puissant, and the strings of life
Began to crack: twice then the trumpets sounded,
And there I left him tranc'd.
Alb.   But who was this?
Edg. Kent, sir, the banish'd Kent; who in disguise
Follow'd his enemy king, and did him service   221
Improper for a slave.

Enter a Gentleman, with a bloody knife.

Gent. Help, help! O, help!
Edg.   What kind of help?
Alb.   Speak, man.
Edg. What means that bloody knife?
Gent.   'T is hot, it smokes;
It came even from the heart of—O! she's dead.
Alb. Who dead? speak, man.
Gent. Your lady, sir, your lady: and her sister
By her is poison'd; she confesses it.

Edm. I was contracted to them both: all three
Now marry in an instant.
Edg.   Here comes Kent.   230
Alb. Produce the bodies, be they alive or dead:—
This judgment of the heavens, that makes us tremble,
Touches us not with pity.   [*Exit Gentleman.*

Enter Kent.

                    O, is this he?
The time will not allow the compliment,
Which very manners urges.
Kent.   I am come
To bid my king and master aye good night;
Is he not here?
Alb.   Great thing of us forgot!—
Speak, Edmund, where's the king? and where's Cor-
        delia?—
Seest thou this object, Kent?
[*The bodies of* GONERIL *and* REGAN *are brought in.*
Kent. Alack! why thus?
Edm.   Yet Edmund was belov'd:
The one the other poison'd for my sake,   241
And after slew herself.
Alb. Even so.—Cover their faces.
Edm. I pant for life:—some good I mean to do,
Despite of mine own nature. Quickly send—
Be brief in it—to the castle; for my writ
Is on the life of Lear, and on Cordelia.—
Nay, send in time.
Alb.   Run, run! O, run!
Edg. To who, my lord?—Who has the office? send
Thy token of reprieve.   250
Edm.   Well thought on: take my sword,
Give it the captain.
Alb.   Haste thee, for thy life.   [*Exit* EDGAR.
Edm. He hath commission from thy wife and me
To hang Cordelia in the prison, and
To lay the blame upon her own despair,
That she fordid herself.
Alb. The gods defend her!—Bear him hence awhile.
                              [EDMUND *is borne off.*

Re-enter LEAR, *with* CORDELIA *dead in his arms;*
        EDGAR, *Officer, and others.*

Lear. Howl, howl, howl, howl!—O! you are men of
        stones:
Had I your tongues and eyes, I'd use them so
That heaven's vault should crack.—She's gone for
        ever.—   260
I know when one is dead, and when one lives;
She's dead as earth.—Lend me a looking-glass;
If that her breath will mist or stain the stone,
Why, then she lives.
Kent.   Is this the promis'd end?
Edg. Or image of that horror?
Alb.   Fall, and cease?
Lear. This feather stirs; she lives! if it be so,
It is a chance which does redeem all sorrows
That ever I have felt.
Kent.   O my good master! [*Kneeling.*
Lear. Pr'ythee, away.
Edg.   'T is noble Kent, your friend.
Lear. A plague upon you, murderers, traitors all!
I might have sav'd her; now, she's gone for ever!—
Cordelia, Cordelia! stay a little. Ha!   272
What is 't thou say'st?—Her voice was ever soft,
Gentle, and low,—an excellent thing in woman.—
I kill'd the slave that was a-hanging thee.
Off. 'T is true, my lords, he did.
Lear.   Did I not, fellow?
I have seen the day, with my good biting falchion
I would have made them skip: I am old now,
And these same crosses spoil me.—Who are you?
Mine eyes are not o' the best:—I 'll tell you straight. 280
Kent. If fortune brag of two she lov'd and hated,
One of them we behold.
Lear. This is a dull sight.—Are you not Kent?
Kent.   The same;
Your servant Kent. Where is your servant Caius?
Lear. He's a good fellow, I can tell you that;
He 'll strike, and quickly too.—He's dead and rotten.
Kent. No, my good lord; I am the very man;—

Lear. I'll see that straight.
  Kent. That from your first of difference and decay
Have follow'd your sad steps—
  Lear.   You are welcome hither.

Enter an Officer.

Off. Edmund is dead, my lord.
  Alb.   That's but a trifle here.—

Lear. "Howl, howl, howl, howl!—O! you are men of stones:
Had I your tongues and eyes, I'd use them so
That heaven's vault should crack.—She's gone for ever."

Kent. Nor no man else.—All's cheerless, dark, and
          deadly: 291
Your eldest daughters have fordone themselves,
And desperately are dead.
  Lear.   Ay, so I think.
  Alb. He knows not what he says, and vain is it,
That we present us to him.
  Edg.   Very bootless.

You lords, and noble friends, know our intent.
What comfort to this great decay may come,
Shall be applied: for us, we will resign,
During the life of this old majesty,   300
To him our absolute power.—[*To* EDGAR *and* KENT.]
          You, to your rights,
With boot, and such addition, as your honours
Have more than merited.—All friends shall taste

The wages of their virtue, and all foes
The cup of their deservings.—O! see, see!
 Lear. And my poor fool is hang'd! No, no, no
  life!
Why should a dog, a horse, a rat, have life,
And thou no breath at all? Thou'lt come no
  more,
Never, never, never, never, never!—
Pray you, undo this button: thank you, sir.— 310
Do you see this? Look on her,—look,—her lips,—
Look there, look there!—   [*Dies.*
 Edg.   He faints!—My lord, my lord!—
 Kent. Break, heart; I pr'ythee, break!
 Edg.   Look up, my lord.
 Kent. Vex not his ghost: O, let him pass! he hates
  him,

That would upon the rack of this tough world
Stretch him out longer.
 Edg.   He is gone, indeed.
 Kent. The wonder is, he hath endur'd so long:
He but usurp'd his life.
 Alb. Bear them from hence.—Our present business
Is general woe.—[*To* KENT *and* EDGAR.] Friends of
  my soul, you twain   320
Rule in this realm, and the gor'd state sustain.
 Kent. I have a journey, sir, shortly to go:
My master calls me; I must not say, no.
 Edg. The weight of this sad time we must obey;
Speak what we feel, not what we ought to say.
The oldest hath borne most: we, that are young,
Shall never see so much, nor live so long.
      [*Exeunt, with a dead march.*

OTHELLO, THE MOOR OF VENICE.

DRAMATIS PERSONÆ.

DUKE OF VENICE.
BRABANTIO, *a Senator.*
Other Senators.
GRATIANO, *Brother to Brabantio.*
LODOVICO, *Kinsman to Brabantio.*
OTHELLO, *a noble Moor in the service of the Venetian state.*
CASSIO, *his Lieutenant.*
IAGO, *his Ancient.*
RODERIGO, *a Venetian Gentleman.*

MONTANO, *Governor of Cyprus.*
Clown, Servant to Othello.

DESDEMONA, *Daughter to Brabantio, and Wife to Othello.*
EMILIA, *Wife to Iago.*
BIANCA, *Mistress to Cassio.*

Sailor, Messengers, Herald, Officers, Gentlemen, Musicians, and Attendants.

SCENE—For the First Act, in VENICE ; during the rest of the Play, at a Sea-port in CYPRUS.

ACT I.

SCENE I.—Venice. A Street.

Enter RODERIGO *and* IAGO.

Roderigo.
TUSH ! never tell me ; I take it much un-
    kindly,
That thou, Iago, who hast had my purse,
As if the strings were thine, shouldst
    know of this.
    Iago. 'Sblood, but you will not hear me :
If ever I did dream of such a matter,
Abhor me.
    Rod. Thou toldst me, thou didst hold
      him in thy hate.
    Iago. Despise me, if I do not. Three
      great ones of the city,
In personal suit to make me his lieutenant,
Off-capp'd to him ; and, by the faith of man,   10
I know my price : I am worth no worse a place ;
But he, as loving his own pride and purposes,
Evades them, with a bombast circumstance,
Horribly stuff'd with epithets of war ;
And, in conclusion,
Nonsuits my mediators ; for, "Certes," says he,
"I have already chose my officer."
And what was he ?
Forsooth, a great arithmetician,
One Michael Cassio, a Florentine,   20
A fellow almost damn'd in a fair wife ;
That never set a squadron in the field,
Nor the division of a battle knows
More than a spinster ; unless the bookish theoric,
Wherein the tongued consuls can propose
As masterly as he : mere prattle, without practice,
Is all his soldiership. But he, sir, had the election :
And I,—of whom his eyes had seen the proof
At Rhodes, at Cyprus, and on other grounds
Christen'd and heathen,—must be be-lee'd and calm'd   31
By debitor-and-creditor ; this counter-caster,
He, in good time, must his lieutenant be,
And I (God bless the mark !) his Moorship's ancient.
    Rod. By Heaven, I rather would have been his
      hangman.
    Iago. But there's no remedy : 't is the curse of ser-
      vice,
Preferment goes by letter, and affection,

And not by old gradation, where each second
Stood heir to the first. Now, sir, be judge yourself,
Whether I in any just term am affin'd
To love the Moor.
    Rod.   I would not follow him then.   40
    Iago. O, sir, content you :
I follow him to serve my turn upon him :
We cannot all be masters, nor all masters
Cannot be truly follow'd. You shall mark
Many a duteous and knee-crooking knave,
That, doting on his own obsequious bondage,
Wears out his time, much like his master's ass,
For nought but provender ; and when he's old,
    cashier'd :
Whip me such honest knaves. Others there are,
Who, trimm'd in forms and visages of duty,   50
Keep yet their hearts attending on themselves,
And, throwing but shows of service on their lords,
Do well thrive by them, and, when they have lin'd
    their coats,
Do themselves homage : these fellows have some soul ;
And such a one do I profess myself.
For, sir,
It is as sure as you are Roderigo,
Were I the Moor, I would not be Iago :
In following him, I follow but myself ;
Heaven is my judge, not I for love and duty,   60
But seeming so, for my peculiar end :
For when my outward action doth demonstrate
The native act and figure of my heart
In complement extern, 't is not long after
But I will wear my heart upon my sleeve
For daws to peck at : I am not what I am.
    Rod. What a full fortune does the thick-lips owe,
If he can carry 't thus !
    Iago.   Call up her father :
Rouse him : make after him, poison his delight,
Proclaim him in the streets : incense her kinsmen,   70
And, though he in a fertile climate dwell,
Plague him with flies : though that his joy be joy,
Yet throw such chances of vexation on 't,
As it may lose some colour.
    Rod. Here is her father's house : I 'll call aloud.

Iago. Do; with like timorous accent, and dire yell,
As when, by night and negligence, the fire
Is spied in populous cities.
Rod. What, ho! Brabantio! Signior Brabantio, ho!
Iago. Awake! what, ho! Brabantio! thieves!
   thieves! thieves!   80
Look to your house, your daughter, and your bags!
Thieves! thieves!

Enter BRABANTIO, *above, at a window.*

Bra. What is the reason of this terrible summons?
What is the matter there?
Rod. Signior, is all your family within?
Iago. Are your doors lock'd?
Bra. Why? wherefore ask you this?
Iago. 'Zounds, sir! you are robb'd; for shame, put
   on your gown;
Your heart is burst, you have lost half your soul:
Even now, now, very now, an old black ram
Is tupping your white ewe. Arise, arise!   90
Awake the snorting citizens with the bell,
Or else the devil will make a grandsire of you.
Arise, I say.
Bra. What! have you lost your wits?
Rod. Most reverend signior, do you know my voice?
Bra. Not I: what are you?
Rod. My name is Roderigo.
Bra. The worser welcome:
I have charg'd thee not to haunt about my doors.
In honest plainness thou hast heard me say,
My daughter is not for thee; and now, in madness,
Being full of supper and distempering draughts, 100
Upon malicious knavery dost thou come
To start my quiet.
Rod. Sir, sir, sir,—
Bra. But thou must needs be sure,
My spirit, and my place, have in them power
To make this bitter to thee.
Rod. Patience, good sir.
Bra. What tell'st thou me of robbing? this is
  Venice;
My house is not a grange.
Rod. Most grave Brabantio,
In simple and pure soul I come to you.   108
Iago. 'Zounds, sir! you are one of those that will
not serve God, if the devil bid you. Because we come
to do you service, and you think we are ruffians, you 'll
have your daughter covered with a Barbary horse;
you 'll have your nephews neigh to you; you 'll have
coursers for cousins, and gennets for germans.
Bra. What profane wretch art thou?
Iago. I am one, sir, that comes to tell you, your
daughter and the Moor are now making the beast
with two backs.
Bra. Thou art a villain.
Iago. You are—a senator.
Bra. This thou shalt answer: I know thee, Roderigo.
Rod. Sir, I will answer anything. But I beseech
  you,   121
If 't be your pleasure, and most wise consent,
(As partly, I find, it is,) that your fair daughter,
At this odd-even and dull watch o' the night,
Transported with no worse nor better guard,
But with a knave of common hire, a gondolier,
To the gross clasps of a lascivious Moor,—
If this be known to you, and your allowance,
We then have done you bold and saucy wrongs;
But if you know not this, my manners tell me, 130
We have your wrong rebuke. Do not believe
That, from the sense of all civility,
I thus would play and trifle with your reverence:
Your daughter, if you have not given her leave,
I say again, hath made a gross revolt;
Tying her duty, beauty, wit, and fortunes,
In an extravagant and wheeling stranger,
Of here and everywhere. Straight satisfy yourself:
If she be in her chamber, or your house,
Let loose on me the justice of the state   140
For thus deluding you.
Bra. Strike on the tinder, ho!
Give me a taper!—call up all my people!—
This accident is not unlike my dream;

Belief of it oppresses me already.—
Light, I say! light!   *[Exit from above.*
Iago.   Farewell; for I must leave you:
It seems not meet, nor wholesome to my place,
To be produc'd (as, if I stay, I shall)
Against the Moor: for, I do know, the state
(However this may gall him with some check)   150
Cannot with safety cast him; for he 's embark'd
With such loud reason to the Cyprus wars
(Which even now stands in act), that, for their souls,
Another of his fathom they have none,
To lead their business: in which regard,
Though I do hate him as I do hell-pains,
Yet, for necessity of present life,
I must show out a flag and sign of love,
Which is indeed but sign. That you shall surely find
  him,
Lead to the Sagittary the raised search;
And there will I be with him. So, farewell. *[Exit.*

Enter, below, BRABANTIO *and Servants with torches.*

Bra. It is too true an evil: gone she is;   161
And what 's to come of my despised time,
Is nought but bitterness.—Now, Roderigo,
Where didst thou see her?—O unhappy girl!—
With the Moor, say'st thou?—Who would be a
  father?—
How didst thou know 't was she?—O! she deceives me
Past thought.—What said she to you?—Get more
  tapers!
Raise all my kindred!—Are they married, think you?
Rod. Truly, I think, they are.
Bra. O Heaven!—How got she out?—O, treason of
  the blood!   170
Fathers, from hence trust not your daughters' minds
By what you see them act.—Is there not charms,
By which the property of youth and maidhood
May be abus'd? Have you not read, Roderigo,
Of some such thing?
Rod. Yes, sir; I have, indeed.
Bra. Call up my brother.—O, would you had had
  her!—
Some one way, some another.—Do you know
Where we may apprehend her and the Moor?
Rod. I think, I can discover him, if you please
To get good guard, and go along with me.   180
Bra. Pray you, lead on. At every house I 'll call;
I may command at most.—Get weapons, ho!
And raise some special officers of might.—
On, good Roderigo;—I 'll deserve your pains. [*Exeunt.*

SCENE II.—The Same. Another Street.

Enter OTHELLO, IAGO, *and Attendants, with torches.*

Iago. Though in the trade of war I have slain men,
Yet do I hold it very stuff o' the conscience,
To do no contriv'd murder: I lack iniquity
Sometimes, to do me service. Nine or ten times
I had thought to have yerk'd him here, under the ribs.
Oth. 'T is better as it is.
Iago. Nay, but he prated,
And spoke such scurvy and provoking terms
Against your honour,
That, with the little godliness I have,
I did full hard forbear him. But, I pray you, sir, 10
Are you fast married? Be assur'd of this,
That the magnifico is much beloved;
And hath, in his effect, a voice potential
As double as the duke's: he will divorce you;
Or put upon you what restraint, or grievance,
The law (with all his might to enforce it on)
Will give him cable.
Oth. Let him do his spite:
My services, which I have done the signiory,
Shall out-tongue his complaints. 'T is yet to know,
(Which, when I know that boasting is an honour, 20
I shall promulgate,) I fetch my life and being
From men of royal siege; and my demerits
May speak, unbonneted, to as proud a fortune
As this that I have reach'd: for know, Iago,

But that I love the gentle Desdemona,
I would not my unhoused free condition
Put into circumscription and confine
For the sea's worth. But, look! what lights come
　　　　yond?
　　Iago. Those are the raised father, and his friends:
You were best go in.
　　Oth.　　　　Not I; I must be found:　　30
My parts, my title, and my perfect soul,
Shall manifest me rightly. Is it they?
　　Iago. By Janus, I think no.

　　Enter CASSIO *and certain Officers with torches.*
　　Oth. The servants of the duke, and my lieutenant.

　　Enter BRABANTIO, RODERIGO, *and Officers, with
　　　　torches and weapons.*

　　Oth.　　　　Holla! stand there!
　　Rod. Signior, it is the Moor.
　　Bra.　　　　Down with him, thief!
　　　　　　[*They draw on both sides.*
　　Iago. You, Roderigo! come, sir, I am for you.
　　Oth. Keep up your bright swords, for the dew will
　　　　rust them.—
Good signior, you shall more command with years, 60
Than with your weapons.
　　Bra. O thou foul thief! where hast thou stow'd my
　　　　daughter?—

　　Oth. "Good signior, you shall more command with years,
　　　　　Than with your weapons."

The goodness of the night upon you, friends!
What is the news?
　　Cas.　　　　The duke does greet you, general;
And he requires your haste-post-haste appearance,
Even on the instant.
　　Oth.　　　　What is the matter, think you?
　　Cas. Something from Cyprus, as I may divine.
It is a business of some heat: the galleys　　40
Have sent a dozen sequent messengers
This very night at one another's heels;
And many of the consuls, rais'd and met,
Are at the duke's already. You have been hotly call'd
　　　　for;
When, being not at your lodging to be found,
The senate hath sent about three several quests,
To search you out.
　　Oth.　　　　'T is well I am found by you.
I will but spend a word here in the house,
And go with you.　　　　　　[*Exit.*
　　Cas.　　　　Ancient, what makes he here?
　　Iago. 'Faith, he to-night hath boarded a land-
　　　　carack:　　50
If it prove lawful prize, he 's made for ever.
　　Cas. I do not understand.
　　Iago.　　　　He 's married.
　　Cas.　　　　To who?

　　Re-enter OTHELLO.

　　Iago. Marry, to—Come, captain, will you go?
　　Oth.　　　　Have with you.
　　Cas. Here comes another troop to seek for you.
　　Iago. It is Brabantio.—General, be advis'd:
He comes to bad intent.

Damn'd as thou art, thou hast enchanted her;
For I 'll refer me to all things of sense,
If she in chains of magic were not bound,
Whether a maid so tender, fair, and happy,
So opposite to marriage, that she shunn'd
The wealthy curled darlings of our nation,
Would ever have, to incur a general mock,
Run from her guardage to the sooty bosom　　70
Of such a thing as thou; to fear, not to delight.
Judge me the world, if 't is not gross in sense,
That thou hast practis'd on her with foul charms;
Abus'd her delicate youth with drugs, or minerals,
That weaken motion.—I 'll have 't disputed on;
'T is probable, and palpable to thinking.
I therefore apprehend and do attach thee,
For an abuser of the world, a practiser
Of arts inhibited and out of warrant.—
Lay hold upon him! if he do resist,　　80
Subdue him at his peril.
　　Oth.　　　　Hold your hands,
Both you of my inclining, and the rest:
Were it my cue to fight, I should have known it
Without a prompter.—Where will you that I go
To answer this your charge?
　　Bra.　　　　To prison; till fit time
Of law, and course of direct session,
Call thee to answer.
　　Oth.　　　　What if I do obey?
How may the duke be therewith satisfied,
Whose messengers are here about my side,
Upon some present business of the state,　　90
To bring me to him?
　　Off.　　　　'T is true, most worthy signior:

The duke's in council, and your noble self,
I am sure, is sent for.
　Bra. 　　　　　　How! the duke in council!
In this time of the night!—Bring him away.
Mine's not an idle cause: the duke himself,
Or any of my brothers of the state,
Cannot but feel this wrong as 't were their own;
For if such actions may have passage free,
Bond-slaves and pagans shall our statesmen be.
　　　　　　　　　　　　　　　[Exeunt.

———

Scene III.—The Same.　A Council Chamber.

The Duke, *and Senators, sitting at a table; Officers
attending.*

　Duke. There is no composition in these news,
That gives them credit.
　1 Sen. 　　　Indeed, they are disproportion'd:
My letters say, a hundred and seven galleys.
　Duke. And mine, a hundred and forty.
　2 Sen. 　　　　　　And mine, two hundred:
But though they jump not on a just account,
(As in these cases, where the aim reports,
'Tis oft with difference,) yet do they all confirm
A Turkish fleet, and bearing up to Cyprus.
　Duke. Nay, it is possible enough to judgment.
I do not so secure me in the error, 　　　　　　10
But the main article I do approve
In fearful sense.
　Sailor. [*Within.*] What, ho! what, ho! what, ho!
　Off. A messenger from the galleys.

Enter a Sailor.

　Duke. 　　　　　　Now, what's the business?
　Sail. The Turkish preparation makes for Rhodes:
So was I bid report here to the state,
By Signior Angelo.
　Duke. How say you by this change?
　1 Sen. 　　　　　　This cannot be,
By no assay of reason: 'tis a pageant,
To keep us in false gaze.　When we consider 　　20
The importance of Cyprus to the Turk;
And let ourselves again but understand,
That, as it more concerns the Turk than Rhodes,
So may he with more facile question bear it,
For that it stands not in such warlike brace,
But altogether lacks the abilities
That Rhodes is dress'd in:—if we make thought of
　　　this,
We must not think the Turk is so unskilful,
To leave that latest which concerns him first,
Neglecting an attempt of ease and gain, 　　　　30
To wake and wage a danger profitless.
　Duke. Nay, in all confidence, he's not for Rhodes.
　1 Off. Here is more news.

Enter a Messenger.

　Mess. The Ottomites, reverend and gracious,
Steering with due course toward the isle of Rhodes,
Have there injointed them with an after fleet.
　1 Sen. Ay, so I thought.—How many, as you guess?
　Mess. Of thirty sail; and now do they re-stem
Their backward course, bearing with frank appear-
　　　ance
Their purposes toward Cyprus.—Signior Montano, 40
Your trusty and most valiant servitor,
With his free duty, recommends you thus,
And prays you to believe him.
　Duke. 'Tis certain then for Cyprus.—
Marcus Luccicos, is not he in town?
　1 Sen. He's now in Florence.
　Duke. Write from us to him: post-post-haste
　　　despatch.
　1 Sen. Here comes Brabantio, and the valiant Moor.

Enter Brabantio, Othello, Iago, Roderigo, *and
Officers.*

　Duke. Valiant Othello, we must straight employ
　　　you
Against the general enemy Ottoman.— 　　　　　50

[*To* Brabantio.] I did not see you; welcome, gentle
　　　signior;
We lack'd your counsel and your help to-night.
　Bra. So did I yours.　Good your grace, pardon me;
Neither my place, nor aught I heard of business,
Hath rais'd me from my bed; nor doth the general
　　　care
Take hold on me, for my particular grief
Is of so flood-gate and o erbearing nature,
That it engluts and swallows other sorrows,
And it is still itself.
　Duke. 　　　　Why, what's the matter?
　Bra. My daughter! O, my daughter!
　Sen. 　　　　　　　　Dead?
　Bra. 　　　　　　　　Ay, to me; 　　61
She is abus'd, stol'n from me, and corrupted
By spells and medicines bought of mountebanks;
For nature so preposterously to err,
Being not deficient, blind, or lame of sense,
Sans witchcraft could not.
　Duke. Whoe'er he be, that in this foul proceeding
Hath thus beguil'd your daughter of herself,
And you of her, the bloody book of law
You shall yourself read in the bitter letter,
After your own sense; yea, though our proper son 70
Stood in your action.
　Bra. 　　　　Humbly I thank your grace.
Here is the man, this Moor; whom now, it seems,
Your special mandate, for the state affairs,
Hath hither brought.
　Duke and Sen. 　　　We are very sorry for it.
　Duke. [*To* Othello.] What, in your own part, can
　　　you say to this?
　Bra. Nothing, but this is so.
　Oth. Most potent, grave, and reverend signiors,
My very noble and approv'd good masters,
That I have ta'en away this old man's daughter,
It is most true; true, I have married her: 　　　80
The very head and front of my offending
Hath this extent, no more.　Rude am I in my speech,
And little bless'd with the soft phrase of peace;
For since these arms of mine had seven years' pith,
Till now, some nine moons wasted, they have us'd
Their dearest action in the tented field;
And little of this great world can I speak,
More than pertains to feats of broil and battle;
And, therefore, little shall I grace my cause,
In speaking for myself.　Yet, by your gracious
　　　patience, 　　　　　　　　　　　　　90
I will a round unvarnish'd tale deliver
Of my whole course of love; what drugs, what
　　　charms,
What conjuration, and what mighty magic,
(For such proceeding I am charg'd withal,)
I won his daughter.
　Bra. 　　　A maiden never bold;
Of spirit so still and quiet, that her motion
Blush'd at herself; and she—in spite of nature,
Of years, of country, credit, everything—
To fall in love with what she fear'd to look on!
It is a judgment maim'd, and most imperfect, 　　100
That will confess, perfection so could err
Against all rules of nature; and must be driven
To find out practices of cunning hell,
Why this should be.　I, therefore, vouch again,
That with some mixtures powerful o'er the blood,
Or with some dram conjur'd to this effect,
He wrought upon her.
　Duke. 　　　To vouch this, is no proof:
Without more wider and more overt test,
Than these thin habits, and poor likelihoods
Of modern seeming, do prefer against him. 　　110
　1 Sen. But, Othello, speak:
Did you by indirect and forced courses
Subdue and poison this young maid's affections;
Or came it by request, and such fair question
As soul to soul affordeth?
　Oth. 　　　　I do beseech you,
Send for the lady to the Sagittary,
And let her speak of me before her father:
If you do find me foul in her report,
The trust, the office, I do hold of you,

Not only take away, but let your sentence   120
Even fall upon my life.
   Duke.   Fetch Desdemona hither.
   Oth. Ancient, conduct them; you best know the
place.—   [*Exeunt* IAGO *and Attendants.*
And, till she come, as truly as to Heaven
I do confess the vices of my blood,
So justly to your grave ears I 'll present
How I did thrive in this fair lady's love,
And she in mine.
   Duke. Say it, Othello.
   Oth. Her father lov'd me; oft invited me;
Still question'd me the story of my life,   130
From year to year; the battles, sieges, fortunes,
That I have pass'd.
I ran it through, even from my boyish days,
To the very moment that he bade me tell it:
Wherein I spake of most disastrous chances,
Of moving accidents by flood and field;
Of hair-breadth scapes i' the imminent-deadly breach;
Of being taken by the insolent foe,
And sold to slavery; of my redemption thence,
And portance in my traveller's history;   140
Wherein of antres vast, and deserts idle,
Rough quarries, rocks, and hills whose heads touch
    heaven,
It was my hint to speak,—such was the process;—
And of the Cannibals that each other eat,
The Anthropophagi, and men whose heads
Do grow beneath their shoulders. This to hear,
Would Desdemona seriously incline:
But still the house-affairs would draw her hence;
Which ever as she could with haste despatch,
She 'd come again, and with a greedy ear   150
Devour up my discourse. Which I observing,
Took once a pliant hour; and found good means
To draw from her a prayer of earnest heart,
That I would all my pilgrimage dilate,
Whereof by parcels she had something heard,
But not intentively: I did consent;
And often did beguile her of her tears,
When I did speak of some distressful stroke,
That my youth suffer'd. My story being done,
She gave me for my pains a world of sighs: 160
She swore,—in faith, 't was strange, 't was passing
    strange;
'T was pitiful, 't was wondrous pitiful:
She wish'd she had not heard it; yet she wish'd
That Heaven had made her such a man: she thank'd
    me;
And bade me, if I had a friend that lov'd her,
I should but teach him how to tell my story,
And that would woo her. Upon this hint I spake
She lov'd me for the dangers I had pass'd,
And I lov'd her, that she did pity them.
This only is the witchcraft I have us'd: 170
Here comes the lady; let her witness it.

     Enter DESDEMONA, IAGO, *and Attendants.*

   Duke. I think, this tale would win my daughter too.
Good Brabantio,
Take up this mangled matter at the best:
Men do their broken weapons rather use,
Than their bare hands.
   Bra.   I pray you, hear her speak:
If she confess that she was half the wooer,
Destruction on my head, if my bad blame
Light on the man!—Come hither, gentle mistress;
Do you perceive in all this noble company,   180
Where most you owe obedience?
   Des.   My noble father,
I do perceive here a divided duty:
To you I am bound for life and education;
My life and education, both do learn me
How to respect you; you are the lord of duty;
I am hitherto your daughter: but here 's my husband;
And so much duty as my mother show'd
To you, preferring you before her father,
So much I challenge that I may profess
Due to the Moor, my lord.
   Bra.   God be with you!—I have done.—
Please it your grace, on to the state affairs: 191

I had rather to adopt a child than get it.—
Come hither, Moor:
I here do give thee that with all my heart,
Which, but thou hast already, with all my heart
I would keep from thee.—For your sake, jewel,
I am glad at soul I have no other child;
For thy escape would teach me tyranny,
To hang clogs on them.—I have done, my lord.
   Duke. Let me speak like yourself, and lay a sen-
    tence,   200
Which, as a grise, or step, may help these lovers
Into your favour.
When remedies are past, the griefs are ended
By seeing the worst, which late on hopes depended.
To mourn a mischief that is past and gone
Is the next way to draw new mischief on.
What cannot be preserv'd when fortune takes,
Patience her injury a mockery makes.
The robb'd, that smiles, steals something from the
    thief;
He robs himself, that spends a bootless grief.   210
   Bra. So let the Turk of Cyprus us beguile:
We lose it not, so long as we can smile.
He bears the sentence well, that nothing bears
But the free comfort which from thence he hears;
But he bears both the sentence and the sorrow,
That, to pay grief, must of poor patience borrow.
These sentences, to sugar, or to gall,
Being strong on both sides, are equivocal:
But words are words; I never yet did hear,   219
That the bruis'd heart was pierced through the ear.
I humbly beseech you, proceed to the affairs of state.
   Duke. The Turk with a most mighty preparation
makes for Cyprus.—Othello, the fortitude of the place
is best known to you; and though we have there a
substitute of most allowed sufficiency, yet opinion, a
sovereign mistress of effects, throws a more safer
voice on you: you must, therefore, be content to
slubber the gloss of your new fortunes with this more
stubborn and boisterous expedition.
   Oth. The tyrant custom, most grave senators,   230
Hath made the flinty and steel couch of war
My thrice-driven bed of down: I do agnise
A natural and prompt alacrity,
I find in hardness; and do undertake
These present wars against the Ottomites.
Most humbly, therefore, bending to your state,
I crave fit disposition for my wife;
Due reference of place, and exhibition;   ✎
With such accommodation, and besort,
As levels with her breeding.   240
   Duke. Why; at her father's.
   Bra.   I 'll not have it so.
   Oth. Nor I.
   Des.   Nor I; I would not there reside,
To put my father in impatient thoughts,
By being in his eye. Most gracious duke,
To my unfolding lend your prosperous ear;
And let me find a charter in your voice,
To assist my simpleness.
   Duke. What would you, Desdemona?
   Des. That I did love the Moor to live with him,   250
My downright violence and storm of fortunes
May trumpet to the world: my heart's subdued
Even to the very quality of my lord:
I saw Othello's visage in his mind;
And to his honours, and his valiant parts,
Did I my soul and fortunes consecrate.
So that, dear lords, if I be left behind,
A moth of peace, and he go to the war,
The rites for why I love him are bereft me,
And I a heavy interim shall support
By his dear absence. Let me go with him.   260
   Oth. Let her have your voice.
Vouch with me, Heaven, I therefore beg it not,
To please the palate of my appetite;
Nor to comply with heat, the young affects,
In my defunct and proper satisfaction;
But to be free and bounteous to her mind:
And Heaven defend your good souls, that you think
I will your serious and great business scant,
For she is with me. No, when light-wing'd toys

Of feather'd Cupid seel with wanton dulness   270
My speculative and offic'd instrument,
That my disports corrupt and taint my business,
Let housewives make a skillet of my helm,
And all indign and base adversities
Make head against my estimation.
   Duke. Be it as you shall privately determine,
Either for her stay, or going. The affair cries haste,
And speed must answer it.
   1 *Sen.* You must away to-night.
   Oth.   With all my heart.
   Duke. At nine i' the morning here we'll meet
again.   280
Othello, leave some officer behind,
And he shall our commission bring to you;
With such things else of quality and respect,
As doth import you.
   Oth.   So please your grace, my ancient;
A man he is of honesty, and trust:
To his conveyance I assign my wife,
With what else needful your good grace shall think
To be sent after me.
   Duke.   Let it be so.—
Good night to every one.—[*To* Brabantio.] And, noble
signior,
If virtue no delighted beauty lack,   290
Your son-in-law is far more fair than black.
   1 *Sen.* Adieu, brave Moor! use Desdemona well.
   Bra. Look to her, Moor, if thou hast eyes to see:
She has deceiv'd her father, and may thee.
           [*Exeunt* Duke, *Senators, Officers, &c.*
   Oth. My life upon her faith!—Honest Iago,
My Desdemona must I leave to thee:
I pr'ythee, let thy wife attend on her;
And bring them after in the best advantage.
Come, Desdemona; I have but an hour
Of love, of worldly matters and direction,   300
To spend with thee: we must obey the time.
          [*Exeunt* Othello *and* Desdemona.
   Rod. Iago!
   Iago. What say'st thou, noble heart?
   Rod. What will I do, think'st thou?
   Iago. Why, go to bed, and sleep.
   Rod. I will incontinently drown myself.
   Iago. Well, if thou dost, I shall never love thee after
it. Why, thou silly gentleman!
   Rod. It is silliness to live, when to live is a torment;
and then have we a prescription to die, when death is
our physician.   311
   Iago. O, villainous! I have looked upon the world
for four times seven years, and since I could distinguish betwixt a benefit and an injury, I never found
a man that knew how to love himself. Ere I would
say, I would drown myself for the love of a Guinea-
hen, I would change my humanity with a baboon.
   Rod. What should I do? I confess, it is my shame
to be so fond; but it is not in my virtue to amend it.
   Iago. Virtue? a fig! 'tis in ourselves that we are
thus, or thus. Our bodies are our gardens, to the
which our wills are gardeners: so that if we will
plant nettles, or sow lettuce; set hyssop, and weed up
thyme; supply it with one gender of herbs, or distract
it with many; either to have it steril with idleness, or
manured with industry; why, the power and corrigible authority of this lies in our wills. If the balance
of our lives had not one scale of reason to poise
another of sensuality, the blood and baseness of our
natures would conduct us to most preposterous conclusions: but we have reason to cool our raging
motions, our carnal stings, our unbitted lusts; whereof
I take this, that you call love, to be a sect, or scion.
   Rod. It cannot be.   334
   Iago. It is merely a lust of the blood, and a permission of the will. Come, be a man: drown thyself?
drown cats, and blind puppies. I have profess'd me
thy friend, and I confess me knit to thy deserving
with cables of perdurable toughness: I could never
better stead thee than now. Put money in thy purse;
follow these wars; defeat thy favour with an usurped
beard; I say, put money in thy purse. It cannot be,
that Desdemona should long continue her love to the
Moor,—put money in thy purse,—nor he his to her: it

was a violent commencement in her, and thou shalt
see an answerable sequestration;—put but money in
thy purse.—These Moors are changeable in their wills;
—fill thy purse with money:—the food that to him
now is as luscious as locusts, shall be to him shortly as
bitter as coloquintida. She must change for youth:
when she is sated with his body, she will find the
error of her choice.—She must have change, she must:
therefore, put money in thy purse.—If thou wilt needs
damn thyself, do it a more delicate way than drowning. Make all the money thou canst. If sanctimony

Iago. "These Moors are changeable in their wills;—fill thy
purse with money."

and a frail vow, betwixt an erring barbarian and a
super-subtle Venetian, be not too hard for my wits,
and all the tribe of hell, thou shalt enjoy her; therefore, make money. A pox of drowning thyself! it is
clean out of the way: seek thou rather to be hanged
in compassing thy joy, than to be drowned and go
without her.   362
   Rod. Wilt thou be fast to my hopes, if I depend on
the issue?
   Iago. Thou art sure of me.—Go, make money.—I
have told thee often, and I re-tell thee again and again,
I hate the Moor: my cause is hearted; thine hath no
less reason. Let us be conjunctive in our revenge
against him: if thou canst cuckold him, thou dost
thyself a pleasure, me a sport. There are many
events in the womb of time, which will be delivered.
Traverse; go: provide thy money. We will have
more of this to-morrow. Adieu.   373
   Rod. Where shall we meet i' the morning?
   Iago. At my lodging.
   Rod. I'll be with thee betimes.
   Iago. Go to; farewell. Do you hear, Roderigo?
   Rod. What say you?
   Iago. No more of drowning, do you hear?
   Rod. I am changed. I'll sell all my land.   380
   Iago. Go to; farewell! put money enough in your
purse.   [*Exit* Roderigo.
Thus do I ever make my fool my purse;
For I mine own gain'd knowledge should profane,
If I would time expend with such a snipe
But for my sport and profit. I hate the Moor;
And it is thought abroad, that 'twixt my sheets
He has done my office: I know not if 't be true;
Yet I, for mere suspicion in that kind,
Will do as if for surety. He holds me well;   390
The better shall my purpose work on him.
Cassio's a proper man: let me see now;
To get his place, and to plume up my will,
In double knavery.—How, how?—Let's see:—
After some time, to abuse Othello's ear,
That he is too familiar with his wife:

He hath a person, and a smooth dispose,
To be suspected ; fram'd to make women false.
The Moor is of a free and open nature,
That thinks men honest, that but seem to be so,   400
And will as tenderly be led by the nose,
As asses are.—
I have 't ;—it is engender'd :—hell and night
Must bring this monstrous birth to the world's light.
                                                    [*Exit.*

ACT II.

Scene I.—A Sea-port Town in Cyprus. A Platform.

Enter Montano *and two Gentlemen.*

Montano.
WHAT from the cape can you discern at
            sea ?
1 *Gent.* Nothing at all : it is a high-
            wrought flood ;
I cannot, 'twixt the heaven and the main,
            Descry a sail.
    Mon. Methinks, the wind hath spoke
            aloud at land ;
A fuller blast ne'er shook our battle-
            ments ;
If it hath ruffian'd so upon the sea,
What ribs of oak, when mountains melt on them,
Can hold the mortise ? What shall we hear of this ?
2 *Gent.* A segregation of the Turkish fleet :   10
For do but stand upon the foaming shore,
The chidden billow seems to pelt the clouds ;
The wind-shak'd surge, with high and monstrous
            mane,
Seems to cast water on the burning bear,
And quench the guards of the ever-fixed pole :
I never did like molestation view
On the enchafed flood.
    Mon.   If that the Turkish fleet
Be not enshelter'd and embay'd, they are drown'd ;
It is impossible to bear it out.

Enter a third Gentleman.

3 *Gent.* News, lads ! our wars are done.   20
The desperate tempest hath so bang'd the Turks,
That their designment halts : a noble ship of Venice
Hath seen a grievous wrack and sufferance
On most part of their fleet.
    Mon. How ! is this true ?
    3 *Gent.*   The ship is here put in,
A Veronessa ; Michael Cassio,
Lieutenant to the warlike Moor, Othello,
Is come on shore : the Moor himself at sea,
And is in full commission here for Cyprus.
    Mon. I am glad on 't ; 'tis a worthy governor.   30
    3 *Gent.* But this same Cassio, though he speak of
            comfort,
Touching the Turkish loss, yet he looks sadly,
And prays the Moor be safe ; for they were parted
With foul and violent tempest.
    Mon.   'Pray heavens he be ;
For I have serv'd him, and the man commands
Like a full soldier. Let 's to the sea-side, ho !
As well to see the vessel that 's come in,
As to throw out our eyes for brave Othello,
Even till we make the main, and the aerial blue,
An indistinct regard.
    3 *Gent.*   Come, let 's do so ;   40
For every minute is expectancy
Of more arrivance.

Enter Cassio.

    Cas. Thanks, you the valiant of this warlike isle,
That so approve the Moor.—O ! let the heavens
Give him defence against the elements,
For I have lost him on a dangerous sea.
    Mon. Is he well shipp'd ?
    Cas. His bark is stoutly timber'd, and his pilot
Of very expert and approv'd allowance ;
Therefore my hopes, not surfeited to death,   50
Stand in bold cure.
    [*Within.*]   A sail, a sail, a sail !

Enter a Messenger.

    Cas. What noise ?
    Mess. The town is empty ; on the brow o' the sea
Stand ranks of people, and they cry, " A sail ! "
    Cas. My hopes do shape him for the governor.
                                              [*Guns heard.*
    2 *Gent.* They do discharge their shot of courtesy ;
Our friends, at least.
    Cas.   I pray you, sir, go forth,
And give us truth who 'tis that is arriv'd.
    2 *Gent.* I shall.   [*Exit.*
    Mon. But, good lieutenant, is your general wiv'd ?   60
    Cas. Most fortunately : he hath achiev'd a maid
That paragons description and wild fame ;
One that excels the quirks of blazoning pens,
And, in the essential vesture of creation,
Does tire the ingener.

Re-enter second Gentleman.

                      How now ! who has put in ?
    2 *Gent.* 'T is one Iago, ancient to the general.
    Cas. He has had most favourable and happy speed :
Tempests themselves, high seas, and howling winds,
The gutter'd rocks, and congregated sands,
Traitors ensteep'd to enclog the guiltless keel,   70
As having sense of beauty, do omit
Their mortal natures, letting go safely by
The divine Desdemona.
    Mon.   What is she ?
    Cas. She that I spake of, our great captain's captain,
Left in the conduct of the bold Iago ;
Whose footing here anticipates our thoughts
A se'nnight's speed.—Great Jove ! Othello guard,
And swell his sail with thine own powerful breath,
That he may bless this bay with his tall ship,
Make love's quick pants in Desdemona's arms,   80
Give renew'd fire to our extinct spirits,
And bring all Cyprus comfort !—

Enter Desdemona, Emilia, Iago, Roderigo, *and*
                      Attendants.

                      O, behold,
The riches of the ship is come on shore !
Ye men of Cyprus let her have your knees.—
Hail to thee, lady ! and the grace of Heaven,
Before, behind thee, and on every hand,
Enwheel thee round !

Des. I thank you, valiant Cassio.
What tidings can you tell me of my lord?
Cas. He is not yet arriv'd: nor know I aught
But that he's well, and will be shortly here.   90
Des. O! but I fear—How lost you company?

Let it not gall your patience, good Iago,
That I extend my manners: 'tis my breeding
That gives me this bold show of courtesy.   100
[*Kissing her.*
Iago. Sir, would she give you so much of her lips,

Cas. "Hail to thee, lady! and the grace of Heaven,
Before, behind thee, and on every hand,
Enwheel thee round!"

Cas. The great contention of the sea and skies
Parted our fellowship. But, hark! a sail.
[*Within.*] A sail, a sail!   [*Guns heard.*
2 Gent. They give their greeting to the citadel:
This likewise is a friend.
Cas.   See for the news!—
[*Exit Gentleman.*
Good ancient, you are welcome.—[*To* EMILIA.] Welcome, mistress.—

As of her tongue she oft bestows on me,
You'd have enough.
Des.   Alas! she has no speech.
Iago. In faith, too much;
I find it still, when I have list to sleep:
Marry, before your ladyship, I grant,
She puts her tongue a little in her heart,
And chides with thinking.
Emil. You have little cause to say so.

Iago. Come on, come on; you are pictures out of
doors,　　　　110
Bells in your parlours, wild cats in your kitchens,
Saints in your injuries, devils being offended,
Players in your housewifery, and housewives in your
beds.
Des. O, fie upon thee, slanderer!
Iago. Nay, it is true, or else I am a Turk:
You rise to play, and go to bed to work.
Emil. You shall not write my praise.
Iago.　　　　　No, let me not.
Des. What wouldst thou write of me, if thou
shouldst praise me?
Iago. O gentle lady, do not put me to 't;
For I am nothing, if not critical.　　　　120
Des. Come on; assay.—There's one gone to the
harbour?
Iago. Ay, madam.
Des. I am not merry; but I do beguile
The thing I am, by seeming otherwise.—
Come, how wouldst thou praise me?
Iago. I am about it; but, indeed, my invention
Comes from my pate, as birdlime does from frize;
It plucks out brains and all: but my Muse labours,
And thus she is deliver'd.
If she be fair and wise,—fairness, and wit,　　　　130
The one's for use, the other useth it.
Des. Well prais'd! How, if she be black and witty?
Iago. If she be black, and thereto have a wit,
She'll find a white that shall her blackness fit.
Des. Worse and worse.
Emil. How, if fair and foolish?
Iago. She never yet was foolish that was fair;
For even her folly help'd her to an heir.
Des. These are old fond paradoxes, to make fools
laugh i' the ale-house. What miserable praise hast
thou for her that's foul and foolish?　　　　141
Iago. There's none so foul, and foolish thereunto,
But does foul pranks which fair and wise ones do.
Des. O heavy ignorance! thou praisest the worst
best. But what praise couldst thou bestow on a
deserving woman indeed? one, that, in the authority
of her merit, did justly put on the vouch of very
malice itself?
Iago. She that was ever fair, and never proud;
Had tongue at will, and yet was never loud;　　　　150
Never lack'd gold, and yet went never gay;
Fled from her wish, and yet said, "Now I may;"
She that, being anger'd, her revenge being nigh,
Bade her wrong stay, and her displeasure fly;
She that in wisdom never was so frail,
To change the cod's head for the salmon's tail;
She that could think, and ne'er disclose her mind,
See suitors following, and not look behind:
She was a wight,—if ever such wights were,—
Des. To do what?　　　　160
Iago. To suckle fools, and chronicle small beer.
Des. O most lame and impotent conclusion!—Do
not learn of him, Emilia, though he be thy husband.—
How say you, Cassio? is he not a most profane and
liberal counsellor?
Cas. He speaks home, madam: you may relish him
more in the soldier, than in the scholar.　　　　167
Iago. [*Aside.*] He takes her by the palm: ay, well
said, whisper: with as little a web as this will I ensnare
as great a fly as Cassio. Ay, smile upon her, do; I will
gyve thee in thine own courtship. You say true, 'tis
so, indeed. If such tricks as these strip you out of
your lieutenantry, it had been better you had not
kissed your three fingers so oft, which now again you
are most apt to play the sir in. Very good; well
kissed, an excellent courtesy! 'tis so, indeed. Yet
again your fingers to your lips? would, they were
clyster-pipes for your sake!—[*A trumpet heard.*] The
Moor! I know his trumpet.
Cas. 'T is truly so.　　　　180
Des. Let's meet him, and receive him.
Cas. Lo, where he comes!

Enter OTHELLO *and Attendants.*

Oth. O my fair warrior!
Des.　　　　　My dear Othello!

Oth. It gives me wonder great as my content,
To see you here before me. O my soul's joy!
If after every tempest come such calms,
May the winds blow till they have waken'd death;
And let the labouring bark climb hills of seas,
Olympus-high, and duck again as low
As hell's from heaven! If it were now to die,　　　　190
'T were now to be most happy; for, I fear,
My soul hath her content so absolute,
That not another comfort like to this
Succeeds in unknown fate.
Des.　　　　　The heavens forbid,
But that our loves and comforts should increase,
Even as our days do grow!
Oth.　　　　　Amen to that, sweet powers!
I cannot speak enough of this content;
It stops me here; it is too much of joy:
And this, and this, the greatest discords be,
[*Kissing her.*
That e'er our hearts shall make!
Iago. [*Aside.*]　　　　O! you are well tun'd now;　　　　200
But I'll set down the pegs that make this music,
As honest as I am.
Oth.　　　　　Come, let us to the castle.—
News, friends: our wars are done, the Turks are
drown'd.
How does my old acquaintance of this isle?
Honey, you shall be well-desir'd in Cyprus;
I have found great love amongst them. O my sweet,
I prattle out of fashion, and I dote
In mine own comforts.—I pr'ythee, good Iago,
Go to the bay, and disembark my coffers.
Bring thou the master to the citadel;　　　　210
He is a good one, and his worthiness
Does challenge much respect.—Come, Desdemona,
Once more well met at Cyprus.
[*Exeunt* OTHELLO, DESDEMONA, *and Attendants.*
Iago. Do thou meet me presently at the harbour.
—Come hither. If thou be'st valiant,—as they say,
base men being in love have then a nobility in their
natures more than is native to them,—list me. The
lieutenant to-night watches on the court of guard.—
First, I must tell thee this,—Desdemona is directly in
love with him.　　　　220
Rod. With him! why, 't is not possible.
Iago. Lay thy finger thus, and let thy soul be instructed. Mark me with what violence she first loved
the Moor, but for bragging, and telling her fantastical
lies; and will she love him still for prating? let not
thy discreet heart think it. Her eye must be fed; and
what delight shall she have to look on the devil?
When the blood is made dull with the act of sport,
there should be, again to inflame it, and to give
satiety a fresh appetite, loveliness in favour, sympathy
in years, manners, and beauties; all which the Moor
is defective in. Now, for want of these required
conveniences, her delicate tenderness will find itself
abused, begin to heave the gorge, disrelish and abhor
the Moor; very nature will instruct her in it, and
compel her to some second choice. Now, sir, this
granted (as it is a most pregnant and unforced position), who stands so eminent in the degree of this
fortune, as Cassio does? a knave very voluble, no
further conscionable than in putting on the mere form
of civil and humane seeming, for the better compassing of his salt and most hidden-loose affection?
why, none; why, none: a slipper and subtle knave;
a finder-out of occasions; that has an eye can stamp
and counterfeit advantages, though true advantage
never present itself: a devilish knave! Besides, the
knave is handsome, young, and hath all those re-
quisites in him, that folly and green minds look after;
a pestilent complete knave: and the woman hath
found him already.　　　　250
Rod. I cannot believe that in her: she is full of most
blessed condition.
Iago. Blessed fig's end! the wine she drinks is made
of grapes: if she had been blessed, she would never
have loved the Moor: bless'd pudding! Didst thou
not see her paddle with the palm of his hand? didst not
mark that?
Rod. Yes, that I did; but that was but courtesy.

Iago. Lechery, by this hand! an index, and obscure prologue to the history of lust and foul thoughts. They met so near with their lips, that their breaths embraced together. Villainous thoughts, Roderigo! when these mutualities so marshal the way, hard at hand comes the master and main exercise, the incorporate conclusion. Pish!—But, sir, be you ruled by me: I have brought you from Venice. Watch you to-night; for the command, I'll lay't upon you: Cassio knows you not:—I'll not be far from you: do you find some occasion to anger Cassio, either by speaking too loud, or tainting his discipline; or from what other course you please, which the time shall more favourably minister.   272

Rod. Well.

Iago. Sir, he is rash, and very sudden in choler, and, haply, may strike at you: provoke him, that he may; for even out of that will I cause these of Cyprus to mutiny, whose qualification shall come into no true taste again, but by the displanting of Cassio. So shall you have a shorter journey to your desires, by the means I shall then have to prefer them; and the impediment most profitably removed, without the which there were no expectation of our prosperity. 282

Rod. I will do this, if you can bring it to any opportunity.

Iago. I warrant thee. Meet me by-and-by at the citadel: I must fetch his necessaries ashore. Farewell.

Rod. Adieu.   [*Exit.*

Iago. That Cassio loves her, I do well believe it;
That she loves him, 't is apt, and of great credit:
The Moor—howbeit that I endure him not—   290
Is of a constant, loving, noble nature;
And, I dare think, he'll prove to Desdemona
A most dear husband. Now, I do love her too;
Not out of absolute lust, (though, peradventure,
I stand accountant for as great a sin,)
But partly led to diet my revenge,
For that I do suspect the lusty Moor
Hath leap'd into my seat; the thought whereof
Doth like a poisonous mineral gnaw my inwards;
And nothing can, or shall, content my soul,   300
Till I am even'd with him, wife for wife;
Or, failing so, yet that I put the Moor
At least into a jealousy so strong
That judgment cannot cure. Which thing to do,—
If this poor trash of Venice, whom I trash
For his quick hunting, stand the putting-on,—
I'll have our Michael Cassio on the hip;
Abuse him to the Moor in the rank garb;—
For I fear Cassio with my night-cap too;—
Make the Moor thank me, love me, and reward me,
For making him egregiously an ass,   311
And practising upon his peace and quiet,
Even to madness. 'T is here, but yet confus'd:
Knavery's plain face is never seen, till us'd. [*Exit.*

SCENE II.—A Street.

*Enter a Herald, with a proclamation; people
following.*

Her. It is Othello's pleasure, our noble and valiant general, that, upon certain tidings now arrived, importing the mere perdition of the Turkish fleet, every man put himself into triumph; some to dance, some to make bonfires, each man to what sport and revels his addiction leads him; for, besides these beneficial news, it is the celebration of his nuptial. So much was his pleasure should be proclaimed. All offices are open; and there is full liberty of feasting, from this present hour of five, till the bell have told eleven. Heaven bless the isle of Cyprus, and our noble general, Othello!

[*Exeunt.*

SCENE III.—A Hall in the Castle.

*Enter OTHELLO, DESDEMONA, CASSIO, and
Attendants.*

Oth. Good Michael, look you to the guard to-night:

Let's teach ourselves that honourable stop,
Not to out-sport discretion.

Cas.   Iago hath direction what to do;
But, notwithstanding, with my personal eye
Will I look to 't.

Oth.   Iago is most honest.
Michael, good night: to-morrow, with your earliest,
Let me have speech with you.—[*To* DESDEMONA.]
            Come, my dear love:
The purchase made, the fruits are to ensue;
That profit's yet to come 'twixt me and you.—   10
Good night.

[*Exeunt* OTHELLO, DESDEMONA, *and Attendants.*

Enter IAGO.

Cas. Welcome, Iago: we must to the watch.

Iago. Not this hour, lieutenant; 't is not yet ten o'clock. Our general cast us thus early for the love of his Desdemona, who let us not therefore blame: he hath not yet made wanton the night with her, and she is sport for Jove.

Cas. She's a most exquisite lady.

Iago. And, I'll warrant her, full of game.

Cas. Indeed, she is a most fresh and delicate creature.   21

Iago. What an eye she has! methinks it sounds a parley to provocation.

Cas. An inviting eye, and yet methinks right modest.

Iago. And, when she speaks, is it not an alarum to love?

Cas. She is, indeed, perfection.

Iago. Well, happiness to their sheets! Come, lieutenant, I have a stoop of wine, and here without are a brace of Cyprus gallants, that would fain have a measure to the health of black Othello.   32

Cas. Not to-night, good Iago. I have very poor and unhappy brains for drinking: I could well wish courtesy would invent some other custom of entertainment.

Iago. O! they are our friends; but one cup: I'll drink for you.

Cas. I have drunk but one cup to-night, and that was craftily qualified too, and, behold, what innovation it makes here. I am unfortunate in the infirmity, and dare not task my weakness with any more.   42

Iago. What, man! 't is a night of revels: the gallants desire it.

Cas. Where are they?

Iago. Here at the door; I pray you, call them in.

Cas. I'll do 't; but it dislikes me.   [*Exit.*

Iago. If I can fasten but one cup upon him,
With that which he hath drunk to-night already,
He'll be as full of quarrel and offence   50
As my young mistress' dog. Now, my sick fool,
Roderigo,
Whom love has turn'd almost the wrong side out,
To Desdemona hath to-night carous'd
Potations pottle-deep; and he's to watch.
Three lads of Cyprus—noble, swelling spirits,
That hold their honours in a wary distance,
The very elements of this warlike isle—
Have I to-night fluster'd with flowing cups,
And they watch too. Now, 'mongst this flock of
                                            drunkards,
Am I to put our Cassio in some action   60
That may offend the isle.—But here they come.
If consequence do but approve my dream,
My boat sails freely, both with wind and stream.

Re-enter CASSIO, *with him* MONTANO, *and Gentlemen.*

Cas. 'Fore Heaven, they have given me a rouse already.

Mon. Good faith, a little one; not past a pint, as I am a soldier.

Iago. Some wine, ho!

[*Sings.*] *And let me the canakin clink, clink;*
            And let me the canakin clink: 70
      A soldier's a man;
      O, man's life's but a span;
      Why then let a soldier drink.
Some wine, boys!   [*Wine brought in.*

Cas. 'Fore Heaven, an excellent song.

Iago. I learned it in England, where, indeed, they are most potent in potting : your Dane, your German, and your swag-bellied Hollander, — drink, ho ! — are nothing to your English.   79

Cas. Is your Englishman so expert in his drinking ?

Iago. Why, he drinks you, with facility, your Dane dead drunk; he sweats not to overthrow your Almain ; he gives your Hollander a vomit, ere the next pottle can be filled.

Cas. To the health of our general !

Cas. "To the health of our general !"

Mon. I am for it, lieutenant; and I 'll do you justice.

Iago. O sweet England !

> King Stephen was a worthy peer,
>   His breeches cost him but a crown;
> He held them sixpence all too dear,   90
>   With that he call'd the tailor—lown.
> He was a wight of high renown,
>   And thou art but of low degree:
> 'T is pride that pulls the country down,
>   Then take thine auld cloak about thee.

Some wine, ho !

Cas. Why, this is a more exquisite song than the other.

Iago. Will you hear 't again ?   99

Cas. No ; for I hold him to be unworthy of his place, that does those things.—Well, Heaven's above all; and there be souls must be saved, and there be souls must not be saved.

Iago. It is true, good lieutenant.

Cas. For mine own part,—no offence to the general, nor any man of quality,—I hope to be saved.

Iago. And so do I too, lieutenant.   107

Cas. Ay; but, by your leave, not before me : the lieutenant is to be saved before the ancient. Let 's have no more of this ; let 's to our affairs.—God forgive us our sins !—Gentlemen, let 's look to our business. Do not think, gentlemen, I am drunk : this is my ancient;—this is my right hand, and this is my left hand.—I am not drunk now ; I can stand well enough, and speak well enough.

All. Excellent well.

Cas. Why, very well then ; you must not think then, that I am drunk.   [*Exit.*

Mon. To the platform, masters : come, let 's set the watch.   120

Iago. You see this fellow, that is gone before :
He is a soldier, fit to stand by Cæsar
And give direction ; and do but see his vice.
'T is to his virtue a just equinox,
The one as long as the other : 't is pity of him.
I fear, the trust Othello puts him in,

On some odd time of his infirmity,
Will shake this island.

Mon.   But is he often thus?

Iago. 'T is evermore the prologue to his sleep :
He 'll watch the horologe a double set,   130
If drink rock not his cradle.

Mon.   It were well,
The general were put in mind of it.
Perhaps, he sees it not ; or his good nature
Prizes the virtue that appears in Cassio,
And looks not on his evils.   Is not this true ?

Enter RODERIGO.

Iago. [*Aside to him.*] How now, Roderigo?
I pray you, after the lieutenant ; go.
                                    [*Exit* RODERIGO.

Mon. And 't is great pity, that the noble Moor
Should hazard such a place, as his own second,
With one of an ingraft infirmity :
It were an honest action to say   141
So to the Moor.

Iago.   Not I, for this fair island :
I do love Cassio well, and would do much
To cure him of this evil.   But hark !   what noise?
                        [*Cry within : " Help ! help !"*

Re-enter CASSIO, *pursuing* RODERIGO.

Cas. You rogue ! you rascal !

Mon.   What 's the matter, lieutenant ?

Cas. A knave teach me my duty !
I 'll beat the knave into a twiggen bottle.

Rod. Beat me !

Cas.   Dost thou prate, rogue ?
                        [*Striking* RODERIGO.

Mon.   Nay, good lieutenant ;
                        [*Staying him.*
I pray you, sir, hold your hand.

Cas.   Let me go, sir,   149
Or I 'll knock you o'er the mazzard.

Mon.   Come, come ; you 're drunk.

Cas. Drunk !   [*They fight.*

Iago. [*Aside to* RODERIGO.] Away, I say ! go out,
    and cry—a mutiny.   [*Exit* RODERIGO.
Nay ! good lieutenant,—God 's will, gentlemen !—
Help, ho !—Lieutenant,—sir,—Montano,—sir ;—
Help, masters !—Here 's a goodly watch, indeed !
                                    [*Bell rings.*
Who 's that which rings the bell ?—*Diablo,* ho !
The town will rise : God's will ! lieutenant, hold !
You will be sham'd for ever.

Enter OTHELLO *and Attendants.*

Oth.   What is the matter here ?

Mon. I bleed still : I am hurt to the death.—He dies !   160

Oth. Hold, for your lives !

Iago. Hold, ho ! Lieutenant, — sir, — Montano, — gentlemen !—
Have you forgot all sense of place and duty ?
Hold ! the general speaks to you : hold, for shame !

Oth. Why, how now, ho ! from whence ariseth this ?
Are we turn'd Turks, and to ourselves do that,
Which Heaven hath forbid the Ottomites ?
For Christian shame, put by this barbarous brawl :
He that stirs next to carve for his own rage,
Holds his soul light ; he dies upon his motion.
Silence that dreadful bell ! it frights the isle   170
From her propriety.—What is the matter, masters ?—
Honest Iago, that look'st dead with grieving,
Speak, who began this ? on thy love, I charge thee.

Iago. I do not know :—friends all but now, even now,
In quarter, and in terms like bride and groom
Devesting them for bed ; and then, but now,

(As if some planet had unwitted men,)
Swords out, and tilting one at other's breast,
In opposition bloody. I cannot speak
Any beginning to this peevish odds; 180
And would in action glorious I had lost
Those legs, that brought me to a part of it!

Oth. How came it, Michael, you are thus forgot?

Cas. I pray you, pardon me; I cannot speak.

Oth. Worthy Montano, you were wont be civil;
The gravity and stillness of your youth
The world hath noted, and your name is great
In mouths of wisest censure: what's the matter,
That you unlace your reputation thus,
And spend your rich opinion, for the name 190
Of a night-brawler? give me answer to it.

Mon. Worthy Othello, I am hurt to danger:
Your officer, Iago, can inform you—
While I spare speech, which something now offends
me,—
Of all that I do know; nor know I aught
By me that's said or done amiss this night,
Unless self-charity be sometime a vice,
And to defend ourselves it be a sin,
When violence assails us.

Oth.　　　　　Now, by Heaven,
My blood begins my safer guides to rule; 200
And passion, having my best judgment collied,
Assays to lead the way. If I once stir,
Or do but lift this arm, the best of you
Shall sink in my rebuke. Give me to know
How this foul rout began, who set it on;
And he that's approv'd in this offence,
Though he had twinn'd with me, both at a birth,
Shall lose me.—What! in a town of war,
Yet wild, the people's hearts brimful of fear,
To manage private and domestic quarrel, 210
In night, and on the court and guard of safety!
'T is monstrous.—Iago, who began it?

Mon. If partially affin'd, or leagu'd in office,
Thou dost deliver more or less than truth,
Thou art no soldier.

Iago.　　　　Touch me not so near:
I had rather have this tongue cut from my mouth,
Than it should do offence to Michael Cassio;
Yet, I persuade myself, to speak the truth
Shall nothing wrong him.—Thus it is, general. 220
Montano and myself being in speech,
There comes a fellow, crying out for help,
And Cassio following him with determin'd sword
To execute upon him. Sir, this gentleman
Steps in to Cassio, and entreats his pause:
Myself the crying fellow did pursue,
Lest by his clamour (as it so fell out)
The town might fall in fright: he, swift of foot,
Outran my purpose; and I return'd, the rather
For that I heard the clink and fall of swords,
And Cassio high in oath, which till to-night 230
I ne'er might say before. When I came back
(For this was brief), I found them close together,
At blow and thrust, even as again they were
When you yourself did part them.
More of this matter can I not report:—
But men are men; the best sometimes forget:
Though Cassio did some little wrong to him,
As men in rage strike those that wish them best,
Yet surely Cassio, I believe, received
From him that fled some strange indignity, 240
Which patience could not pass.

Oth.　　　　　I know, Iago,
Thy honesty and love doth mince this matter,
Making it light to Cassio.—Cassio, I love thee;
But never more be officer of mine.

Re-enter DESDEMONA, *attended.*

Look, if my gentle love be not rais'd up!—
I'll make thee an example.

Des.　　　　　What's the matter?

Oth. All's well now, sweeting; come away to
bed.
Sir, for your hurts, myself will be your surgeon.—
Lead him off.—　　　　　[MONTANO *is led off.*
Iago, look with care about the town, 250

And silence those whom this vile brawl distracted.—
Come, Desdemona; 't is the soldiers' life,
To have their balmy slumbers wak'd with strife.
　　　　　[*Exeunt all but* IAGO *and* CASSIO.

Iago. What, are you hurt, lieutenant?

Cas. Ay; past all surgery.

Iago. Marry, Heaven forbid!

Cas. Reputation, reputation, reputation! O! I have
lost my reputation. I have lost the immortal part of
myself, and what remains is bestial.—My reputation,
Iago, my reputation! 260

Iago. As I am an honest man, I thought you had
received some bodily wound; there is more sense in
that than in reputation. Reputation is an idle and
most false imposition; oft got without merit, and lost
without deserving: you have lost no reputation at all,
unless you repute yourself such a loser. What, man!
there are ways to recover the general again: you are
but now cast in his mood, a punishment more in
policy than in malice; even so as one would beat his
offenceless dog, to affright an imperious lion. Sue to
him again, and he's yours. 271

Cas. I will rather sue to be despised, than to deceive
so good a commander with so slight, so drunken, and
so indiscreet an officer. Drunk? and speak parrot?
and squabble? swagger? swear? and discourse fustian
with one's own shadow?—O thou invisible spirit of
wine! if thou hast no name to be known by, let us call
thee devil.

Iago. What was he that you followed with your
sword? What had he done to you? 280

Cas. I know not.

Iago. Is't possible?

Cas. I remember a mass of things, but nothing distinctly; a quarrel, but nothing wherefore.—O God!
that men should put an enemy in their mouths, to
steal away their brains! that we should, with joy,
pleasance, revel, and applause, transform ourselves
into beasts!

Iago. Why, but you are now well enough: how
came you thus recovered? 290

Cas. It hath pleased the devil drunkenness, to give
place to the devil wrath: one unperfectness shows me
another, to make me frankly despise myself.

Iago. Come, you are too severe a moraler. As the
time, the place, and the condition of this country
stands, I could heartily wish this had not befallen;
but, since it is as it is, mend it for your own good.

Cas. I will ask him for my place again: he shall tell
me, I am a drunkard. Had I as many mouths as
Hydra, such an answer would stop them all. To be
now a sensible man, by-and-by a fool, and presently a
beast! O, strange!—Every inordinate cup is un-
blessed, and the ingredient is a devil. 303

Iago. Come, come; good wine is a good familiar
creature, if it be well used: exclaim no more against
it. And, good lieutenant, I think you think I love
you.

Cas. I have well approved it, sir.—I drunk!

Iago. You, or any man living, may be drunk at some
time, man. I'll tell you what you shall do. Our
general's wife is now the general:—I may say so in
this respect, for that he hath devoted and given up
himself to the contemplation, mark, and denotement
of her parts and graces:—confess yourself freely to
her; importune her; she'll help to put you in your
place again. She is of so free, so kind, so apt, so
blessed a disposition, that she holds it a vice in her
goodness, not to do more than she is requested. This
broken joint, between you and her husband, entreat
her to splinter; and my fortunes against any lay worth
naming, this crack of your love shall grow stronger
than it was before. 322

Cas. You advise me well.

Iago. I protest, in the sincerity of love, and honest
kindness.

Cas. I think it freely; and, betimes in the morning,
I will beseech the virtuous Desdemona to undertake
for me. I am desperate of my fortunes, if they check
me here.

Iago. You are in the right. Good night, lieutenant;
I must to the watch. 331

Cas. Good night, honest Iago.   [*Exit.*
Iago. And what 's he then, that says I play the
    villain?
When this advice is free, I give, and honest,
Probal to thinking, and, indeed, the course
To win the Moor again? For 't is most easy,
The inclining Desdemona to subdue
In any honest suit: she 's fram'd as fruitful
As the free elements. And then for her
To win the Moor,—were 't to renounce his baptism, 340
All seals and symbols of redeemed sin,—
His soul is so enfetter'd to her love,
That she may make, unmake, do what she list,
Even as her appetite shall play the god
With her weak function. How am I then a villain,
To counsel Cassio to this parallel course,
Directly to his good? Divinity of hell!
When devils will their blackest sins put on,
They do suggest at first with heavenly shows,
As I do now; for whiles this honest fool   350
Plies Desdemona to repair his fortunes,
And she for him pleads strongly to the Moor,
I 'll pour this pestilence into his ear,
That she repeals him for her body's lust;
And, by how much she strives to do him good,
She shall undo her credit with the Moor.
So will I turn her virtue into pitch,
And out of her own goodness make the net   358
That shall enmesh them all.

             Re-enter RODERIGO.

               How now, Roderigo?
Rod. I do follow here in the chase, not like a hound
that hunts, but one that fills up the cry. My money is
almost spent: I have been to-night exceedingly well
cudgelled; and, I think, the issue will be, I shall have so
much experience for my pains; and so, with no money
at all, and a little more wit, return again to Venice.
Iago. How poor are they, that have not patience!
What wound did ever heal, but by degrees?
Thou know'st, we work by wit, and not by witchcraft;
And wit depends on dilatory time.
Does 't not go well? Cassio hath beaten thee,   370
And thou, by that small hurt, hast cashier'd Cassio.
Though other things grow fair against the sun,
Yet fruits that blossom first will first be ripe:
Content thyself awhile.—By the mass, 't is morning;
Pleasure and action make the hours seem short.
Retire thee; go where thou art billeted:
Away, I say; thou shalt know more hereafter:
Nay, get thee gone. [*Exit* RODERIGO.] Two things are
    to be done,—
My wife must move for Cassio to her mistress;
I 'll set her on;   380
Myself, the while, to draw the Moor apart,
And bring him jump when he may Cassio find
Soliciting his wife:—ay, that 's the way:
Dull not device by coldness and delay.   [*Exit.*

ACT III.

SCENE I.—Before the Castle.

Enter CASSIO *and some Musicians.*

          Cassio.
ASTERS, play here; I will content your
    pains:
Something that 's brief; and bid, "Good
    morrow, general."   [*Music.*

        Enter Clown.

    Clo. Why, masters, have your instru-
ments been in Naples, that they speak i' the
nose thus?
    1 *Mus.* How, sir, how?
    Clo. Are these, I pray you, called wind-
instruments?
    1 *Mus.* Ay, marry, are they, sir.
    Clo. O! thereby hangs a tail.   10
    1 *Mus.* Whereby hangs a tale, sir?
    Clo. Marry, sir, by many a wind-instrument that I
know. But, masters, here 's money for you; and the
general so likes your music, that he desires you, for
love's sake, to make no more noise with it.
    1 *Mus.* Well, sir, we will not.
    Clo. If you have any music that may not be heard,
to 't again; but, as they say, to hear music the general
does not greatly care.
    1 *Mus.* We have none such, sir.   20
    Clo. Then put up your pipes in your bag, for I 'll
away. Go; vanish into air, away!
                  [*Exeunt Musicians.*
    Cas. Dost thou hear, mine honest friend?
    Clo. No, I hear not your honest friend; I hear you.
    Cas. Pr'ythee, keep up thy quillets. There 's a poor
piece of gold for thee. If the gentlewoman that

attends the general's wife be stirring, tell her there 's
one Cassio entreats her a little favour of speech:
wilt thou do this?
    Clo. She is stirring, sir: if she will stir hither, I
shall seem to notify unto her.   31
    Cas. Do, good my friend.   [*Exit Clown.*

        Enter IAGO.

In happy time, Iago.
    Iago. You have not been a-bed, then?
    Cas. Why, no; the day had broke
Before we parted. I have made bold, Iago,
To send in to your wife: my suit to her
Is, that she will to virtuous Desdemona
Procure me some access.
    Iago.   I 'll send her to you presently;
And I 'll devise a mean to draw the Moor   40
Out of the way, that your converse and business
May be more free.
    Cas. I humbly thank you for 't. [*Exit* IAGO.] I never
    knew
A Florentine more kind and honest.

        Enter EMILIA.

    Emil. Good morrow, good lieutenant: I am sorry
For your displeasure; but all will sure be well.
The general and his wife are talking of it,
And she speaks for you stoutly: the Moor replies,
That he you hurt is of great fame in Cyprus,
And great affinity, and that in wholesome wisdom 50
He might not but refuse you; but he protests he loves
    you,

And needs no other suitor but his likings,
To take the saf'st occasion by the front,
To bring you in again.
　　Cas.　　　　　　Yet, I beseech you,—
If you think fit, or that it may be done,—
Give me advantage of some brief discourse
With Desdemon alone.
　　Emil.　　　　　　Pray you, come in :

Clo. "And the general so likes your music, that he desires you, for love's sake, to make no more noise with it."

I will bestow you where you shall have time
To speak your bosom freely.
　　Cas.　　　　I am much bound to you. [*Exeunt.*

SCENE II.—A Room in the Castle.

Enter OTHELLO, IAGO, *and Gentlemen.*

Oth. These letters give, Iago, to the pilot,
And by him do my duties to the senate :
That done, I will be walking on the works ;
Repair there to me.
　　Iago.　　　Well, my good lord ; I 'll do 't.
Oth. This fortification, gentlemen,—shall we see 't ?
Gent. We 'll wait upon your lordship.　[*Exeunt.*

SCENE III.—The Garden of the Castle.

Enter DESDEMONA, CASSIO, *and* EMILIA.

Des. Be thou assur'd, good Cassio, I will do
All my abilities in thy behalf.
　　Emil. Good madam, do : I warrant it grieves my
　　　　husband,
As if the cause were his.
　　Des. O ! that 's an honest fellow.—Do not doubt,
　　　　Cassio,
But I will have my lord and you again
As friendly as you were.
　　Cas.　　　　　Bounteous madam,
Whatever shall become of Michael Cassio,
He 's never anything but your true servant.
　　Des. I know 't : I thank you.　You do love my
　　　　lord ;　　　　　　　　　　　　　　　10
You have known him long : and be you well assur'd,
He shall in strangeness stand no further off
Than in a politic distance.

Cas.　　　　　　Ay, but, lady,
That policy may either last so long,
Or feed upon such nice and waterish diet,
Or breed itself so out of circumstance,
That, I being absent, and my place supplied,
My general will forget my love and service.
　　Des. Do not doubt that : before Emilia here,
I give thee warrant of thy place.　Assure thee,　20
If I do vow a friendship, I 'll perform it
To the last article : my lord shall never rest ;
I 'll watch him tame, and talk him out of patience ;
His bed shall seem a school, his board a shrift :
I 'll intermingle everything he does
With Cassio's suit.　Therefore, be merry, Cassio ;
For thy solicitor shall rather die,
Than give thy cause away.

Enter OTHELLO *and* IAGO, *at a distance.*

　　Emil. Madam, here comes my lord.
　　Cas. Madam, I 'll take my leave.　　　　　30
　　Des. Why, stay, and hear me speak.
　　Cas. Madam, not now : I am very ill at ease,
Unfit for mine own purposes.
　　Des. Well, do your discretion.　　[*Exit* CASSIO.
　　Iago. Ha ! I like not that.
　　Oth. What dost thou say ?
　　Iago. Nothing, my lord : or if—I know not what.
　　Oth. Was not that Cassio, parted from my wife ?
　　Iago. Cassio, my lord ? No, sure, I cannot think it,
That he would steal away so guilty-like,　　40
Seeing you coming.
　　Oth.　　　　I do believe 't was he.
　　Des. How now, my lord ?
I have been talking with a suitor here,
A man that languishes in your displeasure.
　　Oth. Who is 't you mean ?
　　Des. Why, your lieutenant Cassio.　Good my lord,
If I have any grace, or power to move you,
His present reconciliation take ;
For, if he be not one that truly loves you,
That errs in ignorance, and not in cunning,　50
I have no judgment in an honest face.
I pr'ythee, call him back.
　　Oth.　　　　　Went he hence now ?
　　Des. Ay, sooth ; so humbled,
That he hath left part of his grief with me,
To suffer with him.　Good love, call him back.
　　Oth. Not now, sweet Desdemon ; some other time.
　　Des. But shall 't be shortly ?
　　Oth.　　　　　The sooner, sweet, for you.
　　Des. Shall 't be to-night at supper ?
　　Oth.　　　　　No, not to-night.
　　Des. To-morrow dinner then ?
　　Oth.　　　　I shall not dine at home ;
I meet the captains at the citadel.　　　　60
　　Des. Why then, to-morrow night ; or Tuesday morn ;
On Tuesday noon, or night ; on Wednesday morn :
I pr'ythee, name the time, but let it not
Exceed three days : in faith, he 's penitent ;
And yet his trespass, in our common reason,
(Save that, they say, the wars must make examples
Out of her best,) is not almost a fault
To incur a private check.　When shall he come ?
Tell me, Othello.　I wonder in my soul,
What you could ask me that I should deny,　70
Or stand so mammering on.　What ! Michael Cassio,
That came a-wooing with you, and so many a time,
When I have spoke of you dispraisingly,
Hath ta'en your part ; to have so much to do
To bring him in !　Trust me, I could do much,—
　　Oth. Pr'ythee, no more : let him come when he
　　　　will ;
I will deny thee nothing.
　　Des.　　　　Why, this is not a boon ;
'T is as I should entreat you wear your gloves,
Or feed on nourishing dishes, or keep you warm,
Or sue to you to do a peculiar profit　　80
To your own person : nay, when I have a suit
Wherein I mean to touch your love indeed,
It shall be full of poise and difficult weight,
And fearful to be granted.
　　Oth.　　　　I will deny thee nothing :

Whereon, I do beseech thee, grant me this,
To leave me but a little to myself.
Des. Shall I deny you? no. Farewell, my lord.
Oth. Farewell, my Desdemona: I 'll come to thee
    straight.
Des. Emilia, come.—Be as your fancies teach you;
Whate'er you be, I am obedient. [*Exit, with* Emilia.
Oth. Excellent wretch! Perdition catch my soul, 91
But I do love thee! and when I love thee not,
Chaos is come again.
Iago.   My noble lord,—
Oth.   What dost thou say, Iago?
Iago. Did Michael Cassio, when you woo'd my lady,
Know of your love?
Oth. He did, from first to last : why dost thou ask?
Iago. But for a satisfaction of my thought;
No further harm.
Oth.   Why of thy thought, Iago?
Iago. I did not think, he had been acquainted with
    her.   100
Oth. O, yes; and went between us very oft.
Iago. Indeed?
Oth. Indeed! ay, indeed :—discern'st thou aught in
    that?
Is he not honest?
Iago.   Honest, my lord?
Oth.   Honest! ay, honest.
Iago. My lord, for aught I know.
Oth. What dost thou think?
Iago.   Think, my lord?
Oth.   Think, my lord!
By Heaven, he echoes me,
As if there were some monster in his thought
Too hideous to be shown.—Thou dost mean something.
I heard thee say even now,—thou lik'dst not that, 110
When Cassio left my wife : what didst not like?
And, when I told thee, he was of my counsel
In my whole course of wooing, thou criedst, "Indeed?"
And didst contract and purse thy brow together,
As if thou then hadst shut up in thy brain
Some horrible conceit. If thou dost love me,
Show me thy thought.
Iago. My lord, you know I love you.
Oth.   I think, thou dost;
And,—for I know thou art full of love and honesty,
And weigh'st thy words before thou giv'st them
    breath,—   120
Therefore, these stops of thine fright me the more :
For such things, in a false disloyal knave,
Are tricks of custom; but in a man that 's just,
They 're close delations, working from the heart,
That passion cannot rule.
Iago.   For Michael Cassio,—
I dare be sworn, I think that he is honest.
Oth. I think so too.
Iago.   Men should be what they seem;
Or, those that be not, would they might seem none!
Oth. Certain, men should be what they seem.
Iago. Why then, I think Cassio 's an honest man. 130
Oth. Nay, yet there 's more in this.
I pray thee, speak to me as to thy thinkings,
As thou dost ruminate; and give thy worst of thoughts
The worst of words.
Iago.   Good my lord, pardon me :
Though I am bound to every act of duty,
I am not bound to that all slaves are free to.
Utter my thoughts? Why, say, they are vile and
    false,—
As where 's that palace, whereinto foul things
Sometimes intrude not? who has a breast so pure,
But some uncleanly apprehensions   140
Keep leets, and law-days, and in sessions sit
With meditations lawful?
Oth. Thou dost conspire against thy friend, Iago,
If thou but think'st him wrong'd, and mak'st his ear
A stranger to thy thoughts.
Iago.   I do beseech you,—
Though I, perchance, am vicious in my guess,
(As, I confess, it is my nature's plague
To spy into abuses, and oft my jealousy
Shapes faults that are not,)—that your wisdom yet,
From one that so imperfectly conceits,   150

Would take no notice; nor build yourself a trouble
Out of his scattering and unsure observance.
It were not for your quiet, nor your good,
Nor for my manhood, honesty, and wisdom,
To let you know my thoughts.
Oth.   What dost thou mean?
Iago. Good name in man and woman, dear my lord,
Is the immediate jewel of their souls :
Who steals my purse, steals trash; 't is something,
    nothing;
'T was mine, 't is his, and has been slave to thousands;
But he that filches from me my good name,   160
Robs me of that which not enriches him,
And makes me poor indeed.
Oth. By Heaven, I 'll know thy thoughts.
Iago. You cannot, if my heart were in your hand;
Nor shall not, whilst 't is in my custody.
Oth. Ha!
Iago.   O! beware, my lord, of jealousy;
It is the green-ey'd monster, which doth mock
The meat it feeds on : that cuckold lives in bliss,
Who, certain of his fate, loves not his wronger;
But, O! what damned minutes tells he o'er,   170
Who dotes, yet doubts; suspects, yet soundly loves!
Oth. O misery!
Iago. Poor, and content, is rich, and rich enough;
But riches, fineless, is as poor as winter,
To him that ever fears he shall be poor.—
Good Heaven, the souls of all my tribe defend
From jealousy!
Oth.   Why? why is this?
Think'st thou, I 'd make a life of jealousy,
To follow still the changes of the moon
With fresh suspicions? No : to be once in doubt, 180
Is once to be resolv'd. Exchange me for a goat,
When I shall turn the business of my soul
To such exsufflicate and blown surmises,
Matching thy inference. 'T is not to make me jealous,
To say—my wife is fair, feeds well, loves company,
Is free of speech, sings, plays, and dances well;
Where virtue is, these are more virtuous :
Nor from mine own weak merits will I draw
The smallest fear, or doubt of her revolt;
For she had eyes, and chose me. No, Iago;   190
I 'll see, before I doubt; when I doubt, prove;
And, on the proof, there is no more but this,—
Away at once with love, or jealousy.
Iago. I am glad of it : for now I shall have reason
To show the love and duty that I bear you
With franker spirit : therefore, as I am bound,
Receive it from me. I speak not yet of proof.
Look to your wife; observe her well with Cassio;
Wear your eye thus, not jealous, nor secure :
I would not have your free and noble nature,   200
Out of self-bounty, be abus'd; look to 't.
I know our country disposition well :
In Venice they do let Heaven see the pranks
They dare not show their husbands; their best con-
    science
Is, not to leave 't undone, but keep 't unknown.
Oth. Dost thou say so?
Iago. She did deceive her father, marrying you;
And, when she seem'd to shake and fear your looks,
She lov'd them most.
Oth.   And so she did.
Iago.   Why, go to, then;
She that so young could give out such a seeming, 210
To seel her father's eyes up, close as oak,—
He thought, 't was witchcraft :—but I am much to
    blame;
I humbly do beseech you of your pardon,
For too much loving you.
Oth.   I am bound to thee for ever.
Iago. I see, this hath a little dash'd your spirits.
Oth. Not a jot, not a jot.
Iago.   Trust me, I fear it has.
I hope, you will consider what is spoke
Comes from my love.—But, I do see you 're mov'd :
I am to pray you, not to strain my speech
To grosser issues, nor to larger reach,   220
Than to suspicion.
Oth. I will not.

Iago.   Should you do so, my lord,
My speech should fall into such vile success
As my thoughts aim not at. Cassio's my worthy
    friend—
My lord, I see you're mov'd.
 Oth.   No, not much mov'd.—
I do not think but Desdemona's honest.
 Iago. Long live she so! and long live you to think so!
 Oth. And yet, how nature erring from itself,—
 Iago. Ay, there's the point:—as,—to be bold with
    you,—
Not to affect many proposed matches,   230
Of her own clime, complexion, and degree,
Whereto, we see, in all things nature tends:
Foh! one may smell, in such, a will most rank,
Foul disproportion, thoughts unnatural.—
But pardon me; I do not in position
Distinctly speak of her, though I may fear,
Her will, recoiling to her better judgment,
May fall to match you with her country forms,
And, happily, repent.
 Oth.   Farewell, farewell.
If more thou dost perceive, let me know more;   240
Set on thy wife to observe. Leave me, Iago.
 Iago. My lord, I take my leave.   [*Going.*
 Oth. Why did I marry?—This honest creature,
    doubtless,
Sees and knows more, much more, than he unfolds.
 Iago. [*Returning.*] My lord, I would I might entreat
    your honour
To scan this thing no further; leave it to time.
Although 't is fit that Cassio have his place,
(For, sure, he fills it up with great ability,)
Yet, if you please to hold him off awhile,
You shall by that perceive him and his means: 250
Note, if your lady strain his entertainment
With any strong or vehement importunity;
Much will be seen in that. In the meantime,
Let me be thought too busy in my fears
(As worthy cause I have to fear I am),
And hold her free, I do beseech your honour.
 Oth. Fear not my government.
 Iago. I once more take my leave.   [*Exit.*
 Oth. This fellow's of exceeding honesty,
And knows all qualities, with a learned spirit,   260
Of human dealings; if I do prove her haggard,
Though that her jesses were my dear heart-strings,
I'd whistle her off, and let her down the wind,
To prey at fortune. Haply, for I am black,
And have not those soft parts of conversation
That chamberers have; or, for I am declin'd
Into the vale of years;—yet that's not much:
She's gone, I am abus'd; and my relief
Must be to loathe her. O curse of marriage!
That we can call these delicate creatures ours,   270
And not their appetites. I had rather be a toad,
And live upon the vapour of a dungeon,
Than keep a corner in the thing I love
For others' uses. Yet, 't is the plague of great ones;
Prerogativ'd are they less than the base;
'T is destiny unshunnable, like death:
Even then this forked plague is fated to us,
When we do quicken. Look, where she comes.
If she be false, O! then Heaven mocks itself.
I'll not believe it.

Re-enter DESDEMONA *and* EMILIA.

 Des.   How now, my dear Othello?   280
Your dinner and the generous islanders,
By you invited, do attend your presence.
 Oth. I am to blame.
 Des.   Why do you speak so faintly?
Are you not well?
 Oth. I have a pain upon my forehead here.
 Des. 'Faith, that's with watching; 't will away
    again:
Let me but bind it hard, within this hour
It will be well.
 Oth.   Your napkin is too little;
Let it alone. Come, I'll go in with you.
 Des. I am very sorry that you are not well.   290
     [*Exeunt* OTHELLO *and* DESDEMONA.

 Emil. I am glad I have found this napkin.
This was her first remembrance from the Moor:
My wayward husband hath a hundred times
Woo'd me to steal it; but she so loves the token,
(For he conjur'd her she should ever keep it,)
That she reserves it evermore about her,
To kiss, and talk to. I'll have the work ta'en out,
And give 't Iago:
What he will do with it, Heaven knows, not I;
I nothing, but to please his fantasy.   300

Re-enter IAGO.

 Iago. How now! what do you here alone?
 Emil. Do not you chide; I have a thing for you.

Emil. "What will you do with 't, that you have been so earnest
To have me filch it?"

 Iago. A thing for me?—it is a common thing—
 Emil. Ha?
 Iago. To have a foolish wife.
 Emil. O! is that all? What will you give me now
For that same handkerchief?
 Iago.   What handkerchief?
 Emil. What handkerchief?
Why, that the Moor first gave to Desdemona;
That which so often you did bid me steal.   310
 Iago. Hast stol'n it from her?
 Emil. No, 'faith: she let it drop by negligence;
And, to the advantage, I, being here, took 't up.
Look, here it is.
 Iago.   A good wench; give it me.
 Emil. What will you do with 't, that you have been
    so earnest
To have me filch it?
 Iago.   Why, what's that to you?
        [*Snatching it.*
 Emil. If it be not for some purpose of import,
Give 't me again: poor lady! she'll run mad,
When she shall lack it.
 Iago. Be not acknown on 't; I have use for it.   320
Go, leave me.   [*Exit* EMILIA.
I will in Cassio's lodging lose this napkin,
And let him find it: trifles, light as air,
Are, to the jealous, confirmations strong
As proofs of holy writ. This may do something.
The Moor already changes with my poison:

Dangerous conceits are in their natures poisons,
Which at the first are scarce found to distaste ;
But, with a little act upon the blood,
Burn like the mines of sulphur.—I did say so :—　　330
Look, where he comes !

Re-enter OTHELLO.

　　　　　　Not poppy, nor mandragora,
Nor all the drowsy syrups of the world,
Shall ever medicine thee to that sweet sleep
Which thou ow'dst yesterday.
Oth.　　　　　Ha ! ha ! false to me ?
Iago. Why, how now, general ? no more of that.
Oth. Avaunt ! be gone ! thou hast set me on the
　　　rack.—
I swear, 't is better to be much abus'd,
Than but to know 't a little.
Iago.　　　　　How now, my lord ?
Oth. I saw it not, thought it not, it harm'd not me :　340
I slept the next night well, fed well, was free and
　　　merry ;
I found not Cassio's kisses on her lips :
He that is robb'd, not wanting what is stolen,
Let him not know 't, and he 's not robb'd at all.
Iago. I am sorry to hear this.
Oth. I had been happy, if the general camp,
Pioners and all, had tasted her sweet body,
So I had nothing known. O now, for ever,
Farewell the tranquil mind ! farewell content !
Farewell the plumed troops, and the big wars,　　350
That make ambition virtue ! O, farewell !
Farewell the neighing steed, and the shrill trump,
The spirit-stirring drum, the ear-piercing fife,
The royal banner, and all quality,
Pride, pomp, and circumstance of glorious war !
And O you mortal engines, whose rude throats
The immortal Jove's dread clamours counterfeit,
Farewell ! Othello's occupation 's gone !
Iago. Is it possible ?—My lord,—
Oth. Villain, be sure thou prove my love a whore ;
Be sure of it : give me the ocular proof ;　　361
Or, by the worth of mine eternal soul,
Thou hadst been better have been born a dog,
Than answer my wak'd wrath.
Iago.　　　　　Is it come to this ?
Oth. Make me to see 't ; or, at the least, so prove it,
That the probation bear no hinge, nor loop,
To hang a doubt on : or woe upon thy life !
Iago. My noble lord,—
Oth. If thou dost slander her, and torture me,
Never pray more ; abandon all remorse ;　　370
On horror's head horrors accumulate ;
Do deeds to make heaven weep, all earth amaz'd :
For nothing canst thou to damnation add,
Greater than that.
Iago.　　O grace ! O Heaven forgive me !
Are you a man ? have you a soul, or sense ?—
God be wi' you ; take mine office.—O wretched fool,
That liv'st to make thine honesty a vice !—
O monstrous world ! Take note, take note, O world !
To be direct and honest is not safe.—
I thank you for this profit ; and, from hence,　　380
I 'll love no friend, sith love breeds such offence.
Oth. Nay, stay.—Thou shouldst be honest.
Iago. I should be wise ; for honesty 's a fool,
And loses that it works for.
Oth.　　　　By the world,
I think my wife be honest, and think she is not ;
I think that thou art just, and think thou art not.
I 'll have some proof. Her name, that was as fresh
As Dian's visage, is now begrim'd and black
As mine own face.—If there be cords, or knives,
Poison, or fire, or suffocating streams,　　390
I 'll not endure it.—Would I were satisfied !
Iago. I see, sir, you are eaten up with passion.
I do repent me that I put it to you.
You would be satisfied ?
Oth.　　　　Would ! nay, I will.
Iago. And may ; but how ? how satisfied, my lord ?
Would you, the supervisor, grossly gape on,—
Behold her tupp'd ?

Oth.　　　　　Death and damnation ! O !
Iago. It were a tedious difficulty, I think,
To bring them to that prospect. Damn them then,
If ever mortal eyes do see them bolster,　　400
More than their own ! What then ? how then ?
What shall I say ? Where 's satisfaction ?

Oth. " Make me to see 't ; or, at the least, so prove it,
That the probation bears no hinge, nor loop,
To hang a doubt on : or woe upon thy life !"

It is impossible you should see this,
Were they as prime as goats, as hot as monkeys,
As salt as wolves in pride, and fools as gross
As ignorance made drunk : but yet, I say,
If imputation, and strong circumstances,
Which lead directly to the door of truth,
Will give you satisfaction, you might have it.
Oth. Give me a living reason she 's disloyal.　　410
Iago. I do not like the office ;
But, sith I am enter'd in this cause so far,
Prick'd to 't by foolish honesty and love,
I will go on. I lay with Cassio lately ;
And, being troubled with a raging tooth,
I could not sleep.
There are a kind of men so loose of soul,
That in their sleeps will mutter their affairs :
One of this kind is Cassio.
In sleep I heard him say,—" Sweet Desdemona ;　420
Let us be wary, let us hide our loves !"
And then, sir, would he gripe, and wring my hand,
Cry,—" O sweet creature !" and then kiss me hard,
As if he pluck'd up kisses by the roots,
That grew upon my lips : then laid his leg
Over my thigh, and sigh'd, and kiss'd ; and then
Cried,—" Cursed fate, that gave thee to the Moor !"
Oth. O monstrous ! monstrous !
Iago.　　Nay, this was but his dream.
Oth. But this denoted a foregone conclusion :
'T is a shrewd doubt, though it be but a dream.　430
Iago. And this may help to thicken other proofs,
That do demonstrate thinly.
Oth.　　　　I 'll tear her all to pieces.
Iago. Nay, but be wise : yet we see nothing done ;
She may be honest yet. Tell me but this ;
Have you not sometimes seen a handkerchief,
Spotted with strawberries, in your wife's hand ?
Oth. I gave her such a one : 't was my first gift.
Iago. I know not that : but such a handkerchief

(I am sure it was your wife's) did I to-day
See Cassio wipe his beard with.
Oth.   If it be that,— 440
Iago. If it be that, or any that was hers,
It speaks against her, with the other proofs.
Oth. O, that the slave had forty thousand lives!
One is too poor, too weak for my revenge.
Now do I see 't is true.—Look here, Iago;
All my fond love thus do I blow to heaven:
'T is gone.
Arise, black vengeance, from the hollow hell!
Yield up, O love, thy crown and hearted throne
To tyrannous hate! Swell, bosom, with thy fraught,
For 't is of aspics' tongues!
Iago.   Yet be content. 451
Oth. O, blood, blood, blood!
Iago. Patience, I say; your mind perhaps may
         change.
Oth. Never, Iago. Like to the Pontic sea,
Whose icy current and compulsive course
Ne'er feels retiring ebb, but keeps due on
To the Propontic and the Hellespont:
Even so my bloody thoughts, with violent pace,
Shall ne'er look back, ne'er ebb to humble love,
Till that a capable and wide revenge 460
Swallow them up.—[*Kneeling.*] Now, by yond marble
         heaven,
In the due reverence of a sacred vow
I here engage my words.
Iago.   Do not rise yet.—[*Kneeling.*
Witness, you ever-burning lights above!
You elements that clip us round about!
Witness, that here Iago doth give up
The execution of his wit, hands, heart,
To wrong'd Othello's service! Let him command,
And to obey shall be in me remorse,
What bloody business ever.
Oth.   I greet thy love, 470
Not with vain thanks, but with acceptance bounteous,
And will upon the instant put thee to 't:
Within these three days let me hear thee say,
That Cassio 's not alive.
Iago. My friend is dead; 't is done at your request:
But let her live.
Oth.   Damn her, lewd minx! O, damn her!
Come, go with me apart; I will withdraw,
To furnish me with some swift means of death
For the fair devil. Now art thou my lieutenant.
Iago. I am your own for ever. 480
                                   [*Exeunt.*

SCENE IV.—Before the Castle.

Enter DESDEMONA, EMILIA, *and* CLOWN.

Des. Do you know, sirrah, where Lieutenant Cassio
lies?
Clo. I dare not say he lies anywhere.
Des. Why, man?
Clo. He is a soldier; and for one to say a soldier lies,
is stabbing.
Des. Go to. Where lodges he?
Clo. To tell you where he lodges, is to tell you where
I lie.
Des. Can anything be made of this? 10
Clo. I know not where he lodges; and for me to
devise a lodging, and say, he lies here, or he lies
there, were to lie in mine own throat.
Des. Can you inquire him out, and be edified by
report?
Clo. I will catechise the world for him; that is,
make questions, and by them answer.
Des. Seek him; bid him come hither; tell him, I
have moved my lord in his behalf, and hope, all will
be well. 20
Clo. To do this is within the compass of man's wit;
and therefore I will attempt the doing it. [*Exit.*
Des. Where should I lose that handkerchief,
Emilia?
Emil. I know not, madam.
Des. Believe me, I had rather have lost my purse
Full of cruzadoes; and but my noble Moor

Is true of mind, and made of no such baseness
As jealous creatures are, it were enough
To put him to ill thinking.
Emil.   Is he not jealous? 30
Des. Who? he! I think the sun, where he was born,
Drew all such humours from him.
Emil.   Look, where he comes.
Des. I will not leave him now, till Cassio
Be call'd to him.—

Enter OTHELLO.

         How is 't with you, my lord?
Oth. Well, my good lady.—[*Aside.*] O, hardness to
         dissemble!—
How do you, Desdemona?
Des.   Well, my good lord.
Oth. Give me your hand. This hand is moist, my
         lady.
Des. It yet has felt no age, nor known no sorrow.
Oth. This argues fruitfulness, and liberal heart:
Hot, hot, and moist: this hand of yours requires 40
A sequester from liberty, fasting and prayer,
Much castigation, exercise devout;
For here 's a young and sweating devil here,
That commonly rebels. 'T is a good hand,
A frank one.
Des.   You may, indeed, say so;
For 't was that hand that gave away my heart.
Oth. A liberal hand: the hearts of old gave hands;
But our new heraldry is—hands, not hearts.
Des. I cannot speak of this. Come now, your
         promise.
Oth. What promise, chuck? 50
Des. I have sent to bid Cassio come speak with you.
Oth. I have a salt and sorry rheum offends me.
Lend me thy handkerchief.
Des. Here, my lord.
Oth. That which I gave you.
Des. I have it not about me.
Oth. Not?
Des. No, indeed, my lord.
Oth. That 's a fault. That handkerchief
Did an Egyptian to my mother give; 60
She was a charmer, and could almost read
The thoughts of people: she told her, while she kept it,
'T would make her amiable, and subdue my father
Entirely to her love; but if she lost it,
Or made a gift of it, my father's eye
Should hold her loathed, and his spirits should hunt
After new fancies. She, dying, gave it me;
And bid me, when my fate would have me wived,
To give it her. I did so: and take heed on 't;
Make it a darling like your precious eye; 70
To lose 't or give 't away, were such perdition,
As nothing else could match.
Des.   Is 't possible?
Oth. 'T is true: there 's magic in the web of it.
A sibyl, that had number'd in the world
The sun to course two hundred compasses,
In her prophetic fury sew'd the work;
The worms were hallow'd that did breed the silk,
And it was dy'd in mummy, which the skilful
Conserv'd of maidens' hearts.
Des.   Indeed! is 't true?
Oth. Most veritable; therefore look to 't well. 80
Des. Then would to Heaven that I had never seen 't.
Oth. Ha! wherefore?
Des. Why do you speak so startingly and rash?
Oth. Is 't lost? is 't gone? speak, is it out o' the way?
Des. Heaven bless us!
Oth. Say you?
Des. It is not lost; but what an if it were?
Oth. How?
Des. I say, it is not lost.
Oth. Fetch 't, let me see 't. 90
Des. Why, so I can, sir; but I will not now.
This is a trick, to put me from my suit:
I pray, let Cassio be receiv'd again.
Oth. Fetch me that handkerchief: my mind mis-
         gives.
Des. Come, come;
You 'll never meet a more sufficient man.

Oth. The handkerchief!
Des.   I pray, talk me of Cassio.
Oth. The handkerchief!
Des.   A man that, all his time,
Hath founded his good fortunes on your love;
Shar'd dangers with you;—   100

They eat us hungerly, and when they are full,   109
They belch us.—Look you! Cassio, and my husband.

Enter IAGO *and* CASSIO.

Iago. There is no other way; 't is she must do 't:
And, lo, the happiness! go, and importune her.

Bian.   "O Cassio, whence came this?
This is some token from a newer friend."

Oth. The handkerchief!
Des.   In sooth, you are to blame.
Oth. Away!   [*Exit.*
Emil. Is not this man jealous?
Des. I ne'er saw this before.
Sure, there 's some wonder in this handkerchief:
I am most unhappy in the loss of it.
Emil. 'T is not a year or two shows us a man:
They are all but stomachs, and we all but food;

Des. How now, good Cassio? what 's the news with
    you?
Cas. Madam, my former suit. I do beseech you,
That by your virtuous means I may again
Exist, and be a member of his love,
Whom I, with all the office of my heart,
Entirely honour: I would not be delay'd.
If my offence be of such mortal kind,
That nor my service past, nor present sorrows,   120

Nor purpos'd merit in futurity,
Can ransom me into his love again,
But to know so must be my benefit ;
So shall I clothe me in a forc'd content,
And shut myself up in some other course,
To fortune's alms.
Des.   Alas ! thrice-gentle Cassio,
My advocation is not now in tune ;
My lord is not my lord ; nor should I know him,
Were he in favour, as in humour, alter'd.
So help me every spirit sanctified,   130
As I have spoken for you all my best,
And stood within the blank of his displeasure,
For my free speech. You must awhile be patient :
What I can do, I will ; and more I will,
Than for myself I dare : let that suffice you.
Iago. Is my lord angry ?
Emil.   He went hence but now,
And, certainly, in strange unquietness.
Iago. Can he be angry ? I have seen the cannon,
When it hath blown his ranks into the air,
And, like the devil, from his very arm   140
Puff'd his own brother ;—and can he be angry ?
Something of moment, then : I will go meet him.
There 's matter in 't, indeed, if he be angry.
Des. I pr'ythee, do so. [*Exit* IAGO.]—Something,
     sure, of state—
Either from Venice, or some unhatch'd practice,
Made demonstrable here in Cyprus to him—
Hath puddled his clear spirit ; and, in such cases,
Men's natures wrangle with inferior things,
Though great ones are their object. 'T is even so ; 150
For let our finger ache, and it indues
Our other healthful members ev'n to that sense
Of pain. Nay, we must think, men are not gods ;
Nor of them look for such observancy
As fits the bridal.—Beshrew me much, Emilia,
I was (unhandsome warrior as I am)
Arraigning his unkindness with my soul :
But now I find, I had suborn'd the witness,
And he 's indited falsely.
Emil. Pray Heaven it be state-matters, as you think,
And no conception, nor no jealous toy,   160
Concerning you.
Des. Alas the day ! I never gave him cause.
Emil. But jealous souls will not be answer'd so ;
They are not ever jealous for the cause,
But jealous for they are jealous : 't is a monster
Begot upon itself, born on itself.
Des. Heaven keep that monster from Othello's mind !

Emil. Lady, Amen.
Des. I will go seek him.—Cassio, walk hereabout :
If I do find him fit, I 'll move your suit,   170
And seek to effect it to my uttermost.
Cas. I humbly thank your ladyship.
     [*Exeunt* DESDEMONA *and* EMILIA.

Enter BIANCA.

Bian. Save you, friend Cassio !
Cas.   What make you from home ?
How is it with you, my most fair Bianca ?
I' faith, sweet love, I was coming to your house.
Bian. And I was going to your lodging, Cassio.
What ! keep a week away ? seven days and nights ?
Eight score eight hours ? and lovers' absent hours,
More tedious than the dial eight score times ?
O weary reckoning !
Cas.   Pardon me, Bianca ;   180
I have this while with leaden thoughts been press'd ;
But I shall, in a more continuate time,
Strike off this score of absence. Sweet Bianca,
     [*Giving her* DESDEMONA's *handkerchief.*
Take me this work out.
Bian.   O Cassio, whence came this ?
This is some token from a newer friend.
To the felt absence now I feel a cause.
Is it come to this ? Well, well.
Cas.   Go to, woman !
Throw your vile guesses in the devil's teeth,
From whence you have them. You are jealous now,
That this is from some mistress, some remembrance :
No, in good troth, Bianca.
Bian.   Why, whose is it ?   191
Cas. I know not neither : I found it in my chamber.
I like the work well : ere it be demanded
(As like enough it will), I 'd have it copied :
Take it, and do 't ; and leave me for this time.
Bian. Leave you ! wherefore ?
Cas. I do attend here on the general,
And think it no addition, nor my wish,
To have him see me woman'd.
Bian.   Why, I pray you ?
Cas. Not that I love you not.
Bian.   But that you do not love me.
I pray you, bring me on the way a little ;   201
And say, if I shall see you soon at night.
Cas. 'T is but a little way, that I can bring you,
For I attend here ; but I 'll see you soon.
Bian. 'T is very good : I must be circumstanc'd.
     [*Exeunt.*

ACT IV.

SCENE I.—Before the Castle.

Enter OTHELLO *and* IAGO.

Iago. Will you think so ?
Oth.   Think so, Iago ?
Iago.   What !
To kiss in private ?
Oth.   An unauthoris'd kiss.
Iago. Or to be naked with her friend
     a-bed,
An hour, or more, not meaning any harm ?
Oth. Naked a-bed, Iago, and not mean
     harm ?
It is hypocrisy against the devil :
They that mean virtuously, and yet do so,
The devil their virtue tempts, and they tempt Heaven.

Iago. If they do nothing, 't is a venial slip :
But if I give my wife a handkerchief,—   10
Oth. What then ?
Iago. Why, then 't is hers, my lord ; and, being hers,
She may, I think, bestow 't on any man.
Oth. She is protectress of her honour too :
May she give that ?
Iago. Her honour is an essence that 's not seen ;
They have it very oft, that have it not :
But, for the handkerchief,—
Oth. By Heaven, I would most gladly have forgot it.
Thou saidst,—O ! it comes o'er my memory,   20
As doth the raven o'er the infectious house,
Boding to all,—he had my handkerchief.

Iago. Ay, what of that?
Oth.   That's not so good, now.
Iago. What, if I had said, I had seen him do you
wrong?
Or heard him say,—as knaves be such abroad,
Who, having, by their own importunate suit,
Or voluntary dotage of some mistress,
Convinced or supplied them, cannot choose
But they must blab.
Oth.   Hath he said anything?
Iago. He hath, my lord; but, be you well assur'd, 30
No more than he 'll unswear.
Oth.   What hath he said?
Iago. 'Faith, that he did—I know not what he did.
Oth. What? what?
Iago. Lie—
Oth.   With her?
Iago.   With her, on her; what you will.
Oth. Lie with her! lie on her!—We say, lie on her,
when they belie her. Lie with her! that's fulsome.—
Handkerchief,—confessions,—handkerchief.—To con-
fess, and be hanged for his labour.—First, to be
hanged, and then to confess:—I tremble at it. Nature
would not invest herself in such shadowing passion,
without some instruction. It is not words, that
shakes me thus.—Pish!—Noses, ears, and lips.—Is
it possible?—Confess!—Handkerchief!—O devil!— 43
                              [*Falls in a trance.*

Iago. Work on,
My medicine, work! Thus credulous fools are caught;
And many worthy and chaste dames, even thus,
All guiltless, meet reproach.—What, ho! my lord!
My lord, I say! Othello!—

                Enter CASSIO.
                    How now, Cassio?
Cas. What's the matter?
Iago. My lord is fall'n into an epilepsy: 50
This is his second fit; he had one yesterday.
Cas. Rub him about the temples.
Iago.   No, forbear.
The lethargy must have his quiet course;
If not, he foams at mouth; and, by-and-by,
Breaks out to savage madness. Look, he stirs:
Do you withdraw yourself a little while,
He will recover straight: when he is gone,
I would on great occasion speak with you.—
                              [*Exit* CASSIO.
How is it, general? have you hurt your head?
Oth. Dost thou mock me?
Iago.   I mock you! no, by Heaven.
'Would you would bear your fortune like a man. 61
Oth. A horned man's a monster, and a beast.
Iago. There's many a beast then in a populous city,
And many a civil monster.
Oth. Did he confess it?
Iago.   Good sir, be a man;
Think, every bearded fellow, that's but yok'd,
May draw with you: there's millions now alive,
That nightly lie in those unproper beds,
Which they dare swear peculiar: your case is better.
O! 't is the spite of hell, the fiend's arch-mock,   70
To lip a wanton in a secure couch,
And to suppose her chaste. No, let me know;
And, knowing what I am, I know what she shall be.
Oth. O! thou art wise; 't is certain.
Iago. Stand you awhile apart;
Confine yourself but in a patient list.
Whilst you were here, o'erwhelmed with your grief
(A passion most unsuiting such a man),
Cassio came hither: I shifted him away,
And laid good 'scuse upon your ecstacy;   80
Bade him anon return, and here speak with me;
The which he promis'd. Do but encave yourself,
And mark the fleers, the gibes, and notable scorns,
That dwell in every region of his face;
For I will make him tell the tale anew,
Where, how, how oft, how long ago, and when
He hath, and is again to cope your wife:
I say, but mark his gesture.—Marry, patience;
Or I shall say, you are all in all in spleen,
And nothing of a man.

Oth.   Dost thou hear, Iago?   90
I will be found most cunning in my patience;
But (dost thou hear?) most bloody.
Iago.   That's not amiss;
But yet keep time in all. Will you withdraw?
                              [OTHELLO *withdraws.*
Now will I question Cassio of Bianca,
A housewife, that by selling her desires
Buys herself bread and clothes: it is a creature,
That dotes on Cassio, as 't is the strumpets' plague,
To beguile many, and be beguil'd by one.
He, when he hears of her, cannot refrain
From the excess of laughter.—Here he comes.—   100

            Re-enter CASSIO.
As he shall smile, Othello shall go mad;
And his unbookish jealousy must construe
Poor Cassio's smiles, gestures, and light behaviour
Quite in the wrong.—How do you now, lieutenant?
Cas. The worser, that you give me the addition,
Whose want even kills me.
Iago. Ply Desdemona well, and you are sure on 't.
[*Speaking lower.*] Now, if this suit lay in Bianca's
                              dower,
How quickly should you speed!
Cas.   Alas, poor caitiff!
Oth. [*Aside.*] Look, how he laughs already!   110
Iago. I never knew woman love man so.
Cas. Alas, poor rogue! I think, i' faith, she loves
                              me.
Oth. [*Aside.*] Now he denies it faintly, and laughs
                              it out.
Iago. Do you hear, Cassio?
Oth. [*Aside.*]   Now he importunes him
To tell it o'er. Go to; well said, well said.
Iago. She gives it out, that you shall marry her:
Do you intend it?
Cas. Ha, ha, ha!
Oth. [*Aside.*] Do you triumph, Roman! do you
triumph?   120
Cas. I marry her!—what! a customer? I pr'ythee,
bear some charity to my wit; do not think it so
unwholesome. Ha, ha, ha!
Oth. [*Aside.*] So, so, so, so. They laugh that win.
Iago. 'Faith, the cry goes, that you shall marry
                              her.—
Cas. Pr'ythee, say true.
Iago. I am a very villain else.
Oth. [*Aside.*] Have you scored me? Well.
Cas. This is the monkey's own giving out: she is
persuaded I will marry her, out of her own love and
flattery, not out of my promise.   131
Oth. [*Aside.*] Iago beckons me: now he begins the
story.
Cas. She was here even now; she haunts me in
every place. I was, the other day, talking on the sea-
bank with certain Venetians, and thither comes the
bauble; and, by this hand, she falls me thus about my
neck;—
Oth. [*Aside.*] Crying, O dear Cassio! as it were: his
gesture imports it.   140
Cas. So hangs, and lolls, and weeps upon me; so
hales and pulls me: ha, ha, ha!—
Oth. [*Aside.*] Now he tells, how she plucked him to
my chamber. O! I see that nose of yours, but not
that dog I shall throw it to.
Cas. Well, I must leave her company.
Iago. Before me! look, where she comes.
Cas. 'T is such another fitchew! marry, a perfumed
one.

            Enter BIANCA.
What do you mean by this haunting of me?   150
Bian. Let the devil and his dam haunt you! What
did you mean by that same handkerchief, you gave
me even now? I was a fine fool to take it. I must
take out the work!—A likely piece of work, that you
should find it in your chamber, and know not who left
it there! This is some minx's token, and I must take
out the work! There, give it your hobby-horse:
wheresoever you had it, I 'll take out no work on 't.
Cas. How now, my sweet Bianca! how now, how
now!   160

Oth. [*Aside.*] By Heaven, that should be my hand-
kerchief!
Bian. An you 'll come to supper to-night, you may;
an you will not, come when you are next prepared
for.   [*Exit.*
Iago. After her, after her.
Cas. 'Faith, I must; she 'll rail in the street else.
Iago. Will you sup there?
Cas. 'Faith, I intend so.
Iago. Well, I may chance to see you, for I would
very fain speak with you.   171
Cas. Pr'ythee, come; will you?
Iago. Go to; say no more.   [*Exit* CASSIO.
Oth. [*Advancing.*] How shall I murder him, Iago?
Iago. Did you perceive how he laughed at his vice?
Oth. O, Iago!
Iago. And did you see the handkerchief?
Oth. Was that mine?
Iago. Yours, by this hand: and to see how he prizes
the foolish woman, your wife! she gave it him, and he
hath given it his whore.   181
Oth. I would have him nine years a-killing.—A fine
woman! a fair woman! a sweet woman!
Iago. Nay, you must forget that.
Oth. Ay, let her rot, and perish, and be damned to-
night; for she shall not live. No, my heart is turned
to stone; I strike it, and it hurts my hand. O! the
world hath not a sweeter creature: she might lie by
an emperor's side, and command him tasks.
Iago. Nay, that 's not your way.   190
Oth. Hang her! I do but say what she is.—So deli-
cate with her needle!—An admirable musician! O!
she will sing the savageness out of a bear.—Of so high
and plenteous wit and invention!—
Iago. She 's the worse for all this.
Oth. O! a thousand, a thousand times. And then,
of so gentle a condition!
Iago. Ay, too gentle.
Oth. Nay, that 's certain :—but yet the pity of it,
Iago!—O, Iago! the pity of it, Iago!   200
Iago. If you are so fond over her iniquity, give her
patent to offend: for, if it touch not you, it comes near
nobody.
Oth. I will chop her into messes.—Cuckold me!
Iago. O! 't is foul in her.
Oth. With mine officer!
Iago. That 's fouler.
Oth. Get me some poison, Iago; this night :—I 'll not
expostulate with her, lest her body and beauty unpro-
vide my mind again.—This might, Iago.   210
Iago. Do it not with poison, strangle her in her bed,
even the bed she hath contaminated.
Oth. Good, good: the justice of it pleases; very
good.
Iago. And for Cassio, let me be his undertaker: you
shall hear more by midnight.   [*A trumpet within.*
Oth. Excellent good.—What trumpet is that same?
Iago. Something from Venice, sure. 'T is Lodovico,
Come from the duke; and, see, your wife is with him.

Enter LODOVICO, DESDEMONA, *and Attendants.*

Lod. God save the worthy general!
Oth.   With all my heart, sir.
Lod. The duke and senators of Venice greet you.
                               [*Giving him a packet.*
Oth. I kiss the instrument of their pleasures.   222
                           [*Opens the packet, and reads.*
Des. And what 's the news, good cousin Lodovico?
Iago. I am very glad to see you, signior :
Welcome to Cyprus.
Lod. I thank you. How does Lieutenant Cassio?
Iago. Lives, sir.
Des. Cousin, there 's fall'n between him and my lord
An unkind breach, but you shall make all well.
Oth. Are you sure of that?   230
Des. My lord?
Oth. [*Reading.*] "This fail you not to do, as you
will"—
Lod. He did not call; he 's busy in the paper.
Is there division 'twixt my lord and Cassio?
Des. A most unhappy one: I would do much
To atone them, for the love I bear to Cassio.

Oth. Fire and brimstone!
Des. My lord?
Oth. Are you wise?   210
Des. What! is he angry?
Lod.   May be, the letter mov'd him;
For, as I think, they do command him home,
Deputing Cassio in his government.
Des. Trust me I am glad on 't.
Oth.   Indeed?
Des.   My lord?
Oth. I am glad to see you mad.
Des.   How, sweet Othello?
Oth. Devil!   [*Striking her.*
Des. I have not deserv'd this.
Lod. My lord, this would not be believ'd in Venice,
Though I should swear I saw it. 'T is very much:
Make her amends, she weeps.
Oth.   O devil, devil!   250
If that the earth could teem with woman's tears,
Each drop she falls would prove a crocodile.—
Out of my sight!
Des.   I will not stay to offend you. [*Going.*
Lod. Truly, an obedient lady.—
I do beseech your lordship, call her back.
Oth. Mistress!
Des.   My lord?
Oth.   What would you with her, sir?
Lod. Who, I, my lord?
Oth. Ay; you did wish, that I would make her turn:
Sir, she can turn, and turn, and yet go on,
And turn again; and she can weep, sir, weep;   260
And she 's obedient, as you say,—obedient,—
Very obedient.—Proceed you in your tears.—
Concerning this, sir,—O well-painted passion!—
I am commanded home.—Get you away;
I 'll send for you anon.—Sir, I obey the mandate,
And will return to Venice.—Hence! avaunt!—
                              [*Exit* DESDEMONA.
Cassio shall have my place. And,—sir, to-night,
I do entreat that we may sup together:
You are welcome, sir, to Cyprus. — Goats and
monkeys!   [*Exit.*
Lod. Is this the noble Moor whom our full senate
Call all-in-all sufficient?—Is this the nature   271
Whom passion could not shake? whose solid virtue
The shot of accident, nor dart of chance,
Could neither graze, nor pierce?
Iago.   He is much chang'd.
Lod. Are his wits safe? is he not light of brain?
Iago. He 's that he is: I may not breathe my
censure.
What he might be,—if, what he might, he is not,—
I would to Heaven, he were!
Lod.   What! strike his wife!
Iago. 'Faith, that was not so well; yet 'would I
knew,
That stroke would prove the worst.
Lod.   Is it his use?
Or did the letters work upon his blood,   281
And new-create this fault?
Iago.   Alas, alas!
It is not honesty in me, to speak
What I have seen and known. You shall observe him,
And his own courses will denote him so,
That I may save my speech. Do but go after,
And mark how he continues.
Lod. I am sorry, that I am deceiv'd in him.
                                          [*Exeunt.*

SCENE II.—A Room in the Castle.

Enter OTHELLO *and* EMILIA.

Oth. You have seen nothing then?
Emil. Nor ever heard; nor ever did suspect.
Oth. Yes, you have seen Cassio and she together.
Emil. But then I saw no harm; and then I heard
Each syllable that breath made up between them.
Oth. What, did they never whisper?
Emil.   Never, my lord.
Oth. Nor send you out o' the way?
Emil.   Never.

Oth. To fetch her fan, her gloves, her mask, nor
 nothing?
Emil. Never, my lord.
Oth. That's strange.   10
Emil. I durst, my lord, to wager she is honest,
Lay down my soul at stake: if you think other,
Remove your thought; it doth abuse your bosom.
If any wretch have put this in your head,
Let Heaven requite it with the serpent's curse!
For, if she be not honest, chaste, and true,
There's no man happy; the purest of their wives
Is foul as slander.
 Oth.   Bid her come hither:—go.—
          [*Exit* EMILIA.

Des. "Upon my knees, what doth your speech import?"

She says enough;—yet she's a simple bawd,
That cannot say as much. This is a subtle whore, 20
A closet-lock-and-key of villainous secrets:
And yet she'll kneel, and pray; I have seen her do't.

   Re-enter EMILIA, *with* DESDEMONA.

Des. My lord, what is your will?
Oth.   Pray, chuck, come hither.
Des. What is your pleasure?
Oth.   Let me see your eyes:
Look in my face.
 Des.   What horrible fancy's this?
Oth. [*To* EMILIA.] Some of your function, mistress;
Leave procreants alone, and shut the door;
Cough, or cry hem, if anybody come:
Your mystery, your mystery;—nay, despatch.
         [*Exit* EMILIA.
Des. Upon my knees, what doth your speech
 import?   30
I understand a fury in your words,
But not the words.
Oth. Why, what art thou?
Des. Your wife, my lord; your true and loyal wife.
Oth. Come, swear it, damn thyself;
Lest, being like one of heaven, the devils themselves
Should fear to seize thee: therefore, be double-
 damn'd;
Swear thou art honest.
 Des.   Heaven doth truly know it.
Oth. Heaven truly knows, that thou art false as hell.
Des. To whom, my lord? with whom? how am I
 false?   40
Oth. Ah, Desdemon!—away, away, away!
Des. Alas, the heavy day!—Why do you weep?
Am I the motive of these tears, my lord?
If, haply, you my father do suspect
An instrument of this your calling back,

Lay not your blame on me; if you have lost him,
Why, I have lost him too.
Oth.   Had it pleas'd Heaven
To try me with affliction; had they rain'd
All kinds of sores, and shames, on my bare head;
Steep'd me in poverty to the very lips; 50
Given to captivity me and my utmost hopes;
I should have found in some place of my soul
A drop of patience: but, alas! to make me
The fixed figure, for the time of scorn
To point his slow and moving finger at,—
Yet could I bear that too; well, very well:
But there, where I have garner'd up my heart,
Where either I must live, or bear no life,
The fountain from the which my current
 runs,
Or else dries up; to be discarded thence, 60
Or keep it as a cistern, for foul toads
To knot and gender in!—turn thy com-
 plexion there,
Patience, thou young and rose-lipp'd
 cherubin;
Ay, there, look grim as hell!
 Des. I hope, my noble lord esteems me
 honest.
 Oth. O! ay; as summer flies are in the
 shambles,
That quicken even with blowing. O thou
 weed?
Who art so lovely fair, and smell'st so sweet,
That the sense aches at thee,—'would thou
 hadst ne'er been born!
 Des. Alas! what ignorant sin have I
 committed?   70
 Oth. Was this fair paper, this most
 goodly book,
Made to write whore upon? What com-
 mitted?
Committed!—O thou public commoner!
I should make very forges of my cheeks,
That would to cinders burn up modesty,
Did I but speak thy deeds.—What com-
 mitted?
Heaven stops the nose at it, and the moon
 winks;
The bawdy wind, that kisses all it meets,
Is hush'd within the hollow mine of earth,
And will not hear it. What committed?— 80
Impudent strumpet!
 Des.   By Heaven, you do me wrong.
Oth. Are not you a strumpet?
 Des.   No, as I am a Christian.
If to preserve this vessel for my lord,
From any other foul unlawful touch,
Be not to be a strumpet, I am none.
Oth. What, not a whore?
 Des.   No, as I shall be saved.
Oth. Is it possible?
Des. O, Heaven forgive us!
 Oth.   I cry you mercy then:
I took you for that cunning whore of Venice,
That married with Othello.—You, mistress, 90
That have the office opposite to Saint Peter,
And keep the gate of hell!

     Re-enter EMILIA.

      You, you, ay, you:
We have done our course; there's money for your
 pains.
I pray you, turn the key, and keep our counsel. [*Exit.*
 Emil. Alas! what does this gentleman conceive?—
How do you, madam? how do you, my good lady?
Des. 'Faith, half asleep.
Emil. Good madam, what's the matter with my
 lord?
Des. With who?
Emil. Why, with my lord, madam.   100
Des. Who is thy lord?
Emil.   He that is yours, sweet lady.
Des. I have none: do not talk to me, Emilia:
I cannot weep; nor answer have I none,
But what should go by water. Pr'ythee, to-night

Lay on my bed my wedding sheets,—remember ;—
And call thy husband hither.
  Emil.   Here 's a change, indeed !
                               [*Exit.*
  Des. 'T is meet I should be us'd so, very meet.
How have I been behav'd, that he might stick
The small'st opinion on my least misuse ?

Re-enter EMILIA, *with* IAGO.

  Iago. What is your pleasure, madam ? How is 't
    with you ?   110
  Des. I cannot tell. Those, that do teach young
    babes,
Do it with gentle means and easy tasks :
He might have chid me so ; for, in good faith,
I am a child to chiding.
  Iago.   What 's the matter, lady ?
  Emil. Alas, Iago, my lord hath so bewhor'd her,
Thrown such despite and heavy terms upon her,
As true hearts cannot bear.
  Des. Am I that name, Iago ?
  Iago.   What name, fair lady ?
  Des. Such as she says my lord did say I was.
  Emil. He call'd her whore : a beggar in his drink 120
Could not have laid such terms upon his callat.
  Iago. Why did he so ?
  Des. I do not know ; I am sure, I am none such.
  Iago. Do not weep, do not weep. Alas the day !
  Emil. Hath she forsook so many noble matches,
Her father, and her country, and her friends,
To be call'd whore ? would it not make one weep ?
  Des. It is my wretched fortune.
  Iago.   Beshrew him for 't !
How comes this trick upon him ?
  Des.   Nay, Heaven doth know.
  Emil. I will be hang'd, if some eternal villain,   130
Some busy and insinuating rogue,
Some cogging cozening slave, to get some office,
Have not devis'd this slander ; I 'll be hang'd else.
  Iago. Fie ! there is no such man : it is impossible.
  Des. If any such there be, Heaven pardon him !
  Emil. A halter pardon him, and hell gnaw his
    bones !
Why should he call her whore ? who keeps her com-
    pany ?
What place ? what time ? what form ? what likeli-
    hood ?
The Moor 's abus'd by some most villainous knave,
Some base notorious knave, some scurvy fellow.— 140
O Heaven ! that such companions thou 'dst unfold,
And put in every honest hand a whip,
To lash the rascals naked through the world,
Even from the east to the west !
  Iago.   Speak within door.
  Emil. O, fie upon them ! Some such squire he
    was,
That turn'd your wit the seamy side without,
And made you to suspect me with the Moor.
  Iago. You are a fool ; go to.
  Des.   O good Iago !
What shall I do to win my lord again ?
Good friend, go to him ; for, by this light of heaven,
I know not how I lost him. Here I kneel :—   151
If e'er my will did trespass 'gainst his love,
Either in discourse of thought, or actual deed ;
Or that mine eyes, mine ears, or any sense,
Delighted them in any other form ;
Or that I do not yet, and ever did,
And ever will,—though he do shake me off
To beggarly divorcement,—love him dearly,
Comfort forswear me ! Unkindness may do much ;
And his unkindness may defeat my life,   160
But never taint my love. I cannot say whore :
It does abhor me, now I speak the word ;
To do the act that might the addition earn,
Not the world's mass of vanity could make me.
  Iago. I pray you, be content ; 't is but his humour :
The business of the state does him offence,
And he does chide with you.
  Des. If 't were no other,—
  Iago.   'T is but so, I warrant.
                             [*Trumpets.*

Hark, how these instruments summon to supper !
The messengers of Venice stay the meat.   170
Go in, and weep not ; all things shall be well.
             [*Exeunt* DESDEMONA *and* EMILIA.

Enter RODERIGO.

How now, Roderigo ?
  Rod. I do not find that thou deal'st justly with
me.
  Iago. What in the contrary ?
  Rod. Every day thou daff'st me with some device,
Iago ; and rather, as it seems to me now, keep'st from
me all conveniency, than suppliest me with the least
advantage of hope. I will, indeed, no longer endure
it ; nor am I yet persuaded, to put up in peace what
already I have foolishly suffered.   181
  Iago. Will you hear me, Roderigo ?
  Rod. 'Faith, I have heard too much ; for your words,
and performances, are no kin together.
  Iago. You charge me most unjustly.
  Rod. With nought but truth. I have wasted myself
out of my means. The jewels you have had from me,
to deliver to Desdemona, would half have corrupted a
votarist : you have told me, she hath received them,
and returned me expectations and comforts of sudden
respect and acquaintance ; but I find none.   191
  Iago. Well ; go to ; very well.
  Rod. Very well ! go to ! I cannot go to, man : nor
't is not very well : by this hand, I say, it is very
scurvy ; and begin to find myself fopped in it.
  Iago. Very well.
  Rod. I tell you, 't is not very well. I will make
myself known to Desdemona : if she will return me
my jewels, I will give over my suit, and repent my
unlawful solicitation ; if not, assure yourself, I will
seek satisfaction of you.   201
  Iago. You have said now.
  Rod. Ay, and I have said nothing, but what I
protest intendment of doing.
  Iago. Why, now I see there 's mettle in thee ; and
even, from this instant, do build on thee a better
opinion than ever before. Give me thy hand,
Roderigo : thou hast taken against me a most just
exception ; but yet, I protest I have dealt most
directly in thy affair.   210
  Rod. It hath not appeared.
  Iago. I grant, indeed, it hath not appeared, and
your suspicion is not without wit and judgment. But,
Roderigo, if thou hast that within thee indeed, which
I have greater reason to believe now than ever,—I
mean, purpose, courage, and valour,—this night show
it : if thou the next night following enjoyest not
Desdemona, take me from this world with treachery,
and devise engines for my life.
  Rod. Well, what is it ? is it within reason and
compass ?   221
  Iago. Sir, there is especial commission come from
Venice, to depute Cassio in Othello's place.
  Rod. Is that true ? why, then Othello and Desde-
mona return again to Venice.
  Iago. O, no ! he goes into Mauritania, and takes
away with him the fair Desdemona, unless his abode
be lingered here by some accident ; wherein none can
be so determinate, as the removing of Cassio.
  Rod. How do you mean, removing him ?   230
  Iago. Why, by making him uncapable of Othello's
place ; knocking out his brains.
  Rod. And that you would have me do ?
  Iago. Ay ; if you dare do yourself a profit, and a
right. He sups to-night with a harlotry, and thither
will I go to him : he knows not yet of his honourable
fortune. If you will watch his going thence (which I
will fashion to fall out between twelve and one), you
may take him at your pleasure : I will be near to
second your attempt, and he shall fall between us.
Come, stand not amazed at it, but go along with me ;
I will show you such a necessity in his death, that
you shall think yourself bound to put it on him. It is
now high supper-time, and the night grows to waste :
about it.
  Rod. I will hear further reason for this.
  Iago. And you shall be satisfied.   [*Exeunt.*

SCENE III.—Another Room in the Castle.

Enter OTHELLO, LODOVICO, DESDEMONA, EMILIA, *and Attendants.*

Lod. I do beseech you, sir, trouble yourself no further.

Oth. O! pardon me; 't will do me good to walk.

Lod. Madam, good night; I humbly thank your ladyship.

Des. Your honour is most welcome.

Oth.   Will you walk, sir?—
O!—Desdemona,—

Des. My lord?

Oth. Get you to bed on the instant; I will be returned forthwith: dismiss your attendant there: look it be done.

Des. I will, my lord.   10
 [*Exeunt* OTHELLO, LODOVICO, *and Attendants.*

Emil. How goes it now? he looks gentler than he did.

Des. He says, he will return incontinent;
He hath commanded me to go to bed,
And bade me to dismiss you.

Emil.   Dismiss me!

Des. It was his bidding: therefore, good Emilia,
Give me my nightly wearing, and adieu:
We must not now displease him.

Emil. I would you had never seen him.

Des. So would not I: my love doth so approve him,
That even his stubbornness, his checks, and frowns,—
Pr'ythee, unpin me,—have grace and favour in them.

Emil. I have laid those sheets you bade me on the bed.   22

Des. All 's one.—Good father! how foolish are our minds!—
If I do die before thee, pr'ythee, shroud me
In one of those same sheets.

Emil.   Come, come, you talk.

Des. My mother had a maid call'd Barbara:
She was in love; and he she lov'd prov'd mad,
And did forsake her: she had a song of—willow;
An old thing 't was, but it express'd her fortune,
And she died singing it: that song, to-night,   30
Will not go from my mind; I have much to do,
But to go hang my head all at one side,
And sing it like poor Barbara.   Pr'ythee, despatch.

Emil. Shall I go fetch your night-gown?

Des.   No, unpin me here.—
This Lodovico is a proper man.

Emil. A very handsome man.

Des. He speaks well.

Emil. I know a lady in Venice would have walked barefoot to Palestine, for a touch of his nether lip.

Des. [*Singing.*] *The poor soul sat sighing by a sycamore tree;*   40
Sing all a green willow;
Her hand on her bosom, her head on her knee;
Sing willow, willow, willow:
The fresh streams ran by her, and murmur'd her moans;
Sing willow, willow, willow;
Her salt tears fell from her, and soften'd the stones;
Lay by these.—
Sing willow, willow, willow.
Pr'ythee, hie thee: he 'll come anon.—

Sing all a green willow must be my garland.   50
Let nobody blame him, his scorn I approve,—
Nay, that 's not next.—Hark! who is it that knocks?

Emil. It is the wind.

Des. I call'd my love, false love; but what said he then?
Sing willow, willow, willow:
If I court moe women, you 'll couch with moe men.
So, get thee gone; good night.   Mine eyes do itch;
Doth that bode weeping?

Emil.   'T is neither here nor there.

Des. I have heard it said so.—O, these men, these men!—
Dost thou in conscience think,—tell me, Emilia,— 60
That there be women do abuse their husbands
In such gross kind?

Emil.   There be some such, no question.

Des. Wouldst thou do such a deed for all the world?

Emil. Why, would not you?

Des.   No, by this heavenly light!

Emil. Nor I neither by this heavenly light: I might do 't as well i' the dark.

Des. Wouldst thou do such a thing for all the world?

Emil. The world is a huge thing: 't is a great price For a small vice.

Des.   In troth, I think thou wouldst not. €9

Emil. In troth, I think I should, and undo 't when I had done.   Marry, I would not do such a thing for a joint-ring, nor for measures of lawn, nor for gowns, petticoats, nor caps, nor any petty exhibition; but, for the whole world,—why, who would not make her husband a cuckold, to make him a monarch?   I should venture purgatory for 't.

Des. Beshrew me, if I would do such a wrong For the whole world.

Emil. Why, the wrong is but a wrong i' the world; and, having the world for your labour, 't is a wrong in your own world, and you might quickly make it right.   82

Des. I do not think there is any such woman.

Emil. Yes, a dozen; and as many to the vantage, As would store the world they played for.
But, I do think, it is their husbands' faults,
If wives do fall.   Say, that they slack their duties,
And pour our treasures into foreign laps;
Or else break out in peevish jealousies,
Throwing restraint upon us; or, say, they strike us, 90
Or scant our former having in despite:
Why, we have galls; and, though we have some grace,
Yet have we some revenge.   Let husbands know,
Their wives have sense like them: they see, and smell,
And have their palates, both for sweet and sour,
As husbands have.   What is it that they do,
When they change us for others?   Is it sport?
I think, it is.   And doth affection breed it?
I think, it doth.   Is 't frailty, that thus errs?
It is so too.   And have not we affections,   100
Desires for sport, and frailty, as men have?
Then, let them use us well; else let them know,
The ills we do, their ills instruct us so.

Des. Good night, good night: Heaven me such uses send,
Not to pick bad from bad, but by bad mend!
                                                  [*Exeunt.*

ACT V.

SCENE I.—A Street.

Enter IAGO *and* RODERIGO.

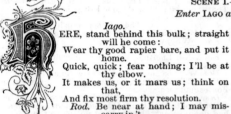

Iago.
ERE, stand behind this bulk; straight
    will he come:
Wear thy good rapier bare, and put it
    home.
Quick, quick; fear nothing; I'll be at
    thy elbow.
It makes us, or it mars us; think on
    that,
And fix most firm thy resolution.
  Rod. Be near at hand; I may mis-
    carry in 't.
  Iago. Here, at thy hand: be bold,
    and take thy stand. [*Retires.*
  Rod. I have no great devotion to the
    deed:
And yet he has given me satisfying reasons.—
'Tis but a man gone:—forth, my sword; he dies. 10
  Iago. I have rubb'd this young quat almost to the
    sense,
And he grows angry. Now, whether he kill Cassio,
Or Cassio him, or each do kill the other,
Every way makes my gain: live Roderigo,
He calls me to a restitution large
Of gold, and jewels, that I bobb'd from him,
As gifts to Desdemona;
It must not be: if Cassio do remain,
He hath a daily beauty in his life,
That makes me ugly; and, besides, the Moor 20
May unfold me to him: there stand I in much peril.
No, he must die:—but, so I hear him coming.

Enter CASSIO.

  Rod. I know his gait; 'tis he.—Villain, thou diest.
    [*Rushing out, and making a pass at* CASSIO.
  Cas. That thrust had been mine enemy indeed,
But that my coat is better than thou know'st:
I will make proof of thine.
     [*Draws, and wounds* RODERIGO.
  Rod.   O, I am slain!
    [IAGO *rushes from his post, cuts* CASSIO
    behind in the leg, and exit.
  Cas. I am maim'd for ever.—Help, ho! murder!
    murder!   [*Falls.*

Enter OTHELLO, *at a distance.*

  Oth. The voice of Cassio:—Iago keeps his word.
  Rod. O, villain that I am!
  Oth.   It is even so.
  Cas. O, help! ho! light! a surgeon!   30
  Oth. 'T is he.—O brave Iago, honest, and just,
That hast such noble sense of thy friend's wrong!
Thou teachest me,—Minion, your dear lies dead,
And your unblest fate hies:—strumpet, I come!
Forth of my heart those charms, thine eyes, are
    blotted;
Thy bed, lust-stain'd, shall with lust's blood be spotted.
                        [*Exit.*

Enter LODOVICO *and* GRATIANO, *at a distance.*

  Cas. What, ho! no watch? no passage? murder!
    murder!
  Gra. 'T is some mischance; the cry is very direful.
  Cas. O, help!
  Lod. Hark!   40

  Rod. O wretched villain!
  Lod. Two or three groan.—It is a heavy night!
These may be counterfeits; let 's think 't unsafe
To come in to the cry without more help.
  Rod. Nobody come? then shall I bleed to death.
  Lod. Hark!

Re-enter IAGO, *with a light.*

  Gra. Here 's one comes in his shirt, with light and
    weapons.
  Iago. Who 's there? whose noise is this, that cries
    on murder?
  Lod. We do not know.
  Iago.   Did not you hear a cry?
  Cas. Here, here! for Heaven's sake, help me!
  Iago.   What 's the matter?
  Gra. This is Othello's ancient, as I take it.   51
  Lod. The same, indeed; a very valiant fellow.
  Iago. What are you here, that cry so grievously?
  Cas. Iago? O! I am spoil'd, undone by villains:
Give me some help.
  Iago. O me, lieutenant! what villains have done
    this?
  Cas. I think that one of them is hereabout,
And cannot make away.
  Iago.   O treacherous villains!—
    [*To* LODOVICO *and* GRATIANO.] What are you there?
    come in, and give some help.
  Rod. O, help me here!   60
  Cas. That 's one of them.
  Iago.   O murderous slave! O villain!
                    [*Stabs* RODERIGO.
  Rod. O damn'd Iago! O inhuman dog!
  Iago. Kill men i' the dark!—Where be these bloody
    thieves?
How silent is this town!—Ho! murder! murder!
What may you be? are you of good, or evil?
  Lod. As you shall prove us, praise us.
  Iago. Signior Lodovico?
  Lod. He, sir.
  Iago. I cry you mercy. Here 's Cassio hurt by
    villains.
  Gra. Cassio?   70
  Iago. How is 't, brother?
  Cas. My leg is cut in two.
  Iago.   Marry, Heaven forbid!—
Light, gentlemen; I 'll bind it with my shirt.

Enter BIANCA.

  Bian. What is the matter, ho? who is 't that cried?
  Iago. Who is 't that cried?
  Bian. O my dear Cassio! my sweet Cassio!
O Cassio, Cassio, Cassio!
  Iago. O notable strumpet!—Cassio, may you suspect
Who they should be, that have thus mangled you?
  Cas. No.   80
  Gra. I am sorry to find you thus: I have been to
    seek you.
  Iago. Lend me a garter:—so.—O, for a chair,
To bear him easily hence!
  Bian. Alas! he faints.—O Cassio, Cassio, Cassio!
  Iago. Gentlemen all, I do suspect this trash
To be a party in this injury.—
Patience awhile, good Cassio.—Come, come.
Lend me a light.—Know we this face, or no?

Alas! my friend, and my dear countryman,
Roderigo? no:—yes, sure. O Heaven! Roderigo.   90
Gra. What, of Venice?
Iago. Even he, sir; did you know him?
Gra.   Know him? ay.
Iago. Signor Gratiano? I cry you gentle pardon:
These bloody accidents must excuse my manners,
That so neglected you.
Gra.   I am glad to see you.
Iago. How do you, Cassio?—O, a chair, a chair!
Gra. Roderigo!
Iago. He, he, 't is he.—[*A chair brought in.*] O!
  that 's well said ;—the chair.—
Some good man bear him carefully from hence;
I 'll fetch the general's surgeon.—[*To* BIANCA.] For
  you, mistress,   100
Save you your labour.—He that lies slain here, Cassio,
Was my dear friend. What malice was between you?
Cas. None in the world; nor do I know the man.
Iago. [*To* BIANCA.] What, look you pale?—O, bear
  him out o' the air.—
  [CASSIO *and* RODERIGO *are borne off.*
Stay you, good gentlemen.—Look you pale, mistress?—
Do you perceive the ghastness of her eye?—
Nay, if you stare, we shall hear more anon.—
Behold her well; I pray you, look upon her:
Do you see, gentlemen? nay, guiltiness will speak,
Though tongues were out of use.   110

Enter EMILIA.

Emil. 'Las! what 's the matter? what 's the matter,
  husband?
Iago. Cassio hath here been set on in the dark
By Roderigo, and fellows that are 'scap'd.
He 's almost slain, and Roderigo dead.
Emil. Alas, good gentleman! alas, good Cassio!
Iago. This is the fruits of whoring.—Pr'ythee, Emilia,
Go know of Cassio where he supp'd to-night.—
What! do you shake at that?
Bian. He supp'd at my house; but I therefore shake
  not.
Iago. O, did he so? I charge you, go with me.   120
Emil. Fie, fie upon thee, strumpet!
Bian. I am no strumpet; but of life as honest,
As you that thus abuse me.
Emil.   As I? foh! fie upon thee!
Iago. Kind gentlemen, let 's go see poor Cassio
  dress'd.—
Come, mistress, you must tell 's another tale.—
Emilia, run you to the citadel,
And tell my lord and lady what hath happ'd.—
Will you go on afore?—[*Aside.*] This is the night,
That either makes me, or fordoes me quite. [*Exeunt.*

SCENE II.—*A Bedchamber.*

DESDEMONA *in bed asleep. A light burning.*

Enter OTHELLO.

Oth. It is the cause, it is the cause, my soul,—
Let me not name it to you, you chaste stars!—
It is the cause.—Yet I 'll not shed her blood;
Nor scar that whiter skin of hers than snow,
And smooth as monumental alabaster.
Yet she must die, else she 'll betray more men.
Put out the light, and then put out the light:
If I quench thee, thou flaming minister,
I can again thy former light restore,
Should I repent me; but once put out thy light,   10
Thou cunning'st pattern of excelling nature,
I know not where is that Promethean heat
That can thy light relume. When I have pluck'd thy
  rose,
I cannot give it vital growth again,
It needs must wither:—I 'll smell it on the tree.—
                          [*Kissing her.*
O balmy breath, that dost almost persuade
Justice to break her sword!—One more, one more.—
Be thus when thou art dead, and I will kill thee,
And love thee after.—One more, and this the last:
So sweet was ne'er so fatal. I must weep,   20

But they are cruel tears: this sorrow 's heavenly;
It strikes where it doth love.—She wakes.
Des. Who 's there? Othello?
Oth.   Ay, Desdemona.
Des. Will you come to bed, my lord?
Oth. Have you pray'd to-night, Desdemon?
Des.   Ay, my lord.
Oth. If you bethink yourself of any crime,
Unreconcil'd as yet to Heaven and grace,
Solicit for it straight.
Des. Alas, my lord! what may you mean by that?
Oth. Well, do it, and be brief; I will walk by: 29
I would not kill thy unprepared spirit;
No,—Heaven forfend!—I would not kill thy soul.
Des. Talk you of killing?
Oth.   Ay, I do.
Des.   Then, Heaven
Have mercy on me!
Oth.   Amen, with all my heart!
Des. If you say so, I hope you will not kill me.
Oth. Hum!
Des. And yet I fear you; for you are fatal then,
When your eyes roll so. Why I should fear, I know not,
Since guiltiness I know not; but yet, I feel I fear.
Oth. Think on thy sins.
Des.   They are loves I bear to you.
Oth. Ay, and for that thou diest.   41
Des. That death 's unnatural, that kills for loving.—
Alas! why gnaw you so your nether lip?—
Some bloody passion shakes your very frame:
These are portents; but yet I hope, I hope,
They do not point on me.
Oth.   Peace, and be still!
Des. I will so. What 's the matter?
Oth. That handkerchief, which I so lov'd and gave
  thee,
Thou gav'st to Cassio.
Des.   No, by my life and soul!
Send for the man, and ask him.
Oth.   Sweet soul, take heed,
Take heed of perjury: thou art on thy death-bed.   51
Des. Ay, but not yet to die.
Oth.   Yes, presently:
Therefore, confess thee freely of thy sin;
For to deny each article with oath
Cannot remove, nor choke, the strong conception,
That I do groan withal. Thou art to die.
Des. Then Lord have mercy on me!
Oth.   I say, Amen.
Des. And have you mercy too!—I never did
Offend you in my life; never lov'd Cassio,
But with such general warranty of Heaven   60
As I might love: I never gave him token.
Oth. By Heaven, I saw my handkerchief in 's hand.
O perjur'd woman! thou dost stone my heart,
And mak'st me call what I intend to do,
A murder, which I thought a sacrifice:
I saw the handkerchief.
Des.   He found it then;
I never gave it him.—Send for him hither;
Let him confess a truth.
Oth.   He hath confess'd.
Des. What, my lord?
Oth. That he hath us'd thee.
Des.   How? unlawfully?   70
Oth. Ay.
Des. He will not say so.
Oth.   No; his mouth is stopp'd:
Honest Iago hath ta'en order for 't.
Des. O, my fear interprets.—What, is he dead?
Oth. Had all his hairs been lives, my great revenge
Had stomach for them all.
Des. Alas! he is betray'd, and I undone.
Oth. Out, strumpet! Weep'st thou for him to my
  face?
Des. O! banish me, my lord, but kill me not.
Oth. Down, strumpet!   80
Des. Kill me to-morrow; let me live to-night.
Oth. Nay, if you strive,—
Des. But half an hour!
Oth.   Being done, there is no pause.
Des. But while I say one prayer.

Oth. It is too late.   [*He smothers her.*
Emil. [*Within.*] My lord, my lord! what, ho! my
          lord, my lord!
Oth. What noise is this?—Not dead? not yet quite
          dead?

Still as the grave.—Shall she come in? Were 't good?—
I think she stirs again :—no.—What 's best to do?
If she come in, she 'll sure speak to my wife :
My wife! my wife! what wife?—I have no wife :
O, insupportable! O heavy hour!   100

Oth. " Yet she must die, else she 'll betray more men."

I, that am cruel, am yet merciful ;
I would not have thee linger in thy pain.—
So, so.   90
     Emil. [*Within.*] What, ho! my lord, my lord!
     Oth.   Who 's there?
     Emil. [*Within.*] O, good my lord! I would speak a
          word with you.
     Oth. Yes ;—'t is Emilia :—by-and-by.—She 's dead.—
'T is like she comes to speak of Cassio's death ;
The noise was high.—Ha! no more moving?

Methinks it should be now a huge eclipse
Of sun and moon, and that the affrighted globe
Should yawn at alteration.
     Emil. [*Within.*] I do beseech you, I may speak with
          you.
O, good my lord!
     Oth. I had forgot thee.   O! come in, Emilia.—
Soft,—by-and-by :—let me the curtains draw.—
Where art thou? What 's the matter with thee now?
                                        [*Unlocks the door.*

Enter EMILIA.

Emil. O, my good lord! yonder's foul murder done.
Oth. What! now? 110
Emil. But now, my lord.
Oth. It is the very error of the moon;
She comes more nearer earth than she was wont,
And makes men mad.
Emil. Cassio, my lord, has kill'd a young Venetian,
Call'd Roderigo.
Oth. Roderigo kill'd!
And Cassio kill'd!
Emil. No; Cassio is not kill'd.
Oth. Not Cassio kill'd? Then murder's out of tune,
And sweet revenge grows harsh.
Des. O, falsely, falsely murder'd!
Emil. Alas! what cry is that?
Oth. That! what? 121
Emil. Out, and alas! that was my lady's voice :—
Help! help, ho! help!—O lady, speak again!
Sweet Desdemona! O, sweet mistress, speak!
Des. A guiltless death I die.
Emil. O, who hath done this deed?
Des. Nobody; I myself: farewell:
Commend me to my kind lord. O, farewell! [*Dies.*
Oth. Why, how should she be murder'd?
Emil. Alas, who knows?
Oth. You heard her say herself, it was not I. 130
Emil. She said so : I must needs report the truth.
Oth. She's like a liar gone to burning hell :
'T was I that kill'd her.
Emil. O! the more angel she,
And you the blacker devil!
Oth. She turn'd to folly, and she was a whore.
Emil. Thou dost belie her, and thou art a devil.
Oth. She was false as water.
Emil. Thou art rash as fire, to say
That she was false : O! she was heavenly true.
Oth. Cassio did tup her; ask thy husband else.
O! I were damn'd beneath all depth in hell, 140
But that I did proceed upon just grounds
To this extremity. Thy husband knew it all.
Emil. My husband?
Oth. Thy husband.
Emil. That she was false to wedlock?
Oth. Ay, with Cassio. Nay, had she been true,
If Heaven would make me such another world
Of one entire and perfect chrysolite,
I'd not have sold her for it.
Emil. My husband?
Oth. Ay, 't was he that told me first :
An honest man he is, and hates the slime 151
That sticks on filthy deeds.
Emil. My husband?
Oth. What needs this iterance, woman? I say, thy
husband.
Emil. O mistress! villainy hath made mocks with
love.—
My husband say, that she was false?
Oth. He, woman;
I say, thy husband : dost understand the word?
My friend, thy husband, honest, honest Iago.
Emil. If he say so, may his pernicious soul
Rot half a grain a day! he lies to the heart :
She was too fond of her most filthy bargain. 160
Oth. Ha!
Emil. Do thy worst :
This deed of thine is no more worthy heaven,
Than thou wast worthy her.
Oth. Peace! you were best.
Emil. Thou hast not half that power to do me
harm,
As I have to be hurt. O gull! O dolt!
As ignorant as dirt! thou hast done a deed,—
I care not for thy sword; I'll make thee known,
Though I lost twenty lives.—Help! help, ho! help!
The Moor has kill'd my mistress! Murder! murder!

Enter MONTANO, GRATIANO, *and* IAGO.

Mon. What is the matter?—How now, general? 171
Emil. O! are you come, Iago? you have done well,
That men must lay their murders on your neck.

Gra. What is the matter?
Emil. Disprove this villain, if thou be'st a man :
He says, thou told'st him that his wife was false.
I know, thou didst not, thou 'rt not such a villain.
Speak, for my heart is full.
Iago. I told him what I thought; and told no more
Than what he found himself was apt and true. 180
Emil. But did you ever tell him, she was false?
Iago. I did.
Emil. You told a lie; an odious, damned lie;
Upon my soul, a lie; a wicked lie.—
She false with Cassio!—Did you say with Cassio?
Iago. With Cassio, mistress. Go to, charm your
tongue.
Emil. I will not charm my tongue; I am bound to
speak.
My mistress here lies murder'd in her bed.
All. O heavens forfend!
Emil. And your reports have set the murder on. 190
Oth. Nay, stare not, masters : it is true, indeed.
Gra. 'T is a strange truth.
Mon. O monstrous act!
Emil. Villainy! villainy! villainy!
I think upon 't,—I think,—I smell 't :—O villainy!
I thought so then :—I'll kill myself for grief.—
O villainy, villainy!
Iago. What! are you mad? I charge you, get you
home.
Emil. Good gentlemen, let me have leave to speak :
'T is proper I obey him, but not now.—
Perchance, Iago, I will ne'er go home. 200
Oth. O! O! O! [*Falling on the bed.*
Emil. Nay, lay thee down, and roar;
For thou hast kill'd the sweetest innocent,
That e'er did lift up eye.
Oth. [*Rising.*] O! she was foul.—
I scarce did know you, uncle. There lies your niece,
Whose breath, indeed, these hands have newly
stopp'd.
I know, this act shows horrible and grim.
Gra. Poor Desdemon! I am glad thy father's dead.
Thy match was mortal to him, and pure grief
Shore his old thread in twain : did he live now,
This sight would make him do a desperate turn, 210
Yea, curse his better angel from his side,
And fall to reprobance.
Oth. 'T is pitiful; but yet Iago knows,
That she with Cassio hath the act of shame
A thousand times committed : Cassio confess'd it;
And she did gratify his amorous works
With that recognisance and pledge of love
Which I first gave her. I saw it in his hand;
It was a handkerchief, an antique token
My father gave my mother. 220
Emil. O Heaven! O heavenly powers!
Iago. Come, hold your peace.
Emil. 'T will out, 't will out :—I hold my peace, sir?
no;
No, I will speak as liberal as the north :
Let Heaven, and men, and devils, let them all,
All, all, cry shame against me, yet I 'll speak.
Iago. Be wise, and get you home.
Emil. I will not.
[IAGO *offers to stab his wife.*
Gra. Fie!
Your sword upon a woman?
Emil. O thou dull Moor! that handkerchief thou
speak'st of,
I found by fortune, and did give my husband;
For often, with a solemn earnestness, 230
(More than, indeed, belong'd to such a trifle,)
He begg'd of me to steal it.
Iago. Villainous whore!
Emil. She give it Cassio! no, alas! I found it,
And I did give 't my husband.
Iago. Filth, thou liest!
Emil. By Heaven, I do not; I do not, gentlemen.—
O murderous coxcomb! what should such a fool
Do with so good a wife?
[IAGO *stabs* EMILIA, *then runs out.*
Oth. Are there no stones in heaven,
But what serve for the thunder?—Precious villain!

Gra. The woman falls : sure, he hath kill'd his wife.
Emil. Ay, ay. O, lay me by my mistress' side ! 240
Gra. He 's gone, but his wife 's kill'd.
Mon. 'T is a notorious villain.   Take you this
                 weapon,
Which I have here recover'd from the Moor.
Come, guard the door without : let him not pass,
But kill him rather.   I 'll after that same villain,
For 't is a damned slave.   [*Exit.*
Oth.   I am not valiant neither,
But every puny whipster gets my sword.
But why should honour outlive honesty ?
Let it go all.

From the possession of this heavenly sight !
Blow me about in winds ! roast me in sulphur !
Wash me in steep-down gulfs of liquid fire !
O Desdemon ! dead, Desdemon ! dead ! O !

Enter LODOVICO, MONTANO, CASSIO, *carried in a
      chair, and Officers, with* IAGO, *prisoner.*

Lod. Where is this rash and most unfortunate
                man ?
Oth. That 's he that was Othello ;—here I am.
Lod. Where is that viper ? bring the villain forth.
Oth. I look down towards his feet ;—but that 's a
                fable :

Gra. " The woman falls : sure, he hath kill'd his wife."

Emil.   What did thy song bode, lady ?
Hark, canst thou hear me ? I will play the swan, 250
And die in music.—[*Singing.*]   *Willow, willow,
      willow.*—
Moor, she was chaste : she lov'd thee, cruel Moor :
So come my soul to bliss, as I speak true ;
So speaking as I think, I die,—I die.   [*Dies.*
Oth. I have another weapon in this chamber ;
It is a sword of Spain, the ice-brook's temper.
O ! here it is.—Uncle, I must come forth.
Gra. If thou attempt it, it will cost thee dear :
Thou hast no weapon, and perforce must suffer.
Oth. Look in upon me then, and speak with me, 260
Or, naked as I am, I will assault thee.
Gra. What is the matter ?
Oth.   Behold ! I have a weapon ;
A better never did itself sustain
Upon a soldier's thigh : I have seen the day,
That with this little arm, and this good sword,
I have made my way through more impediments
Than twenty times your stop.—But, O vain boast !
Who can control his fate ? 't is not so now.—
Be not afraid, though you do see me weapon'd :
Here is my journey's end, here is my butt,   270
And very sea-mark of my utmost sail.
Do you go back dismay'd ? 't is a lost fear ;
Man but a rush against Othello's breast,
And he retires.—Where should Othello go ?—
Now, how dost thou look now ? O ill-starr'd wench !
Pale as thy smock ! when we shall meet at compt,
This look of thine will hurl my soul from heaven,
And fiends will snatch at it. Cold, cold, my girl !
Even like thy chastity.
O, cursed, cursed slave !—Whip me, ye devils,   280

If that thou be'st a devil, I cannot kill thee.
                             [*Wounds* IAGO.
Lod. Wrench his sword from him.
Iago.   I bleed, sir ; but not kill'd.
Oth. I am not sorry neither : I 'd have thee live ; 291
For, in my sense, 't is happiness to die.
Lod. O thou Othello ! that wert once so good,
Fall'n in the practice of a damned slave,
What shall be said to thee ?
Oth.   Why, anything :
An honourable murderer, if you will ;
For nought did I in hate, but all in honour.
Lod. This wretch hath part confessed his villany :
Did you and he consent in Cassio's death ?
Oth. Ay.   300
Cas. Dear general, I never gave you cause.
Oth. I do believe it, and I ask you pardon.
Will you, I pray, demand that demi-devil,
Why he hath thus ensnar'd my soul and body ?
Iago. Demand me nothing : what you know, you
                know :
From this time forth I never will speak word.
Lod. What ! not to pray ?
Gra.   Torments will ope your lips.
Oth. Well, thou dost best.
Lod. Sir, you shall understand what hath befall'n,
Which, as I think, you know not. Here is a letter, 310
Found in the pocket of the slain Roderigo ;
And here another : the one of them imports
The death of Cassio to be undertook
By Roderigo.
Oth. O villain !
Cas.   Most heathenish, and most gross !
Lod. Now, here 's another discontented paper,

Found in his pocket too ; and this, it seems,
Roderigo meant to have sent this damned villain ;
But that, belike, Iago in the interim
Came in and satisfied him.
 Oth.   O thou pernicious caitiff !—
How came you, Cassio, by that handkerchief, 321
That was my wife's ?
 Cas.   I found it in my chamber :
And he himself confess'd, but even now,
That there he dropp'd it, for a special purpose,
Which wrought to his desire.
 Oth.   O fool ! fool ! fool !
 Cas. There is, besides, in Roderigo's letter,
How he upbraids Iago, that he made him
Brave me upon the watch ; whereon it came
That I was cast : and even but now he spake,
After long seeming dead,—Iago hurt him, 330
Iago set him on.
 Lod. You must forsake this room, and go with us :
Your power and your command is taken off,
And Cassio rules in Cyprus. For this slave,—
If there be any cunning cruelty,
That can torment him much, and hold him long,
It shall be his. You shall close prisoner rest,
Till that the nature of your fault be known
To the Venetian state.—Come, bring him away.
 Oth. Soft you ; a word or two, before you go. 340
I have done the state some service, and they know
No more of that.—I pray you, in your letters,
When you shall these unlucky deeds relate,
Speak of me as I am ; nothing extenuate,
Nor set down aught in malice : then must you speak
Of one that lov'd not wisely, but too well ;
Of one not easily jealous, but, being wrought,
Perplex'd in the extreme ; of one, whose hand,
Like the base Indian, threw a pearl away,
Richer than all his tribe ; of one, whose subdu'd
 eyes,
Albeit unused to the melting mood, 351
Drop tears as fast as the Arabian trees
Their medicinable gum. Set you down this ;
And say, besides, that in Aleppo once,
Where a malignant and a turban'd Turk
Beat a Venetian, and traduc'd the state,
I took by the throat the circumcised dog,
And smote him—thus. [*Stabs himself.*
 Lod. O bloody period !
 Gra.   All that 's spoke is marr'd.
 Oth. I kiss'd thee, ere I kill'd thee :—no way but
 this, [*Falling upon* DESDEMONA.
Killing myself to die upon a kiss. [*Dies.*
 Cas. This did I fear, but thought he had no weapon ;
For he was great of heart.
 Lod. [*To* IAGO.] O Spartan dog ! 363
More fell than anguish, hunger, or the sea !
Look on the tragic loading of this bed ;
This is thy work : the object poisons sight ;
Let it be hid.—Gratiano, keep the house,
And seize upon the fortunes of the Moor,
For they succeed on you.—To you, lord governor,
Remains the censure of this hellish villain ; 370
The time, the place, the torture :—O, enforce it !
Myself will straight aboard, and to the state
This heavy act with heavy heart relate. [*Exeunt.*

ANTONY AND CLEOPATRA.

DRAMATIS PERSONÆ.

M. ANTONY,
OCTAVIUS CÆSAR, } *Triumvirs.*
M. ÆMIL. LEPIDUS,
SEXTUS POMPEIUS.
DOMITIUS ENOBARBUS,
VENTIDIUS,
EROS,
SCARUS, } *Friends of Antony.*
DERCETAS,
DEMETRIUS,
PHILO,
MECÆNAS,
AGRIPPA,
DOLABELLA, } *Friends of Cæsar.*
PROCULEIUS,
THYREUS,
GALLUS,

MENAS,
MENECRATES, } *Friends of Pompey.*
VARRIUS,
TAURUS, *Lieutenant-General to Cæsar.*
CANIDIUS, *Lieutenant-General to Antony.*
SILIUS, *an Officer under Ventidius.*
EUPHRONIUS, *an Ambassador from Antony to Cæsar.*
ALEXAS, MARDIAN, SELEUCUS, *and* DIOMEDES, *Attendants on Cleopatra.*
A Soothsayer. A Clown.

CLEOPATRA, *Queen of Egypt.*
OCTAVIA, *Sister to Cæsar, and Wife to Antony.*
CHARMIAN *and* IRAS, *Attendants on Cleopatra.*

Officers, Soldiers, Messengers, and other Attendants.

SCENE—In several Parts of the Roman Empire.

ACT I.

SCENE I.—Alexandria. A Room in CLEOPATRA'S Palace.

Enter DEMETRIUS *and* PHILO.

Philo.
NAY, but this dotage of our general's
O'erflows the measure: those his
  goodly eyes,
That o'er the files and musters of
  the war
Have glow'd like plated Mars,
  now bend, now turn,
The office and devotion of their
  view
Upon a tawny front: his captain's
  heart,
Which in the scuffles of great fights hath burst
The buckles on his breast, reneagues all temper,
And is become the bellows, and the fan,
To cool a gipsy's lust. Look, where they come. 10

Flourish. Enter ANTONY *and* CLEOPATRA, *with their Trains; Eunuchs fanning her.*

Take but good note, and you shall see in him
The triple pillar of the world transform'd
Into a strumpet's fool: behold and see.
  Cleo. If it be love indeed, tell me how much.
  Ant. There's beggary in the love that can be
    reckon'd.
  Cleo. I'll set a bourn how far to be belov'd.
  Ant. Then must thou needs find out new heaven,
    new earth.

Enter an Attendant.

  Att. News, my good lord, from Rome.
  Ant.   Grates me:—the sum.
  Cleo. Nay, hear them, Antony:
Fulvia, perchance, is angry; or, who knows   20
If the scarce-bearded Cæsar have not sent
His powerful mandate to you, "Do this, or this;

Take in that kingdom, and enfranchise that;
Perform 't, or else we damn thee."
  Ant.   How, my love!
  Cleo. Perchance,—nay, and most like,—
You must not stay here longer; your dismission
Is come from Cæsar; therefore hear it, Antony.—
Where's Fulvia's process? Cæsar's, I would say?
    both?—
Call in the messengers.—As I am Egypt's queen,
Thou blushest, Antony, and that blood of thine   30
Is Cæsar's homager; else so thy cheek pays shame,
When shrill-tongu'd Fulvia scolds.—The messengers!
  Ant. Let Rome in Tiber melt, and the wide arch
Of the rang'd empire fall! Here is my space.
Kingdoms are clay; our dungy earth alike
Feeds beast as man: the nobleness of life
Is, to do thus; when such a mutual pair,   [*Embracing.*
And such a twain can do 't, in which I bind,
On pain of punishment, the world to weet,
We stand up peerless.
  Cleo.   Excellent falsehood!   40
Why did he marry Fulvia, and not love her?—
I'll seem the fool I am not; Antony
Will be himself.
  Ant.   But stirr'd by Cleopatra.—
Now, for the love of Love, and her soft hours,
Let's not confound the time with conference harsh:
There's not a minute of our lives should stretch
Without some pleasure now. What sport to-night?
  Cleo. Hear the ambassadors.
  Ant.   Fie, wrangling queen!
Whom everything becomes, to chide, to laugh,
To weep; whose every passion fully strives   50
To make itself, in thee, fair and admir'd.
No messenger; but thine, and all alone,
To-night we'll wander through the streets, and note

The qualities of people. Come, my queen;
Last night you did desire it.—Speak not to us.
                [Exeunt Antony *and* Cleopatra, *with
                        their Train.*
Dem. Is Cæsar with Antonius priz'd so slight?
Phi. Sir, sometimes, when he is not Antony,
He comes too short of that great property
Which still should go with Antony.
Dem.   I am full sorry,
That he approves the common liar, who   60
Thus speaks of him at Rome; but I will hope
Of better deeds to-morrow. Rest you happy.
                                        [Exeunt.

SCENE II.—The Same. Another Room.

Enter Charmian, Iras, Alexas, *and a Soothsayer.*
Char. Lord Alexas, sweet Alexas, most anything

Char. "Good sir, give me good fortune."

Alexas, almost most absolute Alexas, where's the
soothsayer that you praised so to the queen? O! that
I knew this husband, which, you say, must charge his
horns with garlands!
Alex. Soothsayer!
Sooth. Your will?
Char. Is this the man?—Is't you, sir, that know
    things?
Sooth. In nature's infinite book of secrecy
A little I can read.
Alex.   Show him your hand.   10

Enter Enobarbus.

Eno. Bring in the banquet quickly; wine enough,
Cleopatra's health to drink.
Char. Good sir, give me good fortune.
Sooth. I make not, but foresee.
Char. Pray then, foresee me one.
Sooth. You shall be yet far fairer than you are.
Iras. No, you shall paint when you are old.
Char. Wrinkles forbid!
Alex. Vex not his prescience; be attentive.   20
Char. Hush!
Sooth. You shall be more beloving, than belov'd.
Char. I had rather heat my liver with drinking.
Alex. Nay, hear him.
Char. Good now, some excellent fortune! Let me
be married to three kings in a forenoon, and widow
them all: let me have a child at fifty, to whom Herod
of Jewry may do homage: find me to marry me with
Octavius Cæsar, and companion me with my mistress.
Sooth. You shall outlive the lady whom you serve.
Char. O excellent! I love long life better than figs.
Sooth. You have seen and prov'd a fairer former
    fortune,   32
Than that which is to approach.

Char. Then, belike, my children shall have no
names: pr'ythee, how many boys and wenches must
I have?
Sooth. If every of your wishes had a womb,
And fertile every wish, a million.
Char. Out, fool! I forgive thee for a witch.
Alex. You think, none but your sheets are privy to
your wishes.   41
Char. Nay, come; tell Iras hers.
Alex. We'll know all our fortunes.
Eno. Mine, and most of our fortunes, to-night, shall
be—drunk to bed.
Iras. There's a palm presages chastity, if nothing
else.
Char. Even as the o'erflowing Nilus presageth
famine.   49
Iras. Go, you wild bedfellow, you cannot soothsay.
Char. Nay, if an oily palm be not a fruitful prog-
nostication, I cannot scratch mine ear.—Pr'ythee, tell
her but a worky-day fortune.
Sooth. Your fortunes are alike.
Iras. But how? but how? give me particulars.
Sooth. I have said.
Iras. Am I not an inch of fortune better than she?
Char. Well, if you were but an inch of fortune
better than I, where would you choose it?
Iras. Not in my husband's nose.   60
Char. Our worser thoughts heavens mend! Alexas,
—come, his fortune, his fortune.—O! let him marry a
woman that cannot go, sweet Isis, I beseech thee;
and let her die too, and give him a worse; and let
worse follow worse, till the worst of all follow him
laughing to his grave, fifty-fold a cuckold! Good
Isis, hear me this prayer, though thou deny me a
matter of more weight, good Isis, I beseech thee! 68
Iras. Amen. Dear goddess, hear that prayer of the
people; for, as it is a heart-breaking to see a handsome man loose-wived, so it is a deadly sorrow to
behold a foul knave uncuckolded: therefore, dear
Isis, keep decorum, and fortune him accordingly!
Char. Amen.
Alex. Lo, now! if it lay in their hands to make me
a cuckold, they would make themselves whores, but
they'd do't.
Eno. Hush! here comes Antony.
Char.   Not he; the queen.

Enter Cleopatra.

Cleo. Saw you my lord?
Eno. No, lady.   80
Cleo. Was he not here?
Char. No, madam.
Cleo. He was dispos'd to mirth; but, on the sudden,
A Roman thought hath struck him.—Enobarbus,—
Eno. Madam?
Cleo. Seek him, and bring him hither. Where's
Alexas?
Alex. Here, at your service.—My lord approaches.

Enter Antony, *with a Messenger and Attendants.*

Cleo. We will not look upon him: go with us.
        [Exeunt Cleopatra, Enobarbus, Alexas, Iras,
                Charmian, *Soothsayer, and Attendants.*
Mess. Fulvia thy wife first came into the field.
Ant. Against my brother Lucius?   90
Mess. Ay:
But soon that war had end, and the time's state
Made friends of them, jointing their force 'gainst
                                        Cæsar;
Whose better issue in the war, from Italy,
Upon the first encounter, drave them.
Ant.   Well what worst?
Mess. The nature of bad news infects the teller.
Ant. When it concerns the fool, or coward.—On:
Things, that are past, are done with me.—'T is thus:
Who tells me true, though in his tale lie death,
I hear him as he flatter'd.
Mess.   Labienus   100
(This is stiff news) hath with his Parthian force
Extended Asia; from Euphrates
His conquering banner shook, from Syria,
To Lydia, and to Ionia: whilst—

Ant. Antony, thou wouldst say,—
Mess. O, my lord!
Ant. Speak to me home, mince not the general
　　　tongue;
Name Cleopatra as she is call'd in Rome;
Rail thou in Fulvia's phrase; and taunt my faults
With such full license, as both truth and malice　110
Have power to utter. O! then we bring forth weeds,
When our quick winds lie still; and our ills told us,
Is as our earing. Fare thee well awhile.
Mess. At your noble pleasure. 　　　　[*Exit.*
Ant. From Sicyon, ho, the news! Speak there!
1 Att. The man from Sicyon.—Is there such an one?
2 Att. He stays upon your will.
Ant. 　　　　　　　Let him appear.—
These strong Egyptian fetters I must break,
Or lose myself in dotage.

　　　　Enter another Messenger.
　　　　　　　What are you?
2 Mess. Fulvia thy wife is dead.
Ant. 　　　　　　Where died she?　121
2 Mess. In Sicyon:
Her length of sickness, with what else more serious
Importeth thee to know, this bears. [*Giving a letter.*
Ant. 　　　Forbear me.— 　[*Exit Messenger.*
There's a great spirit gone. Thus did I desire it:
What our contempts do often hurl from us,
We wish it ours again; the present pleasure,
By revolution lowering, does become
The opposite of itself: she's good, being gone;
The hand could pluck her back, that shov'd her on.
I must from this enchanting queen break off;　130
Ten thousand harms, more than the ills I know,
My idleness doth hatch.—How now! Enobarbus!

　　　　　Re-enter ENOBARBUS.
Eno. What's your pleasure, sir?
Ant. I must with haste from hence.
Eno. Why, then, we kill all our women. We see
how mortal an unkindness is to them: if they suffer
our departure, death's the word.
Ant. I must be gone. 　　　　　　138
Eno. Under a compelling occasion, let women die:
it were pity to cast them away for nothing; though,
between them and a great cause, they should be
esteemed nothing. Cleopatra, catching but the least
noise of this, dies instantly: I have seen her die
twenty times upon far poorer moment. I do think,
there is mettle in death, which commits some loving
act upon her, she hath such a celerity in dying.
Ant. She is cunning past man's thought.
Eno. Alack, sir! no; her passions are made of
nothing but the finest part of pure love. We cannot
call her winds and waters sighs and tears; they are
greater storms and tempests than almanacs can report: this cannot be cunning in her; if it be, she
makes a shower of rain as well as Jove.　153
Ant. 'Would I had never seen her!
Eno. O, sir! you had then left unseen a wonderful
piece of work; which not to have been blessed withal,
would have discredited your travel.
Ant. Fulvia is dead.
Eno. Sir?
Ant. Fulvia is dead.　　　　　　　160
Eno. Fulvia?
Ant. Dead.
Eno. Why, sir, give the gods a thankful sacrifice.
When it pleaseth their deities to take the wife of a
man from him, it shows to man the tailors of the
earth: comforting therein, that when old robes are
worn out, there are members to make new. If there
were no more women but Fulvia, then had you indeed
a cut, and the case to be lamented: this grief is
crowned with consolation; your old smock brings
forth a new petticoat; and, indeed, the tears live in
an onion, that should water this sorrow.　172
Ant. The business she hath broached in the state
Cannot endure my absence.
Eno. And the business you have broached here
cannot be without you; especially that of Cleopatra's,
which wholly depends on your abode.

Ant. No more light answers. Let our officers
Have notice what we purpose. I shall break
The cause of our expedience to the queen,　　180
And get her love to part. For not alone
The death of Fulvia, with more urgent touches,
Do strongly speak to us, but the letters too
Of many our contriving friends in Rome
Petition us at home. Sextus Pompeius
Hath given the dare to Cæsar, and commands
The empire of the sea: our slippery people
(Whose love is never link'd to the deserver,
Till his deserts are past) begin to throw
Pompey the Great, and all his dignities,　　190
Upon his son: who, high in name and power,
Higher than both in blood and life, stands up
For the main soldier; whose quality, going on,
The sides o' the world may danger. Much is breeding,
Which, like the courser's hair, hath yet but life,
And not a serpent's poison. Say, our pleasure,
To such whose place is under us, requires
Our quick remove from hence.
Eno. 　　　　　　I shall do it. [*Exeunt.*

　　　　　　　─────

SCENE III.—The Same. Another Room.

Enter CLEOPATRA, CHARMIAN, IRAS, *and* ALEXAS.
Cleo. Where is he?
Char. 　　　　I did not see him since.
Cleo. See where he is, who's with him, what he
　　does:—
I did not send you.—If you find him sad,
Say, I am dancing; if in mirth, report
That I am sudden sick: quick, and return.
　　　　　　　　　[*Exit* ALEXAS.
Char. Madam, methinks, if you did love him dearly,
You do not hold the method to enforce
The like from him.
Cleo. 　　　　What should I do, I do not?
Char. In each thing give him way, cross him in
　　nothing.
Cleo. Thou teachest like a fool: the way to lose him.
Char. Tempt him not so too far; I wish, forbear: 11
In time we hate that which we often fear.

　　　　　　Enter ANTONY.
But here comes Antony.
Cleo. 　　　　　　I am sick and sullen.
Ant. I am sorry to give breathing to my purpose.
Cleo. Help me away, dear Charmian; I shall fall:
It cannot be thus long, the sides of nature
Will not sustain it.
Ant. 　　　　　Now, my dearest queen,—
Cleo. Pray you, stand further from me.
Ant. 　　　　　　　　What's the matter?
Cleo. I know, by that same eye, there's some good
　　news.
What says the married woman?—You may go:　20
'Would she had never given you leave to come!
Let her not say, 'tis I that keep you here:
I have no power upon you; hers you are.
Ant. The gods best know,—
Cleo. 　　　　　　O! never was there queen
So mightily betray'd; yet at the first
I saw the treasons planted.
Ant. 　　　　　　　Cleopatra,—
Cleo. Why should I think, you can be mine, and
　　true,
Though you in swearing shake the throned gods,
Who have been false to Fulvia? Riotous madness,　30
To be entangled with those mouth-made vows,
Which break themselves in swearing!
Ant. 　　　　　　　　Most sweet queen,—
Cleo. Nay, pray you, seek no colour for your going,
But bid farewell, and go: when you sued staying,
Then was the time for words; no going then:—
Eternity was in our lips and eyes;
Bliss in our brows' bent; none our parts so poor,
But was a race of heaven: they are so still,
Or thou, the greatest soldier of the world,
Art turn'd the greatest liar.
Ant. 　　　　　　How now, lady!

Cleo. I would I had thy inches; thou shouldst
    know,   40
There were a heart in Egypt.
    Ant.   Hear me, queen.
The strong necessity of time commands
Our services awhile ; but my full heart
Remains in use with you. Our Italy
Shines o'er with civil swords : Sextus Pompeius
Makes his approaches to the port of Rome :
Equality of two domestic powers
Breed scrupulous faction. The hated, grown to
    strength,
Are newly grown to love : the condemn'd Pompey,
Rich in his father's honour, creeps apace   50
Into the hearts of such as have not thriv'd
Upon the present state, whose numbers threaten ;
And quietness, grown sick of rest, would purge
By any desperate change. My more particular,
And that which most with you should safe my
    going,
Is Fulvia's death.
    Cleo. Though age from folly could not give me
    freedom,
It does from childishness.—Can Fulvia die ?
    Ant. She 's dead, my queen.
Look here, and, at thy sovereign leisure, read   60
The garboils she awak'd ; at the last, best,
See, when and where she died.
    Cleo.   O most false love
Where be the sacred vials thou shouldst fill
With sorrowful water ? Now I see, the tears
In Fulvia's death, how mine receiv'd shall be.
    Ant. Quarrel no more, but be prepar'd to know
The purposes I bear ; which are, or cease,
As you shall give the advice. By the fire
That quickens Nilus' slime, I go from hence,
Thy soldier, servant ; making peace, or war,   70
As thou affect'st.
    Cleo.   Cut my lace, Charmian, come ;—
But let it be.—I am quickly ill, and well :
So Antony loves.
    Ant.   My precious queen, forbear ;
And give true evidence to his love, which stands
An honourable trial.
    Cleo.   So Fulvia told me.
I pr'ythee, turn aside, and weep for her ;
Then bid adieu to me, and say, the tears
Belong to Egypt : good now, play one scene
Of excellent dissembling, and let it look
Like perfect honour.
    Ant.   You 'll heat my blood : no more.
    Cleo. You can do better yet, but this is meetly. 81
    Ant. Now, by my sword,—
    Cleo.   And target.—Still he mends ;
But this is not the best. Look, pr'ythee, Char-
    mian,
How this Herculean Roman does become
The carriage of his chafe.
    Ant. I 'll leave you, lady.
    Cleo.   Courteous lord, one word.
Sir, you and I must part,—but that 's not it :
Sir, you and I have lov'd,—but there 's not it ;
That you know well : something it is I would,—
O ! my oblivion is a very Antony,   90
And I am all forgotten.
    Ant.   But that your royalty
Holds idleness your subject, I should take you
For idleness itself.
    Cleo.   'T is sweating labour
To bear such idleness so near the heart,
As Cleopatra this. But, sir, forgive me ;
Since my becomings kill me, when they do not
Eye well to you : your honour calls you hence ;
Therefore, be deaf to my unpitied folly,
And all the gods go with you ! Upon your sword
Sit laurel victory, and smooth success   100
Be strew'd before your feet !
    Ant.   Let us go. Come ;
Our separation so abides, and flies,
That thou, residing here, go'st yet with me,
And I, hence fleeting, here remain with thee.
Away !   [*Exeunt.*

SCENE IV.—Rome.   An Apartment in CÆSAR'S
                        House.

Enter OCTAVIUS CÆSAR, LEPIDUS, *and Attendants.*

    Cæs. You may see, Lepidus, and henceforth know,
It is not Cæsar's natural wise to hate
Our great competitor. From Alexandria
This is the news : he fishes, drinks, and wastes
The lamps of night in revel ; is not more manlike
Than Cleopatra, nor the queen of Ptolemy
More womanly than he ; hardly gave audience, or
Vouchsaf'd to think he had partners : you shall find
    there
A man, who is the abstract of all faults
That all men follow.
    Lep.   I must not think, there are 10
Evils enow to darken all his goodness :
His faults, in him, seem as the spots of heaven,
More fiery by night's blackness ; hereditary,
Rather than purchas'd ; what he cannot change,
Than what he chooses.
    Cæs. You are too indulgent. Let us grant, it is not
Amiss to tumble on the bed of Ptolemy ;
To give a kingdom for a mirth ; to sit
And keep the turn of tippling with a slave ;
To reel the streets at noon, and stand the buffet   20
With knaves that smell of sweat : say, this becomes
    him,
(As his composure must be rare indeed,
Whom these things cannot blemish,) yet must Antony
No way excuse his soils, when we do bear
So great weight in his lightness. If he fill'd
His vacancy with his voluptuousness,
Full surfeits, and the dryness of his bones,
Call on him for 't ; but, to confound such time,
That drums him from his sport, and speaks as loud
As his own state, and ours,—'t is to be chid   30
As we rate boys, who, being mature in knowledge,
Pawn their experience to their present pleasure,
And so rebel to judgment.

                Enter a Messenger.
    Lep.   Here 's more news.
    Mess. Thy biddings have been done ; and every
    hour,
Most noble Cæsar, shalt thou have report
How 't is abroad. Pompey is strong at sea ;
And it appears, he is belov'd of those
That only have fear'd Cæsar : to the ports
The discontents repair, and men's reports
Give him much wrong'd.
    Cæs.   I should have known no less.
It hath been taught us from the primal state,   41
That he, which is, was wish'd, until he were ;
And the ebb'd man, ne'er lov'd, till ne'er worth love,
Comes dear'd by being lack'd. This common body,
Like to a vagabond flag upon the stream,
Goes to, and back, lackeying the varying tide,
To rot itself with motion.
    Mess.   Cæsar, I bring thee word,
Menecrates and Menas, famous pirates,
Make the sea serve them ; which they ear and wound
With keels of every kind : many hot inroads   50
They make in Italy ; the borders maritime
Lack blood to think on 't, and flush youth revolt :
No vessel can peep forth, but 't is as soon
Taken as seen ; for Pompey's name strikes more,
Than could his war resisted.
    Cæs.   Antony,
Leave thy lascivious wassails. When thou once
Wast beaten from Modena, where thou slew'st
Hirtius and Pansa, consuls, at thy heel
Did famine follow ; whom thou fought'st against,
Though daintily brought up, with patience more   60
Than savages could suffer : thou didst drink
The stale of horses, and the gilded puddle,
Which beasts would cough at : thy palate then did
    deign
The roughest berry on the rudest hedge ;
Yea, like the stag, when snow the pasture sheets,
The barks of trees thou browsed'st ; on the Alps,
It is reported, thou didst eat strange flesh,

Which some did die to look on ; and all this
(It wounds thine honour, that I speak it now)
Was borne so like a soldier, that thy cheek   70
So much as lank'd not.
  Lep. 'T is pity of him.
  Cæs. Let his shames quickly
Drive him to Rome. 'T is time we twain
Did show ourselves i' the field ; and, to that end,
Assemble we immediate council : Pompey
Thrives in our idleness.
  Lep. To-morrow, Cæsar,
I shall be furnish'd to inform you rightly
Both what by sea and land I can be able,
To front this present time.
  Cæs. Till which encounter,   80
It is my business too. Farewell.
  Lep. Farewell, my lord. What you shall know
      meantime
Of stirs abroad, I shall beseech you, sir,
To let me be partaker.
  Cæs. Doubt not, sir ;
I knew it for my bond.   *[Exeunt.*

SCENE V.—Alexandria. A Room in the Palace.

Enter CLEOPATRA, CHARMIAN, IRAS, *and* MARDIAN.

  Cleo. Charmian,—
  Char. Madam ?
  Cleo. Ha, ha !—
Give me to drink mandragora.
  Char. Why, madam ?
  Cleo. That I might sleep out this great gap of
      time,
My Antony is away.
  Char. You think of him too much.
  Cleo. O, 't is treason !
  Char. Madam, I trust, not so.
  Cleo. Thou, eunuch Mardian !
  Mar. What 's your highness' pleasure ?
  Cleo. Not now to hear thee sing ; I take no pleasure
In aught an eunuch has. 'T is well for thee,   10
That, being unseminar'd, thy freer thoughts
May not fly forth of Egypt. Hast thou affections ?
  Mar. Yes, gracious madam.
  Cleo. Indeed ?
  Mar. Not in deed, madam ; for I can do nothing,
But what indeed is honest to be done ;
Yet have I fierce affections, and think,
What Venus did with Mars.
  Cleo. O Charmian !
Where think'st thou he is now ? Stands he, or sits he ?
Or does he walk ? or is he on his horse ?   20
O happy horse, to bear the weight of Antony !
Do bravely, horse, for wott'st thou whom thou mov'st ?
The demi-Atlas of this earth, the arm
And burgonet of men.—He 's speaking now,
Or murmuring, " Where 's my serpent of old Nile ?"
For so he calls me. Now I feed myself
With most delicious poison.—Think on me,
That am with Phœbus' amorous pinches black,

And wrinkled deep in time ? Broad-fronted Cæsar,
When thou wast here above the ground, I was   30
A morsel for a monarch ; and great Pompey
Would stand, and make his eyes grow in my brow :
There would he anchor his aspect, and die
With looking on his life.

Enter ALEXAS.

  Alex. Sovereign of Egypt, hail !
  Cleo. How much unlike art thou Mark Antony !
Yet, coming from him, that great medicine hath
With his tinct gilded thee.—
How goes it with my brave Mark Antony ?
  Alex. Last thing he did, dear queen,
He kiss'd—the last of many doubled kisses—   40
This orient pearl.—His speech sticks in my heart.
  Cleo. Mine ear must pluck it thence.
  Alex. " Good friend," quoth he,
" Say, the firm Roman to great Egypt sends
This treasure of an oyster ; at whose foot,
To mend the petty present, I will piece
Her opulent throne with kingdoms : all the east,
Say thou, shall call her mistress." So he nodded,
And soberly did mount an arrogant steed,
Who neigh'd so high, that what I would have spoke
Was beastly dumb'd by him.
  Cleo. What ! was he sad, or merry ?
  Alex. Like to the time o' the year between the
      extremes   51
Of hot and cold : he was nor sad, nor merry.
  Cleo. O well-divided disposition !—Note him,
Note him, good Charmian, 't is the man ; but note
      him :
He was not sad, for he would shine on those
That make their looks by his ; he was not merry,
Which seem'd to tell them, his remembrance lay
In Egypt with his joy ; but between both :
O heavenly mingle !—Be'st thou sad, or merry,
The violence of either thee becomes ;   60
So does it no man else.—Mett'st thou my posts ?
  Alex. Ay, madam, twenty several messengers.
Why do you send so thick ?
  Cleo. Who 's born that day
When I forget to send to Antony,
Shall die a beggar.—Ink and paper, Charmian.—
Welcome, my good Alexas.—Did I, Charmian,
Ever love Cæsar so ?
  Char. O, that brave Cæsar !
  Cleo. Be chok'd with such another emphasis !
Say, the brave Antony.
  Char. The valiant Cæsar !
  Cleo. By Isis, I will give thee bloody teeth,   70
If thou with Cæsar paragon again
My man of men.
  Char. By your most gracious pardon,
I sing but after you.
  Cleo. My salad days,
When I was green in judgment :—cold in blood,
To say as I said then !—But come, away ;
Get me ink and paper :
He shall have every day a several greeting,
Or I 'll unpeople Egypt.   *[Exeunt.*

ACT II.

SCENE I.—Messina. A Room in POMPEY'S House.

Enter POMPEY, MENECRATES, and MENAS.

Pompey.
F' the great gods be just, they shall assist
The deeds of justest men.
  Mene.   Know, worthy Pompey,
That what they do delay, they not deny.
  Pom. Whiles we are suitors to their throne,
   decays
The thing we sue for.
  Mene.   We, ignorant of ourselves,
Beg often our own harms, which the wise
   powers
Deny us for our good ; so find we profit,
By losing of our prayers.
  Pom.   I shall do well :
The people love me, and the sea is mine ;
My powers are crescent, and my auguring hope 10
Says, it will come to the full. Mark Antony
In Egypt sits at dinner, and will make
No wars without doors : Cæsar gets money where
He loses hearts : Lepidus flatters both,
Of both is flatter'd ; but he neither loves,
Nor either cares for him.
  Men.   Cæsar and Lepidus
Are in the field : a mighty strength they carry.
  Pom. Where have you this? 't is false.
  Men.   From Silvius, sir.
  Pom. He dreams : I know, they are in Rome to-
   gether,
Looking for Antony. But all the charms of love, 20
Salt Cleopatra, soften thy wan'd lip !
Let witchcraft join with beauty, lust with both !
Tie up the libertine in a field of feasts,
Keep his brain fuming ; Epicurean cooks
Sharpen with cloyless sauce his appetite,
That sleep and feeding may prorogue his honour,
Even till a Lethe'd dulness !

Enter VARRIUS.

      How now, Varrius ?
  Var. This is most certain that I shall deliver :
Mark Antony is every hour in Rome
Expected ; since he went from Egypt, 't is 30
A space for further travel.
  Pom.   I could have given less matter
A better ear.—Menas, I did not think,
This amorous surfeiter would have donn'd his helm
For such a petty war : his soldiership
Is twice the other twain. But let us rear
The higher our opinion, that our stirring
Can from the lap of Egypt's widow pluck
The ne'er lust-wearied Antony.
  Men.   I cannot hope,
Cæsar and Antony shall well greet together :
His wife that 's dead did trespasses to Cæsar ; 40
His brother warr'd upon him, although, I think,
Not mov'd by Antony.
  Pom.   I know not, Menas,
How lesser enmities may give way to greater.
Were 't not that we stand up against them all,
'T were pregnant they should square between them-
   selves ;
For they have entertained cause enough
To draw their swords : but how the fear of us
May cement their divisions, and bind up
The petty difference, we yet not know.
Be 't as our gods will have 't ! It only stands 50

Our lives upon, to use our strongest hands.
Come, Menas.   [*Exeunt.*

SCENE II.—Rome. A Room in the House of LEPIDUS.

Enter ENOBARBUS and LEPIDUS.

  Lep. Good Enobarbus, 't is a worthy deed,
And shall become you well, to entreat your captain
To soft and gentle speech.
  Eno.   I shall entreat him
To answer like himself : if Cæsar move him,
Let Antony look over Cæsar's head,
And speak as loud as Mars. By Jupiter,
Were I the wearer of Antonius' beard,
I would not shave 't to-day.
  Lep.   'T is not a time
For private stomaching.
  Eno.   Every time
Serves for the matter that is then born in 't. 10
  Lep. But small to greater matters must give way.
  Eno. Not if the small come first.
  Lep.   Your speech is passion :
But, pray you, stir no embers up. Here comes
The noble Antony.

Enter ANTONY and VENTIDIUS.

  Eno.   And yonder, Cæsar.

Enter CÆSAR, MECÆNAS, and AGRIPPA.

  Ant. If we compose well here, to Parthia :
Hark ye, Ventidius.
  Cæs.   I do not know,
Mecænas ; ask Agrippa.
  Lep.   Noble friends,
That which combin'd us was most great, and let not
A leaner action rend us. What 's amiss,
May it be gently heard : when we debate 20
Our trivial difference loud, we do commit
Murder in healing wounds. Then, noble partners,
(The rather, for I earnestly beseech,)
Touch you the sourest points with sweetest terms,
Nor curstness grow to the matter.
  Ant.   'T is spoken well.
Were we before our armies, and to fight,
I should do thus.
  Cæs. Welcome to Rome.
  Ant. Thank you.
  Cæs. Sit. 30
  Ant. Sit, sir.
  Cæs. Nay, then.
  Ant. I learn, you take things ill, which are not so ;
Or, being, concern you not.
  Cæs.   I must be laugh'd at,
If, or for nothing, or a little, I
Should say myself offended ; and with you
Chiefly i' the world ; more laugh'd at, that I should
Once name you derogately, when to sound your name
It not concern'd me.
  Ant.   My being in Egypt, Cæsar,
What was 't to you? 40
  Cæs. No more than my residing here at Rome
Might be to you in Egypt : yet, if you there
Did practise on my state, your being in Egypt
Might be my question.
  Ant.   How intend you, practis'd ?

Cæs. You may be pleas'd to catch at mine intent
By what did here befall me. Your wife, and brother,
Made wars upon me, and their contestation
Was theme for you, you were the word of war.
Ant. You do mistake your business; my brother
    never
Did urge me in his act: I did enquire it;   50
And have my learning from some true reports,
That drew their swords with you. Did he not rather
Discredit my authority with yours,
And make the wars alike against my stomach,
Having alike your cause? Of this my letters
Before did satisfy you. If you 'll patch a quarrel,
As matter whole you have not to make it with,
It must not be with this.
Cæs.   You praise yourself
By laying defects of judgment to me; but
You patch'd up your excuses.
Ant.   Not so, not so;   60
I know you could not lack, I am certain on 't,
Very necessity of this thought, that I,
Your partner in the cause 'gainst which he fought,
Could not with graceful eyes attend those wars
Which fronted mine own peace. As for my wife,
I would you had her spirit in such another:
The third o' the world is yours, which with a snaffle
You may pace easy, but not such a wife.
Eno. 'Would we had all such wives, that the men
might go to wars with the women!   70
Ant. So much uncurbable, her garboils, Cæsar,
Made out of her impatience (which not wanted
Shrewdness of policy too), I grieving grant,
Did you too much disquiet: for that, you must
But say, I could not help it.
Cæs.   I wrote to you,
When rioting in Alexandria; you
Did pocket up my letters, and with taunts
Did gibe my missive out of audience.
Ant.   Sir,
He fell upon me, ere admitted: then
Three kings I had newly feasted, and did want 80
Of what I was i' the morning: but, next day,
I told him of myself, which was as much
As to have ask'd him pardon. Let this fellow
Be nothing of our strife; if we contend,
Out of our question wipe him.
Cæs.   You have broken
The article of your oath, which you shall never
Have tongue to charge me with.
Lep.   Soft, Cæsar.
Ant. No, Lepidus, let him speak:
The honour 's sacred which he talks on now,
Supposing that I lack'd it. But on, Cæsar;— 90
The article of my oath,—
Cæs. To lend me arms and aid when I requir'd
    them,
The which you both denied.
Ant.   Neglected, rather;
And then, when poison'd hours had bound me up
From mine own knowledge. As nearly as I may,
I 'll play the penitent to you; but mine honesty
Shall not make poor my greatness, nor my power
Work without it. Truth is, that Fulvia,
To have me out of Egypt, made wars here;
For which myself, the ignorant motive, do 100
So far ask pardon, as befits mine honour
To stoop in such a case.
Lep.   'T is noble spoken.
Mec. If it might please you, to enforce no further
The griefs between ye: to forget them quite,
Were to remember that the present need
Speaks to atone you.
Lep.   Worthily spoken, Mecænas.
Eno. Or, if you borrow one another's love for the
instant, you may, when you hear no more words of
Pompey, return it again: you shall have time to
wrangle in, when you have nothing else to do. 110
Ant. Thou art a soldier only: speak no more.
Eno. That truth should be silent, I had almost forgot.
Ant. You wrong this presence; therefore, speak no
    more.
Eno. Go to then; your considerate stone.

Cæs. I do not much dislike the matter, but
The manner of his speech; for 't cannot be,
We shall remain in friendship, our conditions
So differing in their acts. Yet, if I knew
What hoop should hold us stanch, from edge to
    edge
O' the world I would pursue it.
Agr.   Give me leave, Cæsar,—
Cæs. Speak, Agrippa. 121
Agr. Thou hast a sister by the mother's side,
Admir'd Octavia: great Mark Antony
Is now a widower.
Cæs.   Say not so, Agrippa:
If Cleopatra heard you, your reproof
Were well deserv'd of rashness.
Ant. I am not married, Cæsar: let me hear
Agrippa further speak.
Agr. To hold you in perpetual amity,
To make you brothers, and to knit your hearts 130
With an unslipping knot, take Antony
Octavia to his wife; whose beauty claims
No worse a husband than the best of men,
Whose virtue and whose general graces speak
That which none else can utter. By this marriage,
All little jealousies, which now seem great,
And all great fears, which now import their dangers,
Would then be nothing: truths would be tales,
Where now half tales be truths: her love to both
Would, each to other, and all loves to both, 140
Draw after her. Pardon what I have spoke,
For 't is a studied, not a present thought,
By duty ruminated.
Ant.   Will Cæsar speak?
Cæs. Not till he hears how Antony is touch'd
With what is spoke already.
Ant.   What power is in Agrippa,
If I would say, "Agrippa, be it so,"
To make this good?
Cæs.   The power of Cæsar, and
His power unto Octavia.
Ant.   May I never
To this good purpose, that so fairly shows,
Dream of impediment!—Let me have thy hand: 150
Further this act of grace, and from this hour
The heart of brothers govern in our loves,
And sway our great designs!
Cæs.   There is my hand.
A sister I bequeath you, whom no brother
Did ever love so dearly: let her live
To join our kingdoms, and our hearts; and never
Fly off our loves again!
Lep.   Happily, Amen!
Ant. I did not think to draw my sword 'gainst
    Pompey;
For he hath laid strange courtesies, and great,
Of late upon me: I must thank him only, 160
Lest my remembrance suffer ill report;
At heel of that, defy him.
Lep.   Time calls upon 's:
Of us must Pompey presently be sought,
Or else he seeks out us.
Ant.   Where lies he?
Cæs. About the Mount Misenum.
Ant. What is his strength by land?
Cæs. Great and increasing; but by sea
He is an absolute master.
Ant.   So is the fame.
'Would we had spoke together! Haste we for it:
Yet, ere we put ourselves in arms, despatch we 170
The business we have talk'd of.
Cæs.   With most gladness;
And do invite you to my sister's view,
Whither straight I 'll lead you.
Ant.   Let us, Lepidus,
Not lack your company.
Lep.   Noble Antony,
Not sickness should detain me.
    [*Flourish. Exeunt* CÆSAR, ANTONY, *and*
    LEPIDUS.
Mec. Welcome from Egypt, sir.
Eno. Half the heart of Cæsar, worthy Mecænas!—
My honourable friend, Agrippa!—

Agr. Good Enobarbus!
Mec. We have cause to be glad, that matters are so
well digested. You stay'd well by it in Egypt.   181
Eno. Ay, sir ; we did sleep day out of countenance,
and made the night light with drinking.
Mec. Eight wild-boars roasted whole at a breakfast,
and but twelve persons there ; is this true?
Eno. This was but as a fly by an eagle : we had
much more monstrous matter of feast, which worthily
deserved noting.
Mec. She's a most triumphant lady, if report be
square to her.   190
Eno. When she first met Mark Antony, she pursed
up his heart, upon the river of Cydnus.
Agr. There she appeared indeed, or my reporter
devised well for her.
Eno. I will tell you.
The barge she sat in, like a burnish'd throne,
Burn'd on the water : the poop was beaten gold ;
Purple the sails, and so perfumed, that
The winds were love-sick with them ; the oars were
    silver ;
Which to the tune of flutes kept stroke, and
    made ·   200
The water, which they beat, to follow faster,
As amorous of their strokes. For her own person,
It beggar'd all description : she did lie
In her pavilion (cloth of gold of tissue),
O'er-picturing that Venus, where we see
The fancy outwork nature : on each side her
Stood pretty dimpled boys, like smiling Cupids,
With divers-colour'd fans, whose wind did seem
To glow the delicate cheeks which they did cool,
And what they undid, did.
Agr.   O, rare for Antony !   210
Eno. Her gentlewomen, like the Nereides,
So many mermaids, tended her i' the eyes,
And made their bends adornings : at the helm
A seeming mermaid steers ; the silken tackle
Swell with the touches of those flower-soft hands,
That yarely frame the office. From the barge
A strange invisible perfume hits the sense
Of the adjacent wharfs. The city cast
Her people out upon her ; and Antony,
Enthron'd i' the market-place, did sit alone,   220
Whistling to the air ; which, but for vacancy,
Had gone to gaze on Cleopatra too,
And made a gap in nature.
Agr.   Rare Egyptian !
Eno. Upon her landing Antony sent to her,
Invited her to supper: she replied,
It should be better he became her guest,
Which she entreated. Our courteous Antony,
Whom ne'er the word of "No" woman heard
    speak,
Being barber'd ten times o'er, goes to the feast ;
And for his ordinary pays his heart   230
For what his eyes eat only.
Agr.   Royal wench !
She made great Cæsar lay his sword to bed ;
He plough'd her, and she cropp'd.
Eno.   I saw her once
Hop forty paces through the public street ;
And having lost her breath, she spoke, and panted,
That she did make defect perfection,
And, breathless, power breathe forth.
Mec. Now Antony must leave her utterly.
Eno. Never ; he will not.
Age cannot wither her, nor custom stale   240
Her infinite variety. Other women cloy
The appetites they feed, but she makes hungry,
Where most she satisfies ; for vilest things
Become themselves in her, that the holy priests
Bless her when she is riggish.
Mec. If beauty, wisdom, modesty, can settle
The heart of Antony, Octavia is
A blessed lottery to him.
Agr.   Let us go.—
Good Enobarbus, make yourself my guest,
Whilst you abide here.
Eno.   Humbly, sir, I thank you. 250
                                   [*Exeunt.*

SCENE III.—The Same. A Room in CÆSAR's House.

Enter CÆSAR, ANTONY, OCTAVIA *between them ;*
    Attendants.

Ant. The world, and my great office, will sometimes
Divide me from your bosom.
Octa.   All which time,
Before the gods my knee shall bow my prayers
To them for you.
Ant.   Good night, sir.—My Octavia,
Read not my blemishes in the world's report :
I have not kept my square ; but that to come
Shall all be done by the rule. Good night, dear lady.—
Good night, sir.
Cæs. Good night.   [*Exeunt* CÆSAR *and* OCTAVIA.

Enter a Soothsayer.

Ant. Now, sirrah : you do wish yourself in Egypt ?
Sooth. 'Would I had never come from thence, nor
you thither !   12
Ant. If you can, your reason ?
Sooth. I see it in my motion, have it not in my
tongue : but yet hie you to Egypt again.
Ant. Say to me, whose fortunes shall rise higher,
Cæsar's or mine ?
Sooth. Cæsar's.
Therefore, O Antony ! stay not by his side :
Thy demon (that's thy spirit which keeps thee) is   20
Noble, courageous, high, unmatchable,
Where Cæsar's is not ; but near him thy angel
Becomes a fear, as being o'erpower'd : therefore,
Make space enough between you.
Ant.   Speak this no more.
Sooth. To none but thee ; no more, but when to thee.
If thou dost play with him at any game,
Thou art sure to lose ; and, of that natural luck,
He beats thee 'gainst the odds : thy lustre thickens,
When he shines by. I say again, thy spirit
Is all afraid to govern thee near him,   30
But, he away, 't is noble.
Ant.   Get thee gone :
Say to Ventidius, I would speak with him.—
                                   [*Exit Soothsayer.*
He shall to Parthia.—Be it art, or hap,
He hath spoken true : the very dice obey him ;
And in our sports my better cunning faints
Under his chance : if we draw lots, he speeds ;
His cocks do win the battle still of mine,
When it is all to nought ; and his quails ever
Beat mine, inhoop'd, at odds. I will to Egypt :
And though I make this marriage for my peace,   40
I' the east my pleasure lies.

Enter VENTIDIUS.

               O ! come, Ventidius,
You must to Parthia : your commission's ready ;
Follow me, and receive 't.   [*Exeunt.*

SCENE IV.—The Same. A Street.

Enter LEPIDUS, MECÆNAS, *and* AGRIPPA.

Lep. Trouble yourselves no further : pray you, hasten
Your generals after.
Agr.   Sir, Mark Antony
Will e'en but kiss Octavia, and we'll follow.
Lep. Till I shall see you in your soldier's dress,
Which will become you both, farewell.
Mec.   We shall,
As I conceive the journey, be at the Mount
Before you, Lepidus.
Lep.   Your way is shorter ;
My purposes do draw me much about :
You'll win two days upon me.
Mec., Agr.   Sir, good success !   9
Lep. Farewell.   [*Exeunt.*

SCENE V.—Alexandria. A Room in the Palace.

Enter CLEOPATRA, CHARMIAN, IRAS, *and* ALEXAS.

Cleo. Give me some music ; music, moody food
Of us that trade in love.
Attend.   The music, ho !

Enter MARDIAN.

Cleo. Let it alone; let's to billiards: come, Charmian.

Char. My arm is sore; best play with Mardian.

Cleo. As well a woman with an eunuch play'd,
As with a woman.—Come, you 'll play with me, sir?

Mar. As well as I can, madam.

Cleo. And when good will is show'd, though 't come too short,
The actor may plead pardon. I 'll none now.—
Give me mine angle,—we 'll to the river: there,   10
My music playing far off, I will betray
Tawny-finn'd fishes; my bended hook shall pierce
Their slimy jaws; and, as I draw them up,
I 'll think them every one an Antony,
And say, Ah, ha! you're caught.

Char.   'T was merry, when
You wager'd on your angling; when your diver
Did hang a salt-fish on his hook, which he
With fervency drew up.

Cleo.   That time—O times!—
I laugh'd him out of patience; and that night
I laugh'd him into patience: and next morn,   20
Ere the ninth hour, I drunk him to his bed;
Then put my tires and mantles on him, whilst
I wore his sword Philippan.

Enter a Messenger.

                        O! from Italy?—
Ram thou thy fruitful tidings in mine ears,
That long time have been barren.

Mess.   Madam, madam,—

Cleo. Antonius dead? if thou say so, villain,
Thou kill'st thy mistress: but well and free,
If thou so yield him, there is gold, and here
My bluest veins to kiss; a hand that kings
Have lipp'd, and trembled kissing.   30

Mes. First, madam, he is well.

Cleo.   Why, there 's more gold.
But, sirrah, mark, we use
To say, the dead are well: bring it to that,
The gold I give thee will I melt, and pour
Down thy ill-uttering throat.

Mess. Good madam, hear me.

Cleo.   Well, go to, I will;
But there 's no goodness in thy face, if Antony
Be free, and healthful:—so tart a favour
To trumpet such good tidings! if not well,
Thou shouldst come like a Fury crown'd with snakes,
Not like a formal man.

Mess.   Will 't please you hear me?   41

Cleo. I have a mind to strike thee, ere thou speak'st:
Yet, if thou say, Antony lives, is well,
Or friends with Cæsar, or not captive to him,
I 'll set thee in a shower of gold, and hail
Rich pearls upon thee.

Mess.   Madam, he 's well.

Cleo.   Well said.

Mess. And friends with Cæsar.

Cleo.   Thou 'rt an honest man.

Mess. Cæsar and he are greater friends than ever.

Cleo. Make thee a fortune from me.

Mess.   But yet, madam,—

Cleo. I do not like "but yet," it does allay   50
The good precedence; fie upon "but yet!"
"But yet" is a gaoler to bring forth
Some monstrous malefactor. Pr'ythee, friend,
Pour out the pack of matter to mine ear,
The good and bad together. He 's friends with Cæsar;
In state of health, thou say'st; and, thou say'st, free.

Mess. Free, madam? no; I made no such report:
He 's bound unto Octavia.

Cleo.   For what good turn?

Mess. For the best turn i' the bed.

Cleo.   I am pale, Charmian.

Mess. Madam, he 's married to Octavia.   60

Cleo. The most infectious pestilence upon thee!
                        [*Strikes him down.*

Mess. Good madam, patience.

Cleo.   What say you?—
                        [*Strikes him again.*
Hence, horrible villain! or I 'll spurn thine eyes
Like balls before me; I 'll unhair thy head.
                        [*She hales him up and down.*
Thou shalt be whipp'd with wire, and stew'd in brine,
Smarting in lingering pickle.

Mess.   Gracious madam,
I, that do bring the news, made not the match.

Cleo. Say, 't is not so, a province I will give thee,
And make thy fortunes proud: the blow thou hadst
Shall make thy peace for moving me to rage;   70
And I will boot thee with what gift beside
Thy modesty can beg.

Mess.   He 's married, madam.

Cleo. Rogue! thou hast liv'd too long.
                        [*Draws a knife.*

Mess.   Nay, then I 'll run.—
What mean you, madam? I have made no fault.
                        [*Exit.*

Char. Good madam, keep yourself within yourself:
The man is innocent.

Cleo. Some innocents 'scape not the thunderbolt.—
Melt Egypt into Nile! and kindly creatures
Turn all to serpents!—Call the slave again:
Though I am mad, I will not bite him.—Call.   80

Char. He is afeard to come.

Cleo.   I will not hurt him.—
                        [*Exit* CHARMIAN.
These hands do lack nobility, that they strike
A meaner than myself; since I myself
Have given myself the cause.

Re-enter CHARMIAN *and Messenger.*

                        Come hither, sir.
Though it be honest, it is never good
To bring bad news; give to a gracious message
An host of tongues; but let ill tidings tell
Themselves, when they be felt.

Mess. I have done my duty.

Cleo.   Is he married?   90
I cannot hate thee worser than I do,
If thou again say, Yes.

Mess.   He 's married, madam.

Cleo. The gods confound thee! dost thou hold there still?

Mess. Should I lie, madam?

Cleo.   O! I would, thou didst;
So half my Egypt were submerg'd, and made
A cistern for scal'd snakes. Go, get thee hence:
Hadst thou Narcissus in thy face, to me
Thou wouldst appear most ugly. He is married?

Mess. I crave your highness' pardon.

Cleo.   He is married?

Mess. Take no offence, that I would not offend
you:
To punish me for what you make me do,   100
Seems much unequal. He is married to Octavia.

Cleo. O! that his fault should make a knave of thee,
That art not what thou 'rt sure of!—Get thee hence:
The merchandise which thou hast brought from Rome,
Are all too dear for me: lie they upon thy hand,
And be undone by 'em!   [*Exit Messenger.*

Char.   Good your highness, patience.

Cleo. In praising Antony, I have dispraised Cæsar.

Char. Many times, madam.

Cleo.   I am paid for 't now.
Lead me from hence;
I faint. O Iras! Charmian!—'T is no matter.—   110
Go to the fellow, good Alexas; bid him
Report the feature of Octavia, her years,
Her inclination, let him not leave out
The colour of her hair: bring me word quickly.—
                        [*Exit* ALEXAS.
Let him for ever go:—let him not—Charmian,
Though he be painted one way like a Gorgon,
The other way 's a Mars.—[*To* MARDIAN.] Bid you
Alexas
Bring me word, how tall she is.—Pity me, Charmian,
But do not speak to me.—Lead me to my chamber.
                        [*Exeunt.*

SCENE VI.—Near Misenum.

Flourish. Enter POMPEY *and* MENAS, *at one side, with drum and trumpet; at another,* CÆSAR, LEPIDUS, ANTONY, ENOBARBUS, MECÆNAS, *with Soldiers marching.*

Pom. Your hostages I have, so have you mine ;
And we shall talk before we fight.

Cæs.   Most meet
That first we come to words ; and therefore have we
Our written purposes before us sent ;
Which if thou hast consider'd, let us know
If 't will tie up thy discontented sword,

Cleo. "Lead me from hence ;
I faint."

And carry back to Sicily much tall youth,
That else must perish here.

Pom.   To you all three,
The senators alone of this great world,
Chief factors for the gods,—I do not know   10
Wherefore my father should revengers want,
Having a son, and friends ; since Julius Cæsar,
Who at Philippi the good Brutus ghosted,
There saw you labouring for him. What was it,
That mov'd pale Cassius to conspire ? And what
Made the all-honour'd, honest, Roman Brutus,
With the arm'd rest, courtiers of beauteous freedom,
To drench the Capitol, but that they would
Have one man but a man ? And that is it
Hath made me rig my navy ; at whose burden   20
The anger'd ocean foams ; with which I meant
To scourge the ingratitude that despiteful Rome
Cast on my noble father.

Cæs.   Take your time.
Ant. Thou canst not fear us, Pompey, with thy sails ;
We 'll speak with thee at sea : at land, thou know'st
How much we do o'er-count thee.

Pom.   At land, indeed,
Thou dost o'er-count me of my father's house :
But, since the cuckoo builds not for himself,
Remain in 't as thou may'st.

Lep.   Be pleas'd to tell us,
(For this is from the present,) how you take   30
The offers we have sent you.

Cæs.   There 's the point.
Ant. Which do not be entreated to, but weigh
What it is worth embrac'd.

Cæs.   And what may follow,
To try a larger fortune.

Pom.   You have made me offer
Of Sicily, Sardinia ; and I must
Rid all the sea of pirates ; then, to send
Measures of wheat to Rome : this 'greed upon,
To part with unhack'd edges, and bear back
Our targes undinted.

Cæs., Ant., Lep. That 's our offer.
Pom.   Know then,   40
I came before you here, a man prepar'd

To take this offer : but Mark Antony
Put me to some impatience.—Though I lose
The praise of it by telling, you must know,
When Cæsar and your brother were at blows,
Your mother came to Sicily, and did find
Her welcome friendly.

Ant.   I have heard it, Pompey ;
And am well studied for a liberal thanks
Which I do owe you.

Pom.   Let me have your hand.
I did not think, sir, to have met you here.   50
Ant. The beds i' the east are soft ; and thanks to
    you,
That call'd me, timelier than my purpose, hither,
For I have gain'd by 't.

Cæs.   Since I saw you last,
There is a change upon you.

Pom.   Well, I know not
What counts harsh fortune casts upon my face ;
But in my bosom shall she never come,
To make my heart her vassal.

Lep.   Well met here.
Pom. I hope so, Lepidus.—Thus we are agreed.
I crave, our composition may be written,
And seal'd between us.

Cæs.   That 's the next to do.   60
Pom. We 'll feast each other ere we part ; and let 's
Draw lots who shall begin.

Ant.   That will I, Pompey.
Pom. No, Antony, take the lot :
But, first or last, your fine Egyptian cookery
Shall have the fame. I have heard, that Julius Cæsar
Grew fat with feasting there.

Ant.   You have heard much.
Pom. I have fair meanings, sir.
Ant.   And fair words to them.
Pom. Then, so much have I heard :
And I have heard, Apollodorus carried—
Eno. No more of that :—he did so.
Pom.   What, I pray you ?
Eno. A certain queen to Cæsar in a mattress.   71
Pom. I know thee now : how far'st thou, soldier ?
Eno.   Well ;
And well am like to do ; for, I perceive,
Four feasts are toward.

Pom.   Let me shake thy hand :
I never hated thee. I have seen thee fight,
When I have envied thy behaviour.

Eno.   Sir,
I never lov'd you much ; but I have prais'd you,
When you have well deserv'd ten times as much
As I have said you did.

Pom.   Enjoy thy plainness,
It nothing ill becomes thee.—   80
Aboard my galley I invite you all :
Will you lead, lords ?

Cæs., Ant., Lep. Show us the way, sir.
Pom.   Come.
    [*Exeunt* POMPEY, CÆSAR, ANTONY, LEPIDUS,
      Soldiers, and Attendants.

Men. [*Aside.*] Thy father, Pompey, would ne'er
have made this treaty.—You and I have known, sir.
Eno. At sea, I think.
Men. We have, sir.
Eno. You have done well by water.
Men. And you by land.
Eno. I will praise any man that will praise me ;
though it cannot be denied what I have done by land.
Men. Nor what I have done by water.   91
Eno. Yes : something you can deny for your own
safety : you have been a great thief by sea.
Men. And you by land.
Eno. There I deny my land service. But give me
your hand, Menas : if our eyes had authority, here
they might take two thieves kissing.
Men. All men's faces are true, whatsoe'er their
hands are.
Eno. But there is never a fair woman has a true
face.   101
Men. No slander ; they steal hearts.
Eno. We came hither to fight with you.
Men. For my part, I am sorry it is turned to a

drinking. Pompey doth this day laugh away his fortune.

Eno. If he do, sure, he cannot weep 't back again.

Men. You have said, sir. We looked not for Mark Antony here. Pray you, is he married to Cleopatra?

Eno. Cæsar's sister is call'd Octavia.   110

Men. True, sir; she was the wife of Caius Marcellus.

Eno. But she is now the wife of Marcus Antonius.

Men. Pray ye, sir?

Eno. 'T is true.

Men. Then is Cæsar and he for ever knit together.

Eno. If I were bound to divine of this unity, I would not prophesy so.

Men. I think, the policy of that purpose made more in the marriage, than the love of the parties.   119

Eno. I think so too: but you shall find, the band that seems to tie their friendship together will be the very strangler of their amity. Octavia is of a holy, cold, and still conversation.

Men. Who would not have his wife so?

Eno. Not he, that himself is not so; which is Mark Antony. He will to his Egyptian dish again: then shall the sighs of Octavia blow the fire up in Cæsar; and, as I said before, that which is the strength of their amity, shall prove the immediate author of their variance. Antony will use his affection where it is: he married but his occasion here.   131

Men. And thus it may be. Come, sir, will you aboard? I have a health for you.

Eno. I shall take it, sir: we have used our throats in Egypt.

Men. Come; let 's away.   [*Exeunt.*

SCENE VII.—On board POMPEY'S Galley, lying near Misenum.

Music. Enter two or three Servants, with a banquet.

1 Serv. Here they 'll be, man. Some o' their plants are ill-rooted already; the least wind i' the world will blow them down.

2 Serv. Lepidus is high-coloured.

1 Serv. They have made him drink alms-drink.

2 Serv. As they pinch one another by the disposition, he cries out, "No more;" reconciles them to his entreaty, and himself to the drink.

1 Serv. But it raises the greater war between him and his discretion.   10

2 Serv. Why, this it is to have a name in great men's fellowship: I had as lief have a reed that will do me no service, as a partisan I could not heave.

1 Serv. To be called into a huge sphere, and not to be seen to move in 't, are the holes where eyes should be, which pitifully disaster the cheeks.

A sennet sounded. Enter CÆSAR, ANTONY, POMPEY, LEPIDUS, AGRIPPA, MECÆNAS, ENOBARBUS, MENAS, *with other Captains.*

Ant. Thus do they, sir. They take the flow o' the Nile
By certain scales i' the pyramid; they know,
By the height, the lowness, or the mean, if dearth
Or foison follow. The higher Nilus swells,   20
The more it promises: as it ebbs, the seedsman
Upon the slime and ooze scatters his grain,
And shortly comes to harvest.

Lep. You have strange serpents there.

Ant. Ay, Lepidus.

Lep. Your serpent of Egypt is bred now of your mud by the operation of your sun: so is your crocodile.

Ant. They are so.

Pom. Sit,—and some wine!—A health to Lepidus!

Lep. I am not so well as I should be, but I'll ne'er out.   32

Eno. Not till you have slept: I fear me, you 'll be in, till then.

Lep. Nay, certainly, I have heard, the Ptolemies' pyramises are very goodly things; without contradiction, I have heard that.

Men. [*Aside.*] Pompey, a word.

Pom. [*Aside.*]   Say in mine ear: what is 't?

Men. [*Aside.*] Forsake thy seat, I do beseech thee. captain,
And hear me speak a word.

Pom. [*Aside.*]   Forbear me till anon.—
This wine for Lepidus.   41

Lep. What manner o' thing is your crocodile?

Ant. It is shaped, sir, like itself, and it is as broad as it hath breadth; it is just so high as it is, and moves with it own organs; it lives by that which nourisheth it; and the elements once out of it, it transmigrates.

Lep. What colour is it of?

Ant. Of it own colour too.

Lep. 'T is a strange serpent.   50

Ant. 'T is so: and the tears of it are wet.

Cæs. Will this description satisfy him?

Ant. With the health that Pompey gives him, else he is a very epicure.

Pom. [*To* MENAS, *aside.*] Go hang, sir, hang! Tell me of that? away!
Do as I bid you.—Where 's this cup I call'd for?

Men. [*Aside.*] If for the sake of merit thou wilt hear me,
Rise from thy stool.

Pom. [*Aside.*] I think, thou 'rt mad. The matter?
[*Walks aside.*

Men. I have ever held my cap off to thy fortunes.

Pom. Thou hast serv'd me with much faith. What 's else to say?—   60
Be jolly, lords.

Ant.   These quick-sands, Lepidus,
Keep off them, for you sink.

Men. Wilt thou be lord of all the world?

Pom.   What say'st thou?

Men. Wilt thou be lord of the whole world? That 's twice.

Pom. How should that be?

Men.   But entertain it,
And, though thou think me poor, I am the man
Will give thee all the world.

Pom.   Hast thou drunk well?

Men. No, Pompey, I have kept me from the cup.
Thou art, if thou dar'st be, the earthly Jove:
Whate'er the ocean pales, or sky inclips,   70
Is thine, if thou wilt ha 't.

Pom.   Show me which way.

Men. These three world-sharers, these competitors,
Are in thy vessel: let me cut the cable;
And, when we are put off, fall to their throats:
All there is thine.

Pom.   Ah! this thou shouldst have done.
And not have spoke on 't. In me, 't is villainy;
In thee, 't had been good service. Thou must know,
'T is not my profit that does lead mine honour;
Mine honour, it. Repent, that e'er thy tongue
Hath so betray'd thine act: being done unknown,   80
I should have found it afterwards well done,
But must condemn it now. Desist, and drink.

Men. [*Aside.*] For this,
I 'll never follow thy pall'd fortunes more.
Who seeks, and will not take, when once 't is offer'd,
Shall never find it more.

Pom.   This health to Lepidus.

Ant. Bear him ashore.—I 'll pledge it for him, Pompey.

Eno. Here 's to thee, Menas.

Men.   Enobarbus, welcome.

Pom. Fill, till the cup be hid.

Eno. There 's a strong fellow, Menas.   90
[*Pointing to the Attendant who carries off* LEPIDUS.

Men. Why?

Eno. 'A bears the third part of the world, man: see'st not?

Men. The third part then is drunk: 'would it were all, That it might go on wheels!

Eno. Drink thou; increase the reels.

Men. Come.

Pom. This is not yet an Alexandrian feast.

Ant. It ripens towards it.—Strike the vessels, ho! Here is to Cæsar.

Cæs.   I could well forbear it.   100
It 's monstrous labour, when I wash my brain,
And it grows fouler.
Ant.   Be a child o' the time.
Cæs. Possess it, I 'll make answer; but I had rather
     fast
From all, four days, than drink so much in one.
Eno. [*To* ANTONY.] Ha, my brave emperor !
Shall we dance now the Egyptian Bacchanals,
And celebrate our drink ?
Pom.   Let 's ha 't, good soldier.
Ant. Come, let us all take hands,
Till that the conquering wine hath steep'd our sense
In soft and delicate Lethe.
Eno.   All take hands.—   110
Make battery to our ears with the loud music ;
The while I 'll place you : then, the boy shall sing ;
The holding every man shall bear, as loud
As his strong sides can volley.
     [*Music plays.* ENOBARBUS *places them hand
          in hand.*
                    SONG.

*Come, thou monarch of the vine,
Plumpy Bacchus, with pink eyne :
In thy vats our cares be drown'd ;
With thy grapes our hairs be crown'd ;
Cup us, till the world go round ;
Cup us, till the world go round !*   120

Cæs. What would you more ? Pompey, good night.
     Good brother,
Let me request you off : our graver business
Frowns at this levity.—Gentle lords, let 's part ;
You see, we have burnt our cheeks. Strong Enobarb
Is weaker than the wine ; and mine own tongue
Splits what it speaks : the wild disguise hath almost
Antick'd us all. What needs more words ? Good
     night.—
Good Antony, your hand.
Pom.   I 'll try you on the shore.
Ant. And shall, sir. Give 's your hand.
Pom.   O Antony !
You have my father's house,—But what ? we are
     friends.   130
Come down into the boat.
Eno.   Take heed you fall not.—
     [*Exeunt* POMPEY, CÆSAR, ANTONY, *and
          Attendants.*
Menas, I 'll not on shore.
Men.   No, to my cabin.—
These drums !—these trumpets, flutes ! what !—
Let Neptune hear, we bid a loud farewell
To these great fellows : sound, and be hang'd !
     sound out !
     [*A flourish of trumpets, with drums.*
Eno. Ho, says 'a !—There 's my cap.
Men. Ho !—Noble captain ! come.   [*Exeunt.*

ACT III.

SCENE I.—A Plain in Syria.

Enter VENTIDIUS, *as it were in triumph, with* SILIUS, *and other Romans, Officers, and Soldiers ; the dead
body of* PACORUS *borne before him.*

          Ventidius.
NOW, darting Parthia, art thou struck ;
          and now
Pleas'd fortune does of Marcus Crassus'
          death
Make me revenger.—Bear the king's son's
          body
Before our army.—Thy Pacorus, Orodes,
Pays this for Marcus Crassus.
Sil.   Noble Ventidius,
Whilst yet with Parthian blood thy sword
          is warm,
The fugitive Parthians follow : spur through
          Media,
Mesopotamia, and the shelters whither
The routed fly : so thy grand captain Antony
Shall set thee on triumphant chariots, and
Put garlands on thy head.
Ven.   O Silius, Silius !   11
I have done enough ; a lower place, note well,
May make too great an act : for learn this, Silius,
Better to leave undone, than by our deed
Acquire too high a fame, when him we serve 's away.
Cæsar and Antony have ever won
More in their officer than person : Sossius,
One of my place in Syria, his lieutenant,
For quick accumulation of renown,
Which he achiev'd by the minute, lost his favour.   20
Who does i' the wars more than his captain can,
Becomes his captain's captain ; and ambition,
The soldier's virtue, rather makes choice of loss,
Than gain which darkens him.
I could do more to do Antonius good,

But 't would offend him ; and in his offence
Should my performance perish.
Sil.   Thou hast, Ventidius, that
Without the which a soldier, and his sword,
Grants scarce distinction. Thou wilt write to Antony ?
Ven. I 'll humbly signify what in his name,   30
That magical word of war, we have effected ;
How, with his banners and his well-paid ranks,
The ne'er-yet-beaten horse of Parthia
We have jaded out o' the field.
Sil.   Where is he now ?
Ven. He purposeth to Athens ; whither, with what
     haste
The weight we must convey with 's will permit,
We shall appear before him.—On, there ; pass along.
     [*Exeunt.*

SCENE II.—Rome. An Ante-chamber in CÆSAR'S House.

Enter AGRIPPA *and* ENOBARBUS, *meeting.*

Agr. What, are the brothers parted ?
Eno. They have despatch'd with Pompey : he is
     gone ;
The other three are sealing. Octavia weeps
To part from Rome ; Cæsar is sad ; and Lepidus,
Since Pompey's feast, as Menas says, is troubled
With the green sickness.
Agr.   'T is a noble Lepidus.
Eno. A very fine one. O, how he loves Cæsar !
Agr. Nay, but how dearly he adores Mark Antony !
Eno. Cæsar ? Why, he 's the Jupiter of men.

Agr. What's Antony? The god of Jupiter. 10
Eno. Spake you of Cæsar? How! the nonpareil!
Agr. O Antony! O thou Arabian bird!
Eno. Would you praise Cæsar, say,—Cæsar;—go no
further.
Agr. Indeed, he plied them both with excellent
praises.
Eno. But he loves Cæsar best;—yet he loves
Antony.
Ho! hearts, tongues, figures, scribes, bards, poets,
cannot
Think, speak, cast, write, sing, number,—ho!
His love to Antony. But as for Cæsar,
Kneel down, kneel down, and wonder.
Agr. Both he loves.
Eno. They are his shards, and he their beetle.
[*Trumpets.*] So,— 20
This is to horse.—Adieu, noble Agrippa.
Agr. Good fortune, worthy soldier; and farewell.

Enter CÆSAR, ANTONY, LEPIDUS, *and* OCTAVIA.

Ant. No further, sir.
Cæs. You take from me a great part of myself:
Use me well in't.—Sister, prove such a wife
As my thoughts make thee, and as my furthest
band
Shall pass on thy approof.—Most noble Antony,
Let not the piece of virtue, which is set
Betwixt us as the cement of our love,
To keep it builded, be the ram to batter 30
The fortress of it; for better might we
Have lov'd without this mean, if on both parts
This be not cherish'd.
Ant. Make me not offended
In your distrust.
Cæs. I have said.
Ant. You shall not find,
Though you be therein curious, the least cause
For what you seem to fear. So, the gods keep
you,
And make the hearts of Romans serve your ends!
We will here part.
Cæs. Farewell, my dearest sister, fare thee well:
The elements be kind to thee, and make 40
Thy spirits all of comfort! fare thee well.
Octa. My noble brother!—
Ant. The April's in her eyes; it is love's spring,
And these the showers to bring it on.—Be cheerful.
Octa. Sir, look well to my husband's house; and—
Cæs. What,
Octavia?
Octa. I'll tell you in your ear.
Ant. Her tongue will not obey her heart, nor can
Her heart inform her tongue; the swan's down-
feather,
That stands upon the swell at the full of tide,
And neither way inclines. 50
Eno. [*Aside to* AGRIPPA.] Will Cæsar weep?
Agr. He has a cloud in's face.
Eno. He were the worse for that, were he a horse;
So is he, being a man.
Agr. Why, Enobarbus,
When Antony found Julius Cæsar dead,
He cried almost to roaring; and he wept,
When at Philippi he found Brutus slain.
Eno. That year, indeed, he was troubled with a
rheum;
What willingly he did confound, he wail'd,
Believe't, till I wept too.
Cæs. No, sweet Octavia,
You shall hear from me still: the time shall not 60
Out-go my thinking on you.
Ant. Come, sir, come;
I'll wrestle with you in my strength of love:
Look, here I have you; thus I let you go,
And give you to the gods.
Cæs. Adieu; be happy!
Lep. Let all the number of the stars give light
To thy fair way!
Cæs. Farewell, farewell. [*Kisses* OCTAVIA.
Ant. Farewell.
[*Trumpets sound. Exeunt.*

SCENE III.—Alexandria. A Room in the Palace.

Enter CLEOPATRA, CHARMIAN, IRAS, *and* ALEXAS.
Cleo. Where is the fellow?
Alex. Half afeard to come.
Cleo. Go to, go to.—Come hither, sir.

Enter the Messenger.
Alex. Good majesty,
Herod of Jewry dare not look upon you,
But when you are well pleas'd.

Cleo. "That's not so good. He cannot like her long."

Cleo. That Herod's head
I'll have: but how, when Antony is gone,
Through whom I might command it?—Come thou
near.
Mess. Most gracious majesty,—
Cleo. Didst thou behold
Octavia?
Mess. Ay, dread queen.
Cleo. Where?
Mess. Madam, in Rome 10
I look'd her in the face; and saw her led
Between her brother and Mark Antony.
Cleo. Is she as tall as me?
Mess. She is not, madam.
Cleo. Didst hear her speak? is she shrill-tongu'd, or
low?
Mess. Madam, I heard her speak: she is low-voic'd.
Cleo. That's not so good. He cannot like her long.
Char. Like her? O Isis! 'tis impossible.
Cleo. I think so, Charmian: dull of tongue, and
dwarfish!—
What majesty is in her gait? Remember,
If e'er thou look'dst on majesty.
Mess. She creeps; 20
Her motion and her station are as one:
She shows a body rather than a life;
A statue, than a breather.
Cleo. Is this certain?
Mess. Or I have no observance.
Char. Three in Egypt
Cannot make better note.
Cleo. He's very knowing,
I do perceive't.—There's nothing in her yet.—
The fellow has good judgment.
Char. Excellent.
Cleo. Guess at her years, I pr'ythee.
Mess. Madam,
She was a widow—
Cleo. Widow?—Charmian, hark.
Mess. And I do think, she's thirty.
Cleo. Bear'st thou her face in mind? is't long, or
round? 30
Mess. Round, even to faultiness.
Cleo. For the most part, too, they are foolish that
are so.—
Her hair, what colour?

Mess.　　　　　Brown, madam ; and her forehead
As low as she would wish it.
　Cleo.　　　　　There 's gold for thee :
Thou must not take my former sharpness ill.
I will employ thee back again : I find thee
Most fit for business. Go, make thee ready ;
Our letters are prepar'd.　　　　*[Exit Messenger.*
　Char.　　　　A proper man.
　Cleo. Indeed, he is so : I repent me much,
That so I harried him. Why, methinks, by him,　40
This creature 's no such thing.
　Char.　　　　Nothing, madam.
　Cleo. The man has seen some majesty, and should
　　　know.
　Char. Hath he seen majesty? Isis else defend,
And serving you so long !
　Cleo. I have one thing more to ask him yet, good
　　　Charmian :
But 't is no matter ; thou shalt bring him to me
Where I will write. All may be well enough.
　Char. I warrant you, madam.　　　　*[Exeunt.*

Scene IV.—Athens. A Room in Antony's House.

Enter Antony *and* Octavia.

　Ant. Nay, nay, Octavia, not only that,—
That were excusable, that, and thousands more
Of semblable import,—but he hath wag'd
New wars 'gainst Pompey ; made his will, and read it
To public ear :
Spoke scantly of me : when perforce he could not
But pay me terms of honour, cold and sickly
He vented them ; most narrow measure lent me ;
When the best hint was given him, he not took 't,
Or did it from his teeth.
　Octa.　　　　O my good lord !　　10
Believe not all ; or, if you must believe,
Stomach not all. A more unhappy lady,
If this division chance, ne'er stood between,
Praying for both parts :
The good gods will mock me presently,
When I shall pray, "O, bless my lord and husband !"
Undo that prayer, by crying out as loud,
"O, bless my brother ! " Husband win, win brother,
Prays, and destroys the prayer ; no midway
'Twixt these extremes at all.
　Ant.　　　　Gentle Octavia,　　20
Let your best love draw to that point, which seeks
Best to preserve it. If I lose mine honour,
I lose myself : better I were not yours,
Than yours so branchless. But, as you requested,
Yourself shall go between us : the meantime, lady,
I 'll raise the preparation of a war
Shall stain your brother. Make your soonest haste :
So your desires are yours.
　Octa.　　　　Thanks to my lord.
The Jove of power make me most weak, most weak,
Your reconciler ! Wars 'twixt you twain would be,
As if the world should cleave, and that slain men　31
Should solder up the rift.
　Ant. When it appears to you where this begins,
Turn your displeasure that way ; for our faults
Can never be so equal, that your love
Can equally move with them. Provide your going ;
Choose your own company, and command what cost
Your heart has mind to.　　　　*[Exeunt.*

Scene V.—The Same. Another Room in the Same.

Enter Enobarbus *and* Eros, *meeting.*

　Eno. How now, friend Eros ?
　Eros. There 's strange news come, sir.
　Eno. What, man ?
　Eros. Cæsar and Lepidus have made wars upon
Pompey.
　Eno. This is old : what is the success ?
　Eros. Cæsar, having made use of him in the wars
'gainst Pompey, presently denied him rivality, would

not let him partake in the glory of the action ; and
not resting here, accuses him of letters he had for-
merly wrote to Pompey ; upon his own appeal, seizes
him : so the poor third is up, till death enlarge his
confine.　　　　　　　　　　　　　　13
　Eno. Then, world, thou hast a pair of chaps, no
　　　more ;
And throw between them all the food thou hast,
They 'll grind the one the other. Where 's Antony ?
　Eros. He 's walking in the garden—thus : and
　　　spurns
The rush that lies before him ; cries, " Fool, Lepidus !"
And threats the throat of that his officer,
That murder'd Pompey.
　Eno.　　　　Our great navy 's rigg'd.　20
　Eros. For Italy, and Cæsar. More, Domitius ;
My lord desires you presently : my news
I might have told hereafter.
　Eno.　　　　'T will be naught ;
But let it be. Bring me to Antony.
　Eros. Come, sir.　　　　　　　　*[Exeunt.*

Scene VI.—Rome. A Room in Cæsar's House.

Enter Cæsar, Agrippa, *and* Mecænas.

　Cæs. Contemning Rome, he has done all this : and
　　　more ;
In Alexandria—here 's the manner of 't—
I' the market-place, on a tribunal silver'd,
Cleopatra and himself in chairs of gold
Were publicly enthron'd : at the feet sat
Cæsarion, whom they call my father's son,
And all the unlawful issue, that their lust
Since then hath made between them. Unto her
He gave the stablishment of Egypt ; made her
Of lower Syria, Cyprus, Lydia,　　　　10
Absolute queen.
　Mec.　　　　This in the public eye ?
　Cæs. I' the common show-place, where they exercise.
His sons he there proclaim'd the kings of kings :
Great Media, Parthia, and Armenia,
He gave to Alexander : to Ptolemy he assign'd
Syria, Cilicia, and Phœnicia. She
In the habiliments of the goddess Isis
That day appear'd ; and oft before gave audience,
As 't is reported, so.
　Mec.　　　　Let Rome be thus
Inform'd.　　　　　　　　　　　　20
　Agr. Who, queasy with his insolence already,
Will their good thoughts call from him.
　Cæs. The people know it ; and have now receiv'd
His accusations.
　Agr.　　　　Whom does he accuse ?
　Cæs. Cæsar : and that, having in Sicily
Sextus Pompeius spoil'd, we had not rated him
His part o' the isle : then does he say, he lent me
Some shipping unrestor'd : lastly, he frets,
That Lepidus of the triumvirate
Should be depos'd ; and, being, that we detain　30
All his revenue.
　Agr.　　　　Sir, this should be answer'd.
　Cæs. 'T is done already, and the messenger gone.
I have told him, Lepidus was grown too cruel ;
That he his high authority abus'd,
And did deserve his change : for what I have con-
　　　quer'd,
I grant him part ; but then, in his Armenia,
And other of his conquer'd kingdoms, I
Demand the like.
　Mec.　　　　He 'll never yield to that.
　Cæs. Nor must not then be yielded to in this.

Enter Octavia, *with her Train.*

　Octa. Hail, Cæsar, and my lord ! hail, most dear
　　　Cæsar !　　　　　　　　　　40
　Cæs. That ever I should call thee castaway !
　Octa. You have not call'd me so, nor have you cause.
　Cæs. Why have you stol'n upon us thus ? You come
　　　not
Like Cæsar's sister : the wife of Antony
Should have an army for an usher, and

The neighs of horse to tell of her approach,
Long ere she did appear; the trees by the way
Should have borne men, and expectation fainted,
Longing for what it had not; nay, the dust
Should have ascended to the roof of heaven,　　　50
Rais'd by your populous troops. But you are come
A market-maid to Rome, and have prevented
The ostentation of our love, which, left unshown,
Is often left unlov'd: we should have met you
By sea and land, supplying every stage
With an augmented greeting.

Octa. 　　　　　　　　　　Good my lord,
To come thus was I not constrain'd, but did it
On my free will. My lord, Mark Antony,
Hearing that you prepar'd for war, acquainted
My grieved ear withal; whereon, I begg'd　　　60
His pardon for return.

Cæs. 　　　　　　　Which soon he granted,
Being an obstruct 'tween his lust and him.

Octa. Do not say so, my lord.

Cæs. 　　　　　　　I have eyes upon him,
And his affairs come to me on the wind.
Where is he now?

Octa. 　　　　　　　My lord, in Athens.

Cæs. No, my most wronged sister; Cleopatra
Hath nodded him to her. He hath given his empire
Up to a whore; who now are levying
The kings o' the earth for war. He hath assembled
Bocchus, the king of Libya; Archelaus,　　　70
Of Cappadocia; Philadelphos, king
Of Paphlagonia; the Thracian king, Adallas;
King Malchus of Arabia; King of Pont;
Herod of Jewry; Mithridates, king
Of Comagene; Polemon and Amintas,
The kings of Mede, and Lycaonia,
With a more larger list of sceptres.

Octa. 　　　　　　　Ah me, most wretched,
That have my heart parted betwixt two friends,
That do afflict each other!

Cæs. 　　　　　　　Welcome hither.
Your letters did withhold our breaking forth,　　　80
Till we perceiv'd, both how you were wrong led,
And we in negligent danger. Cheer your heart.
Be you not troubled with the time, which drives
O'er your content these strong necessities;
But let determin'd things to destiny
Hold unbewail'd their way. Welcome to Rome;
Nothing more dear to me. You are abus'd
Beyond the mark of thought; and the high gods,
To do you justice, make their ministers
Of us and those that love you. Best of comfort;　　　90
And ever welcome to us.

Agr. 　　　　　　　Welcome, lady.

Mec. Welcome, dear madam.
Each heart in Rome does love and pity you:
Only the adulterous Antony, most large
In his abominations, turns you off,
And gives his potent regiment to a trull,
That noises it against us.

Octa. 　　　　　　　Is it so, sir?

Cæs. Most certain. Sister, welcome: pray you,
Be ever known to patience: my dear'st sister!
　　　　　　　　　　　　　　　　　　　　[*Exeunt.*

SCENE VII.—ANTONY'S Camp, near the Promontory
of Actium.

Enter CLEOPATRA *and* ENOBARBUS.

Cleo. I will be even with thee, doubt it not.

Eno. But why, why, why?

Cleo. Thou hast forspoke my being in these wars,
And say'st, it is not fit.

Eno. 　　　　　　　Well, is it, is it?

Cleo. If not, denounc'd against us, why should not
　　　　we
Be there in person!

Eno. [*Aside.*]　　　Well, I could reply:—
If we should serve with horse and mares together,
The horse were merely lost; the mares would bear
A soldier, and his horse.

Cleo. 　　　　　　　What is't you say?

Eno. Your presence needs must puzzle Antony;　　　10
Take from his heart, take from his brain, from's time,
What should not then be spar'd. He is already
Traduc'd for levity; and 'tis said in Rome,
That Photinus, an eunuch, and your maids,
Manage this war.

Cleo. 　　　　　　　Sink Rome; and their tongues rot,
That speak against us! A charge we bear i' the war,
And, as the president of my kingdom, will
Appear there for a man. Speak not against it;
I will not stay behind.

Eno. 　　　　　　　Nay, I have done.
Here comes the emperor.

Enter ANTONY *and* CANIDIUS.

Ant. 　　　　　　　Is't not strange, Canidius,
That from Tarentum, and Brundusium,　　　21
He could so quickly cut the Ionian sea,
And take in Toryne?—You have heard on't, sweet?

Cleo. Celerity is never more admir'd,
Than by the negligent.

Ant. 　　　　　　　A good rebuke,
Which might have well becom'd the best of men,
To taunt at slackness.—Canidius, we
Will fight with him by sea.

Cleo. 　　　　　　　By sea! What else?

Can. Why will my lord do so?

Ant. 　　　　　　　For that he dares us to't.

Eno. So hath my lord dar'd him to single fight.　　　30

Can. Ay, and to wage this battle at Pharsalia,
Where Cæsar fought with Pompey; but these offers,
Which serve not for his vantage, he shakes off;
And so should you.

Eno. 　　　　　　　Your ships are not well mann'd;
Your mariners are muliters, reapers, people
Ingross'd by swift impress: in Cæsar's fleet
Are those, that often have 'gainst Pompey fought:
Their ships are yare; yours, heavy. No disgrace
Shall fall you for refusing him at sea,
Being prepar'd for land.

Ant. 　　　　　　　By sea, by sea.　　　40

Eno. Most worthy sir, you therein throw away
The absolute soldiership you have by land;
Distract your army, which doth most consist
Of war-mark'd footmen; leave unexecuted
Your own renowned knowledge; quite forego
The way which promises assurance, and
Give up yourself merely to chance and hazard,
From firm security.

Ant. 　　　　　　　I'll fight at sea.

Cleo. I have sixty sails, Cæsar none better.

Ant. Our overplus of shipping will we burn;　　　50
And with the rest, full-mann'd, from the head of
　　　　Actium
Beat the approaching Cæsar. But if we fail,
We then can do't at land.

Enter a Messenger.

　　　　　　　　　Thy business?

Mess. The news is true, my lord; he is descried;
Cæsar has taken Toryne.

Ant. Can he be there in person? 'tis impossible;
Strange, that his power should be.—Canidius,
Our nineteen legions thou shalt hold by land,
And our twelve thousand horse:—we'll to our ship.
Away, my Thetis!

Enter a Soldier.

　　　　　　　　　How now, worthy soldier?　　　60

Sold. O noble emperor! do not fight by sea;
Trust not to rotten planks. Do you misdoubt
This sword, and these my wounds? Let the Egyptians
And the Phœnicians go a-ducking; we
Have used to conquer standing on the earth,
And fighting foot to foot.

Ant. 　　　　　　　Well. well.—Away!
　　　[*Exeunt* ANTONY, CLEOPATRA, *and* ENOBARBUS.

Sold. By Hercules, I think, I am i' the right.

Can. Soldier, thou art; but his whole action grows
Not in the power on't: so our leader's led,
And we are women's men.

Sold. 　　　　　　　You keep by land　　　70
The legions and the horse whole, do you not?

Can. Marcus Octavius, Marcus Justeius;
Publicola, and Cælius, are for sea ; ,
But we keep whole by land.　This speed of Cæsar's
Carries beyond belief.
　　Sold.　　　　　　While he was yet in Rome,
His power went out in such distractions, as
Beguil'd all spies.
　　Can.　　　Who's his lieutenant, hear you?
　　Sold. They say, one Taurus.
　　Can.　　　　　Well I know the man.

Enter a Messenger.

Mess. The emperor calls Canidius.
　Can. With news the time's with labour; and throes
forth　　　　　　　　　　　　　　80
Each minute some.　　　　　　　[*Exeunt.*

SCENE VIII.—A Plain near Actium.

Enter CÆSAR, TAURUS, *Officers, and others.*

Cæs. Taurus!
Taur.　　My lord?
Cæs.　　　　　Strike not by land; keep whole :
Provoke not battle, till we have done at sea.
Do not exceed the prescript of this scroll :
Our fortune lies upon this jump.　　[*Exeunt.*

Enter ANTONY and ENOBARBUS.

Ant. Set we our squadrons on yond side o' the hill,
In eye of Cæsar's battle ; from which place
We may the number of the ships behold,
And so proceed accordingly.　　　　[*Exeunt.*

Enter CANIDIUS, *marching with his land Army one
way over the stage; and* TAURUS, *the Lieutenant
of* CÆSAR, *the other way.　After their going in, is
heard the noise of a sea-fight.*

Alarum.　Re-enter ENOBARBUS.

Eno. Naught, naught, all naught ! I can behold no
　longer.
The Antoniad, the Egyptian admiral,　　10
With all their sixty, fly, and turn the rudder :
To see 't, mine eyes are blasted.

Enter SCARUS.

Scar.　　　　Gods, and goddesses,
All the whole synod of them !
　Eno.　　　　What 's thy passion ?
　Scar. The greater cantle of the world is lost
With very ignorance : we have kiss'd away
Kingdoms and provinces.
　Eno.　　　How appears the fight ?
　Scar. On our side like the token'd pestilence,
Where death is sure.　Yon ribaudred nag of Egypt,
Whom leprosy o'ertake ! i' the midst o' the fight,—
When vantage like a pair of twins appear'd,　20
Both as the same, or rather ours the elder,—
The breese upon her, like a cow in June,
Hoists sails, and flies.
　Eno.　　　　That I beheld :
Mine eyes did sicken at the sight, and could not
Endure a further view.
　Scar.　　　　She once being loof'd,
The noble ruin of her magic, Antony,
Claps on his sea-wing, and like a doting mallard,
Leaving the fight in height, flies after her.
I never saw an action of such shame :
Experience, manhood, honour, ne'er before　30
Did violate so itself.
　Eno.　　　　Alack, alack !

Enter CANIDIUS.

Can. Our fortune on the sea is out of breath,
And sinks most lamentably.　Had our general
Been what he knew himself, it had gone well :
O ! he has given example for our flight,
Most grossly, by his own.
　Eno.　　　Ay, are you thereabouts ?
Why then, good night, indeed.
　Can. Towards Peloponnesus are they fled.

Scar. 'T is easy to 't ; and there I will attend
What further comes.
　Can.　　　To Cæsar will I render　46
My legions, and my horse : six kings already
Show me the way of yielding.
　Eno.　　　　I 'll yet follow
The wounded chance of Antony, though my reason
Sits in the wind against me.　　　[*Exeunt.*

SCENE IX.—Alexandria.　A Room in the Palace.

Enter ANTONY and Attendants.

Ant. Hark ! the land bids me tread no more upon 't ;
It is asham'd to bear me.—Friends, come hither :
I am so lated in the world, that I
Have lost my way for ever.—I have a ship
Laden with gold ; take that, divide it ; fly,
And make your peace with Cæsar.
　Att.　　　　Fly ! not we.
　Ant. I have fled myself, and have instructed
　cowards
To run, and show their shoulders.—Friends, be gone ;
I have myself resolv'd upon a course,
Which has no need of you ; be gone :　　10
My treasure 's in the harbour, take it.—O !
I follow'd that I blush to look upon :
My very hairs do mutiny ; for the white
Reprove the brown for rashness, and they them
For fear and doting.—Friends, be gone : you shall
Have letters from me to some friends, that will
Sweep your way for you.　Pray you, look not sad,
Nor make replies of loathness : take the hint
Which my despair proclaims ; let that be left
Which leaves itself : to the sea-side straightway :　20
I will possess you of that ship and treasure.
Leave me, I pray, a little ; 'pray you now :—
Nay, do so ; for, indeed, I have lost command,
Therefore, I pray you.　I 'll see you by-and-by.
　　　　　　　　　　　[*Sits down.*

Enter EROS, *and* CLEOPATRA, *led by* CHARMIAN
and IRAS.

Eros. Nay, gentle madam, to him ; comfort him.
　Iras. Do, most dear queen.
　Char. Do !　Why, what else ?
　Cleo. Let me sit down.　O Juno !
　Ant. No, no, no, no, no.
　Eros. See you here, sir ?　　　　30
　Ant. O fie, fie, fie !
　Char. Madam,—
　Iras. Madam ; O good empress !—
　Eros. Sir, sir,—
　Ant. Yes, my lord, yes.—He, at Philippi, kept
His sword e'en like a dancer ; while I struck
The lean and wrinkled Cassius ; and 't was I
That the mad Brutus ended : he alone
Dealt on lieutenantry, and no practice had
In the brave squares of war : yet now—No matter.　40
　Cleo. Ah ! stand by.
　Eros. The queen, my lord, the queen.
　Iras. Go to him, madam, speak to him :
He is unqualitied with very shame.
　Cleo. Well then,—sustain me :—O !
　Eros. Most noble sir, arise ; the queen approaches :
Her head 's declin'd, and death will seize her, but
Your comfort makes the rescue.
　Ant. I have offended reputation ;
A most unnoble swerving.
　Eros.　　　Sir, the queen.　50
　Ant. O ! whither hast thou led me, Egypt ? See,
How I convey my shame out of thine eyes
By looking back on what I have left behind
'Stroy'd in dishonour.
　Cleo.　　　O my lord, my lord !
Forgive my fearful sails : I little thought
You would have follow'd.
　Ant.　　　Egypt, thou knew'st too well,
My heart was to thy rudder tied by the strings,
And thou shouldst tow me after : o'er my spirit
Thy full supremacy thou knew'st, and that

Thy beck might from the bidding of the gods   60
Command me.
   Cleo.   O, my pardon!
   Ant.   Now I must
To the young man send humble treaties, dodge

SCENE X.--CÆSAR'S Camp in Egypt.

Enter CÆSAR, DOLABELLA, THYREUS, *and others.*
   Cæs. Let him appear that 's come from Antony.--
Know you him?

Eros. "Most noble sir, arise; the queen approaches."

And palter in the shifts of lowness, who
With half the bulk o' the world play'd as I pleas'd,
Making and marring fortunes.   You did know,
How much you were my conqueror; and that
My sword, made weak by my affection, would
Obey it on all cause.
   Cleo.   Pardon, pardon!
   Ant. Fall not a tear, I say: one of them rates
All that is won and lost.   Give me a kiss;   70
Even this repays me.--We sent our schoolmaster;
Is he come back?--Love, I am full of lead.--
Some wine, within there, and our viands!--Fortune
    knows,
We scorn her most when most she offers blows. [*Exeunt.*

   Dol.   Cæsar, 't is his schoolmaster:
An argument that he is pluck'd, when hither
He sends so poor a pinion of his wing,
Which had superfluous kings for messengers,
Not many moons gone by.
          Enter EUPHRONIUS.
   Cæs.   Approach, and speak.
   Euph. Such as I am, I come from Antony:
I was of late as petty to his ends,
As is the morn-dew on the myrtle-leaf
To his grand sea.
   Cæs.   Be 't so.   Declare thine office.   10
   Euph. Lord of his fortunes he salutes thee, and

Requires to live in Egypt; which not granted,
He lessens his requests, and to thee sues
To let him breathe between the heavens and earth,
A private man in Athens. This for him.
Next, Cleopatra does confess thy greatness,
Submits her to thy might, and of thee craves
The circle of the Ptolemies for her heirs,
Now hazarded to thy grace.
　Cæs.　　　　　　　For Antony,
I have no ears to his request. The queen　　20
Of audience, nor desire, shall fail, so she
From Egypt drive her all-disgraced friend,
Or take his life there : this if she perform,
She shall not sue unheard. So to them both.
　Euph. Fortune pursue thee!
　Cæs.　　　　　Bring him through the bands.
　　　　　　　　　　　　[*Exit* EUPHRONIUS.
[*To* THYREUS.] To try thy eloquence, now 't is time ;
　　despatch.
From Antony win Cleopatra : promise,
And in our name, what she requires ; add more,
From thine invention, offers. Women are not
In their best fortunes strong, but want will perjure　30
The ne'er-touch'd vestal. Try thy cunning, Thyreus ;
Make thine own edict for thy pains, which we
Will answer as a law.
　Thyr.　　　　　　Cæsar, I go.
　Cæs. Observe how Antony becomes his flaw,
And what thou think'st his very action speaks
In every power that moves.
　Thyr.　　　　Cæsar, I shall. [*Exeunt.*

————

SCENE XI.—Alexandria. A Room in the Palace.

Enter CLEOPATRA, ENOBARBUS, CHARMIAN, *and*
　IRAS.

　Cleo. What shall we do, Enobarbus?
　Eno.　　　　　　Think, and die.
　Cleo. Is Antony, or we, in fault for this?
　Eno. Antony only, that would make his will
Lord of his reason. What though you fled
From that great face of war, whose several ranges
Frighted each other, why should he follow?
The itch of his affection should not then
Have nick'd his captainship ; at such a point,
When half to half the world oppos'd, he being
The mered question. 'T was a shame no less　　10
Than was his loss, to course your flying flags,
And leave his navy gazing.
　Cleo.　　　　Pr'ythee, peace.

Enter ANTONY, *with* EUPHRONIUS.

　Ant. Is that his answer?
　Euph. Ay, my lord.
　Ant. The queen shall then have courtesy, so she
Will yield us up.
　Euph.　　　　He says so.
　Ant.　　　　　　Let her know 't.
To the boy Cæsar send this grizzled head,
And he will fill thy wishes to the brim
With principalities.
　Cleo.　　　　That head, my lord?
　Ant. To him again. Tell him, he wears the rose　20
Of youth upon him, from which the world should
　　note
Something particular : his coin, ships, legions,
May be a coward's ; whose ministers would prevail
Under the service of a child, as soon
As i' the command of Cæsar : I dare him therefore
To lay his gay comparisons apart,
And answer me declin'd, sword against sword,
Ourselves alone. I 'll write it : follow me.
　　　　　　　[*Exeunt* ANTONY *and* EUPHRONIUS.
　Eno. [*Aside.*] Yes, like enough, high-battled Cæsar
　　will
Unstate his happiness, and be stag'd to the show,　30
Against a sworder!—I see, men's judgments are
A parcel of their fortunes, and things outward
Do draw the inward quality after them,
To suffer all alike. That he should dream,

Knowing all measures, the full Cæsar will
Answer his emptiness!—Cæsar, thou hast subdu'd
His judgment too.

Enter an Attendant.

　Att.　　　　A messenger from Cæsar.
　Cleo. What, no more ceremony?—See, my women!—
Against the blown rose may they stop their nose,
That kneel'd unto the buds.—Admit him, sir.　　40
　Eno. [*Aside.*] Mine honesty and I begin to square.
The loyalty, well held to fools, does make
Our faith mere folly : yet he, that can endure
To follow with allegiance a fall'n lord,
Does conquer him that did his master conquer,
And earns a place i' the story.

Enter THYREUS.

　Cleo.　　　　　Cæsar's will?
　Thyr. Hear it apart.
　Cleo.　　　None but friends : say boldly.
　Thyr. So, haply, are they friends to Antony.
　Eno. He needs as many, sir, as Cæsar has,
Or needs not us. If Cæsar please, our master　　50
Will leap to be his friend : for us, you know
Whose he is, we are, and that 's Cæsar's.
　Thyr.　　　　　　So.—
Thus then, thou most renown'd : Cæsar entreats,
Not to consider in what case thou stand'st,
Further than he is Cæsar.
　Cleo.　　　　Go on : right royal.
　Thyr. He knows, that you embrace not Antony
As you did love, but as you fear'd him.
　Cleo.　　　　　　O!
　Thyr. The scars upon your honour therefore he
Does pity, as constrained blemishes,
Not as deserv'd.
　Cleo.　　　He is a god, and knows　　60
What is most right. Mine honour was not yielded,
But conquer'd merely.
　Eno. [*Aside.*] To be sure of that,
I will ask Antony.—Sir, sir, thou 'rt so leaky,
That we must leave thee to thy sinking, for
Thy dearest quit thee.　　　　　　[*Exit.*
　Thyr.　　　　Shall I say to Cæsar
What you require of him? for he partly begs
To be desir'd to give. It much would please him,
That of his fortunes you should make a staff
To lean upon ; but it would warm his spirits,
To hear from me you had left Antony,　　70
And put yourself under his shroud,
The universal landlord.
　Cleo.　　　　What 's your name?
　Thyr. My name is Thyreus.
　Cleo.　　　　Most kind messenger,
Say to great Cæsar this : in deputation
I kiss his conqu'ring hand : tell him, I am prompt
To lay my crown at his feet, and there to kneel :
Tell him, from his all-obeying breath I hear
The doom of Egypt.
　Thyr.　　　'T is your noblest course.
Wisdom and fortune combating together,
If that the former dare but what it can,　　80
No chance may shake it. Give me grace to lay
My duty on your hand.
　Cleo.　　　Your Cæsar's father oft,
When he hath mus'd of taking kingdoms in,
Bestow'd his lips on that unworthy place
As it rain'd kisses.

Re-enter ANTONY *and* ENOBARBUS.

　Ant.　　　Favours, by Jove that thunders!—
What art thou, fellow?
　Thyr.　　　One, that but performs
The bidding of the fullest man, and worthiest
To have command obey'd.
　Eno. [*Aside.*]　　You will be whipp'd.
　Ant. Approach, there.—Ay, you kite!—Now, gods
　　and devils!
Authority melts from me : of late, when I cried,
　　" Ho!"　　　　　　　　　　90
Like boys unto a muss, kings would start forth,
And cry, " Your will?" Have you no ears?

Enter Attendants.

I am Antony yet. Take hence this Jack, and whip
    him.
 Eno. [*Aside.*] 'T is better playing with a lion's
    whelp,
Than with an old one dying.
 Ant.   Moon and stars!
Whip him.—Were 't twenty of the greatest tributaries
That do acknowledge Cæsar, should I find them

Thyr.   "Give me grace to lay
      My duty on your hand."

So saucy with the hand of—she here (what 's her name,
Since she was Cleopatra ?)—Whip him, fellows,
Till, like a boy, you see him cringe his face,   100
And whine aloud for mercy. Take him hence.
 Thyr. Mark Antony,—
 Ant.   Tug him away : being whipp'd,
Bring him again.—This Jack of Cæsar's shall
Bear us an errand to him.—
                        [*Exeunt Attendants with* THYREUS.
You were half blasted ere I knew you : ha !
Have I my pillow left unpress'd in Rome,
Forborne the getting of a lawful race,
And by a gem of women, to be abus'd
By one that looks on feeders ?
 Cleo.   Good my lord,—
 Ant. You have been a boggler ever :—   110
But when we in our viciousness grow hard,
(O misery on 't !) the wise gods seel our eyes ;
In our own filth drop our clear judgments ; make us
Adore our errors ; laugh at 's, while we strut
To our confusion.
 Cleo.   O ! is 't come to this ?
 Ant. I found you as a morsel cold upon
Dead Cæsar's trencher : nay, you were a fragment
Of Cneius Pompey's ; besides what hotter hours,
Unregister'd in vulgar fame, you have
Luxuriously pick'd out : for, I am sure,   120
Though you can guess what temperance should be,
You know not what it is.
 Cleo.   Wherefore is this ?
 Ant. To let a fellow that will take rewards,
And say, "God quit you !" be familiar with
My playfellow, your hand, this kingly seal,
And plighter of high hearts !—O, that I were
Upon the hill of Basan to outroar,
The horned herd ! for I have savage cause ;
And to proclaim it civilly, were like
A halter'd neck, which does the hangman thank   130
For being yare about him.—

Re-enter Attendants, with THYREUS.

                        Is he whipp'd ?
 1 Att. Soundly, my lord.

 Ant.   Cried he ? and begg'd he pardon ?
 1 Att. He did ask favour.
 Ant. If that thy father live, let him repent
Thou wast not made his daughter ; and be thou sorry
To follow Cæsar in his triumph, since
Thou hast been whipp'd for following him : hence-
    forth,
The white hand of a lady fever thee ;
Shake thou to look on 't. Get thee back to Cæsar,
Tell him thy entertainment : look, thou say,   140
He makes me angry with him ; for he seems
Proud and disdainful, harping on what I am,
Not what he knew I was. He makes me angry ;
And at this time most easy 't is to do 't,
When my good stars, that were my former guides,
Have empty left their orbs, and shot their fires
Into the abysm of hell. If he mislike
My speech, and what is done, tell him, he has
Hipparchus, my enfranched bondman, whom
He may at pleasure whip, or hang, or torture,   150
As he shall like, to quit me. Urge it thou :
Hence, with thy stripes ! be gone ! [*Exit* THYREUS.
 Cleo. Have you done yet ?
 Ant.   Alack ! our terrene moon
Is now eclips'd, and it portends alone
The fall of Antony.
 Cleo.   I must stay his time.
 Ant. To flatter Cæsar, would you mingle eyes
With one that ties his points ?
 Cleo.   Not know me yet ?
 Ant. Cold-hearted toward me ?
 Cleo.   Ah, dear ! if I be so.
From my cold heart let heaven engender hail,
And poison it in the source ; and the first stone   160
Drop in my neck : as it determines, so
Dissolve my life ! The next Cæsarion smite,
Till by degrees the memory of my womb,
Together with my brave Egyptians all,
By the discandying of this pelleted storm,
Lie graveless, till the flies and gnats of Nile
Have buried them for prey !
 Ant.   I am satisfied.
Cæsar sits down in Alexandria, where
I will oppose his fate. Our force by land
Hath nobly held ; our sever'd navy too   170
Have knit again, and fleet, threat'ning most sealike.
Where hast thou been, my heart ?—Dost thou hear,
    lady ?
If from the field I shall return once more
To kiss these lips, I will appear in blood ;
I and my sword will earn our chronicle :
There 's hope in 't yet.
 Cleo.   That 's my brave lord !
 Ant. I will be treble-sinew'd, hearted, breath'd,
And fight maliciously : for when mine hours
Were nice and lucky, men did ransom lives
Of me for jests ; but now, I 'll set my teeth,   180
And send to darkness all that stop me.—Come,
Let 's have one other gaudy night.—Call to me
All my sad captains ; fill our bowls ; once more
Let 's mock the midnight bell.
 Cleo.   It is my birthday :
I had thought to have held it poor ; but, since my lord
Is Antony again, I will be Cleopatra.
 Ant. We will yet do well.
 Cleo. Call all his noble captains to my lord.
 Ant. Do so, we 'll speak to them ; and to-night I 'll
    force
The wine peep through their scars.—Come on, my
    queen ;   190
There 's sap in 't yet. The next time I do fight,
I 'll make death love me, for I will contend
Even with his pestilent scythe.
          [*Exeunt* ANTONY, CLEOPATRA, *and Attendants.*
 Eno. Now he 'll outstare the lightning. To be
    furious,
Is to be frighted out of fear ; and, in that mood,
The dove will peck the estridge : and I see still,
A diminution in our captain's brain
Restores his heart. When valour preys on reason,
It eats the sword it fights with. I will seek
Some way to leave him.   [*Exit.*

ACT IV.

SCENE I.—CÆSAR'S Camp at Alexandria.

Enter CÆSAR, *reading a letter;* AGRIPPA, MECÆNAS, *and others.*

Cæsar.

E calls me boy, and chides, as he
   had power
To beat me out of Egypt; my
   messenger
He hath whipp'd with rods; dares
   me to personal combat,
Cæsar to Antony. Let the old
   ruffian know,
I have many other ways to die;
   meantime,
Laugh at his challenge.
 Mec.   Cæsar must think,
When one so great begins to rage, he's hunted
Even to falling. Give him no breath, but now
Make boot of his distraction. Never anger
Made good guard for itself.
 Cæs.   Let our best heads 10
Know, that to-morrow the last of many battles
We mean to fight. Within our files there are,
Of those that serv'd Mark Antony but late,
Enough to fetch him in. See it done;
And feast the army: we have store to do't,
And they have earn'd the waste. Poor Antony!
           [*Exeunt.*

———

SCENE II.—Alexandria. A Room in the Palace.

Enter ANTONY, CLEOPATRA, ENOBARBUS, CHARMIAN,
 IRAS, ALEXAS, *and others.*

 Ant. He will not fight with me, Domitius.
 Eno.   No.
 Ant. Why should he not?
 Eno. He thinks, being twenty times of better for-
  tune,
He is twenty men to one.
 Ant.   To-morrow, soldier,
By sea and land I'll fight: or I will live,
Or bathe my dying honour in the blood
Shall make it live again. Woo't thou fight well?
 Eno. I'll strike, and cry, "Take all."
 Ant.   Well said; come on.—
Call forth my household servants: let's to-night
Be bounteous at our meal.

Enter Servants.

      Give me thy hand, 10
Thou hast been rightly honest;—so hast thou;—
Thou,—and thou,—and thou:—you have serv'd me
 well,
And kings have been your fellows.
 Cleo. [*Aside to* ENO.]   What means this?
 Eno. [*Aside to* CLEO.] 'Tis one of those odd tricks,
  which sorrow shoots
Out of the mind.
 Ant.   And thou art honest too.
I wish I could be made so many men,
And all of you clapp'd up together in
An Antony, that I might do you service,
So good as you have done.
 Serv.   The gods forbid!
 Ant. Well, my good fellows, wait on me to-night;20
Scant not my cups, and make as much of me,
As when mine empire was your fellow too,
And suffer'd my command.

 Cleo. [*Aside to* ENO.] What does he mean?
 Eno. [*Aside to* CLEO.] To make his followers weep.
 Ant.   Tend me to-night;
May be, it is the period of your duty:
Haply, you shall not see me more; or if,
A mangled shadow: perchance, to-morrow
You'll serve another master. I look on you
As one that takes his leave. Mine honest friends,
I turn you not away; but, like a master 30
Married to your good service, stay till death.
Tend me to-night two hours, I ask no more,
And the gods yield you for 't!
 Eno.   What mean you, sir,
To give them this discomfort? Look, they weep;
And I, an ass, am onion-ey'd: for shame,
Transform us not to women.
 Ant.   Ho, ho, ho!
Now, the witch take me, if I meant it thus!
Grace grow where those drops fall! My hearty
  friends,
You take me in too dolorous a sense,
For I spake to you for your comfort; did desire you 40
To burn this night with torches. Know, my hearts,
I hope well of to-morrow; and will lead you
Where rather I'll expect victorious life,
Than death and honour. Let's to supper, come,
And drown consideration.   [*Exeunt.*

———

SCENE III.—The Same. Before the Palace.

Enter two Soldiers, to their guard.

 1 Sold. Brother, good night: to-morrow is the day.
 2 Sold. It will determine one way: fare you well.
Heard you of nothing strange about the streets?
 1 Sold. Nothing. What news?
 2 Sold. Belike, 'tis but a rumour. Good night to you.
 1 Sold. Well, sir, good night.

Enter two other Soldiers.

 2 Sold.   Soldiers, have careful watch.
 3 Sold. And you. Good night, good night.
     [*The first two place themselves at their posts.*
 4 Sold. Here we: [*they take their posts*] and if to-
  morrow
Our navy thrive, I have an absolute hope
Our landmen will stand up.
 3 Sold.   'T is a brave army, 10
And full of purpose.
    [*Music of hautboys under the stage.*
 4 Sold.   Peace! what noise?
 1 Sold.   List, list!
 2 Sold. Hark!
 1 Sold.   Music i' the air.
 3 Sold.   Under the earth.
 4 Sold. It signs well, does it not?
 3 Sold.   No.
 1 Sold.   Peace, I say!
What should this mean?
 2 Sold. 'T is the god Hercules, whom Antony lov'd,
Now leaves him.
 1 Sold.   Walk: let's see if other watchmen
Do hear what we do. [*They advance to another post.*
 2 Sold.   How now, masters?
 Soldiers. [*Speaking together.*] How now?
How now? do you hear this?

1 Sold.   Ay; is 't not strange?
3 Sold. Do you hear, masters? do you hear?
1 Sold. Follow the noise so far as we have quarter;
Let's see how 't will give off.
Soldiers.   Content. 'T is strange.
                     [*Exeunt.*

SCENE IV.—The Same. A Room in the Palace.

Enter ANTONY *and* CLEOPATRA; CHARMIAN, *and others, attending.*

Ant. Eros! mine armour, Eros!
Cleo.   Sleep a little.
Ant. No, my chuck.—Eros, come; mine armour, Eros!

Enter EROS, *with armour.*

Come, good fellow, put mine iron on:—

Ant.   " Ah, let be, let be! thou art
The armourer of my heart."

If fortune be not ours to-day, it is
Because we brave her.—Come.
Cleo.   Nay, I'll help too.
What's this for?
Ant.   Ah, let be, let be! thou art
The armourer of my heart:—false, false; this, this.
Cleo. Sooth, la! I'll help. Thus it must be.
Ant.   Well, well;
We shall thrive now.—Seest thou, my good fellow?
Go, put on thy defences.
Eros.   Briefly, sir.   10
Cleo. Is not this buckled well?
Ant.   Rarely, rarely:
He that unbuckles this, till we do please
To doff 't for our repose, shall hear a storm.—
Thou fumblest, Eros; and my queen's a squire
More tight at this than thou. Despatch.—O love!
That thou couldst see my wars to-day, and knew'st
The royal occupation! thou shouldst see
A workman in 't.

Enter an armed Soldier.

          Good morrow to thee; welcome:
Thou look'st like him that knows a warlike charge:
To business that we love we rise betime,   20
And go to 't with delight.
Sold.   A thousand, sir,
Early though 't be, have on their riveted trim,
And at the port expect you.
              [*Shout. Trumpets flourish.*

Enter Captains and Soldiers.

Capt. The morn is fair.—Good morrow, general.
All. Good morrow, general.
Ant.   'T is well blown, lads.
This morning, like the spirit of a youth
That means to be of note, begins betimes.—
So, so; come, give me that: this way; well said.

Fare thee well, dame: whate'er becomes of me,
This is a soldier's kiss. [*Kisses her.*] Rebukable,   30
And worthy shameful check it were, to stand
On more mechanic compliment: I'll leave thee
Now, like a man of steel.—You, that will fight,
Follow me close; I'll bring you to 't.—Adieu.
      [*Exeunt* ANTONY, EROS, *Officers, and Soldiers.*
Char. Please you, retire to your chamber.
Cleo.   Lead me.
He goes forth gallantly. That he and Cæsar might
Determine this great war in single fight!
Then Antony—but now—Well, on.   [*Exeunt.*

SCENE V.—ANTONY's Camp near Alexandria.

Trumpets sound. Enter ANTONY *and* EROS; *a Soldier meeting them.*

Sold. The gods make this a happy day to Antony!
Ant. 'Would thou, and those thy scars, had once prevail'd
To make me fight at land!
Sold.   Hadst thou done so,
The kings that have revolted, and the soldier
That has this morning left thee, would have still
Follow'd thy heels.
Ant.   Who's gone this morning?
Sold.   Who?
One ever near thee: call for Enobarbus,
He shall not hear thee; or from Cæsar's camp
Say, "I am none of thine."
Ant.   What say'st thou?
Sold.   Sir,
He is with Cæsar.
Eros.   Sir, his chests and treasure   10
He has not with him.
Ant.   Is he gone?
Sold.   Most certain.
Ant. Go, Eros, send his treasure after; do it:
Detain no jot, I charge thee. Write to him
(I will subscribe) gentle adieus and greetings:
Say, that I wish he never find more cause
To change a master.—O! my fortunes have
Corrupted honest men.—Despatch.—Enobarbus!
                   [*Exeunt.*

SCENE VI.—CÆSAR's Camp before Alexandria.

Flourish. Enter CÆSAR, *with* AGRIPPA, ENOBARBUS, *and others.*

Cæs. Go forth, Agrippa, and begin the fight.
Our will is, Antony be took alive;
Make it so known.
Agr.   Cæsar, I shall.   [*Exit.*
Cæs. The time of universal peace is near:
Prove this a prosperous day, the three-nook'd world
Shall bear the olive freely.

Enter a Messenger.

Mess.   Antony
Is come into the field.
Cæs.   Go, charge Agrippa
Plant those that have revolted in the van,
That Antony may seem to spend his fury   10
Upon himself.   [*Exeunt* CÆSAR *and his Train.*
Eno. Alexas did revolt, and went to Jewry,
On affairs of Antony; there did persuade
Great Herod to incline himself to Cæsar,
And leave his master Antony: for this pains,
Cæsar hath hang'd him. Canidius, and the rest
That fell away, have entertainment, but
No honourable trust. I have done ill,
Of which I do accuse myself so sorely,
That I will joy no more.

Enter a Soldier of CÆSAR's.

Sold.   Enobarbus, Antony   20
Hath after thee sent all thy treasure, with
His bounty overplus: the messenger
Came on my guard, and at thy tent is now
Unloading of his mules.

Eno.   I give it you.
Sold. Mock not, Enobarbus.
I tell you true : best you saf'd the bringer
Out of the host ; I must attend mine office,
Or would have done 't myself. Your emperor
Continues still a Jove.   [*Exit.*
  Eno. I am alone the villain of the earth,   30
And feel I am so most. O Antony !
Thou mine of bounty, how wouldst thou have paid
My better service, when my turpitude
Thou dost so crown with gold ! This blows my heart :
If swift thought break it not, a swifter mean
Shall outstrike thought ; but thought will do 't, I feel.
I fight against thee ?—No : I will go seek
Some ditch, wherein to die : the foul'st best fits
My latter part of life.   [*Exit.*

Scene VII.—Field of Battle between the Camps.

Alarum. Drums and trumpets. Enter AGRIPPA
and others.

  Agr. Retire, we have engag'd ourselves too far.
Cæsar himself has work, and our oppression
Exceeds what we expected.   [*Exeunt.*

Alarum. Enter ANTONY, *and* SCARUS, *wounded.*

  Scar. O my brave emperor, this is fought indeed !
Had we done so at first, we had driven them home
With clouts about their heads.
  Ant.   Thou bleed'st apace.
  Scar. I had a wound here that was like a T,
But now 't is made an H.
  Ant.   They do retire.
  Scar. We 'll beat 'em into bench-holes. I have yet
Room for six scotches more.   10

Enter EROS.

  Eros. They are beaten, sir ; and our advantage
                    serves
For a fair victory.
  Scar.   Let us score their backs,
And snatch 'em up, as we take hares, behind :
'T is sport to maul a runner.
  Ant.   I will reward thee
Once for thy sprightly comfort, and ten-fold
For thy good valour. Come thee on.
  Scar.   I 'll halt after. *Exeunt.*

Scene VIII.—Under the Walls of Alexandria.

Alarum. Enter ANTONY, *marching ;* SCARUS *and
Forces.*

  Ant. We have beat him to his camp. Run one
                    before,
And let the queen know of our guests.—To-morrow,
Before the sun shall see us, we 'll spill the blood
That has to-day escap'd. I thank you all ;
For doughty-handed are you, and have fought
Not as you serv'd the cause, but as it had been
Each man's like mine : you have shown all Hectors.
Enter the city, clip your wives, your friends,
Tell them your feats ; whilst they with joyful tears
Wash the congealment from your wounds, and kiss 10
The honour'd gashes whole.—Give me thy hand :

Enter CLEOPATRA, *attended.*

To this great fairy I 'll commend thy acts,
Make her thanks bless thee.—O thou day o' the world !
Chain mine arm'd neck ; leap thou, attire and all,
Through proof of harness to my heart, and there
Ride on the pants triumphing.
  Cleo.   Lord of lords !
O infinite virtue ! com'st thou smiling from
The world's great snare uncaught ?
  Ant.   My nightingale,
We have beat them to their beds. What, girl ! though
                    grey
Do something mingle with our younger brown, yet
                    ha' we   20
A brain that nourishes our nerves, and can

Get goal for goal of youth. Behold this man ;
Commend unto his lips thy favouring hand :—
Kiss it, my warrior :—he hath fought to-day,
As if a god, in hate of mankind, had
Destroy'd in such a shape.
  Cleo.   I 'll give thee, friend,
An armour all of gold ; it was a king's.
  Ant. He has deserv'd it, were it carbuncled
Like holy Phœbus' car.—Give me thy hand :
Through Alexandria make a jolly march ;   30
Bear our hack'd targets like the men that owe them.
Had our great palace the capacity

Eno.   "O Antony,
Nobler than my revolt is infamous,
Forgive me in thine own particular."

To camp this host, we all would sup together,
And drink carouses to the next day's fate,
Which promises royal peril. –Trumpeters,
With brazen din blast you the city's ear :
Make mingle with our rattling tabourines,
That heaven and earth may strike their sounds to-
                    gether,
Applauding our approach.   [*Exeunt.*

Scene IX.—Cæsar's Camp.

Sentinels on their Post.

  1 *Sold.* If we be not reliev'd within this hour,
We must return to the court of guard. The night
Is shiny, and, they say, we shall embattle
By the second hour i' the morn.
  2 *Sold.*   This last day was
A shrewd one to us.

Enter ENOBARBUS.

  Eno.   O ! bear me witness, night,—
  3 *Sold.* What man is this ?
  2 *Sold.*   Stand close, and list him.
  Eno. Be witness to me, O thou blessed moon,
When men revolted shall upon record
Bear hateful memory, poor Enobarbus did
Before thy face repent !—
  1 *Sold.*   Enobarbus !
  3 *Sold.*   Peace !   10
Hark further.
  Eno. O sovereign mistress of true melancholy,
The poisonous damp of night disponge upon me,
That life, a very rebel to my will,
May hang no longer on me : throw my heart
Against the flint and hardness of my fault,
Which, being dried with grief, will break to powder,
And finish all foul thoughts. O Antony,
Nobler than my revolt is infamous,
Forgive me in thine own particular ;   20
But let the world rank me in register
A master-leaver, and a fugitive.
O Antony ! O Antony !   [*Dies.*

2 *Sold.* Let 's speak to him.
1 *Sold.* Let 's hear him ; for the things he speaks
May concern Cæsar.
3 *Sold.* 　　　　　Let 's do so. But he sleeps.
1 *Sold.* Swoons rather ; for so bad a prayer as his
Was never yet for sleep.
2 *Sold.* 　　　　Go we to him.
3 *Sold.* Awake, sir, awake! speak to us.
2 *Sold.* 　　　　　　Hear you, sir?
1 *Sold.* The hand of death hath raught him. [*Drums
　　　afar off.] Hark! the drums　　　　30
Demurely wake the sleepers. Let us bear him
To the court of guard ; he is of note : our hour
Is fully out.
3 *Sold.* 　　Come on then ;
He may recover yet. 　　　　[*Exeunt with the body.*]

SCENE X.—Between the two Camps.

Enter ANTONY *and* SCARUS, *with Forces, marching.*
Ant. Their preparation is to-day by sea :
We please them not by land.
Scar. 　　　　　For both, my lord.
Ant. I would, they 'd fight i' the fire, or i' the air ;
We 'd fight there too. But this it is : our foot
Upon the hills adjoining to the city
Shall stay with us : order for sea is given ;
They have put forth the haven :
Where their appointment we may best discover,
And look on their endeavour. 　　　[*Exeunt.*]

Enter CÆSAR *and his Forces, marching.*
Cæs. But being charg'd, we will be still by land, 10
Which, as I take 't, we shall ; for his best force
Is forth to man his galleys. To the vales,
And hold our best advantage! 　　[*Exeunt.*]

Re-enter ANTONY *and* SCARUS.
Ant. Yet they are not join'd. Where yond pine does
　　　stand,
I shall discover all : I 'll bring thee word
Straight, how 't is like to go. 　　　[*Exit.*]
Scar. 　　Swallows have built
In Cleopatra's sails their nests : the auguries
Say, they know not,—they cannot tell ;—look grimly,
And dare not speak their knowledge. Antony
Is valiant, and dejected ; and, by starts, 　　20
His fretted fortunes give him hope, and fear,
Of what he has, and has not.
　　　[*Alarum afar off, as at a sea-fight.*]

Re-enter ANTONY.
Ant. 　　　　　All is lost !
This foul Egyptian hath betrayed me :
My fleet hath yielded to the foe ; and yonder
They cast their caps up, and carouse together
Like friends long lost.—Triple-turn'd whore! 't is thou
Hast sold me to this novice, and my heart
Makes only wars on thee.—Bid them all fly ;
For when I am reveng'd upon my charm,
I have done all.—Bid them all fly ; be gone. 　30
　　　　[*Exit* SCARUS.
O sun ! thy uprise shall I see no more :
Fortune and Antony part here ; even here
Do we shake hands.—All come to this ?—The hearts
That spaniel'd me at heels, to whom I gave
Their wishes, do discandy, melt their sweets
On blossoming Cæsar ; and this pine is bark'd,
That overtopp'd them all. Betray'd I am.
O this false soul of Egypt ! this grave charm,—
Whose eye beck'd forth my wars, and call'd them
　　　home,
Whose bosom was my crownet, my chief end,— 　40
Like a right gipsy, hath, at fast and loose,
Beguil'd me to the very heart of loss.—
What, Eros ! Eros !

Enter CLEOPATRA.
　　　Ah, thou spell ! Avaunt !
Cleo. Why is my lord enrag'd against his love ?

Ant. Vanish, or I shall give thee thy deserving,
And blemish Cæsar's triumph. Let him take thee,
And hoist thee up to the shouting plebeians :
Follow his chariot, like the greatest spot
Of all thy sex ; most monster-like, be shown
For poor'st diminutives, for doits ; and let 　　50
Patient Octavia plough thy visage up
With her prepared nails. [*Exit* CLEOPATRA.] 'T is
　　　well thou 'rt gone,
If it be well to live ; but better 't were
Thou fell'st into my fury, for one death
Might have prevented many.—Eros, ho !—
The shirt of Nessus is upon me : teach me,
Alcides, thou mine ancestor, thy rage :
Let me lodge Lichas on the horns o' the moon ;
And with those hands, that grasp'd the heaviest club,
Subdue my worthiest self. The witch shall die : 　60
To the young Roman boy she hath sold me, and I fall
Under this plot ; she dies for 't.—Eros, ho ! 　[*Exit.*]

SCENE XI.—Alexandria. A Room in the Palace.

Enter CLEOPATRA, CHARMIAN, IRAS, *and* MARDIAN.
Cleo. Help me, my women ! O ! he is more mad
Than Telamon for his shield ; the boar of Thessaly
Was never so emboss'd.
Char. 　　　　To the monument !
There lock yourself, and send him word you are dead.
The soul and body rive not more in parting,
Than greatness going off.
Cleo. 　　　　To the monument !—
Mardian, go tell him I have slain myself ;
Say, that the last I spoke was, Antony,
And word it, pr'ythee, piteously. Hence,
Mardian, and bring me how he takes my death. 　10
To the monument ! 　　　　[*Exeunt.*]

SCENE XII.—The Same. Another Room.

Enter ANTONY *and* EROS.
Ant. Eros, thou yet behold'st me ?
Eros. 　　　　　Ay, noble lord.
Ant. Sometime, we see a cloud that 's dragonish,
A vapour, sometime, like a bear, or lion,
A tower'd citadel, a pendant rock,
A forked mountain, or blue promontory
With trees upon 't, that nod unto the world,
And mock our eyes with air : thou hast seen these
　　　signs ;
They are black vesper's pageants.
Eros. 　　　　　Ay, my lord.
Ant. That which is now a horse, even with a
　　　thought
The rack dislimns, and makes it indistinct, 　　10
As water is in water.
Eros. 　　　It does, my lord.
Ant. My good knave, Eros, now thy captain is
Even such a body : here I am Antony ;
Yet cannot hold this visible shape, my knave.
I made these wars for Egypt : and the queen,—
Whose heart, I thought, I had, for she had mine,
Which, whilst it was mine, had annex'd unto 't
A million moe, now lost,—she, Eros, has
Pack'd cards with Cæsar, and false-play'd my glory
Unto an enemy's triumph.— 　　　　20
Nay, weep not, gentle Eros ; there is left us
Ourselves to end ourselves.

Enter MARDIAN.
　　　　O, thy vile lady !
She has robb'd me of my sword.
Mar. 　　　　No, Antony ;
My mistress lov'd thee, and her fortunes mingled
With thine entirely.
Ant. 　　Hence, saucy eunuch ! peace !
She hath betray'd me, and shall die the death.
Mar. Death of one person can be paid but once,
And that she has discharg'd. What thou wouldst do,
Is done unto thy hand : the last she spake

Was, Antony ! most noble Antony !   30
Then in the midst a tearing groan did break
The name of Antony ; it was divided
Between her heart and lips. She render'd life,
Thy name so buried in her.
    Ant.   Dead then ?
    Mar.   Dead.
    Ant. Unarm, Eros : the long day's task is done,
And we must sleep.—That thou depart'st hence safe,
Does pay thy labour richly ; go. [*Exit* MARDIAN.]—
    Off, pluck off :—
The seven-fold shield of Ajax cannot keep
The battery from my heart. O, cleave, my sides !
Heart, once be stronger than thy continent.   40
Crack thy frail case !—Apace, Eros, apace.—
No more a soldier :—bruised pieces, go ;
You have been nobly borne. [*Exit* EROS.]—From me
            awhile.
I will o'ertake thee, Cleopatra, and
Weep for my pardon. So it must be, for now
All length is torture : since the torch is out,
Lie down, and stray no farther. Now all labour
Mars what it does ; yea, very force entangles
Itself with strength : seal then, and all is done.—
Eros !—I come, my queen.—Eros !—Stay for me :   50
Where souls do couch on flowers, we 'll hand in hand,
And with our spritely port make the ghosts gaze :
Dido and her Æneas shall want troops,
And all the haunt be ours.—Come, Eros ! Eros !

             Re-enter EROS.

    Eros. What would my lord ?
    Ant.   Since Cleopatra died,
I have liv'd in such dishonour, that the gods
Detest my baseness. I, that with my sword
Quarter'd the world, and o'er green Neptune's back
With ships made cities, condemn myself to lack
The courage of a woman ; less noble mind   60
Than she, which by her death our Cæsar tells,
" I am conqueror of myself." Thou art sworn, Eros,
That when the exigent should come, (which now
Is come, indeed,) when I should see behind me
The inevitable prosecution of
Disgrace and horror, that on my command
Thou then wouldst kill me : do 't ; the time is come.
Thou strik'st not me, 't is Cæsar thou defeat'st.
Put colour in thy cheek.
    Eros.   The gods withhold me !
Shall I do that which all the Parthian darts,   70
Though enemy, lost aim, and could not ?
    Ant.   Eros,
Wouldst thou be window'd in great Rome, and see
Thy master thus with pleach'd arms, bending down
His corrigible neck, his face subdued
To penetrative shame, whilst the wheel'd seat
Of fortunate Cæsar, drawn before him, branded
His baseness that ensued ?
    Eros.   I would not see 't.
    Ant. Come then ; for with a wound I must be cur'd.
Draw that thy honest sword, which thou hast worn
Most useful for thy country.
    Eros.   O, sir ! pardon me.   80
    Ant. When I did make thee free, swor'st thou not
        then
To do this when I bade thee ? Do it at once,
Or thy precedent services are all
But accidents unpurpos'd. Draw, and come.
    Eros. Turn from me then that noble countenance,
Wherein the worship of the whole world lies.
    Ant. Lo thee !   [*Turning from him.*
    Eros. My sword is drawn.
    Ant.   Then let it do at once
The thing why thou hast drawn it.
    Eros.   My dear master,
My captain, and my emperor, let me say,   90
Before I strike this bloody stroke, farewell.
    Ant. 'T is said, man ; and farewell.
    Eros. Farewell, great chief. Shall I strike now ?
    Ant.   Now, Eros.
    Eros. Why, there then : [*falls on his sword*]—thus
        I do escape the sorrow
Of Antony's death.   [*Dies.*

    Ant.   Thrice-nobler than myself !
Thou teachest me, O valiant Eros, what
I should, and thou couldst not. My queen and Eros
Have, by their brave instruction, got upon me
A nobleness in record : but I will be
A bridegroom in my death, and run into 't   100
As to a lover's bed. Come then ; and, Eros,
Thy master dies thy scholar : to do thus
               [*Falling on his sword.*
I learn'd of thee.—How ! not dead ? not dead ?--
The guard !—ho !—O, despatch me !

Ant.   " Come then ; and, Eros,
Thy master dies thy scholar."

         Enter DERCETAS *and Guard.*

    1 *Guard.*   What 's the noise ?
    Ant. I have done my work ill, friends : O ! make an
        end
Of what I have begun.
    2 *Guard.*   The star is fallen.
    1 *Guard.* And time is at his period.
    All.   Alas, and woe !
    Ant. Let him that loves me strike me dead.
    1 *Guard.*   Not I.
    2 *Guard.* Nor I.
    3 *Guard.* Nor any one.   [*Exeunt Guard.*
    Der. Thy death and fortunes bid thy followers fly.
This sword but shown to Cæsar, with this tidings,   112
Shall enter me with him.

            Enter DIOMEDES,

    Dio. Where 's Antony ?
    Der.   There, Diomed, there.
    Dio.   Lives he ?
Wilt thou not answer, man ?   [*Exit* DERCETAS.
    Ant. Art thou there, Diomed ? Draw thy sword,
        and give me
Sufficient strokes for death.
    Dio.   Most absolute lord,
My mistress Cleopatra sent me to thee.
    Ant. When did she send thee ?
    Dio.   Now, my lord.
    Ant.   Where is she ?
    Dio. Lock'd in her monument. She had a prophesy-
        ing fear   120
Of what hath come to pass ; for when she saw
(Which never shall be found) you did suspect
She had dispos'd with Cæsar, and that your rage
Would not be purg'd, she sent you word she was dead ;
But, fearing since how it might work, hath sent
Me to proclaim the truth ; and I am come,
I dread, too late,
    Ant. Too late, good Diomed. Call my guard, I
        pr'ythee.
    Dio. What, ho ! the emperor's guard ! The guard,
        what, ho !
Come ; your lord calls.   130

Enter some of the Guard.

Ant. Bear me, good friends, where Cleopatra bides:
T is the last service that I shall command you.

SCENE XIII.—The Same.   A Monument.

Enter, above, CLEOPATRA, CHARMIAN, *and* IRAS.
Cleo. O Charmian! I will never go from hence.

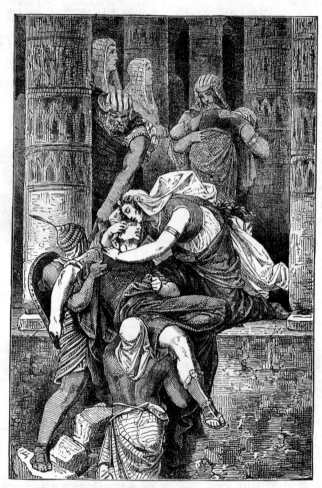

Cleo.   " O! come, come, come;
And welcome, welcome! die, where thou hast liv'd."

1 *Guard.* Woe, woe are we, sir, you may not live
        to wear
All your true followers out.
All.   Most heavy day!
Ant. Nay, good my fellows, do not please sharp
        fate
To grace it with your sorrows : bid that welcome
Which comes to punish us, and we punish it
Seeming to bear it lightly.   Take me up :
I have led you oft : carry me now good friends,
And have my thanks for all.   140
                    [*Exeunt, bearing* ANTONY

Char. Ee comforted, dear madam.
Cleo.   No, I will not.
All strange and terrible events are welcome,
But comforts we despise : our size of sorrow,
Proportion'd to our cause, must be as great
As that which makes it.

Enter, below, DIOMEDES.
                          How now ? is he dead ?
Dio. His death 's upon him, but not dead.
Look out o' the other side your monument ;
His guard have brought him thither.

Enter, below, ANTONY, *borne by the Guard.*

Cleo. O sun,   10
Burn the great sphere thou mov'st in!—darkling stand
The varying shore o' the world. O Antony,
Antony, Antony! Help, Charmian, help, Iras, help:
Help, friends below; let's draw him hither.
Ant.   Peace!
Not Cæsar's valour hath o'erthrown Antony,
But Antony's hath triumph'd on itself.
Cleo. So it should be, that none but Antony
Should conquer Antony; but woe 't is so!
Ant. I am dying, Egypt, dying; only
I here importune death awhile, until   20
Of many thousand kisses the poor last
I lay upon thy lips.
Cleo.   I dare not, dear,
(Dear my lord, pardon,) I dare not,
Lest I be taken: not the imperious show
Of the full-fortun'd Cæsar ever shall
Be brooch'd with me; if knife, drugs, serpents, have
Edge, sting, or operation, I am safe:
Your wife Octavia, with her modest eyes,
And still conclusion, shall acquire no honour
Demuring upon me.—But come, come, Antony,—   30
Help me, my women,—we must draw thee up.—
Assist, good friends.
Ant.   O! quick, or I am gone.
Cleo. Here's sport, indeed!—How heavy weighs my
    lord!
Our strength is all gone into heaviness,
That makes the weight. Had I great Juno's power,
The strong-wing'd Mercury should fetch thee up,
And set thee by Jove's side. Yet come a little,—
Wishers were ever fools.—O! come, come, come;
    [*They draw* ANTONY *up.*
And welcome, welcome! die, where thou hast liv'd:
Quicken with kissing: had my lips that power,   40
Thus would I wear them out.
All.   A heavy sight!
Ant. I am dying, Egypt, dying.
Give me some wine, and let me speak a little.
Cleo. No, let me speak; and let me rail so high,
That the false housewife Fortune break her wheel,
Provok'd by my offence.
Ant.   One word, sweet queen.
Of Cæsar seek your honour with your safety.—O!
Cleo. They do not go together.
Ant.   Gentle, hear me:
None about Cæsar trust, but Proculeius.

Cleo. My resolution, and my hands, I'll trust;   50
None about Cæsar.
Ant. The miserable change now at my end
Lament nor sorrow at: but please your thoughts,
In feeding them with those my former fortunes
Wherein I liv'd, the greatest prince o' the world,
The noblest; and do now not basely die,
Not cowardly put off my helmet to
My countryman, a Roman by a Roman
Valiantly vanquish'd. Now, my spirit is going;
I can no more.
Cleo.   Noblest of men, woo't die?   60
Hast thou no care of me? shall I abide
In this dull world, which in thy absence is
No better than a sty?—O! see, my women,
    [ANTONY *dies.*
The crown o' the earth doth melt.—My lord!—
O! wither'd is the garland of the war,
The soldier's pole is fall'n: young boys and girls
Are level now with men; the odds is gone,
And there is nothing left remarkable
Beneath the visiting moon.
Char.   O, quietness, lady!
Iras. She is dead too, our sovereign.
Char.   Lady!—
Iras.   Madam!—
Char. O madam, madam, madam!
Iras.   Royal Egypt!
Empress!   72
Char. Peace, peace, Iras!
Cleo. No more, but e'en a woman; and commanded
By such poor passion as the maid that milks,
And does the meanest chares.—It were for me
To throw my sceptre at the injurious gods;
To tell them, that this world did equal theirs,
Till they had stol'n our jewel. All 's but naught;
Patience is sottish, and impatience does   80
Become a dog that 's mad: then is it sin,
To rush into the secret house of death,
Ere death dare come to us?—How do you, women?
What, what! good cheer! Why, how now, Charmian?
My noble girls!—Ah, women, women! look,
Our lamp is spent, it 's out.—Good sirs, take heart:
We ll bury him; and then, what's brave, what's noble,
Let's do it after the high Roman fashion,
And make death proud to take us. Come, away:
This case of that huge spirit now is cold.   90
Ah, women, women! Come; we have no friend
But resolution, and the briefest end.
    [*Exeunt; those above bearing off* ANTONY'S *body.*

ACT V.

SCENE I.—CÆSAR's Camp before Alexandria.

Enter CÆSAR, AGRIPPA, DOLABELLA, MECÆNAS, GALLUS, PROCULEIUS, *and others.*

Cæsar.
G O to him, Dolabella, bid him yield;
    Being so frustrate, tell him, he mocks
The pauses that he makes.
Dol.   Cæsar, I shall. [*Exit.*

Enter DERCETAS, *with the sword of*
ANTONY.

Cæs. Wherefore is that? and what art
    thou, that dar'st
Appear thus to us?
Der.   I am call'd Dercetas.
Mark Antony I serv'd, who best was worthy
Best to be serv'd: whilst he stood up, and spoke,

He was my master; and I wore my life,
To spend upon his haters. If thou please
To take me to thee, as I was to him   10
I'll be to Cæsar; if thou pleasest not,
I yield thee up my life.
Cæs.   What is 't thou say'st?
Der. I say, O Cæsar, Antony is dead.
Cæs. The breaking of so great a thing should make
A greater crack: the round world
Should have shook lions into civil streets,
And citizens to their dens. The death of Antony
Is not a single doom: in the name lay
A moiety of the world.
Der.   He is dead, Cæsar,

Not by a public minister of justice,   20
Nor by a hired knife ; but that self hand,
Which writ his honour in the acts it did,
Hath, with the courage which the heart did lend it,
Splitted the heart. This is his sword :
I robb'd his wound of it : behold it stain'd
With his most noble blood.
Cæs.   Look you sad, friends?
The gods rebuke me, but it is tidings
To wash the eyes of kings.
Agr.   And strange it is,
That nature must compel us to lament
Our most persisted deeds.
Mec.   His taints and honours   30
Wag'd equal with him.
Agr.   A rarer spirit never
Did steer humanity ; but you, gods, will give us
Some faults to make us men. Cæsar is touch'd.
Mec. When such a spacious mirror 's set before him,
He needs must see himself.
Cæs.   O Antony !
I have follow'd thee to this :—but we do lance
Diseases in our bodies : I must perforce
Have shown to thee such a declining day,
Or look on thine : we could not stall together
In the whole world. But yet let me lament,   40
With tears as sovereign as the blood of hearts,
That thou, my brother, my competitor
In top of all design, my mate in empire,
Friend and companion in the front of war,
The arm of mine own body, and the heart
Where mine his thoughts did kindle, that our stars,
Unreconciliable, should divide
Our equalness to this.—Hear me, good friends,—

Enter a Messenger.

But I will tell you at some meeter season :
The business of this man looks out of him ;   50
We 'll hear him what he says.—Whence are you?
Mess. A poor Egyptian yet. The queen my mistress,
Confin'd in all she has, her monument,
Of thy intents desires instruction,
That she preparedly may frame herself
To the way she 's forc'd to.
Cæs.   Bid her have good heart :
She soon shall know of us, by some of ours,
How honourable and how kindly we
Determine for her ; for Cæsar cannot live
To be ungentle.
Mess.   So the gods preserve thee !   [Exit.
Cæs. Come hither, Proculeius. Go, and say,   61
We purpose her no shame : give her what comforts
The quality of her passion shall require,
Lest in her greatness by some mortal stroke
She do defeat us : for her life in Rome
Would be eternal in our triumph. Go,
And with your speediest bring us what she says,
And how you find of her.
Pro.   Cæsar, I shall.   [Exit.
Cæs. Gallus, go you along. [Exit GALLUS.]—Where's
Dolabella,
To second Proculeius?
Agr., Mec.   Dolabella !   70
Cæs. Let him alone. I remember now
How he 's employ'd : he shall in time be ready.
Go with me to my tent : where you shall see
How hardly I was drawn into this war ;
How calm and gentle I proceeded still
In all my writings. Go with me, and see
What I can show in this.   [Exeunt.

SCENE II.—Alexandria. The Monument.

Enter CLEOPATRA, CHARMIAN, and IRAS.

Cleo. My desolation does begin to make
A better life. 'T is paltry to be Cæsar :
Not being Fortune, he 's but Fortune's knave,
A minister of her will ; and it is great
To do that thing that ends all other deeds,
Which shackles accidents, and bolts up change ;

Which sleeps, and never palates more the dung,
The beggar's nurse and Cæsar's.

Enter PROCULEIUS, GALLUS, and Soldiers.

Pro. Cæsar sends greeting to the Queen of Egypt ;
And bids thee study on what fair demands   10
Thou mean'st to have him grant thee.
Cleo.   What 's thy name ?
Pro. My name is Proculeius.
Cleo.   Antony
Did tell me of you, bade me trust you ; but
I do not greatly care to be deceiv'd,
That have no use for trusting. If your master
Would have a queen his beggar, you must tell
him,
That majesty, to keep decorum, must
No less beg this a kingdom : if he please
To give me conquer'd Egypt for my son,
He gives me so much of mine own, as I   20
Will kneel to him with thanks.
Pro.   Be of good cheer ;
You are fall'n into a princely hand, fear nothing.
Make your full reference freely to my lord,
Who is so full of grace, that it flows over
On all that need. Let me report to him
Your sweet dependancy, and you shall find
A conqueror, that will pray in aid for kindness,
Where he for grace is kneel'd to.
Cleo.   Pray you, tell him
I am his fortune's vassal, and I send him
The greatness he has got. I hourly learn   30
A doctrine of obedience, and would gladly
Look him i' the face.
Pro.   This I 'll report, dear lady.
Have comfort ; for I know your plight is pitied
Of him that caus'd it.
Gal. You see how easily she may be surpris'd.
  [PROCULEIUS, *and two of the Guard, ascend the
    monument by a ladder, and come behind
    CLEOPATRA. Some of the Guard unbar and
    open the gates.*
[*To* PROCULEIUS *and the Guard.*] Guard her till Cæsar
come.   [Exit.
Iras. Royal queen !
Char. O Cleopatra ! thou art taken, queen !—
Cleo. Quick, quick, good hands. [Drawing a dagger.
Pro.   Hold, worthy lady, hold !
      [Seizes and disarms her.
Do not yourself such wrong, who are in this   40
Reliev'd, but not betray'd.
Cleo.   What, of death too,
That rids our dogs of languish ?
Pro.   Cleopatra,
Do not abuse my master's bounty, by
The undoing of yourself : let the world see
His nobleness well acted, which your death
Will never let come forth.
Cleo.   Where art thou, death ?
Come hither, come ! come, come, and take a queen
Worth many babes and beggars !
Pro.   O, temperance, lady !
Cleo. Sir, I will eat no meat, I 'll not drink, sir ;   50
If idle talk will once be necessary,
I 'll not sleep neither. This mortal house I 'll ruin,
Do Cæsar what he can. Know, sir, that I
Will not wait pinion'd at your master's court,
Nor once be chastis'd with the sober eye
Of dull Octavia. Shall they hoist me up,
And show me to the shouting varletry
Of censuring Rome ? Rather a ditch in Egypt
Be gentle grave to me ! rather on Nilus' mud
Lay me stark nak'd, and let the water-flies   60
Blow me into abhorring ! rather make
My country's high pyramides my gibbet,
And hang me up in chains !
Pro.   You do extend
These thoughts of horror further than you shall
Find cause in Cæsar.

Enter DOLABELLA.

Dol.   Proculeius,
What thou hast done thy master Cæsar knows,

And he hath sent for thee: for the queen,
I 'll take her to my guard.
   Pro.   So, Dolabella,
It shall content me best: be gentle to her.
[*To* CLEOPATRA.] To Cæsar I will speak **what you**
          shall please,
If you 'll employ me to him.
   Cleo.   Say, I would die.   70
           [*Exeunt* PROCULEIUS *and Soldiers.*
   Dol. Most noble empress, you have heard of me?
   Cleo. I cannot tell.
   Dol.   Assuredly, you know me.
   Cleo. No matter, sir, what I have heard or known.
You laugh, when boys or women tell their dreams;
Is 't not your trick?
   Dol.   I understand not, madam.
   Cleo. I dreamt, there was an emperor Antony:
O, such another sleep, that I might see
But such another man!
   Dol.   If it might please ye,—
   Cleo. His face was as the heavens, and therein stuck
A sun and moon, which kept their course, and lighted
The little O, the earth.
   Dol.   Most sovereign creature,— 81
   Cleo. His legs bestrid the ocean; his rear'd arm
Crested the world; his voice was propertied
As all the tuned spheres, and that to friends;
But when he meant to quail and shake the orb,
He was as rattling thunder. For his bounty,
There was no winter in 't; an autumn 't was,
That grew the more by reaping: his delights
Were dolphin-like; they show'd his back above
The element they liv'd in: in his livery   90
Walk'd crowns and crownets; realms and islands were
As plates dropp'd from his pocket.
   Dol.   Cleopatra,—
   Cleo. Think you there was, or might be, such a man
As this I dreamt of?
   Dol.   Gentle madam, no.
   Cleo. You lie, up to the hearing of the gods.
But, if there be, or ever were, one such,
It 's past the size of dreaming: nature wants stuff
To vie strange forms with fancy; yet, to imagine
An Antony, were nature's piece 'gainst fancy,
Condemning shadows quite.
   Dol.   Hear me, good madam.
Your loss is as yourself, great; and you bear it   101
As answering to the weight: 'would I might never
O'ertake pursu'd success, but I do feel,
By the rebound of yours, a grief that smites
My very heart at root.
   Cleo.   I thank you, sir.
Know you what Cæsar means to do with me?
   Dol. I am loath to tell you what I would you knew.
   Cleo. Nay, pray you, sir,—
   Dol.   Though he be honourable,—
   Cleo. He 'll lead me then in triumph?
   Dol. Madam, he will; I know 't.
[*Within.*]   Make way there!—Cæsar!

   Enter CÆSAR, GALLUS, PROCULEIUS, MECÆNAS,
       SELEUCUS, *and Attendants.*

   Cæs. Which is the Queen of Egypt?   111
   Dol. It is the emperor, madam. [CLEOPATRA *kneels.*
   Cæs. Arise, you shall not kneel:
I pray you, rise; rise, Egypt.
   Cleo.   Sir, the gods
Will have it thus: my master and my lord
I must obey.
   Cæs.   Take to you no hard thoughts:
The record of what injuries you did us,
Though written in our flesh, we shall remember
As things but done by chance.
   Cleo.   Sole sir o' the world,
I cannot project mine own cause so well   120
To make it clear; but do confess, I have
Been laden with like frailties, which before
Have often sham'd our sex.
   Cæs.   Cleopatra, know,
We will extenuate rather than enforce:
If you apply yourself to our intents
(Which towards you are most gentle), you shall find

A benefit in this change; but if you seek
To lay on me a cruelty, by taking
Antony's course, you shall bereave yourself
Of my good purposes, and put your children   130
To that destruction which I 'll guard them from,
If thereon you rely. I 'll take my leave.
   Cleo. And may through all the world: 't is yours;
        and we,
Your scutcheons, and your signs of conquest, shall
Hang in what place you please. Here, my good lord.
   Cæs. You shall advise me in all for Cleopatra.
   Cleo. This is the brief of money, plate, and jewels,
I am possess'd of: 't is exactly valued;
Not petty things admitted.—Where 's Seleucus?
   Sel. Here, madam.   140
   Cleo. This is my treasurer: let him speak, my lord,
Upon his peril, that I have reserv'd
To myself nothing. Speak the truth, Seleucus.
   Sel. Madam,
I had rather seal my lips, than, to my peril,
Speak that which is not.
   Cleo.   What have I kept back?
   Sel. Enough to purchase what you have made
        known.
   Cæs. Nay, blush not, Cleopatra; I approve
Your wisdom in the deed.
   Cleo.   See, Cæsar! O, behold,
How pomp is follow'd! mine will now be yours;   150
And, should we shift estates, yours would be mine.
The ingratitude of this Seleucus does
Even make me wild.—O slave, of no more trust
Than love that 's hir'd!—What! goest thou back?
        thou shalt
Go back, I warrant thee; but I 'll catch thine eyes,
Though they had wings. Slave, soulless villain, dog!
O rarely base!
   Cæs.   Good queen, let us entreat you.
   Cleo. O Cæsar! what a wounding shame is this,
That thou, vouchsafing here to visit me,
Doing the honour of thy lordliness   160
To one so meek, that mine own servant should
Parcel the sum of my disgraces by
Addition of his envy! Say, good Cæsar,
That I some lady trifles have reserv'd,
Immoment toys, things of such dignity
As we greet modern friends withal; and say,
Some nobler token I have kept apart
For Livia, and Octavia, to induce
Their mediation; must I be unfolded
With one that I have bred? The gods! it smites me
Beneath the fall I have. [*To* SELEUCUS.] Pr'ythee, go
        hence;   171
Or I shall show the cinders of my spirits
Through the ashes of my chance.—Wert thou a man,
Thou wouldst have mercy on me.
   Cæs.   Forbear, Seleucus. [*Exit* SELEUCUS.
   Cleo. Be it known that we, the greatest, are mis-
        thought
For things that others do; and, when we fall,
We answer others' merits in our name,
Are therefore to be pitied.
   Cæs.   Cleopatra,
Not what you have reserv'd, nor what acknowledg'd,
Put we i' the roll of conquest: still be it yours,   180
Bestow it at your pleasure; and believe,
Cæsar 's no merchant, to make prize with you
Of things that merchants sold. Therefore be cheer'd;
Make not your thoughts your prisons: no, dear queen;
For we intend so to dispose you, as
Yourself shall give us counsel. Feed, and sleep:
Our care and pity is so much upon you,
That we remain your friend; and so, adieu.
   Cleo. My master, and my lord!
   Cæs.   Not so. Adieu.
      [*Flourish. Exeunt* CÆSAR *and his Train.*
   Cleo. He words me, girls, he words me, that I should
        not   190
Be noble to myself: but hark thee, Charmian.
                [*Whispers* CHARMIAN.
   Iras. Finish, good lady; the bright day is done,
And we are for the dark.
   Cleo.   Hie thee again:

I have spoke already, and it is provided;
Go, put it to the haste.
 Char.   Madam, I will.

     Re-enter DOLABELLA.

 Dol. Where is the queen?
 Char.   Behold, sir.   [*Exit.*
 Cleo.   Dolabella!
 Dol. Madam, as thereto sworn by your command,
Which my love makes religion to obey,
I tell you this: Cæsar through Syria
Intends his journey, and within three days 200
You with your children will he send before.
Make your best use of this; I have perform'd
Your pleasure, and my promise.
 Cleo.   Dolabella,
I shall remain your debtor.
 Dol.   I your servant.
Adieu, good queen; I must attend on Cæsar.
 Cleo. Farewell, and thanks. [*Exit* DOLABELLA.]
  Now, Iras, what think'st thou?
Thou, an Egyptian puppet, shalt be shown
In Rome, as well as I: mechanic slaves
With greasy aprons, rules, and hammers, shall
Uplift us to the view: in their thick breaths, 210
Rank of gross diet, shall we be enclouded,
And forc'd to drink their vapour.
 Iras.   The gods forbid!
 Cleo. Nay, 't is most certain, Iras. Saucy lictors
Will catch at us, like strumpets; and scald rhymers
Ballad us out o' tune: the quick comedians
Extemporally will stage us, and present
Our Alexandrian revels. Antony
Shall be brought drunken forth, and I shall see
Some squeaking Cleopatra boy my greatness
I' the posture of a whore.
 Iras.   O, the good gods! 220
 Cleo. Nay, that is certain.
 Iras. I 'll never see it; for, I am sure, my nails
Are stronger than mine eyes.
 Cleo.   Why, that 's the way
To fool their preparation, and to conquer
Their most absurd intents.

     Re-enter CHARMIAN.

      Now, Charmian?—
Show me, my women, like a queen:—go fetch
My best attires:—I am again for Cydnus,
To meet Mark Antony.—Sirrah, Iras, go.—
Now, noble Charmian, we 'll despatch indeed;
And, when thou hast done this chare, I 'll give thee
  leave   230
To play till doomsday.—Bring our crown and all.
     [*Exit* IRAS. *A noise within.*
Wherefore 's this noise?

    Enter one of the Guard.

 Guard.   Here is a rural fellow,
That will not be denied your highness' presence:
He brings you figs.
 Cleo. Let him come in. [*Exit Guard.*] What poor
  an instrument
May do a noble deed! he brings me liberty.
My resolution 's plac'd, and I have nothing
Of woman in me: now from head to foot
I am marble-constant; now the fleeting moon
No planet is of mine.

 Re-enter Guard, with a Clown bringing in a basket.

 Guard. This is the man   240
 Cleo. Avoid, and leave him. [*Exit Guard.*
Hast thou the pretty worm of Nilus there,
That kills and pains not?
 Clown. Truly I have him; but I would not be the
party that should desire you to touch him, for his
biting is immortal: those that do die of it do seldom
or never recover.
 Cleo. Remember'st thou any that have died on 't? 248
 Clown. Very many, men and women too. I heard
of one of them no longer than yesterday: a very
honest woman, but something given to lie, as a woman
should not do but in the way of honesty: how she died
of the biting of it, what pain she felt.—Truly, she

makes a very good report o' the worm; but he that
will believe all that they say, shall never be saved
by half that they do. But this is most fallible, the
worm 's an odd worm.
 Cleo. Get thee hence: farewell.
 Clown. I wish you all joy of the worm.
       [*Sets down the basket.*
 Cleo. Farewell.   260
 Clown. You must think this, look you, that the
worm will do his kind.
 Cleo. Ay, ay; farewell.
 Clown. Look you, the worm is not to be trusted but
in the keeping of wise people; for, indeed, there is no
goodness in the worm.
 Cleo. Take thou no care: it shall be heeded.
 Clown. Very good. Give it nothing, I pray you, for
it is not worth the feeding.
 Cleo. Will it eat me?   270
 Clown. You must not think I am so simple, but I
know the devil himself will not eat a woman: I know
that a woman is a dish for the gods, if the devil dress
her not. But, truly, these same whoreson devils do
the gods great harm in their women, for in every ten
that they make, the devils mar five.
 Cleo. Well, get thee gone: farewell.
 Clown. Yes, forsooth; I wish you joy of the worm.
          [*Exit.*

  Re-enter IRAS, *with a robe, crown, &c.*

 Cleo. Give me my robe, put on my crown; I have
Immortal longings in me. Now, no more 280
The juice of Egypt's grape shall moist this lip.—
Yare, yare, good Iras; quick.—Methinks, I hear
Antony call: I see him rouse himself
To praise my noble act; I hear him mock
The luck of Cæsar, which the gods give men
To excuse their after-wrath. Husband, I come:
Now to that name my courage prove my title!
I am fire and air; my other elements
I give to baser life.—So,—have you done?
Come then, and take the last warmth of my lips. 290
Farewell, kind Charmian:—Iras, long farewell.
   [*Kisses them.* IRAS *falls and dies.*
Have I the aspic in my lips? Dost fall?
If thou and nature can so gently part,
The stroke of death is as a lover's pinch,
Which hurts, and is desir'd. Dost thou lie still?
If thus thou vanishest, thou tell'st the world
It is not worth leave-taking.
 Char. Dissolve, thick cloud, and rain, that I may
  say,
The gods themselves do weep.
 Cleo.   This proves me base: 300
If she first meet the curled Antony,
He 'll make demand of her, and spend that kiss,
Which is my heaven to have. Come, thou mortal
  wretch,
  [*To the asp, which she applies to her breast.*
With thy sharp teeth this knot intrinsicate
Of life at once untie: poor venomous fool,
Be angry, and despatch. O! couldst thou speak,
That I might hear thee call great Cæsar ass
Unpolicied!
 Char.   O eastern star!
 Cleo.   Peace, peace!
Dost thou not see my baby at my breast,
That sucks the nurse asleep?
 Char.   O, break! O, break!
 Cleo. As sweet as balm, as soft as air, as gentle,—
O Antony!—Nay, I will take thee too. 311
   [*Applying another asp to her arm.*
What should I stay— [*Falls on a bed and dies.*
 Char. In this vile world?—So, fare thee well.—
Now boast thee, death, in thy possession lies
A lass unparallel'd.—Downy windows, close;
And golden Phœbus never be beheld
Of eyes again so royal? Your crown 's awry;
I 'll mend it, and then play.

    Enter the Guard, rushing in.

 1 *Guard.* Where is the queen?
 Char.   Speak softly; wake her not.

1 Guard. Cæsar hath sent—
Char.   Too slow a messenger.
                    [*Applies the asp.*
O! come; apace; despatch: I partly feel thee.   321

Char. " Speak softly; wake her not."

1 Guard. Approach, ho! All 's not well: Cæsar 's
    beguil'd.
2 Guard. There 's Dolabella sent from Cæsar: call
    him.
1 Guard. What work is here?—Charmian, is this
    well done?
Char. It is well done, and fitting for a princess
Descended of so many royal kings.
Ah, soldier!   [*Dies.*
            Re-enter DOLABELLA.

Dol. How goes it here?
2 Guard.   All dead.

Dol.   Cæsar, thy thoughts
Touch their effects in this: thyself art coming
To see perform'd the dreaded act, which thou   330
So sought'st to hinder.
    [*Within.*]   A way there! a way for Cæsar!

        Re-enter CÆSAR *and all his Train.*

Dol. O, sir! you are too sure an augurer:
That you did fear, is done.
Cæs.   Bravest at the last:
She levell'd at our purposes, and, being royal,
Took her own way.—The manner of their deaths?
I do not see them bleed.
Dol.   Who was last with them?
1 Guard. A simple countryman that brought her
        figs:
This was his basket.
Cæs.   Poison'd then.
1 Guard.   O Cæsar!
This Charmian liv'd but now; she stood, and
        spake:
I found her trimming up the diadem   340
On her dead mistress; tremblingly she stood,
And on the sudden dropp'd.
Cæs.   O noble weakness!—
If they had swallow'd poison, 't would appear
By external swelling; but she looks like sleep,
As she would catch another Antony
In her strong toil of grace.
Dol.   Here, on her breast,
There is a vent of blood, and something blown:
The like is on her arm.
1 Guard. This is an aspic's trail; and these fig-
        leaves
Have slime upon them, such as the aspic leaves   350
Upon the caves of Nile.
Cæs.   Most probable,
That so she died; for her physician tells me,
She hath pursu'd conclusions infinite
Of easy ways to die.—Take up her bed,
And bear her women from the monument.
She shall be buried by her Antony:
No grave upon the earth shall clip in it
A pair so famous. High events as these
Strike those that make them; and their story is
No less in pity than his glory, which   360
Brought them to be lamented. Our army shall,
In solemn show, attend this funeral,
And then to Rome.—Come, Dolabella, see
High order in this great solemnity.   [*Exeunt.*

CYMBELINE.

DRAMATIS PERSONÆ.

CYMBELINE, *King of Britain.*
CLOTEN, *Son to the Queen by a former Husband.*
LEONATUS POSTHUMUS, *Husband to Imogen.*
BELARIUS, *a banished Lord, disguised under the name of Morgan.*
GUIDERIUS, } *Sons to Cymbeline, disguised under*
ARVIRAGUS, } *the names of Polydore and Cadwal, supposed Sons to Belarius.*
PHILARIO, *Friend to Posthumus,* } *Italians.*
IACHIMO, *Friend to Philario,* }
A French Gentleman, Friend to Philario.
CAIUS LUCIUS, *General of the Roman Forces.*
A Roman Captain.
Two British Captains.

PISANIO, *Servant to Posthumus.*
CORNELIUS, *a Physician.*
Two Gentlemen.
Two Gaolers.

QUEEN, *Wife to Cymbeline.*
IMOGEN, *Daughter to Cymbeline by a former Queen.*
HELEN, *Woman to Imogen.*

Lords, Ladies, Roman Senators, Tribunes, Apparitions, a Soothsayer, a Dutch Gentleman, a Spanish Gentleman, Musicians, Officers, Captains, Soldiers, Messengers, and other Attendants.

SCENE—Sometimes in BRITAIN, sometimes in ITALY.

ACT I.

SCENE I.—Britain. The Garden of CYMBELINE's Palace.

Enter two Gentlemen.

1 Gentleman.
YOU do not meet a man but frowns: our bloods
No more obey the heavens, than our courtiers
Still seem as does the king.
   2 Gent.   But what's the matter?
   1 Gent. His daughter, and the heir of 's kingdom, whom
He purpos'd to his wife's sole son, (a widow,
That late he married,) hath referr'd herself
Unto a poor but worthy gentleman. She's wedded;
Her husband banish'd; she imprison'd: all
Is outward sorrow, though, I think, the king
Be touch'd at very heart.
   2 Gent.   None but the king?
   1 Gent. He that hath lost her, too; so is the queen,   11
That most desir'd the match: but not a courtier,
Although they wear their faces to the bent
Of the king's looks, hath a heart that is not
Glad at the thing they scowl at.
   2 Gent.   And why so?
   1 Gent. He that hath miss'd the princess is a thing
Too bad for bad report; and he that hath her
(I mean, that married her,—alack, good man!—
And therefore banish'd) is a creature such
As, to seek through the regions of the earth   20
For one his like, there would be something failing
In him that should compare. I do not think,
So fair an outward, and such stuff within,
Endows a man but he.
   2 Gent.   You speak him far.
   1 Gent. I do extend him, sir, within himself;
Crush him together, rather than unfold
His measure duly.
   2 Gent.   What's his name, and birth?
   1 Gent. I cannot delve him to the root. His father

Was call'd Sicilius, who did join his honour
Against the Romans with Cassibelan,   30
But had his titles by Tenantius, whom
He serv'd with glory and admir'd success;
So gain'd the sur-addition, Leonatus:
And had, besides this gentleman in question,
Two other sons, who, in the wars o' the time,
Died with their swords in hand; for which their father
(Then old and fond of issue) took such sorrow,
That he quit being; and his gentle lady,
Big of this gentleman, our theme, deceas'd
As he was born. The king, he takes the babe   40
To his protection; calls him Posthumus Leonatus;
Breeds him, and makes him of his bedchamber;
Puts to him all the learnings that his time
Could make him the receiver of; which he took,
As we do air, fast as 't was minister'd,
And in 's spring became a harvest; liv'd in court
(Which rare it is to do) most prais'd, most lov'd;
A sample to the youngest, to the more mature
A glass that feated them; and to the graver
A child that guided dotards: to his mistress,   50
For whom he now is banish'd,—her own price
Proclaims how she esteem'd him and his virtue;
By her election may be truly read
What kind of man he is.
   2 Gent.   I honour him
Even out of your report. But, 'pray you, tell me,
Is she sole child to the king?
   1 Gent.   His only child.
He had two sons: (if this be worth your hearing,
Mark it:) the eldest of them at three years old,
I' the swathing-clothes the other, from their nursery
Were stolen; and to this hour no guess in knowledge
Which way they went.
   2 Gent.   How long is this ago?   61
   1 Gent. Some twenty years.
   2 Gent. That a king's children should be so convey'd,
So slackly guarded, and the search so slow,
That could not trace them!

1 *Gent.*   Howsoe'er 't is strange,
Or that the negligence may well be laugh'd at,
Yet is it true, sir.
2 *Gent.*   I do well believe you.
1 *Gent.*   We must forbear. Here comes the gentleman,
The queen, and princess.   [*Exeunt.*

SCENE II.—The Same.

Enter the QUEEN, POSTHUMUS, *and* IMOGEN.

Queen. No, be assur'd, you shall not find me,
daughter,
After the slander of most stepmothers,
Evil-ey'd unto you: you are my prisoner, but
Your gaoler shall deliver you the keys
That lock up your restraint. For you, Posthumus,
So soon as I can win the offended king,
I will be known your advocate: marry, yet
The fire of rage is in him; and 't were good,
You lean'd unto his sentence, with what patience
Your wisdom may inform you.
Post.   Please your highness,
I will from hence to-day.
Queen.   You know the peril:—   12
I 'll fetch a turn about the garden, pitying
The pangs of barr'd affections; though the king
Hath charg'd you should not speak together. [*Exit.*
Imo. Dissembling courtesy! How fine this
tyrant
Can tickle where she wounds!—My dearest hus-
band,
I something fear my father's wrath; but nothing
(Always reserv'd my holy duty) what
His rage can do on me. You must be gone;
And I shall here abide the hourly shot   20
Of angry eyes; not comforted to live,
But that there is this jewel in the world,
That I may see again.
Post.   My queen! my mistress!
O lady! weep no more, lest I give cause
To be suspected of more tenderness
Than doth become a man. I will remain
The loyal'st husband that did e'er plight troth.
My residence in Rome, at one Philario's;
Who to my father was a friend, to me
Known but by letter: thither write, my queen,   30
And with mine eyes I 'll drink the words you send,
Though ink be made of gall.

Re-enter QUEEN.

Queen.   Be brief, I pray you:
If the king come, I shall incur I know not
How much of his displeasure. [*Aside.*] Yet I 'll move
him
To walk this way. I never do him wrong,
But he does buy my injuries to be friends,
Pays dear for my offences.   [*Exit.*
Post.   Should we be taking leave
As long a term as yet we have to live,
The loathness to depart would grow. Adieu!
Imo. Nay, stay a little.
Were you but riding forth to air yourself,   40
Such parting were too petty. Look here, love:
This diamond was my mother's: take it, heart;
But keep it till you woo another wife,
When Imogen is dead.
Post.   How! how! another?—
You gentle gods, give me but this I have,
And sear up my embracements from a next
With bonds of death!—[*Putting on the ring.*] Remain,
remain thou here
While sense can keep it on. And, sweetest, fairest,
As I my poor self did exchange for you,
To your so infinite loss, so in our trifles   50
I still win of you: for my sake, wear this:
It is a manacle of love; I 'll place it
Upon this fairest prisoner.
                    [*Putting a bracelet on her arm.*
Imo.   O, the gods!
When shall we see again?

Enter CYMBELINE *and Lords.*

Post.   Alack, the king!
Cym. Thou basest thing, avoid! hence, from my
sight!
If after this command thou fraught the court
With thy unworthiness, thou diest. Away!
Thou 'rt poison to my blood.
Post.   The gods protect you,
And bless the good remainders of the court!
I am gone.   [*Exit.*
Imo.   There cannot be a pinch in death   60
More sharp than this is.
Cym.   O disloyal thing,
That shouldst repair my youth, thou heap'st
A year's age on me.

Cym. "If after this command thou fraught the court
With thy unworthiness, thou diest."

Imo.   I beseech you, sir,
Harm not yourself with your vexation:
I am senseless of your wrath; a touch more rare
Subdues all pangs, all fears.
Cym.   Past grace? obedience?
Imo. Past hope, and in despair; that way, past
grace.
Cym. That might'st have had the sole son of my
queen!
Imo. O bless'd, that I might not! I chose an eagle,
And did avoid a puttock.   70
Cym. Thou took'st a beggar; wouldst have made
my throne
A seat for baseness.
Imo.   No; I rather added
A lustre to it.
Cym.   O thou vile one!
Imo.   Sir,
It is your fault that I have lov'd Posthumus:
You bred him as my playfellow; and he is
A man worth any woman; overbuys me
Almost the sum he pays.
Cym.   What! art thou mad?
Imo. Almost, sir: heaven restore me!—'Would I
were
A neat-herd's daughter, and my Leonatus
Our neighbour shepherd's son!
Cym.   Thou foolish thing!—

Re-enter QUEEN.

[*To the* QUEEN.] They were again together: you have
done   81
Not after our command. Away with her,
And pen her up.
Queen.   'Beseech your patience.—Peace!
Dear lady daughter, peace!—Sweet sovereign,

Leave us to ourselves; and make yourself some com-
fort
Out of your best advice.
Cym.   Nay, let her languish
A drop of blood a day; and, being aged,
Die of this folly!   [*Exeunt* CYMBELINE *and Lords.*

Enter PISANIO.

Queen.   Fie!—you must give way.
Here is your servant.—How now, sir? What news?
Pis. My lord your son drew on my master.
Queen.   Ha! 90
No harm, I trust, is done?
Pis.   There might have been,
But that my master rather play'd than fought,
And had no help of anger: they were parted
By gentlemen at hand.
Queen.   I am very glad on 't.
Imo. Your son 's my father's friend; he takes his
          part.—
To draw upon an exile!—O brave sir!
I would they were in Afric both together,
Myself by with a needle, that I might prick
The goer-back.—Why came you from your master?
Pis. On his command. He would not suffer me 100
To bring him to the haven; left these notes
Of what commands I should be subject to,
When 't pleas'd you to employ me.
Queen.   This hath been
Your faithful servant: I dare lay mine honour,
He will remain so.
Pis.   I humbly thank your highness.
Queen. Pray, walk awhile.
Imo.   About some half-hour hence,
Pray you, speak with me. You shall, at least,
Go see my lord aboard: for this time, leave me.
                                        [*Exeunt.*

SCENE III.—A Public Place.

Enter CLOTEN *and two Lords.*

1 Lord. Sir, I would advise you to shift a shirt: the
violence of action hath made you reek as a sacrifice.
Where air comes out, air comes in; there 's none
abroad so wholesome as that you vent.
Clo. If my shirt were bloody, then to shift it. Have
I hurt him?
2 Lord. [*Aside.*] No, faith; not so much as his
patience.
1 Lord. Hurt him? his body 's a passable carcass, if
he be not hurt: it is a thoroughfare for steel, if it be
not hurt.   11
2 Lord. [*Aside.*] His steel was in debt; it went o'
the backside the town.
Clo. The villain would not stand me.
2 Lord. [*Aside.*] No; but he fled forward still,
toward your face.
1 Lord. Stand you! You have land enough of your
own; but he added to your having, gave you some
ground.
2 Lord. [*Aside.*] As many inches as you have
oceans.—Puppies!   21
Clo. I would they had not come between us.
2 Lord. [*Aside.*] So would I, till you had measured
how long a fool you were upon the ground.
Clo. And that she should love this fellow, and
refuse me!
2 Lord. [*Aside.*] If it be a sin to make a true election, she is damned.
1 Lord. Sir, as I told you always, her beauty and
her brain go not together: she 's a good sign, but I
have seen small reflection of her wit.   31
2 Lord. [*Aside.*] She shines not upon fools, lest the
reflection should hurt her.
Clo. Come, I 'll to my chamber. 'Would there had
been some hurt done!
2 Lord. [*Aside.*] I wish not so; unless it had been
the fall of an ass, which is no great hurt.
Clo. You 'll go with us?
1 Lord. I 'll attend your lordship.

Clo. Nay, come, let 's go together.   40
2 Lord. Well, my lord.   [*Exeunt.*

SCENE IV.—A Room in CYMBELINE'S Palace.

Enter IMOGEN *and* PISANIO.

Imo. I would thou grew'st unto the shores o' the
          haven,
And question'dst every sail: if he should write,
And I not have it, 't were a paper lost,
As offer'd mercy is. What was the last
That he spake to thee?
Pis.   It was, his queen, his queen!
Imo. Then wav'd his handkerchief?
Pis.   And kiss'd it, madam.
Imo. Senseless linen, happier therein than I!—
And that was all?
Pis.   No, madam; for so long
As he could make me with this eye or ear
Distinguish him from others, he did keep   10
The deck, with glove, or hat, or handkerchief,
Still waving, as the fits and stirs of his mind
Could best express how slow his soul sail'd on,
How swift his ship.
Imo.   Thou shouldst have made him
As little as a crow, or less, ere left
To after-eye him.
Pis.   Madam, so I did.
Imo. I would have broke mine eye-strings, crack'd
          them, but
To look upon him, till the diminution
Of space had pointed him sharp as my needle;
Nay, follow'd him, till he had melted from   20
The smallness of a gnat to air; and then
Have turn'd mine eye, and wept.—But, good Pisanio,
When shall we hear from him?
Pis.   Be assur'd, madam,
With his next vantage.
Imo. I did not take my leave of him, but had
Most pretty things to say: ere I could tell him,
How I would think on him, at certain hours,
Such thoughts, and such; or I could make him swear
The shes of Italy should not betray
Mine interest and his honour; or have charg'd him, 30
At the sixth hour of morn, at noon, at midnight,
To encounter me with orisons, for then
I am in heaven for him; or ere I could
Give him that parting kiss, which I had set
Betwixt two charming words, comes in my father,
And, like the tyrannous breathing of the north,
Shakes all our buds from growing.

Enter a Lady.

Lady.   The queen, madam,
Desires your highness' company.
Imo. Those things I bid you do, get them des-
          patch'd.—
I will attend the queen.
Pis.   Madam, I shall.   40
                                        [*Exeunt.*

SCENE V.—Rome. An Apartment in PHILARIO'S House.

Enter PHILARIO, IACHIMO, *a Frenchman, a Dutch-man, and a Spaniard.*

Iach. Believe it, sir, I have seen him in Britain: he
was then of a crescent note; expected to prove so
worthy, as since he hath been allowed the name of;
but I could then have looked on him without the help
of admiration, though the catalogue of his endowments had been tabled by his side, and I to peruse
him by items.
Phi. You speak of him when he was less furnished,
than now he is, with that which makes him both
without and within.   10
French. I have seen him in France: we had very
many there could behold the sun with as firm eyes as
he.

Iach. This matter of marrying his king's daughter (wherein he must be weighed rather by her value, than his own) words him, I doubt not, a great deal from the matter.

French. And then his banishment— 18

Iach. Ay, and the approbation of those that weep this lamentable divorce, under her colours, are wonderfully to extend him; be it but to fortify her judgment, which else an easy battery might lay flat, for taking a beggar without less quality. But how comes it, he is to sojourn with you? How creeps acquaintance?

Phi. His father and I were soldiers together; to whom I have been often bound for no less than my life.—Here comes the Briton. Let him be so entertained amongst you, as suits with gentlemen of your knowing, to a stranger of his quality. 30

Enter POSTHUMUS.

I beseech you all, be better known to this gentleman, whom I commend to you, as a noble friend of mine: how worthy he is, I will leave to appear hereafter, rather than story him in his own hearing.

French. Sir, we have known together in Orleans.

Post. Since when I have been debtor to you for courtesies, which I will be ever to pay, and yet pay still.

French. Sir, you o'er-rate my poor kindness. I was glad I did atone my countryman and you: it had been pity you should have been put together with so mortal a purpose, as then each bore, upon importance of so slight and trivial a nature. 42

Post. By your pardon, sir, I was then a young traveller; rather shunned to go even with what I heard, than in my every action to be guided by others' experiences: but, upon my mended judgment, (if I offend not to say it is mended,) my quarrel was not altogether slight.

French. 'Faith, yes, to be put to the arbitrement of swords; and by such two, that would, by all likelihood, have confounded one the other, or have fallen both. 52

Iach. Can we, with manners, ask what was the difference?

French. Safely, I think. 'T was a contention in public, which may, without contradiction, suffer the report. It was much like an argument that fell out last night, where each of us fell in praise of our country mistresses; this gentleman at that time vouching (and upon warrant of bloody affirmation) his to be more fair, virtuous, wise, chaste, constant, qualified, and less attemptable, than any the rarest of our ladies in France. 63

Iach. That lady is not now living; or this gentleman's opinion, by this, worn out.

Post. She holds her virtue still, and I my mind.

Iach. You must not so far prefer her 'fore ours of Italy.

Post. Being so far provoked as I was in France, I would abate her nothing, though I profess myself her adorer, not her friend. 71

Iach. As fair, and as good, (a kind of hand-in-hand comparison,) had been something too fair, and too good, for any lady in Britany. If she went before others I have seen, as that diamond of yours outlustres many I have beheld, I could not but believe she excelled many; but I have not seen the most precious diamond that is, nor you the lady.

Post. I praised her as I rated her; so do I my stone.

Iach. What do you esteem it at? 80

Post. More than the world enjoys.

Iach. Either your unparagoned mistress is dead, or she's outprized by a trifle.

Post. You are mistaken: the one may be sold, or given; or if there were wealth enough for the purchase, or merit for the gift: the other is not a thing for sale, and only the gift of the gods.

Iach. Which the gods have given you?

Post. Which, by their graces, I will keep. 89

Iach. You may wear her in title yours: but, you know, strange fowl light upon neighbouring ponds. Your ring may be stolen too: so, your brace of unprizable estimations; the one is but frail, and the other casual; a cunning thief, or a that way accomplished courtier, would hazard the winning both of first and last.

Post. Your Italy contains none so accomplished a courtier to convince the honour of my mistress; if, in the holding or loss of that, you term her frail. I do nothing doubt you have store of thieves; notwithstanding I fear not my ring. 101

Phi. Let us leave here, gentlemen.

Post. Sir, with all my heart. This worthy signior, I thank him, makes no stranger of me; we are familiar at first.

Iach. With five times so much conversation, I should get ground of your fair mistress: make her go back, even to the yielding, had I admittance, and opportunity to friend.

Post. No, no. 110

Iach. I dare thereupon pawn the moiety of my estate to your ring, which, in my opinion, o'ervalues it something, but I make my wager rather against your confidence than her reputation: and, to bar your offence herein too, I durst attempt it against any lady in the world.

Post. You are a great deal abused in too bold a persuasion; and I doubt not you sustain what you're worthy of by your attempt.

Iach. What's that? 120

Post. A repulse; though your attempt, as you call it, deserve more,—a punishment too.

Phi. Gentlemen, enough of this; it came in too suddenly; let it die as it was born, and, I pray you, be better acquainted.

Iach. 'Would I had put my estate, and my neighbour's, on the approbation of what I have spoke.

Post. What lady would you choose to assail? 128

Iach. Yours; whom in constancy you think stands so safe. I will lay you ten thousand ducats to your ring, that, commend me to the court where your lady is, with no more advantage than the opportunity of a second conference, and I will bring from thence that honour of hers, which you imagine so reserved.

Post. I will wage against your gold, gold to it: my ring I hold dear as my finger; 't is part of it.

Iach. You are a friend, and therein the wiser. If you buy ladies' flesh at a million a dram, you cannot preserve it from tainting. But I see, you have some religion in you, that you fear. 140

Post. This is but a custom in your tongue: you bear a graver purpose, I hope.

Iach. I am the master of my speeches; and would undergo what's spoken, I swear.

Post. Will you?—I shall but lend my diamond till your return. Let there be covenants drawn between's. My mistress exceeds in goodness the hugeness of your unworthy thinking: I dare you to this match. Here's my ring.

Phi. I will have it no lay. 150

Iach. By the gods, it is one.—If I bring you no sufficient testimony, that I have enjoyed the dearest bodily part of your mistress, my ten thousand ducats are yours; so is your diamond too: if I come off, and leave her in such honour as you have trust in, she your jewel, this your jewel, and my gold are yours;—provided, I have your commendation for my more free entertainment. 158

Post. I embrace these conditions; let us have articles betwixt us.—Only, thus far you shall answer: if you make your voyage upon her, and give me directly to understand you have prevailed, I am no further your enemy; she is not worth our debate: if she remain unseduced, (you not making it appear otherwise,) for your ill opinion, and the assault you have made to her chastity, you shall answer me with your sword.

Iach. Your hand: a covenant. We will have these things set down by lawful counsel, and straight away for Britain, lest the bargain should catch cold, and starve. I will fetch my gold, and have our two wagers recorded. 171

Post. Agreed. [*Exeunt* POSTHUMUS *and* IACHIMO.

French. Will this hold, think you?

Phi. Signior Iachimo will not from it. Pray, let us follow 'em. [*Exeunt.*

SCENE VI.—Britain. A Room in CYMBELINE's Palace.

Enter QUEEN, *Ladies, and* CORNELIUS.

Queen. Whiles yet the dew's on ground, gather
 those flowers:
Make haste. Who has the note of them?
1 Lady.   I, madam.
Queen. Despatch.—   [*Exeunt Ladies.*
Now, master doctor, have you brought those drugs?
 Cor. Pleaseth your highness, ay: here they are,
  madam;   [*Presenting a small box.*
But I beseech your grace, without offence,
(My conscience bids me ask,) wherefore you have

Queen. "Now, master doctor, have you brought those drugs?"

Commanded of me these most poisonous compounds,
Which are the movers of a languishing death;
But, though slow, deadly?
 Queen.   I wonder, doctor,   10
Thou ask'st me such a question: have I not been
Thy pupil long? Hast thou not learn'd me how
To make perfumes? distil? preserve? yea, so,
That our great king himself doth woo me oft
For my confections? Having thus far proceeded,
(Unless thou think'st me devilish,) is't not meet
That I did amplify my judgment in
Other conclusions? I will try the forces
Of these thy compounds on such creatures as
We count not worth the hanging (but none human), 21
To try the vigour of them, and apply
Allayments to their act; and by them gather
Their several virtues, and effects.
 Cor.   Your highness
Shall from this practice but make hard your heart:
Besides, the seeing these effects will be
Both noisome and infectious.
 Queen.   O! content thee.—

Enter PISANIO.

[*Aside.*] Here comes a flattering rascal; upon him
Will I first work: he's for his master,
And enemy to my son.—How now, Pisanio!—
Doctor, your service for this time is ended;   30
Take your own way.
 Cor. [*Aside.*]   I do suspect you, madam;
But you shall do no harm.
 Queen. [*To* PISANIO.]   Hark thee, a word.—
 Cor. [*Aside.*] I do not like her. She doth think she
  has
Strange lingering poisons: I do know her spirit,
And will not trust one of her malice with
A drug of such damn'd nature. Those she has
Will stupify and dull the sense awhile;
Which first, perchance, she'll prove on cats and dogs,
Then afterward up higher: but there is   40
No danger in what show of death it makes,
More than the locking up the spirits a time,
To be more fresh, reviving. She is fool'd

With a most false effect; and I the truer,
So to be false with her.
 Queen.   No further service, doctor,
Until I send for thee.
 Cor.   I humbly take my leave. [*Exit.*
 Queen. Weeps she still, say'st thou? Dost thou
  think, in time
She will not quench, and let instructions enter
Where folly now possesses? Do thou work:
When thou shalt bring me word she loves my son,
I'll tell thee, on the instant, thou art then   50
As great as is thy master: greater; for
His fortunes all lie speechless, and his name
Is at last gasp: return he cannot, nor
Continue where he is: to shift his being
Is to exchange one misery with another;
And every day that comes, comes to decay
A day's work in him. What shalt thou expect,
To be depender on a thing that leans;
Who cannot be new built, nor has no friends,
So much as but to prop him?
 [*The* QUEEN *drops the box:* PISANIO *takes it up.*
       Thou tak'st up   60
Thou know'st not what; but take it for thy labour:
It is a thing I made, which hath the king
Five times redeem'd from death: I do not know
What is more cordial:—nay, I pr'ythee, take it;
It is an earnest of a further good
That I mean to thee. Tell thy mistress how
The case stands with her: do't as from thyself.
Think what a chance thou changest on; but think
Thou hast thy mistress still; to boot, my son,
Who shall take notice of thee. I'll move the king 70
To any shape of thy preferment, such
As thou'lt desire; and then myself, I chiefly,
That set thee on to this desert, am bound
To load thy merit richly. Call my women:—
Think on my words. [*Exit* PISANIO.]—A sly and con-
  stant knave,
Not to be shak'd; the agent for his master,
And the remembrancer of her, to hold
The hand-fast to her lord.—I have given him that,
Which, if he take, shall quite unpeople her
Of leigers for her sweet; and which she after,   80
Except she bend her humour, shall be assur'd
To taste of too.—

Re-enter PISANIO *and Ladies.*

      So, so;—well done, well done.
The violets, cowslips, and the primroses,
Bear to my closet.—Fare thee well, Pisanio;
Think on my words. [*Exeunt* QUEEN *and Ladies.*
 Pis.   And shall do;
But when to my good lord I prove untrue,
I'll choke myself: there's all I'll do for you.   [*Exit.*

SCENE VII.—Another Room in the Same.

Enter IMOGEN.

Imo. A father cruel, and a step-dame false;
A foolish suitor to a wedded lady,
That hath her husband banish'd:—O, that husband!
My supreme crown of grief! and those repeated
Vexations of it! Had I been thief-stolen,
As my two brothers, happy! but most miserable
Is the desire that's glorious: blessed be those,
How mean soe'er, that have their honest wills,
Which seasons comfort.—Who may this be? Fie!

Enter PISANIO *and* IACHIMO.

 Pis. Madam, a noble gentleman of Rome,   10
Comes from my lord with letters.
 Iach.   Change you, madam?
The worthy Leonatus is in safety,
And greets your highness dearly. [*Presents a letter.*
 Imo.   Thanks, good sir:
You are kindly welcome.
 Iach. [*Aside.*] All of her that is out of door, most
  rich!
If she be furnish'd with a mind so rare,

She is alone the Arabian bird, and I
Have lost the wager. Boldness be my friend!
Arm me, audacity, from head to foot!
Or, like the Parthian, I shall flying fight;   20
Rather, directly fly.
  Imo. [*Reads.*] "He is one of the noblest note, to
whose kindnesses I am most infinitely tied. Reflect
upon him accordingly, as you value your trust—
           LEONATUS."
So far I read aloud;
But even the very middle of my heart
Is warm'd by the rest, and takes it thankfully.—
You are as welcome, worthy sir, as I
Have words to bid you; and shall find it so   30
In all that I can do.
  Iach.   Thanks, fairest lady.—
What! are men mad? Hath nature given them eyes
To see this vaulted arch, and the rich crop
Of sea and land, which can distinguish 'twixt
The fiery orbs above, and the twinn'd stones
Upon the number'd beach, and can we not
Partition make with spectacles so precious
'Twixt fair and foul?
  Imo.   What makes your admiration?
  Iach. It cannot be i' the eye; for apes and monkeys,   40
'Twixt two such shes, would chatter this way, and
Contemn with mows the other; nor i' the judgment;
For idiots, in this case of favour, would
Be wisely definite; nor i' the appetite;
Sluttery, to such neat excellence oppos'd,
Should make desire vomit emptiness,
Not so allur'd to feed.
  Imo. What is the matter, trow?
  Iach.   The cloyed will,
(That satiate yet unsatisfied desire,
That tub both fill'd and running,) ravening first
The lamb, longs after for the garbage.
  Imo.   What, dear sir,
Thus raps you? Are you well?
  Iach.   Thanks, madam, well.—   52
[*To* PISANIO.] 'Beseech you, sir,
Desire my man's abode where I did leave him;
He 's strange and peevish.
  Pis.   I was going, sir,
To give him welcome.   [*Exit.*
  Imo. Continues well my lord his health, 'beseech
you?
  Iach. Well, madam.
  Imo. Is he dispos'd to mirth? I hope, he is.
  Iach. Exceeding pleasant; none a stranger there
So merry and so gamesome: he is call'd   60
The Briton reveller.
  Imo.   When he was here,
He did incline to sadness; and oft-times
Not knowing why.
  Iach.   I never saw him sad.
There is a Frenchman his companion, one
An eminent monsieur, that, it seems, much loves
A Gallian girl at home; he furnaces
The thick sighs from him, whiles the jolly Briton
(Your lord, I mean) laughs from 's free lungs, cries, "O!
Can my sides hold, to think that man,—who knows   70
By history, report, or his own proof,
What woman is, yea, what she cannot choose
But must be,—will his free hours languish for
Assured bondage?"
  Imo.   Will my lord say so?
  Iach. Ay, madam, with his eyes in flood with
    laughter.
It is a recreation to be by,
And hear him mock the Frenchman: but, heavens
    know,
Some men are much to blame.
  Imo.   Not he, I hope.
  Iach. Not he; but yet heaven's bounty towards him
    might
Be us'd more thankfully. In himself, 't is much;
In you,—which I account his beyond all talents,—   80
Whilst I am bound to wonder, I am bound
To pity too.
  Imo.   What do you pity, sir?
  Iach. Two creatures, heartily.

  Imo.   Am I one, sir?
You look on me. What wreck discern you in me,
Deserves your pity?
  Iach.   Lamentable! What!
To hide me from the radiant sun, and solace
I' the dungeon by a snuff?
  Imo.   I pray you, sir,
Deliver with more openness your answers
To my demands. Why do you pity me?
  Iach. That others do,   90
I was about to say, enjoy your—But
It is an office of the gods to venge it,
Not mine to speak on 't.
  Imo.   You do seem to know
Something of me, or what concerns me: 'pray you,
(Since doubting things go ill often hurts more
Than to be sure they do; for certainties
Either are past remedies, or, timely knowing,
The remedy then born,) discover to me
What both you spur and stop.
  Iach.   Had I this cheek
To bathe my lips upon; this hand, whose touch,   100
Whose every touch, would force the feeler's soul
To the oath of loyalty; this object, which
Takes prisoner the wild motion of mine eye,
Fixing it only here; should I (damn'd then)
Slaver with lips as common as the stairs
That mount the Capitol; join gripes with hands
Made hard with hourly falsehood (falsehood as
With labour); then by-peeping in an eye
Base and inlustrous as the smoky light
That 's fed with stinking tallow: it were fit,   110
That all the plagues of hell should at one time
Encounter such revolt.
  Imo.   My lord, I fear,
Has forgot Britain.
  Iach.   And himself. Not I,
Inclin'd to this intelligence, pronounce
The beggary of his change; but 't is your graces
That, from my mutest conscience, to my tongue,
Charms this report out.
  Imo.   Let me hear no more.
  Iach. O dearest soul! your cause doth strike my
    heart
With pity, that doth make me sick. A lady
So fair, and fasten'd to an empery,   120
Would make the great'st king double, to be partner'd
With tomboys, hir'd with that self exhibition
Which your own coffers yield! with diseas'd ventures,
That play with all infirmities for gold
Which rottenness can lend nature! such boil'd stuff,
As well might poison poison! Be reveng'd:
Or she that bore you was no queen, and you
Recoil from your great stock.
  Imo.   Reveng'd!
How should I be reveng'd? If this be true,
(As I have such a heart, that both mine ears   130
Must not in haste abuse,) if it be true,
How should I be reveng'd?
  Iach.   Should he make me
Live like Diana's priest, betwixt cold sheets,
Whiles he is vaulting variable ramps,
In your despite, upon your purse? Revenge it.
I dedicate myself to your sweet pleasure,
More noble than that runagate to your bed;
And will continue fast to your affection,
Still close, as sure.
  Imo.   What, ho, Pisanio!
  Iach. Let me my service tender on your lips.   140
  Imo. Away!—I do condemn mine ears, that have
So long attended thee.—If thou wert honourable,
Thou wouldst have told this tale for virtue, not
For such an end thou seek'st, as base, as strange.
Thou wrong'st a gentleman, who is as far
From thy report, as thou from honour; and
Solicit'st here a lady, that disdains
Thee and the devil alike.—What, ho, Pisanio!—
The king my father shall be made acquainted
Of thy assault: if he shall think it fit,   150
A saucy stranger, in his court, to mart
As in a Romish stew, and to expound
His beastly mind to us, he hath a court

He little cares for, and a daughter who
He not respects at all.—What, ho, Pisanio!—
　　Iach.　O happy Leonatus! I may say :
The credit, that thy lady hath of thee,
Deserves thy trust ; and thy most perfect goodness
Her assur'd credit.—Blessed live you long !
A lady to the worthiest sir, that ever　　　　160

Imo. " Away!—I do condemn mine ears, that have
So long attended thee."

Country call'd his ; and you his mistress, only
For the most worthiest fit. Give me your pardon.
I have spoke this, to know if your affiance
Were deeply rooted ; and shall make your lord
That which he is, new o'er : and he is one
The truest-manner'd ; such a holy witch,
That he enchants societies into him ;
Half all men's hearts are his.
　　Imo.　　　　　　　You make amends.
　　Iach. He sits 'mongst men like a descended god :
He hath a kind of honour sets him off,　　170

More than a mortal seeming. Be not angry,
Most mighty princess, that I have adventur'd
To try your taking of a false report ; which hath
Honour'd with confirmation your great judgment
In the election of a sir so rare,
Which you know cannot err. The love I bear him
Made me to fan you thus ; but the gods made you,
Unlike all others, chaffless. Pray, your pardon.
　　Imo. All 's well, sir. Take my power i' the court for
　　　　yours.
　　Iach. My humble thanks. I had almost forgot　180
To entreat your gace but in a small request,
And yet of moment too, for it concerns
Your lord ; myself, and other noble friends,
Are partners in the business.
　　Imo.　　　　　　Pray, what is 't?
　　Iach. Some dozen Romans of us, and your lord
(The best feather of our wing), have mingled sums
To buy a present for the emperor ;
Which I, the factor for the rest, have done
In France : 't is plate of rare device, and jewels
Of rich and exquisite form ; their values great ;　190
And I am something curious, being strange,
To have them in safe stowage. May it please you
To take them in protection ?
　　Imo.　　　　　　Willingly ;
And pawn mine honour for their safety : since
My lord hath interest in them, I will keep them
In my bedchamber.
　　Iach.　　　　　They are in a trunk,
Attended by my men ; I will make bold
To send them to you, only for this night :
I must aboard to-morrow.
　　Imo.　　　　　　O ! no, no.
　　Iach. Yes, I beseech ; or I shall short my word,　200
By lengthening my return. From Gallia
I cross'd the seas on purpose, and on promise
To see your grace.
　　Imo.　　　　I thank you for your pains :
But not away to-morrow !
　　Iach.　　　　　O ! I must, madam :
Therefore, I shall beseech you, if you please
To greet your lord with writing, do 't to-night :
I have outstood my time, which is material
To the tender of our present.
　　Imo.　　　　　I will write.
Send your trunk to me : it shall safe be kept,
And truly yielded you. You are very welcome.　210
　　　　　　　　　　　　　　　　　　[*Exeunt.*

ACT II.

SCENE I.—Court before CYMBELINE'S Palace.

Enter CLOTEN *and two Lords.*

　　Cloten.
　　　　AS there ever man had such
　　　　luck ! when I kissed the
　　　　jack, upon an up-cast to be
hit away ! I had a hundred pound on 't :
and then a whoreson jackanapes must
take me up for swearing ; as if I borrowed mine oaths of him, and might
not spend them at my pleasure.
　　1 Lord. What got he by that ? You
have broke his pate with your bowl.　10
　　2 Lord. [*Aside.*] If his wit had been
like him that broke it, it would have
run all out.
　　Clo. When a gentleman is disposed
to swear, it is not for any standers-by
to curtail his oaths : ha ?

　　2 Lord. No, my lord ; [*aside*] nor crop the ears of them.
　　Clo. Whoreson dog !—I give him satisfaction ?
'Would he had been one of my rank !
　　2 Lord. [*Aside.*] To have smelt like a fool.　20
　　Clo. I am not vexed more at anything in the earth.
—A pox on 't ! I had rather not be so noble as I am.
They dare not fight with me, because of the queen
my mother. Every Jack-slave hath his bellyful of
fighting, and I must go up and down like a cock that
nobody can match.
　　2 Lord. [*Aside.*] You are cock and capon too ; and
you crow, cock, with your comb on.
　　Clo. Sayest thou ?
　　2 Lord. It is not fit your lordship should undertake
every companion that you give offence to.　31
　　Clo. No, I know that ; but it is fit I should commit
offence to my inferiors.

2 Lord. Ay, it is fit for your lordship only.
Clo. Why, so I say.
1 Lord. Did you hear of a stranger, that 's come to court to-night?
Clo. A stranger, and I not know on 't!
2 Lord. [*Aside.*] He 's a strange fellow himself, and knows it not.   40
1 Lord. There 's an Italian come; and, 't is thought, one of Leonatus' friends.
Clo. Leonatus! a banished rascal; and he 's another, whatsoever he be. Who told you of this stranger?
1 Lord. One of your lordship's pages.
Clo. Is it fit I went to look upon him? Is there no derogation in 't?
1 Lord. You cannot derogate, my lord.
Clo. Not easily, I think.   50
2 Lord. [*Aside.*] You are a fool granted; therefore your issues, being foolish, do not derogate.
Clo. Come, I 'll go see this Italian. What I have lost to-day at bowls, I 'll win to-night of him. Come, go.
2 Lord. I 'll attend your lordship.—
    [*Exeunt* Cloten *and first Lord.*
That such a crafty devil as is his mother
Should yield the world this ass! a woman, that
Bears all down with her brain; and this her son
Cannot take two from twenty for his heart,   60
And leave eighteen. Alas, poor princess!
Thou divine Imogen, what thou endur'st,
Betwixt a father by thy step-dame govern'd;
A mother hourly coining plots; a wooer
More hateful than the foul expulsion is
Of thy dear husband, than that horrid act
Of the divorce he 'd make! The heavens hold firm
The walls of thy dear honour; keep unshak'd
That temple, thy fair mind; that thou may'st stand,
To enjoy thy banish'd lord, and this great land!   70
    [*Exit.*

Scene II.—*A Bedchamber; in one part of it a Trunk.*

Imogen *reading in her bed; a Lady attending.*

Imo. Who s there? my woman Helen?
Lady.   Please you, madam.
Imo. What hour is it?
Lady.   Almost midnight, madam.
Imo. I have read three hours then: mine eyes are weak;
Fold down the leaf where I have left: to bed.
Take not away the taper, leave it burning;
And if thou canst awake by four o' the clock,
I pr'ythee, call me. Sleep hath seiz'd me wholly.
    [*Exit Lady.*
To your protection I commend me, gods!
From fairies, and the tempters of the night,
Guard me, beseech ye!   10
    [*Sleeps.* Iachimo *comes from the trunk.*
Iach. The crickets sing, and man's o'er-labour'd sense
Repairs itself by rest. Our Tarquin thus
Did softly press the rushes, ere he waken'd
The chastity he wounded.—Cytherea,
How bravely thou becom'st thy bed! fresh lily,
And whiter than the sheets! That I might touch!
But kiss; one kiss!—Rubies unparagon'd,
How dearly they do 't!—'T is her breathing that
Perfumes the chamber thus: the flame o' the taper
Bows toward her, and would under-peep her lids,   20
To see the enclosed lights, now canopied
Under these windows, white and azure, lac'd
With blue of heaven's own tinct.—But my design!
To note the chamber, I will write all down:—
Such and such pictures;—there the window;—such
The adornment of her bed;—the arras, figures,
Why, such, and such;—and the contents o' the story.—
Ah! but some natural notes about her body,
Above ten thousand meaner movables
Would testify, to enrich mine inventory.   30
O sleep, thou ape of death, lie dull upon her!
And be her sense but as a monument,

Thus in a chapel lying!—Come off, come off;—
    [*Taking off her bracelet.*
As slippery, as the Gordian knot was hard!—
'T is mine; and this will witness outwardly,
As strongly as the conscience does within,
To the madding of her lord.—On her left breast
A mole cinque-spotted, like the crimson drops
I' the bottom of a cowslip. Here 's a voucher,
Stronger than ever law could make; this secret   40
Will force him think I have pick'd the lock, and ta'en
The treasure of her honour. No more.—To what end?
Why should I write this down, that 's riveted,
Screw'd to my memory? She hath been reading late
The tale of Tereus; here the leaf 's turn'd down,
Where Philomel gave up.—I have enough:
To the trunk again, and shut the spring of it.
Swift, swift, you dragons of the night, that dawning
May bare the raven's eye! I lodge in fear;
Though this a heavenly angel, hell is here.   50
    [*Clock strikes.*
One, two, three,—time, time!
    [*Goes into the trunk. The scene closes.*

Scene III.—*An Ante-chamber adjoining* Imogen's *Apartment.*

Enter Cloten *and Lords.*

1 Lord. Your lordship is the most patient man in loss, the most coldest that ever turned up ace.
Clo. It would make any man cold to lose.
1 Lord. But not every man patient after the noble temper of your lordship. You are most hot and furious, when you win.
Clo. Winning will put any man into courage. If I could get this foolish Imogen, I should have gold enough. It 's almost morning, is 't not?
1 Lord. Day, my lord.   10
Clo. I would this music would come. I am advised to give her music o' mornings; they say, it will penetrate.

Enter Musicians.

Come on; tune. If you can penetrate her with your fingering, so; we 'll try with tongue too: if none will do, let her remain; but I 'll never give o'er. First, a very excellent good-conceited thing; after, a wonderful sweet air, with admirable rich words to it,—and then let her consider.

Song.

    Hark! hark! the lark at heaven's gate sings,   20
      And Phœbus 'gins arise,
    His steeds to water at those springs
      On chalic'd flowers that lies;
    And winking Mary-buds begin
      To ope their golden eyes;
    With every thing that pretty is,
      My lady sweet, arise;
      Arise, arise!

So, get you gone. If this penetrate, I will consider your music the better: if it do not, it is a vice in her ears, which horse-hairs, and calves'-guts, nor the voice of unpaved eunuch to boot, can never amend.   32
    [*Exeunt Musicians.*
2 Lord. Here comes the king.
Clo. I am glad I was up so late, for that 's the reason I was up so early: he cannot choose but take this service I have done, fatherly.

Enter Cymbeline *and* Queen.

Good morrow to your majesty, and to my gracious mother.
Cym. Attend you here the door of our stern daughter?
Will she not forth?   40
Clo. I have assailed her with musics, but she vouchsafes no notice.
Cym. The exile of her minion is too new;
She hath not yet forgot him: some more time
Must wear the print of his remembrance out,
And then she 's yours.

Queen.   You are most bound to the king,
Who lets go by no vantages that may
Prefer you to his daughter. Frame yourself
To orderly solicits, and be friended
With aptness of the season : make denials   50

Albeit he comes on angry purpose now ;
But that 's no fault of his : we must receive him
According to the honour of his sender ;   60
And towards himself, his goodness forespent on us,
We must extend our notice.—Our dear son,

IACHIMO STEALING THE BRACELET.

Increase your services : so seem, as if
You were inspir'd to do those duties which
You tender to her ; that you in all obey her,
Save when command to your dismission tends,
And therein you are senseless.
Clo.   Senseless? not so.

Enter a Messenger.

Mess. So like you, sir, ambassadors from Rome :
The one is Caius Lucius.
Cym.   A worthy fellow,

When you have given good morning to your mistress
Attend the queen and us ; we shall have need
To employ you towards this Roman.—Come, our
        queen.   [*Exeunt all but* CLOTEN.
Clo. If she be up, I 'll speak with her ; if not,
Let her lie still, and dream.—By your leave, ho !—
                                    [*Knocks.*
I know her women are about her. What
If I do line one of their hands? 'T is gold
Which buys admittance ; oft it doth ; yea, and makes
Diana's rangers false themselves, yield up   71

Their deer to the stand o' the stealer : and 't is gold
Which makes the true man kill'd, and saves the
thief ;
Nay, sometime, hangs both thief and true man.
   What
Can it not do, and undo ? I will make
One of her women lawyer to me ; for
I yet not understand the case myself.
By your leave.   [*Knocks.*

Enter a Lady.

Lady. Who 's there that knocks ?
Clo.   A gentleman.
Lady.   No more ?
Clo. Yes, and a gentlewoman's son.
Lady.   That 's more   80
Than some, whose tailors are as dear as yours,
Can justly boast of. What 's your lordship's pleasure ?
 Clo. Your lady's person : is she ready ?
Lady.   Ay,
To keep her chamber.
 Clo. There 's gold for you ; sell me your good
report.
 Lady. How ! my good name ? or to report of you
What I shall think is good ?—The princess !—   [*Exit.*

Enter Imogen.

Clo. Good morrow, fairest : sister, your sweet
hand.
Imo. Good morrow, sir. You lay out too much
pains
For purchasing but trouble : the thanks I give,   90
Is telling you that I am poor of thanks,
And scarce can spare them.
 Clo.   Still, I swear, I love you.
 Imo. If you but said so, 't were as deep with me :
If you swear still, your recompense is still
That I regard it not.
 Clo.   This is no answer.
 Imo. But that you shall not say I yield, being
silent,
I would not speak. I pray you, spare me : 'faith,
I shall unfold equal discourtesy
To your best kindness. One of your great knowing
Should learn, being taught, forbearance.   100
 Clo. To leave you in your madness, 't were my sin :
I will not.
 Imo. Fools are not mad folks.
 Clo.   Do you call me fool ?
 Imo. As I am mad, I do :
If you 'll be patient, I 'll no more be mad ;
That cures us both. I am much sorry, sir,
You put me to forget a lady's manners,
By being so verbal : and learn now, for all,
That I, which know my heart, do here pronounce
By the very truth of it, I care not for you ;   110
And am so near the lack of charity,
(To accuse myself,) I hate you ; which I had rather
You felt, than make 't my boast.
 Clo.   You sin against
Obedience, which you owe your father. For
The contract you pretend with that base wretch,
(One bred of alms, and foster'd with cold dishes,
With scraps o' the court,) it is no contract, none :
And though it be allow'd in meaner parties,
(Yet who than he more mean ?) to knit their souls
(On whom there is no more dependency   120
But brats and beggary) in self-figur'd knot,
Yet you are curb'd from that enlargement by
The consequence o' the crown, and must not soil
The precious note of it with a base slave,
A hilding for a livery, a squire's cloth,
A pantler, not so eminent.
 Imo.   Profane fellow !
Wert thou the son of Jupiter, and no more
But what thou art besides, thou wert too base
To be his groom : thou wert dignified enough,
Even to the point of envy, if 't were made   130
Comparative for your virtues, to be styl'd
The under-hangman of his kingdom, and hated
For being preferr'd so well.
 Clo.   The south-fog rot him !

Imo. He never can meet more mischance, then
come
To be but nam'd of thee. His meanest garment,
That ever hath but clipp'd his body, is dearer
In my respect, than all the hairs above thee,
Were they all made such men.—How now, Pisanio !

Enter Pisanio.

Clo. His garment ? Now, the devil—
Imo. To Dorothy my woman hie thee presently.—
Clo. His garment ?
Imo.   I am sprighted with a fool ;   141
Frighted, and anger'd worse.—Go, bid my woman
Search for a jewel, that too casually
Hath left mine arm : it was thy master's ; 'shrew me,
If I would lose it for a revenue
Of any king's in Europe. I do think,
I saw 't this morning : confident I am,
Last night 't was on mine arm ; I kiss'd it :
I hope, it be not gone to tell my lord
That I kiss aught but he.
 Pis.   'T will not be lost.   150
 Imo. I hope so : go, and search.   [*Exit* Pisanio.
 Clo.   You have abus'd me :—
His meanest garment ?
 Imo.   Ay ; I said so, sir.
If you will make 't an action, call witness to 't.
 Clo. I will inform your father.
 Imo.   Your mother too :
She 's my good lady, and will conceive, I hope,
But the worst of me. So I leave you, sir,
To the worst of discontent.   [*Exit.*
 Clo.   I 'll be reveng'd.—
His meanest garment ?—Well.   [*Exit.*

Scene IV.—Rome. An Apartment in Philario's
House.

Enter Posthumus *and* Philario.

Post. Fear it not, sir : I would I were so sure
To win the king, as I am bold her honour
Will remain hers.
 Phi.   What means do you make to him ?
 Post. Not any ; but abide the change of time ;
Quake in the present winter's state, and wish
That warmer days would come. In these sear'd
hopes,
I barely gratify your love ; they failing,
I must die much your debtor.
 Phi. Your very goodness, and your company,
O'erpays all I can do. By this, your king   10
Hath heard of great Augustus : Caius Lucius
Will do 's commission throughly ; and, I think,
He 'll grant the tribute, send the arrearages,
Or look upon our Romans, whose remembrance
Is yet fresh in their grief.
 Post.   I do believe,
(Statist though I am none, nor like to be,)
That this will prove a war ; and you shall hear
The legions, now in Gallia, sooner landed
In our not-fearing Britain, than have tidings
Of any penny tribute paid. Our countrymen   20
Are men more order'd, than when Julius Cæsar
Smil'd at their lack of skill, but found their courage
Worthy his frowning at : their discipline
(Now mingled with their courages) will make known
To their approvers, they are people such
That mend upon the world.

Enter Iachimo.

 Phi.   See ! Iachimo !
 Post. The swiftest harts have posted you by land,
And winds of all the corners kiss'd your sails,
To make your vessel nimble.
 Phi.   Welcome, sir.
 Post. I hope, the briefness of your answer made   30
The speediness of your return.
 Iach.   Your lady
Is one of the fairest that I have look'd upon.
 Post. And therewithal the best ; or let her beauty

Look through a casement to allure false hearts,
And be false with them.
Iach.   Here are letters for you.
Post. Their tenor good, I trust.
Iach.   'T is very like.
Phi. Was Caius Lucius in the Britain court,
When you were there?
Iach.   He was expected then,
But not approach'd.
Post.   All is well yet.—
Sparkles this stone as it was wont? or is 't not   40
Too dull for your good wearing?
Iach.   If I have lost it,
I should have lost the worth of it in gold.
I 'll make a journey twice as far, to enjoy
A second night of such sweet shortness, which
Was mine in Britain ; for the ring is won.
Post. The stone 's too hard to come by.
Iach.   Not a whit,
Your lady being so easy.
Post.   Make not, sir,
Your loss your sport : I hope, you know that we
Must not continue friends.
Iach.   Good sir, we must,
If you keep covenant. Had I not brought   50
The knowledge of your mistress home, I grant
We were to question further ; but I now
Profess myself the winner of her honour,
Together with your ring ; and not the wronger
Of her, or you, having proceeded but
By both your wills.
Post.   If you can make 't apparent
That you have tasted her in bed, my hand,
And ring, is yours : if not, the foul opinion
You had of her pure honour, gains, or loses,
Your sword, or mine ; or masterless leaves both   60
To who shall find them.
Iach.   Sir, my circumstances,
Being so near the truth as I will make them,
Must first induce you to believe : whose strength
I will confirm with oath ; which, I doubt not,
You 'll give me leave to spare, when you shall find
You need it not.
Post.   Proceed.
Iach.   First, her bedchamber,
(Where, I confess, I slept not, but profess,
Had that was well worth watching,) it was hang'd
With tapestry of silk and silver ; the story
Proud Cleopatra, when she met her Roman,   70
And Cydnus swell'd above the banks, or for
The press of boats, or pride : a piece of work
So bravely done, so rich, that it did strive
In workmanship, and value ; which I wonder'd
Could be so rarely and exactly wrought,
Since the true life on 't was—
Post.   This is true ;
And this you might have heard of here, by me,
Or by some other.
Iach.   More particulars
Must justify my knowledge.
Post.   So they must,
Or do your honour injury.
Iach.   The chimney   80
Is south the chamber ; and the chimney-piece.
Chaste Dian, bathing : never saw I figures
So likely to report themselves ; the cutter
Was as another nature, dumb ; outwent her,
Motion and breath left out.
Post.   This is a thing
Which you might from relation likewise reap,
Being, as it is, much spoke of.
Iach.   The roof o' the chamber
With golden cherubins is fretted : her andirons
(I had forgot them) were two winking Cupids
Of silver, each on one foot standing, nicely   90
Depending on their brands.
Post.   This is her honour !—
Let it be granted you have seen all this (and praise
Be given to your remembrance), the description
Of what is in her chamber nothing saves
The wager you have laid.
Iach.   Then, if you can,

Be pale : I beg but leave to air this jewel ; see !—
                    [*Pulling out the bracelet.*
And now 't is up again : it must be married
To that your diamond ; I 'll keep them.
Post.   Jove !—
Once more let me behold it. Is it that
Which I left with her ?
Iach.   Sir, (I thank her,) that :   100
She stripp'd it from her arm ; I see her yet ;
Her pretty action did outsell her gift,
And yet enrich'd it too. She gave it me,
And said, she priz'd it once.
Post.   May be, she pluck'd it off,
To send it me.
Iach.   She writes so to you, doth she ?
Post. O ! no, no, no ; 't is true. Here, take this too ;
                    [*Giving the ring.*
It is a basilisk unto mine eye,
Kills me to look on 't.—Let there be no honour,
Where there is beauty ; truth, where semblance ; love,
Where there 's another man : the vows of women   110
Of no more bondage be to where they are made,
Than they are to their virtues, which is nothing.—
O, above measure false !
Phi.   Have patience, sir,
And take your ring again ; 't is not yet won :
It may be probable she lost it ; or,
Who knows, if one of her women, being corrupted,
Hath stol'n it from her ?
Post.   Very true ;
And so, I hope, he came by 't.—Back my ring.—
Render to me some corporal sign about her,
More evident than this ; for this was stolen.   120
Iach. By Jupiter, I had it from her arm.
Post. Hark you, he swears ; by Jupiter he swears.
'T is true :—nay, keep the ring,—'t is true, I am sure
She would not lose it : her attendants are
All sworn, and honourable :—they induc'd to steal it !
And by a stranger !—No, he hath enjoy'd her :—
The cognisance of her incontinency
Is this :—she hath bought the name of whore thus
                    dearly.—
There, take thy hire ; and all the fiends of hell
Divide themselves between you !
Phi.   Sir, be patient.   130
This is not strong enough to be believ'd
Of one persuaded well of—
Post.   Never talk on 't ;
She hath been colted by him.
Iach.   If you seek
For further satisfying, under her breast
(Worthy the pressing) lies a mole, right proud
Of that most delicate lodging : by my life,
I kiss'd it, and it gave me present hunger
To feed again, though full. You do remember
This stain upon her ?
Post.   Ay, and it doth confirm
Another stain, as big as hell can hold,   140
Were there no more but it.
Iach.   Will you hear more ?
Post. Spare your arithmetic : never count the turns ;
Once, and a million !
Iach.   I 'll be sworn,—
Post.   No swearing.
If you will swear you have not done 't, you lie ;
And I will kill thee, if thou dost deny
Thou 'st made me cuckold.
Iach.   I will deny nothing.
Post. O, that I had her here, to tear her limb-meal !
I will go there, and do 't ; i' the court ; before
Her father.—I 'll do something—   [*Exit.*
Phi.   Quite besides
The government of patience !—You have won :   150
Let 's follow him, and pervert the present wrath
He hath against himself.
Iach.   With all my heart. [*Exeunt.*

SCENE V.—The Same. Another Room in the Same.

Enter POSTHUMUS.

Post. Is there no way for men to be, but women

Must be half-workers? We are all bastards;
And that most venerable man, which I
Did call my father, was I know not where
When I was stamp'd; some coiner with his tools
Made me a counterfeit: yet my mother seem'd
The Dian of that time; so doth my wife
The nonpareil of this.—O, vengeance, vengeance!
Me of my lawful pleasure she restrain'd,
And pray'd me oft forbearance; did it with   10
A pudency so rosy, the sweet view on 't
Might well have warm'd old Saturn; that I thought her
As chaste as unsunn'd snow:—O, all the devils!—
This yellow Iachimo, in an hour,—was 't not?—
Or less,—at first; perchance he spoke not, but,
Like a full-acorn'd boar, a German one,
Cried "O!" and mounted; found no opposition
But what he look'd for should oppose, and she

Should from encounter guard. Could I find out
The woman's part in me! For there's no motion   2t
That tends to vice in man, but I affirm
It is the woman's part: be it lying, note it
The woman's; flattering, hers; deceiving, hers;
Lust and rank thoughts, hers, hers; revenges, hers;
Ambitions, covetings, change of prides, disdain,
Nice longing, slanders, mutability,
All faults that may be nam'd, nay, that hell knows,
Why, hers, in part or all: but rather, all;
For even to vice
They are not constant, but are changing still   30
One vice but of a minute old, for one
Not half so old as that. I'll write against them,
Detest them, curse them.—Yet 't is greater skill
In a true hate, to pray they have their will:
The very devils cannot plague them better.   [Exit.

ACT III.

SCENE I.—Britain. A Room of State in CYMBELINE's Palace.

Enter CYMBELINE, QUEEN, CLOTEN, *and Lords, at one door; and at another,* CAIUS LUCIUS *and Attendants.*

Cymbeline.
OW say, what would Augustus Cæsar
with us?
Luc. When Julius Cæsar (whose re-
membrance yet
Lives in men's eyes, and will to ears and
tongues
Be theme and hearing ever) was in this
Britain,
And conquer'd it, Cassibelan, thine uncle,
(Famous in Cæsar's praises, no whit less
Than in his feats deserving it,) for him,
And his succession, granted Rome a
tribute,
Yearly three thousand pounds; which
by thee lately
Is left untender'd.
Queen.   And, to kill the marvel,
Shall be so ever.
Clo.   There be many Cæsars,   11
Ere such another Julius. Britain is
A world by itself; and we will nothing pay
For wearing our own noses.
Queen.   That opportunity,
Which then they had to take from 's, to resume
We have again.—Remember, sir, my liege,
The kings your ancestors, together with
The natural bravery of your isle, which stands
As Neptune's park, ribbed and paled in   20
With rocks unscalable, and roaring waters;
With sands that will not bear your enemies' boats,
But suck them up to the topmast. A kind of con-
quest
Cæsar made here; but made not here his brag
Of "came, and saw, and overcame:" with shame
(The first that ever touch'd him) he was carried
From off our coast, twice beaten; and his shipping
(Poor ignorant baubles!) on our terrible seas,
Like egg-shells mov'd upon their surges, crack'd
As easily 'gainst our rocks: for joy whereof,
The fam'd Cassibelan, who was once at point   30
(O giglot fortune!) to master Cæsar's sword,
Made Lud's town with rejoicing fires bright,
And Britons strut with courage.

Clo. Come, there's no more tribute to be paid. Our
kingdom is stronger than it was at that time; and, as
I said, there is no more such Cæsars: other of them
may have crooked noses; but, to owe such straight
arms, none.
Cym. Son, let your mother end.   39
Clo. We have yet many among us can gripe as hard
as Cassibelan: I do not say, I am one; but I have a
hand.—Why tribute? why should we pay tribute? If
Cæsar can hide the sun from us with a blanket, or
put the moon in his pocket, we will pay him tribute
for light; else, sir, no more tribute, pray you now.
Cym. You must know,
Till the injurious Romans did extort
This tribute from us, we were free; Cæsar's ambition,
(Which swell'd so much, that it did almost stretch
The sides o' the world,) against all colour, here   50
Did put the yoke upon 's; which to shake off
Becomes a warlike people, whom we reckon
Ourselves to be. We do say then to Cæsar,
Our ancestor was that Mulmutius, which
Ordain'd our laws; whose use the sword of Cæsar
Hath too much mangled; whose repair and franchise
Shall, by the power we hold, be our good deed,
Though Rome be therefore angry. Mulmutius made
our laws,
Who was the first of Britain which did put
His brows within a golden crown, and call'd   60
Himself a king.
Luc.   I am sorry, Cymbeline,
That I am to pronounce Augustus Cæsar
(Cæsar, that hath more kings his servants, than
Thyself domestic officers) thine enemy.
Receive it from me, then:—war, and confusion,
In Cæsar's name pronounce I 'gainst thee: look
For fury not to be resisted.—Thus defied,
I thank thee for myself.
Cym.   Thou art welcome, Caius.
Thy Cæsar knighted me; my youth I spent
Much under him; of him I gather'd honour;   70
Which he to seek of me again, perforce,
Behoves me keep at utterance. I am perfect
That the Pannonians and Dalmatians, for
Their liberties, are now in arms; a precedent,

Which not to read would show the Britons cold :
So Cæsar shall not find them.
Luc.　　　　　　　　　　　　Let proof speak.
Clo. His majesty bids you welcome. Make pastime
with us a day or two, or longer : if you seek us after-
wards in other terms, you shall find us in our salt-
water girdle : if you beat us out of it, it is yours. If
you fall in the adventure, our crows shall fare the
better for you ; and there's an end.　　　　　　82
Luc. So, sir.
Cym. I know your master's pleasure, and he mine :
All the remain is, welcome.　　　　　　　　[*Exeunt.*

SCENE II.—Another Room in the Same.

Enter PISANIO, *reading a letter.*

Pis. How! of adultery? Wherefore write you not
What monster's her accuser?—Leonatus!
O master! what a strange infection
Is fall'n into thy ear! What false Italian
(As poisonous tongued as handed) hath prevail'd
On thy too ready hearing?—Disloyal? No :
She's punish'd for her truth ; and undergoes,
More goddess-like than wife-like, such assaults
As would take in some virtue.—O my master!　　10
Thy mind to her is now as low, as were
Thy fortunes.—How! that I should murder her?
Upon the love, and truth, and vows, which I
Have made to thy command?—I, her?—her blood?
If it be so to do good service, never
Let me be counted serviceable. How look I,
That I should seem to lack humanity,
So much as this fact comes to?—"Do't. The letter
That I have sent her, by her own command
Shall give thee opportunity."—O damn'd paper!　　20
Black as the ink that's on thee. Senseless bauble,
Art thou a feodary for this act, and look'st
So virgin-like without? Lo! here she comes.
I am ignorant in what I am commanded.

Enter IMOGEN.

Imo. How now, Pisanio?
Pis. Madam, here is a letter from my lord.
Imo. Who? thy lord? that is my lord : Leonatus.
O! learn'd indeed were that astronomer,
That knew the stars as I his characters ;
He'd lay the future open.—You good gods,
Let what is here contain'd relish of love,　　　30
Of my lord's health, of his content,—yet not,
That we two are asunder,—let that grieve him :
Some griefs are medicinable ; that is one of them,
For it doth physic love :—of his content,
All but in that!—Good wax, thy leave.—Bless'd be
You bees, that make these locks of counsel! Lovers,
And men in dangerous bonds, pray not alike :
Though forfeiters you cast in prison, yet
You clasp young Cupid's tables.—Good news, gods!　39
[*Reads.*] "Justice, and your father's wrath, should
he take me in his dominion, could not be so cruel to
me, as you, O the dearest of creatures, would even
renew me with your eyes. Take notice, that I am in
Cambria, at Milford-Haven : what your own love will
out of this advise you, follow. So, he wishes you all
happiness, that remains loyal to his vow, and your,
increasing in love, 　　　LEONATUS POSTHUMUS."
O, for a horse with wings!—Hear'st thou, Pisanio?
He is at Milford-Haven : read, and tell me
How far 'tis thither. If one of mean affairs　　50
May plod it in a week, why may not I
Glide thither in a day?—Then, true Pisanio,
(Who long'st, like me, to see thy lord ; who long'st,—
O, let me 'bate!—but not like me ;—yet long'st,—
But in a fainter kind :—O! not like me,
For mine's beyond beyond) say, and speak thick,
(Love's counsellor should fill the bores of hearing,
To the smothering of the sense,) how far it is
To this same blessed Milford : and, by the way,
Tell me how Wales was made so happy, as　　60
To inherit such a haven : but, first of all,
How we may steal from hence ; and, for the gap

That we shall make in time, from our hence-going
And our return, to excuse :—but first, how get hence.
Why should excuse be born or ere begot?
We'll talk of that hereafter. Pr'ythee, speak,
How many score of miles may we well ride
'Twixt hour and hour?
Pis.　　　　　　　One score 'twixt sun and sun,
Madam,'s enough for you, and too much too.
Imo. Why, one that rode to's execution, man,　　70
Could never go so slow : I have heard of riding
wagers,
Where horses have been nimbler than the sands
That run i' the clock's behalf.—But this is foolery.—
Go, bid my woman feign a sickness ; say
She'll home to her father ; and provide me, presently,
A riding-suit, no costlier than would fit
A franklin's housewife.
Pis.　　　　　　　Madam, you're best consider.
Imo. I see before me, man ;—nor here, nor here,
Nor what ensues, but have a fog in them,
That I cannot look through. Away, I pr'ythee :　　80
Do as I bid thee. There's no more to say ;
Accessible is none but Milford way.　　　[*Exeunt.*

SCENE III.—Wales. A Mountainous Country, with a
Cave.

Enter BELARIUS, GUIDERIUS, *and* ARVIRAGUS.

Bel. A goodly day not to keep house, with such
Whose roof's as low as ours! Stoop, boys : this gate
Instructs you how to adore the heavens, and bows you
To a morning's holy office : the gates of monarchs
Are arch'd so high, that giants may jet through
And keep their impious turbans on, without
Good morrow to the sun.—Hail, thou fair heaven!
We house i' the rock, yet use thee not so hardly
As prouder livers do.
Gui.　　　　　　Hail, heaven!
Arv.　　　　　　　　　　Hail, heaven!
Bel. Now for our mountain sport. Up to yon hill ;
Your legs are young ; I'll tread these flats. Consider,
When you above perceive me like a crow,　　　12
That it is place which lessens and sets off :
And you may then revolve what tales I have told you
Of courts, of princes, of the tricks in war :
This service is not service, so being done,
But being so allow'd : to apprehend thus,
Draws us a profit from all things we see ;
And often, to our comfort, shall we find
The sharded beetle in a safer hold　　　20
Than is the full-wing'd eagle. O! this life
Is nobler, than attending for a check ;
Richer, than doing nothing for a bribe ;
Prouder, than rustling in unpaid-for silk :
Such gain the cap of him that makes 'em fine,
Yet keeps his book uncross'd. No life to ours.
Gui. Out of your proof you speak : we, poor un-
fledg'd,
Have never wing'd from view o' the nest ; nor know
not
What air's from home. Haply this life is best,
If quiet life be best ; sweeter to you,　　　30
That have a sharper known ; well corresponding
With your stiff age : but unto us it is
A cell of ignorance ; travelling a-bed ;
A prison for a debtor, that not dares
To stride a limit.
Arv.　　　　　　What should we speak of,
When we are old as you? when we shall hear
The rain and wind beat dark December, how,
In this our pinching cave, shall we discourse
The freezing hours away? We have seen nothing :
We are beastly ; subtle as the fox, for prey ;　　40
Like warlike as the wolf, for what we eat :
Our valour is to chase what flies ; our cage
We make a quire, as doth the prison'd bird,
And sing our bondage freely.
Bel.　　　　　　　　How you speak!
Did you but know the city's usuries,
And felt them knowingly : the art o' the court,

As hard to leave, as keep; whose top to climb
Is certain falling, or so slippery, that
The fear's as bad as falling: the toil o' the war,
A pain that only seems to seek out danger   50
I' the name of fame and honour; which dies i' the
    search
And hath as oft a slanderous epitaph,
As record of fair act; nay, many times,
Doth ill deserve by doing well; what's worse,
Must court'sy at the censure.—O boys! this story
The world may read in me: my body's mark'd
With Roman swords, and my report was once
First with the best of note: Cymbeline lov'd me;
And when a soldier was the theme, my name
Was not far off: then was I as a tree,   60
Whose boughs did bend with fruit; but, in one night,
A storm, or robbery, call it what you will,
Shook down my mellow hangings, nay, my leaves,
And left me bare to weather.
  Gui.   Uncertain favour!
  Bel. My fault being nothing (as I have told you oft)
But that two villains, whose false oaths prevail'd
Before my perfect honour, swore to Cymbeline,
I was confederate with the Romans: so,
Follow'd my banishment; and this twenty years
This rock, and these demesnes, have been my world,
Where I have liv'd at honest freedom, paid   71
More pious debts to heaven, than in all
The fore-end of my time.—But, up to the mountains!
This is not hunters' language.—He that strikes
The venison first shall be the lord o' the feast;
To him the other two shall minister;
And we will fear no poison, which attends
In place of greater state. I'll meet you in the valleys.
    [*Exeunt* GUIDERIUS *and* ARVIRAGUS.
How hard it is to hide the sparks of nature!
These boys know little they are sons to the king;   80
Nor Cymbeline dreams that they are alive.
They think they are mine: and, though train'd up
    thus meanly
I' the cave wherein they bow, their thoughts do hit
The roofs of palaces; and nature prompts them,
In simple and low things, to prince it much
Beyond the trick of others. This Polydore,—
The heir of Cymbeline and Britain, whom
The king his father call'd Guiderius,—Jove!
When on my three-foot stool I sit, and tell
The warlike feats I have done, his spirits fly out   90
Into my story: say,—"Thus mine enemy fell;
And thus I set my foot on 's neck,"—even then
The princely blood flows in his cheek, he sweats,
Strains his young nerves, and puts himself in posture
That acts my words. The younger brother, Cadwal,
(Once Arviragus,) in as like a figure,
Strikes life into my speech, and shows much more
His own conceiving. Hark! the game is rous'd.—
O Cymbeline! heaven, and my conscience, knows,
Thou didst unjustly banish me; whereon   100
At three, and two years old, I stole these babes,
Thinking to bar thee of succession, as
Thou reft'st me of my lands. Euriphile,
Thou wast their nurse; they took thee for their
    mother,
And every day do honour to her grave:
Myself, Belarius, that am Morgan call'd,
They take for natural father.—The game is up. [*Exit.*

SCENE IV.—Near Milford-Haven.

Enter PISANIO *and* IMOGEN.

  Imo. Thou told'st me, when we came from horse,
    the place
Was near at hand.—Ne'er long'd my mother so
To see me first, as I have now.—Pisanio! man!
Where is Posthumus? What is in thy mind,
That makes thee stare thus? Wherefore breaks that
    sigh
From the inward of thee? One, but painted thus,
Would be interpreted a thing perplex'd
Beyond self-explication: put thyself

Into a haviour of less fear, ere wildness
Vanquish my staider senses. What's the matter?   10
Why tender'st thou that paper to me, with
A look untender? If it be summer news,
Smile to 't before; if winterly, thou need'st
But keep that countenance still.—My husband's hand!
That drug-damn'd Italy hath out-crafted him,
And he's at some hard point.—Speak, man: thy
    tongue
May take off some extremity, which to read
Would be even mortal to me.
  Pis.   Please you, read;
And you shall find me, wretched man, a thing
The most disdain'd of fortune.   20

Pis.   "Please you, read;
And you shall find me, wretched man, a thing
The most disdain'd of fortune."

  Imo. [*Reads.*] " Thy mistress, Pisanio, hath played
the strumpet in my bed: the testimonies whereof lie
bleeding in me. I speak not out of weak surmises,
but from proof as strong as my grief, and as certain
as I expect my revenge. That part, thou, Pisanio,
must act for me, if thy faith be not tainted with the
breach of hers. Let thine own hands take away her
life; I shall give thee opportunity at Milford-Haven:
she hath my letter for the purpose: where, if thou
fear to strike, and to make me certain it is done, thou
art the pander to her dishonour, and equally to me
disloyal."   32
  Pis. What shall I need to draw my sword? the
    paper
Hath cut her throat already.—No; 't is slander,
Whose edge is sharper than the sword; whose tongue
Outvenoms all the worms of Nile; whose breath
Rides on the posting winds, and doth belie
All corners of the world: kings, queens, and states,
Maids, matrons, nay, the secrets of the grave
This viperous slander enters.—What cheer, madam?
  Imo. False to his bed! What is it to be false?   41
To lie in watch there, and to think on him?
To weep 'twixt clock and clock? if sleep charge
    nature,
To break it with a fearful dream of him,
And cry myself awake? that 's false to 's bed, is it?
  Pis. Alas, good lady!
  Imo. I false? Thy conscience witness, Iachimo:
Thou didst accuse him of incontinency;
Thou then look'dst like a villain; now, methinks,
Thy favour 's good enough.—Some jay of Italy,   50

Whose mother was her painting, hath betray'd him :
Poor I am stale, a garment out of fashion ;
And, for I am richer than to hang by the walls,
I must be ripp'd :—to pieces with me !—O !
Men's vows are women's traitors. All good seeming,
By thy revolt, O husband ! shall be thought
Put on for villainy ; not born where 't grows,
But worn, a bait for ladies.
    Pis.   Good madam, hear me.
    Imo. True honest men being heard, like false Æneas,
Were in his time thought false ; and Sinon's weeping
Did scandal many a holy tear ; took pity   61
From most true wretchedness : so thou, Posthumus,
Wilt lay the leaven on all proper men :
Goodly, and gallant, shall be false, and perjur'd,
From thy great fail.—Come, fellow, be thou honest :
Do thou thy master's bidding. When thou seest him,
A little witness my obedience : look !
I draw the sword myself : take it, and hit
The innocent mansion of my love, my heart.
Fear not ; 't is empty of all things but grief :   70
Thy master is not there, who was, indeed,
The riches of it. Do his bidding ; strike.
Thou may'st be valiant in a better cause,
But now thou seem'st a coward.
    Pis.   Hence, vile instrument !
Thou shalt not damn my hand.
    Imo.   Why, I must die ;
And if I do not by thy hand, thou art
No servant of thy master's. Against self-slaughter
There is a prohibition so divine,
That cravens my weak hand. Come, here 's my
       heart :
Something 's afore 't :—soft, soft ! we 'll no defence ; 80
Obedient as the scabbard.—What is here ?
The scriptures of the loyal Leonatus,
All turn'd to heresy ? Away, away,
Corrupters of my faith ! you shall no more
Be stomachers to my heart. Thus may poor fools
Believe false teachers : though those that are betray'd
Do feel the treason sharply, yet the traitor
Stands in worse case of woe.
And thou, Posthumus, thou that didst set up
My disobedience 'gainst the king my father,   90
And make me put into contempt the suits
Of princely fellows, shalt hereafter find
It is no act of common passage, but
A strain of rareness : and I grieve myself,
To think, when thou shalt be disedg'd by her
That now thou tir'st on, how thy memory
Will then be pang'd by me.—Pr'ythee, despatch :
The lamb entreats the butcher : where 's thy knife ?
Thou art too slow to do thy master's bidding,
When I desire it too.
    Pis.   O gracious lady !   100
Since I receiv'd command to do this business,
I have not slept one wink.
    Imo.   Do 't, and to bed then.
    Pis. I 'll wake mine eye-balls blind first.
    Imo.   Wherefore then
Didst undertake it ? Why hast thou abus'd
So many miles with a pretence ? this place ?
Mine action, and thine own ? our horses' labour ?
The time inviting thee ? the perturb'd court,
For my being absent ; whereunto I never
Purpose return ? Why hast thou gone so far,
To be unbent, when thou hast ta'en thy stand,   110
The elected deer before thee ?
    Pis.   But to win time,
To lose so bad employment ; in the which
I have consider'd of a course. Good lady,
Hear me with patience.
    Imo.   Talk thy tongue weary ; speak :
I have heard I am a strumpet ; and mine ear,
Therein false struck, can take no greater wound,
Nor tent, to bottom that. But speak.
    Pis.   Then, madam,
I thought you would not back again.
    Imo.   Most like,
Bringing me here to kill me.
    Pis.   Not so, neither :
But if I were as wise as honest, then   120

My purpose would prove well. It cannot be,
But that my master is abus'd :
Some villain, ay, and singular in his art,
Hath done you both this cursed injury.
    Imo. Some Roman courtesan ?
    Pis.   No, on my life.
I 'll give but notice you are dead, and send him
Some bloody sign of it ; for 't is commanded
I should do so : you shall be miss'd at court,
And that will well confirm it.
    Imo.   Why, good fellow,
What shall I do the while ? where bide ? how live ?
Or in my life what comfort, when I am   131
Dead to my husband ?
    Pis.   If you 'll back to the court,—
    Imo. No court, no father ; nor no more ado
With that harsh, noble, simple nothing,
That Cloten, whose love-suit hath been to me
As fearful as a siege.
    Pis.   If not at court,
Then not in Britain must you bide.
    Imo.   Where then ?
Hath Britain all the sun that shines ? Day, night,
Are they not but in Britain ? I' the world's volume
Our Britain seems as of it, but not in 't ;   140
In a great pool, a swan's nest. Pr'ythee, think
There 's livers out of Britain.
    Pis.   I am most glad
You think of other place. The ambassador,
Lucius the Roman, comes to Milford-Haven
To-morrow : now, if you could wear a mind
Dark as your fortune is, and but disguise
That which, to appear itself, must not yet be,
But by self-danger, you should tread a course
Pretty, and full of view : yea, haply, near
The residence of Posthumus ; so nigh, at least,   150
That, though his actions were not visible, yet
Report should render him hourly to your ear,
As truly as he moves.
    Imo.   O, for such means,
Though peril to my modesty, not death on 't,
I would adventure.
    Pis.   Well then, here 's the point :
You must forget to be a woman ; change
Command into obedience ; fear, and niceness,
(The handmaids of all women, or more truly,
Woman it pretty self,) into a waggish courage ;
Ready in gibes, quick-answer'd, saucy, and   160
As quarrellous as the weasel : nay, you must
Forget that rarest treasure of your cheek,
Exposing it (but, O, the harder heart !
Alack, no remedy !) to the greedy touch
Of common-kissing Titan ; and forget
Your laboursome and dainty trims, wherein
You made great Juno angry.
    Imo.   Nay, be brief :
I see into thy end, and am almost
A man already.
    Pis.   First, make yourself but like one.
Forethinking this, I have already fit   170
('T is in my cloak-bag) doublet, hat, hose, all
That answer to them : would you, in their serving,
And with what imitation you can borrow
From youth of such a season, 'fore noble Lucius
Present yourself, desire his service, tell him
Wherein you 're happy, (which you 'll make him know,
If that his head have ear in music,) doubtless
With joy he will embrace you ; for he 's honourable,
And, doubling that, most holy. Your means abroad,
You have me, rich ; and I will never fail   180
Beginning nor supplyment.
    Imo.   Thou art all the comfort
The gods will diet me with. Pr'ythee, away :
There 's more to be consider'd, but we 'll even
All that good time will give us. This attempt
I 'm soldier to, and will abide it with
A prince's courage. Away, I pr'ythee.
    Pis. Well, madam, we must take a short farewell,
Lest, being miss'd, I be suspected of
Your carriage from the court. My noble mistress,
Here is a box ; I had it from the queen :   190
What 's in 't is precious ; if you are sick at sea,

Or stomach-qualm'd at land, a dram of this
Will drive away distemper.—To some shade,
And fit you to your manhood.—May the gods
Direct you to the best!
  Imo.   Amen. I thank thee. [*Exeunt.*

Scene V.—A Room in Cymbeline's Palace.

Enter Cymbeline, Queen, Cloten, Lucius, *Lords,
and Attendants.*

Cym. Thus far; and so farewell.
Luc.   Thanks, royal sir.
My emperor hath wrote; I must from hence;
And am right sorry that I must report ye
My master's enemy.
Cym.   Our subjects, sir,
Will not endure his yoke; and for ourself
To show less sovereignty than they, must needs
Appear unkinglike.
Luc.   So, sir, I desire of you
A conduct over land to Milford-Haven.—
Madam, all joy befall your grace, and you!
Cym. My lords, you are appointed for that office; 10
The due of honour in no point omit.
So, farewell, noble Lucius.
Luc.   Your hand, my lord.
Clo. Receive it friendly; but from this time forth
I wear it as your enemy.
Luc.   Sir, the event
Is yet to name the winner. Fare you well.
Cym. Leave not the worthy Lucius, good my lords,
Till he have cross'd the Severn.—Happiness!
              [*Exeunt* Lucius *and Lords.*
Queen. He goes hence frowning; but it honours us,
That we have given him cause.
Clo.   'T is all the better:
Your valiant Britons have their wishes in it. 20
Cym. Lucius hath wrote already to the emperor
How it goes here. It fits us therefore, ripely,
Our chariots and our horsemen be in readiness:
The powers that he already hath in Gallia
Will soon be drawn to head, from whence he moves
His war for Britain.
Queen.   'T is not sleepy business,
But must be look'd to speedily, and strongly.
Cym. Our expectation that it would be thus
Hath made us forward. But, my gentle queen,
Where is our daughter? She hath not appear'd 30
Before the Roman, nor to us hath tender'd
The duty of the day. She looks us like
A thing more made of malice, than of duty:
We have noted it.—Call her before us, for
We have been too slight in sufferance.
                  [*Exit an Attendant.*
Queen.   Royal sir,
Since the exile of Posthumus, most retir'd
Hath her life been; the cure whereof, my lord,
'T is time must do. 'Beseech your majesty,
Forbear sharp speeches to her: she's a lady
So tender of rebukes, that words are strokes, 40
And strokes death to her.

Re-enter Attendant.

Cym.   Where is she, sir? How
Can her contempt be answer'd?
Atten.   Please you, sir,
Her chambers are all lock'd; and there's no answer
That will be given to the loud'st of noise we make.
Queen. My lord, when last I went to visit her,
She pray'd me to excuse her keeping close;
Whereto constrain'd by her infirmity,
She should that duty leave unpaid to you,
Which daily she was bound to proffer: this
She wish'd me to make known, but our great court 50
Made me to blame in memory.
Cym.   Her doors lock'd?
Not seen of late? Grant, heavens, that which I fear
Prove false! [*Exit.*
Queen.   Son, I say, follow the king.

Clo. That man of hers, Pisanio, her old servant,
I have not seen these two days.
Queen.   Go, look after.—[*Exit* Cloten.
Pisanio, thou that stand'st so for Posthumus!—
He hath a drug of mine: I pray, his absence
Proceed by swallowing that, for he believes
It is a thing most precious. But for her,
Where is she gone? Haply, despair hath seiz'd her; 60
Or, wing'd with fervour of her love, she's flown
To her desir'd Posthumus. Gone she is
To death, or to dishonour; and my end
Can make good use of either: she being down,
I have the placing of the British crown.

Re-enter Cloten.

How now, my son?
Clo.   'T is certain, she is fled.
Go in, and cheer the king: he rages; none
Dare come about him.
Queen. [*Aside.*]   All the better: may
This night forestall him of the coming day! [*Exit.*
Clo. I love, and hate her, for she's fair and royal, 70
And that she has all courtly parts, more exquisite
Than lady, ladies, woman: from every one
The best she hath, and she, of all compounded,
Outsells them all. I love her therefore. But,
Disdaining me, and throwing favours on
The low Posthumus, slanders so her judgment,
That what's else rare is chok'd; and, in that point,
I will conclude to hate her; nay, indeed,
To be reveng'd upon her: for, when fools
Shall—

Enter Pisanio.

        Who is here? What! are you packing, sirrah?
Come hither. Ah, you precious pander! Villain, 81
Where is thy lady? In a word, or else
Thou art straightway with the fiends.
Pis.   O, good my lord!
Clo. Where is thy lady? or, by Jupiter,
I will not ask again. Close villain,
I'll have this secret from thy heart, or rip
Thy heart to find it. Is she with Posthumus?
From whose so many weights of baseness cannot
A dram of worth be drawn.
Pis.   Alas, my lord!
How can she be with him? When was she miss'd? 90
He is in Rome.
Clo.   Where is she, sir? Come nearer;
No further halting: satisfy me home,
What is become of her?
Pis. O, my all-worthy lord!
Clo.   All-worthy villain!
Discover where thy mistress is, at once,
At the next word:—no more of worthy lord!—
Speak, or thy silence on the instant is
Thy condemnation and thy death.
Pis.   Then, sir,
This paper is the history of my knowledge
Touching her flight. [*Presenting a letter.*
Clo.   Let's see't.—I will pursue her
Even to Augustus' throne.
Pis. [*Aside.*]   Or this, or perish. 101
She's far enough; and what he learns by this,
May prove his travel, not her danger.
Clo.   Hum!
Pis. [*Aside.*] I'll write to my lord she's dead. O
    Imogen,
Safe may'st thou wander, safe return again!
Clo. Sirrah, is this letter true?
Pis. Sir, as I think. 107
Clo. It is Posthumus' hand; I know't.—Sirrah, if
thou wouldst not be a villain, but do me true service,
undergo those employments, wherein I should have
cause to use thee, with a serious industry,—that is,
what villainy soe'er I bid thee do, to perform it
directly and truly,—I would think thee an honest
man; thou shouldst neither want my means for thy
relief, nor my voice for thy preferment.
Pis. Well, my good lord.
Clo. Wilt thou serve me? For since patiently and
constantly thou hast stuck to the bare fortune of that

beggar Posthumus, thou canst not in the course of
gratitude but be a diligent follower of mine. Wilt
thou serve me?   121
Pis. Sir, I will.
Clo. Give me thy hand; here's my purse. Hast
any of thy late master's garments in thy possession?
Pis. I have, my lord, at my lodging, the same suit
he wore when he took leave of my lady and mistress.
Clo. The first service thou dost me, fetch that suit
hither: let it be thy first service; go.   128
Pis. I shall, my lord.   [*Exit.*
Clo. Meet thee at Milford-Haven!—I forgot to ask
him one thing; I'll remember 't anon.—Even there,
thou villain, Posthumus, will I kill thee.—I would
these garments were come. She said upon a time,
(the bitterness of it I now belch from my heart,) that
she held the very garment of Posthumus in more
respect than my noble and natural person, together
with the adornment of my qualities. With that suit
upon my back, will I ravish her: first kill him, and in
her eyes; there shall she see my valour, which will
then be a torment to her contempt. He on the ground,
my speech of insultment ended on his dead body,—and
when my lust hath dined, (which, as I say, to vex her,
I will execute in the clothes that she so praised,) to
the court I'll knock her back, foot her home again.
She hath despised me rejoicingly, and I'll be merry in
my revenge.

Re-enter PISANIO, *with the clothes.*

Be those the garments?
Pis. Ay, my noble lord.
Clo. How long is't since she went to Milford-
Haven?   150
Pis. She can scarce be there yet.
Clo. Bring this apparel to my chamber; that is the
second thing that I have commanded thee: the third
is, that thou wilt be a voluntary mute to my design.
Be but duteous, and true preferment shall tender
itself to thee.—My revenge is now at Milford:—'would
I had wings to follow it.—Come, and be true. [*Exit.*
Pis. Thou bidd'st me to my loss: for, true to thee,
Were to prove false, which I will never be   160
To him that is most true.—To Milford go,
And find not her whom thou pursu'st. Flow, flow,
You heavenly blessings, on her! This fool's speed
Be cross'd with slowness: labour be his meed! [*Exit.*

SCENE VI.—Before the Cave of BELARIUS.

Enter IMOGEN, *in boy's clothes.*

Imo. I see, a man's life is a tedious one:
I have tir'd myself, and for two nights together
Have made the ground my bed: I should be sick,
But that my resolution helps me.—Milford,
When from the mountain-top Pisanio show'd thee,
Thou wast within a ken. O Jove! I think,
Foundations fly the wretched; such, I mean,
Where they should be reliev'd. Two beggars told
me,
I could not miss my way: will poor folks lie,
That have afflictions on them, knowing 't is   10
A punishment, or trial? Yes; no wonder,
When rich ones scarce tell true: to lapse in fulness
Is sorer, than to lie for need; and falsehood
Is worse in kings, than beggars.—My dear lord!
Thou art one o' the false ones. Now I think on thee,
My hunger 's gone; but even before, I was
At point to sink for food.—But what is this?
Here is a path to 't: 't is some savage hold:
I were best not call; I dare not call; yet famine,
Ere clean it o'erthrow nature, makes it valiant.   20
Plenty, and peace, breeds cowards; hardness ever
Of hardiness is mother.—Ho! Who's here?
If anything that's civil, speak; if savage,
Take, or lend.—Ho!—No answer? then, I'll enter.
Best draw my sword; and if mine enemy
But fear the sword like me, he'll scarcely look on 't.
Such a foe, good heavens!   [*Enters the cave.*

Enter BELARIUS, GUIDERIUS, *and* ARVIRAGUS.

Bel. You, Polydore, have prov'd best woodman,
and
Are master of the feast: Cadwal, and I,
Will play the cook and servant; 't is our match: 30
The sweat of industry would dry, and die,

Imo. "Best draw my sword; and if mine enemy
But fear the sword like me, he'll scarcely look on 't."

But for the end it works to. Come, our stomachs
Will make what's homely, savoury: weariness
Can snore upon the flint, when resty sloth
Finds the down pillow hard.—Now, peace be here,
Poor house, that keep'st thyself!
Gui.   I am throughly weary.
Arv. I am weak with toil, yet strong in appetite.
Gui. There is cold meat i' the cave; we'll browse
on that,
Whilst what we have kill'd be cook'd.
Bel. [*Looking into the cave.*]   Stay: come not in.
But that it eats our victuals, I should think   40
Here were a fairy.
Gui.   What's the matter, sir?
Bel. By Jupiter, an angel! or, if not,
An earthly paragon!—Behold divineness
No elder than a boy!

Re-enter IMOGEN.

Imo. Good masters, harm me not:
Before I enter'd here, I call'd; and thought
To have begg'd, or bought what I have took. Good
troth,
I have stol'n nought; nor would not, though I had
found
Gold strew'd i' the floor. Here's money for my meat:
I would have left it on the board, so soon   50
As I had made my meal, and parted
With prayers for the provider.
Gui.   Money, youth?
Arv. All gold and silver rather turn to dirt!
As 't is no better reckon'd, but of those
Who worship dirty gods.
Imo.   I see, you're angry.
Know, if you kill me for my fault, I should
Have died, had I not made it.
Bel.   Whither bound?
Imo. To Milford-Haven.
Bel.   What's your name?

Imo. Fidele, sir. I have a kinsman, who
Is bound for Italy : he embark'd at Milford ;   60
To whom being going, almost spent with hunger,
I am fall'n in this offence.
   Bel.   Pr'ythee, fair youth.

He is a man : I 'll love him as my brother ;   70
And such a welcome as I 'd give to him
After long absence, such is yours.—Most welcome !
Be sprightly, for you fall 'mongst friends.
   Imo.   'Mongst friends !

IMOGEN IN THE CAVE.

Think us no churls, nor measure our good minds
By this rude place we live in. Well encounter'd !
'T is almost night : you shall have better cheer
Ere you depart ; and thanks, to stay and eat it.—
Boys, bid him welcome.
   Gui.   Were you a woman, youth,
I should woo hard, but be your groom.—In honesty,
I bid for you, as I do buy.
   Arv.   I 'll make 't my comfort,

[*Aside.*] If brothers ! 'Would it had been so, that
       they
Had been my father's sons : then had my prize
Been less ; and so more equal ballasting
To thee, Posthumus.
   Bel.   He wrings at some distress.
   Gui. 'Would I could free 't !
   Arv.   Or I ; whate'er it be,
What pain it cost, what danger. Gods !

Bel.   Hark, boys.   [*Whispering.*
Imo. Great men,   80
That had a court no bigger than this cave,
That did attend themselves, and had the virtue
Which their own conscience seal'd them, (laying by
That nothing gift of differing multitudes,)
Could not out-peer these twain.   Pardon me, gods!
I 'd change my sex to be companion with them,
Since Leonatus' false.
Bel.   It shall be so.
Boys, we 'll go dress our hunt.—Fair youth, come in :
Discourse is heavy, fasting ; when we have supp'd,
We'll mannerly demand thee of thy story,   90
So far as thou wilt speak it.
Gui.   Pray, draw near.
Arv. The night to the owl, and morn to the lark, less welcome.
Imo. Thanks, sir.
Arv.   I pray, draw near.   [*Exeunt.*

SCENE VII.—Rome. A Public Place.

Enter two Senators and Tribunes.

1 Sen. This is the tenor of the emperor's writ :
That since the common men are now in action
'Gainst the Pannonians and Dalmatians,
And that the legions now in Gallia are
Full weak to undertake our wars against
The fall'n-off Britons, that we do incite
The gentry to this business. He creates
Lucius proconsul : and to you, the tribunes,
For this immediate levy, he commends
His absolute commission. Long live Cæsar !   10
Tri. Is Lucius general of the forces ?
2 Sen.   Ay.
Tri. Remaining now in Gallia ?
1 Sen.   With those legions
Which I have spoke of, whereunto your levy
Must be suppliant : the words of your commission
Will tie you to the numbers, and the time
Of their despatch.
Tri.   We will discharge our duty. [*Exeunt.*

ACT IV.

SCENE I.—The Forest, near the Cave.

Enter CLOTEN.

Cloten.
I AM near to the place where they should meet, if Pisanio have mapped it truly. How fit his garments serve me! Why should his mistress, who was made by him that made the tailor, not be fit too? the rather (saving reverence of the word) for 'tis said, a woman's fitness comes by fits. Therein I must play the workman. I dare speak it to myself, (for it is not vain-glory for a man and his glass to confer in his own chamber,) I mean, the lines of my body are as well drawn as his ; no less young, more strong, not beneath him in fortunes, beyond him in the advantage of the time, above him in birth, alike conversant in general services, and more remarkable in single oppositions : yet this imperseverant thing loves him in my despite. What mortality is! Posthumus, thy head, which now is growing upon thy shoulders, shall within this hour be off, thy mistress enforced, thy garments cut to pieces before thy face ; and all this done, spurn her home to her father, who may, haply, be a little angry for my so rough usage, but my mother, having power of his testiness, shall turn all into my commendations. My horse is tied up safe : out, sword, and to a sore purpose ! Fortune, put them into my hand ! This is the very description of their meeting-place ; and the fellow dares not deceive me.   [*Exit.*

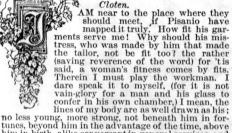

SCENE II.—Before the Cave.

Enter, from the cave, BELARIUS, GUIDERIUS, ARVIRAGUS, *and* IMOGEN.

Bel. [*To* IMOGEN.] You are not well : remain here in the cave ;
We 'll come to you after hunting.
Arv. [*To* IMOGEN.]   Brother, stay here :
Are we not brothers?

Imo.   So man and man should be ;
But clay and clay differs in dignity,
Whose dust is both alike. I am very sick.

Clo. "This is the very description of their meeting-place."

Gui. Go you to hunting ; I 'll abide with him.
Imo. So sick I am not,—yet I am not well ;
But not so citizen a wanton, as
To seem to die, ere sick. So please you, leave me ;
Stick to your journal course : the breach of custom   10
Is breach of all. I am ill ; but your being by me
Cannot amend me : society is no comfort

To one not sociable. I am not very sick,
Since I can reason of it: pray you, trust me here ;
I 'll rob none but myself ; and let me die,
Stealing so poorly.
 Gui. I love thee ; I have spoke it ;
How much the quantity, the weight as much,
As I do love my father.
 Bel.   What ! how ? how ?
 Arv. If it be sin to say so, sir, I yoke me
In my good brother's fault : I know not why 20
I love this youth ; and I have heard you say,
Love's reason 's without reason : the bier at door,
And a demand who is 't shall die, I 'd say,
My father, not this youth.
 Bel. [*Aside.*] O noble strain !
O worthiness of nature ! breed of greatness !
Cowards father cowards, and base things sire base :
Nature hath meal and bran, contempt and grace.
I'm not their father ; yet who this should be,
Doth miracle itself, lov'd before me.—
'T is the ninth hour o' the morn.
 Arv.   Brother, farewell. 30
 Imo. I wish ye sport.
 Arv. You health.—So please you, sir.
 Imo. [*Aside.*] These are kind creatures. Gods, what
    lies I have heard !
Our courtiers say, all 's savage but at court :
Experience, O ! thou disprov'st report.
The imperious seas breed monsters ; for the dish,
Poor tributary rivers as sweet fish.
I am sick still ; heart-sick.—Pisanio,
I 'll now taste of thy drug. [*Swallows some.*
 Gui. I could not stir him :
He said, he was gentle, but unfortunate ;
Dishonestly afflicted, but yet honest. 40
 Arv. Thus did he answer me ; yet said, hereafter
I might know more.
 Bel. To the field, to the field !—
We 'll leave you for this time ; go in, and rest.
 Arv. We 'll not be long away.
 Bel.   Pray, be not sick,
For you must be our housewife.
 Imo. Well, or ill,
I am bound to you.
 Bel. And shalt be ever. [*Exit* IMOGEN.
This youth, howe'er distress'd, appears he hath had
Good ancestors.
 Arv. How angel-like he sings !
 Gui. But his neat cookery ! He cut our roots
In characters ;
And sauc'd our broths, as Juno had been sick, 50
And he her dieter.
 Arv. Nobly he yokes
A smiling with a sigh, as if the sigh
Was that it was, for not being such a smile ;
The smile mocking the sigh, that it would fly
From so divine a temple, to commix
With winds that sailors rail at.
 Gui. I do note,
That grief and patience, rooted in him both,
Mingle their spurs together.
 Arv. Grow, patience !
And let the stinking elder, grief, untwine
His perishing root with the increasing vine ! 60
 Bel. It is great morning. Come away !—Who 's
   there ?

    Enter CLOTEN.

 Clo. I cannot find those runagates : that villain
Hath mock'd me.—I am faint.
 Bel. Those runagates !
Means he not us ? I partly know him ; 't is
Cloten, the son o' the queen. I fear some ambush.
I saw him not these many years, and yet
I know 't is he.—We are held as outlaws :—hence !
 Gui. He is but one. You and my brother search
What companies are near ; pray you, away ;
Let me alone with him.
   [*Exeunt* BELARIUS *and* ARVIRAGUS.
 Clo. Soft ! What are you 70
That fly me thus ? some villain mountaineers ?
I have heard of such.—What slave art thou ?

 Gui.   A thing
More slavish did I ne'er than answering
A slave without a knock.
 Clo. Thou art a robber,
A law-breaker, a villain. Yield thee, thief.
 Gui. To who ? to thee ? What art thou ? Have not I
An arm as big as thine ? a heart as big ?
Thy words, I grant, are bigger ; for I wear not
My dagger in my mouth. Say, what thou art,
Why I should yield to thee ?
 Clo. Thou villain base, 80
Know'st me not by my clothes ?
 Gui. No, nor thy tailor, rascal,
Who is thy grandfather : he made those clothes,
Which, as it seems, make thee.
 Clo. Thou precious varlet,
My tailor made them not.
 Gui. Hence then, and thank
The man that gave them thee. Thou art some fool ;
I am loath to beat thee.
 Clo. Thou injurious thief,
Hear but my name, and tremble.
 Gui. What 's thy name ?
 Clo. Cloten, thou villain.
 Gui. Cloten, thou double villain, be thy name,
I cannot tremble at it : were it toad, or adder, spider,
'T would move me sooner.
 Clo. To thy further fear, 91
Nay, to thy mere confusion, thou shalt know
I 'm son to the queen.
 Gui. I am sorry for 't ; not seeming
So worthy as thy birth.
 Clo. Art not afeard ?
 Gui. Those that I reverence, those I fear, the wise :
At fools I laugh, not fear them.
 Clo. Die the death.
When I have slain thee with my proper hand,
I 'll follow those that even now fled hence,
And on the gates of Lud's town set your heads.
Yield, rustic mountaineer. [*Exeunt, fighting.*

 Re-enter BELARIUS *and* ARVIRAGUS.

 Bel. No companies abroad ? 101
 Arv. None in the world. You did mistake him,
   sure.
 Bel. I cannot tell : long is it since I saw him,
But time hath nothing blurr'd those lines of favour
Which then he wore : the snatches in his voice,
And burst of speaking, were as his. I am absolute,
'T was very Cloten.
 Arv. In this place we left them :
I wish my brother make good time with him,
You say he is so fell.
 Bel. Being scarce made up, 110
I mean, to man, he had not apprehension
Of roaring terrors ; for the effect of judgment
Is oft the cause of fear. But see, thy brother.

 Re-enter GUIDERIUS, *with* CLOTEN'S *head.*

 Gui. This Cloten was a fool, an empty purse,
There was no money in 't. Not Hercules
Could have knock'd out his brains, for he had none ;
Yet I not doing this, the fool had borne
My head, as I do his.
 Bel. What hast thou done ?
 Gui. I am perfect, what : cut off one Cloten's head,
Son to the queen, after his own report ;
Who call'd me traitor, mountaineer ; and swore, 120
With his own single hand he 'd take us in,
Displace our heads, where (thank the gods !) they
   grow,
And set them on Lud's town.
 Bel. We are all undone.
 Gui. Why, worthy father, what have we to lose,
But, that he swore to take, our lives ? The law
Protects not us : then, why should we be tender,
To let an arrogant piece of flesh threat us ;
Play judge, and executioner, all himself,
For we do fear the law ? What company
Discover you abroad ?
 Bel. No single soul 130
Can we set eye on, but in all safe reason

He must have some attendants. Though his humour
Was nothing but mutation; ay, and that
From one bad thing to worse; not frenzy, not
Absolute madness, could so far have rav'd,
To bring him here alone. Although, perhaps,
It may be heard at court, that such as we
Cave here, hunt here, are outlaws, and in time
May make some stronger head: the which he hearing,
(As it is like him,) might break out, and swear   140
He'd fetch us in; yet 't is not probable
To come alone, either he so undertaking,
Or they so suffering: then on good ground we
    fear,
If we do fear this body hath a tail
More perilous than the head.
    Arv.   Let ordinance
Come as the gods foresay it: howsoe'er,
My brother hath done well.
    Bel.   I had no mind
To hunt this day: the boy Fidele's sickness
Did make my way long forth.
    Gui.   With his own sword,
Which he did wave against my throat, I have
    ta'en   150
His head from him: I'll throw 't into the creek
Behind our rock; and let it to the sea,
And tell the fishes, he 's the queen's son, Cloten:
That 's all I reck.   [*Exit.*
    Bel.   I fear, 't will be reveng'd.
'Would, Polydore, thou hadst not done 't; though
    valour
Becomes thee well enough.
    Arv.   'Would I had done 't,
So the revenge alone pursu'd me!—Polydore,
I love thee brotherly, but envy much
Thou hast robb'd me of this deed: I would, revenges,
That possible strength might meet, would seek us
    through,   160
And put us to our answer.
    Bel.   Well, 't is done.
We'll hunt no more to-day, nor seek for danger
Where there 's no profit. I pr'ythee, to our rock:
You and Fidele play the cooks; I'll stay
Till hasty Polydore return, and bring him
To dinner presently.
    Arv.   Poor sick Fidele!
I'll willingly to him: to gain his colour,
I'd let a parish of such Clotens blood,
And praise myself for charity.   [*Exit.*
    Bel.   O thou goddess,
Thou divine Nature, how thyself thou blazon'st   170
In these two princely boys! They are as gentle
As zephyrs, blowing below the violet,
Not wagging his sweet head; and yet as rough,
Their royal blood enchaf'd, as the rud'st wind,
That by the top doth take the mountain pine,
And make him stoop to the vale. 'T is wonder,
That an invisible instinct should frame them
To royalty unlearn'd, honour untaught,
Civility not seen from other, valour
That wildly grows in them, but yields a crop   180
As if it had been sow'd! Yet still it 's strange,
What Cloten's being here to us portends,
Or what his death will bring us.

Re-enter GUIDERIUS.

    Gui.   Where 's my brother?
I have sent Cloten's clotpoll down the stream,
In embassy to his mother: his body 's hostage
For his return.   [*Solemn music.*
    Bel.   My ingenious instrument!
Hark, Polydore, it sounds; but what occasion
Hath Cadwal now to give it motion? Hark!
    Gui. Is he at home?
    Bel.   He went hence even now.
    Gui. What does he mean? since death of my dear'st
    mother   190
It did not speak before. All solemn things
Should answer solemn accidents. The matter?
Triumphs for nothing, and lamenting toys,
Is jollity for apes, and grief for boys.
Is Cadwal mad?

Re-enter ARVIRAGUS, *bearing* IMOGEN *as dead in his
    arms.*

    Bel.   Look! here he comes,
And brings the dire occasion in his arms,
Of what we blame him for.
    Arv.   The bird is dead,
That we have made so much on. I had rather
Have skipp'd from sixteen years of age to sixty,
To have turn'd my leaping-time into a crutch,   200
Than have seen this.

Gui.   "Let us bury him,
And not protract with admiration what
        Is now due debt."

    Gui.   O sweetest, fairest lily!
My brother wears thee not the one half so well,
As when thou grew'st thyself.
    Bel.   O melancholy!
Who ever yet could sound thy bottom? find
The ooze, to show what coast thy sluggish crare
Might easiliest harbour in?—Thou blessed thing!
Jove knows what man thou might'st have made;
    but I,
Thou diedst, a most rare boy, of melancholy.—
How found you him?
    Arv.   Stark, as you see: 210
Thus smiling, as some fly had tickled slumber,
Not as death's dart, being laugh'd at; his right cheek
Reposing on a cushion.
    Gui.   Where?
    Arv.   O' the floor;
His arms thus leagu'd: I thought he slept, and put
My clouted brogues from off my feet, whose rudeness
Answer'd my steps too loud.
    Gui.   Why, he but sleeps;
If he be gone, he'll make his grave a bed:
With female fairies will his tomb be haunted,
And worms will not come to thee.
    Arv.   With fairest flowers,
Whilst summer lasts, and I live here, Fidele,
I'll sweeten thy sad grave: thou shalt not lack   220
The flower that 's like thy face, pale primrose, nor
The azur'd hare-bell, like thy veins; no, nor
The leaf of eglantine, whom not to slander,
Out-sweeten'd not thy breath: the ruddock would,
With charitable bill, (O bill, sore-shaming
Those rich-left heirs, that let their fathers lie
Without a monument!) bring thee all this;

Yea, and furr'd moss besides, when flowers are none,
To winter-ground thy corse.

Gui.   Pr'ythee, have done;
And do not play in wench-like words with that   230
Which is so serious. Let us bury him,
And not protract with admiration what
Is now due debt.—To the grave.

Arv.   Say, where shall 's lay him?

Gui. By good Euriphile, our mother.

Arv.   Be 't so:
And let us, Polydore, though now our voices
Have got the mannish crack, sing him to the
    ground.
As once our mother; use like note, and words,
Save that Euriphile must be Fidele.

Gui. Cadwal,
I cannot sing: I 'll weep, and word it with thee;
For notes of sorrow, out of tune, are worse 241
Than priests and fanes that lie.

Arv.   We 'll speak it then.

Bel. Great griefs, I see, medicine the less; for
    Cloten
Is quite forgot. He was a queen's son, boys;
And, though he came our enemy, remember,
He was paid for that: though mean and mighty,
    rotting
Together, have one dust, yet reverence
(That angel of the world) doth make distinction
Of place 'tween high and low. Our foe was
    princely,
And though you took his life, as being our foe,
Yet bury him as a prince.

Gui.   Pray you, fetch him hither.
Thersites' body is as good as Ajax, 252
When neither are alive.

Arv.   If you 'll go fetch him,
We 'll say our song the whilst.—Brother, begin.
              [*Exit* BELARIUS.

Gui. Nay, Cadwal, we must lay his head to the east;
My father hath a reason for 't.

Arv.   'T is true.

Gui. Come on then, and remove him.

Arv.   So.—Begin.

         SONG.

Gui. Fear no more the heat o' the sun,
    Nor the furious winter's rages;
  Thou thy worldly task hast done,
    Home art gone, and ta'en thy wages: 260
  Golden lads and girls all must,
    As chimney-sweepers, come to dust.

Arv. Fear no more the frown o' the great,
    Thou art past the tyrant's stroke;
  Care no more to clothe, and eat;
    To thee the reed is as the oak:
  The sceptre, learning, physic, must
    All follow this, and come to dust.

Gui. Fear no more the lightning-flash, 270
Arv.   Nor the all-dreaded thunder-tone;
Gui. Fear not slander, censure rash;
Arv.   Thou hast finish'd joy and moan:
Both. All lovers young, all lovers must
    Consign to thee, and come to dust.

Gui. No exorciser harm thee!
Arv. Nor no witchcraft charm thee!
Gui. Ghost unlaid forbear thee!
Arv. Nothing ill come near thee!
Both. Quiet consummation have; 280
    And renowned be thy grave!

Re-enter BELARIUS, *with the body of* CLOTEN.

Gui. We have done our obsequies. Come, lay him
    down.

Bel. Here 's a few flowers; but 'bout midnight,
    more:
The herbs that have on them cold dew o' the night,
Are strewings fitt'st for graves.—Upon their faces.—
You were as flowers, now wither'd; even so
These herblets shall, which we upon you strew.—
Come on, away; apart upon our knees.

The ground, that gave them first, has them again:
Their pleasures here are past, so is their pain. 290
    [*Exeunt* BELARIUS, GUIDERIUS, *and* ARVIRAGUS.

Imo. [*Awaking.*] Yes, sir, to Milford-Haven; which
    is the way?—
I thank you.—By yond bush?—Pray, how far thither?
'Ods pittikins!—can it be six miles yet?—
I have gone all night.—Faith, I 'll lie down and sleep.
But, soft! no bedfellow.—O gods and goddesses!
    [*Seeing the body of* CLOTEN.

Imo. "O, my lord, my lord!"

These flowers are like the pleasures of the world;
This bloody man, the care on 't.—I hope, I dream;
For so I thought I was a cave-keeper,
And cook to honest creatures; but 't is not so: 300
'T was but a bolt of nothing, shot at nothing,
Which the brain makes of fumes. Our very eyes
Are sometimes like our judgments, blind. Good
    faith,
I tremble still with fear: but if there be
Yet left in heaven as small a drop of pity
As a wren's eye, fear'd gods, a part of it!
The dream 's here still: even when I wake, it is
Without me, as within me; not imagin'd, felt.
A headless man!—The garment of Posthumus!
I know the shape of his leg; this is his hand; 310
His foot Mercurial; his Martial thigh;
The brawns of Hercules: but his Jovial face—
Murder in heaven?—How?—'T is gone.—Pisanio,
All curses madded Hecuba gave the Greeks,
And mine to boot, be darted on thee! Thou,
Conspir'd with that irregulous devil, Cloten,
Hast here cut off my lord.—To write and read
Be henceforth treacherous!—Damn'd Pisanio
Hath with his forged letters,—damn'd Pisanio—
From this most bravest vessel of the world 320
Struck the main-top!—O Posthumus! alas,
Where is thy head? where 's that? Ah me! where 's
    that?
Pisanio might have kill'd thee at the heart,
And left this head on.—How should this be? Pisanio?
'T is he, and Cloten: malice and lucre in them
Have laid this woe here. O! 't is pregnant, pregnant.
The drug he gave me, which, he said, was precious
And cordial to me, have I not found it
Murderous to the senses? That confirms it home:
This is Pisanio's deed, and Cloten's: O!—
Give colour to my pale cheek with thy blood, 330
That we the horrider may seem to those
Which chance to find us. O, my lord, my lord!
    [*Falls on the body.*

Enter LUCIUS, *a Captain and other Officers,
and a Soothsayer.*

Cap. To them the legions garrison'd in Gallia,
After your will, have cross'd the sea; attending
You here at Milford-Haven, with your ships:
They are in readiness.

Luc.   But what from Rome?
Cap. The senate hath stirr'd up the confiners,
And gentlemen of Italy : most willing spirits,
That promise noble service, and they come
Under the conduct of bold Iachimo,   340
Sienna's brother.
Luc.   When expect you them?
Cap. With the next benefit o' the wind.
Luc.   This forwardness
Makes our hopes fair. Command, our present
            numbers
Be muster'd ; bid the captains looks to 't.—Now, sir,
What have you dream'd of late of this war's purpose?
Sooth. Last night the very gods show'd me a vision,
(I fast, and pray'd, for their intelligence,) thus :—
I saw Jove's bird, the Roman eagle, wing'd
From the spungy south to this part of the west,
There vanish'd in the sunbeams : which portends 350
(Unless my sins abuse my divination)
Success to the Roman host.
Luc.   Dream often so,
And never false.—Soft, ho ! what trunk is here.
Without his top? The ruin speaks, that sometime
It was a worthy building.—How ! a page!—
Or dead, or sleeping on him? But dead, rather ;
For nature doth abhor to make his bed
With the defunct, or sleep upon the dead.—
Let 's see the boy's face.
Cap.   He 's alive, my lord.
Luc. He 'll then instruct us of this body.—Young
            one,   360
Inform us of thy fortunes ; for, it seems
They crave to be demanded. Who is this,
Thou mak'st thy bloody pillow? Or who was he,
That, otherwise than noble nature did,
Hath alter'd that good picture? What's thy interest
In this sad wrack? How came it? Who is it?
What art thou?
Imo.   I am nothing : or if not,
Nothing to be were better. This was my master,
A very valiant Briton and a good,
That here by mountaineers lies slain.—Alas !   370
There is no more such masters : I may wander
From east to occident, cry out for service,
Try many, all good, serve truly, never
Find such another master.
Luc.   'Lack, good youth !
Thou mov'st no less with thy complaining, than
Thy master in bleeding. Say his name, good friend.
Imo. Richard du Champ. [*Aside.*] If I do lie, and
            do
No harm by it, though the gods hear, I hope
They 'll pardon it.—Say you, sir?
Luc. Thy name?   380
Imo. Fidele, sir.
Luc. Thou dost approve thyself the very same.
Thy name well fits thy faith ; thy faith thy name.
Wilt take thy chance with me? I will not say,
Thou shalt be so well master'd, but, be sure,
No less belov'd. The Roman emperor's letters,
Sent by a consul to me, should not sooner,
Than thine own worth, prefer thee. Go with me.
Imo. I 'll follow, sir. But first, an't please the
            gods,
I 'll hide my master from the flies, as deep   390
As these poor pickaxes can dig : and when
With wild wood-leaves and weeds I ha' strew'd his
            grave,
And on it said a century of prayers,
Such as I can, twice o'er, I 'll weep, and sigh ;
And, leaving so his service, follow you,
So please you entertain me.
Luc.   Ay, good youth ;
And rather father thee, than master thee.—
My friends,
The boy hath taught us manly duties : let us
Find out the prettiest daisied plot we can,   400
And make him with our pikes and partisans
A grave : come, arm him.—Boy, he is preferr'd
By thee to us, and he shall be interr'd,
As soldiers can. Be cheerful ; wipe thine eyes :
Some falls are means the happier to arise. [*Exeunt.*

SCENE III.—A Room in CYMBELINE'S Palace.

Enter CYMBELINE, *Lords,* PISANIO, *and Attendants.*
Cym. Again ; and bring me word how 'tis with her.
                                    [*Exit an Attendant.*
A fever with the absence of her son ;
A madness, of which her life 's in danger.—Heavens,
How deeply you at once do touch me ! Imogen,
The great part of my comfort, gone ; my queen
Upon a desperate bed, and in a time
When fearful wars point at me ; her son gone,
So needful for this present : it strikes me, past
The hope of comfort.—But for thee, fellow,
Who needs must know of her departure, and   10
Dost seem so ignorant, we 'll enforce it from thee
By a sharp torture.
Pis.   Sir, my life is yours,
I humbly set it at your will ; but, for my mistress,
I nothing know where she remains, why gone,
Nor when she purposes return. 'Beseech your
            highness,
Hold me your loyal servant.
1 Lord.   Good my liege,
The day that she was missing he was here :
I dare be bound he 's true, and shall perform
All parts of his subjection loyally. For Cloten,
There wants no diligence in seeking him,   20
And will, no doubt, be found.
Cym.   The time is troublesome.
[*To* PISANIO.] We 'll slip you for a season ; but our
            jealousy
Does yet depend.
1 Lord.   So please your majesty,
The Roman legions, all from Gallia drawn,
Are landed on your coast, with a supply
Of Roman gentlemen, by the senate sent.
Cym. Now for the counsel of my son and queen !
I am amaz'd with matter.
1 Lord.   Good my liege,
Your preparation can affront no less
Than what you hear of : come more, for more you 're
            ready.   30
The want is, but to put those powers in motion,
That long to move.
Cym.   I thank you. Let 's withdraw
And meet the time, as it seeks us. We fear not
What can from Italy annoy us, but
We grieve at chances here.—Away !
                                    [*Exeunt all but* PISANIO.
Pis. I heard no letter from my master, since
I wrote him Imogen was slain : 'tis strange :
Nor hear I from my mistress, who did promise
To yield me often tidings ; neither know I
What is betid to Cloten ; but remain   40
Perplex'd in all : the heavens still must work.
Wherein I am false, I am honest ; not true, to be true.
These present wars shall find I love my country,
Even to the note o' the king, or I 'll fall in them.
All other doubts, by time let them be clear'd ;
Fortune brings in some boats, that are not steer'd.
                                    [*Exit.*

SCENE IV.—Before the Cave.

Enter BELARIUS, GUIDERIUS, *and* ARVIRAGUS.
Gui. The noise is round about us.
Bel.   Let us from it.
Arv. What pleasure, sir, find we in life, to lock it
From action and adventure?
Gui.   Nay, what hope
Have we in hiding us? this way, the Romans
Must or for Britons slay us, or receive us
For barbarous and unnatural revolts
During their use, and slay us after.
Bel.   Sons,
We 'll higher to the mountains ; there secure us.
To the king's party there 's no going : newness
Of Cloten's death (we being not known, not muster'd
Among the bands) may drive us to a render   11
Where we have liv'd ; and so extort from 's that
Which we have done, whose answer would be death
Drawn on with torture.

Gui.   This is, sir, a doubt,
In such a time nothing becoming you,
Nor satisfying us.
    Arv.   It is not likely,
That when they hear the Roman horses neigh,
Behold their quarter'd fires, have both their eyes
And ears so cloy'd importantly as now,
That they will waste their time upon our note,   20
To know from whence we are.
    Bel.   O, I am known
Of many in the army: many years,
Though Cloten then but young, you see, not wore him
From my remembrance. And, besides, the king
Hath not deserv'd my service, nor your loves,
Who find in my exile the want of breeding,
The certainty of this hard life; aye hopeless
To have the courtesy your cradle promis'd,
But to be still hot summer's tanlings, and
The shrinking slaves of winter.
    Gui.   Than be so,   30
Better to cease to be. Pray, sir, to the army:
I and my brother are not known; yourself,
So out of thought, and thereto so o'ergrown,
Cannot be question'd.

    Arv.   By this sun that shines,
I 'll thither: what thing is it, that I never
Did see man die? scarce ever look'd on blood,
But that of coward hares, hot goats, and venison?
Never bestrid a horse, save one that had
A rider like myself, who ne'er wore rowel,
Nor iron, on his heel? I am asham'd   40
To look upon the holy sun, to have
The benefit of his bless'd beams, remaining
So long a poor unknown.
    Gui.   By heavens, I 'll go.
If you will bless me, sir, and give me leave,
I 'll take the better care; but if you will not,
The hazard therefore due fall on me by
The hands of Romans.
    Arv.   So say I. Amen.
    Bel. No reason I, since of your lives you set
So slight a valuation, should reserve
My crack'd one to more care. Have with you, boys.
If in your country wars you chance to die,   51
That is my bed too, lads, and there I 'll lie:
Lead, lead.—[*Aside.*] The time seems long; their
                    blood thinks scorn,
Till it fly out, and show them princes born. [*Exeunt.*

ACT V.

SCENE I.—A Field between the British and Roman Camps.

Enter POSTHUMUS, *with a bloody handkerchief.*

    Posthumus.
EA, bloody cloth, I 'll keep thee; for I
            wish'd
Thou shouldst be colour'd thus. You
            married ones,
If each of you should take this course,
            how many
Must murder wives much better than
            themselves,
For wrying but a little!—O Pisanio!
Every good servant does not all com-
            mands:
No bond, but to do just ones.—Gods! if you
Should have ta'en vengeance on my faults, I
            never
Had liv'd to put on this: so had you saved   10
The noble Imogen to repent, and struck
Me, wretch, more worth your vengeance. But, alack!
You snatch some hence for little faults; that 's
            love,
To have them fall no more: you some permit
To second ills with ills, each elder worse,
And make them dread it, to the doers' thrift.
But Imogen is your own: do your best wills,
And make me bless'd to obey! I am brought hither
Among the Italian gentry, and to fight
Against my lady's kingdom: 't is enough   20
That, Britain, I have kill'd thy mistress. Peace!
I 'll give no wound to thee. Therefore, good
            heavens,
Hear patiently my purpose. I 'll disrobe me
Of these Italian weeds, and suit myself
As does a Briton peasant: so I 'll fight
Against the part I come with; so I 'll die
For thee, O Imogen! even for whom my life
Is, every breath, a death; and thus, unknown,
Pitied nor hated, to the face of peril

Myself I 'll dedicate. Let me make men know
More valour in me, than my habits show.   30
Gods, put the strength o' the Leonati in me!
To shame the guise o' the world, I will begin
The fashion, less without, and more within. [*Exit.*

SCENE II.—The Same.

Enter, at one side, LUCIUS, IACHIMO, *and the Roman Army: at the other side, the British Army;* LEONATUS POSTHUMUS *following, like a poor soldier. They march over and go out. Alarums. Then enter again, in skirmish,* IACHIMO *and* POSTHUMUS: *he vanquisheth and disarmeth* IACHIMO, *and then leaves him.*

    Iach. The heaviness and guilt within my bosom
Takes off my manhood: I have belied a lady,
The princess of this country, and the air on 't
Revengingly enfeebles me. Or could this carl,
A very drudge of nature's, have subdu'd me
In my profession? Knighthoods and honours, borne
As I wear mine, are titles but of scorn.
If that thy gentry, Britain, go before
This lout, as he exceeds our lords, the odds
Is, that we scarce are men, and you are gods. [*Exit.*

The battle continues; the Britons fly; CYMBELINE *is taken: then enter, to his rescue,* BELARIUS, GUIDE- RIUS, *and* ARVIRAGUS.

    Bel. Stand, stand! We have the advantage of the
            ground.   11
The lane is guarded: nothing routs us, but
The villainy of our fears.
    Gui., Arv.   Stand, stand, and fight!

Re-enter POSTHUMUS, *and seconds the Britons; they*
rescue CYMBELINE, *and exeunt. Then re-enter*
LUCIUS, IACHIMO, *and* IMOGEN.

Luc. Away, boy, from the troops, and save thyself;
For friends kill friends, and the disorder's such
As war were hood-wink'd.

Iach.   'T is their fresh supplies.

Luc. It is a day turn'd strangely : or betimes
Let's re-enforce, or fly.   [*Exeunt.*

SCENE III.—Another Part of the Field.

Enter POSTHUMUS *and a British Lord.*

Lord. Cam'st thou from where they made the stand?

Post.   I did ;
Though you, it seems, come from the fliers.

Lord.   I did.

Post. No blame be to you, sir; for all was lost,
But that the heavens fought. The king himself
Of his wings destitute, the army broken,
And but the backs of Britons seen, all flying
Through a strait lane; the enemy full-hearted,
Lolling the tongue with slaughtering, having work
More plentiful than tools to do 't, struck down
Some mortally, some slightly touch'd, some falling 10
Merely through fear ; that the strait pass was damm'd
With dead men, hurt behind, and cowards living
To die with lengthen'd shame.

Lord.   Where was this lane?

Post. Close by the battle, ditch'd, and wall'd with
turf ;
Which gave advantage to an ancient soldier,—
An honest one, I warrant ; who deserv'd
So long a breeding, as his white beard came to,
In doing this for 's country ;—athwart the lane,
He, with two striplings, (lads more like to run 20
The country base, than to commit such slaughter ;
With faces fit for masks, or rather fairer
Than those for preservation cas'd, or shame,)
Made good the passage ; cried to those that fled,
" Our Britain's harts die flying, not our men :
To darkness fleet, souls that fly backwards. Stand !
Or we are Romans, and will give you that
Like beasts, which you shun beastly, and may save,
But to look back in frown : stand, stand !"--These
three,
Three thousand confident, in act as many,
(For three performers are the file, when all 30
The rest do nothing,) with this word, " Stand, stand !"
Accommodated by the place, more charming
With their own nobleness (which could have turn'd
A distaff to a lance), gilded pale looks,
Part shame, part spirit renew'd ; that some, turn'd
coward
But by example, (O, a sin in war,
Damn'd in the first beginners!) 'gan to look
The way that they did, and to grin like lions
Upon the pikes o' the hunters. Then began
A stop i' the chaser, a retire ; anon, 40
A rout, confusion thick : forthwith they fly,
Chickens, the way which they stoop'd eagles ; slaves,
The strides they victors made. And now our cowards
(Like fragments in hard voyages) became
The life o' the need : having found the back-door open
Of the unguarded hearts, heavens, how they wound !
Some slain before ; some dying ; some, their friends,
O'erborne i' the former wave : ten, chas'd by one,
Are now each one the slaughter-man of twenty :
Those that would die or ere resist, are grown 50
The mortal bugs o' the field.

Lord.   This was strange chance :
A narrow lane, an old man, and two boys !

Post. Nay, do not wonder at it : you are made
Rather to wonder at the things you hear,
Than to work any. Will you rhyme upon 't,
And vent it for a mockery? Here is one :
" Two boys, an old man twice a boy, a lane,
Preserv'd the Britons, was the Romans' bane."

Lord. Nay, be not angry, sir.

Post.   'Lack ! to what end?

Who dares not stand his foe, I 'll be his friend ; 60
For if he 'll do, as he is made to do,
I know, he 'll quickly fly my friendship too.
You have put me into rhyme.

Lord.   Farewell ; you 're angry. [*Exit.*

Post. Still going?—This is a lord. O noble misery !
To be i' the field, and ask, what news, of me !
To-day, how many would have given their honours
To have sav'd their carcasses ! took heel to do 't,
And yet died too ! I, in mine own woe charm'd,
Could not find death, where I did hear him groan ;
Nor feel him where he struck : being an ugly monster,
'T is strange he hides him in fresh cups, soft beds, 71
Sweet words ; or hath moe ministers than we
That draw his knives i' the war.—Well, I will find him ;
For, being now a favourer to the Briton,
No more a Briton, I have resum'd again
The part I came in. Fight I will no more,
But yield me to the veriest hind that shall
Once touch my shoulder. Great the slaughter is
Here made by the Roman ; great the answer be
Britons must take. For me, my ransom 's death : 80
On either side I come to spend my breath ;
Which neither here I 'll keep, nor bear again,
But end it by some means for Imogen.

Enter two British Captains, and Soldiers.

1 Cap. Great Jupiter be prais'd ! Lucius is taken.
'T is thought, the old man and his sons were angels.

2 Cap. There was a fourth man, in a silly habit,
That gave the affront with them.

1 Cap.   So 't is reported ;
But none of 'em can be found.—Stand ! who is there?

Post. A Roman,
Who had not now been drooping here, if seconds 90
Had answer'd him.

2 Cap.   Lay hands on him ; a dog !
A leg of Rome shall not return to tell
What crows have peck'd them here. He brags his
service
As if he were of note. Bring him to the king.

Enter CYMBELINE, *attended;* BELARIUS, GUIDERIUS,
ARVIRAGUS, PISANIO, *and Roman Captives. The*
Captains present POSTHUMUS *to* CYMBELINE, *who*
delivers him over to a Gaoler; after which, all go
out.

SCENE IV.—A Prison.

Enter POSTHUMUS *and two Gaolers.*

1 Gaol. You shall not now be stol'n ; you have locks
upon you :
So, graze as you find pasture.

2 Gaol.   Ay, or a stomach.
                   [*Exeunt Gaolers.*

Post. Most welcome, bondage, for thou art a way,
I think, to liberty. Yet am I better
Than one that 's sick o' the gout ; since he had rather
Groan so in perpetuity, than be cur'd
By the sure physician, death, who is the key
To unbar these locks. My conscience, thou art fetter'd
More than my shanks and wrists : you good gods,
give me
The penitent instrument, to pick that bolt ; 10
Then, free for ever ! Is 't enough, I am sorry ?
So children temporal fathers do appease ;
Gods are more full of mercy. Must I repent ?
I cannot do it better than in gyves,
Desir'd, more than constrain'd : to satisfy,
If of my freedom 't is the main part, take
No stricter render of me, than my all.
I know, you are more clement than vile men,
Who of their broken debtors take a third,
A sixth, a tenth, letting them thrive again 20
On their abatement : that 's not my desire.
For Imogen's dear life take mine ; and though
'T is not so dear, yet 't is a life ; you coin'd it :
'Tween man and man they weigh not every stamp ;
Though light, take pieces for the figure's sake :
You rather mine, being yours ; and so, great powers,
If you will take this audit, take this life.

And cancel these cold bonds. O Imogen!
I'll speak to thee in silence.

Solemn music. Enter, as in an apparition, SICILIUS
LEONATUS, *father to* POSTHUMUS, *an old man,
attired like a warrior; leading in his hand an
ancient matron, his wife, and mother to* POSTHU-
MUS, *with music before them. Then, after other
music, follow the two young* LEONATI, *brothers to*
POSTHUMUS, *with wounds as they died in the wars.
They circle* POSTHUMUS *round, as he lies sleeping.*

Sici. No more, thou thunder-master, show 30
  Thy spite on mortal flies;
  With Mars fall out, with Juno chide,
   That thy adulteries
   Rates and revenges.
 Hath my poor boy done aught but well,
  Whose face I never saw?
 I died, whilst in the womb he stay'd
  Attending nature's law.
 Whose father then (as men report,
  Thou orphans' father art) 40
 Thou shouldst have been, and shielded him
  From this earth-vexing smart.

Moth. Lucina lent not me her aid,
  But took me in my throes;
 That from me was Posthumus ript,
  Came crying 'mongst his foes,
   A thing of pity!

Sici. Great nature, like his ancestry,
  Moulded the stuff so fair,
 That he deserv'd the praise o' the world, 50
  As great Sicilius' heir.

1 Bro. When once he was mature for man,
  In Britain where was he,
 That could stand up his parallel,
  Or fruitful object be
 In eye of Imogen, that best
  Could deem his dignity?

Moth. With marriage wherefore was he mock'd,
  To be exil'd, and thrown
 From Leonati' seat, and cast 60
  From her his dearest one,
   Sweet Imogen?

Sici. Why did you suffer Iachimo,
  Slight thing of Italy,
 To taint his nobler heart and brain
  With needless jealousy;
 And to become the geck and scorn
  O' the other's villainy?

2 Bro. For this from stiller seats we came,
  Our parents, and us twain, 70
 That striking in our country's cause
  Fell bravely, and were slain;
 Our fealty, and Tenantius' right,
  With honour to maintain.

1 Bro. Like hardiment Posthumus hath
  To Cymbeline perform'd:
 Then, Jupiter, thou king of gods,
  Why hast thou thus adjourn'd
 The graces for his merits due,
  Being all to dolours turn'd? 80

Sici. Thy crystal window ope; look out:
  No longer exercise
 Upon a valiant race thy harsh
  And potent injuries.

Moth. Since, Jupiter, our son is good,
  Take off his miseries.

Sici. Peep through thy marble mansion; help!
  Or we poor ghosts will cry
 To the shining synod of the rest,
  Against thy deity. 90

2 Bro. Help, Jupiter! or we appeal,
  And from thy justice fly.

JUPITER *descends in thunder and lightning, sitting
upon an eagle: he throws a thunderbolt; the Ghosts
fall on their knees.*

Jup. No more, you petty spirits of region low,

Offend our hearing: hush!—How dare you ghosts
Accuse the thunderer, whose bolt, you know,
 Sky-planted, batters all rebelling coasts?
Poor shadows of Elysium, hence; and rest
 Upon your never-withering banks of flowers:
Be not with mortal accidents opprest;
 No care of yours it is, you know; 'tis ours. 100
Whom best I love, I cross; to make my gift,
 The more delay'd, delighted. Be content;
Your low-laid son our godhead will uplift:
 His comforts thrive, his trials well are spent.
Our Jovial star reign'd at his birth, and in
 Our temple was he married.—Rise, and fade!—
He shall be lord of Lady Imogen,
 And happier much by his affliction made.
This tablet lay upon his breast, wherein
 Our pleasure his full fortune doth confine; 110
And so, away: no further with your din
 Express impatience, lest you stir up mine.—
Mount, eagle, to my palace crystalline. [*Ascends.*
Sici. He came in thunder; his celestial breath
Was sulphurous to smell: the holy eagle
Stoop'd, as to foot us: his ascension is
More sweet than our bless'd fields: his royal bird
Prunes the immortal wing, and cloys his beak,
As when his god is pleas'd.
All.   Thanks, Jupiter!
Sici. The marble pavement closes; he is enter'd 120
His radiant roof.—Away! and, to be blest,
Let us with care perform his great behest.
      [*The Ghosts vanish.*
Post. [*Waking.*] Sleep, thou hast been a grandsire,
    and begot
A father to me; and thou hast created
A mother, and two brothers. But (O scorn!)
Gone! they went hence so soon as they were born:
And so I am awake.—Poor wretches, that depend
On greatness' favour, dream as I have done;
Wake, and find nothing.—But, alas, I swerve:
Many dream not to find, neither deserve, 130
And yet are steep'd in favours; so am I,
That have this golden chance, and know not why.
What fairies haunt this ground? A book? O rare
  one!
Be not, as is our fangled world, a garment
Nobler than that it covers: let thy effects
So follow, to be most unlike our courtiers,
As good as promise. 137
[*Reads.*] " Whenas a lion's whelp shall, to himself
unknown, without seeking find, and be embraced by
a piece of tender air; and when from a stately cedar
shall be lopped branches, which, being dead many
years, shall after revive, be jointed to the old stock,
and freshly grow, then shall Posthumus end his
miseries, Britain be fortunate, and flourish in peace
and plenty."
'T is still a dream, or else such stuff as madmen
Tongue, and brain not; either both, or nothing:
Or senseless speaking, or a speaking such
As sense cannot untie. Be what it is,
The action of my life is like it, which 150
I'll keep, if but for sympathy.

Re-enter Gaoler.

Gaol. Come, sir, are you ready for death?
Post. Over-roasted rather; ready long ago.
Gaol. Hanging is the word, sir: if you be ready for
that, you are well cooked.
Post. So, if I prove a good repast to the spectators,
the dish pays the shot. 157
Gaol. A heavy reckoning for you, sir; but the comfort is, you shall be called to no more payments, fear
no more tavern-bills, which are often the sadness of
parting, as the procuring of mirth. You come in faint
for want of meat, depart reeling with too much drink,
sorry that you have paid too much, and sorry that you
are paid too much; purse and brain both empty: the
brain the heavier for being too light, the purse too
light, being drawn of heaviness. Of this contradiction
you shall now be quit.—O, the charity of a penny cord!
it sums up thousands in a trice: you have no true
debitor-and-creditor but it; of what's past, is, and to

come, the discharge.—Your neck, sir, is pen, book,
and counters; so the acquittance follows. 171
Post. I am merrier to die, than thou art to live.
Gaol. Indeed, sir, he that sleeps feels not the toothache; but a man that were to sleep your sleep, and a
hangman to help him to bed, I think, he would change
places with his officer; for, look you, sir, you know
not which way you shall go.
Post. Yes, indeed do I, fellow. 178
Gaol. Your death has eyes in 's head, then; I have
not seen him so pictured: you must either be directed
by some that take upon them to know, or take upon
yourself that which I am sure you do not know, or
jump the after-inquiry on your own peril: and how
you shall speed in your journey's end, I think you 'll
never return to tell one.
Post. I tell thee, fellow, there are none want eyes to
direct them the way I am going, but such as wink, and
will not use them. 188
Gaol. What an infinite mock is this, that a man
should have the best use of eyes to see the way of
blindness! I am sure, hanging 's the way of winking.

Enter a Messenger.

Mess. Knock off his manacles: bring your prisoner
to the king.
Post. Thou bring'st good news. I am called to be
made free.
Gaol. I 'll be hanged then.
Post. Thou shalt be then freer than a gaoler; no
bolts for the dead. 198
[*Exeunt* POSTHUMUS *and Messenger.*
Gaol. Unless a man would marry a gallows, and
beget young gibbets, I never saw one so prone. Yet,
on my conscience, there are verier knaves desire to
live, for all he be a Roman; and there be some of
them too, that die against their wills: so should I, if I
were one. I would we were all of one mind, and one
mind good: O, there were desolation of gaolers, and
gallowses! I speak against my present profit, but my
wish hath a preferment in 't. [*Exeunt.*

SCENE V.—CYMBELINE'S Tent.

Enter CYMBELINE, BELARIUS, GUIDERIUS, ARVI-
RAGUS, PISANIO, *Lords, Officers, and Attendants.*

Cym. Stand by my side, you whom the gods have
made
Preservers of my throne. Woe is my heart,
That the poor soldier, that so richly fought,
Whose rags sham'd gilded arms, whose naked breast
Stepp'd before targes of proof, cannot be found:
He shall be happy that can find him, if
Our grace can make him so.
Bel. I never saw
Such noble fury in so poor a thing;
Such precious deeds in one that promis'd nought
But beggary and poor looks.
Cym. No tidings of him? 10
Pis. He hath been search'd among the dead and
living,
But no trace of him.
Cym. To my grief, I am
The heir of his reward; which I will add
To you, the liver, heart, and brain of Britain,
By whom, I grant, she lives. 'T is now the time
To ask of whence you are:—report it.
Bel. Sir,
In Cambria are we born, and gentlemen:
Further to boast, were neither true nor modest,
Unless I add, we are honest.
Cym. Bow your knees.
Arise, my knights o' the battle: I create you 20
Companions to our person, and will fit you
With dignities becoming your estates.

Enter CORNELIUS *and Ladies.*

There 's business in these faces.—Why so sadly
Greet you our victory? you look like Romans,
And not o' the court of Britain.
Cor. Hail, great king!
To sour your happiness, I must report
The queen is dead.
Cym. Who worse than a physician
Would this report become? But I consider,
By medicine life may be prolong'd, yet death
Will seize the doctor too.—How ended she? 30
Cor. With horror, madly dying, like her life;
Which, being cruel to the world, concluded
Most cruel to herself. What she confess'd,
I will report, so please you: these her women
Can trip me, if I err, who with wet cheeks
Were present when she finish'd.
Cym. Pr'ythee, say.
Cor. First, she confess'd she never lov'd you; only
Affected greatness got by you, not you:
Married your royalty, was wife to your place;
Abhorr'd your person.
Cym. She alone knew this; 40
And, but she spoke it dying, I would not
Believe her lips in opening it. Proceed.
Cor. Your daughter, whom she bore in hand to love
With such integrity, she did confess,
Was as a scorpion to her sight; whose life,
But that her flight prevented it, she had
Ta'en off by poison.
Cym. O most delicate fiend!
Who is 't can read a woman?—Is there more?
Cor. More, sir, and worse. She did confess, she had
For you a mortal mineral; which, being took, 50
Should by the minute feed on life, and ling'ring
By inches waste you: in which time she purpos'd,
By watching, weeping, tendance, kissing, to
O'ercome you with her show; and in time
(When she had fitted you with her craft) to work
Her son into the adoption of the crown:
But failing of her end by his strange absence,
Grew shameless-desperate; open'd, in despite
Of heaven and men, her purposes; repented
The evils she hatch'd were not effected: so, 60
Despairing, died.
Cym. Heard you all this, her women?
Lady. We did, so please your highness.
Cym. Mine eyes
Were not in fault, for she was beautiful;
Mine ears, that heard her flattery; nor my heart,
That thought her like her seeming; it had been
vicious,
To have mistrusted her: yet, O my daughter!
That it was folly in me, thou may'st say,
And prove it in thy feeling. Heaven mend all!

Enter LUCIUS, IACHIMO, *the Soothsayer, and other
Roman Prisoners, guarded;* POSTHUMUS *behind;
and* IMOGEN.

Thou com'st not, Caius, now for tribute: that 70
The Britons have raz'd out, though with the loss
Of many a bold one; whose kinsmen have made suit,
That their good souls may be appeas'd with slaughter
Of you their captives, which ourself have granted:
So, think of your estate.
Luc. Consider, sir, the chance of war: the day
Was yours by accident; had it gone with us,
We should not, when the blood was cool, have
threaten'd
Our prisoners with the sword. But since the gods
Will have it thus, that nothing but our lives 80
May be call'd ransom, let it come: sufficeth,
A Roman with a Roman's heart can suffer:
Augustus lives to think on 't; and so much
For my peculiar care. This one thing only
I will entreat: my boy, a Briton born,
Let him be ransom'd: never master had
A page so kind, so duteous, diligent,
So tender over his occasions, true,
So feat, so nurse-like. Let his virtue join
With my request, which, I 'll make bold, your high-
ness 90
Cannot deny: he hath done no Briton harm,
Though he have serv'd a Roman. Save him, sir,
And spare no blood beside.
Cym. I have surely seen him:

His favour is familiar to me.—Boy,
Thou hast look'd thyself into my grace,
And art mine own.—I know not why, nor wherefore,
To say, live, boy: ne'er thank thy master; live,
And ask of Cymbeline what boon thou wilt,
Fitting my bounty and thy state, I'll give it;
Yea, though thou do demand a prisoner,   100
The noblest ta'en.
Imo.   I humbly thank your highness.
Luc. I do not bid thee beg my life, good lad,
And yet I know thou wilt.
Imo.   No, no; alack!
There's other work in hand.—I see a thing
Bitter to me as death.—Your life, good master,
Must shuffle for itself.
Luc.   The boy disdains me,
He leaves me, scorns me: briefly die their joys,—
That place them on the truth of girls and boys.—
Why stands he so perplex'd?
Cym.   What wouldst thou, boy?
I love thee more and more; think more and more   110
What's best to ask. Know'st him thou look'st on?
          speak:
Wilt have him live? Is he thy kin? thy friend?
Imo. He is a Roman; no more kin to me,
Than I to your highness; who, being born your vassal,
Am something nearer.
Cym.   Wherefore ey'st him so?
Imo. I'll tell you, sir, in private, if you please
To give me hearing.
Cym.   Ay, with all my heart,
And lend my best attention, What's thy name?
Imo. Fidele, sir.
Cym.   Thou art my good youth, my page;
I'll be thy master: walk with me; speak freely.   120
          [CYMBELINE *and* IMOGEN *converse apart.*
Bel. Is not this boy reviv'd from death?
Arv.   One sand another
Not more resembles: that sweet rosy lad,
Who died, and was Fidele.—What think you?
Gui. The same dead thing alive.
Bel. Peace, peace! see further; he eyes us not:
          forbear;
Creatures may be alike: were't he, I am sure
He would have spoke to us.
Gui.   But we saw him dead.
Bel. Be silent; let's see further.
Pis. [*Aside.*]   It is my mistress!
Since she is living, let the time run on
To good, or bad.
          [CYMBELINE *and* IMOGEN *come forward.*
Cym.   Come, stand thou by our side: 130
Make thy demand aloud.—[*To* IACHIMO.] Sir, step you
          forth;
Give answer to this boy, and do it freely;
Or, by our greatness, and the grace of it,
Which is our honour, bitter torture shall
Winnow the truth from falsehood.—On, speak to him.
Imo. My boon is, that this gentleman may render
Of whom he had this ring.
Post. [*Aside.*]   What's that to him?
Cym. That diamond upon your finger, say,
How came it yours?
Iach. Thou'lt torture me to leave unspoken that 140
Which, to be spoke, would torture thee.
Cym.   How! me?
Iach. I am glad to be constrain'd to utter that
Which torments me to conceal. By villainy
I got this ring: 't was Leonatus' jewel;
Whom thou didst banish; and (which more may
          grieve thee,
As it doth me) a nobler sir ne'er liv'd
'Twixt sky and ground. Wilt thou hear more, my
          lord?
Cym. All that belongs to this.
Iach.   That paragon, thy daughter,
For whom my heart drops blood, and my false spirits
Quail to remember,—Give me leave: I faint.   150
Cym. My daughter! what of her? Renew thy
          strength:
I had rather thou shouldst live while nature will,
Than die ere I hear more. Strive, man, and speak.

Iach. Upon a time, (unhappy was the clock
That struck the hour!) it was in Rome, (accurs'd
The mansion where!) 't was at a feast (O, 'would
Our viands had been poison'd, or at least
Those which I heav'd to head!) the good Posthumus
(What should I say? he was too good to be
Where ill men were, and was the best of all   160
Amongst the rar'st of good ones) sitting sadly,
Hearing us praise our loves of Italy
For beauty, that made barren the swell'd boast
Of him that best could speak: for feature, laming
The shrine of Venus, or straight-pight Minerva,
Postures beyond brief nature; for condition,
A shop of all the qualities that man
Loves woman for; besides that hook of wiving,
Fairness, which strikes the eye.
Cym.   I stand on fire.
Come to the matter.
Iach.   All too soon I shall,   170
Unless thou wouldst grieve quickly.—This Posthumus
(Most like a noble lord in love, and one
That had a royal lover) took his hint;
And, not dispraising whom we prais'd, (therein
He was as calm as virtue,) he began
His mistress' picture; which by his tongue being
          made,
And then a mind put in't, either our brags
Were crack'd of kitchen-trulls, or his description
Prov'd us unspeaking sots.
Cym.   Nay, nay, to the purpose.
Iach. Your daughter's chastity—there it begins. 180
He spake of her as Dian had hot dreams,
And she alone were cold: whereat I, wretch,
Made scruple of his praise; and wager'd with
          him
Pieces of gold 'gainst this, which then he wore
Upon his honour'd finger, to attain
In suit the place of 's bed, and win this ring
By hers and mine adultery. He, true knight,
No lesser of her honour confident
Than I did truly find her, stakes this ring;
And would so, had it been a carbuncle   190
Of Phœbus' wheel; and might so safely, had it
Been all the worth of 's car. Away to Britain
Post I in this design. Well may you, sir,
Remember me at court, where I was taught
Of your chaste daughter the wide difference
'Twixt amorous and villainous. Being thus quench'd
Of hope, not longing, mine Italian brain
'Gan in your duller Britain operate
Most vilely; for my vantage, excellent;
And, to be brief, my practice so prevail'd,   200
That I return'd with simular proof, enough
To make the noble Leonatus mad,
By wounding his belief in her renown
With tokens thus, and thus; averring notes
Of chamber-hanging, pictures, this her bracelet,
(O cunning, how I got it!) nay, some marks
Of secret on her person, that he could not
But think her bond of chastity quite crack'd,
I having ta'en the forfeit. Whereupon,—
Methinks, I see him now,—
Post. [*Coming forward.*] Ay, so thou dost,   210
Italian fiend!—Ah me! most credulous fool,
Egregious murderer, thief, anything
That's due to all the villains past, in being,
To come!—O, give me cord, or knife, or poison,
Some upright justicer! Thou, king, send out
For torturers ingenious: it is I
That all the abhorred things o' the earth amend,
By being worse than they. I am Posthumus, .
That kill'd thy daughter:—villain-like, I lie;
That caus'd a lesser villain than myself,   220
A sacrilegious thief, to do't:—the temple
Of virtue was she; yea, and she herself.
Spit, and throw stones, cast mire upon me; set
The dogs o' the street to bay me: every villain
Be call'd Posthumus Leonatus; and
Be villainy less than 't was! O Imogen!
My queen, my life, my wife! O Imogen,
Imogen, Imogen!
Imo.   Peace, my lord! hear, hear!

Post. Shall 's have a play of this? Thou scornful
 page,
There lie thy part.   [*Striking her : she falls.*
 Pis.   O gentlemen! help   230
Mine, and your mistress.—O, my Lord Posthumus!
You ne'er kill'd Imogen till now.—Help, help!—
Mine honour'd lady!
 Cym.   Does the world go round?
 Post. How come these staggers on me?
 Pis.   Wake, my mistress!
 Cym. If this be so, the gods do mean to strike me
To death with mortal joy.
 Pis.   How fares my mistress?
 Imo. O! get thee from my sight;
Thou gav'st me poison : dangerous fellow, hence!
Breathe not where princes are.
 Cym.   The tune of Imogen!
 Pis. Lady,   240
The gods throw stones of sulphur on me, if
That box I gave you was not thought by me
A precious thing : I had it from the queen.
 Cym. New matter still?
 Imo.   It poison'd me.
 Cor.   O gods!
I left out one thing which the queen confess'd,
Which must approve thee honest : " If Pisanio
Have," said she, " given his mistress that confection
Which I gave him for a cordial, she is serv'd
As I would serve a rat."
 Cym.   What 's this, Cornelius?
 Cor. The queen, sir, very oft importun'd me 250
To temper poisons for her ; still pretending
The satisfaction of her knowledge, only
In killing creatures vile, as cats and dogs
Of no esteem : I, dreading that her purpose
Was of more danger, did compound for her
A certain stuff, which, being ta'en, would cease
The present power of life ; but, in short time,
All offices of nature should again
Do their due functions.—Have you ta'en of it?
 Imo. Most like I did, for I was dead.
 Bel.   My boys, 260
There was our error.
 Gui.   This is, sure, Fidele.
 Imo. Why did you throw your wedded lady from
 you?
Think that you are upon a rock ; and now
Throw me again.   [*Embracing him.*
 Post.   Hang there like fruit, my soul,
Till the tree die!
 Cym.   How now, my flesh, my child!
What! mak'st thou me a dullard in this act?
Wilt thou not speak to me?
 Imo. [*Kneeling.*]   Your blessing, sir.
 Bel. [*To* GUIDERIUS *and* ARVIRAGUS.] Though
  you did love this youth, I blame ye not;
You had a motive for 't.
 Cym.   My tears, that fall,
Prove holy water on thee! Imogen, 270
Thy mother 's dead.
 Imo.   I am sorry for 't, my lord.
 Cym. O! she was naught ; and long of her it was,
That we meet here so strangely : but her son
Is gone, we know not how, nor where.
 Pis.   My lord,
Now fear is from me, I 'll speak troth. Lord Cloten,
Upon my lady's missing, came to me
With his sword drawn ; foam'd at the mouth, and
 swore,
If I discover'd not which way she was gone,
It was my instant death. By accident,
I had a feigned letter of my master's 280
Then in my pocket, which directed him
To seek her on the mountains near to Milford ;
Where, in a frenzy, in my master's garments,
Which he inforced from me, away he posts
With unchaste purpose, and with oath to violate
My lady's honour : what became of him,
I further know not.
 Gui.   Let me end the story :
I slew him there.
 Cym.   Marry, the gods forfend!

I would not thy good deeds should from my lips
Pluck a hard sentence : pr'ythee, valiant youth, 290
Deny 't again.
 Gui.   I have spoke it, and I did it.
 Cym. He was a prince.
 Gui. A most uncivil one. The wrongs he did me
Were nothing prince-like ; for he did provoke me
With language that would make me spurn the sea,
If it could so roar to me. I cut off 's head ;
And am right glad, he is not standing here
To tell this tale of mine.
 Cym.   I am sorry for thee :
By thine own tongue thou art condemn'd, and must
Endure our law. Thou 'rt dead.
 Imo.   That headless man
I thought had been my lord.
 Cym.   Bind the offender, 301
And take him from our presence.
 Bel.   Stay, sir king.
This man is better than the man he slew,
As well descended as thyself ; and hath
More of thee merited, than a band of Clotens
Had ever scar for.—[*To the Guard.*] Let his arms
 alone ;
They were not born for bondage.
 Cym.   Why, old soldier,
Wilt thou undo the worth thou art unpaid for,
By tasting of our wrath? How of descent
As good as we?
 Arv.   In that he spake too far. 310
 Cym. And thou shalt die for 't.
 Bel.   We will die all three :
But I will prove that two on 's are as good
As I have given out him.—My sons, I must
For mine own part unfold a dangerous speech,
Though, haply, well for you.
 Arv.   Your danger 's ours.
 Gui. And our good his.
 Bel.   Have at it then.—By leave ;
Thou hadst, great king, a subject, who was call'd
Belarius.
 Cym.   What of him? he is
A banish'd traitor.
 Bel.   He it is that hath
Assum'd this age : indeed, a banish'd man ; 320
I know not how a traitor.
 Cym.   Take him hence.
The whole world shall not save him.
 Bel.   Not too hot :
First pay me for the nursing of thy sons ;
And let it be confiscate all, so soon
As I have receiv'd it.
 Cym.   Nursing of my sons?
 Bel. I am too blunt, and saucy ; here 's my knee :
Ere I arise I will prefer my sons ;
Then, spare not the old father. Mighty sir,
These two young gentlemen, that call me father,
And think they are my sons, are none of mine : 330
They are the issue of your loins, my liege,
And blood of your begetting.
 Cym.   How! my issue?
 Bel. So sure as you your father's. I, old Morgan,
Am that Belarius whom you sometime banish'd :
Your pleasure was my mere offence, my punishment
Itself, and all my treason ; that I suffer'd
Was all the harm I did. These gentle princes
(For such and so they are) these twenty years
Have I train'd up ; those arts they have, as I
Could put into them : my breeding was, sir, as 340
Your highness knows. Their nurse, Euriphile,
Whom for the theft I wedded, stole these children
Upon my banishment : I mov'd her to 't ;
Having receiv'd the punishment before,
For that which I did then : beaten for loyalty
Excited me to treason. Their dear loss,
The more of you 't was felt, the more it shap'd
Unto my end of stealing them. But, gracious sir,
Here are your sons again ; and I must lose
Two of the sweet'st companions in the world.— 350
The benediction of these covering heavens
Fall on their heads like dew! for they are worthy
To inlay heaven with stars.

Cym. Thou weep'st, and speak'st.
The service, that you three have done, is more
Unlike than this thou tell'st. I lost my children:
If these be they, I know not how to wish
A pair of worthier sons.
Bel. Be pleas'd awhile.
This gentleman, whom I call Polydore,
Most worthy prince, as yours, is true Guiderius;
This gentleman, my Cadwal, Arviragus, 360
Your younger princely son: he, sir, was lapp'd
In a most curious mantle, wrought by the hand
Of his queen mother, which, for more probation,
I can with ease produce.
Cym. Guiderius had
Upon his neck a mole, a sanguine star:
It was a mark of wonder.
Bel. This is he,
Who hath upon him still that natural stamp.
It was wise nature's end in the donation,
To be his evidence now.
Cym. O! what, am I
A mother to the birth of three? Ne'er mother 370
Rejoic'd deliverance more.—Bless'd pray you be,
That, after this strange starting from your orbs,
You may reign in them now.—O Imogen!
Thou hast lost by this a kingdom.
Imo. No, my lord;
I have got two worlds by 't.—O my gentle brothers!
Have we thus met? O! never say hereafter,
But I am truest speaker: you call'd me brother,
When I was but your sister; I you brothers,
When ye were so indeed.
Cym. Did you e'er meet?
Arv. Ay, my good lord.
Gui. And at first meeting lov'd;
Continued so, until we thought he died. 381
Cor. By the queen's dram she swallow'd.
Cym. O rare instinct!
When shall I hear all through? This fierce abridgment
Hath to it circumstantial branches, which
Distinction should be rich in.—Where, how liv'd
you?
And when came you to serve our Roman captive?
How parted with your brothers? how first met them?
Why fled you from the court, and whither? These,
And your three motives to the battle, with
I know not how much more, should be demanded, 390
And all the other by-dependencies,
From chance to chance; but nor the time, nor place,
Will serve our long inter'gatories. See,
Posthumus anchors upon Imogen;
And she, like harmless lightning, throws her eye
On him, her brothers, me, her master, hitting
Each object with a joy: the counterchange
Is severally in all. Let's quit this ground,
And smoke the temple with our sacrifices.—
[*To* Belarius.] Thou art my brother: so we 'll hold
thee ever. 400
Imo. You are my father too; and did relieve me,
To see this gracious season.
Cym. All o'erjoy'd,
Save these in bonds: let them be joyful too,
For they shall taste our comfort.
Imo. My good master,
I will yet do you service.
Luc. Happy be you!
Cym. The forlorn soldier, that so nobly fought,
He would have well becom'd this place, and grac'd
The thankings of a king.
Post. I am, sir,
The soldier that did company these three
In poor beseeming: 't was a fitment for 410
The purpose I then follow'd.—That I was he,
Speak, Iachimo: I had you down, and might
Have made you finish.
Iach. [*Kneeling.*] I am down again;
But now my heavy conscience sinks my knee,
As then your force did. Take that life, 'beseech you,
Which I so often owe; but your ring first,

And here the bracelet of the truest princess,
That ever swore her faith.
Post. Kneel not to me:
The power that I have on you, is to spare you;
The malice towards you, to forgive you. Live, 420
And deal with others better.
Cym. Nobly doom'd.
We 'll learn our freeness of a son-in-law:
Pardon 's the word to all.
Arv. You holp us, sir,
As you did mean indeed to be our brother;
Joy'd are we, that you are.
Post. Your servant, princes. — Good my lord of
Rome,
Call forth your soothsayer. As I slept, methought,
Great Jupiter, upon his eagle back'd,
Appear'd to me, with other spritely shows
Of mine own kindred: when I wak'd, I found 430
This label on my bosom; whose containing
Is so from sense in hardness, that I can
Make no collection of it: let him show
His skill in the construction.
Luc. Philarmonus!
Sooth. Here, my good lord. [*Coming forward.*
Luc. Read, and declare the meaning.
Sooth. [*Reads.*] "Whenas a lion's whelp shall, to
himself unknown, without seeking find, and be em-
braced by a piece of tender air; and when from a
stately cedar shall be lopped branches, which, being
dead many years, shall after revive, be jointed to the
old stock, and freshly grow, then shall Posthumus end
his miseries, Britain be fortunate, and flourish in
peace and plenty." 443
Thou, Leonatus, art the lion's whelp;
The fit and apt construction of thy name,
Being Leo-natus, doth import so much.
[*To* Cymbeline.] The piece of tender air, thy virtuous
daughter,
Which we call *mollis aer*; and *mollis aer*
We term it *mulier*: which *mulier*, I divine,
Is this most constant wife; who, even now, 450
Answering the letter of the oracle,
Unknown to you, unsought, were clipp'd about
With this most tender air.
Cym. This hath some seeming.
Sooth. The lofty cedar, royal Cymbeline,
Personates thee; and thy lopp'd branches point
Thy two sons forth: who, by Belarius stolen,
For many years thought dead, are now reviv'd,
To the majestic cedar join'd, whose issue
Promises Britain peace and plenty.
Cym. Well,
My peace we will begin.—And, Caius Lucius, 460
Although the victor, we submit to Cæsar,
And to the Roman empire; promising
To pay our wonted tribute, from the which
We were dissuaded by our wicked queen;
Whom heavens, in justice, (both on her and hers,)
Have laid most heavy hand.
Sooth. The fingers of the powers above do tune
The harmony of this peace. The vision,
Which I made known to Lucius ere the stroke
Of this yet scarce-cold battle, at this instant 470
Is full accomplish'd; for the Roman eagle,
From south to west on wing soaring aloft,
Lessen'd herself, and in the beams o' the sun
So vanish'd: which foreshow'd our princely eagle,
The imperial Cæsar, should again unite
His favour with the radiant Cymbeline,
Which shines here in the west.
Cym. Laud we the gods;
And let our crooked smokes climb to their nostrils
From our bless'd altars. Publish we this peace
To all our subjects. Set we forward. Let 480
A Roman and a British ensign wave
Friendly together; so through Lud's town march:
And in the temple of great Jupiter
Our peace we 'll ratify; seal it with feasts.—
Set on there.—Never was a war did cease,
Ere bloody hands were wash'd, with such a peace.
[*Exeunt.*

PERICLES.

DRAMATIS PERSONÆ.

ANTIOCHUS, *King of Antioch.*
PERICLES, *Prince of Tyre.*
HELICANUS, ⎱ *Two Lords of Tyre.*
ESCANES, ⎰
SIMONIDES, *King of Pentapolis.*
CLEON, *Governor of Tharsus.*
LYSIMACHUS, *Governor of Mitylene.*
CERIMON, *a Lord of Ephesus.*
THALIARD, *a Lord of Antioch.*
PHILEMON, *Servant to Cerimon.*
LEONINE, *Servant to Dionyza.*
Marshal.

A Pander. BOULT, *his Servant.*
The Daughter of Antiochus.
DIONYZA, *Wife to Cleon.*
THAISA, *Daughter to Simonides.*
MARINA, *Daughter to Pericles and Thaisa.*
LYCHORIDA, *Nurse to Marina.*
A Bawd.
DIANA.
GOWER, *as Chorus.*

Lords, Ladies, Knights, Gentlemen, Sailors,
Pirates, Fishermen, and Messengers.

SCENE—Dispersedly in various Countries.

ACT I.

Enter GOWER.

Before the Palace of Antioch.

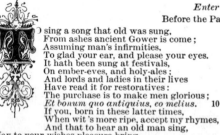

To sing a song that old was sung,
From ashes ancient Gower is come;
Assuming man's infirmities,
To glad your ear, and please your eyes.
It hath been sung at festivals,
On ember-eves, and holy-ales;
And lords and ladies in their lives
Have read it for restoratives:
The purchase is to make men glorious;
Et bonum quo antiquius, eo melius.   10
If you, born in these latter times,
When wit 's more ripe, accept my rhymes,
And that to hear an old man sing,
May to your wishes pleasure bring,
I life would wish, and that I might
Waste it for you, like taper-light.—
This Antioch, then, Antiochus the Great
Built up, this city, for his chiefest seat,
The fairest in all Syria,—
I tell you what my authors say :   20
This king unto him took a pheere,
Who died and left a female heir,
So buxom, blithe, and full of face,
As heaven had lent her all his grace ;
With whom the father liking took,
And her to incest did provoke.
Bad child, worse father ! to entice his own
To evil, should be done by none.
But custom what they did begin
Was, with long use, account no sin.   30
The beauty of this sinful dame
Made many princes thither frame,
To seek her as a bedfellow,
In marriage-pleasures playfellow :
Which to prevent he made a law,
To keep her still, and men in awe,—
That whoso ask'd her for his wife,
His riddle told not, lost his life :
So, for her many a wight did die,
As yon grim looks do testify.   40
What now ensues, to the judgment of your eye
I give, my cause who best can justify.   [*Exit.*

SCENE I.—Antioch. A Room in the Palace.

Enter ANTIOCHUS, PERICLES, *and Attendants.*

Ant. Young Prince of Tyre, you have at large
receiv'd
The danger of the task you undertake.
Per. I have, Antiochus, and, with a soul
Embolden'd with the glory of her praise,
Think death no hazard, in this enterprise.
Ant. Bring in our daughter, clothed like a bride,
For the embracements even of Jove himself;
At whose conception (till Lucina reign'd)
Nature this dowry gave, to glad her presence ;
The senate-house of planets all did sit,   10
To knit in her their best perfections.

Music. Enter the Daughter of ANTIOCHUS.

Per. See, where she comes, apparell'd like the spring,
Graces her subjects, and her thoughts the king
Of every virtue gives renown to men !
Her face, the book of praises, where is read
Nothing but curious pleasures, as from thence
Sorrow were ever raz'd, and testy wrath
Could never be her mild companion.
You gods, that made me man, and sway in love,
That have inflam'd desire in my breast,   20
To taste the fruit of yon celestial tree,
Or die in the adventure, be my helps,
As I am son and servant to your will,
To compass such a boundless happiness !
Ant. Prince Pericles,—
Per. That would be son to great Antiochus.
Ant. Before thee stands this fair Hesperides,
With golden fruit, but dangerous to be touch'd ;
For death-like dragons here affright thee hard :
Her face, like heaven, enticeth thee to view   30
Her countless glory, which desert must gain ;
And which, without desert, because thine eye
Presumes to reach, all thy whole heap must die.
Yon sometime famous princes, like thyself,
Drawn by report, adventurous by desire,
Tell thee with speechless tongues, and semblance pale,

That, without covering, save yon field of stars,
They here stand martyrs, slain in Cupid's wars;
And with dead cheeks advise thee to desist,
For going on death's net, whom none resist.   40
  Per. Antiochus, I thank thee, who hath taught
My frail mortality to know itself,
And by those fearful objects to prepare
This body, like to them, to what I must:
For death remember'd should be like a mirror,
Who tells us, life 's but breath, to trust it, error.
I 'll make my will then; and, as sick men do,
Who know the world, see heaven, but, feeling woe,
Gripe not at earthly joys, as erst they did:
So, I bequeath a happy peace to you,   50
And all good men, as every prince should do;
My riches to the earth from whence they came,
[*To the Daughter of* ANTIOCHUS.] But my unspotted
  fire of love to you.
Thus, ready for the way of life or death,
I wait the sharpest blow.
  Ant. Scorning advice, read the conclusion then;
Which read and not expounded, 't is decreed,
As these before thee, thou thyself shalt bleed.
  Daugh. Of all, 'say'd yet, may'st thou prove pros-
  perous!
Of all, 'say'd yet, I wish thee happiness.   60
  Per. Like a bold champion, I assume the lists,
Nor ask advice of any other thought
But faithfulness, and courage.   [*Reads the riddle.*

I am no viper, yet I feed
On mother's flesh, which did me breed;
I sought a husband, in which labour
I found that kindness in a father.
He's father, son, and husband mild,
I mother, wife, and yet his child.
How they may be, and yet in two,   70
As you will live, resolve it you.

Sharp physic is the last: but, O you powers!
That give heaven countless eyes to view men's acts.
Why cloud they not their sights perpetually,
If this be true, which makes me pale to read it?
Fair glass of light, I lov'd you, and could still,
Were not this glorious casket stor'd with ill:
But I must tell you,—now, my thoughts revolt;
For he's no man on whom perfections wait,
That, knowing sin within, will touch the gate.   80
You 're a fair viol, and your sense the strings,
Who, finger'd to make man his lawful music,
Would draw heaven down and all the gods to hearken;
But being play'd upon before your time,
Hell only danceth at so harsh a chime.
Good sooth, I care not for you.
  Ant. Prince Pericles, touch not, upon thy life,
For that 's an article within our law,
As dangerous as the rest. Your time 's expired:
Either expound now, or receive your sentence.   90
  Per. Great king,
Few love to hear the sins they love to act;
'T would 'braid yourself too near for me to tell it.
Who has a book of all that monarchs do,
He 's more secure to keep it shut, than shown;
For vice repeated is like the wandering wind,
Blows dust in other's eyes, to spread itself;
And yet the end of all is bought thus dear,
The breath is gone, and the sore eyes see clear
To stop the air would hurt them.   The blind mole
  casts   100
Copp'd hills towards heaven, to tell the earth is
  throng'd
By man's oppression; and the poor worm doth die
  for 't.
Kings are earth's gods; in vice their law 's their will;
And if Jove stray, who dares say Jove doth ill?
It is enough you know; and it is fit,
What being more known grows worse, to smother it.
All love the womb that their first being bred,
Then give my tongue like leave to love my head.
  Ant. [*Aside.*] Heaven, that I had thy head! he has
  found the meaning;
But I will gloze with him.—Young Prince of Tyre, 110
Though by the tenor of our strict edict,

Your exposition misinterpreting,
We might proceed to cancel of your days;
Yet hope, succeeding from so fair a tree
As your fair self, doth tune us otherwise.
Forty days longer we do respite you;
If by which time our secret be undone,
This mercy shows, we 'll joy in such a son:
And until then your entertain shall be,
As doth befit our honour, and your worth.   120
                [*Exeunt all but* PERICLES.
  Per. How courtesy would seem to cover sin,
When what is done is like an hypocrite,
The which is good in nothing but in sight!
If it be true that I interpret false,
Then were it certain, you were not so bad,
As with foul incest to abuse your soul;
Where now you 're both a father and a son,
By your untimely claspings with your child,
(Which pleasure fits a husband, not a father,)
And she an eater of her mother's flesh,   130
By the defiling of her parent's bed;
And both like serpents are, who though they feed
On sweetest flowers, yet they poison breed.
Antioch, farewell! for wisdom sees, those men
Blush not in actions blacker than the night,
Will shun no course to keep them from the light:
One sin, I know, another doth provoke;
Murder 's as near to lust, as flame to smoke.
Poison and treason are the hands of sin,
Ay, and the targets, to put off the shame: 140
Then, lest my life be cropp'd to keep you clear,
By flight I 'll shun the danger which I fear.   [*Exit.*
          Re-enter ANTIOCHUS.
  Ant. He hath found the meaning, for which we
  mean
To have his head.
He must not live to trumpet forth my infamy,
Nor tell the world, Antiochus doth sin
In such a loathed manner:
And therefore instantly this prince must die;
For by his fall my honour must keep high.
Who attends us there?
                Enter THALIARD.
  Thal.   Doth your highness call? 150
  Ant. Thaliard!
You 're of our chamber, and our mind partakes
Her private actions to your secrecy;
And for your faithfulness we will advance you.
Thaliard, behold, here 's poison, and here 's gold;
We hate the Prince of Tyre, and thou must kill him:
It fits thee not to ask the reason why,
Because we bid it. Say, is it done?
  Thal. My lord, 't is done.
  Ant. Enough.—   160
          Enter a Messenger.
Let your breath cool yourself, telling your haste.
  Mess. My lord, Prince Pericles is fled.   [*Exit.*
  Ant.   As thou
Wilt live, fly after: and, like an arrow, shot
From a well-experienc'd archer, hits the mark
His eye doth level at, so ne'er return,
Unless thou say, "Prince Pericles is dead."
  Thal. My lord,
If I can get him within my pistol's length,
I 'll make him sure enough: so, farewell to your
  highness.
  Ant. Thaliard, adieu. [*Exit* THALIARD.] — Till
  Pericles be dead,   170
My heart can lend no succour to my head.   [*Exit.*

SCENE II.—Tyre.   A Room in the Palace.
          Enter PERICLES.

  Per. [*To those without.*] Let none disturb us.—Why
  should this change of thoughts,
The sad companion, dull-ey'd melancholy,
Be my so us'd a guest, as not an hour,
In the day's glorious walk, or peaceful night

(The tomb where grief should sleep), can breed me
quiet?
Here pleasures court mine eyes, and mine eyes shun
them,
And danger, which I fear'd, is at Antioch,
Whose arm seems far too short to hit me here ;
Yet neither pleasure's art can joy my spirits,
Nor yet the other's distance comfort me.　10
Then it is thus : the passions of the mind,
That have their first conception by mis-dread,
Have after-nourishment and life by care ;
And what was first but fear what might be done,
Grows elder now, and cares it be not done.
And so with me :—the great Antiochus
('Gainst whom I am too little to contend,
Since he 's so great, can make his will his act)
Will think me speaking, though I swear to silence ,
Nor boots it me to say, I honour him,　20
If he suspect I may dishonour him :
And what may make him blush in being known,
He 'll stop the course by which it might be known.
With hostile forces he 'll o'erspread the land,
And with the ostent of war will look so huge,
Amazement shall drive courage from the state ;
Our men be vanquish'd ere they do resist,
And subjects punish'd that ne'er thought offence :
Which care of them, not pity of myself,
(Who am no more but as the tops of trees,　30
Which fence the roots they grow by, and defend
them,)
Makes both my body pine, and soul to languish,
And punish that before, that he would punish.

Enter HELICANUS *and other Lords.*

1 *Lord.* Joy and all comfort in your sacred breast !
2 *Lord.* And keep your mind, till you return to us,
Peaceful and comfortable !
Hel. Peace, peace ! and give experience tongue.
They do abuse the king that flatter him :
For flattery is the bellows blows up sin ;
The thing which is flatter'd, but a spark,　40
To which that blast gives heat and stronger glowing ;
Whereas reproof, obedient and in order,
Fits kings, as they are men, for they may err :
When Signior Sooth here does proclaim a peace,
He flatters you, makes war upon your life.
Prince, pardon me, or strike me, if you please ;
I cannot be much lower than my knees.
Per. All leave us else ; but let your cares o'erlook
What shipping and what lading 's in our haven,
And then return to us. [*Exeunt Lords.*]—Helicanus,
thou　50
Hast moved us : what seest thou in our looks ?
Hel. An angry brow, dread lord.
Per. If there be such a dart in princes' frowns,
How durst thy tongue move anger to our face ?
Hel. How dare the plants look up to heaven, from
whence
They have their nourishment ?
Per.　Thou know'st I have power
To take thy life from thee.
Hel. [*Kneeling.*]　I have ground the axe myself ;
Do you but strike the blow.
Per.　Rise, pr'ythee, rise ;
Sit down ; thou art no flatterer :
I thank thee for it ; and heaven forbid　60
That kings should let their ears hear their faults hid !
Fit counsellor, and servant for a prince,
Who by thy wisdom mak'st a prince thy servant,
What wouldst thou have me do ?
Hel.　To bear with patience
Such griefs as you yourself do lay upon yourself.
Per. Thou speak'st like a physician, Helicanus,
That minister'st a potion unto me,
That thou wouldst tremble to receive thyself.
Attend me then : I went to Antioch,
Where, as thou know'st, against the face of death　70
I sought the purchase of a glorious beauty
From whence an issue I might propagate,
Are arms to princes, and bring joys to subjects,
Her face was to mine eye beyond all wonder ;
The rest (hark in thine ear) as black as incest :

Which by my knowledge found, the sinful father
Seem'd not to strike, but smooth ; but thou know'st
this,
'T is time to fear, when tyrants seem to kiss,
Which fear so grew in me, I hither fled,
Under the covering of a careful night,　80
Who seem'd my good protector : and, being here,
Bethought me what was past, what might succeed.
I knew him tyrannous ; and tyrants' fears
Decrease not, but grow faster than their years.
And should he doubt it (as no doubt he doth),
That I should open to the listening air,
How many worthy princes' bloods were shed,
To keep his bed of blackness unlaid ope,—
To lop that doubt he 'll fill this land with arms,
And make pretence of wrong that I have done him ;　90
When all, for mine, if I may call 't, offence,
Must feel war's blow, who spares not innocence :
Which love to all, of which thyself art one,
Who now reprovedst me for it,—
Hel.　Alas, sir !
Per. Drew sleep out of mine eyes, blood from my
cheeks,
Musings into my mind, a thousand doubts
How I might stop this tempest ere it came ;
And finding little comfort to relieve them,
I thought it princely charity to grieve them.
Hel. Well, my lord, since you have given me leave
to speak,　100
Freely will I speak. Antiochus you fear,
And justly too, I think, you fear the tyrant,
Who either by public war, or private treason,
Will take away your life.
Therefore, my lord, go travel for a while,
Till that his rage and anger be forgot,
Or till the Destinies do cut his thread of life.
Your rule direct to any ; if to me,
Day serves not light more faithful than I 'll be.
Per. I do not doubt thy faith ;　110
But should he wrong my liberties in my absence ?
Hel. We 'll mingle our bloods together in the earth,
From whence we had our being and our birth.
Per. Tyre, I now look from thee then, and to Tharsus
Intend my travel, where I 'll hear from thee,
And by whose letters I 'll dispose myself.
The care I had, and have, of subjects' good,
On thee I lay, whose wisdom's strength can bear it.
I 'll take thy word for faith, not ask thine oath ;
Who shuns not to break one, will sure crack both.　120
But in our orbs we 'll live so round and safe,
That time of both this truth shall ne'er convince,
Thou show'dst a subject's shine, I a true prince.
[*Exeunt.*

SCENE III.—Tyre. An Ante-chamber in the Palace.

Enter THALIARD.

Thal. So, this is Tyre, and this is the court. Here
must I kill King Pericles ; and if I do not, I am sure
to be hanged at home : 't is dangerous.—Well, I perceive he was a wise fellow, and had good discretion,
that, being bid to ask what he would of the king,
desired he might know none of his secrets : now do I
see he had some reason for 't ; for if a king bid a man
be a villain, he is bound by the indenture of his oath
to be one.—Hush ! here come the lords of Tyre.

Enter HELICANUS, ESCANES, *and other Lords.*

Hel. You shall not need, my fellow peers of Tyre,　10
Further to question me of your king's departure :
His seal'd commission, left in trust with me,
Doth speak sufficiently, he 's gone to travel.
Thal. [*Aside.*] How ! the king gone ?
Hel. If further yet you will be satisfied,
Why, as it were unlicens'd of your loves,
He would depart, I 'll give some light unto you.
Being at Antioch—
Thal. [*Aside.*]　What from Antioch ?
Hel. Royal Antiochus (on what cause I know not)
Took some displeasure at him : at least, he judg'd so ;
And doubting lest that he had err'd or sinn'd,　21

To show his sorrow he'd correct himself;
So puts himself unto the shipman's toil,
With whom each minute threatens life or death.
Thal. [*Aside.*] Well, I perceive
I shall not be hang'd now, although I would;
But since he's gone, the king it sure must please,
He 'scap'd the land, to perish at the sea.—
I'll present myself.—[*To them.*] Peace to the lords of
    Tyre!
Hel. Lord Thaliard from Antiochus is welcome. 30
Thal. From him I come,
With message unto princely Pericles;
But since my landing I have understood,
Your lord has betook himself to unknown travels,
My message must return from whence it came.
Hel. We have no reason to desire it,
Commended to our master, not to us:
Yet, ere you shall depart, this we desire,
As friends to Antioch, we may feast in Tyre.
                        [*Exeunt.*

SCENE IV.—Tharsus. A Room in the Governor's
House.

Enter CLEON, DIONYZA, *and Attendants.*

Cle. My Dionyza, shall we rest us here,
And by relating tales of others' griefs,
See if 't will teach us to forget our own?
Dio. That were to blow at fire in hope to quench it;
For who digs hills because they do aspire,
Throws down one mountain to cast up a higher.
O my distressed lord! even such our griefs are;
Here they 're but felt and seen with mischief's eyes,
But like to groves, being topp'd, they higher rise.
Cle. O Dionyza, 10
Who wanteth food, and will not say he wants it,
Or can conceal his hunger, till he famish?
Our tongues and sorrows do sound deep
Our woes into the air; our eyes do weep,
Till lungs fetch breath that may proclaim them
    louder;
That if heaven slumber, while their creatures want,
They may awake their helps to comfort them.
I'll then discourse our woes, felt several years,
And, wanting breath to speak, help me with tears.
Dio. I'll do my best, sir. 20
Cle. This Tharsus, o'er which I have the government,
A city, on whom plenty held full hand,
For riches strew'd herself even in the street;
Whose towers bore heads so high, they kiss'd the
    clouds,
And strangers ne'er beheld, but wonder'd at;
Whose men and dames so jetted, and adorn'd,
Like one another's glass to trim them by:
Their tables were stor'd full to glad the sight,
And not so much to feed on as delight;
All poverty was scorn'd, and pride so great, 30
The name of help grew odious to repeat.
Dio. O! 't is too true.
Cle. But see what heaven can do! By this our
    change,
These mouths, whom but of late, earth, sea, and air,
Were all too little to content and please,
Although they gave their creatures in abundance,
As houses are defil'd for want of use,
They are now starv'd for want of exercise:
Those palates, who, not yet two summers younger,
Must have inventions to delight the taste, 40
Would now be glad of bread, and beg for it:
Those mothers, who, to nousle up their babes,
Thought nought too curious, are ready now

To eat those little darlings whom they lov'd.
So sharp are hunger's teeth, that man and wife
Draw lots, who first shall die to lengthen life.
Here stands a lord, and there a lady weeping;
Here many sink, yet those which see them fall,
Have scarce strength left to give them burial.
Is not this true? 50
Dio. Our cheeks and hollow eyes do witness it.
Cle. O! let those cities that of plenty's cup
And her prosperities so largely taste,
With their superfluous riots, hear these tears:
The misery of Tharsus may be theirs.

Enter a Lord.

Lord. Where's the lord governor?
Cle. Here.
Speak out thy sorrows which thou bring'st, in haste,
For comfort too too far for us to expect.
Lord. We have descried, upon our neighbouring
    shore, 60
A portly sail of ships make hitherward.
Cle. I thought as much.
One sorrow never comes, but brings an heir
That may succeed as his inheritor;
And so in ours. Some neighbouring nation,
Taking advantage of our misery,
Hath stuff'd these hollow vessels with their power,
To beat us down, the which are down already;
And make a conquest of unhappy me,
Whereas no glory's got to overcome. 70
Lord. That's the least fear; for, by the semblance
Of their white flags display'd, they bring us peace,
And come to us as favourers, not as foes.
Cle. Thou speak'st like him's untutor'd to repeat:
Who makes the fairest snow, means most deceit.
But bring they what they will, and what they can,
What need we fear?
The ground's the lowest, and we're half way there.
Go, tell their general, we attend him here,
To know for what he comes, and whence he comes, 80
And what he craves.
Lord. I go, my lord.   [*Exit.*
Cle. Welcome is peace, if he on peace consist;
If wars, we are unable to resist.

Enter PERICLES, *with Attendants.*

Per. Lord governor, for so we hear you are,
Let not our ships and number of our men
Be, like a beacon fir'd, to amaze your eyes,
We have heard your miseries as far as Tyre,
And seen the desolation of your streets;
Nor come we to add sorrow to your tears, 90
But to relieve them of their heavy load:
And these our ships, you happily may think
Are like the Trojan horse, was stuff'd within
With bloody veins, expecting overthrow,
Are stor'd with corn to make your needy bread,
And give them life whom hunger starv'd half dead.
All. The gods of Greece protect you!
And we will pray for you.
Per.   Arise, I pray you, rise:
We do not look for reverence, but for love,
And harbourage for ourself, our ships, and men. 100
Cle. The which when any shall not gratify,
Or pay you with unthankfulness in thought,
Be it our wives, our children, or ourselves,
The curse of heaven and men succeed their evils!
Till when, (the which, I hope, shall ne'er be seen,)
Your grace is welcome to our town and us.
Per. Which welcome we'll accept; feast here
    awhile,
Until our stars, that frown, lend us a smile. [*Exeunt.*

ACT II.

Enter GOWER.

Gower.
ERE have you seen a mighty king
His child, I wis, to incest bring;
A better prince and benign lord,
That will prove awful both in deed and
    word.
Be quiet then, as men should be,
Till he has pass'd necessity.
I'll show you those in troubles reign,
Losing a mite, a mountain gain.
The good in conversation
(To whom I give my benison)   10
Is still at Tharsus, where each man
Thinks all is writ he spoken can;
And, to remember what he does,
Build his statue to make him glorious:
But tidings to the contrary
Are brought your eyes; what need speak I?

Dumb-show.

Enter, at one door, PERICLES, *talking with* CLEON;
*all the Train with them. Enter, at another door, a
Gentleman, with a letter to* PERICLES: PERICLES
shows the letter to CLEON; *then gives the Messenger
a reward, and knights him. Exeunt* PERICLES,
CLEON, &c., *severally.*

Gow. Good Helicane, that stay'd at home,
Not to eat honey like a drone,
From others' labours; for though he strive
To killen bad, keep good alive;   20
And, to fulfil his prince' desire,
Sends word of all that haps in Tyre:
How Thaliard came full bent with sin,
And hid intent, to murder him;
And that in Tharsus was not best
Longer for him to make his rest.
He, doing so, put forth to seas,
Where when men been, there's seldom ease;
For now the wind begins to blow;
Thunder above, and deeps below,   30
Make such unquiet, that the ship,
Should house him safe, is wrack'd and split;
And he, good prince, having all lost,
By waves from coast to coast is tost.
All perishen of man, of pelf,
Ne ought escapen but himself;
Till fortune, tir'd with doing bad,
Threw him ashore, to give him glad:
And here he comes. What shall be next,
Pardon old Gower; thus long's the text.   40
                          [*Exit.*

SCENE I.—Pentapolis. An Open Place by the Sea-side.

Enter PERICLES, *wet.*

Per. Yet cease your ire, you angry stars of heaven!
Wind, rain, and thunder, remember, earthly man
Is but a substance that must yield to you;
And I, as fits my nature, do obey you.
Alas! the sea hath cast me on the rocks,
Wash'd me from shore to shore, and left me breath,
Nothing to think on, but ensuing death:
Let it suffice the greatness of your powers,
To have bereft a prince of all his fortunes;

And having thrown him from your watery grave, 10
Here to have death in peace is all he'll crave.

Enter three Fishermen.

1 Fish. What, ho, Pilch!
2 Fish. Ho! come, and bring away the nets.
1 Fish. What, Patch-breech, I say!
3 Fish. What say you, master?
1 Fish. Look how thou stirrest now! come away,
or I'll fetch thee with a wannion.
3 Fish. 'Faith, master, I am thinking of the poor
men, that were cast away before us even now. 19
1 Fish. Alas, poor souls! it grieved my heart to
hear what pitiful cries they made to us to help them,
when, well-a-day, we could scarce help ourselves.
3 Fish. Nay, master, said not I as much, when I
saw the porpus, how he bounced and tumbled? they
say, they're half fish, half flesh: a plague on them!
they ne'er come, but I look to be washed. Master, I
marvel how the fishes live in the sea. 27
1 Fish. Why, as men do a-land: the great ones eat
up the little ones. I can compare our rich misers to
nothing so fitly as to a whale; 'a plays and tumbles,
driving the poor fry before him, and at last devours
them all at a mouthful. Such whales have I heard
on o' the land, who never leave gaping, till they've
swallowed the whole parish, church, steeple, bells,
and all.
Per. [*Aside.*] A pretty moral.
3 Fish. But, master, if I had been the sexton, I
would have been that day in the belfry.
2 Fish. Why, man? 39
3 Fish. Because he should have swallowed me too;
and when I had been in his belly, I would have kept
such a jangling of the bells, that he should never
have left, till he cast bells, steeple, church, and parish,
up again. But if the good King Simonides were of
my mind—
Per. [*Aside.*] Simonides?
3 Fish. We would purge the land of these drones,
that rob the bee of her honey.
Per. [*Aside.*] How from the finny subject of the sea
These fishers tell the infirmities of men; 50
And from their watery empire recollect
All that may men approve, or men detect!—
Peace be at your labour, honest fishermen.
2 Fish. Honest! good fellow, what's that? if it be a
day fits you, scratch out of the calendar, and nobody
look after it.
Per. Y' may see, the sea hath cast me upon your
    coast—
2 Fish. What a drunken knave was the sea, to cast
thee in our way!
Per. A man whom both the waters and the wind, 60
In that vast tennis-court, hath made the ball
For them to play upon, entreats you pity him;
He asks of you, that never us'd to beg.
1 Fish. No, friend, cannot you beg? here's them in
our country of Greece, gets more with begging than
we can do with working.
2 Fish. Canst thou catch any fishes then?
Per. I never practis'd it.
2 Fish. Nay, then thou wilt starve, sure; for here's
nothing to be got now-a-days, unless thou canst fish
for 't. 71
Per. What I have been, I have forgot to know;

But what I am, want teaches me to think on :
A man throng'd up with cold ; my veins are chill,
And have no more of life, than may suffice
To give my tongue that heat to ask your help ;
Which if you shall refuse, when I am dead,
For that I am a man, pray see me buried.   78
  1 Fish. Die, quoth-a? Now, gods forbid it ! I have
a gown here ; come, put it on ; keep thee warm.
Now, afore me, a handsome fellow ! Come, thou
shalt go home, and we 'll have flesh for holidays, fish
for fasting days, and moreo'er puddings and flap-
jacks ; and thou shalt be welcome.
  Per. I thank you, sir.
  2 Fish. Hark you, my friend ; you said you could
not beg.
  Per. I did but crave.
  2 Fish. But crave? Then I 'll turn craver too, and
so I shall scape whipping.   90
  Per. Why, are all your beggars whipped then?
  2 Fish. O ! not all, my friend, not all : for if all
your beggars were whipped, I would wish no better
office than to be a beadle. But, master, I 'll go draw
up the net.   [*Exeunt two of the Fishermen.*
  Per. [*Aside.*] How well this honest mirth becomes
their labour !
  1 Fish. Hark you, sir ; do you know where you are?
  Per. Not well.
  1 Fish. Why, I 'll tell you : this is called Pentapolis,
and our king, the good Simonides.   100
  Per. The good King Simonides, do you call him ?
  1 Fish. Ay, sir ; and he deserves to be so called, for
his peaceable reign, and good government.
  Per. He is a happy king, since he gains from his
subjects the name of good by his government. How
far is his court distant from this shore?
  1 Fish. Marry, sir, half a day's journey : and I 'll
tell you, he hath a fair daughter, and to-morrow is
her birthday ; and there are princes and knights come
from all parts of the world, to joust and tourney for
her love.   111
  Per. Were my fortunes equal to my desires, I could
wish to make one there.
  1 Fish. O, sir ! things must be as they may ; and
what a man cannot get, he may lawfully deal for his
wife's soul.

Re-enter the two Fishermen, drawing up a net.

  2 Fish. Help, master, help ! here 's a fish hangs in
the net, like a poor man's right in the law ; 't will
hardly come out. Ha ! bots on 't ; 't is come at last,
and 't is turned to a rusty armour.   120
  Per. An armour, friends ! I pray you, let me see it.
Thanks, Fortune, yet, that after all thy crosses
Thou giv'st me somewhat to repair myself :
And though it was mine own, part of mine heritage,
Which my dead father did bequeath to me,
With this strict charge, (even as he left his life,)
"Keep it, my Pericles, it hath been a shield
'Twixt me and death " (and pointed to this brace) ;
"For that it sav'd me, keep it ; in like necessity,
The which the gods protect thee from ! may defend
thee."   130
It kept where I kept, I so dearly lov'd it,
Till the rough seas, that spare not any man,
Took it in rage, though calm'd have given 't again.
I thank thee for 't : my shipwrack now 's no ill,
Since I have here my father's gift in 's will.
  1 Fish. What mean you, sir?
  Per. To beg of you, kind friends, this coat of worth,
For it was sometime target to a king ;
I know it by this mark. He lov'd me dearly,
And for his sake I wish the having of it :   140
And that you 'd guide me to your sovereign's court,
Where with it I may appear a gentleman :
And if that ever my low fortunes better,
I 'll pay your bounties ; till then, rest your debtor.
  1 Fish. Why, wilt thou tourney for the lady ?
  Per. I 'll show the virtue I have borne in arms.
  1 Fish. Why, do ye take it ; and the gods give thee
good on 't.
  2 Fish. Ay, but hark you, my friend ; 't was we
that made up this garment through the rough seams

of the waters : there are certain condolements, certain
vails. I hope, sir, if you thrive, you 'll remember from
whence you had it.   153
  Per. Believe it, I will.
By your furtherance I am cloth'd in steel ;
And spite of all the rapture of the sea,
This jewel holds his gilding on my arm :
Unto thy value will I mount myself
Upon a courser, whose delightful steps
Shall make the gazer joy to see him tread.—   160
Only, my friends, I yet am unprovided
Of a pair of bases.
  2 Fish. We 'll sure provide : thou shalt have my
best gown to make thee a pair, and I 'll bring thee to
the court myself.
  Per. Then honour be but equal to my will !
This day I 'll rise, or else add ill to ill.   [*Exeunt.*

Scene II.—*The Same. A Public Way or Platform
leading to the Lists. A Pavilion near it, for the
reception of the* King, Princess, *Ladies, Lords,* &c.

Enter Simonides, Thaisa, *Lords, and Attendants.*

  Sim. Are the knights ready to begin the triumph ?
  1 Lord. They are, my liege ;
And stay your coming to present themselves.
  Sim. Return them, we are ready ; and our daughter,
In honour of whose birth these triumphs are,
Sits here, like beauty's child, whom nature gat
For men to see, and seeing wonder at.   [*Exit a Lord.*
  Thai. It pleaseth you, my royal father, to express
My commendations great, whose merit 's less.
  Sim. 'Tis fit it should be so ; for princes are   10
A model, which heaven makes like to itself :
As jewels lose their glory if neglected,
So princes their renown, if not respected.
'T is now your honour, daughter, to explain
The labour of each knight in his device.
  Thai. Which, to preserve mine honour, I 'll per-
form.

*Enter a Knight : he passes over the stage, and his
Squire presents his shield to the* Princess.

  Sim. Who is the first that doth prefer himself ?
  Thai. A knight of Sparta, my renowned father ;
And the device he bears upon his shield
Is a black Ethiop, reaching at the sun ;   20
The word, *Lux tua vita mihi.*
  Sim. He loves you well that holds his life of you.
             [*The second Knight passes over.*
Who is the second that presents himself ?
  Thai. A prince of Macedon, my royal father ;
And the device he bears upon his shield
Is an arm'd knight, that 's conquer'd by a lady ;
The motto thus, in Spanish, *Piu por dulzura que por
fuerza.*   [*The third Knight passes over.*
  Sim. And what 's the third ?
  Thai.   The third of Antioch ;
And his device, a wreath of chivalry ;
The word, *Me pompæ provexit apex.*   30
             [*The fourth Knight passes over.*
  Sim. What is the fourth ?
  Thai. A burning torch, that 's turned upside down ;
The word, *Quod me alit, me extinguit.*
  Sim. Which shows that beauty hath his power and
will,
Which can as well inflame, as it can kill.
             [*The fifth Knight passes over.*
  Thai. The fifth, a hand environed with clouds,
Holding out gold that 's by the touchstone tried ;
The motto thus, *Sic spectanda fides.*
             [*The sixth Knight passes over.*
  Sim. And what 's
The sixth and last, the which the knight himself   40
With such a graceful courtesy deliver'd ?
  Thai. He seems to be a stranger ; but his present is
A wither'd branch, that 's only green at top ;
The motto, *In hac spe vivo.*
  Sim. A pretty moral :

From the dejected state wherein he is,
He hopes by you his fortunes yet may flourish.
1 *Lord.* He had need mean better than his outward
show
Can any way speak in his just commend;
For by his rusty outside he appears
To have practis'd more the whipstock, than the lance.
2 *Lord.* He well may be a stranger, for he comes
To an honour'd triumph strangely furnished.
3 *Lord.* And on set purpose let his armour rust
Until this day, to scour it in the dust.
Sim. Opinion 's but a fool, that makes us scan
The outward habit by the inward man.
But stay, the knights are coming ; we 'll withdraw
Into the gallery.   [*Exeunt.*
[*Great shouts, and all cry, "The mean knight!"*

SCENE III.—The Same. A Hall of State.—A Banquet
prepared.

Enter SIMONIDES, THAISA, *Ladies, Lords, Knights,
and Attendants.*

Sim. Knights,
To say you 're welcome were superfluous.
To place upon the volume of your deeds,
As in a title page, your worth in arms,
Were more than you expect, or more than 's fit,
Since every worth in show commends itself.
Prepare for mirth, for mirth becomes a feast :
You are princes, and my guests.
Thai.   But you, my knight and guest ;
To whom this wreath of victory I give,
And crown you king of this day's happiness.   10
Per. 'T is more by fortune, lady, than by merit.
Sim. Call it by what you will, the day is yours ;
And here, I hope, is none that envies it.
In framing an artist art hath thus decreed,
To make some good, but others to exceed ;
And you 're her labour'd scholar. Come, queen o' the
feast,
(For, daughter, so you are,) here take your place :
Marshal the rest, as they deserve their grace.
Knights. We are honour'd much by good Simonides.
Sim. Your presence glads our days : honour we
love,   20
For who hates honour, hates the gods above.
Marshal. Sir, yonder is your place.
Per.   Some other is more fit.
1 *Knight.* Contend not, sir ; for we are gentlemen,
That neither in our hearts, nor outward eyes,
Envy the great, nor do the low despise.
Per. You are right courteous knights.
Sim.   Sit, sir ; sit.
[*Aside.*] By Jove, I wonder, that is king of thoughts,
These cates resist me, he not thought upon.
Thai. [*Aside.*] By Juno, that is queen of marriage,
All viands that I eat do seem unsavoury,   30
Wishing him my meat. Sure, he 's a gallant gentle-
man.
Sim. [*Aside.*] He 's but a country gentleman :
Has done no more than other knights have done,
Has broken a staff, or so ; so let it pass.
Thai. [*Aside.*] To me he seems like diamond to
glass.
Per. [*Aside.*] Yon king 's to me like to my father's
picture,
Which tells me in that glory once he was ;
Had princes sit, like stars, about his throne,
And he the sun for them to reverence.
None that beheld him, but, like lesser lights   40
Did vail their crowns to his supremacy ;
Where now his son 's like a glow-worm in the night.
The which hath fire in darkness, none in light :
Whereby I see that Time 's the king of men ;
He 's both their parent, and he is their grave,
And gives them what he will, not what they crave.
Sim. What, are you merry, knights?
1 *Knight.* Who can be other in this royal presence ?
Sim. Here, with a cup that 's stor'd unto the brim,

(As you do love, fill to your mistress' lips,)   50
We drink this health to you.
Knights.   We thank your grace.
Sim. Yet pause awhile ;
Yon knight doth sit too melancholy,
As if the entertainment in our court
Had not a show might countervail his worth.
Note it not you, Thaisa ?
Thai. What is 't to me, my father ?
Sim. O ! attend, my daughter :
Princes, in this, should live like gods above,
Who freely give to every one that comes   60
To honour them ;
And princes, not doing so, are like to gnats
Which make a sound, but kill'd are wonder'd at.
Therefore, to make his entrance more sweet,
Here say, we drink this standing-bowl of wine to him.
Thai. Alas, my father ! it befits not me
Unto a stranger knight to be so bold :
He may my proffer take for an offence.
Since men take women's gifts for impudence.
Sim. How !   70
Do as I bid you, or you 'll move me else.
Thai. [*Aside.*] Now, by the gods, he could not
please me better.
Sim. And furthermore tell him, we desire to know
of him,
Of whence he is, his name, and parentage.
Thai. The king my father, sir, has drunk to you.
Per. I thank him.
Thai. Wishing it so much blood unto your life.
Per. I thank both him and you, and pledge him
freely.
Thai. And further he desires to know of you,
Of whence you are, your name, and parentage.   80
Per. A gentleman of Tyre, (my name, Pericles,)
My education been in arts and arms,)
Who, looking for adventures in the world,
Was by the rough seas reft of ships and men,
And after shipwrack driven upon this shore.
Thai. He thanks your grace ; names himself Pericles,
A gentleman of Tyre,
Who only by misfortune of the seas
Bereft of ships and men, cast on this shore.
Sim. Now, by the gods, I pity his misfortune,   90
And will awake him from his melancholy.
Come, gentlemen, we sit too long on trifles,
And waste the time which looks for other revels.
Even in your armours, as you are address'd,
Will very well become a soldier's dance.
I will not have excuse, with saying, this
Loud music is too harsh for ladies' heads,
Since they love men in arms as well as beds.
[*The Knights dance.*
So this was well ask'd, 't was so well perform'd.
Come, sir ; here 's a lady that wants breathing too :
And I have heard, you knights of Tyre   101
Are excellent in making ladies trip,
And that their measures are as excellent.
Per. In those that practise them, they are, my lord.
Sim. O ! that 's as much as you would be denied
Of your fair courtesy. [*The Knights and Ladies
dance.*]—Unclasp, unclasp ;
Thanks, gentlemen, to all ; all have done well,
[*To* PERICLES.] But you the best.—Pages and lights,
to conduct
These knights unto their several lodgings !—Yours,
sir,
We have given order to be next our own.   110
Per. I am at your grace's pleasure.
Sim. Princes, it is too late to talk of love,
And that 's the mark I know you level at :
Therefore, each one betake him to his rest ;
To-morrow all for speeding do their best.   [*Exeunt.*

SCENE IV.—Tyre. A Room in the Governor's House.

Enter HELICANUS *and* ESCANES.

Hel. No, Escanes, know this of me,
Antiochus from incest liv'd not free :

For which, the most high gods not minding longer
To withhold the vengeance that they had in store,
Due to his heinous capital o..ence,
Even in the height and pride of all his glory,
When he was seated in a chariot
Of an inestimable value, and his daughter with him,
A fire from heaven came, and shrivell'd up
Their bodies, even to loathing ; for they so stunk,   10
That all those eyes ador'd them ere their fall,
Scorn now their hand should give them burial.
  Esca. 'T was very strange.
  Hel.   And yet but just ; for though
This king were great, his greatness was no guard
To bar heaven's shaft, but sin had his reward.
  Esca. 'T is very true.

Enter two or three Lords.

  1 Lord. See, not a man, in private conference
Or council, has respect with him but he.
  2 Lord. It shall no longer grieve without reproof.
  3 Lord. And curs'd be he that will not second it.   20
  1 Lord. Come then.—Lord Helicane, a word.
  Hel. With me ? and welcome.—Happy day, my
    lords.
  1 Lord. Know, that our griefs are risen to the top,
And now at length they overflow their banks.
  Hel. Your griefs ! for what ? wrong not the prince
    you love.
  1 Lord. Wrong not yourself then, noble Helicane ;
But if the prince do live, let us salute him,
Or know what ground 's made happy by his breath.
If in the world he live, we 'll seek him out ;
If in his grave he rest, we 'll find him there ;   30
And be resolv'd, he lives to govern us,
Or dead, gives cause to mourn his funeral,
And leaves us to our free election.
  2 Lord. Whose death 's, indeed, the strongest in our
    censure :
And knowing this kingdom is without a head,
(Like goodly buildings left without a roof)
Soon fall to ruin,) your noble self,
That best know how to rule, and how to reign,
We thus submit unto, our sovereign.
  All. Live, noble Helicane !   40
  Hel. For honour's cause forbear your suffrages :
If that you love Prince Pericles, forbear.
Take I your wish, I leap into the seas,
Where 's hourly trouble for a minute's ease.
A twelvemonth longer, let me entreat you
To forbear the absence of your king ;
If in which time expir'd he not return,
I shall with aged patience bear your yoke.
But if I cannot win you to this love,
Go search like nobles, like noble subjects,   50
And in your search spend your adventurous worth ;
Whom if you find, and win unto return,
You shall like diamonds sit about his crown.
  1 Lord. To wisdom he 's a fool that will not yield :
And since Lord Helicane enjoineth us,
We with our travels will endeavour it.
  Hel. Then you love us, we you, and we 'll clasp
    hands :
When peers thus knit, a kingdom ever stands.
                          [*Exeunt.*

Scene V.—Pentapolis. A Room in the Palace.

Enter Simonides, *reading a letter: the Knights*
meet him.

  1 Knight. Good morrow to the good Simonides.
  Sim. Knights, from my daughter this I let you
    know,
That for this twelvemonth she 'll not undertake
A married life.
Her reason to herself is only known,
Which yet from her by no means can I get.
  2 Knight. May we not get access to her, my lord?
  Sim. 'Faith, by no means ; she hath so strictly
Tied her to her chamber, that 't is impossible.
One twelve moons more she 'll wear Diana's livery ;   10

This by the eye of Cynthia hath she vow'd,
And on her virgin honour will not break it.
  3 Knight. Loath to bid farewell, we take our
    leaves.   [*Exeunt Knights.*
  Sim. So,
They 're well despatch'd ; now to my daughter's
    letter.
She tells me here, she 'll wed the stranger knight,
Or never more to view nor day nor light.
'T is well, mistress ; your choice agrees with mine ;
I like that well :—nay, how absolute she 's in 't,
Not minding whether I dislike or no !   20
Well, I commend her choice,
And will no longer have it be delay'd.
Soft ! here he comes : I must dissemble it.

Enter Pericles.

  Per. All fortune to the good Simonides !
  Sim. To you as much, sir ! I am beholding to you
For your sweet music this last night : I do
Protest, my ears were never better fed
With such delightful pleasing harmony.
  Per. It is your grace's pleasure to commend,
Not my desert.
  Sim.   Sir, you are music's master.   30
  Per. The worst of all her scholars, my good lord.
  Sim. Let me ask one thing.
What do you think of my daughter, sir ?
  Per. A most virtuous princess.
  Sim. And she is fair too, is she not ?
  Per. As a fair day in summer ; wondrous fair.
  Sim. My daughter, sir, thinks very well of you ;
Ay, so well, sir, that you must be her master,
And she will be your scholar : therefore, look to it.
  Per. I am unworthy for her schoolmaster.   40
  Sim. She thinks not so ; peruse this writing else.
  Per. [*Aside.*] What 's here ?
A letter, that she loves the knight of Tyre ?
'T is the king's subtilty, to have my life.—
O ! seek not to entrap me, gracious lord,
A stranger and distressed gentleman,
That never aim'd so high to love your daughter,
But bent all offices to honour her.
  Sim. Thou hast bewitch'd my daughter, and thou art
A villain.
  Per.   By the gods, I have not :   50
Never did thought of mine levy offence ;
Nor never did my actions yet commence
A deed might gain her love, or your displeasure.
  Sim. Traitor, thou liest.
  Per.   Traitor !
  Sim.   Ay, traitor.
  Per. Even in his throat, unless it be the king,
That calls me traitor, I return the lie.
  Sim. [*Aside.*] Now, by the gods, I do applaud his
    courage.
  Per. My actions are as noble as my thoughts,
That never relish'd of a base descent.
I came unto your court for honour's cause,   60
And not to be a rebel to her state ;
And he that otherwise accounts of me,
This sword shall prove, he 's honour's enemy.
  Sim. No?
Here comes my daughter, she can witness it.

Enter Thaisa.

  Per. Then, as you are as virtuous as fair,
Resolve your angry father, if my tongue
Did e'er solicit, or my hand subscribe
To any syllable that made love to you ?
  Thai. Why, sir, say if you had,   70
Who takes offence at that would make me glad ?
  Sim. Yea, mistress, are you so peremptory ?—
  [*Aside.*] I am glad on 't with all my heart.—
I 'll tame you ; I 'll bring you in subjection.
Will you, not having my consent,
Bestow your love and your affections
Upon a stranger ? [*aside*] who, for aught I know,
May be (nor can I think the contrary)
As great in blood as I myself.—
Therefore, hear you, mistress ; either frame   80
Your will to mine ; and you, sir, hear you,

Either be rul'd by me, or I will make you—
Man and wife.
Nay, come, your hands and lips must seal it too ;
And being join'd, I 'll thus your hopes destroy ;
And for a further grief,—God give you joy !—
What, are you both pleas'd ?

Thai.   Yes, if you love me, sir.
Per. Even as my life, or blood that fosters it.
Sim. What ! are you both agreed ?
Both. Yes, if 't please your majesty.   90
Sim. It pleaseth me so well, that I will see you wed ;
Then, with what haste you can, get you to bed.
                             [*Exeunt.*

ACT III.

Enter GOWER.

Gower.
NOW sleep yslaked hath the rout ;
No din but snores the house about,
Made louder by the o'er-fed breast
Of this most pompous marriage-feast.
The cat, with eyne of burning coal,
Now couches 'fore the mouse's hole ;
And crickets sing at the oven's mouth,
All the blither for their drouth.
Hymen hath brought the bride to bed,
Where, by the loss of maidenhead,   10
A babe is moulded.—Be attent,
And time, that is so briefly spent,
With your fine fancies quaintly eche ;
What 's dumb in show, I 'll plain with speech.

Dumb-show.

Enter PERICLES *and* SIMONIDES *at one door, with
Attendants ; a Messenger meets them, kneels, and
gives* PERICLES *a letter :* PERICLES *shows it to*
SIMONIDES ; *the Lords kneel to* PERICLES. *Then
enter* THAISA *with child, and* LYCHORIDA : SIMO-
NIDES *shows his daughter the letter ; she rejoices :
she and* PERICLES *take leave of her father, and all
depart.*

Gow. By many a dern and painful perch
Of Pericles the careful search
By the four opposing coigns,
Which the world together joins,
Is made, with all due diligence,
That horse, and sail, and high expense,   20
Can stead the quest. At last from Tyre
(Fame answering the most strange inquire)
To the court of King Simonides
Are letters brought, the tenor these :—
Antiochus and his daughter dead ;
The men of Tyrus on the head
Of Helicanus would set on
The crown of Tyre, but he will none :
The mutiny he there hastes t' oppress ;
Says to 'em, if King Pericles   30
Come not home in twice six moons,
He, obedient to their dooms,
Will take the crown. The sum of this,
Brought hither to Pentapolis,
Yravished the regions round,
And every one with claps can sound,
" Our heir-apparent is a king !
Who dream'd, who thought of such a thing ?"
Brief, he must hence depart to Tyre :
His queen, with child, makes her desire   40
(Which who shall cross ?) along to go :
Omit we all their dole and woe :
Lychorida, her nurse, she takes,
And so to sea. Their vessel shakes
On Neptune's billow ; half the flood

Hath their keel cut : but fortune's mood
Varies again ; the grizzly north
Disgorges such a tempest forth,
That, as a duck for life that dives,
So up and down the poor ship drives.   50
The lady shrieks, and well-a-near
Does fall in travail with her fear :
And what ensues in this fell storm
Shall for itself itself perform.
I nill relate, action may
Conveniently the rest convey,
Which might not what by me is told.
In your imagination hold
This stage the ship, upon whose deck
The sea-tost Pericles appears to speak.   60
                             [*Exit.*

SCENE I.

Enter PERICLES, *on shipboard.*

Per. Thou god of this great vast, rebuke these surges,
Which wash both heaven and hell ; and thou, that hast
Upon the winds command, bind them in brass,
Having call'd them from the deep. O ! still
Thy deafening, dreadful thunders ; gently quench
Thy nimble, sulphurous flashes !—O ! how, Lychorida,
How does my queen ?—Thou storm, venomously
Wilt thou spit all thyself ?—The seaman's whistle
Is as a whisper in the ears of death,
Unheard. Lychorida !—Lucina, O !   10
Divinest patroness, and midwife gentle
To those that cry by night, convey thy deity
Aboard our dancing boat ; make swift the pangs
Of my queen's travails !—Now, Lychorida !

Enter LYCHORIDA, *with an Infant.*

Lyc. Here is a thing too young for such a place,
Who, if it had conceit, would die, as I
Am like to do. Take in your arms this piece
Of your dead queen.
Per.   How, how, Lychorida !
Lyc. Patience, good sir ; do not assist the storm.
Here 's all that is left living of your queen,   20
A little daughter : for the sake of it,
Be manly, and take comfort.
Per.   O you gods !
Why do you make us love your goodly gifts,
And snatch them straight away ? We here below
Recall not what we give, and therein may
Vie honour with you.
Lyc.   Patience, good sir,
Even for this charge.
Per.   Now, mild may be thy life !
For a more blust'rous birth had never babe :

Quiet and gentle thy conditions!
For thou 'rt the rudeliest welcome to this world,   30
That e'er was prince's child.   Happy what follows!
Thou hast as chiding a nativity,
As fire, air, water, earth, and heaven can make,
To herald thee from the womb: even at the first,
Thy loss is more than can thy portage quit,
With all thou canst find here.—Now the good gods
Throw their best eyes upon 't!

Enter two Sailors.

1 Sail. What courage, sir? God save you!
Per. Courage enough.   I do not fear the flaw;
It has done to me the worst.   Yet for the love   40
Of this poor infant, this fresh-new sea-farer,
I would it would be quiet.
1 Sail. Slack the bolins there.   Thou wilt not, wilt
thou?   Blow, and split thyself.
2 Sail. But sea-room, an the brine and cloudy billow
kiss the moon, I care not.
1 Sail. Sir, your queen must overboard: the sea
works high, the wind is loud, and will not lie till the
ship be cleared of the dead.
Per. That 's your superstition.   50
1 Sail. Pardon us, sir; with us at sea it hath been
still observed, and we are strong in custom.   There-
fore briefly yield her, for she must overboard straight.
Per. As you think meet.—Most wretched queen!
Lyc. Here she lies, sir.
Per. A terrible childbed hast thou had, my dear;
No light, no fire: the unfriendly elements
Forgot thee utterly; nor have I time
To give thee hallow'd to thy grave, but straight
Must cast thee, scarcely coffin'd, in the ooze;   60
Where, for a monument upon thy bones,
And aye-remaining lamps, the belching whale,
And humming water, must o'erhelm thy corse,
Lying with simple shells.—O Lychorida!
Bid Nestor bring me spices, ink and paper,
My casket and my jewels; and bid Nicander
Bring me the satin coffer: lay the babe
Upon the pillow.   Hie thee, whiles I say
A priestly farewell to her: suddenly, woman.
                              [*Exit* LYCHORIDA.
2 Sail. Sir, we have a chest beneath the hatches,
caulk'd and bitumed ready.   71
Per. I thank thee.   Mariner, say what coast is this?
2 Sail. We are near Tharsus.
Per. Thither, gentle mariner,
Alter thy course from Tyre.   When canst thou reach
    it?
2 Sail. By break of day, if the wind cease.
Per. O, make for Tharsus.—
There will I visit Cleon, for the babe
Cannot hold out to Tyrus: there I 'll leave it
At careful nursing.—Go thy ways, good mariner: 80
I 'll bring the body presently.   [*Exeunt.*

SCENE II.—Ephesus. A Room in CERIMON'S House.

Enter CERIMON, *a Servant, and some Persons who
have been shipwracked.*

Cer. Philemon, ho!

Enter PHILEMON.

Phil. Doth my lord call?
Cer. Get fire and meat for these poor men:
It has been a turbulent and stormy night.
Serv. I have been in many; but such a night as
this,
Till now I ne'er endur'd.
Cer. Your master will be dead ere you return:
There 's nothing can be minister'd to nature,
That can recover him.—[*To* PHILEMON.] Give this to
        the 'pothecary,
And tell me how it works. [*Exeunt all but* CERIMON.

Enter two Gentlemen.

1 Gent.   Good morrow.   10
2 Gent. Good morrow to your lordship.

Cer.   Gentlemen,
Why do you stir so early?
1 Gent. Sir,
Our lodgings, standing bleak upon the sea,
Shook, as the earth did quake;
The very principals did seem to rend,
And all to topple.   Pure surprise and fear
Made me to quit the house.
2 Gent. That is the cause we trouble you so early;
'T is not our husbandry.
Cer.   O! you say well.   20
1 Gent. But I much marvel that your lordship,
        having
Rich tire about you, should at these early hours
Shake off the golden slumber of repose.
'T is most strange,
Nature should be so conversant with pain,
Being thereto not compell'd.
Cer.   I held it ever,
Virtue and cunning were endowments greater
Than nobleness and riches: careless heirs
May the two latter darken and expend;
But immortality attends the former,   30
Making a man a god.   'T is known, I ever
Have studied physic, through which secret art,
By turning o'er authorities, I have
(Together with my practice) made familiar
To me and to my aid the blest infusions
That dwell in vegetives, in metals, stones;
And I can speak of the disturbances
That nature works, and of her cures; which doth give
        me
A more content in course of true delight,
Than to be thirsty after tottering honour,   40
Or tie my treasure up in silken bags,
To please the fool and death.
2 Gent. Your honour has through Ephesus pour'd
        forth
Your charity, and hundreds call themselves
Your creatures, who by you have been restor'd:
And not your knowledge, your personal pain, but
        even
Your purse, still open, hath built Lord Cerimon
Such strong renown as never shall decay.

Enter two or three Servants, with a chest.

Serv. So; lift there.
Cer.   What is that?
Serv.   Sir, even now
Did the sea toss upon our shore this chest: 50
'T is of some wrack.
Cer.   Set it down; let 's look upon 't.
2 Gent. 'T is like a coffin, sir.
Cer.   Whate'er it be,
'T is wondrous heavy.   Wrench it open straight:
If the sea's stomach be o'ercharg'd with gold,
'T is a good constraint of fortune it belches upon us.
2 Gent. 'T is so, my lord.
Cer.   How close 't is caulk'd and bitum'd!
Did the sea cast it up?
Serv. I never saw so huge a billow, sir,
As toss'd it upon shore.
Cer.   Come, wrench it open.
Soft!—it smells most sweetly in my sense.   60
2 Gent. A delicate odour.
Cer. As ever hit my nostril.   So, up with it.
O you most potent gods! what 's here? a corse!
1 Gent. Most strange!
Cer. Shrouded in cloth of state; balm'd and en-
        treasur'd
With full bags of spices!   A passport too:
Apollo, perfect me i' the characters!
                              [*Reads from a scroll.*

*Here I give to understand,
(If e'er this coffin drive a-land,)
I, King Pericles, have lost*   70
*This queen, worth all our mundane cost.
Who finds her, give her burying;
She was the daughter of a king:
Besides this treasure for a fee,
The gods requite his charity!*

If thou liv'st, Pericles, thou hast a heart
That even cracks for woe!—This chanc'd to-night.
2 Gent. Most likely, sir.
Cer. 　　　　　　　　Nay, certainly to-night;
For look, how fresh she looks.—They were too rough,
That threw her in the sea. Make fire within : 　　80
Fetch hither all the boxes in my closet. [*Exit a Servant.*
Death may usurp on nature many hours,
And yet the fire of life kindle again
The o'erpress'd spirits. I heard
Of an Egyptian, that had nine hours lien dead,
Who was by good appliance recovered.

Re-enter Servant, with boxes, napkins, and fire.

Well said, well said ; the fire and the cloths.—
The rough and woful music that we have,
Cause it to sound, 'beseech you.
The vial once more ;—how thou stirr'st, thou block!—
The music there! I pray you, give her air. 　　91
Gentlemen,
This queen will live : nature awakes ; a warmth
Breathes out of her : she hath not been entranc'd
Above five hours. See, how she 'gins to blow
Into life's flower again !
1 Gent. 　　　　　　　　The heavens,
Through you, increase our wonder, and set up
Your fame for ever.
Cer. 　　　　　　She is alive! behold,
Her eyelids, cases to those heavenly jewels
Which Pericles hath lost, 　　　　　　　　100
Begin to part their fringes of bright gold :
The diamonds of a most praised water
Do appear, to make the world twice rich. Live,
And make us weep to hear your fate, fair creature,
Rare as you seem to be ! 　　　　　　[*She moves.*
Thai. 　　　　　　　　O dear Diana !
Where am I? Where's my lord? What world is this?
2 Gent. Is not this strange?
1 Gent. Most rare.
Cer. Hush, gentle neighbours !
Lend me your hands ; to the next chamber bear her.
Get linen : now this matter must be look'd to, 　　111
For her relapse is mortal. Come, come ;
And Æsculapius guide us !
　　　　　　　[*Exeunt, carrying* THAISA *away.*

SCENE III.—Tharsus. A Room in CLEON's House.

Enter PERICLES, CLEON, DIONYZA, LYCHORIDA,
　　with MARINA *in her arms.*

Per. Most honour'd Cleon, I must needs be gone :
My twelve months are expir'd, and Tyrus stands
In a litigious peace. You, and your lady,
Take from my heart all thankfulness ; the gods
Make up the rest upon you !
Cle. Your shafts of fortune, though they hurt you
　　　　mortally,
Yet glance full wanderingly on us.
Dion. 　　　　　　O your sweet queen !
That the strict fates had pleas'd you had brought her
　　　　hither,
To have bless'd mine eyes with her !

Per. 　　　　　　　　We cannot but obey
The powers above us. Could I rage and roar 　　10
As doth the sea she lies in, yet the end
Must be as 't is. My gentle babe Marina (whom,
For she was born at sea, I have nam'd so) here
I charge your charity withal, and leave her
The infant of your care, beseeching you
To give her princely training, that she may
Be manner'd as she is born.
Cle. 　　　　Fear not, my lord, but think
Your grace, that fed my country with your corn
(For which the people's prayers still fall upon you),
Must in your child be thought on. If neglection 　　20
Should therein make me vile, the common body,
By you reliev'd, would force me to my duty ;
But if to that my nature need a spur,
The gods revenge it upon me and mine,
To the end of generation !
Per. 　　　　　　　I believe you ;
Your honour and your goodness teach me to 't,
Without your vows. Till she be married, madam,
By bright Diana, whom we honour, all
Unscissar'd shall this hair of mine remain,
Though I show ill in 't. So I take my leave. 　　30
Good madam, make me blessed in your care
In bringing up my child.
Dion. 　　　　　　I have one myself,
Who shall not be more dear to my respect,
Than yours, my lord.
Per. 　　　　　　Madam, my thanks and prayers.
Cle. We 'll bring your grace even to the edge o' the
　　　　shore ;
Then give you up to the mask'd Neptune, and
The gentlest winds of heaven.
Per. 　　　　　　　I will embrace
Your offer. Come, dear'st madam.—O ! no tears,
Lychorida, no tears :
Look to your little mistress, on whose grace 　　40
You may depend hereafter.—Come, my lord.
　　　　　　　　　　　　　　[*Exeunt.*

SCENE IV.—Ephesus. A Room in CERIMON's House.

Enter CERIMON *and* THAISA.

Cer. Madam, this letter, and some certain jewels,
Lay with you in your coffer : which are
At your command. Know you the character?
Thai. It is my lord's.
That I was shipp'd at sea, I well remember,
Even on my eaning time ; but whether there
Delivered, by the holy gods,
I cannot rightly say. But since King Pericles,
My wedded lord, I ne'er shall see again,
A vestal livery will I take me to, 　　10
And never more have joy.
Cer. Madam, if this your purpose as ye speak,
Diana's temple is not distant far,
Where you may abide till your date expire.
Moreover, if you please, a niece of mine
Shall there attend you.
Thai. My recompense is thanks, that's all ;
Yet my good will is great, though the gift small.
　　　　　　　　　　　　　　[*Exeunt.*

ACT IV.

Enter GOWER.

Gower.

IMAGINE Pericles arriv'd at Tyre,
Welcom'd and settled to his own desire.
His woful queen we leave at Ephesus,
Unto Diana there a votaress.
Now to Marina bend your mind,
Whom our fast-growing scene must find
At Tharsus, and by Cleon train'd
In music, letters; who hath gain'd
Of education all the grace,
Which makes her both the heart and
     place   10
Of general wonder. But, alack!
That monster envy, oft the wrack
Of earned praise, Marina's life
Seeks to take off by treason's knife.
And in this kind hath our Cleon
One daughter, and a wench full grown,
Even ripe for marriage-rite: this maid
Hight Philoten; and it is said
For certain in our story, she
Would ever with Marina be: 20
Be 't when she weav'd the sleided silk
With fingers long, small, white as milk;
Or when she would with sharp needle wound
The cambric, which she made more sound
By hurting it; or when to the lute
She sung, and made the night-bird mute,
That still records with moan; or when
She would with rich and constant pen
Vail to her mistress Dian; still
This Philoten contends in skill   30
With absolute Marina: so
With the dove of Paphos might the crow
Vie feathers white. Marina gets
All praises, which are paid as debts,
And not as given. This so darks
In Philoten all graceful marks,
That Cleon's wife, with envy rare,
A present murderer does prepare
For good Marina, that her daughter
Might stand peerless by this slaughter.   40
The sooner her vile thoughts to stead,
Lychorida, our nurse, is dead:
And cursed Dionyza hath
The pregnant instrument of wrath
Prest for this blow. The unborn event
I do commend to your content:
Only I carry winged time
Post on the lame feet of my rhyme;
Which never could I so convey,
Unless your thoughts went on my way.—   50
Dionyza doth appear,
With Leonine, a murderer.   [*Exit.*

SCENE I.—Tharsus. *An Open Place near the Sea-shore.*

Enter DIONYZA and LEONINE.

Dion. Thy oath remember: thou hast sworn to do 't:
'T is but a blow, which never shall be known.
Thou canst not do a thing i' the world so soon,
To yield thee so much profit. Let not conscience,
Which is but cold, inflaming love i' thy bosom,
Inflame too nicely; nor let pity, which
Even women have cast off, melt thee, but be
A soldier to thy purpose.
Leon. I 'll do 't; but yet she is a goodly creature.
Dion. The fitter, then, the gods should have her.
     Here   10
She comes weeping for her only mistress' death.
Thou art resolv'd?
Leon.   I am resolv'd.

Enter MARINA, *with a basket of flowers.*

Mar. No, I will rob Tellus of her weed,
To strew thy green with flowers: the yellows, blues,
The purple violets, and marigolds,
Shall as a carpet hang upon thy grave,
While summer-days do last. Ah me, poor maid!
Born in a tempest, when my mother died,
This world to me is like a lasting storm,
Whirring me from my friends.   20
Dion. How now, Marina! why do you keep alone?
How chance my daughter is not with you? Do not
Consume your blood with sorrowing: you have
A nurse of me. Lord! how your favour 's chang'd
With this unprofitable woe! Come,
Give me your flowers, ere the sea mar it.
Walk with Leonine; the air is quick there,
And it pierces and sharpens the stomach. Come,
Leonine, take her by the arm, walk with her.
Mar. No, I pray you;   30
I 'll not bereave you of your servant.
Dion. Come, come;
I love the king your father, and yourself,
With more than foreign heart. We every day
Expect him here: when he shall come, and find
Our paragon to all reports thus blasted,
He will repent the breadth of his great voyage;
Blame both my lord and me, that we have ta'en
No care to your best courses. Go, I pray you;
Walk, and be cheerful once again: reserve   40
That excellent complexion, which did steal
The eyes of young and old. Care not for me;
I can go home alone.
Mar.   Well, I will go;
But yet I have no desire to it.
Dion. Come, come, I know 't is good for you.—
Walk half an hour, Leonine, at the least.
Remember what I have said.
Leon.   I warrant you, madam.
Dion. I 'll leave you, my sweet lady, for a while.
Pray you, walk softly, do not heat your blood:
What! I must have care of you.
Mar.   My thanks, sweet madam.—
                                    [*Exit* DIONYZA.
Is the wind westerly that blows?
Leon.   South-west.   51
Mar. When I was born, the wind was north.
Leon.   Was 't so?
Mar. My father, as nurse said, did never fear,
But cried "Good seamen!" to the sailors, galling
His kingly hands with haling of the ropes;
And, clasping to the mast, endur'd a sea
That almost burst the deck.
Leon. When was this?
Mar. When I was born:
Never were waves nor wind more violent;   60
And from the ladder-tackle washes off
A canvass-climber. "Ha!" says one, "wilt out?"
And with a dropping industry they skip

From stem to stern: the boatswain whistles, and
The master calls, and trebles their confusion.
Leon. Come; say your prayers.
Mar. What mean you?
Leon. If you require a little space for prayer,
I grant it. Pray; but be not tedious,
For the gods are quick of ear, and I am sworn 70
To do my work with haste.
Mar. Why will you kill me?
Leon. To satisfy my lady.
Mar. Why would she have me kill'd?
Now, as I can remember, by my troth,
I never did her hurt in all my life.
I never spake bad word, nor did ill turn
To any living creature: believe me, la,
I never kill'd a mouse, nor hurt a fly:
I trod upon a worm against my will, 80
But I wept for it. How have I offended,
Wherein my death might yield her any profit,
Or my life imply her any danger?
Leon. My commission
Is not to reason of the deed, but do 't.
Mar. You will not do 't for all the world, I hope.
You are well-favour'd, and your looks foreshow
You have a gentle heart. I saw you lately,
When you caught hurt in parting two that fought:
Good sooth, it show'd well in you: do so now: 90
Your lady seeks my life; come you between,
And save poor me, the weaker.
Leon.   I am sworn,
And will despatch.   [*Seizes her.*
            Enter Pirates.
1 *Pir.* Hold, villain!   [LEONINE *runs away.*
2 *Pir.* A prize! a prize!
3 *Pir.* Half-part, mates, half-part. Come, let 's have
her aboard suddenly. [*Exeunt Pirates with* MARINA.

SCENE II.—Near the Same.
            Enter LEONINE.
Leon. These roguing thieves serve the great pirate
Valdes;
And they have seiz'd Marina. Let her go:
There 's no hope she 'll return. I 'll swear she 's dead,
And thrown into the sea.—But I 'll see further;
Perhaps they will but please themselves upon her,
Not carry her aboard. If she remain,
Whom they have ravish'd must by me be slain.[*Exit.*

SCENE III.—Mitylene. A Room in a Brothel.
            Enter Pander, Bawd, and BOULT.
Pand. Boult!
Boult. Sir?
Pand. Search the market narrowly; Mitylene is
full of gallants: we lost too much money this mart,
by being too wenchless.
Bawd. We were never so much out of creatures.
We have but poor three, and they can do no more than
they can do; and they with continual action are even
as good as rotten.
Pand. Therefore, let 's have fresh ones, whate'er
we pay for them. If there be not a conscience to be
used in every trade, we shall never prosper. 12
Bawd. Thou say'st true: 't is not the bringing up of
poor bastards,—as I think, I have brought up some
eleven—
Boult. Ay, to eleven; and brought them down again.
But shall I search the market?
Bawd. What else, man? The stuff we have, a
strong wind will blow it to pieces, they are so pitifully
sodden. 20
Pand. Thou say'st true; they 're too unwholesome,
o' conscience. The poor Transylvanian is dead, that
lay with the little baggage.
Boult. Ay, she quickly pooped him; she made him
roast-meat for worms. But I 'll go search the market.
            [*Exit.*

Pand. Three or four thousand chequins were as
pretty a proportion to live quietly, and so give over.
Bawd. Why to give over, I pray you? is it a shame
to get when we are old? 29
Pand. O! our credit comes not in like the commodity; nor the commodity wages not with the
danger: therefore, if in our youths we could pick up
some pretty estate, 't were not amiss to keep our door
hatched. Besides, the sore terms we stand upon with
the gods, will be strong with us for giving over.
Bawd. Come, other sorts offend as well as we.
Pand. As well as we? ay, and better too; we offend
worse. Neither is our profession any trade; it 's no
calling. But here comes Boult.

Re-enter BOULT, *with the Pirates and* MARINA.
Boult. [*To* MARINA.] Come your ways.—My masters,
you say she 's a virgin? 41
1 *Pir.* O, sir! we doubt it not.
Boult. Master, I have gone through for this piece,
you see: if you like her, so; if not, I have lost my
earnest.
Bawd. Boult, has she any qualities?
Boult. She has a good face, speaks well, and has
excellent good clothes: there 's no further necessity of
qualities can make her be refused.
Bawd. What 's her price, Boult? 50
Boult. I cannot be baited one doit of a thousand
pieces.
Pand. Well, follow me, my masters, you shall have
your money presently. Wife, take her in: instruct
her what she has to do, that she may not be raw in her
entertainment.   [*Exeunt Pander and Pirates.*
Bawd. Boult, take you the marks of her, the colour
of her hair, complexion, height, her age, with warrant
of her virginity; and cry, "He that will give most,
shall have her first." Such a maidenhead were no
cheap thing, if men were as they have been. Get this
done as I command you. 62
Boult. Performance shall follow.   [*Exit.*
Mar. Alack, that Leonine was so slack, so slow!
He should have struck, not spoke; or that these pirates
(Not enough barbarous) had not o'erboard thrown me
For to seek my mother!
Bawd. Why lament you, pretty one?
Mar. That I am pretty.
Bawd. Come, the gods have done their part in you.
Mar. I accuse them not. 71
Bawd. You are light into my hands, where you are
like to live.
Mar. The more my fault,
To scape his hands where I was like to die.
Bawd. Ay, and you shall live in pleasure.
Mar. No.
Bawd. Yes, indeed, shall you, and taste gentlemen
of all fashions. You shall fare well; you shall have
the difference of all complexions. What! do you stop
your ears? 81
Mar. Are you a woman?
Bawd. What would you have me be, an I be not a
woman?
Mar. An honest woman, or not a woman.
Bawd. Marry, whip thee, gosling: I think I shall
have something to do with you. Come, you're a young
foolish sapling, and must be bowed as I would have
you.
Mar. The gods defend me! 90
Bawd. If it please the gods to defend you by men,
then men must comfort you, men must feed you, men
must stir you up.—Boult 's returned.

            Re-enter BOULT.
Now, sir, hast thou cried her through the market?
Boult. I have cried her almost to the number of her
hairs: I have drawn her picture with my voice.
Bawd. And, I pr'ythee, tell me, how dost thou find
the inclination of the people, especially of the younger
sort? 99
Boult. 'Faith, they listened to me, as they would
have hearkened to their father's testament. There
was a Spaniard's mouth so watered, that he went to
bed to her very description.

Bawd. We shall have him here to-morrow with his best ruff on.

Boult. To-night, to-night. But, mistress, do you know the French knight that cowers i' the hams?

Bawd. Who? Monsieur Veroles?   108

Boult. Ay: he offered to cut a caper at the proclamation; but he made a groan at it, and swore he would see her to-morrow.

Bawd. Well, well; as for him, he brought his disease hither: here he does but repair it. I know, he will come in our shadow, to scatter his crowns in the sun.

Boult. Well, if we had of every nation a traveller, we should lodge them with this sign.   117

Bawd. [*To* MARINA.] Pray you, come hither awhile. You have fortunes coming upon you. Mark me: you must seem to do that fearfully, which you commit willingly; to despise profit, where you have most gain. To weep that you live as ye do, makes pity in your lovers: seldom, but that pity begets you a good opinion, and that opinion a mere profit.

Mar. I understand you not.

Boult. O! take her home, mistress, take her home: these blushes of hers must be quenched with some present practice.

Bawd. Thou say'st true, i' faith, so they must; for your bride goes to that with shame, which is her way to go with warrant.   131

Boult. 'Faith, some do, and some do not. But, mistress, if I have bargained for the joint,—

Bawd. Thou may'st cut a morsel off the spit.

Boult. I may so?

Bawd. Who should deny it? Come, young one, I like the manner of your garments well.

Boult. Ay, by my faith, they shall not be changed yet.   139

Bawd. Boult, spend thou that in the town: report what a sojourner we have; you'll lose nothing by custom. When nature framed this piece, she meant thee a good turn; therefore, say what a paragon she is, and thou hast the harvest out of thine own report.

Boult. I warrant you, mistress, thunder shall not so awake the beds of eels, as my giving out her beauty stir up the lewdly-inclined. I'll bring home some to-night.

Bawd. Come your ways: follow me.

Mar. If fires be hot, knives sharp, or waters deep, Untied I still my virgin knot will keep.   151 Diana, aid my purpose!

Bawd. What have we to do with Diana? Pray you, will you go with us?   [*Exeunt.*

SCENE IV.—Tharsus. A Room in CLEON's House.

Enter CLEON *and* DIONYZA.

Dion. Why, are you foolish? Can it be undone?

Cle. O Dionyza! such a piece of slaughter The sun and moon ne'er look'd upon.

Dion.   I think, You'll turn a child again.

Cle. Were I chief lord of all this spacious world, I'd give it to undo the deed. O lady, Much less in blood than virtue, yet a princess To equal any single crown o' the earth, I' the justice of compare! O villain Leonine!   10 Whom thou hast poison'd too. If thou hadst drunk to him, 't had been a kindness Becoming well thy fact: what canst thou say, When noble Pericles shall demand his child?

Dion. That she is dead. Nurses are not the fates, To foster it, nor ever to preserve. She died at night; I'll say so. Who can cross it? Unless you play the pious innocent, And, for an honest attribute, cry out, "She died by foul play."

Cle.   O! go to. Well, well, Of all the faults beneath the heavens, the gods   20 Do like this worst.

Dion.   Be one of those, that think The petty wrens of Tharsus will fly hence, And open this to Pericles. I do shame

---

To think of what a noble strain you are, And of how coward a spirit.

Cle.   To such proceeding Who ever but his approbation added, Though not his prime consent, he did not flow From honourable sources.

Dion.   Be it so, then; Yet none does know, but you, how she came dead, Nor none can know, Leonine being gone.   30 She did distain my child, and stood between Her and her fortunes: none would look on her, But cast their gazes on Marina's face; Whilst ours was blurted at, and held a malkin, Not worth the time of day. It pierc'd me thorough; And though you call my course unnatural, You not your child well loving, yet I find, It greets me as an enterprise of kindness, Perform'd to your sole daughter.

Cle.   Heavens forgive it!

Dion. And as for Pericles,   40 What should he say? We wept after her hearse, And yet we mourn: her monument Is almost finish'd, and her epitaphs In glittering golden characters express A general praise to her, and care in us At whose expense 't is done.

Cle.   Thou art like the harpy, Which, to betray, dost, with thine angel's face, Seize with thine eagle's talons.

Dion. You are like one, that superstitiously Doth swear to the gods, that winter kills the flies: 50 But yet, I know, you'll do as I advise.   [*Exeunt.*

Enter GOWER, *before the monument of* MARINA *at Tharsus.*

Gow. Thus time we waste, and longest leagues make short; Sail seas in cockles, have an wish but for 't; Making (to take your imagination) From bourn to bourn, region to region. By you being pardon'd, we commit no crime To use one language, in each several clime, Where our scenes seem to live. I do beseech you To learn of me, who stand i' the gaps to teach you, The stages of our story. Pericles   60 Is now again thwarting the wayward seas, Attended on by many a lord and knight, To see his daughter, all his life's delight. Old Escanes, whom Helicanus late Advanc'd in time to great and high estate, Is left to govern. Bear you it in mind, Old Helicanus goes along behind. Well-sailing ships, and bounteous winds, have brought This king to Tharsus, (think his pilot thought, So with his steerage shall your thoughts grow on,)   70 To fetch his daughter home, who first is gone. Like motes and shadows see them move awhile; Your ears unto your eyes I'll reconcile.

Dumb-show.

Enter PERICLES, *with his Train, at one door;* CLEON *and* DIONYZA *at the other.* CLEON *shows* PERICLES *the tomb of* MARINA; *whereat* PERICLES *makes lamentation, puts on sackcloth, and in a mighty passion departs.*

Gow. See, how belief may suffer by foul show! This borrow'd passion stands for true old woe; And Pericles, in sorrow all devour'd, With sighs shot through, and biggest tears o'er-show'r'd, Leaves Tharsus, and again embarks. He swears Never to wash his face, nor cut his hairs; He puts on sackcloth, and to sea. He bears   80 A tempest, which his mortal vessel tears, And yet he rides it out. Now please you wit The epitaph is for Marina writ By wicked Dionyza.   [*Reads the inscription on* MARINA'S *monument.*

The fairest, sweet'st, and best, lies here, Who wither'd in her spring of year:

She was of Tyrus the king's daughter,
On whom foul death hath made this slaughter.
Marina was she call'd; and at her birth,
Thetis, being proud, swallow'd some part o' the
   earth: 90
Therefore the earth, fearing to be o'erflow'd,
Hath Thetis' birth-child on the heavens bestow'd:
Wherefore she does (and swears she'll never stint)
Make raging battery upon shores of flint.
No visor does become black villainy
So well as soft and tender flattery.
Let Pericles believe his daughter's dead,
And bear his courses to be ordered
By Lady Fortune; while our scene must play
His daughter's woe and heavy well-a-day, 100
In her unholy service. Patience then,
And think you now are all in Mitylen.   [*Exit.*

SCENE V.—Mitylene. A Street before the Brothel.

Enter, from the brothel, two Gentlemen.

1 *Gent.* Did you ever hear the like?
2 *Gent.* No, nor never shall do in such a place as
this, she being once gone.
1 *Gent.* But to have divinity preached there! did
you ever dream of such a thing?
2 *Gent.* No, no. Come, I am for no more bawdy-
houses. Shall's go hear the vestals sing?
1 *Gent.* I'll do anything now that is virtuous; but I
am out of the road of rutting for ever.   [*Exeunt.*

SCENE VI.—The Same. A Room in the Brothel.

Enter Pander, Bawd, and BOULT.

Pand. Well, I had rather than twice the worth of
her, she had ne'er come here.
Bawd. Fie, fie upon her! she is able to freeze the
god Priapus, and undo a whole generation: we must
either get her ravished, or be rid of her. When she
should do for clients her fitment, and do me the kindness of our profession, she has me her quirks, her
reasons, her master-reasons, her prayers, her knees,
that she would make a puritan of the devil, if he
should cheapen a kiss of her. 10
Boult. 'Faith, I must ravish her, or she'll disfurnish
us of all our cavaliers, and make all our swearers
priests.
Pand. Now, the pox upon her green-sickness for
me!
Bawd. 'Faith, there's no way to be rid on't, but by
the way to the pox. Here comes the Lord Lysimachus,
disguised.
Boult. We should have both lord and lown, if the
peevish baggage would but give way to customers. 20

Enter LYSIMACHUS.

Lys. How now! How a dozen of virginities?
Bawd. Now, the gods to-bless your honour!
Boult. I am glad to see your honour in good health.
Lys. You may so; 't is the better for you that your
resorters stand upon sound legs. How now, whole-
some iniquity! have you that a man may deal withal,
and defy the surgeon?
Bawd. We have here one, sir, if she would—but
there never came her like in Mitylene.
Lys. If she'd do the deed of darkness, thou wouldst
say. 31
Bawd. Your honour knows what 't is to say, well
enough.
Lys. Well; call forth, call forth.
Boult. For flesh and blood, sir, white and red, you
shall see a rose; and she were a rose indeed, if she had
but—
Lys. What, pr'ythee?
Boult. O, sir! I can be modest. 39
Lys. That dignifies the renown of a bawd, no less
than it gives a good report to a number to be chaste.

Enter MARINA.

Bawd. Here comes that which grows to the stalk;—
never plucked yet, I can assure you.—Is she not a fair
creature?
Lys. 'Faith, she would serve after a long voyage at
sea. Well, there's for you: leave us.
Bawd. I beseech your honour, give me leave, a word,
and I'll have done presently.
Lys. I beseech you, do.
Bawd. [*To* MARINA.] First, I would have you note,
this is an honourable man. 51
Mar. I desire to find him so, that I may worthily
note him.
Bawd. Next, he's the governor of this country, and
a man whom I am bound to.
Mar. If he govern the country, you are bound to
him indeed; but how honourable he is in that, I know
not.
Bawd. 'Pray you, without any more virginal fenc-
ing, will you use him kindly? He will line your apron
with gold. 61
Mar. What he will do graciously, I will thankfully
receive.
Lys. Have you done?
Bawd. My lord, she's not paced yet; you must take
some pains to work her to your manage. Come, we
will leave his honour and her together.
Lys. Go thy ways. [*Exeunt Bawd, Pander, and*
BOULT.]—Now, pretty one, how long have you been at
this trade? 70
Mar. What trade, sir?
Lys. Why, I cannot name 't but I shall offend.
Mar. I cannot be offended with my trade. Please
you to name it.
Lys. How long have you been of this profession?
Mar. E'er since I can remember.
Lys. Did you go to it so young? Were you a game-
ster at five, or at seven?
Mar. Earlier too, sir, if now I be one.
Lys. Why, the house you dwell in proclaims you to
be a creature of sale. 81
Mar. Do you know this house to be a place of such
resort, and will come into 't? I hear say, you are of
honourable parts, and are the governor of this place.
Lys. Why, hath your principal made known unto
you who I am?
Mar. Who is my principal?
Lys. Why, your herb-woman; she that sets seed
and roots of shame and iniquity. O! you have heard
something of my power, and so stand aloof for more
serious wooing. But I protest to thee, pretty one, my
authority shall not see thee, or else, look friendly
upon thee. Come, bring me to some private place:
come, come. 94
Mar. If you were born to honour, show it now;
If put upon you, make the judgment good
That, thought you worthy of it.
Lys. How's this? how's this?—Some more:—be sage.
Mar.   For me,
That am a maid, though most ungentle fortune
Hath plac'd me in this sty, where, since I came, 100
Diseases have been sold dearer than physic,—
O, that the gods
Would set me free from this unhallow'd place,
Though they did change me to the meanest bird
That flies i' the purer air!
Lys.   I did not think
Thou couldst have spoke so well; ne'er dream'd thou
      couldst.
Had I brought hither a corrupted mind,
Thy speech had alter'd it. Hold, here's gold for thee:
Persever in that clear way thou goest,
And the gods strengthen thee!
Mar.   The gods preserve you!
Lys. For me, be you thoughten 111
That I came with no ill intent; for to me
The very doors and windows savour vilely.
Farewell. Thou art a piece of virtue, and
I doubt not but thy training hath been noble.
Hold, here's more gold for thee.
A curse upon him, die he like a thief,

That robs thee of thy goodness! If thou dost
Hear from me, it shall be for thy good.

Re-enter BOULT.

Boult. I beseech your honour, one piece for me. 120
Lys. Avaunt, thou damned door-keeper! Your house,
But for this virgin that doth prop it, would
Sink, and overwhelm you. Away! *[Exit.*
Boult. How's this? We must take another course
with you. If your peevish chastity, which is not
worth a breakfast in the cheapest country under the
cope, shall undo a whole household, let me be gelded
like a spaniel. Come your ways.
Mar. Whither would you have me? 129
Boult. I must have your maidenhead taken off, or
the common hangman shall execute it. Come your
way. We'll have no more gentlemen driven away.
Come your ways, I say.

Re-enter Bawd.

Bawd. How now! what's the matter?
Boult. Worse and worse, mistress: she has here
spoken holy words to the Lord Lysimachus.
Bawd. O, abominable!
Boult. She makes our profession as it were to stink
afore the face of the gods.
Bawd. Marry, hang her up for ever! 140
Boult. The nobleman would have dealt with her
like a nobleman, and she sent him away as cold as a
snow-ball; saying his prayers, too.
Bawd. Boult, take her away; use her at thy
pleasure: crack the glass of her virginity, and make
the rest malleable.
Boult. An if she were a thornier piece of ground
than she is, she shall be ploughed.
Mar. Hark, hark, you gods! 149
Bawd. She conjures: away with her! 'Would she
had never come within my doors!—Marry, hang you!
—She's born to undo us.—Will you not go the way of
women-kind? Marry, come up, my dish of chastity
with rosemary and bays! *[Exit.*
Boult. Come, mistress; come your way with me.
Mar. Whither wilt thou have me?
Boult. To take from you the jewel you hold so dear.

Mar. Pr'ythee, tell me one thing first.
Boult. Come now, your one thing.
Mar. What canst thou wish thine enemy to be? 160
Boult. Why, I could wish him to be my master, or
rather, my mistress.
Mar. Neither of these are so bad as thou art,
Since they do better thee in their command.
Thou hold'st a place, for which the pained'st fiend
Of hell would not in reputation change:
Thou art the damned door-keeper to every
Coystril that comes inquiring for his Tib;
To the choleric fisting of every rogue
Thy ear is liable; thy food is such 170
As hath been belch'd on by infected lungs.
Boult. What would you have me do? go to the wars,
would you? where a man may serve seven years for
the loss of a leg, and have not money enough in the
end to buy him a wooden one?
Mar. Do anything but this thou doest. Empty
Old receptacles, or common sewers, of filth;
Serve by indenture to the common hangman:
Any of these ways are yet better than this;
For what thou professest, a baboon, could he speak,
Would own a name too dear. That the gods 181
Would safely deliver me from this place!
Here, here's gold for thee.
If that thy master would gain by me,
Proclaim that I can sing, weave, sew, and dance,
With other virtues, which I'll keep from boast;
And I will undertake all these to teach.
I doubt not but this populous city will
Yield many scholars.
Boult. But can you teach all this you speak of? 190
Mar. Prove that I cannot, take me home again,
And prostitute me to the basest groom
That doth frequent your house.
Boult. Well, I will see what I can do for thee: if I
can place thee, I will.
Mar. But amongst honest women.
Boult. 'Faith, my acquaintance lies little amongst
them. But since my master and mistress have bought
you, there's no going but by their consent; therefore,
I will make them acquainted with your purpose, and
I doubt not but I shall find them tractable enough.
Come; I'll do for thee what I can: come your ways.
[Exeunt.

ACT V.

Enter GOWER.

Gower.
MARINA thus the brothel scapes, and chances
  Into an honest house, our story says.
She sings like one immortal, and she dances
  As goddess-like to her admired lays.
Deep clerks she dumbs; and with her
      needle composes
Nature's own shape, of bud, bird, branch,
      or berry,
That even her art sisters the natural roses;
Her inkle, silk, twin with the rubied cherry:
That pupils lacks she none of noble race,
Who pour their bounty on her; and her gain 10
She gives the cursed bawd. Here we her place,
And to her father turn our thoughts again,
Where we left him, on the sea. We there him lost,
Whence, driven before the winds, he is arriv'd
Here where his daughter dwells: and on this coast
Suppose him now at anchor. The city striv'd
God Neptune's annual feast to keep: from whence

Lysimachus our Tyrian ship espies,
His banners sable, trimm'd with rich expense;
And to him in his barge with fervour hies. 20
In your supposing once more put your sight
Of heavy Pericles; think this his bark:
Where, what is done in action, more, if might,
Shall be discover'd; please you, sit and hark. *[Exit.*

SCENE I.—*On board* PERICLES' *Ship, off Mitylene. A
Pavilion on deck, with a curtain before it;* PERICLES
*within it, reclining on a couch. A barge lying beside
the Tyrian vessel.*

*Enter two Sailors, one belonging to the Tyrian
vessel, the other to the barge; to them* HELICANUS.

Tyr. Sail. [To the Sailor of Mitylene.] Where is
    Lord Helicanus? he can resolve you.
O, here he is.—

Sir, there's a barge put off from Mitylene,
And in it is Lysimachus, the governor,
Who craves to come aboard. What is your will?
Hel. That he have his. Call up some gentlemen.
Tyr. Sail. Ho, gentlemen! my lord calls.

Enter two or three Gentlemen.

1 *Gent.* Doth your lordship call?
Hel. Gentlemen, there is some of worth would
come aboard: I pray, greet them fairly. 10
[*Gentlemen and Sailors descend, and
go on board the barge.*

Enter, from thence, LYSIMACHUS *and Lords ; the
Tyrian Gentlemen and the two Sailors.*

Tyr. Sail. Sir,
This is the man that can in aught you would
Resolve you.
Lys. Hail, reverend sir! the gods preserve you!
Hel. And you, sir, to outlive the age I am,
And die as I would do.
Lys.   You wish me well.
Being on shore, honouring of Neptune's triumphs,
Seeing this goodly vessel ride before us,
I made to it to know of whence you are.
Hel. First, what is your place? 20
Lys. I am the governor of this place you lie before.
Hel. Sir,
Our vessel is of Tyre, in it the king;
A man, who for this three months hath not spoken
To any one, nor taken sustenance,
But to prorogue his grief.
Lys. Upon what ground is his distemperature?
Hel. 'T would be too tedious to repeat ;
But the main grief springs from the loss
Of a beloved daughter and a wife. 30
Lys. May we not see him?
Hel. You may ;
But bootless is your sight: he will not speak
To any.
Lys.   Yet, let me obtain my wish.
Hel. Behold him. [PERICLES *discovered.*] This was
a goodly person,
Till the disaster that, one mortal night,
Drove him to this.
Lys. Sir king, all hail! the gods preserve you!
Hail, royal sir!
Hel. It is in vain ; he will not speak to you! 40
1 *Lord.* Sir, we have a maid in Mitylen, I durst
wager,
Would win some words of him.
Lys.   'T is well bethought.
She, questionless, with her sweet harmony,
And other choice attractions, would allure,
And make a battery through his deafen'd parts,
Which now are midway stopp'd :
She is all happy as the fair'st of all,
And with her fellow-maids is now upon
The leafy shelter that abuts against
The island's side. 50
[*Whispers one of the attendant Lords. Exit Lord.*
Hel. Sure, all effectless ; yet nothing we 'll omit,
That bears recovery's name. But, since your kindness
We have stretch'd thus far, let us beseech you,
That for our gold we may provision have,
Wherein we are not destitute for want,
But weary for the staleness.
Lys.   O, sir, a courtesy,
Which if we should deny, the most just gods
For every graff would send a caterpillar,
And so inflict our province.—Yet once more
Let me entreat to know at large the cause 60
Of your king's sorrow.
Hel.   Sit, sir, I will recount it to you ;—
But see, I am prevented.

Re-enter Lord, with MARINA *and a young Lady.*

Lys.   O! here is
The lady that I sent for.—Welcome, fair one!—
Is 't not a goodly presence?
Hel.   She 's a gallant lady.
Lys. She 's such a one, that were I well assur'd

She came of gentle kind, and noble stock,
I 'd wish no better choice, and think me rarely wed.—
Fair one, all goodness that consists in bounty
Expect even here, where is a kingly patient :
If that thy prosperous and artificial feat 70
Can draw him but to answer thee in aught,
Thy sacred physic shall receive such pay
As thy desires can wish.
Mar.   Sir, I will use
My utmost skill in his recovery, provided
That none but I and my companion maid
Be suffer'd to come near him.
Lys.   Come, let us leave her,
And the gods make her prosperous!—[MARINA *sings.*
Mark'd he your music?
Mar.   No, nor look'd on us.
Lys. See, she will speak to him.
Mar. Hail, sir! my lord, lend ear. 80
Per. Hum! ha!
Mar. I am a maid,
My lord, that ne'er before invited eyes,
But have been gaz'd on like a comet : she speaks,
My lord, that, may be, hath endur'd a grief
Might equal yours, if both were justly weigh'd.
Though wayward fortune did malign my state,
My derivation was from ancestors
Who stood equivalent with mighty kings ;
But time hath rooted out my parentage, 90
And to the world and awkward casualties
Bound me in servitude.—[*Aside.*] I will desist ;
But there is something glows upon my cheek,
And whispers in mine ear, "Go not till he speak."
Per. My fortunes—parentage—good parentage—
To equal mine!—was it not thus? what say you?
Mar. I said, my lord, if you did know my parentage,
You would not do me violence.
Per. I do think so.—Pray you, turn your eyes upon
me.—
You are like something that—What countrywoman?
Here of these shores?
Mar.   No, nor of any shores; 101
Yet I was mortally brought forth, and am
No other than I appear.
Per. I am great with woe, and shall deliver weeping.
My dearest wife was like this maid, and such a one
My daughter might have been : my queen's square
brows ;
Her stature to an inch ; as wand-like straight ;
As silver-voic'd ; her eyes as jewel-like,
And cas'd as richly ; in pace another Juno ;
Who starves the ears she feeds, and makes them
hungry, 110
The more she gives them speech.—Where do you live?
Mar. Where I am but a stranger : from the deck
You may discern the place.
Per.   Where were you bred?
And how achiev'd you these endowments, which
You make more rich to owe?
Mar. If I should tell my history, it would seem
Like lies, disdain'd in the reporting.
Per.   Pr'ythee, speak :
Falseness cannot come from thee, for thou look'st
Modest as justice, and thou seem'st a palace
For the crown'd truth to dwell in. I 'll believe thee,
And make my senses credit thy relation 121
To points that seem impossible ; for thou look'st
Like one I lov'd indeed. What were thy friends?
Didst thou not say, when I did push thee back
(Which was when I perceiv'd thee), that thou cam'st
From good descending?
Mar.   So indeed I did.
Per. Report thy parentage. I think thou saidst
Thou hadst been toss'd from wrong to injury,
And that thou thought'st thy griefs might equal mine,
If both were open'd.
Mar.   Some such thing 130
I said, and said no more but what my thoughts
Did warrant me was likely.
Per.   Tell thy story ;
If thine consider'd prove the thousandth part
Of my endurance, thou art a man, and I
Have suffer'd like a girl : yet thou dost look

Like Patience, gazing on kings' graves, and smiling
Extremity out of act. What were thy friends?
How lost thou them? Thy name, my most kind
    virgin?
Recount, I do beseech thee. Come, sit by me.
  Mar. My name is Marina.
  Per.   O! I am mock'd,   140
And thou by some incensed god sent hither
To make the world to laugh at me.
  Mar.   Patience, good sir,
Or here I 'll cease.
  Per.   Nay, I 'll be patient.
Thou little know'st how thou dost startle me,
To call thyself Marina.
  Mar.   The name
Was given me by one that had some power;
My father, and a king.
  Per.   How! a king's daughter?
And call'd Marina?
  Mar.   You said you would believe me;
But, not to be a troubler of your peace,
I will end here.
  Per.   But are you flesh and blood?   150
Have you a working pulse? and are no fairy?—
Motion!—Well; speak on. Where were you born?
And wherefore call'd Marina?
  Mar.   Call'd Marina,
For I was born at sea.
  Per.   At sea! what mother?
  Mar. My mother was the daughter of a king;
Who died the minute I was born,
As my good nurse Lychorida hath oft
Deliver'd weeping.
  Per.   O! stop there a little.—
[*Aside.*] This is the rarest dream that e'er dull sleep
Did mock sad fools withal; this cannot be.   160
My daughter 's buried.—Well:—where were you bred?
I 'll hear you more, to the bottom of your story,
And never interrupt you.
  Mar. You scorn to believe me; 't were best I did
    give o'er.
  Per. I will believe you by the syllable
Of what you shall deliver. Yet, give me leave :—
How came you in these parts? where were you bred?
  Mar. The king, my father, did in Tharsus leave me,
Till cruel Cleon, with his wicked wife,
Did seek to murder me : and having woo'd   170
A villain to attempt it, who having drawn to do 't,
A crew of pirates came and rescu'd me;
Brought me to Mitylene. But, good sir,
Whither will you have me? Why do you weep? It
    may be,
You think me an impostor : no, good faith ;
I am the daughter to King Pericles,
If good King Pericles be.
  Per. Ho, Helicanus!
  Hel. Calls my lord?
  Per. Thou art a grave and noble counsellor,   180
Most wise in general : tell me, if thou canst,
What this maid is, or what is like to be,
That thus hath made me weep?
  Hel.   I know not ; but
Here is the regent, sir, of Mitylene,
Speaks nobly of her.
  Lys.   She never would tell
Her parentage ; being demanded that,
She would sit still and weep.
  Per. O Helicanus! strike me, honour'd sir ;
Give me a gash, put me to present pain ;
Lest this great sea of joys rushing upon me,   190
O'erbear the shores of my mortality,
And drown me with their sweetness. O! come hither,
Thou that begett'st him that did thee beget ;
Thou that wast born at sea, buried at Tharsus,
And found at sea again.—O Helicanus!
Down on thy knees, thank the holy gods as loud
As thunder threatens us : this is Marina.—
What was thy mother's name? tell me but that,
For truth can never be confirm'd enough,
Though doubts did ever sleep.
  Mar.   First, sir, I pray,   200
What is your title?

  Per. I am Pericles of Tyre : but tell me now
My drown'd queen's name (as in the rest you said
Thou hast been godlike perfect), thou 'rt heir of king-
    doms,
And another life to Pericles thy father.
  Mar. Is it no more to be your daughter, than
To say, my mother's name was Thaisa?
Thaisa was my mother, who did end
The minute I began.
  Per. Now, blessing on thee! rise ; thou art my child.
Give me fresh garments! Mine own, Helicanus ; 211
She is not dead at Tharsus, as she should have been,
By savage Cleon : she shall tell thee all ;
When thou shalt kneel, and justify in knowledge,
She is thy very princess.—Who is this?
  Hel. Sir, 't is the governor of Mitylene,
Who, hearing of your melancholy state,
Did come to see you.
  Per.   I embrace you.—
Give me my robes : I am wild in my beholding.
O heavens, bless my girl ! But hark ! what music?—
Tell Helicanus, my Marina, tell him   221
O'er, point by point, for yet he seems to doubt,
How sure you are my daughter.—But what music?
  Hel. My lord, I hear none.
  Per. None?
The music of the spheres ! List, my Marina.
  Lys. It is not good to cross him : give him way.
  Per. Rarest sounds ! Do ye not hear?—
  Lys. My lord, I hear.   [*Music.*
  Per.   Most heavenly music :
It nips me unto list'ning, and thick slumber   230
Hangs upon mine eyes : let me rest.   [*Sleeps.*
  Lys. A pillow for his head.
    [*The curtain before the pavilion of* Pericles
    is closed.
So, leave him all.—Well, my companion-friends,
If this but answer to my just belief,
I 'll well remember you.
    [*Exeunt* Lysimachus, Helicanus, Marina,
    and attendant Lady.

Scene II.—The Same.

Pericles *on the deck asleep ;* Diana *appearing to
    him in a vision.*

  Dia. My temple stands in Ephesus : hie thee thither,
And do upon mine altar sacrifice.
There, when my maiden priests are met together,
Before the people all,
Reveal how thou at sea didst lose thy wife :
To mourn thy crosses, with thy daughter's, call,
And give them repetition to the life.
Or perform my bidding, or thou liv'st in woe :
Do it, and happy, by my silver bow !
Awake, and tell thy dream.   [*Disappears.*
  Per. Celestial Dian, goddess argentine,   11
I will obey thee !—Helicanus !

    Enter Lysimachus, Helicanus, *and* Marina.

  Hel.   Sir?
  Per. My purpose was for Tharsus, there to strike
The inhospitable Cleon ; but I am
For other service first : toward Ephesus
Turn our blown sails ; eftsoons I 'll tell thee why.—
Shall we refresh us, sir, upon your shore,
And give you gold for such provision
As our intents will need?
  Lys. Sir,   20
With all my heart ; and when you come ashore,
I have another suit.
  Per.   You shall prevail,
Were it to woo my daughter ; for it seems
You have been noble towards her.
  Lys.   Sir, lend your arm.
  Per. Come, my Marina.   [*Exeunt.*

  Enter Gower, *before the Temple of* Diana *at* Ephesus.

  Gow. Now our sands are almost run ;
More a little, and then dumb.

This, my last boon, give me,
For such kindness must relieve me,
That you aptly will suppose 30
What pageantry, what feats, what shows,
What minstrelsy, and pretty din,
The regent made in Mitylen,
To greet the king. So he thriv'd,
That he is promis'd to be wiv'd
To fair Marina; but in no wise
Till he had done his sacrifice,
As Dian bade: whereto being bound,
The interim, pray you, all confound.
In feather'd briefness sails are fill'd, 40
And wishes fall out as they 're will'd.
At Ephesus, the temple see,
Our king, and all his company.
That he can hither come so soon,
Is by your fancy's thankful doom. [*Exit.*

SCENE III.—The Temple of DIANA at Ephesus;
THAISA standing near the altar, as high priestess;
a number of Virgins on each side; CERIMON and
other Inhabitants of Ephesus attending.

Enter PERICLES, *with his Train;* LYSIMACHUS,
HELICANUS, MARINA, *and a Lady.*

Per. Hail, Dian! to perform thy just command,
I here confess myself the King of Tyre;
Who, frighted from my country, did wed,
At Pentapolis, the fair Thaisa.
At sea in childbed died she, but brought forth
A maid-child call'd Marina; who, O goddess!
Wears yet thy silver livery. She at Tharsus
Was nurs'd with Cleon, whom at fourteen years
He sought to murder: but her better stars
Brought her to Mitylene; against whose shore 10
Riding, her fortunes brought the maid aboard us,
Where, by her own most clear remembrance, she
Made known herself my daughter.
Thai. Voice and favour!—
You are, you are—O royal Pericles!— [*Faints.*
Per. What means the woman? she dies: help,
gentlemen!
Cer. Noble sir,
If you have told Diana's altar true,
This is your wife.
Per. Reverend appearer, no:
I threw her overboard with these very arms.
Cer. Upon this coast, I warrant you.
Per. 'T is most certain.
Cer. Look to the lady.—O! she 's but overjoy'd. 21
Early in blust'ring morn this lady was
Thrown on this shore. I op'd the coffin,
Found there rich jewels; recover'd her, and plac'd her
Here in Diana's temple.
Per. May we see them?
Cer. Great sir, they shall be brought you to my
house,
Whither I invite you. Look! Thaisa is
Recovered.
Thai. O, let me look!
If he be none of mine, my sanctity
Will to my sense bend no licentious ear, 30
But curb it, spite of seeing. Like him you speak,
Like him you are. Did you not name a tempest,
A birth, and death?
Per. The voice of dead Thaisa!
Thai. That Thaisa am I, supposed dead
And drown'd.
Per. Immortal Dian!
Thai. Now I know you better.-
When we with tears parted Pentapolis,
The king, my father, gave you such a ring. [*Shews a ring.*
Per. This, this: no more, you gods! your present
kindness

Makes my past miseries sports: you shall do well, 40
That on the touching of her lips I may
Melt, and no more be seen. O! come, be buried
A second time within these arms.
Mar. My heart
Leaps to be gone into my mother's bosom.
[*Kneels to* THAISA.
Per. Look, who kneels here. Flesh of thy flesh,
Thaisa;
Thy burden at the sea, and call'd Marina,
For she was yielded there.
Thai. Bless'd, and mine own!
Hel. Hail, madam, and my queen!
Thai. I know you not.
Per. You have heard me say, when I did fly from
Tyre,
I left behind an ancient substitute: 50
Can you remember what I call'd the man?
I have nam'd him oft.
Thai. 'T was Helicanus then.
Per. Still confirmation!
Embrace him, dear Thaisa; this is he.
Now do I long to hear how you were found,
How possibly preserv'd, and whom to thank,
Besides the gods, for this great miracle.
Thai. Lord Cerimon, my lord; this man,
Through whom the gods have shown their power;
that can
From first to last resolve you.
Per. Reverend sir, 60
The gods can have no mortal officer
More like a god than you. Will you deliver
How this dead queen re-lives?
Cer. I will, my lord:
'Beseech you, first go with me to my house,
Where shall be shown you all was found with her;
How she came placed here in the temple;
No needful thing omitted.
Per. Pure Dian! bless thee for thy vision; I
Will offer night-oblations to thee. Thaisa,
This prince, the fair-betrothed of your daughter, 70
Shall marry her at Pentapolis. And now,
This ornament,
Makes me look dismal, will I clip to form;
And what this fourteen years no razor touch'd,
To grace thy marriage-day, I 'll beautify.
Thai. Lord Cerimon hath letters of good credit, sir,
My father 's dead.
Per. Heavens, make a star of him! Yet there, my
queen,
We 'll celebrate their nuptials, and ourselves
Will in that kingdom spend our following days: 80
Our son and daughter shall in Tyrus reign.
Lord Cerimon, we do our longing stay,
To hear the rest untold.—Sir, lead 's the way.
[*Exeunt.*

Enter GOWER.

Gow. In Antiochus, and his daughter, you have
heard
Of monstrous lust the due and just reward:
In Pericles, his queen, and daughter, seen,
Although assail'd with fortune fierce and keen,
Virtue preserv'd from fell destruction's blast,
Led on by heaven, and crown'd with joy at last.
In Helicanus may you well descry 90
A figure of truth, of faith, of loyalty.
In reverend Cerimon there well appears
The worth that learned charity aye wears.
For wicked Cleon and his wife, when fame
Had spread their cursed deed, and honour'd name
Of Pericles, to rage the city turn;
That him and his they in his palace burn.
The gods for murder seemed so content
To punish them,—although not done, but meant.
So on your patience evermore attending, 100
New joy wait on you! Here our play has ending.
[*Exit.*

THE POEMS

VENUS AND ADONIS.

EVEN as the sun with purple-colour'd face
 Had ta'en his last leave of the weeping
  morn,
Rose-cheek'd Adonis hied him to the
  chase;
Hunting he lov'd, but love he laugh'd to
  scorn:
 Sick-thoughted Venus makes amain
  unto him,
 And like a bold-fac'd suitor 'gins to
  woo him.

"Thrice fairer than myself," thus she began,
"The field's chief flower, sweet above compare,
Stain to all nymphs, more lovely than a man,
More white and red than doves or roses are;   10
 Nature, that made thee, with herself at strife,
 Saith, that the world hath ending with thy life.

"Vouchsafe, thou wonder, to alight thy steed,
And rein his proud head to the saddle-bow;
If thou wilt deign this favour, for thy meed
A thousand honey-secrets shalt thou know:
 Here come and sit, where never serpent hisses;
 And being set, I 'll smother thee with kisses:

"And yet not cloy thy lips with loath'd satiety,
But rather famish them amid their plenty,   20
Making them red and pale with fresh variety;
Ten kisses short as one, one long as twenty:
 A summer's day will seem an hour but short,
 Being wasted in such time-beguiling sport."

With this she seizeth on his sweating palm,
The precedent of pith and livelihood,
And, trembling in her passion, calls it balm,
Earth's sovereign salve to do a goddess good:
 Being so enrag'd, desire doth lend her force
 Courageously to pluck him from his horse.   30

Over one arm the lusty courser's rein,
Under her other was the tender boy,
Who blush'd and pouted in a dull disdain,
With leaden appetite, unapt to toy;
 She red and hot as coals of glowing fire,
 He red for shame, but frosty in desire.

The studded bridle on a ragged bough
Nimbly she fastens; (O, how quick is love!)
The steed is stalled up, and even now
To tie the rider she begins to prove: 40
 Backward she push'd him, as she would be thrust,
 And govern'd him in strength, though not in lust.

So soon was she along, as he was down,
Each leaning on their elbows and their hips:
Now doth she stroke his cheek, now doth he frown,
And 'gins to chide, but soon she stops his lips;
 And kissing speaks, with lustful language broken,
 "If thou wilt chide, thy lips shall never open."

He burns with bashful shame; she with her tears
Doth quench the maiden burning of his cheeks;   50
Then with her windy sighs, and golden hairs,
To fan and blow them dry again she seeks:
 He saith she is immodest, blames her miss;
 What follows more she murders with a kiss.

Even as an empty eagle, sharp by fast,
Tires with her beak on feathers, flesh, and bone,
Shaking her wings, devouring all in haste,
Till either gorge be stuff'd, or prey be gone;
 Even so she kiss'd his brow, his cheek, his chin,
 And where she ends she doth anew begin.   60

Forc'd to content, but never to obey,
Panting he lies, and breatheth in her face;
She feedeth on the steam, as on a prey,
And calls it heavenly moisture, air of grace;
 Wishing her cheeks were gardens full of flowers,
 So they were dew'd with such distilling showers.

Look, how a bird lies tangled in a net,
So fasten'd in her arms Adonis lies;
Pure shame and aw'd resistance made him fret,
Which bred more beauty in his angry eyes: 70
 Rain added to a river that is rank,
 Perforce will force it overflow the bank.

Still she entreats, and prettily entreats,
For to a pretty ear she tunes her tale;
Still is she sullen, still he lours and frets,
'Twixt crimson shame, and anger ashy-pale:
 Being red, she loves him best; and being white,
 Her best is better'd with a more delight.

Look how he can, she cannot choose but love;
And by her fair immortal hand she swears,   80
From his soft bosom never to remove,
Till he take truce with her contending tears,
 Which long have rain'd, making her cheeks all wet;
 And one sweet kiss shall pay this countless debt.

Upon this promise did he raise his chin,
Like a dive-dapper peering through a wave,
Who, being look'd on, ducks as quickly in:
So offers he to give what she did crave;
 But when her lips were ready for his pay,
 He winks, and turns his lips another way.   90

Never did passenger in summer's heat
More thirst for drink than she for this good turn.
Her help she sees, but help she cannot get;
She bathes in water, yet her fire must burn:
 "Oh, pity," 'gan she cry, "flint-hearted boy!
 'T is but a kiss I beg; why art thou coy?

"I have been woo'd, as I entreat thee now,
Even by the stern and direful god of war,
Whose sinewy neck in battle ne'er did bow,
Who conquers where he comes, in every jar;   100
 Yet hath he been my captive and my slave,
 And begg'd for that which thou unask'd shalt have.

" Over my altars hath he hung his lance,
His batter'd shield, his uncontrolled crest,
And for my sake hath learn'd to sport and dance,
To toy, to wanton, dally, smile, and jest ;
　Scorning his churlish drum, and ensign red,
　Making my arms his field, his tent my bed.

" Thus he that overrul'd, I oversway'd,
Leading him prisoner in a red-rose chain :　　110
Strong-temper'd steel his stronger strength obey'd,
Yet was he servile to my coy disdain.
　O ! be not proud, nor brag not of thy might,
　For mastering her that foil'd the god of fight.

" Touch but my lips with those fair lips of thine,-
Though mine be not so fair, yet are they red,—
The kiss shall be thine own as well as mine.
What seest thou in the ground ? hold up thy head :
　Look in mine eyeballs, there thy beauty lies ;
　Then why not lips on lips, since eyes in eyes ?　120

" Art thou asham'd to kiss ? then wink again,
And I will wink ; so shall the day seem night ;
Love keeps his revels where there are but twain ;
Be bold to play, our sport is not in sight :
　These blue-vein'd violets, whereon we lean,
　Never can blab, nor know not what we mean.

" The tender spring upon thy tempting lip
Shows thee unripe, yet may'st thou well be tasted.
Make use of time, let not advantage slip ;
Beauty within itself should not be wasted :　　130
　Fair flowers that are not gather'd in their prime,
　Rot and consume themselves in little time.

" Were I hard-favour'd, foul, or wrinkled-old,
Ill-nurtur'd, crooked, churlish, harsh in voice,
O'erworn, despised, rheumatic, and cold,
Thick-sighted, barren, lean, and lacking juice,
　Then might'st thou pause, for then I were not for
　　thee ;
　But having no defects, why dost abhor me ?

" Thou canst not see one wrinkle in my brow ;
Mine eyes are grey, and bright, and quick in turning ;
My beauty as the spring doth yearly grow,　　141
My flesh is soft and plump ; my marrow burning ;
　My smooth moist hand, were it with thy hand felt,
　Would in thy palm dissolve, or seem to melt.

" Bid me discourse, I will enchant thine ear,
Or like a fairy trip upon the green,
Or like a nymph, with long dishevell'd hair,
Dance on the sands, and yet no footing seen :
　Love is a spirit all compact of fire,
　Not gross to sink, but light, and will aspire.　　150

" Witness this primrose bank whereon I lie ;
These forceless flowers as sturdy trees support me ;
Two strengthless doves will draw me through the sky,
From morn till night, even where I list to sport me :
　Is love so light, sweet boy, and may it be
　That thou shouldst think it heavy unto thee?

" Is thine own heart to thine own face affected?
Can thy right hand seize love upon thy left ?
Then woo thyself, be of thyself rejected ;
Steal thine own freedom, and complain on theft.　160
　Narcissus so himself himself forsook,
　And died to kiss his shadow in the brook.

" Torches are made to light, jewels to wear,
Dainties to taste, fresh beauty for the use,
Herbs for their smell, and sappy plants to bear ;
Things growing to themselves are growth's abuse :
　Seeds spring from seeds, and beauty breedeth
　　beauty ;
　Thou wast begot,—to get it is thy duty.

" Upon the earth's increase why shouldst thou feed,
Unless the earth with thy increase be fed ?　　170

By law of nature thou art bound to breed,
That thine may live, when thou thyself art dead ;
　And so in spite of death thou dost survive,
　In that thy likeness still is left alive."

By this, the love-sick queen began to sweat,
For where they lay the shadow had forsook them,
And Titan, tired in the mid-day heat,
With burning eye did hotly overlook them ;
　Wishing Adonis had his team to guide,
　So he were like him, and by Venus' side.　　180

And now Adonis, with a lazy spright,
And with a heavy, dark, disliking eye,
His louring brows o'erwhelming his fair sight,
Like misty vapours, when they blot the sky,
　Souring his cheeks, cries, " Fie ! no more of love :
　The sun doth burn my face ; I must remove."

" Ah me !" quoth Venus, " young, and so unkind ?
What bare excuses mak'st thou to be gone !
I 'll sigh celestial breath, whose gentle wind
Shall cool the heat of this descending sun :　　190
　I 'll make a shadow for thee of my hairs ;
　If they burn too, I 'll quench them with my tears.

" The sun that shines from heaven shines but warm,
And, lo ! I lie between that sun and thee :
The heat I have from thence doth little harm,
Thine eye darts forth the fire that burneth me ;
　And were I not immortal, life were done
　Between this heavenly and earthly sun.

" Art thou obdurate, flinty, hard as steel ?
Nay, more than flint, for stone at rain relenteth.　200
Art thou a woman's son, and canst not feel
What 't is to love ? how want of love tormenteth ?
　O ! had thy mother borne so hard a mind,
　She had not brought forth thee, but died unkind.

" What am I, that thou shouldst contemn me this ?
Or what great danger dwells upon my suit ?
What were thy lips the worse for one poor kiss ?
Speak, fair ; but speak fair words, or else be mute :
　Give me one kiss, I 'll give it thee again,
　And one for interest, if thou wilt have twain.　　210

" Fie ! lifeless picture, cold and senseless stone,
Well-painted idol, image dull and dead,
Statue contenting but the eye alone,
Thing like a man, but of no woman bred :
　Thou art no man, though of a man's complexion,
　For men will kiss even by their own direction."

This said, impatience chokes her pleading tongue,
And swelling passion doth provoke a pause ;
Red cheeks and fiery eyes blaze forth her wrong :
Being judge in love, she cannot right her cause ;　220
　And now she weeps, and now she fain would speak,
　And now her sobs do her intendments break.

Sometimes she shakes her head, and then his hand ;
Now gazeth she on him, now on the ground ;
Sometimes her arms infold him like a band :
She would, he will not in her arms be bound ;
　And when from thence he struggles to be gone,
　She locks her lily fingers one in one.

" Fondling," she saith, " since I have hemm'd thee here,
Within the circuit of this ivory pale,　　230
I 'll be a park, and thou shalt be my deer ;
Feed where thou wilt, on mountain or in dale ;
　Graze on my lips, and if those hills be dry,
　Stray lower, where the pleasant fountains lie.

" Within this limit is relief enough,
Sweet bottom-grass, and high delightful plain,
Round rising hillocks, brakes obscure and rough,
To shelter thee from tempest, and from rain :
　Then be my deer, since I am such a park ;
　No dog shall rouse thee, though a thousand bark."240

At this Adonis smiles, as in disdain,
That in each cheek appears a pretty dimple:
Love made those hollows, if himself were slain,
He might be buried in a tomb so simple;
Foreknowing well, if there he came to lie,
Why, there Love liv'd, and there he could not die.

These lovely caves, these round enchanting pits,
Open'd their mouths to swallow Venus' liking.
Being mad before, how doth she now for wits?
Struck dead at first, what needs a second striking? 250
Poor queen of love, in thine own law forlorn,
To love a cheek that smiles at thee in scorn!

Now which way shall she turn? what shall she say?
Her words are done! her woes the more increasing;
The time is spent, her object will away,
And from her twining arms doth urge releasing.
" Pity!" she cries, " some favour, some remorse!"
Away he springs, and hasteth to his horse.

But lo! from forth a copse that neighbours by,
A breeding jennet, lusty, young, and proud, 260
Adonis' trampling courser doth espy,
And forth she rushes, snorts, and neighs aloud:
The strong-neck'd steed, being tied unto a tree,
Breaketh his rein, and to her straight goes he.

Imperiously he leaps, he neighs, he bounds,
And now his woven girths he breaks asunder;
The bearing earth with his hard hoof he wounds,
Whose hollow womb resounds like heaven's thunder:
The iron bit he crushes 'tween his teeth,
Controlling what he was controlled with. 270

His ears up-prick'd; his braided hanging mane
Upon his compass'd crest now stand on end;
His nostrils drink the air, and forth again,
As from a furnace, vapours doth he send:
His eye, which scornfully glisters like fire,
Shows his hot courage, and his high desire.

Sometime he trots, as if he told the steps,
With gentle majesty, and modest pride;
Anon he rears upright, curvets and leaps,
As who should say, Lo! thus my strength is tried; 280
And this I do to captivate the eye
Of the fair breeder that is standing by.

What recketh he his rider's angry stir,
His flattering holla, or his " Stand, I say?"
What cares he now for curb, or pricking spur,
For rich caparisons, or trapping gay?
He sees his love, and nothing else he sees,
For nothing else with his proud sight agrees.

Look, when a painter would surpass the life,
In limning out a well-proportion'd steed, 290
His art with nature's workmanship at strife,
As if the dead the living should exceed;
So did this horse excel a common one,
In shape, in courage, colour, pace, and bone.

Round-hoof'd, short-jointed, fetlocks shag and long,
Broad breast, full eye, small head, and nostril wide,
High crest, short ears, straight legs, and passing
strong,
Thin mane, thick tail, broad buttock, tender hide:
Look, what a horse should have, he did not lack,
Save a proud rider on so proud a back. 300

Sometime he scuds far off, and there he stares;
Anon he starts at stirring of a feather:
To bid the wind a base he now prepares,
And where'r he run or fly, they know not whether;
For through his mane and tail the high wind sings,
Fanning the hairs, who wave like feather'd wings.

He looks upon his love, and neighs unto her;
She answers him, as if she knew his mind:

Being proud, as females are, to see him woo her,
She puts on outward strangeness, seems unkind; 310
Spurns at his love, and scorns the heat he feels,
Beating his kind embracements with her heels.

Then, like a melancholy malcontent,
He vails his tail, that, like a falling plume,
Cool shadow to his melting buttock lent:
He stamps, and bites the poor flies in his fume.
His love, perceiving how he is enrag'd,
Grew kinder, and his fury was assuag'd.

His testy master goeth about to take him,
When, lo! the unback'd breeder, full of fear, 320
Jealous of catching, swiftly doth forsake him,
With her the horse, and left Adonis there.
As they were mad, unto the wood they hie them,
Outstripping crows that strive to overfly them.

All swoln with chafing, down Adonis sits,
Banning his boisterous and unruly beast:
And now the happy season once more fits,
That love-sick Love by pleading may be blest;
For lovers say, the heart hath treble wrong,
When it is barr'd the aidance of the tongue. 330

An oven that is stopp'd, or river stay'd,
Burneth more hotly, swelleth with more rage:
So of concealed sorrow may be said;
Free vent of words love's fire doth assuage;
But when the heart's attorney once is mute,
The client breaks, as desperate in his suit.

He sees her coming, and begins to glow
Even as a dying coal revives with wind,
And with his bonnet hides his angry brow;
Looks on the dull earth with disturbed mind, 340
Taking no notice that she is so nigh,
For all askance he holds her in his eye.

O, what a sight it was, wistly to view
How she came stealing to the wayward boy!
To note the fighting conflict of her hue,
How white and red each other did destroy!
But now her cheek was pale, and by-and-by
It flash'd forth fire, as lightning from the sky.

Now was she just before him as he sat,
And like a lowly lover down she kneels; 350
With one fair hand she heaveth up his hat,
Her other tender hand his fair cheek feels:
His tenderer cheek receives her soft hand's print,
As apt as new-fall'n snow takes any dint.

O, what a war of looks was then between them!
Her eyes, petitioners, to his eyes suing;
His eyes saw her eyes as they had not seen them;
Her eyes woo'd still, his eyes disdain'd the wooing:
And all this dumb play had his acts made plain
With tears, which, chorus-like, her eyes did rain.
360

Full gently now she takes him by the hand,
A lily prison'd in a gaol of snow,
Or ivory in an alabaster band;
So white a friend engirts so white a foe:
This beauteous combat, wilful and unwilling,
Show'd like two silver doves that sit a-billing.

Once more the engine of her thoughts began:
" O fairest mover on this mortal round,
'Would thou wert as I am, and I a man,
My heart all whole as thine, thy heart my wound; 370
For one sweet look thy help I would assure thee,
Though nothing but my body's bane would cure
thee."

" Give me my hand," saith he, " why dost thou feel it?"
" Give me my heart," saith she, " and thou shalt have it;
O, give it me, lest thy hard heart do steel it,
And being steel'd, soft sighs can never grave it:
Then love's deep groans I never shall regard,
Because Adonis' heart hath made mine hard."

"For shame !" he cries, "let go, and let me go ;
My day's delight is past, my horse is gone, 380
And 't is your fault I am bereft him so :
I pray you hence, and leave me here alone :
 For all my mind, my thought, my busy care,
 Is how to get my palfrey from the mare."

Thus she replies : " Thy palfrey, as he should,
Welcomes the warm approach of sweet desire :
Affection is a coal that must be cool'd ;
Else, suffer'd, it will set the heart on fire.
 The sea hath bounds, but deep desire hath none ;
 Therefore, no marvel though thy horse be gone. 390

"How like a jade he stood, tied to the tree,
Servilely master'd with a leathern rein !
But when he saw his love, his youth's fair fee,
He held such petty bondage in disdain :
 Throwing the base thong from his bending crest,
 Enfranchising his mouth, his back, his breast.

"Who sees his true-love in her naked bed,
Teaching the sheets a whiter hue than white,
But, when his glutton eye so full hath fed,
His other agents aim at like delight ? 400
 Who is so faint, that dare not be so bold
 To touch the fire, the weather being cold ?

"Let me excuse thy courser, gentle boy,
And learn of him, I heartily beseech thee,
To take advantage on presented joy ;
Though I were dumb, yet his proceedings teach thee.
 O ! learn to love ; the lesson is but plain,
 And once made perfect, never lost again."

"I know not love," quoth he, "nor will not know it,
Unless it be a boar, and then I chase it ; 410
'T is much to borrow, and I will not owe it ;
My love to love is love but to disgrace it ;
 For I have heard it is a life in death,
 That laughs, and weeps, and all but with a breath.

"Who wears a garment shapeless and unfinish'd ?
Who plucks the bud before one leaf put forth ?
If springing things be any jot diminish'd,
They wither in their prime, prove nothing worth :
 The colt that 's back'd and burden'd being young,
 Loseth his pride, and never waxeth strong. 420

"You hurt my hand with wringing ; let us part,
And leave this idle theme, this bootless chat :
Remove your siege from my unyielding heart ;
To love's alarms it will not ope the gate :
 Dismiss your vows, your feigned tears, your
  flattery,
 For where a heart is hard, they make no battery."

"What ! canst thou talk ?" quoth she, "hast thou a
 tongue ?
O, 'would thou hadst not, or I had no hearing !
Thy mermaid's voice hath done me double wrong ;
I had my load before, now press'd with bearing : 430
 Melodious discord, heavenly tune harsh-sounding,
 Ear's deep-sweet music, and heart's deep-sore
  wounding.

"Had I no eyes, but ears, my ears would love
That inward beauty and invisible ;
Or, were I deaf, thy outward parts would move
Each part in me that were but sensible :
 Though neither eyes nor ears, to hear nor see,
 Yet should I be in love by touching thee.

"Say, that the sense of feeling were bereft me,
And that I could not see, nor hear, nor touch, 440
And nothing but the very smell were left me,
Yet would my love to thee be still as much ;
 For from the still'tory of thy face excelling
 Comes breath perfum'd, that breedeth love by
  smelling.

"But, O, what banquet wert thou to the taste,
Being nurse and feeder of the other four :
Would they not wish the feast might ever last,
And bid Suspicion double-lock the door,
 Lest Jealousy, that sour unwelcome guest,
 Should, by his stealing in, disturb the feast ?" 450

Once more the ruby-colour'd portal open'd,
Which to his speech did honey passage yield :
Like a red morn, that ever yet betoken'd
Wrack to the seaman, tempest to the field,
 Sorrow to shepherds, woe unto the birds,
 Gusts and foul flaws to herdmen and to herds.

This ill presage advisedly she marketh :
Even as the wind is hush'd before it raineth,
Or as the wolf doth grin before he barketh,
Or as the berry breaks before it staineth, 460
 Or like the deadly bullet of a gun,
 His meaning struck her ere his words begun.

And at his look she flatly falleth down,
For looks kill love, and love by looks reviveth :
A smile recures the wounding of a frown ;
But blessed bankrupt, that by love so thriveth !
 The silly boy, believing she is dead,
 Claps her pale cheek, till clapping makes it red ;

And all-amaz'd brake off his late intent,
For sharply he did think to reprehend her, 470
Which cunning love did wittily prevent :
Fair fall the wit that can so well defend her !
 For on the grass she lies, as she were slain,
 Till his breath breatheth life in her again.

He wrings her nose, he strikes her on the cheeks,
He bends her fingers, holds her pulses hard,
He chafes her lips, a thousand ways he seeks
To mend the hurt that his unkindness marr'd :
 He kisses her ; and she, by her good will
 Will never rise, so he will kiss her still. 480

The night of sorrow now is turn'd to day :
Her two blue windows faintly she upheaveth,
Like the fair sun, when in his fresh array
He cheers the morn, and all the earth relieveth :
 And as the bright sun glorifies the sky,
 So is her face illumin'd with her eye ;

Whose beams upon his hairless face are fix'd,
As if from thence they borrow'd all their shine.
Were never four such lamps together mix'd,
Had not his clouded with his brow's repine ; 490
 But hers, which through the crystal tears gave light,
 Shone like the moon in water seen by night.

"O ! where am I ?" quoth she, "in earth or heaven,
Or in the ocean drench'd, or in the fire ?
What hour is this ? or morn or weary even ?
Do I delight to die, or life desire ?
 But now I liv'd, and life was death's annoy ;
 But now I died, and death was lively joy.

"O, thou didst kill me ; kill me once again :
Thy eyes' shrew'd tutor, that hard heart of thine, 500
Hath taught them scornful tricks, and such disdain,
That they have murder'd this poor heart of mine ;
 And these mine eyes, true leaders to their queen,
 But for thy piteous lips no more had seen.

"Long may they kiss each other for this cure !
O, never let their crimson liveries wear,
And as they last, their verdure still endure,
To drive infection from the dangerous year !
 That the star-gazers, having writ on death,
 May say, the plague is banish'd by thy breath. 510

"Pure lips, sweet seals in my soft lips imprinted,
What bargains may I make, still to be sealing ?

To sell myself I can be well contented,
So thou wilt buy, and pay, and use good dealing;
  Which purchase if thou make, for fear of slips
  Set thy seal-manual on my wax-red lips.

"A thousand kisses buys my heart from me;
And pay them at thy leisure, one by one.
What is ten hundred touches unto thee?
Are they not quickly told, and quickly gone?   520
  Say, for non-payment that the debt should double,
  Is twenty hundred kisses such a trouble?"

"Fair queen," quoth he, "if any love you owe me,
Measure my strangeness with my unripe years:
Before I know myself, seek not to know me;
No fisher but the ungrown fry forbears:
  The mellow plum doth fall, the green sticks fast,
  Or being early pluck'd is sour to taste.

"Look, the world's comforter, with weary gait,   530
His day's hot task hath ended in the west;
The owl, night's herald, shrieks, 't is very late;
The sheep are gone to fold, birds to their nest,
  And coal-black clouds, that shadow heaven's light,
  Do summon us to part, and bid good night.

"Now let me say good night; and so say you;
If you will say so, you shall have a kiss."
"Good night," quoth she; and, ere he says adieu,
The honey fee of parting tender'd is:
  Her arms do lend his neck a sweet embrace;
  Incorporate then they seem, face grows to face.   540

Till, breathless, he disjoin'd, and backward drew
The heavenly moisture, that sweet coral mouth,
Whose precious taste her thirsty lips well knew,
Whereon they surfeit, yet complain on drouth:
  He with her plenty press'd, she faint with dearth,
  (Their lips together glu'd,) fall to the earth.

Now quick desire hath caught the yielding prey,
And glutton-like she feeds, yet never filleth;
Her lips are conquerors, his lips obey,
Paying what ransom the insulter willeth;   550
  Whose vulture thought doth pitch the price so high,
  That she will draw his lips' rich treasure dry.

And having felt the sweetness of the spoil,
With blindfold fury she begins to forage;
Her face doth reek and smoke, her blood doth boil,
And careless lust stirs up a desperate courage;
  Planting oblivion, beating reason back,
  Forgetting shame's pure blush, and honour's wrack.

Hot, faint, and weary, with her hard embracing,
Like a wild bird being tam'd with too much handling,
Or as the fleet-foot roe that 's tir'd with chasing,   561
Or like the froward infant still'd with dandling,
  He now obeys, and now no more resisteth,
  While she takes all she can, not all she listeth.

What wax so frozen but dissolves with tempering,
And yields at last to every light impression?
Things out of hope are compass'd oft with venturing,
Chiefly in love, whose leave exceeds commission:
  Affection faints not like a pale-fac'd coward,
  But then woos best, when most his choice is
    froward.   570

When he did frown, O! had she then gave over,
Such nectar from his lips she had not suck'd.
Foul words and frowns must not repel a lover;
What though the rose had prickles, yet 't is pluck'd:
  Were beauty under twenty locks kept fast,
  Yet love breaks through, and picks them all at last.

For pity now she can no more detain him;
The poor fool prays her that he may depart:
She is resolv'd no longer to restrain him,
Bids him farewell, and look well to her heart,   580
  The which, by Cupid's bow she doth protest,
  He carries thence incaged in his breast.

"Sweet boy," she says, "this night I 'll waste in sorrow,
For my sick heart commands mine eyes to watch.
Tell me, Love's master, shall we meet to-morrow?
Say, shall we? shall we? wilt thou make the match?"
  He tells her, no; to-morrow he intends
  To hunt the boar with certain of his friends.

"The boar!" quoth she, whereat a sudden pale,   590
Like lawn being spread upon the blushing rose,
Usurps her cheek: she trembles at his tale,
And on his neck her yoking arms she throws;
  She sinketh down, still hanging by his neck,
  He on her belly falls, she on her back.

Now is she in the very lists of love,
Her champion mounted for the hot encounter:
All is imaginary she doth prove,
He will not manage her, although he mount her;   600
  That worse than Tantalus' is her annoy,
  To clip Elysium, and to lack her joy.

Even as poor birds, deceiv'd with painted grapes,
Do surfeit by the eye, and pine the maw,
Even so she languisheth in her mishaps,
As those poor birds that helpless berries saw.
  The warm effects which she in him finds missing,
  She seeks to kindle with continual kissing.

But all in vain; good queen, it will not be:
She hath assay'd as much as may be prov'd;
Her pleading hath deserv'd a greater fee;
She 's Love, she loves, and yet she is not lov'd.   610
  "Fie, fie!" he says, "you crush me; let me go:
  You have no reason to withhold me so."

"Thou hadst been gone," quoth she, "sweet boy, ere
    this,
But that thou toldst me, thou wouldst hunt the boar.
O! be advis'd; thou know'st not what it is
With javelin's point a churlish swine to gore,
  Whose tushes never-sheath'd he whetteth still,
  Like to a mortal butcher, bent to kill.

"On his bow-back he hath a battle set   620
Of bristly pikes, that ever threat his foes;
His eyes like glow-worms shine when he doth fret;
His snout digs sepulchres where'er he goes;
  Being mov'd, he strikes whate'er is in his way,
  And whom he strikes his cruel tushes slay.

"His brawny sides, with hairy bristles arm'd,
Are better proof than thy spear's point can enter;
His short thick neck cannot be easily harm'd;
Being ireful, on the lion he will venture:
  The thorny brambles and embracing bushes,
  As fearful of him, part; through whom he rushes.   630

"Alas! he nought esteems that face of thine,
To which Love's eyes pay tributary gazes;
Nor thy soft hands, sweet lips, and crystal eyne,
Whose full perfection all the world amazes;
  But having thee at vantage, (wondrous dread!)
  Would root these beauties, as he roots the mead.

"O! let him keep his loathsome cabin still;
Beauty hath nought to do with such foul fiends:
Come not within his danger by thy will;
They that thrive well take counsel of their friends.   640
  When thou didst name the boar, not to dissemble,
  I fear'd thy fortune, and my joints did tremble.

"Didst thou not mark my face? was it not white?
Saw'st thou not signs of fear lurk in mine eye?
Grew I not faint? and fell I not downright?
Within my bosom, whereon thou dost lie,
  My boding heart pants, beats, and takes no rest,
  But, like an earthquake, shakes thee on my breast.

"For where Love reigns, disturbing Jealousy
Doth call himself Affection's sentinel;   650
Gives false alarms, suggesteth mutiny,
And in a peaceful hour doth cry, 'Kill, kill!'

Distempering gentle Love in his desire,
As air and water do abate the fire.

"This sour informer, this bate-breeding spy,
This canker that eats up Love's tender spring,
This carry-tale, dissentious Jealousy,
That sometime true news, sometime false doth bring,
　Knocks at my heart, and whispers in mine ear,
　That if I love thee, I thy death should fear;　660

"And, more than so, presenteth to mine eye
The picture of an angry-chafing boar,
Under whose sharp fangs on his back doth lie
An image like thyself, all stain'd with gore;
　Whose blood upon the fresh flowers being shed,
　Doth make them droop with grief, and hang the
　　head.

"What should I do, seeing thee so indeed,
That tremble at the imagination?
The thought of it doth make my faint heart bleed,
And fear doth teach it divination:　670
　I prophesy thy death, my living sorrow;
　If thou encounter with the boar to-morrow.

"But if thou needs wilt hunt, be rul'd by me;
Uncouple at the timorous flying hare,
Or at the fox, which lives by subtlety,
Or at the roe, which no encounter dare:
　Pursue these fearful creatures o'er the downs,
　And on thy well-breath'd horse keep with thy
　　hounds.

"And when thou hast on foot the purblind hare,
Mark the poor wretch, to overshoot his troubles,　680
How he outruns the wind, and with what care
He cranks and crosses with a thousand doubles:
　The many musets through the which he goes,
　Are like a labyrinth to amaze his foes.

"Sometime he runs among a flock of sheep,
To make the cunning hounds mistake their smell;
And sometime where earth-delving conies keep,
To stop the loud pursuers in their yell;
　And sometime sorteth with a herd of deer;
　Danger deviseth shifts; wit waits on fear:　690

"For there his smell with others being mingled,
The hot scent-snuffing hounds are driven to doubt,
Ceasing their clamorous cry, till they have singled
With much ado the cold fault cleanly out;
　Then do they spend their mouths: Echo replies,
　As if another chase were in the skies.

"By this, poor Wat, far off upon a hill,
Stands on his hinder legs with listening ear,
To hearken if his foes pursue him still;
Anon their loud alarums he doth hear;　700
　And now his grief may be compared well
　To one sore sick, that hears the passing-bell.

"Then shalt thou see the dew-bedabbled wretch
Turn, and return, indenting with the way;
Each envious briar his weary legs doth scratch,
Each shadow makes him stop, each murmur stay:
　For misery is trodden on by many,
　And being low, never reliev'd by any.

"Lie quietly, and hear a little more;
Nay, do not struggle, for thou shalt not rise:　710
To make thee hate the hunting of the boar,
Unlike myself thou hear'st me moralise,
　Applying this to that, and so to so;
　For love can comment upon every woe.

"Where did I leave?"—"No matter where," quoth he;
"Leave me, and then the story aptly ends:
The night is spent."--"Why, what of that?" quoth
　she.
"I am," quoth he, "expected of my friends;
　And now 't is dark, and going I shall fall."
　"In night," quoth she, "desire sees best of all.　720

"But if thou fall, O! then imagine this,
The earth, in love with thee, thy footing trips,
And all is but to rob thee of a kiss.
Rich preys make true men thieves; so do thy lips
　Make modest Dian cloudy and forlorn,
　Lest she should steal a kiss, and die forsworn.

"Now, of this dark night I perceive the reason:
Cynthia for shame obscures her silver shine,
Till forging Nature be condemn'd of treason,
For stealing moulds from heaven that were divine,　730
　Wherein she fram'd thee, in high heaven's despite,
　To shame the sun by day, and her by night.

"And therefore hath she brib'd the Destinies,
To cross the curious workmanship of Nature;
To mingle beauty with infirmities,
And pure perfection with impure defeature;
　Making it subject to the tyranny
　Of mad mischances, and much misery;

"As burning fevers, agues pale and faint,
Life-poisoning pestilence, and frenzies wood;　740
The marrow-eating sickness, whose attaint
Disorder breeds by heating of the blood:
　Surfeits, imposthumes, grief, and damn'd despair,
　Swear Nature's death for framing thee so fair.

"And not the least of all these maladies
But in one minute's fight brings beauty under:
Both favour, savour, hue, and qualities,
Whereat the impartial gazer late did wonder,
　Are on the sudden wasted, thaw'd, and done,
　As mountain-snow melts with the mid-day sun.　750

"Therefore, despite of fruitless chastity,
Love-lacking vestals, and self-loving nuns,
That on the earth would breed a scarcity,
And barren dearth of daughters and of sons,
　Be prodigal: the lamp that burns by night
　Dries up his oil to lend the world his light.

"What is thy body but a swallowing grave,
Seeming to bury that posterity
Which by the rights of time thou needs must have,
If thou destroy them not in dark obscurity?　760
　If so, the world will hold thee in disdain,
　Sith in thy pride so fair a hope is slain.

"So in thyself thyself art made away,
A mischief worse than civil home-bred strife,
Or theirs whose desperate hands themselves do slay,
Or butcher-sire that reaves his son of life.
　Foul-cankering rust the hidden treasure frets,
　But gold that 's put to use more gold begets."

"Nay then," quoth Adon, "you will fall again
Into your idle overhandled theme;　770
The kiss I gave you is bestow'd in vain,
And all in vain you strive against the stream;
　For by this black-fac'd night, desire's foul nurse,
　Your treatise makes me like you worse and worse.

"If love have lent you twenty thousand tongues,
And every tongue more moving than your own,
Bewitching like the wanton mermaid's songs,
Yet from mine ear the tempting tune is blown;
　For know, my heart stands armed in mine ear,
　And will not let a false sound enter there;　780

"Lest the deceiving harmony should run
Into the quiet closure of my breast;
And then my little heart were quite undone,
In his bedchamber to be barr'd of rest.
　No, lady, no; my heart longs not to groan,
　But soundly sleeps, while now it sleeps alone.

"What have you urg'd that I cannot reprove?
The path is smooth that leadeth on to danger;

I hate not love, but your device in love,
That lends embracements unto every stranger.   790
You do it for increase : O strange excuse,
When reason is the bawd to lust's abuse !

" Call it not love, for Love to heaven is fled,
Since sweating Lust on earth usurp'd his name ;
Under whose simple semblance he hath fed
Upon fresh beauty, blotting it with blame ;
Which the hot tyrant stains, and soon bereaves,
As caterpillars do the tender leaves.

" Love comforteth like sunshine after rain,
But Lust's effect is tempest after sun ;   800
Love's gentle spring doth always fresh remain,
Lust's winter comes ere summer half be done :
Love surfeits not, Lust like a glutton dies ;
Love is all truth, Lust full of forged lies.

" More I could tell, but more I dare not say ;
The text is old, the orator too green.
Therefore, in sadness, now I will away ;
My face is full of shame, my heart of teen :
Mine ears, that to your wanton talk attended,
Do burn themselves for having so offended. '   810

With this he breaketh from the sweet embrace
Of those fair arms which bound him to her breast,
And homeward through the dark laund runs apace ;
Leaves Love upon her back deeply distress'd.
Look, how a bright star shooteth from the sky,
So glides he in the night from Venus' eye ;

Which after him she darts, as one on shore
Gazing upon a late-embarked friend,
Till the wild waves will have him seen no more,
Whose ridges with the meeting clouds contend :   820
So did the merciless and pitchy night
Fold in the object that did feed her sight.

Whereat amaz'd, as one that unaware
Hath dropp'd a precious jewel in the flood,
Or, 'stonish'd as night-wanderers often are,
Their light blown out in some mistrustful wood ;
Even so confounded in the dark she lay,
Having lost the fair discovery of her way.

And now she beats her heart, whereat it groans,
That all the neighbour-caves, as seeming troubled,   830
Make verbal repetition of her moans :
Passion on passion deeply is redoubled.
"Ah me !" she cries, and twenty times, " Woe, woe!"
And twenty echoes twenty times cry so.

She, marking them, begins a wailing note,
And sings extemp'rally a woful ditty ;
How love makes young men thrall, and old men dote ;
How love is wise in folly, foolish-witty :
Her heavy anthem still concludes in woe,
And still the choir of echoes answer so.   840

Her song was tedious, and outwore the night,
For lovers' hours are long, though seeming short :
If pleas'd themselves, others, they think, delight
In such-like circumstance, with such-like sport :
Their copious stories, oftentimes begun,
End without audience, and are never done.

For who hath she to spend the night withal,
But idle sounds resembling parasites ;
Like shrill-tongu'd tapsters answering every call,
Soothing the humour of fantastic wits ?   850
She says, " 'T is so :" they answer all, " 'T is so ;"
And would say after her, if she said, " No."

Lo ! here the gentle lark, weary of rest,
From his moist cabinet mounts up on high,
And wakes the morning, from whose silver breast
The sun ariseth in his majesty ;
Who doth the world so gloriously behold,
That cedar-tops and hills seem burnish'd gold.

Venus salutes him with this fair good-morrow :
" O thou clear god, and patron of all light,   860
From whom each lamp and shining star doth borrow
The beauteous influence that makes him bright,
There lives a son, that suck'd an earthly mother,
May lend thee light, as thou dost lend to other."

This said, she hasteth to a myrtle grove,
Musing the morning is so much o'erworn ;
And yet she hears no tidings of her love :
She hearkens for his hounds, and for his horn :
Anon she hears them chaunt it lustily,
And all in haste she coasteth to the cry.   870

And as she runs, the bushes in the way
Some catch her by the neck, some kiss her face,
Some twin'd about her thigh to make her stay.
She wildly breaketh from their strict embrace,
Like a milch doe, whose swelling dugs do ache,
Hasting to feed her fawn hid in some brake.

By this she hears the hounds are at a bay,
Whereat she starts, like one that spies an adder
Wreath'd up in fatal folds, just in his way,
The fear whereof doth make him shake and shudder :   881
Even so the timorous yelping of the hounds
Appals her senses, and her spirit confounds.

For now she knows it is no gentle chase,
But the blunt boar, rough bear, or lion proud,
Because the cry remaineth in one place,
Where fearfully the dogs exclaim aloud ;
Finding their enemy to be so curst,
They all strain court'sy who shall cope him first.

This dismal cry rings sadly in her ear,
Through which it enters to surprise her heart ;   890
Who, overcome by doubt and bloodless fear,
With cold-pale weakness numbs each feeling part ;
Like soldiers, when their captain once doth yield,
They basely fly, and dare not stay the field.

Thus stands she in a trembling ecstasy,
Till, cheering up her senses all-dismay'd,
She tells them, 't is a causeless fantasy,
And childish error, that they are afraid ;
Bids them leave quaking, bids them fear no more:—
And with that word she spied the hunted boar ;   900

Whose frothy mouth bepainted all with red,
Like milk and blood being mingled both together,
A second fear through all her sinews spread,
Which madly hurries her she knows not whither :
This way she runs, and now she will no further,
But back retires to rate the boar for murther.

A thousand spleens bear her a thousand ways ;
She treads the path that she untreads again :
Her more than haste is mated with delays,
Like the proceedings of a drunken brain,   910
Full of respects, yet nought at all respecting,
In hand with all things, nought at all effecting.

Here kennell'd in a brake she finds a hound,
And asks the weary caitiff for his master ;
And there another licking of his wound,
'Gainst venom'd sores the only sovereign plaster ;
And here she meets another sadly scowling,
To whom she speaks, and he replies with howling.

When he hath ceas'd his ill-resounding noise,
Another flap-mouth'd mourner, black and grim,   920
Against the welkin volleys out his voice ;
Another and another answer him,
Clapping their proud tails to the ground below,
Shaking their scratch'd ears, bleeding as they go.

Look, how the world's poor people are amaz'd
At apparitions, signs, and prodigies,

Whereon with fearful eyes they long have gaz'd,
Infusing them with dreadful prophecies :
  So she at these sad signs draws up her breath,
  And, sighing it again, exclaims on Death.   930

" Hard-favour'd tyrant, ugly, meagre, lean,
Hateful divorce of love," (thus chides she Death,)
" Grim-grinning ghost, earth's worm, what dost thou
         mean,
To stifle beauty, and to steal his breath,
  Who when he liv'd, his breath and beauty set
  Gloss on the rose, smell to the violet?

" If he be dead,—O no ! it cannot be,
Seeing his beauty, thou shouldst strike at it ;—
O yes ! it may ; thou hast no eyes to see,
But hatefully at random dost thou hit.   940
  Thy mark is feeble age ; but thy false dart
  Mistakes that aim, and cleaves an infant's heart.

" Hadst thou but bid beware, then he had spoke,
And hearing him thy power had lost his power.
The Destinies will curse thee for this stroke ;
They bid thee crop a weed, thou pluck'st a flower.
  Love's golden arrow at him should have fled,
  And not Death's ebon dart, to strike him dead.

"Dost thou drink tears, that thou provok'st such
       weeping?
What may a heavy groan advantage thee?   950
Why hast thou cast into eternal sleeping
Those eyes that taught all other eyes to see?
  Now Nature cares not for thy mortal vigour,
  Since her best work is ruin'd with thy rigour."

Here overcome, as one full of despair,
She vail'd her eyelids, who, like sluices, stopp'd
The crystal tide that from her two cheeks fair
In the sweet channel of her bosom dropp'd ;
  But through the flood-gates breaks the silver rain,
  And with his strong course opens them again.   960

O, how her eyes and tears did lend and borrow !
Her eyes seen in the tears, tears in her eye ;
Both crystals, where they view'd each other's sorrow,
Sorrow that friendly sighs sought still to dry ;
  But like a stormy day, now wind, now rain,
  Sighs dry her cheeks, tears make them wet again.

Variable passions throng her constant woe,
As striving who should best become her grief ;
All entertain'd, each passion labours so,
That every present sorrow seemeth chief,   970
  But none is best ; then join they all together,
  Like many clouds consulting for foul weather.

By this, far off she hears some huntsman holla ;
A nurse's song ne'er pleas'd her babe so well :
The dire imagination she did follow
This sound of hope doth labour to expel ;
  For now reviving joy bids her rejoice,
  And flatters her it is Adonis' voice.

Whereat her tears began to turn their tide,
Being prison'd in her eye, like pearls in glass ;   980
Yet sometimes falls an orient drop beside,
Which her cheek melts, as scorning it should pass,
  To wash the foul face of the sluttish ground,
  Who is but drunken when she seemeth drown'd.

O hard-believing love, how strange it seems
Not to believe, and yet too credulous !
Thy weal and woe are both of them extremes ;
Despair and hope make thee ridiculous :
  The one doth flatter thee in thoughts unlikely,
  In likely thoughts the other kills thee quickly.   990

Now she unweaves the web that she hath wrought ;
Adonis lives, and Death is not to blame :

It was not she that call'd him all-to-naught ;
Now she adds honours to his hateful name ;
  She clepes him king of graves, and grave for kings,
  Imperious supreme of all mortal things.

" No, no," quoth she, " sweet Death, I did but jest ;
Yet pardon me, I felt a kind of fear,
Whenas I met the boar, that bloody beast,
Which knows no pity, but is still severe ;   1000
  Then, gentle shadow, (truth I must confess,)
  I rail'd on thee, fearing my love's decease.

" 'T is not my fault : the boar provok'd my tongue ;
Be wreak'd on him, invisible commander ;
'T is he, foul creature, that hath done thee wrong ;
I did but act, he 's author of thy slander.
  Grief hath two tongues, and never woman yet
  Could rule them both, without ten women's wit."

Thus hoping that Adonis is alive,
Her rash suspect she doth extenuate ;   1010
And that his beauty may the better thrive,
With Death she humbly doth insinuate :
  Tells him of trophies, statues, tombs, and stories
  His victories, his triumphs, and his glories.

" O Jove !" quoth she, " how much a fool was I,
To be of such a weak and silly mind,
To wail his death, who lives, and must not die
Till mutual overthrow of mortal kind ;
  For he being dead, with him is beauty slain,
  And, beauty dead, black chaos comes again.   1020

" Fie, fie, fond love ! thou art so full of fear,
As one with treasure laden, hemm'd with thieves :
Trifles, unwitnessed with eye or ear,
Thy coward heart with false bethinking grieves."
  Even at this word she hears a merry horn,
  Whereat she leaps that was but late forlorn.

As falcon to the lure, away she flies :
The grass stoops not, she treads on it so light ;
And in her haste unfortunately spies
The foul boar's conquest on her fair delight :   1030
  Which seen, her eyes, as murder'd with the view,
  Like stars asham'd of day, themselves withdrew.

Or, as the snail, whose tender horns being hit,
Shrinks backward in his shelly cave with pain,
And there, all smother'd up, in shade doth sit,
Long after fearing to creep forth again :
  So, at his bloody view, her eyes are fled
  Into the deep-dark cabins of her head :

Where they resign their office and their light
To the disposing of her troubled brain ;   1040
Who bids them still consort with ugly night,
And never wound the heart with looks again ;
  Who, like a king perplexed in his throne,
  By their suggestion gives a deadly groan,

Whereat each tributary subject quakes ;
As when the wind, imprison'd in the ground,
Struggling for passage, earth's foundation shakes,
Which with cold terror doth men's minds confound.
  This mutiny each part doth so surprise,
  That from their dark beds once more leap her eyes :   1050

And, being open'd, threw unwilling light
Upon the wide wound that the boar had trench'd
In his soft flank ; whose wonted lily white
With purple tears, that his wound wept, was drench'd :
  No flower was nigh, no grass, herb, leaf, or weed,
  But stole his blood, and seem'd with him to bleed.

This solemn sympathy poor Venus noteth,
Over one shoulder doth she hang her head,
Dumbly she passions, franticly she doteth ;
She thinks he could not die, he is not dead :   1060
  Her voice is stopp'd, her joints forget to bow,
  Her eyes are mad that they have wept till now.

Upon his hurt she looks so steadfastly,
That her sight dazzling makes the wound seem three;
And then she reprehends her mangling eye,
That makes more gashes where no breach should be:
His face seems twain, each several limb is doubled;
For oft the eye mistakes, the brain being troubled.

" My tongue cannot express my grief for one,
And yet," quoth she, " behold two Adons dead! 1070
My sighs are blown away, my salt tears gone,
Mine eyes are turn'd to fire, my heart to lead:
Heavy heart's lead, melt at mine eyes' red fire!
So shall I die by drops of hot desire.

" Alas, poor world, what treasure hast thou lost!
What face remains alive that 's worth the viewing?
Whose tongue is music now? what canst thou boast
Of things long since, or anything ensuing?
The flowers are sweet, their colours fresh and trim;
But true-sweet beauty liv'd and died with him. 1080

" Bonnet nor veil henceforth no creature wear!
Nor sun nor wind will ever strive to kiss you:
Having no fair to lose, you need not fear;
The sun doth scorn you, and the wind doth hiss you:
But when Adonis liv'd, sun and sharp air
Lurk'd like two thieves, to rob him of his fair:

" And therefore would he put his bonnet on,
Under whose brim the gaudy sun would peep;
The wind would blow it off, and, being gone,
Play with his locks: then would Adonis weep, 1090
And straight, in pity of his tender years,
They both would strive who first should dry his
    tears.

" To see his face, the lion walk'd along
Behind some hedge, because he would not fear him;
To recreate himself when he hath sung,
The tiger would be tame, and gently hear him;
If he had spoke, the wolf would leave his prey,
And never fright the silly lamb that day.

" When he beheld his shadow in the brook,
The fishes spread on it their golden gills; 1100
When he was by, the b rds such pleasure took,
That some would sing, some other in their bills
Would bring him mulberries, and ripe-red cherries;
He fed them with his sight, they him with berries.

" But this foul, grim, and urchin-snouted boar,
Whose downward eye still looketh for a grave,
Ne'er saw the beauteous livery that he wore;
Witness the entertainment that he gave:
If he did see his face, why then, I know,
He thought to kiss him, and hath kill'd him so. 1110

" 'T is true, 't is true; thus was Adonis slain:
He ran upon the boar with his sharp spear,
Who did not whet his teeth at him again,
But by a kiss thought to persuade him there;
And nuzzling in his flank, the loving swine
Sheath'd, unaware, the tusk in his soft groin.

" Had I been tooth'd like him, I must confess,
With kissing him I should have kill'd him first:
But he is dead, and never did he bless
My youth with his; the more am I accurst." 1120
With this she falleth in the place she stood,
And stains her face with his congealed blood.

She looks upon his lips, and they are pale;
She takes him by the hand, and that is cold;
She whispers in his ears a heavy tale,
As if they heard the woful words she told;
She lifts the coffer-lids that close his eyes,
Where, lo! two lamps, burnt out, in darkness lies:

Two glasses, where herself herself beheld
A thousand times, and now no more reflect; 1130
Their virtue lost, wherein they late excell'd,
And every beauty robb'd of his effect:
" Wonder of time," quoth she, " this is my spite,
That, thou being dead, the day should yet be light.

" Since thou art dead, lo! here I prophesy,
Sorrow on love hereafter shall attend:
It shall be waited on with jealousy,
Find sweet beginning, but unsavoury end;
Ne'er settled equally, but high or low;
That all love's pleasure shall not match his woe.1140

" It shall be fickle, false, and full of fraud;
Bud and be blasted in a breathing-while;
The bottom poison, and the top o'erstraw'd
With sweets, that shall the truest sight beguile:
The strongest body shall it make most weak,
Strike the wise dumb, and teach the fool to speak.

" It shall be sparing, and too full of riot,
Teaching decrepit age to tread the measures;
The staring ruffian shall it keep in quiet,
Pluck down the rich, enrich the poor with treasures;
It shall be raging mad, and silly-mild, 1151
Make the young old, the old become a child.

" It shall suspect, where is no cause of fear;
It shall not fear, where it should most mistrust;
It shall be merciful, and too severe,
And most deceiving, when it seems most just:
Perverse it shall be, where it shows most toward;
Put fear to valour, courage to the coward.

" It shall be cause of war and dire events,
And set dissension 'twixt the son and sire; 1160
Subject and servile to all discontents,
As dry combustious matter is to fire:
Sith in his prime death doth my love destroy,
They that love best, their loves shall not enjoy."

By this, the boy, that by her side lay kill'd,
Was melted like a vapour from her sight,
And in his blood, that on the ground lay spill'd,
A purple flower sprung up, chequer'd with white;
Resembling well his pale cheeks, and the blood
Which in round drops upon their whiteness stood. 1170

She bows her head, the new-sprung flower to smell,
Comparing it to her Adonis' breath;
And says, within her bosom it shall dwell,
Since he himself is reft from her by death:
She crops the stalk, and in the breach appears
Green-dropping sap, which she compares to tears.

" Poor flower," quoth she, " this was thy father's guise,
Sweet issue of a more sweet-smelling sire,
For every little grief to wet his eyes:
To grow unto himself was his desire, 1180
And so 't is thine; but know, it is as good
To wither in my breast, as in his blood.

" Here was thy father's bed, here in my breast;
Thou art the next of blood, and 't is thy right:
Lo! in this hollow cradle take thy rest,
My throbbing heart shall rock thee day and night:
There shall not be one minute in an hour,
Wherein I will not kiss my sweet love's flower."

Thus weary of the world, away she hies,
And yokes her silver doves; by whose swift aid 1190
Their mistress mounted through the empty skies
In her light chariot quickly is convey'd;
Holding their course to Paphos, where their queen
Means to immure herself and not be seen.

LUCRECE.

ROM the besieged Ardea all in post,
Borne by the trustless wings of false desire,
Lust-breathed Tarquin leaves the Roman host,
And to Collatium bears the lightless fire
Which, in pale embers hid, lurks to aspire,
And girdle with embracing flames the waist
Of Collatine's fair love, Lucrece the chaste.

Haply that name of chaste unhappily set
This bateless edge on his keen appetite;
When Collatine unwisely did not let   10
To praise the clear unmatched red and white
Which triumph'd in that sky of his delight;
Where mortal stars, as bright as heaven's beauties,
With pure aspects did him peculiar duties.

For he the night before, in Tarquin's tent,
Unlock'd the treasure of his happy state;
What priceless wealth the heavens had him lent
In the possession of his beauteous mate;
Reckoning his fortune at such high-proud rate,
That kings might be espoused to more fame,   20
But king nor peer to such a peerless dame.

O happiness enjoy'd but of a few!
And, if possess'd, as soon decay'd and done,
As is the morning's silver-melting dew
Against the golden splendour of the sun;
An expir'd date, cancell'd ere well begun:
Honour and beauty, in the owner's arms,
Are weakly fortress'd from a world of harms.

Beauty itself doth of itself persuade
The eyes of men without an orator;   30
What needeth then apologies be made
To set forth that which is so singular?
Or why is Collatine the publisher
Of that rich jewel he should keep unknown
From thievish ears, because it is his own?

Perchance his boast of Lucrece' sovereignty
Suggested this proud issue of a king:
For by our ears our hearts oft tainted be:
Perchance that envy of so rich a thing,
Braving compare, disdainfully did sting   40
His high-pitch'd thoughts, that meaner men should vaunt
That golden hap which their superiors want.

But some untimely thought did instigate
His all-too-timeless speed, if none of those:
His honour, his affairs, his friends, his state,
Neglected all, with swift intent he goes
To quench the coal which in his liver glows.
O rash-false heat, wrapp'd in repentant cold,
Thy hasty spring still blasts, and ne'er grows old!

When at Collatium this false lord arriv'd,   50
Well was he welcom'd by the Roman dame,
Within whose face beauty and virtue striv'd
Which of them both should underprop her fame:
When virtue bragg'd, beauty would blush for shame;
When beauty boasted blushes, in despite
Virtue would stain that or with silver white.

But beauty, in that white intituled,
From Venus' doves doth challenge that fair field;
Then virtue claims from beauty beauty's red,
Which virtue gave the golden age to gild   60
Their silver cheeks, and call'd it then their shield;
Teaching them thus to use it in the fight,—
When shame assail'd, the red should fence the white.

This heraldry in Lucrece' face was seen,
Argu'd by beauty's red, and virtue's white:
Of either's colour was the other queen,
Proving from world's minority their right:
Yet their ambition makes them still to fight;
The sovereignty of either being so great,
That oft they interchange each other's seat.   70

This silent war of lilies and of roses,
Which Tarquin view'd in her fair face's field,
In their pure ranks his traitor eye encloses;
Where, lest between them both it should be kill'd,
The coward captive vanquished doth yield
To those two armies, that would let him go,
Rather than triumph in so false a foe.

Now thinks he, that her husband's shallow tongue—
The niggard prodigal that prais'd her so—
In that high task hath done her beauty wrong,   80
Which far exceeds his barren skill to show:
Therefore that praise which Collatine doth owe
Enchanted Tarquin answers with surmise,
In silent wonder of still-gazing eyes.

This earthly saint, adored by this devil,
Little suspecteth the false worshipper;
For unstain'd thoughts do seldom dream on evil;
Birds never lim'd no secret bushes fear:
So guiltless she securely gives good cheer,
And reverent welcome to her princely guest,   90
Whose inward ill no outward harm express'd:

For that he colour'd with his high estate,
Hiding base sin in plaits of majesty;
That nothing in him seem'd inordinate,
Save sometime too much wonder of his eye,
Which, having all, all could not satisfy;
But, poorly rich, so wanteth in his store,
That, cloy'd with much, he pineth still for more.

But she, that never cop'd with stranger eyes,
Could pick no meaning from their parling looks,   100
Nor read the subtle-shining secrecies
Writ in the glassy margents of such books:
She touch'd no unknown baits, nor fear'd no hooks;
Nor could she moralise his wanton sight,
More than his eyes were open'd to the light.

He stories to her ears her husband's fame,
Won in the fields of fruitful Italy;
And decks with praises Collatine's high name,
Made glorious by his manly chivalry
With bruised arms and wreaths of victory: 110
Her joy with heav'd-up hand she doth express,
And, wordless, so greets heaven for his success.

Far from the purpose of his coming thither,
He makes excuses for his being there:
No cloudy show of stormy blustering weather
Doth yet in his fair welkin once appear;
Till sable Night, mother of dread and fear,
Upon the world dim darkness doth display,
And in her vaulty prison stows the Day.

For then is Tarquin brought unto his bed,   120
Intending weariness with heavy spright:
For after supper long he questioned
With modest Lucrece, and wore out the night:
Now leaden slumber with life's strength doth fight,
And every one to rest themselves betake,
Save thieves, and cares, and troubled minds, that
    wake.

As one of which doth Tarquin lie revolving
The sundry dangers of his will's obtaining;
Yet ever to obtain his will resolving,
Though weak-built hopes persuade him to abstaining:
Despair to gain doth traffic oft for gaining;   131
And when great treasure is the meed propos'd,
Though death be adjunct, there's no death suppos'd.

Those that much covet are with gain so fond,
That what they have not, that which they possess,
They scatter and unloose it from their bond,
And so, by hoping more, they have but less;
Or, gaining more, the profit of excess
Is but to surfeit, and such griefs sustain,
That they prove bankrupt in this poor-rich gain. 140

The aim of all is but to nurse the life
With honour, wealth, and ease, in waning age;
And in this aim there is such thwarting strife,
That one for all, or all for one we gage;
As life for honour in fell battles' rage;
Honour for wealth; and oft that wealth doth cost
The death of all, and all together lost.

So that in venturing ill we leave to be
The things we are for that which we expect;
And this ambitious foul infirmity,   150
In having much, torments us with defect
Of that we have: so then we do neglect
The thing we have; and, all for want of wit,
Make something nothing, by augmenting it.

Such hazard now must desperate Tarquin make,
Pawning his honour to obtain his lust,
And for himself himself he must forsake:
Then where is truth, if there be no self-trust?
When shall he think to find a stranger just,
When he himself himself confounds, betrays   160
To slanderous tongues, and wretched hateful days?

Now stole upon the time the dead of night,
When heavy sleep had clos'd up mortal eyes;
No comfortable star did lend his light,
No noise but owls' and wolves' death-boding cries:
Now serves the season that they may surprise
The silly lambs; pure thoughts are dead and still,
While lust and murder wakes to stain and kill.

And now this lustful lord leap'd from his bed,
Throwing his mantle rudely o'er his arm;   170
Is madly toss'd between desire and dread;
Th' one sweetly flatters, th' other feareth harm;
But honest Fear, bewitch'd with lust's foul charm,
Doth too-too oft betake him to retire,
Beaten away by brain-sick rude Desire.

His falchion on a flint he softly smiteth,
That from the cold stone sparks of fire do fly,
Whereat a waxen torch forthwith he lighteth,
Which must be lode-star to his lustful eye;
And to the flame thus speaks advisedly: 180
"As from this cold flint I enforc'd this fire,
So Lucrece must I force to my desire."

Here pale with fear he doth premeditate
The dangers of his loathsome enterprise,
And in his inward mind he doth debate
What following sorrow may on this arise:
Then looking scornfully, he doth despise
His naked armour of still-slaughter'd lust,
And justly thus controls his thoughts unjust.

"Fair torch, burn out thy light, and lend it not   190
To darken her whose light excelleth thine;
And die, unhallow'd thoughts, before you blot
With your uncleanness that which is divine;
Offer pure incense to so pure a shrine:
Let fair humanity abhor the deed
That spots and stains love's modest snow-white
    weed.

"O shame to knighthood and to shining arms!
O foul dishonour to my household's grave!
O impious act, including all foul harms!
A martial man to be soft fancy's slave!   200
True valour still a true respect should have;
Then my digression is so vile, so base,
That it will live engraven in my face.

"Yea, though I die, the scandal will survive,
And be an eyesore in my golden coat;
Some loathsome dash the herald will contrive,
To cipher me how fondly I did dote;
That my posterity, sham'd with the note,
Shall curse my bones, and hold it for no sin
To wish that I their father had not bin.   210

"What win I, if I gain the thing I seek?
A dream, a breath, a froth of fleeting joy.
Who buys a minute's mirth to wail a week,
Or sells eternity to get a toy?
For one sweet grape who will the vine destroy?
Or what fond beggar, but to touch the crown,
Would with the sceptre straight be strucken down?

"If Collatinus dream of my intent,
Will he not wake, and in a desperate rage
Post hither, this vile purpose to prevent?   220
This siege that hath engirt his marriage,
This blur to youth, this sorrow to the sage,
This dying virtue, this surviving shame,
Whose crime will bear an ever-during blame?

"O! what excuse can my invention make,
When thou shalt charge me with so black a deed?
Will not my tongue be mute, my frail joints shake,
Mine eyes forego their light, my false heart bleed?
The guilt being great, the fear doth still exceed;
And extreme fear can neither fight nor fly,   230
But coward-like with trembling terror die.

"Had Collatinus kill'd my son or sire,
Or lain in ambush to betray my life,
Or were he not my dear friend, this desire
Might have excuse to work upon his wife,
As in revenge or quittal of such strife;
But as he is my kinsman, my dear friend,
The shame and fault finds no excuse nor end.

"Shameful it is;—ay, if the fact be known:
Hateful it is;—there is no hate in loving: .240
I'll beg her love;—but she is not her own:
The worst is but denial, and reproving.
My will is strong, past reason's weak removing:
Who fears a sentence, or an old man's saw,
Shall by a painted cloth be kept in awe."

Thus, graceless, holds he disputation
'Tween frozen conscience and hot-burning will,
And with good thoughts makes dispensation,
Urging the worser sense for vantage still;
Which in a moment doth confound and kill   250
All pure effects, and doth so far proceed,
That what is vile shows like a virtuous deed.

Quoth he : " She took me kindly by the hand,
And gaz'd for tidings in my eager eyes,
Fearing some hard news from the warlike band,
Where her beloved Collatinus lies:
O, how her fear did make her colour rise !
  First red as roses that on lawn we lay,
  Then white as lawn, the roses took away.

" And how her hand, in my hand being lock'd,   260
Forc'd it to tremble with her loyal fear !
Which struck her sad, and then it faster rock'd,
Until her husband's welfare she did hear ;
Whereat she smiled with so sweet a cheer,
  That had Narcissus seen her as she stood,
  Self-love had never drown'd him in the flood.

" Why hunt I then for colour or excuses?
All orators are dumb when beauty pleadeth :
Poor wretches have remorse in poor abuses ;
Love thrives not in the heart that shadows dreadeth :
Affection is my captain, and he leadeth ;   271
  And when his gaudy banner is display'd,
  The coward fights, and will not be dismay'd.

" Then, childish fear, avaunt ! debating, die !
Respect and reason, wait on wrinkled age !
My heart shall never countermand mine eye :
Sad pause and deep regard beseem the sage.
My part is youth, and beats these from the stage.
  Desire my pilot is, beauty my prize ;
  Then, who fears sinking where such treasure
  lies ?"   280

As corn o'ergrown by weeds, so heedful fear
Is almost chok'd by unresisted lust.
Away he steals with open listening ear,
Full of foul hope, and full of fond mistrust ;
Both which, as servitors to the unjust,
  So cross him with their opposite persuasion,
  That now he vows a league, and now invasion.

Within his thought her heavenly image sits,
And in the selfsame seat sits Collatine :
That eye which looks on her confounds his wits ; 290
That eye which him beholds, as more divine,
Unto a view so false will not incline :
  But with a pure appeal seeks to the heart,
  Which, once corrupted, takes the worser part

And therein heartens up his servile powers,
Who, flatter'd by their leader's jocund show,
Stuff up his lust, as minutes fill up hours ;
And as their captain, so their pride doth grow,
Paying more slavish tribute than they owe.
  By reprobate desire thus madly led,   300
  The Roman lord marcheth to Lucrece' bed.

The locks between her chamber and his will,
Each one by him enforc'd, retires his ward ;
But as they open they all rate his ill.
Which drives the creeping thief to some regard :
The threshold grates the door to have him heard ;
  Night-wandering weasels shriek, to see him there ;
  They fright him, yet he still pursues his fear.

As each unwilling portal yields him way,
Through little vents and crannies of the place   310
The wind wars with his torch, to make him stay,
And blows the smoke of it into his face,
Extinguishing his conduct in this case ;
  But his hot heart, which fond desire doth scorch,
  Puffs forth another wind that fires the torch :

And being lighted, by the light he spies
Lucretia's glove, wherein her needle sticks :
He takes it from the rushes where it lies,
And griping it, the needle his finger pricks ;
As who should say, " This glove to wanton tricks 320
  Is not inur'd ; return again in haste ;
  Thou seest our mistress' ornaments are chaste."

But all these poor forbiddings could not stay him ;
He in the worst sense construes their denial :
The doors, the wind, the glove, that did delay him,
He takes for accidental things of trial,
Or as those bars which stop the hourly dial,
  Who with a ling'ring stay his course doth let,
  Till every minute pays the hour his debt.

" So, so," quoth he ; " these lets attend the time, 330
Like little frosts that sometime threat the spring,
To add a more rejoicing to the prime,
And give the sneaped birds more cause to sing.
Pain pays the income of each precious thing ;
  Huge rocks, high winds, strong pirates, shelves and
    sands,
  The merchant fears, ere rich at home he lands."

Now is he come unto the chamber-door,
That shuts him from the heaven of his thought,
Which with a yielding latch, and with no more,
Hath barr'd him from the blessed thing he sought. 340
So from himself impiety hath wrought,
  That for his prey to pray he doth begin,
  As if the heavens should countenance his sin.

But in the midst of his unfruitful prayer,
Having solicited the eternal power
That his foul thoughts might compass his fair fair,
And they would stand auspicious to the hour,
Even there he starts :—quoth he, " I must deflower :
  The powers to whom I pray abhor this fact,
  How can they then assist me in the act ?   350

" Then Love and Fortune be my gods, my guide !
My will is back'd with resolution :
Thoughts are but dreams, till their effects be tried ;
The blackest sin is clear'd with absolution ;
Against love's fire fear's frost hath dissolution.
  The eye of heaven is out, and misty night
  Covers the shame that follows sweet delight."

This said, his guilty hand pluck'd up the latch,
And with his knee the door he opens wide.
The dove sleeps fast that this night-owl will catch :
Thus treason works ere traitors be espied.   361
Who sees the lurking serpent steps aside ;
  But she, sound sleeping, fearing no such thing,
  Lies at the mercy of his mortal sting.

Into the chamber wickedly he stalks,
And gazeth on her yet unstained bed.
The curtains being close, about he walks,
Rolling his greedy eye-balls with his head :
By their high treason is his heart misled ;
  Which gives the watchword to his hand full soon,
  To draw the cloud that hides the silver moon.   371

Look, as the fair and fiery-pointed sun,
Rushing from forth a cloud, bereaves our sight ;
Even so, the curtain drawn, his eyes begun
To wink, being blinded with a greater light :
Whether it is that she reflects so bright,
  That dazzleth them, or else some shame supposed,
  But blind they are, and keep themselves enclosed.

O ! had they in that darksome prison died,
Then had they seen the period of their ill :   380
Then Collatine again, by Lucrece' side,
In his clear bed might have reposed still ;
But they must ope, this blessed league to kill,
  And holy-thoughted Lucrece to their sight
  Must sell her joy, her life, her world's delight.

Her lily hand her rosy cheek lies under,
Cozening the pillow of a lawful kiss ;
Who, therefore angry, seems to part in sunder,
Swelling on either side, to want his bliss ;
Between whose hills her head entombed is :   390
  Where, like a virtuous monument, she lies,
  To be admir'd of lewd unhallow'd eyes.

Without the bed her other fair hand was,
On the green coverlet ; whose perfect white
Show'd like an April daisy on the grass,
With pearly sweat, resembling dew of night.
Her eyes, like marigolds, had sheath'd their light,
And canopied in darkness sweetly lay,
Till they might open to adorn the day.

Her hair, like golden threads, play'd with her breath ;
O modest wantons ! wanton modesty !   401
Showing life's triumph in the map of death,
And death's dim look in life's mortality :
Each in her sleep themselves so beautify,
As if between them twain there were no strife,
But that life liv'd in death, and death in life.

Her breasts, like ivory globes circled with blue,
A pair of maiden worlds unconquered,
Save of their lord no bearing yoke they knew,
And him by oath they truly honoured.   410
These worlds in Tarquin new ambition bred ;
Who, like a foul usurper, went about
From this fair throne to heave the owner out.

What could he see, but mightily he noted ?
What did he note, but strongly he desir'd ?
What he beheld, on that he firmly doted,
And in his will his wilful eye he tir'd.
With more than admiration he admir'd
Her azure veins, her alabaster skin,
Her coral lips, her snow-white dimpled chin.   420

As the grim lion fawneth o'er his prey,
Sharp hunger by the conquest satisfied,
So o'er this sleeping soul doth Tarquin stay,
His rage of lust by gazing qualified ;
Slack'd, not suppress'd ; for standing by her sid
His eye, which late this mutiny restrains,
Unto a greater uproar tempts his veins :

And they, like straggling slaves for pillage fighting,
Obdurate vassals, fell exploits effecting,
In bloody death and ravishment delighting,   430
Nor children's tears, nor mothers' groans respecting,
Swell in their pride, the onset still expecting :
Anon his beating heart, alarum striking,
Gives the hot charge, and bids them do their liking.

His drumming heart cheers up his burning eye,
His eye commends the leading to his hand ;
His hand, as proud of such a dignity,
Smoking with pride, march'd on to make his stand
On her bare breast, the heart of all her land,
Whose ranks of blue veins, as his hand did scale,
Left their round turrets destitute and pale.   441

They, mustering to the quiet cabinet
Where their dear governess and lady lies,
Do tell her she is dreadfully beset,
And fright her with confusion of their cries :
She, much amaz'd, breaks ope her lock'd-up eyes,
Who, peeping forth this tumult to behold,
Are by his flaming torch dimm'd and controll'd.

Imagine her as one in dead of night
From forth dull sleep by dreadful fancy waking,   450
That thinks she hath beheld some ghastly sprite,
Whose grim aspect set every joint a-shaking ;
What terror 'tis ! but she, in worser taking,
From sleep disturbed, heedfully doth view
The sight which makes supposed terror true.

Wrapp'd and confounded in a thousand fears,
Like to a new-kill'd bird she trembling lies ;
She dares not look ; yet, winking, their appears
Quick-shifting anticks, ugly in her eyes :
Such shadows are the weak brain's forgeries ;   460
Who, angry that the eyes fly from their lights,
In darkness daunts them with more dreadful sights.

His hand, that yet remains upon her breast,
(Rude ram to batter such an ivory wall,)
May feel her heart (poor citizen !) distress'd,
Wounding itself to death, rise up and fall,
Beating her bulk, that his hand shakes withal.
This moves in him more rage, and lesser pity,
To make the breach, and enter this sweet city.

First, like a trumpet, doth his tongue begin   470
To sound a parley to his heartless foe ;
Who o'er the white sheet peers her whiter chin,
The reason of this rash alarm to know,
Which he by dumb demeanour seeks to show ;
But she with vehement prayers urgeth still,
Under what colour he commits this ill.

Thus he replies : " The colour in thy face,
That even for anger makes the lily pale,
And the red rose blush at her own disgrace,
Shall plead for me, and tell my loving tale ;   480
Under that colour am I come to scale
Thy never-conquer'd fort : the fault is thine,
For those thine eyes betray thee unto mine.

" Thus I forestall thee, if thou mean to chide :
Thy beauty hath ensnar'd thee to this night,
Where thou with patience must my will abide,
My will, that marks thee for my earth's delight,
Which I to conquer sought with all my might ;
But as reproof and reason beat it dead,
By thy bright beauty was it newly bred.   490

" I see what crosses my attempt will bring ;
I know what thorns the growing rose defends ;
I think the honey guarded with a sting :
All this, beforehand, counsel comprehends ;
But will is deaf, and hears no heedful friends :
Only he hath an eye to gaze on beauty,
And dotes on what he looks, 'gainst law or duty.

" I have debated, even in my soul,
What wrong, what shame, what sorrow I shall breed ;
But nothing can affection's course control,   500
Or stop the headlong fury of his speed.
I know repentant tears ensue the deed,
Reproach, disdain, and deadly enmity ;
Yet strive I to embrace mine infamy."

This said, he shakes aloft his Roman blade,
Which, like a falcon towering in the skies
Coucheth the fowl below with his wings' shade,
Whose crooked beak threats, if he mount he dies :
So under his insulting falchion lies
Harmless Lucretia, marking what he tells   510
With trembling fear, as fowl hear falcon's bells.

" Lucrece," quoth he, " this night I must enjoy thee :
If thou deny, then force must work my way,
For in thy bed I purpose to destroy thee :
That done, some worthless slave of thine I 'll slay,
To kill thine honour with thy life's decay ;
And in thy dead arms do I mean to place him,
Swearing I slew him, seeing thee embrace him.

" So thy surviving husband shall remain
The scornful mark of every open eye ;   520
Thy kinsmen hang their heads at this disdain,
Thy issue blurr'd with nameless bastardy :
And thou, the author of their obloquy,
Shalt have thy trespass cited up in rhymes,
And sung by children in succeeding times.

" But if thou yield, I rest thy secret friend :
The fault unknown is as a thought unacted ;
A little harm, done to a great good end,
For lawful policy remains enacted.
The poisonous simple sometimes is compacted   530
In a pure compound ; being so applied,
His venom in effect is purified.

" Then for thy husband and thy children's sake,
Tender my suit : bequeath not to their lot
The shame that from them no device can take,
The blemish that will never be forgot ;
Worse than a slavish wipe, or birth-hour's blot :
   For marks descried in men's nativity
   Are nature's faults, not their own infamy."

Here with a cockatrice' dead-killing eye   540
He rouseth up himself, and makes a pause ;
While she, the picture of pure piety,
Like a white hind under the gripe's sharp claws,
Pleads in a wilderness, where are no laws,
   To the rough beast that knows no gentle right,
   Nor aught obeys but his foul appetite.

But when a black-fac'd cloud the world doth threat
In his dim mist the aspiring mountains hiding,
From earth's dark womb some gentle gust doth get,
Which blows these pitchy vapours from their biding,
Hindering their present fall by this dividing :   551
   So his unhallowed haste her words delays,
   And moody Pluto winks, while Orpheus plays.

Yet, foul night-waking cat, he doth but dally,
While in his hold-fast foot the weak mouse panteth :
Her sad behaviour feeds his vulture folly,
A swallowing gulf that even in plenty wanteth.
His ear her prayers admits, but his heart granteth
   No penetrable entrance to her plaining :
   Tears harden lust, though marble wear with raining.

Her pity-pleading eyes are sadly fix'd   561
In the remorseless wrinkles of his face ;
Her modest eloquence with sighs is mix'd,
Which to her oratory adds more grace.
She puts the period often from his place ;
   And 'midst the sentence so her accent breaks,
   That twice she doth begin, ere once she speaks.

She conjures him by high almighty Jove,
By knighthood, gentry, and sweet friendship's oath,
By her untimely tears, her husband's love,   570
By holy human law, and common troth,
By heaven and earth, and all the power of both,
   That to his borrow'd bed he make retire,
   And stoop to honour, not to foul desire.

Quoth she : " Reward not hospitality
With such black payment as thou hast pretended ;
Mud not the fountain that gave drink to thee ;
Mar not the thing that cannot be amended ;
End thy ill aim before thy shoot be ended :
   He is no woodman that doth bend his bow   580
   To strike a poor unseasonable doe.

" My husband is thy friend, for his sake spare me ;
Thyself art mighty, for thine own sake leave me ;
Myself a weakling, do not then ensnare me ;
Thou look'st not like deceit, do not deceive me :
My sighs, like whirlwinds, labour hence to heave thee.
   If ever man were mov'd with woman's moans,
   Be moved with my tears, my sighs, my groans.

" All which together, like a troubled ocean,
Beat at thy rocky and wrack-threatening heart,   590
To soften it with their continual motion ;
For stones dissolv'd to water do convert.
O, if no harder than a stone thou art,
   Melt at my tears and be compassionate !
   Soft pity enters at an iron gate.

" In Tarquin's likeness I did entertain thee ;
Hast thou put on his shape to do him shame ?
To all the host of heaven I complain me,
Thou wrong'st his honour, wound'st his princely name :
Thou art not what thou seem'st ; and if the same,   600
   Thou seem'st not what thou art, a god, a king ;
   For kings like gods should govern everything.

" How will thy shame be seeded in thine age,
When thus thy vices bud before thy spring ?
If in thy hope thou dar'st do such outrage,
What dar'st thou not, when once thou art a king ?
O, be remember'd ! no outrageous thing
   From vassal actors can be wip'd away ;
   Then kings' misdeeds cannot be hid in clay.

" This deed will make thee only lov'd for fear ;   610
But happy monarchs still are fear'd for love :
With foul offenders thou perforce must bear,
When they in thee the like offences prove :
If but for fear of this, thy will remove ;
   For princes are the glass, the school, the book,
   Where subjects' eyes do learn, do read, do look.

" And wilt thou be the school where Lust shall learn ?
Must he in thee read lectures of such shame ?
Wilt thou be glass, wherein it shall discern
Authority for sin, warrant for blame,   620
To privilege dishonour in thy name ?
   Thou back'st reproach against long-living laud,
   And mak'st fair reputation but a bawd.

" Hast thou command ? by him that gave it thee,
From a pure heart command thy rebel will
Draw not thy sword to guard iniquity,
For it was lent thee all that brood to kill.
Thy princely office how canst thou fulfil,
   When, pattern'd by thy fault, foul Sin may say,
   He learn'd to sin, and thou didst teach the way ? 630

" Think but how vile a spectacle it were,
To view thy present trespass in another.
Men's faults do seldom to themselves appear ;
Their own transgressions partially they smother :
This guilt would seem death-worthy in thy brother.
   O, how are they wrapp'd in with infamies,
   That from their own misdeeds askance their eyes !

" To thee, to thee, my heav'd-up hands appeal,
Not to seducing lust, thy rash relier ;
I sue for exil'd majesty's repeal ;   640
Let him return, and flattering thoughts retire :
His true respect will prison false desire,
   And wipe the dim mist from thy doting eyne,
   That thou shalt see thy state, and pity mine."

" Have done," quoth he : " my uncontrolled tide
Turns not, but swells the higher by this let.
Small lights are soon blown out, huge fires abide,
And with the wind in greater fury fret :
The petty streams, that pay a daily debt
   To their salt sovereign with their fresh falls' haste,
   Add to his flow, but alter not his taste."   651

" Thou art," quoth she, " a sea, a sovereign king ;
And, lo ! there falls into thy boundless flood
Black lust, dishonour, shame, misgoverning,
Who seek to stain the ocean of thy blood.
If all these petty ills shall change thy good,
   Thy sea within a puddle's womb is hears'd,
   And not the puddle in thy sea dispers'd.

" So shall these slaves be king, and thou their slave ; 660
Thou nobly base, they basely dignified ;
Thou their fair life, and they thy fouler grave :
Thou loathed in their shame, they in thy pride :
The lesser thing should not the greater hide ;
   The cedar stoops not to the base shrub's foot,
   But low shrubs wither at the cedar's root.

" So let thy thoughts, low vassals to thy state "—
" No more," quoth he ; " by Heaven, I will not hear
   thee ;
Yield to my love ; if not, enforced hate,
Instead of love's coy touch, shall rudely tear thee ;
That done, despitefully I mean to bear thee   670
   Unto the base bed of some rascal groom,
   To be thy partner in this shameful doom."

This said, he sets his foot upon the light,
For light and lust are deadly enemies :
Shame folded up in blind concealing night,
When most unseen, then most doth tyrannise.
The wolf hath seiz'd his prey, the poor lamb cries ;
   Till with her own white fleece her voice controll'd
   Entombs her outcry in her lips' sweet fold :

For with the nightly linen that she wears   680
He pens her piteous clamours in her head,
Cooling his hot face in the chastest tears
That ever modest eyes with sorrow shed.
O, that prone lust should stain so pure a bed !
   The spots whereof could weeping purify,
   Her tears should drop on them perpetually.

But she hath lost a dearer thing than life,
And he hath won what he would lose again ;
This forced league doth force a further strife ;
This momentary joy breeds months of pain :   690
This hot desire converts to cold disdain.
   Pure Chastity is rifled of her store,
   And Lust, the thief, far poorer than before.

Look, as the full-fed hound, or gorged hawk,
Unapt for tender smell, or speedy flight,
Make slow pursuit, or altogether balk
The prey wherein by nature they delight:
So surfeit-taking Tarquin fares this night:
   His taste delicious, in digestion souring,
   Devours his will, that liv'd by foul devouring.   700

O deeper sin than bottomless conceit
Can comprehend in still imagination !
Drunken Desire must vomit his receipt,
Ere he can see his own abomination.
While Lust is in his pride, no exclamation
   Can curb his heat, or rein his rash desire,
   Till, like a jade, Self-will himself doth tire.

And then, with lank and lean discolour'd cheek,
With heavy eye, knit brow, and strengthless pace,
Feeble Desire, all recreant, poor, and meek,   710
Like to a bankrupt beggar wails his case :
The flesh being proud, Desire doth fight with Grace,
   For there it revels ; and when that decays,
   The guilty rebel for remission prays.

So fares it with this faultful lord of Rome,
Who this accomplishment so hotly chas'd ;
For now against himself he sounds this doom,—
That through the length of times he stands disgrac'd ;
Besides, his soul's fair temple is defac'd :
   To whose weak ruins muster troops of cares,   720
   To ask the spotted princess how she fares.

She says, her subjects with foul insurrection
Have batter'd down her consecrated wall,
And by their mortal fault brought in subjection
Her immortality, and made her thrall
To living death, and pain perpetual :
   Which in her prescience she controlled still,
   But her foresight could not forestall their will.

Even in this thought through the dark night he
      stealeth
A captive victor that hath lost in gain ;   730
Bearing away the wound that nothing healeth,
The scar that will despite of cure remain ;
Leaving his spoil perplex'd in greater pain.
   She bears the load of lust he left behind,
   And he the burden of a guilty mind.

He, like a thievish dog, creeps sadly thence,
She like a wearied lamb lies panting there ;
He scowls, and hates himself for his offence,
She desperate with her nails her flesh doth tear ;
He faintly flies, sweating with guilty fear,   740
   She stays, exclaiming on the direful night :
   He runs, and chides his vanish'd, loath'd delight.

He thence departs a heavy convertite,
She there remains a hopeless castaway ;
He in his speed looks for the morning light,
She prays she never may behold the day ;
" For day," quoth she, " night's scapes doth open lay,
   And my true eyes have never practis'd how
   To cloak offences with a cunning brow.

" They think not but that every eye can see   750
The same disgrace which they themselves behold,
And therefore would they still in darkness be,
To have their unseen sin remain untold ;
For they their guilt with weeping will unfold,
   And grave, like water that doth eat in steel,
   Upon my cheeks what helpless shame I feel."

Here she exclaims against repose and rest,
And bids her eyes hereafter still be blind.
She wakes her heart by beating on her breast,
And bids it leap from thence where it may find   760
Some purer chest to close so pure a mind.
   Frantic with grief, thus breathes she forth her
      spite
   Against the unseen secrecy of night :

" O comfort-killing Night, image of hell !
Dim register and notary of shame !
Black stage for tragedies and murders fell !
Vast sin-concealing chaos ! nurse of blame !
Blind muffled bawd ! dark harbour for defame !
   Grim cave of death, whispering conspirator
   With close-tongu'd treason and the ravisher !   770

" O hateful, vaporous, and foggy Night !
Since thou art guilty of my cureless crime,
Muster thy mists to meet the eastern light,
Make war against proportion'd course of time :
Or if thou wilt permit the sun to climb
   His wonted height, yet ere he go to bed,
   Knit poisonous clouds about his golden head.

" With rotten damps ravish the morning air ;
Let their exhal'd unwholesome breaths make sick
The life of purity, the supreme fair,   780
Ere he arrive his weary noontide prick ;
And let thy misty vapours march so thick,
   That in their smoky ranks his smother'd light
   May set at noon, and make perpetual night.

" Were Tarquin Night, as he is but Night's child,
The silver-shining queen he would distain ;
Her twinkling handmaids too, by him defil'd,
Through Night's black bosom should not peep again :
So should I have co-partners in my pain ;
   And fellowship in woe doth woe assuage,   790
   As palmers' chat makes short their pilgrimage.

" Where now I have no one to blush with me,
To cross their arms, and hang their heads with mine,
To mask their brows, and hide their infamy ;
But I alone alone must sit and pine,
Seasoning the earth with showers of silver brine ;
   Mingling my talk with tears, my grief with groans,
   Poor wasting monuments of lasting moans.

" O Night, thou furnace of foul-reeking smoke,
Let not the jealous Day behold that face   800
Which underneath thy black all-hiding cloak
Immodestly lies martyr'd with disgrace :
Keep still possession of thy gloomy place,
   That all the faults which in thy reign are made
   May likewise be sepulchred in thy shade.

" Make me not object to the tell-tale Day !
The light will show, character'd in my brow,
The story of sweet chastity's decay,
The impious breach of holy wedlock vow :
Yea, the illiterate, that know not how   810
   To cipher what is writ in learned books,
   Will quote my loathsome trespass in my looks.

"The nurse, to still her child, will tell my story,
And fright her crying babe with Tarquin's name;
The orator, to deck his oratory,
Will couple my reproach to Tarquin's shame;
Feast-finding minstrels, tuning my defame,
　　Will tie the hearers to attend each line,
　　How Tarquin wronged me, I Collatine.

"Let my good name, that senseless reputation,　820
For Collatine's dear love be kept unspotted:
If that be made a theme for disputation,
The branches of another root are rotted,
And undeserv'd reproach to him allotted,
　　That is as clear from this attaint of mine,
　　As I ere this was pure to Collatine.

"O unseen shame! invisible disgrace!
O unfelt sore! crest-wounding, private scar!
Reproach is stamp'd in Collatinus' face,
And Tarquin's eye may read the mot afar,　830
How he in peace is wounded, not in war.
　　Alas, how many bear such shameful blows,
　　Which not themselves, but he that gives them
　　　　knows.

"If, Collatine, thine honour lay in me,
From me by strong assault it is bereft.
My honey lost, and I, a drone-like bee,
Have no perfection of my summer left,
But robb'd and ransack'd by injurious theft:
　　In thy weak hive a wandering wasp hath crept,
　　And suck'd the honey which thy chaste bee kept. 840

"Yet am I guilty of thy honour's wrack;—
Yet for thy honour did I entertain him;
Coming from thee, I could not put him back,
For it had been dishonour to disdain him;
Besides, of weariness he did complain him,
　　And talk'd of virtue:—O unlook'd-for evil,
　　When virtue is profan'd in such a devil!

"Why should the worm intrude the maiden bud,
Or hateful cuckoos hatch in sparrows' nests?
Or toads infect fair founts with venom mud?　850
Or tyrant folly lurk in gentle breasts?
Or kings be breakers of their own behests?
　　But no perfection is so absolute,
　　That some impurity doth not pollute.

"The aged man that coffers-up his gold,
Is plagu'd with cramps, and gouts, and painful fits,
And scarce hath eyes his treasure to behold,
But like still-pining Tantalus he sits,
And useless barns the harvest of his wits;
　　Having no other pleasure of his gain,　860
　　But torment that it cannot cure his pain.

"So then he hath it, when he cannot use it,
And leaves it to be master'd by his young;
Who in their pride do presently abuse it:
Their father was too weak, and they too strong,
To hold their cursed-blessed fortune long.
　　The sweets we wish for turn to loathed sours,
　　Even in the moment that we call them ours.

"Unruly blasts wait on the tender spring;
Unwholesome weeds take root with precious flowers;
The adder hisses where the sweet birds sing;　871
What virtue breeds, iniquity devours:
We have no good that we can say is ours,
　　But ill-annexed Opportunity
　　Or kills his life, or else his quality.

"O Opportunity! thy guilt is great:
'T is thou that execut'st the traitor's treason;
Thou sett'st the wolf where he the lamb may get;
Whoever plots the sin, thou point'st the season;
'T is thou that spurn'st at right, at law, at reason;　880
　　And in thy shady cell, where none may spy him,
　　Sits Sin to seize the souls that wander by him.

"Thou mak'st the vestal violate her oath;
Thou blow'st the fire, when temperance is thaw'd;
Thou smother'st honesty, thou murder'st troth:
Thou foul abettor! thou notorious bawd!
Thou plantest scandal, and displacest laud:
　　Thou ravisher, thou traitor, thou false thief,
　　Thy honey turns to gall, thy joy to grief!

"Thy secret pleasure turns to open shame,　890
Thy private feasting to a public fast,
Thy smoothing titles to a ragged name,
Thy sugar'd tongue to bitter wormwood taste:
Thy violent vanities can never last.
　　How comes it then, vile Opportunity,
　　Being so bad, such numbers seek for thee?

"When wilt thou be the humble suppliant's friend,
And bring him where his suit may be obtain'd?
When wilt thou sort an hour great strifes to end,
Or free that soul which wretchedness hath chain'd?
Give physic to the sick, ease to the pain'd?　901
　　The poor, lame, blind, halt, creep, cry out for
　　　　thee,
　　But they ne'er meet with Opportunity.

"The patient dies while the physician sleeps;
The orphan pines while the oppressor feeds;
Justice is feasting while the widow weeps;
Advice is sporting while infection breeds:
Thou grant'st no time for charitable deeds:
　　Wrath, envy, treason, rape, and murder's rages,
　　Thy heinous hours wait on them as their pages. 910

"When Truth and Virtue have to do with thee
A thousand crosses keep them from thy aid:
They buy thy help; but Sin ne'er gives a fee;
He gratis comes, and thou art well-appay'd
As well to hear as grant what he hath said.
　　My Collatine would else have come to me,
　　When Tarquin did; but he was stay'd by thee.

"Guilty thou art of murder and of theft;
Guilty of perjury and subornation;
Guilty of treason, forgery, and shift;　920
Guilty of incest, that abomination:
An accessary by thine inclination
　　To all sins past, and all that are to come,
　　From the creation to the general doom.

"Misshapen Time, copesmate of ugly Night,
Swift-subtle post, carrier of grisly care,
Eater of youth, false slave to false delight,
Base watch of woes, sin's pack-horse, virtue's snare;
Thou nursest all, and murder'st all that are.
　　O, hear me then, injurious, shifting Time!　930
　　Be guilty of my death, since of my crime.

"Why hath thy servant, Opportunity,
Betray'd the hours thou gav'st me to repose?
Cancell'd my fortunes, and enchained me
To endless date of never-ending woes?
Time's office is to fine the hate of foes;
　　To eat up errors by opinion bred,
　　Not spend the dowry of a lawful bed.

"Time's glory is to calm contending kings,
To unmask falsehood, and bring truth to light,　940
To stamp the seal of time in aged things,
To wake the morn, and sentinel the night,
To wrong the wronger till he render right,
　　To ruinate proud buildings with thy hours,
　　And smear with dust their glittering golden towers:

"To fill with worm-holes stately monuments,
To feed oblivion with decay of things,
To blot old books, and alter their contents,
To pluck the quills from ancient ravens' wings,
To dry the old oak's sap, and cherish springs,　950
　　To spoil antiquities of hammer'd steel,
　　And turn the giddy round of Fortune's wheel:

" To show the bedlam daughters of her daughter,
To make the child a man, the man a child,
To slay the tiger that doth live by slaughter,
To tame the unicorn and lion wild,
To mock the subtle, in themselves beguil'd,
　To cheer the ploughman with increaseful crops,
　And waste huge stones with little water-drops.

" Why work'st thou mischief in thy pilgrimage,　960
Unless thou couldst return to make amends?
One poor retiring minute in an age
Would purchase thee a thousand thousand friends,
Lending him wit, that to bad debtors lends :
　O, this dread night, wouldst thou one hour come
　　back,
　I could prevent this storm, and shun thy wrack!

" Thou ceaseless lackey to eternity,
With some mischance cross Tarquin in his flight :
Devise extremes beyond extremity,
To make him curse this cursed crimeful night :　970
Let ghastly shadows his lewd eyes affright,
　And the dire thought of his committed evil
　Shape every bush a hideous shapeless devil.

" Disturb his hours of rest with restless trances,
Afflict him in his bed with bedrid groans ;
Let there bechance him pitiful mischances,
To make him moan, but pity not his moans :
Stone him with harden'd hearts, harder than stones ;
　And let mild women to him lose their mildness,
　Wilder to him than tigers in their wildness.　980

" Let him have time to tear his curled hair,
Let him have time against himself to rave,
Let him have time of time's help to despair,
Let him have time to live a loathed slave,
Let him have time a beggar's orts to crave,
　And time to see one that by alms doth live
　Disdain to him disdained scraps to give.

" Let him have time to see his friends his foes,
And merry fools to mock at him resort ;
Let him have time to mark how slow time goes　990
In time of sorrow, and how swift and short
His time of folly, and his time of sport :
　And ever let his unrecalling crime
　Have time to wail the abusing of his time.

" O Time, thou tutor both to good and bad,
Teach me to curse him that thou taught'st this ill !
At his own shadow let the thief run mad,
Himself himself seek every hour to kill !
Such wretched hands such wretched blood should spill ;
　For who so base would such an office have　1000
　As slanderous death's-man to so base a slave?

" The baser is he, coming from a king,
To shame his hope with deeds degenerate :
The mightier man, the mightier is the thing
That makes him honour'd, or begets him hate ;
For greatest scandal waits on greatest state.
　The moon being clouded presently is miss'd,
　But little stars may hide them when they list.

" The crow may bathe his coal-black wings in mire,
And unperceiv'd fly with the filth away ;　1010
But if the like the snow-white swan desire,
The stain upon his silver down will stay.
Poor grooms are sightless night, kings glorious day.
　Gnats are unnoted wheresoe'er they fly,
　But eagles gaz'd upon with every eye.

" Out, idle words ! servants to shallow fools,
Unprofitable sounds, weak arbitrators !
Busy yourselves in skill-contending schools ;
Debate where leisure serves with dull debaters ;
To trembling clients be you mediators :　1020
　For me, I force not argument a straw,
　Since that my case is past the help of law.

" In vain I rail at Opportunity,
At Time, at Tarquin, and uncheerful Night ;
In vain I cavil with mine infamy,
In vain I spurn at my confirm'd despite ;
This helpless smoke of words doth me no right.
　The remedy indeed to do me good,
　Is to let forth my foul-defiled blood.

" Poor hand, why quiver'st thou at this decree ?　1030
Honour thyself to rid me of this shame ;
For if I live, my honour lives in thee,
But if I live, thou liv'st in my defame :
Since thou couldst not defend thy loyal dame,
　And wast afear'd to scratch her wicked foe,
　Kill both thyself and her for yielding so."

This said, from her be-tumbled couch she starteth,
To find some desperate instrument of death ;
But this no-slaughter-house no tool imparteth,
To make more vent for passage of her breath ;　1040
Which, thronging through her lips, so vanisheth
　As smoke from Ætna, that in air consumes,
　Or that which from discharged cannon fumes.

" In vain," quoth she, " I live, and seek in vain
Some happy mean to end a hapless life :
I fear'd by Tarquin's falchion to be slain,
Yet for the selfsame purpose seek a knife :
But when I fear'd, I was a loyal wife.
　So am I now :—O no ! that cannot be ;
　Of that true type hath Tarquin rifled me.　1050

" O ! that is gone, for which I sought to live,
And therefore now I need not fear to die.
To clear this spot by death, at least I give
A badge of fame to slander's livery ;
A dying life to living infamy.
　Poor helpless help, the treasure stol'n away,
　To burn the guiltless casket where it lay !

" Well, well, dear Collatine, thou shalt not know
The stained taste of violated troth ;
I will not wrong thy true affection so,　1060
To flatter thee with an infringed oath ;
This bastard graff shall never come to growth :
　He shall not boast, who did thy stock pollute,
　That thou art doting father of his fruit.

" Nor shall he smile at thee in secret thought,
Nor laugh with his companions at thy state ;
But thou shalt know thy interest was not bought
Basely with gold, but stol'n from forth thy gate.
For me, I am the mistress of my fate,
　And with my trespass never will dispense,　1070
　Till life to death acquit my forc'd offence.

" I will not poison thee with my attaint,
Nor fold my fault in cleanly-coin'd excuses ;
My sable ground of sin I will not paint,
To hide the truth of this false night's abuses :
My tongue shall utter all ; mine eyes, like sluices,
　As from a mountain-spring that feeds a dale,
　Shall gush pure streams to purge my impure tale."

By this, lamenting Philomel had ended
The well-tun'd warble of her nightly sorrow,　1080
And solemn night with slow-sad gait descended
To ugly hell ; when, lo ! the blushing morrow
Lends light to all fair eyes that light will borrow ·
　But cloudy Lucrece shames herself to see,
　And therefore still in night would cloister'd be.

Revealing day through every cranny spies,
And seems to point her out where she sits weeping ;
To whom she sobbing speaks : " O eye of eyes !
Why pry'st thou through my window? leave thy
　　peeping ;
Mock with thy tickling beams eyes that are sleeping :
　Brand not my forehead with thy piercing light, 1091
　For day hath nought to do what's done by night."

Thus cavils she with everything she sees:
True grief is fond and testy as a child,
Who wayward once, his mood with nought agrees:
Old woes, not infant sorrows, bear them mild;
Continuance tames the one; the other wild,
  Like an unpractis'd swimmer plunging still,
  With too much labour drowns for want of skill.

So she, deep-drenched in a sea of care,   1100
Holds disputation with each thing she views,
And to herself all sorrow doth compare:
No object but her passion's strength renews,
And as one shifts, another straight ensues:
  Sometime her grief is dumb, and hath no words;
  Sometime 't is mad, and too much talk affords.

The little birds that tune their morning's joy
Make her moans mad with their sweet melody:
For mirth doth search the bottom of annoy;
Sad souls are slain in merry company;   1110
Grief best is pleas'd with grief's society:
  True sorrow then is feelingly suffic'd,
  When with like semblance it is sympathis'd.

'T is double death to drown in ken of shore;
He ten times pines that pines beholding food;
To see the salve doth make the wound ache more;
Great grief grieves most at that would do it good;
Deep woes roll forward like a gentle flood,
  Who, being stopp'd, the bounding banks o'erflows;
  Grief dallied with nor law nor limit knows.   1120

"You mocking birds," quoth she, "your tunes entomb
Within your hollow-swelling feather'd breasts,
And in my hearing be you mute and dumb!—
My restless discord loves no stops nor rests;
A woful hostess brooks not merry guests.—
  Relish your nimble notes to pleasing ears;
  Distress likes dumps, when time is kept with tears.

"Come, Philomel, that sing'st of ravishment,
Make thy sad grove in my dishevell'd hair:
As the dank earth weeps at thy languishment,   1130
So I at each sad strain will strain a tear,
And with deep groans the diapason bear;
  For burden-wise I 'll hum on Tarquin still,
  While thou on Tereus descant'st better skill.

"And whiles against a thorn thou bear'st thy part,
To keep thy sharp woes waking, wretched I,
To imitate thee well, against my heart
Will fix a sharp knife, to affright mine eye,
Who, if it wink, shall thereon fall and die.
  These means, as frets upon an instrument,   1140
  Shall tune our heart-strings to true languishment.

"And for, poor bird, thou sing'st not in the day,
As shaming any eye should thee behold,
Some dark-deep desert, seated from the way,
That knows not parching heat nor freezing cold,
Will we find out; and there we will unfold
  To creatures stern sad tunes, to change their kinds:
  Since men prove beasts, let beasts bear gentle minds."

As the poor frighted deer, that stands at gaze,
Wildly determining which way to fly,   1150
Or one encompass'd with a winding maze,
That cannot tread the way out readily;
So with herself is she in mutiny,
  To live or die which of the twain were better,
  When life is sham'd, and death reproach's debtor.

"To kill myself," quoth she, "alack! what were it,
But with my body my poor soul's pollution?
They that lose half, with greater patience bear it,
Than they whose whole is swallow'd in confusion.
That mother tries a merciless conclusion,   1160
  Who, having two sweet babes, when death takes one,
  Will slay the other, and be nurse to none.

"My body or my soul, which was the dearer,
When the one pure, the other mad divine?
Whose love of either to myself was nearer,
When both were kept for heaven and Collatine?
Ah me! the bark peel'd from the lofty pine,
  His leaves will wither, and his sap decay;
  So must my soul, her bark being peel'd away.

"Her house is sack'd, her quiet interrupted,   1170
Her mansion batter'd by the enemy;
Her sacred temple spotted, spoil'd, corrupted,
Grossly engirt with daring infamy:
Then let it not be call'd impiety,
  If in this blemish'd fort I make some hole,
  Through which I may convey this troubled soul.

"Yet die I will not, till my Collatine
Have heard the cause of my untimely death,
That he may vow, in that sad hour of mine,
Revenge on him that made me stop my breath.   1180
My stained blood to Tarquin I 'll bequeath,
  Which by him tainted shall for him be spent,
  And as his due writ in my testament.

"My honour I 'll bequeath unto the knife
That wounds my body so dishonoured.
'T is honour to deprive dishonour'd life;
The one will live, the other being dead:
So of shame's ashes shall my fame be bred;
  For in my death I murder shameful scorn:
  My shame so dead, mine honour is new-born.   1190

"Dear lord of that dear jewel I have lost,
What legacy shall I bequeath to thee?
My resolution, love, shall be thy boast,
By whose example thou reveng'd may'st be.
How Tarquin must be us'd, read it in me:
  Myself, thy friend, will kill myself, thy foe,
  And for my sake serve thou false Tarquin so.

"This brief abridgment of my will I make:—
My soul and body to the skies and ground;
My resolution, husband, do thou take;   1200
Mine honour be the knife's that makes my wound;
My shame be his that did my fame confound;
  And all my fame that lives disbursed be
  To those that live, and think no shame of me.

"Thou, Collatine, shalt oversee this will;
How was I overseen that thou shalt see it!
My blood shall wash the slander of mine ill;
My life's foul deed, my life's fair end shall free it.
Faint not, faint heart, but stoutly say, "So be it:"
  Yield to my hand; my hand shall conquer thee: 1210
  Thou dead, both die, and both shall victors be."

This plot of death when sadly she had laid,
And wip'd the brinish pearl from her bright eyes,
With untun'd tongue she hoarsely calls her maid,
Whose swift obedience to her mistress hies;
For fleet-wing'd duty with thought's feathers flies.
  Poor Lucrece' cheeks unto her maid seem so,
  As winter meads when sun doth melt their snow.

Her mistress she doth give demure good-morrow,
With soft-slow tongue, true mark of modesty,   1220
And sorts a sad look to her lady's sorrow,
For why her face wore sorrow's livery;
But durst not ask of her audaciously
  Why her two suns were cloud-eclipsed so,
  Nor why her fair cheeks over-wash'd with woe.

But as the earth doth weep, the sun being set,
Each flower moisten'd like a melting eye,
Even so the maid with swelling drops 'gan wet
Her circled eyne, enforc'd by sympathy
Of those fair suns set in her mistress' sky,   1230
  Who in a salt-wav'd ocean quench their light,
  Which makes the maid weep like the dewy night.

A pretty while these pretty creatures stand,
Like ivory conduits coral cisterns filling:
One justly weeps, the other takes in hand
No cause but company of her drops spilling:
Their gentle sex to weep are often willing,
   Grieving themselves to guess at others' smarts,
   And then they drown their eyes, or break their
      hearts:

For men have marble, women waxen minds,   1240
And therefore are they form'd as marble will;
The weak oppress'd, the impression of strange kinds
Is form'd in them by force, by fraud, or skill:
Then call them not the authors of their ill,
   No more than wax shall be accounted evil,
   Wherein is stamp'd the semblance of a devil.

Their smoothness, like a goodly champaign plain,
Lays open all the little worms that creep;
In men, as in a rough-grown grove, remain
Cave-keeping evils that obscurely sleep.   1250
Through crystal walls each little mote will peep:
   Though men can cover crimes with bold stern looks,
   Poor women's faces are their own faults' books.

No man inveigh against the wither'd flower,
But chide rough winter that the flower hath kill'd:
Not that devour'd, but that which doth devour,
Is worthy blame. O! let it not be hild
For women's faults, that they are so fulfill'd
   With men's abuses: those proud lords, to blame,
   Make weak-made women tenants to their shame.

The precedent whereof in Lucrece view,   1261
Assail'd by night, with circumstances strong
Of present death, and shame that might ensue
By that her death, to do her husband wrong:
Such danger to resistance did belong,
   That dying fear through all her body spread;
   And who cannot abuse a body dead?

By this, mild patience bid fair Lucrece speak
To the poor counterfeit of her complaining:
"My girl," quoth she, "on what occasion break   1270
Those tears from thee, that down thy cheeks are
      raining?
If thou dost weep for grief of my sustaining,
   Know, gentle wench, it small avails my mood:
   If tears could help, mine own would do me good.

"But tell me, girl, when went"—(and there she stay'd
Till after a deep groan)—"Tarquin from hence?"
"Madam, ere I was up," replied the maid;
"The more to blame my sluggard negligence:
Yet with the fault I thus far can dispense,—
   Myself was stirring ere the break of day,   1280
   And, ere I rose, was Tarquin gone away.

"But, lady, if your maid may be so bold,
She would request to know your heaviness."
"O, peace!" quoth Lucrece: "if it should be told,
The repetition cannot make it less;
For more it is than I can well express:
   And that deep torture may be call'd a hell,
   When more is felt than one hath power to tell.

"Go, get me hither paper, ink, and pen,—
Yet save that labour, for I have them here.   1290
What should I say?—One of my husband's men
Bid thou be ready by-and-by, to bear
A letter to my lord, my love, my dear:
   Bid him with speed prepare to carry it;
   The cause craves haste, and it will soon be writ."

Her maid is gone, and she prepares to write,
First hovering o'er the paper with her quill.
Conceit and grief an eager combat fight;
What wit sets down is blotted straight with will:
This is too curious-good, this blunt and ill: 1300
   Much like a press of people at a door
   Throng her inventions, which shall go before.

At last she thus begins: "Thou worthy lord
Of that unworthy wife that greeteth thee,
Health to thy person! next, vouchsafe t' afford
(If ever, love, thy Lucrece thou wilt see)
Some present speed to come and visit me.
   So I commend me from our house in grief:
   My woes are tedious, though my words are brief."

Here folds she up the tenor of her woe,   1310
Her certain sorrow writ uncertainly.
By this short schedule Collatine may know
Her grief, but not her grief's true quality:
She dares not thereof make discovery,
   Lest he should hold it her own gross abuse,
   Ere she with blood had stain'd her stain'd excuse.

Besides, the life and feeling of her passion
She hoards, to spend when he is by to hear her;
When sighs and groans and tears may grace the
      fashion
Of her disgrace, the better so to clear her   1320
From that suspicion which the world might bear
      her.
   To shun this blot, she would not blot the letter
   With words, till action might become them better.

To see sad sights moves more than hear them told;
For then the eye interprets to the ear
The heavy motion that it doth behold,
When every part a part of woe doth bear;
'T is but a part of sorrow that we hear:
   Deep sounds make lesser noise than shallow fords,
   And sorrow ebbs, being blown with wind of words.

Her letter now is seal'd, and on it writ,   1331
"At Ardea to my lord, with more than haste."
The post attends, and she delivers it,
Charging the sour-fac'd groom to hie as fast
As lagging fowls before the northern blast:
   Speed more than speed but dull and slow she deems:
   Extremity still urgeth such extremes.

The homely villain court'sies to her low;
And, blushing on her, with a steadfast eye
Receives the scroll, without or yea or no,   1340
And forth with bashful innocence doth hie:
But they whose guilt within their bosoms lie
   Imagine every eye beholds their blame;
   For Lucrece thought he blush'd to see her shame:

When, silly groom! God wot, it was defect
Of spirit, life, and bold audacity.
Such harmless creatures have a true respect
To talk in deeds, while others saucily
Promise more speed, but do it leisurely:
   Even so this pattern of the worn-out age   1350
   Pawn'd honest looks, but laid no words to gage.

His kindled duty kindled her mistrust,
That two red fires in both their faces blaz'd;
She thought he blush'd, as knowing Tarquin's lust,
And, blushing with him, wistly on him gaz'd;
Her earnest eye did make him more amaz'd:
   The more she saw the blood his cheeks replenish,
   The more she thought he spied in her some blemish.

But long she thinks till he return again,
And yet the duteous vassal scarce is gone.   1360
The weary time she cannot entertain,
For now 't is stale to sigh, to weep, and groan:
So woe hath wearied woe, moan tired moan,
   That she her plaints a little while doth stay,
   Pausing for means to mourn some newer way.

At last she calls to mind where hangs a piece
Of skilful painting, made for Priam's Troy;
Before the which is drawn the power of Greece,
For Helen's rape the city to destroy,
Threat'ning cloud-kissing Ilion with annoy;   1370
   Which the conceited painter drew so proud,
   As heaven, it seem'd, to kiss the turrets bow'd.

A thousand lamentable objects there,
In scorn of nature, art gave lifeless life.
Many a dry drop seem'd a weeping tear,
Shed for the slaughter'd husband by the wife:
The red blood reek'd, to show the painter's strife;
  And dying eyes gleam'd forth their ashy lights,
  Like dying coals burnt out in tedious nights.

There might you see the labouring pioner   1380
Begrim'd with sweat, and smeared all with dust;
And from the towers of Troy there would appear
The very eyes of men through loop-holes thrust,
Gazing upon the Greeks with little lust:
  Such sweet observance in this work was had,
  That one might see those far-off eyes look sad.

In great commanders grace and majesty
You might behold, triumphing in their faces;
In youth quick bearing and dexterity;
And here and there the painter interlaces   1390
Pale cowards, marching on with trembling paces:
  Which heartless peasants did so well resemble,
  That one would swear he saw them quake and
      tremble.

In Ajax and Ulysses, O, what art
Of physiognomy might one behold!
The face of either cipher'd either's heart;
Their face their manners most expressly told:
In Ajax' eyes blunt rage and rigour roll'd;
  But the mild glance that sly Ulysses lent
  Show'd deep regard and smiling government.   1400

There pleading might you see grave Nestor stand,
As 't were encouraging the Greeks to fight;
Making such sober action with his hand,
That it beguil'd attention, charm'd the sight.
In speech, it seem'd, his beard, all silver white,
  Wagg'd up and down, and from his lips did fly
  Thin winding breath, which purl'd up to the sky.

About him were a press of gaping faces,
Which seem'd to swallow up his sound advice;
All jointly listening, but with several graces,   1410
As if some mermaid did their ears entice:
Some high, some low, the painter was so nice,
  The scalps of many, almost hid behind,
  To jump up higher seem'd, to mock the mind.

Here one man's hand lean'd on another's head,
His nose being shadow'd by his neighbour's ear;
Here one, being throng'd, bears back, all boll'n and red;
Another, smother'd, seems to pelt and swear;
And in their rage such signs of rage they bear,
  As, but for loss of Nestor's golden words,   1420
  It seem'd they would debate with angry swords.

For much imaginary work was there;
Conceit deceitful, so compact, so kind,
That for Achilles' image stood his spear,
Grip'd in an armed hand: himself behind
Was left unseen, save to the eye of mind.
  A hand, a foot, a face, a leg, a head,
  Stood for the whole to be imagined.

And from the walls of strong-besieged Troy
When their brave hope, bold Hector, march'd to field,
Stood many Trojan mothers, sharing joy   1431
To see their youthful sons bright weapons wield;
And to their hope they such odd action yield,
  That through their light joy seemed to appear
  (Like bright things stain'd) a kind of heavy fear.

And from the strond of Dardan, where they fought,
To Simois' reedy banks the red blood ran,
Whose waves to imitate the battle sought
With swelling ridges; and their ranks began
To break upon the galled shore, and than   1440
  Retire again, till meeting greater ranks
  They join, and shoot their foam at Simois' banks.

To this well-painted piece is Lucrece come,
To find a face where all distress is stell'd.
Many she sees, where cares have carved some,
But none where all distress and dolour dwell'd,
Till she despairing Hecuba beheld,
  Staring on Priam's wounds with her old eyes,
  Which bleeding under Pyrrhus' proud foot lies.

In her the painter had anatomis'd   1450
Time's ruin, beauty's wrack, and grim care's reign:
Her cheeks with chaps and wrinkles were disguis'd;
Of what she was no semblance did remain:
Her blue blood chang'd to black in every vein,
  Wanting the spring that those shrunk pipes had fed,
  Show'd life imprison'd in a body dead.

On this sad shadow Lucrece spends her eyes,
And shapes her sorrow to the beldam's woes,
Who nothing wants to answer her but cries,
And bitter words to ban her cruel foes: 1460
The painter was no god to lend her those;
  And therefore Lucrece swears he did her wrong,
  To give her so much grief, and not a tongue.

"Poor instrument," quoth she, "without a sound,
I'll tune thy woes with my lamenting tongue,
And drop sweet balm in Priam's painted wound,
And rail on Pyrrhus that hath done him wrong,
And with my tears quench Troy, that burns so long,
  And with my knife scratch out the angry eyes
  Of all the Greeks that are thine enemies.   1470

"Show me the strumpet that began this stir,
That with my nails her beauty I may tear.
Thy heat of lust, fond Paris, did incur
This load of wrath that burning Troy doth bear:
Thine eye kindled the fire that burneth here;
  And here, in Troy, for trespass of thine eye,
  The sire, the son, the dame, and daughter, die.

"Why should the private pleasure of some one
Become the public plague of many moe?
Let sin, alone committed, light alone   1480
Upon his head that hath transgressed so;
Let guiltless souls be freed from guilty woe.
  For one's offence why should so many fall,
  To plague a private sin in general?

"Lo! here weeps Hecuba, here Priam dies,
Here manly Hector faints, here Troilus swounds,
Here friend by friend in bloody channel lies,
And friend to friend gives unadvised wounds,
And one man's lust these many lives confounds:
  Had doting Priam check'd his son's desire,   1490
  Troy had been bright with fame, and not with fire."

Here feelingly she weeps Troy's painted woes;
For sorrow, like a heavy-hanging bell,
Once set on ringing, with his own weight goes;
Then little strength rings out the doleful knell:
So Lucrece, set a-work, sad tales doth tell
  To pencill'd pensiveness and colour'd sorrow;
  She lends them words, and she their looks doth
      borrow.

She throws her eyes about the painting round,   1500
And who she finds forlorn she doth lament:
At last she sees a wretched image bound,
That piteous looks to Phrygian shepherds lent;
His face, though full of cares, yet show'd content.
  Onward to Troy with the blunt swains he goes,
  So mild, that Patience seem'd to scorn his woes.

In him the painter labour'd with his skill
To hide deceit, and give the harmless show
An humble gait, calm looks, eyes wailing still,
A brow unbent that seem'd to welcome woe;   1510
Cheeks neither red nor pale, but mingled so
  That blushing red no guilty instance gave,
  Nor ashy pale the fear that false hearts have.

But, like a constant and confirmed devil,
He entertain'd a show so seeming-just,
And therein so ensconc'd his secret evil,
That jealousy itself could not mistrust
False-creeping craft and perjury should thrust
　Into so bright a day such black-fac'd storms,
　Or blot with hell-born sin such saint-like forms.

The well-skill'd workman this mild image drew　1520
For perjur'd Sinon, whose enchanting story
The credulous old Priam after slew;
Whose words like wild-fire burnt the shining glory
Of rich-built Ilion, that the skies were sorry,
　And little stars shot from their fixed places,
　When their glass fell wherein they view'd their faces.

This picture she advisedly perus'd,
And chid the painter for his wondrous skill,
Saying, some shape in Sinon's was abus'd;
So fair a form lodg'd not a mind so ill :　　1530
And still on him she gaz'd, and gazing still,
　Such signs of truth in his plain face she spied,
　That she concludes the picture was belied.

" It cannot be," quoth she, " that so much guile"—
She would have said " can lurk in such a look ;"
But Tarquin's shape came in her mind the while,
And from her tongue " can lurk " from " cannot " took ;
" It cannot be " she in that sense forsook,
　And turn'd it thus : " It cannot be, I find,
　But such a face should bear a wicked mind :　1540

" For even as subtle Sinon here is painted,
So sober-sad, so weary, and so mild,
(As if with grief or travail he had fainted,)
To me came Tarquin armed; so beguil'd
With outward honesty, but yet defil'd
　With inward vice : as Priam him did cherish,
　So did I Tarquin ; so my Troy did perish.

" Look, look, how listening Priam wets his eyes,
To see those borrow'd tears that Sinon sheds !
Priam, why art thou old, and yet not wise ?　1550
For every tear he falls a Trojan bleeds;
His eye drops fire, no water thence proceeds ;
　Those round clear pearls of his, that move thy pity,
　Are balls of quenchless fire to burn thy city.

" Such devils steal effects from lightless hell ;
For Sinon in his fire doth quake with cold,
And in that cold hot-burning fire doth dwell ;
These contraries such unity do hold,
Only to flatter fools, and make them bold :
　So Priam's trust false Sinon's tears doth flatter, 1560
　That he finds means to burn his Troy with water."

Here, all enrag'd, such passion her assails,
That patience is quite beaten from her breast.
She tears the senseless Sinon with her nails,
Comparing him to that unhappy guest
Whose deed hath made herself herself detest :
　At last she smilingly with this gives o'er ;
　"Fool ! fool !" quoth she, "his wounds will not be
　　sore."

Thus ebbs and flows the current of her sorrow,
And time doth weary time with her complaining. 1570
She looks for night, and then she longs for morrow,
And both she thinks too long with her remaining.
Short time seems long in sorrow's sharp sustaining :
　Though woe be heavy, yet it seldom sleeps ;
　And they that watch see time how slow it creeps.

Which all this time hath overslipp'd her thought,
That she with painted images hath spent,
Being from the feeling of her own grief brought
By deep surmise of others' detriment ;
Losing her woes in shows of discontent.　　1580
　It easeth some, though none it ever cur'd,
　To think their dolour others have endur'd.

But now the mindful messenger, come back,
Brings home his lord and other company;
Who finds his Lucrece clad in mourning black ;
And round about her tear-distained eye
Blue circles stream'd, like rainbows in the sky :
　These water-galls in her dim element
　Foretell new storms to those already spent.

Which when her sad-beholding husband saw,　1590
Amazedly in her sad face he stares :
Her eyes, though sod in tears, look'd red and raw ;
Her lively colour kill'd with deadly cares.
He hath no power to ask her how she fares ;
　Both stood like old acquaintance in a trance,
　Met far from home, wondering each other's chance.

At last he takes her by the bloodless hand,
And thus begins : " What uncouth ill event
Hath thee befall'n, that thou dost trembling stand ?
Sweet love, what spite hath thy fair colour spent ? 1600
Why art thou thus attir'd in discontent ?
　Unmask, dear dear, this moody heaviness,
　And tell thy grief, that we may give redress."

Three times with sighs she gives her sorrow fire,
Ere once she can discharge one word of woe :
At length address'd to answer his desire,
She modestly prepares to let them know
Her honour is ta'en prisoner by the foe ;
　While Collatine and his consorted lords
　With sad attention long to hear her words.　1610

And now this pale swan in her watery nest
Begins the sad dirge of her certain ending.
" Few words," quoth she, " shall fit the trespass best,
Where no excuse can give the fault amending :
In me moe woes than words are now depending ;
　And my laments would be drawn out too long,
　To tell them all with one poor tired tongue.

" Then be this all the task it hath to say :
Dear husband, in the interest of thy bed
A stranger came, and on that pillow lay　　1620
Where thou wast wont to rest thy weary head ;
And what wrong else may be imagined
　By foul enforcement might be done to me,
　From that, alas ! thy Lucrece is not free.

" For in the dreadful dead of dark midnight,
With shining falchion in my chamber came
A creeping creature, with a flaming light,
And softly cried : ' Awake, thou Roman dame,
And entertain my love ; else lasting shame
　On thee and thine this night I will inflict,　1630
　If thou my love's desire do contradict.

" ' For some hard-favour'd groom of thine,' quoth he,
' Unless thou yoke thy liking to my will,
I 'll murder straight, and then I 'll slaughter thee,
And swear I found you where you did fulfil
The loathsome act of lust, and so did kill
　The lechers in their deed : this act will be
　My fame, and thy perpetual infamy.'

" With this I did begin to start and cry,
And then against my heart he set his sword,　1640
Swearing, unless I took all patiently,
I should not live to speak another word ;
So should my shame still rest upon record,
　And never be forgot in mighty Rome
　The adulterate death of Lucrece and her groom.

" Mine enemy was strong, my poor self weak,
And far the weaker with so strong a fear :
My bloody judge forbade my tongue to speak ;
No rightful plea might plead for justice there :
His scarlet lust came evidence to swear　　1650
　That my poor beauty had purloin'd his eyes ;
　And when the judge is robb'd, the prisoner dies.

" O ! teach me how to make mine own excuse,
Or, at the least, this refuge let me find :
Though my gross blood be stain'd with this abuse,
Immaculate and spotless is my mind ;
That was not forc'd ; that never was inclin'd
    To accessary yieldings, but still pure
    Doth in her poison'd closet yet endure."

Lo ! here the hopeless merchant of this loss,   1660
With head declin'd, and voice damm'd up with woe,
With sad-set eyes, and wretched arms across,
From lips new-waxen pale begins to blow
The grief away, that stops his answer so :
    But, wretched as he is, he strives in vain ;
    What he breathes out, his breath drinks up again.

As through an arch the violent roaring tide
Outruns the eye that doth behold his haste,
Yet in the eddy boundeth in his pride
Back to the strait that forc'd him on so fast,   1670
In rage sent out, recall'd in rage, being past :
    Even so his sighs, his sorrows, make a saw,
    To push grief on, and back the same grief draw.

Which speechless woe of his poor she attendeth,
And his untimely frenzy thus awaketh :
" Dear lord, thy sorrow to my sorrow lendeth
Another power ; no flood by raining slaketh.
My woe too sensible thy passion maketh
    More feeling-painful : let it then suffice
    To drown one woe, one pair of weeping eyes.   1680

" And for my sake, when I might charm thee so,
For she that was thy Lucrece, now attend me :
Be suddenly revenged on my foe,
Thine, mine, his own : suppose thou dost defend me
From what is past : the help that thou shalt lend me
    Comes all too late, yet let the traitor die ;
    For sparing justice feeds iniquity.

" But ere I name him, you, fair lords," quoth she
(Speaking to those that came with Collatine),
" Shall plight your honourable faiths to me,   1690
With swift pursuit to venge this wrong of mine ;
For 't is a meritorious fair design,
    To chase injustice with revengeful arms :
    Knights, by their oaths, should right poor ladies'
        harms."

At this request, with noble disposition
Each present lord began to promise aid,
As bound in knighthood to her imposition,
Longing to hear the hateful foe bewray'd ;
But she, that yet her sad task hath not said,
    The protestation stops.   " O ! speak," quoth she, 1700
    " How may this forced stain be wip'd from me ?

" What is the quality of mine offence,
Being constrain'd with dreadful circumstance ?
May my pure mind with the foul act dispense,
My low-declined honour to advance ?
May any terms acquit me from this chance ?
    The poison'd fountain clears itself again ;
    And why not I from this compelled stain ?"

With this, they all at once began to say,
Her body's stain her mind untainted clears ;   1710
While with a joyless smile she turns away
The face, that map which deep impression bears
Of hard misfortune, carv'd in it with tears.
    " No, no," quoth she ; " no dame, hereafter living,
    By my excuse shall claim excuse's giving."

Here with a sigh, as if her heart would break,
She throws forth Tarquin's name : " He, he," she
        says,
But more than " he " her poor tongue could not speak ;
Till after many accents and delays,
Untimely breathings, sick and short assays,   1720
    She utters this : " He, he, fair lords, 't is he,
    That guides this hand to give this wound to me."

Even here she sheathed in her harmless breast
A harmful knife, that thence her soul unsheathed :
That blow did bail it from the deep unrest
Of that polluted prison where it breathed ;
Her contrite sighs unto the clouds bequeathed
    Her winged spright, and through her wounds doth
        fly
    Life's lasting date from cancell'd destiny.

Stone-still astonish'd with this deadly deed,   1730
Stood Collatine and all his lordly crew ;
Till Lucrece' father, that beholds her bleed,
Himself on her self-slaughter'd body threw ;
And from the purple fountain Brutus drew
    The murderous knife, and, as it left the place,
    Her blood, in poor revenge, held it in chase ;

And bubbling from her breast, it doth divide
In two slow rivers, that the crimson blood
Circles her body in on every side,
Who like a late-sack'd island vastly stood,   1740
Bare and unpeopled, in this fearful flood.
    Some of her blood still pure and red remain'd,
    And some look'd black, and that false Tarquin
        stain'd.

About the mourning and congealed face
Of that black blood a watery rigol goes,
Which seems to weep upon the tainted place :
And ever since, as pitying Lucrece' woes,
Corrupted blood some watery token shows ;
    And blood untainted still doth red abide,
    Blushing at that which is so putrified.   1750

" Daughter, dear daughter !" old Lucretius cries,
" That life was mine, which thou hast here depriv'd.
If in the child the father's image lies,
Where shall I live, now Lucrece is unliv'd ?
Thou wast not to this end from me deriv'd.
    If children pre-decease progenitors,
    We are their offspring, and they none of ours.

" Poor broken glass, I often did behold
In thy sweet semblance my old age new-born ;
But now that fair fresh mirror, dim and old,   1760
Shows me a bare-bon'd death by time outworn.
O ! from thy cheeks my image thou hast torn,
    And shiver'd all the beauty of my glass,
    That I no more can see what once I was.

" O time ! cease thou thy course, and last no longer,
If they surcease to be that should survive.
Shall rotten death make conquest of the stronger,
And leave the faltering feeble souls alive ?
The old bees die, the young possess their hive :
    Then live, sweet Lucrece ; live again, and see   1770
    Thy father die, and not thy father thee !"

By this starts Collatine as from a dream,
And bids Lucretius give his sorrow place ;
And then in key-cold Lucrece' bleeding stream
He falls, and bathes the pale fear in his face,
And counterfeits to die with her a space ;
    Till manly shame bids him possess his breath,
    And live to be revenged on her death.

The deep vexation of his inward soul
Hath serv'd a dumb arrest upon his tongue ;   1780
Who, mad that sorrow should his use control,
Or keep him from heart-easing words so long,
Begins to talk ; but through his lips do throng
    Weak words so thick, come in his poor heart's aid,
    That no man could distinguish what he said.

Yet sometime " Tarquin " was pronounced plain,
But through his teeth, as if the name he tore.
This windy tempest, till it blow up rain,
Held back his sorrow's tide to make it more ;
At last it rains, and busy winds give o'er :   1790
    Then son and father weep with equal strife,
    Who should weep most, for daughter or for wife.

The one doth call her his, the other his,
Yet neither may possess the claim they lay.
The father says: "She 's mine." "O! mine she is,"
Replies her husband, "do not take away
My sorrow's interest; let no mourner say
  He weeps for her, for she was only mine,
  And only must be wail'd by Collatine."

"O!" quoth Lucretius, "I did give that life,   1800
Which she too early and too late hath spill'd."
"Woe, woe!" quoth Collatine, "she was my wife,
I ow'd her, and 't is mine that she hath kill'd."
"My daughter" and "My wife" with clamours fill'd
  The dispers'd air, who, holding Lucrece' lite,
  Answer'd their cries, "My daughter" and "My
     wife."

Brutus, who pluck'd the knife from Lucrece' side,
Seeing such emulation in their woe,
Began to clothe his wit in state and pride,
Burying in Lucrece' wound his folly's show.   1810
He with the Romans was esteemed so
As silly-jeering idiots are with kings,
  For sportive words, and uttering foolish things:

But now he throws that shallow habit by,
Wherein deep policy did him disguise,
And arm'd his long-hid wits advisedly,
To check the tears in Collatinus' eyes.
"Thou wronged lord of Rome," quoth he, "arise:
  Let my unsounded self, suppos'd a fool,
  Now set thy long-experienc'd wit to school.   1820

Why, Collatine, is woe the cure for woe?
Do wounds help wounds, or grief help grievous deeds?
Is it revenge to give thyself a blow,
For his foul act by whom thy fair wife bleeds?
Such childish humour from weak minds proceeds;
  Thy wretched wife mistook the matter so,
  To slay herself, that should have slain her foe.

"Courageous Roman, do not steep thy heart
In such relenting dew of lamentations,
But kneel with me, and help to bear thy part,   1830
To rouse our Roman gods with invocations,
That they will suffer these abominations,
  Since Rome herself in them doth stand disgrac'd,
  By our strong arms from forth her fair streets
     chas'd.

"Now, by the Capitol that we adore,
And by this chaste blood so unjustly stain'd,
By heaven's fair sun that breeds the fat earth's store,
By all our country rights in Rome maintain'd,
And by chaste Lucrece' soul, that late complain'd
  Her wrongs to us, and by this bloody knife,   1840
  We will revenge the death of this true wife."

This said, he struck his hand upon his breast,
And kiss'd the fatal knife to end his vow;
And to his protestation urg'd the rest,
Who, wondering at him, did his words allow:
Then jointly to the ground their knees they bow;
  And that deep vow which Brutus made before,
  He doth again repeat, and that they swore.

When they had sworn to this advised doom,
They did conclude to bear dead Lucrece thence; 1850
To show her bleeding body thorough Rome,
And so to publish Tarquin's foul offence:
Which being done with speedy diligence,
  The Romans plausibly did give consent
  To Tarquin's everlasting banishment.

A LOVER'S COMPLAINT.

FROM off a hill whose concave womb re-worded
A plaintful story from a sistering vale,
My spirits to attend this double voice accorded,
And down I laid to list the sad-tun'd tale ;
Ere long espied a fickle maid full pale,
Tearing of papers, breaking rings a-twain,
Storming her world with sorrow's wind and rain.

Upon her head a platted hive of straw,
Which fortified her visage from the sun, 10
Whereon the thought might think sometime it saw
The carcass of a beauty spent and done ;
Time had not scythed all that youth begun,
Nor youth all quit ; but, spite of Heaven's fell rage,
Some beauty peep'd through lattice of sear'd age.

Oft did she heave her napkin to her eyne,
Which on it had conceited characters,
Laundering the silken figures in the brine
That season'd woe had pelleted in tears,
And often reading what content it bears ;
As often shrieking undistinguish'd woe 20
In clamours of all size, both high and low.

Sometimes her levell'd eyes their carriage ride,
As they did battery to the spheres intend ;
Sometime, diverted, their poor balls are tied
To the orbed earth ; sometimes they do extend
Their view right on ; anon their gazes lend
To every place at once, and nowhere fix'd,
The mind and sight distractedly commix'd.

Her hair, nor loose, nor tied in formal plat,
Proclaim'd in her a careless hand of pride ; 30
For some, untuck'd, descended her sheav'd hat,
Hanging her pale and pined cheek beside ;
Some in her threaden fillet still did bide,
And, true to bondage, would not break from thence,
Though slackly braided in loose negligence.

A thousand favours from a maund she drew
Of amber, crystal, and of beaded jet,
Which one by one she in a river threw,
Upon whose weeping margent she was set ;
Like usury, applying wet to wet, 40
Or monarchs' hands, that let not bounty fall
Where want cries some, but where excess begs all.

Of folded schedules had she many a one,
Which she perus'd, sigh'd, tore, and gave the flood ;
Crack'd many a ring of posied gold and bone,
Bidding them find their sepulchres in mud ;
Found yet more letters sadly penn'd in blood,
With sleided silk feat and affectedly
Enswath'd, and seal'd to curious secrecy.

These often bath'd she in her fluxive eyes, 50
And often kiss'd, and often 'gan to tear ;
Cried, " O false blood, thou register of lies,
What unapproved witness dost thou bear !
Ink would have seem'd more black and damned here."
This said, in top of rage the lines she rents,
Big discontent so breaking their contents.

A reverend man that graz'd his cattle nigh,—
Sometime a blusterer, that the ruffle knew
Of court, of city, and had let go by
The swiftest hours, observed as they flew,— 60
Towards this afflicted fancy fastly drew ;
And, privileged by age, desires to know
In brief the grounds and motives of her woe.

So slides he down upon his grained bat,
And comely-distant sits he by her side ;
When he again desires her, being sat,
Her grievance with his hearing to divide :
If that from him there may be aught applied,
Which may her suffering ecstacy assuage,
'T is promis'd in the charity of age. 70

" Father," she says, " though in me you behold
The injury of many a blasting hour,
Let it not tell your judgment I am old ;
Not age, but sorrow, over me hath power :
I might as yet have been a spreading flower,
Fresh to myself, if I had self-applied
Love to myself, and to no love beside.

"But woe is me ! too early I attended
A youthful suit,—it was to gain my grace,—
Of one by nature's outwards so commended, 80
That maidens' eyes stuck over all his face.
Love lack'd a dwelling, and made him her place ;
And when in his fair parts she did abide,
She was new lodg'd, and newly deified.

" His browny locks did hang in crooked curls,
And every light occasion of the wind
Upon his lips their silken parcels hurls.
What's sweet to do, to do will aptly find :
Each eye that saw him did enchant the mind ;
For on his visage was in little drawn, 90
What largeness thinks in Paradise was sawn.

"Small show of man was yet upon his chin :
His phœnix down began but to appear,
Like unshorn velvet, on that termless skin,
Whose bare out-bragg'd the web it seem'd to wear ;
Yet show'd his visage by that cost most dear,
And nice affections wavering stood in doubt
If best were as it was, or best without.

" His qualities were beauteous as his form,
For maiden-tongu'd he was, and thereof free ; 100
Yet, if men mov'd him, was he such a storm
As oft 'twixt May and April is to see,
When winds breathe sweet, unruly though they be.
His rudeness so, with his authoris'd youth,
Did livery falseness in a pride of truth.

" Well could he ride, and often men would say,
'That horse his mettle from his rider takes:
Proud of subjection, noble by the sway,
What rounds, what bounds, what course, what stop
      he makes!'
And controversy hence a question takes,   110
Whether the horse by him became his deed,
Or he his manage by the well-doing steed.

" But quickly on this side the verdict went:
His real habitude gave life and grace
To appertainings and to ornament,
Accomplish'd in himself, not in his case:
All aids, themselves made fairer by their place,
Came for additions, yet their purpos'd trim
Piec'd not his grace, but were all grac'd by him.

" So on the tip of his subduing tongue   120
All kind of arguments and question deep,
All replication prompt, and reason strong,
For his advantage still did wake and sleep:
To make the weeper laugh, the laugher weep,
He had the dialect and different skill,
Catching all passions in his craft of will:

" That he did in the general bosom reign
Of young, of old, and sexes both enchanted,
To dwell with him in thoughts, or to remain
In personal duty, following where he haunted: 130
Consents bewitch'd, ere he desire, have granted,
And dialogu'd for him what he would say,
Ask'd their own wills, and made their wills obey.

" Many there were that did his picture get,
To serve their eyes, and in it put their mind;
Like fools that in the imagination set
The goodly objects which abroad they find
Of lands and mansions, theirs in thought assign'd;
And labouring in moe pleasures to bestow them,
Than the true gouty landlord which doth owe them.

" So many have, that never touch'd his hand,   141
Sweetly suppos'd them mistress of his heart.
My woful self, that did in freedom stand,
And was my own fee-simple (not in part),
What with his art in youth, and youth in art,
Threw my affections in his charmed power,
Reserv'd the stalk, and gave him all my flower.

" Yet did I not, as some my equals did,
Demand of him, nor, being desired, yielded;
Finding myself in honour so forbid,   150
With safest distance I mine honour shielded.
Experience for me many bulwarks builded
Of proofs new-bleeding, which remain'd the foil
Of this false jewel, and his amorous spoil.

" But, ah! who ever shunn'd by precedent
The destin'd ill she must herself assay?
Or forc'd examples, 'gainst her own content,
To put the by-pass'd perils in her way?
Counsel may stop awhile what will not stay;
For when we rage, advice is often seen   160
By blunting us to make our wits more keen.

" Nor gives it satisfaction to our blood,
That we must curb it upon others' proof;
To be forbod the sweets that seem so good,
For fear of harms that preach in our behoof.
O appetite, from judgment stand aloof!
The one a palate hath that needs will taste,
Though Reason weep, and cry, 'It is thy last.'

" For further I could say, 'This man's untrue,'
And knew the patterns of his foul beguiling;   170
Heard where his plants in others' orchards grew,
Saw how deceits were gilded in his smiling;
Knew vows were ever brokers to defiling;
Thought characters, and words, merely but art,
And bastards of his foul adulterate heart.

" And long upon these terms I held my city,
Till thus he 'gan besiege me: 'Gentle maid,
Have of my suffering youth some feeling pity,
And be not of my holy vows afraid:
That 's to ye sworn, to none was ever said;   180
For feasts of love I have been call'd unto,
Till now did ne'er invite, nor never woo.

" ' All my offences that abroad you see,
Are errors of the blood, none of the mind;
Love made them not: with acture they may be,
Where neither party is nor true nor kind:
They sought their shame that so their shame did find,
And so much less of shame in me remains,
By how much of me their reproach contains.

" ' Among the many that mine eyes have seen,   190
Not one whose flame my heart so much as warm'd,
Or my affection put to the smallest teen,
Or any of my leisures ever charm'd:
Harm have I done to them, but ne'er was harm'd;
Kept hearts in liveries, but mine own was free,
And reign'd, commanding in his monarchy.

" ' Look here, what tributes wounded fancies sent me,
Of paled pearls, and rubies red as blood;
Figuring that they their passions likewise lent me
Of grief and blushes, aptly understood   200
In bloodless white and the encrimson'd mood;
Effects of terror and dear modesty,
Encamp'd in hearts, but fighting outwardly.

" ' And, lo! behold these talents of their hair,
With twisted metal amorously impleach'd,
I have receiv'd from many a several fair
(Their kind acceptance weepingly beseech'd),
With the annexions of fair gems enrich'd,
And deep-brain'd sonnets, that did amplify
Each stone's dear nature, worth, and quality.   210

" ' The diamond, why, 't was beautiful and hard,
Whereto his invis'd properties did tend;
The deep-green emerald, in whose fresh regard
Weak sights their sickly radiance do amend;
The heaven-hued sapphire, and the opal blend
With objects manifold: each several stone,
With wit well blazon'd, smil'd, or made some moan.

" ' Lo! all these trophies of affections hot,
Of pensiv'd and subdued desires the tender,
Nature hath charg'd me that I hoard them not,   220
But yield them up where I myself must render;
That is, to you, my origin and ender:
For these, of force, must your oblations be,
Since I their altar, you enpatron me.

" ' O! then advance of yours that phraseless hand,
Whose white weighs down the airy scale of praise;
Take all these similes to your own command,
Hallow'd with sighs that burning lungs did raise;
What me, your minister, for you obeys,
Works under you; and to your audit comes   230
Their distract parcels in combined sums.

" ' Lo! this device was sent me from a nun,
Or sister sanctified, of holiest note;
Which late her noble suit in court did shun,
Whose rarest havings made the blossoms dote:
For she was sought by spirits of richest coat,
But kept cold distance, and did thence remove,
To spend her living in eternal love.

" ' But O, my sweet! what labour is 't to leave
The thing we have not, mastering what not strives?
Paling the place which did no form receive;   241
Playing patient sports in unconstrained gyves?
She that her fame so to herself contrives,
The scars of battle scapeth by the flight,
And makes her absence valiant, not her might.

"'O, pardon me, in that my boast is true!
The accident which brought me to her eye,
Upon the moment did her force subdue,
And now she would the caged cloister fly ;
Religious love put out religion's eye :   250
Not to be tempted, would she be immur'd,
And now, to tempt all, liberty procur'd.

"'How mighty then you are, O, hear me tell!
The broken bosoms that to me belong
Have emptied all their fountains in my well,
And mine I pour your ocean all among :
I strong o'er them, and you o'er me being strong,
Must for your victory us all congest,
As compound love to physic your cold breast.

"'My parts had power to charm a sacred nun,   260
Who, disciplin'd, ay, dieted in grace,
Believ'd her eyes, when they to assail begun,
All vows and consecrations giving place.
O most potential love! vow, bond, nor space,
In thee hath neither sting, knot, nor confine,
For thou art all, and all things else are thine.

"'When thou impressest, what are precepts worth
Of stale example? When thou wilt inflame,
How coldly those impediments stand forth
Of wealth, of filial fear, law, kindred, fame!   270
Love's arms are peace, 'gainst rule, 'gainst sense,
          'gainst shame ;
And sweetens, in the suffering pangs it bears,
The aloes of all forces, shocks, and fears.

"'Now, all these hearts that do on mine depend,
Feeling it break, with bleeding groans they pine,
And supplicant their sighs to you extend,
To leave the battery that you make 'gainst mine,
Lending soft audience to my sweet design,
And credent soul to that strong-bonded oath,
That shall prefer and undertake my troth.'   280

"This said, his watery eyes he did dismount,
Whose sights till then were levell'd on my face;
Each cheek a river running from a fount
With brinish current downward flow'd apace.
O, how the channel to the stream gave grace!
Who glaz'd with crystal gate the glowing roses
That flame through water which their hue encloses.

"O father, what a hell of witchcraft lies
In the small orb of one particular tear!
But with the inundation of the eyes   290
What rocky heart to water will not wear?
What breast so cold that is not warmed here?
O cleft effect! cold modesty, hot wrath,
Both fire from hence and chill extincture hath!

"For, lo! his passion, but an art of craft,
Even there resolv'd my reason into tears;
There my white stole of chastity I daff'd ;
Shook off my sober guards, and civil fears :
Appear to him, as he to me appears,
All melting ; though our drops this difference bore,
His poison'd me, and mine did him restore.   301

"In him a plenitude of subtle matter,
Applied to cautels, all strange forms receives,
Of burning blushes, or of weeping water,
Or swounding paleness ; and he takes and leaves,
In either's aptness, as it best deceives
To blush at speeches rank, to weep at woes,
Or to turn white, and swound at tragic shows :

"That not a heart which in his level came
Could scape the hail of his all-hurting aim,   310
Showing fair nature is both kind and tame ;
And, veil'd in them, did win whom he would maim :
Against the thing he sought he would exclaim ;
When he most burn'd in heart-wish'd luxury,
He preach'd pure maid, and prais'd cold chastity.

"Thus merely with the garment of a Grace
The naked and concealed fiend he cover'd ;
That the unexperient gave the tempter place,
Which, like a cherubin, above them hover'd.
Who, young and simple, would not be so lover'd ?   320
Ah me! I fell ; and yet do question make,
What I should do again for such a sake.

"O, that infected moisture of his eye!
O, that false fire, which in his cheek so glow'd!
O, that forc'd thunder from his heart did fly!
O, that sad breath his spungy lungs bestow'd!
O, all that borrow'd motion, seeming ow'd,
Would yet again betray the fore-betray'd,
And new pervert a reconciled maid!'"

THE PASSIONATE PILGRIM.

I.

WHEN my love swears that she is made of truth,
I do believe her, though I know she lies,
That she might think me some untutor'd youth,
Unskilful in the world's false forgeries.
Thus vainly thinking that she thinks me young,
Although I know my years be past the best,
I smiling credit her false-speaking tongue,
Outfacing faults in love with love's ill rest.
But wherefore says my love that she is young?
And wherefore say not I that I am old?   10
O! love's best habit is a soothing tongue,
And age, in love, loves not to have years to'd.
Therefore I'll lie with love, and love with me,
Since that our faults in love thus smother'd be.

II.

Two loves I have of comfort and despair,
Which like two spirits do suggest me still:
The better angel is a man, right fair,
The worser spirit a woman, colour'd ill.
To win me soon to hell, my female evil
Tempteth my better angel from my side,   20
And would corrupt a saint to be a devil,
Wooing his purity with her fair pride:
And whether that my angel be turn'd fiend,
Suspect I may, but not directly tell:
For being both to me, both to each friend,
I guess one angel in another's hell.
The truth I shall not know, but live in doubt,
Till my bad angel fire my good one out.

III.

Did not the heavenly rhetoric of thine eye,
'Gainst whom the world could not hold argument, 30
Persuade my heart to this false perjury?
Vows for thee broke deserve not punishment.
A woman I forswore; but I will prove,
Thou being a goddess, I forswore not thee:
My vow was earthly, thou a heavenly love;
Thy grace being gain'd cures all disgrace in me.
My vow was breath, and breath a vapour is:
Then thou, fair sun, that on this earth dost shine,
Exhale this vapour vow; in thee it is:
If broken, then it is no fault of mine.   40
If by me broke, what fool is not so wise
To break an oath, to win a paradise?

IV.

Sweet Cytherea, sitting by a brook,
With young Adonis, lovely, fresh, and green,
Did court the lad with many a lovely look,
Such looks as none could look but beauty's queen.
She told him stories to delight his ear;
She show'd him favours to allure his eye;
To win his heart, she touch'd him here and there:
Touches so soft still conquer chastity.   50

But whether unripe years did want conceit,
Or he refus'd to take her figur'd proffer,
The tender nibbler would not touch the bait
But smile and jest at every gentle offer:
Then fell she on her back, fair queen, and toward:
He rose and ran away; ah, fool too froward!

V.

If love make me forsworn, how shall I swear to love?
O! never faith could hold, if not to beauty vow'd:
Though to myself forsworn, to thee I'll constant prove;
Those thoughts, to me like oaks, to thee like osiers bow'd. 60
Study his bias leaves, and makes his book thine eyes,
Where all those pleasures live, that art can comprehend.
If knowledge be the mark, to know thee shall suffice;
Well learned is that tongue that well can thee commend;
All ignorant that soul that sees thee without wonder,
Which is to me some praise, that I thy parts admire:
Thine eye Jove's lightning seems, thy voice his dreadful thunder,
Which (not to anger bent) is music and sweet fire.
Celestial as thou art, O! do not love that wrong,
To sing heaven's praise with such an earthly tongue.

VI.

Scarce had the sun dried up the dewy morn,   71
And scarce the herd gone to the hedge for shade,
When Cytherea, all in love forlorn,
A longing tarriance for Adonis made,
Under an osier growing by a brook,
A brook, where Adon us'd to cool his spleen:
Hot was the day; she hotter that did look
For his approach, that often there had been.
Anon he comes, and throws his mantle by,
And stood stark naked on the brook's green brim: 80
The sun look'd on the world with glorious eye,
Yet not so wistly as this queen on him:
He, spying her, bounc'd in, whereas he stood:
"O Jove," quoth she, "why was not I a flood?"

VII.

Fair is my love, but not so fair as fickle;
Mild as a dove, but neither true nor trusty;
Brighter than glass, and yet, as glass is, brittle;
Softer than wax, and yet as iron rusty:
A lily pale, with damask dye to grace her,
None fairer, nor none falser to deface her.   90

Her lips to mine how often hath she join'd,
Between each kiss her oaths of true love swearing!
How many tales to please me hath she coin'd,
Dreading my love, the loss whereof still fearing!
Yet in the midst of all her pure protestings,
Her faith, her oaths, her tears, and all were jestings.

She burn'd with love, as straw with fire flameth;
She burn'd out love, as soon as straw out-burneth;
She fram'd the love, and yet she foil'd the framing;
She bade love last, and yet she fell a-turning. 100

Was this a lover, or a lecher whether?
Bad in the best, though excellent in neither.

VIII.

If music and sweet poetry agree,
As they must needs, the sister and the brother,
Then must the love be great 'twixt thee and me,
Because thou lov'st the one, and I the other.
Dowland to thee is dear, whose heavenly touch
Upon the lute doth ravish human sense;
Spenser to me, whose deep conceit is such,
As, passing all conceit, needs no defence. 110
Thou lov'st to hear the sweet melodious sound
That Phœbus' lute (the queen of music) makes;
And I in deep delight am chiefly drown'd
Whenas himself to singing he betakes.
  One god is god of both, as poets feign;
  One knight loves both, and both in thee remain.

IX.

Fair was the morn, when the fair queen of love,
  *   *   *   *   *   *   *   *   *
Paler for sorrow than her milk-white dove,
For Adon's sake, a youngster proud and wild;
Her stand she takes upon a steep-up hill: 120
Anon Adonis comes with horn and hounds;
She, silly queen, with more than love's good will,
Forbade the boy he should not pass those grounds.
"Once," quoth she, "did I see a fair sweet youth
Here in these brakes deep-wounded with a boar,
Deep in the thigh, a spectacle of ruth!
See, in my thigh," quoth she, "here was the sore."
She showed hers; he saw more wounds than one,
And blushing fled, and left her all alone.

X.

Sweet rose, fair flower, untimely pluck'd, soon vaded,
Pluck'd in the bud, and vaded in the spring! 131
Bright orient pearl, alack, too timely shaded!
Fair creature, kill'd too soon by death's sharp sting!
Like a green plum that hangs upon a tree,
And falls, through wind, before the fall should be.

I weep for thee, and yet no cause I have;
For why thou left'st me nothing in thy will:
And yet thou left'st me more than I did crave;
For why I craved nothing of thee still:
  O yes, dear friend, I pardon crave of thee; 140
  Thy discontent thou didst bequeath to me.

XI.

Venus, with young Adonis sitting by her,
Under a myrtle shade, began to woo him:
She told the youngling how god Mars did try her,
And as he fell to her, so she fell to him.
"Even thus," quoth she, "the warlike god embrac'd
  me;"
And then she clipp'd Adonis in her arms:
"Even thus," quoth she, "the warlike god unlac'd
  me,"
As if the boy should use like loving charms.
"Even thus," quoth she, "he seized of my lips," 150
And with her lips on his did act the seizure;
And as she fetched breath, away he skips,
And would not take her meaning, nor her pleasure.
  Ah! that I had my lady at this bay,
  To kiss and clip me till I ran away!

XII.

Crabbed age and youth cannot live together:
Youth is full of pleasance, age is full of care;
Youth like summer morn, age like winter weather;
Youth like summer brave, age like winter bare.
Youth is full of sport, age's breath is short; 160
  Youth is nimble, age is lame:
Youth is hot and bold, age is weak and cold;
  Youth is wild, and age is tame.

Age, I do abhor thee; youth, I do adore thee;
  O, my love, my love is young!
Age, I do defy thee; O, sweet shepherd! hie thee,
  For methinks thou stay'st too long.

XIII.

Beauty is but a vain and doubtful good;
A shining gloss that vadeth suddenly;
A flower that dies, when first it 'gins to bud; 170
A brittle glass, that's broken presently:
  A doubtful good, a gloss, a glass, a flower,
  Lost, vaded, broken, dead within an hour.

And as goods lost are seld or never found,
As vaded gloss no rubbing will refresh,
As flowers dead lie wither'd on the ground,
As broken glass no cement can redress,
  So beauty blemish'd once 's for ever lost,
  In spite of physic, painting, pain, and cost.

XIV.

Good night, good rest. Ah! neither be my share: 180
She bade good night, that kept my rest away;
And daff'd me to a cabin hang'd with care,
To descant on the doubts of my decay.
  "Farewell," quoth she, "and come again to-
    morrow:"
  Fare well I could not, for I supp'd with sorrow.

Yet at my parting sweetly did she smile,
In scorn or friendship, nill I construe whether:
'T may be, she joy'd to jest at my exile,
'T may be, again to make me wander thither:
  "Wander," a word for shadows like thyself, 190
  As take the pain, but cannot pluck the pelf.

XV.

Lord, how mine eyes throw gazes to the east!
My heart doth charge the watch; the morning rise
Doth cite each moving sense from idle rest.
Not daring trust the office of mine eyes,
  While Philomela sits and sings, I sit and mark,
  And wish her lays were tuned like the lark;

For she doth welcome daylight with her ditty,
And drives away dark dreaming night:
The night so pack'd, I post unto my pretty; 200
Heart hath his hope, and eyes their wished sight;
  Sorrow chang'd to solace, solace mix'd with sorrow:
  For why she sigh'd, and bade me come to-morrow.

Were I with her, the night would post too soon;
But now are minutes added to the hours;
To spite me now, each minute seems a moon;
Yet not for me, shine sun to succour flowers!
  Pack night, peep day; good day, of night now
    borrow:
  Short, night, to-night, and length thyself to-morrow.

XVI.

It was a lording's daughter, the fairest one of three, 210
That liked of her master as well as well might be,
Till looking on an Englishman, the fair'st that eye
    could see,
  Her fancy fell a-turning.

Long was the combat doubtful, that love with love
    did fight,
To leave the master loveless, or kill the gallant knight:
To put in practice either, alas! it was a spite
  Unto the silly damsel.

But one must be refused; more mickle was the pain,
That nothing could be used, to turn them both to gain;
For of the two the trusty knight was wounded with
    disdain: 220
  Alas, she could not help it.

Thus art with arms contending was victor of the day,
Which by a gift of learning did bear the maid away;
Then lullaby, the learned man hath got the lady gay;
For now my song is ended.

XVII.

On a day (alack the day!)
Love, whose month was ever May,
Spied a blossom passing fair,
Playing in the wanton air:
Through the velvet leaves the wind, 230
All unseen, 'gan passage find;
That the lover (sick to death)
Wish'd himself the heaven's breath.
"Air," quoth he, "thy cheeks may blow;
Air, would I might triumph so!
But, alas! my hand hath sworn
Ne'er to pluck thee from thy thorn:
Vow, alack! for youth unmeet.
Youth, so apt to pluck a sweet.
Thou for whom Jove would swear 240
Juno but an Ethiop were;
And deny himself for Jove,
Turning mortal for thy love."

XVIII.

My flocks feed not,
My ewes breed not,
My rams speed not,
All is amiss:
Love's denying,
Faith's defying,
Heart's renying, 250
Causer of this.
All my merry jigs are quite forgot,
All my lady's love is lost, God wot:
Where her faith was firmly fix'd in love,
There a nay is plac'd without remove.
One silly cross
Wrought all my loss:
O frowning Fortune, cursed, fickle dame!
For now I see
Inconstancy 260
More in women than in men remain.

In black mourn I,
All fears scorn I,
Love hath forlorn me,
Living in thrall:
Heart is bleeding,
All help needing,
O cruel speeding!
Fraughted with gall.
My shepherd's pipe can sound no deal, 270
My wether's bell rings doleful knell;
My curtail dog, that wont to have play'd,
Plays not at all, but seems afraid;
My sighs so deep
Procure to weep,
In howling wise, to see my doleful plight.
How sighs resound
Through heartless ground,
Like a thousand vanquish'd men in bloody fight!

Clear wells spring not, 280
Sweet birds sing not,
Green plants bring not
Forth their dye;
Herds stand weeping,
Flocks all sleeping,
Nymphs back peeping
Fearfully:
All our pleasure known to us poor swains,
All our merry meetings on the plains,
All our evening sport from us is fled, 290
All our love is lost, for Love is dead.
Farewell, sweet lass,
Thy like ne'er was
For a sweet content, the cause of all my moan:

Poor Corydon
Must live alone,
Other help for him I see that there is none.

XIX.

Whenas thine eye hath chose the dame,
And stall'd the deer that thou shouldst strike,
Let reason rule things worthy blame, 300
As well as fancy, partial wight:
Take counsel of some wiser head,
Neither too young, nor yet unwed.

And when thou com'st thy tale to tell,
Smooth not thy tongue with filed talk,
Lest she some subtle practice smell;
A cripple soon can find a halt:
But plainly say thou lov'st her well,
And set thy person forth to sell.

What though her frowning brows be bent, 310
Her cloudy looks will clear ere night;
And then too late she will repent
That thus dissembled her delight;
And twice desire, ere it be day,
That which with scorn she put away.

What though she strive to try her strength,
And ban and brawl, and say thee nay,
Her feeble force will yield at length,
When craft hath taught her thus to say,—
"Had women been so strong as men, 320
In faith, you had not had it then."

And to her will frame all thy ways:
Spare not to spend, and chiefly there
Where thy desert may merit praise,
By ringing in thy lady's ear:
The strongest castle, tower, and town,
The golden bullet beats it down.

Serve always with assured trust,
And in thy suit be humble true;
Unless thy lady prove unjust, 330
Seek never thou to choose anew.
When time shall serve, be thou not slack
To proffer, though she put thee back.

The wiles and guiles that women work,
Dissembled with an outward show,
The tricks and toys that in them lurk,
The cock that treads them shall not know.
Have you not heard it said full oft,
A woman's nay doth stand for nought?

Think, women love to match with men 340
And not to live so like a saint;
Here is no heaven; they holy then
Begin when age doth them attaint.
Were kisses all the joys in bed,
One woman would another wed.

But, soft! enough,—too much, I fear;
For if my mistress hear my song,
She will not stick to ring my ear,
To teach my tongue to be so long:
Yet will she blush, here be it said, 350
To hear her secrets so bewray'd.

XX.

Live with me, and be my love,
And we will all the pleasures prove,
That hills and valleys, dales and fields,
And all the craggy mountains yields.

There will we sit upon the rocks,
And see the shepherds feed their flocks,
By shallow rivers, to whose falls
Melodious birds sing madrigals.

There will I make thee a bed of roses,   360
With a thousand fragrant posies ;
A cap of flowers, and a kirtle
Embroider'd all with leaves of myrtle.

A belt of straw and ivy buds,
With coral clasps and amber studs ;
And if these pleasures may thee move,
Then live with me, and be my love.

LOVE'S ANSWER.

If that the world and love were young,
And truth in every shepherd's tongue,
These pretty pleasures might me move,   370
To live with thee and be thy love.

XXI.

As it fell upon a day
In the merry month of May,
Sitting in a pleasant shade,
Which a grove of myrtles made,
Beasts did leap, and birds did sing,
Trees did grow, and plants did spring ;
Everything did banish moan,
Save the nightingale alone ;
She, poor bird, as all forlorn,   380
Lean'd her breast up-till a thorn,
And there sung the dolefull'st ditty,
That to hear it was great pity.
" Fie, fie, fie !" now would she cry ;
" Tereu, Tereu !" by-and-by ;
That to hear her so complain,
Scarce I could from tears refrain ;
For her griefs, so lively shown,
Made me think upon mine own.
Ah ! thought I, thou mourn'st in vain,   390
None takes pity on thy pain :

Senseless trees they cannot hear thee,
Ruthless beasts they will not cheer thee.
King Pandion, he is dead,
All thy friends are lapp'd in lead,
All thy fellow-birds do sing,
Careless of thy sorrowing.

XXII.

Whilst as fickle Fortune smil'd,
Thou and I were both beguil'd :
Every one that flatters thee   400
Is no friend in misery.
Words are easy, like the wind ;
Faithful friends are hard to find :
Every man will be thy friend,
Whilst thou hast wherewith to spend ;
But if store of crowns be scant,
No man will supply thy want.
If that one be prodigal,
Bountiful they will him call,
And with such like flattering,   410
" Pity but he were a king."
If he be addict to vice,
Quickly him they will entice ;
If to women he be bent,
They have him at commandement :
But if Fortune once do frown,
Then, farewell his great renown ;
They that fawn'd on him before
Use his company no more.
He that is thy friend indeed,   420
He will help thee in thy need :
If thou sorrow, he will weep ;
If thou wake, he cannot sleep :
Thus of every grief in heart
He with thee does bear a part.
These are certain signs to know
Faithful friend from flattering foe.

THE PHŒNIX AND TURTLE.

ET the bird of loudest lay,
On the sole Arabian tree,
Herald sad and trumpet be,
To whose sound chaste wings obey.

But thou shrieking harbinger,
Foul precurrer of the fiend,
Augur of the fever's end,
To this troop come thou not near.

From this session interdict
Every fowl of tyrant wing,   10
Save the eagle, feather'd king:
Keep the obsequy so strict.

Let the priest in surplice white,
That defunctive music can,
Be the death-divining swan,
Lest the *requiem* lack his right.

And thou, treble-dated crow,
That thy sable gender mak'st
With the breath thou giv'st and tak'st,
'Mongst our mourners shalt thou go.   20

Here the anthem doth commence:
Love and constancy is dead;
Phœnix and the turtle fled
In a mutual flame from hence.

So they lov'd, as love in twain
Had the essence but in one;
Two distincts, division none:
Number there in love was slain.

Hearts remote, yet not asunder;
Distance, and no space was seen   30
'Twixt the turtle and his queen:
But in them it were a wonder.

So between them love did shine,
That the turtle saw his right
Flaming in the phœnix' sight:
Either was the other's mine.

Property was thus appall'd,
That the self was not the same
Single nature's double name
Neither two nor one was call'd.

Reason, in itself confounded,
Saw division grow together;
To themselves yet either neither,
Simple were so well compounded,

That it cried, how true a twain
Seemeth this concordant one!
Love hath reason, reason none,
If what parts can so remain.

Whereupon it made this threne
To the phœnix and the dove,   50
Co-supremes and stars of love,
As chorus to their tragic scene.

THRENOS.

Beauty, truth, and rarity,
Grace in all simplicity,
Here inclos'd in cinders lie.

Death is now the phœnix' nest;
And the turtle's loyal breast
To eternity doth rest,

Leaving no posterity:
'T was not their infirmity,   60
It was married chastity.

Truth may seem, but cannot be;
Beauty brag, but 't is not she;
Truth and beauty buried be.

To this urn let those repair
That are either true or fair;
For these dead birds sigh a prayer.

THE SONNETS

SONNETS.

I.

FROM fairest creatures we desire increase,
  That thereby beauty's rose might never
      die,
But as the riper should by time decease,
  His tender heir might bear his memory:
But thou, contracted to thine own bright
      eyes,
  Feed'st thy light's flame with self-sub-
      stantial fuel,
Making a famine where abundance lies,
  Thyself thy foe, to thy sweet self too cruel.
Thou that art now the world's fresh
      ornament,
And only herald to the gaudy spring,
Within thine own bud buriest thy content,
And, tender churl, mak'st waste in niggarding.
  Pity the world, or else this glutton be,
  To eat the world's due, by the grave and thee.

II.

When forty winters shall besiege thy brow,
And dig deep trenches in thy beauty's field,
Thy youth's proud livery, so gaz'd on now,
Will be a tatter'd weed, of small worth held:
Then being ask'd where all thy beauty lies,
Where all the treasure of thy lusty days,
To say, within thine own deep-sunken eyes,
Were an all-eating shame, and thriftless praise.
How much more praise deserv'd thy beauty's use,
If thou couldst answer,—"This fair child of mine
Shall sum my count, and make my old excuse,"—
Proving his beauty by succession thine!
  This were to be new-made, when thou art old,
  And see thy blood warm, when thou feel'st it cold.

III.

Look in thy glass, and tell the face thou viewest,
Now is the time that face should form another;
Whose fresh repair if now thou not renewest,
Thou dost beguile the world, unbless some mother.
For where is she so fair, whose unear'd womb
Disdains the tillage of thy husbandry?
Or who is he so fond, will be the tomb
Of his self-love, to stop posterity?
Thou art thy mother's glass, and she in thee
Calls back the lovely April of her prime:
So thou through windows of thine age shalt see,
Despite of wrinkles, this thy golden time.
  But if thou live, remember'd not to be,
  Die single, and thine image dies with thee.

IV.

Unthrifty loveliness, why dost thou spend
Upon thyself thy beauty's legacy?
Nature's bequest gives nothing, but doth lend;
And, being frank, she lends to those are free.
Then, beauteous niggard, why dost thou abuse
The bounteous largess given thee to give?
Profitless usurer, why dost thou use
So great a sum of sums, yet canst not live?
For, having traffic with thyself alone,
Thou of thyself thy sweet self dost deceive.

Then how, when nature calls thee to be gone,
What acceptable audit canst thou leave?
  Thy unus'd beauty must be tomb'd with thee,
  Which, used, lives th'executor to be.

V.

Those hours, that with gentle work did frame
The lovely gaze where every eye doth dwell,
Will play the tyrants to the very same,
And that unfair which fairly doth excel:
For never-resting time leads summer on
To hideous winter, and confounds him there;
Sap check'd with frost, and lusty leaves quite gone,
Beauty o'ersnow'd, and bareness everywhere:
Then, were not summer's distillation left,
A liquid prisoner pent in walls of glass,
Beauty's effect with beauty were bereft,
Nor it, nor no remembrance what it was:
  But flowers distill'd, though they with winter meet,
  Leese but their show; their substance still lives
      sweet.

VI.

Then let not winter's ragged hand deface
In thee thy summer, ere thou be distill'd:
Make sweet some vial; treasure thou some place
With beauty's treasure, ere it be self-kill'd.
That use is not forbidden usury,
Which happies those that pay the willing loan;
That's for thyself to breed another thee,
Or ten times happier, be it ten for one:
Ten times thyself were happier than thou art,
If ten of thine ten times refigur'd thee.
Then what could death do if thou shouldst depart,
Leaving thee living in posterity?
  Be not self-will'd, for thou art much too fair
  To be Death's conquest, and make worms thine heir.

VII.

Lo! in the orient when the gracious light
Lifts up his burning head, each under eye
Doth homage to his new-appearing sight,
Serving with looks his sacred majesty;
And having climb'd the steep-up heavenly hill,
Resembling strong youth in his middle age,
Yet mortal looks adore his beauty still,
Attending on his golden pilgrimage:
But when from high-most pitch with weary car,
Like feeble age, he reeleth from the day,
The eyes, 'fore duteous, now converted are
From his low tract, and look another way.
  So thou, thyself outgoing in thy noon,
  Unlook'd on diest, unless thou get a son.

VIII.

Music to hear, why hear'st thou music sadly?
Sweets with sweets war not, joy delights in joy.
Why lov'st thou that which thou receiv'st not gladly,
Or else receiv'st with pleasure thine annoy?
If the true concord of well-tuned sounds,
By unions married, do offend thine ear,
They do but sweetly chide thee, who confounds
In singleness the parts that thou shouldst bear.

Mark, how one string, sweet husband to another,
Strikes each in each, by mutual ordering;
Resembling sire and child and happy mother,
Who, all in one, one pleasing note do sing:
  Whose speechless song, being many, seeming one,
  Sings this to thee,—"Thou single wilt prove none."

IX.

Is it for fear to wet a widow's eye,
That thou consum'st thyself in single life?
Ah! if thou issueless shalt hap to die,
The world will wail thee, like a makeless wife;
The world will be thy widow, and still weep,
That thou no form of thee hast left behind,
When every private widow well may keep,
By children's eyes, her husband's shape in mind.
Look, what an unthrift in the world doth spend,
Shifts but his place, for still the world enjoys it;
But beauty's waste hath in the world an end,
And, kept unus'd, the user so destroys it.
  No love toward others in that bosom sits,
  That on himself such murderous shame commits.

X.

For shame! deny that thou bear'st love to any,
Who for thyself art so unprovident.
Grant, if thou wilt, thou art belov'd of many,
But that thou none lov'st is most evident;
For thou art so possess'd with murderous hate,
That 'gainst thyself thou stick'st not to conspire,
Seeking that beauteous roof to ruinate,
Which to repair should be thy chief desire.
O, change thy thought, that I may change my mind!
Shall hate be fairer lodg'd than gentle love?
Be, as thy presence is, gracious and kind,
Or to thyself, at least, kind-hearted prove:
  Make thee another self, for love of me,
  That beauty still may live in thine or thee.

XI.

As fast as thou shalt wane, so fast thou grow'st
In one of thine, from that which thou departest;
And that fresh blood which youngly thou bestow'st,
Thou may'st call thine, when thou from youth convertest.
Herein lives wisdom, beauty, and increase;
Without this, folly, age, and cold decay:
If all were minded so, the times should cease,
And threescore year would make the world away.
Let those whom Nature hath not made for store,
Harsh, featureless, and rude, barrenly perish:
Look, whom she best endow'd, she gave thee more;
Which bounteous gift thou shouldst in bounty cherish.
  She carv'd thee for her seal, and meant thereby,
  Thou shouldst print more, not let that copy die.

XII.

When I do count the clock that tells the time,
And see the brave day sunk in hideous night;
When I behold the violet past prime,
And sable curls all silver'd o'er with white;
When lofty trees I see barren of leaves,
Which erst from heat did canopy the herd,
And summer's green all girded up in sheaves,
Borne on the bier with white and bristly beard;
Then of thy beauty do I question make,
That thou among the wastes of time must go,
Since sweets and beauties do themselves forsake,
And die as fast as they see others grow;
  And nothing 'gainst Time's scythe can make defence,
  Save breed, to brave him, when he takes thee hence.

XIII.

O, that you were yourself! but, love, you are
No longer yours, than you yourself here live:
Against this coming end you should prepare,
And your sweet semblance to some other give:
So should that beauty which you hold in lease
Find no determination; then you were
Yourself again, after yourself's decease,
When your sweet issue your sweet form should bear.

Who lets so fair a house fall to decay,
Which husbandry in honour might uphold
Against the stormy gusts of winter's day,
And barren rage of death's eternal cold?
  O! none but unthrifts. Dear my love, you know,
  You had a father: let your son say so.

XIV.

Not from the stars do I my judgment pluck,
And yet, methinks, I have astronomy,
But not to tell of good or evil luck,
Of plagues, of dearths, or seasons' quality;
Nor can I fortune to brief minutes tell,
Pointing to each his thunder, rain, and wind;
Or say with princes if it shall go well,
By oft predict that I in heaven find:
But from thine eyes my knowledge I derive,
And, constant stars, in them I read such art,
As truth and beauty shall together thrive,
If from thyself to store thou wouldst convert;
  Or else of thee this I prognosticate,
  Thy end is truth's and beauty's doom and date.

XV.

When I consider every thing that grows
Holds in perfection but a little moment;
That this huge stage presenteth nought but shows,
Whereon the stars in secret influence comment;
When I perceive that men as plants increase,
Cheered and check'd even by the selfsame sky,
Vaunt in their youthful sap, at height decrease,
And wear their brave state out of memory;
Then the conceit of this inconstant stay
Sets you most rich in youth before my sight,
Where wasteful Time debateth with Decay,
To change your day of youth to sullied night;
  And, all in war with Time, for love of you,
  As he takes from you, I engraft you new.

XVI.

But wherefore do not you a mightier way
Make war upon this bloody tyrant, Time,
And fortify yourself in your decay
With means more blessed than my barren rhyme?
Now stand you on the top of happy hours,
And many maiden gardens, yet unset,
With virtuous wish would bear your living flowers,
Much liker than your painted counterfeit:
So should the lines of life that life repair,
Which this, Time's pencil, or my pupil pen,
Neither in inward worth, nor outward fair,
Can make you live yourself in eyes of men.
  To give away yourself keeps yourself still,
  And you must live, drawn by your own sweet skill.

XVII.

Who will believe my verse in time to come,
If it were fill'd with your most high deserts?
Though yet, Heaven knows, it is but as a tomb
Which hides your life, and shows not half your parts.
If I could write the beauty of your eyes,
And in fresh numbers number all your graces,
The age to come would say, "This poet lies;
Such heavenly touches ne'er touch'd earthly faces."
So should my papers, yellow'd with their age,
Be scorn'd, like old men of less truth than tongue,
And your true rights be term'd a poet's rage,
And stretched metre of an antique song:
  But were some child of yours alive that time,
  You should live twice,—in it, and in my rhyme.

XVIII.

Shall I compare thee to a summer's day?
Thou art more lovely and more temperate:
Rough winds do shake the darling buds of May,
And summer's lease hath all too short a date.
Sometime too hot the eye of heaven shines,
And often is his gold complexion dimm'd;
And every fair from fair sometime declines,
By chance, or nature's changing course, untrimm'd;

But thy eternal summer shall not fade,
Nor lose possession of that fair thou owest;
Nor shall Death brag thou wander'st in his shade,
When in eternal lines to time thou growest.
　So long as men can breathe, or eyes can see,
　So long lives this, and this gives life to thee.

XIX.

Devouring Time, blunt thou the lion's paws,
And make the earth devour her own sweet brood;
Pluck the keen teeth from the fierce tiger's jaws,
And burn the long-liv'd phœnix in her blood;
Make glad and sorry seasons as thou fleets,
And do whate'er thou wilt, swift-footed Time,
To the wide world, and all her fading sweets;
But I forbid thee one most heinous crime:
O! carve not with thy hours my love's fair brow,
Nor draw no lines there with thine antique pen;
Him in thy course untainted do allow,
For beauty's pattern to succeeding men.
　Yet, do thy worst, old Time: despite thy wrong,
　My love shall in my verse ever live young.

XX.

A woman's face, with Nature's own hand painted,
Hast thou, the master-mistress of my passion;
A woman's gentle heart, but not acquainted
With shifting change, as is false women's fashion;
An eye more bright than theirs, less false in rolling,
Gilding the object whereupon it gazeth;
A man in hue, all hues in his controlling,
Which steals men's eyes, and women's souls amazeth;
And for a woman wert thou first created;
Till Nature, as she wrought thee, fell a-doting,
And by addition me of thee defeated,
By adding one thing to my purpose nothing.
　But since she prick'd thee out for women's pleasure,
　Mine be thy love, and thy love's use their treasure.

XXI.

So is it not with me, as with that Muse,
Stirr'd by a painted beauty to his verse,
Who heaven itself for ornament doth use,
And every fair with his fair doth rehearse;
Making a couplement of proud compare,
With sun and moon, with earth and sea's rich gems,
With April's first-born flowers, and all things rare
That heaven's air in this huge rondure hems.
O! let me, true in love, but truly write,
And then believe me, my love is as fair
As any mother's child, though not so bright
As those gold candles fix'd in heaven's air:
　Let them say more that like of hearsay well;
　I will not praise, that purpose not to sell.

XXII.

My glass shall not persuade me I am old,
So long as youth and thou are of one date;
But when in thee time's furrows I behold,
Then look I death my days should expiate.
For all that beauty that doth cover thee
Is but the seemly raiment of my heart,
Which in thy breast doth live, as thine in me:
How can I then be elder than thou art?
O! therefore, love, be of thyself so wary,
As I, not for myself, but for thee will,
Bearing thy heart, which I will keep so chary
As tender nurse her babe from faring ill.
　Presume not on thy heart, when mine is slain;
　Thou gav'st me thine, not to give back again.

XXIII.

As an unperfect actor on the stage,
Who with his fear is put besides his part,
Or some fierce thing replete with too much rage,
Whose strength's abundance weakens his own heart;
So I, for fear of trust, forget to say
The perfect ceremony of love's rite,
And in mine own love's strength seem to decay,
O'ercharg'd with burden of mine own love's might.

O! let my books be then the eloquence
And dumb presagers of my speaking breast,
Who plead for love, and look for recompense,
More than that tongue that more hath more express'd.
　O! learn to read what silent love hath writ:
　To hear with eyes belongs to love's fine wit.

XXIV.

Mine eye hath play'd the painter, and hath stell'd
Thy beauty's form in table of my heart:
My body is the frame wherein 't is held,
And perspective it is best painter's art:
For through the painter must you see his skill,
To find where your true image pictur'd lies,
Which in my bosom's shop is hanging still,
That hath his windows glazed with thine eyes.
Now see what good turns eyes for eyes have done:
Mine eyes have drawn thy shape, and thine for me
Are windows to my breast, where-through the sun
Delights to peep, to gaze therein on thee;
　Yet eyes this cunning want to grace their art,
　They draw but what they see, know not the heart.

XXV.

Let those who are in favour with their stars
Of public honour and proud titles boast,
Whilst I, whom fortune of such triumph bars,
Unlook'd for joy in that I honour most.
Great princes' favourites their fair leaves spread
But as the marigold at the sun's eyes;
And in themselves their pride lies buried,
For at a frown they in their glory die.
The painful warrior, famoused for fight,
After a thousand victories once foil'd,
Is from the book of honour razed quite,
And all the rest forgot for which he toil'd:
　Then happy I, that love and am belov'd,
　Where I may not remove, nor be remov'd.

XXVI.

Lord of my love, to whom in vassalage
Thy merit hath my duty strongly knit,
To thee I send this written embassage,
To witness duty, not to show my wit:
Duty so great, which wit so poor as mine
May make seem bare, in wanting words to show it,
But that I hope some good conceit of thine
In thy soul's thought, all naked, will bestow it;
Till whatsoever star that guides my moving
Points on me graciously with fair aspect,
And puts apparel on my tatter'd loving,
To show me worthy of thy sweet respect:
　Then may I dare to boast how I do love thee;
　Till then, not show my head where thou may'st
　　　prove me.

XXVII.

Weary with toil I haste me to my bed,
The dear repose for limbs with travel tired;
But then begins a journey in my head,
To work my mind, when body's work 's expired:
For then my thoughts (from far where I abide)
Intend a zealous pilgrimage to thee,
And keep my drooping eyelids open wide,
Looking on darkness which the blind do see:
Save that my soul's imaginary sight
Presents thy shadow to my sightless view,
Which, like a jewel hung in ghastly night,
Makes black night beauteous, and her old face new.
　Lo! thus by day my limbs, by night my mind,
　For thee, and for myself, no quiet find.

XXVIII.

How can I then return in happy plight,
That am debarr'd the benefit of rest?
When day's oppression is not eas'd by night,
But day by night, and night by day, oppress'd?
And each, though enemies to either's reign,
Do in consent shake hands to torture me;
The one by toil, the other to complain
How far I toil, still farther off from thee.

I tell the day, to please him thou art bright,
And dost him grace when clouds do blot the heaven:
So flatter I the swart-complexion'd night,
When sparkling stars twire not, thou gild'st the even.
  But day doth daily draw my sorrows longer,
  And night doth nightly make grief's strength seem
     stronger.

XXIX.

When, in disgrace with fortune and men's eyes,
I all alone beweep my outcast state,
And trouble deaf heaven with my bootless cries,
And look upon myself, and curse my fate,
Wishing me like to one more rich in hope,
Featur'd like him, like him with friends possess'd,
Desiring this man's art, and that man's scope,
With what I most enjoy contented least;
Yet in these thoughts myself almost despising,
Haply I think on thee, and then my state
(Like to the lark at break of day arising
From sullen earth) sings hymns at heaven's gate;
  For thy sweet love remember'd such wealth brings,
  That then I scorn to change my state with kings.

XXX.

When to the sessions of sweet silent thought
I summon up remembrance of things past,
I sigh the lack of many a thing I sought,
And with old woes new wail my dear time's waste:
Then can I drown an eye, unus'd to flow,
For precious friends hid in death's dateless night,
And weep afresh love's long-since cancell'd woe,
And moan the expense of many a vanish'd sight.
Then can I grieve at grievances foregone,
And heavily from woe to woe tell o'er
The sad account of fore-bemoaned moan,
Which I new pay, as if not paid before:
  But if the while I think on thee, dear friend,
  All losses are restor'd, and sorrows end.

XXXI.

Thy bosom is endeared with all hearts,
Which I by lacking have supposed dead,
And there reigns love, and all love's loving parts,
And all those friends which I thought buried.
How many a holy and obsequious tear
Hath dear religious love stol'n from mine eye,
As interest of the dead, which now appear
But things remov'd, that hidden in thee lie!
Thou art the grave where buried love doth live,
Hung with the trophies of my lovers gone,
Who all their parts of me to thee did give;
That due of many now is thine alone:
  Their images I lov'd I view in thee,
  And thou (all they) hast all the all of me.

XXXII.

If thou survive my well-contented day,
When that churl Death my bones with dust shall
    cover,
And shalt by fortune once more re-survey
These poor rude lines of thy deceased lover,
Compare them with the bettering of the time,
And though they be outstripp'd by every pen,
Reserve them for my love, not for their rhyme,
Exceeded by the height of happier men.
O! then vouchsafe me but this loving thought:
" Had my friend's Muse grown with this growing age,
A dearer birth than this his love had brought,
To march in ranks of better equipage:
  But since he died, and poets better prove,
  Theirs for their style I 'll read, his for his love.'

XXXIII.

Full many a glorious morning have I seen
Flatter the mountain-tops with sovereign eye,
Kissing with golden face the meadows green,
Gilding pale streams with heavenly alchymy;
Anon permit the basest clouds to ride
With ugly rack on his celestial face,
And from the forlorn world his visage hide,
Stealing unseen to west with this disgrace.
Even so my sun one early morn did shine,
With all-triumphant splendour on my brow;
But out, alack! he was but one hour mine,
The region cloud hath mask'd him from me now.
  Yet him for this my love no whit disdaineth;
  Suns of the world may stain, when heaven's sun
    staineth.

XXXIV.

Why didst thou promise such a beauteous day,
And make me travel forth without my cloak,
To let base clouds o'ertake me in my way,
Hiding thy bravery in their rotten smoke?
'T is not enough that through the cloud thou break,
To dry the rain on my storm-beaten face,
For no man well of such a salve can speak,
That heals the wound, and cures not the disgrace:
Nor can thy shame give physic to my grief;
Though thou repent, yet I have still the loss:
The offender's sorrow lends but weak relief
To him that bears the strong offence's cross.
  Ah! but those tears are pearl, which thy love sheds,
  And they are rich and ransom all ill deeds.

XXXV.

No more be griev'd at that which thou hast done;
Roses have thorns, and silver fountains mud;
Clouds and eclipses stain both moon and sun,
And loathsome canker lives in sweetest bud.
All men make faults, and even I in this,
Authorising thy trespass with compare;
Myself corrupting, salving thy amiss,
Excusing thy sins more than thy sins are:
For to thy sensual fault I bring in sense,—
Thy adverse party is thy advocate,—
And 'gainst myself a lawful plea commence.
Such civil war is in my love and hate,
  That I an accessary needs must be
  To that sweet thief which sourly robs from me.

XXXVI.

Let me confess that we two must be twain,
Although our undivided loves are one:
So shall these blots that do with me remain,
Without thy help by me be borne alone.
In our two loves there is but one respect,
Though in our lives a separable spite,
Which though it alter not love's sole effect,
Yet doth it steal sweet hours from love's delight.
I may not evermore acknowledge thee,
Lest my bewailed guilt should do thee shame;
Nor thou with public kindness honour me,
Unless thou take that honour from thy name:
  But do not so; I love thee in such sort,
  As, thou being mine, mine is thy good report.

XXXVII.

As a decrepit father takes delight
To see his active child do deeds of youth,
So I, made lame by fortune's dearest spite,
Take all my comfort of thy worth and truth;
For whether beauty, birth, or wealth, or wit,
Or any of these all, or all, or more,
Entitled in thy parts do crowned sit,
I make my love engrafted to this store:
So then I am not lame, poor, nor despis'd,
Whilst that this shadow doth such substance give,
That I in thy abundance am suffic'd,
And by a part of all thy glory live.
  Look, what is best, that best I wish in thee:
  This wish I have; then ten times happy me!

XXXVIII.

How can my Muse want subject to invent,
While thou dost breathe, that pour'st into my verse
Thine own sweet argument, too excellent
For every vulgar paper to rehearse?
O! give thyself the thanks, if aught in me
Worthy perusal stand against thy sight;

For who's so dumb that cannot write to thee,
When thou thyself dost give invention light?
Be thou the tenth Muse, ten times more in worth
Than those old nine which rhymers invocate;
And he that calls on thee, let him bring forth
Eternal numbers to outlive long date.
   If my slight Muse do please these curious days,
   The pain be mine, but thine shall be the praise.

XXXIX.

O! how thy worth with manners may I sing,
When thou art all the better part of me?
What can mine own praise to mine own self bring?
And what is 't but mine own, when I praise thee?
Even for this let us divided live,
And our dear love lose name of single one,
That by this separation I may give
That due to thee which thou deserv'st alone.
O absence, what a torment wouldst thou prove,
Were it not thy sour leisure gave sweet leave
To entertain the time with thoughts of love,
Which time and thoughts so sweetly doth deceive,
   And that thou teachest how to make one twain,
   By praising him here, who doth hence remain!

XL.

Take all my loves, my love, yea, take them all:
What hast thou then more than thou hadst before?
No love, my love, that thou may'st true love call:
All mine was thine before thou hadst this more.
Then, if for my love thou my love receivest,
I cannot blame thee for my love thou usest;
But yet be blam'd, if thou thyself deceivest
By wilful taste of what thyself refusest.
I do forgive thy robbery, gentle thief,
Although thou steal thee all my poverty;
And yet love knows, it is a greater grief
To bear love's wrong, than hate's known injury.
   Lascivious grace, in whom all ill well shows,
   Kill me with spites; yet we must not be foes.

XLI.

Those petty wrongs that liberty commits,
When I am sometime absent from thy heart,
Thy beauty and thy years full well befits,
For still temptation follows where thou art.
Gentle thou art, and therefore to be won,
Beauteous thou art, therefore to be assail'd;
And when a woman woos, what woman's son
Will sourly leave her till she have prevail'd?
Ah me! but yet thou mightst my seat forbear,
And chide thy beauty and thy straying youth,
Who lead thee in their riot even there
Where thou art forc'd to break a two-fold truth:
   Hers, by thy beauty tempting her to thee,
   Thine, by thy beauty being false to me.

XLII.

That thou hast her, it is not all my grief,
And yet it may be said, I lov'd her dearly;
That she hath thee, is of my wailing chief,
A loss in love that touches me more nearly.
Loving offenders, thus I will excuse ye:—
Thou dost love her, because thou know'st I love her;
And for my sake even so doth she abuse me,
Suffering my friend for my sake to approve her.
If I lose thee, my loss is my love's gain,
And losing her, my friend hath found that loss;
Both find each other, and I lose both twain,
And both for my sake lay on me this cross:
   But here 's the joy; my friend and I are one;
   Sweet flattery! then she loves but me alone.

XLIII.

When most I wink, then do mine eyes best see,
For all the day they view things unrespected;
But when I sleep, in dreams they look on thee,
And darkly bright are bright in dark directed.
Then thou, whose shadow shadows doth make bright,
How would thy shadow's form form happy show
To the clear day with thy much clearer light,
When to unseeing eyes thy shade shines so?
How would, I say, mine eyes be blessed made
By looking on thee in the living day,
When in dead night thy fair imperfect shade
Through heavy sleep on sightless eyes doth stay?
   All days are nights to see, till I see thee,
   And nights bright days, when dreams do show thee me.

XLIV.

If the dull substance of my flesh were thought,
Injurious distance should not stop my way;
For then, despite of space, I would be brought,
From limits far remote, where thou dost stay.
No matter then, although my foot did stand
Upon the farthest earth remov'd from thee:
For nimble thought can jump both sea and land,
As soon as think the place where he would be.
But, ah! thought kills me, that I am not thought,
To leap large lengths of miles when thou art gone,
But that, so much of earth and water wrought,
I must attend time's leisure with my moan:
   Receiving nought by elements so slow
   But heavy tears, badges of either's woe.

XLV.

The other two, slight air and purging fire,
Are both with thee, wherever I abide;
The first my thought, the other my desire,
These present-absent with swift motion slide:
For when these quicker elements are gone
In tender embassy of love to thee,
My life, being made of four, with two alone
Sinks down to death, oppress'd with melancholy;
Until life's composition be recur'd
By those swift messengers return'd from thee,
Who even but now come back again, assur'd
Of thy fair health, recounting it to me:
   This told, I joy; but then, no longer glad,
   I send them back again, and straight grow sad.

XLVI.

Mine eye and heart are at a mortal war,
How to divide the conquest of thy sight;
Mine eye my heart thy picture's sight would bar,
My heart mine eye the freedom of that right.
My heart doth plead that thou in him dost lie,
(A closet never pierc'd with crystal eyes,)
But the defendant doth that plea deny,
And says in him thy fair appearance lies.
To 'cide this title is impannelled
A quest of thoughts, all tenants to the heart;
And by their verdict is determined
The clear eye's moiety, and the dear heart's part:
   As thus; mine eye's due is thine outward part,
   And my heart's right thine inward love of heart.

XLVII.

Betwixt mine eye and heart a league is took,
And each doth good turns now unto the other.
When that mine eye is famish'd for a look,
Or heart in love with sighs himself doth smother,
With my love's picture then my eye doth feast,
And to the painted banquet bids my heart;
Another time mine eye is my heart's guest,
And in his thoughts of love doth share a part:
So, either by thy picture or my love,
Thyself away art present still with me;
For thou not farther than my thoughts canst move,
And I am still with them, and they with thee;
   Or, if they sleep, thy picture in my sight
   Awakes my heart to heart's and eye's delight.

XLVIII.

How careful was I, when I took my way,
Each trifle under truest bars to thrust;
That to my use it might unused stay
From hands of falsehood, in sure wards of trust
But thou, to whom my jewels trifles are,
Most worthy comfort, now my greatest grief,

Thou, best of dearest, and mine only care,
Art left the prey of every vulgar thief.
Thee have I not lock'd up in any chest,
Save where thou art not, though I feel thou art,
Within the gentle closure of my breast,
From whence at pleasure thou may'st come and part;
  And even thence thou wilt be stol'n, I fear,
  For truth proves thievish for a prize so dear.

XLIX.

Against that time, if ever that time come,
When I shall see thee frown on my defects,
Whenas thy love hath cast his utmost sum,
Call'd to that audit by advis'd respects;
Against that time, when thou shalt strangely pass,
And scarcely greet me with that sun, thine eye;
When love, converted from the thing it was,
Shall reasons find of settled gravity;
Against that time do I ensconce me here
Within the knowledge of mine own desert,
And this my hand against myself uprear,
To guard the lawful reasons on thy part:
  To leave poor me thou hast the strength of laws,
  Since why to love I can allege no cause.

L.

How heavy do I journey on the way,
When what I seek (my weary travel's end)
Doth teach that ease and that repose to say,
" Thus far the miles are measur'd from thy friend!"
The beast that bears me, tired with my woe,
Plods dully on, to bear that weight in me,
As if by some instinct the wretch did know,
His rider lov'd not speed, being made from thee.
The bloody spur cannot provoke him on
That sometimes anger thrusts into his hide,
Which heavily he answers with a groan,
More sharp to me than spurring to his side;
  For that same groan doth put this in my mind,
  My grief lies onward, and my joy behind.

LI.

Thus can my love excuse the slow offence
Of my dull bearer, when from thee I speed:
From where thou art why should I haste me thence?
Till I return, of posting is no need.
O! what excuse will my poor beast then find,
When swift extremity can seem but slow?
Then should I spur, though motion on the wind;
In winged speed no motion shall I know:
Then can no horse with my desire keep pace;
Therefore desire (of perfect'st love being made)
Shall neigh (no dull flesh) in his fiery race;
But love, for love, thus shall excuse my jade;
  Since from thee going he went wilful-slow,
  Towards thee I 'll run, and give him leave to go.

LII.

So am I as the rich, whose blessed key
Can bring him to his sweet up-locked treasure,
The which he will not every hour survey,
For blunting the fine point of seldom pleasure.
Therefore are feasts so solemn and so rare,
Since seldom coming, in the long year set
Like stones of worth, they thinly placed are,
Or captain jewels in the carcanet.
So is the time that keeps you as my chest,
Or as the wardrobe which the robe doth hide,
To make some special instant special-blest,
By new unfolding his imprison'd pride.
  Blessed are you, whose worthiness gives scope,
  Being had, to triumph, being lack'd, to hope.

LIII.

What is your substance, whereof are you made,
That millions of strange shadows on you tend?
Since every one hath, every one, one shade,
And you, but one, can every shadow lend.
Describe Adonis, and the counterfeit
Is poorly imitated after you;

On Helen's cheek all art of beauty set,
And you in Grecian tires are painted new:
Speak of the spring, and foison of the year,
The one doth shadow of your beauty show,
The other as your bounty doth appear;
And you in every blessed shape we know.
  In all external grace you have some part,
  But you like none, none you, for constant heart.

LIV.

O, how much more doth beauty beauteous seem
By that sweet ornament which truth doth give!
The rose looks fair, but fairer we it deem
For that sweet odour which doth in it live.
The canker-blooms have full as deep a dye
As the perfumed tincture of the roses;
Hang on such thorns, and play as wantonly
When summer's breath their masked buds discloses
But, for their virtue only is their show,
They live unwoo'd, and unrespected fade;
Die to themselves. Sweet roses do not so;
Of their sweet deaths are sweetest odours made,
  And so of you, beauteous and lovely youth,
  When that shall vade, by verse distils your truth.

LV.

Not marble, nor the gilded monuments
Of princes, shall outlive this powerful rhyme;
But you shall shine more bright in these contents
Than unswept stone, besmear'd with sluttish time.
When wasteful war shall statues overturn,
And broils root out the work of masonry,
Nor Mars his sword, nor war's quick fire shall burn
The living record of your memory.
'Gainst death and all-oblivious enmity
Shall you pace forth: your praise shall still find room
Even in the eyes of all posterity,
That wear this world out to the ending doom.
  So, till the judgment that yourself arise,
  You live in this, and dwell in lovers' eyes.

LVI.

Sweet love, renew thy force: be it not said,
Thy edge should blunter be than appetite,
Which but to-day by feeding is allay'd,
To-morrow sharpen'd in his former might:
So, love, be thou; although to-day thou fill
Thy hungry eyes, even till they wink with fulness,
To-morrow see again, and do not kill
The spirit of love with a perpetual dulness.
Let this sad interim like the ocean be
Which parts the shore, where two contracted-new
Come daily to the banks, that, when they see
Return of love, more blest may be the view;
  Or call it winter, which, being full of care,
  Makes summer's welcome thrice more wish'd, more
     rare.

LVII.

Being your slave, what should I do but tend
Upon the hours and times of your desire?
I have no precious time at all to spend,
Nor services to do, till you require.
Nor dare I chide the world-without-end hour,
Whilst I, my sovereign, watch the clock for you,
Nor think the bitterness of absence sour,
When you have bid your servant once adieu;
Nor dare I question with my jealous thought,
Where you may be, or your affairs suppose;
But, like a sad slave, stay and think of nought,
Save, where you are how happy you make those.
  So true a fool is love, that in your will
  (Though you do anything) he thinks no ill.

LVIII.

That God forbid, that made me first your slave,
I should in thought control your times of pleasure,
Or at your hand the account of hours to crave,
Being your vassal, bound to stay your leisure!
O! let me suffer (being at your beck)
The imprison'd absence of your liberty;

And patience, tame to sufferance, bide each check,
Without accusing you of injury.
Be where you list; your charter is so strong,
That you yourself may privilege your time
To what you will; to you it doth belong
Yourself to pardon of self-doing crime.
 I am to wait, though waiting so be hell,
 Not blame your pleasure, be it ill or well.

LIX.

If there be nothing new, but that which is
Hath been before, how are our brains beguil'd,
Which, labouring for invention, bear amiss
The second burden of a former child?
O! that record could with a backward look,
Even of five hundred courses of the sun,
Show me your image in some antique book,
Since mind at first in character was done:
That I might see what the old world could say
To this composed wonder of your frame;
Whether we are mended, or whe'r better they,
Or whether revolution be the same.
 O! sure I am, the wits of former days
 To subjects worse have given admiring praise.

LX.

Like as the waves make towards the pebbled shore,
So do our minutes hasten to their end;
Each changing place with that which goes before,
In sequent toil all forwards do contend.
Nativity, once in the main of light,
Crawls to maturity, wherewith being crown'd,
Crooked eclipses 'gainst his glory fight,
And Time, that gave, doth now his gift confound.
Time doth transfix the flourish set on youth,
And delves the parallels in beauty's brow;
Feeds on the rarities of nature's truth,
And nothing stands but for his scythe to mow:
 And yet to times in hope my verse shall stand,
 Praising thy worth, despite his cruel hand.

LXI.

Is it thy will thy image should keep open
My heavy eyelids to the weary night?
Dost thou desire my slumbers should be broken,
While shadows, like to thee, do mock my sight?
Is it thy spirit that thou send'st from thee
So far from home, into my deeds to pry;
To find out shames and idle hours in me,
The scope and tenor of thy jealousy?
O no! thy love, though much, is not so great:
It is my love that keeps mine eye awake;
Mine own true love that doth my rest defeat,
To play the watchman ever for thy sake:
 For thee watch I, whilst thou dost wake elsewhere,
 From me far off, with others all-too-near.

LXII.

Sin of self-love possesseth all mine eye,
And all my soul, and all my every part;
And for this sin there is no remedy,
It is so grounded inward in my heart.
Methinks no face so gracious is as mine,
No shape so true, no truth of such account;
And for myself mine own worth do define,
As I all other in all worths surmount.
But when my glass shows me myself indeed,
Beated and chopp'd with tann'd antiquity,
Mine own self-love quite contrary I read;
Self so self-loving were iniquity.
 'T is thee (myself) that for myself I praise,
 Painting my age with beauty of thy days.

LXIII.

Against my love shall be, as I am now,
With Time's injurious hand crush'd and o'erworn,
When hours have drain'd his blood, and fill'd his brow
With lines and wrinkles; when his youthful morn
Hath travell'd on to age's steepy night;
And all those beauties, whereof now he 's king,

Are vanishing, or vanish'd out of sight,
Stealing away the treasure of his spring;
For such a time do I now fortify
Against confounding age's cruel knife,
That he shall never cut from memory
My sweet love's beauty, though my lover's life:
 His beauty shall in these black lines be seen,
 And they shall live, and he in them still green.

LXIV.

When I have seen by Time's fell hand defac'd
The rich-proud cost of outworn buried age;
When sometime lofty towers I see down-raz'd,
And brass eternal, slave to mortal rage:
When I have seen the hungry ocean gain
Advantage on the kingdom of the shore,
And the firm soil win of the watery main,
Increasing store with loss, and loss with store:
When I have seen such interchange of state,
Or state itself confounded to decay,
Ruin hath taught me thus to ruminate,—
That Time will come and take my love away.
 This thought is as a death, which cannot choose
 But weep to have that which it fears to lose.

LXV.

Since brass, nor stone, nor earth, nor boundless sea,
But sad mortality o'ersways their power,
How with this rage shall beauty hold a plea,
Whose action is no stronger than a flower?
O! how shall summer's honey breath hold out
Against the wrackful siege of battering days,
When rocks impregnable are not so stout,
Nor gates of steel so strong, but Time decays?
O fearful meditation! where, alack,
Shall Time's best jewel from Time's chest lie hid?
Or what strong hand can hold his swift foot back?
Or who his spoil of beauty can forbid?
 O, none, unless this miracle have might,
 That in black ink my love may still shine bright.

LXVI.

Tir'd with all these, for restful death I cry;—
As, to behold desert a beggar born,
And needy nothing trimm'd in jollity,
And purest faith unhappily forsworn,
And gilded honour shamefully misplac'd,
And maiden virtue rudely strumpeted,
And right perfection wrongfully disgrac'd,
And strength by limping sway disabled,
And art made tongue-tied by authority,
And folly (doctor-like) controlling skill,
And simple truth miscall'd simplicity,
And captive good attending captain ill:
 Tir'd with all these, from these would I be gone,
 Save that, to die, I leave my love alone.

LXVII.

Ah! wherefore with infection should he live,
And with his presence grace impiety,
That sin by him advantage should achieve,
And lace itself with his society?
Why should false painting imitate his cheek,
And steal dead seeing of his living hue?
Why should poor beauty indirectly seek
Roses of shadow, since his rose is true?
Why should he live, now Nature bankrupt is,
Beggar'd of blood to blush through lively veins?
For she hath no exchequer now but his,
And, proud of many, lives upon his gains.
 O! him she stores, to show what wealth she had
 In days long since, before these last so bad.

LXVIII.

Thus is his cheek the map of days outworn,
When beauty liv'd and died as flowers do now,
Before these bastard signs of fair were born,
Or durst inhabit on a living brow;
Before the golden tresses of the dead,
The right of sepulchres, were shorn away,

To live a second life on second head;
Ere beauty's dead fleece made another gay.
In him those holy antique hours are seen,
Without all ornament, itself, and true,
Making no summer of another's green,
Robbing no old to dress his beauty new;
    And him as for a map doth Nature store,
    To show false Art what beauty was of yore.

LXIX.

Those parts of thee that the world's eye doth view,
Want nothing that the thought of hearts can mend;
All tongues (the voice of souls) give thee that due,
Uttering bare truth, even so as foes commend.
Thy outward thus with outward praise is crown'd;
But those same tongues that give thee so thine own,
In other accents do this praise confound,
By seeing farther than the eye hath shown.
They look into the beauty of thy mind,
And that, in guess, they measure by thy deeds;
Then (churls) their thoughts, although their eyes were
    kind,
To thy fair flower add the rank smell of weeds:
    But why thy odour matcheth not thy show,
    The soil is this,—that thou dost common grow.

LXX.

That thou art blam'd shall not be thy defect,
For slander's mark was ever yet the fair;
The ornament of beauty is suspect,
A crow that flies in heaven's sweetest air.
So thou be good, slander doth but approve
Thy worth the greater, being woo'd of time;
For canker vice the sweetest buds doth love,
And thou present'st a pure unstained prime.
Thou hast pass'd by the ambush of young days,
Either not assail'd, or victor being charg'd;
Yet this thy praise cannot be so thy praise,
To tie up envy, evermore enlarg'd:
    If some suspect of ill mask'd not thy show,
    Then thou alone kingdoms of hearts shouldst owe.

LXXI.

No longer mourn for me when I am dead,
Than you shall hear the surly sullen bell
Give warning to the world that I am fled
From this vile world, with vilest worms to dwell:
Nay, if you read this line, remember not
The hand that writ it; for I love you so,
That I in your sweet thoughts would be forgot,
If thinking on me then should make you woe.
O! if (I say) you look upon this verse,
When I perhaps compounded am with clay,
Do not so much as my poor name rehearse,
But let your love even with my life decay;
    Lest the wise world should look into your moan,
    And mock you with me after I am gone.

LXXII.

O! lest the world should task you to recite
What merit liv'd in me, that you should love
After my death,—dear love, forget me quite,
For you in me can nothing worthy prove;
Unless you would devise some virtuous lie,
To do more for me than mine own desert,
And hang more praise upon deceased I,
Than niggard truth would willingly impart.
O! lest your true love may seem false in this,
That you for love speak well of me untrue,
My name be buried where my body is,
And live no more to shame nor me nor you.
    For I am sham'd by that which I bring forth,
    And so should you, to love things nothing worth.

LXXIII.

That time of year thou may'st in me behold,
When yellow leaves, or none, or few, do hang
Upon those boughs which shake against the cold,
Bare ruin'd choirs, where late the sweet birds sang.
In me thou seest the twilight of such day
As after sunset fadeth in the west,

Which by-and-by black night doth take away,
Death's second self, that seals up all in rest:
In me thou seest the glowing of such fire,
That on the ashes of his youth doth lie,
As the death-bed whereon it must expire,
Consum'd with that which it was nourish'd by.
    This thou perceiv'st, which makes thy love more
      strong,
    To love that well which thou must leave ere long:

LXXIV.

But be contented: when that fell arrest
Without all bail shall carry me away,
My life hath in this line some interest,
Which for memorial still with thee shall stay.
When thou reviewest this, thou dost review
The very part was consecrate to thee.
The earth can have but earth, which is his due;
My spirit is thine, the better part of me:
So then thou hast but lost the dregs of life,
The prey of worms, my body being dead;
The coward conquest of a wretch's knife,
Too base of thee to be remembered.
    The worth of that is that which it contains,
    And that is this, and this with thee remains.

LXXV.

So are you to my thoughts, as food to life,
Or as sweet-season'd showers are to the ground;
And for the peace of you I hold such strife
As 'twixt a miser and his wealth is found:
Now proud as an enjoyer, and anon
Doubting the filching age will steal his treasure;
Now counting best to be with you alone,
Then better'd that the world may see my pleasure:
Sometime all full with feasting on your sight,
And by-and-by clean starved for a look;
Possessing or pursuing no delight,
Save what is had or must from you be took.
    Thus do I pine and surfeit day by day;
    Or gluttoning on all, or all away.

LXXVI.

Why is my verse so barren of new pride,
So far from variation or quick change?
Why, with the time, do I not glance aside
To new-found methods, and to compounds strange?
Why write I still all one, ever the same,
And keep invention in a noted weed,
That every word doth almost tell my name,
Showing their birth, and where they did proceed?
O! know, sweet love, I always write of you,
And you and love are still my argument;
So, all my best is dressing old words new,
Spending again what is already spent:
    For as the sun is daily new and old,
    So is my love, still telling what is told.

LXXVII.

Thy glass will show thee how thy beauties wear,
Thy dial how thy precious minutes waste;
The vacant leaves thy mind's imprint will bear,
And of this book this learning may'st thou taste:
The wrinkles which thy glass will truly show,
Of mouthed graves will give thee memory;
Thou by thy dial's shady stealth may'st know
Time's thievish progress to eternity.
Look, what thy memory cannot contain,
Commit to these waste blanks, and thou shalt find
Those children nurs'd, deliver'd from thy brain,
To take a new acquaintance of thy mind.
    These offices, so oft as thou wilt look,
    Shall profit thee, and much enrich thy book.

LXXVIII.

So oft have I invok'd thee for my Muse,
And found such fair assistance in my verse,
As every alien pen hath got my use,
And under thee their poesy disperse.
Thine eyes that taught the dumb on high to sing,
And heavy ignorance aloft to fly,

Have added feathers to the learned's wing,
And given grace a double majesty.
Yet be most proud of that which I compile,
Whose influence is thine, and born of thee :
In others' works thou dost but mend the style,
And arts with thy sweet graces graced be ;
   But thou art all my art, and dost advance
   As high as learning my rude ignorance.

LXXIX.

Whilst I alone did call upon thy aid,
My verse alone had all thy gentle grace :
But now my gracious numbers are decay'd,
And my sick Muse doth give another place.
I grant, sweet love, thy lovely argument
Deserves the travail of a worthier pen ;
Yet what of thee thy poet doth invent,
He robs thee of, and pays it thee again.
He lends thee virtue, and he stole that word
From thy behaviour ; beauty doth he give,
And found it in thy cheek ; he can afford
No praise to thee but what in thee doth live.
   Then thank him not for that which he doth say,
   Since what he owes thee thou thyself dost pay.

LXXX.

O ! how I faint when I of you do write,
Knowing a better spirit doth use your name,
And in the praise thereof spends all his might,
To make me tongue-tied, speaking of your fame :
But since your worth (wide as the ocean is)
The humble as the proudest sail doth bear,
My saucy bark, inferior far to his,
On your broad main doth wilfully appear.
Your shallowest help will hold me up afloat,
Whilst he upon your soundless deep doth ride ;
Or, being wrack'd, I am a worthless boat,
He of tall building, and of goodly pride :
   Then, if he thrive, and I be cast away,
   The worst was this,—my love was my decay.

LXXXI.

Or I shall live your epitaph to make,
Or you survive when I in earth am rotten :
From hence your memory death cannot take,
Although in me each part will be forgotten.
Your name from hence immortal life shall have,
Though I, once gone, to all the world must die :
The earth can yield me but a common grave,
When you entombed in men's eyes shall lie.
Your monument shall be my gentle verse,
Which eyes not yet created shall o'erread ;
And tongues to be your being shall rehearse,
When all the breathers of this world are dead ;
   You still shall live (such virtue hath my pen),
   Where breath most breathes, even in the mouths of
     men.

LXXXII.

I grant thou wert not married to my Muse,
And therefore may'st without attaint o'erlook
The dedicated words which writers use
Of their fair subject, blessing every book.
Thou art as fair in knowledge as in hue,
Finding thy worth a limit past my praise ;
And therefore art enforc'd to seek anew
Some fresher stamp of the time-bettering days.
And do so, love ; yet when they have devis'd
What strained touches rhetoric can lend,
Thou, truly fair, wert truly sympathis'd
In true plain words, by thy true-telling friend ;
   And their gross painting might be better us'd
   Where cheeks need blood : in thee it is abus'd.

LXXXIII.

I never saw that you did painting need,
And therefore to your fair no painting set ;
I found, or thought I found, you did exceed
The barren tender of a poet's debt :
And therefore have I slept in your report,
That you yourself, being extant, well might show

How far a modern quill doth come too short,
Speaking of worth, what worth in you doth grow.
This silence for my sin you did impute,
Which shall be most my glory, being dumb ;
For I impair not beauty being mute,
When others would give life, and bring a tomb.
   There lives more life in one of your fair eyes,
   Than both your poets can in praise devise.

LXXXIV.

Who is it that says most ? which can say more
Than this rich praise, that you alone are you ?
In whose confine immured is the store,
Which should example where your equal grew.
Lean penury within that pen doth dwell,
That to his subject lends not some small glory ;
But he that writes of you, if he can tell
That you are you, so dignifies his story,
Let him but copy what in you is writ,
Not making worse what nature made so clear,
And such a counterpart shall fame his wit,
Making his style admired everywhere.
   You to your beauteous blessings add a curse,
   Being fond on praise, which makes your praises
     worse.

LXXXV.

My tongue-tied Muse in manners holds her still,
While comments of your praise, richly compil'd,
Reserve their character with golden quill,
And precious phrase by all the Muses fil'd.
I think good thoughts, whilst others write good words,
And, like unletter'd clerk, still cry " Amen "
To every hymn that able spirit affords,
In polish'd form of well-refined pen.
Hearing you prais'd, I say, " 'T is so, 't is true,"
And to the most of praise add something more ;
But that is in my thought, whose love to you,
Though words come hindmost, holds his rank before :
   Then others for the breath of words respect,
   Me for my dumb thoughts, speaking in effect.

LXXXVI.

Was it the proud full sail of his great verse,
Bound for the prize of all-too-precious you,
That did my ripe thoughts in my brain inhearse,
Making their tomb the womb wherein they grew ?
Was it his spirit, by spirits taught to write
Above a mortal pitch, that struck me dead ?
No, neither he, nor his compeers by night
Giving him aid, my verse astonished.
He, nor that affable familiar ghost,
Which nightly gulls him with intelligence,
As victors of my silence cannot boast.
I was not sick of any fear from thence ;
   But when your countenance fil'd up his line,
   Then lack'd I matter ; that enfeebled mine.

LXXXVII.

Farewell ! thou art too dear for my possessing,
And like enough thou know'st thy estimate :
The charter of thy worth gives thee releasing ;
My bonds in thee are all determinate.
For how do I hold thee but by thy granting ?
And for that riches where is my deserving ?
The cause of this fair gift in me is wanting,
And so my patent back again is swerving.
Thyself thou gav'st, thy own worth then not knowing,
Or me, to whom thou gav'st it, else mistaking ;
So thy great gift, upon misprision growing,
Comes home again, on better judgment making.
   Thus have I had thee, as a dream doth flatter,
   In sleep a king, but waking no such matter.

LXXXVIII.

When thou shalt be dispos'd to set me light,
And place my merit in the eye of scorn,
Upon thy side against myself I 'll fight,
And prove thee virtuous, though thou art forsworn :
With mine own weakness being best acquainted,
Upon thy part I can set down a story

Of faults conceal'd, wherein I am attainted,
That thou, in losing me, shalt win much glory:
And I by this will be a gainer too;
For bending all my loving thoughts on thee,
The injuries that to myself I do,
Doing thee vantage, double-vantage me.
  Such is my love, to thee I so belong,
  That for thy right myself will bear all wrong.

LXXXIX.

Say that thou didst forsake me for some fault,
And I will comment upon that offence;
Speak of my lameness, and I straight will halt,
Against thy reasons making no defence.
Thou canst not, love, disgrace me half so ill,
To set a form upon desired change,
As I'll myself disgrace: knowing thy will,
I will acquaintance strangle, and look strange;
Be absent from thy walks; and in my tongue
Thy sweet-beloved name no more shall dwell,
Lest I (too much profane) should do it wrong,
And haply of our old acquaintance tell.
  For thee, against myself I'll vow debate,
  For I must ne'er love him whom thou dost hate.

XC.

Then hate me when thou wilt; if ever, now:
Now, while the world is bent my deeds to cross,
Join with the spite of fortune, make me bow,
And do not drop in for an after-loss.
Ah! do not, when my heart hath scap'd this sorrow,
Come in the rearward of a conquer'd woe;
Give not a windy night a rainy morrow,
To linger out a purpos'd overthrow.
If thou wilt leave me, do not leave me last,
When other petty griefs have done their spite,
But in the onset come: so shall I taste
At first the very worst of fortune's might;
  And other strains of woe, which now seem woe,
  Compar'd with loss of thee, will not seem so.

XCI.

Some glory in their birth, some in their skill,
Some in their wealth, some in their body's force,
Some in their garments, though new-fangled ill,
Some in their hawks and hounds, some in their horse;
And every humour hath his adjunct pleasure,
Wherein it finds a joy above the rest;
But these particulars are not my measure:
All these I better in one general best.
Thy love is better than high birth to me,
Richer than wealth, prouder than garments' cost,
Of more delight than hawks or horses be;
And having thee, of all men's pride I boast:
  Wretched in this alone, that thou may'st take
  All this away, and me most wretched make.

XCII.

But do thy worst to steal thyself away,
For term of life thou art assured mine;
And life no longer than thy love will stay,
For it depends upon that love of thine.
Then need I not to fear the worst of wrongs,
When in the least of them my life hath end.
I see a better state to me belongs
Than that which on thy humour doth depend.
Thou canst not vex me with inconstant mind,
Since that my life on thy revolt doth lie.
O! what a happy title do I find,
Happy to have thy love, happy to die:
  But what's so blessed-fair that fears no blot?
  Thou may'st be false, and yet I know it not:

XCIII.

So shall I live, supposing thou art true,
Like a deceived husband; so love's face
May still seem love to me, though alter'd-new;
Thy looks with me, thy heart in other place:
For there can live no hatred in thine eye;
Therefore in that I cannot know thy change.

In many's looks the false heart's history
Is writ in moods, and frowns, and wrinkles strange;
But Heaven in thy creation did decree,
That in thy face sweet love should ever dwell;
Whate'er thy thoughts or thy heart's workings be,
Thy looks should nothing thence but sweetness tell.
  How like Eve's apple doth thy beauty grow,
  If thy sweet virtue answer not thy show!

XCIV.

They that have power to hurt, and will do none
That do not do the thing they most do show,
Who, moving others, are themselves as stone,
Unmoved, cold, and to temptation slow;
They rightly do inherit heaven's graces,
And husband nature's riches from expense;
They are the lords and owners of their faces,
Others but stewards of their excellence.
The summer's flower is to the summer sweet,
Though to itself it only live and die;
But if that flower with base infection meet,
The basest weed outbraves his dignity;
  For sweetest things turn sourest by their deeds
  Lilies that fester smell far worse than weeds.

XCV.

How sweet and lovely dost thou make the shame,
Which, like a canker in the fragrant rose,
Doth spot the beauty of thy budding name!
O, in what sweets dost thou thy sins enclose!
That tongue that tells the story of thy days,
(Making lascivious comments on thy sport,)
Cannot dispraise but in a kind of praise;
Naming thy name blesses an ill report.
O! what a mansion have those vices got,
Which for their habitation chose out thee,
Where beauty's veil doth cover every blot,
And all things turn to fair that eyes can see!
  Take heed, dear heart, of this large privilege;
  The hardest knife ill-us'd doth lose his edge.

XCVI.

Some say, thy fault is youth, some wantonness;
Some say, thy grace is youth, and gentle sport;
Both grace and faults are lov'd of more and less:
Thou mak'st faults graces that to thee resort.
As on the finger of a throned queen
The basest jewel will be well esteem'd,
So are those errors that in thee are seen
To truths translated, and for true things deem'd.
How many lambs might the stern wolf betray,
If like a lamb he could his looks translate!
How many gazers mightst thou lead away,
If thou wouldst use the strength of all thy state!
  But do not so; I love thee in such sort,
  As, thou being mine, mine is thy good report.

XCVII.

How like a winter hath my absence been
From thee, the pleasure of the fleeting year!
What freezings have I felt, what dark days seen,
What old December's bareness everywhere!
And yet this time remov'd was summer's time;
The teeming autumn, big with rich increase,
Bearing the wanton burden of the prime,
Like widow'd wombs after their lords' decease:
Yet this abundant issue seem'd to me
But hope of orphans, and unfather'd fruit;
For summer and his pleasures wait on thee,
And, thou away, the very birds are mute;
  Or, if they sing, 'tis with so dull a cheer,
  That leaves look pale, dreading the winter's near.

XCVIII.

From you have I been absent in the spring,
When proud-pied April, dress'd in all his trim,
Hath put a spirit of youth in everything,
That heavy Saturn laugh'd and leap'd with him:
Yet nor the lays of birds, nor the sweet smell
Of different flowers in odour and in hue,

Could make me any summer's story tell,
Or from their proud lap pluck them where they grew:
Nor did I wonder at the lily's white,
Nor praise the deep vermilion in the rose;
They were but sweet, but figures of delight,
Drawn after you, you pattern of all those.
    Yet seem'd it winter still, and, you away,
    As with your shadow I with these did play:

XCIX.

The forward violet thus did I chide :—
Sweet thief, whence didst thou steal thy sweet that
    smells,
If not from my love's breath ? The purple pride
Which on thy soft cheek for complexion dwells,
In my love's veins thou hast too grossly dy'd.
The lily I condemned for thy hand,
And buds of marjoram had stol'n thy hair:
The roses fearfully on thorns did stand,
One blushing shame, another white despair;
A third, nor red nor white, had stol'n of both,
And to this robbery had annex'd thy breath;
But, for his theft, in pride of all his growth
A vengeful canker eat him up to death.
    More flowers I noted, yet I none could see,
    But sweet or colour it had stol'n from thee.

C.

Where art thou, Muse, that thou forgett'st so long
To speak of that which gives thee all thy might?
Spend'st thou thy fury on some worthless song,
Darkening thy power to lend base subjects light?
Return, forgetful Muse, and straight redeem
In gentle numbers time so idly spent:
Sing to the ear that doth thy lays esteem,
And gives thy pen both skill and argument.
Rise, resty Muse, my love's sweet face survey,
If Time have any wrinkle graven there;
If any, be a satire to decay,
And make Time's spoils despised everywhere.
    Give my love fame faster than Time wastes life;
    So thou prevent'st his scythe and crooked knife.

CI.

O truant Muse! what shall be thy amends
For thy neglect of truth in beauty dy'd?
Both truth and beauty on my love depends;
So dost thou too, and therein dignified.
Make answer, Muse : wilt thou not haply say,
" Truth needs no colour, with his colour fix'd,
Beauty no pencil, beauty's truth to lay;
But best is best, if never intermix'd?"
Because he needs no praise, wilt thou be dumb?
Excuse not silence so; for 't lies in thee
To make him much outlive a gilded tomb,
And to be prais'd of ages yet to be.
    Then do thy office, Muse : I teach thee how
    To make him seem long hence as he shows now.

CII.

My love is strengthen'd, though more weak in seem-
    ing;
I love not less, though less the show appear:
That love is merchandis'd, whose rich esteeming
The owner's tongue doth publish everywhere.
Our love was new, and then but in the spring,
When I was wont to greet it with my lays;
As Philomel in summer's front doth sing,
And stops her pipe in growth of riper days:
Not that the summer is less pleasant now,
Than when her mournful hymns did hush the night,
But that wild music burdens every bough,
And sweets grown common lose their dear delight.
    Therefore, like her, I sometime hold my tongue,
    Because I would not dull you with my song.

CIII.

Alack, what poverty my Muse brings forth,
That having such a scope to show her pride,
The argument, all bare, is of more worth,
Than when it hath my added praise beside!

O! blame me not, if I no more can write :
Look in your glass, and there appears a face,
That over-goes my blunt invention quite,
Dulling my lines, and doing me disgrace.
Were it not sinful then, striving to mend,
To mar the subject that before was well?
For to no other pass my verses tend,
Than of your graces and your gifts to tell;
    And more, much more, than in my verse can sit,
    Your own glass shows you, when you look in it.

CIV.

To me, fair friend, you never can be old,
For as you were when first your eye I ey'd,
Such seems your beauty still. Three winters cold
Have from the forests shook three summers' pride;
Three beauteous springs to yellow autumn turn'd
In process of the seasons have I seen;
Three April perfumes in three hot Junes burn'd,
Since first I saw you fresh, which yet are green.
Ah! yet doth beauty, like a dial-hand,
Steal from his figure, and no pace perceiv'd;
So your sweet hue, which methinks still doth stand,
Hath motion, and mine eye may be deceiv'd:
    For fear of which, hear this, thou age unbred,—
    Ere you were born was beauty's summer dead.

CV.

Let not my love be call'd idolatry,
Nor my beloved as an idol show,
Since all alike my songs and praises be,
To one, of one, still such, and ever so.
Kind is my love to-day, to-morrow kind,
Still constant in a wondrous excellence;
Therefore my verse to constancy confin'd,
One thing expressing, leaves out difference.
Fair, kind, and true, is all my argument,
Fair, kind, and true, varying to other words;
And in this change is my invention spent,
Three themes in one, which wondrous scope affords.
    Fair, kind, and true, have often liv'd alone,
    Which three, till now, never kept seat in one.

CVI.

When in the chronicle of wasted time
I see descriptions of the fairest wights,
And beauty making beautiful old rhyme,
In praise of ladies dead, and lovely knights,
Then, in the blazon of sweet beauty's best,
Of hand, of foot, of lip, of eye, of brow,
I see their antique pen would have express'd
Even such a beauty as you master now.
So all their praises are but prophecies
Of this our time, all you prefiguring;
And for they look'd but with divining eyes,
They had not skill enough your worth to sing:
    For we, which now behold these present days,
    Have eyes to wonder, but lack tongues to praise.

CVII.

Not mine own fears, nor the prophetic soul
Of the wide world, dreaming on things to come,
Can yet the lease of my true love control,
Suppos'd as forfeit to a confin'd doom.
The mortal moon hath her eclipse endur'd,
And the sad augurs mock their own presage;
Incertainties now crown themselves assur'd,
And peace proclaims olives of endless age.
Now, with the drops of this most balmy time
My love looks fresh, and death to me subscribes,
Since, spite of him, I 'll live in this poor rhyme,
While he insults o'er dull and speechless tribes:
    And thou in this shalt find thy monument,
    When tyrants' crests and tombs of brass are spent.

CVIII.

What 's in the brain that ink may character,
Which hath not figur'd to thee my true spirit?
What 's new to speak, what new to register,
That may express my love, or thy dear merit?

Nothing, sweet boy; but yet, like prayers divine,
I must each day say o'er the very same,
Counting no old thing old, thou mine, I thine,
Even as when first I hallow'd thy fair name.
So that eternal love, in love's fresh case,
Weighs not the dust and injury of age;
Nor gives to necessary wrinkles place,
But makes antiquity for aye his page;
 Finding the first conceit of love there bred,
 Where time and outward form would show it dead.

CIX.

O! never say that I was false of heart,
Though absence seem'd my flame to qualify.
As easy might I from myself depart,
As from my soul, which in thy breast doth lie.
That is my home of love: if I have ranged,
Like him that travels, I return again,
Just to the time, not with the time exchanged,
So that myself bring water for my stain.
Never believe, though in my nature reign'd
All frailties that besiege all kind of blood,
That it could so preposterously be stain'd,
To leave for nothing all thy sum of good;
 For nothing this wide universe I call,
 Save thou, my rose; in it thou art my all.

CX.

Alas! 't is true, I have gone here and there,
And made myself a motley to the view;
Gor'd mine own thoughts, sold cheap what is most
   dear,
Made old offences of affections new:
Most true it is, that I have look'd on truth
Askance and strangely; but, by all above,
These blenches gave my heart another youth,
And worse essays prov'd thee my best of love.
Now all is done, have what shall have no end:
Mine appetite I never more will grind
On newer proof, to try an older friend,
A god in love, to whom I am confin'd.
 Then give me welcome, next my heaven the best,
 Even to thy pure and most most loving breast.

CXI.

O! for my sake do you with Fortune chide,
The guilty goddess of my harmful deeds,
That did not better for my life provide,
Than public means, which public manners breeds:
Thence comes it that my name receives a brand;
And almost thence my nature is subdu'd
To what it works in, like the dyer's hand.
Pity me then, and wish I were renew'd;
Whilst, like a willing patient, I will drink
Potions of eisel 'gainst my strong infection;
No bitterness that I will bitter think,
Nor double penance, to correct correction.
 Pity me then, dear friend, and I assure ye,
 Even that your pity is enough to cure me.

CXII.

Your love and pity doth the impression fill
Which vulgar scandal stamp'd upon my brow;
For what care I who calls me well or ill,
So you o'ergreen my bad, my good allow?
You are my all-the-world, and I must strive
To know my shames and praises from your tongue;
None else to me, nor I to none alive,
That my steel'd sense or changes right or wrong.
In so profound abysm I throw all care
Of others' voices, that my adder's sense
To critic and to flatterer stopped are.
Mark how with my neglect I do dispense:—
 You are so strongly in my purpose bred,
 That all the world besides methinks they 're dead.

CXIII.

Since I left you, mine eye is in my mind,
And that which governs me to go about
Doth part his function, and is partly blind,
Seems seeing, but effectually is out;

For it no form delivers to the heart
Of bird, of flower, or shape, which it doth latch:
Of his quick objects hath the mind no part,
Nor his own vision holds what it doth catch;
For if it see the rud'st or gentlest sight,
The most sweet favour, or deformed'st creature,
The mountain or the sea, the day or night,
The crow or dove, it shapes them to your feature:
 Incapable of more, replete with you,
 My most true mind thus maketh mine untrue.

CXIV.

Or whether doth my mind, being crown'd with you,
Drink up the monarch's plague, this flattery?
Or whether shall I say, mine eye saith true,
And that your love taught it this alchymy,
To make of monsters and things indigest
Such cherubins as your sweet self resemble,
Creating every bad a perfect best,
As fast as objects to his beams assemble?
O! 't is the first: 't is flattery in my seeing,
And my great mind most kingly drinks it up:
Mine eye well knows what with his gust is 'greeing,
And to his palate doth prepare the cup:
 If it be poison'd, 't is the lesser sin
 That mine eye loves it, and doth first begin.

CXV.

Those lines that I before have writ, do lie,
Even those that said I could not love you dearer;
Yet then my judgment knew no reason why
My most full flame should afterwards burn clearer.
But reckoning Time, whose million'd accidents
Creep in 'twixt vows, and change decrees of kings,
Tan sacred beauty, blunt the sharp'st intents,
Divert strong minds to the course of altering things:
Alas! why, fearing of Time's tyranny,
Might I not then say, "Now I love you best,"
When I was certain o'er incertainty,
Crowning the present, doubting of the rest?
 Love is a babe; then might I not say so,
 To give full growth to that which still doth grow?

CXVI.

Let me not to the marriage of true minds
Admit impediments. Love is not love
Which alters when it alteration finds,
Or bends with the remover to remove:
O, no! it is an ever-fixed mark,
That looks on tempests, and is never shaken
It is the star to every wandering bark,
Whose worth 's unknown, although his height be
   taken.
Love 's not Time's fool, though rosy lips and cheeks
Within his bending sickle's compass come;
Love alters not with his brief hours and weeks,
But bears it out even to the edge of doom.
 If this be error, and upon me prov'd,
 I never writ, nor no man ever lov'd.

CXVII.

Accuse me thus: that I have scanted all
Wherein I should your great deserts repay;
Forgot upon your dearest love to call,
Whereto all bonds do tie me day by day;
That I have frequent been with unknown minds,
And given to time your own dear-purchas'd right;
That I have hoisted sail to all the winds
Which should transport me farthest from your sight:
Book both my wilfulness and errors down,
And on just proof surmise accumulate:
Bring me within the level of your frown,
But shoot not at me in your waken'd hate;
 Since my appeal says, I did strive to prove
 The constancy and virtue of your love.

CXVIII.

Like as, to make our appetites more keen,
With eager compounds we our palate urge;
As, to prevent our maladies unseen,
We sicken to shun sickness, when we purge;

Even so, being full of your ne'er-cloying sweetness,
To bitter sauces did I frame my feeding;
And, sick of welfare, found a kind of meetness
To be diseas'd, ere that there was true needing.
Thus policy in love, to anticipate
The ills that were not, grew to faults assur'd,
And brought to medicine a healthful state,
Which, rank of goodness, would by ill be cur'd;
  But thence I learn, and find the lesson true,
  Drugs poison him that so fell sick of you.

CXIX.

What potions have I drunk of Siren tears,
Distill'd from limbecks foul as hell within,
Applying fears to hopes, and hopes to fears,
Still losing when I saw myself to win!
What wretched errors hath my heart committed,
Whilst it hath thought itself so blessed never!
How have mine eyes out of their spheres been fitted,
In the distraction of this madding fever!
O benefit of ill! now I find true,
That better is by evil still made better;
And ruin'd love, when it is built anew,
Grows fairer than at first, more strong, far greater.
  So I return rebuk'd to my content,
  And gain by ill thrice more than I have spent.

CXX.

That you were once unkind, befriends me now,
And for that sorrow, which I then did feel,
Needs must I under my transgression bow,
Unless my nerves were brass or hammer'd steel.
For if you were by my unkindness shaken,
As I by yours, you've pass'd a hell of time;
And I, a tyrant, have no leisure taken
To weigh how once I suffer'd in your crime.
O! that our night of woe might have remember'd
My deepest sense, how hard true sorrow hits;
And soon to you, as you to me, then tender'd
The humble salve which wounded bosoms fits!
  But that your trespass now becomes a fee;
  Mine ransoms yours, and yours must ransom me.

CXXI.

'T is better to be vile, than vile-esteem'd,
When not to be receives reproach of being,
And the just pleasure lost, which is so deem'd
Not by our feeling, but by others' seeing.
For why should others' false adulterate eyes
Give salutation to my sportive blood?
Or on my frailties why are frailer spies,
Which in their wills count bad what I think good?
No, I am that I am; and they that level
At my abuses, reckon up their own:
I may be straight, though they themselves be bevel;
By their rank thoughts my deeds must not be shown;
  Unless this general evil they maintain,—
  All men are bad, and in their badness reign.

CXXII.

Thy gift, thy tables, are within my brain
Full character'd with lasting memory,
Which shall above that idle rank remain,
Beyond all date, even to eternity;
Or, at the least, so long as brain and heart
Have faculty by nature to subsist;
Till each to raz'd oblivion yield his part
Of thee, thy record never can be miss'd.
That poor retention could not so much hold,
Nor need I tallies, thy dear love to score;
Therefore to give them from me was I bold,
To trust those tables that receive thee more:
  To keep an adjunct to remember thee,
  Were to import forgetfulness in me.

CXXIII.

No! Time, thou shalt not boast that I do change:
Thy pyramids, built up with newer might,
To me are nothing novel, nothing strange;
They are but dressings of a former sight.

Our dates are brief, and therefore we admire
What thou dost foist upon us that is old,
And rather make them born to our desire,
Than think that we before have heard them told.
Thy registers and thee I both defy,
Not wondering at the present, nor the past;
For thy records and what we see do lie,
Made more or less by thy continual haste.
  This I do vow, and this shall ever be,
  I will be true, despite thy scythe and thee:

CXXIV.

If my dear love were but the child of state,
It might for Fortune's bastard be unfather'd,
As subject to Time's love, or to Time's hate,
Weeds among weeds, or flowers with flowers gather'd.
No, it was builded far from accident;
It suffers not in smiling pomp, nor falls
Under the blow of thralled discontent,
Whereto the inviting time our fashion calls:
It fears not policy, that heretic,
Which works on leases of short-number'd hours,
But all alone stands hugely politic,
That it nor grows with heat, nor drowns with
    showers.
  To this I witness call the fools of time,
  Which die for goodness, who have liv'd for crime.

CXXV.

Were 't aught to me I bore the canopy,
With my extern the outward honouring,
Or laid great bases for eternity,
Which prove more short than waste or ruining?
Have I not seen dwellers on form and favour
Lose all, and more, by paying too much rent;
For compound sweet foregoing simple savour,
Pitiful thrivers, in their gazing spent?
No, let me be obsequious in thy heart,
And take thou my oblation, poor but free,
Which is not mix'd with seconds, knows no art,
But mutual render, only me for thee.
  Hence, thou suborn'd informer! a true soul,
  When most impeach'd, stands least in thy control.

CXXVI.

O thou, my lovely boy, who in thy power
Dost hold Time's fickle glass, his sickle, hour;
Who hast by waning grown, and therein show'st
Thy lovers withering, as thy sweet self grow'st;
If Nature, sovereign mistress over wrack,
As thou goest onwards, still will pluck thee back,
She keeps thee to this purpose, that her skill
May time disgrace, and wretched minutes kill.
Yet fear her, O thou minion of her pleasure!
She may detain, but not still keep her treasure:
  Her audit, though delay'd, answer'd must be,
  And her quietus is to render thee.

CXXVII.

In the old age black was not counted fair,
Or if it were, it bore not beauty's name;
But now is black beauty's successive heir,
And beauty slander'd with a bastard shame;
For since each hand hath put on nature's power,
Fairing the foul with art's false borrow'd face,
Sweet beauty hath no name, no holy bower,
But is profan'd, if not lives in disgrace.
Therefore my mistress' eyes are raven black,
Her eyes so suited, and they mourners seem
At such, who, not born fair, no beauty lack,
Slandering creation with a false esteem:
  Yet so they mourn, becoming of their woe,
  That every tongue says, beauty should look so.

CXXVIII.

How oft, when thou, my music, music play'st,
Upon that blessed wood, whose motion sounds
With thy sweet fingers, when thou gently sway'st
The wiry concord that mine ear confounds,
Do I envy those jacks, that nimble leap
To kiss the tender inward of thy hand,

Whilst my poor lips, which should that harvest reap,
At the wood's boldness by thee blushing stand !
To be so tickled, they would change their state
And situation with those dancing chips,
O'er whom thy fingers walk with gentle gait,
Making dead wood more bless'd than living lips.
  Since saucy jacks so happy are in this,
  Give them thy fingers, me thy lips to kiss.

CXXIX.

The expense of spirit in a waste of shame
Is lust in action ; and till action, lust
Is perjur'd, murderous, bloody, full of blame,
Savage, extreme, rude, cruel, not to trust ;
Enjoy'd no sooner but despised straight ;
Past reason hunted ; and no sooner had,
Past reason hated, as a swallow'd bait,
On purpose laid to make the taker mad :
Mad in pursuit, and in possession so ;
Had, having, and in quest to have, extreme ;
A bliss in proof,—and prov'd, a very woe ;
Before, a joy propos'd ; behind, a dream.
  All this the world well knows ; yet none knows well
  To shun the heaven that leads men to this hell.

CXXX.

My mistress' eyes are nothing like the sun ;
Coral is far more red than her lips' red ;
If snow be white, why then her breasts are dun ;
If hairs be wires, black wires grow on her head.
I have seen roses damask'd, red and white,
But no such roses see I in her cheeks ;
And in some perfumes is there more delight
Than in the breath that from my mistress reeks.
I love to hear her speak, yet well I know
That music hath a far more pleasing sound :
I grant I never saw a goddess go ;
My mistress, when she walks, treads on the ground :
  And yet, by Heaven, I think my love as rare
  As any she belied with false compare.

CXXXI.

Thou art as tyrannous, so as thou art,
As those whose beauties proudly make them cruel ;
For well thou know'st, to my dear-doting heart
Thou art the fairest and most precious jewel.
Yet, in good faith, some say that thee behold,
Thy face hath not the power to make love groan :
To say they err, I dare not be so bold,
Although I swear it to myself alone.
And, to be sure that is not false I swear,
A thousand groans, but thinking on thy face,
One on another's neck, do witness bear,
Thy black is fairest in my judgment's place.
  In nothing art thou black, save in thy deeds,
  And thence this slander, as I think, proceeds.

CXXXII.

Thine eyes I love, and they, as pitying me,
Knowing thy heart torments me with disdain,
Have put on black, and loving mourners be,
Looking with pretty ruth upon my pain.
And truly not the morning sun of heaven
Better becomes the grey cheeks of the east,
Nor that full star that ushers in the even
Doth half that glory to the sober west,
As those two mourning eyes become thy face.
O ! let it then as well beseem thy heart
To mourn for me, since mourning doth thee grace,
And suit thy pity like in every part :
  Then will I swear, beauty herself is black,
  And all they foul that thy complexion lack.

CXXXIII.

Beshrew that heart that makes my heart to groan
For that deep wound it gives my friend and me !
Is 't not enough to torture me alone,
But slave to slavery my sweet'st friend must be ?
Me from myself thy cruel eye hath taken,
And my next self thou harder hast engross'd :

Of him, myself, and thee, I am forsaken ;
A torment thrice threefold thus to be cross'd.
Prison my heart in thy steel bosom's ward,
But then my friend's heart let my poor heart bail ;
Whoe'er keeps me, let my heart be his guard ;
Thou canst not then use rigour in my gaol :
  And yet thou wilt ; for I, being pent in thee,
  Perforce am thine, and all that is in me.

CXXXIV.

So, now I have confess'd that he is thine,
And I myself am mortgag'd to thy will,
Myself I'll forfeit, so that other mine
Thou wilt restore, to be my comfort still :
But thou wilt not, nor he will not be free,
For thou art covetous, and he is kind ;
He learn'd but, surety-like, to write for me,
Under that bond that him as fast doth bind.
The statute of thy beauty thou wilt take,
Thou usurer, that putt'st forth all to use,
And sue a friend, came debtor for my sake ;
So him I lose through my unkind abuse.
  Him have I lost ; thou hast both him and me :
  He pays the whole, and yet am I not free.

CXXXV.

Whoever hath her wish, thou hast thy *Will*,
And *Will* to boot, and *Will* in overplus ;
More than enough am I, that vex thee still,
To thy sweet will making addition thus.
Wilt thou, whose will is large and spacious,
Not once vouchsafe to hide my will in thine ?
Shall will in others seem right gracious,
And in my will no fair acceptance shine ?
The sea, all water, yet receives rain still,
And in abundance addeth to his store ;
So thou, being rich in *Will*, add to thy *Will*
One will of mine, to make thy large *Will* more.
  Let no unkind, no fair beseechers kill ;
  Think all but one, and me in that one *Will*.

CXXXVI.

If thy soul check thee that I come so near,
Swear to thy blind soul that I was thy *Will*,
And will, thy soul knows, is admitted there ;
Thus far for love, my love-suit, sweet, fulfil.
Will will fulfil the treasure of thy love,
Ay, fill it full with wills, and my will one.
In things of great receipt with ease we prove,
Among a number one is reckon'd none :
Then in the number let me pass untold,
Though in thy stores' account I one must be ;
For nothing hold me, so it please thee hold
That nothing me, a something sweet to thee :
  Make but my name thy love, and love that still,
  And then thou lov'st me,—for my name is *Will*.

CXXXVII.

Thou blind fool, Love, what dost thou to mine eyes,
That they behold, and see not what they see ?
They know what beauty is, see where it lies,
Yet what the best is, take the worst to be.
If eyes, corrupt by over-partial looks,
Be anchor'd in the bay where all men ride,
Why of eyes' falsehood hast thou forged hooks,
Whereto the judgment of my heart is tied ?
Why should my heart think that a several plot,
Which my heart knows the wide world's common
    place ?
Or mine eyes seeing this, say, this is not,
To put fair truth upon so foul a face ?
  In things right-true my heart and eyes have err'd,
  And to this false plague are they now transferr'd.

CXXXVIII.

When my love swears that she is made of truth,
I do believe her, though I know she lies,
That she might think me some untutor'd youth,
Unlearned in the world's false subtleties,
Thus vainly thinking that she thinks me young,
Although she knows my days are past the best,

Simply I credit her false-speaking tongue :
On both sides thus is simple truth suppress'd.
But wherefore says she not, she is unjust?
And wherefore say not I, that I am old?
O! love's best habit is in seeming trust,
And age in love loves not to have years told :
    Therefore I lie with her, and she with me,
    And in our faults by lies we flatter'd be.

CXXXIX.

O! call not me to justify the wrong,
That thy unkindness lays upon my heart ;
Wound me not with thine eye, but with thy tongue ;
Use power with power, and slay me not by art.
Tell me thou lov'st elsewhere ; but in my sight,
Dear heart, forbear to glance thine eye aside :
What need'st thou wound with cunning, when thy might
Is more than my o'erpress'd defence can 'bide?
Let me excuse thee : ah ! my love well knows
Her pretty looks have been mine enemies,
And therefore from my face she turns my foes,
That they elsewhere might dart their injuries.
    Yet do not so ; but since I am near slain,
    Kill me outright with looks, and rid my pain.

CXL.

Be wise as thou art cruel ; do not press
My tongue-tied patience with too much disdain ;
Lest sorrow lend me words, and words express
The manner of my pity-wanting pain.
If I might teach thee wit, better it were,
Though not to love, yet, love, to tell me so ;
As testy sick men, when their deaths be near,
No news but health from their physicians know :
For, if I should despair, I should grow mad,
And in my madness might speak ill of thee ;
Now this ill-wresting world is grown so bad,
Mad slanderers by mad ears believed be.
    That I may not be so, nor thou belied,
    Bear thine eyes straight, though thy proud heart go wide.

CXLI.

In faith, I do not love thee with mine eyes,
For they in thee a thousand errors note ;
But 't is my heart that loves what they despise,
Who in despite of view is pleas'd to dote.
Nor are mine ears with thy tongue's tune delighted ;
Nor tender feeling, to base touches prone,
Nor taste, nor smell, desire to be invited
To any sensual feast with thee alone :
But my five wits nor my five senses can
Dissuade one foolish heart from serving thee,
Who leaves unsway'd the likeness of a man,
Thy proud heart's slave and vassal wretch to be :
    Only my plague thus far I count my gain,
    That she that makes me sin awards me pain.

CXLII.

Love is my sin, and thy dear virtue hate,
Hate of my sin, grounded on sinful loving.
O ! but with mine compare thou thine own state,
And thou shalt find it merits not reproving ;
Or, if it do, not from those lips of thine,
That have profan'd their scarlet ornaments,
And seal'd false bonds of love as oft as mine,
Robb'd others' beds' revenues of their rents.
Be it lawful I love thee, as thou lov'st those
Whom thine eyes woo as mine importune thee :
Root pity in thy heart, that when it grows,
Thy pity may deserve to pitied be.
    If thou dost seek to have what thou dost hide,
    By self-example may'st thou be denied !

CXLIII.

Lo ! as a careful housewife runs to catch
One of her feather'd creatures broke away,
Sets down her babe, and makes all swift despatch
In pursuit of the thing she would have stay ;
Whilst her neglected child holds her in chase,
Cries to catch her whose busy care is bent

To follow that which flies before her face,
Not prizing her poor infant's discontent :
So runn'st thou after that which flies from thee,
Whilst I, thy babe, chase thee afar behind ;
But if thou catch thy hope, turn back to me,
And play the mother's part, kiss me, be kind :
    So will I pray that thou may'st have thy *Will*,
    If thou turn back, and my loud crying still.

CXLIV.

Two loves I have of comfort and despair,
Which like two spirits do suggest me still :
The better angel is a man, right fair,
The worser spirit a woman, colour'd ill.
To win me soon to hell, my female evil
Tempteth my better angel from my side,
And would corrupt my saint to be a devil,
Wooing his purity with her foul pride.
And whether that my angel be turn'd fiend,
Suspect I may, yet not directly tell ;
But being both from me, both to each friend,
I guess one angel in another's hell :
    Yet this shall I ne'er know, but live in doubt,
    Till my bad angel fire my good one out.

CXLV.

Those lips that Love's own hand did make,
Breath'd forth the sound that said, "I hate,"
To me that languish'd for her sake ;
But when she saw my woful state,
Straight in her heart did mercy come,
Chiding that tongue, that ever sweet
Was us'd in giving gentle doom,
And taught it thus anew to greet :
"I hate," she alter'd with an end,
That follow'd it as gentle day
Doth follow night, who, like a fiend,
From heaven to hell is flown away :
    "I hate" from hate away she threw,
    And sav'd my life, saying—"not you."

CXLVI.

Poor soul, the centre of my sinful earth,
Fool'd by these rebel powers that thee array,
Why dost thou pine within, and suffer dearth,
Painting thy outward walls so costly gay?
Why so large cost, having so short a lease,
Dost thou upon thy fading mansion spend?
Shall worms, inheritors of this excess,
Eat up thy charge? is this thy body's end?
Then, soul, live thou upon thy servant's loss,
And let that pine to aggravate thy store ;
Buy terms divine in selling hours of dross ;
Within be fed, without be rich no more :
    So shalt thou feed on Death, that feeds on men,
    And, Death once dead, there 's no more dying then.

CXLVII.

My love is as a fever, longing still
For that which longer nurseth the disease ;
Feeding on that which doth preserve the ill,
The uncertain-sickly appetite to please.
My reason, the physician to my love,
Angry that his prescriptions are not kept,
Hath left me, and I desperate now approve,
Desire is death, which physic did except.
Past cure I am, now reason is past care,
And frantic-mad with evermore unrest :
My thoughts and my discourse as madmen's are,
At random from the truth vainly express'd ;
    For I have sworn thee fair, and thought thee bright,
    Who art as black as hell, as dark as night.

CXLVIII.

O me ! what eyes hath Love put in my head,
Which have no correspondence with true sight !
Or, if they have, where is my judgment fled,
That censures falsely what they see aright?
If that be fair whereon my false eyes dote,
What means the world to say it is not so?

If it be not, then love doth well denote
Love's eye is not so true as all men's : no,
How can it ?   O ! how can Love's eye be true,
That is so vex'd with watching and with tears?
No marvel then though I mistake my view ;
The sun itself sees not, till heaven clears.
  O cunning Love ! with tears thou keep'st me blind,
  Lest eyes well-seeing thy foul faults should find.

CXLIX.

Canst thou, O cruel ! say, I love thee not,
When I, against myself, with thee partake?
Do I not think on thee, when I forgot
Am of myself, all tyrant, for thy sake?
Who hateth thee that I do call my friend ?
On whom frown'st thou that I do fawn upon ?
Nay, if thou lour'st on me, do I not spend
Revenge upon myself with present moan ?
What merit do I in myself respect,
That is so proud thy service to despise,
When all my best doth worship thy defect,
Commanded by the motion of thine eyes?
  But, love, hate on, for now I know thy mind :
  Those that can see thou lov'st, and I am blind.

CL.

O ! from what power hast thou this powerful might,
With insufficiency my heart to sway ?
To make me give the lie to my true sight,
And swear that brightness doth not grace the day ?
Whence hast thou this becoming of things ill,
That in the very refuse of thy deeds
There is such strength and warrantise of skill,
That in my mind thy worst all best exceeds?
Who taught thee how to make me love thee more,
The more I hear and see just cause of hate?
O ! though I love what others do abhor,
With others thou shouldst not abhor my state :
  If thy unworthiness rais'd love in me,
  More worthy I to be belov'd of thee.

CLI.

Love is too young to know what conscience is ;
Yet who knows not, conscience is born of love ?
Then, gentle cheater, urge not my amiss,
Lest guilty of my faults thy sweet self prove :
For, thou betraying me, I do betray
My nobler part to my gross body's treason ;
My soul doth tell my body that he may
Triumph in love ; flesh stays no farther reason,
But, rising at thy name, doth point out thee
As his triumphant prize.   Proud of this pride,

He is contented thy poor drudge to be,
To stand in thy affairs, fall by thy side.
  No want of conscience hold it, that I call
  Her love, for whose dear love I rise and fall.

CLII.

In loving thee thou know'st I am forsworn,
But thou art twice forsworn, to me love swearing
In act thy bed-vow broke, and new faith torn,
In vowing new hate after new love bearing.
But why of two oaths' breach do I accuse thee,
When I break twenty ?   I am perjur'd most ;
For all my vows are oaths but to misuse thee,
And all my honest faith in thee is lost :
For I have sworn deep oaths of thy deep kindness,
Oaths of thy love, thy truth, thy constancy ;
And, to enlighten thee, gave eyes to blindness,
Or made them swear against the thing they see ;
  For I have sworn thee fair : more perjur'd I,
  To swear, against the truth, so foul a lie !

CLIII.

Cupid laid by his brand, and fell asleep :
A maid of Dian's this advantage found,
And his love-kindling fire did quickly steep
In a cold valley-fountain of that ground ;
Which borrow'd from this holy fire of Love
A dateless lively heat, still to endure,
And grew a seething bath, which yet men prove
Against strange maladies a sovereign cure.
But at my mistress' eye Love's brand new-fir'd,
The boy for trial needs would touch my breast ;
I, sick withal, the help of bath desir'd,
And thither hied, a sad-distemper'd guest,
  But found no cure : the bath for my help lies
  Where Cupid got new fire,—my mistress' eyes.

CLIV.

The little Love-god lying once asleep,
Laid by his side his heart-inflaming brand,
Whilst many nymphs, that vow'd chaste life to keep,
Came tripping by ; but in her maiden hand
The fairest votary took up that fire
Which many legions of true hearts had warm'd :
And so the general of hot desire
Was, sleeping, by a virgin hand disarm'd.
This brand she quenched in a cool well by,
Which from Love's fire took heat perpetual,
Growing a bath, and healthful remedy
For men diseas'd ; but I, my mistress' thrall,
  Came there for cure, and this by that I prove,
  Love's fire heats water, water cools not love.